Standard Normal Distribution Table

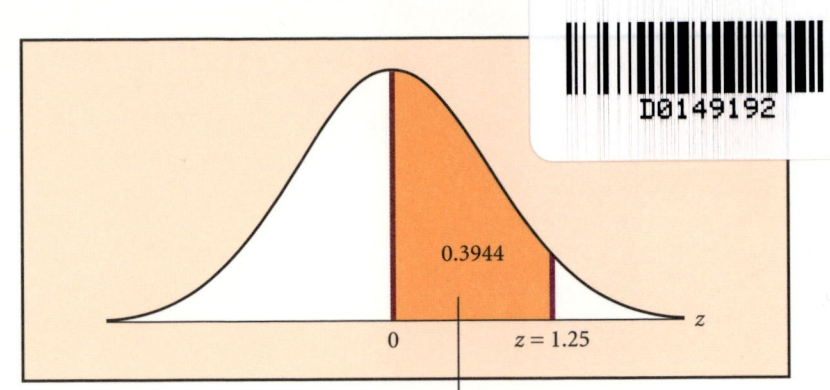

Z	0	0.01	0.02	0.03	0.04	0.05	0.06	0.07	0.08	0.09
0.0	0.0000	0.0040	0.0080	0.0120	0.0160	0.0199	0.0239	0.0279	0.0319	0.0359
0.1	0.0398	0.0438	0.0478	0.0517	0.0557	0.0596	0.0636	0.0675	0.0714	0.0753
0.2	0.0793	0.0832	0.0871	0.0910	0.0948	0.0987	0.1026	0.1064	0.1103	0.1141
0.3	0.1179	0.1217	0.1255	0.1293	0.1331	0.1368	0.1406	0.1443	0.1480	0.1517
0.4	0.1554	0.1591	0.1628	0.1664	0.1700	0.1736	0.1772	0.1808	0.1844	0.1879
0.5	0.1915	0.1950	0.1985	0.2019	0.2054	0.2088	0.2123	0.2157	0.2190	0.2224
0.6	0.2257	0.2291	0.2324	0.2357	0.2389	0.2422	0.2454	0.2486	0.2517	0.2549
0.7	0.2580	0.2611	0.2642	0.2673	0.2704	0.2734	0.2764	0.2794	0.2823	0.2852
0.8	0.2881	0.2910	0.2939	0.2967	0.2995	0.3023	0.3051	0.3078	0.3106	0.3133
0.9	0.3159	0.3186	0.3212	0.3238	0.3264	0.3289	0.3315	0.3340	0.3365	0.3389
1.0	0.3413	0.3438	0.3461	0.3485	0.3508	0.3531	0.3554	0.3577	0.3599	0.3621
1.1	0.3643	0.3665	0.3686	0.3708	0.3729	0.3749	0.3770	0.3790	0.3810	0.3830
1.2	0.3849	0.3869	0.3888	0.3907	0.3925	0.3944	0.3962	0.3980	0.3997	0.4015
1.3	0.4032	0.4049	0.4066	0.4082	0.4099	0.4115	0.4131	0.4147	0.4162	0.4177
1.4	0.4192	0.4207	0.4222	0.4236	0.4251	0.4265	0.4279	0.4292	0.4306	0.4319
1.5	0.4332	0.4345	0.4357	0.4370	0.4382	0.4394	0.4406	0.4418	0.4429	0.4441
1.6	0.4452	0.4463	0.4474	0.4484	0.4495	0.4505	0.4515	0.4525	0.4535	0.4545
1.7	0.4554	0.4564	0.4573	0.4582	0.4591	0.4599	0.4608	0.4616	0.4625	0.4633
1.8	0.4641	0.4649	0.4656	0.4664	0.4671	0.4678	0.4686	0.4693	0.4699	0.4706
1.9	0.4713	0.4719	0.4726	0.4732	0.4738	0.4744	0.4750	0.4756	0.4761	0.4767
2.0	0.4772	0.4778	0.4783	0.4788	0.4793	0.4798	0.4803	0.4808	0.4812	0.4817
2.1	0.4821	0.4826	0.4830	0.4834	0.4838	0.4842	0.4846	0.4850	0.4854	0.4857
2.2	0.4861	0.4864	0.4868	0.4871	0.4875	0.4878	0.4881	0.4884	0.4887	0.4890
2.3	0.4893	0.4896	0.4898	0.4901	0.4904	0.4906	0.4909	0.4911	0.4913	0.4916
2.4	0.4918	0.4920	0.4922	0.4925	0.4927	0.4929	0.4931	0.4932	0.4934	0.4936
2.5	0.4938	0.4940	0.4941	0.4943	0.4945	0.4946	0.4948	0.4949	0.4951	0.4952
2.6	0.4953	0.4955	0.4956	0.4957	0.4959	0.4960	0.4961	0.4962	0.4963	0.4964
2.7	0.4965	0.4966	0.4967	0.4968	0.4969	0.4970	0.4971	0.4972	0.4973	0.4974
2.8	0.4974	0.4975	0.4976	0.4977	0.4977	0.4978	0.4979	0.4979	0.4980	0.4981
2.9	0.4981	0.4982	0.4982	0.4983	0.4984	0.4984	0.4985	0.4985	0.4986	0.4986
3.0	0.4987	0.4987	0.4987	0.4988	0.4988	0.4989	0.4989	0.4989	0.4990	0.4990

Fourth Edition
A COURSE IN
BUSINESS STATISTICS

David F. Groebner
Boise State University

Patrick W. Shannon
Boise State University

Phillip C. Fry
Boise State University

Kent D. Smith
California Polytechnic University at San Luis Obispo

PEARSON
Prentice Hall

Prentice Hall, Upper Saddle River, New Jersey 07458

Library of Congress Cataloging-in-Publication Data

A course in business statistics / Patrick W. Shannon ... [et al.].—4th ed.
    p. cm.
Includes bibliographical references and index.
ISBN 0-13-153687-7 (alk. paper)
    1. Commercial statistics. I. Title: Business statistics. II. Shannon, Patrick W.

HF1017 .C66 2004
519.5—dc22

                                                                2004042351

AVP/Executive Editor: Mark Pfaltzgraff
Senior Sponsoring Editor: Alana Bradley
Editorial Director: Jeff Shelstad
AVP/Executive Marketing Manager: Debbie Clare
Senior Media Manager: Nancy Welcher
Senior Editorial Assistant: Jane Avery
Managing Editor (Production): Cynthia Regan
Production Editor: Carol Samet
Marketing Assistant: Joanna Sabella
Permissions Supervisor: Charles Morris
Manufacturing Buyer: Arnold Vila
Design Manager: Maria Lange
Designer: Blair Brown
Interior Design: Blair Brown
Cover Design: Kim Nickisher
Multimedia Specialist: Cybele Pruksa
Director, Image Resource Center: Melinda Reo
Manager, Rights and Permissions: Zina Arabia
Manager, Visual Research: Beth Brenzel
Manager, Cover Visual Research & Permissions: Karen Sanatar
Manager, Multimedia Production: Richard Bretan
Composition/Full Service Project Management: GGS Book Services, Atlantic Highlands
Printer/Binder: Courier–Kendallville
Typeface: 10/12 Minion

Credits and acknowledgments borrowed from other sources and reproduced, with permission, in this textbook appear on appropriate page within text.

Microsoft® and Windows® are registered trademarks of the Microsoft Corporation in the U.S.A. and other countries. Screen shots and icons reprinted with permission from the Microsoft Corporation. This book is not sponsored or endorsed by or affiliated with the Microsoft Corporation.

Pearson Education LTD.   Pearson Education Australia PTY, Limited
Pearson Education Singapore, Pte. Ltd   Pearson Education North Asia Ltd
Pearson Education, Canada, Ltd   Pearson Educación de Mexico, S.A. de C.V.
Pearson Education–Japan   Pearson Education Malaysia, Pte. Ltd

10 9 8 7 6 5 4 3 2 1
ISBN 0-13-153687-7

To Jane and my family, who survived the process one more time.

David F. Groebner

To Kathy, my wife and best friend; to our children, Jackie and Jason; and to my parents, John and Ruth Shannon.

Patrick W. Shannon

To my wonderful family: Susan, Alex, Allie, Candace, and Courtney.

Phillip C. Fry

To Dottie, my loving wife, who dances much better than I write.

Kent D. Smith

ABOUT THE AUTHORS

David F. Groebner is a Professor of Production Management in the College of Business and Economics at Boise State University. He has bachelor's and master's degrees in Engineering and a Ph.D. in Business Administration. After working as an engineer, he has taught statistics and related subjects for 27 years. In addition to writing textbooks and academic papers, he has worked extensively with both small and large organizations, including Hewlett-Packard, Boise Cascade, Albertson's, and Ore-Ida. He has worked with numerous government agencies, including Boise City and the U.S. Air Force.

Patrick W. Shannon, Ph.D. is Professor of Production and Operations Management in the College of Business and Economics at Boise State University. He teaches graduate and undergraduate courses in business statistics, quality management, and production and operations management. In addition, Dr. Shannon has lectured and consulted in the statistical analysis and quality management areas for over 20 years. Listed among his consulting clients are Boise Cascade Corporation, Hewlett-Packard; PowerBar, Inc.; Potlatch Corporation; Woodgrain Millwork, Inc.; J.R. Simplot Company; Zilog Corporation; and numerous other public- and private-sector organizations. Professor Shannon has co-authored several university-level textbooks and has published numerous articles in such journals as *Business Horizons, Interfaces, Journal of Simulation, Journal of Production and Inventory Control, Quality Progress,* and *Journal of Marketing Research.* He obtained B.S. and M.S. degrees from the University of Montana and a Ph.D. in Statistics and Quantitative Methods from the University of Oregon.

 **Phillip C. Fry** is a Professor in the College of Business and Economics at Boise State University, where he has taught since 1988. Phil received his B.A. and M.B.A degrees from the University of Arkansas, and his M.S. and Ph.D. degrees from Louisiana State University. His teaching and research interests are in the areas of business statistics, production management, and quantitative business modeling. In addition to his academic responsibilities, Phil has consulted with and provided training to small and large organizations, including Boise Cascade Corporation; Hewlett-Packard Corporation; The J.R. Simplot Company; United Water of Idaho; Woodgrain Millwork, Inc.; Boise City; and Micron Electronics.

Phil spends most of his free time with his wife Susan and his four children, Phillip Alexander, Alejandra Johanna, and twins, Courtney Rene and Candace Marie.

 **Kent D. Smith** received a Ph.D. in Applied Statistics from the University of California, Riverside in 1981. He holds a Master of Science degree in Statistics from the University of California, Riverside and a Master of Science degree in Systems Analysis from the Air Force Institute of Technology. His Bachelor of Arts degree in Mathematics was obtained from the University of Utah. Dr. Smith has served as a University Statistical Consultant at the University of California, Riverside and at California Polytechnic State University, San Luis Obispo. While at the University of California, he served as a consultant for the Biometrical Services Unit of the Biometrical Project at the University of California, Riverside. His private consulting has ranged from serving as an expert witness in legal cases, survey sampling for corporations and private researchers, medical and orthodontic research, and assisting graduate students with analysis required for master and doctoral degrees in various disciplines.

Dr. Smith began teaching as a part-time lecturer at the California State University, San Bernardino. While completing his doctoral dissertation, he served as a lecturer at the University of California, Riverside. Currently, he is a Professor of Statistics at the California Polytechnic State University, San Luis Obispo, one of the minority of universities that offer an undergraduate degree in statistics. The subjects he teaches include upper-division courses in regression, analysis of variance, nonparametrics, linear models, and probability and mathematical statistics, as well as a full array of service courses.

BRIEF CONTENTS

CONTENTS

1-3 SPECIAL REVIEW SECTION 121

4 USING PROBABILITY AND PROBABILITY DISTRIBUTIONS 127

PREFACE

In today's workplace, graduating students can have an immediate competitive edge over existing employees by applying statistical analysis skills to real-world decision-making problems.

Our intent in writing the fourth edition of *A Course in Business Statistics* was to build on the strengths of past editions (captivating writing style; extensive use of real-world business applications; decision-making focus emphasizing the interpretation of data; and thorough computer integration of both Microsoft Excel and Minitab) and to take the text to a new level of excellence with *new* built-in study tools aimed at helping students develop the statistical skills necessary to meet the needs of business. Throughout the text the discussion of statistical techniques is reinforced with practical business applications to help students see the relevance of statistics to their daily lives.

All the authors share a passion for the subject as well as a devotion to teaching, and have significant consulting experience in applying the statistical tools in business and industry settings. Based on reviewer and student feedback, we have made substantive changes to this revision to further enhance an understanding of fundamental statistical concepts and techniques. Here are some of the highlights.

KEY CONTENT CHANGES

- Increased emphasis on using box plots for descriptive analyses and to check distribution assumptions
- Expanded emphasis on the assumptions behind the statistical tests
- Enhanced focus on the importance of using random sampling in the estimation and hypothesis testing sections
- New section on weighted means
- Special section on expected values and variances for the sum of two discrete random variables
- New discussion on covariance
- Introduction to the hypergeometric distribution
- New section on hypothesis testing for μ when σ is known
- Revised approach using the *t*-distribution for estimation and hypothesis testing when σ is unknown
- Integration of Minitab 14.0 including call-out boxes that provide step-by-step Minitab commands
- Special review sections following the descriptive and inferential sections of the text, containing flow diagrams that help the students select appropriate statistical tools

NEW FEATURES

● NEW—SUMMARY BOXES

Throughout each chapter major techniques are summarized in easy-to-find boxes to clearly reinforce fundamental concepts and techniques. The methods for employing the statistical techniques are highlighted in an easy to follow step-by-step format.

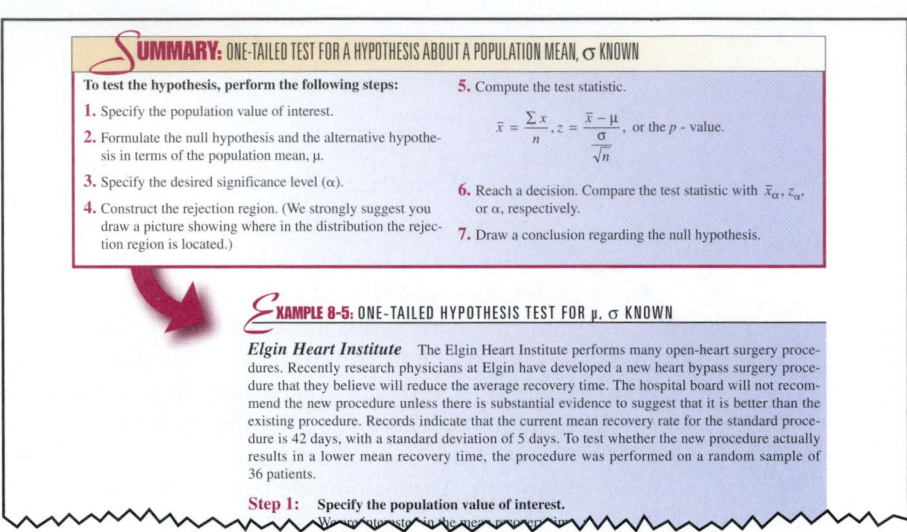

● NEW— STEP-BY-STEP EXAMPLES

New examples added throughout the text provide the step-by-step details to enable students to follow solution techniques easily and then to solve other problems. These specially marked examples are provided in addition to the vast array of business applications that were so widely praised in past editions.

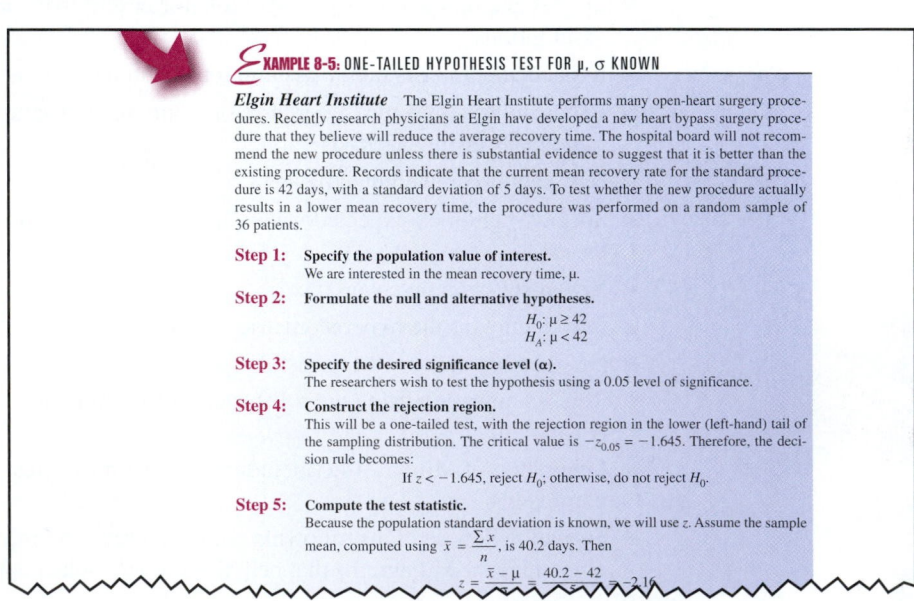

● NEW— EXERCISE SETS

The new edition includes a better balance of easy-to-advanced problems with more computational exercises and easier application exercises. The exercises at the end of each section and chapter involve realistic decision-making situations requiring the application of the statistical concepts introduced in the chapter. In addition to expanding the range of exercises, the exercises have been organized into the following three categories for ease of use and assignment purposes:

■ Skill Development   ■ Business Applications   ■ Advanced Business Applications

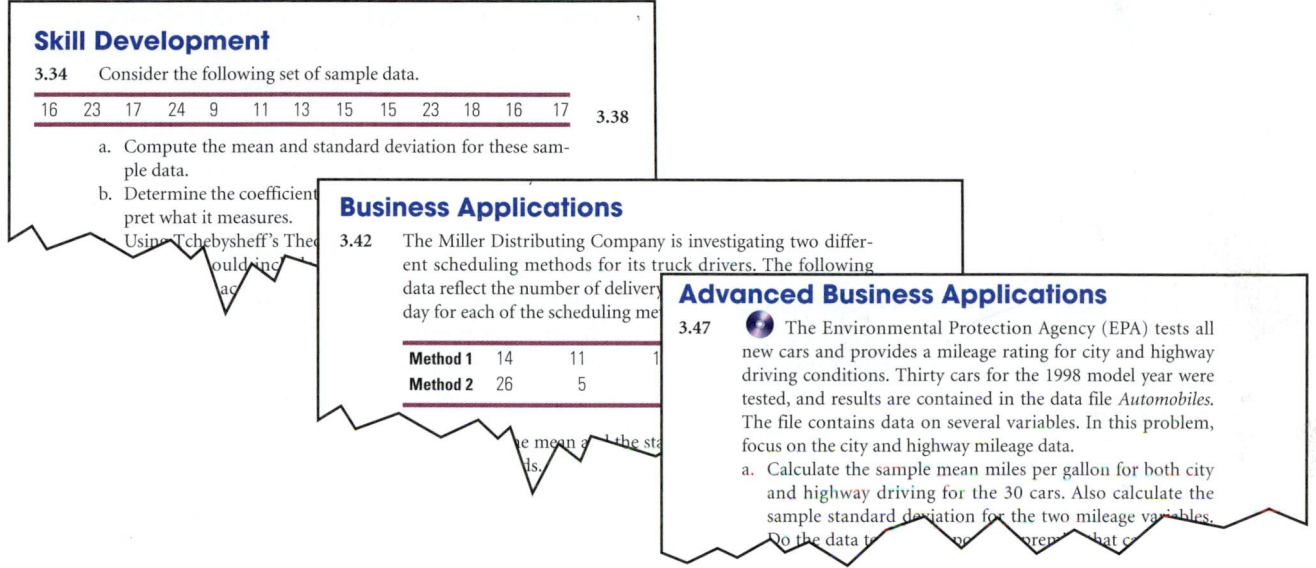

Skill Development

3.34   Consider the following set of sample data.

| 16 | 23 | 17 | 24 | 9 | 11 | 13 | 15 | 15 | 23 | 18 | 16 | 17 |

a. Compute the mean and standard deviation for these sample data.
b. Determine the coefficient ...
    pret what it measures.
    Using Tchebysheff's Theo...

3.38

Business Applications

3.42   The Miller Distributing Company is investigating two different scheduling methods for its truck drivers. The following data reflect the number of delivery ... day for each of the scheduling me...

| Method 1 | 14 | 11 | 1 |
| Method 2 | 26 | 5 | |

e mean a... the st...
ds.

Advanced Business Applications

3.47   The Environmental Protection Agency (EPA) tests all new cars and provides a mileage rating for city and highway driving conditions. Thirty cars for the 1998 model year were tested, and results are contained in the data file *Automobiles*. The file contains data on several variables. In this problem, focus on the city and highway mileage data.
a. Calculate the sample mean miles per gallon for both city and highway driving for the 30 cars. Also calculate the sample standard deviation for the two mileage variables. Do the data t...

In addition to many exercises that can be worked manually, the text contains an extensive number of exercises that have computer data files and can be worked using Excel, Minitab, or other statistical software.

● NEW— SPECIAL REVIEW SECTIONS

Strategically placed at key points in the text, these Special Review Sections reinforce concepts learned in the immediately preceding chapters. Students are provided with flow diagrams and explanations that emphasize the principles, relationships, and properties of the techniques and procedures. These sections conclude with a set of comprehensive exercises that give students the opportunity to practice choosing the correct analytical technique for problem solving from diverse sections of the text.

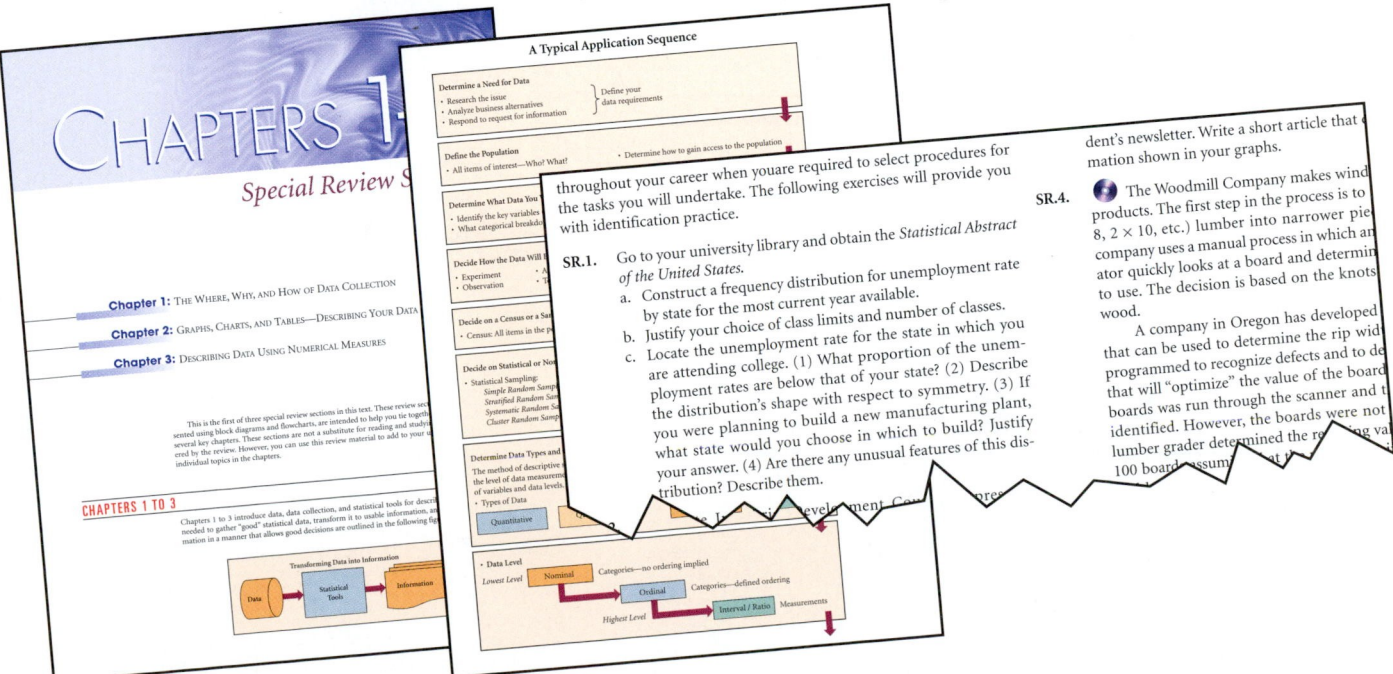

Special Review for Chapters 1-3: This section provides a summary and review of the key issues and statistical techniques associated with data, data collection and sampling, graphical descriptive analysis, and numerical descriptive analysis. These key topics are reviewed using block diagrams and flowcharts. Integrative questions and exercises are included that ask the student to demonstrate his or her comprehension of the topics covered in Chapters 1-3.

Special Review for Chapters 7-11: This section summarizes the key concepts associated with estimation and hypothesis testing. Through a series of color-coded flow diagrams, the students are provided with a template for determining which inferential technique to apply depending on the situation at hand. The summary covers one-, two-, and multiple-population situations. Integrative exercises and project assignments are included to provide the students with the opportunity to demonstrate their comprehension of estimation and hypothesis testing.

● NEW— ONLINE HOMEWORK AND ASSESSMENT SYSTEM (PH GradeAssist)

Prentice Hall is pleased to offer PH GradeAssist in our OneKey courses. PH GradeAssist allows students to go online and work a nearly unlimited number of practice problems tied to the text. Many of the problems are algorithmically generated so each student receives a slightly different problem with a different answer. Students either submit answers online for automatic grading and immediate feedback, or print out problems and submit complete solutions to their instructor. Students prefer the PH GradeAssist system because it provides immediate, individualized performance feedback and the opportunity to generate unlimited practice so they can "Ace" the course.

For instructors, this online homework system allows professors to create, assign, and grade homework assignments quickly and easily. They can select problems from the text, create problems themselves, or use algorithmic variations of both. Plus, by registering and using the site, professors can post assignments, receive grades electronically from students' completed quizzes, and build detailed information regarding overall class performance on assignments. PHGradeAssist is easy to use and helps faculty manage their classes. Contact your local Prentice Hall representative for more details or a presentation.

Picking questions for an assignment is easy.

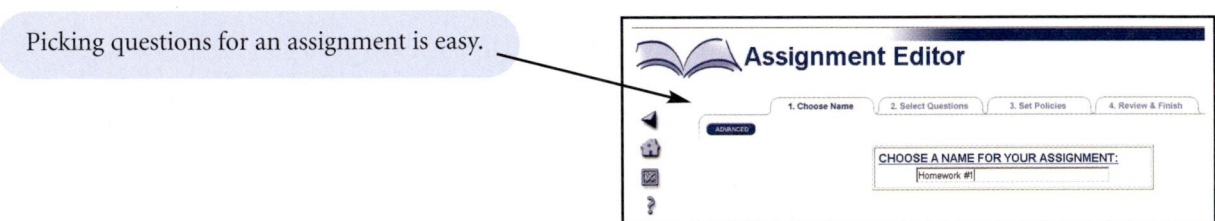

Here's a typical question.

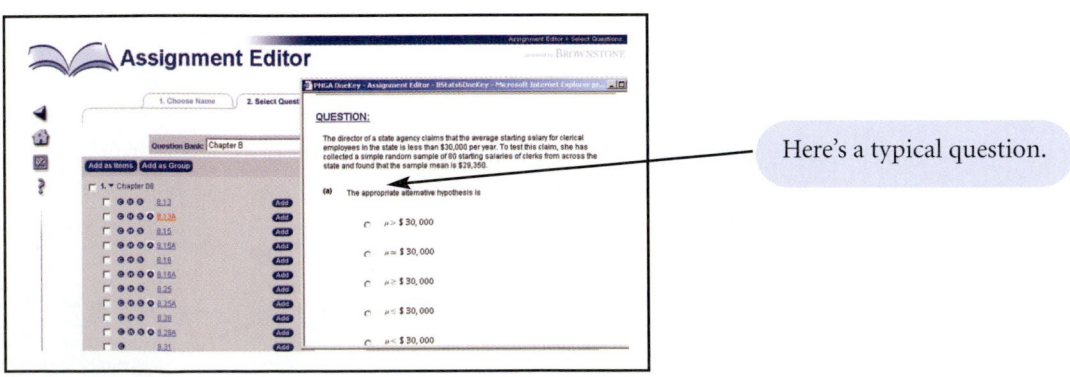

OneKey with PH GradeAssist: OneKey offers the best online teaching and learning resources all in one place. These digital resources are conveniently organized to help save time and help students reinforce and apply what they've learned in class. Prentice Hall's OneKey platform is all you need for anytime online access to our new supplemental course materials. It is available in CourseCompass, Blackboard, and WebCT. The resources are broken down into two categories.

Student Learning Resources folder contains links to a variety of resources for the course:

❏ **PH GradeAssist**–This powerful online homework resource allows students to get additional practice and feedback using preloaded text exercises with algorithmic variables and/or test item file content.

❏ **Excel, Minitab, SPSS, SAS, ASCII data files**–Included for the examples, cases, and exercises in the text.

❏ **PHStat download**–PHStat2 is a statistical add-in for Microsoft Excel. PHStat includes a wide range of topics, and easy to use dialog boxes. Students can now easily perform statistical analysis on many procedures not included in standard Microsoft Excel.

❏ **PHStat Site**–Upgrades, tech support and system requirement information, and a Frequently Asked Questions page are available at www.prenhall.com/phstat to enrich your experience with PHStat2.

❏ **Additional chapters & topics**–Four complete additional chapters are included covering: Decision Analysis, Time-Series and Forecasting, Nonparametric Statistics, and Statistical Quality Control. In addition, special topics reinforce additional statistical concepts. These include: Chapter 11, Experimental Design and Tukey's Method of Multiple Comparison; Chapter 13, Backward Elimination Regression; and Chapter 15, Regression-Based Forecasting Models. This material is also available on the Student CD-ROM.

❏ **Excel Simulations**–Excel Simulations illustrate key statistical topics and allow students to do "what if" scenarios.

❏ **Link to our Companion Website**–Valuable resources include an online study guide, useful statistical tables at our websites.

Chapter Specific folders contain the following resources:

❏ **PowerPoint Lecture Notes**–These PowerPoint Lecture Notes allow students to review and reinforce key points in each chapter. These same PowerPoints can be found in Faculty Resources.

❏ **Guide to Using Excel Tutorial**–These Excel Tutorials show the exact steps needed to replicate all of the computer examples in each chapter.

❏ **Guide to Using Minitab 14.0 Tutorial**–These Minitab Tutorials show the exact steps needed to replicate all of the computer examples in the chapter.

❏ **Self Study Quizzes**–Multiple Choice, True or False, and Essay Self-Study Quizzes are available to students to use for self-practice. Students can assess their understanding, receive immediate feedback, then email the results to their faculty member.

Instructors can access all of our valuable instructor support materials, in addition to the text's images (figures, tables and screen captures), in OneKey.

Setting rules and policies is quick and easy.

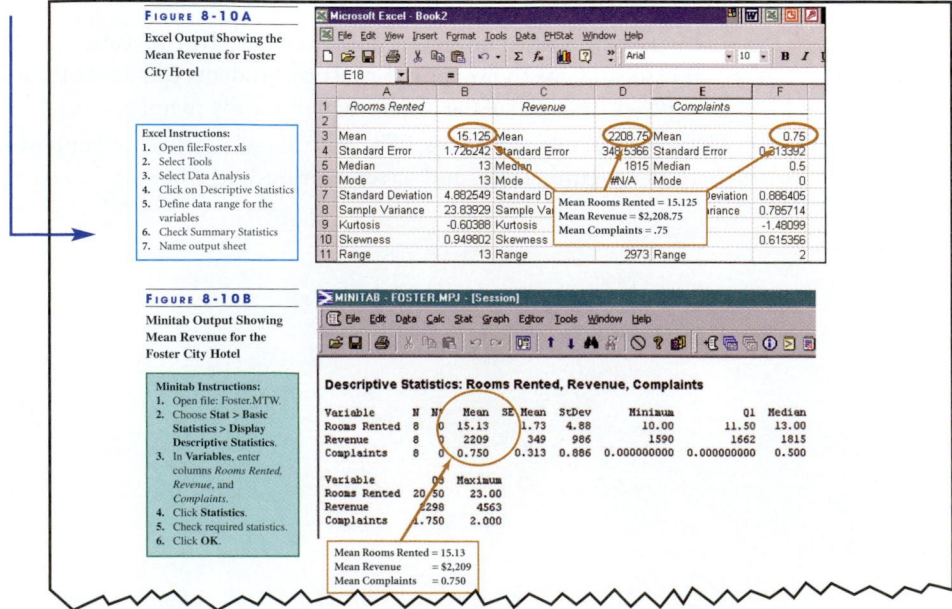

REAL-WORLD BUSINESS APPLICATIONS

Not only do the chapters focus on real companies, actual applications, and rich data sets, but increased effort has been placed on providing the student with an understanding of the role business statistics plays in decision making. Every effort has been made to communicate ideas using a nontechnical, nonthreatening, conversational writing style to stimulate student interest and involvement. This text is designed to help instructors create a climate in which students are motivated to learn statistical techniques in an applied context.

COMPUTER INTEGRATION

Unlike some business statistics texts that provide only end-of-chapter computer instructions, this text seamlessly integrates computer applications with the text examples, always focusing on interpreting the output. The goal is for the students to appreciate the role of spreadsheets and statistical software as business statistics tools.

Microsoft Excel and Minitab are extensively featured throughout the textbook. Chapter examples, exercises, and case studies are based on real industry data or data motivated by real-world examples. This approach helps students gain a greater understanding of what statistical tools to use, when and how to apply them, and how to interpret the results of their analyses to decision making. Special call-outs, positioned next to most of the text examples and output screen shots highlight key instructions and/or key points.

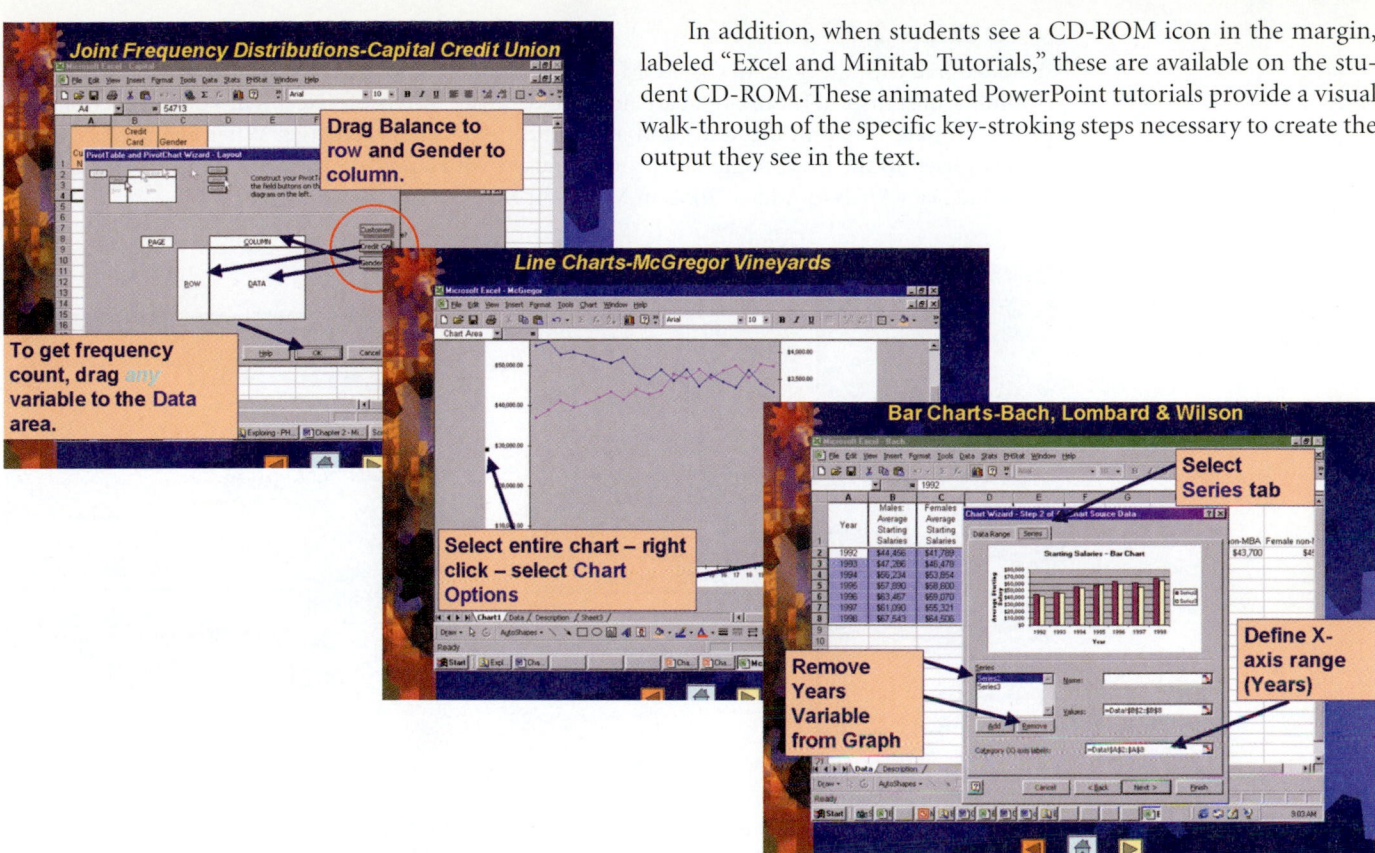

In addition, when students see a CD-ROM icon in the margin, labeled "Excel and Minitab Tutorials," these are available on the student CD-ROM. These animated PowerPoint tutorials provide a visual walk-through of the specific key-stroking steps necessary to create the output they see in the text.

CHAPTER CASES

Most chapters contain short cases that are designed to provide the students with an opportunity to apply the statistical tools to an unstructured situation. These cases challenge the student to define the problem, determine the appropriate statistical tools to use, apply those tools, and write a summary report.

STUDENT CD-ROM

This CD-ROM contains all the resources and tools your students need to succeed in the course:

❏ *Lecture PowerPoints*

Allow students to review and reinforce key points.

Excel and Minitab Tutorial

❏ *Excel and Minitab 14.0 Tutorials*

Customized PowerPoint tutorials for both Minitab and Excel, illustrated above, which use data sets from text examples, are included on the CD-ROM. Students who need additional instruction in Excel or Minitab can access the menu-driven tutorial, which will show the exact steps needed to replicate all computer examples in the text.

❏ *Data Files*

An extensive number of data files for examples, cases, and exercises in the text are included on the CD-ROM in Excel, Minitab, SPSS, SAS, and ASCII formats. The text references these data files with a CD-ROM icon.

Optional CD-ROM Topic

❏ *CD-ROM*

Four complete chapters are included on the CD-ROM. These cover Decision Analysis, Time-Series and Forecasting, Nonparametric Statistics, and Statistical Quality Control. In addition, special CD-ROM topics reinforce additional statistical concepts. Examples of topics include: Chapter 11, Experimental Design and Tukey's Method of Multiple Comparison; Chapter 13, Backward Elimination Regression; and Chapter 15, Regression-Based Forecasting Models.

Excel Simulation

❏ *Excel Simulations*

Several interactive simulations illustrate key statistical topics and allow students to do "what-if" scenarios.

❏ *PHStat2*

Included free with the Student CD-ROM is a specially developed Excel add-in package that contains a number of statistical features that are not included with Microsoft Excel. The added functions and procedures are useful in the study and application of business statistics. When installed, PHStat2 attaches itself to the Excel menu bar, providing users with a pull-down menu of topics that supplement the Data Analysis Add-in Tools in Microsoft Excel.

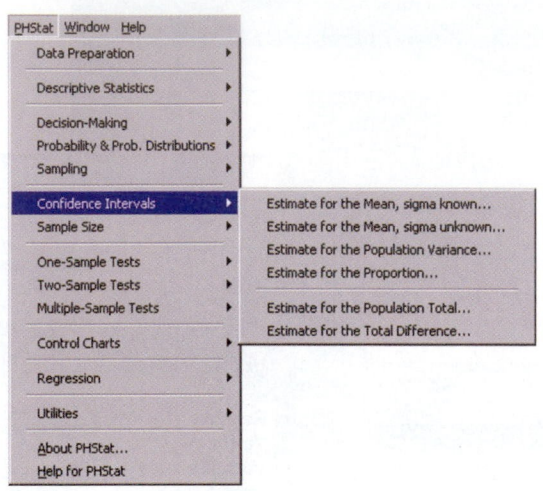
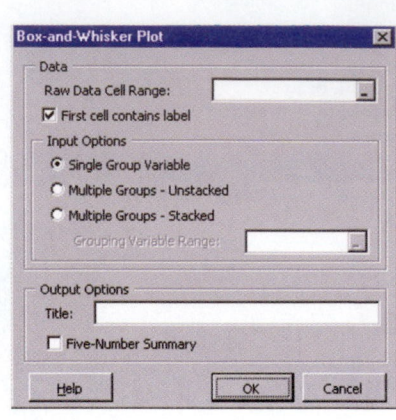

PHStat2 uses a set of simple and consistent dialog boxes that allow students to specify values and options for almost 50 tools included in the software. PHStat2 produces Excel worksheets organized into areas for the input data, intermediate calculations, and the results of the analysis. Unlike some competitors' add-ins, most of these worksheets contain live formulas that allow students to engage immediately in further "what-if" explorations of the data. (Where applicable, these worksheets contain special cell tints that distinguish the cells that contain user-modifiable input values from the cells containing the results, making "what-if" analysis even easier.) Completing the package is an excellent **online help system**.

ANCILLARIES

INSTRUCTOR'S SOLUTIONS MANUAL

The Instructor's Solutions Manual contains the worked-out solutions to all the problems and cases in the text. The manual can also be downloaded from Prentice Hall's Web site at *http://www.prenhall.com/groebner.*

TEST ITEM FILE

The Test Item File, created by Patrick W. Shannon, contains a variety of true/false, multiple choice, and short answer questions for each chapter. The Test Item File can also be downloaded from Prentice Hall's Web site at *http://www.prenhall.com/groebner.*

NEW TESTGEN SOFTWARE

The print Test Item File is designed for use with the TestGen test generating software. This computerized package allows instructors to custom design, save, and generate classroom tests. The test program permits instructors to edit, add, or delete questions from the test banks; edit existing graphics and create new graphics; analyze test results; and organize a database of tests and student results. This new software allows for greater flexibility and ease of use. It provides many options for organizing and displaying tests, along with a search and sort feature.

POWERPOINT PRESENTATION

An extensive set of PowerPoint Presentations, created by Dirk Yandell of the University of San Diego, is available for each chapter. These slides can also be downloaded from Prentice Hall's Web site at *http://www.prenhall.com/groebner.*

INSTRUCTOR'S RESOURCE CD-ROM

The Instructor's Resource CD-ROM provides the electronic files for the entire Instructor's Solutions Manual (in MS Word), PowerPoint presentations (in PowerPoint), Test Item File (in MS Word), and the computerized test bank (TestGen).

STUDENT SOLUTIONS MANUAL

The Student Solutions Manual contains worked-out solutions to all the odd-numbered problems in the text. More than just showing the answer, the Solutions Manual shows the detailed process that students should use to work each problem. The manual also provides interpretation of the answers and serves as a valuable learning tool for the student.

THE COMPANION WEB SITE

The Companion Web site features valuable resources for:

❏ *Online Study Guide*

Extensive quizzes provide a great review of text material with an assortment of multiple choice, true/false, and essay questions.

❏ *Interactive Excel Tutorials*

Dynamic video tutorials animate step-by-step demonstrations on how to use Excel for more than 20 statistical techniques.

❏ *In the News Articles*

Current events articles are added throughout the year. Each article is summarized by a team of experts and is fully supported by exercises, activities, and instructor material.

❏ *Internet Exercises*

Comprehensive exercises and activities expose students to the most current and relevant information on the Internet.

❏ *Instructor Resources*

Downloadable instructor supplements are available on the Web site.

ACKNOWLEDGMENTS

Publishing a textbook is a team effort and involves many people. At the risk of overlooking someone, we take this space to express our appreciation to many of the key contributors to our sixth edition for their helpful suggestions which paved the way for the revision of our brief fourth edition text. Many faculty members from across the country have taken time from their busy schedules to provide valuable input and suggestions for improvement. We offer thanks to:

Suad Alwan
Chicago State University
Mary E. Camp
Indiana University
Cali M. Davis
University of Alabama
John Dutton
North Carolina State University
James Flynn
Cleveland State University
Kelly Haverstick
Brandeis University
John Janke
College of the Cariboo
Chun Jin
Central Connecticut State University
John Lawrence
California State University–Fullerton
Walt McCoy
University of Nebraska—Omaha
Thomas McCullough
University of California—Berkeley

Elaine McGivern
Duquesne University
Dick Morris
Winthrop University
John Nash
University of Ottawa
Pornpilai Ongardanunkul
Boston College
Ranjna Patel
Bethune Cookman College
Robert Patterson
Penn State—Erie
Robert Potter
University of Central Florida
Harold F. Rahmlow
St. Joseph's University
Farhad Raiszadeh
University of Tennessee—Chattanooga
Walter Rom
Cleveland State University
Mary Anne Rothermel
University of Akron

Farhad Saboori
Albright College
William Seaver
University of Tennessee–Knoxville
Gary Smith
Florida State University
David Stewart
Winston-Salem State University
Debra K. Stiver
University of Nevada–Reno
Joaquin Tadeo
University of Texas at El Paso

Mari Yetimyan
San Jose State University
W. F. Younkin
University of Miami
Oliver Yu
San Jose State University
Jiankang Zhang
Carleton University
George Zheng
Western Washington
Zhiwei Zhu
University of Louisiana at Lafayette

A special thanks goes to Frank Purcell at Twin Prime Editorial, who conscientiously read every page of this manuscript and provided valuable suggestions for improving this book in many ways. Thanks also to David Stephan for his expert work in developing the PHStat add-in for Excel.

We want to thank Dirk Yandell, at the University of San Diego, for preparing the best PowerPoint slides we have ever seen. They make teaching this course much easier and students will find them very helpful for their own review.

Accuracy checking a book of this scope is tremendously important, and we especially want to thank those who did a very careful job of reading the manuscript and supplements and carefully screening them for errors. Professor Jackie McLellan at Frostberg State University in Maryland, did a terrific job of accuracy checking the final pages, the instructor's solutions manual, and student solutions manual. Geoff Willis, at the University of Central Oklahoma checked the test questions, which were written by the authors. Jim Zimmer, of Chattanooga State Technical Community College wrote the Interactive Study Guide, also found on the Companion Website.

The team of professionals at Prentice Hall is the finest publishing group with whom we have had the pleasure of working. Carol Samet oversaw the production end of the publishing process and kept us on schedule; Blair Brown created the handsome book design; Nancy Welcher coordinated the CD-ROM materials; Alana Bradley and Jane Avery supervised the preparation of supplements; and Debbie Clare handled the very important marketing component with great creativity and enthusiasm.

—David F. Groebner
—Patrick W. Shannon
—Phillip C. Fry
—Kent D. Smith

CHAPTER 1

The Where, Why, and How of Data Collection

CHAPTER OUTCOMES

After studying the material in Chapter 1, you should:

- Know the key data collection methods.
- Know the difference between a population and a sample.
- Understand how to categorize data by type and level of measurement.
- Understand the similarities and differences between different sampling methods.

WHY YOU NEED TO KNOW

This is a good time to be entering the business world. Never before have the opportunities been so numerous. Global markets have opened up literally a world of possibilities, and job functions in businesses are changing to meet the dynamic business environment. Organizations are scrambling to find people who have the knowledge, skills, and abilities to meet the ever increasing competitive challenges faced by businesses. Although businesses have always looked to colleges and universities to help provide them with the talent they need, the trend in this direction is stronger than ever. However, these businesses are not just seeking educated people. They are seeking individuals who have the ability to understand and apply key decision-making tools to the complexities of the business environment.

Many organizations have access to massive amounts of data, but decision makers have a difficult time using these data effectively. **Business statistics** offers students the necessary tools to effectively convert sets of data into usable information. This is why business statistics is a required course at any accredited business school.

Business statistics offers some very important tools for data conversion. You will have the opportunity to learn about these statistical tools from your professor and from this text. This text focuses on the practical application of statistics: We do not develop the statistical theory you could find in a mathematical statistics course. Will you need to use mathematics in this course? Yes, but it will be mainly basic concepts derived from college algebra.

Statistics does have its own terminology. You will need to learn various terms that have special statistical meaning. You will also learn certain do's and don'ts related to statistics. But most importantly, you will learn specific methods to effectively convert data into information. In all cases, the best way to learn is by doing. The text contains numerous problems and exercises that reinforce the concepts and methods in the chapters. Don't try to memorize the concepts; rather, go to the next level of learning, called *understanding*. Once you understand the underlying concepts, you will be able to *think statistically*.

We have taught business statistics for many years, and we are well aware that you may be approaching this course with a certain degree of apprehension. That's certainly understandable. Anything that is new is uncomfortable at first. However, we promise that once you are under way in this course, you will begin to see that business statistics is actually a logical subject that is applicable to all business areas. When you can think statistically, you will have truly set yourself apart from many others in the business world, and this will give you a competitive advantage for the rest of your life.

1-1 WHAT IS BUSINESS STATISTICS?

Every day, your local newspaper contains stories that report descriptors such as stock prices, crime rates, and government agency budgets. Such descriptors can be found in many places. However, these descriptors are just a small part of a discipline that shares the name of statistics. Statistics as a discipline provides a wide variety of methods to assist in data analysis and decision making. Business is one important area of application for these methods. Business statistics is defined as follows:

Business Statistics

A collection of tools and techniques that are used to convert data into meaningful information in a business environment.

DESCRIPTIVE STATISTICS

The tools and techniques that comprise business statistics include those specially designed to *describe data*, such as charts, graphs, and numerical measures. Also included are inferential tools that help decision makers *draw inferences* from a set of data. Inferential tools include estimation and hypothesis testing. A brief discussion of these tools and techniques follows. The examples illustrate data that have been entered into the Microsoft Excel and Minitab software packages.

Baker City Hospital—Because health care companies in the United States are facing increased competition, hospital administrators must become more efficient in managing operations. This demand means they must better understand their customers.

The financial vice president for Baker City Hospital recently collected data for 138 patients. The VP has entered these data into an Excel spreadsheet, as illustrated in Figure 1-1. Each column in the figure corresponds to a different factor for which data were collected. Each row corresponds

FIGURE 1-1

Excel Spreadsheet of Baker
City Hospital Patient Data

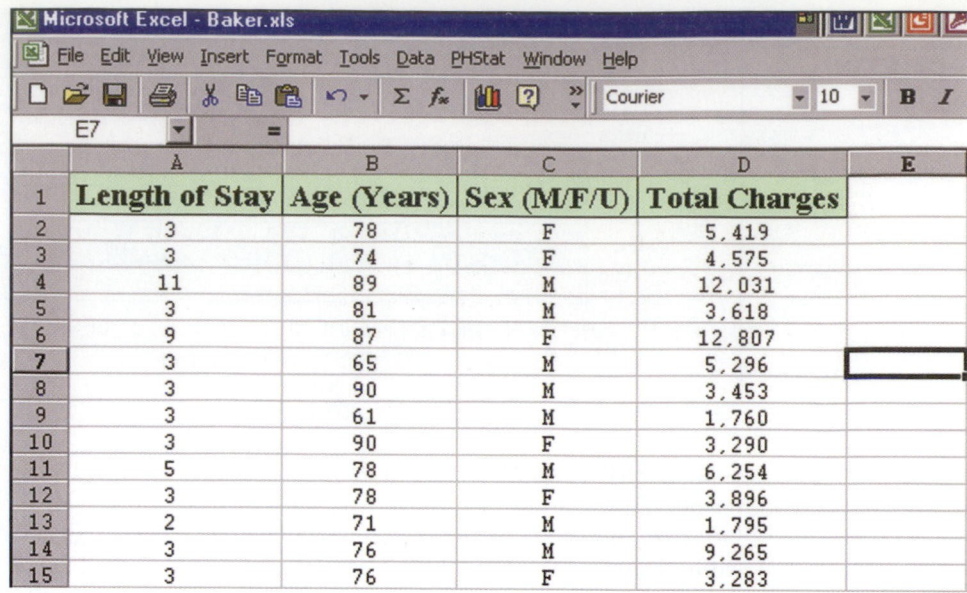

FIGURE 1-1

Excel Spreadsheet of Baker
City Hospital Patient Data

to a different patient. Many statistical tools might help the VP describe these patients' data, including *charts*, *graphs*, and *numerical measures*.

Charts and Graphs

Although we develop an extensive variety of methods to describe data using graphs and charts in Chapter 2, a few examples are offered here to give you an idea of what is possible. Figure 1-2 shows a graph called a *histogram*. This graph gives us some insight into how long patients stay at the Baker City Hospital by visually showing how many patients appear in each length-of-stay category. It describes the shape and spread of the patient length-of-stay distribution. The *bar chart* shown in Figure 1-3 breaks down the patient data showing the percentage of male and female patients. We can tell, looking at this chart, that the mix of patients has a higher number of females.

These are only a few of the graphical techniques that the Baker City Hospital VP might use to help describe her patient population. In Chapter 2 you will learn about these techniques.

FIGURE 1-2

Histogram

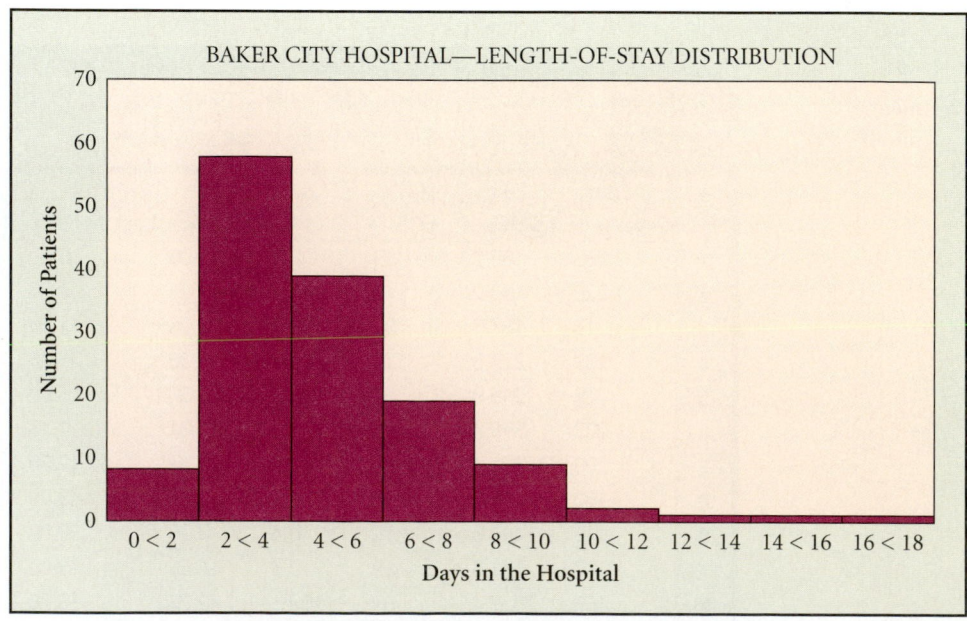

FIGURE 1-3

Bar Chart of Baker City
Hospital

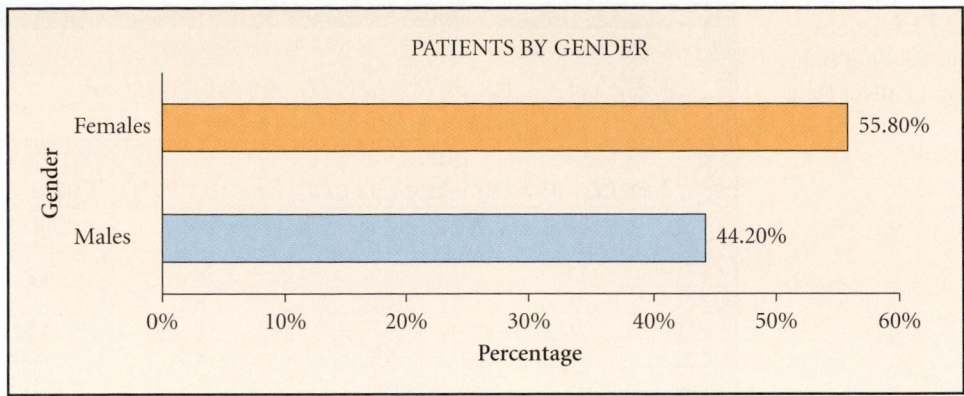

Crown Investments—During the 1990s and early 2000s, many major changes occurred in the financial services industry. Numerous banks merged. Money flowed into the stock market at rates far surpassing anything the U.S. economy had previously witnessed. The international financial world fluctuated greatly. All these developments have spurred the need for more financial analysts who can critically evaluate financial data and explain them to customers.

At Crown Investments, a senior analyst is preparing to present data to upper management on the 100 fastest growing companies on the Hong Kong Stock Exchange. Figure 1-4 shows a Minitab worksheet containing a subset of the data. The columns correspond to the different items of interest (growth percentage, sales, and so on). The data for each company are in a single row.

In addition to preparing appropriate graphs, the analyst will compute important numerical measures. One of the most basic and most useful measures in business statistics is one with which you are already familiar: the **arithmetic mean** or **average**.

Average

The sum of all the values divided by the number of values. In equation form:

where:

$$\text{Average} = \frac{\sum_{i=1}^{N} x_i}{N} = \frac{\text{sum of all data values}}{\text{number of data values}}$$

$N = $ Number of data values

$x_i = i$th data value

FIGURE 1-4

Crown Investment
Example—Minitab
Worksheet

MINITAB - FAST100.MPJ - [Fast100.MTW ***]

File   Edit   Data   Calc   Stat   Graph   Editor   Tools   Window   Help

	C5	C6	C7	C8	C9	C10	C11	C12
	Growth %	Sales	EPS	Profits	Stk-Price	Last Yr Price	P/E ratio	Stk Market
1	256	185.3	-99	6.8	18.00	8.50	17	1
2	228	183.2	243	43.2	42.25	12.50	31	1
3	215	187.5	-99	26.5	21.25	11.13	17	1
4	209	229.8	129	35.4	27.38	26.25	16	1
5	209	249.9	97	8.9	23.38	15.00	53	2
6	203	399.7	18	4.2	2.31	1.13	17	1
7	200	731.4	95	77.7	11.63	10.00	24	2
8	180	93.0	116	8.6	6.63	-99.00	21	2
9	179	440.9	72	8.4	8.25	-99.00	9	1
10	167	131.8	-99	3.7	16.50	-99.00	66	1
11	156	2319.4	-99	102.1	40.25	56.88	4	3

FIGURE 1-5

The Role of Business
Statistics

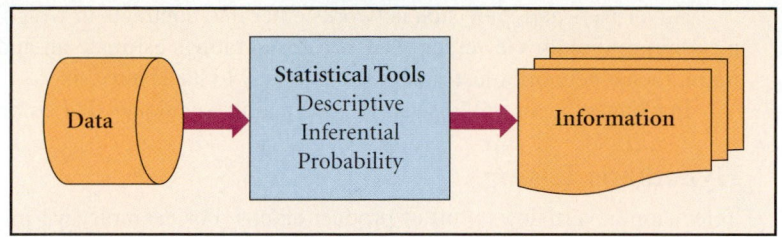

The analyst may be interested in the average profit (that is, the mean of the column labeled *Profits*) for the 100 companies. The total profit calculated for the 100 companies is $3,193.60, but profits are given in millions of dollars, so the total profit amount is actually $3,193,600,000. The average is found by dividing this total by the number of companies:

$$\text{Average} = \frac{\$3,193,600,000}{100} = \$31,936,000, \text{ or } \$31.936 \text{ million dollars}$$

As we will discuss in greater depth in Chapter 3, the average or mean is a measure of the center of the data. In this case, the analyst may use the average profit as an indicator—firms with above-average profits are rated higher than firms with below-average profits.

The graphical and numerical measures illustrated here are only some of the many descriptive tools that will be introduced in Chapters 2 and 3. The key to remember is that the purpose of the descriptive tools is to describe data. Your task will be to select the tool or tools that best accomplish this. As Figure 1-5 reminds you, the role of statistics is to convert data into meaningful information.

INFERENTIAL TOOLS

How do television networks determine which programs people prefer to watch? How does the network that carries the Super Bowl know how many people were watching the game? Advertisers pay for TV ads based on the audience level, so these numbers are important; millions of dollars are at stake. Clearly the networks don't check with everyone in the country. Instead, they use an area of statistics called **statistical inference** to come up with the information.

> ***Statistical Inference Tools***
>
> Tools that allow a decision maker to reach a conclusion about a population of data based on a subset of data from the population.

There are two primary categories of statistical inference tools: *estimation* and *hypothesis testing*. These tools are closely related but serve very different purposes.

Estimation

In situations in which we would like to know about all the data in a large data set but it is impractical to work with all the data, decision makers can use techniques to estimate what the larger data set looks like. The estimates are formed by looking closely at a subset of the larger data set.

TV Ratings—The television networks cannot know for sure how many people watched last year's Super Bowl. They cannot possibly ask everyone what he or she saw that day on television. Instead, the networks rely on organizations that conduct surveys to supply program ratings. For example, the Nielsen Company asks people from only a small number of homes across the country what shows they watched, and then it uses that information to estimate the number of viewers per show for the entire population.

Consider this article, which appeared in newspapers across the country on May 16, 1998:

NEW YORK—Jerry and his three misfit friends ended "Seinfeld" arguing in a prison cell watched by an estimated 76 million people.

Ratings for the comedy's final episode were below the finals for "Cheers" and "M*A*S*H*" and a shade below NBC's predictions.

Advertisers and television networks enter into contracts in which each price per ad is based on a certain minimum viewership. If the Nielsen ratings estimate an audience smaller than this minimum, then a network must refund some money to its advertisers.

In Chapter 7, we will discuss the estimating techniques that companies such as Nielsen use.

Hypothesis Testing

Television advertising is full of product claims. For example, we might hear that "Goodyear tires will last at least 60,000 miles," or that "More doctors recommend Bayer Aspirin than any other brand." Other claims might include statements that "General Electric lightbulbs last longer than any other brand," or that "Customers prefer Burger King over McDonald's." Are these just idle boasts, or are they based on actual data? Probably some of both! However, consumer research organizations such as *Consumer Reports* regularly test these types of claims. For example, in the hamburger case, *Consumer Reports* might select a sample of customers who would be asked to blind taste test Burger King's and McDonald's hamburgers, under the hypothesis that there is no difference in customer preferences between the two restaurants. If the sample data showed a difference in preferences, then the hypothesis of no difference would be rejected. If only a slight difference in preferences were detected, then *Consumer Reports* writers could not reject the hypothesis. Chapters 8 and 9 introduce basic hypothesis-testing techniques that are used to test claims about products and services using information taken from samples.

1-1: EXERCISES

Skill Development

1.1 Describe the difference between a histogram and a bar chart.

1.2 Calculate the average of the total charges listed in Figure 1-1.

1.3 Calculate the averages of the total charges for men and for women in Figure 1-1. What conclusion might you draw concerning the difference in the average charges between the two genders?

1.4 Calculate the average of the ages of the patients listed in Figure 1-1.

1.5 For the data in Figure 1-1, calculate the average total charges for patients older than 75 and younger than 75. What conclusion might you draw about the difference in the average charges between the two age groups?

1.6 Using only the data given in Figure 1-4, construct a bar chart showing the average stock price for each stock market listed in column C12.

1.7 In your own terms, define what is meant by statistical estimation. Provide an example from your own experiences in which estimation is used.

1.8 Define what is meant by hypothesis testing. Provide an example in which you personally have tested a hypothesis (even if you didn't use formal statistical techniques to do so).

1.9 It is important to know when to employ estimation and when to employ hypothesis testing. Explain under what circumstances you would use hypothesis testing, as opposed to an estimation procedure.

Business Applications

1.10 Locate a business periodical, such as *Fortune* or *Forbes*, or a business newspaper, such as *The Wall Street Journal*. Find three examples of the use of a graph to display data. For each graph,
   a. Give the name, date, and page number of the periodical in which the graph appeared.
   b. Describe the main point made by the graph.
   c. Analyze the effectiveness of the graph.

1.11 A group of executives at a local company is considering introducing a new product into a market area. It is important to know the characteristics of the ages of the people in the market area.
   a. If the executives wish to calculate a number that would characterize the "center" of the age data, what statistical technique would you suggest? Explain your answer.
   b. The executives need to know the percentage of people in the market area who are senior citizens. Name the basic category of statistical inference tools they would use to provide this information.
   c. Describe a hypothesis upon which the executives might wish to conduct a test concerning the percentage of senior citizens in the market area.

1.12 An agribusiness company currently uses one brand of commercial fertilizer. However, a new fertilizer is available that the manufacturer says will produce higher-than-average crop yields.
   a. Name the basic category of statistical inference tools they would use to provide this information.
   b. Describe a hypothesis that a manufacturer might use to conduct a test concerning the relative effectiveness of the new fertilizer.

1.13 Locate an example from a business periodical or newspaper in which estimation has been used.
a. What specifically was estimated?
b. What conclusion was reached using the estimation?
c. Describe how the data were extracted and how the data were used to produce the estimation.

d. Keeping in mind the goal of the estimation, discuss whether you believe that the estimation was successful and why.
e. Describe what inferences were drawn as a result of the estimation.

1-2 TOOLS FOR COLLECTING DATA

We have defined business statistics as a set of tools that are used to transform data into information. Before you learn how to use statistical tools, it is important that you become familiar with different types of data collection methods.

DATA COLLECTION METHODS

There are many methods and tools available for collecting data. The following are considered some of the most useful and frequently used data collection methods:

- experiments
- telephone surveys
- mail questionnaires
- direct observation and personal interviews

Experiments

Food Processing—A company often must conduct a specific experiment or set of experiments to get the data managers need to make informed decisions. For example, the J. R. Simplot Company in Idaho is a primary supplier of french fries to companies such as McDonald's. At its Caldwell factory, Simplot has a tech center that, among other things, houses a mini–french fry plant used to conduct experiments on its potato manufacturing process. McDonald's has strict standards on the quality of the french fries it buys. One important attribute is the color of the fries after cooking. They should be "golden brown"—uniformly not too light or too dark.

French fries are made from potatoes that are peeled, sliced into strips, blanched, partially cooked, and then freeze-dried—not a simple process. Because potatoes differ in many ways (such as sugar content and moisture), blanching time, cooking temperature, and other factors vary from batch to batch.

Simplot tech-center employees start their **experiments** by grouping the raw potatoes into batches with similar characteristics. They run some of the potatoes through the line with blanch time and temperature settings set at specific levels defined by an **experimental design**. After measuring one or more output variables for that run, they change the settings and run another batch, again measuring the output variables.

Experiment

Any process that generates data as its outcome.

Experimental Design

A plan for performing an experiment in which the variable of interest is defined. One or more factors are identified to be manipulated or changed so that the impact (or influence) on the variable of interest can be measured or observed.

Figure 1-6 shows a typical data collection form. The output variable (for example, percentage of fries without dark spots) for each combination of potato category, blanch time, and temperature is recorded in the appropriate cell in the table. Chapter 11 introduces the fundamental concepts related to experimental design and analysis.

FIGURE 1-6

Experiment Data Layout

		Potato Category			
Blanch Time	Blanch Temperature	1	2	3	4
10 minutes	100°				
	110°				
	120°				
15 minutes	100°				
	110°				
	120°				
20 minutes	100°				
	110°				
	120°				
25 minutes	100°				
	110°				
	120°				

Telephone Surveys

Public Issues—One common method of obtaining data about people and their opinions is the telephone survey. Chances are that you have been on the receiving end of one. "Hello. My name is Mary Jane and I represent the XYZ organization. I am conducting a survey on. . . ." Political groups use telephone surveys to poll people about candidates and issues.

Telephone surveys are a relatively inexpensive and efficient data collection tool. Of course, some people will refuse to respond to a survey, others are not home when the calls come, and a small percentage of people do not have phones or cannot be reached by phone for one reason or another.

Figure 1-7 shows the major steps in conducting a telephone survey. This example survey was run by a Seattle television station to determine public support for using tax dollars to build a new football stadium for the NFL Seattle Seahawks. The survey was aimed at property-tax payers only.

Because most people will not stay on the line very long, the phone survey must be short—usually 1 to 3 minutes. The questions are generally what are called **closed-end questions**.

Closed-End Questions

Questions that require the respondent to select from a short list of defined choices.

For example, a closed-end question might be, "To which political party do you belong? Republican? Democrat? Or other?" The survey instrument should have a short statement at the beginning explaining the purpose of the survey and reassuring the respondent that his or her responses will remain confidential. The initial section of the survey should contain questions relating to the central issue of the survey. The last part of the survey should contain **demographic questions** (such as gender, income level, and education level) that will allow you to break down the responses and look deeper into the survey results.

Demographic Questions

Questions relating to the respondents' own characteristics, backgrounds, and attributes.

A survey budget must be considered. For example, if you have $3,000 to spend on calls and each call costs $10 to make, you obviously are limited to making 300 calls. However, keep in mind that 300 calls may not result in 300 usable responses.

The phone survey should be conducted in a short time period. Typically, the prime calling time for a voter survey is between 7:00 P.M. and 9:00 P.M. However, some people are not home in the evening and will be excluded from the survey unless there is a plan for conducting callbacks.

FIGURE 1-7

**Major Steps for a
Telephone Survey**

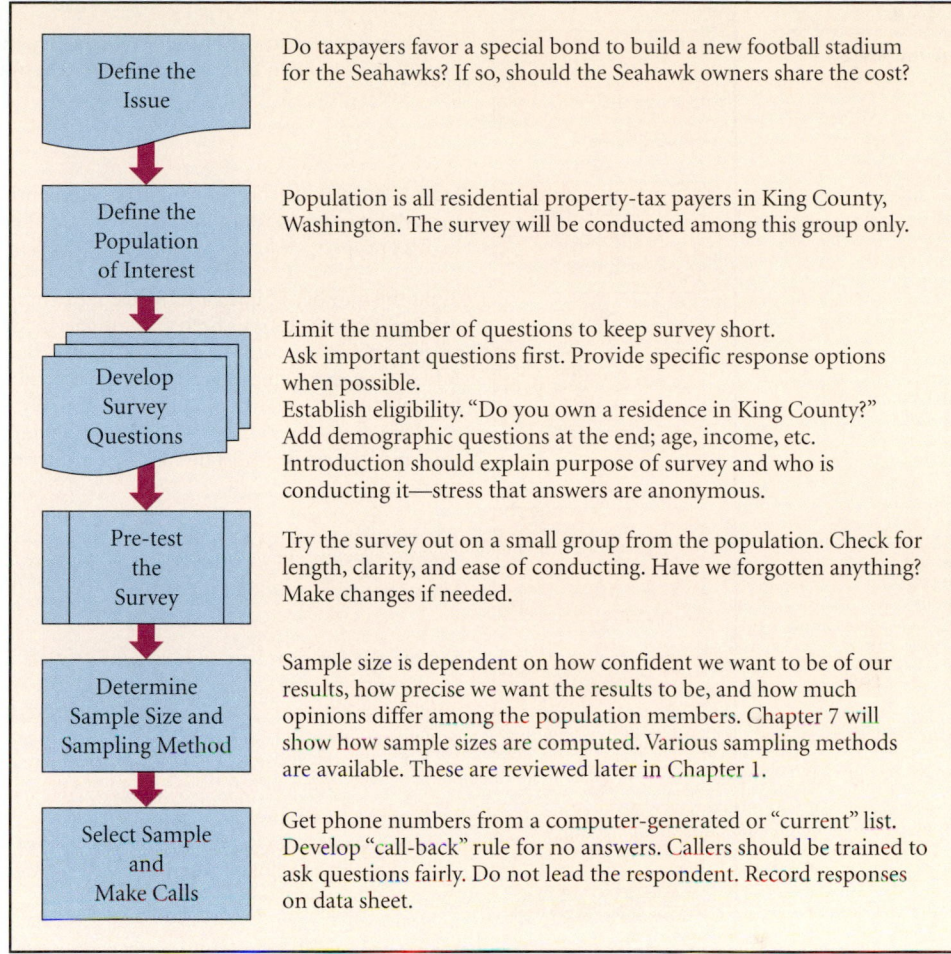

Define the
Issue — Do taxpayers favor a special bond to build a new football stadium for the Seahawks? If so, should the Seahawk owners share the cost?

Define the
Population
of Interest — Population is all residential property-tax payers in King County, Washington. The survey will be conducted among this group only.

Develop
Survey
Questions — Limit the number of questions to keep survey short.
Ask important questions first. Provide specific response options when possible.
Establish eligibility. "Do you own a residence in King County?"
Add demographic questions at the end; age, income, etc.
Introduction should explain purpose of survey and who is conducting it—stress that answers are anonymous.

Pre-test
the
Survey — Try the survey out on a small group from the population. Check for length, clarity, and ease of conducting. Have we forgotten anything? Make changes if needed.

Determine
Sample Size and
Sampling Method — Sample size is dependent on how confident we want to be of our results, how precise we want the results to be, and how much opinions differ among the population members. Chapter 7 will show how sample sizes are computed. Various sampling methods are available. These are reviewed later in Chapter 1.

Select Sample
and
Make Calls — Get phone numbers from a computer-generated or "current" list. Develop "call-back" rule for no answers. Callers should be trained to ask questions fairly. Do not lead the respondent. Record responses on data sheet.

Mail Questionnaires and Other Written Surveys

The most frequently used method to collect opinions and factual data from people is a written survey. In some instances, the surveys are in the form of a mail questionnaire. At other times, the surveys are administered directly to the potential respondents. Written questionnaires are generally the least expensive means of collecting survey data. If the survey is mailed, the major costs include postage to and from the respondents, questionnaire development and printing costs, and data analysis.

Figure 1-8 shows the major steps in conducting a written survey. Note how written surveys are similar to telephone surveys; however, written surveys can be slightly more involved and, therefore, take more time to complete than those used for a telephone survey. However, you must be careful to construct a questionnaire that can be easily completed without requiring too much time.

A written survey can contain both closed-end and **open-end questions**.

Open-End Questions

Questions that allow respondents the freedom to respond with any value, words, or statements of their own choosing.

Open-end questions provide the respondent with greater flexibility in answering a question, however the responses can be difficult to analyze. Note, telephone surveys can use open-end questions, too. However, the caller may have to transcribe a potentially long response and may misinterpret what is being said.

Written surveys also should be formatted to make it easy for the respondent to provide accurate and reliable data. This means that proper space must be provided for the responses. The directions must be clear about how the survey is to be completed. A written survey needs to be pleasing to the eye. How it looks will affect the response rate, so it must look professional.

FIGURE 1-8

Written Survey Steps

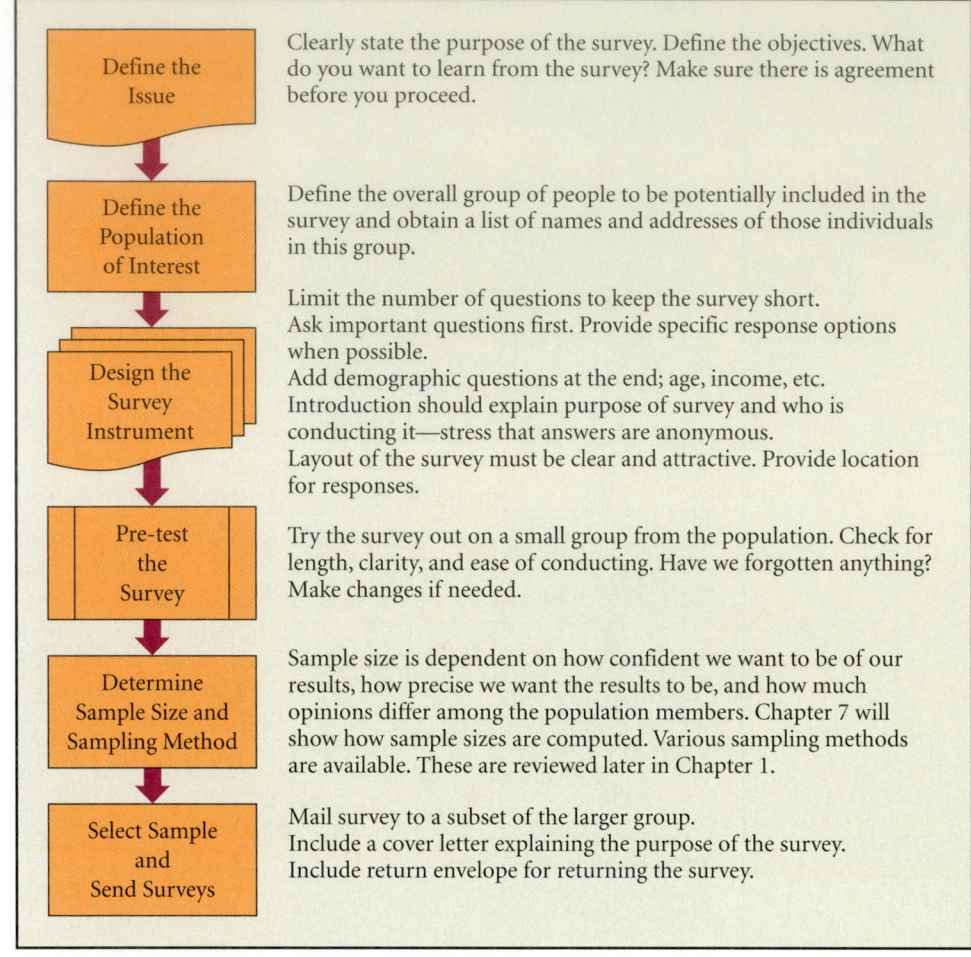

You also must decide whether to manually enter or scan the data gathered from your written survey. The survey design will be affected by the approach you take. If you are administering a large number of surveys, scanning is preferred. It cuts down on data entry errors and speeds up the data gathering process. However, you may be limited in the form of responses that are possible if you use scanning.

If the survey is administered directly to the desired respondents, you can expect a high response rate. For example, you probably have been on the receiving end of a written survey many times in your college career, when you were asked to fill out a course evaluation form at the end of the term. Most students will complete the form. On the other hand, if a survey is administered through the mail, you can expect a low response rate—typically 5% to 20%. Therefore, if you want 200 responses, you should mail out 1,000 to 4,000 questionnaires.

Overall, written surveys can be a low-cost, effective means of collecting data if you can overcome the problems of low response. Be careful to pretest the survey and spend extra time on the format and look of the survey instrument.

Direct Observation and Personal Interviews

Direct observation is another tool that is often used to collect data. As implied by the name, this technique requires that the process from which the data are being collected is physically observed and the data are recorded based on what takes place in the process.

Possibly the most basic way to gather data on human behavior is to watch people. If you are trying to decide whether a new method of displaying your product at the supermarket will be more pleasing to customers, change a few displays and watch customers' reactions.

If, as a member of a state's transportation department, you want to determine how well motorists are complying with the state's seat belt laws, place observers at key spots throughout the state to monitor people's seat belt habits. If, as a movie producer, you want information on whether your new movie will be a success, hold a preview showing and observe the reactions and comments of the movie patrons as they exit the screening. The major constraints when collecting observations are the time and money it takes to carry out the observations. For observations to be effective, trained observers must be used, which increases the cost. Personal observation is also time-consuming. Finally, personal perception is subjective. There is no guarantee that different observers will see a situation in the same way, much less report it the same way.

Personal interviews are often used to gather data from people. Interviews can be either **structured** or **unstructured**, depending on the objectives, and they can utilize either open-end or closed-end questions.

Structured Interview	*Unstructured Interview*
Interviews in which the questions are scripted.	Interviews that begin with one or more broadly stated questions, with further questions being based on the responses.

Regardless of the tool used for data collection, care must be taken that the data collected are accurate and reliable and that they are the right data for the purpose at hand.

OTHER DATA COLLECTION METHODS

Data collection methods that take advantage of new technologies are becoming more prevalent all the time. For example, many people believe that Wal-Mart is the best company in the world at collecting and using data about the buying habits of its customers. Most of the data are collected automatically as checkout clerks scan the UPC bar codes on the products customers purchase. Not only are Wal-Mart's inventory records automatically updated, information about the buying habits of customers is recorded. The data help managers organize their stores to increase sales. For instance, Wal-Mart apparently decided to locate beer and disposable diapers close together when it discovered that many male customers also purchase beer when they are sent to the store for diapers.

Bar code scanning is used in many different data collection applications. In a DRAM wafer fabrication plant, lots of silicon wafers have bar codes. As the lots travel through the plant's work stations, their progress and quality are tracked through the data that are automatically obtained through scanning.

Every time you use your credit card, data are automatically collected by the retailer and the bank. Computer information systems are developed to store the data and to provide decision makers with tools to access the data.

DATA COLLECTION ISSUES

There are several data collection issues of which you need to be aware. When you need data to make a decision, we suggest that you first see if appropriate data have already been collected, because it is usually faster and less expensive to use existing data than to collect data yourself. However, before you rely on data that were collected by someone else for another purpose, you need to check out the source to make sure that the data were collected and recorded properly.

The *Value Lines* and *Fortune* magazines of the world have built their reputations on providing quality data. Although data errors are occasionally encountered, they are few and far between. You really need to be concerned with data that come from sources with which you are not familiar. This is an issue for many sources on the World Wide Web. Any organization, or any individual, can post data to the Web. Just because the data are there doesn't mean they are accurate. Be careful.

There are other general issues associated with data collection. One of these is the potential for *bias* in the data collection. There are many types of bias. For example, in a personal interview, the interviewer can interject bias (either accidentally or on purpose) by the way she asks the questions, by the tone of her voice, or by the way she looks at the subject being interviewed. We recently allowed ourselves to be interviewed at a trade show. The interviewer began by telling us that he would only get credit for the interview if we answered all of the questions. Next, he asked us to indicate our satisfaction with a particular display. He wasn't satisfied with our less-than-enthusiastic rating and kept asking us if we really meant what we said. He even asked us if we would consider upgrading our rating! How reliable do you think these data will be?

Another source of bias that can be interjected into a survey data collection process is called *nonresponse bias*. We stated earlier that mail surveys suffer from a high percentage of unreturned surveys. Phone calls don't always get through, or people refuse to answer. Subjects of personal interviews may refuse to be interviewed. There is a problem with nonresponse. Those who respond may provide data that are quite different from the data that would be supplied by those who chose not to respond. If you aren't careful, the responses may be heavily weighted by people who feel strongly one way or another on an issue.

Bias can be interjected through the way subjects are selected for data collection. This is referred to as *selection bias*. A study on the virtues of increasing the student athletic fee at your university might not be best served by collecting data from students attending a football game. Sometimes, the problem is more subtle. If we do a telephone survey during the evening hours, we will miss all of the people who work nights. Do they share the same views, income, education levels, and so on as people who work days? If not, the data are biased.

Written and phone surveys and personal interviews can also yield flawed data if the interviewees *lie* in response to questions. For example, people commonly give inaccurate data about such sensitive matters as income. Sometimes, the data errors are not due to lies. The respondents may not know or have accurate information to provide the correct answer.

Measurement error is another problem that can be encountered in data collection. A few years ago we were working with a window manufacturer. The company was having a quality problem with one of its saws. A study was developed to measure the width of boards that had been cut by the saw. Two people were trained to use digital calipers and record the data. This caliper is a U-shaped tool that measures distance (in inches) to three decimal places. The caliper was placed around the board and squeezed tightly against the sides. The width was indicated on the display. Each person measured 500 boards during an eight-hour day. When the data were analyzed, it looked like the widths were coming from two different saws; one set showed considerably wider widths than the other. Upon investigation, we learned that the person with the narrower width measurements was pressing down on the calipers much more firmly. The soft wood reacted to the pressure and gave narrower readings. Fortunately, we had kept the data from the two data collectors separate. Had they been merged, the measurement error might have gone undetected.

Data collection through personal observation is also subject to problems. People tend to view the same event or item differently. This is referred to as *observer bias*. One area in which this can easily occur is in safety check programs in companies. An important part of behavioral-based safety programs is the safety observation. Trained data collectors periodically conduct a safety observation on a worker to determine what, if any, unsafe acts might be taking place. We have seen situations in which two observers will conduct an observation on the same worker at the same time, yet record different safety data. This is especially true in areas in which judgment is required on the part of the observer, such as the distance a worker is from an exposed gear mechanism. People judge distance differently.

An extensive discussion of how to measure the magnitude of bias and how to reduce bias and other data collection problems is beyond the scope of this text. However, you should be aware that data may be biased or otherwise flawed. Always pose questions about the potential for bias and determine what steps have been taken to reduce its affect.

1-2: EXERCISES

Skill Development

1.14 Name one data collection method that is not subject to nonresponse bias. Explain and give an example.

1.15 In selecting between a telephone survey and a mail questionnaire, which is more adaptable to open-end questions? Explain.

1.16 *USA Today* (Dec. 15, 1998) reported that 8 out of 10 adults said that they would give to charities during the Christmas season. What data collection method do you think was used to collect this data? Explain your answer.

1.17 What type of data collection is used most frequently for political polls? Explain why.

1.18 If a bank wishes to determine the level of customer satisfaction with its services, would it likely be appropriate to conduct an experiment? Explain.

1.19 Which type of bias is most common when mail questionnaires are used as the data collection tool? Explain.

1.20 What type of bias is most likely to occur when a personal interview is conducted? Explain.

1.21 If an experiment is conducted in a factory to determine the time it takes to assemble a product using different sequences, what type of bias is most likely to occur? Explain.

Business Applications

1.22 The U.S. Department of Agriculture (USDA) estimates that Southern fire ants spread at a rate of 4 to 5 miles a year. What data collection method do you think was used to collect these data? Explain your answer.

1.23 The Blacker's Furniture Store general manager is interested in knowing how long customers spend shopping in his store. If the plan is to start a stopwatch when a customer enters the store and stop it when the customer leaves, what type of bias could occur in the data collection process?

1.24   Assume that you have been given the task of conducting a survey of basketball season ticket holders at your university to determine their satisfaction with the concessions. Describe the method of data collection you would recommend, and outline the steps you would take to conduct the survey.

1.25   What are the advantages and disadvantages of using a mail questionnaire to survey cable TV customers regarding their preferences for a new all-sports channel?

1.26   As production manager for a personal computer maker, you want to set up a data collection process to help deal with the warranty returns problem facing your company. It has been suggested that you use a written survey. Develop an appropriate survey form.

Advanced Business Applications

1.27   As manager of a department store in a local retail mall, you are interested in surveying your customers to determine whether they are pleased with the layout changes that have been made in the store. You wish to examine their attitudes concerning organization of the merchandise in the store, the ease of accessibility, locations of checkout stands, and the position of walkways.
a. State which of the four methods of collection given on page 7 you would use to collect your data.
b. Indicate the advantages and shortcomings of the method you chose.
c. Brainstorm a list of questions that you will ask.
d. Design the survey instrument, keeping in mind the method you plan to use for data collection.

1.28   Assume that you work as a checker in a grocery store. At a meeting you were advised that the store will be conducting a study of customer satisfaction. Your supervisor has suggested that you simply survey the customers as they come through the checkout line. Indicate any bias that might be introduced by this method. To reduce the potential for this type of bias, indicate what method you would suggest for performing the customer satisfaction survey.

1.29   The athletic department at your university is interested in determining why some people who hold season basketball tickets don't come to games. Suppose you were to use a mail questionnaire to contact ticket holders who did not attend.
a. List at least two open-end questions you would place on the survey.
b. Describe how you would transfer the answers to the open-end questions into computer-readable form.

1.30   The administrator of a major Detroit hospital has asked you to assist in a study of the hospital's medical staff. The study is trying to determine how satisfied these employees are and to learn what changes could be made to increase satisfaction. Suppose you choose to obtain your data using personal interviews.
a. Adapt the six steps in Figure 1-7 to develop your personal interviews and explain how this method would be implemented at the hospital.
b. Discuss the advantages and disadvantages of the method you have selected over other potential data collection methods.

1.31   In your position as assistant manager for the University Food Service Company, you have been asked to collect data regarding customer behavior in the food line at the university cafeteria. Specifically, you are interested in the beverage and dessert selections. The cafeteria offers (the same!) 10 dessert selections every day. Develop a form to collect the data on dessert selections made by food line customers. Use mock data to show what a completed form would look like.

1-3 POPULATIONS, SAMPLES, AND SAMPLING TECHNIQUES

POPULATIONS AND SAMPLES

Two of the most important terms in statistics are **population** and **sample**.

Population	*Sample*
The set of all objects or individuals of interest or the measurements obtained from all objects or individuals of interest.	A subset of the population.

The list of all objects or individuals of interest is referred to as the *frame*. The choice of the frame depends on what objects or individuals you wish to study and on the availability of the list of these objects or individuals. Once the frame is defined, it forms the list of sampling units. The next example illustrates what we mean.

CPA Firm—We can use a certified public accounting (CPA) firm to illustrate the difference between a population and a sample. When preparing to audit the financial records of a business, a CPA firm must determine the number of accounts to examine. Until recently, good accounting practice dictated that the auditors verify the balance of every account and each financial transaction. Though this is still done in some audits, the size and complexity of most businesses have forced accountants to select only some accounts and some transactions to audit.

Suppose one part of the financial audit is to verify the accounts receivable balances. By definition, a population includes measurements made on all the items of interest to the data gatherer. In our example, the accountant would define the population as *all accounts receivable balances* on record. The list of these accounts, possibly by account number, forms the frame. If she examines the entire population, she is taking a **census**. But suppose there are too many accounts receivable balances to work through. The CPA would then select a subset of the accounts, called a *sample*. The accountant uses the sample results to make inferences about the population. If the sample balances look good, she might conclude that the population balances also are acceptable. How inferences are drawn will be discussed at greater length in later chapters.

> **Census**
>
> An enumeration of the entire set of measurements taken from the whole population.

There are trade-offs between taking a census and taking a sample. Usually the main trade-off is whether the information gathered in a census is worth the extra cost. In organizations in which data are stored on computer files, the additional time and effort of taking a census may not be substantial. However, if there are many accounts that must be manually checked, a census may be impractical.

Another consideration is that the measurement error in census data may be greater than in sample data. A person obtaining data from fewer sources tends to be more complete and thorough in both gathering and tabulating the data. As a result, with a sample there are likely to be fewer human errors.

Parameters and Statistics

Descriptive numerical measures, such as an average or a percentage, that are computed from an entire population are called *parameters*. Corresponding measures for a sample are called *statistics*. In the previous example, if the CPA examined every accounts receivable balance, the percentage of correct balances would be a parameter, because it reflects the value for the population. However, if she selected a ample of balances from the population, the percentage of accurate balances in this sample is a statistic. These concepts are more fully discussed in Chapters 3 and 6.

SAMPLING TECHNIQUES

Once a manager decides to gather information by sampling, he can use a sampling technique that falls into one of two categories: **statistical** or **nonstatistical**.

> **Nonstatistical Sampling Techniques**
>
> Those methods of selecting samples using convenience, judgment, or other nonchance processes.

> **Statistical Sampling Techniques**
>
> Those sampling methods that use selection techniques based on chance selection.

Both nonstatistical and statistical sampling techniques are commonly used by decision makers. Regardless of which technique is used, the decision maker has the same objective—to obtain a sample that is a close representative of the population. There are some advantages to using a statistical sampling technique, as we will discuss at many places throughout this text. However, in many cases, nonstatistical sampling represents the only feasible way to sample, as illustrated in the following example.

Nonstatistical Sampling

Carpenter Orchards—Carpenter Orchards in central Washington State is a large fruit producer. Like other fruit producers in the region, Carpenter Orchards is part of a cooperative. When fruit is harvested, it is trucked to the packing plant. The growers are paid by weight, but higher quality fruit brings higher per pound prices. As the fruit is unloaded in 20-pound boxes, a sample of fruit in each box is collected by selecting one or two pieces from the top of the box. The sampled fruit is taken to a lab to be analyzed for quality characteristics. Based on these findings, the entire truckload is assigned a quality rating and priced accordingly. Because of the volume of fruit, the packing plant uses a nonstatistical sampling method called **convenience sampling**. In doing so, the quality analysts are assuming that the fruit is evenly distributed within each box and between the boxes on the truck.

Convenience Sampling

A sampling technique that selects the items from the population based on accessibility and ease of selection.

There are other nonstatistical sampling methods, such as *judgment sampling* and *ratio sampling*, which we will not discuss here. Instead, we now turn your attention to the most frequently used statistical sampling techniques.

Statistical Sampling

Statistical sampling methods (also called *probability sampling*) allow every item in the population to have a known or calculable chance of being included in the sample. The fundamental statistical sample is called a *simple random sample*. Other types of statistical sampling discussed in this text include *stratified random sampling*, *systematic sampling*, and *cluster sampling*.

Simple Random Sampling

Baird Life and Casualty—A salesperson at Baird Life and Casualty in Charleston, West Virginia, wishes to estimate the percentage of people in a local subdivision who already have life insurance policies. The result would indicate the potential market. The population of interest consists of all families living in the subdivision.

For this example, we simplify the situation by saying that there are only five families in the subdivision: James, Sanchez, Lui, White, and Fitzpatrick. We will let N be the population size and n be the sample size. From the five families ($N = 5$), we select three ($n = 3$) for the sample. There are 10 possible samples of size 3 that could be selected.

{James, Sanchez, Lui}	{James, Sanchez, White}	{James, Sanchez, Fitzpatrick}
{James, Lui, White}	{James, Lui, Fitzpatrick}	{James, White, Fitzpatrick}
{Sanchez, Lui, White}	{Sanchez, Lui, Fitzpatrick}	{Sanchez, White, Fitzpatrick}
{Lui, White, Fitzpatrick}		

Note that no family is selected more than once in a given sample. This method is called *sampling without replacement* and is the most commonly used random sampling method. If the families could be selected more than once, the method would be called *sampling with replacement*.

Simple random sampling is the method most people think of when they think of random sampling.

Simple Random Sampling

A method of selecting items from a population such that *every possible sample of a specified size has an equal chance of being selected*.

In a correctly performed simple random sample, each of these samples would have an equal chance of being selected. A simplified way of doing this would be to put each sample of three names on a piece of paper in a bowl and then blindly reach in and select one piece of paper. This method would be difficult to do if the number of possible samples were large. For example, if $N = 50$ and a sample of size $n = 10$ is to be selected, there are more than 10 billion possible samples. Try finding a bowl big enough to hold those!

Simple random samples can be obtained in a variety of ways. We will present several examples to illustrate how simple random samples are selected in practice.

Nordstrom's Payroll—Suppose the personnel manager at Nordstrom's Department Store in Seattle is considering changing the payday from once a month to once every two weeks. Before making any decisions, he wants to survey a sample of 10 employees from the store's 300 employees. He first assigns employees a number (001 to 300). He can then use the random number function in either Excel or Minitab to determine which employees to include in the sample. Figure 1-9, shows the results when Excel chooses 10 random numbers. The first employee sampled is number 115, followed by 31, and so forth. The important thing to remember is that assigning each employee a number and then randomly selecting a sample from those numbers gives each possible sample an equal chance of being selected.

If you don't have access to computer software such as Excel or Minitab, the items in the population to be sampled can be determined by using the *random numbers table* in Appendix A. Start by selecting a starting point in the random numbers table (row and column). Suppose we use row 5, column 8 as the starting point. Go down 5 rows and over 8 digits. Verify that the digit in this location is 1. Ignoring the blanks between columns that are there only to make the table more readable, the first three-digit number is 149. Employee number 149 is the first one selected in the sample. Each subsequent random number is obtained from the random numbers in the next row down. For instance, the second number is 127. The procedure continues selecting numbers from top to bottom in each subsequent column. Numbers exceeding 300 and duplicate numbers are eliminated. When enough numbers are found for the desired sample size, the process is completed. Employees whose numbers are chosen are then surveyed.

Stratified Random Sampling

Excel and Minitab Tutorial

Federal Reserve Bank—Sometimes, the sample size required to obtain a certain level of information from a simple random sampling may be greater than our budget permits. At other times it may take more time to collect than is available. **Stratified random sampling** is an alternative method that has the potential to provide the desired information with a smaller sample size. The following example illustrates how stratified sampling is performed.

Stratified Random Sampling

A statistical sampling method in which the population is divided into subgroups called *strata* so that each population item belongs to only one stratum. The objective is to form strata such that the population values of interest within each stratum are as much alike as possible. Sample items are selected from each stratum using the simple random sampling method.

Each year, the Federal Reserve Board asks its staff to estimate the total cash holdings of U.S. financial institutions as of July 1. The staff must base its estimate on a sample. Note that not all financial institutions (banks, credit unions, and the like) are the same size. A majority are small, some are medium-sized, and only a few are large. However, the few large institutions have a substantial percentage of the total cash on hand. To make sure that a simple random sample includes an appropriate number of small, medium, and large institutions, the sample size might have to be quite large.

FIGURE 1-9

Excel Output of Random Numbers for Nordstrom's Example

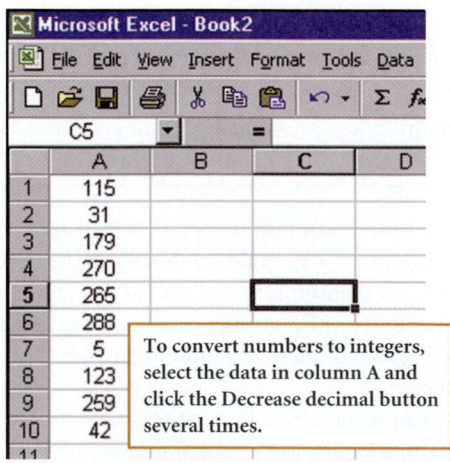

	A
1	115
2	31
3	179
4	270
5	265
6	288
7	5
8	123
9	259
10	42

To convert numbers to integers, select the data in column A and click the Decrease decimal button several times.

Excel Instructions:
1. Click on the **Tools** tab.
2. Select the **Data Analysis** option.
3. Select **Random Number Generation** option.
4. Select **Uniform** as the distribution.
5. Define range as between 1 and 300.
6. Indicate where the results are to go.
7. Click **OK**.

Minitab Instructions (for similar results):
1. Choose **Calc > Random Data > Integer.**
2. In **Generate _ rows of data**, enter sample size.
3. In **Store in column(s)**, enter destination column.
4. In **Minimum value** enter 1.
5. In **Maximum value** enter 300.
6. Click **OK.**

FIGURE 1-10

Stratified Sampling
Example

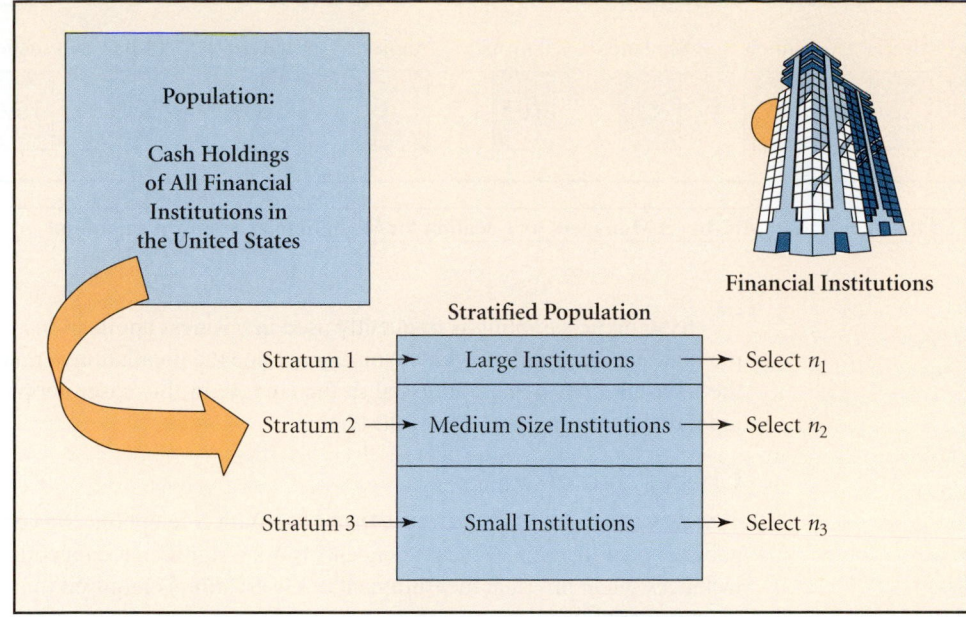

As an alternative to the simple random sample, the Federal Reserve staff could divide the institutions into three groups called *strata*: small, medium, and large. Staff members could then select a simple random sample of institutions from each stratum and estimate the total cash on hand for all institutions from this combined sample. Figure 1-10 shows the stratified random sampling concept. Note that the combined sample size ($n_1 + n_2 + n_3$) is the sum of the simple random samples taken from each stratum.

The key behind stratified sampling is to develop strata that, for the characteristic of interest (such as cash on hand), have items that are quite *homogeneous*. In this example, the size of the financial institution may be a good factor to use in stratifying. Here the combined sample size ($n_1 + n_2 + n_3$) will be less than the sample size that would have been required if no stratification had occurred. Because sample size is directly related to cost (in both time and money), a stratified sample can be more cost-effective than a simple random sample.

Multiple layers of stratification can further reduce the overall sample size. For example, the Federal Reserve might break the three strata in Figure 1-10 into *substrata* based on type of institution: state bank, interstate bank, credit union, and so on.

Most large-scale market research studies use stratified random sampling. The well-known political polls, such as the Gallup and Harris polls, use this technique also. For instance, the Gallup poll typically samples between 1,800 and 2,500 people nationwide to estimate how more than 60 million people will vote in a presidential election.

Systematic Random Sampling

National Association of Accountants—A few years ago, the National Association of Accountants (NAA) considered establishing a code of ethics. To determine the opinion of its 20,000 members, a questionnaire was sent to a sample of 500 members. Although simple random sampling could have been used, an alternative method called **systematic random sampling** was chosen.

Systematic Random Sampling

A statistical sampling technique that involves selecting every kth item in the population after a randomly selected starting point between 1 and k. The value of k is determined as the ratio of the population size over the desired sample size.

The NAA's systematic random sampling plan called for it to send the questionnaire to every fortieth member (20,000/500 = 40) from the list of members. The list was in alphabetical order. They could have begun by using Excel or Minitab to generate a single random number in the range 1 to 40. Suppose this value was 25. The twenty-fifth person in their alphabetic list would be selected. After that, every fortieth member would be selected (25, 65, 105, 145, . . .) until they had 500 NAA members.

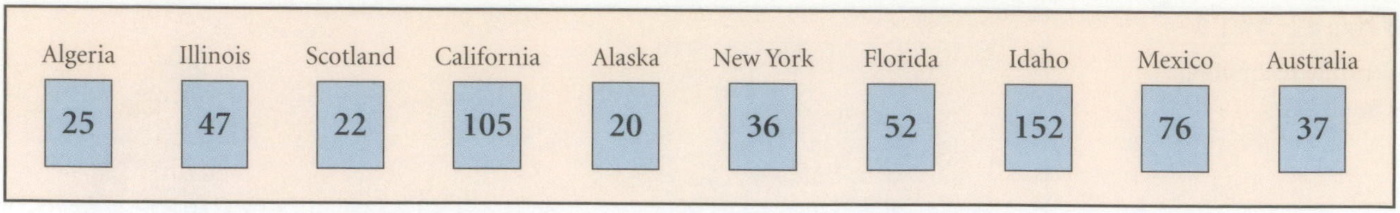

Algeria	Illinois	Scotland	California	Alaska	New York	Florida	Idaho	Mexico	Australia
25	47	22	105	20	36	52	152	76	37

FIGURE 1-11   **Mid-Level Managers by Location for Washington Group International**

Systematic sampling is frequently used in business applications. Use it as an alternative to simple random sampling only when you can assume the population is randomly ordered with respect to the measurement being addressed in the survey. In this case, peoples' views on ethics are likely unrelated to the spelling of their last name.

Cluster Sampling

Washington Group International—With a telephone survey or a mail questionnaire, the geographical location of the respondents is not a significant data collection issue. However, in some instances when physical measurement or observation is required to collect the data, location can be an important issue.

Suppose Washington Group International, a large worldwide construction company, wants to develop a new corporate bidding strategy. Upper management wants input on possible new strategies from its middle-level managers. Assume that Figure 1-11 illustrates the current distribution of middle-level managers throughout the world. For example, there are 25 middle-level managers in Algeria, 47 in Illinois, and so forth. Upper management decides to hold face-to-face personal interviews with a sample of these mid-level managers.

One sampling technique is to select a simple random sample of size n from the population of middle managers. Unfortunately, this technique would likely require the interviewer(s) go to each state or country in which Washington Group International has middle-level managers. This would prove to be an expensive and time-consuming process. A systematic or stratified sampling procedure also would probably require visiting each location. The geographical spread in this case causes problems.

A sampling technique that overcomes the traveling (time and money) problem is **cluster sampling**.

Cluster Sampling

A method by which the population is divided into groups, or clusters, that are each intended to be mini-populations. A simple random sample of m clusters is selected. The items selected from a cluster can be selected using any probability sampling technique.

Ideally, the clusters would each have the same characteristics as the population as a whole. In the Washington Group International example, the states or countries where the company has managers would be the clusters.

After the clusters have been defined, a sample of m clusters is selected at random from the list of possible clusters. The number of clusters to select depends on various factors, including our survey budget. Suppose WGI selects $m = 3$ clusters randomly as follows:

Scotland   Florida   Illinois

These are the *primary clusters*. Next, the company can either survey all the managers in each cluster or select a simple random sample of managers from each cluster, depending on time and budget considerations.

1-3: EXERCISES

Skill Development

1.32 The U.S. Department of Transportation reported the average number of mishandled bags per 1,000 passengers for October was 4.39. State whether this number is a statistic or a population parameter. Explain your answer.

1.33 What conditions must hold in order for a sampling technique to be considered a statistical sample?

1.34 Explain the difference between stratified random sampling and cluster sampling.

1.35 Why is it that systematic random sampling can be considered a statistical sampling technique?

1.36 If a manager surveys a sample of 100 customers to determine how many miles they live from the store, is the mean travel distance for this sample considered a parameter or a statistic? Explain.

1.37 Using row 20, column 18 in the random numbers table in Appendix A, what are the first 3 five-digit numbers that would be used to select a random sample from a population with 52,000 items.

1.38 Explain why a census does not necessarily have to involve a population of people. Use an example to illustrate.

1.39 Use Excel or Minitab to generate five random numbers between 1 and 900.

Business Applications

1.40 An Ernst & Young survey of 1,363 consumers and more than 120 retailers and consumer-goods manufacturers indicated that in 2001, 12% of retailers sold online to consumers. Is this percentage a statistic? Explain.

1.41 On October 31, Reuters news service announced that housing starts in November are estimated to be 1.68 million. They were 1.695 million for October. Indicate which number is a population parameter and give your reasons for your selection.

1.42 The Standard & Poor's 500 index on May 11, 2000, stood at 1,383.05. Give the general statistical term that is used to describe the set of measurements that was used to obtain this index.

1.43 Give the name of the kind of sampling that was most likely used in each of the following cases:
   a. A *Washington Post*/ABC News Poll of 2,000 people to determine the President's approval rating.
   b. A poll taken of each of the General Motor dealerships in Ohio in December 1999 to determine an estimate of the average number of 1999-model Chevrolets not yet sold by GM dealerships in the United States.
   c. A quality assurance procedure within a B. F. Goodrich manufacturing plant that takes every thousandth tire produced to test for cord strength of the tire.
   d. A sampling technique in which a random sample from each of the tax brackets is obtained by the Internal Revenue Service to audit tax returns.

1.44 A student has suggested that one could use a systematic sampling technique to sample from the primary clusters of a cluster sampling scheme. Explain why this is either a good or a bad idea.

1.45 What are the potential advantages of stratified random sampling over simple random sampling? Explain with an example of your own how this advantage might be realized.

Advanced Business Applications

1.46 The U.S. Forest Service plans to survey backcountry hikers to determine the quality of their outdoor experience. They will ask randomly selected hikers to rate the quality on a scale from 1 to 5. One indicates total dissatisfaction; 5 indicates total satisfaction.
   a. Define the population of interest. Be sure to specify the measurement of interest as part of your definition. Assume a sample of 200 is to be obtained.
   b. Describe an approach you would suggest to take a statistical sample from the population. State which sampling technique you would use.
   c. Assuming the population of hikers is 1,500, use either Excel or Minitab to generate the list of hikers to be selected in the sample.

1.47 The Ritz-Carlton hotel chain wishes to select a random sample of guests who stayed at their Atlanta hotel on February 11. They have a list of 742 guests and their mailing addresses. Each guest is given an identification number from 001 to 742. Use Excel or Minitab to generate a list of 30 guest identification numbers so the guests with those numbers can be surveyed.

1.48 Suppose the Ritz-Carlton wishes to personally interview guests who will stay at their hotels throughout the United States next March 20.
   a. Describe an approach for using cluster sampling to select the sample.
   b. What are the potential advantages of using cluster sampling in this case instead of simple random sampling?
   c. Would it be possible to conduct a census in this situation? Why or why not?

1.49 The Fairview Title Company has more than 4,000 customer files listed alphabetically in its computer system. The office manager wants to survey a statistical sample of these customers to determine how satisfied they were with service provided by the title company. She plans to use a telephone survey of 100 customers.
   a. Describe how you would attach identification numbers to the customer files (e.g., how many digits (and which digits) would you use to indicate the first customer file)?
   b. Describe how the first random number would be obtained to begin a simple random sample method.
   c. How many random digits would you need for each random number you selected?
   d. Use Excel or Minitab to generate the list of customers to be surveyed.

1.50 The Craigthorp Company is a statewide food distributor to restaurants, universities, and other establishments that prepare and sell food. The company has a very large warehouse where food is stored until it is pulled from the shelves to be delivered to customers. The warehouse has 64 storage racks numbered 1 to 64. Each rack has three shelves, labeled A, B, and C. The shelves are divided into 80 sections, numbered 1 to 80.

Products are located by rack number, shelf letter, and section number. For example, breakfast cereal is located at 43-A-52 (rack 43, shelf A, section 52).

Each week, employees perform an inventory for a sample of products. Certain products are selected and counted. The *actual count* is compared to the *book count* (the quantity in the records that should be in stock). To simplify things, assume that the company has selected breakfast cereals to inventory. Also, suppose that cereals occupy racks 1 through 5, only.

a. Assume that you plan to use simple random sampling to select the sample. Use Excel or Minitab to determine the sections on each of the five racks to be sampled.

b. Assume that you wish to use cluster random sampling to select the sample. Discuss the steps you would take to carry out the sampling.

c. In this case, why might cluster sampling be preferred over simple random sampling? Discuss.

1.51 A major retail store plans to select a sample of people entering the store on a given Saturday morning. The purpose of the sample is to determine which mode of advertising drew the customer to the store. Assume that the store manager does not care whether the survey is done using statistical or nonstatistical methods.

a. Give reasons why you might choose a nonstatistical method for this survey.

b. Assume 100 customers are to be sampled. Give details of how you would select the customers needed for the survey.

c. Discuss any bias issues you considered in constructing your survey method.

1-4 DATA TYPES AND DATA MEASUREMENT LEVELS

Chapters 2 and 3 will introduce a variety of techniques for describing data and transforming the data into information. As you will see in those chapters, the statistical techniques deal with different forms of data. The level of measurement may vary greatly from application to application. In general, there are four types of data: *quantitative, qualitative, time series, and cross-sectional.* A discussion of each follows.

QUANTITATIVE AND QUALITATIVE DATA

In some cases, data values are best expressed in purely numerical, or **quantitative** terms, such as in dollars, pounds, inches, or percentages.

Quantitative Data

Measurements whose values are inherently numerical.

As an example, a study of college students at your campus might obtain data on the number of hours each week that students work at a paying job and the income level of the students' parents.

In other cases, the observation may signify only the category to which an item belongs. Categorical data are referred to as **qualitative** data.

Qualitative Data

Data whose measurement scale is inherently categorical.

For example, a study might be interested in the class standings—*freshman, sophomore, junior, senior,* or *graduate*—of college students. The same study also might ask the students to judge the quality of their education as *very good, good, fair, poor,* or *very poor.* Note, even if the students are asked to record a number (1 to 5) to indicate the quality level at which the numbers correspond to a category, the data would still be considered qualitative because the numbers are just codes for the categories.

TIME-SERIES DATA AND CROSS-SECTIONAL DATA

Data may also be classified as being either **time-series** or **cross-sectional**.

Time-Series Data

A set of ordered data values observed at successive points in time.

Cross-Sectional Data

A set of data values observed at a fixed point in time.

The data collected from the study of college students about their quality ratings would be cross-sectional because the data from each student relates to a fixed point in time. In another case, if we sampled 100 stocks from the stock market and determined the closing stock price on March 15, the data would be considered cross-sectional because all measurements corresponded to one point in time.

On the other hand, Ford Motor Company tracks the sales of its Taurus automobiles on a monthly basis. Data values observed at intervals over time are referred to as time-series data. If we determined the closing stock price for a particular stock on a daily basis for a year, the stock prices would be time-series data.

DATA MEASUREMENT LEVELS

Data can also be identified by their *level of measurement*. This is important because the higher the data level, the more sophisticated the analysis that can be performed. This will be clear when you study the material in the remaining chapters of this text.

We shall discuss and give examples of four levels of data measurements: *nominal, ordinal, interval, and ratio*. Figure 1-12 illustrates the hierarchy among these data levels, with nominal data being the lowest level.

Nominal Data

Nominal data are the lowest form of data, yet you will encounter this type of data many times. Assigning codes to categories generates nominal data. For example, a survey question that asks for marital status provides the following responses:

1. Married   2. Single   3. Divorced   4. Other

For each person, a code of 1, 2, 3, or 4 would be recorded. These codes are nominal data. Note that the values of the code numbers have no specific meaning, because the order of the categories is arbitrary. We might have shown it this way:

1. Single   2. Divorced   3. Married   4. Other

With nominal data we also have complete control over what codes are used. For example, we could have used:

88. Single   11. Divorced   33. Married   55. Other

All that matters is that you know which code stands for which category. Recognize also that the codes need not be numeric. We might use:

S = Single   D = Divorced   M = Married   O = Other

Ordinal Data

Ordinal, or rank, data are one notch above nominal data on the measurement hierarchy. At this level, the data elements can be rank-ordered on the basis of some relationship among them, with the assigned values indicating this order. For example, a typical market-research technique is to offer

FIGURE 1-12

Data Level Hierarchy

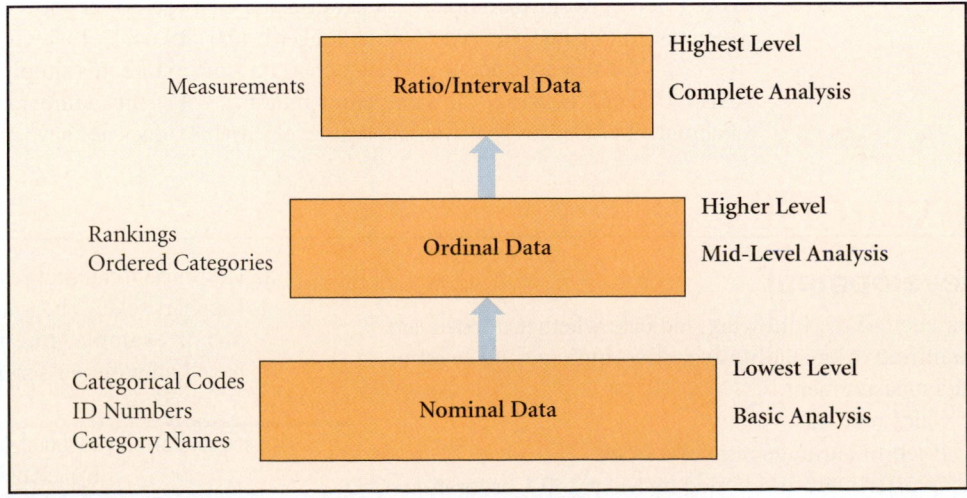

potential customers the chance to use two unidentified brands of a product. The customers are then asked to indicate which brand they prefer. The brand eventually offered to the general public depends on how often it was the preferred test brand. The fact that an ordering of items took place makes this an ordinal measure.

Bank loan applicants are asked to indicate the category corresponding to their household incomes:

_____ Under $20,000	_____ $20,000 to $40,000	_____ over $40,000
(1)	(2)	(3)

The codes 1, 2, and 3 refer to the particular income categories, with higher codes assigned to higher incomes.

Ordinal measurement allows decision makers to equate two or more observations, or to rank-order the observations. In contrast, nominal data can be compared only for equality. You cannot order nominal measurements. Thus, a primary difference between ordinal and nominal data is that ordinal data contain both an equality (=) and a greater than (>) relationship, whereas nominal data contain only an equality (=) relationship.

Interval Data

If the distance between two data items can be measured on some scale and the data have ordinal properties (>, <, or =), the data are said to be **interval data**. The best example of interval data is the temperature scale. Both the Fahrenheit and Celsius temperature scales have ordinal properties of ">" and "=." In addition, the distances between equally spaced points are preserved. For example, $32°F > 30°F$, and $80°C > 78°C$. The difference between $32°F$ and $30°F$ is the same as the difference between $80°F$ and $78°F$, two degrees in each case. Thus, interval data allow us to precisely measure the difference between any two values. With ordinal data this is not possible, because all we can say is that one value is larger than another.

Ratio Data

Data that have all the characteristics of interval data but also have a true zero point (at which zero means "none") are called **ratio data**. Ratio measurement is the highest level of measurement.

Packagers of frozen foods encounter ratio measures when they pack their products by weight. Weight, whether measured in pounds or grams, is a ratio measurement because it has a unique zero point—zero meaning no weight. Many other types of data encountered in business environments involve ratio measurements, for example, distance, money, and time.

The difference between interval and ratio measurements can be confusing because it involves the definition of a true zero. If you have $5 and your brother has $10, he has twice as much money as you. If you convert your dollars to pounds, lire, yen, or marks, your brother will still have twice as much. If your money is lost or stolen, you have no dollars. Money has a true zero. Likewise, if you travel 100 miles today and 200 miles tomorrow, the ratio of distance traveled will be 2/1, even if you convert the distance to kilometers. If on the third day you rest, you have traveled no miles. Distance has a true zero. Conversely, if today's temperature is $35°F$ ($1.67°C$) and tomorrow's is $70°F$ ($21.11°C$), is tomorrow twice as warm as today? The answer is no. One way to see this is to convert the Fahrenheit temperature to Celsius: The ratio will no longer be 2/1 (12.64/1). Likewise, if the temperature reads $0°F$ ($-17.59°C$), this does not imply that there is no temperature. It's simply colder than $10°F$ ($-12.22°C$). Also, $0°C$ ($32°F$) is not the same temperature as $0°F$. Thus, temperature, measured with either the Fahrenheit or Celsius scale (an interval-level variable), does not have a true zero.

1-4: EXERCISES

Skill Development

1.52 For each of the following, indicate whether the data are quantitative or qualitative. Also indicate the level of data measurement.
  a. Sales regions.
  b. Price-to-earnings ratio of a stock.
  c. Quarterly profit reported by Microsoft Corporation.

  d. Response to market research survey measured on the Likehart scale. The scale is in integer steps from 1 to 5. For example, rate the level of satisfaction you have had with our service department as

  (1) exceptional, (2) very good, (3) good, (4) satisfactory, or (5) unsatisfactory

e. Market share captured by Intel Corporation's Pentium II processor.

f. Quarterly dividend paid by Paine Webber Group, Inc.

1.53 Indicate whether each of the following is cross-sectional or time-series data.

a. your income last year

b. weekly defect rate for one assembly line over past 52 weeks

c. yearly size of the population of your city since 1970

d. customer bank balances on December 1

e. students' grade point averages for the 1999 fall term

f. annual student enrollment from 1970 to 2000

1.54 For each of the following variables, indicate what the level of data measurement is.

a. number of years of education

b. hair color

c. type of business

d. salaries of the CEOs of the Fortune 500 companies

e. temperature of furnaces in steel smelteries

f. job classification

Business Applications

1.55 The company for which you work wishes to determine the percentage of Internet sales made by the companies with which it competes. You are assigned this task. You are deciding between two survey questions to use: (1) List the percentage of your sales obtained through the Internet; or (2) The percentage of your sales obtained through the Internet is (1) 0 to 10, (2) 10 to 20, . . . , (10) 90 to 100.

a. State the level of measurement the responses would be to each of these survey questions.

b. State whether each of the survey question responses would be qualitative or quantitative.

c. Which of these two survey questions would allow you to calculate the average percentage of sales obtained through the Internet?

1.56 In a study of Internet sales, the following question appears on a survey instrument: The percentage of your sales obtained through the Internet is (1) 0 to 10, (2) 10 to 20, . . . , (10) 90 to 100. Your supervisor tells you to assign the number in parentheses corresponding to each customer's response. He then instructs you to calculate the average of these assigned numbers and then transform the number obtained back to the appropriate category to find the average percentage of sales through the Internet.

a. Respond to your supervisor's idea by classifying the assigned numbers as qualitative or quantitative data.

b. Does an assigned number of 4 indicate twice as large a percentage of sales through the Internet than a 2? Explain.

c. What is the level of measurement for these assigned numbers?

d. Would such data be classified as time-series or cross-sectional data?

1.57 As part of a marketing survey, you ask customers to list the number of children they have by placing a check by the appropriate category: ____0, ____1, ____2, ____3, ____>3.

a. Specify the level of measurement that such responses exhibit.

b. Would it be possible to calculate the average number of children for the respondents to this survey? Indicate how you would modify the survey so you could calculate such a statistic.

1.58 The manufacturer of a top-selling brand of laser printers has a support center where customers can call to get information about their printers. The manager in charge of this support center has recently conducted a study in which she surveyed 2,300 customers. The customers who called the support center were transferred to a third party, who asked the customers a series of questions.

a. Indicate whether the data that will be generated from this study will be considered cross-sectional or time series. Explain why.

b. One of the questions asked the customers to indicate approximately how many minutes they had been on hold waiting to get through to a support person. What level of data measurement is obtained from this question? Explain.

c. Another question asked the customers to rate the service on a scale of 1 to 7, with 1 being the worst possible service and 7 being the best possible service. What level of data measurement is achieved from this question? Will the data be quantitative or qualitative? Explain.

Summary and Conclusions

Business statistics is about converting data into useful information. There are three main components in this process: *descriptive statistics*, *probability*, and *inferential statistics*. The tools for descriptive statistics include graphs, charts, tables, and various numerical measures. Chapters 2 and 3 will introduce the important descriptive tools.

Probability is the way decision makers express their uncertainty about whether some event will take place. We use probability distributions as a means of defining the chances of any outcome occurring based on a set of business conditions. Chapters 4 and 5 introduce the key rules and concepts you will need to work effectively with probability.

Drawing inferences about a population based on sample data takes up a good portion of the remainder of the text. We will introduce you to a variety of inferential tools to help you learn to think statistically. Figure 1-13 summarizes the differences between populations and samples and the different types of sampling techniques you may have reason to use.

FIGURE 1-13

Sampling Techniques

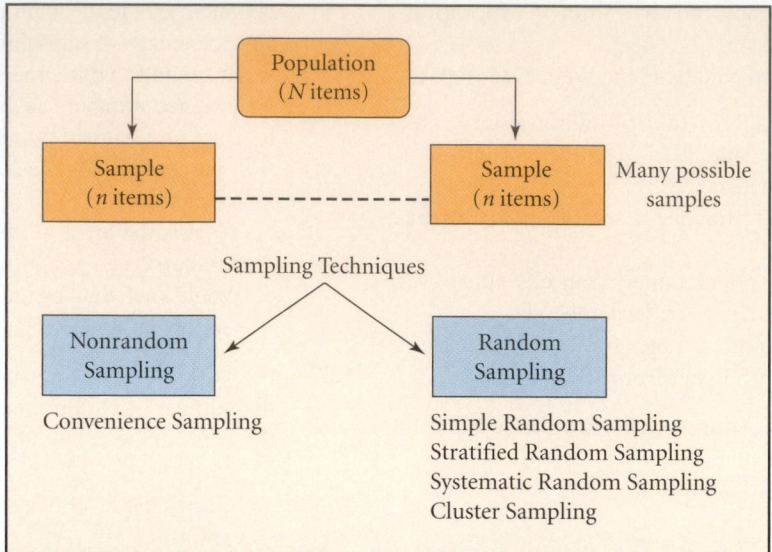

Sampling Techniques

FIGURE 1-14

Data Collection Techniques

Data Collection Method	Advantages	Disadvantages
Experiments	Provide controls Preplanned objectives	Costly Time consuming Requires planning
Telephone Surveys	Timely Relatively inexpensive	Poor reputation Limited scope and length
Mail Questionnaires Written Surveys	Inexpensive Can expand length Can use open-ended questions	Low response rate Requires exceptional clarity
Direct Observation Personal Interview	No respondent bias Expands analysis opportunities	Potential observer bias

FIGURE 1-15

Data Classification

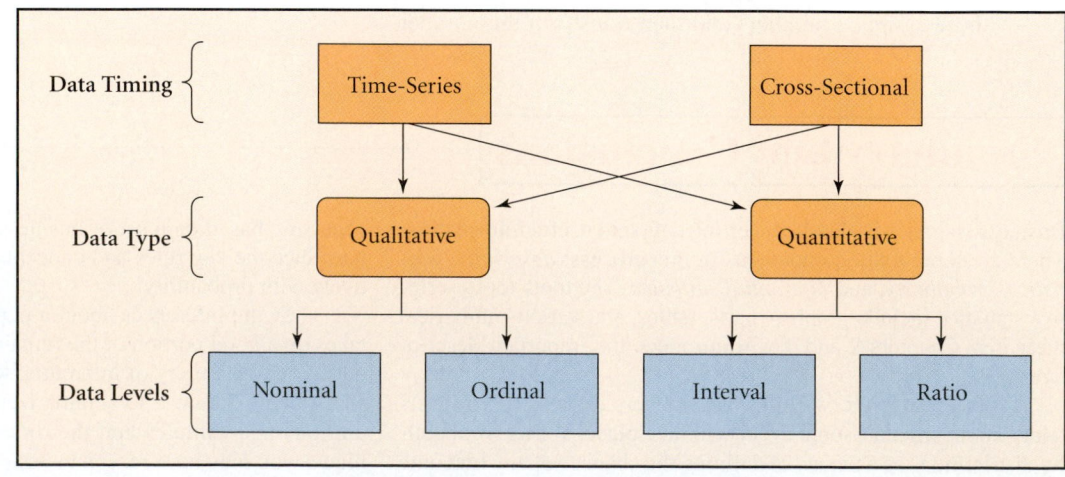

Businesses have access to more data than ever. Much of this data they generate internally through normal operations. In other cases the data they need is found outside the organization. We have discussed the fact that there are numerous ways to gather data. *Surveys* (phone or written) are effective when gathering data from people. Observation and direct measurement are appropriate when collecting data from a process. Figure 1-14 summarizes the most frequently used data collection techniques and the advantages and disadvantages of each.

The type of data that is collected varies, too. The data may be *quantitative* or *qualitative*, it may be *time series* or *cross-sectional*, and it may be *nominal*, *ordinal*, *interval*, or *ratio* level. The type and level of data that we have is important in determining the type of analysis we can perform. Please refer to Figure 1-15 for a quick summary of the ways in which we classify data.

Many of the things you will be doing in this course can be better done using computer software. The software selected for this text is Microsoft Excel and Minitab. Although not a special-purpose statistics software package, Excel contains a great many tools and techniques for performing descriptive and inferential statistical analysis. Minitab is a fully functional statistics package with a spreadsheet look and feel. You will find that whichever software package is used during this course it will be a valuable tool that will free you from tedious computations, allowing you more time to analyze and interpret the output to make better business decisions.

Key Terms

Arithmetic Mean, or average, 4
Business statistics, 2
Census, 14
Closed-end questions, 8
Cluster sampling, 18
Convenience sampling, 15
Cross-sectional data, 20
Demographic questions, 8
Experiment, 7

Experimental design, 7
Nonstatistical sampling, 14
Open-end questions, 9
Population, 13
Qualitative data, 20
Quantitative data, 20
Ratio data, 22
Sample, 13

Simple random sampling, 15
Statistical inference tools, 5
Statistical sampling techniques, 14
Stratified random sampling, 16
Structured interview, 11
Systematic random sampling, 17
Time-series data, 20
Unstructured interview, 11

CHAPTER EXERCISES

Business Applications

1.59 The Ford Motor Company has been advertising a series of comparisons between its cars and competitors' cars. What level of data measurement would each of the following be?
a. the sound level measured in decibels inside the car
b. drivers' ratings of the handling characteristics of the car
c. the mileage ratings in miles per gallon for the cars
d. the indication of whether a stereo radio is standard equipment on a car

1.60 A local television station has asked its viewers to call in and respond to the question, "Do you believe police officers are using too much force in routine traffic stops?"
a. Would the results of this phone-in survey be considered a random sample?
b. What type of bias might be associated with a data collection system such as this? Discuss what options might be used to reduce this bias potential.

1.61 At the start of 1997, 41% of the nearly 900 independent beer distributors affiliated with Anheuser-Busch carried only its brand. The data set that resulted in this summary parameter consists of the distributors' names and the brands of beer they carry. Indicate the data level for each of the two variables in the data set.

1.62 A company financial manager recently made a presentation that showed that during the previous 16 quarters (three months per quarter) the company recorded a profit 12 times and a loss 4 times.
a. Give the level of data for the data used in this presentation.
b. Are these data considered time series or cross-sectional? Explain.

Advanced Business Applications

1.63 The maker of Creamy Good Ice Cream is concerned about the quality of ice cream produced by its Illinois plant. The particular trait of concern is the texture of the ice cream in each carton.
a. Discuss a plan by which Creamy Good managers might determine the percentage of cartons of ice cream believed to have an unacceptable texture by potential purchasers of a particular brand of their ice cream. Define (1) the sampling procedure to be used, (2) the randomization method to be used to select the sample, and (3) the measurement to be obtained.
b. Explain why it would or wouldn't be feasible (or, perhaps, possible) to take a census to address this issue.

1.64 The makers of a particular brand of skiing equipment selected a random sample of skiers at the Aspen Ski Resort. Their method for selecting the sample required that individuals waiting in one of the lift lines be asked questions about various brands of skiing equipment.
a. Reconsider the data collection issues in Section 1-2 of this chapter. Comment on the sampling method employed in this problem.

b. Suggest a better sampling method and explain why it is a better method.

c. Indicate the level of data measurement you will be obtaining.

d. Specify whether the data is qualitative or quantitative.

1.65 A beer manufacturer is considering abandoning can containers and going exclusively to bottles because the sales manager believes beer drinkers prefer drinking beer

from bottles. However, the vice president in charge of marketing is not convinced the sales manager is correct.

a. Indicate the data collection method you would use.

b. Indicate what procedures you would follow to apply this technique in this setting.

c. State which level of data measurement applies to the data you would collect. Justify your answer.

d. Is the data qualitative or quantitative? Explain.

General References

1. Berenson, Mark L., and David M. Levine, *Basic Business Statistics: Concepts and Applications*, 7th ed. (Upper Saddle River, NJ: Prentice Hall, 1999).

2. Cryer, Jonathan D., and Robert B. Miller, *Statistics for Business: Data Analysis and Modeling*, 2nd ed. (Belmont, CA: Duxbury Press, 1994).

3. Dodge, Mark, and Craig Stinson, *Running Microsoft Excel 2000* (Redmond, WA: Microsoft Press, 1999).

4. Groves, R. M., *Survey Errors and Survey Costs* (New York: John Wiley & Sons, 1989).

5. Hildebrand, David, and R. Lyman Ott, *Statistical Thinking for Managers*, 4th ed. (Belmont, CA: Duxbury Press, 1998).

6. Kenkel, James L., *Introductory Statistics for Management and Economics*, 4th ed. (Belmont, CA: Duxbury Press, 1996).

7. *Microsoft Excel 2000* (Redmond, WA: Microsoft Corp., 1999)

8. *Minitab for Windows Version 14* (State College, PA: Minitab, 2003).

9. Pelosi, Marilyn K., and Theresa M. Sandifer, *Doing Statistics for Business with Excel*. (New York: John Wiley & Sons, 2000).

10. Scheaffer, Richard L., William Mendenhall, and Lyman Ott, *Elementary Survey Sampling*, 5th ed. (Belmont, CA: Duxbury Press, 1996).

11. Siegel, Andrew F., *Practical Business Statistics*, 4th ed. (Burr Ridge, IL: Irwin, 2000).

CHAPTER 2

Graphs, Charts, and Tables— Describing Your Data

CHAPTER OUTCOMES

After studying the material in Chapter 2, you should:

- Be able to construct frequency distributions both manually and with your computer.
- Be able to construct and interpret a frequency histogram.
- Know how to construct and interpret various types of bar charts.
- Be able to build a stem and leaf diagram.
- Be able to create a line chart and interpret the trend in the data.
- Be able to construct a scatter plot and interpret it.
- Be able to develop and interpret joint frequency tables.

WHY YOU NEED TO KNOW

Several years ago, a vice president for General Motors spoke at the University of Montana's spring alumni and scholarship banquet. After his speech, a student asked him what factor he considered to be the most important in his rise to the vice presidency of one of the world's largest companies. He responded that a short time after joining GM he took part in a presentation to a group of upper-level managers. He previously had been taught the skills to *effectively organize and present* complex data. His ability to translate the data into meaningful information caught the attention of the company's senior managers. A short time later, he was asked to coordinate another presentation. He stated that he was certain that upper management remembered his presentations for their effective display of business data. When they needed someone to lead a special project, he was selected. The success of that project led to a significant promotion, and the rest was history.

Although you may not end up working at a company as large as General Motors, we are absolutely convinced that you will have numerous opportunities to organize, summarize, analyze, and present data. In fact, of all the tools and techniques introduced in this text, you very likely will use those discussed in this chapter and Chapter 3 more than any others.

Not only will you be called on to actually do the data analysis necessary to make sense out of data, you will find yourself on the receiving end of many statistical reports. Therefore, not only should you be able to perform appropriate data analysis, but you also need to be able to question the accuracy and validity of the charts, graphs, and analysis you receive from others.

Business periodicals, such as *Fortune* and *Business Week*, use graphs and charts extensively in conjunction with their articles to help readers better understand key concepts. Many advertisements will even use graphs and charts to effectively convey their message. What better proof of the potential value of descriptive statistics than to observe ads costing $50,000 or more per page using the concepts we will be discussing in this text?

This chapter introduces some of the most frequently used tools and techniques for describing data with graphs, charts, and tables. Although this analysis can be done manually, we will provide output from Excel and Minitab showing that these software packages can be used as tools for doing the analysis easily, quickly, and with a finished quality that once required a graphic artist.

2-1 FREQUENCY DISTRIBUTIONS AND HISTOGRAMS

Next time you are in your statistics class, look around at your classmates. How many hours a week do they spend studying? How are the students' ages distributed? How is income distributed among the students? How many credits have they completed? A simple survey of the students would provide data to answer each of these questions. However, the data alone would not be enough. You would need to perform a descriptive analysis of the data.

FREQUENCY DISTRIBUTION

One of the first steps would be to construct a **frequency distribution** for each of the variables.

Frequency Distribution

A summary of a set of data that displays the number of observations in each of the distribution's distinct categories or classes.

Books and Music—Consider a national book and music retailer that is considering locating into one of two cities (say, City 1 and City 2). To obtain data to aid in the decision process, the retailer has conducted a marketing study in the two cities. Among the questions asked of individuals is how many years of college they have completed. Experience in other markets indicates that cities with higher-educated populations are more-profitable locations. The variable, years of college, is **discrete** because the possible responses (1, 2, 3, 4, etc.) can be counted.

Discrete Data

Data whose possible values are countable.

TABLE 2-1

Frequency Distribution of Years of College

CITY 1 YEARS OF COLLEGE	FREQUENCY
0	35
1	21
2	24
3	22
4	31
5	13
6	6
7	5
8	3
Total	**160**

TABLE 2-2

Frequency Distribution of Years of College

CITY 2 YEARS OF COLLEGE	FREQUENCY
0	187
1	62
2	34
3	19
4	14
5	7
6	3
7	4
Total	**330**

To construct the frequency distribution for City 1, we need only count the number of times individuals in that city indicate each of these possible responses (years of education). The results are shown in Table 2-1. This frequency distribution shows that, of the 160 people in the survey, few (35 out of 160) have spent less than one year in college.

Suppose now we wished to compare the college years variable for City 1 with the same variable for City 2. The data for City 2 can be organized into the frequency distribution shown in Table 2-2. How do the two market areas compare? Do you see any difficulties in making this comparison? Because the surveys contained a different number of people, it is difficult to compare the frequencies of each category directly. When the number of total observations differs, comparisons are aided if **relative frequencies** are computed. Equation 2-1 is used to compute the relative frequencies.

Relative Frequency

The proportion of total observations that are in a given category. Relative frequency is computed by dividing the frequency in a category by the total number of observations. The relative frequencies can be converted to percentages by multiplying by 100.

$$\text{Relative frequency} = \frac{f_i}{n} \qquad \textbf{2-1}$$

where:

f_i = Frequency of the ith value of the discrete variable

$$n = \sum_{i=1}^{k} f_i$$

k = The number of different values for the discrete variable

Table 2-3 shows the relative frequencies for each market area. This makes a comparison of the two market areas much easier. We see that City 2 has relatively more people without any college (56.7%) or one year of college (18.8%) than City 1 (21.9% and 13.1%). At all other levels of education, City 1 has relatively more people than City 2.

TABLE 2-3

Relative Frequency Distribution for the Book and Music Example

Years of College	CITY 1 Frequency	CITY 1 Relative Frequency	CITY 2 Frequency	CITY 2 Relative Frequency
0	35	35/160 = 0.219	187	187/330 = 0.567
1	21	21/60 = 0.131	62	62/330 = 0.188
2	24	24/160 = 0.150	34	34/330 = 0.103
3	22	22/160 = 0.138	19	19/330 = 0.058
4	31	31/160 = 0.194	14	14/330 = 0.042
5	13	13/160 = 0.081	7	7/330 = 0.021
6	6	6/160 = 0.038	3	3/330 = 0.009
7	5	5/160 = 0.031	4	4/330 = 0.012
8	3	3/160 = 0.019	0	0/330 = 0.00
Total	160		330	

SUMMARY: DEVELOPING FREQUENCY AND RELATIVE FREQUENCY DISTRIBUTIONS FOR DISCRETE DATA

To develop a discrete data frequency distribution, perform the following steps:

1. List all possible values of the variable. If the variable is quantitative, order the possible values from low to high.

2. Count the number of occurrences at each value of the variable and place this value in a column labeled "frequency."

To develop a relative frequency distribution, do the following:

3. Use Equation 2-1 and divide each frequency count by the total number of data values and place in a column headed "relative frequency."

EXAMPLE 2-1: FREQUENCY AND RELATIVE FREQUENCY DISTRIBUTIONS

International Airline Travel Following the tragic events of September 11, 2001, there was a sharp reduction in international travel by U.S. citizens. A travel magazine recently surveyed 16 business executives to determine how many international trips they made in 2002. The following data were observed:

3	0	0	1
1	2	2	0
0	2	1	0
2	1	4	2

The editors wish to construct a frequency distribution and a relative frequency distribution for the number of international trips taken by these executives.

Step 1: **List the possible values.**
The possible values listed in order for the discrete variable are 0, 1, 2, 3, 4.

Step 2: **Count the number of occurrences at each value.**
The frequency distribution follows:

International Trips	Frequency	Relative Frequency
0	5	5/16 = .3125
1	4	4/16 = .2500
2	5	5/16 = .3125
3	1	1/16 = .0625
4	1	1/16 = .0625
	Total = 16	1.0000

Step 3: **Determine the relative frequencies.**
The relative frequencies are determined by dividing each frequency by 16, as shown. Thus, just over 31% of those responding took no trips during 2002.

EXAMPLE 2-2: FREQUENCY DISTRIBUTION FOR QUALITATIVE DATA

Lawn Care Companies A subdivision in northern California has 20 homes. Recently a survey was conducted to determine which lawn service the homeowners used last summer. Fifteen homeowners responded to the survey with the following results:

Emerald	Green Thumb	Green Thumb	Self	Self
Master Care	Emerald	Self	Master Care	Green Thumb
Emerald	Self	Master Care	Emerald	Self

The frequency distribution for this qualitative variable is found as follows:

Step 1:   **List the possible values.**
The possible values for the variable are Emerald, Green Thumb, Master Care, and Self.

Step 2:   **Count the number of occurrences at each value.**
The frequency distribution is:

Lawn Company	Frequency
Emerald	4
Green Thumb	3
Master Care	3
Self	5
	Total = 15

Excel and Minitab Tutorial

Athletic Shoe Survey—In recent years, a status symbol for many students has been the brand and style of athletic shoes they wear. Companies such as Nike, Adidas, and Reebok compete for the top position in the sport shoe market. A survey was recently conducted in which 100 college students at a southern state school were asked a number of questions, including how many pairs of Nike shoes they currently own. The data are in a file called *SportsShoes* on the CD-ROM that comes with this text.

The variable *Number of Nike* is a discrete quantitative variable. Figures 2-1 and 2-2 show frequency distributions (Excel and Minitab versions) for the number of Nike shoes owned by those surveyed. These frequency distributions show that, although a few people own more than six pairs of Nike shoes, the bulk of those surveyed own two or fewer pairs.

GROUPING DATA BY CLASSES

Cox Enterprises—In the previous examples, the variable of interest was a discrete variable and the number of possible values for the variable was limited to only a few. However, there are many instances in which the variable of interest will be either **continuous** (weight, time, length) or discrete and have many possible outcomes (age, income, stock prices), yet we want to describe the variable using a frequency distribution.

Continuous Data

Data whose possible values are uncountable and which may assume any value in an interval.

FIGURE 2-1

Excel Output—Nike Shoes Frequency Distribution

Excel Instructions:
1. Open file: SportsShoes.xls
2. Enter the Possible Values for the Variable; i.e., 0, 1, 2, 3, 4.
3. Select the cells to contain the Frequency values.
4. Click on the f_n button.
5. Select the **Statistics—FREQUENCY** function.
6. Enter the range of data and the bin range (the cells containing the possible number of shoes.
7. Press **ctrl-shift-enter** to determine the frequency values.

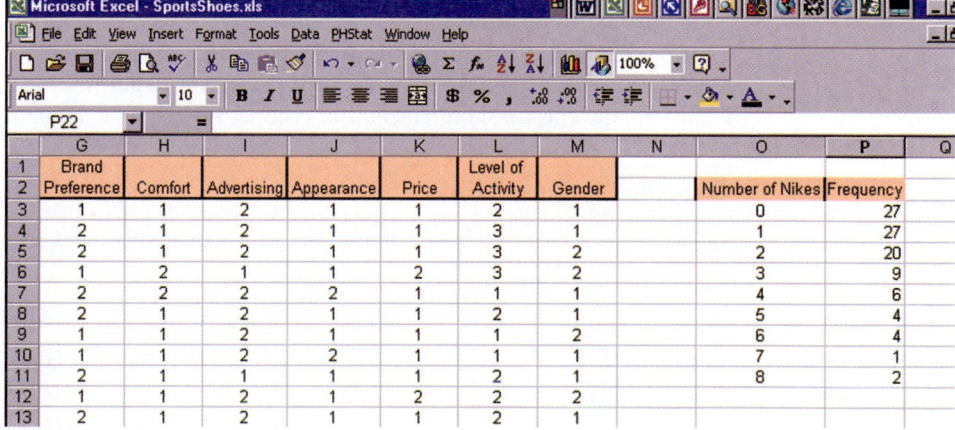

	G	H	I	J	K	L	M	N	O	P	Q
1	Brand					Level of					
2	Preference	Comfort	Advertising	Appearance	Price	Activity	Gender		Number of Nikes	Frequency	
3	1	1	2	1	1	2	1		0	27	
4	2	1	2	1	1	3	1		1	27	
5	2	1	2	1	1	3	2		2	20	
6	1	2	1	1	2	3	2		3	9	
7	2	2	2	2	1	1	1		4	6	
8	2	1	2	1	1	2	1		5	4	
9	1	1	2	1	1	1	2		6	4	
10	1	1	2	2	1	1	1		7	1	
11	2	1	1	1	1	2	1		8	2	
12	1	1	2	1	2	2	2				
13	2	1	2	1	1	2	1				

FIGURE 2-2

Minitab Output—Nike
Shoes Frequency
Distribution

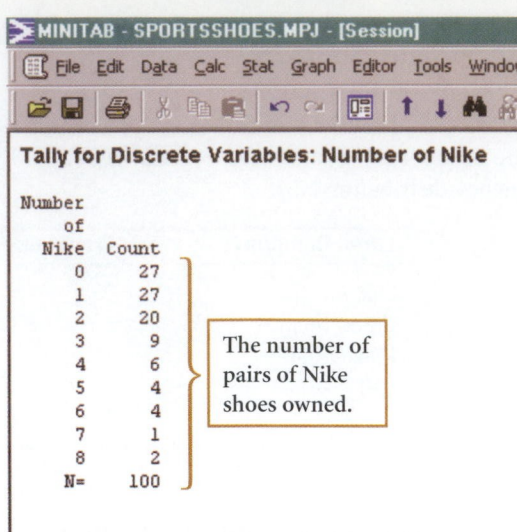

Cox Enterprises owns and operates a large cattle feedlot operation in the plains of west Texas. The company purchases young steer calves at auctions and from cattle ranchers. The company keeps the calves on feedlots for approximately six months before selling them to packing plants.

The more weight the cattle gain on the feedlots, the greater Cox's profit. Cox managers constantly study calves' growth patterns to determine which species offer the best profit potential. Table 2-4 shows the weight gains in pounds, to the nearest tenth of a pound, for a sample of 100 polled Hereford steers. The range for this continuous quantitative variable is 131.3 to 205.6 pounds.

The data have been sorted in order of weight from low to high, forming a **data array**.

Data Array

Data that have been sorted in ascending or descending order.

Even sorted, the weight-gain data provide little information about these cattle. However, a good first step in understanding the data would be to construct a frequency distribution.

The variable, weight gain, can assume many different weights in these data. If we counted the number of values at each weight, we would have many frequencies of 1 and 2. This would provide little new information. Instead, we need to group the data into *classes* and then count the number of cattle that had weight gains in each class.

The first step in this procedure is to form data groups (or classes). Care needs to be taken when constructing these classes to ensure each data point is put into one, and only one, possible class. Therefore, the classes should meet four criteria. First, they must be **mutually exclusive**.

Mutually Exclusive Classes

Classes that do not overlap so that a data value can be placed in only one class.

TABLE 2-4

Cox Enterprises Cattle Weight Gain

131.3	148.3	155.9	160.2	164.5	168.7	173.2	179.3	183.0	191.7
137.2	149.4	156.2	160.5	164.6	169.5	173.7	179.6	183.1	191.7
138.2	150.8	156.3	161.5	165.1	169.6	174.8	180.1	183.5	194.9
142.3	150.8	157.3	162.1	165.2	170.0	176.7	180.4	186.4	196.0
143.4	152.0	157.4	162.3	165.3	170.4	176.8	180.7	186.7	198.3
143.9	153.3	157.7	163.2	165.5	171.1	177.0	181.4	188.0	198.8
144.6	153.7	158.4	163.6	166.4	171.7	177.3	181.4	188.6	199.6
145.8	154.2	159.0	163.9	166.5	172.0	178.1	182.4	189.1	202.9
146.6	154.6	159.6	164.3	167.2	172.0	178.4	182.4	189.6	203.1
147.2	155.3	160.2	164.4	168.7	172.1	178.9	182.9	190.1	205.6

Second, they must be **all inclusive**.

All-Inclusive Classes

A set of classes that contains all the possible data values.

Third, if at all possible, they should be of **equal-width**.

Equal-Width Classes

The distance between the lowest possible value and the highest possible value in each class is equal for all classes.

Equal-width classes make analyzing and interpreting the frequency distribution easier. However, there are some instances in which the presence of extreme high or low values makes it necessary to have an open-ended class. For example, annual family incomes in the United States are mostly between $15,000 and $200,000. However, there are some families with much higher family incomes. In order to best accommodate these high incomes, you might consider having the highest income class be "over $200,000" or "$200,000 and over" as a catchall for the high-income families.

Fourth, avoid **empty classes** if possible. Empty classes are those for which there are no data values. If this occurs, it may be because you have set up classes that are too narrow.

Steps for Grouping Data into Classes

There are four steps for grouping data, such as that found in Table 2-4, into classes.

Step 1: Determine the number of groups or classes to use. Although there is no absolute right or wrong number of classes, the rule of thumb is to have *between 5 and 20 classes*. A formula known as **Sturges's Rule** is often used to provide a guideline for determining the number of classes for a given number of data values, *n*, as shown in Equation 2-2:

Sturges's Rule

$$\text{Classes} = 1 + 3.322 \, [\log_{10}(n)] \qquad \textbf{2-2}$$

where:

$$n = \text{Number of data values}$$

In the Cox Enterprises example, for $n = 100$ values, using Sturges's rule we get:

$$1 + 3.322 \times \log_{10}(100)$$

This formula returns the value 7.644, or 8 classes.

Remember, this is only a guideline for the number of classes. There is no specific right or wrong number. In general, use fewer classes for smaller data sets; more classes for larger data sets. However, using too few classes tends to condense data too much, and information is lost. Using too many classes spreads out the data so much that little advantage is gained over the original raw data.

Step 2: Establish the class width.

Class Width

The distance between the lowest possible value and the highest possible value for a frequency class.

The minimum **class width** is determined by Equation 2-3.

Class Width

$$W = \frac{\text{Largest Value} - \text{Smallest Value}}{\text{Number of Classes}} \qquad \textbf{2-3}$$

For the Cox Enterprises data using eight classes, we get:

$$W = \frac{205.6 - 131.3}{8} = \frac{74.3}{8} = 9.288$$

This means we could construct eight classes that are each 9.288 pounds wide to provide mutually exclusive and all-inclusive classes. However, because our purpose is to make the data more understandable, we suggest that you *round up to a more convenient class width*, such as 10 pounds or even 15 pounds. A major concern in determining class widths is to select ones that are readily understandable. Be aware, people tend to do better with multiples of 2 and 5 than they do with multiples of 3 or 4, so 10 is a better choice than 12.

Step 3: Determine the class boundaries for each class.

Class Boundaries

The upper and lower values of each class.

The **class boundaries** determine the lowest possible value and the highest possible value for each class. In the Cox Enterprises example, if we start the first class at 130 pounds, we get the class boundaries shown in the first column of Table 2-5.

Notice the classes have been formed to be *mutually exclusive* and *all inclusive*. The weight data were recorded in pounds to one decimal place. For instance, a weight value of 149.9 pounds will fall in the second class. A value of 150 pounds will fall in the third class.

Step 4: Count the number of values in each class. From the raw data in Table 2-4, we count the number of steers with weight gains in each class. The results are shown in the Frequency column in Table 2-5. This shows that more steers (24) gained from 160.1 to 170 pounds than any other single category. The vast majority of steers (77 out of 100) in the sample gained from 150.1 pounds to 190 pounds. If the company had multiple feedlots, we might need to compute relative frequencies, as shown in the Relative Frequency column in Table 2-5.

The relative frequencies can be transformed into percentages, which would mean, for example, that 19% of the steers in the sample gained from 170.1 to 180 pounds.

Another step we can take to help analyze the steer weight-gain data is to construct a **cumulative frequency distribution** and a **cumulative relative frequency distribution**.

Cumulative Frequency Distribution

A summary of a set of data that displays the number of observations with values less than or equal to the upper limit of each of its classes.

Cumulative Relative Frequency Distribution

A summary of a set of data that displays the proportion of observations with values less than or equal to the upper limit of each of its classes.

The cumulative frequency distribution is shown in the Cumulative Frequency column of Table 2-5. We can then form the cumulative relative frequency distribution as shown in the Cumulative

TABLE 2-5

Cattle Weight Gain Data for Cox Enterprises

CLASSES	FREQUENCY	RELATIVE FREQUENCY	CUMULATIVE FREQUENCY	CUMULATIVE RELATIVE FREQUENCY
130.1 to 140.0 lbs.	3	3/100 = 0.03	3	0.03
140.1 to 150.0 lbs.	9	9/100 = 0.09	12	0.12
150.1 to 160.0 lbs.	17	17/100 = 0.17	29	0.29
160.1 to 170.0 lbs.	24	24/100 = 0.24	53	0.53
170.1 to 180.0 lbs.	19	19/100 = 0.19	72	0.72
180.1 to 190.0 lbs.	17	17/100 = 0.17	89	0.89
190.1 to 200.0 lbs.	8	8/100 = 0.08	97	0.97
200.1 to 210.0 lbs.	3	3/100 = 0.03	100	1.00
	$\Sigma = 100$	$\Sigma = 1.00$		

Relative Frequency column of Table 2-5. The cumulative relative frequency distribution indicates, as an example, that 72% of the sample steers had weight gains of 180 pounds or less.

SUMMARY: DEVELOPING FREQUENCY DISTRIBUTIONS FOR CONTINUOUS VARIABLES

To develop a continuous data frequency distribution, perform the following steps:

1. Determine the desired number of classes or groups. The rule of thumb is to use 5 to 20 classes. Sturges's rule can be used.

2. Determine the minimum class width using:

$$W = \frac{\text{Largest Value} - \text{Smallest Value}}{\text{Number of Classes}}$$

Round the class width up to a more convenient value.

3. Define the class boundaries, making sure that the classes that are formed are *mutually exclusive* and *all inclusive*. Ideally, the classes should have equal widths and should all contain at least one observation.

4. Count the number of values in each class.

EXAMPLE 2-3: FREQUENCY DISTRIBUTION FOR CONTINUOUS VARIABLES

Airport Security Screening   Example 2-1 referred to the international travel difficulties after the September 11, 2001, attack on the World Trade Center in New York City. As a result, airports throughout the world have stepped up their security, and passengers have had to spend more time waiting to pass through security screening. At the Miami, Florida, airport, officials each week select a random sample of passengers. For each person selected, the time spent in the security screening line is recorded. The waiting times (already sorted from high to low), in seconds, for one such sample of 72 passengers are as follows:

35	339	650	864	1,025	1,261
38	340	655	883	1,028	1,280
48	395	669	883	1,036	1,290
53	457	703	890	1,044	1,312
70	478	730	934	1,087	1,341
99	501	763	951	1,091	1,355
138	521	788	969	1,126	1,357
164	556	789	985	1,176	1,360
220	583	789	993	1,199	1,414
265	595	802	997	1,199	1,436
272	596	822	999	1,237	1,479
312	604	851	1,018	1,242	1,492

The airport security manger wishes to construct a frequency distribution for the time passengers wait for security screening. The frequency distribution is determined as follows:

Step 1: **Group the data into classes.**

The number of classes is arbitrary but typically will be between 5 and 20, depending on the volume of data. Sturges's rule can be used as a guideline. In this example, we have $n = 72$ data items.

$$\text{Classes} = 1 + 3.322 \times \log_{10}(72) = 7.170$$

We might round this down to 7 classes.

Step 2: **Determine the class width.**

$$W = \frac{\text{Largest Value} - \text{Smallest Value}}{\text{Number of Classes}} = \frac{1,492 - 35}{7} = 208.1429 \Rightarrow 225$$

Note, we have rounded the class width up from the minimum required value of 208.1429 to the more convenient value of 225.

Step 3:   **Define the class boundaries.**

0	and under	225
225	and under	450
450	and under	675
675	and under	900
900	and under	1,125
1,125	and under	1,350
1,350	and under	1,575

These classes are mutually exclusive, all inclusive, and have equal width.

Step 4:   **Count the number of values in each class.**

Waiting Time	Frequency
0 and under 225	9
225 and under 450	6
450and under 675	12
675and under 900	13
900and under 1,125	14
1,125and under 1,350	11
1,350and under 1,575	7

This frequency distribution shows that for this sample of passengers, most people wait between 450 and 1,350 seconds.

HISTOGRAMS

Although frequency distributions are useful in analyzing large sets of data, they are in table format and may not be as visually informative as a graph. A graph called a **frequency histogram** can be used to transform a frequency distribution into a visually appealing format.

> **Frequency Histogram**
>
> A graph of a frequency distribution with the horizontal axis showing the classes, the vertical axis showing the frequency count, and (for equal class widths) the rectangles having a height equal to the frequency in each class.

A histogram shows three general types of information:

1. It provides a visual indication of where the approximate center of the data is. Look for the center point along the horizontal axes in the histograms in Figure 2-3. Even though the shapes of the histograms are the same, there is a clear difference in where the data are centered.
2. We can gain an understanding of the degree of spread (or variation) in the data. The more the data cluster around the center, the smaller the variation in the data. If the data are spread out from the center, the data exhibit greater variation. The examples in Figure 2-4 all have the same center but are different in terms of spread.
3. We can observe the shape of the distribution. Is it reasonably flat, is it weighted to one side or the other, is it balanced around the center, or is it bell-shaped?

Capital Credit Union—Even for applications with small amounts of data, such as the Cox Enterprises cattle weight-gain example, constructing grouped data frequency distributions and histograms is a time-consuming process. Decision-makers may hesitate to try different numbers of classes and different class limits because of the effort involved and the "best" presentation of the data may be missed.

Excel and Minitab Tutorial

We showed earlier that Excel and Minitab both provide the capability of constructing frequency distributions. Both software packages are also quite capable of generating grouped data frequency distributions and histograms.

Consider Capital Credit Union (CCU) in Mobile, Alabama, which recently began issuing a new credit card. Managers at CCU have been wondering how customers have been using the card, so a

FIGURE 2-3

**Histograms Showing
Different Centers**

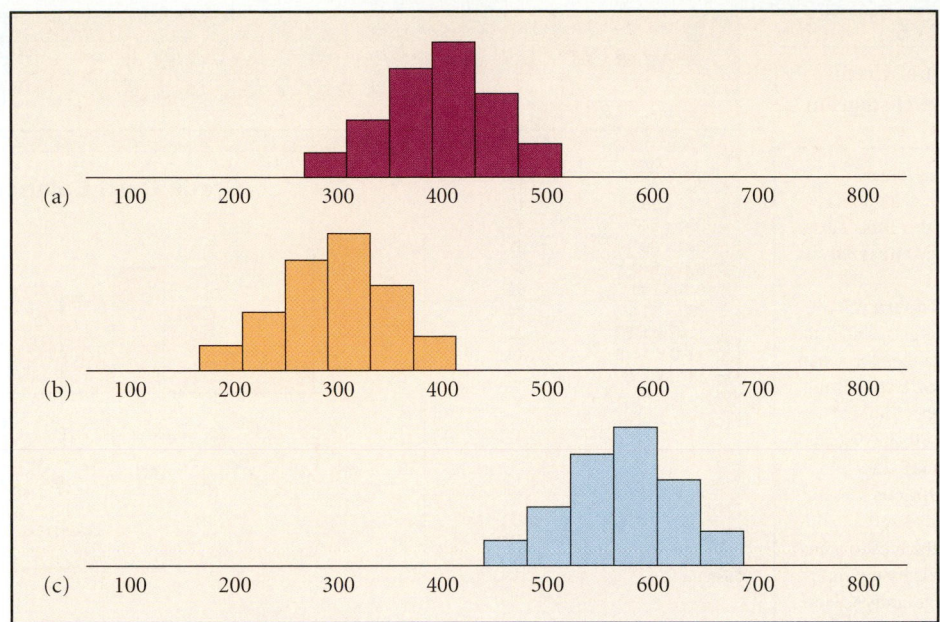

sample of 300 customers was selected. Data on the current credit card balance (rounded to the nearest dollar) and the genders of the cardholders appear in the file *Capital*, which is stored on your CD-ROM.

As with the manual process, the first step in Excel or Minitab is to determine the number of classes. Recall that the rule of thumb is to use between 5 and 20 classes, depending on the amount of data. Suppose we decide to use 10 classes.

Next, we determine the class width using Equation 2-3. The highest account balance in the sample is $1,493.00. The minimum is $99.00. Thus, the class width is

$$W = \frac{1,493.00 - 99.00}{10} = 139.40$$

which we round up to $150.00.

Our classes will be

$90 <$240 (includes all balances between $90.00 and $239.99)

$240 < $390

$390 < $540

etc.

FIGURE 2-4

**Histograms—Same Center,
Different Spread**

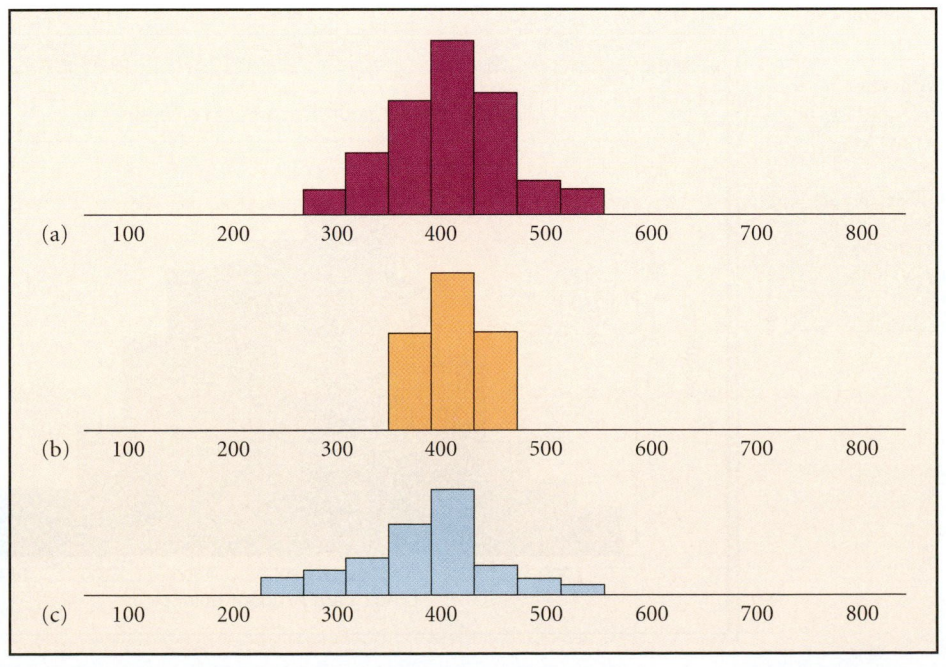

FIGURE 2-5

**Excel Output of Credit
Card Balance Histogram**

Excel Instructions:
1. Open file: Capital.xls
2. Click on the **Tools** tab.
3. Select the **Data Analysis**
   option.
4. Select **Histogram**.
5. **Input Range** specifies the
   cells containing the actual
   data values. Define Bin
   range (upper limit of each
   class 239.99, 389.99, etc.).
6. Use **Format Data
   Series**, **Options**, to set
   gap width to zero.
7. Convert the bins to actual
   class labels by typing
   labels in column A. Note,
   the bin 239.99 is labeled
   < 240, etc.

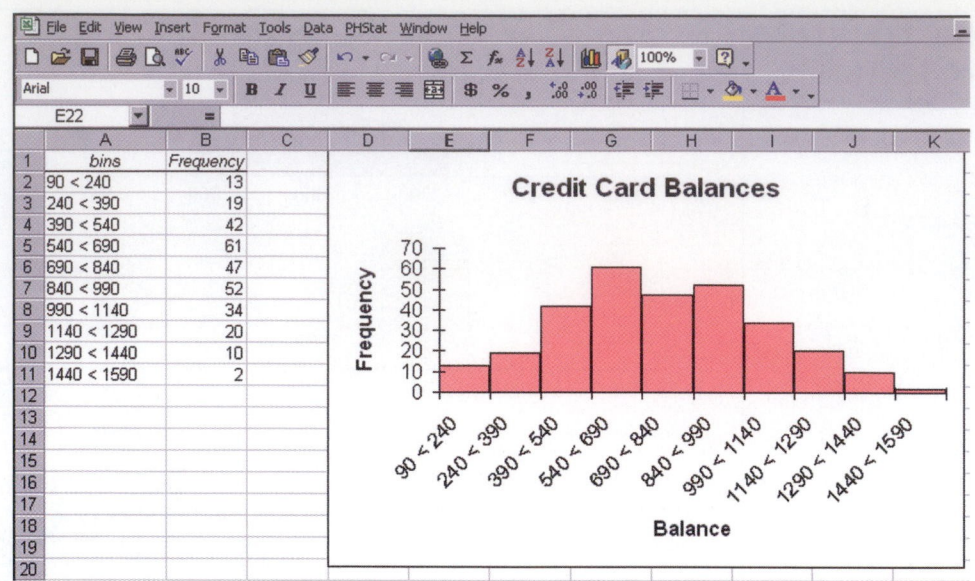

The resulting histogram in Figure 2-5 shows that the data are centered between $690 and $840. The customers vary considerably in their credit card balances, but the distribution is quite symmetrical and bell-shaped. Capital Credit Union managers must decide whether the usage rate for the credit card is sufficient to warrant the cost of maintaining the credit card accounts.

ISSUES WITH EXCEL

If you use Excel to construct a histogram as indicated in the instructions in Figure 2-5, the initial graph will come up with gaps between the bars. Because histograms illustrate the distribution of data across the range of all possible values for the variable, *histograms do not have gaps*. Therefore, to get the proper histogram format, you need to close these gaps by setting the gap width to zero, as indicated in the Excel instructions shown in Figure 2-5. Minitab provides no gaps with its default output, as shown in Figure 2-6.

FIGURE 2-6

**Minitab Output of Credit
Card Balance Histogram**

Minitab Instructions:
1. Open file: Capital.MTW.
2. Choose **Graph >
   Histogram**.
3. Click **Simple**.
4. Click **OK.**
5. In **Graph variables,**
   enter data column.
6. Click **OK.**

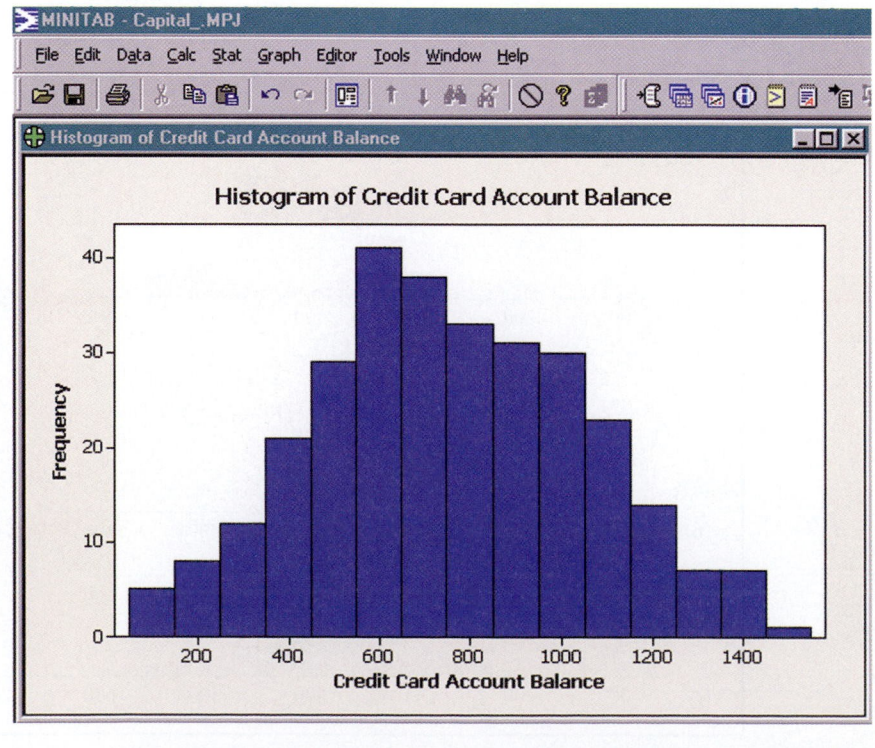

SUMMARY: CONSTRUCTING FREQUENCY HISTOGRAMS

To construct a frequency histogram, perform the following steps:

1. Follow the steps for constructing a frequency distribution (see Examples 2-1 or 2-3).

2. Use the horizontal axis to represent the variable of interest. Use the vertical axis to represent the frequency in each class.

3. Draw vertical bars for each class or data value so that the heights of the bars correspond to the frequencies. Make sure there are no gaps between the bars. (Note, if the classes do not have equal widths, the bar height should be adjusted to make the area of the bar proportional to the frequency.)

4. Label the histogram appropriately.

EXAMPLE 2-4: FREQUENCY HISTOGRAMS

Emergency Response Times   The director of emergency responses in Montreal, Canada, is interested in analyzing the time needed for response teams to reach their destinations in emergency situations after leaving their stations. She has acquired the response times for 1,220 calls last month. To develop the frequency histogram, perform the following steps:

Step 1: **Construct a frequency distribution.**
Because response time is a continuous variable measured in seconds, the data should be broken down into classes and the steps given in Example 2-3 should be used. The following frequency distribution with 10 classes was developed:

Response Time	Frequency	Response Time	Frequency
0 < 30	36	180 < 210	145
30 < 60	68	210 < 240	80
60 < 90	195	240 < 270	43
90 < 120	180	270 < 300	31
120 < 150	260		1,220
150 < 180	182		

Step 2: **Construct the axes for the histogram.**
The horizontal axis will be response time and the vertical axis will be frequency

Step 3: **Construct bars with heights corresponding to the frequency of each class and label appropriately.**
This is shown as follows:

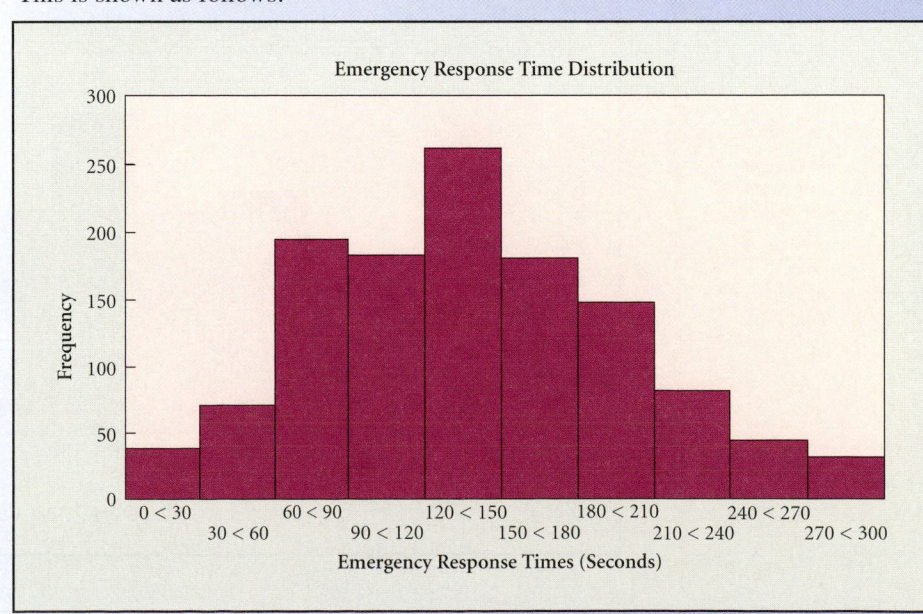

This histogram indicates that the response times vary considerably. The center is somewhere in the range of 120 to 180 seconds.

RELATIVE FREQUENCY HISTOGRAMS AND OGIVES

Histograms can also be used to display relative frequency distributions and cumulative relative frequency distributions. A relative frequency histogram is formed in the same manner as a frequency histogram, but relative frequencies are used rather than frequencies. The cumulative relative frequency is presented using a graph called an **ogive**. Example 2-5 illustrates each of these graphical tools.

*E*XAMPLE 2-5: RELATIVE FREQUENCY HISTOGRAMS AND OGIVES

Emergency Response Times (continued)   Example 2-4 introduced the situation facing the emergency response manager in Montreal. In that example, she formed a frequency distribution for a sample of 1,220 response times. She is now interested in graphing the relative frequencies and the cumulative relative frequencies. To do so, use the following steps:

Step 1:   **Convert the frequency distribution into relative frequencies and cumulative relative frequencies.**

Response Time	Frequency	Relative Frequency	Cumulative Relative Frequency
0 < 30	36	36/1220 = 0.0295	0.0295
30 < 60	68	68/1220 = 0.0557	0.0852
60 < 90	195	195/1220 = 0.1598	0.2451
90 < 120	180	180/1220 = 0.1475	0.3926
120 < 150	260	260/1220 = 0.2131	0.6057
150 < 180	182	182/1220 = 0.1492	0.7549
180 < 210	145	145/1220 = 0.1189	0.8738
210 < 240	80	80/1220 = 0.0656	0.9393
240 < 270	43	43/1220 = 0.0352	0.9746
270 < 300	31	31/1220 = 0.0254	1.0000
	1,220	1.0000	

Step 2:   **Construct the relative frequency histogram.**
Place the quantitative variable on the horizontal axis and the relative frequencies on the vertical axis. The vertical bars are drawn to heights corresponding to the relative frequencies of the classes.

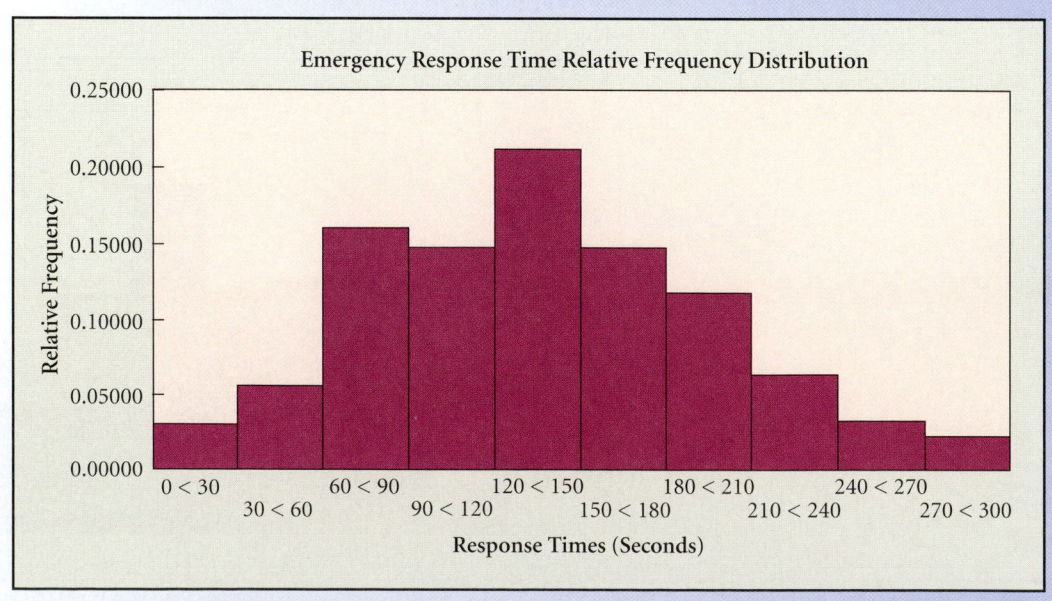

Note the relative frequency histogram has exactly the same shape as the frequency histogram. However, the vertical axis has a different scale.

Step 3:   **Construct the ogive.**

Draw a line connecting the points plotted above the *upper limit* of each class at a height corresponding to the cumulative relative frequency.

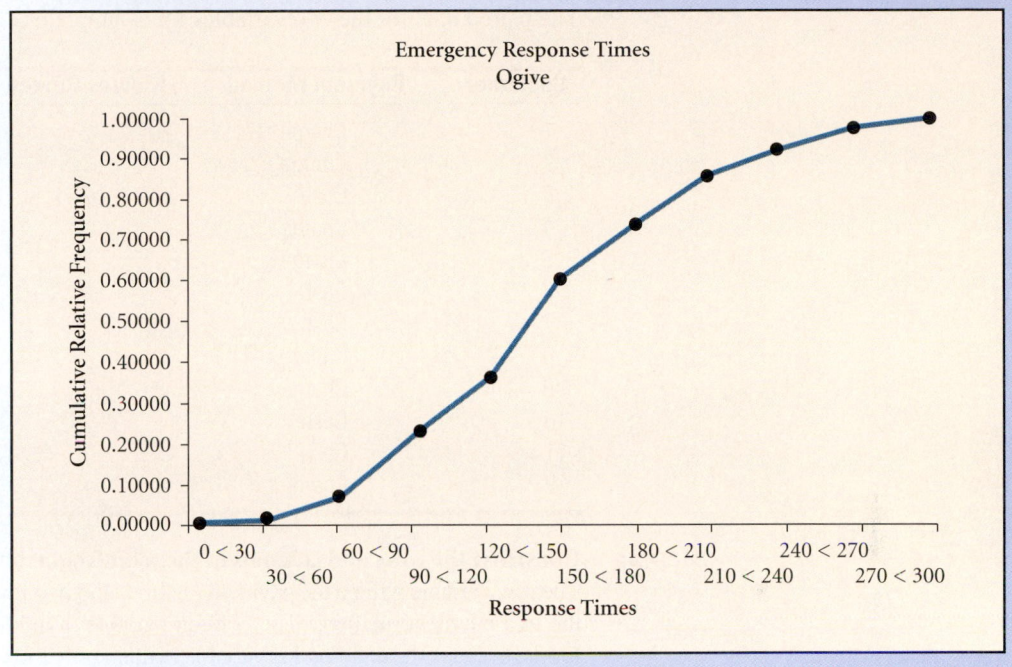

JOINT FREQUENCY DISTRIBUTIONS

Frequency distributions are effective tools for describing data. Thus far we have discussed how to develop grouped and ungrouped frequency distributions for one variable at a time. For instance, in the Capital Credit Union example, we were interested in customer credit card balances for all customers. We constructed a frequency distribution and histogram for that variable. However, often we need to examine the data more closely. This may involve constructing a *joint frequency distribution* for two variables.

Joint frequency distributions can be constructed for qualitative or quantitative variables.

SUMMARY: CONSTRUCTING JOINT FREQUENCY DISTRIBUTIONS

A joint frequency distribution is constructed using the following steps:

1. Obtain a set of data consisting of paired responses for two variables. The responses can be qualitative or quantitative. If the responses are quantitative, they can be discrete or continuous.

2. Construct a table with *r* rows and *c* columns, in which the number of rows represents the number of categories (or numeric classes) of one variable and the number of columns corresponds to the number of categories (or numeric classes) of the second variable.

3. Count the number of joint occurrences at each row level and each column level for all combinations of row and column values and place these frequencies in the appropriate cells.

4. Compute the row and column totals, which are called the marginal frequencies.

5. If a joint relative frequency distribution is desired, divide each cell frequency by the total number of paired observations.

EXAMPLE 2-6: JOINT FREQUENCY DISTRIBUTION

VideoLand   VideoLand is a national chain that rents VHS and DVD movies for home use. Recently, the sales manager at a Minnesota store collected data dealing with customer purchases. Among the data collected were two variables: payment method (cash or charge) and number of movies rented. The manager wishes to develop a joint frequency distribution to better understand the buying habits of his customers. To do this, he can use the following steps:

Step 1: **Obtain the data.**

The paired data for the two variables for a sample of 12 customers are obtained.

Customer	Payment Method	Movies Rented
1	Charge	2
2	Charge	1
3	Cash	2
4	Charge	2
5	Charge	1
6	Cash	1
7	Cash	3
8	Charge	1
9	Charge	3
10	Cash	2
11	Cash	1
12	Charge	1

Step 2: **Construct the rows and columns of the joint frequency table.**

The row variable will be the payment method, and two rows will be used, corresponding to the two payment methods. The column variable is movies rented, and it will have three levels, because the data for this variable contain only the values 1, 2, and 3. (Note, if a variable is continuous, classes should be formed using the methods discussed in Example 2-3.)

		Movies Rented		
		1	2	3
Payment	Charge			
	Cash			

Step 3: **Count the number of joint occurrences at each row level and each column level for all combinations of row and column values and place these frequencies in the appropriate cells.**

		Movies Rented			
		1	2	3	Total
Payment	Charge	4	2	1	7
	Cash	2	2	1	5
	Total	6	4	2	12

Step 4: **Calculate the row and column totals (see Step 3).**

The manager can now see that for this sample, most people charged their purchase (seven people) and most people rented only one movie (six people). Likewise, four people both rented one movie and charged their purchase.

Capital Credit Union (continued)—Recall that the Capital Credit Union discussed earlier was interested in evaluating the success of its new credit card. Figures 2-5 and 2-6 showed the frequency distribution and histogram for a sample of customer credit card balances. Although this information is useful, the managers would like to know more. Specifically, what does the credit card balance distribution look like for male versus female cardholders?

One way to approach this is to sort the data by the gender variable and develop frequency distributions and histograms for males and females separately. You could then make a visual compari-

Excel and Minitab Tutorial

FIGURE 2-7

Excel Output of the Capital Credit Union Joint Frequency Distribution

Excel Instructions:
1. Place Cursor anywhere in the table
2. Right click - select **Wizard**
3. Select **Layout**
4. Double click on **Data** field item
5. For "Show Data As – select % of Column
6. Click **OK**.

Microsoft Excel - Capital.xls

	A	B		C	D
3	Count of Credit Card Account Balance	Gender	1 = Male 2 = Female		
4	Credit Card Account Balance		1	2	Grand Total
5	90-239		4.74%	2.94%	4.33%
6	240-389		6.90%	4.41%	6.33%
7	390-539		14.22%	13.24%	14.00%
8	540-689		19.40%	23.53%	20.33%
9	690-839		15.09%	17.65%	15.67%
10	840-989		17.67%	13.24%	16.67%
11	990-1139		12.07%	11.76%	12.00%
12	1140-1289		6.03%	8.82%	6.67%
13	1290-1439		3.45%	2.94%	3.33%
14	1440-1589		0.43%	1.47%	0.67%
15	Grand Total		100.00%	100.00%	100.00%

Minitab Instructions (for similar results):
1. Open file: Capital.MTW
2. Click on **Data > Code > Numeric to Text**.
3. Under **Code data from columns**, select data column.
4. Under **Into columns**, specify destination column: *Classes*.
5. In **Original values**, define each data class range.
6. In **New**, specify code for each class.
7. Click **OK**.
8. Click on **Stat > Tables > Cross Tabulation and Chi-square**.
9. Under **Categorical variables For rows** enter *Classes* column and **For columns** enter *Gender* column.
10. Under **Display** check **Counts**.
11. Click **OK**.

son of the two to determine what, if any, difference exists between males and females. However, an alternative approach is to jointly analyze the two variables: gender and credit card balance.

Although the process is different for Excel and Minitab, both software packages provide methods for analyzing two variables jointly. In Figure 2-5, we constructed the frequency distribution for the 300 credit card balances using 10 classes. The class width was set at $150. Figure 2-7 shows a table that is called a *joint frequency distribution*. This type of table is also called a *cross-tabulation* table.[1]

The Capital Credit Union managers can use a joint frequency table to analyze the credit card balances for males versus females. For instance, for the 61 customers with balances of $540 to $689, Figure 2-7 shows that 45 were males and 16 were females. Previously, we discussed the concept of relative frequency (proportions, which Excel converts to percentages) as a useful tool for making comparisons between two data sets. In this example, comparisons between males and females would be easier if the frequencies were converted to proportions (or percentages). The result is the *joint relative frequency table* shown in Figure 2-8. Notice that the percentages in each cell are percentages of the total 300 people in the survey. For example, the $540-to-$689 class had 20.33% (61) of the 300 customers.

FIGURE 2-8

Excel Output of the Joint Relative Frequencies

Excel Instructions (for similar results):
1. Place Cursor anywhere in the table.
2. Right click and select **Wizard**.
3. Select **Layout**.
4. Double click on **Data** field item.
5. For "Show Data As _ select % of Column.
6. Click **OK**.

Microsoft Excel - Capital.xls

	A	B		C	D
3	Count of Credit Card Account Balance	Gender	1 = Male 2 = Female		
4	Credit Card Account Balance		1	2	Grand Total
5	90-239		3.67%	0.67%	4.33%
6	240-389		5.33%	1.00%	6.33%
7	390-539		11.00%	3.00%	14.00%
8	540-689		15.00%	5.33%	20.33%
9	690-839		11.67%	4.00%	15.67%
10	840-989		13.67%	3.00%	16.67%
11	990-1139		9.33%	2.67%	12.00%
12	1140-1289		4.67%	2.00%	6.67%
13	1290-1439		2.67%	0.67%	3.33%
14	1440-1589		0.33%	0.33%	0.67%
15	Grand Total		77.33%	22.67%	100.00%

In Figure 2-8 we have used the **Data Field Options** of the Excel PivotTable to represent the data as percentages.

---

[1]In Excel, the joint frequency distribution is developed using a tool called Pivot tables. In Minitab, the joint frequency distributions are constructed using the Cross Tabulation option.

FIGURE 2-9

Minitab Output of the Joint
Relative Frequencies
Distribution

Minitab Instructions:
1. Open file: Capital.MTW.
2. Steps 2 – 7 as in
   Figure 2-7.
3. Click on **Stat > Tables >
   Cross Tabulation and
   Chi-square.**
4. Under **Categorical variables For rows** enter
   Classes column and **For
   columns** enter *Gender*
   column.
5. Under **Display** check
   Total percents.
6. Click **OK.**

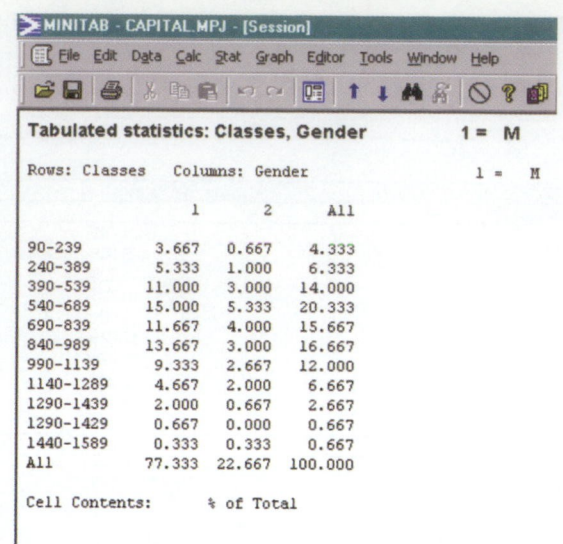

```
MINITAB - CAPITAL.MPJ - [Session]
File  Edit  Data  Calc  Stat  Graph  Editor  Tools  Window  Help

Tabulated statistics: Classes, Gender        1 = M

Rows: Classes    Columns: Gender             1 =   M

                    1        2       All

90-239           3.667    0.667     4.333
240-389          5.333    1.000     6.333
390-539         11.000    3.000    14.000
540-689         15.000    5.333    20.333
690-839         11.667    4.000    15.667
840-989         13.667    3.000    16.667
990-1139         9.333    2.667    12.000
1140-1289        4.667    2.000     6.667
1290-1439        2.000    0.667     2.667
1290-1429        0.667    0.000     0.667
1440-1589        0.333    0.333     0.667
All             77.333   22.667   100.000

Cell Contents:        % of Total
```

The male customers with balances in the $540-to-$689 range constituted 15% (45) of the 300 customers, whereas females with that balance level made up 5.33% (16) of all 300 customers. On the surface, this result seems to indicate a big difference between males and females at this credit balance level.

Suppose we really wanted to focus on the male-versus-female issue and control for the fact that
there are far more male customers than female. We could compute the percentages differently.
Rather than using a base of 300 (the entire sample size), we might instead be interested in the percentages of the males who have balances at each level, and the same data for females.[2] Figure 2-9
shows the relative frequencies converted to percentages of the column total. In general, there seems
to be little difference in the male and female distributions with respect to credit card balances.

There are many options for transferring data into useful information. Thus far, we have introduced frequency distributions, joint frequency tables, and histograms. In the next section, we discuss one of the most useful graphical tools: the bar chart.

2-1: EXERCISES

Skill Development

2.1   A data set has a maximum value of 700 and a minimum
value of 300. Using 10 classes, show the class limits
you would use for the first three classes using a format
similar to:
a. "130 to <145 lbs."
b. "130 to 144.99 lbs."

2.2   A data set has 200 observations. The maximum value in
the data set is $16,300, and the minimum value is $11,500.
a. Use Sturges's rule to determine the number of
classes that you will use.
b. Based on the number of classes determined in part a,
indicate the class width for each class.
c. Show the class limits for the first five classes, using a
format similar to "130 to <145 lbs."

2.3   A data set has 160 observations. The maximum value is
3.25 and the minimum value is −2.80.
a. Use Sturges's rule to determine the number of
classes that you will use.

b. Based on the number of classes determined in part a,
indicate the class width for each class.
c. Show the class limits for the first three classes. Use a format similar to "225 and under 450 seconds" on page 36.

2.4   You are given the following data.

6	10	6	4	9	5
5	5	5	7	6	2
5	5	5	4	5	7
6	7	8	6	8	4
7	5	5	5	5	7
8	7	6	7	5	4
6	4	4	7	4	6
6	7	8	6	7	6
7	8	5	6	5	7
3	6	4	7	4	4

a. Construct a frequency distribution for these data.
b. Based on the frequency distribution, develop a
histogram.

[2] Such distributions are known as *marginal distributions*.

c. Construct a relative frequency distribution.
d. Develop a relative frequency histogram.
e. Compare the two histograms. Why do they look alike?

2.5 Use the data from problem 2.4.
a. Construct a relative frequency distribution of the data. Use Sturges's rule to determine the number of classes.
b. Construct a cumulative frequency distribution of the data.
c. Construct a relative frequency histogram.
d. Construct an ogive.

2.6 Consider these two sets of data.

Value	2	3	4	5	6	7	8	9	10
Frequency	5	3	10	10	10	10	5	1	6

Value	2	3	4	5	6	7	8	9	10
Frequency	1	1	10	15	13	13	5	1	1

a. Construct a frequency distribution for these two sets of data using the same classes.
b. Which distribution appears to have the largest "center" value?
c. Which distribution appears to have the greatest variation?

2.7 You have been given the following joint frequency distribution. Convert the frequencies to relative frequencies.

		Years of College			
Income	None	1–2 Years	3–4 Years	5–6 Years	>6 Years
<$20,000	16	33	30	6	4
$20,000 to <$40,000	22	28	40	26	5
$40,000 to <$60,000	9	12	21	46	9
≥$60,000	3	5	15	13	6

a. Determine the proportion of those having at least five years of college who earn at least $40,000. Compare this proportion to a similar proportion for those having fewer than five years of college.
b. Determine the proportion of those who make at least $60,000 who have more than four years of college.
c. Determine the proportion of the entire sample who make less than $20,000. Compare this to the proportion of those who have not gone to college who make less than $20,000.
d. Calculate the proportion of those who have not gone to college who make at least $60,000. Calculate a similar proportion for each of the years-of-college categories.

Business Applications

2.8 One strategy that some investors take is to invest in local companies. Each day, the city newspaper carries the daily closing stock prices for some of the local com-

panies. On a recent day the closing prices for 37 companies were listed as follows:

61.00	50.06	6.50	45.56	22.13	13.88	18.13	38.75	26.94	91.44
28.38	64.56	7.13	59.94	72.94	37.88	27.75	73.19	25.88	25.38
60.06	14.63	28.88	27.31	52.75	1.69	30.25	52.38	31.81	72.98
118.00	19.88	45.31	31.00	72.63	120.00	25.88			

a. Create a data array for these data.
b. Develop a frequency distribution with five classes for these data. Use zero as the lower limit of the first class.
c. Develop a histogram based on the frequency distribution.
d. Determine the proportion of stock highs that are greater than $50.
e. Write a short statement that describes the stock price data.

2.9 Each month the American Automobile Association (AAA) generates a report on gasoline prices that they distribute to the newspapers throughout the state. On February 17th, AAA called a random sample of 51 stations to determine the price of unleaded gasoline that day. The resulting data are shown as follows:

1.07	1.31	1.18	1.01	1.23	1.09	1.29	1.10	1.16	1.08
0.96	1.66	1.21	1.09	1.02	1.04	1.01	1.03	1.09	1.11
1.11	1.17	1.04	1.09	1.05	0.96	1.32	1.09	1.26	1.11
1.03	1.20	1.21	1.05	1.10	1.04	0.97	1.21	1.07	1.17
0.98	1.10	1.04	1.03	1.12	1.10	1.03	1.18	1.11	1.09
1.06									

a. Create a data array with the gasoline price data.
b. Construct two histograms for this data set, using 5 classes for the first and 15 classes for the second. Use $0.95 as the lower limit of the first class.
c. A local radio station has reported that 30% of the gas stations are charging $1.15 a gallon or more for gasoline. (1) Use one of the histograms you have produced to respond to this report. (2) Which histogram did you use? Why?

2.10 The American Automobile Association study discussed in problem 2.9 produced the following data on unleaded gasoline prices:

1.07	1.31	1.18	1.01	1.23	1.09	1.29	1.10	1.16	1.08
0.96	1.66	1.21	1.09	1.02	1.04	1.01	1.03	1.09	1.11
1.11	1.17	1.04	1.09	1.05	0.96	1.32	1.09	1.26	1.11
1.03	1.20	1.21	1.05	1.10	1.04	0.97	1.21	1.07	1.17
0.98	1.10	1.04	1.03	1.12	1.10	1.03	1.18	1.11	1.09
1.06									

Using $0.90 as the lower limit of the first class, construct the following distributions using seven classes.
a. a frequency distribution.
b. a relative frequency distribution.
c. a cumulative frequency distribution and a cumulative relative frequency distribution.

2.11 The loan officer at Money First National Bank wants to obtain information about the loans she has made over the past five years. She is preparing a report for the bank's regional spring conference. As part of the report, she has decided to develop a distribution showing the loan frequency by size of loan. The data indicates that the smallest loan she made was for $1,000 and the largest loan was $25,000.

a. If she wants to have 10 classes in her distribution, define the 10 classes in terms of lower and upper limits.

b. She knows that other loan officers will also be making similar presentations. If she wishes to compare the information in her distribution with that of the others, what kind of distribution do you recommend? Give your reasons.

2.12 ⊙ The data file *Wallingford* contains a sample of 60 accounts receivable balances selected from accounts at the Wallingford Department Store. Each week, the sales manager asks to summarize the current status of the accounts receivable.

a. Using 10 classes and 5.00 as the lower limit of the first class, develop a frequency distribution and histogram for the accounts receivable.

b. Write a one-paragraph statement describing the accounts receivable balances as reflected by the sample. Specifically, (1) state the range of the account balances, (2) identify any account balances that may warrant more scrutiny by the collections department, and (3) determine the proportion of accounts larger than $100. Describe any other significant features of the data of which the manager should be made aware. (Remember that in business, report writing is an important way of conveying information.)

2.13 In a survey conducted by NFO Interactive, investors were asked to rate how knowledgeable they felt they were as investors. Both online and traditional investors were included in the survey. The survey resulted in the following data:

a. Of the online investors, 8%, 55%, and 37% responded they were "savvy," "experienced," and "novice," respectively.

b. Of the traditional investors, the percentages were 4%, 29%, and 67%, respectively.

Six hundred investors were surveyed, of which 200 were traditional investors.

a. Use this information to construct a joint frequency distribution.

b. Use the information to construct a joint relative frequency distribution.

c. Determine the proportion of investors who were both online investors and rated themselves experienced.

d. Calculate the proportion of investors who were online investors.

2.14 The makers of the PowerChew Energy Bar recently weighed 10 bars from each of their two production lines. The following data were observed:

Line	1	1	1	1	1	1	1	1	1	1
Weight	2.78	2.95	3.03	2.89	3.04	2.97	3.04	2.99	2.95	3.10
Line	2	2	2	2	2	2	2	2	2	2
Weight	3.02	3.11	2.98	2.90	3.02	3.05	3.01	2.97	2.98	3.00

a. Develop a joint frequency distribution showing manufacturing line and the weights broken into two categories: under 3.00 and 3.00 and over.

b. Referring to part a, convert the joint frequency distribution to a joint relative frequency distribution.

c. Write a short paragraph using the information in parts a and b to describe the output for the PowerChew company.

Advanced Business Applications

2.15 ⊙ Lotteries have become very popular across the nation. Information regarding lottery sales between July 1, 1996, and June 30, 1997, are provided in the file *Lottery*. This data set was provided by the North American Association of State and Provincial Lotteries, as reported in the March 15, 1998, issue of the *Idaho Statesman*.

a. Develop a frequency distribution for the lottery sales using five classes and zero as lower limit of first class.

b. Develop a frequency distribution for the state profit. Determine an appropriate number of classes, determine the frequency of each class, and calculate the relative frequency of each class.

c. Develop a frequency distribution for the per capita spending. Determine an appropriate number of classes, determine the frequency of each class, and calculate the relative frequency and the cumulative relative frequency of each class.

d. Develop histograms for parts a, b, and c.

2.16 ⊙ The Franklin Tire Company is interested in demonstrating the durability of their steel-belted radial tires. To do this, the managers have decided to put 4 tires on 100 different sport utility vehicles and drive them throughout Alaska. The data collected indicate the number of miles (rounded to the nearest 1,000 miles) that each of the SUVs traveled before one of the tires on the vehicle did not meet minimum federal standards for tread thickness. The data file is called *Franklin*.

a. Construct a frequency distribution and histogram using eight classes. Use 51 as the lower limit of the first class.

b. The marketing department wishes to know the tread life of at least 50% of the tires, the 10% with the longest tread life, and the longest tread life of these tires. Provide this information to the marketing department. Also provide any other significant items that point out the desirability of this line of steel-belted tires.

c. Construct a frequency distribution and a histogram using 12 classes, with 51 as the lower limit of the first class. Compare your results with those in parts a and b. Which distribution gives the best information about the desirability of this line of steel-belted tires?

2.17 A research project conducted by the State Transportation Department has as its objective determining whether a truck scale that will weigh a truck while it is moving down the highway (WIM scale) could be used to augment the traditional Port-of-Entry scale (POE scale) for enforcement and data-collection purposes. A portion of the data collected in this study is contained in the file called *Trucks*. Two of the variables collected in the study are POE length and WIM length.

a. Develop a frequency distribution for POE length using eight classes.

b. Develop a relative frequency distribution for POE length.

c. Construct both a frequency histogram and an ogive for POE length.

d. Develop a frequency distribution and a histogram for WIM length of trucks. Use the same classes as those used for the POE length-of-trucks distribution so you can compare them. How do the two distributions compare? Discuss.

e. Construct a joint frequency distribution using POE length as the row variable and WIM length as the column variable. Based on this distribution, would you recommend that the WIM truck lengths be used in place of the POE truck lengths? Are there any systematic differences between the two distributions? Write a short report that discusses the similarities and differences between these two length variables.

2.18 The High Desert Banking Company is a small bank that specializes in making consumer loans, small commercial loans, and real estate loans (both home improvement and new-home construction). The data file *High-Desert-Banking* contains the loans made by the bank last year. The loan-type codes are 1 = Consumer, 2 = Commercial, and 3 = Real Estate.

In your position as an intern at the bank, you have been given the task of developing a presentation to the bank's loan officers. You are planning to include the following in your presentation:

a. A frequency distribution of loans by type of loan.

b. A relative frequency distribution.

c. A frequency distribution of loan amounts using class intervals of width equal to $15,000.

d. A histogram of loan amounts using the frequency distribution in part c.

e. A joint frequency distribution of loan amount and type of loan using class intervals of $15,000 for loan amount.

f. Develop a written report that fully discloses the loan data. This report should be developed using word processing. The various frequency distributions and histograms should be pasted into the document and clearly labeled. Make sure your report points out differences and similarities among the various distributions of loan data in the regions of the country. For instance, examine which regions have the largest loans, which regions have similar distributions, and how the regions' distributions are different.

2.19 The research and development department at Hydronics, Inc., has developed two weight-loss systems that they are considering introducing on the market. One month ago, the managers conducted a study in which they put a sample of people into three separate programs: 1, 2, and a placebo. They then recorded the number of pounds each person gained or lost during the month. These data are recorded in the file called *Hydronics*.

You have been asked to analyze the weight-loss data using the following statistical tools:

a. Develop a frequency distribution for each program and the placebo. Use 5-pound class widths.

b. Based on the results in part a, develop histograms for each program and the placebo.

c. Produce relative frequency distributions for each program and for the placebo.

d. Prepare a report that summarizes the information generated in parts a, b, and c. You must include in your report a recommendation concerning which weight-loss system they should introduce and the reasons for the recommendation.

2-2 BAR CHARTS, PIE CHARTS, AND STEM AND LEAF DIAGRAMS

BAR CHARTS

Section 2-1 introduced some of the basic tools for describing numerical variables, both discrete and continuous, when the data were in their raw form. However, in many instances, you will be working with categorical data or data that have already been summarized to some extent. In this case, an effective presentation tool is often a **bar chart**.

Bar Chart

A graphical representation of a categorical data set in which a rectangle or bar is drawn over each category or class. The length of each bar represents the frequency or percentage of observations, or some other measure associated with the category. The bars may be vertical or horizontal. The bars may all be the same color or they may be different colors depicting different categories. Additionally, multiple variables can be graphed on the same bar chart.

TABLE 2-6

1997 U.S. Income from Emerging-Market Countries

Brazil	$4.55	Malaysia	$1.21
Mexico	$3.97	Venezuela	$0.87
Indonesia	$1.74	Argentina	$0.85
Panama	$1.30	China	$0.81
Chile	$1.22	Nigeria	$0.78

Note: Data are in billions of dollars, U.S. currency.

International Banking—In today's business climate, the U.S. economy is closely linked to the international marketplace. Recently an executive for the Wall Street brokerage house Hoenig & Co. gave a speech at an international economic summit in New York City. The talk centered on Brazil, the world's ninth-largest economy, and one that by many accounts is in great peril.[3]

In preparing the speech, the Hoenig executive assembled the data in Table 2-6, which shows the 1997 income, in billions of dollars, derived by U.S. businesses from emerging-market countries.

Although the table format contains the data and is informative, a graphical presentation is often desirable. A bar chart would work well in this instance. Recall that the bars can be vertical or horizontal. Figure 2-10 shows an example. Note, because Brazil is the focus, that bar is high-lighted with a different shading than the other countries. The bar chart shows very clearly how important Brazil is to the United States as a source of income. Do you agree that the chart makes the point more effectively than the table?

People sometimes confuse histograms and bar charts. Although there are some similarities, they are two very different graphical tools. Histograms are used to represent a frequency distribution associated with a quantitative (ratio or interval-level) variable. Refer to the histogram illustrations in Section 2-1. In every case, the variable on the horizontal axis was numerical, with values moving from low to high. There are no gaps between the histogram bars. On the other hand, bar charts are used when the variable of interest is categorical, as in this case in which the category is country.

FIGURE 2-10

Bar Chart of U.S. Income from Emerging Countries

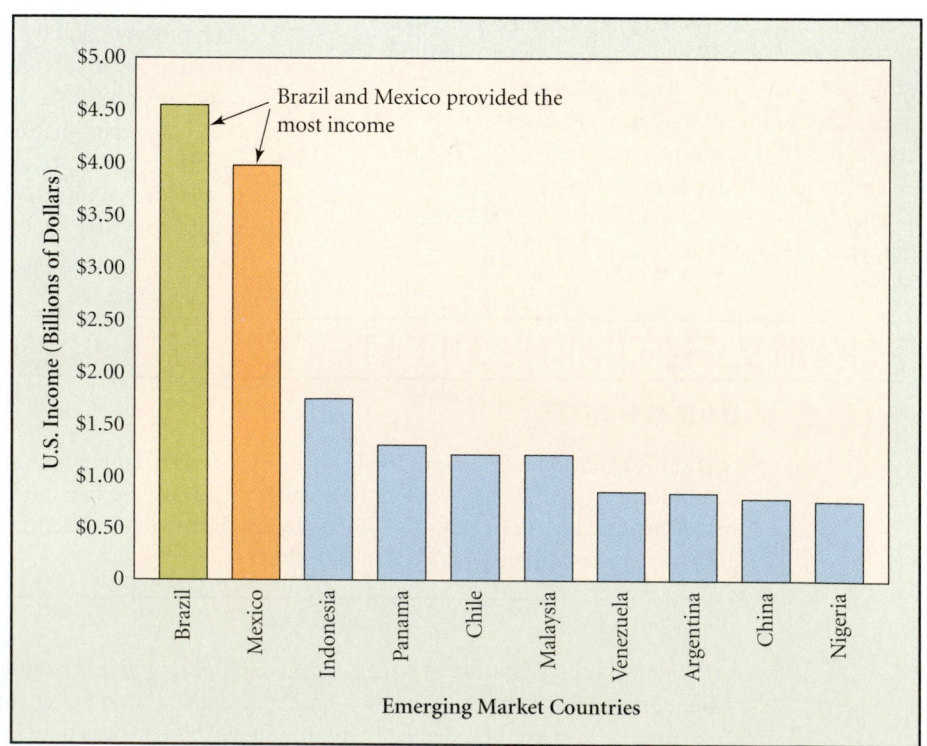

[3]Fox, Justin, "A Prayer for Brazil," *Fortune*, November 9, 1998, pp. 30–31.

SUMMARY: CONSTRUCTING BAR CHARTS

A bar chart is constructed using the following steps:

1. Define the categories for the variable of interest.

2. For each category, determine the appropriate measure or value.

3. For a vertical bar chart, locate the categories on the horizontal axis. The vertical axis is set to a scale correspond-

ing to the values in the categories. For a horizontal bar chart, place the categories on the vertical axis and set the scale of the horizontal axis in accordance with the values in the categories. Then construct bars, either vertical or horizontal, for each category such that the height corresponds to the value for the category.

EXAMPLE 2-7: BAR CHARTS

Attending Higher Education in Idaho   The fact that you are taking this course means that you are pursuing a higher education, either in the United States or internationally. However, not everyone does. A study conducted in Idaho in January 2002 addressed the issue of percentage of high school graduates who continue their education. The objective is to display the data effectively. A bar chart can be conducted using the following steps:

Step 1: **Define the categories.**
Data are available for four years and for three factors, as shown in the following table.

	% Higher Ed	% in Idaho	% Out of State
1992	48	36	12
1994	47	35	12
1996	47	34	13
1998	49	36	13

The main category is the year. For each year, there are three values of interest: percentage of Idaho high school graduates who enroll in higher education; the percentage who enroll in Idaho higher education institutions; and the percentage who go out of state.

Step 2: **Determine the appropriate measure.**
The measure for each category is the percentage of high school graduates.

Step 3: **Develop the bar chart.**
The vertical bar chart that is developed is shown as follows. Note, each percentage value is assigned a different color, and the data are displayed over the four different years.

This bar chart illustrates that the percentage of Idaho's high school graduates who go on to higher education has been fairly stable at just under 50 percent. It also shows that most Idaho students who do enroll tend to stay in state for their higher education.

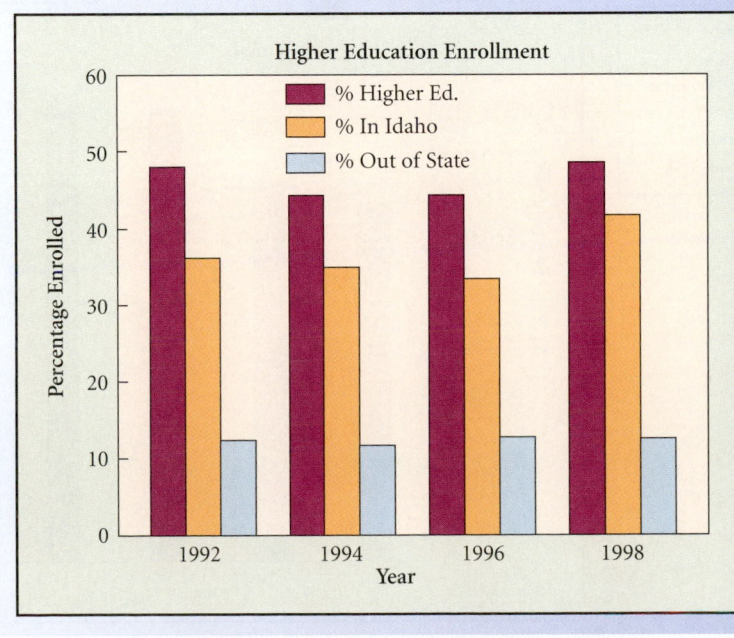

TABLE 2-7

Salary Data for Bach, Lombard, & Wilson

YEAR	MALES: AVERAGE STARTING SALARIES	FEMALES: AVERAGE STARTING SALARIES
1992	$44,456	$41,789
1993	$47,286	$46,478
1994	$56,234	$53,854
1995	$57,890	$58,600
1996	$63,467	$59,070
1997	$61,090	$55,321
1998	$67,543	$64,506

Excel and Minitab Tutorial

Bach, Lombard, & Wilson—One of the most useful features of bar charts is that they can display multiple issues. Consider Bach, Lombard, & Wilson, the New England law firm. Recently, the firm handled a case in which a woman was suing her employer, a major electronics firm, claiming the company gave higher starting salaries to men than to women. Consequently, she stated, even though the company tended to give equal percentage raises to women and men, the gap between the two groups widened.

Attorneys at Bach, Lombard, & Wilson had their staff assemble massive amounts of data. Table 2-7 provides an example of the type of data they collected.

A bar chart is a more effective way to convey this information, as Figure 2-11 shows. From this graph we can quickly see that in all years except 1995 the starting salaries for males did exceed females. The bar chart also illustrates that the general trend in starting salaries for both groups has been increasing, though with a slight downturn in 1997. Do you think the information in Figure 2-11 alone is sufficient to rule in favor of the claimant in this lawsuit?

Suppose other data are available showing the percentage of new hires having MBA degrees by gender, as illustrated in Table 2-8. The bar charts in Figure 2-12a and Figure 2-12b present these data clearly. These charts show that every year the percentage of new hires with MBA degrees was substantially higher for male hires than for female hires. What might this imply about the reason for the difference in starting salaries?

FIGURE 2-11

Excel Output—Bar Chart of Starting Salaries

Excel Instructions:
1. Open file: Bach.xls
2. Click on **Chart Wizard**.
3. Select **Column** type.
4. Define **Data Range**.
5. Label chart as desired.

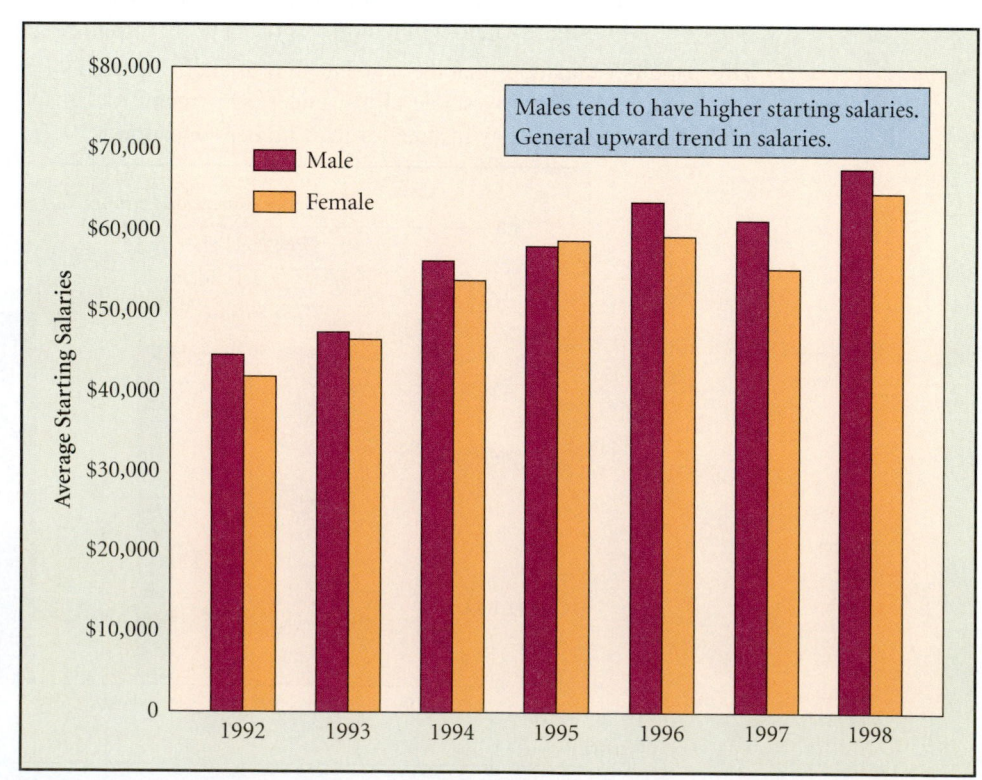

T A B L E   2 - 8

Salary Data for the
Bach, Lombard, &
Wilson Example

YEAR	MALES: AVERAGE STARTING SALARIES	MALES: PERCENTAGE WITH MBA	FEMALES: AVERAGE STARTING SALARIES	FEMALES: PERCENTAGE WITH MBA
1992	$44,456	35	$41,789	18
1993	$47,286	39	$46,478	20
1994	$56,234	49	$53,854	22
1995	$57,890	40	$58,600	30
1996	$63,467	46	$59,070	25
1997	$61,090	32	$55,321	24
1998	$67,543	48	$64,506	26

F I G U R E   2 - 1 2 A

Excel Output—Bar Chart
of MBA Hire Data

Excel Instructions:
1. Open file: Bach.xls
2. Click on **Chart Wizard**.
3. Select **Bar type**.
4. Define **Data Range**.
5. Label chart as desired.

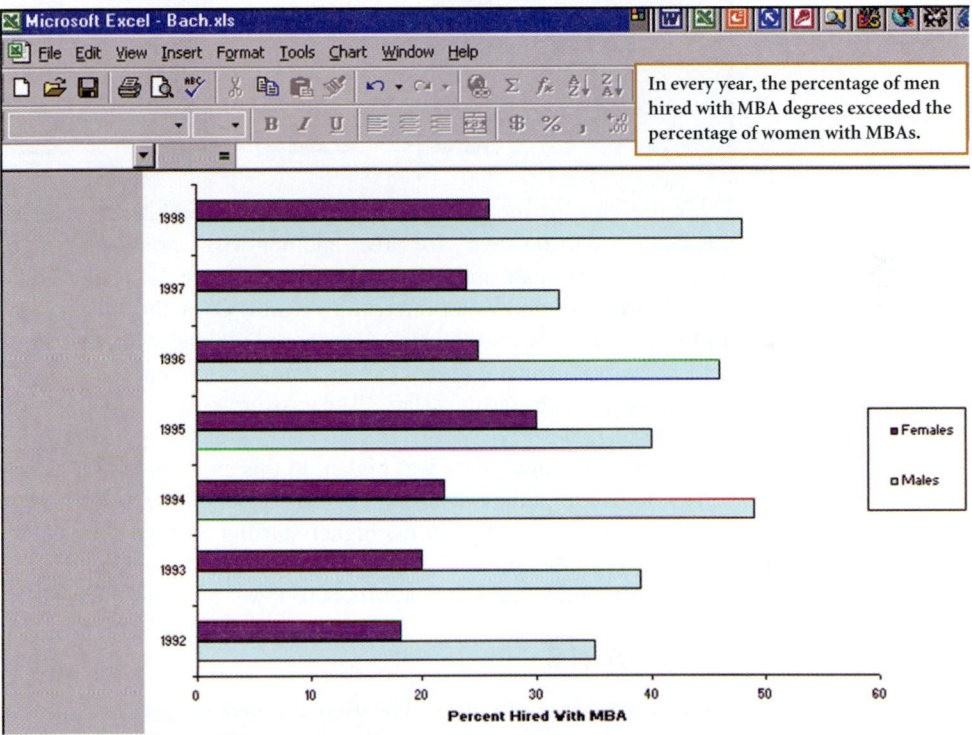

F I G U R E   2 - 1 2 B

Minitab Output—Bar
Chart of MBA Hire Data

Minitab Instructions:
(0. Create stacked columns
for *Percent Hired*, *Years*,
and *Gender*.)
1. Open file: Bach.MTW.
2. Click on **Graph >Bar
Graph**.
3. Under **Bars represent**,
select *Values from a table*.
4. Under **One column of
values**, select *Cluster*,
click **OK**.
5. In **Graph variables**, enter
Percent Hired column.
6. In **Categorical variables
for grouping (1-4 outer-
most first)**, enter *Years*
and *Gender* columns.
7. Click **OK**.

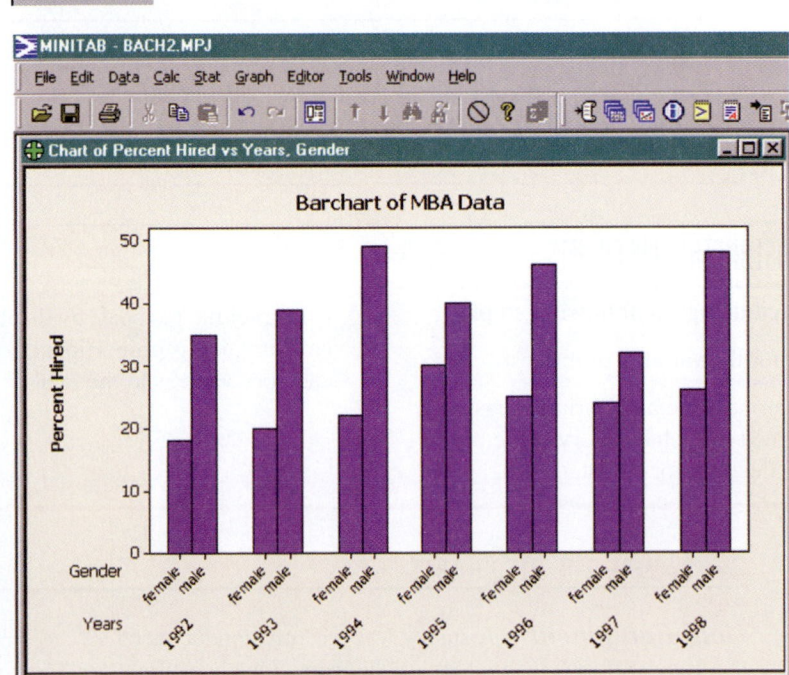

FIGURE 2-13

Excel Output—Bar Chart
of Average Salaries by
Degree Type

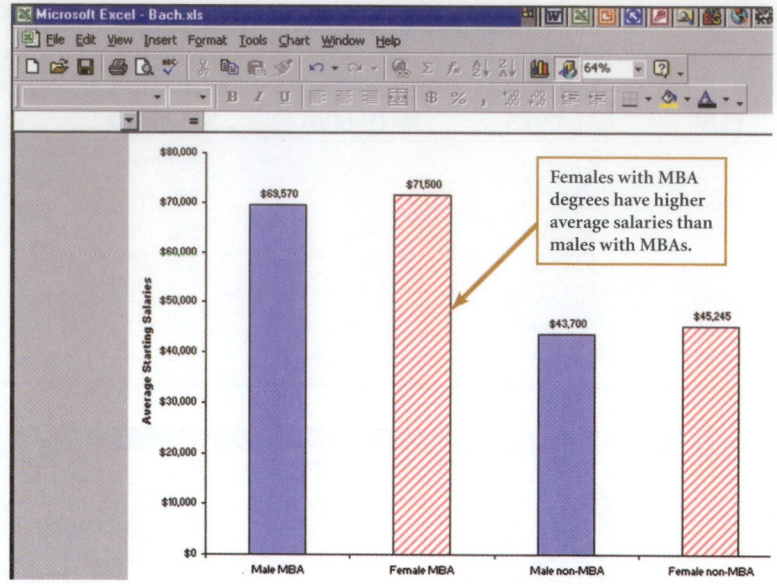

After viewing the bar charts in Figures 2-12a and 2-12b, the lead attorney had her staff look at the average starting salary for MBA and non-MBA graduates for the combined seven-year period, broken down by male and female employees. Figure 2-13 shows the bar chart for those data.

Figure 2-13 shows an interesting result. Over the seven-year period, females actually had higher starting salaries than males for those with and without MBA degrees. Then how can Figure 2-11 be correct, when it shows that in almost every year the male average starting salary exceeded the female average starting salary? The answer lies in Figure 2-12, which shows that far more of the newly hired males have MBAs. Because MBAs tend to get substantially higher starting salaries, the overall male average salary was higher. In this case, the initial data looked like the electronics firm had been discriminating against females by paying lower starting salaries. After digging deeper, we see that females actually get the higher starting average salaries with and without MBA degrees. However, does this prove that the company is not discriminating in its hiring practices? Perhaps it purposefully hires fewer female MBAs or fewer females in general. More research is needed.

PIE CHARTS

Another graphical tool that can be used to transform data into information is the **pie chart**.

> **Pie Chart**
>
> A graph in the shape of a circle. The circle is divided into "slices" corresponding to the categories or classes to be displayed. The size of each slice is proportional to the magnitude of the displayed variable associated with each category or class.

SUMMARY: CONSTRUCTING PIE CHARTS

A pie chart is constructed using the following steps:

1. Define the categories for the variable of interest.

2. For each category, determine the appropriate measure or value. The value assigned to each category is the proportion the category is to the total for all categories.

3. Construct the pie chart by displaying one slice for each category that is proportional in size to the proportion the category value is to the total of all categories.

EXAMPLE 2-8: PIE CHARTS

Gold Equipment   A survey was recently conducted of 300 golfers that asked questions about the impact of new technology on the game. One question asked the golfers to indicate which area of golf equipment is most responsible for improving an amateur golfer's game. The following data were obtained:

Equipment	Frequency
Golf Ball	81
Club Head Material	66
Shaft Material	63
Club Head Size	63
Shaft Length	3
Don't Know	24

To display these data in pie-chart form, use the following steps:

Step 1:   **Define the categories.**
The categories are the six equipment-response categories.

Step 2:   **Determine the appropriate measure.**
The appropriate measure is the proportion of the golfers surveyed. The proportion for each category is determined by dividing the number of golfers in a category by the total sample size. For example, for the category golf ball, the percentage is $81/300 = 0.27$.

Step 3:   **Construct the pie chart.**
The pie chart is constructed by dividing a circle into six slices (one for each category) such that each slice is proportional to the percentage of golfers in the category.

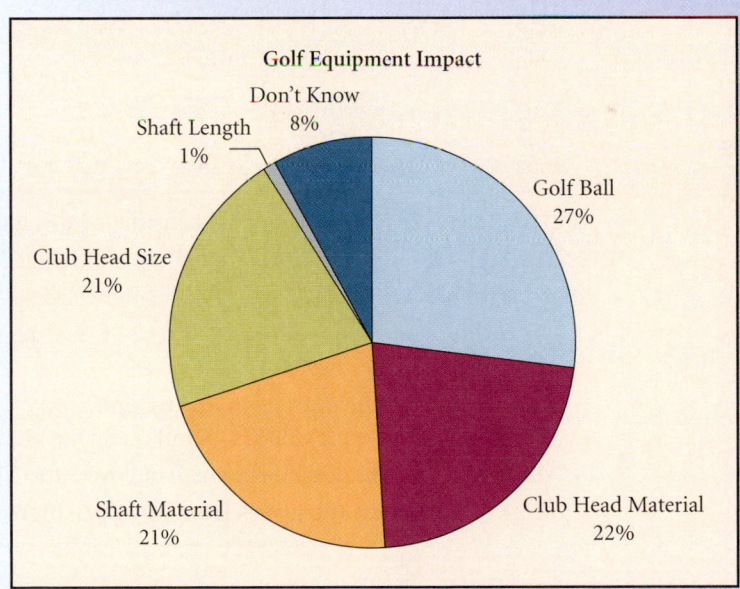

STEM AND LEAF DIAGRAMS

Another graphical technique that is useful for doing a preliminary analysis of quantitative data is called the *stem and leaf diagram*. The stem and leaf diagram is similar to the histogram introduced in Section 2-1 in that it displays the distribution for the quantitative variable. However, unlike the histogram, in which the individual values of the data are lost if the variable of interest is broken into classes, the stem and leaf diagram shows the individual data values.

Minitab has a procedure for constructing stem and leaf diagrams. Although Excel does not have a stem and leaf procedure, the PHStat add-ins to Excel that are included on the CD-ROM do have a stem and leaf procedure.

SUMMARY: CONSTRUCTING STEM AND LEAF DIAGRAMS

To construct the stem and leaf diagram for a quantitative variable, use the following steps:

1. Analyze the data for the variable of interest to determine how you wish to split the values into a stem and a leaf.

2. Sort the data from low to high.

3. List all possible stems in a single column between the lowest and highest values in the data.

4. For each stem, list all leaves associated with the stem.

EXAMPLE 2-9: STEM AND LEAF DIAGRAMS

Regis Auto Rental   The operations manager for Regis Auto Rental is interested in performing an analysis of the miles driven for the cars the company rents on weekends. A quick method for analyzing the data for a sample of 200 rentals is the stem and leaf diagram. The following data represent the miles driven in the cars.

113	112	63	127	110	129	142	115	192	94
165	121	105	140	85	93	105	140	93	126
183	118	67	104	162	110	76	109	91	132
88	96	132	80	144	112	57	139	123	124
172	149	198	114	88	111	133	117	138	134
53	147	108	109	153	89	159	99	130	93
161	118	115	117	128	98	125	184	134	132
117	127	166	72	122	109	124	92	82	69
110	128	151	67	142	177	135	121	143	89
160	115	138	79	104	76	89	110	44	140
117	103	59	109	145	117	162	108	141	139
148	175	107	117	87	87	150	152	80	168
88	127	131	85	143	101	137	111	128	147
110	81	111	149	154	90	150	117	101	116
153	176	112	147	87	177	190	66	62	154
143	122	176	153	97	106	86	62	146	98
134	135	127	118	109	143	146	152	140	95
102	137	158	69	122	135	136	129	91	136
135	86	131	154	132	59	136	85	142	137
155	190	120	154	102	109	97	157	144	149

The stem and leaf diagram is constructed using the following steps:

Step 1: **Split the values into a stem and leaf.**

Stem = tens place   leaf = units place

For example, for the value 113, the stem is 11 and the leaf is 3. We are keeping one digit for the leaf.

Step 2: **Sort the data from low to high.**
The lowest value is 44 miles and the highest value is 198 miles.

Step 3: **List all possible stems from lowest to highest.**

Step 4: **Itemize the leaves from lowest to highest and place next to the appropriate stems.**

4	4
5	3 7 9 9
6	2 2 3 6 7 7 9 9
7	2 6 6 9
8	0 0 1 2 5 5 5 6 6 7 7 7 8 8 8 9 9 9
9	0 1 1 2 3 3 3 4 5 6 7 7 8 8 9
10	1 1 2 2 3 4 4 5 5 6 7 8 8 9 9 9 9 9 9
11	0 0 0 0 0 1 1 1 2 2 2 3 4 5 5 5 6 7 7 7 7 7 7 7 8 8 8
12	0 1 1 2 2 2 3 4 4 5 6 7 7 7 7 8 8 8 9 9
13	0 1 1 2 2 2 2 3 4 4 4 5 5 5 5 6 6 6 7 7 7 8 8 9 9
14	0 0 0 0 1 2 2 2 3 3 3 3 4 4 5 6 6 7 7 7 8 9 9 9
15	0 0 1 2 2 3 3 3 4 4 4 4 5 7 8 9
16	0 1 2 2 5 6 8
17	2 5 6 6 7 7
18	3 4
19	0 0 2 8

The stem and leaf diagram shows that most people drive the rental car between 80 and 160 miles, with the most frequent value in the 110- to 120-mile range.

2-2: EXERCISES

Skill Development

2.20 You are given the following data reflecting the number of people in a study having each of the particular investments.

Investments	No. of People
Mutual Fund	357
Savings Account	506
Certificate of Deposit	158
Individual Stocks	347
Bonds	86
Real Estate	169
Other	41

You wish to demonstrate which investments are the most popular. Based on these data, construct a bar chart to effectively display the data.

2.21 Given the following data on gasoline prices, construct a bar chart that displays the data effectively.

Year	Average Unleaded Price	Average Premium Price
1999	$1.22	$1.34
2000	$1.29	$1.39
2001	$1.37	$1.48
2002	$1.21	$1.31

2.22 A mutual fund recently sent a letter to its customers outlining the planned capital-gains distributions for the current year. The following values reflect the per share capital-gains allocation for each type of fund managed by the company:

Fund	Capital Gains Distributions
Balanced	$0.13
Equity Income	$0.75
Growth	$0.19
Select	$0.91
Utilities	$0.63

Construct a chart that will effectively display these data.

2.23 You are given the following data reflecting the number of people in a study having each of the particular investments.

Investments	No. of People
Mutual Fund	357
Savings Account	506
Certificate of Deposit	158
Individual Stocks	347
Bonds	86
Real Estate	169
Other	41

Construct a pie chart showing the percentage of people having each type of investment.

2.24 Given the following data, construct a stem and leaf diagram.

79	104	76	89	110
109	145	117	162	108
117	87	87	150	152
85	143	101	137	111
149	154	90	150	117
147	87	177	190	66
153	97	106	86	62

2.25 Given the following data, construct a stem and leaf diagram.

0.7	1.7
0.8	1.8
1.0	2.0
1.1	2.1
1.4	2.4
2.0	3.0
2.8	3.8
3.3	4.3
4.4	5.4
5.3	6.3
5.4	6.4

2.26 A university has the following number of students at each grade level.

Freshman	3,450	Senior	1,980
Sophomore	3,190	Graduate	750
Junior	2,780		

a. Construct a bar chart that effectively displays these data.
b. Construct a pie chart to display these data.
c. Referring to the graphs constructed in parts a and b, which would you favor as the most effective way of presenting these data? Discuss.

Business Applications

2.27 Ed Christianson has been asked by the director of marketing to make a presentation at next week's annual meeting of the Brown Manufacturing Company. The presentation concerns the company's advertising budget for the past year and the projected budget for the next year. In preparing for the meeting, Ed has obtained the following data:

Medium	This Year's Expense	Next Year's Budget
Newspaper	$35,000	$40,000
Television	$60,000	$80,000
Trade Publications	$25,000	$25,000
Miscellaneous	$10,000	$10,000

a. Use these data to develop a bar chart that effectively shows both this year's expenses for advertising and next year's proposed budget.

b. Develop two pie charts that show the dollar allocation to each media for the two years.

c. Referring to parts a and b, indicate whether bar charts or pie charts are more effective in displaying the media spending data. Discuss.

2.28   Growing companies must make regular capital expenditures to update and improve their production facilities. The following information, taken from the 1997 annual report of Flowers Industries, Inc., shows the capital expenditures made to renovate, automate, and modernize the firm's bakeries.

Year	Capital Expenditures (millions of dollars)
1992	34
1993	52
1994	64
1995	73
1996	76
1997	78
1998 estimated	40

Prepare a bar chart using this information. Comment on the pattern of capital expenditures since 1992.

2.29   Real estate investment trusts (REITs) were created by Congress in 1960 so small investors could invest in real estate as shareholders rather than as landlords. Using information taken from Paine Webber and SEC filings, the *Orlando Sentinel* on April 5, 1998, reported the following proportions of REIT money invested in different categories:

Category	Percentage
Shopping Centers	20
Multifamily	18
Office	17
Health Care	8
Hotels	8
Industrials	7
Mixed Industrial/Office	5
Mortgage Backed	5
Diversified	5
Self-Storage	4
Specialty	3

a. Present this information graphically using a pie chart and, alternatively, a bar chart.

b. Which do you feel is most effective? Why?

2.30   Real estate investment trusts provided investors with a convenient way to invest in real estate. Of the more than 300 U.S. REITs, 210 are publicly traded on the following exchanges:

Where Traded	Number
NYSE	158
AMEX	37
NASDAQ	15

Source: Paine Webber, SEC Filings, *Orlando Sentinel* (April 5, 1998).

Summarize this information using a bar chart and a pie chart. Discuss.

2.31   The Pennsylvania State Retirement Fund is overseen by an advisory board. At a recent meeting, the funds director suggested investing a sizable amount of money in a well-known mutual fund. As part of her presentation, she collected weekly closing prices for the fund over the past 52 weeks. These data are shown as follows:

41.0	27.4	31.9	29.4	30.0	39.9	27.9	37.4	32.3	33.4
37.0	36.0	32.2	29.1	30.1	36.2	27.1	28.8	16.7	32.0
27.7	30.6	24.8	33.4	28.7	42.5	38.5	35.7	34.7	36.9
33.3	26.7	27.9	29.7	33.0	28.8	31.2	37.3	39.6	26.3
36.6	29.8	32.4	26.0	31.8	34.1	34.9	33.4	33.2	35.8
33.7	30.5								

Construct a stem and leaf diagram for these data and write a short report indicating what this diagram shows.

Advanced Business Applications

2.32   The Celltone Company is a provider of cellular phone service. They have two plans, a basic plan and a business plan. Recently, the local Celltone store manager examined the accounts for 200 customers. The manager was interested in the total number of minutes of cell calls used by customers on each plan. He needed the information presented in an effective way for a sales meeting the next week. Use the file *Celltone* located on your CD-ROM.

a. Develop a bar chart to display the data, and write a short statement that describes the graph.

b. Develop two stem and leaf diagrams, one for the basic plan users and one for the business plan users, which show the distribution of cell phone minutes used. Discuss.

2.33   The real estate loan manager for Citizens Bank uses three appraisal companies to appraise residential property when a customer wants a home mortgage or wants to refinance an existing mortgage. Recently he conducted a test by having three companies appraise the same five properties. The results (in thousands of dollars) are in the file called *Citizens*.

After completing the test, the manager would like your help in displaying the data in an effective way. (Hint, you might consider using total appraisal values.) Provide a graphical display to oblige the manager.

2.34   The Future Vision Company is thinking of opening a TV-dish franchise in a new market area. However, prior to securing a location and taking other necessary steps to make the move, they conducted a survey of 548 residents in the market area. The data from this survey is in the file called *Future-Vision*. As site selection manager, you have been asked to develop a presentation for next week's staff meeting.

  a. First, develop a chart that effectively displays the total number of residents in the following two categories: cable subscriber and not a cable subscriber. Be sure to do a good job of labeling the graph.

  b. Develop a bar chart that shows number of households that subscribe to cable and do not subscribe broken down by family size. Use the following family size categories: 1 to 3, 4 to 6, and 7 to 10.

2.35   The file *Home-Prices* contains data on median home prices (the point below which 50% of the house prices fall) for 100 different U.S. cities. In your job with Farm-Life Insurance, you have been asked to break the cities into regions (North, South, East, and West). Prepare a graphical presentation that compares the median prices by region. Write a short summary report on your findings. Which region tends to have the highest home prices?

2.36   In your capacity as assistant to the administrator at Freedom Hospital, you have been asked to develop a graphical presentation that focuses on the insurance carried by the geriatric patients at the hospital. The data file *Patients* contains data for a sample of geriatric patients. In developing your presentation, please do the following:

  a. Construct a pie chart that shows the percentage of patients with each health insurance payer.

  b. Develop a bar chart that shows total charges for patients by insurance payer.

  c. Develop a stem and leaf diagram for the length-of-stay variable.

  d. Develop a bar chart that shows the number of males and females by insurance carrier.

2-3 LINE CHARTS AND SCATTER DIAGRAMS

LINE CHARTS

Most of the examples that have been presented thus far have involved *cross-sectional data*, or data gathered from many observations, all taken at the same time. However, if you have data that are measured over time (e.g., monthly, quarterly, or annually), an effective tool for presenting such data is a **line chart**.

> **Line Chart**
>
> A two-dimensional chart showing time on the horizontal axis and the variable of interest on the vertical axis.

McGregor Vineyards—McGregor Vineyards owns and operates a winery in the Sonoma Valley in northern California. At a recent company meeting, the financial manager expressed concern about the company's profit trend over the past 20 weeks. He presented weekly profit and sales data to McGregor management personnel. The data are on the CD-ROM that accompanies this text in the file *McGregor*.

Excel and Minitab Tutorial

Initially, the financial manager developed two separate line charts for this data: one for sales, the other for profits. These are displayed in Figures 2-14a and 2-14b. These line charts provide an indication that, although sales have been increasing, the profit trend is downward. But to fit both graphs on one page, he had to compress the size of the graphs. This "flattened" the lines somewhat, masking the magnitude of the problem.

What the financial manager needed is one graph with both profits and sales. Figure 2-15 shows his first attempt. This is better, but there still is a problem: The sales and profit variables are of different magnitudes. This results in the profit line being flattened out to almost a straight line. The profit trend is hidden.

To overcome this problem, the financial manager needed to construct his graph using two scales, one for each variable. Figure 2-16 shows the improved graph. We can now clearly see that although sales are moving steadily higher, profits are headed downhill. For some reason, costs are rising faster than revenues, and this graph should motivate McGregor Vineyards to look into the problem.

FIGURE 2-14A

**Excel Output Showing
McGregor Line Charts**

Excel Instructions:
1. Open file: McGregor.xls
2. Select the Data to be Graphed.
3. Click on the **Chart Wizard**.
4. Select **Line Graph** (option with data points shown).
5. Select **Series** Tab.
6. Define the X Axis Labels.
7. Remove unneeded variables.
8. Click **Next**.
9. Define **Titles**.
10. Click **Finish**.

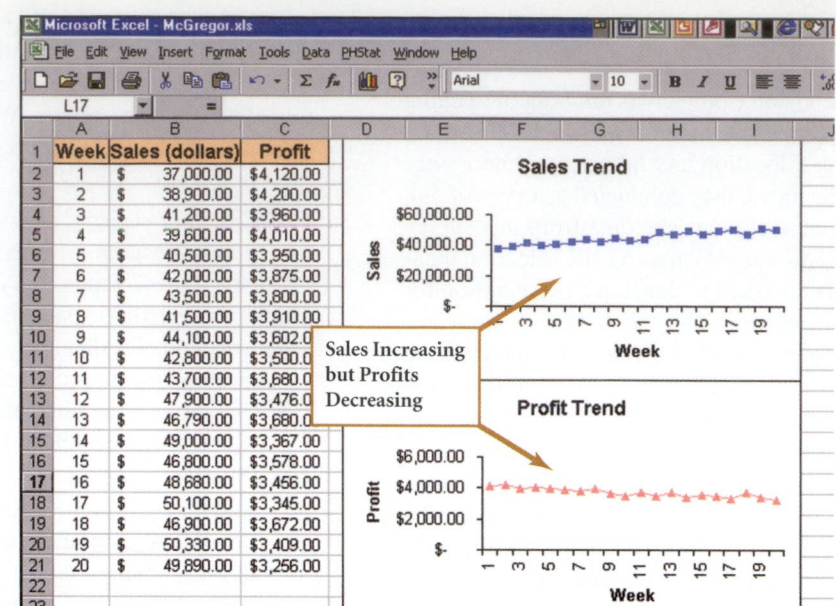

FIGURE 2-14B

**Minitab Output Showing
McGregor Line Charts**

Minitab Instructions:
1. Open file: McGregor.MTW.
2. Choose **Graph > Time Series Plot**.
3. Select **Simple**.
4. Click **OK**.
5. In **Series**, enter *Sales* and *Profit* columns.
6. Select **Multiple Graphs**.
7. Under **Show Graph Variables**, select **In separate panels of the same graph**.
8. Click **OK. OK.**

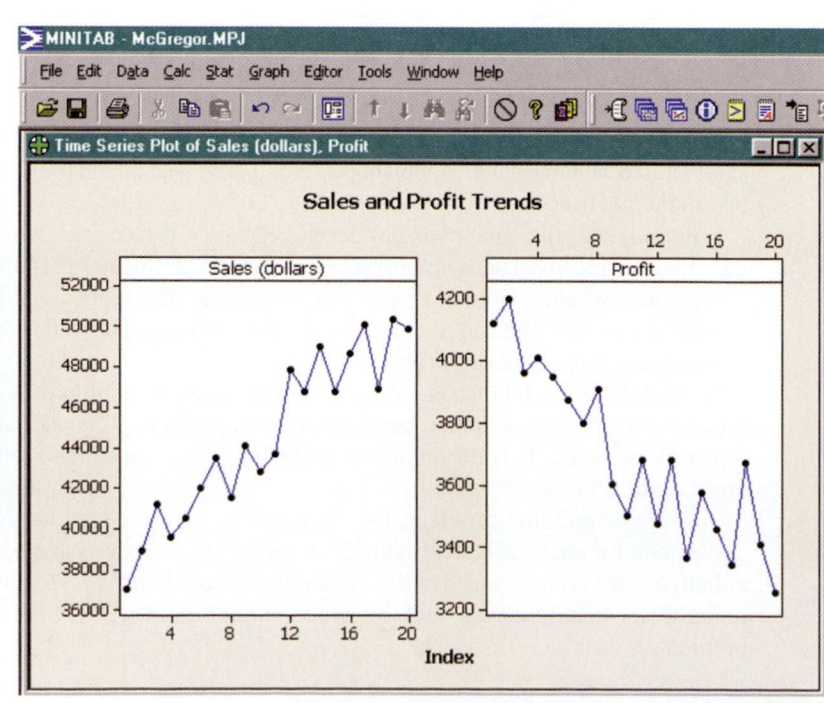

FIGURE 2-15

Excel Line Charts of McGregor Profit and Sales

Excel Instructions:
1. Open File McGregor.xls
2. Select the two variables to be graphed.
3. Go to the **Chart Wizard**.
4. Select the **Line Chart** Option.
5. Add **Titles** and **Labels**.

Minitab Instructions (for similar results):
1. Open File: McGregor.MTW.
2. Choose **Graph > Time Series Plot**.
3. Select **Simple**.
4. Click **OK**.
5. In **Series**, enter *Sales* and *Profit* columns.
6. Select **Multiple Graphs**.
7. Under **Show Graph Variables**, select **Overlaid on the same graph**.
8. Click **OK. OK.**

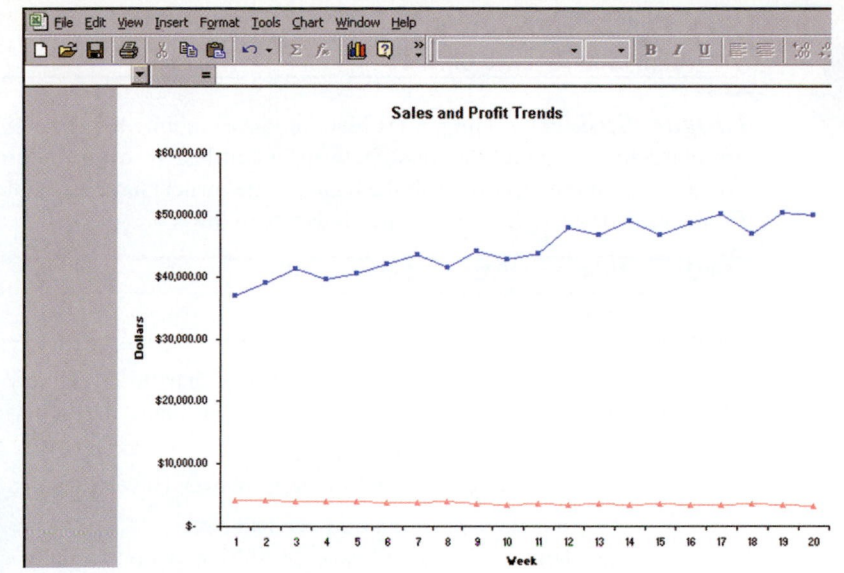

FIGURE 2-16

Excel Sales and Profits Line Chart

Excel Instructions:
1. Select the two variables to be graphed.
2. Go to the **Chart Wizard**.
3. Click on the **Custom Types** Tab.
4. Select **Lines on 2 Axes**.
5. Finish **Line Chart**.

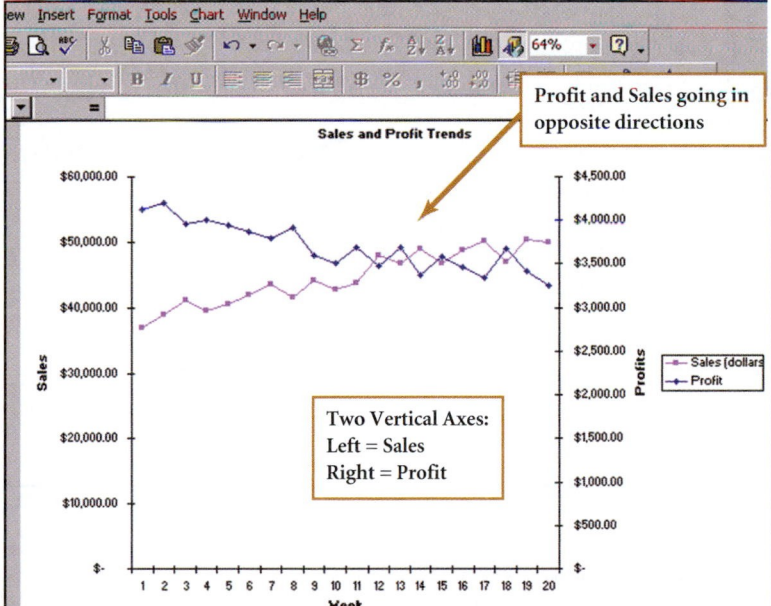

Minitab Instructions (for similar results):
1. Open File: McGregor.MTW.
2. Choose **Graph > Times Series Plot**.
3. Select **Multiple**.
4. Click **OK**.
5. In **Series**, enter *Sales* and *Profit* columns.
6. Select **Multiple Graphs**.
7. Click **OK. OK.**

Page: 1
Note: The Minitab graph is different than the Excel graph. Minitab does not allow different axes on the same graph.

SUMMARY: CONSTRUCTING LINE CHARTS

A line chart, also commonly called a *trend chart*, is developed using the following steps:

1. Identify the time-series variable of interest and determine the maximum value and the range of time periods covered in the data.

2. Construct the horizontal axis for the time periods using equal spacing between each time period. Construct the ver-tical axis with a scale appropriate for the range of values of the time-series variable.

3. Plot the points on the graph and connect the points with straight lines.

*E*XAMPLE 2-10: LINE CHARTS

Grogan Builders   Grogan Builders produces mobile homes in Alberta, Canada. The owners are planning to expand the manufacturing facilities. To do so requires additional financing. In preparation for the meeting with the bankers, the owners have assembled data on total annual sales for the past 10 years. These data are shown as follows:

1993	1994	1995	1996	1997	1998	1999	2000	2001	2002
1,426	1,678	2,591	2,105	2,744	3,068	2,755	3,689	4.003	3,997

The owners wish to present these data in a line chart to effectively show the company's sales growth over the 10-year period. To construct the line chart, the following steps are used:

Step 1:   **Identify the time-series variable.**
The time-series variable is measured over 10 years, with a maximum value of 4,003.

Step 2:   **Lay out the horizontal and vertical axes.**
The horizontal axis will have the 10 time periods equally spaced. The vertical axis will start at zero and go to a value exceeding 4,003. We will use 4,500. The vertical axis will also be divided into 500-unit increments.

Step 3:   **Plot the data values on the graph and connect the points with straight lines.**

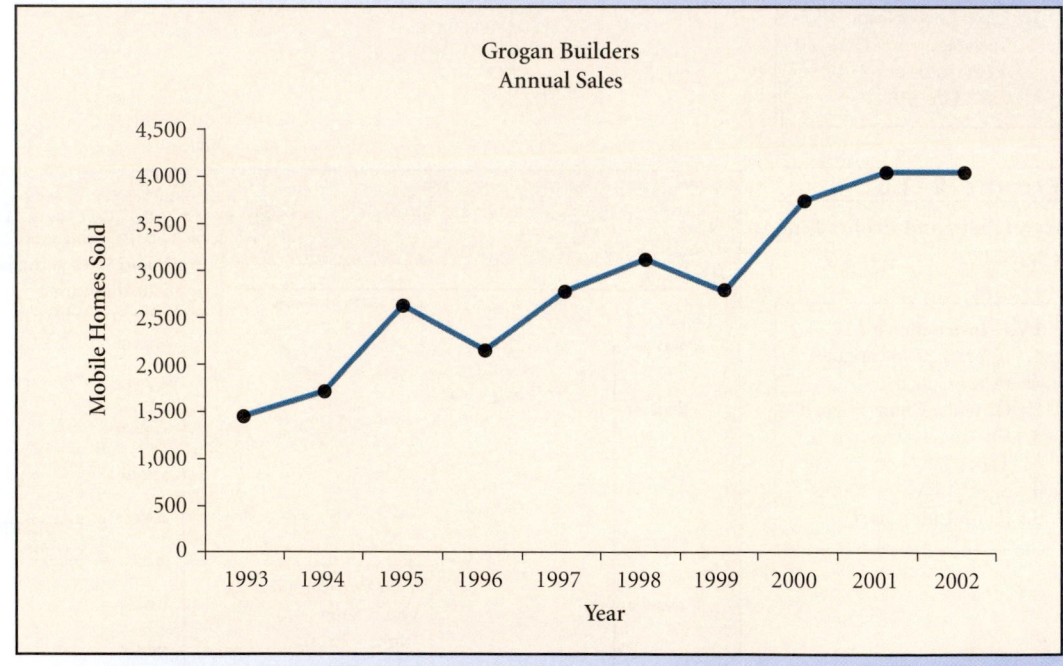

SCATTER DIAGRAMS

In Section 2-1 we introduced a set of statistical tools known as joint frequency distributions that allow the decision maker to examine two variables at the same time. Another tool used to study two variables simultaneously is the **scatter diagram**, or the **scatter plot**.

Scatter Diagram

A two-dimensional graph of plotted points in which the vertical axis represents values of one variable and the horizontal axis represents values of the other. Each plotted point has coordinates whose values are obtained from the respective variables.

There are many situations in which we are interested in understanding the *bivariate* relationship between two *quantitative* variables. For example, a company would like to know the relationship between sales and advertising. A bank might be interested in the relationship between savings-

FIGURE 2-17

**Scatter Diagrams Showing
Relationships Between *X*
and *Y***

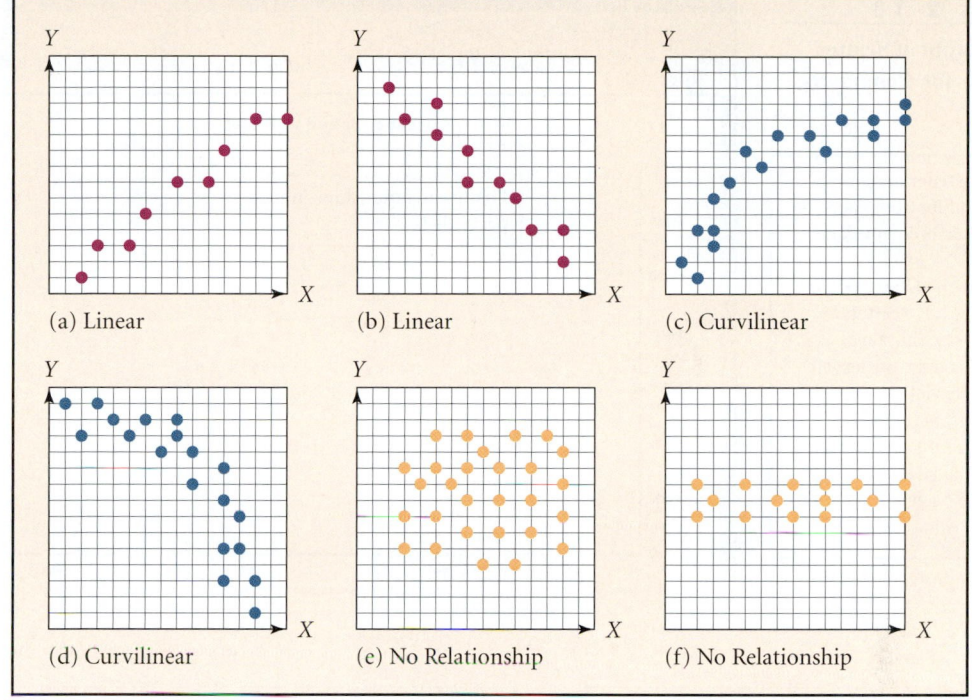

(a) Linear   (b) Linear   (c) Curvilinear

(d) Curvilinear   (e) No Relationship   (f) No Relationship

account balances and credit-card balances for its customers. A real estate agent might wish to know the relationship between the selling price of houses and the number of days that the houses have been on the market. The list of possibilities is almost limitless.

Regardless of the variables involved, there are several key relationships we are looking for when we develop a scatter diagram. Figure 2-17 shows scatter diagrams representing some key bivariate relationships that might exist between two quantitative variables.

Chapters 12 and 13 make extensive use of scatter diagrams. They introduce a statistical tool called *regression analysis* that focuses on the relationship between two variables. These variables are known as **dependent** and **independent variables**.

Dependent Variable

A variable whose values are thought to be a function of, or dependent on, the values of another variable called the *independent variable*. On a scatter plot, the dependent variable is placed on the y axis and is often called the response variable.

Independent Variable

A variable whose values are thought to impact the values of the *dependent variable*. The independent variable, or explanatory variable, is often within the direct control of the decision maker. On a scatter plot, the independent variable, or explanatory variable, is graphed on the X axis.

Excel and Minitab Tutorial

Personal Computers—Can you think of any product that has increased in quality and capability as rapidly as personal computers? Not that long ago an 8-MB RAM system with a 486 processor and a 640 K hard drive sold for the mid-$2500 range. Now the same money would buy a 2.4GHz or faster machine with a 40+ GB hard drive and 512-MB RAM or more!

In December 1998, a PC industry analyst for one of the major business publications wrote an article on computer capability and price. She looked at the relationship between PC cost and such factors as RAM and processor speed. A data file called *Computers* contains price and other information for 36 of the best-known PCs on the market.[4] The dependent variable is the price. One potential independent variable of interest is processor speed. Figure 2-18 illustrates the Excel scatter diagram for price and processor speed. The relationship is positive (that is, as the processor speed increases, so does the price) and somewhat linear.

[4]*Fortune*, December 7, 1998, special computer-hardware supplement.

FIGURE 2-18

Excel Output of Scatter Diagrams for Computers Data

Excel Instructions:
1. Open file: Computers.xls
2. Put cursor in any data cell.
3. Go to the **Chart Wizard**.
4. Select **XY Scatter Plot**—default type.
5. Click on the **Series** tab.
6. Remove all but one variable from series list.
7. Define X and variable data ranges.
8. Go to **Next**.
9. Add Titles, etc.

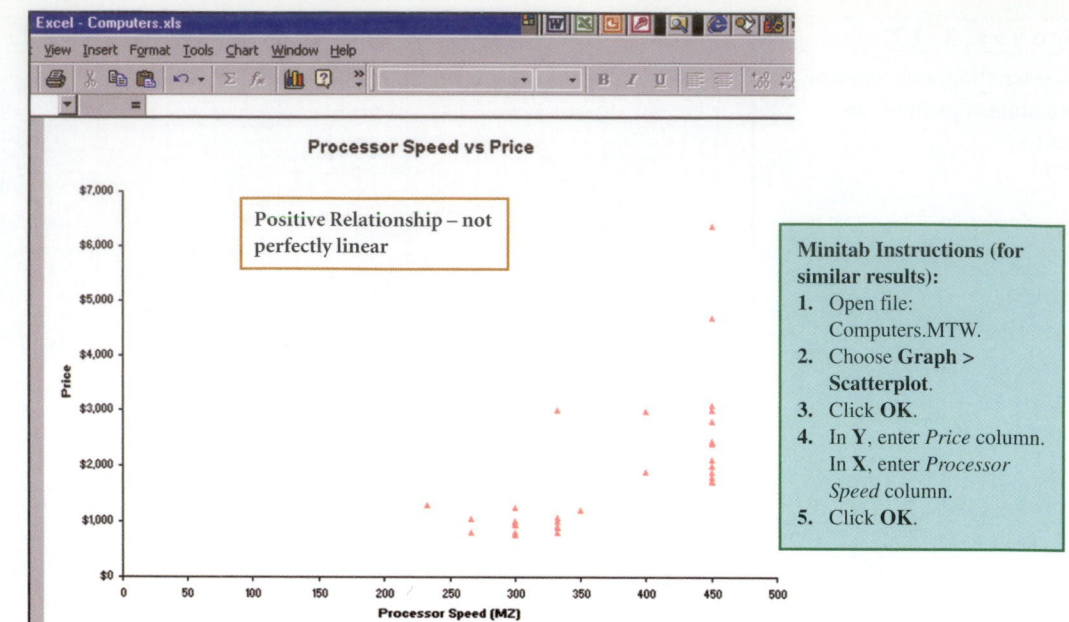

Minitab Instructions (for similar results):
1. Open file: Computers.MTW.
2. Choose **Graph > Scatterplot**.
3. Click **OK**.
4. In **Y**, enter *Price* column. In **X**, enter *Processor Speed* column.
5. Click **OK**.

SUMMARY: CONSTRUCTING SCATTER DIAGRAMS

A scatter diagram is a two-dimensional graph showing the joint values for two quantitative variables. It is constructed using the following steps:

1. Identify the two quantitative variables and collect paired responses for the two variables.

2. Determine which variable will be placed on the vertical axis and which variable will be placed on the horizontal axis. Often the vertical axis can be considered the dependent variable (y) and the horizontal axis can be considered the independent variable (x).

3. Define the range of values for each variable and define the appropriate scale for the x and y axes.

4. Plot the joint values for the two variables by placing a point in the x,y space. Do not connect the points.

EXAMPLE 2-11: SCATTER DIAGRAMS

Fortune's Best Eight Companies   Each year, *Fortune* Magazine surveys employees regarding job satisfaction to try to determine which companies are the "best" companies to work for in the United States. *Fortune* also collects a variety of data associated with these companies. For example, the table here shows data for the top eight companies on three variables: number of U.S. employees; number of training hours per year per employee; and total revenue in millions of dollars.

Company	U.S. Employees	Training Hrs/Yr.	Revenues
Southwest Airlines	24,757	15	$3,400
Kingston Technology	552	100	$1,300
SAS Institute	3,154	32	$653
Fel-Pro	2,577	60	$450
TD Industries	976	40	$127
MBNA	18,050	48	$3,300
W.L. Gore	4,118	27	$1,200
Microsoft	14,936	8	$8,700

To better understand these companies, we might be interested in the relationship between number of U.S. employees and revenue, and between training hours per year and revenue. To construct these scatter diagrams, we can use the following steps:

Step 1:   **Identify the two variables of interest.**
In the first case, one variable is U.S. employees and the second is revenue. In the second case, one variable is training hours and the other is revenue.

Step 2:   **Identify the dependent variable.**
In each case, think of revenue as the dependent (y) variable. Thus,

Case 1: y = revenue (vertical axis)   x = U.S. employees (horizontal axis)

Case 2: y = revenue (vertical axis)   x = training hours (horizontal axis)

Step 3:   **Establish the scales for the vertical and horizontal axes.**
The maximum value for each variable is

revenue = $8,700   U.S. employees = 24,757   training hours = 100

Step 4:   **Plot the joint values for the two variables by placing a point in the x, y space.**

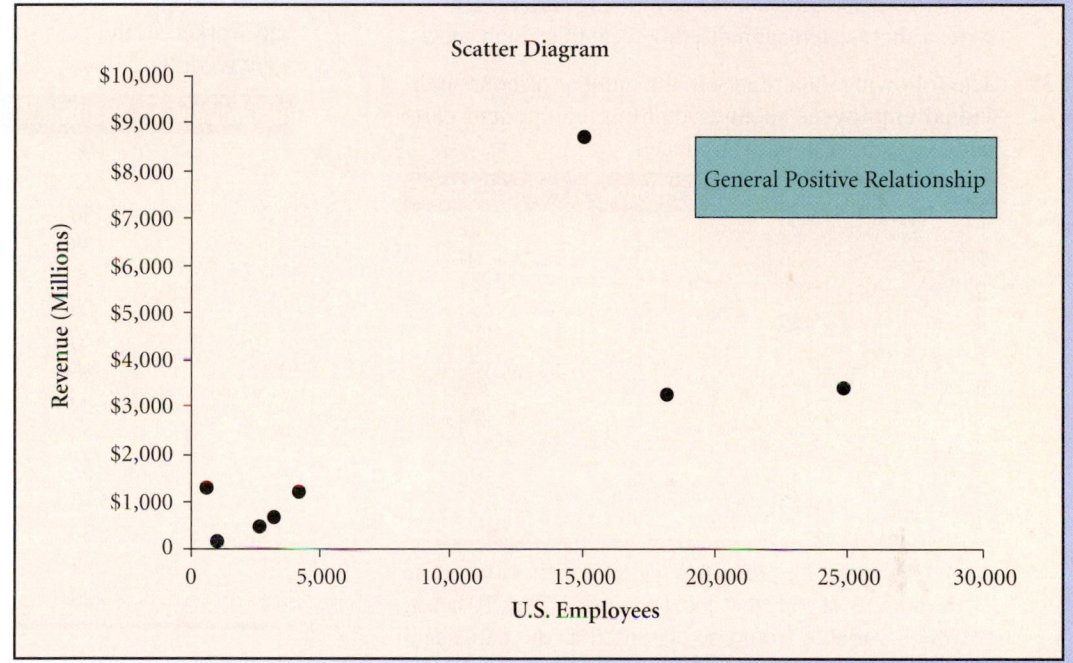

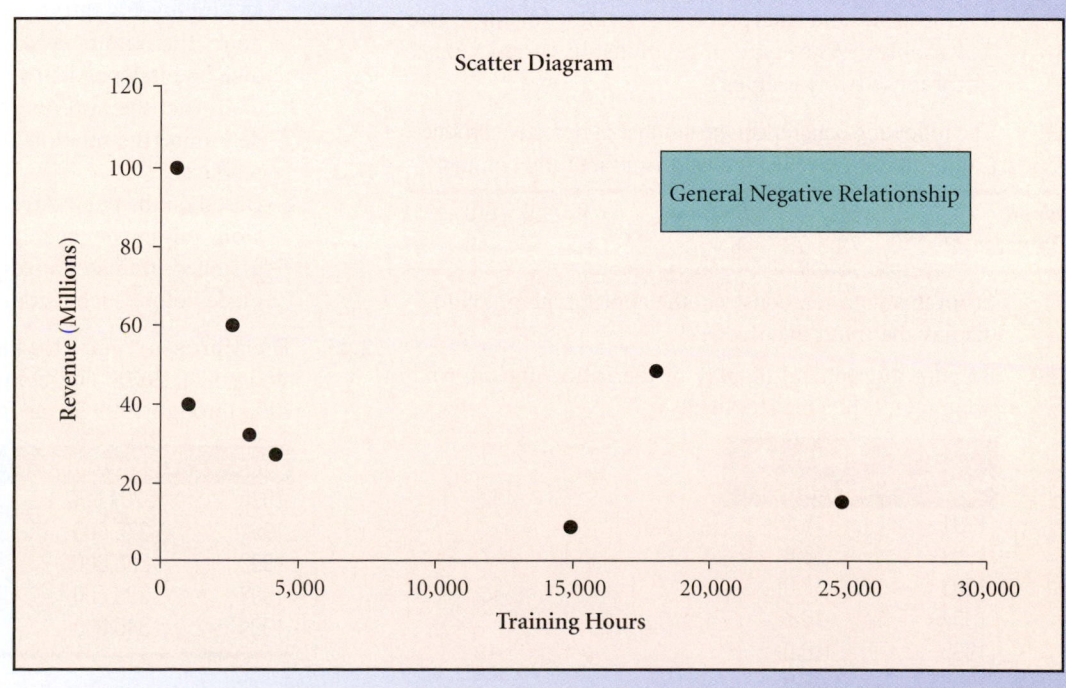

2-3: EXERCISES

Skill Development

2.37 The following data represent expenditures on advertising from 1989 to 1999 by the Swanson Lumber Company.

Year	Advertising	Year	Advertising
1989	$12,500	1995	18,790
1990	14,600	1996	23,500
1991	16,250	1997	24,000
1992	19,800	1998	25,600
1993	23,700	1999	27,800
1994	22,700		

Construct a line graph of the advertising variable and write a short statement indicating what this graph shows.

2.38 The following data represent the number of hours individual employees spent assembling component parts and the number of parts produced.

Hours	Parts Made	Hours	Parts Made
5	192	3	122
3	135	2	97
2	100	4	161
4	148	6	225
6	213	2	94
4	154	8	280
3	123	6	224
2	102	3	130
2	98	3	135
1	63		

a. Assuming that the production manager wishes to estimate the number of parts that could be made in, say, 10 hours, which variable would be classified as the dependent variable and which would be the independent variable?

b. Construct and interpret a scatter plot for these two variables. What type of relationship (if any) exists for these two variables?

2.39 The following data reflect the number of defective products produced each week at a local manufacturing company.

Week:	1	2	3	4	5	6	7	8	9	10	11
Defects:	80	76	79	72	68	70	64	60	64	58	52

From this data set, construct the appropriate graph to display the trend in defects.

2.40 Prepare a graphical display of the following information on U.S. bicycle shipments.

Year	Shipments (in Millions)
1991	15.1
1992	15.4
1993	17.0
1994	16.7
1995	16.0
1996	15.5

2.41 Given the following data, construct a scatter diagram and indicate what, if any, relationship exists between the two variables.

y:	40	33	27	50	18	40	56	70	27	19	30	18	42	11
x:	8	9	3	12	9	18	7	12	6	10	8	10	20	7

Business Applications

2.42 A company's human resources department recently selected a sample of 15 people. They compared the employees' performance ratings (based on a 100-point scale) and the number of overtime hours the employees had worked in the past six months. The following data were recorded:

Employee	Rating	Overtime Hours
1	87	50
2	67	30
3	90	100
4	88	95
5	80	70
6	60	20
7	40	25
8	95	72
9	80	65
10	75	50
11	82	68
12	70	48
13	50	33
14	89	80
15	96	85

a. The human resources department wishes to estimate an employee's rating using the number of overtime hours the employee compiled. Identify the dependent and independent variables.

b. Construct the appropriate chart that can be used to determine the relationship between rating and hours worked.

c. Based on the chart developed in part b, what conclusion might be reached about how ratings are assigned in this company. What cautions need to be made before such a conclusion is reached?

2.43 The Morrison Center for the Performing Arts has operated since 1990. The center's annual ticket sales for 1990 through 1999 are as follows:

Year	Ticket Sales	Year	Ticket Sales
1990	$204,000	1995	368,000
1991	275,000	1996	401,000
1992	280,000	1997	344,000
1993	299,000	1998	359,000
1994	345,000	1999	405,000

a. Prepare a line graph for the sales data.

b. The director of the Morrison Center initially only had data from 1990 to 1996, before the downturn in 1997. He had set a goal to reach ticket sales of $500,000. If the trend in the data from 1990 to 1996 had continued, in what year could the director have expected to meet his goal?

c. Consider the magnitude of the 1997 downturn. Also note that the upturn from 1997 on seems to have approximately the same slope as that from 1990 to 1996. Using this information, estimate the year in which the director will reach his goal.

2.44 Increasing dividends over time is an important factor for many investors when considering whether to purchase a company's stock. Shown here are net income and dividends paid per share of common stock for Flowers Industries, Inc., for 1987 to 1997.

Year	Net Income	Dividends
1987	$0.350	$0.163
1988	0.530	0.191
1989	0.380	0.227
1990	0.370	0.262
1991	0.310	0.291
1992	0.410	0.309
1993	0.470	0.327
1994	0.350	0.345
1995	0.500	0.362
1996	0.360	0.383
1997	0.720	0.413

Source: Flowers Industries, Inc., 1997 annual report.

a. Use this information to prepare a line graph to illustrate the pattern of dividends paid per share of common stock for 1987 to 1997.

b. Prepare a scatter plot that shows whether a relationship exists between net income per share of common stock and dividends per share of common stock. Does there appear to be a relationship between these two variables? If so, briefly describe the relationship.

c. Construct a line chart showing both net income and dividends on the same graph. Does there appear to be a relationship between these two variables?

Would you prefer a line chart or a scatter plot to determine such a relationship? Give reasons for your choice.

Advanced Business Applications

2.45 As part of a study on the banking industry, the data in the file *Banks* has been collected. As part of your study, construct the appropriate graph to determine the relationship between bank revenues and bank profits based on these data. Discuss your results. Discuss whether there are any decreasing economies of scale in the relationship between revenues and profits. That is, does the increase in profit get smaller as bank revenues get larger?

2.46 Chapman Bakery sells a variety of bakery products at its San Jose location. The data file *Bakery* contains information for a sample of daily sales. Of particular interest to the managers is determining the relationship between the number of wheat loaves and the number of white loaves. Construct an appropriate graph to identify the relationship.

2.47 The Ajax Taxi Company has collected data on the number of miles their cabs travel each week. Suppose four cabs are singled out and over a period of 40 weeks the miles that each is driven is recorded. The data are in the file *Ajax*.

a. Combine all four taxis together by summing the miles. Construct a line graph for the total miles. Do the total miles traveled by the cabs seem to be increasing or decreasing over time?

b. Construct a line graph that shows the pattern for each individual taxi over the 40 weeks.

2.48 The State Department of Commerce is in the process of generating a plan to attract new businesses to the state. You have been assigned to this team. At last week's meeting, you were given a data file called *Best-Companies*. The team leader has asked you to prepare a descriptive summary of the data. Specifically, she wants you to examine the relationship between new jobs added and the companies' revenues. In addition, prepare any other graphs or tables that you think would be helpful to better understand the data.

Summary and Conclusions

This chapter has introduced some of the most commonly used statistical techniques for organizing data and presenting them in a meaningful way to aid in the decision-making process. Organizing raw data into a frequency distribution is a major step in transforming data into information. We have outlined the steps for developing frequency distributions and for producing histograms.

The chapter also has introduced other graphical techniques for displaying data to make them more usable to a decision maker. The choices for effective graphical data displays are numerous. Bar charts, pie charts, stem and leaf diagrams, scatter diagrams, and line graphs are among the more commonly used techniques. Figure 2-19 summarizes the conditions under which each descriptive technique is appropriate.

Software packages, such as Excel and Minitab, have made graphical representation of data much easier. You are now able to analyze large volumes of data quickly and easily. The output from these packages can be pasted directly into word-processing documents to create professional-looking business reports.

FIGURE 2-19

Summary: Descriptive Statistical Techniques

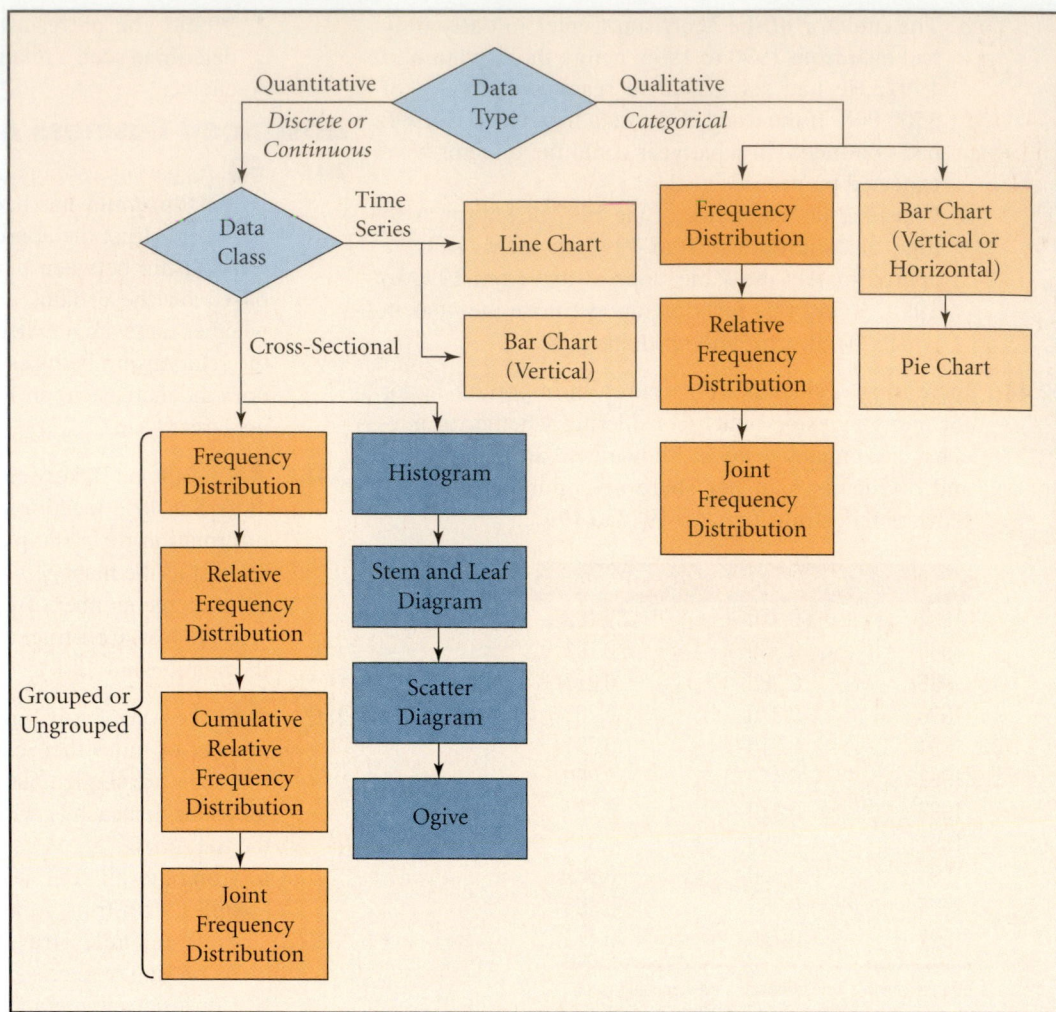

EQUATIONS

Relative Frequency

$$RF = \frac{f_i}{n} \qquad \textbf{2-1}$$

Sturges's Rule

$$\text{Classes} = 1 + 3.322\,[\log_{10}(n)] \qquad \textbf{2-2}$$

Class Width

$$W = \frac{\text{Largest Value} - \text{Smallest Value}}{\text{Number of Classes}} \qquad \textbf{2-3}$$

Key Terms

All-Inclusive Classes, 33	**Data Array,** 32	**Mutually Exclusive Classes,** 32
Bar Chart, 47	**Dependent Variable,** 61	**Pie Chart,** 52
Class Boundaries, 34	**Discrete Data,** 28	**Relative Frequency,** 29
Class Width, 33	**Equal-Width Classes,** 33	**Scatter Diagram,** 60
Continuous Data, 31	**Frequency Distribution,** 28	
Cumulative Frequency Distribution, 34	**Frequency Histogram,** 36	
Cumulative Relative Frequency Distribution, 34	**Independent Variable,** 61	
	Line Chart, 57	

CHAPTER EXERCISES

Business Applications

2.49   The Green Glow Lawn Company spreads liquid fertilizer on lawns. It charges by square footage of the lawn, so it has records of the lawn sizes of its customers. The company is now in the process of planning for next year and assumes the yard-size distribution will probably be much like it was this year. Raw data on yard sizes has been converted to the following frequency distribution:

Class	Frequency
Lawn Size (sq. ft.)	f_i
0 to less than 400	8
400 to less than 800	12
800 to less than 1,200	20
1,200 to less than 1,600	50
1,600 to less than 2,000	125
2,000 to less than 2,400	103
2,400 to less than 2,800	24

a. Develop a histogram from the frequency distribution.
b. Determine the relative frequency distribution for the lawn sizes. Explain why it is often useful to convert a frequency distribution to a relative frequency distribution.
c. Develop a cumulative relative frequency distribution and construct an ogive.

2.50 The Minnesota State Fishing Bureau has contracted with a university biologist to study the length of walleyes (fish) caught in Minnesota lakes. The biologist has collected data on a sample of 1,000 fish caught and has developed the following relative frequency distribution.

Class	Relative Frequency
Length (inches)	f_i
8 to less than 10	0.22
10 to less than 12	0.15
12 to less than 14	0.25
14 to less than 16	0.24
16 to less than 18	0.06
18 to less than 20	0.05
20 to less than 22	0.03

a. Construct a frequency distribution from this relative frequency distribution and then produce a histogram based on the frequency distribution.
b. Construct a pie chart from the relative frequency distribution. Discuss which of the two graphs, the pie chart or histogram, you think is more effective in presenting the fish length data.

2.51 Kronos (NASDAQ: KRON) is a leader in providing employee time and attendance systems to industry. Its 1997 annual report reported the following figures for primary net income per common share for 1993 to 1997.

1993	1994	1995	1996	1997
$0.50	$0.62	$1.03	$1.37	$1.34

Source: 1997 Kronos annual report.

a. Draw a bar chart to present these earnings-per-share values.
b. Develop a line chart for these data.
c. Which do you prefer in this case, a bar chart or a line chart? Discuss why.

2.52 Wendy Harrington is a staff accountant at a regional accounting firm in Miami, Florida. One of her clients has had a problem with balancing the cash register at the end of the day. Wendy has made a study of the ending shortage (indicated with parentheses) or overage for the past 30 days when the cash register did not balance, and she has recorded the following data.

30-Day Study of Cash Shortage or Overage									
12.00	(2.55)	13.05	(55.20)	10.00	(18.00)	(11.00)	6.35	(19.02)	(33.00)
11.00	14.00	(10.00)	9.50	23.00	16.00	8.30	2.00	(24.00)	2.38
20.01	(43.50)	17.20	(41.04)	11.00	(19.33)	23.01	(0.34)	1.01	(23.04)

a. Develop a frequency distribution and a histogram for these data.
b. Develop a stem and leaf diagram for these data. Explain the differences between a histogram and a steam and leaf diagram.

2.53 The following data represent the commuting distances for employees of the Pay-and-Carry department store.

Commuting Distance (Miles)												
3.5	2.0	4.0	2.5	0.3	1.0	12.0	17.5	3.0	3.5	6.5	9.0	3.0
4.0	9.0	16.0	3.5	0.5	2.5	1.0	0.7	1.5	1.4	12.0	9.2	8.3
1.0	3.0	7.5	3.2	2.0	1.0	3.5	3.6	1.9	2.0	3.0	1.5	0.4
6.4	11.0	2.5	2.4	2.7	4.0	2.0	2.0	3.0				

a. The personnel manager for Pay-and-Carry would like you to develop a frequency distribution and a histogram for these data.
b. Develop a stem and leaf diagram for these data.
c. Break the data into three groups: under 3.0 miles; 3.0 and under 6 miles; and 6 miles and over. Construct a pie chart to illustrate the proportion of employees in each category.
d. Referring to part c, construct a bar chart to depict the proportion of employees in each category.

2.54 A local branch of the Government Employees' Credit Union has been keeping track of the types of errors its tellers have been making. You are responsible for providing training to reduce these errors. The following data show the categories of errors and the frequency of each for the past month.

Category of Errors	Frequency
Errors posting debits/credits	182
Errors posting other entries	158
Entries not posted	77
Cash letter errors	31
Claims	24
Adjustment tickets	16
Multiple postings	9
Incorrect totals	7

Use these data to select and justify the areas in which you will start your training effort. Construct a Pareto chart to display the data effectively.

2.55 A computer software company has been looking at the amount of time customers spend on hold after their calls are answered by the central switchboard. The company would like to have only 2% of the callers have to wait more than 2 minutes. The company's calling service has provided the following data showing how long each of last month's callers spent on hold.

Class	Number
Less than 15 seconds	456
15 to less than 30 seconds	718
30 to less than 45 seconds	891
45 to less than 60 seconds	823
60 to less than 75 seconds	610
75 to less than 90 seconds	449
90 to less than 105 seconds	385
105 to less than 120 seconds	221
120 to less than 150 seconds	158
150 to less than 180 seconds	124
180 to less than 240 seconds	87
More than 240 seconds	153

a. Develop a relative frequency distribution and an ogive for these data.
b. The company estimates it loses an average of $30 in business from callers who must wait more than 2 minutes before receiving assistance. The company thinks that last month's distribution of waiting times is typical. Estimate how much money the company is losing in business per month because people have to wait too long before receiving assistance.

2.56 The marketing director of a company manufacturing small disk drives for notebook computers has directed her sales force to accept orders based on a projected production rate of 3,000 disk drives per day. The production manager objected strongly when hearing this and presented the following frequency distribution to support his claim that this goal was impossible, given the present production process.

Production Rate	Frequency
2,000 to 2,499	3
2,500 to 2,749	7
2,750 to 2,999	10
3,000 to 3,249	15
3,250 to 3,499	22
3,500 to 3,999	11
4,000 or more	2

a. Construct a histogram to display these data. Discuss the three factors that can be addressed by examining a histogram.
b. Discuss whether it is possible to construct a stem and leaf diagram from the data in the form supplied here.

2.57 The regional sales manager for American Toys, Inc., recently collected data on weekly sales (in dollars) for the 15 stores in his region. He also collected data on the number of sales-clerk work hours during the week for each of the stores. The data are as follows:

Store	Sales	Hours	Store	Sales	Hours
1	23,300	120	9	27,886	140
2	25,600	135	10	54,156	300
3	19,200	96	11	34,080	254
4	10,211	102	12	25,900	180
5	19,330	240	13	36,400	270
6	35,789	190	14	25,760	175
7	12,540	108	15	31,500	256
8	43,150	234			

a. Develop a scatter plot of these data. Determine which variable should be the dependent variable and which should be the independent variable.
b. Based on the scatter plot, what, if any, conclusions might the sales manager reach with respect to the relationship between sales and number of clerk hours worked? Do any stores stand out as being different? Discuss.

Advanced Business Applications

2.58 🖴 *The Wall Street Journal* reported retail sales for February 1997 and February 1998 for many top retailers. The file *Retailers* contains sales figures for 26 different retailers divided into four categories. In your capacity as marketing manager for a major department store, you plan to develop a report and a presentation on the retail industry using these data. To make your report complete, you plan to do the following:

a. Develop grouped frequency distributions for each year and then develop a histogram from each frequency distribution.
b. Create bar charts comparing the two years' February sales for the stores in each category. This means that you will have four different bar charts.
c. Create a pie chart for the Department Store category for February 1997.
d. Create a bar chart for the Apparel category for February 1998.
e. Using the information generated in parts a through d, create a report on the retail industry.

2.59 🖴 The data file *McCormick* contains selected information from the annual report for McCormick & Company, Inc., the leader in the manufacture, marketing, and distribution of spices, seasonings, and flavors for the food industry. Use the data to perform the following:

a. For 1988 through 1997, construct a line chart of net sales. Determine the relationship between year and net sales.
b. For 1988 through 1997, construct a scatter plot of net sales and capital expenditures. Briefly describe the relationship between net sales and capital expenditures for these years.
c. Develop a line chart that displays both net sales and long-term debt. Do you prefer this display to that

produced in part b? Discuss which of them gives a better presentation of the relationship between the two variables.

2.60 The following information, taken from the 1997 annual report of McCormick & Company, Inc., reports the company's consumer sales (in millions) by region.

Region	Consumer Sales
Americas	$596.4
Europe	$221.2
Asia/Pacific	$43.2

a. Construct a bar chart of this data.
b. Construct a pie chart of this data.
c. Which graphical summary, the bar chart or the pie chart, better describes the relative proportion of total sales by geographic region? Explain the reasons that support your opinion.

2.61 The file *Home-Prices* contains information about single-family housing prices in 100 metropolitan areas in the United States.
a. Construct a frequency distribution and a histogram of 1997 median single-family home prices. Use Sturges's Rule to determine the appropriate number of classes.
b. Construct a cumulative relative frequency distribution and an ogive for 1997 median single-family home prices.
c. Repeat parts a and b but this time use five class intervals. What was the impact of using more class intervals?

2.62 Stock investors often look to beat the performance of the S&P 500 Index, which generally serves as a proxy for the market as a whole. The following table shows a comparison of five-year cumulative total shareholder returns for Idaho Power Company common stock (NYSE symbol: IDA), the S&P 500 Index, and the Edison Electric Institute (EEI) 100 Electric Utilities Index. The data assume that $100 was invested on December 31, 1992, with returns compounded monthly.

Year	Idaho Power	S&P 500	EEI 100 Electric Utilities
1992	$100.00	$100.00	$100.00
1993	117.38	110.08	111.15
1994	97.62	111.53	98.29
1995	134.11	153.45	128.78
1996	147.92	188.69	130.32
1997	189.73	251.63	166.00

Source: Idaho Power Company, *1997 Notice of Annual Meeting of Shareholders*, p. 34.

a. Construct a graph that illustrates the performance of the three investment options for 1992 through 1997.
b. How well has Idaho Power Company performed during this period compared with the S&P 500?
c. How well has it performed relative to its industry?

2.63 Elliel's Department Store tracks its inventory on a monthly basis. Monthly data for 1996 through 2000 are in the file *Elliels*.
a. Construct a line chart showing the monthly inventory over the five years. Discuss what this graph implies about inventory.
b. Sum the monthly inventory figures for each year. Present the sums in bar-chart form. Discuss whether you think this is an appropriate graph to describe the inventory situation at Elliel's.

2.64 The commercial banking industry is undergoing rapid changes due to advances in technology and competitive pressures in the financial services sector. The data file *Banks* contains selected information tabulated by *Fortune* magazine concerning the revenues, profitability, and number of employees for the 51 largest U.S. commercial banks in terms of revenues. Use the information in this file to do the following:
a. Construct a chart to determine whether there is a relationship between revenues and number of employees. Briefly comment on your findings.
b. Develop a frequency distribution and a histogram for profits per employee. (Hint: Construct a new variable from the existing variables.) What does the histogram imply?

CASE 2-A:

AJ's Fitness Center

When A. J. Reeser signed papers to take ownership of the fitness center previously known as The Park Center Club, he realized that he had just taken the biggest financial step in his life. Every asset he could pull together had been pledged against the mortgage. If the new AJ's Fitness Center didn't succeed, he would be in really bad shape financially. But A. J. didn't plan on failing. After all, he had never failed at anything.

As a high school football All-American, A. J. had been heavily recruited by major colleges around the country. Although he loved football, he and his family had always put academics ahead of sports. Thus, he surprised almost everyone other than those who knew him

best when he chose to attend an Ivy League university not particularly noted for its football success. Although he excelled at football and was a member of two winning teams, he also succeeded in the classroom and graduated in four years. He spent six years working for McKinsey & Company, a major consulting firm, in which he gained significant experience in a broad range of business situations.

He was hired away from McKinsey & Company by the Dryden Group, a management services company that specializes in running health and fitness operations and recreational resorts throughout the world. After eight years of leading the Fitness Center section at Dryden, A. J. found that earning a high salary and the perks associated with corporate life were not satisfying him.

Besides, the travel was getting old now that he had married and had two young children. When the opportunity to purchase The Park Center Club came, he decided that the time was right to control his own destiny.

A key aspect of the deal was that AJ's Fitness Club would keep its existing clientele, consisting of 1,833 memberships. One of the things that A. J. was very concerned about was whether these members would stay with the club after the sale or move on to other fitness clubs in the area. He knew that keeping existing customers is a lot less expensive than attracting new customers.

Within days of assuming ownership, A. J. developed a survey that was mailed to all 1,833 members. The letter that accompanied the survey discussed A. J.'s philosophy and asked several key questions regarding the current level of satisfaction. Survey respondents were eligible to win a free lifetime membership in a drawing—an inducement that was no doubt responsible for the 1,214 usable responses.

To get help with the analysis of the survey data, A. J. approached the College of Business at a local university with the idea of having a senior student serve as an intern at AJ's Fitness Center. In addition to an hourly wage, the intern would get free use of the fitness facilities for the rest of the academic year.

The intern's first task was to key the data from the survey into a file that could be analyzed using a spreadsheet or a statistical software package. The survey contained eight questions that were keyed into eight columns as follows:

Column 1: Satisfaction with the club's weight- and exercise-equipment facilities

Column 2: Satisfaction with the club's staff
Column 3: Satisfaction with the club's exercise programs (aerobics, etc.)
Column 4: Satisfaction with the club's overall service

Note, Columns 1 through 4 were coded on an ordinal scale as follows:

1	2	3	4	5
Very Unsatisfied	Unsatisfied	Neutral	Satisfied	Very Satisfied

Column 5: Number of years that the respondent had been a member at this club
Column 6: Gender (1 = Male, 2 = Female)
Column 7: Typical number of visits to the club per week
Column 8: Age

The data, saved in the file *AJFitness*, were clearly too much for anyone to comprehend in raw form. At yesterday's meeting, A. J. asked the intern to "make some sense of the data." When the intern asked for some direction, A. J.'s response was, "That's what I'm paying you the big bucks for. I just want you to develop a descriptive analysis of these data. For now, let's limit it to whatever charts, graphs, and tables that will help us understand our customers. After we see what that shows, maybe we will do some other analysis. For right now, give me a report that discusses the data. Why don't we set a time to get together next week to review your report?"

CASE 2-B:

Westbrook Graphic Arts

Lisa Westbrook founded Westbrook Graphic Arts in 1997, right after her graduation. Throughout college Lisa had worked part time for a local graphics arts company and had gained significant experience in the business. She had a job offer to stay with the same company and several other offers from graphics companies in the area, but her independent spirit pushed her to go out on her own. Business has been slow to develop. However, she has been able to pay her bills and sock a few dollars away for a trip to Europe she promised herself as a graduation present.

As Lisa looked at her e-mail messages in her small office on 13th Street, the phone rang. It was Charles Eddy, who works for the State Department of Commerce in the International Division. Charles had called Lisa yesterday about a possible project and had promised to call back when he had more information about what his boss wanted. Charles explained that C. J. Riley, the director of the Department of Commerce, was going to give an address at a

national conference. The director wanted to contrast the United States with a number of other developed countries around the world. Charles added that he had collected quite a bit of data on various issues for each country. He, however, had not had time to create the presentation for his boss. He wanted Westbrook Graphics to prepare the presentation and the speaker notes.

As Charles hung up, Lisa knew that this was a tremendous opportunity. If she could do a good job on this project, there very likely would be other work coming to her from the Department of Commerce. Charles had agreed to e-mail the data. Charles gave her total leeway in designing the presentation, but he did say that C. J. was big on graphs and charts. The data are in a file called *Westbrook*. Charles had indeed collected some interesting data for each country.

Lisa sent a reply to Charles telling him that she had received the data (which she stored in the file *Countries*) and would have the presentation by next Tuesday. As she leaned back in her chair, she wondered where she should begin.

General References

1. Albright, Christian S., Wayne L. Winston, and Christopher Zappe, *Data Analysis and Decision Making with Microsoft Excel* (Pacific Grove, CA: Duxbury, 1999).
2. Berenson, Mark L., and David M. Levine, *Basic Business Statistics: Concepts and Applications*, 7th ed. (Upper Saddle River, NJ: Prentice Hall, 1999).
3. Cleveland, William, S., "Graphs in Scientific Publications," *The American Statistician* 38 (November 1984), pp. 261–269.
4. Cleveland, William S., and R. McGill, "Graphical Perception: Theory, Experimentation, and Application to the Development of Graphical Methods," *Journal of the American Statistical Association* 79 (September 1984), pp. 531–554.

5. Cryer, Jonathan D., and Robert B. Miller, *Statistics for Business: Data Analysis and Modeling*, 2nd ed. (Belmont, CA: Duxbury Press, 1994).

6. Dodge, Mark, and Craig Stinson, *Running Microsoft Excel 2000* (Redmond, WA: Microsoft Press, 1999).

7. *Microsoft Excel 2000* (Redmond, WA: Microsoft Corp., 1999).

8. *Minitab for Windows Version 14* (State College, PA: Minitab, 2003).

9. Siegel, Andrew F., *Practical Business Statistics,* 4th ed. (Burr Ridge, IL: Irwin, 2000).

10. Tufte, Edward R., *Envisioning Information* (Cheshire, CT: Graphics Press, 1990).

11. Tufte, Edward R., *The Visual Display of Quantitative Information*, reprint ed. (Cheshire, CT: Graphics Press, 1992).

12. Tukey, John W., *Exploratory Data Analysis* (Reading, MA: Addison-Wesley, 1977).

CHAPTER 3

Describing Data Using Numerical Measures

CHAPTER OUTCOMES

After studying the material in Chapter 3, you should be able to:

- Compute the mean, weighted average, median, and mode for a set of data and understand what these values represent.
- Compute the range, variance, and standard deviation and know what these values mean.
- Know how to construct a box and whisker graph and be able to interpret it.
- Compute the coefficient of variation and z scores and understand how they are applied in decision-making situations.
- Use numerical measures along with graphs, charts, and tables to effectively describe data.

WHY YOU NEED TO KNOW

Graphs and charts provide effective tools for transforming data into information; however, they are only a starting point. Graphs and charts do not reveal all the information contained in a set of data. To make your descriptive tool-kit complete, you need to become familiar with the key descriptive measures that quantify the center of the data and its spread.

Suppose you are an advertising manager for a major tire company and you want to develop an ad campaign touting how much longer your company's tires last than the competition's. You must be careful that your claims are valid. First, the Federal Trade Commission (FTC) is charged with regulating advertising and requires that advertising be truthful. Second, customers who could show that they were misled by an incorrect claim about

your tires could sue you and your company. You have no choice. You must use statistical procedures to determine the validity of any claim you might want to make about your tires.

You might start by sampling tires from your company and from the competition. You could measure the number of miles each tire lasts before a specified portion of the tread is depleted. You might graph the data for each company as a histogram, but a clear comparison with this graph might be difficult. Instead, you could compute the mileage numbers for the various tires and show these values side-by-side, perhaps in a bar chart. Thus, to effectively describe data, you will need to combine the graphical tools discussed in Chapter 2 with the numerical measures introduced in this chapter.

3-1 MEASURES OF CENTER AND LOCATION

You learned in Chapter 2 that frequency histograms are an effective way of converting quantitative data into useful information. The histogram provides a visual indication of where data are centered and how much spread there is in the data around the center. However, to fully describe a quantitative variable, we can compute measures of its center and spread. These measures can then be coupled with the histogram to give a clear picture of the variable's distribution. This section focuses on measures of the center of data. Section 3-2 introduces measures of the spread of data.

PARAMETERS AND STATISTICS

Depending on whether we are working with a population or a sample, a numerical measure is either a **parameter** or a **statistic**.

Parameter	***Statistic***
A measure computed from the entire population. As long as the population does not change, the value of the parameter will not change.	A measure computed from a sample that has been selected from a population. The value of the statistic will depend on which sample is selected.

POPULATION MEAN

There are three important measures of the center of a set of data. The first of these is the **mean**, or average of the data. To find the mean, we sum the values and divide the sum by the number of data values, as shown in Equation 3-1.

Mean

A numerical measure of the center of a set of quantitative measures computed by dividing the sum of the values by the number of values in the data.

The **population mean** is represented by the Greek symbol μ, pronounced "mu." The formal notation in the numerator for the sum of the x values reads:

$$\sum_{i=1}^{N} x_i \rightarrow \text{sum each } x_i \text{ value where } i \text{ goes from 1 to } N$$

Population Mean

$$\mu = \frac{\sum\limits_{i=1}^{N} x_i}{N}$$

3-1

where:

μ = Population mean (mu)
N = Population size
x_i = ith individual value of variable x

In other words, we are summing all N values in the population.

Because you almost always sum all the data values, to simplify notation in this text, we generally will drop the subscripts after the first time we introduce a formula. Thus the formula for the population mean will be written as

$$\mu = \frac{\sum x}{N}$$

Foster City Hotel—The manager of a small hotel in Foster City, California, was asked by the corporate vice president to analyze the Sunday night registration information for the past eight weeks. Data on three variables were collected:

x_1 = Total number of rooms rented
x_2 = Total dollar revenue from the room rentals
x_3 = Number of customer complaints that came from guests each Sunday

These data are shown in Table 3-1. They are a population because they include all data that interest the vice president.

Figure 3-1 shows the frequency histogram for the number of rooms rented. If the manager wants to describe the data further, she can locate the center of the data by finding the balance point for the histogram. Think of the horizontal axis as a plank and the histogram bars as weights proportional to their area. The center of the data would be the point at which the plank would balance. As shown in Figure 3-1, the balance point seems to be about 15 rooms.

Eyeing the histogram might yield a reasonable approximation of the center. However, computing a numerical measure of the center directly from the data is preferable. The most frequently used measure of the center is the mean.

The population mean for number of rooms rented is computed using Equation 3-1 as follows.

$$\mu = \frac{\sum x}{N} = \frac{22 + 13 + 10 + 16 + 23 + 13 + 11 + 13}{8}$$
$$= \frac{121}{8}$$
$$\mu = 15.125$$

	WEEK	ROOMS RENTED	REVENUE	COMPLAINTS
TABLE 3-1	1	22	$1,870	0
Foster City Hotel Data	2	13	$1,590	2
	3	10	$1,760	1
	4	16	$2,345	0
	5	23	$4,563	2
	6	13	$1,630	1
	7	11	$2,156	0
	8	13	$1,756	0

FIGURE 3-1

Balance Point, Rooms Rented at Foster City Hotel

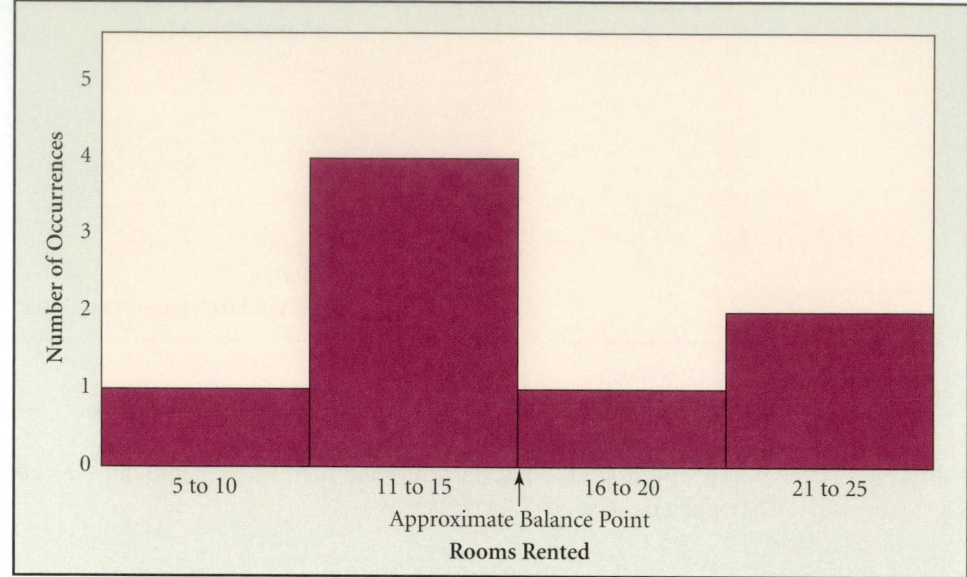

Thus, the average number of rooms rented each Sunday for the past eight weeks is 15.125. This is the true balance point for the data. Turn to Table 3-2, where we find what is called a *deviation* $(x - \mu)$ by subtracting the mean from each value.

Note that the sum of the deviations of the data from the mean is zero. This is not a coincidence. *For any set of data, the sum of the deviations around the mean will be zero.*

SUMMARY: COMPUTING THE POPULATION MEAN

When the available data constitute the population of interest, the population mean is computed using the following steps:

1. Collect the data for the variable of interest for all items in the population. The data must be quantitative and can be discrete or continuous.

2. Sum all values in the population ($\sum x$).

3. Divide the sum ($\sum x$) by the number of values (N) in the population to get the population mean. The formula for the population mean is

$$\mu = \frac{\sum x}{N}$$

EXAMPLE 3-1: COMPUTING THE POPULATION MEAN

Viking Distributors Viking Distributors sells equipment and supplies to companies in the airline maintenance business. During the past year, Viking has made 10 sales to a customer in Spain. The sales manager is interested in knowing the mean dollar value of sales to this customer. These 10 sales constitute the population of interest. The population mean is computed using the following steps:

Step 1: **Collect the data for the quantitative variable of interest.**
In this case, the variable is dollar value of the sale for each of the 10 sales made. These are recorded as follows:

$x =$ \$42,000   \$23,900   \$115,600   \$13,800   \$7,900
\$41,000   \$52,900   \$76,100   \$5,800   \$33,200

Step 2: **Add the data values.**
$\sum x =$ \$42,000 + \$23,900 + \$115,600 + \$13,800 + \$7,900 + \$41,000
+ \$52,900 + \$76,100 + \$5,800 + \$33,200 = \$412,200

Step 3: **Divide the sum by the number of values in the population.**

$$\mu = \frac{\sum x}{N} = \frac{\$412,200}{10} = \$41,220$$

Thus, the mean sales amount to this company in Spain is \$41,220.

TABLE 3-2

Centering Concept of the Mean Using Hotel Data

x	x − μ
22	22 − 15.125 = 6.875
13	13 − 15.125 = −2.125
10	10 − 15.125 = −5.125
16	16 − 15.125 = 0.875
23	23 − 15.125 = 7.875
13	13 − 15.125 = −2.125
11	11 − 15.125 = −4.125
13	13 − 15.125 = −2.125
	Σ = 0.000

Excel and Minitab Tutorial

Foster City Hotel (continued)—In addition to collecting data on the number of rooms rented on Sunday nights, the Foster City Hotel manager also collected data on the room-rental revenue generated, and the number of complaints, on Sunday nights. Both Excel and Minitab have procedures for computing numerical measures such as the mean. Because these data are the population of all nights of interest to the hotel manager, she can compute the population mean, μ, revenue per night. The population mean is μ = $2,208.75 (rounded to $2,209 in Minitab), as shown in the Excel and Minitab outputs in Figure 3-2a and 3-2b. Likewise, the mean number of complaints is μ = 0.75 per night. (Note, there are other measures shown in the figures. We will discuss several of these later in the chapter.)

Now, for these eight Sunday nights, the manager can report to the corporate vice president that the mean number of rooms rented is 15.125. This level of business generated an average nightly revenue of $2,208.75. The number of complaints averaged 0.75 (less than one) per night. These values are the true means for the population and are, therefore, called parameters.

SAMPLE MEAN

The data for the Foster City Hotel constituted the population of interest. Thus, μ = 15.125 nights is the parameter measure. However, if we have a sample rather than a population, the mean for the sample is computed using Equation 3-2. Notice, Equation 3-2 is the same as Equation 3-1 *except* that we sum the sample values, not the population values, and divide by the sample size, not the population size.

FIGURE 3-2A

Excel Output Showing Mean Revenue for the Foster City Hotel

Excel Instructions:
1. Open file: Foster.xls
2. Select **Tools.**
3. Select **Data Analysis.**
4. Click on **Descriptive Statistics.**
5. Define data range for the variables.
6. Check **Summary Statistics.**
7. Name output sheet.

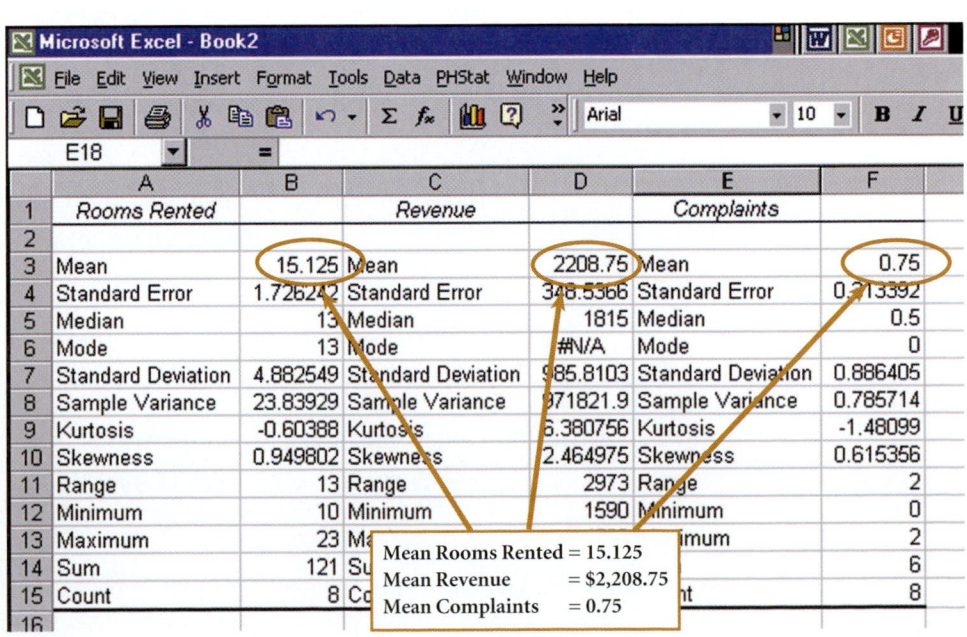

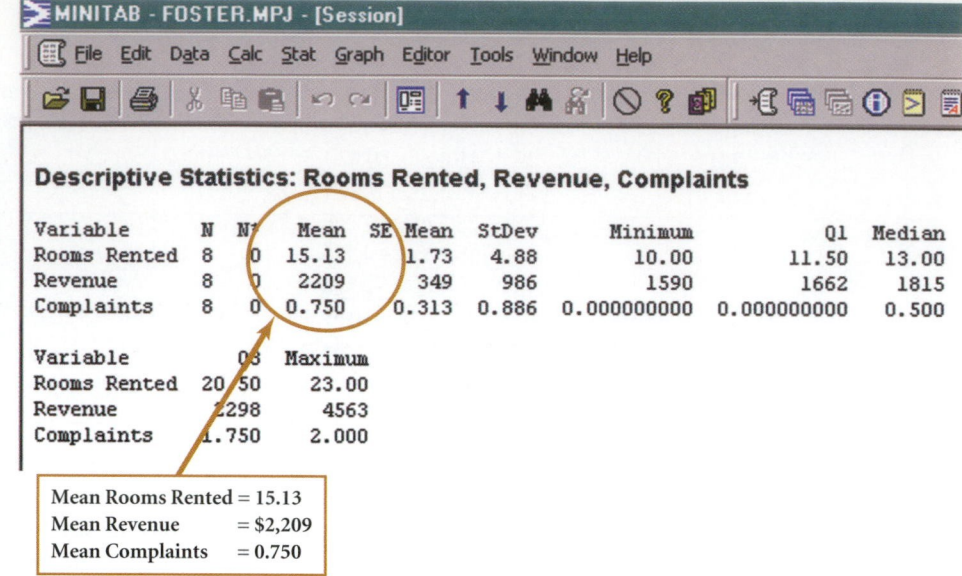

Descriptive Statistics: Rooms Rented, Revenue, Complaints

Variable	N	N*	Mean	SE Mean	StDev	Minimum	Q1	Median
Rooms Rented	8	0	15.13	1.73	4.88	10.00	11.50	13.00
Revenue	8	0	2209	349	986	1590	1662	1815
Complaints	8	0	0.750	0.313	0.886	0.000000000	0.000000000	0.500

Variable	Q3	Maximum
Rooms Rented	20.50	23.00
Revenue	3298	4563
Complaints	1.750	2.000

Mean Rooms Rented = 15.13
Mean Revenue   = $2,209
Mean Complaints = 0.750

Sample Mean

$$\bar{x} = \frac{\sum_{i=1}^{n} x_i}{n}$$

3-2

where:

$\bar{x}$ = Sample mean (pronounced "x-bar")
n = Sample size

The notation for the sample mean is $\bar{x}$. Sample descriptors (statistics) are usually assigned a Roman character. (Recall that population values usually are assigned a Greek character.)

EXAMPLE 3-2: COMPUTING A SAMPLE MEAN

Housing Prices   Consider a sample of seven house prices in Modesto, California. The real estate agency is interested in computing the mean price for this sample of homes. The following steps can be used:

Step 1:   **Collect the sample data.**

$\{x_i\}$ = {house prices} = {$144,000; $98,000; $204,000; $177,000; $155,000; $316,000; $100,000}

Step 2:   **Add the values in the sample.**

$\sum x$ = $144,000 + 98,000 + 204,000 + 177,000 + 155,000 + 316,000 + 100,000
= $1,194,000

Step 3:   **Divide the sum by the sample size (Equation 3-2).**

$$\bar{x} = \frac{\sum x}{n} = \frac{\$1,194,000}{7} = \$170,571.43$$

Therefore, the mean price for the sample of seven houses in Modesto is $170,571.43.

THE IMPACT OF EXTREME VALUES ON THE MEAN

The mean (population or sample) is the balance point for data, so using the mean as a measure of the center generally makes sense. However, the mean does have one potential disadvantage: *The mean can be highly affected by extreme values.* There are many instances in business when this may occur. For example, in a population or sample of income data, there likely will be extremes on the high end that will pull the mean upward from the center. Example 3-3 illustrates how an extreme value can affect the mean. In these situations, a second measure called the *median* may be more appropriate.

EXAMPLE 3-3: IMPACT OF EXTREME VALUES

Housing Prices   Suppose the sample of house prices in Modesto (see Example 3-2) had been slightly different. If the house recorded as $316,000 had actually been $1,000,000, how would the mean be affected? We can see the impact as follows:

Step 1:   **Collect the sample data.**

$$\{x_i\} = \{\text{house prices}\} = \{\$144,000; \$98,000; \$204,000; \$177,000;$$
$$\$155,000; \$1,000,000; \$100,000\}$$

extreme value

Step 2:   **Add the values.**

$$\Sigma x = \$144,000 + 98,000 + 204,000 + 177,000 + 155,000 + 1,000,000 + 100,000$$
$$= \$1,878,000$$

Step 3:   **Divide the sum by the number of values in the sample.**

$$\bar{x} = \frac{\Sigma x}{n} = \frac{\$1,878,000}{7} = \$268,285.71$$

Recall, in Example 3-2, the sample mean was $170,571.43.

With only one value in the sample changed, the mean is now substantially higher than before. Because the mean is affected by extreme values, it may be a misleading measure of the data's center.

MEDIAN

Another measure of the center is called the **median**.

Median

The median is a center value that divides a data array into two halves. We use $\tilde{\mu}$ to denote the population median and M_d to denote the sample median.

The median is found by first arranging data in numerical order from smallest to largest. Data that are sorted in order are referred to as a **data array**.

Data Array

Data that have been arranged in numerical order.

After the data have been sorted, we locate the value that is halfway from either end. This middle value is the median. If the number of data points in the array is odd, then the median is the middle value in the ordered list. However, if the number of data points is even, then the median is the average of the two middle values.[1]

---

[1] A more-precise definition of the median exists. In that definition the median is defined as a data value (or possibly, set of data values) for which at least half of the data are at least as large as the data value and at least half of the data are as small or smaller than that data value. The definition we present in this text does, however, identify one median and will suffice as an introductory definition.

EXAMPLE 3-4: COMPUTING THE MEDIAN

Housing Prices   Consider again the original Modesto, California, house-price data shown in Example 3-2. The median for these data is computed using the following steps:

Step 1:   Collect the sample data.

$$\{x_i\} = \{\text{house prices}\} = \{\$144,000; \$98,000; \$204,000; \$177,000; \$155,000;$$
$$\$316,000; \$100,000\}$$

Step 2:   Sort the data from smallest to largest, forming a data array.

$$\{x_i\} = \{\$98,000; \$100,000; \$144,000; \$155,000; \$177,000; \$204,000; \$316,000\}$$

Step 3:   Locate the middle value in the data.

Because we have seven houses in the sample, the median is the fourth value from either end of the data array.

$$\{x_i\} = \{\$98,000; \$100,000; \$144,000; \$155,000; \$177,000; \$204,000; \$316,000\}$$

$$\text{fourth value} = M_d$$

The median price house is $155,000. The notation for the sample median is M_d.

Note, if the number of data values in a sample or population is an even number, the median is the average of the two middle values. (See Example 3-6.)

SKEWED AND SYMMETRIC DISTRIBUTIONS

Data in a population or sample can be either **symmetric** or **skewed**, depending on how the data are distributed around the center.

Symmetric Data	***Skewed Data***
Data sets whose values are evenly spread around the center. For symmetric data, the mean and median are equal.	Data sets that are not symmetric. For skewed data, the mean will be larger or smaller than the median.

In the original Modesto house-price example (Examples 3-2), the mean for the sample of seven homes was $170,571.43. In Example 3-4, the median home price was $155,000. Thus, for these data the mean and the median are not equal. This sample data set is **right skewed**, because $\bar{x} = \$170,571.43 > M_d = \$155,000$.

Right-Skewed Data	***Left-Skewed Data***
A data distribution is right skewed if the mean for the data is larger than the median.	A data distribution is left skewed if the mean for the data is smaller than the median.

Figure 3-3 illustrates examples of right-skewed, left-skewed, and symmetric distributions. The greater the difference between the mean and the median, the more skewed the distribution. *Example 3-5 shows that an advantage of the median over the mean is that the median is not affected by extreme values.* Thus, the median is particularly useful as a measure of the center when the data are highly skewed.[2]

---

[2]Excel's Descriptive Statistics tool outputs a skewness statistic. The sign on the skewness statistic implies the direction of skewness. The higher the absolute value, the more the data are skewed.

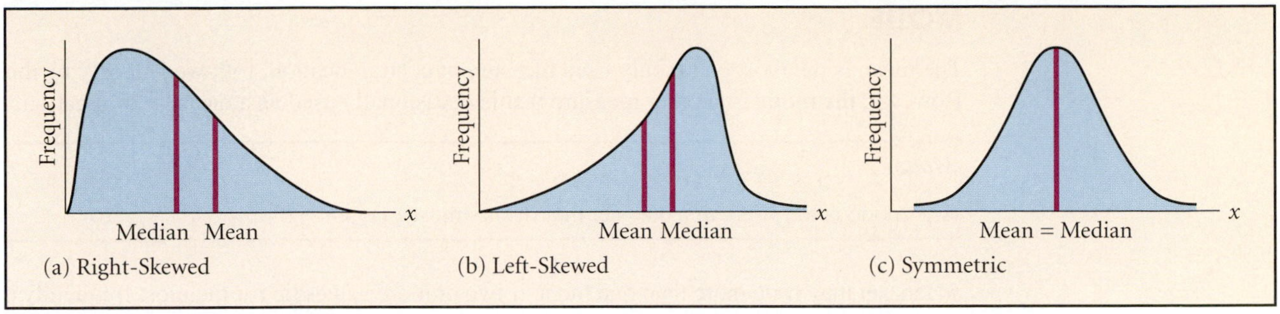

FIGURE 3-3   Skewed and Symmetric Distributions

$\mathcal{E}$XAMPLE 3-5: IMPACT OF EXTREME VALUES ON THE MEDIAN

Housing Prices (Continued)   In Example 3-3, when we substituted a $1,000,000 price for the house priced at $316,000, the sample mean increased from $170,571.43 to $268,285.71. What will happen to the median? The median is determined using the following steps:

Step 1:   **Collect the sample data.** The sample house-price data (including the extremely high-priced house) are

$$\{x_i\} = \{\text{house prices}\} = \{\$144,000; \$98,000; \$204,000; \$177,000;$$
$$\$155,000; \$1,000,000; \$100,000\}$$

Step 2:   **Sort the data from smallest to largest, forming a data array.**

$$\{x_i\} = \{\$98,000; \$100,000; \$144,000; \$155,000; \$177,000; \$204,000; \$1,000,000\}$$

Step 3:   **Locate the middle value in the data.**

Because we have seven houses in the sample, the median is the fourth value from either end of the data array.

$$\{x_i\} = \{\$98,000; \ \$100,000; \ \$144,000; \ \$155,000; \ \$177,000; \ \$204,000; \ \$1,000,000\}$$

$$\text{fourth value} = M_d$$

The median-price house is $155,000, the same value as in Example 3-4, when the high house price was not included in the data.

When the sample or population has an even number of data values, the median can be approximated by the average of the two middle values. Example 3-6 illustrates this.

$\mathcal{E}$XAMPLE 3-6: COMPUTING THE MEDIAN FOR AN EVEN NUMBER OF VALUES

Clonninger's Texaco   Clonninger's Texaco in Canton, Ohio, offers a free car wash when a customer fills his or her car with gas. The manager is interested in knowing the median number of gallons of gasoline that are purchased when a car wash is given out. A sample of 10 customers has been randomly selected. The median is approximated as follows:

Step 1:   **Collect the sample data.**

$$\{x_i\} = \{\text{gallons}\} = \{13.5, 17.9, 11.5, 22.1, 15.0, 16.9, 29.6, 9.6, 17.7, 20.5\}$$

Step 2:   **Sort the data from smallest to largest, forming a data array.**

$$\{x_i\} = \{\text{gallons}\} = \{9.6, 11.5, 13.5, 15.0, 16.9, 17.7, 17.9, 20.5, 22.1, 29.6\}$$

Step 3:   **Locate the middle value in the data.**

Because we have an even number of values, the median is approximated by finding the average of the middle two data values. Thus, we would average the fifth and sixth data values from either end.

$$\{x_i\} = \{\text{gallons}\} = \{9.6, 11.5, 13.5, 15.0, 16.9, 17.7, 17.9, 20.5, 22.1, 29.6\}$$

$$M_d = \frac{16.9 + 17.7}{2} = 17.3 \text{ gallons}$$

MODE

The mean is the most commonly used measure of central location, followed closely by the median. However, the **mode** is another measure that is occasionally used as a measure of location.

Mode

The mode is the value in a data set that occurs most frequently.

A data set may have more than one mode if two or more values tie for the most frequently occurring value. Example 3-7 illustrates this concept and shows how the mode is determined.

EXAMPLE 3-7: DETERMINING THE MODE

Smoky Mountain Pizza   The owners of Smoky Mountain Pizza are planning to expand their restaurant to include an open-air patio. Before finalizing the design, the managers want to know what the most frequently occurring group size is so that they can organize the seating arrangements to best meet demand. They wish to know the mode, which can be calculated using the following steps:

Step 1:   **Collect the sample data.**
A sample of 20 groups was selected at random. These data are

$$\{x_i\} = \{people\} = \{2, 4, 1, 2, 3, 2, 4, 2, 3, 6, 8, 4, 2, 1, 7, 4, 2, 4, 4, 3\}$$

Step 2:   **Organize the data into a frequency distribution.**

x_i	Frequency
1	2
2	6
3	3
4	6
5	0
6	1
7	1
8	1
	Total = 20

Step 3:   **Determine the value that occurs most frequently.**
In this case, there are two modes, because the values 2 and 4 each occurred six times. Thus the modes are 2 and 4.

A common mistake is to state the mode as being the frequency of the most frequently occurring value. In Example 3-6, you might be tempted to say that the mode = 6 because that was the highest frequency. Instead there were two modes, 2 and 4, both of which occurred six times.

If no value occurs more frequently than any other, the data set is said to not have a mode. The mode might be particularly useful in describing the central location value for clothes sizes. For example, shoes come in full and half sizes. Consider the following sample data that have been sorted from low to high:

$$\{x\} = \{7.5, 8.0, 8.5, 9.0, 9.0, 10.0, 10.0, 10.0, 10.5, 10.5, 11.0, 11.5\}$$

The mean for these sample data is

$$\bar{x} = \frac{\sum x}{n} = \frac{7.5 + 8.0 + \cdots + 11.5}{12} = \frac{115.50}{12} = 9.625$$

Although 9.625 is the numerical average, the mode is 10, because more people wore that size shoe than any other. In making purchasing decisions, a shoe store manager would order more shoes at the modal size than at any other size. The mean isn't of any particular value in her purchasing decision.

Excel and Minitab Tutorial

APPLYING THE MEASURES OF CENTRAL TENDENCY

Weigh in Motion—The state transportation department is experimenting with a system called weigh in motion (WIM) that can weigh trucks as they drive down a highway. It may prove to be a substitute for traditional static scales at ports of entry (POE), which require trucks to stop to be weighed. In the experiment, trucks have been weighed on two scales: WIM and POE. The sample data are on your CD-ROM in the file, *Trucks*. Weights were recorded to the nearest pound.

The issue of interest in this study is whether the WIM scale produces measurements that are close to POE measurements. The POE weight is assumed to be accurate. For the purposes of this discussion, we focus on two variables: WIM gross weight and POE gross weight.

Figures 3-4 and 3-5 show the frequency histograms generated for these two variables using Excel. We have used the same class intervals for both variables. The histograms are a good place to start our analysis of whether the WIM scale weighs trucks accurately. What is your initial conclusion based on the histograms in Figures 3-4 and 3-5? Do the truck-weight distributions from the two scales look alike? Are the distributions symmetric or skewed?

We can extend our analysis by computing the appropriate statistical measures. Specifically, we want to look at measures of central location. Figure 3-6 illustrates the Excel output, with the descriptive measures for both WIM and POE gross weight.[3]

We first focus on the primary measures of central location: the mean and the median.

Measures	WIM Weight	POE Weight
Mean	64,171.15 lbs	61,057.25 lbs
Median	71,380.00 lbs.	67,655.00 lbs.

FIGURE 3-4

Excel Frequency Histogram—WIM Gross Weight

Excel Instructions:
1. Open file: Trucks.xls
2. Identify data and bins range.
3. Define bins (upper limit of each class).
4. Click on **Tools**.
5. Select **Data Analysis**.
6. Select **Histogram**.
7. Identify Output Sheet name.
8. Check "Chart Output."
9. Close Gaps (Format Data Series, Options, Gap Width).
10. Modify Class Labels.

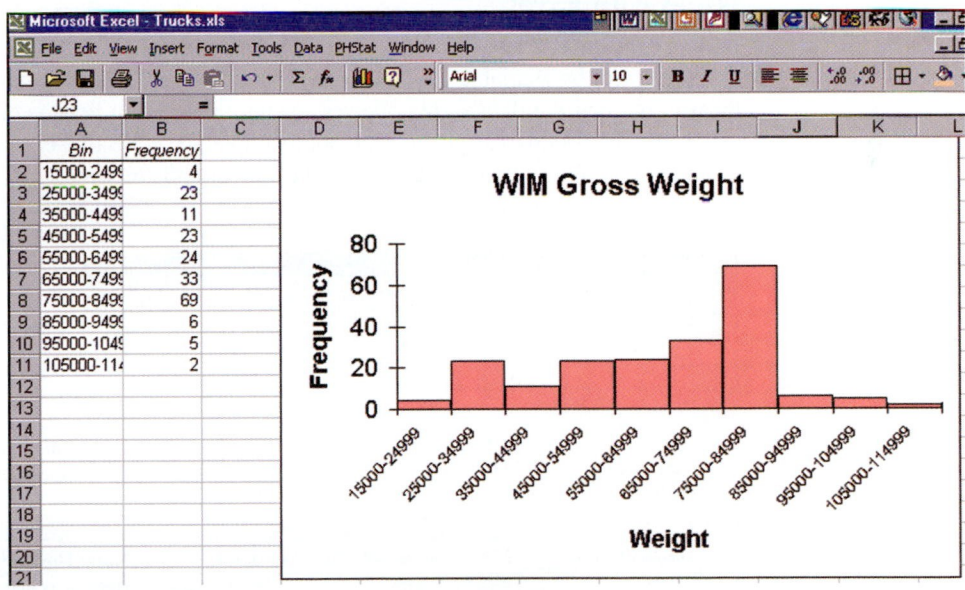

Minitab Instructions (for similar results):
1. Open file: Trucks.MTW.
2. Choose **Graph > Histogram**.
3. Click **Simple**.
4. Click **OK**.
5. In **Graph variables**, enter data column *WIM Gross Wgt*.
6. Click **OK**.

[3]*Note:* The Descriptive Statistics tool in Excel and Minitab provides additional statistical measures beyond the mean, the median and the mode. Several of these will be discussed later in this chapter.

FIGURE 3-5

Excel Frequency
Histogram—POE Gross
Weight

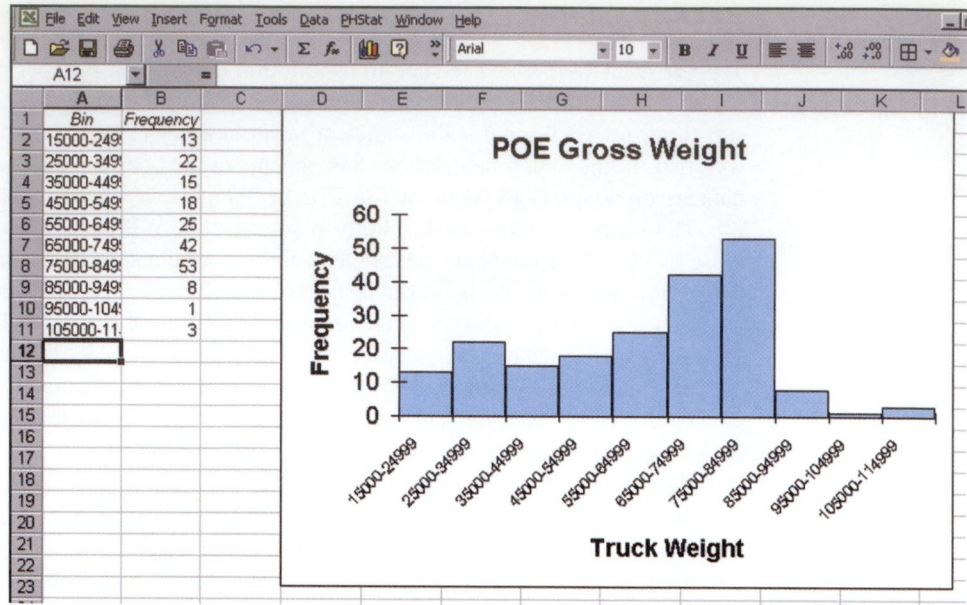

These statistics indicate that, for the sample data, the WIM scale weights are, on average, heavier than the POE scale. Likewise, the median WIM weight exceeds the median POE weight. In both cases, the means are less than the medians. Thus, the sample data from both scales are left skewed.

Issues with Excel

In many instances, data files will have "missing values." That is, the values for one or more variables may not be available for some of the observations. The data have been lost, or they were not measured when the data were collected. Many times when you receive data like this, the missing values will be coded in a special way. For example, the code "N/A" might be used or a "−99" might be entered to signify that the data for that observation is missing.

FIGURE 3-6

Excel Descriptive Statistics
Output

Excel Instructions:
1. Open file: Trucks.xls
2. Click on the **Tools** button.
3. Select **Data Analysis** option.
4. Choose **Descriptive Statistics** and select the appropriate data ranges.
5. Click on "Summary Statistics."

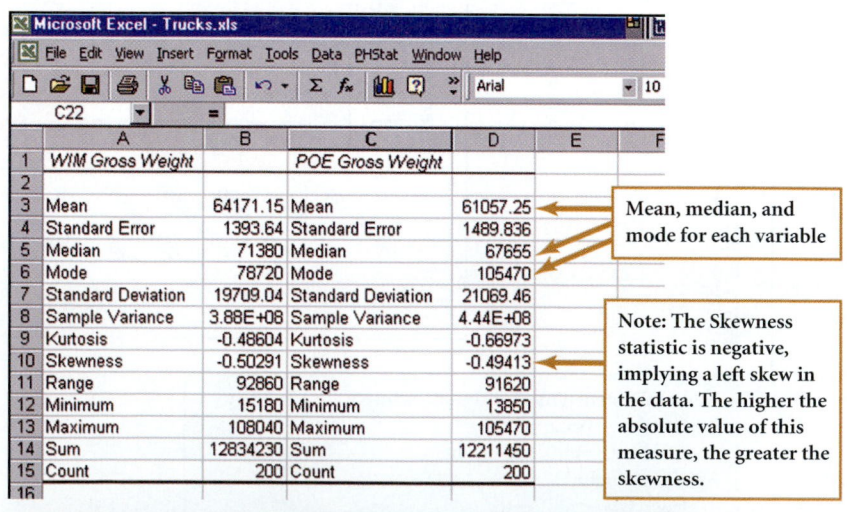

Minitab Instructions (for similar results):
1. Open file: Trucks.MTW.
2. Choose **Stat > Basic Statistics > Display Descriptive Statistics**.
3. In **Variables**, enter columns *WIM Gross Weight* and *POE Gross Weight*.
4. Click **Statistics**.
5. Check required statistics.
6. Click **OK. OK.**

Statistical software packages typically have flexible procedures for dealing with missing data. Minitab provides you with missing data options and properly adjusts the results to account for the missing data. *However, Excel does not contain a missing-value option.* If you attempt to use certain data-analysis options in Excel, such as Descriptive Statistics, in the presence of nonnumeric ("N/A") data, you will get an error message. When that happens you must clear the missing values, generally by deleting all rows with missing values. In some instances, you can save the good data in the row by using **Edit-Clear-All** for the cell in question. However, a bigger problem exists when the missing value has been coded as an arbitrary numeric value (-99). In this case, unless you go into the data and clear these values, Excel will use the -99 values in the computations as if they are real values. The result will be incorrect calculations.

Also, if a data set contains more than one mode, Excel will only show the first mode in the list of modes and will not warn you that multiple modes exist. (Minitab does not have a mode output option in its Descriptive Statistics tool.)

OTHER MEASURES OF LOCATION

Weighted Mean

The arithmetic mean is the most frequently used measure of central location. Equations 3-1 and 3-2 are used when you have either a population or a sample. For instance, the sample mean is computed using

$$\bar{x} = \frac{\sum x}{n} = \frac{x_1 + x_2 + x_3 + \cdots + x_n}{n}$$

In this case, each x value is given an equal weight in the computation of the mean. However, in some applications there is reason to weight the data values differently. In that case, we need to compute a **weighted mean**.

Weighted Mean

The mean value of data values that have been weighted according to their relative importance.

Equations 3-3 and 3-4 are used to find the weighted mean (or weighted average) for a population and for a sample, respectively.

Weighted Mean for a Population		Weighted Mean for a Sample	
$\mu_W = \dfrac{\sum w_i x_i}{\sum w_i}$	**3-3**	$\bar{x}_w = \dfrac{\sum w_i x_i}{\sum w_i}$	**3-4**
		where:	
		w_i = The weight of the ith data value	
		x_i = The ith data value	

$\mathcal{E}$XAMPLE 3-8: CALCULATING A WEIGHTED POPULATION MEAN

Fallon & Associates   Recently, the law firm of Fallon & Associates was involved in a discrimination suit concerning ski instructors at a ski resort in Colorado. One ski instructor from Germany had sued the operator of the ski resort, claiming that he had not received equitable pay compared with the other ski instructors from Norway and the United States. In preparing a defense, the Fallon attorneys planned to compute the mean annual salary for all seven Norwegian ski instructors at the resort. However, because these instructors worked different numbers of days during the ski season, a weighted mean needed to be computed. This was done using the following steps:

Step 1:   **Collect the desired data and determine the weight to be assigned to each data value.**
In this case, the variable of interest was the salary of the ski instructors. The population consisted of seven Norwegian instructors. The weights were the number of days that the instructors worked. The following data and weights were determined:

x_i = Salary:						
$7,600	$3,900	$5,300	$4,000	$7,200	$2,300	$5,100
w_i = Days:						
50	30	40	25	60	15	50

Step 2:   **Multiply each weight by the data value and sum these.**

$$\sum w_i x_i = (50)(\$7,600) + (30)(\$3,900) + \cdots + (50)(\$5,100) = \$1,530,500$$

Step 3:   **Sum the weights for all values** (the weights are the days).

$$\sum w_i = 50 + 30 + 40 + 25 + 60 + 15 + 50 = 270$$

Step 4:   **Compute the weighted mean.**
Divide the weighted sum by the sum of the weights. Because we are working with the population, the result will be the population weighted mean.

$$\mu_W = \frac{\sum w_i x_i}{\sum w_i} = \frac{\$1,530,500}{270} = \$5,668.519$$

Thus, taking into account the number of days worked, the Norwegian ski instructors had a mean salary of $5,668.52.

One weighted-mean example that you are probably very familiar with is your college grade point average (GPA). At most schools, A = 4 points, B = 3 points, and so forth. Each class has a certain number of credits (usually 1 to 5). The credits are the weights. Your GPA is computed by summing the product of points earned in a class times the credits for the class, and then dividing this sum by the total number of credits earned.

Percentiles

In some applications, we might wish to describe the location of the data in terms other than the center of the data. For example, prior to enrolling at your university you took the SAT or ACT test and received a **percentile** score in math and verbal skills.

If you received word that your standardized exam score was at the 90th percentile, it means that you scored as high or higher than 90% of the other students who took the exam. The score at the 50th percentile would indicate that you were at the median, where at least 50% scored at or below and at least 50% scored at or above your score.[4]

Percentiles

The pth percentile in a data array is a value that divides the data set into two parts. The lower segment contains at least $p\%$, and the upper segment contains at least $(100 - p)\%$, of the data. The 50th percentile is the median.

To illustrate how to manually approximate a percentile value, consider a situation in which you have 309 customers enter a bank during the course of a day. The time (rounded to the nearest minute) that each customer spends in the bank is recorded. If we wish to approximate the 10th percentile, we would begin by first sorting the data into order from low to high. Assign each data value a location indicator from 1 to 309. Next determine the location indicator that corresponds to the 10th percentile using Equation 3-5.

---

[4]More rigorously, the percentile is that value (or set of values) such that at least $p\%$ of the data is as small or smaller than that value and at least $(100 - p)\%$ of the data is at least as large as that value. For introductory courses, a convention has been adopted to average the largest and smallest values that qualify as a certain percentile. This is why the median was defined as it was earlier for data sets with an even number of data values.

Percentile Location Value

$$i = \frac{p}{100}(n+1)$$ 3-5

where:

p = Desired percentile
n = Number of values in the data set

   If i is an integer, then the pth percentile is the value in location i. If i is not an integer, then use interpolation.

   Thus, the location of the 10th percentile is

$$i = \frac{p}{100}(n+1) = \frac{10}{100}(309+1) = 31$$

Because i is an integer, the 10th percentile is approximated by the value in the 31st position from the low end of the sorted data.
   The location for the 26th percentile is

$$i = \frac{p}{100}(n+1) = \frac{26}{100}(309+1) = 80.60$$

Because 80.60 is not an integer, we interpolate 60% of the way between the 80th and 81st value in the data. For instance suppose the 80th data value is 5 minutes and the 81st value is 7 minutes, the 26th percentile would be $5 + 0.60(7 - 5) = 6.2$ minutes.

SUMMARY: CALCULATING PERCENTILES

To calculate a specific percentile for a set of quantitative data, you can use the following steps:

1. Sort the data into order from the lowest to highest value.

2. Determine the percentile location value, i, using Equation 3-5.

$$i = \frac{p}{100}(n+1)$$

where
p = desired percentile
n = number of values in the data set

3. If i is not an integer, then interpolate between the integer portion of i and the next value.

EXAMPLE 3-9: CALCULATING PERCENTILES

Henson Trucking   The Henson Trucking Company is a small company that is in the business of moving people from one home to another within the Dallas, Texas, area. Historically, the owners have charged the customers on an hourly basis, regardless of the distance of the move within the Dallas city limits. However, they are now considering adding a surcharge for moves over a certain distance. They have decided to base this charge on the 80th percentile. They have a sample of travel-distance data for 30 moves. These data are as follows:

13.5	8.6	16.2	21.4	21.0	23.7	4.1	13.8	20.5	9.6
11.5	6.5	5.8	10.1	11.1	4.4	12.2	13.0	15.7	13.2
13.4	13.1	21.7	14.6	14.1	12.4	24.9	19.3	26.9	11.7

The 80th percentile can be computed using these steps.

Step 1:   **Sort the data from lowest to highest.**

4.1	4.4	5.8	6.5	8.6	9.6	10.1	11.1	11.5	11.7
12.2	12.4	13.0	13.1	13.2	13.4	13.5	13.8	14.1	14.6
15.7	16.2	19.3	20.5	21.0	21.4	21.7	23.7	24.9	26.9

Step 2:   **Determine percentile location value, i, using Equation 3-5.**
The 80th percentile location value is:

$$i = \frac{p}{100}(n+1) = \frac{80}{100}(30+1) = 24.80$$

Step 3:   **Interpolate if necessary.**
Because $i = 24.80$ is not an integer value, the 80th percentile is found by interpolation. First locate the 24th value, which is 20.5. The next higher value is 21.0. The 80th percentile is

$$20.5 + .80(21.0 - 20.5) = 20.90$$

Therefore, any customer with a move distance exceeding 20.90 miles will receive a surcharge.

Quartiles

Quartiles are another location measure that can be used to describe data.

Quartiles

Quartiles in a data array are those values that divide the data set into four equal-sized groups. The median corresponds to the second quartile.

The first quartile corresponds to the 25th percentile. That is, it is the value at or below which there is at least 25% (one quarter) of the data and at or above which there is at least 75% of the data. The third quartile is also the 75th percentile. It is the value at or below which there is at least 75% of the data and at or above which there is at least 25% of the data. The second quartile is the 50th percentile and is also the median.

A quartile value can be approximated manually using the same method as for percentiles with Equation 3-5. For the 309 bank customer-service times mentioned earlier, the location of the first-quartile (25th percentile) value is found, after sorting the data, as

$$i = \frac{p}{100}(n+1) = \frac{25}{100}(309+1) = 77.5$$

Because 77.5 is not an integer value, the first quartile is approximated by interpolating between the values in the 77th and the 78th locations from the lower end of the sorted data.

Issues with Excel

The procedure that Excel uses to compute quartiles *is not standard*. Therefore, the quartile and percentile values from Excel will be slightly different from those we found using Equation 3-5 and from what other statistical software packages, including Minitab, will provide. For example, referring to Example 3-9, when Excel is used to compute the 80th percentile for the moving distances, the value returned is 20.58 miles. This is slightly different than the 20.90 we found in Example 3-9. Equation 3-5, the method used by Minitab, is generally accepted by statisticians to be correct. Therefore, if you need precise values for quartiles, use software such as Minitab. However, Excel will give reasonably close percentile and quartile values.

BOX AND WHISKER PLOTS

A descriptive tool that many decision makers like to use is called a **box and whisker plot** (or a box plot). The box and whisker plot incorporates the median and the quartiles to graphically display quantitative data. It is also used to identify *outliers* that are extremely small or large data values that lie mostly by themselves.

Box and Whisker Plot

A graph that is composed of two parts: a box and the whiskers. The box has a width that ranges from the first quartile (Q_1) to the third quartile (Q_3). A vertical line through the box is placed at the median. Limits are located at a value that is 1.5 times the difference between Q_1 and Q_3 below Q_1 and above Q_3. The whiskers extend to the left to the lowest value within the limits and to the right to the highest value within the limits.

SUMMARY: CONSTRUCTING A BOX AND WHISKER PLOT

A box and whisker plot is graphical summary of a quantitative variable. It is constructed using the following steps:

1. Sort the data values from low to high.

2. Use Equation 3-5 to find the 25th percentile ($Q1$ = first quartile), the 50th percentile ($Q2$ = median), and the 75th percentile ($Q3$ = third quartile).

3. Draw a box so that the ends of the box are at $Q1$ and $Q3$. This box will contain the middle 50% of the data values in the population or sample.

4. Draw a vertical line through the box at the median. Half the data values in the box will be on either side of the median.

5. Calculate the *interquartile range* ($IQR = Q3 - Q1$). (The interquartile range will be discussed more fully in Section 3-2.) Compute the lower limit for the box and whisker plot as $Q1 - 1.5(Q3 - Q1)$. The upper limit is $Q3 + 1.5(Q3 - Q1)$. Any data values outside these limits are referred to as outliers.

6. Extend dashed lines (called the whiskers) from each end of the box to the lowest and highest value within the limits.

7. Any value outside the limits (outlier) found in 5 is marked with an asterisk (*).

EXAMPLE 3-10: CONSTRUCTING A BOX AND WHISKER PLOT

Rolling Hills Golf Course Rolling Hills is a semiprivate golf club in rural North Carolina. Like most golf courses, Rolling Hills constantly battles the slow-play issue. Recently, the course manager collected a random sample of times for 18-hole rounds at the course. He plans to make a presentation to the board of directors and wishes to construct a box and whisker plot as part of the presentation. The sorted sample data (time measured in minutes) for 45 rounds are shown as follows:

231	236	241	242	242	243	243	243	248
248	249	250	251	251	252	252	254	255
255	256	256	257	259	260	260	260	260
262	262	264	265	265	265	266	268	268
270	276	277	277	280	286	300	324	345

The box and whisker plot is computed using the following steps:

Step 1: **Sort the data from low to high.**

Step 2: **Calculate the 25th percentile ($Q1$), the 50th percentile (median), and the 75th percentile ($Q3$).**
The location for $Q1$ is

$$i = \frac{p}{100}(n + 1) = \frac{25}{100}(45 + 1) = 11.50$$

Thus, $Q1$ will be halfway between the 11th and 12th values, which is $249 + 0.50(250 - 249) = 249.50$.
    The median location is

$$i = \frac{p}{100}(n + 1) = \frac{50}{100}(45 + 1) = 23$$

In the sorted data, the median is the 23rd value, which has a value of 259 minutes. The third-quartile location is

$$i = \frac{p}{100}(n + 1) = \frac{75}{100}(45 + 1) = 34.50$$

Thus, $Q3$ is halfway between the 34th and 35th data values. This is $266 + 0.50(268 - 266) = 267$.

Step 3:   **Draw the box so the ends correspond to $Q1$ and $Q3$.**

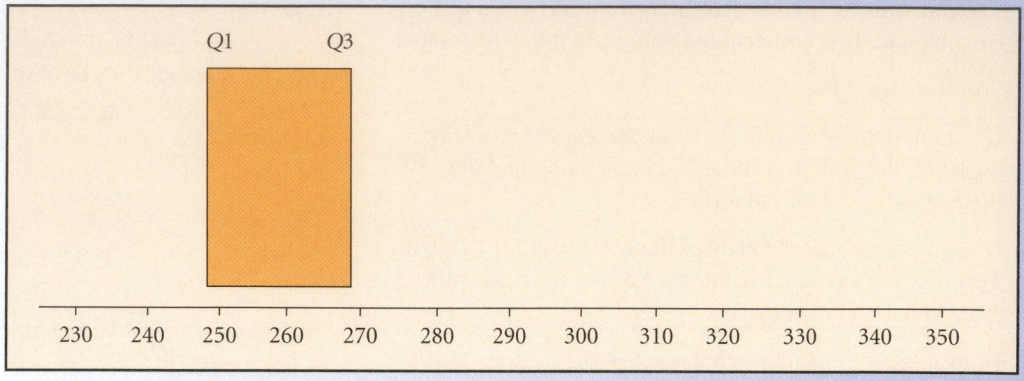

Step 4:   **Draw a vertical line through the box at the median.**

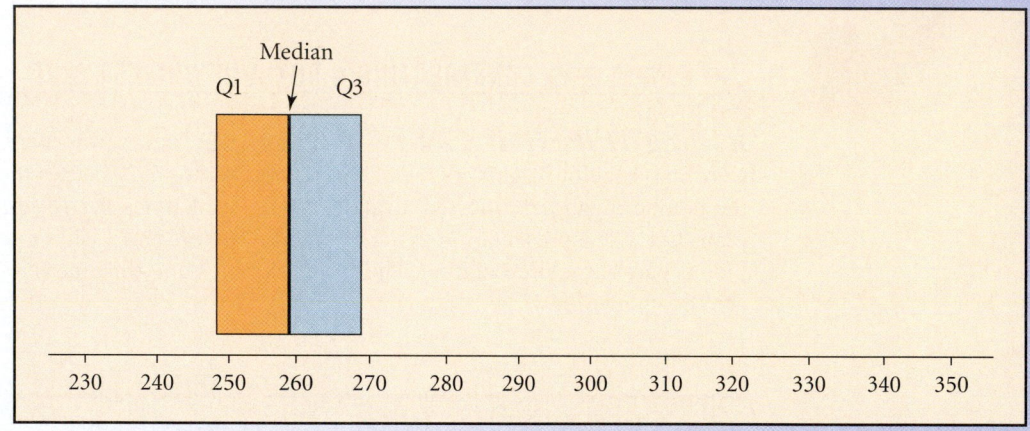

Step 5:   **Compute the upper and lower limits.**
The lower limit is computed as $Q1 - 1.5(Q3 - Q1)$. This is

$$\text{Lower Limit} = 249.50 - 1.5(267 - 249.5) = 223.25$$

The upper limit is $Q3 + 1.5(Q3 - Q1)$. This is

$$\text{Upper Limit} = 267 + 1.5(267 - 249.5) = 293.25$$

Any value outside these limits is identified as an outlier.

Step 6:   **Draw the whiskers.**
The whiskers are drawn to the smallest and largest values inside the limits.

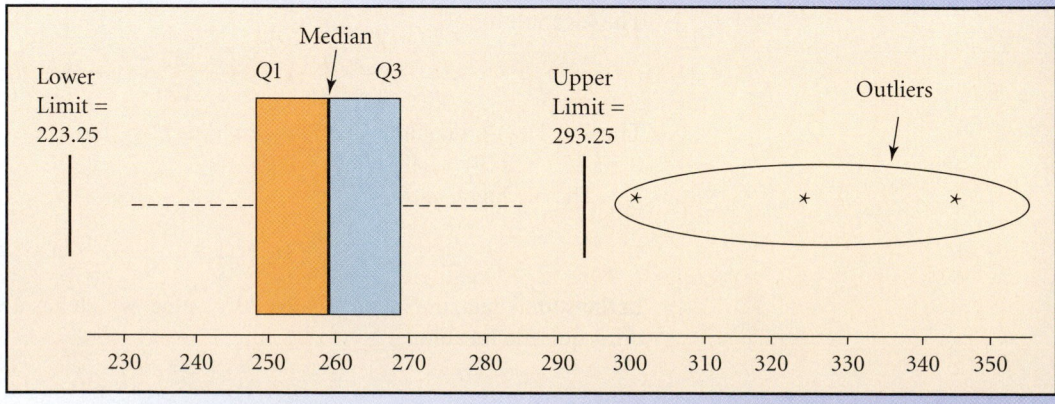

Step 7:   **Plot the outliers.**
The outliers are plotted as values outside the limits.

DATA-LEVEL ISSUES

You need to be very aware of the level of data you are working with before computing the numerical measures introduced in this chapter. A common mistake is to compute means on nominal-level data. For example, a major electronics manufacturer recently surveyed a sample of customers to determine whether they preferred black, white, or colored stereo cases. The data were coded as follows.

$$1 = \text{black}$$
$$2 = \text{white}$$
$$3 = \text{colored}$$

A few of the responses are

$$\text{Color code} = \{1, 1, 3, 2, 1, 2, 2, 2, 3, 1, 1, 1, 3, 2, 2, 1, 2\}$$

Using these codes, the sample mean is

$$\bar{x} = \frac{\sum x}{n}$$

$$= \frac{30}{17} = 1.765$$

As you can see, reporting that customers prefer a color somewhere between black and white but closer to white would be meaningless. The mean should not be used with nominal data. This type of mistake tends to happen when people use computer software to perform their calculations. It is easy to ask Excel, Minitab, or other statistical software to compute mean, median, and so on for all the variables in the data set. Then a table is created and, before long, the meaningless measures creep into your report.

There is also some disagreement about whether means should be computed on ordinal data. For example, in market research a 5- or 7-point scale is often used to measure customers' attitudes about products or TV commercials. For example, we might set up the following scale:

$$1 = \text{Strongly Agree}$$
$$2 = \text{Agree}$$
$$3 = \text{Neutral}$$
$$4 = \text{Disagree}$$
$$5 = \text{Strongly Disagree}$$

Customer responses to a particular question are obtained on this scale from 1 to 5. For a sample of $n = 10$ people, we might get the following responses to a question.

$$\text{Response} = \{2, 2, 1, 3, 3, 1, 5, 2, 1, 3\}$$

The mean rating is 2.3. We could then compute the mean for a second issue and compare the means. However, what exactly do we have? First, when we compute a mean for a scaled variable, we are making two basic assumptions:

1. We are assuming the distance between a rating of 1 and 2 is the same as the distance between 2 and 3. We are also saying these distances are exactly the same for the second issue's variable to which you wish to compare it. Although from a numerical standpoint this is true, in terms of what the scale is measuring, is the difference between strongly agree and agree the same as the difference between agree and neutral? If not, is the mean really a meaningful measure?
2. We are also assuming people who respond to the survey have the same definition of what "strongly agree" means or what "disagree" means. When you mark a 4 (disagree) on your survey, are you applying the same criteria as someone else who also marks a 4 on the same issue? If not, then the mean might be misleading.

Although these difficulties exist with ordinal data, we see many examples in which means are computed and used for decision purposes. In fact, we once had a dean who focused on one particular question on the course evaluation survey that was administered in every class each semester. This question was "Considering all factors of importance to you, how would you rate this instructor?"

1 = Excellent   2 = Good   3 = Average   4 = Poor   5 = Very Poor

The dean then had his staff compute means for each class and for each professor. He then listed classes and faculty in order based on the mean values, and he based a significant part of the performance

FIGURE 3-7

**Descriptive Measures
of the Center**

Descriptive Measure	Computation Method	Data Level	Advantages/ Disadvantages
Mean	Sum of values divided by the number of values	Ratio Interval	• Numerical center of the data • Sum of deviations from the mean is zero • Sensitive to extreme values
Median	Middle value for data that have been sorted	Ratio Interval Ordinal	• Not sensitive to extreme values • Computed only from the center values • Does not use information from all the data
Mode	Value(s) that occur most frequently in the data	Ratio Interval Ordinal Nominal	• May not reflect the center • May not exist • Might have multiple modes

evaluation on where a faculty member stood with respect to mean score on this one question. By the way, he carried the calculations for the mean out to three decimal places!

In general, the median is the preferred measure of central location for ordinal data instead of the mean.

Figure 3-7 summarizes the three measures of the center that have been discussed in this section.

3-1: EXERCISES

Skill Development

3.1 The number of cars that have gone through a car wash during the noon hour over each of the past eight days are shown as follows:

6	3	9	6	6	5	4	1

Compute the mean, median, and mode for these sample data.

3.2 The following data are the average per-hour wages in dollars, after deductions, for the workers in an orthodontist's office:

17.87	19.95	22.95	18.74	9.95
11.22	21.98	14.52	16.65	14.98

Determine the mean, median, and mode for the data.

3.3 Another orthodontist's office employees receive the following hourly wages, in dollars.

15.67	23.45	18.95	20.79	25.49	
25.49	20.79	25.49	18.95	23.45	15.67

a. Using measures of central tendency, determine the shape of this data.
b. Determine the first and third quartiles for this data.

3.4 During one weekend, 11 houses were sold in Half Moon Bay, California. The prices paid for these houses are given here (in thousands of dollars).

264	305	287	325	298	271
112	317	293	325	289	

a. Compute the mean, median, and mode for this population. Which measure of central tendency would you use to describe the "center" of these data?
b. Calculate the quartiles for this data.

3.5 The number of hot dogs sold by 12 randomly selected hot dog vendors in a large city park on July 4 are as follows:

142	97	105	76	90	83
123	115	92	94	73	104

Compute the mean, median, first quartile, and third quartile for these sample data.

3.6 Five wheat farms have been selected at random from those in a particular county. The following crop yields (total bushels of wheat) are given for each of the five, along with the number of acres on each farm.

Yield	15,030	43,400	10,260	13,200	89,200
Acres	80	60	75	55	140

a. Compute the mean yield for this sample of five farms.
b. Taking into account the number of acres on each farm, compute a weighted mean for this sample.

3.7 The following frequency distribution is given for the ages of students at a small private university.

Age	Frequency
18 to 20	345
21 to 22	560
23 to 25	200
26 to 28	80

a. Compute the mean age at this university. (Hint: use the midpoint of each age class to represent all values in the class. Find a weighted mean.)

b. What is the median age at this university?

3.8 The following data constitute a sample of hours of Internet usage per week by students.

5	4	3	10	8	5	2
6	9	6	9	7	6	12
9	11	10	9	7	7	6
9	9	3	7	11	5	11
7	6	4	10	7	3	5

a. Comptue the mean, median, and mode for these data.

b. Develop a box and whisker plot for these data.

3.9 The following data reflect the number of books sold at a used book store in Brooklyn, New York, each day for a random sample of 45 days

17	18	19	20	16	15	17	22	16
16	19	21	15	14	17	21	19	15
19	15	15	19	18	22	13	14	17
18	21	15	13	10	13	20	12	15
21	15	16	16	14	19	15	16	13

a. Develop a box and whisker plot. Are there any outliers in this sample?

b. What number of books constitutes the 60th percentile for this sample?

3.10 The following set of data is the number of employees at 1/30th of the franchises of a prominent fast-food restaurant:

16	23	17	24	9	11	13	15
18	21	16	23	17	16	10	14

a. Determine the mean, median, and mode for the data.

b. Indicate whether the data are skewed or symmetric.

3.11 A question appears on a job application for sales persons at a national insurance company. It asks the applicants to rate their gregariousness on a scale from 1 to 10. The answers obtained from 18 such applications appear here:

8	6	9	9	7	10	7	8	9
8	7	7	10	9	8	5	6	10

a. Consider the type of data carefully and calculate the most appropriate measure of central tendency for this data. Explain your answer.

b. Calculate the interquartile range for this data.

3.12 Examine the following data:

23	65	45	19	35	28	39	100	50	26	25	27
24	17	12	106	23	19	39	70	20	18	44	31

a. Compute the quartiles.

b. Calculate the 90th percentile.

c. Develop a box and whisker plot.

d. Calculate the 20th and 30th percentiles.

Business Applications

3.13 Gayle Pooley, the marketing director for South East Insurance, has been worried about the increasing age of the company's policyholder base. She wants to determine whether the new advertising campaign has had the desired effect of attracting a larger number of younger customers. As a first step in this analysis, she has selected two samples of customers. The first sample is from the customer base before the new advertising campaign. The data are the ages of the customers at the time the policies went into effect. The second sample was taken from the customers who were added after the advertising campaign.

Pre-Advertising		Post-Advertising	
33	30	23	34
44	40	31	40
52	29	40	28
34	55	28	25
25	36	26	29

a. Determine the mean, median, and mode for each sample.

b. Discuss whether either of the two data sets is skewed and show why or why not.

c. Is there any indication from these two samples that the new policyholders may tend to be younger? Write a short report that uses the findings in parts a and b to justify your answer.

3.14 The Soccer Shoppe was recently opened in Sonoma, California, to provide soccer equipment and supplies to players and teams in the area. During the first month that it was open, the managers kept track of the number of customers who entered the store each day. The following data were collected.

21	19	21	19	19	20	18	12	20	19	17	14
21	22	25	21	22	23	10	19	25	14	17	18

a. Compute the mean, median, and mode for these data.

b. Indicate whether the data are skewed or symmetrical.

c. Construct a box and whisker plot for these data. Referring to your answer in part a, does the box plot support your conclusion about skewness? Discuss.

3.15 One of the leading business periodicals recently conducted a study of its subscribers to determine the total credit card debt for each customer. A sample of 50 subscribers responded to the survey, with the following results, in dollars.

$1,366	$0	$1,692	$2,973	$2,426	$2,090	$2,429	$3,306	$3,050	$2,085
3,269	2,261	3,011	3,617	2,273	2,960	3,203	347	0	2,441
2,516	3,727	2,085	2,010	700	2,301	2,096	2,008	2,653	3,088
2,257	8,345	2,523	1,948	2,685	3,393	2,591	1,209	3,621	300
3,612	2,380	0	2,681	2,506	3,076	4,065	2,218	3,287	3,712

a. Develop a box and whisker plot for these sample data.

b. Based on the box and whisker plot, does it appear that the distribution of credit card debt is skewed? If so, in which direction is it skewed? Discuss.

3.16   The Ollander Corporation operates five food processing plants in western Europe. Recently, the company was considering modifying its financial reward system for the plant managers. In doing the analysis, the director of human resources collected information on the profits (in thousands of U.S. dollars) generated from each plant last year. She also collected data on the number of employees at the plants. These data are shown as follows:

Profits	$7,400	$14,400	$12,300	$6,200	$3,100
Employees	123	402	256	109	67

a. Compute the weighted mean profit for these five plants using the number of employees as the weights.

b. Explain why the human resources director would want a weighted average to be computed in this situation rather than a simple numeric average.

Advanced Business Applications

3.17   The Golden Calendar Company produces a variety of specialized calendars that it sells to commercial customers, who then resell the calendars. The sales manager at Golden has selected a sample of 16 major customers and recorded the total number of calendars purchased by each customer last year. The data here list the number of calendars purchased. The data are in a file called *Golden* on your CD-ROM.

a. Compute the mean and median for these sales data.

b. Develop a box and whisker plot for these sales data.

c. Write a short statement that describes these sales data using the information generated in parts a and b. Make special note of any unusually low or high number of calendar purchases, because these accounts often require more attention. The company wishes to increase sales to the low accounts and keep clients who purchase large amounts.

3.18   The Cozine Corporation operates a garbage hauling business. Up to this point, the company has been charged a flat fee for each of its garbage trucks that enters the county landfill. The flat fee is based on an assumed truck weight of 45,000 pounds. In two weeks, the company is required to appear before the county commissioners to discuss a rate adjustment. In preparation for this meeting, Cozine has hired an independent company to weigh a sample of Cozine's garbage trucks just before they enter the landfill. The data file *Cozine* shows the data the company has collected.

a. Based on the sample data, what percentile does the 45,000-pound weight fall closest to?

b. Compute appropriate measures of central location for the data.

c. Construct a frequency histogram based on the sample data. Use Sturges' rule (see Chapter 2) to determine the number of classes. Also, construct a box and whisker plot for these data. Discuss the relative advantages of histograms and box and whisker plots for presenting these data.

d. Use the information determined in parts a, b, and c to develop a presentation to the county commissioners. Make sure the presentation attempts to answer the question of whether Cozine deserves a rate reduction.

3.19   The High Desert Bank loan manager recently selected a random sample of loan files from the bank's loan portfolio. Her objective in selecting the sample is to gain a better understanding of the relationship between commercial and real estate loans. In particular, she wishes to analyze the loan amounts by type of loan. The data file *High-Desert* contains the data on a sample of 350 loans. Determine appropriate measures of central location for the overall sample.

a. Compute the measures of central location for each category of loan.

b. Develop a box and whisker plot for loan amount for each type of loan. Compare these.

3-2 MEASURES OF VARIATION

Bryce Lumber Company—Consider the situation involving two manufacturing facilities for the Bryce Lumber Company. The division vice president asked the two plant managers to record their production output for five days. The resulting sample data are shown in Table 3-3.

Instead of reporting these raw data, the managers reported only the mean and median for their data. The following are the computed statistics for the two plants:

TABLE 3-3

Manufacturing Output for Bryce Lumber

PLANT A	PLANT B
15 units	23 units
25 units	26 units
35 units	25 units
20 units	24 units
30 units	27 units

Plant A	Plant B
$\bar{x} = 25$ units	$\bar{x} = 25$ units
$M_d = 25$ units	$M_d = 25$ units

The division vice president looked at these statistics and concluded:

1. Average production is the same at both plants.

2. At both plants, the output is at or more than 25 units half the time and at or fewer than 25 units half the time.

3. Because the mean and median are equal, the distribution of production output at the two plants is symmetrical.

4. Based on these statistics, there is no reason to believe that the two plants are any different in terms of their production output.

However, if he had taken a closer look at the raw data, he would have seen there is a very big difference between the two plants. The difference is the production **variation** from day to day. Plant B is very stable, producing almost the same amount every day. Plant A varies considerably, with some high-output days and some low-output days. Thus, looking at only measures of the data's central location can be misleading.

To fully describe a set of data, we need a measure of variation or spread.

Variation

A set of data exhibits variation if all the data are not the same value.

There is variation in everything that is made by humans or that occurs in nature. The variation may be small, but it is there. Given a fine enough measuring instrument, we can detect the variation. Variation is either a natural part of a process (or inherent to a product) or can be attributed to a special cause that is not considered random.

There are several different measures that are used in business decision-making. In this section, we introduce four of these measures: range, interquartile range, variance, and standard deviation.

RANGE

The simplest measure of variation is the **range**. It is both easy to compute and easy to understand.

Range

The range is a measure of variation that is computed by finding the difference between the maximum and minimum values in a data set.

The range is computed using Equation 3-6.

Range

$$R = \text{Maximum Value} - \text{Minimum Value}$$ **3-6**

Bryce Lumber (continued)—Table 3-3 showed the production-volume data for the two Bryce Lumber Company plants. The range for each plant is determined using Equation 3-6 as follows:

Plant A	Plant B
$R = \text{Maximum} - \text{Minimum}$	$R = \text{Maximum} - \text{Minimum}$
$R = 35 - 15$	$R = 27 - 23$
$R = 20$	$R = 4$

We see plant A has a range that is five times as great as plant B.

Although the range is quick and easy to compute, it does have some limitations. First, because we use only the high and low values to compute the range, it is very sensitive to extreme values in the data. Second, regardless of how many values are in the sample or population, the range is computed from only two of these values. For these reasons, it is considered a weak measure of variation.

INTERQUARTILE RANGE

A measure of variation that tends to overcome the range's susceptibility to extreme values is called the **interquartile range**.

Interquartile Range

The interquartile range is a measure of variation that is determined by computing the difference between the third and first quartiles.

Equation 3-7 is used to compute the interquartile range.

Interquartile Range

$$\text{Interquartile Range} = \text{Third Quartile} - \text{First Quartile} \qquad \textbf{3-7}$$

EXAMPLE 3-11: COMPUTING THE INTERQUARTILE RANGE

D.C. Hilton Investment Company The D.C. Hilton Investment Company, headquartered in New Orleans, has a number of individual clients who have recently opened a Roth IRA. Each client must decide on how much they will contribute on a monthly basis. The manager in charge of Roth investments at D.C. Hilton has collected a random sample of 100 clients who make monthly contributions to a Roth IRA. He has recorded the net dollars, after brokerage fees, that each client deposits into his or her account. He wishes to analyze the variation in these data by computing the range and the interquartile range. He could use the following steps to do so:

Step 1: **Sort the data into a data array from lowest to highest.**
The 100 sorted deposit values, in dollars, are shown as follows:

$33	$164	$173	$184	$190	$197	$207	$216	$224	$237
53	164	175	186	191	197	207	217	225	240
150	164	175	186	191	198	208	217	225	240
152	166	175	186	192	200	208	217	229	240
157	166	178	187	193	200	208	219	231	250
160	168	178	188	193	201	210	222	231	251
161	169	179	188	194	202	211	223	234	259
162	171	180	188	194	204	212	223	234	270
162	171	182	190	196	205	213	223	235	379
163	172	183	190	196	205	216	224	236	479

Step 2: **Compute the range using Equation 3-6.**

$$R = \text{Maximum Value} - \text{Minimum Value}$$
$$R = \$479 - \$33 = \$446$$

Note, the range is sensitive to extreme values. The small value of $33 and the high value of $479 cause the range value to be very large.

Step 3: **Compute the first and third quartiles.**
Equation 3-5 can be used to find the location of the third quartile (75th percentile) and the first quartile (25th percentile).

For $Q3$, the location is $\dfrac{75}{100}(100 + 1) = 75.75$

Thus, $Q3$ is .75 of the way between the 75th and 76th data values, which is found as follows:

$$Q3 = 219 + 0.75(222 - 219) = \$221.25$$

For $Q1$, the location is $\dfrac{25}{100}(100 + 1) = 25.25$

Then $Q1$ is a quarter of the way between the 25th and 26th data values, which is found as follows:

$$Q1 = 178 + 0.25(178 - 178) = \$178$$

Step 4:   **Compute the interquartile range.**
The interquartile range overcomes the range's sensitivity problem. It is computed using Equation 3-7:

$$\text{Interquartile Range} = Q3 - Q1$$
$$= \$221.25 - \$178 = \$43.2$$

Note, the interquartile range would be unchanged even if the values on the high or low end of the distribution were even more extreme than those shown in these sample data.

POPULATION VARIANCE AND STANDARD DEVIATION

Although the range is easy to compute and understand and the interquartile range is designed to overcome the range's sensitivity to extreme values, neither measure uses all the available data in its computation. Thus, both measures ignore potentially valuable information in data.

Two measures of variation that incorporate all the values in a data set are the **variance** and the **standard deviation**.

Variance	*Standard Deviation*
The population variance is the average of the squared distances of the data values from the mean.	The standard deviation is the positive square root of the variance.

These two measures are closely related. The standard deviation is the square root of the variance. The standard deviation is in the original units (dollars, pounds, etc.), whereas the units of measure in the variance are squared. Because dealing with original units is easier than dealing with the square of the units, we usually use the standard deviation to measure variation in a population or sample.

Bryce Lumber (continued)—Recall the Bryce Lumber example, in which we compared the production output for two of the company's plants. Table 3-3 showed the data, which are considered a population for our purposes here.

Previously we examined the variability in the output from these two plants by computing the ranges. Although those results gave us some sense of how much more variable Plant A is than Plant B, we also pointed out some of the deficiencies of the range. The variance and standard deviation offer alternatives to the range for measuring variation in data.

Equation 3-8 is the formula for the population variance. Like the population mean, the population variance and standard deviation are assigned a Greek symbol.

Population Variance

$$\sigma^2 = \frac{\sum_{i=1}^{N} (x_i - \mu)^2}{N}$$

3-8

where:

μ = Population mean
N = Population size
σ^2 = Population variance (sigma squared)

We begin by computing the variance for the output data from Plant A. The first step in manually calculating the variance is to find the mean using Equation 3-1.

$$\mu = \frac{\sum x}{N} = \frac{15 + 25 + 35 + 20 + 30}{5} = \frac{125}{5} = 25$$

Next, subtract the mean from each value, as shown in Table 3-4. Notice the sum of the deviations from the mean is 0. Recall from Section 3-1 that this will be true for any set of data. The

TABLE 3-4

**Computing the
Population Variance:
Squaring the Deviations**

x	$(x - \mu)$	$(x - \mu)^2$
15	$15 - 25 = -10$	100
25	$25 - 25 = 0$	0
35	$35 - 25 = 10$	100
20	$20 - 25 = -5$	25
30	$30 - 25 = 5$	25
	$\Sigma = 0$	$\Sigma = 250$

positive differences are cancelled out by the negative differences. To overcome this fact when computing the variance, we square each of the differences and then sum the squared differences. These calculations are also shown in Table 3-4.

The final step in computing the population variance is to divide the sum of the squared differences by the population size, $N = 5$.

$$\sigma^2 = \frac{\Sigma(x - \mu)^2}{N} = \frac{250}{5} = 50$$

The population variance is 50 *products-squared*.

Manual calculations for the population variance may be easier if you use an alternative formula for σ^2 that is the algebraic equivalent. This is shown as Equation 3-9.

Population Variance Shortcut

$$\sigma^2 = \frac{\Sigma(x - \mu)^2}{N} = \frac{\Sigma x^2 - \frac{(\Sigma x)^2}{N}}{N}$$

3-9

Example 3-12 will illustrate the application of Equation 3-9 for the population variance.

Because we squared the deviations to keep the plus values and minus values from canceling, the units of measure were also squared, but the term *products-squared* doesn't have a meaning. To get back to the original units of measure, take the square root of the variance. The result is the standard deviation. Equation 3-10 shows the formula for the population standard deviation.

Population Standard Deviation

$$\sigma = \sqrt{\sigma^2} = \sqrt{\frac{\sum_{i=1}^{N}(x_i - \mu)^2}{N}}$$

3-10

Therefore, the population standard deviation of Plant A's production output is

$$\sigma = \sqrt{50}$$
$$\sigma = 7.07 \text{ products}$$

The population standard deviation is a parameter and will not change unless the population values change.

We could repeat this process using the data for Plant B, which also had a mean output of 25 products. You should verify that the population variance is

$$\sigma^2 = \frac{\Sigma(x - \mu)^2}{N} = \frac{10}{5} = 2$$

The standard deviation is found by taking the square root of the variance.

$$\sigma = \sqrt{2}$$
$$\sigma = 1.414 \text{ products}$$

Thus, Plant A has an output standard deviation that is five times larger than Plant B. The fact that Plant A's range was also five times larger than the range for Plant B is merely a coincidence.

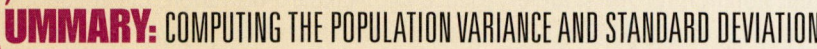

SUMMARY: COMPUTING THE POPULATION VARIANCE AND STANDARD DEVIATION

The population variance and standard deviation are computed using the following steps:

1. Collect quantitative data for the variable of interest for the entire population.

2. Use either Equation 3-8 or Equation 3-9 to compute the variance. If Equation 3-9 is used:

3. Find the sum of the x values ($\sum x$) and then square this sum $(\sum x)^2$

4. Square each x value and sum these squared values ($\sum x^2$)

5. Compute the variance using

$$\sigma^2 = \frac{\sum x^2 - \frac{(\sum x)^2}{N}}{N}$$

6. Compute the standard deviation by taking the square root of the variance:

$$\sigma = \sqrt{\sigma^2}$$

EXAMPLE 3-12: COMPUTING A POPULATION VARIANCE AND A STANDARD DEVIATION

Boydson Shipping Company   Boydson Shipping Company owns and operates a fleet of tanker ships that carry commodities between the countries of the world. In the past six months, the company has had seven contracts that called for shipments between Vancouver, Canada, and London, England. For many reasons, the travel time varies between these two locations. The scheduling manager is interested in knowing the variance and standard deviation in shipping times for these seven shipments. To find these values, he can follow these steps:

Step 1:   **Collect the data for the population.**
These shipping times are shown as follows:

$$x = \text{shipping weeks}$$
$$= \{5, 7, 5, 9, 7, 4, 6\}$$

Step 2:   **Select Equation 3-9 to find the population variance.**

$$\sigma^2 = \frac{\sum x^2 - \frac{(\sum x)^2}{N}}{N}$$

Step 3:   **Add the x values and square the sum.**
$$\sum x = 5 + 7 + 5 + 9 + 7 + 4 + 6 = 43$$
$$(\sum x)^2 = (43)^2 = 1{,}849$$

Step 4:   **Square each of the x values and sum these squares.**
$$\sum x^2 = 5^2 + 7^2 + 5^2 + 9^2 + 7^2 + 4^2 + 6^2 = 281$$

Step 5:   **Compute the population variance.**

$$\sigma^2 = \frac{\sum x^2 - \frac{(\sum x)^2}{N}}{N} = \frac{281 - \frac{1{,}849}{7}}{7} = 2.4082$$

The variance is in units squared, so in this example the population variance is 2.4082 weeks squared.

Step 6:   **Calculate the standard deviation as the square root of the variance.**

$$\sigma = \sqrt{\sigma^2} = \sqrt{2.4082} = 1.5518 \text{ weeks}$$

Thus, the standard deviation for the number of shipping days between Vancouver and London for the seven shipments is 1.5518 weeks.

SAMPLE VARIANCE AND STANDARD DEVIATION

Equations 3-8, 3-9, and 3-10 are the equations for the population variance and standard deviation. Any time you are working with a population, these are the equations that are used. However, in most instances, you will be describing sample data that have been selected from the population. In addition to using different notation for the sample variance and standard deviation, the equations are also slightly different. Equations 3-11 and 3-12 can be used to find the sample variance. Note that Equation 3-12 is considered the shortcut formula for manual computations.

Sample Variance

$$s^2 = \frac{\sum\limits_{i=1}^{n}(x_i - \bar{x})^2}{n - 1}$$

3-11

Sample Variance Shortcut

$$s^2 = \frac{\sum x^2 - \dfrac{(\sum x)^2}{n}}{n - 1}$$

3-12

where:

n = Sample size
$\bar{x}$ = Sample mean
s^2 = Sample variance

The sample standard deviation is found by taking the square root of the sample variance, as shown in Equation 3-13.

Sample Standard Deviation

$$s = \sqrt{s^2} = \sqrt{\frac{\sum\limits_{i=1}^{n}(x_i - \bar{x})^2}{n - 1}}$$

3-13

Take note in Equations 3-11, 3-12, and 3-13 that the denominator is $n - 1$ (sample size minus 1). This may seem strange, given that the denominator for the population variance and the standard deviation is simply N, the population size. The mathematical justification for the $n - 1$ divisor is outside the scope of this text. However, the general reason for this is that we want the average sample variance to equal the population variance. If we were to select all possible samples of size n from a given population and for each sample we computed the sample variance using Equation 3-11 or Equation 3-12, the average of all the sample variances would equal σ^2 (the population variance), provided we used $n - 1$ as the divisor. Using n instead of $n - 1$ in the denominator would produce an average sample variance that would be smaller than σ^2, the population variance. Because we do not want an estimator on average to underestimate the population variance, we use $n - 1$ in the denominator of s^2.

*E*XAMPLE 3-13: COMPUTING A SAMPLE VARIANCE AND STANDARD DEVIATION

Red Line Taxi   The managers at Red Line Taxi selected a random sample of 10 taxicabs and recorded the number of round-trips made to the local international airport on November 15. The manager can find the sample variance and the sample standard deviation using the following steps:

Step 1:   **Select the sample and record the data for the variable of interest.**

Cab	Round-Trips = x
1	4
2	7
3	1
4	0
5	5
6	0
7	3
8	2
9	6
10	2

Step 2: **Select either Equation 3-11 or Equation 3-12 to compute the sample variance.**
If we use Equation 3-11,

$$s^2 = \frac{\sum(x - \bar{x})^2}{n - 1}$$

Step 3: **Compute $\bar{x}$.**
The sample mean number of trips is

$$\bar{x} = \frac{\sum x}{n} = \frac{30}{10} = 3.0$$

Step 4: **Determine the sum of the squared deviations of each x value from $\bar{x}$.**

Cab	Round Trips = x	$(x - \bar{x})$	$(x - \bar{x})^2$
1	4	1	1
2	7	4	16
3	1	−2	4
4	0	−3	9
5	5	2	4
6	0	−3	9
7	3	0	0
8	2	−1	1
9	6	3	9
10	2	−1	1
		$\sum = 0$	$\sum = 54$

Step 5: **Compute the sample variance using Equation 3-11.**

$$s^2 = \frac{\sum(x - \bar{x})^2}{n - 1} = \frac{54}{9} = 6$$

The sample variance is measured in squared units. Thus, the variance in this example is 6 trips squared.

Step 6: **Compute the sample standard deviation by taking the square root of the variance (see Equation 3-13):**

$$s = \sqrt{\frac{\sum(x - \bar{x})^2}{n - 1}} = \sqrt{\frac{54}{9}} = \sqrt{6}$$

$$s = 2.4495 \text{ trips}$$

This sample standard deviation measures the variation in the sample data for daily round-trips to the airport for Red Line Taxi.

Weigh in Motion (continued)—The state transportation department has conducted a study to determine whether the Weigh-in-Motion scale can substitute for the static scale located at a port of entry. (See page 83.) The state collected data on a sample of $n = 200$ trucks over several months. Each truck was weighed on both scales.

Previously, we computed measures of central tendency and constructed histograms to better understand the sample data. We focused on the WIM gross vehicle weight and the POE gross vehicle weight. We saw that there were only "small" differences in the mean and median values for the two variables.

We now turn our attention to measures of variability. The question is whether the two scales provide weight distributions of similar variability. The range (maximum − minimum) is one measure of variability, and Excel and Minitab can compute the range. Figures 3-8a and 3-8b show the Excel and Minitab descriptive statistics results for POE and WIM gross weights.

FIGURE 3-8A

Excel Descriptive Statistics Output—Truck Weight Data

Excel Instructions:
1. Open file: Trucks.xls
2. Click on the **Tools** button.
3. Select the **Data Analysis** option.
4. Choose **Descriptive Statistics** and select the appropriate data ranges.
5. Click on "Summary Statistics."

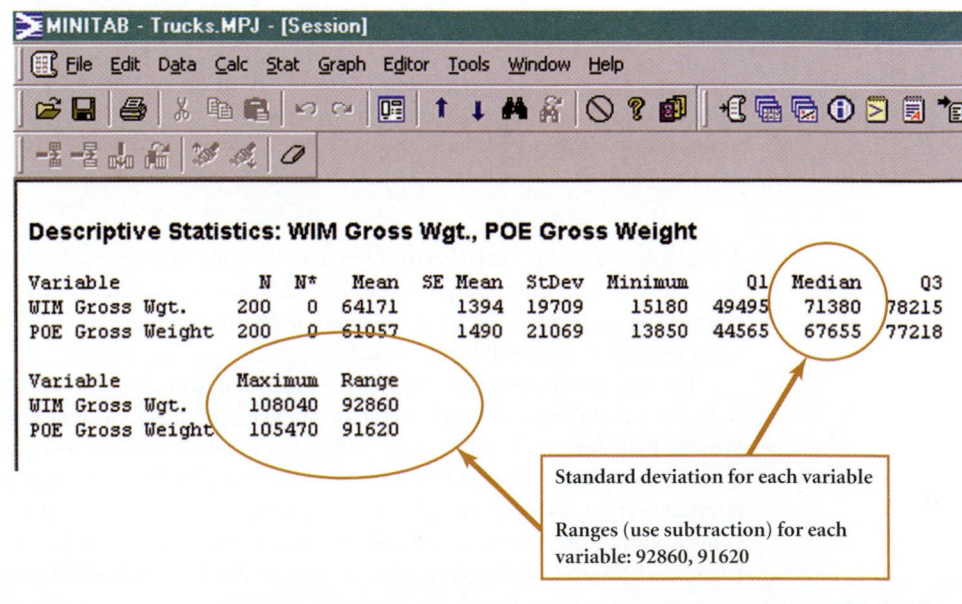

Excel and Minitab Tutorial

The values based on the sample data are

$$\text{WIM scale gross weight:} \quad R = 92{,}860 \text{ pounds}$$
$$\text{POE scale gross weight:} \quad R = 91{,}620 \text{ pounds}$$

The ranges are reasonably close in value, which seems to indicate that the variability in weights for the two scales is similar.

The standard deviation is a more-powerful measure of variation because it measures the deviation of all the values around the center. Again, Excel and Minitab have options for computing the standard deviation. The standard deviations for the two scales are

$$\text{WIM scale gross weight:} \quad s = 19{,}709.04 \text{ pounds}$$
$$\text{POE scale gross weight:} \quad s = 21{,}069.46 \text{ pounds}$$

These statistics show there is variation between truck weights. (Recall that the mean weights for trucks over both scales were less than 65,000 pounds.) These data also indicate that the WIM scale provided slightly less variation than the POE scale.

Up to this point, considering the graphical analyses we did in Chapter 2 and this numerical descriptive analysis, what are your conclusions about the effectiveness of the weigh-in-motion process? Are the measures given by the two scales close enough to use? The answer probably depends on how close the weights must be to be useful to the engineers at the transportation department. Table 3-5 summarizes the descriptive statistics.

FIGURE 3-8B

Minitab Descriptive Statistics Output—Truck Weight Data

Minitab Instructions:
1. Open file: Trucks.MTW.
2. Choose **Stat > Basic Statistics > Display Descriptive Statistics**.
3. In **Variables**, enter columns *WIM Gross Weight* and *POE Gross Weight*.
4. Click **Statistics**.
5. Check required statistics.
6. Click **OK. OK**.

	STATISTICAL MEASURE	WIM SCALE	POE SCALE
TABLE 3-5	Mean	64,171 lbs.	61,057 lbs.
Summary Statistics—	Median	71,380	67,655
WIM versus POE	Mode	78,720	105,470
Weights	1st Quartile	49,885	45,255
	3rd Quartile	78,125	77,112
	Range	92,860	91,620
	Standard Deviation	19,709	21,069

3-2: EXERCISES

Skill Development

3.20 Assume the following data set represents the population:

16	23	17	24	9	11	13	15
18	21	16	23	17	16	10	14

Determine the range, variance, and standard deviation for the data set.

3.21 The following data are a sample from a larger population.

33	42	39	17	27	32	40	37
30	35	37	19	34	37	41	35

Calculate the mean, median, range, interquartile range, variance, and standard deviation.

3.22 You are given the following data for the number of times a population of six families dined out during the previous month:

4	6	9	4	5	7

a. Compute the range for these data.
b. Compute the variance and the standard deviation.
c. Assume that these data represented a sample rather than a population. Compute the variance and the standard deviation. Discuss the difference between the values computed here and in part b.

3.23 For the following set of sample sales data, in dollars, compute the range, interquartile range, variance, and standard deviation.

$17.87	19.95	22.95	18.74	9.95
11.22	21.98	14.52	16.65	14.98

3.24 Assume the following sample represents vehicle speeds.

51	43	58	67	67	69	40	52
66	44	47	41	41	45	47	41

a. Determine the proportion of this data set that is within one standard deviation of the mean.
b. Determine the proportion of this data set that is within two standard deviations of the mean.

c. Determine the proportion of this data set that is within three standard deviations of the mean.

Business Applications

3.25 The Price Corporation has built six homes during the past year. The number of square feet in each home (treated as the population of interest) is listed as follows:

square feet = {1,560; 2,340; 1,990; 1,750; 4,000; 2,200}

a. Compute the range.
b. Compute the variance.
c. Compute the standard deviation.
d. Write a short paragraph that describes these data. Please feel free to also compute measures of the center and include these values in your discussion.

3.26 The Stop N' Go convenience chain recently selected a random sample of 10 customers. The store monitored the number of times each customer made a purchase at the store over a two-month period. The following data were collected.

10	19	17	19	12	20	20	15	16	13

Store executives are considering a promotion in which they reward frequent purchases with a small gift. They have decided that they will only give gifts to those shoppers whose number of visits in the previous two-month period is above the mean plus one standard deviation. Find the minimum number of visits required to receive a prize.

3.27 The marketing director for South East Insurance (see Problem 3.13) continues to worry about the increasing age of the company's policyholders. She wants to determine whether the new advertising campaign has helped retain younger customers. She has taken a sample of ten renewed policies and has found the following ages:

32	22	24	27	27
33	28	23	24	21

a. Compute the range, the interquartile range, and the standard deviation for these data.
b. Before the new advertising campaign, the average age of the customers was 37.8. Based on your calculations in part a, has the advertising campaign been effective in reducing the average age of the customers?

3.28 Grover's Pay n' Pak sells hardware supplies to "do-it-your-selfers." One of the things the company prides itself on is fast service. It uses a number system and takes customers in the order in which they arrive at the store. Recently, the assistant manager tracked the time customers spent in the store from the time they took a number until they left. A sample of 16 customers was selected, and the following data (measured in minutes) were recorded.

15	14	16	14	14	14	13	8
12	9	7	17	10	15	16	16

a. Compute the mean, median, mode, range, interquartile range, and standard deviation.
b. Develop a box and whisker plot for these data.

3.29 Welton Corporation makes dynamic random access memory chips (DRAMS) for use in personal computers. DRAMS are made on silicon wafers. The company's goal is to yield as many good chips from each wafer as possible in order to make more profit from its production operations. The following data represent the number of usable DRAM chips (yield) from each of the wafers:

488	449	510	551	548	569	413	491
544	457	472	432	426	461	469	415
477	484	505	485	487	485	554	497
493	479	579	535	595	474	566	436

a. Compute the following numerical measures for these yield data: (a) mean, (b) median, (c) mode, (d) range, (e) quartiles, (f) interquartile range, (g) variance, and (h) standard deviation.
b. Develop a box and whisker plot for these data.
c. Write a short report that describes the yield data.

Advanced Business Applications

3.30 A complaint was recently filed in Nevada by a California resident who claimed that drivers with California license plates on their cars were being unfairly singled out by Nevada law enforcement officers and given speeding tickets. The court ordered a study done in which the speeds on a particular section of Nevada highway were monitored with speed-measurement equipment. Speeds for only Nevada and California cars were recorded. The data for this test is in the file called *Speed-Test*.
a. For each state, construct a box and whisker plot.
b. Calculate the mean and median speed for vehicles from each state.

c. Compute the sample standard deviation, the range, and the interquartile range for vehicles from each state.
d. Write a report using the information generated in parts a, b, and c to inform the court about the speeds of vehicles from California and Nevada.

3.31 The B.T. Longmont Department Store has recently conducted a study related to the losses it has incurred due to shoplifting. The file called *Longmont* contains data that show the dollar losses over the past 17 months. Consider these data to be the population of interest.
a. Compute the mean, median, mode, range, variance, and standard deviation for these data.
b. Construct a box and whisker plot for the data.
c. Constuct a line chart for the 17 months.
d. Write a short report to the management of B.T. Longmont describing the shoplifting data.

3.32 The Amalgamated Sugar Company is in the process of revamping their maintenance program. As part of that effort, employees at the plant have collected equipment-downtime data for a sample of days from last year's records. Downtime is measured in seconds for each of the three shifts. The data are in the file called *Amalgamated*.
a. Compute the mean, median, mode, range, variance, and standard deviation for the downtime data for each shift individually.
b. Compute a box and whisker plot for each shift.
c. Write a short report that describes the data for the three shifts. Indicate whether the data seem to imply a difference between the three shifts in terms of equipment downtime.

3.33 The managers at the Capital Credit Union have to issue a report to the State Bank Commission regarding credit card balances for their customers. In response to this request, the managers have selected a random sample of their customers and have determined current credit card balances and genders of the cardholders. The resulting data are contained in the file called *Capital*.
a. Compute the mean, median, range, interquartile range, variance, and standard deviation of credit card balances for all customers in the sample.
b. Compute the mean, median, range, interquartile range, variance, and standard deviation of credit card balances for males and for females separately.
c. Draft a report to the State Bank Commission that describes the credit card balances. Specifically address any notable or systematic differences in the distribution of credit card balances between males and females.

3-3 USING THE MEAN AND THE STANDARD DEVIATION TOGETHER

In the previous sections, we introduced several important descriptive measures that are useful for transforming data into meaningful information. Two of the most important of these measures are the mean and the standard deviation. In this section, we discuss several statistical tools that combine these two.

COEFFICIENT OF VARIATION

The standard deviation measures the variation in a set of data. For decision makers, the standard deviation indicates how spread out a distribution is. For distributions having the same mean, the distribution with the largest standard deviation has the greatest relative spread. When two or more distributions have different means, the relative spread cannot be determined by merely comparing standard deviations.

The **coefficient of variation**, (*CV*), is used to measure the relative variation for distributions with different means.

Coefficient of Variation

The ratio of the standard deviation to the mean expressed as a percentage. The coefficient of variation is used to measure the relative variation in data.

The coefficient of variation for a population is computed using Equation 3-14, whereas Equation 3-15 is used for sample data.

Population Coefficient of Variation

$$CV = \frac{\sigma}{\mu} (100)$$

3-14

Sample Coefficient of Variation

$$CV = \frac{s}{\bar{x}} (100)$$

3-15

When the coefficients of variation for two or more distributions are compared, the distribution with the largest CV is said to have the greatest relative spread.

In finance, the CV measures the relative risk of a stock portfolio. Assume portfolio A has a collection of stocks that average a 12% return with a standard deviation of 3% and portfolio B has an average return of 6% with a standard deviation of 2%. We can compute the CV values for each as follows:

$$CV(A) = \frac{3}{12}(100) = 25\%$$

and

$$CV(B) = \frac{2}{6}(100) = 33\%$$

Even though portfolio B has a lower standard deviation, it would be considered more risky than portfolio A because B's CV is 33% and A's CV is 25%.

*E*XAMPLE 3-14: COMPUTING THE COEFFICIENT OF VARIATION

Agra-Tech Industries   Agra-Tech Industries has recently introduced feed supplements for both cattle and hogs that will increase the rate at which the animals gain weight. Three years of feedlot tests indicate that steers fed the supplement will weigh an average of 125 pounds more than those not fed the supplement. However, not every steer on the supplement has the same weight gain; results vary. The standard deviation in weight gain advantage for the steers in the three-year study has been 10 pounds.

Similar tests with hogs indicate those fed the supplement average 40 additional pounds compared with hogs not given the supplement. The standard deviation for the hogs was also 10 pounds. Even though the standard deviation is the same for both cattle and hogs, the mean added weight differs. Therefore the coefficient of variation is needed to compare relative variability. The coefficient of variation for each is computed using the following steps:

Step 1:   **Collect the sample (or population) of data for the variable of interest.**
In this case, we have two sets of data: weight gain for cattle and weight gain for hogs.

Step 2: **Compute the mean and the standard deviation.**
For the two data sets in this example, we get

$$\text{Cattle: } \bar{x} = 125 \text{ lbs. and } s = 10 \text{ lb}$$

$$\text{Hogs: } \bar{x} = 40 \text{ lbs. and } s = 10 \text{ lb}$$

Step 3: **Compute the coefficient of variation using Equation 3-14 (for populations) or Equation 3-15 (for samples).**
Because the data in this example is from a sample, the *CV* is computed using

$$CV = \frac{s}{\bar{x}}(100)$$

For each data set, we get

$$CV(\text{cattle}) = \frac{10}{125}(100) = 8\%$$

$$CV(\text{hogs}) = \frac{10}{40}(100) = 25\%$$

These results indicate that hogs exhibit much greater relative variability in weight gain compared with cattle.

Excel and Minitab Tutorial

THE EMPIRICAL RULE

A tool that is helpful in describing data in certain circumstances is called the **Empirical Rule**. In order for the Empirical Rule to be used, the frequency distribution must be bell-shaped, such as the one shown in Figure 3-9.

Empirical Rule

If the data distribution is bell-shaped, then the interval:

$\mu \pm 1\sigma$ contains approximately 68% of the values
$\mu \pm 2\sigma$ contains approximately 95% of the values
$\mu \pm 3\sigma$ contains virtually all of the data values

Burger n' Brew—The standard deviation can be thought of as a measure of distance from the mean. Consider the Phoenix Burger n' Brew restaurant chain, which records the number of each hamburger option it sells each day at each location. The number of chili burgers sold each day for

<caption>**FIGURE 3-9**

Illustrating the Empirical Rule for the Bell-Shaped Distribution</caption>

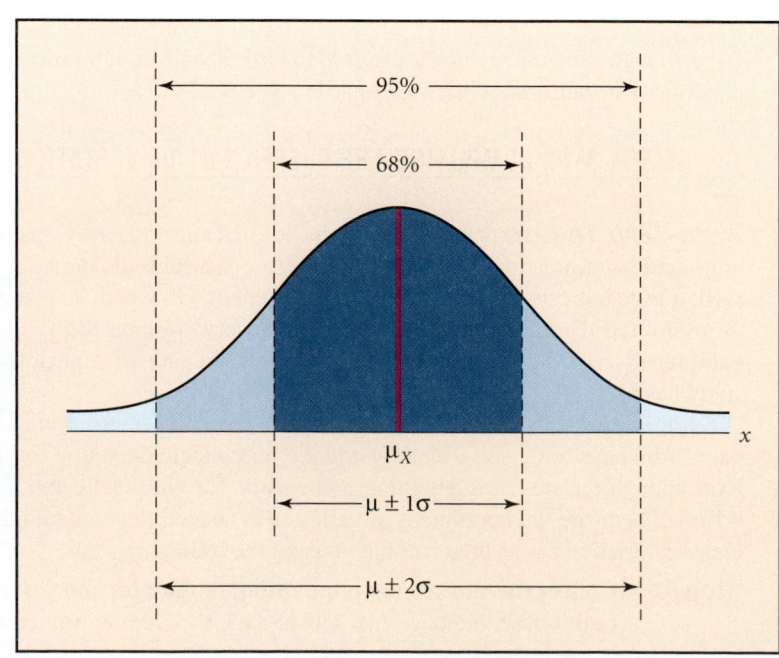

the past 365 days are in the file called *BurgerNBrew*. Figure 3-10 shows the frequency histogram for those data. The distribution is nearly *symmetrical* and approximately *bell-shaped*. The mean number of chili burgers sold was 15.1, with a standard deviation of 3.1.

The Empirical Rule is a very useful statistical concept for helping us understand the data in a bell-shaped distribution. In the Burger n' Brew example, with $\bar{x} = 15.1$ and $s = 3.1$, if we move one standard deviation in each direction from the mean, *approximately* 68% of the data should lie within the range:

$$15.1 \pm 1(3.1)$$

$$12.0 - - - - - - - - - - - - -18.2$$

The actual number of days Burger n' Brew sold between 12 and 18 chili burgers is 262. Thus, out of 365 days, 72% of the days Burger n' Brew sold between 12 and 18 chili burgers. (The reason that we didn't get exactly 68% is that the distribution in Figure 3-12 is not perfectly bell-shaped.)

If we look at the interval two standard deviations from either side of the mean, we would expect approximately 95% of the data. The interval is

$$15.1 \pm 2(3.1)$$
$$15.1 \pm 6.2$$

$$8.9 - - - - - - - - - - - - -21.30$$

Counting the values between these limits, we find 353 of the 365 values, or 97%. Again this is close to what the Empirical Rule predicted. Finally, according to the Empirical Rule, we would expect almost all of the data to fall within three standard deviations. The interval is

$$15.1 \pm 3(3.1)$$
$$15.1 \pm 9.3$$

$$5.80 - - - - - - - - - - - - -24.40$$

Looking at the data in Figure 3-10, we find that in fact all the data do fall within this interval.

FIGURE 3-10

Excel Histogram for Burger n' Brew Data

Excel Instructions:
1. Open file: BurgerNBrew.xls
2. Set up Bins (upper limit of each class)
3. Click on **Tools—Data Analysis—Histogram**.
4. Supply data range and bin range.
5. Check **Chart Output**.

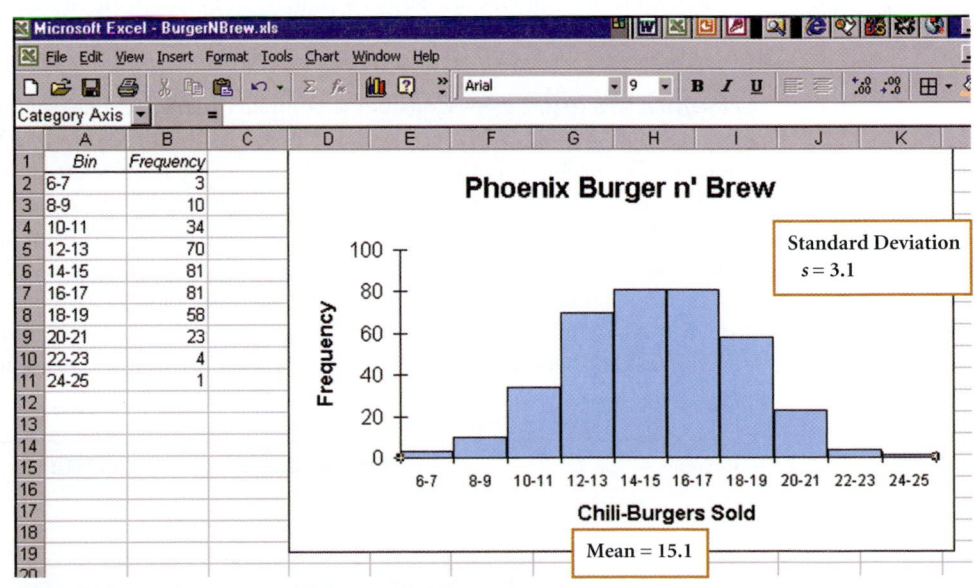

Minitab Instructions (for similar results):
1. Open file: BurgerNBrew.MTW.
2. Choose **Graph > Histogram**.
3. Click **Simple**.
4. Click **OK**.
5. In **Graph variables**, enter data column *Chili-Burgers Sold*.
6. Click **OK**.

Therefore, if we know only the mean and the standard deviation for a set of data, the Empirical Rule gives us a tool for describing how the data are distributed, if the distribution is bell-shaped.

TCHEBYSHEFF'S THEOREM

The Empirical Rule applies when a distribution is bell-shaped. But what about the many situations when a distribution is skewed and not bell-shaped? In these cases, we can use **Tchebysheff's theorem**.

Tchebysheff's Theorem

Regardless of how data are distributed, *at least* $(1 - 1/k^2)$ of the values will fall within k standard deviations of the mean. For example:

At least $(1 - \frac{1}{1}^2) = 0 = 0\%$ of the values will fall within $k = 1$ standard deviation of the mean.

At least $(1 - \frac{1}{2}^2) = \frac{3}{4} = 75\%$ of the values will lie within $k = 2$ standard deviations of the mean.

At least $(1 - \frac{1}{3}^2) = \frac{8}{9} = 89\%$ of the values will lie within $k = 3$ standard deviations of the mean.

Tchebysheff's theorem is conservative. It tells us nothing about the data within one standard deviation of the mean. Tchebysheff indicates that *at least* 75% of the data will fall within two standard deviations—it could be more. If we applied Tchebysheff's theorem to bell-shaped distributions, the percentage estimates are very low. The thing to remember is that Tchebysheff's theorem applies to *any distribution*. This gives it great flexibility.

STANDARDIZED DATA VALUES

When you are dealing with quantitative data, you will sometimes want to convert the measures to a form called **standardized data values**. This is especially useful when we wish to compare data from two or more distributions when the data scales for the two distributions are substantially different.

Standardized Data Values

The number of standard deviations a value is from the mean. Standardized data values are sometimes referred to as z-scores.

Human Resources—Consider a company that uses placement exams as part of its hiring process. The company currently will accept scores from either of two tests: AIMS Hiring and BHS-Screen. The problem is that the AIMS Hiring test has an average score of 2,000 and a standard deviation of 200, whereas the BHS-Screen test has an average score of 80 with a standard deviation of 12. (These means and standard deviations were developed from a large number of people who have taken the two tests.) How can the company compare applicants when the average scores and measures of spread are so different for the two tests? One approach is to *standardize* the test scores.

Suppose the company is considering two applicants, John and Mary. John took the AIMS Hiring test and scored 2,344, whereas Mary took the BHS-Screen and scored 95. Their scores can be standardized using Equation 3-16.

Standardized Population Data

$$z = \frac{x - \mu}{\sigma}$$

3-16

where:

x = Original data value
μ = Population mean
σ = Population standard deviation
z = Standard score (number of standard deviations x is from μ)

If you are working with sample data rather than a population, Equation 3-17 can be used to standardize the values.

Standardized Sample Data

$$z = \frac{x - \bar{x}}{s}$$

3-17

where:

z = The standard score
$\bar{x}$ = Sample mean
s = Sample standard deviation
x = Original data value

We can standardize the test scores for John and Mary using

$$z = \frac{x - \mu}{\sigma}$$

For AIMS Hiring test, the mean, μ, is 2,000, and the standard deviation, σ, equals 200. John's score of 2,344 converts to

$$z = \frac{2{,}344 - 2{,}000}{200}$$
$$z = 1.72$$

The BHS Screen has $\mu = 80$ and $\sigma = 12$. Mary's score of 95 converts to

$$z = \frac{95 - 80}{12}$$
$$z = 1.25$$

Compared to the average score on the AIMS Hiring test, John's score is 1.72 standard deviations higher. Mary's score is only 1.25 standard deviations higher than the average score on the BHS-Screen test. Therefore, even though the two tests used different scales, standardizing the data allows us to conclude John scored relatively better on his test than Mary did on her test.

 SUMMARY: CONVERTING DATA TO STANDARDIZED VALUES

For a set of quantitative data, each data value can be converted to a corresponding standardized value by determining how many standard deviations the value is from the mean. Here are the steps to do this.

1. Collect the population or sample values for the quantitative variable of interest.

2. Compute the population mean and standard deviation or the sample mean and standard deviation.

3. Convert the values to standardized z values using Equation 3-16 or Equation 3-17. For populations,

$$z = \frac{x - \mu}{\sigma}$$

For samples,

$$z = \frac{x - \bar{x}}{s}$$

 **EXAMPLE 3-15: CONVERTING DATA TO STANDARDIZED VALUES**

SAT and ACT Exams   Many colleges and universities require students to submit either SAT or ACT scores or both. One eastern university requires both exam scores. However, in assessing whether to admit a student, the university uses whichever exam score favors the student among all the applicants. Suppose the school receives 4,000 applications for admission. To determine which exam will be used for each student, the school will standardize the exam scores from both tests. To do this, it can use the following steps:

Step 1:   **Collect data.**
The university will collect the data for the 4,000 SAT scores and the 4,000 ACT scores for those students who applied for admission.

Step 2:   **Compute the mean and standard deviation.**
Assuming that these data reflect the population of interest for the university, the population mean is computed using

$$\text{SAT:} \quad \mu = \frac{\Sigma x}{N} = 1{,}255 \qquad \text{ACT:} \quad \mu = \frac{\Sigma x}{N} = 28.3$$

The standard deviation is computed using

$$\text{SAT:} \quad \sigma = \sqrt{\frac{\Sigma(x - \mu)^2}{N}} = 72 \qquad \text{ACT:} \quad \sigma = \sqrt{\frac{\Sigma(x - \mu)^2}{N}} = 2.4$$

Step 3: **Standardize the data.**

Convert the x values to z values using

$$z = \frac{x - \mu}{\sigma}$$

Suppose a particular applicant has an SAT score of 1,228 and an ACT score of 27. These test scores can be converted to standardized scores.

$$\text{SAT:} \quad z = \frac{x - \mu}{\sigma} = \frac{1{,}228 - 1{,}255}{72} = -0.375$$

$$\text{ACT:} \quad z = \frac{x - \mu}{\sigma} = \frac{27 - 28.3}{2.4} = -0.5417$$

The negative z values indicate that this student is below the mean on both the SAT and ACT exams. Because the university wishes to use the score that most favors the student, it will use the SAT score. The student is only 0.375 standard deviations below the SAT mean, compared with 0.5417 standard deviations below the ACT mean.

3-3: EXERCISES

Skill Development

3.34 Consider the following set of sample data.

16	23	17	24	9	11	13	15	15	23	18	16	17

a. Compute the mean and standard deviation for these sample data.

b. Determine the coefficient of variation for the set and interpret what it measures.

c. Using Tchebysheff's Theorem, determine the range of values that should include at least 75% of the data. Count how many actually fell into this interval and discuss whether your interval range was, in fact, conservative.

d. Assume that the distribution of values is bell-shaped and determine the range of values that should contain approximately 68% of the data values.

3.35 Two distributions of data are being analyzed. Distribution A has a mean of 500 and a standard deviation equal to 100. Distribution B has a mean of 10 and a standard deviation equal to 4.0. Based on this information, use the coefficient of variation to determine which distribution has a greater relative variation.

3.36 If a sample mean is known to be 500 and the sample standard deviation is 75, what is the standardized value for a value of $x = 615$?

3.37 Two distributions have the following characteristics:

Distribution A	Distribution B
$\mu = 45{,}600$	$\mu = 33.40$
$\sigma = 6{,}333$	$\sigma = 4.05$

If a value from distribution A is 50,000 and a value from distribution B is 40, convert each value to a standardized z value and indicate which one is relatively closer to its respective mean.

3.38 A population of unknown shape has a mean of 3,000 and a standard deviation of 200.

a. Find the minimum proportion of observations in the population that are in the range 2,600 to 3,400.

b. Determine the maximum proportion of the observations that are greater than 3,600.

c. What statement could you make concerning the proportion of observations that are smaller than 2,400?

3.39 Consider the following data representing samples from two populations.

A	B
191	1,135
162	996
207	1,219
238	935
236	952
252	974
134	930
193	968

a. Compute the standard deviation for each sample. Which has the largest dispersion (or spread) according to the standard deviation?

b. Now compute the coefficient of variation for each variable and indicate which one has the greatest *relative* variation.

3.40 A sample contains 1,000 values. The histogram for this sample is bell-shaped. Approximately 950 values in the sample are known to be within $100 of the mean. Suppose the mean is $5,000. Use the Empirical Rule to perform the following:

a. Calculate a value for the standard deviation.
b. Determine the data value that is the 97.5th percentile.
c. Calculate the z-score for the 16th percentile.

3.41 A population has a mean of 400 and a standard deviation of 30.

a. Calculate the standardized z-score for the number 455 from this population.
b. Determine the z-score for the mean value of 400.
c. Find the proportion of data that have z–scores between -2 and 2 when the population is bell-shaped. Next, find the proportion of data that have z-scores between -2 and 2 when the population is highly skewed. Does this make a difference in your answer?

Business Applications

3.42 The Miller Distributing Company is investigating two different scheduling methods for its truck drivers. The following data reflect the number of delivery miles each driver drove per day for each of the scheduling methods.

Method 1	14	11	19	6	10
Method 2	26	5	9	6	14

a. Compute the mean and the standard deviation for each of these methods. Assume the data are sample data.
b. Compute the coefficient of variation for each method and discuss which scheduling method seems to provide the least relative variability in the distances traveled.
c. Referring to part b, in this case would it be acceptable to compare standard deviations directly to compare relative variability? Explain your answer.

3.43 Sportway Manufacturing has been experimenting with new materials to use for golf ball covers. Two recently developed compounds have been shown to be equally resistant to cutting, and the development lab is now looking at the distance the balls will travel during a simulated drive. However, both distance and consistency are important for a golf ball. A sample of 10 balls with each type of cover was selected, and the following distances were measured (in yards) using a mechanical driver that struck each ball with the same force.

Type A	298	291	290	310	296	299	300	305	289	285
Type B	297	315	291	292	301	286	287	290	302	323

a. A new technician records the next ball hit as traveling only 274. He says the ball was a Type B ball. Do you believe the technician? Use Tchebysheff's Theorem to provide calculations and reasoning to support your answer.
b. The technician also recorded a ball hit 312 yards. However, he does not remember which type of ball it was. Help the technician decide which type of ball he

used for this experiment. Give reasons and calculations to support your answer. Use Tchebysheff's Theorem.

c. Do you believe it is likely that one of these types of balls can be hit 325 yards? Explain your answer.

3.44 The Rippon Investment Company offers two different mutual funds. The stocks in the Growth Fund have generated an average return of 8%, with a standard deviation of 2%. The stocks in the Specialized Fund have generated an average return of 18%, with a standard deviation of 6%.

a. Based on the data provided, which of these funds has exhibited greater relative variability? Use the proper statistical measure to make your determination.
b. Suppose and investor who is very risk averse is interested in one of these two funds. Based strictly on relative variability, which fund would you recommend? Discuss.
c. Suppose the distributions for the two stock funds had a bell-shaped distribution with the means and standard deviations previously indicated. Which fund would appear to be the best investment, assuming future returns will mimic past returns? Explain.

3.45 The division manager for Northern Pipe and Steel Company decided to implement a new incentive system for the managers of Northern's three plants. The plan called for a bonus to be paid the next month to the manager whose plant had the greatest relative improvement over the average monthly production volume. The following data reflected the historical production volumes at the three plants.

Plant 1	Plant 2	Plant 3
$\mu = 700$	$\mu = 2,300$	$\mu = 1,200$
$\sigma = 200$	$\sigma = 350$	$\sigma = 30$

At the close of the next month, the monthly output for the three plants was

Plant 1 = 810	Plant 2 = 2,600	Plant 3 = 1,320

Suppose the division manager awarded the bonus to the manager of Plant 2 because her plant increased its production by 300 units over the mean. This was a bigger increase than that of any of the other managers. Do you agree with who received the bonus this month? Explain, using the appropriate statistical measures to support your position.

3.46 Each week for the past 40 weeks the Ajax Taxi Company has collected data on the miles driven by four taxis. These data are in the file called *Ajax*. Combine the data from the four taxis into one variable with $n = 160$ observations.

a. Develop a frequency distribution for this new variable.
b. Standardize the data (z-values) and develop a frequency distribution for the standardized data values. Compare this distribution to the one computed for the raw scores in part a.
c. Produce a box plot and determine if any of the taxis are being driven unusually small or large amounts. (Hint: Identify the mild and extreme outliers.)

Advanced Business Applications

3.47 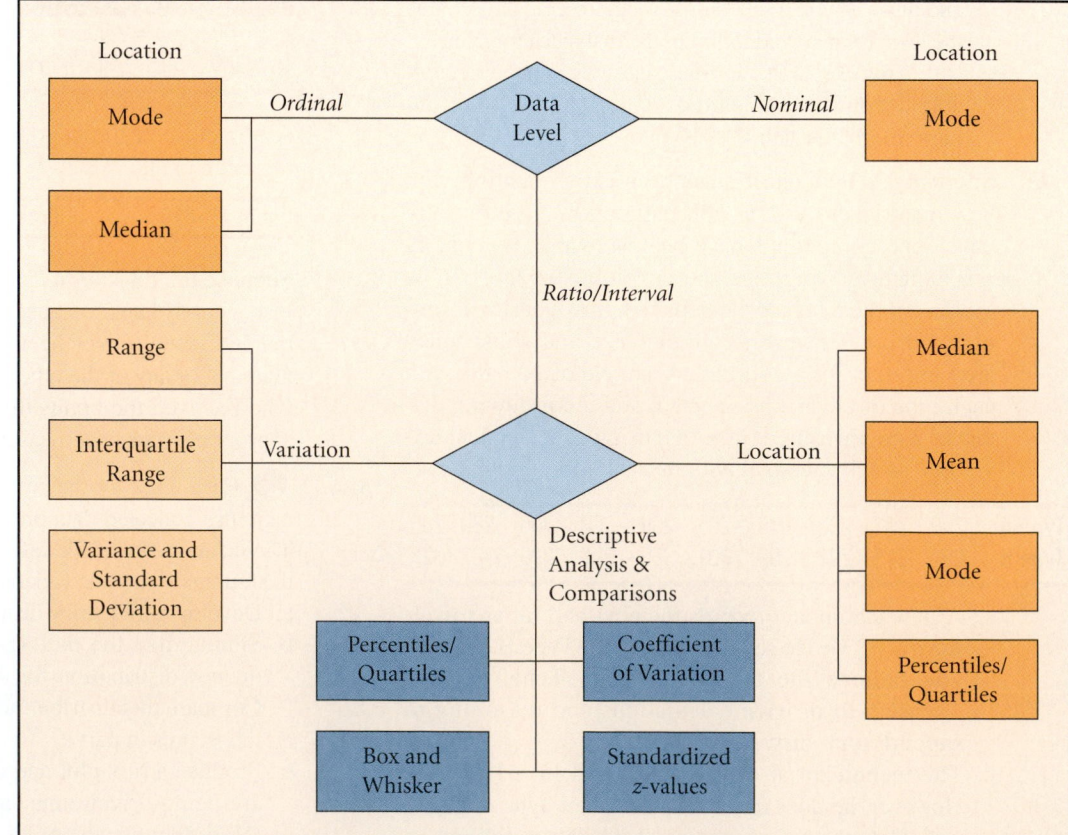 The Environmental Protection Agency (EPA) tests all new cars and provides a mileage rating for city and highway driving conditions. Thirty cars for the 1998 model year were tested, and results are contained in the data file *Automobiles*. The file contains data on several variables. In this problem, focus on the city and highway mileage data.

a. Calculate the sample mean miles per gallon for both city and highway driving for the 30 cars. Also calculate the sample standard deviation for the two mileage variables. Do the data tend to support the premise that cars will get better mileage on the highway than around town? Discuss.

b. Referring to part a, what can the EPA conclude about the relative variability between car models for highway versus city driving? (Hint: Compute the appropriate measure to compare relative variability.)

c. Assume that mileage ratings are approximately bell-shaped. Approximately what proportion of cars get at least as good a mileage in city driving conditions as the mean mileage for highway driving for all cars?

3.48 Zepolle's Bakery makes a variety of bread types that it sells to supermarket chains in the area. One of Zepolle's problems is the number of loaves of each type of bread sold each day by the chain stores varies considerably, making it difficult to know how many loaves to make. A sample of daily demand data is contained in the file called *Bakery*.

a. Which bread type has the highest average daily demand?

b. Develop a frequency distribution for each bread type.

c. Which bread type has the highest standard deviation in demand?

d. Which bread type has the greatest relative variability? Which type has the lowest relative variability?

e. Assuming that these sample data are representative of demand during the year, determine how many loaves of each type of bread should be made so demand would be met on at least 75% of the days during the year.

f. Create a new variable called Total Loaves Sold. On which day of the week is the average for total loaves sold the highest?

Summary and Conclusions

Transforming data into useful information is an important activity for business decision makers. Chapter 3 has introduced a variety of numerical measures that can be used either by themselves or in conjunction with the graphical techniques introduced in Chapter 2.

These measures can be computed for the population as a whole or from a sample taken from the population.

Two main categories of measures were introduced. These were measures of the center and measures of spread or variation.

FIGURE 3-11

Summary of Numerical Statistical Measures

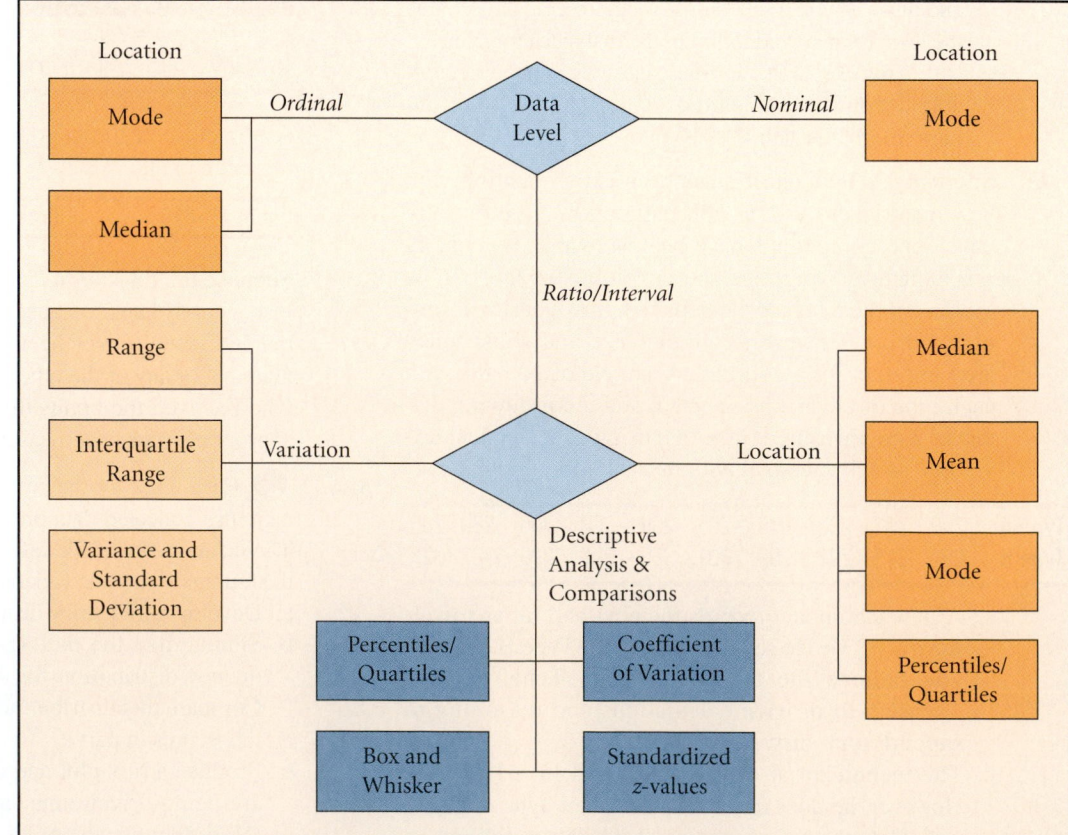

The two most frequently used measures of central location are the mean and the median. Generally, the mean is preferred. However, when the data are highly skewed or when the data level is ordinal, the median is preferred. Other measures of location, including the mode, percentiles, and quartiles, were introduced.

The most frequently used measure of variation is the standard deviation. This measure uses all the data and measures the spread of the individual observations around the mean. Other measures include the range and the interquartile range. Figure 3-11 summarizes the measures of location and spread that were discussed in this chapter.

When the numerical measures introduced in this chapter are effectively combined with the graphical techniques from Chapter 2, you will have the capability of transforming data into information. These concepts and skills will be utilized throughout the remainder of this text and will be highly valuable to you in other classes and in your careers after graduation.

EQUATIONS

Population Mean

$$\mu = \frac{\sum_{i=1}^{N} x_i}{N} \qquad \text{3-1}$$

Sample Mean

$$\bar{x} = \frac{\sum_{i=1}^{n} x_i}{n} \qquad \text{3-2}$$

Weighted Mean for a Population

$$\mu_W = \frac{\sum w_i x_i}{\sum w_i} \qquad \text{3-3}$$

Weighted Mean for a Sample

$$\bar{x}_w = \frac{\sum w_i x_i}{\sum w_i} \qquad \text{3-4}$$

Percentile Location Value

$$i = \frac{p}{100}(n+1) \qquad \text{3-5}$$

Range

$$R = \text{Maximum Value} - \text{Minimum Value} \qquad \text{3-6}$$

Interquartile Range

Interquartile Range = Third Quartile − First Quartile   **3-7**

Population Variance

$$\sigma^2 = \frac{\sum_{i=1}^{N}(x_i - \mu)^2}{N} \qquad \text{3-8}$$

Population Variance Shortcut

$$\sigma^2 = \frac{\sum(x-\mu)^2}{N} = \frac{\sum x^2 - \frac{(\sum x)^2}{N}}{N} \qquad \text{3-9}$$

Population Standard Deviation

$$\sigma = \sqrt{\sigma^2} = \sqrt{\frac{\sum_{i=1}^{N}(x_i - \mu)^2}{N}} \qquad \text{3-10}$$

Sample Variance

$$s^2 = \frac{\sum_{i=1}^{n}(x_i - \bar{x})^2}{n-1} \qquad \text{3-11}$$

Sample Variance Shortcut

$$s^2 = \frac{\sum x^2 - \frac{(\sum x)^2}{n}}{n-1} \qquad \text{3-12}$$

Sample Standard Deviation

$$s = \sqrt{s^2} = \sqrt{\frac{\sum_{i=1}^{n}(x_i - \bar{x})^2}{n-1}} \qquad \text{3-13}$$

Population Coefficient of Variation

$$CV = \frac{\sigma}{\mu}(100) \qquad \text{3-14}$$

Sample Coefficient of Variation

$$CV = \frac{s}{\bar{x}}(100) \qquad \text{3-15}$$

Standardized Population Data

$$z = \frac{x - \mu}{\sigma} \qquad \text{3-16}$$

Standardized Sample Data

$$z = \frac{x - \bar{x}}{s} \qquad \text{3-17}$$

Key Terms

Box and Whisker Plots, 88
Coefficient of Variation, 105
Data Array, 79
Empirical Rule, 106

Interquartile Range, 96
Left-Skewed Data, 80
Mean, 74
Median, 79

Mode, 82
Parameter, 74
Percentiles, 86
Quartiles, 88

CHAPTER EXERCISES

Conceptual Questions

3.49 Discuss the circumstances under which you would prefer the median to the mean as a measure of location.

3.50 Considering the relative positions of the mean, median, and mode,
   a. Draw a symmetrical distribution and label the three measures of location.
   b. Draw a left-skewed distribution and label the three measures of location.
   c. Draw a right-skewed distribution and label the three measures of location.

3.51 The marketing manager for Sweetright Cola has just received the results of two separate marketing studies performed in the Ohio Valley market region. One study was based on a random sample of 300 people, and it indicated that the mean income is $2,450 per month. The second study was based on a random sample of 400 people, and it indicated that the mean income in the region is $2,375 per month. The manager is confused. Should he have expected the two samples to yield exactly the same mean? Why or why not? Also, is it reasonable to believe that a sample mean should exactly equal the mean of the population? Discuss.

3.52 Discuss the advantages and disadvantages of using a range as a measure of spread in a set of data.

3.53 At almost every university in the United States, the university computes student grade point averages. The following scale is typically used by universities:

| A = 4 points | B = 3 points | C = 2 points | D = 1 point | F = 0 points |

Discuss what, if any, problems might exist when GPAs for two students are compared? What about comparing GPAs for students from two different universities?

3.54 Why is it inappropriate to compare the standard deviations of two or more distributions with different means? What measure is more appropriate? Discuss this measure and indicate what large versus small values of the measure imply.

3.55 Explain in your own terms, and through an example that you develop, why the standard deviation is considered a measure of dispersion.

Business Applications

3.56 Ivan Horton is a building contractor whose company builds many homes every year. In planning for each job, Ivan needs some idea about the direct labor hours required to build a home. He has collected sample information on the labor hours for 10 jobs during the past year.

| 645 | 802 | 791 | 651 | 653 | 542 | 418 | 695 | 552 | 575 |

a. Calculate the mean for this sample and explain what it means.
b. Calculate the median for this sample.
c. Calculate the variance and the standard deviation.
d. If Ivan had to select the mean or the median as the measure of location for direct labor hours, what factors about each should he consider before making the decision? Which measure would you suggest he use?

3.57 The Hillside Bowling Alley manager selected a random sample of his league customers. He asked them to record the number of lines they bowl during December, including league and open bowling. The reason for his interest in this data is that he is planning to offer a special discount to customers who bowl more than a specified number of games each month. The sample of eight people produced the following data:

| 13 | 32 | 12 | 9 | 16 | 17 | 16 | 12 |

a. Compute the mean for these sample data.
b. Compute the median for these sample data.
c. Compute the mode for these sample data.
d. Calculate the variance and the standard deviation for these sample data.
e. Note that one person bowled 32 lines. What effect, if any, does this large value have on each of the three measures of location? Discuss.
f. For these sample data, which measure of location provides the best measure of the center of the data? Discuss.
g. Given the sample data, suppose the manager wishes to give discounts to bowlers in the top quartile. What should the minimum number of games bowled be in order to receive a discount?

3.58 After performing the analysis on the Hillside Bowling Alley, the manager in the previous exercise collected data for a second bowling alley owned by his company. These data showed an average lines bowled of 10, with a standard deviation of 2. Do the bowlers at this second alley exhibit relatively more variation in the number of games bowled in December than those at the Hillside alley? Use the appropriate measures to make your point.

3.59 The Wilnet Development Company proposed building a new housing development in Warwick, Rhode Island. The city's planning department required that the developer conduct a traffic study as part of project planning. One part of that traffic study involved analyzing the trips from home made by residents in the "impact area" located near the proposed project location. The Wilnet Company selected 15 families at random from those in the impact area and asked them to keep track of their trips from home during the next week. The data returned to the Wilnet Company are shown.

| 38 | 44 | 11 | 26 | 19 | 13 | 45 | 27 | 11 | 19 | 19 | 26 | 20 | 19 | 34 |

a. Compute the mean for these data and describe what it measures.

b. Compute the median for these data and compare it with the mean found in part a.

c. Compute the mode for these data.

d. Compute the sample standard deviation and discuss what it measures.

e. Compute the interquartile range for these data and discuss why it is often preferred as a measure of variation over the range.

f. Use the values computed in previous parts of this problem to develop a box and whisker plot. Write a short statement explaining what the plot shows.

3.60 The Indiana Transportation Department recently set up a speed-check station on one of the interstate highways and collected speed data on 12 vehicles selected at random during a four-hour period. The data collected (in miles per hour) are

62	75	81	64	81	66	70	70	69	73	72	75

a. Compute the average speed for the sample.

b. Compute the median speed for the sample data.

c. Compute the mode speed for these sample data.

d. Compute the variance and the standard deviation of these sample data.

3.61 The Norton Oil Company has 20 oil wells operating in the Gulf of Mexico. The output of these wells has been recorded in terms of barrels per day pumped, as follows.

800	100	230	700	1,900	300	400	700	250	500
340	670	340	250	450	700	500	200	75	1,200

a. Compute the mean daily production for these 20 wells. Assume the data represent the population of interest.

b. Determine the median oil production per day for this population.

c. Norton Oil will cease oil production in those oil wells that are below the 33rd percentile. Determine which oil wells will be closed.

3.62 A simple random sample of six oil wells was selected from the population of 20 Norton Oil Company wells shown in Exercise 3-61. This sample was

700	700	670	700	1,200	450

a. Describe the method that is used to determine such a sample.

b. Compute the median for the sample.

c. Compute the mean for the sample.

d. Does it trouble you that there are three "700s" contained in the sample? Before answering this question, make sure that you review the definition of a random sample. Explain why you are either troubled or not troubled.

3.63 Since deregulation has taken place, the airline industry has undergone substantial changes with respect to ticket prices. Many discount fares are available if a customer knows how to obtain the discounts. Many travelers complain that they get a different price every time they call. The American Consumer Institute recently priced tickets between Spokane, Washington, and St. Louis, Missouri. The passenger was to fly coach class, round-trip, and stay seven days. Calls were made directly to airlines and to travel agents with the following results. Note that the data reflect round-trip airfare.

$229	$345	$599	$229	$429	$605
$339	$339	$229	$279	$344	$407

a. Compute the mean quoted airfare.

b. Compute the variance and the standard deviation in airfares quoted. Treat the data as a sample.

3.64 The C. A. Whitman Investment Company recently offered two mutual funds to its customers. A mutual fund is a group of stocks and bonds that is managed by an investment company. Individuals purchase shares of the mutual fund, and the investment company uses the money to buy stocks. Many investors feel comfortable with a mutual fund because their money is not tied up in one or two stocks but is spread over many stocks, thereby, they hope, reducing the risk.

Each of the two mutual funds offered by C. A. Whitman currently has 60 stocks. During the past six months, the average increase in stock prices in fund A has been $3.30, with a standard deviation of $1.25. The stocks in fund B have shown an average increase of $8.00, with a standard deviation of $3.50.

a. Based on this information, which of the two funds has stocks that have shown the greater relative variability?

b. Compute the appropriate measures and explain why we cannot simply compare standard deviations in this case.

3.65 A survey of local airline passengers shows that the mean height of male passengers is 69.5 inches, with a standard deviation of 2.5 inches. The mean weight is 177 pounds, with a standard deviation of 12 pounds. Which of the two distributions has the greater relative variability?

3.66 The data in the file named *Fast100* was collected by D. L. Green & Associates, a regional investment management company that specializes in working with clients who wish to invest in smaller companies with high growth potential. To aid the investment firm in locating appropriate investments for its clients, Sandra Williams, an assistant client manager, put together the database on 100 fast-growing companies. The data were compiled in the late summer of 2001. The database consists of data on eight variables for each of the 100 companies. Note that in some cases data are not available. A code of −99 has been used to signify missing data. These data must be omitted from any calculations.

a. Select the variable Sales. Develop a frequency distribution and histogram for Sales.

b. Compute the mean, median, and standard deviation for the Sales variable.

c. Determine the interquartile range for the Sales variable.

d. Construct a box and whisker plot for the Sales variable. Identify any outliers. Discard the outliers and recalculate the measures in b.

e. Each year a goal is set for sales. Next year's goal will be to have an average sales level that is at this year's 65th percentile. Identify next year's sales goal.

3.67 The file *McCormick* contains selected information from the 1997 annual report for McCormick & Company, Inc., the leader in the manufacture, marketing, and distribution of spices, seasonings, and flavors for the food industry. Use the table data to answer the following questions. (All values are in millions of dollars.)

a. For 1988 to 1997, compute the mean, median, and standard deviation for each variable, assuming that the 10 years represent a sample.

b. Convert each value to a z-value. Then analyze the z-values for each year. Treating all variables as being on an equal footing, which year seems to stand out as most unique from the others?

3.68   The file *Industrial Rents* contains the average annual cost per square foot for Class A warehouses in 51 selected cities for the fourth quarter for 1996 and 1997. Use this information to:

a. Construct a histogram of square-footage costs for each time period.

b. Compute the mean, median, and standard deviation for cost per square foot.

c. Devlop a box and whisker plot for cost per square foot.

d. Use the information generated in parts a, b, and c to prepare a report on the square-footage costs for Class A warehouses in the 51 cities in the sample.

Advanced Business Applications

3.69   The manager of the Clark Fork Station Restaurant recently selected a random sample of 18 customers and kept track of how long the customers were required to wait from the time they arrived at the restaurant until they were actually served dinner. This study resulted from several complaints the manager had received from customers saying that their wait time was unduly long and that it appeared that the objective was to keep people waiting in the lounge for as long as possible to increase the lounge business. The following data were recorded, with time measured in minutes.

34	24	43	56	74	20	19	33	55
43	54	34	27	34	36	24	54	39

a. Compute the mean waiting time for this sample of customers.

b. Compute the median waiting time for this sample of customers.

c. Compute the variance and standard deviation of waiting time for this sample of customers.

d. Develop a frequency distribution using six classes each with a class width of 10. Make the lower limit of the first class 15.

e. Develop a frequency histogram for the frequency distribution.

f. Constuct a box and whisker plot of this data.

g. The manager is considering giving a complimentary drink to customers whose waiting time is longer than the third quartile. Determine the minimum number of minutes a customer would have to wait in order to receive a complimentary drink.

3.70   Stock investors often look to beat the performance of the S&P 500 Index, which generally serves as a yardstick for the market as a whole. The following table shows a comparison of five-year cumulative total shareholder returns for Idaho Power Company common stock (NYSE Symbol: IDA), the S&P 500 Index, and the Edison Electric Institute (EEI) 100 Electric Utilities Index. The data assumes that $100 was invested on December 31, 1992, with returns compounded monthly. Construct appropriate statistical measures that illustrate the performance of the three investment options for

1992 through 1997. How well has Idaho Power Company performed during this period compared with the S&P 500? How well has it performed relative to its industry?

Year	Idaho Power	S&P 500	EEI 100 Electric Utilities
1992	$100.00	$100.00	$100.00
1993	117.38	110.08	111.15
1994	97.62	111.53	98.29
1995	134.11	153.45	128.78
1996	147.92	188.69	130.32
1997	189.73	251.63	166.00

3.71   The Smithfield Agricultural Company operates in the Midwest. The company owns and leases a total of 34,000 acres of prime farmland. Most of the crops are grain. Because of its size, the company can afford to do a great amount of testing to determine what seed types produce greatest yields. Recently, the company tested three types of corn seed on test plots. The following values were observed after the first year.

	Seed Type A	Seed Type B	Seed Type C
Mean bushels/acre	88	56	100
Standard deviation	25	15	16

a. Based on the results of this testing, which seed seems to produce the greatest average yield per acre? Comment on the type of testing controls that should have been used to make this study valid.

b. Suppose the company is interested in consistency. Which seed type shows the least relative variability?

c. Using the Empirical Rule, describe the production distribution for each of the three seed types.

d. Suppose you were a farmer and had to obtain at least 135 bushels per acre to escape bankruptcy. Which seed type would you plant? Explain your choice.

e. Rework your answer to part d assuming the farmer needed 115 bushels per acre instead.

3.72   The B. L. Williams Company makes tennis balls. The company has two manufacturing plants. The plant in Portland, Maine, is a unionized plant with an average daily production of 34,000 tennis balls. The output varies, with a standard deviation of 4,500 tennis balls per day. The San Antonio, Texas, plant is nonunion and is quite a bit smaller than the Portland plant. The San Antonio plant averages 12,000 tennis balls per day, with a standard deviation of 3,000.

Recently, the production manager was giving a speech to the Association of Sporting Goods Manufacturers. In that speech he stated that the B. L. Williams Company has been having real problems with its union plant maintaining consistency in production output and that the problem is not as large at the nonunion plant.

Based on the production data, was the manager justified in drawing the conclusions he made in the speech? Discuss and support your discussion with any appropriate calculations.

3.73   The Internal Revenue Service has come under a great deal of criticism in recent years for various actions it is purported to have taken against U.S. citizens related to collecting federal income taxes. The IRS is also criticized for the complexity of the tax code, although the tax laws are actually written by congressional staff and passed by Congress. For the past few years, one of the country's biggest tax-preparation companies has sponsored an event in which 50 certified public accountants from all sizes of CPA firms are asked to determine the tax owed for a fictitious citizen. The IRS is also asked to determine the "correct" tax owed. Last year, the "correct" figure stated by the IRS was $11,560. The file *Taxes* contains the data for the 50 accountants.

a. Compute a new variable that is the difference between the IRS number and the number determined by each accountant.

b. For the new variable computed in part a, develop a frequency distribution.

c. For the new variable computed in part a, determine the mean, median, and standard deviation.

d. Determine the percentile that would be attached to the "correct" tax figure if the IRS figure were one of the CPA's estimated tax figures. Describe what this implies about the agreement between the IRS and tax consultants around the country.

3.74 The Soft-Sole Shoe Company is considering opening a new shoe outlet in a U.S. city. As part of the company's analysis, the managers have gained access to data on a target group of cities. To avoid bias, the names of the cities have been omitted from the data file *Cities*. The first step in the analysis is to analyze the populations of these potential franchise locations.

a. Compute the appropriate descriptive statistical measures for this variable.

b. Construct a frequency histogram.

c. The company is only interested in locating outlets in cities with populations above the 84th percentile. Determine this value for the data.

d. If the populations were bell-shaped, determine the 84th percentile. Discuss what this says about whether this data could be assumed to be bell-shaped.

3.75 The Soft-Sole Shoe Company referred to in the previous problem knows that income levels in a city will be important to the success of the new store. Using the data file *Cities*, locate the income variables for manufacturing workers and white-collar workers.

a. Develop a frequency histogram for both variables.

b. Compute the mean, median, and mode for each variable.

c. Convert each income to a z-score within its own group.

d. If the Soft-Sole Shoe Company will consider only companies with white-collar and manufacturing incomes over two standard deviations above the mean for the entire group, which cities (by number) are still in the running?

3.76 Continuing to work with the data file *Cities* and the Soft-Sole Shoe Company's location decision, locate the income variables for manufacturing workers and for white-collar workers.

a. Compute a new variable that is the paired difference between manufacturing and white-collar incomes.

b. Construct a frequency distribution for the paired difference variable.

c. Compute the descriptive measures for this new variable and write a short report that summarizes your findings. Discuss primarily what your measures indicate about whether manufacturing jobs are more lucrative than white-collar incomes, any outliers, and the proportion of cities in which manufacturing incomes are larger than white-collar incomes.

3.77 Sandra Williams of D. L. Green & Associates has been asked to prepare an analysis on the earnings per share for the companies located in the *Fast 100* database.

a. Select the variable EPS. Develop a frequency distribution and histogram for EPS.

b. Compute the mean, median, and standard deviation for EPS.

c. Determine the interquartile range for EPS.

d. Constuct a box and whisker plot for EPS.

e. Sandra Williams is certain that the number of negative earnings per share will stand out in the data. She, therefore, wishes to determine the largest negative value and its percentile. Provide these measures to her for her report.

3.78 The file *Home-Prices* contains information about single-family housing prices in 100 metropolitan areas in the United States. The price variable represents the median price of homes in each area. In preparation for a speech to a national real estate association, you plan to use these data to illustrate real estate patterns. Discuss why it might be appropriate to have recorded the median price home in each area rather than the mean.

a. Compute the mean of the median home prices. Is this a reasonable measure to compute? Why or why not?

b. Construct a frequency histogram for the annualized price-change variable for 1993 to 1998.

c. Referring to part b, compute the mean, median, and standard deviation for the annualized price change of homes in the sampled areas.

d. As an investment, you have purchased a house that just happened to sell for the median price in your metropolitan area of $109,333. You were hoping that you could obtain a quick profit and sell your house for $120,000. Considering the analysis you have performed previously, do you think this is realistic? Support your answer with reasons and calculations.

CASE 3-A:

Wilson Corporation

The certified letter was delivered about 4:00 P.M. to Andrew Wilson, CEO and principle owner of the Wilson Corporation. It was from the state Department of Environmental Services, and it sent shivers down Andrew's spine. In bold-faced type at the top of the letter was the message:

"Notice of Water Quality Violation—Wilson Corporation"

The letter went on to outline the situation. The state had performed tests at the outflow location from Wilson's main processing plant and had found problems with nitrates and pH levels. A hearing was scheduled in two weeks to outline the issues and to assess damages to be paid by the Wilson Corp. In the

FIGURE 3-12

Excel Worksheet for Water Samples Data

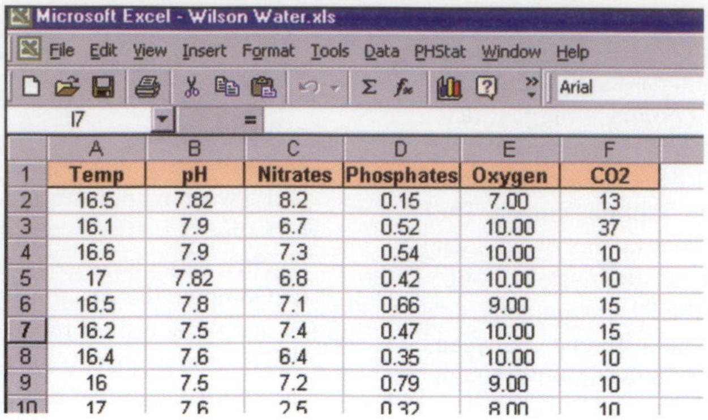

	Temp	pH	Nitrates	Phosphates	Oxygen	CO2
2	16.5	7.82	8.2	0.15	7.00	13
3	16.1	7.9	6.7	0.52	10.00	37
4	16.6	7.9	7.3	0.54	10.00	10
5	17	7.82	6.8	0.42	10.00	10
6	16.5	7.8	7.1	0.66	9.00	15
7	16.2	7.5	7.4	0.47	10.00	15
8	16.4	7.6	6.4	0.35	10.00	10
9	16	7.5	7.2	0.79	9.00	10

meantime, all effluent from the plant was to be immediately halted.

Accompanying the letter was a computer disk file containing data from 95 water samples selected at the Wilson plant over a three-week period. The file is labeled *Wilson Water*. Figure 3-12 illustrates the type of data that was included in the file.

Andrew reached for his phone to make two calls. The first was to Randy Glover, his production scheduler. He explained the problem and told Randy to immediately stop production and schedule an employee meeting at 8:00 the next morning.

The second call went to Jennifer Scranton, the company's environmental liaison. Andrew explained the essence of the letter and the action he was taking. He wanted Jennifer to halt all other work and immediately perform an analysis on the sample data supplied by the state. Andrew wanted a comprehensive descriptive analysis as soon as possible so he could prepare for the hearing.

CASE 3-B:

Holcome Financial Planners

Marsha Holcome founded Holcome Financial Planners almost three years ago, after working for Merrill Lynch for more than 14 years. Although she was able to bring several clients with her, she found that getting the business started was pretty much a "chicken and egg" problem. Potential customers would ask her how much money she had under management. When she responded with a relatively small number, the customers would tell her to call back when she had a bigger portfolio and a better track record. However, without customers she couldn't have much money under management, so it was a circular problem.

Marsha countered this problem by attempting to provide superior service to major brokerage firms. One talent on which she prided herself was her ability to analyze an industry. Recently she had met with a potential client who was interested in the computer industry. At the close of the meeting, Marsha agreed to prepare an industry analysis to show the client what she could do.

Marsha's assistant collected appropriate data using Standard and Poor's industry publications and generated a data file called *Computer Industry*. Figure 3-13 illustrates the types of data collected. Now Marsha had to get to work. She wanted to prepare a first-rate descriptive analysis of the data using graphs, charts, and appropriate numerical measures. It would be important to break out the analysis by type of computer company, too. She decided to develop a clear written narrative to go along with the descriptive information. A key to success was the way the finished product looked. It had to have "eye appeal," as well as be informative.

FIGURE 3-13

Excel Worksheet for Computer Industry Financial Data

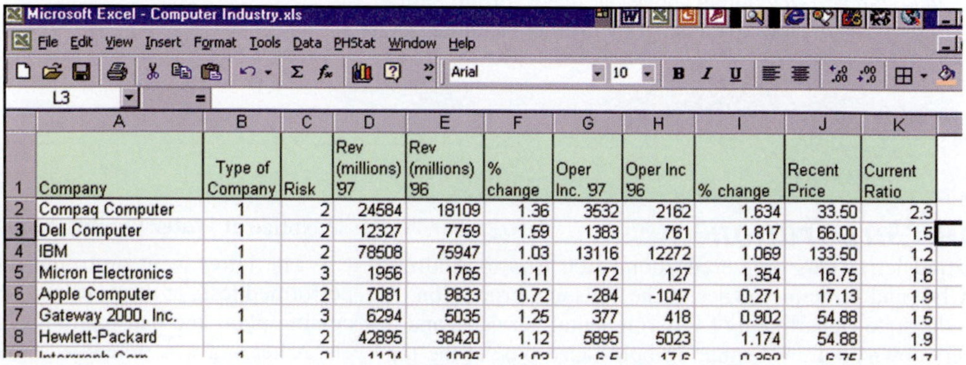

	Company	Type of Company	Risk	Rev (millions) 97	Rev (millions) 96	% change	Oper Inc. 97	Oper Inc 96	% change	Recent Price	Current Ratio
2	Compaq Computer	1	2	24584	18109	1.36	3532	2162	1.634	33.50	2.3
3	Dell Computer	1	2	12327	7759	1.59	1383	761	1.817	66.00	1.5
4	IBM	1	2	78508	75947	1.03	13116	12272	1.069	133.50	1.2
5	Micron Electronics	1	3	1956	1765	1.11	172	127	1.354	16.75	1.6
6	Apple Computer	1	2	7081	9833	0.72	-284	-1047	0.271	17.13	1.9
7	Gateway 2000, Inc.	1	3	6294	5035	1.25	377	418	0.902	54.88	1.5
8	Hewlett-Packard	1	2	42895	38420	1.12	5895	5023	1.174	54.88	1.9

CASE 3-C:

AJ's Fitness Center

A. J. Reeser was mildly surprised at the quality of the report that the intern from the local university had prepared for him. (Refer to Case 2-A in Chapter 2. The data file is *AJFitness*.) The report contained a wide variety of informative charts and graphs that effectively displayed the data. When A. J. had given the assignment, he had asked the intern to limit the descriptive analysis to charts and graphs. He wasn't sure what to expect. Now that he could see how good "this kid" was, he wanted more analysis.

When the knock on the door came, A. J. realized how quickly time had passed as he was reading the survey report. As the intern settled into the chair to the right of A. J.'s desk, the phone rang but A. J. ignored it. He stretched out his hand to the young intern and congratulated him on such a fine job.

"Now that I know how good you are, I need you to take this project a step further," A. J. said with a big grin. "What I need you to do now is combine the graphical analysis you have already done with a complete numerical analysis of the data. I want you to fully analyze this survey using whatever statistics will help, and then put your work in a full report."

After discussing the graphs and charts for a few minutes, A. J. said he would like the revised report next week. He suggested that they meet for dinner next Thursday to take a look at it.

General References

1. Albright, Christian S., Wayne L. Winston, and Christopher Zappe, *Data Analysis and Decision Making With Microsoft Excel* (Pacific Grove, CA: Duxbury, 1999).
2. Berenson, Mark L., and David M. Levine, *Basic Business Statistics: Concepts and Applications*, 7th ed. (Upper Saddle River, NJ: Prentice Hall, 1999).
3. Dodge, Mark, and Craig Stinson, *Running Microsoft Excel 2000* (Redmond, WA: Microsoft Press, 1999).
4. *Microsoft Excel 2000* (Redmond, WA: Microsoft Corp., 1999).
5. *Minitab for Windows Version 14* (State College, PA: Minitab, 2003).
6. Siegel, Andrew F., *Practical Business Statistics*, 4th ed. (Burr Ridge, IL: Irwin, 2000).
7. Tukey, John W., *Exploratory Data Analysis* (Reading, MA: Addison-Wesley, 1977).

CHAPTERS 1-3

Special Review Section

This is the first of two special review sections in this text. These sections, which are presented using block diagrams and flowcharts, are intended to help you tie together the material from several key chapters. These sections are not a substitute for reading and studying the chapters covered by the review. However, you can use this review material to add to your understanding of the individual topics in the chapters.

CHAPTERS 1–3

Chapters 1 to 3 introduce data, data collection, and statistical tools for describing data. The steps needed to gather "good" statistical data, transform it to usable information, and present the information in a manner that allows good decisions are outlined in the following figures.

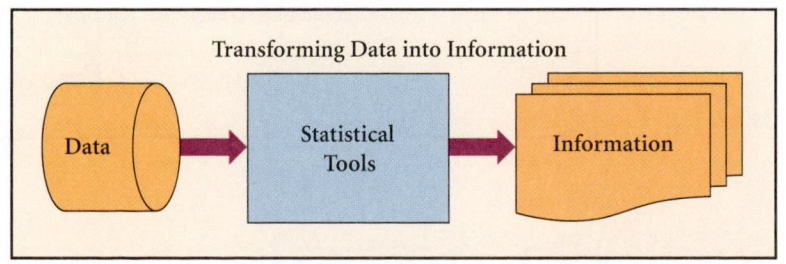

Transforming Data into Information

Data → Statistical Tools → Information

A Typical Application Sequence

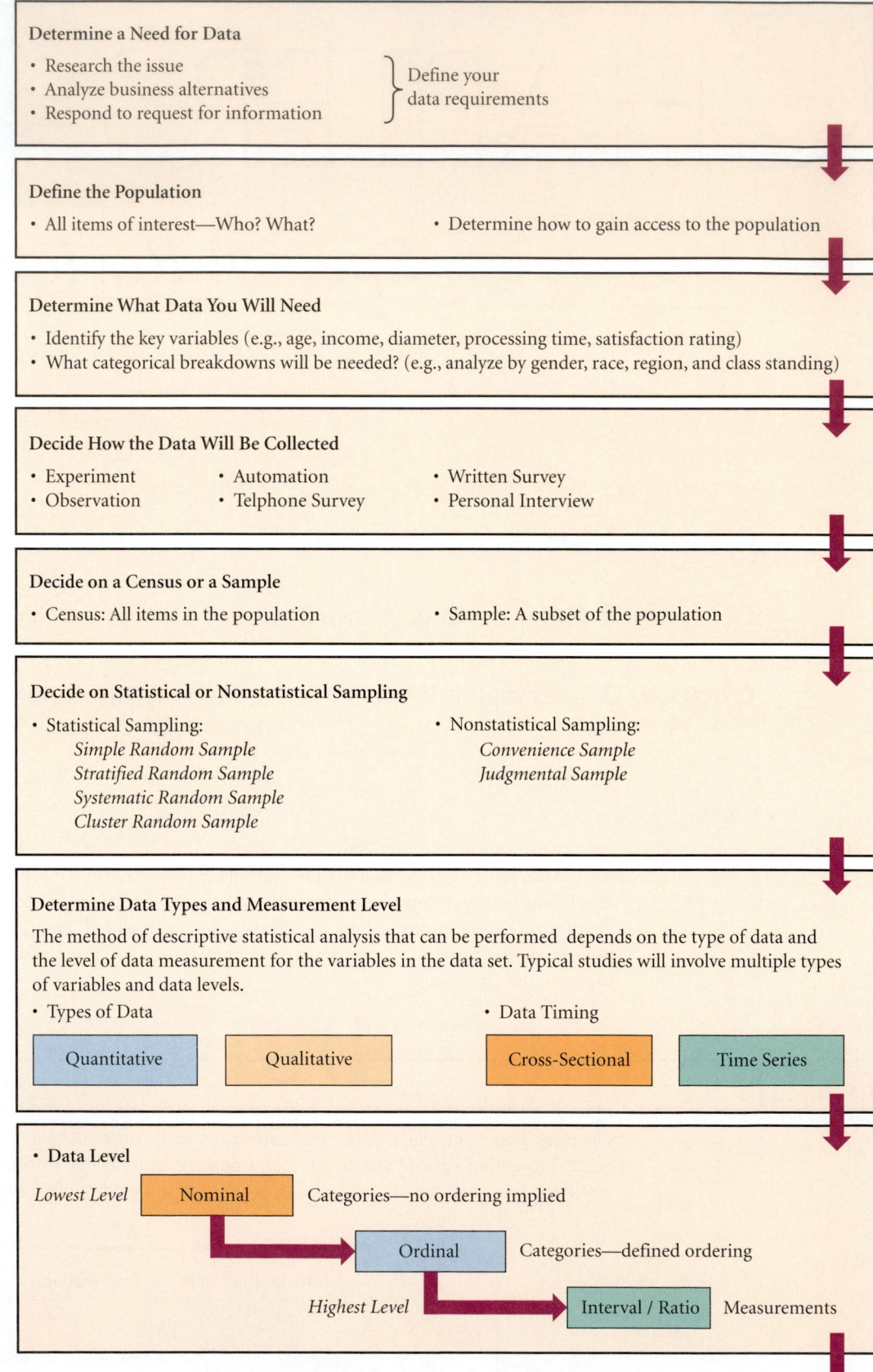

Determine a Need for Data

- Research the issue
- Analyze business alternatives
- Respond to request for information

} Define your data requirements

Define the Population

- All items of interest—Who? What?
- Determine how to gain access to the population

Determine What Data You Will Need

- Identify the key variables (e.g., age, income, diameter, processing time, satisfaction rating)
- What categorical breakdowns will be needed? (e.g., analyze by gender, race, region, and class standing)

Decide How the Data Will Be Collected

- Experiment
- Observation
- Automation
- Telephone Survey
- Written Survey
- Personal Interview

Decide on a Census or a Sample

- Census: All items in the population
- Sample: A subset of the population

Decide on Statistical or Nonstatistical Sampling

- Statistical Sampling:
  - *Simple Random Sample*
  - *Stratified Random Sample*
  - *Systematic Random Sample*
  - *Cluster Random Sample*
- Nonstatistical Sampling:
  - *Convenience Sample*
  - *Judgmental Sample*

Determine Data Types and Measurement Level

The method of descriptive statistical analysis that can be performed depends on the type of data and the level of data measurement for the variables in the data set. Typical studies will involve multiple types of variables and data levels.

- Types of Data

  Quantitative   Qualitative

- Data Timing

  Cross-Sectional   Time Series

- Data Level

Lowest Level   Nominal   Categories—no ordering implied

Ordinal   Categories—defined ordering

Highest Level   Interval / Ratio   Measurements

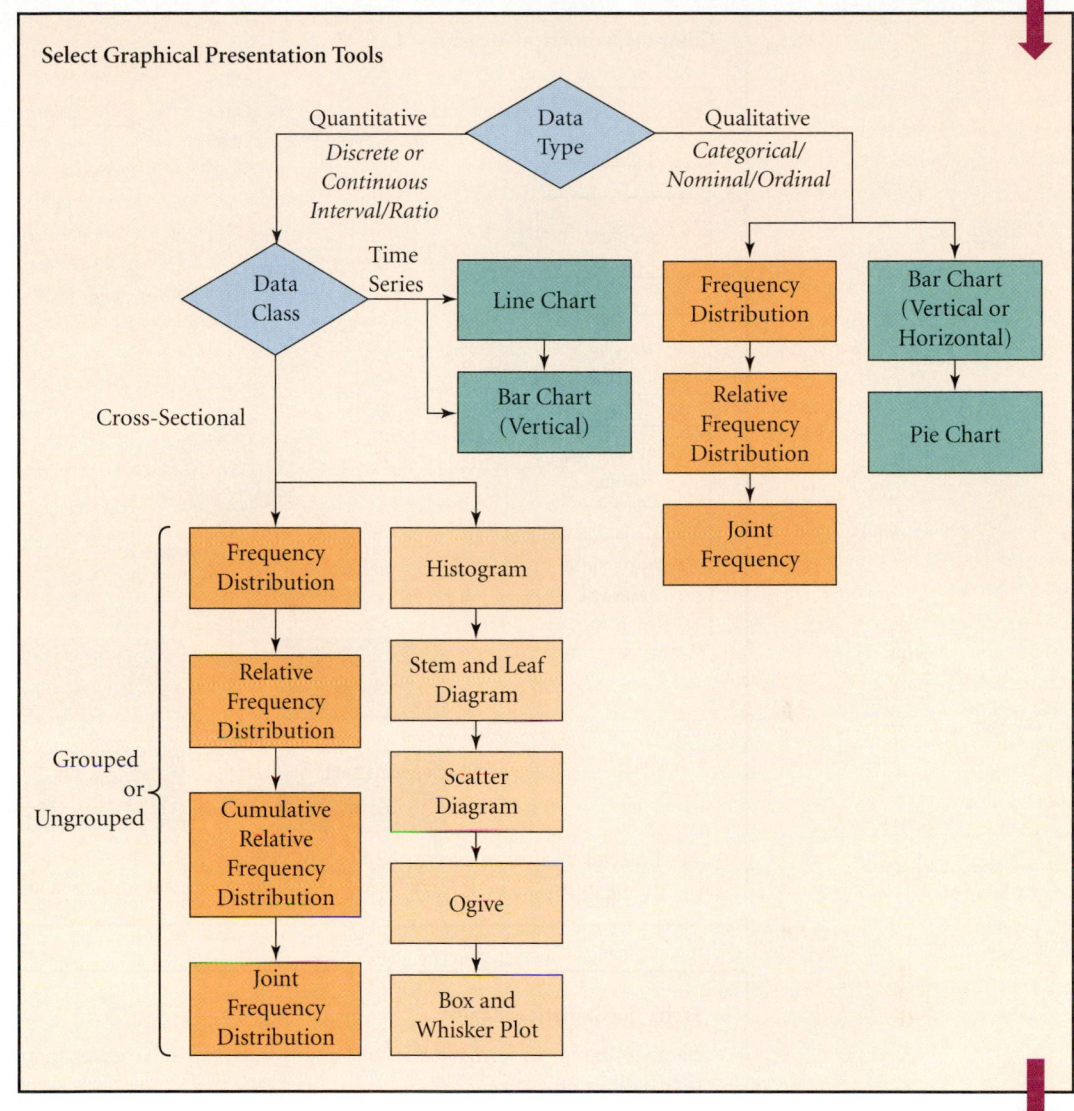

Select Graphical Presentation Tools

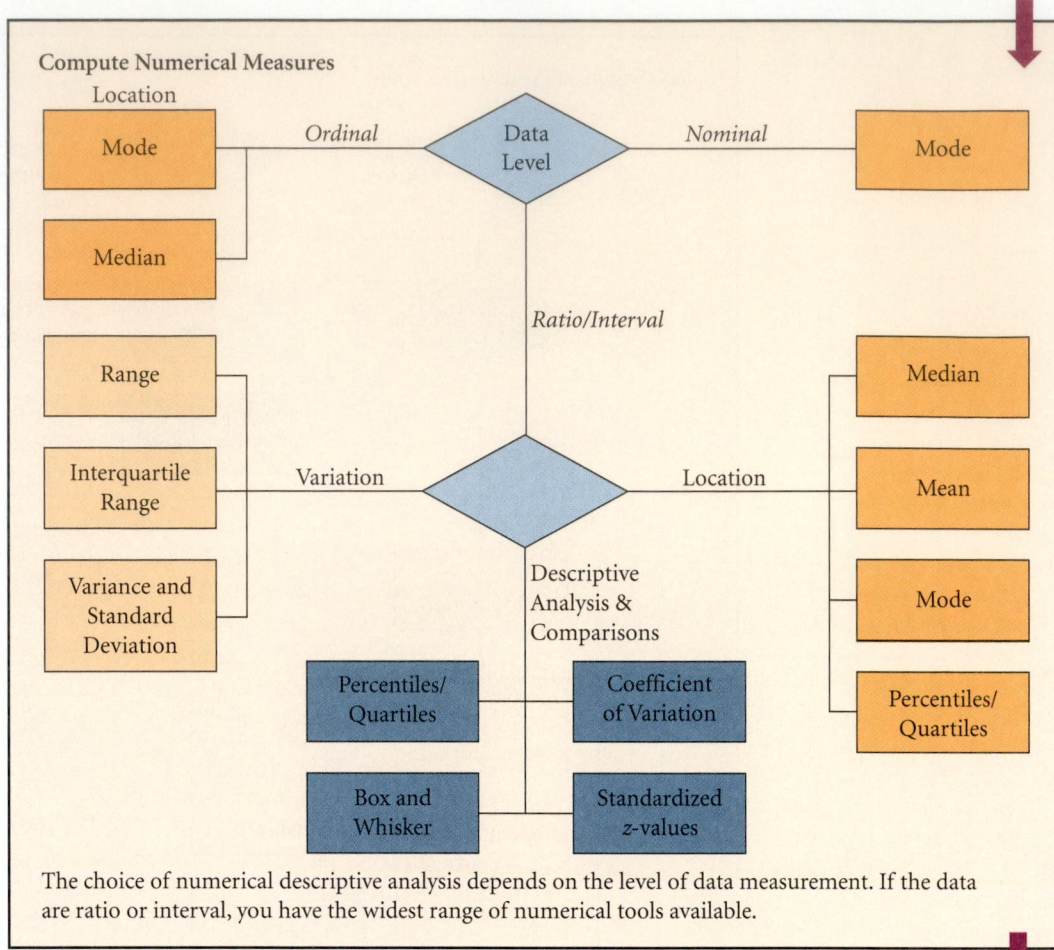

The choice of numerical descriptive analysis depends on the level of data measurement. If the data are ratio or interval, you have the widest range of numerical tools available.

Write the Statistical Report

There is no one set format for writing a statistical report. However, there are a few suggestions you may find useful.

- *Lay the foundation:*
  Provide background and motivation for the analysis.

- *Describe the data collection methodology:*
  Explain how the data were gathered and the sampling techniques were used.

- *Use a logical sequence:*
  Follow a systematic plan for presenting your findings and analysis.

- *Label figures and tables by number:*
  Employ a consistent numbering and labeling format.

EXERCISES

Integrative Application Exercises

Chapters 1 to 3 have introduced you to the basics of descriptive statistics. Many of the business application problems, advanced business application problems, and cases in these chapters will give you practice at performing descriptive statistical analysis. However, too often you are told which procedure you should use, or you can surmise which to use by the location of the exercise. It is important that you learn to identify the appropri-

ate procedure on your own in order to solve problems for test purposes. But more important, this ability is essential throughout your career when you are required to select procedures for the tasks you will undertake. The following exercises will provide you with identification practice.

SR.1   Go to your university library and obtain the *Statistical Abstract of the United States*.
   a. Construct a frequency distribution for unemployment rate by state for the most current year available.

b. Justify your choice of class limits and number of classes.

c. Locate the unemployment rate for the state in which you are attending college. (1) What proportion of the unemployment rates are below that of your state? (2) Describe the distribution's shape with respect to symmetry. (3) If you were planning to build a new manufacturing plant, what state would you choose in which to build? Justify your answer. (4) Are there any unusual features of this distribution? Describe them.

SR.2   The State Industrial Development Council is presently working on a financial services brochure to send to out-of-state companies. It is hoped that the brochure will be helpful in attracting companies to relocate to your state. You are given the following frequency distribution on banks in your state:

Deposit Size (in Millions)	Number of Banks	Total Deposits (in Millions)
Less than 5	2	7.2
5 to less than 10	7	52.1
10 to less than 25	6	111.5
25 to less than 50	3	95.4
50 to less than 100	2	166.6
100 to less than 500	2	529.8
Over 500	2	1663.0

a. Does this frequency distribution violate any of the rules of construction for frequency distributions? If so, re-construct the frequency distribution to remedy this violation.

b. The Council wishes to target companies that would require financial support from banks that have at least $25 million in deposits. Reconstruct the frequency distribution to attract such companies to relocate to your state. Do this by considering different classes that would accomplish such a goal.

c. Reconstruct the frequency distribution to attract companies that require financial support from banks that have between $5 million and $25 million in deposits.

d. Present an eye-catching, two-paragraph summary of what the data would mean to a company that is considering moving to the state. Your boss has said you need to include relative frequencies in this presentation.

SR.3   As an intern for the Intel company, suppose you have been asked to help the vice president prepare a newsletter to the shareholders. You have been given access to the data in a file called *Intel* that contains Intel Corporation financial data for the years 1987–1996. Go to the Internet or to Intel's annual report and update the file to include the same variables for the years 1997 to present. Then, use graphs to effectively present the data in a format that would be usable for the vice president's newsletter. Write a short article that discusses the information shown in your graphs.

SR.4   The Woodmill Company makes windows and door trim products. The first step in the process is to rip dimension (2 × 8, 2 × 10, etc.) lumber into narrower pieces. Currently, the company uses a manual process in which an experienced operator quickly looks at a board and determines what rip widths to use. The decision is based on the knots and defects in the wood.

A company in Oregon has developed an optical scanner that can be used to determine the rip widths. The scanner is programmed to recognize defects and to determine rip widths that will "optimize" the value of the board. A test run of 100 boards was run through the scanner and the rip widths were identified. However, the boards were not actually ripped. A lumber grader determined the resulting values for each of the 100 boards assuming that the rips determined by the scanner had been made. Next, the same 100 boards were manually ripped using the normal process. The grader then determined the value for each board after the manual rip process was completed. The resulting data in the file, *Woodmill*, consist of manual rip values and scanner rip values for each of the 100 boards.

a. Develop a frequency distribution for the board values for the scanner and the manual process.

b. Compute appropriate descriptive statistics for both manual and scanner values. Use these data along with the frequency distribution developed in part (a) to prepare a written report that describes the results of the test. Be sure to include in your report a conclusion regarding whether the scanner outperforms the manual process.

c. Which process, scanner, or manual generated the most values that were more than two standard deviations from the mean?

d. Which of the 2 processes has the least relative variability?

SR.5   The commercial banking industry is undergoing rapid changes due to advances in technology and competitive pressures in the financial services sector. The data file *Banks* contains selected information tabulated by *Fortune* magazine concerning the revenues, profitability, and number of employees for the 51 largest U.S. commercial banks in terms of revenues. Use the information in this file to complete the following:

a. Compute the mean, median, and standard deviation for the three variables, Revenues, Profits, and Number of Employees.

b. Convert the data for each variable to a z-value. Consider Mellon Bank Corporation headquartered in Pittsburgh. How does it compare to the average bank in the study on the three variables? Discuss.

c. As you can see by examining the data and by looking at the statistics computed in part (a), not all banks had the same revenue, same profit, or the same number of employees. Which variable had the greatest relative variation among the banks in the study?

d. Calculate a new variable: profits per employee. Develop a frequency distribution and a histogram for this new variable. Also compute the mean, median, and standard deviation for the new variable. Write a short report that describes the profits per employee for the banks.

e. Referring to part d, how many Banks had a profit per employee ratio which exceeded 2 standard deviations from the mean?

Here is an integrative case study designed to give you additional experience. In addition, we have included several term project assignments that require you to collect and analyze data.

REVIEW CASE 1:

State Department of Insurance

This case study describes the efforts undertaken by the director of the Department of Insurance Division to assess the magnitude of the uninsured motorist problem in a western state. The objective of the case study is to introduce you to a data collection application and show how one organization developed a database. The database on your data diskette called *Liabins* is a subset of the data actually collected by the state department.

The impetus for the case came from the Legislative Transportation Committee, which heard much testimony during the recent legislative session about the problems that occur when an uninsured motorist is involved in a traffic accident where damages to individuals and property occur. The state's law enforcement officers also testified that a large number of vehicles are not covered by liability insurance.

Because of both political pressure and a sense of duty to do what is right, the legislative committee spent many hours wrestling with what to do about drivers who do not carry the mandatory liability insurance. Because the actual magnitude of the problem was unknown, the committee finally arrived at a compromise plan, which required the State Insurance Division to perform random audits of vehicles to determine whether the vehicle was covered by liability insurance. The audits are to be performed on approximately 1% of the state's 1 million registered vehicles each month. If a vehicle is found not to have liability insurance, the vehicle license and the owner's driver's license will be revoked for 3 months and a $250 fine will be imposed.

However, before actually implementing the audit process, which is projected to cost $1.5 million per year, Herb Kriner, director of the Insurance Department, was told to conduct a preliminary study of the uninsured motorists problem in the state and to report back to the legislative committee in 6 months.

The Study

A random sample of twelve counties in the state was selected in a manner that gave the counties with higher numbers of registered vehicles proportionally higher chances of being selected. Two locations were selected in each county and the State Police set up roadblocks on a randomly selected day. Vehicles with in-state license plates were stopped at random until approximately 100 vehicles had been stopped at each location. The target total was about 2,400 vehicles statewide.

The issue of primary interest was whether the vehicle was insured. This was determined by observing whether the vehicle was carrying the required certificate of insurance. If so, the officer took down the insurance company name and address and the policy number. If the certificate was not in the car, but the owner stated that insurance was carried, the owner was given a postcard to return within 5 days supplying the required information. A vehicle was determined to be uninsured if no postcard was returned or if, subsequently, the insurance company reported that the policy was not valid on the day of the survey.

In addition to the issue of insurance coverage, Herb Kriner wanted to collect other information about the vehicle and the owner. This was done using a personal interview during which the police officer asked a series of questions and observed certain things such as seat belt usage and driver's and vehicle license expiration status. Also, the owners' driving records were obtained through the Transportation Department's computer division and added to the information gathered by the State Police.

The Data

The data are contained in the file *Liabins*. The sheet, titled Description, contains an explanation of the data set and the variables.

Issues to Address

Herb Kriner has two weeks before making a presentation to the Legislative subcommittee that has been dealing with the liability insurance issue. As Herb's chief analyst, your job is to perform a comprehensive analysis of the data and to prepare the report that Herb will deliver to the Legislature. Remember, this report will go a long way in determining whether the state should spend the $1.5 million to implement a full liability insurance audit system.

Term Project Assignments

For the project selected, you are to devise a sampling plan, collect appropriate data, and carry out a full descriptive analysis aimed at shedding light on the key issues for the project. The finished project will include a written report of a length and format specified by your professor.

Project A:

Issue: Your College of Business and Economics seeks input from business majors regarding class scheduling. Some potential issues are:

- Day or evening
- Morning or afternoon
- 1-day, 2-day, or 3-day schedules
- Weekend
- Location (on or off campus)

Project B:

Issue: Intercollegiate athletics is a part of any major university. Revenue from attendance at major sporting events is one key to financing the athletic program. Investigate the drivers of attendance at your university's men's basketball and football games. Some potential issues:

- Game times
- Game days (basketball)
- Ticket prices
- Athletic booster club memberships
- Competition for entertainment dollars

Project C:

Issue: The department of your major is interested in surveying department alumni. Some potential issues are

- Satisfaction with degree
- Employment Status
- Job satisfaction
- Suggestions for improving course content

CHAPTER 4

Using Probability and Probability Distributions

CHAPTER OUTCOMES

After studying the material in Chapter 4, you should:

- Understand the three approaches to assessing probabilities.
- Be able to apply the common rules of probability.
- Know how to use Bayes' Theorem for applications involving conditional probabilities.
- Be able to distinguish the difference between discrete and continuous probability distributions.
- Be able to compute the expected value and standard deviation for a discrete probability distribution.

WHY YOU NEED TO KNOW

Business managers frequently must choose a course of action from among several alternatives to move their companies closer to their goals and objectives. For example, suppose the quality control manager at the American Plywood plant examines three pieces of plywood to determine whether the thickness of the boards meets specifications. The manager records her findings by labeling a good piece of plywood "*G*" and a defective piece of plywood "*D*." For three pieces of plywood she has just sampled, she obtains the following results: *G, D, G*. How can this sample help her decide between the two alternatives of closing the plant to make adjustments to the production equipment or keeping the plant operating as it is?

Consider a second example in which an accountant randomly examines 15 accounts and finds that 14 of them are accurate. What does this tell him about whether the firm has major problems in its accounting information system?

In both of these cases someone had to make a decision—about equipment operation in one case and an accounting information system in the other. Decision making means selecting among two or more alternatives. To make good decisions, managers must establish general criteria for deciding among alternatives. Certainly the criteria must somehow be related to the objective of the decision-making situation. This objective may involve revising a plant operation, updating an accounting system, analyzing a profit or sales level, or even creating an orderly situation from near chaos. In addition, good decisions must be based on correctly using available information. This chapter explores how to use information.

Chapter 1 described how managers must often operate with sample information collected from the population of interest. They are uncertain about the population, but they know a great deal about the sample. This is the case in our previous examples, in which we know the number of good sheets of plywood and the number of accurate accounts in the samples. Probability theory allows managers to use this sample information to make inferences about a population and to have confidence in these inferences.

In Chapter 2, we saw how a frequency distribution transforms raw data into a useful form that provides meaningful insight into the data. Frequency distributions are one way in which decision makers deal with uncertainty in their decision environments. Because all managers operate in an uncertain environment, they must be able to make the connection between descriptive statistics and probability. Moving from frequency distributions to *probability distributions* makes this connection.

Constructing and analyzing a frequency distribution for every decision-making situation would be time-consuming. Just deciding on the correct data-gathering procedures, the appropriate class intervals, and the right methods of presenting the data are not trivial issues. Fortunately, many physical and organizational events that appear to be unrelated have the same underlying characteristics and can be described by the same probability distribution. If decision makers are dealing with an application described by a predetermined *theoretical* probability distribution, they can use a great deal of developmental statistical work already known and can save considerable personal effort in analyzing their situation. Therefore, decision makers need to become comfortable with probability distributions if they are to apply them effectively. Fortunately for both the quality control manager and the accountant, their situations can be described by a well-known probability distribution.

4-1 THE BASICS OF PROBABILITY

Before we can apply *probability* to the decision-making process, we must understand what it means. The mathematical study of probability originated more than 300 years ago. The Chevalier de Méré, a French nobleman (who today would probably own a gaming house in Monte Carlo), began asking questions about games of chance. He was mostly interested in the probability of observing various outcomes (a pair of ones in 24 tosses of a pair of dice or a one in four tosses of a die) when dice were repeatedly rolled. The French mathematician Blaise Pascal (you may remember studying Pascal's triangle in a mathematics class) with the help of his friend Pierre de Fermat was able to answer de Méré's questions. Of course, Pascal began asking more and more complicated questions of himself and his colleagues, and the formal study of probability began.

IMPORTANT PROBABILITY TERMS

Several explanations of what probability is have come out of this mathematical study. However, the definition of probability is quite basic.

Probability

The chance that a particular event will occur.

The probability of an event will be a value in the range 0 to 1. A value of 0 means the event will not occur. A probability of 1 means the event will occur. Anything between 0 and 1 reflects the uncertainty of the event occurring. The definition given is for a countable number of events.

Events and Sample Space

As discussed in Chapter 1, data come in many forms and are gathered in many ways. In a business environment, when a sample is selected or a decision is made, there are generally many possible outcomes. In probability language, the process that produces the outcomes is an **experiment**. In business situations, the experiment can range from an investment decision to a personnel decision to a choice of warehouse location.

Experiment

A process that produces a single outcome whose result cannot be predicted with certainty.

The individual outcomes from an experiment are called **elementary events**.

Elementary Events

The most rudimentary outcomes resulting from a simple experiment.

The collection of the most elementary events is called the **sample space**.

Sample Space

The collection of all elementary outcomes that can result from a selection, decision, or experiment.

The sample space for an experiment consists of all the elementary events that the experiment can produce.

XAMPLE 4-1: DEFINING THE SAMPLE SPACE

Able Accounting   A partner for Able Accounting, a large regional accounting firm, is analyzing the performance of her many audit teams. She is particularly interested in whether the audits are finished by the projected completion date. She is interested in determining the sample space (possible outcomes) under different circumstances. To do this, she can use the following steps:

Step 1: **Define the experiment.**
The experiment is the audit. Of interest is the status of an audit completion.

Step 2: **Define the elementary events for one trial of the experiment.**
The partner can define the elementary events to be

$$e_1 = \text{Audit done early}$$
$$e_2 = \text{Audit done on time}$$
$$e_3 = \text{Audit done late}$$

The sample space (SS) for an experiment involving a single audit is

$$SS = \{e_1, e_2, e_3\}$$

If the experiment is expanded to include two audits, the sample space is

$$SS = \{e_1, e_2, e_3, e_4, e_5, e_6, e_7, e_8, e_9\}$$

where the events include what happens on both audits and are defined as:

Elementary Event	Audit 1	Audit 2
e_1	early	early
e_2	early	on time
e_3	early	late
e_4	on time	early
e_5	on time	on time
e_6	on time	late
e_7	late	early
e_8	late	on time
e_9	late	late

EXAMPLE 4-2: DEFINING THE SAMPLE SPACE

Lincoln Marketing Research　Recently, Lincoln Marketing Research in Lincoln, Nebraska, was retained to interview television viewers to determine whether they objected to having ads for hard liquor on TV. The analyst assigned to the project is interested in listing the sample space (possible outcomes). To do this, he can use the following steps:

Step 1:　**Define the experiment.**
　　　　The experiment involves selecting a television viewer and posing the question: "Would you object to hard-liquor advertisements on television?"

Step 2:　**Determine the elementary events for a single trial of the simple experiment.**
　　　　The possible outcomes when one person is interviewed are

$$e_1 = no$$
$$e_2 = yes$$

Step 3:　**Define the sample space.**
　　　　If three people (3 trials) are interviewed, the sample space (possible outcomes) is

Viewer 1	Viewer 2	Viewer 3
no	no	no
no	no	yes
no	yes	no
no	yes	yes
yes	no	no
yes	no	yes
yes	yes	no
yes	yes	yes

Using Tree Diagrams

A tree diagram is often a useful way to define the sample space for an experiment that helps ensure that no elementary events are omitted. Example 4-3 illustrates how a tree diagram is used.

EXAMPLE 4-3: USING A TREE DIAGRAM TO DEFINE THE SAMPLE SPACE

Lincoln Marketing Research　In Example 4-2, Lincoln Marketing Research was involved in a project in which television viewers were asked whether they objected to hard-liquor advertisements being shown on television. The analyst is interested in listing the sample space, using a tree diagram as an aid, when three viewers are interviewed. The following steps can be used:

Step 1:　**Define the experiment.**
　　　　Three people are interviewed and asked, "Would you object to hard-liquor advertisements on television?" Thus, the experiment consists of three trials.

Step 2:　**Define the elementary events for a single trial of the experiment.**
　　　　The possible outcomes when one person is interviewed are:

$$e_1 = no$$
$$e_2 = yes$$

Step 3:　**Define the sample space for three trials using a tree diagram.**
　　　　Begin by determining the elementary events for a single trial. Illustrate these with tree branches beginning on the left side of the page:

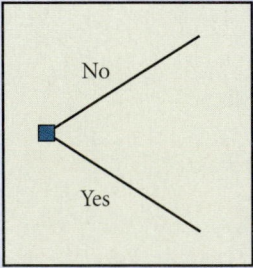

For each of these branches, add branches depicting the outcomes for a second trial. Continue until the tree has the number of sets of branches corresponding to the number of trials:

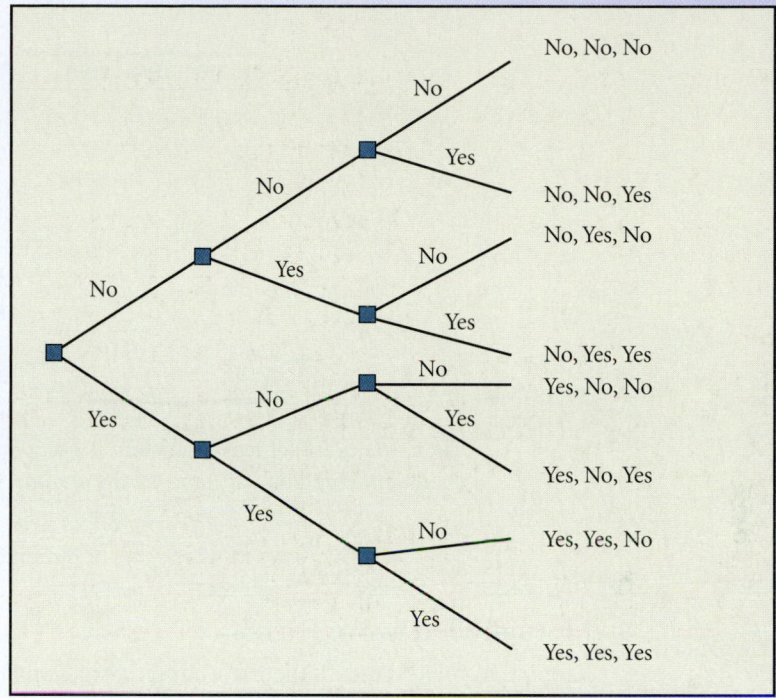

A collection of elementary events is called an **event**. An example will help clarify these terms.

Event

A collection of elementary events.

$\mathcal{E}$XAMPLE 4-4: DEFINING AN EVENT OF INTEREST

Able Accounting   The Able Accounting firm in Example 4-1 is interested in the sample space for an audit experiment in which the outcome of interest is the audit's completion status. The sample space is the list of all possible elementary events from the experiment. The accounting firm is also interested in specifying the elementary events that make up an event of interest. This can be done using the following steps:

Step 1:   **Define the experiment.**
The experiment is the audit.

Step 2:   **List the elementary events associated with one trial of the experiment.**
For a single audit the following completion-status possibilities exist:

$$e_1 = \text{Audit done early}$$
$$e_2 = \text{Audit done on time}$$
$$e_3 = \text{Audit done late}$$

The sample space (SS) for an experiment involving a single audit is

$$SS = \{e_1, e_2, e_3\}$$

Step 3:   **Define the event of interest.**
For two audits (two trials), the event of interest is at least one audit is completed late. Here, each elementary event consists of the combined outcomes of audit 1 and audit 2. We define the sample space for two trials:

Elementary Event	Audit 1	Audit 2
e_1	early	early
e_2	early	on time
e_3	early	late
e_4	on time	early
e_5	on time	on time
e_6	on time	late
e_7	late	early
e_8	late	on time
e_9	late	late

Then, the event (at least one audit is completed late) is composed of all the elementary events in which one or more audits are late. This event (E) is

$$E = \{e_3, e_6, e_7, e_8, e_9\}$$

There are five ways in which one or more audits are completed late.

Mutually Exclusive Events

Keeping in mind the definitions for *experiment, sample space, elementary events*, and *events*, we introduce two additional concepts. The first is **mutually exclusive events**.

Mutually Exclusive Events

Two events are mutually exclusive if the occurrence of one event precludes the occurrence of the other event.

Able Accounting (continued)—Consider again the Able Accounting firm example. The possible elementary events for different audits done by two teams are

Elementary Event	Audit 1	Audit 2
e_1	early	early
e_2	early	on time
e_3	early	late
e_4	on time	early
e_5	on time	on time
e_6	on time	late
e_7	late	early
e_8	late	on time
e_9	late	late

Suppose we define one event as consisting of the elementary events in which at least one of the two audits is late.

$$E_1 = \{e_3, e_6, e_7, e_8, e_9\}$$

Further, suppose we define two more events as follows:

$$E_2 = \text{neither audit is late} = \{e_1, e_2, e_4, e_5\}.$$
$$E_3 = \text{both audits are finished at the same time} = \{e_1, e_5, e_9\}$$

Events E_1 and E_2 are mutually exclusive: If E_1 occurs, E_2 cannot occur; if E_2 occurs, E_1 cannot occur. That is, if at least one audit is late, then it is not possible for neither audit to be late. We can verify this fact by observing that no elementary events in E_1 appear in E_2. This observation provides another way of defining mutually exclusive events: Two events are mutually exclusive if they have no common elementary events.

Independent and Dependent Events

The second additional probability concept is that of **independent** versus **dependent** events.

Independent Events

Two events are independent if the occurrence of one event in no way influences the probability of the occurrence of the other event.

Dependent Events

Two events are dependent if the occurrence of one event impacts the probability of the other event occurring.

Mobile Exploration—Mobile Exploration is a subsidiary of the Mobile Corporation and is responsible for oil and natural gas exploration worldwide. During the exploration phase, seismic surveys are conducted that provide information about the earth's underground formations. Based on past history, the company knows that if the seismic readings are favorable, oil or gas more likely will be discovered than if the seismic readings are not favorable. However, the readings are not perfect indicators. Suppose the company currently is exploring in the eastern part of Australia. The elementary events for the seismic survey are defined as:

$$e_1 = \text{favorable}$$
$$e_2 = \text{unfavorable}$$

If the company decides to drill, the elementary events are defined as:

$$e_3 = \text{strike oil or gas}$$
$$e_4 = \text{dry hole}$$

If we let the Event A be that the seismic survey is favorable and Event B be that the hole is dry, we can say that the events A and B are not mutually exclusive, because if one event occurs, it does not preclude the other event from occurring. We can also say that the two events are dependent because the chance of a dry hole depends on whether the seismic survey is favorable or unfavorable.

$\mathcal{E}$XAMPLE 4-5: INDEPENDENT, DEPENDENT, AND MUTUALLY EXCLUSIVE EVENTS

Barcelona Assembly   Barcelona Assembly, located in Barcelona, Spain, does contract assembly work for Hewlett-Packard. Each item produced on the assembly line can be thought of as an experimental trial. The managers at this facility can analyze their process to determine whether the events of interest are mutually exclusive and are independent or dependent using the following steps:

Step 1:   **Define the experiment.**
The experiment is producing a part on an assembly line.

Step 2:   **Define the elementary events for a single trial.**
On each trial the outcome is either a *good* or a *defective* item. Thus, the sample space for a single trial is
$$SS = \{\text{good, defective}\}$$

Step 3:   **Determine whether the events are mutually exclusive.**
If two products are produced (two trials), the following sample space is defined:

good	good
good	defective
defective	good
defective	defective

Let Event A be defined as both products produced are good (good, good), and let Event B be defined as at least one product is defective.

good	defective
defective	good
defective	defective

Then Events *A* and *B* are determined to be mutually exclusive because the two events have no elementary events in common. Having two good items and at the same time having at least one defective item is not possible.

Step 4:   **An analysis of whether events are independent or dependent is made based on whether the occurrence of one event affects the probability of the second event occurring.**

As long as the machine is properly adjusted, it may produce some good outcomes and some defective outcomes with no apparent pattern, or dependency, between trials. That is, the production of one item, good or bad, has no influence on the probability of the outcome of subsequent trials. In that case, the events (defective item and good item) would be independent. However, if the machine goes out of adjustment, one item made defective because of maladjustment may cause still further adjustment problems and increase the chances that subsequent items will be defective. In this case, the trials are dependent, because the probability of the outcome of one trial is in some way influenced by the outcome of a previous trial.

METHODS OF ASSIGNING PROBABILITY

Part of the confusion surrounding probability may be due to the fact that probability means different things to different people. There are three common ways to assign probability to events: *classical probability assessment, relative frequency of occurrence*, and *subjective probability assessment.* The following notation is used when we refer to the probability of an event:

$$P(E_i) = \text{probability of event } E_i \text{ occurring}$$

Classical Probability Assessment

The first method of probability measurement is **classical probability**, or *a priori* probability.

Classical Probability Assessment

The method of determining probability based on the ratio of the number of ways the event of interest can occur to the number of ways *any* event can occur when the individual elementary events are equally likely.

You are probably already familiar with classical probability. It had its beginning with games of chance and is still most often discussed in those terms.

In those situations in which all possible elementary events are *equally likely*, the classical probability measurement is defined in Equation 4-1.

Classical Probability Measurement

$$P(E_i) = \frac{\text{Number of ways } E_i \text{ can occur}}{\text{Total number of elementary events}} \qquad \textbf{4-1}$$

$\mathcal{E}$XAMPLE 4-6: CLASSICAL PROBABILITY ASSESSMENT

Galaxy Furniture   The managers at Galaxy Furniture plan to hold a special promotion over Labor Day Weekend. Each customer making a purchase exceeding $100 will qualify to select an envelope from a large drum. Inside the envelope are coupons for percentage discounts off the purchase total. At the beginning of the weekend, there were 500 coupons. Four hundred of these were for 10% discount, 50 were for 20% discount, 45 were for 30%, and 5 were for 50% discount. Customers were interested in determining the probability of getting a particular discount amount. The probabilities can be determined using classical assessment with the following steps:

Step 1:   **Determine whether the elementary events are equally likely.**
In this case, the envelopes with the different discount amounts are unmarked from the outside and are thoroughly mixed in the drum. Thus, any one coupon has the same probability of being selected as any other coupon.

Step 2: **Determine the total number of elementary events.**
There are 500 envelopes in the drum.

Step 3: **Define the event of interest.**
We might be interested in assessing the probability that a customer will get a 20% discount.

Step 4: **Determine the number of elementary events associated with the event of interest.**
There are 50 coupons with a discount of 20% marked on them.

Step 5: **Compute the classical probability using Equation 4-1:**

$$P(E_i) = \frac{\text{Number of ways } E_i \text{ can occur}}{\text{Total number of elementary events}}$$

$$P(20\% \text{ Discount}) = \frac{\text{Number of ways 20\% can occur}}{\text{Total number of elementary events}} = \frac{50}{500} = 0.10$$

Note: After each customer selects an envelope from the drum, the probability that the next customer will get a particular discount will change, because the values in both the numerator and the denominator will change.

As you can see, the classical approach to probability measurement is fairly straightforward. Many games of chance are based on classical probability assessment. However, classical probability assessment is difficult to apply to most business situations. Rarely are the elementary events equally likely. For instance, you might be thinking of starting a business. The sample space listing the elementary events is

$$SS = \{\text{Succeed, Fail}\}$$

Would it be reasonable to use classical assessment to determine the probability that your business will succeed? We would make the following assessment:

$$P(\text{Succeed}) = \frac{1}{2}$$

If this were true, then the chance of any business succeeding would be 0.50. Of course, this is not true. Too many factors go into determining the success or failure of a business. The elementary events (Succeed, Failure) are not equally likely. Instead, we need another method of assessment in these situations.

Relative Frequency of Occurrence

The **relative frequency of occurrence** approach is based on actual observations.

Relative Frequency of Occurrence

The method that defines probability as the number of times an event occurs divided by the total number of times an experiment is performed in a large number of trials.

Equation 4-2 shows how the relative frequency of occurrence can assess these probabilities.

Relative Frequency of Occurrence

$$\text{Relative frequency of } E_i = \frac{\text{Number of times } E_i \text{ occurs}}{N} \qquad \textbf{4-2}$$

where:

$$E_i = \text{The event of interest}$$
$$N = \text{Number of trials}$$

Hathaway Heating & Air Conditioning—The sales manager at Hathaway Heating & Air Conditioning has recently developed the customer profile shown in Table 4-1. The profile is based on a random sample of 500 customers. As a promotion for the company, the sales manager plans to randomly select a customer once a month and do a free service to the customer's system. What is the

TABLE 4-1	CUSTOMER CATEGORY		
Hathaway Heating & Air Conditioning Co.	**Commercial**	**Residential**	**Total**
Heating Systems	55	145	200
Air Conditioning Systems	45	255	300
Total	100	400	500

probability that the customer selected is a residential customer? What is the probability that the customer has a heating system?

To determine the probability that the customer selected is residential, we determine from Table 4-1 the number of residential customers and divide by the total number of customers, both residential and commercial.

$$P(\text{Residential}) = RF(\text{Residential}) = \frac{400}{500} = 0.80$$

Thus, there is an 80% chance the customer selected will be a residential customer.

The probability the customer selected has a heating system is determined by the ratio of the number of customers with heating systems to the number of total customers.

$$P(\text{Heating}) = RF(\text{Heating}) = \frac{200}{500} = 0.40$$

There is a 40% chance the randomly selected customer will have a heating system.

The sales manager hopes the customer selected is a residential customer with a heating system. Because there are 145 customers in this category, the relative frequency of occurrence method assesses the probability of this event occurring as follows:

$$P(\text{Residential with Heating}) = \frac{145}{500} = 0.29$$

There is a 29% chance the customer selected will be a residential customer with a heating system.

ℰXAMPLE 4-7: RELATIVE FREQUENCY OF OCCURRENCE PROBABILITY ASSESSMENT

Thomas' Dairy Bar   Thomas' Dairy Bar is located in a busy mall in Pittsburgh, Pennsylvania. Thomas' sells ice cream and frozen yogurt products. One of the difficulties in this business is knowing how much of a given product to prepare for the day. The manager is interested in determining the probability that a customer will select yogurt over ice cream. She has maintained records of customer purchases for the past three weeks. The probability can be assessed using relative frequency of occurrence with the following steps:

Step 1:   **Define the events of interest.**
The manager is interested in two events: customer selects yogurt and customer selects ice cream.

Step 2:   **Determine the total number of occurrences.**
In this case, she has observed 2,250 sales of ice cream and yogurt in the past three weeks.

Step 3:   **For the event of interest, determine the number of occurrences.**
In the past three weeks, 1,570 sales were for yogurt and 680 were ice cream.

Step 4:   The probability that a customer will purchase yogurt is found using Equation 4-2.

$$\text{Relative frequency of } E_i = \frac{\text{Number of times } E_i \text{ occurs}}{N} = \frac{1,570}{2,250} = 0.6978$$

Thus, based on past history, the chance that a customer will purchase yogurt is just under 0.70.

Subjective Probability Assessment

Unfortunately, even though managers may have some past experience to guide their decision making, there always will be new factors affecting each decision that make that experience only an approximate guide to the future. In other cases, managers may have little or no past experience and, therefore, may not be able to use a relative frequency of occurrence as even a starting point in assessing the desired probability. When past experience is not available, decision makers must make a **subjective probability assessment**. A subjective probability is a measure of a personal conviction that an outcome will occur. Therefore, in this instance, probability represents a person's belief that an event will occur.

Subjective Probability Assessment

The method that defines probability of an event as reflecting a decision maker's state of mind regarding the chances that the particular event will occur.

Harrison Construction—The Harrison Construction Company is preparing a bid for a road construction project. The company's engineers are very good at defining all the elements of the projects (labor, materials, and so on) and know the costs of these with a great deal of certainty. In finalizing the bid amount, the managers add a profit markup to the projected costs. The problem is how much markup to add. If they add too much, they won't be the low bidder and may lose the contract. If they don't mark it up enough, they may get the project and make less profit than they might have made had they used a higher markup. The managers are considering four possible markup values, stated as percentages of base costs:

| 10% | 12% | 15% | 20% |

To make their decision, the managers need to figure the probability of winning the contract at each of these markup levels. Because they have never done another project exactly like this one, they can't rely on relative frequency of occurrence. Instead, they must subjectively assess the probability based on whatever information they currently have available, such as who the other bidders are, the rapport Harrison has with the potential client, and so forth.

After considering these values, the Harrison managers make the following assessments:

$$P(\text{Win at } 10\%) = 0.30$$
$$P(\text{Win at } 12\%) = 0.25$$
$$P(\text{Win at } 15\%) = 0.15$$
$$P(\text{Win at } 20\%) = 0.05$$

These assessments indicate the managers' state of mind regarding the chances of winning the contract. If new information (for example, a competitor drops out of the bidding) becomes available before the bid is submitted, these assessments could change.

Each of the three methods by which probabilities are assigned to events has specific advantages and specific applications. Regardless of how decision makers arrive at a probability assessment, the rules by which people use these probabilities in decision making are the same.

4-1: EXERCISES

Skill Development

4.1 The following table reflects data that have been collected on a store's customers.

Age	Male	Female
under 20	168	208
20 to 40	340	290
over 40	170	160

a. Using the relative frequency of occurrence approach, what is the probability that a customer is a male?

b. What is the probability that a customer is 20 to 40 years old?

c. What is the joint probability of a customer being 20 to 40 years old and a male?

d. Calculate the probability that a customer selected from the male customers would be under 20 years old. Calculate the same for the female customers. Does it appear that gender is independent of age. Support your answer with calculations and reasons.

4.2 The following data refer to products produced by a company.

Model	Color		
	Blue	Brown	White
XB-50	302	105	200
YZ-99	40	205	130

a. Based on the relative frequency of occurrence method, what is the probability that an item manufactured is brown?

b. What is the probability that the product manufactured is a YZ-99?

c. What is the joint probability that a product manufactured is a YZ-99 and brown?

d. Suppose a product is chosen at random. Consider two events: the event that model YZ-99 was chosen and the event that a white product was chosen. Are these two events mutually exclusive? Explain.

4.3 A room contains four empty chairs. One chair is red. Assuming that the next person who enters the room will select a chair at random, what is the chance that the red chair will be the one selected?

4.4 If a paper carrier has delivered his route for 50 days and during that time has been shorted papers by the publisher five times, what is the probability that he will be shorted tomorrow?

4.5 A study of weather data in a particular area reveals that measurable precipitation has occurred on 25 of the 200 days studied. Based upon this information, what is the probability that it will not rain tomorrow?

4.6 If two customers are asked their opinions on a new product and if their opinion is confined to "Like It" or "Don't Like It," list the sample space of possible responses from the customers. How many of these events indicate a customer likes the product?

4.7 Two thousand people were recently interviewed by a marketing consulting company. Six hundred indicated that they currently smoke. If a follow-up study is to be conducted, what is the probability that a person selected at random from the 2,000 will be a smoker?

Business Applications

4.8 A study of the classified advertisements in a local newspaper shows that 204 are help-wanted ads, 520 are real estate ads, and 306 are for other ads.

a. If the newspaper plans to select an ad at random each week to be published free, what is the probability that the ad for a specific week will be a help-wanted ad?

b. What method of probability assessment is used to determine the probability in part a?

c. Are the events that a help-wanted ad is chosen and that an ad for other types of products or services is chosen for this promotion on a specific week mutually exclusive? Explain?

4.9 A major airline has tracked its on-time status during the past year for flights originating in San Francisco and Los Angeles. The following data reflect the data for 400 flights.

Origination	On-Time Status		
	Early	On Time	Late
San Francisco	25	50	100
Los Angeles	50	100	75

a. Based on these data, what is the probability that a flight from one of the two cities will arrive early?

b. What is the probability that a flight will have originated in Los Angeles?

c. Given that the flight originated in Los Angeles, determine the probability that it will arrive early. What would this probability have to be if the event arriving early were independent from the event in Los Angeles?

d. If three flights are selected at random, list the sample space indicating the possible "on-time" status for all three.

4.10 The manager at Filger's Furniture Store is in the process of negotiating a contract with a new supplier for dining tables. He has assessed the probability that the supplier will take the price he is willing to offer to be 0.70.

a. Explain what type of probability assessment method the manager would use to assess this probability.

b. Would it make sense to use the classical probability assessment approach in this case? Explain.

4.11 The Skateworld Company operates ice rinks in several major cities throughout the United States. During each session of open skating, one customer is selected at random to receive a free pass for a future open skating session. At a recent session there were 150 males and 130 females skating.

a. What is the probability that the person selected for the free pass will be a female?

b. Referring to part a, what method of probability assessment is used to determine the probability?

c. Suppose the company decides to give free passes to two customers. Are the events that a female received the first pass and a male received the second pass independent? Why or why not?

Advanced Business Applications

4.12 A shipping company can send a package through one of three cities (A, B, or C) before it gets to its final destination. Two packages are sent by the company. An elementary event will designate which city each package goes through [e.g., (A, B) will indicate the first package goes through city A and the second through city B]. Assume the package is equally likely to go through any of the cities. List the sample space for the possible cities through which the two packages might go.

a. Using classical probability assessment, determine the probability the first package did go and the second package did not go through city A.

b. Using classical probability assessment, determine the probability that neither of the packages went through city A.

4.13 A gasoline filling station recently began a promotion on its full-service island. If the dollar value shown on the pump stops at $9.99 when the pump clicks off, the customer will get the gasoline free.

a. If we define three events, one for each digit, can we conclude that the three events are independent? Why or why not?

b. Are the three events referred to in part a considered to be mutually exclusive? Why or why not?

c. What is the relationship between mutually exclusive events and independent events? (Hint: Consider two events that are mutually exclusive. If one occurs what is the probability that the other will occur?)

4.14 A Courtyard Hotel by Marriott conducted a survey of its guests. Sixty-two surveys were completed. The data can be found in the file named *CourtyardSurvey*. Based on the survey data, determine the following probabilities using the relative frequency of occurrence method:

a. What is the probability a customer either *probably will* or *definitely will* stay at a Courtyard again?

b. What is the probability the customer is on a business trip?

c. What is the probability that the customer previously has stayed at a Courtyard?

d. What is the joint probability of a customer being on a business trip and rating the hotel *better* than other hotels in the area?

4.15 The ECCO company makes backup alarms for machinery such as forklifts and commercial trucks. When a customer returns one of the alarms under warranty, the quality manager logs data on the product. Using the available data in the file named *ECCO*, use relative frequency of occurrence to find the following probabilities:

a. What is the probability the product was made at the Atlanta plant?

b. What is the probability that the customer returned the product due to a wiring problem?

c. What is the joint probability the returned item was from the Atlanta plant and had a wiring-related problem?

d. What is the probability that a returned item was made on the day shift at the Atlanta plant and had a cracked lens problem?

e. If an item was returned, what is the most likely profile for the item, including plant location, shift, and cause of problem?

4-2 THE RULES OF PROBABILITY

MEASURING PROBABILITIES

The probability attached to an event represents the likelihood the event will occur on a specified trial of an experiment. This probability also measures the perceived uncertainty about whether the event will occur.

Possible Values and Sum

The probability of any event will be between 0 and 1 inclusively. If we are certain about the outcome of an event, we will assign the event a probability of 0 or 1, where $P(E_i) = 0$ indicates the event E_i will not occur, and $P(E_i) = 1$ means that E_i will definitely occur. If we are uncertain about the result of an experiment, we measure this uncertainty by assigning a probability between 0 and 1. Probability Rule 1 shows that the probability of an event occurring is always between 0 and 1.

Probability Rule 1

For any event E_i,

$$0 \le P(E_i) \le 1 \quad \text{for all } i \qquad \text{4-3}$$

All possible elementary events associated with an experiment form the sample space. Therefore, the sum of the probabilities of all possible elementary events is 1, as shown by Probability Rule 2.

Probability Rule 2

$$\sum_{i=1}^{k} P(e_i) = 1 \qquad \text{4-4}$$

where:

k = Number of elementary events in the sample
e_i = ith elementary event

Addition Rule for Elementary Events

If a single event is composed of two or more elementary events, then the probability of the event is found by summing the probabilities of the elementary events. This is illustrated by Probability Rule 3.

Probability Rule 3: Addition Rule for Elementary Events

The probability of an event E_i is equal to the *sum* of the probabilities of the elementary events forming E_i. For example, if

$$E_i = \{e_1, e_2, e_3\}$$

then

$$P(E_i) = P(e_1) + P(e_2) + P(e_3)$$

4-5

Veronica's Cineplex—Veronica's Cineplex is considering opening a 20-screen complex in Lansing, Michigan, and has recently performed a resident survey as part of its decision-making process. One question of particular interest is how often a respondent goes to a movie. Table 4-2 shows the results of the survey for this question.

The sample space for the experiment for each respondent is

$$SS = \{e_1, e_2, e_3, e_4\}$$

where:

$$e_1 = \geq 10 \text{ movies}$$
$$e_2 = 3 \text{ to } 9 \text{ movies}$$
$$e_3 = 1 \text{ to } 2 \text{ movies}$$
$$e_4 = 0 \text{ movies}$$

Using the relative frequency of occurrence approach, we assign the following probabilities.

$$
\begin{aligned}
P(e_1) &= 400/5{,}000 = 0.08 \\
P(e_2) &= 1{,}900/5{,}000 = 0.38 \\
P(e_3) &= 1{,}500/5{,}000 = 0.30 \\
P(e_4) &= 1{,}200/5{,}000 = \underline{0.24} \\
&\phantom{= 1{,}200/5{,}000 =} \Sigma = 1.00
\end{aligned}
$$

Assume we are interested in the event "respondent attends 1 to 9 movies per month."

$$E = \text{Respondent attends 1 to 9 movies}$$

The elementary events that make up E are

$$E = (e_2, e_3)$$

We can find the probability $P(E)$ by using Probability Rule 3, as follows:

$$
\begin{aligned}
P(E) &= P(e_2) + P(e_3) \\
&= 0.38 + 0.30 \\
&= 0.68
\end{aligned}
$$

TABLE 4-2

Veronica's Cineplex Survey Results

Movies Per Month	Frequency	Relative Frequency
≥10	400	0.08
3 to 9	1,900	0.38
1 to 2	1,500	0.30
0	1,200	0.24
Total	5,000	1.00

EXAMPLE 4-8: THE ADDITION RULE FOR ELEMENTARY EVENTS

Cranston Forest Products   The inventory manager at the Cranston Forest Products Company has reported the following data on boards in inventory:

	Dimension		
Length	2″ × 4″	2″ × 6″	2″ × 8″
8 feet	1,400	1,500	1,100
10 feet	2,000	3,500	2,500
12 feet	1,600	2,000	2,400

The manager plans to select one board at random from the inventory to show visiting customers. He is interested in the probability that he will get a $2″ × 4″$ board that is 10 or more feet long. To do this he can employ the following steps.

Step 1:   **Define the elementary events of interest.**
The elementary events of interest deal with the $2″ × 4″$ board length. The following elementary events are defined: e_1 = 8-foot $2″ × 4″$, e_2 = 10-foot $2″ × 4″$, and e_3 = 12-foot $2″ × 4″$.

Step 2:   **Determine the probability of each elementary event.**
The probabilities can be assessed using classical probability assessment. There are 18,000 boards in inventory. Of these, 1,400 are $2″ × 4″$ 8 feet long, 2,000 are $2″ × 4″$ 10 feet long, and 1,600 are $2″ × 4″$ 12 feet long. The probabilities of the three events are

$$P(e_1) = \frac{1,400}{18,000} = 0.0778$$

$$P(e_2) = \frac{2,000}{18,000} = 0.1111$$

$$P(e_3) = \frac{1,600}{18,000} = 0.0889$$

Step 3:   **Define the event for which the probability is desired.**
In this case, the manager is interested in the $2″ × 4″$ boards that are 10 feet or 12 feet long. The elementary events making up this event are

$$2″ × 4″ \text{ boards 10 or more feet} = E = \{e_2, e_3\}$$

Step 4:   **Use Probability Rule 3 to find the desired probability.**
$$P(E) = P(e_2) + P(e_3)$$
$$= 0.1111 + 0.0889$$
$$= 0.2000$$

Complement Rule

Closely connected with Probability Rules 1 and 2 is the **complement** of an event. The complement of an event E is the collection of all possible elementary events not contained in event E. The complement of event E is represented by $\overline{E}$. Thus, the Complement Rule is a corollary to Probability Rules 1 and 2.

Complement Rule

$$P(\overline{E}) = 1 - P(E)$$

4-6

That is, the probability of the complement of event E is 1 minus the probability of event E.

EXAMPLE 4-9: THE COMPLEMENT RULE

Haupert Machinery The sales manager for Haupert Machinery in Medford, Oregon, is preparing to call on a new customer, a building contractor. The sales manager wants to sell the contractor some equipment. Before making the presentation, the manager lists four possible outcomes and his subjectively assessed probabilities related to the sales prospect.

Events (Sales)	P(Sales)
$ 0	0.70
$ 2,000	0.20
$15,000	0.07
$50,000	0.03
	1.00

Note that each probability is between 0 and 1 and that the sum of the probabilities is 1, as required by Rules 1 and 2.

The owner is interested in knowing the probability of sales >$0. This can be found using the complement rule with the following steps:

Step 1: **Determine the probabilities for the events.**

$$P(\$0) = 0.70$$
$$P(\$2,000) = 0.20$$
$$P(\$15,000) = 0.07$$
$$P(\$50,000) = 0.03$$

Step 2: **Find the desired probability.**
Let E be the event sales = $0. The probability of not selling anything to the building contractor is

$$P(E) = 0.70$$

The complement, $\bar{E}$, is all sales >$0. Using the Complement Rule, the probability of sales >$0 is

$$P(\text{Sales} > \$0) = 1 - P(\text{sales} = \$0)$$
$$P(\text{Sales} > \$0) = 1 - 0.70$$
$$P(\text{Sales} > \$0) = 0.30$$

Based on his subjective assessment, there is a 30% chance the sales manager will sell something to the building contractor.

Addition Rule for Two Events

Veronica's Cineplex (continued)—Suppose the people who conducted the survey for Veronica's Cineplex also asked questions about the respondents' ages. The company's managers consider age important in deciding on location because its theaters do better in areas with a younger population base. Table 4-3 shows the breakdown of the sample by age group and by the number of times a respondent goes to a movie per month.

TABLE 4-3

Veronica's Cineplex

MOVIES PER MONTH	E_5 Less than 30	E_6 30 to 50	E_7 Over 50	TOTAL
	AGE GROUP			
E_1 ≥10 Movies	e_1 200	e_2 100	e_3 100	400
E_2 3 to 9 Movies	e_4 600	e_5 900	e_6 400	1,900
E_3 1 to 2 Movies	e_7 400	e_8 600	e_9 500	1,500
E_4 0 Movies	e_{10} 700	e_{11} 500	e_{12} 0	1,200
TOTAL	1,900	2,100	1,000	5,000

TABLE 4-4

Veronica's Cineplex—
Joint Probability Table

MOVIES PER MONTH	AGE GROUP			
	E_5 Less than 30	E_6 30 to 50	E_7 Over 50	TOTAL
E_1 ≥10 Movies	e_1 200/5,000 = 0.04	e_2 100/5,000 = 0.02	e_3 100/5,000 = 0.02	400/5,000 = 0.08
E_2 3 to 9 Movies	e_4 600/5,000 = 0.12	e_5 900/5,000 = 0.18	e_6 400/5,000 = 0.08	1,900/5,000 = 0.38
E_3 1 to 2 Movies	e_7 400/5,000 = 0.08	e_8 600/5,000 = 0.12	e_9 500/5,000 = 0.10	1,500/5,000 = 0.30
E_4 0 Movies	e_{10} 700/5,000 = 0.14	e_{11} 500/5,000 = 0.10	e_{12} 0/5,000 = 0	1,200/5,000 = 0.24
TOTAL	1,900/5,000 = 0.38	2,100/5,000 = 0.42	1,000/5,000 = 0.20	5,000/5,000 = 1

Table 4-3 illustrates two important concepts in data analysis: *joint frequencies* and *marginal frequencies*. Joint frequencies, which were discussed in Chapter 2, are the values inside the table. They provide information on age group and movie viewing jointly. Marginal frequencies are the row and column totals. These values give information on only the age group or only movie attendance.

For example, 2,100 people in the survey are in the 30 to 50 year age group. This column total is a marginal frequency for the age group 30 to 50 years, which is represented by E_6. Now notice that 600 respondents are younger than 30 years old and attend a movie three to nine times a month. The 600 is a joint frequency whose elementary event is represented by e_4. The joint frequencies are the number of times their associated elementary events occur.

Table 4-4 shows the relative frequencies for the data in Table 4-3. These values are the probabilities of the events and elementary events.

Suppose we wish to find the probability of E_4 (0 movies) **or** E_6 (being in the 30-to-50 age group). That is,

$$P(E_4 \text{ or } E_6) = ?$$

To find this probability, we must use Probability Rule 4.

Probability Rule 4: Addition Rule for Any Two Events, E_1 and E_2

$$P(E_1 \text{ or } E_2) = P(E_1) + P(E_2) - P(E_1 \text{ and } E_2) \qquad \text{4-7}$$

The key word in knowing when to use Rule 4 is *or*. The word *or* indicates addition. (You may have covered this concept as a *union* in a math class. $P(E_1 \text{ or } E_2) = P(E_1 \cup E_2)$.). Figure 4-1 is a Venn diagram that illustrates the application of the Addition Rule for Two Events. Notice that the overlap between the two events, E_1 and E_2, is double counted when E_1 is added to E_2. Thus, the overlap, which is E_1 and E_2, needs to be subtracted to avoid the double counting.

FIGURE 4-1

Venn Diagram—Addition
Rule for Two Events

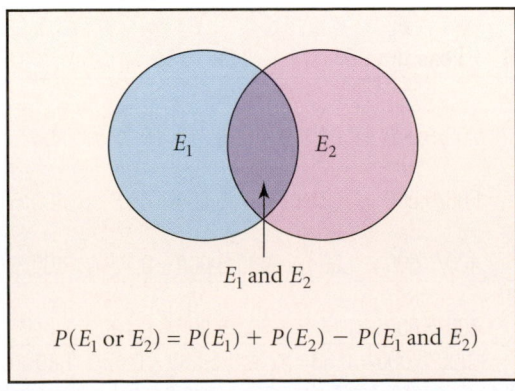

$$P(E_1 \text{ or } E_2) = P(E_1) + P(E_2) - P(E_1 \text{ and } E_2)$$

MOVIES PER MONTH	AGE GROUP			TOTAL
	E_5 Less than 30	E_6 30 to 50	E_7 Over 50	
E_1 $\geq$10 Movies	e_1 200/5,000 = 0.04	e_2 100/5,000 = 0.02	e_3 100/5,000 = 0.02	400/5,000 = 0.08
E_2 3 to 9 Movies	e_4 600/5,000 = 0.12	e_5 900/5,000 = 0.18	e_6 400/5,000 = 0.08	1,900/5,000 = 0.38
E_3 1 to 2 Movies	e_7 400/5,000 = 0.08	e_8 600/5,000 = 0.12	e_9 500/5,000 = 0.10	1,500/5,000 = 0.30
E_4 0 Movies	e_{10} 700/5,000 = 0.14	e_{11} 500/5,000 = 0.10	e_{12} 0/5,000 = 0	1,200/5,000 = 0.24
TOTAL	1,900/5,000 = 0.38	2,100/5,000 = 0.42	1,000/5,000 = 0.20	5,000/5,000 = 1

Referring to the Veronica Cineplex situation, suppose we wish to find the probability of E_4 (0 movies) *or* E_6 (being in the 30-to-50 age group). That is,

$$P(E_4 \text{ or } E_6) = ?$$

Table 4-5 shows the relative frequencies with the events of interest shaded. The overlap corresponds to the *joint occurrence* (intersection) of attending 0 movies *and* being in the 30-to-50 age group. The probability of the overlap is represented by $P(E_4 \text{ and } E_6)$ and must be subtracted. This is done to avoid double counting the probabilities of the elementary events that are in both E_4 and E_6 when calculating the $P(E_4 \text{ or } E_6)$. Thus

$$P(E_4 \text{ or } E_6) = P(E_4) + P(E_6) - P(E_4 \text{ and } E_6)$$
$$= 0.24 + 0.42 - 0.10$$
$$= 0.56$$

Therefore, the probability that a respondent will either be in the 30-to-50 age group or attend a movie less than once a month is 0.56.

What is the probability a respondent will go to 0 movies *or* be in the over-50 age group? Again, we can use Rule 4:

$$P(E_4 \text{ or } E_7) = P(E_4) + P(E_7) - P(E_4 \text{ and } E_7)$$

Table 4-6 shows the relative frequencies for these events. We have

$$P(E_4 \text{ or } E_7) = 0.24 + 0.20 - 0 = 0.44$$

In this case, there were no joint occurrences, so $P(E_4 \text{ and } E_7)$ was assessed as 0, using the relative frequency approach.

MOVIES PER MONTH	AGE GROUP			TOTAL
	E_5 Less than 30	E_6 30 to 50	E_7 Over 50	
E_1 $\leq$10 Movies	e_1 200/5,000 = 0.04	e_2 100/5,000 = 0.02	e_3 100/5,000 = 0.02	400/5,000 = 0.08
E_2 3 to 9 Movies	e_4 600/5,000 = 0.12	e_5 900/5,000 = 0.18	e_6 400/5,000 = 0.08	1,900/5,000 = 0.38
E_3 1 to 2 Movies	e_7 400/5,000 = 0.08	e_8 600/5,000 = 0.12	e_9 500/5,000 = 0.10	1,500/5,000 = 0.30
E_4 0 Movies	e_{10} 700/5,000 = 0.14	e_{11} 500/5,000 = 0.10	e_{12} 0/5,000 = 0	1,200/5,000 = 0.24
TOTAL	1,900/5,000 = 0.38	2,100/5,000 = 0.42	1,000/5,000 = 0.20	5,000/5,000 = 1

EXAMPLE 4-10: ADDITION RULE FOR TWO EVENTS

Cranston Forest Products In Example 4-8, the inventory manager at the Cranston Forest Products Company reported the following data on boards in inventory:

Length	Dimension		
	$2'' \times 4''$	$2'' \times 6''$	$2'' \times 8''$
8 feet	1,400	1,500	1,100
10 feet	2,000	3,500	2,500
12 feet	1,600	2,000	2,400

He will be selecting one board at random from the inventory to show a visiting customer. He is interested in the probability that the board selected will be 8 feet long or a $2'' \times 6''$. To find this probability, he can use the following steps:

Step 1: **Define the events of interest.**
The manager is interested in boards that are 8 feet long.

$$E_1 = \text{8-foot boards}$$

He is also interested in the $2'' \times 6''$ dimension, so

$$E_2 = 2'' \times 6'' \text{ boards}$$

Step 2: **Determine the probability for each event.**
There are 18,000 boards in inventory, and 4,000 of these are 8 feet long, so

$$P(E_1) = \frac{4,000}{18,000} = 0.2222$$

Of the 18,000 boards, 7,000 are $2'' \times 6''$, so the probability is

$$P(E_2) = \frac{7,000}{18,000} = 0.3889$$

Step 3: **Determine whether the two events overlap and if so, compute the joint probability.**
Of the 18,000 total boards, 1,500 are 8 feet long and $2'' \times 6''$. Thus the joint probability is

$$P(E_1 \text{ and } E_2) = \frac{1,500}{18,000} = 0.0833$$

Step 4: **Compute the desired probability using Probability Rule 4.**
$$P(E_1 \text{ or } E_2) = P(E_1) + P(E_2) - P(E_1 \text{ and } E_2)$$
$$P(E_1 \text{ or } E_2) = 0.2222 + 0.3889 - 0.0833$$
$$= 0.5278$$

The chance of selecting an 8-foot board or a $2'' \times 6''$ is just under 0.53.

Addition Rule for Mutually Exclusive Events

We indicated previously that when two events are mutually exclusive, both events cannot occur at the same time. Thus for mutually exclusive events,

$$P(E_1 \text{ and } E_2) = 0$$

Therefore when you are dealing with mutually exclusive events, the addition rule assumes a special form, shown as Rule 5.

Probability Rule 5: Addition Rule for Mutually Exclusive Events

For two mutually exclusive events E_1 and E_2:

$$P(E_1 \text{ or } E_2) = P(E_1) + P(E_2)$$

4-8

Figure 4-2 is a Venn diagram illustrating the application of the Addition Rule for Mutually Exclusive Events.

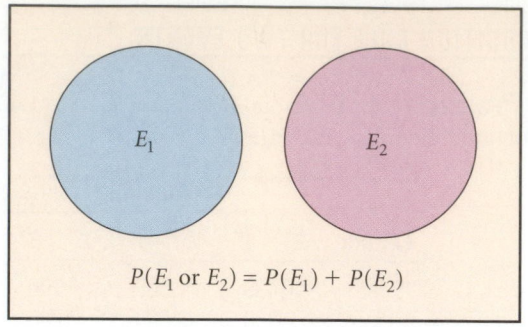

$$P(E_1 \text{ or } E_2) = P(E_1) + P(E_2)$$

CONDITIONAL PROBABILITY

In dealing with probabilities, you will often need to determine the chances of two or more events occurring either at the same time or in succession. For example, a quality control manager for a manufacturing company may be interested in the probability of selecting two successive defective products from an assembly line. If the probability of this event is low, the quality control manager will be surprised when it occurs and might readjust the production process. In other instances, the decision-maker might know that an event has occurred and may want to know the probability of a second event occurring. For instance, suppose that an oil company geologist who believes oil will be found at a certain drilling site makes a favorable report. Because oil is not always found at locations with a favorable report, the oil company's exploration vice president might well be interested in the probability of finding oil, given the favorable report.

Situations such as this refer to a probability concept known as **conditional probability**.

Conditional Probability

The probability that an event will occur *given* that some other event has already happened.

Probability Rule 6 offers a general rule for conditional probability. The notation, $P(E_1|E_2)$, reads probability of event E_1 *given* event E_2 has occurred. Thus, the probability of one event is conditional upon a second event having occurred.

Probability Rule 6: Conditional Probability for Any Two Events

For any two events E_1, E_2:

$$P(E_1|E_2) = \frac{P(E_1 \text{ and } E_2)}{P(E_2)}$$

4-9

where:

$$P(E_2) > 0$$

Rule 6 uses a *joint probability*, $P(E_1 \text{ and } E_2)$, and *a marginal probability*, $P(E_2)$, to calculate the conditional probability $P(E_1|E_2)$. Note that to find a conditional probability, we find the ratio of how frequently E_1 occurs to the total number of observations, given that we restrict our observations to only those cases in which E_2 has occurred.

West.net—West.net, an Internet service provider, is in an increasingly competitive industry. The company has studied its customers' Internet habits. Among the information collected are the data shown in Table 4-7.

TABLE 4-7

West.net Example

HOURS PER MONTH	GENDER		
	E_4 Female	E_5 Male	TOTAL
E_1 <20	e_1 450	e_2 500	950
E_2 20 to 40	e_3 300	e_4 800	1,100
E_3 >40	e_5 100	e_6 350	450
TOTAL	850	1,650	2,500

TABLE 4-8

West.net Example

HOURS PER MONTH	GENDER E_4 Female	E_5 Male	TOTAL
E_1 <20	e_1 450/2,500 = 0.18	e_2 500/2,500 = 0.2	950/2,500 = 0.38
E_2 20 to 40	e_3 300/2,500 = 0.12	e_4 800/2,500 = 0.32	1,100/2,500 = 0.44
E_3 >40	e_5 100/2,500 = 0.04	e_6 350/2,500 = 0.14	450/2,500 = 0.18
TOTAL	850/2,500 = 0.34	1,650/2,500 = 0.66	2,500/2,500 = 1.00

The company is focusing on high-volume users, and one of the factors that will influence West.net's marketing strategy is whether time spent using the Internet is related to a customer's gender. For example, suppose the company knows a user is female and wants to know the chances this woman will spend between 20 and 40 hours a month on the Internet. Let:

$$E_2 = \{e_3,\ e_4\} = \text{Event: Person uses services 20 to 40 hours per month}$$
$$E_4 = \{e_1,\ e_3,\ e_5\} = \text{Event: User is female}$$

A marketing analyst needs to know the probability of E_2 *given* E_4.

Table 4-8 shows the frequencies and relative frequencies of interest. One way to find the desired probability is as follows.

1. We know E_4 has occurred (customer is female). There are 850 females in the survey.
2. Of the 850 females, 300 use Internet services 20 to 40 hours per month.
3. Then,

$$P(E_2|E_4) = \frac{300}{850}$$
$$= 0.35$$

However, we can also apply Rule 6, as follows:

$$P(E_2|E_4) = \frac{P(E_2 \text{ and } E_4)}{P(E_4)}$$

From Table 4-8, we get the joint probability $P(E_2 \text{ and } E_4) = 0.12$ and

$$P(E_4) = 0.34$$

Then,

$$P(E_2|E_4) = \frac{0.12}{0.34} = 0.35$$

EXAMPLE 4-11: COMPUTING CONDITIONAL PROBABILITIES

Retirement Planning   After the Enron Corporation collapse in late fall, 2001, in which thousands of Enron employees lost most or all of their retirement savings, many people began to take a closer look at how their own retirement money is invested. A recent survey conducted by a major financial publication yielded the following table.

AGE OF INVESTOR	PERCENTAGE OF RETIREMENT INVESTMENTS IN THE STOCK MARKET <5%	5 < 10%	10 < 30%	30 < 50%	50% or More	TOTAL
<30 years	70	240	270	80	55	715
30 < 50 years	90	300	630	1,120	1,420	3,560
50 < 65 years	110	305	780	530	480	2,205
65+ years	200	170	370	260	65	1,065
TOTAL	470	1,015	2,050	1,990	2,020	7,545

The publication's editors are interested in knowing the probability that someone 65 or older will have 50% or more of their retirement funds invested in the stock market. Assuming the data collected in this study reflect the population of investors, the editors can find this conditional probability using the following steps:

Step 1:   **Define the events of interest.**
In this case, we are interested in two events:

$$E_1 = 65 \text{ years or older}$$
$$E_2 = 50\% \text{ or more in stocks}$$

Step 2:   **Define the probability statement of interest.**
The editors are interested in:

$$P(E_2 \mid E_1) = \text{probability of } 50\% \text{ stocks } given \text{ 65 and older}$$

Step 3:   **Convert the data to probabilities using the relative frequency of occurrence method of assessment.**
We begin with the event that is given to have occurred (E_1). A total of 1,065 people in the study were 65+ years of age. Of the 1,065 people, 65 had 50% or more of their retirement funds in the stock market.

$$P(E_2 \mid E_1) = \frac{65}{1,065} = 0.061$$

Thus, the conditional probability that someone 65 or older will have 50% or more of their retirement assets in the stock market is 0.061. This value can be found using Step 4 as well.

Step 4:   **Use Probability Rule 6 to find the conditional probability.**

$$P(E_2 \mid E_1) = \frac{P(E_1 \text{ and } E_2)}{P(E_1)}$$

The necessary probabilities are found using the relative frequency of occurrence method

$$P(E_1) = \frac{1,065}{7,545} = 0.1412$$

and the joint probability is

$$P(E_1 \text{ and } E_2) = \frac{65}{7,545} = 0.0086$$

Then using Probability Rule 6 we get:

$$P(E_2 \mid E_1) = \frac{P(E_1 \text{ and } E_2)}{P(E_1)} = \frac{0.0086}{0.1412} = 0.061$$

Tree Diagrams

Another way of organizing the events of an experiment that aids in the calculation of probabilities is the *tree diagram*.

West.net (cont.)—Figure 4-3 illustrates the tree diagram for West.net. Note that the branches at each node in the tree diagram represent mutually exclusive events. Moving from left to right, the first two branches indicate the two customer types (male and female—mutually exclusive events). Three branches grow from each of these original branches, representing the three possible categories for Internet use. The probabilities for the events male and female are shown on the first two branches. The probabilities shown on the right of the tree are the joint probability for each combination of gender and hours of use. These figures are found using Table 4-8, which was shown earlier. The probabilities on the branches following the male and female branches showing hours of

FIGURE 4-3

Tree Diagram for West.net

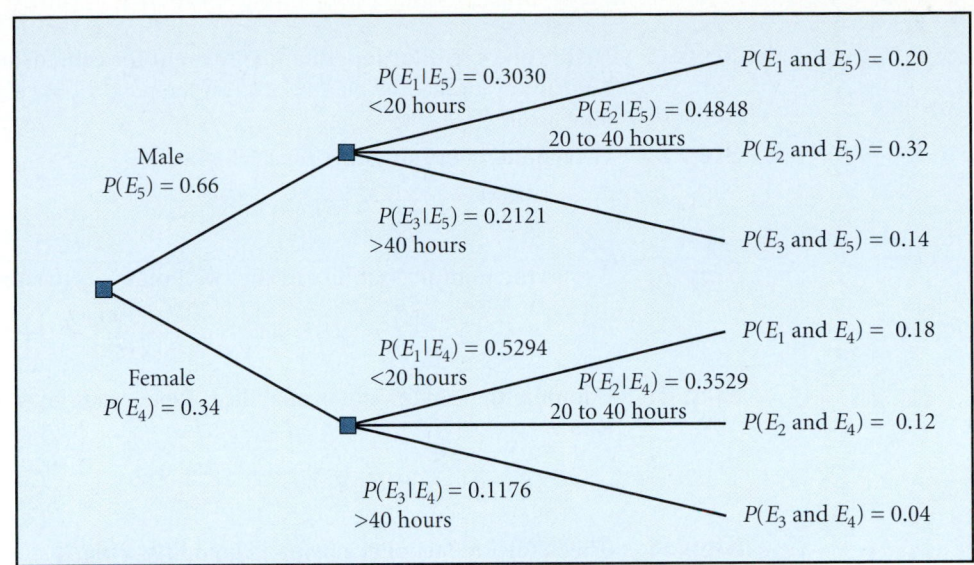

use are conditional probabilities. For example, we can find the probability that a male customer (E_5) will spend more than 40 hours on the Internet (E_3) by

$$P(E_3|E_5) = \frac{P(E_3 \text{ and } E_5)}{P(E_5)} = \frac{0.14}{0.66} = 0.2121$$

Conditional Probability for Independent Events

We earlier discussed that two events are independent if the occurrence of one event has no bearing on the probability that the second event occurs. Therefore, when two events are independent, the rule for conditional probability takes a special form, as indicated in Probability Rule 7.

Probability Rule 7: Conditional Probability for Independent Events

For independent events E_1, E_2:

$$P(E_1|E_2) = P(E_1); \quad P(E_2) > 0 \qquad \textbf{4-10}$$

and

$$P(E_2|E_1) = P(E_2); \quad P(E_1) > 0$$

As Rule 7 shows, the conditional probability of one event occurring, given a second independent event has already occurred, is simply the probability of the first occurring.

EXAMPLE 4-12: CHECKING FOR INDEPENDENCE

Cranston Forest Products   In Examples 4-8 and 4-10, the inventory manager at the Cranston Forest Products Company reported the following data on boards in inventory:

Length	Dimension $2'' \times 4''$	$2'' \times 6''$	$2'' \times 8''$
8 feet	1,400	1,500	1,100
10 feet	2,000	3,500	2,500
12 feet	1,600	2,000	2,400

He will be selecting one board at random from the inventory to show a visiting customer. Of interest is whether the length of the board is independent of the dimension. This can be determined using the following steps:

Step 1: **Define one event for length and one event for dimension.**
Let E_1 = event that the board is 10 feet long and E_2 = event that the board is a $2'' \times 6''$ dimension.

Step 2: **Determine the probability for each event.**

$$P(E_1) = \frac{8,000}{18,000} = 0.4444 \qquad \text{and} \qquad P(E_2) = \frac{7,000}{18,000} = 0.3889$$

Step 3: **Assess the joint probability of the two events occurring.**

$$P(E_1 \text{ and } E_2) = \frac{3,500}{18,000} = 0.1944$$

Step 4: **Compute the conditional probability of one event given the other using Probability Rule 6.**

$$P(E_1 | E_2) = \frac{P(E_1 \text{ and } E_2)}{P(E_2)} = \frac{0.1944}{0.3889} = 0.4999$$

Step 5: **Check for independence using Probability Rule 7.**
Because $P(E_1 | E_2) = 0.4999 \neq P(E_1) = 0.4444$, the two events are not independent and, therefore, board length and board dimension are not independent.

MULTIPLICATION RULES

We needed the joint probability of two events in the discussion on addition of two events and in the discussion on conditional probability. We were able to find $P(E_1 \text{ and } E_4)$ simply by examining the joint relative frequency tables. However, we often need to find $P(E_1 \text{ and } E_2)$ when we do not know the joint relative frequencies. When this is the case, we can use the multiplication rule for two events.

Multiplication Rule for Two Events

Probability Rule 8: Multiplication Rule for Any Two Events

For two events, E_1 and E_2:

$$P(E_1 \text{ and } E_2) = P(E_1)P(E_2 | E_1) \qquad \textbf{4-11}$$

Real Computer Co.—To illustrate how to find a joint probability, consider an example involving classical probability. Real Computer Co., a manufacturer of personal computers, uses two suppliers for CD-ROM drives. These parts are intermingled in the manufacturing-floor inventory rack. When a computer is assembled, the CD-ROM unit is pulled randomly from inventory without regard to which company made it. Recently a customer ordered two personal computers. At the time of assembly, the CD-ROM inventory contained 30 MATX units and 50 Quinex units. What is the probability that both computers ordered by this customer will have MATX units?

To answer this question, we must recognize that two events are required to form the desired outcome. Therefore, let

E_1 = Event: MATX CD-ROM on first computer
E_2 = Event: MATX CD-ROM on second computer

The probability that both computers contain MATX units is written as $P(E_1 \text{ and } E_2)$. The key word here is *and*, as contrasted with the addition rule, in which the key word is *or*. The *and* signifies that we are interested in the joint probability of two events, as noted by $P(E_1 \text{ and } E_2)$. To find this probability, we employ Probability Rule 8.

$$P(E_1 \text{ and } E_2) = P(E_1)P(E_2 | E_1)$$

We start by assuming that each CD-ROM in the inventory has the same chance of being selected for assembly. For the first computer,

$$P(E_1) = \frac{\text{Number of MATX units}}{\text{Number of CD-ROMs in inventory}}$$

$$= \frac{30}{80} = 0.375$$

Then, because we are not replacing the first CD-ROM, we find $P(E_2|E_1)$ by

$$P(E_2|E_1) = \frac{\text{Number of remaining MATX units}}{\text{Number of remaining CD-ROM units}}$$

$$= \frac{29}{79} = 0.3671$$

Now, by Rule 8,

$$P(E_1 \text{ and } E_2) = P(E_1)P(E_2|E_1) = (0.375)(0.3671)$$
$$= 0.1377$$

Therefore, there is a 13.77% chance the two personal computers will get MATX CD-ROM drives.

Using a Tree Diagram

Real Computer (continued)—A tree diagram can be used to display the situation facing the computer manufacturer. The two branches on the left side of the tree in Figure 4-4 show the possible CD-ROM options for the first computer. The two branches coming from each of the first branches show the possible CD-ROM options for the second computer. The probabilities at the far right are the joint probabilities for the CD-ROM options for the two computers. As we determined previously, the probability that both computers will get a MATX unit is 0.1377, as shown on the top right on the tree diagram.

We can use the multiplication rule and the addition rule in one application when we determine the probability that two systems will have different CD-ROMs. Looking at Figure 4-4, we see there are two ways this can happen.

$$P[(\text{MATX and Quinex}) \textit{ or } (\text{Quinex and MATX})] = ?$$

If the first CD-ROM is a MATX and the second one is a Quinex, then the first cannot be a Quinex and the second a MATX. These two events are mutually exclusive and, therefore, Rule 6 can be used to calculate the required probability. The joint probabilities (generated from the multiplication rule) are shown on the right side of the tree. To find the desired probability, using Rule 6 we can add the two joint probabilities:

$$P[(\text{MATX and Quinex}) \textit{ or } (\text{Quinex and MATX})] =$$
$$0.2373 \qquad + \qquad 0.2373 \qquad = 0.4746$$

The chance that a customer buying two computers will get two different CD-ROMs is 47.46%.

FIGURE 4-4

**Tree Diagram for
the CD-Rom Example**

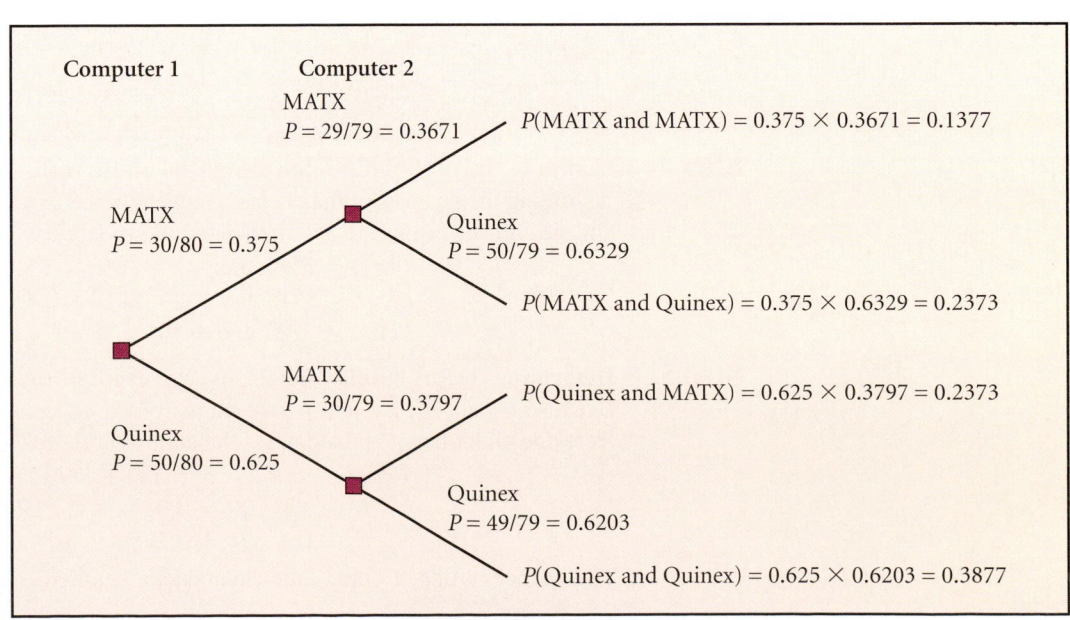

Multiplication Rule for Independent Events

When we determined the probability that two computers would have an MATX CD-ROM unit, we used the general multiplication rule (Rule 8). The general multiplication rule requires that conditional probability be used because the result for the second computer depends on the CD-ROM selected for the first computer. The chance of obtaining a MATX was lowered from 30/80 to 29/79, given the first CD-ROM was a MATX.

However, if the two events of interest are *independent*, the imposed condition does not alter the probability, and the multiplication rule takes the form shown in Probability Rule 9.

Probability Rule 9: Multiplication Rule for Independent Events

For independent events E_1, E_2:

$$P(E_1 \text{ and } E_2) = P(E_1)P(E_2)$$

4-12

The joint probability of two independent events is simply the product of the marginal probabilities of the two events. Rule 9 is the primary way that you can determine whether any two events are independent. If the product of the probabilities of the two events equals the joint probability, then the events are independent.

$\mathcal{E}$XAMPLE 4-13: USING THE MULTIPLICATION RULE AND THE ADDITION RULE

Medlin Accounting   Medlin Accounting prepares tax returns for individuals and companies. Over the years, the firm has tracked its clients and has discovered that 12% of the individual returns have been selected for audit by the Internal Revenue Service. On one particular day, the firm signed two new individual tax clients. The firm is interested in the probability that at least one of these clients will be audited. This probability can be found using the following steps:

Step 1:   **Define the overall event of interest.**
The event that Medlin Accounting is interested in is
$$E = \text{at least one client is audited}$$

Step 2:   **Define the elementary events.**
For a single client, the following elementary events are defined:
$$A = \text{audit}$$
$$N = \text{no audit}$$
For each of the clients, we define the elementary events as:

Client 1: A_1	and	N_1
Client 2: A_2	and	N_2

Step 3:   **List the sample space for the events of interest.**
The possible outcomes for which at least one client will be audited are as follows:

E_1:	A_1	A_2	both are audited
E_2:	A_1	N_2	} one client is audited
E_3:	N_1	A_2	

Step 4:   **Compute the probabilities for the events of interest.**
Assuming the chances of the clients being audited are independent of each other, probabilities for the events are determined using Probability Rule 9 for independent events:
$$P(E_1) = P(A_1 \text{ and } A_2) = 0.12 \times 0.12 = 0.0144$$
$$P(E_2) = P(A_1 \text{ and } N_2) = 0.12 \times 0.88 = 0.1056$$
$$P(E_3) = P(N_1 \text{ and } A_2) = 0.88 \times 0.12 = 0.1056$$

Step 5:   **Determine the probability for the overall event of interest.**
Because events E_1, E_2, and E_3 are mutually exclusive, compute the probability of at least one client being audited using the addition rule for mutually exclusive events:
$$P(E_1 \text{ or } E_2 \text{ or } E_3) = P(E_1) + P(E_2) + P(E_3)$$
$$= 0.0144 + 0.1056 + 0.1056$$
$$= 0.2256$$
The chance of one or both of the clients being audited is 0.2256.

BAYES' THEOREM

As decision makers, you will often encounter situations that require you to assess probabilities for events of interest. Your assessment may be based on relative frequency of occurrence or subjectivity. However, you may then come across new information that causes you to revise the probability assessment. For example, a human resource manager who has interviewed a person for a sales job might assess a low probability that the person will succeed in sales. However, after seeing the person's very high score on the company's sales aptitude test, the manager might revise her assessment upward. A medical doctor might assign an 80% chance that a patient has a particular disease. However, after seeing positive results from a lab test, he might increase his assessment to 95%.

In these situations, you will need a way to formally incorporate the new information. One very useful tool for doing this is called *Bayes' Theorem,* which is named for the Reverend Thomas Bayes, who developed the special application of conditional probability in the 1700s. Letting event B be an event that is given to have occurred, the conditional probability of event E_i occurring can be computed using Equation 4-9:

$$P(E_i \mid B) = \frac{P(E_i \text{ and } B)}{P(B)}$$

The numerator can be reformulated using the multiplication rule (Equation 4-11) as:

$$P(E_i \text{ and } B) = P(E_i)P(B \mid E_i)$$

The conditional probability is then:

$$P(E_i \mid B) = \frac{P(E_i)P(B \mid E_i)}{P(B)}$$

The denominator, $P(B)$, can be found by adding the probability of the k ways that event B can occur. This is

$$P(B) = P(E_1)P(B \mid E_1) + P(E_2)P(B \mid E_2) + \cdots + P(E_k)P(B \mid E_k)$$

Then Bayes' Theorem is formulated as Equation 4-13.

Bayes' Theorem

$$P(E_i \mid B) = \frac{P(E_i)P(B \mid E_i)}{P(E_1)P(B \mid E_1) + P(E_2)P(B \mid E_2) + \cdots + P(E_k)P(B \mid E_k)} \qquad \text{4-13}$$

where:

$$E_i = i \text{th event of interest of the } k \text{ possible events}$$
$$B = \text{Event that has occurred that might impact } P(E_i)$$

Events E_1 to E_k are mutually exclusive and collectively exhaustive.

Varden Soap Co.—The Varden Soap Company has two production facilities, one in Ohio and one in Virginia. The company makes the same type of soap at both facilities. The Ohio plant makes 60% of the company's total soap output, and the Virginia plant 40%. All soap from the two facilities is sent to a central warehouse, where it is intermingled. After extensive sampling, the quality assurance manager has determined that 5% of the soap produced in Ohio and 10% of the soap produced in Virginia is unusable due to quality problems. When the company sells a defective product, it incurs not only the cost of replacing the item but also the loss of goodwill. The vice president for production would like to allocate these costs fairly between the two plants. To do so, he knows he must first determine the probability that a defective item was produced by a particular production line. Specifically, he needs to answer these questions:

1. What is the probability that the soap was produced at the Ohio plant, given that the soap is defective?
2. What is the probability that the soap was produced at the Virginia plant, given that the soap is defective?

In notation form, with D representing the occurrence of a defective item, what the manager wants to know is

$$P(\text{Ohio plant} \mid D) = ?$$
$$P(\text{Virginia plant} \mid D) = ?$$

We can use Bayes' Theorem to determine these probabilities, as follows.

$$P(Ohio|D) = \frac{P(Ohio)P(D|Ohio)}{P(D)}$$

We know that D(defective soap) can happen if it is made in either Ohio or Virginia. Thus,

$$P(D) = P(Ohio)P(D|Ohio) + P(Virginia)P(D|Virginia)$$

We already know that 60% of the soap comes from Ohio and 40% from Virginia. So, $P(Ohio) = 0.60$ and $P(Virginia) = 0.40$. These are called the *prior* probabilities. Without Bayes' Theorem, we would likely allocate the total cost of defects in a 60/40 split between Ohio and Virginia, based on total production. However, the new information about the quality from each line is

$$P(D|Ohio) = 0.05 \quad \text{and} \quad P(D|Virginia) = 0.10$$

which can be used to properly allocate the cost of defects. This is done using Bayes' Theorem.

$$P(Ohio|D) = \frac{P(Ohio)P(D|Ohio)}{P(Ohio)P(D|Ohio) + P(Virginia)P(D|Virginia)}$$

then,

$$P(Ohio|D) = \frac{(0.60)(0.05)}{(0.60)(0.05) + (0.40)(0.10)} = 0.4286$$

and

$$P(Virginia|D) = \frac{P(Virginia)P(D|Virginia)}{P(Virginia)P(D|Virginia) + P(Ohio)P(D|Ohio)}$$

$$P(Virginia|D) = \frac{(0.40)(0.10)}{(0.40)(0.10) + (0.60)(0.05)} = 0.5714$$

These probabilities are called the *revised* probabilities. The prior probabilities have been revised given the new quality information. We now see that 42.86% of the cost of defects should be allocated to the Ohio plant, and 57.14% should be allocated to the Virginia plant.

Note, the denominator $P(D)$ is the overall probability of defective soap. This probability is

$$\begin{aligned}P(D) &= P(Ohio)P(D|Ohio) + P(Virginia)P(D|Virginia) \\ &= (0.60)(0.05) + (0.40)(0.10) \\ &= 0.03 + 0.04 \\ &= 0.07\end{aligned}$$

Thus, 7% of all the soap made by Varden is defective.

You might prefer to use a tabular approach like that shown in Table 4-9 when you apply Bayes' Theorem. Another alternative is to use a tree diagram, as illustrated in the following example.

Bayes' Theorem Using a Tree Diagram

IRS Audit—This year experts project that 20% of all taxpayers will file an incorrect tax return. The Internal Revenue Service (IRS) itself is not perfect. IRS audits indicate there is an error when no problem exists about 10% of the time. The audits also indicate no error with a tax return when in fact there really is a problem about 30% of the time.

The IRS has just notified a taxpayer there is an error in his return. What is the probability that the return actually has an error? We use the following notation:

$$\begin{aligned}E &= \text{the return actually contains an error} \\ NE &= \text{the return contains no error} \\ AE &= \text{audit says an error exists} \\ ANE &= \text{audit says no error}\end{aligned}$$

TABLE 4-9 Bayes' Theorem Calculations for Varden Soap	Events	Prior Probabilities	Conditional Probabilities	Joint Probability	Revised Probability
	Ohio	0.60	0.05	(0.60)(0.05) = 0.03	0.03/0.07 = 0.4286
	Virginia	0.40	0.10	(0.40)(0.10) = 0.04	0.04/0.07 = 0.5714
				0.07	1.0000

FIGURE 4-5

Tree Diagram for the IRS
Audit Example

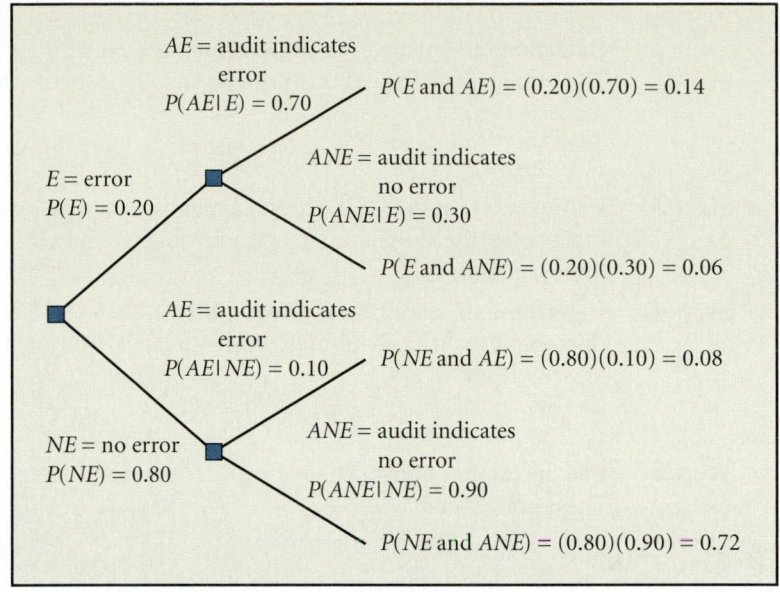

Then, we are interested in determining the following:

$$P(E \mid AE) = ?$$

We know the following:

$$P(E) = 0.20 \qquad P(ANE \mid E) = 0.30 \qquad P(AE \mid NE) = 0.10$$
$$P(ANE \mid NE) = 0.90 \qquad P(AE \mid E) = 0.70$$

We need to use Bayes' Theorem to determine the probability of interest. A tree diagram can be used to do this. Figure 4-5 shows the tree diagram and probabilities. Now,

$$P(E \mid AE) = \frac{P(E \text{ and } AE)}{P(AE)} = ?$$

From Figure 4-5 we see that $P(E \text{ and } AE) = 0.14$. To find $P(AE)$, we add the probabilities of the ways in which AE occurs (audit says an error occurred), because those two ways are mutually exclusive.

$$P(AE) = P(E \text{ and } AE) + P(NE \text{ and } AE) = 0.14 + 0.08 = 0.22$$

Then,

$$P(E \mid AE) = \frac{P(E \text{ and } AE)}{P(AE)} = \frac{0.14}{0.22} = 0.6364$$

The probability that the return contains an error, given that the IRS audit indicates an error exists, is 63.64%.

EXAMPLE 4-14: BAYES' THEOREM

Techtronics Equipment Corporation   The Techtronics Equipment Corporation has developed a new electronic device that it would like to sell to the U.S. military for use in fighter aircraft. The sales manager believes there is a 0.60 chance that the military will place an order. However, after making an initial sales presentation, military officials will often ask for a second presentation to other military decision makers. Historically, 70% of successful companies are asked to make a second presentation, whereas 50% of unsuccessful companies are asked back a second time. Suppose Techtronics Equipment has just been asked to make a second presentation, what is the revised probability that the company will make the sale? This probability can be determined using the following steps:

Step 1:   **Define the events.**
In this case, there are two events:

$$S = \text{sale} \qquad N = \text{no sale}$$

Step 2: **Determine the prior probabilities for the events.**
The probability of the events prior to knowing whether a second presentation will be requested are

$$P(S) = 0.60 \qquad P(N) = 0.40$$

Step 3: **Define an event that if it occurs, could alter the prior probabilities.**
In this case, the altering event is the invitation to make a second presentation. We label this event as SP.

Step 4: **Determine the conditional probabilities.**
The conditional probabilities are associated with being invited to make a second presentation:

$$P(SP \mid S) = 0.70 \qquad P(SP \mid N) = 0.50$$

Step 5: **Use the tabular approach for Bayes' Theorem to determine the *revised probabilities*.** These correspond to

$$P(S \mid SP) \qquad \text{and} \qquad P(N \mid SP)$$

Event	Prior Probability	Conditional Probability	Joint Probability	Revised Probability
S = sale	0.60	$P(SP\|S) = 0.70$	$P(S)P(SP\|S) = (0.60)(0.70) = 0.42$	0.42/0.62 = 0.6774
N = no sale	0.40	$P(SP\|N) = 0.50$	$P(S)P(SP\|S) = (0.40)(0.50) = \underline{0.20}$	0.20/0.62 = $\underline{0.3226}$
			0.62	1.0000

Thus, using Bayes' Theorem, if Techtronics Equipment gets a second presentation opportunity, the probability of making the sale is revised upward from 0.60 to 0.6774.

4-2: EXERCISES

Skill Development

4.16 You are given the following table:

	A	B	C
D	100	150	50
E	600	150	150
F	300	300	300

a. What is the probability of event A?
b. What is the probability of event A and B?
c. What is the probability of event B and F?
d. What is the probability of event E given that event A has occurred?
e. What is the probability of event A or event F?

4.17 Historically, on Christmas the weather in a certain Midwest city has occurred according to the following distribution:

Event	Relative Frequency
Clear and dry	0.20
Cloudy and dry	0.30
Rain	0.40
Snow	0.10

a. Based on these data, what is the probability that next Christmas will be dry?
b. Based on the data, what is the probability that next Christmas will be rainy or cloudy and dry?
c. Suppose next Christmas is dry, determine the probability that it will also be cloudy.

4.18 The television schedule lists three different sitcoms in each of three consecutive 30-minute time slots on channels 2, 6, and 7.
a. What is the probability that a person will randomly select programs using all three stations over the course of the 1.5 hours?
b. Suppose you know that the person who will randomly select programs will watch at least two of the sitcoms on the same channel. Determine the probability that the person will watch all three sitcoms on the same channel.

4.19 Your neighbor has just returned from a trip to Atlantic City and claims to have a foolproof method to make money on the roulette wheel. She knows the odds are slightly with the house on any single spin. However, she claims that all you need to do is to watch the wheel and any time three successive rolls have the same color bet the next roll on the opposite color. Comment on her technique.

4.20 A store carries sweaters in three colors (brown, gray, and red). Assume the store has an unlimited number of sweaters and that customers select color at random.
  a. What is the probability that three customers will select the same color?
  b. Determine the probability that the three customers will not all select the same color.

4.21 A paint store carries three brands of paint. A customer arrives and wants to buy another gallon of paint to match paint that she purchased at the store previously. She can't recall the brand name and does not wish to return home to find the old can of paint. She selects two of the three brands of paint at random and buys them.
  a. What is the probability that she matched the paint?
  b. Her husband also goes to the paint store and fails to remember what brand to buy. He also purchases two of the three brands of paint at random. Determine the probability that both the woman and her husband fail to get the correct brand of paint. (Hint: Are the two events independent?)

4.22 A fast-food restaurant has determined that the chance that a customer will order a soft drink is 0.90. The chance that a customer will order a hamburger is 0.60. The chance that a customer will order French fries is 0.50.
  a. If a customer places an order, what is the probability that the order will include a soft drink and no fries if these two events are independent?
  b. The restaurant has also determined that if a customer orders a hamburger the chance the customer will also order fries is 0.80. Determine the probability that the order will include a hamburger and fries.

4.23 If 15 of the Fortune 500 companies have their headquarters in Michigan and 6 have their headquarters in Maryland, what is the probability that of 2 firms selected at random from the 500, one would have Michigan headquarters and one would have Maryland headquarters?

Business Applications

4.24 The Fortune 500 ranks the 500 largest U.S. corporations. The 1998 list revealed that 30 firms have their headquarters in Ohio. What is the probability that a firm selected at random from the list would have its headquarters in Ohio?

4.25 A local ski area offers private ski lessons with professionally qualified ski instructors. There are three ski instructors available. One is Austrian, one is German, and the third is from the United States. According to company policy, the instructors are assigned randomly. Thus, when a customer calls, a random selection is made and the selected instructor is scheduled with that customer.
  a. On a given day, five customers call for lessons. Of these, four are assigned to the German instructor and one to the American. What is the probability of this happening if the assignments are random?
  b. On a different day, three customers call for lessons and all three are assigned to the German instructor. What is the probability of this happening?
  c. Referring to parts a and b, compute the probability that both the outcomes for day one and day two happen. Based on this probability, is there any cause for concern that the ski-lesson assignment may not be random? Explain.

4.26 A local photocopy shop has three black-and-white copy machines and two color copiers. Based on historical data, the chance that each black-and-white copier will be down for repairs is 0.10. The color copiers are more of a problem and are down 20% of the time each.
  a. Based on this information, what is the probability that, if a customer needs a color copy, both color machines will be down for repairs?
  b. If a customer wants both a color copy and a black-and-white copy, what is the probability that the necessary machines will be available? (Assume that the color copier can also be used to make a black-and-white copy if needed.)
  c. If the manager wants to have at least a 99% chance of being able to furnish a black-and-white copy upon demand, is the present configuration sufficient? (Assume that the color copier can also be used to make a black-and-white copy if needed.) Back up your answer with appropriate probability computations.
  d. What is the probability that all five copies will be up and running at the same time? Suppose the manager added a fourth black-and-white copier, how would the probability of all copiers being ready at any one time be affected?

4.27 Refer to Exercise 4.26. The owners of the photocopy shop are going to open a new photocopy store. They wish to meet the increasing demand for color photocopies and have more reliable service. As a goal, they would like to have at least a 99.9% chance of being able to furnish a black-and-white copy or a color copy upon demand. They also wish to purchase only four copiers. They have asked for your advice regarding the mix of black-and-white and color copiers. Supply them with your advice. Provide calculations and reasons to support your advice.

4.28 The Skiwell Manufacturing Company gets materials for its cross-country skis from two suppliers. Supplier A's materials make up 30% of what is used, with supplier B providing the rest. Past records indicate that 15% of supplier A's materials are defective, and 10% of B's are defective. Because it is impossible to tell which supplier the materials came from once they are in inventory, the manager wants to know which supplier most likely supplied the defective materials the foreman has brought to his attention. Provide the manager this information.

4.29 Alpine Cannery is currently processing vegetables from the summer harvest. The manager has found a case of cans that has not been properly sealed. There are three lines that processed cans of this type, and the manager wants to know which line is most likely to be responsible for this mistake. Provide the manager this information.

Line	Contribution to Total	Proportion Defective
1	0.40	0.05
2	0.35	0.10
3	0.25	0.07

4.30 Cascade paint mixes paint in three separate plants and then ships the unmarked cans to a central warehouse. Plant A supplies 50% of the paint, and past records indicate that the paint is incorrectly mixed 10% of the time. Plant B contributes 30%, with a defective rate of 5%. Plant C supplies 20%, with paint mixed incorrectly 20% of the time. If Cascade guarantees its product and spent $10,000 replacing improperly mixed paint last year, how should the cost be distributed among the three plants?

4.31 The Chocolate House specializes in hand-dipped chocolates for special occasions. Recently, several long-time customers have complained about the quality of the chocolates. It seems there are several partially covered chocolates in each box. The defective chocolates should have been caught when the boxes were packed. The manager is wondering which of the three packers is not doing the job properly. Clerk 1 packs 40% of the boxes and usually has a 2% defective rate. Clerk 2 packs 30% with a 2.5% defective rate. Clerk 3 boxes 30% of the chocolates, and her defective rate is 1.5%. Which clerk is most likely responsible for the boxes that raised the complaints?

4.32 As the owner of the Union Nursery, Kelly is concerned about the quality of some of the plants purchased from a local wholesaler but is not certain why the problem has suddenly cropped up. The company has been buying plants from this particular wholesaler for years, and the quality has always been excellent. A new employee of Kelly's who worked for the wholesaler explains that just before he left his previous position, the wholesaler started purchasing plants from a new grower in order to meet demand. The old grower has a good reputation and only 2% of his plants are unusable. The new grower's plants are of poor quality 30% of the time. The old grower currently supplies 80% of the wholesaler's plants. If Kelly buys a plant that is poor quality, which grower most likely supplied the plants?

4.33 The Carlisle Medical Clinic has five doctors on staff. The doctors have agreed to keep the office open on Saturdays but with only three doctors. The office manager has decided to make up Saturday schedules in such a way that no set of three doctors will be in the office together more than once. How many weeks can be covered by this schedule? (Hint: Use a tree diagram to list the sample space.)

4.34 In the late 1960s, the U.S. government instituted a lottery system for determining how young men 18 to 26 years old would be drafted into military service. Balls, each marked with a different day of the year (365 of them), were placed in a large drum and mixed. Balls were selected from the drum randomly.
   a. What is the probability that the first two balls selected were for birthdays in March?
   b. What is the probability that the first ball selected was a December birthday or a birthday on the first of any month?
   c. If the first ball selected was a March birthday, what is the probability that the second ball selected was a June birthday?
   d. What is the probability that the first three balls selected were for birthdays in the same month?

4.35 The Ace Construction Company has submitted a bid on a state government project in Delaware. The price of the bid was predetermined in the bid specifications. The contract is to be awarded on the basis of a blind drawing from those who have bid. Five other companies have also submitted bids.
   a. What is the probability of Ace Construction winning the bid?
   b. Suppose that there are two contracts to be awarded by a blind draw. What is the probability of Ace winning both contracts?
   c. Referring to part b, what is the probability of Ace not winning either contract?
   d. Referring to part b, what is the probability of Ace winning exactly one contract?
   e. Referring to part b, what is the probability of Ace winning at least one contract?

Advanced Business Applications

4.36 A manager of a gasoline filling station is thinking about a promotion that she hopes will bring in more business to the full-service island. She is considering the option that when a customer requests a fill-up, if the pump stops with the dollar amount at $9.99, the customer will get the gasoline free. Previous studies show that 70% of customers pay $10.00 or more when they fill up their gas tanks, so they would not be eligible for the free gas. What is the probability that a customer will get free gas at this station if the promotion is implemented?

4.37 Referring to Exercise 4.36, suppose the manager is concerned about alienating customers who buy $10.00 or more, because they would not be eligible to win free gas under the original concept. To overcome this, she is thinking about changing the contest. A customer will get free gas if any of the following happens:

$9.99	$11.11	$12.22	$13.33	$14.44	$15.55
$16.66	$17.77	$18.88	$19.99		

Past data show that only 5% of all customers spend $20.00 or more. If one of these big-volume customers arrives, he or she will get a blind draw of a ball from a box containing 100 balls (99 red, 1 white). If the white ball is picked, the customer will get a free tank of gas. Considering this new promotion, what is the probability that a customer will get free gas?

4.38 🔘 A Courtyard Hotel by Marriott conducted a survey of its guests. Sixty-two surveys were completed. Based upon the data from the survey, found in the file named *CourtyardSurvey*, determine the following probabilities using the relative frequency of occurrence method.
a. Two customers are selected. What is the probability that both will be on a business trip?
b. What is the probability that a customer will be on a business trip or will experience a hotel problem during a stay at the Courtyard?
c. What is the probability that a customer on business will have an in-state-area-code phone number?

d. Based on the data, can the Courtyard manager conclude that a customer's rating regarding staff attentiveness is independent of whether he or she is traveling on business, pleasure, or both? Use the rules of probability to make this determination.

4.39 🔘 The ECCO company makes backup alarms for machinery, such as forklifts and commercial trucks. When a customer returns one of the alarms under warranty, the quality manager logs data on the product. Using the available data in the *ECCO* file, use relative frequency of occurrence to find the following probabilities.
a. If a part was made in the Atlanta plant, what is the probability the cause of the returned part was due to wiring?
b. If the company incurs a $30 cost for each returned alarm, what percentage of the cost should be assigned to each plant?

4-3 INTRODUCTION TO PROBABILITY DISTRIBUTIONS

RANDOM VARIABLES

As discussed earlier in this chapter, when a random experiment or trial is performed, some outcome, or event, must occur. When the trial or experiment has a quantitative characteristic, we can associate a number with each outcome. For example, an inspector who examines three sheets of plywood can judge each sheet as "acceptable" or "unacceptable." The outcome of the experiment defines a **random variable** in which the specific number of acceptable sheets of plywood is

$$x = \{0, 1, 2, 3\}$$

Although the inspector knows these are the possible values for the variable before she samples, she does not know which will occur in any given trial. Further, the value of the random variable may vary each time three plywood sheets are inspected.

Random Variable

A variable that assigns a numerical value to each outcome of a random experiment or trial.

Two classes of random variables exist: **discrete random variables** and **continuous random variables**. For instance, if a bank auditor randomly examines 15 accounts to verify the accuracy of the balances, the number of inaccurate account balances can be represented by a discrete random variable with the following values:

$$x = \{0, 1, \ldots 15\}$$

Discrete Random Variable

A random variable that can only assume a countable number of values.

In another situation, 10 employees were recently hired by a major electronics company. The number of females in that group can be described as a discrete random variable with possible values equal to:

$$x = \{0, 1, 2, 3, \ldots 10\}$$

Notice that the value for a discrete random variable is often determined by counting. In the bank auditing example, the variable, x, is determined by counting the number of accounts with errors. In the hiring example, the value for the variable, x, is determined by counting the number of females hired.

In other situations, the random variable is said to be continuous.

Continuous Random Variables

Random variables that can assume any value in an interval.

For example the exact time it takes a trainee to perform a job task may be any value between two points, say 1 minute and 10 minutes. If x is the time required, then x is continuous because, if measured precisely enough, the possible values, x, can be any value in the interval 1 to 10 minutes.[1] Other examples of continuous variables include measures of distance and measures of weight when measured precisely. A continuous random variable is generally defined by measuring, which is contrasted with a discrete random variable, whose value is typically determined by counting.

Comparing Discrete and Continuous Probability Distributions Graphically

The probability distribution for a discrete random variable is composed of the values the variable can assume and the probabilities associated with the variable assuming those values. For example, if three parts are tested to determine if they are defective, the probability distribution for number of defectives might be

x = Number of Defectives	$P(x)$
0	0.10
1	0.30
2	0.40
3	0.20
	1.00

Graphically, the discrete probability distribution associated with these defectives can be represented by the areas of rectangles in which the base is one unit wide and the height corresponds to the probability. The areas of the rectangles sum to 1.

The probability distribution of a continuous random variable is represented by a probability density function that defines a curve. The area under the curve corresponds to the probabilities for the random variable. Figure 4-6 illustrates the relationship of discrete probability distributions and a typical probability density function. Figure 4-6(a) shows a discrete random variable with only three possible outcomes. Figure 4-6(b) shows the probability distribution for a discrete variable that has 21 possible outcomes. Note, as the number of possible outcomes increases, the distribution becomes smoother. In Figure 4-6(c), the graph of the continuous variable is a smooth curve. This smooth curve represents the probability density function for a continuous variable.

The total area (probability) under the density function curve is equal to 1. In addition, the probability that the variable will have a value between any two points $P(a < x < b)$, on the continuous scale equals the area under the curve between these two points. However, for any chosen x value, $P(x) = 0$. This indicates the probability that a continuous random variable will assume a specific value is zero. Thus, when dealing with continuous random variables, we will determine probabilities for ranges of values and not for specific values. For instance, we might ask, "What is the probability of a student in this class weighing 160 pounds?" If we mean exactly 160.0000 pounds, the probability is zero. But we could find the probability of a weight between 159.5 and 160.5 pounds by finding the area under the probability density function between these two values. If we want the probability of a student weighing less than 160 pounds, we would need to find the area under the probability density function to the left of 160 pounds.

Both discrete and continuous probability distributions have extensive applications in business decision-making situations. In the remainder of this section we discuss several important issues that are of particular importance to discrete probability distributions. We will follow this in Chapter 5 with further discussion of discrete and continuous distributions.

---

[1]If the time were observed to the nearest minute, then there would only be 10 possible values (a countable number) for the random variable. It would then be considered a discrete random variable.

FIGURE 4-6

**Probability Density
Functions Versus Discrete
Probability Distributions**

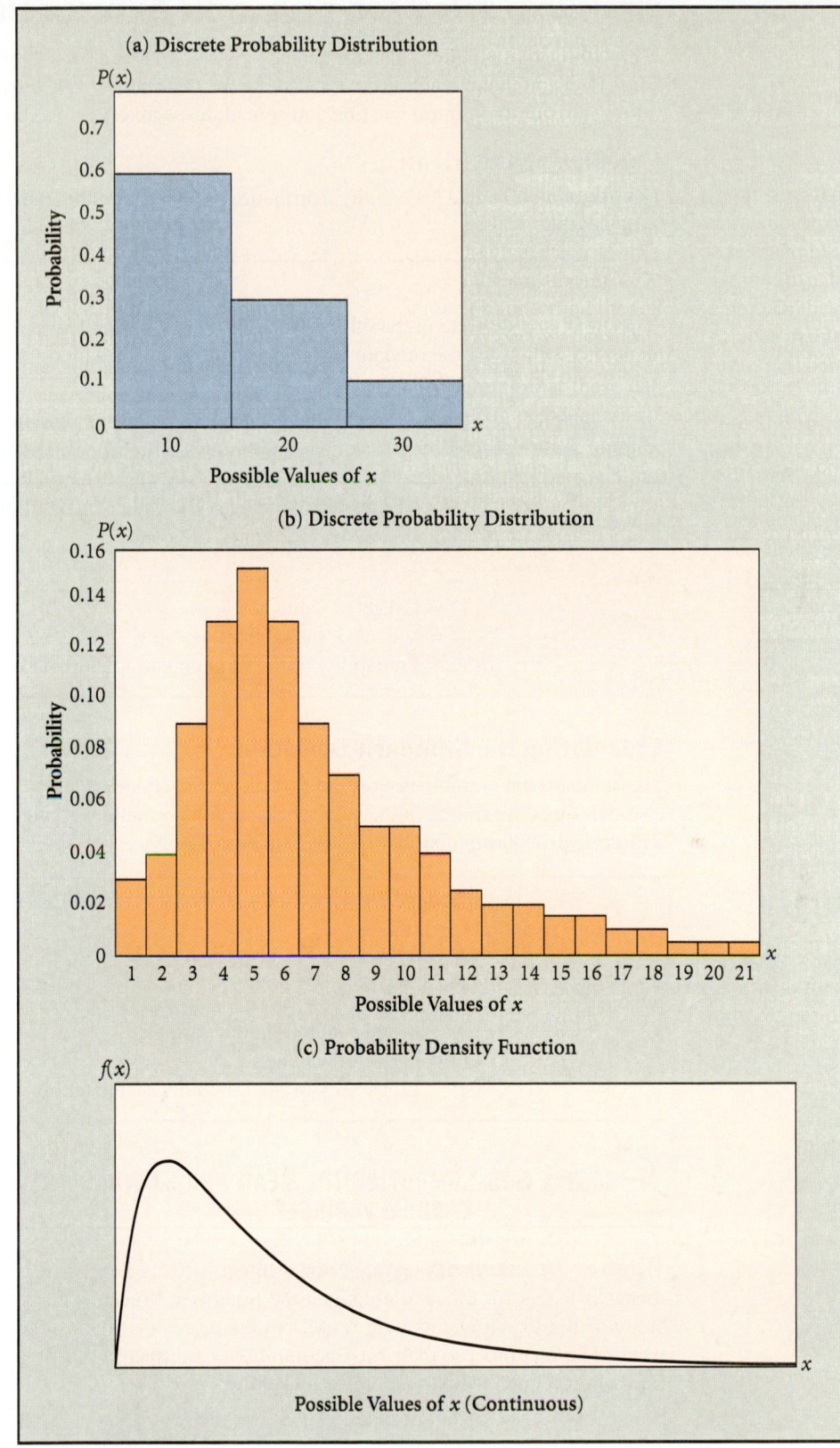

(a) Discrete Probability Distribution

(b) Discrete Probability Distribution

(c) Probability Density Function

MEAN AND STANDARD DEVIATION OF DISCRETE DISTRIBUTIONS

A probability distribution, like a frequency distribution, can be only partially described by a graph. Often decision makers will need to calculate the distribution's *mean* and *standard deviation*. These values measure the central location and spread, respectively, of the probability distribution.

Calculating the Mean

The mean of a discrete probability distribution is also called the **expected value** of the discrete random variable.

Expected Value

The mean of a discrete probability distribution. The average value when the experiment that generates values for the random variable is repeated over the long run.

The expected value is actually a *weighted average* of the random variable values, in which the weights are the probabilities assigned to the values. The expected value is given in Equation 4-14.

Expected Value of a Discrete Distribution

$$E(x) = \sum x P(x)$$

4-14

where:

$E(x)$ = Expected value of x

x = Values of the random variable

$P(x)$ = Probability of the random variable taking on the value x

Calculating the Standard Deviation

The standard deviation measures the spread, or dispersion, in a set of data. The standard deviation also measures the spread in the values of a random variable. To calculate the standard deviation for a discrete probability distribution, use Equation 4-15.

Standard Deviation of a Discrete Probability Distribution

$$\sigma_x = \sqrt{\sum [x - E(x)]^2 P(x)}$$

4-15

where:

x = Values of the random variable

$E(x)$ = Expected value of x

$P(x)$ = Probability of the random variable taking on the value x

EXAMPLE 4-15: COMPUTING THE MEAN AND STANDARD DEVIATION OF A DISCRETE RANDOM VARIABLE

Wagner Investments   Wagner Investment is located in Fairfax, West Virginia. The company manages assets for clients throughout the Southeast. Recently the managing partner conducted a study of the firm's clients with respect to the number of their stock transactions during the past week. The random variable, x, is the number of transactions per client, ranging from 0 to 3. The following frequency distribution was developed.

x	Frequency
0	120
1	72
2	30
3	78
	$\sum = 300$

Assuming that these data reflect the typical week, the manager wishes to develop a discrete probability distribution and compute the mean and standard deviation for the distribution. This can be done using the following steps:

Step 1: **Convert the frequency distribution into a probability distribution using the relative frequency of occurrence method.**

x	Frequency
0	120/300 = 0.40
1	72/300 = 0.24
2	30/300 = 0.10
3	78/300 = 0.26
	Σ = 1.00

Step 2: **Compute the expected value using Equation 4-14.**

$$E(x) = \Sigma\, xP(x)$$
$$E(x) = 0(0.40) + 1(0.24) + 2(0.10) + 3(0.26)$$
$$= 1.22$$

The expected number of stock trades per week is 1.22 per client.

Step 3: **Compute the standard deviation using Equation 4-15 or the shortcut algebraic equivalent.**

$$\sigma_x = \sqrt{\Sigma[x - E(x)]^2 P(x)} \;\; = \sqrt{\Sigma\, x^2 P(x) - [E(x)]^2}$$
$$= \sqrt{0^2(0.40) + 1^2(0.24) + 2^2(0.10) + 3^2(0.26) - [1.22]^2}$$
$$= 1.2213$$

The expected value and the standard deviation are virtually the same for this probability distribution.

WORKING WITH TWO DISCRETE RANDOM VARIABLES

So far we have discussed the basics of discrete random variables, including how to find the expected value and standard deviation. Each example and application has focused on a single random variable. However, there are many instances in which business decision making will involve working with two or more random variables simultaneously. Decision makers need tools for working with two discrete random variables.

Expected Value of the Sum of Two Discrete Random Variables

The expected value of a random variable was defined previously as the mean outcome for the random variable, and it is computed using Equation 4-14.

$$E(x) = \Sigma\, xP(x)$$

If we have two random variables, x and y, and we wish to know the expected value of the sum of the two variables, Equation 4-16 is used.

Expected Value of the Sum of Two Random Variables

$$E(x + y) = E(x) + E(y)$$ **4-16**

The expected value of the sum of two random variables is the sum of the two expected values.

$\mathcal{E}$XAMPLE 4-16: FINDING THE EXPECTED VALUE OF THE SUM OF TWO RANDOM VARIABLES

White, Barney & Associates   At White, Barney & Associates, investment clients are offered opportunities to invest in both stock and bond mutual funds. Suppose an individual has $10,000 to invest and is considering splitting the investment equally between a stock fund and a bond fund.

The returns that will be earned on each of these investments are thought to be related to what will happen to interest rates during the coming year. After discussions with her broker, the investor has subjectively assessed the following probability distribution for interest rates and the associated return for each investment that will occur during the coming year:

Interest Rate	Probability	x Stock Return	y Bond Return
Increase	0.20	−$1,000	$300
No Change	0.30	$ 400	$500
Decrease	0.50	$ 900	−$200

The investor is interested in knowing the expected total return if she invests in both the stock fund and the bond fund. To determine this, she can use the following steps:

Step 1: **Compute the expected value of each random variable using Equation 4-14.**
For variable x, the stock-fund return, we use $E(x) = \sum xP(x)$, and for variable y, the bond fund, we use $E(y) = \sum yP(y)$. These expected values are

x	$P(x)$	$xP(x)$	y	$P(y)$	$yP(y)$
−$1,000	0.20	−$200	$300	0.20	$ 60
$ 400	0.30	$120	$500	0.30	$150
$ 900	0.50	$450	−$200	0.50	−$100
		$\sum = \$370$			$\sum = \$110$

Thus, $E(x) = \$370$ and $E(y) = \$110$.

Step 2: **Add the expected values.**
Using Equation 4-16, we get:

$$E(x + y) = E(x) + E(y)$$
$$= \$370 + \$110$$
$$= \$480$$

The investor can expect to earn $480 from the two investments.

Covariance of Two Discrete Random Variables

You may also be interested in determining the extent to which two discrete random variables are jointly related. That is, to what extent do the values of the two variables move together? A measure of this joint relationship is called the **covariance**. Equation 4-17 can be used to compute the covariance.

Covariance

$$\sigma_{xy} = \sum [x_i - E(x)][y_j - E(y)]P(x_i y_j)$$

4-17

where:

x_i = Possible values of the x discrete random variable
y_j = Possible values of the y discrete random variable
$P(x_i y_j)$ = Joint probability of values of x_i and y_j occurring

---

The covariance can be positive or negative depending on whether the two variables move together in the same or opposite directions. If the covariance is zero or close to zero, this implies that the two variables do not move closely together.

EXAMPLE 4-17: COMPUTING THE COVARIANCE

White, Barney & Associates Example 4-16 introduced an investor at White, Barney & Associates who was planning to invest in both a stock fund and a bond fund. She assessed the following probability distributions for the returns that would be earned on the investments over the coming year:

Interest Rate	P(xy) Probability	x Stock Return	y Bond Return
Increase	0.20	−$1,000	$300
No Change	0.30	$ 400	$500
Decrease	0.50	$ 900	−$200

She determined that her total expected return for the two investments was $480. Now she is interested in determining the extent to which the returns on these two investments move together. This is measured by the covariance and can be computed using the following steps.

Step 1: **Compute the expected values of each random variable.**
Refer to Example 4-16, in which we found:

$$E(x) = \$370 \quad \text{and} \quad E(y) = \$110$$

Step 2: **Find the joint probabilities for all possible pairs of outcomes for the two discrete random variables.**
In this example, because returns were tied to interest rate movements, the joint probabilities are given. For example, the joint probability of $x = -\$1,000$ and $y = \$300$ (associated with an increase in interest rates) is assessed as 0.20. Thus, in the above table, $P(xy)$ are the joint probabilities for each combination of x and y.

Step 3: **Use Equation 4-17 to compute the covariance.**

$$\sigma_{xy} = \Sigma[x_i - E(x)][y_j - E(y)]P(x_i y_j)$$

x	y	P(xy)	x − E(x)	y − E(y)	[x − E(x)][y − E(y)]	[x − E(x)][y − E(y)]P(xy)
−1,000	300	0.20	−1,370	190	−260,300	−52,060
400	500	0.30	30	390	11,700	3,510
900	−200	0.50	530	−310	−164,300	−82,150
						$\sigma_{xy} = -130,700$

The covariance for these two investments is −130,700. The negative sign indicates the two variables tend to move in opposite directions as interest rates change. Note, the covariance is not in the original units (dollars) because it was computed using the product of two dollar amounts.

Correlation Between Two Discrete Random Variables

As Example 4-17 showed, the covariance between two random variables provides information about whether the two variables move in the same or opposite directions. However, the covariance alone does not measure the strength of the relationship between the two variables. Instead, a measure called the **correlation coefficient** is used to measure the strength of the linear relationship between two variables.

Correlation Coefficient

A quantitative measure of the strength of the linear relationship between two variables. The correlation ranges from −1.0 to +1.0. A correlation of ±1.0 indicates a perfect linear relationship, whereas a correlation of 0.0 indicates no linear relationship.

If two variables have a strong linear relationship, the correlation will be close to ±1.0, depending on whether they move in the same or opposite directions. The correlation coefficient is computed using Equation 4-18. Note, the numerator in the correlation coefficient equation is the covariance between the two variables. Therefore, if the covariance is positive, the correlation will be positive and vice versa.

Correlation Coefficient

$$\rho = \frac{\sigma_{xy}}{\sigma_x \sigma_y}$$

4-18

where:

ρ = Correlation coefficient (rho)

σ_{xy} = Covariance between variables x and y

σ_x = Standard deviation of variable x

σ_y = Standard deviation of variable y

EXAMPLE 4-18: COMPUTING THE CORRELATION COEFFICIENT

White, Barney & Associates   Examples 4-16 and 4-17 introduced an investor who was going to invest in a stock fund and a bond fund. She assessed the following probability distributions for the return on each investment at different interest rates. These distributions are shown as follows:

Interest Rate	P(xy) Probability	x Stock Return	y Bond Return
Increase	0.20	−$1,000	$300
No Change	0.30	$ 400	$500
Decrease	0.50	$ 900	−$200

The investor is interested in measuring the strength of the linear relationship between these two investment options. To do this, she can compute the correlation coefficient using the following steps:

Step 1:   **Compute the covariance between the two variables using Equation 4-17.**
Refer to Example 4-17, in which the covariance was computed using

$$\sigma_{xy} = \Sigma[x_i - E(x)][y_j - E(y)]P(x_i y_j)$$

The value for the covariance was −130,700, which indicated that the relationship between the two variables is negative.

Step 2:   **Compute the standard deviation for each discrete random variable using Equation 4-15.**
Recall from Example 4-16 that the expected values of variables x and y were

$$E(x) = 370 \qquad \text{and} \qquad E(y) = 110$$

Then the standard deviations are

$$\sigma_x = \sqrt{\Sigma[x_i - E(x)]^2 P(x_i)} = \sqrt{(-1,000 - 370)^2(.20) + (400 - 370)^2(.30) + (900 - 370)^2(.50)}$$
$$= \sqrt{516,100} = 718.401$$

$$\sigma_y = \sqrt{\Sigma[y_j - E(y)]^2 P(y_j)} = \sqrt{(300 - 110)^2(.20) + (500 - 110)^2(.30) + (-200 - 110)^2(.50)}$$
$$= \sqrt{100,900} = 317.648$$

Step 3:   **Compute the correlation coefficient using Equation 4-18.**

$$\rho = \frac{\sigma_{xy}}{\sigma_x \sigma_y} = \frac{-130,700}{(718.401)(317.648)} = -0.573$$

The correlation between the stock and bond investments is −0.573, indicating a negative linear relationship.

4-3: EXERCISES

Skill Development

4.40 Examine this discrete probability distribution.

x	P(x)
10	0.05
15	0.20
25	0.40
40	0.35

a. Find the expected value, variance, and standard deviation.
b. Develop a graphical picture of the discrete probability distribution.

4.41 Given this discrete probability distribution:

x	P(x)
100	0.30
150	0.40
160	0.30

a. Find the expected value of x.
b. Find the variance of x.
c. Find the standard deviation of x.

4.42 Four possible prizes are being awarded by a real estate developer to people who will look at new property. The prizes are being awarded based on a blind drawing with the following probability distribution:

x	P(x)
$ 10	0.80
$ 20	0.10
$ 100	0.08
$1,000	0.02

a. What is the expected prize award?
b. What is the standard deviation for the prize award?
c. If one person is allowed to have two chances at the drawing and keep the highest prize, what is the probability that she will leave with at least $100?

4.43 At one Las Vegas casino, if you bet $5 that a 12 will come up as the total points on two dice, and you win, you will get back $50. If any total other than 12 comes up, you get back $0. Based on the assumption that the dice are fair, what is the expected payoff for placing this bet?

4.44 An investment opportunity has the following possible net returns and associated probabilities:

x = return	P(x)
$ 500	0.25
$ 1,000	0.40
$ 5,000	0.30
$10,000	0.05

a. If you have the opportunity to participate in this investment opportunity, what is your expected net return?

b. Suppose you have the opportunity to participate in this investment situation twice. What is the probability that you will have a total net return of more than $10,000?

4.45 The following probability distributions are given for two discrete random variables, x and y.

x	y	P(x)	P(y)
100	500	0.25	0.25
200	300	0.40	0.40
300	400	0.20	0.20
400	600	0.15	0.15

Find the expected value for the sum of the two random variables.

4.46 The following probability distributions are given for two discrete random variables, x and y.

x	y	P(x)	P(y)	P(xy)
100	500	0.25	0.25	0.10
200	300	0.40	0.40	0.50
300	400	0.20	0.20	0.30
400	600	0.15	0.15	0.10

Determine the covariance for the two random variables. Is the relationship positive or negative?

4.47 The following probability distributions are given for two discrete random variables, x and y.

x	y	P(x)	P(y)	P(xy)
100	500	0.25	0.25	0.10
200	300	0.40	0.40	0.50
300	400	0.20	0.20	0.30
400	600	0.15	0.15	0.10

Compute the correlation coefficient and indicate what it means with respect to these two variables.

Business Applications

4.48 For the past four years, Armonco Manufacturing has been offering a three-year limited warranty on all appliances it manufactures. Although all appliances are given a unique serial number when manufactured, until this year Armonco had no capability of determining how often any appliance was brought to an authorized service facility. At the beginning of the year, the long-promised computer database linking all service facilities with a central system was finally operational. A preliminary report shows the following results for one of the appliances Armonco manufactures.

Times Brought for Repair	Probability
0	0.55
1	0.25
2	0.14
3	0.04
4	0.02

a. Find the expected number of repairs for this appliance.
b. Find the standard deviation of this repair distribution.
c. If the average cost of a service call is $40, provide an estimate for the average cost of a warranty for Armonco per year for this appliance.

4.49 The Seremonte Emergency Medical Department has recorded the number of emergency calls received each day for the past 200 days. These data are shown in this frequency distribution.

Calls	Number of Days
0	22
1	20
2	40
3	55
4	28
5	20
6	5
7	10
	200

a. Determine the probability distribution based on the frequency distribution.
b. What is the mean of the probability distribution?
c. What is the standard deviation of the probability distribution?
d. Compute the coeffiecient of variation.
e. Each emergency call requires a team of three individuals to respond. How many employees must Seremonte have so they can respond to at least 75% of the emergency calls?

4.50 The Nu-Look Car Wash recently opened at a new location. The manager at this location is concerned about staffing levels, so he has taken a sample of 100 days from the company's other location and has found the following frequency distribution.

Cars	Frequency
0 and under 10	10
10 and under 20	17
20 and under 30	35
30 and under 40	22
40 and under 50	16
	100

a. Use the midpoints of each class to develop a probability distribution for the number of cars arriving at the car wash.
b. Determine the expected number of cars.
c. Determine the variance and standard deviation.
d. Two employees wash each car. It takes approximately 20 minutes to wash each car. Determine the number of employees the manager must have on hand each day to meet demand at least 85% of the days.

4.51 Refer to Exercise 4.50. The manager of Nu-Look Car Wash has had complaints from his employees. He pays them each $2 a car. However, on some days there just aren't very many cars to wash and on others there are lots of cars. The employees' wages vary substantially. The manager, therefore, has offered a salary of $6 an hour to any employee who wishes to accept. Suppose you are advising the employees. What would you advise them to do? (Hint: You may wish to calculate the probability distribution, average dollars earned, and standard deviation under the two systems of pay.)

4.52 Adams Car Sales owns two used-car dealerships in suburban Detroit. The following table is a joint frequency distribution for the number of cars sold each day at the two dealerships. Note, the sample consists of 1,100 days.

		Location A				
		0	1	2	3	4	Total
	0	10	40	50	50	50	200
	1	30	60	90	50	20	250
Location B	2	20	60	50	70	100	300
	3	10	30	40	20	50	150
	4	30	10	70	10	80	200
	Total	100	200	300	200	300	1,100

a. Using the relative frequency of occurrence approach for assessing probabilities, convert the joint frequency distri-bution table to a joint probability distribution.
b. Compute the expected number of cars sold per day at each of the two locations.
c. Compute the expected value for the sum of cars sold at the two dealerships.
d. Compute the covariance.
e. Compute the correlation coefficient and discuss what it means.

Summary and Conclusions

Probability provides decision makers a quantitative measure of the chance a particular outcome will occur. Probability allows decision makers to quantify uncertainty. The objectives of this chapter have been to discuss the various types of probability and to provide the basic rules that govern probability operations. In addition, we have introduced the basic concepts associated with discrete probability distributions, including how to compute the expected value and standard deviation for discrete distributions.

By understanding the basic rules of probability, you will be able to effectively measure the chances of events of interest occurring. If you need to combine probabilities, the addition rule and the multiplication rule are useful in specific instances. Bayes' Theorem helps when dealing with conditional probabilities in special circumstances and in revising prior probabilities based on new information. Table 4-10 presents a summary classification of several of the basic rules of probability.

TABLE 4-10

Probability Rules Summary

Event Type	KEYWORD "OR" Addition Rule	KEYWORD "AND" Multiplication Rule	KEYWORD "GIVEN" Conditional Rule
Mutually Exclusive	$P(A \text{ or } B) = P(A) + P(B)$	$P(A \text{ and } B) = 0$	$P(A \mid B) = 0$
Independent	$P(A \text{ or } B) = P(A) + P(B) - P(A \text{ and } B)$	$P(A \text{ and } B) = P(A) \times P(B)$	$P(A \mid B) = P(A)$
Dependent	$P(A \text{ or } B) = P(A) + P(B) - P(A \text{ and } B)$	$P(A \text{ and } B) = P(A)P(B \mid A)$	$P(A \mid B) = \dfrac{P(A \text{ and } B)}{P(B)}$

Chapter 5 expands on the discussion of probability and introduces several very useful discrete and continuous probability distributions, including the binomial, Poisson, hypergeometric and normal distributions, which will be used throughout the remainder of the text.

EQUATIONS

Classical Probability Measurement

$$P(E_i) = \frac{\text{Number of ways } E_i \text{ can occur}}{\text{Total number of elementary events}} \qquad \textbf{4-1}$$

Relative Frequency of Occurrence

$$RF(E_i) = \frac{\text{Number of times } E_i \text{ occurs}}{N} \qquad \textbf{4-2}$$

Probability Rule 1
For any event E_i

$$0 \le P(E_i) \le 1 \quad \text{for all } i \qquad \textbf{4-3}$$

Probability Rule 2

$$\sum_{i=1}^{k} P(e_i) = 1 \qquad \textbf{4-4}$$

Probability Rule 3
Addition rule for elementary events:

The probability of an event E_i is equal to the *sum* of the probabilities of the elementary events forming E_i. For example, if

$$E_i = \{e_1, e_2, e_3\}$$

then

$$P(E_i) = P(e_1) + P(e_2) + P(e_3) \qquad \textbf{4-5}$$

Complement Rule

$$P(\overline{E}) = 1 - P(E) \qquad \textbf{4-6}$$

Probability Rule 4
Addition rule for any two events E_1 and E_2:

$$P(E_1 \text{ or } E_2) = P(E_1) + P(E_2) - P(E_1 \text{ and } E_2) \quad \textbf{4-7}$$

Probability Rule 5
Addition rule for mutually exclusive events E_1, E_2:

$$P(E_1 \text{ or } E_2) = P(E_1) + P(E_2) \qquad \textbf{4-8}$$

Probability Rule 6
Conditional probability for any two events E_1, E_2:

$$P(E_1 \mid E_2) = \frac{P(E_1 \text{ and } E_2)}{P(E_2)} \qquad \textbf{4-9}$$

Probability Rule 7
Conditional probability for independent events E_1, E_2:

$$P(E_1 \mid E_2) = P(E_1); \qquad P(E_2) > 0 \qquad \textbf{4-10}$$

and

$$P(E_2 \mid E_1) = P(E_2); \qquad P(E_1) > 0$$

Probability Rule 8
Multiplication rule for two events, E_1 and E_2:

$$P(E_1 \text{ and } E_2) = P(E_1)P(E_2 \mid E_1) \qquad \textbf{4-11}$$

Probability Rule 9
Multiplication rule for independent events E_1, E_2:

$$P(E_1 \text{ and } E_2) = P(E_1)P(E_2) \qquad \textbf{4-12}$$

Bayes' Theorem

$$P(E_i \mid B) = \frac{P(E_i)P(B \mid E_i)}{P(E_1)P(B \mid E_1) + P(E_2)P(B \mid E_2) + \ldots + P(E_k)P(B \mid E_k)}$$

$$\textbf{4-13}$$

Expected Value of a Discrete Distribution

$$E(x) = \sum xP(x) \qquad \textbf{4-14}$$

Standard Deviation of a Discrete Probability Distribution

$$\sigma_x = \sqrt{\sum [x - E(x)]^2 P(x)} \qquad \textbf{4-15}$$

Expected Value of the Sum of Two Random Variables

$$E(x + y) = E(x) + E(y) \qquad \textbf{4-16}$$

Covariance

$$\sigma_{xy} = \sum [x_i - E(x)][y_j - E(y)]P(x_iy_j) \qquad \textbf{4-17}$$

Correlation Coefficient

$$\rho = \frac{\sigma_{xy}}{\sigma_x \sigma_y} \qquad \textbf{4-18}$$

Key Terms

CHAPTER EXERCISES

Conceptual Questions

4.53 Discuss what is meant by the relative frequency of occurrence approach to probability assessment. Provide a business-related example, other than those given in the text, in which this method of probability assessment might be used.

4.54 Discuss what is meant by *subjective probability*. Provide a business-related example in which subjective probability assessment would likely be used. Also provide an example of when you have personally used subjective probability assessment.

4.55 Discuss what is meant by *classical probability assessment* and indicate why classical assessment is not often used in business applications.

4.56 Based on your experience thus far in this class, what is the probability that you will receive an "A" grade? Discuss the factors you have used in arriving at this probability assessment. Do you believe that all students in your class will arrive at the same probability assessment as you? Why or why not?

4.57 Define and list five business examples of each of the following:
a. Mutually exclusive events
b. Independent events

4.58 How old is your statistics instructor? Rather than trying to pick an exact age, assess a probability to each of the following categories. Make sure that the sum of the probabilities you assess equals 1.0.

Under 30
30 to 40
41 to 50
51 to 60
Over 60

Business Applications

4.59 There are four defective power supplies in a package of 10. If two power supplies are randomly selected one after another, what is the probability of
a. One defective and one good power supply being selected?
b. Two good power supplies being selected?

4.60 A small town has two ambulances. Records indicate that the first ambulance is in service 60% of the time and the second one is in service 40% of the time.
a. What is the probability that when an ambulance is needed, one will not be available?
b. What is the probability that at least one ambulance will be available?

4.61 The Goldberg Construction Company recently bid on three contracts, each of which the company could be either awarded or not awarded.

a. Define the elementary events for a given bid.
b. List the sample space for a bid on one contract.
c. List the sample space for all three contracts.

4.62 The Harrison Corporation manufactures electronic components for the U.S. government. One particular component can be made without defect, with a minor defect, or with a major defect. If the company makes only one of these components, list the sample space.

4.63 Assume that the outcomes of a lottery are equally likely.
a. What is the probability that an individual will win if he or she holds one ticket out of 500 sold?
b. What is the probability of winning if he or she holds three tickets out of 500 sold?
c. What method of probability assessment did you use to answer parts a and b?

4.64 Gossage's Beverages recently sent a special advertisement to a large number of people in its marketing area. It offered a special price on root beer for purchases of one to four packages of six bottles or cans. In planning for the special promotion, Jane Gossage assessed the probability distribution of the number of packages of six that each customer would buy during the promotion as follows:

Number of Packages	
x	P(x)
0	0.30
1	0.10
2	0.10
3	0.05
4	0.45

Based on the probability assessments, what is the expected number of packages to be sold per customer? Comment on whether any particular customer is likely to purchase exactly this amount.

4.65 Amstar Airlines has just supplied data to the U.S. government indicating that out of 10,000 flights, 4,900 arrived on time (within 5 minutes of schedule), 4,000 arrived late, and the remaining flights arrived early.
a. Using the relative frequency of occurrence method, provide an assessment of the chances that an Amstar Airlines flight will arrive on time.
b. Assess the probability that a flight will be late.
c. Assess the chances that a flight will be early.
d. Comment on some of the potential problems associated with using relative frequency of occurrence probability assessment in this kind of case.

4.66 The Harris Newspaper Company sometimes makes printing errors in its advertising and is forced to provide corrected advertising in the next issue of the paper. The managing editor has done a study of this problem and has found the following data:

No. of Errors x	Relative Frequency
0	0.56
1	0.21
2	0.13
3	0.07
4	0.03

a. Using the relative frequencies as probabilities, what is the expected number of errors? Interpret what this value means to the managing editor.

b. Compute the variance and standard deviation for the number of errors and explain what these values measure.

4.67 Suppose you are given a three-question multiple-choice quiz in which each question has four optional answers.

a. What is the probability of getting a perfect score if you are forced to guess at each question?

b. Suppose it takes at least two correct answers out of three to pass the test. What is the probability of passing if you are forced to guess at each question? What does this indicate about studying for such an exam?

c. Suppose through some late-night studying you are able to correctly eliminate two answers on each question. Now answer parts a and b.

4.68 The Aims Photo Company sends photographers around to various department stores in the South to take pictures of children. The company charges only $0.99 for a sitting, which consists of six poses. The company then makes up three packages that are offered to the parents, who have a choice of buying zero, one, two, or all three of the packages. Based on his experience in the business, Samuel Aims has assessed the following probabilities of the number of packages that might be purchased by a parent.

Number of Packages	
x	P(x)
0	0.30
1	0.40
2	0.20
3	0.10

a. What is the expected number of packages to be purchased by each parent?

b. What is the standard deviation for the random variable, x?

c. Suppose all of the picture packages are to be priced at the same level. How much should they be priced if the Aims Company wants to break even? Assume that the production costs are $3.00 per package. Remember that the sitting charge is $0.99.

4.69 The Iverson Investment Company recently gave a public seminar in which its representative discussed a number of issues, including investment risk analysis. In that seminar the company reminded people that the coefficient of variation often can be used as a measure of an investment's risk. To demonstrate its point, it used two hypothetical stocks as examples. It let x equal the change in assets for a $1,000 investment in stock 1 and y reflect the change in assets for a $1,000 investment in stock 2. It showed the seminar participants the following probability distributions:

x	P(x)	y	P(y)
−$1,000	0.10	−$1,000	0.20
0	0.10	0	0.40
500	0.30	500	0.30
1,000	0.30	1,000	0.05
2,000	0.20	2,000	0.05

a. Compute the expected values for random variables x and y.

b. Compute the standard deviations for x and y.

c. Recalling that the coefficient of variation is determined by the ratio of the standard deviation over the mean, compute the coefficient of variation for each random variable.

d. Referring to part c, suppose the seminar director said that the first stock was more risky, because its standard deviation was greater than the standard deviation of the second stock. How would you respond? (Hint: What do the coefficients of variation imply?)

4.70 The Bentfield Electronics Company purchases parts from a variety of vendors. In each case the company is particularly concerned with the quality of the products it purchases. Part number 34-78D is used in the company's new laser printer. The parts are sensitive to dust and can easily be damaged in shipment, even if they are acceptable when they leave the vendor's plant. In a shipment of four parts, the purchasing agent has assessed the following probability distribution for the number of defective products.

x	P(x)
0	0.20
1	0.20
2	0.20
3	0.20
4	0.20

a. What is the expected number of defectives in a shipment of four parts? Discuss what this value really means to Bentfield.

b. Compute and interpret the standard deviation of the number of defective parts in a shipment of four.

c. Examine the probabilities as assessed and indicate what this probability distribution is called. Provide some reasons why the probabilities might all be equal, as they are in this case.

4.71 If the probability of a particular stock increasing in value is assessed at 0.60 and the probability of a second stock increasing is 0.70, are the two stocks independent if the probability of both stocks increasing is 0.15? Discuss.

4.72 Approximately 90% of executives indicate that Microsoft Windows is standard software at their companies (Source: 1997 Olsten Forum and **www.usatoday.com/snapshot/money/msnap039.htm**). What is the probability that a sample of 3 executives would reveal:
a. At least two using Microsoft Windows?
b. None using Microsoft Windows?
c. Exactly one uses Microsoft Windows?

4.73 In the sales business, repeat calls to finalize a sale are common. Suppose a particular salesperson has a 0.70 probability of selling on the first call and that the probability of selling drops by 0.10 on each successive call. If the salesperson is willing to make up to four calls on any client, what is the probability of a sale?

Advanced Business Applications

4.74 Recreational developers are considering opening a skiing area near a western U.S. town. They are trying to decide whether to open an area catering to family skiers or to some other group. To help make their decision, they gather the following information. If

A_1 = Family will ski
A_2 = Family will not ski
B_1 = Family has children but none in the 8-to-16 age group
B_2 = Family has children in the 8-to-16 age group
B_3 = Family has no children

Then, for this location,

$$P(A_1) = 0.40$$
$$P(B_2) = 0.35$$
$$P(B_1) = 0.25$$
$$P(A_1|B_2) = 0.70$$
$$P(A_1|B_1) = 0.30$$

a. Use the probabilities given to construct a joint probability distribution table.
b. What is the probability a family will ski *and* have children who are not in the 8-to-16 age group? How do you write this probability?
c. What is the probability a family with children in the 8-to- 16 age group will not ski?
d. Are the categories *skiing* and *family composition* independent?

4.75 A company is considering changing its starting hour from 8:00 A.M. to 7:30 A.M. A census of the company's 1,200 office and production workers shows 370 of its 750 production workers favor the change and a total of 715 workers favor the change. To further assess worker opinion, the region manager decides to talk with randomly selected workers.
a. What is the probability a randomly selected worker will be in favor of the change?
b. What is the probability a randomly selected worker will be against the change *and* be an office worker?

c. Is the relationship between job type and opinion independent? Explain.

4.76 Bill Jones and Herman Smith are long-time business associates. They know that regular exercise improves their productivity and have made a practice of playing either tennis or golf every Saturday for the past 10 years. Jones enjoys tennis, but Smith prefers golf. Each Saturday they flip a coin to decide which sport to play. Jones beats Smith at tennis 80% of the time, whereas he beats Smith at golf only 30% of the time.
a. Suppose Jones walks into the Monday morning staff meeting and announces he beat Smith on Saturday. What sport do you think they played and why?
b. Assume open tennis courts are hard to find on Saturday, so instead of flipping a coin, Smith and Jones always first look for a tennis court. If they find one open, they play tennis; if not, they play golf. Further, suppose the chance of finding an open court is 30%. Given this, what sport do you think they played on Saturday, given that Jones won?

4.77 A marketing research team is considering using a mailing list for an advertising campaign. They know that 40% of the people on the list have only a MasterCard and that 10% have only an American Express card. Another 20% hold both MasterCard and American Express. Finally, 30% of those on the list have neither card. Suppose a person on the list is known to have a MasterCard. What is the probability that person also has an American Express card?

4.78 American International Drilling Company explores for oil worldwide. Recently, the company was considering drilling for oil in Fiji. Based on the best analysis of the company's engineers, the company believes that there is a 30% chance of striking oil. Before drilling, there is an expensive, but imperfect, test that can be conducted. The final reading of the test will indicate "positive" or "negative," depending on the data recorded during the test. This test will show a positive result 70% of the time when it turns out that there actually is oil. The test also will show a negative result 80% of the time when it turns out that there is no oil. Suppose American International Drilling has just run the test on the Fiji site and the result is negative. What is the revised probability of oil at the site?

4.79 The American Society for Quality is preparing to host their 40th annual Spring Quality Conference. Leaders of the conference feel that there is a 0.90 chance that the registration revenues will exceed the conference costs and the group will make money. In the past, when the conference has been a financial success, the governor has appeared on the program 80% of the time. When the conference has not been a financial success, the governor has been on the program 60% of the time. Suppose the conference chairman has just received a call from the governor's office indicating that the governor will be unable to attend this year. What will be the revised thinking on the probability that this year's conference will be a financial success?

CHAPTER 5

Discrete and Continuous Probability Distributions

CHAPTER OUTCOMES

After studying the material in Chapter 5, you should:

- Be able to apply the binomial distribution to business decision-making situations.
- Be able to compute probabilities for the Poisson and hypergeometric distributions.
- Be able to discuss the important properties of the normal probability distribution.
- Recognize when the normal distribution might apply in a decision-making process.
- Be able to calculate probabilities using the normal distribution table and be able to apply the normal distribution in appropriate business situations.
- Recognize situations in which the uniform and exponential distributions apply.

WHY YOU NEED TO KNOW

Consider a major wood-products company that has perfected a new strain of disease-resistant Douglas fir tree. Even though the tree seeds are clones of each other, company biologists find the trees exhibit different growth rates. Also consider a tire manufacturer that has developed a new tread design for sport utility vehicles. The testing team, measuring tread life by the number of miles driven, has found that the tires don't all wear at the same rate, even when they are tested on the same vehicle.

In addition to the discrete random variable examples introduced in Chapter 4, there are many situations in which a variable of interest is not restricted to discrete, integer values. For example, the growth rates of trees can take on any value between zero and some large number, and tire tread life, measured in miles driven, could also take on values between zero and some large number. Variables that are measured in units of length, time, weight, volume, or distance are often assumed to be *continuous* variables.

Technically, a continuous variable is one that can take on an infinitely uncountable number of values (measured to as many decimal places as necessary). Because of measuring limitations, some argue that there is no such thing as a truly continuous variable. They consider all variables discrete even though they can take on values containing several decimal values. However, if a variable of interest is measured such that it takes on a very large number of possible values in a specified interval, we might make the assumption that it is continuous. It depends on the situation. For instance, if the time required to complete a small project that will last less than a day is tracked in hours, the time variable is not assumed to be continuous. However, if the time is measured in seconds, we would be justified in treating the variable as continuous.

Because many business applications involve discrete and continuous or quasi-continuous variables, decision makers need to become acquainted with both discrete and continuous probability distributions and learn how to use them in decision making.

5-1 THE BINOMIAL PROBABILITY DISTRIBUTION

In Chapter 4 you learned that variables can be classified as either **discrete** or **continuous**, depending on the number of values that the variable can assume.

Discrete Random Variable	*Continuous Random Variable*
A random variable that can assume only a countable number of possible values.	Random variables that can assume any value in an interval.

In most instances, the value of a discrete random variable is determined by counting. For instance, the number of customers who arrive at a store is a discrete variable. Its value is determined by counting the customers.

In many other instances, decision makers will be faced with variables that can take on a seemingly unlimited number of values. The values for these continuous random variables are typically determined by measurement instead of counting. Examples include:

Time required to perform a job	Interest rates
Financial ratios	Income levels
Product weights	Distances between two points
Volume of soft drink in a can	

In general, *measurement* is required to determine the value for a continuous random variable, whereas the value for a discrete random variable comes from *counting*.

Several theoretical discrete distributions have extensive application in business decision making. A probability distribution is called *theoretical* when the mathematical properties of its random variable are used to produce its probabilities. Such distributions are different than the distributions that are obtained subjectively or from observation.

Sections 5-1 and 5-2 focus on theoretical discrete probability distributions, whereas Sections 5-3 and 5-4 introduce important theoretical continuous probability distributions.

THE BINOMIAL DISTRIBUTION

The simplest theoretical probability distribution we will consider is one that describes processes whose trials have only two possible outcomes. The physical events described by this type of process are widespread. For instance, a quality control system in a manufacturing plant labels each tested item as either defective or acceptable. A firm bidding for a contract either will or will not get the contract. A marketing research firm may receive responses to a questionnaire in the form of "Yes, I will buy" or "No, I will not buy." The personnel manager in an organization is faced with a two-stage process each time he offers a job—either the applicant accepts the offer or rejects it.

CHARACTERISTICS OF THE BINOMIAL DISTRIBUTION

These examples are all situations that can be described by a discrete probability distribution called the **binomial distribution.**

Binomial Probability Distribution Characteristics

A distribution that gives the probability of x successes in n trials in a process that meets the following conditions.
1. A trial has only two possible outcomes: a success or a failure.
2. There is a fixed number, n, of identical trials.
3. The trials of the experiment are independent of each other. This means that if one outcome is a success, this does not influence the chance of another outcome being a success.
4. The process must be consistent in generating successes and failures. That is, the probability, p, associated with a success remains constant from trial to trial.
5. If p represents the probability of a success, then $(1 - p) = q$ is the probability of a failure.

The binomial distribution requires that the experiment trials be independent. This can be assured in a finite population if the sampling is performed with replacement. This means that an item is sampled from a population and returned to the population, after its characteristic(s) have been recorded, before the next item is sampled. However, sampling with replacement is the exception rather than the rule in business applications. Most often the sampling is performed without replacement. Strictly speaking, when sampling is performed without replacement, the conditions for the binomial distribution cannot be satisfied. However, the conditions are approximately satisfied if the sample selected is quite small relative to the size of the population from which the sample is selected.

A commonly used rule of thumb is that the binomial distribution can be applied if the sample size is at most 5% of the population size.

Household Security—Household Security produces and installs 300 custom-made home security units every week. The units are priced to include one-day installation service by two technicians. A unit with either a design or production problem must be modified on site and will require more than one day to install.

Household Security has completed an extensive study of its design and manufacturing systems. The information shows that if the company is operating at standard quality, 10% of the security systems will have problems and will require more than one day to install.

The binomial distribution applies to this situation because the following conditions exist.

1. There are only two possible outcomes when a unit is sold: it is good or it is defective (will take more than one day to install). Finding a defective system in this application will be considered a success. A success occurs when we observe the outcome of interest.
2. Each unit is designed and made in the same way.
3. The outcome of a security system (good or defective) is independent of whether the preceding system was good or defective.
4. The probability of a defective system, $p = 0.10$, remains constant from unit to unit.
5. The probability of a good system, $q = 1 - p = 0.90$, remains constant from unit to unit.

To determine the likely cause of defects—design or manufacturing—the quality assurance group at Household Security has developed a plan for dismantling a random sample of four security systems each week. Because the sample size is small (4/300 = 1.33%) relative to the size of the population (300 units per week), the conditions of independence and constant probability will be approximately satisfied because the sample is less than 5% of the population.

We let the number of defective units be the random variable of interest. The number of defectives is limited to discrete values, $x = 0, 1, 2, 3,$ or 4. We can determine the probability that the random variable will have any of the discrete values. One way is to list the sample space, as shown in

TABLE 5-1

Sample Space

RESULTS	NO. OF DEFECTIVES	NO. OF WAYS
G,G,G,G	0	1
G,G,G,D	1	
G,G,D,G		
G,D,G,G,		4
D,G,G,G		
G,G,D,D	2	
G,D,G,D		
D,G,G,D		
G,D,D,G		6
D,G,D,G		
D,D,G,G		
D,D,D,G	3	
D,D,G,D		
D,G,D,D		4
G,D,D,D		
D,D,D,D	4	1

Table 5-1. We can find the probability of zero defectives, for instance, by employing the multiplication rule for independent events.

$$P(x = 0 \text{ defectives}) = P(G \text{ and } G \text{ and } G \text{ and } G)$$

where:

$$G = \text{Unit is good (not defective)}$$

Here

$$P(G) = 0.90$$

and we have assumed the units are independent. Using the multiplication rule for independent events introduced in Chapter 4 (Rule 4-12):

$$P(G \text{ and } G \text{ and } G \text{ and } G) = P(G)P(G)P(G)P(G) = (0.90)(0.90)(0.90)(0.90)$$
$$= 0.90^4$$
$$= 0.6561.$$

We can also find the probability of exactly one defective in a sample of four. This is accomplished using both the multiplication rule for independent events and the addition rule for mutually exclusive events, which was also introduced in Chapter 4 (Rule 4-8):

$$P \text{ (1 defective)} = P(G \text{ and } G \text{ and } G \text{ and } D) + P(G \text{ and } G \text{ and } D \text{ and } G) + P(G \text{ and } D \text{ and } G \text{ and } G) + P(D \text{ and } G \text{ and } G \text{ and } G)$$

where:

$$P(G \text{ and } G \text{ and } G \text{ and } D) = P(G)P(G)P(G)P(D) = (0.90)(0.90)(0.90)(0.10)$$
$$= (0.90^3)(0.10)$$

Likewise:

$$P(G \text{ and } G \text{ and } D \text{ and } G) = (0.90^3)(0.10)$$
$$P(G \text{ and } D \text{ and } G \text{ and } G) = (0.90^3)(0.10)$$
$$P(D \text{ and } G \text{ and } G \text{ and } G) = (0.90^3)(0.10)$$

Then:

$$P(1 \text{ defective}) = (0.90^3)(0.10) + (0.90^3)(0.10) + (0.90^3)(0.10) + (0.90^3)(0.10)$$
$$= (4)(0.90^3)(0.10)$$
$$= 0.2916$$

Note that each of the four possible ways of finding one defective unit has the same probability $[(.90^3)(.10)]$. We determine the probability of one of the ways to obtain one defective unit and multiply this value by the number of ways (four) of obtaining one defective unit. This produces the overall probability of one defective unit.

Combinations

In this relatively simply application, we can fairly easily list the sample space and from that count the number of ways that each possible number of defectives can occur. However, for larger examples, this approach is inefficient. A more effective method exists for counting the number of ways binomial events can occur. This method is called the **counting rule for combinations**. This rule is used to count the number of outcomes from an experiment in which x objects are to be selected from a group of n objects. Equation 5-1 is used to find the combinations.

Counting Rule for Combinations

$$C_x^n = \frac{n!}{x!(n-x)!}$$

5-1

where:

C_x^n = Number of combinations of x objects selected from n objects
$n! = n(n-1)(n-2)\ldots(2)(1)$
$0! = 1$ by definition

Using Equation 5-1, we find the number of ways that $x = 2$ defectives can occur in a sample of $n = 4$ as:

$$C_x^n = \frac{n!}{x!(n-x)!} = \frac{4!}{2!(4-2)!} = \frac{(4)(3)(2)(1)}{(2)(1)(2)(1)} = \frac{24}{4} = 6 \text{ ways}$$

Refer to Table 5-1 to see that this is the same value obtained by listing the sample space.

Now we can find the probabilities of two defectives.

$$P(2 \text{ defectives}) = (6)(0.90^2)(0.10^2)$$
$$= 0.0486$$

Use this method to verify the following:

$$P(3 \text{ defectives}) = (4)(0.90)(0.10^3)$$
$$= 0.0036$$
$$P(4 \text{ defectives}) = (1)(0.10^4)$$
$$= 0.0001$$

The key to developing the probability distribution for a binomial process is first to determine the probability of any one way the event of interest can occur and then to multiply this probability by the number of ways that event can occur. Table 5-2 shows the binomial probability distribution for the number of defective security units in a sample size of 4 when the probability of any individual unit being defective is 0.10. The probability distribution is graphed in Figure 5-1. Most samples would contain zero or one defective units when the production system is functioning as designed.

Binomial Formula

The steps that we have taken to develop this binomial probability distribution can be summarized through a formula called the **binomial formula**, shown as Equation 5-2. Note, this formula is composed of two parts: the combinations of x items selected from n items and the probability of one of the ways that x items can occur.

TABLE 5-2

Binomial Distribution for Household Security: $n = 4$, $p = 0.10$

x = # OF DEFECTS	$P(x)$
0	0.6561
1	0.2916
2	0.0486
3	0.0036
4	0.0001
$\Sigma\, P(x) =$	1.0000

FIGURE 5-1

Binomial Distribution
for Household Security

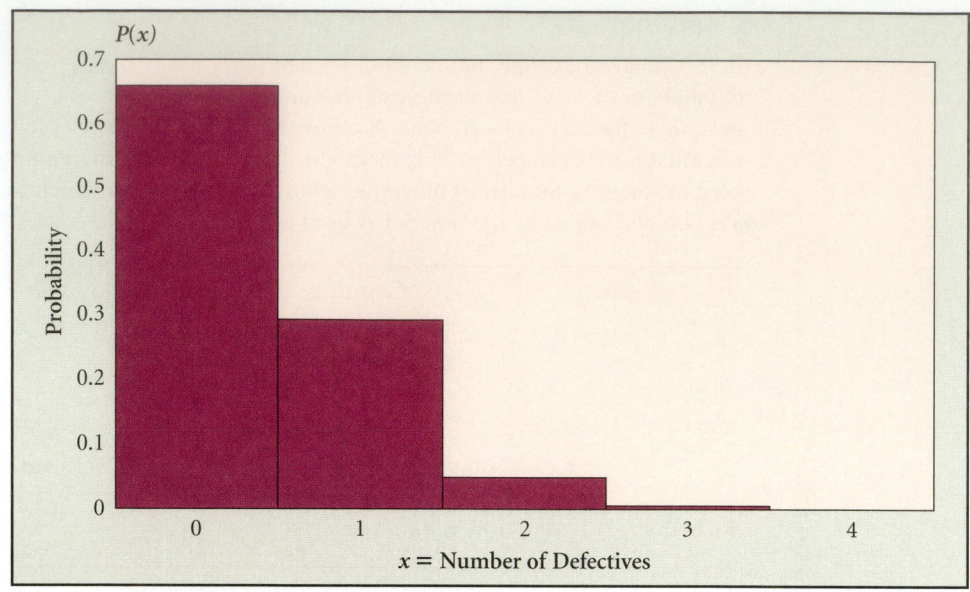

Binomial Formula

$$P(x) = \frac{n!}{x!(n-x)!} p^x q^{n-x}$$

5-2

where:

n = Random sample size
x = Number of successes (when a success is what we are looking for)
$n - x$ = Number of failures
p = Probability of a success
$q = 1 - p$ = Probability of a failure
$n! = n(n-1)(n-2)(n-3)\cdots 1$
$0! = 1$ by definition

Applying Equation 5-2 to the security system example for $n = 4$, $p = 0.10$, and $x = 2$ defects, we get:

$$P(x) = \frac{n!}{x!(n-x)!} p^x q^{n-x}$$

$$P(x = 2) = \frac{4!}{2!\,2!}(0.10^2)(0.90^2) = 6(0.10^2)(0.90^2) = 0.0486$$

This is the same value we obtained earlier when we listed out the sample space.

EXAMPLE 5-1: USING THE BINOMIAL FORMULA

Hanson's Car Wash   Hanson's Car Wash offers a full refund to anyone who is not satisfied with the way their car looks after it is washed. The owners believe the wash results from car to car are independent and that the probability that a customer will ask for a refund is 0.20. Suppose a random sample of six cars is observed. In four instances, the owner has asked for a refund. The owner might be interested in the probability of four refunds in six cars. If the binomial distribution applies, the probability can be found using the following steps:

Step 1:   **Define the characteristics of the binomial distribution.**
In this case, the characteristics are
$$n = 6, p = 0.20, q = 1 - p = 0.80$$

Step 2:   **Determine the probability of x successes in n trials using the binomial formula, Equation 5-2.**

In this case, $n = 6$, $p = 0.20$, $q = 0.80$, and we are interested in the probability of $x = 4$ successes.

$$P(x) = \frac{n!}{x!(n-x)!} p^x q^{n-x}$$

$$P(4) = \frac{6!}{4!(6-4)!} (0.20^4)(0.80^{6-4})$$

$$P(4) = 15(0.20^4)(0.80^2)$$

$$P(4) = 0.0154$$

There is only a 0.0154 chance that exactly four customers will want a refund in a sample of six if the chance that any one of the customers will want a refund is 0.20.

Using the Binomial Distribution Table

Using Equation 5-2 to develop the binomial distribution is not difficult, but it can be time-consuming. To make binomial probabilities easier to find, you can use the binomial table in Appendix B. This table is constructed to give individual probabilities for different sample sizes and probabilities of success. Each column is headed by a probability, p, which is the probability associated with a success. The column headings correspond to probabilities of success ranging from 0.01 to 0.50. Down the left side of the table are integer values that correspond to the number of successes, x, for the specified sample size, n. If we are dealing with probabilities ranging from 0.51 to 1.0, we use the values of p located at the bottom of the columns. The corresponding values of x are on the right side of the table, running from bottom to top.

U.S. Bio—U.S. Bio, a pharmaceutical company, has developed a drug to restore hair growth in men. Like most drugs, this product has potential side effects. One of these is increased blood pressure. The company is willing to market the drug if there are blood-pressure increases in 2% or fewer of the men using the drug.

The company plans to conduct a clinical test with 10 randomly selected men. The number of men with increased blood pressure will be $x = 0, 1, 2, \ldots 10$. We can use the binomial table in Appendix B to develop the probability distribution. Table 5-3 shows the portion of the binomial table we need for $p = 0.02$ and $n = 10$. Go to the column for $p = 0.02$. The values of x are listed down the left side of the table. For example, the probability of 3 occurrences is 0.0008. This means that it is extremely unlikely that 3 men, in a sample of 10, would exhibit increased blood pressure if the overall fraction having this side effect is 0.02. Note, in Table 5-3, the probabilities for all values of $x > 3$ is 0.0000. So, to four decimal places, the probability of four men experiencing increased blood pressure is zero. The true probability is not zero but is very small. Then:

$$P(x \geq 3) = 0.0008 + 0.0000 + 0.0000 + \ldots + 0.0000 = 0.0008$$

There are about 8 chances in 10,000 that we would find three or more men with increased blood pressure if the probability of it happening for any one person is $p = 0.02$. If the test did show that

TABLE 5-3

Binomial Table ($n = 10$)

					$n = 10$						
x	p = 0.01	p = 0.02	p = 0.03	p = 0.04	p = 0.05	p = 0.06	p = 0.07	p = 0.08	p = 0.09	p = 0.10	
0	0.9044	0.8171	0.7374	0.6648	0.5987	0.5386	0.4840	0.4344	0.3894	0.3487	10
1	0.0914	0.1667	0.2281	0.2770	0.3151	0.3438	0.3643	0.3777	0.3851	0.3874	9
2	0.0042	0.0153	0.0317	0.0519	0.0746	0.0988	0.1234	0.1478	0.1714	0.1937	8
3	0.0001	0.0008	0.0026	0.0058	0.0105	0.0168	0.0248	0.0343	0.0452	0.0574	7
4	0.0000	0.0000	0.0001	0.0004	0.0010	0.0019	0.0033	0.0052	0.0078	0.0112	6
5	0.0000	0.0000	0.0000	0.0000	0.0001	0.0001	0.0003	0.0005	0.0009	0.0015	5
6	0.0000	0.0000	0.0000	0.0000	0.0000	0.0000	0.0000	0.0000	0.0001	0.0001	4
7	0.0000	0.0000	0.0000	0.0000	0.0000	0.0000	0.0000	0.0000	0.0000	0.0000	3
8	0.0000	0.0000	0.0000	0.0000	0.0000	0.0000	0.0000	0.0000	0.0000	0.0000	2
9	0.0000	0.0000	0.0000	0.0000	0.0000	0.0000	0.0000	0.0000	0.0000	0.0000	1
10	0.0000	0.0000	0.0000	0.0000	0.0000	0.0000	0.0000	0.0000	0.0000	0.0000	0
	p = 0.99	p = 0.98	p = 0.97	p = 0.96	p = 0.95	p = 0.94	p = 0.93	p = 0.92	p = 0.91	p = 0.90	x

three men had elevated blood pressure after taking the new drug, the true rate of high blood pressure likely exceeds 2%, and the company should have serious doubts about marketing the drug.

EXAMPLE 5-2: USING THE BINOMIAL TABLE

Nielsen TV Ratings   The Nielsen Company is the best-known television ratings company. On Tuesday after the 2002 Masters Golf Tournament in Augusta, Georgia, which Tiger Woods won, the company announced that slightly more than 9% of all televisions were tuned to the final round on Sunday. Assuming that the 9% rating is correct, what is the probability that in a random sample of 20 television sets, two or fewer would have been tuned to the Masters? This question can be answered, assuming that the binomial distribution applies, using the following steps:

Step 1:   **Define the characteristics of the binomial distribution.**
In this case, the characteristics are
$$n = 20, p = 0.09, q = 1 - p = 0.91$$

Step 2:   **Go to the binomial table in Appendix B. Locate the appropriate column for p and the appropriate section in the table for the sample size, n.**
In this case, we locate the section of the table corresponding to sample size equal to $n = 20$ and go to the column headed $p = 0.09$. The probabilities from the binomial table are

x	P(x)
0	0.1516
1	0.3000
2	0.2818
3	0.1672
4	0.0703
5	0.0222
6	0.0055
7	0.0011
8	0.0002

Step 3:   **Define the event of interest and obtain the probabilities from the binomial table.**
We are interested in the probability of two or fewer sets tuned to the Masters. This is
$$P(x \leq 2) = P(x = 0) + P(x = 1) + P(x = 2)$$
From the binomial table we get:
$$P(x \leq 2) = 0.1516 + 0.3000 + 0.2818$$
$$= 0.7334$$
Thus, there is a 0.7334 chance that two or fewer sets in a random sample of 20 were tuned to the Masters.

EXAMPLE 5-3: USING THE BINOMIAL DISTRIBUTION

Naumann Research   Naumann Research is a full-service marketing research consulting firm. Recently it was retained to do a project for a major U.S. airline. The airline was considering changing from an assigned-seating reservation system to one in which fliers would be able to take any seat they wished on a first-come-first-served basis. The airline believes that 80% of its fliers would like this change if it was accompanied with a reduction in ticket prices. Naumann Research will survey a large number of customers on this issue, but prior to conducting the full research, it has selected a random sample of 20 customers and determined that 12 like the proposed change. What is the probability of finding 12 or fewer who like the change if the probability is 0.80 that a customer will like the change?

If we assume the binomial distribution applies, we can use the following steps to answer this question.

Step 1:   **Define the characteristics of the binomial distribution.**
In this case, the characteristics are
$$n = 20, p = 0.80, q = 1 - p = 0.20$$

Step 2: **Go to the binomial table in Appendix B. Locate the appropriate column for p and the appropriate section in the table for the sample size, *n*.**
First, locate the section of the table corresponding to sample size equal to $n = 20$. Then, because $p > 0.50$, we find the desired column by looking to the p values at the bottom of each column. Locate the column for $p = 0.80$.

Step 3: **Define the event of interest.**
We are interested in knowing:
$$P(x \le 12) = P(x = 12) + P(x = 11) + \cdots + P(x = 0)$$

Step 4: **Locate the desired probabilities in the binomial table and sum them.**
Since $p > 0.50$, the values of x are in the far right column of the binomial table. Go to the row corresponding to $x = 12$ and the column for $p = 0.80$ in the section of the table for $n = 20$ to get:
$$P(x = 12) = 0.0222$$

Repeat this for the values of x from 12 down to 0:
$$P(x \le 12) = 0.0222 + 0.0074 + 0.0020 + 0.0005 + 0.0001 + 0.0000 + \cdots + 0.0000$$
$$= 0.0322$$

Thus, it is quite unlikely that if 80% of customers like the new seating plan that 12 or fewer in a sample of 20 would like it. The airline may want to rethink its plan.

MEAN AND STANDARD DEVIATION OF THE BINOMIAL DISTRIBUTION

In Chapter 4 we stated the mean of a discrete probability distribution is also referred to as the *expected value*. The expected value of a discrete random variable, x, is found using Equation 5-3.

Expected Value of a Discrete Random Variable

$$\mu_x = E(x) = \sum xP(x)$$ **5-3**

where:

x = Values of the random variable
$P(x)$ = Probability of the random variable taking on the value of x

---

Mean of a Binomial Distribution

Equation 5-3 can be used with any discrete probability distribution, including the binomial. However, if we are working with a binomial distribution, the mean can be found more easily by using Equation 5-4.

Expected Value of a Binomial Distribution

$$\mu_x = E(x) = np$$ **5-4**

where:

n = Sample size
p = Probability of a success

Excel and Minitab Tutorial

Catalog Sales—Catalog sales have been a part of the U.S. economy for many years, and in the 1990s companies such as Lands' End, L.L. Bean, and Eddie Bauer enjoyed increased business. One feature that has made mail-order buying so popular is the ease with which customers can return merchandise. Nevertheless, one mail-order catalog has the goal of having no more than 11% of all purchased items returned.

FIGURE 5-2A

Output for Mail-Order
Sales Returns

Excel Instructions:
1. Click on f_x on tool bar.
2. Select **Statistical** and then **BINOMDIST** options.
3. Fill in requested information.
4. **"True"** indicates Cumulative Probabilities.

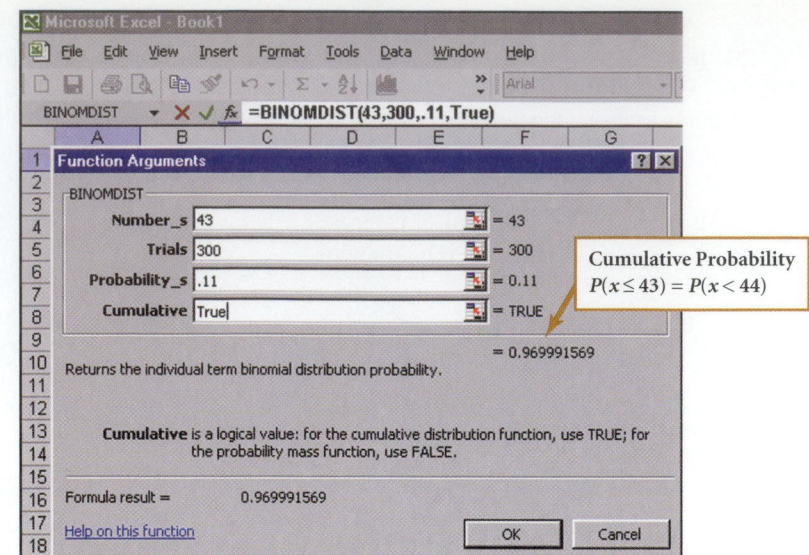

The binomial distribution can describe the number of items returned. For instance, in a given hour the company shipped 300 items. If the probability of an item being returned is $p = 0.11$, the expected number of items (mean) to be returned is

$$\mu_x = E(x) = np$$
$$\mu_x = E(x) = (300)(0.11) = 33.0$$

Thus, the average number of returned items for each 300 items shipped is 33.

Suppose the company sales manager wants to know if the return rate is stable at 11%. To test this, she monitors a random sample of 300 items and finds that 44 have been returned. This return rate exceeds the mean of 33 units, which concerns her. However, before reaching a conclusion, she will be interested in the probability of observing 44 or more returns in a sample of 300.

$$P(x \geq 44) = 1 - P(x < 44)$$

The binomial table in Appendix B does not contain sample sizes of 300. Instead, we can use Excel's **BINOMDIST** function or the binomial tool in Minitab's **CALC—Probability Distribution** menu to find the probability. The Excel and Minitab output in Figures 5-2a and Figure 5-2b show the cumulative probability of 43 or fewer is equal to

$$P(x \leq 43) = P(x < 44) = 0.9700$$

Then the probability of 44 or more returns is

$$P(x \geq 44) = 1 - 0.9700 = 0.0300$$

There is only a 3% chance of 44 or more items being returned if the 11% return rate is still in effect. This low probability suggests that the return rate may have increased above 11%.

FIGURE 5-2B

Minitab Output for
Mail-Order Sales Return

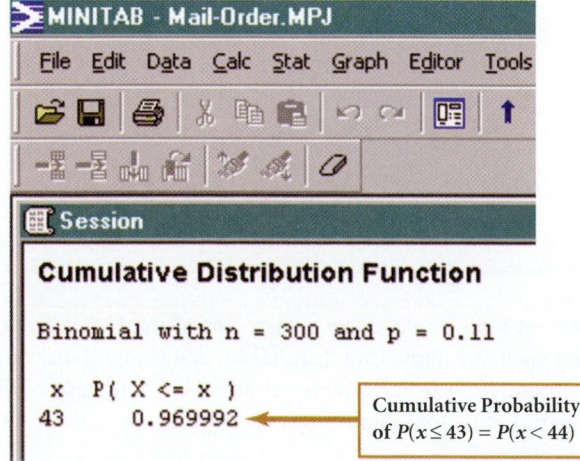

Minitab Instructions:
1. Choose **Calc > Probability Distribution > Binomial**.
2. Choose **Cumulative probability**.
3. In **Number of trials** enter sample size.
4. In **Probability of success** enter p.
5. In **Input constant** enter the number of successes: x.
6. Click **OK**.

EXAMPLE 5-4: FINDING THE MEAN OF THE BINOMIAL DISTRIBUTION

Naumann Research   In Example 5-3, Naumann Research had been hired to do a study for a major airline that is planning to change from a designated-seat assignment plan to an open-seating system. The company believes that 80% of its customers approve of the idea. Naumann Research interviewed a sample of $n = 20$ and found 12 who like the proposed change. If the airline is correct in its assessment of the probability, what is the expected number of people in a sample of $n = 20$ who will like the change? We can find this using the following steps:

Step 1:   **Define the characteristics of the binomial distribution.**
In this case, the characteristics are
$$n = 20, p = 0.80, q = 1 - p = 0.20$$

Step 2:   **Use Equation 5-4 to find the expected value.**
$$\mu_x = E(x) = np$$
$$E(x) = 20(0.80) = 16$$

The average number who would say they like the proposed change is 16 in a sample of 20.

Standard Deviation of a Binomial Distribution

In Chapter 4, we introduced the standard deviation for a discrete probability distribution and showed how it is calculated. Equation 5-5 can be used to compute the standard deviation for any discrete probability distribution.

Standard Deviation of a Discrete Random Variable

$$\sigma_x = \sqrt{\sum [x - E(x)]^2 P(x)}$$

5-5

where:

$x =$ Value for the random variable
$E(x) =$ Expected value of the random variable
$P(x) =$ Probability of the random variable taking on the value of x

---

If a discrete probability distribution meets the binomial distribution conditions, the standard deviation is defined by Equation 5-6.

Standard Deviation of the Binomial Distribution

$$\sigma = \sqrt{npq}$$

5-6

where:

$n =$ Sample size
$p =$ Probability of a success
$q = 1 - p =$ Probability of a failure

EXAMPLE 5-5: FINDING THE STANDARD DEVIATION OF A BINOMIAL DISTRIBUTION

Naumann Research   Refer to Examples 5-3 and 5-4, in which Naumann Research surveyed a sample of $n = 20$ airline customers about changing the way seats are assigned on flights. The airline believes that 80% of its customers approve of the proposed change. Example 5-4 showed that if the airline is correct in its assessment, the expected number in a sample of 20 who would like the change is 16. However, there are other possible outcomes if 20 customers are surveyed. What is the standard deviation of the random variable, x, in this case? We can find the standard deviation for the binomial distribution using the following steps.

Step 1:   **Define the characteristics of the binomial distribution.**
In this case, the characteristics are

$$n = 20, p = 0.80, q = 1 - p = 0.20$$

Step 2:   **Use Equation 5-6 to calculate the standard deviation.**

$$\sigma = \sqrt{npq} = \sqrt{20(0.80)(0.20)} = 1.7889$$

ADDITIONAL INFORMATION ABOUT THE BINOMIAL DISTRIBUTION

At this point, several comments about the binomial distribution are worth making. If p, the probability of a success, is 0.50, the binomial distribution is *symmetrical* and bell-shaped, regardless of the sample size. This is illustrated in Figure 5-3, which shows frequency histograms for samples of $n = 5$, $n = 10$, and $n = 50$. Notice that all three distributions are centered at the expected value, $E(x) = \mu_x$.

When the value of p differs from 0.50 in either direction, the binomial distribution is skewed. The skewness will be most pronounced when n is small and p approaches 0 or 1. However, the binomial distribution becomes more bell-shaped as n increases. The frequency histograms shown in Figure 5-4 bear this out.

FIGURE 5-3   **The Binomial Distribution with Varying Sample Sizes ($p = 0.50$)**

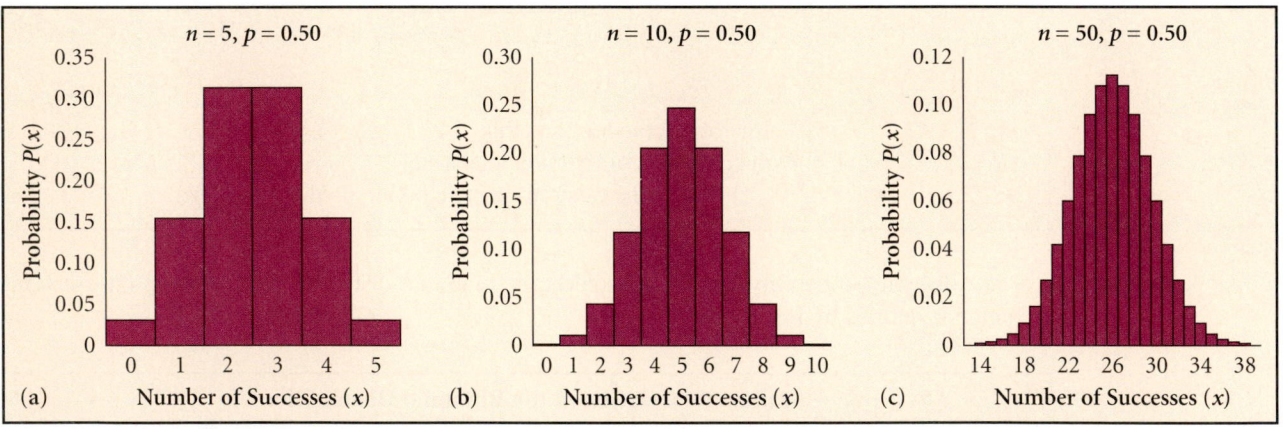

FIGURE 5-4   **The Binomial Distribution with Varying Sample Sizes ($p = 0.05$)**

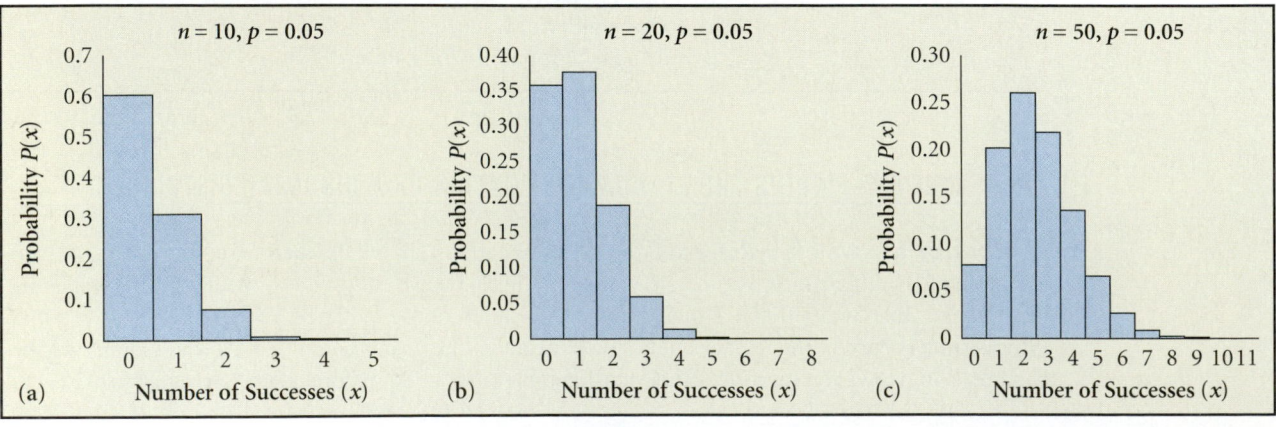

5-1: EXERCISES

Skill Development

5.1 Use the binomial formula to develop the probability distribution for an experiment in which $n = 4$ and $p = 0.2$.

5.2 Use the binomial formula to calculate the following probabilities for an experiment in which $n = 5$ and $p = 0.4$.
a. the probability that x is at most one
b. the probability that x is at least four
c. the probability that x is less than one

5.3 Use the binomial distribution table to calculate the following probabilities for a binomial random variable where $n = 20$ and $p = 0.40$.
a. $P(x = 10)$
b. $P(7 < x < 12)$
c. $P(x \geq 12)$

5.4 For a binomial distribution with $n = 10$ and $p = 0.70$, determine:
a. $P(x > 7)$
b. $P(x < E(x))$

5.5 Use the counting rule for combinations to determine:
a. the number of ways 4 items can be selected from 8 items
b. the number of ways 6 items can be selected from 10 items
c. the number of ways 3 items can be selected from 10 items
d. the number of ways 7 items can be selected from 10 items

5.6 For a sample of $n = 10$, assuming that the binomial probability distribution applies, find the following.
a. the probability of 3 successes if the probability of a success is 0.20
b. the probability of 3 successes if the probability of a success is 0.80

5.7 Assuming that the binomial distribution applies, if a sample size of $n = 5$ is selected and the probability of a success is 0.40,
a. What is the probability of 4 successes?
b. What is the probability of 4 or more successes?
c. What is the expected value and standard deviation for the number of successes?

5.8 Assuming that the binomial distribution applies, given a sample size of $n = 20$, find the following.
a. the probability of 5 successes if the probability of a success is 0.75
b. the probability of 4 or fewer failures if the probability of a success is 0.20
c. the probability of 11 successes if the probability of a failure is 0.33

5.9 If a binomial distribution applies with a sample size of $n = 20$, find
a. the probability of 5 successes if the probability of a success is 0.40

b. the probability of at least 7 successes if the probability of a success is 0.25
c. the expected value, $n = 20$, p = .20
d. the standard deviation, $n = 20$, p = .20

5.10 A binomial random variable, x, has parameters $n = 250$ and $p = 0.70$. Find the mean, variance, standard deviation, and coefficient of variation of the random variable, x.

5.11 The following probability distribution is provided for a binomial random variable with $n = 4$ and $p = 0.20$:

x	P(x)
0	0.4096
1	0.4096
2	0.1536
3	0.0256
4	0.0016

a. Use Equation 5-3 to compute the expected value of this probability distribution.
b. Use Equation 5-4 to find the expected value.

5.12 Indicate the conditions under which a binomial distribution will be symmetric. Under what conditions will a binomial distribution be skewed? Discuss the role that sample size plays in determining whether a binomial distribution is skewed or symmetric.

Business Applications

5.13 A credit card company knows that 70% of its customers are males. The company is considering randomly selecting five people each month to receive a free vacation.
a. What is the probability in a given month that all five people selected will be males?
b. Suppose that in a given month, all five people selected are females. What is the probability of this happening?

5.14 An auto parts store in Chicago believes that it has parts in inventory to meet the needs of 90% of its customers. If a random sample of 10 customers is selected, what is the probability that the store will have parts for all of them? Discuss the conditions in this situation that are required to assume that the binomial distribution applies.

5.15 The Lexington School Board has agreed to help the A. P. Stevens School Furniture Company test a new type of elementary school chair. Using the present school furniture, school administrators have found that 15% of the chairs must be replaced each year. A. P. Stevens claims its chair will average a 10% replacement rate. Assume that characteristics for a binomial distribution apply.
a. Calculate the probability that 2 or more of the A. P. Stevens' chairs will have to be replaced each year. Assume its claim of a 10% replacement rate is correct and that there are 10 chairs.

b. Calculate the probability that 2 or more currently used chairs will have to be replaced each year. Assume the school administrators' claim of a 15% replacement rate is correct and that there are 10 chairs sampled.

c. Assume 10 Stevens chairs are tested for one year and 2 need to be replaced. Comment on Stevens' claim that this proves its chair is superior to the present brand. Support your comments with probabilities and reasons.

5.16   The 1997 Tenth Planet Teachers and Technology Survey reported that 21% of elementary teachers use the Web. If five teachers are selected at random, what is the probability that

a. exactly three of the teachers use the Web

b. fewer than four teachers use the Web

c. more than one teacher uses the Web

5.17   A survey by KRC Research for *U.S. News* reported that 37% of people plan to spend more on eating out after they retire. If eight people are randomly selected, determine the following probabilities.

a. Exactly five people plan to spend more on eating out after they retire.

b. Fewer than four people plan to spend more on eating out after they retire.

c. More than two plan to spend more on eating out after they retire.

5.18   Gateway 2000, Inc., receives large shipments of microprocessors from Intel Corp. It must try to ensure that the proportion of microprocessors that are defective is small. Suppose Gateway decides to test five microprocessors out of a shipment of thousands of them. Suppose that if at least one of the microprocessors is defective, the shipment is returned.

a. If Intel Corp.'s shipment contains 10% defective microprocessors, calculate the probability the entire shipment will be returned.

b. If Intel and Gateway agree that Intel will not provide more than 5% defective chips, calculate the probability that the entire shipment will be returned even though only 5% are defective.

c. Calculate the probability that the entire shipment will be kept by Gateway even though the shipment has 10% defective microprocessors.

5.19   A CBS News survey reported that 67% of adults said the U.S. Treasury should continue making pennies. If six adults are selected at random, determine the expected number of adults who will say the U.S. Treasury should continue making pennies.

5.20   A CBS News survey reported that 67% of adults said the U.S. Treasury should continue making pennies. What is the probability that for six adults selected at random

a. Exactly five adults would want the Treasury to continue making pennies?

b. Three or fewer adults would want the Treasury to continue making pennies?

c. More than two adults would want the Treasury to continue making pennies?

5.21   The 1997 Tenth Planet Teachers and Technology Survey reported that 21% of elementary teachers use the Web. If five teachers are selected at random, determine the

a. expected number of these teachers who use the Web

b. standard deviation of these teachers who use the Web

5.22   A survey by KRC Research for *U.S. News* reported that 37% of people plan to spend more on eating out after they retire. If eight people are randomly selected, then determine

a. the expected number of people who plan to spend more eating out after they retire

b. the standard deviation of the individuals who plan to spend more eating out after they retire

c. the probability that two or fewer in the sample indicate that they actually plan to spend more on eating out after retirement.

Advanced Business Applications

5.23   The Ziteck Corporation buys parts from international suppliers. One part is currently being purchased from a Malaysian supplier under a contract that calls for at most 5% of the 10,000 parts to be defective. When a shipment arrives, Ziteck randomly samples 10 parts. If they find 2 or fewer defectives in the sample, they keep the shipment; otherwise they return the entire shipment to the supplier.

a. Assuming that the conditions for the binomial distribution are satisfied, what is the probability that the sample will lead Ziteck to keep the shipment if the defect rate is actually 0.05?

b. Suppose the supplier is actually sending Ziteck 10% defects, what is the probability that the sample will lead Ziteck to accept the shipment anyway?

c. Comment on this sampling plan (sample size and accept/reject point.) Do you think it favors either Ziteck or the supplier? Discuss.

5.24   A food-packaging business in California has a process that fills tomato juice into 24-ounce containers. When the process is in control, half the cans actually contain more than 24 ounces and half contain less. Suppose a quality inspector has just randomly sampled nine cans and has found that all nine had more than 24 ounces. Calculate the probability that this would occur if the filling process was in control. Based on this probability, what conclusion might be reached? Discuss.

5.25   In addition to microprocessors, Intel also supplies Gateway with memory modules (RAM). An important issue for Gateway is the proportion of defective modules it receives. Gateway must be very careful to negotiate a contract with Intel that will ensure the quality of its own product. Suppose that Gateway can tolerate 2.5% of its computers being returned because of failures in the memory modules. Assume each computer has three memory modules installed. If any one of the modules malfunctions, the computer will be returned for repair. Define x to be the random variable, whose value equals the number of defective memory modules in a randomly chosen Gateway computer.

a. Does the random variable (*x*) have a binomial distribution? If so, list the parameters that define this specific binomial distribution.

b. If Gateway negotiates a contract that allows Intel to send shipments in which 5% of the modules are defective, calculate the probability that a randomly chosen Gateway computer with these memory modules installed will be returned for repair. Is this probability larger than the 0.025 (2.5%) required by Gateway?

c. If the contract negotiated in part b doesn't meet with Gateway's approval, suggest a defect rate that Intel can deliver so that no more than 2.5% of Gateway's computers are returned for repairs.

5.26 Suppose a training program for electronics repair technicians has a goal that 70% of those who complete the program will be able to carry out a standard set of repairs on a personal computer. Five individuals who are believed to have completed the training are assigned the task of making the PC repairs. Of the five, one is successful.

a. What is the expected number of technicians who should be successful?

b. Assuming that these individuals did complete the training and that the 70% goal was met, what is the probability that one or fewer would be able to make the repairs? What might this result imply? Discuss some of the optional scenarios.

5-2 OTHER DISCRETE PROBABILITY DISTRIBUTIONS

The binomial distribution is very useful in many business situations, as indicated by the examples and applications presented in the previous section. However, as we pointed out, there are several requirements that must hold before we can use the binomial distribution to determine probabilities. If those conditions are not satisfied, there may be other theoretical probability distributions that could be employed. In this section we introduce two other very useful discrete probability distributions: the Poisson distribution and the hypergeometric distribution.

THE POISSON DISTRIBUTION

To use the binomial distribution, we must be able to count the number of successes and the number of failures. Although in many situations you may be able to count the number of successes, you often cannot count the number of failures. For example, suppose a company builds freeways in Vermont. The company could count the number of chuckholes that develop per mile (here a chuckhole is a success because it is what we are looking for), but how could it count the number of non-chuckholes? Or what about a hospital supplying emergency medical services in Los Angeles? It could easily count the number of emergencies its units respond to in one hour, but how could it determine how many calls it did not receive? Obviously, in these cases the number of possible outcomes (successes + failures) is difficult, if not impossible, to determine. If the total number of possible outcomes cannot be determined, the binomial distribution cannot be applied. In these cases you may be able to use the Poisson distribution.

Characteristics of the Poisson Distribution

The Poisson distribution[1] describes a process that extends over time or space. The outcomes of interest, such as emergency calls or chuckholes, occur at random, and we count the number of outcomes that occur in a given segment of time or space. We might count the number of emergency calls in a 15-minute period or the number of chuckholes in a two-mile stretch of freeway. As we did with the binomial distribution, we will call these outcomes *successes* even though (like chuckholes) they might be undesirable.

The possible counts are the integers 0, 1, 2, . . . and we would like to know the probability of each of these values. For example, what is the chance of getting exactly 4 emergency calls in a particular quarter hour? What is the chance that a chosen two-mile stretch of freeway will contain 0 chuckholes?

We can use the Poisson probability distribution to answer these questions if we make the following assumptions.

1. We know λ, the average number of successes in a segment of *unit* size. For example, we know that there is an average of 8 emergency calls per hour ($\lambda = 8$), or an average of 15 chuckholes per mile of freeway ($\lambda = 15$).

2. The probability of *x* successes in a segment is the same for all segments of the same size. For example, the probability distribution of emergency calls is the same for any 15-minute period of time at the hospital.

3. What happens in one segment has no influence on any nonoverlapping segment. For example, the number of calls arriving between 9:30 P.M. and 9:45 P.M. has no influence on the number of calls between 10:00 P.M. and 10:15 P.M.

---

[1]The Poisson distribution can be derived as the limiting distribution of the binomial distribution as the number of trials, *n*, tends to infinity. It serves as a good approximation to the binomial when *n* is large.

4. We imagine dividing time or space into tiny subsegments. Then the chance of *more* than one success in a subsegment is negligible and the chance of exactly one success in a tiny subsegment of length t is λt. For example, the chance of two emergency calls in the same second is essentially 0, and if $\lambda = 8$ calls per hour, the chance of a call in any given second is $(8)(1/3600) \approx 0.0022$.

Once λ has been determined, we can calculate the average occurrence rate for a segment of any size t. This is λt. Note that λ and t must be in compatible units. If we have $\lambda = 20$ arrivals per hour, the segments must be in hours or fractional parts of an hour.

That is, if we have $\lambda = 20$ per hour and we wish to work with half-hour time periods, the segment would be

$$t = \tfrac{1}{2} \text{ hour};$$

not $t = 30$ minutes.

Although the Poisson distribution is often used to describe situations such as the number of customers who arrive at a hospital emergency room per hour or the number of calls the Hewlett-Packard LaserJet printer service center receives in a 30-minute period, the segments need not be time intervals. Poisson distributions are also used to describe such random variables as the number of knots in a sheet of plywood or the number of contaminants in a certain volume of lake water. The segments would be the sheet of plywood and the volume of water.

Another important point is that λt, the average number in a segment of size t, is not necessarily the number we will see if we observe the process for one segment. We might expect an average of 20 people to arrive at a checkout stand in any given hour, but we do not expect to find exactly that number arriving every hour. The actual arrivals will form a distribution with an expected value, or mean, equal to λt. So, for the Poisson distribution,

$$\mu_x = \lambda t$$

Once λ and t have been specified, the probability for any discrete value in the Poisson distribution can be found using Equation 5-7.

Poisson Probability Distribution

$$P(x) = \frac{(\lambda t)^x \, e^{-\lambda t}}{x!}$$

5-7

where:

t = Size of the segment of interest

x = Number of successes in the segment of interest

λ = Expected number of successes in a segment of unit size

e = Base of the natural logarithm system (2.71828...)

First City Bank—A study conducted at First City Bank shows that the average number of arrivals to the teller section of the bank per hour is 15. Further, the distribution for the number of arrivals is considered to be Poisson distributed. Figure 5-5 shows the shape of the Poisson distribution for $\lambda = 15$. The probability of each possible number of customers arriving can be computed using Equation 5-7. For example, we can find the probability of $x = 12$ customers in one hour ($t = 1$) as follows.

$$P(x = 12) = \frac{(\lambda t)^x e^{-\lambda t}}{x!} = \frac{15^{12} e^{-15}}{12!} = 0.0829$$

Poisson Probability Distribution Table

As was the case with the binomial distribution, a table of probabilities exists for the Poisson distribution. (The full Poisson table appears in Appendix C.) The Poisson table shows the probabilities for different λt values. We can use the following business example to illustrate how to use the Poisson table.

Acme Taxi Service—The Acme Taxi Service has studied the demand for taxis at the local airport and has found that, on average, six taxis are demanded per hour. Thus, $\lambda = 6/\text{hour}$. If the company is considering locating six taxis at the airport during each hour, what is the probability that demand will exceed six and people will have to wait for taxi service?

To answer this question, we recognize that the segment of interest, t, equals one hour, so $\lambda t = 6$. We are interested in

$$P(x > 6) = 1 - P(x \le 6)$$

FIGURE 5-5

Poisson Distribution for
Bank Customer Arrivals
with λ = 15

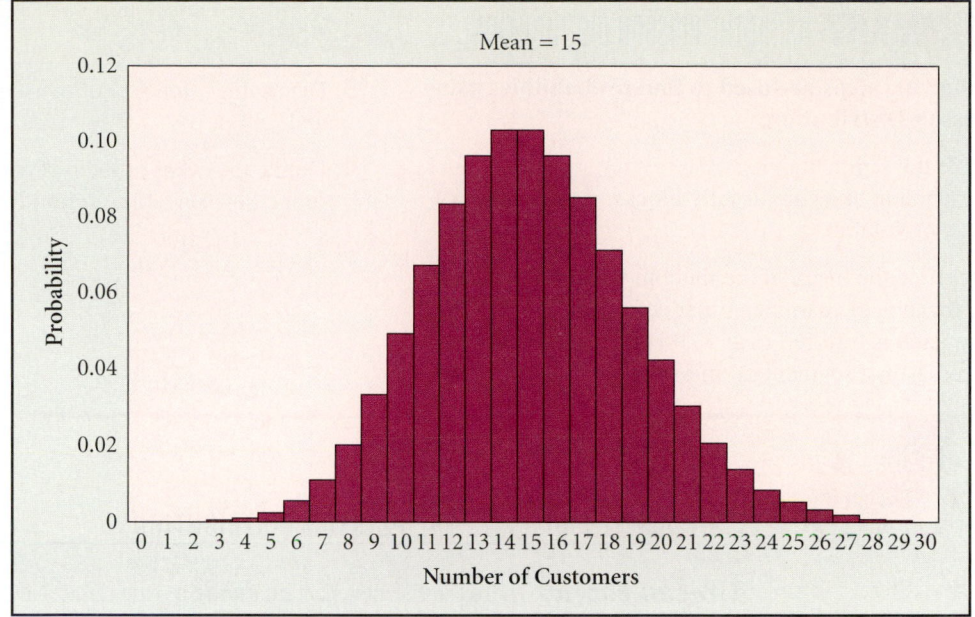

To use the Poisson probability tables, turn to Appendix C and locate the column with $\lambda t = 6$. Table 5-4 shows the portion of the Poisson table that we will need. Locate the values of x down the left-hand side of the table. We first wish to determine the sum of the probabilities for $x = 0$ to $x = 6$. This sum is found by adding the probabilities under the column for $\lambda t = 6$ from $x = 0$ through $x = 6$. Doing this, we get:

$$P(x \leq 6) = 0.0025 + 0.0149 + 0.0446 + 0.0892 + 0.1339 + 0.1606 + 0.1606$$
$$= 0.6063$$

Therefore, the desired probability is

$$P(x > 6) = 1 - P(x \leq 6)$$
$$= 1 - 0.6063$$
$$= 0.3937$$

Thus, there is a 0.3937 probability that demand for taxis at the airport will exceed supply if the company puts only six taxis at the airport. This means that in almost 4 of every 10 hours, at least one more cab will be demanded than Acme will have available.

TABLE 5-4

Poisson Distribution Table

					λt					
x	5.10	5.20	5.30	5.40	5.50	5.60	5.70	5.80	5.90	6.00
0	.0061	.0055	.0050	.0045	.0041	.0037	.0033	.0030	.0027	.0025
1	.0311	.0287	.0265	.0244	.0225	.0207	.0191	.0176	.0162	.0149
2	.0793	.0746	.0701	.0659	.0618	.0580	.0544	.0509	.0477	.0446
3	.1348	.1293	.1239	.1185	.1133	.1082	.1033	.0985	.0938	.0892
4	.1719	.1681	.1641	.1600	.1558	.1515	.1472	.1428	.1383	.1339
5	.1753	.1748	.1740	.1728	.1714	.1697	.1678	.1656	.1632	.1606
6	.1490	.1515	.1537	.1555	.1571	.1584	.1594	.1601	.1605	.1606
7	.1086	.1125	.1163	.1200	.1234	.1267	.1298	.1326	.1353	.1377
8	.0692	.0731	.0771	.0810	.0849	.0887	.0925	.0962	.0998	.1033
9	.0392	.0423	.0454	.0486	.0519	.0552	.0586	.0620	.0654	.0688
10	.0200	.0220	.0241	.0262	.0285	.0309	.0334	.0359	.0386	.0413
11	.0093	.0104	.0116	.0129	.0143	.0157	.0173	.0190	.0207	.0225
12	.0039	.0045	.0051	.0058	.0064	.0073	.0082	.0092	.0102	.0113
13	.0015	.0018	.0021	.0024	.0028	.0032	.0036	.0041	.0046	.0052
14	.0006	.0007	.0008	.0009	.0011	.0013	.0015	.0017	.0019	.0022
15	.0002	.0002	.0003	.0003	.0004	.0005	.0006	.0007	.0008	.0009
16	.0001	.0001	.0001	.0001	.0001	.0002	.0002	.0002	.0003	.0003
17	.0000	.0000	.0000	.0000	.0000	.0001	.0001	.0001	.0001	.0001

SUMMARY: USING THE POISSON DISTRIBUTION

The following steps are used to find probabilities using the Poisson Distribution:

1. Define the segment units.
The segment units are usually blocks of time, areas of space, or volume.

2. Determine the mean of the random variable.
The mean is the parameter that defines the Poisson distribution and is referred to as λ. It is the average number of successes in a segment of unit size.

3. Determine t, the size of the segments to be considered, and λt.

4. Define the event of interest and use the Poisson formula or the Poisson tables to find the probability.

EXAMPLE 5-6: USING THE POISSON DISTRIBUTION

Grogan Fabrics   Grogan Fabrics, headquartered in Auckland, New Zealand, makes wool fabrics for export to many other countries around the world. Before shipping, fabric-quality tests are performed. The industry standards call for the average number of defects per fabric bolt to not exceed 5. During a recent test, the inspector selected a 30-yard bolt at random and carefully examined the first 3 yards finding 3 defects. To determine the probability of this event occurring if the fabric meets the industry standards, assuming that the Poisson distribution applies, the company can perform the following steps:

Step 1: **Define the segment unit.**
Because the mean was stated as 5 defects per fabric bolt, the segment unit in this case is one 30-yard fabric bolt.

Step 2: **Determine the mean of the random variable.**
In this case if the company meets the industry standards, the mean will be:
$$\lambda = 5$$

Step 3: **Determine the segment size t.**
The company quality inspectors analyzed 3 yards from a 30-yard bolt, which is equal to .1 units. So $t = .1$. Then
$$\lambda t = 5(.1) = .5$$
When looking at 3 yards, the company would expect to find .5 defects if the industry standards are being met.

Step 4: **Define the event of interest and use the Poisson formula or the Poisson tables to find the probability.**
In this case, 3 defects were observed. Because 3 exceeds the expected number ($\lambda t = .5$) the company would want to find:
$$P(x \geq 3) = P(x = 3) + P(x = 4) + \cdots$$
The Poisson table in Appendix C is used to determine these probabilities. Locate the desired probability under the column headed $\lambda t = .5$. Then find the values of x down the left-hand column.

$$P(x \geq 3) = 0.0126 + 0.0016 + 0.0002$$
$$= 0.0144$$

This low probability may cause the company some concern about whether it is actually meeting the quality standards.

The Mean and Standard Deviation of the Poisson Distribution

The mean of the Poisson distribution is λt. This is the value we use to specify which Poisson distribution we are using. We must know the mean before we can find probabilities for a Poisson distribution.

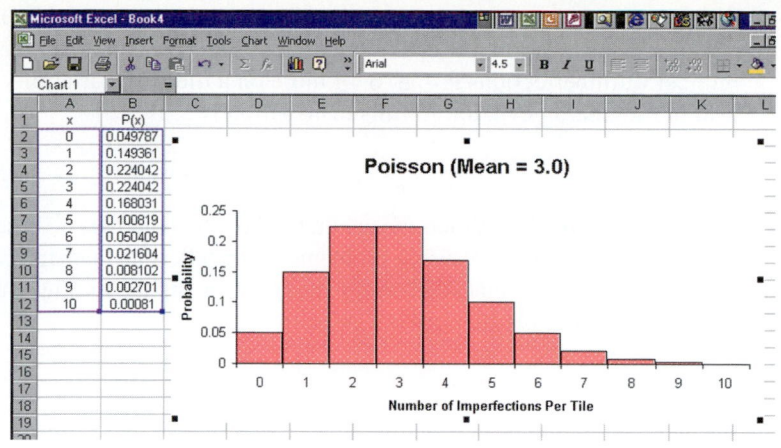

Figure 5-5 illustrated that the outcome of a Poisson distribution variable is subject to variation. Like any other discrete probability distribution, the standard deviation for the Poisson can be computed using Equation 5-5:

$$\sigma_x = \sqrt{\sum [x - E(x)]^2 P(x)}$$

However, for a Poisson distribution, the standard deviation also can be found using Equation 5-8.

Standard Deviation of the Poisson Distribution

$$\sigma = \sqrt{\lambda t}$$

5-8

The standard deviation of the Poisson distribution is simply the square root of the mean. Therefore, if you are working with a Poisson process, reducing the mean can reduce the variability also.

Excel and Minitab Tutorial

Heritage Tile—To illustrate the importance of the relationship between the mean and standard deviation of the Poisson distribution, consider Heritage Tile in New York City. The company makes ceramic tile for kitchens and bathrooms. The quality standards call for the number of imperfections in tile to average 3 or fewer. The distribution of imperfections is thought to be Poisson. Both Minitab and Excel generate Poisson probabilities in much the same way as for the binomial distribution, which was discussed in Section 5-1. If we assume that the company is meeting the standard, Figure 5-6a and Figure 5-6b show the Poisson probability

FIGURE 5-6B

Minitab Output for Heritage Tile Example

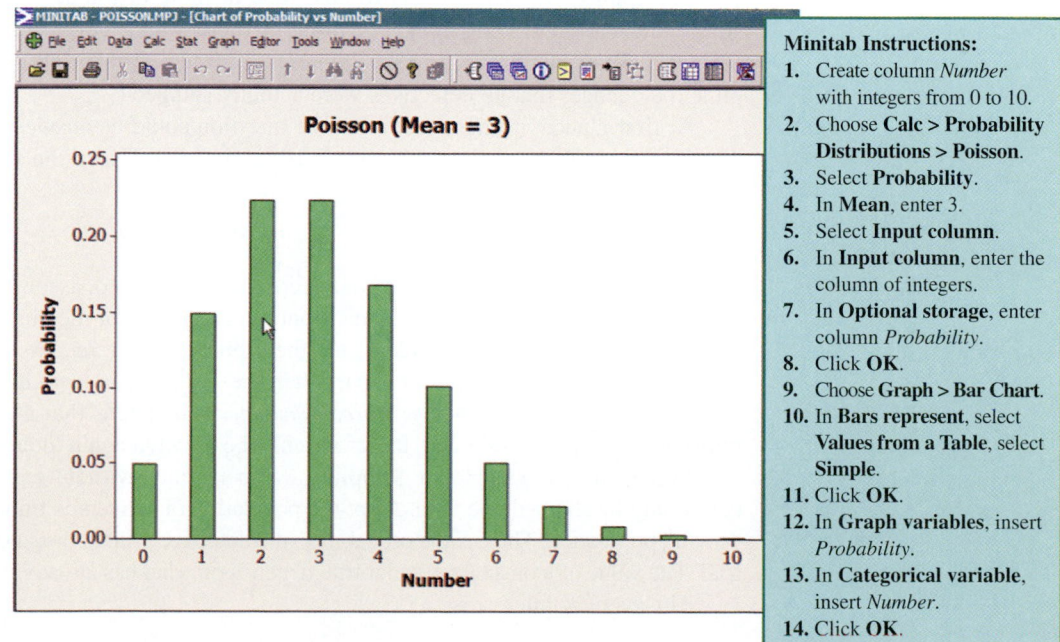

distribution generated using Excel and Minitab when $\lambda t = 3.0$. Even though the average number of defects is 3, the manager is concerned about the large number of instances in which the number of imperfections is 4, 5, 6, or more on a tile. The variability is too great. Using Equation 5-8, the standard deviation for this distribution is

$$\sigma = \sqrt{3.0} = 1.732$$

This large standard deviation means that although some tiles will have few if any imperfections, others will have several, causing problems for installers and unhappy customers.

A quality improvement effort directed at reducing the average number of imperfections to 2.0 would also reduce the standard deviation to

$$\sigma = \sqrt{2.0} = 1.414$$

Further reductions in the average would also reduce variation in the number of imperfections between tiles. This would mean more consistency for installers and higher customer satisfaction.

THE HYPERGEOMETRIC DISTRIBUTION

Although the binomial and Poisson distributions are very useful in many business decision-making situations, they both require that the trials be independent. For instance, in binomial applications the probability of a success on one trial must be the same as the probability of a success on any other trial. Although there are certainly times when this assumption can be satisfied, or at least approximated, in instances in which the population is fairly small and we are sampling without replacement, the condition of independence will not hold. In these cases, a discrete probability distribution referred to as the *hypergeometric distribution* can be useful.

Lindell Corporation—The Lindell Corporation manufactures high-speed line printers for computer systems. Lindell printers are compatible with most of the major computer vendors' hardware. Because of the intense competition in the marketplace for printers and other peripherals, Lindell has made every attempt to make a high-quality printer. However, a recent production run of 20 printers contained two printers that tested out as defective. The problem was traced to a shipment of defective cables that Lindell received shortly before the production run started.

The production manager ordered that the entire batch of 20 printers be isolated from other production output until further testing could be completed. Unfortunately, a new shipping clerk packaged 10 of these isolated printers and shipped them to the California State Purchasing Department to fill an order that was already overdue. By the time the production manager noticed what had happened, the printers were already in transit.

The immediate concern was whether one or more of the defectives had been included in the shipment. The new shipping clerk thought there was a good chance that no defectives were included. Short of reinspecting the remaining printers, how might the Lindell Corporation determine the chances that no defectives were actually shipped?

At first glance, it might seem that the question could be answered by employing the binomial distribution with $n = 10$, $p = 2/20 = 0.10$, and $x = 0$. Using the binomial distribution table in Appendix B we get:

$$P(x = 0) = 0.3487$$

There is a 0.3487 chance that no defectives were shipped, assuming the selection process satisfied the requirements of a binomial distribution. However, for the binomial distribution to be applicable, the trials must be independent, and the probability of a success, p, must remain constant from trial to trial. In order for this to occur when the sampling is from a "small," *finite* population, the sampling must be performed with *replacement*. This means that after each item is selected, it is returned to the population and, therefore, may be selected again later in the sampling.

In the Lindell example the sampling was performed without replacement because each printer could only be shipped one time. Also, the population of printers is finite with size $N = 20$, which is a "small" population. Thus, p, the probability of a defective printer, does not remain equal to 0.10 on each trial. The value of p on any particular trial depends on what has already been selected on previous trials.

The event of interest is

$$G\,G\,G\,G\,G\,G\,G\,G\,G\,G$$

The probability that the first printer selected for shipment would be good would be 18/20, because there were 18 good printers in the batch of 20. Now, assuming the first printer selected was good, the probability the second printer was good is 17/19, because we then had only 19 printers to select from and 17 of those would be good. The probability that all 10 printers selected were good is

$$\frac{18}{20} \times \frac{17}{19} \times \frac{16}{18} \times \frac{15}{17} \times \frac{14}{16} \times \frac{13}{15} \times \frac{12}{14} \times \frac{11}{13} \times \frac{10}{12} \times \frac{9}{11} = 0.2368$$

This value is not the same as the 0.3847 probability we got when the binomial distribution was used. This demonstrates that when sampling is performed without replacement from finite populations, the binomial distribution *cannot* be used to compute exact probabilities unless the sample is small relative to the size of the population. Under that circumstance, the value of p will not change very much as the sample is selected, and the binomial distribution will be a reasonable approximation to the actual probability distribution.

In those cases in which the sample is large relative to the size of the population, a discrete probability distribution, called the hypergeometric distribution is the correct distribution for computing probabilities for the random variable of interest.

The hypergeometric distribution is formed by the ratio of the number of ways an event of interest can occur over the total number of ways any event can occur. The number of ways these events can occur can be determined by listing the sample space or, more simply, by using Equation 5-1 for combinations.

$$C_x^n = \frac{n!}{x!(n-x)!}$$

We then use the formula for counting combinations to form the equation for computing probabilities for the hypergeometric distribution when each trial has two possible outcomes (success and failure), as defined in Equation 5-9.

Hypergeometric Distribution (Two Possible Outcomes per Trial)

$$P(x) = \frac{C_{n-x}^{N-X} \cdot C_x^X}{C_n^N} \qquad \text{5-9}$$

where:

N = Population size
X = Number of successes in the population
n = Sample size
x = Number of successes in the sample
$n - x$ = Number of failures in the sample

Notice that the numerator of Equation 5-9 is the product of the number of ways you can select x successes in a random sample out of the X successes in the population and the number of ways you can select $n - x$ failures in a sample from the $N - X$ failures in the population. The denominator in the equation is the number of ways the sample can be selected from the population.

In the Lindell example, the probability of zero defectives being shipped ($x = 0$) is

$$P(x = 0) = \frac{C_{10-0}^{20-2} \cdot C_0^2}{C_{10}^{20}}$$

$$P(x = 0) = \frac{C_{10}^{18} \cdot C_0^2}{C_{10}^{20}}$$

Carrying out the arithmetic, we get

$$P(x) = \frac{(43{,}758)(1)}{184{,}756} = 0.2368$$

As we found before, the probability that zero defectives were included in the shipment is 0.2368, or approximately 24%.

The probabilities of $x = 1$ and $x = 2$ defectives can also be found by using Equation 5-9, as follows:

$$P(x = 1) = \frac{C_{10-1}^{20-2} \cdot C_1^2}{C_{10}^{20}} = 0.5264$$

and

$$P(x = 2) = \frac{C_{10-2}^{20-2} \cdot C_2^2}{C_{10}^{20}} = 0.2368$$

Thus, the hypergeometric probability distribution for the number of defective printers in a random selection of 10 is

x	P(x)
0	0.2368
1	0.5264
2	0.2368
	$\Sum = 1.0000$

EXAMPLE 5-7: THE HYPERGEOMETRIC DISTRIBUTION (TWO OUTCOMES PER TRIAL)

Gender Equity   One of the biggest changes in U.S. business practice in the past few decades has been the inclusion of women into the management ranks of companies. Tom Peters, management consultant and author of such books as *In Search of Excellence*, recently stated that one of the reasons the Middle Eastern countries have suffered economically compared with countries such as the United States is that they have not included women in their economic system. However, there are still issues in U.S. business. Consider a situation in which a Maryland company needed to downsize one department having 30 people—12 women and 18 men. Ten people were laid off, and upper management said the layoffs were done randomly. Of the 10 laid off, 8 were women. By chance, 40% (12/30) of the layoffs would be women. A labor attorney is interested in the probability of 8 or more women being laid off by chance alone. This can be done using the following steps:

Step 1: **Determine the population size and the combined sample size.**
The population size and sample size are
$$N = 30 \quad \text{and} \quad n = 10$$

Step 2: **Define the event of interest.**
The attorney is interested in the event:
$$P(x \geq 8) = ?$$
What are the chances that 8 or more women would be selected?

Step 3: **Determine the number of successes in the population and the number of successes in the sample.**
In this situation, a success is the event that a woman is selected. There are $X = 12$ women in the population and $x \geq 8$ in the sample. We will break this down as $x = 8$, $x = 9$, $x = 10$.

Step 4: **Compute the desired probabilities using Equation 5-9.**
$$P(x) = \frac{C_{n-x}^{N-X} \cdot C_x^X}{C_n^N}$$

We want:[2]

$$P(x \geq 8) = P(x = 8) + P(x = 9) + P(x = 10)$$

$$P(x = 8) = \frac{C_{10-8}^{30-12} \cdot C_8^{12}}{C_{10}^{30}} = \frac{C_2^{18} \cdot C_8^{12}}{C_{10}^{30}} = 0.0025$$

$$P(x = 9) = \frac{C_1^{18} \cdot C_9^{12}}{C_{10}^{30}} = 0.0001$$

$$P(x = 10) = \frac{C_0^{18} \cdot C_{10}^{12}}{C_{10}^{30}} \approx 0.0000$$

Therefore, $P(x \geq 8) = 0.0025 + 0.0001 + 0.0000 = 0.0026$
The chances that 8 or more women would have been selected among the 10 people chosen for layoff strictly due to chance is 0.0026. The attorney will likely wish to challenge the layoffs based on this extremely low probability.

[2]Note, you can use Excel's HYPGEOMDIST function to compute these probabilities.

THE HYPERGEOMETRIC DISTRIBUTION WITH MORE THAN TWO POSSIBLE OUTCOMES PER TRIAL

Equation 5-9 assumes that on any given sample selection or trial only one of two possible outcomes will occur. However, the hypergeometric distribution can easily be extended to consider any number of possible categories of outcomes on a given trial by employing Equation 5-10.

Hypergeometric Distribution (k Possible Outcomes per Trial)

$$P(x_1, x_2, x_3, \ldots, x_k) = \frac{C_{x_1}^{X_1} \cdot C_{x_2}^{X_2} \cdot C_{x_3}^{X_3} \cdot \cdots \cdot C_{x_k}^{X_k}}{C_n^N}$$ 5-10

where:

$$\sum_{i=1}^{k} X_i = N$$

$$\sum_{i=1}^{k} x_i = n$$

N = Population size
n = Total sample size
X_i = Number of items in the population with outcome i
x_i = Number of items in the sample with outcome i

$\mathcal{E}$XAMPLE 5-8: THE HYPERGEOMETRIC DISTRIBUTION FOR MULTIPLE OUTCOMES

Brand Preference Study   Consider a marketing study that involves placing toothpaste made by four different companies in a basket at the exit to a drugstore. A sign on the basket invites customers to take one tube free of charge. At the beginning of the study, the basket contains the following:

> 5 brand A tubes
> 4 brand B tubes
> 6 brand C tubes
> 4 brand D tubes

The researchers were interested in the brand selection patterns for customers who could select without regard to price. Suppose six customers were observed and three selected brand B, two selected brand D, and one selected brand C. No one selected brand A. The probability of this selection mix, assuming the customers were selecting entirely at random without replacement from a finite population, can be found using the following steps:

Step 1: **Determine the population size and the combined sample size.**
The population size and sample size are

$$N = 19 \quad \text{and} \quad n = 6$$

Step 2: **Define the event of interest.**
The event of interest is

$$P(x_1 = 0; x_2 = 3; x_3 = 1; x_4 = 2) = ?$$

Step 3: **Determine the number in each category in the population and the number in each category in the sample.**

$X_1 = 5$	(brand A)	$x_1 = 0$
$X_2 = 4$	(brand B)	$x_2 = 3$
$X_3 = 6$	(brand C)	$x_3 = 1$
$X_4 = 4$	(brand D)	$x_4 = 2$
$N = 19$		$n = 6$

Step 4:   **Compute the desired probability using Equation 5-10.**

$$P(x_1, x_2, x_3, \ldots, x_k) = \frac{C_{x_1}^{X_1} \cdot C_{x_2}^{X_2} \cdot C_{x_3}^{X_3} \cdot \ldots \cdot C_{x_k}^{X_k}}{C_n^N}$$

$$P(0, 3, 1, 2) = \frac{C_0^5 \cdot C_3^4 \cdot C_1^6 \cdot C_2^4}{C_6^{19}}$$

$$= \frac{(1)(4)(6)(6)}{27{,}132} = \frac{144}{27{,}132}$$

$$= 0.0053$$

There are slightly more than five chances in 1,000 of this exact selection occurring by random chance.

5-2: EXERCISES

Skill Development

5.27 If the mean value of a Poisson-distributed variable is 5.0, find the following:
   a. $P(x = 5) =$
   b. $P(x \leq 5) =$
   c. $P(x \geq 3) =$

5.28 If $\lambda t = 3.5$ for a Poisson-distributed variable, find the following:
   a. $P(2 \leq x \leq 5) =$
   b. $P(x = 3) =$
   c. $P(x \geq 1) =$

5.29 If $\lambda = 5$ and $t = 2$ for a Poisson distribution,
   a. Determine the mean and standard deviation of this Poisson distribution.
   b. What is the probability of three or fewer successes?

5.30 If $\lambda = 18$ and $t = \frac{1}{3}$ for a Poisson distribution,
   a. Find the expected value, variance, and standard deviation of this Poisson distribution.
   b. Determine the probability of exactly zero successes.

5.31 A sample of 4 is taken from a population of 20 containing 4 defective items. Determine the probability distribution that defines the defectives that can be found in the sample.

5.32 A sample of 3 is taken from a population of 12 engines, 5 of which are built to metric standards and 7 of which are built to English standards. Determine the probability distribution that defines the number of English standard engines that could be found in the sample.

5.33 A population consists of 40 items. Ten of these are red, 15 are green, and 15 are yellow. If a sample of size 10 is randomly selected from the population, what is the probability that sample will contain two red, two green, and six yellow?

5.34 A gathering contained 15 people, six of whom were Republicans, five were Democrats, and the rest were Independents. If three of these people were selected at random to give a speech to the group, what is the probability that the three would consist of one Democrat, one Republican, and one Independent?

Business Applications

5.35 East-West Translations publishes textbooks of ancient Oriental teachings for English-speaking universities. The company currently is testing a computer-based translation service. Because Oriental symbols are difficult to translate, East-West assumes the computer program will make some errors, but then so do human translators. The computer service claims its error rate will average 3 per 400 words of translation. East-West randomly selects a 1,200-word passage. Assuming the computer company's claim is accurate and the Poisson distribution applies,
   a. Determine the probability no errors will be found.
   b. Calculate the probability more than 14 errors will be found.
   c. Find the probability that fewer than 9 errors will be found.
   d. If 15 errors are found in the 1,200-word passage, what would you conclude about the computer company's claim? Why?

5.36 Your company president has told you that your company experiences product returns at the rate of two per month, distributed as a Poisson random variable. Determine the probability that next month there will be
   a. No returns.
   b. One return.
   c. Two returns.
   d. More than two returns.
   e. In the past three months your company has only had one month in which the number of returns was at most two. Calculate the probability of this event occurring. What will you tell the president of your company concerning the return rate for your company? Make sure you support your statement with something other than opinion.

5.37 The Defense Department has recently advertised for bids for producing a new night-vision binocular. Vista Optical decided to submit a bid for the contract. The first step was to supply a sample of binoculars for the army to test at its Kentucky development grounds. Vista makes a superior night-vision binocular. However, the four sent for testing were taken from a development-lab project of 20 units that contained four defectives. The army has indicated it will reject any manufacturer that submits one or more defective binoculars. What is the probability that this mistake has cost Vista any chance for the contract?

5.38 An inventory of kitchen ranges contains 11 white, 9 almond, and 6 salmon pink. Five new homes are being built in a subdivision by five different builders, and the kitchen ranges will be taken randomly from this inventory.

  a. What is the probability that three of the homes will have a white range and the other two almond?

  b. What is the probability that all five ranges will be the same color?

c. What is the probability that three ranges will be white and the other two will be of the same color but not white?

5.39 The Farmhill Nursery sells trees and other yard and garden items. Currently, the nursery has 10 fruit trees, 8 pine trees, and 14 maple trees. It plans to give 4 trees away at next Saturday's lawn and garden show in the city park. The four winners can select which type of tree they want. Assume they select randomly.

  a. What is the probability that all four winners will select the same type of tree?

  b. What is the probability that three winners will select pine trees and the other tree will be a maple?

  c. What is the probability that no fruit trees and two of each of the others will be selected?

5-3 THE NORMAL PROBABILITY DISTRIBUTION

THE NORMAL DISTRIBUTION

You will encounter many business situations in which the random variable of interest will be treated as a continuous variable. There are several continuous distributions that are frequently used to describe physical situations. The most useful continuous probability distribution is the **normal distribution**.[3] The reason is that the output from a great many processes (both man-made and natural) are normally distributed.

Normal Distribution

The normal distribution is a bell-shaped distribution with the following properties:
1. It is *unimodal*; that is, the normal distribution peaks at a single value.
2. It is *symmetrical*; this means that the two areas under the curve between the mean and any two points equidistant on either side of the mean are identical. One side of the distribution is the mirror image of the other side.
3. The mean, median, and mode are equal.
4. The normal approaches the horizontal axis on either side of the mean toward plus and minus infinity (∞). In more formal terms, the normal distribution is *asymptotic* to the x-axis.
5. The amount of variation in the random variable determines the width of the normal distribution.

Figure 5-7 illustrates a typical normal distribution and highlights the normal distribution's characteristics. All normal distributions have the same general shape as the one shown in Figure 5-7.

FIGURE 5-7

Characteristics of the Normal Distribution

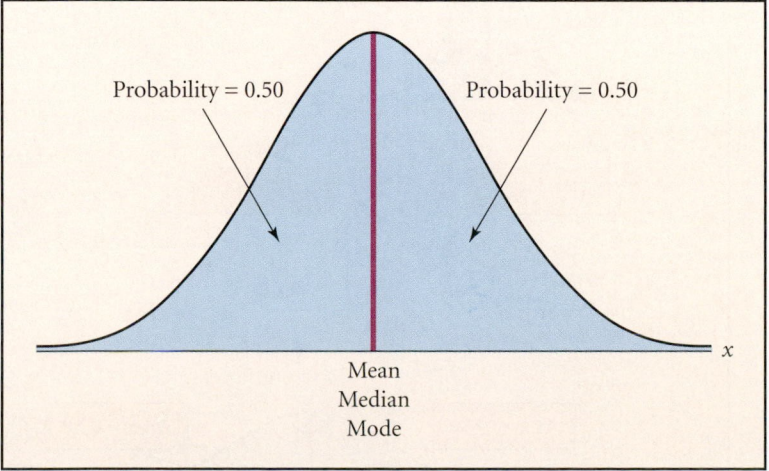

[3]It is common to refer to the very large family of normal distributions as "*the* normal distribution." Keep in mind, however, that "the normal distribution" really is a very large family of distributions.

However, they can differ in their mean value and their variation, depending on the situation being considered. The process being represented determines the scale of the horizontal axis. It may be pounds, inches, dollars, or any other physical attribute with a continuous measurement. Figure 5-8 shows several normal distributions with different centers and different spreads. Note that the total area (probability) under each normal curve equals 1.

The normal distribution is described by the rather-complicated-looking probability density function, shown in Equation 5-11.

Normal Distribution Density Function

$$f(x) = \frac{1}{\sigma\sqrt{2\pi}} e^{-(x-\mu)^2/2\sigma^2}$$

5-11

where:

x = Any value of the continuous random variable
σ = Population standard deviation
e = Base of the natural log $\simeq 2.71828\ldots$
μ = Population mean

To graph the normal distribution, we need to know the mean, μ, and the standard deviation, σ. Placing μ, σ, and a value of the variable, x, into the probability density function, we can calculate a height, $f(x)$, of the density function. If we try enough x values, we will get a curve like those shown in Figures 5-7 and 5-8.

The area under the normal curve corresponds to probability. The probability, $P(x)$, is equal to 0 for any particular x. However, we can find the probability for a range of values between x_1 and x_2 by finding the area under the curve between these two values. Integral calculus is used to find areas under a curve. Alternatively, a special normal distribution called the *standard normal distribution* is also used to find areas (probabilities) for a normal distribution.

THE STANDARD NORMAL DISTRIBUTION

The trick to finding probabilities for a normal distribution is to convert the normal distribution to a **standard normal distribution**.

FIGURE 5-8

Difference Between Normal Distributions

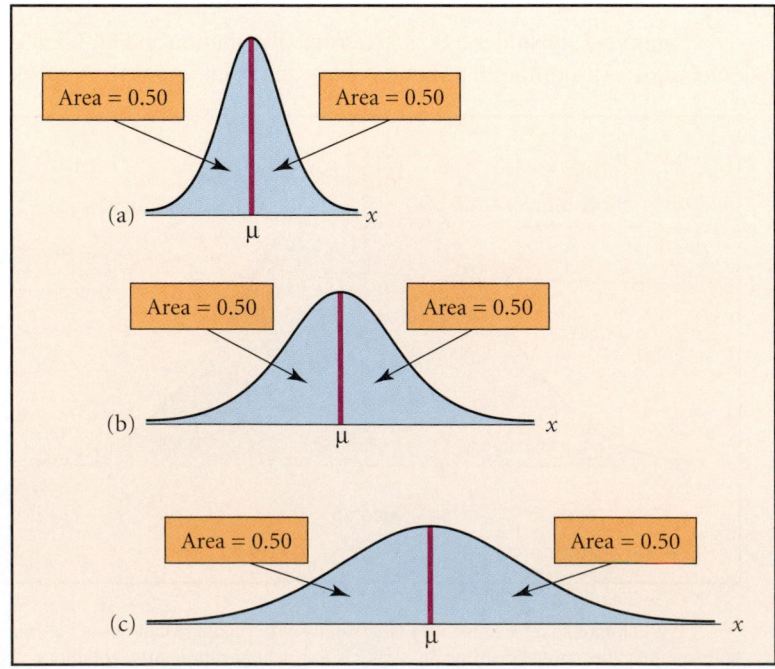

Standard Normal Distribution

A normal distribution that has a mean = 0.0 and a standard deviation = 1.0. The horizontal axis is scaled in z-values that measure the number of standard deviations a point is from the mean. Values above the mean have positive z-values. Values below the mean have negative z-values.

To convert a normal distribution to a standard normal distribution, the values (x) of the random variable are standardized as outlined previously in Chapter 3. The conversion formula is shown as Equation 5-12.

Standardized Normal z-Value

$$z = \frac{x - \mu}{\sigma}$$

5-12

where:

z = Scaled value (the number of standard deviations a point x is from the mean)
x = Any point on the horizontal axis
μ = Mean of the normal distribution
σ = Standard deviation of the normal distribution

Equation 5-12 *rescales* any normal distribution axis from its true units (time, weight, dollars, barrels, and so forth) to the standard measure referred to as a *z-value*. Thus, any value of the normally distributed continuous random variable can be represented by a unique z-value.

Westex Oil Company—Westex Oil, headquartered in Midland, Texas, budgets most of its cash flow from wells it owns on maturing oil fields. Most oil fields in the lower 48 states are maturing and facing declining production, but substantial oil often remains, though it is not recoverable by conventional means. Some companies inject water into a well to force out this additional oil. Westex management is considering adding a newly developed enzyme to the injected water to increase the amount of oil extracted, but they will do so only if the increased production covers the additional costs. Suppose the new enzyme will increase oil output by an average of 50 barrels a day, but because of differences in rock structures, this output varies with a standard deviation of 10 barrels a day.

Assume data suggest that the number of barrels of oil is described by the normal distribution with $\mu = 50$ and a standard deviation of $\sigma = 10$. Equation 5-11 will determine the height of the normal distribution curve for each possible value of the random variable. Figure 5-9 shows the resulting distribution.

Suppose in the Westex situation we select a level of

$$x = 50$$

barrels per day. (Note that 50 is also μ, the mean increase.) We can find the z-value for this point using Equation 5-12:

$$z = \frac{x - \mu}{\sigma} = \frac{50 - 50}{10} = 0$$

The z-value corresponding to the population mean, μ, is zero. This indicates that the mean is 0 standard deviations from itself.

FIGURE 5-9

Distribution of Oil Barrels Produced per Day for Westex Oil

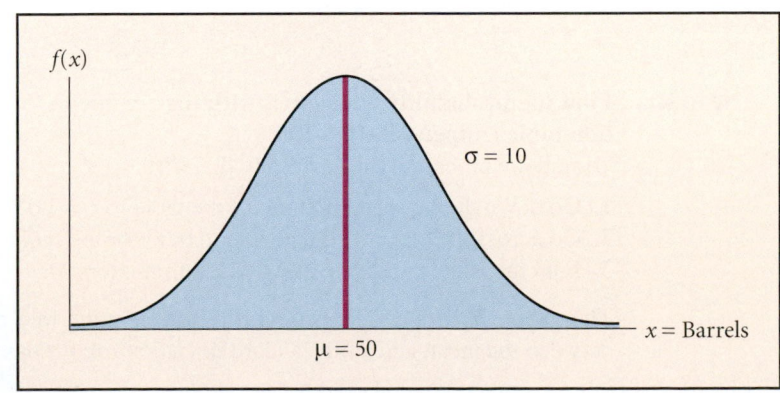

Next, we select

$$x = 60$$

barrels per day. The z-value for this point is

$$z = \frac{x - \mu}{\sigma} = \frac{60 - 50}{10} = \frac{10}{10} = 1$$

Thus, for this distribution, the value, 60 barrels is 1 standard deviation above the mean of 50. A value,

$$x = 35$$

has a standardized z-value $= -1.50$, as follows:

$$z = \frac{x - \mu}{\sigma} = \frac{35 - 50}{10} = \frac{-15}{10} = -1.50$$

This indicates that the value, 35 barrels is 1.50 standard deviations below the mean of 50 barrels. Verify for yourself that $x = 40$ barrels per day corresponds to a z-value of -1. Note that a negative z-value indicates that the specified value of x is less than the mean.

The z-value represents the number of standard deviations a point, x, is away from the population mean. In this Westex Oil example, the standard deviation is 10 barrels per day. Therefore, an output increase to 60 barrels per day is 1 standard deviation above the mean of 50 barrels per day. Likewise, an output increase to 70 barrels per day is 2 standard deviations above the mean. Figure 5-10 shows the standard normal distribution for the Westex Company example.

Using the Standard Normal Table

The *standard normal table* in Appendix D provides probabilities (or areas under the normal curve) for many different z-values. The standard normal table is constructed so that the probabilities provided represent the chance of a value falling between the z-value and the population mean.

The standard normal table is also reproduced in Table 5-5. This table provides probabilities for z-values between $z = 0.00$ and $z = 3.09$.

EXAMPLE 5-9: USING THE STANDARD NORMAL TABLE

Employee Commute Time   After completing a study, a company in Kansas City concluded the time its employees spend commuting to work each day is normally distributed with a mean equal to 15 minutes and a standard deviation equal to 3.5 minutes. One employee has indicated that she commutes 22 minutes per day. To find the probability that an employee would commute 22 or more minutes per day, you can use the following steps:

Step 1:   **Determine the mean and standard deviation for the random variable.**
The parameters of the probability distribution are
$$\mu = 15 \quad \text{and} \quad \sigma = 3.5$$

Step 2:   **Define the event of interest.**
The employee has a commute time of 22 minutes. We wish to find:
$$P(x \geq 22) = ?$$

Step 3:   **Convert the random variable to a standardized value using Equation 5-12.**
$$z = \frac{x - \mu}{\sigma} = \frac{22 - 15}{3.5} = 2.00$$

Step 4:   **Find the probability associated with the z-value in the standard normal distribution table (Appendix D).**
To find the probability for $z = 2.00$, [i.e., $P(0 \leq z \leq 2.00)$], do the following:

1. Go down the left-hand column of the table to $z = 2.0$.
2. Go across the top row of the table to 0.00 for the second decimal place in $z = 2.00$.
3. Find the value where the row and column intersect.

The value, 0.4772, is the probability that a value in a normal distribution will lie between the mean and 2.00 standard deviations above the mean.

FIGURE 5-10

Standard Normal Distribution

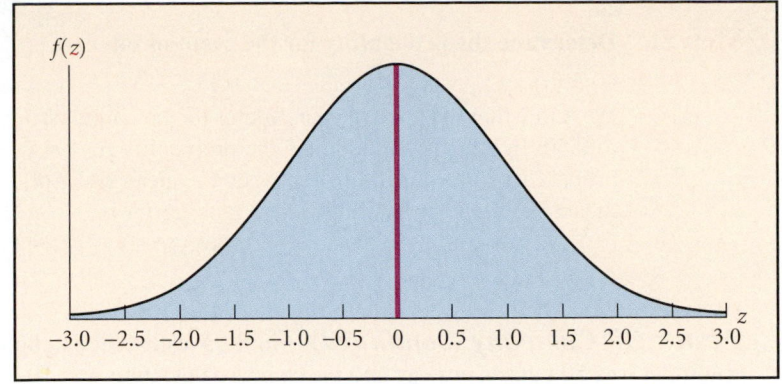

TABLE 5-5

Standard Normal Distribution Table

To illustrate: 19.85% of the area under a normal curve lies between the mean, μ, and a point 0.52 standard deviation units away.

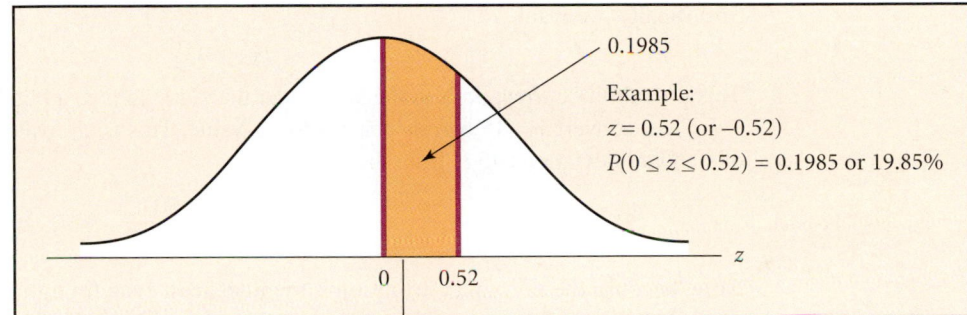

0.1985

Example:
$z = 0.52$ (or -0.52)
$P(0 \leq z \leq 0.52) = 0.1985$ or 19.85%

z	.00	.01	.02	.03	.04	.05	.06	.07	.08	.09
0.0	.0000	.0040	.0080	.0120	.0160	.0199	.0239	.0279	.0319	.0359
0.1	.0398	.0438	.0478	.0517	.0557	.0596	.0636	.0675	.0714	.0753
0.2	.0793	.0832	.0871	.0910	.0948	.0987	.1026	.1064	.1103	.1141
0.3	.1179	.1217	.1255	.1293	.1331	.1368	.1406	.1443	.1480	.1517
0.4	.1554	.1591	.1628	.1664	.1700	.1736	.1772	.1808	.1844	.1879
0.5	.1915	.1950	.1985	.2019	.2054	.2088	.2123	.2157	.2190	.2224
0.6	.2257	.2291	.2324	.2357	.2389	.2422	.2454	.2486	.2517	.2549
0.7	.2580	.2611	.2642	.2673	.2704	.2734	.2764	.2794	.2823	.2852
0.8	.2881	.2910	.2939	.2967	.2995	.3023	.3051	.3078	.3106	.3133
0.9	.3159	.3186	.3212	.3238	.3264	.3289	.3315	.3340	.3365	.3389
1.0	.3413	.3438	.3461	.3485	.3508	.3531	.3554	.3577	.3599	.3621
1.1	.3643	.3665	.3686	.3708	.3729	.3749	.3770	.3790	.3810	.3830
1.2	.3849	.3869	.3888	.3907	.3925	.3944	.3962	.3980	.3997	.4015
1.3	.4032	.4049	.4066	.4082	.4099	.4115	.4131	.4147	.4162	.4177
1.4	.4192	.4207	.4222	.4236	.4251	.4265	.4279	.4292	.4306	.4319
1.5	.4332	.4345	.4357	.4370	.4382	.4394	.4406	.4418	.4429	.4441
1.6	.4452	.4463	.4474	.4484	.4495	.4505	.4515	.4525	.4535	.4545
1.7	.4554	.4564	.4573	.4582	.4591	.4599	.4608	.4616	.4625	.4633
1.8	.4641	.4649	.4656	.4664	.4671	.4678	.4686	.4693	.4699	.4706
1.9	.4713	.4719	.4726	.4732	.4738	.4744	.4750	.4756	.4761	.4767
2.0	.4772	.4778	.4783	.4788	.4793	.4798	.4803	.4808	.4812	.4817
2.1	.4821	.4826	.4830	.4834	.4838	.4842	.4846.	.4850	.4854	.4857
2.2	.4861	.4864	.4868	.4871	.4875	.4878	.4881	.4884	.4887	.4890
2.3	.4893	.4896	.4898	.4901	.4904	.4906	.4909	.4911	.4913	.4916
2.4	.4918	.4920	.4922	.4925	.4927	.4929	.4931	.4932	.4934	.4936
2.5	.4938	.4940	.4941	.4943	.4945	.4946	.4948	.4949	.4951	.4952
2.6	.4953	.4955	.4956	.4957	.4959	.4960	.4961	.4962	.4963	.4964
2.7	.4965	.4966	.4967	.4968	.4969	.4970	.4971	.4972	.4973	.4974
2.8	.4974	.4975	.4976	.4977	.4977	.4978	.4979	.4979	.4980	.4981
2.9	.4981	.4982	.4982	.4983	.4984	.4984	.4985	.4985	.4986	.4986
3.0	.4987	.4987	.4987	.4988	.4988	.4989	.4989	.4989.	.4990	.4990

Step 5: **Determine the probability for the event of interest.**

$$P(x \geq 22) = ?$$

We know that the area on each side of the mean under the normal distribution is equal to 0.50. In Step 4 we computed the probability for $z = 2.00$ to be 0.4772, which is the probability of a value falling between the mean and 2.00 standard deviations above the mean. Then, the probability we are looking for is

$$P(x \geq 22) = P(z \geq 2.00) = 0.5000 - 0.4772 = 0.0228$$

Westex Oil Company (continued)—In the Westex Oil example, recall the mean increase in oil output was 50 barrels per day and the standard deviation was 10 barrels per day. Company cost accountants have estimated that the output level must be increased by at least 45 barrels per day to pay for the additional cost of the enzyme injection. Therefore, if the enzyme is tried on one well, we are interested in the probability that production will be increased by 45 or more barrels per day. Specifically, we want

$$P(x \geq 45).$$

This probability corresponds to the area under the curve to the right of $x = 45$ barrels per day.

First, convert $x = 45$ barrels per day to a z-value. This is equivalent to determining the number of standard deviations 45 is from the mean.

$$z = \frac{x - \mu}{\sigma} = \frac{45 - 50}{10} = -0.50$$

Note, because the normal distribution is symmetrical, even though the z-value is a negative 0.50, we find the probability by looking for a z-value of positive 0.50. From the standard normal table, the

$$P(-0.50 \leq z \leq 0) = 0.1915.$$

This is shown as the area between $x = 45$ and $\mu = 50$ in Figure 5-11. The normal curve is symmetrical, and half the total area lies on each side of the mean. By adding 0.1915 to 0.5000, we can find

$$P(x \geq 45 \text{ barrels per day}) = 0.1915 + 0.5000 = 0.6915$$

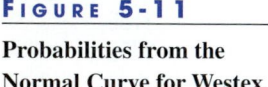

FIGURE 5-11

Probabilities from the Normal Curve for Westex

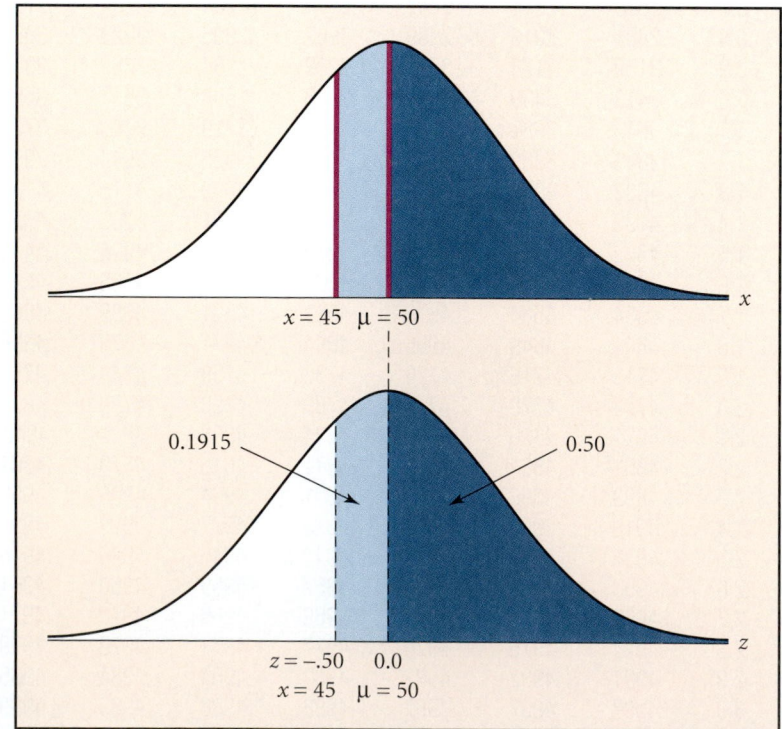

So

$$P(x \geq 45) = P(z \geq -0.50)$$

Therefore, based on the mean and standard deviation values, the probability that the well will increase production by 45 or more gallons per day is 0.6915. Conversely,

$$P(x < 45 \text{ barrels per day}) = 1 - 0.6915 = 0.3085$$

is the probability that increased production will be less than 45 barrels, thus unprofitable for Westex Oil.

Longlife Battery Company—Several states, predominately California, have passed legislation requiring automakers to sell a certain percentage of zero-emissions cars within their borders. One current alternative is battery-powered cars. The major problem with battery-operated cars is the limited time they can be driven before the batteries must be recharged. Longlife Battery, a start-up company, has developed a battery pack it claims will power a car at a sustained speed of 45 miles per hour for an average of 8 hours. But of course there will be variations: Some battery packs will last longer and some shorter than 8 hours. Current data indicate that the standard deviation of battery operation time before a charge is needed is 0.4 hours. Data show a normal distribution of uptime on these battery packs. Automakers are concerned that batteries may run short. For example, drivers might find an "8-hour" battery that lasts 7.5 hours or less unacceptable. What are the chances of this happening with the Longlife battery pack?

To calculate the probability the batteries will last 7.5 hours or less, find the appropriate area under the normal curve shown in Figure 5-12. There is approximately 1 chance in 10 that a battery will last 7.5 hours or less when the vehicle is driven at 45 miles per hour.

Suppose this level of reliability is unacceptable to the automakers. Instead of a 10% chance of an "8-hour" battery lasting 7.5 hours or less, the automakers will accept no more than a 2% chance. Longlife Battery asks the question, what would the mean uptime have to be to meet the 2% requirement?

Assuming that uptime is normally distributed, we can answer this question by using the standard normal distribution. However, instead of using the standard normal table to find a probability, we use it in reverse to find the z-value that corresponds to a known probability. Figure 5-13 shows the uptime distribution for the battery packs. Note, the 2% probability is shown in the left tail of the distribution. This is the allowable chance of a battery lasting 7.5 hours or less. We must solve for μ, the mean uptime that will meet this requirement.

1. Go to the body of the standard normal table, where the probabilities are located, and find the probability as close to 0.48 as possible. This is 0.4798.

FIGURE 5-12

Longlife Battery Company

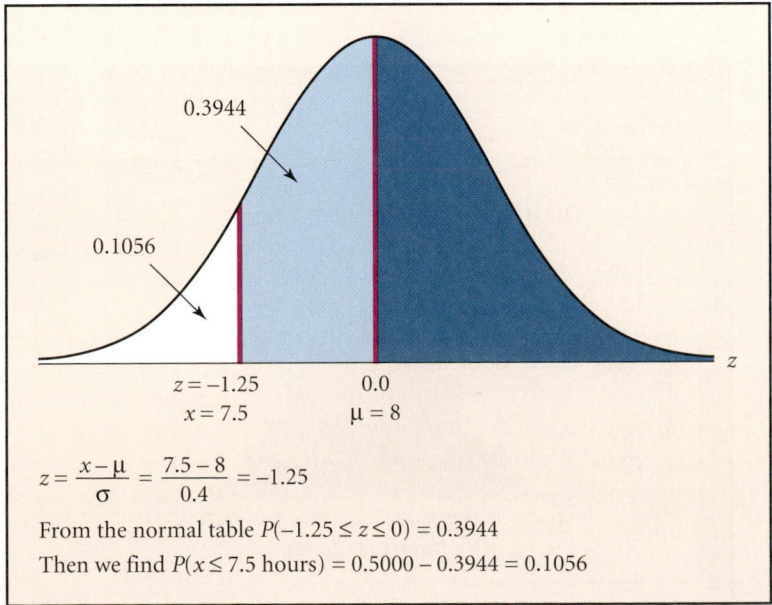

$$z = \frac{x - \mu}{\sigma} = \frac{7.5 - 8}{0.4} = -1.25$$

From the normal table $P(-1.25 \leq z \leq 0) = 0.3944$

Then we find $P(x \leq 7.5 \text{ hours}) = 0.5000 - 0.3944 = 0.1056$

FIGURE 5-13

Longlife Battery Company, Solving for the Mean

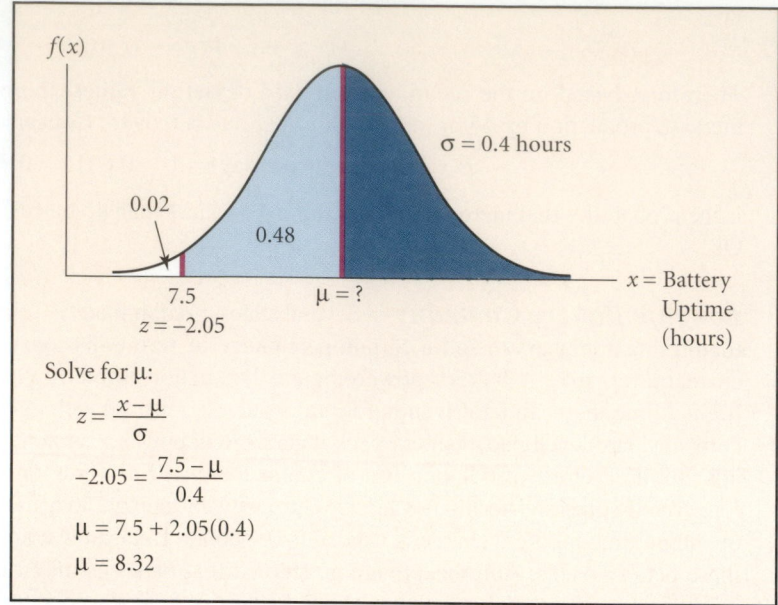

2. Determine the z-value associated with 0.4798. This is $z = 2.05$. Because we are below the mean, the z is negative. Thus, $z = -2.05$.
3. The formula for z is

$$z = \frac{x - \mu}{\sigma}$$

4. Substituting the known values, we get

$$-2.05 = \frac{7.5 - \mu}{0.4}$$

5. Solve for μ:

$$\mu = 7.5 + 2.05(0.4) = 8.32 \text{ hours}$$

Longlife Battery will need to increase the mean life of the battery pack to 8.32 hours to meet the automakers' requirement that no more than 2% of the batteries fail in 7.5 hours or less.

FIGURE 5-14

Excel Output for State Bank and Trust Service Times

Excel Instructions:
1. Open file: **State Bank.xls**
2. Define Bins upper limit of each class.
3. Select **Tools > Data Analysis**.
4. Click on **Histogram**.
5. Identify Data range and bin range.
6. Check **Chart Output**.
7. Define output location.
8. Click **OK**.

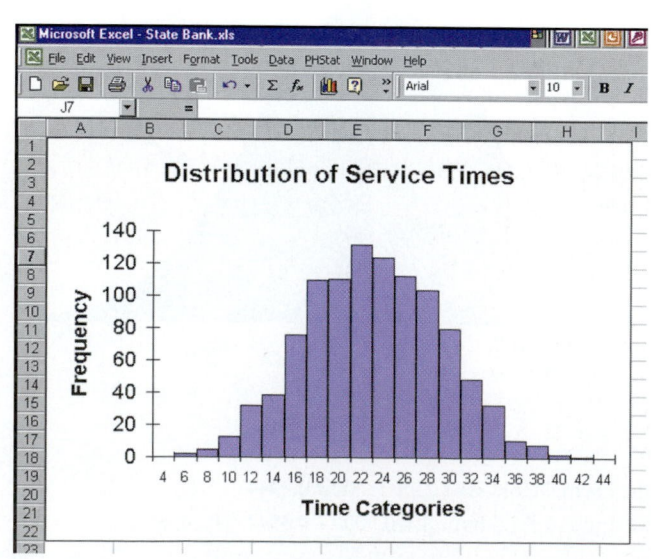

Minitab Instructions (for similar results):
1. Open file: State Bank.MTW.
2. Choose **Graph > Histogram**.
3. Click **Simple**.
4. Click **OK**.
5. In **Graph variables**, enter data column *Service Time*.
6. Click **OK**.

FIGURE 5-15

Normal Distribution for the State Bank Example

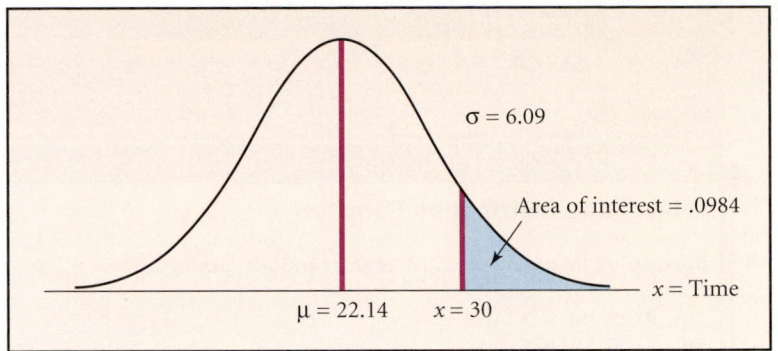

FIGURE 5-15

Normal Distribution for the State Bank Example

Excel and Minitab Tutorial

State Bank and Trust—The director of operations for the State Bank and Trust recently performed a study of the time bank customers spent from the time they arrived in the parking lot until they exited the parking lot after completing their banking. The data file, *State Bank*, contains the data for a sample of 1,045 customers randomly observed over a four-week period. The customers in the survey were limited to those who were there for "basic bank business," such as making a deposit or a withdrawal, or cashing a check. The histogram in Figure 5-14 shows that the times appear to be distributed quite closely to a normal distribution.[4]

The mean service for the 1,045 customers was 22.14 minutes, with a standard deviation equal to 6.09 minutes.

On the basis of these data, the manager assumes that the service times are normally distributed with $\mu = 22.14$ and $\sigma = 6.09$. Given these assumptions, the manager is considering providing a gift certificate to a local restaurant to any customer who is required to spend more than 30 minutes in the service process for basic bank business. Before doing this, she is interested in the probability of having to pay off on this offer.

Figure 5-15 shows the theoretical distribution, with the area of interest identified.

The manager is interested in finding

$$P(x > 30 \text{ minutes})$$

This can be done manually or with Excel or Minitab. Figure 5-16a and Figure 5-16b show the output. The cumulative probability is

$$P(x \le 30) = 0.9016$$

Then to find the probability of interest, we subtract this value from 1.0, giving

$$P(x > 30 \text{ minutes}) = 1.0 - 0.9016 = 0.0984$$

Thus, there are just under 10 chances in 100 that the bank would have to give out a gift certificate. Suppose the manager believes this policy is too liberal. She wants to set the time limit so that the chance

---

[4]A statistical technique known as the chi-square goodness-of-fit test is introduced in Chapter 12 that can be used to determine statistically whether the data follow a normal distribution.

FIGURE 5-16A

Excel Output for State Bank and Trust

Excel Instructions:
1. Select the Function Wizard.
2. Click on **Statistical**.
3. Select **NORMDIST**.
4. Enter the mean, standard deviation, and *x* value.
5. Set Cumulative equal to True.
6. Click **OK**.

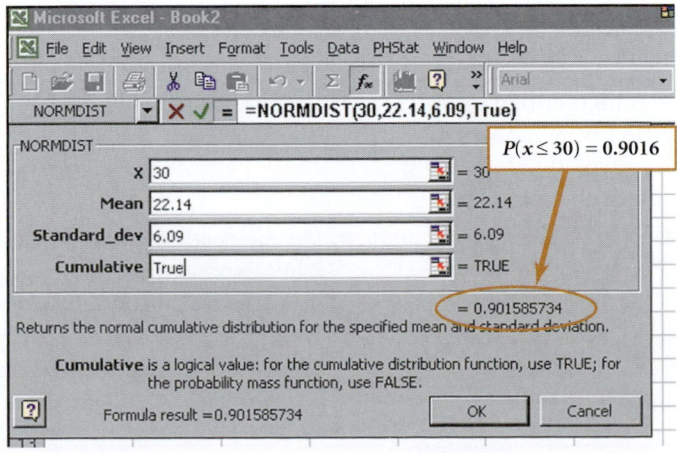

FIGURE 5-16B

Minitab Output for State Bank and Trust

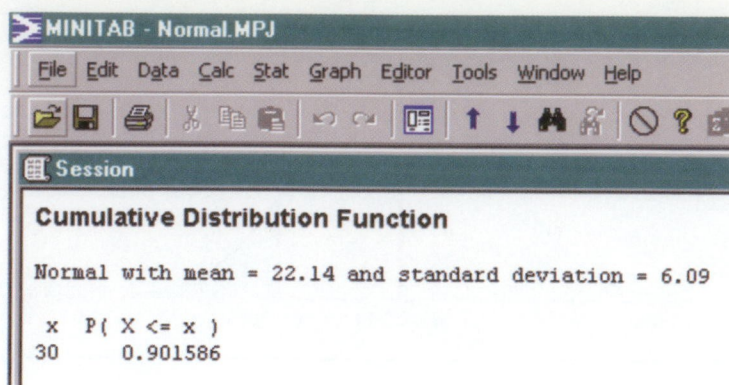

Minitab Instructions:
1. Choose **Calc > Probability Distribution > Normal**.
2. Choose **Cumulative probability**.
3. In **Mean**, enter μ.
4. In **Standard deviation**, enter σ.
5. In **Input constant**, enter x.
6. Click **OK**.

of giving out the gift is only 5%. You can use the standard normal table, the **Probability Distribution** command in Minitab, or the **NORMSINV** function in Excel to find the new limit.[5] To use the table, we first consider that the manager wants a 5% area in the upper tail of the normal distribution. This will leave

$$0.50 - 0.05 = 0.45$$

between the new time limit and the mean. Now go to the body of the standard normal table, where the probabilities are, and locate the value as close to 0.45 as possible (0.4495 or 0.4505). Next, determine the z-value that corresponds to this probability. Because 0.45 lies midway between 0.4495 and 0.4505, we interpolate halfway between $z = 1.64$ and $z = 1.65$ to get

$$z = 1.645$$

Now, we know

$$z = \frac{x - \mu}{\sigma}$$

We then substitute the known values and solve for x:

$$1.645 = \frac{x - 22.14}{6.09}$$
$$x = 22.14 + 1.645(6.09)$$
$$x = 32.158 \text{ minutes}$$

Therefore, any customer required to wait more than 32.158 (or 32) minutes will receive the gift. This should result in about 5% of the customers getting the restaurant certificate. Obviously, the bank will work to reduce the average service time or standard deviation so even fewer customers will have to be in the bank for more than 32 minutes.

[5]The function is =NORMSINV(.95) in Excel. This will return the z-value corresponding to the area to left of the upper tail equaling .05.

SUMMARY: USING THE NORMAL DISTRIBUTION

If a continuous random variable is distributed as a normal distribution, the distribution is symmetrically distributed around the mean, or expected value, and is described by the mean and standard deviation. To find probabilities associated with a normally distributed random variable, use the following steps:

1. Determine the mean, μ, and the standard deviation, σ.

2. Define the event of interest, such as $P(x \geq x_1)$.

3. Convert the normal distribution to the standard normal distribution using Equation 5-12:

$$z = \frac{x - \mu}{\sigma}$$

4. Use the standard normal distribution tables to find the probability associated with the calculated z-value. The table gives the probability of value between the z-value and the mean.

5. Determine the desired probability using the knowledge that the probability of a value being on either side of the mean is 0.50 and the total probability under the normal distribution is 1.0.

EXAMPLE 5-10: USING THE NORMAL DISTRIBUTION

McMillin Assembly   McMillin Assembly has a contract to assemble components for radar systems to be used by the U.S. military. The time required to complete one part of the assembly is thought to be normally distributed, with a mean equal to 30 hours and a standard deviation equal to 4.7 hours. In order to keep the assembly flow moving on schedule, this assembly step needs to be completed in 26 to 35 hours. To determine the probability of this happening, use the following steps:

Step 1:   **Determine the mean, μ, and the standard deviation, σ.**
The mean assembly time for this step in the process is thought to be 30 hours, and the standard deviation is thought to be 4.7 hours.

Step 2:   **Define the event of interest.**
We are interested in determining the following:
$$P(26 \leq x \leq 35) = ?$$

Step 3:   **Convert the normal distribution to the standard normal distribution using Equation 5-12:**
$$z = \frac{x - \mu}{\sigma}$$

We need to find the z-value corresponding to $x = 26$ and to $x = 35$.
$$z = \frac{x - \mu}{\sigma} = \frac{26 - 30}{4.7} = -0.85 \quad \text{and} \quad z = \frac{35 - 30}{4.7} = 1.06$$

Step 4:   **Use the standard normal table to find the probabilities associated with each z-value.**
For $z = -0.85$, the probability is 0.3023.
For $z = 1.06$, the probability is 0.3554.

Step 5:   **Determine the desired probability for the event of interest.**
$$P(26 \leq x \leq 35) = 0.3023 + 0.3554 = 0.6577$$

Thus, there is a 0.6577 chance that this step in the assembly process will stay on schedule.

Approximate Areas Under the Normal Curve

In Figure 3-9 we introduced the empirical rule for probabilities with bell-shaped distributions. For the normal distribution we can make this rule more precise. Knowing the area under the normal curve between $\pm 1\sigma$, $\pm 2\sigma$, and $\pm 3\sigma$ provides a useful benchmark for estimating probabilities and checking reasonableness of results. Figure 5-17 shows these benchmark areas for any normal distribution.

FIGURE 5-17

Approximate Areas Under the Normal Curve

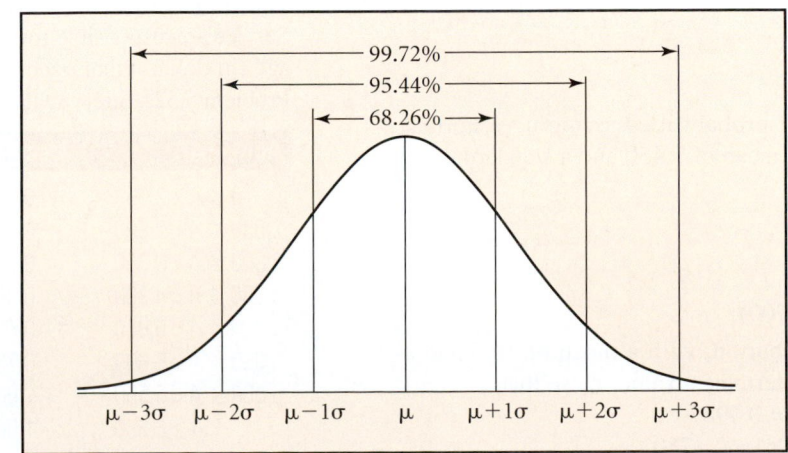

5-3: EXERCISES

Skill Development

5.40 Assuming that we have a normal distribution, find the following probabilities if the mean is 60 and the standard deviation is 10.
a. $P(x > 60)$
b. $P(x \geq 70)$
c. $P(50 \leq x \leq 70)$
d. $P(x \leq 40)$

5.41 Assume a normal distribution, with a mean of 15 and a standard deviation of 2.5.
a. Determine the probability of a value exceeding 18.7.
b. Calculate the distribution's 90th percentile.
c. Determine the probability of a value being within two standard deviations of the mean.

5.42 A variable is distributed as a normal distribution, with a standard deviation equal to 2.5.
a. If the probability of a value being larger than 16.3 is to be set at 0.10, what must the mean value be? (Assume the standard deviation remains at 2.5.)
b. Suppose the mean of the distribution is 13. Determine the value of the standard deviation so that the probability that a value is larger than 16.3 is 0.10.

5.43 For a standardized normal distribution, calculate the following probabilities:
a. $P(0.00 < z \leq 2.33)$
b. $P(-1.00 < z \leq 1.00)$
c. $P(1.78 < z < 2.34)$

5.44 For a standardized normal distribution, determine a value, say z_0, so that
a. $P(0 < z < z_0) = 0.4772$
b. $P(-z_0 \leq z < 0) = 0.45$
c. $P(-z_0 \leq z \leq z_0) = 0.95$
d. $P(z > z_0) = 0.025$
e. $P(z \leq z_0) = 0.01$

5.45 For a normal distribution with a mean of 7.5 and a variance of 9, find the following probabilities:
a. $P(x \geq 8.5)$
b. $P(x \geq 6.5)$
c. $P(x \geq 9.5)$
d. $P(3 \leq x \leq 5.5)$

5.46 Find the following probabilities assuming a normal distribution, with a mean of 7,450 and a standard deviation of 300:
a. $P(x \leq 7,000)$
b. $P(x \geq 8,000)$
c. $P(x \geq 8,250)$
d. $P(7,400 \leq x \leq 7,700)$

5.47 For a normal distribution, with a mean of 10.5 and a variance of 16.7, determine a value, x_0, so that
a. $P(10.5 < x < x_0) = 0.4987$
b. $P(-x_0 \leq x < 10.25) = 0.4750$

5.48 A distribution has a normal distribution, with a mean of 109 and a standard deviation of 23.5.
a. Calculate the probability of a value being less than 101.3.
b. Determine the probability of a value being more than two standard deviations above the mean.
c. Suppose three values are randomly sampled from this distribution. Calculate the probability that at least two out of the three values are more than two standard deviations above the mean.

5.49 A variable is normally distributed with $\sigma = 9.3$.
a. If the probability of a value being less than 23 is to be set at 0.13, what must the mean value be?
b. If the mean of this variable is 12.5, determine the probability that at least four out of five randomly chosen values are more than one standard deviation below the mean.

5.50 A variable is normally distributed with a mean equal to 100 and a standard deviation equal to 15. One value, x_A, is on the high side of the mean. Another value, x_B, is the same distance from the mean as x_A, but on the low side of the mean. If the probability of a value falling between x_A and x_B is 0.70, what are the values for x_A and x_B?

5.51 Assume a normal distribution with a mean of 22. If the probability of a value being greater than 17 is 0.75, calculate the standard deviation.

Business Applications

5.52 The average number of acres burned by forest and range fires in a large New Mexico county is 4,300 acres per year, with a standard deviation of 750 acres. The distribution of the number of acres burned is normal.
a. Compute the probability in any year that more than 5,000 acres will be burned.
b. Determine the probability in any year that fewer than 4,000 acres will be burned.
c. What is the probability that between 2,500 and 4,200 acres will be burned?
d. In those years when more than 5,500 acres are burned, help is needed from eastern-region fire teams. Determine the probability help will be needed in any year.

5.53 The Bureau of Land Management and the U.S. Forest Service are responsible for estimating the amount of damage (in dollars) that occurs as a result of such fires (see Problem 5.52). Suppose the damage is estimated to be

Acres (A)	Cost ($M)	# Firefighters (F)
$0 \leq A < 2,050$	0.05	25
$2,050 \leq A < 2,800$	0.15	50
$2,800 \leq A < 3,550$	0.25	100
$3,550 \leq A < 4,300$	0.35	130
$4,300 \leq A < 5,050$	0.40	150
$5,050 \leq A < 5,600$	0.75	160
$5,600 \leq A < 6,550$	1.00	175
$A \geq 6,550$	1.50	200

a. Calculate the average monetary damage occurring as a result of a forest fire.

b. Calculate the average number of fire fighters needed as a result of a forest fire.

c. If it is desired to have enough firefighters on hand for 75% of the fires, how many firefighters are required?

d. If only 160 firefighters are available, calculate the percentage of fires that can be fought successively.

5.54 Micron Electronics makes both desktop and laptop personal computers that they sell directly to customers by phone or over the Internet. In addition to making the computers, Micron provides customer support via a 1-800 number. Recently, the manager of the service department conducted a study of the time customers spent on hold waiting for a Micron representative to become available. The data showed that the distribution of time spent on hold is approximately normally distributed, with a mean of 18 minutes and a standard deviation of 4 minutes.

a. Based on this information, what is the probability that a customer will have to wait more than 11.3 minutes?

b. Considering the data collected in this study, what is the probability that a customer will wait less than 2 minutes?

c. Suppose a customer has complained to the customer service manager that she was on hold for 22 minutes. Based on the data collected in the study, how would you respond to this customer? Do you think that the customer is accurate with her claim?

d. The service manager wants to make sure (for all practical purposes) that no one waits longer than 18 minutes. Determine the standard deviation that would be required to meet this goal.

5.55 A commuter airline has studied the passenger counts on a flight between Boston and Atlanta and has found that the number of passengers who purchase tickets for this flight is approximately normally distributed, with a mean of 72 and a standard deviation of 4. The data were determined for all days, regardless of the number of tickets sold on the flight. Keep in mind, some people do not show up for their flight.

a. If the capacity on the plane is 85, what percentage of the time should the flight be full?

b. The catering manager who is responsible for snack and beverage provisions on the flight plans to stock 90 snack packs. What is the probability that there will be 8 or fewer left over, assuming that each passenger gets one snack pack?

c. Comment on the potential problems in assuming that the number of fliers on a flight is normally distributed? What type of variable is the number of fliers? Discuss.

5.56 J & G Painting has been gathering data on its painting speed in an effort to be more accurate in submitting bids. Based on data gathered after considering washing, taping, painting, and cleanup, one person can paint an average of 100 square feet of indoor wall space per hour (because of extra taping time, doors and windows are counted as plain wall space), with a standard deviation of 12 square feet. The distribution of square feet painted is considered to be normally distributed.

A painter has just started an 8-foot-wide-by-10-foot-long room at 2:00 P.M. (assume an 8-foot-high ceiling). The painter will be paid overtime if she is not finished by 5:00 P.M. The ceiling is not to be painted.

a. Determine the probability overtime will not be paid.

b. Calculate the earliest she can expect to be finished with the room.

5.57 The Nelson Company makes the machines that automatically dispense soft drinks into cups. Many national fast food chains such as McDonald's and Burger King use these machines. A study by the company shows that the actual volume of soft drink that goes into a 16-ounce cup per fill is normally distributed, with a mean of 16 ounces and a standard deviation 0.35 ounces. A new 16-ounce cup that is being considered actually holds 16.7 ounces of drink.

a. Calculate the proportion of cups that will be "overfilled" by the filling machine.

b. They wish to adjust the machine so that the overfill percentage is no greater than 0.5%. Determine the mean required to fulfill this wish.

c. If the mean is set at 16 ounces, calculate the standard deviation that would be required to meet the stipulation in part b.

d. Which of the two procedures described in parts b and c do you prefer? Explain your answer.

5.58 Referring to the Nelson Company example in Exercise 5.57, suppose the managers wish to have no more than 1 cup in 1,000 overfill. What should the mean fill setting on the machine be to assure that this takes place? (Assume the standard deviation stays at 0.35 ounces.)

5.59 Once a machine has been set at the value determined in Exercise 5.58, the machine is put into use. After a period of time, the mean amount of soft drink dispensed changes. It is important to know when this occurs so that the machine can be serviced and the mean level of soft drink dispensed can be adjusted. One of the decision rules developed for quality control would have the machine shut down if two out of three observations are outside (and on the same side of the mean) two standard deviations from the mean.

a. Calculate the value that is two standard deviations above the mean.

b. Calculate the probability that the amount of liquid dispensed in one cup is above the value found in part a.

c. Now calculate the probability that at least two out of three observations are above the value found in a. (Hint: You are counting something that assumes one of two things per trial.) For this calculation assume that the mean has not changed (i.e., the mean is still 16 oz.).

5.60   A new filter system for swimming pools is designed to filter out certain harmful particles that can get into the water. A study shows that the number of particles per gallon of water is normally distributed, with a mean of 20,000 and a standard deviation of 3,000. The filter is designed to catch 25,000 particles per gallon.

a. Determine the probability that the filter will allow some particles to escape back into the pool.

b. The manufacturer of the filter claims that the filter removes 90% of the particles from the water. Is this statement correct? Support your answer with probability calculations and reasons.

c. If the filter fulfilled the claim made by the manufacturer, how many particles per gallon of water would the filter remove?

5.61   The Edward's Theater chain has studied its movie customers to determine how much they spend on concessions. The study based on a large number of customers shows that the spending distribution is approximately normally distributed, with a mean of $4.11 and a standard deviation of $1.37.

a. Compute the probability that a customer will spend more than $7.50 on concessions.

b. Suppose the manager would like the chances that a customer will spend less than $3.50 on concessions to be at most 5%. If the standard deviation remains at $1.37, what would the mean spending value need to be?

5.62   The length of french fries made by the J. R. Simplot Company for one of its biggest customers is normally distributed, with a mean of 4.2 inches and a standard deviation of 0.5 inch. The customer purchases the fries by the pound but sells to its customers by volume. Thus, it prefers the longer fries and wants no more than a 5% chance that a fry will be shorter than 3.5 inches. Based on the current data, does the Simplot Company meet the customer's requirements? Show why or why not.

5.63   The Simplot Company, which produces french fries, is considering changing its purchasing standards for raw potatoes in an effort to change the average length of fries. If the standard deviation for fries is to remain at 0.50 inches, what will the average fry length have to be to meet Simplot's customer's requirement that no more than 5% of the fries be shorter than 3.5 inches?

Advanced Business Applications

5.64   The Hydronics Company is in the business of developing health supplements. Recently, the company's R&D department came up with two weight-loss plans that included products produced by Hydronics. To determine whether these products are effective, the company has conducted a test. A total of 300 people who each were 30 pounds or more overweight were recruited to participate in the study. Of these, 100 people were given a placebo supplement, 100 people were given plan 1, and 100 people were given plan 2. As might be expected, some people dropped out before the four-week study period was completed. The weight loss (or gain) for each individual is listed in the data file called *Hydronics*. Note, positive values indicate that the individual actually gained weight during the study period.

a. Develop a frequency histogram for the weight loss (or gain) for those people on plan 1. Does it appear from this graph that weight loss is approximately normally distributed?

b. Referring to part a, assuming that a normal distribution does apply, compute the mean and standard deviation weight loss for the plan 1 subjects.

c. Referring to parts a and b, assuming that the weight-change distribution for plan 1 users is normally distributed and that the sample mean and standard deviation are used to directly represent the population mean and standard deviation. Then, what is the probability that a plan 1 user will lose more than 12 pounds in a four-week period?

d. Referring to your answer in part c, would it be appropriate for the company to claim that plan 1 users can expect to lose as much as 12 pounds in four weeks? Discuss.

5.65   Refer to the Hydronics Company in Exercise 5.64. Using the data set in the file *Hydronics*:

a. Develop a frequency histogram for the weight loss (or gain) for those people on plan 2. Does it appear from this graph that weight loss is approximately normally distributed?

b. Referring to part a, assuming that a normal distribution does apply, compute the mean and standard deviation weight loss for the plan 2 subjects.

c. Referring to parts a and b, assume that the weight-change distribution for plan 2 users is normally distributed and that the sample mean and standard deviation are used to directly represent the population mean and standard deviation. Then, what is the probability that a plan 2 user will lose more than 12 pounds in a four-week period?

d. Referring to your answer in part c, would it be appropriate for the company to claim that plan 2 users can expect to lose as much as 12 pounds in four weeks? Discuss.

5.66   Refer to Exercise 5.65.

a. Twin sisters were part of this study. One was put on plan 1 and the other on plan 2. Determine the probability that at least one of the sisters will lose 12 pounds.

b. Provide the number of pounds lost such that 10% will lose at least that many pounds on plan 2.

5.67   The Future-Vision Cable TV Company recently surveyed its customers. A total of 548 responses were received. Among other things, the respondents were asked to indicate their household income. The data from the survey are found in the file *Future-Vision*.

a. Develop a frequency histogram for the income variable. Does it appear from the graph that income is approximately normally distributed? Discuss.

b. Compute the mean and standard deviation for the income variable.

c. Referring to parts a and b and assuming that income is normally distributed and the sample mean and standard deviation are good substitutes for the population values, what is the probability that a Future-Vision customer will have an income exceeding $40,000?

d. Suppose that Future-Vision managers are thinking about offering a monthly discount to customers who have a household income below a certain level. If the management wants to grant discounts to no more than 7% of the customers, what income level should be used for the cutoff?

5.68 Refer to the Future-Vision managers of Exercise 5.67. The company targets the $40,000 through $60,000 income group with special advertising. As part of the program, it offers a discount coupon of $10 off of next month's cable bill. Of those in the $40,000 to $60,000 category, 75% return the coupons. Determine the percentage of Future-Visions' customers who both receive the promotion and send in the coupon.

5-4 OTHER CONTINUOUS PROBABILITY DISTRIBUTIONS

The normal distribution is the most frequently used continuous probability distribution in statistics. However, there are other continuous distributions that apply to business decision-making. This section introduces two of these: the uniform distribution and the exponential distribution.

UNIFORM PROBABILITY DISTRIBUTION

The **uniform distribution** is sometimes referred to as the *distribution of little information*, because the probability over any interval of the continuous random variable is the same as for any other interval of the same width.

Equation 5-13 defines the *continuous uniform distribution*.

Continuous Uniform Distribution

$$f(x) = \begin{cases} \dfrac{1}{b-a} & \text{if } a \le x \le b \\ 0 & \text{otherwise} \end{cases}$$ **5-13**

where:

$f(x)$ = Value of the density function at any x value
a = Lower limit of the interval from a to b
b = Upper limit of the interval from a to b

Figure 5-18 illustrates two examples of uniform probability distributions with different a to b intervals. Note the height of the probability distribution is the same for all values of x between a and b for a given distribution. The graph of the uniform distribution is a rectangle.

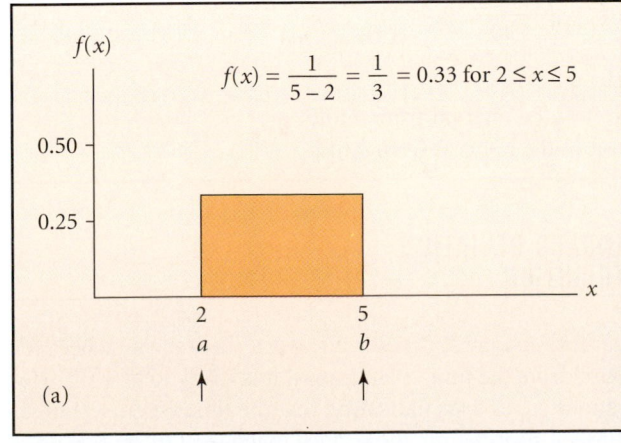

(a)

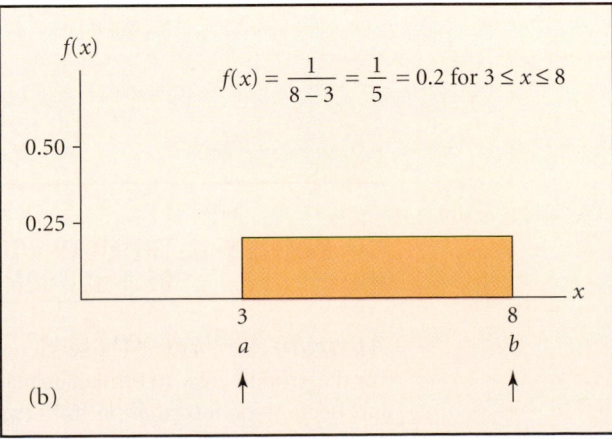

(b)

FIGURE 5-18 Uniform Distributions

EXAMPLE 5-11: USING THE UNIFORM DISTRIBUTION

Stern Manufacturing Company   The Stern Manufacturing Company makes seat-belt buckles for all types of vehicles. The inventory level for the spring mechanism used in producing the buckles is only enough to continue production for two more hours. The purchasing clerk estimates that the springs will be delivered one to four hours from the time they are ordered. Because the dispatcher offers no other information about the pending delivery schedule, the time it will take to replenish the inventory is said to be *uniformly distributed* over the interval of one-to-four hours. We are interested in the probability that the company will run out of parts due to the shipment taking more than two hours. The probability can be determined using the following steps:

Step 1:   **Define the probability distribution.**

The height of the probability rectangle, $f(x)$, for the delivery time interval one-to-four hours is determined using Equation 5-13, as follows:

$$f(x) = \frac{1}{b - a}$$

$$f(x) = \frac{1}{4 - 1} = \frac{1}{3} = 0.33$$

Step 2:   **Define the event of interest.**

The production scheduler is specifically concerned that shipment will take longer than two hours to arrive. We determine the probability as follows:

$$
\begin{aligned}
P(x > 2.0) &= 1 - P(x \leq 2.0) \\
&= 1 - f(x)(2.0 - 1.0) \\
&= 1 - 0.33(1.0) \\
&= 1 - 0.33 \\
&= 0.67
\end{aligned}
$$

Thus, there is a 67% chance that production will be delayed because the shipment is more than two hours late.

Like the normal distribution, the uniform distribution can be further described by specifying the mean and the standard deviation. These values are computed using Equations 5-14 and 5-15.

Mean and Standard Deviation of a Uniform Distribution

Mean (Expected Value):

$$E(x) = \mu = \frac{a + b}{2} \qquad\qquad \textbf{5-14}$$

Standard Deviation:

$$\sigma = \sqrt{\frac{(b - a)^2}{12}} \qquad\qquad \textbf{5-15}$$

where:

a = Lower limit of the interval from a to b
b = Upper limit of the interval from a to b

EXAMPLE 5-12: THE MEAN AND STANDARD DEVIATION OF A UNIFORM DISTRIBUTION

Austrian Airlines   The service manager for Austrian Airlines is uncertain about the time needed for the ground crew to turn an airplane around from the time it lands until it is ready to take off. He has been given information from the operations supervisor indicating that the times seem to range between 15 and 45 minutes. Without any further information, the service manager will apply a uniform distribution to the turnaround. Based on this, he can determine the mean and standard deviation for the airplane turnaround times using the following steps:

Step 1:   **Define the probability distribution.**

Equation 5-13 can be used to define the distribution:

$$f(x) = \frac{1}{b-a} = \frac{1}{45-15} = \frac{1}{30} = 0.0333$$

Step 2:   **Compute the mean of the probability distribution using Equation 5-14.**

$$\mu = \frac{a+b}{2} = \frac{15+45}{2} = 30$$

Thus, the mean turnaround time is 30 minutes.

Step 3:   **Compute the standard deviation using Equation 5-15.**

$$\sigma = \sqrt{\frac{(b-a)^2}{12}} = \sqrt{\frac{(45-15)^2}{12}} = \sqrt{75} = 8.66$$

The standard deviation is 8.66 minutes.

THE EXPONENTIAL PROBABILITY DISTRIBUTION

Another continuous probability distribution that is frequently used in business situations is called the **exponential distribution**. The exponential distribution is used to measure the time that elapses between two occurrences of an event, such as the time between "hits" on an Internet homepage. The exponential distribution might also be used to describe the time between arrivals of customers at a bank drive-in teller window or the time between failures of an electronic component.

Equation 5-16 shows the probability density function for the exponential distribution.

Exponential Distribution

A continuous random variable that is exponentially distributed has the probability density function given by

$$f(x) = \lambda e^{-\lambda x}, x \geq 0 \qquad \textbf{5-16}$$

where:

$$e = 2.71828\ldots$$
$$1/\lambda = \text{the mean time between events } (\lambda > 0)$$

Note, the parameter that defines the exponential distribution is λ (lambda). You should recall from Section 5-2 that λ is the mean value for the Poisson distribution. If the number of occurrences per time period is known to be Poisson distributed with a mean of λ, then the time between occurrences will be exponentially distributed with a mean time of $1/\lambda$.

If we select a value for λ, we can graph the exponential distribution by substituting λ and different values for x into Equation 5-16. For instance, Figure 5-19 shows exponential distributions for $\lambda = 0.5$, $\lambda = 1.0$, $\lambda = 2.0$, and $\lambda = 3.0$. Note in Figure 5-19 that for any exponential distribution, with density function $f(x)$, $f(0) = \lambda$, and as x increases, $f(x)$ approaches zero. It can also be shown that *the standard deviation of any exponential distribution is equal to the mean, $1/\lambda$.*

As with any continuous probability distribution, the probability that a value will fall within an interval is the area under the graph between the two points defining the interval.[6] Equation 5-17 is used to find the probability that a value will be equal to or less than a particular value for an exponential distribution.

Exponential Probability

$$P(0 \leq x \leq a) = 1 - e^{-\lambda a} \qquad \textbf{5-17}$$

---

[6]Integral calculus is used to find the area.

FIGURE 5-19 **Exponential Distributions**

FIGURE 5-19 **Exponential Distributions**

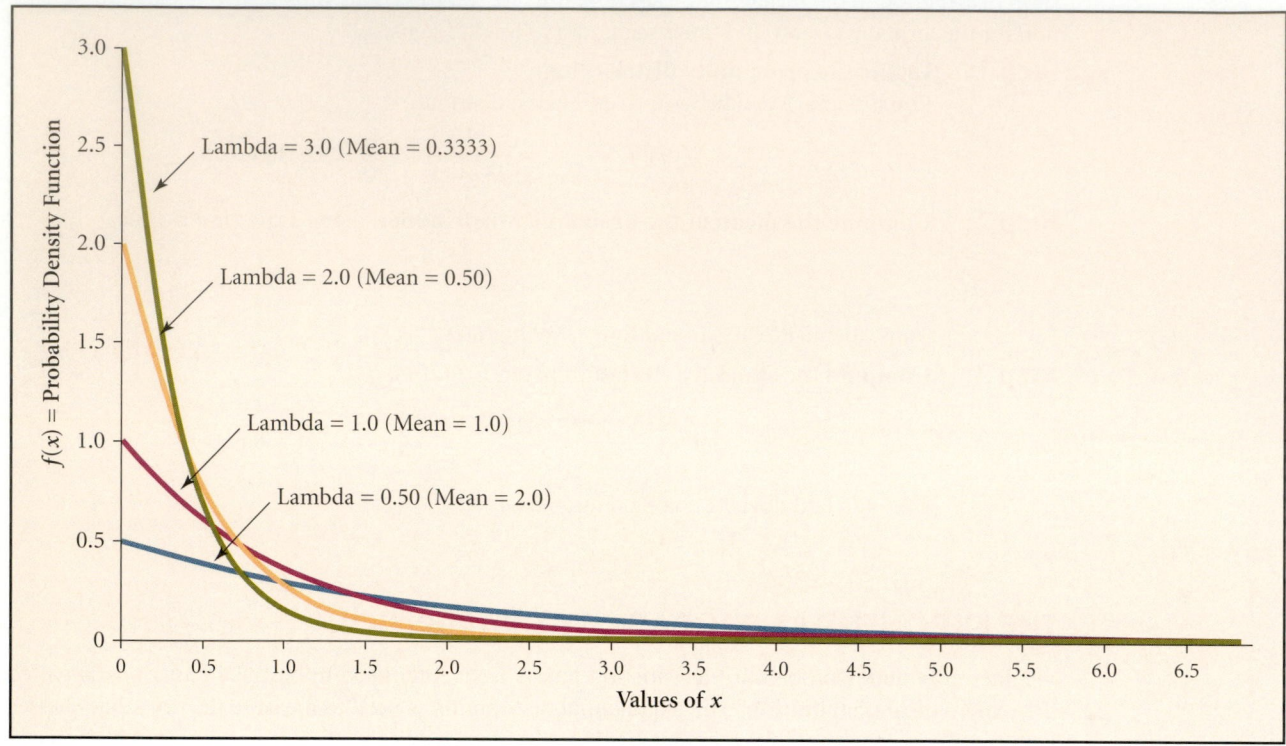

Appendix E contains a table of $e^{-\lambda a}$ values for different values of λa. You can use this table and Equation 5-17 to find the probabilities when the λa of interest is contained in the table. You can also use Minitab or Excel to find exponential probabilities, as the following application illustrates.

Excel and Minitab Tutorial

Haines Internet Services—The Haines Internet Services Company has determined that the number of customers who attempt to connect to the Internet per hour is Poisson distributed with $\lambda = 30$ per hour. The time between connect requests is exponentially distributed with a mean time between calls of 2.0 minutes, computed as follows:

$$\lambda = 30 \text{ per } 60 \text{ minutes} = 0.50 \text{ per minute}$$

The mean time between calls, then, is

$$1/\lambda = 1/0.50 = 2.0 \text{ minutes.}$$

Because of the system that Haines uses, if customer requests are too close together—45 seconds (0.75 minutes) or less—some customers fail to connect. The managers at Haines are analyzing whether they should purchase new equipment that will eliminate this problem. They need to know the probability that a customer will fail to connect. Thus they want:

$$P(x \leq 0.75 \text{ minutes}) = ?$$

FIGURE 5-20A

Excel Exponential Probability Output for Haines Internet Services

Excel Instructions:
1. Click on Function Wizard.
2. Select **Statistics**.
3. Select **EXPONDIST** function.
4. Supply x and lamda.
5. Set **Cumulative =** **TRUE** for cumulative probability.

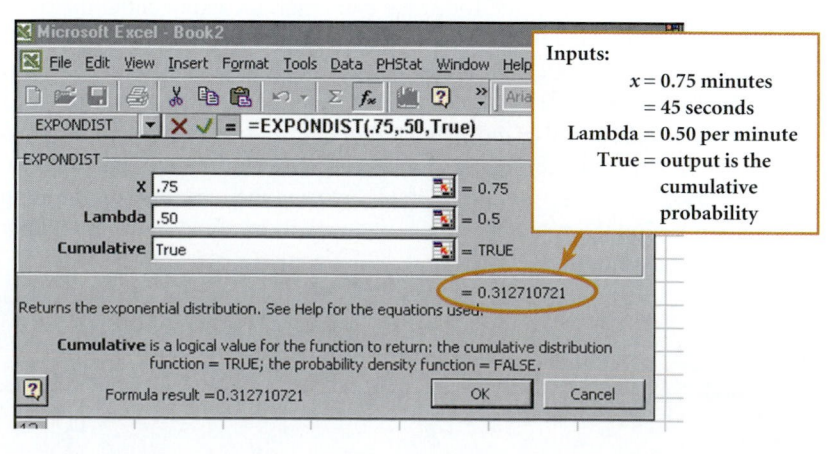

Inputs:
$x = 0.75$ minutes
$= 45$ seconds
Lambda $= 0.50$ per minute
True $=$ output is the cumulative probability

FIGURE 5-20B

Minitab Exponential
Probability Output for
Haines Internet Services

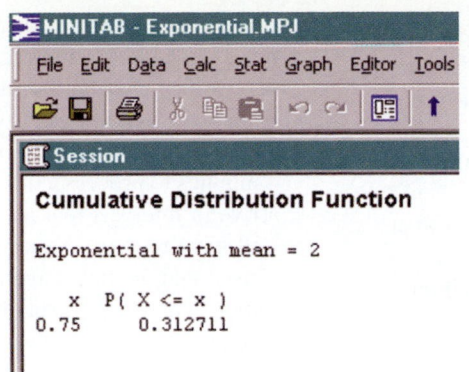

Minitab Instructions:
1. Choose **Calc > Probability Distribution > Exponential.**
2. Choose **Cumulative probability.**
3. In **Scale**, enter μ.
4. In **Input constant**, enter x.
5. Click **OK**.

To find this probability using a calculator, we need to first determine λa. In this example, $\lambda = 0.50$ and $a = 0.75$. Then

$$\lambda a = (0.50)(0.75) = 0.3750.$$

We find the desired probability is:

$$1 - e^{-\lambda a} = 1 - e^{-0.3750}$$
$$= 0.3127$$

The managers can also use the **EXPONDIST** function in Excel or the **Probability Distributions** command in Minitab to compute the precise value for the desired probability.[7] Figure 5-20a and Figure 5-20b show that the chance of failing to connect is 0.3127. This means that nearly one-third of the customers will experience a problem with the current system.

5-4: EXERCISES

Skill Development

5.69 A continuous random variable is uniformly distributed between 20 and 60.
a. What is the probability a randomly selected value will be above 50?
b. Calculate the probability a randomly selected value will be exactly 45.
c. Determine the probability that a randomly selected value will be between 25 and 35.
d. Find the probability that a randomly selected value will be less than 34.

5.70 A random variable is known to be exponentially distributed, with a mean time between occurrences equal to 2.0 minutes.
a. What is the probability that the time between the next two occurrences is more than 2.0 minutes?
b. Determine the probability that the time between the next two occurrences is between 1.0 and 2.0 minutes. [Hint, find $P(x \le 1.0)$ and subtract from $P(x \le 2.0)$].
c. Calculate the probability that the time between the next two occurrences is greater than 2.5 minutes.

5.71 A continuous random variable is uniformly distributed between 100 and 400.
a. Determine the probability a randomly selected value will be above 200.
b. Calculate the probability a randomly selected value will be between 150 and 300.
c. What is the probability that a randomly selected value will fall between 260 and 180?

5.72 A variable is uniformly distributed between the values 300 and 1,000.
a. Draw a graph that describes the probability distribution.
b. Find the probability of a value exceeding 700.
c. Find the probability that a randomly selected value is less than 650.
d. What is the probability that a randomly selected value exceeds 500?

5.73 A variable is uniformly distributed between the values -0.40 and 1.7.
a. Draw a graph that describes the probability distribution.
b. Find the probability of a value exceeding 0.0.

5.74 The Poisson distribution is known to describe the number of occurrences for a random variable with $\lambda = 60$ arrivals per hour.
a. What is the probability that the time between arrivals will exceed 1.0 minute?
b. Determine the probability that the time between arrivals will be between 45 and 75 seconds.

5.75 The time between occurrences for a random variable is known to be exponentially distributed with $\lambda = 4$ seconds.
a. Find the probability that the time between occurrences is between 0.10 and 0.60 seconds.
b. Calculate the probability that the time between occurrences will exceed the mean.
c. Determine the probability that the time between occurrences will be greater than 0.30 seconds.

[7]The Excel EXPONDIST function requires that λ be inputted rather than $1/\lambda$.

Business Applications

5.76 When only the value-added time is considered, the time it takes to build a laser printer is thought to be uniformly distributed between 8 and 15 hours.

a. What are the chances that it will take more than 10 value-added hours to build a printer?

b. How likely is it that a printer will require fewer than 9 value-added hours?

c. Suppose a single customer orders two printers. Determine the probability that the first and second printer each will require fewer than 9 value-added hours to complete.

5.77 In western Oregon, the growth distribution for a pine tree is thought to be uniformly distributed between 5 and 8.5 inches per year. A forest-products company is building a computer simulation model that they will use to help determine how many trees should be harvested each year.

a. The modelers are thinking of using a constant growth rate of 7.0 inches per year. Based on the growth distribution, what is the probability that a tree will grow fewer than 7.0 inches in a year? Comment on the potential impact of using this growth level in the model. Would the model tend to understate or overstate the actual pine tree growth? Discuss.

b. Suppose the modelers are also considering using a growth rate of 6.0 inches per year. What is the probability that a tree will grow more than 6.0 inches per year? If they use this as their model input, what might be the general impact on tree-growth projections by the model? Discuss?

5.78 The Sea Pines Golf Course is preparing for a major LPGA golf tournament. Because parking near the course is extremely limited (room for only 500 cars), the course officials have contracted with the local community to provide parking and a bus shuttle service. Sunday, the final day of the tournament, will draw the largest crowd, and the officials estimate they will have between 8,000 and 12,000 cars needing parking spaces. However, they think no value is more likely than another. The tournament committee is discussing how many parking spots to contract from the city. If they want to limit the chance of not having enough parking to 10%, how many spaces do they need from the city on Sunday?

5.79 The manager for Select-a-Seat, a company that sells tickets to athletic games, concerts, and other events, has determined that the number of people arriving at the Broadway location on a typical day is Poisson distributed with a mean of 12 per hour. It takes approximately 4 minutes to process a ticket request. Thus, if customers arrive in intervals that are shorter than 4 minutes, they will have to wait. Assuming that a customer has just arrived and the ticket agent is starting to serve that customer, what is the probability that the next customer who arrives will have to wait in line?

5.80 The Barineer Hospital in Sarasota, Florida, has determined that the time between patient arrivals to the emergency room is exponentially distributed with a mean time between arrivals of 11 minutes. Processing a patient into the hospital requires 5 minutes. A person has just begun to be processed and there are no other patients waiting.

a. What is the probability that the next arriving patient will have to wait to be processed? What does this imply about the hospital's need to add another check-in station in the emergency room? Discuss.

b. The emergency room often has several patients arriving at once as a result of a traffic accident or fire. Suppose the emergency room has five patients from a traffic accident arrive at the same time. How many other patients will arrive at the emergency room while the original five are being processed? (Hint: Recall the relationship between the Poisson distribution and the exponential distribution.) Can you visualize why at times it takes a long time to see a doctor in a hospital's emergency room?

5.81 The time to failure for a power supply unit used in a particular brand of personal computer is thought to be exponentially distributed with a mean of 4,000 hours, as per the contract between the vendor and the PC maker. The PC manufacturer has just had a warranty return from a customer who had the power supply fail after 2,100 hours of use.

a. What is the probability that the power supply would fail at 2,100 hours or fewer? Based on this probability, do you feel the PC maker has a right to require that the power supply maker refund the money on this unit?

b. Assuming that the PC maker has sold 100,000 computers with this power supply, approximately how many should be returned due to failure at 2,100 hours or fewer?

Summary and Conclusions

This chapter introduced several discrete and continuous probability distributions, including the binomial, Poisson, hypergeometric, normal, uniform, and exponential distributions. All of these distributions are used by decision makers. The choice of which distribution to use depends on whether the random variable of interest is discrete or continuous. Figure 5-21 summarizes the different distributions introduced in this chapter.

The binomial distribution is useful when the value of a discrete random variable is based on independent trials when on a given trial there are two possible outcomes and we can count the number of successes and failures. The Poisson distribution, also a discrete distribution, deals with situations in which the trials are independent but we are able to count only the successes. The final discrete distribution introduced in this chapter is the hypergeomet-

FIGURE 5-21

Probability Distribution Summary

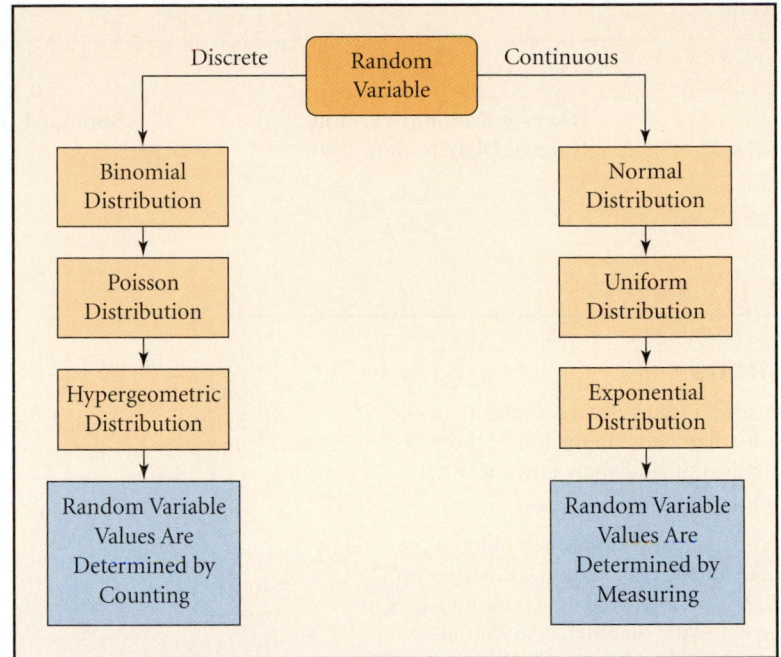

ric distribution. This distribution applies when the trials are dependent and the sample size is large relative to the size of the finite population.

In Section 5-3, we showed that the normal distribution, with its special properties, is used extensively in statistical decision making. The chapter discussed in some detail the standard normal distribution. It showed how the standard normal can be used to produce probability characteristics of any normal distribution. We also illustrated the use of Excel and Minitab to find probabilities for the normal and exponential distributions. The exponential and uniform distributions are also continuous distributions that have specific application in business situations.

Subsequent chapters will introduce other continuous probability distributions. Among these will be the *t distribution*, the *chi-square distribution*, and the *F distribution*. These additional distributions play important roles in statistical decision making. The basic concept that the area under a continuous curve is equivalent to the probability is true for all continuous distributions.

EQUATIONS

Counting Rule for Combinations

$$C_x^n = \frac{n!}{x!\,(n-x)!} \qquad \textbf{5-1}$$

Binomial Formula

$$P(x) = \frac{n!}{x!\,(n-x)!}\,p^x q^{n-x} \qquad \textbf{5-2}$$

Expected Value of a Discrete Random Variable

$$E(x) = \sum xP(x) \qquad \textbf{5-3}$$

Expected Value of a Binomial Distribution

$$\mu_x = E(x) = np \qquad \textbf{5-4}$$

Standard Deviation of a Discrete Random Variable

$$\sigma_x = \sqrt{\sum [x - E(x)]^2\, P(x)} \qquad \textbf{5-5}$$

Standard Deviation of the Binomial Distribution

$$\sigma = \sqrt{npq} \qquad \textbf{5-6}$$

Poisson Probability Distribution

$$P(x) = \frac{(\lambda t)^x\, e^{-\lambda t}}{x!} \qquad \textbf{5-7}$$

Standard Deviation of the Poisson Distribution

$$\sigma = \sqrt{\lambda t} \qquad \textbf{5-8}$$

Hypergeometric Distribution (Two Possible Outcomes per Trial)

$$P(x) = \frac{C_{n-x}^{N-X} \cdot C_x^X}{C_n^N} \qquad \textbf{5-9}$$

Hypergeometric Distribution (k Possible Outcomes per Trial)

$$P(x_1, x_2, x_3, \ldots, x_k) = \frac{C_{x_1}^{X_1} \cdot C_{x_2}^{X_2} \cdot C_{x_3}^{X_3} \cdot \ldots \cdot C_{x_k}^{X_k}}{C_n^N} \qquad \textbf{5-10}$$

Normal Distribution Density Function

$$f(x) = \frac{1}{\sigma\sqrt{2\pi}}\, e^{-(x-\mu)^2/2\sigma^2} \qquad \textbf{5-11}$$

Standardized Normal z-Value

$$z = \frac{x - \mu}{\sigma} \qquad \textbf{5-12}$$

Continuous Uniform Distribution

$$f(x) = \begin{cases} \dfrac{1}{b-a} & \text{if } a \le x \le b \\ 0 & \text{otherwise} \end{cases} \qquad \textbf{5-13}$$

Mean of the Uniform Distribution

$$E(x) = \mu = \frac{a+b}{2} \qquad \textbf{5-14}$$

Standard Deviation of the Uniform Distribution

$$\sigma = \sqrt{\frac{(b-a)^2}{12}} \qquad \textbf{5-15}$$

Exponential Distribution

$$f(x) = \lambda e^{-\lambda x},\ x \ge 0 \qquad \textbf{5-16}$$

Exponential Probability

$$P(0 \le x \le a) = 1 - e^{-\lambda a} \qquad \textbf{5-17}$$

Key Terms

CHAPTER EXERCISES

Conceptual Questions

5.82 Discuss the characteristics that must be present for the binomial probability distribution to apply. Relate these to a particular business application and show how the application meets the binomial requirements.

5.83 Discuss why, in the strictest sense, if the sampling is performed without replacement, the binomial distribution does not apply. Also, indicate under what conditions it is considered acceptable to use the binomial distribution even when the sampling is without replacement. Identify a business application that supports your answer.

5.84 How is the shape of a binomial distribution changed for a given sample size as p approaches 0.50 from either side? Discuss.

5.85 How is the shape of the binomial distribution changed for a given value of p as the sample size is increased? Discuss.

5.86 Discuss the basic differences and similarities between the binomial distribution and the Poisson distribution.

5.87 Through an example, discuss why, if the mean of the Poisson distribution can be reduced, the spread of the distribution can also be reduced.

5.88 The probability that a value for a normally distributed random variable will exceed the mean is 0.50. The same is true for the uniform distribution. Why is this not necessarily true for the exponential distribution? Discuss and show examples to illustrate your point.

5.89 One of your fellow students tells you that when working with a continuous distribution, it does not make sense to try to compute the probability of any specific value because it will be zero. She then says that this can't be true because when the experiment is performed some value must occur, so the probability can't be zero. Your task is to respond to her statement and in doing so explain why it is appropriate to find the probability for specific ranges of values for a continuous distribution.

5.90 Discuss the difference between discrete and continuous probability distributions. Discuss two situations in which a variable of interest may be considered either continuous or discrete.

Business Applications

5.91 The American Testing Service has determined that examination scores on the Indiana real estate exam are uniformly distributed between scores of 40% and 80% correct.
a. Develop a graph of the probability distribution.
b. Determine the probability of a score under 65% correct on the exam.
c. What is the probability of scoring 70% correct or better on the exam?
d. What is the probability of scoring between 60% and 75% correct on the exam?
e. Determine the score you would need to achieve the 90th percentile on this test.

5.92 The manager of a local convenience-food and gasoline store has observed that the number of customers failing to pay for their gasoline is Poisson distributed, with a mean of five per week.
a. What is the probability that during a given week, no customers fail to pay?
b. Suppose that during the initial week of a new employee's hire, more than nine people failed to pay for their gasoline. Based on the probability of this happening, what should the store manager conclude about the distribution of the people who fail to pay?

5.93 Assuming that the customer arrivals at the Fidelity Credit Union drive-through window are Poisson distributed, with a mean of five per hour, find
a. the probability that in a given hour more than eight customers will arrive at the drive-through window
b. the probability that between three and six customers, inclusive, will arrive at the drive-through window in a given hour.
c. the probability that fewer than three customers will arrive at the window in a given 30-minute period.

5.94 The manager for the Inland Food Market chain has determined that the occurrence of spoiled fruit is Poisson distributed, with a mean of 4 pieces per case.
a. What is the probability that in two cases more than 10 pieces of spoiled fruit will be discovered?
b. Suppose a new employee has been assigned the task of unpacking two cases of fruit and he reports that none of the pieces were spoiled. What are some conclusions you might reach and why?

5.95 The Hilgren Map Company produces topographical maps covering all parts of Utah, Arizona, and New Mexico. Past studies have indicated that the number of errors per map is Poisson distributed, with an average of 0.5 error per map.
a. What is the probability that a map will contain no errors?
b. What is the probability that a map will contain fewer than three errors?
c. What is the probability that a series of three maps will contain no errors?
d. What is the probability that a map will have five or more errors? What would you conclude if this did occur? Discuss.

5.96 A new battery designed especially for children's toys has been found to have a lifetime between 2.5 hours and 7 hours, with probabilities uniformly distributed between these two points.
  a. Develop a graph showing the probability distribution.
  b. Determine the probability that a battery will last more than 6 hours.
  c. What is the probability that a battery will last between 3.5 and 5.5 hours?
  d. You have been given the task of deciding whether to purchase these batteries for the toy manufacturer. Your firm will purchase the batteries if you can verify the lifetime distribution claimed. A sample of 10 batteries is tested. Only 1 battery lasted longer than 6 hours. Discuss what you will report to your superiors concerning your decision to purchase these batteries. Include probability calculations in your discussion.

5.97 Suppose a study performed at St. Jude's Hospital shows that 30% of all patients arriving at the emergency room are subsequently admitted to the hospital for at least one night. Assuming that in a sample of seven who arrived at the emergency room the number of people needing to be admitted to the hospital meets the requirements for the binomial distribution:
  a. What is the probability that five or more in the sample of seven will require admittance to the hospital?
  b. What is the expected number of patients in the sample who will require admittance to the hospital?

5.98 It has been determined that vehicles arriving at a drive-through pharmacy window arrive according to a Poisson distribution at the rate of 12 per hour.
  a. In a half-hour time period, what is the probability that three or fewer cars will arrive at the window?
  b. In a 15-minute period, what is the probability that three or fewer cars will arrive at the window?
  c. If the pharmacist can serve 4 cars per half-hour, what is the probability that during the first half-hour of business a customer will not be served and will still be waiting in line when the half-hour ends?

5.99 The Telephone Company of America recently made the claim that only 10% of the people who have telephones in their residences make enough local calls during a month to justify paying their monthly bills if the calls would be billed at a rate of $0.25 per call. A consumer agency decided to follow up this claim by selecting a random sample of 15 people who have telephones.
  a. Assuming the binomial distribution applies, what is the probability that the survey will show fewer than 7 people actually making the necessary number of calls to justify their phone bills if in fact the true percentage in the population is 10%, as claimed by the Telephone Company of America?
  b. If the binomial distribution applies, what is the probability that no customer in the sample will be found to be making enough calls to justify their bill at the rate of $0.25 per call?

5.100 A typist in Austin Company's typing pool makes errors periodically. In fact, a study has shown that errors made are random and independent of each other at an average rate of three per page ($\lambda = 3$).
  a. Develop the appropriate probability distribution for the number of errors made by the typist on a particular page.
  b. Based on the distribution developed in part a, determine the average number of errors the typist will make per page.
  c. Compute the variance and standard deviation for the probability distribution in part a.

5.101 The manager of consumer loans at Farwest National Bank has indicated that the distribution of account balances is a normal distribution.
  a. He has determined that the average credit card account balance is $700, with a median balance of $600. Comment on this conclusion.
  b. Having seen your comments in a, he recounts and says, "I was mistaken. It is the standard deviation that is $600." Comment on this conclusion.

5.102 Suppose personal daily water usage in California is normally distributed, with a mean of 18 gallons and a standard deviation of 6 gallons.
  a. What percentage of the population uses more than 18 gallons.
  b. What percentage of the population uses between 10 and 20 gallons?
  c. What is the probability of finding a person who uses fewer than 10 gallons?
  d. La Niña (the little sister weather pattern of her more famous brother, el Niño) has been cited as the cause of drought conditions in the southern portion of the United States. The city manager of Morro Bay, California (population: 14,500), has been trying to gain support for Morro Bay's participation in a state water project to bring water from northern to southern California. He contends that the city's population has grown to the point that the city's water needs cannot be met. Recently, he noted that the city's current water sources could provide only 350,000 gallons of water a day. Do you see a need for additional water for Morro Bay? Provide statistical evidence to support your views.

5.103 Referring to Exercise 5.102, the daily water usage in California was thought to be normally distributed, with a mean of 18 gallons and a standard deviation of 6 gallons. Because of a perpetual water shortage in California, the governor wants to give a tax rebate to the 20% of the population who use the least amount of water.
  a. What should the governor use as the maximum water limit for a person to qualify for a tax rebate?
  b. Referring to your answer in part a, suppose the governor's proposed tax rebate causes a shift in the average water usage from 18 gallons to 14 gallons per person per day, but it causes no change in the standard deviation. What percentage of the water users will now get a rebate? Assume the tax rebates will be given to those using less water than you specified in part a.

5.104 Cattle are often fattened in a feedlot before being shipped to a slaughterhouse. Suppose the weight gain per steer at a feedlot averages 1.5 pounds per day, with a standard deviation of 0.25 pound. Assume a normal distribution.
  a. What is the probability a steer will gain more than 2 pounds on a given day?

b. Determine the probability a steer will gain between 1 and 2 pounds in any given day.

c. Provide the probability of selecting two steers that both gain fewer than 1.5 pounds on a given day, assuming the two are independent.

d. Compute the probabilities found in parts a, b, and c, assuming a standard deviation of 0.2 pound. Why are these probabilities different?

5.105 The dollar amount of dairy products consumed per week by adults is thought to be normally distributed, with a mean of $4.50 and a standard deviation of $1.10.

a. What is the probability that an individual adult from the population will consume more than $4.90 in dairy products in a week?

b. Determine the probability that an individual selected at random from the population will consume less than $6.25 in dairy products in a week.

c. Compute the probability that a person will consume between $3.25 and $5.75 in dairy products in a week.

5.106 The Town-Pump service station has performed an analysis of its customers and has found that 80% pay on credit and the rest pay cash. If five customers are sampled, what is the probability that three or fewer of them will pay on credit?

5.107 The makers of Time-Tell digital watches claim that their watches are of very high quality. Specifically, they have claimed that no more than 10% of their watches will fail within the first six months of use. Suppose the distribution of watch failures in a sample of 10 watches has a binomial distribution.

a. What is the mean of the probability distribution? Interpret this value.

b. What is the standard deviation of the random variable? Interpret this value.

5.108 Jamieson Airlines has a central office that takes reservations for all flights flown by the airline. The calls received during any week are approximately normally distributed, with a mean of 12,000 and a standard deviation of 2,500.

a. During what percentage of weeks does the airline receive more than 11,000 calls?

b. During what percentage of weeks does it receive fewer than 12,300 calls?

c. During what percentage of weeks does it receive between 10,800 an 13,400 calls?

d. During the past year, the manager of the central office has kept track of the number of calls received each week. She has determined that the smallest number of calls was 10,800 and the largest number of calls was 13,400. If the calls received are normally distributed, determine the mean and standard deviations this data suggests.

Advanced Business Applications

5.109 The Ziegler Lumber Company sets the cut length on its 2 x 12 lumber a little longer than the specified length because its trim saw is fairly old. The mill foreman discovered that the saw would cut any set length short by an average of 3 inches, with a standard deviation of 1.5 inches. Fortunately, the errors seem to be normally distributed.

a. If the foreman is setting up the trim saw to cut 2 x 12 boards 10 feet long, what should the trim-saw length setting be if he wants no more than a 5% chance of a board being shorter than 10 feet?

b. Suppose the machine can be fixed so that the standard deviation in cut error can be controlled to a specified level. What would the standard deviation have to be so that trim length could be set 1 inch shorter than the answer to part a?

5.110 Exercise 5.109 refers to the Ziegler Lumber Company, which discovered its old trim saw would cut any length short by an average of 3 inches, with a standard deviation of 1.5 inches. The errors seen are normally distributed. Suppose an adjustment is made to the machine that reduces the average error to 2 inches but increases the standard deviation to 2 inches.

a. Determine the trim-saw length setting if the foreman wants no more than a 5% chance of a board being cut shorter than 10 feet.

b. The foreman has kept track of the complaints concerning the length of the 10-foot boards. He is convinced that about 10% of the boards are more than 4.56 inches shorter than they were intended to be. About 5% of the boards are cut longer than they were intended to be. Do these figures convince you that the supposed adjustment really was made? Provide statistical evidence with your opinion?

5.111 The personnel manager for a large company is interested in the distribution of sick-leave hours for employees of her company. A recent study revealed the distribution to be approximately normal, with a mean of 58 hours per year and a standard deviation of 14 hours.

An office manager in one division has reason to believe that during the past year, two of his employees have taken excessive sick leave relative to everyone else. The first employee used 74 hours of sick leave, and the second used 90 hours. What would you conclude about the office manager's claim and why?

5.112 Exercise 5.111 considers a company's allocation of sick-leave hours for its employees. The personnel manager has found the distribution of time lost per year due to illness to be approximately normal, with a mean of 58 hours per year and a standard deviation of 14 hours. Suppose the company grants 40 hours of paid sick leave per year. Given the distribution of time lost due to illness, what would you conclude about the adequacy of the company's sick-leave policy? Why?

5.113 The Bryce Brothers Lumber Company is considering buying a machine that planes lumber to the correct thickness. The machine is advertised to produce "6-inch lumber" having a thickness that is normally distributed, with a mean of 6 inches and a standard deviation of 0.10 inch.

a. If building standards in the industry require a 99% chance of a board being between 5.85 and 6.15 inches, should Bryce Brothers purchase this machine? Why or why not?

b. To what level would the company that manufactures the machine have to reduce the standard deviation for the machine to conform to industry standards?

5.114 After a recent freeze in Florida, the Sweetbrand Citrus Company was concerned about the quality of its grapefruit. Estimates by the U.S. Department of Agriculture (USDA) indicated that 25% of the grapefruit were damaged by the freeze. The problem is that there seems to be no pattern to indicate which grapefruit suffered freeze damage. For instance, given two grapefruit growing side by side on a tree, one could be perfect and the other damaged. Suppose the Sweetbrand Company selected a random sample of 50 grapefruit.

a. What conditions must be satisfied so that the number of damaged grapefruit has a probability distribution described by the binomial distribution?

b. Assuming that the binomial distribution does apply, what is the probability of finding fewer than 5 damaged grapefruit, given that the 25% estimate is correct?

c. Assuming that the binomial distribution applies, what is the probability of finding more than 20 damaged grapefruit if the 25% estimate is correct?

d. Referring to your answer in part c, suppose that the company actually did observe more than 20 damaged grapefruit in a sample of 50. What might be concluded about the USDA's 25% estimate? Discuss.

5.115 The Bayhill City Council claims that 40% of the parking spaces downtown are used by employees of the downtown businesses. A sample of 5 parking spaces was selected from the 4,000 parking spaces.

a. Suppose the sample results showed 4 or more of the spaces were filled by employees. What would you conclude about the council's claim? Discuss.

b. What is the expected number of employees' cars in a sample of 5 parking spaces?

5.116 The Milky-Way Dairy buys milk bottles in lots of 5,000. According to the supplier, 80% of the bottles will be acceptable for use without any additional cleaning by the company's "scrubber." Assuming that the binomial distribution applies:

a. In a sample of 200 bottles, what is the expected number of bottles that will need to be cleaned by the scrubber?

b. In a sample of 100 bottles, what is the expected number of bottles that will not require additional cleaning by the Milky-Way Dairy?

c. Suppose it costs the Milky-Way Dairy $0.03 per bottle to use the scrubber. What is the expected cost of scrubbing for a sample of 300 bottles?

d. Compute the standard deviation of the probability distribution for a sample of 100 bottles, when x_1 is defined as the number of bottles that require scrubbing. Assume that the estimate of 80%-acceptable clean bottles applies.

5.117 The manager at the Town Square Movie Theater has determined that in the 15 minutes prior to the start of a movie, the number of customers who go to the concession stand to make a purchase averages 45 and the distribution for the number of arrivals is Poisson distributed. Based upon this information, determine each of the following:

a. Find the probability that the time between arrivals for any two customers is less than 20 seconds.

b. Determine the probability that the time between two customers arriving is more than 30 seconds.

c. What is the probability that the time between arrivals for two customers is between 30 seconds and 1 minute?

5.118 One of the production steps for a company that makes equipment for the semiconductor industry involves polishing. The polishing machine requires a polishing disk. The amount of time this disk lasts varies from disk to disk. Once a disk wears to a certain point, it must be replaced with a new one. Experience indicates that the time to failure is exponentially distributed, with a mean of 4.5 hours. The operators are required to log the amount of time each disk lasts. One operator reported the following times for her machine on her 12-hour shift: 2.4 hours, 1.5 hours, 2.8 hours, and 3.1 hours. (Note, the fifth disk was still okay when she went off shift after 12 hours.)

a. What is the probability that an operator would find four successive disks with time to failure under 3.1 hours?

b. Based on your answers to part a, comment on whether you think there is evidence to suggest that the disks currently being used are not meeting the 4.5-hour mean life.

5.119 Referring to semiconductor equipment company of Exercise 5.118, suppose the shift supervisor is concerned that this operator is changing polishing disks too quickly. Explain how the probabilities computed in Exercise 5.118 could be used to help analyze the situation and reach a conclusion about the operator. How might the supervisor determine whether the problem was with the disks or with the operator? Discuss.

5.120 The Askot Publishing Company publishes paperback romance novels. At the page-proof stage, it has been determined that spelling errors appear randomly and are independent of each other at an average rate of 1.3 errors per page ($\lambda = 1.3$). Suppose a proofreader has been hired to read a new book.

a. If the proofreader does a perfect job, what is the average number of errors he will find for each two pages read?

b. What is the variance of the number of errors per two pages? What is the standard deviation?

c. Suppose a proofreader has just finished four pages and has found no errors. What are some of the possible conclusions you might reach and why?

5.121 The Dade County Emergency Services dispatcher is trained to determine from the call received whether an emergency exists or whether the problem can be handled on a nonemergency basis. Past evidence indicates that 50% of calls are true emergencies.

a. If the binomial distribution applies, develop the probability distribution for a sample of 10, and graph the distribution in histogram form. Does the distribution appear to be symmetric? Discuss.

b. Referring to part a, suppose that the probability of a call being a true emergency is actually 70%. Develop the probability distribution, and graph the distribution in histogram form. Compare the distribution in part a with this one in terms of symmetry. Discuss.

5.122 A small private ambulance service in Oklahoma has determined that the time between emergency calls is exponentially distributed, with a mean of 41 minutes. When a unit goes on call, it is out of service for 60 minutes. If a unit is busy when an emergency call is received, the call is immediately routed to another service. The company is considering buying a second ambulance. However, before doing so, the owners are interested in determining the probability that a call will come in before the ambulance is back in service. Without knowing the costs involved in this situation, does this probability tend to support the need for a second ambulance? Discuss.

5.123 The Stevens Company in Seattle, Washington, recently conducted a study regarding customer satisfaction with its winter boots, which are marketed throughout the United States. A basic premise that the company has been operating under for the past several years is that 90% of its customers have been satisfied with the boots they purchased. However, H. B. Stevens, the company president, felt that a survey should be taken to see if this was, in fact, the case.

a. Assuming that the characteristics of the binomial distribution are satisfied, what is the probability of finding fewer than 90 satisfied customers in a sample of 100 if the company's assumption about consumer satisfaction is correct?

b. Assuming that the binomial distribution is applicable, what is the probability of finding more than 10 dissatisfied customers in a sample of 100 if the probability of any 1 customer being satisfied is 90%?

c. Suppose the sample reveals 78 satisfied customers. What is the probability of exactly 78 satisfied customers if the probability of a customer being satisfied is 90%?

5.124 The Cozine Corporation runs the land fill operation outside Little Rock, Arkansas. Each day, each of the company's trucks makes several trips from the city to the land fill. On each entry the truck is weighed. The data file *Cozine* contains a sample of 200 truck weights. Determine the mean and standard deviation for the garbage truck weights. Assuming that these sample values are representative of the population of all Cozine garbage trucks, and assuming that the distribution is normally distributed,

a. Determine the probability that a truck will arrive at the landfill weighing in excess of 46,000 pounds.

b. Compare the probability in part a to the proportion of trucks in the sample that weighed over 46,000 pounds. What does this imply to you?

c. Suppose the managers are concerned that trucks are returning to the landfill before they are fully loaded. If they have set a minimum weight of 38,000 pounds before a truck returns to the landfill, what is the probability that a truck will fail to meet the minimum standard?

5.125 The St. Maries plywood plant is part of the Potlatch Corporation's Northwest Division. The plywood superintendent organized a study of the diameters of trees that are being shipped to the mill. After collecting a large amount of data on diameters, he concluded that the distribution is approximately normally distributed, with a mean of 14.25 inches and a standard deviation of 2.92 inches. Because of the way plywood is made, there is a certain amount of waste on each log because the peeling process leaves a core that is approximately 3 inches thick. For this reason, he feels that any log that is less than 10 inches in diameter is not profitable for making plywood.

a. Based on the data he has collected, what is the probability that a log will be unprofitable?

b. An alternative is to peel the log and then sell the core as "peeler logs." These peeler logs are sold as fence posts and for various landscape projects. There is not as much profit in these peeler logs, however. The superintendent has determined that he can make a profit if a peeler log's diameter is not more than 32% of the diameter of the log. Using this additional information, calculate the proportion of logs that will be unprofitable.

5.126 Referring to the plywood plant discussed in the previous problem, suppose the manager of the plywood mill wants no more than a 3% chance that any log will be unprofitable (fewer than 10 inches in diameter). One way to get to this value is to have the tree cutters do a better job sorting the logs, to reduce the standard deviation. Assume that the mean diameter does not change.

a. What standard deviation would have to be achieved to meet the manager's requirements?

b. Answer part a, if the peeler logs defined in Exercise 5.125 are included.

CASE 5-A:

East Mercy Medical Center

Dorothy Jacobs recently was hired as assistant administrator of the East Mercy Medical Center. She is a new graduate of a well-regarded master's degree program in hospital administration and is expected to incorporate some advanced thinking into the apparently lax practices at East Mercy.

Hospitals have recently been under increasing pressure from both government and local sources because of escalating costs. Although members of the board of directors of East Mercy feel that cost considerations are secondary to quality care, its members also are sensitive to the increasing public pressure.

East Mercy is located in a rapidly growing area and is experiencing capacity limitations. In particular, according to staff personnel, the obstetrics, adult medical/surgical, and pediatric wards are "bursting at the seams." East Mercy is considering an extensive expansion program, including expansion of the obstetric, adult medical/surgical, and pediatric wards. The board has allocated a total of $400,000 for new beds in these three wards. Dorothy is currently trying to determine how many beds current demand levels justify for each ward and how many beds to add, given the $400,000 cost constraint.

Dorothy and her staff have computed statistics based on the current year's patient census data in each of the three wards. These figures are as follows:

WARD	AVERAGE NO. BEDS USED PER DAY	STANDARD DEVIATION
Obstetrics	24	6.1
Surgery	13	4.3
Pediatrics	19	4.7

Histogram plots of bed usage show a close approximation to a normal distribution for each department.

The present capacity of each ward is

Obstetrics:	30
Surgery:	20
Pediatrics:	24

The hospital's architects have given the following estimates for the cost of adding one bed and all necessary supporting equipment to each of the wards:

Obstetrics:	$20,000
Surgery:	$26,000
Pediatrics:	$15,500

It is possible for a ward to exceed its capacity, but according to state guidelines, this should not occur more than 5% of the time.

Dorothy is in the process of preparing a report to the administrator showing how many beds are to be added to each of the three wards.

CASE 5-B:

Rutledge Collections

Bob and Lisa Rutledge have operated a small collection company in New Hampshire for 14 years. Throughout this time, they have worked as agents for various companies in the area doing debt collection work. For example, they currently are under contract with Dalton Chevrolet to collect past due accounts for Dalton's service department. As with most of their contracts, Rutledge gets a percentage of all money collected. This has worked well over the years, and the Rutledges have earned a decent income.

However, Bob and Lisa are now facing a major decision that involves significant risk and significant reward, as well. The Bell Home Furnishings Company in Vermont recently declared bankruptcy. At the time, Bell had more than 8,000 receivable accounts that had balances that were more than 90 days late. This delay in collecting payments from so many customers put a cash flow strain on the company, causing their lenders to call due Bell's short-term loans.

The bankruptcy judge handling the case has ordered the delinquent accounts to be sold. Bob and Lisa have the opportunity to purchase these accounts at a fraction of their face value. If they do, then any money they collect will be theirs. Bob has figured that if they can collect on 30% or more of the accounts, they will make a sizable profit. However, if the collection rate is 20% or less, they will be in big trouble themselves. The judge has agreed to allow the Rutledges the opportunity to test their collection process on a random sample of 50 of Bell's accounts. Bob and Lisa agree that if they are able to collect 15 or more, they will take the deal. If they are successful on 14 or fewer, they will walk away from the opportunity.

However, they are both uneasy about this plan. If they would actually be successful in collecting on 30% or more of the accounts, they don't want to miss out. On the other hand, if the collection rate is really as low as 20%, they don't want the deal. Bob wonders how effective the proposed sampling plan might be. He decides to make a call to the local university to see if he can get some advice.

CASE 5-C:

American Oil Company

Chad Williams, field geologist for the American Oil Company, settled into his first-class seat on the Sun-Air flight between Los Angeles and Oakland, California. Earlier that afternoon, he had attended a meeting with the design engineering group at the Los Angeles New Product Division. He was now on his way to the home office in Oakland. He was looking forward to the one-hour flight because it would give him a chance to reflect on a problem that surfaced during the meeting. It would also give him a chance to think about the exciting opportunities that lay ahead in Australia.

Chad works with a small group of highly trained people at American Oil who literally walk the earth looking for new sources of oil. They make use of the latest in electronic equipment to take a wide range of measurements from many thousands of feet below the earth's surface. It is one of these electronic machines that is the source of Chad's current problem. Engineers in Los Angeles have designed a sophisticated enhancement that will greatly improve the equipment's ability to detect oil. The enhancement requires 800 capacitors, which must operate within ± 0.50 microns from the specified standard of 12 microns.

The problem is that the supplier can provide capacitors that operate according to a normal distribution, with a mean of 12 microns and a standard deviation of 1 micron. Thus, Chad knows that not all capacitors will meet the specifications required by the new piece of exploration equipment. This will mean that in order to have at least 800 usable capacitors, American Oil will have to order more than 800 from the supplier. However, these items are very expensive, so he wants to order as few as possible to meet their needs. At the meeting, the group agreed that they wanted a 98% chance that any order of capacitors would contain the sufficient number of usable items. If the project is to remain on schedule, Chad must place the order by tomorrow. He wants the new equipment ready to go by the time he leaves for an exploration trip in Australia. As he reclined in his seat, sipping a cool lemonade, he wondered whether a basic statistical technique could be used to help determine how many capacitors to order.

CASE 5-D:

Boise Cascade Corporation

At the Boise Cascade Corporation, lumber mill logs arrive by truck and are scaled (measured to determine the number of board feet) before they are dumped into a log pond. Figure 5-22 illustrates the basic flow. The mill manager must determine how many scale stations to have open during various times of the day. If he has too many stations open, the scalers will have excessive idle time and the cost of scaling will be unnecessarily high. On the other hand, if too few scale stations are open, some log trucks will have to wait.

The manager has studied the truck arrival patterns and has determined that during the first open hour (7:00–8:00 A.M.), the trucks randomly arrive at 12 per hour on average. Each scale sta-

tion can scale 6 trucks per hour (10 minutes each). If the manager knew how many trucks would arrive during the hour, he would know how many scale stations to have open.

0 to 6 trucks:	open 1 scale station
7 to 12 trucks:	open 2 scale stations
etc.	

However, the number of trucks is a random variable and is uncertain. Your task is to provide guidance to the decision.

FIGURE 5-22

Truck Flow for Boise Cascade Mill Example

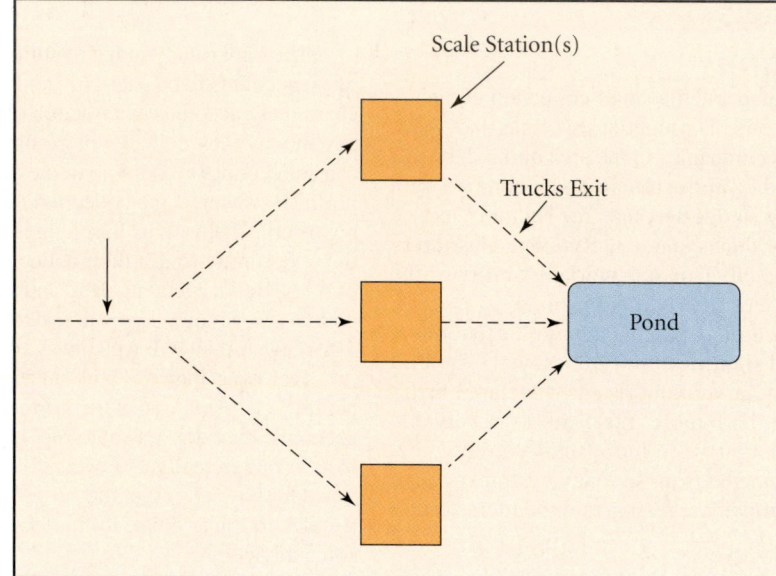

General References

1. Albright, Christian S., Wayne L. Winston, and Christopher Zappe, *Data Analysis and Decision Making with Microsoft Excel* (Pacific Grove, CA: Duxbury, 1999).
2. Dodge, Mark, and Craig Stinson, *Running Microsoft Excel 2000* (Redmond, WA: Microsoft Press, 1999).
3. Hogg, R. V., and Elliot A. Tanis, *Probability and Statistical Inference*, 5th ed. (Upper Saddle River, NJ: Prentice Hall, 1997).
4. Marx, Moriss L., and Richard J. Larsen, *Mathematical Statistics and Its Applications*, 3rd ed. (Upper Saddle River, NJ: Prentice Hall, 2000).
5. *Microsoft Excel 2000* (Redmond, WA: Microsoft Corp., 1999).
6. *Minitab for Windows Version 14* (State College, PA: Minitab, 2003).
7. Siegel, Andrew F., *Practical Business Statistics*, 4th ed. (Burr Ridge, IL: Irwin, 2000).

CHAPTER 6

Introduction to Sampling Distributions

CHAPTER OUTCOMES

After studying the material in Chapter 6, you should be able to:

- Understand the concept of sampling error.
- Determine the mean and standard deviation for the sampling distribution of $\bar{x}$.
- Determine the mean and standard deviation for the sampling distribution of the sample proportion, $\bar{p}$.
- Understand the importance of the Central Limit Theorem.
- Apply sampling distributions for both $\bar{x}$ and $\bar{p}$.

WHY YOU NEED TO KNOW

A marketing research executive receives a summary report from her analyst that indicates the mean dollars spent by adults on winter-sports recreation activities per year is $302.45. As she reads further, she learns that the mean value is based on a statistical sample of 540 adults in Vermont. The $302.45 is a *statistic*, not a *parameter*, because it is based on a sample rather than an entire population. If you were this marketing executive, you might have several questions:

- Is the actual population mean equal to $302.45?
- If the population mean is not $302.45, how close is $302.45 to the true population mean?
- Is a sample of 540 taken from a population of several million sufficient to provide a "good" estimate of the population mean?

A major manufacturer of personal computers selects a random sample of computers boxed and ready for shipment to customers. These computers are unboxed and inspected to see whether what is in the box matches exactly what the customer order specifies. This past week, 233 systems were sampled and 18 had one or more discrepancies. This is a 7.7% defect rate. Should the quality engineer conclude that exactly 7.7% of the 13,300 computers made this week reached the customer with one or more order discrepancies? Is the actual percentage higher or lower than 7.7%, and by

how much? Should the quality engineer request that more computers be sampled?

The questions facing the marketing executive and the quality engineer are common to those faced by people in business everywhere. If you haven't already, you will almost assuredly find yourself in a similar situation many times in the future. To help answer these questions, you need to have an understanding of *sampling distributions*. Whenever decisions are based on samples rather than an entire population, questions about the sample results exist. Anytime we sample from a population, there are many, many possible samples that could have been selected. Each sample will contain different items. Because of this, the sample means for each possible sample can be different, or the sample percentages can be different. The sampling distribution describes the distribution of possible sample outcomes. If you know what this distribution looks like, it will help you understand the specific result you have obtained from the one sample you have selected.

This chapter introduces you to sampling error and sampling distributions and discusses how you can use this knowledge to help answer the questions facing the marketing executive and the quality engineer. The information presented here provides an essential building block to understanding statistical estimation and hypothesis testing, which will be covered in upcoming chapters.

6-1 SAMPLING ERROR: WHAT IT IS AND WHY IT HAPPENS

As discussed in previous chapters, you will encounter many situations in business in which a sample will be taken from a population and you will be required to analyze the sample data. Chapter 1 introduced several different statistical sampling techniques. Chapters 2 and 3 introduced a variety of descriptive tools that are useful in analyzing sample data. The objective of sampling is to gather data that mirror a population. Then when analysis is performed on the sample data, the results will be as though we had worked with all the population data. However, we very rarely know if our objective has been achieved. To be able to determine if a sample mirrors the population, we must know the entire population, and if that is the case, we do not need to sample. We can just census the population. Because we do not know the population, we require that our sample be random so that bias is not introduced into an already difficult task.

CALCULATING SAMPLING ERROR

Regardless of how careful we are in using proper sampling methods, the sample may not be a perfect reflection of the population. For example a *statistic* such as $\bar{p}$ might be computed for sample data. Unless the sample is a mirror image of the population, the statistic will likely not equal the *parameter*, μ. In this case, the difference between the sample mean and the population mean is called **sampling error**. In the case in which we are interested in the mean value, the sampling error is computed using Equation 6-1.

Sampling Error

The difference between a value computed from a sample (a statistic) and the corresponding value computed from the population (a parameter).

Sampling Error of the Sample Mean

$$\text{Sampling Error} = \bar{x} - \mu \qquad \qquad \textbf{6-1}$$

where:

$\bar{x} = $ sample mean
$\mu = $ population mean

Kornfield, Harrington & Sandmeyer—The architectural firm of Kornfield, Harrington & Sandmeyer (KH&S) has designed 12 shopping centers. Table 6-1 shows a list of the 12 projects and the total square footage of each project.

Because these 12 projects are all the shopping centers the company has worked on, the square-feet area for all 12 projects, shown in Table 6-1, is a population. Equation 6-2 is used to compute the mean square feet in the population of projects.

Population Mean

$$\mu = \frac{\sum x}{N} \qquad \qquad \textbf{6-2}$$

where:

$\mu = $ Population mean
$x = $ Values in the population
$N = $ Population size

The mean square feet for the 12 shopping centers is

$$\mu = \frac{114{,}560 + 202{,}300 + \cdots + 125{,}200 + 156{,}900}{12}$$

$$\mu = 158{,}972 \text{ square feet}$$

The average-size shopping center designed by the firm is 158,972 square feet. This value is a **parameter**. No matter how many times we compute the value, assuming no arithmetic mistakes, we will get the same value for the population mean.

Parameter

A measure computed from the entire population.

KH&S is a finalist to be the architect for a new shopping center in Orlando, Florida. The developers who will hire the architect plan to select a **simple random sample** of $n = 5$ projects from

TABLE 6-1

Square Feet for Shopping Center Projects

PROJECT	SQUARE FEET
1	114,560
2	202,300
3	78,600
4	156,700
5	134,600
6	88,200
7	177,300
8	155,300
9	214,200
10	303,800
11	125,200
12	156,900

those that the finalists have completed. The developers will travel to these shopping centers and examine the designs and interview owners and shoppers. (You may want to refer to Chapter 1 to review the material on simple random samples.)

Simple Random Sample

A sample selected in such a manner that each possible sample of a given size has an equal chance of being selected.

Refer to the shopping center data in Table 6-1, and suppose the developers randomly select the following five KH&S projects from the population:

Project	Square Feet
5	134,600
4	156,700
1	114,560
8	155,300
9	214,200

Key in the selection process is the finalists' past performance on large projects, so the developers might be interested in the mean size of the shopping centers that the finalists have designed. Equation 6-3 is used to compute the sample mean.

Sample Mean

$$\bar{x} = \frac{\sum x}{n}$$

6-3

where:

$\bar{x}$ = Sample mean
x = Sample value selected from the population
n = Sample size

The sample mean is:

$$\bar{x} = \frac{134,600 + 156,700 + 114,560 + 155,300 + 214,200}{5} = \frac{775,360}{5} = 155,072$$

The average number of square feet in the sample of five shopping centers selected by the developers is 155,072. This value is a *statistic* based on the sample.

Recall the mean for the population:

$$\mu = 158,972 \text{ square feet}$$

The sample mean is

$$\bar{x} = 155,072 \text{ square feet}$$

As you can see, the sample mean does not equal the population mean. This difference is called *sampling error*. Using Equation 6-1, we compute the sampling error as follows.

$$\text{Sampling error} = \bar{x} - \mu$$
$$= 155,072 - 158,972 = -3,900 \text{ square feet}$$

The sample mean for the sample of $n = 5$ shopping centers is 3,900 square feet less than the population mean. Regardless of how carefully you construct your sampling plan, you can expect to see sampling error. A sample will almost never be a perfect mirror image of its population. The sample value and the population value will most likely be different.

Suppose the developer who selected the random sample throws these five projects back into the stack and selects a second sample of five as follows:

Project	Square Feet
9	214,200
6	88,200
5	134,600
12	156,900
10	303,800

The mean for this sample is

$$\bar{x} = \frac{214{,}200 + 88{,}200 + 134{,}600 + 156{,}900 + 303{,}800}{5} = \frac{897{,}700}{5} = 179{,}540 \text{ square feet}$$

This time, the sample mean is higher than the population mean. This time the sampling error is

$$\bar{x} - \mu = 179{,}540 - 158{,}972 = 20{,}568 \text{ square feet}$$

This illustrates some useful fundamental concepts.

- The size of the sampling error depends on which sample is selected.
- The sampling error may be positive or negative.
- There is potentially a different $\bar{x}$ for each possible sample.

If the developers wanted to use the sample mean to estimate the population mean, in one case they would be 3,900 square feet too low and in the other, they would be 20,568 square feet too high.

$\mathcal{E}$XAMPLE 6-1: COMPUTING THE SAMPLING ERROR

Jim's Appliances   Jim's Appliances is a discount appliance dealer that specializes in kitchen appliances. On Saturday morning, among the store's inventory were 10 electric ranges. The retail prices, in dollars, on these 10 ranges were:

$479	$569	$599	$649	$649	$699	$699	$749	$799	$799

Suppose the manager wished to do a quick analysis of the electric range inventory and randomly sampled $n = 4$ ranges. The ranges selected had retail prices of:

$569	$649	$799	$799

Assuming that the manager was hoping that the sampled ranges would be representative of the population, the sampling error can be computed using the following steps:

Step 1:   **Determine the population mean using Equation 6-2:**

$$\mu = \frac{\sum x}{N} = \frac{479 + 569 + 599 + \cdots + 799 + 799}{10} = \frac{6{,}690}{10} = \$669$$

Step 2:   **Compute the sample mean using Equation 6-3:**

$$\bar{x} = \frac{\sum x}{n} = \frac{569 + 649 + 799 + 799}{4} = \frac{2{,}816}{4} = \$704$$

Step 3:   **Compute the sampling error using Equation 6-1:**

$$\bar{x} - \mu = 704 - 669 = \$35$$

This sample of four has a sampling error of $35. The sample of electric ranges has a slightly larger mean than the population as a whole.

THE ROLE OF SAMPLE SIZE IN SAMPLING ERROR

Kornfield, Harrington & Sandmeyer (continued)—Previously, we selected potential samples of size 5 and computed the resulting sampling error. There are actually 792 possible samples of size 5 taken from 12 projects. This value is found using the counting rule for combinations, which was discussed in Chapter 5.[1]

---

[1]The number of combinations of x items from a sample of n is $\dfrac{n!}{(x)!\,(n-x)!}$.

In actual situations, only one sample is selected, and the decision maker uses the sample value to estimate the population value. A "small" sampling error may be acceptable. However, if the sampling error is "too large," conclusions about the population value could be misleading.

We can look at the extremes on either end to evaluate the potential for extreme sampling error. The population of square feet for the 12 projects is:

Project	Square Feet
1	114,560
2	202,300
3	78,600
4	156,700
5	134,600
6	88,200
7	177,300
8	155,300
9	214,200
10	303,800
11	125,200
12	156,900

Suppose, by chance, the developers ended up with the five smallest shopping centers in their sample. These would be

Project	Square Feet
3	78,600
6	88,200
1	114,560
11	125,200
5	134,600

The mean of this sample is

$$\bar{x} = 108,232 \text{ square feet}$$

Of all the possible samples, this one provides the smallest sample mean. The sampling error is

$$\bar{x} - \mu = 108,232 - 158,972 = -50,740 \text{ square feet}$$

Thus, if this sample had been selected, the sampling error would be $-50,740$ square feet.

On the other extreme, suppose the sample contained the five largest shopping centers, as follows.

Project	Square Feet
10	303,800
9	214,200
2	202,300
7	177,300
12	156,900

The mean for this sample is $\bar{x} = 210,900$.

This is the largest possible sample mean from all the possible samples. The sampling error in this case would be

$$\bar{x} - \mu = 210,900 - 158,972 = 51,928 \text{ square feet}$$

The potential for extreme sampling error ranges from

$$-50,740 \text{ to } +51,928 \text{ square feet}$$

TABLE 6-2

Shopping Center Example for $n = 3$ (Extreme Samples)

SMALLEST SHOPPING CENTERS		LARGEST SHOPPING CENTERS	
Project	**Square Feet**	**Project**	**Square Feet**
3	78,600	10	303,800
6	88,200	9	214,200
1	114,560	2	202,300

$\bar{x} = 93,786.67$ sq. feet
Sampling Error:
$93,786.67 - 158,972 = -65,185.33$ square feet

$\bar{x} = 240,100$ sq. feet
Sampling Error:
$240,100 - 158,972 = 81,128$ square feet

The remaining possible samples will provide sampling error between these limits.

What happens if the sample size is larger or smaller? Suppose the developers scale back their sample size to $n = 3$ shopping centers. Table 6-2 shows the extremes. By reducing the sample size from 5 to 3, the range of potential sampling error has increased from

$$(-50,740 \cdots +51,928 \text{ square feet})$$

to

$$(-65,185.33 \cdots +81,128 \text{ square feet})$$

This illustrates that the potential for extreme sampling error is greater when smaller-sized samples are used.

Although larger sample sizes reduce the potential for extreme sampling error, there is no guarantee that the larger sample size will always give the smallest sampling error. For example, Table 6-3 shows two further applications of the shopping center data. As illustrated, the sample of 3 had a sampling error of $-2,672$ square feet, whereas the sample of 5 had a sampling error of 16,540 square feet. In this case, the smaller sample was "better" than the larger sample. However, in Section 6-2, you will learn that, on average, the sampling error produced by large samples will be less than the sampling error from small samples.

TABLE 6-3

Shopping Center Example with Different Sample Sizes

$n = 5$		$n = 3$	
Project	**Square Feet**	**Project**	**Square Feet**
4	156,700	12	156,900
1	114,560	8	155,300
7	177,300	4	156,700
11	125,200		
10	303,800		

$\bar{x} = 175,512$ sq. feet
Sampling Error:
$175,512 - 158,972 = 16,540$ square feet

$\bar{x} = 156,300$ sq.feet
Sampling Error:
$156,300 - 158,972 = -2,672$ square feet

6-1: EXERCISES

Skill Development

6.1 Consider the following data to be a population of $N = 20$ values.

5	3	2	6	6	7	3	3	6	7
7	9	7	5	3	12	6	10	7	2

a. Compute the population mean.
b. A random sample of $n = 6$ produced the following numbers: 6, 12, 10, 3, 2, 2. Find the sample mean and determine the sampling error for this sample.

c. Find the range of extreme sampling error for a sample of 6. (Hint: Find the lowest possible sample mean and highest possible sample mean.)

6.2 Consider the following values to represent a population

29	33	10	20	50	10	10	30	19	40	20
11	40	60	20	20	13	20	20	19	30	20

a. If a random sample of $n = 8$ items includes the following, compute the sampling error.

33	20	20	11	19	10	20	29

b. Determine the range for the possible sampling error when a sample of size $n = 8$ is used. (Hint: find the sampling error for the eight smallest values and the sampling error for the eight largest values.)

c. Refer to part b and determine the range of potential sampling error if the sample size is reduced to 5. Discuss the impact of sample size on the potential for extreme sampling error.

6.3   Consider the following values to represent a population:

129	330	100	200	150	105	100	130	190	400	120

a. If a random sample of $n = 3$ items includes the following, compute the sampling error.

150	100	400

b. Determine the range for the possible sampling error when a sample of size $n = 3$ is used. (Hint: find the sampling error for the three smallest values and the sampling error for the three largest values.)

c. Refer to part b and determine the range of potential sampling error if the sample size is increased to 5. Discuss the impact of sample size on the potential for extreme sampling error.

6.4   A population is known to have a mean value of 112,000. If a random sample of 6 items had the following values, what is the sampling error for this sample?

105,000	112,900	104,600	120,700	115,000	106,000

Business Applications

6.5   The Patterson Real Estate Company has 20 listings for homes in Fresno, California. The number of days that each house has been on the market without selling is shown as follows:

26	45	16	77	33	50	19	23	55	107
88	15	7	19	30	60	80	66	31	17

a. Considering these 20 values to be the population of interest, what is the mean of the population?

b. The company is making a sales brochure and wishes to feature five homes selected at random from the list. The number of days the five sampled homes have been on the market is:

77	60	15	31	23

If these five houses were used to estimate the mean for all 20, what would the sampling error be?

c. What is the range of possible sampling error if five homes are selected at random from the population?

6.6   Holland Management Services manages apartment complexes in Tucson, Arizona. They currently have 30 units available for rent. The monthly rental prices, in dollars, for this population of 30 units are

455	690	450	495	550	780	800	395	500	405
675	550	490	495	700	995	650	550	400	750
600	780	650	905	415	600	600	780	575	750

a. What is the range of possible sampling error if a random sample of size $n = 6$ is selected from the population?

b. What is the range of possible sampling error if a random sample of size $n = 10$ is selected? Compare your answers to parts a and b and explain why the difference exists.

6.7   The owner of Miller's Union 76 in Rochester, New York, has tracked gasoline sales for several years and is confident that the true mean sale is 16.9 gallons. Assuming that this is the population mean, if a random sample of 10 fill-ups is collected, what is the sampling error if the gallons per fill are

13.3	19.8	22.6	15.0	19.3	9.7	17.5	22.4	18.0	13.0

6.8   A major airline has stated that the mean ticket price for a round-trip flight between Dallas, Texas, and Atlanta, Georgia, is $337. Suppose a travel agency has recently selected a random sample of seven round-trip tickets for this trip with the following prices recorded in dollars.

176	459	379	588	467	802	198

Given this sample, how much sampling error exists? Discuss whether you would expect more or less sampling error if the sample size were increased to 20 tickets.

Advanced Business Applications

6.9   The State Transportation Department has conducted a study of drivers to determine whether they were carrying proof of liability insurance in their cars. The data are located in the CD-ROM file called *Liabins*. Treat the data in this file as a population. The State Insurance Department is interested in the ages of the participants in the study.

A simple random sample of 10 drivers was selected from the population. It produced the following ages: 18, 18, 68, 58, 42, 22, 55, 61, 31, 36.

Compute the sample mean. Discuss how this value compares with the population mean.

6.10   The Golden Calendar Company has a population of 16 customers. These customers are brokers who sell the calendars to stores and catalogs. The following data reflect the number of calendars sold to each of the 16 customers last year. These data are also contained in the CD-ROM file called *Golden*.

41,591	48,600	48,348	60,977
26,226	51,269	21,519	20,124
36,526	51,836	40,444	43,572
47,091	31,444	39,580	67,452

a. Compute the population mean and standard deviation.

b. Suppose that Golden managers selected four customers to take part in a special promotional test. The test is designed to increase the number of calendars that each customer will purchase next year. The simple random sample of four was obtained from this population. The data were

40,444	21,519	67,452	47,091

1. Calculate the sample mean number of calendars sold.
2. How much sampling error is present in this sample?

c. A second simple random sample of 4 was obtained from the population of 16 customers. The data obtained were

| 36,526 | 51,836 | 20,124 | 43,572 |

1. Determine the sampling error for this sample.
2. Explain why sampling error occurs and why the sampling error in part c is different than the sampling error in part b.
3. Discuss the ramifications of sampling error. What problems might it cause in this case, in which the promotion is intended to increase calendar sales next year?

d. Take a sample of size $n = 8$ from the original population.
1. Compute the sampling error.
2. Compare the sampling error for this sample with those for the two samples of size $n = 4$.
3. Without regard to the results you obtained here, explain why it is possible for a smaller sample to have a smaller sampling error than a larger sample from the same population.

(Hint: In Excel, use the Sampling feature under Tools—Data Analysis. In Minitab, use the Calc—Random Data—Sample from Columns options.)

6-2 SAMPLING DISTRIBUTION OF THE MEAN

Section 6-1 introduced the fundamental concepts of sampling error. A sample selected from a population will not perfectly match the population. This means that the sample value (statistic) likely will not equal the population value (parameter). If this difference arises because the sample is not a perfect representation of the population, it is called sampling error.

In business applications, decision makers select a single sample from a population. They compute the sample value and use it to make decisions about the entire population. For example, the Nielsen Company takes a single sample of television viewers to determine the percentage who are watching a particular program during a particular week. Of course, the sample selected is only one of many possible samples that could have been selected from the same population. The sampling error will differ depending on which sample is selected. If, in theory, you were to select all possible random samples of a given size and compute the sample means for each one, these means would vary above and below the true population mean. If we graphed these values as a frequency distribution, the graph would be the **sampling distribution**.

> **Sampling Distribution**
>
> A distribution of the possible values of a statistic for a given-size random sample selected from a population.

In this section, we introduce the basic concepts of sampling distributions. We will use an Excel tool to select repeated samples from the same population for demonstration purposes only. The same thing can be done using Minitab.

SIMULATING THE SAMPLING DISTRIBUTION FOR $\bar{x}$

Excel and Minitab Tutorial

Aims Investment Company—Aims Investment Company handles employee retirement funds, primarily for small companies. The CD-ROM file called *AIMS* contains data on the number of mutual funds in each client's portfolio. The file contains data for all 200 Aims customers, so it is a population. Figure 6-1 shows a graph of the population distribution and important numerical measures for the population.

The mean number of mutual funds in a portfolio is 2.505 funds. The standard deviation is 1.507 funds. The graph in Figure 6-1 indicates that the population is spread between 0 and 6 funds, with more customers owning 2 funds than any other number.

Suppose the controller at Aims plans to select a random sample of 10 accounts. In Excel, we can use the **Sampling** tool to generate the random sample.[2] Figure 6-2 shows the resulting sample of the

---

[2]The same thing can be achieved in Minitab by using the **Sample from Columns** option under **Calc–Random Data** options.

FIGURE 6-1

Distribution of Mutual
Funds for the Aims
Investment Company

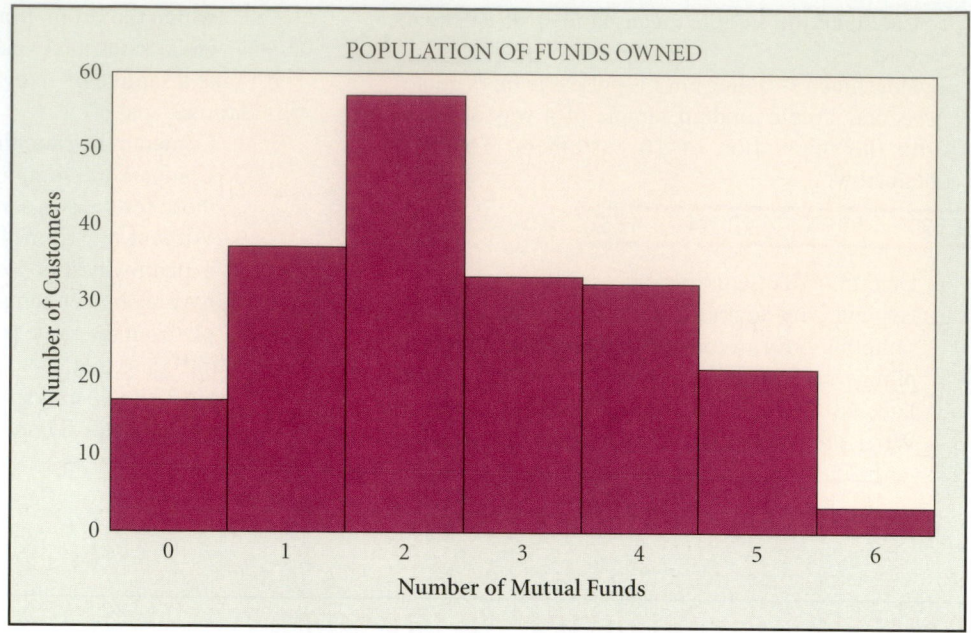

Population Mean = μ = 2.505 funds owned
Population Standard Deviation = σ = 1.507 funds owned

number of mutual funds owned for a random sample of 10 clients. The sample mean of 1.8 is also shown. To illustrate the sampling distribution, we repeat this process 500 times, generating 500 different samples of size 10. After each sample, we compute the sample mean. Figure 6-3 shows the frequency histogram for these sample means. Note that the horizontal axis represents the $\bar{x}$ values. The graph in Figure 6-3 is not a complete sampling distribution because it is based on only 500 samples out of the many possible samples that could be selected. However, this simulation gives us an idea of what the sampling distribution looks like.

Look again at the population distribution in Figure 6-1 and compare it with the shape of the frequency distribution in Figure 6-3. Although the population distribution is somewhat skewed, the sampling distribution is taking the shape of a bell curve, or normal distribution.

Note also that the population mean for the 200 individual customers in the population is 2.505 mutual funds. If we average the 500 sample means in Figure 6-3, we get 2.41. This value is the *mean of the sample means.* It is reasonably close to the population mean. Although beyond the scope of this text, it can be shown that the average of all possible sample means will equal the population mean. When the average of all possible values of the sample statistic equals a parameter, we call that statistic an *unbiased estimator* of the parameter.

FIGURE 6-2

Excel Output for the Aims
Investment Company
First Sample Size *n* = 10

	Microsoft Excel - AIMS.xls
	File Edit View Insert Format Tools Data PHStat

	A	B	C	D
1	Cutomer Number	Number of Mutual Fund Accounts		Sample n = 10
2	19100	4		2
3	5034	4		1
4	29824	1		3
5	44955	0		1
6	44230	5		0
7	47923	5		4
8	725	2		2
9	20371	3		1
10	43162	4		1
11	6929	1		3
12	12252	4		
13	2274	2	Mean =	1.8
14	1619	0		

Excel Instructions:
1. Open file: AIMS.xls
2. Click on the **Tools** tab.
3. Select the **Data Analysis** option.
4. Select **Sampling**.
5. Indicate the population data range (B2:B201).
6. Select **Random sampling** and indicate the number of samples (10 = sample size).
7. Select **Output Option**.
8. Click **OK**.

Minitab Instructions (for similar results):
1. Open file: AIMS.MTW.
2. Choose **Calc > Random Data > Sample From Columns**.
3. In **Sample**, enter the sample size.
4. In box following **row from column(s)**, enter data column: *Number of Mutual Fund Accounts.*
5. In **Store Samples in**, enter sample's storage column.
6. Click **OK**.
7. Choose **Calc > Calculator**.
8. In **Store Result in Variable**, enter column to store mean.
9. Choose **Mean** from **Functions**. **Expression: Mean(Sample Column)**.
10. Repeat Steps 2–9 to form the sampling distribution.
11. Click **OK**.

FIGURE 6-3

Aims Investment Company, Histogram of Sample Means

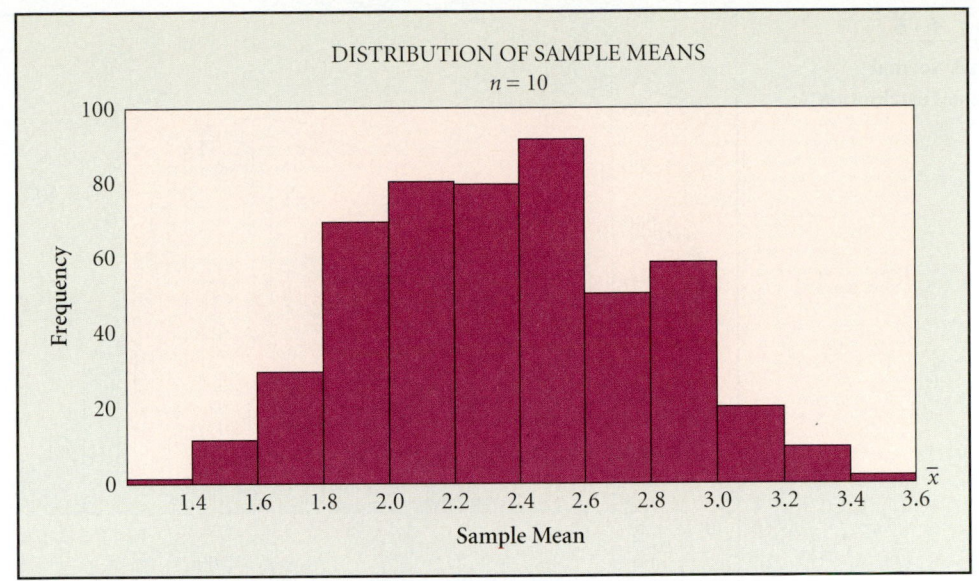

Unbiased Estimator

A characteristic of certain statistics in which the average of all possible values of the sample statistic equals a parameter.

Also, the population standard deviation is 1.507 mutual funds. This measures the variation in the number of mutual funds between individual customers. When we compute the standard deviation of the 500 sample means, we get 0.421, which is considerably smaller than the population standard deviation. As we will show shortly, this will always be the case.

Now suppose we increased the sample size from $n = 10$ to $n = 20$ and selected 500 different samples. Figure 6-4 shows the distribution of the 500 different sample means.

The distribution in Figure 6-4 is even more bell-shaped than what we observed in Figure 6-3. As sample size increases, the distribution of sample means will become shaped more like a normal distribution. The average sample mean for these 500 samples is 2.53, and the standard deviation of the different sample means is 0.376.

Keep in mind the distributions shown in Figures 6-3 and 6-4 are not true sampling distributions because they are developed from only 500 sample means. A true sampling distribution would be developed from the sample means of all possible random samples of a given size that could be selected from the population.

FIGURE 6-4

Aims Investment Company, Histogram of Sample Means

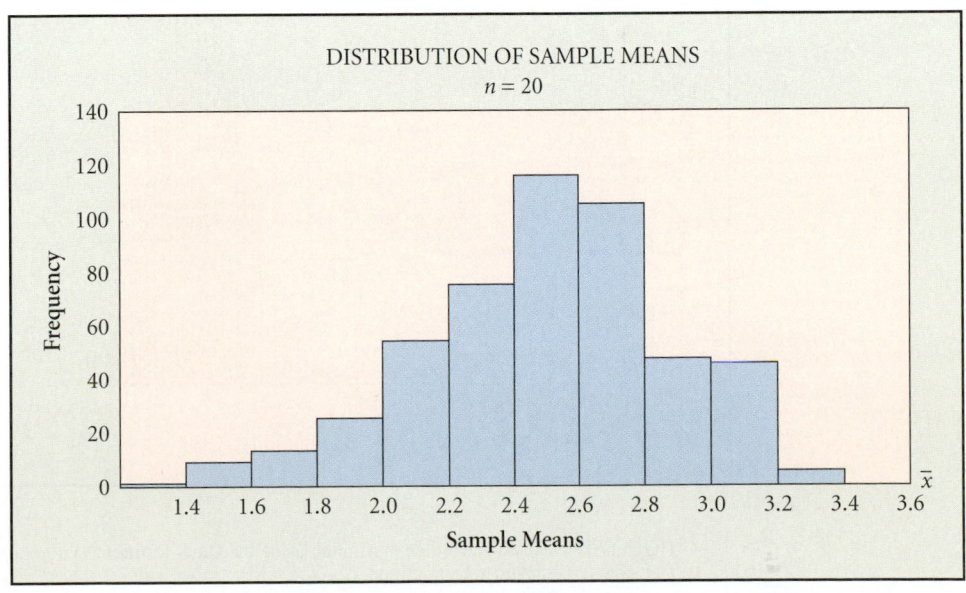

FIGURE 6-5

Simulated Normal
Population Distribution

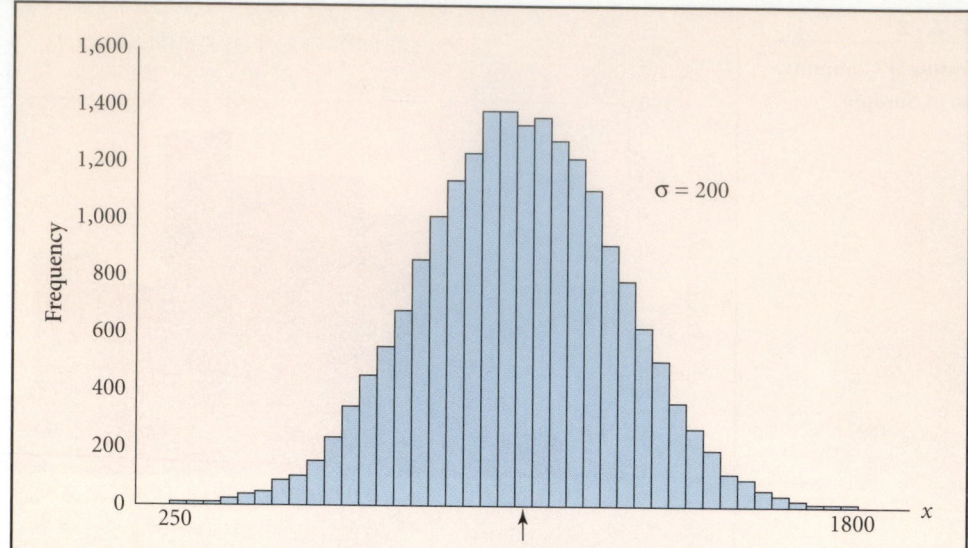

Sampling from Normal Populations

We can again use Excel or Minitab to illustrate some additional sampling distribution concepts by first generating a normally distributed population.[3] Recall from Chapter 5 that many populations appear to closely approximate a normal distribution, so you may find yourself sampling from such a distribution.

Figure 6-5 shows a simulated population that is normally distributed with a mean equal to 1,000 and a standard deviation equal to 200. The data range is from 250 to 1,800.

Next, we simulate the selection of 2,000 samples of size 10 from the population and compute the sample mean for each sample. These sample means can then be graphed as a frequency histogram, as shown in Figure 6-6. This histogram represents the sampling distribution. It, too, is approximately normally distributed.

FIGURE 6-6

Approximated Sampling
Distribution ($n = 10$)

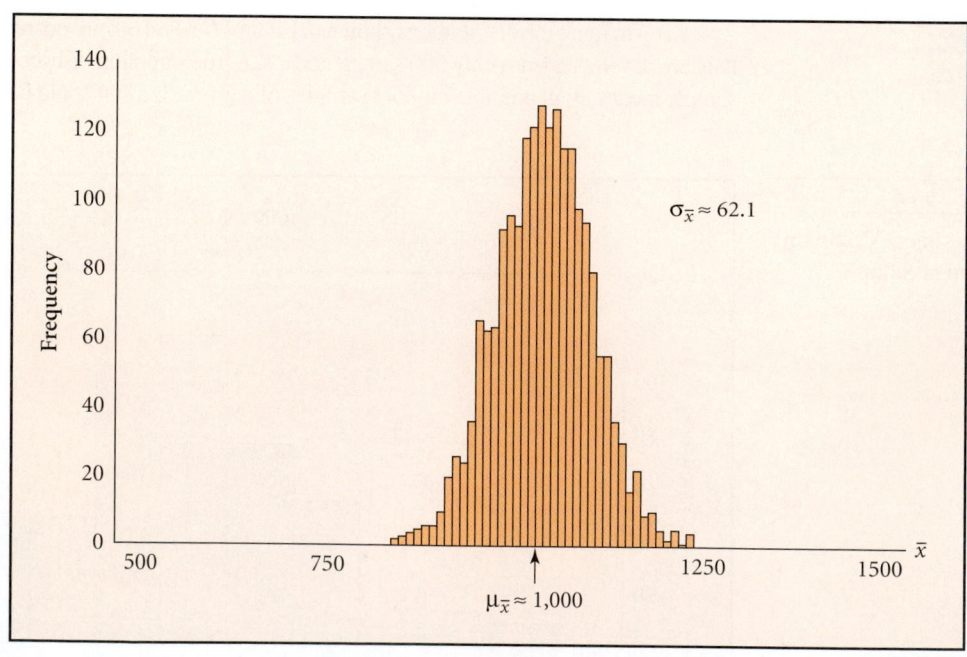

[3]The same task can be performed in Minitab using the **Calc–Random Data** option. However, you will have to generate each sample individually, which will take time.

We next compute the average of the 2,000 sample means and use it to approximate $\mu_{\bar{x}}$ as follows.

$$\mu_{\bar{x}} \approx \frac{\Sigma \bar{x}}{2,000} = \frac{2,000,178}{2,000} \approx 1,000$$

The mean of these sample means is approximately 1,000. This is the same as the population mean. We also approximate the standard deviation of the sample means as follows.

$$\sigma_{\bar{x}} \approx \sqrt{\frac{\Sigma(\bar{x} - \mu_{\bar{x}})^2}{2,000}} = 62.1$$

We see the standard deviation of the sample means is 62.1. This is much smaller than the population standard deviation, which is 200. The largest sample mean was just more than 1,212, and the smallest sample mean was just less than 775. Recall, however, that the population ranged from 250 to 1,800. The variation in the sample means always will be less than the variation for the population as a whole.

We have used this simulated example to illustrate how a sampling distribution is developed. However, in actual practice we only select one sample from the population, and we know this sample is subject to sampling error. The sample mean may be either larger or smaller than the population mean. Currently, we are assuming the population is normally distributed. Because the population forms a continuous distribution and has an uncountable number of values, we could not possibly obtain all possible samples from this population. As a result, we would be unable to construct the true sampling distribution. Figure 6-6 is an approximation based on 2,000 samples. Fortunately, an important statistical theorem exists that overcomes this obstacle: **Theorem 6-1**.

Theorem 6-1

If a population is normally distributed, with mean μ and a standard deviation σ, the sampling distribution of the sample mean $\bar{x}$ is also normally distributed with a mean equal to the population mean ($\mu_{\bar{x}} = \mu$) and a standard deviation equal to the population standard deviation divided by the square root of the sample

size $\left(\sigma_{\bar{x}} = \dfrac{\sigma}{\sqrt{n}} \right)$.

In Theorem 6-1, the quantity $\sigma_{\bar{x}} = \dfrac{\sigma}{\sqrt{n}}$ is the *standard deviation of the sampling distribution.* Another term that is given to this is the *standard error of* $\bar{x}$, because it is the measure of the standard deviation of the potential sampling error.

Suppose we again use the simulated population shown in Figure 6-5, with $\mu = 1,000$ and $\sigma = 200$. We are interested in seeing what the sampling distribution will look like for different size samples. For example, if the sample size is 10 (as we simulated earlier), Theorem 6-1 indicates that the sampling distribution will have a mean equal to 1,000 and a standard deviation equal to

$$\sigma_{\bar{x}} = \frac{200}{\sqrt{10}} = 63.2$$

For the 2,000 random samples, the mean, $\bar{x}$, is almost exactly 1,000, and the standard deviation of the $\bar{x}$ values is 62.1, close to the theoretical value of 63.2.

If we were to take a random sample of 5, Theorem 6-1 indicates the sampling distribution would be normal, with a mean equal to 1,000 and a standard deviation equal to

$$\sigma_{\bar{x}} = \frac{200}{\sqrt{5}} = 89.4$$

For a sample size of 20, the sampling distribution will be centered at $\mu_{\bar{x}} = 1,000$, with a standard deviation equal to

$$\sigma_{\bar{x}} = \frac{200}{\sqrt{20}} = 44.7$$

FIGURE 6-7

Theorem 6-1 Examples

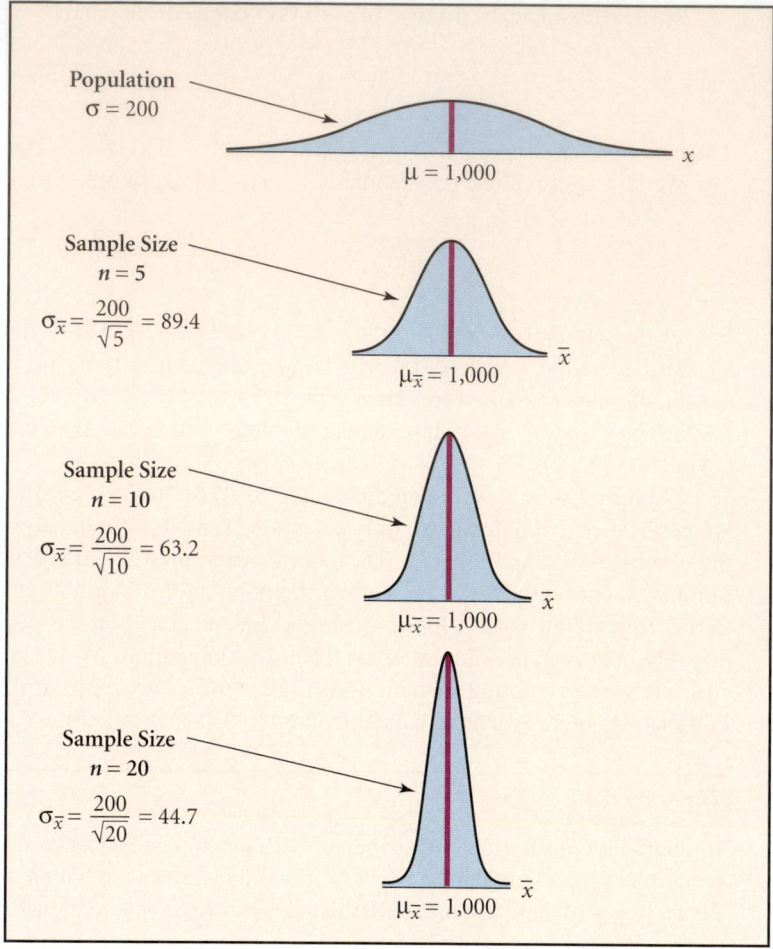

Notice, as the sample size is increased, the standard deviation of the sampling distribution is reduced. This means the potential for extreme sampling error is reduced when larger sample sizes are used. Figure 6-7 shows sampling distributions for sample sizes of 5, 10, and 20. When the population is normally distributed, the sampling distribution of $\bar{x}$ will always be normal and centered at the population mean. Only the spread in the distribution will change as the sample size changes.

The sampling distribution is composed of all possible sample means. Half the sample means will lie above the center of the sampling distribution and half will lie below. The relative distance that a given sample mean is from the center can be determined by *standardizing* the sampling distribution. As discussed in Chapter 5, a standardized value is determined by converting the value from its original units into a *z*-value. A *z*-value measures the number of standard deviations a value is from the mean. This same concept can be used when working with a sampling distribution. Equation 6-4 shows how the *z*-values are computed.

z-Value for Sampling Distribution of $\bar{x}$

$$z = \frac{\bar{x} - \mu}{\frac{\sigma}{\sqrt{n}}}$$

6-4

where:

$\bar{x}$ = Sample mean
μ = Population mean
σ = Population standard deviation
n = Sample size

Note, if the sample that is being selected is large relative to the size of the population (greater than 5 percent of the population size), and the sampling is being done without replacement, we need to modify how we compute the standard deviation of the sampling distribution and z-value using what is known as the **finite population correction factor** as shown in Equation 6-5.

---

z-Value Adjusted for the Finite Population Correction Factor

$$z = \frac{\bar{x} - \mu}{\frac{\sigma}{\sqrt{n}} \sqrt{\frac{N-n}{N-1}}}$$

6-5

where:

$$N = \text{Population size}$$
$$n = \text{Sample size}$$

$$\sqrt{\frac{N-n}{N-1}} = \text{Finite correction factor}$$

The finite population correction factor is used to calculate the standard deviation of the sampling distribution when the sampling is performed without replacement and when the sample size is greater than 5% of the population size.

EXAMPLE 6-2: FINDING THE PROBABILITY THAT $\bar{x}$ IS IN A GIVEN RANGE

Vextronix Manufacturing   Vextronix Manufacturing makes precision parts for the personal computer industry. One part is used in making the motor unit for PCs. When the production process is operating according to specifications, the diameter of the parts is normally distributed, with a mean equal to 1.5 inches and a standard deviation of 0.05 inches. Before shipping a large batch of these parts, Vextronix quality analysts have selected a random sample of 8 parts with the following diameters:

1.57	1.59	1.48	1.60	1.59	1.62	1.55	1.52

The analysts want to use these measurements to determine if the process is no longer operating within the specifications. The following steps can be used.

Step 1:   **Compute the mean for this sample.**

$$\bar{x} = \frac{\sum x}{n} = \frac{12.52}{8} = 1.565 \text{ inches}$$

Step 2:   **Define the sampling distribution for $\bar{x}$ using Theorem 6-1.**
Theorem 6-1 indicates that if the population is normally distributed, the sampling distribution for $\bar{x}$ will also be normally distributed, with

$$\mu_{\bar{x}} = \mu \text{ and } \sigma_{\bar{x}} = \frac{\sigma}{\sqrt{n}}$$

Thus, in this case, the mean of the sampling distribution should be 1.50 inches, and the standard deviation should be $\frac{0.05}{\sqrt{8}} = 0.0177$ inches

Step 3:   **Define the event of interest.**
Because the sample mean is $\bar{x} = 1.565$, which is greater than the mean of the sampling distribution, we want to find

$$P(\bar{x} \geq 1.565 \text{ inches}) = ?$$

Step 4:   **Convert the sample mean to a standardized z-value, using Equation 6-4.**

$$z = \frac{\bar{x} - \mu}{\frac{\sigma}{\sqrt{n}}} = \frac{1.565 - 1.50}{\frac{0.05}{\sqrt{8}}} = \frac{0.065}{0.0177} = 3.67$$

Step 5: **Use the standard normal distribution table to determine the desired probability.**

$$P(z \geq 3.67) = ?$$

The standard normal distribution table in Appendix D does not show z-values as high as 3.67. This implies that $P(z \geq 3.67) \approx 0.00$. So, if the production process is working properly, there is virtually no chance that a random sample of eight items will have a mean diameter of 1.565 inches or greater. Because the analysts at Vextronix did find this sample result, there is a very good chance that something is wrong with the process.

THE CENTRAL LIMIT THEOREM

Theorem 6-1 applies when the population distribution is a normal (bell-shaped) distribution. Although there are many situations in business when this will be the case, there are also many situations when the population is not normal. For example, incomes in a region tend to be right-skewed. Some distributions, such as people's weight, are bimodal (a peak weight group for males and another peak weight group for females).

What does the sampling distribution of $\bar{x}$ look like when a population is not normally distributed? The answer is . . . it depends. It depends on what the shape of the population is and what size sample is selected. To illustrate, suppose we have a U-shaped population, such as the one in Figure 6-8, with mean = 14.00 and standard deviation equal to 3.00. Now, we select 3,000 simple random samples of size 3 and compute the mean for each sample. These $\bar{x}$ values are graphed in the histogram shown in Figure 6-9.

The number of all possible random samples of size 3 obtained from the population is, of course, considerably larger than 3,000. Therefore, we would not expect that these samples would produce exactly the same results as if we had actually taken all the possible random samples of size 3. However, the results would be reasonably close to the value that would be obtained for the average of all the possible means. The average of these 3,000 sample means is

$$\frac{\sum \bar{x}}{3,000} \approx \mu_{\bar{x}} = 14.02$$

Notice this value is approximately equal to the population mean of 14.00. Next we compute the standard deviation as

$$\sigma_{\bar{x}} \approx \sqrt{\frac{\sum(\bar{x} - \mu_{\bar{x}})^2}{3,000}} = 1.82$$

The standard deviation of the sampling distribution is less than the standard deviation for the population, which was 3.00. This will always be the case.

FIGURE 6-8

Simulated Nonnormal Population

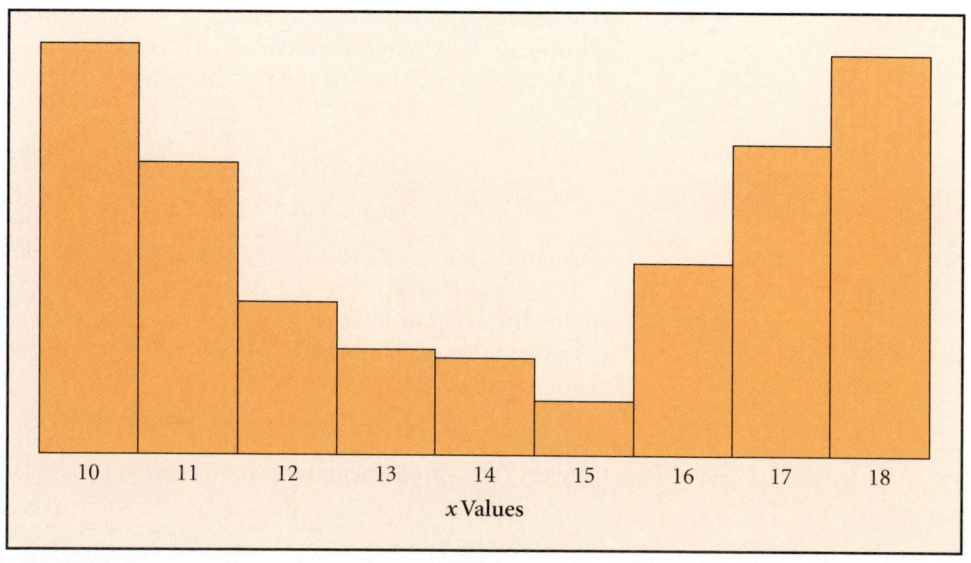

x Values

$\mu = 14.00$
$\sigma = 3.00$

FIGURE 6-9

Frequency Distribution of
$\bar{x}$'s ($n = 3$)

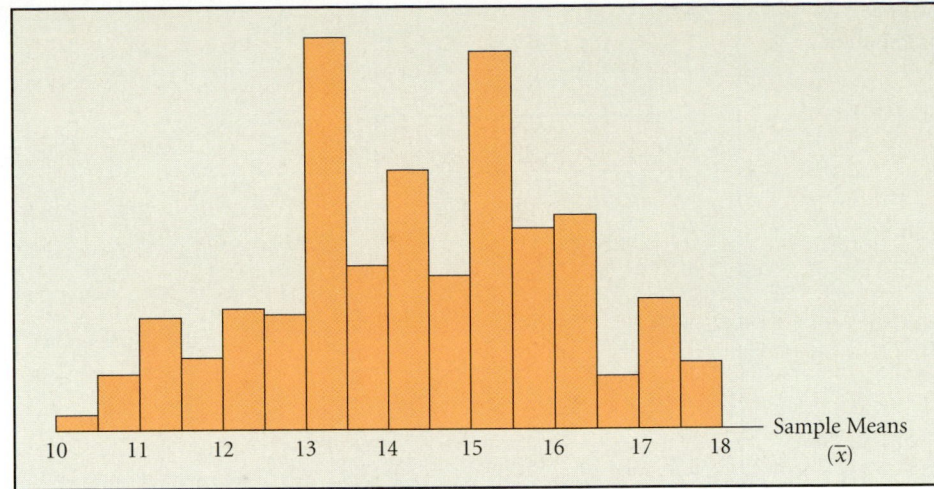

14.02 = Average of sample means

1.82 = Standard deviation of sample means

The frequency distribution of $\bar{x}$ values for the 3,000 samples of 3 looks different than the population distribution, which is U-shaped. Suppose we increase the sample size to 10 and take 3,000 samples from the same U-shaped population. The resulting frequency distribution of $\bar{x}$ values is shown in Figure 6-10. Now the frequency distribution looks very much like a normal distribution. The average of the sample means is still equal to 14.02, which is virtually equal to the population mean. The standard deviation for this sampling distribution is now reduced to 0.97.

This example is not a special case. Instead, it illustrates a very important statistical concept called the **Central Limit Theorem**.

Theorem 6-2: The Central Limit Theorem

For simple random samples of n observations taken from a population with mean μ and standard deviation σ, regardless of the population's distribution, provided the sample size is sufficiently large, the distribution of the sample means, $\bar{x}$, will be approximately normal with a mean equal to the population mean ($\mu_{\bar{x}} = \mu$) and a standard deviation equal to the population standard deviation divided by the square root of the sample size $\left(\sigma_{\bar{x}} = \dfrac{\sigma}{\sqrt{n}} \right)$. The larger the sample size, the better the approximation to the normal distribution.

FIGURE 6-10

Frequency Distribution
($n = 10$)

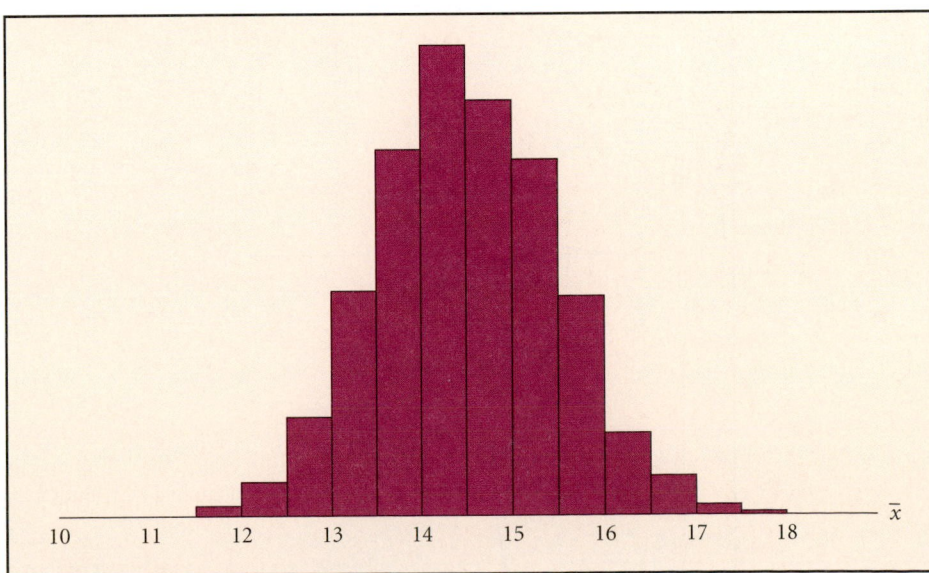

14.02 = Average of sample means

0.97 = Standard deviation of sample means

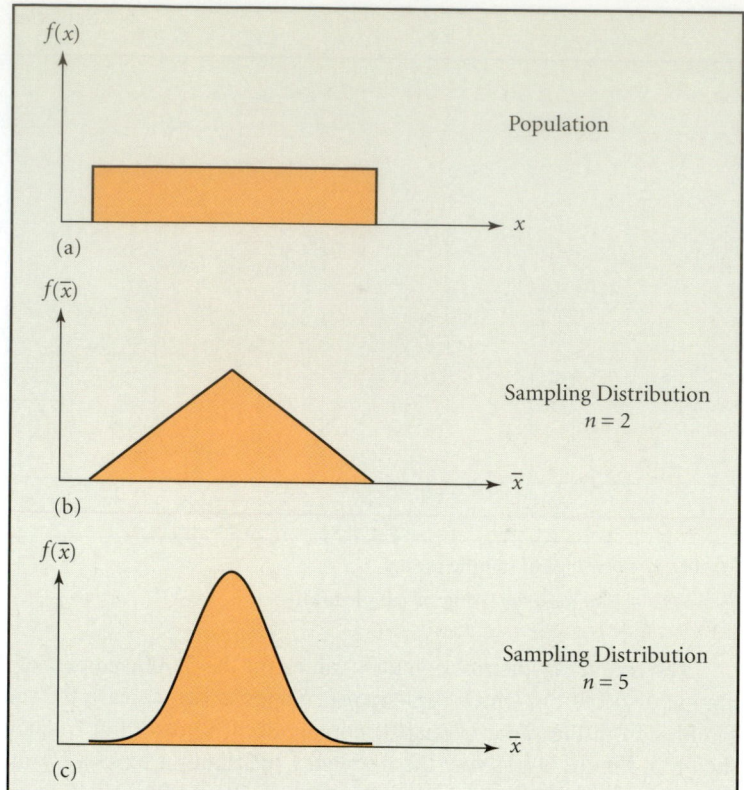

FIGURE 6-12

Central Limit Theorem
with Triangular Population

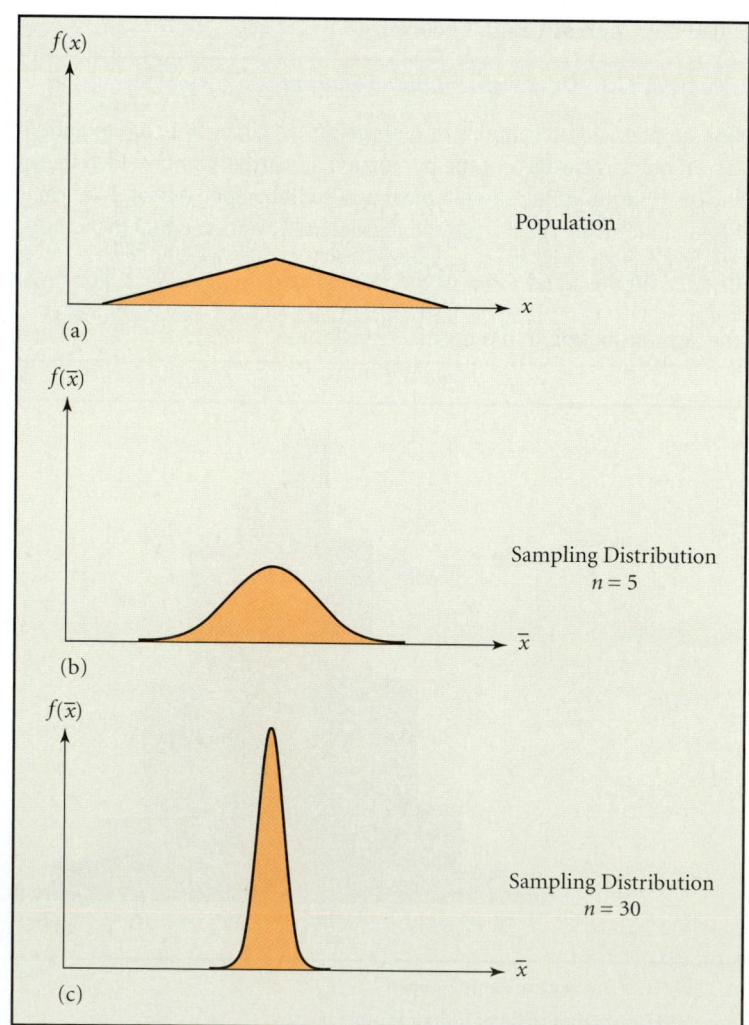

FIGURE 6-13

Central Limit Theorem
with a Skewed Population

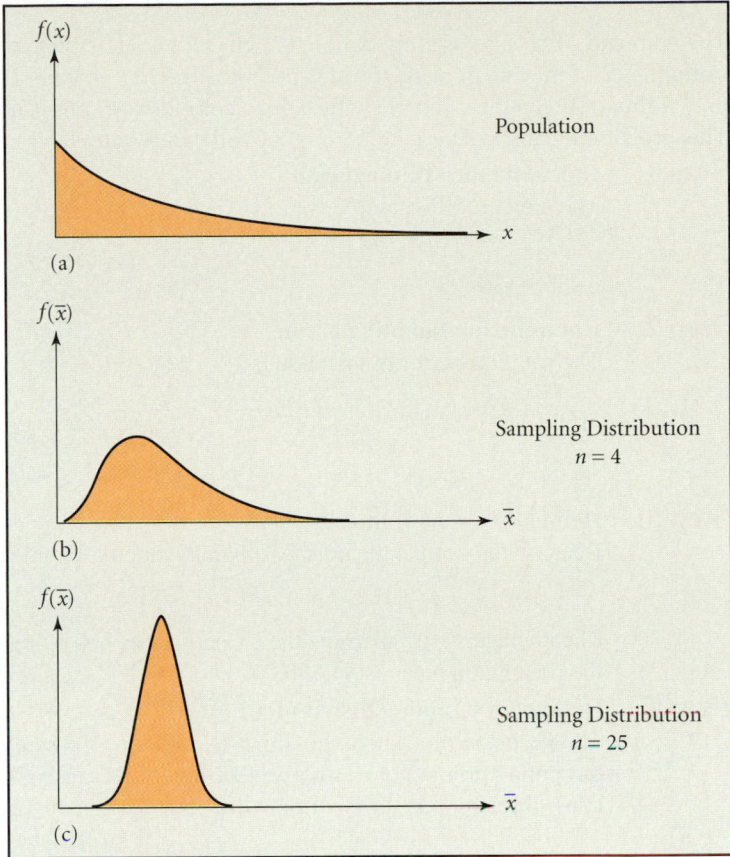

The Central Limit Theorem is very important because with it we know the shape of the sampling distribution even though we may not know the shape of the population distribution. The one catch is that the sample size must be "sufficiently large." What is a sufficiently large sample size?

The answer depends on the shape of the population. If the population is quite symmetric, then sample sizes as small as 2 or 3 will provide a normally distributed sampling distribution. If the population is highly skewed or otherwise irregularly shaped, the required sample size will be larger. Recall the example of the U-shaped population. The frequency distribution obtained from samples of 3 was shaped differently than the population, but not like a normal distribution. However, for samples of 10, the frequency distribution was a very close approximation to a normal distribution. Figures 6-11, 6-12, and 6-13 show some examples of the Central Limit Theorem concept. Simulation studies indicate that even for very strange-looking populations, samples of 25 to 30 produce sampling distributions that are approximately normal. Thus, *a conservative definition of a sufficiently large sample size is $n \geq 30$.* The Central Limit Theorem is illustrated in the following examples.

EXAMPLE 6-3: FINDING THE PROBABILITY THAT $\bar{x}$ IS IN A GIVEN RANGE

Moline Insurance   Moline Insurance recently conducted a study of car damages. Past history has shown that the damage distribution is right-skewed, with $\mu = \$4,560$ and $\sigma = \$600$. A simple random sample of 100 automobile claim files was selected from the large population of claims in Moline's files. The dollar damages paid to repair the cars were recorded, as follows:

Insurance Payments for 100 Claims									
$4,483.95	$4,992.97	$3,906.07	$4,197.44	$5,718.97	$4,484.87	$3,800.40	$5,500.79	$4,402.45	$4,613.89
5,190.25	4,487.37	4,118.90	5,841.33	4,570.86	5,475.73	3,851.05	4,157.62	3,563.31	5,256.10
5,105.74	5,545.20	4,523.56	4,207.26	5,082.41	4,820.87	4,493.93	4,309.38	4,409.71	4,146.40
4,765.37	3,915.06	5,041.89	4,191.81	4,166.32	4,424.53	5,374.26	3,753.40	4,185.92	5,173.52
4,665.91	3,833.69	4,605.51	3,736.42	4,819.91	4,845.52	4,307.68	5,075.28	3,312.88	4,248.25
5,175.07	3,323.43	4,711.53	4,550.84	4,763.23	3,717.65	4,813.38	3,730.37	5,670.43	4,440.64
4,751.75	3,982.61	3,456.37	4,687.57	3,850.04	4,670.01	4,835.79	4,630.92	3,889.10	3,642.36
5,347.96	5,297.90	4,765.81	3,786.70	4,949.20	5,145.17	4,696.74	4,423.50	4,750.20	4,836.45
5,012.67	4,005.24	6,009.68	4,804.32	4,235.20	3,781.62	4,087.37	5,050.94	4,090.43	3,825.02
4,604.22	4,875.80	4,102.92	3,722.66	3,870.87	5,539.77	4,835.68	4,066.16	3,611.93	5,649.96

The company wishes to use this sample to help set its rate structure, but managers worry that the sampling error may be too large for this population. The company is interested in determining the probability of obtaining a sample with as much or more sampling error as obtained in this sample. This probability can be determined using the following steps.

Step 1:   **Calculate the sample mean.**
The mean for this sample is

$$\bar{x} = \frac{\sum x}{100} = \$4,527.77$$

Step 2:   **Compute the sampling error.**
The sampling error in this case is

$$\begin{aligned} \text{sampling error} &= \bar{x} - \mu \\ &= \$4,527.77 - \$4,560.00 \\ &= -\$32.23 \end{aligned}$$

Step 3:   **Define the event of interest.**
Because the sample mean is less than the population mean, the event of interest is

$$P(\bar{x} \leq 4,527.77) = ?$$

The managers wish to know the probability of observing an $\bar{x} \leq \$4,527.77$, given that the population mean is \$4,560.00.

Step 4:   **Define the sampling distribution.**
The Central Limit Theorem allows us to define the sampling distribution even though the population is not normally distributed. Because the sample size is $n = 100$, we know the sampling distribution will be approximately normal, with

$$\mu_{\bar{x}} = \mu = \$4,560$$

and

$$\sigma_{\bar{x}} = \frac{\sigma}{\sqrt{n}} = \frac{600}{\sqrt{100}} = \$60$$

Step 5:   **Use the standard normal distribution to find the probability of interest.**
To find $P(\bar{x} \leq \$4,527.77)$, we use the concepts introduced in Chapter 5 for finding probabilities with a normal distribution. We begin by converting to the standard normal distribution using Equation 6-4.

$$z = \frac{\bar{x} - \mu}{\dfrac{\sigma}{\sqrt{n}}} = \frac{4,527.77 - 4,560}{\dfrac{600}{\sqrt{100}}} = \frac{-32.23}{60} = -0.537$$

Now go to the standard normal table in Appendix D for $z = -0.54$. We find $P(-0.54 \leq z \leq 0) = 0.2054$. Subtract this from 0.50 to get the desired probability of 0.2946, as shown:

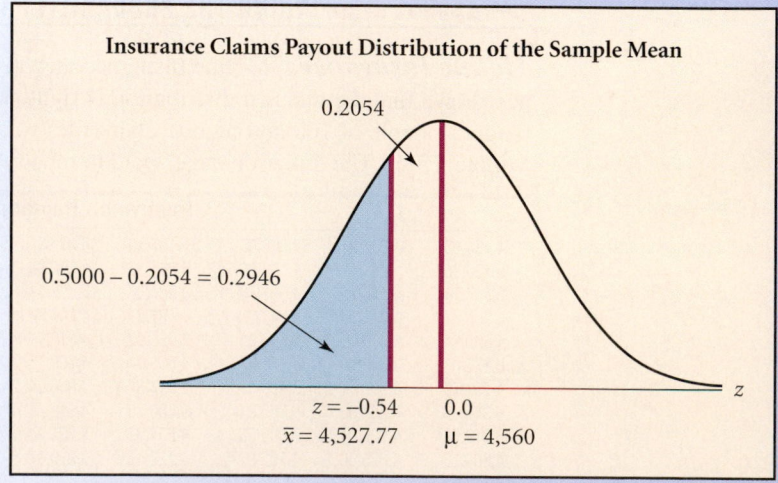

Insurance Claims Payout Distribution of the Sample Mean

0.2054

$0.5000 - 0.2054 = 0.2946$

$z = -0.54$ 0.0
$\bar{x} = 4,527.77$ $\mu = 4,560$

Therefore, there is nearly a 30% chance of getting a sample mean as small or smaller than $4,527.77 from this population. Although the managers might want to look at other characteristics of the sample, this evidence suggests this sampling error is not unusual for the population of all claim values.

SUMMARY: SAMPLING DISTRIBUTION OF $\bar{x}$

To find probabilities associated with a sampling distribution of $\bar{x}$ for samples of size n from a population with mean μ and standard deviation σ, use the following steps.

1. Compute the sample mean using

$$\bar{x} = \frac{\sum x}{n}$$

2. Define the sampling distribution.
If the population is normally distributed, the sampling distribution also will be normally distributed for any size sample. If the population is not normally distributed but the sample size is sufficiently large, the sampling distribution will be approximately normal. In either case, the sampling distribution will have:

$$\mu_{\bar{x}} = \mu \quad \text{and} \quad \sigma_{\bar{x}} = \frac{\sigma}{\sqrt{n}}.$$

3. Define the event of interest.
We are interested in finding the probability of some range of sample means, such as

$$P(\bar{x} \geq 25) =$$

4. Use the standard normal distribution to find the probability for the event of interest, using Equation 6-4 or 6-5 to convert the sample mean to a corresponding z-value.

$$z = \frac{\bar{x} - \mu}{\dfrac{\sigma}{\sqrt{n}}} \quad \text{or} \quad z = \frac{\bar{x} - \mu}{\dfrac{\sigma}{\sqrt{n}} \sqrt{\dfrac{N-n}{N-1}}}$$

Then use the standard normal table to find the probability associated with the calculated z-value.

EXAMPLE 6-4: FINDING THE PROBABILITY THAT $\bar{x}$ IS IN A GIVEN RANGE

Fairway Stores, Inc. Past sales records indicate that sales at the store are right-skewed, with a population mean of $12.50 per customer and a standard deviation of $5.50. The store manager has selected a random sample of 100 sales receipts. She is interested in determining the probability of getting a sample mean between $12.25 and $13.00 from this population. To find this probability, she can use the following steps.

Step 1: **Compute the sample mean.**
In this case, two sample means are being considered:
$$\bar{x} = \$12.25 \quad \text{and} \quad \bar{x} = \$13.00$$

Step 2: **Define the sampling distribution.**
The Central Limit Theorem can be used because the sample size is large enough ($n = 100$) to determine that the sampling distribution will be approximately normal (even though the population is right-skewed), with

$$\mu_{\bar{x}} = \$12.50 \quad \text{and} \quad \sigma_{\bar{x}} = \frac{\$5.50}{\sqrt{100}} = \$0.55$$

Step 3: **Define the event of interest.**
The manager is interested in:
$$P(\$12.25 \leq \bar{x} \leq \$13.00) = ?$$

Step 4: **Use the standard normal distribution to find the probability of interest.**
Assuming the population of sales records is quite large, we use Equation 6-4 to convert the sample means to corresponding z-values.

$$z = \frac{\bar{x} - \mu}{\dfrac{\sigma}{\sqrt{n}}} = \frac{12.25 - 12.50}{\dfrac{5.50}{\sqrt{100}}} = -0.46 \quad \text{and} \quad z = \frac{\bar{x} - \mu}{\dfrac{\sigma}{\sqrt{n}}} = \frac{13.00 - 12.50}{\dfrac{5.50}{\sqrt{100}}} = 0.91$$

From the standard normal table in Appendix D, the probability associated with $z = -0.46$ is 0.1772, and the probability for $z = 0.91$ is 0.3186. Therefore,

$$P(\$12.25 \leq \bar{x} \leq \$13.00) = P(-0.46 \leq z \leq 0.91) = 0.1772 + 0.3186 = 0.4958$$

There is nearly a 0.50 chance that the sample mean will fall in the range $12.25 to $13.00.

6-2: EXERCISES

Skill Development

6.11 A population is normally distributed, with a mean of 1,000 and a standard deviation equal to 200.
  a. Determine the probability that a random sample of size 5 selected from this population will have a sample mean less than 970.
  b. Referring to part a, suppose a second sample of size 10 is selected. What is the probability that this sample will have a mean that is less than 970?
  c. Why are the answers to parts a and b different? Discuss.

6.12 A population is known to have a mean equal to 6,000 and a standard deviation of 1,300. If a sample of size 50 is selected, what is the probability that the sample mean will be between 5,950 and 6,050? Does it matter what the distribution of the population is?

6.13 A population is normally distributed, with a mean of 400 and a standard deviation equal to 50.
  a. Determine the probability of selecting a single value from the population that exceeds 450.
  b. Calculate the probability of selecting a random sample of size 3 that has a sample mean that exceeds 450.
  c. Explain why the probabilities are different.

6.14 A population is thought to be normally distributed, with a mean of 500 and a standard deviation equal to 40. A sample of size 6 items is randomly selected from the population, with the following values:

570	430	600	520	480	500

Find the probability of getting a sample mean as large or larger than the one for these sample data.

6.15 A population is thought to be somewhat skewed, with a mean equal to 24.90 and a standard deviation of 1.30. A simple random sample of 40 items has been selected with the following values:

24.3	23.2	25.0	26.2	26.1	26.8	22.1	24.4	26.0	23.4
23.9	22.7	22.5	23.5	23.8	22.2	24.0	24.2	24.9	24.3
24.3	24.3	26.3	24.6	24.5	24.1	27.1	25.7	27.6	23.9
26.7	22.8	25.3	25.8	27.0	24.6	24.1	25.5	24.2	25.6

  a. What is the sampling error for this sample if you want to estimate the population mean?

  b. What is the probability of getting a sample mean as small or smaller than the one computed from this sample?

6.16 A population has a distribution of unknown shape. The mean of the population is 3,500, and the standard deviation is 600.
  a. If a sample of 100 values is selected randomly from this population, what is the probability that the sample mean will exceed 3,600?
  b. If a sample of 200 is selected from the population, what is the probability that the sample mean will exceed 3,600?
  c. Compare your answers to parts a and b and explain why the two probabilities are different.

6.17 A random sample of 100 items is selected from a population of size 350. What is the probability that the sample mean will exceed 200 if the population mean is 195 and the population standard deviation equals 20? (Hint: Use the finite correction factor, because the sample size is more than 5% of the population size.)

6.18 A population with a mean of 1.35 and a standard deviation of 0.40 is known to be very irregularly shaped. If a random sample of 49 items is selected from the population, calculate the probability that the sample mean will be less than 1.45

Business Applications

6.19 The Adam's Food King chain employs more than 3,000 people. The workers' ages are approximately normally distributed, with a mean of 31 years and a standard deviation of 4.3 years. The company is thinking of introducing a health-care package, and its insurance company wants to sample 25 workers before quoting a price.
  a. Calculate the probability that the sample of 25 will have an average age less than 31.
  b. Determine the value of the standard error associated with this sample.
  c. What can the insurance company do to reduce the standard error? Focus your answer on issues related to sampling concepts.

6.20 SeaFair Fashions relies on its sales force of 220 to do an initial screening of all new fashions. The company is bringing out a new line of swimwear and has invited 40 salespeople to its Orlando, Florida, home office. An issue of constant concern to the SeaFair sales office is the volume of orders generated by each salesperson. Last year the overall company average was $417,330, with a standard deviation of $45,285. (Hint: The finite correction factor, Equation 6-5, is required.)

a. Determine the probability the random sample of 40 will have a sales average less than $400,000.

b. What shape do you think the distribution of all possible sample means of 40 will have? Discuss.

c. Determine the value of the standard deviation of the distribution of the sample means of all possible samples of size 40.

d. How would the answers to parts a, b, and c change if the home office brought 60 salespeople to Orlando? Provide the respective answers for this sample size.

e. Each year SeaFair invites the sales personnel with sales greater than the 85th percentile to enjoy a complimentary vacation in Hawaii. Determine the smallest average salary for the sales personnel who were in Hawaii last year. (Assume the distribution of sales was normally distributed last year.)

6.21 A recent study by a midwestern university has concluded that the time adults spend watching television each week averages 14.6 hours, with a standard deviation of 4.3 hours.

a. Assuming these values are the population parameters, determine the probability that a sample of 100 adults from the population will average more than 15 hours of television per week. Does it seem likely that the university's conclusion concerning the population mean could be correct? Support your answer.

b. The university obtained three random samples of 100 adults, and each sample had an average greater than 15 hours. How likely is this assuming the university's conclusions about the population parameters are correct? Answer part a with this new information.

6.22 Draper, Inc., makes particleboard for the building industry. Particleboard is built by mixing wood chips and resins together, forming the mix into 4-feet-by-8-feet sheets, and pressing the sheets under extreme heat and pressure to form a 4-by-8 sheet that is used as a substitute for plywood. The strength of a particleboard is tied to the board's weight. Boards that are too light are brittle and do not meet the quality standard for strength. Boards that are too heavy are strong but are difficult for customers to use. The company knows that there will be variation in its boards' weight. Product specifications call for the weight per sheet to average 10 pounds, with a standard deviation of 1.75 pounds. During each shift, Draper employees select and weigh a random sample of 25 boards. The boards are thought to have a normally distributed weight distribution.

If the average of the sample slips below 9.60 pounds, an adjustment is made to the process to add more moisture and resins to increase the weight (and hopefully the strength).

a. Assuming that the process is operating correctly according to specifications, what is the probability that a sample will indicate that an adjustment is needed?

b. Assume the population mean weight per sheet slips to 9 pounds. Determine the probability that the sample will indicate an adjustment is not needed.

c. Assuming that 10 pounds is the mean weight, what should be the cutoff if the company wants no more than a 5% chance that a sample of 25 boards will have an average weight less than this cutoff?

6.23 Armstrong Windows makes windows for use in homes and commercial buildings. The standards for glass thickness call for the glass to average 0.375 inches, with a standard deviation of 0.050 inches. Suppose a random sample of $n = 50$ windows yields a sample mean of 0.392 inches.

a. What is the probability of $\bar{x} \geq 0.392$ if the windows meet the standards?

b. Based on your answer to part a, what would you conclude about the population of windows? Are they meeting the standards?

Advanced Business Applications

6.24 ⊙ The Jordeen Beverage Company bottles soft drinks and distributes them in the St. Louis area. Every week, a Missouri state inspector comes to the plant (on randomly selected days during the week) to test whether the average fill in the cans and bottles is acceptable. The state inspector, in looking out for consumers, selects a random sample of cans and bottles from the plant inventory that day. Each can (or bottle) is supposed to contain 12 ounces, but there will always be a certain amount of inherent variability from can to can. If the mean of the sample of 50 cans is less than 11.98 ounces, the company is given a $1,000 citation and the state inspector comes back the next day and reinspects. The process continues until the company meets the standard.

Jordeen controls the mean fill per can with a machine adjustment. They always have this set at 12 ounces. The machine does put slightly different amounts into each can. The CD-ROM file called *Jordeen* contains the actual fill amounts for each of the 5,000 cans in inventory the day the state inspector arrives.

a. Assuming that the data represent the population of cans, compute the population mean fill and population standard deviation. (Note, if you are using Minitab, you will need to use the **Stack Columns** under the **Manip** menu item.)

b. Compute the probability that a sample mean from a random sample of 50 cans from this population will be less than 11.98 ounces.

c. Suppose the Jordeen managers wish to limit their chances of getting fined to no more than 5%. If the state will not change its procedure and assuming that the standard deviation in the fill amount can't be changed, what specifically must the company do to reach the 5% level? Discuss the ramifications of making this change, assuming that company fills 5,000 cans every week for 52 weeks a year.

d. Suppose the Jordeen managers are unwilling to adjust their average fill to any value higher than 12 ounces. Instead, they can purchase a new filling machine that will have an adjustable mean but also will have a different standard deviation in fill amount than the current machine. What would the new machine's standard deviation have to be if the company wants no more than a 5% chance of being fined and assuming that the average fill is exactly 12 ounces?

6.25 Open the CD-ROM file named *Fast100*. The second column contains total sales for the past four quarters for these 100 companies. Assume that these 100 companies represent the population of interest.
a. Compute the population mean and population standard deviation.
b. Develop a frequency distribution for these data using eight classes, and indicate whether the population data appear to be normally distributed.
c. Select a random sample of 30 companies from this population. Compute the mean sales for this sample of companies. If you were asked to write a report using these 30 companies that would have characteristics (such as the mean) similar to those of the population, would you use this sample? Why or why not? (Hint: Compute the probability of getting a sample mean as extreme or more extreme than the one you have. Remember to use the finite correction factor.)

6.26 Open the CD-ROM file called *Trucks*. This file contains data on trucks that have been weighed on two weigh scales: the in-ground scale at the Port of Entry (POE) and a scale that is located in the highway before the POE turnoff. This latter scale allows the trucks to be weighed as they move along the road and is referred to as a Weigh-in-Motion scale (WIM). Assuming that data for these 200 trucks represent the population of interest,

create a new variable that is the difference between front-axle WIM weight and front-axle POE weight.
a. Develop a frequency histogram for this new variable using six classes. Does this population distribution look approximately normally distributed? Describe the shape of the distribution.
b. Compute the population mean and population standard deviation for this new variable.
c. Select a random sample of 25 trucks. Compute the sample mean. What is the probability of getting a sample mean as extreme or more extreme than the one you have?

6.27 Referring to Exercise 6.26, suppose the data in the *Trucks* file represent a random sample from a bigger population of trucks rather than a population. Consider the new variable (difference between WIM front-axle and POE front-axle weights). Suppose the bigger population of all trucks has an average difference equal to 0 pounds, with a standard deviation equal to 2,000 pounds. Suppose the objective is being met. Determine the probability that the random sample mean difference between WIM and POE front-axle weight will be as large or larger than the one you computed in Exercise 6.26. Discuss.

6.28 The CD-ROM file called *Cities* contains data on a random sample of 100 U.S. cities. Assume the population mean unemployment rate is 5%.
a. Calculate the probability of a sample of 100 cities having a mean unemployment rate as small or smaller than the one you have computed. (Hint: In your computation, substitute the sample standard deviation for σ.)
b. Based upon your calculation in part a, do you believe the population mean is the value it was assumed to be? Provide a rationale for your statement.

6-3 SAMPLING DISTRIBUTION OF A PROPORTION

WORKING WITH PROPORTIONS

In many instances, the objective of sampling is to estimate a population proportion. For instance, an accountant may be interested in determining the proportion of accounts payable balances that are correct. A production supervisor may wish to determine the percentage of product that is defect free. A marketing research department might want to know the proportion of potential customers who will purchase a particular product. In all these instances, the decision makers could select a sample, compute the sample proportion, and make their decision based on the sample results.

Sample proportions are subject to sampling error, just as are sample means. The concept of sampling distributions provides us a way to assess the potential magnitude of the sampling error for proportions in given situations.

Lincoln Research—Consider Lincoln Research, a market research firm that surveyed every customer in a certain region who purchased a specific brand of tires during the first week of March last year. The key question in the survey was: "Are you satisfied with the tires and service received at this tire store?"

The population size was 80 customers. The number of customers who answered "Yes" to the question was 72. The value of interest in this example is the **population proportion**. Equation 6-6 is used to compute a population proportion.

Population Proportion

The fraction of values in a population that have a specific attribute.

$$p = \frac{X}{N}$$

6-6

where:

p = Population proportion
X = Number of items in the population having the attribute
N = Population size

The proportion of customers in the population who are satisfied with the tires and service is

$$p = \frac{72}{80} = 0.90$$

Therefore, 90% of the population responded "Yes" to the survey question. This is the *parameter*. It is a measurement taken from the population. It is the "true value."

Now, suppose that the market research firm wishes to do a follow-up survey for a simple random sample of $n = 20$ of the customers. What fraction of this sample will be people who had previously responded "Yes" to the satisfaction question?

The answer depends on which sample is selected. There are many possible samples of 20 that could be selected from 80 people. However, the marketing research firm will select only one of these possible samples. At one extreme, suppose the 20 people selected for the sample included all 8 who answered "No" to the satisfaction question and 12 others who answered "Yes." The sample proportion is computed using Equation 6-7.

Sample Proportion

The fraction of items in a sample that have the attribute of interest.

$$\bar{p} = \frac{x}{n}$$

6-7

where:

$\bar{p}$ = Sample proportion
x = Number of items in the sample with the attribute
n = Sample size

For the tire store example, the sample proportion of "Yes" responses is

$$\bar{p} = \frac{12}{20} = 0.60$$

The sample proportion of "Yes" responses is 0.60, whereas the population proportion is 0.90. The difference between the sampling value and the population value is sampling error. Equation 6-8 is used to compute the sampling error involving a single proportion.

Single-Proportion Sampling Error

$$\text{Sampling error} = \bar{p} - p$$

6-8

where:

p = Population proportion
$\bar{p}$ = Sample proportion

Then for this extreme situation we get

$$\text{Sampling error} = 0.60 - 0.90 = -0.30$$

If a sample on the other extreme had been selected and all 20 people came from the original list of 72 who had responded "Yes" in the original survey, the sample proportion would be

$$\bar{p} = \frac{20}{20} = 1.00$$

For this sample, the sampling error is

$$\text{Sampling error} = 1.00 - 0.90 = 0.10$$

Thus, the range of sampling error in this example is from -0.30 to 0.10. As with any sampling situation, you can expect some sampling error. The sample proportion will probably not equal the population proportion because the sample selected will not be a perfect mirror image of the population.

EXAMPLE 6-5: SAMPLING ERROR FOR A PROPORTION

Hewlett-Packard–Compaq Merger As you may recall, in 2002 a proxy fight took place between the management of Hewlett-Packard (HP) and Walter Hewlett, the son of one of HP's founders, over whether the merger between HP and Compaq should be approved. Each outstanding share of common stock was allocated one vote. After the vote in March 2002, the initial tally showed that the proportion of shares in the approval column was 0.51. After the vote, a lawsuit was filed by a group led by Walter Hewlett, which claimed improprieties by the HP management team. Suppose the attorneys for the Hewlett faction randomly selected 40 shares from the millions of total shares outstanding. The intent was to interview the owners of these shares to determine whether they felt undue pressure to vote for the merger. Of these shares in the sample, 26 carried an "Approval" vote. The attorneys can use the following steps to assess the sampling error.

Step 1: **Determine the population proportion.**
In this case, the proportion of votes cast in favor of the merger is
$$p = 0.51$$
This is the number of approval votes divided by the total number of shares.

Step 2: **Compute the sample proportion using Equation 6-7.**
The sample proportion is

$$\bar{p} = \frac{x}{n} = \frac{26}{40} = 0.65$$

Step 3: **Compute the sampling error using Equation 6-8.**
$$\text{Sampling error} = \bar{p} - p = 0.65 - 0.51 = 0.14$$

The proportion of "Approval" votes from the shares in this sample exceeds the population proportion by 0.14.

SAMPLING DISTRIBUTION OF $\bar{p}$

In many applications you will be interested in determining the proportion (p) of all items that possess a particular attribute. The best estimate of this population proportion will be $\bar{p}$, the sample proportion. However, any inference about how close your estimate is to the true population value will be based on the distribution of this sample proportion, $\bar{p}$, whose underlying distribution is the binomial. However, if the sample size is sufficiently large such that

$$np \geq 5 \quad \text{and} \quad n(1 - p) \geq 5$$

then the normal distribution can be used as a reasonable approximation to the discrete binomial distribution.[4] Providing we have a large enough sample size, the distribution of all possible sample proportions will be approximately normally distributed. In addition to being normally distributed, the sampling distribution will have a mean and standard error as indicated in Equations 6-9 and 6-10.

---

[4]An application of the Central Limit Theorem provides the rationale for this statement. Recall that $\bar{p} = \dfrac{x}{n}$ where x is the sum of random variables (x_i) whose values are 0 and 1. Thus, $\dfrac{x}{n} = \dfrac{\sum x_i}{n}$. Therefore, $\bar{p}$ is in reality just a sample mean. Each of these x_i can be thought of as binomial random variables from a sample of size $n = 1$. Thus, they each have a mean of $\mu = np = p$ and a variance of $\sigma^2 = np(1 - p) = p(1 - p)$. As we have seen from the Central Limit Theorem, the sample mean has an expected value of μ and a variance of $\dfrac{\sigma^2}{n}$. Thus, the sample proportion has an expected value of $\mu = p$ and a variance of $\sigma^2 = \dfrac{p(1 - p)}{n}$.

Sampling Distribution of $\bar{p}$

$$\text{Mean} = \mu_{\bar{p}} = p \qquad \qquad \textbf{6-9}$$

and

$$\text{Standard error} = \sigma_{\bar{p}} = \sqrt{\frac{p(1-p)}{n}} \qquad \qquad \textbf{6-10}$$

where:

p = Population proportion
n = Sample size
$\bar{p}$ = Sample proportion

Heaton Manufacturing—Heaton Manufacturing makes Christmas ornaments that it ships to retailers throughout the United States. Heaton executives have observed that 15% of the ornaments, even when specially packed, are damaged before reaching the retailer. There appears to be no particular pattern to the damage. Whether one ornament breaks seems independent of whether any other ornament breaks.

Suppose that Heaton heard from a retail customer who claimed that 18% of the 500 ornaments she purchased were damaged. Assume the general damage rate of

$$p = 0.15$$

holds for the population of all ornaments. How likely is it that a sample of

$$n = 500$$

units will contain 18% or more broken items? To answer this question, we first check to determine if the sample size is sufficiently large. Because both

$$n(p) = 500(0.15) = 75 \geq 5 \text{ and } n(1-p) = 500(0.85) = 425 \geq 5$$

we can safely conclude that the sampling distribution of sample proportions will be approximately normal. Using Equations 6-9 and 6-10, we can compute the mean and standard error for the sampling distribution as follows.

$$\mu_{\bar{p}} = 0.15$$

and

$$\sigma_{\bar{p}} = \sqrt{\frac{(0.15)(0.85)}{500}} = 0.016$$

Equation 6-11 is used to convert the sample proportion to a standardized z-value.

---

z-Value for Proportions

$$z = \frac{\bar{p} - p}{\sigma_{\bar{p}}} \qquad \qquad \textbf{6-11}$$

where:

z = Number of standard errors $\bar{p}$ is from p
$\bar{p}$ = Sample proportion
$\sigma_{\bar{p}} = \sqrt{\frac{p(1-p)}{n}}$ = Standard error of the sampling distribution[5]
p = Mean of sample proportions

---

[5]If the sample size n is greater than 5% of the population size, the standard error of the sampling distribution should be computed using the finite population correction as $\sigma_{\bar{p}} = \sqrt{\frac{p(1-p)}{n}}\sqrt{\frac{N-n}{N-1}}$.

FIGURE 6-14

Standard Normal
Distribution for Heaton
Manufacturing

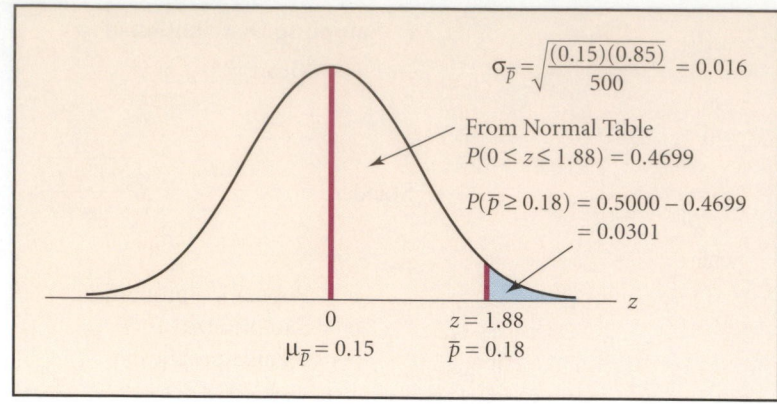

From Equation 6-11 we get

$$z = \frac{\bar{p} - p}{\sigma_{\bar{p}}} = \frac{0.18 - 0.15}{\sqrt{\dfrac{(0.15)(0.85)}{500}}} = 1.88$$

Therefore the 0.18 damage rate reported by the customer is 1.88 standard deviations above the average rate of 0.15. Figure 6-14 illustrates that the chances of a damage rate of 0.18 or more is

$$P(\bar{p} \geq 0.18) = 0.0301$$

Because this is a very low probability, the Heaton managers might want to see if there was something unusual about how this shipment was packed.

SUMMARY: SAMPLING DISTRIBUTION OF p̄

To find probabilities associated with a sampling distribution for a single-population proportion, the following steps can be used.

1. Determine the population proportion, p, using:

$$p = \frac{x}{N}$$

2. Calculate the sample proportion using:

$$\bar{p} = \frac{x}{n}$$

3. Determine the mean and standard deviation of the sampling distribution using:

$$\mu_{\bar{p}} = p \quad \text{and} \quad \sigma_{\bar{p}} = \sqrt{\frac{p(1 - p)}{n}}$$

4. Define the event of interest. For example:

$$P(\bar{p} \geq 0.30) = ?$$

5. If np and $n(1 - p)$ are both ≥ 5, then convert $\bar{p}$ to a standardized z-value using:

$$z = \frac{\bar{p} - p}{\sigma_{\bar{p}}}$$

6. Use the standard normal distribution table in Appendix D to determine the required probability.

EXAMPLE 6-6: FINDING THE PROBABILITY THAT p̄ IS IN A GIVEN RANGE

The Daily Statesman   The classified-advertisement manager for the *Daily Statesman* newspaper believes that the proportion of "apartment for rent" ads that are placed in the paper that result in a rental within two weeks is 0.80 or higher. She would like to make this claim as part of the paper's promotion of its classified section. Before doing this, she has selected a simple random sample of 100 "apartment for rent" ads. Of these, 73 resulted in a rental within the two-week period. To determine the probability of this result or something more extreme, she can use the following steps.

Step 1:   **Determine the population proportion, p.**
The population proportion is believed to be $p = 0.80$, based upon the manager's experience.

Step 2:   **Calculate the sample proportion.**
In this case, a sample of $n = 100$ ads was selected, with 73 having the attribute of interest. Thus,

$$\bar{p} = \frac{x}{n} = \frac{73}{100} = 0.73$$

Step 3:   **Determine the mean and standard deviation of the sampling distribution.**
The mean of the sampling distribution is equal to p, the population proportion. So
$$\mu_{\bar{p}} = 0.80$$

The standard deviation of the sampling distribution for p is computed using:

$$\sigma_{\bar{p}} = \sqrt{\frac{p(1-p)}{n}} = \sqrt{\frac{0.80(1-0.80)}{100}} = 0.0400$$

Step 4:   **Define the event of interest.**
In this case, because 0.73 is less than 0.80, we are interested in
$$P(\bar{p} \leq 0.73) = ?$$

Step 5:   **If np and $n(1-p)$ are both ≥ 5, then convert $\bar{p}$ to a standardized z-value.**
Checking, we get
$$np = 100(0.80) = 80 \geq 5 \text{ and } n(1-p) = 100(0.20) = 20 \geq 5$$
then we convert p to a standardized z-value using:

$$z = \frac{\bar{p} - p}{\sigma_{\bar{p}}} = \frac{0.73 - 0.80}{\sqrt{\dfrac{0.80(1-0.80)}{100}}} = -1.75$$

Step 6:   **Use the standard normal distribution table in Appendix D to determine the probability for the event of interest.**
We want

$$P(\bar{p} \leq 0.73) \quad \text{or} \quad P(z \leq -1.75)$$

From the normal distribution table for $z = -1.75$, we get 0.4599, which corresponds to the probability of a z-value between -1.75 and 0.0. To get the probability of interest, we subtract 0.4599 from 0.5000, giving 0.0401. There is only a 4% chance that a random sample of $n = 100$ would produce a sample proportion of $\bar{p} \leq 0.73$ if the population proportion is 0.80. She might want to use caution before making this claim.

6-3: EXERCISES

Skill Development

6.29   Assume the following data represent a population of 50 values. Values equal to 1 indicate that a particular attribute is present. A value equal to 0 indicates the attribute is not present.

1	1	1	1	1	1	1	1	0	0
0	1	1	0	0	1	1	1	0	1
0	1	1	1	1	1	1	1	1	0
1	1	1	1	1	1	1	0	1	1
0	1	1	1	1	1	1	1	1	1

a. Compute the population proportion.
b. A random sample of 15 items produced the following numbers: 1, 1, 1, 0, 0, 1, 0, 0, 1, 1, 0, 0, 0, 1, 0.

Compute the sample proportion and the sampling error present in your sample.
c. What is the range of extreme sampling error for a sample of 15 taken from this population?
d. How would the range of extreme sampling error change if the sample size was set to 30? Discuss the advantages of having a larger sample size.

6.30   Given a population in which the proportion of items with a desired attribute is $p = 0.25$, if a sample of 400 is taken:
a. What is the standard deviation of the sampling distribution of $\bar{p}$?
b. What is the probability the proportion of successes in the sample will be greater than 0.22?

6.31 Given a population in which the proportion of items with a desired attribute is $p = 0.65$, if a sample of 100 is taken:

a. Determine the probability the proportion of successes in the sample will be less than 0.63.

b. Referring to part a, suppose the sample size is increased to $n = 200$, what is the probability that the sample proportion will be less than 0.63? Discuss why the answers in parts a and b differ.

6.32 Given a population in which the proportion of items with a desired attribute is $p = 0.50$, if a sample of 200 is taken:

a. Find the probability the proportion of successes in the sample will be between 0.47 and 0.51.

b. Referring to part a, what would the probability be if the sample size were 100?

6.33 Thirty percent of the items in a population are known to possess a particular attribute. If a random sample of 60 items is selected, what is the probability that the sample proportion of items with the attribute will exceed 0.33?

6.34 Suppose 95% of the items in a population have a particular characteristic. Find the chance that a sample of 100 items will have fewer than 90 items with that same characteristic.

6.35 Given a population in which the probability of a success is $p = 0.40$, if a sample of 1,000 is taken:

a. Calculate the probability the proportion of successes in the sample will be less than 0.42.

b. What is the probability the proportion of successes in the sample will be greater than 0.44?

Business Applications

6.36 Tom Marley and Jennifer Griggs have recently started a marketing research firm in Jacksonville, Florida. They have contacted the Florida Democratic Party with a proposal to do all political polling for the party. Because they have just started their company, the state party chairman is reluctant to sign a contract without some test of their accuracy and has asked them to do a trial poll in a central Florida county known to have 60% registered Democratic Party voters. The poll itself had many questions. However, for the test of accuracy, only the proportion of registered Democrats was considered. Tom and Jennifer report back that from a random sample of 760 respondents, 395 were registered Democrats.

a. Determine the probability that such a random sample would result in 395 or fewer Democrats in the sample.

b. Based on your calculations in part a, would you recommend that the Florida Democratic Party (or anyone else for that matter) contract with the Marley/Griggs marketing research firm. Explain your answer.

6.37 A golf-equipment catalog company regularly inserts in the catalogs coupons that can be redeemed for merchandise in local businesses. Historically, 8% of the coupons are redeemed. Recently the company enclosed a new style of coupon in a sample of 300 catalogs. It then determined that 35 of these coupons were redeemed.

a. What is the probability that if the new coupon has the same redemption rate as the old, the company would find 35 or more new coupons redeemed in a sample of 300?

b. Based on the answer to part a, would you recommend adoption of the new coupon? Justify your answer.

6.38 Micron Electronics makes personal computers that are sold directly over the phone and the Internet. One of the most critical factors in the success of PC makers is how fast they can turn their inventory of parts. Faster inventory turns mean lower average inventory cost. Recently at a meeting, the vice president of manufacturing said that there is no reason to continue offering hard disk drives that have less than a 20 GB storage capacity because only 10% of Micron customers ask for the smaller hard disks. After much discussion and debate about the accuracy of the VP's figure, it was decided to sample 100 orders from the past week's sales. This sample revealed 14 requests for drives with less than 20 GB capacity.

a. Determine the probability of finding 14 or more requests like this if the VP's assertion is correct. Do you believe that the proportion of customers requesting hard drives with storage capacity is as small as 0.10? Explain.

b. Suppose a second sample of 100 customers is selected. This sample again yields 14 requests for a hard drive with less than 20 GB of storage. Combining this sample information with that found in part a, what conclusion would you now reach regarding the VP's 10% claim? Base your answer on probability.

6.39 One of the major video rental chains recently made a change in its rental policies, allowing movies to be rented for three nights instead of one. The marketing team that made this decision reasoned that at least 70% of the customers would return the movie by the second night anyway. A sample of 500 customers found 68% returned the movie before the third night.

a. Given the marketing team's estimate, what would be the probability of a sample result with 68% or fewer returns before the third night?

b. Based on your calculations, would you recommend the adoption of the new rental policy? Support your answer with statistical reasoning and calculations.

6.40 The file on your CD-ROM called *Patients* contains information for a random sample of geriatric patients. During a meeting, one hospital administrator indicated that 70% of the geriatric patients are males.

a. What is the sample proportion of male patients?

b. Assuming that the administrator is correct, what is the probability that a sample of this size would have a sample proportion as extreme or more extreme than the one you found in part a?

c. Would you conclude that the administrator's assertion concerning the proportion of male geriatric patients is correct? Justify your answer.

Advanced Business Applications

6.41 Referring to Exercise 6.40, the belief is that 80% of all geriatric patients are covered by Medicare (Code = CARE). Assuming that the data in the *Patients* file represents a random sample of all hospital geriatric patients,

    a. What proportion of patients in the sample are covered by Medicare?

    b. Determine probability of getting a sample proportion as extreme or more extreme than this one if the administrator's 80% figure is correct.

    c. Based on the probability you computed in part b, what conclusion should the hospital administrator reach concerning the proportion of geriatric patients covered by Medicare? Discuss.

6.42 The data file *Trucks* contains a sample of 200 trucks that were weighed on two scales. The WIM (Weigh-in-Motion) scale weighs trucks as they drive down the highway. The POE scale weighs trucks while they are stopped in a port-of-entry station. The makers of the WIM scale believe that their scale will weigh heavier than the POE scale 60% of the time when gross weight is considered.

    a. Create a new variable that has a value equal to 1 when the WIM gross weight is greater than POE gross weight, and 0 otherwise.

    b. Determine the sample proportion of times the WIM gross weight exceeds the POE gross weight.

    c. Based on this sample, what is the probability of finding a proportion less than that found in part b? For this calculation, assume the WIM maker's assertion is correct.

    d. Based on the probability found in part c, what should the WIM maker conclude? Is his 60% figure reasonable?

6.43 Refer to Exercise 6.42. The *Trucks* file also contains data that indicate the speed the trucks were traveling when they crossed the WIM scale.

    a. Determine the percentage of the trucks in the sample that were exceeding 55 mph when they crossed the WIM scale.

    b. If the state highway patrol has indicated in the past that 30% of all trucks exceed the 55 mph speed limit on this section of highway, do the sample data tend to support or refute the highway patrol? (Hint: Compute the probability of getting the sample proportion equal to or more extreme than the one you computed. Base your response on this probability.)

6.44 Guidian Manufacturing supplies parts to Standard Generator, which incorporates the parts in its generators. Standard wishes to negotiate a contract with Guidian concerning the proportion of defective parts it receives. It wishes the defective rate to be no larger than 0.05. Guidian has established from past performance that its defective rate is 0.076.

    a. Standard managers propose a way of checking to determine that the defective rate (p) does not exceed 0.05. They propose sampling 150 of the parts. If more than 5 are defective, they will conclude that $p > 0.05$ and cancel the contract. Calculate the probability that Standard will cancel the contract even if the defective rate is 0.05. After examining this probability, Guidian refuses to sign this contract and instead proposes that the contract only be cancelled if more than 10 are defective. Calculate the probability the contract isn't cancelled if the defective rate is what Guidian knows it to be (i.e., 0.076).

    b. Write a report to both companies discussing the issues.

Summary and Conclusions

When a manager selects a sample, it is only one of many samples that could have been selected. Consequently the sample mean, $\bar{x}$, is only one of the many possible sample means that could have been found. There is no reason to believe that the single $\bar{x}$ value will equal the population mean, μ. The difference between $\bar{x}$ and μ is called sampling error. Because sampling error exists, decision makers must be aware of how the sample means are distributed in order to discuss the potential for extreme sampling error.

This chapter introduced two important theorems. These theorems describe the distribution of sample means taken from any population. The more important of these theorems is the Central Limit Theorem. The concepts of estimation and hypothesis testing depend heavily on the Central Limit Theorem. The important aspect of the Central Limit Theorem is that no matter how the population is distributed, if the sample size is large enough, the sampling distribution will be approximately normal.

The chapter also presented several new statistical terms, which are listed in the Key Terms section. Be sure you understand these concepts and how they apply to the material in this chapter. You will encounter these terms many times as you continue in this text.

EQUATIONS

Sampling Error of the Sample Mean

$$\text{Sampling error} = \bar{x} - \mu \qquad \textbf{6-1}$$

Population Mean

$$\mu = \frac{\sum x}{N} \qquad \textbf{6-2}$$

Sample Mean

$$\bar{x} = \frac{\sum x}{n} \qquad \textbf{6-3}$$

z-Value for Sampling Distribution of $\bar{x}$

$$z = \frac{\bar{x} - \mu}{\dfrac{\sigma}{\sqrt{n}}} \qquad \textbf{6-4}$$

z-Value Adjusted for the Finite Population Correction Factor

$$z = \frac{\bar{x} - \mu}{\dfrac{\sigma}{\sqrt{n}} \sqrt{\dfrac{N-n}{N-1}}} \qquad \textbf{6-5}$$

Population Proportion

$$p = \frac{X}{N} \qquad \textbf{6-6}$$

Sample Proportion

$$\bar{p} = \frac{x}{n} \qquad \textbf{6-7}$$

Single-Proportion Sampling Error

$$\text{Sampling error} = \bar{p} - p \qquad \textbf{6-8}$$

Mean of the Sampling Distribution of $\bar{p}$

$$\text{Mean} = \mu_{\bar{p}} = p \qquad \textbf{6-9}$$

Standard Deviation of the Sampling Distribution of $\bar{p}$

$$\sigma_{\bar{p}} = \sqrt{\frac{p(1-p)}{n}} \qquad \textbf{6-10}$$

z-Value for Proportions

$$z = \frac{\bar{p} - p}{\sigma_{\bar{p}}} \qquad \textbf{6-11}$$

Key Terms

Central Limit Theorem, 242
Finite Population Correction Factor, 241
Parameter, 251

Population Proportion, 251
Sampling Distribution, 235
Sampling Error, 228

Simple Random Sample, 230
Theorem 6-1, 239
Unbiased Estimator, 236

CHAPTER EXERCISES

Conceptual Questions

6.45 Explain in your own words what is meant by the term *sampling distribution*.

6.46 Discuss why the sampling distribution will be less variable than the population distribution. Give a short example to illustrate your answer.

6.47 Discuss why the standard error of a sampling distribution is considered a measure of average sampling error.

6.48 Discuss (using your own examples) what effect the finite correction factor has on the computation of the standard error of the sampling distribution as the sample size gets small relative to the size of the population.

6.49 The Central Limit Theorem indicates that the sampling distribution of $\bar{x}$ will have a standard deviation of $\sigma_{\bar{x}} = \dfrac{\sigma}{\sqrt{n}}$.

Discuss why the sampling distribution of $\bar{x}$ should have less dispersion than the population distribution.

6.50 Under what conditions should the finite correction factor be used in determining the standard error of a sampling distribution?

6.51 A researcher has collected all possible samples of a size of 150 from a population and has listed the sample means for each of these samples.
  a. If the average of the sample means is 450.55, what would be the numerical value of the true population mean? Discuss.
  b. If the standard deviation of the sample means is 12.25, determine the standard deviation of the model from which the samples came. To perform this calculation, assume the population has a size of 1,250.

6.52 In Exercise 6.51, a researcher collected all possible samples of a given size and found that the average of the sample means was 450.55. The researcher recognized that the sample means will vary around the true population mean. Consequently, she found the standard deviation of the sample means to be 30.56.

  a. Discuss this number. What term is used to describe this number?
  b. Based on the 30.56 value, determine the population standard deviation.

6.53 Suppose we are told the sampling distribution developed from a sample of size 400, has a mean of 56.78, and has a standard error of 9.6. If the population is known to be normally distributed, what are the population mean and the population standard deviation? Discuss how these values relate to the values for the sampling distribution.

6.54 If a population is known to be normally distributed, what size sample is required to ensure that the sampling distribution is normally distributed?

6.55 Suppose a population is normally distributed. What is the probability of finding a sample mean, $\bar{x}$, that is greater than the population mean?

Business Applications

6.56 The Hardcone Baking Company recently performed a market study from a sample of 400. It asked people how much they spent on bakery products per week. The average of this sample was $3.45.
  a. Calculate the probability that a sample of 400 would produce a sample mean exactly equal to $3.45.
  b. Calculate the probability that two samples of 400 would both produce sample means of $3.45.
  c. Review the answers to parts a and b. Is it reasonable to expect that another sample of size 400 would result in the same sample average? Discuss why or why not.

6.57 Recently, a school system in the Midwest performed a study of its students' performance on mathematics examinations. If the population of all examination scores is thought to be normally distributed, with a mean of 68 points and a standard deviation of 12 points,
  a. What are the mean and standard deviation for the sampling distribution of $\bar{x}$ if the sample size is 100? Discuss why the sampling distribution has a smaller standard deviation that the population.

b. Suppose the school system takes a second sample of size 500. What is the relationship between the sampling distributions of the two sample means? Illustrate using graphs.

6.58 The time it takes a mechanic to tune an engine is known to be normally distributed, with a mean of 45 minutes and a standard deviation of 14 minutes.
  a. Determine the mean and standard error of a sampling distribution for a sample size of 20 tune-ups. Draw a picture of the sampling distribution.
  b. Calculate the largest sampling error you would expect to make in estimating the population mean with the sample size of 20 tune-ups.

6.59 The money spent by individuals for recreation in a particular target population is normally distributed.
  a. How much will the standard error be reduced if the sample size is doubled? Discuss.
  b. The z-value for a particular person's expenditure for recreation is 2.50. Determine the proportion of individuals who spend more on recreation than this individual.

6.60 Suppose the interest earned on savings accounts by individuals at a particular bank has a distribution that may be skewed to the right. The bank asserts that the population mean is $450 earned per year, with a standard deviation of $67.
  a. Describe the sampling distribution for a sample of size 100. Also show the sampling distribution in graphical form.
  b. An audit has been conducted on the bank's savings accounts. One hundred accounts were randomly sampled. The mean of the sample was $443. Do you believe the bank's assertion to be an exaggeration? Support your answer with calculation and statistical reasoning.

6.61 The population distribution for family incomes in the Canadian province of British Columbia is unknown, but it has a mean of $21,500 and a standard deviation of $1,700.
  a. A sample of size 200 is to be selected and the sample mean calculated. Describe the sampling distribution in terms of its general shape and descriptive measures.
  b. If the sample size were actually 60 instead of 200, how would the sampling distribution be affected? Illustrate with a graph, indicating the mean and standard error.
  c. What is the probability that a sample of 60 selected randomly from the population will have a mean equal to or greater than $21,300?

6.62 The Galusha CPA firm performs audits for the Alien Tool Company. As part of an audit, the accountant in charge selected a random sample of 300 accounts from the 2,000 accounts receivable on Alien's books. He was particularly interested in the average account balance.
  a. If the computer records indicate that the true average balance for all 2,000 accounts if $786.98, with a standard deviation of $356.75, describe the sampling distribution of the sample mean. (Hint: Use the finite correction factor.)
  b. Draw an illustration of the sampling distribution.
  c. Describe the sampling distribution for the mean if the accountant changes the sample size to 500 accounts. Also discuss why it is not necessary to know the shape of the population distribution.

d. The accountant's sample of 500 produced a mean of $795.20. If the computer records are correct with regard to the standard deviation of the account balances, do you believe the figure given for the average of the account balances? Support you answer with probability calculations and rationale.

6.63 The Chair Company repairs old furniture and restores it to "better than original" condition. Records indicate the time it takes to refinish and otherwise restore a standard dining room set is normally distributed, with a mean of 30 hours and a standard deviation of 5 hours. Recently a customer complained that he was charged too much for work performed. To settle the argument, the manager of the company offered the customer the following option. The company will select a random sample of past work performed on tables similar to the customer's table. If the sample mean based on five randomly selected work times turns out to be less than the time required for his table, the Chair Company will refund his money. If the mean of this sample turns out to be greater than or equal to his billed time, he will pay the company half again the amount of the bill.
  a. Taking into account the average and standard deviation of all work times on file, do you think the manager is wise to make such an offer if this customer's billed time was 26 hours? Discuss why or why not.
  b. What would be your response if the customer's billed time was 28 hours? Supply probability calculations and statistical reasoning to support your answer.

6.64 The Swim and Racquet Club is in the process of establishing a policy for how long a court may be reserved at any one time. The club pro has said that he thinks the average time required to complete a tennis match is 90 minutes, with a standard deviation of 10 minutes. To help make the policy, club managers have selected a random sample of 100 tennis matches and have determined that the mean time for completion is 75 minutes. The managers' spokesperson maintains that this data supports the club's pro and says the managers are preparing to put the maximum time to reserve a court to be 90 minutes. They argue that it is quite understandable that a sample of size 100 would produce a sample mean of 75 minutes. After all, 75 is only 1.5 standard deviations below the mean of 90 minutes.
  a. Calculate the probability that a sample mean of 75 or less would occur if the club pro were correct in his assessment of mean and standard deviation.
  b. Based on your answer to part a, does it appear that the 90-minute limit will be sufficient? Explain.

6.65 The Environmental Protection Agency (EPA) requires all U.S. automobile makers to test their cars for mileage in the city and on the highway. One company has indicated that a certain model will get 25 miles per gallon (mpg) in the city and 32 mpg on the highway. However, not all cars of a given model will get the same mileage; these mileage ratings are simply averages. Furthermore, because there is variation among cars, the manufacturer has discovered that the standard deviation is 3 mpg for city driving and 2 mpg for highway driving.
  a. Given this information, suppose the San Francisco Police Department has purchased a random sample of 64 cars from this company. The police officers have driven these cars exclusively in the city and have recorded

an average of 24.25 mpg. Based on this sample information, what would you conclude about the EPA city-driving average mileage rating for this car? Base your response on the probability of getting a sample mean of 24.25 mpg or less.

b. The police chief has asked his officers to drive the cars to Los Angeles and back to determine how the cars perform in highway driving. The 64 cars averaged 34 mpg. What can the chief conclude about the advertised highway mileage? Explain your answer.

Advanced Business Applications

6.66 The Sullivan Advertising Agency has determined that the average cost to develop a 30-second commercial is $20,000. The standard deviation is $3,000. Suppose a random sample of 50 commercials is selected and the average cost is $20,300.

a. What are the chances of finding a sample mean this high or higher?

b. Sullivan's has budgeted $2,250,000 to finance the development of its next 100 commercials. Is this a realistic figure? Determine the chances that Sullivan's will overrun their budget. (Assume the 100 commercials constitute a simple random sample.)

6.67 Referring to Exercise 6.66, suppose the Sullivan Advertising Agency is interested in establishing a pricing policy for prospective customers of 30-second commercials. Recall the mean cost is $20,000, with a standard deviation of $3,000.

a. What are the chances of a given commercial costing between $19,500 and $22,000?

b. What is the probability of a sample of 36 commercials having an average cost between $19,500 and $22,000? Explain why these probabilities are different.

6.68 The Baily Hill Bicycle Shop sells mountain bikes and offers a maintenance program to its customers. The manager has found the average repair bill during the maintenance program's first year to be $15.30, with a standard deviation of $7.00.

a. What is the probability a random sample of 40 customers will have a mean repair cost exceeding $16.00?

b. What is the probability the mean repair cost for a sample of 100 customers will be between $15.10 and $15.80?

c. The manager has decided to offer a Spring Special. He is aware of the mean and standard deviation for repair bills last year. Therefore, he has decided to randomly select and repair 50 bicycles for $14 each. He notes that this is not even one standard deviation below the mean price to make such repairs. He asks your advice. Is this a risky thing to do? Based on the probability of the mean repair bill being $14.00 or less, what would you recommend? Discuss.

6.69 As part of a marketing study, the Food King Supermarket chain has randomly sampled 150 customers. The average dollar volume purchased by the customers in this sample was $31.14.

Before sampling, the company assumed that the distribution of customer purchases had a mean of $30.00 and a standard deviation of $8.00. If these figures are correct, what is the probability of observing a sample mean of $31.14 or greater? What would this probability indicate to you concerning the assumed distribution of customer purchases?

6.70 The Bendbo Corporation has a total of 300 employees in its two manufacturing locations and the headquarters office. A study conducted five years ago showed the average commuting distance to work for Bendbo employees was 6.2 miles, with a standard deviation of 3 miles. Recently, a follow-up study based on a random sample of 100 employees indicated an average travel distance of 5.9 miles.

a. Assuming that the mean and standard deviation of the original study hold, what is the probability of obtaining a sample mean of 5.9 miles or less?

b. Based on this probability, do you think the average travel distance may have decreased?

c. A second random sample of 40 was selected. This sample produced a mean travel distance of 5.9 miles. If the mean for all employees is 6.2 miles and the standard deviation is 3 miles, what is the probability of observing a sample mean of 5.9 miles or less?

d. Discuss why the probabilities differ even though the sample results were the same in each case.

6.71 An automatic saw at a local lumber mill cuts 2-by-4s to an average length of 120 inches. However, because the saw is a mechanical device, not all the boards are 120 inches long. In fact, the distribution of lengths has a variance of 0.64. The saw operator took a sample of 36 boards.

a. If the saw is set correctly, what is the probability the average length of the sample boards is more than 120.2 inches?

b. What is the probability the sample mean length is less than 119.73 inches?

c. What should the saw operator conclude if she finds the sample to have an average length of 120.3 inches?

d. An order has been received for 1,000 2-by-4s. However, the purchaser has declared that he will refuse the shipment if any boards are more than 1.5 inches different than your stated average. Is this a good proposition for the lumber company? Support your opinion with statistical calculations and reasoning. You may have to make some assumptions to justify your calculations. Do so, but specify what they are.

6.72 The manager for quality control at Bixby Electronics recently reviewed a contract the company has with one of the suppliers of a particular component part. According to the contract, the defective rate in the components is to be no more than 7%. A large quantity of the components has just arrived at Bixby Electronics. As part of the regular receiving process, a random sample of 100 parts was selected. In this sample 12% of the parts were found to be defective.

a. What is the probability of 12% or more of the components being defective if the true percentage defective in the population is actually 7%?

b. Based on the probability you have computed, what should the quality control manager conclude about the entire shipment of components with respect to the 7% defective limit?

c. Calculate the value for control limits for the quality control procedure. The control limits are established at 3 standard deviations from the mean. (Assume $n = 100$.)

d. Determine the probability that a sample proportion from a sample of size 100 would be beyond the control limits if the true rate of defective items is 7%.

6.73 The Republican Election Committee maintains that 34% of the members of the AFL-CIO labor union are registered Republicans, but a random sample of 300 members shows a sample proportion of 28% registered Republicans.
a. What statistical term is given to the difference between the 28% and the 34%?
b. Also, how likely is it that a sample of this size would contain 28% or fewer Republicans if the 34% figure is correct?

6.74 The average of all accounts payable for a large national electronics firm has been determined to be $2,755, with a standard deviation of $375.
a. Determine the probability that a random sample of 36 accounts payable would have a sample mean (1) greater than $2,850, (2) less than $2,700, or (3) between $2,650 and $2,750?
b. Determine the largest accounts payable that the electronics firm has experienced. Assume that these accounts have a normal distribution.

6.75 Suppose it is thought that 45% of all computer users in Seattle have made at least one purchase using the Internet. You have just conducted a random sample of 49 computer users in Seattle and have found that 18 of them have made at least one purchase using the Internet.
a. Does your sample proportion surprise you? How likely are you to see a sample proportion this small or smaller if the true population proportion is 0.45?
b. Using your knowledge of the normal distribution, determine the maximum sampling error you could experience in such a sample.

6.76 The file *High Desert Banking* contains information regarding consumer, real estate, and small commercial loans made last year by the bank. Use your computer software to
a. Construct a frequency histogram using eight classes for dollar values of loans made last year. Does the population distribution appear to be normally distributed?
b. Compute the population mean for all loans made last year.
c. Compute the population standard deviation for all loans made last year.
d. Select a simple random sample of 36 loans. Compute the sample mean. By how much does the sample mean differ from the population mean? Use the Central Limit Theorem to determine the probability that you would have a sample mean this small or smaller and the probability that you would have a sample mean this large or larger.

6.77 Marketing research indicates that 37% of all customers of a nationwide pizza chain are college students.
a. What is the probability that a random sample of 625 customers of the pizza chain would contain 250 or more people who are college students?
b. A local pizzeria wishes to attract college students. The pizzeria advertises in the college newspaper that it will give a coffee mug displaying the local college's insignia to every customer who presents a student ID from that college on a certain Saturday. Normally the pizzeria has approximately 100 customers on Saturdays. If the pizzeria stocks 50 coffee mugs, determine the probability that it will have enough coffee mugs to give to the students if the advertisement doesn't work (i.e., doesn't attract a larger percentage of students). (Assume that the 100 customers constitutes a random sample of the population of customers.)

6.78 The file *Best-Companies* contains selected information from the 100 best companies for U.S. employees as determined by *Fortune* magazine. Use this file to perform the following:
a. Calculate the average number of U.S. employees for all 100 companies.
b. Calculate the population standard deviation for the variable number of U.S. employees.
c. Select a simple random sample of 36 companies. Compute the average number of U.S. employees for the sample. Is the sample mean identical to the population mean? Would you expect it to be? Why or why not?
d. Compute the standard error of the sampling distribution of the mean for a sample size of 36. Is this value larger than or smaller than the population standard deviation?
e. What is the probability that for a sample of 36 you would get a sample mean that is at least 15,000 employees?

6.79 A sample of 500 business professionals found that 30% chose an airline based on price.
a. If the population proportion of all business professionals who select an airline based on price is 0.27, then what is the probability that we would find a sample proportion of 0.30 or more?
b. If the population proportion of all business professionals who select an airline based on price is 0.29, then what is the probability that we would find a sample proportion of 0.30 or more?
c. If you had to decide whether the proportion of business professionals who select an airline based on price was at most 0.27 or greater than 0.27, what would you conclude? Justify your answer statistically.

6.80 When its ovens are working properly, the time required to bake fruit pies at Ellardo Bakeries is normally distributed, with a mean of 45 minutes and a standard deviation of 5 minutes. Yesterday, a random sample of 16 had an average baking time of 50 minutes.
a. If Ellardo's ovens are working correctly, how likely is it that a sample of 16 pies would have an average baking time of 50 minutes or more?
b. Would you recommend that Ellardo inspect its ovens to see if they are working properly? Justify your answer.

6.81 If the true proportion of home computer users who would purchase an additional telephone line for Internet use is 0.27, then what is the probability that a random sample of 500 computer users would produce a sample proportion between 0.25 and 0.29?

6.82 The CD-ROM file called *Cozine* contains data on weights of garbage trucks. Assume these data represent the population of interest. Suppose the landfill manager plans to select a random sample of 30 truck weights and from that will develop a report to the county commissioners.
a. Determine the population mean and population standard deviation.

b. Develop a frequency histogram for these data.

c. Write a paragraph that describes the population.

d. Select a random sample of 30 weights. Compute the sample mean weight.

e. Compute the probability of getting a sample mean as extreme or more extreme than the one you calculated.

f. Based on the probability computed in part e, does it appear that this sample may have attributes, such as the mean, similar to those of the population, or is the sampling error too great? Discuss.

6.83   The Celltone company offers cell phone service with two plans for customers: Basic Plan and Business Plan.

When the owners first devised the idea of offering the two plans, they felt that 70% of all customers would select the Business Plan. The data file *Celltone* contains data for a random sample of 200 customers.

a. Compute the sample proportion of Business Plan customers.

b. What is the probability that a sample will contain a proportion as extreme or more extreme than the one computed in part a if the 70% figure is correct for the population?

c. Based on the result in part b, what conclusion should the owner reach about his assumption regarding Business Plan customers? Discuss.

CASE 6-A:

Carpita Bottling Company

Don Carpita owns and operates Carpita Bottling Company in Lakeland, Wisconsin. The company bottles soda pop and beer and distributes the products in the counties surrounding Lakeland.

The company has four bottling machines, which can be adjusted to fill bottles at any mean fill level between 2 ounces and 72 ounces. The machines exhibit some variation in actual fill from the mean setting. For instance, if the mean setting is 16 ounces, the actual fill may be slightly more or less than that amount.

Three of the four filling machines are relatively new, and their fill variation is not as great as that of the older machine. Don has observed that the standard deviation in fill for the three new machines is about 1% of the mean fill level when the mean fill is set at 16 ounces or less, and it is 0.5% of the mean at settings exceeding 16 ounces. The older machine has a standard deviation of about 1.5% of the mean setting regardless of the mean fill setting. However, the older machine tends to underfill bottles more than overfill, so the older machine is set at a mean fill slightly in excess of the desired mean to compensate for the propensity to underfill. For example, when 16-ounce bottles are to be filled, the machine is set at a mean fill level of 16.05 ounces.

The company can simultaneously fill bottles with two brands of soda pop using two machines, and it can use the other two machines to bottle beer. Although each filling machine has its own

warehouse and the products are loaded from the warehouse directly on a truck, products from two or more filling machines may be loaded on the same truck. However, an individual store almost always receives bottles on a particular day from just one machine.

On Saturday morning Don received a call at home from the J. R. Summers Grocery store manager. She was very upset because the shipment of 16-ounce bottles of beer received yesterday contained several bottles that were not adequately filled. The manager wanted Don to replace the entire shipment at once.

Don gulped down his coffee and prepared to head to the store to check out the problem. He started thinking how he could determine which machine was responsible for the problem. If he could at least determine whether it was the old machine or one of the new ones, he could save his maintenance people a lot of time and effort checking all the machines.

His plan was to select a sample of 64 bottles of beer from the store and measure the contents. Don figures that he might be able to determine, on the basis of the average contents, whether it is more likely that the beer was bottled by a new machine or by the old one.

The results of the sampling showed an average of 15.993 ounces. Now Don needs some help in determining whether a sample mean of 15.993 ounces or less is more likely to come from the new machines or the older machine.

CASE 6-B:

Truck Safety Inspection

The Idaho Department of Law Enforcement, in conjunction with the federal government, recently began a truck inspection program in Idaho. The current inspection effort is limited to an inspection of only those trucks that visually appear to have some defect when they stop at one of the weigh stations in the state. The proposed inspection program will not be limited to the trucks with visible defects, but it will potentially subject all trucks to a comprehensive safety inspection.

Jane Lund of the Department of Law Enforcement is in charge of the new program. She has stated that the ultimate objective of the new

truck inspection program is to reduce the number of trucks with safety defects operating in Idaho. Ideally, all trucks passing through, or operating within, Idaho would be inspected once a month, and substantial penalties would be applied to operators if safety defects were discovered. Ms. Lund is confident that such an inspection program would, without fail, reduce the number of defective trucks operating on Idaho's highways. However, each safety inspection takes about an hour, and because of limited money to hire inspectors, she realizes that all trucks cannot be inspected. She also knows it is unrealistic to have trucks wait to be inspected until trucks ahead of them have been checked. Such delays would cause problems with the drivers.

In meetings with her staff, Jane has suggested that before the inspection program begins, the number of defective trucks currently operating in Idaho should be estimated. This estimate can be compared with later estimates to see if the inspection program has been effective. To arrive at this initial estimate, Jane thinks that some sort of sampling plan to select representative trucks from the population for all trucks in the state must be developed. She has suggested that this sampling be done at the eight weigh stations near Idaho's borders, but she is unsure how to establish a statistically sound sampling plan that is practical to implement.

CASE 6-C:

Houston Nut and Candy Company

Bruce Houston wanted to get away from the office and start on a much-needed vacation that he and his family had been planning for some time. He really needed to get his packing done if they were going to make their 8:00 P.M. flight for Honolulu. But he also knew that he needed to get a potential problem straightened out before he left or he wouldn't be able to enjoy the sun and beaches of Hawaii.

Earlier in the day, Helen Stahl in quality assurance had dropped by his office with three e-mails she had received from customers in the past few days. The e-mail messages all contained essentially the same message: "Your gourmet mixed nuts contain too many peanuts!" Helen indicated that as far as she knew, there was nothing wrong with the production process. The company's standard calls for no more than 30% peanuts in the gourmet mix. Obviously, some cans will contain more, some less, but overall the proportion should not exceed 30%. The production line controls this by starting with fixed quantities of nuts that go into the storage vats that lead to the filling machine.

Helen assured Bruce that the vats started with 30% peanuts, 30% cashews, and 40% walnuts and other varieties. These nuts are thoroughly mixed and then the cans are filled. According to Helen, the contents of each can be considered a random sample of the total production.

While Helen waited in his office, Bruce called one of the unhappy customers to find out the basis of his complaint. This customer indicated that of the 345 nuts in a can, there were 125 peanuts when they would have expected no more than 103. A call to a second customer indicated that of 360 nuts in a can, 144 were peanuts. Bruce called the third customer and heard similar results.

After Helen left, Bruce decided to assign Helen three tasks. First he wanted her to determine the chances of other customers getting the results that were reported by the unhappy customers if the process proportion of peanuts was really 30%. Second, Bruce reasoned that if the vats started out with 30% peanuts, about half the cans would have more than 30% and half would have less than 30% by chance. He decided to have Helen open a random sample of 100 cans. For each can, she was to record whether the can contained more than 30% peanuts. Then, he wanted her to compute the probability of finding whatever result she recorded assuming that the proportion of cans with more than 30% peanuts was equal to 0.50. Finally, he wanted her to write him a short report summarizing the results along with suggestions for how they might improve things if improvement was needed. (The data file Nuts contains the results of the sample of 100 cans.)

Bruce e-mailed these instructions to Helen, shut off his lights, said good-bye to Gladys at the front desk, and headed for home.

General References

1. Albright, S. Christian, Wayne L. Winston, and Christopher Zappe, *Data Analysis and Decision Making with Microsoft Excel* (Pacific Grove, CA: Duxbury, 1999).
2. Berenson, Mark L., and David M. Levine, *Basic Business Statistics: Concepts and Applications*, 7th ed. (Upper Saddle River, NJ: Prentice Hall, 1999).
3. Cochran, William G., *Sampling Techniques*, 3rd ed. (New York: Wiley, 1977).
4. Dodge, Mark, and Craig Stinson, *Running Microsoft Excel 2000* (Redmond, WA: Microsoft Press, 1999).
5. Hogg, R. V., and Elliot A. Tanis, *Probability and Statistical Inference*, 5th ed. (Upper Saddle River, NJ: Prentice Hall, 1997).
6. Johnson, Richard A., and Dean W. Wichern, *Business Statistics: Decision Making with Data* (New York: Wiley, 1997).
7. *Microsoft Excel 2000* (Redmond, WA: Microsoft Corp., 1999).
8. *Minitab for Windows Version 14* (State College, PA: Minitab, 2003).

CHAPTER 7

Estimating Population Values

CHAPTER OUTCOMES

After studying the material in Chapter 7, you should be able to:

- Distinguish between a point estimate and a confidence interval estimate.
- Construct and interpret a confidence interval estimate for a single population mean using both the standard normal and *t* distributions.
- Determine the required sample size for estimating a single population mean.
- Establish and interpret a confidence interval estimate for a single population proportion.

WHY YOU NEED TO KNOW

Wherever you find yourself working, you may need to know population values (*parameters*) to help you make decisions. An accountant needs to know the percentage of accounts with correct balances. A marketing manager needs to know the average income in her target-market area. A manufacturing manager needs to know the average machine downtime in his plant. The programming manager at a major television network needs to know the percentage of people watching each of his shows so he can cancel the poor performers. A restaurant manager needs to know the percentage of customers who will order the daily special so she will know how many orders to have available.

In these cases and many others like them, decision makers need to know a population parameter. However, gaining access to an entire population is extremely expensive and time-consuming and, in many cases, infeasible. Therefore, an alternative approach is to select a sample from the population. The sample data are used to compute a desired statistic that forms an estimate of the corresponding population parameter.

Chapter 1 discussed various sampling techniques, including statistical and nonstatistical methods. Chapter 6 introduced the concepts of sampling error and sampling distributions. Chapter 7 builds on these concepts and introduces the steps needed to develop and interpret statistical estimations of various population values. The concepts introduced here will be very useful. You will undoubtedly need to estimate population parameters as a regular part of your managerial decision-making activities. In addition, you will receive estimates that other people have developed that you will need to evaluate before relying on them as inputs to your decision-making process. Was the sample size sufficiently large to provide valid estimates of the population parameter? How confident can I be that the estimate matches the population parameter of interest? These and similar questions can all be answered using the concepts and tools presented in this chapter.

7-1 POINT AND CONFIDENCE INTERVAL ESTIMATES FOR A POPULATION MEAN

POINT ESTIMATES AND CONFIDENCE INTERVALS

You, no doubt, have either been a respondent to, or have seen the results of a political poll taken during an election year. These polls attempt to determine the percentage of voters who will favor a particular candidate or a particular issue. For example, suppose a poll indicates that 62% of the people older than 18 in your state favor limiting property taxes to 1% of the market value of the property. The pollsters have not contacted every person in the state, but rather they have sampled only a relatively few people to arrive at the 62% figure. In statistical terminology, the 62% is the **point estimate** for the true population percentage of people who favor the property-tax limitation.

Point Estimate

A statistic, determined from a sample, that is used to estimate the corresponding population parameter.

The Environmental Protection Agency (EPA) tests the mileage of automobiles sold in the United States. The resulting EPA mileage rating is actually a point estimate for the true average mileage of all cars of a given model.

Cost accountants study their company's production processes to determine product costs. Often the accountants select a sample of items and follow each one through a complete production process. The costs at each step in the process are measured and summed to determine the total cost. This figure is the point estimate for the true average cost of all the items produced. The point estimate is used in assigning a selling price to the finished product.

Which point estimator the decision maker uses depends on the population characteristic the decision maker wishes to estimate. However, regardless of the population value being estimated, we always expect **sampling error**.

Sampling Error

The difference between a value (a statistic) computed from a sample and the corresponding value (a parameter) computed from the population.

Chapter 6 discussed sampling error. We cannot eliminate sampling error, but we can deal with it in our decision process. For example, when cost accountants use $\bar{x}$, the average cost of a sample of items, to establish the average cost of production, the point estimate, $\bar{x}$, will most likely not equal the population mean, μ. But with $\bar{x}$ as their only information, they will have no way of determining how much in error it is.

To overcome this problem with point estimates, the most common procedure is to calculate an interval estimate known as a **confidence interval**.

Confidence Interval

An interval developed from sample values such that if all possible intervals of a given width were constructed, a percentage of these intervals, known as the confidence level, would include the true population parameter.

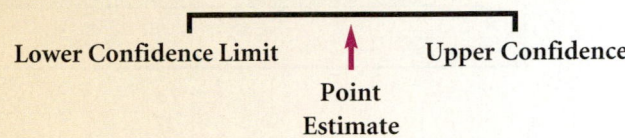

Lower Confidence Limit   Upper Confidence

Point
Estimate

An example will help to make this definition clear.

Excel and Minitab Tutorial

Nagel Beverage Company—The Nagel Beverage Company has recently installed a new soft-drink filling machine that allows the operator to adjust the mean fill quantity. However, no matter what the mean setting, the actual volume of the liquid in each can will vary. The machine has been carefully tested and is known to fill cans with a standard deviation of $\sigma = 0.2$ ounce.

The filling machine has been adjusted to fill cans at an average of 12 ounces. After running the machine for several hours, a simple random sample of 100 cans is selected and the volume of soda in each can is measured in the company's quality lab. Figure 7-1 shows the frequency histogram of the sample data. (The data are in a file on your CD-ROM called *Nagel-Beveragea*.) Notice that the distribution seems to be centered at a point higher than 12 ounces. The manager wishes to use the sample data to estimate the mean fill amount for all cans filled by this machine.

FIGURE 7-1

Excel Histogram for Nagel Beverage

Excel Instructions:
1. Open file: Nagel Beverage
2. Create bins (upper limit of each class).
3. Select **Tools**.
4. Select **Histogram**.
5. Define data and bin ranges.
6. Check **Chart Output**.

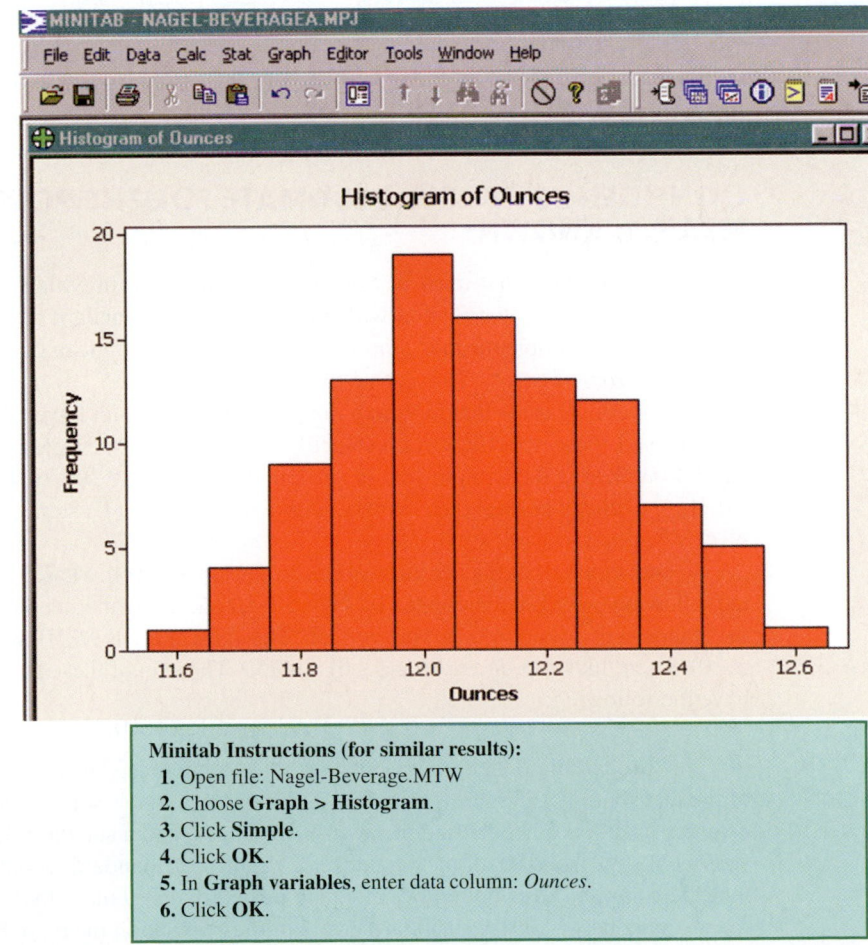

Minitab Instructions (for similar results):
1. Open file: Nagel-Beverage.MTW
2. Choose **Graph > Histogram**.
3. Click **Simple**.
4. Click **OK**.
5. In **Graph variables**, enter data column: *Ounces*.
6. Click **OK**.

FIGURE 7-2

Sampling Distribution of $\bar{x}$

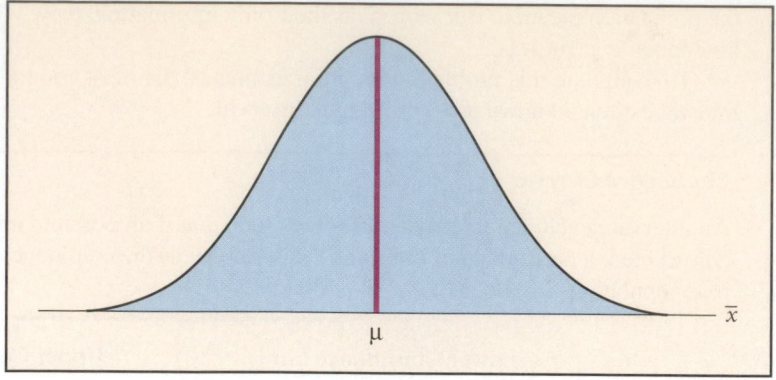

The sample mean computed from 100 cans is $\bar{x}$ = 12.09 ounces. This is the *point estimate* of the population mean, μ. Because of the potential for sampling error, the manager should not expect a particular $\bar{x}$ to equal μ. However, as discussed in Chapter 6, the Central Limit Theorem indicates that the distribution of all possible sample means will be approximately normally distributed around the population mean, as illustrated in Figure 7-2.

Although the sample mean is 12.09 ounces, the manager knows the true population mean may be higher or lower than this number. To account for the potential for sampling error, the manager can develop a *confidence interval estimate* for μ. This estimate will take the form:

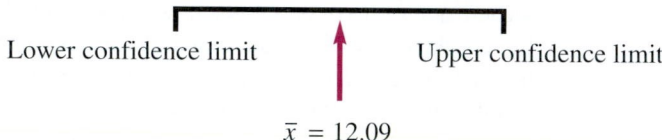

$\bar{x}$ = 12.09

The key now is to determine the upper and lower limits of the interval. The specific method for computing these values depends on whether the population standard deviation, σ, is known or unknown. We first take up the case in which σ is known.

CONFIDENCE INTERVAL ESTIMATE FOR THE POPULATION MEAN, σ KNOWN

There are two cases that must be considered. In the case in which the simple random sample is drawn from a normal distribution with a mean of μ and a standard deviation of σ, the sampling distribution of the sample mean is a normal distribution with a mean of μ and a standard deviation (or *standard error*) of $\sigma/\sqrt{n}$. This is true for any sample size.

The second case is that in which the population does not have a normal distribution. Chapter 6 addressed these specific circumstances. Recall that in such cases the Central Limit Theorem can be invoked if the sample size is sufficiently large ($n \geq 30$). In such cases, the sampling distribution is also a normal distribution, with a mean of μ and a standard deviation (standard error) of $\sigma/\sqrt{n}$.

In both cases, a confidence interval can be constructed from a basic probability statement. Consider the following equation, represented by Figure 7-3, concerning the standard normal distribution. Look at the standard distribution table for $z = 1.96$. The value there is .4750, which corresponds to $P(1.96 \leq z \leq 0)$. Then, likewise, $P(-1.96 \leq z \leq 0) = .4750$. The sum of these two probabilities = .95. Thus we have the following:

$$P(-1.96 \leq z \leq 1.96) = 0.95$$

The probability 0.95 corresponds to a $1 - \alpha$ confidence level where $\alpha/2$ is the area in each tail of the distribution. In Figure 7-3, $\alpha/2 = .025$. Thus $z_{\alpha/2} = z_{.025} = 1.96$ and $-z_{\alpha/2} = -z_{.025} = -1.96$. The z-values have a normal distribution, with a mean of 0 and a standard deviation of 1. Therefore, this statement says that 95% of the z-values are within 1.96 standard deviations of their mean, 0. Given that the sampling distribution of $\bar{x}$ is also normally distributed, then 95% of the possible sample means must be within 1.96 standard errors of the population mean, μ. Because the standard error is

FIGURE 7-3

Critical Value for a 95%
Confidence Interval

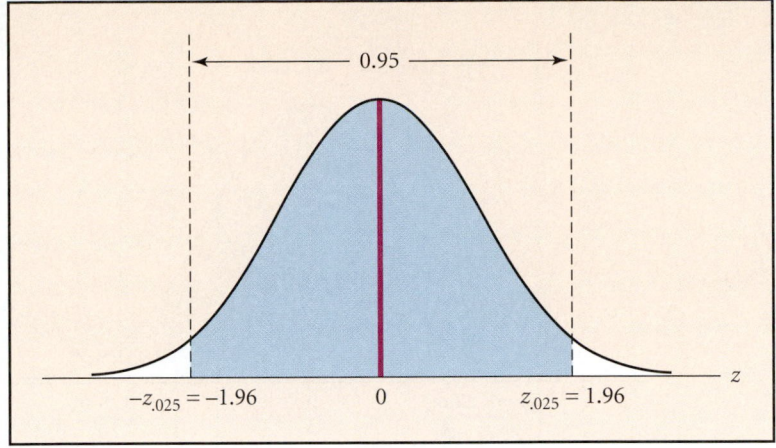

$\dfrac{\sigma}{\sqrt{n}}$, 95% of the sample means will be within $\pm1.96\ \dfrac{\sigma}{\sqrt{n}}$ of the population mean, μ. Thus, 95% of all interval estimates formed as

$$\bar{x} - 1.96\,\dfrac{\sigma}{\sqrt{n}} \ \text{--------------------}\ \bar{x} + 1.96\,\dfrac{\sigma}{\sqrt{n}}$$

will contain the population mean. Figure 7-4 illustrates this concept. This concept can be generalized to any probability by replacing the value 1.96 by the appropriate *z*-value. The *z*-value is referred to as the *critical value*.

Confidence Interval Calculation

All confidence interval estimates can be constructed using the same general format shown in Equation 7-1.

Confidence Interval General Format

Point estimate ± (Critical Value)(Standard Error)   **7-1**

The first step in developing a confidence interval estimate is to specify the **confidence level** that is needed to determine the critical value.

Confidence Level

A percentage less than 100 that corresponds to the percentage of all possible confidence intervals, based on a given sample size, that will contain the true population parameter.

Confidence Coefficient

The confidence level divided by 100%—that is, the decimal equivalent of a confidence level.

Suppose the Nagel Beverage manager specifies a 95% confidence level. This means the width of the interval estimate will be computed so that of all the possible confidence intervals that could be created from a given sample size, 95% will contain the true mean fill level for the population of all cans. The higher the confidence level, the better we feel about the one interval estimate that we will compute.

Once we decide on the confidence level, the next step is to determine the critical value. If the population standard deviation is known, and the population is normally distributed, or if the sample size is large enough to comply with the Central Limit Theorem requirements, the critical value is a *z*-value from the standard normal table. Equation 7-2 shows a modified form of the general format for a confidence interval.

Confidence Interval, General Format, σ Known

Point estimate ± *z* (Standard Error)   **7-2**

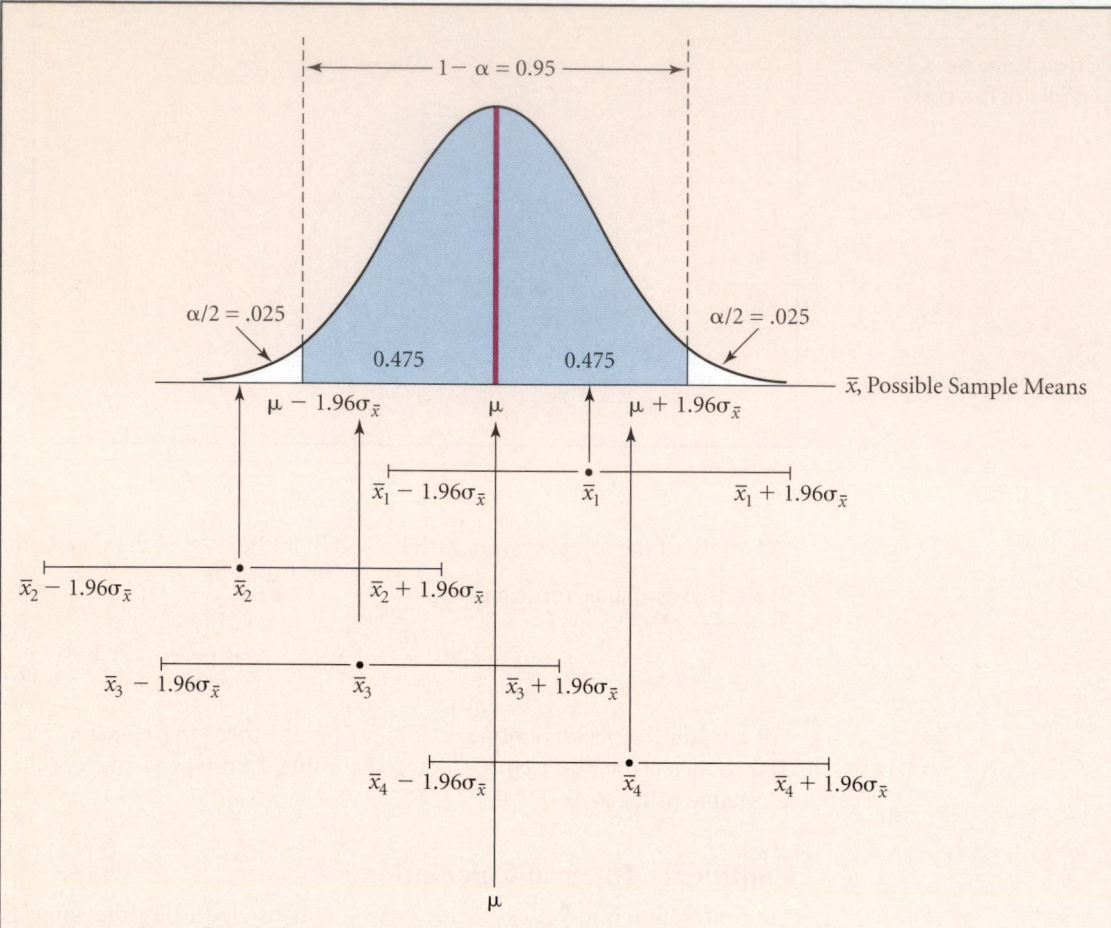

Note: Most intervals include μ and some do not. Those intervals that do not contain the population mean are developed from sample means that fall in either tail of the sampling distribution. If enough intervals were constructed, 95% would include μ.

FIGURE 7-4 **Confidence Intervals from Selected Random Samples**

In Figure 7-3 you can see that the confidence coefficient defines an area that is the middle 95% of the distribution. Therefore, to find the z-value, divide the confidence coefficient by 2, giving:

$$\frac{0.95}{2} = 0.475$$

Then go to the standard normal table in Appendix D. Inside the table, where the probabilities are located, find the value that is as close to 0.475 as possible and determine the corresponding z-value. Here we find that the z-value that corresponds to a probability of 0.475 is 1.96:

$$P(0 \le z \le 1.96) = 0.475$$

A sample mean that falls within 1.96 standard deviations of the population mean will produce a 95% confidence interval that includes the population mean.

Note, instead of using the standard normal table, you can also find the critical z-value using Excel's **NORMSINV** function or Minitab's **Calc > Probability Distribution** command. In Excel, a probability equal to $\alpha/2$ is inserted where $(1 - \alpha)100\%$ is equal to the confidence level. For example, for a 95% confidence interval, $\alpha = 0.05$ and $\alpha/2 = 0.025$. The critical z-value is the absolute value of the function result. Then **NORMSINV(0.025)** $= -1.96$. The critical z is 1.96. Minitab requires the use of the inverse-cumulative probability equal to $1 - \alpha/2$. However, the same critical z is obtained.

The next step is to compute the standard error. In Chapter 6, you learned the standard error of the sampling distribution for $\bar{x}$ is $\frac{\sigma}{\sqrt{n}}$. Then Equation 7-3 is used to compute the confidence interval estimate of a single population mean.

Confidence Interval Estimate for μ, σ Known

$$\bar{x} \pm z_{\alpha/2} \frac{\sigma}{\sqrt{n}}$$

7-3

where:

$z_{\alpha/2}$ = Critical value from standard normal table for a $1 - \alpha$ confidence level
σ = Population standard deviation
n = Sample size

Nagel Beverage Company (continued)—Recall that the sample of 100 cans produced a sample mean of $\bar{x} = 12.09$ ounces and the Nagel manager knows that $\sigma = 0.2$ ounces. Thus, the 95% confidence interval estimate for the population mean is

$$\bar{x} \pm z_{.025} \frac{\sigma}{\sqrt{n}}$$

$$12.09 \pm 1.96 \frac{0.2}{\sqrt{100}}$$

$$12.09 \pm 0.039$$

12.051 ounces ------------------------- 12.129 ounces

Based on this sample information, the Nagel manager believes that the true mean fill for all cans is within the following range:

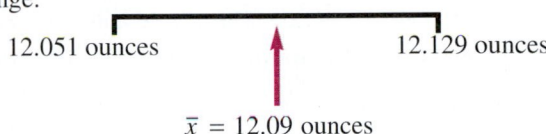

12.051 ounces   12.129 ounces

$\bar{x} = 12.09$ ounces

Because this interval does not contain the target mean of 12 ounces, the manager should conclude that the filling equipment is out of adjustment and is putting in too much soda, on average.

SUMMARY: CONFIDENCE INTERVAL ESTIMATE FOR μ WITH σ KNOWN

Computing a confidence interval estimate for the population mean when the population standard deviation is assumed known and the population is normally distributed or the sample size is sufficiently large so the Central Limit Theorem applies:

1. Define the population of interest and select a simple random sample of size *n*.

2. Specify the confidence level.

3. Compute the sample mean using:

$$\bar{x} = \frac{\sum x}{n}$$

4. Determine the standard error of the sampling distribution using:

$$\sigma_{\bar{x}} = \frac{\sigma}{\sqrt{n}}$$

5. Determine the critical value, *z*, from the standard normal table.

6. Compute the confidence interval estimate using:

$$\bar{x} \pm z_{\alpha/2} \frac{\sigma}{\sqrt{n}}$$

EXAMPLE 7-1: CONFIDENCE INTERVAL ESTIMATE FOR μ, σ KNOWN

Saint Regis Hospital   Administrators at Saint Regis Hospital wish to know the mean dollars spent on medical expenses for the patients who were admitted to the hospital during the previous year. To do this, they could use the following steps.

Step 1:   **Define the population of interest and select a simple random sample of size *n*.**
The population is all patients who were admitted to the hospital during the previous year. A simple random sample of 200 patients will be selected.

Step 2:   **Specify the confidence level.**
The administrators want to develop a 90% confidence interval estimate. Thus, 90% of all possible intervals will contain the population mean.

Step 3:   **Compute the sample mean.**

After the sample has been selected and the dollars spent on medical care last year have been recorded for each of the 200 people sampled, the sample mean is computed using:

$$\bar{x} = \frac{\sum x}{n}$$

Assume the sample mean is $5,230.

Step 4:   **Determine the standard error of the sampling distribution.**

Suppose past studies have indicated that the population standard deviation is

$$\sigma = \$500$$

Then the standard error of the sampling distribution is computed using:

$$\sigma_{\bar{x}} = \frac{\sigma}{\sqrt{n}} = \frac{\$500}{\sqrt{200}} = \$35.36$$

Step 5:   **Determine the critical value, z, from the standard normal table.**

Because the sample size is large, the Central Limit Theorem applies. The sampling distribution will be normally distributed, and the critical value will be a z-value from the standard normal distribution. The administrators want 90% confidence, so the z-value is determined by finding a probability in Appendix D corresponding to $\frac{0.90}{2} = 0.45$. We find 0.4495 and 0.4505, so the correct z-value is between $z = 1.64$ and $z = 1.65$. The critical value is $z = 1.645$.

Step 6:   **Compute the confidence interval estimate.**

The 90% confidence interval estimate for the population mean is

$$\bar{x} \pm z_{.05}\frac{\sigma}{\sqrt{n}}$$

$$\$5,230 \pm 1.645\frac{500}{\sqrt{200}}$$

$$\$5,230 \pm \$58.16$$

$$\$5,171.84 \text{ --------------------------------- } \$5,288.16$$

Thus, based on the sample results, with 90% confidence, the administrators at Saint Regis Hospital believe that the true population mean for dollars spent on medical care last year is between $5,171.84 and $5,288.16.

Special Message About Interpreting Confidence Intervals

There is a subtle distinction to be made here. Beginning students often wonder if it is permissible to say, "There is a 0.95 probability that the population mean is between $5,171.84 and $5,288.16." This may seem to be the logical consequence of constructing a confidence interval. However, we must be very careful to attribute probability only to random events or variables. Because the population mean is a fixed value, there can be no probability statement about the population mean. The confidence interval we have computed will either contain the population mean or it will not. If you were to produce all the possible confidence intervals using the mean of each possible sample from the population, 95% of these intervals would contain the population mean.

Impact of the Confidence Level on the Interval Estimate

Nagel Beverage (continued)—In the Nagel Beverage example, the manager specified a 95% confidence level. The resulting confidence interval estimate for the population mean was

$$\bar{x} \pm z_{.025}\frac{\sigma}{\sqrt{n}}$$

$$12.09 \pm 1.96\frac{0.2}{\sqrt{100}}$$

$$12.09 \pm 0.039$$

$$12.051 \text{ ounces } \text{------------------------ } 12.129 \text{ ounces}$$

The quantity, 0.039, on the right of the ± sign above is called the **margin of error**. This is illustrated in Equation 7-4. The margin of error defines the relationship between the sample mean and the population mean.

Margin of Error

The amount that is added and subtracted to the point estimate to determine the endpoints of the confidence interval.

Margin of Error for Estimating μ, σ Known

$$e = z_{\alpha/2}\frac{\sigma}{\sqrt{n}}$$

7-4

where:

$$e = \text{Margin of error}$$
$$z_{\alpha/2} = \text{Critical value}$$
$$\frac{\sigma}{\sqrt{n}} = \text{Standard error of the sampling distribution}$$

Now suppose the manager at Nagel is willing to settle for 80% confidence. This will impact the critical value. To determine the new value, divide 0.80 by 2, giving 0.40. Go to the standard normal table and locate a probability value (area under the curve) that is as close to 0.40 as possible. The corresponding z-value is 1.28.[1] The 80% confidence interval estimate is

$$\bar{x} \pm z_{0.10}\frac{\sigma}{\sqrt{n}}$$
$$12.09 \pm (1.28)\frac{0.2}{\sqrt{100}}$$
$$12.09 \pm 0.026$$
$$12.064 \text{ ounces} \text{ -------------------- } 12.116 \text{ ounces}$$

Based on this sample information and the 80% confidence interval, we believe that the true average fill level is between 12.064 ounces and 12.116 ounces.

By lowering the confidence level, the method used to produce the interval is less likely to contain the population mean. However, on the positive side, the margin of error has been reduced from 0.039 ounces to 0.026 ounces. For equivalent samples from a population:

1. If the confidence level is decreased, the margin of error is reduced.
2. If the confidence level is increased, the margin of error is increased.

The Nagel manager will need to decide which is more important, a higher confidence level or a lower margin of error.

ℰXAMPLE 7-2: IMPACT OF CHANGING THE CONFIDENCE LEVEL

DuVall Services   DuVall Services operates a garbage hauling company in a south Florida city. Each year, the company must apply for a new contract with the city. The contract is in part based on the pounds of garbage hauled. Part of the analysis that goes into contract development is an estimate of the mean pounds of garbage put out by each customer in the city. The city has asked for both 99% and 90% confidence interval estimates for the mean. The steps used to generate these estimates follow.

Step 1:   **Define the population of interest and select a simple random sample of size *n*.**
The population is the collection of all of Duvall's customers, and a simple random sample of $n = 100$ customers is selected.

Step 2:   **Specify the confidence level.**
The city requires 99% and 90% confidence interval estimates.

---

[1]You can also use Excel's NORMSINV function = NORMSINV(.10) = 1.281.

Step 3: **Compute the sample mean.**

After the sample has been selected and the pounds of garbage have been determined for each of the 100 customers sampled, the sample mean is computed using:

$$\bar{x} = \frac{\sum x}{n}$$

Suppose the sample mean is 40.78 pounds.

Step 4: **Determine the standard error of the sampling distribution.**

Suppose, from past years, the population standard deviation is known to be $\sigma = 12.6$ pounds. Then the standard error of the sampling distribution is computed using:

$$\sigma_{\bar{x}} = \frac{\sigma}{\sqrt{n}} = \frac{12.6}{\sqrt{100}} = 1.26 \text{ pounds}$$

Step 5: **Determine the critical value, z, from the standard normal table.**

First, the city wants a 99% confidence interval estimate so the z-value is determined by finding a probability in Appendix D corresponding to $\frac{0.99}{2} = 0.495$. The correct z-value is between $z = 2.57$ and $z = 2.58$. We split the difference to get the critical value: $z_{.005} = 2.575$. For 90% confidence, the critical z is determined to be 1.645.

Step 6: **Compute the confidence interval estimate.**

The 99% confidence interval estimate for the population mean is

$$\bar{x} \pm z_{.005} \frac{\sigma}{\sqrt{n}}$$

$$40.78 \pm 2.575 \frac{12.6}{\sqrt{100}}$$

$$40.78 \pm 3.24$$

37.54 pounds ----------------------------- 44.02 pounds

The margin of error at 99% confidence is ±3.24 pounds.
The 90% confidence interval estimate for the population mean is

$$\bar{x} \pm z_{.05} \frac{\sigma}{\sqrt{n}}$$

$$40.78 \pm 1.645 \frac{12.6}{\sqrt{100}}$$

$$40.78 \pm 2.07$$

38.71 pounds ----------------------------- 42.85 pounds

The margin of error is only 2.07 pounds when the confidence level is reduced from 99% to 90%. The margin of error will be smaller when the confidence level is smaller.

Lowering the confidence level is one way to reduce the margin of error. However, by examining Equation 7-4, you will note there are two other values that affect the margin of error. One of these is the population standard deviation. The more the population's standard deviation, σ, can be reduced, the smaller the margin of error will be. In a business environment, large standard deviations for measurements related to the quality of a product are not desired. In fact, corporations spend considerable effort to decrease the variation in their products either by changing their process or by controlling variables that cause the variation. Typically all avenues for reducing the standard deviation should be pursued before thoughts of reducing the confidence level are entertained.

Unfortunately, there are many situations in which reducing the population standard deviation is not possible. In these cases, another step that can be taken to reduce the margin of error is to increase the sample size. As you learned in Chapter 6, an increase in sample size reduces the standard error of the sampling distribution. This can be the most direct way of reducing the margin of error as long as obtaining an increased sample is not prohibitively costly or unattainable for other reasons.

Impact of the Sample Size on the Interval Estimate

Nagel Beverage (continued)—Suppose the Nagel Beverage Company production manager decided to increase the sample to 400 cans. This is a four-fold increase over the original sample size. We learned in Chapter 6 that an increase in sample size reduces the standard error of the sampling distribution because the standard error is computed as $\frac{\sigma}{\sqrt{n}}$. Thus, without adversely affecting his confidence level, the manager can reduce the margin of error by increasing his sample size.

Assume that the sample mean for the larger sample size also happens to be $\bar{x} = 12.09$ ounces. The new 95% confidence interval estimate is

$$12.09 \pm 1.96\frac{0.2}{\sqrt{400}}$$

$$12.09 \pm 0.02$$

12.07 ounces -------------------- 12.11 ounces

Notice that by increasing the sample size to 400 cans, the margin of error is reduced from the original 0.04 ounces to 0.02 ounces. The production manager now believes that his sample mean is within ±0.02 ounces of the true population mean.

He was able to reduce the margin of error without reducing the confidence level. However, the downside is that a sample of 400 cans instead of 100 cans will cost more money and take more time. That's the trade-off. Absent the possibility of reducing the population standard deviation, if he wants to reduce the margin of error, he must either reduce the confidence level or increase the sample size, or some combination of each. If he is unwilling to do so, he will have to accept the larger margin of error.

CONFIDENCE INTERVAL ESTIMATES FOR THE POPULATION MEAN, σ UNKNOWN

In the Nagel Beverage Company example, the manager was dealing with a filling machine that had a known standard deviation in fill volume. You may encounter situations in which the standard deviation is known. However, in most cases, if you do not know the population mean, you also will not know the standard deviation. When this occurs you need to make a minor, but important, modification to the confidence interval estimation process.

STUDENT'S *t*-DISTRIBUTION

When the population standard deviation is known, the sampling distribution of the mean has only one unknown parameter: its mean, μ. This is estimated by $\bar{x}$. However, when the population standard deviation is unknown, there are two unknown parameters, μ and σ, which must be estimated by $\bar{x}$ and s, respectively. This estimation doesn't affect the general format for a confidence interval, as shown earlier in Equation 7-1:

Point Estimate ± (Critical Value)(Standard Error)

However, not knowing the population standard deviation does affect the critical value. Recall that when σ is known and the population is normally distributed or the Central Limit Theorem applies, the critical value is a *z*-value taken from the standard normal table. But when σ is not known, the critical value is a *t*-value taken from a distribution called the **Student's *t*-distribution**.

Student's t-Distribution

A family of distributions that is bell-shaped and symmetric like the standard normal distribution but with greater area in the tails. Each distribution in the *t*-family is defined by its degrees of freedom. As the degrees of freedom increase, the *t*-distribution approaches the normal distribution.

Because the specific *t*-distribution chosen is based upon its *degrees of freedom*, it is important to understand what degrees of freedom means. Recall that the sample standard deviation is an estimate of the population's standard deviation and is defined as

$$s = \sqrt{\frac{\sum(x - \bar{x})^2}{n - 1}}$$

Therefore, if we wish to estimate the population standard deviation, we must first calculate the sample mean. The sample mean is itself an estimator of a parameter, namely the population mean. The sample mean is obtained from a sample of n randomly chosen (and, therefore, independent) data values. Once the sample mean has been obtained, there are only $n - 1$ independent pieces of data information left in the sample.

To illustrate, examine a sample of size $n = 3$ in which the sample mean is calculated to be 12. This implies that the sum of the three data values equals 36 (3×12). If you know that the first two data values are 10 and 8, respectively, then the third data value is determined to be 18. Similarly, if you know that the first two data values are 18 and 7, respectively, the third data value must be 11. You are free to choose any two of the three data values. In general, if you must estimate k parameters before you are able to estimate the population's standard deviation from a sample of n data values, you have the freedom to choose any $n - k$ data values before the remaining k values are determined. This value $n - k$ is called the **degrees of freedom**.

Degrees of Freedom

The number of independent data values available to estimate the population's standard deviation. If k parameters must be estimated before the population's standard deviation can be calculated from a sample of size n, the degrees of freedom are equal to $n - k$.

When the population is normally distributed, the t-value represents the number of standard errors $\bar{x}$ is from μ, as shown in Equation 7-5. Appendix F contains a table of standardized t-values that correspond to specified tail areas and different degrees of freedom. The t-table is used to determine the critical value when we do not know the population standard deviation. Note, in Equation 7-5, we use the sample standard deviation, s, to estimate the population standard deviation, σ. The fact that we are estimating σ is the reason the t-distribution is more spread out (i.e., has a larger standard deviation) than the normal distribution (see Figure 7-5). By estimating σ, we are introducing more uncertainty into the estimation process; therefore, to achieve the same level of confidence requires a larger number of standard deviations. As the sample size increases, our estimate of σ becomes better and the t-distribution converges to the z-distribution.

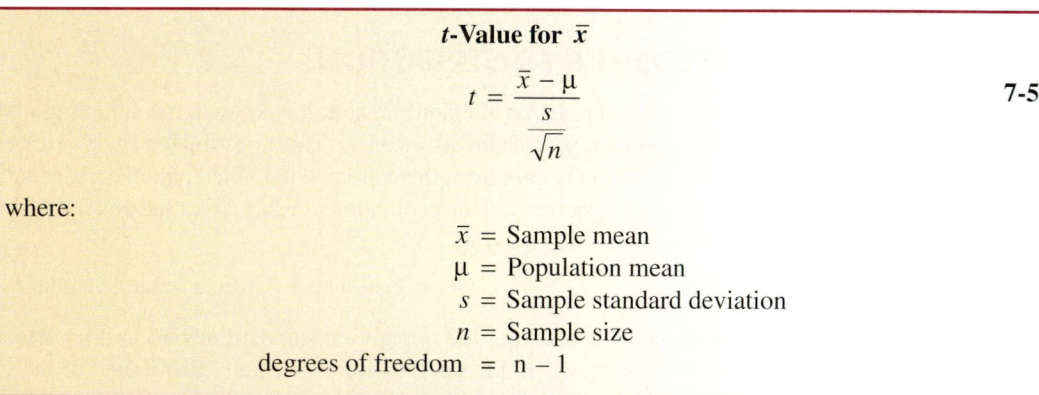

t-Value for $\bar{x}$

$$t = \frac{\bar{x} - \mu}{\dfrac{s}{\sqrt{n}}}$$

7-5

where:

$\bar{x}$ = Sample mean
μ = Population mean
s = Sample standard deviation
n = Sample size
degrees of freedom = $n - 1$

FIGURE 7-5

t **Distribution and Normal Distribution**

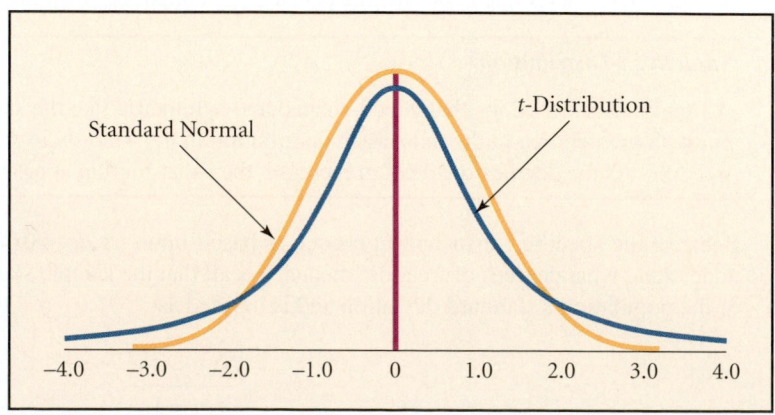

We should emphasize that the *t*-distribution is based on the assumption that the population is normally distributed. Although beyond the scope of this text, it can be shown that as long as the population is reasonably symmetric, the *t*-distribution can be used.

Excel and Minitab Tutorial

Heritage Software—Heritage Software, a maker of educational and business software, operates a service center in Tulsa, Oklahoma, where employees respond to customer calls about questions and problems with the company's software packages. Recently, a team of Heritage employees was asked to study the average length of time service representatives spend with customers. The team decided that a simple random sample of 25 calls would be collected and the population mean call time would be estimated based on the sample data. Not only did the team not know the average length of time, μ, but it also didn't know the standard deviation of length of service time, σ.

Table 7-1 shows the sample data for 25 calls, along with a box and whisker diagram. (These data are on your CD-ROM in a file called *Heritage*.) After examining the box and whisker diagram for the sample data and observing that the median is approximately equidistant between the first and third quartiles and that the whiskers extend about the same distance in each direction, the managers at Heritage Software are willing to assume the population of call times is approximately normal.

Heritage's sample mean and standard deviation are

$$\bar{x} = 7.088 \text{ minutes}$$
$$s = 4.64 \text{ minutes}$$

If the managers need a single-valued estimate of the population mean, they would use the point estimate, $\bar{x} = 7.088$ minutes. However, they should realize that this point estimate is subject to sampling error. To take the sampling error into account, the managers can construct a confidence interval estimate. Equation 7-6 shows the formula for the confidence interval estimate for the population mean when the population standard deviation is unknown.

Confidence Interval Estimate for μ, σ Unknown

$$\bar{x} \pm t_{\alpha/2} \frac{s}{\sqrt{n}}$$

7-6

where:

$\bar{x}$ = Sample mean

$t_{\alpha/2}$ = Critical value from the *t*-distribution with $n - 1$ degrees of freedom for a $1 - \alpha$ level

s = Sample standard deviation

n = Sample size

TABLE 7-1

Sample Call Times for Heritage Software

7.1	11.6	12.4	8.5	0.4
13.6	1.7	11.0	6.1	11.0
1.4	16.9	3.7	3.3	0.8
3.6	2.6	14.6	6.1	6.4
1.9	7.7	8.8	6.9	9.1

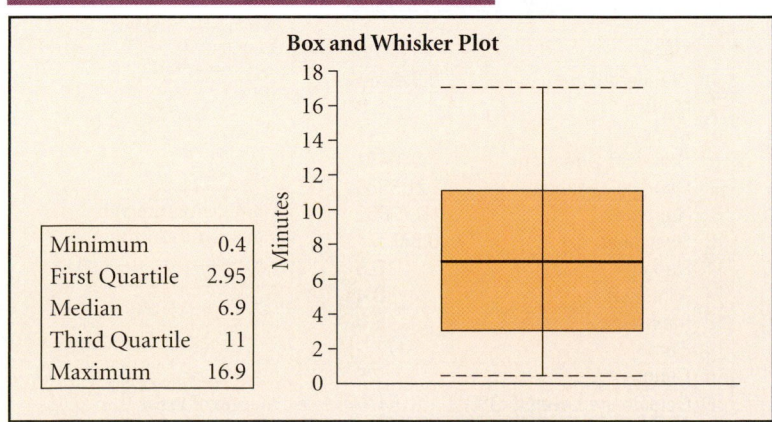

Box and Whisker Plot

Minimum	0.4
First Quartile	2.95
Median	6.9
Third Quartile	11
Maximum	16.9

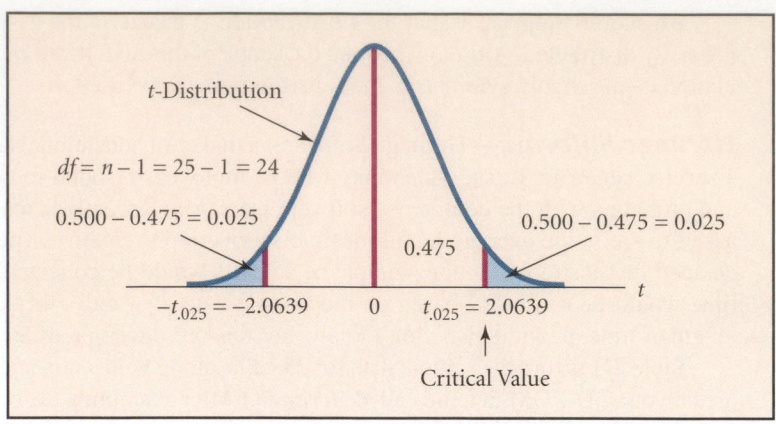

The first step is to specify the desired confidence level. For example, suppose the Heritage team specifies a

95% confidence level.

To get the critical *t*-value from the *t*-table in Appendix F, go to the top of the table to the row labeled *Conf. Level*. Locate the column headed 0.95. Next, go to the row corresponding to

$n - 1 = 25 - 1 = 24$ degrees of freedom.

The critical *t*-value for 95% confidence and 24 degrees of freedom is

$$t_{\alpha/2} = 2.0639.$$

Figure 7-6 illustrates the *t*-distribution and the critical value. You can get the *t* critical value by using Excel's **TINV** function. For this example, enter **TINV(0.05,24)** to get 2.0639. (Note: The **TINV** function requires that α be used while the **NORMSINV** function requires $\alpha/2$.) You can also insert the cumulative probability 0.975 into Minitab's **Calc > Probability Distribution > *t*** command.

The Heritage team can now compute the 95% confidence interval estimate using Equation 7-6, as follows:

$$\bar{x} \pm t_{.025} \frac{s}{\sqrt{n}}$$

$$7.088 \pm 2.0639 \frac{4.64}{\sqrt{25}}$$

$$7.088 \pm 1.915$$

5.173 min. ------------------------ 9.003 min.

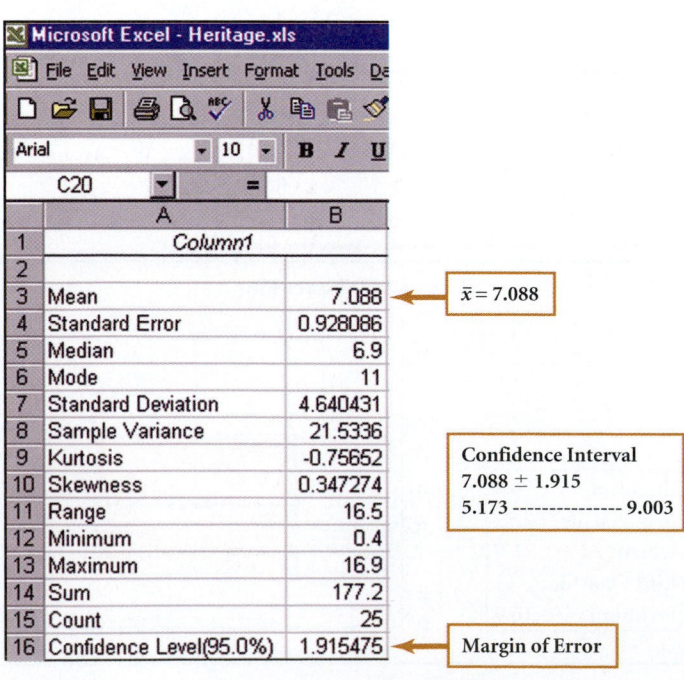

FIGURE 7-8

Minitab Output for the Heritage Example

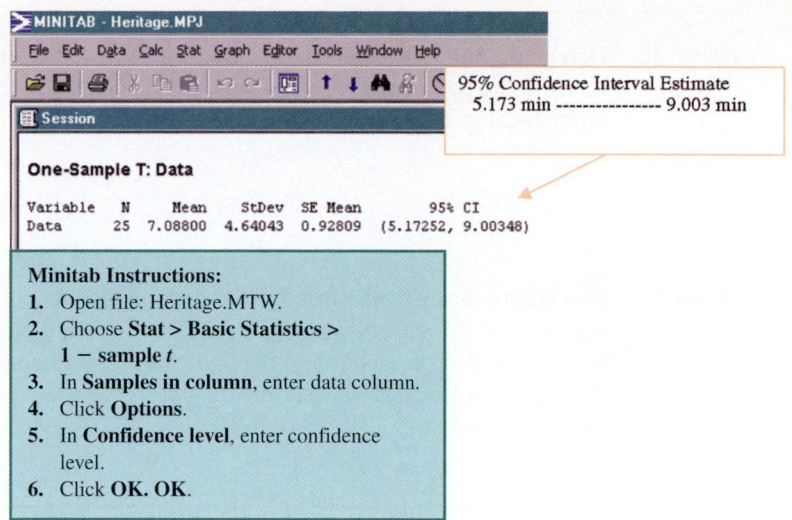

Therefore, based on the random sample of 25 calls and the 95% confidence interval, the Heritage Software team has estimated the true average time per call to be between 5.173 minutes and 9.003 minutes.

Excel and Minitab have procedures for computing the confidence interval estimate of the population mean. The Excel output is shown in Figure 7-7. Note, the margin of error is printed. You will have to use it and the sample mean to compute the upper and lower limits. Figure 7-8 shows the results when Minitab is used to compute the 95% confidence interval estimate for the Heritage Company.

EXAMPLE 7-3: CONFIDENCE INTERVAL ESTIMATE FOR μ, σ UNKNOWN

Medlin & Associates   Medlin & Associates is a regional CPA firm located near Minneapolis. Recently a team conducted an audit for a discount chain. One part of the audit involved developing an estimate for the mean dollar error in total charges that occur during the checkout process. They wish to develop a 90% confidence interval estimate for the population mean. To do so, they can use the following steps.

Step 1:   **Define the population and select a simple random sample of size n from the population.**
In this case, the population consists of errors made in all customers' bills at the discount chain store in a given week. A simple random sample of $n = 20$ is selected, with the following data (Note: Positive values indicate that the customer was overcharged.)

| $0.00 | $1.20 | $0.43 | $1.00 | $1.47 | $0.83 | $0.50 | $3.34 | $1.58 | $1.46 |
| −$0.36 | −$1.10 | $2.60 | $0.00 | $0.00 | −$1.70 | $0.83 | $1.99 | $0.00 | $1.34 |

Step 2:   **Specify the confidence level.**
A 90% confidence interval estimate is desired.

Step 3:   **Compute the sample mean and sample standard deviation.**
After the sample has been selected and the billing errors have been determined for each of the 20 customers sampled, the sample mean is computed using:

$$\bar{x} = \frac{\sum x}{n} = \frac{\$15.41}{20} = \$0.77$$

The sample standard deviation is computed using:

$$s = \sqrt{\frac{\sum(x - \bar{x})^2}{n - 1}} = \sqrt{\frac{(0.00 - 0.77)^2 + (1.20 - 0.77)^2 + \cdots + (1.34 - 0.77)^2}{20 - 1}} = \$1.194$$

Step 4: **Determine the standard error of the sampling distribution.**
Because the population standard deviation is unknown, the standard error of the sampling distribution is estimated using:

$$\sigma_{\bar{x}} \approx \frac{s}{\sqrt{n}} = \frac{1.194}{\sqrt{20}} = \$0.27$$

Step 5: **Determine the critical value for the desired level of confidence.**
Because we do not know the population standard deviation, the critical value will come from the *t*-distribution, providing we can assume that the population is normally distributed. A box and whisker diagram can give some insight about how the population might look.

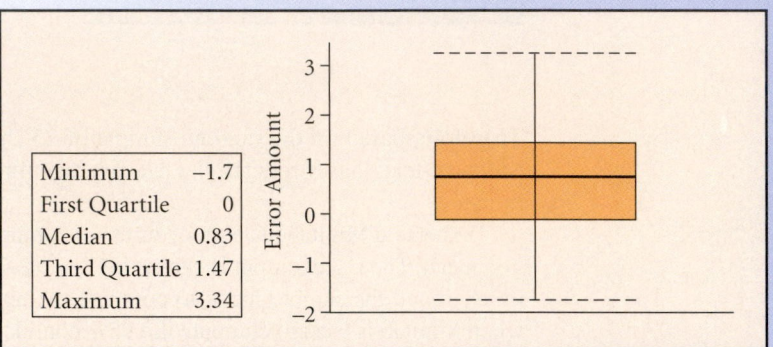

Minimum	−1.7
First Quartile	0
Median	0.83
Third Quartile	1.47
Maximum	3.34

This diagram does not indicate that there is any serious skewness or other abnormality in the data, so we will continue with the normal distribution assumption.

Then the critical value for 90% confidence and 20 − 1 = 19 degrees of freedom is found in the *t*-distribution table as $t = 1.7291$.

Step 6: **Compute the confidence interval estimate.**
The 90% confidence interval estimate for the population mean is

$$\bar{x} \pm t_{.05} \frac{s}{\sqrt{n}}$$

$$0.77 \pm 1.7291 \frac{1.194}{\sqrt{20}}$$

$$0.77 \pm 0.46$$

$$\$0.31 \text{ -------------------------------- } \$1.23$$

Thus, based upon the sample data, with 90% confidence, the auditors can conclude that the population mean dollar error at the checkout is between $0.31 and $1.23.

Estimation with Larger Sample Sizes

We saw earlier that a change in sample size can affect the margin of error in a statistical estimation situation when the population standard deviation is known. This is also true in applications in which the standard deviation is not known. In fact, the effect of a change is compounded because the change in sample size affects both the calculation of the standard error and the critical value from the *t*-distribution.

The *t*-distribution table in Appendix F shows degrees of freedom up to 30 and then incrementally to 500. Observe that for any confidence level, as the degrees of freedom increase, the *t*-value gets smaller as it approaches a limit equal to the *z*-value from the standard normal table in Appendix D for the same confidence level.

If your degrees of freedom is not shown in the t-distribution table use Excel **TINV** function or Minitab's **Calc > Probability Distribution > t** command to get the critical t-value for any specified degrees of freedom and then use Equation 7-6.

You should have noticed that the format for confidence interval estimates for μ is essentially the same, regardless of whether the population standard deviation is known. The basic format is always

Point Estimate ± (Critical Value)(Standard Error)

Later in this chapter, we introduce estimation examples in which the population value of interest is p, the population proportion. Regardless of the parameter of interest, the same confidence interval format is used. In addition, the trade-offs between margin of error, confidence level, and sample size that were discussed in this section also apply to every other estimation situation.

SUMMARY: CONFIDENCE INTERVAL ESTIMATES FOR A SINGLE POPULATION MEAN

A confidence interval estimate for a single population mean can be developed using the following steps.

1. Define the population of interest and the variable for which you wish to estimate the population mean.

2. Determine the sample size and select a simple random sample.

3. Compute the confidence interval as follows, depending on the conditions that exist:

■ If σ is known and the population is normally distributed or the sample size is large ($n \geq 30$), use:

$$\bar{x} \pm z_{\alpha/2} \frac{\sigma}{\sqrt{n}}$$

■ If σ is unknown, and we can assume that the population distribution is approximately normal, use:

$$\bar{x} \pm t_{\alpha/2} \frac{s}{\sqrt{n}}$$

7-1: EXERCISES

Skill Development

7.1 Assume a sample of size n has been obtained from a normal distribution. Determine the critical value from a t-distribution when you wish to estimate the population mean in each of the following cases:
   a. Confidence coefficient = 0.95, $n = 26$
   b. Confidence coefficient = 0.90, $n = 31$
   c. Confidence coefficient = 0.98, $n = 15$
   d. Confidence coefficient = 0.99, $n = 19$
   e. Confidence coefficient = 0.80, $n = 21$
   f. Confidence coefficient = 0.90, $n = 17$

7.2 Assuming that the population standard deviation is known, compute the critical values from the standard normal distribution table in each of the following cases:
   a. Confidence coefficient = 0.95, $n = 31$
   b. Confidence coefficient = 0.90, $n = 31$
   c. Confidence coefficient = 0.98, $n = 15$
   d. Confidence coefficient = 0.99, $n = 36$
   e. Confidence coefficient = 0.88, $n = 56$
   f. Confidence coefficient = 0.90, $n = 41$

7.3 Determine the 90% confidence interval estimate for the population mean.
   a. $\bar{x} = 102.36$, $n = 17$, $\sigma = 1.26$
   b. $\bar{x} = 56.33$, $n = 21$, $s = 22.4$

7.4 Determine the 95% confidence interval estimate for a population mean of a normal distribution, given the following information:
   a. $\bar{x} = 13.56$, $n = 300$, $\sigma = 12.6$
   b. $\bar{x} = 2.45$, $n = 31$, $s = 22.3$

7.5 For each of the following situations, determine the margin of error
   a. Confidence coefficient = 0.98, $\bar{x} = 2.47$, $n = 12$, $\sigma = 6.58$
   b. Confidence coefficient = 0.95, $\bar{x} = 13.9$, $n = 21$, $s = 2.33$
   c. Confidence coefficient = 0.80, $\bar{x} = 114.7$, $n = 500$, $s = 15.6$

7.6 Determine the 99% confidence interval estimate for the population mean of a normal distribution given $n = 500$, $\sigma = 1.22$, and $\bar{x} = 34.6$.

7.7   Determine the margin of error for a confidence interval estimate for the population mean of a normal distribution, given the following information:
a. Confidence coefficient = 0.98, $n = 13$, $s = 15.68$
b. Confidence coefficient = 0.99, $n = 25$, $\sigma = 3.47$
c. Confidence coefficient = 0.98, standard error = 2.356

7.8   Determine the margin of error for a confidence interval estimate for the population mean of a normal distribution, given the following information:
a. Confidence coefficient = 0.80, $n = 11$, $s = 114.7$
b. Confidence coefficient = 0.98, $n = 3$, $s = 26.96$

7.9   Given the following data from a simple random sample for the population of interest, compute the 95% confidence interval estimate. (What assumption must be made about the population?)

114	97	107	101	84	84	85	66	108	76

7.10   The following data were collected in a simple random sample from a normally distributed population. Construct a 90% confidence interval estimate for the population mean.

11	14	10	12	11	11	12	12	15

Business Applications

7.11   Mortimor's is a nice, upscale restaurant specializing in seafood dishes. The owner is interested in estimating the mean dollars spent per table on appetizers. He has selected a simple random sample of 200 sales receipts from the past year's receipts and has calculated the mean and standard deviation for the dollar amount of each bill that was allocated to appetizers. These results are

$$\bar{x} = \$4.22 \qquad s = \$2.59$$

a. Based on these sample data, what is the point estimate for the mean amount spent on appetizers per table at Mortimor's?
b. Construct and interpret a 95% confidence interval estimate for the true mean amount spent per table on appetizers.

7.12   Presto Pizza delivers pizzas throughout its local market area at no charge to the customer. However, customers often tip the driver. The owner is interested in estimating the mean tip income per delivery. To do this, she has selected a simple random sample of 12 deliveries and has recorded the tips that were received by the drivers. These data are

$2.25	$2.50	$2.25	$2.00	$2.00	$1.50
$0.00	$2.00	$1.50	$2.00	$3.00	$1.50

a. Based on these sample data, what is the best point estimate to use as an estimate of the true mean tip per delivery?

b. Suppose the owner is interested in developing a 90% confidence interval estimate. Given the fact that the sample size is small and the population standard deviation is unknown, what distribution will be used to obtain the critical value?
c. Referring to part b, what assumption is required to use the specified distribution to obtain the critical value? Develop a box and whisker diagram to illustrate whether this assumption seems to be reasonably satisfied.
d. Referring to parts b and c, construct and interpret the 90% confidence interval estimate for the population mean.

7.13   The Traveler Rent-A-Car Company is interested in estimating the mean number of miles its cars are driven on a particular holiday. From the 23,000 cars it owns nationwide, analysts have selected a simple random sample of 200 cars on the holiday in question. The mileage for each car was recorded. The data computed from the sample data were

$$\bar{x} = 54.5 \text{ miles}$$
$$s = 14.0 \text{ miles}$$

a. Produce a 95% confidence interval estimate for the mean miles driven by all 23,000 vehicles owned by the company.
b. Traveler's vice president of operations received a report from the company's southwestern region. It indicated the region had rented 200 cars during the holiday and had received $2,500 in fees charged for mileage. Assume Traveler's charges 25 cents per mile as a mileage fee. On the basis of the confidence interval calculated in part a, would you say that the vice president should investigate the billing practices of the southwestern region? Support your opinion with statistical reasoning and logic.
c. Suppose the Traveler Rent-A-Car Company wishes to decrease the margin of error in the estimate for average miles driven per car per day. Discuss the three options available to the managers, and provide examples for each case that demonstrate that your options actually do decrease the margin of error.

7.14   The First National Bank is considering a survey of its customers to estimate the mean number of checks written per month. A sample of 360 customers was selected. The sample values were

$$\bar{x} = 33.4$$
$$s = 11.2$$

a. Provide a 90% confidence interval estimate for the mean number of checks written and interpret the estimate.
b. Suppose a clerical mistake was made in recording the number of customers who were surveyed and the actual sample size was 36, not 360. Recompute the 90% confidence interval estimate and compare it to the estimate developed in part a. Why are the esti-

mates different even though the sample mean and standard deviation did not change?

7.15 Agri-Beef, Inc., is a large midwestern farming operation. The company has been a leader in employing statistical analysis techniques in its business. Recently, John Goldberg, operations manager, requested that a random sample of cattle be selected and fed a special diet. The cattle were weighed before the start of the new feeding program and at the end. John wished to estimate the average daily weight gain for cattle on the new program. Two hundred cattle were tested, and the sample results were

$$\bar{x} = 1.2 \text{ lb. per day gain}$$
$$s = 0.50 \text{ lb}$$

a. Obtain a 95% confidence interval estimate for the true average daily weight gain.
b. Provide a 90% confidence interval estimate for the true average daily weight gain.
c. Discuss the difference between the estimates found in parts a and b and indicate the advantages and disadvantages of each.

7.16 The Evergreen Company operates retail pharmacies in 10 eastern states. Recently, the company's internal audit department selected a random sample of 300 prescriptions filled throughout the system. The objective of the sampling was to estimate the average dollar value of all prescriptions filled by the company. The data collected were

$$\bar{x} = \$14.23$$
$$s = 3.00$$

a. Determine the 90% confidence interval estimate for the true average sales value for prescriptions filled. Interpret the interval estimate.
b. One of its retail outlets recently reported that it had monthly revenue of $7,392 from 528 prescriptions. Are such results to be expected? Do you believe that the retail outlet should be audited? Support your answer with calculations and logic.

7.17 Marine World–Africa USA is a facility located near San Francisco, California, where people can see animals from the ocean and from Africa on display and performing in shows. Customers pay for a full-day ticket. The management is interested in determining the average length of time customers actually spend at the park. They select a simple random sample of customers and ask them their arrival time as they leave the park, from which they determine the length of stay for each customer. A total of 144 customers were selected at random, and the sample results were

$$\bar{x} = 311 \text{ minutes}$$
$$s = 72 \text{ minutes}$$

a. Obtain a 90% confidence interval estimate for the mean time spent at the park. Interpret the interval estimate.

b. If park administration wishes to reduce the margin of error from that which you determined in part a, what options exist to do so? Discuss.

7.18 The Apex Entertainment Company owns and operates movie theaters in Wyoming. The president of the company is concerned that home videocassette recorders are hurting business because people can simply rent a movie and watch it at home. He has directed a staff member to estimate the mean number of movies rented by people in Wyoming in December. A phone survey involving a random sample of 300 homes was conducted, and the results were

$$\bar{x} = 2.4 \text{ movies}$$
$$s = 1.6 \text{ movies}$$

a. Develop and interpret the 95% confidence interval estimate for the true mean number of movies rented by people in Wyoming in December.
b. Develop and interpret a 90% confidence interval estimate for the mean number of movies rented per month. Discuss why the width of this interval is smaller than the one you constructed in part a.

7.19 A major American pharmaceutical company has randomly sampled 14 customers who have used one of their new painkilling drugs for two months. There is concern that the drug may elevate the user's heart rate. Each of the customers in the sample had their heart rate measured after using the drug for one week. All people in the sample had heart rates of 55 prior to taking the drug. The following data were recorded for the 14 customers:

50	70	60	70	90	72	50
80	85	55	66	70	80	40

a. Suppose that you have just started working in the marketing department of the pharmaceutical company. You were given the following instructions: "Based on these sample data, construct a 90% confidence interval estimate for the true mean heart rate for the company's drug customers. Interpret the estimate." Follow these instructions.
b. Referring to your answer in part a, can the estimate be applied to all potential drug customers? Explain why or why not.
c. Refer to your calculations in part a. (1) Was the concern expressed justified? Explain your answer. (2) If the average heart rate did increase, determine the probability that a sample mean at least as large as the one obtained in your sample could have been obtained assuming the beginning mean rate is 55.

7.20 The Simmons Furniture Company selected a random sample of nine sofas that were made at its Memphis factory. Each sofa was subjected to a test process that simulated people sitting on the cushions. The test requires that a heavy object be repeatedly dropped on the cushion until the fabric wears out. The following data reflect the number of drops that were recorded for each of the nine sofas:

13,356	12,742	15,345
9,459	10,634	14,309
14,098	11,245	12,652

a. Obtain a 95% confidence interval estimate for the mean number of drops until the sofa cushions wear out. Interpret the result.

b. Simmons wishes to advertise that the sofa fabric will last at least 20 years. If a sofa is sat upon an average of once a day, could Simmons justify their proposed advertisement? Explain your answer.

Advanced Business Applications

7.21 The Aims Investment Company is interested in estimating the average number of mutual funds its customers have in their portfolios. A random sample of investment customers is located in the CD-ROM file called *Aims*.

a. Based on the sample data, construct a 90% confidence interval estimate for the mean number of mutual funds for all their customers. Interpret this interval.

b. Suppose that the interval estimate that you computed in part a has a margin of error that is greater than Aims management wants. Discuss what options are open to Aims. What are the advantages and disadvantages of each option?

7.22 The Ecco Company makes electronics products for distribution throughout the world. As quality manager, you are interested in the warranty claims that are made by customers who have experienced problems with Ecco products. The CD-ROM file called *Ecco* contains data for a random sample of warranty claims.

a. You are to develop and interpret a 90% confidence interval estimate for the mean dollar claim.

b. Develop and interpret a 95% confidence interval estimate for the mean warranty claim amount for only those products that were made on the graveyard shift (shift 3 in the data file). There has been some concern within Ecco management that the graveyard shift's workmanship is not of the caliber of the other two shifts. Using the confidence interval you have calculated and any other statistical techniques required, address this issue.

7.23 Refer to Exercise 7.22. Ecco's quality control manager has been concerned with the source of what he believes to be high warranty claims at the Boise site. He believes that corrosion may be the source.

a. Develop and interpret a 95% confidence interval estimate for the mean warranty claim amount for products produced at the Boise site. Do this for each of the complaint sources (complaint codes 1 to 4). (You must produce four separate confidence intervals.) Now compute the 95% confidence interval estimate for mean warranty claims for Boise that were based on corrosion complaints. How do these two interval estimates compare?

b. Write a letter to the quality control manager that addresses his concern about the source of the high warranty claims. Identify, if possible, what complaint is producing the highest warranty claims. Discuss the implications of the four confidence intervals concerning the average warranty claims for each complaint type.

7.24 Clair's Deli serves many types of sandwiches, soups, and salads. All sandwiches are made fresh at the time of the order. Customers can eat inside at tables or use the drive-through window to order food to go. The manager is interested in estimating the mean time customers spend in the drive-through line. The CD-ROM file called *Clairs Deli* contains data from a simple random sample of 50 drive-through customers. These data, measured in minutes, are also shown here.

6.6	6.9	6.4	12.2	11.3
9.0	11.1	9.5	9.9	12.5
11.9	16.3	9.4	2.5	13.2
4.4	7.4	10.8	9.7	13.2
9.8	10.1	8.2	8.2	9.0
9.1	7.4	9.9	14.5	8.9
6.2	9.3	9.8	5.7	6.2
9.3	8.2	15.9	9.8	7.0
7.9	18.4	14.1	10.2	9.3
11.5	8.2	18.7	11.5	11.1

a. Develop a box and whisker diagram and discuss whether the sample data appear to come from a population that is approximately normally distributed.

b. Regardless of your conclusions in part a, develop and interpret a 95% confidence interval estimate for the mean time the customers wait in the drive-through line.

7-2 DETERMINING THE REQUIRED SAMPLE SIZE FOR ESTIMATING THE POPULATION MEAN

We have discussed the basic trade-offs that are present in all statistical estimations: the desire to have a high confidence level, a low margin of error, and a small sample size. The problem is these three objectives conflict. For a given sample size, a high confidence level will tend to generate a large margin of error. For a given confidence level, a small sample size will result in an increased margin of error. Reducing the margin of error requires either reducing the confidence level or increasing the sample size or both.

A common question from business decision makers who are planning an estimation application is, "How large a sample size do I really need?" To answer this question, we usually begin by asking a couple of questions of our own:

1. How much money do you have budgeted to do the sampling?
2. How much will it cost to select each item in the sample?

The answers to these questions provide the upper limit on the sample size that can be selected. For instance, if the decision maker indicates that she has a $2,000 budget for selecting the sample and the cost will be about $10 per unit to collect the sample, the sample size's upper limit is $2,000 ÷ $10 = 200 units.

Keeping in mind the estimation trade-offs discussed earlier, the issue should be fully discussed with the decision maker. For instance, is a sample of 200 sufficient to give the desired margin of error at a specified confidence level? Is 200 more than is needed to achieve the desired margin of error?

Therefore, before we can give a definite answer about what sample size is needed, the decision maker must specify her confidence level and a desired margin of error. Then the required sample size can be computed.

DETERMINING THE REQUIRED SAMPLE SIZE FOR ESTIMATING μ, σ KNOWN

Mission Valley Power Company—Consider the Mission Valley Power Company (MVP) in northwest Michigan, which has more than 6,000 residential customers. In response to a request by the Michigan Public Utility Commission, MVP needs to estimate the average kilowatts of electricity used by customers on February 1. The only way to get this number is to select a random sample of customers and take a meter reading after 5:00 P.M. on January 31 and again after 5:00 P.M. on February 1. The commission has specified that any estimate presented in the utility's report must be based on a 95% confidence level. Further, the margin of error must not exceed ±30 kilowatts. Given these requirements, what size sample is needed?

To answer this question, if the population standard deviation is known, we start with Equation 7-4, the equation for calculating the margin of error.

$$e = z_{\alpha/2} \frac{\sigma}{\sqrt{n}}$$

We next substitute into this equation the values we know. For example, the margin of error was specified to be

$$e = 30 \text{ kilowatts}$$

The confidence level was specified to be 95%. The z-value for 95% is 1.96. (Refer to the standard normal table in Appendix D.) This gives us

$$30 = 1.96 \frac{\sigma}{\sqrt{n}}$$

We need to know the population standard deviation. MVP might know this value from other studies that it has conducted in the past or from similar studies done by other utility companies. Assume for this example that σ, the population standard deviation, is 200 kilowatts. We can now substitute

$$\sigma = 200$$

into the equation for e, as follows,

$$30 = 1.96 \frac{200}{\sqrt{n}}$$

We now have a single equation with one unknown, n, the sample size. Doing the algebra to solve for n, we get

$$n = \left(\frac{1.96\,(200)}{30}\right)^2 = 170.73 \approx 171 \text{ customers}$$

Thus, to meet the requirements of the utility commission, a sample of $n = 171$ customers should be selected. Equation 7-7 is used to determine the required sample size for estimating a single population mean when σ is known.

Sample Size Requirement for Estimating μ, σ Known

$$n = \left(\frac{z_{\alpha/2}\sigma}{e}\right)^2 = \frac{z_{\alpha/2}^2\sigma^2}{e^2}$$

7-7

where:

$z_{\alpha/2}$ = Critical value for the specified $1 - \alpha$ confidence level
e = Desired margin of error
σ = Population standard deviation

Always round up to the next highest integer when solving for n.

If MVP feels that the cost of sampling 171 customers will be too high, it might appeal to the commission to allow for a higher margin of error or a lower confidence level. For example, if the confidence level is lowered to 90%, the z-value is lowered to 1.645, as found in the standard normal table.[2]

We can now use Equation 7-7 to determine the revised sample-size requirement.

$$n = \frac{1.645^2 (200)^2}{30^2} = 120.27 \approx 121$$

MVP will need to sample only 121 (120.27 rounded up) customers for a confidence level of 90% rather than 95%.

EXAMPLE 7-4: DETERMINING THE REQUIRED SAMPLE SIZE, σ KNOWN

Gordon's Self-Service Gasoline   The general manager for Gordon's Self-Service Gasoline is interested in estimating the mean number of gallons of gasoline that are purchased by customers at his Kansas City location. He would like his estimate to be within plus or minus 0.50 gallons, and he would like the estimate to be at the 99% confidence level. Past studies have shown that the standard deviation for purchase amount is 4.0 gallons. To determine the required sample size, he can use the following steps.

Step 1:   Specify the desired margin of error.
The manager wishes to have his estimate be within ±0.50 gallons, so the margin of error is
$$e = 0.50 \text{ gallons}$$

Step 2:   Determine the population standard deviation.
Based on other studies, the manager is willing to conclude that the population standard deviation is known. Thus,
$$\sigma = 4.0$$

Step 3:   Determine the critical value for the desired level of confidence.
The critical value will be a z-value from the standard normal table for 99% confidence. This is
$$z_{0.005} = 2.575$$

---

[2]You can also use the Excel function, NORMSINV, to determine the z-value.

Step 4:   **Compute the required sample size using Equation 7-7.**
The required sample size is

$$n = \frac{z_{\alpha/2}^2\sigma^2}{e^2} = \frac{2.575^2 4.0^2}{0.50^2} = 424.36 = 425 \text{ customers}$$

Note: The sample size is always rounded up to the next integer value.

DETERMINING THE REQUIRED SAMPLE SIZE FOR ESTIMATING μ, σ UNKNOWN

Equation 7-7 assumes that you know the population standard deviation. Although this may be the case in some situations, most likely we won't know the population standard deviation. To get around this problem, two approaches can be used. One is to use a value for σ that is considered to be at least as large as the true σ. This will provide a conservatively large sample size.

The second option is to select a **pilot sample**, a sample from the population that is used explicitly to estimate σ.

Pilot Sample

A sample taken from the population of interest that is used to provide an estimate for the population standard deviation.

$\mathcal{E}$XAMPLE 7-5: DETERMINING THE REQUIRED SAMPLE SIZE σ UNKNOWN

Georgia Lumber Mill   Consider a Georgia lumber mill manager who wishes to know the average diameter of logs the mill cuts. Not only does she not know μ, she also does not know the population standard deviation. She wants a 90% confidence level and is willing to have a margin of error of 0.50 inch in estimating the true mean diameter. The required sample size can be determined using the following steps.

Step 1:   **Specify the desired margin of error.**
The manager wants the estimate to be within ±0.50 inch of the true mean. Thus,
$$e = 0.50$$

Step 2:   **Determine an estimate for the population standard deviation.**
The manager will select a pilot sample of $n = 20$ logs and measure the diameter of each. These values are

18.9	22.4	24.6	25.7	26.3	28.4	21.7	31.0	19.0	31.7
17.4	25.5	20.1	34.3	25.9	20.3	21.6	25.8	31.6	28.8

The estimate for the population standard deviation is the sample standard deviation for the pilot sample. This is computed using:

$$s = \sqrt{\frac{\sum(x-\bar{x})^2}{n-1}} = \sqrt{\frac{(18.9-25.05)^2 + (22.4-25.05)^2 + \cdots + (28.8-25.05)^2}{20-1}} = 4.85$$

We will use
$$\sigma \approx 4.85$$

Step 3:   **Determine the critical value for the desired level of confidence.**
The critical value will be a z-value from the standard normal table. The 90% confidence level gives
$$z_{.05} = 1.645$$

Step 4:   **Calculate the required sample size using Equation 7-7.**
The required sample size is

$$n = \frac{z_{\alpha/2}^2 \sigma^2}{e^2} = \frac{(1.645^2)(4.85^2)}{0.50^2} = 254.61 = 255$$

The required sample size is 255, but we can use the pilot sample as part of this total. Thus, the net required sample size in this case is $255 - 20 = 235$.

7-2: EXERCISES

Skill Development

7.25   Suppose it is known that the population standard deviation is 40. If you wish to estimate the population mean using a 95% confidence interval estimate with a margin of error of ± 2.5, what sample size will be required?

7.26   If you wish to estimate a population mean and have your estimate be within ±0.25 of the true value and you wish to have a confidence level of 99%, what sample size will be required if the population standard deviation is known to be 1.20?

7.27   Suppose, as part of your job, you are asked to estimate a population mean using a 90% confidence interval and a margin of error of 60. What size sample is required if the following pilot sample is used to determine a value to use for the population standard deviation?

3,239	3,144	2,960	2,507	2,842
3,134	3,249	2,908	2,754	2,715

7.28   A sample size must be determined for estimating a population mean, given the confidence level is to be 90%, and the desired margin of error is 0.30. The largest value in the population is thought to be 15, and the smallest value is thought to be 5.
   a. Calculate the sample size required to estimate the population using a conservatively large sample size. (Hint: Use the range ÷ 4 option.)
   b. If a smaller sample size is desired (use the range ÷ 6 option), calculate the required sample size. Discuss why the answers in parts a and b are different.

7.29   The required sample size for estimating a population mean is to be calculated, given that the desired margin of error is 40 and a pilot sample of 30 items indicated a sample standard deviation of 900.
   a. Determine the required sample size if the confidence level is to be 90%.
   b. Increase the confidence level to 95% and determine the percentage change in the resulting sample size.

7.30   A sample size is required for estimating a population mean, given that the confidence level is to be 99%, the desired margin of error is 2, and a pilot sample of 50 items indicated a sample standard deviation of 46.5. Calculate the number of additional items that must be

sampled to provide the required estimation of the population mean.

7.31   There are trade-offs that exist when estimating a single population mean.
   a. For a given sample size, what must be done to decrease the margin of error?
   b. What will be affected if the confidence level is to be increased for a given sample size?
   c. How can the confidence level increase and the margin of error decrease at the same time?

7.32   The standard deviation of a population is thought to be somewhere in the interval (250, 300). The population mean is to be estimated using a confidence interval with a 90% confidence level. The desired margin of error is 20.
   a. Calculate the required sample size using the smallest value of the standard deviation perceived to be possible.
   b. Repeat the calculation in part a using the largest value of the standard deviation perceived to be possible.
   c. Discuss why the sample size requirements would be greater when a population has a larger variation.

Business Applications

7.33   A study is being planned to estimate the mean number of inches that trees will grow per year in a forest. The analysts wish to have 90% confidence and want to estimate the mean within ±0.20 inch. A pilot study was conducted that showed a sample standard deviation equal to 0.80 inch. What size sample is needed for this study?

7.34   The Longmont Computer Leasing Company leases computers and peripherals such as laser printers. The printers have a counter that keeps track of the number of pages that are printed. The company wishes to estimate the mean number of pages that will be printed in a month on their leased printers. The plan is to select a random sample of printers and record the number on each printer's counter at the beginning of May. At the end of May, the number on the counter will be recorded again, and the difference will be the number of copies on that printer for the month. The company wants the estimate to be within ±100 pages of the true mean, with a 95% confidence level.

a. The standard deviation in pages printed is thought to be about 1,400 pages. How many printers should be sampled?

b. Suppose that the conjecture concerning the size of the standard deviation is off (plus or minus) by as much as 10%. What percentage change in the required sample size would this produce?

7.35 Arco Manufacturing makes electronic pagers. As part of the company's quality efforts, the company wishes to estimate the mean number of days the pager is used before repair is needed. A pilot sample of 40 pagers indicates a sample standard deviation of 200 days. The company wishes its estimate to have a margin of error of no more than 50 days, and the confidence level must be 95%.

a. Given this information, how many additional pagers should be sampled?

b. The pilot study was initiated because of the costs involved in sampling. Each sampled observation costs approximately $10 to obtain. Originally, it was thought that the population's standard deviation might be as large as 300. Determine the amount of money saved by obtaining the pilot sample. (Hint: Figure the total cost of obtaining the required samples for both methods.)

7.36 The Northwest Pacific Phone Company wishes to estimate the average number of minutes its customers spend on long-distance calls per month. The company wants the estimate made with 99% confidence and a margin of error of no more than 5 minutes.

a. A previous study indicated that the standard deviation for long-distance calls is 21 minutes per month. What should the sample size be?

b. Determine the required sample size if the confidence level were changed from 99% to 90%.

c. What would the required sample size be if the confidence level was 95% and the margin of error was 8 minutes?

7.37 ◉ The quality manager for a major automobile manufacturer is interested in estimating the mean number of paint defects in cars produced by the company. She wishes to have her estimate be within ± 0.10 of the true mean and wants 98% confidence in the estimate. The data in the CD-ROM file called *CarPaint* contains a pilot sample that was conducted for the purpose of determining a value to use for the population standard deviation. How many additional cars need to be sampled to provide the estimate required by the quality manager?

Advanced Business Applications

7.38 ◉ The quality manager at Ecco Company, a maker of back-up alarms for use on industrial vehicles such as forklifts, is interested in estimating the mean dollar volume for warranty claims for products made in Boise on the day shift. He has taken a pilot sample. The data for the pilot sample are in a CD-ROM file called *ECCO*.

a. Assuming that the manager wishes to estimate the mean warranty amount to within ±$8.00 with 90%

confidence, how many additional claims must be selected to develop the estimate?

b. Suppose the sample size determined in part a is more than the manager is willing to use. What options are open to the manager? Discuss.

c. Referring to parts a and b, suppose the manager wishes to cut the total sample size in half. For each option available to the manger, show specifically what must be done to achieve the reduction in sample size.

7.39 ◉ The loan manager at High-Desert Bank wishes to estimate the mean loan amount for the commercial customers of his bank. A couple of weeks ago, an intern from the nearby college collected a random sample of customers (commercial and retail). These data are in a file called *High-Desert Bank*.

a. Use the data in this sample to develop a 95% confidence interval estimate for the population mean loan amount for commercial customers. The manager's promotion program had a goal of raising the average loan amount for commercial customers to $67,500. Has the manager reached this goal? Explain your answer.

b. Referring to part a, suppose the loan manager would like to maintain the 95% confidence interval but with a margin of error that is 40% of the existing margin of error. How many, if any, additional loan customers must be sampled?

c. Refer to parts a and b. Suppose the manager feels the new required sample size is too large but does not want to increase the margin of error, what must he do? Assume he wants to cut the required sample size by 15% of that found in part b, what specifically will be required? Discuss the impact of these trade-offs.

7.40 ◉ The state Department of Transportation is experimenting with a new scale for weighing trucks. This new scale is called a Weigh-in-Motion (WIM) scale because it weighs trucks while they are driving down the highway. The traditional method is a static scale that is at the port of entry (POE). The trucks pull into the scale, stop, and are weighed. The POE scale is assumed to provide accurate weights. The state has set up a test area on one stretch of highway. The WIM scale is located about a half-mile before the POE scale. A sample of trucks are weighed on the WIM scale and then on the POE scale. Some trucks were weighed in each of several months beginning in February. These data are in the file called *Trucks*.

a. Suppose that the department's objective is to estimate the mean difference between WIM gross weight and POE gross weight for those trucks that were weighed in February. (Note, February trucks have a Month Code = 2.) The estimate is to be based on a 95% confidence level. Using the sample data, develop this estimate and interpret it. (Hint: Compute a new variable that is WIM gross − POE gross.)

b. Referring to part a, suppose the department wants the margin of error reduced to no more than 50 pounds, with 95% confidence. Using the sample data already collected as a pilot sample, how many more trucks would be needed to estimate the February mean difference? Comment on this result.

c. Suppose the department wishes to estimate the speed of vehicles crossing the WIM scale with 99% confidence and with a margin of error equal to ±1.5 mph. Use the data in the file as a pilot sample. How many additional trucks must be sampled to meet the estimation requirements?

7-3 ESTIMATING A POPULATION PROPORTION

The previous sections have illustrated the methods for developing confidence interval estimates when the population value of interest is the mean. However, you will encounter many situations in which the value of interest is the proportion of items in the population that possess a particular attribute. For example, you may wish to estimate the proportion of customers who are satisfied with the service provided by your company. The notation for the *population proportion* is *p*. The point estimate for *p* is the *sample proportion, $\bar{p}$*, which is computed using Equation 7-8.

Sample Proportion

$$\bar{p} = \frac{x}{n}$$

7-8

where:

x = Number of occurrences
n = Sample size

In Chapter 6, we introduced the sampling distribution for proportions. We indicated then that when the sample size is sufficiently large [$np \geq 5$ and $n(1 - p) \geq 5$], the sampling distribution can be approximated by a normal distribution centered at *p*, with a standard error for $\bar{p}$ computed using Equation 7-9.

Standard Error for $\bar{p}$

$$\sigma_{\bar{p}} = \sqrt{\frac{p(1 - p)}{n}}$$

7-9

where:

p = Population proportion
n = Sample size

CONFIDENCE INTERVAL ESTIMATE FOR A POPULATION PROPORTION

To develop the confidence interval estimate for a population proportion, *p*, we use Equation 7-1, the basic equation for establishing all confidence intervals:

Point Estimate ± (Critical Value)(Standard Error)

Using Equations 7-8 and 7-9 as the point estimator and standard error, we find the confidence interval estimate for *p* in Equation 7-10.

Theoretical Confidence Interval Estimate for *p*

$$\bar{p} \pm z_{\alpha/2}\sqrt{\frac{p(1 - p)}{n}}$$

7-10

where:

$\bar{p}$ = Point estimate for $p \left(\bar{p} = \dfrac{x}{n} \right)$
n = Sample size
p = Population proportion
$z_{\alpha/2}$ = Critical value from the standard normal distribution for a $1 - \alpha$ confidence level

Equation 7-10 creates a conflict. We are trying to estimate p, yet the standard error requires that p be known. To overcome this, we must estimate the standard error by substituting the sample proportion, $\bar{p}$, for the population proportion, p. Therefore, the specific format for *confidence intervals involving the population proportion* is shown in Equation 7-11.

Confidence Interval Estimate for p

$$\bar{p} \pm z_{\alpha/2}\sqrt{\frac{\bar{p}(1 - \bar{p})}{n}}$$

7-11

where:

$\bar{p}$ = Sample proportion

n = Sample size

z = Critical value from the standard normal distribution for a $1 - \alpha$ confidence level

---

SUMMARY: DEVELOPING A CONFIDENCE INTERVAL ESTIMATE FOR A POPULATION PROPORTION

Here are the steps necessary to develop a confidence interval estimate for a population proportion.

1. Define the population of interest and the variable for which to estimate the population proportion.

2. Determine the sample size and select a simple random sample. Note, the sample must be large enough so that $np \geq 5$ and $n(1 - p) \geq 5$.

3. Specify the level of confidence and obtain the critical value from the standard normal distribution table.

4. Calculate $\bar{p}$, the sample proportion.

5. Construct the interval estimate using Equation 7-11.

$$\bar{p} \pm z_{\alpha/2}\sqrt{\frac{\bar{p}(1 - \bar{p})}{n}}$$

EXAMPLE 7-6: CONFIDENCE INTERVAL FOR A POPULATION PROPORTION

Quick Lube   The Quick Lube Company operates a chain of oil-change outlets in several states. When a customer comes in for service, the date of service and the mileage on the car are recorded. A computer program tracks the customers, and when three months have almost passed, a reminder card is sent to the customer.

The marketing manager is interested in estimating the *proportion* of customers who return after getting a card. Of a simple random sample of 100 customers, 62 returned within one month after the card was mailed. A confidence interval estimate for the true population proportion is found using the following steps.

Step 1:   **Define the population and the variable of interest.**
The population is all customers who have their oil changed at Quick Lube, and the variable of interest is the number who respond to a reminder card that is mailed to them.

Step 2:   **Determine the sample size.**
A simple random sample of $n = 100$ customers receive cards. (Note, as long as $p \geq 0.05$, a sample size of 100 will meet the requirements that $np \geq 5$ and $n(1 - p) \geq 5$.

Step 3:   **Specify the desired level of confidence and determine the critical value.**
Assuming that a 95% confidence level is desired, the critical value from the standard normal distribution table (Appendix D) will be $z = 1.96$.

Step 4:   **Compute the point estimate based on the sample data.**
Equation 7-8 is used to compute the sample proportion.

$$\bar{p} = \frac{x}{n} = \frac{62}{100} = 0.62$$

Step 5:   **Compute the confidence interval using Equation 7-11.**
The 95% confidence interval estimate is

$$\bar{p} \pm z_{.025} \sqrt{\frac{\bar{p}(1 - \bar{p})}{n}}$$

$$.62 \pm 1.96 \sqrt{\frac{.62(1 - .62)}{100}}$$

$$0.62 \pm 0.095$$

$$0.525 \text{ ----------------------------- } 0.715$$

Using the sample of 100 customers and a 95% confidence interval, the manager estimates that the true percentage of customers who will respond to the reminder card will be between 52.5% and 71.5%.

DETERMINING THE REQUIRED SAMPLE SIZE FOR ESTIMATING A POPULATION PROPORTION

Changing the confidence level affects the interval width. Likewise, changing the sample size will affect the interval width. An increase in sample size will reduce the standard error and reduce the interval width. A decrease in the sample size will have the opposite effect. For many applications, decision makers would like to determine a required sample size before doing the sampling. As was the case for estimating the population mean, the required sample size in a proportion application is based on the desired margin of error, the desired confidence level, and the variation in the population. The **margin of error**, e, is computed using Equation 7-12.

Margin of Error for Estimating p

$$e = z_{\alpha/2} \sqrt{\frac{p(1 - p)}{n}}$$

7-12

where:

p = Population proportion
$z_{\alpha/2}$ = Critical value from standard normal distribution for a $1 - \alpha$ confidence level
n = Sample size

Equation 7-13 is used to determine the required sample size for a given confidence level and margin of error.

Sample Size for Estimating p

$$n = \frac{z_{\alpha/2}^2 p(1 - p)}{e^2}$$

7-13

where:

p = Value used to represent the population proportion
e = Desired margin of error
$z_{\alpha/2}$ = Critical value from standard normal distribution for a $1 - \alpha$ confidence level

---

Quick Lube (continued)—Referring to Example 7-6, recall that the marketing manager developed a confidence interval estimate for the proportion of customers who would respond to a reminder card. This interval was

$$0.62 \pm 1.96 \sqrt{\frac{0.62(1 - 0.62)}{100}}$$

$$0.62 \pm 0.095$$

$$0.525 \text{ ----------------------------- } 0.715$$

The margin of error in this situation is 0.095. Suppose the marketing manager wants the margin of error reduced to $e = \pm0.04$ at a 95% confidence level. This will require an increase in sample size. To apply Equation 7-13, the margin of error and the confidence level are specified by the decision maker. However, the population proportion, p, is not something you can control. In fact, if you already knew the value for p, you wouldn't need to estimate it and the sample-size issue wouldn't come up.

Two methods overcome this problem. First, you can select a *pilot sample* and compute the sample proportion, $\bar{p}$, and substitute $\bar{p}$ for p. Then once the sample size is computed, the pilot sample can be used as part of the overall required sample.

Second, you can select a conservative value for p. The closer p is to 0.50, the greater is the variation because $p(1 - p)$ is greatest when $p = 0.50$. For example, if the manager has reason to believe that the population proportion, p, will be about 0.60, he could use a value for p a little closer to 0.50—say, 0.55. If he doesn't have a good idea of what p is, he could conservatively use $p = 0.50$, which will give a sample size at least large enough to meet requirements.

Suppose the Quick Lube manager selects a pilot sample of $n = 100$ customers and sends these people cards. Further suppose $x = 62$ of these customers respond to the mailing. Then

$$\bar{p} = \frac{62}{100} = 0.62$$

is substituted for p in Equation 7-13. For a 95% confidence level, the z-value is

$$z = 1.96,$$

and the margin of error is equal to

$$e = 0.04.$$

Substitute these values into Equation 7-13 and solve for the required sample size.

$$n = \frac{1.96^2(0.62)(1 - 0.62)}{0.04^2} = 565.676 = 566$$

Because the pilot sample of 100 can be included, the Quick Lube manager needs to send out an additional 466 cards to randomly selected customers. If this is more than the company can afford or wishes to include in the sample, the margin of error can be increased or the confidence level can be reduced.

EXAMPLE 7-7: SAMPLE SIZE DETERMINATION FOR ESTIMATING p

The Newsday Times   The managing editor for the The Newsday Times paper is interested in estimating the proportion of the paper's customers who like the new design for the sports page. She wishes to develop a 90% confidence interval estimate and would like to have the estimate be within ±0.05 of the true population proportion. To determine the required sample size, she can use the following steps.

Step 1:   **Define the population of interest.**
The population is all customers of the newspaper.

Step 2:   **Determine the level of confidence and find the critical z-value using the standard normal distribution table.**
The desired confidence level is 90%. The z-value for 90% confidence is the z-value that corresponds to $\frac{0.90}{2} = 0.45$. This is $z = 1.645$.

Step 3:   **Determine the desired margin of error.**
The editor wishes the margin of error to be 0.05.

Step 4:   **Arrive at a value to use for p.**
Two options can be used to obtain a value for p:

   1. Use a pilot sample and compute p, the sample proportion. Use $\bar{p}$ to represent p.
   2. Select a value for p that is closer to 0.50 than you actually believe the value to be. If you have no idea what p might be, use $p = 0.50$ to give a conservatively large sample size.

In this case, suppose the editor has no idea what the p is but wants to make sure that her sample is sufficiently large to meet her estimation requirements. Then she will use $p = 0.50$.

Step 5:   **Use Equation 7-13 to determine the sample size.**

$$n = \frac{z_{\alpha/2}^2 p(1-p)}{e^2} = \frac{1.645^2(0.50)(1-0.50)}{0.05^2} = 270.6025 = 271$$

The editor should randomly survey 271 customers.

7-3: EXERCISES

Skill Development

7.41   Compute the 95% confidence interval estimate for p based on a sample size of 400 when the sample proportion, $\bar{p}$, is equal to 0.30.

7.42   Determine the required sample size needed to estimate a population proportion when the desired margin of error is ±0.03, the confidence level is 95%, and p is set at 0.50.

7.43   A sample of $n = 300$ items has been randomly selected. Of these, 55 contain the attribute of interest. Based on this information, compute a 90% confidence interval estimate for the proportion of items in the population that have this attribute.

7.44   A simple random sample of 150 items provides a sample proportion having a specific attribute of 0.23.
   a.   What is the point estimate for the population proportion having the attribute?
   b.   Develop a 99% confidence interval estimate for the proportion of items in the population having the attribute.

7.45   A pilot sample of $n = 50$ items reveals that 11 items have the attribute of interest. Using this information, determine how many more items must be sampled to obtain a confidence interval estimate for the population proportion if the confidence level is 98% and the margin of error is ±0.03.

7.46   A random sample of 900 items was selected from a population. The sample contained 750 items with a particular attribute.
   a.   Based on the sample data, construct a 90% confidence interval estimate and interpret the estimate.
   b.   Referring to your answer in part a, what size sample would be needed to cut the margin of error in half? (Hint: Use the 900 units as a pilot sample.)

7.47   Assume that we wish to have 95% confidence and a margin of error of ±0.03.
   a.   What sample size is needed to estimate the population proportion if it is thought that p will be approximately 0.70?
   b.   Suppose that p were 0.30 instead. How would this change the required sample size? Does this answer surprise you? Explain why the sample sizes came out as they did.

7.48   A sample of size 100 was selected from a population. Out of this sample, 47 had a particular attribute.
   a.   Is the sample size large enough so that the sampling distribution of the sample proportion can be approximated with a normal distribution? Support your answer with calculations and reasons.
   b.   Based on these sample data, construct and interpret the 95% confidence interval estimate for the population proportion.

7.49   A random sample of 300 items was selected from a population. Of this sample, 88 items possessed a desired attribute. Construct and interpret the 85% confidence interval estimate for the population proportion.

7.50   Assume that a decision maker wants to estimate a population proportion with 90% confidence and a margin of error of ±0.03. The decision maker has obtained a pilot sample of 10. This pilot sample's proportion is 0.50. What sample size will be sure to achieve the desired results? How many additional observations must the decision maker obtain?

7.51   Suppose a pilot sample of 50 items was selected and 22 items had the attribute of interest. How many more items must be sampled to develop a 90% confidence level with a 0.05 margin of error?

Business Applications

7.52   A bank in Midland, Texas, is interested in estimating the proportion of customers who have credit cards with one or more other banks. A simple random sample of 200 customers showed that 144 have these credit cards. If the bank wishes the estimate to be made with a 95% confidence level, what are the upper and lower limits of the confidence interval estimate?

7.53   An export–import shop in Seattle, Washington, recently sent a buyer to China to purchase glass dinnerware products from a company. The buyer is interested in estimating the proportion of the glassware that contains visual defects. A simple random sample of 130 items is selected, and 13 are found to have a visual defect.
   a.   Based on this information, what is the 90% confidence interval estimate for the proportion of all products made by the company?
   b.   Suppose the buyer would like to reduce the margin of error for the estimate found in part a, what options does he have? Discuss.

7.54   A survey of 499 women for the American Orthopedic Foot and Ankle Society revealed that 38% wear flats to work.
   a.   Use this sample information to develop a 99% confidence interval for the population proportion of women who wear flats to work.

b. Suppose the society wished to estimate the proportion of women who wear athletic shoes to work and the proportion of women who wear flats to work within a margin of error of 0.01 with 95% confidence. Determine the sample size required if only one sample is to be obtained.

7.55 Watson, Harris & Tonkin is a CPA firm in Columbus, Ohio. As part of an audit of a large retail company, the firm wishes to estimate the proportion of credit card accounts that are past due. They want this estimate to have a margin of error no greater than 0.03, and they wish to use a 95% confidence interval estimate.

  a. What size sample should they select if they have no idea what the percentage might be and they want to make sure the sample size is large enough to meet their requirements?

  b. Suppose that the sample size determined in part a is used and the sample proportion is 0.18. Construct the confidence interval estimate for the population.

  c. Referring to parts a and b, discuss why the margin of error obtained in the interval estimate is actually smaller than what the firm wanted.

7.56 A local radio station is interested in estimating the percentage of people in a target market who have a favorable impression of its morning show. The marketing department wishes to estimate this proportion within ±0.03 of the true population value and have a confidence level of 98%. A pilot sample of 40 people is selected, and the proportion in this sample with a favorable impression is 0.45. Based on this information, how many more people must be surveyed?

Advanced Business Applications

7.57 The corporate operations manager for the Phillips Oil Company has his staff working on a new service-station layout plan that would potentially alter the ratio of regular unleaded pumps to other gasoline pumps (premium, super premium, etc.) that are placed at a station. As part of the staff's analysis, they are interested in estimating the difference in the population proportion of customers who purchase unleaded regular gasoline in eastern states versus western states. They have considerably more experience with the eastern states. The proportion of customers who purchase unleaded regular gasoline in the eastern states is known to be 0.75. They have sampled 900 western-state customers; 643 of the western-state customers purchased regular unleaded gasoline.

  a. Using a 95% confidence level, determine the estimate for the population proportion of western-state customers who purchase unleaded regular.

  b. On the basis of this confidence interval, would you recommend that Phillips Oil use a different ratio of regular unleaded pumps in the western states than in the eastern states? Support your answer with the confidence interval and the logic that accompanies it.

  c. Referring to part a, what is the margin of error for the confidence interval?

  d. Discuss the options that exist to reduce the margin of error.

7.58 Most major airlines allow passengers to carry two pieces of luggage (of a certain maximum size) onto a plane.

However, their studies show that the more carry-on bags passengers have, the longer it takes the plane to unload and load passengers. One regional airline is considering changing its policy to allow only one carry-on per passenger. Before doing so, it decided to collect some data. Specifically, a random sample of 1,000 passengers was selected. The passengers were observed and the number of bags carried on the plane was noted. Out of the 1,000 passengers, 345 had more than one bag.

  a. Based on this sample, develop and interpret a 95% confidence interval estimate for the proportion of the traveling population who would have been impacted if the "one-bag" limit had been in effect. Discuss your result.

  b. The domestic version of Boeing's 747 has a capacity for 568 passengers. Determine an interval estimate of the number of passengers you would expect to board the plane carrying more than one piece of luggage. Assume the plane is at its passenger capacity.

  c. Suppose the airline also noted whether the passengers were male or female. Out of the 1,000 passengers observed, 690 were males. Of this group, 280 had more than one bag. Using this data, obtain and interpret a 95% confidence interval estimate for the proportion of male passengers in the population who would have been affected by the one-bag limit. Discuss.

  d. Suppose the airline decides to conduct a survey of its customers to determine their opinion of the proposed one-bag limit. The plan calls for a random sample of customers on different flights to be given a short written survey to complete during the flight. One key question on the survey will be: "Do you approve of limiting the number of carry-on bags to a maximum of one bag?" Airline managers expect that only about 15% will say yes. Based on this assumption, what size sample should the airline take if it wants to develop a 95% confidence interval estimate for the population proportion who will say "yes" with a margin of error of ±0.02?

7.59 A major manufacturer of athletic footwear is considering a new marketing campaign directed at working women. The idea is to create the impression that athletic footwear is comfortable and appropriate to wear to work. Part of the motivation for this idea came from a survey of 499 women conducted for the American Orthopedic Foot and Ankle Society. This survey revealed that 23% wear athletic shoes to work.

  a. Use this information to develop a 90% confidence interval estimate for the population proportion of women who wear athletic shoes to work. Interpret your findings.

  b. The mass media usually references the information contained in a confidence interval by reciting the point estimate for the parameter of interest, followed by a specification of the margin of error. Write a short description of the media release summarizing the confidence in part a.

  c. Suppose the station manager can't afford to survey that many people and has indicated that the maximum sample size can be 300 people. Assuming that the sample size is cut to 300, without changing the confidence level, indicate specifically what must be changed and by how much.

Summary and Conclusions

By the time you have reached this point, you may be wondering how you are ever going to keep all these different estimation processes straight. If you try to memorize them, you probably won't be able to do it. However, if you develop an understanding of the basic logic of estimation, it is very manageable.

Remember, your first objective is to estimate a population value based on information from a sample. There are two types of estimates: point estimates and interval estimates. Point estimates are subject to potential sampling error. Point estimates are almost always different than the population value. A confidence interval estimate takes into account the potential for sampling error and provides a range within which we believe the true population value falls. There is a common format for all confidence interval estimates:

Point Estimate ± (Critical Value)(Standard Error)

The point estimate is at the center of the interval. The amount that we add and subtract to the point estimate is called the margin of error.

Although this format is always used, there are slightly different formulas that we use depending on what population value we are estimating and certain other conditions. You shouldn't try to memorize these formulas. Instead, you should focus on sorting out the characteristics of the situation at hand. Once you do that, you can locate the appropriate formula to determine the interval estimate. The key will be on correctly interpreting the results and applying these results to your decision situation.

Figure 7-9 contains a diagram that you should find useful as you work the problems and cases at the end of this chapter and later on when you encounter estimation applications in your work.

EQUATIONS

Confidence Interval General Format
Point Estimate ± (Critical Value)(Standard Error)   **7-1**

Confidence Interval General Format—σ Known
Point Estimate ± z(Standard Error)   **7-2**

Confidence Interval Estimate for μ, σ Known

$$\bar{x} \pm z_{\alpha/2} \frac{\sigma}{\sqrt{n}}$$ **7-3**

Margin of Error for Estimating μ, σ Known

$$e = z_{\alpha/2} \frac{\sigma}{\sqrt{n}}$$ **7-4**

t-Value for $\bar{x}$

$$t = \frac{\bar{x} - \mu}{\frac{s}{\sqrt{n}}}$$ **7-5**

Confidence Interval Estimate for μ, σ Unknown

$$\bar{x} \pm t_{\alpha/2} \frac{s}{\sqrt{n}}$$ **7-6**

Sample Size Requirement for Estimating μ, σ Known

$$n = \left(\frac{z_{\alpha/2}\sigma}{e}\right)^2 = \frac{z_{\alpha/2}^2 \sigma^2}{e^2}$$ **7-7**

Sample Proportion

$$\bar{p} = \frac{x}{n}$$ **7-8**

Standard Error for $\bar{p}$

$$\sigma_{\bar{p}} = \sqrt{\frac{p(1-p)}{n}}$$ **7-9**

Theoretical Confidence Interval Estimate for p

$$\bar{p} \pm z_{\alpha/2} \sqrt{\frac{p(1-p)}{n}}$$ **7-10**

Confidence Interval Estimate for p

$$\bar{p} \pm z_{\alpha/2} \sqrt{\frac{\bar{p}(1-\bar{p})}{n}}$$ **7-11**

Margin of Error for Estimating p

$$e = z_{\alpha/2} \sqrt{\frac{p(1-p)}{n}}$$ **7-12**

Sample Size for Estimating p

$$n = \frac{z_{\alpha/2}^2 p(1-p)}{e^2}$$ **7-13**

FIGURE 7-9

Flow Diagram for Confidence Interval Estimation Alternatives

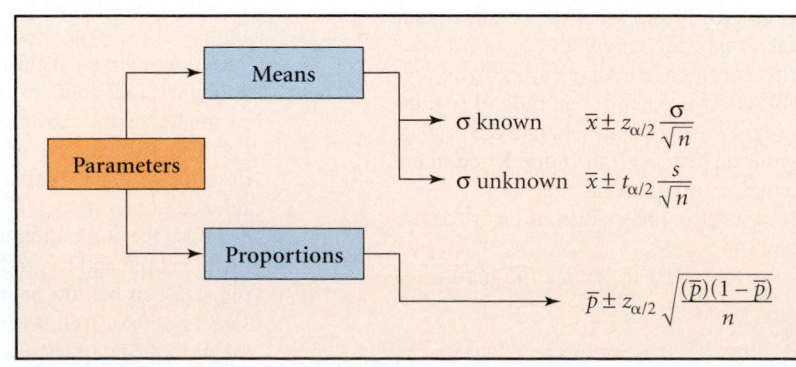

CHAPTER EXERCISES

Conceptual Questions

7.60 In a situation in which our objective is to estimate the population mean, if a small sample is used and the population standard deviation is unknown, we are hit with a "double whammy" when it comes to the margin of error. Explain what the double whammy is and why it occurs. (Hint: Consider the sources of variation in the margin of error.)

7.61 When a decision maker is interested in estimating a single population proportion, why is the margin of error greater when the sample proportion is near 0.50 for a given confidence level? (Note: If you have had a calculus class, you may wish to use the tools acquired there to prove the result. If not, a few sample calculations of the margin of error for various sample proportions should point the way.)

7.62 An insurance company in Iowa recently conducted a survey of its automobile-policy customers to estimate the mean miles these customers commute to work each day. The result based on a random sample of 300 policyholders indicated the population mean was between 3.5 and 6.7 miles. This interval estimate was constructed using 95% confidence.
   a. After receiving this result, one of the managers was overheard telling a colleague that 95% of all customers commute between 3.5 and 6.7 miles to work each day. How would you respond to this statement? Is it correct? Why or why not? Discuss.
   b. Another manager was overheard to say that he was 95% confident that the mean of the 300 policyholders was between 3.5 and 6.7. How would you respond to this statement? Is it correct? Why or why not? Discuss.

7.63 Referring to Exercise 7.62, suppose a third manager is overheard telling another colleague that there is a 95% chance that the true average commute for all policyholders is between 3.5 and 6.7 miles per day. Comment on this statement. Is it a correct statement? Discuss why or why not.

Business Applications

7.64 A survey of 619 working adults revealed that 38% of them favored allowing the federal government to invest a portion of the Social Security Trust Fund in the stock market (*USA Today*, July 27, 1998). Use this information to construct a 99% confidence interval for the proportion of working adults who favor such investments.

7.65 A random sample of 48 individuals who purchased items over the Internet revealed an average purchase amount of $178, with a standard deviation of $27. Use this sample information and a 95% confidence level to provide the following:
   a. a point estimate of the average purchase amount
   b. the margin of error of the point estimate you have provided
   c. an interval estimate for the population mean

7.66 Chambre Corporation makes a variety of products, including electrical surge protectors. They are considering developing a special model surge protector that will be mounted internally in a PC at the time of manufacture. However, before doing this, the company needs convincing data to make the sale to the computer makers. The company contracted with a national survey research firm to conduct a survey of PC owners to determine several issues related to PC ownership and the need for a surge protector. A key question on the survey asked the respondents to indicate the total value of the PCs that they had purchased most recently. The objective now is to develop a 95% confidence interval estimate for the mean value for all PCs owned in the market. The desired margin of error is not to exceed ±$100. A previous study has indicated that the standard deviation for PC value is approximately $300. Based on this, what size random sample should be taken? Explain why this required sample size is this small.

7.67 Suppose the survey research firm selected a simple random sample of 300 people for the purposes of estimating their mean weekly income and found the sample information was $\bar{x} = \$1,345.78$ and $s = \$257.90$.
   a. Compute the desired confidence interval estimate and interpret the estimate.
   b. Indicate what options exist to reduce the margin of error.
   c. Based on the sample information above, determine the smallest and largest prices being paid for a PC.
   d. What assumption about the distribution of the PC prices allows you to produce these estimates?

7.68 A U.S. senator has asked her staff to conduct a study to determine whether people would be in favor of raising the retirement age as a way to save the Social Security system.
   a. If you seek to have a 95% confidence interval for your estimate, with a margin of error of 4 percentage points, how large a sample should you select? Produce a conservatively high sample size.

b. Suppose when the survey was conducted in the senator's home state using the sample size determined in part a, 37.9% indicated that they would favor the proposal. Use this information to construct the confidence interval estimate. Interpret the estimate.

7.69 A company wishes to obtain the sample size required to determine a company's average ordering lead time to within 1 day with 95% confidence. If the standard deviation of lead times is known to be 7 days, determine the required sample size.

7.70 A random sample of 25 sports utility vehicles (SUVs) for the same year and model revealed the following miles per gallon (MPG) values:

12.40	13.00	12.60	12.10	13.10
13.00	12.00	13.10	11.40	12.60
9.50	13.25	12.40	10.70	11.70
10.00	14.00	10.90	9.90	10.20
11.00	11.90	9.90	12.00	11.30

Assume that the population distribution for MPG for this model year is normally distributed.
a. Use the sample results to develop a 95% confidence interval estimate for the population mean MPG.
b. Determine the average number of gallons of gasoline the SUVs described here would use to travel between Los Angeles and San Francisco, California—a distance of approximately 400 miles.
c. Another sample of the same size is to be obtained. If you know that the average MPG in the second sample will be larger than the one obtained in part a, determine the probability that the sample mean will be larger than the upper confidence limit of the confidence interval you calculated.

7.71 A travel agency would like to estimate the proportion of domestic travelers who select an airline based on the price of the ticket to the desired destination. If the travel agency would like to be 94% confident of being within ±4% of the true population proportion, then what size sample should they take? (Assume that they have no knowledge about what the proportion might be and want to make sure they have a large enough sample size to meet their needs.)

Advanced Business Applications

7.72 💿 The Future-Vision Company is considering applying for a franchise to market satellite television dish systems in a Florida market area. As part of the company's research into this opportunity, staff in the New Acquisitions Department conducted a survey of 548 homes selected at random in the market area. They asked a number of questions on the survey. The data for some of the variables are in the CD-ROM file called *Future-Vision*. One key question asked whether the household was currently connected to cable TV.
a. Using the sample information, what is the 95% confidence interval estimate for the true proportion of households in the market area that subscribe to cable television?
b. Based on the sample data, develop a 95% confidence interval estimate for the mean income and interpret this estimate.

7.73 💿 The Jordeen Bottling Company recently did an extensive sampling of its soft drink inventory in which 5,000 cans were sampled. Employees weighed each can and used weight to determine the fluid ounces in the cans. The data are in a file on your CD-ROM called *Jordeen*. Based on this sample data, should the company conclude that the mean volume is 12 ounces? Base your conclusion on a 95% confidence interval estimate and discuss.

7.74 A survey was taken to determine the average amount young professionals living in Denver have invested in stock mutual funds outside of retirement accounts. The survey results showed lower and upper confidence interval limits of $25,114 and $26,068. respectively. If the confidence interval was based on a sample size of 1,024 young professionals and a known population standard deviation of $7,543, then what is the confidence level for the estimate of the population mean amount invested?

7.75 A survey conducted by the NPD Group for Quaker Oats (*USA Today*) revealed that 70% of those people who use oatmeal as a cereal put something on it. Suppose this estimate was based on a sample of 1,024 people who eat oatmeal for breakfast.
a. Use the study's findings to calculate the 95% confidence interval for the true proportion of breakfast oatmeal eaters who put something on their oats.
b. Calculate the largest the margin of error could possibly be when estimating the proportion of oatmeal eaters who put something on it with the sample proportion given above.

7.76 A sample of 441 shoppers selected from people in San Luis Obispo, California, revealed that 76% made at least one purchase at a discount store last month.
a. Based on this sample information, what is the 90% confidence interval for the population proportion of shoppers who made at least one discount store purchase last month?
b. San Luis Obispo has a population of 35,000 people. It does not have a discount store. Therefore, shoppers travel outside of the city to buy at discount stores. Determine a 90% confidence interval for the number of shoppers who made at least one discount store purchase last month.

7.77 💿 Open the CD-ROM file *High-Desert Banking*. Assume that these data reflect the population of all loans in the bank's portfolio.
a. Select a random sample of 49 loans. Use this sample to construct a 90% confidence interval for the population mean of all loans in the High Desert Bank's portfolio. (Hint: Remember to use the finite correction factor, because the sample is large relative to the size of the population.)
b. Repeat this process nine more times, for a total of 10 samples, each of size 49.

c. Compute the actual population mean for all loans in the portfolio. How many of the 10 confidence intervals that you constructed contain the population mean? How many intervals would you expect to contain the true population mean in the long run?

7.78   Paper-R-Us is a national distributor of printer and copier paper for commercial use. The data file called *Sales* contains the annual, year-to-date sales values for each of the company's customers. Suppose the internal audit department has decided to audit a sample of 36 of these accounts. However, before they actually conduct the in-depth audit (a process that involves tracking all transactions for each sampled account), they want to be sure that the sample they have selected is representative of the population.

a. Compute the population mean.
b. Use all the data in the population to develop a frequency distribution and histogram.
c. Calculate the proportion of accounts for customers in each region of the country.
d. Select a random sample of accounts. Develop a frequency distribution for this sample data. Compare this distribution to that of the population. (Hint: You might want to consider using relative frequencies for comparison purposes.)
e. Construct a 95% confidence interval estimate for the population mean sales per customer. Discuss how you would use this interval estimate to help determine whether the sample is a good representative of the population. (Hint: You may want to use the finite correction factor, because the sample is large relative to the size of the population.)
f. Use the information developed in parts a through e to draw a conclusion about whether the sample is a representative sample of the population. What other information would be desirable? Discuss.

7.79   In 1998, the University of Michigan conducted a study of college basketball players in the United States. A total of 758 people responded to the survey. Among these, 316 were female athletes. The study found that 546 athletes admitted to gambling since entering college. Of the females, 187 said they had gambled. Two hundred sixty-five of the respondents said they had placed bets on sports, and 266 of the male athletes said they had bet on sports. Finally, 22 of the male athletes admitted to providing inside information for gambling purposes, betting on a game in which they were playing, or shaving points for money. (Source: *Idaho Statesman* and Associated Press, January 12, 1999.)

a. Develop a 95% confidence interval estimate for the proportion of all athletes who have gambled on sports while in college. Interpret.
b. Develop a 99% confidence interval estimate for the proportion of male athletes who have gambled on sports while in college. Interpret.
c. Construct and interpret a 95% confidence interval estimate for the proportion of male students who have shaved points, provided inside information, or bet on their own game.

d. Based on your responses to parts a, b, and c, write a short report to the NCAA on the subject of gambling by student athletes.

7.80   The president of Morgan Fabrics, a nationwide manufacturer of fabric material for the garment industry, has recommitted the company to better serving its customers. One key measure of customer satisfaction is the proportion of on-time deliveries. The company did not use this measure in the past, so the president has no idea right now of what the company's past on-time delivery rate has been. To establish this benchmark, the customer service manager has sampled 400 customer orders from the past year. Of these, 310 showed that the delivery had reached the customer by the promised date. Use this sample data to construct a 90% confidence interval of the true proportion of on-time deliveries for this company. Interpret this interval and discuss whether you feel this will be a good benchmark against which they can compare their future on-time delivery performance.

7.81   One of the major U.S. producers of household products recently surveyed 64 adults in order to estimate the proportion of adults who prefer mint-flavored toothpaste to plain toothpaste. The motive behind the survey was to aid in its production planning efforts. The results of the survey are contained in a file called *Toothpaste*.

a. Use this sample data to construct a 99% confidence interval of the population proportion of adults who prefer mint-flavored toothpaste. Explain how this might help the company plan its toothpaste production.
b. Suppose that you are the production manager for a relatively small toothpaste-manufacturing company. You only produce mint-flavored and plain toothpaste. You are trying to decide what proportion of each of these you should produce. You would like the proportion of production to match that of the consumers' preferences. You do, however, have a slightly larger profit margin on plain toothpaste. Determine the proportions of each type of toothpaste that you will produce. Support you answer with statistical reasoning related to the above confidence interval.

7.82   The brokerage firm of Gallusha, Higgins & Morton is considering buying another brokerage firm in the Northeast. One factor that plays a part in the price it would be willing to pay for this firm is the cash balances of the current clients. The data file called *Gallusha* contains cash balance data as of a particular point in time for a sample of customers in the firm.

a. Assuming the population of cash account balances from which this sample was taken is normally distributed, construct a 95% confidence interval of the mean cash balance for all accounts for this firm.
b. Suppose that Gallusha representatives look at the confidence interval computed in part a and feel that the margin of error is too large. If they want to reduce the margin of error by 40%, what would be the required sample size, assuming that no change in confidence level takes place? (Hint: Use the sample standard deviation from part a in solving for the required sample size.)

CASE 7-A:

Duro Industries, Inc.

Rochelle Phillips was more nervous than she had been for a long time. Today was the day she would have to prepare an interim report to management on the new production process she had been testing at Duro Industries, Inc., a producer of bricks and paver blocks. Rochelle had started work at the company's Memphis plant right out of college and had worked her way up to assistant plant manager in charge of production during her 22 years with the company.

She knew her report could result in significant changes at Duro Industries. The company had been in business for 75 years and had established a solid regional reputation for quality and reliability in the manufacturing and delivery of its products. But the brick industry was changing rapidly. In addition to competition from other regional companies, Duro was facing increased competition from large foreign firms that were looking for ways to take Duro's best customers. Furthermore, there were fundamental changes underway in how brick companies managed their production processes.

Brick companies had traditionally relied on manual labor to move bricks through the manufacturing process. Duro was not different, employing hundreds of workers to help move bricks and paver blocks through the various manufacturing steps. But some foreign competitors, most notably Australian firms, were using vector drives to provide the precision motion control necessary to automatically move different quantities and configurations through the process accurately and repeatedly, with less manual labor than before. This produced both cost savings and faster production times. If domestic firms adopted the same technology, the resulting costs savings could give them a competitive advantage in price and delivery times over Duro.

The CEO of Duro had notified Rochelle that her plant would be expected to evaluate the feasibility of undertaking this new approach to moving product through the process. If successful, Rochelle would head up the implementation team at the other Duro facilities in the United States. She was concerned that the implementation would be difficult and expensive. Furthermore, she was uncertain whether the expenditure on the vector drives would have a quick enough payback. Duro was convinced that the company had to at least investigate the feasibility of such a process, and the company was initially interested in the productivity improvements that might arise from such a plan.

Rochelle contacted a company that produced electric motors and vector drives, and its consultants told her that it would be possible to set up an experiment that would allow her to estimate whether the new process could increase production. Rochelle began to plan for the test. She decided that once the new equipment was in place and the workers were trained in the new process, the experiment would run for 50 days. Each day's output would be recorded. The CD-ROM file called *Duro* contains the production output each day at the Memphis plant.

Rochelle needs to prepare a report that analyzes the data for the test period at the Memphis plant. The financial analysts at Duro headquarters believe the purchase can be justified if the equipment will lead to an average increase in production of at least 10,000 bricks per day. (Note, in Chapter 9, Rochelle will be asked to compare the output at the Memphis plant to that at a comparable plant in Birmingham, Alabama.)

CASE 7-B:

Management Solutions, Inc.

The round-trip to the "site" was just under 360 miles, which gave Fred Kitchener and Mike Kyte plenty of time to discuss the next steps in the project. The site is a rural stretch of highway in Idaho where two visibility sensors are located. The project is part of a contract Fred's company, Management Solutions, Inc., has with the state of Idaho and the Federal Highway Administration. Under the contract, among other things, Management Solutions is charged with evaluating the performance of a new technology for measuring visibility. The larger study involves determining whether visibility sensors can be effectively tied to electronic message signs that would warn motorists of upcoming visibility problems in rural areas.

Mike Kyte, a transportation engineer and professor at the University of Idaho, has been involved with the project as a consultant to Fred's company since the initial proposal. Mike is very knowledgeable about visibility sensors and traffic systems. Fred's expertise is in managing projects like this one, in which it is important to get people from multiple organizations to work together effectively.

As the pair headed back toward Boise from the site, Mike was more excited than Fred had seen him in a long time. Fred reasoned that the source of excitement was that they had finally been successful in getting solid data to compare the two visibility sensors in a period of low visibility. The previous day at the site had been very foggy. The Scorpion Sensor is a tested technology that Mike has worked with for some time in urban applications. However, it has never before been installed in such a remote location at this stretch of highway I-84, which connects Idaho and Utah. The other sensor produced by the Vanguard Company measures visibility in a totally new way using laser technology.

The data that had excited Mike so much were collected by the two sensors and fed back to a computer system at the port of entry near the test site. The measurements were collected every five minutes for the 24-hour day. As Fred took advantage of the 75 mph speed limit through southern Idaho, Mike kept glancing at the data on the printout he had made of the first few 5-minute time periods. The Scorpion system had not only provided visibility readings, but it also had provided other weather-related data, such as temperature, wind speed, wind direction, and humidity.

Mike's eyes went directly to the two visibility columns. Ideally, the visibility readings for the two sensors would be the same at any 5-minute period, but they weren't. After a few exclamations of surprise from Mike, Fred suggested that they come up with an outline for the report they would have to make from these data for the project team meeting next week. Both agreed that a full descriptive analysis of all the data, including graphs and numerical measures, was necessary. In addition, Fred wanted to use these early data to provide an estimate for the mean visibility provided by the two sensors. They agreed that estimates were needed for the day as a whole and also for only those periods when the Scorpion system showed visibility under 1.0 mile. They also felt that the analysis should look at the other weather factors, too, but they weren't sure just what was needed.

As the lights in the Boise Valley became visible, Mike agreed to work up a draft of the report, including a narrative based on the data in the CD-ROM file called *Visibility*. Fred said that he would set up the project team meeting agenda, and Mike could make the presentation. Both men agreed that the data were strictly a sample and that more low-visibility data would be collected when conditions occurred.

General References

1. Berenson, Mark L., and David M. Levine, *Basic Business Statistics Concepts and Applications*, 7th ed. (Upper Saddle River, NJ: Prentice Hall, 1999).
2. Dodge, Mark, and Craig, Stinson, *Running Microsoft Excel 2000* (Redmond, WA: Microsoft Press, 1999).
3. Hogg, Robert V., and Elliot A. Tanis, *Probability and Statistical Inference*, 5th ed. (Upper Saddle River, NJ: Prentice Hall, 1997).
4. Marx, Morris L., and Richard J. Larsen, *Mathematical Statistics and Its Applications*, 3rd ed. (Upper Saddle River, NJ: Prentice Hall, 2000).
5. *Microsoft Excel 2000* (Redmond, WA: Microsoft Corp., 1999).
6. *Minitab for Windows Version 14* (State College, PA: Minitab, 2003).
7. Siegel, Andrew F., *Practical Business Statistics*, 4th ed. (Burr Ridge, IL: Irwin, 2000).

CHAPTER 8

Introduction to Hypothesis Testing

CHAPTER OUTCOMES

After studying the material in Chapter 8, you should be able to:

- Formulate null and alternative hypotheses for applications involving a single population mean or proportion.
- Correctly formulate a decision rule for testing a null hypothesis.
- Know how to use the test statistic, critical value, and *p*-value approaches to test the null hypothesis.
- Know what Type I and Type II errors are.
- Compute the probability of a Type II error.

WHY YOU NEED TO KNOW

Chapter 7 introduced the steps required to estimate the value of a population mean or proportion based on data from a simple random sample. Based on those estimates, decision makers are able to draw inferences about a population without having to conduct a costly and time-consuming census. Estimation is required when the decision maker has no specific knowledge of a population value but seeks to gain that knowledge.

However, many times managers know what a population value should be because of a company policy or a contract specification, and they must be able to use sample information to determine whether the policy or contract specification is being satisfied. For instance, large metropolitan areas are required to report air pollution levels on a daily basis. They cannot possibly sample all the air in the metropolitan area, yet they are required to report whether the city's air quality meets federal standards. When CPA firms perform audits, they issue a final report stating whether the audited firm followed Generally Accepted Accounting Procedures. They are unable to audit every transac-

tion, so they must make the statement based on a sample of transactions. Even construction crews pouring foundations for large buildings need to determine whether the concrete meets specifications. Taking core samples (long cylinders cut from the poured foundation) and testing these samples does this. The core samples provide information that building inspectors and construction managers use to decide whether construction work can continue, or whether foundations must be further reinforced.

Imagine for a moment that you are the buyer for a company that makes home thermostats, which are used to regulate the heating and cooling systems in homes. A new producer of a major electronic component that is used in your thermostats claims that no more than 3% of its components will have a sensing error of two degrees or more. Before you buy 100,000 units, you might want to test the manufacturer's claim. Because you could not feasibly test each component, you would select a sample and use the sample information to decide whether to make the purchase.

This chapter introduces statistical techniques used to test claims about population values. All decision makers need to have a solid understanding of these techniques in order to use sample information effectively in their decision making.

8-1   HYPOTHESIS TESTS FOR MEANS

By now you know that information contained in a sample is subject to sampling error. The sample mean likely will not equal the population mean. Therefore, in situations in which you need to test a claim about a population mean by using the sample mean, you can't simply compare the sample mean to the claim and reject the claim if $\bar{x}$ and the claim are different. Instead, you need a testing procedure that incorporates the potential for sampling error.

Statistical hypothesis testing provides managers with a structured analytical method for making decisions of this type. It lets them make decisions in such a way that the probability of decision errors can be controlled, or at least measured. Even though statistical hypothesis testing does not eliminate the uncertainty in the managerial environment, the techniques involved often allow managers to identify and control the level of uncertainty.

The techniques presented in this chapter assume the data are selected using an appropriate statistical sampling process and that the data are interval or ratio level. In short, we assume we are working with good data.

FORMULATING THE HYPOTHESES

Null and Alternative Hypotheses

In hypothesis testing, two hypotheses are formulated. One is the **null hypothesis**.

Null Hypothesis

The statement about the population value that will be tested. The null hypothesis will be rejected only if the sample data provide substantial contradictory evidence.

The null hypothesis is represented by H_0 and should contain an equality sign, such as "=," "≤," or "≥." The second hypothesis is the **alternative hypothesis** (represented by H_A).

Alternative Hypothesis

The hypothesis that includes all population values not covered by the null hypothesis. The alternative hypothesis is deemed to be true if the null hypothesis is rejected.

Based on the sample data, we either reject H_0 or we do not reject H_0.

State Insurance Fund—The State Insurance Fund administers the workmen's compensation system. The agency is under legislative inquiry because of complaints from companies covered by the fund. The major objection is that the average processing time exceeds the legally mandated average of 25 days. The fund managers, however, believe they are within the 25-day average response, although they admit that some complicated claims may take longer.

Because the legislative committee has requested a quick reply, fund managers cannot gather information from all claims filed this year and, therefore, must formulate a response based on a sample of claims. As indicated earlier, when a decision is based on sample results, sampling error must be expected. Without considering the effect of sampling error, the managers can't simply say that if the sample mean is 25 days or less, then the population mean is also. Likewise, if the sample mean exceeds 25 days, that does not automatically indicate that the population mean exceeds 25 days.

To account for the potential sampling error, the managers need to formally test whether the sample mean supports the conclusion that the population mean is less than or equal to 25 days or the conclusion that the average time exceeds 25 days. The first step is to express these two possibilities using formal hypothesis-testing terms.

In this example, the status quo is that no change is needed and that the mean processing time is less than or equal to 25 days. If this is rejected and the data indicate that the mean processing time is greater than 25 days, the fund managers would need to change procedures. In this case, the null and alternative hypotheses are stated as:

Null hypothesis $\quad\quad\quad\quad$ $H_0: \mu \leq 25$ days

Alternative hypothesis $\quad\quad$ $H_A: \mu > 25$ days

where μ is the mean claim-processing time.

Determining the null and alternative hypotheses is often a difficult task for students. The null hypothesis represents the situation that is assumed to be true unless the evidence is strong enough to convince the decision maker it is not true. A common analogy is with a legal system, in which a defendant is assumed innocent unless the evidence convinces a jury that the person is guilty. A little bit of evidence is not sufficient. The proof must be substantial. In the case of the State Insurance Fund, the formulation for the null and alternative hypotheses puts the burden of proof on those filing the complaint. Unless the sample mean is "substantially" greater than 25 days, no action will be taken to change the system.

EXAMPLE 8-1: FORMULATING THE NULL AND ALTERNATIVE HYPOTHESES

Student Work Hours   In today's economy, many university students work many hours, often full time, to help pay for the high costs of a college education. Suppose a university in the Midwest was considering changing its class schedule to accommodate students working long hours. The registrar has stated a change was needed because the mean number of hours worked by undergraduate students at the university is more than 20 per week. The following steps can be taken to establish the appropriate null and alternative hypotheses.

Step 1:   **Determine the population value of interest.**
In this case, the population value of interest is the mean hours worked, μ. The null and alternative hypotheses must be stated in terms of the population value.

Step 2:   **Define the situation that is assumed to be true unless substantial information exists to suggest otherwise.**
Because changing the class scheduling system would be expensive and time consuming, the assumption is made that the mean hours worked is less than or equal to 20

hours per week. Thus, the burden of proof is placed on the registrar to justify her claim that the mean exceeds 20 hours.

Step 3: **Formulate the null and alternative hypotheses.**
Keep in mind that the equality goes in the null hypothesis.

$$H_0: \mu \leq 20 \text{ hours}$$
$$H_A: \mu > 20 \text{ hours (claim)}$$

Example 8-2 illustrates another example of how the null and alternative hypotheses are formulated.

EXAMPLE 8-2: FORMULATING THE NULL AND ALTERNATIVE HYPOTHESES

Chips N' Snacks Company   The Chips N' Snacks Company produces several snack and food products that are sold in food stores throughout Colorado and New Mexico. The company uses an automatic filling machine to fill the sacks with the desired weight. For instance, when the company is running potato chips on the fill line, the machine is set to fill the sacks with 20 ounces. Thus, if the machine is working properly, the mean fill will be 20 ounces. Each hour, a sample of sacks is collected and weighed, and the technicians determine whether the machine is still operating correctly or whether it needs adjustment. The following steps can be used to establish the null and alternative hypotheses to be tested.

Step 1: **Determine the population value of interest.**
In this case, the population value of interest is the mean weight per sack, μ.

Step 2: **Define the situation that is assumed to be true unless substantial information exists to suggest otherwise.**
The status quo is that the machine is filling the sacks with the proper amount, which is $\mu = 20$ ounces. We will believe this to be true unless we find evidence to suggest otherwise. If such evidence exists, it means that the filling process needs to be adjusted.

Step 3: **Formulate the null and alternative hypotheses.**
Keep in mind that the equality goes in the null hypothesis.
The null and alternative hypotheses are

$$H_0: \mu = 20 \text{ ounces}$$
$$H_A: \mu \neq 20 \text{ ounces}$$

The Research Hypothesis

Another way to think about formulating the null and alternative hypotheses is to consider research applications. Companies such as Intel, Gillette, Dell Computers, and 3M continually bring out new and improved products. However, before introducing a new product, the companies want to be sure it is superior to the old product. They want sufficient evidence of the new product's superiority. The default position is that the existing product or process is at least as good as the new one. The burden of proof rests with the new idea. Only if the sample test results are substantially better for the new product or process will it be deemed superior. In these situations, when the decision maker has control over how the null and alternative hypotheses are stated, the alternative hypothesis should be the **research hypothesis**.

Research Hypothesis

The hypothesis the decision maker attempts to demonstrate to be true. Because this is the hypothesis deemed to be the most important to the decision maker, it will not be declared true unless the sample data strongly indicate that it is true.

If the research hypothesis forms the alternative hypothesis, a decision to reject the null hypothesis would indicate that there is statistical evidence to believe that the research hypothesis is true.

SUMMARY: FORMULATING THE NULL AND ALTERNATIVE HYPOTHESES

We find that some students have a difficult time formulating the null and alternative hypotheses. The previous discussion hopefully has clarified the process. However, we might offer the following suggestions and reminders.

1. The null and alternative hypotheses must be stated in terms of the population value of interest (e.g., μ or p).

2. The null hypothesis represents the status quo, it should contain an equality sign. It represents the condition that will be assumed to exist unless sufficient evidence is presented to show the condition has changed.

3. If you have a choice in formulating the null and alternative hypotheses, construct them so that the null hypothesis contains an equality sign and the alternative hypothesis contains what you wish to show. That way, if the null hypothesis is rejected, you have statistical support for your position.

4. In a research situation, construct the null and alternative hypotheses so that the burden of proof is placed on the research study. This means that the null hypothesis will be the status quo and the alternative will contain the "new" outcome.

You will encounter situations in which it may seem impossible to adhere to this broad set of rules. For instance, someone else may want the burden of proof to be placed on a claim containing an equality, such as $\mu \geq 20$. In such cases you must reason with the individual. For all continuous and many discrete variables, the chances that the population mean would equal exactly, say, 20 are so small that such an eventuality can be disregarded. The claim may be restated to be $\mu > 20$ without tainting the hypothesis test or the intent of the research.

Types of Statistical Errors

Because of the potential for extreme sampling error, two possible errors can occur when a hypothesis is tested: **Type I** and **Type II errors**. These errors show the relationship between what actually exists (a state of nature) and the decision made based on the sample information.

Type I Error	Type II Error
Rejecting the null hypothesis when it is, in fact, true.	*Failing to reject* the null hypothesis when it is, in fact, false.

Figure 8-1 shows the possible actions and states of nature associated with any hypothesis-testing application. As you can see, there are three possible outcomes: no error (correct decision), Type I error, and Type II error. *Only one of these outcomes will occur for a hypothesis test.* From Figure 8-1, if the null hypothesis is true and an error is made, it must be a Type I error. On the other hand, if the null hypothesis is false and an error is made, it must be a Type II error.

Many statisticians argue that you should never use the phrase "accept the null hypothesis." Instead you should use "*do not reject* the null hypothesis." Thus, the only two hypothesis-testing decisions would be *reject H_0* or *do not reject H_0*. This is why in a jury verdict to acquit a defendant, the verdict is "not guilty" rather than innocent. Just because the evidence is insufficient to convict does not necessarily mean that the defendant is innocent.

FIGURE 8-1

The Relationship Between Decisions and States of Nature

		State of Nature	
		Null Hypothesis True	Null Hypothesis False
Decision	Conclude Null True (Don't reject H_0)	Correct Decision	Type II Error
	Conclude Null False (Reject H_0)	Type I Error	Correct Decision

This thinking is appropriate when hypothesis testing is employed in situations in which some future action is not dependent on the results of the hypothesis test. However, in most business applications, the purpose of the hypothesis test is to direct the decision maker to take one action or another, based on the test results. For instance, in the State Insurance Fund example, if the sample data do not lead the managers to reject that $\mu \leq 25$ days, the fund managers will write a report to the legislature indicating that the customer assertions are not supported. Therefore, no changes will be made in the claims-evaluation process. Although they have "not rejected" the null hypothesis, their actions are consistent with what would have taken place if they had "accepted" the null hypothesis. So, in this text, when hypothesis testing is applied to decision-making situations, *not rejecting* the null hypothesis is essentially the same as *accepting* it.[1]

State Insurance Fund (continued)—In the State Insurance Fund hypothesis test, a Type I error would occur if the sample data led the managers to conclude that $\mu > 25$ days (H_0 is rejected) when the truth is that $\mu \leq 25$ days. The result would be that the managers would undertake an effort to change the system when no changes were required. This would be a costly waste of resources.

A Type II error would occur if the sample evidence led the managers to incorrectly conclude that $\mu \leq 25$ days (H_0 is not rejected) when the truth is the mean response time exceeds 25 days. The outcome is that nothing would be done to the system when changes were needed.

SIGNIFICANCE LEVEL AND CRITICAL VALUE

The objective of a hypothesis test is to use sample information to decide whether to reject the null hypothesis about a population parameter. How do decision makers determine whether the sample information supports or refutes the null hypothesis? The answer to this question is the key to understanding statistical hypothesis testing.

In hypotheses tests for a single population mean, the sample mean, $\bar{x}$, is used to test the hypotheses under consideration. Depending on how the null and alternative hypotheses are formulated, certain values of $\bar{x}$ will tend to support the null hypothesis, whereas other values will appear to contradict it. In the State Insurance Fund example, the null and alternative hypotheses were formulated as:

$$H_0: \mu \leq 25 \text{ days}$$
$$H_A: \mu > 25 \text{ days}$$

Values of $\bar{x}$ less than or equal to 25 days would tend to support the null hypothesis. By contrast, values of $\bar{x}$ greater than 25 days would tend to refute the null hypothesis. The larger the value of $\bar{x}$, the greater the evidence that the null hypothesis should be rejected. However, because we expect some sampling error, do we want to reject H_0 for any value of $\bar{x}$ that is greater than 25 days? Probably not. But should we reject H_0 if $\bar{x} = 26$ days, or $\bar{x} = 30$ days, or $\bar{x} = 35$ days? At what point do we stop attributing the result to sampling error?

In order to perform the hypothesis test we need to select a *cutoff* point that is the demarcation between rejecting and not rejecting the null hypothesis. Our *decision rule* is then

If $\bar{x} >$ cutoff, reject H_0
If $\bar{x} \leq$ cutoff, do not reject H_0

If $\bar{x}$ is greater than the cutoff, we will reject H_0 and conclude that the average processing time *does* exceed the mandated value of 25 days. If $\bar{x}$ is less than or equal to the cutoff, we will not reject H_0; in this case our test does not give evidence that the processing time exceeds 25 days.

Recall from the Central Limit Theorem (see Chapter 6) that, for large samples, the distribution of the possible sample means is approximately normal, with a center at the population mean μ. The null hypothesis in our example is $\mu \leq 25$ days. Figure 8-2 shows the sampling distribution for $\bar{x}$ assuming that $\mu = 25$. The shaded region on the right is called the *rejection region*. The area of the rejection region gives the probability of getting an $\bar{x}$ larger than the cutoff when μ is really 25, so it is the probability of making a Type I statistical error. This probability is called the **significance level** of the test and is given the symbol α.

---

[1]Whichever language you use, you should make an effort to understand both arguments and make an informed choice. If your instructor requests that you reference the action in a particular way, it would behoove you to follow the instructions. Having gone through this process ourselves, we prefer to state the choice as "don't reject the null hypothesis." This terminology will be used throughout this text.

FIGURE 8-2

Sampling Distribution of $\bar{x}$ for the State Insurance Fund

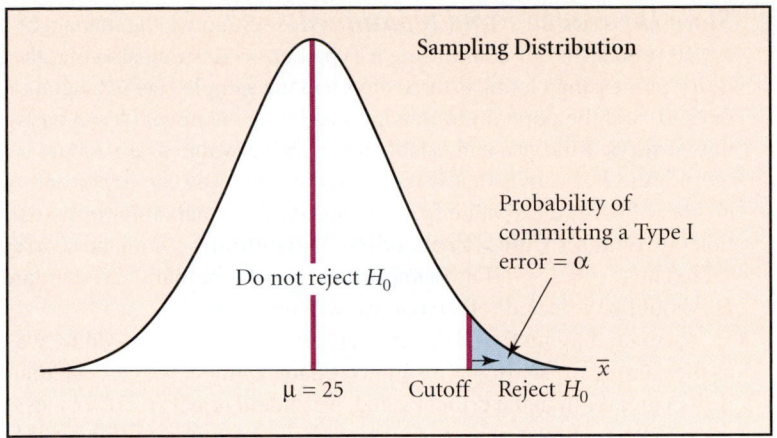

FIGURE 8-2

Sampling Distribution of $\bar{x}$ for the State Insurance Fund

---

Significance Level

The maximum allowable probability of committing a Type I statistical error. The probability is denoted by the symbol α.

The decision maker carrying out the test specifies the significance level, α. The value of α is determined based on the costs involved in committing a Type I error. If making a Type I error is costly, we will want the probability of a Type I error to be small. If a Type I error is less costly, then we can allow a higher probability of a Type I error.

However, in determining α, we must also take into account the probability of making a Type II error, which is given the symbol β (*beta*). The two error probabilities, α and β, are inversely related.[2] That is, if we reduce α, then β will increase. Thus, in setting α, you must consider both sides of the issue.

Calculating the specific dollar costs associated with making the Type I and Type II errors is often difficult and may require a subjective management decision. Therefore, any two managers might well arrive at different alpha levels. However, in the end, the choice for alpha must reflect the decision maker's best estimate of the costs of these two errors.[3]

Having chosen a significance level α, the decision maker then must calculate the corresponding cutoff point, which is called a **critical value**.

Critical Value

The value of a statistic corresponding to a given significance level. This cutoff value determines the boundary between those samples resulting in a test statistic that leads to rejecting the null hypothesis and those that lead to a decision not to reject the null hypothesis.

HYPOTHESIS TEST FOR μ, σ KNOWN

Calculating Critical Values

To calculate critical values corresponding to a chosen α, we need to know the sampling distribution of the sample mean $\bar{x}$. If the population is approximately normally distributed or the sample size n is large ($n \geq 30$) and we know the population standard deviation σ, then the sampling distribution of $\bar{x}$ is normal with mean equal to the population mean μ and standard deviation $\frac{\sigma}{\sqrt{n}}$. With this information we can calculate a critical z-value, called z_α, or a critical $\bar{x}$-value, called $\bar{x}_\alpha$. We illustrate both calculations in the State Insurance Fund example.

---

[2]The sum of alpha and beta may coincidently equal one. However, in general, the sum of these two error probabilities does not equal one.

[3]We will discuss Type II errors more fully later in this chapter. Contrary to the Type I situation in which we specify the desired alpha level, beta is computed based on certain assumptions. Methods for computing beta are shown later.

State Insurance Fund (continued)—Suppose the managers decide they are willing to incur a 0.10 probability of committing a Type I error. Assume also that the population standard deviation, σ, for processing claims is three days and the sample size is 64 claims. Since the sample size is large ($n \geq 30$) and the population standard deviation is known ($\sigma = 3$ days), we can state the critical value in two ways. First, we can establish the critical value as a z-value.

Figure 8-3 shows that if the rejection region on the upper end of the sampling distribution has an area of 0.10, the z-value from the standard normal table (or by using Excel's **NORMSINV** function or Minitab's **Calc > Probability Distributions** command) corresponding to the critical value is 1.28. Thus, $z_\alpha = 1.28$. If the sample mean lies more than 1.28 standard deviations above $\mu = 25$ days, H_0 should be rejected; otherwise we will not reject H_0.

Second, having found the critical value in terms of a z-value, we can express it in the same units as the sample mean. In the Insurance Fund example, we can calculate a critical $\bar{x}$ value, $\bar{x}_\alpha$, so that if $\bar{x}$ is greater than the critical value, we should reject H_0. If $\bar{x}$ is less than or equal to $\bar{x}_\alpha$, we should not reject H_0. Equation 8-1 shows how $\bar{x}_\alpha$ is computed. Figure 8-4 illustrates the use of Equation 8-1 for computing the critical value, $\bar{x}_\alpha$.

$\bar{x}_\alpha$ **for Hypothesis Tests, σ Known**

$$\bar{x}_\alpha = \mu + z_\alpha \frac{\sigma}{\sqrt{n}}$$

8-1

where:

μ = Hypothesized value for the population mean
z_α = Critical value from the standard normal distribution
σ = Population standard deviation
n = Sample size

If $\bar{x} > 25.48$ days, H_0 should be rejected and changes made in the process; otherwise, H_0 should not be rejected and the process should not be changed. Any sample mean between 25.48 and 25 days would be attributed to sampling error, and the null hypothesis would not be rejected. A sample mean of 25 or fewer will support the null hypothesis.

Decision Rules and Test Statistics

To conduct a hypothesis test, you can use two approaches. You can calculate a z-value and compare it to the critical value, z_α. Alternatively, you can calculate the sample mean, $\bar{x}$, and compare it to the critical value, $\bar{x}_\alpha$. It makes no difference which approach you use in establishing the critical value as long as you use the corresponding statistic to make your decision.

Suppose $\bar{x} = 26$ days. How we test the null hypothesis depends on the procedure we used to establish the critical value. First, using the z-value method, we establish the following decision rule.

Hypotheses

$$H_0: \mu \leq 25 \text{ days}$$
$$H_A: \mu > 25 \text{ days}$$
$$\alpha = 0.10$$

FIGURE 8-3

Determining the Critical Value as a z-Value

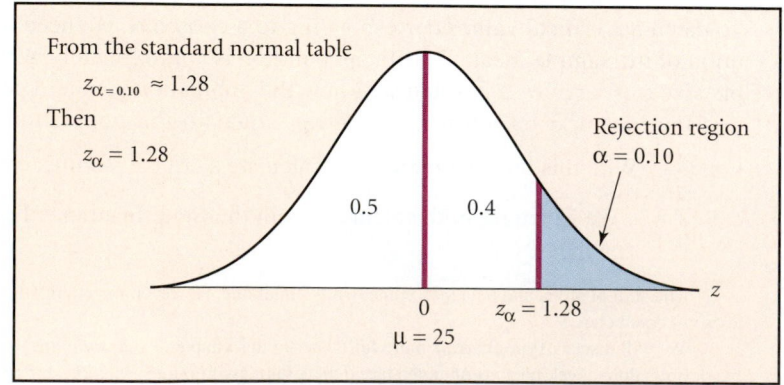

FIGURE 8-4

Determining the Critical Value as an $\bar{x}$-Value, State Insurance Fund Example

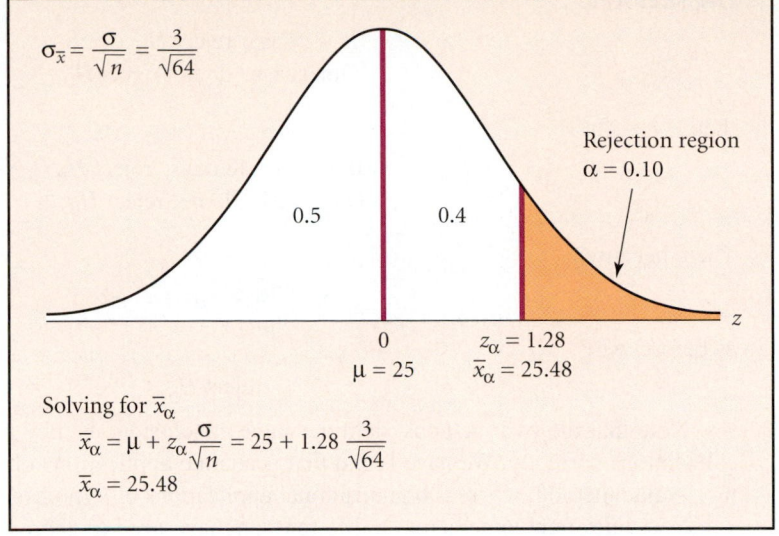

Decision Rule

If $z > z_\alpha$, reject H_0.

If $z \leq z_\alpha$, do not reject H_0.

where:

$$z_\alpha = 1.28$$

Recall that the number of claims tested is 64 and the population standard deviation is assumed known at 3 days. The calculated z-value is called the **test statistic**.

Test Statistic

A function of the sampled observations that provides a basis for testing a statistical hypothesis.

The z test statistic is computed using Equation 8-2.

---

z Test Statistic for Hypothesis Tests, σ Known

$$z = \frac{\bar{x} - \mu}{\dfrac{\sigma}{\sqrt{n}}}$$

8-2

where:

$\bar{x}$ = Sample mean

μ = Hypothesized value for the population mean

σ = Population standard deviation

n = Sample size

Applying Equation 8-2 we get:

$$z = \frac{\bar{x} - \mu}{\dfrac{\sigma}{\sqrt{n}}} = \frac{26 - 25}{\dfrac{3}{\sqrt{64}}} = 2.67$$

The sample mean is 2.67 standard deviations above the hypothesized mean. Because z is greater than the critical value

$$z = 2.67 > z_\alpha = 1.28,$$

we clearly

reject H_0.

Now we use the second approach, which established (see Figure 8-4) a decision rule, as follows.

Decision Rule

$$\text{If } \bar{x} > \bar{x}_\alpha, \text{ reject } H_0$$
$$\text{Otherwise, do not reject } H_0$$

then

$$\text{If } \bar{x} > 25.48 \text{ days, reject } H_0$$
$$\text{Otherwise, do not reject } H_0.$$

Then, because

$$\bar{x} = 26 > \bar{x}_\alpha = 25.48,$$

as before, we

$$\text{reject } H_0.$$

Note that the two methods yield the same conclusion, as they always will if you perform the calculations correctly. We have found that academic applications of hypothesis testing tend to use the z-value method, whereas organizational applications of hypothesis testing use the $\bar{x}$ approach.

You will often come across a different language used to express the outcome of a hypothesis test. For instance, a statement for the hypothesis test presented above would be "The hypothesis test was significant at an α (or significance level) of 0.10." This simply means that the null hypothesis was rejected using a significance level of 0.10.

EXAMPLE 8-3: HYPOTHESIS TEST FOR μ, σ KNOWN

Employee Commute Time   A study in southern California claimed that the mean commute time for all employees working in Orange County exceeds 40 minutes. This figure is higher than what has been assumed in the past. The plan is to test this claim using an alpha level equal to 0.05 and a sample size of $n = 100$ commuters. Based on previous studies, suppose that the population standard deviation is known to be $\sigma = 8$ minutes. The hypothesis test can be conducted using the following steps.

Step 1:   **Specify the population value of interest.**
The population value of interest is the mean commute time, μ.

Step 2:   **Formulate the null and alternative hypotheses.**
The new claim is that $\mu > 40$. Because this is different from past studies, it will become the alternative hypothesis. Thus, the null and alternative hypotheses are

$$H_0: \mu \leq 40 \text{ minutes}$$
$$H_A: \mu > 40 \text{ minutes (claim)}$$

Step 3:   **Specify the significance level.**
The alpha level is specified to be 0.05.

Step 4:   **Construct the rejection region.**
Because we have a large sample and the population standard deviation is known, alpha is the area under the standard normal distribution to the right of the critical value. The critical z-value, z_α, is found by locating the z-value that corresponds to an area equal to $0.50 - 0.05 = 0.45$. The critical z-value from the standard normal table is 1.645.

Step 5:   **Compute the test statistic.**
Suppose that the sample of 100 commuters showed a sample mean of 43.5 minutes. Because the sample size is large and the population standard deviation is known to be 8 minutes, the test statistic is a z-value computed using:

$$z = \frac{\bar{x} - \mu}{\dfrac{\sigma}{\sqrt{n}}} = \frac{43.5 - 40}{\dfrac{8}{\sqrt{100}}} = 4.38$$

The sample mean is 4.38 standard deviations higher than the hypothesized mean.

Step 6:   Reach a decision.
The decision rule is

If $z > 1.645$, reject H_0
Otherwise, do not reject.

Because $z = 4.38 > 1.645$, we reject H_0.

Step 7:   Draw a conclusion.
Conclude that the mean commute distance does exceed 40 minutes.

p-Values

In addition to the two methods discussed previously, a third approach for conducting hypothesis tests also exists. This third approach uses a ***p*-value** instead of a critical value.

---

p-Value

The probability (assuming the null hypothesis is true) of obtaining a test statistic at least as extreme as the test statistic we calculated from the sample. The *p*-value is also known as the *observed significance level.*

If the calculated *p*-value is smaller than the probability in the rejection region (α), then the null hypothesis is rejected. If the calculated *p*-value is greater than or equal to α, then the hypothesis will not be rejected. The *p*-value approach is popular today because *p*-values are usually computed by statistical software packages, including Excel and Minitab. The advantage to reporting test results using a *p*-value is that it provides more information than simply stating whether the null hypothesis is rejected. The decision maker is presented with a measure of the degree of significance of the result (i.e., the *p*-value). This allows the reader the opportunity to evaluate the *extent* to which the data disagree with the null hypothesis, not just whether they disagree.

$\mathcal{E}$XAMPLE 8-4: HYPOTHESIS TEST USING p-VALUES, σ KNOWN

Cardio-Fitness Club   The manager at the Cardio-Fitness Club believes that the recent remodeling project has greatly improved the club's appeal for members and that they now stay longer at the club per visit than before the remodeling. Studies show that the previous mean time per visit was 36 minutes, with a standard deviation equal to 11 minutes. A simple random sample of $n = 200$ visits is selected, and the current sample mean is 36.8 minutes. To test the manager's claim, and partially justify the remodeling project, using an alpha = 0.05 level, the following steps can be used.

Step 1:   Specify the population value of interest.
The manager is interested in the mean time per visit, μ.

Step 2:   Formulate the null and alternative hypotheses.
Based on the manager's claim that the current mean stay is longer than before the remodeling, the null and alternative hypotheses are

H_0: $\mu \leq 36$ minutes
H_A: $\mu > 36$ minutes (claim)

Step 3:   Specify the significance level.
The alpha level specified for this test is $\alpha = 0.05$.

Step 4:   Compute the test statistic.
Because the sample size is large and the population standard deviation is assumed known, the test statistic will be a *z*-value, which is computed as follows:

$$z = \frac{\bar{x} - \mu}{\frac{\sigma}{\sqrt{n}}} = \frac{36.8 - 36}{\frac{11}{\sqrt{200}}} = 1.0285 = 1.03$$

Step 5: **Calculate the p-value.**

In this example, the p-value is the probability of a z-value from the standard normal distribution being at least as large as 1.03. This is stated as:

$$p\text{-value} = p\,(z \geq 1.03)$$

From the standard normal distribution table in Appendix D:

$$P(z \geq 1.03) = 0.5000 - 0.3485 = 0.1515$$

Step 6: **Reach a decision.**

The decision rule is:

$$\text{If } p\text{-value} < \alpha = 0.05, \text{ reject } H_0$$
$$\text{Otherwise, do not reject } H_0.$$

Because the p-value $= 0.1515 > \alpha = 0.05$, do not reject the null hypothesis.

Step 7: **Draw a conclusion.**

The difference between the sample mean and the hypothesized population mean is not large enough to attribute the difference to anything but sampling error.

Why do we need three methods to test the same hypothesis when they all give the same result? The answer is that we don't. However, you need to be aware of all three methods because you will encounter each in business situations. The p-value approach is especially important because many statistical software packages provide a p-value that you can use to test a hypothesis quite easily, and using a p-value means you don't need probability distribution tables. This text will use both test-statistic approaches, as well as the p-value approach to hypothesis testing.

TYPES OF HYPOTHESIS TESTS

Hypothesis tests are formulated as either one-tailed tests or two-tailed tests depending on how the null and alternative hypotheses are presented.

One-Tailed Test

A hypothesis test in which the entire rejection region is located in one tail of the sampling distribution. In a one-tailed test, the entire alpha level is located in one tail of the distribution.

For instance, in the State Insurance Fund application, the null and alternative hypotheses are:

Null hypothesis　　　　　　　　　H_0: $\mu \leq 25$ days
Alternative hypothesis　　　　　　H_A: $\mu > 25$ days

This hypothesis test is one-tailed because the entire rejection region is located in the upper tail and the null hypothesis will be rejected only when the sample mean falls in the extreme upper tail of the sampling distribution (see Figure 8-5). In this application, it will take a sample mean substantially larger than 25 days in order to reject the null hypothesis.

Two-Tailed Test

A hypothesis test in which the entire rejection region is split into the two tails of the sampling distribution. In a two-tailed test, the alpha level is typically split evenly between the two tails.

In Example 8-2 involving the Chips N' Snack Company, the null and alternative hypotheses involving the mean fill of potato chip sacks is:

$$H_0\text{: } \mu = 20 \text{ ounces}$$
$$H_A\text{: } \mu \neq 20 \text{ ounces}$$

In this two-tailed hypotheses case, the null hypothesis will be rejected if the sample mean is extremely large (upper tail) or extremely small (lower tail). The alpha level would be split evenly between the two tails.

SUMMARY: ONE-TAILED TEST FOR A HYPOTHESIS ABOUT A POPULATION MEAN, σ KNOWN

To test the hypothesis, perform the following steps:

1. Specify the population value of interest.

2. Formulate the null hypothesis and the alternative hypothesis in terms of the population mean, μ.

3. Specify the desired significance level (α).

4. Construct the rejection region. (We strongly suggest you draw a picture showing where in the distribution the rejection region is located.)

5. Compute the test statistic.

$$\bar{x} = \frac{\Sigma x}{n}, z = \frac{\bar{x} - \mu}{\frac{\sigma}{\sqrt{n}}}, \text{ or the } p\text{ - value.}$$

6. Reach a decision. Compare the test statistic with $\bar{x}_\alpha$, z_α, or α, respectively.

7. Draw a conclusion regarding the null hypothesis.

EXAMPLE 8-5: ONE-TAILED HYPOTHESIS TEST FOR μ, σ KNOWN

Elgin Heart Institute   The Elgin Heart Institute performs many open-heart surgery procedures. Recently research physicians at Elgin have developed a new heart bypass surgery procedure that they believe will reduce the average recovery time. The hospital board will not recommend the new procedure unless there is substantial evidence to suggest that it is better than the existing procedure. Records indicate that the current mean recovery rate for the standard procedure is 42 days, with a standard deviation of 5 days. To test whether the new procedure actually results in a lower mean recovery time, the procedure was performed on a random sample of 36 patients.

Step 1:   **Specify the population value of interest.**
We are interested in the mean recovery time, μ.

Step 2:   **Formulate the null and alternative hypotheses.**
$$H_0: \mu \geq 42$$
$$H_A: \mu < 42$$

Step 3:   **Specify the desired significance level (α).**
The researchers wish to test the hypothesis using a 0.05 level of significance.

Step 4:   **Construct the rejection region.**
This will be a one-tailed test, with the rejection region in the lower (left-hand) tail of the sampling distribution. The critical value is $-z_{0.05} = -1.645$. Therefore, the decision rule becomes:
If $z < -1.645$, reject H_0; otherwise, do not reject H_0.

Step 5:   **Compute the test statistic.**
Because the population standard deviation is known, we will use z. Assume the sample mean, computed using $\bar{x} = \frac{\Sigma x}{n}$, is 40.2 days. Then
$$z = \frac{\bar{x} - \mu}{\frac{\sigma}{\sqrt{n}}} = \frac{40.2 - 42}{\frac{5}{\sqrt{36}}} = -2.16$$

Step 6:   **Reach a decision.** (See Figure 8-5.)
The decision rule is
If $z < -1.645$, reject H_0
Otherwise, do not reject.
Because $-2.16 < -1.645$, reject H_0.

Step 7:   **Draw a conclusion.**
There is sufficient evidence to conclude that the new bypass procedure does result in a shorter average recovery period.

FIGURE 8-5

Elgin Heart Institute
Hypothesis Test

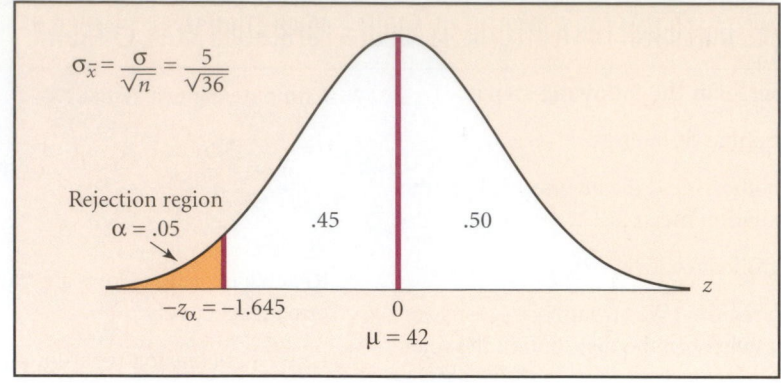

p-VALUE FOR TWO-TAILED TESTS

In the previous examples, the rejection region was located in one tail of the sampling distribution. In those cases, the null hypothesis was of the ≥ or ≤ format. However, sometimes the null hypothesis will be stated as a direct equality.

Cranston Peanuts—Consider the Cranston Peanut Company, which grows and packages salted and unsalted, unshelled peanuts in 16-ounce sacks. The company's filling process strives for an average fill amount equal to 16 ounces. Therefore, Cranston would test the following null and alternative hypotheses:

$$H_0: \mu = 16 \text{ ounces}$$
$$H_A: \mu \neq 16 \text{ ounces}$$

The null hypothesis will be rejected if the test statistic falls in either tail of the sampling distribution. The size of the rejection region is determined by α. Each tail has an area equal to $\alpha/2$.

The *p*-value for the two-tailed test is computed in a manner similar to that for a one-tailed test. First, determine the *z* test statistic as follows:

$$z = \frac{\bar{x} - \mu}{\dfrac{\sigma}{\sqrt{n}}}$$

Suppose for this situation, Cranston managers calculated a $z = 3.32$. Next, find $P(z > 3.32)$ using either the standard normal table in Appendix D, Excel's **NORMSDIST** function, or Minitab's **Calc > Probability Distributions** command. In this case, because $z = 3.32$ exceeds the table values, we will use Excel or Minitab to obtain

$$P(z \leq 3.32) = 0.9995.$$

Then

$$P(z > 3.32) = 1 - 0.9995 = 0.0005.$$

However, because this is a two-tailed hypothesis test, the *p*-value is found by multiplying the 0.0005 value by 2 (to account for the chance that our sample result could have been on either side of the distribution). This is

$$p\text{-value} = 2(0.0005) = 0.0010.$$

Assuming an alpha = 0.10 level, then since the

$$p\text{-value} = 0.0010 < \alpha = 0.10, \text{ we reject } H_0.$$

Figure 8-6 illustrates the two-tailed test for the Cranston Peanuts example.

FIGURE 8-6

Two-Tailed Test—Cranston Peanut Example

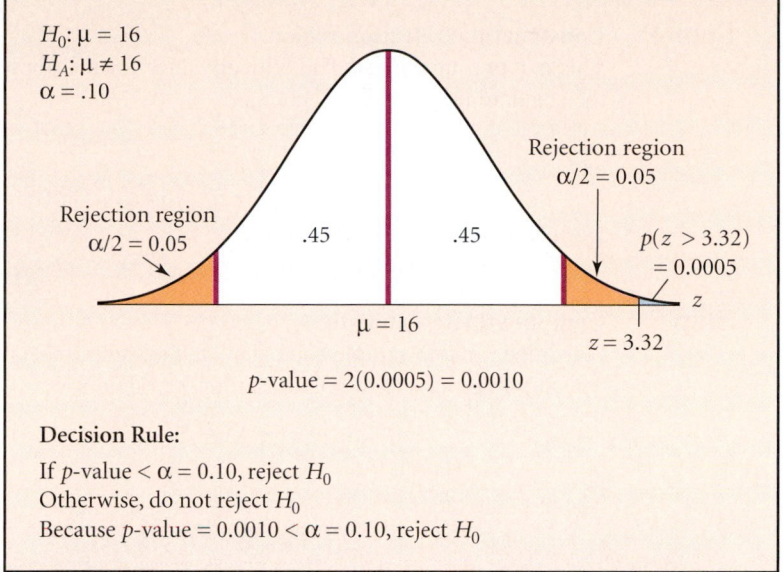

$H_0: \mu = 16$
$H_A: \mu \neq 16$
$\alpha = .10$

Rejection region $\alpha/2 = 0.05$

Rejection region $\alpha/2 = 0.05$

.45   .45

$p(z > 3.32) = 0.0005$

z

$\mu = 16$

$z = 3.32$

p-value $= 2(0.0005) = 0.0010$

Decision Rule:

If p-value $< \alpha = 0.10$, reject H_0
Otherwise, do not reject H_0
Because p-value $= 0.0010 < \alpha = 0.10$, reject H_0

SUMMARY: TWO-TAILED TEST FOR A HYPOTHESIS ABOUT A POPULATION MEAN, σ KNOWN

To conduct a two-tailed hypothesis test when the population standard deviation is known, you can perform the following steps.

1. Specify the population value of interest.

2. Formulate the null and alternative hypotheses in terms of the population mean, μ.

3. Specify the desired significance level, α.

4. Construct the rejection region.
   Determine the critical values for each tail, $z_{\alpha/2}$ and $-z_{\alpha/2}$, from the standard normal table. If needed, calculate $\bar{x}_{(\alpha/2)L}$ and $\bar{x}_{(\alpha/2)U}$.

Define the two-tailed decision rule using one of the following:

- If $z > z_{\alpha/2}$, or if $z < -z_{\alpha/2}$ reject H_0; otherwise, do not reject H_0.
- If, $\bar{x} < \bar{x}_{(\alpha/2)L}$, or $\bar{x} > \bar{x}_{(\alpha/2)U}$, reject H_0; otherwise, do not reject H_0.
- If p-value $< \alpha$, reject H_0; otherwise, do not reject H_0.

5. Compute the test statistic, $z = \dfrac{\bar{x} - \mu}{\dfrac{\sigma}{\sqrt{n}}}$, $\bar{x} = \dfrac{\sum x}{n}$ or find the p-value.

6. Reach a decision.

7. Draw a conclusion.

EXAMPLE 8-6: TWO-TAILED HYPOTHESIS TEST FOR μ, σ KNOWN

The Wilson Glass Company   The Wilson Glass Company has a contract to supply plate glass for home and commercial windows. The contract specifies that the mean thickness of the glass must be 0.375 inches. The standard deviation, σ, is known to be 0.05 inch. Before sending the first shipment, Wilson managers wish to test whether they are meeting the requirements by selecting a random sample of $n = 100$ thickness measurements.

Step 1:   Specify the population value of interest.
The mean thickness of glass is of interest.

Step 2:   Formulate the null and the alternative hypotheses.
The null and alternative hypotheses are:

$$H_0: \mu = 0.375 \text{ inch}$$
$$H_A: \mu \neq 0.375 \text{ inch}$$

Step 3:   Specify the desired significance level (α).
The managers wish to test the hypothesis using an $\alpha = 0.05$.

Step 4:   **Construct the rejection region.**
This is a two-tailed test. The critical values for the upper and lower tails are found in the standard normal table. These are:

$$-z_{\alpha/2} = -z_{0.05/2} = -z_{0.025} = -1.96$$

and

$$z_{\alpha/2} = z_{0.05/2} = z_{0.025} = 1.96$$

Define the two-tailed decision rule:

If $z > 1.96$, or if $z < -1.96$, reject H_0; otherwise, do not reject H_0.

Step 5:   **Compute the test statistic.**
Select the random sample and calculate the sample mean.
Suppose that the sample mean for the random sample of 100 measurements is:

$$\bar{x} = \frac{\sum x}{n} = 0.378 \text{ inch}$$

The test statistic is

$$z = \frac{\bar{x} - \mu}{\dfrac{\sigma}{\sqrt{n}}} = \frac{0.378 - 0.375}{\dfrac{0.05}{\sqrt{100}}} = 0.60$$

Step 6:   **Reach a decision.**
Because $-1.96 < z = 0.60 < 1.96$, do not reject the null hypothesis.

Step 7:   **Draw a conclusion.**
The Wilson Company does not have sufficient evidence to conclude that they are not meeting the contract.

HYPOTHESIS TEST FOR μ, σ UNKNOWN

In Chapter 7, we introduced situations in which the objective was to estimate a population mean when the population standard deviation was unknown. In those cases, the t-distribution was used to determine the critical value, rather than the standard normal distribution. The same logic is used again, together with Equation 8-3, to compute the test statistic when testing hypotheses about a population mean for cases in which σ is unknown.

---

t Test Statistic for Hypothesis Test, σ Unknown

$$t = \frac{\bar{x} - \mu}{\dfrac{s}{\sqrt{n}}}$$ **8-3**

where:

$\bar{x}$ = Sample mean
μ = Hypothesized value for the population mean
s = Sample standard deviation $s = \sqrt{\dfrac{\sum(x - \bar{x})^2}{n - 1}}$
n = Sample size

In order to employ the t-distribution, we must make the following assumption:

SSUMPTION   The population is normally distributed.

If the population from which the simple random sample is selected is normal or approximately normal, the t test statistic computed using Equation 8-3 will be distributed according to a t-distribution with $n - 1$ degrees of freedom.

EXAMPLE 8-7: HYPOTHESIS TEST FOR μ, σ UNKNOWN

Dairy Fresh Ice Cream   The Dairy Fresh Ice Cream plant in Pittsburgh, Pennsylvania, uses a filling machine for its 64-ounce cartons. There is some variation in the actual amount of ice cream that goes into the carton. The machine can go out of adjustment and put a mean amount either less or more than 64 ounces in the cartons. To monitor the filling process, the production manager selects a simple random sample of 16 filled ice cream cartons each day. He can test whether the machine is still in adjustment using the following steps.

Step 1: **Specify the population value of interest.**
The manager is interested in the mean amount of ice cream.

Step 2: **Formulate the appropriate null and alternative hypotheses.**
The status quo is that the machine continues to fill ice cream cartons with a mean equal to 64 ounces. Thus, the null and alternative hypotheses are:

$$H_0: \mu = 64 \text{ ounces (Machine is in adjustment.)}$$
$$H_A: \mu \neq 64 \text{ ounces (Machine is out of adjustment.)}$$

Step 3: **Specify the desired level of significance.**
The test will be conducted using an alpha level equal to 0.05.

Step 4: **Construct the rejection region.**
We first produce a box and whisker plot for a rough check on the normality assumption. The sample data are

62.7	64.7	64.0	64.5	64.6	65.0	64.4	64.2
64.6	65.5	63.6	64.7	64.0	64.2	63.0	63.6

The box and whisker diagram is:

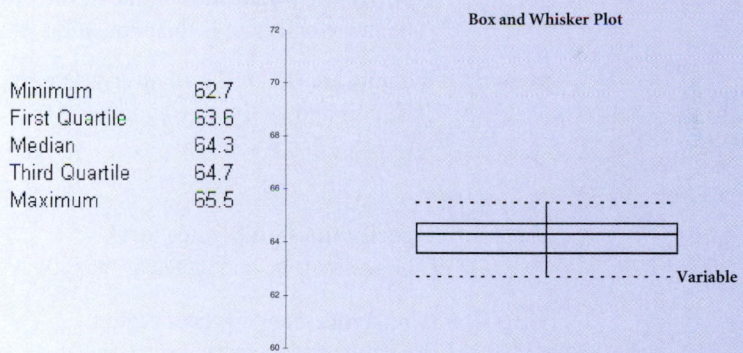

Minimum	62.7
First Quartile	63.6
Median	64.3
Third Quartile	64.7
Maximum	65.5

Box and Whisker Plot

The box and whisker diagram does not indicate that the population distribution is unduly skewed. Thus, the normal distribution assumption is reasonable based on these sample data.

Now we determine the critical values from the *t*-distribution.

Based on the null and alternative hypotheses, this test is two-tailed. Thus, we will split the alpha into two tails and determine the critical value from the *t*-distribution with $n - 1$ degrees of freedom. Using Appendix F, the critical *t* for $\alpha/2 = 0.025$, and $16 - 1 = 15$ degrees of freedom is $t = \pm 2.1315$.

The decision rule for this two-tailed test is

If $t < -2.1315$ or $t > 2.1315$, reject H_0
Otherwise, do not reject H_0.

Step 5: **Compute the test statistic using Equation 8-3.**
The sample mean is

$$\bar{x} = \frac{\sum x}{n} = \frac{1,027.3}{16} = 64.2$$

The sample standard deviation is

$$s = \sqrt{\frac{\sum(x - \bar{x})^2}{n - 1}} = 0.72$$

The test statistic is

$$t = \frac{\bar{x} - \mu}{\frac{s}{\sqrt{n}}} = \frac{64.2 - 64}{\frac{0.72}{\sqrt{16}}} = 1.11$$

Step 6: **Reach a decision.**
Because $t = 1.11$ is not less than -2.1315 and not greater than 2.1315, we do not reject the null hypothesis.

Step 7: **Draw a conclusion.**
Based on these sample data, the company has no reason to believe that the filling machine is out of adjustment.

EXAMPLE 8-8: TESTING THE HYPOTHESIS FOR μ, σ UNKNOWN

The Qwest Company The Qwest Company operates service centers in various cities where customers can call to get answers to questions about their bills. Previous studies indicate that the distribution of time required for each call is normally distributed, with a mean equal to 540 seconds. Company officials have selected a random sample of 16 calls and wish to determine whether the mean call time is now fewer than 540 seconds after a training program given to call-center employees.

Step 1: **Specify the population value of interest.**
The mean call time is the population value of interest.

Step 2: **Formulate the null and alternative hypotheses.**
The null and alternative hypotheses are

$$H_0: \mu \geq 540 \text{ seconds}$$
$$H_A: \mu < 540 \text{ seconds}$$

Step 3: **Specify the significance level.**
The test will be conducted at the 0.01 level of significance. Thus, $\alpha = 0.01$.

Step 4: **Construct the rejection region.**
Because this is a one-tailed test and the rejection region is in the lower tail, the critical value from the t-distribution with $16 - 1 = 15$ degrees of freedom is $-t_\alpha = -t_{.01} = -2.6025$.

Step 5: **Compute the test statistic.**
The sample mean for the random sample of 16 calls is $\bar{x} = \frac{\sum x}{n} = 510$ seconds, and

the sample standard deviation is $s = \sqrt{\frac{\sum(x - \bar{x})^2}{n - 1}} = 45$ seconds. Assuming that the

population distribution is approximately normal, the test statistic is

$$t = \frac{\bar{x} - \mu}{\frac{s}{\sqrt{n}}} = \frac{510 - 540}{\frac{45}{\sqrt{16}}} = -2.67$$

Step 6: **Reach a decision.**
Because $t = -2.67 < -2.6025$, the null hypothesis should be rejected.

Step 7: **Draw a conclusion.**
Qwest can conclude that the mean time for service calls has been reduced below 540 seconds.

FIGURE 8-7

FIGURE 8-7

**Tires Test Data for Franklin
Tire Company**

Excel Instructions:
1. Open file: Franklin.xls
2. Select **PHStat**.
3. Select **Box and Whisker
   Plot**.
4. Define **Data Range**.
5. Select **5-Number
   Summary**.

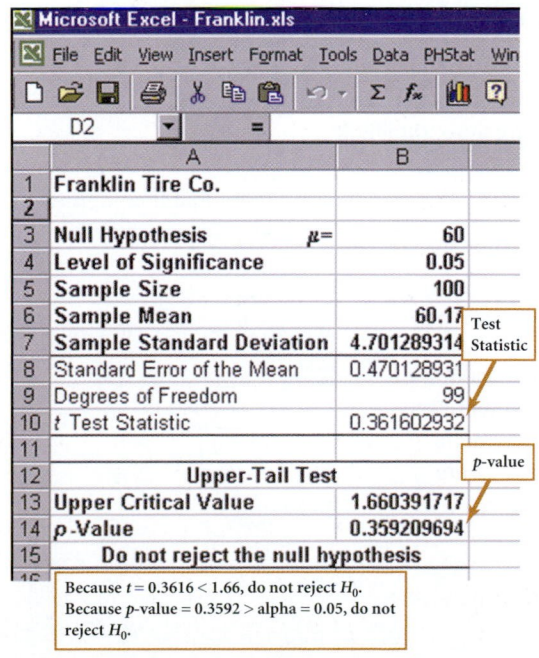

Franklin Tire Company—The Franklin Tire Company recently conducted a test on a new tire design to determine whether the company could make the claim that the mean tire mileage would exceed 60,000 miles. The test was conducted in Alaska. A simple random sample of 100 tires was tested, and the number of miles each tire lasted until it no longer met the federal government minimum tread thickness was recorded. Figure 8-7 shows some of the sample data in an Excel spreadsheet format and a box and whisker diagram. The data (shown in thousands of dollars) are in the CD-ROM file called *Franklin*.

The null and alternative hypotheses to be tested are

$$H_0: \mu \leq 60$$
$$H_A: \mu > 60$$
$$\alpha = 0.05$$

Excel does not have a special procedure for testing hypotheses for single population means. However, the Excel add-ins software called PHStat on the CD-ROM that accompanies this text has the necessary hypothesis-testing tools. Figure 8-8a and Figure 8-8b show the Excel PHStat and the Minitab outputs.[4]

We denote the critical value of an upper (lower) tail test with a significance level of α as t_α $(-t_\alpha)$. The critical value for $\alpha = 0.05$ and 99 degrees of freedom is $t_\alpha = 1.66$. Using the critical value approach, the decision rule is

If the test statistic $> 1.66 = t_\alpha$, reject H_0; otherwise, do not reject H_0.

FIGURE 8-8A

**Excel (PHStat) Output for
Franklin Tire Hypothesis
Test Results**

**Excel (PHStat)
Instructions:**
1. Open file: Franklin.xls
2. Click on **PHStat** tab.
3. Select **One Sample
   Tests**, *t-test for Mean,
   Sigma Unknown*.
4. Enter Hypothesized
   Mean.
5. Check "**Sample
   Statistics Unknown.**"
6. Check **One-Tailed Test**.

[4]This test can be done in Excel without the benefit of the PHStat add-ins. Please refer to the Excel tutorial on your CD-ROM for the specifics.

FIGURE 8-8B

Minitab Output for Franklin Tire Hypothesis Test Results

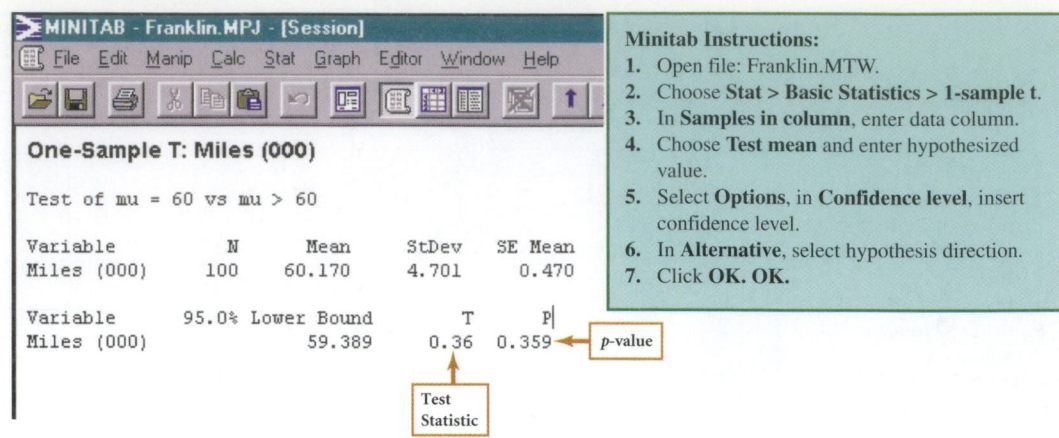

The sample mean, based on a sample of 100 tires is $\bar{x} = 60.17$ (60,170 miles), and the sample standard deviation is $s = 4.701$ (4,701 miles). The t test statistics shown in Figures 8-8a and 8-8b are computed as follows:

$$t = \frac{\bar{x} - \mu}{\frac{s}{\sqrt{n}}} = \frac{60.17 - 60}{\frac{4.701}{\sqrt{100}}} = 0.3616$$

Because

$$t = 0.3616 < 1.66 = t_{\alpha},$$

we do not reject the null hypothesis.

Thus, based upon the sample data, the evidence is insufficient to conclude that the new tires have an average life exceeding 60,000 miles. Based on this test, the company would not be justified in making the claim.

Franklin managers could also use the p-value approach to test the null hypothesis because the output shown in Figures 8-8a and 8-8b provide the p-value. In this case, the p-value = 0.3592. The decision rule for a test is

If p-value $< \alpha$ reject H_0; otherwise, do not reject H_0.

Because

$$p\text{-value} = 0.3592 > 0.05 = \alpha,$$

we do not reject the null hypothesis. This is the same conclusion we reached using the critical value approach.

SUMMARY: ONE- OR TWO-TAILED TESTS FOR μ, σ UNKNOWN

1. Specify the population value of interest, μ.

2. Formulate the null hypothesis and the alternative hypothesis.

3. Specify the desired significance level (α).

4. Construct the rejection region.
   If it is a two-tailed test, determine the critical values for each tail, $t_{\alpha/2}$ and $-t_{\alpha/2}$, from the t-distribution table. If the test is a one-tailed test, find either t_{α} or $-t_{\alpha}$, depending on the tail of the rejection region. Degrees of freedom are $n - 1$. If desired, the critical t-values can be used to find the appropriate $\bar{x}_{\alpha}$ or the $\bar{x}_{\alpha/2}$ and $\bar{x}_{\alpha/2}$ values.
   Define the decision rule.
   a. If the test statistic falls into the rejection region, reject H_0; otherwise, do not reject H_0.
   b. If the p-value is less than α, reject H_0; otherwise, do not reject H_0.

5. Assuming that the population is approximately normal, compute the test statistic.
   Select the random sample and calculate the sample mean, $\bar{x} = \frac{\sum x}{n}$, and the sample standard deviation,

$$s = \sqrt{\frac{\sum(x - \bar{x})^2}{n - 1}}.$$ Then calculate

$$t = \frac{\bar{x} - \mu}{\frac{s}{\sqrt{n}}} \text{ or } p\text{-value}$$

6. Reach a decision.

7. Draw a conclusion.

This section has introduced the basic concepts of hypothesis testing. There are several ways to test a null hypothesis. Each method will yield the same result, however computer software such as Minitab and Excel show the p-values automatically. Therefore, decision makers increasingly use the p-value approach.

8-1: EXERCISES

Skill Development

8.1 For each of the following claims, list the appropriate null and alternative hypotheses:
a. The mean is larger than 20.
b. The mean equals 50.
c. The mean is at least 35.
d. The mean is more than 87.
e. The mean is at most 6.

8.2 Determine the p-values associated with the following test statistics for a two-tailed test.
a. $z = 2.97$
b. $z = 1.98$
c. $z = 3.01$
d. $z = 4.58$
e. $z = -1.58$

8.3 Given the following null and alternative hypotheses,

$$H_0: \mu \leq 200$$
$$H_A: \mu > 200$$
$$\alpha = 0.05$$

and

$$\bar{x} = 204.50 \qquad \sigma = 45.00 \qquad n = 200$$

a. Establish the appropriate decision rule for $\bar{x}$ and z.
b. Indicate the appropriate decision based on the sample information and each of the decision rules.
c. Which of the hypotheses will not be declared true unless the sample data strongly indicate that it is true?

8.4 Given the following null and alternative hypotheses,

$$H_0: \mu \leq 24.78$$
$$H_A: \mu > 24.78$$
$$\alpha = 0.03$$

and

$$\bar{x} = 24.85 \qquad \sigma = 9.00 \qquad n = 50$$

a. Establish the appropriate decision rule for the p-value and z.
b. Indicate the appropriate decision based on the sample information and each of the decision rules.

8.5 Given the following null and alternative hypotheses,

$$H_0: \mu \geq 4{,}000$$
$$H_A: \mu < 4{,}000$$
$$\alpha = 0.05$$

and

$$\bar{x} = 3{,}980 \qquad s = 205 \qquad n = 100$$

a. Establish the appropriate decision rule.

b. Indicate the appropriate decision based on the sample information, using both the p-value and $\bar{x}$.
c. Provide the two research hypotheses that could have produced the null and alternative hypotheses in this problem.

8.6 Determine the p-values associated with the following test statistic for an upper-tail test.
a. $z = 1.45$
b. $z = 2.33$
c. $z = -1.87$
d. $z = 0$
e. $z = -4.59$

8.7 For each of the following, indicate which of the two errors associated with hypothesis testing could occur.
a. The null hypothesis was rejected.
b. The null hypothesis was not rejected.
c. The null hypothesis, in reality, was true.
d. The alternative hypothesis, in reality, was true.

8.8 Given the following null and alternative hypotheses,

$$H_0: \mu = 1{,}346$$
$$H_A: \mu \neq 1{,}346$$
$$\alpha = 0.05$$

and

$$\bar{x} = 1{,}338 \qquad \sigma = 90 \qquad n = 64$$

a. Establish the appropriate decision rule based on z as a test statistic.
b. Indicate the appropriate decision based on the sample information and the decision rule.
c. Given the decision you reached, which of the two types of errors associated with hypothesis tests could you have made?

8.9 Determine the p-value for each of the following hypothesis scenarios:
a. $H_0: \mu = 1{,}346$ versus $H_A: \mu \neq 1{,}346$ and $z = 2.36$.
b. $H_0: \mu \geq 4{,}000$ versus $H_A: \mu < 4{,}000$ and $z = -1.85$.
c. $H_0: \mu \leq 24.78$ versus $H_A: \mu > 24.78$ and $z = 0.84$.
d. $H_0: \mu \leq 200$ versus $H_A: \mu > 200$ and $z = -2.06$ (be careful here).

8.10 Determine the critical value(s), z_α (or $\pm z_{\alpha/2}$), for each of the following situations.
a. $\alpha = 0.05$, upper-tail test
b. $\alpha = 0.025$, upper-tail test
c. $\alpha = 0.01$, lower-tail test
d. $\alpha = 0.05$, two-tailed test
e. $\alpha = 0.10$, two-tailed test

8.11   Given the following null and alternative hypotheses,

$$H_0: \mu = 4{,}450$$
$$H_A: \mu \neq 4{,}450$$
$$\alpha = 0.1$$

and

$$\bar{x} = 4{,}475.6 \qquad s = 940 \qquad n = 30$$

a. Establish the appropriate decision rule in terms of $\bar{x}$.

b. Indicate the appropriate decision based on the sample information and the decision rule.

Business Applications

8.12   Peterson Automotive is the Honda automobile dealership in a western U.S. city. They recently stated in an advertisement that Honda owners average more than 85,000 miles before trading in or selling their Hondas. To test this, an independent agency selected a simple random sample of 80 Honda owners who have either traded or sold their Hondas and determined the number of miles on the cars when the owners parted with them. They plan to test Peterson's claim at the alpha = 0.05 level.

a. State the appropriate null and alternative hypotheses.

b. If the sample mean is 86,200 miles and the sample standard deviation is 12,000 miles, what conclusion should be reached about the claim?

8.13   The director of a state agency claims that the average starting salary for clerical employees in the state is less than $30,000 per year. To test this claim, she has collected a simple random sample of 100 starting salaries of clerks from across the state and found that the sample mean is $29,750.

a. State the appropriate null and alternative hypotheses.

b. Assuming the population standard deviation is known to be $2,500 and the significance level for the test is 0.05, what is the critical value?

c. Referring to your answer in part b, what conclusion should be reached with respect to the null hypothesis?

d. Referring to your answer in part c, which of the two statistical errors might have been made in this case? Explain.

8.14   A telemarketing company located in Los Angeles has established a guideline that states that the average time for each completed call should be 4 minutes or less. Recently the operations manager was concerned that calls were taking too long. The operations manager did not wish to assert that the calls were taking too long if the sample data did not strongly indicate this. A sample of 12 calls was selected and the following times (in seconds) were recorded.

| 194 | 278 | 302 | 140 | 245 | 234 | 268 | 208 | 102 | 190 | 220 | 255 |

a. Construct the appropriate null and alternative hypotheses.

b. Based on the sample data, what should the operations manager conclude? Test at the 0.10 significance level.

c. Suppose you wished to conduct the test in part b using $\bar{x}$ as the test statistic. Calculate the critical value, $\bar{x}_\alpha$.

8.15   A mail-order business prides itself in its ability to fill customers' orders in six calendar days or fewer, on the average. Periodically, the operations manager selects a random sample of customer orders and determines the number of days required to fill the orders. Based on this sample information, he decides whether the desired standard is being met. He will assume that the average number of days to fill customers' orders is six or fewer unless the data suggest strongly otherwise.

a. Establish the appropriate null and alternative hypotheses.

b. On one occasion when a sample of 40 customers was selected, the average number of days was 6.65, with a sample standard deviation of 1.5 days. Can the operations manager conclude that his mail-order business is achieving its goal? Use a significance level of 0.025 to answer this question.

c. Calculate the p-value for this test. Conduct the test using this p-value.

d. The operations manager wishes to monitor the efficiency of his mail-order service often. Therefore, he does not wish to repeatedly calculate z-values to conduct the hypothesis tests. Obtain the critical value, $\bar{x}_\alpha$, so that the manager can simply compare the sample mean to this value to conduct the test. Use $\bar{x}$ as the test statistic to conduct the test.

8.16   The makers of Mini-Oats Cereal have an automated packaging machine that can be set at any targeted fill level between 12 and 32 ounces. Every box of cereal is not expected to contain exactly the targeted weight, but the average of all boxes filled should. At the end of every shift (8 hours), 16 boxes are selected at random and the mean and standard deviation of the sample are computed. Based on these sample results, the production control manager determines whether the filling machine needs to be readjusted or it remains all right to operate. Use $\alpha = 0.05$.

a. Establish the appropriate null and alternative hypotheses to be tested for boxes that are supposed to have an average of 24 ounces.

b. At the end of a particular shift during which the machine was filling 24-ounce boxes of Mini-Oats, the sample mean of 16 boxes was 24.32 ounces, with a standard deviation of 0.70 ounce. Assist the production control manager in determining if the machine is achieving its targeted average.

c. Why do you suppose the production control manager would prefer to make this hypothesis test a two-tailed test? Discuss.

d. Conduct the test using a p-value as the test statistic.

e. Considering the result of the test, which of the two types of errors in hypothesis testing could you have made?

8.17   Bowman Electronics sells electronic components for car stereos. They claim that the average life of a component exceeds 4,000 hours. To test this claim, they have selected a random sample of $n = 12$ of their components and have traced the life between installation and failure. The following data were obtained:

| 1,973 | 4,838 | 3,805 | 4,494 | 4,738 | 5,249 |
| 4,459 | 4,098 | 4,722 | 5,894 | 3,322 | 4,800 |

a. State the appropriate null and alternative hypotheses.
b. Assuming that the test is to be conducted using a 0.05 level of significance, what conclusion should be reached based on these sample data? Be sure to examine the required normality assumption.

8.18 The makers of a new home furnace system claim that if the furnace is installed, homeowners will observe an average fuel bill of less than $80.00 per month during January if their house has between 2,200 and 2,400 square feet of heated living space. A consumer agency plans to test this claim by taking a random sample of homes of this size where the new furnace has just been installed.
a. (1) Suppose the consumer agency conducts this test and declares that the manufacturer's claim is not correct. Would you expect the manufacturer to take legal action?
(2) Suppose, now, that the consumer agency states that the manufacturer's claim is correct. Would you expect the same type and magnitude of consequences?
(3) Taking your answers to (1) and (2), determine the research hypothesis for the consumer agency's test.
b. Establish the appropriate null and alternative hypotheses.
c. If the desired significance level for the test is 0.05, what should be concluded about the company's claim if the following sample results are observed?

$$\bar{x} = \$78.60 \qquad s^2 = 625 \qquad n = 64$$

Use the p-value to conduct this hypothesis test.

Advanced Business Applications

8.19 The Cell Tone Company sells cellular phones and airtime in several northwestern states. At a recent meeting, the marketing manager stated that the average age of Cell Tone customers is under 40 years. This came up in conjunction with a proposed advertising plan that is to be directed toward a young audience. Before actually completing the advertising plan, Cell Tone decided to randomly sample customers. Among the questions asked in the survey of 50 customers in the Jacksonville, Florida, area was the customers' ages. The age data are available in the CD-ROM file called *Cell Phone Survey*.
a. Based on the statement made by the marketing manager, formulate the appropriate null and alternative hypotheses.
b. The marketing manager must support his statement concerning average customer age in an upcoming board meeting. Using a significance level of 0.10, provide this support for the marketing manager.

c. Consider the result of the hypothesis test you conducted in part b. Which of the two types of hypothesis test errors could you have committed? How could you discover if you had, indeed, made this error?

8.20 Reconsider Exercise 8.19.
a. Calculate the critical value, $\bar{x}_\alpha$.
b. Determine the p-value and conduct the test using the p-value.
c. Note that the sample data lists the customers' ages to the nearest year.
(1) If we denote a randomly selected customer's age (to the nearest year) as x_i, is x_i a continuous or discrete random variable? (2) Is it possible that x_i has a normal distribution? (3) Consider your answers to (1) and (2) and the fact that $\bar{x}$ must have a normal distribution to facilitate the calculation in part b. Does this mean that the calculation you have performed in part b is inappropriate? Explain your answer.

8.21 The Haines Lumber Company makes plywood for the furniture industry. One product it makes is $\frac{3}{4}$-inch oak veneer panels. It is very important that the panels conform to specifications. One specification calls for the panels to be made to an average thickness of 0.75 inch. Each hour, 5 panels are selected at random and measured. After 20 hours, a total of 100 panels have been measured. These data are in the CD-ROM file called *Haines*.
a. Formulate the appropriate null and alternative hypotheses relative to the thickness specification.
b. Based on the sample data, what should the company conclude about the status of its product meeting the thickness specification? Test at a significance level of 0.01. Discuss your results in a report to the production manager.
c. The production manager has looked at the results of your test. He wishes to repeat this sampling process and wants a rule to compare future $\bar{x}$ values. Furnish this information to the manager.
d. The manager wishes to know what error in part b could have been made. He also wishes to know how you could be certain whether such an error could have been made. Provide this information to the manager.

8.22 The Wilson Company uses a great deal of water in the process of making industrial milling equipment. To comply with the federal clean-water laws, it has a water purification system that all wastewater goes through before being discharged into a settling pond on the company's property. To determine whether the company is complying with federal requirements, sample measures are taken every so often. One requirement is that the average pH level not exceed 7.4. A sample of 95 pH measures has been taken. The data for these measures are shown in the file *Wilson Water*.

a. Considering the requirement for pH level, state the appropriate null and alternative hypotheses.
b. Discuss why it is appropriate to form the hypotheses with the federal standard as the alternative hypothesis.

c. Based on the sample data of pH level, what should the company conclude about its current status on meeting the federal requirement? Test the hypothesis at the 0.05 level. Discuss your results in a memo to the company's environmental relations manager.

8-2 HYPOTHESIS TESTS FOR PROPORTIONS

So far this chapter has focused on hypothesis tests about a single population mean. Although many decision problems involve a test of a population mean, there are also cases in which the value of interest is the population proportion. For example, a production manager might consider the proportion of defective items produced on an assembly line in order to determine whether the line should be restructured. Likewise, a life insurance salesperson's performance assessment might include the proportion of existing clients who renew their policies.

TESTING A HYPOTHESIS ABOUT A SINGLE POPULATION PROPORTION

The basic concept of hypothesis testing for proportions is the same as for means.

1. The null and alternative hypotheses are stated in terms of a population parameter, now p instead of μ, and the sample statistic becomes $\bar{p}$ instead of $\bar{x}$.
2. The null hypothesis should be a statement concerning the parameter that includes the equality.
3. The significance level of the hypothesis again determines the size of the rejection region.
4. The test can be one- or two-tailed, depending on how the alternative hypothesis is formulated.

First American Bank and Title—The internal auditors at First American Bank and Title Company routinely test the bank's system of internal controls. Recently, the audit manager examined the documentation on the bank's 22,500 outstanding automobile loans. The bank's procedures require that the file on each auto loan account contain certain specific documentation, such as a list of applicant assets, statement of monthly income, list of liabilities, and certificate of automobile insurance. If an account contains all the required documentation, then it complies with bank procedures.

The audit manager has established a 1% noncompliance rate as the bank's standard. If more than 1% of the 22,500 loans do not have appropriate documentation, then the internal controls are not effective and the bank needs to improve the situation. The audit staff does not have enough time to examine all 22,500 files to determine the noncompliance rate. As a result, the audit staff selects a random sample of 600 files, examines them, and determines the number of files not in compliance with bank documentation requirements. The sample findings will tell the manager if the bank is exceeding the 1% noncompliance rate for the population of all 22,500 loan files. The manager will not act unless the noncompliance rate exceeds 1%. The default position is that the internal controls are effective. Thus, the null and alternative hypotheses are

$$H_0: p \leq 0.01 \text{ (Internal Controls Are Effective)}$$
$$H_A: p > 0.01 \text{ (Internal Controls Are Not Effective)}$$

Suppose the sample of 600 accounts uncovered 9 files with inadequate loan documentation. The question is whether 9 out of 600 is sufficient to conclude that the bank has a problem. To answer this question statistically, we need to recall a lesson from Chapter 6.

REQUIREMENT

The sample size, n, is large such that $np \geq 5$ and $n(1 - p) \geq 5$.

If this requirement is satisfied, the sampling distribution is approximately normal with mean $= p$ and standard deviation $= \sqrt{\dfrac{p(1 - p)}{n}}$.

The bank's auditors have a general policy of performing these tests with a significance level of $\alpha = 0.02$.

They are willing to reject a true null hypothesis 2% of the time. In this case, if a Type I statistical error is committed, the internal controls will be considered ineffective when, in fact, they are working as intended.

Once the null and alternative hypotheses and the significance level have been specified, we can formulate the decision rule for this test. Figure 8-9 shows how the decision rule is developed. Notice the critical value, $\bar{p}_\alpha$, is 2.05 standard deviations above $p = 0.01$. Thus, if the sample proportion, $\bar{p}$, exceeds

$$\bar{p}_\alpha = 0.0182,$$

the null hypothesis should be rejected.

Because there were 9 deficient files in the sample of 600 files, this means that

$$\bar{p} = 9/600 = 0.015.$$

Because

$$\bar{p} = 0.015 < 0.0182 = \bar{p}_\alpha$$

the null hypothesis H_0 should not be rejected, based on these sample data. Therefore, the auditors will conclude the system of internal controls is working effectively.

Alternatively, we could have based the test on a test statistic (z) with a standardized normal distribution. This test statistic is calculated using Equation 8-4.

---

z Test Statistic for Proportions

$$z = \frac{\bar{p} - p}{\sqrt{\dfrac{p(1 - p)}{n}}}$$

8-4

where:

$\bar{p}$ = Sample proportion
p = Hypothesized population proportion
n = Sample size

The z-value for this test statistic is

$$z = \frac{0.015 - 0.01}{0.004} = 1.25.$$

As was established in Figure 8-9, the critical value,

$$z_\alpha = 2.05.$$

FIGURE 8-9

Decision Rule for First American Bank and Title Example

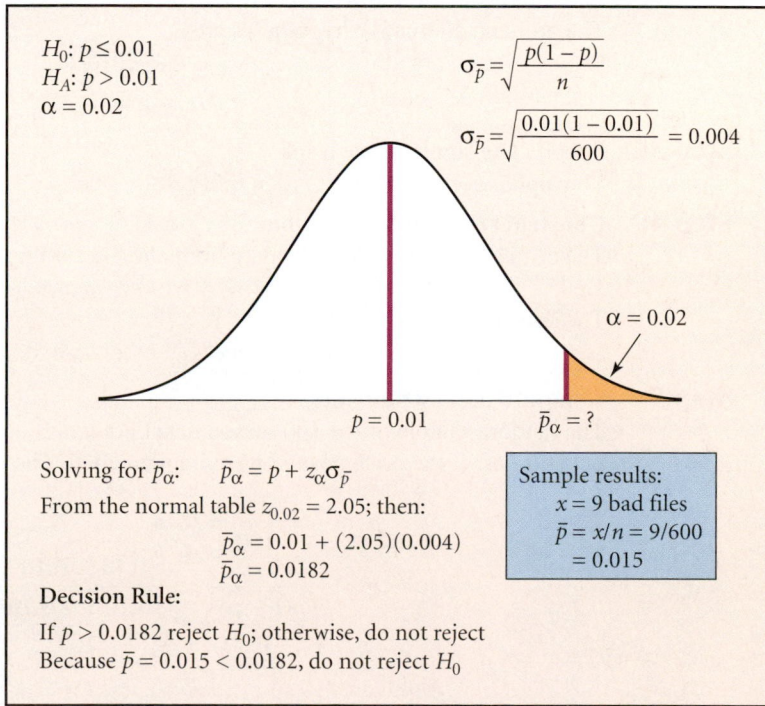

$H_0: p \leq 0.01$
$H_A: p > 0.01$
$\alpha = 0.02$

$\sigma_{\bar{p}} = \sqrt{\dfrac{p(1 - p)}{n}}$

$\sigma_{\bar{p}} = \sqrt{\dfrac{0.01(1 - 0.01)}{600}} = 0.004$

$\alpha = 0.02$

$p = 0.01$ $\bar{p}_\alpha = ?$

Solving for $\bar{p}_\alpha$: $\bar{p}_\alpha = p + z_\alpha \sigma_{\bar{p}}$
From the normal table $z_{0.02} = 2.05$; then:

$$\bar{p}_\alpha = 0.01 + (2.05)(0.004)$$
$$\bar{p}_\alpha = 0.0182$$

Sample results:
$x = 9$ bad files
$\bar{p} = x/n = 9/600$
$= 0.015$

Decision Rule:

If $p > 0.0182$ reject H_0; otherwise, do not reject
Because $\bar{p} = 0.015 < 0.0182$, do not reject H_0

We reject the null hypothesis only if $z > z_\alpha$. Because

$$z = 1.25 < 2.05$$

we

don't reject the null hypothesis.

This, of course, was the same conclusion we reached when we used $\bar{p}$ as the test statistic. Both test statistics must yield the same decision.

$\mathcal{S}$UMMARY: TESTING HYPOTHESES ABOUT A SINGLE POPULATION PROPORTION

1. Specify the population value of interest.

2. Formulate the null and alternative hypotheses.

3. Specify the significance level for testing the null hypothesis.

4. Construct the rejection region.
   For a one-tail test, determine the critical value, z_α, from the standard normal distribution table or

$$\bar{p}_\alpha = p + z_\alpha \sqrt{\frac{p(1-p)}{n}}$$

For a two-tail test, determine the critical values

$$\pm z_{\alpha/2} \text{ or } \bar{p}_{\alpha/2} = p \pm z_{\alpha/2}\sqrt{\frac{p(1-p)}{n}}$$

5. Compute the test statistic, $\bar{p} = \dfrac{x}{n}$ or $z = \dfrac{\bar{p} - p}{\sqrt{\dfrac{p(1-p)}{n}}}$

6. Reach a decision by comparing z to z_α or $\bar{p}$ to $\bar{p}_\alpha$.

7. Draw a conclusion.

$\mathcal{E}$XAMPLE 8-9: TESTING HYPOTHESES FOR SINGLE POPULATION PROPORTIONS

Season Ticket Sales   A major university is considering increasing the season ticket prices for basketball games. The athletic director is concerned that some people will terminate their ticket orders if this change occurs. If more than 10% of the season ticket orders would be terminated, the AD does not want to implement the changes. To test this, a random sample of ticket holders are surveyed and asked what they would do if the prices were increased.

Step 1:   **Specify the population value of interest.**
The parameter of interest is the population proportion.

Step 2:   **Formulate the null and alternative hypotheses.**
The null and alternative hypotheses are

$$H_0: p \le 0.10$$
$$H_A: p > 0.10$$

Step 3:   **Specify the significance level.**
The alpha level for this test is $\alpha = 0.05$.

Step 4:   **Construct the rejection region.**
The critical value from the standard normal table for this upper-tailed test is $z_\alpha = z_{.05} = 1.645$.
The decision rule is

If $z > 1.645$, reject H_0; otherwise, do not reject.

Step 5:   **Compute the test statistic.**
The random sample of $n = 100$ season ticket holders showed that 14 would cancel their ticket orders if the price change were implemented. The sample proportion is

$$\bar{p} = \frac{x}{n} = \frac{14}{100} = 0.14$$

$$z = \frac{\bar{p} - p}{\sqrt{\dfrac{p(1-p)}{n}}} = \frac{0.14 - 0.10}{\sqrt{\dfrac{0.10(1 - 0.10)}{100}}} = 1.33$$

Step 6:   **Reach a decision.**
Because $z = 1.33 < 1.645$, do not reject H_0.

Step 7:   **Draw a conclusion.**
Based on the sample data, the athletic director does not have sufficient evidence to conclude that more than 10% of the season ticket holders will cancel their ticket orders.

8-2: EXERCISES

Skill Development

8.23 Calculate the critical values for the following situations:
a. $H_A: p > 0.4$, $n = 150$, $\alpha = 0.05$
b. $H_A: p < 0.7$, $n = 200$, $\alpha = 0.10$
c. $H_A: p \neq 0.85$, $n = 100$, $\alpha = 0.10$

8.24 Given the following null and alternative hypotheses,

$$H_0: p = 0.20$$
$$H_A: p \neq 0.20$$

test the null hypothesis based on a random sample of 100, where $p = 0.23$.
a. Use the p-value approach to test the hypothesis. State the decision rule.
b. Use z as the test statistic to test the hypothesis. Assume an $\alpha = 0.05$ level. Be sure to show clearly the decision rule.

8.25 Given the following null and alternative hypotheses,

$$H_0: p = 0.70$$
$$H_A: p \neq 0.70$$

test the null hypothesis based on a random sample of 100, where $\bar{p} = 0.64$. Assume an $\alpha = 0.07$ level. Use the p-value approach to test the hypothesis. Be sure to show clearly the decision rule.

8.26 Given the following null and alternative hypotheses,

$$H_0: p \leq 0.45$$
$$H_A: p > 0.45$$

test the null hypothesis based on a random sample of $n = 500$, where $\bar{p} = 0.49$. Assume an $\alpha = 0.05$ level. Use the critical value approach to test the hypothesis. Be sure to show clearly the decision rule.

8.27 Given the following null and alternative hypotheses,

$$H_0: p \leq 0.24$$
$$H_A: p > 0.24$$

test the null hypothesis based on a random sample of $n = 100$, where $\bar{p} = 0.27$. Assume an $\alpha = 0.05$ level.
a. Use $\bar{p}_\alpha$ as the test statistic to test the hypothesis. Be sure to show clearly the decision rule.
b. Use z as the test statistic to test the hypothesis.

8.28 Given the following null and alternative hypotheses,

$$H_0: p \geq 0.50$$
$$H_A: p < 0.50$$

test the null hypothesis based on a random sample of 200, where $\bar{p} = 0.47$. Use $\alpha = 0.10$.
a. Use the p-value approach to test the hypothesis. State the decision rule.
b. Use $\bar{p}_\alpha$ as the test statistic to conduct the test of hypothesis.

Business Applications

8.29 The College of Business at a state university has a computer-literacy requirement for all graduates: Students must show proficiency with a spreadsheet software package and with a word-processing software package. To assess whether students are computer literate, a test is given at the end of each semester. The test is designed so that at least 70% of all students who have taken a special microcomputer course will pass the test. Suppose that, in a random sample of 100 students who have recently finished the microcomputer course, 63 pass the proficiency test.
a. Using a significance level of 0.05, what conclusions should the administrators make regarding the difficulty of the test?
b. Describe a Type II error in the context of this problem.

8.30 A shopping center developer claims in a presentation to a potential client that at least 40% of the adult female population in a community visit the mall one or more times a week. To test this claim, the developer selected a random sample of 100 households with an adult female present and asked if they visit the mall at least one day per week. Thirty-eight of the 100 respondents replied "yes" to the question.
  Based on the sample data and a significance level of 0.05, what should be concluded about the developer's claim? Show the decision rule and your analysis clearly.

8.31 A large number of complaints have been received in the past six months regarding airlines losing fliers' baggage. The airlines claim the problem is much smaller than newspaper articles have indicated. In fact, one airline spokesman claimed that fewer than 1% of all bags fail to arrive at their destinations with the passengers. To test this claim, 800 bags were randomly selected at various airports in the United States when they were checked with this airline. Of these, 6 failed to reach their destinations when their owners arrived.
a. Is this sufficient evidence to support the airline spokesman's claim? Test using a significance level of 0.05. Discuss.

b. Estimate the proportion of bags that fail to arrive at the proper destinations using a technique for which 95% confidence applies.

8.32 Evan Huntsman & Associates owns and operates a lawn maintenance service in Trenton, New Jersey. The company is considering expanding into a nearby community. The managers believe that the proportion of homes in this new community that are currently using a professional lawn service is less than 0.40. To test this, the company plans to select a simple random sample of 120 homes and interview the homeowners to determine their lawn care status.
 a. State the appropriate null and alternative hypotheses.
 b. Using a significance level of 0.05, conduct the hypothesis test, assuming that 45 of those interviewed indicated that they are already using a lawn service. Discuss your results.

8.33 Suppose that at your university, administrators believe that the proportion of students preferring to take classes at night exceeds 0.30. To test this, a simple random sample of 200 students is selected, and 66 indicate that they prefer night classes.
 a. State the appropriate null and alternative hypotheses.
 b. If an alpha level equal to 0.10 is used, conduct the hypothesis test and discuss your results.

8.34 A major issue facing many states is whether to legalize casino gambling. Suppose the governor of one state believes that more than 55% of the state's registered voters would favor some form of legal casino gambling. However, before backing a proposal to allow such gambling, the governor instructed his aides to conduct a statistical test on the issue. To do this, the aides hired a consulting firm to survey a simple random sample of 300 voters. Of these 300 voters, 175 actually favor legalized gambling.
 a. State the appropriate null and alternative hypotheses.
 b. Assuming that a significance level of 0.05 is used, what conclusion should the governor reach based on these sample data? Discuss.

8.35 In a March 2002 article, *Golf Digest* reported on a survey in which 300 golfers were asked their views about the impact of new technologies on the game of golf. Before the study, a group of United States Golf Association officials believed that 50% or fewer of golfers believed that professional golfers should have different equipment rules than amateurs. The survey found 67% did not favor different equipment rules.
 a. If the claim made by the USGA is to be tested, what should be the null and alternative hypotheses?
 b. Based on the sample data and an alpha level equal to 0.05, use the *p*-value approach to conduct the hypothesis test.

Advanced Business Applications

8.36 💿 The AJ Fitness Center has surveyed 1,214 of its customers. Of particular interest is whether more than

60% of the customers who express overall service satisfaction with the club (represented by codes 4 or 5) are female. If this is not the case, the promotions director feels she must initiate new exercise programs that are designed specifically for women. Should the promotions director initiate the new exercise programs? Support your answer with the relevant hypothesis test, utilizing a *p*-value to perform the test. The data are found in the CD-ROM file *AJ Fitness* ($\alpha = 0.05$).

8.37 💿 A computer manufacturer has a dial-up 800 number that customers can use to call for help with problems related to their computer. The service manager expects that the proportion of calls that will be answered within 5 minutes exceeds 0.80. Recently a survey was conducted of 70 calls. The data file *Customer Service* contains the evaluation (Yes or No) on whether the call was answered within 5 minutes.
 a. State the appropriate null and alternative hypotheses.
 b. Carry out the hypothesis test using a significance level of 0.10. Show the decision rule and the result of the test.
 c. Construct a 90% confidence interval for the proportion of calls that were answered in 5 minutes. Do you see any relationship between the confidence interval you constructed and the test you conducted in part b? State any generalization you may determine.

8.38 💿 At the annual meeting of the Golf Equipment Manufacturers' Association, a speaker made the claim that fewer than 30% of all golf clubs being used by nonprofessional United States Golf Association members are knockoffs. These knockoffs are clubs that look very much like the more-expensive originals, such as Big Bertha drivers, but they are actually nonauthorized copies that are sold at a very reduced rate. This claim prompted the association to conduct a study to see if the speaker was correct. A random sample of 400 golfers was selected from the USGA. The players were called and asked to indicate the brand of clubs that they used, along with several other questions. Data were collected from 294 golfers. Based on the response to club brand, a determination was made about whether the clubs were "original" or a "copy." The data are in a CD-ROM file called *Golf Survey*.
 a. Based on the sample data, what conclusion should be reached if the hypothesis is tested at a significance level of 0.05? Show the decision rule.
 b. Determine whether a Type I or Type II error for this hypothesis test would be more severe. Given your determination, would you advocate raising or lowering the significance level for this test? Explain your reasoning.

8.39 💿 Referring to Exercise 8.38, one of the USGA officials has stated that the use of knockoff golf clubs is greater among the high-handicap players. He went on to say that at least 40% of all golfers with handicaps 20 and above use unauthorized copies. This claim will be accepted unless the sample data indicate strongly that it is incorrect. Use the data in the file *Golf Survey* to test this claim.

a. Confirm that the sample proportion's distribution can be approximated by a normal distribution.

b. Based on the sample data and a significance level of 0.05, what should the USGA conclude about the use of knockoff clubs by the high-handicap golfers? Is the official's statement justified?

8-3 TYPE II ERRORS

Sections 8-1 and 8-2 provided several examples that illustrated how hypotheses and decision rules for tests of the population mean are formulated. In these examples, we determined the critical values by first specifying the significance level, alpha: the maximum allowable probability of committing a Type I error. As we indicated, if the cost of committing a Type I error is high, the decision maker will want to specify a small significance level.

This logic provides a basis for establishing the critical value for the hypothesis test. However, it ignores the possibility of committing a Type II error. Recall that a Type II error occurs if a false null hypothesis is accepted. The probability of a Type II error is given the symbol β, the Greek letter beta. We discussed in Section 8-1 that α and β are inversely related. That is, if we make α smaller, β will increase. However, the two are not proportional. A case in point: cutting α in half will not necessarily double β.

CALCULATING BETA

Once α has been specified for a hypothesis test involving a particular sample size, β cannot also be specified. Rather, the β value is fixed, and all the decision maker can do is calculate it. However, β is not a single value. Because a Type II error occurs when a false null hypothesis is accepted (refer to Figure 8-1), there is a β value for each possible population value for which the null hypothesis is false. To calculate beta, we must first specify a "what if" value for the true population value. Then, β is computed conditional on that population value being true. Keep in mind that β is computed before the sample is taken, so its value is not dependent on the sample outcome.

For instance, if the null hypothesis is the mean income for a population is equal to or greater than $30,000, then β could be calculated for any value of μ less than $30,000. We would get a different β for each value of μ. An example will help clarify this concept.

American Lighting Company—The American Lighting Company has developed a new light bulb designed to last more than 700 hours on average. If a hypothesis test could confirm this, the company would use the "greater than 700 hour" claim in its advertising. The null and alternative hypotheses are:

$$H_0: \mu \leq 700 \text{ hours}$$
$$H_A: \mu > 700 \text{ hours}$$

Therefore, the null hypothesis is false for all possible values of $\mu > 700$ hours. Thus, for each of the infinite number of possibilities, a value of β can be determined. (Note: σ is assumed to be 15 hours.)

Figure 8-10 shows how β is determined if the value of μ selected from H_A is 701 hours. By specifying the significance level to be 0.05 and a sample size of 100 bulbs, the chance of committing a Type II error is approximately 0.8365. This means that if the true population mean is 701 hours, there is nearly an 84% chance that the sampling plan American Lighting is using will not reject the assumption that the mean is 700 hours or less.

Figure 8-11 shows that if the "what if" mean value ($\mu = 704$) is farther from the hypothesized mean ($\mu = 700$), beta becomes smaller. The greater the difference between the mean specified in H_0 and the mean selected from H_A, the easier it is to tell the two apart, and the less likely we are to not reject the null hypothesis when it is actually false. Of course the opposite is also true. As the mean selected from H_A moves increasingly closer to the mean specified in H_0, the harder it is for the hypothesis test to distinguish between the two.

CONTROLLING ALPHA AND BETA

Ideally, we want both alpha and beta to be as small as possible. Although we can set alpha at any desired level, for a specified sample size and standard deviation, the calculated value of beta depends on the population mean chosen from the alternative hypothesis and the significance level.

FIGURE 8-10

Beta Calculation for True
$\mu = 701$

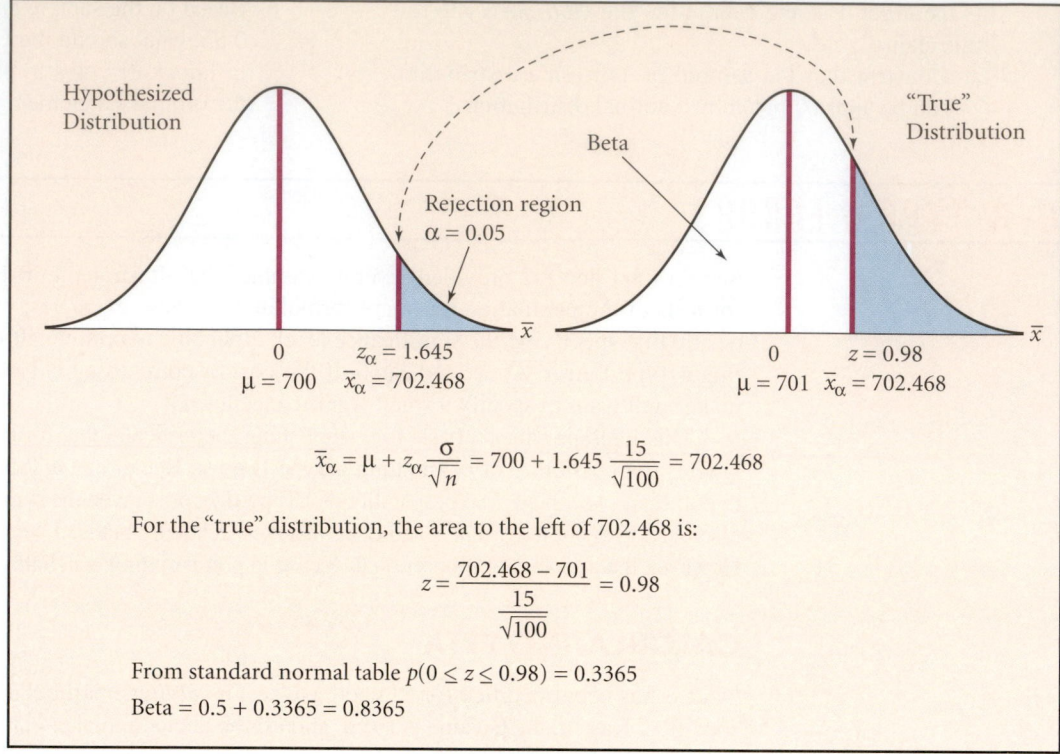

$$\bar{x}_\alpha = \mu + z_\alpha \frac{\sigma}{\sqrt{n}} = 700 + 1.645 \frac{15}{\sqrt{100}} = 702.468$$

For the "true" distribution, the area to the left of 702.468 is:

$$z = \frac{702.468 - 701}{\frac{15}{\sqrt{100}}} = 0.98$$

From standard normal table $p(0 \leq z \leq 0.98) = 0.3365$

Beta $= 0.5 + 0.3365 = 0.8365$

For a specified sample size, reducing alpha will increase beta. However, we can control the size of both alpha and beta if we are willing to increase the sample size.

The American Lighting Company planned to take a sample of 100 light bulbs. In Figure 8-10, we showed that beta = 0.8365 when the "true" population mean was 701 hours. This is a very large probability and would be unacceptable to the company. However, if the company is willing to incur the cost associated with a sample size of 500 bulbs, the probability of a Type II error could be reduced to 0.5596, as shown in Figure 8-12. This is a big improvement and is due to the fact that the standard error $\left(\frac{\sigma}{\sqrt{n}} \right)$ is reduced because of the increased sample size.

FIGURE 8-11

Beta Calculation for True
$\mu = 704$

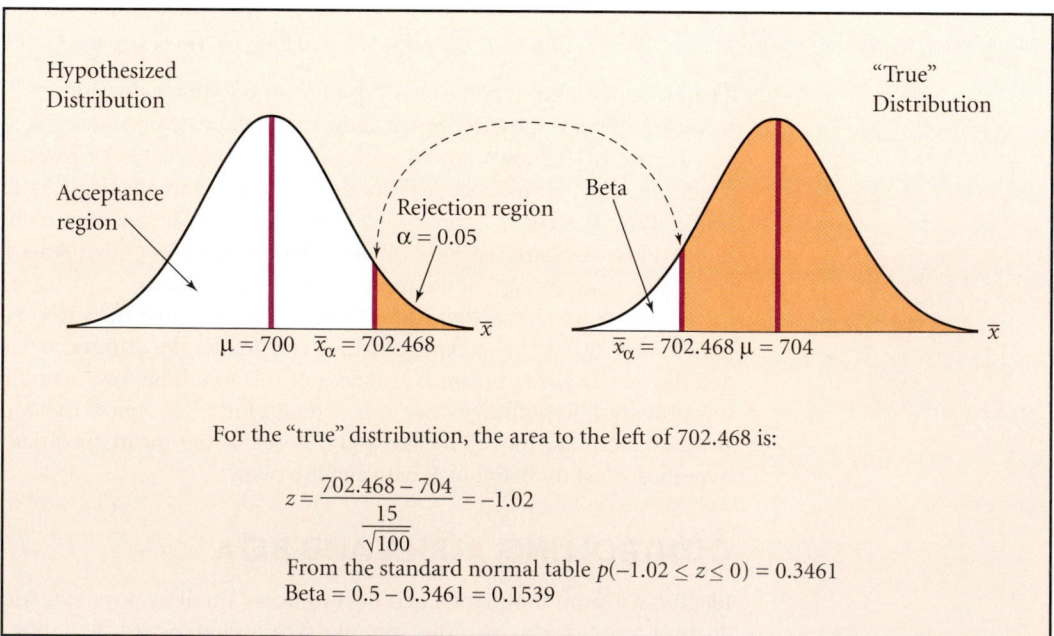

For the "true" distribution, the area to the left of 702.468 is:

$$z = \frac{702.468 - 704}{\frac{15}{\sqrt{100}}} = -1.02$$

From the standard normal table $p(-1.02 \leq z \leq 0) = 0.3461$

Beta $= 0.5 - 0.3461 = 0.1539$

FIGURE 8-12

Beta Calculation for True μ and *n* = 500

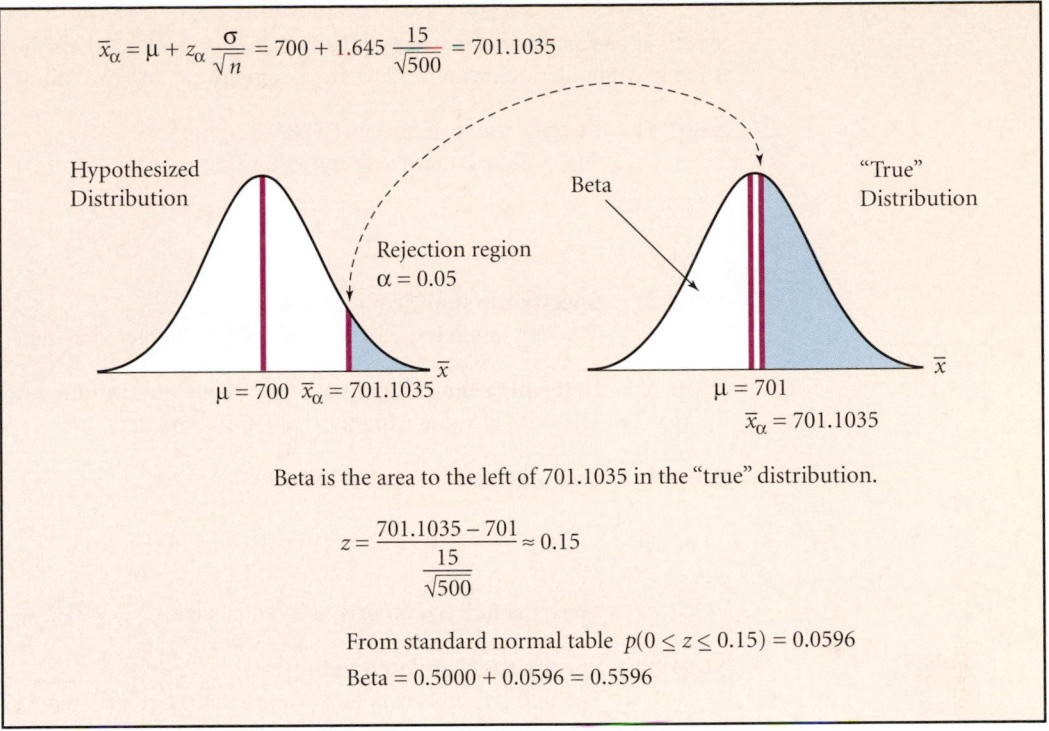

$$\bar{x}_\alpha = \mu + z_\alpha \frac{\sigma}{\sqrt{n}} = 700 + 1.645 \frac{15}{\sqrt{500}} = 701.1035$$

Hypothesized Distribution

"True" Distribution

Beta

Rejection region α = 0.05

μ = 700 $\bar{x}_\alpha$ = 701.1035

μ = 701
$\bar{x}_\alpha$ = 701.1035

Beta is the area to the left of 701.1035 in the "true" distribution.

$$z = \frac{701.1035 - 701}{\frac{15}{\sqrt{500}}} \approx 0.15$$

From standard normal table $p(0 \le z \le 0.15) = 0.0596$

Beta = 0.5000 + 0.0596 = 0.5596

SUMMARY: CALCULATING BETA

The probability of committing a Type II error can be calculated using the following steps.

1. Formulate the null and alternative hypotheses.

2. Specify the significance level. (Hint: Draw a picture of the hypothesized sampling distribution showing the rejection region(s) and the acceptance region found by specifying the significance level.)

3. Determine the critical value, z_α, from the standard normal distribution.

4. Determine the critical value, $\bar{x}_\alpha = \mu + z_\alpha \frac{\sigma}{\sqrt{n}}$ for an

upper-tail test, or $\bar{x}_\alpha = \mu - z_\alpha \frac{\sigma}{\sqrt{n}}$ for a lower-tail test.

5. Specify the stipulated value for μ, the population mean for which you wish to compute β.

6. Compute the test statistic based on the stipulated population mean as:

$$z = \frac{\bar{x}_\alpha - \mu}{\frac{\sigma}{\sqrt{n}}}$$

7. Use the standard normal table to find β, the probability associated with "accepting" the null hypothesis when it is false.

EXAMPLE 8-10: COMPUTING BETA

Wright Tax Assistance, Inc.   Wright Tax Assistance, Inc., a major income tax preparation company, has claimed its clients save an average of more than $200 each by using the company's services. A consumer's group plans to randomly sample 64 customers to test this claim. The standard deviation of the amount saved is assumed to be $100. Before testing, the consumer's group is interested in knowing the probability that they will mistakenly conclude that the mean savings is less than or equal to $200 when, in fact, it does exceed $200, as the company claims. To find beta if the true population mean is $210, the company can use the following steps.

Step 1: **Specify the null and alternative hypotheses.**
The null and alternative hypotheses are

$$H_0: \mu \le \$200$$
$$H_A: \mu > \$200$$

Step 2: **Specify the significance level.**
The one-tailed hypothesis test will be conducted using $\alpha = 0.05$.

Step 3: **Determine the critical value, z_α, from the standard normal distribution.**
The critical value from the standard normal is $z_\alpha = z_{0.05} = 1.645$.

Step 4: **Calculate the critical value.**

$$\bar{x}_\alpha = \mu + z_\alpha \frac{\sigma}{\sqrt{n}} = 200 + 1.645 \frac{100}{\sqrt{64}} = 220.56$$

Thus, the null hypothesis will be rejected if $\bar{x} > 220.56$.

Step 5: **Specify the stipulated value for μ.**
The null hypothesis is false for all values greater than $200. What is beta if the stipulated mean is $210?

Step 6: **Compute the test statistic based on the stipulated population mean.**
The test statistic based on stipulated population mean is

$$z = \frac{\bar{x}_\alpha - \mu}{\frac{\sigma}{\sqrt{n}}} = \frac{220.56 - 210}{\frac{100}{\sqrt{64}}} = 0.84$$

Step 7: **Determine beta.**
From the standard normal table, the probability associated with $z = 0.84$ is 0.2995. Then $\beta = 0.5000 + 0.2995 = 0.7995$. There is a 0.7995 probability that the hypothesis test will lead the consumer agency to mistakenly believe that the mean tax savings is less than or equal to $200 when, in fact, the mean savings is $210.

POWER OF THE TEST

In the previous examples, we have been concerned about the chance of making a Type II error. We would like beta to be as small as possible. If the null hypothesis is false, we want to reject it. Another way to look at this is that we would like the hypothesis test to have a high probability of rejecting a false hypothesis. This concept is expressed by what is called the **power** of the test.

Power

The probability that the hypothesis test will reject the null hypothesis when the null hypothesis is false.

When the alternative hypothesis is true, the power of the test is computed using Equation 8-5.

Power

$$\text{Power} = 1 - \beta$$

8-5

8-3: EXERCISES

Skill Development

8.40 You are given the following null and alternative hypotheses:

$$H_0: \mu \le 4{,}000$$
$$H_A: \mu > 4{,}000$$
$$\alpha = 0.05$$

a. If the population mean is 4,004, determine the value of beta. Assume that the population standard deviation is known to be 20 and the sample size is 40.

b. Referring to part a, calculate the power of the test.

c. Referring to parts a and b, what could be done to increase power and reduce beta if the true population mean is 4,004? Discuss.

d. Indicate clearly the decision rule that would be used to test the null hypothesis and determine what decision should be made if the sample mean were 4,002.

8.41 You are given the following null and alternative hypotheses:

$$H_0: \mu = 1.20$$
$$H_A: \mu \ne 1.20$$
$$\alpha = 0.10$$

a. If the true population mean is 1.25, determine the value of beta. Assume the population standard deviation is known to be 0.50 and the sample size is 60.

b. Referring to part a, calculate the power of the test.

c. Referring to parts a and b, what could be done to increase power and reduce beta when the true population mean is 1.25? Discuss.

d. Indicate clearly the decision rule that would be used to test the null hypothesis and determine what decision should be made if the sample mean were 1.23.

8.42 You are given the following null and alternative hypotheses:

$$H_0: \mu \ge 88$$
$$H_A: \mu < 88$$
$$\alpha = 0.10$$

a. If the true population mean is 86, determine the value of beta. Assume that the population standard deviation is known to be 12 and the sample size is 64.

b. Referring to part a, calculate the power of the test.

c. Referring to parts a and b, what could be done to increase power and reduce beta when the true population mean is 86? Discuss.

d. Indicate clearly the decision rule that would be used to test the null hypothesis and determine what decision should be made if the sample mean were 85.66.

8.43 You are given the following null and alternative hypotheses:

$$H_0: \mu \ge 4{,}350$$
$$H_A: \mu < 4{,}350$$
$$\alpha = 0.05$$

a. If the true population mean is 4,345, determine the value of beta. Assume the population standard deviation is known to be 200 and the sample size is 100.

b. Referring to part a, calculate the power of the test.

c. Referring to parts a and b, what could be done to increase power and reduce beta when the true population mean is 4,345? Discuss.

d. Indicate clearly the decision rule that would be used to test the null hypothesis and determine what decision should be made if the sample mean were 4,337.50.

8.44 You are given the following null and alternative hypotheses:

$$H_0: \mu \le 256$$
$$H_A\ \mu > 256$$
$$\alpha = 0.05$$

a. If the true population mean is 260, determine the value of beta. Assume the population standard deviation is known to be 40 and the sample size is 100.

b. Referring to part a, calculate the power for this test.

c. Suppose that the true mean is 262. Determine the value of the power and beta. Indicate why these values changed compared with those found in parts a and b.

d. Suppose the true population mean is 260, but the alpha level for the test is 0.10 rather than 0.05, what will be the impact on the beta value? Will power increase or decrease?

Business Applications

8.45 The Arrow Tire and Rubber Company plans to warranty its new mountain bike tire for 12 months. However, before it does this, the company wants to be sure that the mean lifetime of the tires is at least 18 months under normal operations. It will put the warranty in place unless the sample data strongly suggest that the mean lifetime of the tires is less than 18 months. The company plans to test this statistically using a random sample of tires. The test will be conducted using an alpha level of 0.03.

a. If the population mean is actually 16.5 months, determine the probability the hypothesis test will lead to incorrectly accepting the null hypothesis. Assume that the population standard deviation is known to be 2.4 months and the sample size is 60.

b. If the population mean is actually 17.3, calculate the chance of committing a Type II error. This is a specific example of a generalization relating the probability of committing a Type II error and the parameter being tested. State this generalization.

c. Without calculating the probability, state whether the probability of a Type II error would be larger or smaller than that calculated in part b if you were to calculate it for a hypothesized mean of 15 months. Justify your answer.

d. Suppose the company decides to increase the sample size from 60 to 100 tires. What can you expect to happen to the probabilities calculated previously?

8.46 The union negotiations between labor and management at the Stone Container paper mill in Minnesota hit a snag when management asked labor to take a cut in health insurance coverage. As part of its justification, management claimed that the average amount of insurance claims filed by union employees did not exceed $250 per employee. The union's chief negotiator requested that a sample of 100 employees' records be selected and that this claim be tested statistically. The claim would be accepted if the sample data did not strongly suggest otherwise. The significance level for the test was set at 0.10.

a. State the null and alternative hypotheses.

b. Before the sample was selected, the negotiator was interested in knowing the power of this test if the mean amount of insurance claims was $260. (Assume the standard deviation in claims is $70, as determined in a similar study at another plant location.) Calculate this probability for the negotiator.

c. Referring to part b, how will the power of the test change if alpha = 0.05 is used?

d. Suppose alpha is left at 0.10, but the standard deviation of the population is $50 rather than $70, what will be the power of the test? State the generalization that explains the relationship between the answers to parts b and d.

e. Referring to part d, based on the probability computed, if you were the negotiator, would you be satisfied with the sampling plan in this situation? Explain why or why not. What steps could be taken to improve the sampling plan?

8.47 The makers of Mini-Oats Cereal have an automated packaging machine that can be set at any targeted fill level between 12 and 32 ounces. At the end of every shift (8 hours), 16 boxes are selected at random and the mean and standard deviation of the sample are computed. Based on these sample results, the production control manager determines whether the filling machine needs to be readjusted or whether it remains all right to operate. Previous data suggest the fill level has a normal distribution, with a standard deviation of 0.65 ounces. Use $\alpha = 0.05$. The test is a two-sided test to determine if the mean fill level is equal to 24 ounces.

a. Calculate the probability that the test procedure will detect that the average fill level is not equal to 24 ounces when in fact it equals 24.5 ounces.

b. On the basis of your calculation in part a, would you suggest a change in the test procedure? Explain what change you would make and the reasons you would make this change.

8.48 The Wainwright Lawn and Garden Company's marketing manager believes that the average income for the company's customers is less than $30,000. This claim was made by the manager as he defended his selection of brands aimed at lower-income customers. To verify the claim, a simple random sample of 400 customers was selected and a survey was conducted to determine income levels. It is assumed that σ is equal to $4,000. The significance level is 0.10. If the actual mean income is $29,800, determine the probability that the test will mistakenly lead the managers to "accept" the null hypothesis.

Summary and Conclusions

This chapter has introduced the fundamentals of hypothesis testing. The concepts presented in this chapter provide decision makers with tools for using sample information to decide whether a given null hypothesis should be rejected.

In this chapter we have concentrated on examples of sample hypothesis tests involving a single population mean and a population proportion. In subsequent chapters you will see that the hypothesis testing methodology is basically the same for all situations. The central issue is always to determine whether the sample information tends to support or refute the null hypothesis.

We have emphasized the importance of recognizing that when a hypothesis is tested, an error might occur. Type I and Type II statistical errors have been discussed. We have shown how to calculate the probability of committing each type of error for applications involving a single population mean.

You have probably noticed that the statistical estimation techniques discussed in Chapter 7 and hypothesis testing have much in common. Both estimation and hypothesis testing are used extensively by business decision makers. Estimation procedures are most useful when decision makers have little or no idea of the value of a population parameter and are primarily interested in determining these values. On the other hand, hypothesis testing is used when a claim about a population value needs to be tested. Estimation and hypothesis testing are the central components of statistical inference and will be used throughout the remaining chapters of this text. Figure 8-13 on the next page is a flow diagram that should help you determine which hypothesis testing procedure to use in various situations. Note: Figure 8-13 assumes a right-tailed hypothesis test. Table 8-1 provides a matrix format to help you determine which statistical tools to apply in specific situations.

EQUATIONS

$\bar{x}_\alpha$ for Hypothesis Tests, σ Known, Large Samples

$$\bar{x}_\alpha = \mu + z_\alpha \frac{\sigma}{\sqrt{n}} \qquad \textbf{8-1}$$

z Test Statistic for Hypothesis Tests for μ, σ Known

$$z = \frac{\bar{x} - \mu}{\frac{\sigma}{\sqrt{n}}}$$ **8-2**

t Test Statistic for Hypothesis Tests for μ, σ Unknown

$$t = \frac{\bar{x} - \mu}{\frac{s}{\sqrt{n}}}$$ **8-3**

z Test Statistic for Proportions

$$z = \frac{\bar{p} - p}{\sqrt{\frac{p(1 - p)}{n}}}$$ **8-4**

Power

$$\text{Power} = 1 - \beta$$ **8-5**

FIGURE 8-13

Deciding Which Hypothesis Testing Procedure to Use

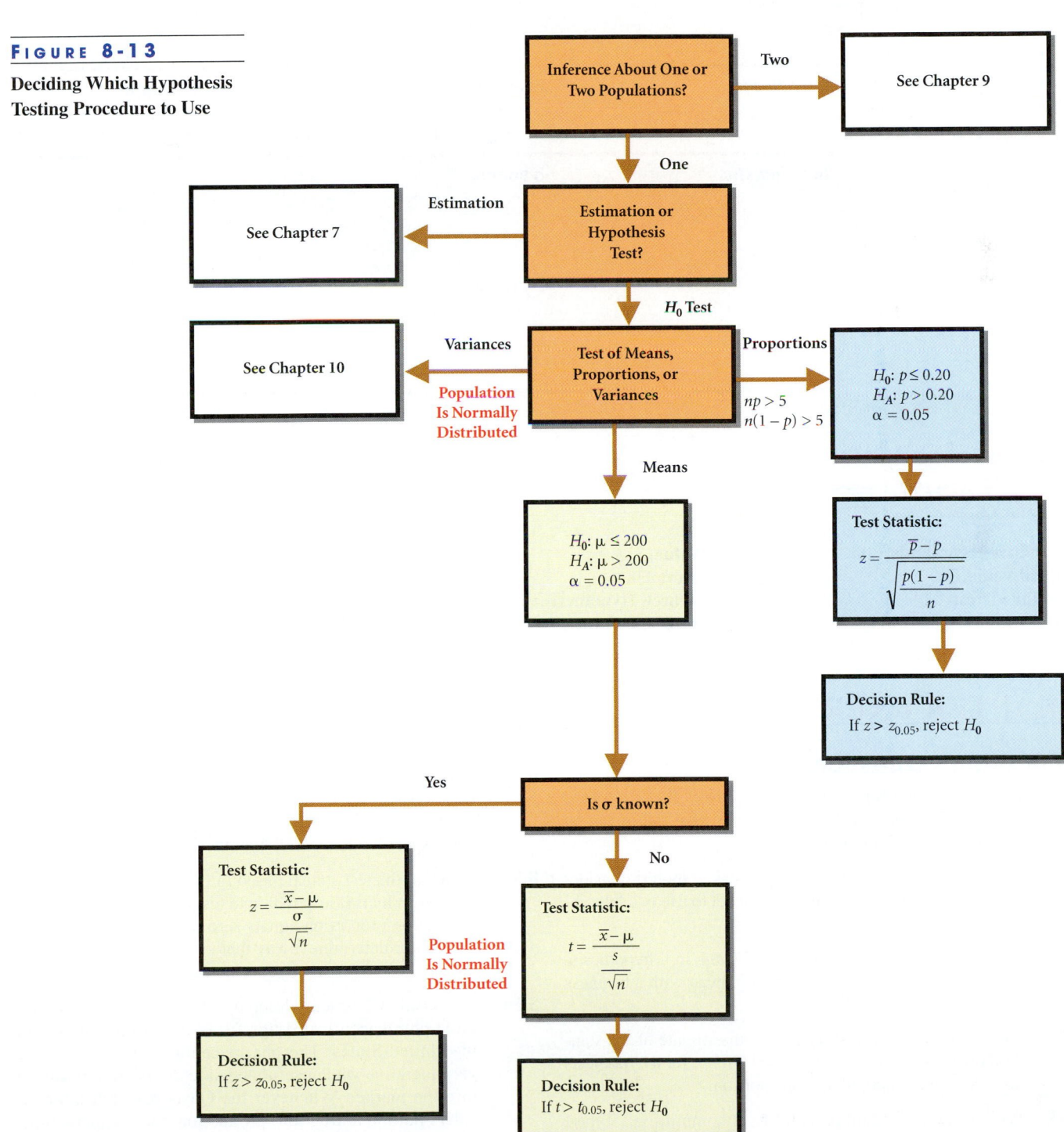

TABLE 8-1

Statistical Inference
Tools—One Sample
Situations

	Population Mean μ	Population Proportion p
Statistic	$\bar{x} = \dfrac{\sum x}{n}$	$\bar{p} = \dfrac{x}{n}$
Confidence Interval	σ **known:** $\bar{x} \pm z_{\alpha/2} \dfrac{\sigma}{\sqrt{n}}$ σ **unknown** $\bar{x} \pm t_{\alpha/2} \dfrac{s}{\sqrt{n}}$	$\bar{p} \pm z\sqrt{\dfrac{\bar{p}(1-\bar{p})}{n}}$
Hypotheses	**Example** $H_0: \mu \leq 200$ $H_A: \mu > 200$	**Example** $H_0: p \geq 0.60$ $H_A: p < 0.60$
Test Statistic	σ **known:** $z = \dfrac{\bar{x} - \mu}{\dfrac{\sigma}{\sqrt{n}}}$ σ **unknown** $t = \dfrac{\bar{x} - \mu}{\dfrac{s}{\sqrt{n}}}$	$z = \dfrac{\bar{p} - p}{\sqrt{\dfrac{p(1-p)}{n}}}$

Key Terms

Alternative Hypothesis, 305	**p-Value,** 313	**Two-Tailed Test,** 314
Critical Value, 309	**Power,** 334	**Test Statistic,** 311
One-Tailed Test, 314	**Research Hypothesis,** 306	**Type I Error,** 307
Null Hypothesis, 304	**Significance Level,** 309	**Type II Error,** 307

CHAPTER EXERCISES

Conceptual Questions

8.49   Discuss the two types of statistical errors that can occur when a hypothesis is tested. Illustrate what you mean by using a business example for each.

8.50   Discuss the issues that a decision maker should consider when determining the significance level to use in a hypothesis test.

8.51   What is meant by the term *critical value* in a hypothesis-testing situation? Illustrate what you mean with a business example.

8.52   Discuss why it is necessary to use an estimate of the standard error for a confidence interval but not for a hypothesis test concerning a population proportion.

8.53   What is the maximum probability of committing a Type I error called? How is this probability determined? Discuss.

8.54   Recall that the power of the test is the probability that the null hypothesis is rejected when H_0 is false. Explain whether power is definable if the given parameter is the value specified in the null hypothesis.

8.55   Examine the test statistic used in testing a population proportion. Why is it impossible to test the hypothesis that the population proportion equals zero using such a test statistic? Try to determine a way that such a test could be conducted.

8.56   The Oasis Chemical Company develops and manufactures pharmaceutical drugs for distribution and sale in the United States. The pharmaceutical business can be very lucrative when useful and safe drugs are introduced into the market. Whenever the Oasis research lab considers putting a drug into production, the company must establish the following sets of null and alternative hypotheses:

Set 1	Set 2
H_0: The drug is safe.	H_0: The drug is effective.
H_A: The drug is not safe.	H_A: The drug is not effective.

Take each set of hypotheses separately.

a. Discuss the considerations that should be made in establishing alpha and beta.

b. For each set of hypotheses, describe what circumstances would suggest that a Type I error would be of more concern.

c. For each set of hypotheses, describe what circumstances would suggest that a Type II error would be of more concern.

Business Applications

8.57 The Ohio State Tax Commission attempts to set up payroll-tax withholding tables so that by the end of a year, an employee's income-tax withholding is about $100 below his or her actual income tax owed to the state. The commission director claims that when all the Ohio tax returns are in, the average additional payment will be less than $100.

A random sample of 50 accounts revealed, on average, an additional payment of $114, with a sample standard deviation of $50.

a. Testing at a significance level of 0.10, do the sample data refute the director's claim?

b. Determine the largest sample mean (with the same sample size and standard deviation) that would fail to refute the director's claim.

8.58 The TSR Testing Service prepares real estate license examinations for several states. Wisconsin officials are considering hiring this company to devise a test for their real estate brokers' license requirements. Wisconsin requires that the average test score be exactly 70 points. In order to evaluate the test prepared by TSR Testing, Wisconsin officials selected a random sample of 60 potential brokers and administered the exam. They found that the mean score was 68.55 points.

a. State the appropriate null and alternative hypotheses.

b. Assuming that the true standard deviation is 10 points and the hypothesis is to be tested at a significance level of 0.08, on the basis of the sample data, should the Wisconsin officials consider requiring TSR to restructure its test? Describe what a Type II error would be in the context of this problem.

8.59 The Cherry Hill Growers Association operates a fruit warehouse in California. Because of the volume of cherries that arrive at the warehouse during the picking season, the growers have agreed that instead of weighing each box of cherries, they would assume that the average box weighs 20 pounds. The total weight is then simply the number of boxes times 20 pounds.

Past studies have shown that the standard deviation of weight from box to box is 0.5 pound. Suppose the warehouse manager has decided to select a random sample of 70 boxes of cherries from a particular grower's crop. He suspects that the grower may be underfilling the boxes and is concerned about detecting this, if it is the case. He is not concerned if the average box contains more than 20 pounds.

a. Would the warehouse manager be justified in concluding that underfilling of the boxes is occurring if the sample mean is 19.62? Use a significance level of 0.05.

b. Determine the probability that a sample mean less than or equal to 19.62 would be obtained from a sample of size 70 if the population mean were 20 pounds. What is the statistical term for the value you calculated?

c. Discuss which type of hypothesis testing error would be more important to the warehouse manager.

d. Discuss which type of error would be more important to the grower.

8.60 The Lazer Company has a contract to produce a part for Boeing Corporation that must have an average diameter of 6 inches and a standard deviation of 0.10 inch. Lazer has developed a process that will meet the specifications with respect to the standard deviation, but it is still trying to meet the mean specifications. A test run (considered a random sample) of parts was produced and the company wishes to determine whether this latest process that produced the sample will produce parts meeting the requirement of average diameter equal to 6 inches.

a. Specify the appropriate null and alternative hypotheses.

b. Develop the decision rule assuming that the sample size is 200 parts and the significance level is 0.01.

c. What should Lazer conclude if the sample mean diameter for the 200 parts is 6.03 inches? Discuss.

8.61 Tom Morgan operates a gas station in a suburban area of Boston. He is thinking of installing a mechanism on his self-service pumps that will not allow more than 10 gallons to be pumped without having the pump restarted. He hopes this will cut down on theft without making honest customers angry.

The marketing representative for the new mechanism claims that if Tom's station is typical, the average fill-up is no more than 10 gallons. Tom has decided to select a random sample of 200 customers and test to determine whether the marketing representative's claim is true. He is willing to accept the claim unless the data strongly indicate that it is not true.

a. If the sample results show a mean of 10.32 gallons per fill-up, with a sample standard deviation of 2.9 gallons, what should Tom conclude about the population mean? Use a significance level of 0.05. Discuss your results.

b. Calculate a 95% confidence interval for the average fill-up.

8.62 The owners of Fit and Trim, a fitness and diet club, would like to advertise that their clients lose more than 10 pounds on average during their first three months of membership at the club. A sample resulted in the following summary statistics:

$$\bar{x} = 10.9 \text{ lb.}$$
$$s = 0.4 \text{ lb.}$$
$$n = 20$$

a. If the desired significance level is 0.05, what should be concluded about this claim if the above results are observed? Be sure to first set up the appropriate decision rule.

b. What assumption(s) must you make about the population's distribution so that your results in part a are valid?

8.63 The personnel manager for a large airline has claimed that, on the average, workers are asked to work no more than 3 hours overtime per week. Past studies show the standard deviation in overtime hours per worker to be 1.2 hours.

Suppose union negotiators wish to test this claim by sampling payroll records for 250 employees. They believe that the personnel manager's claim is untrue, but they want to base their conclusion on the sample results.

a. State the null and alternative hypotheses, and discuss the meaning of Type I and Type II errors in the context of this case.

b. Establish the appropriate decision rule if the union wishes to have no more than a 0.01 chance of a Type I error.

c. The payroll records produced a sample mean of 3.15 hours. Do the union negotiators have a basis for a grievance against the airline? Support your answer with a relevant statistical procedure.

8.64   A major U.S. tire manufacturer has developed a new design that will allow an owner to drive on a punctured tire for some miles without having to stop and change the tire. The R&D engineers claim that the average miles should exceed 50. However, they do not wish to assert this claim to the public if the sample data indicate otherwise. To conduct a test, a sample of 25 tires is selected with the following results:

$$\bar{x} = 51.05$$
$$s = 14.2$$

a. State the appropriate null and alternative hypotheses.

b. What conclusion should the company reach, assuming they want to test the hypothesis with a significance level of 0.05?

8.65   At a recent meeting of the budget committee at the Winter Corporation, the marketing manager made a pitch for a larger department budget by stating that more money was needed in advertising to improve the company's image. This prompted the company president to establish a task force to measure public opinion about the company.

This task force planned to use a well-established instrument for measuring public perception of companies such as Winter. Past studies using this particular instrument indicate that a company should receive at least an average 40-point overall rating to consider that it has a positive image in the public eye. They will assume that the company's image is positive unless the sample data indicate otherwise.

The task force randomly sampled 300 people within the market area and found that the average rating received was 38.98, with a sample standard deviation of 5.3 points.

a. Establish the appropriate null and alternative hypotheses.

b. Assuming that the test is to be conducted with a significance level equal to 0.10, what conclusion should the Winter Corporation reach about its average company rating by all the members of the population? Discuss.

c. Reflect on Type I and Type II errors in the context of this problem. Which of these do you think would be of most importance to the task force? Explain your reasoning.

8.66   A major U.S. tire manufacturer has developed a new design that will allow the owner to drive on a punctured tire for several miles without having to change the tire. The R&D department head claims that more than 90% of the tires will last for more than 30 miles before needing to be changed. However, he wishes to test this claim before going public with the statement. A simple random sample

of 100 tires with punctures revealed that 93 lasted longer than 30 miles.

a. State the appropriate null and alternative hypotheses.

b. What conclusion should the department head reach, based on the sample data, if the test is to be conducted using an alpha level equal to 0.05?

8.67   In a recent management-union negotiating process at a large, national, tire manufacturing company, one of the points made by management was that the average number of dollars in health-care benefits used per worker was $417 per year or less. It also indicated that the standard deviation was $200 per employee. Assuming that the standard deviation figure was correct, the union decided to select a random sample of 100 employee health records and test to determine whether the management assertion was correct. It planned to test at a significance level of 0.05.

a. Set up the correct null and alternative hypotheses.

b. Discuss why this hypothesis test is considered a one-tailed hypothesis test.

c. If the sample mean for the 100 workers was $433, what should the union conclude about the claim made by management? Discuss.

8.68   The Bell Corporation is a parent corporation that franchises automobile lube-and-oil-change centers around the United States. The standard set forth by Bell is that the average time to lube and change oil in a car is 10 minutes or less.

Periodically, Bell representatives visit the franchises and perform a compliance test on this standard. They randomly select 15 cars (without the local operator's knowledge) and record how long it takes to service each car. Then, based on the sample mean, they will determine whether the franchise is operating within the standard.

a. Establish the appropriate null and alternative hypotheses.

b. Determine the decision rule, assuming that the company performs the compliance test using a significance level of 0.05.

c. Determine if the franchise is operating within its standard if the sample average service time is 10.30 minutes and standard deviation = 2.0 minutes.

8.69   The maker of Quick Lite, ready-to-light charcoal briquettes, bases its claim to fame on the premise that its product, on average, will ignite within three tries. A consumer-awareness group would like to test the charcoal maker's claim and reach its own opinion about the product.

A sample of 20 buyers was asked to use the charcoal and record how many times it took before the briquettes caught fire. The sample revealed that an average of 3.15 tries, with a sample standard deviation of 0.2, was the norm.

a. Testing at a significance level of 0.05, decide what the consumer group should conclude about Quick Lite's claim.

b. Which type of error associated with hypothesis tests would the consumer-awareness group be most interested in avoiding? Explain your reasoning.

8.70   A manufacturer of computer monitors claims that its product will last at least 50 weeks on average without needing repairs. The Quast Corporation is considering purchasing a great many of these computer monitors. However, it does not wish to purchase the computer monitors if the manufacturer's claim is untrue. A Quast data-processing manager has determined that, given the price of the monitor and the total dollars involved, Quast should ask for some quality control records from the manufacturer.

Suppose the manufacturer produces records of a random sample of 30 monitors. The average time before the first breakdown was 48 weeks, with a standard deviation equal to 12 weeks.

a. Establish the appropriate null and alternative hypotheses.
b. Determine the appropriate decision rule and indicate whether the sample information justifies rejecting the manufacturer's claim. Use a significance level of 0.05.
c. Discuss the ramifications of this decision and the potential costs of being wrong.
d. Which type of hypothesis test error would Quast be most interested in avoiding? Explain your reasons.

Advanced Business Applications

8.71 The Softsoap Company recently developed a new soap product designed for use in automatic washing machines. The marketing department would like to claim in its advertisements that the new soap will save the average homeowner at least 10 ounces of soap per month. Before setting up the advertising plan, it decided to test the product in a random sample of 70 homes for a period of one month. The selected homeowners were asked to record how much soap they had used the previous month. Then they were asked to keep track of their soap usage with the new Softsoap product, while keeping their washing procedures the same as before the test.

a. Establish the null and alternative hypotheses to be tested, considering the objectives of the marketing department.
b. Assuming that the population standard deviation is known to be 3 ounces saved per month, what is the decision rule for the hypothesis test if the test is to be conducted with a significance level of 0.10?
c. Suppose the sample shows that the average savings is 9.5 ounces. What conclusion should the Softsoap marketing department reach with respect to its desired advertising claim? Discuss.
d. With respect to the decision reached in part c, comment on which statistical error may have been committed and what it would mean to the Softsoap Company.

8.72 The Rainbow Company operates coin-operated candy machines in Lincoln, Nebraska. When the company started using the so-called "talking" machines, it expected daily revenue per machine to exceed $63, on the average. Suppose a sample of 100 machines was selected in the Lincoln area over a period of time after the new machines were installed and the average revenue per machine was $66.05 with a standard deviation of $12.40.

a. Formulate the appropriate null and alternative hypotheses for this situation.
b. Establish the critical value and decision rule using the z-value approach, assuming the significance level is 0.05.
c. Determine if the Rainbow Company's expectations have been met.
d. If the average daily revenue were in fact $63, determine the probability that the sample mean would be at most $66.05. Give the statistical term that refers to the probability calculated.

8.73 The Inland Empire Food Store Company has stated in its advertising that the average shopper will save more than $3.00 per week by shopping at Inland stores. A consumer group has decided to test this assertion by sampling 50 shoppers who currently shop at other stores. It selects the customers and then notes each item purchased at their regular store. These same items are then priced at an Inland store, and the total bill is compared. The data in a file called *Inland Foods* on the CD-ROM reflect savings at Inland for the 50 shoppers. Those cases in which the bill was higher at Inland are marked with a minus sign.

a. Set up the appropriate null and alternative hypotheses to test Inland's claim.
b. Using a significance level of 0.05, develop the decision rule and test the hypothesis. Can Inland Empire support its advertising claim?
c. Which type of hypothesis error would the consumer group be most interested in controlling? Which type of hypothesis error would the company be most interested in controlling? Explain your reasoning.

8.74 The Falcon Speed-Reading Course advertises that the average increase in reading speed for graduates of the course is more than 200 words per minute.

a. What should an independent reviewer conclude if a sample of 15 graduates showed an average improvement of 210 words per minute, with a standard deviation equal to 40? Test at the significance level of 0.10.
b. Consider the facts that you do not know the population's standard deviation and that the sample size is small. What assumption must you make concerning the population to validate your analysis in part a?
c. Suppose the sample standard deviation is 20 words per minute rather than 40. Assuming that the sample mean and the significance level are unchanged, what conclusion should be reached with respect to the speed-reading course offered by Falcon?
d. Discuss why the change in standard deviation would have this effect on the conclusion reached, considering that the sample mean did not change.

8.75 The Cajun King restaurant manager is thinking about running a coupon advertisement in the local newspaper offering a free soft drink with the purchase of a meal. He hopes that more than 30% of the coupons will be redeemed. Before running the ad, he has a student group at a local high school distribute 200 coupons to a random sample of homes in the market area. Seventy-four coupons are redeemed.

a. What should the owner conclude concerning his preconception of the redemption rate, assuming that the test is based on a significance level of 0.10? Be sure to state the appropriate null and alternative hypotheses.
b. Construct a 90% confidence interval for the proportion of coupons that will be redeemed. Suppose it costs the owner of Cajun King 10 cents for each free soft drink and that he distributes 5,000 coupons. Determine the minimum and maximum cost of the free drink offer to the owner.

8.76 A story ran recently in a major newspaper that claimed that more than 70% of all employees call in sick at least one time a year when they are not actually sick. The story described this as a way for employees to get extra vacation days. Suppose a follow-up study is conducted in which 400 employees are selected at random and asked (confidentially) to indicate whether they had called in sick when they were not sick during the past year. A total of 292 employees admit that they had done this.

a. State the appropriate null and alternative hypotheses to test the claim made in the newspaper story.

b. Based on the sample data and a significance level of 0.05, what should be concluded about the newspaper's claim? Use the p-value approach to test the hypothesis.

8.77 Assuming the data in the CD-ROM file *Cities* is a random sample of cities in the United States, use this data to test an economist's claim that the average of 1998 white-collar earnings in U.S. cities was less than $25,000. Testing at a significance level of 0.05, do these sample data support or refute this contention? Discuss your results.

8.78 Referring to Exercise 8.77, the same economist has claimed that the average manufacturing salary in U.S. cities in 1998 exceeded $26,100. Based on the sample data, can this claim be supported or refuted at a significance level of 0.05? Discuss your conclusion.

8.79 A market research company was recently hired to conduct a survey of cell phone owners to determine whether the Nokia brand had a market share greater than 35%. Use the sample data contained in the file *Cell Phone Survey* to reach a conclusion, using a significance level of 0.05. Be sure to state the null and alternative hypotheses.

8.80 A study was conducted by the State Transportation Department to determine whether a weigh-in-motion (WIM) scale could be used in place of the static scale currently used at port-of-entry (POE) locations across the state. The WIM scale weighs trucks as they drive over a scale, rather than making them stop at a POE to be weighed. It is thought that the mean speed of trucks crossing the WIM scale would be less than the posted speed limit of 65 miles per hour.

a. Based on the sample data in the file *Trucks*, what conclusion can be reached concerning the preconception about the average speed? Test at an $\alpha = 0.10$.

b. A published report indicates the WIM scale average truck length on the state highway exceeds 60 feet. Based on the sample data, can this claim be supported or refuted? Test at an $\alpha = 0.05$.

c. Compute a new variable that is the difference between X_7 and X_4. It is thought that, if the WIM scale were effective, the average difference would be 0. Based on these sample data, what can be concluded? Test at an $\alpha = 0.05$.

CASE 8-A:

Campbell Brewery, Inc., Part 1

Don Campbell and his younger brother, Edward, purchased Campbell Brewery from their father in 1983. The brewery makes and bottles beer under two labels and distributes it throughout the Southwest. Since purchasing the brewery, Don has been instrumental in modernizing operations.

One of the latest acquisitions is a filling machine that can be adjusted to fill at any average fill level desired. Because the bottles and cans filled by the brewery are exclusively the 12-ounce size, when they received the machine Don set the fill level to 12 ounces and left it that way. According to the manufacturer's specifications, the machine will fill bottles or cans around the average, with a standard deviation of 0.15 ounce.

Don just returned from a brewery convention in which he attended a panel discussion related to problems with filling machines. One brewery representative discussed a problem her company had. It failed to learn that its machine's average fill went out of adjustment until several months later, when its cost accounting department reported some problems with beer production in bulk not matching output in bottles and cans. It turns out that the machine's average fill had increased from 12 ounces to 12.07 ounces. With large volumes of production, this deviation meant a substantial loss in profits.

Another brewery reported the same type of problem, but in the opposite direction. Its machine began filling bottles with slightly less than 12 ounces on the average. Although the consumers could not detect the shortage in a given bottle, the state and federal agencies responsible for checking the accuracy of packaged products discovered the problem in their testing and substantially fined the brewery for the underfill.

These problems were a surprise to Don Campbell. He had not considered the possibility that the machine might go out of adjustment and pose these types of problems. In fact, he became very concerned because the problems of losing profits and potentially being fined by the government were ones that he wished to avoid, if possible. After the convention, Don and Ed decided to hire a consulting firm with expertise in these matters to assist them in setting up a procedure for monitoring the performance of the filling machine.

The consultant suggested that they set up a sampling plan in which once a month they would sample some number of bottles and measure their volumes precisely. If the average of the sample deviated too much from 12 ounces, they would shut the machine down and make the necessary adjustments. Otherwise, they would let the filling process continue. The consultant identified two types of problems that could occur from this sort of sampling plan:

1. They might incorrectly decide to adjust the machine when it was not really necessary to do so.

2. They might incorrectly decide to allow the filling process to continue when, in fact, the true average had deviated from 12 ounces.

After carefully considering what the consultant told them, Don indicated that he wanted no more than a 0.02 chance of the first problem occurring because of the costs involved. He also decided that if the true average fill had slipped to 11.99 ounces, he wanted no more than a 0.05 chance of not detecting this with his sampling plan. He wanted to avoid problems with state and federal agencies. Finally, if the true average fill had actually risen to 12.007 ounces, he wanted to be able to detect this 98% of the time with his sampling plan. Thus, he wanted to avoid the lost profits that would result from such a problem.

In addition, Don needs to determine how large a sample size is necessary to meet his requirements.

General References

1. Berenson, Mark L., and David M. Levine, *Basic Business Statistics Concepts and Applications*, 7th ed. (Upper Saddle River, NJ: Prentice Hall, 1999).

2. Dodge, Mark, and Craig Stinson, *Running Microsoft Excel 2000* (Redmond, WA: Microsoft Press, 1999).

3. Hogg, Robert V., and Elliot A. Tanis, *Probability and Statistical Inference*, 5th ed. (Upper Saddle River, NJ: Prentice Hall, 1997).

4. Marx, Morris L., and Richard J. Larsen, *Mathematical Statistics and Its Applications*, 3rd ed. (Upper Saddle River, NJ: Prentice Hall, 2000).

5. *Microsoft Excel 2000* (Redmond, WA: Microsoft Corp., 1999).

6. *Minitab for Windows Version 14* (State College, PA: Minitab, 2003).

7. Siegel, Andrew F., *Practical Business Statistics*, 4th ed. (Burr Ridge, IL: Irwin, 2000).

CHAPTER 9

Estimation and Hypothesis Testing for Two Population Parameters

CHAPTER OUTCOMES

After studying the material in Chapter 9, you should be able to:

- Discuss the logic behind, and demonstrate the techniques for, using sample data to test hypotheses and develop interval estimates about the difference between two population means for both independent and paired samples.
- Carry out hypothesis tests and establish interval estimates, using sample data, for the difference between two population proportions.

WHY YOU NEED TO KNOW

Chapter 8 introduced the concepts of hypothesis testing and illustrated its application through examples involving a single population parameter. However, in many business decision-making situations, managers must decide between two or more alternatives. For example, farmers must decide which of several brands and types of wheat to plant. Fleet managers in large companies must decide which model and make of car to purchase next year. Airlines must decide whether to purchase replacement planes from Boeing or Airbus. When deciding on a new advertising campaign, a company may need to evaluate proposals from competing advertising agencies. Hiring decisions may require a personnel director to select one employee from a list of applicants. Production managers are often confronted with decisions concerning whether to change a produc-

tion process or leave it alone. Each day consumers purchase a product from among several competing brands.

The difficulty in such situations is that the decision maker must make the decision based on limited (sample) information. Fortunately, there are statistical tools that can help decision makers use sample information to compare different populations (alternative choices). In this chapter, we introduce these tools and techniques by discussing methods that can be used to make statistical comparisons between two populations. Later, we will discuss some methods to extend this comparison to more than two populations. Whether we are discussing cases involving two populations or those with more than two populations, the techniques we present are all extensions of the statistical tools involving a single population parameter introduced in Chapters 7 and 8.

9-1 ESTIMATION FOR TWO POPULATION MEANS

In this section, we build on the concepts introduced in Chapters 7 and 8 and examine situations in which we are interested in the difference between two population means. We look first at the case where our samples from the two populations are **independent**.

Independent Samples

Samples selected from two or more populations in such a way that the occurrence of values in one sample has no influence on the probability of the occurrence of values in the other sample(s).

We will introduce techniques for estimating the difference between two population means in the following situations:

1. The population standard deviations are known and the samples are independent.
2. The population standard deviations are unknown and the samples are independent.
3. The samples are not independent.

ESTIMATING THE DIFFERENCE BETWEEN TWO MEANS WHEN σ_1 AND σ_2 ARE KNOWN, INDEPENDENT SAMPLES

Recall that in our Chapter 7 discussion of estimation involving a single population mean we introduced procedures that applied when the population standard deviation was assumed to be known. The standard normal distribution z-values were used in establishing the critical value and developing the interval estimate. The general format for a confidence interval estimate is shown in Equation 9-1. This same format applies when we are interested in estimating the difference between two population means.

Confidence Interval, General Format

Point Estimate ± (Critical Value)(Standard Error) **9-1**

You will often be interested in estimating the difference between two population means. For instance, you may wish to estimate the difference in mean starting salaries between males and females, the difference in mean production in union and nonunion factories, or the difference in mean service times at two different fast-food businesses. In these situations, the best point estimate for $\mu_1 - \mu_2$ is

$$\text{Point Estimate} = \bar{x}_1 - \bar{x}_2$$

When independent samples are selected from two populations that are approximately normal, or both samples are large ($n_1 \geq 30$ and $n_2 \geq 30$), and when the population standard deviations are known, the critical value will be a z-value from the standard normal table for the desired level of confidence. Under these same conditions, Equation 9-2 gives the standard error of the sampling distribution.

Standard Error of $\bar{x}_1 - \bar{x}_2$ When σ_1 and σ_2 Are Known

$$\sigma_{\bar{x}_1 - \bar{x}_2} = \sqrt{\frac{\sigma_1^2}{n_1} + \frac{\sigma_2^2}{n_2}} \qquad \text{9-2}$$

where:

$$\sigma_1^2 = \text{variance of population 1}$$
$$\sigma_2^2 = \text{variance of population 2}$$
$$n_1 \text{ and } n_2 = \text{sample sizes from populations 1 and 2}$$

Then the confidence interval estimate for the difference between the two population means when σ_1 and σ_2 are known is given by Equation 9-3.

Confidence Interval Estimate for $\mu_1 - \mu_2$ When σ_1 and σ_2 Are Known, Independent Samples

$$(\bar{x}_1 - \bar{x}_2) \pm z_{\alpha/2} \sqrt{\frac{\sigma_1^2}{n_1} + \frac{\sigma_2^2}{n_2}} \qquad \text{9-3}$$

$\mathcal{E}$XAMPLE 9-1: CONFIDENCE INTERVAL ESTIMATE FOR $\mu_1 - \mu_2$ WHEN σ_1 AND σ_2 ARE KNOWN, INDEPENDENT SAMPLES

Crawford & Associates   Crawford & Associates was recently retained to survey customers of one of the nation's largest food chains to estimate the difference in mean time spent in the store per visit between men and women shoppers. Previous studies indicate that the standard deviation is 11 minutes for males and 16 minutes for females. To develop a 95% confidence interval estimate, the following steps are taken.

Step 1:   **Define the population value of interest.**
In this case, the company is interested in estimating the difference in mean time spent in the store between males and females. The measure of interest is $\mu_1 - \mu_2$.

Step 2:   **Specify the desired confidence level and determine the critical value.**
The interval estimate will be developed using a 95% confidence interval. Because the population standard deviations are known, the critical value is a z-value from the standard normal table. The critical value is

$$z_{\alpha/2} = z_{0.025} = 1.96.$$

Step 3:   **Select independent samples from the two populations and compute the point estimate.**
The company has selected simple random samples of 100 males and 100 females at different times in different stores owned by the food chain. The resulting sample means are

Males: $\bar{x}_1 = 34.5$ minutes   Females: $\bar{x}_2 = 42.4$ minutes

The point estimate is

$$\bar{x}_1 - \bar{x}_2 = 34.5 - 42.4 = -7.9 \text{ minutes}$$

Women spent 7.9 minutes longer, on average, shopping at the stores.

Step 4:   **Develop the confidence interval estimate using Equation 9-3.**

$$(\bar{x}_1 - \bar{x}_2) \pm z_{\alpha/2}\sqrt{\frac{\sigma_1^2}{n_1} + \frac{\sigma_2^2}{n_2}}$$

$$-7.9 \pm 1.96\sqrt{\frac{11^2}{100} + \frac{16^2}{100}}$$

$$-7.9 \pm 3.8056$$

The 95% confidence interval estimate for the difference in mean time spent in the chain's food stores between men and women is

$$-11.7056 \text{ minutes} \text{-----------------------}-4.0944 \text{ minutes}$$

Thus, based on the sample data, women spend on average between 4.09 and 11.71 minutes more at the food stores.

ESTIMATING THE DIFFERENCE BETWEEN TWO MEANS WHEN σ_1 AND σ_2 ARE UNKNOWN, INDEPENDENT SAMPLES

In Chapter 7, you learned that when estimating a single population mean when the population standard deviation is unknown, the critical value is a t-value from the t-distribution. This is also the case when you are interested in estimating the difference between two population means, if three conditions hold:

- The populations are normally distributed.
- The populations have equal variances.
- The samples are independent.

The following application illustrates how a confidence interval estimate is developed using the t-distribution.

Retirement Investing—A major political issue for the past decade has focused on the long-term future of the U.S. Social Security system. Many people who have entered the workforce in the past 20 years believe the system will not be solvent when they retire, so they are actively investing in their own retirement accounts. One investment alternative is a tax-sheltered annuity (TSA) marketed by life insurance companies. Certain people, depending on occupation, qualify to invest part of their paychecks in a TSA and pay no federal income tax on this money until it is withdrawn. While the money is invested, the insurance companies invest it in either stock or bond portfolios. A second alternative open to many people is a plan known as a 401(k), in which employees contribute a portion of their paychecks to purchase stocks, bonds, or mutual funds. In some cases, employers match all or part of the employee contributions. In many 401(k) systems, the employees can control how their funds are invested.

A recent study in North Carolina was interested in estimating the difference in mean annual contributions for individuals covered by the two plans [TSA or 401(k)]. A simple random sample of 15 people from the population of adults who are eligible for a TSA investment was selected. A second sample of 15 people was selected from the population of adults in North Carolina who have 401(k) plans. The variable of interest is the dollar amount of money invested in the retirement plan during the previous year. Specifically, we are interested in estimating $\mu_1 - \mu_2$ using a 95% confidence interval estimate where:

μ_1 = Mean dollars invested by the TSA-eligible population during the past year
μ_2 = Mean dollars invested by the 401(k)-eligible population during the past year

The sample results are

TSA-Eligible	401(k)-Eligible
$n_1 = 15$	$n_2 = 15$
$\bar{x}_1 = \$2,119.70$	$\bar{x}_2 = \$1,777.70$
$s_1 = \$709.70$	$s_2 = \$593.90$

FIGURE 9-1

Investment Study—Sample
Information

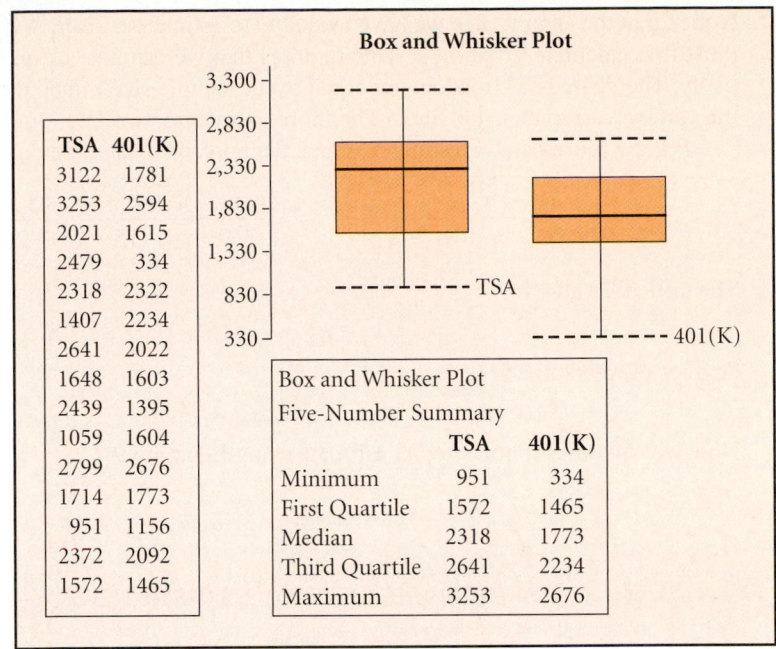

Before applying the *t*-distribution, we need to determine whether the assumptions are likely to be satisfied. First, the samples are considered independent because the amount invested by one group should have no influence on the amount invested by the other.

Next, Figure 9-1 shows the sample data and the box and whisker diagrams for the two samples. These diagrams exhibit characteristics that are reasonably consistent with those that might be associated with normal distributions and approximately equal variances. While using a box and whisker plot to check the *t*-distribution assumptions may seem to be imprecise, fortunately studies have shown the *t*-distribution to be applicable even when there are small violations of the assumptions. This is particularly the case when the sample sizes are approximately equal.[1]

Equation 9-4 can be used to develop the confidence interval estimate for the difference between two population means when you have independent samples.

Confidence Interval Estimate for $\mu_1 - \mu_2$ When σ_1 and σ_2 Are Unknown, Small Independent Samples

$$(\bar{x}_1 - \bar{x}_2) \pm t_{\alpha/2} s_p \sqrt{\frac{1}{n_1} + \frac{1}{n_2}}$$

9-4

where:

$$s_p = \sqrt{\frac{(n_1 - 1)s_1^2 + (n_2 - 1)s_2^2}{n_1 + n_2 - 2}} = \text{pooled standard deviation}$$

$t_{\alpha/2} = $ critical *t*-value from the *t*-distribution, with degrees of freedom equal to $n_1 + n_2 - 2$

To use Equation 9-4, we must compute the pooled standard deviation, s_p. If the equal-variance assumption holds, then both s_1^2 and s_2^2 are estimators of the same population variance, σ^2. To only use one of these, say s_1^2, to estimate σ^2 would be disregarding the information obtained from the other sample. To use the average of s_1^2 and s_2^2, if the sample sizes were different, would ignore the fact that more information about σ^2 is obtained from the sample having the larger sample size. We, therefore, use a weighted average of s_1^2 and s_2^2, denoted as s_p^2 to estimate σ^2, where the weights are the degrees of freedom associated with each sample. The square root of s_p^2 is known as the *pooled standard deviation* and is computed using:

$$s_p = \sqrt{\frac{(n_1 - 1)s_1^2 + (n_2 - 1)s_2^2}{n_1 + n_2 - 2}}$$

[1]Chapter 10 introduces a statistical procedure for testing whether two populations have equal variances.

Notice that the sample size we have available to estimate σ^2 is $n_1 + n_2$. However, to produce s_p, we must first calculate s_1^2 and s_2^2. This requires that we estimate μ_1 and μ_2 using $\bar{x}_1$ and $\bar{x}_2$, respectively. The degrees of freedom are equal to the sample size minus the parameters estimated before the variance estimate is obtained. Therefore, our degrees of freedom must equal $n_1 + n_2 - 2$.

For the retirement investing example, the pooled standard deviation is:

$$s_p = \sqrt{\frac{(n_1 - 1)s_1^2 + (n_2 - 1)s_2^2}{n_1 + n_2 - 2}} = \sqrt{\frac{(15 - 1)(709.7)^2 + (15 - 1)(593.9)^2}{15 + 15 - 2}} = 654.37$$

The critical t-value for

$$n_1 + n_2 - 2 = 15 + 15 - 2 = 28$$

degrees of freedom and 95% confidence is

$$t_{\alpha/2} = 2.0484.$$

Now we can develop the interval estimate using Equation 9-4.

$$(\bar{x}_1 - \bar{x}_2) \pm t_{\alpha/2} s_p \sqrt{\frac{1}{n_1} + \frac{1}{n_2}}$$

$$(2119.70 - 1777.70) \pm 2.0484(654.37) \sqrt{\frac{1}{15} + \frac{1}{15}}$$

$$342 \pm 489.45$$

Thus, the 95% confidence interval estimate for the difference in mean dollars for people who invest in a TSA versus those who invest in a 401(k) is

$$-\$147.45 \text{ ------------------ } \$831.45$$

The fact that this interval crosses zero indicates that there may be no difference in the mean investment by the two groups of investors.

$\mathcal{E}$XAMPLE 9-2: CONFIDENCE INTERVAL ESTIMATE FOR $\mu_1 - \mu_2$ WHEN σ_1 AND σ_2 ARE UNKNOWN, INDEPENDENT SAMPLES

Sneva Pharmaceutical Research The head of research and development at Sneva Pharmaceutical Research is interested in estimating the difference between males and females with respect to the mean time from when a patient takes a new medication until the medication can be detected in the blood. A simple random sample of six males and eight females participated in the study. The estimate can be developed using the following steps.

Step 1: **Define the population value of interest.**
The objective here is to estimate the difference in mean time between males and females with respect to the speed at which the medication reaches the blood. The parameter of interest is $\mu_1 - \mu_2$.

Step 2: **Select independent samples from the two populations, verify that the assumptions are satisfied, and compute the point estimate.**
The research lab has selected simple random samples of six males and eight females. Because the impact of the medication in one person does not influence the impact in another person, the samples are independent. The resulting sample means and sample standard deviations are

Males: $\bar{x}_1 = 13.6$ minutes   Females: $\bar{x}_2 = 11.2$ minutes

$s_1 = 3.1$ minutes $s_2 = 5.0$ minutes

Although not shown here, the box and whisker diagrams were not inconsistent with the normal distribution and equal variance assumptions.

Step 3: **Compute the point estimate.**
The point estimate is

$$\bar{x}_1 - \bar{x}_2 = 13.6 - 11.2 = 2.4 \text{ minutes.}$$

Step 4: **Specify the desired confidence level and determine the critical value.**
The research manager wishes to have a 95% confidence interval estimate. Because the samples are small, the critical value will be a t-value from the t-distribution as long as the population variances are equal and the populations are normally distributed.

Because we have established that the assumptions are reasonable in this case, we can use the t-distribution to obtain the critical value. The critical t for 95% confidence and $6 + 8 - 2 = 12$ degrees of freedom is

$$t_{\alpha/2} = 2.1788.$$

Step 5: **Develop a confidence interval using Equation 9-4.**

$$(\bar{x}_1 - \bar{x}_2) \pm t_{\alpha/2} s_p \sqrt{\frac{1}{n_1} + \frac{1}{n_2}}$$

where:

$$s_p = \sqrt{\frac{(n_1 - 1)s_1^2 + (n_2 - 1)s_2^2}{n_1 + n_2 - 2}} = \sqrt{\frac{(6 - 1)3.1^2 + (8 - 1)5^2}{6 + 8 - 2}} = 4.31$$

Then the interval estimate is

$$2.4 \pm 2.1788(4.31) \sqrt{\frac{1}{6} + \frac{1}{8}}$$

$$2.4 \pm 5.0715$$

$$-2.6715 \text{ ------------------------------ } 7.4715$$

Because the interval crosses zero, the research manager cannot conclude that a difference exists between males and females with respect to the mean time needed for the medication to be detected in the blood.

What If the Population Variances Are Not Equal?

If you have reason to believe that the population variances are substantially different, Equation 9-5 is not appropriate for computing the confidence interval. Instead of computing the pooled standard deviation as part of the confidence interval formula, we use Equation 9-5.

Confidence Interval for the Difference Between Two Means When σ_1 and σ_2 Are Unknown and Not Equal, Small Independent Samples

$$(\bar{x}_1 - \bar{x}_2) \pm t_{\alpha/2} \sqrt{\frac{s_1^2}{n_1} + \frac{s_2^2}{n_2}}$$

9-5

where:

$t_{\alpha/2} = t$-value from the t-distribution with degrees of freedom computed using:

$$df = \frac{(s_1^2/n_1 + s_2^2/n_2)^2}{\left(\dfrac{(s_1^2/n_1)^2}{n_1 - 1} + \dfrac{(s_2^2/n_2)^2}{n_2 - 1} \right)}$$

INTERVAL ESTIMATION FOR PAIRED SAMPLES

The previous examples in this section introduced the methods by which decision makers can estimate the difference between the means for two populations when the two samples are independent. In each example, the samples were independent because the sample values from one population did not have the potential to influence the probability that values would be selected from the second population.

However, there are instances in business in which you would want to use **paired samples** to control for sources of variation that might otherwise distort the conclusions of a study.

Paired Samples

Samples that are selected in such a way that values in one sample are matched with the values in the second sample for the purpose of controlling for extraneous factors. Another term for paired samples is dependent samples.

Testing Engine Oil—A major oil company wanted to estimate the difference in average mileage for cars using a regular engine oil compared with cars using a synthetic-oil product. The company used a paired-sample approach to control any variation in mileage arising because of different cars and drivers. A random sample of 10 motorists (and their cars) was selected. Each car was filled with gasoline, the oil was drained and new, regular oil was added. The car was driven 200 miles on a specified route. The car then was filled with gasoline and the miles per gallon were computed. After the 10 cars completed this process, the same steps were performed using synthetic oil. Because the same cars and drivers tested both types of oil, the miles-per-gallon measurements for synthetic oil and regular engine oil will most likely be related. The two samples are not independent, but are instead considered paired samples. Thus, we will compute d, the **paired difference** between the values from each sample, using Equation 9-6.

Paired Difference

$$d = x_1 - x_2$$

9-6

where:

d = Paired difference
x_1 and x_2 = Values from sample 1 and 2, respectively

FIGURE 9-2

Excel Worksheet for Engine Oil Study

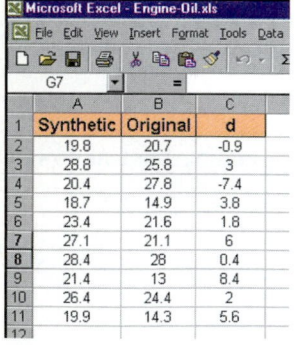

Excel Instructions:
1. Open file: Engine Oil.xls

Figure 9-2 shows the Excel spreadsheet for this engine oil study with the paired differences computed. The data are in the file on your CD-ROM called *Engine-Oil*.

The first step to develop the interval estimate is to compute the *mean paired difference*, $\bar{d}$, using Equation 9-7. This value is the best point estimate for the population mean paired difference, μ_d.

Point Estimate for the Population Mean Paired Difference, μ_d

$$\bar{d} = \frac{\sum_{i=1}^{n} d_i}{n}$$

9-7

where:

d_i = ith paired difference value
n = Number of paired differences

Using Equation 9-7, we determine $\bar{d}$ as follows.

$$\bar{d} = \frac{\sum d}{n} = \frac{22.7}{10} = 2.27$$

The next step is to compute the sample *standard deviation for the paired differences* using Equation 9-8.

Sample Standard Deviation for Paired Differences

$$s_d = \sqrt{\frac{\sum_{i=1}^{n} (d_i - \bar{d})^2}{n-1}}$$

9-8

where:

$$d_i = i\text{th paired difference}$$
$$\bar{d} = \text{Mean paired difference}$$

The sample standard deviation for the paired differences is

$$s_d = \sqrt{\frac{\Sigma(d - \bar{d})^2}{n - 1}} = \sqrt{\frac{172.8}{10 - 1}} = 4.38$$

Assuming that the population of paired differences is normally distributed, the confidence interval estimate for the population mean paired difference is computed using Equation 9-9.

Confidence Interval Estimate for Population Mean Paired Difference, μ_d

$$\bar{d} \pm t_{\alpha/2} \frac{s_d}{\sqrt{n}} \qquad \qquad \textbf{9-9}$$

where:

$$t_{\alpha/2} = \text{Critical } t\text{-value from } t\text{-distribution with } n - 1 \text{ degrees of freedom}$$
$$\bar{d} = \text{Sample mean paired difference}$$
$$s_d = \text{Sample standard deviation of paired differences}$$
$$n = \text{Number of paired differences (sample size)}$$

For a 95% confidence interval with $10 - 1 = 9$ degrees of freedom, we use a critical t from the t-distribution of

$$t_{\alpha/2} = 2.2622$$

The interval estimate obtained from Equation 9-9 is

$$\bar{d} \pm t_{\alpha/2} \frac{s_d}{\sqrt{n}}$$

$$2.27 \pm 2.2622 \frac{4.38}{\sqrt{10}}$$

$$2.27 \pm 3.13$$

$$-.86 \text{ mpg} \text{ -------------------------- } 5.40 \text{ mpg}$$

$\mathcal{E}$XAMPLE 9-3: CONFIDENCE INTERVAL ESTIMATE FOR μ_d

Golf Ball Testing   Technology has done more to change golf than possibly any other sport in recent years. Titanium woods and irons and new golf ball designs have impacted professional and amateur golfers alike. A maker of golf balls has developed a new ball technology and is interested in estimating the mean difference in driving distance for this new ball versus its existing best-seller. To conduct the test, the developers selected six professional golfers and had each golfer hit each ball one time. Here are the steps necessary to develop a confidence interval estimate for the mean paired difference.

Step 1:   Define the population value of interest.
Because the same golfers hit each golf ball, the company is controlling for the variation in the golfers' ability to hit a golf ball. The samples are paired, and the population value of interest is μ_d, the mean paired difference in distance. We assume that the population of paired differences is normally distributed.

Step 2:   Specify the desired confidence level and determine the appropriate critical value.
For a 95% confidence interval, the critical value is a t-value from the t-distribution with $n - 1 = 5$ degrees of freedom. From the t-table, we get
$$t_{\alpha/2} = 2.5706$$

Step 3: **Collect the sample data and compute the point estimate, $\bar{d}$, and the standard deviation, s_d.**
The sample data, paired differences, are shown as follows.

Golfer	Existing Ball	New Ball	d
1	278	285	−7
2	299	301	−2
3	280	276	4
4	295	300	−5
5	268	273	−5
6	301	299	2

The point estimate is computed using Equation 9-7.

$$\bar{d} = \frac{\Sigma d}{n} = \frac{-13}{6} = -2.17 \text{ yards}$$

The standard deviation for the paired differences is computed using Equation 9-8.

$$s_d = \sqrt{\frac{\Sigma(d - \bar{d})^2}{n - 1}} = 4.36 \text{ yards}$$

Step 4: **Compute the confidence interval estimate using Equation 9-9.**

$$\bar{d} \pm t_{\alpha/2} \frac{s_d}{\sqrt{n}}$$

$$-2.17 \pm 2.5706 \frac{4.36}{\sqrt{6}}$$

$$-2.17 \pm 4.58$$

$$-6.75 \text{ yards} \text{ ------------------------ } 2.41 \text{ yards}$$

The key in deciding whether to use paired samples is to determine whether a factor exists that might adversely influence the results of the estimation. In the engine-oil test example, we controlled for potential outside influence by using the same cars to test both oils. In Example 9-3, we controlled for golfer ability by having the same golfers hit both golf balls. If you determine that there is no need to control for an outside source of variation, then independent samples should be used, as discussed earlier in this section.

9-1: EXERCISES

Skill Development

9.1 Given the following information:

$$n_1 = 100 \qquad n_2 = 150$$
$$\bar{x}_1 = 50 \qquad \bar{x}_2 = 65$$
$$s_1 = 6 \qquad s_2 = 8$$

a. Determine the 90% confidence interval estimate for the difference between population means. Interpret the estimate.

b. Determine the 98% confidence interval estimate for the difference between population means. Interpret the estimate.

c. What are the advantages and disadvantages of using a higher confidence level to estimate the difference between the two population means?

9.2 Given the following information:

$$n_1 = 25 \qquad n_2 = 25$$
$$\bar{x}_1 = 0.145 \qquad \bar{x}_2 = 0.107$$
$$s_1 = 0.06 \qquad s_2 = 0.08$$

a. Determine the 90% confidence interval estimate for the difference between population means. Interpret the estimate.

b. Determine the 95% confidence interval estimate for the difference between population means. Interpret the estimate.

c. How would the answers to parts a and b differ if the sample sizes were doubled? Discuss what factors affect your answer.

9.3 You are given the following results of a paired difference test:

$$\bar{d} = 344$$
$$s_d = 34$$
$$n = 23$$

a. Construct and interpret a 95% confidence interval estimate for the paired difference in mean values.

b. Construct and interpret a 90% confidence interval estimate for the paired difference in mean values.

c. Discuss why the two estimates are different. What are the advantages and disadvantages of using a lower confidence level?

9.4 You are given the following results of a paired difference test:

$$\bar{d} = -4.6$$
$$s_d = 0.25$$
$$n = 16$$

a. Construct and interpret a 99% confidence interval estimate for the paired difference in mean values.

b. Construct and interpret a 90% confidence interval estimate for the paired difference in mean values.

c. The variances of the two dependent samples are $s_1^2 = 0.060$ and $s_2^2 = 0.065$. Calculate a 90% confidence interval as though the samples were obtained independently. Comment on any differences you see in the two intervals obtained in parts b and c.

9.5 Given the following information:

Sample 1	Sample 2
$n_1 = 36$	$n_2 = 45$
$s_1 = 32$	$s_2 = 80$
$\bar{x}_1 = 2{,}456$	$\bar{x}_2 = 2{,}460$

a. Develop a 90% confidence interval estimate for the difference in the population means.

b. Develop a 98% confidence interval estimate for the difference in the population means.

9.6 Given the following information:

Sample 1	Sample 2
$n_1 = 25$	$n_2 = 20$
$s_1 = 20$	$s_2 = 24$
$\bar{x}_1 = 430$	$\bar{x}_2 = 405$

a. Develop a 95% confidence interval estimate for the difference in the population means.

b. Develop a 99% confidence interval estimate for the difference in the population means.

Business Applications

9.7 Wilson Construction and Concrete Company is known as a very progressive company that is willing to try new ideas to improve its products and service. One of the key factors of importance in concrete work is the time it takes for the concrete to "set up." The company is considering a new additive that can be put in concrete mix to help reduce the set-up time. Before going ahead with the additive, the company tested it against the current additive. To do this, 14 batches of concrete were mixed using each of the additives. The following results were observed:

Old Additive	New Additive
$\bar{x} = 17.2$ hours	$\bar{x} = 15.9$ hours
$s = 2.5$ hours	$s = 1.8$ hours

a. Use these sample data to construct a 90% confidence interval estimate for the difference in mean set-up time for the two concrete additives. On the basis of the confidence interval produced, do you agree that the new additive helps reduce the set-up time for cement? Explain your answer.

b. Assuming that the new additive is slightly more expensive than the old additive, do the data support switching to the new additive if the managers of the company are primarily interested in reducing average set-up time?

9.8 A random sample of 256 credit unions that offer credit cards revealed that the average annual fee charged by a credit union was $12.56, with a standard deviation of $2.33. A random sample of 225 federally chartered banks offering credit cards showed that the average annual fee was $22.48, with a standard deviation of $6.18.

a. Construct 90% and 95% confidence interval estimates for the true difference in means between the annual fees charged by credit unions and federally chartered banks.

b. Could the federally chartered banks be accused of having an average annual fee that is $10 more than that of credit unions? Support your answer using your knowledge of probability and statistics.

9.9 The ECCO company makes back-up alarms for equipment such as forklifts. As its quality manager, you are concerned about how large the difference is in average warranty claims for products made at the Boise location versus the Atlanta location. Sample warranty data are contained in a file called *ECCO* on your CD-ROM. Develop a 98% confidence interval estimate for the difference in mean warranty amounts for the two locations. Interpret your results. Do these results suggest that the manager needs to focus on one location or the other? Discuss.

9.10 The CD-ROM file *Banks* contains data on a sample of U.S. banks. You are asked to develop a 95% confidence interval estimate for the difference in mean number of employees per bank for banks that had profits greater than $1 billion versus those that had profits less than $1 billion. (Data listed under "Profits" in the data file are in units of thousands of dollars.) Interpret your results. Do these data provide evidence to suggest that there is a difference between the two groups of banks? Discuss. (Hint: You may need to reorganize the data prior to developing the interval estimate.)

9.11   The marketing manager for the Capital Credit Union is considering developing an advertising campaign directed at female credit card customers. However, before continuing, she wants to know what the difference in average credit card balances is between male and female customers. She asked the database manager to select a random sample of 300 customers. These data are in the CD-ROM file *Capital*.

a. Use the sample data to construct a 95% confidence interval estimate for the difference in mean credit card balances for males and females.

b. Interpret the interval estimate and write a business letter to the marketing manager discussing the conclusions that could be reached from this estimate.

9.12   Freedom Hospital is in the midst of contract negotiations with its resident physicians. There has been a lot of discussion about the hospital's ability to pay and the way patients are charged. The doctors' negotiator recently mentioned that the geriatric charge system does not make sense and there may be a difference in the way males are charged versus females. To look into this, the hospital has collected a random sample of patient data for 138 patients. The data are in a CD-ROM file called *Patients*. The operations manager wants to use this data to develop an estimate for the difference in average charges between males and females.

a. Construct a 95% confidence interval estimate for the difference in average charges. What does this imply about how male and female patients are charged? Is there anything to what the negotiator is saying? Discuss.

b. The manager is now interested in estimating the difference between average charges for male and female patients, but only for patients who have Medicare as their principal payer. Construct the 95% confidence interval estimate. Is there a difference in how male and female patients are charged for this group?

Advanced Applications

9.13   The CD-ROM file *Cities* contains a random sample of cities in the United States. Use this sample data to estimate the difference in average SAT scores for city versus suburban dwellers. (Hint: Are the samples independent or paired?)

a. Compute the point estimate for the difference in mean SAT scores. On the basis of this point estimate alone, could you conclude that there are as many as 150 points of difference in the average

SAT scores for those living in the suburbs? Explain your answer.

b. Based on the sample data, calculate a 95% confidence interval estimate for the difference between mean SAT scores for city versus suburban dwellers. On the basis of this confidence interval alone, could you conclude that there are as many as 150 points of difference in the average SAT scores for those living in the suburbs? Explain your answer.

c. Referring to part b, suppose the confidence level is changed to 80%. What is the impact on the interval estimate? Discuss why this impact occurred.

9.14   The owner of Fortee Bakery is interested in determining the difference between mean purchase amounts per customer at his two locations. To estimate the difference, he has selected a random sample of 50 customer receipts at each location. The following data are available:

Location 1	Location 2
$\bar{x} = \$5.26$	$\bar{x} = \$6.19$
$s = \$0.89$	$s = \$1.05$

a. What is the point estimate for the difference between mean purchase amounts at the two locations? Comment on the advantages and disadvantages of using a point estimate only in this case?

b. Assuming that the owner wishes to develop a 95% confidence interval estimate for the difference in mean purchase amounts, what will the standard error be?

c. Compute the 95% confidence interval estimate. Determine if there is a difference in the average purchase amounts per customer at his two locations.

d. Referring to parts c and d, suppose the owner wishes to reduce the margin of error, what are his options? Discuss.

9.15   Two companies that manufacture batteries for electronics products have submitted their products to an independent testing agency. The agency tested 200 of each company's batteries and recorded the length of time the batteries lasted before failure. The following results were determined:

Company A	Company B
$\bar{x} = 41.5$ hours	$\bar{x} = 39.0$ hours
$s = 3.6$	$s = 5.0$

a. Based on these data, determine the 95% confidence interval to estimate the difference in average lives of the batteries for the two companies. Do these data indicate that one company's batteries will outlast the other company's batteries on average? Explain.

b. Suppose the manufacturers of each of these batteries wished to warranty their batteries. One small company to which they both ship batteries receives shipments of 200 batteries weekly. If the average length of time to failure of the batteries is less than a specified number, the manufacturer will refund the company's purchase price of that set of batteries. What value should each manufacturer set if they wish to refund money to at most 5% of the shipments?

9.16 Referring to Exercise 9-7, suppose Wilson's managers repeat the test with 14 more batches of concrete, using each additive. They then combined the information from the two tests, giving a sample size of 28 batches. The following results were observed.

Old Additive	New Additive
$\bar{x} = 18.4$ hours	$\bar{x} = 15.2$ hours
$s = 2.9$ hours	$s = 1.6$ hours

a. Use these sample data to construct a 90% confidence interval estimate for the difference in mean set-up time for the two concrete additives. On the basis of this confidence interval, do you agree that the new additive helps reduce the set-up time for cement? Explain your answer.

b. Compare this interval with the one computed in Exercise 9-7. Discuss why the standard error for the estimate is lower when the samples are combined.

c. Assuming that the new additive is slightly more expensive than the old additive, do the data support switching to the new additive if the managers of the company are primarily interested in reducing average set-up time?

9-2 HYPOTHESIS TESTS FOR THE DIFFERENCE BETWEEN TWO POPULATION MEANS

You will encounter many business situations such as those illustrated in Section 9-1, in which you will be interested in the difference between two population means. However, you will also encounter many other situations that will require you to test whether two populations have equal means, or whether one population mean is larger (smaller) than another. These hypothesis-testing applications are just an extension of the hypothesis-testing process introduced in Chapter 8 for a single population mean. They also build directly on the estimation process introduced in Section 9-1.

In this section, we will introduce hypothesis-testing techniques for the difference between two population means in the following situations:

1. The population standard deviations are known and the samples are large and independent.
2. The population standard deviations are not known and the sample sizes are large and independent.
3. The population standard deviations are unknown and the sample sizes are small and independent.
4. The samples are not independent.

SUMMARY: THE HYPOTHESIS-TESTING PROCESS

The hypothesis-testing process for tests involving two population means introduced in this section is essentially the same as for a single population mean. The process is composed of the following steps:

1. Specify the population value of interest.

2. Formulate the appropriate null and alternative hypotheses. The null hypothesis should contain the equality. Possible formats for testing whether two populations have equal means are

$H_0: \mu_1 - \mu_2 = 0.0$ $H_0: \mu_1 - \mu_2 \leq 0.0$ $H_0: \mu_1 - \mu_2 \geq 0.0$

$H_A: \mu_1 - \mu_2 \neq 0.0$ $H_A: \mu_1 - \mu_2 > 0.0$ $H_A: \mu_1 - \mu_2 < 0.0$

two-tailed test   one-tailed test   one-tailed test

3. Specify the significance level (α) for testing the hypothesis. Alpha is the maximum probability of committing a Type I statistical error.

4. Construct the rejection region and develop the decision rule.

5. Compute the test statistic. Of course, you must first select simple random samples from each population and compute the sample means.

6. Reach a decision. Apply the decision rule to determine whether to reject the null hypothesis. Note that you can also compute the p-value and compare it to α.

7. Draw a conclusion.

The logic of all hypothesis tests is that if the sample value (statistic) is "substantially" different from the hypothesized population value (parameter), the null hypothesis should be rejected. If the sample values are consistent with the hypothesized population value, the null hypothesis will not be rejected. Two possible errors can occur:

Type I Error: Rejecting H_0 when it is true. (Alpha error)

Type II Error: Not rejecting H_0 when it is false. (Beta error)

The probability of a Type I error is controlled by the decision maker by the choice of α. Recall from Section 8-3 that α and β are inversely related. If we reduce α, β is increased, assuming everything else remains constant.

The remainder of this section presents examples of hypothesis tests under different situations.

TESTING FOR $\mu_1 - \mu_2$ WHEN σ_1 AND σ_2 ARE KNOWN, INDEPENDENT SAMPLES

In Section 9-1, we said that *independent samples* occur when the samples from the two populations are taken in such a way that the values in one sample are in no way influenced by the values in the second sample. In special cases in which the population standard deviations are known and the samples are independent, the test statistic is a z-value computed using Equation 9-10.

---

z Test Statistic for $\mu_1 - \mu_2$ When σ_1 and σ_2 Are Known, Independent Samples

$$z = \frac{(\bar{x}_1 - \bar{x}_2) - (\mu_1 - \mu_2)}{\sqrt{\dfrac{\sigma_1^2}{n_1} + \dfrac{\sigma_2^2}{n_2}}}$$

9-10

If the calculated z-value using Equation 9-10 exceeds the critical z-value from the standard normal distribution, the null hypothesis is rejected. Example 9-4 illustrates the use of this test statistic.

$\mathcal{E}$XAMPLE 9-4: HYPOTHESIS TEST FOR $\mu_1 - \mu_2$ WHEN σ_1 AND σ_2 ARE KNOWN, INDEPENDENT SAMPLES

Phillips Systems   Phillips Systems is an Ohio-based company that makes parts for the automotive industry. One part is a bolt used in the engine manifold system. The company has two machines that make these bolts. It is well established that the standard deviation for bolts made by machine one is 0.025 inches and the standard deviation for machine two is 0.034 inches. At question is whether machine 2 also provides bolts with higher average diameters. To test this, you can use these steps.

Step 1:   **Specify the population value of interest.**
            This is $\mu_1 - \mu_2$, the difference in population means.

Step 2:   **Formulate the appropriate null and alternative hypotheses.**
            We are interested in determining whether the mean diameter for machine two exceeds that for machine one. The following null and alternative hypotheses are specified:

$$H_0: \mu_1 - \mu_2 \geq 0.0$$
$$H_A: \mu_1 - \mu_2 < 0.0$$

Step 3:   **Specify the significance level for the test.**
            The test will be conducted using alpha = 0.05.

Step 4:   **Determine the rejection region and state the decision rule.**
            Because the population standard deviations are assumed to be known, the critical value is a z-value from the standard normal distribution. This test is a one-tailed lower-tail test, with $\alpha = 0.05$. From the standard normal distribution, the critical z-value is

$$z_{0.05} = -1.645$$

The decision rule is

If $z < -1.645$, reject the null hypothesis;
Otherwise, do not reject the null hypothesis.

Alternatively, you can state the decision rule in terms of a p-value, as follows:

If p-value $< \alpha = 0.05$, reject the null hypothesis;
Otherwise, do not reject the null hypothesis.

Step 5:   **Compute the test statistic.**

Select simple random samples from the two populations and compute the sample means. A simple random sample of 100 bolts is selected from machine one's production, and another simple random sample of 100 bolts is selected from machine two. The samples are independent because the diameters of bolts made by one machine can in no way influence the diameter of bolts made by the other machine. The means computed from the samples are

$$\bar{x}_1 = 0.501 \text{ inches and } \bar{x}_2 = 0.509 \text{ inches}$$

The test statistic is obtained using Equation 9-10.

$$z = \frac{(\bar{x}_1 - \bar{x}_2) - (\mu_1 - \mu_2)}{\sqrt{\dfrac{\sigma_1^2}{n_1} + \dfrac{\sigma_2^2}{n_2}}}$$

$$z = \frac{(0.501 - 0.509) - 0}{\sqrt{\dfrac{0.025^2}{100} + \dfrac{0.034^2}{100}}} = -1.90$$

Step 6:   **Reach a decision.**

Applying the decision rule,

Because $z = -1.90 < -1.645$, reject the null hypothesis.

Step 7:   **Draw a conclusion.**

There is statistical evidence to conclude that the bolts made by machine two have a larger mean diameter than those made by machine one.

Using *p*-values

The z test statistic computed in Example 9-4 indicates the difference in sample means is 1.90 standard errors below the hypothesized difference of zero. Because this falls below the z critical level of -1.645, the null hypothesis was rejected. You could have also tested this hypothesis using the *p*-value approach introduced in Chapter 8. The *p*-value for this one-tailed test is the probability of a z-value in a standard normal distribution being less than -1.90. From the standard normal table, the probability associated with $z = -1.90$ is 0.4713. Then the *p*-value is

$$p\text{-value} = 0.5000 - 0.4713 = 0.0287$$

The decision rule to use with *p*-values is

If *p*-value $< \alpha = 0.05$, reject the null hypothesis;
Otherwise, do not reject the null hypothesis.

Because
$$p\text{-value} = 0.0287 < \alpha = 0.05,$$

reject the null hypothesis and conclude that the population means are different.

TESTING $\mu_1 - \mu_2$ WHEN σ_1 AND σ_2 ARE UNKNOWN, INDEPENDENT SAMPLES

In Section 9-1 we showed that to develop a confidence interval estimate for the difference between two population means when the standard deviations are unknown, we used the *t*-distribution to obtain the critical value. As you might suspect, this same approach is taken for hypothesis-testing situations. Equation 9-11 shows the t-test statistic that will be used when σ_1 and σ_2 are unknown and the samples are small.

***t* Test Statistic for $\mu_1 - \mu_2$ When σ_1 and σ_2 Are Unknown, Independent Samples**

$$t = \frac{(\bar{x}_1 - \bar{x}_2) - (\mu_1 - \mu_2)}{s_p\sqrt{\dfrac{1}{n_1} + \dfrac{1}{n_2}}}, \qquad df = n_1 + n_2 - 2 \qquad\qquad \textbf{9-11}$$

where:

$$\bar{x}_1 \text{ and } \bar{x}_2 = \text{Sample means from populations 1 and 2}$$
$$\mu_1 - \mu_2 = \text{Hypothesized difference}$$
$$n_1 \text{ and } n_2 = \text{Sample sizes from the two populations}$$
$$s_p = \text{Pooled standard deviation}$$

The test statistic in Equation 9-11 is based on three assumptions:

ASSUMPTIONS

1. Each population has a normal distribution.
2. The two population variances, σ_1^2 and σ_2^2, are equal.
3. The samples are independent.

Notice that in Equation 9-11 we are using the pooled estimate for the common population standard deviation that we developed in Section 9-1.

Retirement Investing—Recall the earlier example discussing a recent study in North Carolina involving retirement investing. The leaders of the study are interested in determining whether there is a difference in mean annual contributions for individuals covered by tax-sheltered annuities (TSA) and those with 401(k) retirement programs. A simple random sample of 15 people from the population of adults who are eligible for a TSA investment was selected. A second sample of 15 people was selected from the population of adults in North Carolina who have 401(k) plans. The variable of interest is the dollar amount of money invested in the retirement plan during the previous year.

Specifically, we are interested in testing the following null and alternative hypotheses:

$$H_0: \mu_1 - \mu_2 = 0.0$$
$$H_A: \mu_1 - \mu_2 \neq 0.0$$

$$\mu_1 = \text{Mean dollars invested by the TSA-eligible population during the past year}$$
$$\mu_2 = \text{Mean dollars invested by the 401(k)-eligible population during the past year}$$

The leaders of the study select a significance level of $\alpha = 0.05$. Refer to Figure 9-1 on page 350 for the sample data and the box and whisker diagrams.

The sample results are

TSA-Eligible	401(k)-Eligible
$n_1 = 15$	$n_2 = 15$
$\bar{x}_1 = \$2,119.70$	$\bar{x}_2 = \$1,777.70$
$s_1 = \$709.70$	$s_2 = \$593.90$

Because the investments by individuals with TSA accounts is in no way influenced by investments by individuals with 401(k) accounts, the samples are considered independent. The box and whisker diagrams shown earlier in Figure 9-1 are consistent with what might be expected if the populations have equal variances and are approximately normally distributed.

We are now in a position to complete the hypothesis test to determine whether the mean dollar amount invested by TSA employees is equal to the mean amount invested by 401(k) employees. We first determine the critical value from the t-distribution table in Appendix F (or use Excel's **TINV** function or Minitab's **Calc > Probability Distributions** command) with degrees of freedom equal to

$$n_1 + n_2 - 2 = 15 + 15 - 2 = 28,$$

and alpha = 0.05 for the two-tailed test. The appropriate *t*-value is

$$t_{\alpha/2} = 2.0484.$$

To continue the hypothesis test, we compute the pooled standard deviation.

$$s_p = \sqrt{\frac{(n_1 - 1)s_1^2 + (n_2 - 1)s_2^2}{n_1 + n_2 - 2}} = \sqrt{\frac{(15 - 1)(709.7)^2 + (15 - 1)(593.9)^2}{15 + 15 - 2}} = 654.37$$

Note that the pooled standard deviation is partway between the two sample standard deviations. Now, keeping in mind that the hypothesized difference between μ_1 and μ_2 is zero, we compute the t test statistic using Equation 9-11, as follows.

$$t = \frac{(\bar{x}_1 - \bar{x}_2) - (\mu_1 - \mu_2)}{s_p \sqrt{\frac{1}{n_1} + \frac{1}{n_2}}} = \frac{(2{,}119.70 - 1{,}777.70) - 0.0}{654.37 \sqrt{\frac{1}{15} + \frac{1}{15}}} = 1.4313$$

This indicates that the difference in sample means is 1.4313 standard errors above the hypothesized difference of zero. Because

$$t = 1.4313 < t_{\alpha/2} = 2.0484,$$

the null hypothesis should not be rejected.

The difference in sample means is attributed to sampling error. Figure 9-3 summarizes this hypothesis test. Based on the sample data, there is no statistical justification to believe that the mean annual investment by individuals who are eligible for the tax-sheltered annuity option is different than for those individuals who are eligible for the 401(k) plan.

Excel and Minitab Tutorial

SUV Vehicle Mileage—Both Excel and Minitab have procedures for performing the necessary calculations to test hypotheses involving two population means. Consider a national car rental company that is interested in testing to determine whether there is a difference in mean mileage for sport-utility vehicles (SUVs) driven in town versus those driven on the highway. Based on its experience with regular automobiles, the company believes the mean highway mileage will exceed the mean city mileage.

To test this belief, the company has randomly selected 25 SUV rentals driven only on the highway and another random sample of 25 SUV rentals driven only in the city. The vehicles were

FIGURE 9-3

Hypothesis Test for the Equality of the Two Population Means for the North Carolina Investment Study

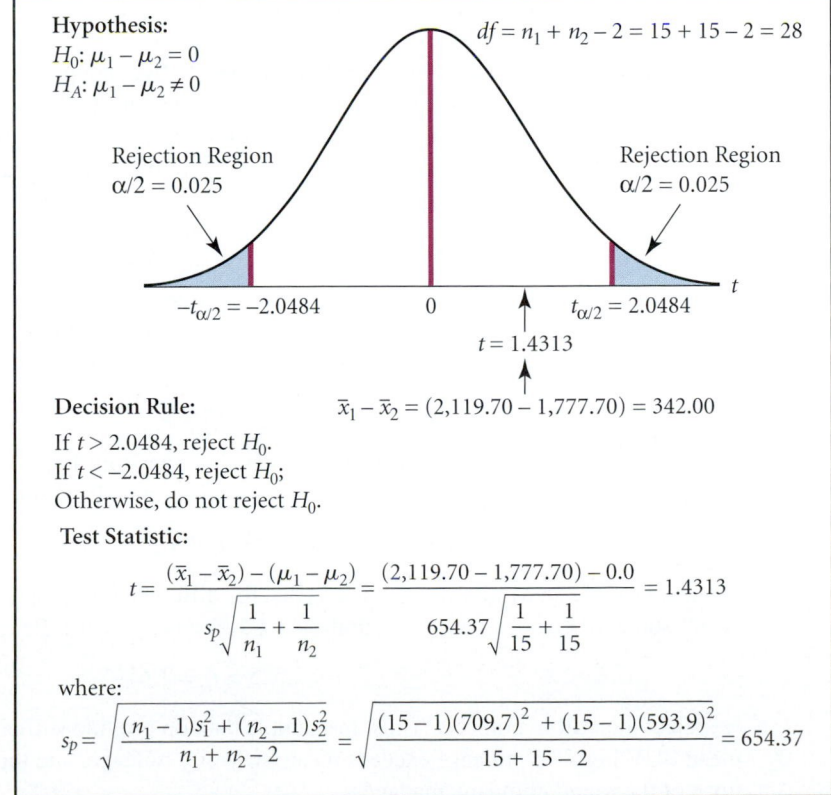

Hypothesis:
$H_0: \mu_1 - \mu_2 = 0$
$H_A: \mu_1 - \mu_2 \neq 0$

$df = n_1 + n_2 - 2 = 15 + 15 - 2 = 28$

Rejection Region
$\alpha/2 = 0.025$

Rejection Region
$\alpha/2 = 0.025$

$-t_{\alpha/2} = -2.0484$ 0 $t_{\alpha/2} = 2.0484$ t

$t = 1.4313$

$\bar{x}_1 - \bar{x}_2 = (2{,}119.70 - 1{,}777.70) = 342.00$

Decision Rule:
If $t > 2.0484$, reject H_0.
If $t < -2.0484$, reject H_0;
Otherwise, do not reject H_0.

Test Statistic:

$$t = \frac{(\bar{x}_1 - \bar{x}_2) - (\mu_1 - \mu_2)}{s_p \sqrt{\frac{1}{n_1} + \frac{1}{n_2}}} = \frac{(2{,}119.70 - 1{,}777.70) - 0.0}{654.37 \sqrt{\frac{1}{15} + \frac{1}{15}}} = 1.4313$$

where:

$$s_p = \sqrt{\frac{(n_1 - 1)s_1^2 + (n_2 - 1)s_2^2}{n_1 + n_2 - 2}} = \sqrt{\frac{(15 - 1)(709.7)^2 + (15 - 1)(593.9)^2}{15 + 15 - 2}} = 654.37$$

FIGURE 9-4

Excel Output—SUV
Mileage Descriptive
Statistics

	A	B	C	D
1	Highway Mileage		City Mileage	
2				
3	Mean	19.6468	Mean	16.146
4	Standard Error	0.85938907	Standard Error	1.088235881
5	Median	19.54	Median	16.62
6	Mode	#N/A	Mode	#N/A
7	Standard Deviation	4.296945349	Standard Deviation	5.441179406
8	Sample Variance	18.46373933	Sample Variance	29.60643333
9	Kurtosis	-0.417874222	Kurtosis	-0.722382196
10	Skewness	0.19290028	Skewness	-0.382880482
11	Range	15.66	Range	18.43
12	Minimum	12.27	Minimum	5.89
13	Maximum	27.93	Maximum	24.32
14	Sum	491.17	Sum	403.65
15	Count	25	Count	25

filled with 14 gallons of gasoline. The company then asked each customer to drive their car until it ran out of gasoline. At that point, the elapsed miles were noted and the miles per gallon (mpg) were recorded. For their trouble, the customers received free use of the SUV and a coupon valid for one week's free rental. The results of the experiment are contained in the CD-ROM file *Mileage*.

Both Excel and the PHStat add-ins that accompany this text contain procedures for performing the calculations we will need to determine whether the manager's belief about SUV highway mileage can be justified. We first formulate the null and alternative hypotheses to be tested.

$$H_0: \mu_1 - \mu_2 \le 0.0$$
$$H_A: \mu_1 - \mu_2 > 0.0$$

Population 1 represents highway mileage, and Population 2 represents city mileage. The test is conducted using a significance level of $0.05 = \alpha$.

Figure 9-4 shows the descriptive statistics for the two independent samples.

Figure 9-5a displays the box and whisker diagrams for the two samples, and Figure 9-5b shows the Minitab boxplot diagrams. Based on these diagrams, the normal distribution and equal variance assumptions appear reasonable. We will proceed with the test of means assuming normal distributions and equal variances and use Equation 9-11.

Both Excel and Minitab have procedures for carrying out this hypothesis test. Figure 9-6a and Figure 9-6b show the outputs from these procedures. The mean highway mileage is 19.6468 mpg, whereas the mean for city driving is 16.146. At issue is whether this difference in sample means (19.6468 − 16.146 = 3.5008 mpg) is sufficient to conclude the population means are not equal. The one-tail *t* critical value for alpha = 0.05 is shown in Figure 9-6a to be

$$t_{\alpha} = 1.6772.$$

Figures 9-6a and 9-6b show that the "*t*-Stat" value from Excel and the *t*-value from Minitab, which are the calculated test statistics (or *t*-values, based on Equation 9-13), are equal to

$$t = 2.525$$

(rounded to 2.52 in Minitab). This means that the difference in sample means (3.5008 mpg) is 2.525 (2.52) standard errors above the hypothesized difference of zero. Because the test statistic

$$t = 2.525 > t_{\alpha} = 1.6772,$$

we reject the null hypothesis. Thus, the sample data do provide sufficient evidence to conclude that mean SUV highway mileage exceeds mean SUV city mileage, and this study confirms the expectations of the rental company managers.

FIGURE 9-5A

Excel Output (PHStat Add-in) Box and Whisker Diagram—SUV Mileage Test

Excel Instructions:
1. Open file: Mileage.xls
2. Select **PHStat tab**.
3. Select **Box and Whisker Plot**.
4. Define data range (both columns).
5. Check **Multiple Groups—Unstacked**.

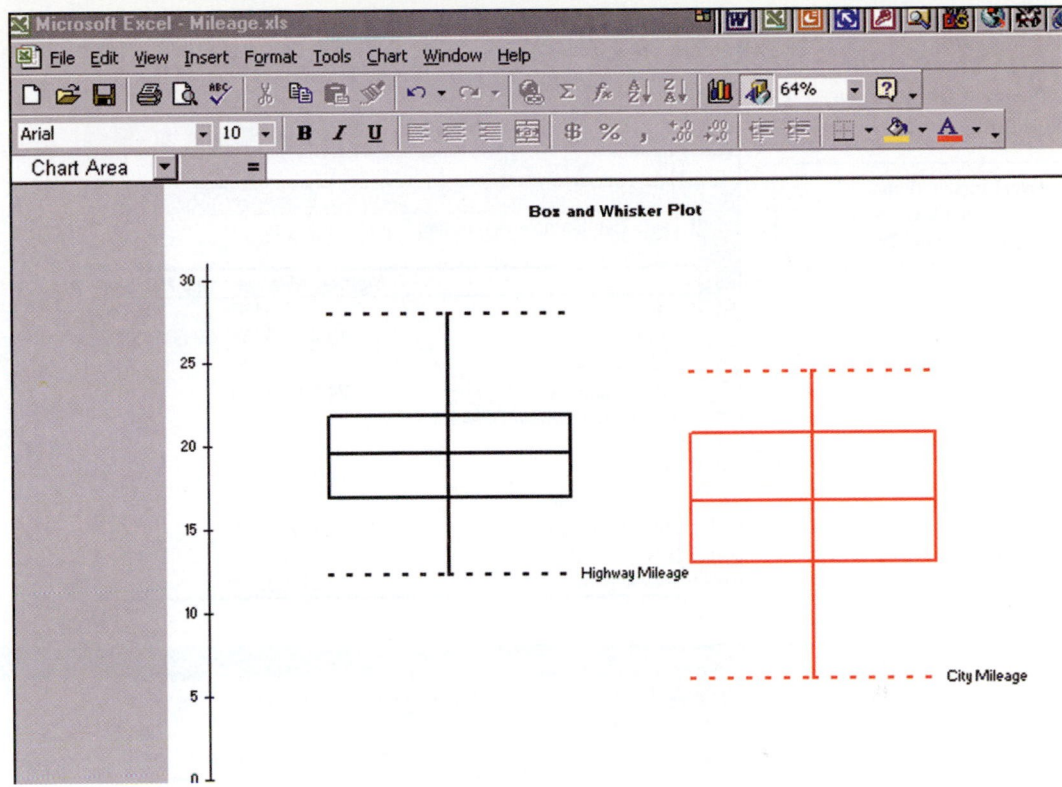

The outputs shown in Figures 9-6a and 9-6b also provide the p-value for the one-tailed test, which can also be used to test the null hypothesis. Recall, if the calculated p-value is less than alpha, the null hypothesis should be rejected. The decision rule is

$$\text{If } p\text{-value} < 0.05, \text{ reject } H_0;$$
$$\text{Otherwise, do not reject } H_0.$$

The p-value for the one-tailed test is 0.00747. Because $0.00747 < 0.05$, the null hypothesis is rejected. This is the same conclusion as the one we reached using the test statistic approach.

FIGURE 9-5B

Minitab Output Boxplot Diagrams—SUV Mileage Test

Minitab Instructions:
1. Open file: Mileage.MTW.
2. Choose **Graph > Boxplot**.
3. Under **Multiple Ys**, select **Simple**.
4. Click **OK**.
4. In **Graph variables**, enter data columns.
5. Click **OK**.

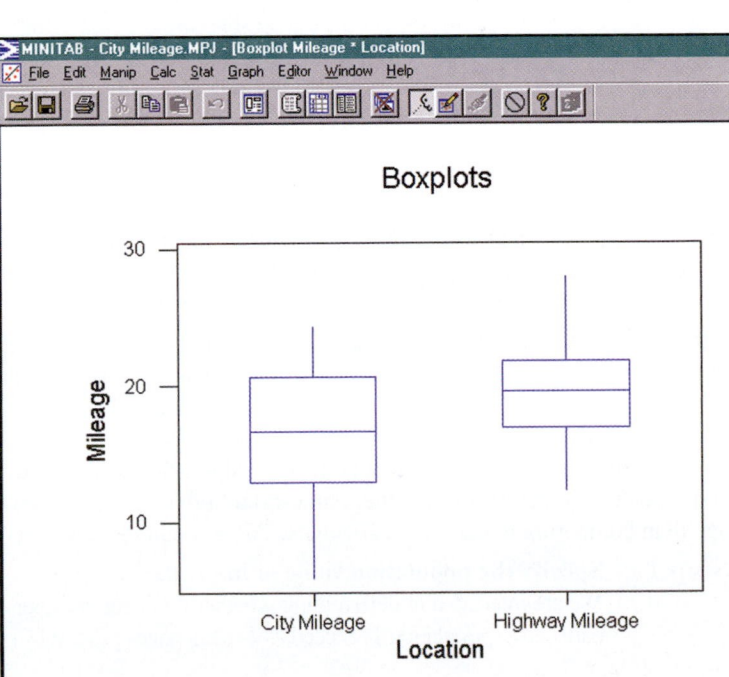

FIGURE 9-6A

Excel Output—SUV Mileage *t*-Test for Two Population Means

Excel Instructions:
1. Select **Tools** tab.
2. Select t-test: **Two-Sample** Assuming Equal **Variances**.
3. Define data ranges.
4. Set Hypothesized Mean Difference to 0.0.
5. Set alpha at 0.05.

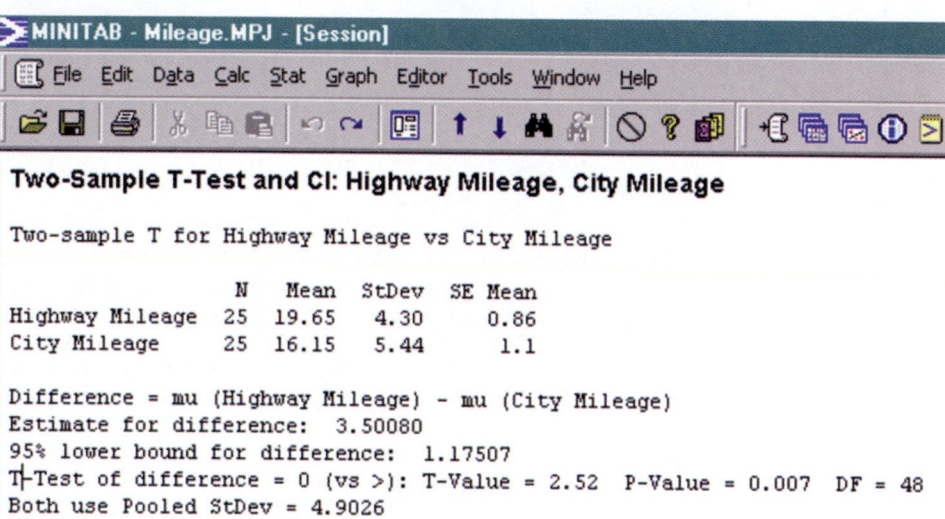

	A	B	C
1	t-Test: Two-Sample Assuming Equal Variances		
2			
3		*Highway Mileage*	*City Mileage*
4	Mean	19.6468	16.146
5	Variance	18.46373933	29.60643333
6	Observations	25	25
7	Pooled Variance	24.03508633	
8	Hypothesized Mean Difference	0	
9	df	48	
10	t Stat	2.524640028	
11	P(T<=t) one-tail	0.007470767	
12	t Critical one-tail	1.677224191	
13	P(T<=t) two-tail	0.014941533	
14	t Critical two-tail	2.01063358	

FIGURE 9-6B

Minitab Output—SUV Mileage *t*-Test for Two Population Means

Minitab Instructions:
1. Open file: Mileage.MTW.
2. Choose **Stat > Basic Statistics > 2-Sample t.**
3. Choose **Samples in different columns.**
4. In **First**, enter the first data column.
5. In **Second**, enter the other data column.
6. Check **Assume equal variances.**
7. Click **Options** and enter $1 - \alpha$ in **Confidence level.**
8. In **Alternative**, choose *greater than.*
9. Click **OK. OK.**

Two-Sample T-Test and CI: Highway Mileage, City Mileage

```
Two-sample T for Highway Mileage vs City Mileage

                   N    Mean   StDev   SE Mean
Highway Mileage   25   19.65    4.30     0.86
City Mileage      25   16.15    5.44     1.1


Difference = mu (Highway Mileage) - mu (City Mileage)
Estimate for difference:  3.50080
95% lower bound for difference:  1.17507
T-Test of difference = 0 (vs >): T-Value = 2.52   P-Value = 0.007   DF = 48
Both use Pooled StDev = 4.9026
```

EXAMPLE 9-5: HYPOTHESIS TEST FOR $\mu_1 - \mu_2$ WHEN σ_1 AND σ_2 ARE UNKNOWN, INDEPENDENT SAMPLES

Color Printer Ink Cartridges An Associated Press news story out of Brussels, Belgium, on May 16, 2002, indicated the European Union was considering a probe of computer makers after consumers complained that they were being overcharged for ink cartridges. Companies such as Cannon, Hewlett-Packard, and Epson are the printer market leaders and make most of their printer-related profits by selling replacement ink cartridges. Suppose an independent test agency wishes to conduct a test to determine whether name-brand ink cartridges generate more color pages on average than competing generic ink cartridges. The test can be conducted using the following steps:

Step 1: **Specify the population value of interest.**
We are interested in determining whether the mean number of pages printed by name-brand cartridges (population 1) exceeds the mean pages printed by generic cartridges (population 2).

Step 2: **Formulate the appropriate null and alternative hypotheses.**
The following null and alternative hypotheses are specified:

$$H_0: \mu_1 - \mu_2 \leq 0.0$$
$$H_A: \mu_1 - \mu_2 > 0.0$$

Step 3: **Specify the significance level for the test.**
The test will be conducted using $\alpha = 0.05$.

When the population standard deviations are unknown, the critical value is a t-value from the t-distribution if the populations are assumed to be normally distributed.

A simple random sample of 10 users was selected, and the users were given a name-brand cartridge. A second sample of 8 users was given generic cartridges. Both groups used their printers until the ink ran out. The number of pages printed was recorded. The samples are independent because the pages printed by users in one group did not in any way influence the pages printed by users in the second group. The means computed from the samples are

$$\bar{x}_1 = 322.5 \text{ pages} \quad \text{and} \quad \bar{x}_2 = 298.3 \text{ pages}.$$

Because we do not know the population standard deviations, these values are computed from the sample data and are

$$s_1 = 48.3 \text{ pages} \quad \text{and} \quad s_2 = 53.3 \text{ pages}.$$

Suppose previous studies have shown that the number of pages printed by both types of cartridge tend to be approximately normal with equal variances.

Step 4: **Construct the rejection region.**
Based on a one-tailed test with $\alpha = 0.05$, the critical value is a t-value from the t-distribution with $10 + 8 - 2 = 16$ degrees of freedom. From the t-table, the critical t-value is

$$t_{0.05} = 1.7459.$$

The decision rule is

If $t > 1.7459$, reject the null hypothesis;
Otherwise, do not reject the null hypothesis.

Step 5: **Compute the test statistic using Equation 9-11.**

$$t = \frac{(\bar{x}_1 - \bar{x}_2) - (\mu_1 - \mu_2)}{s_p \sqrt{\dfrac{1}{n_1} + \dfrac{1}{n_2}}}$$

The pooled standard deviation is

$$s_p = \sqrt{\frac{(n_1 - 1)s_1^2 + (n_2 - 1)s_2^2}{n_1 + n_2 - 2}} = \sqrt{\frac{(10 - 1)48.3^2 + (8 - 1)53.3^2}{10 + 8 - 2}} = 50.55$$

Then the t-test statistic is

$$t = \frac{(322.5 - 298.3) - 0.0}{50.55 \sqrt{\dfrac{1}{10} + \dfrac{1}{8}}} = 1.0093$$

Step 6: **Reach a decision.**
Because

$$t = 1.0093 < t_{\alpha/2} = 1.7459,$$

do not reject the null hypothesis.

Step 7: **Draw a conclusion.**
Based on these sample data, there is insufficient evidence to conclude that the mean number of pages produced by name-brand ink cartridges exceeds the mean for generic cartridges.

What If the Population Variances Are Not Equal?

In the previous examples, we assumed that the population variances were equal, and we carried out the hypothesis test for two population means using Equation 9-11. Even in cases where the population variances are not equal, the t-test as specified in Equation 9-11 is appropriate as long as the sample sizes are equal. However, if the sample sizes are not equal and if the sample data lead us to suspect that the variances are not equal, the t test statistic must be approximated using Equation 9-12. In cases where the variances are not equal, the degrees of freedom are computed using Equation 9-13.

t Test Statistic for $\mu_1 - \mu_2$ When Population Variances Are Not Equal

$$t = \frac{(\bar{x}_1 - \bar{x}_2) - (\mu_1 - \mu_2)}{\sqrt{\frac{s_1^2}{n_1} + \frac{s_2^2}{n_2}}}$$

9-12

Degrees of Freedom for t Test Statistic When Population Variances Are Not Equal

$$\frac{(s_1^2/n_1 + s_2^2/n_2)^2}{\left(\frac{(s_1^2/n_1)^2}{n_1 - 1} + \frac{(s_2^2/n_2)^2}{n_2 - 1}\right)}$$

9-13

HYPOTHESIS TESTING FOR PAIRED SAMPLES

In Section 9-1, we discussed the difference between independent and paired samples. As we indicated, there will be instances when paired samples can be used to control for an outside source of variation. For instance in Example 9-5 involving the ink cartridges, the original test of whether name-brand cartridges yield a higher mean number of printed pages than generic cartridges involved different users for the two types of cartridges, so the samples were independent. However, different users may use more or less ink as a rule; therefore, we could control for that source of variation by having a sample of people use both types of cartridges in a paired test format.

If a paired sample experiment is used, the test statistic is computed using Equation 9-14.

t-Test Statistic for Paired Sample Test

$$t = \frac{\bar{d} - \mu_d}{\frac{s_d}{\sqrt{n}}} \qquad df = (n - 1)$$

9-14

where:

$\bar{d}$ = Mean paired difference = $\dfrac{\sum d}{n}$

μ_d = Hypothesized population mean paired difference

s_d = Sample standard deviation for paired differences = $\sqrt{\dfrac{\sum(d - \bar{d})^2}{n - 1}}$

n = Number of paired values in the sample

EXAMPLE 9-6: HYPOTHESIS TEST FOR μ_d, PAIRED SAMPLES

Color Printer Ink Cartridges　　Referring to Example 9-5, suppose the experiment regarding ink cartridges is conducted differently. Instead of having different samples of users use name-brand and generic cartridges, the test is done using paired samples. This means that the same people will use both types of cartridges, and the pages printed in each case will be recorded. The test under this paired sample scenario can be conducted using the following steps. Six randomly selected people have agreed to participate.

Step 1:   **Specify the population value of interest.**
In this case we will form paired differences by subtracting the generic pages from the name-brand pages. We are interested in determining whether name-brand cartridges produce more printed pages, on average, than generic cartridges, so we would expect the paired difference to be positive. We assume that the paired differences are normally distributed.

Step 2:   **Formulate the null and alternative hypotheses.**
The null and alternative hypotheses are

$$H_0: \mu_d \leq 0.0$$
$$H_A: \mu_d > 0.0$$

Step 3:   **Specify the significance level for the test.**
The test will be conducted using $\alpha = 0.01$.

Step 4:   **Construct the rejection region.**
The critical value is a t-value from the t-distribution, with alpha = 0.01 and $6 - 1 = 5$ degrees of freedom. The critical value is

$$t_{0.01} = 3.3649.$$

The decision rule is

If $t > 3.3649$, reject the null hypothesis;
Otherwise, do not reject the null hypothesis.

Step 5:   **Compute the test statistic.**
Select the random sample and compute the mean and standard deviation for the paired differences.

In this case a random sample of six people tests each type of cartridge. The following data and paired differences were observed:

Printer User	Name-Brand	Generic	d
1	306	300	6
2	256	260	−4
3	402	357	45
4	299	286	13
5	306	290	16
6	257	260	−3

The mean paired difference is

$$\bar{d} = \frac{\Sigma d}{n} = \frac{73}{6} = 12.17$$

The standard deviation for the paired differences is

$$s_d = \sqrt{\frac{\Sigma(d - \bar{d})^2}{n - 1}} = 18.02$$

The test statistic is calculated using Equation 9-16.

$$t = \frac{\bar{d} - \mu_d}{\dfrac{s_d}{\sqrt{n}}} = \frac{12.17 - 0.0}{\dfrac{18.02}{\sqrt{6}}} = 1.6543$$

Step 6:   **Reach a decision.**
Because $t = 1.6543 < t_\alpha = 3.3649$, do not reject the null hypothesis.

Step 7:   **Draw a conclusion.**
Based on these sample data, there is insufficient evidence to conclude that name-brand ink cartridges produce more pages on average than generic brands.

9-2: EXERCISES

Skill Development

9.17 Given two independent samples with the following information:

Item	Sample 1	Sample 2
1	19.6	21.3
2	22.1	17.4
3	19.5	19.0
4	20.0	21.2
5	21.5	20.1
6	20.2	23.5
7	17.9	18.9
8	23.0	22.4
9	12.5	14.3
10	19.0	17.8

Based on these samples, test at the 0.10 significance level whether the true average difference is 0.

9.18 The following sample data have been collected from two independent samples from two populations. The claim is that the second population mean will exceed the first population mean.

Sample 1	Sample 2
12	9
21	18
12	16
11	17
11	13
13	7
12	12
9	17

a. State the appropriate null and alternative hypotheses.
b. Based on the sample data, what should you conclude about the null hypothesis? Test using an $\alpha = 0.05$. Perform the test using both a critical value and a p-value.

9.19 Given the following null and alternative hypotheses:

$$H_0: \mu_1 - \mu_2 \geq 0$$
$$H_A: \mu_1 - \mu_2 < 0$$

and this sample information:

Sample 1	Sample 2
$n_1 = 16$	$n_2 = 25$
$s_1 = 32$	$s_2 = 30$
$\bar{x}_1 = 2{,}456$	$\bar{x}_2 = 2{,}460$

a. Develop the appropriate decision rule, assuming a significance level of 0.05 is to be used.
b. Use the appropriate test to determine whether the two populations have equal means.

9.20 Given the following null and alternative hypotheses:

$$H_0: \mu_1 - \mu_2 = 0$$
$$H_A: \mu_1 - \mu_2 \neq 0$$

and the following sample information:

Sample 1	Sample 2
$n_1 = 25$	$n_2 = 20$
$s_1 = 20$	$s_2 = 24$
$\bar{x}_1 = 430$	$\bar{x}_2 = 405$

a. Develop the appropriate decision rule, assuming a significance level of 0.05 is to be used.
b. Test the null hypothesis and indicate whether the sample information leads you to reject or fail to reject the null hypothesis. Use the test-statistic approach.

9.21 Given the following null and alternative hypotheses:

$$H_0: \mu_1 - \mu_2 = 0$$
$$H_A: \mu_1 - \mu_2 \neq 0$$

and the following sample information:

Sample 1	Sample 2
$n_1 = 125$	$n_2 = 120$
$s_1 = 31$	$s_2 = 38$
$\bar{x}_1 = 130$	$\bar{x}_2 = 105$

a. Develop the appropriate decision rule, assuming a significance level of 0.05 is to be used.
b. Test the null hypothesis and indicate whether the sample information leads you to reject or fail to reject the null hypothesis. Use the test-statistic approach.

9.22 Given the following null and alternative hypotheses:

$$H_0: \mu_1 - \mu_2 \leq 0$$
$$H_A: \mu_1 - \mu_2 > 0$$

and the following sample information:

Sample 1	Sample 2
$n_1 = 75$	$n_2 = 80$
$s_1 = 2.20$	$s_2 = 2.644$
$\bar{x}_1 = 5.30$	$\bar{x}_2 = 5.10$

a. Develop the appropriate decision rule, assuming a significance level of 0.05 is to be used.
b. Test the null hypothesis and indicate whether the sample information leads you to reject or fail to reject the null hypothesis.

9.23 The following sample data have been collected from a paired sample from two populations. The claim is that the first population mean will be at least as large as the mean of the second population. This claim will be assumed to be true unless the data strongly suggest otherwise.

Sample 1	Sample 2
4.4	3.7
2.7	3.5
1.0	4.0
3.5	4.9
2.8	3.1
2.6	4.2
2.4	5.2
2.0	4.4
2.8	4.3

a. State the appropriate null and alternative hypotheses.
b. Based on the sample data, what should you conclude about the null hypothesis? Test using $\alpha = 0.10$. Test using both a critical value and a p-value.
c. Calculate a 90% confidence interval for the difference in the population means. Are the results from the confidence interval consistent with the outcome of your hypothesis test? Explain.

9.24 The following sample data have been collected from a paired sample from two populations. The claim is that the first population mean will exceed the second population mean.

Sample 1	Sample 2
50	38
47	44
44	38
48	37
40	43
36	44
43	31
46	38
72	39
40	54
55	41
38	40

a. State the appropriate null and alternative hypotheses.
b. Based on the sample data, what should you conclude about the null hypothesis? Test at a significance level of 0.01.
c. Suppose these samples had been obtained independently. Conduct the test and determine if the results would be different.

Business Applications

9.25 The State College registrar is interested in determining whether female students exceed male students by an average of more than one credit hour taken during a term. She has selected a random sample of 60 males and 60 females and has observed the following sample information:

Male	Female
$\bar{x} = 13.24$ credits	$\bar{x} = 14.65$ credits
$s = 1.2$ credits	$s = 1.56$ credits

Provide the registrar with the information she is seeking by performing a hypothesis test based on a 0.05 significance level.

9.26 The marketing manager for a major retail grocery chain is wondering about the location of the stores' dairy products. She believes that the mean amount spent by customers on dairy products per visit is higher in stores in which the dairy section is in the central part of the store, compared with stores that have the dairy section at the rear. To consider relocating the dairy products, the manager feels that the increase in the mean amount spent by customers must be more than 25 cents. To determine whether relocation is justified, her staff selected a random sample of 25 customers at stores in which the dairy section is central in the store. A second sample of 25 customers was selected in stores with the dairy section at the rear of the store. The following sample results were observed:

Central Dairy	Rear Dairy
$\bar{x}_1 = \$3.74$	$\bar{x}_2 = \$3.26$
$s_1 = \$0.87$	$s_2 = \$0.79$

a. Conduct a hypothesis test with a significance level of 0.05 to determine if the manager should relocate the dairy products in those stores displaying their dairy products in the rear.
b. If a statistical error associated with hypothesis testing were made in this hypothesis test, what error could it have been? Explain.

9.27 The makers of ink cartridges for color ink-jet printers have developed a new system for storing the ink. They think the new system will result in a longer lasting product. In order to determine whether this is the case, a test was developed in which a sample of 35 of the new cartridges was selected. They were put in a printer, and test pages were run until the cartridge was empty. The same thing was done for a sample of 32 —original cartridges. The following data were observed:

New Cartridge	Existing Cartridge
$\bar{x}_1 = 288$ pages	$\bar{x}_2 = 279$ pages
$s_1 = 16.3$ pages	$s_2 = 15.91$ pages

a. Based on the sample data and a significance level equal to 0.10, determine if the new system will result in a longer lasting product. Write a short statement that discusses the results of the test.
b. Calculate a 90% confidence interval for the difference between these two population means. Are the results of the hypothesis test consistent with the confidence interval you produced? Explain.

9.28 The managers of a regional bank in Florida believe that customers who regularly use their ATM cards (regular is defined as at least one time per week) are more profitable to the bank overall than customers who do not regularly use their ATM cards. A sample of 200 of the bank's customers in each category was selected. An accounting was performed to determine the 1999 profit generated from each customer. The following sample data were observed?

Regular ATM	Non-ATM Users
$\bar{x}_1 = \$142.76$	$\bar{x}_2 = \$133.19$
$s_1 = \$30.31$	$s_2 = \$33.92$

a. Using an alpha level equal to 0.05, what conclusion should the bank's managers reach based on the sample data? Discuss your results in a short written statement.

b. Calculate a 95% confidence interval for the difference of the average profit produced by these two groups. If you were one of the bank's managers, which of the two (hypothesis test or confidence interval) statistical inference procedures would you prefer in this situation? Explain.

9.29   The First Night Stage Company operates a small nonprofit theater group in Milwaukee, Wisconsin. Each year the company markets Christmas candy to help fund its operations. This year, it has obtained the help of a marketing research company in the city. This company has proposed two different candy brochures. Brochure B costs an average of 35 cents more to produce than brochure A. The theater group is trying to determine which brochure will produce the higher sales. To determine this, a random sample of 20 people was selected to receive brochure A and another random sample of 20 people was selected to receive brochure B. The sales data (including sales tax) are contained in the CD-ROM file called *First-Night*.

a. Based on these sample data, which brochure should the First Night Company adopt? Use $\alpha = 0.01$ for whatever statistical inference techniques you use.

b. Referring to the statistical inference techniques you used in part a, what assumptions are required?

9.30   The California State Highway Patrol recently conducted a study on a stretch of interstate highway south of San Francisco to determine whether the mean speed for California vehicles exceeded the mean speed for out-of-state vehicles. It would consider any average hike of more than 5 mph to be a significant increase in speed. A total of 140 California cars were included in the study, whereas 75 out-of-state cars were included. Radar was used to measure speed. The CD-ROM file called *Speed-Test* contains the data collected by the California Highway Patrol.

a. Determine the research hypothesis. Specify the alternative and null hypotheses that would be derived from the research hypothesis.

b. Using a significance level equal to 0.10, would the average speed of California drivers be considered to be "significantly higher" by the California Highway Patrol? Use both the *p*-value and critical value to perform the test. Are the conclusions consistent?

c. Discuss the results of this test in a short written statement.

9.31   For years there has been a debate about whether children who are in child care facilities while their parents work experience negative effects. A recent study, discussed in the March 1999 issue of *Developmental Psychology*, of 6,000 children found "no permanent negative effects caused by their mothers' absence." In fact, the study indicated that there might be some positive benefits from the day care experience. To investigate this premise, a nonprofit organization called Child Care Connections conducted a small study in which children were observed playing in a neutral setting (not at home or at a day care center). Over a period of 20 hours of observation, 15 children who did not go to day care and 21 children who had spent much time in day care were observed. The variable of interest was the total minutes of play in which each child was actively interacting with other students. Child Care Connections leaders hoped to show that the children who had been in day care would have a higher mean time in interactive situations than the stay-at-home children. The CD-ROM file called *Children* contains the study results.

a. Test the hypothesis that the children who had been in day care had a higher mean time in interactive situations than the stay-at-home children. Use a significance level of 0.05.

b. Based on the outcome of the hypothesis test, which statistical error might have been committed?

Advanced Applications

9.32   A regional airport is considering the purchase of a new visibility sensor system to be used in conjunction with air traffic control equipment. The managers have narrowed the choices down to two suppliers: Vangaurd and Scorpion. To help make the final selection, the two suppliers agreed to participate in a test. The two sensors were temporarily installed side by side at the airport. Visibility readings from each sensor were recorded on 5-minute intervals for a 24-hour period. The resulting data are in a CD-ROM file called *Visibility*.

a. Discuss whether the samples can be treated as independent, or if they are in fact paired samples. Be sure to state your reasoning.

b. Perform the hypothesis test using a *p*-value, assuming that samples are independent, and using a significance level of 0.05. Discuss the results.

c. Perform the hypothesis test assuming that the samples are paired. Use a significance level of 0.05 and discuss your results. How does the conclusion compare with the one reached in part b?

9.33   The Sunbeam Corporation makes a wide variety of appliances for the home. One product is a digital blood pressure gauge. For obvious reasons, the blood pressure readings made by the monitor need to be accurate. When a new model is being designed, one of the steps is to test it. To do this, a sample of people is selected. Each person has his or her systolic blood pressure taken by a highly respected physician. They then immediately have their systolic blood pressure taken using the Sunbeam monitor. If the mean blood pressure is the same for the monitor as that determined by the physician, then the monitor passes the test.

In a recent test, 15 people were randomly selected to be in the sample. The blood pressure readings for these people using both methods are contained in the data file called *Sunbeam*.

Physician	Monitor
112	126
109	108
139	116
141	123
120	138
99	123
128	119
118	122
116	116
120	118
111	114
123	108
114	130
121	123
132	127

a. Based on the sample data and a significance level equal to 0.05, what conclusion should the Sunbeam engineers reach regarding the latest blood pressure monitor? Discuss your answer in a short written statement.

b. Consider the context of this problem. Does it make sense to you that any deviation from the equality between the mean blood pressure readings would be of interest? Examine the data to determine a, perhaps, more reasonable criterion.

c. Calculate a 95% confidence interval for the paired difference between the two mean blood pressure readings. Based on your criterion of part b, would you consider the Sunbeam blood pressure monitor to be a good substitute for a doctor's blood pressure reading? Explain.

d. Comment on whether it would be possible to reach a different conclusion using a paired sample test versus a test assuming independent samples. Why could this happen?

9-3 ESTIMATION AND HYPOTHESIS TESTS FOR TWO POPULATION PROPORTIONS

The previous section illustrated the methods for testing hypotheses involving two population means. There are many business situations in which these methods can be applied. However, there are other instances involving two populations in which the measures of interest are not the population means. For example, Chapter 8 introduced the methodology for testing hypotheses involving a single population proportion. This section extends that methodology to tests involving hypotheses about the difference between two population proportions. First, we will look at a confidence interval estimation involving two population proportions.

ESTIMATING THE DIFFERENCE BETWEEN TWO POPULATION PROPORTIONS

V. C. Elroy Agency—Advertising agencies spend a significant amount of time determining whether proposed advertisements will appeal to different market segments before the ads run on national media. Recently, the V. C. Elroy Agency in Chicago developed an advertising campaign for a national fast-food chain. Among the many issues the ad managers were interested in was the difference in how appealing males and females would find the ads.

Obviously, there was no way to gauge the attitudes of the entire population of men and women who would eventually see or hear the ads. Instead, the Elroy agency showed the ad campaign to a random sample of 425 men and 370 women. In the results that follow, the variable x indicates the number in the sample who said they liked the campaign.

Men	Women
$n_1 = 425$	$n_2 = 370$
$x_1 = 240$	$x_2 = 196$

Based on these sample data, the sample proportions are

$$\bar{p}_1 = \frac{240}{425} = 0.565 \text{ and } \bar{p}_2 = \frac{196}{370} = 0.530.$$

The point estimate for the difference in population proportions is

$$\bar{p}_1 - \bar{p}_2 = 0.565 - 0.530 = 0.035.$$

So, the single best estimate for the difference in the proportion of men versus women who liked the ad campaign is 0.035. However, all point estimates are subject to sampling error. A confidence interval estimate for the difference in population proportions can be developed using Equation 9-15, providing the sample sizes are sufficiently large. A rule of thumb for "sufficiently large" is that, as with hypothesis testing, $n\bar{p}$ and $n(1 - \bar{p})$ are greater than or equal to 5 for both samples.

Confidence Interval Estimate for $p_1 - p_2$

$$(\bar{p}_1 - \bar{p}_2) \pm z_{\alpha/2} \sqrt{\frac{(\bar{p}_1)(1 - \bar{p}_1)}{n_1} + \frac{(\bar{p}_2)(1 - \bar{p}_2)}{n_2}} \qquad \text{9-15}$$

where:

$\bar{p}_1$ = Sample proportion from population 1
$\bar{p}_2$ = Sample proportion from population 2
$z_{\alpha/2}$ = Critical value from the standard normal table

---

The Elroy managers can substitute the sample results into Equation 9-15 to establish a 95% confidence interval estimate, as follows.

$$(.565 - .530) \pm 1.96 \sqrt{\frac{(.565)(1 - .565)}{425} + \frac{(.530)(1 - .530)}{370}}$$

$$0.035 \pm 0.069$$

$$-0.034 \text{ ---------------------------- } 0.104$$

Thus, based on the sample data and using a 95% confidence interval, the managers estimate that the true difference in proportion of males versus females who like the ad campaign is between −0.034 and 0.104. At one extreme, 3.4% more females like the ad than males. At the other extreme, 10.4% more males like the ad than females. Because zero is included in the interval, there may be no difference between males and females based on these data. Consequently, the managers are not able to conclude that one group or the other has a stronger preference for the fast-food ad campaign.

HYPOTHESIS TESTS FOR THE DIFFERENCE BETWEEN TWO POPULATION PROPORTIONS

Excel and Minitab Tutorial

Pomona Fabrications—Pomona Fabrication, Inc., produces handheld hair dryers that several major retailers sell as in-house brands. A critical component of a handheld hair dryer is the motor-heater unit, which accounts for most of the dryer's cost and also for most of the product's reliability problems. Product reliability is important to Pomona because the company offers a 1-year warranty. Of course, Pomona is also interested in reducing production costs.

Ponoma's research and development department has recently created a new motor-heater unit with fewer parts than the current unit, which would lead to a 15% cost savings per hair dryer. However, the company's vice president of product development is unwilling to authorize the new component unless it is more reliable than the current motor-heater.

The research and development department has decided to test samples of both units to see which motor-heater is more reliable. Two hundred fifty units of each type will be tested under conditions that simulate one year's use, and the proportion of each type that fails within that time will be recorded. This leads to the formulation of the following null and alternative hypotheses:

$$H_0: p_1 - p_2 \geq 0.0$$
$$H_A: p_1 - p_2 < 0.0$$

where:

p_1 = Population proportion of new dryer type that fails in simulated one-year period
p_2 = Population proportion of existing dryer type that fails in simulated one-year period

The null hypothesis states that the new motor-heater is no better than the old, or current, motor-heater. The alternative states that the new unit has a smaller proportion of failures within one year than the current unit. In other words, the alternative states that the new unit is more reliable. The company wants clear evidence before changing units. If the null hypothesis is rejected, the company will conclude that the new motor-heater unit is more reliable than the old unit and should be used in producing the hair dryers. To test the null hypothesis, we can use the test statistic approach.

The test statistic is based on the sampling distribution of $\bar{p}_1 - \bar{p}_2$. In Chapter 6 we showed that when $np \geq 5$ and $n(1 - p) \geq 5$, the sampling distribution of the sample proportion is approximately normally distributed, with a mean equal to p and a variance equal to $\dfrac{p(1 - p)}{n}$.

Likewise, in the two-sample case, the sampling distribution of $\bar{p}_1 - \bar{p}_2$ will also be approximately normal if

$$n_1 p_1 \geq 5, \ n_1(1 - p_1) \geq 5, \ n_2 p_2 \geq 5, \quad \text{and} \quad n_2(1 - p_2) \geq 5$$

Because p_1 and p_2 are unknown, we substitute the sample proportions, $\bar{p}_1$ and $\bar{p}_2$, to determine whether the sample size requirements are satisfied.

The mean of the sampling distribution of $\bar{p}_1 - \bar{p}_2$ is the difference of the population proportions, $p_1 - p_2$. The variance is, however, the sum of the variances, $\dfrac{p_1(1 - p_1)}{n_1} + \dfrac{p_2(1 - p_2)}{n_2}$.

Because the test is conducted using the assumption that the null hypothesis is true, we assume that $p_1 = p_2 = p$ and estimate their common value, p, using a pooled estimate, as shown in Equation 9-16. The z test statistic for the difference between two proportions is given as Equation 9-17.

Pooled Estimator for Overall Proportion

$$\bar{p} = \frac{n_1 \bar{p}_1 + n_2 \bar{p}_2}{n_1 + n_2} = \frac{x_1 + x_2}{n_1 + n_2}$$

9-16

where:

x_1 and x_2 = number from samples 1 and 2 with the characteristic of interest

---

z Test Statistic for Difference between Population Proportions

$$z = \frac{(\bar{p}_1 - \bar{p}_2) - (p_1 - p_2)}{\sqrt{\bar{p}(1 - \bar{p})\left(\dfrac{1}{n_1} + \dfrac{1}{n_2}\right)}}$$

9-17

where:

$(p_1 - p_2)$ = Hypothesized difference in proportions from populations 1 and 2, respectively
$\bar{p}_1$ and $\bar{p}_2$ = Sample proportions for samples selected from populations 1 and 2
$\bar{p}$ = Pooled estimator for the overall proportion for both populations combined

---

The reason for taking a weighted average in Equation 9-16 is to give more weight to the larger sample. Note that the numerator is the total number of items with the characteristic of interest in the two samples, and the denominator is the total sample size. Again, the pooled estimator, $\bar{p}$, is used when the null hypothesis is that there is no difference between the population proportions.

Assume that Pomona is willing to use a significance level of 0.05 and that 55 of the new motor-heaters and 75 of the originals failed the one-year test. Figure 9-7 illustrates the decision-rule development and the hypothesis test. As you can see, Pomona should reject the null hypothesis based on the sample data. Thus, the firm should conclude that the new motor-heater is more reliable than the old one. Because the new one is also less costly, the company should now use the new unit in the production of hair dryers.

The p-value approach to hypothesis testing could also have been used to test Pomona's hypothesis. In this case, the calculated value of the test statistic, $z = -2.04$, results in a p-value of 0.0207 $(0.5 - 0.4793)$ from the standard normal table. Because this p-value is smaller than the significance level of 0.05, we would reject the null hypothesis. Remember, whenever your p-value is smaller than the alpha value, your sample contains evidence to reject the null hypothesis.

FIGURE 9-7

Hypothesis Test of Two Population Proportions for Pomona Fabrications

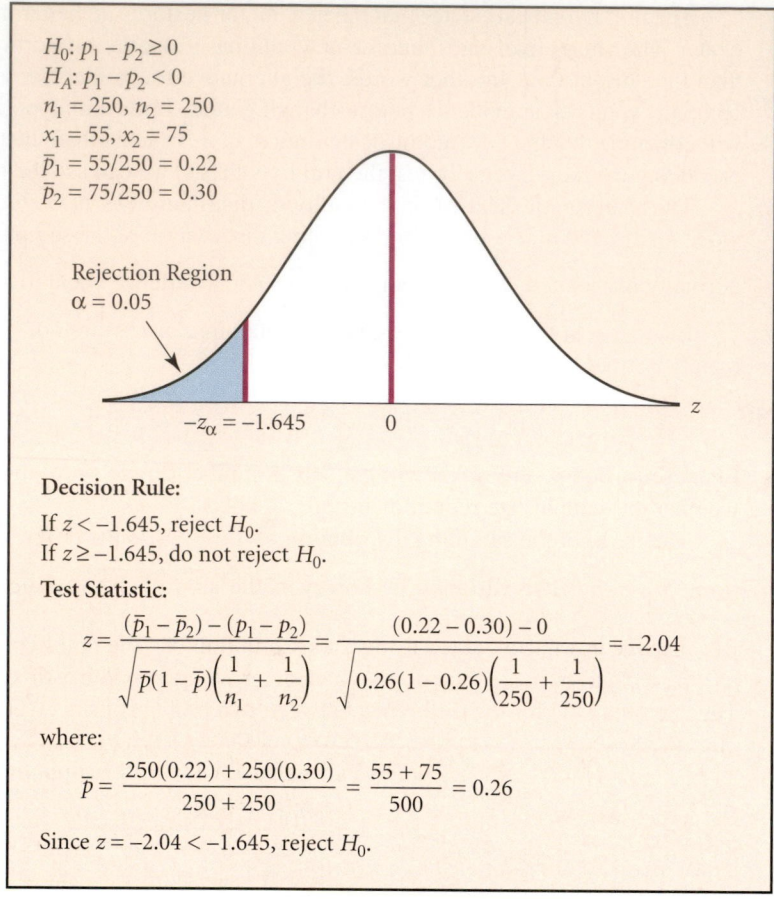

$H_0: p_1 - p_2 \geq 0$
$H_A: p_1 - p_2 < 0$
$n_1 = 250, n_2 = 250$
$x_1 = 55, x_2 = 75$
$\bar{p}_1 = 55/250 = 0.22$
$\bar{p}_2 = 75/250 = 0.30$

Rejection Region
$\alpha = 0.05$

$-z_\alpha = -1.645$ 0 z

Decision Rule:

If $z < -1.645$, reject H_0.
If $z \geq -1.645$, do not reject H_0.

Test Statistic:

$$z = \frac{(\bar{p}_1 - \bar{p}_2) - (p_1 - p_2)}{\sqrt{\bar{p}(1-\bar{p})\left(\dfrac{1}{n_1} + \dfrac{1}{n_2}\right)}} = \frac{(0.22 - 0.30) - 0}{\sqrt{0.26(1-0.26)\left(\dfrac{1}{250} + \dfrac{1}{250}\right)}} = -2.04$$

where:

$$\bar{p} = \frac{250(0.22) + 250(0.30)}{250 + 250} = \frac{55 + 75}{500} = 0.26$$

Since $z = -2.04 < -1.645$, reject H_0.

Both Minitab and the PHStat add-ins to Excel contain procedures for performing hypothesis tests involving two population proportions. Figures 9-8a and 9-8b show the PHStat output and the Minitab output for the Pomona example. The output contains both the z test statistic and the p-value. As we observed from our manual calculations, the difference in sample proportions is sufficient to reject the null hypothesis that there is no difference in population proportions.

FIGURE 9-8A

Excel (PHStat) Output of the Two Proportions Test for Pomona Fabrications

Excel (PHStat) Instructions:

1. Click on the PHStat tab.
2. Select the **Two-Sample Tests** option.
3. Select **Z Test for Differences in Two Proportions**.
4. Enter sample size and number of occurrences for each population.

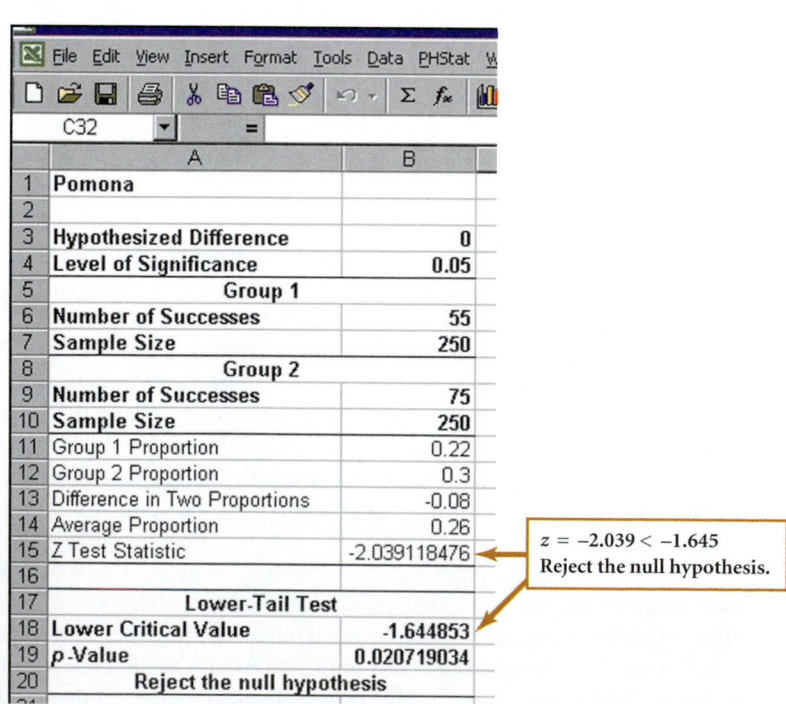

	A	B
1	Pomona	
2		
3	Hypothesized Difference	0
4	Level of Significance	0.05
5	Group 1	
6	Number of Successes	55
7	Sample Size	250
8	Group 2	
9	Number of Successes	75
10	Sample Size	250
11	Group 1 Proportion	0.22
12	Group 2 Proportion	0.3
13	Difference in Two Proportions	-0.08
14	Average Proportion	0.26
15	Z Test Statistic	-2.039118476
16		
17	Lower-Tail Test	
18	Lower Critical Value	-1.644853
19	p-Value	0.020719034
20	Reject the null hypothesis	

$z = -2.039 < -1.645$
Reject the null hypothesis.

FIGURE 9-8B

Minitab Output of the Two Proportions Test for Pomona Fabrications

Minitab Instructions:
1. Choose **Stat > Basic Statistics >2 Proportions**.
2. Choose **Summarized data**.
3. In **First**, enter Trials and Events for sample 1 (e.g., 250 and 55).
4. In **Second**, enter Trials and Events for sample 2 (e.g., 250 and 75).
5. Select **Options**, insert 1 − α in **Confidence level**.
6. In **Alternative**, select *less than*.
7. Check **Use pooled estimate of p for test**.
8. Click **OK. OK**.

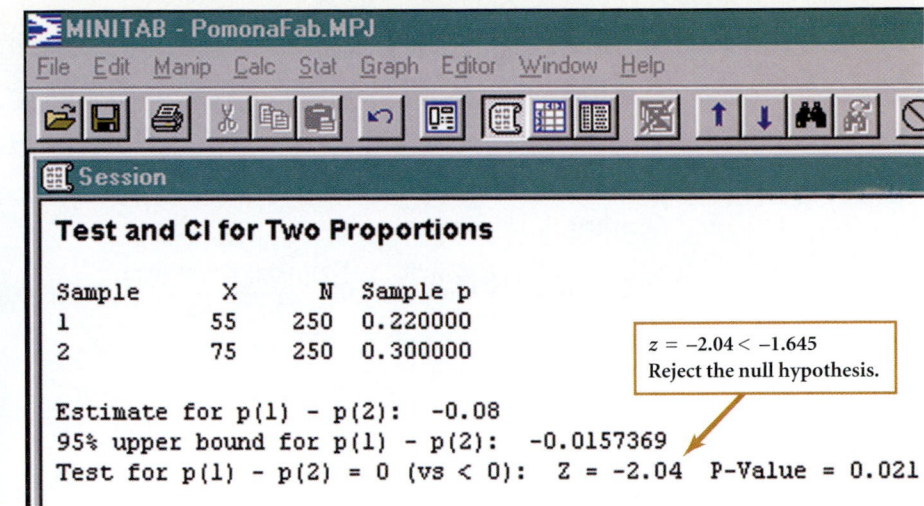

FIGURE 9-8B

Minitab Output of the Two Proportions Test for Pomona Fabrications

Minitab Instructions:
1. Choose **Stat > Basic Statistics >2 Proportions**.
2. Choose **Summarized data**.
3. In **First**, enter Trials and Events for sample 1 (e.g., 250 and 55).
4. In **Second**, enter Trials and Events for sample 2 (e.g., 250 and 75).
5. Select **Options**, insert 1 − α in **Confidence level**.
6. In **Alternative**, select *less than*.
7. Check **Use pooled estimate of p for test**.
8. Click **OK. OK**.

EXAMPLE 9-7: HYPOTHESIS TEST FOR THE DIFFERENCE BETWEEN TWO POPULATION PROPORTIONS

Gregston Ticketing   Gregston Ticketing is evaluating two suppliers of a scanning system it is considering purchasing. Both scanners are designed to detect forged tickets for sporting events. High quality scanners and printers and home computers have made forged tickets an increasing industry problem. The company is interested in determining whether there is a difference in the proportion of forged tickets detected by the two suppliers. To conduct this test, use the following steps.

Step 1:   **Specify the population value of interest.**
In this case, the population value of interest is the population proportion of detected forged tickets. At issue is whether there is a difference between the two suppliers in terms of the proportion of forged tickets detected.

Step 2:   **Formulate the appropriate null and alternative hypotheses.**
The null and alternative hypotheses are

$$H_0: p_1 - p_2 = 0.0$$
$$H_A: p_1 - p_2 \neq 0.0$$

Step 3:   **Specify the significance level.**
The test will be conducted using an $\alpha = 0.02$.

Step 4:   **Construct the rejection region.**
For a two-tailed test, the critical values for each side of the distribution are

$$-z_{0.02/2} = -2.33 \text{ and } z_{0.02/2} = 2.33.$$

The decision rule based on the z test statistic is:

If $z < -2.33$ or $z > 2.33$, reject the null hypothesis;

Otherwise, do not reject the null hypothesis.

Step 5:   **Compute the z test statistic using Equation 9-17 and apply it to the decision rule.**
Two hundred known forged tickets will be randomly selected and scanned by systems from each supplier. For supplier one, 186 forgeries are detected, and for supplier two, 168 are detected. The sample proportions are

$$\bar{p}_1 = \frac{x_1}{n_1} = \frac{186}{200} = 0.93 \qquad \bar{p}_2 = \frac{x_2}{n_2} = \frac{168}{200} = 0.84$$

The test statistic is then calculated using Equation 9-17.

$$z = \frac{(\bar{p}_1 - \bar{p}_2) - (p_1 - p_2)}{\sqrt{\bar{p}(1 - \bar{p})\left(\dfrac{1}{n_1} + \dfrac{1}{n_2}\right)}}$$

where:

$$\bar{p} = \frac{n_1\bar{p}_1 + n_2\bar{p}_2}{n_1 + n_2} = \frac{200(0.93) + 200(0.84)}{200 + 200} = 0.885 \quad \text{(see Equation 9-18)}$$

Then:

$$z = \frac{(0.93 - .084) - 0.0}{\sqrt{0.885(1 - 0.885)\left(\dfrac{1}{200} + \dfrac{1}{200}\right)}} = 2.8211$$

Step 6:　**Reach a decision.**
Because $z = 2.8211 > z_{\alpha/2} = 2.33$, reject the null hypothesis.

Step 7:　**Draw a conclusion.**
The difference between the two sample proportions does provide sufficient evidence to allow us to conclude a difference exists between the two suppliers.

9-3: EXERCISES

9.34　Note the following null and alternative hypotheses:

$$H_0: p_1 = p_2$$
$$H_A: p_1 \neq p_2$$

and this sample information:

Sample 1	Sample 2
$n_1 = 100$	$n_2 = 100$
$x_1 = 30$	$x_2 = 34$

Using an $\alpha = 0.05$ and the sample information, what should be concluded with respect to the null and alternative hypotheses? Conduct the hypothesis test using a p-value approach. Be sure to clearly show the decision rule.

9.35　Given the following null and alternative hypotheses:

$$H_0: p_1 - p_2 = 0.0$$
$$H_A: p_1 - p_2 \neq 0.0$$

and this sample information:

Sample 1	Sample 2
$n_1 = 200$	$n_2 = 150$
$x_1 = 87$	$x_2 = 80$

Using an $\alpha = 0.10$ and the sample information, what should be concluded with respect to the null and alternative hypotheses? Be sure to clearly show the decision rule.

9.36　Given the following null and alternative hypotheses:

$$H_0: p_1 - p_2 \geq 0.0$$
$$H_A: p_1 - p_2 < 0.0$$

and this sample information:

Sample 1	Sample 2
$n_1 = 100$	$n_2 = 100$
$x_1 = 70$	$x_2 = 75$

a. Based on $\alpha = 0.05$ and the sample information, what should be concluded with respect to the null and alternative hypotheses? Be sure to clearly show the decision rule.

b. Calculate a 95% confidence interval for the difference between the two population proportions.

c. Compare the standard error obtained in the confidence interval to that in the test statistic. Why are these two standard errors different?

9.37　Given the following null and alternative hypotheses:

$$H_0: p_1 - p_2 \leq 0.0$$
$$H_A: p_1 - p_2 > 0.0$$

and this sample information:

Sample 1	Sample 2
$n_1 = 60$	$n_2 = 80$
$x_1 = 30$	$x_2 = 24$

a. Based on $\alpha = 0.02$ and the sample information, what should be concluded with respect to the null and alternative hypotheses? Be sure to clearly show the decision rule.

b. Calculate the p-value for this hypothesis test. Based on the p-value, would the null hypothesis be rejected? Support your answer with calculations and/or reasons.

9.38 The following information was obtained from samples of two populations:

Population 1	Population 2
$n_1 = 300$	$n_2 = 400$
$x_1 = 88$	$x_2 = 136$

a. Determine if the sample sizes are large enough so that the sampling distribution of the difference between the sample proportions is approximately normally distributed.

b. Calculate and interpret an 80% confidence interval estimate for the difference between the two population proportions.

Business Applications

9.39 Recently a nationwide television network commissioned a polling service to poll homeowners across the United States. Among the issues to be addressed in the survey was whether there is a difference in the proportions of households that watch a national news broadcast depending on whether the household is headed by a man or a woman. The study surveyed 1,200 households. In 745 of these, the head of household was listed as a man. In the others, the household head was a woman. The survey results showed that 62% of the households headed by men tuned into a national network news program, whereas 49% of those homes headed by women did so.

a. Can the distribution of the difference between the sample proportions of households headed by men and women that tune into a national network news program be approximated by a normal distribution? Provide calculations and reasons for your answer.

b. Based on these data, what could the network conclude overall? State the null and alternative hypotheses, and test at a significance level equal to 0.05.

9.40 The United Way raises money for community charity activities. Recently in one community, the fund-raising committee was concerned with whether there is a difference in the proportion of employees who give to the United Way, depending on whether their employer is a private business or a government agency. A random sample of people who had been contacted about contributing last year was selected. Of those contacted, 70 worked for a private business and 50 worked for a government agency. Of the 70 private-sector employees, 22 had contributed some amount to United Way, and 19 of the government employees in the sample had contributed.

a. Based on these sample data and $\alpha = 0.05$, what should be concluded? Be sure to show the decision rule.

b. Construct a 95% confidence interval for the difference between the proportion of private-business and government-agency employees who contribute to United Way. Do the hypothesis test and the confidence interval produce compatible results? Explain and give reasons for your answer.

9.41 Most major airlines allow passengers to carry two pieces of luggage (of a certain maximum size) onto the plane. However, their studies show that the more carry-on baggage passengers have, the longer it takes the plane to unload and load passengers. One regional airline is considering changing its policy to allow only one carry-on per passenger. Before doing so, it decided to collect some data. Specifically, a random sample of 1,000 passengers was selected. The passengers were observed, and the number of bags each carried onto the plane was counted. The passengers are divided into two groups: those with fewer than two bags and those with two or more bags. Suppose 404 passengers had fewer than two bags each. Of these, 181 people responded "yes" to a question about whether the airline should limit the number of bags to one. Of those in the group with two bags, 123 indicated "yes" to the question. Using this information, construct and interpret a 95% confidence interval estimate for the difference in proportion of "yes" responses for the two groups. Do you find the results surprising?

Advanced Applications

9.42 Vintner Mortgage Company in Chicago, Illinois, markets residential and commercial loans to customers in the region. Recently, the company's board of directors asked whether the company had experienced a difference in the proportion of loan defaults between residential and commercial customers. To answer this question, company officials selected a random sample of 200 residential loans and 105 commercial loans that had been issued before 1995. The loans were analyzed to determine their status. A loan that was still being paid was labeled "Active," whereas a default loan was labeled "Default." The resulting data are in a CD-ROM file called *Vintner*.

a. Based on the sample data and a significance level equal to 0.05, does there appear to be a difference in the proportion of loan defaults between residential and commercial customers?

b. Prepare a short response to the Vintner board of directors. Include a graph of the data that supports your statistical analysis in your report.

c. Consider the outcome of the hypothesis test in part a. In the last five audits, 10 residential and 10 commercial customers were selected. In three of the audits, there were more residential than commercial loan defaults. Determine the probability of such an occurrence.

9-4 INTRODUCTION TO CONTINGENCY ANALYSIS

Thus far you have been introduced to hypothesis tests involving one and two population proportions. Although these techniques are useful in many cases, you will also encounter many situations involving multiple population proportions. For example, a major mutual fund company offers six different mutual funds. The president of the company may wish to determine if the proportion of customers selecting each mutual fund is related to the four sales regions in which the customers reside. A hospital administrator who collects service-satisfaction data from patients might be interested in determining whether there is a significant difference in patient rating by hospital department. A personnel manager for a large corporation might be interested in determining whether there is a relationship between level of employee job satisfaction and job classification. In each of these cases, the proportions relate to characteristic categories of the variable of interest. The six mutual funds, four sales regions, hospital departments, and job classifications are the specific categories.

These situations involving categorical data call for a new statistical tool known as *contingency analysis* to help make decisions when multiple proportions are involved. Contingency analysis can be used when a level of data measurement is either nominal or ordinal and the values are determined by counting the number of occurrences in each category.

2 × 2 CONTINGENCY TABLES

Dalgarno Photo, Inc.—Dalgarno Photo, Inc., gets much of its business from taking photographs for college yearbooks. Dalgarno hired a first-year MBA student to develop the survey it mailed to 850 yearbook representatives at the colleges and universities in its market area. The representatives were unaware that Dalgarno Photo had developed the survey.

The survey asked about the photography and publishing activities associated with yearbook development. For instance, what photographer and publisher services did the schools use, and what factors were most important in selecting services? The survey instrument contained 30 questions, which were coded into 137 separate variables.

Among his many interests in this study, Dalgarno's marketing manager questioned whether funding source and gender of the yearbook editor were related in some manner. To analyze this issue, we examine these two variables more closely. Source of university funding is a categorical variable, coded as follows:

$$1 = \text{Private funding}$$
$$2 = \text{State-funded}$$

Of the 221 respondents who provided data for this variable, 155 came from privately funded colleges or universities and 66 were from publicly funded institutions.

The second variable, sex of the yearbook editor, is also a categorical variable, with two response categories, coded as follows:

$$1 = \text{Male}$$
$$2 = \text{Female}$$

Of the 221 responses to the survey, 164 were from females and 57 were from males.

In cases in which the variables of interest are both categorical and the decision maker is interested in determining whether a relationship exists between the two, a statistical technique known as contingency analysis is useful. We first set up a two-dimensional table called a **contingency table**. The contingency table for these two variables is shown in Table 9-1.

TABLE 9-1

Contingency Table for Dalgarno Photo

GENDER	SOURCE OF FUNDING		
	Private	State	
Male	14	43	57
Female	141	23	164
	155	66	221

> **Contingency Table**
>
> A table used to classify sample observations according to two or more identifiable characteristics. It is also called a *crosstabulation table*.

Table 9-1 shows that 14 of the respondents were males from schools that are privately funded. The numbers at the extreme right and along the bottom are called the *marginal frequencies*. For example, 57 respondents were males, and 155 respondents were from privately funded institutions.

The issue of whether there is a relationship between responses to these two variables is formally addressed through a hypothesis test, in which the null and alternative hypotheses are stated as follows:

TABLE 9-2

Contingency Table for Dalgarno Photo

	SOURCE OF FUNDING		
GENDER	**Private**	**State**	
Male	$o_{11} = 14$ $e_{11} = 39.98$	$o_{12} = 43$ $e_{12} = 17.02$	57
Female	$o_{21} = 141$ $e_{21} = 115.02$	$o_{22} = 23$ $e_{22} = 48.98$	164
	155	66	221

H_0: Gender of yearbook editor is independent of the college's funding source.
H_A: Gender of yearbook editor *is not* independent of the college's funding source.

If the null hypothesis is true, the population proportion of yearbook editors from private institutions who are males should be equal to the proportion of male editors from state-funded institutions. These two proportions should also equal the population proportion of male editors without regard to a school's funding source. To illustrate, we can use the sample data to determine the sample proportion of male editors as follows:

$$P_M = \frac{\text{Number of male editors}}{\text{Number of respondents}} = \frac{57}{221}$$
$$= 0.2579$$

Then, if the null hypothesis is true, we would expect 25.79% of the 155 privately funded schools, or 39.98 schools, to have a male yearbook editor. We would also expect 25.79% of the 66 state-funded schools, or 17.02, to have male yearbook editors. (Note that the expected numbers need not be integer values. Note also that the sum of expected frequencies in any column or row add to the marginal frequency.) We can use this reasoning to determine the expected number of respondents in each cell of the contingency table, as shown in Table 9-2.

You can simplify the calculations needed to produce the expected values for each cell. Note that the first cell's expected value, 39.98, was obtained by the following calculation:

$$e_{11} = 0.2579(155) = 39.98$$

However, because the probability, 0.2579, is calculated by dividing the row total, 57, by the grand total, 221, the calculation can be represented as

$$e_{11} = \frac{(\text{Row total})(\text{Column total})}{\text{Grand total}} = \frac{(57)(155)}{221} = 39.98$$

As a further example, we can calculate the expected value for the next cell in the same row. The expected number of male yearbook editors in state-funds schools is

$$e_{12} = \frac{(\text{Row total})(\text{Column total})}{\text{Grand total}} = \frac{(57)(66)}{221} = 17.02$$

Keep in mind that the row and column totals (the marginal frequencies) must be the same for the expected values as for the observed values. Therefore, when there is only one cell left in a row or a column for which you must calculate an expected value, you can obtain it by subtraction. So, as an example, the expected value, e_{12}, could have been calculated as

$$e_{12} = 57 - 39.98 = 17.02$$

Allowing for sampling error, we would expect the actual frequencies in each cell to approximately match the corresponding expected cell frequencies when the null hypothesis is true. The greater the difference between the actual and the expected frequencies, the more likely the null hypothesis of independence is false and should be rejected. The statistical test to determine whether the sample data support or refute the null hypothesis is given by Equation 9-18. Do not be confused by the double summation in Equation 9-18; it merely indicates that all rows and columns must be used in calculating χ^2. The degrees of freedom are the number of independent data values obtained from the experiment. In any given row, once you know $c - 1$ of the data values, the remaining data value is determined. For instance, once you know that 14 of the 57 male editors were from privately funded institutions, you know that 43 were from state-funded institutions.

Chi-Square Contingency Test Statistic

$$\chi^2 = \sum_{i=1}^{r} \sum_{j=1}^{c} \frac{(o_{ij} - e_{ij})^2}{e_{ij}} \quad \text{with } df = (r-1)(c-1) \qquad \text{9-18}$$

where:

$$o_{ij} = \text{Observed frequency in cell } (i, j)$$
$$e_{ij} = \text{Expected frequency in cell } (i, j)$$
$$r = \text{Number of rows}$$
$$c = \text{Number of columns}$$

Similarly, once $r - 1$ data values in a column are known, the remaining data value is determined. Therefore, the degrees of freedom are obtained by the expression $(r - 1)(c - 1)$.

Figure 9-9 presents the hypotheses and test results for this example. The test statistic has a distribution that can be approximated by the chi-square distribution if the expected values are

FIGURE 9-9

Chi-Square Contingency Analysis Test for Dalgarno Photo

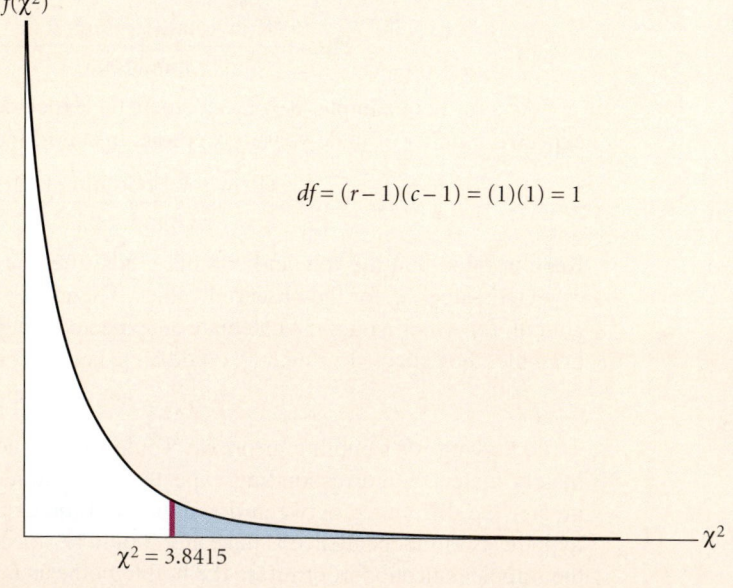

Hypotheses:

H_0: Gender of yearbook editor is independent of college's funding source.
H_A: Gender of yearbook editor is not independent of college's funding source.
$\alpha = 0.05$

	Private	Public
Male	$o_{11} = 14$ $e_{11} = 39.98$	$o_{12} = 43$ $e_{12} = 17.02$
Female	$o_{21} = 141$ $e_{21} = 115.02$	$o_{22} = 23$ $e_{22} = 48.98$

Test Statistic:

$$\chi^2 = \sum_{i=1}^{r} \sum_{j=1}^{c} \frac{(o_{ij} - e_{ij})^2}{e_{ij}} = \frac{(14 - 39.98)^2}{39.98} + \frac{(43 - 17.02)^2}{17.02}$$
$$+ \frac{(141 - 115.02)^2}{115.02} + \frac{(23 - 48.98)^2}{48.98} = 76.19$$

$f(\chi^2)$

$df = (r-1)(c-1) = (1)(1) = 1$

$\chi^2 = 3.8415$

χ^2

Decision Rule:

If $\chi^2 > 3.8415$, reject H_0
Otherwise, do not reject H_0
Because $76.19 > 3.8415$, reject H_0

larger than 5. Note that the calculated chi-square statistic is compared to the tabled value of chi-square from Appendix G for an $\alpha = 0.05$ and degrees of freedom $= (2 - 1)(2 - 1) = 1$. Because $\chi^2 = 76.19 > 3.8415$, the null hypothesis of independence should be rejected. Dalgarno Photo representatives should conclude that the sex of the yearbook editor and each school's source of funding are not independent. By examining the data in Figure 9-9, you can see that private schools are more likely to have female editors, whereas state schools are more likely to have male yearbook editors.

EXAMPLE 9-8: 2 × 2 CONTINGENCY ANALYSIS

Barger Advertising   Before releasing a major advertising campaign to the media, Barger Advertising runs a test on the material. Recently, it randomly called 100 people and asked them to listen to a commercial that was slated to run nationwide on the radio. At the end of the commercial, the respondents were asked to name the company that was in the ad. The company is interested in determining whether there is a relationship between gender and a person's ability to recall the company name. To test this, the following steps can be used.

Step 1: **Specify the null and alternative hypotheses.**
The company is interested in testing whether a relationship exists between gender and recall ability. Here are the appropriate null and alternative hypotheses.

H_0: Ability to correctly recall the company name is independent of gender.
H_A: Recall ability and gender are not independent.

Step 2: **Determine the significance level.**
The test will be conducted using a 0.01 level of significance.

Step 3: **Determine the critical value.**
The critical value for this test will be the chi-square value, with $(r - 1)(c - 1) = (2 - 1)(2 - 1) = 1$ degree of freedom with an $\alpha = 0.01$. From Appendix G, the critical value is 6.6349.

Step 4: **Collect the sample data and compute the chi-square test statistic using Equation 9-18.**
The following contingency table shows the results of the sampling.

	Female	Male	Total
Correct Recall	33	25	58
Incorrect Recall	22	20	42
Total	55	45	100

The expected cell frequencies are determined by multiplying the row total by the column and dividing by the overall sample size. For example, for the cell corresponding to female and correct recall, we get:

$$\text{Expected} = \frac{58 \times 55}{100} = 31.90$$

The expected cell values for all cells are

	Female	Male	Total
Correct Recall	$o = 33$	$o = 25$	58
	$e = 31.90$	$e = 26.10$	
Incorrect Recall	$o = 22$	$o = 20$	42
	$e = 23.10$	$e = 18.9$	
Total	55	45	100

The test statistic is computed using Equation 9-18.

$$\chi^2 = \sum_{i=1}^{r} \sum_{j=1}^{c} \frac{(o_{ij} - e_{ij})^2}{e_{ij}}$$

$$= \frac{(33 - 31.9)^2}{31.9} + \frac{(25 - 26.10)^2}{26.10} + \frac{(22 - 23.10)^2}{23.10} + \frac{(20 - 18.9)^2}{18.9} = 0.20$$

Step 5: **Reach a decision.**
Because $\chi^2 = 0.20 < 6.6349$, do not reject the null hypothesis.

Step 6: **Draw a conclusion.**
Based on the sample data there is no reason to believe that being able to recall the name of the company in the ad is related to gender.

Excel and Minitab Tutorial

$r \times c$ CONTINGENCY TABLES

Benton Industries—Benton Industries manufactures carpets and draperies in the Atlanta area. It pays market wages, provides competitive benefits, and offers attractive options for employees in an effort to create a satisfied workforce and reduce turnover. Recently, however, several supervisors have complained that employee absenteeism is becoming a problem. In response to these complaints, the human resources manager studied a random sample of 500 employees. One aim of this study was to determine whether there is a relationship between absenteeism and marital status. Absenteeism during the past year was broken down into three levels:

1. zero absences
2. 1 to 5 absences
3. over 5 absences

Marital status was divided into four categories:

1. single   2. married

3. divorced   4. widowed

Table 9-3 shows the contingency table for the sample of 500 employees. The table is also shown in the CD-ROM file *Benton*. The null and alternative hypotheses to be tested are

H_0: Absentee behavior is independent of marital status.
H_A: Absentee behavior is *not* independent of marital status.

As with 2×2 contingency analysis, the test for independence can be made using the chi-square test, where the expected cell frequencies are compared to the actual cell frequencies and the test statistic shown as Equation 9-18 is used. The logic of the test says that if the actual and expected frequencies closely match, then the null hypothesis of independence is not rejected. However, if the actual and expected cell frequencies are substantially different overall, the null hypothesis of independence is rejected. The calculated chi-square statistic is compared to a table critical value for the desired significance and degrees of freedom equal to $(r - 1)(c - 1)$.

The expected cell frequencies are determined assuming that the row and column variables are independent. This means, for example, that the probability of a married person being absent more than 5 days during the year is the same as the probability of any employee being absent more than 5 days. An easy way to compute the expected cell frequencies, e_{ij}, is given by Equation 9-19.

TABLE 9-3

Contingency Table for Benton Industries

	ABSENTEE RATE			
Marital Status	**Zero**	**1–5**	**Over 5**	**Row Totals**
Single	84	82	34	200
Married	50	64	36	150
Divorced	50	34	16	100
Widowed	16	20	14	50
Column Total	200	200	100	500

Expected Cell Frequencies

$$e_{ij} = \frac{(i\text{th Row total})\,(j\text{th Column total})}{\text{Total sample size}}$$

9-19

For example, the expected cell frequency for row 1, column 1 is

$$e_{11} = \frac{(200)(200)}{500} = 80$$

and the expected cell frequency for row 2, column 3 is

$$e_{23} = \frac{(100)(150)}{500} = 30$$

Figures 9-10a and 9-10b show the completed contingency table with the actual and expected cell frequencies. The calculated chi-square test value is computed as follows:

$$\chi^2 = \sum_{i=1}^{r} \sum_{j=1}^{c} \frac{(o_{ij} - e_{ij})^2}{e_{ij}}$$

$$= \frac{(84 - 80)^2}{80} + \frac{(82 - 80)^2}{80} + \ldots + \frac{(20 - 20)^2}{20} + \frac{(14 - 10)^2}{10}$$

$$= 10.88$$

The degrees of freedom are $(r - 1)(c - 1) = (4 - 1)(3 - 1) = 6$. You can use the chi-square table in Appendix G to get the chi-square critical value for $\alpha = 0.05$ and 6 degrees of freedom, or you can use Minitab's **Probability Distributions** command or Excel's **CHIINV** function (CHIINV(0.05,6) = 12.5916). Because the calculated chi-square value (10.88) shown in Figure 9-10a is less than 12.5916, we cannot reject the null hypothesis. Based on these sample data, there is *insufficient evidence* to conclude that absenteeism and marital status are not independent.

CHI-SQUARE TEST LIMITATIONS

The chi-square distribution is only an approximation for the true distribution for contingency analysis. We use the chi-square approximation because the true distribution is impractical to compute in most instances. However, the approximation (and, therefore, the conclusion reached) is quite good when all expected cell frequencies are at least 5.0. When expected cell frequencies drop below 5.0, the calculated chi-square value tends to be inflated and may inflate the true probability of Type I error beyond the stated significance level. As a rule, if the null hypothesis is not rejected, you do not need to worry when the expected cell frequencies drop below 5.0.

FIGURE 9-10A

Excel Output—Benton Industries Contingency Analysis Test

Excel Instructions:
1. Open file: Benton.xls
2. Compute expected cell frequencies using Excel formula.
3. Compute chi-square statistic using Excel formula.

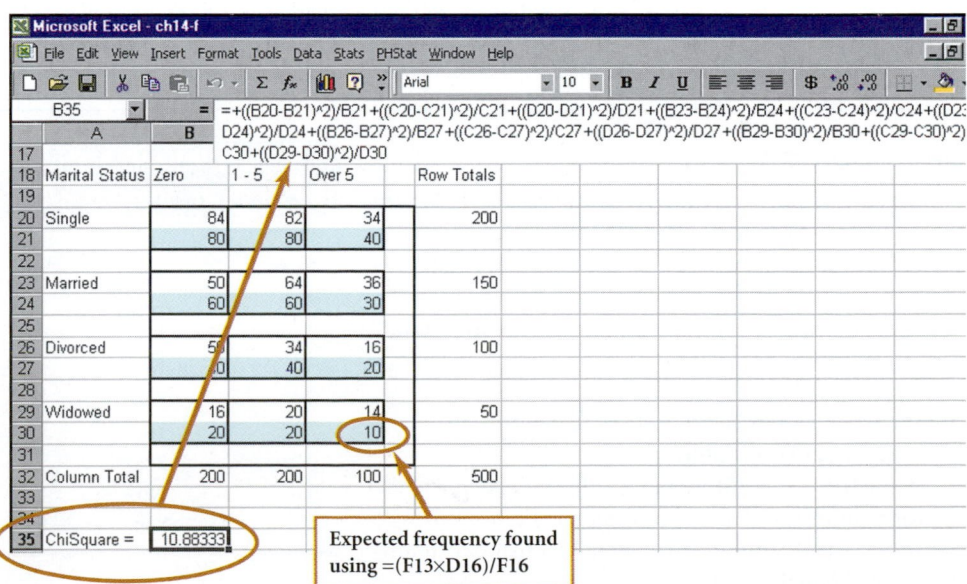

FIGURE 9-10B

Minitab Output—Benton
Industries Contingency
Analysis Test

Minitab Instructions:
1. Open file: Benton.MTW.
2. Choose **Stat > Tables > Chi-Square Test**.
3. In **Columns containing the table**, enter data columns.
4. Click **OK**.

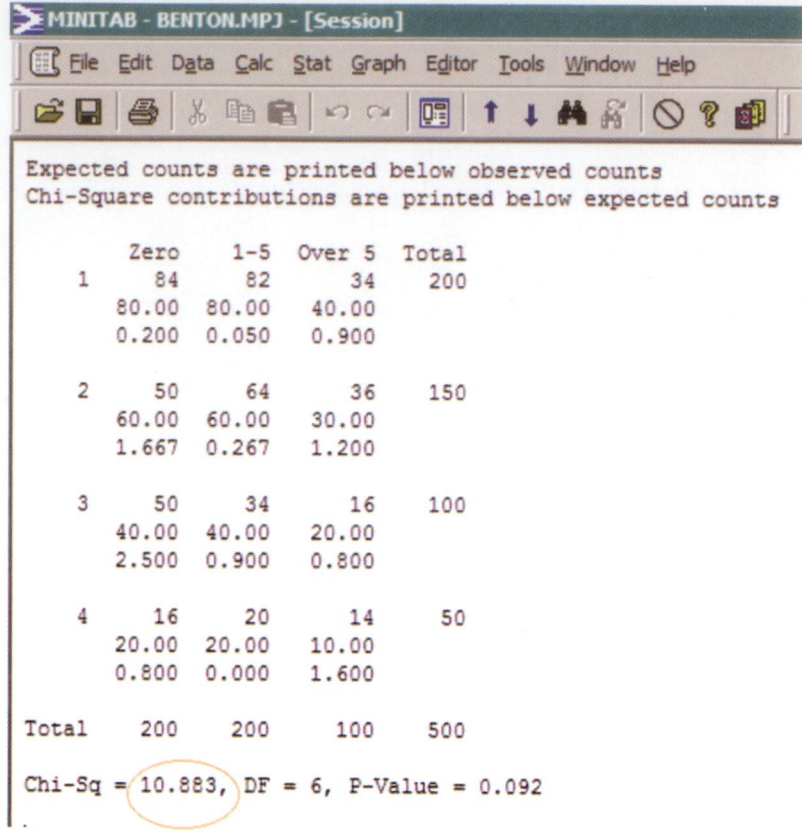

There are two alternatives that can be used to overcome the small expected-cell-frequency problem. The first is to increase the sample size. This may increase the marginal frequencies in each row and column enough to increase the expected cell frequencies. The second option is to combine the categories of the row and/or column variables. If you do decide to group categories together, there should be some logic behind the resulting categories. You don't want to lose the meaning of the results through poor groupings. You will need to examine each situation individually to determine whether the option of grouping classes to increase expected cell frequencies makes sense.

9-4: EXERCISES

Skill Development

9.43 A survey has been conducted at a local company in which various questions about the workplace environment were asked. Two of the questions are listed as follows:
1. Do you mind if people smoke in the office area? _____Yes _____No
2. Do you smoke? _____Yes _____No

Shown is a random sample of 30 responses that came back on these two variables.

Construct a contingency table and perform the appropriate test to determine whether the responses to questions 1 and 2 are independent. Test using a significance level equal to 0.05.

Respondent (R)	Question 1 (Q1)	Question 2 (Q2)	R	Q1	Q2	R	Q1	Q2
1	Yes	No	11	No	No	21	No	Yes
2	Yes	Yes	12	No	No	22	Yes	Yes
3	No	Yes	13	No	Yes	23	Yes	No
4	No	Yes	14	Yes	No	24	Yes	No
5	No	No	15	Yes	Yes	25	No	Yes
6	Yes	No	16	Yes	Yes	26	Yes	Yes
7	Yes	No	17	No	Yes	27	Yes	No
8	Yes	Yes	18	No	No	28	No	No
9	No	No	19	No	Yes	29	Yes	No
10	Yes	No	20	Yes	No	30	Yes	No

9.44 Referring to Exercise 9.43, suppose 200 people in the company respond to the survey and the following contingency table is constructed from the responses.

Do You Care About Smoking in the Office?	Do You Smoke?	
	Yes	No
Yes	11	139
No	29	21

Based on these data, is attitude about smoking in the office independent of whether an individual smokes? Use the chi-square test and test at an $\alpha = 0.10$ level. Discuss the results.

9.45 Jack O'Connell, chief of officials for the National Basketball Association, reviews films of all games to evaluate calls made by the referees. Jack rates each call "good" or "bad." For games played during a one-week period, Jack found the following distribution of calls for two officials:

Call	Official A	Official B
Good	463	518
Bad	51	38

a. Do these data indicate that the proportion of bad calls is the same for each official?
b. Test the data using a chi-square statistic with an $\alpha = 0.05$.
c. Compare the test in part b with the z-test for the difference between two population proportions. Determine the relationship between the two test statistics.

9.46 Develop a data-collection form on which you can collect measurements for two variables from students in one of your other classes (not this statistics course). The two variables are GPA and number of hours per week spent working at a paying job. Obtain a sample size of at least 25 students, and assume that these responses represent a random sample of all students at your college or university. Using the sample data that you have collected, apply contingency analysis to determine whether GPA is independent of number of hours worked. Break GPA into four categories and hours worked into five categories. Test at an $\alpha = 0.05$ level.

9.47 A contingency analysis table has been constructed from data obtained in a phone survey of customers in a market area in which respondents were asked to indicate whether they owned a domestic or foreign car and whether they were a member of a union. The following contingency table is provided.

Car	Union	
	Yes	No
Domestic	155	470
Foreign	40	325

a. Use the chi-square approach to test whether type of car owned (domestic or foreign) is independent of union membership. Test using an $\alpha = 0.05$ level.
b. Calculate the p-value for this hypothesis test.

9.48 In a recent study of college graduates, it was hypothesized that income was independent of number of different employers a person had worked for since graduation. The data collected were as follows:

Income Level	Number of Employers				
	1	2	3	4	5 or more
Under $20,000	3	4	3	2	3
$20,000–$30,000	5	3	7	3	2
$30,000–$40,000	2	5	3	6	1
$40,000–$50,000	1	7	9	3	4
Over $50,000	1	3	11	7	4

Assuming that these data reflect observed frequencies, what can be concluded about the hypothesis? Test at an $\alpha = 0.05$ level.

Business Applications

9.49 A study of automobile drivers was conducted to determine whether the number of traffic citations issued during a three-year period was independent of the sex of the driver. The following data were collected.

Citations Issued	Sex of Driver	
	Male	Female
0	240	160
1	80	40
2	32	18
3	11	9
Over 3	5	4

a. Using an $\alpha = 0.05$ level, determine whether the two variables are independent.
b. A friend of yours claims to know a person who was included in the study. He says his friend had more than one citation during the study period. Calculate the probability that your friend's acquaintance is a female.

9.50 A bank in Midvale, Wisconsin, recently did a study of its customers to determine whether the number of transactions in a checking account was independent of the marital status of the customer. The following data were obtained.

Marital Status	Number of Transactions				
	0–10	11–20	21–30	31–40	Over 40
Single	13	23	19	20	11
Married	6	15	33	45	27
Divorced	4	19	22	20	15
Other	2	11	8	5	2

a. Based on these data, what should the bank conclude? Test at an $\alpha = 0.05$ level.
b. (1) Are there any cells that have expected values smaller than 5? (2) Suggest an appropriate way to combine cells in a meaningful way so that the expected cell frequencies are at least 5. (3) Repeat part a using the reconstructed contingency table.

c. Given the decision reached in part a, was it necessary to implement the procedure indicated in part b? When is it unnecessary to combine cells even though some of them have expected values smaller than 5?

9.51 In a recent labor negotiation, union officials collected data from a sample of union members regarding how long they had been with the company and how long they would be willing to stay out on strike if a strike were called. The following data were collected.

	Strike-Length Toleration		
Time with Company	Under 1 Week	1–4 Weeks	Over 4 Weeks
Under 1 year	23	6	3
1–2 years	19	15	8
2–5 years	20	23	19
5–10 years	4	21	29
Over 10 years	2	5	18

a. Based on these data, can the union conclude that strike-length toleration is independent of time with the company? Test at the $\alpha = 0.05$ level.

b. Consider two groups: those employed with the company at most 5 years, and those employed with the company more than 10 years. Do the data suggest that the proportion of employees who would be willing to stay out on strike for at least a week is larger for the first group? Conduct an appropriate hypothesis test to determine this.

9.52 The table here classifies a stock's price change as up, down, or no change for both today's and yesterday's prices. Price changes were examined for 100 days. A financial theory states that stock prices follow what is called a "random walk." This means, in part, that the price change today for a stock must be independent of yesterday's price change. Test the hypothesis that daily stock-price changes for this stock are independent. Let $\alpha = 0.05$.

		Price Change Previous Day		
		Up	No Change	Down
	Up	14	16	12
Price Change Today	No Change	6	8	6
	Down	16	14	8

9.53 An AceCo Precision Products metal-fabrication shop operates three shifts. The accompanying data give the distribution of accidents among the three shifts by type of accident.

		Accident Type	
		Behavior-Based	Equipment-Related
	Day	270	80
Shift	Swing	190	25
	Graveyard	96	24

Test the hypothesis that shift and accident type are unrelated. Let $\alpha = 0.01$.

9.54 A random sample of 980 heads of households was taken from the customer list for State Bank and Trust. Those sampled were asked to classify their own attitudes and their parents' attitudes toward borrowing money, as follows:

A: Borrow only for real estate and car purchases.
B: Borrow for short-term purchases such as appliances and furniture.
C: Never borrow money.

The following table indicates the responses from those in the study.

		Respondent		
		A	B	C
	A	240	80	20
Parent	B	180	120	40
	C	180	80	40

a. Test the hypothesis that the respondents' borrowing habits are independent from what they believe their parents' attitudes to be. Let $\alpha = 0.01$.

b. Calculate a 99% confidence interval for the difference between the proportion of respondents who never borrow money and whose parents never borrowed money and the proportion of respondents who never borrow money and whose parents borrowed money for short-term purchases. (Hint: See the discussion of the difference between two population proportions in Chapter 9). Are the results of this confidence interval compatible with the conclusion you reached in part a?

9.55 A major appliance manufacturer provides four washing machine models: standard, deluxe, superior, and XLT. The marketing manager has recently conducted a study on the purchasers of the washing machines. The study recorded the model of appliance purchased and the credit account balance of each customer at the time of purchase. The sample data are in the table here. Based on these data, is there evidence of a relationship between the account balance and the model of washer purchased? Use a significance level of 0.02. Conduct the test using a p-value approach.

		Washer Model Purchased			
		Standard	Deluxe	Superior	XLT
	Under $200	10	16	40	5
Credit Balance	$200–$800	8	12	24	15
	Over $800	16	12	16	30

Advanced Applications

9.56 ECCO (Electronic Controls Company) makes back-up alarms that are used on such equipment as forklifts and delivery trucks. The quality manager recently performed a study involving a random sample of 100 warranty claims. One of the questions the manager wanted to answer was whether there is a relationship between the type of warranty complaint and the plant at which an alarm was made. The data are in the CD-ROM file *ECCO*.

a. Calculate the expected values for the cells in this analysis. Suggest a way in which cells can be combined to assure that the expected value of each cell is at least 5 so that as many level combinations of the two variables as possible are retained.

b. Using a significance level of 0.01, conduct a relevant hypothesis test and provide an answer to the manager's question.

c. Can the quality control manager conclude that the type of warranty problem is independent of the shift on which an alarm was manufactured? Test using a significance level of 0.05. Discuss your results.

Summary and Conclusions

The process of using sample information to reach conclusions about the population from which the sample was selected is used extensively in business decision making. This inferential analysis takes on two forms: estimation and hypothesis testing. Chapter 7 introduced the fundamentals of statistical estimation. There we discussed how to formulate and interpret confidence interval estimates for a variety of population values involving one and two populations.

Chapter 8 introduced hypothesis testing in which we were interested in a single population value. It presented the basic concepts and discussed the types of statistical errors that can be made when a hypothesis is tested using sample information. In Chapter 9, we have extended the discussion of hypothesis testing to situations involving two populations. We specifically looked at situations in which the difference between two population means was the issue of concern. In some instances, the samples from the two populations are considered independent. In other cases, to control for potential sources of variation, we paired the samples and used a paired-sample test to determine whether the population means were different.

In addition to tests about the difference in population means, this chapter introduced hypothesis testing for the difference in two population proportions.

You may have difficulty in determining which procedure to use in a given situation. Figure 9-11 shows a flow diagram that you might find useful. As you work the problems at the end of the chapter, you might use this diagram to help you sort through the options.

EQUATIONS

Confidence Interval Format

Point Estimate $\pm$ (Critical Value)(Standard Error) **9-1**

Standard Error of $\bar{x}_1 - \bar{x}_2$ When σ_1 and σ_2 Are Known

$$\sigma_{\bar{x}_1 - \bar{x}_2} = \sqrt{\frac{\sigma_1^2}{n_1} + \frac{\sigma_2^2}{n_2}} \qquad \textbf{9-2}$$

Confidence Interval Estimate for $\mu_1 - \mu_2$ When σ_1 and σ_2 Are Known, Independent Samples

$$(\bar{x}_1 - \bar{x}_2) \pm z_{\alpha/2}\sqrt{\frac{\sigma_1^2}{n_1} + \frac{\sigma_2^2}{n_2}} \qquad \textbf{9-3}$$

Confidence Interval Estimate for $\mu_1 - \mu_2$ When σ_1 and σ_2 Are Unknown, Independent Samples

$$(\bar{x}_1 - \bar{x}_2) \pm t_{\alpha/2}s_p\sqrt{\frac{1}{n_1} + \frac{1}{n_2}} \qquad \textbf{9-4}$$

Confidence Interval Estimate for $\mu_1 - \mu_2$ When σ_1 and σ_2 Are Unknown and Not Equal, Independent Samples

$$(\bar{x}_1 - \bar{x}_2) \pm t_{\alpha/2}\sqrt{\frac{s_1^2}{n_1} + \frac{s_2^2}{n_2}} \qquad \textbf{9-5}$$

Paired Difference

$$d = x_1 - x_2 \qquad \textbf{9-6}$$

Point Estimate for the Population Mean Paired Difference, μ_d

$$\bar{d} = \frac{\sum_{i=1}^{n} d_i}{n} \qquad \textbf{9-7}$$

Sample Standard Deviation for Paired Differences

$$s_d = \sqrt{\frac{\sum_{i=1}^{n}(d_i - \bar{d})^2}{n-1}} \qquad \textbf{9-8}$$

Confidence Interval Estimate for Population Mean Paired Difference, μ_d

$$\bar{d} \pm t_{\alpha/2}\frac{s_d}{\sqrt{n}} \qquad \textbf{9-9}$$

z Test Statistic for $\mu_1 - \mu_2$ When σ_1 and σ_2 Are Known, Independent Samples

$$z = \frac{(\bar{x}_1 - \bar{x}_2) - (\mu_1 - \mu_2)}{\sqrt{\frac{\sigma_1^2}{n_1} + \frac{\sigma_2^2}{n_2}}} \qquad \textbf{9-10}$$

t Test Statistic for $\mu_1 - \mu_2$ When σ_1 and σ_2 Are Unknown, Independent Samples

$$t = \frac{(\bar{x}_1 - \bar{x}_2) - (\mu_1 - \mu_2)}{s_p\sqrt{\frac{1}{n_1} + \frac{1}{n_2}}}, \qquad df = n_1 + n_2 - 2 \qquad \textbf{9-11}$$

t Test Statistic for $\mu_1 - \mu_2$ When Population Variances Are Not Equal

$$t = \frac{(\bar{x}_1 - \bar{x}_2) - (\mu_1 - \mu_2)}{\sqrt{\frac{s_1^2}{n_1} + \frac{s_2^2}{n_2}}} \qquad \textbf{9-12}$$

Estimation and Hypothesis Testing Flow Diagram

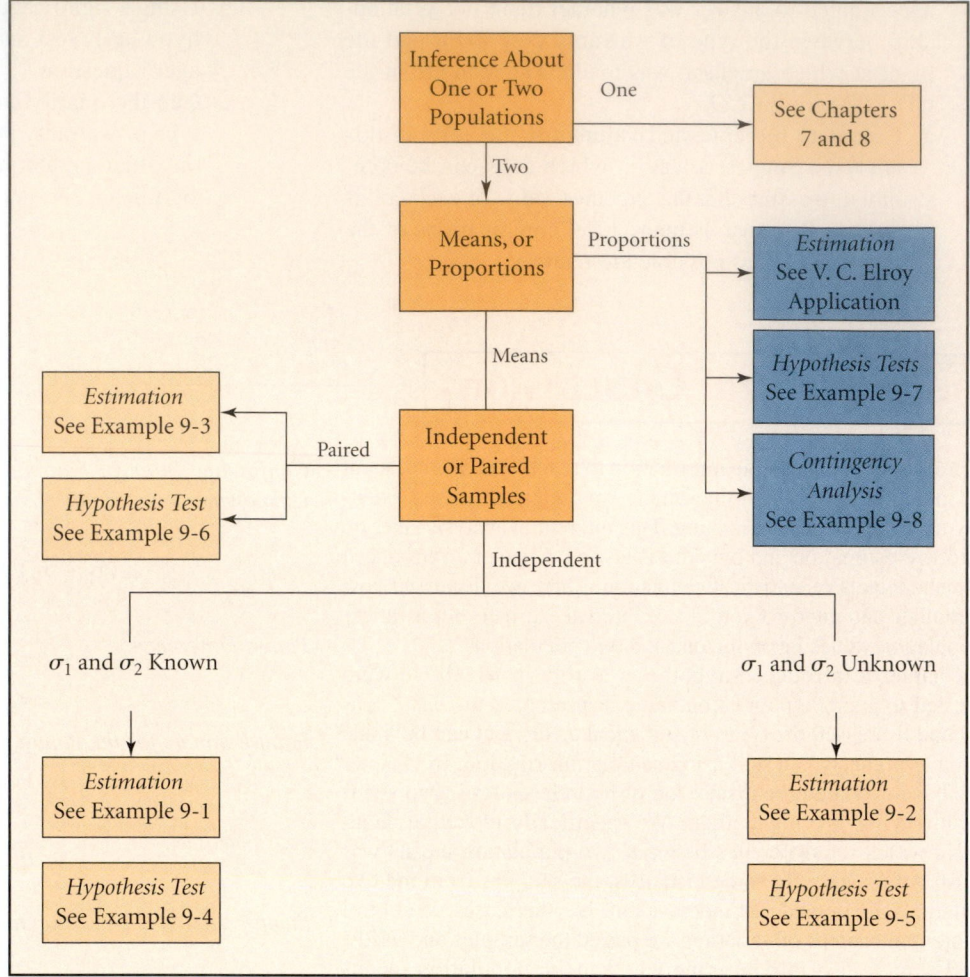

Degrees of Freedom for t Test Statistic When Population Variances Are Not Equal

$$\frac{(s_1^2/n_1 + s_2^2/n_2)^2}{\left(\dfrac{(s_1^2/n_1)^2}{n_1 - 1} + \dfrac{(s_2^2/n_2)^2}{n_2 - 1}\right)} \qquad \textbf{9-13}$$

t Test Statistic for Paired Sample Test

$$t = \frac{\bar{d} - \mu_d}{\dfrac{s_d}{\sqrt{n}}} \qquad df = (n - 1) \qquad \textbf{9-14}$$

Confidence Interval Estimate for $p_1 - p_2$

$$(\bar{p}_1 - \bar{p}_2) \pm z_{\alpha/2} \sqrt{\frac{(\bar{p}_1)(1 - \bar{p}_1)}{n_1} + \frac{(\bar{p}_2)(1 - \bar{p}_2)}{n_2}} \qquad \textbf{9-15}$$

Pooled Estimator for Overall Proportion

$$\bar{p} = \frac{n_1 \bar{p}_1 + n_2 \bar{p}_2}{n_1 + n_2} = \frac{x_1 + x_2}{n_1 + n_2} \qquad \textbf{9-16}$$

z Test Statistic for Difference Between Population Proportions

$$z = \frac{(\bar{p}_1 - \bar{p}_2) - (p_1 - p_2)}{\sqrt{\bar{p}(1 - \bar{p})\left(\dfrac{1}{n_1} + \dfrac{1}{n_2}\right)}} \qquad \textbf{9-17}$$

Chi-Square Contingency Test Statistic

$$\chi^2 = \sum_{i=1}^{r} \sum_{j=1}^{c} \frac{(o_{ij} - e_{ij})^2}{e_{ij}} \quad \text{with } df = (r - 1)(c - 1) \textbf{ 9-18}$$

Expected Cell Frequencies

$$e_{ij} = \frac{(i\text{th Row total}) \, (j\text{th Column total})}{\text{Total sample size}} \qquad \textbf{9-19}$$

Key Terms

CHAPTER EXERCISES

Business Applications

9.57 Recently at a sales meeting of the Fitness Service Company, the statement was made that there is no difference in the average whole life insurance coverage for clients in the two states. Managers decided a test of this statement should be made because the conclusion could affect the sales promotion that was being planned.

To test the claim, a random sample of 65 clients was selected from Wisconsin and another sample of 85 clients was selected from Ohio. The sample was analyzed, with these results:

Wisconsin	Ohio
$\bar{x}_1 = \$58,740$	$\bar{x}_2 = \$54,900$
$s_1 = \$24,800$	$s_2 = \$27,920$

Assuming that a significance level equal to 0.05 is used, based on the sample data, what should the Fitness Service Company conclude? Conduct the hypothesis test using a p-value approach. Discuss.

9.58 A book publisher claims that undergraduates are more likely to buy used textbooks than graduate students. The publisher's marketing department selected two random samples of 200 undergraduate students and 100 graduate students, respectively, at Arizona State University. The students were asked whether they had purchased a used textbook this term. Of the undergraduates, 138 said "yes," whereas 59 of the graduates said "yes."
a. Using a significance level of 0.05, what should the publisher conclude?
b. Based on the results of this survey, should the publisher extend its conclusions to all undergraduates and graduates at any university? Discuss.

9.59 A college official claimed that there is no difference between athletes and nonathletes in terms of the proportion of credits taken that apply toward graduation. To test this, two random samples were selected. First a random sample of 200 courses taken by athletes was selected. Of these, 144 were judged to count toward the degree of the person taking the course. The second sample consisted of 500 courses taken by nonathletes. Of these, 402 were deemed to apply toward the graduation requirements of the students involved. Using a significance level equal to 0.05, what conclusion should be reached about the official's claim regarding athletes and nonathletes?

9.60 Hamilton Bank & Trust operates banks throughout Wisconsin. Management is very concerned about making sure that a standard of quality service is achieved. For instance, they are interested in whether there is a difference in standard deviation in service times for customers who use the drive-up window versus those who go inside to the teller windows.

One branch in Madison recently was the subject of evaluation. A sample of 13 drive-up customers was selected, and a sample of 9 inside-counter customers was selected. The time (in minutes) it took each customer to be served was recorded. The following statistics were computed from the sample data.

Drive-Up	Walk-In
$\bar{x}_1 = 8.5$	$\bar{x}_2 = 8.4$
$s_1 = 2.0$	$s_2 = 1.2$

Suppose the managers are also interested in testing whether there is a difference in average time it takes to service the two types of customers. State the appropriate null and alternative hypotheses and test using $\alpha = 0.05$. Based on part a, comment on the validity of this latter test concerning the population means.

9.61 Last year the city of Bellingham in Selina County, Georgia, undertook a campaign to consolidate the city and county governments. The premise was that proportionately more people in the city would favor the concept than in the outlying county area. This was because the county residents might expect a tax increase from the consolidation even though the proponents of the plan promised a tax reduction in the long run. A polling agency was hired to conduct a study of this issue. It randomly selected 100 people in the city and 75 people in the county. It found 62 city dwellers favored the idea and 36 county residents favored the plan. Based on the sample results, what should be concluded about the proportions favoring the consolidation when the city residents are compared with the county residents? Use a significance level of 0.10.

9.62 A local restaurant is interested in determining whether the dollar amount of lunches ordered by males has greater variability than those ordered by females. To conduct the test, random samples of 25 males and 25 females were selected from people who had lunch during the last month. The following statistics were computed from the sample data:

Males	Females
$\bar{x}_1 = \$12.40$	$\bar{x}_2 = \$8.92$
$s_1 = \$2.50$	$s_2 = \$1.34$

Suppose the manager is also interested in determining whether there is a significant difference in the average dollar amount spent on lunch between men and women. The manager believes that only a difference of $1.00 or more would be considered significant. State the appropriate null and alternative hypotheses and test using $\alpha = 0.05$.

9.63 The owners of Campbell Electronics decided to place an advertisement on television to be shown three times during a live broadcast of the local university's football game. They hope that their average sales per day would increase so that they would recoup the cost of the advertisements during any seven randomly selected days after the football game. The advertisements cost a total of $3,500. The sales for each of the seven days after the ad was placed were to be compared with the sales for the seven days immediately before the ad ran. The following data, representing the total dollar sales each day, were collected:

Sales Before the Ad	Sales After the Ad
$1,765	$2,045
1,543	2,456
2,867	2,590
1,490	1,510
2,800	2,850
1,379	1,255
2,097	2,255

a. What assumptions must be made about the population distributions in order to test the hypothesis using the t-distribution?
b. Based on the sample data, what conclusions should be reached with respect to average sales before versus after the advertisement?

9.64 The Wilcox Company sells breakable china through a mail-order system that has been very profitable. One of its major problems is freight damage. Wilcox insures the items at shipping, but the inconvenience to the customer when a piece gets broken can cause the customer not to place another order in the future. Thus, packaging is important to Wilcox.

In the past, the company has purchased two different packaging materials from two suppliers. The assumption was that there would be no difference in proportion of damaged shipments resulting from use of either packaging material. The sales manager recently decided a study of this issue should be done. Therefore, a random sample of 300 orders using shipping material 1 and a random sample of 250 orders using material 2 were pulled from the files. The number of damaged parcels, x, was recorded for each material, as follows:

Material 1	Material 2
$n_1 = 300$	$n_2 = 250$
$x_1 = 19$	$x_2 = 12$

a. Is the normal distribution a good approximation for the distribution of the difference between the sample proportions? Provide support for your answer.
b. Based on the sample information and an alpha = 0.03 level, what should the Wilcox Company conclude?

9.65 The makers of Hot Mix Chili in Houston, Texas, have a product that, by seasoning standards, is one of the hottest on the market. They have marketed this product under the assumption that there is no difference between men and women in their preference for spicy foods. The marketing manager decided that she would test this assumption by taking two samples of 280 men and 280 women, respectively, and letting them taste Hot Mix Chili and a milder variety offered by a competitor. The people were asked to select which chili they liked better based on the seasoning. The results showed that 81 men preferred Hot Mix Chili and 74 women preferred Hot Mix Chili.
a. Determine if the sample difference of the proportion of women and men who prefer Hot Mix Chili can be properly approximated with a normal distribution.
b. Using a significance level of 0.10, what conclusions should the marketing manager reach based on these sample data?

9.66 Ralph Rogers has developed a highly successful practice as an acupuncture specialist. Ralph's success is built on his money-back guarantee. If his treatment wears off, he will treat you again. His accountant, in trying to set up an allowance for the future-visits account, hypothesizes that whether a patient will demand a retreatment is related to the price of the original treatment. The following data show the relationship between price and return treatment:

		Price		
		High	Medium	Low
Retreatment	In less than 2 years	46	53	56
	In 2–5 years	83	75	92
	None in 5 years	127	119	149

a. What should the accountant conclude regarding the hypothesis? (Use $\alpha = 0.05$.)
b. What factors that the accountant apparently has not considered might be important to the analysis?

9.67 The J. Scholten CPA firm performed a study of last year's income-tax business. In one part of the study, the accountants collected data on their clients' gross taxable incomes and the associated tax payments. These data are shown in the following table, where, for example, there are 50 clients whose gross incomes were below $10,000 and who paid $3,000 or less in taxes.

	Taxes			
Gross Income	$0-$3,000	$3,001–$5,000	$5,001–10,000	Over $10,000
$0–$10,000	50	0	0	0
$10,001–$20,000	42	30	0	0
$20,001–$40,000	40	65	33	28
Over $40,000	28	52	47	39

a. Based on these data, can Scholten conclude that its clients' gross incomes are independent of the income taxes paid? Test at $\alpha = 0.05$.
b. If the taxes paid and income earned are not independent, then based on an examination of the data, what conclusions do you reach? Discuss.

9.68 Scholten also studied the time its accountants took to complete each client's tax return and related this time to the taxes paid by the client. Scholten managers were interested in determining whether a relationship exists between these two variables or whether they could consider the two variables independent. The following data are available.

	Taxes			
No. Work Hours	$0-$3,000	$3,001–$5,000	$5,001–$10,000	Over $10,000
0–2	52	55	30	27
0–4	47	55	30	31
Over 4	35	37	55	35

Based on these data, what should the Scholten firm conclude? Use $\alpha = 0.10$.

9.69 The manager of a local engine repair service is considering mailing out a large number of discount coupons. Two types of coupons would be mailed. The first offers discounts on engine tune-ups. The second offers discounts on brake work. Before doing the mass mailing, a sample of 90 potential customers was selected to receive the tune-up coupon, and a sample of 90 potential customers received the brake-work coupon. A total of 11 engine tune-up coupons were redeemed, and 15 brake-work coupons were redeemed. The owner is interested in determining whether this sample information indicates that there will be a difference in the proportion of coupons of the two types that will be redeemed after the mass mailing is sent.

a. Based on the sample data and a significance level equal to 0.05, what conclusion should the owner reach? Conduct the hypothesis test using the *p*-value approach.

b. Discuss in terms that the shop owner can understand what Type I and Type II errors are as they relate to this situation. Also discuss the relative costs associated with each type of error. Which type of error might have been committed in this case?

9.70 U.S. automakers have been criticized in some circles for the poor quality of U.S. cars when compared with their foreign competitors. In fact, one trade publication has indicated that the percentage of U.S.-made cars having serious mechanical troubles within two years from purchase is greater than that for foreign cars after five years of ownership. If this allegation were to be substantiated, it would be a severe blow to the U.S. automakers' efforts to contradict their poor quality image. To test this claim, a random sample of 60 U.S.-car owners and another sample of 70 foreign-car owners were selected. It found that 12 owners of U.S. cars had severe mechanical problems within the first two years, and 13 foreign-car owners had severe mechanical problems within the first five years of ownership.

a. Discuss what a Type I and a Type II error would be in this situation, and provide an assessment of the relative costs of each.

b. Based on a significance level of 0.02, what conclusion should be reached? Discuss.

9.71 The makers of Bounce Back glass backboards for basketball gymnasiums have claimed that their board is more durable, on the average, than the leading backboard made by Swoosh Company. Products Testing Services of Des Moines, Iowa, was hired to verify this claim. It selected a random sample of 50 backboards of each type and subjected the boards to a pressure test to determine how much weight is needed to break each company's backboard. The following results were determined from the testing process:

Swoosh	Bounce Back
$\bar{x}_1 = 653$ lbs	$\bar{x}_2 = 691$ lbs
$s_1 = 112$ lbs	$s_2 = 105$ lbs

a. Assuming that the more pounds it takes to break the backboard, the better it is, state the appropriate null and alternative hypotheses.

b. At a significance level of 0.01, what conclusion should be reached with respect to the claim made by the Bounce Back Company? Discuss.

c. Suppose the hypothesis test were conducted at a significance level of 0.10, instead of 0.01. Would this change the conclusion reached based on the sample data? If so, discuss why; if not, discuss why not.

9.72 The Barton Family Bakery makes and sells a variety of specialty breads at its Fifth Street location. The production scheduler believes that white bread outsells wheat bread. Specifically, he believes that the average number of white loaves sold per day exceeds the average number for wheat bread. To test this, a sample of past days' sales was selected. The data are contained in the CD-ROM file called *Bakery*.

a. Based on the sample data, what conclusions should the production manager reach about the sales of white and wheat bread? Test the hypothesis using a significance level of 0.05.

b. Discuss your results in a report that uses appropriate graphs.

9.73 The Capital Bank marketing department has recently conducted a study of a sample of the bank's customers. At issue is whether there is a difference between the mean credit card balance between female and male customers. If they find that the two groups differ, they will target the lower group with a marketing campaign designed to increase their use of the credit card. The sample data for this study are in the CD-ROM file called *Capital*.

Based on the sample data, what conclusion should the Capital Bank reach about the mean balances for males and females? Test using a significance level of 0.05.

9.74 The makers of a new chemical fertilizer claim that hay yields will average 0.40 tons more per acre if its fertilizer is used than if the leading brand is used. The agricultural testing service at Oregon State University was retained to test this claim. A random sample of 52 acre-sized plots was selected, and the new fertilizer was applied. A second sample of 40 acre-sized plots was selected, and the leading fertilizer was used. The following sample data (in tons per acre) were observed:

Current Leading Brand	New Product
$n_1 = 40$	$n_2 = 52$
$\bar{x}_1 = 4.3$ tons/acre	$\bar{x}_2 = 5.2$ tons/acre
$s_1 = 0.8$ tons	$s_2 = 0.7$ tons

a. If alpha is set at 0.05, what conclusion should be reached with respect to the claim made by the makers of the new fertilizer? Discuss.

b. Determine the largest significance level at which this test could indicate the new hay yields would average more than 0.40 tons per acre more if this fertilizer were used than if the leading brand is used.

9.75 In planning for graduation, the university graduation chairperson based her seat assignments on the assumption that the proportion of undergraduates attending would exceed the proportion of graduate students attending. A member of the graduation committee suggested that before making firm plans, they should survey students to see whether the assumption of the chairperson is correct. A sample of 80 undergraduates showed that 46 planned to attend, whereas a sample of 60 graduate students showed 26 planned to attend.

a. Based on the sample data, what conclusions should the committee reach concerning the proportion of graduate and undergraduates who plan to attend the ceremony? Assume they plan to test the hypothesis using a significance level of 0.05. Discuss.

b. Suppose there are 2,000 undergraduates and 500 graduates who are eligible to graduate. Determine the number of seats that should be reserved for the graduate and undergraduate students. Explain your answer.

Advanced Applications

9.76   Refer to the data in the *Cities* file.

a. Break the variables, labor-market stress index and 1998 unemployment rate, into a different set of categories: three equal-sized intervals for the stress index and four for the unemployment rate. Conduct the test again.

b. Did the results change this time? Discuss why it is possible for the contingency analysis results to differ depending on how the categories are formed for a continuous random variable.

CASE 9-A:

Green Valley Assembly Company

The Green Valley Assembly Company assembles consumer electronics products for manufacturers that need temporary extra production capacity. As such, it has periodic product changes. Because the products Green Valley assembles are marketed under the label of well-known manufacturers, high quality is a must.

Tom Bradley of the Green Valley personnel department has been very impressed by recent research concerning job-enrichment programs. In particular, he has been impressed with the increases in quality that seem to be associated with these programs. However, some studies have shown no significant increase in quality, and they imply that the money spent on such programs has not been worthwhile.

Tom has talked to Sandra Hansen, the production manager, about instituting a job-enrichment program in the assembly operation at Green Valley. Sandra was somewhat pessimistic about the potential, but she agreed to introduce the program. The plan was to implement the program in one wing of the plant and continue with the current method in the other wing. The procedure was to be in effect for six months. After that period, a test would be made to determine the effectiveness of the job-enrichment program.

After the six-month trial period, a random sample of employees from each wing produced the following output measures:

OLD	JOB-ENRICHED
$n_1 = 50$	$n_2 = 50$
$\bar{x}_1 = 11/hr$	$\bar{x}_2 = 9.7/hr$
$s_1 = 1.2/hr$	$s_2 = 0.9/hr$

Both Sandra and Tom wonder whether the job-enrichment program has affected production output. They would like to use these sample results to determine whether the average output has changed and to determine whether the employees' consistency has been affected by the new program.

A second sample from each wing was selected. The measure was the quality of the products assembled. In the "old" wing, 79 products were tested and 12% were found to be defectively assembled. In the "job-enriched" wing, 123 products were examined and 9% were judged defectively assembled.

With all these data, Sandra and Tom are beginning to get a little confused. However, they realize that there must be some way to use the information in order to make a judgment about the effectiveness of the job-enrichment program.

CASE 9-B:

U-Need-It Rental Agency

Richard Fundt has operated the U-Need-It rental agency in a northern Wisconsin city for the past five years. One of the biggest rental items has always been chainsaws; lately, the demand for these saws has increased dramatically. Richard buys chainsaws at a special industrial rate and then rents them for $10 per day. The chainsaws are used an average of 50 to 60 days per year. Although Richard makes money on any chainsaw, he obviously makes more on those saws that last the longest.

Richard worked for a time as a repairperson and can make most repairs on the equipment he rents, including chainsaws. However, he would also like to limit the time he spends making repairs. U-Need-It is currently stocking two types of saws: North Woods and Accu-Cut. Richard has an impression that one of the models, Accu-Cut, does not seem to break down as much as the other. Richard presently has 8 North Woods saws and 11 Accu-Cut

saws. He decides to keep track of the number of hours each is used between major repairs. He finds the following values, in hours:

ACCU-CUT		NORTH WOODS	
48	46	48	78
39	88	44	94
84	29	72	59
76	52	19	52
41	57		
24			

The North Woods sales representative has stated that the company may be raising the price of its saws in the near future. This will make them slightly more expensive than the Accu-Cut models. However, the prices have tended to move with each other in the past.

CASE 9-C:

Bentford Electronics, Part 1

On Saturday morning, Jennifer Bentford received a call at her home from the production supervisor at Bentford Electronics Plant 1. The supervisor indicated that she and the supervisors from Plants 2, 3, and 4 had agreed that something must be done to improve company morale and, thereby, increase the production output of their plants. Jennifer Bentford, president of Bentford Electronics, agreed to set up a Monday morning meeting with the supervisors to see if they could arrive at a plan for accomplishing these objectives.

By Monday each supervisor had compiled a list of several ideas, including a four-day work week and interplant competitions of various kinds. A second meeting was set for Wednesday to discuss the issue further.

Following the Wednesday afternoon meeting, Jennifer Bentford and her plant supervisors agreed to implement a weekly contest called the NBE Game of the Week. The plant producing the most each week would be considered the NBE Game of the Week winner and would receive 10 points. The second-place plant would receive 7 points, and the third- and fourth-place plants would receive 3 points and 1 point, respectively. The contest would last 26 weeks. At the end of that period, a $200,000 bonus would be divided among the employees in the four plants proportional to the total points accumulated by each plant.

The announcement of the contest created a lot of excitement and enthusiasm at the four plants. No one complained about the rules because the four plants were designed and staffed to produce equally.

At the close of the contest, Jennifer Bentford called the supervisors into a meeting, at which time she asked for data to determine whether the contest had significantly improved productivity. She indicated that she had to know this before she could authorize a second contest. The supervisors, expecting this response, had put together the following data:

UNITS PRODUCED (4 PLANTS COMBINED)	BEFORE-CONTEST FREQUENCY	DURING-CONTEST FREQUENCY
0–2,500	11	0
2,501–8,000	23	20
8,001–15,000	56	83
15,001–20,000	15	52
	105 days	155 days

Jennifer examined the data and indicated that it looked like the contest was a success, but she wanted to base her decision to continue the contest on more than just an observation of the data. "Surely there must be some way to statistically test the worthiness of this contest," Jennifer stated. "I have to see the results before I will authorize the second contest."

General References

1. Berenson, Mark L., and David M. Levine, *Basic Business Statistics Concepts and Applications*, 7th ed. (Upper Saddle River, NJ: Prentice Hall, 1999).
2. Cryer, Jonathan D., and Robert B. Miller, *Statistics for Business: Data Analysis and Modeling*, 2nd ed. (Belmont, CA: Duxbury Press, 1994).
3. Johnson, Richard A. and Dean W. Wichern, *Business Statistics: Decision Making with Data* (New York: John Wiley & Sons, 1997).
4. Larsen, Richard J., Morris L. Marx, and Bruce Cooil, *Statistics for Applied Problem Solving and Decision Making* (Pacific Grove, CA: Duxbury Press, 1997).
5. *Microsoft Excel 2000* (Redmond, WA: Microsoft Corp., 1999).
6. *Minitab for Windows Version 14* (State College, PA: Minitab, 2003).
7. Siegel, Andrew F., *Practical Business Statistics*, 4th ed. (Burr Ridge, IL: Irwin, 2000).

CHAPTER 10

Hypothesis Tests for One and Two Population Variances

CHAPTER OUTCOMES

After studying the material in Chapter 10, you should be able to:

- Formulate and carry out hypothesis tests for a single population variance.
- Formulate and carry out hypothesis tests for the difference between two population variances.

WHY YOU NEED TO KNOW

Chapters 8 and 9 introduced the concepts of hypothesis testing for one and two population means and proportions. There are also business situations where decision makers must reach a conclusion about the value of a single population variance, or about the relationship between two population variances. For example, knowing that a machine fills soda bottles with a specific average fill rate may not be enough. The manager must also be concerned about the variability in the fill rate. If the machine is too variable, then some bottles may be underfilled and will cause problems with consumers who believe they have been cheated. If the machine overfills the bottles, then soda is wasted and unnecessary costs are incurred in the bottling process. The manager in this case must monitor both the average fill and the variation in the fill of the bottling process. A manager may also be required to decide if there is a difference in the variability of sales between two different sales territories, or if the output of one production process is more or less variable than another. Just as we have tools and techniques for tests involving population means and proportions, we also have tools and techniques for testing a single population variance and two population variances. In this chapter we discuss methods that can be used to make inferences concerning one and two population variances. The techniques presented in this chapter will also introduce new distributions that will be used in later chapters of the textbook. When reading this chapter keep in mind that the techniques discussed here are extensions of the hypothesis testing concepts introduced in Chapters 8 and 9.

10-1 HYPOTHESES TESTS FOR A SINGLE POPULATION VARIANCE

In the previous two chapters, we concentrated on examples involving population means or proportions. However, in many cases you will be as interested in the spread of a population as in its central location. For instance, military planes designed to penetrate enemy defenses have a ground-following radar system. The radar tells the pilot exactly how far the plane is above the ground. A radar unit that is correct *on the average* is useless if the readings are distributed widely around the average value. Many airport shuttle systems have stopping sensors to deposit passengers at the correct spot in a terminal. A sensor that, *on the average*, lets passengers off at the correct point could leave many irritated people long distances up and down the track. Therefore, many product specifications involve both an average value and some limit on the dispersion that the individual values can have. For example, the specification for a steel push pin may be an average length of 1.78 inches plus or minus 0.01 inch. A company using these pins would be interested in both the average length and how much these pins vary in length.

Usually when we think of measuring variation, the standard deviation is used as the measure because it is measured in the same units as the mean. Ideally, in the ground-following radar example, we would want to test to see whether the standard deviation exceeds a certain level, as determined by the product specifications. Unfortunately, there is no statistical test that directly tests the standard deviation. However, there is a test called the chi-square test that can be used to test the population variance. We can convert any standard deviation application into one involving the variance, as shown in the following example.

CHI-SQUARE TEST FOR A ONE POPULATION VARIANCE

H & L Machines—H & L Machines services copy machines. Looking at past records and manufacturer recommendations, the company determined the mean service time for a properly trained staff working on a Kodak Image Source 85 should be 2 hours, with a standard deviation not to exceed 0.5 hour. Past data indicate that the 2-hour average is being achieved. However, variability may be excessive. The service schedule is built around the assumptions of $\mu = 2$ hours and $\sigma = 0.5$ hour. If the service-time standard deviation exceeds 0.5 hour, the service schedule gets disrupted.

The service manager has decided to select a sample of service calls and use the sample data to determine whether the service-time standard deviation exceeds 0.5 hour. The methodology for conducting such a test is generally the same as for testing a population mean or proportion.

Ideally, the manager would like to test the following null and alternative hypotheses.

$$H_0: \sigma \le 0.5$$
$$H_A: \sigma > 0.5$$

Because there is no statistical technique for directly testing hypotheses about a population standard deviation, she will use a test for a population variance. We first convert the standard deviation to a variance by squaring the standard deviation, and then restate the null and alternative hypotheses as follows:

$$H_0: \sigma^2 \le 0.25$$
$$H_A: \sigma^2 > 0.25$$

As with all hypothesis tests, the decision to reject or accept the null hypothesis will be based on the value computed from the sample. In testing hypotheses about a single population variance, the appropriate sample value is s^2, the *sample variance*.

To test a null hypothesis about a population variance, we compare s^2 with the hypothesized population variance, σ^2. To do this, we need to standardize the distribution of the sample variance in much the same way as we used the z-distribution and the t-distribution when testing hypotheses about the population mean.

 **SSUMPTION**

If the random sample is from a normally distributed population, the distribution for the standardized sample variance is a *chi-square distribution*.

The chi-square distribution is a continuous distribution of a standardized random variable, computed by using Equation 10-1.

Chi-Square Test for a Single Population Variance

$$\chi^2 = \frac{(n-1)s^2}{\sigma^2}$$

10-1

where:

χ^2 = Standardized chi-square variable
n = Sample size
s^2 = Sample variance
σ^2 = Hypothesized variance

Examining Equation 10-1, you will note that this test statistic can be rewritten as

$$\chi^2 = \frac{(n-1)s^2}{\sigma^2} = \frac{(n-1)\dfrac{\Sigma(x-\bar{x})^2}{n-1}}{\sigma^2} = \frac{\Sigma(x-\bar{x})^2}{\sigma^2} = \Sigma\left(\frac{x-\bar{x}}{\sigma}\right)^2$$

If the sample is obtained from a normal distribution, the last expression inside the parentheses is essentially a z-value. Recall that $z = \dfrac{x-\mu}{\sigma}$. Therefore, χ^2 is the sum of squared z-values. When a z-value from a normal distribution is squared, it produces a chi-squared variable with one degree of freedom. The sum of n independent chi-squared variables is also a chi-squared random variable with n degrees of freedom. Here, however, we must estimate the population mean using the sample mean (because μ is unknown) before we estimate the population variance using s^2. You may recall from the discussion concerning degrees of freedom in Chapter 7 that this reduces the degrees of freedom by one. Therefore, the distribution of χ^2 is a chi-squared distribution with $n-1$ degrees of freedom.

The central location and shape of the chi-square distribution depends only on the degrees of freedom, $n-1$. Figure 10-1 illustrates chi-square distributions for various degrees of freedom. Note that as the degrees of freedom increase, the chi-square distribution becomes more symmetrical.

Returning to the H & L Machines example, suppose the dispatch manager took a sample of 20 service calls and found a variance of 0.33 hours squared. Figure 10-2 illustrates the hypothesis test at a significance level of 0.10.

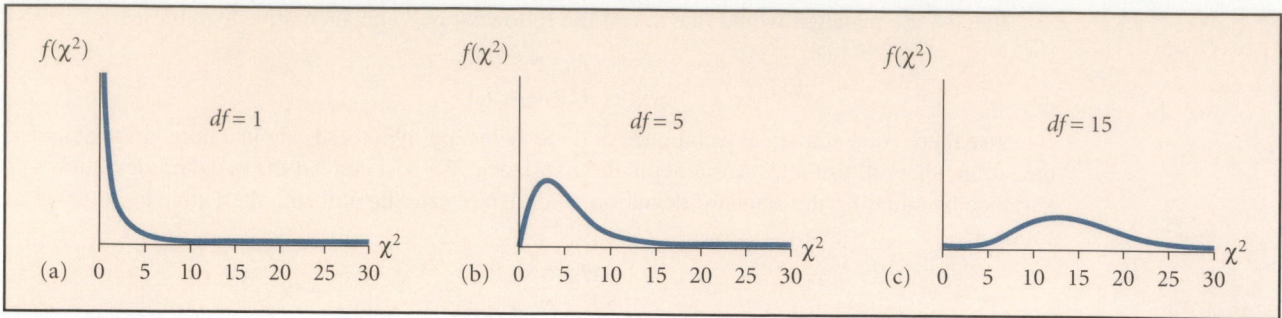

FIGURE 10-1

Chi-Square Distributions

Appendix G contains a table of chi-square values for various probabilities and degrees of freedom. The use of the chi-square table is similar to the use of the t-distribution table. For example, to find the critical value, χ_α^2, for the H & L Machines example, determine the

degrees of freedom, $n - 1 = 20 - 1 = 19$, and
the desired significance level, 0.10.

Now go to the chi-square table under the column headed 0.10 and find the χ^2 value in this column that intersects the row corresponding to the appropriate degrees of freedom. You should find the critical value of $\chi_\alpha^2 = 27.204$.

As you can see in Figure 10-2, the chi-square test statistic, calculated using Equation 10-1, is

$$\chi^2 = 25.08.$$

This falls to the left of the rejection region, meaning the manager should not reject the null hypothesis based on these sample data. Thus, based on these results, there is insufficient evidence to conclude that the service representatives should complete their service calls with a standard deviation of more than 0.5 hours.

FIGURE 10-2

Chi-square Test for One
Population Variance for the
H & L Machines Example

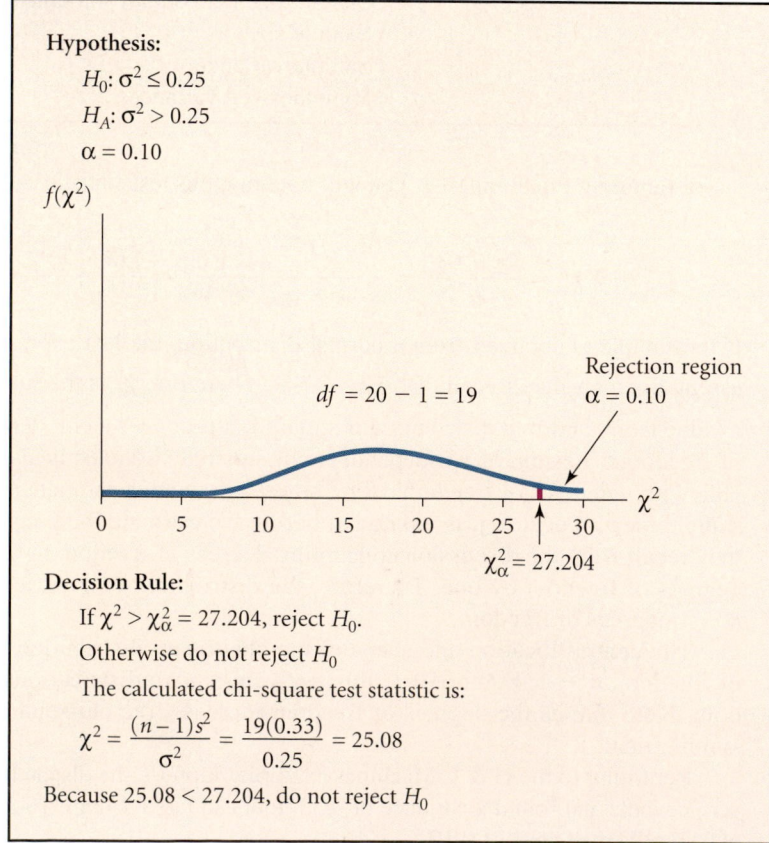

Hypothesis:

$H_0: \sigma^2 \le 0.25$
$H_A: \sigma^2 > 0.25$
$\alpha = 0.10$

$f(\chi^2)$

$df = 20 - 1 = 19$

Rejection region
$\alpha = 0.10$

$\chi_\alpha^2 = 27.204$

Decision Rule:

If $\chi^2 > \chi_\alpha^2 = 27.204$, reject H_0.

Otherwise do not reject H_0

The calculated chi-square test statistic is:

$$\chi^2 = \frac{(n-1)s^2}{\sigma^2} = \frac{19(0.33)}{0.25} = 25.08$$

Because $25.08 < 27.204$, do not reject H_0

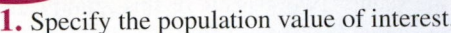

SUMMARY: HYPOTHESES TESTS FOR A POPULATION VARIANCE

1. Specify the population value of interest.

2. Formulate the null and alternative hypotheses in terms of σ^2, the population variance.

3. Specify the level of significance for the hypothesis test.

4. Construct the rejection region.

Obtain the critical value, χ_α^2, from the chi-square distribution table.

5. Compute the test statistic.
Select a random sample and compute the sample variance,

$$s^2 = \frac{\sum(x - \bar{x})^2}{n - 1}$$

Based on the sample variance, $\chi^2 = \frac{(n-1)s^2}{\sigma^2}$

6. Reach a decision.

7. Draw a conclusion.

EXAMPLE 10-1: HYPOTHESES TESTS FOR A POPULATION VARIANCE

Abo Manufacturing Company   One specification listed in the contract between the Abo Manufacturing Company and its customers concerns the variability in the diameter of the part being supplied. Before shipping a batch of parts, Abo employees take a random sample of 20 parts from the batch and test to see whether the standard deviation exceeds the 0.05-inch specification. This can be done using the following steps.

Step 1: **Specify the population value of interest.**
The variability in the diameter of a part is the value of interest.

Step 2: **Specify the null and alternative hypotheses.**
The null and alternative hypotheses must be stated in terms of the population variance, so we convert the specification, $\sigma = 0.05$, to the variance, $\sigma^2 = 0.0025$. The null and alternative hypotheses are

$$H_0: \sigma^2 \leq 0.0025$$
$$H_A: \sigma^2 > 0.0025$$

Step 3: **Specify the significance level.**
The hypothesis test will be conducted using $\alpha = 0.05$.

Step 4: **Construct the rejection region.**
The critical value from the chi-square distribution with $20 - 1 = 19$ degrees of freedom and 0.05 level of significance is

$$\chi_\alpha^2 = \chi_{0.05}^2 = 30.1435$$

The decision rule is stated as:

If $\chi^2 > \chi_{0.05}^2 = 30.1435$, reject H_0; otherwise, do not reject.

Step 5: **Compute the test statistic.**
The random sample of $n = 20$ parts gives a sample variance for part diameter of

$$s^2 = \frac{\sum(x - \bar{x})^2}{n - 1} = 0.0108.$$

The test statistic is

$$\chi^2 = \frac{(n-1)s^2}{\sigma^2} = \frac{(20-1)0.0108}{0.0025} = 82.08$$

Step 6: **Reach a decision.**
Because $\chi^2 = 82.08 > 30.1435$, reject the null hypothesis.

Step 7: **Draw a conclusion.**
Conclude that the variance of the population does exceed the 0.0025 limit. The company appears to have a problem with its product variation.

10-1: EXERCISES

Skill Development

10.1 Find the critical value of the chi-square distribution for each of the following situations:
a. H_A: $\sigma^2 > 0.25$, $n = 10$, $\alpha = 0.05$
b. H_A: $\sigma^2 > 20$, $n = 20$, $\alpha = 0.025$
c. H_A: $\sigma^2 \neq 0.25$, $n = 10$, $\alpha = 0.10$

10.2 Determine the p-value for each of the following situations:
a. H_A: $\sigma^2 > 0.25$, $n = 10$,
and test statistic $\chi^2 = 16.919$
b. H_A: $\sigma^2 > 13$, $n = 21$,
and test statistic $\chi^2 = 35.0196$
c. H_A: $\sigma^2 \neq 7.80$, $n = 23$,
and test statistic $\chi^2 = 35.1725$

10.3 Given the following null and alternative hypotheses,

$$H_0: \sigma^2 \leq 12$$
$$H_A: \sigma^2 > 12$$

a. Test if $n = 13$, $s = 4.5$, and $\alpha = 0.10$. Be sure to show the decision rule.
b. Test if $n = 30$, $s^2 = 21$, and $\alpha = 0.05$. Show the decision rule.

10.4 Given the following null and alternative hypotheses,

$$H_0: \sigma^2 \leq 40$$
$$H_A: \sigma^2 > 40$$

a. Test if $n = 10$, $s = 7$, and $\alpha = 0.05$. Be sure to show the decision rule.
b. Test if $n = 30$, $s^2 = 54$, and $\alpha = 0.10$. Show the decision rule.

10.5 Given the following null and alternative hypotheses,

$$H_0: \sigma^2 \leq 300$$
$$H_A: \sigma^2 > 300$$

a. Test if $n = 20$, $s = 20$, and $\alpha = 0.05$. Be sure to show the decision rule.
b. Test if $n = 15$, $s^2 = 367$, and $\alpha = 0.10$. Show the decision rule.

Business Applications

10.6 TranCo operates the city bus service for a large southern city. One of the keys to satisfying bus riders is that the buses run on schedule. One important part of this requires that the variation in travel time for the bus route be controlled. Suppose on one particular bus route, the company wants the standard deviation in travel time to be no greater than 2 minutes. To test this, a random sample of 15 trips is selected.
a. State the appropriate null and alternative hypotheses. (Remember, there is not a test procedure for testing the standard deviations directly.)
b. Assuming that the company wishes to test the null hypothesis in part a using a significance level equal to 0.05, what conclusion should be reached if the sample standard deviation is 2.86 minutes? Discuss your result.

10.7 One dimension of quality for a city fire department is the time it takes from when a call for help arrives until a crew is on the scene. Two aspects of this quality measure are important: the mean time to arrival and the variance of time to arrival. Suppose the fire chief wishes the variance for response time to be no greater than 2,025 seconds squared.
a. State the appropriate null and alternative hypotheses.
b. Assume that a simple random sample of 20 calls results in a sample variance of 3,000 seconds squared. Based on this sample value and a significance level equal to 0.10, what should the chief conclude? Discuss.

10.8 The Hagluud Corporation manufactures paint and stain products for interior and exterior home and commercial applications. The new "Apple Wood Stain" product is thought to be a real improvement over some of the company's previous products. One criterion of a quality stain is the consistency of coverage per gallon. Hagluud hopes the standard deviation of the new stain will not exceed 20 square feet per gallon. The company R&D Department will assume the standard deviation does not exceed 20 square feet unless the data strongly suggest otherwise. To test this, they selected a random sample of 12 gallons and found the following coverage in square feet:

245	302	240	280	255	300	290	240	300	270	230	300

Perform a hypothesis test to determine if the consistency of coverage for the stain is as desired by Hagluud's R&D Department. Write one paragraph for the manager stating your conclusions concerning the stain's coverage consistency.

10.9 Airlines face the challenging task of keeping their planes on schedule. One key measure is the number of minutes a plane deviates from the targeted arrival time. Ideally, the measure for each arrival will be zero minutes, indicating that the plane arrived exactly on time. However, experience indicates that even under the best of circumstances there will be inherent variability. Suppose one major airline has set standards that require its planes to arrive, on average, on time, with a standard deviation not to exceed 2 minutes. To determine whether these standards are being met, each month the airline selects a random sample of 12 airplane arrivals and determines the number of minutes early or late each flight is. For last month, the times, rounded to the nearest minute, are

3	−7	4	2	−2	5	11	−3	4	6	−4	1

a. State the appropriate null and alternative hypotheses for testing the standard regarding the mean value. Test the hypothesis using a significance level equal to 0.05. What assumption will be required?
b. State the appropriate null and alternative hypotheses regarding the standard deviation. Use the sample data to conduct the hypothesis test with $\alpha = 0.05$.
c. Discuss the results of both tests. What should the airline conclude regarding its arrival standards? What factors could influence the arrival times of flights?

10.10 A software design firm has recently developed a prototype educational computer game for children. One of the important factors in the success of a game such as this is the time it takes a child to play the game. Two factors are important: the mean time it takes to play and the variability in time required from child to child. Experience indicates that the mean time should be 10 minutes or less, and the standard deviation should not exceed 4 minutes. The company decided to test this prototype with 10 children selected at random from the local school district. The following values represent the time (rounded to the nearest minute) each child spent completing the game.

9	14	11	8	13	15	11	10	7	12

a. The software developers will assume the mean time to completion of the game is 10 minutes or less unless the data strongly suggest otherwise. State the appropriate null and alternative hypotheses for testing the requirement regarding the mean value.
b. Referring to part a, test the hypothesis using a significance level equal to 0.10. What assumption will be required?
c. The software developers will assume the standard deviation of the time to completion of the game does not exceed 4 minutes unless the data strongly suggest otherwise. State the appropriate null and alternative hypotheses regarding the standard deviation. Use the sample data to conduct the hypothesis test with a significance level = 0.10.

Advanced Business Applications

10.11 The Fillmore Institute has established a service designed to help charities increase the amount of money they collect from their direct mail solicitations. Its consulting is aimed at increasing the mean dollar amount returned from each giver and also at reducing the variation in amount contributed from giver to giver. The Badke Foundation collects money for heart disease research. Over the past eight years, records show that the average contribution per returned envelope is $14.25, with a standard deviation of $6.44. Badke Foundation directors decided to try the Fillmore services on a test basis. They used the recommended letters and other request materials and sent out 1,000 requests. From these, 166 were returned. The data showing the dollars returned per giver are in the CD-ROM file *Badke*.

Based on the sample data, what conclusions should the Badke Foundation reach regarding the Fillmore consulting services? Use appropriate hypothesis tests with a significance level = 0.05 to reach your conclusions. (Hint: Use Excel's ChiInv function or Minitab's Calc > Probability Distributions command to obtain the critical value for the chi-square distribution.)

10-2 HYPOTHESIS TESTS FOR TWO POPULATION VARIANCES

F-TEST FOR TWO POPULATION VARIANCES

The previous section introduced a method for testing hypotheses involving a single population standard deviation. Recall that in order to conduct the test, we had to first convert the standard deviation to the variance. Then we used the chi-square distribution to determine whether the sample variance led us to reject the null hypothesis. However, decision makers are often faced with decision problems involving two population standard deviations. Although there is no hypothesis test that directly tests standard deviations, there is a procedure that can be used to test whether two populations have equal variances. We can formulate null and alternative hypotheses of the following forms. Note, the two different forms are equivalent and may be used interchangeably, depending on your preference.

Two-Tailed Test	Upper One-Tailed Test	Lower One-Tailed Test
Format 1		
$H_0:\ \sigma_1^2 - \sigma_2^2 = 0$ $H_A:\ \sigma_1^2 - \sigma_2^2 \neq 0$	$H_0:\ \sigma_1^2 - \sigma_2^2 \leq 0$ $H_A:\ \sigma_1^2 - \sigma_2^2 > 0$	$H_0:\ \sigma_1^2 - \sigma_2^2 \geq 0$ $H_A:\ \sigma_1^2 - \sigma_2^2 < 0$
Format 2		
$H_0:\ \sigma_1^2 = \sigma_2^2$ $H_A:\ \sigma_1^2 \neq \sigma_2^2$	$H_0:\ \sigma_1^2 \leq \sigma_2^2$ $H_A:\ \sigma_1^2 > \sigma_2^2$	$H_0:\ \sigma_1^2 \geq \sigma_2^2$ $H_A:\ \sigma_1^2 < \sigma_2^2$

In order to test a hypothesis involving two population variances, we first compute the sample variances. We then compute the test statistic shown as Equation 10-2.

F Test Statistic for Testing Whether Two Populations Have Equal Variances

$$F = \frac{s_i^2}{s_j^2} \quad (df: D_1 = n_i - 1 \quad \text{and} \quad D_2 = n_j - 1)$$

10-2

where:

n_i = Sample size from ith population

n_j = Sample size from jth population

s_i^2 = Sample variation from the ith population

s_j^2 = Sample variation from the jth population

Analyzing this test statistic requires that we introduce the *F*-distribution. Although it is beyond the scope of this book, statistical theory shows the *F*-distribution is equal to the ratio of two independent chi-square distributions. Like the chi-square and the *t*-distributions, the appropriate *F*-distribution is determined by its degrees of freedom. However, the *F*-distribution has two degrees of freedom, D_1 and D_2, that depend on the sample sizes for the variances in the numerator and denominator, respectively, in Equation 10-2.

In order to apply the *F*-distribution to test whether two population variances are equal, the following assumptions must be made:

SSUMPTIONS

- The populations are normally distributed.
- The sample variances are independent.

Independent sample variances will occur when the sample data are obtained in such a way that the values in one sample are in no way influenced by the values in the second sample.

Independent Samples

Samples selected from two or more populations in such a way that the occurrence of values in one sample has no influence on the probability of the occurrence of values in the other sample(s).

The test statistic shown in Equation 10-2 is formed as the ratio of two sample variances. There are two key points to remember when formulating this ratio.

1. For a two-tailed test, always place the larger sample variance in the numerator. This will make the calculated *F*-value greater than 1.0 and push the *F*-value toward the upper tail of the *F*-distribution.
2. For the one-tailed test, look to the alternative hypothesis. For the population that is *predicted* (based on the alternative hypothesis) to have the larger variance, place that sample variance in the numerator.

The following applications and examples will illustrate the specific methods used for testing for a difference between two population variances.

E. Coli Bacteria Testing—Recent years have seen several national scares involving contaminated meat carrying *E. coli* bacteria. The recommended preventative measure is to cook the meat at a required temperature. However, different meat patties cooked for the same amount of time will have different final internal temperatures because of variations in the patties and variations in burner temperatures. A regional fast-food chain will replace its current burners with one of two new digitally controlled models.

The chain's purchasing agents have arranged to sample 11 batches of meat cooked by burner model 1 and 13 batches of meat cooked by burner model 2 to learn if there is a difference in temperature variation between the two models. If a difference exists, the chain's managers have decided to select the model that provides the smaller variation in final internal meat temperature. Ideally, they would like a test that compares standard deviations, but no such test exists. Instead they must convert the standard deviations to variances. The hypotheses are

Hypotheses:

$$H_0: \sigma_1^2 = \sigma_2^2$$
$$H_A: \sigma_1^2 \neq \sigma_2^2$$

The null and alternative hypotheses are formulated as a two-tailed test. Intuitively, you might reason that if the two population variances are actually equal, the sample variances should be approximately equal also. That would mean that the ratio of the two sample variances should be approximately one. We will reject the null hypothesis if one sample variance is significantly larger than the other and if the ratio of sample variances is significantly greater than one. The managers will use a significance level of $\alpha = 0.10$.

The next step is to collect the sample data. Figure 10-3 shows the sample data and the box and whisker diagram. The assumption of independence is met because the two burners were used to cook different meat patties and the temperature measures are not related. The box and whiskers diagrams provide no evidence to suggest that the distributions are highly skewed, so the assumption that populations are normally distributed seems reasonable.

The sample variances are computed using Equation 10-3.

Sample Variance

$$s^2 = \frac{\Sigma(x - \bar{x})^2}{n - 1}$$

10-3

where:

$$\bar{x} = \frac{\Sigma x}{n} = \text{Sample mean}$$

$$n = \text{Sample size}$$

Based on the sample data shown in Figure 10-3, the sample variances are:

$$s_1^2 = 6.7 \quad \text{and} \quad s_2^2 = 2.5.$$

The null hypothesis is that the two population variances are equal, making this a two-tailed test. Thus, we form the test statistic using Equation 10-3 by placing the larger sample variance in the numerator. Thus, the calculated F-value is

$$F = \frac{s_1^2}{s_2^2} = \frac{6.7}{2.5} = 2.68$$

If the calculated F-value exceeds the critical value, then the null hypothesis is rejected. The critical F-value is determined by locating the appropriate F-distribution table for the desired alpha level and the correct degrees of freedom. This requires the following thought process:

1. If the test is two-tailed, use the table corresponding to $\alpha/2$. For example, if $\alpha = 0.10$ for a two-tailed test, the appropriate F table is the one with the upper tail equal to 0.05.

FIGURE 10-3

E. Coli **Bacteria Testing**

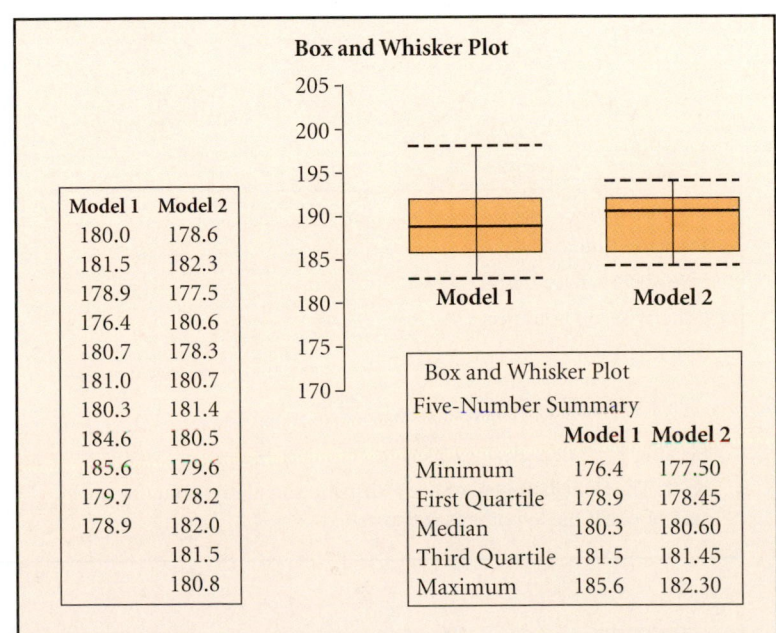

Model 1	Model 2
180.0	178.6
181.5	182.3
178.9	177.5
176.4	180.6
180.7	178.3
181.0	180.7
180.3	181.4
184.6	180.5
185.6	179.6
179.7	178.2
178.9	182.0
	181.5
	180.8

Box and Whisker Plot

Box and Whisker Plot
Five-Number Summary

	Model 1	Model 2
Minimum	176.4	177.50
First Quartile	178.9	178.45
Median	180.3	180.60
Third Quartile	181.5	181.45
Maximum	185.6	182.30

2. If the test is one-tailed, use the F table corresponding to the significance level. If $\alpha = 0.05$ for a one-tailed test, use the table with the upper-tail area equal to 0.05.

In this example, the test is two-tailed and α is 0.10. Thus, we go to the F-distribution table in Appendix H for the upper-tail area equal to 0.05.

The next step is to determine the appropriate degrees of freedom. In Chapter 7, we showed that the degrees of freedom of any test statistic are equal to the number of independent data values available to estimate the population variance. We lose one degree of freedom for each parameter we are required to estimate. For both the numerator and denominator in Equation 10-2, we must estimate the population mean using $\bar{x}$ before we calculate s^2. In each case, we lose one degree of freedom. Therefore, we have two distinct degrees of freedom, D_1 and D_2, where D_1 is equal to the sample size for the variance in the numerator of the F test statistic minus one $(n_1 - 1)$ and D_2 is equal to the sample size for the variance in the denominator minus one $(n_2 - 1)$. Recall that for a two-tailed test, the larger sample variance is placed in the numerator. In this example, burner 1 has the larger sample variance, so model 1 is placed in the numerator with a sample size of 11 so $D_1 = 11 - 1 = 10$ and $D_2 = 13 - 1 = 12$.

Locate the page of the F table corresponding to the desired upper-tail area. In this text we have three options (0.05, 0.025, and 0.01). The F table is arranged in columns and rows. The columns correspond to the D_1 degrees of freedom, and the rows correspond to the D_2 degrees of freedom. For this example, the critical F-value at the intersection of $D_1 = 10$ and $D_2 = 12$ degrees of freedom is 2.753. If you prefer you can use Excel's **FINV** function or Minitab's **Calc > Probability Distributions** command to determine the critical F-value.[1]

Figure 10-4 summarizes the hypothesis test. Note that the decision rule is

If the calculated $F > 2.753$, reject H_0;

Otherwise, do not reject H_0.

Because the F-value $= 2.68 < 2.753$, the conclusion is that the null hypothesis is not rejected based on these sample data; that is, we cannot conclude that there is a difference in the population variances.

FIGURE 10-4

F-Test for the *E. Coli* Example

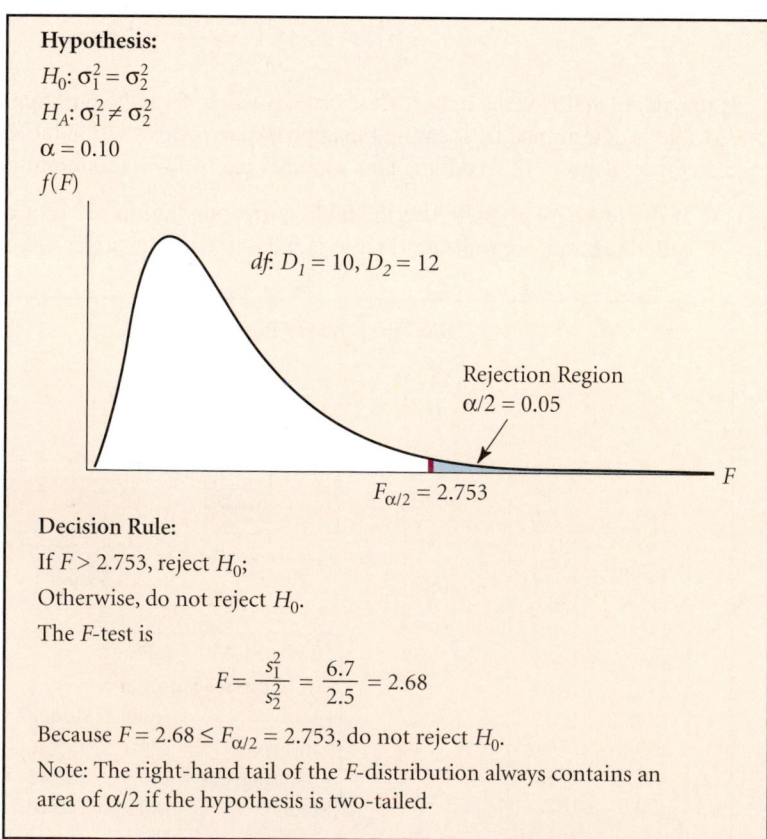

Hypothesis:

$H_0: \sigma_1^2 = \sigma_2^2$

$H_A: \sigma_1^2 \neq \sigma_2^2$

$\alpha = 0.10$

$f(F)$

df: $D_1 = 10$, $D_2 = 12$

Rejection Region
$\alpha/2 = 0.05$

$F_{\alpha/2} = 2.753$

Decision Rule:

If $F > 2.753$, reject H_0;

Otherwise, do not reject H_0.

The F-test is

$$F = \frac{s_1^2}{s_2^2} = \frac{6.7}{2.5} = 2.68$$

Because $F = 2.68 \leq F_{\alpha/2} = 2.753$, do not reject H_0.

Note: The right-hand tail of the F-distribution always contains an area of $\alpha/2$ if the hypothesis is two-tailed.

---

[1]The FINV function is = FINV(.05,10,12) = 2.753.

EXAMPLE 10-2: TWO-TAILED TEST FOR TWO POPULATION VARIANCES

Airport Security   Since the September 11 tragedy in New York City, airport security has been tightened substantially around the world. The federal government has taken over the management of airport security in U.S. airports, and private security companies have been replaced by federal employees. Suppose that the security manager at O'Hare airport in Chicago is concerned about the waiting time for passengers required to pass through security checks before being admitted to the departure gates. Of particular interest is whether there is a difference in the variability of waiting time at concourses A and B. The following steps can be used to test to determine whether there is a difference in population variances.

Step 1:   **Specify the population value of interest.**

The population value of interest is the variation in waiting times at the two concourses.

Step 2:   **Formulate the appropriate null and alternative hypotheses.**

Because we are interested in determining if a difference exists in variances and because neither concourse is predicted to have a higher variance, the test will be two-tailed, and the hypotheses are established as:

$$H_0: \sigma_A^2 = \sigma_B^2$$
$$H_A: \sigma_A^2 \neq \sigma_B^2$$

Step 3:   **Specify the level of significance.**

The test will be conducted using an alpha = 0.02 level.

Step 4:   **Construct the rejection region.**

Select simple random samples from each population of interest, determine whether the assumptions have been satisfied, and compute the test statistic.

Random samples of 25 passengers from Concourse A and 31 passengers from Concourse B were selected and the waiting time for each passenger was recorded. There is no connection between the two samples, so the assumption of independence is satisfied. The stem and leaf diagrams do not dispute the assumption of normality.

Stem and Leaf Display for Concourse A Stem unit: 1		Stem and Leaf Display for Concourse B Stem unit: 1
Statistics	8| 9	**Statistics**
Sample Size 25	9| 0	Sample Size 31
Mean 14.58191	10| 2 3 7 9	Mean 16.24597
Median 14.15696	11| 9	Median 15.77023
Std. Deviation 3.765897	12| 2 4	Std. Deviation 4.785841
Minimum 8.889582	13| 2	Minimum 4.70353
Maximum 22.16486	14| 0 0 2 2	Maximum 24.37963

Concourse A stem and leaf (continued):
```
 8| 9
 9| 0
10| 2 3 7 9
11| 9
12| 2 4
13| 2
14| 0 0 2 2
15| 5 6 9
16| 2
17| 0 4
18| 2 4
19|
20| 8
21| 5
22| 2
```

Concourse B stem and leaf:
```
 4| 7
 5|
 6| 3
 7|
 8|
 9|
10| 8
11| 1 4 7
12| 2 4
13|
14| 2 2 2 8
15| 1 3 7 8
16|
17| 0 5
18| 3 6
19| 0 1 3 3
20| 4
21| 8 8
22| 1 4 9
23|
24| 4
```

To determine the critical value from the F-distribution, we can use either Excel's FINV function, Minitab's **Calc > Probability Distributions** command, or the F table in Appendix H. The degrees of freedom are D_1 = numerator sample size − 1, and D_2 = denominator sample size − 1. As shown in the statistics section of the stem and leaf display, Concourse B has the larger standard deviation, thus we get:

$$D_1 = n_B - 1 = 31 - 1 = 30 \quad \text{and} \quad D_2 = n_A - 1 = 25 - 1 = 24$$

Then for $\alpha/2 = 0.01$, we get a critical $F = 2.577$. The null hypothesis is rejected if $F > F_{\alpha/2} = 2.577$. Otherwise, do not reject the null hypothesis.

Step 5: **Compute the test statistic.**

The test statistic is formed by the ratio of the two sample variances. Because this is a two-tailed test, the large sample variance is placed in the numerator.

$$F = \frac{4.786^2}{3.766^2} = 1.615$$

Step 6: **Reach a decision.**

Compare the test statistic to the critical value and reach a conclusion with respect to the null hypothesis.

Because $F = 1.615 < F_{\alpha/2} = 2.577$, do not reject the null hypothesis.

Step 7: **Draw a conclusion.**

There is no reason to conclude that there is a difference in the variability of waiting time at concourses A and B.

Excel and Minitab Tutorial

Bank ATM Machines—One-tailed tests on two population variances are performed much like two-tailed tests. Consider the systems development group for a midwestern bank, which has developed a new software algorithm for its ATM machines. Although reducing average transaction time is an objective, the systems programmers also want to reduce the variability in transaction speed. They believe the standard deviation for transaction time will be less with the new software (population 2) than it was with the old algorithm (population 1). For their analysis, the programmers have performed 7 test runs using the original software and 11 test runs using the new system. Although the managers want to determine the standard deviation of transaction time, they must perform the test as a test of variances because no method exists for testing standard deviations directly. Thus, the null and alternative hypotheses are

$$H_0: \ \sigma_1^2 \leq \sigma_2^2 \quad \text{or} \quad \sigma_1^2 - \sigma_2^2 \leq 0$$
$$H_A: \ \sigma_1^2 > \sigma_2^2 \quad \text{or} \quad \sigma_1^2 - \sigma_2^2 > 0$$

The hypothesis is to be tested using a significance level of $\alpha = 0.01$.

In order to use the F-test to test whether these sample variances come from populations with equal variances, we need to make sure that the sample variances are independent and the populations are approximately normally distributed. Because the test runs using the two algorithms were unique, the variances are independent. The following box and whisker plots give no reason to indicate that, based on these small samples, the populations are not approximately normal.

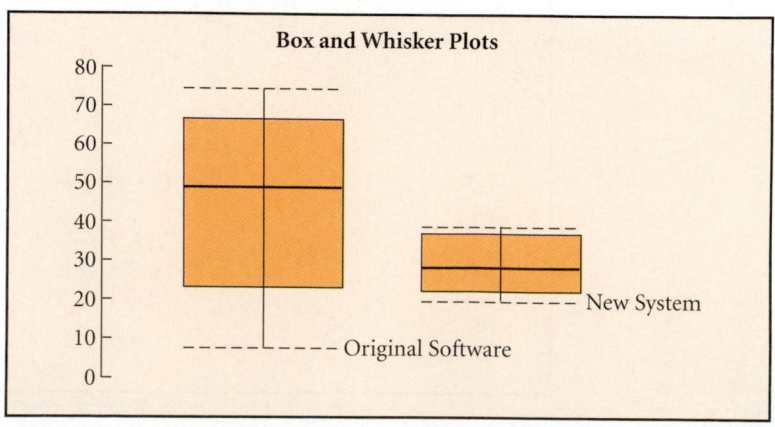

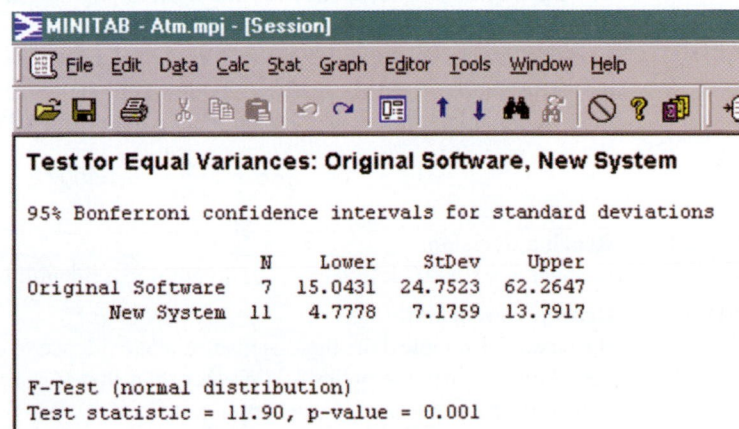

Microsoft Excel - ATM.xls

File Edit View Insert Format Tools Data PHStat Window Help

Arial   10   B U

E13   =

	A	B	C	D	E	F
1	Original Software	New System		F-Test Two-Sample for Variances		
2	38.9	22.8				
3	23.2	20			Original Software	New System
4	49.2	26.5		Mean	46.55714286	29.8
5	66.8	37.9		Variance	612.6761905	51.494
6	65.5	27.2		Observations	7	11
7	74.6	39.6		df	6	10
8	7.7	34.1		F	11.89801123	
9		39.4		P(F<=f) one-tail	0.000473972	
10		20.9		F Critical one-tail	5.38580025	
11		30.3				
12		29.1				

> Because the calculated $F = 11.898 > F_{.01} = 5.39$, we reject the null hypothesis and conclude that the variance for population 1 exceeds the population 2 variance.

Figure 10-5a and Figure 10-5b illustrate the one-tailed hypothesis test for this situation using a significance level of 0.01. Recall that in a two-tailed test, placing the largest sample variance in the numerator and the smallest variance in the denominator forms the *F*-ratio. In a one-tailed test, we look to the alternative hypothesis to determine which sample variance should go in the numerator. In this example, population 1 (the original software) is thought to have the larger variance. Then the sample variance from population 1 forms the numerator, regardless of the size of the sample variances. Excel and Minitab correctly compute the calculated *F*-ratio.

If you are performing the test manually, the *F*-ratio needs to be formed correctly for two reasons. First, the correct *F*-ratio will be computed. Second, the correct degrees of freedom will be used to determine the critical value to test the null hypothesis. In this one-tailed example, the numerator represents population 1, and the denominator represents population 2. This means that the degrees of freedom are

$$D_1 = n_1 - 1 = 7 - 1 = 6 \quad \text{and} \quad D_2 = n_2 - 1 = 11 - 1 = 10.$$

Using the *F*-distribution table in Appendix H, Minitab's **Calc > Probability Distributions** command, or Excel's **FINV** function, you can determine

$$F_{0.01} = 5.39$$

for this one-tailed test with a $\alpha = 0.01$.

The sample data for the test runs are in a CD-ROM file called *ATM*. The sample variances are

$$s_1^2 = 612.68$$
$$s_2^2 = 51.49$$

Thus, the calculated *F*-ratio is

$$F = \frac{612.68}{51.49} = 11.898$$

MINITAB - Atm.mpj - [Session]

File Edit Data Calc Stat Graph Editor Tools Window Help

Test for Equal Variances: Original Software, New System

95% Bonferroni confidence intervals for standard deviations

	N	Lower	StDev	Upper
Original Software	7	15.0431	24.7523	62.2647
New System	11	4.7778	7.1759	13.7917

F-Test (normal distribution)
Test statistic = 11.90, p-value = 0.001

Excel and Minitab have a procedure for performing this test. As shown in Figures 10- 10-5b, the calculated

$$F = 11.898 > F_{0.01} = 5.39,$$

so the null hypothesis,

$$H_0, \text{ is rejected.}$$

Based on the sample data, the systems programmers have evidence to support their claim new ATM algorithm will result in reduced transaction-time variability.

There are many business decision-making applications in which you will need to test w two populations have equal variances.

EXAMPLE 10-3: ONE-TAILED TEST FOR TWO POPULATION VARIANCES

Thomas Supply   Thomas Supply has a contract to assemble component parts that will b by a leading maker of personal computers. One critical part is available from two supplier Thomas will purchase from supplier 1 because its parts are less expensive, if the variation in ness is less than or equal to that for supplier 2. The following steps can be used to conduct a t the two suppliers.

Step 1:   **Specify the population value of interest.**

Thomas Supply is concerned with the variation in thickness. Therefore, the popu parameter of interest is the variance, σ^2.

Step 2:   **Formulate the appropriate null and alternative hypotheses.**

Because Thomas managers are concerned with whether supplier 1's varianc exceed that of supplier 2, the test will be one-tailed, and the null and alter hypotheses are formed as follows:

$$H_0: \sigma_1^2 \leq \sigma_2^2$$
$$H_A: \sigma_1^2 > \sigma_2^2$$

Step 3:   **Specify the significance level.**

The test will be conducted using an alpha level equal to 0.05.

Step 4:   **Construct the rejection region.**

Based on sample sizes of 11 parts from each supplier, the critical value for tailed test with alpha = 0.05 and $D_1 = 10$ and $D_2 = 10$ degrees of freedom is The null hypothesis is rejected if $F > F_\alpha = 2.98$. Otherwise, do not reject th hypothesis.

Step 5:   **Compute the test statistic.**

A simple random sample of 11 parts was selected from each supplier with the variances of

$$s_1^2 = 0.799 \quad \text{and} \quad s_2^2 = 0.547.$$

The assumptions of independence and normal populations are believed to be s in this case.

The test statistic is an F-ratio formed by placing the variance that is predict larger (as shown in the alternative hypothesis) in the numerator. Supplier 1 is p to have the larger variance in the alternative hypothesis. Thus the test statistic i

$$F = \frac{0.799}{0.547} = 1.4607$$

Step 6:   **Reach a decision.**

Because $F = 1.4607 < 2.98 = F_{0.05}$, do not reject the null hypothesis.

Step 7:   **Draw a conclusion.**

Based on the sample data, there is insufficient evidence to conclude that the va part thickness from supplier 1 is greater than that for supplier 2. Therefore will continue to purchase from supplier 1.

EXAMPLE 10-2: TWO-TAILED TEST FOR TWO POPULATION VARIANCES

Airport Security   Since the September 11 tragedy in New York City, airport security has been tightened substantially around the world. The federal government has taken over the management of airport security in U.S. airports, and private security companies have been replaced by federal employees. Suppose that the security manager at O'Hare airport in Chicago is concerned about the waiting time for passengers required to pass through security checks before being admitted to the departure gates. Of particular interest is whether there is a difference in the variability of waiting time at concourses A and B. The following steps can be used to test to determine whether there is a difference in population variances.

Step 1:   Specify the population value of interest.
The population value of interest is the variation in waiting times at the two concourses.

Step 2:   Formulate the appropriate null and alternative hypotheses.
Because we are interested in determining if a difference exists in variances and because neither concourse is predicted to have a higher variance, the test will be two-tailed, and the hypotheses are established as:

$$H_0: \sigma_A^2 = \sigma_B^2$$
$$H_A: \sigma_A^2 \neq \sigma_B^2$$

Step 3:   Specify the level of significance.
The test will be conducted using an alpha = 0.02 level.

Step 4:   Construct the rejection region.
Select simple random samples from each population of interest, determine whether the assumptions have been satisfied, and compute the test statistic.

Random samples of 25 passengers from Concourse A and 31 passengers from Concourse B were selected and the waiting time for each passenger was recorded. There is no connection between the two samples, so the assumption of independence is satisfied. The stem and leaf diagrams do not dispute the assumption of normality.

	Stem and Leaf Display for Concourse A Stem unit: 1			Stem and Leaf Display for Concourse B Stem unit: 1
	8 | 9			4 | 7
Statistics	9 | 0	**Statistics**		5 |
Sample Size 25	10 | 2 3 7 9	Sample Size 31		6 | 3
Mean 14.58191	11 | 9	Mean 16.24597		7 |
Median 14.15696	12 | 2 4	Median 15.77023		8 |
Std. Deviation 3.765897	13 | 2	Std. Deviation 4.785841		9 |
Minimum 8.889582	14 | 0 0 2 2	Minimum 4.70353		10 | 8
Maximum 22.16486	15 | 5 6 9	Maximum 24.37963		11 | 1 4 7
	16 | 2			12 | 2 4
	17 | 0 4			13 |
	18 | 2 4			14 | 2 2 2 8
	19 |			15 | 1 3 7 8
	20 | 8			16 |
	21 | 5			17 | 0 5
	22 | 2			18 | 3 6
				19 | 0 1 3 3
				20 | 4
				21 | 8 8
				22 | 1 4 9
				23 |
				24 | 4

To determine the critical value from the F-distribution, we can use either Excel's FINV function, Minitab's **Calc > Probability Distributions** command, or the F table in Appendix H. The degrees of freedom are D_1 = numerator sample size − 1, and D_2 = denominator sample size − 1. As shown in the statistics section of the stem and leaf display, Concourse B has the larger standard deviation, thus we get:

$$D_1 = n_B - 1 = 31 - 1 = 30 \quad \text{and} \quad D_2 = n_A - 1 = 25 - 1 = 24$$

Then for $\alpha/2 = 0.01$, we get a critical $F = 2.577$. The null hypothesis is rejected if $F > F_{\alpha/2} = 2.577$. Otherwise, do not reject the null hypothesis.

Step 5: **Compute the test statistic.**

The test statistic is formed by the ratio of the two sample variances. Because this is a two-tailed test, the large sample variance is placed in the numerator.

$$F = \frac{4.786^2}{3.766^2} = 1.615$$

Step 6: **Reach a decision.**

Compare the test statistic to the critical value and reach a conclusion with respect to the null hypothesis.

Because $F = 1.615 < F_{\alpha/2} = 2.577$, do not reject the null hypothesis.

Step 7: **Draw a conclusion.**

There is no reason to conclude that there is a difference in the variability of waiting time at concourses A and B.

Excel and Minitab Tutorial

***Bank ATM Machines*—**One-tailed tests on two population variances are performed much like two-tailed tests. Consider the systems development group for a midwestern bank, which has developed a new software algorithm for its ATM machines. Although reducing average transaction time is an objective, the systems programmers also want to reduce the variability in transaction speed. They believe the standard deviation for transaction time will be less with the new software (population 2) than it was with the old algorithm (population 1). For their analysis, the programmers have performed 7 test runs using the original software and 11 test runs using the new system. Although the managers want to determine the standard deviation of transaction time, they must perform the test as a test of variances because no method exists for testing standard deviations directly. Thus, the null and alternative hypotheses are

$$H_0 : \quad \sigma_1^2 \leq \sigma_2^2 \quad \text{or} \quad \sigma_1^2 - \sigma_2^2 \leq 0$$
$$H_A : \quad \sigma_1^2 > \sigma_2^2 \quad \text{or} \quad \sigma_1^2 - \sigma_2^2 > 0$$

The hypothesis is to be tested using a significance level of $\alpha = 0.01$.

In order to use the F-test to test whether these sample variances come from populations with equal variances, we need to make sure that the sample variances are independent and the populations are approximately normally distributed. Because the test runs using the two algorithms were unique, the variances are independent. The following box and whisker plots give no reason to indicate that, based on these small samples, the populations are not approximately normal.

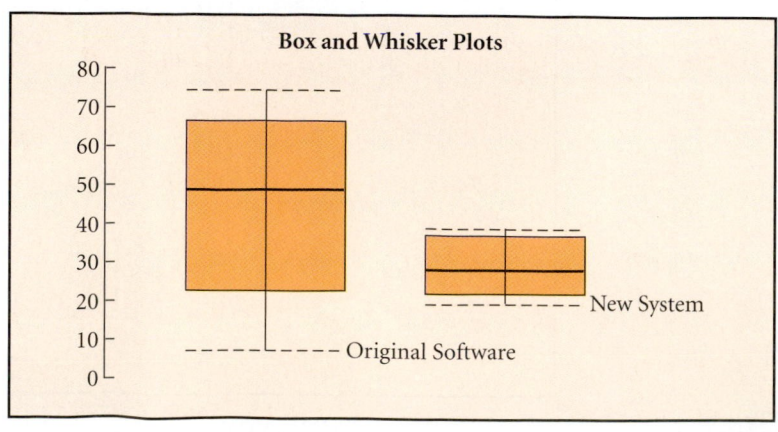

FIGURE 10-5A

Excel Output *F*-Test Example of ATM Transaction Time

Excel Instructions:
1. Open file: ATM.xls
2. Click on **Tools**.
3. Select **Data Analysis**.
4. Select *F*-**Test Two Sample for Variances**.
5. Define data ranges.
6. Indicate significance level = 0.01.

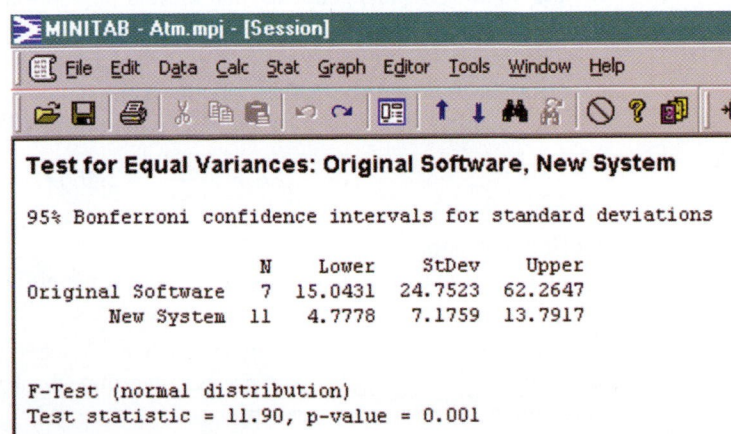

	A	B	C	D	E	F
1	Original Software	New System		F-Test Two-Sample for Variances		
2	38.9	22.8				
3	23.2	20			Original Software	New System
4	49.2	26.5		Mean	46.55714286	29.8
5	66.8	37.9		Variance	612.6761905	51.494
6	65.5	27.2		Observations	7	11
7	74.6	39.6		df	6	10
8	7.7	34.1		F	11.89801123	
9		39.4		P(F<=f) one-tail	0.000473972	
10		20.9		F Critical one-tail	5.38580025	
11		30.3				
12		29.1				

> Because the calculated $F = 11.898 > F_{.01} = 5.39$, we reject the null hypothesis and conclude that the variance for population 1 exceeds the population 2 variance.

Figure 10-5a and Figure 10-5b illustrate the one-tailed hypothesis test for this situation using a significance level of 0.01. Recall that in a two-tailed test, placing the largest sample variance in the numerator and the smallest variance in the denominator forms the *F*-ratio. In a one-tailed test, we look to the alternative hypothesis to determine which sample variance should go in the numerator. In this example, population 1 (the original software) is thought to have the larger variance. Then the sample variance from population 1 forms the numerator, regardless of the size of the sample variances. Excel and Minitab correctly compute the calculated *F*-ratio.

If you are performing the test manually, the *F*-ratio needs to be formed correctly for two reasons. First, the correct *F*-ratio will be computed. Second, the correct degrees of freedom will be used to determine the critical value to test the null hypothesis. In this one-tailed example, the numerator represents population 1, and the denominator represents population 2. This means that the degrees of freedom are

$$D_1 = n_1 - 1 = 7 - 1 = 6 \quad \text{and} \quad D_2 = n_2 - 1 = 11 - 1 = 10.$$

Using the *F*-distribution table in Appendix H, Minitab's **Calc > Probability Distributions** command, or Excel's **FINV** function, you can determine

$$F_{0.01} = 5.39$$

for this one-tailed test with a $\alpha = 0.01$.

The sample data for the test runs are in a CD-ROM file called *ATM*. The sample variances are

$$s_1^2 = 612.68$$
$$s_2^2 = 51.49$$

Thus, the calculated *F*-ratio is

$$F = \frac{612.68}{51.49} = 11.898$$

FIGURE 10-5B

Minitab Output *F*-Test Example of ATM Transaction Time

MINITAB - Atm.mpj - [Session]

File Edit Data Calc Stat Graph Editor Tools Window Help

Test for Equal Variances: Original Software, New System

95% Bonferroni confidence intervals for standard deviations

```
                      N    Lower    StDev    Upper
Original Software     7  15.0431  24.7523  62.2647
      New System     11   4.7778   7.1759  13.7917
```

F-Test (normal distribution)
Test statistic = 11.90, p-value = 0.001

Minitab Instructions:
1. Open file: ATM.MTW.
2. Choose **Stat > Basic Statistics > 2 Variances**.
3. Select **Samples in different columns**, enter one data column in **First** and another in **Second**.
4. Click on **Options**.
5. In **Confidence Level**, enter $1 - \alpha$.
6. Click **OK. OK.**

Excel and Minitab have a procedure for performing this test. As shown in Figures 10-5a and 10-5b, the calculated

$$F = 11.898 > F_{0.01} = 5.39,$$

so the null hypothesis,

$$H_0, \text{ is rejected.}$$

Based on the sample data, the systems programmers have evidence to support their claim that the new ATM algorithm will result in reduced transaction-time variability.

There are many business decision-making applications in which you will need to test whether two populations have equal variances.

EXAMPLE 10-3: ONE-TAILED TEST FOR TWO POPULATION VARIANCES

Thomas Supply   Thomas Supply has a contract to assemble component parts that will be used by a leading maker of personal computers. One critical part is available from two suppliers, and Thomas will purchase from supplier 1 because its parts are less expensive, if the variation in thickness is less than or equal to that for supplier 2. The following steps can be used to conduct a test for the two suppliers.

Step 1:   **Specify the population value of interest.**
Thomas Supply is concerned with the variation in thickness. Therefore, the population parameter of interest is the variance, σ^2.

Step 2:   **Formulate the appropriate null and alternative hypotheses.**
Because Thomas managers are concerned with whether supplier 1's variance will exceed that of supplier 2, the test will be one-tailed, and the null and alternative hypotheses are formed as follows:

$$H_0: \sigma_1^2 \leq \sigma_2^2$$
$$H_A: \sigma_1^2 > \sigma_2^2$$

Step 3:   **Specify the significance level.**
The test will be conducted using an alpha level equal to 0.05.

Step 4:   **Construct the rejection region.**
Based on sample sizes of 11 parts from each supplier, the critical value for a one-tailed test with alpha = 0.05 and $D_1 = 10$ and $D_2 = 10$ degrees of freedom is 2.98. The null hypothesis is rejected if $F > F_\alpha = 2.98$. Otherwise, do not reject the null hypothesis.

Step 5:   **Compute the test statistic.**
A simple random sample of 11 parts was selected from each supplier with the sample variances of

$$s_1^2 = 0.799 \quad \text{and} \quad s_2^2 = 0.547.$$

The assumptions of independence and normal populations are believed to be satisfied in this case.

The test statistic is an F-ratio formed by placing the variance that is predicted to be larger (as shown in the alternative hypothesis) in the numerator. Supplier 1 is predicted to have the larger variance in the alternative hypothesis. Thus the test statistic is:

$$F = \frac{0.799}{0.547} = 1.4607$$

Step 6:   **Reach a decision.**
Because $F = 1.4607 < 2.98 = F_{0.05}$, do not reject the null hypothesis.

Step 7:   **Draw a conclusion.**
Based on the sample data, there is insufficient evidence to conclude that the variance of part thickness from supplier 1 is greater than that for supplier 2. Therefore, Thomas will continue to purchase from supplier 1.

Additional *F*-test Considerations

Recall that in Chapter 9, the *t*-test for the difference between two population means with independent samples assumed that the two populations have equal variances. Often times, decision makers use the *F*-test introduced in this section to test whether the assumption of equal variances is satisfied. However, studies have shown that the *F*-test may not be particularly effective in detecting certain differences in population variances that can adversely affect the *t*-test. Therefore, other tests for equality of variances such as the Aspen-Welch test may be preferred as preliminary tests to the *t*-test for two population means. (See the Markowski reference at the end of this chapter.)

10-2: EXERCISES

Skill Development

10.12 Find the appropriate critical *F*-value, F_α, from the *F*-distribution table for each of the following assuming one-tailed tests:
   a. $D_1 = 10, D_2 = 14, \alpha = 0.05$
   b. $D_1 = 8, D_2 = 8, \alpha = 0.01$
   c. $D_1 = 14, D_2 = 10, \alpha = 0.05$

10.13 Find the appropriate critical *F*-value, F_α, from the *F*-distribution table for each of the following assuming one-tailed tests:
   a. $D_1 = 16, D_2 = 14, \alpha = 0.01$
   b. $D_1 = 5, D_2 = 12, \alpha = 0.05$
   c. $D_1 = 16, D_2 = 20, \alpha = 0.01$

10.14 Given the following null and alternative hypotheses:

$$H_0: \sigma_1^2 = \sigma_2^2$$
$$H_A: \sigma_1^2 \neq \sigma_2^2$$

and the following sample information:

Sample 1	Sample 2
$n_1 = 11$	$n_2 = 21$
$s_1 = 19$	$s_2 = 23$

   a. If $\alpha = 0.02$, state the decision rule for the hypothesis.
   b. Test the hypothesis and indicate whether the null hypothesis should be rejected.
   c. If you are able to obtain it from suitable computer software, determine the *p*-value for this hypothesis test. Otherwise, place a bound on the *p*-value using Appendix H.

10.15 Given the following null and alternative hypotheses:

$$H_0: \sigma_1^2 \leq \sigma_2^2$$
$$H_A: \sigma_1^2 > \sigma_2^2$$

and the following sample information:

Sample 1	Sample 2
$n_1 = 15$	$n_2 = 11$
$s_1 = 230$	$s_2 = 210$

   a. If $\alpha = 0.05$, state the decision rule for the hypothesis.
   b. Test the hypothesis and indicate whether the null hypothesis should be rejected.

10.16 Given the following null and alternative hypotheses:

$$H_0: \sigma_1^2 \leq \sigma_2^2$$
$$H_A: \sigma_1^2 > \sigma_2^2$$

and the following sample information:

Sample 1	Sample 2
$n_1 = 13$	$n_2 = 21$
$s_1^2 = 1{,}450$	$s_2^2 = 1{,}320$

   a. If $\alpha = 0.05$, state the decision rule for the hypothesis.
   b. Test the hypothesis and indicate whether the null hypothesis should be rejected.

10.17 Given the following null and alternative hypotheses:

$$H_0: \sigma_1^2 \leq \sigma_2^2$$
$$H_A: \sigma_1^2 > \sigma_2^2$$

and the following sample information:

Sample 1	Sample 2
$n_1 = 21$	$n_2 = 13$
$s_1^2 = 345.7$	$s_2^2 = 745.2$

   a. If $\alpha = 0.01$, state the decision rule for the hypothesis. (Be careful to pay attention to the alternative hypothesis to construct this decision rule.)
   b. Test the hypothesis and indicate whether the null hypothesis should be rejected.

10.18 You are given two random samples with the following information:

Item	Sample 1	Sample 2
1	19.6	21.3
2	22.1	17.4
3	19.5	19.0
4	20.0	21.2
5	21.5	20.1
6	20.2	23.5
7	17.9	18.9
8	23.0	22.4
9	12.5	14.3
10	19.0	17.8

a. Based on these samples, test at $\alpha = 0.10$ whether the true difference in population variances is equal to zero.

b. If you are able to obtain it from suitable computer software, determine the p-value for this hypothesis test. Otherwise, place a bound on the p-value using Appendix H.

Business Applications

10.19 The McBurger Company operates fast-food stores throughout the United States and in 14 other countries. Management is very concerned about making sure that a standard of quality service is achieved. For instance, they are interested in whether there is a difference in standard deviation in service times for customers who use the drive-through window versus those who go inside to the service counter.

   The McBurger store in Knoxville, Tennessee, was recently analyzed. A sample of 13 drive-through customers was selected, and a sample of 9 inside-counter customers was selected. The time (in minutes) it took each customer to be served was recorded. The following statistics were computed from the sample data.

Drive-Through	Walk-In
$\bar{x} = 4.5$	$\bar{x} = 4.0$
$s = 2.0$	$s = 1.2$

Based on a significance level of 0.10, determine if there is a difference in standard deviation in service times for customers who use the drive-through window versus those who go inside to the service counter.

10.20 A national TV telethon committee is interested in determining whether males' donations have greater variability in amount than females' donations. To test this, random samples of 25 males and 25 females were selected from people who donated during last year's telethon. The following statistics were computed from the sample data:

Males	Females
$\bar{x} = \$12.40$	$\bar{x} = \$8.92$
$s = \$2.50$	$s = \$1.34$

Based on a significance level of 0.05, does it appear that donations by males have greater variability than donations by females?

10.21 ⊙ The First Night Stage Company operates a small nonprofit theater group in Milwaukee, Wisconsin. Each year the Company solicits donations to help fund its operations. This year, it obtained the help of a marketing research company in the city. This company's representatives proposed two different solicitation brochures. They are interested in determining whether there is a difference in the standard deviation of dollars returned between the two brochures. To test this, a random sample of 20 people was selected to receive brochure A, and another random sample of 20 people was selected to receive brochure B. The data are contained in the CD-ROM file *First-Night*. Based on these sample data, what should the First Night Company conclude about the two brochures with respect to their variability? Test using a significance level of 0.02. Use both the p-value and critical-value approaches.

10.22 ⊙ The Celltone Company is in the business of providing cellular phone coverage. Recently it conducted a study of its customers who have purchased either the "Basic Plan" or the "Business Plan" service. At issue is the number of minutes of use by the customers during the midnight to 7:00 A.M. time period, Monday through Friday, over a four-week period. The belief by Celltone managers is that the standard deviation in minutes used by Business Plan customers will be less than that for Basic Plan customers. Data for this study are in the CD-ROM file *Celltone*. Assume that the managers wish to test this using a 0.05 level of significance.

   Determine if the standard deviation in minutes used by Business Plan customers is less than that for the Basic Plan customers, using an alpha level equal to 0.05.

Advanced Applications

10.23 The Fister Corporation makes ribbons for computer printers. It is currently considering changing from its current ribbon to a new ribbon expected to last just as long, on the average, as the current ribbon. However, the new ribbon is thought to be more consistent in terms of how long it will last.

   To test this claim, random samples of 21 current and 17 new ribbons were selected and tested on the company's quality-testing equipment. The following results (measured in tens of thousands of characters) were recorded.

Current	New
$n = 21$	$n = 17$
$s = 3.45$	$s = 2.87$

Be sure to state clearly the null hypothesis, alternative hypothesis, and decision rule. Test the hypotheses using $\alpha = 0.05$. Also discuss the results.

10.24 As purchasing agent for the Horner-Williams Company, you have primary responsibility for securing high-quality raw materials at the best possible price. One particular material that the Horner-Williams Company uses a great deal is aluminum. After careful study, you have been able to reduce the prospective vendors to two. It is unclear whether these two vendors produce aluminum that is equally durable.

To compare durability, the recommended procedure is to put pressure on an aluminum sample until it cracks. The vendor whose aluminum requires the greatest average pressure will be judged to be the one that provides the most durable product.

To carry out this test, 14 pieces of aluminum from vendor 1 and 14 pieces from vendor 2 are selected at random. The following results in pounds per square inch were noted.

Vendor 1	Vendor 2
$n_1 = 14$	$n_2 = 14$
$\bar{x}_1 = 2{,}345$ psi	$\bar{x}_2 = 2{,}411$ psi
$s_1 = 300$	$s_2 = 250$

Before testing the hypothesis about difference in population means, suppose the purchasing agent for the company is concerned about whether the assumption of equal population variances is satisfied.

a. Based on the sample data, what would you tell him if you tested at the significance level of 0.10?

b. Would your conclusion differ if you tested at the significance level of 0.02? Discuss.

c. What would be the largest significance level that would cause the null hypothesis to be rejected?

10.25 The production control manager at Ashmore Manufacturing is interested in determining whether there is a difference in standard deviation of product diameter for part #XC-343 for units made at the Trenton, New Jersey, plant versus those made at the Atlanta, Georgia, plant. The Trenton plant is highly automated and thought to provide better quality control. Thus, the parts produced there should be less variable than those made in Atlanta.

A random sample of 15 parts was selected from those produced last week at Trenton. The standard deviation for these parts was 0.14 inch. A sample of 13 parts was selected from those made in Atlanta. The sample standard deviation for these parts was 0.202 inch.

a. Based on these sample data, is there sufficient evidence to conclude that the Trenton plant produces parts that are less variable than those of the Atlanta plant? Test using $\alpha = 0.05$.

b. Consider the scenario in which the Trenton plant is discovered to have a smaller variability than the Atlanta plant. Management, on this basis, decides that they must expend a large amount of money to upgrade the machinery in Atlanta. Suppose also that, in reality, the difference in the observed variability between the two plants is a result of sampling error. Under these conditions, specify the type of error associated with this hypothesis test. How would you modify the hypothesis procedure to guard against such an error?

Summary and Conclusions

There are many business situations where the decision maker must reach a conclusion about a single population variance or about the relationship between two population variances. Chapter 10 introduced two hypothesis tests, the first using the chi-square distribution for testing a single population variance and the second using the F-distribution for testing the relationship between two population variances. Together, these procedures provide the decision maker with powerful tools for making inferences concerning one and two population variances. Combining the techniques presented in Chapter 10 with the hypothesis testing procedures in Chapters 8 and 9 gives the decision maker useful techniques for testing population parameters for one and two populations. Furthermore, Chapter 10 introduced two probability distributions, the chi-square distribution and the F-distribution. The chi-square distribution will again be used in Chapter 12 where goodness of fit and contingency analysis are discussed. The F-distribution will be used extensively in the analysis of variance and regression analysis chapters.

EQUATIONS

Chi-Square Test for a Single Population Variance

$$\chi^2 = \frac{(n-1)s^2}{\sigma^2} \qquad \textbf{10-1}$$

F Test Statistic for Testing Whether Two Populations Have Equal Variances

$$F = \frac{s_i^2}{s_j^2} \, (df = D_1 = n_i - 1 \quad \text{and} \quad D_2 = n_j - 1) \quad \textbf{10-2}$$

Sample Variance

$$s^2 = \frac{\sum(x - \bar{x})^2}{n-1} \qquad \textbf{10-3}$$

Key Term

Independent Samples, 402

CHAPTER EXERCISES

Business Applications

10.26 Maher Saddles, Inc. produces bicycle seats. Among the many seats produced by the company is a seat for the high-end mountain bicycle market. Maher is interested in knowing whether changes to the production process will reduce the variability in the assembly time for this bicycle seat, as measured by the standard deviation for assembly times. Before changes were made to the production process the standard deviation of assembly times was 3.27 minutes. To evaluate whether the changes made to the production process are effective in reducing the variability in assembly times, Maher produced 36 seats using the new production methods and found the sample standard deviation to be 3.12 minutes. Based on the sample results, and using a significance level of 0.05, can Maher conclude that the new production methods have reduced the variation in the seat's assembly time?

10.27 A medical research group is investigating what differences might exist between the two pain killing drugs, Azerlieve and Zynumbic. The researchers have already established that there is no difference between the two drugs in terms of the average amount of time required before the drugs take effect. However, they are also interested in knowing if there is any difference between the variability of time until pain relief occurs. A random sample of 24 patients using Azerlieve and 32 patients using Zynumbic yielded the following results:

Azerlieve	Zynumbic
$n_1 = 24$	$n_2 = 32$
$s_1 = 37.5$ sec	$s_2 = 41.3$ sec

At the 0.05 level of significance, can the researchers conclude that there is a significant difference in the effect time variability between the two drugs?

10.28 Marsha and Greg operate two jewelry stores in Denver, one located downtown and one located in a suburban mall. While both stores report approximately the same average monthly sales figures, Marsha and Greg would like to know if the downtown store has higher variability in monthly sales than the suburban mall store. A random sample of 36 monthly sales reports from the downtown store and 39 monthly sales reports from the suburban store produced the following results:

Downtown	Mall
$n_1 = 36$	$n_2 = 39$
$s_1 = \$687$	$s_2 = \$521$

Based on the sample data, can Marsha and Greg conclude that the downtown store has greater variability in monthly sales than their suburban mall store? Conduct your analysis using a level of significance of 0.10.

10.29 In the production of its Nutty Toffee, Cordum Candies must carefully control the temperature of its cooking process. If there is too much variation in the cooking temperature then the taste and consistency of the toffee is compromised. Historically the standard deviation of the cooking temperature has been 0.90° F. A random sample of 27 batches of toffee was selected yesterday and the standard deviation of the temperature was computed to be 1.15° F. At the 0.05 level of significance does the sample data support the conclusions that there has been an increase in the variability of the toffee cooking temperature?

10.30 The production control supervisor at a fish cannery in Alaska is concerned with the variability in the fill rates for cans of salmon. The current canning process for 12 oz cans of salmon has a standard deviation in the fill rate of 0.05 oz. Following changes to the canning process the production control supervisor samples 36 12-oz cans of salmon and computes a sample standard deviation of 0.04 oz. Based on these sample results can the production control supervisor conclude that the production process changes have reduced the variability in the fill rate for 12-oz cans of salmon? Use a level of significance of 0.10.

10.31 Ozarka Lumber uses two types of saws to cut 2-×-6 boards. Both saws cut to the correct dimension on the average, but there is variability in the cutting process. A random sample of 29 2-×-6 boards cut using Saw 1 and 33 2-×-6 boards cut using Saw 2 produced the following results:

Saw 1	Saw 2
$n_1 = 29$	$n_2 = 33$
$s_1 = 0.0061$	$s_2 = 0.00593$

At the 0.10 level of significance can Ozarka conclude that there is more variability in the length of 2-×-6 boards cut using Saw 1 than in 2-×-6 boards cut using Saw 2?

10.32 The Automotive Research Group (ARG) provides independent testing for a variety of automobile-related products. Recently, ARG tested two gasoline additives that are designed to increase the average miles per gallon for automobiles that use the additive. The additives had similar effects on mean miles per gallon, but ARG is interested in determining if there is a difference in the variability between the two additives. Random samples of automobiles using the additives were selected and the following results were reported:

Additive 1	Additive II
$n_1 = 30$	$n_2 = 30$
$s_1 = 1.53$ miles	$s_2 = 0.98$ miles

Based on the sample results, can ARG conclude that there is a significant difference in the variability between the two additives? Conduct the analysis at the 0.05 level of significance.

10.33 Crestline Bank has instituted a new check clearing procedure. Historically, the bank's standard deviation in the number of checks cleared daily has been 29.2. Crestline is interested in knowing if the new check clearing procedure has reduced the variation in the number of checks cleared each day as measured by the standard deviation. A sample standard deviation of 22.8 was computed based on a random sample of 45 days checks. Based on this sample result, can Crestline conclude that the variation in the number of daily checks cleared has been reduced? Conduct the analysis at a 0.05 level of significance.

10.34 A company produces an O-ring that must have a diameter of 200.0 millimeters. The company has worked to improve its manufacturing process and believes that it can meet the product specifications. However, the company must regularly monitor its output to ensure that process variability is within limits. The company's engineers have determined that output variation, measured as the variance in the ring's diameter, should not be greater than 2.25 millimeters squared. A recent sample of 23 O-rings was selected and a sample standard deviation of 1.65 millimeters was calculated. Based on this sample, is the process variation too high? Use a level of significance of 0.01 to conduct the analysis.

10.35 Poultry growers are concerned with both the average weight and the variability in weight of the chickens they grow. A new feed supplement is being tested by a poultry research group to determine if it will reduce the variability in weights of chickens when compared to the currently marketed supplement. A random sample of 34 growers using the new supplement and a random sample of 43 growers using the current supplement were tested with the following results:

Current Supplement	New Supplement
$n_1 = 43$	$n_2 = 34$
$s_1 = 6.1$ oz	$s_2 = 4.2$ oz

At the 0.05 level of significance, can the researchers conclude that the new supplement significantly reduces the variation in the weight of chickens?

Advanced Business Applications

10.36 The X-John Company makes batteries for cellular telephones. Recently the R&D department has developed a new battery that it believes will be less expensive to produce. The R&D engineers are concerned, however, about the consistency in the lasting power of the battery. If there is too much variability in battery life, cellular phone users will be unwilling to buy X-John batteries even if they are less expensive. Engineers have specified that the standard deviation of battery life must be less than 5 hours. Treat the measurements in the file *X-John* as a random sample of 100 of the new batteries. Based on this sample, is there evidence that the standard deviation of battery life is less than 5 hours? Conduct the appropriate hypothesis test using a level of significance of 0.01. Report the p-value for this test and be sure to state a conclusion in business terms.

10.37 The operations manager for Cozine Corporation is concerned with variation in the number of pounds of garbage collected per truck. If this variation is too high, the manager will change the garbage truck pickup routes to try to better balance the garbage truck loads. The manager believes that the current truck routing system provides for consistent garbage pickup per truck and is unwilling to reroute the trucks unless the variability, measured by the standard deviation in pounds per truck, is greater than 3,900 pounds. The data file *Cozine* contains 200 truck weights. Assuming that the data represent a random sample of 200 trucks selected from Cozine's daily garbage pickup operations, is there evidence that the manager needs to change the garbage pickup routes to better balance the loads? Conduct your analysis using a level of significance of 0.10. Be sure to state your conclusion in terms of the operations manager's decision.

10.38 Freedom Hospital is in the midst of negotiations with its resident physicians. There has been a lot of discussion about the hospital's ability to pay and the way patients are charged for services. The physicians' negotiator recently mentioned that the geriatric charge system did not make sense. The negotiator is concerned that there is a greater variability in the total charges for males than in the total charges for females. To investigate this issue the hospital has randomly selected 138 patient files. These data are contained in the file *Patients*. Using the data for total charges, conduct the appropriate test to respond to the negotiator's concern. Use a significance level of 0.05. State your conclusion in terms that address the issue raised by the negotiator.

10.39 A retail analyst is examining February sales for several different types of retailers. The data that she has collected for February 1997 and February 1998 by retail group are contained in the file *Retailers*.
a. Assuming that the sales data are a random sample, conduct the appropriate test to determine if February sales for discounters are less variable in 1997 than in 1998. Use a level of significance of 0.05.
b. Assuming that the sales data are a random sample, conduct the appropriate test to determine if February 1998 miscellaneous sales are less variable than February 1998 department store sales. Use a level of significance of 0.05.

10.40 The California State Highway Patrol recently conducted a study on a stretch of interstate highway south of San Francisco to determine what differences, if any, existed in driving speeds of cars licensed in California and cars licensed in Nevada. One of the issues to be examined was whether there was a difference in the variability of driving speeds between cars licensed in the two states. The data file *Speed-Test* contains speeds of 140 randomly selected California cars and 75 randomly selected Nevada cars. Based on these sample results, can you conclude at the 0.05 level of significance that there is a difference between the variations in driving speeds for cars licensed in the two states?

10.41 Solontactics, a large law firm in New York City, uses couriers to deliver business documents to their clients and other lawyers in and around Wall Street. Recently, they have become concerned about the variability in the delivery times by some of the couriers. A random sample of average delivery times in minutes of several of the couriers can be found in the data file *Solontactics*.
a. Solontactics requires that the variability in delivery times, as measured by the standard deviation, must be less than 2.5 minutes for any courier service that it uses. For each courier service conduct the appropriate statistical test at the 0.10 level of significance to determine if Solontactics' requirement is met.
b. Based on the sample results can Solontactics conclude that there is less variability in the delivery times of Blazers courier service than in the delivery times of Time Warps courier service? Use a level of significance of 0.10 to conduct the appropriate test. Be certain to state your conclusion in terms of Solontactics' question.

10.42   Jason Enterprises produces two different products, Product 1 and Product 2. Among the concerns of the production engineers is whether there is less variation in the production of Product I than in Product II. The data file *Jason Enterprises* contains the time in minutes required to produce the two products using three different production processes: Current, Cellular, and Flex-Flow. Assuming that the data in the file *Jason Enterprises* is a random sample of the times required to produce the two products, conduct the appropriate statistical test to determine whether there is less variation in the production time required for Product 1 than for Product 2 for the Current production process. Use a level of significance of 0.05.

10.43   Hypos, a marketer of computer games, sells its products online (using the Internet), by telephone, through the mail (catalog), and through the company's retail stores. Assume that the file *Hypos* contains a random sample of the dollar sales of computer games for the different sales channels. The marketing department is interested in understanding more about the buying decisions of its customers.

a. Based on the sample of Internet sales, can Hypos conclude that the variability in Internet sales as measured by the standard deviation is less than $10.00 per order? Use a level of significance of 0.05 to conduct the appropriate test. Be sure to state a conclusion that answers Hypos' question.

b. Based on the sample data for Phone/Catalog sales and In-Store sales can Hypos conclude that there is a difference in the variability of sales between the two sales channels? Use a level of significance of 0.05 to conduct the appropriate statistical analysis. State your conclusion in terms of the marketing issue of interest.

10.44   Phone Solutions provides assistance to users of a personal finance software package. Users of the software call Phone Solutions with their questions and trained consultants provide answers and information. One concern that Phone Solutions must deal with is the staffing of its call centers. As a part of the staffing issues Phone Solutions seeks to reduce the average variability in the amount of time that a consultant spends on each caller. A study of this issue is currently being undertaken by the operations managers of Phone Solutions three call centers. Each call center manager has randomly sampled 50 days of calls and the collected times, in minutes, are in the file *Phone Solutions*.

a. Call Center 1 has set the goal that the average variation in phone calls, measured in standard deviation of the length of phone calls in minutes, should be less than 3.5 minutes. Using the data in the *Phone Solutions* file, can the operations manager of Call Center 1 conclude that her consultants are meeting the goal? Use a level of significance of 0.10.

b. Can the managers conclude that there is greater variability in the average length of phone calls for Call Center 3 than for Call Center 2? Use a level of significance of 0.10 to conduct the appropriate test.

10.45   To determine whether there is a difference between the average variation in computer usage by college major, the manager of the computer laboratories at a state university in North Dakota randomly sampled observations from the computer records kept in the computer laboratories. When students enter a computer laboratory they must enter a code that indicates their college: (1) for Engineering; (2) for Arts and Sciences; and (3) for Business. A computer then keeps track of each student's start and stop time. At the end of the semester the computer laboratory manager randomly selected the 155 records contained in the file labeled *Lab-Time* from all the students who used the computer laboratories that semester.

a. Based on the sample data is there evidence to conclude at the 0.05 level of significance that the variability in computer lab usage as measured by the standard deviation is greater than 1.5 minutes for Business students?

b. Based on the sample data is there evidence to conclude at the 0.05 level of significance that there is greater variability in usage for Arts and Sciences than for Engineering students?

General References

1. Berenson, Mark L., and David M. Levine, *Basic Business Statistics Concepts and Applications*, 7th ed. (Upper Saddle River, NJ: Prentice Hall, 1999).
2. Cryer, Jonathan D., and Robert B. Miller, *Statistics for Business: Data Analysis and Modeling*, 2nd ed. (Belmont, CA: Duxbury Press, 1994).
3. Duncan, Acheson, J., *Quality Control and Industrial Statistics*, 5th Edition (Burr Ridge, IL: Irwin, 1986).
4. Johnson, Richard A. and Dean W. Wichern, *Business Statistics: Decision Making with Data* (New York: John Wiley & Sons, 1997).
5. Larsen, Richard J., Morris L. Marx, and Bruce Cooil, *Statistics for Applied Problem Solving and Decision Making* (Pacific Grove, CA: Duxbury Press, 1997).
6. Markowski, Carol, and Edmund Markowski, *Conditions for the Effectiveness of a Preliminary Test of Variance*, The American Statistician, November, 1990, No. 4, pp. 322–326.
7. *Microsoft Excel 2000* (Redmond, WA: Microsoft Corp., 1999).
8. *Minitab for Windows Version 14* (State College, PA: Minitab, 2003).
9. Siegel, Andrew F., *Practical Business Statistics*, 4th ed. (Burr Ridge, IL: Irwin, 2000).

CHAPTER 11

Analysis of Variance

CHAPTER OUTCOMES

After studying the material in Chapter 11, you should be able to:

- Recognize situations that call for the use of analysis of variance.
- Understand the basic logic of analysis of variance.
- Be aware of several different analysis of variance designs and understand when to use each.
- Perform a single-factor hypothesis test using analysis of variance manually and with the aid of Excel or Minitab software.
- Conduct and interpret post-analysis of variance pairwise comparisons procedures.
- Recognize when randomized blocks analysis of variance is useful and be able to perform randomized blocks analysis.

WHY YOU NEED TO KNOW

Chapters 8, 9, and 10 introduced the basics of hypothesis testing. By now you should understand that, regardless of the population parameter in question, hypothesis-testing steps are basically the same.

1. Specify the population value of interest.
2. Formulate the null and alternative hypothesis.
3. Specify the level of significance.
4. Determine a decision rule defining the rejection and "acceptance" regions.
5. Select a random sample of data from the population(s). Compute the appropriate sample statistic(s). Finally, calculate the test statistic.
6. Reach a decision. Reject the null hypothesis, H_0, if the sample statistic falls in the rejection region; otherwise, do not reject the null hypothesis. If the test is conducted using the p-value approach, H_0 is rejected whenever the p-value is smaller than the significance level; otherwise H_0 is not rejected.
7. Draw a conclusion. State the result of your hypothesis test in the context of the exercise or analysis of interest.

Chapter 8 focused on hypothesis tests involving a single population. Chapter 9 expanded the hypothesis-testing process to include applications in which differences between two populations are involved. However, you will encounter many instances involving more than two populations. For example, the vice pres-ident of operations at Farber Rubber, Inc., oversees production at Farber's six different U.S. manufacturing plants. Because each plant uses slightly different manufacturing processes, the vice president needs to know if there are any differences in average strength of the products produced at the different plants.

Similarly, *Golf Digest*, a major publisher of articles about golf, might wish to determine which of five major brands of golf balls have the highest mean distance off the tee. The Environmental Protection Agency (EPA) might conduct a test to determine if there is a difference in the average miles-per-gallon performance of cars manufactured by the Big Three U.S. auto-mobile producers. In each of these cases, testing a hypothesis involving more than two population means could be required.

This chapter introduces a tool called analysis of variance (ANOVA), which can be used to test whether there are differences among three or more population means. There are several ANOVA procedures, depending on the type of test that is being conducted. Our aim in this chapter is to introduce you to the basics of ANOVA and to illustrate how to use Microsoft Excel or Minitab to help conduct hypothesis tests involving three or more population parameters. You will almost certainly need either to apply ANOVA in future decision-making situations or to inter-pret the results of an ANOVA study performed by someone else. Thus, you need to be familiar with this powerful statistical tool.

11-1 ONE-WAY ANALYSIS OF VARIANCE

In Chapter 9 we introduced the *t*-test for testing whether two populations have equal means when the sam-ples from the two populations are independent. However, you will often encounter situations in which you are interested in determining whether three or more populations have equal means. To conduct this test, you will need a new tool called *analysis of variance* (*ANOVA*). There are many different analysis of vari-ance designs to fit different situations. The simplest ANOVA design is **one-way analysis of variance**.

> **One-Way Analysis of Variance**
>
> An analysis of variance design in which independent samples are obtained from k levels of a single factor for the purpose of testing whether the k levels have equal means.

THE LOGIC BEHIND ONE-WAY ANOVA

Bayhill Marketing Company—The Bayhill Marketing Company is a full-service marketing and advertising firm in San Francisco, California. Although Bayhill provides many different marketing services, one of its most lucrative is coupon design. Companies that wish to increase sales often mail coupons to potential customers in their marketing areas. These companies hope that people will redeem them and overall sales will increase. Bayhill's account managers help client companies design their coupons for maximum effectiveness. Of course, some coupon designs are more effective than others.

For example, a major greeting card company wants to work with Bayhill in developing a coupon offer for its "Special Events" card set. The card company has negotiated a deal with the American Express credit card company to include its coupon in every American Express cardholder's monthly statement. Now the company must decide what the coupon should offer and how it will look to max-imize its effectiveness. Coupon effectiveness can be determined by the percentage of coupons redeemed or by the dollar value of the greeting card sets purchased with a redeemed coupon.

Through a series of meetings with the client and focus-group sessions with potential customers, Bayhill has developed four coupon designs. Bayhill has arranged with American Express to test these

TABLE 11-1

Bayhill Marketing Company Coupon Order Data

Customer	COUPON DESIGN				
	1	2	3	4	
1	$ 4.10	$ 6.90	$ 4.60	$12.50	
2	5.90	9.10	11.40	7.50	
3	10.45	13.00	6.15	6.25	
4	11.55	7.90	7.85	8.75	
5	5.25	9.10	4.30	11.15	
6	7.75	13.40	8.70	10.25	
7	4.78	7.60	10.20	6.40	
8	6.22	5.00	10.80	9.20	
					Grand Mean
Mean	$ 7.00	$ 9.00	$ 8.00	$ 9.00	$8.25
Variance	7.341	8.423	7.632	5.016	

Note: Data are dollar value of card sets ordered with each coupon.

designs by sending out 200 of each coupon type to randomly selected cardholders. Bayhill will then select a random sample from redeemed coupons and determine the dollar value of greeting card sets purchased with each coupon. Table 11-1 shows the data for a sample of eight redemptions for each design. The values in the table are the dollar values of greeting card sets ordered by each customer.

In this example, we are interested in whether the different coupon designs result in different order sizes. In other words, we are trying to determine if "coupon designs" are one of the possible causes of the variation in the dollar value of the card sets ordered (the response variable). In this case, coupon design is called a **factor**.

Factor

A quantity under examination in an experiment as a possible cause of variation in the response variable.

The *single factor* of interest is coupon design. This factor has four categories, measurements, or strata, called **levels**.

Levels

The categories, measurements, or strata of a factor of interest in the current experiment.

These four levels are the four designs: 1, 2, 3, and 4. Because we are using only one factor here, each dollar value of card sets ordered is associated with only one level (that is, with coupon design—type 1, 2, 3, or 4), as you can see in Table 11-1. Each level is a population of interest.

The null and alternative hypotheses to be tested are

$$H_0: \mu_1 = \mu_2 = \mu_3 = \mu_4$$
$$H_A: \text{At least two of the population means are different.}$$

The experimental design producing the data for this experiment is called a **completely randomized design**.

Completely Randomized Design

An experiment is completely randomized if it consists of the independent random selection of observations representing each level of one factor.

The appropriate statistical tool for conducting the hypothesis test related to this experimental design is ANOVA. Because this ANOVA addresses an experiment with only one factor, it is a one-way ANOVA, or a one-factor ANOVA. Because the sample size for each coupon design (level) is the same, the experiment has a **balanced design**.

Balanced Design

An experiment has a balanced design if the factor levels have equal sample sizes.

ANOVA tests the null hypothesis that three or more populations have the same mean. The test is based on three assumptions:

SSUMPTIONS

1. All populations are normally distributed.
2. The population variances are equal.
3. The observations are independent—that is, the occurrence of any one individual value does not affect the probability that any other observation will occur.

If the null hypothesis is true, the populations have identical distributions. If so, the sample means for random samples from each population should be close in value. The basic logic of ANOVA is the same as the two-sample t-test introduced in Chapter 9: The null hypothesis should be rejected only if the sample means are substantially different.

You may be surprised to learn that the hypothesis test for equality of the population means is in fact an F-test involving two variances. To show you what we mean, consider that in Chapter 6 we showed that the distribution of sample means for a sample of size n taken from a normally distributed population has a standard deviation, $\sigma_{\bar{x}} = \dfrac{\sigma}{\sqrt{n}}$. From this, the variance of the $\bar{x}$ values is $\sigma_{\bar{x}}^2 = \dfrac{\sigma^2}{n}$.

Figure 11-1 illustrates what the sampling distribution of $\bar{x}$ values would look like. If the null hypothesis is true, the sample means from each population can be thought of as values coming from the sampling distribution in Figure 11-1. The average value of the sample means would be an estimate for μ, the mean of the sampling distribution. Likewise, the variation in the sample means would be the estimate for the variance of the sampling distribution, $\sigma_{\bar{x}}^2$.

If, as assumed, the populations have the same variance, σ^2, we can solve for σ^2 as:

$$n\sigma_{\bar{x}}^2 = \sigma^2$$

where n is the common sample size from each population. Consider the data in Table 11-1. The sample means are shown for sample sizes of eight. Also shown is the average of the sample means, 8.25. Then the estimate for $\sigma_{\bar{x}}^2$ is

$$s_{\bar{x}}^2 = \frac{(7 - 8.25)^2 + (9 - 8.25)^2 + (8 - 8.25)^2 + (9 - 8.25)^2}{4 - 1} = 0.91667$$

It follows that an estimate of σ^2 is

$$n\left(s_{\bar{x}}^2\right) = 8(0.91667) = 7.333$$

This value is referred to as the *between-levels (or treatments) estimate of* σ^2, and it is based on the premise that the null hypothesis is true and the means of the respective populations are equal.

Another approach to estimating the common variance, σ^2, is to use a pooled estimate. Because we assume that all k populations have the same variance, the average of the population variances is equal to the common population variance:

$$\sigma^2 = \frac{\sigma_1^2 + \sigma_2^2 + \cdots + \sigma_k^2}{k} = \frac{\sigma^2 + \sigma^2 + \cdots + \sigma^2}{k} = \frac{k\sigma^2}{k}$$

FIGURE 11-1

Sampling Distribution of $\bar{x}$

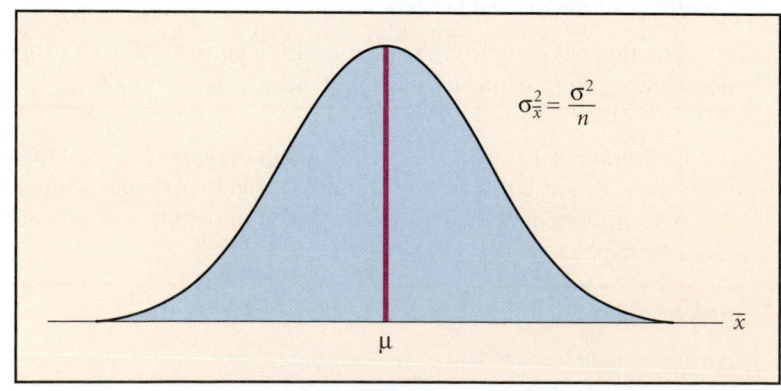

FIGURE 11-2

Variation in Sample Means

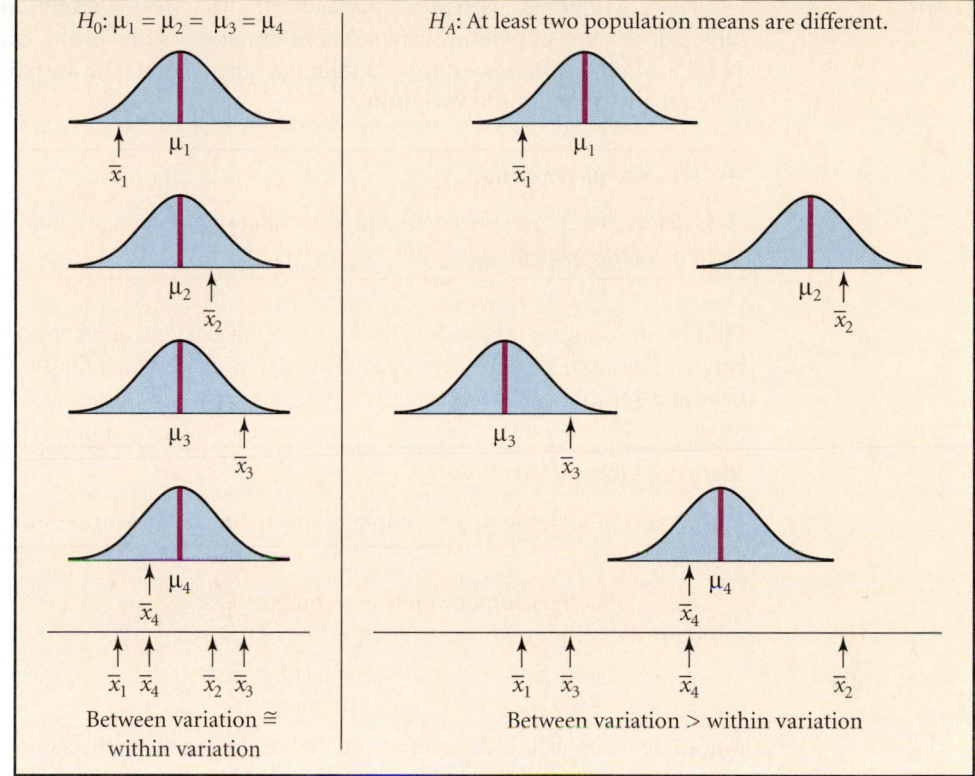

However, each population variance is a measure of the variation within that specific population and is not dependent on whether the means of the populations are equal. Thus, given equal sample sizes from each population, the *within-levels estimate of* σ^2 is

$$s^2 = \frac{s_1^2 + s_2^2 + \cdots + s_k^2}{k}$$

Based on the data in Table 11-1 for the Bayhill Marketing Company, the within-levels estimate for σ^2 is

$$s^2 = \frac{7.341 + 8.423 + 7.632 + 5.016}{4} = 7.103$$

Now, we have two estimates for the same population variance. The two estimates should have approximately the same value if the null hypothesis of equal means is true. However, if the populations have unequal means, the *between-levels estimate* for σ^2 will be greater than the *within-levels estimate* because the sample means will tend to differ substantially from one another. This is illustrated in Figure 11-2.

Thus, to test whether the population means are equal, we actually compare these two variance estimates. As we learned in Chapter 10, the *F*-distribution is used to test whether two variances are equal. As we will illustrate shortly, in ANOVA, the *F*-ratio is formed by taking the ratio of the between level estimate over the within level estimate. If this *F*-ratio gets too large, the null hypothesis of equal means is rejected.

PARTITIONING THE SUM OF SQUARES

Refer again to the sample data in Table 11-1. In order to understand the logic of ANOVA, you should take note of several things about the data. First, the dollar values of the orders are different throughout the data table. Some values are higher; others are lower. Thus, variation exists across all customer orders. This variation is called the **total variation** in the data.

Total Variation

The aggregate dispersion of the individual data values across the various factor levels is called the *total variation* in the data.

Next, within any particular coupon design (i.e., factor levels), not all customers ordered the same dollar value of greeting card sets. For instance, within level 1, order size ranged from \$4.10 to \$11.55. Similar differences occur within the other levels. The variation within each factor level is called the **within-sample variation**.

Within-Sample Variation

The dispersion that exists among the data values within a particular factor level is called the *within-sample variation*.

Finally, the sample means for the four coupon designs are not all equal. Thus, variation exists between the four designs' averages. This variation between the factor levels is referred to as the **between-sample variation**.

Between-Sample Variation

Dispersion among the factor sample means is called the *between-sample variation*.

Recall that the sample variance is computed as:

$$s^2 = \frac{\Sigma(x - \bar{x})^2}{n - 1}$$

The sample variance is the sum of squared deviations from the sample mean divided by its degrees of freedom. When all the data from all the samples are included, s^2 is the estimator of the *total variation*. The numerator of this estimator is called the *total sum of squares* (SST) and can be partitioned into the sum of squares associated with the estimators of the between-sample variation and the within-sample variation, as shown in Equation 11-1.

Partitioned Sum of Squares

$$SST = SSB + SSW$$ **11-1**

where:

SST = Total Sum of Squares
SSB = Sum of Squares Between
SSW = Sum of Squares Within

After separating the sum of squares, they are divided by their degrees of freedom to produce the respective variance estimators previously discussed. If the between-sample portion of the total variation is large relative to the within-sample variation, the ANOVA procedure will lead us to reject the null hypothesis and conclude the population means are different. The question is: How can we determine at what point any difference is statistically significant?

THE ANOVA ASSUMPTIONS

Bayhill Marketing Company (continued)—Recall that Bayhill is testing whether the four coupon designs generate orders of equal average dollar value. The null and alternative hypotheses are

$$H_0: \mu_1 = \mu_2 = \mu_3 = \mu_4$$
$$H_A: \text{At least two population means are different.}$$

Before we jump into the ANOVA calculations, recall the three basic assumptions of ANOVA:

1. All populations are normally distributed.
2. The population variances are equal.
3. The sampled observations are independent.

Figure 11-3 demonstrates the first two assumptions. The populations are normally distributed and the spread (variance) is the same for each population. However, in this case, the populations

FIGURE 11-3

Normal Populations with Equal Variances and Unequal Means

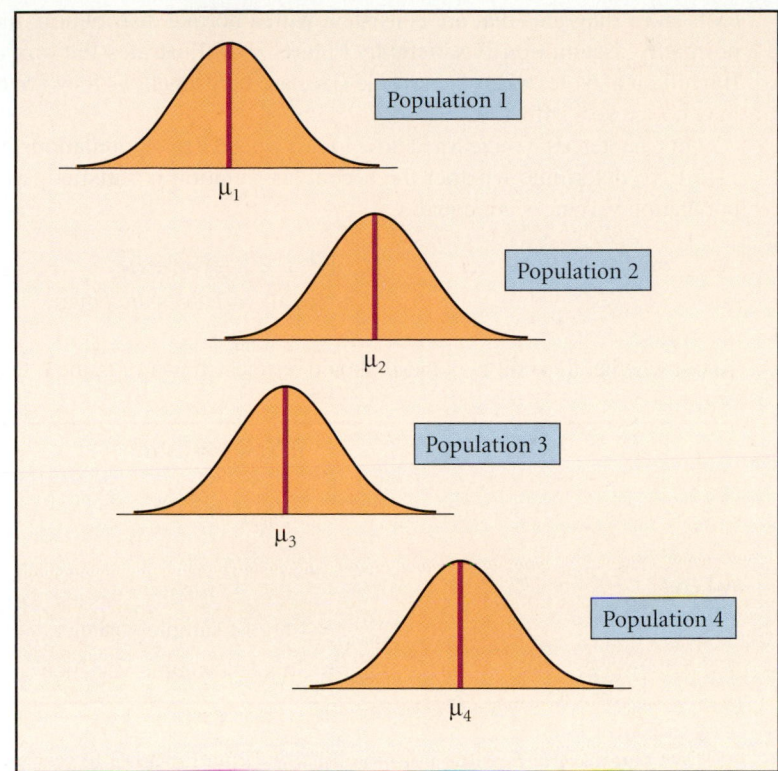

have different means—and the null hypothesis is false. Figure 11-4 demonstrates the same assumptions but in a case in which the population means are equal; therefore, the null hypothesis is true.

You can do a rough check to determine whether the normality assumption is satisfied by developing graphs of the sample data from each population. Histograms are probably the best tool for checking the normality assumption, but they require a fairly large sample size. The stem and leaf and box and whisker diagrams are good alternatives when sample sizes are smaller. If the graphical

FIGURE 11-4

Normal Populations with Equal Variances and Means

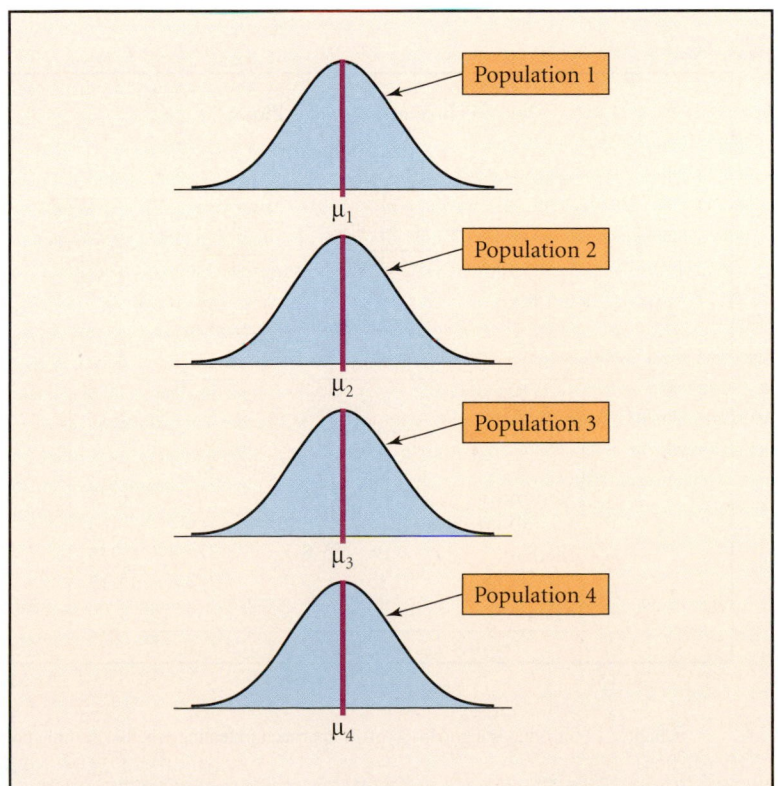

tools show diagrams that are consistent with a normal distribution, then that evidence suggests the normality assumption is satisfied.[1] Figure 11-5 illustrates the box and whisker diagram for the Bayhill data. Note, when the sample sizes are very small, as they are here, the graphical techniques may not be very effective.

In Chapter 10, you learned how to test whether two populations have equal variances using the F-test. To determine whether the second assumption is satisfied, we can hypothesize that all the population variances are equal:

$$H_0: \sigma_1^2 = \sigma_2^2 = \cdots = \sigma_k^2$$
$$H_A: \text{Not all variances are equal.}$$

To test whether this null hypothesis should be rejected, we form the F test statistic using Equation 11-2.

F Test Statistic

$$F_{max} = \frac{s_{max}^2}{s_{min}^2}$$

11-2

where:

$$s_{max}^2 = \text{Largest sample variance}$$
$$s_{min}^2 = \text{Smallest sample variance}$$

We can use the F-value computed using Equation 11-2 to test whether the variances are equal by comparing the calculated F to a critical value from a distribution known as *Hartley's F_{max} distribution*, which appears in Appendix I.[2] For the Bayhill example, the computed variance for each of the four samples is

$$s_1^2 = 7.341 \quad s_2^2 = 8.423 \quad s_3^3 = 7.632 \quad s_4^2 = 5.016$$

Using Equation 11-2, we compute the F_{max} value as

$$F_{max} = \frac{8.423}{5.016} = 1.679$$

FIGURE 11-5

Box and Whisker Diagram—Bayhill Marketing Company

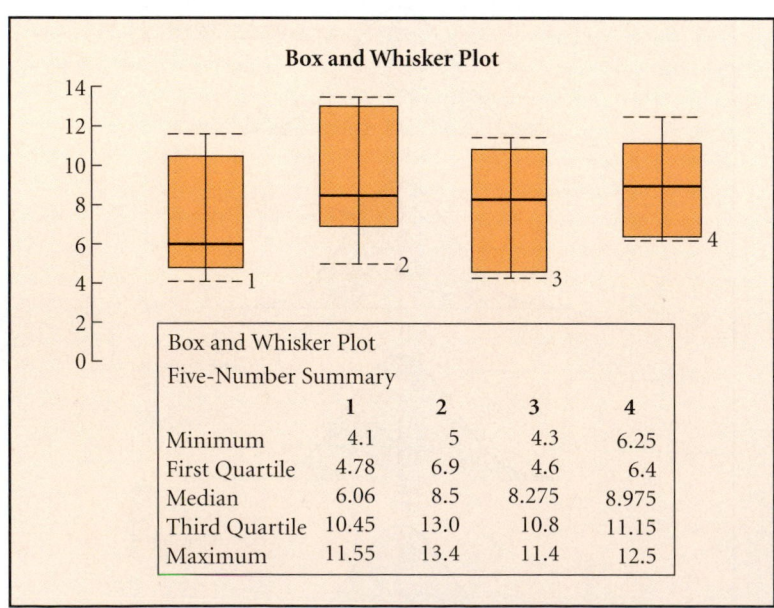

Box and Whisker Plot Five-Number Summary	1	2	3	4
Minimum	4.1	5	4.3	6.25
First Quartile	4.78	6.9	4.6	6.4
Median	6.06	8.5	8.275	8.975
Third Quartile	10.45	13.0	10.8	11.15
Maximum	11.55	13.4	11.4	12.5

[1]Chapter 12 introduces a goodness-of-fit approach to testing whether sample data come from a normally distributed population.

[2]Other tests for equal variances exist. For example, Minitab has a procedure that uses Bartlett and Levine's test.

This value is now compared to the critical F_α from the table in Appendix I for $\alpha = 0.05$, with $k = 4$ and $\bar{n} - 1 = 7$ degrees of freedom. The value, k, is the number of populations ($k = 4$). The value $\bar{n}$ is the average sample size, which equals 8 in this example. If $\bar{n}$ is not an integer value, then set $\bar{n}$ equal to the integer portion of the computed $\bar{n}$. If $F_{max} > F_\alpha$, reject the null hypothesis of equal variances. If $F_{max} \le F_\alpha$, do not reject. From the Hartley's F_{max} distribution table, the critical $F = 8.44$. Because $F_{max} = 1.679 \le 8.44$, the null hypothesis of equal variances is not rejected.[3]

If you are unsure whether you meet the ANOVA assumptions or if your tests indicate that you do not, Chapter 16 introduces an alternative ANOVA procedure called the Kruskal-Wallis one-way ANOVA, which does not require these restrictive assumptions. However, for the examples presented in this chapter, we will consider the ANOVA assumptions to be satisfied.

APPLYING ONE-WAY ANOVA

Although the previous discussion covers the essence of ANOVA, to determine whether the null hypothesis should be rejected requires that we actually determine values of the estimators for the total variation, between-sample variation, and within-sample variation. Most ANOVA tests are done using a computer, but we will illustrate the manual computational approach once. Because software such as Excel and Minitab can be used to perform all calculations, future examples will be done using the computer. The software packages will do all the computations while we focus on interpreting the results.

Bayhill Marketing Company (continued)—Now we are ready to perform the necessary one-way ANOVA computations for the Bayhill example. Recall from Equation 11-1 that we can partition the total sum of squares into two components:

$$SST = SSB + SSW$$

The *total sum of squares* is computed as shown in Equation 11-3.

Total Sum of Squares

$$SST = \sum_{i=1}^{k} \sum_{j=1}^{n_i} (x_{ij} - \bar{\bar{x}})^2$$

11-3

where:

SST = Total sum of squares
k = Number of populations (treatments)
n_i = Sample size from population i
x_{ij} = jth measurement from population i
$\bar{\bar{x}}$ = Grand mean (mean of all the data values)

Equation 11-3 is not as complicated as it appears. Manually applying Equation 11-3 to the Bayhill data shown in Table 11-1 on page 409 (grand mean = $\bar{\bar{x}} = 8.25$), we can compute SST as follows.

$$SST = (4.10 - 8.25)^2 + (5.90 - 8.25)^2 + (10.45 - 8.25)^2 + \cdots + (9.20 - 8.25)^2$$
$$SST = 220.88$$

Thus, the sum of the squared deviations of all values from the grand mean is 220.88. Equation 11-3 can also be restated as:

$$SST = \sum_{i=1}^{k} \sum_{j=1}^{n_i} (x_{ij} - \bar{\bar{x}})^2 = (N - 1)s^2$$

where s^2 is the sample variance for all data combined, and N is the sum of the combined sample sizes.

---

[3]Hartley's F_{max} test is very dependent on the populations being normally distributed and should not be used if the populations' distributions are skewed. Note also in Hartley's F_{max} table, $c = k$ and $v = \bar{n} - 1$.

We now need to determine how much of this total sum of squares is due to between-sample sum of squares and how much is due to within-sample sum of squares. The between-sample portion is called the *sum of squares between* and is found using Equation 11-4.

Sum of Squares Between

$$SSB = \sum_{i=1}^{k} n_i (\bar{x}_i - \bar{\bar{x}})^2$$

11-4

where:

SSB = Sum of squares between samples
k = Number of populations
n_i = Sample size from population i
$\bar{x}_i$ = Sample mean from population i
$\bar{\bar{x}}$ = Grand mean

We can use Equation 11-4 to manually compute the sum of squares between for the Bayhill data, as follows.

$$SSB = 8(7 - 8.25)^2 + 8(9 - 8.25)^2 + 8(8 - 8.25)^2 + 8(9 - 8.25)^2$$
$$SSB = 22$$

Once both the *SST* and *SSB* have been computed, the *sum of squares within* (also called the sum of squares error, *SSE*) is easily computed using Equation 11-5. The sum of squares within can also be computed directly using Equation 11-6.

Sum of Squares Within
$$SSW = SST - SSB$$

11-5

or

Sum of Squares Within

$$SSW = \sum_{i=1}^{k} \sum_{j=1}^{n_i} (x_{ij} - \bar{x}_i)^2$$

11-6

where:

SSW = Sum of squares within samples
k = Number of populations
n_i = Sample size from population i
$\bar{x}_i$ = Sample mean from population i
x_{ij} = jth measurement from population i

TABLE 11-2	SOURCE OF VARIATION	SS	df	MS	F-RATIO
One-Way ANOVA Table: The Basic Format	Between samples	SSB	$k - 1$	MSB	$\dfrac{MSB}{MSW}$
	Within samples	SSW	$N - k$	MSW	
	Total	SST	$N - 1$		

where:

k = Number of populations
N = Sum of the sample sizes from all populations
df = Degrees of freedom
MSB = Mean square between = $\dfrac{SSB}{k - 1}$

MSW = Mean square within = $\dfrac{SSW}{N - k}$

TABLE 11-3	SOURCE OF VARIATION	SS	df	MS	F-RATIO
One-Way ANOVA Table for the Bayhill Marketing Co.	Between samples	22.00	3	7.3333	$\dfrac{7.3333}{7.10286} = 1.03244$
	Within samples	198.88	28	7.10286	
	Total	220.88	31		

where:

$$MSB = \text{Mean square between} = \frac{SSB}{k-1} = \frac{22}{3} = 7.3333$$

$$MSW = \text{Mean square within} = \frac{SSW}{N-k} = \frac{198.88}{28} = 7.10286$$

For the Bayhill example, the SSW is

$$SSW = 220.88 - 22.00$$
$$= 198.88$$

These computations are the essential first steps in performing the ANOVA test to determine whether the population means are equal. Table 11-2 illustrates the ANOVA table format that is used to conduct the test.

The format shown in Table 11-2 is the standard ANOVA table layout. For the Bayhill example, we substitute the numerical values for SSB, SSW, and SST, and complete the ANOVA table, as shown in Table 11-3.

The Mean Square column contains the MSB (mean square between-samples) and the MSW (mean square within-samples).[4] These values are computed by dividing the sum of squares by their respective degrees of freedom, as shown in Table 11-3. They are actually the estimates of the respective variances that we computed earlier.

Restating the null and alternative hypotheses for the Bayhill example:

$H_0: \mu_1 = \mu_2 = \mu_3 = \mu_4$
$H_A:$ At least one pair of populations has different means.

Glance back at Figures 11-3 and 11-4. If the null hypothesis is true (that is, all the means are equal—Figure 11-4), MSW and MSB will be equal, except for the presence of sampling error. However, the more the sample means differ (Figure 11-3), the larger the MSB becomes. As the MSB increases, it will tend to get larger than the MSW. When this difference gets too large, we will conclude that the population means must not be equal, and the null hypothesis will be rejected. But how do we determine what "too large" is? How do we know when the difference is due to more than just sampling error?

To answer these questions, recall from Chapter 10 and from the development in "The Logic Behind the One-Way ANOVA" that the F-distribution is used to test whether two populations have the same variance. In the ANOVA test, if the null hypothesis is true, the ratio of MSB over MSW forms an F-distribution with $D_1 = k - 1$ and $D_2 = N - k$ degrees of freedom. If the calculated F-ratio in Table 11-3 gets too large, the null hypothesis is rejected.

Figure 11-6 illustrates the hypothesis test for a significance level of 0.05. Because the calculated F-ratio = 1.03244 is less than the critical $F = 2.95$ from the F-table with 3 and 28 degrees of freedom, the null hypothesis cannot be rejected. The F-ratio indicates that the between-levels estimate and the within-levels estimate are not different enough to conclude that the population means are significantly different. This means there is insufficient statistical evidence to conclude that any one of the four coupon designs will generate higher average dollar values of orders than any of the other four designs. Therefore, the choice of which coupon design to use can be based on other factors, such as printing cost.

---

[4] MSW is also known as the *mean square for error* (MSE).

FIGURE 11-6

Bayhill Company
Hypothesis Test

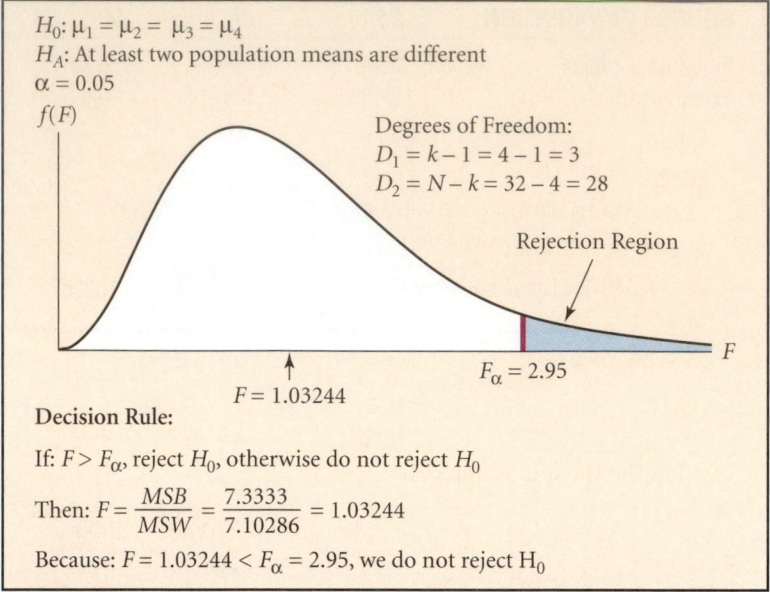

$H_0: \mu_1 = \mu_2 = \mu_3 = \mu_4$
$H_A:$ At least two population means are different
$\alpha = 0.05$

$f(F)$

Degrees of Freedom:
$D_1 = k - 1 = 4 - 1 = 3$
$D_2 = N - k = 32 - 4 = 28$

Rejection Region

$F = 1.03244$

$F_\alpha = 2.95$

F

Decision Rule:

If: $F > F_\alpha$, reject H_0, otherwise do not reject H_0

Then: $F = \dfrac{MSB}{MSW} = \dfrac{7.3333}{7.10286} = 1.03244$

Because: $F = 1.03244 < F_\alpha = 2.95$, we do not reject H_0

EXAMPLE 11-1: ONE-WAY ANALYSIS OF VARIANCE

Westfall Relocation Company   The Westfall Relocation Company, located in Denver, Colorado, contracts with major corporations forced to lay off employees. Westfall provides a variety of services, including job searches, specialized training, and resume development. Westfall then bills the corporation for the services. It currently operates in three regions: west, southwest, and northwest. Recently, Westfall's general manager questioned whether the company's mean billing amount differed by region. To determine this, the following steps can be performed.

Step 1:   **Specify the parameter(s) of interest.**
The parameter of interest is the mean dollars billed in each region.

Step 2:   **Formulate the null and alternative hypotheses.**
The appropriate null and alternative hypotheses are

$$H_0: \mu_W = \mu_{SW} = \mu_{NW}$$
$H_A:$ Not all populations have the same mean.

Step 3:   **Specify the significance level (α) for testing the hypothesis.**
The test will be conducted using an $\alpha = 0.05$.

Step 4:   **Select independent simple random samples from each population, and compute the sample means and the grand mean.**
There are three regions. Simple random samples of employees served in these regions have been selected: 10 in the west, 8 in the southwest, and 12 in the northwest. The following sample data were collected:

West	Southwest	Northwest
$3,700	$3,300	$2,900
2,900	2,100	4,300
4,100	2,600	5,200
4,900	2,100	3,300
4,900	3,600	3,600
5,300	2,700	3,300
2,200	4,500	3,700
3,700	2,400	2,400
4,800		4,400
3,000		3,300
		4,400
		3,200

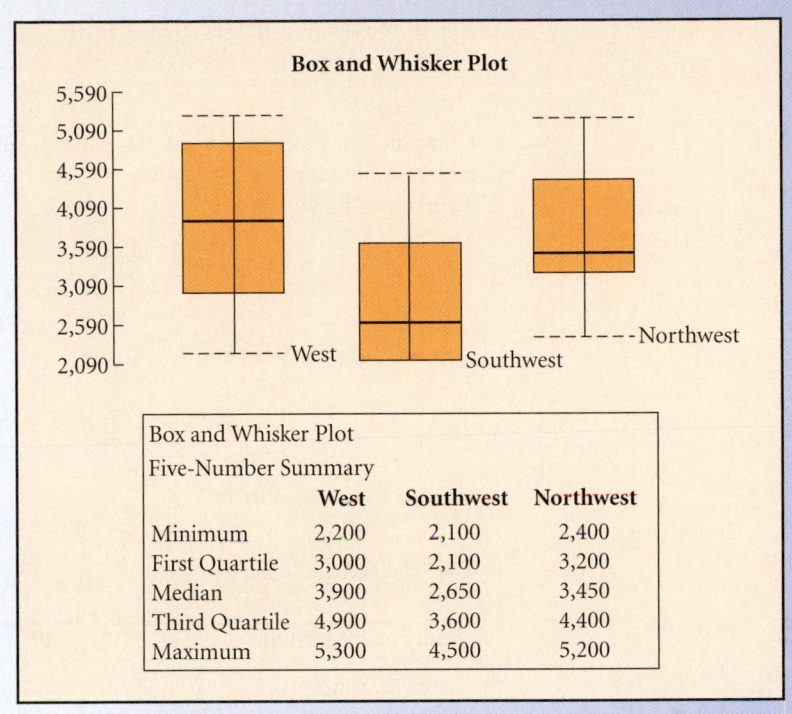

Box and Whisker Plot

Box and Whisker Plot Five-Number Summary	West	Southwest	Northwest
Minimum	2,200	2,100	2,400
First Quartile	3,000	2,100	3,200
Median	3,900	2,650	3,450
Third Quartile	4,900	3,600	4,400
Maximum	5,300	4,500	5,200

Step 5: **Check to see that the normality and equal variance assumptions have been satisfied.**
Because of the small sample size, the box and whisker diagram is used.

As long as we assume that the populations are normally distributed, Hartley's F_{max} test can be used to test whether the three populations have equal variances. The test statistic is

$$F_{max} = \frac{s_{max}^2}{s_{min}^2}$$

The three variances are computed using:

$$s_W^2 = \frac{\sum(x - \bar{x})^2}{n - 1} = 1,062,778 \quad s_{SW}^2 = 695,535.7 \quad s_{NW}^2 = 604,242.4$$

$$\text{Hartley's } F_{max} = \frac{1,062,778}{604,242.4} = 1.7589$$

From the F_{max} table in Appendix I, the critical value for $\alpha = 0.05$, $c = 3$, and $v = 9$ ($v = \bar{n} - 1$) is 5.34. Because $1.7589 \leq 5.34$, we conclude that the population variances could be equal.

Step 6: **Construct the rejection region.**
The F critical value from the F-distribution table in Appendix H for $D_1 = 2$ and $D_2 = 27$ degrees of freedom is a value between 3.316 and 3.403. The exact value $F = 3.354$ can be found using Excel's **FINV** function or Minitab's **Calc > Probability Distributions** command.

The decision rule is

If $F > 3.354$, reject the null hypothesis;
Otherwise, do not reject the null hypothesis.

Step 7: **Compute the test statistic.**
The sample means are

$$\bar{x}_W = \frac{\sum x}{n} = \frac{\$39,500}{10} = \$3,950 \quad \bar{x}_{SW} = \frac{\$23,300}{8} = \$2,912.50$$

$$\bar{x}_{NW} = \frac{\$44,000}{12} = \$3,666.67$$

The grand mean is the mean of the data from all samples combined:

$$\bar{\bar{x}} = \frac{\sum \sum x}{N} = \frac{\$3,700 + \$2,900 + \cdots + \$3,200}{30} = \frac{\$106,800}{30} = \$3,560$$

Compute the total sum of squares, sum of squares between, and sum of squares within, and complete the ANOVA table.

Total Sum of Squares

$$SST = \sum_{i=1}^{k} \sum_{j=1}^{n_i} (x_{ij} - \bar{\bar{x}})^2 = 26,092,000$$

Sum of Squares Between

$$SSB = \sum_{i=1}^{k} n_i (\bar{x}_i - \bar{\bar{x}})^2 = 5,011,583$$

Sum of Squares Within

$$SSW = SST - SSB = 21,080,417$$

The ANOVA table is

Source of Variation	SS	df	MS	F-Ratio
Between samples	5,011,583	2	2,505,792	$\frac{2,505,792}{780,756.2} = 3.2094$
Within samples	21,080,417	27	780,756.2	
Total	26,092,000	29		

Step 8: **Reach a decision.**
Because the F test statistic = 3.2094 < F_α = 3.354, we do not reject the null hypothesis based on these sample data.

Step 9: **Draw a conclusion.**
We are not able to detect a difference in the mean billing per customer by region.

Excel and Minitab Tutorial

Hydronics Corporation—The Hydronics Corporation makes and distributes health products. Currently the company's research department is experimenting with two new herb-based weight-loss-enhancing products. To gauge their effectiveness, researchers at the company conducted a test using 300 human subjects over a six-week period. All the people in the study were between 30 and 40 pounds overweight.

One-third of the subjects were randomly selected to receive a placebo—in this case, a pill containing only vitamin C. One-third of the subjects were randomly selected and given Product 1. The remaining 100 people received Product 2. The subjects did not know which pill they had been assigned. Each person was asked to take the pill regularly for six weeks and otherwise observe his or her normal routine. At the end of six weeks, the subjects' weight loss was recorded. The company was hoping to find statistical evidence that at least one of the products is an effective weight-loss aid.

The CD-ROM file *Hydronics* shows the study data. Positive values indicate that the subject lost weight, whereas negative values indicate that the subject gained weight during the six-week study period. As often happens in studies involving human subjects, people drop out. Thus, at the end of six weeks, only 89 placebo subjects, 91 Product 1 subjects, and 83 Product 2 subjects with valid data remained. Consequently, this experiment resulted in an unbalanced design. (Note, though, one-way ANOVA applies to both balanced and unbalanced designs.)

The null and alternative hypotheses to be tested using a significance level of 0.05 are

$$H_0: \mu_1 = \mu_2 = \mu_3$$
$$H_A: \text{At least two population means are different.}$$

The experimental design is completely randomized. The factor is diet supplement, which has three levels: placebo, Product 1, and Product 2. We will use a significance level of

$$\alpha = 0.05$$

FIGURE 11-7A

Excel Output: Hydronics Weight Loss ANOVA Results

Excel Instructions
1. Open file: Hydronics.xls
2. Select **Tools**.
3. Click on **Data Analysis**.
4. Select **ANOVA: Single Factor**.
5. Define data range.
6. Specify alpha level.

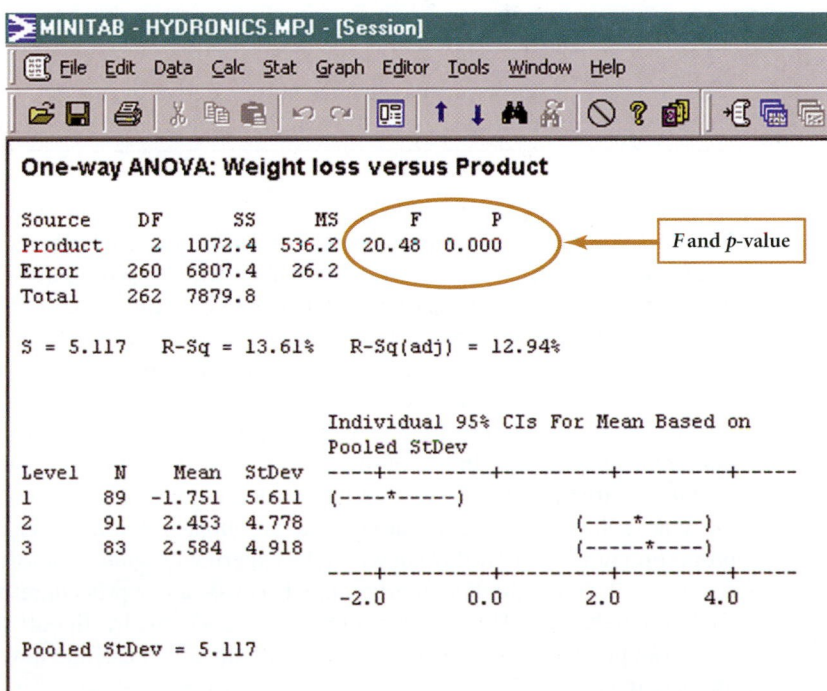

Figure 11-7a and Figure 11-7b show the Excel and Minitab analysis of variance results. The top section of the Excel ANOVA and the bottom section of the Minitab ANOVA output in Figure 11-7b provide descriptive information for the three levels. The ANOVA table is the other half of the output. These tables look like the one we generated manually in the Bayhill example. However, Excel and Minitab also compute the p-value. In addition, Excel displays the critical value, F-critical, from the F-distribution table. Thus, you can test the null hypothesis by comparing the calculated F to the F-critical or by comparing the p-value to the significance level.

The decision rule is

$$\text{If } F > F_\alpha = 3.03, \text{ reject } H_0;$$
$$\text{Otherwise, do not reject } H_0.$$

or

$$\text{If } p\text{-value} < \alpha, \text{ reject } H_0;$$
$$\text{Otherwise, do not reject } H_0.$$

FIGURE 11-7B

Minitab Output: Hydronics Weight Loss ANOVA Results

Minitab Instructions:
1. Open file: Hydronics.MTW.
2. Choose **Stat > ANOVA > One-way**.
3. In **Response**, enter data column, *Loss*.
4. In **Factor**, enter factor column, *Program*.
5. Click **OK**.

```
MINITAB - HYDRONICS.MPJ - [Session]

File  Edit  Data  Calc  Stat  Graph  Editor  Tools  Window  Help

One-way ANOVA: Weight loss versus Product

Source     DF      SS      MS       F       P
Product     2   1072.4   536.2   20.48   0.000       F and p-value
Error     260   6807.4    26.2
Total     262   7879.8

S = 5.117   R-Sq = 13.61%   R-Sq(adj) = 12.94%


                              Individual 95% CIs For Mean Based on
                              Pooled StDev
Level   N     Mean   StDev   ----+---------+---------+---------+-----
1      89   -1.751   5.611   (----*-----)
2      91    2.453   4.778                      (----*-----)
3      83    2.584   4.918                      (-----*----)
                              ----+---------+---------+---------+-----
                              -2.0       0.0       2.0       4.0


Pooled StDev = 5.117
```

Because

$$F = 20.48 > F_\alpha = 3.03 \text{ (or because } p\text{-value} = 5.51 \text{ E-09} < \alpha = 0.05)$$

we reject the null hypothesis
and conclude there is a difference in the mean weight loss for people on the three treatments. At least two of the populations have different means. The top portion of Figure 11-7a shows the descriptive measures for the sample data. For example, the subjects who took the placebo actually gained an average of 1.75 pounds. Subjects on Product 1 lost an average of 2.45 pounds, and subjects on Product 2 lost an average of 2.58 pounds.

The Tukey-Kramer Procedure for Multiple Comparisons

What does this conclusion imply about which treatment results in greater weight loss? One approach for answering this question is to use confidence interval estimates for all possible pairs of population means, based on the pooling of the two relevant sample variances, as introduced in Chapter 9.

$$s_p = \sqrt{\frac{(n_1 - 1)s_1^2 + (n_2 - 1)s_2^2}{n_1 + n_2 - 2}}$$

These confidence intervals are constructed using the formula also given in Chapter 9, Equation 9-5:

$$(\bar{x}_1 - \bar{x}_2) \pm t_{\alpha/2} \, s_p \sqrt{\frac{1}{n_1} + \frac{1}{n_2}}$$

It uses a weighted average of only the two sample variances corresponding to the two sample means in the confidence interval. However, in the Hydronics example, we have three samples, and thus three variances involved. If we were to use the pooled standard deviation, s_p shown here, we would be disregarding one-third of the information available to estimate the common population variance. Instead, we use confidence intervals based on the pooled standard deviation obtained from the square root of *MSW*. This is the square root of the weighted average of all (three in this example) sample variances. This is preferred to the interval estimate shown here because we are assuming that each of the three sample variances is an estimate of the common population variance.

A superior method for testing which populations have different means after the one-way ANOVA has led us to reject the null hypothesis is called the *Tukey-Kramer procedure for multiple comparisons*. To understand why the Tukey-Kramer procedure is superior, we introduce the concept of an **experiment-wide error rate**.

Experiment-Wide Error Rate

The proportion of experiments in which at least one of the set of confidence intervals constructed does not contain the true value of the population parameter being estimated.

The Tukey-Kramer procedure is based on the simultaneous construction of confidence intervals for all differences of pairs of treatment means. In this example, there are three different pairs of means ($\mu_1 - \mu_2, \mu_1 - \mu_3, \mu_2 - \mu_3$). The Tukey-Kramer procedure simultaneously constructs three different confidence intervals for a specified confidence level, say 95%. Intervals that do not contain zero imply that a difference exists between the associated population means.

Suppose we repeat the study a large number of times. Each time, we construct the Tukey-Kramer 95% confidence intervals. The Tukey-Kramer method assures us that in 95% of these experiments, the three confidence intervals constructed will include the true difference between the population means, $\mu_i - \mu_j$. In 5% of the experiments, at least one of the confidence intervals will not contain the true difference between the population means. Thus in 5% of the situations, we would make at least one mistake in our conclusions about which populations have different means. This proportion of errors (0.05) is known as the experiment-wide error rate.

For a 95% confidence interval, the Tukey-Kramer procedure controls the experiment-wide error to a 0.05 level. However, because we are concerned with only this one experiment (with one set of sample data), the error rate associated with any one of the three confidence intervals is actually less than 0.05.

The Tukey-Kramer procedure allows us to simultaneously examine all pairs of populations *after* the ANOVA test has been completed without increasing the true alpha level.[5] Because these comparisons are made after the ANOVA *F*-test, the procedure is called a post-test procedure.

The first step in using the Tukey-Kramer procedure is to compute the absolute differences between each pair of sample means. Using the results shown in Figure 11-7a, we get the following differences.

$$|\bar{x}_1 - \bar{x}_2| = |-1.75 - 2.45| = 4.20$$
$$|\bar{x}_1 - \bar{x}_3| = |-1.75 - 2.58| = 4.33$$
$$|\bar{x}_2 - \bar{x}_3| = |2.45 - 2.58| = 0.13$$

The Tukey-Kramer procedure requires us to compare these absolute differences to the *critical range* that is computed using Equation 11-7.

Tukey-Kramer Critical Range

$$\text{Critical Range} = q_\alpha \sqrt{\frac{MSW}{2}\left(\frac{1}{n_i} + \frac{1}{n_j}\right)} \qquad \textbf{11-7}$$

where:

q_α = Value from studentized range table (Appendix J), with $D_1 = k$ and $D_2 = N - k$ degrees of freedom for the desired level of α [k = number of groups or factor levels, and N = total number of data values from all populations (levels) combined]

MSW = Mean square within

n_i and n_j = Sample sizes from populations (levels) i and j, respectively

---

A critical range is computed for each pairwise comparison, but if the samples sizes are equal, only one critical-range calculation is necessary because the quantity under the radical in Equation 11-7 will be the same for all comparisons. If the calculated pairwise comparison value is greater than the critical-range value, we conclude the difference is significant.

The q value from the studentized range table in Appendix J for a significance level equal to

$$\alpha = 0.05$$

and

$$k = 3 \text{ and } N - k = 260 \text{ degrees of freedom}$$

is approximately

$$q_\alpha = 3.31$$

For $D_2 = N - k = 260$ degrees of freedom, we use the row labeled ∞. Then, for the placebo versus Product 1 comparison,

$$n_1 = 89 \text{ and } n_2 = 91$$

We use Equation 11-7 to compute the critical range, as follows:

$$\text{Critical Range} = q_\alpha \sqrt{\frac{MSW}{2}\left(\frac{1}{n_i} + \frac{1}{n_j}\right)}$$

$$\text{Critical Range} = 3.31\sqrt{\frac{26.18}{2}\left(\frac{1}{89} + \frac{1}{91}\right)} = 1.785$$

Because

$$|\bar{x}_1 - \bar{x}_2| = 4.20 > 1.785$$

we conclude that

$$\mu_1 \neq \mu_2$$

---

[5]There are a variety of other methods for performing multiple-comparison tests in ANOVA.

TABLE 11-4

Hydronics Pairwise Comparisons—Tukey-Kramer Test

	$|\bar{x}_i - \bar{x}_j|$	CRITICAL RANGE	SIGNIFICANT?
Placebo vs. Product 1	4.20	1.785	Yes
Placebo vs. Product 2	4.33	1.827	Yes
Product 1 vs. Product 2	0.13	1.818	No

The mean weight loss for the placebo group is not equal to the mean for the Product 1 group. Table 11-4 summarizes the results for the three pairwise comparisons.

From the table we see that Product 1 and Product 2 both offer significantly higher average weight loss than the placebo. However, the sample data do not indicate a difference in the average weight loss between Product 1 and Product 2.

EXAMPLE 11-2: THE TUKEY-KRAMER PROCEDURE FOR MULTIPLE COMPARISON

Digitron, Inc.   Digitron, Inc., makes disc brakes for automobiles. Digitron's R&D department recently tested four brake systems to determine if there is a difference in the average stopping distance among them. Forty identical mid-sized cars were driven on a test track. Ten cars were fitted with Brake A, 10 with Brake B, and so forth. An electronic, remote switch was used to apply the brakes at exactly the same point on the road. The number of feet required to bring the car to a full stop was recorded. The data are in the CD-ROM file *Digitron*. Because we care to determine only whether the four brake systems have the same or different mean stopping distances, the test is a one-way (single factor) test with four levels and can be completed using the following steps.

Step 1: **Specify the parameter(s) of interest.**
The parameter of interest is the mean stopping distance for each brake type. The company is interested in knowing whether a difference exists in mean stopping distance for the four brake types.

Step 2: **Formulate the appropriate null and alternative hypotheses.**
The appropriate null and alternative hypotheses are

$$H_0: \mu_1 = \mu_2 = \mu_3 = \mu_4$$
$$H_A: \text{At least two population means are different.}$$

Step 3: **Specify the significance level for the test.**
The test will be conducted using $\alpha = 0.05$.

Step 4: **Select independent simple random samples from each population.**

Step 5: **Check to see that the normality and equal-variance assumptions have been satisfied.**
Because of the small sample size, the box and whisker diagram is used.

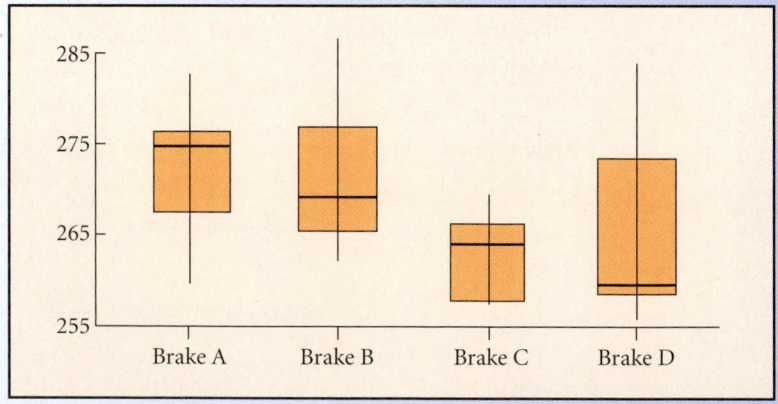

The box plots indicate some skewness in the samples and question the assumption of equality of variances. However, if we assume that the populations are normally distributed, Hartley's F_{max} test can be used to test whether the four populations have equal variances. The test statistic is

$$F_{max} = \frac{s_{max}^2}{s_{min}^2}$$

The four variances are computed using $s_1^2 = \dfrac{\Sigma(x - \bar{x})^2}{n - 1} = 49.9001$

$$s_1^2 = 49.9001 \quad s_2^2 = 61.8557 \quad s_3^2 = 21.7356 \quad s_4^2 = 106.4385$$

Hartley's $F_{max} = \dfrac{106.4385}{21.7356} = 4.8970$

From the F_{max} table in Appendix I, the critical value for alpha = 0.05, $k = 4$, and $\bar{n} - 1 = 9$ is 6.31. Because $4.8970 < 6.31$, we conclude that the population variances could be equal. We might perform other confirmatory tests, such as the chi-square goodness-of-fit test, to determine if the populations have normal distributions. However, of the two assumptions, equality of variances is the most pressing concern. Because we have concluded that the population variances are equal, we proceed with the analysis.

Step 6: **Determine the decision rule.**

Because $k - 1 = 3$ and $N - k = 36$, $F_\alpha = 2.866$. The decision rule is

If the calculated $F > F_\alpha = 2.866$, reject H_0, or
If the p-value $< \alpha = 0.05$, reject H_0;
Otherwise, do not reject H_0.

Step 7: **Use Excel or Minitab to construct the ANOVA table.**

Figure 11-8 shows the Excel output for the ANOVA.

Step 8: **Reach a decision.**

From Figure 11-8, we see that

$$F = 3.89 > F_\alpha = 2.866, \text{ and}$$
$$p\text{-value} = 0.0167 < 0.05.$$

We reject the null hypothesis.

Step 9: **Draw a conclusion.**

We conclude that not all population means are equal. But which systems are different? Is one system superior to all the others?

FIGURE 11-8

Excel One-Way ANOVA Output for the Digitron Example

Excel Instructions:
1. Open file: Digitron.xls
2. Click on **Tools** tab.
3. Select **Data Analysis** option.
4. Select **ANOVA: Single Factor**.
5. Enter significance level and data ranges.

Minitab Instructions (for similar results):
1. Open file: Digitron.MTW.
2. Choose **Stat > ANOVA > One-way**.
3. In **Response**, enter data column, *Distance*.
4. In **Factor**, enter factor level column, *Brake*.
5. Click **OK**.

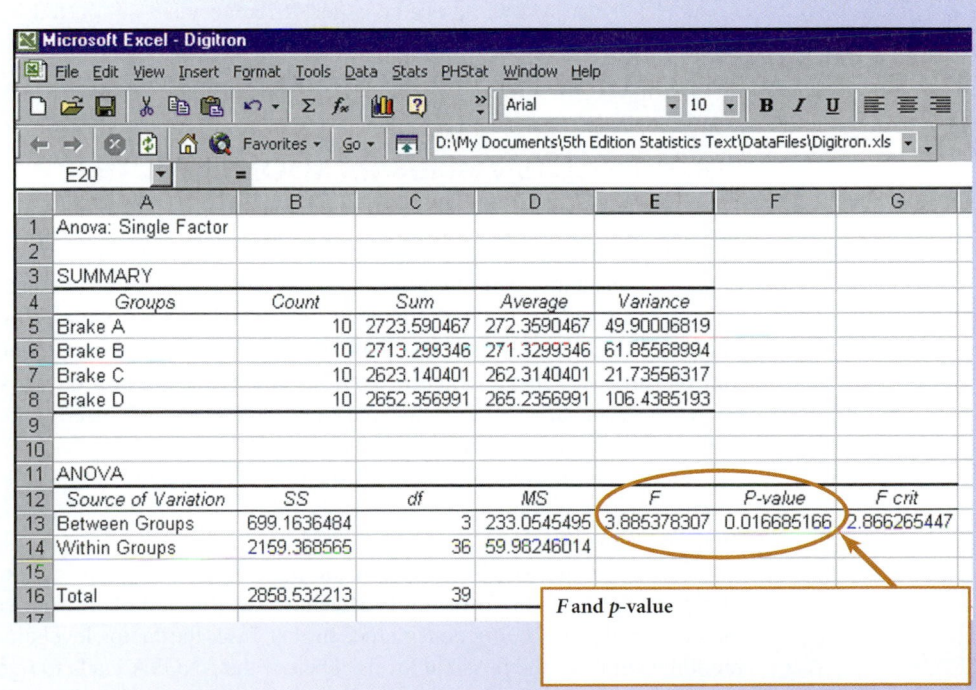

Anova: Single Factor

SUMMARY

Groups	Count	Sum	Average	Variance
Brake A	10	2723.590467	272.3590467	49.90006819
Brake B	10	2713.299346	271.3299346	61.85568994
Brake C	10	2623.140401	262.3140401	21.73556317
Brake D	10	2652.356991	265.2356991	106.4385193

ANOVA

Source of Variation	SS	df	MS	F	P-value	F crit
Between Groups	699.1636484	3	233.0545495	3.885378307	0.016685166	2.866265447
Within Groups	2159.368565	36	59.98246014			
Total	2858.532213	39				

F and *p*-value

Step 10: **Use the Tukey-Kramer test to determine which populations have different means.** Because we have rejected the null hypothesis of equal means, we need to perform a post-ANOVA multiple comparison test. Using Equation 11-7 to construct the critical range to compare to the absolute differences in all possible pairs of sample means. The critical range is[6]

$$\text{Critical Range} = q_\alpha \sqrt{\frac{MSW}{2} \left(\frac{1}{n_i} + \frac{1}{n_j} \right)} = 3.79 \sqrt{\frac{59.98}{2} \left(\frac{1}{10} + \frac{1}{10} \right)}$$

Critical Range = 9.282

Only one critical range is necessary because all of the sample sizes are equal. If any pair of sample means has an absolute difference, $|\bar{x}_i - \bar{x}_j|$, greater than the critical range, we can infer that a difference exists in those population means. The possible pairwise comparisons (part of a family of comparisons called *contrasts*) are

Contrast	Conclusions
$|\bar{x}_1 - \bar{x}_2| = |272.359 - 271.3299| = 1.029 < 9.282$	
$|\bar{x}_1 - \bar{x}_3| = |272.359 - 262.314| = 10.045 > 9.282$	$\mu_1 \neq \mu_3$
$|\bar{x}_1 - \bar{x}_4| = |272.359 - 265.2357| = 7.123 < 9.282$	
$|\bar{x}_2 - \bar{x}_3| = |271.3299 - 262.314| = 9.016 < 9.282$	
$|\bar{x}_2 - \bar{x}_4| = |271.3299 - 265.2357| = 6.094 < 9.282$	
$|\bar{x}_3 - \bar{x}_4| = |262.314 - 265.2357| = 2.922 < 9.282$	

Therefore, based on the Tukey-Kramer procedure, we can infer that population 1 (brake system A) and population 3 (brake system C) have different mean stopping distances. Because short stopping distances are preferred, system C would be preferred over system A, but no other differences are supported by these sample data. For the other contrasts, the difference between the two sample means is insufficient to conclude that a difference in population means exists.

FIXED EFFECTS VERSUS RANDOM EFFECTS IN ANALYSIS OF VARIANCE

In the Digitron brake example, the company was testing four brake systems. These were the only brake systems under consideration. The ANOVA was intended to determine whether there was a difference in these four brake systems only. In the Hydronics weight loss example, the company was interested in determining whether there was a difference in mean weight loss for two supplements and the placebo. In the Bayhill example involving coupon designs, the company narrowed its choices to four different designs, and the ANOVA test was used to determine whether there was a difference in means for these four designs only.

Thus, in each of these examples, the inferences extend only to the factor levels being analyzed, and the levels are assumed to be the only levels of interest. This type of test is called a *fixed effects analysis of variance test*.

Suppose in the Bayhill coupon example that instead of paring the list of possible coupons to a final four, the company had simply selected a random sample of four coupon designs from all possible coupon designs being considered. In that case, the factor levels included in the test would be a random sample of the possible levels. Then, if the ANOVA leads to rejecting the null hypothesis, the

---

[6]The q-value from the studentized range table with alpha = 0.05 and degrees of freedom equal to $k = 4$ and $N - k = 36$ must be approximated using degrees of freedom 4 and 40 because the table does not show degrees of freedom of 4 and 36. This value is 3.79.

conclusion applies to all possible coupon designs. The assumption is the possible levels have a normal distribution and the tested levels are a random sample from this distribution. When the factor levels are selected through random sampling, the analysis of variance test is called a *random effects test*.

11-1: EXERCISES

Skill Development

11.1 Respond to each of the following questions using this partially completed one-way ANOVA table.

Source of Variation	SS	df	MS	F-Ratio
Between samples	1,745			
Within samples	___	240		
Total	6,504	246		

a. How many different populations are being considered in this analysis?
b. Fill in the ANOVA table with the missing values.
c. State the appropriate null and alternative hypotheses.
d. Based on the ANOVA F-test, what conclusion should be reached regarding the null hypothesis? Test using a significance level of 0.01.

11.2 Respond to each of the following questions using this partially completed one-way ANOVA table.

Source of Variation	SS	df	MS	F-Ratio
Between samples		3		
Within samples	405		___	
Total	888	31		

a. How many different populations are being considered in this analysis?
b. Fill in the ANOVA table with the missing values.
c. State the appropriate null and alternative hypotheses.
d. Based on the ANOVA F-test, what conclusion should be reached regarding the null hypothesis? Test using an $\alpha = 0.05$ level.

11.3 Given the following sample data:

Item	Group 1	Group 2	Group 3
1	10.1	8.2	13.7
2	9.3	6.1	12.2
3	11.4	8.6	12.4
4	12.0	9.5	11.6
5	13.5	10.3	13.1
6	12.8	10.4	15.1

a. State the appropriate null and alternative hypotheses for determining whether a difference exists in the average value for the three populations.
b. Compute the sum of squares-between for the sample data.
c. Compute the sum of squares within for the sample data.
d. Based on the computations in parts b and c, develop the ANOVA table and test the null hypothesis using $\alpha = 0.05$. Use the test-statistic approach.

11.4 Given the following sample data:

Item	Group 1	Group 2	Group 3	Group 4
1	20.9	28.2	17.8	21.2
2	27.2	26.2	15.9	23.9
3	26.6	21.6	18.4	19.5
4	22.1	29.7	20.2	17.4
5	25.3	30.3	14.1	
6	30.1	25.9		
7		23.8		

a. Based on the computations for the within- and between-sample variations, develop the ANOVA table and test the appropriate null hypothesis using an $\alpha = 0.05$. Use the p-value approach.
b. Use the Tukey-Kramer procedure to determine which populations have different means. Use $\alpha = 0.05$.

Business Applications

11.5 The Green-Checker Cab Company operates 12 taxis in Seattle, Washington. The manager is interested in determining whether there is a difference in average fares collected for the day, swing, and graveyard shifts. To test whether a difference exists, she has collected a random sample of 10 observations from each shift. The following summary values have been computed from the sample data:

$$SST = 156.764 \quad SSB = 55.600$$

a. Develop the appropriate ANOVA table to reach the determination of interest to the manager. Test the hypothesis using an $\alpha = 0.05$.
b. How would your conclusion change if you used a significance level of 0.01? Discuss why this change would occur.

11.6 Channel 9 television in Colville, Washington, recently conducted a study of television news viewers. One item of interest to Channel 9 management was whether the average age of viewers watching Channel 9 was the same as for the other two stations in Colville. The sample included 24 viewers of each station, with $SST = 2,903.27$ and $SSW = 713.56$.

Using a significance level of 0.05, what should Channel 9 conclude about the average ages of news viewers of the three stations? Discuss.

11.7 The Savouy Corporation recently purchased a bicycle manufacturing plant formerly owned by the American Traveling Company. American had been outfitting its bikes with tires produced by the Leach Corporation. Savouy management is considering whether to stay with Leach tires or to change to another brand. Three other brands are being considered, all of which cost about the same as the Leach tire. The criterion for tire selection will be average tread life.

Samples of 20 have been selected from the Leach tires and from brands A, B, and C. The following results were found:

$$\bar{x}_{Leach} = 111 \text{ hours} \quad \bar{x}_A = 126 \text{ hours}$$
$$\bar{x}_B = 100 \text{ hours} \quad \bar{x}_C = 105 \text{ hours}$$
$$SST = 19,620$$

(Note that the sample means represent the mean hours of use until the tread was reduced to a specified level, at which time the tires were discarded.)

Based on the sample data and using $\alpha = 0.05$ level, what conclusion should the Savouy Corporation reach regarding the different brands of bicycle tires? Discuss.

Advanced Applications

11.8 Suppose as part of your job you are responsible for installing emergency lighting in a series of state office buildings. Bids have been received from four manufacturers of battery-operated emergency lights. The costs are about equal, so the decision will be based on the length of time the lights last before failing. A sample of four lights from each manufacturer has been tested, with the following values (time in hours) recorded for each manufacturer:

Type A	Type B	Type C	Type D
1,024	1,270	1,121	923
1,121	1,325	1,201	983
1,250	1,426	1,190	1,087
1,022	1,322	1,122	1,121

a. Using a significance level equal to 0.01, what conclusion should you reach about the four manufacturer's battery-operated emergency lights? Explain.

b. If the test conducted in part a reveals that the null hypothesis should be rejected, what manufacturer should be used to supply the lights? Is there one or more manufacturers that you can eliminate based on these data? Use the appropriate test for multiple comparisons. Discuss.

11.9 A large metropolitan police force is considering changing from full-size cars to intermediates. The police force sampled cars from each of three manufacturers. The number of cars sampled represents the number the manufacturer was able to provide for the test. Each car was driven for 5,000 miles, and the operating cost per mile was computed. The operating costs, in cents per mile, for the cars are provided in the CD-ROM file *Police*.

a. Perform an analysis of variance on these data. Assume an alpha level of 0.05. Do the experimental data provide evidence that the average operating costs per mile for the three types of police cars are different? Use a *p*-value approach.

b. Referring to part a, based on the sample data and the appropriate test for multiple comparisons, what conclusions should be reached concerning which type of car the police force should adopt? Discuss and prepare a report to the police chief.

c. Provide an estimate for the maximum and minimum differences in average savings per year if the police chief chooses the "best" versus the "worst" car, using operating costs as a criterion. Assume that police cars are driven 30,000 miles a year. Use a 90% confidence interval.

11.10 A nationwide moving company is considering five different types of nylon tie-down straps. The purchasing department randomly selected straps from each company and determined their breaking strengths in pounds. The sample data are contained in the CD-ROM file called *Nylon*.

a. (1) Determine if the variance of the breaking strength measurements for each of the companies can be considered equal. Use a significance level of 0.05. (2) State any additional assumptions you would need to make to justify the use of a one-way ANOVA procedure to determine that the mean strength of the aluminum was the same for each vendor. (3) Construct histograms for the data for each company. Do these samples appear to have come from normal distributions? Explain your reasons.

b. Based on your analysis, with a Type I error rate of 0.05, can you conclude that a difference in breaking strengths exists among the types of nylon ropes?

c. Based on the sample data, make a recommendation regarding which company should be selected based on mean strength of the nylon straps. Discuss in a report to the purchasing manager.

11.11 A leading brewer of beer is considering five different types of advertising displays for a new low-calorie beer. Each display type is tested in five different randomly selected stores. A total of 25 stores are in the sample. The mean monthly sales figures (in cases) and variances for each type of display are as follows:

Display Type	Sample Mean	Sample Variance
A	98	100.75
B	77	83.00
C	84	64.75
D	103	144.35
E	91	101.00

a. Based on these sample data, can the brewery conclude that it makes a difference which type of display is used? Test using a significance level of 0.05. (Hint: Use the means and variances to determine the SSB and SSW values.)

b. Comment on the sampling method used for this study. Specifically, address any assumptions that are violated and are necessary for the ANOVA to be valid.

c. Use the Tukey-Kramer procedure to determine which display type is preferred. Discuss your conclusions in a short report to the marketing manager.

11-2 RANDOMIZED COMPLETE BLOCK ANALYSIS OF VARIANCE

Section 11-1 introduced one-way ANOVA for testing hypotheses involving three or more population means. This ANOVA method is appropriate as long as we are interested in analyzing one factor at a time and we select independent random samples from the populations. For instance, Example 11-2 involving brake assembly systems at the Digitron Corporation (Figure 11-8) illustrated a situation in which we were interested in only one factor: type of brake assembly system. The measurement of interest was the stopping distance with each brake system. To test the hypothesis that the four brake systems were equal with respect to average stopping distance, four groups of the same make and model cars were assigned to each brake system independently. Thus, the one-way ANOVA design was appropriate.

There are, however, situations in which another factor affects the observed response in a one-way design. Often this additional factor is unknown. This is the reason for randomization within the experiment. However, there are also situations in which we know the factor that is impinging on the response variable of interest. Chapter 9 introduced the concept of paired samples and indicated that there are instances when you will want to test for differences in two population means by controlling for sources of variation that might adversely affect the analysis. For instance, in the Digitron example, we might be concerned that, even though we used the same make and model of car in the study, the cars themselves may interject a source of variability that could affect the result. To control for this, we could use the concept of *paired samples* by using the same 10 cars for each of the four brake systems. When an additional factor with two or more levels is involved, a design technique called *blocking* can be used to eliminate its effect on the statistical analysis of the main factor of interest.

RANDOMIZED COMPLETE BLOCK ANOVA

Excel and Minitab Tutorial

Citizen's State Bank—At Citizen's State Bank, homeowners can borrow money against the equity they have in their homes. To determine equity the bank values the home and subtracts the mortgage balance. The maximum loan is 90% of the equity.

The bank outsources the home appraisals to three companies: Allen & Associates, Heist Appraisal, and Appraisal International. The bank managers know that appraisals are not exact. Some appraisal companies may overvalue homes on average, whereas others might undervalue homes.

Bank managers wish to test the hypothesis that there is no difference in the average house appraisal among the three different companies. The managers could select a random sample of homes for Allen & Associates to appraise, a second sample of homes for Heist Appraisal to work on, and a third sample of homes for Appraisal International. One-way ANOVA would be used to compare the sample means. Obviously a problem could occur if, by chance, one company received larger, higher-quality homes located in better neighborhoods than the other companies. This company's appraisals would naturally be higher on average, not because it tended to appraise higher, but because the homes were simply more expensive.

Citizen's State Bank officers need to control for the variation in size, quality, and location of homes to fairly test that the three companies' appraisals are equal on the average. To do this, they select a random sample of properties and have each company appraise the same properties. In this case, the properties are called *blocks*, and the test design is called a *randomized complete block design*.

The data in Table 11-5 were obtained when each appraisal company was asked to appraise the same five properties. The bank managers wish to test the following hypothesis.

$$H_0: \mu_1 = \mu_2 = \mu_3$$
$$H_A: \text{At least two populations have different means.}$$

The randomized block design requires the following assumptions:

**SSUMPTIONS**

1. The populations are normally distributed.
2. The populations have equal variances.
3. The observations within samples are independent.

You can check these assumptions using graphical methods (e.g., histograms and box and whisker diagrams) and the Hartley's *F*-test if you have sufficient sample sizes from each population.

Because the managers have chosen to have the same properties appraised by each company (block on property), the samples are not independent, and a method known as *randomized complete block ANOVA* must be employed to test the hypothesis. This method is similar to the one-way

TABLE 11-5

Citizen's State Bank Property Appraisals (in thousands of dollars)

Property (Block)	APPRAISAL COMPANY Allen & Associates	Heist Appraisal	Appraisal International	Block Mean
1	78	82	79	79.67
2	102	102	99	101.00
3	68	74	70	70.67
4	83	88	86	85.67
5	95	99	92	95.33
Factor Level Mean	85.2	89	85.2	86.47 = Grand Mean

ANOVA in Section 11-1. However, there is one more source of variation to be accounted for, the block variation. As was the case in Section 11-1, we must find estimators for each source of variation. Identifying the appropriate sums of squares and then dividing each by its degrees of freedom does this. As was the case in the one-way ANOVA, the sums of squares are obtained by partitioning the total sum of squares (SST). However, in this case the *SST* is divided into three components instead of two, as shown in Equation 11-8.

Sum of Squares Partitioning for Randomized Complete Block Design

$$SST = SSB + SSBL + SSW \qquad \textbf{11-8}$$

where:

SST = Total sum of squares
SSB = Sum of squares between factor levels
$SSBL$ = Sum of squares between blocks
SSW = Sum of squares within levels

Both *SST* and *SSB* are computed just as we did with one-way ANOVA, using Equations 11-3 and 11-4. The *sum of squares for blocking (SSBL)* is computed using Equation 11-9.

Sum of Squares for Blocking

$$SSBL = \sum_{j=1}^{b} k(\bar{x}_j - \bar{\bar{x}})^2 \qquad \textbf{11-9}$$

where:

k = Number of levels for the factor
b = Number of blocks
$\bar{x}_j$ = The mean of the *j*th block
$\bar{\bar{x}}$ = Grand mean

Finally, the *sum of squares within (SSW)* is computed using Equation 11-10. This sum of squares is what remains (the residual) after the variation for all known factors has been removed. This residual sum of squares may be due to the inherent variability of the data, measurement error, or other unidentified sources of variation. Therefore, the sum of squares within is also known as the sum of squares of error, *SSE*.

Sum of Squares Within

$$SSW = SST - (SSB + SSBL) \qquad \textbf{11-10}$$

The effect of computing *SSBL* and subtracting it from *SST* in Equation 11-9 is that *SSW* is reduced. Also, if the corresponding variation in the blocks is significant, the variation within the factor levels will be significantly reduced. This can make it easier to detect a difference in the population means if such a difference actually exists. If it does, the estimator for the within variability will in all likelihood be reduced and, thus, the denominator for the *F* test statistic will be smaller. This will pro-

	SOURCE OF VARIATION	SS	df	MS	F-RATIO
TABLE 11-6	Between blocks	SSBL	$b - 1$	MSBL	$\dfrac{MSBL}{MSW}$
Basic Format for the Randomized Block ANOVA Table	Between samples	SSB	$k - 1$	MSB	$\dfrac{MSB}{MSW}$
	Within samples	SSW	$(k - 1)(b - 1)$	MSW	
	Total	SST	$N - 1$		

where:

$$k = \text{Number of levels}$$
$$b = \text{Number of blocks}$$
$$df = \text{Degrees of freedom}$$
$$N = \text{Combined sample size}$$
$$MSB = \text{Mean square between} = \frac{SSB}{k - 1}$$
$$MSBL = \text{Mean square blocking} = \frac{SSBL}{b - 1}$$
$$MSW = \text{Mean square within} = \frac{SSW}{(k - 1)(b - 1)}$$

Note: Some randomized block ANOVA tables put *SSB* first, followed by *SSBL*.

duce a larger F test statistic, which will more likely lead to rejecting the null hypothesis. This will depend, of course, on the relative size of *SSBL* and the respective changes in the degrees of freedom.

Table 11-6 shows the completely randomized block ANOVA table format and equations for degrees of freedom, mean squares, and F-ratios. As you can see, we now have two F-ratios. The reason for this is that we test not only to determine whether the population means are equal, but also to obtain an indication of whether the blocking was necessary by examining the ratio of the mean square for blocks to the mean square within.

Although you could manually compute the necessary values for the randomized block design, both Excel and Minitab contain a procedure that will do all the computations and build the ANOVA table. The Citizen's State Bank appraisal data are included in your data diskette in the file *Citizens*. (Note that the first column contains labels for each block.)

Figures 11-9a and 11-9b show the ANOVA output. Using Excel or Minitab to perform the computations frees the decision maker to focus on interpreting the results. Note that Excel refers to the randomized block ANOVA as Two-Factor ANOVA without replication. Minitab refers to randomized block ANOVA as Two-Way ANOVA.

The main issue is to determine whether the three appraisal companies differ in average appraisal values. The primary test is

$$H_0: \mu_1 = \mu_2 = \mu_3$$
$$H_A: \text{At least two populations have different means.}$$
$$\alpha = 0.05$$

Using the output presented in Figures 11-9a and 11-9b, you can test this hypothesis two ways. First, we can use the F-distribution approach. Figure 11-10 shows the results of this test. Based on the sample data, we reject the null hypothesis and conclude that the three appraisal companies do not provide equal average values for properties.

The second approach to testing the null hypothesis is the p-value approach. The decision rule in an ANOVA application for p-values is

If p-value $< \alpha$, reject H_0;
Otherwise, do not reject H_0.

In this case,

$$\alpha = 0.05$$

and the p-value in Figure 11-9a is 0.0103. Because

$$p\text{-value} = 0.0103 < \alpha = 0.05$$

we

reject the null hypothesis

Both the F-distribution approach and the p-value approach give the same result, as they must.

FIGURE 11-9A

Excel Output: Citizen's State Bank Analysis of Variance

Excel Instructions:
1. Open file: Citizens.xls
2. Click on the **Tools** tab.
3. Select the **Data Analysis** option.
4. Select **ANOVA: Two-Factor Without Replication**.
5. Specify the data range.
6. Determine the desired alpha level.

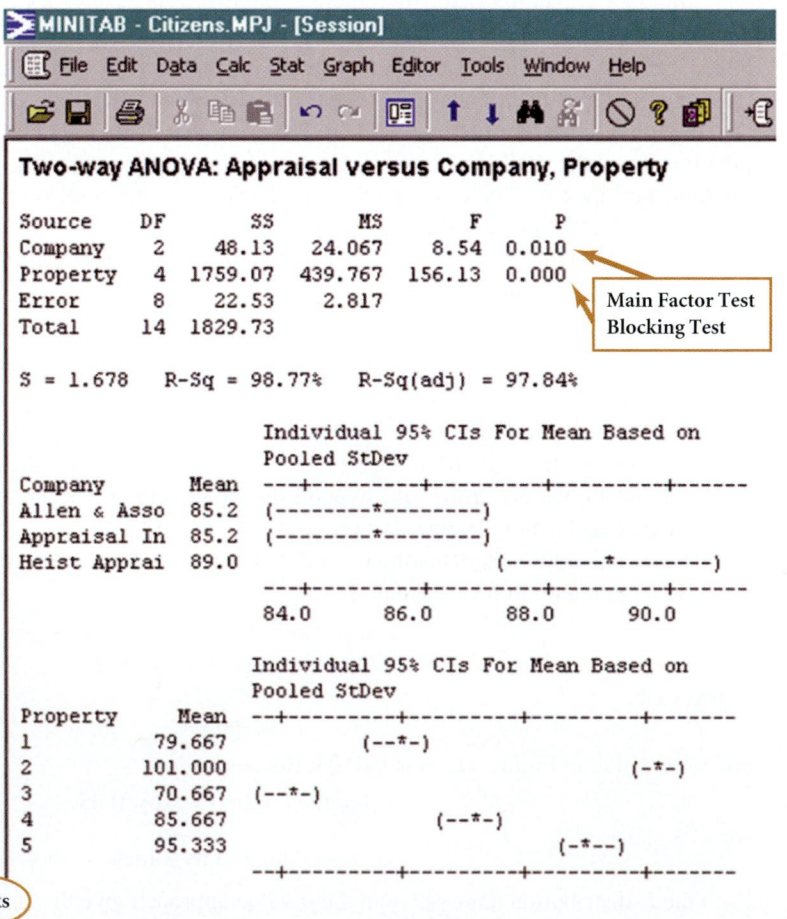

FIGURE 11-9B

Minitab: Citizen's State Bank Analysis of Variance Output

Minitab Instructions:
1. Open file: Citizens.MTW.
2. Choose **Stat > ANOVA > Two-way**.
3. In **Response**, enter the data column (*Appraisal*).
4. In **Row Factor**, enter main factor indicator column (*Company*) and select **Display Means**.
5. In **Column Factor**, enter the block indicator column (*Property*) and select **Display Means**.
6. Choose **Fit additive model**.
7. Click **OK**.

FIGURE 11-10

Appraisal Company
Hypothesis Test for Citizens
State Bank

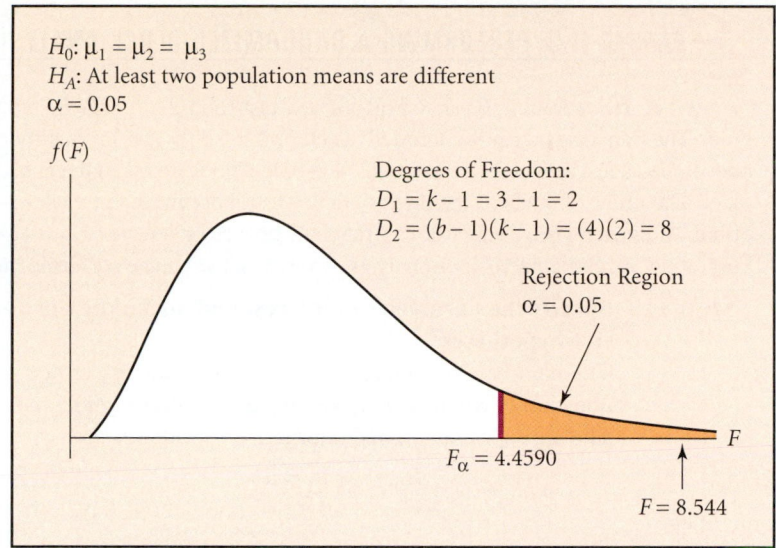

$H_0: \mu_1 = \mu_2 = \mu_3$
H_A: At least two population means are different
$\alpha = 0.05$

$f(F)$

Degrees of Freedom:
$D_1 = k - 1 = 3 - 1 = 2$
$D_2 = (b - 1)(k - 1) = (4)(2) = 8$

Rejection Region
$\alpha = 0.05$

$F_\alpha = 4.4590$

$F = 8.544$

Was Blocking Necessary?

Before we take up the issue of determining which company provides the highest mean property values, we need to discuss one other issue. Recall that the bank managers chose to control for variation between properties by having each appraisal company evaluate the same five properties. This restriction is called blocking, and the properties are the blocks. The ANOVA output in Figure 11-9a contains information that allows us to test whether blocking was necessary.

If the blocking was necessary, it would mean that appraisal values are in fact influenced by the particular property being appraised. The blocks then form a second factor of interest, and we formulate a secondary hypothesis test for this factor, as follows.

$$H_0: \mu_{b1} = \mu_{b2} = \mu_{b3} = \mu_{b4} = \mu_{b5}$$
$$H_A: \text{Not all block means are equal.}$$

Note that we are using μ_{bj} to represent the mean of the jth block.

It seems only natural to use a test statistic that consists of the ratio of the mean square for blocks to the mean square within. However, certain (randomization) restrictions placed on the complete block design make this proposed test statistic invalid from a theoretical-statistics point of view. As an approximate procedure, however, the examination of the ratio $MSBL/MSW$ is certainly reasonable. If it is large, it implies that the blocks had a large effect on the response variable and that they were probably helpful in improving the precision of the F-test for primary factor's means.[7] In performing the analysis of variance, we may also conduct a pseudo-test to see whether the average appraisals for each property are equal. If the null hypothesis is "rejected," we have an indication that the blocking is necessary and the randomized block design is justified. However, we should be careful to present this only as an indication and not a precise test of hypothesis for the blocks. The output in Figure 11-9a provides the F-value and p-value for this pseudo-test to determine if the blocking was a necessity. Because $F = 156.1302 > F_\alpha = 3.837$, we definitely have an indication that the blocking design was necessary.

If a hypothesis test indicates blocking is not necessary, the chance of a Type II error for the primary hypothesis has been unnecessarily increased by the use of blocking. The reason is that by blocking we not only partition the sum of squares, we also partition the degrees of freedom. Therefore, the denominator of MSW is decreased, and MSW will most likely increase. If blocking isn't needed, the MSW will tend to be relatively larger than if we had run a one-way design with independent samples. This can lead to failing to reject the null hypothesis for the primary test when it actually should have been rejected.

Therefore, if blocking is indicated to be unnecessary, follow these rules:

1. If the primary H_0 is rejected, proceed with your analysis and decision making. There is no concern.
2. If the primary H_0 is not rejected, redo the study without using blocking. Run a one-way ANOVA with independent samples.

---

[7]Many authors argue that the randomization restriction imposed by using blocks means that the F-ratio really is a test for the equality of the block means plus the randomization restriction. For a summary of this argument and references, see Montgomery, D. C., *Design and Analysis of Experiments*, 4th ed. (New York: John Wiley & Sons, 1997) pp. 175–176.

EXAMPLE 11-3: PERFORMING A RANDOMIZED BLOCK ANALYSIS OF VARIANCE

Fresh & Fun Inc.   Fresh & Fun is a new fast-food chain with three outlets in a midwestern community. The franchise owner is interested in determining if the service quality at the three is the same. She has developed a test in which she selected 14 people who were asked to eat at each of the three fast-food outlets. The order of visits to the three outlets was randomized, but each customer visited each outlet one time. After each visit, each customer rated the service on a scale of 1 to 1,000, with 1,000 being the highest rating. A randomized block analysis of variance test can be performed using the following steps.

Step 1:   **Specify the parameter of interest and formulate the appropriate null and alternative hypotheses.**

The parameter of interest is the mean customer-service rating for each outlet, and the question is whether there is a difference between the mean ratings at the three outlets. The appropriate null and alternative hypotheses are

$$H_0: \mu_1 = \mu_2 = \mu_3$$
$$H_A: \text{At least two populations have different means.}$$

In this case, the franchise owner wants to control for variation in customer standards by having the same customers visit each outlet. The ratings will be independent because the rating assigned by one customer does not influence the ratings assigned by other customers. Here the customers are the blocks.

Step 2:   **Select simple random samples from each population, check the normality and equal-variance assumptions, and compute treatment means, block means, and the grand mean.**

The following sample data were observed:

Customer	Outlet 1	Outlet 2	Outlet 3	Block Means
1	830	647	630	702.33
2	743	840	786	789.67
3	652	747	730	709.67
4	885	639	617	713.67
5	814	943	632	796.33
6	733	916	410	686.33
7	770	923	727	806.67
8	829	903	726	819.33
9	847	760	648	751.67
10	878	856	668	800.67
11	728	878	670	758.67
12	693	990	825	836.00
13	807	871	564	747.33
14	901	980	719	866.67
Treatment Means	793.57	849.50	668.00	770.36 = grand mean

Step 3:   **Compute the sums of squares and complete the ANOVA table.**

Four sums of squares are required:

Total Sum of Squares (Equation 11-3)

$$SST = \sum_{i=1}^{k} \sum_{j=1}^{n_i} (x_{ij} - \bar{\bar{x}})^2 = 614{,}641.6$$

Sum of Squares Between (Equation 11-4)

$$SSB = \sum_{i=1}^{k} n_i (\bar{x}_i - \bar{\bar{x}})^2 = 241{,}912.7$$

Sum of Squares Blocking (Equation 11-9)

$$SSBL = \sum_{j=1}^{b} k(\bar{x}_j - \bar{\bar{x}})^2 = 116{,}605$$

Sum of Squares Within (Equation 11-10)

$$SSW = SST - (SSB + SSBL) = 256,123.90$$

The ANOVA table is (see Table 11-6 format):

Source	SS	df	MS	F-Ratio
Between blocks	116,605.0	13	8,969.6	0.9105
Between samples	241,912.7	2	120,956.4	12.279
Within samples	256,123.9	26	9,850.9	
Total	614,641.6	41		

Step 4:   **Specify the level of significance for conducting the tests.**
The tests will be conducted using an $\alpha = 0.05$.

Step 5:   **Test to determine whether blocking is effective.**
Fourteen people were used to evaluate and rate customer service. These constitute the blocks, so if blocking is effective, the mean rating across the three fast-food outlets will not be the same for all 14 customers. The null and alternative hypotheses are

$$H_0: \mu_1 = \mu_2 = \mu_3 = \ldots = \mu_{14}$$
$$H_A: \text{Not all means are equal (blocking is effective).}$$

As shown in Step 3, the F test statistic to test this null hypothesis is formed by:

$$F = \frac{MSBL}{MSW} = \frac{8,969.6}{9,850.9} = 0.9105$$

The F-critical from the F-distribution, with alpha $= 0.05$ and $D_1 = 13$ and $D_2 = 26$ degrees of freedom, can be approximated using the F-distribution table in Appendix H as

$$F_{\alpha=.05} \approx 2.15$$

The exact F-critical can be found using the **FINV** function in Excel or the **Calc > Probability Distributions** command in Minitab as $F = 2.119$. Then, because

$$F = 0.9105 < F_{\alpha=.05} = 2.119, \text{ do not reject the null hypothesis}$$

This means that based on these sample data we cannot conclude that blocking was effective.

Step 6:   **Conduct the main hypothesis test to determine whether the treatments have equal means.**
We have three outlet locations. At issue is whether the mean service rating is equal for the three outlets. The appropriate null and alternative hypotheses are

$$H_0: \mu_1 = \mu_2 = \mu_3$$
$$H_A: \text{At least two populations have different means.}$$

As shown in the ANOVA table in step 3, the F test statistic for this null hypothesis is formed by:

$$F = \frac{MSB}{MSW} = \frac{120,956.4}{9,850.9} = 12.279$$

The F-critical from the F-distribution, with alpha $= 0.05$ and $D_1 = 2$ and $D_2 = 26$ degrees of freedom, can be approximated using the F-distribution table in Appendix H as

$$F_{\alpha=.05} \approx 3.40$$

The exact F-critical can be found using the **FINV** function in Excel or the **Calc > Probability Distributions** command in Minitab as $F = 3.369$. Then, because

$$F = 12.279 > F_{\alpha=.05} = 3.369, \text{ reject the null hypothesis}$$

Even though in step 5 we concluded that blocking was not effective, the sample data still lead us to reject the primary null hypothesis and conclude that the three outlets do not all have the same mean service rating.

FISHER'S LEAST SIGNIFICANT DIFFERENCE TEST

An analysis of variance test can be used to test whether the populations of interest have different means. However, even if the null hypothesis of equal population means is rejected, the ANOVA does not specify which population means are different. In Section 11-1, we showed how the Tukey–Kramer multiple comparisons procedure is used to determine where the population differences occur for a one-way ANOVA design. Likewise, *Fisher's least significant difference test* is one test for multiple comparisons that we can use for a randomized block ANOVA design.

If the primary null hypothesis has been rejected, then we can compare the absolute differences in sample means from any two populations to the *least significant difference (LSD)*, as computed using Equation 11-11.

Fisher's Least Significant Difference

$$LSD = t_{\alpha/2}\sqrt{MSW}\sqrt{\frac{2}{b}}$$

11-11

where:

$t_{\alpha/2}$ = One-tailed value from student's t-distribution for
$\dfrac{\alpha}{2}$ and $(k-1)(b-1)$ degrees of freedom

MSW = Mean square within from ANOVA table

b = Number of blocks

k = Number of levels of the main factor

ℰXAMPLE 11-4: APPLYING FISHER'S LEAST SIGNIFICANT DIFFERENCE TEST

Fresh & Fun Inc. Recall that in Example 11-3 the franchise operators for the three Fresh & Fun fast-food outlets used a randomized block ANOVA design to conclude that three outlets do not all have the same mean customer-service rating. To determine which populations have different means, you can use the following steps.

Step 1: **Compute the *LSD* statistic using Equation 11-11.**

$$LSD = t_{\alpha/2}\sqrt{MSW}\sqrt{\frac{2}{b}}$$

Using a significance level equal to 0.05, the t-critical for $(3-1)(14-1) = 26$ degrees of freedom is

$$t_{.05/2} = 2.0555$$

The mean square within from the ANOVA table (see Example 11-3, step 3) is
$$MSW = 9,850.9$$

The *LSD* is

$$LSD = t_{\alpha/2}\sqrt{MSW}\sqrt{\frac{2}{b}} = 2.0555\sqrt{9,850.9}\sqrt{\frac{2}{14}} = 77.1092$$

Step 2: **Compute the sample means from each population.**

$$\bar{x}_1 = \frac{\sum x}{n} = 793.57 \quad \bar{x}_2 = \frac{\sum x}{n} = 849.50 \quad \bar{x}_3 = \frac{\sum x}{n} = 668$$

Step 3: **Form all possible contrasts by finding the absolute differences between all pairs of sample means. Compare these to the LSD value.**

Absolute Difference	Comparison	Conclusion
$\lvert \bar{x}_1 - \bar{x}_2 \rvert = \lvert 793.57 - 849.50 \rvert = 55.93$	$55.93 < 77.1092$	
$\lvert \bar{x}_1 - \bar{x}_3 \rvert = \lvert 793.57 - 668 \rvert = 125.57$	$125.57 > 77.1092$	$\mu_1 \neq \mu_3$
$\lvert \bar{x}_2 - \bar{x}_3 \rvert = \lvert 849.50 - 668 \rvert = 181.50$	$181.50 > 77.1092$	$\mu_2 \neq \mu_3$

We infer, based on the sample data, that the mean customer-service rating for outlet 1 exceeds the mean for outlet 3, and the mean for outlet 2 exceeds the mean for outlet 3.

11-2: EXERCISES

Skill Development

11.12 The following data were collected for a randomized block ANOVA design with four populations and eight blocks:

	Group 1	Group 2	Group 3	Group 4
Block 1	56	44	57	84
Block 2	34	30	38	50
Block 3	50	41	48	52
Block 4	19	17	21	30
Block 5	33	30	35	38
Block 6	74	72	78	79
Block 7	33	24	27	33
Block 8	56	44	56	71

a. State the appropriate null and alternative hypotheses for both groups and blocks.
b. Construct the appropriate ANOVA table.
c. Using a significance level equal to 0.05, can you conclude that blocking was necessary in this case? Use a test-statistic approach.
d. Based on the data and a significance level equal to 0.05, is there a difference in population means for the four groups? Use a p-value approach.
e. If you found that a difference exists in part d, use the LSD approach to determine which populations have different means.

11.13 The following data were collected for a randomized block ANOVA design with three groups and 10 blocks:

	Group 1	Group 2	Group 3
Block 1	67	56	60
Block 2	45	42	41
Block 3	61	53	51
Block 4	30	29	24
Block 5	44	42	38
Block 6	85	84	81
Block 7	44	36	30
Block 8	67	56	59
Block 9	99	77	56
Block 10	35	60	67

a. Construct the appropriate ANOVA table.

b. Using a significance level equal to 0.05, can you conclude that blocking was effective in this case?
c. Based on the data and a significance level equal to 0.05, is there a difference in population means for the four groups?
d. If you found that a difference exists in part c, use the LSD approach to determine which populations have different means.

11.14 A randomized block ANOVA was performed, and the following partially completed ANOVA table is available:

Source of Variation	SS	df	MS	F-Ratio
Between blocks	4,560	7		
Between samples	8,900	3		
Within samples	____			—
Total	23,400			

a. How many populations are being tested? How many blocks were used?
b. Using a significance level equal to 0.05, what conclusion have you reached about whether blocking was necessary in this case? Be sure to state the appropriate null and alternative hypotheses.
c. What conclusion should be reached with respect to the primary null hypothesis? Test using a significance level equal to 0.05. Be sure to state the appropriate null and alternative hypotheses.
d. Given your results in part c, is it appropriate to perform a post-ANOVA multiple comparison test to determine which populations have different means? Discuss. If so, conduct the appropriate test and discuss the results.

11.15 A randomized block ANOVA was performed and the following partially completed ANOVA table is available:

Source of Variation	SS	df	MS	F-Ratio
Between blocks		14	2464.2857	
Between samples		6		
Within samples	56,900			—
Total	133,100			

a. How many populations are being tested?

b. How many blocks were used in this analysis of variance?

c. What is the calculated F-value for testing whether blocking was effective?

d. Based on your response to part c, using an alpha equal to 0.05, what conclusion have you reached about whether blocking was effective in this case? Be sure to state the appropriate null and alternative hypotheses.

e. What is the calculated F-value for testing the main hypothesis?

f. Based on your response to part e, what conclusion should be reached with respect to the primary null hypothesis? Test using an alpha level equal to 0.05. Be sure to state the appropriate null and alternative hypotheses.

11.16 A complete randomized block ANOVA has been performed on four populations using a three-blocks data set. It produces the following summary statistics: $SSBL = 25.667$, $SSB = 38.50$, $SSW = 5.333$, $\bar{x}_1 = 9.40$, $\bar{x}_2 = 9.425$, $\bar{x}_3 = 9.725$, and $\bar{x}_4 = 9.95$.

a. Without determining whether blocks should be included in the model, you are requested to conduct a completely randomized ANOVA on this data. Produce the ANOVA table for this experiment.

b. Turning now to the randomized block design, determine if the blocks should be used in this model.

c. If you determined in part b that the blocks should be included in the design, conduct a hypothesis test that the main factor's means are all equal to each other. If you concluded that blocks were not necessary, determine which of the main factor's means differ.

d. Use Fisher's LSD procedure to determine which of the main factor's means differ.

Business Application

11.17 Weekly cash sales records have been collected for four drive-in restaurants in Topeka, Kansas, for a six-week period. The following data were collected and are also contained in the CD-ROM file *Topeka*.

Week	Drive-in			
	1	2	3	4
1	$1,430	$ 980	$1,780	$2,300
2	2,200	1,400	2,890	2,680
3	1,140	1,200	1,500	2,000
4	880	1,300	1,470	1,900
5	1,670	1,300	2,400	2,540
6	990	550	1,600	1,900

a. If the assumptions of a one-way ANOVA design are satisfied in this case, what should be concluded about the average sales at the four drive-in restaurants in Topeka? Use a significance level of 0.05.

b. Discuss whether you think the assumptions of a one-way ANOVA are satisfied in this case and indicate why or why not. If they are not, what design is appropriate? Discuss.

c. Perform a randomized block ANOVA test using a significance level of 0.05 to determine whether the mean sales for the four drive-ins are equal.

d. Comment on any differences between these results and those in part a.

e. Suppose blocking was necessary and the researcher chose not to use blocks. Discuss what impact this could have on the results of the ANOVA.

f. Use Fisher's LSD procedure to determine which, if any, drive-ins have different true average weekly sales.

Advanced Applications

11.18 There are three commercial tax-preparation offices in Benbde, Minnesota. The local Better Business Bureau has been receiving some complaints that one of the offices does not understand tax law well enough to provide expert advice. The complaints state that to safeguard itself, the preparing office overstates the tax due by the payer and thus avoids later problems with the IRS.

The Better Business Bureau has decided to invest several hundred dollars in grant money to test the claim. It has selected eight people at random and has asked that they allow each of the three offices to prepare their taxes using the same information. The following data show the tax bills as figured by each office. The data are also located in the CD-ROM file *Tax-test*.

Return	Office 1	Office 2	Office 3
1	4,376.20	5,100.10	4,988.03
2	5,678.45	6,234.23	5,489.23
3	2,341.78	2,242.60	2,121.90
4	9,875.33	10,300.30	9,845.60
5	7,650.20	8,002.90	7,590.88
6	1,324.80	1,450.90	1,356.89
7	2,345.90	2,356.90	2,345.90
8	15,468.75	16,080.78	15,376.70

a. Discuss why the Better Business Bureau set this test up as a randomized block design. Why did it think it was important to have all three offices do the returns for each of the eight people?

b. Test to determine whether the blocking was necessary in this situation. Use a significance level of 0.01. State the null and alternative hypotheses.

c. Based on the sample data, can the Better Business Bureau conclude that there is a difference in the mean taxes due on tax returns? Test using a significance level of 0.01. State the appropriate null and alternative hypotheses.

d. Referring to part c, if you did conclude that a difference exists, use Fisher's LSD approach to determine which office has the highest mean tax due.

11.19 In a local community there are three grocery chain stores. The three have been carrying out a spirited advertising campaign in which each claims to have the lowest prices. A local news station recently sent a reporter to the three stores to check prices on several items. She found that for certain items each store had the lowest price. This survey didn't really answer the question for consumers. Thus, the station set up a test in which 20 shoppers were given different lists of grocery items and were sent to each of the three chain stores. The sales receipts from each of the three stores were recorded in the CD-ROM file called *Groceries*.

a. Why should this price test be conducted using the design that the television station used? What was it attempting to achieve by having the same shopping lists used at each of the three grocery stores?

b. Based on a significance level of 0.05 and these sample data, test to determine whether blocking was nec-

essary in this example. State the null and alternative hypotheses. Use a test-statistic approach.

c. Based on these sample data, can you conclude the three grocery stores have different sample means? Test using a significance level of 0.05. State the appropriate null and alternative hypotheses. Use a *p*-value approach.

d. Based on the sample data, which store has the highest average prices? Use Fisher's LSD test if appropriate.

Summary and Conclusions

Chapter 11 has illustrated through a wide variety of examples that there are many instances in business in which we are interested in testing to determine whether three or more populations have equal means. The technique for performing such tests is called analysis of variance. ANOVA is an extension of the two-sample *t*-test procedure introduced in Chapter 9. The basic logic is that if the sample means tend to be substantially different, then the hypothesis of equal means is rejected.

Depending upon the experimental design employed, there are different hypothesis tests that must be used. The most elementary of these experimental designs is the one-way design, which is used to test whether three or more populations have equal mean values when the samples from the populations are considered to be independent. If we need to control for an outside source of variation (analogous to forming paired samples in Chapter 9), we can use the randomized complete block design.

Regardless of which method is used, if the null hypothesis of equal means is rejected, methods exist to determine which pairs of populations have different means. Methods such as the Tukey-Kramer and Fisher's LSD method allow us to examine all possible contrasts without expanding the experiment-wide significance level.

Analysis of variance is actually an array of statistical techniques used to test hypotheses related to these (and more) experimental designs. By completing this chapter, you will have been introduced to some of the most popular ANOVA techniques.

EQUATIONS

Partitioned Sum of Squares
$$SST = SSB + SSW \qquad \textbf{11-1}$$

F Test Statistic
$$F_{max} = \frac{s^2_{max}}{s^2_{min}} \qquad \textbf{11-2}$$

Total Sum of Squares
$$SST = \sum_{i=1}^{k}\sum_{j=1}^{n_i}(x_{ij} - \bar{\bar{x}})^2 \qquad \textbf{11-3}$$

Sum of Squares Between
$$SSB = \sum_{i=1}^{k} n_i(\bar{x}_i - \bar{\bar{x}})^2 \qquad \textbf{11-4}$$

Sum of Squares Within
$$SSW = SST - SSB \qquad \textbf{11-5}$$
or
$$SSW = \sum_{i=1}^{k}\sum_{j=1}^{n_i}(x_{ij} - \bar{x}_i)^2 \qquad \textbf{11-6}$$

Tukey-Kramer Critical Range
$$\text{Critical Range} = q_\alpha \sqrt{\frac{MSW}{2}\left(\frac{1}{n_i}+\frac{1}{n_j}\right)} \qquad \textbf{11-7}$$

Sum of Squares Partitioning for Randomized Complete Block Design
$$SST = SSB + SSBL + SSW \qquad \textbf{11-8}$$

Sum of Squares for Blocking
$$SSBL = \sum_{j=1}^{b} k(\bar{x}_j - \bar{\bar{x}})^2 \qquad \textbf{11-9}$$

Sum of Squares Within
$$SSW = SST - (SSB + SSBL) \qquad \textbf{11-10}$$

Fisher's Least Significant Difference
$$LSD = t_{\alpha/2}\sqrt{MSW}\sqrt{\frac{2}{b}} \qquad \textbf{11-11}$$

Key Terms

CHAPTER EXERCISES

Conceptual Questions

11.20 Explain in your own terms the logic of analysis of variance.

11.21 Discuss why in some circumstances it is appropriate to use the randomized complete block design. Give an example other than those discussed in the text in which this design could be used.

11.22 In a randomized complete block's ANOVA, the conclusion might be reached that blocking is not necessary.
a. What does this imply to the decision maker?
b. Why can this happen?
c. What should be done if it does happen? Discuss.

11.23 Consider some decision-making situations in your major and describe two or more in which tests of three or more population means are important.

11.24 Discuss in your own words each of the following:
a. Within-group variation
b. Between-group variation
c. Total sum of squares
d. Degrees of freedom

11.25 A one-way analysis of variance has just been performed. The conclusion reached is that the null hypothesis stating that the population means are equal has not been rejected. What would you expect the Tukey-Kramer procedure for multiple comparisons to show if it were performed for all pairwise comparisons? Discuss.

11.26 A one-way and a randomized complete block's ANOVA have been conducted on the same set of data.
a. Explain the relative sizes of both analysis of variances' sum of squares and degrees of freedom.
b. If the randomized complete block's ANOVA concluded that blocking was unnecessary, what would you expect to be the relative size of SSB in the two ANOVAs? Explain your answer.
c. When blocking is used unnecessarily, what impact does this have on the components of the ANOVA? Support your answer with reasons.

11.27 In any of the multiple-comparison techniques (Tukey-Kramer, LSD, etc.), the estimate of the within-sample variance uses data from the entire experiment. However, if one were to do a two-sample t-test to determine if there were a difference between any two means, the estimate of the population variances would only include data from the two specific samples under consideration. Explain this seeming discrepancy.

Business Applications

11.28 In an effort to improve the academic preparation of junior-high school students in the Dallas–Fort Worth metroplex, a group of concerned parents examined the number of hours per week spent doing homework by ninth-grade boys and girls attending public, private (nonreligious), and religious junior-high schools in the area. A random sample of 15 boys and 15 girls from the three types of schools were monitored during the semester and the average number of weekly hours that each spent doing homework was recorded. The data are in the CD-ROM file *Homework*.

The parents would like to know if the type of school makes a difference in the amount of hours students spend on homework. They would also like to determine if there is a difference in the average number of hours spent on homework by boys and girls.
a. Is there a significant interaction effect between the type of school and each student's gender? Justify and explain your answer.
b. At the 0.05 level of significance, is there evidence of a difference in the average number of hours spent on homework by type of school? Does one type of school require significantly fewer hours of homework per week? If so, identify the type of school.
c. At the 0.05 level of significance, is there a difference in the average number of hours spent on homework by gender?

11.29 Gordon Manufacturing produces golf balls. Recently, Gordon developed a golf ball made from a space-age material. This new golf ball promises greater distance off the tee. To test Gordon Manufacturing's claim, a test was set up to measure the average distance of four different golf balls (the New Gordon, Competitor 1, Competitor 2, and Competitor 3) hit by a driving machine. The results (rounded to the nearest yard) are listed in the CD-ROM file *Gordon*. Conduct a test to determine if there are significant differences due to type of golf ball. Use an alpha value = 0.05.

11.30 The materials planning group at Selser Industries is responsible for managing the inventory for all component parts and subassemblies used in the manufacturer of the firm's products. Because the group monitors more than 100,000 stock keeping units (SKUs), they must use a computer to assist them in their inventory control efforts. For example, the group uses the computer to calculate the requirements for all component parts of the firm's production plans. These material requirements planning (MRP) calculations are time-consuming, and Selser is currently evaluating six MRP software packages to determine if there are significant differences in the time required by each to calculate materials requirements. Each software package was installed on Selser's computer and used to calculate the material requirements for a random sample of production plans. The results that were reported are included in the CD-ROM file *Selser*.
a. (1) Determine if the variances in the time required by different software packages to calculate materials requirements can be considered equal. Use a significance level of 0.05. (2) Assume the distributions of the time required by different software packages to calculate materials requirements are normal. Comment on whether you would be justified in using a one-way ANOVA procedure to determine that the times required by different software packages to calculate materials requirements were the same.
b. At the 0.01 level of significance, would the materials planning group conclude that the software package

makes a difference in the average time required to calculate the material plans? Use the test-statistic approach.

c. (1) At the 0.01 level of significance, is there evidence to conclude that Accumat calculates material requirements plans faster than Explode? (2) Is it possible to identify a clear winner on the basis of speed of calculation, or will Selser need to examine other criteria to decide on the "best" package?

Advanced Applications

11.31 PhoneEx provides call center services for many different companies. A large increase in its business has made it necessary to establish a new call center. One of four cities will be selected: Little Rock, Wichita, Tulsa, and Memphis. The new center will employ approximately 1,500 workers, and PhoneEx will transfer 75 managers from its Omaha center to the new location. One concern in the choice of where to locate the new center is the cost of housing for the managers who will be moving there. To help determine whether significant housing-cost differences exist across the competing sites, PhoneEx has asked a real estate broker in each city to randomly select a list of 33 homes between 5 and 15 years old and ranging in size between 1,975 and 2,235 square feet. The prices (in dollars) that were recorded for each city are contained in the CD-ROM file *PhoneEx*.

a. At the 0.05 level of significance, is there evidence to conclude that average price of houses between 5 and 15 years old and ranging in size between 1,975 and 2,235 square feet is not the same in the four cities? Use the *p*-value approach.

b. At the 0.05 level of significance, is there a difference in average housing price between Wichita and Little Rock? Between Little Rock and Tulsa? Between Tulsa and Memphis?

c. Determine the sample size required to estimate the average housing price in Wichita to within $500 with a 95% confidence level. Assume the required parameters' estimates are sufficient for this calculation.

11.32 GroBros, a regional grocery store chain located in the intermountain West, is considering upgrading to a new series of price scanners for its checkout lanes. Although scanners can save checkers a great deal of time, scanners will sometimes misread an item's price code. Before investing in one of three new systems, GroBros would like to determine if there is a difference in scanner accuracy. To investigate possible differences, 30 shopping baskets were randomly selected from customers at the Boise store. The 30 baskets differed from each other in the number and types of items each contained. The items in each basket were then scanned by the three new scanners under consideration, as well as by the scanner type used in all GroBros stores, at a specially designed scanner set up for the analysis. Each item was also checked manually, and a count was kept of the number of scanning errors made by each scanner for each basket. Each of the scannings was repeated 30 times, and the average number of scanning errors was determined. The sample data are in the CD-ROM file *GroBros*.

a. What type of experimental design did GroBros use to test for differences among scanners? Why was this type of design selected?

b. State the primary hypotheses of interest for this test.

c. At the 0.01 level of significance, is there a difference in the average number of errors among the four different scanners?

d. (1) Is there a difference in the average number of errors by shopping basket? (2) Was GroBros correct in blocking by shopping basket?

e. If you determined that there is a difference in the average number of errors among the four different scanners, identify where those differences exist.

f. Do you think that GroBros should upgrade from its existing scanner to Scanner A, Scanner B, or Scanner C? What other factors may it want to consider before making a decision?

11.33 Phone Solutions provides assistance to users of a personal-finance software package. Users call Phone Solutions with their questions, and trained consultants provide answers and information. One concern that Phone Solutions must deal with regularly is the staffing of its call centers. If the centers are understaffed, callers seeking help must wait for long periods before reaching a consultant. Many callers are unwilling to wait for more than a couple of minutes before hanging up. If the centers are overstaffed, some consultants will be idle for a large part of their shift. Phone Solutions has invested heavily in a technology to help route calls to each of its three centers so that a uniform number of calls is being handled at each center each day. However, the number of calls can differ depending on the day. Also, if one center takes a great deal more time to handle each caller's request, then there will be a need to redirect calls and perhaps personnel, so that a more-uniform usage pattern across centers is maintained. Phone Solutions has collected data on the average lengths of phone calls (in minutes) for the three centers on 50 randomly selected days. These sample data are in the CD-ROM file *Phone Solutions*.

Phone Solutions would like to determine if there is a difference in the average lengths of phone calls among the three call centers.

a. State the null and alternative hypotheses of interest to Phone Solutions.

b. Is there an effect due to the day a call is made? Was Phone Solutions right in using this experimental design?

c. At the 0.05 level of significance, is there sufficient evidence to conclude that there is a difference in the average lengths of calls by call center?

d. If there is a difference in the average length of a call to a center, which center takes the greatest amount of time to handle calls?

e. What might Phone Solutions do to equalize the amount of time across centers?

11.34 In order to determine whether differences exist in grocery prices charged by three supermarket chains located in a small city in the southwestern United States, a consumer group purchased a "typical" shopping basket of groceries from each of the three stores every week for 26 weeks. The typical basket of groceries was the same for all three stores in any week. The price for each basket by store for each of the 26 weeks is shown in the CD-ROM file *Grocery Store*.

a. (1) Determine if the variance in the average price paid for the typical shopping basket among the three stores is equal. Use a significance level of 0.05. (2) Assume that the distributions of the average prices paid for the typical shopping basket among the three stores are normal. Comment on whether you would be justified if you were to use a one-way ANOVA procedure.

b. At the 0.05 level of significance, is there evidence of a significant difference in the average price paid for the typical shopping basket among the three stores?

c. Which pairs of stores differ in the average price of the typical shopping basket? Does one store clearly appear to be more expensive than the others? If so, which store?

d. Are there significant differences in the price of the shopping basket from week to week?

11.35 To determine whether there is a difference in average weekly hours of computer usage by college major, the manager of the computer laboratories at a state university in North Dakota randomly samples 155 observations from computer records kept at the lab. When entering the lab, student computer users must enter a code that indicates their college: (1) for Engineering; (2) for Arts and Sciences; and (3) for Business. The computer then keeps track of each student's start and stop time. At the end of the semester, the lab manager randomly selected the 155 records contained in the CD-ROM file *Lab-Time*.

a. State the null and alternative hypotheses of interest to the computer laboratory manager.

b. At the 0.01 level of significance, is there a significant difference in the average hours of weekly laboratory use by major?

c. What is the *p*-value for the test you conducted in part b?

d. If the average weekly amount of computer usage were actually the same for Engineering and Business, determine the probability that a difference in the sample means as large or larger than observed would occur. Assume the estimates for the relevant population parameters obtained in this problem are sufficient for this purpose.

11.36 Hypos, a marketer of computer games, is interested in determining whether there is a difference in the average dollar amount spent on its games. It wishes to know if this difference depends on whether the customer places an order online (using the Internet), over the telephone, by mail (catalog), or in one of the company's retail stores. Hypos hopes to use this information to determine how best to advertise and market its products. The VP of marketing for Hypos randomly selected sales receipts from Internet orders, phone and catalog orders, and in-store sales. These data are contained in the CD-ROM file *Hypos*.

a. Based on the sample data, what would be your conclusion about the average purchase amounts by customers from the different sources at the 0.01 level of significance?

b. If you concluded that differences in population means differ, identify which pairs of means differ.

c. How could Hypos use this information in its marketing and advertising programs?

CASE 11-A:

Consumer Information Association

Yolanda Carson is a newly hired research assistant for the Consumer Information Association. The association is a non-profit group whose major purpose is to supply information necessary to help consumers make better-informed decisions. Yolanda has been assigned to work with the group studying consumer practices in the banking industry.

Yolanda is aware of studies that indicate that the interest banks charge for loans is related to demographic factors such as the size of the city in which the banks are located and whether the state allows branch banks. She has been asked to determine whether there is a difference in consumer loan charges between major sections of the country.

Yolanda has been assured the cooperation of the American Banking Institute and has been given access to any data the institute has. However, she knows that loan charges may depend on many factors, and she feels compelled to study banks firsthand. In particular, she has decided to randomly select banks in all parts of the country and to apply for an automobile loan at each bank selected. She has decided to make the test during two time periods six months apart.

Because consumer interest rates have been changing rapidly lately, Yolanda has recorded all rates in terms of the prime rate plus a certain percentage. (The prime rate is the rate large banks charge their largest corporate customers.) In the first test, Yolanda found the following values charged. These data are also contained in the data file *Consumer Interest*.

NORTHEAST	SOUTHEAST	MIDWEST	WEST
3.2	2.7	3.4	3.7
2.9	2.9	3.5	3.6
2.8	3.0	2.9	3.6
3.5	2.0	3.7	3.9
3.4	2.8	3.4	4.0
4.0	2.5	3.5	3.8
3.2	2.7	3.0	3.4
	2.9		3.8

The executive director of the Consumer Information Association will be holding a news conference in a few days to discuss the work the organization has been doing. He would like to be able to cite Yolanda's study as an example of its services.

CASE 11-B:

West Coast Bell System 💿

James Todd is the recently appointed director of employee benefits for West Coast Bell, a regional telephone system. The West Coast Bell medical-benefits system insures more than 60,000 employees and dependents. Over the last five years its medical costs have been increasing by more than 20% annually. James knows that many companies, when facing these annual increases, have tried to pass some of the medical costs to their employees, generally by increasing the deductible allowance for each treatment visit. He has decided to look into the possibility of developing a managed-care network. Managed-care networks are a recent development in health care. They involve a company contracting with a group of physicians and hospitals to provide a variety of health care services. The company monitors the cost of the care provided to its employees and holds discussions with those whose costs are high. In some cases, the relationship between the company and either a hospital or physician will be terminated. Some companies using managed-care networks have held their health care cost increases to less than one-third of the previous levels.

James has recently read a study that reported on the cost of an outpatient procedure that determines the extent to which a patient's arteries are closed. One hospital in Kansas City charged more than $5,000 for the operation, whereas a second, also in Kansas City, charged less than $3,000. James decided to use this operation to determine whether categories of hospitals tended to charge less for this procedure. The four categories of hospitals he identified were university-related, religious-affiliated, municipally owned, and profit-making. He contacted 10 hospitals on the West Coast in each category, asking what they charged for this operation. Not all responded, and some who did provided data that could not readily be compared with that provided by the majority of respondents. The reported costs are shown here and are also contained in the CD-ROM file *Hospitals*.

UNIVERSITY-RELATED	RELIGIOUS-AFFILIATED	MUNICIPALLY-OWNED	PRIVATELY-HELD
$6,120	$4,010	$4,320	$5,100
5,960	3,770	4,650	4,920
6,300	3,960	4,575	5,200
6,500	3,620	4,440	5,345
6,250	3,280	4,900	4,875
6,695	3,680	4,560	5,330
6,475	3,350	4,610	5,415
6,250	3,250	4,850	5,150
6,880	3,400		5,380
6,550			

James plans to prepare a report on this study for presentation to the West Coast Bell committee on health and benefits.

General References

1. Berenson, Mark L., and David M. Levine, *Basic Business Statistics: Concepts and Applications*, 7th ed. (Upper Saddle River, NJ: Prentice Hall, 1999).
2. Bowerman, Bruce L., and Richard T. O'Connell, *Linear Statistical Models: An Applied Approach*, 2nd ed. (Belmont, CA: Duxbury Press, 1990).
3. Cox, D. R., *Planning of Experiments*, (New York: John Wiley & Sons, 1992).
4. Cryer, Jonathan D., and Robert B. Miller, *Statistics for Business: Data Analysis and Modeling*, 2nd ed. (Belmont, CA: Duxbury Press, 1994).
5. *Microsoft Excel 2000* (Redmond, WA: Microsoft Corp., 1999).
6. *Minitab for Windows Version 14* (State College, PA: Minitab, 2003).
7. Montgomery, D. C., *Design and Analysis of Experiments*, 4th ed. (New York: John Wiley & Sons, 1997).
8. Neter, John, Michael H. Kutner, Christopher J. Nachtsheim, and William Wasserman, *Applied Linear Statistical Models*, 4th ed. (Homewood, IL: Richard D. Irwin, 1996).
9. Searle, S. R., and R. F. Fawcett (1970). "Expected Mean Squares in Variance Component Models Having Finite Populations." *Biometrics*, Vol. 26, pp. 243–254.

CHAPTERS 7-11

Special Review Section

This review section, which is presented using block diagrams and flowcharts, is intended to help you tie together the material from several key chapters. This section is not a substitute for reading and studying the chapters covered by the review. However, you can use this review material to add to your understanding of the individual topics in the chapters.

CHAPTERS 7 TO 11

Statistical inference is the process of reaching conclusions about a population based on a random sample selected from the population. Chapters 7 to 11 introduced the fundamental concepts of statistical inference involving two major categories of inference, *estimation and hypothesis testing*. These chapters have covered a fairly wide range of different situations that for beginning students can sometimes seem overwhelming. The following diagrams will hopefully help you better identify which specific estimation or hypothesis-testing technique to use in a given situation. These diagrams form something resembling an expert system that you should be able to use as a guide through the estimation and hypothesis-testing processes.

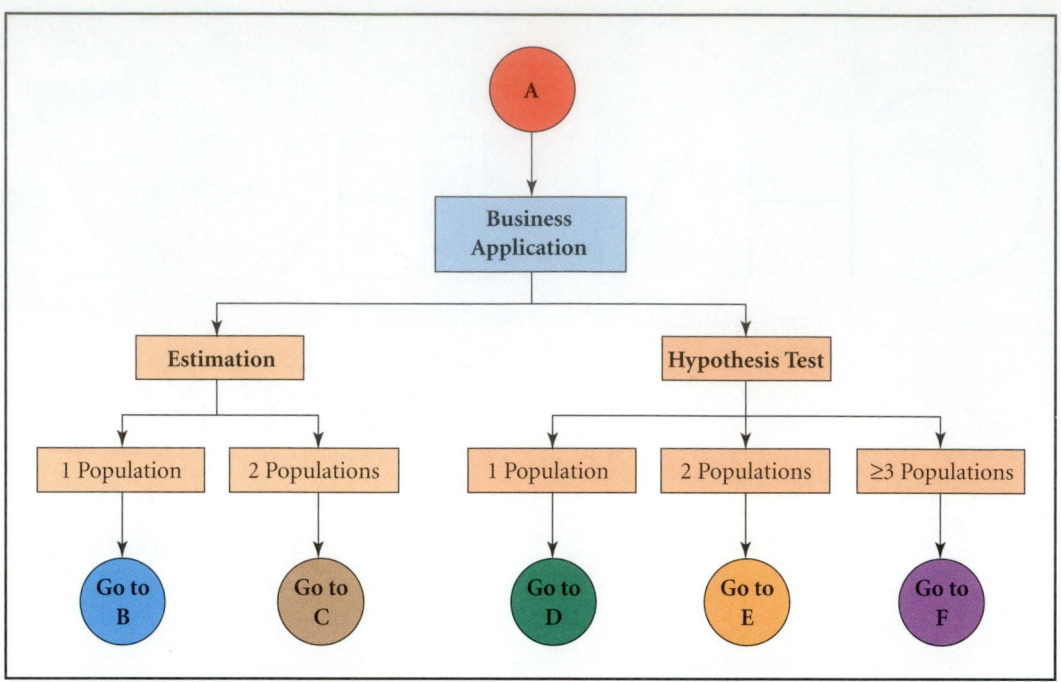

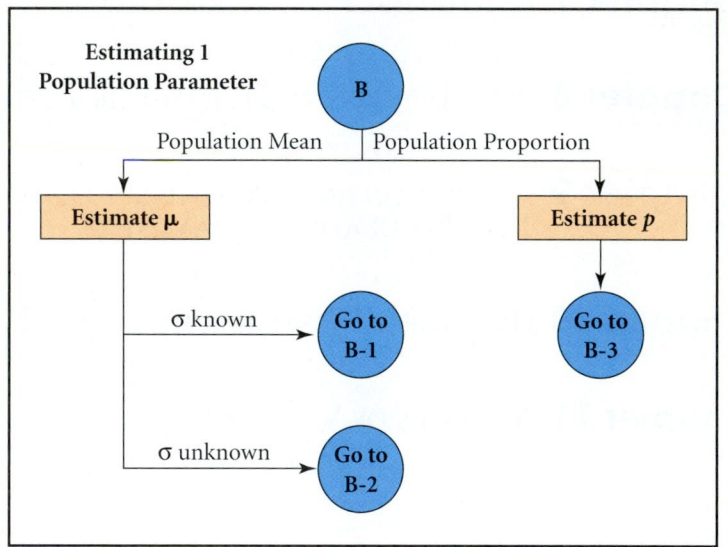

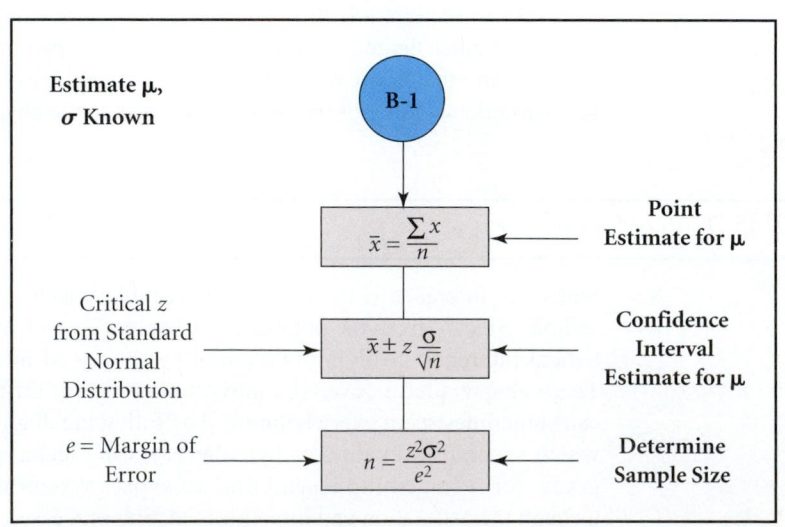

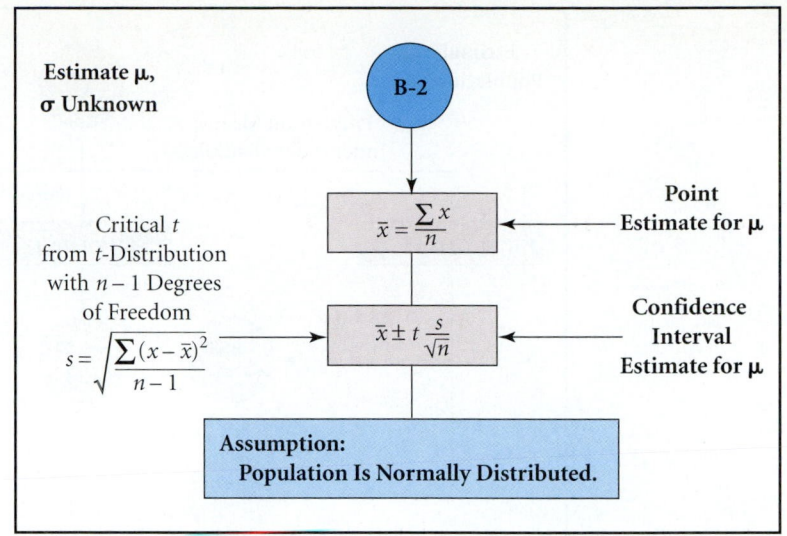

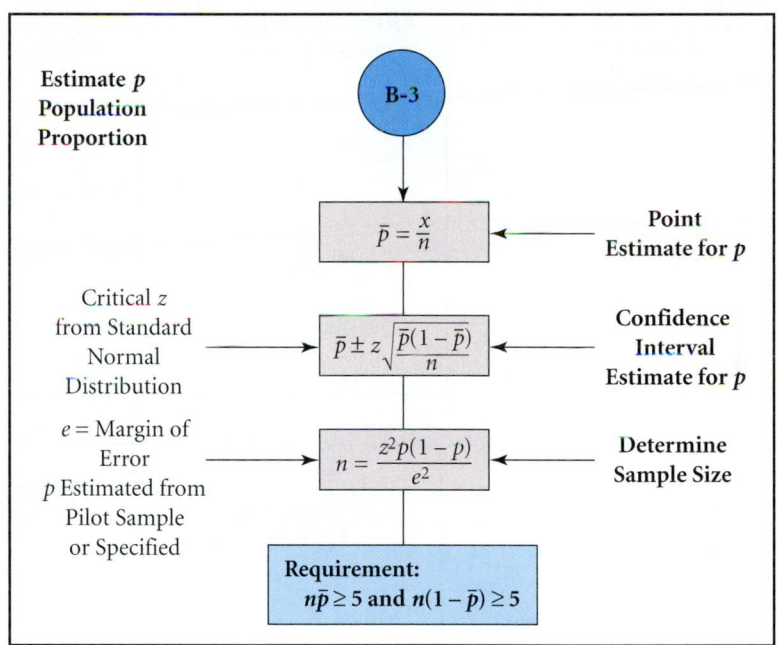

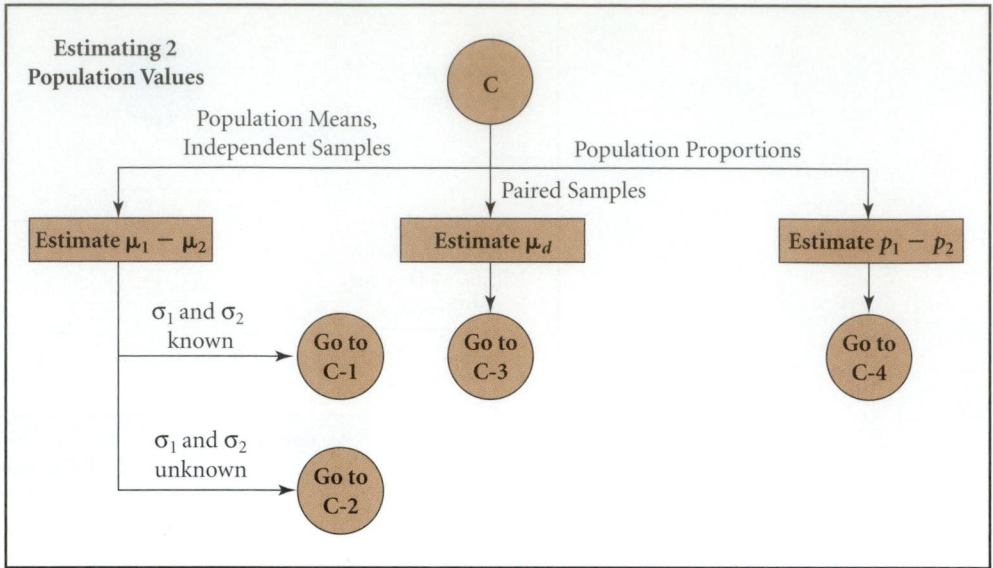

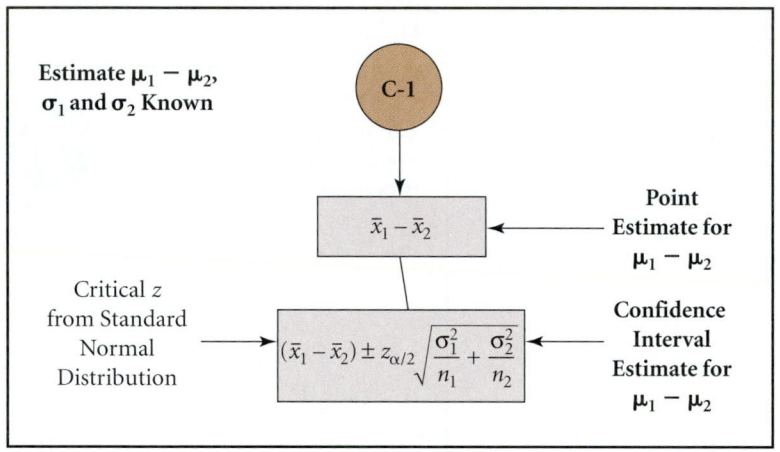

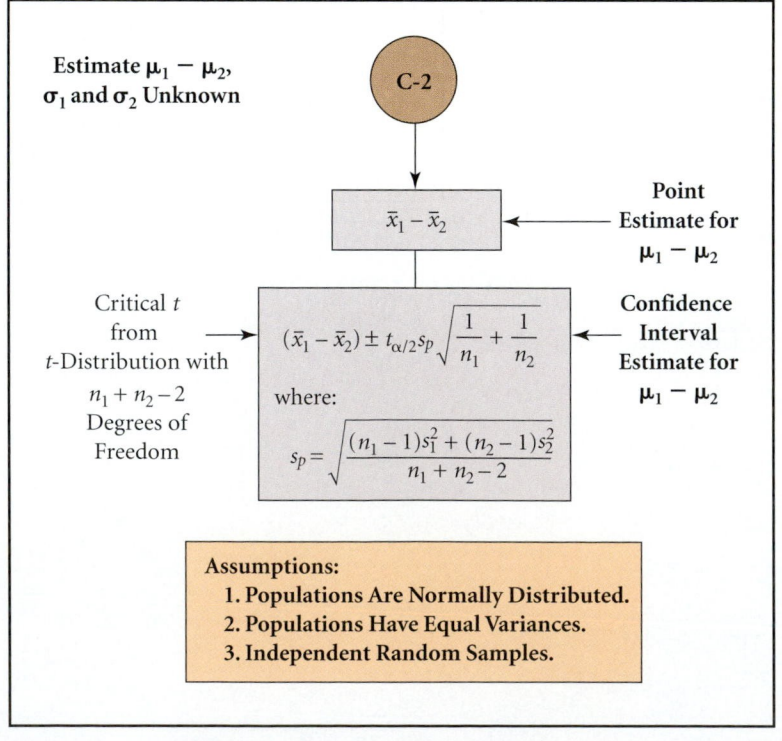

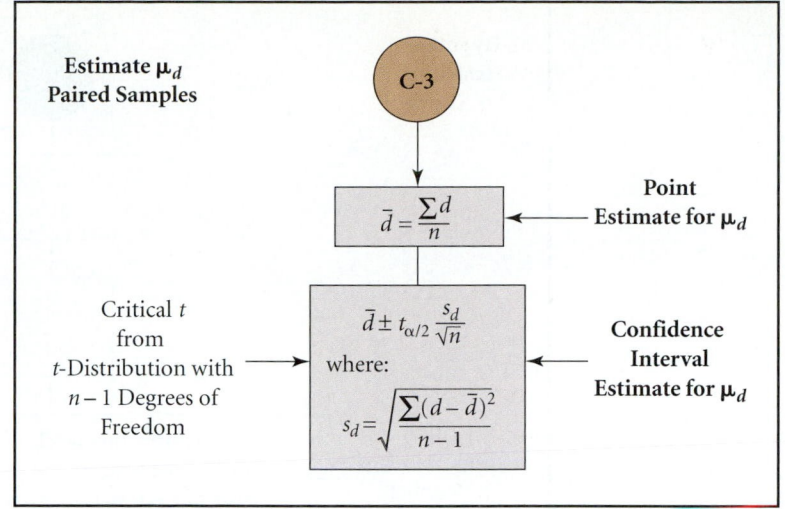

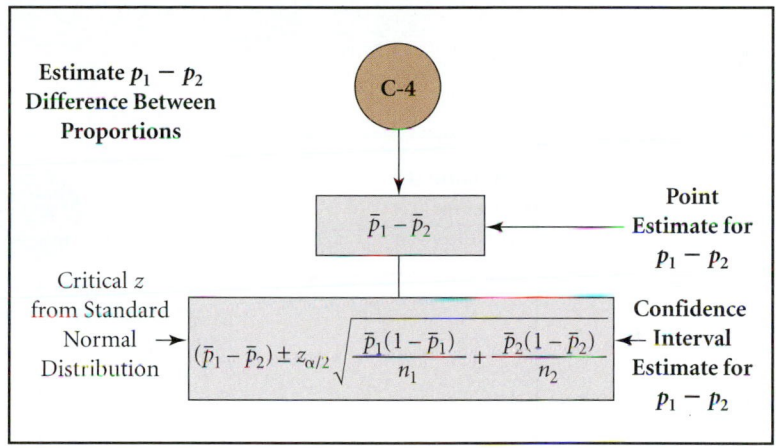

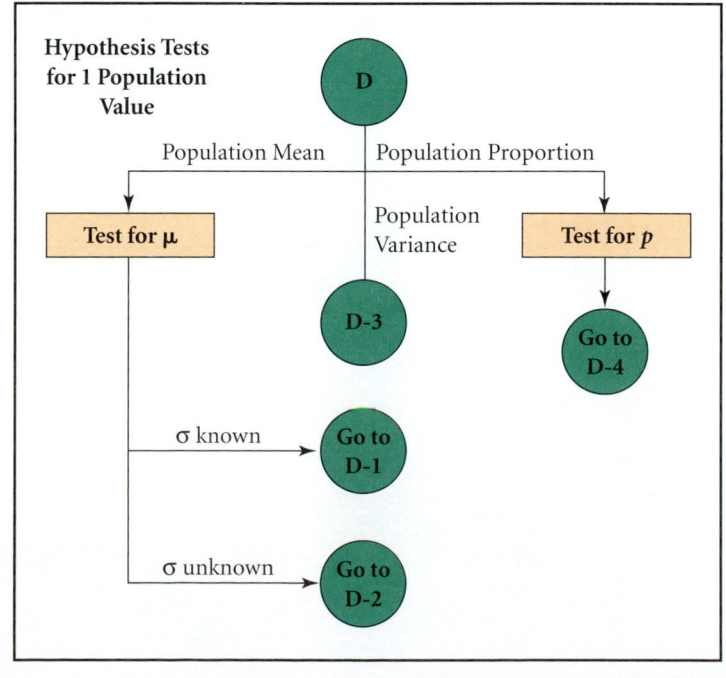

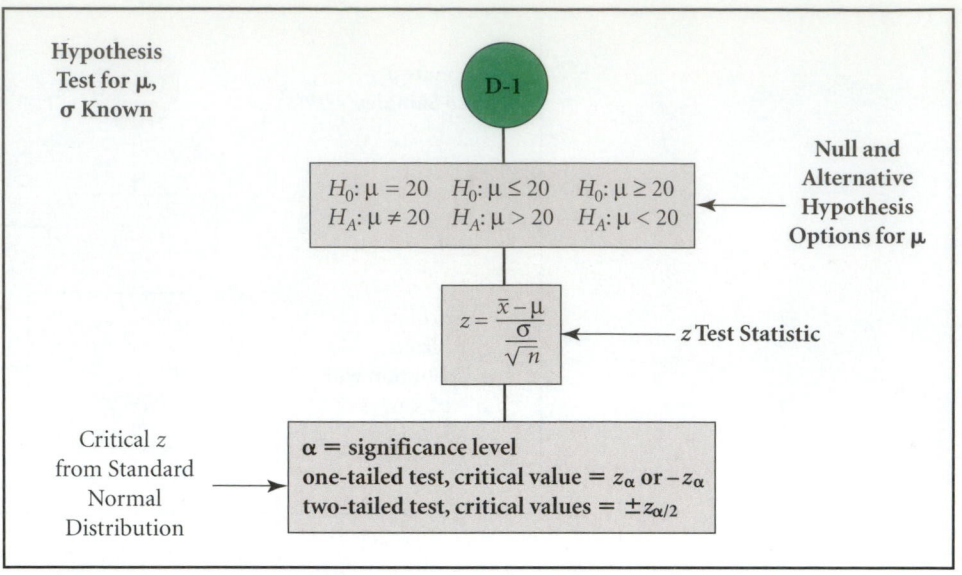

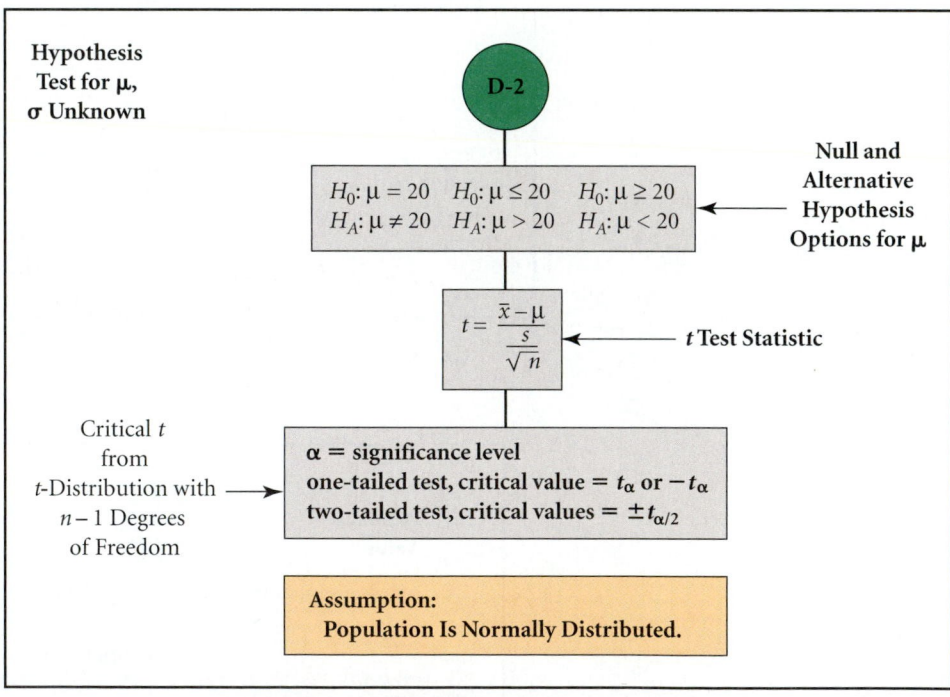

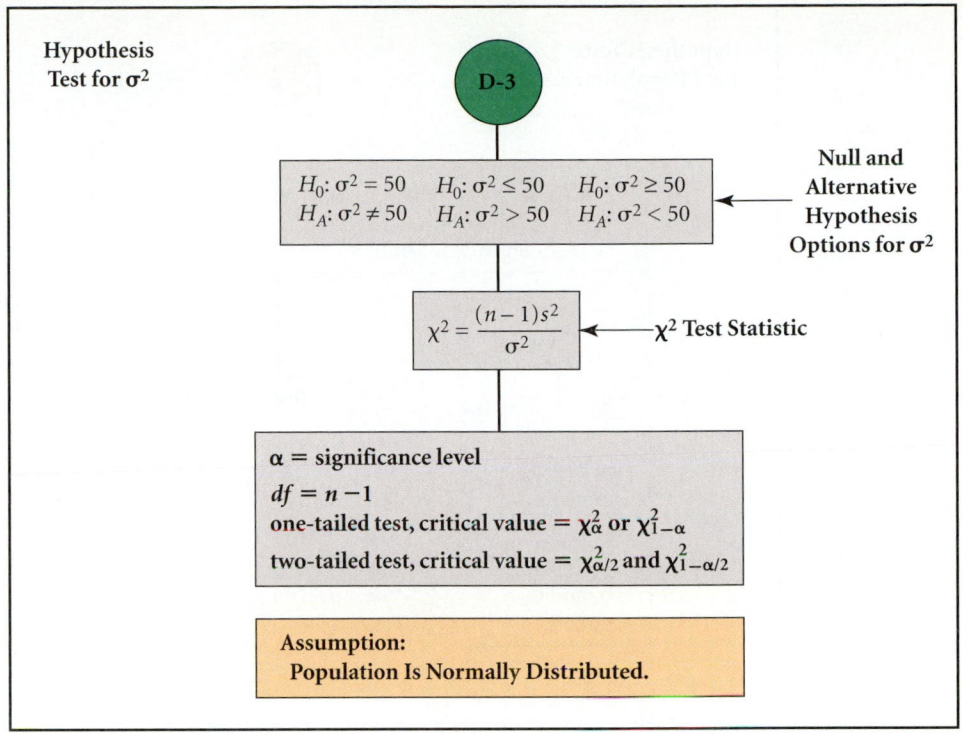

Hypothesis
Test for σ^2

D-3

$$H_0: \sigma^2 = 50 \quad H_0: \sigma^2 \le 50 \quad H_0: \sigma^2 \ge 50$$
$$H_A: \sigma^2 \ne 50 \quad H_A: \sigma^2 > 50 \quad H_A: \sigma^2 < 50$$

Null and
Alternative
Hypothesis
Options for σ^2

$$\chi^2 = \frac{(n-1)s^2}{\sigma^2}$$

χ^2 Test Statistic

α = significance level

$df = n - 1$

one-tailed test, critical value = χ^2_α or $\chi^2_{1-\alpha}$

two-tailed test, critical value = $\chi^2_{\alpha/2}$ and $\chi^2_{1-\alpha/2}$

Assumption:
Population Is Normally Distributed.

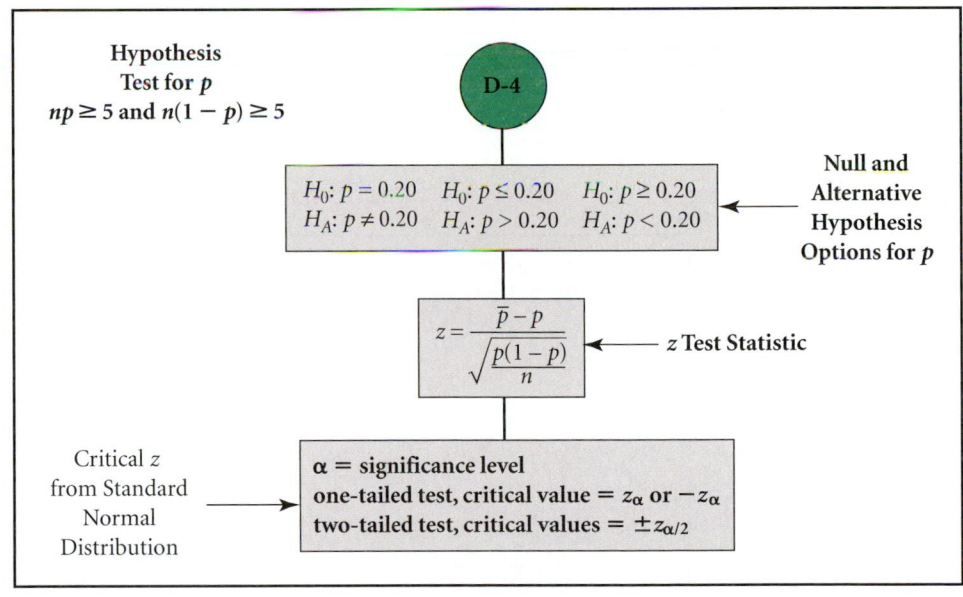

Hypothesis
Test for p
$np \ge 5$ and $n(1-p) \ge 5$

D-4

$$H_0: p = 0.20 \quad H_0: p \le 0.20 \quad H_0: p \ge 0.20$$
$$H_A: p \ne 0.20 \quad H_A: p > 0.20 \quad H_A: p < 0.20$$

Null and
Alternative
Hypothesis
Options for p

$$z = \frac{\bar{p} - p}{\sqrt{\dfrac{p(1-p)}{n}}}$$

z Test Statistic

Critical z
from Standard
Normal
Distribution

α = significance level

one-tailed test, critical value = z_α or $-z_\alpha$

two-tailed test, critical values = $\pm z_{\alpha/2}$

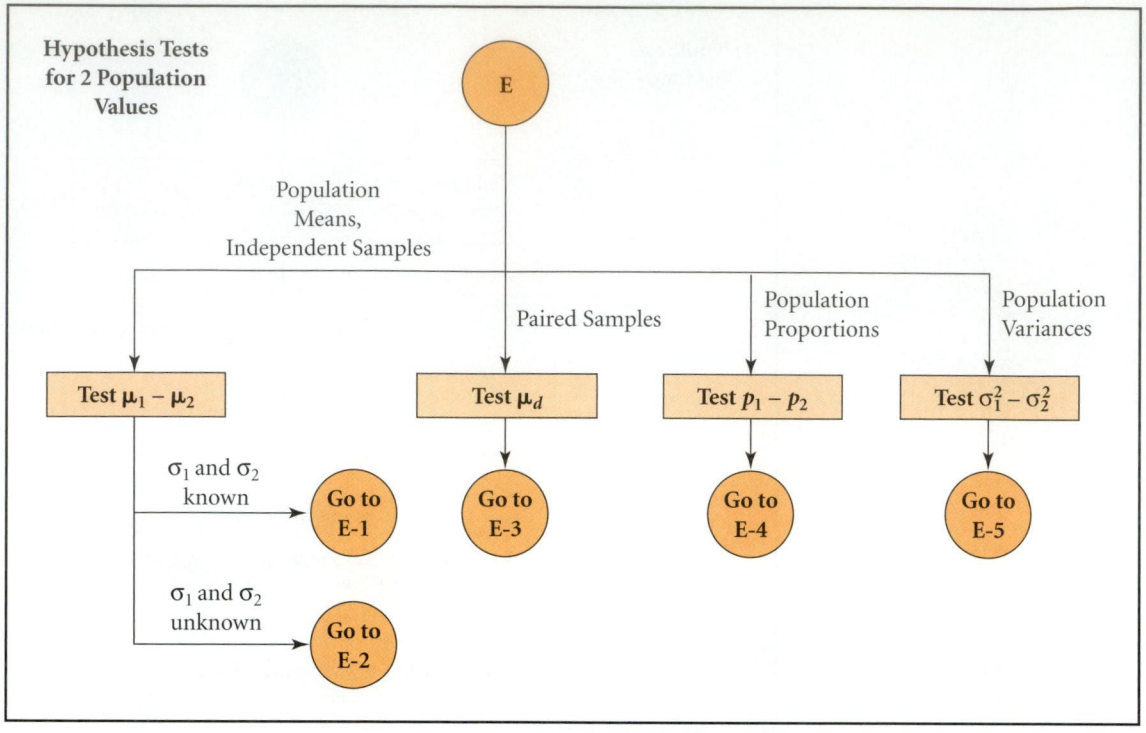

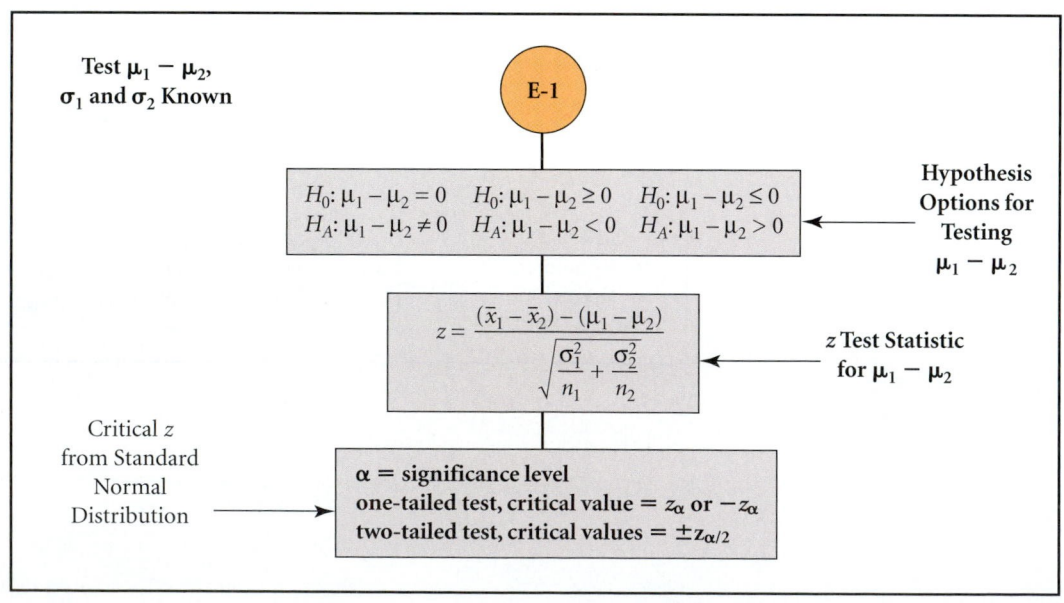

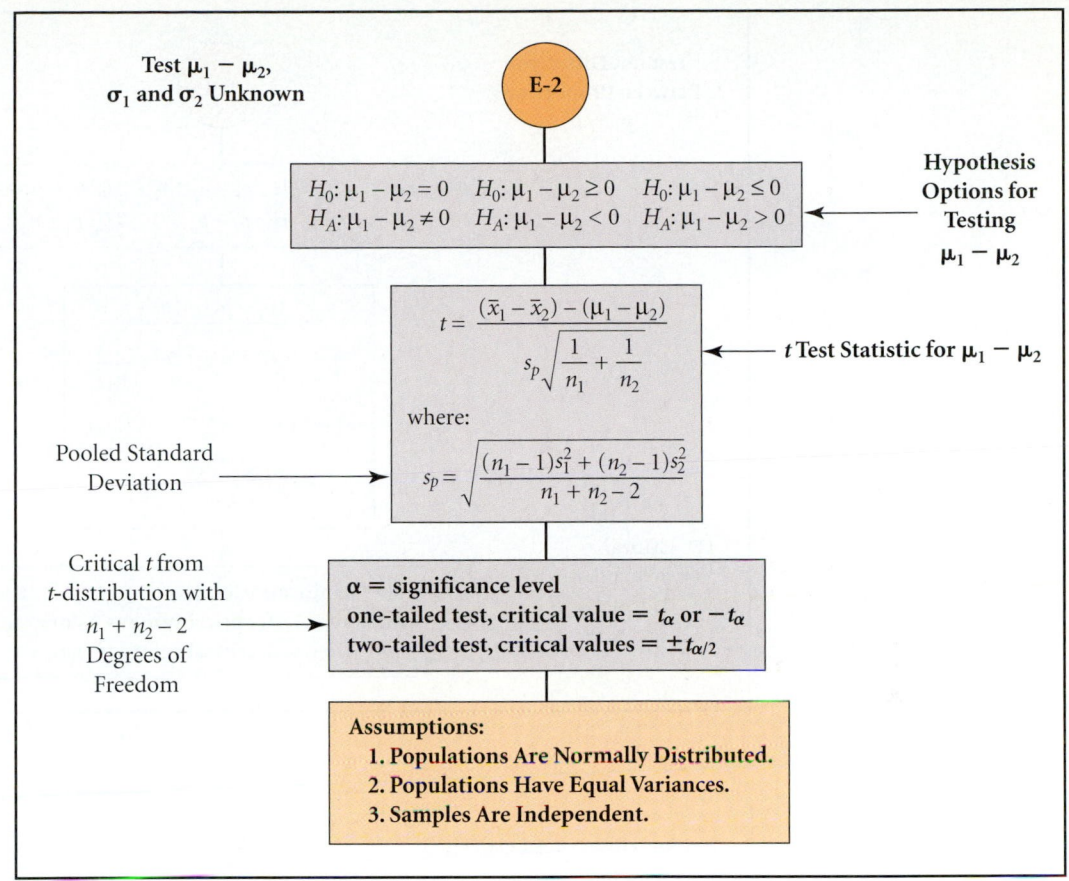

Test $\mu_1 - \mu_2$,
σ_1 and σ_2 Unknown

E-2

$H_0: \mu_1 - \mu_2 = 0$ $H_0: \mu_1 - \mu_2 \geq 0$ $H_0: \mu_1 - \mu_2 \leq 0$
$H_A: \mu_1 - \mu_2 \neq 0$ $H_A: \mu_1 - \mu_2 < 0$ $H_A: \mu_1 - \mu_2 > 0$

Hypothesis
Options for
Testing
$\mu_1 - \mu_2$

$$t = \frac{(\bar{x}_1 - \bar{x}_2) - (\mu_1 - \mu_2)}{s_p\sqrt{\dfrac{1}{n_1} + \dfrac{1}{n_2}}}$$

t Test Statistic for $\mu_1 - \mu_2$

where:

Pooled Standard
Deviation

$$s_p = \sqrt{\frac{(n_1 - 1)s_1^2 + (n_2 - 1)s_2^2}{n_1 + n_2 - 2}}$$

Critical t from
t-distribution with
$n_1 + n_2 - 2$
Degrees of
Freedom

α = **significance level**
one-tailed test, critical value = t_α or $-t_\alpha$
two-tailed test, critical values = $\pm t_{\alpha/2}$

Assumptions:
1. **Populations Are Normally Distributed.**
2. **Populations Have Equal Variances.**
3. **Samples Are Independent.**

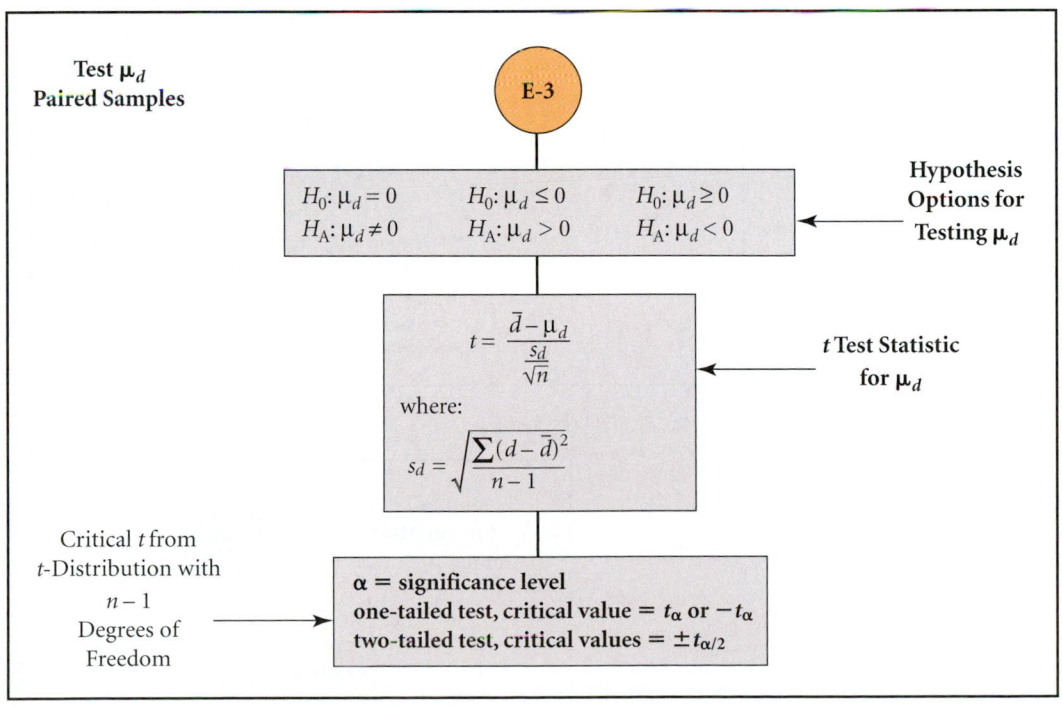

Test μ_d
Paired Samples

E-3

$H_0: \mu_d = 0$ $H_0: \mu_d \leq 0$ $H_0: \mu_d \geq 0$
$H_A: \mu_d \neq 0$ $H_A: \mu_d > 0$ $H_A: \mu_d < 0$

Hypothesis
Options for
Testing μ_d

$$t = \frac{\bar{d} - \mu_d}{\dfrac{s_d}{\sqrt{n}}}$$

t Test Statistic
for μ_d

where:

$$s_d = \sqrt{\frac{\sum(d - \bar{d})^2}{n - 1}}$$

Critical t from
t-Distribution with
$n - 1$
Degrees of
Freedom

α = **significance level**
one-tailed test, critical value = t_α or $-t_\alpha$
two-tailed test, critical values = $\pm t_{\alpha/2}$

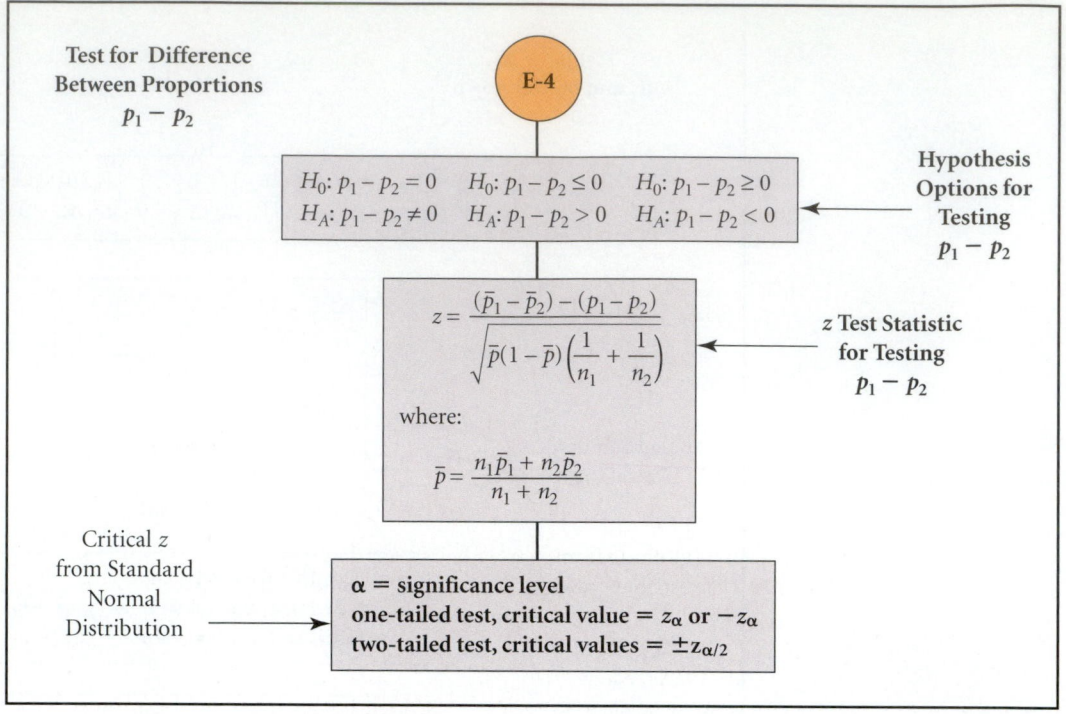

Test for Difference Between Proportions
$p_1 - p_2$

E-4

$H_0: p_1 - p_2 = 0$ $H_0: p_1 - p_2 \leq 0$ $H_0: p_1 - p_2 \geq 0$
$H_A: p_1 - p_2 \neq 0$ $H_A: p_1 - p_2 > 0$ $H_A: p_1 - p_2 < 0$

Hypothesis Options for Testing $p_1 - p_2$

$$z = \frac{(\bar{p}_1 - \bar{p}_2) - (p_1 - p_2)}{\sqrt{\bar{p}(1 - \bar{p})\left(\frac{1}{n_1} + \frac{1}{n_2}\right)}}$$

where:

$$\bar{p} = \frac{n_1\bar{p}_1 + n_2\bar{p}_2}{n_1 + n_2}$$

z Test Statistic for Testing $p_1 - p_2$

Critical z from Standard Normal Distribution

α = significance level
one-tailed test, critical value = z_α or $-z_\alpha$
two-tailed test, critical values = $\pm z_{\alpha/2}$

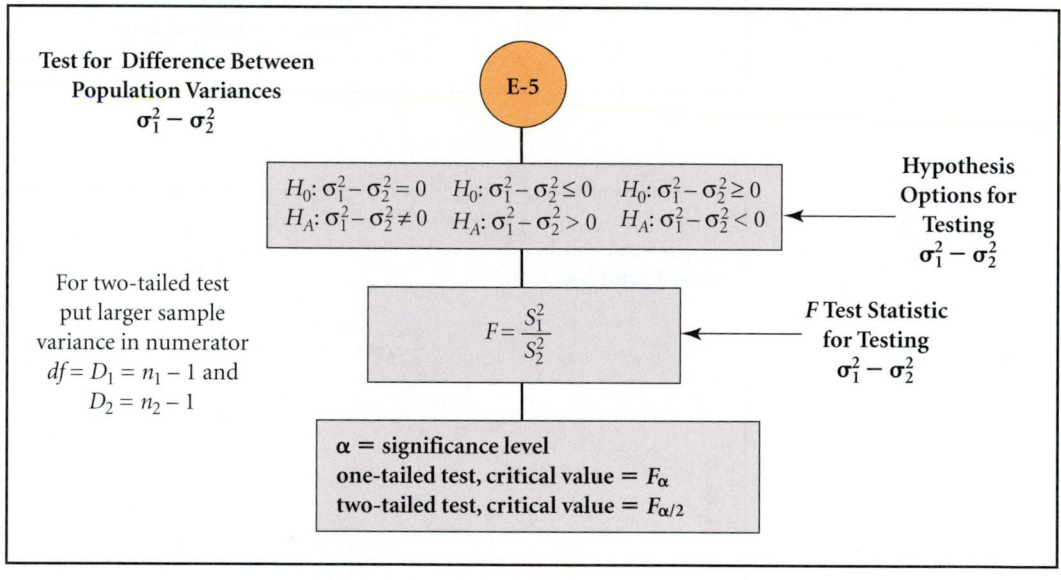

Test for Difference Between Population Variances
$\sigma_1^2 - \sigma_2^2$

E-5

$H_0: \sigma_1^2 - \sigma_2^2 = 0$ $H_0: \sigma_1^2 - \sigma_2^2 \leq 0$ $H_0: \sigma_1^2 - \sigma_2^2 \geq 0$
$H_A: \sigma_1^2 - \sigma_2^2 \neq 0$ $H_A: \sigma_1^2 - \sigma_2^2 > 0$ $H_A: \sigma_1^2 - \sigma_2^2 < 0$

Hypothesis Options for Testing $\sigma_1^2 - \sigma_2^2$

For two-tailed test put larger sample variance in numerator
$df = D_1 = n_1 - 1$ and $D_2 = n_2 - 1$

$$F = \frac{S_1^2}{S_2^2}$$

F Test Statistic for Testing $\sigma_1^2 - \sigma_2^2$

α = significance level
one-tailed test, critical value = F_α
two-tailed test, critical value = $F_{\alpha/2}$

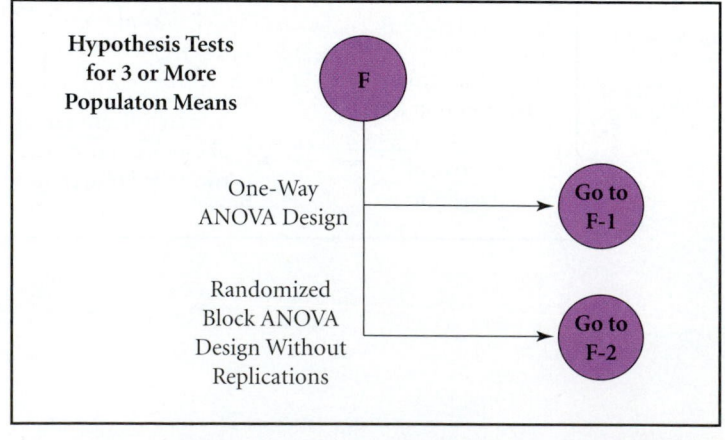

Hypothesis Tests for 3 or More Populaton Means

F

One-Way ANOVA Design

Go to F-1

Randomized Block ANOVA Design Without Replications

Go to F-2

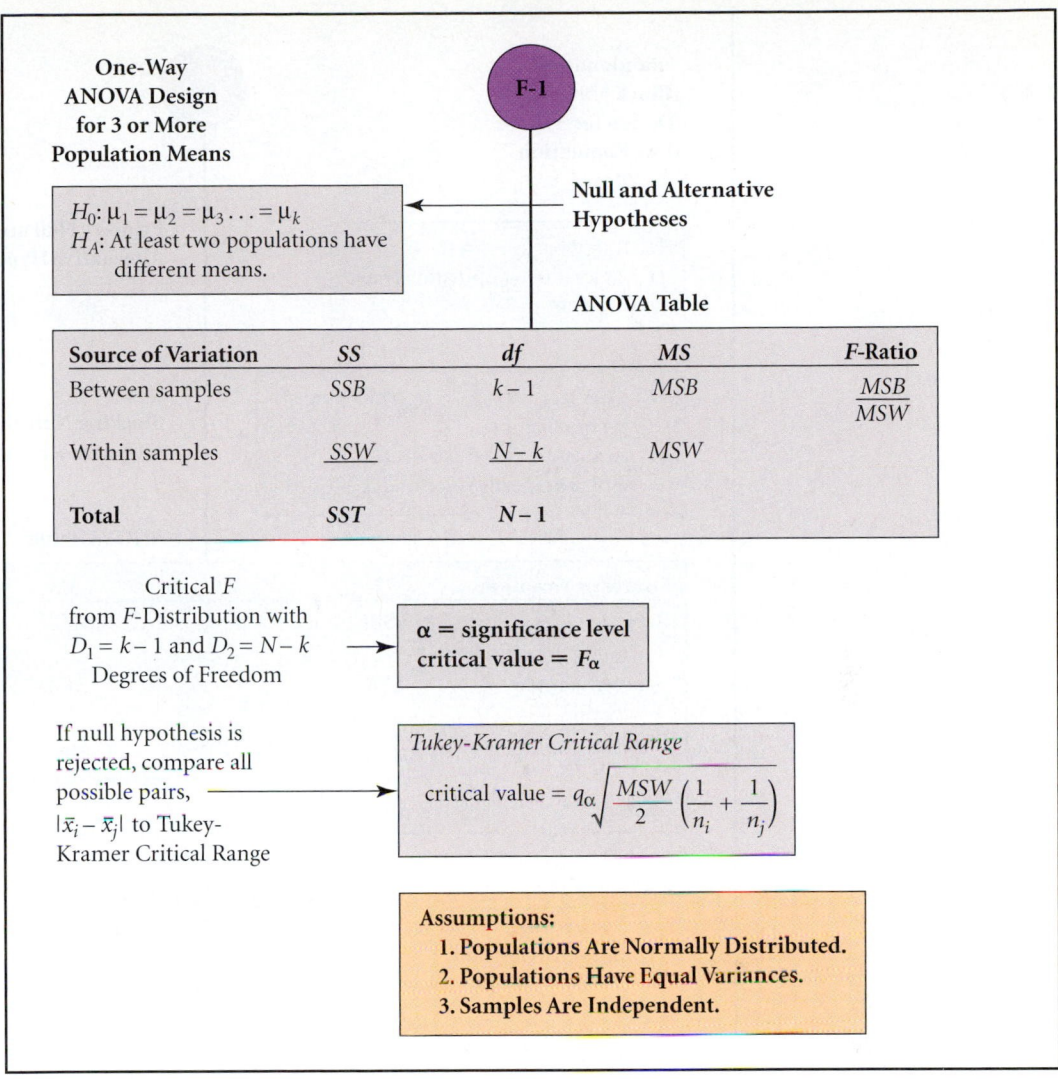

One-Way ANOVA Design for 3 or More Population Means

$H_0: \mu_1 = \mu_2 = \mu_3 \ldots = \mu_k$
H_A: At least two populations have different means.

F-1

Null and Alternative Hypotheses

ANOVA Table

Source of Variation	SS	df	MS	F-Ratio
Between samples	SSB	$k-1$	MSB	$\dfrac{MSB}{MSW}$
Within samples	SSW	$N-k$	MSW	
Total	SST	$N-1$		

Critical F from F-Distribution with $D_1 = k-1$ and $D_2 = N-k$ Degrees of Freedom

α = significance level
critical value = F_α

If null hypothesis is rejected, compare all possible pairs, $|\bar{x}_i - \bar{x}_j|$ to Tukey-Kramer Critical Range

Tukey-Kramer Critical Range

$$\text{critical value} = q_\alpha \sqrt{\frac{MSW}{2}\left(\frac{1}{n_i} + \frac{1}{n_j}\right)}$$

Assumptions:
1. Populations Are Normally Distributed.
2. Populations Have Equal Variances.
3. Samples Are Independent.

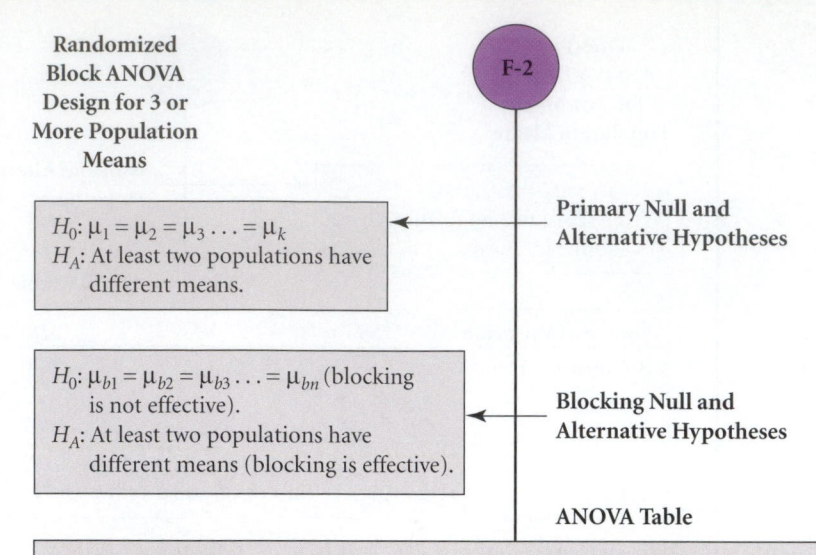

Randomized
Block ANOVA
Design for 3 or
More Population
Means

F-2

$H_0: \mu_1 = \mu_2 = \mu_3 \ldots = \mu_k$
H_A: At least two populations have different means.

Primary Null and
Alternative Hypotheses

$H_0: \mu_{b1} = \mu_{b2} = \mu_{b3} \ldots = \mu_{bn}$ (blocking is not effective).
H_A: At least two populations have different means (blocking is effective).

Blocking Null and
Alternative Hypotheses

ANOVA Table

Source of Variation	SS	df	MS	F-Ratio
Between blocks	SSBL	$b - 1$	MSBL	$\dfrac{MSBL}{MSW}$
Between samples	SSB	$k - 1$	MSB	$\dfrac{MSB}{MSW}$
Within samples	SSW	$(k-1)(b-1)$	MSW	
Total	SST	$N - 1$		

Critical F
from F-Distribution

α = significance level
Blocking critical value = F_α
$df = D_1 = b - 1$ and $D_2 = (k - 1)(b - 1)$
Primary critical value = F_α, $df = D_1 = k - 1$ and $D_2 = (k - 1)(b - 1)$

Assumptions:
1. **Populations Are Normally Distributed.**
2. **Populations Have Equal Variances.**
3. **Observations Within Samples Are Independent.**

If null is rejected, compare all $|\bar{x}_i - \bar{x}_j|$ to Fisher's

$$LSD = t_{\alpha/2} \sqrt{MSW} \sqrt{\frac{2}{b}}$$

USING THE FLOW DIAGRAMS

Example Problem: A travel agency in Florida is interested in determining whether there is a difference in the total out-of-pocket costs incurred by customers on two major cruise lines. To test this, she has selected a simple random sample of 20 customers who have taken cruise line I and has asked these people to track their costs over and above the fixed price of the cruise. She did the same for a second simple random sample of 15 people who took cruise line II.

You can use the flow diagrams to direct you to the appropriate statistical tool.

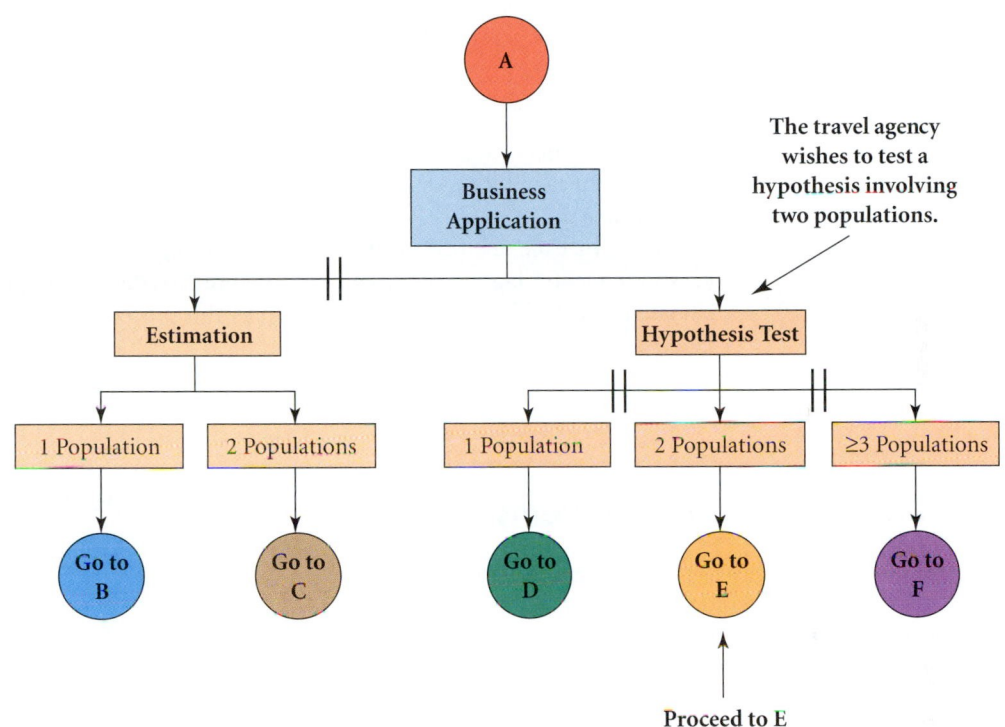

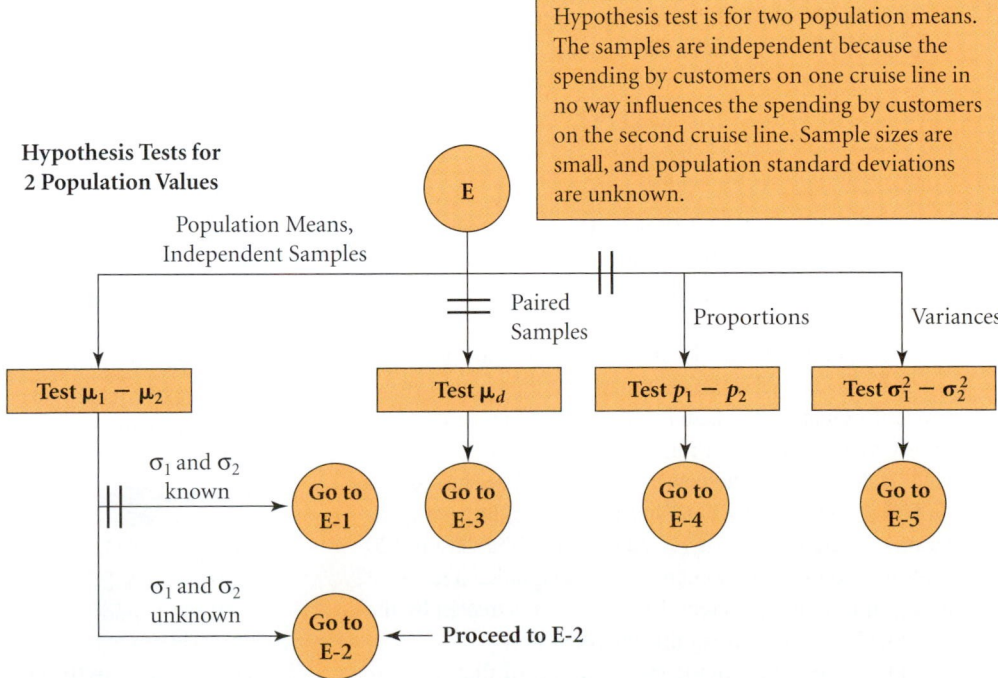

At E-2, we determine the null hypothesis to be

$$H_0: \mu_1 - \mu_2 = 0$$

$$H_A: \mu_1 - \mu_2 \neq 0$$

Next, we establish the test statistic as

$$t = \frac{(\bar{x}_1 - \bar{x}_2) - (\mu_1 - \mu_2)}{s_p \sqrt{\dfrac{1}{n_1} + \dfrac{1}{n_2}}}$$

where:

$$s_p = \sqrt{\frac{(n_1 - 1)s_1^2 + (n_2 - 1)s_2^2}{n_1 + n_2 - 2}}$$

Finally, the critical value is a t-value from the t-distribution with $20 + 15 - 2 = 33$ degrees of freedom. Note, if the degrees of freedom are not shown in the t table, use Excel's **TINV** or use Minitab to determine the t-value.

Thus, by using the flow diagrams and answering a series of basic questions, you should be successful in identifying the statistical tools required to address any problem or application covered in Chapters 7 to 11. You are encouraged to apply this process to the application problems and projects listed here.

EXERCISES

Integrative Application Problems

SR.1 Brandon Outdoor Advertising supplies neon signs to retail stores. A major complaint from their clients is that letters in the signs can burn out and leave the signs looking silly, depending on which letters stop working. The primary cause of neon letters not working is the failure of the starter unit attached to each letter. Starter units fail primarily based on turn-on/turn-off cycles. The present unit bought by Brandon averages 1,000 cycles before failure. A new manufacturer has approached Brandon claiming to have a model that is superior to the present unit. Brandon is skeptical but agrees to sample 50 starter units. It says it will buy from the new supplier if the sample results indicated the new unit is better. The sample of 50 gives the following values:

Sample mean = 1,010 cycles
Sample standard deviation = 48 cycles

Would you recommend changing suppliers?

SR.2 PestFree Chemicals has developed a new fungus preventative that may have a significant market among potato growers. Unfortunately, the actual extent of the fungus problem in any year depends on rainfall, temperature, and many other factors. To test the new chemical, PestFree has used it on 500 acres of potatoes and has used the leading competitor on an additional 500 acres. At the end of the season, 120 acres treated by the new chemical show significant levels of fungus infestation, whereas 160 of the acres treated by the leading chemical show significant infestation.

Do these data provide statistical proof that the new product is superior to the leading competitor?

SR.3 Last year Tucker Electronics decided to try to do something about turnover among assembly line workers at its several plants. It implemented two trial personnel policies, one based on an improved hiring policy and the other based on increasing worker responsibility. These policies were put into effect at two different plants, with the following results:

	Plant 1	Plant 2
	Improved Hiring	*Increased Responsibility*
Workers in trial group	800	900
Turnover proportion	0.05	0.09

Do these data provide evidence that there is a difference between the turnover rates for the two trial policies?

SR.4 A Big 10 University has been approached by Wilson Sporting Goods. Wilson has developed a football designed specifically for practice sessions. Wilson would like to claim the ball will last for 500 practice hours before it needs to be replaced. Wilson has supplied six balls for use during spring and fall practice. The following data has been gathered on the time used before the ball must be replaced.

Hours	
551	511
479	435
440	466

Do you see anything wrong with Wilson claiming the ball will last 500 hours?

SR.5 The management of a chain of movie theaters believes the average weekend attendance at their downtown theater is greater than at their suburban theater. The following sample results were found from their accounting data.

	Downtown	Suburban
Number of weekends	11	10
Average attendance	855	750
Sample variance	1,684	1,439

Do these data provide sufficient evidence to indicate there is a difference in average attendances? The company is also interested in whether there is a significant difference in the variability of attendance.

SR.6 A large mail-order company has placed an order for 5,000 thermal-powered fans to sit on wood-burning stoves from a supplier in Canada, with the stipulation that no more than 2% of the units will be defective. To check the shipment, the company tests a random sample of 400 fans and finds 11 defective. Should this sample evidence lead the company to conclude the supplier has violated the terms of the contract?

SR.7 A manufacturer of automobile shock absorbers is interested in comparing the durability of its shocks with that of its two biggest competitors. To make the comparison, a set of one each of the manufacturer's and of the competitor's shocks were randomly selected and installed on the rear wheels of each of six randomly selected cars of the same type. After the cars had been driven 20,000 miles, the strength of each test shock was measured, coded, and recorded.

Car number	Manufacturer's	Competitor 1	Competitor 2
1	8.8	9.3	8.6
2	10.5	9.0	13.7
3	12.5	8.4	11.2
4	9.7	13.0	9.7
5	9.6	12.0	12.2
6	13.2	10.1	8.9

Do these data present sufficient evidence to conclude there is a difference in the mean strength of the two types of shocks after 20,000 miles?

SR.8 AstraZeneca is the maker of the stomach medicine Prilosec, which is the second-best-selling drug in the world. Recently the company has come under close scrutiny concerning the cost of their medicines. The company's internal audit department selected a random sample of 300 prescriptions issued for Prilosec. They wished to characterize how much is being spent on this medicine. In the sample, the mean price per 20 milligram tablet of Prilosec was $2.70. The sample had a standard deviation of $0.30. Determine an estimate that will characterize the average range of values charged for a tablet of Prilosec.

SR.9 The Vilmore Corporation is considering two word processors for its PCs. One factor that will influence its decision is the ease of use in preparing a business report. Consequently, Jody Vilmore selected a random sample of nine typists from the clerical pool and asked them to type a typical report using both word processors. The typists then were timed (in seconds) to determine how quickly they could type one of the frequently used forms. The results were as follows.

Typist	Processor 1	Processor 2
1	82	75
2	76	80
3	90	70
4	55	58
5	49	53
6	82	75
7	90	80
8	45	45
9	70	80

Jody wishes to have an estimate of the smallest and biggest differences that might exist in the average time required for typing the business form using the two processors. Provide this information.

SR.10 The research department of an appliance manufacturing firm has developed a solid-state switch for its blender that the department claims will reduce the percentage of appliances being returned under the one-year full warranty by from 3% to 6%. To determine if the claim can be supported, the testing department selects a group of the blenders manufactured with the new switch and the old switch and subjects them to a normal year's worth of wear. Out of 250 blenders tested with the new switch, nine would have been returned. Sixteen would have been returned out of the 250 blenders with the old switch. Use a statistical procedure to verify or refute the department's claim.

SR.11 The Ecco Company makes electronics products for distribution throughout the world. As a member of the quality department, you are interested in the warranty claims that are made by customers who have experienced problems with Ecco products. The file on your CD-ROM called *Ecco* contains data for a random sample of warranty claims. Large warranty claims not only cost the company money but also provide adverse publicity. The quality manager has asked you to provide her with a range of values that would represent the percentage of warranty claims filed for more than $300. Provide this information for your quality manager.

Term Project Assignment

Investigate whether there are differences in grocery prices for three or more stores in your city.

a. Specify the type of testing procedure you will use.

b. What type of experimental design will be used? Why?

c. Develop a "typical" market basket of at least 10 items that you will price-check. Collect price data on these items at three or more different stores that sell groceries.

d. Analyze your price data using the testing procedure and experimental design you specified in parts 1 and 2.

e. Present your findings in a report. Did you find differences in average prices of the "market basket" across the different grocery stores?

CHAPTER 12

Introduction to Linear Regression and Correlation Analysis

CHAPTER OUTCOMES

After studying the material in Chapter 12, you should be able to:

- Calculate and interpret the simple correlation between two variables.
- Determine whether the correlation is significant.
- Calculate the simple linear regression equation for a set of data and know the basic assumptions behind regression analysis.
- Determine whether a regression model is significant.
- Calculate and interpret confidence intervals for the regression coefficients.
- Recognize regression analysis applications for purposes of prediction and description.
- Recognize some potential problems if regression analysis is used incorrectly.
- Recognize several nonlinear relationships between two variables and be able to introduce the appropriate transformation to apply linear regression analysis.

WHY YOU NEED TO KNOW

Although some business situations involve only one variable, others require decision makers to consider the relationship between two or more variables. For example, an investment broker might be interested in the relationship between stock prices and the dividends issued by a publicly traded company. A marketing manager would be interested in examining the relationship between product sales and the amount of money spent on advertising. Finally, consider a real estate appraiser who is interested in determining the fair market value of a home or business. He would begin by collecting data on a sample of "comparable properties" that have sold recently. In addition to the selling price, he would collect data on other factors, such as the size and age of the property. He might then analyze the relationship between the price and the other variables and use this relationship to determine an appraised price for the property in question.

Simple linear regression and correlation analysis, which are introduced in this chapter, are statistical techniques the broker, marketing director, and appraiser will need in their analysis. These techniques are important to decision makers who need to determine the relationship between two variables. In Chapter 13, we will extend the discussion to include three or more variables. Regression analysis and correlation analysis are two of the most often applied statistical tools for business decision making.

12-1 SCATTER PLOTS AND CORRELATION

In those situations in which you are interested in analyzing the relationship between two variables, the **scatter plot**, or *scatter diagram*, introduced in Chapter 2 is very useful.

> *Scatter Plot*
>
> A two-dimensional plot showing the values for the joint occurrence of two variables. The scatter plot may be used to graphically represent the relationship between two variables. It is also known as a scatter diagram.

Figure 12-1 shows scatter plots that depict several potential relationships between values of a dependent variable, y, and an independent variable, x. A **dependent** (or *response*) **variable** is the variable whose variation we wish to explain. An **independent** (or *explanatory*) **variable** is a vari-

FIGURE 12-1   **Two-Variable Relationships**

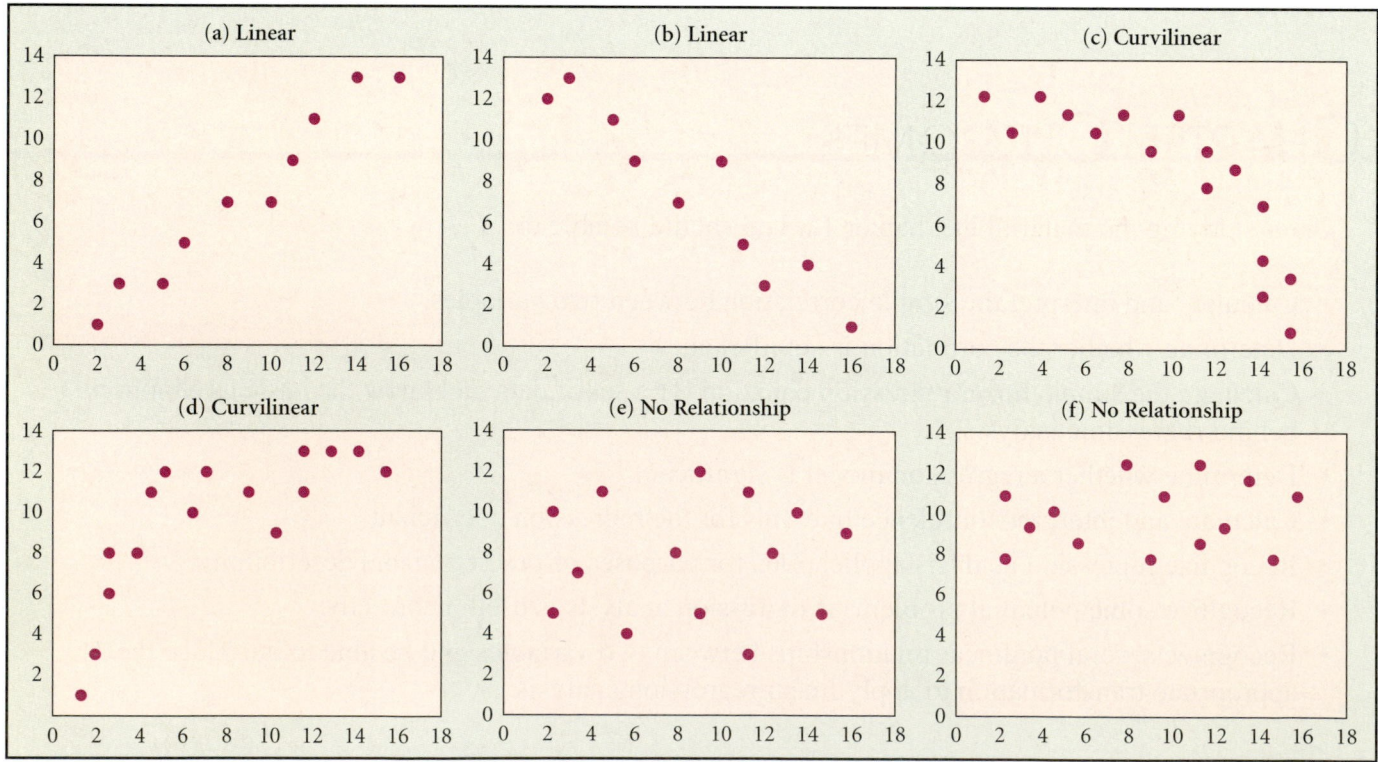

able used to explain variation in the dependent variable. The independent variable may or may not have random variation, but it is not of primary interest. In Figure 12-1, (a) and (b) are examples of strong *linear* relationships between x and y. This means that for each unit change in the independent variable, x, the corresponding change in the dependent variable, y, will tend to be a fairly consistent amount. Note that this systematic change in y can be positive (y increases as x increases) or negative (y decreases as x increases). The degree of linearity exhibited depends on the degree of consistency in the change of the y variable when the independent variable, x, changes.

Figures 12-1 (c) and (d) illustrate situations in which the relationship between the x and y variable are nonlinear. There are many possible nonlinear relationships that can occur. The scatter plot is very useful for visually identifying the nature of the relationship.

Figures 12-1 (e) and (f) show examples in which there is no identifiable relationship between the two variables. This means that as x increases, y sometimes increases and sometimes decreases but with no particular pattern.

CORRELATION VERSUS REGRESSION

In analyzing the relationship between two variables, there are two basic models that we can use, depending on the conditions under which the data are collected. These models are the subjects of this chapter. The first model is referred to as the *regression model*, in which the relationship between x and y assumes that the x variable takes on known values specifically selected from all the possible values for x. The y variable is a random variable observed at the different levels of x.

The second model is referred to as the *correlation model* and is used in applications in which both the x and the y variables are considered to be random variables. These two models, regression versus correlation, arise in practice by the way in which the data are obtained. Consider models that might apply to the relationship between the amount of daily sunscreen sold, y, as a function of the day's high temperature, x. We could select a random sample of 36 days and record the amount of sunscreen sold and the day's maximum temperature. In this case, the measurements obtained for both variables are observations from a joint distribution of x and y. An analysis of these data would be done using the correlation model approach.

Suppose instead that we decide to collect data for days with maximum temperatures of 75, 80, 85, 90, 95, and 100. We would measure the amount of daily sunscreen sold (y) for several randomly chosen days in which the maximum temperature is at each of these preselected temperatures. That is, we might pick six days at random from a population of days that have a maximum temperature of 75 degrees and observe the amount of sunscreen sold, and so on. Now each observation of y is from the distribution of y for a fixed x value. The analysis of these data would be done using the regression model approach.

We stress the two types of sampling because there are important differences in what can be estimated using these two methods. As we will illustrate later in this chapter, when the data have been collected at specific levels of the x variable, as was suggested in the second situation, our estimates for the y variable will be conditional on the value of x we are using.[1]

THE CORRELATION COEFFICIENT

In addition to analyzing the relationship between two variables graphically, we can also measure the strength of the linear relationship between two variables using a measure called the **correlation coefficient**. We introduced this concept in Chapter 4.

Correlation Coefficient

A quantitative measure of the strength of the linear relationship between two variables. The correlation ranges from -1.0 to $+1.0$. A correlation of ± 1.0 indicates a perfect linear relationship, whereas a correlation of 0 indicates no linear relationship.

---

[1]See Neter et al., *Applied Linear Statistical Models*, 4th ed., p. 85, and Draper, N. R., and Smith, H., *Applied Regression Analysis*, 3rd ed., p. 89, for more discussion on this subject.

The correlation coefficient for two variables can be estimated from sample data using Equation 12-1 or the algebraic equivalent, Equation 12-2.[2]

Sample Correlation Coefficient

$$r = \frac{\sum(x - \bar{x})(y - \bar{y})}{\sqrt{[\sum(x - \bar{x})^2][\sum(y - \bar{y})^2]}}$$

12-1

or the algebraic equivalent:

$$r = \frac{n\sum xy - \sum x \sum y}{\sqrt{[n(\sum x^2) - (\sum x)^2][n(\sum y^2) - (\sum y)^2]}}$$

12-2

where:

r = Sample correlation coefficient
n = Sample size
x = Value of the independent variable
y = Value of the dependent variable

The sample correlation coefficient computed using Equations 12-1 and 12-2 is called the *Pearson Product Moment Correlation*. The sample correlation coefficient, r, can range from a perfect positive correlation, +1.0, to a perfect negative correlation, −1.0. A perfect correlation is one in which a given change in the value of the x variable is accompanied by a specific uniform amount of change in the y variable. Graphically, the x,y points will plot on a straight line. If two variables have no linear relationship, the correlation between them is 0 and there is no linear relationship between the change in x and y. Consequently, the more the correlation differs from 0.0, the stronger the linear relationship between the two variables. The sign of the correlation coefficient indicates the direction of the relationship, but it does not aid in determining the strength.

Figure 12-2 illustrates some examples of correlation between two variables. Note for the correlation coefficient to equal plus or minus 1.0, all the (x,y) points form a perfectly straight line. The

FIGURE 12-2   Correlation Between Two Variables

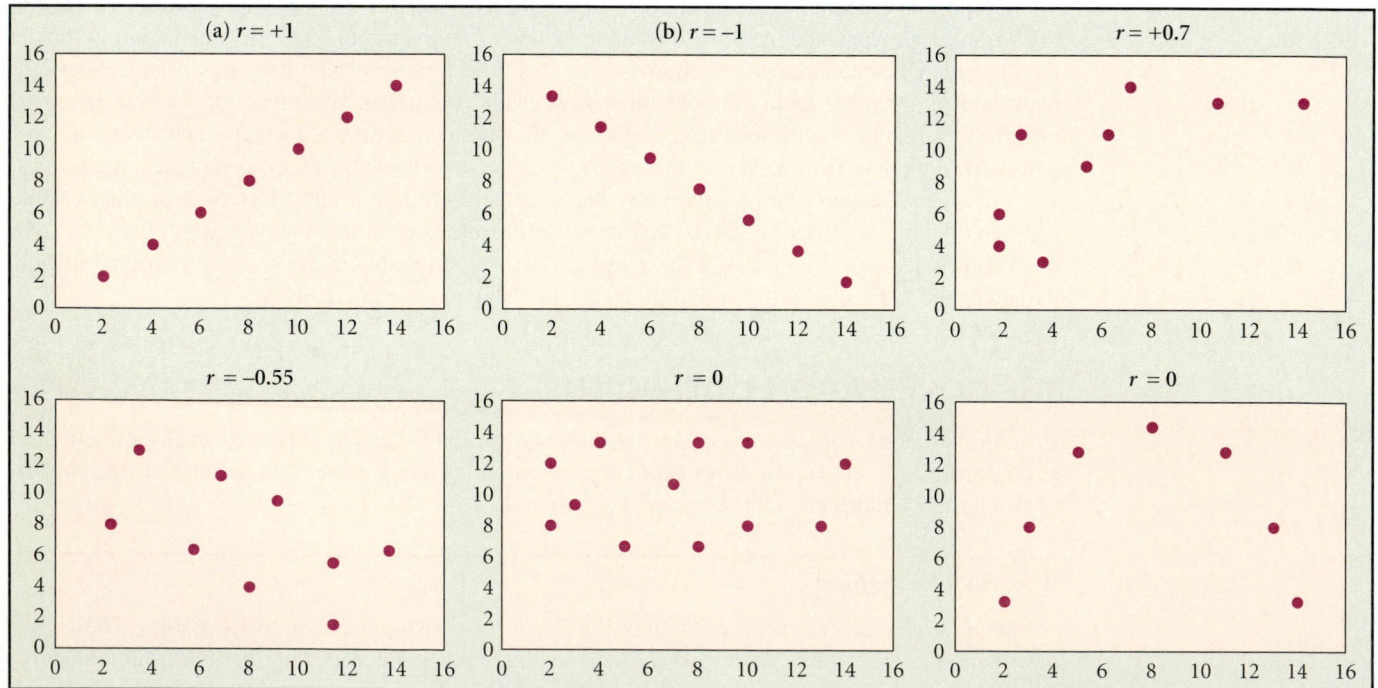

[2]Refer to Section 4-3 in Chapter 4 for a discussion of covariance between two variables and the explanation that the population correlation coefficient can be computed using Equation 4-18,

$$\rho = \frac{\sigma_{xy}}{\sigma_x \sigma_y}$$

more the points depart from a straight line, the weaker (closer to 0.0) the correlation is between the two variables.

Excel and Minitab Tutorial

Midwest Distribution Company—Midwest Distribution supplies soft drinks and snack foods to convenience stores in Michigan, Illinois, and Iowa. Although Midwest Distribution has been profitable, the director of marketing has been concerned about the rapid turnover in her sales force. In the course of exit interviews, she discovered a major concern with the compensation structure.

Midwest Distribution has a two-part wage structure: a base salary and a commission computed on monthly sales. Typically, about half of the total wages paid comes from the base salary, which increases with longevity with the company. This portion of the wage structure is not an issue. The concern expressed by departing employees is that new employees tend to be given parts of the sales territory previously covered by existing employees and are assigned prime customers as a recruiting inducement.

At issue, then, is the relationship between sales (on which commissions are paid) and number of years with the company. The data for a random sample of 12 sales representatives are in the file called *Midwest* on your CD-ROM. The first step is to develop a scatter plot of the data. Both Excel and Minitab have procedures for constructing a scatter plot (refer to Chapter 2) and computing the correlation coefficient.

The scatter plot for the Midwest data is shown in Figure 12-3. Based on this plot, total sales and years with the company appear to be linearly related. However, the strength of this relationship is uncertain. That is, how close do the points come to falling on a straight line? To answer this question, we need a quantitative measure of the strength of the linear relationship between the two variables. That measure is the correlation coefficient.

Equation 12-1 is used to determine the correlation between sales and years with the company. Table 12-1 shows the manual calculations necessary to determine the correlation coefficient that equals 0.8325. However, because the calculations are rather tedious and long, we almost always use computer software to perform the computation, as shown in Figure 12-4. The $r = 0.8325$ indicates that there is a fairly strong, positive correlation between these two variables for the sample data.

Significance Test for the Correlation

Although a correlation coefficient of 0.8325 seems quite high (relative to 0), you should remember that this value is based on a sample of 12 data points and is subject to sampling error. To illustrate

FIGURE 12-3

Excel Scatter Plot of Sales vs. Years with Midwest Distribution

Minitab Instructions (for similar results):
1. Open file: Midwest.MTW.
2. Choose **Graph > Scatterplot**.
3. Under **Scatterplot**, choose **Simple. OK.**
4. In **Y variable**, enter *y* column.
5. In **X variable**, enter *x* column.
6. Click **OK**.

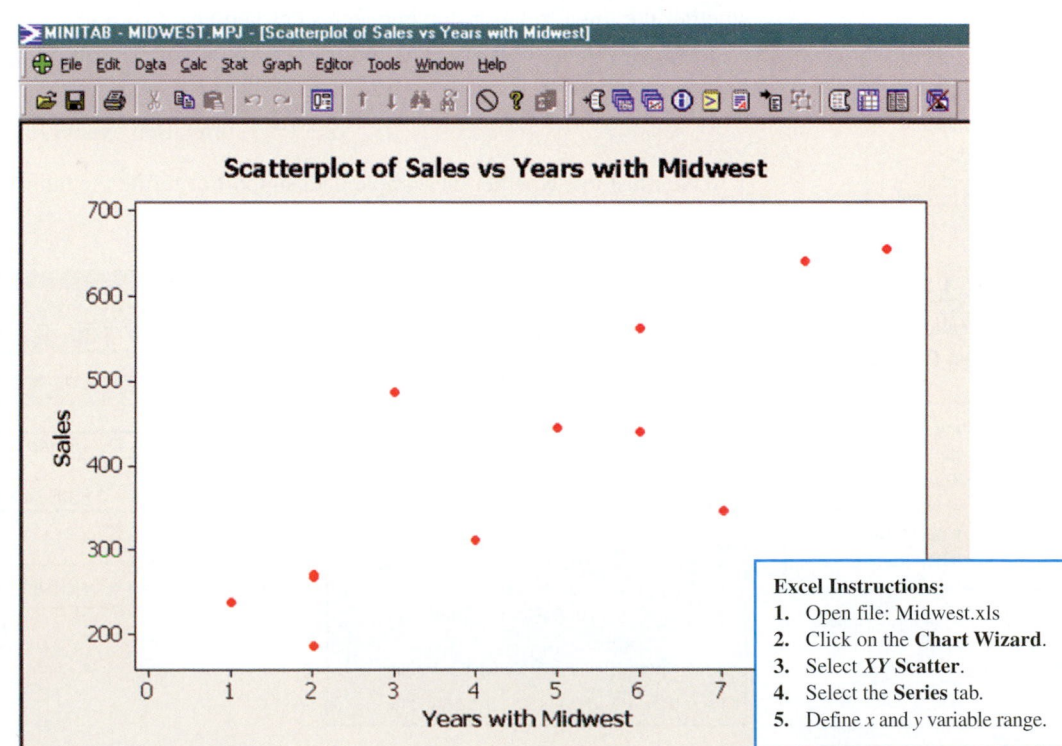

Excel Instructions:
1. Open file: Midwest.xls
2. Click on the **Chart Wizard**.
3. Select *XY* **Scatter**.
4. Select the **Series** tab.
5. Define *x* and *y* variable range.

Sales	Years			
y	x	xy	y^2	x^2
487	3	1,461	237,169	9
445	5	2,225	198,025	25
272	2	544	73,984	4
641	8	5,128	410,881	64
187	2	374	34,969	4
440	6	2,640	193,600	36
346	7	2,422	119,716	49
238	1	238	56,644	1
312	4	1,248	97,344	16
269	2	538	72,361	4
655	9	5,895	429,025	81
563	6	3,378	316,969	36
$\Sigma = 4,855$	$\Sigma = 55$	$\Sigma = 26,091$	$\Sigma = 2,240,687$	$\Sigma = 329$

$$r = \frac{n\sum xy - \sum x \sum y}{\sqrt{[n(\sum x^2) - (\sum x)^2][n(\sum y^2) - (\sum y)^2]}}$$

$$r = \frac{12(26,091) - 55(4,855)}{\sqrt{[12(329) - (55)^2][12(2,240,687) - (4,855)^2]}}$$

$$= 0.8325$$

what can happen, consider the scatter plot for the hypothetical situation shown in Figure 12-5. The scatter plot for the population of values indicates there is no linear relationship between the two variables. The population correlation coefficient for these data is 0. We use the Greek symbol ρ (rho), to represent the population correlation coefficient. Now, suppose a random sample of values is selected from the population (see circled values in Figure 12-5.) These sample values appear to have a fairly strong linear relationship. In fact, the correlation coefficient, r, is 0.952 based on these sample data. In this case, the sample correlation coefficient is very high, yet the two variables for the population as a whole are not correlated. This could happen if the sample data exhibit extreme sampling error. Therefore, a formal hypothesis-testing procedure is needed to determine whether the linear relationship between sales and years with the company is significant.

The null and alternative hypotheses to be tested are

$$H_0: \rho = 0 \quad \text{(no correlation)}$$
$$H_A: \rho \neq 0 \quad \text{(correlation exists)}$$

We must test whether the sample data support or refute the null hypothesis. The test procedure utilizes the t test statistic in Equation 12-3.

FIGURE 12-4

Excel Correlation Output for Midwest Distribution

Excel Instructions:
1. Open file: Midwest.xls
2. Select **Tools**.
3. Click on **Data Analysis**.
4. Select **Correlation**.
5. Define Data Range.

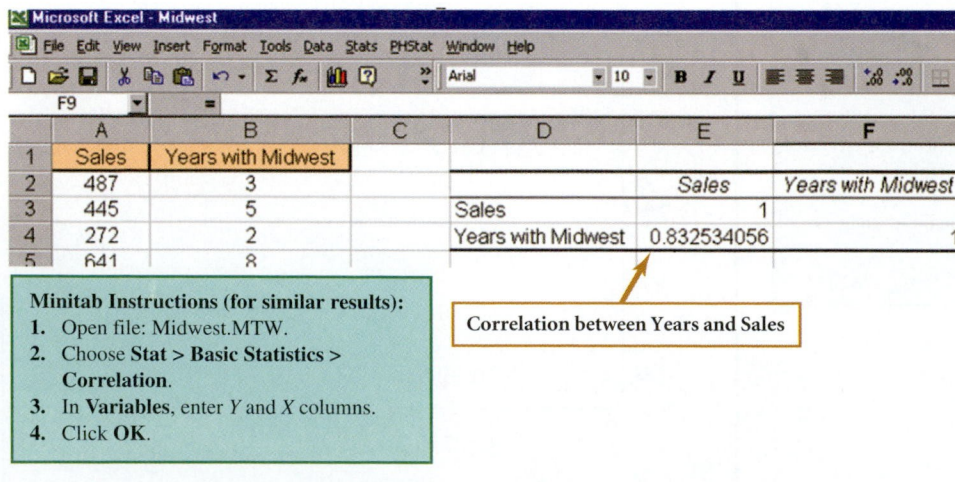

Minitab Instructions (for similar results):
1. Open file: Midwest.MTW.
2. Choose **Stat > Basic Statistics > Correlation**.
3. In **Variables**, enter Y and X columns.
4. Click **OK**.

Correlation between Years and Sales

FIGURE 12-5

Scatter Plot—Hypothetical Data

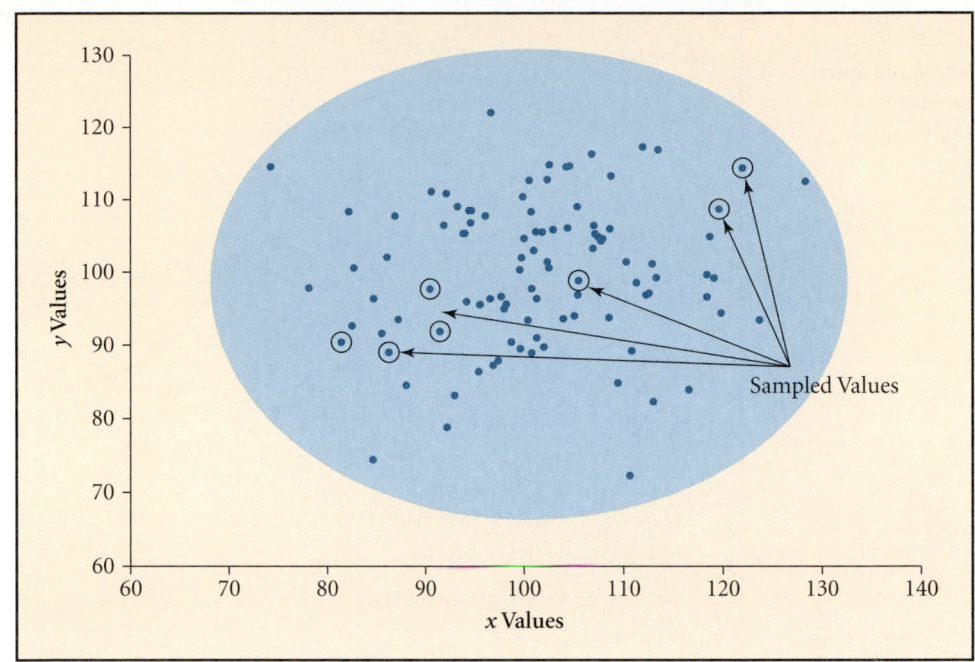

Test Statistic for Correlation

$$t = \frac{r}{\sqrt{\dfrac{1 - r^2}{n - 2}}} \qquad df = n - 2$$

12-3

where:

t = Number of standard deviations r is from 0
r = Simple correlation coefficient
n = Sample size

The degrees of freedom for this test are $n - 2$, because we lose one degree of freedom for each of the two sample means that are used to estimate the population means for the two variables.

Figure 12-6 shows the hypothesis test for the Midwest Distribution example using an alpha level of 0.05. Recall that the sample correlation coefficient was $r = 0.8325$. Based on these sample data, we should conclude there is a significant, positive linear relationship in the population between years of experience and total sales for Midwest Distribution sales representatives. The implication is that the more years an employee has been with the company, the more sales that representative generates. This runs counter to the claims made by some of the departing employees. The manager will probably want to look further into the situation to see whether a problem might exist in certain regions.

The t test for determining whether the population correlation is significantly different from 0.0 requires the following assumptions.

SSUMPTIONS

1. The data are interval- or ratio-level.
2. The two variables (y and x) are distributed as a *bivariate normal* distribution.

Although the formal mathematical representation is beyond the scope of this text, *two variables are bivariate normal if their joint distribution is normally distributed*. Although the t test assumes a bivariate normal distribution, it is robust—that is, correct inferences can be reached even with slight departures from the normal-distribution assumption. (See Neter et al., *Applied Linear Statistical Models* for further discussion of bivariate normal distributions.)

F I G U R E   1 2 - 6

**Correlation Significance
Test for the Midwest
Distribution Example**

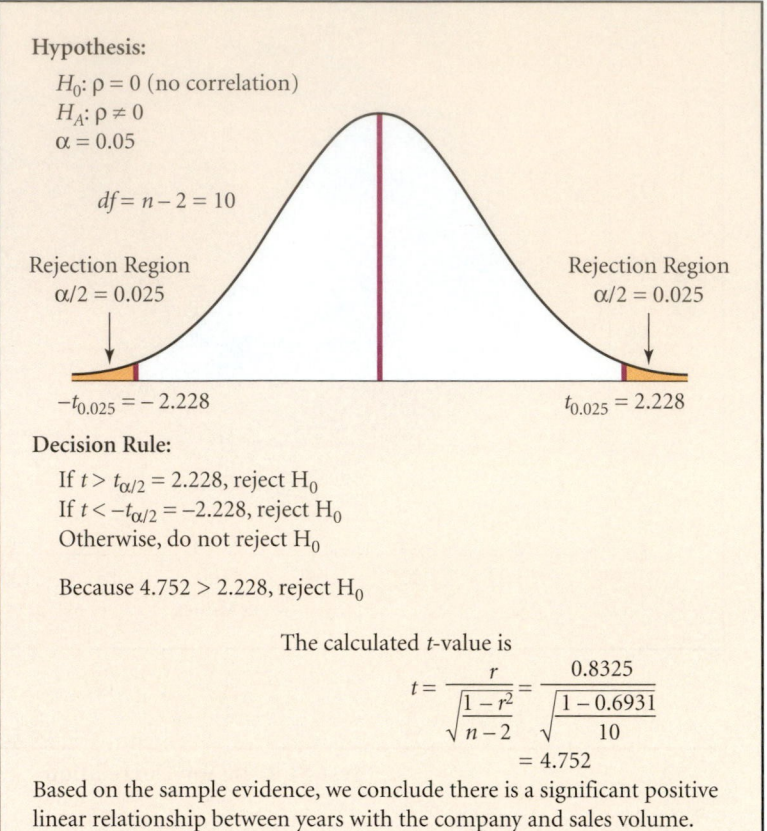

Hypothesis:

H_0: $\rho = 0$ (no correlation)
H_A: $\rho \neq 0$
$\alpha = 0.05$

$df = n - 2 = 10$

Rejection Region
$\alpha/2 = 0.025$

Rejection Region
$\alpha/2 = 0.025$

$-t_{0.025} = -2.228$ $t_{0.025} = 2.228$

Decision Rule:

If $t > t_{\alpha/2} = 2.228$, reject H_0
If $t < -t_{\alpha/2} = -2.228$, reject H_0
Otherwise, do not reject H_0

Because $4.752 > 2.228$, reject H_0

The calculated t-value is

$$t = \frac{r}{\sqrt{\dfrac{1-r^2}{n-2}}} = \frac{0.8325}{\sqrt{\dfrac{1-0.6931}{10}}}$$

$$= 4.752$$

Based on the sample evidence, we conclude there is a significant positive linear relationship between years with the company and sales volume.

ℰXAMPLE 12-1: CORRELATION ANALYSIS

Yellow Page Advertising   Recently a publisher of a regional telephone book surveyed a simple random sample of 10 of its commercial yellow-page advertising customers in an attempt to determine whether the size of their advertisements, in square inches (x), were positively correlated with the proportion of calls to the businesses that were generated by the ads (y). For a one-month period, each commercial customer asked each caller to their business if they had learned about the business through the yellow pages. To determine whether there is a statistically significant correlation between the two variables, the following steps can be employed.

Step 1:   Specify the population value of interest.
The publisher wishes to determine whether the size of an ad is positively correlated with the proportion of calls to the business that were generated by the ad. The parameter of interest is, therefore, the population correlation, ρ.

Step 2:   Formulate the appropriate null and alternative hypotheses.
Because the regional phone company is interested in establishing a positive relationship between ad size and proportion of calls generated from the ad, the test will be one-tailed, as follows:

$$H_0: \rho \leq 0$$
$$H_A: \rho > 0$$

Step 3:   Specify the level of significance.
A significance level of 0.05 is chosen.

Step 4:   Construct the rejection region.
For an alpha level equal to 0.05, the one-tailed, upper-tail, critical value for $n - 2 = 10 - 2 = 8$ degrees of freedom is $t = 1.8595$. The decision rule is

If $t > 1.8595$, reject the null hypothesis;
Otherwise, do not reject the null hypothesis.

Step 5:   **Compute the correlation coefficient and the test statistic.**
Compute the sample correlation coefficient using Equation 12-1 or 12-2, or by using software such as Excel or Minitab.
The following sample data were obtained:

Square Inches	Proportion of Calls Generated by Ad
9	0.13
16	0.16
25	0.21
16	0.18
20	0.18
16	0.19
20	0.15
20	0.17
16	0.13
9	0.11

Using Equation 12-1, we get:

$$r = \frac{\Sigma(x - \bar{x})(y - \bar{y})}{\sqrt{[\Sigma(x - \bar{x})^2][\Sigma(y - \bar{y})^2]}} = 0.7796$$

Compute the t test statistic using Equation 12-3.

$$t = \frac{r}{\sqrt{\dfrac{1 - r^2}{n - 2}}} = \frac{0.7796}{\sqrt{\dfrac{1 - 0.7796^2}{10 - 2}}} = 3.52$$

Step 6:   **Reach a decision.**
Because

$$t = 3.52 > 1.8595, \text{ reject the null hypothesis.}$$

Step 7:   **Draw a conclusion.**
Because the null hypothesis is rejected, the sample data do support the contention that there is a positive linear relationship between ad size and the proportion of calls that were generated by the ad.

Cause-and-Effect Interpretations

Care must be used when interpreting the correlation results. For example, even though we found a significant linear relationship between years of experience and sales for the Midwest Distribution sales force, the correlation does not imply cause and effect. Although an increase in experience may, in fact, cause sales to change, simply because the two variables are correlated does not guarantee a cause-and-effect situation. Two seemingly unconnected variables will often be highly correlated. For example, over a period of time, teachers' salaries in North Dakota might be highly correlated with the price of grapes in Spain. Yet, we doubt that a change in grape prices will *cause* a corresponding change in salaries for teachers in North Dakota, or vice versa. When a correlation exists between two seemingly unrelated variables, the correlation is said to be a **spurious correlation**. You should take great care to avoid basing conclusions on spurious correlations.

The Midwest Distribution marketing director has a logical reason to believe that years of experience with the company and total sales are related. That is, sales theory and customer feedback hold that product knowledge is a major component in successfully marketing a product. However, a statistically significant correlation alone does not prove that this cause-and-effect relationship exists. When two seemingly unrelated variables are correlated, they may both be responding to changes in some third variable. For example, the observed correlation could be the effect of a company policy of giving better sales territories to more senior salespeople.

12-1: EXERCISES

Skill Development

12.1 Develop a scatter plot for the following data.

y	x
100	88
200	120
150	200
75	100
140	100
160	90
230	125

Based on the scatter plot, describe what, if any, relationship exists between these two variables.

12.2 Develop individual scatter plots for the variable y against variables x_1 and x_2.

y	x_1	x_2
25	4	7
29	3	9
40	1	13
20	6	6
24	5	8
18	7	5
30	3	11
25	3	5

Describe what, if any, relationship is present in each of the scatter plots.

12.3 If two variables have a negative linear relationship, what will the value of y tend to do when the corresponding value of x increases substantially? Show with an example.

12.4 If the scatter plot of two variables shows a weak positive linear relationship, what will be the general change in y associated with a downward change in x? Show with an example.

12.5 If a scatter plot shows that two variables have a curvilinear relationship showing y increasing at a decreasing rate as x increases, what might the scatter plot look like? Describe two variables that might exhibit such a relationship? Explain your reasoning.

12.6 You are given the following data for variables x and y:

x	y
3.0	1.5
2.0	0.5
2.5	1.0
3.0	1.8
2.5	1.2
4.0	2.2
1.5	0.4
1.0	0.3
2.0	1.3
2.5	1.0

a. Plot these variables in scatter-plot format. Based on this plot, what type of relationship appears to exist between the two variables?

b. Compute the correlation coefficient for these sample data. Indicate what the correlation coefficient measures.

c. Test to determine whether the population correlation coefficient is positive. Use the $\alpha = 0.01$ level to conduct the test. Be sure to state the null and alternative hypotheses, and show the test statistic and decision rule clearly.

12.7 You are given the following data for variables x and y:

x	y
20	16
18	12
24	18
20	17
22	21
14	10
18	10

a. Plot these variables in scatter-plot format. Based on this plot, what type of relationship appears to exist between the two variables?

b. Compute the correlation coefficient for these sample data. Indicate what the correlation coefficient measures.

c. Test to determine whether the population correlation coefficient is zero. Use the $\alpha = 0.05$ level to conduct the test. Be sure to state the null and alternative hypotheses, and show the test statistic and decision rule clearly.

d. Refer to part c. Describe the type of hypothesis test error that could have been made.

12.8 You are given the following data for variables x and y:

x	y
100	80
110	90
90	75
100	90
110	80
80	60
90	90
90	70

a. (1) Compute the correlation coefficient for these sample data. Indicate what the correlation coefficient measures. (2) Divide the x variable by 10 and the y by 5. Recalculate the correlation coefficient. What is the mathematical relationship between the two correlation coefficients?

b. Test to determine whether the population correlation coefficient is negative. Use the $\alpha = 0.05$ level to conduct the test. Be sure to state the null and alternative hypotheses, and show the test statistic and decision rule clearly.

Business Applications

12.9 A sample of 32 people was randomly selected, and height and weight measurements were made for each person. The correlation coefficient for the two variables was 0.80.

a. Discuss in your own words what $r = 0.80$ means with respect to the variables height and weight. Determine whether each of the variables is a fixed or a randomly selected value. Explain your answer.

b. Using an $\alpha = 0.10$ level, test to determine if a correlation exists between height and weight in the population. Be sure to state the null and alternative hypotheses.

12.10 A random sample of 50 bank accounts was selected from a local branch bank. Account balance and number of deposits and withdrawals during the past month were the two variables recorded. The correlation coefficient for the two variables was -0.23.

a. Discuss what $r = -0.23$ measures. Make sure to frame your discussion in terms of the two variables discussed here.

b. Using an $\alpha = 0.10$ level, test to determine whether there is a significant linear relationship between account balance and the number of transactions to an account during the past month. State the null and alternative hypotheses and show the decision rule.

c. Consider the decision you reached in part b. Describe the type of error you could have made in the context of this problem.

12.11 Consider these two scenarios:

a. The number of new workers hired per week in your county has a high positive correlation with the average weekly temperature. Can you conclude that an increase in temperature causes an increase in the number of new hires? Discuss.

b. Suppose the stock price and the common dividends declared for a certain company have a high positive correlation. Are you safe in concluding on the basis of the correlation coefficient that an increase in the common dividends declared causes an increase in the stock price? Present other reasons than the correlation coefficient that might lead you to conclude that an increase in common dividends declared causes an increase in the stock price.

Advanced Applications

12.12 The following information taken from the 1998 annual report of Baldor Electric Company shows Net Sales and Working Capital (in thousands of dollars) for 1988 to 1998. The data are also contained in the CD-ROM file *Baldor*.

Year	Net Sales	Working Capital
1988	$234,463	67,168
1989	281,462	69,788
1990	294,030	75,306
1991	286,495	84,740
1992	318,930	97,343
1993	356,595	108,601
1994	418,152	118,550
1995	473,103	145,069
1996	502,875	146,975
1997	557,940	141,268
1998	589,406	176,126

a. Plot the variables Net Sales (y) and Working Capital (x) in scatter-plot format. What type of relationship appears to exist between Working Capital and Net Sales? Indicate whether a regression model or a correlation model would be more appropriate. Give statistical reasons for your answer.

b. Compute the correlation coefficient between Working Capital and Net Sales. What does the correlation coefficient measure?

c. Test to determine if when Net Sales declines, Working Capital will also decline. (Hint: Think what this indicates for the value of the population correlation coefficient.) Clearly state your null and alternative hypotheses. Conduct your test at a significance level of 0.05. Be sure to state a conclusion for your test.

12.13 The following basic earnings per share (EPS) and common dividends declared for 1989 to 1998 were taken from the 1998 annual report of McCormick & Company. The data are also contained in the CD-ROM file *McCormick Dividends*.

Year	Basic EPS	Common Dividends Declared
1989	$1.59	$0.19
1990	0.86	0.24
1991	1.01	0.31
1992	1.19	0.40
1993	0.90	0.45
1994	0.75	0.49
1995	1.20	0.53
1996	0.52	0.57
1997	1.30	0.61
1998	1.42	0.65

a. Plot the variables EPS and dividends in scatter-plot format. What, if any, kind of relationship appears to exist between them? Would a regression model or a correlation model be more appropriate for this data? Explain your answer.

b. Compute the correlation coefficient between EPS and dividends. Provide an interpretation of this coefficient.

c. Does it appear that as EPS increases, dividends decrease? Conduct a hypothesis test of the relevant parameter to answer this question. Conduct your test at a significance level of 0.025. Conduct this hypothesis test using the *p*-value approach.

12-2 SIMPLE LINEAR REGRESSION ANALYSIS

In the Midwest Distribution example, we determined that the relationship between years of experience and total sales is linear and statistically significant, based on the correlation analysis performed in the previous section. Because hiring and training costs have been increasing, we would like to use this relationship to help formulate a more-acceptable wage package for the sales force.

The statistical method we will use to analyze the relationship between years of experience and total sales is *regression analysis*. When we have only two variables—a dependent variable, such as sales, and an independent variable, such as years with the company—the technique is referred to as *simple regression analysis*. When the relationship between the dependent variable and the independent variable is linear, the technique is **simple linear regression**.

THE REGRESSION MODEL AND ASSUMPTIONS

The objective of simple linear regression (which we shall call *regression analysis*) is to represent the relationship between values of *x* and *y* with a model of the form shown in Equation 12-4.

Simple Linear Regression Model (Population Model)

$$y = \beta_0 + \beta_1 x + \varepsilon \qquad \qquad \textbf{12-4}$$

where:

y = Value of the dependent variable
x = Value of the independent variable
β_0 = Population's *y*-intercept
β_1 = Slope of the population regression line
ε = Error term, or residual (i.e., the difference between the actual *y* value and the value of *y* predicted by the population model)

The simple linear regression population model described in Equation 12-4 has four assumptions:

1. Individual values of the error terms, ε, are statistically independent of one another, and these values represent a random sample from the population of possible values at each level of *x*.
2. For a given value of *x*, there can exist many values of *y* and therefore many values of ε. Further, the distribution of possible ε values for any *x* value is normal.
3. The distributions of possible ε values have equal variances for all values of *x*.
4. The means of the dependent variable, *y*, for all specified values of the independent variable, $(\mu_{y|x})$, can be connected by a straight line called the population regression model.

Figure 12-7 illustrates assumptions 2, 3, and 4. The regression model (straight line) connects the average of the *y* values for each level of the independent variable, *x*. The actual *y* values for each level of *x* are normally distributed around the mean of *y*. Finally, observe that the spread of possible *y* values is the same regardless of the level of *x*. The population regression line is determined by two values, β_0 and β_1. These values are known as the population *regression coefficients*. Value β_0 identifies the *y*-intercept and β_1 the slope of the regression line. Under the regression assumptions, the coefficients define the true population model. For each observation, the actual value of the dependent variable, *y*, for any *x*, is the sum of two components:

$$y = \underbrace{\beta_0 + \beta_1 x}_{\text{Linear Component}} + \underbrace{\varepsilon}_{\text{Random Error Component}}$$

The random error component, ε, may be positive, zero, or negative, depending on whether a single value of *y* for a given *x* falls above, on, or below the population regression line.

FIGURE 12-7

Graphical Display of Linear Regression Assumptions

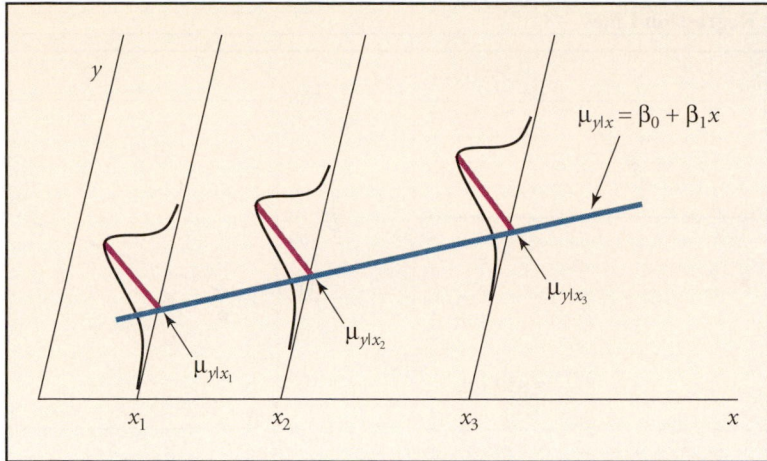

$$\mu_{y|x} = \beta_0 + \beta_1 x$$

$\mu_{y|x_1}$ $\mu_{y|x_2}$ $\mu_{y|x_3}$

x_1 x_2 x_3 x

MEANING OF THE REGRESSION COEFFICIENTS

Coefficient β_1, the **regression slope coefficient** of the population regression line, measures the average change in the value of the dependent variable, y, for each unit change in x. The population slope can be either positive, zero, or negative, depending on the relationship between x and y. For example, a positive population slope of 12 ($\beta_1 = 12$) means that for a 1-unit increase in x, we can expect an average 12-unit increase in y. Correspondingly, if the population slope is negative 12 ($\beta_1 = -12$), we can expect an average decrease of 12 units in y for a 1-unit increase in x.

Regression Slope Coefficient

The average change in the dependent variable for a unit increase in the independent variable. The slope coefficient may be positive or negative, depending on the relationship between the two variables.

The population's y-intercept, β_0, indicates the mean value of y when x is 0. However, this interpretation holds only if the population could have x values equal to 0. When this cannot occur, β_0 does not have a meaningful interpretation in the regression model.

Midwest Distribution (continued)—The Midwest Distribution marketing manager has data for a sample of 12 sales representatives. In Section 12-1, she has established that a significant linear relationship exists between years of experience and total sales using correlation analysis. (Recall that the correlation between the two variables was $r = 0.8325$.) Now she would like to estimate the regression equation that defines the *true* linear relationship (that is, the population's linear relationship) between years of experience and sales. Figure 12-3 shows the scatter plot for two variables: years with the company and sales. We need to use the sample data to estimate β_0 and β_1, the true intercept and slope of the line representing the relationship between two variables. The *regression line* through the sample data is the best estimate of the population regression line. However, there are an infinite number of possible regression lines for a set of points. For example, Figure 12-8 shows three of the possible different lines that pass through Midwest Distribution data. Which line should be used to estimate the true regression model?

We must establish a criterion for selecting the best line. The criterion used is the **least squares criterion**.[3]

Least Squares Criterion

The criterion for determining a regression line that minimizes the sum of squared residuals.

To understand the least squares criterion, you need to know about prediction error, or **residual**, the distance between the y-coordinate of an (x,y) point and the estimate of that y-coordinate produced by the regression line. Figure 12-9 shows how the prediction error is calculated for the employee

---

[3]The reason that we are using the sum of the squared residuals is that the sum of the residuals will be zero for the best regression line (the positive values will balance the negative values).

FIGURE 12-8   Possible Regression Lines

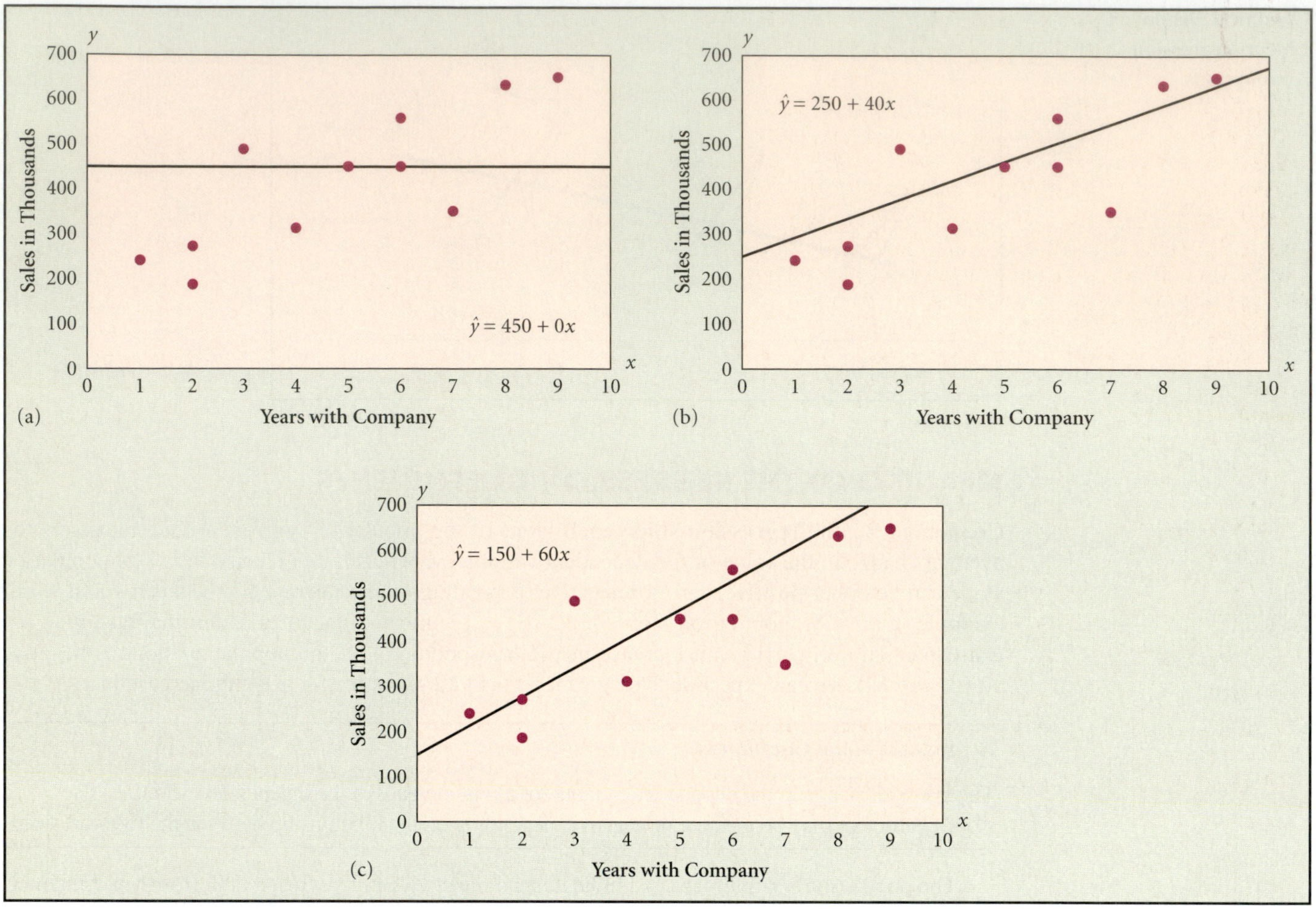

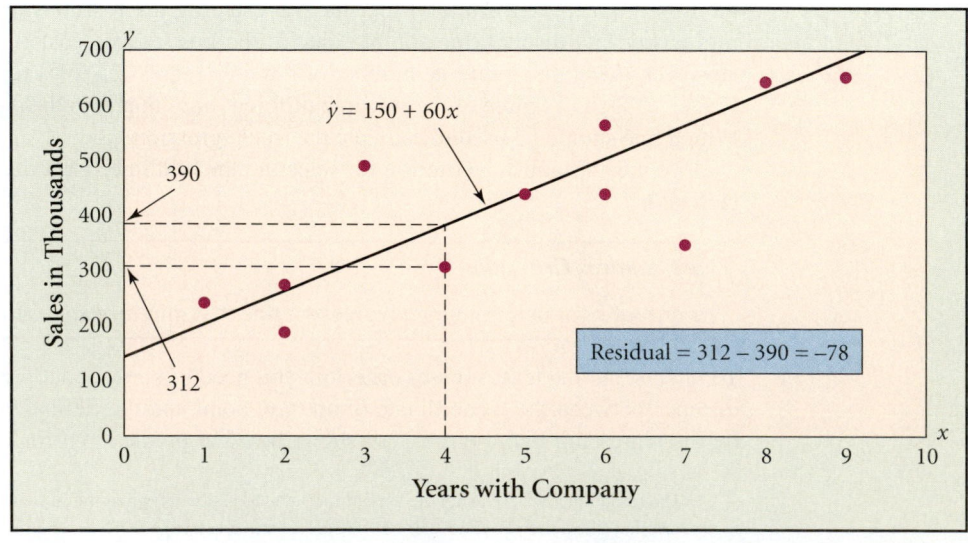

who was with Midwest for 4 years ($x = 4$) using one possible regression line: $\hat{y} = 150 + 60x$ (where $\hat{y}$ is the estimated sales value). The predicted sales value is

$$\hat{y} = 150 + 60(4) = 390$$

However, the actual sales (y) for this employee were 312. Thus, when $x = 4$, the difference between the observed, $y = 312$, and the regression line value, $\hat{y} = 390$, is $312 - 390 = -78$. The residual (or prediction error) for this case when $x = 4$ is -78. Table 12-2 shows the calculated errors

FIGURE 12-9

Computation of Regression Error for the Midwest Distribution Example

TABLE 12-2

Sum of Squared Errors for Three Linear Equations for Midwest Distribution

From Figure 12-8(a):

$\hat{y} = 450 + 0x$

			RESIDUAL	
x	$\hat{y}$	y	$y - \hat{y}$	$(y - \hat{y})^2$
3	450	487	37	1,369
5	450	445	−5	25
2	450	272	−178	31,684
8	450	641	191	36,481
2	450	187	−263	69,169
6	450	440	−10	100
7	450	346	−104	10,816
1	450	238	−212	44,944
4	450	312	−138	19,044
2	450	269	−181	32,761
9	450	655	205	42,025
6	450	563	113	12,769
				$\Sigma = 301{,}187$

From Figure 12-8(b):

$\hat{y} = 250 + 40x$

			RESIDUAL	
x	$\hat{y}$	y	$y - \hat{y}$	$(y - \hat{y})^2$
3	370	487	117	13,689
5	450	445	−5	25
2	330	272	−58	3,364
8	570	641	71	5,041
2	330	187	−143	20,449
6	490	440	−50	2,500
7	530	346	−184	33,856
1	290	238	−52	2,704
4	410	312	−98	9,604
2	330	269	−61	3,721
9	610	655	45	2,025
6	490	563	73	5,329
				$\Sigma = 102{,}307$

From Figure 12-8(c):

$\hat{y} = 150 + 60x$

			RESIDUAL	
x	$\hat{y}$	y	$y - \hat{y}$	$(y - \hat{y})^2$
3	330	487	157	24,649
5	450	445	−5	25
2	270	272	2	4
8	630	641	11	121
2	270	187	−83	6,889
6	510	440	−70	4,900
7	570	346	−224	50,176
1	210	238	28	784
4	390	312	−78	6,084
2	270	269	−1	1
9	690	655	−35	1,225
6	510	563	53	2,809
				$\Sigma = 97{,}667$

and sum of squared errors for each of the three regression lines shown in Figure 12-8. Of these three potential regression models, the line with the equation $\hat{y} = 150 + 60x$ has the smallest sum of squared errors. However, is this line the best of all possible lines? That is, would $\sum_{i=1}^{n}(y_i - \hat{y}_i)^2$ be smaller than for any other line? One way to determine this is to calculate the sum of squared errors for all other regression lines. However, because there are an infinite number of these lines, this approach is not feasible. Fortunately, through the use of calculus, equations can be derived to directly determine the slope and intercept estimates such that $\sum_{i=1}^{n}(y_i - \hat{y}_i)^2$ is minimized.[4] This is accomplished by letting the estimated regression model be of the form shown in Equation 12-5.

Estimated Regression Model (Sample Model)

$$\hat{y} = b_0 + b_1 x \qquad\qquad \textbf{12-5}$$

where:

$\hat{y}$ = Estimated, or predicted, y value

b_0 = Unbiased estimate of the regression intercept, found using Equation 12-8

b_1 = Unbiased estimate of the regression slope, found using Equation 12-6 or 12-7

x = Value of the independent variable

Equations 12-6 and 12-8 are referred to as the *least squares equations* because they provide the slope and intercept that minimize the sum of squared errors. Equation 12-7 is the algbraic equivalent of Equation 12-6 and is easier to use when the computation is performed using a calculator.

Least Squares Equations (Sample Values)

$$b_1 = \frac{\Sigma(x - \bar{x})(y - \bar{y})}{\Sigma(x - \bar{x})^2} \qquad\qquad \textbf{12-6}$$

algebraic equivalent:

$$b_1 = \frac{\Sigma xy - \dfrac{\Sigma x \, \Sigma y}{n}}{\Sigma x^2 - \dfrac{(\Sigma x)^2}{n}} \qquad\qquad \textbf{12-7}$$

and

$$b_0 = \bar{y} - b_1 \bar{x} \qquad\qquad \textbf{12-8}$$

Table 12-3 shows the manual calculations, which are subject to rounding, for the least squares estimates for the Midwest Distribution example. However, you will almost always use a software package such as Excel or Minitab to perform these computations. Figures 12-10a and 12-10b show the regression output. In this case, the "best" regression line, given the least squares criterion, is $\hat{y} = 175.8288 + 49.9101(x)$. Figure 12-11 shows the predicted sales values and the residuals and squared residuals associated with this best simple linear regression line. Keep in mind that the residuals are also referred to as *errors* or *prediction errors*. From Figure 12-11, the sum of the squared errors is 84,834.29. This is the smallest sum of squared residuals possible for this set of sample data. No other simple linear regression line through these 12 (x,y) points will produce a smaller sum of squared residuals. Equation 12-9 presents a formula that can be used to calculate the sum of squared errors manually.

---

[4]The calculus derivation of the least squares equations is contained on the CD-ROM that accompanies this text under the Chapter 12 folder.

TABLE 12-3

Manual Calculations for Least Squares Regression Coefficients for the Midwest Distribution Example

y	x	xy	x^2	y^2
487	3	1,461	9	237,169
445	5	2,225	25	198,025
272	2	544	4	73,984
641	8	5,128	64	410,881
187	2	374	4	34,969
440	6	2,640	36	193,600
346	7	2,422	49	119,716
238	1	238	1	56,644
312	4	1,248	16	97,344
269	2	538	4	72,361
655	9	5,895	81	429,025
563	6	3,378	36	316,969
$\Sigma y = 4{,}855$	$\Sigma x = 55$	$\Sigma xy = 26{,}091$	$\Sigma x^2 = 329$	$\Sigma y^2 = 2{,}240{,}687$

$$\bar{y} = \frac{\Sigma y}{n} = \frac{4{,}855}{12} = 404.58 \qquad \bar{x} = \frac{\Sigma x}{n} = \frac{55}{12} = 4.58$$

$$b_1 = \frac{\Sigma xy - \dfrac{\Sigma x \Sigma y}{n}}{\Sigma x^2 - \dfrac{(\Sigma x)^2}{n}} = \frac{26{,}091 - \dfrac{55(4{,}855)}{12}}{329 - \dfrac{(55)^2}{12}}$$

$$= 49.91$$

Then,

$$b_0 = \bar{y} - b_1 \bar{x} = 404.58 - 49.91(4.58) = 175.83$$

The least squares regression line is, therefore,

$$\hat{y} = 175.83 + 49.91(x)$$

FIGURE 12-10A

Excel Midwest Distribution Regression Results

Excel Instructions:
1. Open file Midwest.xls
2. Select **Tools**.
3. Click on **Data Analysis**.
4. Select **Regression Analysis**.
5. Define x and y variable data range.
6. Select output location.
7. Click **Residuals**.

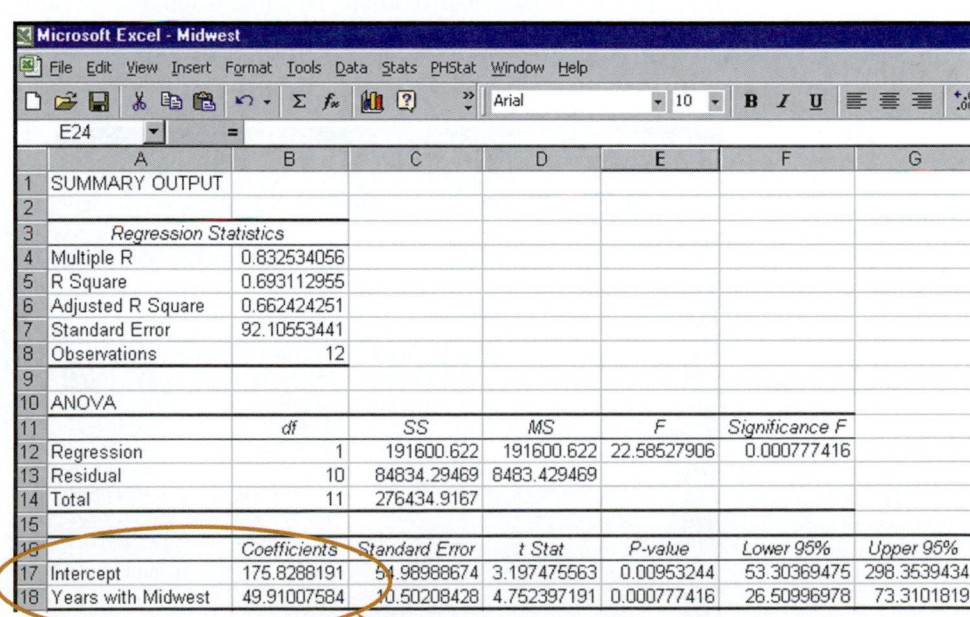

Estimated regression equation is
$\hat{y} = 175.8288 = 49.9101(x)$

FIGURE 12-10B

**Minitab Midwest
Distribution Regression
Results**

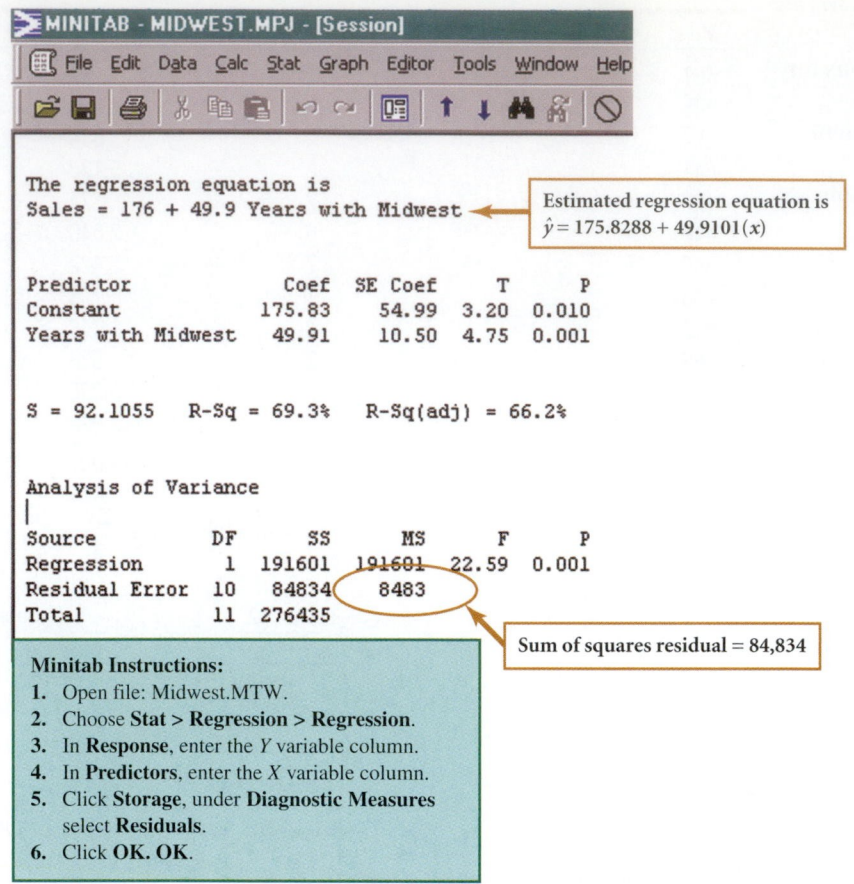

Minitab Instructions:
1. Open file: Midwest.MTW.
2. Choose **Stat > Regression > Regression**.
3. In **Response**, enter the Y variable column.
4. In **Predictors**, enter the X variable column.
5. Click **Storage**, under **Diagnostic Measures** select **Residuals**.
6. Click **OK. OK**.

Sum of Squared Errors

$$SSE = \Sigma\, y^2 - b_0\, \Sigma\, y - b_1\, \Sigma\, xy$$

12-9

Figure 12-12 shows the scatter plot of sales and years experience and the least squares regression line for Midwest Distribution. This line is the *best fit* for these sample data. Note that the regression line passes through the point corresponding to $(\bar{x}, \bar{y})$.

FIGURE 12-11

**Residuals and Squared
Residuals for the Midwest
Distribution Example**

Excel Instructions:
1. Create Squared Residuals using Excel formula.

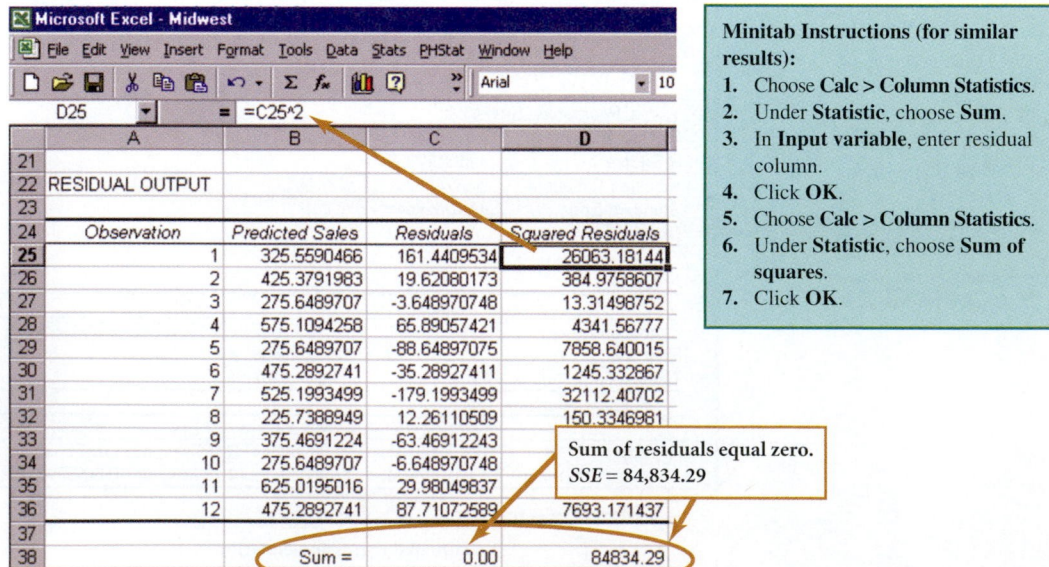

Minitab Instructions (for similar results):
1. Choose **Calc > Column Statistics**.
2. Under **Statistic**, choose **Sum**.
3. In **Input variable**, enter residual column.
4. Click **OK**.
5. Choose **Calc > Column Statistics**.
6. Under **Statistic**, choose **Sum of squares**.
7. Click **OK**.

FIGURE 12-12

Least Squares Regression
Line for Midwest
Distribution

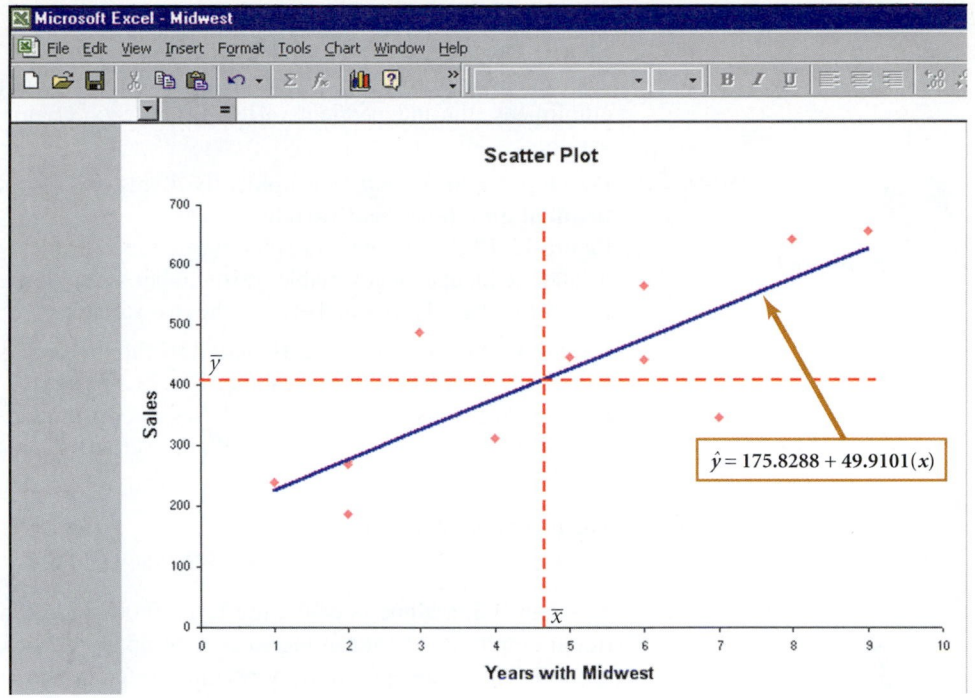

LEAST SQUARES REGRESSION PROPERTIES

Figure 12-11 illustrates several important properties of least squares regression.

1. The sum of the residuals from the least squares regression line is 0 (Equation 12-10). The total underprediction by the regression model is exactly offset by the total overprediction.

Sum of Residuals

$$\sum_{i=1}^{n} (y_i - \hat{y}_i) = 0$$

12-10

2. The sum of the squared residuals is a minimum (Equation 12-11).

Sum of Squared Residuals (Errors)

$$SSE = \sum_{i=1}^{n} (y_i - \hat{y}_i)^2$$

12-11

This property provided the basis for developing the equations for b_0 and b_1.

3. The simple regression line always passes through the mean of the y variable, $\bar{y}$, and the mean of the x variable, $\bar{x}$. This is illustrated in Figure 12-12. So, to manually draw any simple linear regression line, all you need to do is to draw a line connecting the least squares y-intercept with the $(\bar{x}, \bar{y})$ point.

4. The least squares coefficients are unbiased estimates of β_0 and β_1. Thus, the expected values of b_0 and b_1 equal β_0 and β_1, respectively.

$\mathcal{E}$XAMPLE 12-2: SIMPLE LINEAR REGRESSION AND CORRELATION

Fitzpatrick & Associates   The investment firm Fitzpatrick & Associates wants to manage the pension fund of a major Chicago retailer. For their presentation to the retailer, the Fitzpatrick analysts want to use simple linear regression to model the relationship between profits and numbers of employees for 50 Fortune 500 companies in the firm's portfolio. The data for the analysis is contained in the CD-ROM file *Fortune 50*. This analysis can be done using the following steps.

Excel and Minitab Tutorial

Step 1:   Specify the independent and dependent variables.
The object in this example is to model the linear relationship between number of employees (the independent variable) and each company's profits (the dependent variable).

Step 2:   Develop a scatter plot to graphically display the relationship between the independent and dependent variables.
Figure 12-13 shows the scatter plot, where the dependent variable, y, is company profits and the independent variable, x, is number of employees. There appears to be slight positive linear relationship between the two variables.

Step 3:   Calculate the correlation coefficient and the linear regression equation.
Do either manually using Equations 12-1, 12-6, and 12-8, respectively, or by using Excel or Minitab software. Figure 12-14 shows the regression results. The sample correlation coefficient (called multiple R in Excel) is

$$r = 0.3638$$

The regression equation is

$$\hat{y} = 2556.88 + 0.0048x$$

The regression slope is estimated to be 0.0048, which means that for each additional employee, the mean increase in company profit is 0.0048 million dollars, or $4,800. The intercept can only be interpreted when a value equal to zero for the x variable (employees) is plausible. Clearly no company has zero employees, so the intercept in this case has no meaning other than it locates the height of the regression line for $x = 0$.

FIGURE 12-13

Excel Scatter Plot for Fitzpatrick & Associates

Excel Instructions:
1. Open file: Fortune 50.xls
2. Click on **Chart Wizard**.
3. Select **XY Scatter**.
4. Click on **Series** Tab.
5. Define x and y variable range.

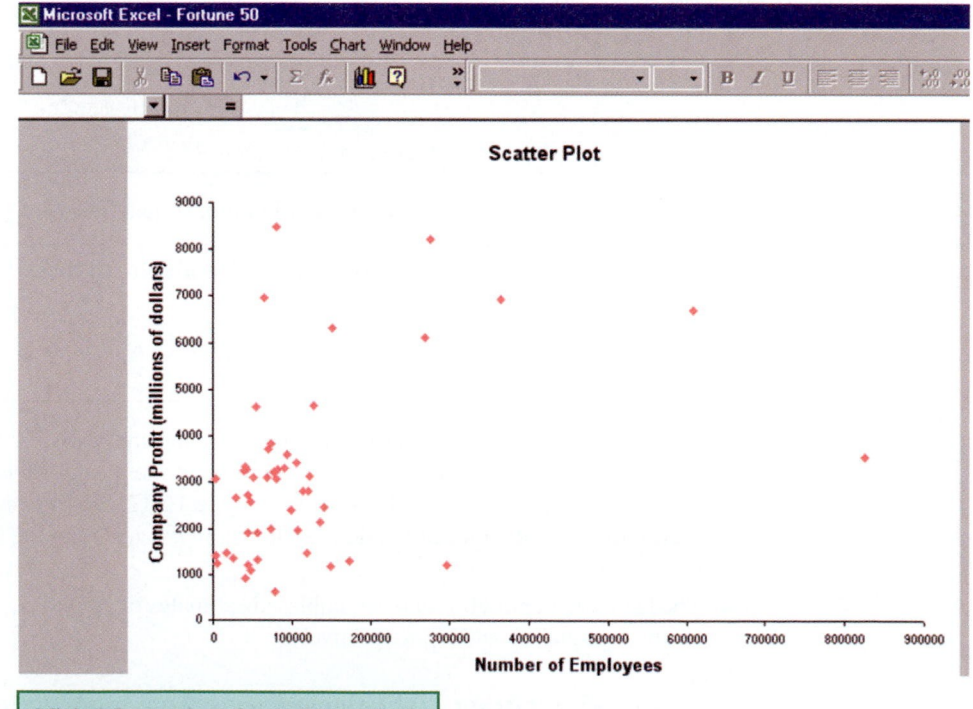

Minitab Instructions (for similar results):
1. Open file: Fortune 50.MTW.
2. Choose **Graph > Scatterplot**.
3. Under **Scatterplot**, choose **Simple. OK**.
4. Under **Y variable**, enter y column.
5. In **X variable**, enter x column.
6. Click **OK**.

FIGURE 12-14

Excel Regression Results for Fitzpatrick & Associates

Excel Instructions:
1. Open file: Fortune 50.xls
2. Click on **Tools** tab.
3. Select **Regression**.
4. Define *x* and *y* variable data range.

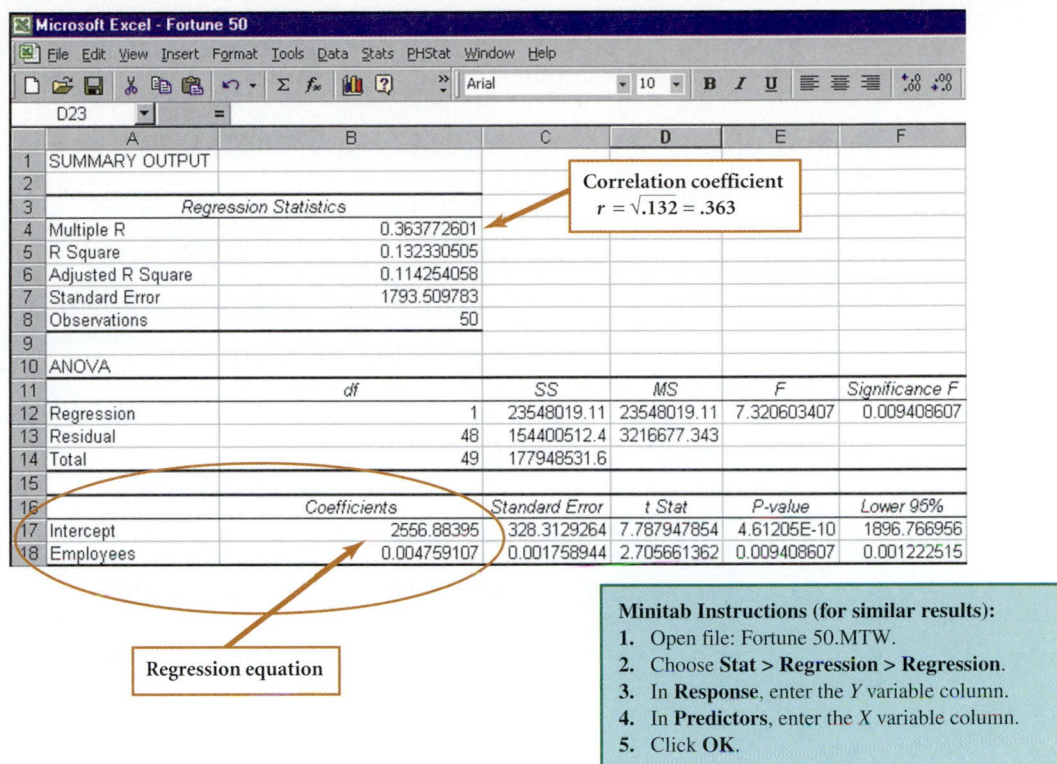

Correlation coefficient
$r = \sqrt{.132} = .363$

Regression equation

Minitab Instructions (for similar results):
1. Open file: Fortune 50.MTW.
2. Choose **Stat > Regression > Regression**.
3. In **Response**, enter the *Y* variable column.
4. In **Predictors**, enter the *X* variable column.
5. Click **OK**.

SIGNIFICANCE TESTS IN REGRESSION ANALYSIS

In Section 12-1, we pointed out that the correlation coefficient computed from sample data is a point estimate of the population correlation coefficient and is subject to sampling error. We also introduced a test of significance for the correlation coefficient. Likewise, the regression coefficients developed from a sample of data are also point estimates of the true regression coefficients for the population. The regression coefficients are subject to sampling error. For example, due to sampling error the estimated slope coefficient may be positive or negative while the population slope is really zero. Therefore, we need a test procedure to determine whether the regression slope coefficient is statistically significant. As you will see in this section, the test for the simple linear regression slope coefficient is equivalent to the test for the correlation coefficient. That is, if the correlation between two variables is found to be significant, then the regression slope coefficient will also be significant.

The Coefficient of Determination, R^2

Midwest Distribution (continued)—Recall that the Midwest Distribution marketing manager was analyzing the relationship between the number of years an employee had been with the company (independent variable) and the sales generated by the employee (dependent variable). We note when looking at the sample data for 12 employees (see Table 12-3) that sales vary between employees. Regression analysis aims to determine the extent to which an independent variable can explain this variation. In this case, does number of years with the company help explain the variation in sales from employee to employee?

The *SST* (total sum of squares) can be used in measuring the variation in the dependent variable. *SST* is computed using Equation 12-12. For Midwest Distribution, the total sum of squares for sales is provided in the output generated by Excel or Minitab as shown in Figure 12-15a and Figure 12-15b. As you can see, the total sum of squares in sales that needs to be explained is 276,434.9. Note that the *SST* value is in squared units and has no particular meaning.

Total Sum of Squares

$$SST = \sum_{i=1}^{n} (y_i - \bar{y})^2$$

12-12

where:

SST = Total sum of squares
n = Sample size
y_i = ith value of the dependent variable
$\bar{y}$ = Average value of the dependent variable

The *SST* is the sum of two other sum of squares, the sum of squares error (*SSE*) and the sum of squares regression (*SSR*). Thus,

$$SST = SSE + SSR$$

The least squares regression line is computed so that the sum of squared residuals is minimized (recall the discussion of the least squares equations). The sum of squares residuals is also called the *sum of squares error* (*SSE*) and is defined by Equation 12-13.

Sum of Squares Error

$$SSE = \sum_{i=1}^{n} (y_i - \hat{y}_i)^2$$

12-13

where:

n = Sample size
y_i = ith value of the dependent variable
$\hat{y}_i$ = ith predicted value of y given the ith value of x

SSE represents the amount of the total sum of squares in the dependent variable that *is not explained* by the least squares regression line. Excel refers to *SSE* as *sum of squares residual*. This value is contained in the regression output shown in Figure 12-15a and Figure 12-15b.

$$SSE = \Sigma(y - \hat{y})^2 = 84,834.29$$

FIGURE 12-15A

Excel Regression Results for Midwest Distribution

Excel Instructions:
1. Open file: Midwest.xls
2. Click on **Tools** tab.
3. Select **Regression**.
4. Define x and y variable data range.

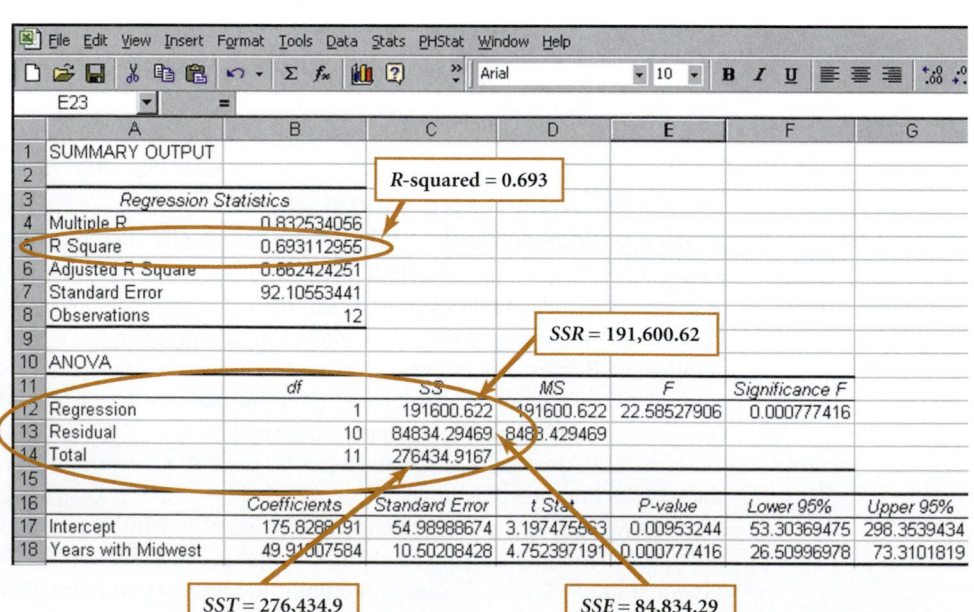

R-squared = 0.693

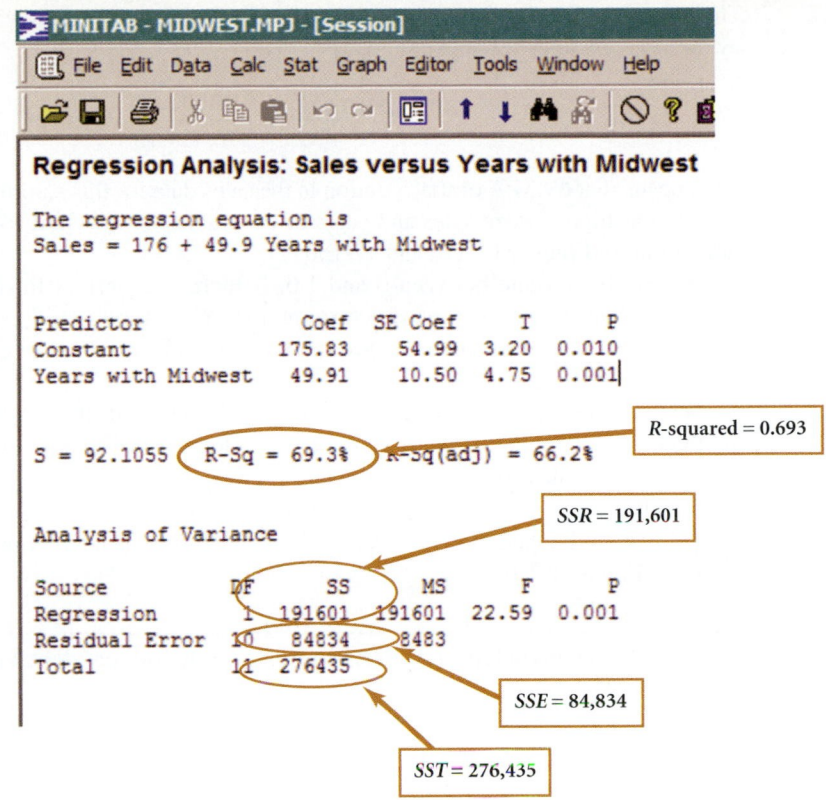

F I G U R E 12-15B

Minitab Regression Results for Midwest Distribution

Minitab Instructions:
1. Open file: Midwest.MTW.
2. Choose **Stat > Regression > Regression**.
3. In **Response**, enter the *y* variable column.
4. In **Predictors**, enter the *x* variable column.
5. Click **OK**.

Thus, of the total sum of squares (*SST* = 276,434.9), the regression model leaves *SSE* = 84,834.29 unexplained. Then, the portion of the total sum of squares that *is explained* by the regression line is called the *sum of squares regression* (*SSR*) and is calculated by Equation 12-14.

Sum of Squares Regression

$$SSR = \sum_{i=1}^{n} (\hat{y}_i - \bar{y})^2$$

12-14

where:

$$\hat{y}_i = \text{Estimated value of } y \text{ for each value of } x$$
$$\bar{y} = \text{Average value of the } y \text{ variable}$$

The sum of squares regression (*SSR* = 191,600.62) is also provided in the regression output shown in Figure 12-15a.

We can use these calculations to compute an important measure in regression analysis called the **coefficient of determination**.

Coefficient of Determination

The portion of the total variation in the dependent variable that is explained by its relationship with the independent variable. The coefficient of determination is also called *R*-squared and is denoted as R^2.

The coefficient of determination is calculated using Equation 12-15.

Coefficient of Determination, R^2

$$R^2 = \frac{SSR}{SST}$$

12-15

Then, for the Midwest Distribution example, the fraction of variation in sales that can be explained by the years of sales force experience is

$$R^2 = \frac{SSR}{SST} = \frac{191,600.62}{276,434.90} = 0.6931$$

This means that 69.31% of the variation in the sales data for this sample can be explained by the linear relationship between sales and years of experience. Notice that R-squared is part of the regression output in Figures 12-15a and 12-15b.

R^2 can be a value between 0 and 1.0. If there is a perfect linear relationship between two variables, then the coefficient of determination, R^2, will be 1.0. This would correspond to a situation in which the least squares regression line would pass through each of the points in the scatter plot.

R^2 is the measure used by many decision makers to indicate how well the linear regression line fits the (x,y) data points. The better the fit, the closer R^2 will be to 1.0. R^2 will be close to 0 when there is a weak linear relationship.

Finally, when you are employing *simple linear regression* (a linear relationship between the independent and dependent variables in the model), there is an alternative way of computing R^2, as shown in Equation 12-16.

Coefficient of Determination, Single Independent Variable Case

$$R^2 = r^2 \qquad \textbf{12-16}$$

where:

R^2 = Coefficient of determination
r = Simple correlation coefficient

Therefore, by squaring the correlation coefficient, we can get R^2 for the simple regression model. Figure 12-15a shows the correlation, $r = 0.8325$, which is referred to as Multiple R in Excel. Then using Equation 12-16, we get R^2.

$$R^2 = r^2$$
$$= 0.8325^2$$
$$= 0.6931$$

Significance of the Slope Coefficient

Before we use the regression model to analyze the relationship between sales and years of experience, we need to determine if the overall model is statistically significant. For a simple linear regression model (one independent variable), there are two equivalent methods.

1. Test for significance of the correlation between x and y.
2. Test for significance of the regression slope coefficient.

In Section 12-1, we discussed the first method, in which a t test is used to determine whether the population correlation coefficient is equal to 0.0. In simple regression, if the null hypothesis of zero correlation is rejected, we conclude that the two variables have a significant linear relationship. If that is the case, then the resulting regression model will also be statistically significant. However, you can directly test for the significance of the regression model with the null and alternative hypotheses as

$$H_0: \beta_1 = 0$$
$$H_A: \beta_1 \neq 0$$

To test the significance of the simple linear regression model, we test to determine whether the population regression slope coefficient is 0. A slope of 0 would imply that a linear relationship between x and y variables is of no use in explaining the variation in y. If the linear relationship is useful, then we should reject the hypothesis that the regression slope is 0. However, because the estimated regression slope coefficient, b_1, is calculated from sample data, it is subject to sampling error. Therefore, even though b_1 is not 0, we must determine whether its difference from 0 is greater than would generally be attributed to sampling error.

If we selected several samples from the same population and for each sample determined the least squares regression line, we would likely get regression lines with different slopes and different y-intercepts. This is analogous to getting different sample means from different samples. Just as the distribution of possible sample means has a standard deviation, the possible regression slopes have a standard deviation, which is given in Equation 12-17.

Standard Deviation of the Regression Slope Coefficient (Population)

$$\sigma_{b_1} = \frac{\sigma_\varepsilon}{\sqrt{\sum(x - \bar{x})^2}}$$

12-17

where:

σ_{b_1} = Standard deviation of the regression slope
(called the *standard error of the slope*)
σ_ε = Population standard error of the estimate

Equation 12-17 requires that we know the **standard error of the estimate**. It measures the dispersion of the dependent variable about its mean value at each value of the dependent variable in the original units of the dependent variable. However, because we are sampling from the population, we can estimate σ_ε as shown in Equation 12-18.

Estimator for the Standard Error of the Estimate

$$s_\varepsilon = \sqrt{\frac{SSE}{n - k - 1}}$$

12-18

where:

SSE = Sum of squares error
n = Sample size
k = Number of independent variables in the model

Equation 12-17, the standard deviation of the regression slope, applies when we are dealing with a population. However, in most cases, such as the Midwest Distribution example, we are dealing with a sample from the population. Thus, we need to estimate the regression slope's standard deviation using Equation 12-19.

Estimator for the Standard Deviation of the Regression Slope

$$s_{b_1} = \frac{s_\varepsilon}{\sqrt{\sum(x - \bar{x})^2}} = \frac{s_\varepsilon}{\sqrt{\sum x^2 - \frac{(\sum x)^2}{n}}}$$

12-19

where:

s_{b_1} = Estimate of the standard error of the least squares slope

$s_\varepsilon = \sqrt{\dfrac{SSE}{n - 2}}$ = Sample standard error of the estimate (the measure
of deviation of the actual y values around the regression line)

FIGURE 12-16A

Excel Regression Results for Midwest Distribution

Excel Instructions:
1. Open file: Midwest.xls
2. Click on **Tools** tab.
3. Select **Regression**.
4. Define *x* and *y* variable data range.

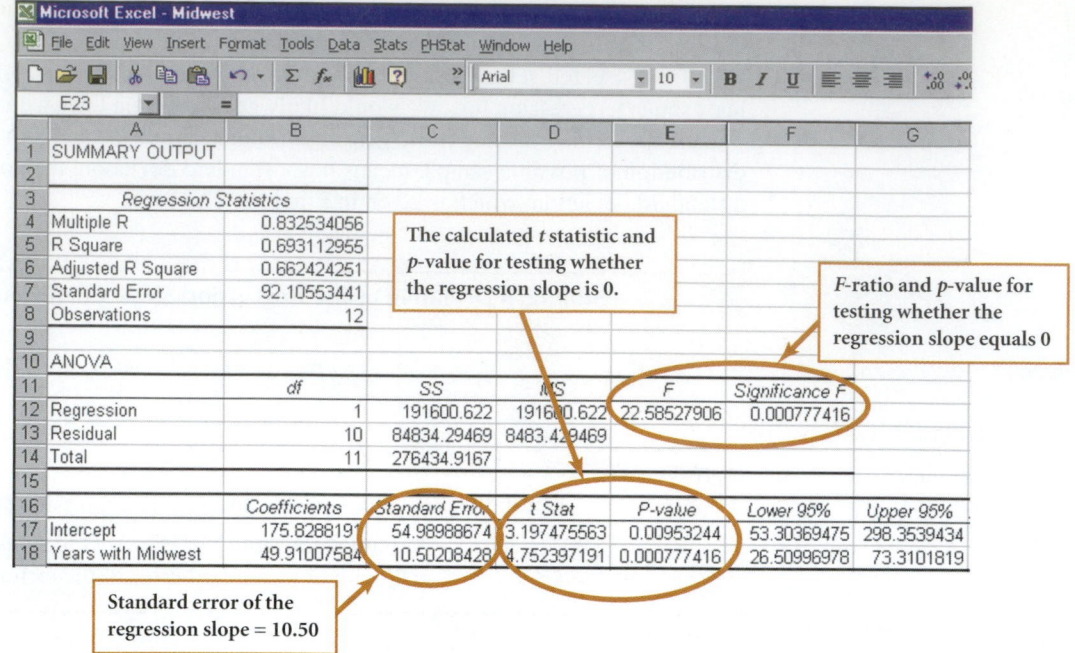

Midwest Distribution (continued)—For Midwest Distribution, the regression outputs in Figure 12-16a and Figure 12-16b show $b_1 = 49.91$. The question is whether this value is different enough from zero to have not been caused by sampling error. We find the answer by looking at the value of the estimate of the standard error of the slope, calculated using Equation 12-19, which is also shown in Figure 12-16a. The standard error of the slope coefficient is 10.50.

If the standard error of the slope is large, then the value of b_1 will be quite variable from sample to sample. Conversely, if σ_{b_1} is small, the slope values will be less variable. However, regardless of the standard error of the slope, the average value of b_1 will equal β_1, the true

FIGURE 12-16B

Minitab Regression Results for Midwest Distribution

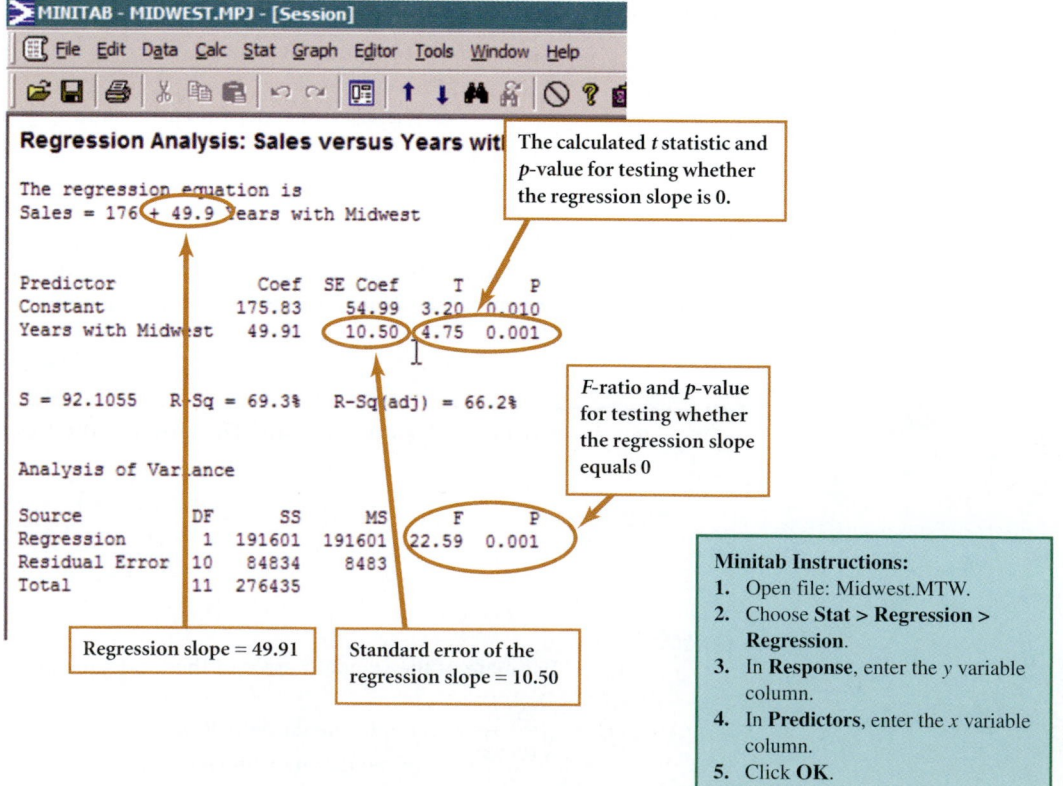

Minitab Instructions:
1. Open file: Midwest.MTW.
2. Choose **Stat > Regression > Regression**.
3. In **Response**, enter the *y* variable column.
4. In **Predictors**, enter the *x* variable column.
5. Click **OK**.

FIGURE 12-17   **Standard Error of the Slope**

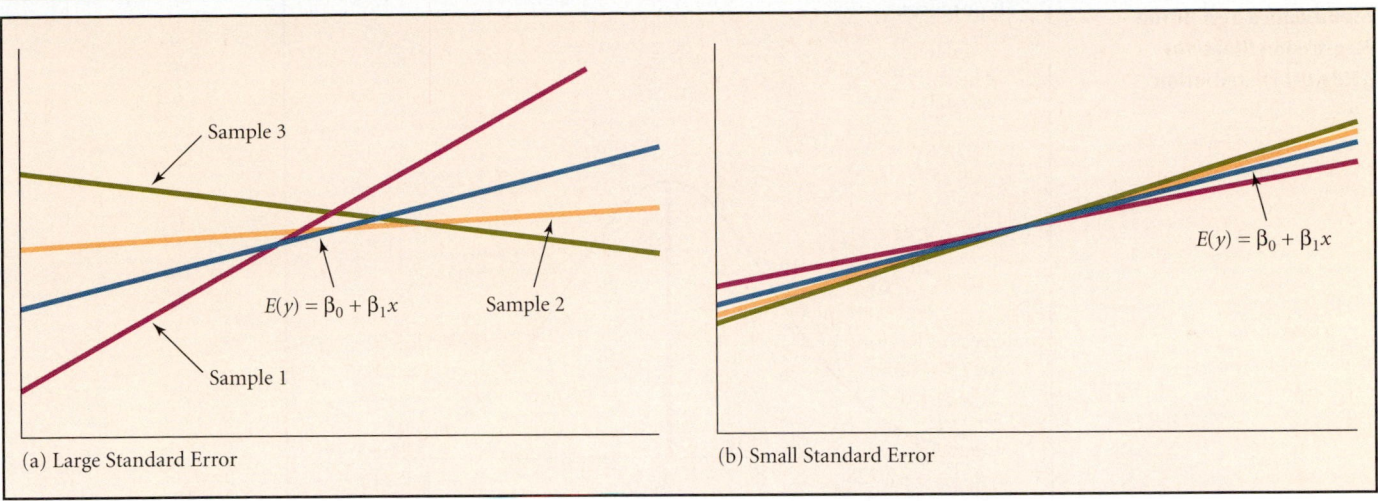

(a) Large Standard Error

(b) Small Standard Error

regression slope, if the assumptions of the regression analysis are satisfied. Figure 12-17 illustrates what this means. Notice that when the standard error of the slope is large, the sample slope can take on values *much* different from the true population slope. As Figure 12-17a shows, a sample slope and the true population slope can even have different signs. However, when σ_{b_1} is small, the sample regression lines will cluster closely around the true population line (Figure 12-17b).

Because the sample regression slope will most likely not equal the true population slope, we must test to determine whether the true slope could possibly be 0. A slope of 0 in the linear model means that the independent variable will not explain any variation in the dependent variable, nor will it be useful in predicting the dependent variable. The null and alternative hypotheses to be tested at the 0.05 level of significance are

$$H_0: \beta_1 = 0$$
$$H_A: \beta_1 \neq 0$$

To test the significance of a slope coefficient, we use the *t* test value in Equation 12-20.

Test Statistic for Test of the Significance of the Regression Slope, Simple Linear Regression

$$t = \frac{b_1 - \beta_1}{s_{b_1}} \qquad df = n - 2 \qquad\qquad \textbf{12-20}$$

where:

$$b_1 = \text{Sample regression slope coefficient}$$
$$\beta_1 = \text{Hypothesized slope}$$
$$s_{b_1} = \text{Estimator of the standard error of the slope}$$

Figure 12-18 illustrates this test for the Midwest Distribution example. The calculated *t*-value of 4.753 exceeds the critical value from the *t*-distribution with 10 degrees of freedom and $\alpha/2 = 0.025$. This indicates that we should reject the hypothesis that the true regression slope is 0. Thus, years of experience can be used to help explain the variation in an individual representative's sales. (Note that the calculated *t* is the same value that we found in Figure 12-6 for the test of the correlation coefficient.)

The output shown in Figures 12-16a and 12-16b also contain the calculated *t* statistic. The *p*-value for the calculated *t* statistic is also provided. As with other situations involving two-tailed hypothesis tests, if the *p*-value is less than α, the null hypothesis is rejected. In this case, because *p*-value = 0.0008 < 0.05, we reject the null hypothesis.

FIGURE 12-18

**Significance Test of the
Regression Slope for
Midwest Distribution**

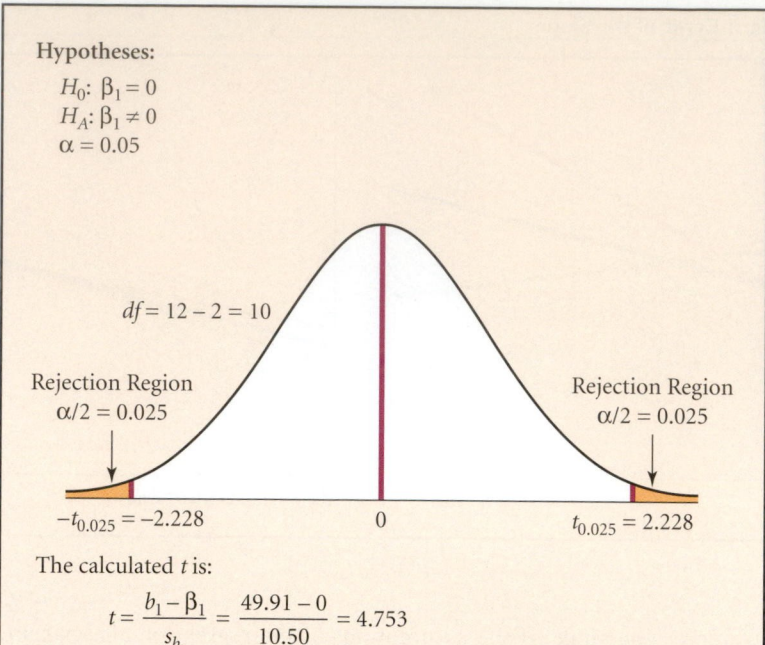

Hypotheses:

H_0: $\beta_1 = 0$
H_A: $\beta_1 \neq 0$
$\alpha = 0.05$

$df = 12 - 2 = 10$

Rejection Region
$\alpha/2 = 0.025$

Rejection Region
$\alpha/2 = 0.025$

$-t_{0.025} = -2.228$ 0 $t_{0.025} = 2.228$

The calculated t is:

$$t = \frac{b_1 - \beta_1}{s_{b_1}} = \frac{49.91 - 0}{10.50} = 4.753$$

Decision Rule:

If $t > t_{\alpha/2} = 2.228$, reject H_0
If $t < -t_{\alpha/2} = -2.228$, reject H_0
Otherwise, do not reject H_0

Because 4.753 > 2.228, we should reject the null hypothesis and conclude that the true slope is not zero. Thus, the simple linear relationship that utilizes the independent variable, years with the company, is useful in explaining the variation in the dependent variable, sales volume.

SUMMARY: SIMPLE LINEAR REGRESSION ANALYSIS

The following steps outline the process that can be used in developing a simple linear regression model and the various hypotheses tests used to determine the significance of a simple linear regression model.

1. Define the independent (x) and dependent (y) variables and select a simple random sample of pairs of x,y values.

2. Develop a scatter plot of y and x. You are looking for a linear relationship between the two variables.

3. Compute the correlation coefficient for the sample data.

4. Calculate the least squares regression line for the sample data and the simple coefficient of determination, R^2. The coefficient of determination measures the proportion of variation in the dependent variable explained by the independent variable.

5. Conduct either of the following tests for determining whether the regression model is statistically significant.

a. Test to determine whether the true regression slope is 0. The test statistic with $df = n - 2$ is

$$t = \frac{b_1 - \beta_1}{s_{b_1}} = \frac{b_1 - 0}{s_{b_1}}$$

b. Test to see whether ρ is significantly different from 0. The test statistic is

$$t = \frac{r}{\sqrt{\dfrac{1 - r^2}{n - 2}}}$$

6. Reach a decision.

7. Draw a conclusion.

Excel and Minitab Tutorial

$\mathscr{E}$XAMPLE 12-3: SIMPLE LINEAR REGRESSION ANALYSIS

Vantage Electronic Systems   Consider the example involving Vantage Electronic Systems in Deerfield, Michigan, which started out supplying electronic equipment for the automobile industry, but in recent years has ventured into other areas. One area is visibility sensors that are used by airports to provide takeoff and landing information and by transportation departments to detect low visibility on roadways during fog and snow. The recognized leader in the visibility sensor business is the SCR Company, which makes a sensor called the Scorpion. The R&D department at Vantage has recently performed a test on its new unit by locating a Vanguard sensor and a Scorpion sensor side-by-side. Various data, including visibility measurements, were collected at randomly selected points in time over a two-week period. These data are contained in a CD-ROM file called *Vantage*.

Step 1: **Define the independent (*x*) and dependent (*y*) variables.**

The analysis included a simple linear regression using the Scorpion visibility measurement as the dependent variable, *y*, and the Vanguard visibility measurement as the independent variable, *x*.

Step 2: **Develop a scatter plot of *y* and *x*.**

The scatter plot is shown in Figure 12-19. There does not appear to be a strong linear relationship.

Step 3: **Compute the correlation coefficient for the sample data.**

Equation 12-1 or 12-2 can be used for manual computation, or we can use Excel or Minitab. The correlation coefficient is

$$r = 0.5778$$

Step 4: **Calculate the least squares regression line for the sample data and the simple coefficient of determination, R^2.**

Equations 12-7 and 12-8 can be used to manually compute the regression slope coefficient and intercept, respectively, and Equation 12-15 or 12-16 can be used to manually compute R^2. Excel and Minitab can also be used to eliminate the computational burden. The coefficient of determination is

$$R^2 = r^2 = 0.5778^2 = 0.3339$$

Thus, approximately 33% of the variation in the Scorpion visibility measures is explained by knowing the corresponding Vanguard system visibility measure. The least squares regression equation is

$$\hat{y} = 0.586 + 3.017x$$

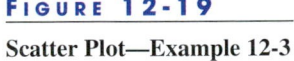

FIGURE 12-19

Scatter Plot—Example 12-3

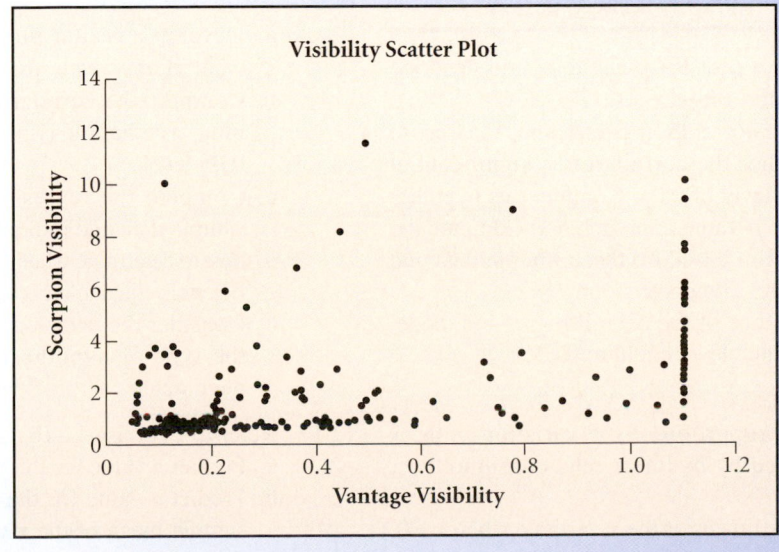

Step 5: **Conduct a test to determine whether the regression model is statistically significant (or whether the population correlation is equal to zero).**
The null and alternative hypotheses to test the correlation coefficient are

$$H_0: \rho = 0$$
$$H_A: \rho \neq 0$$

The t test statistic is

$$t = \frac{r}{\sqrt{\dfrac{1 - r^2}{n - 2}}} = \frac{0.5778}{\sqrt{\dfrac{1 - 0.5778^2}{280 - 2}}} = 11.81$$

The $t = 11.81$ exceeds the critical t (or the normal approximation to it) for any reasonable level of α for 278 degrees of freedom, so the null hypothesis is rejected and we conclude that there is a statistically significant linear relationship between visibility measures for the two visibility sensors.

Alternatively, the null and alternative hypotheses to test the regression slope coefficient are

$$H_0: \beta_1 = 0$$
$$H_A: \beta_1 \neq 0$$

The t test statistic is

$$t = \frac{b_1 - \beta_1}{s_{b_1}} = \frac{3.017 - 0}{0.256} = 11.81$$

Step 6: **Reach a decision.**
The t test statistic of 11.81 exceeds the t-critical (or normal approximation to it) for any reasonable level of α for 278 degrees of freedom.

Step 7: **Draw a conclusion.**
The regression slope coefficient is not equal to zero.

12-2: EXERCISES

Skill Development

12.14 You are given the following sample data for variables y and x:

y	140.1	120.3	80.8	100.7	130.2	90.6	110.5	120.2	130.4	130.3	100.1
x	5	3	2	4	5	4	4	5	6	5	4

a. Develop a scatter plot for these data and describe what, if any, relationship exists.
b. (1) Compute the correlation coefficient. (2) Test to determine whether the correlation is significant at the significance level of 0.05. Conduct this hypothesis test using the p-value approach. (3) Compute the regression equation based on these sample data and interpret the regression coefficients.
c. Test the significance of the overall regression model using a significance level equal to 0.05.

12.15 Refer to Exercise 12.14.
a. Determine the proportion of the variation in the y variable explained by its linear relationship to the x variable.
b. (1) Provide an estimate for the y variable when $x = 0$. (2) There is a name associated with this particular y value. Provide this name.

12.16 You are given the following sample data for variables y and x:

y	12.5	9.0	13.0	7.5	9.0	6.2	3.5	14	15
x	100	120	100	90	110	160	200	95	80

a. Develop a scatter plot for these data and describe what, if any, relationship exists.
b. Compute the correlation coefficient. Test to determine whether the correlation is significant at the $\alpha = 0.05$ level.
c. Compute the regression equation based on these sample data and interpret the regression coefficients.
d. Test to determine whether the true regression slope coefficient is equal to zero. Use a significance level of 0.02.
e. Consider the decision you made in part d. Describe the type of hypothesis test error that could have been made.

12.17 Refer to Exercise 12.16.
a. Predict a value for the y variable when x equals 10.
b. Predict a value for the y variable when x equals the sample mean of the x values. Which of the two predictions produced in part a and in part b, respectively, would have the largest margin of error.

12.18 You are given the following results from computations pertaining to a simple linear regression application:

$$\hat{y} = 23.0 + 1.45x$$
$$SSE = 45,000$$
$$n = 25$$
$$\sum(x - \bar{x})^2 = 4,000$$

a. Based on the statistics supplied, can you conclude that there is a significant linear relationship between x and y? Test at the $\alpha = 0.05$ level.

b. Interpret the slope coefficient.

Business Applications

12.19 At State University, a study was done to establish whether a relationship existed between a student's GPA when graduating and SAT score when entering the university. The sample data are reported as follows:

GPA	2.5	3.2	3.5	2.8	3.0	2.4	3.4	2.9	2.7	3.8
SAT	640	700	550	540	620	490	710	600	505	710

a. Develop a scatter plot for these data and describe what, if any, relationship exists between the two variables, GPA and SAT score.

b. (1) Compute the correlation coefficient.
(2) Does it appear that the success of students at State University is related to the SAT scores of those students? Conduct a statistical procedure to answer this question. Use a significance level of 0.01.

c. (1) Compute the regression equation based on these sample data if you wish to predict the university GPA using the students' SAT scores.
(2) Interpret the regression coefficients.

12.20 One of the editors of a major automobile publication has collected data on 30 of the best-selling cars in the United States. The data are in a CD-ROM file called *Automobiles*. The editor is particularly interested in the relationship between highway mileage and curb weight of the vehicles.

a. Develop a scatter plot for these data. Discuss what the plot implies about the relationship between two variables. Assume that you wish to predict highway mileage by using vehicle curb weight.

b. Compute the correlation coefficient for the two variables and test to determine whether there is a linear relationship between the curb weight and the highway mileage of automobiles.

c. (1) Compute the linear regression equation based on the sample data. (2) Cadillac's 1999 Sedan DeVille weighs approximately 4,012 pounds. Provide an estimate of the average highway mileage you would expect to obtain from this model.

12.21 An accountant who is performing an audit of the parts inventory for a machinery company has collected the following data. The dependent variable, y, is the actual level of inventory (in hundreds of dollars) determined by the accountant. The independent variable, x, is the inventory level on the computer inventory record.

y	233.23	10.56	24.45	56.87	78.10	102.23	90.94	200.23	344.41	120.53	18.62
x	245.51	12.43	22.52	56.84	90.31	103.85	85.56	190.86	320.74	120.25	23.88

Of course, the accountant wishes to know whether these sample data show a high level of agreement between the measure of inventory level determined during the audit and the levels indicated on the company records. Calculate a value that would give the accountant an indication of the level of agreement between these two measures. Is this measure, based on sample information, statistically significant? Be careful to consider the type and direction of the appropriate measurement.

12.22 The Skeleton Manufacturing Company recently did a study of its customers. A random sample of 50 customer accounts was pulled from the computer records. Two variables were observed:

y = Total dollar volume of business this year
x = Miles customer is from corporate headquarters

The following statistics were computed:

$$\hat{y} = 2,140.23 - 10.12x$$
$$s_{b_1} = 3.12$$

a. Interpret the regression slope coefficient.

b. Using a significance level of 0.01, test to determine whether it is true that the farther a business is from the corporate headquarters the smaller is the total dollar volume of business.

12.23 The data shown here and in the CD-ROM file *McCormick* contain information (measured in millions of dollars) from the 1998 McCormick Company annual report.

Year	Net Sales	Capital Expenditures	Current Debt	Long-Term Debt	Shareholders' Equity
1988	$1,099.10	$50.40	$49.50	$229.40	$294.30
1989	1,110.20	53.40	20.30	210.50	346.20
1990	1,166.20	58.40	30.40	311.50	364.40
1991	1,276.30	73.00	78.20	207.60	389.20
1992	1,323.90	79.30	122.60	201.00	437.90
1993	1,400.90	76.10	84.70	346.40	466.80
1994	1,529.40	87.70	214.00	374.30	490.00
1995	1,691.10	82.10	297.30	349.10	519.30
1996	1,732.50	74.70	108.90	291.20	450.00
1997	1,801.00	43.90	121.30	276.50	393.10

a. Compute the linear regression model based on the sample data if net sales are to be predicted using capital expenditures.

b. Conduct a test to determine whether the relationship between McCormick's net sales and capital expenditures is significant. Interpret the meaning of this measure.

c. Refer to part b. Describe the type of hypothesis test error that could have been made in the context of this problem.

d. Provide a brief financial explanation of the regression slope coefficient.

12.24 The data in the CD-ROM file *Baldor* are from that company's 1998 annual report.

a. Compute the linear regression model based on the sample data using net sales as the independent variable and working capital as the dependent variable.

b. Conduct a test to determine whether net sales can be used to predict working capital for Baldor Electric. Conduct this hypothesis test using the *p*-value approach.

c. Compute the *R*-squared value and discuss how well you believe Baldor will be able to predict its working capital using its net sales.

Advanced Applications

12.25 Referring again to the automobile magazine editor discussed in Exercise 12.20, the editor now wants to examine the relationship between price of the vehicle and the horsepower of the engine.

a. (1) Develop a scatter plot for these data. (2) Discuss what the plot implies about the relationship between the two variables. Use price as the dependent (*y*) variable.

b. Compute the correlation coefficient for the two variables.

c. Compute the linear regression equation based on the sample data.

d. Toyota's 1999 Camry four-cylinder model generates 133 horsepower. Provide an estimate of the price of the 1999 Camry. Toyota's suggested retail price for the Camry LE 4A model was $20,278. Calculate the appropriate residual for this model of Camry.

e. (1) Compute the *R*-squared value and discuss what this value means. (2) At a significance level of 0.01, can you conclude that engine horsepower is a good predictor of the price of an automobile?

12.26 A 1998 article in Fortune magazine titled *The 100 Best Companies to Work For in America* (January 12, 1998) contained selected characteristics on the 100

companies. These data are included in the CD-ROM file *Best-Companies*. Two variables of interest are the revenues of each company and the number of hours of training per year per employee. (Note: You will need to omit companies with data marked N.A. before completing the analysis.)

a. Develop a scatter plot for these data. Discuss what the plot implies about the relationship between the two variables.

b. Provide a measurement that will provide an indication of the strength of the linear relationship between revenues and the number of hours of training for employees.

c. Compute the linear regression equation based on the sample data if you wish to use the revenue of a company to predict the number of hours of training per year per employee. Interpret the slope and intercept coefficients.

d. Using a significance level of 0.01, test to determine whether the true regression slope is zero. Do your test results suggest that if companies stop training their employees that their revenues will not suffer? Does the result of your test indicate that there is no relationship whatsoever between revenues and the number of hours of training for employees? Discuss these two related questions.

e. Refer to part d. Describe the type of hypothesis test error that could have been made in the context of this problem.

12.27 A study has been conducted for a sample of cities in the United States. Among the data collected for each city were the 1995 population and the 1998 unemployment rate. The data are contained in the CD-ROM file *Cities*.

a. Develop a scatter plot for these data. Discuss what the plot implies about the relationship between the two variables. Assume you wish to predict the unemployment rate using the population of the city.

b. Compute the correlation coefficient for the two variables.

c. (1) Compute the linear regression equation based on the sample data. (2) Conduct a statistical procedure to determine if cities with larger populations in 1995 had higher employment rates in 1998.

12-3 USES FOR REGRESSION ANALYSIS

Regression analysis is a statistical tool that is used for two main purposes: description and prediction. This section discusses these two applications.

REGRESSION ANALYSIS FOR DESCRIPTION

Excel and Minitab Tutorial

Car Mileage—In the spring of 2000, gasoline prices soared to record levels in the United States, heightening customers' concern for fuel economy. Analysts at a major automobile company collected data on a variety of variables for a sample of 30 different cars and small trucks. Included among those data were the EPA highway mileage rating and the horsepower of each vehicle. What is the relationship between horsepower (x) and highway mileage (y)? The data are contained in the file *Automobiles* on the CD-ROM.

A simple linear regression model can be developed using Excel or Minitab, as shown in Figure 12-20. For these sample data, the coefficient of determination, $R^2 = 0.3016$ indicates that knowing the horsepower of the vehicle explains 30.16% of the variation in the highway mileage. The estimated regression equation is

$$\hat{y} = 31.1658 - 0.0286x$$

Before the analysts attempt to describe the relationship between horsepower and highway mileage, they first need to test whether there is a statistically significant linear relationship between the two variables. To do this, they can apply the t test described in Section 12-2 to test the following null and alternative hypotheses:

$$H_0: \beta_1 = 0$$
$$H_A: \beta_1 \neq 0$$

at the significance level

$$\alpha = 0.05$$

The calculated t statistic and the corresponding p-value are shown in Figure 12-20. Because the

$$p\text{-value} = 0.0017 < 0.05$$

the null hypothesis

$$H_0 \text{ is rejected,}$$

and the analysts can conclude that the population regression slope is not equal to zero.

The sample slope, b_1, equals -0.0286. This means that for each one-unit increase in horsepower, the highway mileage decreases by an average of 0.0286 miles per gallon. However, b_1 is subject to sampling error and is considered a *point estimate* for the true regression slope coefficient. From earlier discussions about point estimates in Chapters 7 and 9, we expect that $b_1 \neq \beta_1$. Therefore, to fully describe the relationship between the independent variable, horsepower, and the dependent variable, highway miles per gallon, we need to develop a *confidence interval estimate* for β_1. Equation 12-21 is used to do this.

FIGURE 12-20

Excel Regression Results for the Automobile Mileage Study

Excel Instructions:
1. Open file: Automobiles.xls
2. Select **Tools**.
3. Click on **Regression**.
4. Define y variable range.
5. Define x variable range.

Minitab Instructions (for similar results):
1. Open file: Automobiles.MTW.
2. Choose **Stat > Regression > Regression**.
3. In **Response**, enter the y variable column.
4. In **Predictors**, enter the x variable column.
5. Click **OK**.

Microsoft Excel - Automobiles

	A	B	C	D	E	F	G
1	SUMMARY OUTPUT						
2							
3	*Regression Statistics*						
4	Multiple R	0.549172956					
5	R Square	0.301590935					
6	Adjusted R Square	0.276647754					
7	Standard Error	3.553224834					
8	Observations	30					
9							
10	ANOVA						
11		*df*	*SS*	*MS*	*F*	*Significance F*	
12	Regression	1	152.6552784	152.6552784	12.09111768	0.001672558	
13	Residual	28	353.5113883	12.62540672			
14	Total	29	506.1666667				
15							
16		*Coefficients*	*Standard Error*	*t Stat*	*P-value*	*Lower 95%*	*Upper 95%*
17	Intercept	31.16576391	1.933210883	16.12124377	1.06194E-15	27.20575648	35.12577134
18	Horse Power	-0.028563061	0.008214318	-3.477228448	0.001672558	-0.045389348	-0.011736774

Regression equation
$\hat{y} = 31.1658 - 0.0286(x)$

Confidence Interval Estimate for the Regression Slope, Simple Linear Regression

$$b_1 \pm t_{\alpha/2} s_{b_1}$$

12-21

or equivalently,

$$b_1 \pm t_{\alpha/2} \frac{s_\varepsilon}{\sqrt{\Sigma(x - \bar{x})^2}} \qquad df = n - 2$$

where:

s_{b_1} = Standard error of the regression slope coefficient

s_ε = Standard error of the estimate

The regression output shown in Figure 12-20 contains the 95% confidence interval estimate for the slope coefficient, which is

$$-0.045 \; \text{-----------------} -0.012$$

Thus, at the 95% confidence level, based on the sample data, the analysts for the car company can conclude that a one-unit increase in horsepower will result in an average drop in mileage by an average amount between 0.012 and 0.045 miles per gallon.

There are many other situations in which the prime purpose of regression analysis is description. Economists use regression analysis for descriptive purposes as they search for a way of explaining the economy. Market researchers also use regression analysis, among other techniques, in an effort to describe the factors that influence the demand for products.

EXAMPLE 12-4: DEVELOPING A CONFIDENCE INTERVAL ESTIMATE FOR THE REGRESSION SLOPE

Home Prices   Home values are determined by a variety of factors. One factor is the size of the house (square feet). Recently a study was conducted by First City Real Estate aimed at estimating the average value of each additional square foot of space in a house. A simple random sample of 319 homes that were sold within the past year was collected. The data are in a file called *First-City* on the CD-ROM. Here are the steps required to compute a confidence interval estimate for the regression slope coefficient.

Step 1:   Define the *y* (dependent) and *x* (independent) variables.
The dependent variable is sales price, and the independent variable is square feet.

Step 2:   Obtain the sample data.
The study consists of sales prices and corresponding square feet for a sample of 319 homes.

Step 3:   Compute the regression equation and the standard error of the slope coefficient.
These computations can be performed manually using Equations 12-7 and 12-8 for the regression model and Equation 12-19 for the standard error of the slope. Alternatively, we can use Excel or Minitab to obtain these values.

	Coefficients	Standard Error
Intercept (b_0)	39838.48333	7304.951587
Square Feet (b_1)	75.69512354	3.775610524

The point estimate for the regression slope coefficient is $75.70. Thus, for a one-square-foot increase in the size of a house, house prices increase by an average of $75.70. This is a point estimate and is subject to sampling error.

Step 4:   Construct and interpret the confidence interval estimate for the regression slope using Equation 12-21.
The confidence interval estimate is

$$b_1 \pm t_{\alpha/2} s_{b_1}$$

where the degrees of freedom for the critical t is $319 - 2 = 317$. The critical t for a 95% confidence interval estimate is approximately 1.96, and the interval estimate is

$$\$75.70 \pm 1.96(\$3.78)$$
$$\$75.70 \pm \$7.41$$
$$\$68.29 \text{ -------------------- } \$83.11$$

So, for a one-square-foot increase in house size, at the 95% confidence level, homes increase in price by an average of between $68.29 and $83.11.

REGRESSION ANALYSIS FOR PREDICTION

Freedom Hospital—One of the main uses of regression analysis is *prediction*. You may need to predict the value of the dependent variable based on the value of the independent variable. Consider the administrator for Freedom Hospital, who has been asked by the hospital's board of directors to develop a model to predict the total charges for a geriatric patient. The CD-ROM file *Patients* contains the data that the administrator has collected.

Although the Regression tool in Excel works well for generating the simple linear regression equation and other useful information, it does not provide predicted values for the dependent variable. However, both Minitab and the PHStat add-ins do provide predictions. We will illustrate the Minitab output, which is formatted somewhat differently than the Excel output but contains the same basic information.

The administrator is attempting to construct a simple linear regression model, with total charges as the dependent (y) variable and length of stay as the independent (x) variable. Figure 12-21 shows the Minitab regression output. The least squares regression equation is

$$\hat{y} = 528 + 1,353x$$

As shown in the figure, the regression slope coefficient is significantly different from zero ($t = 14.17$; p-value = 0.000). The model explains 59.6% of the variation in the total charges (R-squared = 59.6%). Notice in Figure 12-21 that Minitab has rounded the regression coefficient. The more-precise values are provided in the column headed "Coef" and are

$$\hat{y} = 527.6 + 1,352.80x$$

FIGURE 12-21

Minitab Regression Output for Freedom Hospital

Minitab Instructions:
1. Open file: Patients.MTW.
2. Choose **Stat > Regression > Regression**.
3. In **Response**, enter the y variable column.
4. In **Predictors**, enter the x variable column.
5. Click **OK**.

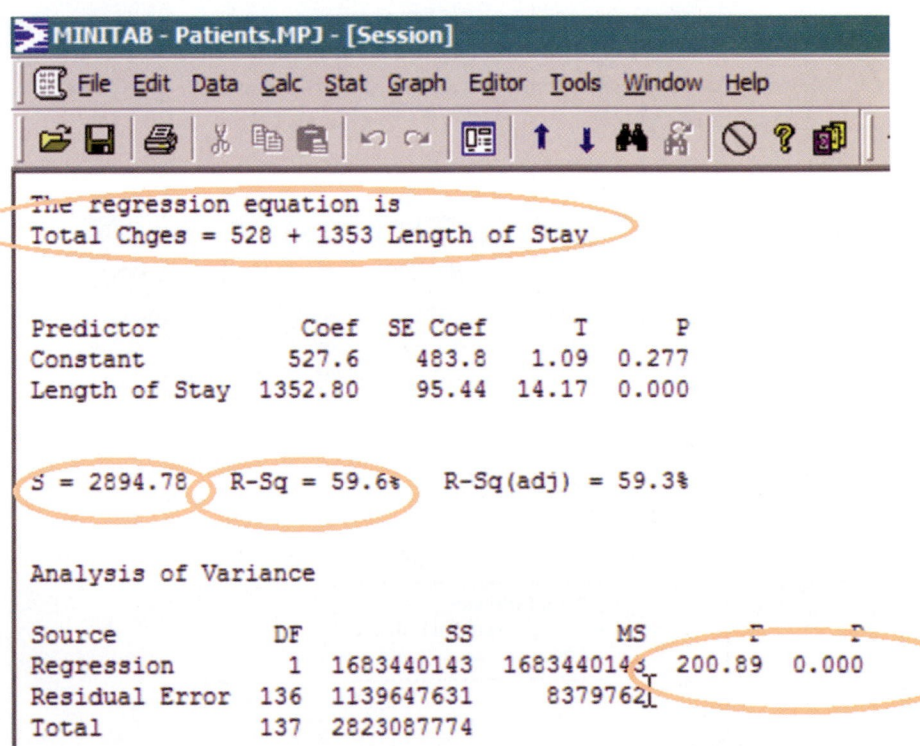

The administrator could use this equation to predict total charges by substituting the length of stay into the regression equation for x. For example, suppose a patient has a five-day stay. The predicted total charges are

$$\hat{y} = 527.6 + 1,352.80(5)$$
$$\hat{y} = \$7,291.60$$

Note that this predicted value is a *point estimate* of the actual charges for this patient. The true charges will be either higher or lower than this amount. The administrator can develop a prediction interval, which is similar to the confidence interval estimates developed in Chapter 7.

Excel and Minitab Tutorial

Confidence Interval for the Average *y*, Given *x*

The marketing manager might like a 95% confidence interval for *average* charges for all patients who stay in the hospital five days. The confidence interval for the expected value of a dependent variable, given a specific level of the independent variable, is determined by Equation 12-22. Observe that the specific value of x used to provide the prediction is denoted as x_p.

Confidence Interval for $E(y)|x_p$

$$\hat{y} \pm t_{\alpha/2} s_\varepsilon \sqrt{\frac{1}{n} + \frac{(x_p - \bar{x})^2}{\Sigma(x - \bar{x})^2}}$$

12-22

where:

$\hat{y}$ = Point estimate of the dependent variable
t = Critical value with $n - 2$ *df*
n = Sample size
x_p = Specific value of the independent variable
$\bar{x}$ = Mean of the independent variable observations in the sample
s_ε = Estimate of the standard error of the estimate

Although the confidence interval estimate can be manually computed using Equation 12-22, using your computer is much easier. For instance, both PHStat and Minitab have built-in options to generate the confidence interval estimate for the dependent variable for a given value of the x variable. Figure 12-22 shows the Minitab results when length of stay, x, equals five days. Given this length of stay, the point estimate for the mean total charges is rounded by Minitab to $7,292, and at the 95% confidence level, the administrators believe the mean total charges will be in the interval $6,790 to $7,794.

FIGURE 12-22

Minitab Output: Freedom Hospital Confidence Interval Estimate

Minitab Instructions:
1. Use instructions in Figure 12-21 to get regression results.
2. Before clicking **OK**, select **Options**.
3. In **Prediction Interval for New Observations**, enter value(s) of x variable.
4. In **Confidence level**, enter $(1 - \alpha)100$.
5. Click **OK. OK**.

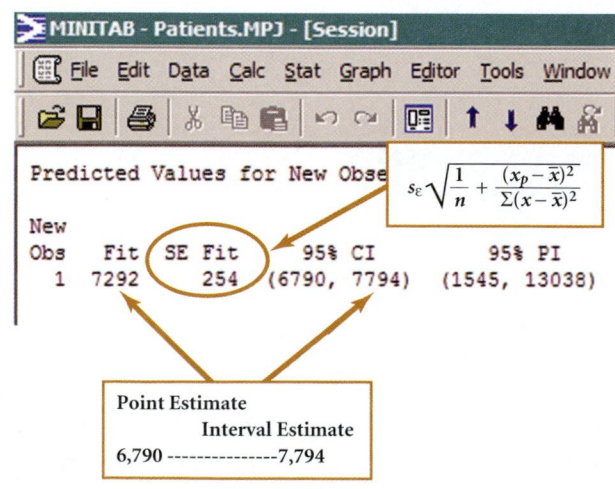

Excel and Minitab Tutorial

Prediction Interval for a Particular *y*, Given *x*

The confidence interval shown in Figure 12-22 is for the average value of *y* given x_p. The administrator might also be interested in predicting the total charges for a *particular* patient with a five-day stay, rather than the average of the charges for all patients staying five days. Developing this 95% prediction interval requires only a slight modification to Equation 12-22. This prediction interval is given by Equation 12-23.

Prediction Interval for $y|x_p$

$$\hat{y} \pm t_{\alpha/2}s_\varepsilon\sqrt{1 + \frac{1}{n} + \frac{(x_p - \bar{x})^2}{\Sigma(x - \bar{x})^2}}$$

12-23

As was the case with the confidence interval application discussed previously, the manual computations required to use Equation 12-23 can be onerous. We recommend using your computer and software such as Minitab or PHStat to find the prediction interval. Figure 12-23 shows the PHStat results. Note that the same PHStat process generates both the prediction and confidence interval estimates.

Based on this regression model, at the 95% confidence level, the hospital administrators can predict total charges for any patient with length of stay of five days to be between $1,545 and $13,038.

As you can see, this prediction has extremely poor precision. We doubt any hospital administrator will use a prediction interval that is so wide. Although the regression model explains a significant proportion of variation in the dependent variable, it is relatively imprecise for predictive purposes. To improve the precision, we might decrease the confidence requirements or increase the sample size and redevelop the model.

The prediction interval for a specific value of the dependent variable is wider (less precise) than the confidence interval for predicting the average value of the dependent variable. This will always be the case, as seen in Equations 12-22 and 12-23. From an intuitive viewpoint, we should expect to come closer to predicting an average value than a single value.

Note, the term $(x_p - \bar{x})^2$ has a particular effect on the confidence interval determined by both Equations 12-22 and 12-23. The farther x_p (the value of the independent variable used to predict *y*), is from $\bar{x}$, the greater $(x_p - \bar{x})^2$ becomes. Figure 12-24 shows two regression lines developed from two samples with the same set of *x* values. We have made both lines pass through the same $(\bar{x}, \bar{y})$

FIGURE 12-23

Excel (PHStat) Prediction Interval for Freedom Hospital

Excel (PHStat) Instructions:
1. Open file: Patients.xls
2. Select **PHStat**.
3. Click on **Regression**.
4. Select **Simple Linear Regression**.
5. Specify *y* and *x* data ranges.
6. Define x_p.
7. Specify confidence level for intervals.

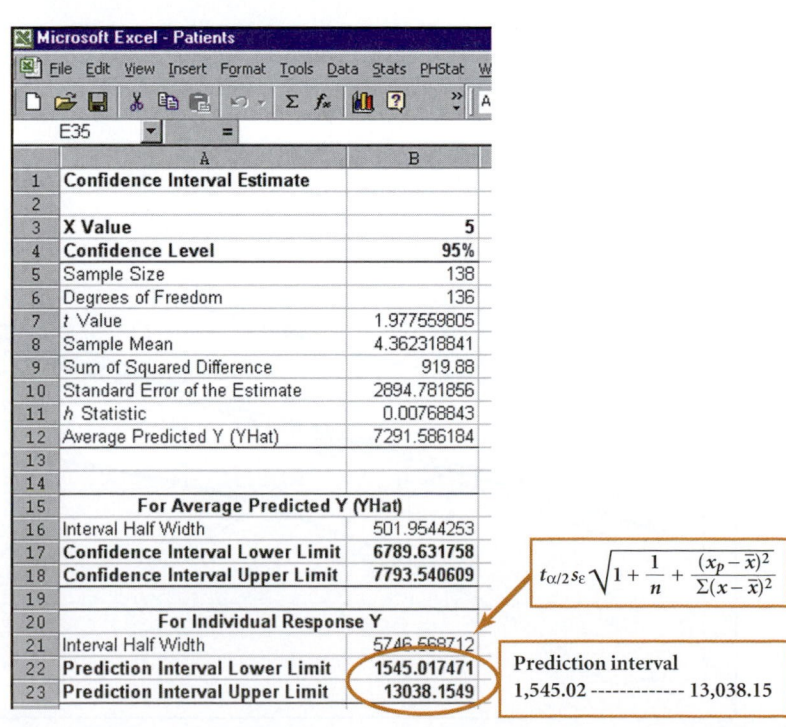

FIGURE 12-24

**Regression Lines
Illustrating the Increase in
Potential Variation in y as
x_p Moves Farther from $\bar{x}$**

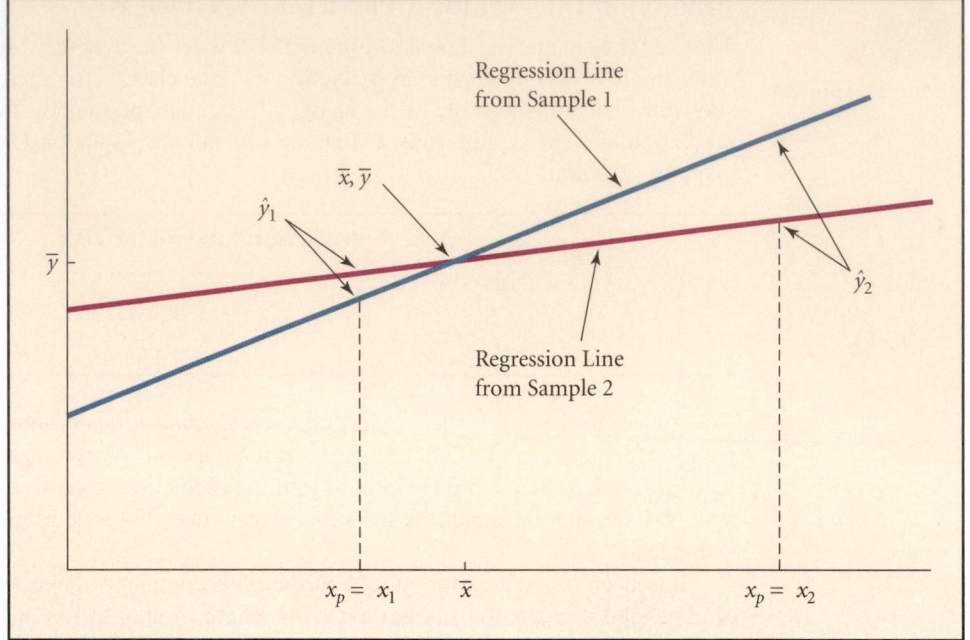

point; however, they have different slopes and intercepts. At $x_p = x_1$, the two regression lines give predictions of y that are close to each other. However, for $x_p = x_2$, the predictions of y are quite different. Thus, when x_p is close to $\bar{x}$, the problems caused by variations in regression slopes are not as great as when x_p is far from $\bar{x}$. Figure 12-25 shows the prediction intervals over the range of possible x_p values. The band around the estimated regression line bends away from the regression line as x_p moves in either direction from $\bar{x}$.

RESIDUAL ANALYSIS

Recall two important assumptions associated with linear regression analysis.

SSUMPTIONS

1. The model errors are normally distributed.
2. The model errors have a constant variance at all levels of the independent variable.

FIGURE 12-25

**Confidence Intervals for
$y|x_p$ and $E(y)|x_p$**

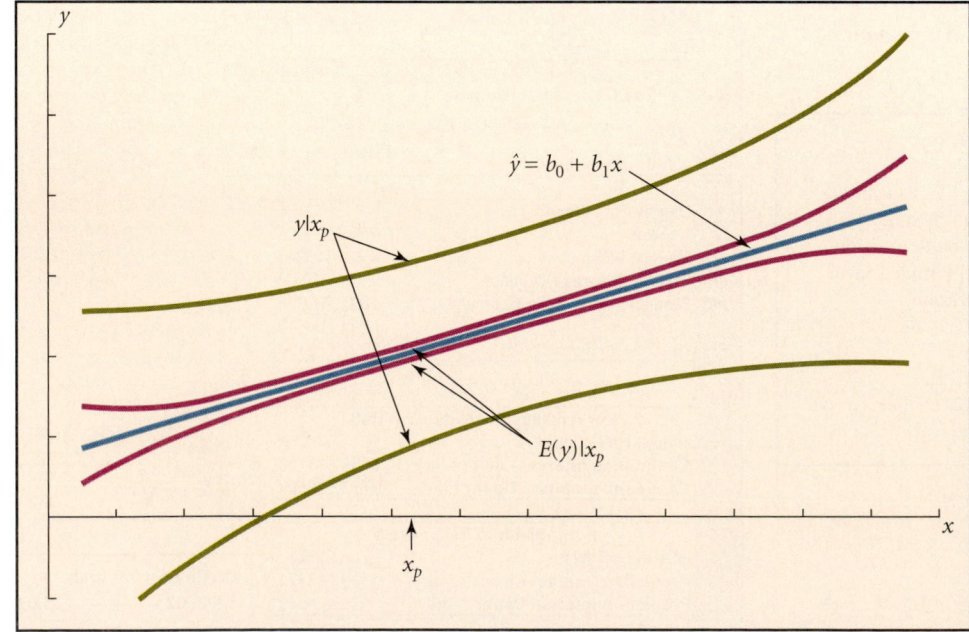

Before using a regression model for description or prediction, you should check to see if these assumptions are satisfied. One way to do this is by examining graphs called *residual plots*. Both Excel and Minitab can be used to generate residual plots.

Excel and Minitab Tutorial

Freedom Hospital (continued)—Previously we showed the regression model constructed by the administrator at Freedom Hospital. He wanted to predict the total patient charges by knowing the patient length of stay. The resulting model was statistically significant. However, before the hospital actually uses this model, the administrator might develop two different residual plots. The first is a *residual frequency histogram*, which is shown in Figure 12-26. As you can see, the histogram closely resembles a normal distribution, which is one indication that the normality assumption is satisfied.

The second residual plot charts the residuals against the *x* variable, as shown in Figure 12-27. Chapter 13 discusses this type of plot more fully. For now, you will be looking for a result in which the residuals have approximately the same spread at all levels of *x*. In Figure 12-27, the plot illustrates that for short lengths of stay, the spread in the residuals is less than when stays are longer. This implies that the assumption of equal variances in the residuals is violated. We will discuss this in more detail in Chapter 13 and suggest possible steps for improving the regression model.

COMMON PROBLEMS USING REGRESSION ANALYSIS

Regression is perhaps the most widely used statistical tool other than descriptive statistical techniques. Because it is so widely used, you need to be aware of the common problems found when the technique is employed.

One potential problem occurs when decision makers apply regression analysis for predictive purposes. The conclusions and inferences made from a regression line are statistically valid only over the range of the data contained in the sample used to develop the regression line. For instance, in the Midwest Distribution example, we analyzed the performance of sales representatives with one to nine years of experience. Therefore, predicting sales levels for employees with one to nine years of experience would be justified. However, if we were to try to predict the sales performance of someone with more than nine years of experience, the relationship between sales and experience might be different. Because no observations were taken for experience levels beyond the one- to nine-year range, we have no information about what might happen outside that range. Figure 12-28

FIGURE 12-26

Minitab Residual Histogram for Freedom Hospital

Minitab Instructions:
1. Open file: Patients.MTW.
2. Choose **Stat > Regression > Regression**.
3. In **Response**, enter the *y* variable column.
4. In **Predictors**, enter the *x* variable column.
5. Click **Storage**, under **Diagnostic Measures** select **Residuals**.
6. Click **OK**.
7. Choose **Graphs > Histogram of Residuals**.
8. Click **OK. OK.**

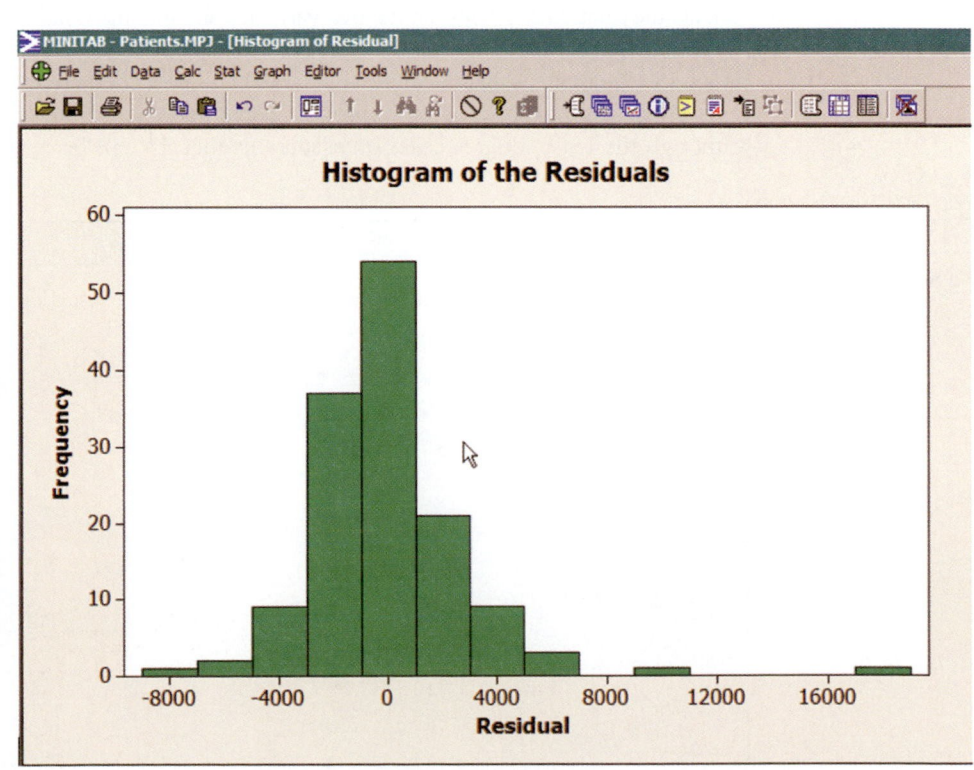

FIGURE 12-27

Minitab Residual Plot for
Freedom Hospital Example

Minitab Instructions:
1. Open file: Patients.MTW.
2. Choose **Stat > Regression > Regression**.
3. In **Response**, enter the y variable column.
4. In **Predictors**, enter the x variable column.
5. Select **Graphs**.
6. In **Residuals versus the variables**: enter the x variable column.
7. Click **OK. OK**.

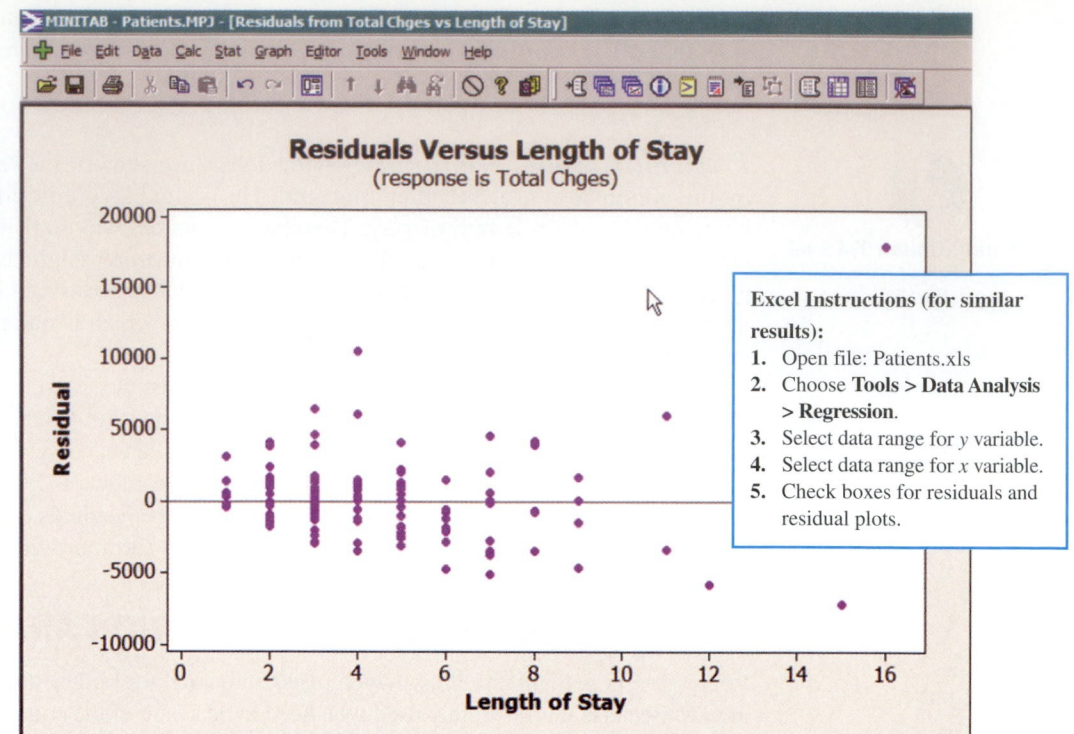

shows a case in which the true relationship between sales and experience reaches a peak value at about 20 years and then starts to decline. If a linear regression equation were used to predict sales based on experience levels beyond the relevant range of data, large prediction errors could occur.

A second important consideration, one that was discussed earlier, involves correlation and causation. The fact that a significant linear relationship exists between two variables does not imply that one variable causes the other. Although there may be a cause-and-effect relationship, you should not infer that such a relationship is present based only on regression and/or correlation analysis. You should also recognize that a cause-and-effect relationship between two variables is not necessary for regression analysis to be an effective tool. What matters is that the regression model accurately reflects the relationship between the two variables and that the relationship remains stable.

Finally, many users of regression analysis mistakenly believe that a high coefficient of determination (R^2) guarantees that the regression model will be a good predictor. You should remember that R^2 is a measure of the variation in the dependent variable explained by the independent variable. Although the least squares criterion assures us that R^2 will be maximized (because the sum of

FIGURE 12-28

Graph for a Sales Peak at
20 Years

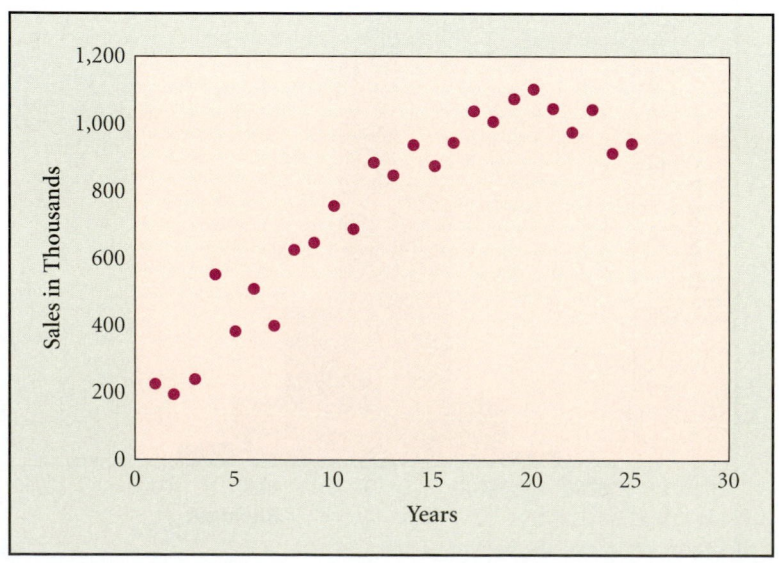

squares error is a minimum) for the given set of sample data, the value applies only to those data used to develop the model. Thus, R^2 measures the fit of the regression line to the sample data. There is no guarantee that there will be an equally good fit with new data. The only true test of a regression model's predictive ability is how well the model actually predicts.

Finally, we should mention that you might find a large R^2 with a large sum of squares error. This can happen if total sum of squares is large in comparison to the SSE. Then, even though R^2 is relatively large, so too is the estimate of the model's standard error. Thus, confidence and prediction errors may be simply too wide for the model to be used in many situations.

12-3: EXERCISES

Skill Development

12.28 You are given the following results from computations pertaining to a simple linear regression application:

$$\hat{y} = 5,723.0 + 145x$$
$$n = 25$$
$$s_{b_1} = 10.80$$

a. Based on the statistics supplied, can you conclude that there is a significant linear relationship between x and y? Test at a significance level of 0.05.
b. Interpret the slope coefficient.
c. Develop a 95% confidence interval estimate for the true regression slope and interpret the estimate.

12.29 The following data have been collected by an accountant who is performing an audit of paper products at a large office supply company. The dependent variable, y, is the time taken (in minutes) by the accountant to count the units. The independent variable, x, is the number of units on the computer inventory record.

y	23.1	100.5	242.9	56.4	178.7	10.5	94.2	200.4	44.2	128.7	180.5
x	24	120	228	56	190	13	85	190	32	120	230

a. Develop a scatter plot for these data.
b. Determine the regression equation representing this data. Is the model significant? Test using a significance level of 0.10 and the p-value approach.
c. Develop a 90% confidence interval estimate for the true regression slope and interpret this interval estimate. Based on this interval, could you conclude the accountant takes an additional minute to count each additional unit?

12.30 You are given the following summary statistics from a regression analysis:

$$\hat{y} = 200 + 150x$$
$$SSE = 25.25$$
$$SSX = \text{Sum of squares } x = \Sigma x^2 - \frac{(\Sigma x)^2}{n} = 99,645$$
$$n = 18$$
$$x = 52.0$$

a. Determine the point estimate for y if $x_p = 48$ is used.
b. Provide a 95% confidence interval estimate for the average y, given $x_p = 48$.
c. Provide a 95% prediction interval estimate for a particular y, given $x_p = 48$.

d. Discuss the difference between the estimates provided in parts b and c.

12.31 The following summary statistics were obtained from a regression analysis:

$$\hat{y} = 9,784 - 345.50x$$
$$SSE = 800.25$$
$$SSX = \text{Sum of squares } x = \Sigma x^2 - \frac{(\Sigma x)^2}{n} = 145,789$$
$$\bar{x} = 67.20$$
$$n = 20$$

a. Provide a 90% confidence interval estimate for the average y, given $x_p = 80$.
b. An estimate of a particular y is required for a given $x_p = 80$. Determine the largest error $y_i - \hat{y}_i$ you would expect from estimating the independent variable with a 90% confidence interval.

12.32 You are given the following summary statistics from a regression analysis:

$$\hat{y} = 1,200 + 0.878x$$
$$SSE = 145.40$$
$$SSX = \text{Sum of squares } x = 134,679$$
$$\bar{x} = 40,000$$
$$n = 8$$

a. Provide a 95% prediction interval estimate for the average y, given $x_p = 40,000$.
b. Provide a 95% prediction interval estimate for a particular y, given $x_p = 40,000$.
c. (1) What would happen to the precision of the estimate if the value of x_p were increased to 43,000? Discuss. (2) What value of x_p would produce the greatest precision?

Business Applications

12.33 The Shelton Manufacturing Company recently did a study of its customers. A random sample of 50 customer accounts was pulled from the computer records. Two variables were observed:

y = Total dollar volume of business this year
x = Miles customer is from corporate headquarters

The following quantities were computed:

$$\hat{y} = 2,140.23 - 10.12x$$
$$s_{b_1} = 3.12$$

a. Interpret the regression slope coefficient in the context of this problem.
b. Develop a 95% confidence interval estimate of the change in the amount of total dollar volume you would expect to see if a company relocated to a site that was an additional 100 miles from Shelton's corporate headquarters.
c. Construct a 90% prediction interval for the change in total dollar volume if the firm in part b relocated an additional 50 miles from Shelton's corporate headquarters.

12.34 The state Department of Transportation has conducted a study of 100 randomly selected vehicles in which the speed of each vehicle and the age of the driver were measured. The data were collected from a stretch of highway that produces an unusually high accident rate. A regression model was developed with vehicle speed being predicted, using age as the independent variable. The results obtained were

$$\hat{y} = 56.78 + 0.124x$$
$$s_{b_1} = 2.88$$

a. Develop a 95% interval estimate for the true regression slope and interpret.
b. Based on your response to part a, can you conclude that age and speed are linearly related? Explain your answer.

12.35 The following data have been collected by an accountant who is performing an audit of account balances for a major retail company. The population from which the data were collected represented those accounts for which the customer had indicated the balance was incorrect. The dependent variable, y, is the actual account balance as verified by the accountant. The independent variable, x, is the computer account balance.

y	233	10	24	56	78	102	90	200	344	120	18
x	245	12	22	56	90	103	85	190	320	120	33

a. Compute the least squares regression equation.
b. If a computer account balance were 100, what would you expect to be the actual account balance as verified by the accountant?
c. The computer balance for Timothy Jones is listed as 100 in the computer account record. Provide a 90% interval estimate for Mr. Jones's actual account balance.
d. Provide a 90% interval estimate for the average of all customers' actual account balances in which a computer account balance is the same as that of Mr. Jones. Interpret.

Advanced Applications

12.36 One of the editors of a major automobile publication has collected data on 30 of the best-selling cars in the United States. The data are in the CD-ROM file *Automobiles*. The editor is particularly interested in the relationship between highway mileage and curb weight of the vehicles.

a. Develop a linear regression model in which highway mileage is to be predicted by using curb weight.
b. The editor just purchased a Cadillac Sedan DeVille, which weighs 4,012 lbs. His previous car was a Toyota Camry, which weighed 3,241 lbs. He wonders how much of a decrease in gas mileage he should expect. Give the editor an idea of the maximum and minimum decreases in gas mileage he should expect. You should use a procedure that will allow you to be 90% confident of your answer.
c. Provide an estimate of the gasoline mileage the editor should expect from his newly purchased car. Suppose the estimate you just provided is the true average mpg for cars that weigh the same as the Cadillac. Cadillac advertises that the Sedan DeVille has a mileage rating of 26 mpg. Determine the percentile for the DeVille's mileage rating.
d. The individual from whom the editor purchased the Cadillac said this car got the exceptional gas mileage of 29 mpg. Construct an appropriate 95% interval estimate that would indicate whether the seller of the Cadillac was stretching the truth. Comment on the seller's veracity.

12.37 Refer to Exercise 12.36, in which a major automobile publication has collected data on 30 of the best-selling cars in the United States. The data are in the CD-ROM file *Automobiles*. The editor is particularly interested in the relationship between highway mileage and curb weight of the vehicles.

a. The editor often takes his entire family to visit relatives in a nearby state. The combined weight of his family is 570 lbs. Combining the weight of the editor's new Cadillac and that of his family, provide an estimate for the gas mileage the editor should expect to get on a trip to visit these relatives.
b. Calculate a 95% prediction interval for the average highway mileage for a car with a curb weight equal to the weight of the Cadillac when the editor's family is inside.
c. Compute a 95% prediction interval for the actual highway mileage of this particular Cadillac carrying the editor's family.
d. Compare the prediction intervals computed in this problem to that computed in part d of Exercise 12.36. Discuss why the intervals are different widths even though the same confidence level is used.
e. Suppose an editor for the publication wishes to predict the highway mileage of vehicles with a curb weight of 6,000 pounds. What cautions should be made before using this regression model to make that prediction? Discuss.
f. Finally, Toyota considered increasing the horsepower in its Camry motor by 10% (recall that the horsepower for the 1999 Camry was 133). Give advice on how much the cost of the automobile should increase,

based solely on the increase in horsepower. Provide minimum and maximum amounts of increase you would expect with a 90% probability.

12.38 💿 A 1998 article in *Fortune* magazine titled *The 100 Best Companies to Work For in America* (January 12, 1998) contained data on the 100 companies. These data are included in the CD-ROM file *Best-Companies*. Three variables of interest are the revenues of each company, the number of hours of training per year per employee and the number of employees. (Note: You will need to omit companies with data marked N.A. before completing the analysis.)

a. Compute the linear regression equation based on the sample data if the revenue of each company is to be used to predict the number of hours of training per year per employee.

b. Would you feel comfortable using the revenue of one of the 100 companies to determine the number of hours of training per year per employee with a sim-

ple linear regression model? Conduct a statistical procedure to answer this question.

c. Synovus Financial has 8,827 employees. Predict the number of hours of training per year per employee for Synovus.

d. Referring to part c, develop and interpret a 90% prediction interval for the average training hours per employee for companies with 8,827 employees.

e. Referring to part d, what is the 90% confidence interval for average training hours per employee for companies with 40,000 employees? Compare this interval with the one computed in part d and discuss why the widths of the two are different.

f. Referring to parts d and e, at what number of employees would the width of a 90% prediction interval for average training hours be minimized?

g. Referring to parts d and e, develop and interpret a 90% prediction interval for the actual training hours per employee for Synovus.

Summary and Conclusions

Correlation and regression analysis are two of the most frequently used statistical techniques for business decision makers. This chapter has introduced the basics of these two topics. The discussion of regression analysis has been limited to situations in which you have one dependent variable and one independent variable. In these cases, the technique for modeling the linear relationship between the two variables is referred to as simple linear regression analysis.

If two variables are correlated, then they are said to be linearly related. When that's the case, the resulting simple linear regression model will be statistically significant, which means that the fraction of variation in the dependent variable that is explained by the independent variable (R-squared) is significant and the predictions for the y variable based on values of x will be superior to using the mean of y as the predictor.

This chapter introduced the methods used to test whether a correlation is zero and whether a regression slope coefficient is zero. We also introduced you to the uses of regression for descriptive and predictive purposes and showed how to construct confidence interval estimates for the true regression slope coefficient and prediction intervals.

Chapter 13 will extend the discussion of regression analysis by showing how two or more independent variables are included in the analysis. The focus of that chapter will be on building a model for explaining the variation in the dependent variable. However, the basic concepts presented in this chapter will be carried forward.

EQUATIONS

Sample Correlation Coefficient

$$r = \frac{\Sigma(x - \bar{x})(y - \bar{y})}{\sqrt{[\Sigma(x - \bar{x})^2][\Sigma(y - \bar{y})^2]}} \qquad \textbf{12-1}$$

or the algebraic equivalent:

$$r = \frac{n \Sigma xy - \Sigma x \Sigma y}{\sqrt{[n(\Sigma x^2) - (\Sigma x)^2][n(\Sigma y^2) - (\Sigma y)^2]}} \qquad \textbf{12-2}$$

Test Statistic for Correlation

$$t = \frac{r}{\sqrt{\frac{1 - r^2}{n - 2}}} \qquad df = n - 2 \qquad \textbf{12-3}$$

Simple Linear Regression Model (Population Model)

$$y = \beta_0 + \beta_1 x + \varepsilon \qquad \textbf{12-4}$$

Estimated Regression Model (Sample Model)

$$\hat{y} = b_0 + b_1 x \qquad \textbf{12-5}$$

Least Squares Equations (Sample Values)

$$b_1 = \frac{\Sigma(x - \bar{x})(y - \bar{y})}{\Sigma(x - \bar{x})^2} \qquad \textbf{12-6}$$

algebraic equivalent:

$$b_1 = \frac{\Sigma xy - \frac{\Sigma x \Sigma y}{n}}{\Sigma x^2 - \frac{(\Sigma x)^2}{n}} \qquad \textbf{12-7}$$

and

$$b_0 = \bar{y} - b_1 \bar{x} \qquad \textbf{12-8}$$

Sum of Squared Errors

$$SSE = \Sigma y^2 - b_0 \Sigma y - b_1 \Sigma xy \qquad \textbf{12-9}$$

Sum of Residuals

$$\sum_{i=1}^{n} (y_i - \hat{y}_i) = 0 \qquad \text{12-10}$$

Sum of Squared Residuals

$$SSE = \sum_{i=1}^{n} (y_i - \hat{y}_i)^2 \qquad \text{12-11}$$

Total Sum of Squares

$$SST = \sum_{i=1}^{n} (y_i - \bar{y})^2 \qquad \text{12-12}$$

Sum of Squares Error

$$SSE = \sum_{i=1}^{n} (y_i - \hat{y}_i)^2 \qquad \text{12-13}$$

Sum of Squares Regression

$$SSR = \sum_{i=1}^{n} (\hat{y}_i - \bar{y})^2 \qquad \text{12-14}$$

Coefficient of Determination, R^2

$$R^2 = \frac{SSR}{SST} \qquad \text{12-15}$$

Coefficient of Determination, Single Independent Variable Case

$$R^2 = r^2 \qquad \text{12-16}$$

Standard Deviation of the Regression Slope Coefficient (Population)

$$\sigma_{b_1} = \frac{\sigma_\varepsilon}{\sqrt{\sum(x - \bar{x})^2}} \qquad \text{12-17}$$

Estimator for the Standard Error of the Estimate

$$s_\varepsilon = \sqrt{\frac{SSE}{n - k - 1}} \qquad \text{12-18}$$

Estimator for the Standard Deviation of the Regression Slope

$$s_{b_1} = \frac{s_\varepsilon}{\sqrt{\sum(x - \bar{x})^2}} = \frac{s_\varepsilon}{\sqrt{\sum x^2 - \frac{(\sum x)^2}{n}}} \qquad \text{12-19}$$

Test Statistic for Test of the Significance of the Regression Slope

$$t = \frac{b_1 - \beta_1}{s_{b_1}} \qquad df = n - 2 \qquad \text{12-20}$$

Confidence Interval Estimate for the Regression Slope, Simple Linear Regression

$$b_1 \pm t_{\alpha/2} s_{b_1} \qquad \text{12-21}$$

or equivalently,

$$b_1 \pm t_{\alpha/2} \frac{s_\varepsilon}{\sqrt{\sum(x - \bar{x})^2}} \qquad \text{with } df = n - 2$$

Confidence Interval for $E(y)|x_p$

$$\hat{y} \pm t_{\alpha/2} s_\varepsilon \sqrt{\frac{1}{n} + \frac{(x_p - \bar{x})^2}{\sum(x - \bar{x})^2}} \qquad \text{12-22}$$

Prediction Interval for $y|x_p$

$$\hat{y} \pm t_{\alpha/2} s_\varepsilon \sqrt{1 + \frac{1}{n} + \frac{(x_p - \bar{x})^2}{\sum(x - \bar{x})^2}} \qquad \text{12-23}$$

Key Terms

Coefficient of Determination, 491
Correlation Coefficient, 471
Dependent Variable, 470
Independent Variable, 470

Least Squares Criterion, 481
Regression Coefficients, 480
Regression Slope Coefficient, 481
Residual, 481

Scatter Plot, 470
Simple Linear Regression, 480
Spurious Correlation, 477
Standard Error of the Estimate, 493

CHAPTER EXERCISES

Conceptual Questions

12.39 Think of two variables that you believe would be negatively related in a linear manner. Describe what is meant by a negative linear relationship.

12.40 A statistics student was recently working on a class project that required him to compute a correlation coefficient for two variables. After careful work, he arrived at a correlation coefficient of 0.45. Interpret this correlation coefficient for the student who did the calculations.

12.41 Referring to Exercise 12.40, another student in the same class computed a regression equation relating the two variables. The slope of the equation was found to be −0.735.

After trying several times and always coming up with the same result, she felt that she must have been doing something wrong because the value was negative and she knew that this could not be right. Comment on this student's conclusion.

12.42 If we select a random sample of data for two variables and, after computing the correlation coefficient, conclude that the two variables may have zero correlation, can we say that there is no relationship between the two variables? Discuss.

12.43 Discuss why prediction intervals that attempt to predict a particular y value are less precise than confidence intervals for predicting an average y.

Business Applications

12.44 The Farmington City Council recently commissioned a study of park users in their community. Data were collected on the age of each person surveyed and the amount of hours he or she had spent in the park in the past month. The data collected were as follows:

Time in Park	Age
7.2	16
3.5	15
6.6	28
5.4	16
1.5	29
2.3	38
4.4	48
8.8	18
4.9	24
5.1	33
1.0	56

a. Draw a scatter plot for these data and discuss what, if any, relationship appears to be present between the two variables.
b. Compute the correlation coefficient between age and the amount of time spent in the park. Provide an explanation to the Farmington City Council explaining what the correlation measures.
c. Test to determine whether the amount of time spent in the park increases with the ages of the park users. Use a significance level of 0.10. Use a p-value approach to conduct this hypothesis test.

12.45 A marketing research study performed by the marketing division of the Klondike Company surveyed the income levels and expenditures on recreation for a sample of 20 people. Measurements recorded the expenditures on recreation during the previous year, y, and the total annual family income, x.

y	x	y	x
$1,425	$21,300	$900	$17,600
1,675	30,200	1,000	16,890
1,356	31,500	2,450	28,000
4,530	45,900	650	14,300
3,200	34,600	300	9,800
1,060	17,800	1,500	24,700
4,090	53,600	890	20,500
1,200	17,400	2,300	31,700
1,800	26,800	3,100	47,800
700	15,700	100	8,400

a. Draw a scatter plot for these data and discuss what, if any, relationship appears to exist between the variables, based on the scatter plot.
b. Compute the correlation coefficient for the two variables, income and dollars spent on recreation.
c. Test to determine whether the amount spent on recreation increases as the annual family income increases. Use a significance level of 0.025.

12.46 The Savemore Brokerage Firm of Spokane, Washington, recently studied a random sample of companies whose stocks are sold on the New York Stock Exchange. Among other things, it collected data on stock price, y, and the pre-

vious year's profits, x. The following data were collected. (The x variable is measured in thousands of dollars.)

y	x	y	x
$18.70	$40,000	$12.60	$12,500
34.50	24,900	43.60	9,000
25.70	102,000	33.50	23,900
8.90	44,000	71.80	15,000
25.90	123,700	15.00	45,000
11.11	36,900	6.78	99,500
21.00	3,700	21.70	45,300
3.50	145,900	44.70	23,600

Draw a scatter plot for these data and discuss what, if any, relationship appears to exist between the two variables. Also comment on what other factors might be important to consider when studying stock price and earnings of a company.

12.47 A company that makes a cattle feed supplement has studied 335 cattle and found the correlation between the amount of supplement feed and the daily weight gain to be 0.104 ($r = 0.104$). Based on these results, can you conclude that increasing the amount of supplemental feed is associated with an increase in the daily weight gain? Test using an alpha level of 0.01. Comment on the results.

12.48 The Smithfield Tobacco Company recently studied a random sample of 30 of its distributors and found the correlation between sales and advertising dollars to be 0.67.
a. Can it conclude that there is a significant linear relationship between sales and advertising? If so, is it fair to conclude that advertising causes sales to increase?
b. If a regression model were developed using sales as the dependent variable and advertising as the independent variable, determine the proportion of the variation in sales that would be explained by its relationship to advertising. Discuss what this says about the usefulness of using advertising to predict sales.

12.49 The American Airline Company recently performed a customer survey in which it asked a random sample of 100 passengers to indicate their incomes and the total cost of the airfares they purchased for pleasure trips in the past year. A regression model was developed to determine whether income could be used as a variable to explain the variation in number of times individuals fly on airlines in a year. The following regression results were obtained.

$$\hat{y} = 0.25 + 0.0150x$$
$$s_\varepsilon = 721.44$$
$$R^2 = 0.65$$
$$s_{b_1} = 0.000122$$

a. Produce an estimate of the maximum and minimum amounts of difference in the amounts allocated to purchase airline tickets by two families who have a difference of $20,000 in family income. Assume that you wish to use a 90% confidence level.
b. Can the intercept of the regression equation be interpreted in this case, assuming that no one who was surveyed had an income of 0 dollars? Explain.
c. Use the information provided to perform a test of the significance of regression model. Discuss your results, assuming the test is performed at the significance level of 0.05.

12.50 A manager for a major manufacturing company recently delivered a speech to other managers from around the United States. During the course of the speech, he was explaining a study his company had done with respect to sales and price of a particular product. He said that it had developed a simple regression model and had found the regression slope coefficient to be $-3,456.98$. He then said that this meant that increasing price by 1 dollar would cause sales to drop by 3,456.98 units. Comment on this statement, indicating with what, if anything, about the statement you agree or disagree.

12.51 Briggs Bank and Trust recently performed a study of its checking account customers. One objective of the study was to determine whether it is possible to explain a variation in average checking account balance by knowing the number of checks written per month per account. The sample data selected are contained in the CD-ROM file *Briggs*.
a. Draw a scatter plot for these data.
b. Develop the least squares regression equation for these data.
c. Develop the 90% interval estimate for the change in the average checking account balance when a person who formerly wrote 25 checks a month increased to 50 checks a month.
d. Test to determine if an increase in the number of checks written by an individual can be used to predict the checking account balance of that individual. Use $\alpha = 0.05$. Comment on this result and the result of part c.

12.52 An economist for the state of Mississippi recently collected the data contained in the CD-ROM file *Mississippi* on the percentage of people unemployed in the state at randomly selected times over the past 25 years and the interest rate of treasury bills offered by the federal government at those times.
a. (1) Develop a plot showing the relationship between the two variables. (2) Describe the relationship as being either linear or curvilinear.
b. (1) Develop a simple linear regression model with unemployment rate as the dependent variable. (2) Write a short report describing the model and indicating the important measures.

12.53 The Cooley Service Center polishes and cleans automobiles. It has major accounts such as the Bayview Taxi Service and Bayview Police Department. It also does work for the general public by appointment. Recently, the manager decided to survey customers to determine how satisfied they were with the work performed by Cooley. He devised a rating scale between 0 and 100, with 0 being poor and 100 being excellent service. He selected a random sample of 14 customers and asked the customers when they picked up their cars to rate the service. He also recorded the amount of time spent on each customer's car. These data are in the CD-ROM file *Cooley*.
a. (1) Draw a scatter plot showing these two variables, with the y variable on the vertical axis and the x variable on the horizontal axis. (2) Describe the relationship between these two variables.
b. (1) Develop a linear regression model to explain the variation in the service rating. (2) Write a short report describing the model and showing the results of pertinent hypothesis tests, using a significance level of 0.10.

Advanced Applications

Exercises 12.54 through 12.57 refer to the Harris Corporation, which has recently done a study of homes that have sold in the Detroit area within the past 18 months. Data were recorded for the asking price (x) and the number of weeks (y) each home was on the market before it sold. The data collected are in the CD-ROM file *Harris*.

12.54 Produce a graphical representation of this data to determine if a simple linear relationship exists between variables. Specify the relationship indicated by the graph you produced.

12.55 For the Harris data:
a. Compute the correlation coefficient for the number of weeks each house has been on the market and the asking price of the house.
b. Test at a significance level of 0.10 to determine whether it is true that the more expensive a house is, the longer it will take to sell. Discuss your results.

12.56 For the Harris data:
a. Develop a regression model using asking price of a home as the independent variable and weeks on the market as the dependent variable.
b. Provide an interpretation for the regression slope coefficient.
c. Use the t test statistic to determine whether the more expensive a house is, the longer it will take to sell. Use a significance level of 0.01.
d. Use a p-value approach to conduct the test relating expense to time to sell. Comment on the relationship between this hypothesis test and the one conducted in part c.

12.57 For the regression model developed showing the relationship between time to sell and expense, develop a 95% interval estimate to determine how much longer it will take to sell a house if its price is increased by $10,000. (Hint: Be very careful that you determine the parameter you are estimating and its interpretation. This parameter measures the change in the y variable for an increase in a certain number of units of the x variable. Ask yourself how many units that is.)

12.58 Grinfield Service Company's marketing director is interested in analyzing the relationship between her company's sales and the advertising dollars spent. In the course of her analysis, she selected a random sample of 20 weeks and recorded the sales for each week and the amount spent on advertising. These data are contained in the CD-ROM file *Grinfield*.
a. Identify the independent and dependent variables.
b. Draw a scatter plot with the dependent variable on the vertical axis and the independent variable on the horizontal axis.
c. The marketing director wishes to know if increasing the amount spent on advertising increases sales. As a first attempt, use a statistical test that will provide the required information. Use a significance level of 0.025. Upon careful consideration, the marketing manager realizes that it takes a certain amount of time for the effect of advertising to register in terms of increased sales. She, therefore, asks you to calculate a correlation coefficient for sales of the current week against amount of advertising spent in the previous week and conduct a hypothesis test to determine if, under this model, increasing the amount spent on advertising increases sales. Again, use a significance of 0.025.

12.59   Refer to the Grinfield Service Company discussed in Exercise 12.58.

a. Develop the least squares regression equation for these variables. Plot the regression line on the scatter plot.

b. Develop a 95% confidence interval estimate for the increase in sales resulting from increasing the advertising budget by $50. Interpret the interval.

c. Discuss whether it is appropriate to interpret the intercept value of this model. Under what conditions is it appropriate? Discuss.

d. Develop a 90% confidence interval for the mean sales amount achieved during all weeks in which advertising is $200 for the week.

e. Suppose you are asked to use this regression model to predict the weekly sales when advertising will be $100. What would you reply to the request? Discuss.

12.60   The Rio-River Railroad, headquartered in Santa Fe, New Mexico, is trying to devise a method for allocating fuel costs to individual railroad cars on a particular route between Denver and Santa Fe. The railroad thinks that fuel consumption will increase as more cars are added to the train, but it is uncertain about how much cost should be assigned to each additional car. In an effort to deal with this problem, the cost-accounting department has randomly sampled 10 trips between the two cities and has recorded the data in the CD-ROM file *Rio-River*.

a. Draw a scatter plot for these two variables and comment on the apparent relationship between fuel consumption and the number of rail cars on the train.

b. (1) Compute the correlation coefficient between fuel consumption and the number of rail cars. (2) Test Rio-River's preconception of the relation between fuel consumption and the number of rail cars, using a significance level of 0.025. (3) Comment on the results of this test. Do these results necessarily indicate that adding more cars will increase the fuel usage?

c. Develop the least square regression model to help explain the variation in fuel consumption.

d. Write a report that interprets the regression results. In the report, address the issue of, on average, how much the addition of another rail car will increase fuel consumption. Also, calculate the average fuel consumption, average number of cars per train, and average fuel consumption per car for the data given. Does this average equal the average increase in fuel consumption from adding an additional car using the regression model? Explain any difference.

12.61   Sanders Company's production manager, Bill Hendley, is performing a productivity study of the employees at the Black Hills plant. As part of this study, he selected a random sample of 20 employees who have worked for the company for four years or longer. For each employee, he measured the number of hours of special training the employee had taken and the employee's production rate in pieces produced per day. The following summary data are available:

$$y = \text{Pieces produced per day}$$
$$x = \text{Hours of special training}$$
$$\bar{x} = 13.50$$
$$s_\varepsilon = 11.0$$
$$\bar{y} = 125.0$$
$$\hat{y} = 88.5 + 1.5x$$
$$\Sigma(x - \bar{x})^2 = 1,245.0$$

a. Bill has been having trouble with one of the employees at Black Hills: Jim Svede. Jim often takes naps during working hours. When questioned about this behavior, Jim asserts that these naps make him more alert and productive than other employees. Develop a 95% confidence interval for the average daily production for people, such as Jim, who have taken 15 hours of training. Jim has an average daily production rate of 118 pieces a day. Does his assertion carry any weight?

b. Develop a 95% prediction interval for a particular individual who has taken 15 hours of special training courses. Does this interval shed any more light on Jim Svede's assertion? Which of the two interval estimates is more appropriate to address Jim's assertion? Discuss.

12.62   A company is considering recruiting new employees from a particular college and plans to place a great deal of emphasis on each student's college grade point average. However, the company is aware that not all schools have the same grading standards, so it is possible that a student at this school might have a lower (or higher) grade point average than a student from another school, yet really be on par with the other student. To make this comparison between schools, the company has devised a test that it has administered utilizing a sample size of 400. With the results of the test, it has developed a regression model that it uses to predict student grade point average. The following equation represents the model:

$$\hat{y} = 1.0 + 0.028x$$

The R^2 for this model is 0.88, and the standard error of the estimate is 0.20, based on the sample data used to develop the model. Note that the dependent variable is the grade point average, and the independent variable is the test score, where this score can range from 0 to 100. For the sample data used to develop the model, the following values are known.

$$\bar{y} = 2.76$$
$$\bar{x} = 68$$
$$\Sigma(x - \bar{x})^2 = 148,885.73$$

a. Based on the information contained in this problem, can you conclude that as a test score increases, the GPA will also increase, using a significance level of 0.05?

b. Suppose a student interviews with this company, takes the company test, and scores 80% correct. What is the 90% prediction interval estimate for this student's grade point average? Interpret the interval.

c. Suppose the student in part b actually has a 2.90 grade point average at this school. Based on this evidence, what might be concluded about this person's actual grade point average compared with other students at other schools with the same grade point average? Discuss the limitations you might place on this conclusion.

d. Suppose a second student with a 2.45 grade point average took the test and scored 65% correct. What is the 90% prediction interval for this student's "real" grade point average? Interpret.

12.63   Suppose the company that developed the test discussed in Exercise 12.62 is interested in developing a 95% confidence interval estimate for the average grade point average for students who score 88% correct on this test. Calculate this interval and interpret it.

CASE 12-A:

Alamar Industries

While driving home in northern Kentucky at 8:00 P.M., Juan Alamar wondered whether his father had done him any favor by retiring early and letting him take control of the family machine-tool-restoration business. When his father started the business of overhauling machine tools (both for resale and on a contract basis), American companies dominated the tool manufacturing market. During the past 30 years, however, the original equipment industry had been devastated, first by competition from Germany and then from Japan. Although foreign competition had not yet invaded the overhaul segment of the business, Juan had heard about foreign companies establishing operations on the West Coast.

The foreign competitors were apparently stressing the high-quality service and operations that had been responsible for their great inroads into the original equipment market. Last week Juan had attended a daylong conference on total quality management that had discussed the advantages of competing for the Baldrige Award, the national quality award established in 1987. Presenters from past Baldrige winners, including Xerox, Federal Express, Cadillac, and Motorola, stressed the positive effects on their companies of winning and said similar effects would be possible for any company. This assertion of only positive effects was what Juan questioned. He was certain that the effect on his remaining free time would not be positive.

The Baldrige Award considers seven corporate dimensions of quality. Although the award is not based on a numerical score, an overall score is calculated. The maximum score is 1,000, with most recent winners scoring about 800. Juan did not doubt the award was good for the winners, but he wondered about the nonwinners. In particular, he wondered about any relationship between attempting to improve quality according to the Baldrige dimensions and company profitability. Individual company scores are not released, but Juan was able to talk to one of the conference presenters who shared some anonymous data, such as companies' scores in the year they applied, their returns on investment in the year applied, and returns on investment in the year after application. Juan decided to commit the company to a total quality management process if the data provided evidence that the process would lead to increased profitability.

BALDRIGE SCORE	ROI APPLICATION YEAR	ROI NEXT YEAR
470	11%	13%
520	10	11
660	14	15
540	12	12
600	15	16
710	16	16
580	11	12
600	12	13
740	16	16
610	11	14
570	12	13
660	17	19

CASE 12-B:

Continental Trucking

Norm Painter is the newly hired cost analyst for Continental Trucking. Continental is a nationwide trucking firm, and, until recently, most of its routes were driven under regulated rates. These rates were set to allow small trucking firms to earn an adequate profit, leaving little incentive to work to reduce costs by efficient management techniques. In fact, the greatest effort was made to try to influence regulatory agencies to grant rate increases.

A recent rash of deregulation moves has made the long-distance trucking industry more competitive. Norm has been hired to analyze Continental's whole expense structure. As part of this study, Norm is looking at truck repair costs. Because the trucks are involved in long hauls, they inevitably break down. In the past, little preventive maintenance was done, and if a truck broke down in the middle of a haul, either a replacement tractor was sent or an independent contractor finished the haul. The truck was then repaired at the nearest local shop. Norm is sure this procedure has led to more expense than if major repairs had been made before the trucks failed.

Norm thinks that some method should be found for determining when preventive maintenance is needed. He believes that fuel consumption is a good indicator of possible breakdowns, and as the trucks begin running badly, they will consume more fuel. Unfortunately, the major determinants of fuel consumption are the weight of a truck and head winds. Norm picks a sample of a single truck model and gathers data relating fuel consumption to truck weight. All trucks in the sample are in good condition. He separates the data by direction of the haul, realizing that winds tend to blow predominantly out of the west.

EAST–WEST HAUL		WEST–EAST HAUL	
Miles/Gallon	Haul Weight	Miles/Gallon	Haul Weight
4.1	41,000 lbs.	4.3	40,000 lbs.
4.7	36,000	4.5	37,000
3.9	37,000	4.8	36,000
4.3	38,000	5.2	38,000
4.8	32,000	5.0	35,000
5.1	37,000	4.7	42,000
4.3	46,000	4.9	37,000
4.6	35,000	4.5	36,000
5.0	37,000	5.2	42,000
		4.8	41,000

Although he can rapidly gather future data on fuel consumption and haul weight, now that Norm has these data, he is not quite sure what to do with them.

General References

1. Berenson, Mark L., and David M. Levine *Basic Business Statistics: Concepts and Applications*, 7th ed. (Upper Saddle River, NJ: Prentice-Hall, 1999).

2. Cryer, Jonathan D., and Robert B. Miller, *Statistics for Business: Data Analysis and Modeling*, 2nd ed. (Belmont, CA: Duxbury Press, 1994).

3. Draper, Norman R., and Harry Smith, *Applied Regression Analysis*, 3rd ed. (New York: John Wiley and Sons, 1998).

4. Frees, Edward W., *Data Analysis Using Regression Models: The Business Perspective* (Englewood Cliffs, NJ: Prentice-Hall, 1996).

5. Kleinbaum, David G., Lawrence L. Kupper, Keith E. Muller, and Azhar Nizam, *Applied Regression Analysis and Other Multivariable Methods*, 3rd ed. (Belmont, CA: Duxbury Press, 1998).

6. *Microsoft Excel 2000* (Redmond, WA: Microsoft Corp., 1999).

7. *Minitab for Windows Version 14* (State College, PA: Minitab, 2003).

8. Neter, John, Michael H. Kutner, Christopher J. Nachtsheim, and William Wasserman, *Applied Linear Statistical Models*, 4th ed. (Homewood, IL: Richard D. Irwin, 1996).

CHAPTER 13

Multiple Regression Analysis and Model Building

CHAPTER OUTCOMES

After studying the material in Chapter 13, you should be able to:

- Understand the general concepts behind model building using multiple regression analysis.
- Use variable transformations to model nonlinear relationships in a regression model.
- Apply multiple regression analysis to business decision-making situations.
- Analyze the computer output for a multiple regression model and interpret the regression results.
- Test hypotheses about the significance of a multiple regression model and test the significance of the independent variables in the model.
- Recognize potential problems when using multiple regression analysis and take steps to correct the problems.
- Incorporate qualitative variables into a regression model by using dummy variables.

WHY YOU NEED TO KNOW

Chapter 12 pointed out that decision-makers often need to consider the relationship between two variables when analyzing a problem. Simple linear regression and correlation analyses provide a basis for analyzing the relationship between two variables. If the two variables are correlated, there is a linear relationship between them, and linear regression analysis can be used to model that relationship.

As you might expect, business problems are not limited to linear relationships involving only two variables. Many practical situations involve analyzing the relationships among three or more variables, and these relationships may be nonlinear. For example, a vice president of planning for an automobile manufacturer would be interested in the relationship between her company's automobile sales and the variables that influence those sales. Included in her analysis might be such independent or explanatory variables as automobile price, competitors' sales, and advertising, as well as such economic variables as disposable personal income, the inflation rate, and the unemployment rate.

When multiple independent variables are to be included in an analysis simultaneously, the technique introduced in this chapter—multiple linear regression—is very useful. When a relationship between variables is nonlinear, we may be able to apply variable transformations that allow us to use multiple linear regression analysis to construct a model. This chapter examines the general topic of model building by extending the concepts of simple linear regression analysis. The background information provided in Chapter 12 will be very helpful in understanding and applying multiple regression analysis to business decision-making situations.

13-1 INTRODUCTION TO MULTIPLE REGRESSION ANALYSIS

Chapter 12 introduced the concept of simple linear regression analysis involving a dependent variable and a single independent, or explanatory, variable. In those situations, we attempt to model the relationship in a population between two variables as shown in Equation 13-1.

Simple Linear Regression Model (Population Model)

$$y = \beta_0 + \beta_1 x + \varepsilon \qquad \text{13-1}$$

where:

y = Value of the dependent variable in the population
x = Value of the independent variable in the population
β_0 = The population regression coefficient representing the y intercept
β_1 = The population regression slope coefficient
ε = Error term, or residual

When we have a random sample of data, the regression model represented by Equation 13-1 is estimated in the form shown as Equation 13-2.

Estimated Simple Linear Regression Model

$$\hat{y} = b_0 + b_1 x \qquad \text{13-2}$$

where:

$\hat{y}$ = Estimated, or predicted value of y
b_0 = Estimated y intercept
b_1 = Estimated slope coefficient
x = Value of the independent variable

The simple regression model is characterized by two variables: y, the *dependent variable*, and x, the *independent*, or *explanatory*, *variable*. The single independent variable explains some variation in the dependent variable, but unless x and y are perfectly correlated, the proportion explained will be less than 100%. This also means that the predicted (or fitted) y values will often not equal the actual *y* values. This means that prediction error, *e*, will be present. Another word for prediction error is **residual**.

Residual (Prediction Error)

The difference between the actual value of *y* and the predicted value of *y*, which is given by:

$$e = y - \hat{y}$$

Chapter 12 indicated that the model's random error (ε) is assumed to have a mean of 0 and a standard deviation called the *standard error of the estimate*. If this standard error of the estimate is too large, the regression model may not be very useful for prediction.

In multiple regression analysis, additional independent variables are added to the regression model to explain some of the yet-unexplained variation in the dependent variable. Adding appropriate independent variables should reduce the sum of squares of error for the regression equation.

You will note as we proceed that multiple regression is merely an extension of simple regression analysis. However, as we expand the model for the population from one independent variable to two or more, there are some new considerations.

The general format of a **multiple regression model for the population** is given by Equation 13-3.

Multiple Regression Model (Population Model)

$$y = \beta_0 + \beta_1 x_1 + \beta_2 x_2 + \ldots + \beta_k x_k + \varepsilon \qquad \textbf{13-3}$$

where:

β_0 = Population's regression constant
β_j = Population's regression coefficient for variable *x*; $j = 1, 2, \ldots k$
k = Number of independent variables
ε = Model error

There are four general assumptions of the linear multiple regression model.

**SSUMPTIONS**

1. The regression model errors are normally distributed.
2. The mean of the model error terms is 0.
3. The model error terms have a constant variance, σ_ε^2, for all combinations of values of the independent variables.
4. The model error terms are independent.

Equation 13-3 represents the multiple regression model for the population. However, in most instances, you will be working with a random sample from the population. Given the above assumptions, the estimated multiple regression model, based on the sample data, is of the form shown in Equation 13-4.

Estimated Multiple Regression Model

$$\hat{y} = b_0 + b_1 x_1 + b_2 x_2 + \ldots + b_k x_k \qquad \textbf{13-4}$$

This estimated model is an extension of the estimated simple regression model shown in Equation 13-2. The principal difference is that, whereas the estimated simple regression model is the equation for a straight line in a two-dimensional space, the estimated multiple regression model forms a hyperplane (or response surface) through multidimensional space. Each regression coefficient represents a different slope. Therefore, for a decision maker, using Equation 13-2 means a value of the dependent variable can be estimated using a value of one independent variable, but a multiple regression model requires values of two or more (*k*) independent variables to be known. The **regression hyperplane** represents the relationship between the dependent variable and the many independent variables.

(A) ONE INDEPENDENT VARIABLE		(B) TWO INDEPENDENT VARIABLES		
y	x_1	y	x_1	x_2
564.99	50	564.99	50	10
601.06	60	601.06	60	13
560.11	40	560.11	40	14
616.41	50	616.41	50	12
674.96	60	674.96	60	15
630.58	45	630.58	45	16
554.66	53	554.66	53	14

Regression Hyperplane

The multiple regression equivalent of the simple regression line. The plane has a different slope for each independent variable.

For example, Table 13-1a shows sample data for a dependent variable, y, and one independent variable, x_1. Figure 13-1 shows a scatter plot and the regression line for the simple regression analysis for y and x_1. The points are plotted in two-dimensional space, and the regression model is represented by a line through the points such that the sum of squares of error $[SSE = \Sigma(y - \hat{y})^2]$ is minimized.

If we add variable x_2 to the model, as shown in Table 13-1b, the resulting multiple regression equation becomes

$$\hat{y} = 307.71 + 2.85x_1 + 10.94x_2$$

For the time being don't worry about how this equation was computed. That will be discussed shortly. Note, however, that the (y, x_1, x_2) points are plotted in three-dimensional space, as shown in Figure 13-2. The regression equation forms a slice (hyperplane) through the data such that $\Sigma(y - \hat{y})^2$ is minimized. This is the same *least squares criterion* that is used with simple linear regression.

The mathematics for developing the least squares regression equation for simple linear regression involves differential calculus. The same is true for the multiple regression equation. Because the least squares regression coefficients are determined using matrix algebra, the mathematical derivation is beyond the scope of this test.[1]

Multiple regression analysis is virtually always performed with the aid of a computer and appropriate software. Both Minitab and Excel contain procedures for performing multiple regres-

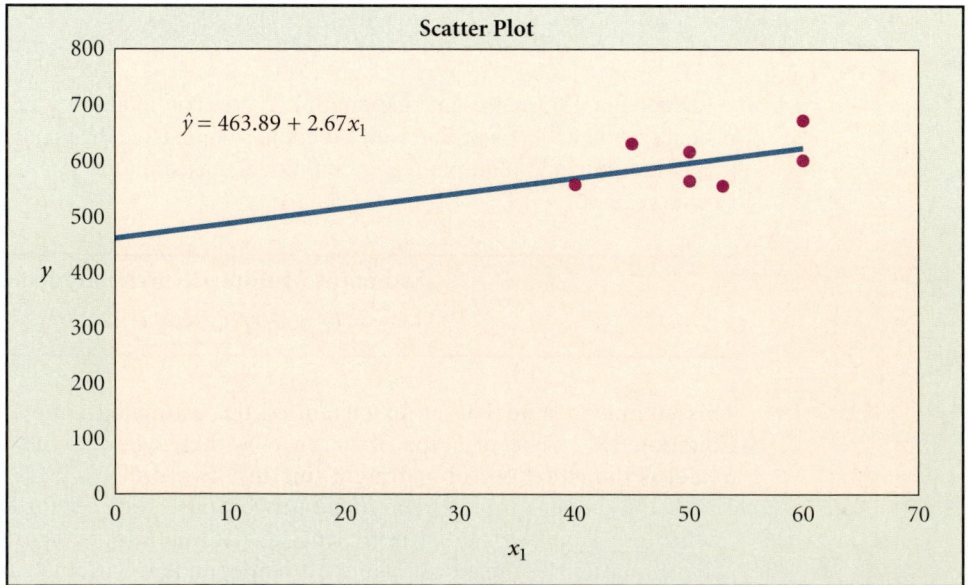

Scatter Plot

$\hat{y} = 463.89 + 2.67x_1$

[1]For a complete treatment of the matrix algebra approach for estimating multiple regression coefficients, consult *Applied Linear Statistical Models* by Neter et al.

FIGURE 13-2

Multiple Regression Hyperplane for Population

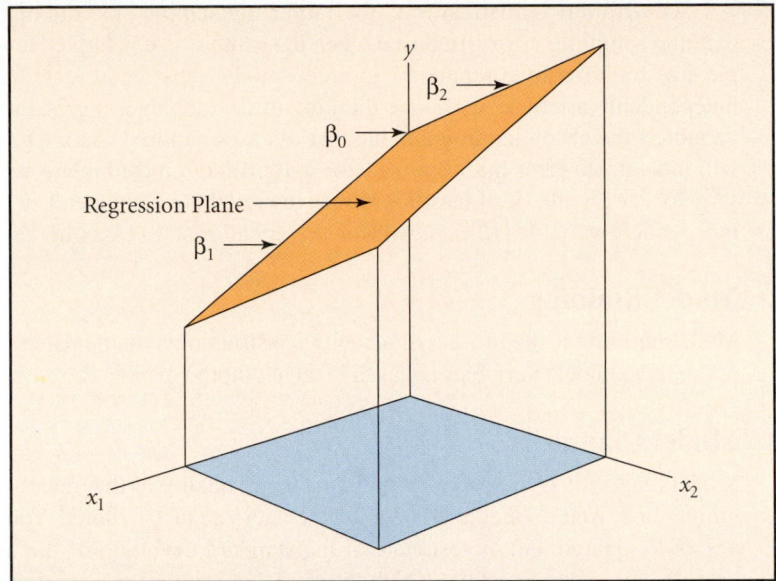

sion. Minitab has a far-more-complete regression procedure. However, the PHStat Excel add-ins expand Excel's capabilities. Each software package presents the results in a slightly different format; however, the same basic information will appear in all regression output.

BASIC MODEL-BUILDING CONCEPTS

An important activity in business decision making is referred to as **model** building.

Model

A representation of an actual system using either a physical or a mathematical portrayal.

Models are often used to test changes in a system without actually having to change the real system. Models are also used to help describe a system or to predict the output of a system based on certain specified inputs. You are probably quite aware of physical models. Airlines use flight simulators to train pilots. Wind tunnels are used to determine the aerodynamics of automobile designs. Golf ball makers use a physical model of a golfer called "Iron Mike" that can be set to swing golf clubs in a very controlled manner to determine how far a golf ball will fly. Although physical models are very useful in business decision making, our emphasis in this chapter is on mathematical models. In particular, we are interested in statistical models that are developed using multiple regression analysis.

People involved in model building frequently conclude that it is both an art and a science. Determining an appropriate model is a challenging task, but it can be made manageable by employing a model-building process consisting of the following three components: model specification, model fitting, and model diagnosis.

Model Specification

Model specification, or model identification, is the process of determining the dependent variable and deciding which independent variables should be included in the model.

SUMMARY: MODEL SPECIFICATION

In the context of the statistical models discussed in this chapter, this component involves the following three steps:

1. Decide what question you want to ask. The question being asked usually indicates the dependent variable. In the previous chapter we discussed how simple linear regression

analysis could be used to describe the relationship between a dependent and an independent variable.

2. List the potential independent variables for your model. Here, your knowledge of the situation you are modeling guides you in identifying potential independent variables.

3. Gather the sample data (observations) for all variables.

As with any statistical tool, the larger the sample size the better, because the potential for extreme sampling error is reduced when the sample size is large. However, at a minimum, the sample size required to compute a regression model must be at least one greater than the number of independent variables.[2] If we are thinking of developing a regression model with five independent variables, the absolute minimum number of cases required is six. Otherwise, the computer software will indicate an error has been made or will print out meaningless values. As a practical matter, the sample size should be at least four times the number of independent variables. Thus, if we had five independent variables ($k = 5$), we would want at least 20 cases to develop the regression model.

Model Building

Model building is the process of actually constructing a mathematical equation in which some or all of the independent variables are used in an attempt to explain the variation in the dependent variable.

Model Diagnosis

Model diagnosis is the process of analyzing the quality of the model you have constructed by determining how well a specified model fits the data you just gathered. You will examine such output values as R-squared and the estimate of the standard deviation of the model error. At this stage, you will also assess the extent to which the model's assumptions appear to be satisfied. (Section 13-5 is devoted to examining whether a model meets the regression analysis assumptions.) If the model is unacceptable in any of these areas, you will be forced to revert to the model-specification step and begin again. However, you will be the final judge of whether the model provides acceptable results, and you will always be constrained by time and cost considerations.

An important consideration in practical situations is to use the simplest available model that will meet your needs. The objective of model building is to help you make better decisions. You do not need to feel that a sophisticated model is better if a simpler one will provide acceptable results.

SUMMARY: DEVELOPING A MULTIPLE REGRESSION MODEL

The following steps are employed in developing a multiple regression model.

1. Specify the model by determining the dependent variable and potential independent variables.

2. Formulate the model. This is done by computing the correlation coefficients for the dependent variable and each independent variable and for each independent variable with all other independent variables. The multiple regression equation is also computed. The computations are performed using computer software such as Excel or Minitab.

3. Perform diagnostic checks on the model to determine how well the specified model fits the data and how well the model appears to meet the multiple regression assumptions.

EXAMPLE 13-1: DEVELOPING A MULTIPLE REGRESSION MODEL

Excel and Minitab Tutorial

First City Real Estate   First City Real Estate executives recently decided to make the firm more responsive to inquiries from people thinking about selling their houses. They wish to build a model to predict sales prices for residential property. This can be done using the following steps.

Step 1:   Specify the model.
The question being asked is how can the real estate firm determine what the selling price for a house should be? Thus, the dependent variable is the sales price. This is what the managers want to be able to predict. The managers met in a brainstorming session to derive a list of possible independent (explanatory) variables. Some variables, such as "condition of the house" were eliminated because of lack of data. Others such as "curb appeal" (the appeal of the house to people as they drive by) were eliminated because the values for these variables would be too subjective and difficult to

---

[2]There are mathematical reasons for this sample-size requirement that are beyond the scope of this text. In essence, Equation 13-4 can't be computed if the sample size is not at least one larger than the number of independent variables.

quantify. From a wide list of possibilities, the managers selected the following variables as good candidates:

$$x_1 = \text{Home size (in square feet)}$$
$$x_2 = \text{Age of house}$$
$$x_3 = \text{Number of bedrooms}$$
$$x_4 = \text{Number of bathrooms}$$
$$x_5 = \text{Garage size (number of cars)}$$

Data were obtained for a sample of 319 residential properties that had sold within the previous two months in an area served by two of First City's offices. For each house in the sample, the sales price and values for each potential independent variable were collected. The data are in the CD-ROM file *First City*.

Step 2:   Formulate the model.
The regression model is developed by including independent variables from among those for which you have complete data. There is no way to determine whether an independent variable will be a good predictor variable by analyzing the individual variable's descriptive statistics, such as the mean and standard deviation. Instead, we need to look at the correlation between the independent variables and the dependent variable, which is measured by the **correlation coefficient**.

Correlation Coefficient

A quantitative measure of the strength of the linear relationship between two variables. The correlation coefficient, r, ranges from -1.0 to $+1.0$.

When we have multiple independent variables and one dependent variable, we can look at the correlation between all pairs of variables by developing a **correlation matrix**. Each correlation is computed using one of the equations in Equation 13-5. The appropriate formula is determined by whether the correlation is being calculated for an independent variable and the dependent variable or for two independent variables, respectively.

Correlation Matrix

A table showing the pairwise correlations between all variables (dependent and independent).

Correlation Coefficient

$$r = \frac{\sum(x - \bar{x})(y - \bar{y})}{\sqrt{\sum(x - \bar{x})^2 \, \sum(y - \bar{y})^2}} \quad \text{or} \quad r = \frac{\sum(x_1 - \bar{x}_1)(x_2 - \bar{x}_2)}{\sqrt{\sum(x_1 - \bar{x}_1)^2 \, \sum(x_2 - \bar{x}_2)^2}}$$

One x variable with y One x variable with another x **13-5**

The actual calculations are done using Excel's correlation tool or Minitab's correlation command, and the results are shown in Figure 13-3a and Figure 13-3b. The output provides the correlation between y and each x variable and between each pair of independent variables.[3] Recall that in Chapter 12, a t-test (see Equation 12-3) was used to test whether the correlation coefficient is statistically significant.

$$H_0: \rho = 0$$
$$H_A: \rho \neq 0$$

---

[3]Minitab, in addition to providing the correlation matrix, provides the p-values for each correlation. If the p-value is less than the desired alpha, the correlation is statistically significant.

FIGURE 13-3A

Excel Results Showing First City Real Estate Correlation Matrix

Excel Instructions:
1. Open file: First City.xls
2. Click on **Tools > Data Analysis**.
3. Select **Correlation**.
4. Define data range and output location.

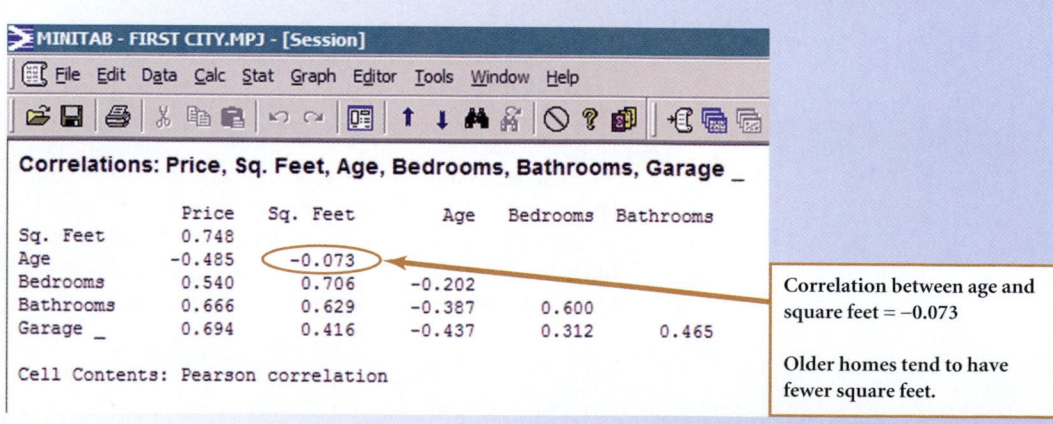

	A	B	C	D	E	F	G
1		*Price*	*Sq. Feet*	*Age*	*Bedrooms*	*Bathrooms*	*Garage #*
2	Price	1					
3	Sq. Feet	0.747711972	1				
4	Age	-0.485221836	-0.072883413	1			
5	Bedrooms	0.540087962	0.705860253	-0.202401652	1		
6	Bathroom	0.665504255	0.629289554	-0.387104876	0.599640313	1	
7	Garage #	0.693538499	0.416261286	-0.437379482	0.312034317	0.464601539	1

Correlation between age and square feet = −0.07288

Older homes tend to have fewer square feet.

We will conduct the test with a significance level of

$$\alpha = 0.05$$

Given degrees of freedom equal to

$$n - 2 = 319 - 2 = 317$$

the critical t (see Appendix E) for a two-tailed test is approximately

$$t_{\alpha/2} = 1.96^4$$

Any correlation coefficient generating a t-value > 1.96 or less than -1.96 is determined to be significant.

For now, we will focus on the correlations in the first column in Figures 13-3a and 13-3b, which measure the strength of the linear relationship between each independent variable and the dependent variable, sales price. For example, the t statistic for price and square feet is

$$t = \frac{r}{\sqrt{\dfrac{1 - r^2}{n - 2}}} = \frac{0.7477}{\sqrt{\dfrac{1 - 0.7477^2}{319 - 2}}} = 20.048$$

Because

$$t = 20.048 > 1.96$$

the correlation between sales price and square feet is statistically significant. We reject H_0.

Similar calculations for the other independent variables with price show that all variables are statistically correlated with price. This indicates that a significant linear relationship exists between each independent variable and sales price. Variable x_1, square feet, has the highest correlation at 0.748. Variable x_2, age of the house, has the lowest correlation at -0.485. The negative correlation implies that older homes tend to have lower sales prices.

FIGURE 13-3B

Minitab Results Showing First City Real Estate Correlation Matrix

Minitab Instructions:
1. Open file: First City.MTW.
2. Choose **Stat > Basic Statistics > Correlation**.
3. In **Variables**, enter variable columns.
4. Click **OK**.

Correlations: Price, Sq. Feet, Age, Bedrooms, Bathrooms, Garage _

	Price	Sq. Feet	Age	Bedrooms	Bathrooms
Sq. Feet	0.748				
Age	-0.485	-0.073			
Bedrooms	0.540	0.706	-0.202		
Bathrooms	0.666	0.629	-0.387	0.600	
Garage _	0.694	0.416	-0.437	0.312	0.465

Cell Contents: Pearson correlation

Correlation between age and square feet = −0.073

Older homes tend to have fewer square feet.

---

[4] You can use the Excel TINV function to get the precise t-value, which is 1.967.

As we discussed in Chapter 12, it is always a good idea to develop scatter plots to visually see the relationship between two variables. Figure 13-4 shows the scatter plots for each independent variable and the dependent variable, sales price. In each case, the plots indicate a linear relationship between the independent variable and the dependent variable. Note that several of the independent variables (bedrooms, bathrooms, garage size) are quantitative but discrete. The scatter plots for these variables show points at each level of the independent variable rather than over a continuum of values.

Computing the Regression Equation

First City's goal is to develop a regression model to predict the appropriate selling price for a home, using certain measurable characteristics. The first attempt at developing the model will be to run a multiple regression computer program using all available independent variables. The regression outputs from Excel and Minitab are shown in Figure 13-5a and Figure 13-5b.

The estimate of the multiple regression model given in Figure 13-5a is

$$\hat{y} = 31,127.6 + 63.1(\text{sq. feet}) - 1,144.4(\text{age}) - 8,410.4(\text{bedrooms}) + 3,522.0(\text{bathrooms}) + 28,203.5(\text{garage})$$

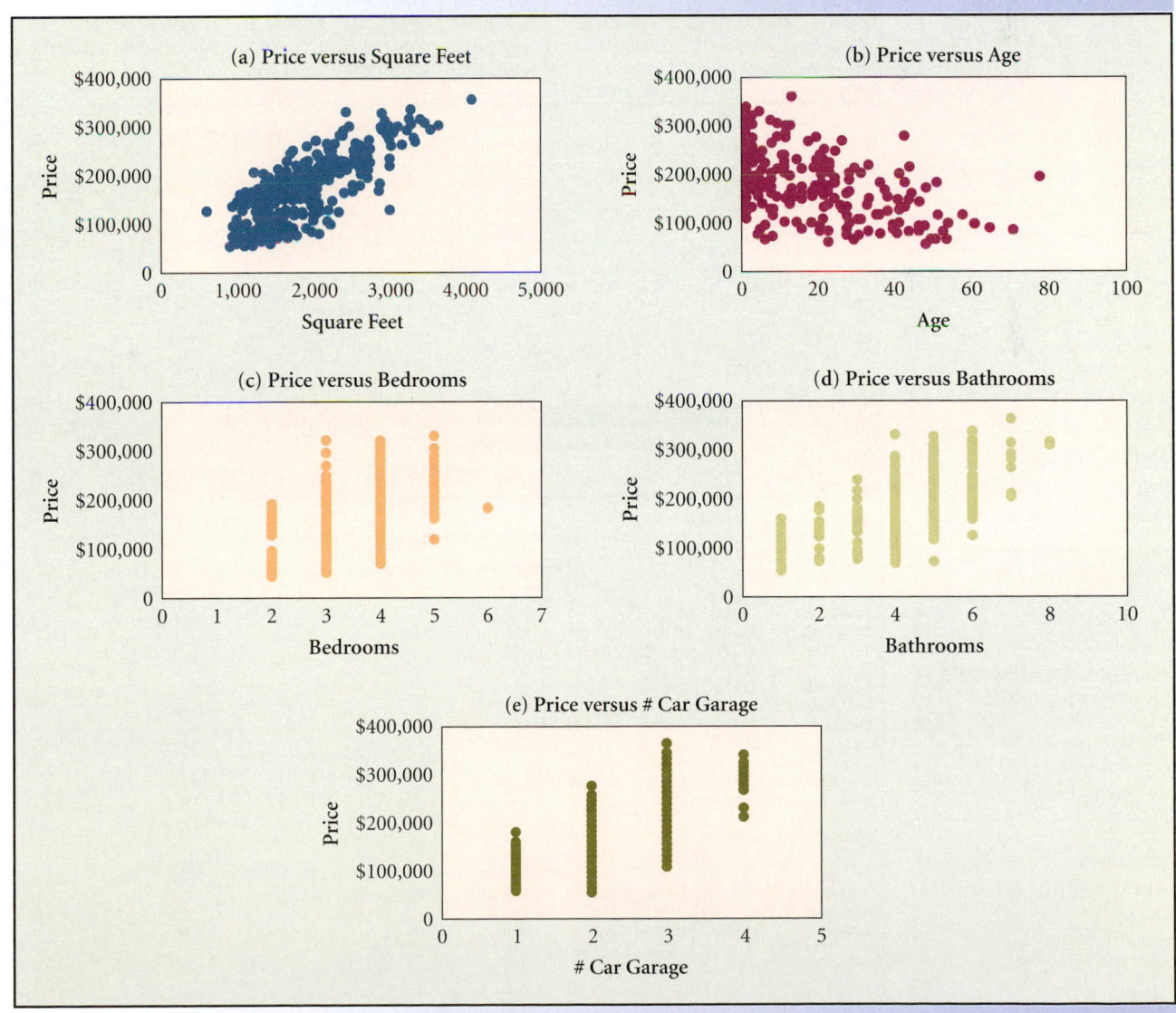

FIGURE 13-4   First City Real Estate Scatter Plots

FIGURE 13-5A

Excel Multiple Regression Model Results for First City Real Estate

Excel Instructions:
1. Open file: First City.xls
2. Click on **Tools > Data Analysis**.
3. Select **Regression**.
4. Define dependent and independent variable range.
5. Determine output location.
6. Click **OK**.

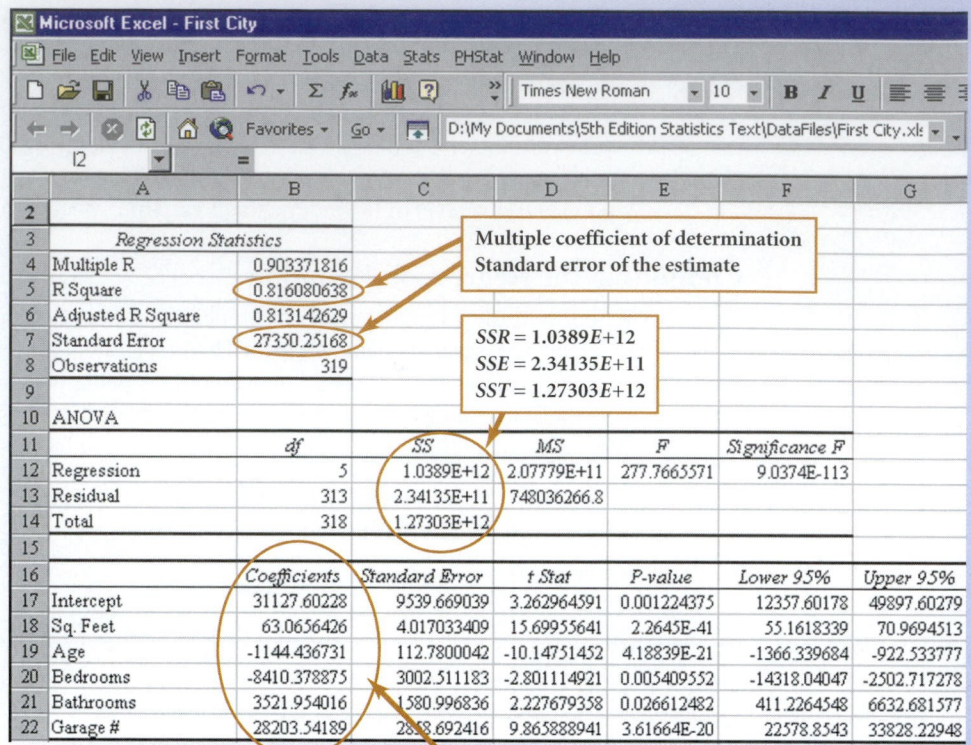

FIGURE 13-5B

Minitab Multiple Regression Model Results for First City Real Estate

Minitab Instructions:
1. Open file: First City.MTW.
2. Choose **Stat > Regression > Regression**.
3. In **Response**, enter dependent (Y) variable.
4. In **Predictors**, enter independent (X) variables.
5. Click **OK**.

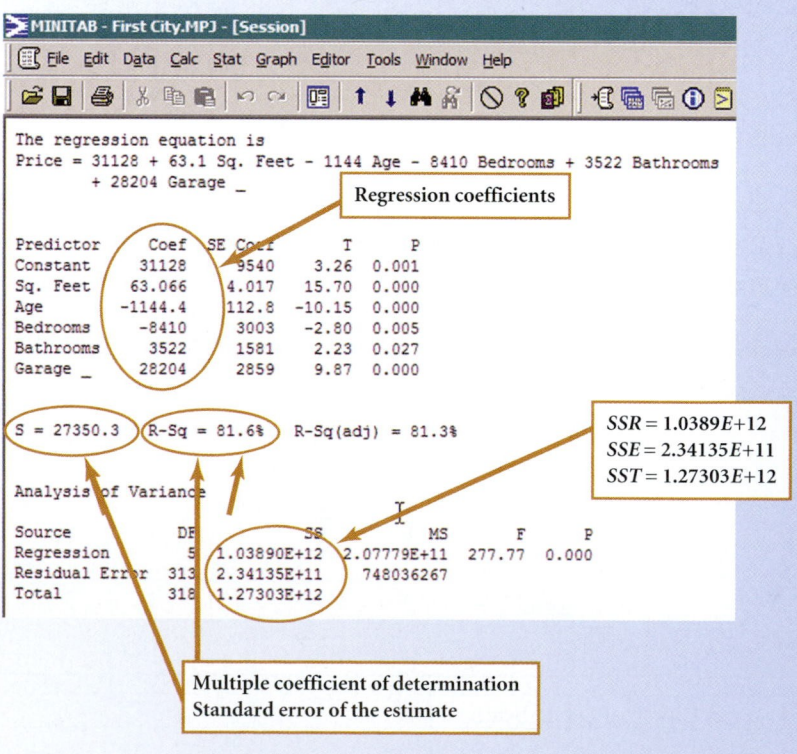

The coefficients for each independent variable represent an estimate of the average change in the dependent variable for a one-unit change in the independent variable, all other independent variables remaining constant. For example, for houses of the same age, with the same number of bedrooms, baths, and garages, a one-square-foot increase in the size of the house is estimated to increase its price by an average of $63.10. Likewise, for houses with the same size, bedrooms, bathrooms, and garages, a one-year increase in the age of the house is estimated to result in an average drop in sales price of $1,144.40. The other coefficients are interpreted in the same way. Note, in each case, we are interpreting the regression coefficient for one independent variable while holding the other variables constant.

To estimate the value of a residential property, First Real Estate brokers would substitute values for the independent variables into the regression equation. For example, suppose a house with the following characteristics is considered.

$$x_1 = \text{Square feet} = 2,100$$
$$x_2 = \text{Age} = 15$$
$$x_3 = \text{Number of bedrooms} = 4$$
$$x_4 = \text{Number of baths} = 3$$
$$x_5 = \text{Size of garage} = 2$$

The point estimate for the sales price is

$$\hat{y} = 31,127.6 + 63.1(\text{sq. feet}) - 1,144.4(\text{age}) - 8,410.4(\text{bedrooms}) + 3,522.0(\text{baths})$$
$$\quad + 28,203.5(\text{garages})$$
$$\hat{y} = 31,127.6 + 63.1(2,100) - 1,144.4(15) - 8,410.4(4) + 3,522.0(3) + 28,203.5(2)$$
$$\hat{y} = \$179,802.70$$

The Coefficient of Determination

You learned in Chapter 12 that the *coefficient of determination*, R^2, measures the fraction of variation in the dependent variable that can be explained by the dependent variable's relationship to a single independent variable. When there are multiple independent variables in a model, R^2 is also used to determine the proportion of variation in the dependent variable that is explained by the dependent variable's relationship to all the independent variables in the model. However, R^2 is now called the **multiple coefficient of determination**. Equation 13-6 is used to compute R^2 for a multiple regression model.

Multiple Coefficient of Determination (R^2)

$$R^2 = \frac{\text{Sum of squares regression}}{\text{Total sum of squares}} = \frac{SSR}{SST}$$

13-6

As shown in Figure 13-5a, $R^2 = 0.816$. Both SSR and SST are also included in the output. Therefore, you can use Equation 13-6 to get R^2, as follows:

$$\frac{SSR}{SST} = \frac{1.0389E+12}{1.27303E+12} = 0.816$$

More than 81% of the variation in sales price can be explained by the linear relationship of the five independent variables in the regression model to the dependent variable. However, as we shall shortly see, not all independent variables are equally important to the model's ability to explain this variation.

Step 3:   **Diagnose the model.**

Before First City actually uses this regression model to estimate the sales price of a house, there are several questions that should be answered.

1. Is the overall model significant?
2. Are the individual variables significant?
3. Is the standard deviation of the model error too large to provide meaningful results?
4. Is multicollinearity a problem?
5. Have the regression analysis assumptions been satisfied?

We shall answer the first four questions in order. We will have to wait until Section 13-5 before we have the tools to answer the fifth important question.

Is the Model Significant?

You should keep in mind that the regression model we constructed is based on a sample of data from the population and is subject to sampling error. Therefore, we need to test the statistical significance of the overall regression model. We have previously discussed the multiple coefficient of determination, R^2, which is a measure of how much of the variation in the dependent variable can be explained by the regression model. Because R^2 is a sample statistic, it can be used to make inferences about whether the overall model is statistically significant in explaining the variation in the dependent variable. The specific null and alternative hypotheses tested for First City Real Estate are

$$H_0: \beta_1 = \beta_2 = \beta_3 = \beta_4 = \beta_5 = 0$$
$$H_A: \text{At least one } \beta_i \text{ does not equal zero.}$$

If the null hypothesis is true and all the slope coefficients are simultaneously equal to zero, the overall regression model is not useful for predictive or descriptive purposes.

The analysis of variance F-test is a method for testing whether the regression model explains a significant proportion of the variation in the dependent variable (and whether the overall model is significant). The F test statistic for a multiple regression model is shown in Equation 13-7.

F Test Statistic

$$F = \frac{\dfrac{SSR}{k}}{\dfrac{SSE}{n-k-1}}$$

13-7

where:

$$SSR = \text{Sum of squares regression} = \Sigma(\hat{y} - \bar{y})^2$$
$$SSE = \text{Sum of squares error} = \Sigma(y - \hat{y})^2$$
$$n = \text{Number of data points}$$
$$k = \text{Number of independent variables}$$
$$\text{Degrees of freedom} = D_1 = k \text{ and } D_2 = (n - k - 1)$$

The ANOVA portion of the output shown in Figure 13-5a contains values for *SSR*, *SSE*, and the *F* value. The general format of the ANOVA table in a regression analysis is shown as follows:

ANOVA

	df	SS	MS	F	Significance F
Regression	k	SSR	$MSR = SSR/k$	MSR/MSE	computed p-value
Residual	$n - k - 1$	SSE	$MSE = SSE/(n - k - 1)$		
Total	$n - 1$	SST			

The ANOVA portion of the output from Figure 13-5a is shown as follows:

ANOVA

	df	SS	MS	F	Significance F
Regression	5	$1.0389E+12$	$2.07779E+11$	277.7665571	$9.0374E-113$
Residual	313	$2.34135E+11$	748036266.8		
Total	318	$1.27303E+12$			

We can test the model's significance.

$$H_0: \beta_1 = \beta_2 = \beta_3 = \beta_4 = \beta_5 = 0$$
$$H_A: \text{At least one } \beta_i \neq \text{zero.}$$

by either comparing the calculated F-value, 277.77, with a table value for a given alpha level

$$\alpha = 0.01$$

and $k = 5$ and $n - k - 1 = 313$ degrees of freedom ($F = 3.079$), or compare the p-value in the output with a specified alpha level. Because

$$F = 277.77 > 3.079, \text{ reject } H_0$$

or because

$$p\text{-value} \approx 0.0 < 0.01, \text{ reject } H_0$$

Therefore, we should conclude that the regression model *does* explain a significant proportion of the variation is sales price. Thus, the overall model is statistically significant. This indicates that for estimating house sales prices, this multiple regression model is superior to using the mean house price as the estimate.

Excel and Minitab also provide a measure called the R-sq(adj), which is the **adjusted R-squared** value (see Figure 13-5a and 13-5b). It is calculated by Equation 13-8.

Adjusted R-Squared

A measure of the percentage of explained variation in the dependent variable that takes into account the relationship between the sample size and the number of independent variables in the regression model.

$$R\text{-sq(adj)} = R_A^2 = 1 - (1 - R^2)\left(\frac{n - 1}{n - k - 1}\right) \qquad \textbf{13-8}$$

where:

$$n = \text{Sample size}$$
$$k = \text{Number of independent variables}$$

Adding independent variables to the regression model will always increase R^2, even if these variables have no relationship to the dependent variable. Therefore, as the number of independent variables is increased (regardless of the quality of the variables), R^2 will increase. However, each additional variable results in the loss of one degree of freedom. This is viewed as part of the cost of adding the specified variable. The addition to R^2 may not justify the reduction in degrees of freedom. The R_A^2 value takes into account this cost and adjusts the R_A^2 value accordingly. R_A^2 will always be less than R^2. When a variable is added that does not contribute its fair share to the explanation of the dependent variable, the R_A^2 will actually decline, even though R^2 will increase. The adjusted R-squared is a particularly important measure when the number of independent variables is large relative to the sample size. It takes into account the relationship between sample size and number of variables. R^2 may appear artificially high if the number of variables is large compared with the sample size.

In this example, in which the sample size is quite large relative to the number of independent variables, the adjusted R-squared is 81.3%, only slightly less than $R^2 = 81.6\%$.

Are the Individual Variables Significant?

We have concluded that the overall model is significant. This means that *at least* one independent variable explains a significant proportion of the variation in sales price. This does not mean that *all* the variables are significant, however. To determine which variables are significant, we test the following hypotheses.

$$H_0 : \beta_j = 0$$
$$H_A : \beta_j \neq 0 \qquad \text{for all } j$$

We can test the significance of each independent variable using significance level

$$\alpha = 0.05$$

and a t-test, as discussed in Chapter 12. The calculated t-values should be compared to the critical t-value with

$$n - k - 1 = 319 - 5 - 1 = 313$$

degrees of freedom, which is approximately

$$t_{\alpha/2} \approx 1.96$$

for $\alpha = 0.05$. The calculated t-value for each variable is provided on the computer printout in Figures 13-5a and 13-5b. Recall that the t statistic is determined by dividing the regression coefficient by the estimator of the standard deviation of the regression coefficient, as shown in Equation 13-9.

---

t-Test for Significance of Each Regression Coefficient

$$t = \frac{b_j - 0}{s_{b_j}} \qquad df = n - k - 1 \qquad \qquad \textbf{13-9}$$

where:

b_j = Sample slope coefficient for the jth independent variable

s_{b_j} = Estimate of the standard error for the jth sample slope coefficient

---

For example, the t-value for square feet shown in Figure 13-5a is 15.699. This was computed using Equation 13-9, as follows:

$$t = \frac{b_j - 0}{s_{b_j}} = \frac{63.06564 - 0}{4.01703} = 15.699$$

Because

$$t = 15.699 > 1.96, \text{ we reject } H_0,$$

the hypothesis that the regression slope for square feet is zero.

We can also look at the Excel or Minitab output and compare the p-value for each regression slope coefficient with alpha. If the p-value is less than alpha, we reject the null hypothesis and conclude that the independent variable is statistically significant in the model. Both the t-test and the p-value techniques will give the same results.

You should consider that these t-tests are *conditional* tests. This means the null hypothesis is that *the value of each slope coefficient is 0, given that the other independent variables are already in the model*.[5] Figure 13-6 shows the hypothesis tests for each independent variable using a 0.05 significance level. We conclude that all five independent variables in the model are significant. When a regression model is to be used for prediction, the model should contain no insignificant variables. If insignificant variables are present, they should be dropped and a new regression equation obtained before the model is used for prediction purposes. We will have more to say about this later.

Is the Standard Deviation of the Regression Model Too Large?

The purpose of developing the First City regression model is to be able to determine values of the dependent variable when corresponding values of the independent variables are known. An indication of how good the regression model is can be found by looking at the relationship between the measured values of the dependent variable and those values that would be predicted by the regression model. The standard deviation of the regression model (also called the **standard error of the estimate**), measures the dispersion of observed home sale values, y, around values predicted by the regression model. The estimate for this standard deviation of the model error, shown in Figure 13-5a, can be computed using Equation 13-10.

---

[5]Note that the t-tests may be affected if the independent variables in the model are themselves correlated. A procedure known as the *sum of squares drop F test*, discussed by Neter et. al. in *Applied Linear Statistical Models*, should be used in this situation. Each t-test considers only the marginal contribution of the independent variables and may indicate that none of the variables in the model are significant, even though the ANOVA procedure indicates otherwise.

FIGURE 13-6

Significance Tests for Each Independent Variable in the First City Real Estate Example

Note: The degrees of freedom for the t-distribution is $(n - k - 1)$, where k is the total number of independent variables in the model.

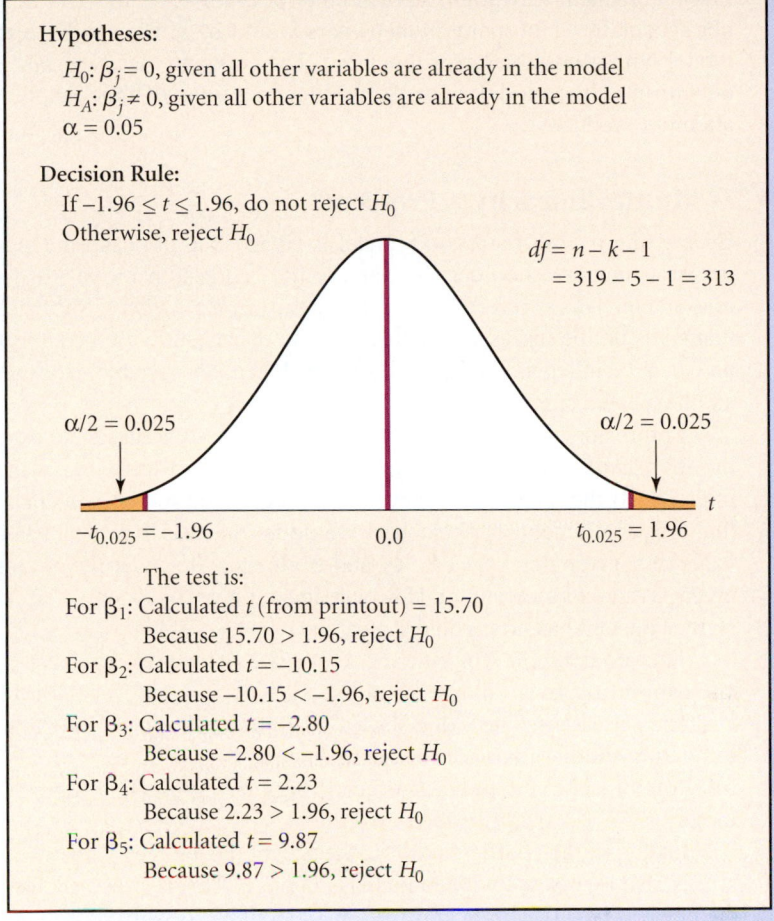

Hypotheses:

H_0: $\beta_j = 0$, given all other variables are already in the model
H_A: $\beta_j \neq 0$, given all other variables are already in the model
$\alpha = 0.05$

Decision Rule:

If $-1.96 \leq t \leq 1.96$, do not reject H_0
Otherwise, reject H_0

$df = n - k - 1$
$= 319 - 5 - 1 = 313$

$\alpha/2 = 0.025$ $\alpha/2 = 0.025$

$-t_{0.025} = -1.96$ 0.0 $t_{0.025} = 1.96$ t

The test is:
For β_1: Calculated t (from printout) $= 15.70$
  Because $15.70 > 1.96$, reject H_0
For β_2: Calculated $t = -10.15$
  Because $-10.15 < -1.96$, reject H_0
For β_3: Calculated $t = -2.80$
  Because $-2.80 < -1.96$, reject H_0
For β_4: Calculated $t = 2.23$
  Because $2.23 > 1.96$, reject H_0
For β_5: Calculated $t = 9.87$
  Because $9.87 > 1.96$, reject H_0

Estimate for the Standard Deviation of the Model

$$s_\varepsilon = \sqrt{\frac{SSE}{n - k - 1}} = \sqrt{MSE}$$

13-10

where:

SSE = Sum of squares error (residual)
n = Sample size
k = Number of independent variables

Examining Equation 13-10 closely, we see that this standard deviation is the square root of the mean square error of the residuals found in the analysis of variance table.

Sometimes, even though a model has a high R^2, the estimate of the standard deviation of the model error will be too large to provide adequate precision for confidence and prediction intervals. A rule of thumb that we have found useful is to examine the range $\pm 2s_\varepsilon$.[6] If this range is acceptable from a practical viewpoint, the estimate of the standard deviation of the model error might be considered acceptable.

In this First City Real Estate Company example, the model error's estimated standard deviation, shown in Figure 13-5a, is \$27,350. Thus, the rough prediction range for the price of an individual home is

$$\pm 2(\$27,350)$$
$$\pm \$54,700$$

[6]The actual confidence interval for prediction of a new observation requires the use of matrix algebra. However, when the sample size is large and dependent variable values near the means of the dependent variables are used, the rule of thumb given here is a close approximation. Refer to *Applied Linear Statistical Models* by Neter et al. for further discussion.

From a practical viewpoint, a potential error of $54,700 above or below the true value is probably not acceptable. Not many homeowners would be willing to have their appraisal value set by a model with a possible error this large. The company needs to take steps to reduce the standard deviation of the model error. Subsequent sections of this chapter discuss some ways we can attempt to reduce it.

Is Multicollinearity a Problem?

Even if the overall regression model is significant and each independent variable is significant, decision makers should still examine the regression model to determine whether it appears reasonable. This is referred to as checking for *face validity*. Specifically, you should check to see that signs on the regression coefficients are consistent with the signs on the correlation coefficient between the independent variable and the dependent variable. Does any regression coefficient have an unexpected sign?

Before answering this question for the First City Real Estate example, we should review what the regression coefficients mean. First, the constant term, b_0, is the estimate of the model's y-intercept. If the data used to develop the regression model contain values of x_1, x_2, x_3, x_4, and x_5 that are simultaneously 0 (such as would be the case for vacant land), the constant is the mean value of y, given that x_1, x_2, x_3, x_4, and x_5 all equal 0. Under these conditions b_0 would estimate the average value of a vacant lot. However, in the First City example, no vacant land was in the sample, so the constant has no particular meaning.

The coefficient for square feet, b_1, estimates the average change in sales price corresponding to a change in house size of 1 square foot, holding the other independent variables constant. The value shown in Figure 13-5a for b_1 is 63.1. The coefficient is positive, indicating that an increase in square footage is associated with an increase in sales price. This relationship is expected. All other things being equal, bigger houses should sell for more money.

Likewise, the coefficient for x_5, the size of the garage, is positive, indicating that an increase in size is also associated with an increase in price. This is expected. The coefficient for x_2, the age of the house is negative, indicating that an older house is worth less than a similar younger house. This also seems reasonable. However, the coefficient for variable x_3, the number of bedrooms, is $-\$8,410.4$ meaning that, if we hold the other variables constant but increase the number of bedrooms by one, the average price will *drop* by $8,410.40. This would appear to run counter to conventional thinking about the housing market. Finally, variable x_4 for bathrooms has the expected positive sign.

Referring to the correlation matrix that was shown earlier in Figure 13-3, the correlation between variable x_3, bedrooms, and y, the sales price, is +0.540. This indicates that, without considering the other independent variables, the linear relationship between number of bedrooms and sales price is positive. But why does the regression coefficient turn out negative in the model? The answer lies in what is called **multicollinearity**.

Multicollinearity

A high correlation between two independent variables such that the two variables contribute redundant information to the model. When highly correlated independent variables are included in the regression model, they can adversely affect the regression results.

Multicollinearity occurs when independent variables overlap with respect to the information they provide in explaining the variation in the dependent variable. For example, x_3 and the other independent variables have the following correlations.

$$r_{x_3,x_1} = 0.706$$
$$r_{x_3,x_2} = -0.202$$
$$r_{x_3,x_4} = 0.600$$
$$r_{x_3,x_5} = 0.312$$

All four correlations have t-values indicating a significant linear relationship. Refer to the correlation matrix in Figure 13-3 to see that other independent variables are also correlated with each other.

The problems caused by multicollinearity, and how to deal with them, continue to be of prime concern to statisticians. From a decision maker's viewpoint, you should be aware that multicollinearity can (and usually does) exist and recognize the basic problems it can cause. Some of the most obvious problems and indications of severe multicollinearity are the following:

1. Incorrect signs on the coefficients.
2. A sizable change in the values of the previous coefficients when a new variable is added to the model.
3. A variable that was previously significant in the regression model becomes insignificant when a new independent variable is added.
4. The estimate of the standard deviation of the model error increases when a variable is added to the model.

Mathematical approaches exist for dealing with multicollinearity and reducing its impact. Although these procedures are beyond the scope of this text, one suggestion is to eliminate the variables that are the chief cause of the multicollinearity problems.

If the independent variables in a regression model are correlated and multicollinearity is present, another potential problem is that the t-tests for the significance of the individual independent variables may be misleading. That is, a t-test may indicate that the variable is not statistically significant when in fact it is.

One method of measuring multicollinearity is known as the **variance inflation factor (VIF)**.

Variance Inflation Factor

A measure of how much the variance of an estimated regression coefficient increases if the independent variables are correlated. A VIF equal to 1.0 for a given independent variable indicates that this independent variable is not correlated with the remaining independent variables in the model. The greater the multicollinearity, the larger the VIF.

Equation 13-11 is used to compute the VIF for each independent variable.

Variance Inflation Factor

$$VIF = \frac{1}{(1 - R_j^2)}$$

13-11

where:

R_j^2 = Coefficient of determination when the jth independent variable is regressed against the remaining $k - 1$ independent variables.

Both the PHStat add-ins to Excel and Minitab contain options that provide VIF values.[7]

Figure 13-7 shows the Excel (PHStat) output of the variance inflation factors for the First City Real Estate example. The effect of multicollinearity is to decrease the test statistic, thus reducing the probability that the variable will be declared significant. A related impact is to increase the width of the confidence interval estimate of the slope coefficient in the regression model. Generally, if the VIF < 5 for a particular independent variable, multicollinearity is not considered a problem for that variable. VIF values ≥ 5 imply that the correlation between the independent variables is too extreme and should be dealt with by dropping variables from the model. As Figure 13-7 illustrates, the VIF values for each independent variable are less than 5, so based on variance inflation factors, even though the sign on the variable, bedrooms, is incorrect, the other multicollinearity issues do not exist among these independent variables.

---

[7]Excel's Regression procedure in the Data Analysis Tools area does not provide VIF values directly. Without PHStat, you would need to compute each regression analysis individually and record the R-squared value to compute the VIF.

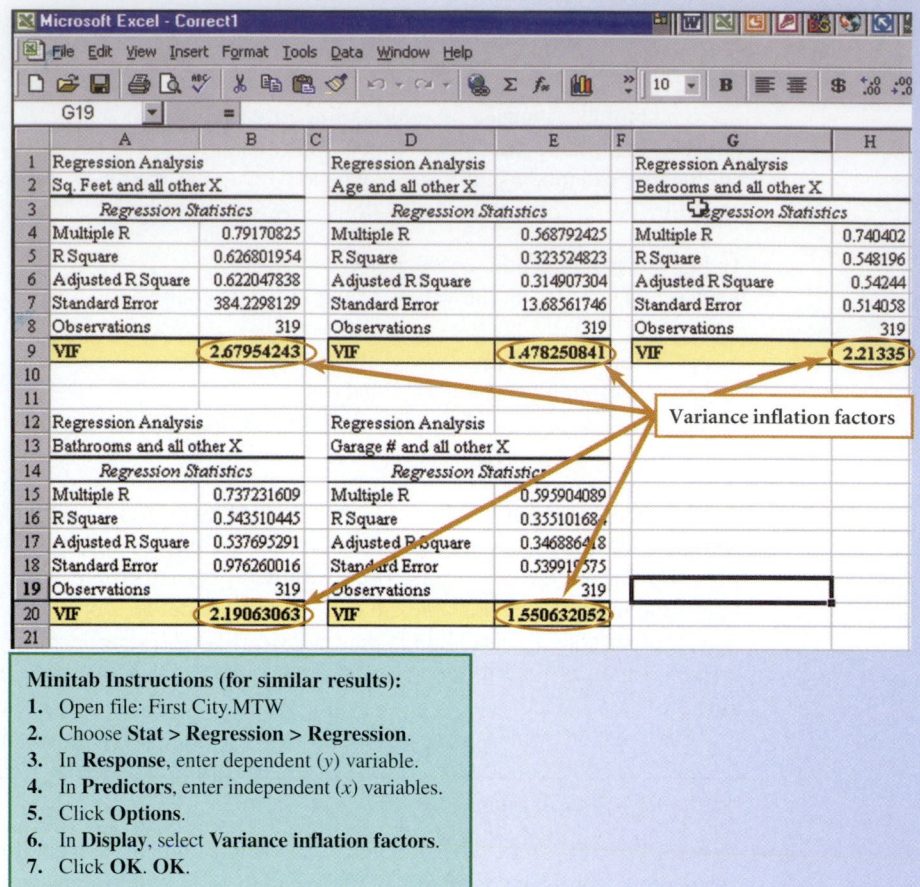

Minitab Instructions (for similar results):
1. Open file: First City.MTW
2. Choose **Stat > Regression > Regression**.
3. In **Response**, enter dependent (*y*) variable.
4. In **Predictors**, enter independent (*x*) variables.
5. Click **Options**.
6. In **Display**, select **Variance inflation factors**.
7. Click **OK. OK**.

Confidence Interval Estimation for Regression Coefficients

Previously we showed how to determine whether the regression coefficients are statistically significant. This was necessary because the estimates of the regression coefficients are developed from sample data and are subject to sampling error. The issue of sampling error also comes into play when interpreting the slope coefficients.

Consider the regression models for First City Real Estate shown in Figures 13-8a and 13-8b. The regression coefficients shown are *point estimates* for the true regression coefficients. For example, the coefficient for the variable, square feet, is $b_1 = 63.07$. We interpret this to mean that, holding the other variables constant, for each increase in the size of a home by one square foot, the price of a house is estimated to increase by $63.07. But like all point estimates, this is subject to sampling error. In Chapter 12 you were introduced to the concept of confidence interval estimates for the regression coefficients. That same concept applies in multiple regression models. Equation 13-12 is used to develop the confidence interval estimate for the regression coefficients.

Confidence Interval Estimate for the Regression Slope

$$b_j \pm t_{\alpha/2} s_{b_j}$$

13-12

where:

b_j = Point estimate for the regression coefficient for x_j

$t_{\alpha/2}$ = Critical *t*-value for a $1 - \alpha$ confidence interval

s_{b_j} = The standard error of the *j*th regression coefficient

---

FIGURE 13-8A

Excel Multiple Regression Model—First City Real Estate

Excel Instructions:
1. Open file: First City.xls
2. Select **Tools**.
3. Select **Data Analysis**.
4. Select **Regression**.
5. Define *y* variable range.
6. Define *x* variable range.

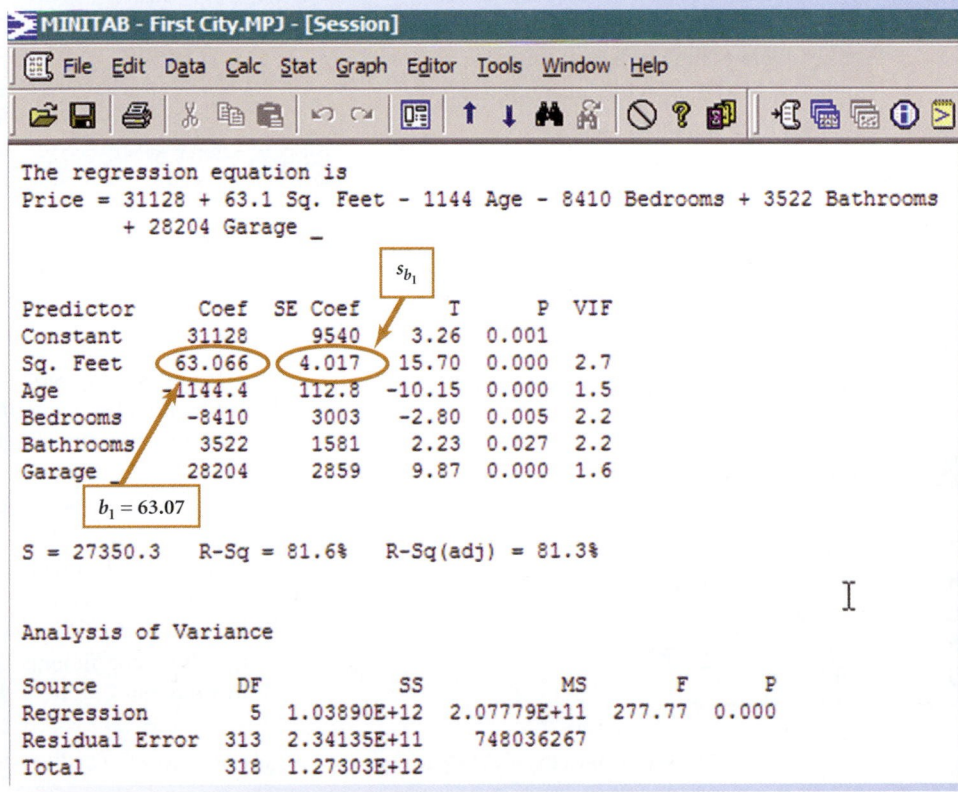

The Excel output in Figure 13-8a provides the confidence interval estimates for each regression coefficient. For example, the 95% interval estimate for square feet is

$$\$55.16 \text{ ———— } \$70.97$$

Minitab does not have a command to generate confidence intervals for the individual regression parameters. However, statistical quantities are provided on the Minitab output in Figure 13-8b to allow the manual calculation of these confidence intervals. As an example, the

FIGURE 13-8B

Minitab Multiple Regression Model—First City Real Estate

Minitab Instructions:
1. Open file: First City.MTW.
2. Choose **Stat > Regression > Regression**.
3. In **Response**, enter dependent (*y*) variable.
4. In **Predictors**, enter independent (*x*) variables.
5. Click **OK**.

```
The regression equation is
Price = 31128 + 63.1 Sq. Feet - 1144 Age - 8410 Bedrooms + 3522 Bathrooms
           + 28204 Garage _


Predictor     Coef   SE Coef        T       P   VIF
Constant     31128      9540     3.26   0.001
Sq. Feet    63.066     4.017    15.70   0.000   2.7
Age         -1144.4     112.8   -10.15   0.000   1.5
Bedrooms     -8410      3003    -2.80   0.005   2.2
Bathrooms     3522      1581     2.23   0.027   2.2
Garage       28204      2859     9.87   0.000   1.6


S = 27350.3   R-Sq = 81.6%   R-Sq(adj) = 81.3%


Analysis of Variance

Source          DF          SS           MS        F       P
Regression       5  1.03890E+12  2.07779E+11   277.77   0.000
Residual Error 313  2.34135E+11    748036267
Total          318  1.27303E+12
```

s_{b_1}

$b_1 = 63.07$

confidence interval for the coefficient associated with the square feet variable can be computed using Equation 13-12 as:

$$b_1 \pm t_{\alpha/2}s_{b_1}$$
$$63.07 \pm 1.96\,(4.017)$$
$$63.07 \pm 7.90$$
$$\$55.17 \text{----------------} \$70.97\,[8]$$

We interpret this interval as follows: Holding the other variables constant, using a 95% confidence level, a change in square feet by one foot is estimated to generate an average change in home price of between $55.17 and $70.97. Each of the other regression coefficients can be interpreted in the same manner.

13-1: EXERCISES

Skill Development

13.1 You are given the following estimated regression equation involving a dependent and two independent variables.

$$\hat{y} = 12.67 + 4.14x_1 + 8.72x_2$$

a. Interpret the values of the slope coefficients in this equation.
b. Estimate the value of the dependent variable when $x_1 = 4$ and $x_2 = 9$.

13.2 In working for a local retail store, you have developed the following estimated regression equation:

$$\hat{y} = 22{,}167 - 412x_1 + 818x_2 - 93x_3 - 71x_4$$

where:

y = Weekly sales
x_1 = Local unemployment rate
x_2 = Weekly average high temperature
x_3 = Number of activities in the local community
x_4 = Average gasoline price

a. Interpret the values of b_1, b_2, b_3, and b_4 in this estimated regression equation.
b. What are the estimated sales if the unemployment rate is 5.7%, the average high temperature is 61°, there were 14 activities, and the average gasoline price was $1.39?

13.3 Given the following data for a dependent and two independent variables:

y	x_1	x_2
22	9	14
17	6	15
28	12	17
35	14	18
25	15	15
30	16	17

a. Estimate the regression equation relating the dependent variable to the first independent variable.
b. Estimate the regression equation relating the dependent variable to the second independent variable.
c. Estimate the regression relating the dependent variable to both independent variables.

13.4 The following output is associated with a multiple regression model with three independent variables.

	df	SS	MS	F	Significance F
Regression	3	16646.09124	5548.697	5.327561	0.006890815
Residual	21	21871.66876	1041.508		
Total	24	38517.76			

	Coefficients	Standard Error	t Stat	p-value
Intercept	87.789729	25.46767899	3.447104	0.002415
x_1	−0.9704675	0.586041665	−1.65597	0.112596
x_2	0.0023343	0.000745097	3.132828	0.005028
x_3	−8.7233223	7.495492501	−1.16381	0.257554

	Lower 95%	Upper 95%	Lower 90.0%	Upper 90.0%
Intercept	34.82678246	140.75268	43.96638607	131.613073
x_1	−2.189208073	0.2482731	−1.97889489	0.03795989
x_2	0.000784747	0.0038838	0.001052141	0.00361638
x_3	−24.31105497	6.8644104	−21.6211424	4.1744978

a. What is the regression model associated with this data?
b. Is the model statistically significant?
c. How much of the variation in the dependent variable can be explained by the model?
d. Are all of the independent variables in the model significant? If not, which are not and how can you tell?
e. How much of a change in the dependent variable will be associated with a one-unit change in x_2? In x_3?
f. Do any of the 95% confidence interval estimates of the slope coefficients contain zero? If so, what does this indicate?

---

[8]Note, we used Excel's TINV function to get the precise t-value of 1.967. The t-distribution table in Appendix E gives an approximate t-value = 1.96 for large degrees of freedom.

13.5 The following correlation matrix is associated with the same data used to build the regression model in Exercise 13-4.

	y	x_1	x_2	x_3
y	1			
x_1	-0.405743076	1		
x_2	0.459099549	0.051276	1	
x_3	-0.244495858	0.503749	0.271800482	1

Does this output indicate any potential multicollinearity problems with the analysis?

Business Applications

13.6 ◉ Commercial Federal Savings and Loan has been trying to gain a foothold in the southern United States. Initial plans are to open several branches throughout that region in the next five years. In deciding whether to go ahead with the expansion, the board of directors is trying to determine whether the expanding number of S&L offices nationwide has lead to an increase or decrease in overall profitability. One of the board members has recently come across the article "Entry and Probability in Rate-Free Savings and Loan Market" (*Quarterly Review of Economics and Business* (1978) pp. 87–95). The article relates the overall profit margin of savings and loan companies (y) to their net revenues in that year (x_1, in million dollars) and the number of branch offices (x_2). The data that were presented in the article are in the CD-ROM file *Profit*.

a. Produce scatter plots of each independent variable versus the dependent variable in this data set. On the basis of these plots, determine the relationship between each independent variable and the dependent variable.

b. Determine whether the board can use a multiple regression model containing both net revenue and number of branch offices to predict the profit margins of savings and loans companies. Use a hypothesis test with a significance level of 0.10.

c. Which, if any, of the independent variables is statistically significant? Use a significance level of $\alpha = 0.10$ and the p-value approach to conduct these tests.

d. Use a rule of thumb to determine if the standard deviation of the model error is too large for this model. Explain your reasoning in the context of this exercise.

13.7 ◉ The Western States Tourist Association gives out pamphlets, maps, and other tourist-related information to people who call a toll-free number and request the information. The association orders the packets of information from a document-printing company and likes to have enough available to meet immediate needs without having too many sitting around taking up space. The marketing manager decided to develop a multiple regression model to be used in predicting the number of calls that will be received in the coming week. A ran-

dom sample of 12 weeks is selected, with the following variables:

y = Number of calls
x_1 = Number of advertisements placed the previous week
x_2 = Number of calls received the previous week
x_3 = Number of airline tour bookings into western cities for the current week

The data that were collected are in the CD-ROM file *Western States*.

a. Produce the correlation matrix and scatter plots for each independent variable versus the dependent variable.

b. Based on the scatter plots and the correlation matrix, specify the relationship that exists between each independent variable and the dependent variable, then comment on whether you think a multiple regression model will be effectively developed from these data.

c. Specify three simple linear regression equations, one for each of the respective independent variables, and then determine the estimate of each model obtained from the sample data.

d. Indicate which of the models in part c is preferred. Provide statistical analysis and reasoning to support your answer.

13.8 ◉ Refer to the Western States Tourist Association situation described in Exercise 13-7.

a. Specify and then use the data to estimate a multiple regression model that contains all three independent variables.

b. What percentage of the total variation in the dependent variable is explained by the model containing the three independent variables?

c. Test to determine whether the overall model is statistically significant. Use $\alpha = 0.05$ and the p-value approach to conduct this test.

d. Which, if any, of the independent variables is statistically significant? Test using a significance level of 0.05.

e. Determine the adjusted R-squared and comment on what it means.

f. Determine an estimate of the standard error of the estimate and discuss whether this regression model is acceptable as a means of predicting the number of calls that will come to Western Tourist in a given week.

g. Indicate what, if any, evidence there is of multicollinearity problems with this multiple regression model. Discuss problems multicollinearity could cause in this example.

h. Determine the *VIF* for each variable and determine whether this measure results in different conclusions regarding the significance of the independent variables. Do the *VIF* calculations imply that a multicollinearity problem exists? Discuss.

Advanced Application

13.9 ◉ The athletic director of State University is interested in developing a multiple regression model that might be used to explain the variation in attendance at football games at his school. A sample of 16 games was selected from home games played during the past 10 seasons. Data for the following factors were determined.

y = Game attendance
x_1 = Team win/loss percentage to date
x_2 = Opponent win/loss percentage to date
x_3 = Games played this season
x_4 = Temperature at game time

The data that were collected are in the CD-ROM file *Football*.

a. Produce the scatter plots for each independent variable versus the dependent variable. Based on the scatter plots, produce a model that you believe represents the relationship between the dependent variable and the group of predictor variables represented in the scatter plots.

b. Based on the correlation matrix developed from this data, comment on whether you think a multiple regression model will be effectively developed from these data.

c. Use the sample data to estimate a multiple regression model that contains all four independent variables.

d. What percentage of the total variation in the dependent variable is explained by the four independent variables in the model?

e. Test to determine whether the overall model is statistically significant. Use $\alpha = 0.05$.

f. Which, if any, of the independent variables is statistically significant? Use a significance level of $\alpha = 0.08$ and the *p*-value approach to conduct these tests.

g. Estimate the standard deviation of the model error and discuss whether this regression model is acceptable as a means of predicting the football attendance at State University at any given game.

h. Define the term *multicollinearity* and indicate the potential problems that multicollinearity can cause for this model. Indicate what, if any, evidence there is of multicollinearity problems with this regression model. Use the variance inflation factor to assist you in this analysis.

i. Develop a 95% confidence interval estimate for each of the regression coefficients and interpret each estimate. Comment on whether the interpretation of the intercept is relevant in this situation.

13-2 USING QUALITATIVE INDEPENDENT VARIABLES

In Example 13-1 involving the First City Real Estate Company, the independent variables were quantitative and ratio level. However, you will encounter many situations in which you may wish to use a qualitative, lower-level, variable as an explanatory variable.

If a variable is nominal, and numerical codes are assigned to the categories, you already know not to perform mathematical calculations using those data. The results would be meaningless. Yet, we may wish to use marital status, gender, or geographical location as an independent variable in a regression model. If the variable of interest is coded as an ordinal variable, such as education level or job performance ranking, computing means and variances is also inappropriate. Then how are these variables incorporated into a multiple regression analysis? The answer lies in using what are called **dummy** (or indicator) **variables**.

Dummy Variables

A variable that is assigned a value equal to either zero or one, depending on whether the observation possesses a given characteristic.

For instance, consider the variable gender, which can take on two possible values:

male or female

Gender can be converted to a dummy variable as follows:

$$x_1 = 1 \text{ if female}$$
$$x_1 = 0 \text{ if male}$$

Thus, a data set consisting of males and females will have corresponding values for x_1 equal to 0s and 1s, respectively. Note that it makes no difference which gender is coded 1 and which is coded 0.

If a categorical variable has more than two mutually exclusive outcome possibilities, multiple dummy variables must be created. Consider the variable, marital status, with the following possible outcomes:

never married   married   divorced   widowed

In this case, marital status has four values. To account for all the possibilities, you would create three dummy variables, one less than the number of possible outcomes for the original variable. They could be coded as follows.

$$x_1 = 1 \text{ if never married}, 0 \text{ if not}$$
$$x_2 = 1 \text{ if married}, 0 \text{ if not}$$
$$x_3 = 1 \text{ if divorced}, 0 \text{ if not}$$

Note that we don't need the fourth variable because we would know that a person is widowed if $x_1 = 0$, $x_2 = 0$, and $x_3 = 0$. If the person isn't single, married, or divorced, he or she must be widowed. *Always use one fewer dummy variables than categories.* The mathematical reason that the number of dummy variables must be one less than the number of possible responses is called the *dummy variable trap.* Perfect multicollinearity is introduced, and the least squares regression estimates cannot be obtained, if the number of dummy variables equals the number of possible categories.

EXAMPLE 13-2: INCORPORATING DUMMY VARIABLES

Business Executive Salaries   To illustrate the effect of incorporating dummy variables into a regression model, consider the sample data displayed in the scatter plot in Figure 13-9. The population from which the sample was selected consists of executives between the ages of 24 and 60 who are working in U.S. manufacturing businesses. Data for annual salary (y) and age (x_1) are available. The objective is to determine whether a model can be generated to explain the variation in annual salary for business executives. Even though age and annual salary are significantly correlated ($r = 0.686$) at the $\alpha = 0.05$ level, the coefficient of determination is only 47%. Therefore, we would likely search for other independent variables that could help us to further explain the variation in annual salary.

Suppose we can determine which of the 16 people in the sample had an MBA degree. Figure 13-10 shows the scatter plot for these same data, with the MBA data represented by triangles. To incorporate a qualitative variable into the analysis, use the following steps.

Step 1:   **Code the qualitative variable as a dummy variable.**
Create a new variable, x_2, which is a dummy variable coded as

$$x_2 = 1 \text{ if MBA, } 0 \text{ if not}$$

The data with the new variable are shown in Table 13-2.

Step 2:   **Develop a multiple regression model with the dummy variables incorporated as independent variables.**
The two-variable population multiple regression model has the following form:

$$y = \beta_0 + \beta_1 x_1 + \beta_2 x_2 + \varepsilon$$

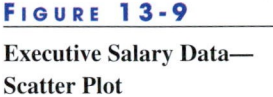

FIGURE 13-9

Executive Salary Data— Scatter Plot

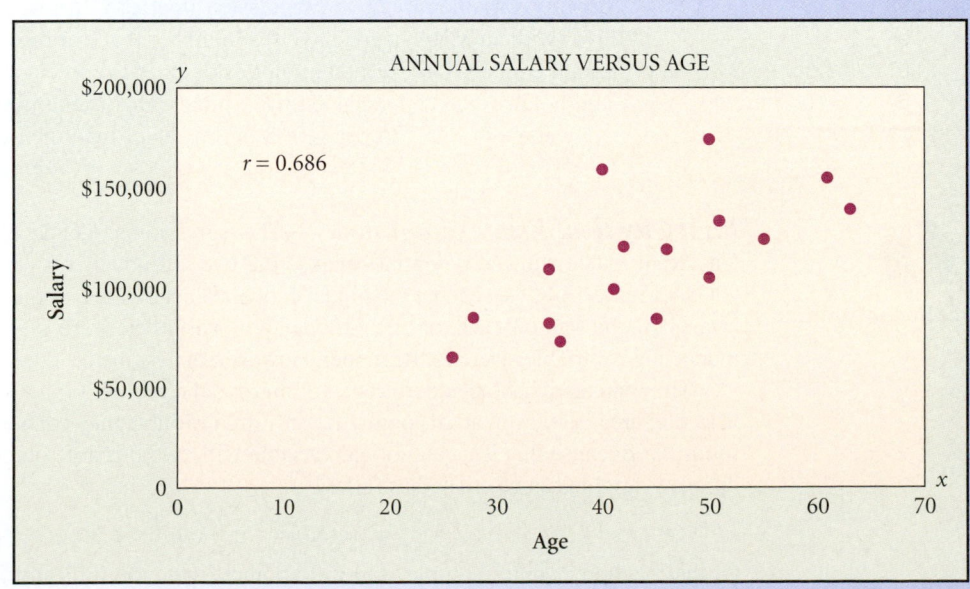

FIGURE 13-10

Impact of a Dummy
Variable

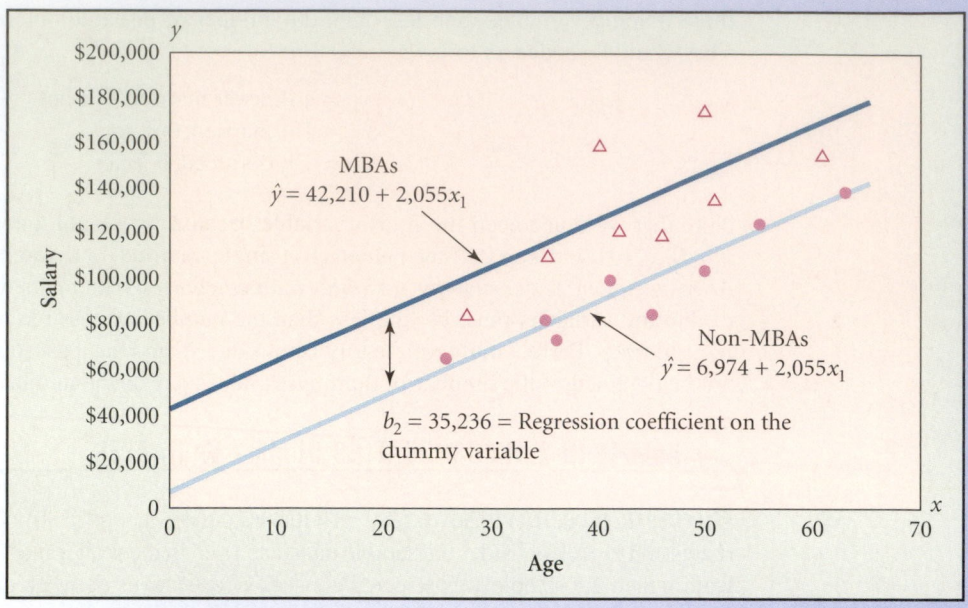

TABLE 13-2

Executive Salary Data
Including MBA Variable

SALARY	AGE	MBA
$ 65,000	26	0
85,000	28	1
74,000	36	0
83,000	35	0
110,000	35	1
160,000	40	1
100,000	41	0
122,000	42	1
85,000	45	0
120,000	46	1
105,000	50	0
135,000	51	1
125,000	55	0
175,000	50	1
156,000	61	1
140,000	63	0

Using either Excel or Minitab, we get the following regression equation as an estimate of the population model.

$$\hat{y} = 6{,}974 + 2{,}055x_1 + 35{,}236x_2$$

Because the dummy variable, x_2, has been coded 0 or 1 depending on degree status, incorporating it into the regression model is like having two simple linear regression lines with the same slopes, but different intercepts. For instance, when $x_2 = 0$, the regression equation is

$$\hat{y} = 6{,}974 + 2{,}055x_1 + 35{,}236(0)$$
$$= 6{,}974 + 2{,}055x_1$$

This line is shown in Figure 13-10.
However, when $x_2 = 1$ (the executive has an MBA), the regression equation is

$$\hat{y} = 6{,}974 + 2{,}055x_1 + 35{,}236(1)$$
$$= 42{,}210 + 2{,}055x_1$$

This regression line is also shown in Figure 13-10. As you can see, incorporating the dummy variable affects the regression intercept. In this case, the intercept for executives with an MBA degree is $35,236 higher than for those without an MBA. We interpret the regression coefficient on this dummy variable as follows: Based on these data, and holding age (x_1) constant, we estimate that executives with an MBA degree make an average of $35,236 per year more in salary than their non-MBA counterparts.

Excel and Minitab Tutorial

First City Real Estate (continued)—The regression model developed in Example 13-1 for First City Real Estate showed potential because the overall model was statistically significant. Looking back at Figure 13-8, we see that the model explained nearly 82% of the variation in sales prices for the homes in the sample. All of the independent variables were significant, given that the other independent variables were in the model. However, the estimate of the standard error was quite large.

The managers have decided to try to improve the model. First, they have decided to add a new variable: area. However, at this point, the only area variable they can get is whether the house is in the foothills. Because this is a categorical variable with two possible outcomes (foothills or flatland), a dummy variable can be created as follows:

$$x_6 \text{ (area)} = 1 \text{ if foothills, 0 if not}$$

Of the 319 homes in the sample, 249 were homes in the foothills and 70 were in the flatland. Figure 13-11 shows the revised Minitab multiple regression with the variable, area, added. This model is bet-

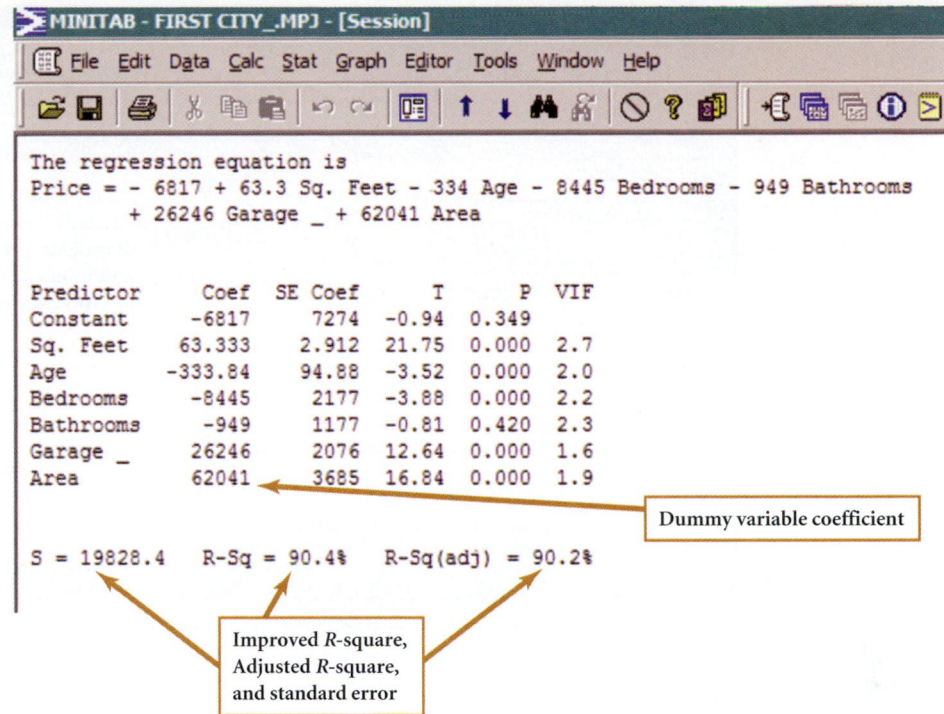

FIGURE 13-11

Minitab Output—First City
Real Estate Revised
Regression Model

Minitab Instructions:
1. Open file: First
   City.MTW.
2. Choose **Stat >
   Regression > Regression.**
3. In **Response**, enter
   dependent (*y*) variable.
4. In **Predictors**, enter
   independent (*x*)
   variables.
5. Click **Options.**
6. In **Display**, select
   **Variance inflation
   factors.**
7. Click **OK. OK.**

```
The regression equation is
Price = - 6817 + 63.3 Sq. Feet - 334 Age - 8445 Bedrooms - 949 Bathrooms
            + 26246 Garage _ + 62041 Area


Predictor       Coef  SE Coef      T      P   VIF
Constant       -6817     7274  -0.94  0.349
Sq. Feet      63.333    2.912  21.75  0.000   2.7
Age          -333.84    94.88  -3.52  0.000   2.0
Bedrooms       -8445     2177  -3.88  0.000   2.2
Bathrooms       -949     1177  -0.81  0.420   2.3
Garage _       26246     2076  12.64  0.000   1.6
Area           62041     3685  16.84  0.000   1.9



S = 19828.4    R-Sq = 90.4%    R-Sq(adj) = 90.2%
```

Dummy variable coefficient

Improved *R*-square,
Adjusted *R*-square,
and standard error

ter than the original model because the adjusted R-squared has increased from 0.813 to 0.904, and the estimate of the standard error of the estimate has decreased from \$27,350 to \$19,828. The conditional t-tests show that all of the regression model's slope coefficients, except that for the variable bathrooms, differ significantly from 0. Because the variance inflation factors are all less than 5.0, we don't need to be too concerned about the t-tests understating the significance of the regression coefficients. (See the Excel Tutorial on the CD-ROM for this example to get the full *VIF* output from PHStat.)

The resulting regression model is

$$\hat{y} = -6{,}817 + 63.333(\text{sq. feet}) - 333.84(\text{age}) - 8{,}445(\text{bedrooms}) - 949(\text{bathrooms})$$
$$+ 26{,}246(\text{garages}) + 62{,}041(\text{area})$$

Because the variable, bathrooms, is not significant in the presence of the other variables, we can remove the variable and rerun the multiple regression. The resulting model is

$$\text{Price} = -7{,}050 + 62.5(\text{sq. feet}) - 322(\text{age}) - 8{,}830(\text{bedrooms}) + 26{,}054(\text{garage})$$
$$+ 61{,}370(\text{area})$$

Based on the sample data and this regression model, we estimate that a house with the same characteristics (square feet, age, bedrooms, and garages) is worth an average of \$61,370 more if it is located in the foothills (based on how the dummy variable was coded).

There are still signals of multicollinearity problems. The coefficient on the independent variable, bedrooms, is negative, when we would expect homes with more bedrooms to sell for more. Also, the estimate of the standard error of the estimate is still too large (\$19,817) to provide the precision the managers need to set prices for homes. More work needs to be done before the model is complete.

Possible Improvements to the First City Appraisal Model

Because the standard error of the estimate is still too high, we look to improve the model. We could start by identifying possible problems:

1. Useful independent variables may have been omitted.
2. Independent variables may have been included that should not have been included.

There is no sure way of determining the correct model specification. However, a recommended approach is for the decision maker to try adding variables or removing variables from the model.

We begin by removing the bedrooms variable, which has the incorrect sign on the regression slope coefficient. (Note: If the regression model's sole purpose is for prediction, independent variables with unexpected signs do not automatically pose a problem and do not necessarily need to be

FIGURE 13-12A

Excel Output for the First City Real Estate Revised Model

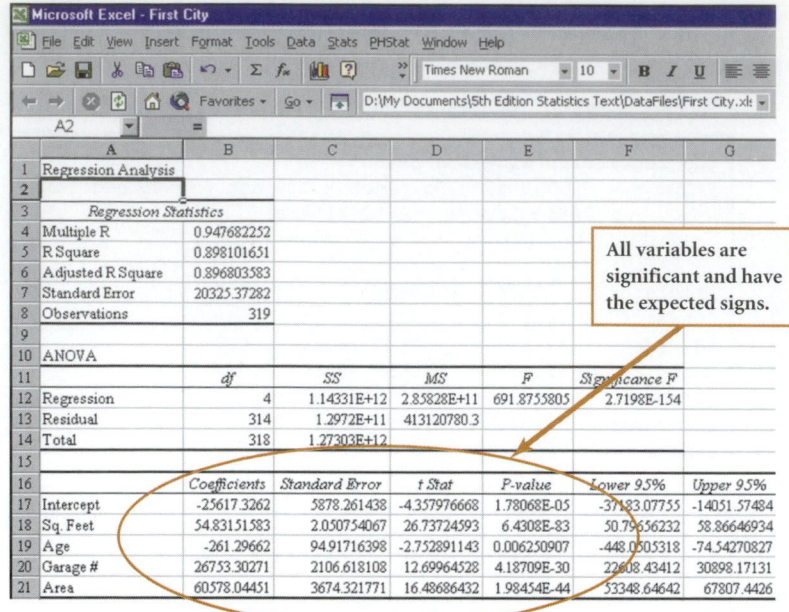

deleted. However, insignificant variables should be deleted.) The resulting model is shown in Figures 13-12a and 13-12b. Now all the variables in the model have the expected signs. However, the estimate of the model's standard error has increased slightly.

Adding other explanatory variables might help. For instance, consider whether the house has central air conditioning, which might affect sales. If we can identify whether a house has air conditioning, we could add a dummy variable coded as follows:

$$\text{If air conditioning, } x_7 = 1$$
$$\text{If no air conditioning, } x_7 = 0$$

Other potential independent variables might include a more-detailed location variable, a measure of the physical condition, or whether the house has one or two stories. Can you think of others?

The First City example illustrates that even though a regression model may pass the statistical tests of significance, it may not be functional. Good appraisal models can be developed using multi-

FIGURE 13-12B

Minitab Output for the First City Real Estate Revised Model

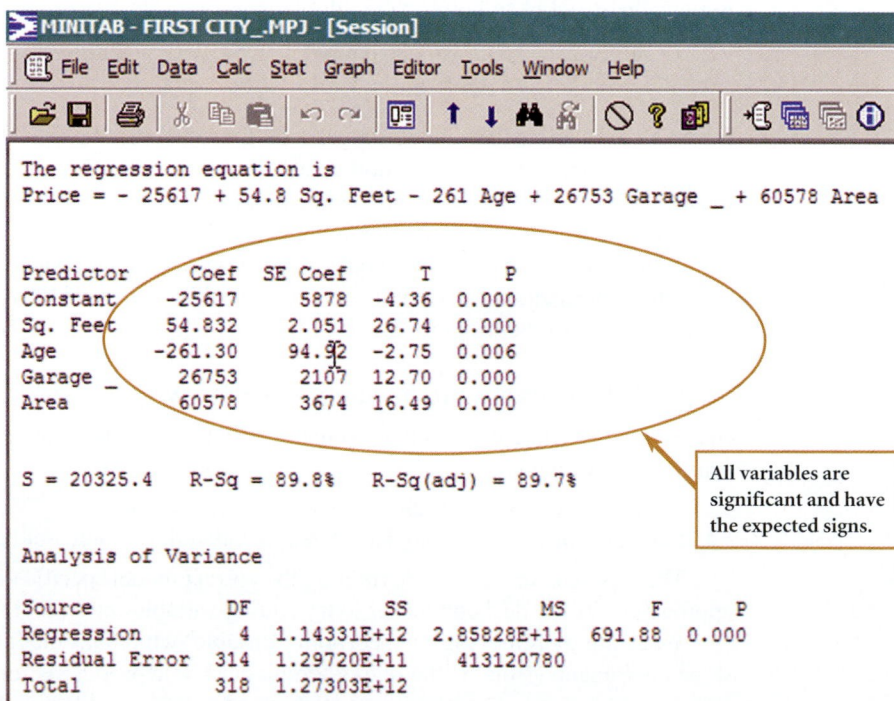

ple regression analysis, provided more detail is available about such characteristics as finish quality, landscaping, location, neighborhood characteristics, and so forth. The cost and effort required to obtain these data can be relatively high.

Developing a multiple regression model is more of an art than a science. The real decisions revolve around how to select the best set of independent variables for the model.

13-2: EXERCISES

Skill Development

13.10 You are considering developing a regression equation relating a dependent variable to two independent variables. One of the variables can be measured on a ratio scale, but the other is a categorical variable with two possible levels.
   a. Write a multiple regression model relating the dependent variable to the independent variables.
   b. Interpret the meaning of the coefficients in the regression model.

13.11 You are considering developing a regression model relating a dependent variable to two independent variables. One of the variables can be measured on a ratio scale, but the other is a categorical variable with four possible levels.
   a. How many dummy variables are needed to represent the categorical variable?
   b. Write a multiple regression model relating the dependent variable to the independent variables.
   c. Interpret the meaning of the coefficients in the regression model.

13.12 A manager is considering incorporating a new variable into her regression model. This variable measures educational level of the respondent. The variable has been measured on four levels, as follows:
   1. No high school degree
   2. High school degree
   3. Some college courses
   4. College degree
   a. She is considering this variable and plans to use the codes 1, 2, 3, and 4 to determine which educational level the respondent has achieved. Comment on this.
   b. How many dummy variables would you set up to handle this situation? Specify the values each dummy variable could assume and what each value would represent.

Business Applications

13.13 The Polk Utility Corporation is developing a multiple regression model that it plans to use to predict customers' utility usage. The analyst currently has three quantitative variables (x_1, x_2, and x_3) in the model, but she is dissatisfied with the R-squared and the estimate of the standard deviation of the model's error. Two variables that she thinks might be useful are whether a house has a gas or an electric water heater and whether a house was constructed before or after the 1974 energy crisis.

Provide the model she should use to predict customers' utility usage. Specify the dummy variables to

be used, the values these variables can assume, and what each value will represent.

13.14 A study was recently performed by the American Automobile Association in which it attempted to develop a regression model to explain variation in EPA mileage ratings of new cars. At one stage of the analysis, the estimate of the model took the following form:

$$\hat{y} = 34.20 - 0.003x_1 + 4.56x_2$$

where:

$$x_1 = \text{Vehicle weight}$$
$$x_2 = 1 \text{ if standard transmission}$$
$$= 0 \text{ if automatic transmission}$$

   a. Interpret the regression coefficient for variable x_1.
   b. Interpret the regression coefficient for variable x_2.
   c. Present an estimate of a model that would predict the average EPA mileage rating for an automobile with standard transmission as a function of the vehicle's weight.
   d. Cadillac's 1999 Sedan Deville with automatic transmission weighs approximately 4,012 pounds. Provide an estimate of the average highway mileage you would expect to obtain from this model.
   e. Discuss the effect of a dummy variable being incorporated into a regression equation like this one. Use a graph if it is helpful.

13.15 A recent study by the U.S. Department of Agriculture attempted to develop a multiple regression model to explain variation in farm income. At one stage of development, the estimate of the model took the following form:

$$\hat{y} = -23,200 + 4.2x_1 + 2,345x_2 + 4,670x_3$$

where:

$$x_1 = \text{Number of acres farmed}$$
$$x_2 = 1 \text{ if land is row-irrigated}$$
$$= 0 \text{ if not}$$
$$x_3 = 1 \text{ if land is sprinkler-irrigated}$$
$$= 0 \text{ if not}$$

   a. Interpret the regression coefficient for variable x_1.
   b. Interpret the regression coefficient for variable x_2.
   c. Interpret the regression coefficient for variable x_3.
   d. Present a model that would predict the average farm income for a 1,000-acre farm that irrigated using sprinklers.

Advanced Applications

13.16 Gilmore Accounting collected the data here in an effort to explain variation in client profitability. The data also are in the CD-ROM file *Gilmore*.

y	x_1	x_2
2,345	45	1
4,200	56	2
278	26	3
1,211	56	2
1,406	24	2
500	23	3
−700	34	3
3,457	45	1
2,478	47	1
1,975	24	2
206	32	3

where:

y = Net profit earned from the client
x_1 = Number of hours spent working with the client
x_2 = Type of client:
    1 if manufacturing
    2 if service
    3 if governmental

a. Develop a scatter plot of each independent variable against the client-income variable. Comment on what, if any, relationship appears to exist in each case.
b. Run a simple linear regression analysis using only variable x_1 as the independent variable. Describe the resulting estimate fully.
c. Test to determine if the number of hours spent working with a client is useful in predicting the net profit earned by that client.

13.17 Use the data from Gilmore Accounting found in the CD-ROM file *Gilmore*. (See Exercise 13.16.)
a. Incorporate the client type into the regression analysis using dummy variables. Describe the resulting multiple regression estimate.
b. Test to determine if this model is useful in predicting the net profit earned by a client.
c. Test to determine if the number of hours spent working with a client is useful in this model in predicting the net profit earned by that client.
d. Considering the tests you have performed, construct a model and its estimate for predicting the net profit earned by a client.
e. Predict the average difference in profit if a client is governmental versus manufacturing. Also state this in terms of a 95% confidence interval estimate. (Refer to Chapter 12 if needed.)

13.18 One of the editors of a major automobile publication has collected data on 30 of the best-selling cars in the United States. The data are in the CD-ROM file *Automobiles*. The editor is particularly interested in the relationship between price of a vehicle and the horsepower of the engine. She thinks another variable that might have an impact on price would be the type of vehicle.
a. Specify a model that characterizes the relationship between vehicle price, horsepower, and vehicle type. Specify the dummy variables to be used, the values these variables can assume, and what each value will represent. Note that there are three types of vehicles.
b. Produce an estimate of the model presented in part a.
c. Which of the independent variables from part b are significant? Is the overall model significant?

13-3 WORKING WITH NONLINEAR RELATIONSHIPS

Section 12-1 in Chapter 12 showed there are a variety of ways in which two variables can be related. Correlation and regression analysis techniques are tools for measuring and modeling linear relationships between variables. Many situations in business have a linear relationship between two variables, and regression equations that model that relationship will be appropriate to use in these situations. However, there are also many instances in which the relationship between two variables will be curvilinear, rather than linear. For instance, demand for electricity has grown at an almost exponential rate relative to the population growth in some areas. Advertisers believe that a diminishing-returns relationship will occur between sales and advertising if advertising is allowed to grow too large. These two situations are shown in Figures 13-13 and 13-14, respectively. They represent just two of the great many possible curvilinear relationships that could exist between two variables.

As you will soon see, models with nonlinear relationships become more complicated than models showing only linear relationships. Although complicated models are sometimes necessary, decision makers should use them with caution for several reasons. First, management researchers and authors have written that people use decision aids they understand and don't use those they don't understand. So, the more complicated a model is, the less likely it is to be used. Second, the scientific principle of parsimony suggests using the simplest model possible that provides a reasonable fit of the data, because complex models typically do not reflect the underlying phenomena that produce the data in the first place.

FIGURE 13-13

Exponential Relationship of
Increased Demand for
Electricity versus
Population Growth

FIGURE **13-13**

Exponential Relationship of
Increased Demand for
Electricity versus
Population Growth

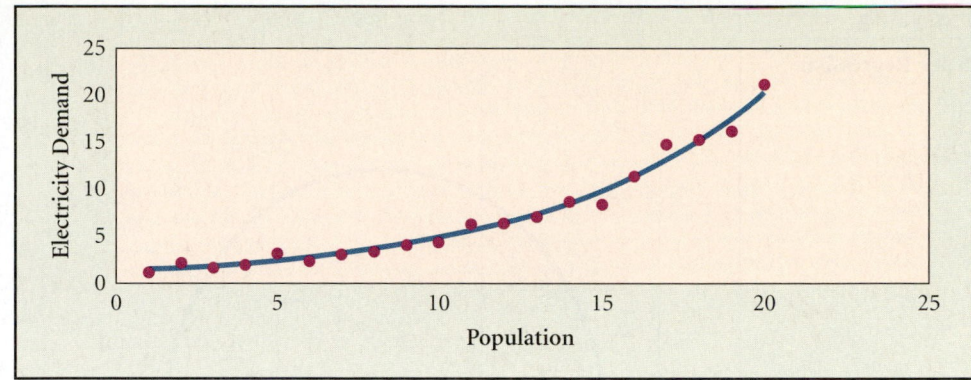

This section provides a brief introduction into how linear regression analysis can be used in dealing with curvilinear relationships. In order to model such curvilinear relationships, we must incorporate terms into the multiple regression model that will create "curves" in the model we are building. Including terms whose independent variable has an exponent larger than one generates these curves. When a model possesses such terms we refer to it as a **polynomial model**. The general equation for a polynomial with one independent variable is given in Equation 13-13.

Polynomial Population Regression Model

$$y = \beta_0 + \beta_1 x + \beta_2 x^2 + \ldots + \beta_p x^p + \varepsilon$$
                                                                        13-13

where:

β_0 = Population's regression constant

β_j = Population's regression coefficient for variable x^j; $j = 1, 2, \ldots p$

p = Order (or degree) of the polynomial

ε = Model error

The order, or degree, of the model is determined by the largest exponent of the independent variable in the model. For instance, the model

$$y = \beta_0 + \beta_1 x + \beta_2 x^2 + \varepsilon$$

is a second-order polynomial because the largest exponent in any term of the polynomial is two. You will note that this model contains terms of all orders less than or equal to two. A polynomial with this property is said to be a *complete* polynomial. Therefore, the previous model would be referred to as a complete *second-order regression model*.

A second-order model produces a parabola. The parabola either opens upward ($\beta_2 > 0$) or downward ($\beta_2 < 0$), shown in Figure 13-15. You will notice that the models in Figures 13-13 and 13-14 both possess a single curve.

As more curves appear in the data, the order of the polynomial must be increased. A general (complete) third-order polynomial is given by the equation

$$y = \beta_0 + \beta_1 x + \beta_2 x^2 + \beta_3 x^3 + \varepsilon$$

FIGURE **13-14**

Diminishing Returns
Relationship of Advertising
versus Sales

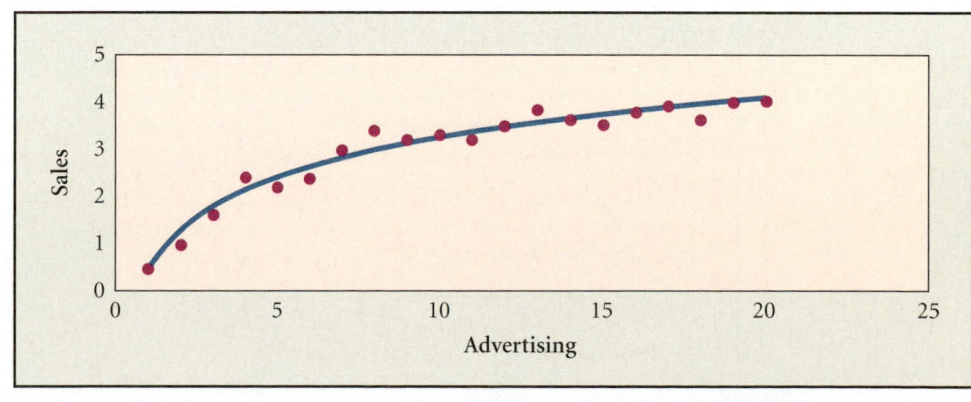

FIGURE **13-15**

Second-Order Regression
Models

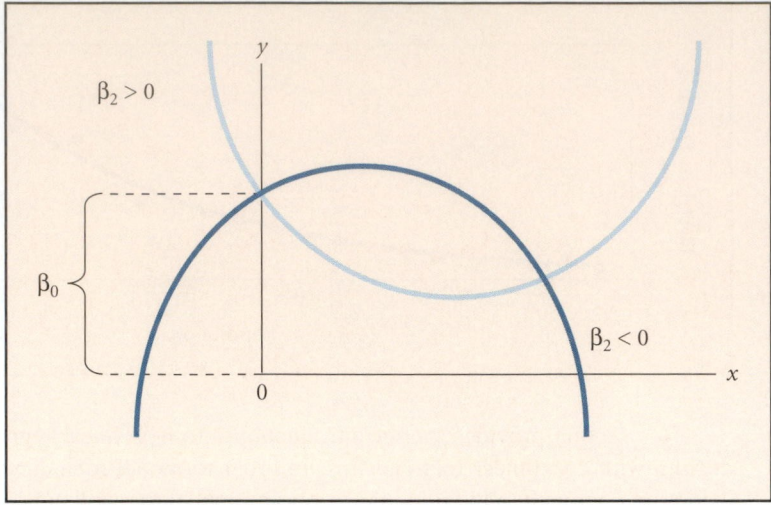

This model produces a curvilinear model that reverses the direction of the initial curve to produce a second curve, as shown in Figure 13-16. Note that there are two curves in the third-order model. In general a *p*th-order polynomial will exhibit $p - 1$ curves.

Our discussion of polynomials has, thus far, concerned only models with one independent variable raised to a power. When more than one independent variable is involved, the same terminology is used. However, we must use the sum of the exponents of the independent variables in any one term to determine the order of that term. As an example, a term of the form $\beta_i x_1^2 x_2^3$ would be a fifth-order term, because the sum of the independent variables' exponents $(2 + 3)$ equals 5. Using similar logic, the term *complete pth-order polynomial* implies that the polynomial contains all those terms of order p and all orders smaller than p as well. Therefore, the model

$$y = \beta_0 + \beta_1 x_1 + \beta_2 x_2 + \beta_3 x_1^2 + \beta_4 x_2^2 + \beta_5 x_1 x_2 + \varepsilon$$

is a complete second-order model involving the independent variables x_1 and x_2. The model

$$y = \beta_0 + \beta_1 x_1 + \beta_2 x_2 + \beta_3 x_1^2 + \beta_4 x_2^2 + \varepsilon$$

is a second-order model. However, it is not a complete second-order model because it does not contain the term $\beta_5 x_1 x_2$, whose exponents of the independent variables sum to two.

Although polynomials of all orders exist in the business sector, perhaps second-order polynomials are the most common. Sharp reversals in the curvature of a relationship between variables in the business environment usually point to some unexpected or, perhaps, severe changes that were not foreseen. The vast majority of organizations try to avoid such reverses. For this reason, and the fact that this is an introductory business statistics course, we will direct most of our attention to second-order polynomials.

FIGURE **13-16**

**Third-Order Regression
Models**

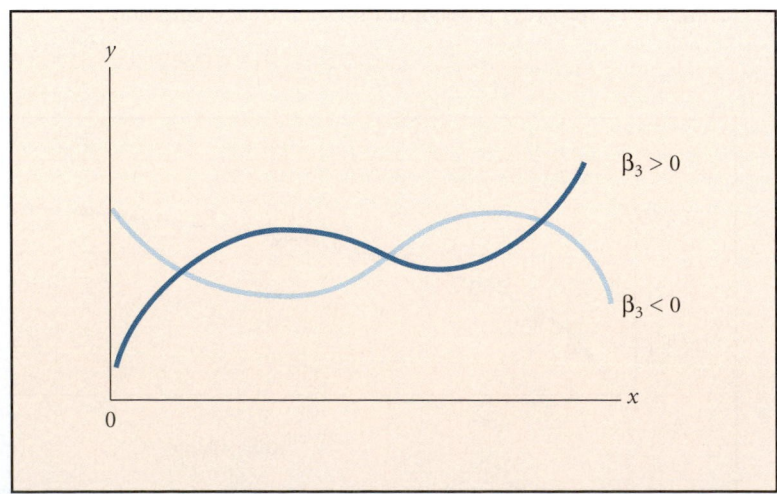

The following examples illustrate two of the most common instances in which curvilinear relationships can be used in decision making. They should give you an idea of how to approach similar situations.

EXAMPLE 13-3: MODELING CURVILINEAR RELATIONSHIPS

Excel and Minitab Tutorial

Ashley Investment Services   Ashley Investment Services has been severely shaken by a recent downturn in the stock market. To maintain profitability and save as many jobs as possible, everyone has been busy analyzing new investment opportunities. The director of personnel has noticed an increased number of people suffering from "burnout," in which physical and emotional fatigue hurt job performance. Although he cannot change the job's pressures, he has read that the more time a person spends socializing with coworkers away from the job, the more likely a higher degree of burnout. With the help of the human resources lab at the local university, the personnel director has administered a questionnaire to company employees. A burnout index has been computed from the responses to the survey. Likewise, the survey responses are used to determine quantitative measures of socialization. Sample data from questionnaires are contained in the file *Ashley* on the CD-ROM. The following steps can be used to model the relationship between the socialization index and the burnout index for Ashley employees:

Step 1:   **Specify the model by determining the dependent and potential independent variables.**
The dependent variable is the burnout index. The company wishes to explain the variation in burnout level. One potential independent variable is the socialization index.

Step 2:   **Formulate the model.**
We begin by proposing that a linear relationship exists between the two variables. Figures 13-17a and 13-17b show the linear regression analysis results using Excel and Minitab. The correlation between the two variables is $r = 0.818$, which is statistically different from zero at any reasonable significance level. The estimate of the population linear regression model shown in Figure 13-17a is

$$\hat{y} = -66.164 + 9.5889x$$

Step 3:   **Perform diagnostic checks on the model.**
The sample data and the regression line are plotted in Figure 13-18. The line appears to fit the data. However, a closer inspection reveals instances where several consecutive points lie above or below the line. The points are not randomly dispersed around the regression line, as we would expect given the regression analysis assumptions. (In Chapter 12 we briefly discussed the concept of residual analysis. Section 13-5 expands the residual analysis discussion.)

FIGURE 13-17A

Excel Output of a Simple Linear Regression for Ashley Investment Services

Excel Instructions:
1. Open file: Ashley.xls
2. Select **Tools**.
3. Click on **Data Analysis**.
4. Select **Regression**.
5. Define *y* and *x* variable range.
6. Specify output location.
7. Click **OK**.

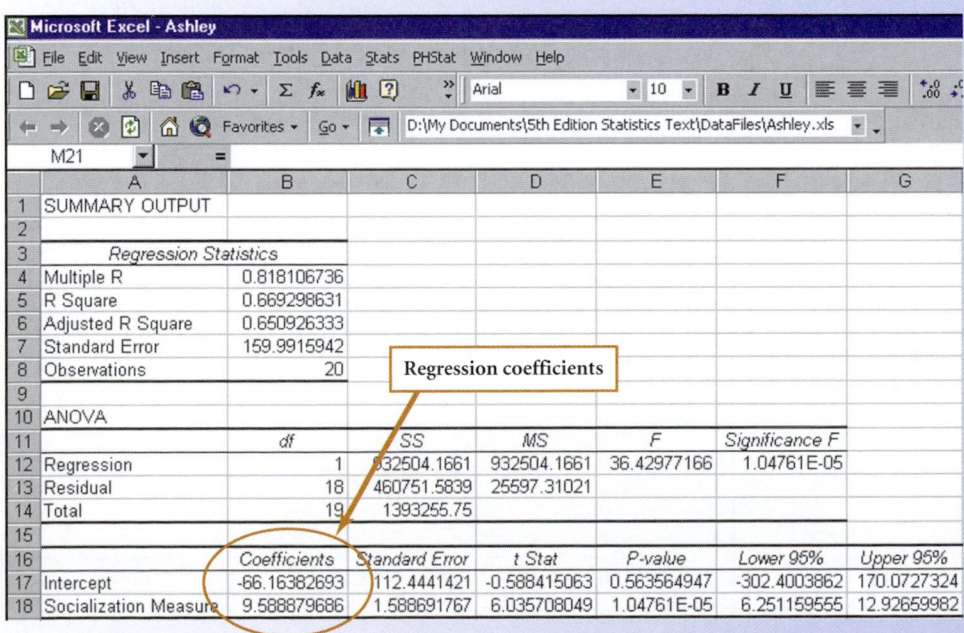

FIGURE **13-17B**

Minitab Output of a Simple Linear Regression for Ashley Investment Services

Minitab Instructions:
1. Open file: Ashley.MTW.
2. Choose **Stat > Regression > Regression**.
3. In **Response**, enter the *y* variable column.
4. In **Predictors**, enter the *x* variable column.
5. Click **OK**.

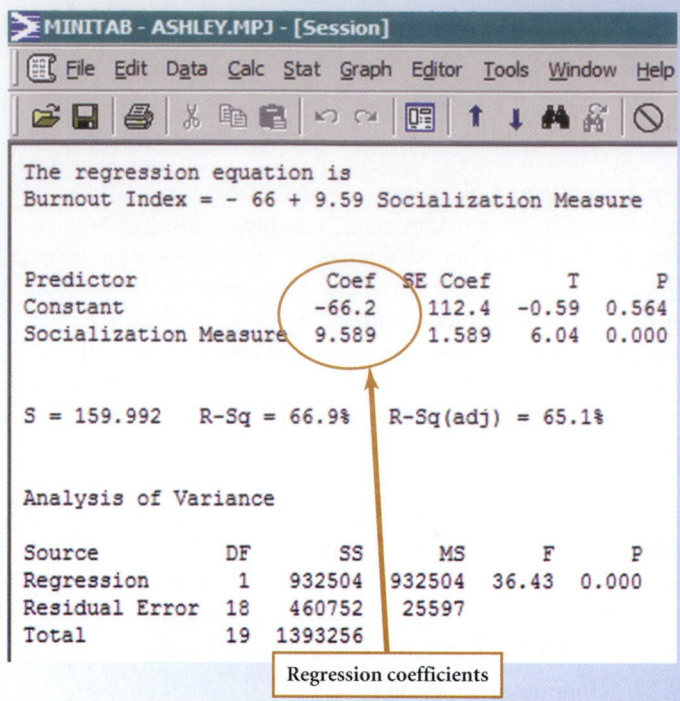

As you will recall from earlier discussions, we can use analysis of variance to test whether a regression line explains a significant amount of variation in the dependent variable.

$$H_0{:}\beta_1 = 0$$
$$H_A{:}\beta_1 \neq 0$$

From the output in Figure 13-17a,

$$F = 36.43$$

which has a *p*-value < 0.0001.

Thus, we conclude that the simple linear model is statistically significant. However, we should also examine the data to determine if any curvilinear relationships may be present.

Step 4: **Model the curvilinear relationship.**

Finding instances of nonrandom patterns in the residuals for a regression model indicates the possibility of using a curvilinear relationship rather than a linear one. One

FIGURE **13-18**

Plot of Regression Line for the Ashley Investment Services Example

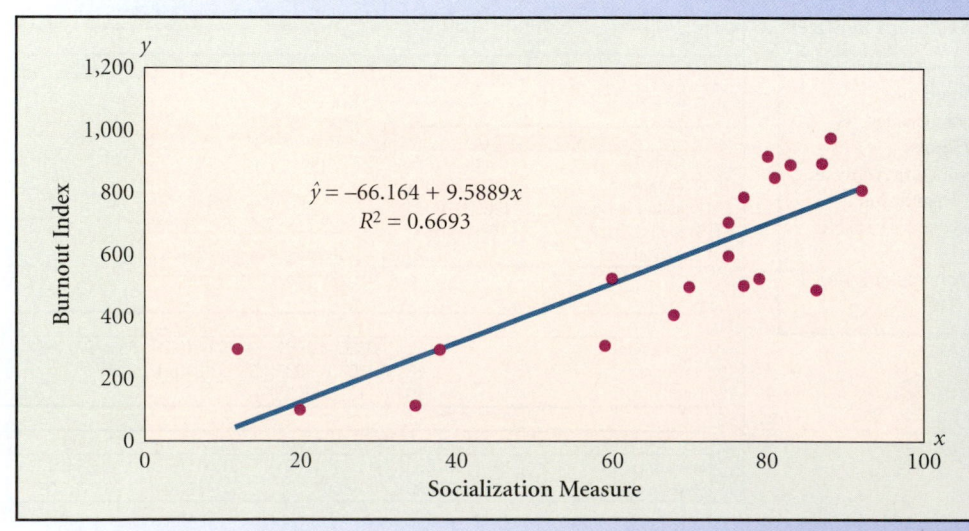

FIGURE 13-19A

Excel Output of a Second-Order Polynomial Fit for Ashley Investment

Excel Instructions:
1. Open file: Ashley.xls
2. Click on **Tools**.
3. Select **Data Analysis**.
4. Select **Regression**.
5. Define y and x variable ranges.
6. Click **OK**.

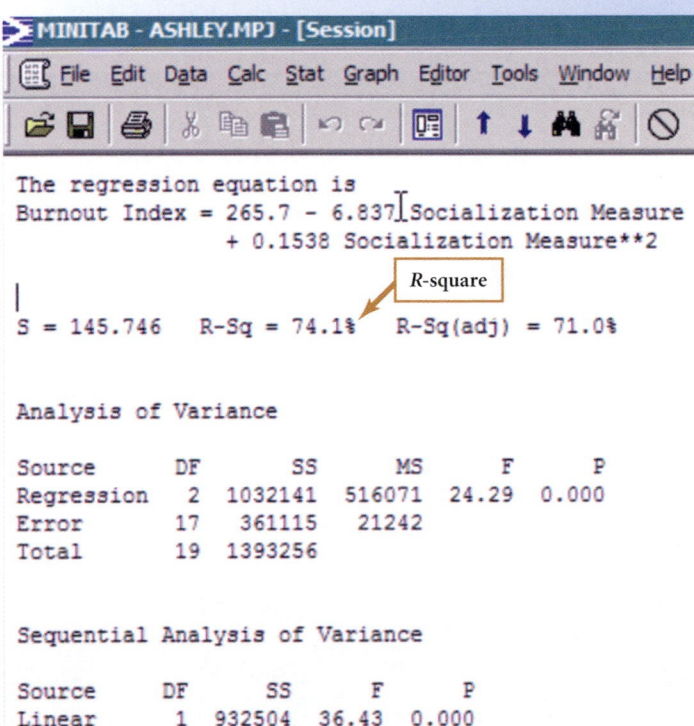

possible approach to modeling the curvilinear nature of the data in the Ashley Investments example is with the use of polynomials. From Figure 13-18, we can see that there is one curve in the data. This suggests fitting the second-order polynomial

$$y = \beta_0 + \beta_1 x + \beta_2 x^2 + \varepsilon$$

Before fitting the estimate for this population model, you will need to create the new independent variable by squaring the socialization measure variable. In Excel, use the formula option, or in Minitab, use the **Calc > Calculator** command to create the new variable. Figures 13-19a and 13-19b show the output after fitting this second-order polynomial model.

Step 5:   Perform diagnostics on the revised curvilinear model.

Notice the second-order polynomial provides a model whose estimated regression equation has an R^2 of 0.741. This is higher than the R^2 of 0.6693 for the linear model. Figure

FIGURE 13-19B

Minitab Output of a Second-Order Polynomial Fit for Ashley Investment

Minitab Instructions:
1. Open file: Ashley.MTW.
2. Choose **Stat > Regression > Fitted Line Plot**.
3. In **Response**, enter y variable.
4. In **Predictor**, enter x variable.
5. Under **Type of Regression Model**, choose **Quadratic**.
6. Click **OK**.

13-20 shows the plot of the second-order polynomial model. Comparing Figure 13-20 with Figure 13-18, we can see that the polynomial model does appear to fit the sample data better than the linear model.

FIGURE 13-20

Plot of Second-Order Polynomial Model—Ashley Investment Example

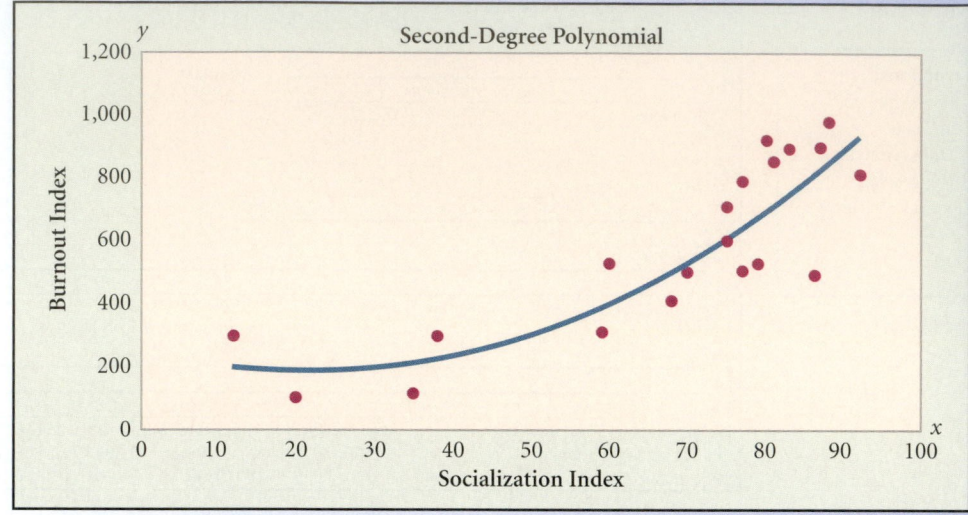

ANALYZING INTERACTION EFFECTS

Excel and Minitab Tutorial

Ashley Investment Services (continued)—Referring again to Example 13-3 involving Ashley Investment Services, the director of personnel wondered if the effects of burnout differ among male and female workers. He therefore identified the gender of the previously surveyed employees (see the CD-ROM file *Ashley-2*). A multiple scatter plot of the data appears as Figure 13-21.

The personnel director tried to visualize the relationship between the burnout index and socialization measure for men and women. The sketches of the result are presented in Figure 13-21. Note that both relationships appear to be curvilinear with a similarly shaped curve. As we showed earlier, curvilinear shapes often can be modeled by the second-order polynomial

$$\hat{y} = b_0 + b_1 x_1 + b_2 x_1^2$$

FIGURE 13-21

Excel Multiple Scatter Plot for Ashley Investment Services

Excel Instructions:
1. Open file: Ashley-2.mtw
2. Click on **Chart Wizard**.
3. Select **Scatter Plot**.
4. Use **Series** Tab.
5. Identify the *y* Variable Range for males.
6. Identify the *x* Variable Range for males.
7. Repeat steps 5 and 6 for females.
8. Right click on each series and select **Add Trend Lines**, exponential option.

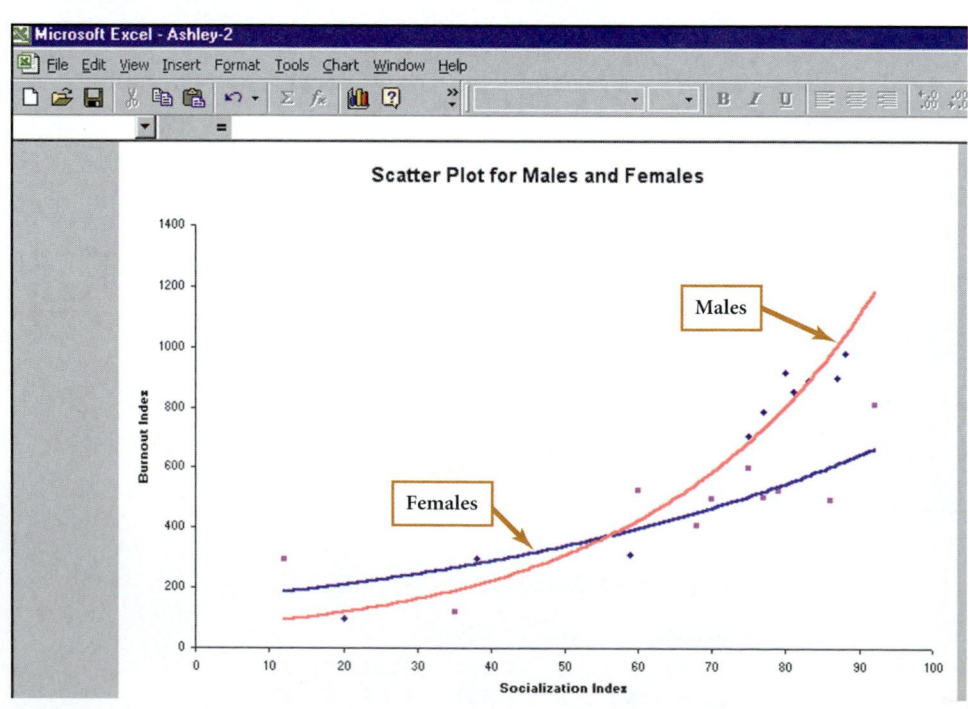

However, the regression equations that estimate this second-order polynomial for men and women are not the same. The two equations seem to have different locations and different rates of curvature. Whether an employee is a man or woman seems to change the basic relationship between burnout index (y) and socialization measure (x_1). In order to represent this difference, the equation's coefficients b_0, b_1, and b_2 must be different for men and women employees. Thus, we could use two models, one for each gender. Alternatively, we could use one model for both males and females by incorporating a dummy independent variable with two levels, which is shown as:

$$x_2 = 1 \text{ if a male, } 0 \text{ if a female}$$

As x_2 changes values from 0 to 1, it affects the values of the coefficients b_0, b_1, and b_2. When the director fitted the second-order model for the female employees only, he obtained the following regression equation:

$$\hat{y} = 291.70 - 4.62x_1 + 0.102x_1^2$$

The equation for the male employees only was

$$\hat{y} = 149.59 - 4.40x_1 + 0.160x_1^2$$

To explain how a change in gender can cause this kind of change, we must introduce the concept of **interaction**.

Interaction

The case in which one independent variable (such as x_2) affects the relationship between another independent variable (x_1) and a dependent variable (y).

Therefore, in our example, gender (x_2) interacts with the relationship between socialization measure (x_1) and burnout index (y). The question is how do we obtain the interaction terms to model such a relationship? To answer this question, we first obtain the model for the basic relationship between the x_1 and the y variables. The population model is

$$y = \beta_0 + \beta_1 x_1 + \beta_2 x_1^2 + \varepsilon$$

To obtain the interaction terms, multiply the terms on the right-hand side of this equation by the variable that is interacting with this relationship between y and x_1. In this case, that interacting variable is x_2. Then the interaction terms would be

$$\beta_3 x_2 + \beta_4 x_1 x_2 + \beta_5 x_1^2 x_2$$

Notice that we have changed the coefficient subscripts so we do not duplicate those in the original model. Then the interaction terms are added to the original model to produce the **composite model**.

$$y = \beta_0 + \beta_1 x_1 + \beta_2 x_1^2 + \beta_3 x_2 + \beta_4 x_1 x_2 + \beta_5 x_1^2 x_2 + \varepsilon$$

Composite Model

The model that contains both the basic terms and the interaction terms.

Note, the model for women is obtained by substituting $x_2 = 0$ into the composite model. This gives:

$$y = \beta_0 + \beta_1 x_1 + \beta_2 x_1^2 + \beta_3(0) + \beta_4 x_1(0) + \beta_5 x_1^2(0) + \varepsilon$$
$$= \beta_0 + \beta_1 x_1 + \beta_2 x_1^2 + \varepsilon$$

Similarly, for men we substitute the value of $x_2 = 1$. The model then becomes

$$y = \beta_0 + \beta_1 x_1 + \beta_2 x_1^2 + \beta_3(1) + \beta_4 x_1(1) + \beta_5 x_1^2(1) + \varepsilon$$
$$= (\beta_0 + \beta_3) + (\beta_1 + \beta_4)x_1 + (\beta_2 + \beta_5)x_1^2 + \varepsilon$$

This illustrates how the coefficients are changed for different values of x_2, and, therefore, how x_2 is interacting with the relationship between x_1 and y. Once we know β_3, β_4, and β_5, we know the effect of the interaction of gender on the original relationship between the burnout index (y) and the socialization measure (x_1). In order to estimate the composite model, we need to create the required variables, as shown in Figure 13-22. Figures 13-23a and 13-23b show the regression for the composite model. The estimate for the composite model is

$$\hat{y} = 291.706 - 4.615x_1 + 0.102x_1^2 - 142.113x_2 + 0.215x_1 x_2 + 0.058x_1^2 x_2$$

We obtain the model for females by substituting $x_2 = 0$, giving

$$\hat{y} = 291.706 - 4.615x_1 + 0.102x_1^2 - 142.113(0) + 0.215x_1(0) + 0.058x_1^2(0)$$
$$\hat{y} = 291.706 - 4.615x_1 + 0.102x_1^2$$

For males, we substitute $x_2 = 1$, giving

$$\hat{y} = 291.706 - 4.615x_1 + 0.102x_1^2 - 142.113(1) + 0.215x_1(1) + 0.058x_1^2(1)$$
$$\hat{y} = 149.593 - 4.40x_1 + 0.160x_1^2$$

Note that these equations for males and females are the same as what we found earlier when we generated two separate regression models, one for each gender.

In this example we have looked at a case in which a dummy variable interacts with the relationship between another independent variable and the dependent variable. However, the interact-

FIGURE 13-22

Data Preparation for Estimating Interactive Effects for Second-Order Model for Ashley Investment

Excel Instructions:
1. Open file: Ashley-2.xls
2. Use Excel formulas to create new variables.

Minitab Instructions (for similar results):
1. Open file: Ashley-2.MTW.
2. Use Minitab **Calc** menu to create new variables.

Microsoft Excel - Ashley-2

File Edit View Insert Format Tools Data Stats PHStat Window Help

G22

	A	B	C	D	E	F
	Burnout Index	Socialization Measure	Socialization Squared	Gender		
1	y	x_1	x_1^2	x_2	$x_1 x_2$	$x_1^2 x_2$
2	100	20	400	1	20	400
3	980	88	7744	1	88	7744
4	310	59	3481	1	59	3481
5	900	87	7569	1	87	7569
6	920	80	6400	1	80	6400
7	892	83	6889	1	83	6889
8	855	81	6561	1	81	6561
9	709	75	5625	1	75	5625
10	791	77	5929	1	77	5929
11	300	38	1444	1	38	1444
12	810	92	8464	0	0	0
13	120	35	1225	0	0	0
14	525	60	3600	0	0	0
15	410	68	4624	0	0	0
16	296	12	144	0	0	0
17	501	70	4900	0	0	0
18	506	77	5929	0	0	0
19	493	86	7396	0	0	0
20	527	79	6241	0	0	0
21	600	75	5625	0	0	0

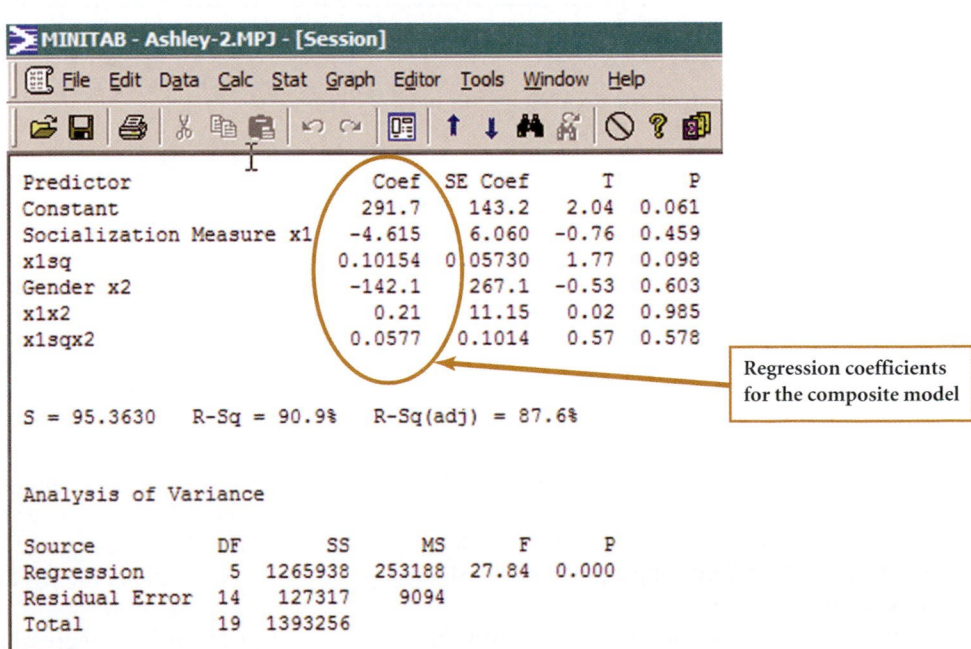

FIGURE 13-23A

Excel Composite Model for Ashley Investment Services

Excel Instructions:
1. Continue from previous figure.
2. Click on **Tools**.
3. Select **Data Analysis**.
4. Select **Regression**.
5. Define *y* and *x* variable ranges.
6. Click **OK**.

ing variable need not be a dummy variable. It can be any independent variable. Also, strictly speaking, interaction is not said to exist if the only effect of the interaction variable is to change the *y*-intercept of the equation relating another independent variable to the dependent variable. Therefore, when you search a scatter plot to detect interaction, you are trying to determine if the relationships produced, when the interaction variable changes values, are parallel or not. If the relationships are parallel, that indicates that only the *y*-intercept is being affected by the change of the interacting variable and that interaction does not exist. Figure 13-24 demonstrates this concept graphically.

FIGURE 13-23B

Minitab Composite Model for Ashley Investments

Minitab Instructions:
1. Continue from previous figure.
2. Choose **Stat > Regression > Regression**.
3. In **Response**, enter dependent (*y*) variable.
4. In **Predictors**, enter independent (*x*) variables.
5. Click **OK**.

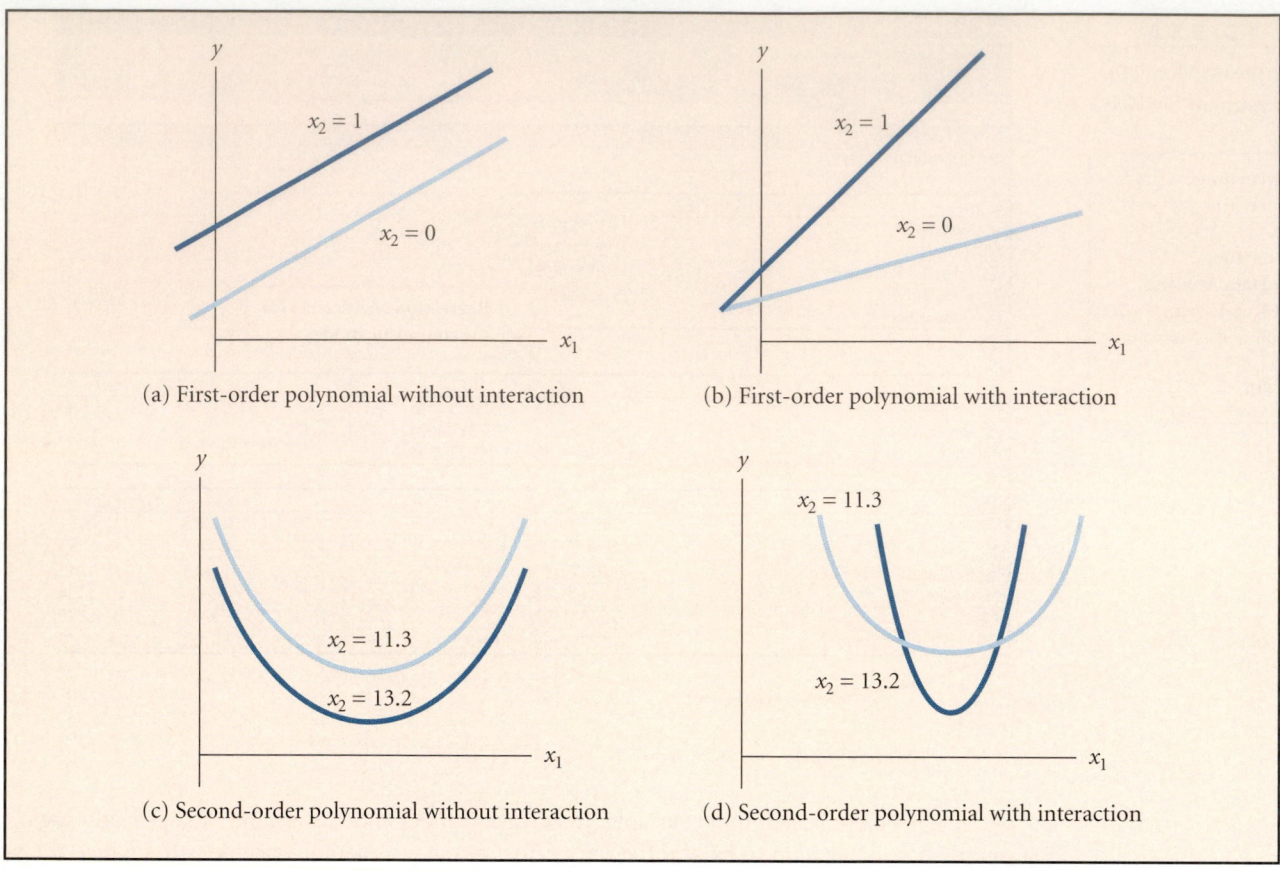

FIGURE 13-24 **Graphical Evidence of Interaction**

13-3: EXERCISES

Skill Development

13.19 Consider the following values for dependent and independent variables:

y	x
8	4
14	8
20	10
18	16
16	18

a. Develop a scatter plot of the data. Does the plot suggest a linear or nonlinear relationship between the dependent and independent variables?

b. Develop an estimated linear regression equation for these data. Is the relationship significant? Test at an $\alpha = 0.05$ level.

c. Develop a regression equation of the form $b_1x + b_2x^2$. Does this equation provide a better fit to the data than that found in part b?

13.20 Consider the following values for dependent and independent variables:

x	y
5	10
15	15
40	25
50	44
60	79
80	112

a. Develop a scatter plot of the data. Does the plot suggest a linear or nonlinear relationship between the dependent and independent variables?

b. Develop an estimated linear regression equation for these data. Is the relationship significant? Test at an $\alpha = 0.05$ level.

c. Develop a regression equation of the form $\hat{y} = b_0 + b_1x + b_2x^2$. Does this equation provide a better fit to the data than that found in part b?

13.21 Consider the following values for dependent and independent variables:

x	y
6	5
9	20
14	28
18	30
22	33
27	35

a. Develop a scatter plot of the data. Does the plot suggest a linear or nonlinear relationship between the dependent and independent variables?

b. Develop an estimated linear regression equation for these data. Is the relationship significant? Test at an $\alpha = 0.05$ level.

c. Develop a regression equation of the form $\hat{y} = b_0 + b_1 \ln(x)$. Does this equation provide a better fit to the data than that found in part b?

Business Applications

13.22 Gilmore Accounting collected the following in an effort to explain variation in client profitability. The data are also in the CD-ROM file *Gilmore*.

y	x_1	x_2
2,345	45	1
4,200	56	2
278	26	3
1,211	56	2
1,406	24	2
500	23	3
−700	34	3
3,457	45	1
2,478	47	1
1,975	24	2
206	32	3

where:

y = Net profit earned from the client
x_1 = Number of hours spent working with the client
x_2 = Type of client:
    1 if manufacturing
    2 if service
    3 if governmental

Gilmore has asked if it needs the client type in addition to the number of hours spent working with the client to predict the net profit earned from the client. You are asked to provide this information.

a. Fit a model to the data that incorporates the number of hours spent working with the client and the type of client as independent variables. (Hint: Client type has three levels.)

b. Fit a second-order model to the data, again using dummy variables for client type. Does this model provide a better fit than that found in part a? Which model would you recommend be used?

13.23 McCullom's International Grains is constantly searching out areas in which to expand its market. Such markets present different challenges because tastes in the international market are different than domestic tastes. India is one country on which McCullom's has recently focused. Paddy is a grain used widely in India, but its characteristics are unknown to McCullom's. Charles Walters has been assigned to take charge of the handling of this grain. He has researched its characteristics. During his research, he came across the article "Determination of Biological Maturity and Effect of Harvesting and Drying Conditions on Milling Quality of Paddy" [*Journal of Agricultural Engineering Research* (1975), pp. 353–361]. The article examines the relationship between y, the yield (kg/ha) of paddy, as a function of x, the number of days after flowering at which harvesting took place. The accompanying data appeared in the article and are in the CD-ROM file *Paddy*.

y	x	y	x
2,508	16	3,823	32
2,518	18	3,646	34
3,304	20	3,708	36
3,423	22	3,333	38
3,057	24	3,517	40
3,190	26	3,241	42
3,500	28	3,103	44
3,883	30	2,776	46

a. Construct a scatter plot of the yield (kg/ha) of paddy as a function of the number of days after flowering at which harvesting took place. Display at least two models that would explain the relationship you see in the scatter plot.

b. Conduct tests of hypotheses to determine if the models you selected are useful in predicting the yield of paddy.

c. Consider a model that includes the second-order term x^2. Would a simple linear regression model be preferable to the model containing the second-order term? Conduct a hypothesis test using the p-value approach to arrive at your answer.

d. Which model should Charles use to predict the yield of paddy? Explain your answer.

13.24 Badeaux Brothers Louisiana Treats ships packages of Louisiana coffee, cakes, and Cajun spices to individual customers around the United States. The cost to ship these products depends primarily on the weight of the package being shipped. Badeaux charges customers for shipping and then ships the product itself. As a part of a study of whether it is economically feasible to continue to ship products, Badeaux sampled 20 recent shipments to determine what, if any, relationship exists between shipping costs and package weight. These data are in the CD-ROM file *Badeaux*.

a. Develop a scatter plot of the data with the dependent variable, cost, on the vertical axis and the independent variable, weight, on the horizontal axis. Does there appear to be a relationship between the two variables? Is the relationship linear?

b. Compute the sample correlation coefficient between the two variables. Conduct a test, using a significance level of 0.05, to determine whether the population correlation coefficient is significantly different from zero.

c. Badeaux Brothers has been using a simple linear regression equation to predict the cost of shipping various items. Would you recommend they use a second-order polynomial model instead? Is the second-order polynomial model a significant improvement over the simple linear regression equation?

d. Badeaux Brothers has made a decision to stop shipping products if the shipping charges exceed $100. They have asked you to determine the maximum weight for future shipments. Do this for both the first- and second-order models you have developed.

13.25   The State Tax Commission must download information files each morning. The time to download the files primarily depends on the size of the file. The Tax Commission has asked your computer consulting firm to determine what, if any, relationship exists between download time and size of files. The Tax Commission randomly selected a sample of 20 days and provided the information to your firm in the CD-ROM file *Tax Commission*.

a. Develop a scatter plot of the data with the dependent variable, download time, on the vertical axis and the independent variable, size, on the horizontal axis. Specify the relationship between the two variables by supplying a model that describes this relationship.

b. Compute the sample correlation coefficient between the two variables. Conduct a test, using a significance level of 0.025, to determine whether the population correlation coefficient is significantly different from zero. Use a p-value approach to conduct this test.

c. Estimate the simple linear regression model for this data. Plot the simple linear regression model together with the data. Would a nonlinear model better fit the sample data? Explain the reasons for your answer.

d. Estimate a nonlinear model and plot the model against the data. Does the nonlinear model provide a better fit than the linear model developed in part c? Describe the criterion you used to reach your conclusion.

13.26   First City Real Estate is an established, family-owned firm located in the Midwest. First City management wishes to build a model that can be used to predict sales price for residential property. From a wide list of possibilities, the managers selected the following as good candidates: x_1 = home size in square feet, x_2 = age of house, x_3 = number of bedrooms, x_4 = number of bathrooms, and x_5 = garage size (number of cars).

Data were obtained for a sample of 319 residential properties that had sold within the previous two months in an area served by two of First City's offices. For each house in the sample, the sales price and values for all potential independent variables were collected. The data are in the CD-ROM file *First City*.

a. Construct a model that would use home size to predict a home's selling price.

b. Use a statistical technique to determine if the number of bathrooms in a home affects the relationship between the selling price of the home and its size (Hint: What type of terms measure such an effect?)

13.27   Refer to Exercise 13-26. Recently managers have begun to suspect that the age of a house has an unusual relationship to its price. They conjecture that the price decreases at a decreasing rate as a function of age until the house is almost 50 years old. Then the price begins to increase at an increasing rate.

a. From the description given above, construct a model that would describe the relationship between the price and the age of a home. Produce an estimate of such a model.

b. Construct a scatter plot of the price versus the age of a home.

c. The manager indicates that the scatter plot seems to say that there is only a linear relationship between the price and age of a home. Produce an estimate of such a model.

13-4 STEPWISE REGRESSION

One option in regression analysis is to bring all possible independent variables into the model in one step. This is what we have done in the previous sections. We use the term *full regression* to describe this approach. Another method for developing a regression model is called *stepwise regression*. Stepwise regression, as the name implies, develops the least squares regression equation in steps, either through *forward selection*, *backward elimination*, or *standard stepwise* regression.

FORWARD SELECTION

The forward selection procedure begins by selecting a single independent variable from all those available. The independent variable selected at step 1 is the variable that is most highly correlated with the dependent variable. An F-test is used to determine if this variable explains a significant amount of the variation in the dependent variable. The F-value that defines the beginning of the rejection region here is known as the *F-to-enter*. If the variable does explain a significant amount of the dependent variable's variation, it is selected to be part of the final model used to predict the dependent variable. If it does not, the process is terminated. If no variables are found to be significant, the researcher will have to search for different independent variables than the ones already tested.

At step 2, a second independent variable is selected based on its ability to explain the remaining unexplained variation in the dependent variable. The independent variable selected in the second, and each subsequent, step is the variable with the highest **coefficient of partial determination**.

Coefficient of Partial Determination

The measure of the marginal contribution of each independent variable, given that other independent variables are in the model.

Recall that the coefficient of determination (R^2) measures the proportion of variation explained by all of the independent variables in the model. Thus, after the first variable (say, x_1) is selected, R^2 will indicate the percentage of variation explained by this variable. The forward selection routine will then compute all possible two-variable regression models, with x_1 included, and determine the R^2 for each model. The coefficient of partial determination at step 2 is the proportion of unexplained variation (after x_1 is in the model) that is explained by the additional variable. The independent variable that adds the most to R^2, given the variable(s) already in the model, is the one selected. Then an *F*-test is conducted to determine if the proportion of unexplained variation that is explained by the additional variable is significant. This process continues until either all independent variables have been entered or the remaining independent variables do not add appreciably to R^2.

Backward elimination is just the reverse of the forward selection procedure. In the backward elimination procedure, all variables are forced into the model to begin the process. Variables are removed one at a time until no more insignificant variables are found. Once a variable has been removed from the model, it cannot be reentered. For the forward selection procedure, the model begins with no variables. Variables are entered one at a time, and after a variable is entered, it cannot be removed.

EXAMPLE 13-4: APPLYING FORWARD SELECTION STEPWISE REGRESSION ANALYSIS

B. T. Longmont Company   The B. T. Longmont Company operates a large retail department store in Macon, Georgia. Like other department stores, Longmont has incurred heavy losses due to shoplifting and employee pilferage. The store's security manager wants to develop a regression model to explain the monthly dollar loss. The following steps can be used when developing a multiple regression model using stepwise regression.

Step 1:   **Specify the model by determining the dependent variable and potential independent variables.**

The dependent variable (*y*) is the monthly dollar losses due to shoplifting and pilferage. The security manager has identified the following potential independent variables:

x_1 = Average monthly temperature (degrees Fahrenheit)
x_2 = Number of sales transactions
x_3 = Dummy variable for holiday month (1 if holiday during month, 0 if not)
x_4 = Number of persons on the store's monthly payroll

The data are contained in a CD-ROM file called *Longmont*.

Step 2:   **Formulate step 1 of the regression model.**

The correlation matrix for the data is presented in Figure 13-25. The forward selection procedure will select the independent variable most highly correlated with the dependent variable. By examining the bottom row in the correlation matrix in Figure 13-25, you can see the variable x_2, number of sales transactions, is most highly correlated ($r = 0.6307$) with dollars lost. Once this variable is entered into the model, the remaining

FIGURE 13-25

**Excel Correlation Matrix
Output for Longmont**

Excel Instructions:
1. Open file: Longmont.xls
2. Click on **Tools**.
3. Select **Data Analysis**.
4. Select **Correlation**.
5. Define data range.

	Month	Average Temperature	Number of Sales Transactions	Holiday	Employees	Shoplifting Loss
Month	1					
Average Temperature	-0.068525647	1				
Number of Sales Transactions	0.815085742	-0.024107419	1			
Holiday	0.144337567	-0.143178951	0.062559195	1		
Employees	0.816495224	-0.082057775	0.918479738	-0.19655	1	
Shoplifting Loss	0.476151389	0.285757558	0.63074948	0.136069	0.41324611	1

Minitab Instructions (for similar results):
1. Open file: Longmont.MTW
2. Choose **Stat > Basic Statistics > Correlation**.
3. In **Variables**, enter variable columns.
4. Click **OK**.

independent variables will be entered based on their ability to explain the remaining variation in the dependent variable.

Figure 13-26a shows the PHStat stepwise regression output, and Figure 13-26b has the Minitab output. At step 1, variable x_2, number of monthly sales transactions, enters the model.

Step 3: **Perform diagnostic checks on the model.**

Although PHStat does not provide R^2 or the estimate of the standard error of the estimate directly, they can be computed from the output in the ANOVA section of the printout. Recall from Chapter 12 that R^2 is computed as

$$R^2 = \frac{SSR}{SST} = \frac{1{,}270{,}172.193}{3{,}192{,}631.529} = 0.398$$

This one independent variable explains 39.8% ($R^2 = 0.398$) of the variation in the dependent variable. The estimate of the standard error of the estimate is the square root of the mean square residual.

$$s_\varepsilon = \sqrt{MSE} = \sqrt{MS\ \text{Residual}} = \sqrt{128{,}163.96} = 358$$

Now at step 1, we test the following:

$$H_0: \beta_2 = 0 \ (\text{Slope for variable } x_2 = 0)$$
$$H_A: \beta_2 \neq 0$$
$$\alpha = 0.05$$

FIGURE 13-26A

**Excel (PHStat) Forward
Selection Results for
Longmont Co.—Step 1**

**Excel (PHStat)
Instructions:**
1. Open file: Longmont.xls
2. Select the **PHStat** tab.
3. Define the y variable data range.
4. Define the x variables data range.
5. Select **Forward Stepwise** option.
6. Select **p-value** (or t-value) criteria.
7. Set p-value or t-value to enter.

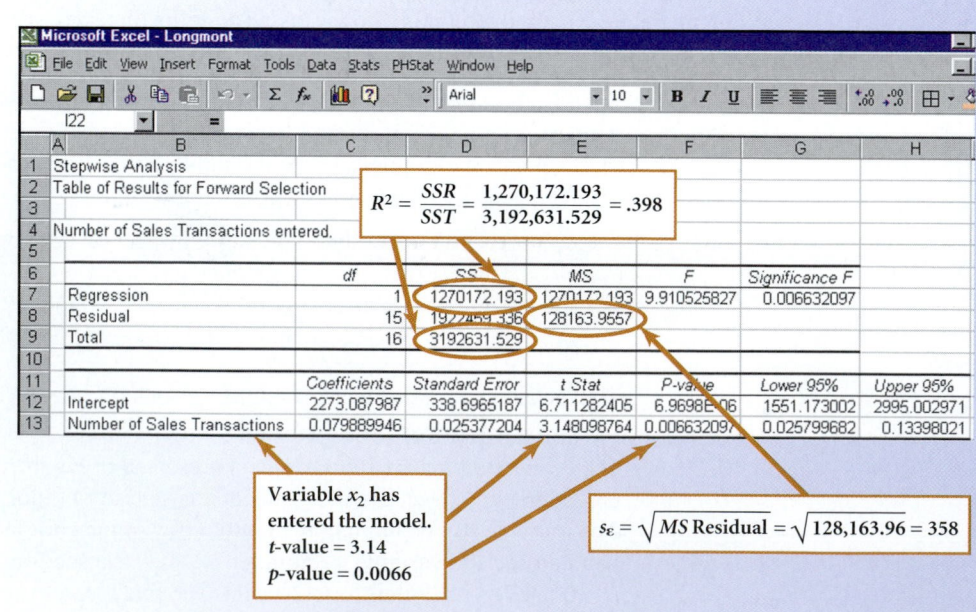

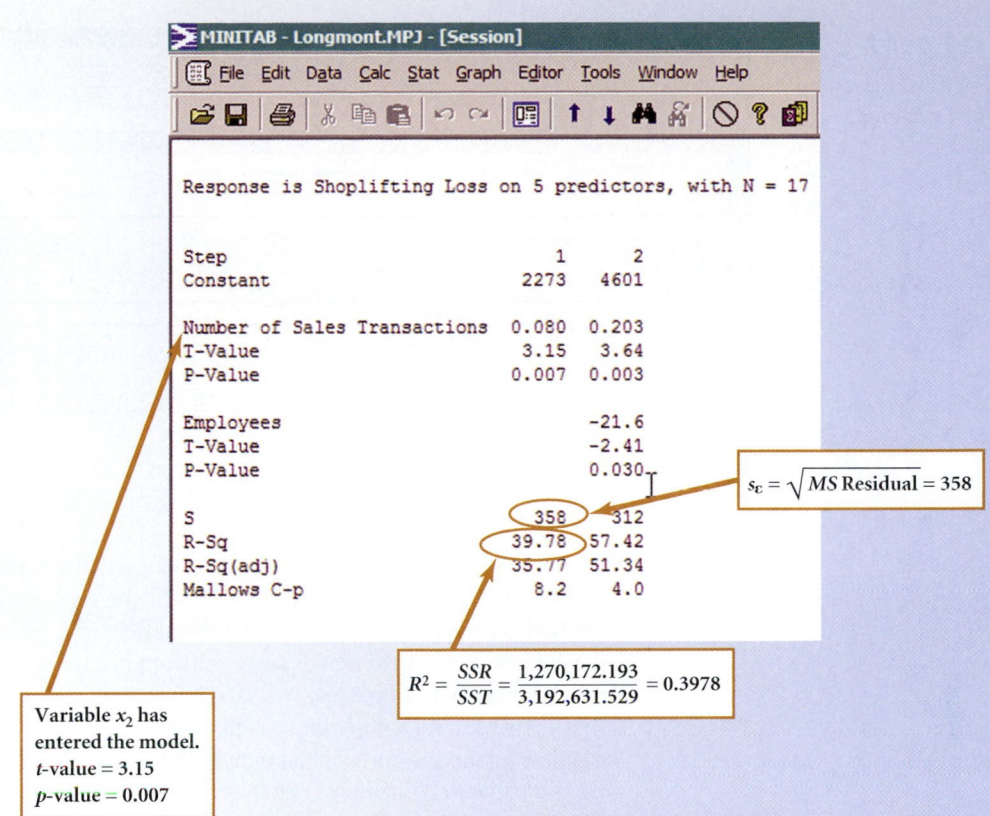

FIGURE 13-26B

Minitab Forward Selection
Results for Longmont
Co.—Step 1

Minitab Instructions:
1. Open file:
   Longmont.MTW.
2. Choose **Stat >
   Regression > Stepwise**.
3. In **Response**, enter
   dependent variable (y).
4. In **Predictors**, enter independent variables (x).
5. Select **Methods**.
6. Select **Forward selection**, enter α in **Alpha to
   enter** an F in **F to enter**.
7. Click **OK**.

```
MINITAB - Longmont.MPJ - [Session]

File  Edit  Data  Calc  Stat  Graph  Editor  Tools  Window  Help

Response is Shoplifting Loss on 5 predictors, with N = 17


Step                             1       2
Constant                      2273    4601

Number of Sales Transactions  0.080   0.203
T-Value                        3.15    3.64
P-Value                        0.007   0.003

Employees                             -21.6
T-Value                               -2.41
P-Value                               0.030

S                               358     312
R-Sq                          39.78   57.42
R-Sq(adj)                     35.77   51.34
Mallows C-p                     8.2     4.0
```

$s_\varepsilon = \sqrt{MS\,Residual} = 358$

$$R^2 = \frac{SSR}{SST} = \frac{1{,}270{,}172.193}{3{,}192{,}631.529} = 0.3978$$

Variable x_2 has
entered the model.
t-value = 3.15
p-value = 0.007

As shown in Figures 13-26a and 13-26b, the calculated t-value is 3.15. We compare this to the critical value from the t-distribution for $\dfrac{\alpha}{2} = \dfrac{0.05}{2} = 0.025$ and degrees of freedom equal to

$$n - k - 1 = 17 - 1 - 1 = 15$$

This critical value is

$$t_{\alpha/2} = 2.131$$

Because

$$t = 3.15 > 2.131$$

we

reject the null hypothesis

and conclude that the regression slope coefficient for the variable, number of sales transactions, is not zero. Note also, because the

$$p\text{-value} = 0.0066 < \alpha = 0.05$$

we would reject the null hypothesis.

Step 4:   Continue to formulate and diagnose the model by adding other independent variables.

The next variable to be selected will be the one that can do the most to increase R^2. If you were doing this manually, you would try each variable to see which one yields the highest R^2, given that the transactions variable is already in the model. Both the PHStat add-in software and Minitab do this automatically. As shown in Figure 13-27, the variable selected in step 2 is x_4, number of employees. Using the ANOVA section, we can determine R^2 and s_ε as before.

$$R^2 = \frac{SSR}{SST} = \frac{1{,}833{,}270.524}{3{,}192{,}631.529} = 0.5742 \qquad \text{and}$$

$$s_\varepsilon = \sqrt{MS\,Residual} = \sqrt{97{,}097.22} = 311.6$$

FIGURE 13-27

PHStat Forward Selection Results for Longmont Co.—Step 2

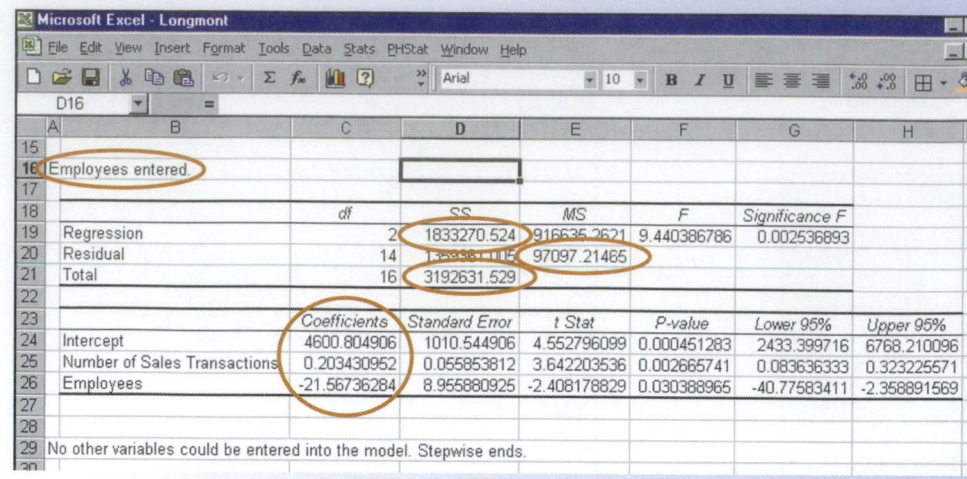

The model now explains 57.42% of the variation in the dependent variable. The *t*-values for both slope coefficients exceed $t = 2.145$ (the critical value from the *t*-distribution table with a one-tailed area equal to 0.025 and $17 - 2 - 1 = 14$ degrees of freedom), so we conclude that both variables are significant in explaining the variation in the dependent variable, shoplifting loss.

The forward selection routine continues to enter variables as long as each additional variable explains a significant amount of the remaining variation in the dependent variable. Note that PHStat allows you to set the significance level in terms of a *p*-value or in terms of the *t* statistic. Then as long as the calculated *p*-value for an incoming variable is less than your limit, the variable is allowed to enter the model. Likewise, if the calculated statistic exceeds your *t* limit, the variable is allowed to enter.

In this example, with the *p*-value limit set at 0.05, neither of the two remaining independent variables would explain a significant amount of the remaining variation in the dependent variable.

The procedure is, therefore, terminated. The resulting regression equation provided by forward selection is

$$\hat{y} = 4600.8 + 0.203x_2 - 21.57x_4$$

Note that the dummy variables for holiday and temperature did not enter the model. This implies that, given the other variables, knowing whether the month in question has a holiday or knowing its average temperature does not add significantly to the model's ability to explain the variation in the dependent variable.

The Longmont Company can now use this regression model to explain variation in shoplifting losses based on knowing the number of sales transactions and the number of employees.

STANDARD STEPWISE REGRESSION

The standard stepwise procedure (sometimes referred to as forward stepwise regression—not to be confused with forward selection) combines attributes of both backward elimination and forward selection. The forward stepwise method serves one more important function. If two or more variables overlap, a variable selected in an early step may become insignificant when other variables are added at later steps. The forward stepwise procedure will drop this insignificant variable from the model. Forward stepwise regression also offers a means of observing multicollinearity problems, because we can see how the regression model changes as each new variable is added to it.

The forward stepwise procedure is widely used in decision-making applications and is generally recognized as a useful regression method. However, care should be exercised when using this procedure because it is easy to rely too heavily on the automatic selection process. Remember, the order of variable selection is conditional, based on the variables already in the model. There is no guarantee that stepwise regression will lead you to the best set of independent variables from those available. Decision makers still must use common sense in applying regression analysis to make sure they have usable regression models.

BEST SUBSETS REGRESSION

Another method for developing multiple regression models is called the *best subsets* method. As the name implies, the best subsets method works by trying possible subsets from the list of possible independent variables. The user can then select the "best" model based on such measures as R-squared or the estimate of the standard deviation of the model error. Both Minitab and PHStat contain procedures for performing best subsets regression.

OPTIONAL CD-ROM TOPICS BACKWARD ELIMINATION, STEPWISE REGRESSION

You can also perform stepwise regression analysis by starting out with all the independent variables in the model and then removing the variables one at a time. For more information, go to the CD-ROM.

13-4: EXERCISES

Skill Development

13.28 You are given the following set of data:

y	x_1	x_2	x_3
33	9	192	40
44	11	397	47
34	10	235	37
60	13	345	61
20	11	245	23
30	7	235	35
45	12	296	52
25	9	235	27
53	10	295	57
45	13	335	50
37	11	243	41
44	13	413	51

a. Determine the appropriate correlation matrix and use it to predict which variable will enter in the first step of a stepwise regression model.
b. Use forward stepwise regression to construct a regression equation, entering all significant variables.
c. Construct an estimate of the full regression model. What are the differences between the estimate of this model and the equation in part b? Which equation explains the most variation in the dependent variable?

13.29 You are given the following set of data:

y	x_1	x_2	x_3
45	40	41	39
41	31	41	35
43	45	49	39
38	43	41	41
50	42	42	51
39	48	40	42
50	44	44	41
45	42	39	37
43	37	52	41
34	40	47	40
49	35	44	44
45	39	40	45
40	43	30	42
43	53	34	34

a. Determine the appropriate correlation matrix and use it to predict which variable will enter in the first step of a stepwise regression model.
b. Use forward stepwise regression to construct a regression equation. Initiate the procedure using all three independent variables.
c. Construct an estimate of the full regression model. What are the differences between the estimate of this model and the equation in part b? Which equation

explains the most variation in the dependent variable?

13.30 Suppose you have four potential independent variables, x_1, x_2, x_3, and x_4, from which you want to develop an estimate of a multiple regression model. Using stepwise regression, x_2 and x_4 enter the regression equation.

a. Why did only two variables enter the equation? Discuss.

b. Suppose a regression equation with only variables x_2 and x_4 had been constructed. Would the resulting equation be different from the stepwise equation that included only these two variables? Discuss.

c. Now suppose an estimate of a full regression model was developed, with all four independent variables in the equation. Which would have the higher R^2 value, the estimate of the full regression model or the stepwise regression equation? Discuss.

Business Applications

13.31 The Western States Tourist Association gives out pamphlets, maps, and other tourist-related information to people who call a toll-free number and request the information. The association orders the packets of information from a document-printing company and likes to have enough available to meet its immediate needs without having too many sitting around taking up space. The marketing manager decided to develop a multiple regression model to be used in predicting the number of calls that will be received in the coming week. A random sample of 12 weeks is selected, with the following variables:

y = Number of calls
x_1 = Number of advertisements placed the previous week
x_2 = Number of calls received the previous week
x_3 = Number of airline tour bookings into western cities for the current week

These data are in the CD-ROM file *Western States*.

a. Develop an estimate of the multiple regression model for predicting the number of calls received, using backward elimination stepwise regression. (Review the CD-ROM topic.)

b. At the final step of the analysis, how many variables are in the equation?

c. Discuss why the variables were removed from the equation in the order shown by the stepwise regression.

13.32 Refer to Exercise 13-31.

a. Develop the correlation matrix that includes all independent variables and the dependent variable. Predict the order that the variables will be selected into the regression equation if forward selection stepwise regression is used.

b. Use forward selection stepwise regression to develop an estimate of a model for predicting the number of calls that the company will receive. Write a report that describes what has taken place at each step of the regression process.

c. Compare the results of the forward selection stepwise regression results in part b and the backward elimination results determined in Exercise 13-31. Which regression equation would you choose? Explain your answer.

13.33 The athletic director at State University is interested in developing a multiple regression model for explaining the variation in home-game football attendance. Use forward stepwise regression to develop a regression equation to estimate the model. (The data are in the CD-ROM file *Football*.)

a. Which variable entered the regression equation at step 1? Discuss why this variable entered.

b. Indicate the order of variables entering the stepwise regression equation. What happens to R^2 and the estimate of the standard error of the estimate for each variable entering?

c. Discuss the regression equation at the final step. Also discuss why the procedure stopped at this step.

d. Test the overall significance of the regression model at the final step. Also test whether each regression coefficient is statistically significant. Use an $\alpha = 0.05$ level.

Advanced Application

13.34 Lands' End is a leading direct merchant of traditionally styled casual clothing for men, women, and children, as well as soft luggage and products for the home. *Catalog Age* ranked Lands' End as the 12th largest mail-order company and the second largest for apparel only. Its R&D department is constantly looking for ways to improve its products. Jeremy Walters, one of its consulting scientists, recently read an article titled "Applying Stepwise Multiple Regression Analysis to the Reaction of Formaldehyde with Cotton Cellulose" (*Textile Research Journal*, 1984, pp. 157–165). This article attempted to establish a relationship between the durable-press rating of cotton and the formaldehyde concentration (HCHO, x_1), the catalyst ratio (x_2), the curing temperature (x_3), and the curing time (x_4) to which the cotton was subjected. The data are in the CD-ROM file *Cotton*.

a. Construct scatter plots of each of the independent variables versus the durable-press rating. Specify the model that would describe the relationship of each of these variables to the dependent variable.

b. Whether or not your scatter plots indicated such a relationship, develop a model using stepwise regression that could include all the dependent variables ($x_1 \ldots x_4$), their squares ($x_1^2 \ldots x_4^2$), and all possible (second-order) interaction terms ($x_1 x_2 \ldots x_3 x_4$).

c. Perform backward elimination on the data used for the stepwise regression procedure in part b. Which of the resulting equations would you suggest in order to predict the durable-press rating? Explain and give statistical reasons for your answer. (This exercise can only be done using Minitab. Excel cannot handle the number of independent variables required.)

13-5 DETERMINING THE APTNESS OF THE MODEL

In Section 13-1 we discussed the basic steps involved in building a multiple regression model. These are

1. Specify the model.
2. Formulate the model.
3. Perform diagnostic checks on the model.

The final step is the diagnostic step in which you examine the model to determine how well it performs. In Section 13-2, we discussed several statistics that you need to consider when performing the diagnostic step, including analyzing R^2, adjusted R^2, and the estimate of the standard error of the estimate. In addition, we discussed the concept of multicollinearity and the impacts that can occur when multicollinearity is present. Section 13-3 introduced another diagnostic step that involves looking for potential curvilinear relationships between the independent variables and the dependent variable. We presented some basic data transformation techniques for dealing with curvilinear situations. However, a major part of the diagnostic process involves an analysis of how well the model fits the regression analysis assumptions.

The basic assumptions of multiple regression include the following.

ASSUMPTIONS

1. The relationship between the dependent and independent variables is linear.
2. The variance of the model errors is constant over the range of the values of the independent variables.
3. The model errors are independent from observation to observation.
4. The model errors are normally distributed.

The degree to which a regression model satisfies these assumptions is called **aptness**.

ANALYSIS OF RESIDUALS

The **residual**, the difference between the actual value of the dependent variables and the value predicted by the regression model, is defined by Equation 13-14:

Residual

$$e_i = y_i - \hat{y}_i$$

13-14

A residual value can be computed for each observation in the data set. A great deal can be learned about the aptness of the regression model by analyzing the residuals. The principal means of residual analysis is a study of residual plots. The following problems can be inferred through graphical analysis of residuals.

1. The regression function is not linear.
2. The model errors do not have a constant variance.
3. The model errors are not independent.
4. The model error terms are not normally distributed.

We will address each of these in order. The regression options in both Minitab and Excel provide extensive residual analysis. In Excel, the residual options are shown on the Regression drop-down box. In Minitab, they are accessed in the Regression window by clicking on either the Graphs or Results buttons.

Checking for Linearity

A plot of the residuals (on the vertical axis) against the independent variable (on the horizontal axis) is useful for detecting whether a linear function is the appropriate regression function. Figure 13-28 illustrates two different residual plots. Figure 13-28a shows residuals that systematically depart from 0. When x is small, the residuals are negative. When x is in the midrange, the residuals are positive; and for large x values, the residuals are negative again. This type of plot suggests that the relationship between y and x is nonlinear. Figure 13-28b shows a plot in which residuals do not show a systematic variation from 0, implying that the relationship between x and y is linear.

If a linear model is appropriate, we expect the residuals to band around 0 with no systematic pattern displayed. If the residual plot shows a systematic pattern, it may be possible to transform the

FIGURE 13-28

Residual Plots Showing Linear and Nonlinear Patterns

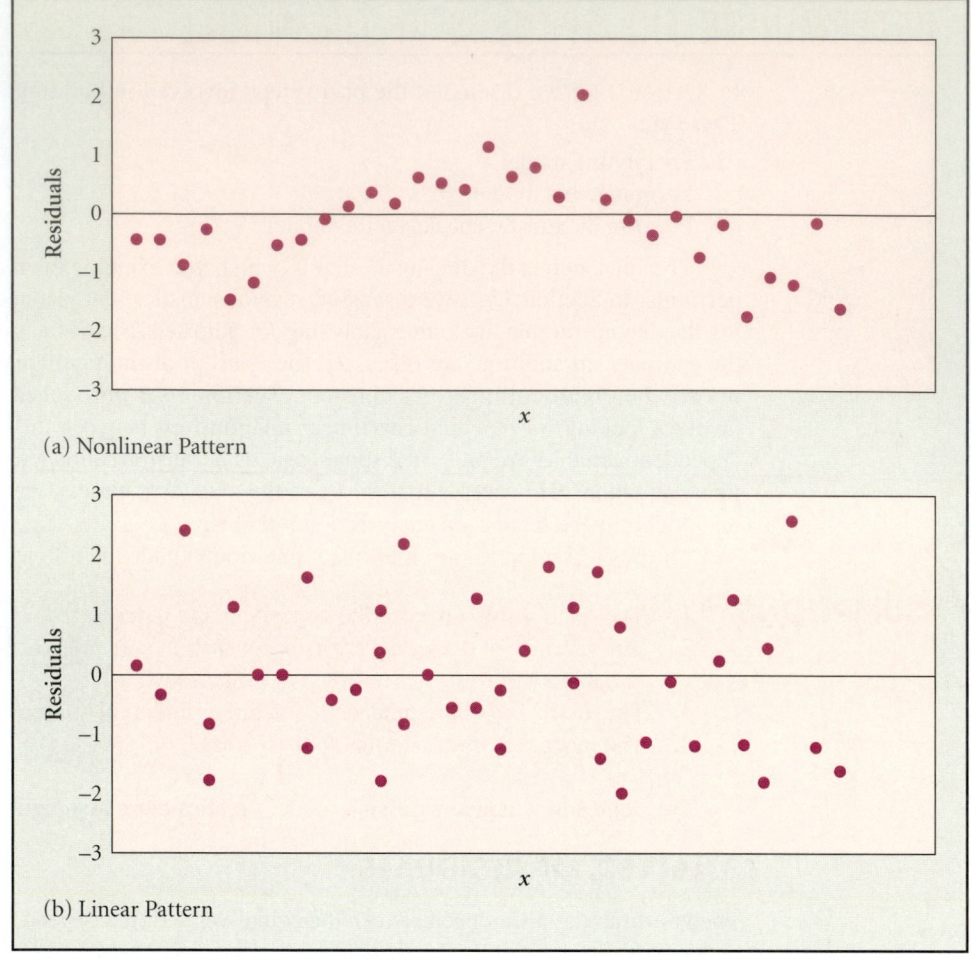

(a) Nonlinear Pattern

(b) Linear Pattern

independent variable (refer to Section 13-3) so that the revised model will produce residual plots that will not systematically vary from 0.

Excel and Minitab Tutorial

First City Real Estate (continued)—We have been using First City Real Estate to introduce multiple regression tools throughout this chapter. Remember, the managers wish to develop a multiple regression model for predicting the sales prices of homes in their market. Suppose that the most current model incorporates a transformation of the lot size variable as log of lot size. The output for this model is shown in Figure 13-29. Notice the model now has a R^2 value of 96.9%.

There are currently four independent variables in the model: square feet, bedrooms, garages, and the log of lot size. Both Minitab and Excel provide procedures for automatically producing residual plots. Figure 13-30 shows the plots of the residuals against each of the independent variables. The transformed variable, log lot size, has a residual pattern that shows a systematic pattern. The residuals are positive for small values of log lot size, negative for intermediate values of log lot size, and positive again for large values of log lot size. This pattern suggests that the curvature of the relationship between sales prices of homes and lot size is even more pronounced than the logarithm implies. Potentially, a second- or third-degree polynomial in the lot size should be pursued.

Do the Residuals Have a Constant Variance?

Residual plots also can be used to determine whether the residuals have a constant variance. Consider Figure 13-31, in which the residuals are plotted against an independent variable. The plot in Figure 13-31a shows an example in which, as x increases, the residuals become less variable. Figure 13-31b shows the opposite situation. When x is small, the residuals are tightly packed around 0, but as x increases, the residuals become more variable. Figure 13-31c shows an example in which the residuals exhibit a constant variance around the zero mean.

When a multiple regression model has been employed, we can analyze the constant variance assumption by plotting the residuals against the fitted ($\hat{y}$) values. When the residual plot is cone-

FIGURE 13-29

Minitab Output of First City Real Estate Appraisal Model

Minitab Instructions:
1. Open file: First City-3.MTW.
2. Choose **Stat > Regression > Regression**.
3. In **Response**, enter dependent (*y*) variable.
4. In **Predictors**, enter independent (*x*) variables.
5. Click **OK**.

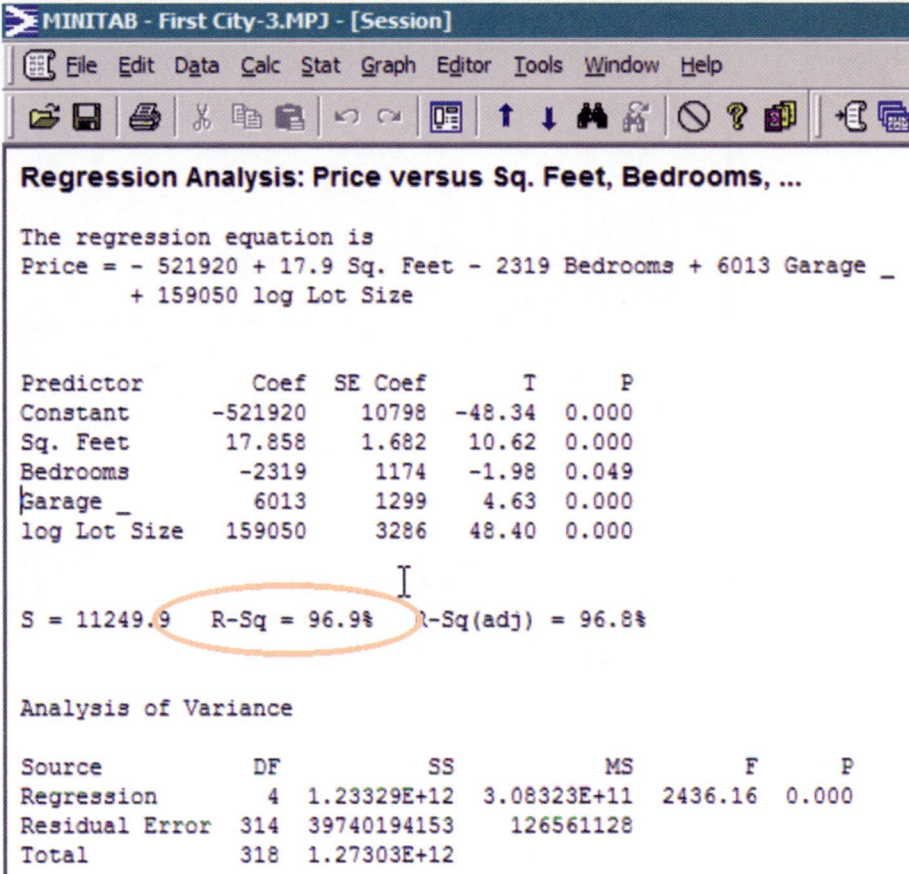

MINITAB - First City-3.MPJ - [Session]

File Edit Data Calc Stat Graph Editor Tools Window Help

Regression Analysis: Price versus Sq. Feet, Bedrooms, ...

The regression equation is
Price = - 521920 + 17.9 Sq. Feet - 2319 Bedrooms + 6013 Garage _
        + 159050 log Lot Size

Predictor	Coef	SE Coef	T	P
Constant	-521920	10798	-48.34	0.000
Sq. Feet	17.858	1.682	10.62	0.000
Bedrooms	-2319	1174	-1.98	0.049
Garage _	6013	1299	4.63	0.000
log Lot Size	159050	3286	48.40	0.000

S = 11249.9   R-Sq = 96.9%   R-Sq(adj) = 96.8%

Analysis of Variance

Source	DF	SS	MS	F	P
Regression	4	1.23329E+12	3.08323E+11	2436.16	0.000
Residual Error	314	39740194153	126561128		
Total	318	1.27303E+12			

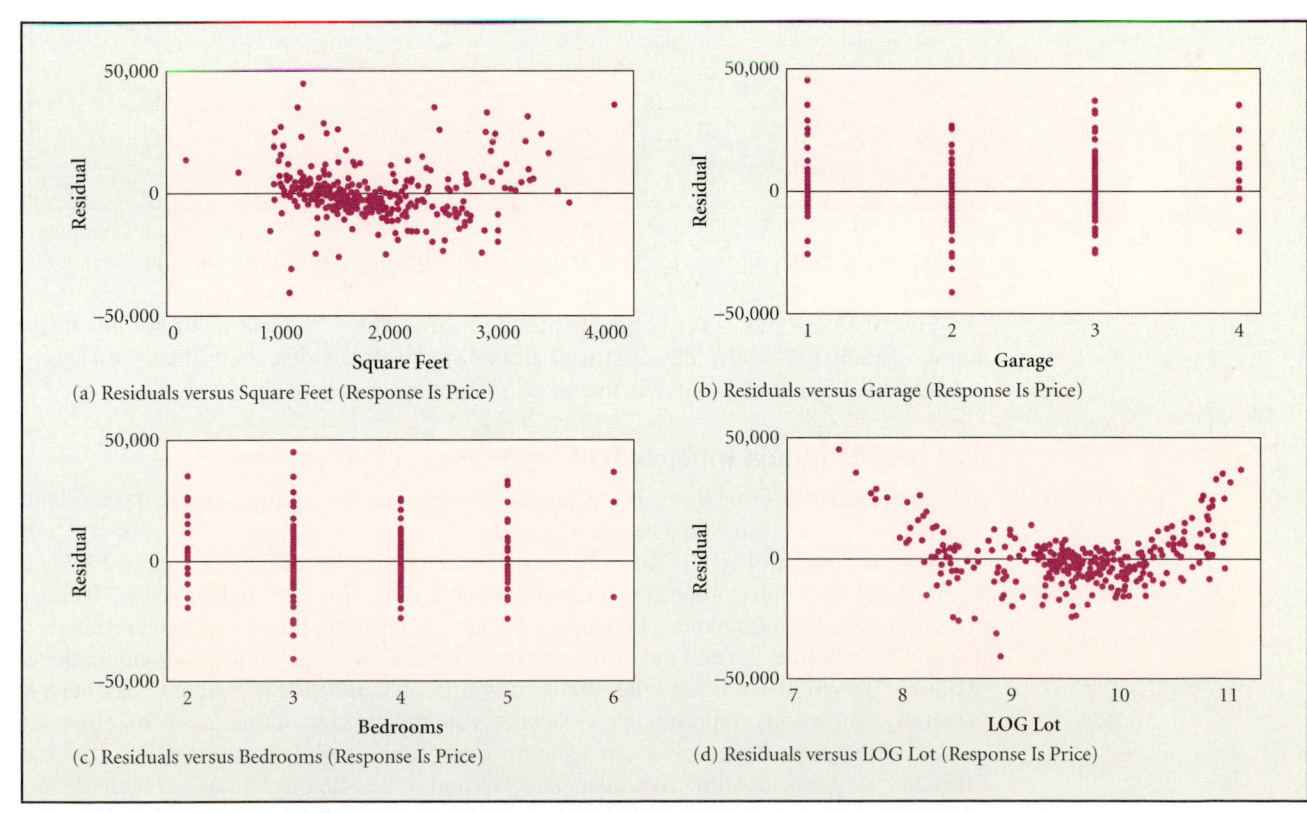

(a) Residuals versus Square Feet (Response Is Price)

(b) Residuals versus Garage (Response Is Price)

(c) Residuals versus Bedrooms (Response Is Price)

(d) Residuals versus LOG Lot (Response Is Price)

FIGURE 13-30   First City Real Estate Residual Plots versus the Independent Variables

FIGURE 13-31

Residual Plots Showing
Constant and Nonconstant
Variances

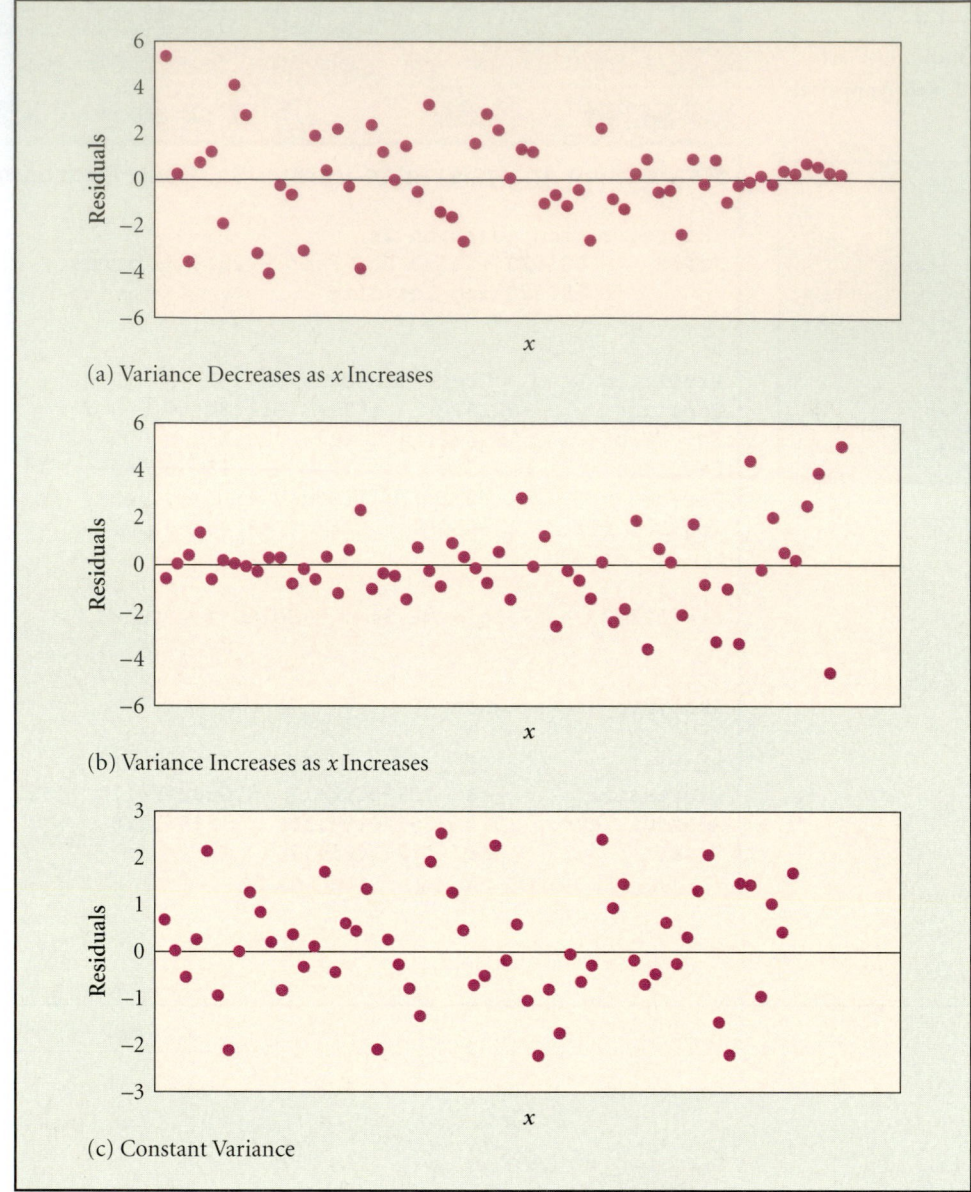

(a) Variance Decreases as x Increases

(b) Variance Increases as x Increases

(c) Constant Variance

shaped, as in either Figure 13-32 it suggests that the assumption of constant variance has been violated.

Figure 13-33 shows the residuals plotted against the $\hat{y}$ values for First City Real Estate's appraisal model. We have drawn a band around the residuals that shows that the variance of the residuals stays quite constant over the range of the fitted values.

Are the Residuals Independent?

If the data used to develop the regression model are measured over time, a plot of the residuals against time is used to determine whether the residuals are correlated. Figure 13-34a shows an example in which the residual plot against time suggests independence. The residuals in Figure 13-34a appear to be randomly distributed around the mean of zero over time. However, in Figure 13-34b, the plot suggests that the residuals are not independent, because in the early time periods the residuals are negative and in later time periods the residuals are positive. This, or any other nonrandom pattern in the residuals over time, indicates that the assumption of independent residuals has been violated. Generally, this means some variable associated with the passage of time has been omitted from the model. Often, time is used as a surrogate for other time-related variables in a regression model. Chapter 15 will discuss time series data analysis and forecasting techniques in more detail and will address the issue of incorporating the time variable into the model. In Chapter 15, we introduce a procedure called the Durbin-Watson test to determine whether residuals are correlated over time.

FIGURE 13-32

Residual Plots Against the Fitted ($\hat{y}$) Values

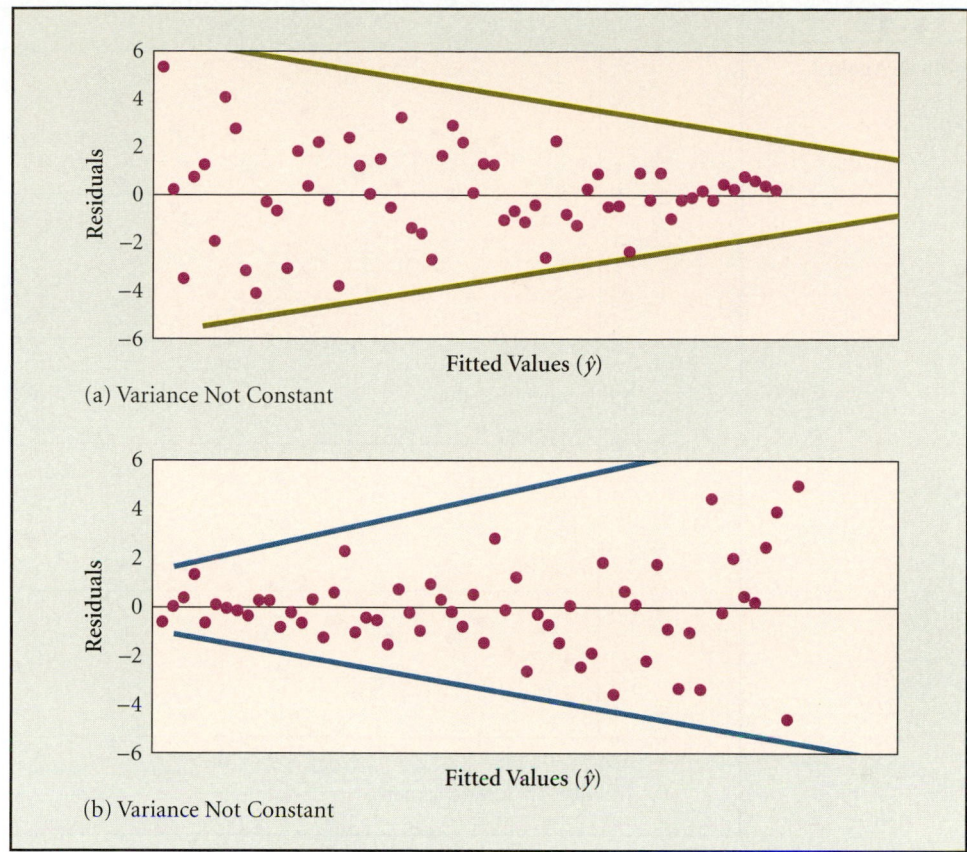

(a) Variance Not Constant

(b) Variance Not Constant

Checking for Normally Distributed Error Terms

The need for normally distributed model errors occurs when we want to test a hypothesis about the regression model. Small departures from normality do not cause serious problems. However, if the model errors depart dramatically from a normal distribution, there is cause for concern. Examining the sample residuals will allow us to detect such dramatic departures. One method for graphically

FIGURE 13-33

Minitab Plot of Residuals versus Fitted Values for First City Real Estate

Minitab Instructions:
1. Open file: First City-3.MTW.
2. Choose **Stat > Regression > Regression**.
3. In **Response**, enter dependent (y) variable.
4. In **Predictors**, enter independent (x) variables.
5. Choose **Graphs**.
6. Under **Residual Plots**, select **Residuals versus fits**.
7. Click **OK. OK.**

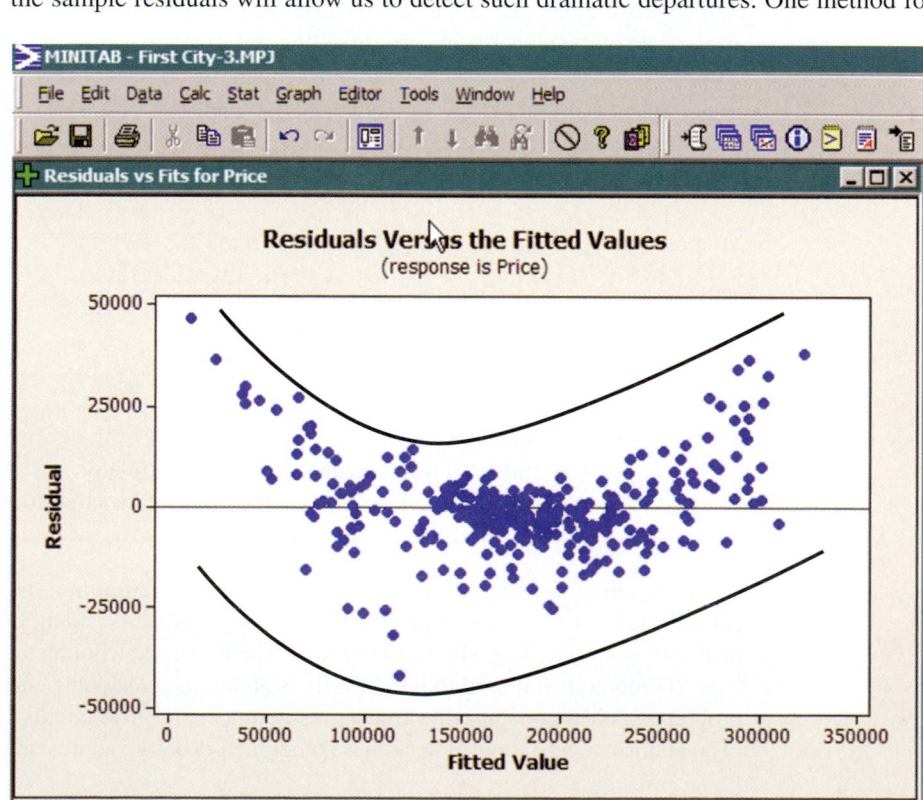

FIGURE 13-34

Plot of Residuals Against
Time

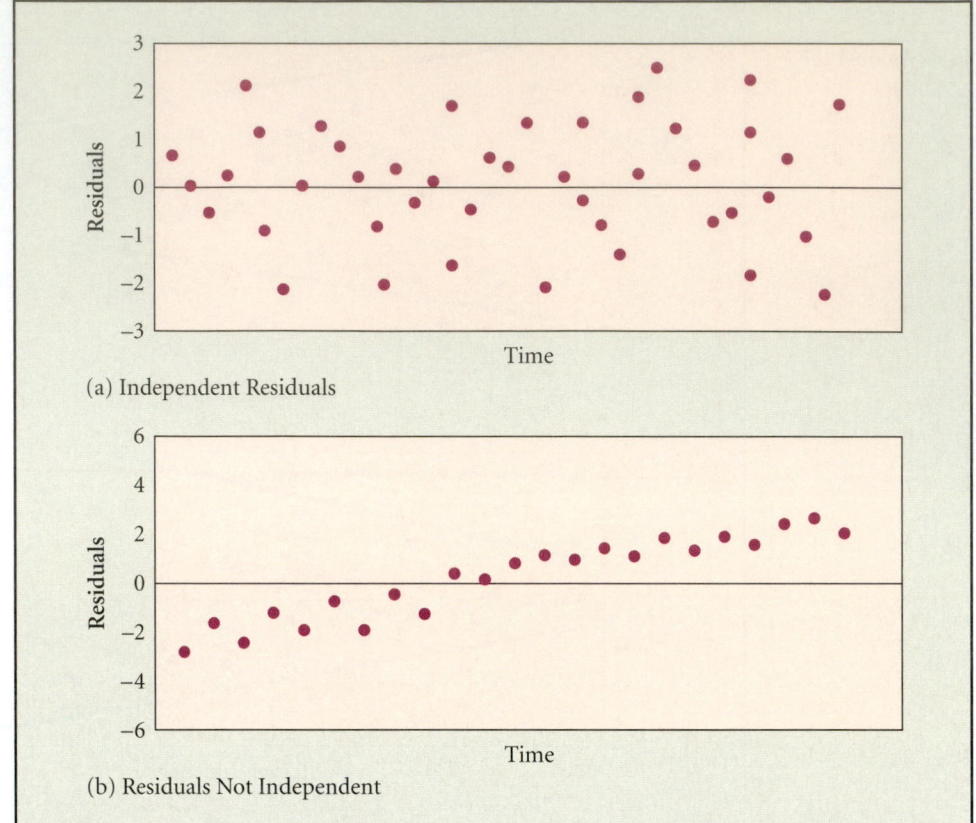

(a) Independent Residuals

(b) Residuals Not Independent

analyzing the residuals is to form a frequency histogram of the residuals to determine whether the general shape is normal. The chi-square goodness-of-fit test presented in Chapter 9 can be used to test whether the residuals fit a normal distribution.

Another method for determining normality is to calculate and plot the **standardized residuals**. In Chapter 3 you learned that a random variable is standardized by subtracting its mean and dividing the result by its standard deviation. The mean of the residuals is zero. Therefore, dividing each residual by an estimate of its standard deviation gives the standardized residual.[9] Although the proof is beyond the scope of this text, it can be shown that the standardized residual for any particular observation for a simple linear regression model is found using Equation 13-15.

Standardized Residual—Simple Linear Regression

$$s_{e_i} = \frac{e_i}{s_\varepsilon \sqrt{1 + \dfrac{1}{n} + \dfrac{(x_i - \bar{x})^2}{\sum x^2 - \dfrac{(\sum x)^2}{n}}}}$$

13-15

where:

e_i = ith residual value

s_ε = Estimate of the standard error of the estimate

x_i = Value of x used to generate the predicted y value for the ith observation

Computing the standardized residual for an observation in a multiple regression model is too complicated to be done by hand. However, the standardized residuals are generated from most statistical software, including Minitab and Excel. The Excel and Minitab tutorials on your CD-ROM illustrate the methods required to generate the standardized residuals and residual plots. Because other problems such as nonconstant variance and nonindependent residuals can result in residuals that seem to be abnormal, you should check these other factors before addressing the normality assumption.

[9]The standardized residual is also referred to as the studentized residual.

FIGURE 13-35

Minitab Histogram of Residuals for First City Real Estate

Minitab Instructions:
1. Open file: First City-3.MTW.
2. Choose **Stat > Regression > Regression**.
3. In **Response**, enter dependent (*y*) variable.
4. In **Predictors**, enter independent (*x*) variables.
5. Choose **Graphs**.
6. Under **Residual Plots**, select **Histogram of residuals**.
7. Click **OK. OK**.

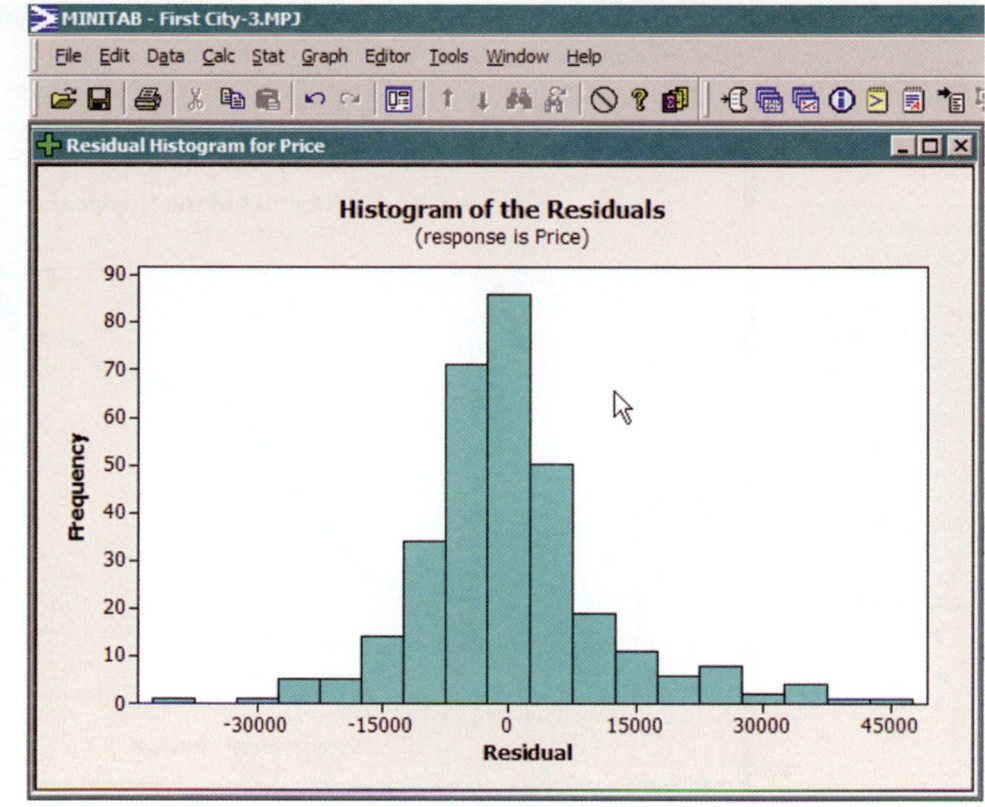

Recall that for a normal distribution, approximately 68% of the values will fall within one standard deviation of the mean, 95% within two standard deviations of the mean, and virtually all values will fall within three standard deviations of the mean.

Figure 13-35 illustrates the histogram of the residuals for the First City Real Estate example. The distribution of residuals looks to be close to a normal distribution. Figure 13-36 shows the his-

FIGURE 13-36

Minitab Histogram of Standardized Residuals for First City Real Estate

Minitab Instructions:
1. Open file: First City-3.MTW.
2. Choose **Stat > Regression > Regression**.
3. In **Response**, enter dependent (*y*) variable.
4. In **Predictors**, enter independent (*x*) variables.
5. Choose **Graphs**.
6. Under **Residual for Plots**, select **Standardized**.
7. Under **Residual Plots**, select **Histogram of residuals**.
8. Click **OK. OK**.

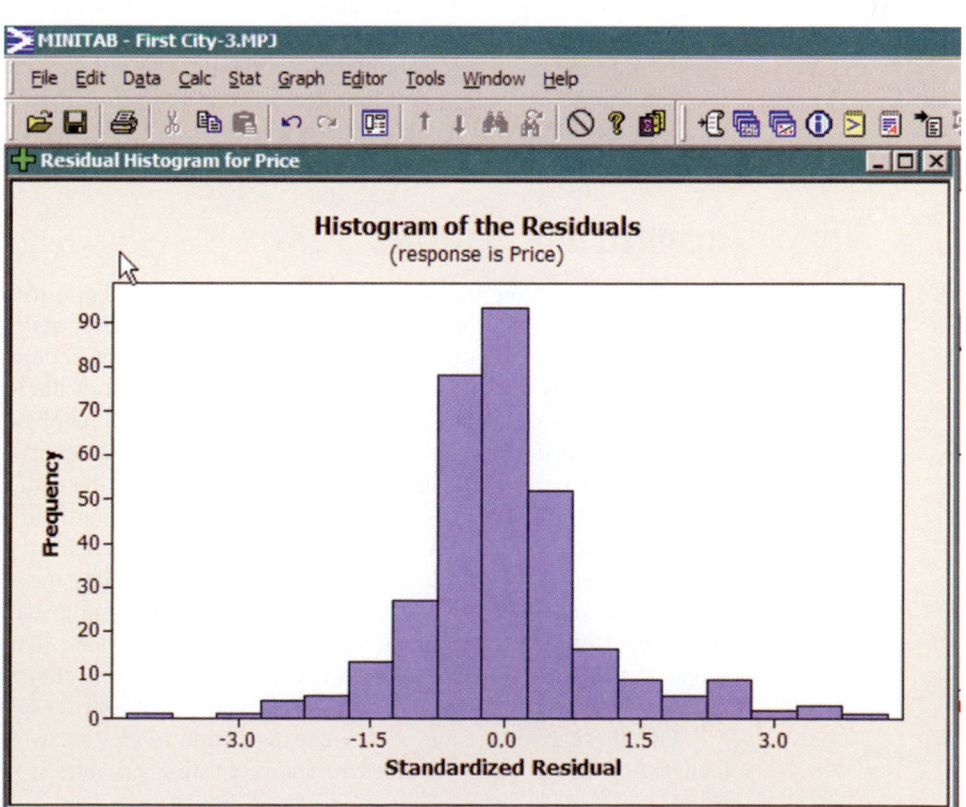

FIGURE 13-37

Minitab Normal
Probability Plot of
Residuals for First City
Real Estate

Minitab Instructions:
1. Open file: First City-3.MTW.
2. Choose **Stat > Regression > Regression**.
3. In **Response**, enter dependent (y) variable.
4. In **Predictors**, enter independent (x) variables.
5. Choose **Graphs**.
6. Under **Residual Plots**, select **Normal plot of residuals**.
7. Click **OK. OK.**

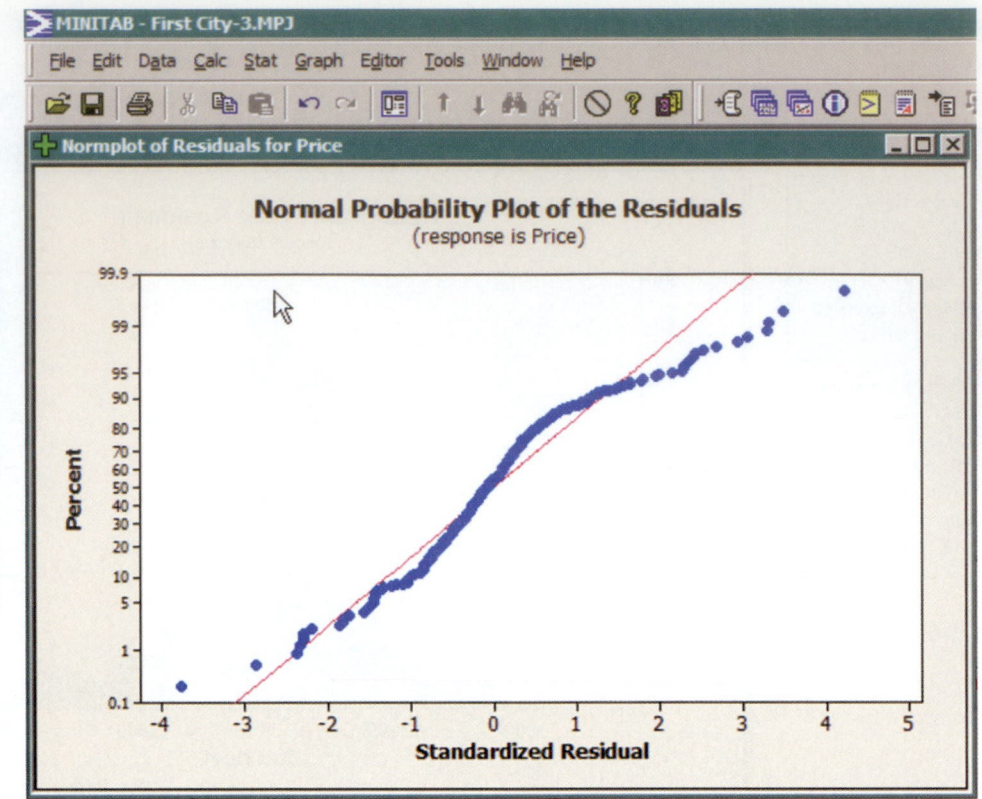

togram for the standardized residuals, which will have the same basic shape as the residual distribution in Figure 13-35.

Another approach for checking for normality of the residuals is to form a *probability plot*. We start by arranging the residuals in numerical order from smallest to largest. The standardized residuals are plotted on the horizontal axis, and the corresponding expected value for the standardized residual is plotted on the vertical axis. Although we won't delve into how the expected value is computed, you can examine the normal probability plot to see whether the plot forms a straight line. The closer the line is to linear, the closer the residuals are to being normally distributed. Figure 13-37 shows the normal probability plot for the First City Real Estate Company example.

You should be aware that Minitab and Excel format their residual plots slightly differently. However, the same general information is conveyed, and you can look for the same signs of problems with the regression model.

CORRECTIVE ACTIONS

If, based on analyzing the residuals, you decide the model constructed is not appropriate, but you still want a regression-based model, some corrective action may be warranted. There are three approaches that may work: transform some of the existing independent variables; remove some variables from the model; or start over in the development of the regression model.

Earlier in this chapter, we discussed a basic approach involved in variable transformation. In general, the transformations of the independent variables (such as raising x to a power, taking the square root of x, or taking the log of x) are used to make the data better conform to a linear relationship. If the model suffers from non-linearity and if the residuals have a non-constant variance, you may want to transform both the independent and dependent variables. In cases in which the normality assumption is not satisfied, transforming the dependent variable is often useful. In many instances, a log transformation works. In some instances a transformation involving the product of two independent variables will help. A more detailed discussion is beyond the scope of this text. However, you can read more about this subject in the Neter et al. reference listed at the end of the chapter.

The alternative of using a different regression model means that we respecify the model to include new independent variables or remove existing variables from the model. In most modeling situations, we are in a continual state of model respecification. We are always seeking to improve the regression model by finding new independent variables.

13-5: EXERCISES

Skill Development

13.35 Consider the following values for dependent and independent variables:

x	y
6	5
9	20
14	28
18	30
22	33
27	35
33	45

a. Determine the estimated linear regression equation relating the dependent and independent variables.
b. Is the regression equation you found significant? Test at the $\alpha = 0.05$ level.
c. Determine both the residuals and standardized residuals. Is there anything about the residuals that would lead you to question whether the assumptions necessary to use regression analysis are satisfied?

13.36 Consider the following values for dependent and independent variables:

x	y
6	5
9	20
14	28
18	15
22	27
27	31
33	32
50	60
61	132
75	160

a. Determine the estimated linear regression equation relating the dependent and independent variables.
b. Is the regression equation you found significant? Test at the $\alpha = 0.05$ level.
c. Determine both the residuals and standardized residuals. Is there anything about the residuals that would lead you to question whether the assumptions necessary to use regression analysis are satisfied?

13.37 Consider the following values for dependent and independent variables:

x	y
16	15
19	20
24	28
28	15
32	35
37	20
43	55
60	25
71	32
75	40

a. Determine the estimated linear regression equation relating the dependent and independent variables.
b. Is the regression equation you found significant? Test at the $\alpha = 0.10$ level.
c. Determine both the residuals and standardized residuals. Plot the residuals. Is there anything about the residuals that would lead you to question whether the assumptions necessary to use regression analysis are satisfied?

13.38 Under what conditions is it desirable to plot the residuals against the predicted y values? Discuss.

13.39 In a multiple regression model, if we wish to determine whether the residuals have a constant variance, is it appropriate to plot the residuals against each x variable individually? If not, what should be done?

Business Applications

13.40 The Western States Tourist Association gives out pamphlets, maps, and other tourist-related information to people who call a toll-free number and request the information. The association orders the packets of information from a document-printing company and likes to have enough available to meet immediate needs without having too many sitting around taking up space. The marketing manager decided to develop a multiple regression model to be used in predicting the number of calls that will be received in the coming week. A random sample of 12 weeks is selected, with the following variables:

y = Number of calls
x_1 = Number of advertisements placed the previous week
x_2 = Number of calls received the previous week
x_3 = Number of airline tour bookings into western cities for the current week

The data are in the CD-ROM file *Western States*.
a. Construct a multiple regression model using all three independent variables. Write a short report discussing the model.
b. Based on the appropriate residual plots, what can you conclude about the constant variance assumption? Discuss.
c. Based on the appropriate residual analysis, does it appear that the residuals are independent? Discuss.
d. Use an appropriate analysis of the residuals to determine whether the regression model meets the assumption of normally distributed error terms. Discuss.

13.41 ⊙ The athletic director of State University is interested in developing a multiple regression model that might be used to explain variations in attendance at football games at his school. A sample of 16 games was selected from home games played during the past 10 seasons. Data for the following factors were determined.

$$y = \text{Game attendance}$$
$$x_1 = \text{Team win/loss percentage to date}$$
$$x_2 = \text{Opponent win/loss percentage to date}$$
$$x_3 = \text{Games played this season}$$
$$x_4 = \text{Temperature at game time}$$

The sample data are in the CD-ROM file *Football*.
a. Build an estimate of a multiple regression model using all four independent variables. Write a short report that outlines the characteristics of this model.
b. Develop a table of residuals for this model. What is the average residual value? Why do you suppose it came out to this value? Discuss.
c. Based on the appropriate residual plot, what can you conclude about the constant variance assumption? Discuss.
d. Based on the appropriate residual analysis, does it appear that the model errors are independent? Discuss.
e. Can you conclude, based on the appropriate method of analysis, that the model error terms are approximately normally distributed?

Advanced Applications

13.42 ⊙ Charles Walters has been assigned to take charge of the handling of paddy, an Indian grain. He has researched the various characteristics of the grain. During his research he came across the article "Determination of

Biological Maturity and Effect of Harvesting and Drying Conditions on Milling Quality of Paddy" [*Journal of Agricultural Engineering Research* (1975) pp. 353–361]. The article examines the relationship between y, the yield (kg/ha) of paddy, as a function of x, the number of days after flowering at which harvesting took place. The data are in the CD-ROM file *Paddy* and are shown as follows:

y	x	y	x
2,508	16	3,823	32
2,518	18	3,646	34
3,304	20	3,708	36
3,423	22	3,333	38
3,057	24	3,517	40
3,190	26	3,241	42
3,500	28	3,103	44
3,883	30	2,776	46

a. Fit a simple linear regression model to this data. Calculate the residuals associated with the resulting regression equation.
b. Plot the residuals against the independent variable. On the basis of this plot, determine if a linear function is the appropriate regression function to use for this data, and if the residuals demonstrate a constant variance. Be sure to explain your answers using statistical concepts as support.
c. Whether you determined that a linear model is appropriate or had to select another model to fit the data, conduct a hypothesis test to determine if that model is significant.

13.43 ⊙ Refer to Exercise 13-42. Use a curvilinear model to fit the data.
a. Construct a scatter plot of the residuals versus the independent variable. Determine if the residuals possess a constant variance for each value of the independent variables. Explain your answer using statistical reasoning.
b. Produce a histogram of the residuals. Based on this histogram, do the residuals seem to possess a normal distribution? Explain your answer.
c. Determine the percentages of the residuals that are one standard deviation, two standard deviations, or three standard deviations from their mean. On this basis, do the residuals seem to possess a normal distribution? Explain your answer.

Summary and Conclusions

Multiple regression is an extension of simple regression analysis. In multiple regression, two or more independent variables are used to explain the variation in the dependent variable. Just as a manager searches for the best combination of employees to perform a job, the decision maker using multiple regression analysis searches for the best combination of independent variables to explain variation in the dependent variable.

The presentation of multiple regression analysis has largely been an analysis of computer printouts. As a decision maker, you will almost assuredly not be required to manually develop the regression model, but you will have to judge its applicability based on a computer printout. The Excel and Minitab software we have used in Chapters 12 and 13 are representative of the many software packages that are available. You no doubt will encounter printouts that look somewhat different from those shown in this text and some of the terms used may differ slightly. However, the basic information will be the same, as will be the inferences you can make from the model.

This chapter has discussed the difference between R^2 and adjusted R^2, as well as the difference between statistical significance and practical significance. As a decision maker, you must recognize that a regression model can be statistically significant yet have no practical use because the standard error of the estimate is too large or multicollinearity impacts too heavily.

As you continue your study of business, you will find that multiple regression is one of the most widely used statistical tools. You will find it applied particularly to the areas of production, finance, accounting, and economics.

EQUATIONS

Simple Linear Regression Model
$$y = \beta_0 + \beta_1 x + \varepsilon \qquad \text{13-1}$$

Estimated Simple Linear Regression Model
$$\hat{y} = b_0 + b_1 x \qquad \text{13-2}$$

Population Multiple Regression Model
$$y = \beta_0 + \beta_1 x_1 + \beta_2 x_2 + \ldots + \beta_k x_k + \varepsilon \qquad \text{13-3}$$

Estimated Multiple Regression Model
$$\hat{y} = b_0 + b_1 x_1 + b_2 x_2 + \ldots + b_k x_k \qquad \text{13-4}$$

Correlation Coefficient
$$r = \frac{\sum (x - \bar{x})(y - \bar{y})}{\sqrt{\sum (x - \bar{x})^2 \sum (y - \bar{y})^2}}$$

$$\text{or} \quad r = \frac{\sum (x_1 - \bar{x}_1)(x_2 - \bar{x}_2)}{\sqrt{\sum (x_1 - \bar{x}_1)^2 \sum (x_2 - \bar{x}_2)^2}} \qquad \text{13-5}$$

Multiple Coefficient of Determination (R^2)
$$R^2 = \frac{\text{Sum of squares regression}}{\text{Total sum of squares}} = \frac{SSR}{SST} \qquad \text{13-6}$$

F Test Statistic
$$F = \frac{\dfrac{SSR}{k}}{\dfrac{SSE}{n - k - 1}} \qquad \text{13-7}$$

Adjusted R-Squared
$$R\text{-sq(adj)} = R_A^2 = 1 - (1 - R^2)\left(\frac{n - 1}{n - k - 1}\right) \quad \text{13-8}$$

t-Test for Significance of Each Regression Coefficient
$$t = \frac{b - 0}{s_b} \qquad df = n - k - 1 \qquad \text{13-9}$$

Estimate for the Standard Deviation of the Model (Standard Error of the Estimate)
$$s_\varepsilon = \sqrt{\frac{SSE}{n - k - 1}} = \sqrt{MSE} \qquad \text{13-10}$$

Variance Inflation Factor
$$VIF = \frac{1}{(1 - R_j^2)} \qquad \text{13-11}$$

Confidence Interval Estimate for the Regression Slope
$$b \pm t_{\alpha/2} s_b \qquad \text{13-12}$$

Polynomial Regression Model
$$y = \beta_0 + \beta_1 x + \beta_2 x^2 + \ldots + \beta_p x^p + \varepsilon \quad \text{13-13}$$

Residual
$$e_i = y_i - \hat{y}_i \qquad \text{13-14}$$

Standardized Residual
$$s_{e_i} = \frac{e_i}{s_\varepsilon \sqrt{1 + \dfrac{1}{n} + \dfrac{(x_i - \bar{x})^2}{\sum x^2 - \dfrac{(\sum x)^2}{n}}}} \qquad \text{13-15}$$

Key Terms

CHAPTER EXERCISES

Conceptual Questions

13.44 Discuss in your own terms the similarities and differences between simple linear regression analysis and multiple regression analysis.

13.45 Discuss what is meant by the least squares criterion as it pertains to multiple regression analysis. Is the least squares criterion any different for simple regression analysis? Discuss.

13.46 List the basic assumptions of regression analysis and discuss in your own terms what each means.

13.47 What does it mean if we have developed a multiple regression model and have concluded that the model is apt?

13.48 Go to the library, or use the Internet, to locate three articles using a regression model with more than one independent variable. For each article, write a short summary covering the following points:
a. purpose for using the model
b. how the variables in the model were selected
c. how the data in the model were selected
d. any possible violations of the needed assumptions
e. the conclusions drawn from using the model

13.49 Select a company in your area that you think might use a regression model and interview a decision maker in that company. If the company uses a regression model, outline its use. If the company does not use a regression model, discuss the alternate tools used.

13.50 A financial analyst for a Wall Street firm recently collected a random sample of 24 companies and recorded their year-end stock prices. He hopes to be able to develop a regression model that can be used to explain the variation in stock prices for these 24 firms. He plans to use financial ratios such as the debt/equity ratio as independent variables. What would you suggest to him as the maximum number of independent variables to use in the model? Discuss.

Business Applications

13.51 The managerial development director of a major corporation is trying to determine what personal abilities are necessary for a manager to move from middle- to upper-level management. Although she has been relatively successful predicting who will move rapidly from lower- to middle-management levels, she has had difficulty determining the characteristics necessary to move to the next major level. For a long time, the director has heard that the most glaring deficiency in college graduates entering the company is in communication skills, so she decides to measure whether these skills may be a determining factor.

The director decides to try to develop a multiple regression relationship between job ratings and communication ability. She picks a random sample of middle-level managers who have been in their present positions fewer than five years but more than one year. These managers are given a series of cases to analyze and are asked to present both written and oral recommendations. They are rated by a group of top-level managers on their analyses and on their written and oral presentations. These ratings are then compared with the latest employee ratings. The data are listed in the CD-ROM file *Job Rating*.

Determine the multiple regression equation for these data. Write a report that summarizes the characteristics of the model.

13.52 Refer to the situation described in Exercise 13-51. One of the assumptions of multiple regression is that the independent variables are not correlated with each other. Is this assumption satisfied for these data? What do you check to see if multicollinearity is a problem? Use a significance level of 0.05.

13.53 Refer to the situation described in Exercise 13-51.
a. Does the multiple regression model you have estimated show a significant relationship between job ratings and each of the three independent variables measured? How did you measure this significance? Test with a significance level of 0.05.
b. If a middle manager were to ask you which of the three variables is most important for his chances of getting promoted, what would you respond?

13.54 Referring to Exercise 13-51, if you were a middle-level manager, would you be willing to have your job rating determined only on the basis of your performance on these three independent variables? Explain in statistical terms why or why not.

13.55 Referring to the regression model you developed in Exercise 13-53, respond to each of the following:
a. Discuss how much of the variation in job rating is explained by the three independent variables. How do you measure this factor?
b. As a test, the development director gives the same cases to a group of middle-level managers without knowing their job ratings. One of the managers received the following scores:

Case analysis	9.1
Written presentations	9.4
Verbal presentations	9.3

Based on these data, what is the best estimate of the job rating this manager received?
c. One manager who participated in this study is concerned with his job rating and would like to know how much his job rating should change if his written presentation score increased by a full point. You are to develop a 95% confidence interval for the regression coefficient for the independent variable, written presentation. Be sure to interpret this interval.

The following information applies to Exercises 13-56, 13-57, and 13-58.

A publishing company in New York is attempting to develop a model that it can use to help predict textbook sales for books it is considering for future publication. The marketing department has collected data on several variables from a random sample of 15 books. These data are given in the CD-ROM file *Textbook*.

13.56 Develop the correlation matrix showing the correlation between all possible pairs of variables. Test statistically to determine which independent variables are significantly correlated with the dependent variable, book sales. Use a significance level of 0.05.

13.57 Develop a multiple regression model containing all four independent variables. Show clearly the regression coefficients. Write a short report discussing the model. In your report make sure you cover the following issues:

a. How much of the total variation in book sales can be explained by these four independent variables? Would you conclude that the model is significant at the 0.05 level?

b. Develop a 95% confidence interval for each regression coefficient and interpret these confidence intervals.

c. Which of the independent variables can be concluded to be significant in explaining the variation in book sales? Test using an alpha level of 0.05.

d. How much, if any, does adding one more page to the book impact the sales volume of the book? Develop and interpret a 95% confidence interval estimate to answer this question.

e. Perform the appropriate analysis to determine the aptness of this regression model. Discuss your results and conclusions.

13.58 The publishing company recently came up with some additional data for the 15 books in the original sample. Two new variables, production expenditures (x_5) and number of prepublication reviewers (x_6), have been added. These additional data are as follows:

Book	x_5	x_6	Book	x_5	x_6
1	$38,000	5	9	$51,000	4
2	86,000	8	10	34,000	6
3	59,000	3	11	20,000	2
4	80,000	9	12	80,000	5
5	29,500	3	13	60,000	5
6	31,000	3	14	87,000	8
7	40,000	5	15	29,000	3
8	69,000	4			

Incorporating this additional data, calculate the correlation between each of these additional variables and the dependent variable, book sales. Then respond to each of the following questions in the form of a report to the chief editor.

a. Test the significance of the correlation coefficients, using an alpha level of 0.05. Comment on your results.

b. Develop a multiple regression model that includes all six independent variables. Which, if any, variables would you recommend be retained if this model is going to be used to predict book sales for the publishing company? For any statistical tests you might perform, use a significance level of 0.05. Discuss your results.

c. Use the ANOVA approach to test the null hypothesis that all slope coefficients are 0. Test with a significance level of 0.05. What do these results mean? Discuss.

d. Do multicollinearity problems appear to be present in the model? Discuss the potential consequences of multicollinearity with respect to the regression model.

e. Discuss whether the standard error of the estimate is small enough to make this model useful for predicting the sales of textbooks.

f. Plot the residuals against the predicted value of y, and comment on what this plot means relative to the aptness of the model.

g. Compute the standardized residuals and form these into a frequency histogram. What does this indicate about the normality assumption?

h. Comment on the overall aptness of this model and indicate what might be done to improve the model.

The following information applies to Exercises 13-59 through 13-68.

The J. J. McCracken Company has authorized its marketing research department to make a study of customers who have been issued a McCracken charge card. The marketing research department hopes to be able to identify the significant variables that explain the variations in purchases. Once these variables are determined, the department intends to try to attract new customers who would be predicted to have a high volume of purchases.

Twenty-five customers were selected at random, and values for the following variables were recorded in the CD-ROM file *McCracken*.

y = Average monthly purchases (in dollars) at McCracken
x_1 = Customer age
x_2 = Customer family income
x_3 = Family size

13.59 A first step in regression analysis often involves developing a scatter plot of the data. Develop the scatter plots of all the possible pairs of variables, and with a brief statement indicate what each plot says about the relationship between the two variables.

13.60 Compute the correlation matrix for these data. Develop the decision rule for testing the significance of each coefficient. Which, if any, correlations are not significant? Use an alpha level of 0.05.

13.61 Use forward selection stepwise regression to develop the multiple regression model. The variable x_2, family income, was brought into the model. Discuss why this happened.

13.62 Test the significance of the regression model at step 1 of the computer printout. Justify the significance level you have selected.

13.63 Develop a 95% confidence level for the slope coefficient for the family income variable at step 1 of the model. Be sure to interpret this confidence interval.

13.64 Describe the regression model at step 2 of the analysis. In your discussion, be sure to discuss the effect of adding a new variable on the standard error of the estimate and on R^2.

13.65 Referring to Exercise 13-64, suppose the manager of McCracken's marketing department questions the appropriateness of adding a second variable. How would you respond to her question?

13.66 Looking carefully at the stepwise regression model, you can see that the value of the slope coefficient for variable x_2, family income, changes each time a new variable is added to the regression model. Discuss why this change takes place.

13.67 Analyze the regression model at step 3 and the intermediate results at steps 1 and 2. Write a report to the marketing manager pointing out the strengths and weaknesses of the model. Be sure to comment on the department's goal of being able to use the model to predict customers who will purchase high volumes from McCracken.

13.68 Plot the residuals against the predicted value of y, and comment on what this plot means relative to the aptness of the model.
  a. Compute the standardized residuals and form these in a frequency histogram. What does this indicate about the normality assumption?
  b. Comment on the overall aptness of this model, and indicate what might be done to improve the model.

Advanced Applications

13.69 Refer to the State Department of Transportation file on the CD-ROM, *Liabins*. The department was interested in determining the rate of compliance with the state's mandatory liability insurance law, as well as other things. *Assume the data were collected using a simple random sampling process.* Develop the best possible estimated linear regression model using driving citations as the dependent variable and any or all of the other variables as potential independent variables. Assume that your objective is to develop a predictive model. Write a report that discusses the steps you took to develop the estimate of the final model. Include a correlation matrix and all appropriate statistical tests. Use an $\alpha = 0.05$. If you are using a nominal or ordinal variable, remember that you must make sure it is in the form of one or more dummy variables.

13.70 Refer to the Department of Transportation CD-ROM file described in the previous exercise. Develop the best possible estimated linear regression model using number of years of formal education as the dependent variable and any or all of the other variables as potential independent variables. Assume that your objective is to develop a predictive model. Write a report that discusses the steps you took to develop the estimate of the final model. Include a correlation matrix and all appropriate statistical tests. Use an $\alpha = 0.05$. If you are using a nominal or ordinal variable, remember that you must make sure it is in the form of one or more dummy variables.

13.71 Refer to the CD-ROM file *Cities*, in which an economist from a major East Coast bank has collected data on major cities in the United States. You are to develop an estimate of a multiple regression model that would allow you to predict the labor market stress index, x_8, based on the other variables in the database. (Note: Be careful about the SAT/ACT variables.)
  a. Develop a correlation matrix for all relevant variables and write a short report that discusses the correlation results. Be sure to indicate which potential independent variables appear to have the most promise in the model.
  b. Bring all the relevant independent variables into the model at one time. Show an estimate of the model,

including the intercept and regression coefficients. Look at the signs on the coefficients and indicate which, if any, seem to have inappropriate signs. Discuss.
  c. Is the overall model significant? State clearly the null and alternative hypotheses and show your test procedure. Test at the $\alpha = 0.05$ level. Discuss.
  d. What is the coefficient of determination? Does the model explain a significant proportion of the variation in the dependent variable? Test at an $\alpha = 0.05$ level.
  e. Test each of the regression slope coefficients individually to determine which variables are significant in the model. Test at an $\alpha = 0.05$ level. Write a short report describing your results.

13.72 Referring to the data collected by the economist discussed in Exercise 13-71, use forward stepwise regression to develop the regression model using appropriate independent variables. Write a complete report describing step-by-step what took place as the variables were entered into the model. In your analysis, perform any appropriate tests of significance. Would you recommend that this model be used to predict a city's labor stress market index? Explain.

13.73 The objective set forth in a recent staff meeting at D. L. Green & Associates is to develop a regression model for predicting company stock price. The CD-ROM file *FAST100* contains data on several potential independent variables. Construct a correlation matrix that shows the correlation between the independent variables and the dependent variable and between all possible pairs of independent variables. Write a report that discusses the correlation matrix. Which variables appear to have most promise as predictors of stock price? Discuss.

13.74 Referring to the D. L. Green data discussed in the previous exercise, develop an estimate of a multiple regression model with stock price as the dependent variable. Bring in all appropriate independent variables.
  a. Identify the regression equation, including the intercept and slope coefficients. Comment on whether these coefficients look reasonable given the correlations in the previous exercise. Discuss.
  b. Is the overall model significant? State clearly the null and alternative hypotheses and show your test procedure. Test at the $\alpha = 0.10$ level. Discuss.
  c. What is the coefficient of determination? Does the model explain a significant proportion of the variation in the dependent variable? Test at an $\alpha = 0.10$ level.
  d. Test each of the regression slope coefficients individually to determine which variables are significant in the model. Test at an $\alpha = 0.10$ level. Write a short report describing your results.

13.75 Referring to the D. L. Green data discussed in the previous exercise, use forward stepwise regression to develop the estimated regression model using appropriate independent variables. Write a complete report describing step-by-step what took place as the variables were entered into the model's estimate. Be sure to indicate what, if any, evidence of multicollinearity is present in the model. In your analysis, perform any appropriate tests of significance. Would you recommend that this model be used as a predictive tool? Explain. (This problem can only be done using Minitab.)

CASE 13-A:

Dynamic Scales, Inc.

In 1985, Stanley Ahlon and three financial partners formed Dynamic Scales, Inc. The company was based on an idea Stanley had for developing a scale to weigh trucks in motion and thus eliminate the need for every truck to stop at weigh stations along highways. This dynamic scale would be placed in the highway approximately one-quarter mile from the regular weigh station. The scale would have a minicomputer that would automatically record truck speed, axle weights, and climate variables, including temperature, wind, and moisture. Stanley Ahlon and his partners believed that state transportation departments in the United States would be the primary market for such a scale.

Like many technological advances, developing the dynamic scale has been difficult. When the scale finally proved accurate for trucks traveling 40 miles per hour, it would not perform for trucks traveling at higher speeds. However, eight months ago, Stanley announced that the dynamic scale was ready to be field-tested by the Nebraska State Department of Transportation under a grant from the federal government. Stanley explained to his financial partners, and to Nebraska transportation officials, that the dynamic weight would not exactly equal the static weight (truck weight on a static scale). However he was sure a statistical relationship between dynamic weight and static weight could be determined, which would make the dynamic scale useful.

Nebraska officials, along with people from Dynamic Scales, installed a dynamic scale on a major highway in Nebraska. Each month for six months, data were collected for a random sample of trucks weighed on both the dynamic scale and a static scale. Table 13-3 presents these data.

Once the data were collected, the next step was to determine whether, based on this test, the dynamic scale measurements could be used to predict static weights. A complete report will be submitted to the U.S. government and to Dynamic Scales.

TABLE 13-3					
Test Data for the Dynamic Scales Example	MONTH	FRONT-AXLE STATIC WEIGHT	FRONT-AXLE DYNAMIC WEIGHT	TRUCK SPEED	TEMPERATURE	MOISTURE
	January	1,800 lbs.	1,625 lbs.	52 mph	21°F	0.00%
		1,311	1,904	71	17	0.15
		1,504	1,390	48	13	0.40
		1,388	1,402	50	19	0.10
		1,250	1,100	61	24	0.00
	February	2,102	1,950	55	26	0.10
		1,410	1,475	58	32	0.20
		1,000	1,103	59	38	0.15
		1,430	1,387	43	24	0.00
		1,073	948	59	18	0.40
	March	1,502	1,493	62	34	0.00
		1,721	1,902	67	36	0.00
		1,113	1,415	48	42	0.21
		978	983	59	29	0.32
		1,254	1,149	60	48	0.00
	April	994	1,052	58	37	0.00
		1,127	999	52	34	0.21
		1,406	1,404	59	40	0.40
		875	900	47	48	0.00
		1,350	1,275	68	51	0.00
	May	1,102	1,120	55	52	0.00
		1,240	1,253	57	57	0.00
		1,087	1,040	62	63	0.00
		993	1,102	59	62	0.10
		1,408	1,400	67	68	0.00
	June	1,420	1,404	58	70	0.00
		1,808	1,790	54	71	0.00
		1,401	1,396	49	83	0.00
		933	1,004	62	88	0.40
		1,150	1,127	64	81	0.00

General References

1. Berenson, Mark L., and David M. Levine, *Basic Business Statistics: Concepts and Applications*, 7th ed. (Upper Saddle River, NJ: Prentice-Hall, 1999).

2. Bowerman, Bruce L., and Richard T. O'Connell, *Linear Statistical Models: An Applied Approach*, 2d ed. (Belmont, CA: Duxbury Press, 1990).

3. Cryer, Jonathan D., and Robert B. Miller, *Statistics for Business: Data Analysis and Modeling*, 2d ed. (Belmont, CA: Duxbury Press, 1994).

4. Demmert, Henry, and Marshall Medoff, "Game-Specific Factors and Major League Baseball Attendance: An Econometric Study," *Santa Clara Business Review* (1977) pp. 49–56.

5. Draper, Norman R., and Harry Smith, *Applied Regression Analysis*, 3rd ed. (New York: John Wiley and Sons, 1998).

6. Frees, Edward W., *Data Analysis Using Regression Models: The Business Perspective* (Englewood Cliffs, NJ: Prentice-Hall, 1996).

7. Gloudemans, Robert J., and Dennis Miller, "Multiple Regression Analysis Applied to Residential Properties." *Decision Sciences 7* (April 1976) pp. 294–304.

8. Kleinbaum, David G., Lawrence L. Kupper, Keith E. Muller, and Azhar Nizam, *Applied Regression Analysis and Other Multivariable Methods*, 3rd ed. (Belmont, CA: Duxbury Press, 1998).

9. *Microsoft Excel 2000* (Redmond, WA: Microsoft Corp. 1999).

10. *Minitab for Windows Version 14* (State College, PA: Minitab, 2004).

11. Neter, John, Michael H. Kutner, Christopher J. Nachtsheim, and William Wasserman, *Applied Linear Statistical Models*, 4th ed. (Homewood, IL: Richard D. Irwin, 1996).

LIST OF APPENDIX TABLES

Random Numbers Table

1511	4745	8716	2793	9142	4958	5245	8312	8925
6249	7073	0460	0819	0729	6806	2713	6595	5149
2587	4800	3455	7565	1196	7768	6137	4941	0488
0168	1379	7838	7487	7420	5285	8045	6679	1361
9664	9021	4990	5570	4697	7939	5842	5353	7503
1384	4981	2708	6437	2298	6230	7443	9425	5384
6390	8953	4292	7372	7197	2121	6538	2093	7629
6944	8134	0704	8500	6996	3492	4397	8802	3253
3610	3119	7442	6218	7623	0546	8394	3286	4463
9865	0028	1783	9029	2858	8737	7023	0444	8575
7044	6712	7530	0018	0945	8803	4467	0979	1342
9304	4857	5476	8386	1540	5760	9815	7191	3291
1717	8278	0072	2636	3217	1693	6081	1330	3458
2461	3598	5173	9666	6165	7438	6805	2357	6994
8240	9856	0075	7599	8468	7653	6272	0573	4344
1697	6805	1386	2340	6694	9786	0536	6423	1083
4695	2251	8962	5638	9459	5578	0676	2276	4724
3056	8558	3020	7509	5105	4283	5390	5715	8405
6887	9035	8520	6571	3233	7175	2859	1615	3349
1267	8824	5588	2821	1247	0967	4355	1385	0727
4369	9267	9377	8205	6479	7002	0649	4731	7086
2888	0333	5347	4849	5526	2975	5295	5071	6011
9893	7251	6243	4617	9256	4039	4800	9393	3263
8927	3977	6054	5979	8566	8120	2566	4449	2414
2676	7064	2198	3234	3796	5506	4462	5121	9052
0775	7316	2249	5606	9411	3818	5268	7652	6098
3828	9178	3726	0743	4075	3560	9542	3922	7688
3281	3419	6660	7968	1238	2246	2164	4567	1801
0328	7471	5352	2019	5842	1665	5939	6337	9102
8406	1826	8437	3078	9068	1425	1232	0573	7751
7076	8418	6778	1292	2019	3506	7474	0141	6544
0446	8641	3249	5431	4068	6045	1939	5626	1867
3719	9712	7472	1517	8850	6862	6990	5475	6227
5648	0563	6346	1981	9512	0659	5694	6668	2563
3694	8582	3434	4052	8392	3883	5126	0477	4034
3554	9876	4249	9473	9085	6594	2434	9453	8883
4934	8446	4646	2054	1136	1023	6295	6483	9915
7835	1506	0019	5011	0563	4450	1466	6334	2606
1098	2113	8287	3487	8250	2269	1876	3684	8856
1186	2685	7225	8311	3835	8059	9163	2539	6487
4618	1522	0627	0448	0669	4086	4083	0881	4270
5529	4173	5711	7419	2535	5876	8435	2564	3031
0754	5808	8458	2218	9180	6213	5280	4753	0696
5865	0806	2070	7986	4800	3076	2866	0515	7417
6168	8963	0235	1514	7875	2176	3095	1171	7892
7479	4144	6697	2255	5465	7233	4981	3553	8144
4608	6576	9422	4198	2578	1701	4764	7460	3509
0654	2483	6001	4486	4941	1500	3502	9693	1956
3000	9694	6616	5599	7759	1581	9896	2312	8140
2686	3675	5760	2918	0185	7364	9985	5930	9869
4713	4121	5144	5164	8104	0403	4984	3877	8772
9281	6522	7916	8941	6710	1670	1399	5961	4714
5736	9419	5022	6955	3356	5732	1042	0527	7441
2383	0408	2821	7313	5781	6951	7181	0608	2864
8740	8038	7284	6054	2246	1674	9984	0355	0775

APPENDIX B

Binomial Distribution Table

$$P(x) = \frac{n!}{x!(n-x)!} p^x (1-p)^{n-x}$$

$n = 1$

x	p = 0.01	p = 0.02	p = 0.03	p = 0.04	p = 0.05	p = 0.06	p = 0.07	p = 0.08	p = 0.09	
0	0.9900	0.9800	0.9700	0.9600	0.9500	0.9400	0.9300	0.9200	0.9100	1
1	0.0100	0.0200	0.0300	0.0400	0.0500	0.0600	0.0700	0.0800	0.0900	0
	p = 0.99	p = 0.98	p = 0.97	p = 0.96	p = 0.95	p = 0.94	p = 0.93	p = 0.92	p = 0.91	x

x	p = 0.10	p = 0.15	p = 0.20	p = 0.25	p = 0.30	p = 0.35	p = 0.40	p = 0.45	p = 0.50	
0	0.9000	0.8500	0.8000	0.7500	0.7000	0.6500	0.6000	0.5500	0.5000	1
1	0.1000	0.1500	0.2000	0.2500	0.3000	0.3500	0.4000	0.4500	0.5000	0
	p = 0.90	p = 0.85	p = 0.80	p = 0.75	p = 0.70	p = 0.65	p = 0.60	p = 0.55	p = 0.50	x

$n = 2$

x	p = 0.01	p = 0.02	p = 0.03	p = 0.04	p = 0.05	p = 0.06	p = 0.07	p = 0.08	p = 0.09	
0	0.9801	0.9604	0.9409	0.9216	0.9025	0.8836	0.8649	0.8464	0.8281	2
1	0.0198	0.0392	0.0582	0.0768	0.0950	0.1128	0.1302	0.1472	0.1638	1
2	0.0001	0.0004	0.0009	0.0016	0.0025	0.0036	0.0049	0.0064	0.0081	0
	p = 0.99	p = 0.98	p = 0.97	p = 0.96	p = 0.95	p = 0.94	p = 0.93	p = 0.92	p = 0.91	x

x	p = 0.10	p = 0.15	p = 0.20	p = 0.25	p = 0.30	p = 0.35	p = 0.40	p = 0.45	p = 0.50	
0	0.8100	0.7225	0.6400	0.5625	0.4900	0.4225	0.3600	0.3025	0.2500	2
1	0.1800	0.2550	0.3200	0.3750	0.4200	0.4550	0.4800	0.4950	0.5000	1
2	0.0100	0.0225	0.0400	0.0625	0.0900	0.1225	0.1600	0.2025	0.2500	0
	p = 0.90	p = 0.85	p = 0.80	p = 0.75	p = 0.70	p = 0.65	p = 0.60	p = 0.55	p = 0.50	x

$n = 3$

x	p = 0.01	p = 0.02	p = 0.03	p = 0.04	p = 0.05	p = 0.06	p = 0.07	p = 0.08	p = 0.09	
0	0.9703	0.9412	0.9127	0.8847	0.8574	0.8306	0.8044	0.7787	0.7536	3
1	0.0294	0.0576	0.0847	0.1106	0.1354	0.1590	0.1816	0.2031	0.2236	2
2	0.0003	0.0012	0.0026	0.0046	0.0071	0.0102	0.0137	0.0177	0.0221	1
3	0.0000	0.0000	0.0000	0.0001	0.0001	0.0002	0.0003	0.0005	0.0007	0
	p = 0.99	p = 0.98	p = 0.97	p = 0.96	p = 0.95	p = 0.94	p = 0.93	p = 0.92	p = 0.91	x

x	p = 0.10	p = 0.15	p = 0.20	p = 0.25	p = 0.30	p = 0.35	p = 0.40	p = 0.45	p = 0.50	
0	0.7290	0.6141	0.5120	0.4219	0.3430	0.2746	0.2160	0.1664	0.1250	3
1	0.2430	0.3251	0.3840	0.4219	0.4410	0.4436	0.4320	0.4084	0.3750	2
2	0.0270	0.0574	0.0960	0.1406	0.1890	0.2389	0.2880	0.3341	0.3750	1
3	0.0010	0.0034	0.0080	0.0156	0.0270	0.0429	0.0640	0.0911	0.1250	0
	p = 0.90	p = 0.85	p = 0.80	p = 0.75	p = 0.70	p = 0.65	p = 0.60	p = 0.55	p = 0.50	x

$n = 4$

x	p = 0.01	p = 0.02	p = 0.03	p = 0.04	p = 0.05	p = 0.06	p = 0.07	p = 0.08	p = 0.09	
0	0.9606	0.9224	0.8853	0.8493	0.8145	0.7807	0.7481	0.7164	0.6857	4
1	0.0388	0.0753	0.1095	0.1416	0.1715	0.1993	0.2252	0.2492	0.2713	3
2	0.0006	0.0023	0.0051	0.0088	0.0135	0.0191	0.0254	0.0325	0.0402	2
3	0.0000	0.0000	0.0001	0.0002	0.0005	0.0008	0.0013	0.0019	0.0027	1
4	0.0000	0.0000	0.0000	0.0000	0.0000	0.0000	0.0000	0.0000	0.0001	0
	p = 0.99	p = 0.98	p = 0.97	p = 0.96	p = 0.95	p = 0.94	p = 0.93	p = 0.92	p = 0.91	x

x	p = 0.10	p = 0.15	p = 0.20	p = 0.25	p = 0.30	p = 0.35	p = 0.40	p = 0.45	p = 0.50	
0	0.6561	0.5220	0.4096	0.3164	0.2401	0.1785	0.1296	0.0915	0.0625	4
1	0.2916	0.3685	0.4096	0.4219	0.4116	0.3845	0.3456	0.2995	0.2500	3
2	0.0486	0.0975	0.1536	0.2109	0.2646	0.3105	0.3456	0.3675	0.3750	2
3	0.0036	0.0115	0.0256	0.0469	0.0756	0.1115	0.1536	0.2005	0.2500	1
4	0.0001	0.0005	0.0016	0.0039	0.0081	0.0150	0.0256	0.0410	0.0625	0
	p = 0.90	p = 0.85	p = 0.80	p = 0.75	p = 0.70	p = 0.65	p = 0.60	p = 0.55	p = 0.50	x

$n = 5$

x	p = 0.01	p = 0.02	p = 0.03	p = 0.04	p = 0.05	p = 0.06	p = 0.07	p = 0.08	p = 0.09	
0	0.9510	0.9039	0.8587	0.8154	0.7738	0.7339	0.6957	0.6591	0.6240	5
1	0.0480	0.0922	0.1328	0.1699	0.2036	0.2342	0.2618	0.2866	0.3086	4
2	0.0010	0.0038	0.0082	0.0142	0.0214	0.0299	0.0394	0.0498	0.0610	3
3	0.0000	0.0001	0.0003	0.0006	0.0011	0.0019	0.0030	0.0043	0.0060	2
4	0.0000	0.0000	0.0000	0.0000	0.0000	0.0001	0.0001	0.0002	0.0003	1
5	0.0000	0.0000	0.0000	0.0000	0.0000	0.0000	0.0000	0.0000	0.0000	0
	p = 0.99	p = 0.98	p = 0.97	p = 0.96	p = 0.95	p = 0.94	p = 0.93	p = 0.92	p = 0.91	x

x	p = 0.10	p = 0.15	p = 0.20	p = 0.25	p = 0.30	p = 0.35	p = 0.40	p = 0.45	p = 0.50	
0	0.5905	0.4437	0.3277	0.2373	0.1681	0.1160	0.0778	0.0503	0.0313	5
1	0.3281	0.3915	0.4096	0.3955	0.3602	0.3124	0.2592	0.2059	0.1563	4
2	0.0729	0.1382	0.2048	0.2637	0.3087	0.3364	0.3456	0.3369	0.3125	3
3	0.0081	0.0244	0.0512	0.0879	0.1323	0.1811	0.2304	0.2757	0.3125	2
4	0.0005	0.0022	0.0064	0.0146	0.0284	0.0488	0.0768	0.1128	0.1563	1
5	0.0000	0.0001	0.0003	0.0010	0.0024	0.0053	0.0102	0.0185	0.0313	0
	p = 0.90	p = 0.85	p = 0.80	p = 0.75	p = 0.70	p = 0.65	p = 0.60	p = 0.55	p = 0.50	x

$n = 6$

x	p = 0.01	p = 0.02	p = 0.03	p = 0.04	p = 0.05	p = 0.06	p = 0.07	p = 0.08	p = 0.09	
0	0.9415	0.8858	0.8330	0.7828	0.7351	0.6899	0.6470	0.6064	0.5679	6
1	0.0571	0.1085	0.1546	0.1957	0.2321	0.2642	0.2922	0.3164	0.3370	5
2	0.0014	0.0055	0.0120	0.0204	0.0305	0.0422	0.0550	0.0688	0.0833	4
3	0.0000	0.0002	0.0005	0.0011	0.0021	0.0036	0.0055	0.0080	0.0110	3
4	0.0000	0.0000	0.0000	0.0000	0.0001	0.0002	0.0003	0.0005	0.0008	2
5	0.0000	0.0000	0.0000	0.0000	0.0000	0.0000	0.0000	0.0000	0.0000	1
6	0.0000	0.0000	0.0000	0.0000	0.0000	0.0000	0.0000	0.0000	0.0000	0
	p = 0.99	p = 0.98	p = 0.97	p = 0.96	p = 0.95	p = 0.94	p = 0.93	p = 0.92	p = 0.91	x

x	p = 0.10	p = 0.15	p = 0.20	p = 0.25	p = 0.30	p = 0.35	p = 0.40	p = 0.45	p = 0.50	
0	0.5314	0.3771	0.2621	0.1780	0.1176	0.0754	0.0467	0.0277	0.0156	6
1	0.3543	0.3993	0.3932	0.3560	0.3025	0.2437	0.1866	0.1359	0.0938	5
2	0.0984	0.1762	0.2458	0.2966	0.3241	0.3280	0.3110	0.2780	0.2344	4
3	0.0146	0.0415	0.0819	0.1318	0.1852	0.2355	0.2765	0.3032	0.3125	3
4	0.0012	0.0055	0.0154	0.0330	0.0595	0.0951	0.1382	0.1861	0.2344	2
5	0.0001	0.0004	0.0015	0.0044	0.0102	0.0205	0.0369	0.0609	0.0938	1
6	0.0000	0.0000	0.0001	0.0002	0.0007	0.0018	0.0041	0.0083	0.0156	0
	p = 0.90	p = 0.85	p = 0.80	p = 0.75	p = 0.70	p = 0.65	p = 0.60	p = 0.55	p = 0.50	x

$n = 7$

x	p = 0.01	p = 0.02	p = 0.03	p = 0.04	p = 0.05	p = 0.06	p = 0.07	p = 0.08	p = 0.09	
0	0.9321	0.8681	0.8080	0.7514	0.6983	0.6485	0.6017	0.5578	0.5168	7
1	0.0659	0.1240	0.1749	0.2192	0.2573	0.2897	0.3170	0.3396	0.3578	6
2	0.0020	0.0076	0.0162	0.0274	0.0406	0.0555	0.0716	0.0886	0.1061	5
3	0.0000	0.0003	0.0008	0.0019	0.0036	0.0059	0.0090	0.0128	0.0175	4
4	0.0000	0.0000	0.0000	0.0001	0.0002	0.0004	0.0007	0.0011	0.0017	3
5	0.0000	0.0000	0.0000	0.0000	0.0000	0.0000	0.0000	0.0001	0.0001	2
6	0.0000	0.0000	0.0000	0.0000	0.0000	0.0000	0.0000	0.0000	0.0000	1
	p = 0.99	p = 0.98	p = 0.97	p = 0.96	p = 0.95	p = 0.94	p = 0.93	p = 0.92	p = 0.91	x

x	p = 0.10	p = 0.15	p = 0.20	p = 0.25	p = 0.30	p = 0.35	p = 0.40	p = 0.45	p = 0.50	
0	0.4783	0.3206	0.2097	0.1335	0.0824	0.0490	0.0280	0.0152	0.0078	7
1	0.3720	0.3960	0.3670	0.3115	0.2471	0.1848	0.1306	0.0872	0.0547	6
2	0.1240	0.2097	0.2753	0.3115	0.3177	0.2985	0.2613	0.2140	0.1641	5
3	0.0230	0.0617	0.1147	0.1730	0.2269	0.2679	0.2903	0.2918	0.2734	4
4	0.0026	0.0109	0.0287	0.0577	0.0972	0.1442	0.1935	0.2388	0.2734	3
5	0.0002	0.0012	0.0043	0.0115	0.0250	0.0466	0.0774	0.1172	0.1641	2
6	0.0000	0.0001	0.0004	0.0013	0.0036	0.0084	0.0172	0.0320	0.0547	1
7	0.0000	0.0000	0.0000	0.0001	0.0002	0.0006	0.0016	0.0037	0.0078	0
	p = 0.90	p = 0.85	p = 0.80	p = 0.75	p = 0.70	p = 0.65	p = 0.60	p = 0.55	p = 0.50	x

$n = 8$

x	p = 0.01	p = 0.02	p = 0.03	p = 0.04	p = 0.05	p = 0.06	p = 0.07	p = 0.08	p = 0.09	
0	0.9227	0.8508	0.7837	0.7214	0.6634	0.6096	0.5596	0.5132	0.4703	8
1	0.0746	0.1389	0.1939	0.2405	0.2793	0.3113	0.3370	0.3570	0.3721	7
2	0.0026	0.0099	0.0210	0.0351	0.0515	0.0695	0.0888	0.1087	0.1288	6
3	0.0001	0.0004	0.0013	0.0029	0.0054	0.0089	0.0134	0.0189	0.0255	5
4	0.0000	0.0000	0.0001	0.0002	0.0004	0.0007	0.0013	0.0021	0.0031	4
5	0.0000	0.0000	0.0000	0.0000	0.0000	0.0000	0.0001	0.0001	0.0002	3
6	0.0000	0.0000	0.0000	0.0000	0.0000	0.0000	0.0000	0.0000	0.0000	2
	p = 0.99	p = 0.98	p = 0.97	p = 0.96	p = 0.95	p = 0.94	p = 0.93	p = 0.92	p = 0.91	x

x	p = 0.10	p = 0.15	p = 0.20	p = 0.25	p = 0.30	p = 0.35	p = 0.40	p = 0.45	p = 0.50	
0	0.4305	0.2725	0.1678	0.1001	0.0576	0.0319	0.0168	0.0084	0.0039	8
1	0.3826	0.3847	0.3355	0.2670	0.1977	0.1373	0.0896	0.0548	0.0313	7
2	0.1488	0.2376	0.2936	0.3115	0.2965	0.2587	0.2090	0.1569	0.1094	6
3	0.0331	0.0839	0.1468	0.2076	0.2541	0.2786	0.2787	0.2568	0.2188	5
4	0.0046	0.0185	0.0459	0.0865	0.1361	0.1875	0.2322	0.2627	0.2734	4
5	0.0004	0.0026	0.0092	0.0231	0.0467	0.0808	0.1239	0.1719	0.2188	3
6	0.0000	0.0002	0.0011	0.0038	0.0100	0.0217	0.0413	0.0703	0.1094	2
7	0.0000	0.0000	0.0001	0.0004	0.0012	0.0033	0.0079	0.0164	0.0313	1
8	0.0000	0.0000	0.0000	0.0000	0.0001	0.0002	0.0007	0.0017	0.0039	0
	p = 0.90	p = 0.85	p = 0.80	p = 0.75	p = 0.70	p = 0.65	p = 0.60	p = 0.55	p = 0.50	x

$n = 9$

x	p = 0.01	p = 0.02	p = 0.03	p = 0.04	p = 0.05	p = 0.06	p = 0.07	p = 0.08	p = 0.09	
0	0.9135	0.8337	0.7602	0.6925	0.6302	0.5730	0.5204	0.4722	0.4279	9
1	0.0830	0.1531	0.2116	0.2597	0.2985	0.3292	0.3525	0.3695	0.3809	8
2	0.0034	0.0125	0.0262	0.0433	0.0629	0.0840	0.1061	0.1285	0.1507	7
3	0.0001	0.0006	0.0019	0.0042	0.0077	0.0125	0.0186	0.0261	0.0348	6
4	0.0000	0.0000	0.0001	0.0003	0.0006	0.0012	0.0021	0.0034	0.0052	5
5	0.0000	0.0000	0.0000	0.0000	0.0000	0.0001	0.0002	0.0003	0.0005	4
6	0.0000	0.0000	0.0000	0.0000	0.0000	0.0000	0.0000	0.0000	0.0000	3
7	0.0000	0.0000	0.0000	0.0000	0.0000	0.0000	0.0000	0.0000	0.0000	2
	p = 0.99	p = 0.98	p = 0.97	p = 0.96	p = 0.95	p = 0.94	p = 0.93	p = 0.92	p = 0.91	x

x	p = 0.10	p = 0.15	p = 0.20	p = 0.25	p = 0.30	p = 0.35	p = 0.40	p = 0.45	p = 0.50	
0	0.3874	0.2316	0.1342	0.0751	0.0404	0.0207	0.0101	0.0046	0.0020	9
1	0.3874	0.3679	0.3020	0.2253	0.1556	0.1004	0.0605	0.0339	0.0176	8
2	0.1722	0.2597	0.3020	0.3003	0.2668	0.2162	0.1612	0.1110	0.0703	7
3	0.0446	0.1069	0.1762	0.2336	0.2668	0.2716	0.2508	0.2119	0.1641	6
4	0.0074	0.0283	0.0661	0.1168	0.1715	0.2194	0.2508	0.2600	0.2461	5
5	0.0008	0.0050	0.0165	0.0389	0.0735	0.1181	0.1672	0.2128	0.2461	4
6	0.0001	0.0006	0.0028	0.0087	0.0210	0.0424	0.0743	0.1160	0.1641	3
7	0.0000	0.0000	0.0003	0.0012	0.0039	0.0098	0.0212	0.0407	0.0703	2
8	0.0000	0.0000	0.0000	0.0001	0.0004	0.0013	0.0035	0.0083	0.0176	1
9	0.0000	0.0000	0.0000	0.0000	0.0000	0.0001	0.0003	0.0008	0.0020	0
	p = 0.90	p = 0.85	p = 0.80	p = 0.75	p = 0.70	p = 0.65	p = 0.60	p = 0.55	p = 0.50	x

$n = 10$

x	p = 0.01	p = 0.02	p = 0.03	p = 0.04	p = 0.05	p = 0.06	p = 0.07	p = 0.08	p = 0.09	
0	0.9044	0.8171	0.7374	0.6648	0.5987	0.5386	0.4840	0.4344	0.3894	10
1	0.0914	0.1667	0.2281	0.2770	0.3151	0.3438	0.3643	0.3777	0.3851	9
2	0.0042	0.0153	0.0317	0.0519	0.0746	0.0988	0.1234	0.1478	0.1714	8
3	0.0001	0.0008	0.0026	0.0058	0.0105	0.0168	0.0248	0.0343	0.0452	7
4	0.0000	0.0000	0.0001	0.0004	0.0010	0.0019	0.0033	0.0052	0.0078	6
5	0.0000	0.0000	0.0000	0.0000	0.0001	0.0001	0.0003	0.0005	0.0009	5
6	0.0000	0.0000	0.0000	0.0000	0.0000	0.0000	0.0000	0.0000	0.0001	4
7	0.0000	0.0000	0.0000	0.0000	0.0000	0.0000	0.0000	0.0000	0.0000	3
	p = 0.99	p = 0.98	p = 0.97	p = 0.96	p = 0.95	p = 0.94	p = 0.93	p = 0.92	p = 0.91	x

x	p = 0.10	p = 0.15	p = 0.20	p = 0.25	p = 0.30	p = 0.35	p = 0.40	p = 0.45	p = 0.50	
0	0.3487	0.1969	0.1074	0.0563	0.0282	0.0135	0.0060	0.0025	0.0010	10
1	0.3874	0.3474	0.2684	0.1877	0.1211	0.0725	0.0403	0.0207	0.0098	9
2	0.1937	0.2759	0.3020	0.2816	0.2335	0.1757	0.1209	0.0763	0.0439	8
3	0.0574	0.1298	0.2013	0.2503	0.2668	0.2522	0.2150	0.1665	0.1172	7
4	0.0112	0.0401	0.0881	0.1460	0.2001	0.2377	0.2508	0.2384	0.2051	6
5	0.0015	0.0085	0.0264	0.0584	0.1029	0.1536	0.2007	0.2340	0.2461	5
6	0.0001	0.0012	0.0055	0.0162	0.0368	0.0689	0.1115	0.1596	0.2051	4
7	0.0000	0.0001	0.0008	0.0031	0.0090	0.0212	0.0425	0.0746	0.1172	3
8	0.0000	0.0000	0.0001	0.0004	0.0014	0.0043	0.0106	0.0229	0.0439	2
9	0.0000	0.0000	0.0000	0.0000	0.0001	0.0005	0.0016	0.0042	0.0098	1
10	0.0000	0.0000	0.0000	0.0000	0.0000	0.0000	0.0001	0.0003	0.0010	0
	p = 0.90	p = 0.85	p = 0.80	p = 0.75	p = 0.70	p = 0.65	p = 0.60	p = 0.55	p = 0.50	x

n = 11

x	p = 0.01	p = 0.02	p = 0.03	p = 0.04	p = 0.05	p = 0.06	p = 0.07	p = 0.08	p = 0.09	
0	0.8953	0.8007	0.7153	0.6382	0.5688	0.5063	0.4501	0.3996	0.3544	11
1	0.0995	0.1798	0.2433	0.2925	0.3293	0.3555	0.3727	0.3823	0.3855	10
2	0.0050	0.0183	0.0376	0.0609	0.0867	0.1135	0.1403	0.1662	0.1906	9
3	0.0002	0.0011	0.0035	0.0076	0.0137	0.0217	0.0317	0.0434	0.0566	8
4	0.0000	0.0000	0.0002	0.0006	0.0014	0.0028	0.0048	0.0075	0.0112	7
5	0.0000	0.0000	0.0000	0.0000	0.0001	0.0002	0.0005	0.0009	0.0015	6
6	0.0000	0.0000	0.0000	0.0000	0.0000	0.0000	0.0000	0.0001	0.0002	5
7	0.0000	0.0000	0.0000	0.0000	0.0000	0.0000	0.0000	0.0000	0.0000	4
	p = 0.99	p = 0.98	p = 0.97	p = 0.96	p = 0.95	p = 0.94	p = 0.93	p = 0.92	p = 0.91	x

x	p = 0.10	p = 0.15	p = 0.20	p = 0.25	p = 0.30	p = 0.35	p = 0.40	p = 0.45	p = 0.50	
0	0.3138	0.1673	0.0859	0.0422	0.0198	0.0088	0.0036	0.0014	0.0005	11
1	0.3835	0.3248	0.2362	0.1549	0.0932	0.0518	0.0266	0.0125	0.0054	10
2	0.2131	0.2866	0.2953	0.2581	0.1998	0.1395	0.0887	0.0513	0.0269	9
3	0.0710	0.1517	0.2215	0.2581	0.2568	0.2254	0.1774	0.1259	0.0806	8
4	0.0158	0.0536	0.1107	0.1721	0.2201	0.2428	0.2365	0.2060	0.1611	7
5	0.0025	0.0132	0.0388	0.0803	0.1321	0.1830	0.2207	0.2360	0.2256	6
6	0.0003	0.0023	0.0097	0.0268	0.0566	0.0985	0.1471	0.1931	0.2256	5
7	0.0000	0.0003	0.0017	0.0064	0.0173	0.0379	0.0701	0.1128	0.1611	4
8	0.0000	0.0000	0.0002	0.0011	0.0037	0.0102	0.0234	0.0462	0.0806	3
9	0.0000	0.0000	0.0000	0.0001	0.0005	0.0018	0.0052	0.0126	0.0269	2
10	0.0000	0.0000	0.0000	0.0000	0.0000	0.0002	0.0007	0.0021	0.0054	1
11	0.0000	0.0000	0.0000	0.0000	0.0000	0.0000	0.0000	0.0002	0.0005	0
	p = 0.90	p = 0.85	p = 0.80	p = 0.75	p = 0.70	p = 0.65	p = 0.60	p = 0.55	p = 0.50	x

n = 12

x	p = 0.01	p = 0.02	p = 0.03	p = 0.04	p = 0.05	p = 0.06	p = 0.07	p = 0.08	p = 0.09	
0	0.8864	0.7847	0.6938	0.6127	0.5404	0.4759	0.4186	0.3677	0.3225	12
1	0.1074	0.1922	0.2575	0.3064	0.3413	0.3645	0.3781	0.3837	0.3827	11
2	0.0060	0.0216	0.0438	0.0702	0.0988	0.1280	0.1565	0.1835	0.2082	10
3	0.0002	0.0015	0.0045	0.0098	0.0173	0.0272	0.0393	0.0532	0.0686	9
4	0.0000	0.0001	0.0003	0.0009	0.0021	0.0039	0.0067	0.0104	0.0153	8
5	0.0000	0.0000	0.0000	0.0001	0.0002	0.0004	0.0008	0.0014	0.0024	7
6	0.0000	0.0000	0.0000	0.0000	0.0000	0.0000	0.0001	0.0001	0.0003	6
7	0.0000	0.0000	0.0000	0.0000	0.0000	0.0000	0.0000	0.0000	0.0000	5
	p = 0.99	p = 0.98	p = 0.97	p = 0.96	p = 0.95	p = 0.94	p = 0.93	p = 0.92	p = 0.91	x

x	p = 0.10	p = 0.15	p = 0.20	p = 0.25	p = 0.30	p = 0.35	p = 0.40	p = 0.45	p = 0.50	12
0	0.2824	0.1422	0.0687	0.0317	0.0138	0.0057	0.0022	0.0008	0.0002	12
1	0.3766	0.3012	0.2062	0.1267	0.0712	0.0368	0.0174	0.0075	0.0029	11
2	0.2301	0.2924	0.2835	0.2323	0.1678	0.1088	0.0639	0.0339	0.0161	10
3	0.0852	0.1720	0.2362	0.2581	0.2397	0.1954	0.1419	0.0923	0.0537	9
4	0.0213	0.0683	0.1329	0.1936	0.2311	0.2367	0.2128	0.1700	0.1208	8
5	0.0038	0.0193	0.0532	0.1032	0.1585	0.2039	0.2270	0.2225	0.1934	7
6	0.0005	0.0040	0.0155	0.0401	0.0792	0.1281	0.1766	0.2124	0.2256	6
7	0.0000	0.0006	0.0033	0.0115	0.0291	0.0591	0.1009	0.1489	0.1934	5
8	0.0000	0.0001	0.0005	0.0024	0.0078	0.0199	0.0420	0.0762	0.1208	4
9	0.0000	0.0000	0.0001	0.0004	0.0015	0.0048	0.0125	0.0277	0.0537	3
10	0.0000	0.0000	0.0000	0.0000	0.0002	0.0008	0.0025	0.0068	0.0161	2
11	0.0000	0.0000	0.0000	0.0000	0.0000	0.0001	0.0003	0.0010	0.0029	1
12	0.0000	0.0000	0.0000	0.0000	0.0000	0.0000	0.0000	0.0001	0.0002	0
	p = 0.90	p = 0.85	p = 0.80	p = 0.75	p = 0.70	p = 0.65	p = 0.60	p = 0.55	p = 0.50	x

n = 13

x	p = 0.01	p = 0.02	p = 0.03	p = 0.04	p = 0.05	p = 0.06	p = 0.07	p = 0.08	p = 0.09	13
0	0.8775	0.7690	0.6730	0.5882	0.5133	0.4474	0.3893	0.3383	0.2935	13
1	0.1152	0.2040	0.2706	0.3186	0.3512	0.3712	0.3809	0.3824	0.3773	12
2	0.0070	0.0250	0.0502	0.0797	0.1109	0.1422	0.1720	0.1995	0.2239	11
3	0.0003	0.0019	0.0057	0.0122	0.0214	0.0333	0.0475	0.0636	0.0812	10
4	0.0000	0.0001	0.0004	0.0013	0.0028	0.0053	0.0089	0.0138	0.0201	9
5	0.0000	0.0000	0.0000	0.0001	0.0003	0.0006	0.0012	0.0022	0.0036	8
6	0.0000	0.0000	0.0000	0.0000	0.0000	0.0001	0.0001	0.0003	0.0005	7
7	0.0000	0.0000	0.0000	0.0000	0.0000	0.0000	0.0000	0.0000	0.0000	6
8	0.0000	0.0000	0.0000	0.0000	0.0000	0.0000	0.0000	0.0000	0.0000	5
	p = 0.99	p = 0.98	p = 0.97	p = 0.96	p = 0.95	p = 0.94	p = 0.93	p = 0.92	p = 0.91	x

x	p = 0.10	p = 0.15	p = 0.20	p = 0.25	p = 0.30	p = 0.35	p = 0.40	p = 0.45	p = 0.50	13
0	0.2542	0.1209	0.0550	0.0238	0.0097	0.0037	0.0013	0.0004	0.0001	13
1	0.3672	0.2774	0.1787	0.1029	0.0540	0.0259	0.0113	0.0045	0.0016	12
2	0.2448	0.2937	0.2680	0.2059	0.1388	0.0836	0.0453	0.0220	0.0095	11
3	0.0997	0.1900	0.2457	0.2517	0.2181	0.1651	0.1107	0.0660	0.0349	10
4	0.0277	0.0838	0.1535	0.2097	0.2337	0.2222	0.1845	0.1350	0.0873	9
5	0.0055	0.0266	0.0691	0.1258	0.1803	0.2154	0.2214	0.1989	0.1571	8
6	0.0008	0.0063	0.0230	0.0559	0.1030	0.1546	0.1968	0.2169	0.2095	7
7	0.0001	0.0011	0.0058	0.0186	0.0442	0.0833	0.1312	0.1775	0.2095	6
8	0.0000	0.0001	0.0011	0.0047	0.0142	0.0336	0.0656	0.1089	0.1571	5
9	0.0000	0.0000	0.0001	0.0009	0.0034	0.0101	0.0243	0.0495	0.0873	4
10	0.0000	0.0000	0.0000	0.0001	0.0006	0.0022	0.0065	0.0162	0.0349	3
11	0.0000	0.0000	0.0000	0.0000	0.0001	0.0003	0.0012	0.0036	0.0095	2
12	0.0000	0.0000	0.0000	0.0000	0.0000	0.0000	0.0001	0.0005	0.0016	1
13	0.0000	0.0000	0.0000	0.0000	0.0000	0.0000	0.0000	0.0000	0.0001	0
	p = 0.90	p = 0.85	p = 0.80	p = 0.75	p = 0.70	p = 0.65	p = 0.60	p = 0.55	p = 0.50	x

n = 14

x	p = 0.01	p = 0.02	p = 0.03	p = 0.04	p = 0.05	p = 0.06	p = 0.07	p = 0.08	p = 0.09	14
0	0.8687	0.7536	0.6528	0.5647	0.4877	0.4205	0.3620	0.3112	0.2670	14
1	0.1229	0.2153	0.2827	0.3294	0.3593	0.3758	0.3815	0.3788	0.3698	13
2	0.0081	0.0286	0.0568	0.0892	0.1229	0.1559	0.1867	0.2141	0.2377	12
3	0.0003	0.0023	0.0070	0.0149	0.0259	0.0398	0.0562	0.0745	0.0940	11
4	0.0000	0.0001	0.0006	0.0017	0.0037	0.0070	0.0116	0.0178	0.0256	10
5	0.0000	0.0000	0.0000	0.0001	0.0004	0.0009	0.0018	0.0031	0.0051	9
6	0.0000	0.0000	0.0000	0.0000	0.0000	0.0001	0.0002	0.0004	0.0008	8
7	0.0000	0.0000	0.0000	0.0000	0.0000	0.0000	0.0000	0.0000	0.0001	7
8	0.0000	0.0000	0.0000	0.0000	0.0000	0.0000	0.0000	0.0000	0.0000	6
	p = 0.99	p = 0.98	p = 0.97	p = 0.96	p = 0.95	p = 0.94	p = 0.93	p = 0.92	p = 0.91	x

x	p = 0.10	p = 0.15	p = 0.20	p = 0.25	p = 0.30	p = 0.35	p = 0.40	p = 0.45	p = 0.50	
0	0.2288	0.1028	0.0440	0.0178	0.0068	0.0024	0.0008	0.0002	0.0001	14
1	0.3559	0.2539	0.1539	0.0832	0.0407	0.0181	0.0073	0.0027	0.0009	13
2	0.2570	0.2912	0.2501	0.1802	0.1134	0.0634	0.0317	0.0141	0.0056	12
3	0.1142	0.2056	0.2501	0.2402	0.1943	0.1366	0.0845	0.0462	0.0222	11
4	0.0349	0.0998	0.1720	0.2202	0.2290	0.2022	0.1549	0.1040	0.0611	10
5	0.0078	0.0352	0.0860	0.1468	0.1963	0.2178	0.2066	0.1701	0.1222	9
6	0.0013	0.0093	0.0322	0.0734	0.1262	0.1759	0.2066	0.2088	0.1833	8
7	0.0002	0.0019	0.0092	0.0280	0.0618	0.1082	0.1574	0.1952	0.2095	7
8	0.0000	0.0003	0.0020	0.0082	0.0232	0.0510	0.0918	0.1398	0.1833	6
9	0.0000	0.0000	0.0003	0.0018	0.0066	0.0183	0.0408	0.0762	0.1222	5
10	0.0000	0.0000	0.0000	0.0003	0.0014	0.0049	0.0136	0.0312	0.0611	4
11	0.0000	0.0000	0.0000	0.0000	0.0002	0.0010	0.0033	0.0093	0.0222	3
12	0.0000	0.0000	0.0000	0.0000	0.0000	0.0001	0.0005	0.0019	0.0056	2
13	0.0000	0.0000	0.0000	0.0000	0.0000	0.0000	0.0001	0.0002	0.0009	1
14	0.0000	0.0000	0.0000	0.0000	0.0000	0.0000	0.0000	0.0000	0.0001	0
	p = 0.90	p = 0.85	p = 0.80	p = 0.75	p = 0.70	p = 0.65	p = 0.60	p = 0.55	p = 0.50	x

n = 15

x	p = 0.01	p = 0.02	p = 0.03	p = 0.04	p = 0.05	p = 0.06	p = 0.07	p = 0.08	p = 0.09	
0	0.8601	0.7386	0.6333	0.5421	0.4633	0.3953	0.3367	0.2863	0.2430	15
1	0.1303	0.2261	0.2938	0.3388	0.3658	0.3785	0.3801	0.3734	0.3605	14
2	0.0092	0.0323	0.0636	0.0988	0.1348	0.1691	0.2003	0.2273	0.2496	13
3	0.0004	0.0029	0.0085	0.0178	0.0307	0.0468	0.0653	0.0857	0.1070	12
4	0.0000	0.0002	0.0008	0.0022	0.0049	0.0090	0.0148	0.0223	0.0317	11
5	0.0000	0.0000	0.0001	0.0002	0.0006	0.0013	0.0024	0.0043	0.0069	10
6	0.0000	0.0000	0.0000	0.0000	0.0000	0.0001	0.0003	0.0006	0.0011	9
7	0.0000	0.0000	0.0000	0.0000	0.0000	0.0000	0.0000	0.0001	0.0001	8
	p = 0.99	p = 0.98	p = 0.97	p = 0.96	p = 0.95	p = 0.94	p = 0.93	p = 0.92	p = 0.91	x

x	p = 0.10	p = 0.15	p = 0.20	p = 0.25	p = 0.30	p = 0.35	p = 0.40	p = 0.45	p = 0.50	
0	0.2059	0.0874	0.0352	0.0134	0.0047	0.0016	0.0005	0.0001	0.0000	15
1	0.3432	0.2312	0.1319	0.0668	0.0305	0.0126	0.0047	0.0016	0.0005	14
2	0.2669	0.2856	0.2309	0.1559	0.0916	0.0476	0.0219	0.0090	0.0032	13
3	0.1285	0.2184	0.2501	0.2252	0.1700	0.1110	0.0634	0.0318	0.0139	12
4	0.0428	0.1156	0.1876	0.2252	0.2186	0.1792	0.1268	0.0780	0.0417	11
5	0.0105	0.0449	0.1032	0.1651	0.2061	0.2123	0.1859	0.1404	0.0916	10
6	0.0019	0.0132	0.0430	0.0917	0.1472	0.1906	0.2066	0.1914	0.1527	9
7	0.0003	0.0030	0.0138	0.0393	0.0811	0.1319	0.1771	0.2013	0.1964	8
8	0.0000	0.0005	0.0035	0.0131	0.0348	0.0710	0.1181	0.1647	0.1964	7
9	0.0000	0.0001	0.0007	0.0034	0.0116	0.0298	0.0612	0.1048	0.1527	6
10	0.0000	0.0000	0.0001	0.0007	0.0030	0.0096	0.0245	0.0515	0.0916	5
11	0.0000	0.0000	0.0000	0.0001	0.0006	0.0024	0.0074	0.0191	0.0417	4
12	0.0000	0.0000	0.0000	0.0000	0.0001	0.0004	0.0016	0.0052	0.0139	3
13	0.0000	0.0000	0.0000	0.0000	0.0000	0.0001	0.0003	0.0010	0.0032	2
14	0.0000	0.0000	0.0000	0.0000	0.0000	0.0000	0.0000	0.0001	0.0005	1
15	0.0000	0.0000	0.0000	0.0000	0.0000	0.0000	0.0000	0.0000	0.0000	0
	p = 0.90	p = 0.85	p = 0.80	p = 0.75	p = 0.70	p = 0.65	p = 0.60	p = 0.55	p = 0.50	x

n = 20

x	p = 0.01	p = 0.02	p = 0.03	p = 0.04	p = 0.05	p = 0.06	p = 0.07	p = 0.08	p = 0.09	
0	0.8179	0.6676	0.5438	0.4420	0.3585	0.2901	0.2342	0.1887	0.1516	20
1	0.1652	0.2725	0.3364	0.3683	0.3774	0.3703	0.3526	0.3282	0.3000	19
2	0.0159	0.0528	0.0988	0.1458	0.1887	0.2246	0.2521	0.2711	0.2818	18
3	0.0010	0.0065	0.0183	0.0364	0.0596	0.0860	0.1139	0.1414	0.1672	17
4	0.0000	0.0006	0.0024	0.0065	0.0133	0.0233	0.0364	0.0523	0.0703	16
5	0.0000	0.0000	0.0002	0.0009	0.0022	0.0048	0.0088	0.0145	0.0222	15
6	0.0000	0.0000	0.0000	0.0001	0.0003	0.0008	0.0017	0.0032	0.0055	14
7	0.0000	0.0000	0.0000	0.0000	0.0000	0.0001	0.0002	0.0005	0.0011	13
8	0.0000	0.0000	0.0000	0.0000	0.0000	0.0000	0.0000	0.0001	0.0002	12
9	0.0000	0.0000	0.0000	0.0000	0.0000	0.0000	0.0000	0.0000	0.0000	11
	p = 0.99	p = 0.98	p = 0.97	p = 0.96	p = 0.95	p = 0.94	p = 0.93	p = 0.92	p = 0.91	x

x	p = 0.10	p = 0.15	p = 0.20	p = 0.25	p = 0.30	p = 0.35	p = 0.40	p = 0.45	p = 0.50	
0	0.1216	0.0388	0.0115	0.0032	0.0008	0.0002	0.0000	0.0000	0.0000	20
1	0.2702	0.1368	0.0576	0.0211	0.0068	0.0020	0.0005	0.0001	0.0000	19
2	0.2852	0.2293	0.1369	0.0669	0.0278	0.0100	0.0031	0.0008	0.0002	18
3	0.1901	0.2428	0.2054	0.1339	0.0716	0.0323	0.0123	0.0040	0.0011	17
4	0.0898	0.1821	0.2182	0.1897	0.1304	0.0738	0.0350	0.0139	0.0046	16
5	0.0319	0.1028	0.1746	0.2023	0.1789	0.1272	0.0746	0.0365	0.0148	15
6	0.0089	0.0454	0.1091	0.1686	0.1916	0.1712	0.1244	0.0746	0.0370	14
7	0.0020	0.0160	0.0545	0.1124	0.1643	0.1844	0.1659	0.1221	0.0739	13
8	0.0004	0.0046	0.0222	0.0609	0.1144	0.1614	0.1797	0.1623	0.1201	12
9	0.0001	0.0011	0.0074	0.0271	0.0654	0.1158	0.1597	0.1771	0.1602	11
10	0.0000	0.0002	0.0020	0.0099	0.0308	0.0686	0.1171	0.1593	0.1762	10
11	0.0000	0.0000	0.0005	0.0030	0.0120	0.0336	0.0710	0.1185	0.1602	9
12	0.0000	0.0000	0.0001	0.0008	0.0039	0.0136	0.0355	0.0727	0.1201	8
13	0.0000	0.0000	0.0000	0.0002	0.0010	0.0045	0.0146	0.0366	0.0739	7
14	0.0000	0.0000	0.0000	0.0000	0.0002	0.0012	0.0049	0.0150	0.0370	6
15	0.0000	0.0000	0.0000	0.0000	0.0000	0.0003	0.0013	0.0049	0.0148	5
16	0.0000	0.0000	0.0000	0.0000	0.0000	0.0000	0.0003	0.0013	0.0046	4
17	0.0000	0.0000	0.0000	0.0000	0.0000	0.0000	0.0000	0.0002	0.0011	3
18	0.0000	0.0000	0.0000	0.0000	0.0000	0.0000	0.0000	0.0000	0.0002	2
	p = 0.90	p = 0.85	p = 0.80	p = 0.75	p = 0.70	p = 0.65	p = 0.60	p = 0.55	p = 0.50	x

n = 25

x	p = 0.01	p = 0.02	p = 0.03	p = 0.04	p = 0.05	p = 0.06	p = 0.07	p = 0.08	p = 0.09	
0	0.7778	0.6035	0.4670	0.3604	0.2774	0.2129	0.1630	0.1244	0.0946	25
1	0.1964	0.3079	0.3611	0.3754	0.3650	0.3398	0.3066	0.2704	0.2340	24
2	0.0238	0.0754	0.1340	0.1877	0.2305	0.2602	0.2770	0.2821	0.2777	23
3	0.0018	0.0118	0.0318	0.0600	0.0930	0.1273	0.1598	0.1881	0.2106	22
4	0.0001	0.0013	0.0054	0.0137	0.0269	0.0447	0.0662	0.0899	0.1145	21
5	0.0000	0.0001	0.0007	0.0024	0.0060	0.0120	0.0209	0.0329	0.0476	20
6	0.0000	0.0000	0.0001	0.0003	0.0010	0.0026	0.0052	0.0095	0.0157	19
7	0.0000	0.0000	0.0000	0.0000	0.0001	0.0004	0.0011	0.0022	0.0042	18
8	0.0000	0.0000	0.0000	0.0000	0.0000	0.0001	0.0002	0.0004	0.0009	17
9	0.0000	0.0000	0.0000	0.0000	0.0000	0.0000	0.0000	0.0001	0.0002	16
10	0.0000	0.0000	0.0000	0.0000	0.0000	0.0000	0.0000	0.0000	0.0000	15
	p = 0.99	p = 0.98	p = 0.97	p = 0.96	p = 0.95	p = 0.94	p = 0.93	p = 0.92	p = 0.91	x

x	p = 0.10	p = 0.15	p = 0.20	p = 0.25	p = 0.30	p = 0.35	p = 0.40	p = 0.45	p = 0.50	
0	0.0718	0.0172	0.0038	0.0008	0.0001	0.0000	0.0000	0.0000	0.0000	25
1	0.1994	0.0759	0.0236	0.0063	0.0014	0.0003	0.0000	0.0000	0.0000	24
2	0.2659	0.1607	0.0708	0.0251	0.0074	0.0018	0.0004	0.0001	0.0000	23
3	0.2265	0.2174	0.1358	0.0641	0.0243	0.0076	0.0019	0.0004	0.0001	22
4	0.1384	0.2110	0.1867	0.1175	0.0572	0.0224	0.0071	0.0018	0.0004	21
5	0.0646	0.1564	0.1960	0.1645	0.1030	0.0506	0.0199	0.0063	0.0016	20
6	0.0239	0.0920	0.1633	0.1828	0.1472	0.0908	0.0442	0.0172	0.0053	19
7	0.0072	0.0441	0.1108	0.1654	0.1712	0.1327	0.0800	0.0381	0.0143	18
8	0.0018	0.0175	0.0623	0.1241	0.1651	0.1607	0.1200	0.0701	0.0322	17
9	0.0004	0.0058	0.0294	0.0781	0.1336	0.1635	0.1511	0.1084	0.0609	16
10	0.0001	0.0016	0.0118	0.0417	0.0916	0.1409	0.1612	0.1419	0.0974	15
11	0.0000	0.0004	0.0040	0.0189	0.0536	0.1034	0.1465	0.1583	0.1328	14
12	0.0000	0.0001	0.0012	0.0074	0.0268	0.0650	0.1140	0.1511	0.1550	13
13	0.0000	0.0000	0.0003	0.0025	0.0115	0.0350	0.0760	0.1236	0.1550	12
14	0.0000	0.0000	0.0001	0.0007	0.0042	0.0161	0.0434	0.0867	0.1328	11
15	0.0000	0.0000	0.0000	0.0002	0.0013	0.0064	0.0212	0.0520	0.0974	10
16	0.0000	0.0000	0.0000	0.0000	0.0004	0.0021	0.0088	0.0266	0.0609	9
17	0.0000	0.0000	0.0000	0.0000	0.0001	0.0006	0.0031	0.0115	0.0322	8
18	0.0000	0.0000	0.0000	0.0000	0.0000	0.0001	0.0009	0.0042	0.0143	7
19	0.0000	0.0000	0.0000	0.0000	0.0000	0.0000	0.0002	0.0013	0.0053	6
20	0.0000	0.0000	0.0000	0.0000	0.0000	0.0000	0.0000	0.0003	0.0016	5
21	0.0000	0.0000	0.0000	0.0000	0.0000	0.0000	0.0000	0.0001	0.0004	4
22	0.0000	0.0000	0.0000	0.0000	0.0000	0.0000	0.0000	0.0000	0.0001	3
	p = 0.90	p = 0.85	p = 0.80	p = 0.75	p = 0.70	p = 0.65	p = 0.60	p = 0.55	p = 0.50	x

APPENDIX C

Poisson Probability Distribution Table

Values of $P(x) = \dfrac{(\lambda t)^x e^{-\lambda t}}{x!}$

λt

x	0.005	0.01	0.02	0.03	0.04	0.05	0.06	0.07	0.08	0.09
0	0.9950	0.9900	0.9802	0.9704	0.9608	0.9512	0.9418	0.9324	0.9231	0.9139
1	0.0050	0.0099	0.0196	0.0291	0.0384	0.0476	0.0565	0.0653	0.0738	0.0823
2	0.0000	0.0000	0.0002	0.0004	0.0008	0.0012	0.0017	0.0023	0.0030	0.0037
3	0.0000	0.0000	0.0000	0.0000	0.0000	0.0000	0.0000	0.0001	0.0001	0.0001

λt

x	0.10	0.20	0.30	0.40	0.50	0.60	0.70	0.80	0.90	1.00
0	0.9048	0.8187	0.7408	0.6703	0.6065	0.5488	0.4966	0.4493	0.4066	0.3679
1	0.0905	0.1637	0.2222	0.2681	0.3033	0.3293	0.3476	0.3595	0.3659	0.3679
2	0.0045	0.0164	0.0333	0.0536	0.0758	0.0988	0.1217	0.1438	0.1647	0.1839
3	0.0002	0.0011	0.0033	0.0072	0.0126	0.0198	0.0284	0.0383	0.0494	0.0613
4	0.0000	0.0001	0.0003	0.0007	0.0016	0.0030	0.0050	0.0077	0.0111	0.0153
5	0.0000	0.0000	0.0000	0.0001	0.0002	0.0004	0.0007	0.0012	0.0020	0.0031
6	0.0000	0.0000	0.0000	0.0000	0.0000	0.0000	0.0001	0.0002	0.0003	0.0005
7	0.0000	0.0000	0.0000	0.0000	0.0000	0.0000	0.0000	0.0000	0.0000	0.0001

λt

x	1.10	1.20	1.30	1.40	1.50	1.60	1.70	1.80	1.90	2.00
0	0.3329	0.3012	0.2725	0.2466	0.2231	0.2019	0.1827	0.1653	0.1496	0.1353
1	0.3662	0.3614	0.3543	0.3452	0.3347	0.3230	0.3106	0.2975	0.2842	0.2707
2	0.2014	0.2169	0.2303	0.2417	0.2510	0.2584	0.2640	0.2678	0.2700	0.2707
3	0.0738	0.0867	0.0998	0.1128	0.1255	0.1378	0.1496	0.1607	0.1710	0.1804
4	0.0203	0.0260	0.0324	0.0395	0.0471	0.0551	0.0636	0.0723	0.0812	0.0902
5	0.0045	0.0062	0.0084	0.0111	0.0141	0.0176	0.0216	0.0260	0.0309	0.0361
6	0.0008	0.0012	0.0018	0.0026	0.0035	0.0047	0.0061	0.0078	0.0098	0.0120
7	0.0001	0.0002	0.0003	0.0005	0.0008	0.0011	0.0015	0.0020	0.0027	0.0034
8	0.0000	0.0000	0.0001	0.0001	0.0001	0.0002	0.0003	0.0005	0.0006	0.0009
9	0.0000	0.0000	0.0000	0.0000	0.0000	0.0000	0.0001	0.0001	0.0001	0.0002

λt

x	2.10	2.20	2.30	2.40	2.50	2.60	2.70	2.80	2.90	3.00
0	0.1225	0.1108	0.1003	0.0907	0.0821	0.0743	0.0672	0.0608	0.0550	0.0498
1	0.2572	0.2438	0.2306	0.2177	0.2052	0.1931	0.1815	0.1703	0.1596	0.1494
2	0.2700	0.2681	0.2652	0.2613	0.2565	0.2510	0.2450	0.2384	0.2314	0.2240
3	0.1890	0.1966	0.2033	0.2090	0.2138	0.2176	0.2205	0.2225	0.2237	0.2240
4	0.0992	0.1082	0.1169	0.1254	0.1336	0.1414	0.1488	0.1557	0.1622	0.1680
5	0.0417	0.0476	0.0538	0.0602	0.0668	0.0735	0.0804	0.0872	0.0940	0.1008
6	0.0146	0.0174	0.0206	0.0241	0.0278	0.0319	0.0362	0.0407	0.0455	0.0504
7	0.0044	0.0055	0.0068	0.0083	0.0099	0.0118	0.0139	0.0163	0.0188	0.0216
8	0.0011	0.0015	0.0019	0.0025	0.0031	0.0038	0.0047	0.0057	0.0068	0.0081
9	0.0003	0.0004	0.0005	0.0007	0.0009	0.0011	0.0014	0.0018	0.0022	0.0027
10	0.0001	0.0001	0.0001	0.0002	0.0002	0.0003	0.0004	0.0005	0.0006	0.0008
11	0.0000	0.0000	0.0000	0.0000	0.0000	0.0001	0.0001	0.0001	0.0002	0.0002
12	0.0000	0.0000	0.0000	0.0000	0.0000	0.0000	0.0000	0.0000	0.0000	0.0001

x	3.10	3.20	3.30	3.40	3.50	3.60	3.70	3.80	3.90	4.00
0	0.0450	0.0408	0.0369	0.0334	0.0302	0.0273	0.0247	0.0224	0.0202	0.0183
1	0.1397	0.1304	0.1217	0.1135	0.1057	0.0984	0.0915	0.0850	0.0789	0.0733
2	0.2165	0.2087	0.2008	0.1929	0.1850	0.1771	0.1692	0.1615	0.1539	0.1465
3	0.2237	0.2226	0.2209	0.2186	0.2158	0.2125	0.2087	0.2046	0.2001	0.1954
4	0.1733	0.1781	0.1823	0.1858	0.1888	0.1912	0.1931	0.1944	0.1951	0.1954
5	0.1075	0.1140	0.1203	0.1264	0.1322	0.1377	0.1429	0.1477	0.1522	0.1563
6	0.0555	0.0608	0.0662	0.0716	0.0771	0.0826	0.0881	0.0936	0.0989	0.1042
7	0.0246	0.0278	0.0312	0.0348	0.0385	0.0425	0.0466	0.0508	0.0551	0.0595
8	0.0095	0.0111	0.0129	0.0148	0.0169	0.0191	0.0215	0.0241	0.0269	0.0298
9	0.0033	0.0040	0.0047	0.0056	0.0066	0.0076	0.0089	0.0102	0.0116	0.0132
10	0.0010	0.0013	0.0016	0.0019	0.0023	0.0028	0.0033	0.0039	0.0045	0.0053
11	0.0003	0.0004	0.0005	0.0006	0.0007	0.0009	0.0011	0.0013	0.0016	0.0019
12	0.0001	0.0001	0.0001	0.0002	0.0002	0.0003	0.0003	0.0004	0.0005	0.0006
13	0.0000	0.0000	0.0000	0.0000	0.0001	0.0001	0.0001	0.0001	0.0002	0.0002
14	0.0000	0.0000	0.0000	0.0000	0.0000	0.0000	0.0000	0.0000	0.0000	0.0001

λt

x	4.10	4.20	4.30	4.40	4.50	4.60	4.70	4.80	4.90	5.00
0	0.0166	0.0150	0.0136	0.0123	0.0111	0.0101	0.0091	0.0082	0.0074	0.0067
1	0.0679	0.0630	0.0583	0.0540	0.0500	0.0462	0.0427	0.0395	0.0365	0.0337
2	0.1393	0.1323	0.1254	0.1188	0.1125	0.1063	0.1005	0.0948	0.0894	0.0842
3	0.1904	0.1852	0.1798	0.1743	0.1687	0.1631	0.1574	0.1517	0.1460	0.1404
4	0.1951	0.1944	0.1933	0.1917	0.1898	0.1875	0.1849	0.1820	0.1789	0.1755
5	0.1600	0.1633	0.1662	0.1687	0.1708	0.1725	0.1738	0.1747	0.1753	0.1755
6	0.1093	0.1143	0.1191	0.1237	0.1281	0.1323	0.1362	0.1398	0.1432	0.1462
7	0.0640	0.0686	0.0732	0.0778	0.0824	0.0869	0.0914	0.0959	0.1002	0.1044
8	0.0328	0.0360	0.0393	0.0428	0.0463	0.0500	0.0537	0.0575	0.0614	0.0653
9	0.0150	0.0168	0.0188	0.0209	0.0232	0.0255	0.0281	0.0307	0.0334	0.0363
10	0.0061	0.0071	0.0081	0.0092	0.0104	0.0118	0.0132	0.0147	0.0164	0.0181
11	0.0023	0.0027	0.0032	0.0037	0.0043	0.0049	0.0056	0.0064	0.0073	0.0082
12	0.0008	0.0009	0.0011	0.0013	0.0016	0.0019	0.0022	0.0026	0.0030	0.0034
13	0.0002	0.0003	0.0004	0.0005	0.0006	0.0007	0.0008	0.0009	0.0011	0.0013
14	0.0001	0.0001	0.0001	0.0001	0.0002	0.0002	0.0003	0.0003	0.0004	0.0005
15	0.0000	0.0000	0.0000	0.0000	0.0001	0.0001	0.0001	0.0001	0.0001	0.0002

λt

x	5.10	5.20	5.30	5.40	5.50	5.60	5.70	5.80	5.90	6.00
0	0.0061	0.0055	0.0050	0.0045	0.0041	0.0037	0.0033	0.0030	0.0027	0.0025
1	0.0311	0.0287	0.0265	0.0244	0.0225	0.0207	0.0191	0.0176	0.0162	0.0149
2	0.0793	0.0746	0.0701	0.0659	0.0618	0.0580	0.0544	0.0509	0.0477	0.0446
3	0.1348	0.1293	0.1239	0.1185	0.1133	0.1082	0.1033	0.0985	0.0938	0.0892
4	0.1719	0.1681	0.1641	0.1600	0.1558	0.1515	0.1472	0.1428	0.1383	0.1339
5	0.1753	0.1748	0.1740	0.1728	0.1714	0.1697	0.1678	0.1656	0.1632	0.1606
6	0.1490	0.1515	0.1537	0.1555	0.1571	0.1584	0.1594	0.1601	0.1605	0.1606
7	0.1086	0.1125	0.1163	0.1200	0.1234	0.1267	0.1298	0.1326	0.1353	0.1377
8	0.0692	0.0731	0.0771	0.0810	0.0849	0.0887	0.0925	0.0962	0.0998	0.1033
9	0.0392	0.0423	0.0454	0.0486	0.0519	0.0552	0.0586	0.0620	0.0654	0.0688
10	0.0200	0.0220	0.0241	0.0262	0.0285	0.0309	0.0334	0.0359	0.0386	0.0413
11	0.0093	0.0104	0.0116	0.0129	0.0143	0.0157	0.0173	0.0190	0.0207	0.0225
12	0.0039	0.0045	0.0051	0.0058	0.0065	0.0073	0.0082	0.0092	0.0102	0.0113
13	0.0015	0.0018	0.0021	0.0024	0.0028	0.0032	0.0036	0.0041	0.0046	0.0052
14	0.0006	0.0007	0.0008	0.0009	0.0011	0.0013	0.0015	0.0017	0.0019	0.0022
15	0.0002	0.0002	0.0003	0.0003	0.0004	0.0005	0.0006	0.0007	0.0008	0.0009
16	0.0001	0.0001	0.0001	0.0001	0.0001	0.0002	0.0002	0.0002	0.0003	0.0003
17	0.0000	0.0000	0.0000	0.0000	0.0000	0.0001	0.0001	0.0001	0.0001	0.0001

λt

x	6.10	6.20	6.30	6.40	6.50	6.60	6.70	6.80	6.90	7.00
0	0.0022	0.0020	0.0018	0.0017	0.0015	0.0014	0.0012	0.0011	0.0010	0.0009
1	0.0137	0.0126	0.0116	0.0106	0.0098	0.0090	0.0082	0.0076	0.0070	0.0064
2	0.0417	0.0390	0.0364	0.0340	0.0318	0.0296	0.0276	0.0258	0.0240	0.0223
3	0.0848	0.0806	0.0765	0.0726	0.0688	0.0652	0.0617	0.0584	0.0552	0.0521
4	0.1294	0.1249	0.1205	0.1162	0.1118	0.1076	0.1034	0.0992	0.0952	0.0912
5	0.1579	0.1549	0.1519	0.1487	0.1454	0.1420	0.1385	0.1349	0.1314	0.1277
6	0.1605	0.1601	0.1595	0.1586	0.1575	0.1562	0.1546	0.1529	0.1511	0.1490
7	0.1399	0.1418	0.1435	0.1450	0.1462	0.1472	0.1480	0.1486	0.1489	0.1490
8	0.1066	0.1099	0.1130	0.1160	0.1188	0.1215	0.1240	0.1263	0.1284	0.1304
9	0.0723	0.0757	0.0791	0.0825	0.0858	0.0891	0.0923	0.0954	0.0985	0.1014
10	0.0441	0.0469	0.0498	0.0528	0.0558	0.0588	0.0618	0.0649	0.0679	0.0710
11	0.0244	0.0265	0.0285	0.0307	0.0330	0.0353	0.0377	0.0401	0.0426	0.0452
12	0.0124	0.0137	0.0150	0.0164	0.0179	0.0194	0.0210	0.0227	0.0245	0.0263
13	0.0058	0.0065	0.0073	0.0081	0.0089	0.0099	0.0108	0.0119	0.0130	0.0142
14	0.0025	0.0029	0.0033	0.0037	0.0041	0.0046	0.0052	0.0058	0.0064	0.0071
15	0.0010	0.0012	0.0014	0.0016	0.0018	0.0020	0.0023	0.0026	0.0029	0.0033
16	0.0004	0.0005	0.0005	0.0006	0.0007	0.0008	0.0010	0.0011	0.0013	0.0014
17	0.0001	0.0002	0.0002	0.0002	0.0003	0.0003	0.0004	0.0004	0.0005	0.0006
18	0.0000	0.0001	0.0001	0.0001	0.0001	0.0001	0.0001	0.0002	0.0002	0.0002
19	0.0000	0.0000	0.0000	0.0000	0.0000	0.0000	0.0001	0.0001	0.0001	0.0001

λt

x	7.10	7.20	7.30	7.40	7.50	7.60	7.70	7.80	7.90	8.00
0	0.0008	0.0007	0.0007	0.0006	0.0006	0.0005	0.0005	0.0004	0.0004	0.0003
1	0.0059	0.0054	0.0049	0.0045	0.0041	0.0038	0.0035	0.0032	0.0029	0.0027
2	0.0208	0.0194	0.0180	0.0167	0.0156	0.0145	0.0134	0.0125	0.0116	0.0107
3	0.0492	0.0464	0.0438	0.0413	0.0389	0.0366	0.0345	0.0324	0.0305	0.0286
4	0.0874	0.0836	0.0799	0.0764	0.0729	0.0696	0.0663	0.0632	0.0602	0.0573
5	0.1241	0.1204	0.1167	0.1130	0.1094	0.1057	0.1021	0.0986	0.0951	0.0916
6	0.1468	0.1445	0.1420	0.1394	0.1367	0.1339	0.1311	0.1282	0.1252	0.1221
7	0.1489	0.1486	0.1481	0.1474	0.1465	0.1454	0.1442	0.1428	0.1413	0.1396
8	0.1321	0.1337	0.1351	0.1363	0.1373	0.1381	0.1388	0.1392	0.1395	0.1396
9	0.1042	0.1070	0.1096	0.1121	0.1144	0.1167	0.1187	0.1207	0.1224	0.1241
10	0.0740	0.0770	0.0800	0.0829	0.0858	0.0887	0.0914	0.0941	0.0967	0.0993
11	0.0478	0.0504	0.0531	0.0558	0.0585	0.0613	0.0640	0.0667	0.0695	0.0722
12	0.0283	0.0303	0.0323	0.0344	0.0366	0.0388	0.0411	0.0434	0.0457	0.0481
13	0.0154	0.0168	0.0181	0.0196	0.0211	0.0227	0.0243	0.0260	0.0278	0.0296
14	0.0078	0.0086	0.0095	0.0104	0.0113	0.0123	0.0134	0.0145	0.0157	0.0169
15	0.0037	0.0041	0.0046	0.0051	0.0057	0.0062	0.0069	0.0075	0.0083	0.0090
16	0.0016	0.0019	0.0021	0.0024	0.0026	0.0030	0.0033	0.0037	0.0041	0.0045
17	0.0007	0.0008	0.0009	0.0010	0.0012	0.0013	0.0015	0.0017	0.0019	0.0021
18	0.0003	0.0003	0.0004	0.0004	0.0005	0.0006	0.0006	0.0007	0.0008	0.0009
19	0.0001	0.0001	0.0001	0.0002	0.0002	0.0002	0.0003	0.0003	0.0003	0.0004
20	0.0000	0.0000	0.0001	0.0001	0.0001	0.0001	0.0001	0.0001	0.0001	0.0002
21	0.0000	0.0000	0.0000	0.0000	0.0000	0.0000	0.0000	0.0000	0.0001	0.0001

λt

x	8.10	8.20	8.30	8.40	8.50	8.60	8.70	8.80	8.90	9.00
0	0.0003	0.0003	0.0002	0.0002	0.0002	0.0002	0.0002	0.0002	0.0001	0.0001
1	0.0025	0.0023	0.0021	0.0019	0.0017	0.0016	0.0014	0.0013	0.0012	0.0011
2	0.0100	0.0092	0.0086	0.0079	0.0074	0.0068	0.0063	0.0058	0.0054	0.0050
3	0.0269	0.0252	0.0237	0.0222	0.0208	0.0195	0.0183	0.0171	0.0160	0.0150
4	0.0544	0.0517	0.0491	0.0466	0.0443	0.0420	0.0398	0.0377	0.0357	0.0337
5	0.0882	0.0849	0.0816	0.0784	0.0752	0.0722	0.0692	0.0663	0.0635	0.0607
6	0.1191	0.1160	0.1128	0.1097	0.1066	0.1034	0.1003	0.0972	0.0941	0.0911
7	0.1378	0.1358	0.1338	0.1317	0.1294	0.1271	0.1247	0.1222	0.1197	0.1171
8	0.1395	0.1392	0.1388	0.1382	0.1375	0.1366	0.1356	0.1344	0.1332	0.1318
9	0.1256	0.1269	0.1280	0.1290	0.1299	0.1306	0.1311	0.1315	0.1317	0.1318
10	0.1017	0.1040	0.1063	0.1084	0.1104	0.1123	0.1140	0.1157	0.1172	0.1186
11	0.0749	0.0776	0.0802	0.0828	0.0853	0.0878	0.0902	0.0925	0.0948	0.0970
12	0.0505	0.0530	0.0555	0.0579	0.0604	0.0629	0.0654	0.0679	0.0703	0.0728
13	0.0315	0.0334	0.0354	0.0374	0.0395	0.0416	0.0438	0.0459	0.0481	0.0504
14	0.0182	0.0196	0.0210	0.0225	0.0240	0.0256	0.0272	0.0289	0.0306	0.0324
15	0.0098	0.0107	0.0116	0.0126	0.0136	0.0147	0.0158	0.0169	0.0182	0.0194
16	0.0050	0.0055	0.0060	0.0066	0.0072	0.0079	0.0086	0.0093	0.0101	0.0109
17	0.0024	0.0026	0.0029	0.0033	0.0036	0.0040	0.0044	0.0048	0.0053	0.0058
18	0.0011	0.0012	0.0014	0.0015	0.0017	0.0019	0.0021	0.0024	0.0026	0.0029
19	0.0005	0.0005	0.0006	0.0007	0.0008	0.0009	0.0010	0.0011	0.0012	0.0014
20	0.0002	0.0002	0.0002	0.0003	0.0003	0.0004	0.0004	0.0005	0.0005	0.0006
21	0.0001	0.0001	0.0001	0.0001	0.0001	0.0002	0.0002	0.0002	0.0002	0.0003
22	0.0000	0.0000	0.0000	0.0000	0.0001	0.0001	0.0001	0.0001	0.0001	0.0001

λt

x	9.10	9.20	9.30	9.40	9.50	9.60	9.70	9.80	9.90	10.00
0	0.0001	0.0001	0.0001	0.0001	0.0001	0.0001	0.0001	0.0001	0.0001	0.0000
1	0.0010	0.0009	0.0009	0.0008	0.0007	0.0007	0.0006	0.0005	0.0005	0.0005
2	0.0046	0.0043	0.0040	0.0037	0.0034	0.0031	0.0029	0.0027	0.0025	0.0023
3	0.0140	0.0131	0.0123	0.0115	0.0107	0.0100	0.0093	0.0087	0.0081	0.0076
4	0.0319	0.0302	0.0285	0.0269	0.0254	0.0240	0.0226	0.0213	0.0201	0.0189
5	0.0581	0.0555	0.0530	0.0506	0.0483	0.0460	0.0439	0.0418	0.0398	0.0378
6	0.0881	0.0851	0.0822	0.0793	0.0764	0.0736	0.0709	0.0682	0.0656	0.0631
7	0.1145	0.1118	0.1091	0.1064	0.1037	0.1010	0.0982	0.0955	0.0928	0.0901
8	0.1302	0.1286	0.1269	0.1251	0.1232	0.1212	0.1191	0.1170	0.1148	0.1126
9	0.1317	0.1315	0.1311	0.1306	0.1300	0.1293	0.1284	0.1274	0.1263	0.1251
10	0.1198	0.1210	0.1219	0.1228	0.1235	0.1241	0.1245	0.1249	0.1250	0.1251
11	0.0991	0.1012	0.1031	0.1049	0.1067	0.1083	0.1098	0.1112	0.1125	0.1137
12	0.0752	0.0776	0.0799	0.0822	0.0844	0.0866	0.0888	0.0908	0.0928	0.0948
13	0.0526	0.0549	0.0572	0.0594	0.0617	0.0640	0.0662	0.0685	0.0707	0.0729
14	0.0342	0.0361	0.0380	0.0399	0.0419	0.0439	0.0459	0.0479	0.0500	0.0521
15	0.0208	0.0221	0.0235	0.0250	0.0265	0.0281	0.0297	0.0313	0.0330	0.0347
16	0.0118	0.0127	0.0137	0.0147	0.0157	0.0168	0.0180	0.0192	0.0204	0.0217
17	0.0063	0.0069	0.0075	0.0081	0.0088	0.0095	0.0103	0.0111	0.0119	0.0128
18	0.0032	0.0035	0.0039	0.0042	0.0046	0.0051	0.0055	0.0060	0.0065	0.0071
19	0.0015	0.0017	0.0019	0.0021	0.0023	0.0026	0.0028	0.0031	0.0034	0.0037
20	0.0007	0.0008	0.0009	0.0010	0.0011	0.0012	0.0014	0.0015	0.0017	0.0019
21	0.0003	0.0003	0.0004	0.0004	0.0005	0.0006	0.0006	0.0007	0.0008	0.0009
22	0.0001	0.0001	0.0002	0.0002	0.0002	0.0002	0.0003	0.0003	0.0004	0.0004
23	0.0000	0.0001	0.0001	0.0001	0.0001	0.0001	0.0001	0.0001	0.0002	0.0002
24	0.0000	0.0000	0.0000	0.0000	0.0000	0.0000	0.0000	0.0001	0.0001	0.0001

λt

x	11.00	12.00	13.00	14.00	15.00	16.00	17.00	18.00	19.00	20.00
0	0.0000	0.0000	0.0000	0.0000	0.0000	0.0000	0.0000	0.0000	0.0000	0.0000
1	0.0002	0.0001	0.0000	0.0000	0.0000	0.0000	0.0000	0.0000	0.0000	0.0000
2	0.0010	0.0004	0.0002	0.0001	0.0000	0.0000	0.0000	0.0000	0.0000	0.0000
3	0.0037	0.0018	0.0008	0.0004	0.0002	0.0001	0.0000	0.0000	0.0000	0.0000
4	0.0102	0.0053	0.0027	0.0013	0.0006	0.0003	0.0001	0.0001	0.0000	0.0000
5	0.0224	0.0127	0.0070	0.0037	0.0019	0.0010	0.0005	0.0002	0.0001	0.0001
6	0.0411	0.0255	0.0152	0.0087	0.0048	0.0026	0.0014	0.0007	0.0004	0.0002
7	0.0646	0.0437	0.0281	0.0174	0.0104	0.0060	0.0034	0.0019	0.0010	0.0005
8	0.0888	0.0655	0.0457	0.0304	0.0194	0.0120	0.0072	0.0042	0.0024	0.0013
9	0.1085	0.0874	0.0661	0.0473	0.0324	0.0213	0.0135	0.0083	0.0050	0.0029
10	0.1194	0.1048	0.0859	0.0663	0.0486	0.0341	0.0230	0.0150	0.0095	0.0058
11	0.1194	0.1144	0.1015	0.0844	0.0663	0.0496	0.0355	0.0245	0.0164	0.0106
12	0.1094	0.1144	0.1099	0.0984	0.0829	0.0661	0.0504	0.0368	0.0259	0.0176
13	0.0926	0.1056	0.1099	0.1060	0.0956	0.0814	0.0658	0.0509	0.0378	0.0271
14	0.0728	0.0905	0.1021	0.1060	0.1024	0.0930	0.0800	0.0655	0.0514	0.0387
15	0.0534	0.0724	0.0885	0.0989	0.1024	0.0992	0.0906	0.0786	0.0650	0.0516
16	0.0367	0.0543	0.0719	0.0866	0.0960	0.0992	0.0963	0.0884	0.0772	0.0646
17	0.0237	0.0383	0.0550	0.0713	0.0847	0.0934	0.0963	0.0936	0.0863	0.0760
18	0.0145	0.0255	0.0397	0.0554	0.0706	0.0830	0.0909	0.0936	0.0911	0.0844
19	0.0084	0.0161	0.0272	0.0409	0.0557	0.0699	0.0814	0.0887	0.0911	0.0888
20	0.0046	0.0097	0.0177	0.0286	0.0418	0.0559	0.0692	0.0798	0.0866	0.0888
21	0.0024	0.0055	0.0109	0.0191	0.0299	0.0426	0.0560	0.0684	0.0783	0.0846
22	0.0012	0.0030	0.0065	0.0121	0.0204	0.0310	0.0433	0.0560	0.0676	0.0769
23	0.0006	0.0016	0.0037	0.0074	0.0133	0.0216	0.0320	0.0438	0.0559	0.0669
24	0.0003	0.0008	0.0020	0.0043	0.0083	0.0144	0.0226	0.0328	0.0442	0.0557
25	0.0001	0.0004	0.0010	0.0024	0.0050	0.0092	0.0154	0.0237	0.0336	0.0446
26	0.0000	0.0002	0.0005	0.0013	0.0029	0.0057	0.0101	0.0164	0.0246	0.0343
27	0.0000	0.0001	0.0002	0.0007	0.0016	0.0034	0.0063	0.0109	0.0173	0.0254
28	0.0000	0.0000	0.0001	0.0003	0.0009	0.0019	0.0038	0.0070	0.0117	0.0181
29	0.0000	0.0000	0.0001	0.0002	0.0004	0.0011	0.0023	0.0044	0.0077	0.0125
30	0.0000	0.0000	0.0000	0.0001	0.0002	0.0006	0.0013	0.0026	0.0049	0.0083
31	0.0000	0.0000	0.0000	0.0000	0.0001	0.0003	0.0007	0.0015	0.0030	0.0054
32	0.0000	0.0000	0.0000	0.0000	0.0001	0.0001	0.0004	0.0009	0.0018	0.0034
33	0.0000	0.0000	0.0000	0.0000	0.0000	0.0001	0.0002	0.0005	0.0010	0.0020
34	0.0000	0.0000	0.0000	0.0000	0.0000	0.0000	0.0001	0.0002	0.0006	0.0012
35	0.0000	0.0000	0.0000	0.0000	0.0000	0.0000	0.0000	0.0001	0.0003	0.0007
36	0.0000	0.0000	0.0000	0.0000	0.0000	0.0000	0.0000	0.0001	0.0002	0.0004
37	0.0000	0.0000	0.0000	0.0000	0.0000	0.0000	0.0000	0.0000	0.0001	0.0002
38	0.0000	0.0000	0.0000	0.0000	0.0000	0.0000	0.0000	0.0000	0.0000	0.0001
39	0.0000	0.0000	0.0000	0.0000	0.0000	0.0000	0.0000	0.0000	0.0000	0.0001

APPENDIX D

Standard Normal Distribution Table

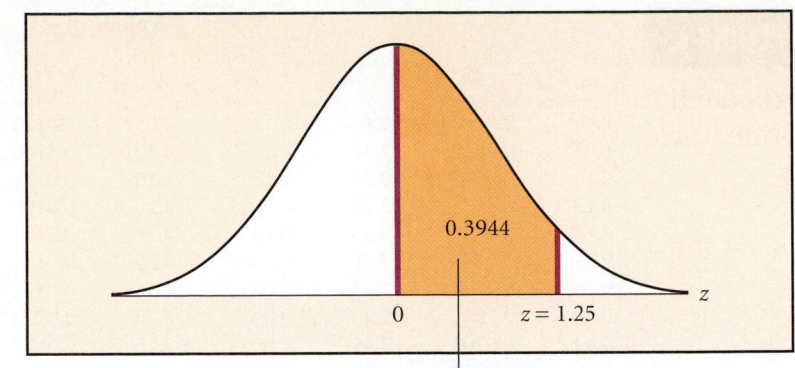

z	0	0.01	0.02	0.03	0.04	0.05	0.06	0.07	0.08	0.09
0.0	0.0000	0.0040	0.0080	0.0120	0.0160	0.0199	0.0239	0.0279	0.0319	0.0359
0.1	0.0398	0.0438	0.0478	0.0517	0.0557	0.0596	0.0636	0.0675	0.0714	0.0753
0.2	0.0793	0.0832	0.0871	0.0910	0.0948	0.0987	0.1026	0.1064	0.1103	0.1141
0.3	0.1179	0.1217	0.1255	0.1293	0.1331	0.1368	0.1406	0.1443	0.1480	0.1517
0.4	0.1554	0.1591	0.1628	0.1664	0.1700	0.1736	0.1772	0.1808	0.1844	0.1879
0.5	0.1915	0.1950	0.1985	0.2019	0.2054	0.2088	0.2123	0.2157	0.2190	0.2224
0.6	0.2257	0.2291	0.2324	0.2357	0.2389	0.2422	0.2454	0.2486	0.2517	0.2549
0.7	0.2580	0.2611	0.2642	0.2673	0.2704	0.2734	0.2764	0.2794	0.2823	0.2852
0.8	0.2881	0.2910	0.2939	0.2967	0.2995	0.3023	0.3051	0.3078	0.3106	0.3133
0.9	0.3159	0.3186	0.3212	0.3238	0.3264	0.3289	0.3315	0.3340	0.3365	0.3389
1.0	0.3413	0.3438	0.3461	0.3485	0.3508	0.3531	0.3554	0.3577	0.3599	0.3621
1.1	0.3643	0.3665	0.3686	0.3708	0.3729	0.3749	0.3770	0.3790	0.3810	0.3830
1.2	0.3849	0.3869	0.3888	0.3907	0.3925	0.3944	0.3962	0.3980	0.3997	0.4015
1.3	0.4032	0.4049	0.4066	0.4082	0.4099	0.4115	0.4131	0.4147	0.4162	0.4177
1.4	0.4192	0.4207	0.4222	0.4236	0.4251	0.4265	0.4279	0.4292	0.4306	0.4319
1.5	0.4332	0.4345	0.4357	0.4370	0.4382	0.4394	0.4406	0.4418	0.4429	0.4441
1.6	0.4452	0.4463	0.4474	0.4484	0.4495	0.4505	0.4515	0.4525	0.4535	0.4545
1.7	0.4554	0.4564	0.4573	0.4582	0.4591	0.4599	0.4608	0.4616	0.4625	0.4633
1.8	0.4641	0.4649	0.4656	0.4664	0.4671	0.4678	0.4686	0.4693	0.4699	0.4706
1.9	0.4713	0.4719	0.4726	0.4732	0.4738	0.4744	0.4750	0.4756	0.4761	0.4767
2.0	0.4772	0.4778	0.4783	0.4788	0.4793	0.4798	0.4803	0.4808	0.4812	0.4817
2.1	0.4821	0.4826	0.4830	0.4834	0.4838	0.4842	0.4846	0.4850	0.4854	0.4857
2.2	0.4861	0.4864	0.4868	0.4871	0.4875	0.4878	0.4881	0.4884	0.4887	0.4890
2.3	0.4893	0.4896	0.4898	0.4901	0.4904	0.4906	0.4909	0.4911	0.4913	0.4916
2.4	0.4918	0.4920	0.4922	0.4925	0.4927	0.4929	0.4931	0.4932	0.4934	0.4936
2.5	0.4938	0.4940	0.4941	0.4943	0.4945	0.4946	0.4948	0.4949	0.4951	0.4952
2.6	0.4953	0.4955	0.4956	0.4957	0.4959	0.4960	0.4961	0.4962	0.4963	0.4964
2.7	0.4965	0.4966	0.4967	0.4968	0.4969	0.4970	0.4971	0.4972	0.4973	0.4974
2.8	0.4974	0.4975	0.4976	0.4977	0.4977	0.4978	0.4979	0.4979	0.4980	0.4981
2.9	0.4981	0.4982	0.4982	0.4983	0.4984	0.4984	0.4985	0.4985	0.4986	0.4986
3.0	0.4987	0.4987	0.4987	0.4988	0.4988	0.4989	0.4989	0.4989	0.4990	0.4990

APPENDIX E

Exponential Distribution Table

Values of $e^{-\lambda a}$

λa	$e^{-\lambda a}$	λa	$e^{-\lambda a}$	λa	$e^{-\lambda a}$	λa	$e^{-\lambda a}$	λa	$e^{-\lambda a}$
0.00	1.0000	2.05	0.1287	4.05	0.0174	6.05	0.0024	8.05	0.0003
0.05	0.9512	2.10	0.1225	4.10	0.0166	6.10	0.0022	8.10	0.0003
0.10	0.9048	2.15	0.1165	4.15	0.0158	6.15	0.0021	8.15	0.0003
0.15	0.8607	2.20	0.1108	4.20	0.0150	6.20	0.0020	8.20	0.0003
0.20	0.8187	2.25	0.1054	4.25	0.0143	6.25	0.0019	8.25	0.0003
0.25	0.7788	2.30	0.1003	4.30	0.0136	6.30	0.0018	8.30	0.0002
0.30	0.7408	2.35	0.0954	4.35	0.0129	6.35	0.0017	8.35	0.0002
0.35	0.7047	2.40	0.0907	4.40	0.0123	6.40	0.0017	8.40	0.0002
0.40	0.6703	2.45	0.0863	4.45	0.0117	6.45	0.0016	8.45	0.0002
0.45	0.6376	2.50	0.0821	4.50	0.0111	6.50	0.0015	8.50	0.0002
0.50	0.6065	2.55	0.0781	4.55	0.0106	6.55	0.0014	8.55	0.0002
0.55	0.5769	2.60	0.0743	4.60	0.0101	6.60	0.0014	8.60	0.0002
0.60	0.5488	2.65	0.0707	4.65	0.0096	6.65	0.0013	8.65	0.0002
0.65	0.5220	2.70	0.0672	4.70	0.0091	6.70	0.0012	8.70	0.0002
0.70	0.4966	2.75	0.0639	4.75	0.0087	6.75	0.0012	8.75	0.0002
0.75	0.4724	2.80	0.0608	4.80	0.0082	6.80	0.0011	8.80	0.0002
0.80	0.4493	2.85	0.0578	4.85	0.0078	6.85	0.0011	8.85	0.0001
0.85	0.4274	2.90	0.0550	4.90	0.0074	6.90	0.0010	8.90	0.0001
0.90	0.4066	2.95	0.0523	4.95	0.0071	6.95	0.0010	8.95	0.0001
0.95	0.3867	3.00	0.0498	5.00	0.0067	7.00	0.0009	9.00	0.0001
1.00	0.3679	3.05	0.0474	5.05	0.0064	7.05	0.0009	9.05	0.0001
1.05	0.3499	3.10	0.0450	5.10	0.0061	7.10	0.0008	9.10	0.0001
1.10	0.3329	3.15	0.0429	5.15	0.0058	7.15	0.0008	9.15	0.0001
1.15	0.3166	3.20	0.0408	5.20	0.0055	7.20	0.0007	9.20	0.0001
1.20	0.3012	3.25	0.0388	5.25	0.0052	7.25	0.0007	9.25	0.0001
1.25	0.2865	3.30	0.0369	5.30	0.0050	7.30	0.0007	9.30	0.0001
1.30	0.2725	3.35	0.0351	5.35	0.0047	7.35	0.0006	9.35	0.0001
1.35	0.2592	3.40	0.0334	5.40	0.0045	7.40	0.0006	9.40	0.0001
1.40	0.2466	3.45	0.0317	5.45	0.0043	7.45	0.0006	9.45	0.0001
1.45	0.2346	3.50	0.0302	5.50	0.0041	7.50	0.0006	9.50	0.0001
1.50	0.2231	3.55	0.0287	5.55	0.0039	7.55	0.0005	9.55	0.0001
1.55	0.2122	3.60	0.0273	5.60	0.0037	7.60	0.0005	9.60	0.0001
1.60	0.2019	3.65	0.0260	5.65	0.0035	7.65	0.0005	9.65	0.0001
1.65	0.1920	3.70	0.0247	5.70	0.0033	7.70	0.0005	9.70	0.0001
1.70	0.1827	3.75	0.0235	5.75	0.0032	7.75	0.0004	9.75	0.0001
1.75	0.1738	3.80	0.0224	5.80	0.0030	7.80	0.0004	9.80	0.0001
1.80	0.1653	3.85	0.0213	5.85	0.0029	7.85	0.0004	9.85	0.0001
1.85	0.1572	3.90	0.0202	5.90	0.0027	7.90	0.0004	9.90	0.0001
1.90	0.1496	3.95	0.0193	5.95	0.0026	7.95	0.0004	9.95	0.0000
1.95	0.1423	4.00	0.0183	6.00	0.0025	8.00	0.0003	10.00	0.0000
2.00	0.1353								

APPENDIX F

Values of *t* for Selected Probabilities

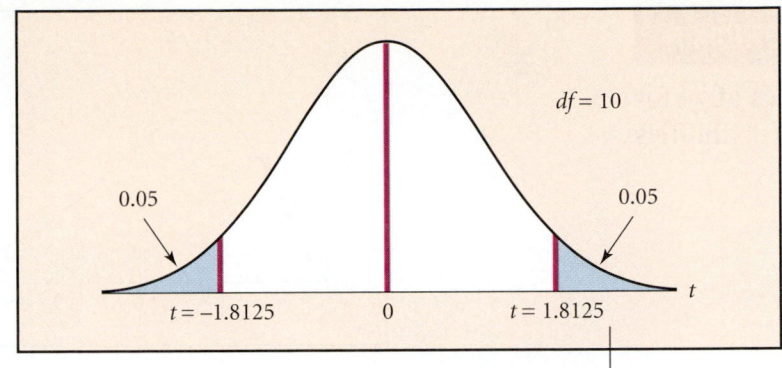

$df = 10$

0.05

0.05

$t = -1.8125$ 0 $t = 1.8125$

t

PROBABILITES (OR AREAS UNDER *t*-DISTRIBUTION CURVE)

Conf. Level One Tail Two Tails	0.1 0.45 0.9	0.3 0.35 0.7	0.5 0.25 0.5	0.7 0.15 0.3	0.8 0.1 0.2	0.9 0.05 0.1	0.95 0.025 0.05	0.98 0.01 0.02	0.99 0.005 0.01
df					*Values of t*				
1	0.1584	0.5095	1.0000	1.9626	3.0777	6.3137	12.7062	31.8210	63.6559
2	0.1421	0.4447	0.8165	1.3862	1.8856	2.9200	4.3027	6.9645	9.9250
3	0.1366	0.4242	0.7649	1.2498	1.6377	2.3534	3.1824	4.5407	5.8408
4	0.1338	0.4142	0.7407	1.1896	1.5332	2.1318	2.7765	3.7469	4.6041
5	0.1322	0.4082	0.7267	1.1558	1.4759	2.0150	2.5706	3.3649	4.0321
6	0.1311	0.4043	0.7176	1.1342	1.4398	1.9432	2.4469	3.1427	3.7074
7	0.1303	0.4015	0.7111	1.1192	1.4149	1.8946	2.3646	2.9979	3.4995
8	0.1297	0.3995	0.7064	1.1081	1.3968	1.8595	2.3060	2.8965	3.3554
9	0.1293	0.3979	0.7027	1.0997	1.3830	1.8331	2.2622	2.8214	3.2498
10	0.1289	0.3966	0.6998	1.0931	1.3722	1.8125	2.2281	2.7638	3.1693
11	0.1286	0.3956	0.6974	1.0877	1.3634	1.7959	2.2010	2.7181	3.1058
12	0.1283	0.3947	0.6955	1.0832	1.3562	1.7823	2.1788	2.6810	3.0545
13	0.1281	0.3940	0.6938	1.0795	1.3502	1.7709	2.1604	2.6503	3.0123
14	0.1280	0.3933	0.6924	1.0763	1.3450	1.7613	2.1448	2.6245	2.9768
15	0.1278	0.3928	0.6912	1.0735	1.3406	1.7531	2.1315	2.6025	2.9467
16	0.1277	0.3923	0.6901	1.0711	1.3368	1.7459	2.1199	2.5835	2.9208
17	0.1276	0.3919	0.6892	1.0690	1.3334	1.7396	2.1098	2.5669	2.8982
18	0.1274	0.3915	0.6884	1.0672	1.3304	1.7341	2.1009	2.5524	2.8784
19	0.1274	0.3912	0.6876	1.0655	1.3277	1.7291	2.0930	2.5395	2.8609
20	0.1273	0.3909	0.6870	1.0640	1.3253	1.7247	2.0860	2.5280	2.8453
21	0.1272	0.3906	0.6864	1.0627	1.3232	1.7207	2.0796	2.5176	2.8314
22	0.1271	0.3904	0.6858	1.0614	1.3212	1.7171	2.0739	2.5083	2.8188
23	0.1271	0.3902	0.6853	1.0603	1.3195	1.7139	2.0687	2.4999	2.8073
24	0.1270	0.3900	0.6848	1.0593	1.3178	1.7109	2.0639	2.4922	2.7970
25	0.1269	0.3898	0.6844	1.0584	1.3163	1.7081	2.0595	2.4851	2.7874
26	0.1269	0.3896	0.6840	1.0575	1.3150	1.7056	2.0555	2.4786	2.7787
27	0.1268	0.3894	0.6837	1.0567	1.3137	1.7033	2.0518	2.4727	2.7707
28	0.1268	0.3893	0.6834	1.0560	1.3125	1.7011	2.0484	2.4671	2.7633
29	0.1268	0.3892	0.6830	1.0553	1.3114	1.6991	2.0452	2.4620	2.7564
30	0.1267	0.3890	0.6828	1.0547	1.3104	1.6973	2.0423	2.4573	2.7500
40	0.1265	0.3881	0.6807	1.0500	1.3031	1.6839	2.0211	2.4233	2.7045
50	0.1263	0.3875	0.6794	1.0473	1.2987	1.6759	2.0086	2.4033	2.6778
60	0.1262	0.3872	0.6786	1.0455	1.2958	1.6706	2.0003	2.3901	2.6603
70	0.1261	0.3869	0.6780	1.0442	1.2938	1.6669	1.9944	2.3808	2.6479
80	0.1261	0.3867	0.6776	1.0432	1.2922	1.6641	1.9901	2.3739	2.6387
90	0.1260	0.3866	0.6772	1.0424	1.2910	1.6620	1.9867	2.3685	2.6316
100	0.1260	0.3864	0.6770	1.0418	1.2901	1.6602	1.9840	2.3642	2.6259
250	0.1258	0.3858	0.6755	1.0386	1.2849	1.6510	1.9695	2.3414	2.5956
500	0.1257	0.3855	0.6750	1.0375	1.2832	1.6479	1.9647	2.3338	2.5857
∞					See Normal Distribution				

Values of χ^2 for Selected Probabilities

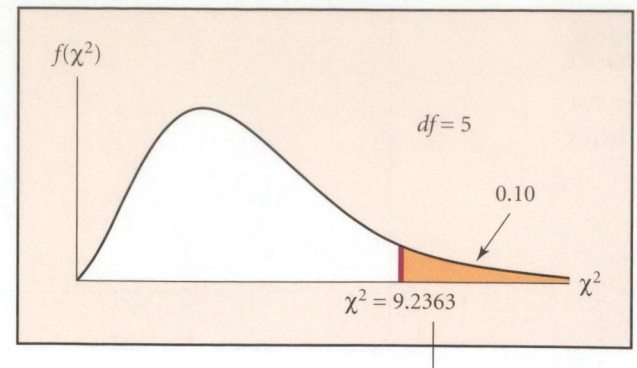

PROBABILITIES (OR AREAS UNDER CHI-SQUARE DISTRIBUTION CURVE ABOVE GIVEN CHI-SQUARE VALUES)

df	0.995	0.99	0.975	0.95	0.90	0.10	0.05	0.025	0.01	0.005
					Values of Chi-Squared					
1	0.0000	0.0002	0.0010	0.0039	0.0158	2.7055	3.8415	5.0239	6.6349	7.8794
2	0.0100	0.0201	0.0506	0.1026	0.2107	4.6052	5.9915	7.3778	9.2104	10.5965
3	0.0717	0.1148	0.2158	0.3518	0.5844	6.2514	7.8147	9.3484	11.3449	12.8381
4	0.2070	0.2971	0.4844	0.7107	1.0636	7.7794	9.4877	11.1433	13.2767	14.8602
5	0.4118	0.5543	0.8312	1.1455	1.6103	9.2363	11.0705	12.8325	15.0863	16.7496
6	0.6757	0.8721	1.2373	1.6354	2.2041	10.6446	12.5916	14.4494	16.8119	18.5475
7	0.9893	1.2390	1.6899	2.1673	2.8331	12.0170	14.0671	16.0128	18.4753	20.2777
8	1.3444	1.6465	2.1797	2.7326	3.4895	13.3616	15.5073	17.5345	20.0902	21.9549
9	1.7349	2.0879	2.7004	3.3251	4.1682	14.6837	16.9190	19.0228	21.6660	23.5893
10	2.1558	2.5582	3.2470	3.9403	4.8652	15.9872	18.3070	20.4832	23.2093	25.1881
11	2.6032	3.0535	3.8157	4.5748	5.5778	17.2750	19.6752	21.9200	24.7250	26.7569
12	3.0738	3.5706	4.4038	5.2260	6.3038	18.5493	21.0261	23.3367	26.2170	28.2997
13	3.5650	4.1069	5.0087	5.8919	7.0415	19.8119	22.3620	24.7356	27.6882	29.8193
14	4.0747	4.6604	5.6287	6.5706	7.7895	21.0641	23.6848	26.1189	29.1412	31.3194
15	4.6009	5.2294	6.2621	7.2609	8.5468	22.3071	24.9958	27.4884	30.5780	32.8015
16	5.1422	5.8122	6.9077	7.9616	9.3122	23.5418	26.2962	28.8453	31.9999	34.2671
17	5.6973	6.4077	7.5642	8.6718	10.0852	24.7690	27.5871	30.1910	33.4087	35.7184
18	6.2648	7.0149	8.2307	9.3904	10.8649	25.9894	28.8693	31.5264	34.8052	37.1564
19	6.8439	7.6327	8.9065	10.1170	11.6509	27.2036	30.1435	32.8523	36.1908	38.5821
20	7.4338	8.2604	9.5908	10.8508	12.4426	28.4120	31.4104	34.1696	37.5663	39.9969
21	8.0336	8.8972	10.2829	11.5913	13.2396	29.6151	32.6706	35.4789	38.9322	41.4009
22	8.6427	9.5425	10.9823	12.3380	14.0415	30.8133	33.9245	36.7807	40.2894	42.7957
23	9.2604	10.1957	11.6885	13.0905	14.8480	32.0069	35.1725	38.0756	41.6383	44.1814
24	9.8862	10.8563	12.4011	13.8484	15.6587	33.1962	36.4150	39.3641	42.9798	45.5584
25	10.5196	11.5240	13.1197	14.6114	16.4734	34.3816	37.6525	40.6465	44.3140	46.9280
26	11.1602	12.1982	13.8439	15.3792	17.2919	35.5632	38.8851	41.9231	45.6416	48.2898
27	11.8077	12.8785	14.5734	16.1514	18.1139	36.7412	40.1133	43.1945	46.9628	49.6450
28	12.4613	13.5647	15.3079	16.9279	18.9392	37.9159	41.3372	44.4608	48.2782	50.9936
29	13.1211	14.2564	16.0471	17.7084	19.7677	39.0875	42.5569	45.7223	49.5878	52.3355
30	13.7867	14.9535	16.7908	18.4927	20.5992	40.2560	43.7730	46.9792	50.8922	53.6719

APPENDIX H

F-Distribution Table: Upper 5% Probability (or 5% Area) Under *F*-Distribution Curve

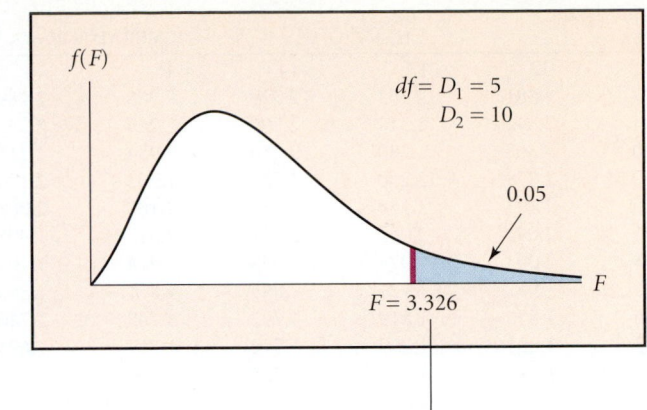

$df = D_1 = 5$
$D_2 = 10$

0.05

$F = 3.326$

DENOMINATOR
$df = D_2$

NUMERATOR $df = D_1$

	1	2	3	4	5	6	7	8	9	10
1	161.446	199.499	215.707	224.583	230.160	233.988	236.767	238.884	240.543	241.882
2	18.513	19.000	19.164	19.247	19.296	19.329	19.353	19.371	19.385	19.396
3	10.128	9.552	9.277	9.117	9.013	8.941	8.887	8.845	8.812	8.785
4	7.709	6.944	6.591	6.388	6.256	6.163	6.094	6.041	5.999	5.964
5	6.608	5.786	5.409	5.192	5.050	4.950	4.876	4.818	4.772	4.735
6	5.987	5.143	4.757	4.534	4.387	4.284	4.207	4.147	4.099	4.060
7	5.591	4.737	4.347	4.120	3.972	3.866	3.787	3.726	3.677	3.637
8	5.318	4.459	4.066	3.838	3.688	3.581	3.500	3.438	3.388	3.347
9	5.117	4.256	3.863	3.633	3.482	3.374	3.293	3.230	3.179	3.137
10	4.965	4.103	3.708	3.478	3.326	3.217	3.135	3.072	3.020	2.978
11	4.844	3.982	3.587	3.357	3.204	3.095	3.012	2.948	2.896	2.854
12	4.747	3.885	3.490	3.259	3.106	2.996	2.913	2.849	2.796	2.753
13	4.667	3.806	3.411	3.179	3.025	2.915	2.832	2.767	2.714	2.671
14	4.600	3.739	3.344	3.112	2.958	2.848	2.764	2.699	2.646	2.602
15	4.543	3.682	3.287	3.056	2.901	2.790	2.707	2.641	2.588	2.544
16	4.494	3.634	3.239	3.007	2.852	2.741	2.657	2.591	2.538	2.494
17	4.451	3.592	3.197	2.965	2.810	2.699	2.614	2.548	2.494	2.450
18	4.414	3.555	3.160	2.928	2.773	2.661	2.577	2.510	2.456	2.412
19	4.381	3.522	3.127	2.895	2.740	2.628	2.544	2.477	2.423	2.378
20	4.351	3.493	3.098	2.866	2.711	2.599	2.514	2.447	2.393	2.348
24	4.260	3.403	3.009	2.776	2.621	2.508	2.423	2.355	2.300	2.255
30	4.171	3.316	2.922	2.690	2.534	2.421	2.334	2.266	2.211	2.165
40	4.085	3.232	2.839	2.606	2.449	2.336	2.249	2.180	2.124	2.077
50	4.034	3.183	2.790	2.557	2.400	2.286	2.199	2.130	2.073	2.026
100	3.936	3.087	2.696	2.463	2.305	2.191	2.103	2.032	1.975	1.927
200	3.888	3.041	2.650	2.417	2.259	2.144	2.056	1.985	1.927	1.878
300	3.873	3.026	2.635	2.402	2.244	2.129	2.040	1.969	1.911	1.862

DENOMINATOR
$df = D_2$

NUMERATOR $df = D_1$

	11	12	13	14	15	16	17	18	19	20
1	242.981	243.905	244.690	245.363	245.949	246.466	246.917	247.324	247.688	248.016
2	19.405	19.412	19.419	19.424	19.429	19.433	19.437	19.440	19.443	19.446
3	8.763	8.745	8.729	8.715	8.703	8.692	8.683	8.675	8.667	8.660
4	5.936	5.912	5.891	5.873	5.858	5.844	5.832	5.821	5.811	5.803
5	4.704	4.678	4.655	4.636	4.619	4.604	4.590	4.579	4.568	4.558
6	4.027	4.000	3.976	3.956	3.938	3.922	3.908	3.896	3.884	3.874
7	3.603	3.575	3.550	3.529	3.511	3.494	3.480	3.467	3.455	3.445
8	3.313	3.284	3.259	3.237	3.218	3.202	3.187	3.173	3.161	3.150
9	3.102	3.073	3.048	3.025	3.006	2.989	2.974	2.960	2.948	2.936
10	2.943	2.913	2.887	2.865	2.845	2.828	2.812	2.798	2.785	2.774
11	2.818	2.788	2.761	2.739	2.719	2.701	2.685	2.671	2.658	2.646
12	2.717	2.687	2.660	2.637	2.617	2.599	2.583	2.568	2.555	2.544
13	2.635	2.604	2.577	2.554	2.533	2.515	2.499	2.484	2.471	2.459
14	2.565	2.534	2.507	2.484	2.463	2.445	2.428	2.413	2.400	2.388
15	2.507	2.475	2.448	2.424	2.403	2.385	2.368	2.353	2.340	2.328
16	2.456	2.425	2.397	2.373	2.352	2.333	2.317	2.302	2.288	2.276

(continued)

DENOMINATOR
$df = D_2$

NUMERATOR $df = D_1$

	11	12	13	14	15	16	17	18	19	20
17	2.413	2.381	2.353	2.329	2.308	2.289	2.272	2.257	2.243	2.230
18	2.374	2.342	2.314	2.290	2.269	2.250	2.233	2.217	2.203	2.191
19	2.340	2.308	2.280	2.256	2.234	2.215	2.198	2.182	2.168	2.155
20	2.310	2.278	2.250	2.225	2.203	2.184	2.167	2.151	2.137	2.124
24	2.216	2.183	2.155	2.130	2.108	2.088	2.070	2.054	2.040	2.027
30	2.126	2.092	2.063	2.037	2.015	1.995	1.976	1.960	1.945	1.932
40	2.038	2.003	1.974	1.948	1.924	1.904	1.885	1.868	1.853	1.839
50	1.986	1.952	1.921	1.895	1.871	1.850	1.831	1.814	1.798	1.784
100	1.886	1.850	1.819	1.792	1.768	1.746	1.726	1.708	1.691	1.676
200	1.837	1.801	1.769	1.742	1.717	1.694	1.674	1.656	1.639	1.623
300	1.821	1.785	1.753	1.725	1.700	1.677	1.657	1.638	1.621	1.606

DENOMINATOR
$df = D_2$

NUMERATOR $df = D_1$

	24	30	40	50	100	200	300
1	249.052	250.096	251.144	251.774	253.043	253.676	253.887
2	19.454	19.463	19.471	19.476	19.486	19.491	19.492
3	8.638	8.617	8.594	8.581	8.554	8.540	8.536
4	5.774	5.746	5.717	5.699	5.664	5.646	5.640
5	4.527	4.496	4.464	4.444	4.405	4.385	4.378
6	3.841	3.808	3.774	3.754	3.712	3.690	3.683
7	3.410	3.376	3.340	3.319	3.275	3.252	3.245
8	3.115	3.079	3.043	3.020	2.975	2.951	2.943
9	2.900	2.864	2.826	2.803	2.756	2.731	2.723
10	2.737	2.700	2.661	2.637	2.588	2.563	2.555
11	2.609	2.570	2.531	2.507	2.457	2.431	2.422
12	2.505	2.466	2.426	2.401	2.350	2.323	2.314
13	2.420	2.380	2.339	2.314	2.261	2.234	2.225
14	2.349	2.308	2.266	2.241	2.187	2.159	2.150
15	2.288	2.247	2.204	2.178	2.123	2.095	2.085
16	2.235	2.194	2.151	2.124	2.068	2.039	2.030
17	2.190	2.148	2.104	2.077	2.020	1.991	1.981
18	2.150	2.107	2.063	2.035	1.978	1.948	1.938
19	2.114	2.071	2.026	1.999	1.940	1.910	1.899
20	2.082	2.039	1.994	1.966	1.907	1.875	1.865
24	1.984	1.939	1.892	1.863	1.800	1.768	1.756
30	1.887	1.841	1.792	1.761	1.695	1.660	1.647
40	1.793	1.744	1.693	1.660	1.589	1.551	1.537
50	1.737	1.687	1.634	1.599	1.525	1.484	1.469
100	1.627	1.573	1.515	1.477	1.392	1.342	1.323
200	1.572	1.516	1.455	1.415	1.321	1.263	1.240
300	1.554	1.497	1.435	1.393	1.296	1.234	1.210

(continued)

F-Distribution Table: Upper 2.5% Probability (or 2.5% Area) Under F-Distribution Curve

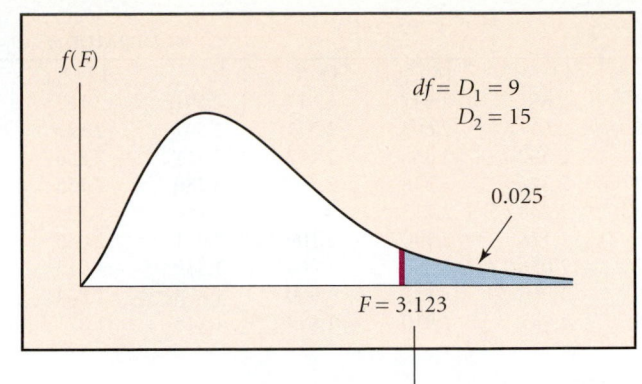

$f(F)$

$df = D_1 = 9$
$D_2 = 15$

0.025

$F = 3.123$

DENOMINATOR $df = D_2$

NUMERATOR $df = D_1$

$df = D_2$	1	2	3	4	5	6	7	8	9	10	11
1	647.793	799.482	864.151	899.599	921.835	937.114	948.203	956.643	963.279	968.634	973.028
2	38.506	39.000	39.166	39.248	39.298	39.331	39.356	39.373	39.387	39.398	39.407
3	17.443	16.044	15.439	15.101	14.885	14.735	14.624	14.540	14.473	14.419	14.374
4	12.218	10.649	9.979	9.604	9.364	9.197	9.074	8.980	8.905	8.844	8.794
5	10.007	8.434	7.764	7.388	7.146	6.978	6.853	6.757	6.681	6.619	6.568
6	8.813	7.260	6.599	6.227	5.988	5.820	5.695	5.600	5.523	5.461	5.410
7	8.073	6.542	5.890	5.523	5.285	5.119	4.995	4.899	4.823	4.761	4.709
8	7.571	6.059	5.416	5.053	4.817	4.652	4.529	4.433	4.357	4.295	4.243
9	7.209	5.715	5.078	4.718	4.484	4.320	4.197	4.102	4.026	3.964	3.912
10	6.937	5.456	4.826	4.468	4.236	4.072	3.950	3.855	3.779	3.717	3.665
11	6.724	5.256	4.630	4.275	4.044	3.881	3.759	3.664	3.588	3.526	3.474
12	6.554	5.096	4.474	4.121	3.891	3.728	3.607	3.512	3.436	3.374	3.321
13	6.414	4.965	4.347	3.996	3.767	3.604	3.483	3.388	3.312	3.250	3.197
14	6.298	4.857	4.242	3.892	3.663	3.501	3.380	3.285	3.209	3.147	3.095
15	6.200	4.765	4.153	3.804	3.576	3.415	3.293	3.199	3.123	3.060	3.008
16	6.115	4.687	4.077	3.729	3.502	3.341	3.219	3.125	3.049	2.986	2.934
17	6.042	4.619	4.011	3.665	3.438	3.277	3.156	3.061	2.985	2.922	2.870
18	5.978	4.560	3.954	3.608	3.382	3.221	3.100	3.005	2.929	2.866	2.814
19	5.922	4.508	3.903	3.559	3.333	3.172	3.051	2.956	2.880	2.817	2.765
20	5.871	4.461	3.859	3.515	3.289	3.128	3.007	2.913	2.837	2.774	2.721
24	5.717	4.319	3.721	3.379	3.155	2.995	2.874	2.779	2.703	2.640	2.586
30	5.568	4.182	3.589	3.250	3.026	2.867	2.746	2.651	2.575	2.511	2.458
40	5.424	4.051	3.463	3.126	2.904	2.744	2.624	2.529	2.452	2.388	2.334
50	5.340	3.975	3.390	3.054	2.833	2.674	2.553	2.458	2.381	2.317	2.263
100	5.179	3.828	3.250	2.917	2.696	2.537	2.417	2.321	2.244	2.179	2.124
200	5.100	3.758	3.182	2.850	2.630	2.472	2.351	2.256	2.178	2.113	2.058
300	5.075	3.735	3.160	2.829	2.609	2.451	2.330	2.234	2.156	2.091	2.036

DENOMINATOR $df = D_2$

NUMERATOR $df = D_1$

$df = D_2$	12	13	14	15	16	17	18	19	20	24	30
1	976.725	979.839	982.545	984.874	986.911	988.715	990.345	991.800	993.081	997.272	1001.405
2	39.415	39.421	39.427	39.431	39.436	39.439	39.442	39.446	39.448	39.457	39.465
3	14.337	14.305	14.277	14.253	14.232	14.213	14.196	14.181	14.167	14.124	14.081
4	8.751	8.715	8.684	8.657	8.633	8.611	8.592	8.575	8.560	8.511	8.461
5	6.525	6.488	6.456	6.428	6.403	6.381	6.362	6.344	6.329	6.278	6.227
6	5.366	5.329	5.297	5.269	5.244	5.222	5.202	5.184	5.168	5.117	5.065
7	4.666	4.628	4.596	4.568	4.543	4.521	4.501	4.483	4.467	4.415	4.362
8	4.200	4.162	4.130	4.101	4.076	4.054	4.034	4.016	3.999	3.947	3.894
9	3.868	3.831	3.798	3.769	3.744	3.722	3.701	3.683	3.667	3.614	3.560
10	3.621	3.583	3.550	3.522	3.496	3.474	3.453	3.435	3.419	3.365	3.311
11	3.430	3.392	3.359	3.330	3.304	3.282	3.261	3.243	3.226	3.173	3.118
12	3.277	3.239	3.206	3.177	3.152	3.129	3.108	3.090	3.073	3.019	2.963
13	3.153	3.115	3.082	3.053	3.027	3.004	2.983	2.965	2.948	2.893	2.837
14	3.050	3.012	2.979	2.949	2.923	2.900	2.879	2.861	2.844	2.789	2.732
15	2.963	2.925	2.891	2.862	2.836	2.813	2.792	2.773	2.756	2.701	2.644
16	2.889	2.851	2.817	2.788	2.761	2.738	2.717	2.698	2.681	2.625	2.568
17	2.825	2.786	2.753	2.723	2.697	2.673	2.652	2.633	2.616	2.560	2.502
18	2.769	2.730	2.696	2.667	2.640	2.617	2.596	2.576	2.559	2.503	2.445

(*continued*)

DENOMINATOR $df = D_2$	NUMERATOR $df = D_1$										
	12	**13**	**14**	**15**	**16**	**17**	**18**	**19**	**20**	**24**	**30**
19	2.720	2.681	2.647	2.617	2.591	2.567	2.546	2.526	2.509	2.452	2.394
20	2.676	2.637	2.603	2.573	2.547	2.523	2.501	2.482	2.464	2.408	2.349
24	2.541	2.502	2.468	2.437	2.411	2.386	2.365	2.345	2.327	2.269	2.209
30	2.412	2.372	2.338	2.307	2.280	2.255	2.233	2.213	2.195	2.136	2.074
40	2.288	2.248	2.213	2.182	2.154	2.129	2.107	2.086	2.068	2.007	1.943
50	2.216	2.176	2.140	2.109	2.081	2.056	2.033	2.012	1.993	1.931	1.866
100	2.077	2.036	2.000	1.968	1.939	1.913	1.890	1.868	1.849	1.784	1.715
200	2.010	1.969	1.932	1.900	1.870	1.844	1.820	1.798	1.778	1.712	1.640
300	1.988	1.947	1.910	1.877	1.848	1.821	1.797	1.775	1.755	1.688	1.616

DENOMINATOR $df = D_2$	NUMERATOR $df = D_1$				
	40	**50**	**100**	**200**	**300**
1	1005.596	1008.098	1013.163	1015.724	1016.539
2	39.473	39.478	39.488	39.493	39.495
3	14.036	14.010	13.956	13.929	13.920
4	8.411	8.381	8.319	8.288	8.278
5	6.175	6.144	6.080	6.048	6.037
6	5.012	4.980	4.915	4.882	4.871
7	4.309	4.276	4.210	4.176	4.165
8	3.840	3.807	3.739	3.705	3.693
9	3.505	3.472	3.403	3.368	3.357
10	3.255	3.221	3.152	3.116	3.104
11	3.061	3.027	2.956	2.920	2.908
12	2.906	2.871	2.800	2.763	2.750
13	2.780	2.744	2.671	2.634	2.621
14	2.674	2.638	2.565	2.526	2.513
15	2.585	2.549	2.474	2.435	2.422
16	2.509	2.472	2.396	2.357	2.343
17	2.442	2.405	2.329	2.289	2.275
18	2.384	2.347	2.269	2.229	2.215
19	2.333	2.295	2.217	2.176	2.162
20	2.287	2.249	2.170	2.128	2.114
24	2.146	2.107	2.024	1.981	1.966
30	2.009	1.968	1.882	1.835	1.819
40	1.875	1.832	1.741	1.691	1.673
50	1.796	1.752	1.656	1.603	1.584
100	1.640	1.592	1.483	1.420	1.397
200	1.562	1.511	1.393	1.320	1.293
300	1.536	1.484	1.361	1.285	1.255

(continued)

F-Distribution Table: Upper 1% Probability (or 1% Area) Under F-Distribution Curve

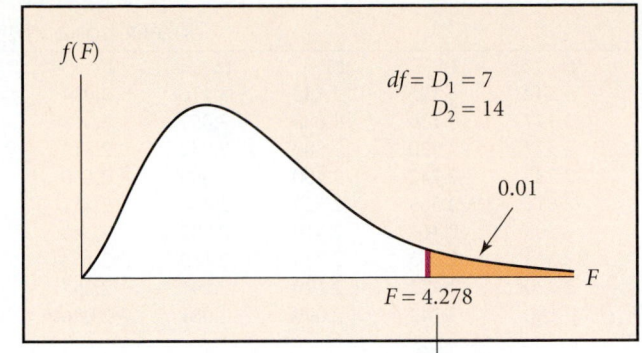

DENOMINATOR
$df = D_2$

NUMERATOR $df = D_1$

	1	2	3	4	5	6	7	8	9	10	11
1	4052.185	4999.340	5403.534	5624.257	5763.955	5858.950	5928.334	5980.954	6022.397	6055.925	6083.399
2	98.502	99.000	99.164	99.251	99.302	99.331	99.357	99.375	99.390	99.397	99.408
3	34.116	30.816	29.457	28.710	28.237	27.911	27.671	27.489	27.345	27.228	27.132
4	21.198	18.000	16.694	15.977	15.522	15.207	14.976	14.799	14.659	14.546	14.452
5	16.258	13.274	12.060	11.392	10.967	10.672	10.456	10.289	10.158	10.051	9.963
6	13.745	10.925	9.780	9.148	8.746	8.466	8.260	8.102	7.976	7.874	7.790
7	12.246	9.547	8.451	7.847	7.460	7.191	6.993	6.840	6.719	6.620	6.538
8	11.259	8.649	7.591	7.006	6.632	6.371	6.178	6.029	5.911	5.814	5.734
9	10.562	8.022	6.992	6.422	6.057	5.802	5.613	5.467	5.351	5.257	5.178
10	10.044	7.559	6.552	5.994	5.636	5.386	5.200	5.057	4.942	4.849	4.772
11	9.646	7.206	6.217	5.668	5.316	5.069	4.886	4.744	4.632	4.539	4.462
12	9.330	6.927	5.953	5.412	5.064	4.821	4.640	4.499	4.388	4.296	4.220
13	9.074	6.701	5.739	5.205	4.862	4.620	4.441	4.302	4.191	4.100	4.025
14	8.862	6.515	5.564	5.035	4.695	4.456	4.278	4.140	4.030	3.939	3.864
15	8.683	6.359	5.417	4.893	4.556	4.318	4.142	4.004	3.895	3.805	3.730
16	8.531	6.226	5.292	4.773	4.437	4.202	4.026	3.890	3.780	3.691	3.616
17	8.400	6.112	5.185	4.669	4.336	4.101	3.927	3.791	3.682	3.593	3.518
18	8.285	6.013	5.092	4.579	4.248	4.015	3.841	3.705	3.597	3.508	3.434
19	8.185	5.926	5.010	4.500	4.171	3.939	3.765	3.631	3.523	3.434	3.360
20	8.096	5.849	4.938	4.431	4.103	3.871	3.699	3.564	3.457	3.368	3.294
24	7.823	5.614	4.718	4.218	3.895	3.667	3.496	3.363	3.256	3.168	3.094
30	7.562	5.390	4.510	4.018	3.699	3.473	3.305	3.173	3.067	2.979	2.906
40	7.314	5.178	4.313	3.828	3.514	3.291	3.124	2.993	2.888	2.801	2.727
50	7.171	5.057	4.199	3.720	3.408	3.186	3.020	2.890	2.785	2.698	2.625
100	6.895	4.824	3.984	3.513	3.206	2.988	2.823	2.694	2.590	2.503	2.430
200	6.763	4.713	3.881	3.414	3.110	2.893	2.730	2.601	2.497	2.411	2.338
300	6.720	4.677	3.848	3.382	3.079	2.862	2.699	2.571	2.467	2.380	2.307

DENOMINATOR
$df = D_2$

NUMERATOR $df = D_1$

	12	13	14	15	16	17	18	19	20	24	30
1	6106.682	6125.774	6143.004	6156.974	6170.012	6181.188	6191.432	6200.746	6208.662	6234.273	6260.350
2	99.419	99.422	99.426	99.433	99.437	99.441	99.444	99.448	99.448	99.455	99.466
3	27.052	26.983	26.924	26.872	26.826	26.786	26.751	26.719	26.690	26.597	26.504
4	14.374	14.306	14.249	14.198	14.154	14.114	14.079	14.048	14.019	13.929	13.838
5	9.888	9.825	9.770	9.722	9.680	9.643	9.609	9.580	9.553	9.466	9.379
6	7.718	7.657	7.605	7.559	7.519	7.483	7.451	7.422	7.396	7.313	7.229
7	6.469	6.410	6.359	6.314	6.275	6.240	6.209	6.181	6.155	6.074	5.992
8	5.667	5.609	5.559	5.515	5.477	5.442	5.412	5.384	5.359	5.279	5.198
9	5.111	5.055	5.005	4.962	4.924	4.890	4.860	4.833	4.808	4.729	4.649
10	4.706	4.650	4.601	4.558	4.520	4.487	4.457	4.430	4.405	4.327	4.247
11	4.397	4.342	4.293	4.251	4.213	4.180	4.150	4.123	4.099	4.021	3.941
12	4.155	4.100	4.052	4.010	3.972	3.939	3.910	3.883	3.858	3.780	3.701
13	3.960	3.905	3.857	3.815	3.778	3.745	3.716	3.689	3.665	3.587	3.507
14	3.800	3.745	3.698	3.656	3.619	3.586	3.556	3.529	3.505	3.427	3.348
15	3.666	3.612	3.564	3.522	3.485	3.452	3.423	3.396	3.372	3.294	3.214
16	3.553	3.498	3.451	3.409	3.372	3.339	3.310	3.283	3.259	3.181	3.101
17	3.455	3.401	3.353	3.312	3.275	3.242	3.212	3.186	3.162	3.083	3.003
18	3.371	3.316	3.269	3.227	3.190	3.158	3.128	3.101	3.077	2.999	2.919

(continued)

DENOMINATOR
$df = D_2$

NUMERATOR $df = D_1$

	12	13	14	15	16	17	18	19	20	24	30
19	3.297	3.242	3.195	3.153	3.116	3.084	3.054	3.027	3.003	2.925	2.844
20	3.231	3.177	3.130	3.088	3.051	3.018	2.989	2.962	2.938	2.859	2.778
24	3.032	2.977	2.930	2.889	2.852	2.819	2.789	2.762	2.738	2.659	2.577
30	2.843	2.789	2.742	2.700	2.663	2.630	2.600	2.573	2.549	2.469	2.386
40	2.665	2.611	2.563	2.522	2.484	2.451	2.421	2.394	2.369	2.288	2.203
50	2.563	2.508	2.461	2.419	2.382	2.348	2.318	2.290	2.265	2.183	2.098
100	2.368	2.313	2.265	2.223	2.185	2.151	2.120	2.092	2.067	1.983	1.893
200	2.275	2.220	2.172	2.129	2.091	2.057	2.026	1.997	1.971	1.886	1.794
300	2.244	2.190	2.142	2.099	2.061	2.026	1.995	1.966	1.940	1.854	1.761

DENOMINATOR
$df = D_2$

NUMERATOR $df = D_1$

	40	50	100	200	300
1	6286.427	6302.260	6333.925	6349.757	6355.345
2	99.477	99.477	99.491	99.491	99.499
3	26.411	26.354	26.241	26.183	26.163
4	13.745	13.690	13.577	13.520	13.501
5	9.291	9.238	9.130	9.075	9.057
6	7.143	7.091	6.987	6.934	6.916
7	5.908	5.858	5.755	5.702	5.685
8	5.116	5.065	4.963	4.911	4.894
9	4.567	4.517	4.415	4.363	4.346
10	4.165	4.115	4.014	3.962	3.944
11	3.860	3.810	3.708	3.656	3.638
12	3.619	3.569	3.467	3.414	3.397
13	3.425	3.375	3.272	3.219	3.202
14	3.266	3.215	3.112	3.059	3.040
15	3.132	3.081	2.977	2.923	2.905
16	3.018	2.967	2.863	2.808	2.790
17	2.920	2.869	2.764	2.709	2.691
18	2.835	2.784	2.678	2.623	2.604
19	2.761	2.709	2.602	2.547	2.528
20	2.695	2.643	2.535	2.479	2.460
24	2.492	2.440	2.329	2.271	2.251
30	2.299	2.245	2.131	2.070	2.049
40	2.114	2.058	1.938	1.874	1.851
50	2.007	1.949	1.825	1.757	1.733
100	1.797	1.735	1.598	1.518	1.490
200	1.694	1.629	1.481	1.391	1.357
300	1.660	1.594	1.441	1.346	1.309

APPENDIX I

Critical Values of Hartley's F_{max} Test

$$F_{max} = \frac{S^2_{largest}}{S^2_{smallest}} \sim F_{max_{1-a(c,v)}}$$

UPPER 5% POINTS ($\alpha = 0.05$)

v \ c	2	3	4	5	6	7	8	9	10	11	12
2	39.0	87.5	142	202	266	333	403	475	550	626	704
3	15.4	27.8	39.2	50.7	62.0	72.9	83.5	93.9	104	114	124
4	9.60	15.5	20.6	25.2	29.5	33.6	37.5	41.1	44.6	48.0	51.4
5	7.15	10.8	13.7	16.3	18.7	20.8	22.9	24.7	26.5	28.2	29.9
6	5.82	8.38	10.4	12.1	13.7	15.0	16.3	17.5	18.6	19.7	20.7
7	4.99	6.94	8.44	9.70	10.8	11.8	12.7	13.5	14.3	15.1	15.8
8	4.43	6.00	7.18	8.12	9.03	9.78	10.5	11.1	11.7	12.2	12.7
9	4.03	5.34	6.31	7.11	7.80	8.41	8.95	9.45	9.91	10.3	10.7
10	3.72	4.85	5.67	6.34	6.92	7.42	7.87	8.28	8.66	9.01	9.34
12	3.28	4.16	4.79	5.30	5.72	6.09	6.42	6.72	7.00	7.25	7.48
15	2.86	3.54	4.01	4.37	4.68	4.95	5.19	5.40	5.59	5.77	5.93
20	2.46	2.95	3.29	3.54	3.76	3.94	4.10	4.24	4.37	4.49	4.59
30	2.07	2.40	2.61	2.78	2.91	3.02	3.12	3.21	3.29	3.36	3.39
60	1.67	1.85	1.96	2.04	2.11	2.17	2.22	2.26	2.30	2.33	2.36
∞	1.00	1.00	1.00	1.00	1.00	1.00	1.00	1.00	1.00	1.00	1.00

UPPER 1% POINTS ($\alpha = 0.01$)

v \ c	2	3	4	5	6	7	8	9	10	11	12
2	199	448	729	1036	1362	1705	2063	2432	2813	3204	3605
3	47.5	85	120	151	184	21(6)	24(9)	28(1)	31(0)	33(7)	36(1)
4	23.2	37	49	59	69	79	89	97	106	113	120
5	14.9	22	28	33	38	42	46	50	54	57	60
6	11.1	15.5	19.1	22	25	27	30	32	34	36	37
7	8.89	12.1	14.5	16.5	18.4	20	22	23	24	26	27
8	7.50	9.9	11.7	13.2	14.5	15.8	16.9	17.9	18.9	19.8	21
9	6.54	8.5	9.9	11.1	12.1	13.1	13.9	14.7	15.3	16.0	16.6
10	5.85	7.4	8.6	9.6	10.4	11.1	11.8	12.4	12.9	13.4	13.9
12	4.91	6.1	6.9	7.6	8.2	8.7	9.1	9.5	9.9	10.2	10.6
15	4.07	4.9	5.5	6.0	6.4	6.7	7.1	7.3	7.5	7.8	8.0
20	3.32	3.8	4.3	4.6	4.9	5.1	5.3	5.5	5.6	5.8	5.9
30	2.63	3.0	3.3	3.4	3.6	3.7	3.8	3.9	4.0	4.1	4.2
60	1.96	2.2	2.3	2.4	2.4	2.5	2.5	2.6	2.6	2.7	2.7
∞	1.00	1.0	1.0	1.0	1.0	1.0	1.0	1.0	1.0	1.00	1.0

Note: $S^2_{largest}$ is the largest and $s^2_{smallest}$ the smallest in a set of c independent mean squares, each based on v degrees of freedom.

Source: Reprinted from E. S. Pearson and H. O. Hartley, eds., *Biometrika Tables for Statisticians*, 3d ed., 1966, by permission of the Biometrika Trustees.

Distribution of the Studentized Range (q-values)

$p = 0.95$

D_2 \ D_1	2	3	4	5	6	7	8	9	10
1	17.97	26.98	32.82	37.08	40.41	43.12	45.40	47.36	49.07
2	6.08	8.33	9.80	10.88	11.74	12.44	13.03	13.54	13.99
3	4.50	5.91	6.82	7.50	8.04	8.48	8.85	9.18	9.46
4	3.93	5.04	5.76	6.29	6.71	7.05	7.35	7.60	7.83
5	3.64	4.60	5.22	5.67	6.03	6.33	6.58	6.80	6.99
6	3.46	4.34	4.90	5.30	5.63	5.90	6.12	6.32	6.49
7	3.34	4.16	4.68	5.06	5.36	5.61	5.82	6.00	6.16
8	3.26	4.04	4.53	4.89	5.17	5.40	5.60	5.77	5.92
9	3.20	3.95	4.41	4.76	5.02	5.24	5.43	5.59	5.74
10	3.15	3.88	4.33	4.65	4.91	5.12	5.30	5.46	5.60
11	3.11	3.82	4.26	4.57	4.82	5.03	5.20	5.35	5.49
12	3.08	3.77	4.20	4.51	4.75	4.95	5.12	5.27	5.39
13	3.06	3.73	4.15	4.45	4.69	4.88	5.05	5.19	5.32
14	3.03	3.70	4.11	4.41	4.64	4.83	4.99	5.13	5.25
15	3.01	3.67	4.08	4.37	4.59	4.78	4.94	5.08	5.20
16	3.00	3.65	4.05	4.33	4.56	4.74	4.90	5.03	5.15
17	2.98	3.63	4.02	4.30	4.52	4.70	4.86	4.99	5.11
18	2.97	3.61	4.00	4.28	4.49	4.67	4.82	4.96	5.07
19	2.96	3.59	3.98	4.25	4.47	4.65	4.79	4.92	5.04
20	2.95	3.58	3.96	4.23	4.45	4.62	4.77	4.90	5.01
24	2.92	3.53	3.90	4.17	4.37	4.54	4.68	4.81	4.92
30	2.89	3.49	3.85	4.10	4.30	4.46	4.60	4.72	4.82
40	2.86	3.44	3.79	4.04	4.23	4.39	4.52	4.63	4.73
60	2.83	3.40	3.74	3.98	4.16	4.31	4.44	4.55	4.65
120	2.80	3.36	3.68	3.92	4.10	4.24	4.36	4.47	4.56
∞	2.77	3.31	3.63	3.86	4.03	4.17	4.29	4.39	4.47

D_2 \ D_1	11	12	13	14	15	16	17	18	19	20
1	50.59	51.96	53.20	54.33	55.36	56.32	57.22	58.04	58.83	59.56
2	14.39	14.75	15.08	15.38	15.65	15.91	16.14	16.37	16.57	16.77
3	9.72	9.95	10.15	10.35	10.52	10.69	10.84	10.98	11.11	11.24
4	8.03	8.21	8.37	8.52	8.66	8.79	8.91	9.03	9.13	9.23
5	7.17	7.32	7.47	7.60	7.72	7.83	7.93	8.03	8.12	8.21
6	6.65	6.79	6.92	7.03	7.14	7.24	7.34	7.43	7.51	7.59
7	6.30	6.43	6.55	6.66	6.76	6.85	6.94	7.02	7.10	7.17
8	6.05	6.18	6.29	6.39	6.48	6.57	6.65	6.73	6.80	6.87
9	5.87	5.98	6.09	6.19	6.28	6.36	6.44	6.51	6.58	6.64
10	5.72	5.83	5.93	6.03	6.11	6.19	6.27	6.34	6.40	6.47
11	5.61	5.71	5.81	5.90	5.98	6.06	6.13	6.20	6.27	6.33
12	5.51	5.61	5.71	5.80	5.88	5.95	6.02	6.09	6.15	6.21
13	5.43	5.53	5.63	5.71	5.79	5.86	5.93	5.99	6.05	6.11
14	5.36	5.46	5.55	5.64	5.71	5.79	5.85	5.91	5.97	6.03
15	5.31	5.40	5.49	5.57	5.65	5.72	5.78	5.85	5.90	5.96
16	5.26	5.35	5.44	5.52	5.59	5.66	5.73	5.79	5.84	5.90
17	5.21	5.31	5.39	5.47	5.54	5.61	5.67	5.73	5.79	5.84
18	5.17	5.27	5.35	5.43	5.50	5.57	5.63	5.69	5.74	5.79
19	5.14	5.23	5.31	5.39	5.46	5.53	5.59	5.65	5.70	5.75
20	5.11	5.20	5.28	5.36	5.43	5.49	5.55	5.61	5.66	5.71
24	5.01	5.10	5.18	5.25	5.32	5.38	5.44	5.49	5.55	5.59
30	4.92	5.00	5.08	5.15	5.21	5.27	5.33	5.38	5.43	5.47
40	4.82	4.90	4.98	5.04	5.11	5.16	5.22	5.27	5.31	5.36
60	4.73	4.81	4.88	4.94	5.00	5.06	5.11	5.15	5.20	5.24
120	4.64	4.71	4.78	4.84	4.90	4.95	5.00	5.04	5.09	5.13
∞	4.55	4.62	4.68	4.74	4.80	4.85	4.89	4.93	4.97	5.01

Note: $D_1 = K$ populations and $D_2 = N - K$.

$p = 0.99$

D_2 \ D_1	2	3	4	5	6	7	8	9	10
1	90.03	135.0	164.3	185.6	202.2	215.8	227.2	237.0	245.6
2	14.04	19.02	22.29	24.72	26.63	28.20	29.53	30.68	31.69
3	8.26	10.62	12.17	13.33	14.24	15.00	15.64	16.20	16.69
4	6.51	8.12	9.17	9.96	10.58	11.10	11.55	11.93	12.27
5	5.70	6.98	7.80	8.42	8.91	9.32	9.67	9.97	10.24
6	5.24	6.33	7.03	7.56	7.97	8.32	8.61	8.87	9.10
7	4.95	5.92	6.54	7.01	7.37	7.68	7.94	8.17	8.37
8	4.75	5.64	6.20	6.62	6.96	7.24	7.47	7.68	7.86
9	4.60	5.43	5.96	6.35	6.66	6.91	7.13	7.33	7.49
10	4.48	5.27	5.77	6.14	6.43	6.67	6.87	7.05	7.21
11	4.39	5.15	5.62	5.97	6.25	6.48	6.67	6.84	6.99
12	4.32	5.05	5.50	5.84	6.10	6.32	6.51	6.67	6.81
13	4.26	4.96	5.40	5.73	5.98	6.19	6.37	6.53	6.67
14	4.21	4.89	5.32	5.63	5.88	6.08	6.26	6.41	6.54
15	4.17	4.84	5.25	5.56	5.80	5.99	6.16	6.31	6.44
16	4.13	4.79	5.19	5.49	5.72	5.92	6.08	6.22	6.35
17	4.10	4.74	5.14	5.43	5.66	5.85	6.01	6.15	6.27
18	4.07	4.70	5.09	5.38	5.60	5.79	5.94	6.08	6.20
19	4.05	4.67	5.05	5.33	5.55	5.73	5.89	6.02	6.14
20	4.02	4.64	5.02	5.29	5.51	5.69	5.84	5.97	6.09
24	3.96	4.55	4.91	5.17	5.37	5.54	5.69	5.81	5.92
30	3.89	4.45	4.80	5.05	5.24	5.40	5.54	5.65	5.76
40	3.82	4.37	4.70	4.93	5.11	5.26	5.39	5.50	5.60
60	3.76	4.28	4.59	4.82	4.99	5.13	5.25	5.36	5.45
120	3.70	4.20	4.50	4.71	4.87	5.01	5.12	5.21	5.30
∞	3.64	4.12	4.40	4.60	4.76	4.88	4.99	5.08	5.16

D_2 \ D_1	11	12	13	14	15	16	17	18	19	20
1	253.2	260.0	266.2	271.8	277.0	281.8	286.3	290.4	294.3	298.0
2	32.59	33.40	34.13	34.81	35.43	36.00	36.53	37.03	37.50	37.95
3	17.13	17.53	17.89	18.22	18.52	18.81	19.07	19.32	19.55	19.77
4	12.57	12.84	13.09	13.32	13.53	13.73	13.91	14.08	14.24	14.40
5	10.48	10.70	10.89	11.08	11.24	11.40	11.55	11.68	11.81	11.93
6	9.30	9.48	9.65	9.81	9.95	10.08	10.21	10.32	10.43	10.54
7	8.55	8.71	8.86	9.00	9.12	9.24	9.35	9.46	9.55	9.65
8	8.03	8.18	8.31	8.44	8.55	8.66	8.76	8.85	8.94	9.03
9	7.65	7.78	7.91	8.03	8.13	8.23	8.33	8.41	8.49	8.57
10	7.36	7.49	7.60	7.71	7.81	7.91	7.99	8.08	8.15	8.23
11	7.13	7.25	7.36	7.46	7.56	7.65	7.73	7.81	7.88	7.95
12	6.94	7.06	7.17	7.26	7.36	7.44	7.52	7.59	7.66	7.73
13	6.79	6.90	7.01	7.10	7.19	7.27	7.35	7.42	7.48	7.55
14	6.66	6.77	6.87	6.96	7.05	7.13	7.20	7.27	7.33	7.39
15	6.55	6.66	6.76	6.84	6.93	7.00	7.07	7.14	7.20	7.26
16	6.46	6.56	6.66	6.74	6.82	6.90	6.97	7.03	7.09	7.15
17	6.38	6.48	6.57	6.66	6.73	6.81	6.87	6.94	7.00	7.05
18	6.31	6.41	6.50	6.58	6.65	6.73	6.79	6.85	6.91	6.97
19	6.25	6.34	6.43	6.51	6.58	6.65	6.72	6.78	6.84	6.89
20	6.19	6.28	6.37	6.45	6.52	6.59	6.65	6.71	6.77	6.82
24	6.02	6.11	6.19	6.26	6.33	6.39	6.45	6.51	6.56	6.61
30	5.85	5.93	6.01	6.08	6.14	6.20	6.26	6.31	6.36	6.41
40	5.69	5.76	5.83	5.90	5.96	6.02	6.07	6.12	6.16	6.21
60	5.53	5.60	5.67	5.73	5.78	5.84	5.89	5.93	5.97	6.01
120	5.37	5.44	5.50	5.56	5.61	5.66	5.71	5.75	5.79	5.83
∞	5.23	5.29	5.35	5.40	5.45	5.49	5.54	5.57	5.61	5.65

Source: Reprinted with permission from E. S. Pearson and H. O. Hartley, *Biometrika Tables for Statisticians* (New York: Cambridge University Press, 1954).

APPENDIX K

Critical Values of r in the Runs Test

a. Lower Tail: Too Few Runs

n_1 \ n_2	2	3	4	5	6	7	8	9	10	11	12	13	14	15	16	17	18	19	20
2											2	2	2	2	2	2	2	2	2
3					2	2	2	2	2	2	2	2	2	3	3	3	3	3	3
4			2	2	2	3	3	3	3	3	3	3	3	3	4	4	4	4	4
5			2	2	3	3	3	3	3	4	4	4	4	4	4	4	5	5	5
6		2	2	3	3	3	3	4	4	4	4	5	5	5	5	5	5	6	6
7		2	2	3	3	3	4	4	5	5	5	5	5	6	6	6	6	6	6
8		2	3	3	3	4	4	5	5	5	6	6	6	6	6	7	7	7	7
9		2	3	3	4	4	5	5	5	6	6	6	7	7	7	7	8	8	8
10		2	3	3	4	5	5	5	6	6	7	7	7	7	8	8	8	8	9
11		2	3	4	4	5	5	6	6	7	7	7	8	8	8	9	9	9	9
12	2	2	3	4	4	5	6	6	7	7	7	8	8	8	9	9	9	10	10
13	2	2	3	4	5	5	6	6	7	7	8	8	9	9	9	10	10	10	10
14	2	2	3	4	5	5	6	7	7	8	8	9	9	9	10	10	10	11	11
15	2	3	3	4	5	6	6	7	7	8	8	9	9	10	10	11	11	11	12
16	2	3	4	4	5	6	6	7	8	8	9	9	10	10	11	11	11	12	12
17	2	3	4	4	5	6	7	7	8	9	9	10	10	11	11	11	12	12	13
18	2	3	4	5	5	6	7	8	8	9	9	10	10	11	11	12	12	13	13
19	2	3	4	5	6	6	7	8	8	9	10	10	11	11	12	12	13	13	13
20	2	3	4	5	6	6	7	8	9	9	10	10	11	12	12	13	13	13	14

b. Upper Tail: Too Many Runs

n_1 \ n_2	2	3	4	5	6	7	8	9	10	11	12	13	14	15	16	17	18	19	20
2																			
3																			
4				9	9														
5			9	10	10	11	11												
6			9	10	11	12	12	13	13	13	13								
7				11	12	13	13	14	14	14	14	15	15	15					
8				11	12	13	14	14	15	15	16	16	16	16	17	17	17	17	17
9					13	14	14	15	16	16	16	17	17	18	18	18	18	18	18
10					13	14	15	16	16	17	17	18	18	18	19	19	19	20	20
11					13	14	15	16	17	17	18	19	19	19	20	20	20	21	21
12					13	14	16	16	17	18	19	19	20	20	21	21	21	22	22
13						15	16	17	18	19	19	20	20	21	21	22	22	23	23
14						15	16	17	18	19	20	20	21	22	22	23	23	23	24
15						15	16	18	18	19	20	21	22	22	23	23	24	24	25
16							17	18	19	20	21	21	22	23	23	24	25	25	25
17							17	18	19	20	21	22	23	23	24	25	25	26	26
18							17	18	19	20	21	22	23	24	25	25	26	26	27
19							17	18	20	21	22	23	23	24	25	26	26	27	27
20							17	18	20	21	22	23	24	25	25	26	27	27	28

Source: Adapted from Frieda S. Swed and C. Eisenhart, "Tables for testing randomness of grouping in a sequence of alternatives," *Ann. Math. Statist.* 14 (1943): 83–86, with the permission of the publisher.

APPENDIX L

Mann-Whitney U Test Probabilities ($n < 9$)

$n_2 = 3$

U \ n_1	1	2	3
0	.250	.100	.050
1	.500	.200	.100
2	.750	.400	.200
3		.600	.350
4			.500
5			.650

$n_2 = 4$

U \ n_1	1	2	3	4
0	.200	.067	.028	.014
1	.400	.133	.057	.029
2	.600	.267	.114	.057
3		.400	.200	.100
4		.600	.314	.171
5			.429	.243
6			.571	.343
7				.443
8				.557

$n_2 = 5$

U \ n_1	1	2	3	4	5
0	.167	.047	.018	.008	.004
1	.333	.095	.036	.016	.008
2	.500	.190	.071	.032	.016
3	.667	.286	.125	.056	.028
4		.429	.196	.095	.048
5		.571	.286	.143	.075
6			.393	.206	.111
7			.500	.278	.155
8			.607	.365	.210
9				.452	.274
10				.548	.345
11					.421
12					.500
13					.579

$n_2 = 6$

U \ n_1	1	2	3	4	5	6
0	.143	.036	.012	.005	.002	.001
1	.286	.071	.024	.010	.004	.002
2	.428	.143	.048	.019	.009	.004
3	.571	.214	.083	.033	.015	.008
4		.321	.131	.057	.026	.013
5		.429	.190	.086	.041	.021
6		.571	.274	.129	.063	.032
7			.357	.176	.089	.047
8			.452	.238	.123	.066
9			.548	.305	.165	.090
10				.381	.214	.120
11				.457	.268	.155
12				.545	.331	.197
13					.396	.242
14					.465	.294
15					.535	.350
16						.409
17						.469
18						.531

$n_2 = 7$

U \ n_1	1	2	3	4	5	6	7
0	.125	.028	.008	.003	.001	.001	.000
1	.250	.056	.017	.006	.003	.001	.001
2	.375	.111	.033	.012	.005	.002	.001
3	.500	.167	.058	.021	.009	.004	.002
4	.625	.250	.092	.036	.015	.007	.003
5		.333	.133	.055	.024	.011	.006
6		.444	.192	.082	.037	.017	.009
7		.556	.258	.115	.053	.026	.013
8			.333	.158	.074	.037	.019
9			.417	.206	.101	.051	.027
10			.500	.264	.134	.069	.036
11			.583	.324	.172	.090	.049
12				.394	.216	.117	.064
13				.464	.265	.147	.082
14				.538	.319	.183	.104
15					.378	.223	.130
16					.438	.267	.159
17					.500	.314	.191
18					.562	.365	.228
19						.418	.267
20						.473	.310
21						.527	.355
22							.402
23							.451
24							.500
25							.549

$n_2 = 8$

U \ n_1	1	2	3	4	5	6	7	8	t	Normal
0	.111	.022	.006	.002	.001	.000	.000	.000	3.308	.001
1	.222	.044	.012	.004	.002	.001	.000	.000	3.203	.001
2	.333	.089	.024	.008	.003	.001	.001	.000	3.098	.001
3	.444	.133	.042	.014	.005	.002	.001	.001	2.993	.001
4	.556	.200	.067	.024	.009	.004	.002	.001	2.888	.002
5		.267	.097	.036	.015	.006	.003	.001	2.783	.003
6		.356	.139	.055	.023	.010	.005	.002	2.678	.004
7		.444	.188	.077	.033	.015	.007	.003	2.573	.005
8		.556	.248	.107	.047	.021	.010	.005	2.468	.007
9			.315	.141	.064	.030	.014	.007	2.363	.009
10			.387	.184	.085	.041	.020	.010	2.258	.012
11			.461	.230	.111	.054	.027	.014	2.153	.016
12			.539	.285	.142	.071	.036	.019	2.048	.020
13				.341	.177	.091	.047	.025	1.943	.026
14				.404	.217	.114	.060	.032	1.838	.033
15				.467	.262	.141	.076	.041	1.733	.041
16				.533	.311	.172	.095	.052	1.628	.052
17					.362	.207	.116	.065	1.523	.064
18					.416	.245	.140	.080	1.418	.078
19					.472	.286	.168	.097	1.313	.094
20					.528	.331	.198	.117	1.208	.113
21						.377	.232	.139	1.102	.135
22						.426	.268	.164	.998	.159
23						.475	.306	.191	.893	.185
24						.525	.347	.221	.788	.215
25							.389	.253	.683	.247
26							.433	.287	.578	.282
27							.478	.323	.473	.318
28							.522	.360	.368	.356
29								.399	.263	.396
30								.439	.158	.437
31								.480	.052	.481
32								.520		

Source: Reproduced from H. B. Mann and D. R. Whitney, "On a test of whether one of two random variables is stochastically larger than the other," *Ann. Math Statist*, 18 (1947): 52–54, with the permission of the publisher.

APPENDIX M

Mann-Whitney U Test Critical Values ($9 \leq n \leq 20$)

Critical Values of U for a One-Tailed Test at $\alpha = 0.001$ or for a Two-Tailed Test at $\alpha = 0.002$

n_1 \ n_2	9	10	11	12	13	14	15	16	17	18	19	20
1												
2												
3									0	0	0	0
4		0	0	0	1	1	1	2	2	3	3	3
5	1	1	2	2	3	3	4	5	5	6	7	7
6	2	3	4	4	5	6	7	8	9	10	11	12
7	3	5	6	7	8	9	10	11	13	14	15	16
8	5	6	8	9	11	12	14	15	17	18	20	21
9	7	8	10	12	14	15	17	19	21	23	25	26
10	8	10	12	14	17	19	21	23	25	27	29	32
11	10	12	15	17	20	22	24	27	29	32	34	37
12	12	14	17	20	23	25	28	31	34	37	40	42
13	14	17	20	23	26	29	32	35	38	42	45	48
14	15	19	22	25	29	32	36	39	43	46	50	54
15	17	21	24	28	32	36	40	43	47	51	55	59
16	19	23	27	31	35	39	43	48	52	56	60	65
17	21	25	29	34	38	43	47	52	57	61	66	70
18	23	27	32	37	42	46	51	56	61	66	71	76
19	25	29	34	40	45	50	55	60	66	71	77	82
20	26	32	37	42	48	54	59	65	70	76	82	88

Critical Values of U for a One-Tailed Test at $\alpha = 0.01$ or for a Two-Tailed Test at $\alpha = 0.02$

n_1 \ n_2	9	10	11	12	13	14	15	16	17	18	19	20
1												
2					0	0	0	0	0	0	1	1
3	1	1	1	2	2	2	3	3	4	4	4	5
4	3	3	4	5	5	6	7	7	8	9	9	10
5	5	6	7	8	9	10	11	12	13	14	15	16
6	7	8	9	11	12	13	15	16	18	19	20	22
7	9	11	12	14	16	17	19	21	23	24	26	28
8	11	13	15	17	20	22	24	26	28	30	32	34
9	14	16	18	21	23	26	28	31	33	36	38	40
10	16	19	22	24	27	30	33	36	38	41	44	47
11	18	22	25	28	31	34	37	41	44	47	50	53
12	21	24	28	31	35	38	42	46	49	53	56	60
13	23	27	31	35	39	43	47	51	55	59	63	67
14	26	30	34	38	43	47	51	56	60	65	69	73
15	28	33	37	42	47	51	56	61	66	70	75	80
16	31	36	41	46	51	56	61	66	71	76	82	87
17	33	38	44	49	55	60	66	71	77	82	88	93
18	36	41	47	53	59	65	70	76	82	88	94	100
19	38	44	50	56	63	69	75	82	88	94	101	107
20	40	47	53	60	67	73	80	87	93	100	107	114

Critical Values of U for a
One-Tailed Test at $\alpha = 0.025$
or for a Two-Tailed Test at
$\alpha = 0.05$

n_1 \ n_2	9	10	11	12	13	14	15	16	17	18	19	20
1												
2	0	0	0	1	1	1	1	1	2	2	2	2
3	2	3	3	4	4	5	5	6	6	7	7	8
4	4	5	6	7	8	9	10	11	11	12	13	13
5	7	8	9	11	12	13	14	15	17	18	19	20
6	10	11	13	14	16	17	19	21	22	24	25	27
7	12	14	16	18	20	22	24	26	28	30	32	34
8	15	17	19	22	24	26	29	31	34	36	38	41
9	17	20	23	26	28	31	34	37	39	42	45	48
10	20	23	26	29	33	36	39	42	45	48	52	55
11	23	26	30	33	37	40	44	47	51	55	58	62
12	26	29	33	37	41	45	49	53	57	61	65	69
13	28	33	37	41	45	50	54	59	63	67	72	76
14	31	36	40	45	50	55	59	64	67	74	78	83
15	34	39	44	49	54	59	64	70	75	80	85	90
16	37	42	47	53	59	64	70	75	81	86	92	98
17	39	45	51	57	63	67	75	81	87	93	99	105
18	42	48	55	61	67	74	80	86	93	99	106	112
19	45	52	58	65	72	78	85	92	99	106	113	119
20	48	55	62	69	76	83	90	98	105	112	119	127

Critical Values of U for a
One-Tailed Test at $\alpha = 0.05$
or for a Two-Tailed Test at
$\alpha = 0.10$

n_1 \ n_2	9	10	11	12	13	14	15	16	17	18	19	20
1											0	0
2	1	1	1	2	2	2	3	3	3	4	4	4
3	3	4	5	5	6	7	7	8	9	9	10	11
4	6	7	8	9	10	11	12	14	15	16	17	18
5	9	11	12	13	15	16	18	19	20	22	23	25
6	12	14	16	17	19	21	23	25	26	28	30	32
7	15	17	19	21	24	26	28	30	33	35	37	39
8	18	20	23	26	28	31	33	36	39	41	44	47
9	21	24	27	30	33	36	39	42	45	48	51	54
10	24	27	31	34	37	41	44	48	51	55	58	62
11	27	31	34	38	42	46	50	54	57	61	65	69
12	30	34	38	42	47	51	55	60	64	68	72	77
13	33	37	42	47	51	56	61	65	70	75	80	84
14	36	41	46	51	56	61	66	71	77	82	87	92
15	39	44	50	55	61	66	72	77	83	88	94	100
16	42	48	54	60	65	71	77	83	89	95	101	107
17	45	51	57	64	70	77	83	89	96	102	109	115
18	48	55	61	68	75	82	88	95	102	109	116	123
19	51	58	65	72	80	87	94	101	109	116	123	130
20	54	62	69	77	84	92	100	107	115	123	130	138

Source: Adapted and abridged from Tables 1, 3, 5, and 7 of D. Auble, "Extended tables for the Mann-Whitney statistic," *Bulletin of the Institute of Educational Research at Indiana University* 1, No. 2 (1953) with the permission of the publisher.

APPENDIX N

Critical Values of *T* in the Wilcoxon Matched-Pairs Signed-Ranks Test ($n \leq 25$)

n	LEVEL OF SIGNIFICANCE FOR ONE-TAILED TEST		
	0.025	0.01	0.005
	LEVEL OF SIGNIFICANCE FOR TWO-TAILED TEST		
	0.05	0.02	0.01
6	0	—	—
7	2	0	—
8	4	2	0
9	6	3	2
10	8	5	3
11	11	7	5
12	14	10	7
13	17	13	10
14	21	16	13
15	25	20	16
16	30	24	20
17	35	28	23
18	40	33	28
19	46	38	32
20	52	43	38
21	59	49	43
22	66	56	49
23	73	62	55
24	81	69	61
25	89	77	68

Source: Adapted from Table 1 of F. Wilcoxon, *Some Rapid Approximate Statistical Procedures* (New York: American Cyanamid Company, 1949), 13, with the permission of the publisher.

Critical Values d_L and d_U of the Durbin-Watson Statistic D (Critical Values Are One-Sided)

$\alpha = .05$

n	P = 1		P = 2		P = 3		P = 4		P = 5	
	d_L	d_U	d_L	d_U	d_L	d_U	d_L	d_U	d_L	d_U
15	1.08	1.36	.95	1.54	.82	1.75	.69	1.97	.56	2.21
16	1.10	1.37	.98	1.54	.86	1.73	.74	1.93	.62	2.15
17	1.13	1.38	1.02	1.54	.90	1.71	.78	1.90	.67	2.10
18	1.16	1.39	1.05	1.53	.93	1.69	.82	1.87	.71	2.06
19	1.18	1.40	1.08	1.53	.97	1.68	.86	1.85	.75	2.02
20	1.20	1.41	1.10	1.54	1.00	1.68	.90	1.83	.79	1.99
21	1.22	1.42	1.13	1.54	1.03	1.67	.93	1.81	.83	1.96
22	1.24	1.43	1.15	1.54	1.05	1.66	.96	1.80	.86	1.94
23	1.26	1.44	1.17	1.54	1.08	1.66	.99	1.79	.90	1.92
24	1.27	1.45	1.19	1.55	1.10	1.66	1.01	1.78	.93	1.90
25	1.29	1.45	1.21	1.55	1.12	1.66	1.04	1.77	.95	1.89
26	1.30	1.46	1.22	1.55	1.14	1.65	1.06	1.76	.98	1.88
27	1.32	1.47	1.24	1.56	1.16	1.65	1.08	1.76	1.01	1.86
28	1.33	1.48	1.26	1.56	1.18	1.65	1.10	1.75	1.03	1.85
29	1.34	1.48	1.27	1.56	1.20	1.65	1.12	1.74	1.05	1.84
30	1.35	1.49	1.28	1.57	1.21	1.65	1.14	1.74	1.07	1.83
31	1.36	1.50	1.30	1.57	1.23	1.65	1.16	1.74	1.09	1.83
32	1.37	1.50	1.31	1.57	1.24	1.65	1.18	1.73	1.11	1.82
33	1.38	1.51	1.32	1.58	1.26	1.65	1.19	1.73	1.13	1.81
34	1.39	1.51	1.33	1.58	1.27	1.65	1.21	1.73	1.15	1.81
35	1.40	1.52	1.34	1.58	1.28	1.65	1.22	1.73	1.16	1.80
36	1.41	1.52	1.35	1.59	1.29	1.65	1.24	1.73	1.18	1.80
37	1.42	1.53	1.36	1.59	1.31	1.66	1.25	1.72	1.19	1.80
38	1.43	1.54	1.37	1.59	1.32	1.66	1.26	1.72	1.21	1.79
39	1.43	1.54	1.38	1.60	1.33	1.66	1.27	1.72	1.22	1.79
40	1.44	1.54	1.39	1.60	1.34	1.66	1.29	1.72	1.23	1.79
45	1.48	1.57	1.43	1.62	1.38	1.67	1.34	1.72	1.29	1.78
50	1.50	1.59	1.46	1.63	1.42	1.67	1.38	1.72	1.34	1.77
55	1.53	1.60	1.49	1.64	1.45	1.68	1.41	1.72	1.38	1.77
60	1.55	1.62	1.51	1.65	1.48	1.69	1.44	1.73	1.41	1.77
65	1.57	1.63	1.54	1.66	1.50	1.70	1.47	1.73	1.44	1.77
70	1.58	1.64	1.55	1.67	1.52	1.70	1.49	1.74	1.46	1.77
75	1.60	1.65	1.57	1.68	1.54	1.71	1.51	1.74	1.49	1.77
80	1.61	1.66	1.59	1.69	1.56	1.72	1.53	1.74	1.51	1.77
85	1.62	1.67	1.60	1.70	1.57	1.72	1.55	1.75	1.52	1.77
90	1.63	1.68	1.61	1.70	1.59	1.73	1.57	1.75	1.54	1.78
95	1.64	1.69	1.62	1.71	1.60	1.73	1.58	1.75	1.56	1.78
100	1.65	1.69	1.63	1.72	1.61	1.74	1.59	1.76	1.57	1.78

(continued)

n = number of observations; P = number of independent variables.

Source: This table is reproduced from *Biometrika*, 41 (1951): 173 and 175, with the permission of the *Biometrika* Trustees.

$\alpha = .01$

n	P = 1		P = 2		P = 3		P = 4		P = 5	
	d_L	d_U	d_L	d_U	d_L	d_U	d_L	d_U	d_L	d_U
15	.81	1.07	.70	1.25	.59	1.46	.49	1.70	.39	1.96
16	.84	1.09	.74	1.25	.63	1.44	.53	1.66	.44	1.90
17	.87	1.10	.77	1.25	.67	1.43	.57	1.63	.48	1.85
18	.90	1.12	.80	1.26	.71	1.42	.61	1.60	.52	1.80
19	.93	1.13	.83	1.26	.74	1.41	.65	1.58	.56	1.77
20	.95	1.15	.86	1.27	.77	1.41	.68	1.57	.60	1.74
21	.97	1.16	.89	1.27	.80	1.41	.72	1.55	.63	1.71
22	1.00	1.17	.91	1.28	.83	1.40	.75	1.54	.66	1.69
23	1.02	1.19	.94	1.29	.86	1.40	.77	1.53	.70	1.67
24	1.04	1.20	.96	1.30	.88	1.41	.80	1.53	.72	1.66
25	1.05	1.21	.98	1.30	.90	1.41	.83	1.52	.75	1.65
26	1.07	1.22	1.00	1.31	.93	1.41	.85	1.52	.78	1.64
27	1.09	1.23	1.02	1.32	.95	1.41	.88	1.51	.81	1.63
28	1.10	1.24	1.04	1.32	.97	1.41	.90	1.51	.83	1.62
29	1.12	1.25	1.05	1.33	.99	1.42	.92	1.51	.85	1.61
30	1.13	1.26	1.07	1.34	1.01	1.42	.94	1.51	.88	1.61
31	1.15	1.27	1.08	1.34	1.02	1.42	.96	1.51	.90	1.60
32	1.16	1.28	1.10	1.35	1.04	1.43	.98	1.51	.92	1.60
33	1.17	1.29	1.11	1.36	1.05	1.43	1.00	1.51	.94	1.59
34	1.18	1.30	1.13	1.36	1.07	1.43	1.01	1.51	.95	1.59
35	1.19	1.31	1.14	1.37	1.08	1.44	1.03	1.51	.97	1.59
36	1.21	1.32	1.15	1.38	1.10	1.44	1.04	1.51	.99	1.59
37	1.22	1.32	1.16	1.38	1.11	1.45	1.06	1.51	1.00	1.59
38	1.23	1.33	1.18	1.39	1.12	1.45	1.07	1.52	1.02	1.58
39	1.24	1.34	1.19	1.39	1.14	1.45	1.09	1.52	1.03	1.58
40	1.25	1.34	1.20	1.40	1.15	1.46	1.10	1.52	1.05	1.58
45	1.29	1.38	1.24	1.42	1.20	1.48	1.16	1.53	1.11	1.58
50	1.32	1.40	1.28	1.45	1.24	1.49	1.20	1.54	1.16	1.59
55	1.36	1.43	1.32	1.47	1.28	1.51	1.25	1.55	1.21	1.59
60	1.38	1.45	1.35	1.48	1.32	1.52	1.28	1.56	1.25	1.60
65	1.41	1.47	1.38	1.50	1.35	1.53	1.31	1.57	1.28	1.61
70	1.43	1.49	1.40	1.52	1.37	1.55	1.34	1.58	1.31	1.61
75	1.45	1.50	1.42	1.53	1.39	1.56	1.37	1.59	1.34	1.62
80	1.47	1.52	1.44	1.54	1.42	1.57	1.39	1.60	1.36	1.62
85	1.48	1.53	1.46	1.55	1.43	1.58	1.41	1.60	1.39	1.63
90	1.50	1.54	1.47	1.56	1.45	1.59	1.43	1.61	1.41	1.64
95	1.51	1.55	1.49	1.57	1.47	1.60	1.45	1.62	1.42	1.64
100	1.52	1.56	1.50	1.58	1.48	1.60	1.46	1.63	1.44	1.65

n = number of observations; P = number of independent variables.

Source: This table is reproduced from *Biometrika*, 41 (1951): 173 and 175, with the permission of the *Biometrika* Trustees.

	One-Tailed: $\alpha = .05$ Two-Tailed: $\alpha = .10$	$\alpha = .025$ $\alpha = .05$	$\alpha = .01$ $\alpha = .02$	$\alpha = .005$ $\alpha = .01$
n		(Lower, Upper)		
5	0,15	—,—	—,—	—,—
6	2,19	0,21	—,—	—,—
7	3,25	2,26	0.28	—,—
8	5,31	3,33	1,35	0,36
9	8,37	5,40	3,42	1,44
10	10,45	8,47	5,50	3,52
11	13,53	10,56	7,59	5,61
12	17,61	13,65	10,68	7,71
13	21,70	17,74	12,79	10,81
14	25,80	21,84	16,89	13,92
15	30,90	25,95	19,101	16,104
16	35,101	29,107	23,113	19,117
17	41,112	34,119	27,126	23,130
18	47,124	40,131	32,139	27,144
19	53,137	46,144	37,153	32,158
20	60,150	52,158	43,167	37,173

APPENDIX P

Lower and Upper Critical Values W of Wilcoxon Signed-Ranks Test

Source: Adapted from Table 2 of F. Wilcoxon and R. A. Wilcox, *Some Rapid Approximate Statistical Procedures* (Pearl River, NY: Lederle Laboratories, 1964), with permission of the American Cyanamid Company.

Control Chart Factors

Number of Observations in Sample	d_2	d_3	D_3	D_4	A_2
2	1.128	0.853	0	3.267	1.880
3	1.693	0.888	0	2.575	1.023
4	2.059	0.880	0	2.282	0.729
5	2.326	0.864	0	2.114	0.577
6	2.534	0.848	0	2.004	0.483
7	2.704	0.833	0.076	1.924	0.419
8	2.847	0.820	0.136	1.864	0.373
9	2.970	0.808	0.184	1.816	0.337
10	3.078	0.797	0.223	1.777	0.308
11	3.173	0.787	0.256	1.744	0.285
12	3.258	0.778	0.283	1.717	0.266
13	3.336	0.770	0.307	1.693	0.249
14	3.407	0.763	0.328	1.672	0.235
15	3.472	0.756	0.347	1.653	0.223
16	3.532	0.750	0.363	1.637	0.212
17	3.588	0.744	0.378	1.622	0.203
18	3.640	0.739	0.391	1.609	0.194
19	3.689	0.733	0.404	1.596	0.187
20	3.735	0.729	0.415	1.585	0.180
21	3.778	0.724	0.425	1.575	0.173
22	3.819	0.720	0.435	1.565	0.167
23	3.858	0.716	0.443	1.557	0.162
24	3.895	0.712	0.452	1.548	0.157
25	3.931	0.708	0.459	1.541	0.153

Source: Reprinted from ASTM-STP 15D by kind permission of the American Society for Testing and Materials.

ANSWERS TO SELECTED ODD-NUMBERED PROBLEMS

Worked-out solutions to all the odd-numbered problems are in the Student Solutions Manual that accompanies this text. Please note solutions were done using Excel, which outputs answers to several decimal places. The precision shown may be more than required in some instances.

CHAPTER 1

1-1 A histogram is a graph showing the distribution of a quantitative variable. The horizontal axis contains the individual possible values for the variable or classes containing the possible values. The vertical bars have a height corresponding to the frequency of occurrence of each value or class. A bar chart is used to graphically describe a variable that has been broken down into distinct categories. The bars represent the value of the variable at each category level. The bars can be vertical or horizontal.

1-3 Males: average = $5,434.00; females: average = $5,545.00. For these data, females tended to have higher total charges than males.

1-5 Under 75 years: average = $3,356.50. Over 75 years: Average = $6,331.60. Based on these results it seems that older patients have higher average total charges at the hospital than do younger patients.

1-7 Estimation is a technique by which we can know about all the data in a data set whenever the data set is so large that it is impractical for us to work with all the data. By looking at a subset of the larger data set estimates are formed that give us some insight into the larger data set.

1-9 Hypothesis testing is used whenever one is interested in testing claims that concern a population. Using information taken from samples, hypothesis testing evaluates the claim and makes a conclusion about the population from which the sample was taken. Estimation is used when we are interested in knowing something about all the data, but the population is too large, or the data set is too big for us to work with all the data. In estimation, no claim is being made or tested.

1-11 a A commonly used measure of the center of the data is the mean or average. **b** To determine a value for the percentage of people in the market area that are senior citizens, the executives would rely on estimation—a set of statistical techniques that allow one to know something about a data set by using a subset of the data whenever the data set is too large to work with all the data. **c** The executives might want to test the hypothesis that the percentage of senior citizens in the market area is greater than the percentage of senior citizens nationwide. The executives could also test the hypothesis that the percentage of senior citizens is greater than or less than a specific value, say 27%.

1-13 Some representative examples might include estimates of the number of CEOs who will vote for a particular candidate, estimates of the percentage increase in wages for factory workers, estimates of the average dollar advertising expenditures for pharmaceutical companies in a specific year, and the expected increase in R&D expenditures for the coming quarter.

1-15 Both telephone surveys and mail questionnaires can use open-end questions.

1-17 Telephone surveys are most frequently used for political polls. The reason is that the survey can be conducted in a shorter time span (usually over a 24-hour period).

1-19 Nonresponse bias is the most common type of bias when mail surveys are used. Most surveys end up with between a 5 and 10 percent return rate. Those that don't respond may have different opinions or provide different results than those that do respond.

1-21 The bias that might be interjected in an experiment of this kind is measurement error. The times might be recorded incorrectly or different data collectors might use different start and end points resulting in measurement error.

1-23 Measurement error is the most likely bias because it would be very possible to make a mistake in timing a customer. Selection bias is another possibility because the data collector may target certain customers who may not be representative of the general population.

1-25 Among the advantages of using a mail questionnaire are the relatively low cost and the avoidance of any interviewer injected bias. However, mail questionnaires often suffer from low response rates (nonresponse bias) and in some cases people who feel strongly one way or the other on an issue may heavily weight responses. Written surveys may also suffer from inaccurate responses when people refuse to tell the truth about sensitive matters such as age and income.

1-27 a Student answers will vary, but most likely a personal interview would be used. **b** The advantages are that the interviewer can meet directly with the customer and get immediate feedback after the customer is in the store. The disadvantages include the high cost of conducting the personal interviews and the time required on the part of the customer who may be in a hurry to get home or to another store in the mall.

1-29 b It would be necessary to read the open-end response and code the response into one of several general categories and assign a number or letter to the response based on the judgment of the person reading the response.

1-31

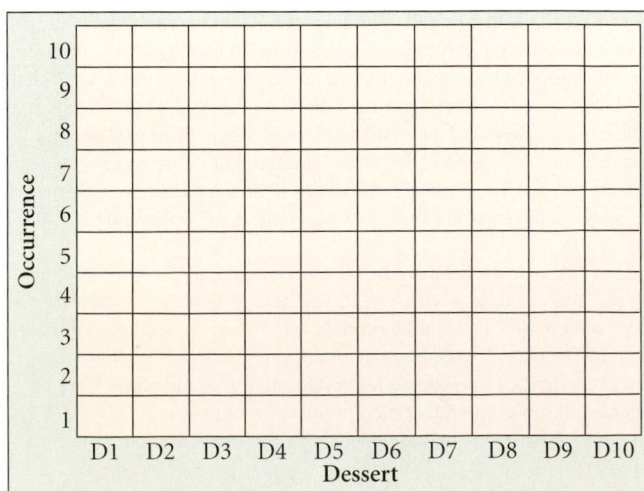

1-33 The basic requirement for a sample to be considered a statistical sample is that the items selected must be selected randomly. Some system of randomness must be in place to assure that the possible samples have an equal chance of being selected at the onset. Different statistical sampling techniques exist including simple random sampling, stratified random sampling, cluster random sampling, and systematic random sampling.

1-35 Even though the term systematic implies that some prior plan is being used to select the items, systematic (or sequential) random sampling is still considered a statistical sampling because the starting point is randomly determined. Thus, all possible samples have the same chance of being selected at the onset of the sampling.

1-37 The first three random numbers would be: 24709; 47970; 25640.

1-39 The resulting random numbers generated are:

$$344.4182$$
$$91.51183$$
$$537.2394$$
$$809.2961$$
$$796.264$$

Note: Students' answers will differ because Excel generates different streams of random numbers each time it is used. Also, if the application requires integer numbers, the **Decrease Decimal** option can be used.

1-41 The November value is an estimate so it is not a parameter; rather, it is a statistic. The value for October is a known value so it is a population parameter.

1-43 a Stratified random sampling **b** Simple random sampling or possibly cluster random sampling **c** Systematic random sampling **d** Stratified random sampling

1-45 There may be cases where the sample size required to obtain a certain desired level of information from a simple random sample is greater than time or money will allow. In such cases, stratified random sampling has the potential to provide the desired information with a smaller sample size.

Student responses will vary but a possible example could involve a market research study looking at consumer expenditures for a product by family income. By dividing the population into the three income strata—low, medium, and high—the desired information can be obtained using a smaller sample size than would be the case with simple random sampling.

1-47 Student answers will vary. In Excel, use either the method outlined in solution to problem 1-39 or the **RANDBETWEEN** function.

1-49 a Because there are 4,000 customer files we could give each file a unique identification number consisting of 4 digits. The first file would be given the identification number "0001." The last file would be given the identification number of "4000." By assigning each employee a number and randomly selecting the number allows each possible sample an equal chance of being selected. **b** Either use a random number table (randomly select the starting row and column), or use a computer program, such as Microsoft Excel or Minitab, which has a random number generator. **c** Because each employee is assigned a 4-digit identification number, we would need a 4-digit random number for each random number selected.

1-51 a Ease of use and timeliness **b** Assuming you want to use a nonstatistical method you could actually survey the first 100 people entering the store or you could wander around the store and just ask any 100 people that you happen to observe. **c** Student answers will vary but they should consider bias of how people are selected and bias by evaluators.

1-53 a Cross-sectional data **b** Time-series data **c** Time-series data **d** Cross-sectional data **e** Cross-sectional data **f** Time-series data

1-55 a Question 1 would be ratio data; question 2 would be ordinal data **b** Question 1 would be quantitative; question 2 is qualitative since it is divided into categories **c** Question 1 would allow you to calculate it more accurately but Question 2 would also allow you to do this if you assume that all values would be at the midpoint of the interval.

1-57 a Because the top category is greater than three this would have to be considered ordinal data. **b** No, not as the survey is currently constructed. Because the last category < 3 does not allow us to identify the exact number of children that belong to customers checking this category we cannot calculate the average number of children. We could modify the survey so that the question is open-ended, such as "How many children do you have?" _____. By allowing for a specific numeric response, rather than the > 3 category, we can calculate the average number of children.

1-59 a Ratio data **b** Ordinal data **c** Ratio data **d** Nominal data

1-61 If the data were collected and used by Anheuser–Busch they would be primary data. If the data were then used by competitors they would be considered secondary data: distributor name—nominal; brands carried—nominal

1-63 a They would probably want to sample the cartons as they come off the assembly line at the Illinois plant for a specified time period. They would want to use a random sample. One method would be to take a systematic random sample. They could then calculate the percentage of the sample that had an unacceptable texture. **b** The product is going to be ruined after testing it. You would not want to ruin the entire product that comes off the assembly line.

1-65 a Student answers will vary but one method would be personal observation at grocery stores or another method would be to simply look at their sales. Are suppliers of the beer ordering bottles or cans? **b** If using personal observation just have people at grocery stores observe people over a specified period of time and note which are selecting cans and which are selecting bottles and look at the percentages of each. **c** You would be looking at ratio data because you could have a true 0 if, for example, no one purchased bottles. **d** The data are quantitative.

CHAPTER 2

2-1 40 is the minimum width for each class. The following classes could be developed: 300 to < 340; 340 to < 380; 380 to < 420; etc.

2-3 a Classes = $1 + 3.322 (\log_{10}(160)) = 1 + 3.322 (2.204) = 8.32 = 9$ **b** Round this up to 0.68 or maybe even to 0.70 for clarity. **c** Using 0.70 as the class width we get: -2.80 to < -2.10; -2.10 to < -1.40; etc.

2-5 a 6.907 rounds to 7; class width is 1.14, which we round up to 2.0. The relative frequency distribution is:

Class	Frequency	Relative Frequency
2–3	2	0.0333
4–5	25	0.4167
6–7	26	0.4333
8–9	6	0.1000
10–11	1	0.0167

b The cumulative frequency distribution is:

Class	Frequency	Cumulative Frequency
2–3	2	2
4–5	25	27
6–7	26	53
8–9	6	59
10–11	1	60

c

Class	Frequency	Relative Frequency	Cumulative Relative Frequency
2–3	2	0.0333	0.0333
4–5	25	0.4167	0.4500
6–7	26	0.4333	0.8833
8–9	6	0.1000	0.9833
10–11	1	0.0167	1.0000

d The ogive is a graph of the cumulative relative frequency distribution.

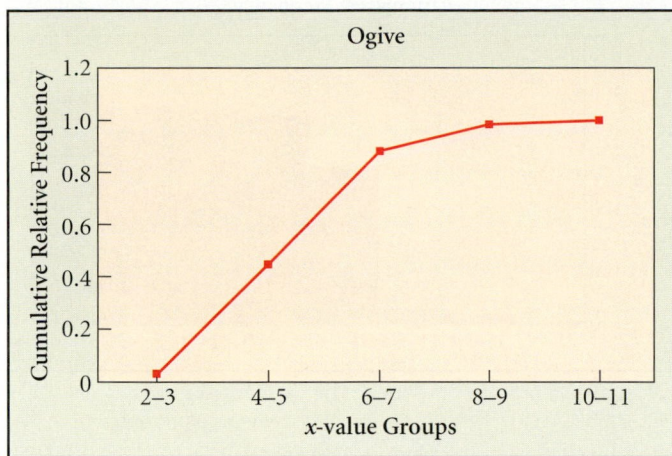

Classes	Frequency
0.95 < 1.00	4
1.00 < 1.05	11
1.05 < 1.10	12
1.10 < 1.15	9
1.15 < 1.20	5
1.20 < 1.25	5
1.25 < 1.30	2
1.30 < 1.35	2
1.35 < 1.40	0
1.40 < 1.45	0
1.45 < 1.50	0
1.50 < 1.55	0
1.55 < 1.60	0
1.60 < 1.65	0
1.65 < 1.70	1

2-7 a The proportion of those having at least five years of college that earn at least \$40,000 = 0.2120. The proportion of those having less than 5 years of college and earning at least \$40,000 = 0.1862. **b** The proportion of those having more than four years of college that earn at least \$60,000 = 0.0544. **c** Proportion that make less than \$20,000 = 0.2550. Of those that have not gone to college the proportion that makes less than \$20,000 = 16/50 = 0.32 **d** The proportion that have not gone to college that make at least \$60,000 = 3/50 = 0.06. The proportion that went to college 1–2 years that makes ≥ \$60,000 = 5/78 = 0.0641. The proportion that went to college 3–4 years that makes ≥ \$60,000 = 15/106 = 0.1415. The proportion that went to college 5–6 years that makes ≥ \$60,000 = 13/91 = 0.1429. The proportion that went to college more than 6 years that makes ≥ \$60,000 = 6/24 = 0.25.

2-9 a Data array in ascending order:

0.96	0.96	0.97	0.98	1.01	1.01	1.02	1.03	1.03	1.03
1.03	1.04	1.04	1.04	1.04	1.05	1.05	1.06	1.07	1.07
1.08	1.09	1.09	1.09	1.09	1.09	1.09	1.10	1.10	1.10
1.10	1.11	1.11	1.11	1.11	1.12	1.16	1.17	1.17	1.18
1.18	1.20	1.21	1.21	1.21	1.23	1.26	1.29	1.31	1.32
1.66									

b Frequency distribution and histogram with five classes: Class width = (1.66 − 0.96)/5 = 0.14 round to 0.15

Classes	Frequency
0.95 < 1.10	27
1.10 < 1.25	19
1.25 < 1.40	4
1.40 < 1.55	0
1.55 < 1.70	1

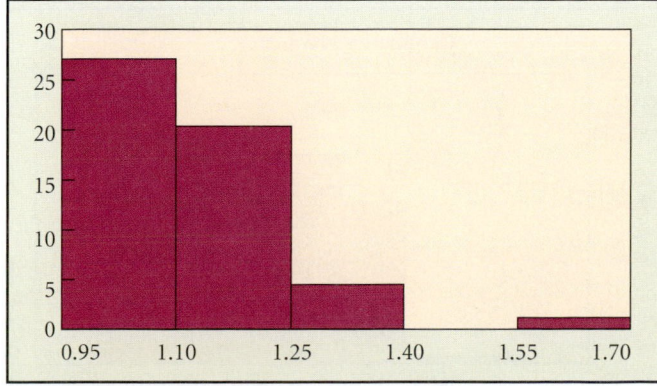

Frequency distribution and histogram with 15 classes:
Class width = (1.66 − 0.96)/15 = 0.0467 round to 0.05

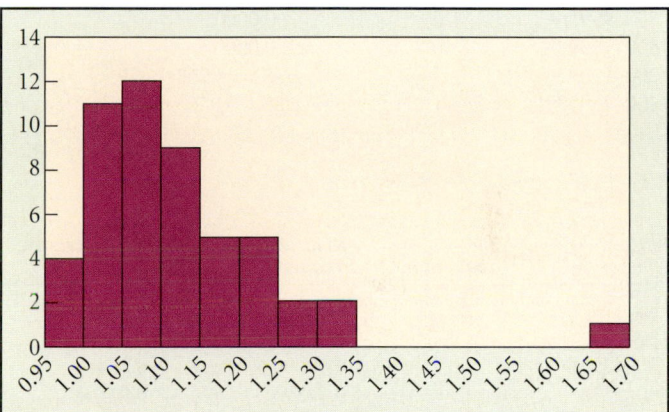

2-11 Class width = 2,400 round to 2,500. *Note:* rounding up is not required.

Class

Class
1,000 < 3,500
3,500 < 6,000
6,000 < 8,500
8,500 < 11,000
11,000 < 13,500
13,500 < 16,000
16,000 < 18,500
18,500 < 21,000
21,000 < 23,500
23,500 < 26,000

2-13 a

	KNOWLEDGE LEVEL			
	Savvy	*Experienced*	*Novice*	*Total*
Online Investors	32	220	148	400
Traditional Investors	8	58	134	200
	40	278	282	600

b

	KNOWLEDGE LEVEL		
	Savvy	*Experienced*	*Novice*
Online Investors	0.0533	0.3667	0.2467
Traditional Investors	0.0133	0.0967	0.2233

c 0.3667 **d** 0.6667

2-15 a

Classes	Frequency
0–799.99	25
800–1599.99	3
1600–2399.99	7
2400–3199.99	0
3200–3999.99	3

b

Classes	Frequency	Relative Frequency
0–199.99	23	23/38 = 0.6053
200–399.99	4	4/38 = 0.1053
400–599.99	3	3/38 = 0.0789
600–799.99	6	6/38 = 0.1579
800–999.99	0	0.0000
1000–1199.99	0	0.0000
1200–1399.99	1	1/38 = 0.0263
1400–1599.99	1	1/38 = 0.0263

c

Classes	Frequency	Relative Frequency	Cumulative Relative Frequency
30–179.99	25	0.65789	0.65789
180–329.99	9	0.23684	0.89473
330–479.99	0	0.00000	0.89473
480–629.99	3	0.07895	0.97368
630–779.99	1	0.02632	1.00000

2-17 a and **b**

Classes	Frequency	Relative Frequency
21–30	3	1.50%
31–40	5	2.50%
41–50	5	2.50%
51–60	125	62.50%
61–70	44	22.00%
71–80	5	2.50%
81–90	1	0.50%
91–100	12	6.00%

c.

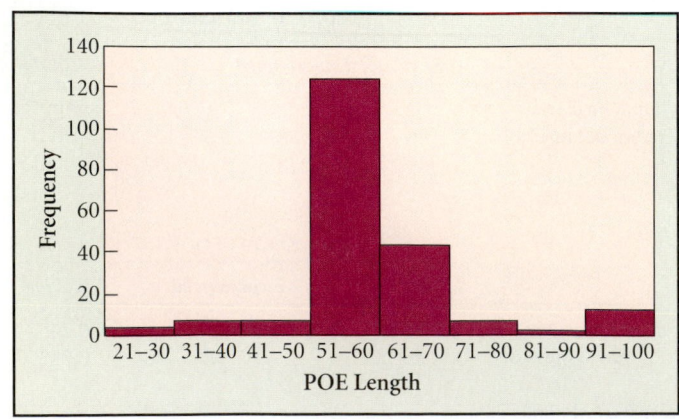

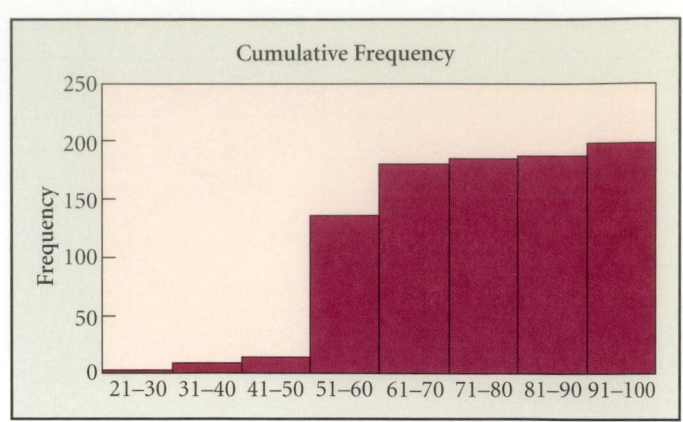

d WIM length

Classes	Frequency	Relative Frequency
21–30	4	2.01%
31–40	4	2.01%
41–50	2	1.01%
51–60	133	66.83%
61–70	38	19.10%
71–80	3	1.51%
81–90	2	1.01%
91–100	13	6.53%

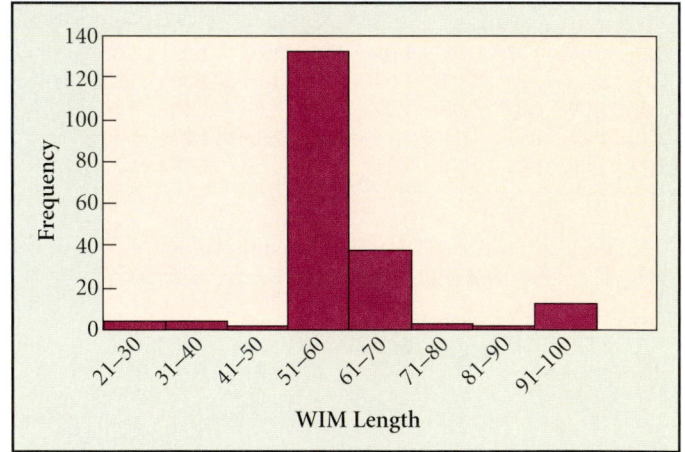

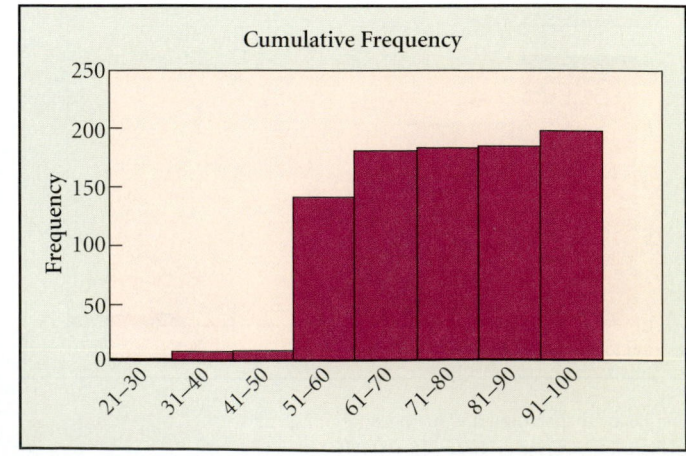

e

Sum of Month Code	WIM Tot									
POE Total Length	21-30	31-40	41-50	51-60	61-70	71-80	81-90	91-100	101-110	Grand Total
21-30	16									16
31-40	3	16						8		27
41-50		5	12	2	5					24
51-60				639	12			8		659
61-70				40	146	7		8		201
71-80					18	10				28
81-90							8			8
91-100							8	73	8	89
Grand Total	19	21	12	681	181	17	16	97	8	1052

Doc1.xls — Sheet1 / Sheet2 / Sheet3

2-19 a

Product 1 Classes	Frequency
−14.99 through −10.00	1
−9.99 through −5.00	5
−4.99 through 0.00	20
0.01 through 5.00	34
5.01 through 10.00	28
10.01 through 15.00	3

Product 2 Classes	Frequency
−9.99 through −5.00	3
−4.99 through 0.00	29
0.01 through 5.00	23
5.01 through 10.00	23
10.01 through 15.00	3
15.01 through 20.00	2

Placebo Classes	Frequency
−14.99 through −10.00	7
−9.99 through −5.00	19
−4.99 through 0.00	29
0.01 through 5.00	23
5.01 through 10.00	10
10.01 through 15.00	1

b

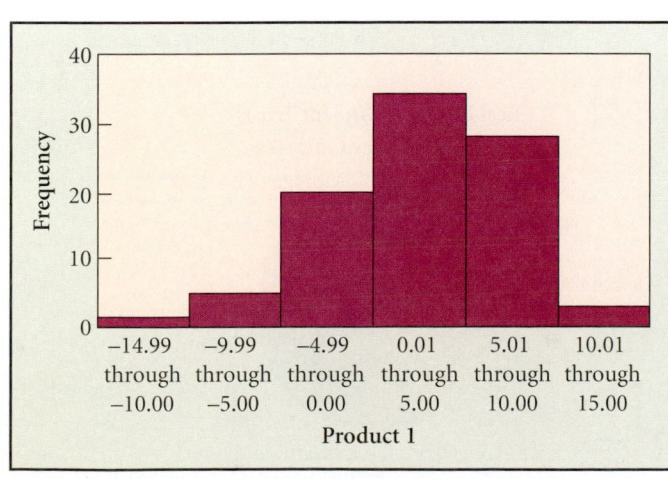

Product 1

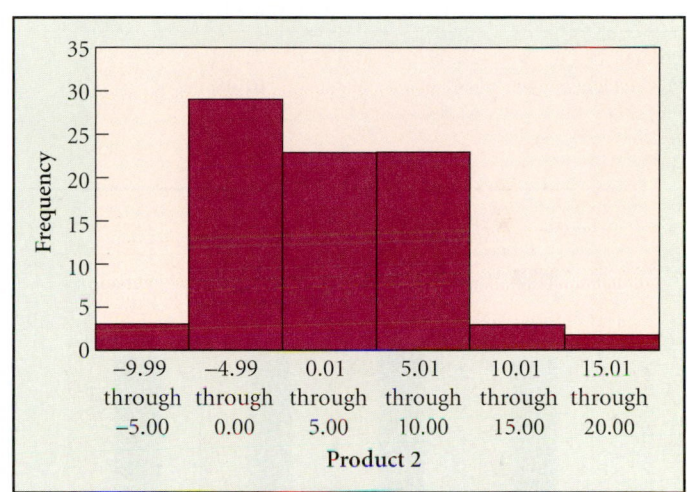

Product 2

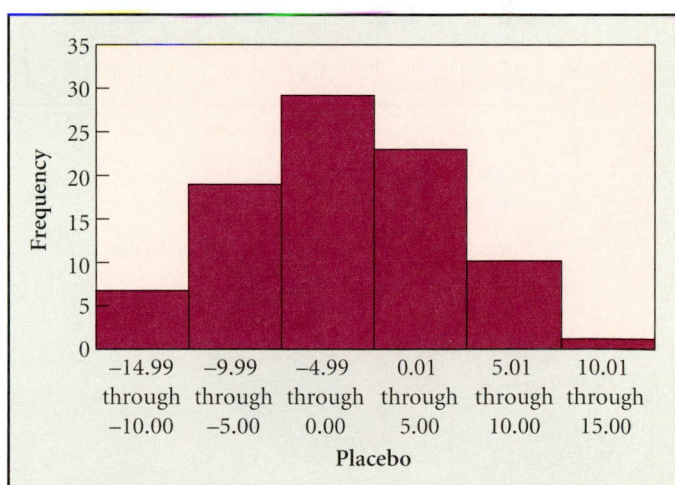

Placebo

c

Product 1 Classes	Frequency	Relative Frequency
−14.99 through −10.00	1	0.0110
−9.99 through −5.00	5	0.0549
−4.99 through 0.00	20	0.2198
0.01 through 5.00	34	0.3736
5.01 through 10.00	28	0.3077
10.01 through 15.00	3	0.0330

Product 2 Classes	Frequency	Relative Frequency
−9.99 through −5.00	3	0.0361
−4.99 through 0.00	29	0.3494
0.01 through 5.00	23	0.2771
5.01 through 10.00	23	0.2771
10.01 through 15.00	3	0.0361
15.01 through 20.00	2	0.0241

Placebo Classes	Frequency	Relative Frequency
−14.99 through −10.00	7	0.0787
−9.99 through −5.00	19	0.2135
−4.99 through 0.00	29	0.3258
0.01 through 5.00	23	0.2584
5.01 through 10.00	10	0.1124
10.01 through 15.00	1	0.0112

d

Plan	Lost Weight	Gained Weight
Product 1	28.6%	71.4%
Product 2	38.6%	61.4%
Placebo	61.8%	38.2%

2-21

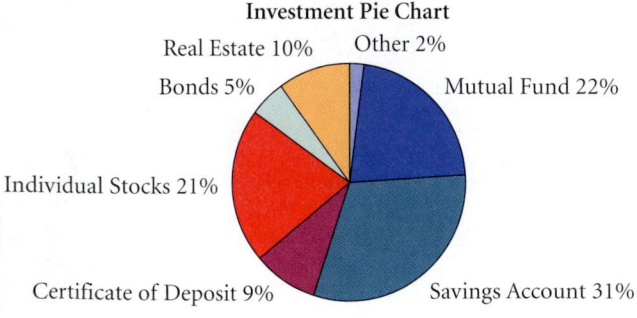

2-23

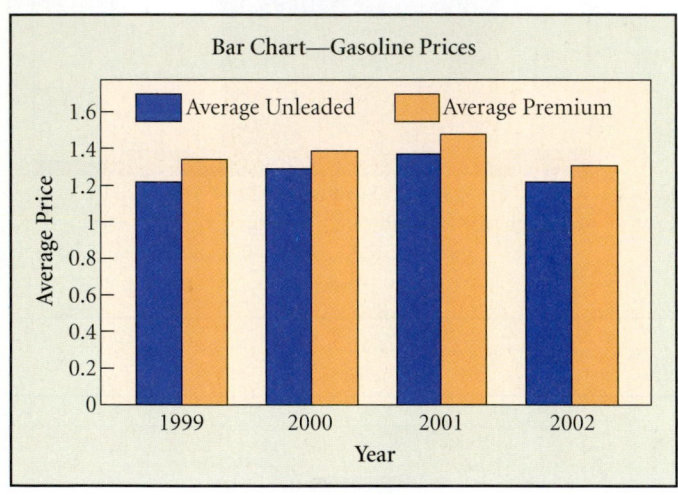

2-25

STEM AND LEAF DISPLAY

Stem Unit	1
0	7 8
1	0 1 4 7 8
2	0 0 1 4 8
3	0 3 8
4	3 4
5	3 4 4
6	3 4

2-27 a

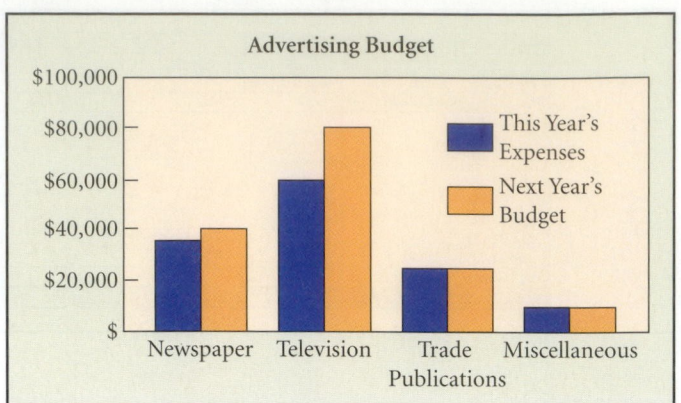

b

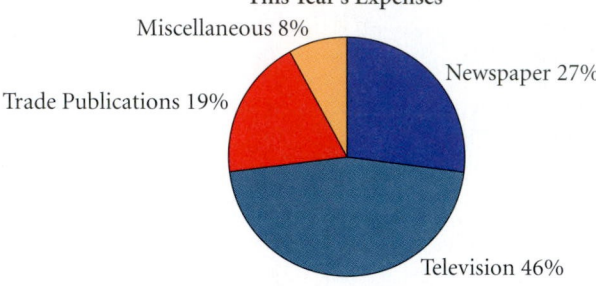

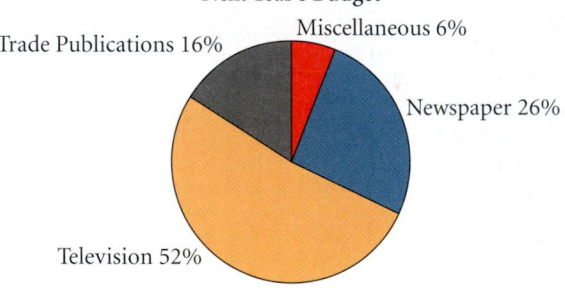

2-29 a

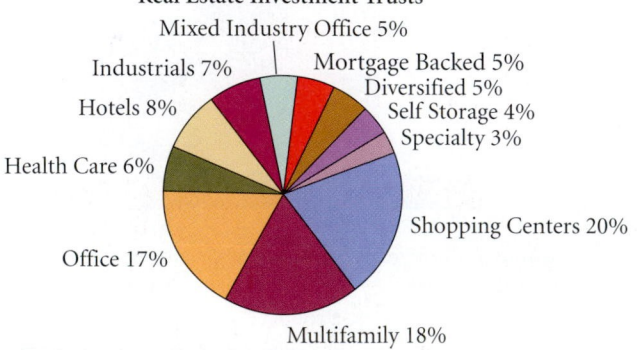

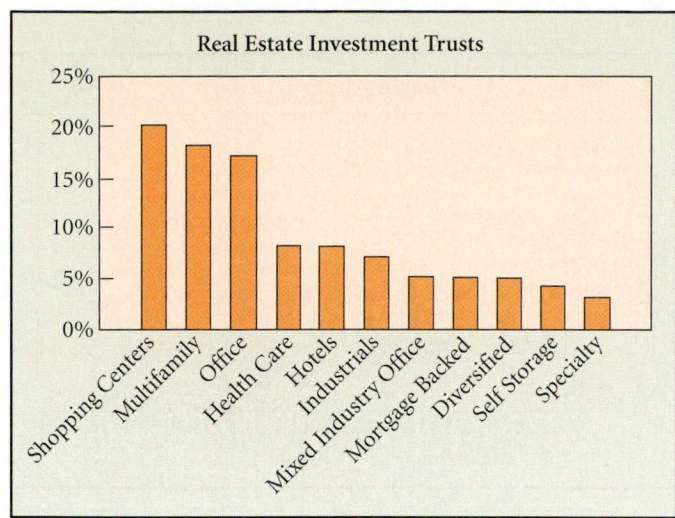

Real Estate Investment Trusts

(Bar chart showing percentages for: Shopping Centers ~20%, Multifamily ~18%, Office ~17%, Health Care ~8%, Hotels ~8%, Industrials ~7%, Mixed Industry Office ~5%, Mortgage Backed ~5%, Diversified ~5%, Self Storage ~4%, Specialty ~3%)

b The pie chart may be more effective because we are looking at percentages.

2-31

STEM AND LEAF DISPLAY

Stem Unit	10
1	7
2	5 6 6 7 7 7 8 8 8 9 9 9 9 10 10
3	0 0 1 1 1 2 2 2 2 2 2 3 3 3 3 3 4 4 5 5 6 6 6 7 7 7 7 9 10 10
4	1 3

2-33

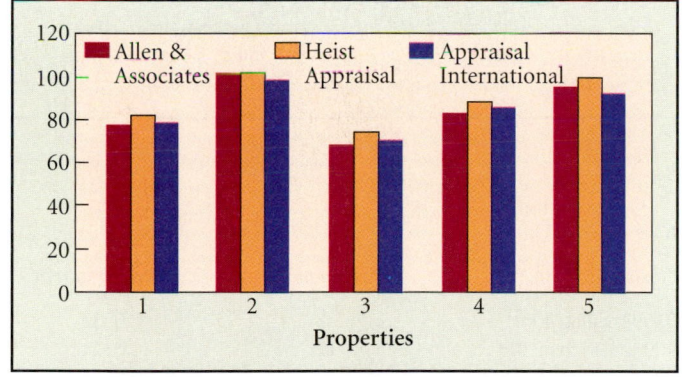

(Grouped bar chart with legend: Allen & Associates, Heist Appraisal, Appraisal International; x-axis "Properties" 1–5)

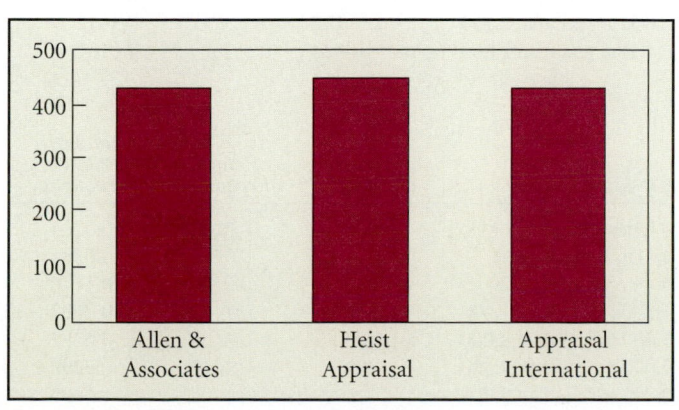

(Bar chart with three bars: Allen & Associates ~430, Heist Appraisal ~450, Appraisal International ~430)

2-35

1997 Median Price	East	North	South	West	Grand Total
70000–109999	10	15	18	4	47
110000–149999	9	6	11	9	35
150000–189999	4	2		5	11
190000–229999	2			1	3
230000–269999				2	2
270000–309999				1	1
310000–349999				1	1
Grand Total	25	23	29	23	100

COUNT OF 1997 MEDIAN PRICE / REGION

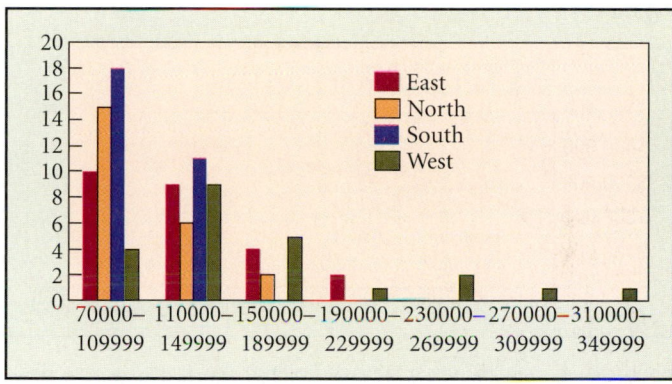

(Grouped bar chart with legend: East, North, South, West across median price ranges)

2-37

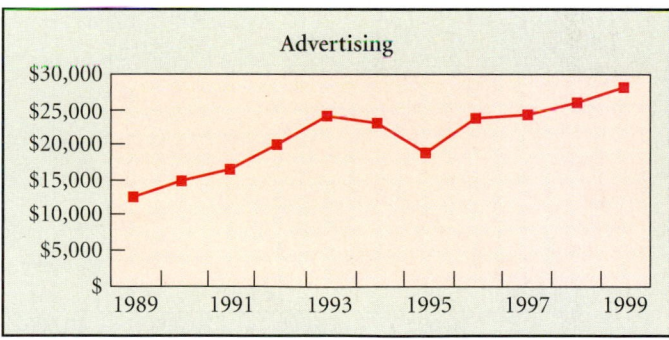

Advertising

(Line chart from 1989 to 1999 showing advertising values increasing from ~$12,500 to ~$28,000)

2-39

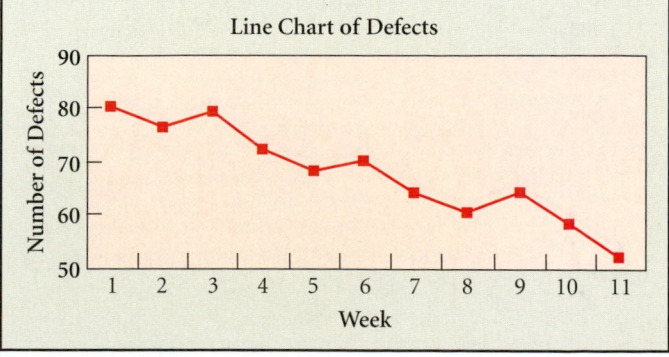

Line Chart of Defects

(Line chart, Number of Defects on y-axis vs Week 1–11, decreasing trend from ~80 to ~52)

2-41

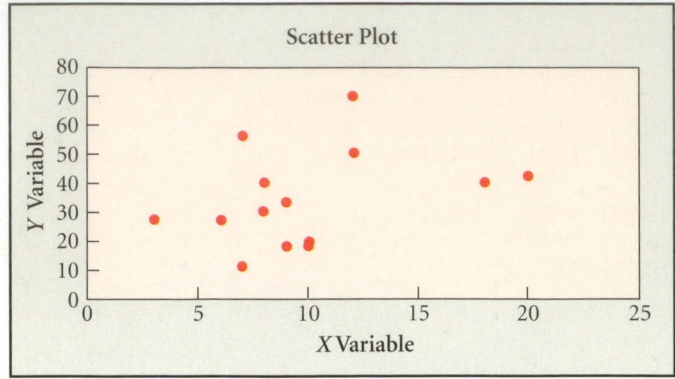

Scatter Plot

2-43 a

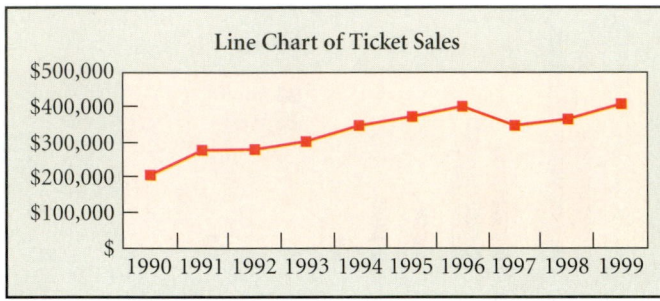

Line Chart of Ticket Sales

b Based on the trend before 1997 he would have reached his goal in about 1999. c The director should reach his goal now in about 2002.

2-45 It appears that profits increase by about $100,000–$150,000 for every $1,000,000 increase in revenue. Because the trend line is approximately at a 45% angle there does not appear to be decreasing economies of scale in the relationship.

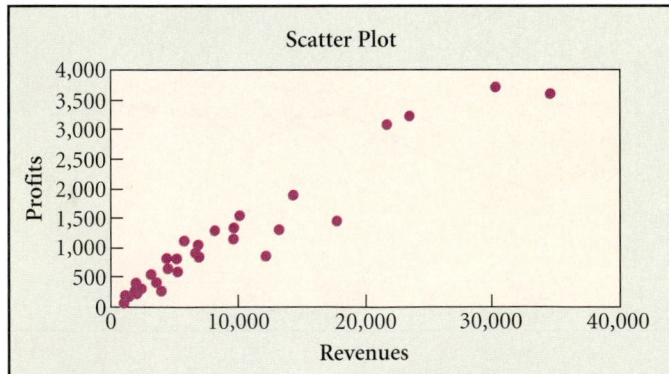

Scatter Plot

2-47 a

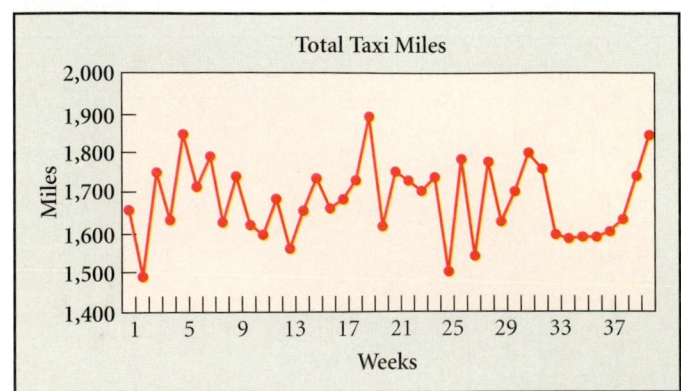

Total Taxi Miles

b

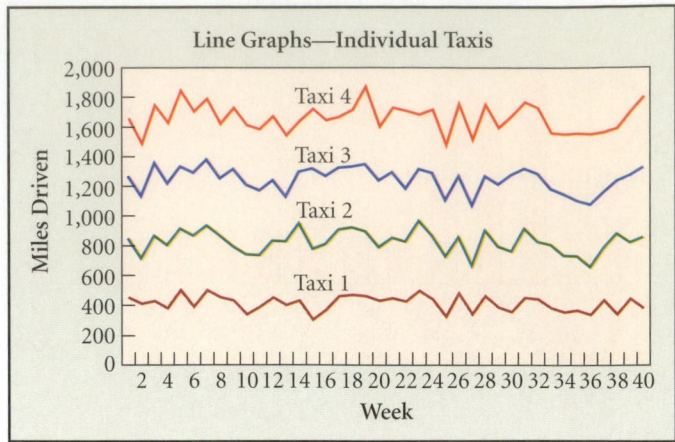

Line Graphs—Individual Taxis

2-49 a

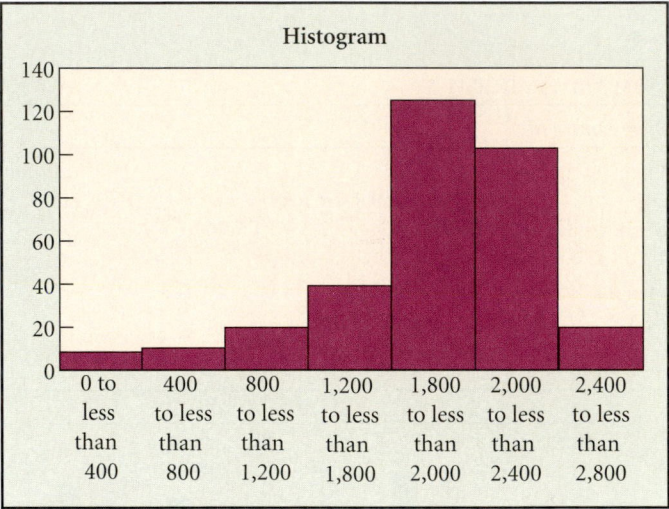

Histogram

b

Classes	Frequency	Relative Frequency
0 to less than 400	8	0.0234
400 to less than 800	12	0.0351
800 to less than 1,200	20	0.0585
1,200 to less than 1,600	50	0.1462
1,600 to less than 2,000	125	0.3655
2,000 to less than 2,400	103	0.3012
2,400 to less than 2,800	24	0.0702

c

Classes	Frequency	Relative Frequency	Cumulative Relative Frequency
0 to less than 400	8	0.0234	0.0234
400 to less than 800	12	0.0351	0.0585
800 to less than 1,200	20	0.0585	0.1170
1,200 to less than 1,600	50	0.1462	0.2632
1,600 to less than 2,000	125	0.3655	0.6287
2,000 to less than 2,400	103	0.3012	0.9299
2,400 to less than 2,800	24	0.0702	1.0000

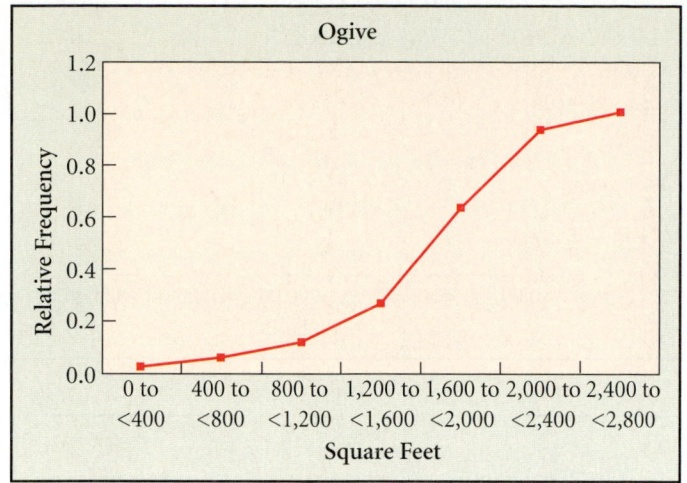

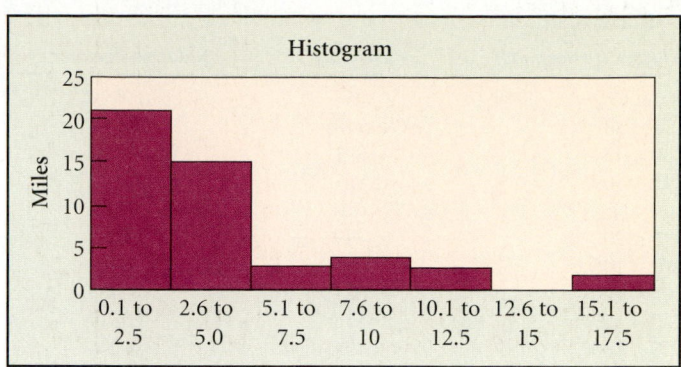

b

Stem and Leaf Display

Stem Unit   1

0	3 4 5 7
1	0 0 0 0 4 5 5 9
2	0 0 0 0 0 4 5 5 5 7
3	0 0 0 0 0 2 5 5 5 5 6
4	0 0 0
5	
6	4 5
7	5
8	3
9	0 0 2
10	
11	0
12	0 0
13	
14	
15	
16	0
17	5

2-51 a

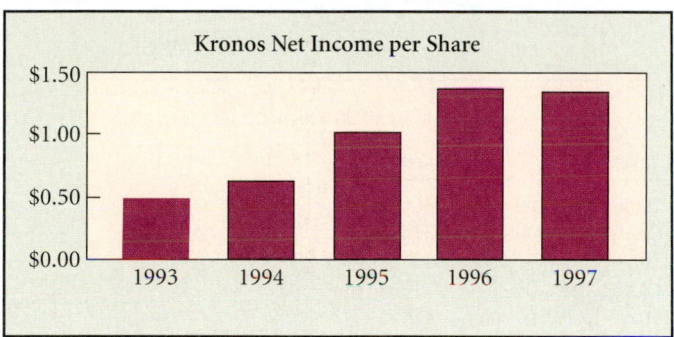

c

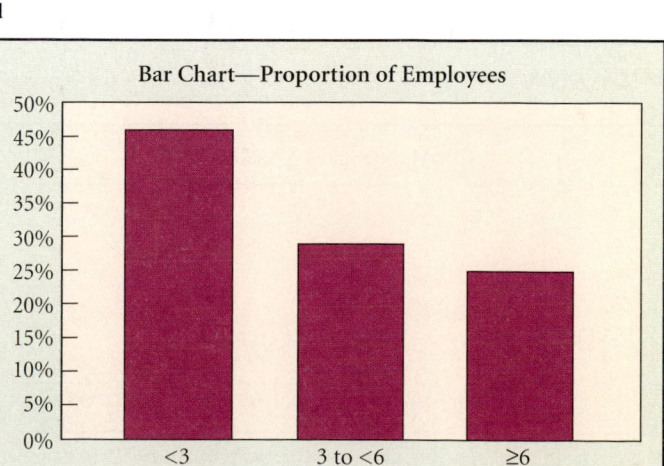

b

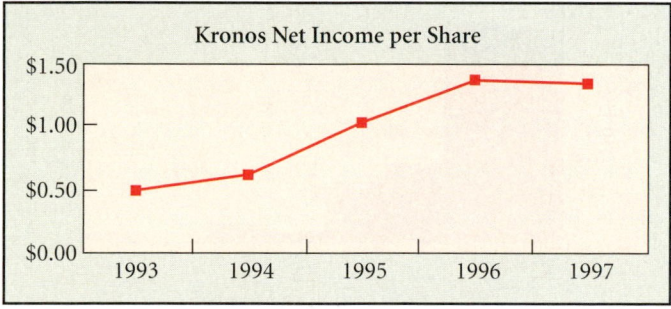

2-53 a Using Sturges's rule = 6.5851 or 7 classes. To determine the class width $(17.5 - 0.3)/7 = 2.46$ so round up to 2.5 to make it easier.

Classes	Frequency
0.1 to 2.5	21
2.6 to 5.0	15
5.1 to 7.5	3
7.6 to 10	4
10.1 to 12.5	3
12.6 to 15	0
15.1 to 17.5	2

d

2-55 a 0.1029

Classes (in seconds)	Number	Relative Frequency
<15	456	0.0899
15 < 30	718	0.1415
30 < 45	891	0.1756
45 < 60	823	0.1622
60 < 75	610	0.1202
75 < 90	449	0.0885
90 < 105	385	0.0759
105 < 120	221	0.0435
120 < 150	158	0.0311
150 < 180	124	0.0244
180 < 240	87	0.0171
≥240	153	0.0301

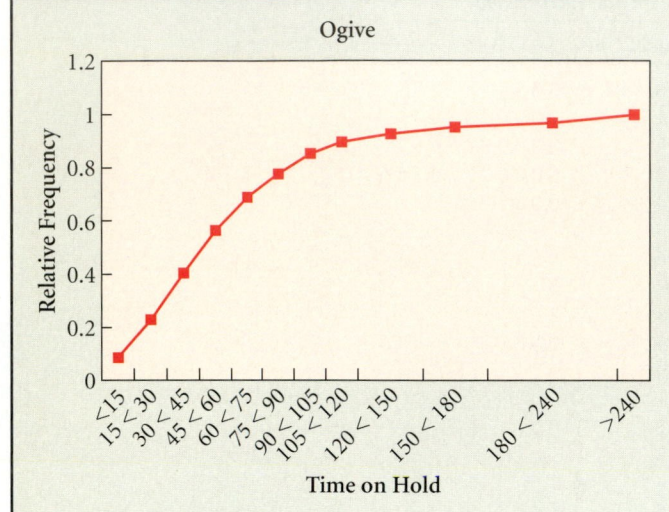

b 522 × $30 = $15,660 month.

2-57 a

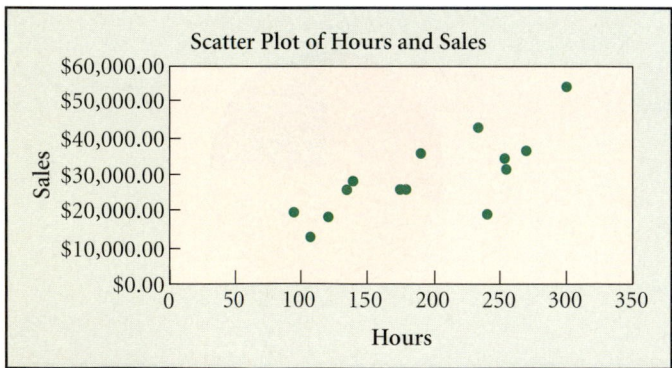

b It appears there is a linear relationship between hours worked and weekly sales.

2-59 a

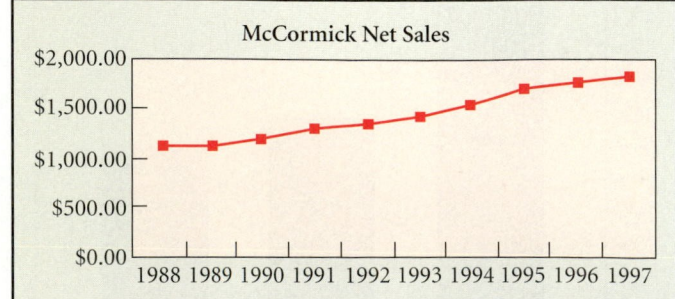

There is an upward trend in sales during the years 1988–1997. **b** It appears that capital expenditures increase as net sales increase in most instances.

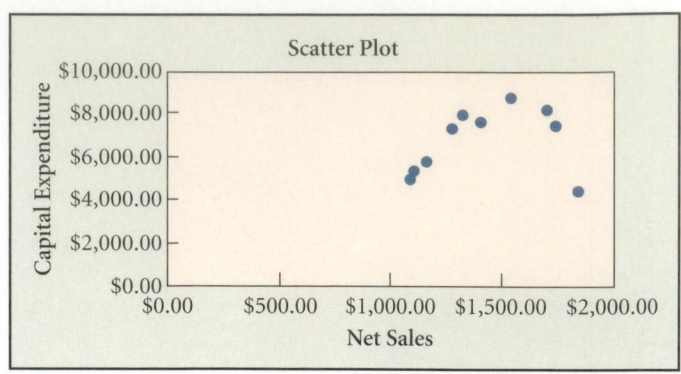

c

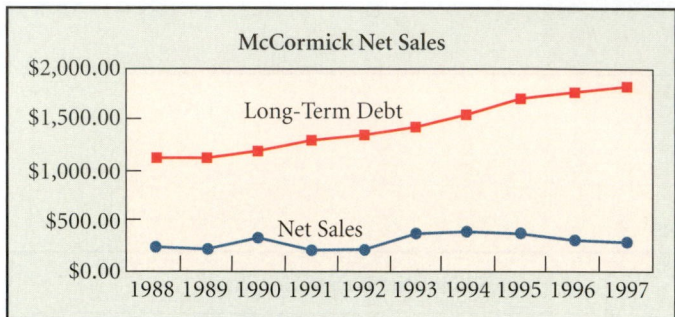

2-61 a Using Sturges's rule: = 30,004 round to 30,100.

Classes	Frequency
70,001–100,100	36
100,101–130,200	37
130,201–160,300	13
160,301–190,400	7
190,401–220,500	2
220,501–250,600	3
250,601–280,700	0
280,701–310,800	2

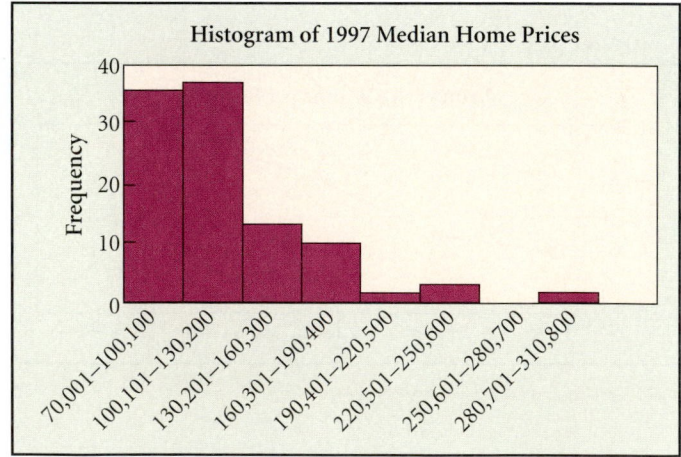

b

Classes	Frequency	Relative Frequency	Cumulative Relative Frequency
70,001–100,100	36	0.36	0.36
100,101–130,200	37	0.37	0.73
130,201–160,300	13	0.13	0.86
160,301–190,400	7	0.07	0.93
190,401–220,500	2	0.02	0.95
220,501–250,600	3	0.03	0.98
250,601–280,700	0	0	0.98
280,701–310,800	2	0.02	1.00

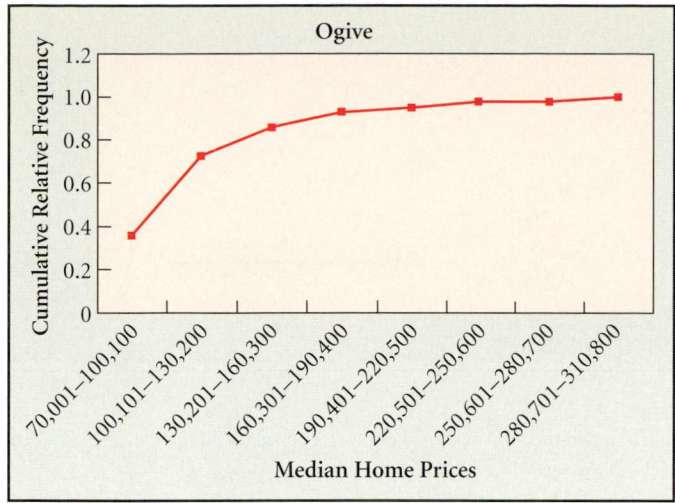

b

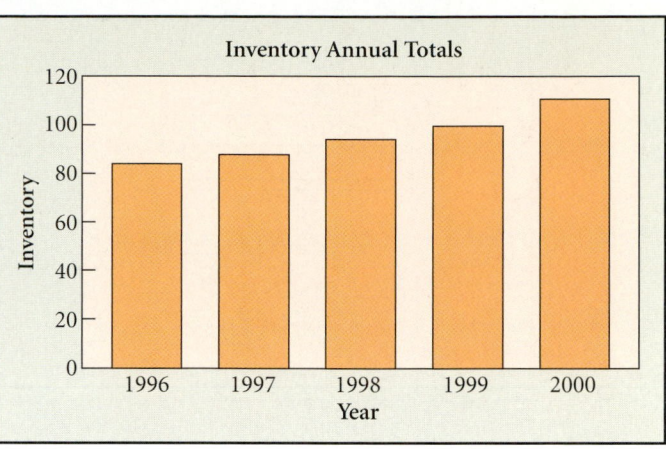

c

Classes	Frequency
70,001–120,000	65
120,001–170,000	23
170,001–220,000	8
220,001–270,000	3
270,001–320,000	2

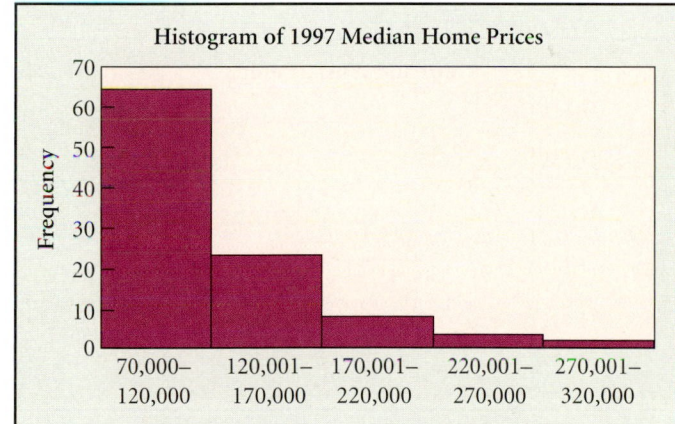

CHAPTER 3

3-1 $\mu = \dfrac{\sum x}{N} = 40/8 = 5$; median $= (5 + 6)/2 = 5.5$; mode $= 6$

3-3 a $\mu = \dfrac{\sum x}{N} = 234.19/11 = \$21.29$; median $= \$20.79$; mode $= \$25.49$;

because the mean (21.29) is greater than the median (20.79) these data are right-skewed. **b** The 1st quartile is equal to the 25th percentile,

$i = \dfrac{p}{100}(n + 1) = (25/100)(12) = 3$ or 3rd observation $= 18.95$; the 3rd

quartile is equal to the 75th percentile, $i = \dfrac{p}{100}(n + 1) = (75/100)(12) = 9$
or 9th observation $= 25.49$

3-5 $\mu = \dfrac{\sum x}{N} = 1194/12 = 99.5$; median $= (94 + 97)/2 = 95.5$; no mode;

$Q1 = 84.75$, $Q2 = 112.50$

3-7 a $\bar{x}_W = \dfrac{\sum w_i x_i}{\sum w_i} = 24,995/1,185 = 21.09$ **b** median $= 21.5$

2-63 a

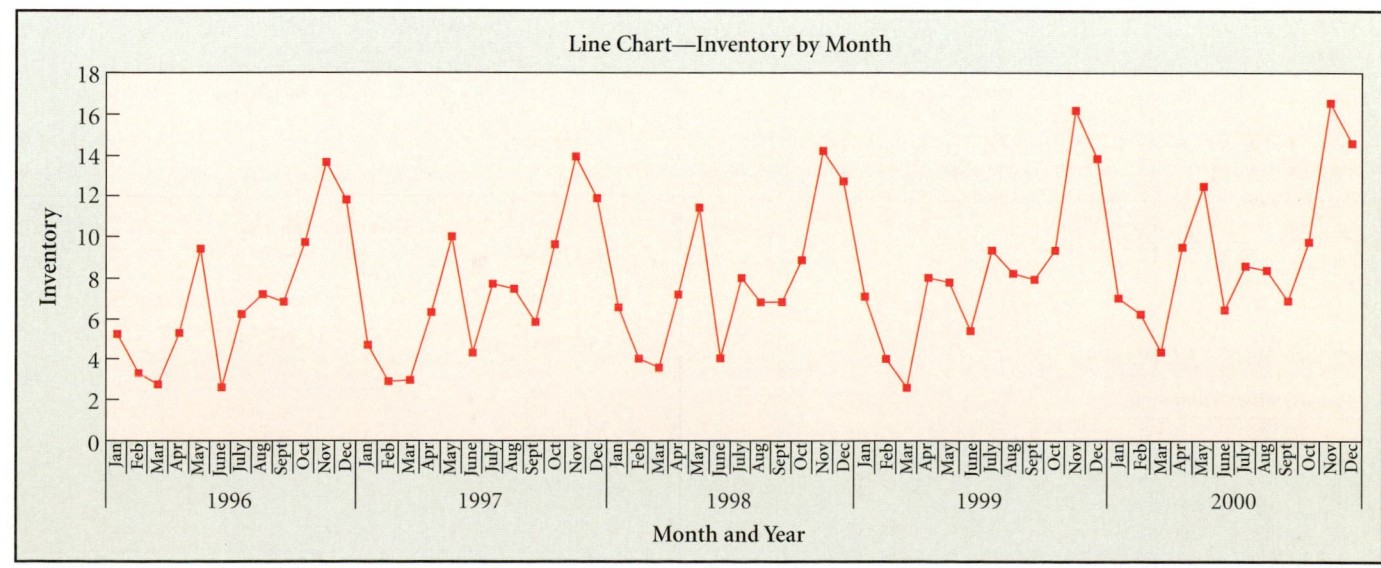

3-9 a Box and whisker plot done using PHStat.

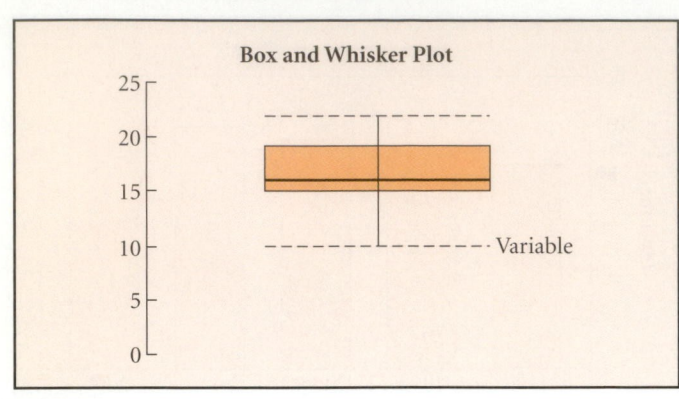

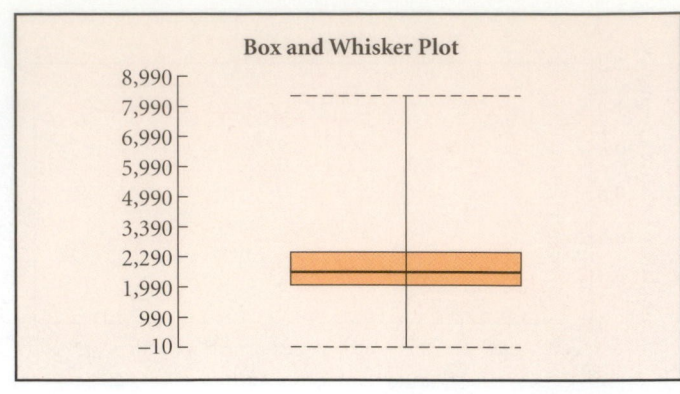

b Based on the box and whisker plot, it appears that the data are skewed.

3-17 a Mean = 42,350; median = 42,582

b

BOX AND WHISKER PLOT

Five-Number Summary

Minimum	21124
First Quartile	31444
Median	42581.5
Third Quartile	51269
Maximum	67452

BOX AND WHISKER PLOT

Five-Number Summary

Minimum	10
First Quartile	15
Median	16
Third Quartile	19
Maximum	22

The lower limit is computed as $Q1 - 1.5(Q3 - Q1) = 15 - 1.5 \times (19 - 15) = 9$; the upper limit is $Q3 + 1.5(Q3 - Q1) = 19 + 1.5 \times (19 - 15) = 25.0$. Because no value is less than 9 nor greater than 25, there are no outliers in these data.
b Thus, the 60th percentile is somewhere between the 27th and 28th value from the top of the data sorted from low to high. This value is 17.
3-11 a Because the data are ordinal level, the median is a preferred measure of the center. The median is the center value when the data have been arranged in numerical order. The median is 8. **b** The interquartile range is: $Q3 - Q1$; $Q3 = 9$ and $Q1 = 7$; $IQR = 9 - 7 = 2$.

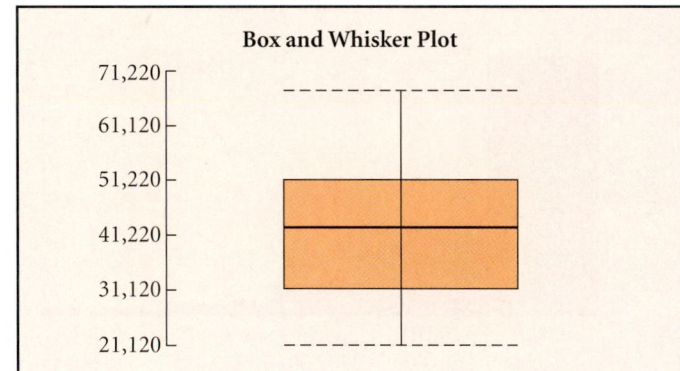

3-13 a Pre-advertising sample: $\bar{x} = \dfrac{\sum x}{n} = 378/10 = 37.8$ years; median = (34 + 36)/2 = 35 years. Because no values are repeated there is no mode. Post-advertising sample: $\bar{x} = \dfrac{\sum x}{n} = 304/10 = 30.4$ years; median = (28 + 29)/2 = 28.5 years. These data are bi-modal because 28 occurs twice and 40 occurs twice. **b** The pre-advertising sample is right-skewed because the mean > median. The post-advertising sample is right-skewed because the mean > median.

3-19 a

Category	Mean	Median
Commercial	61,780.70	65,000.00
Consumer	61,439.66	60,250.00
Real Estate	72,896.83	74,000.00

b

3-15 a

BOX AND WHISKER PLOT

Five-Number Summary

Minimum	0
First Quartile	2085
Median	2506
Third Quartile	3145.5
Maximum	8345

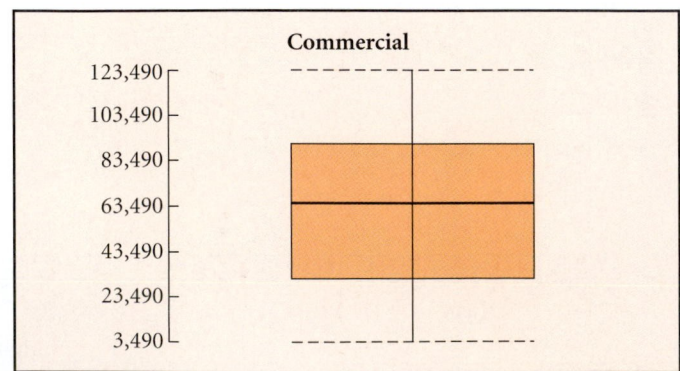

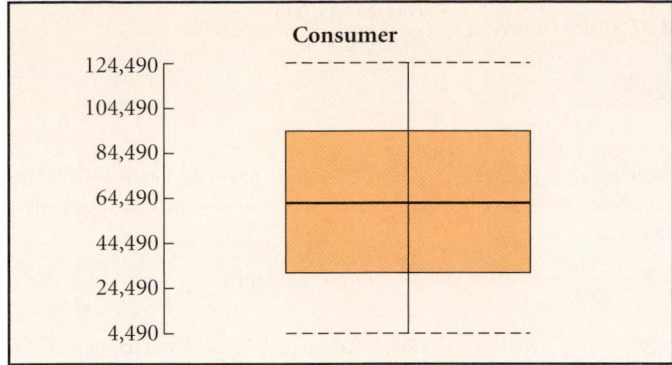

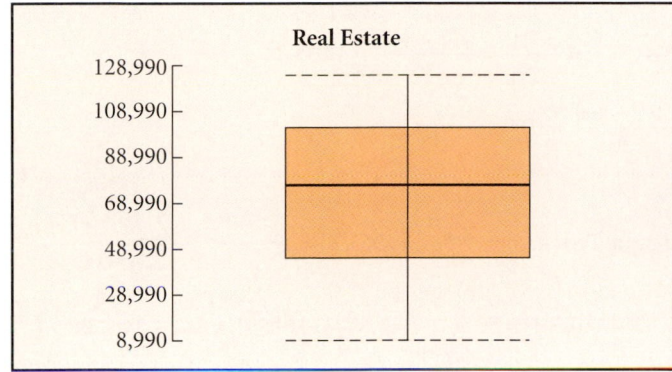

3-21 Range = high − low = 42 − 17 = 25; variance = $s^2 = \dfrac{\sum(x-\bar{x})^2}{n-1}$

= 48.87; standard deviation = $s = \sqrt{s^2} = \sqrt{48.87} = 6.99$

3-23 a Range = 22.95 − 9.95 = 13, $\bar{x} = \dfrac{\sum x}{n} = 168.81/10 = 16.881$;

b $s^2 = \dfrac{\sum(x-\bar{x})^2}{n-1} = 166.0125/(10-1) = 18.4458$;

$s = \sqrt{s^2} = \sqrt{18.4458} = 4.2949$ **c** $Q3 = 19.95 + 0.25(21.98 - 19.95) =$ 20.46. For $Q1 = 11.22 + 0.75(14.52 - 11.22) = 13.70$. Then the interquartile range is $Q3 - Q1 = 20.46 - 13.70 = 6.76$.

3-25 a Range = 4,000 − 1,560 = 2,440 **b** $\sigma^2 = \dfrac{\sum(x-\mu)^2}{N} =$

3,847,533/6 = 641,255.5 **c** $\sigma = \sqrt{\sigma^2} = \sqrt{641,255.5} = 800.7843$

3-27 a Range = 33 − 21 = 12; $\bar{x} = \dfrac{\sum x_i}{n} = 261/10 = 26.1$;

$s^2 = \dfrac{\sum(x-\bar{x})^2}{n-1} = 148.9/(10-1) = 16.5444$; $s = \sqrt{s^2} = \sqrt{16.5444}$

= 4.0675; interquartile range = 28 − 23 = 5

3-29 a $\bar{x} = \dfrac{\sum x_i}{n} = 15,826/32 = 494.5625$; to compute the median,

rank the observations and compute the average of the middle two; median = (485 + 487)/2 = 486; mode = 485; range = 541.75 − 463 = 78.75; interquartile

range = 540.75 − 463 = 77.75; $s^2 = \dfrac{\sum(x-\bar{x})^2}{n-1} = 2,388.8347$;

$s = \sqrt{s^2} = \sqrt{2,388.83} = 48.88$
b

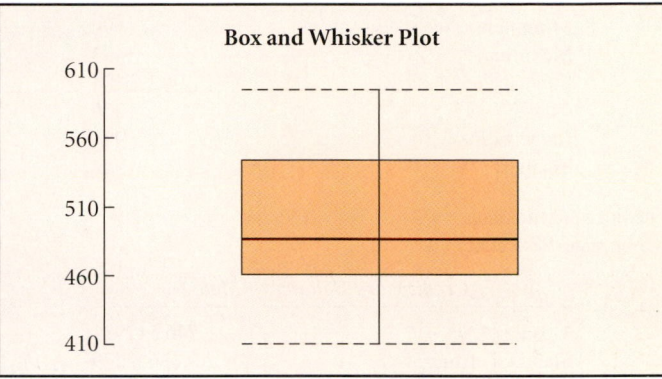

3-31 a Median = $3,125; there is no mode; range = $1,660; population variance = 187,801.9; population standard deviation = 433.36.
b PHStat's box and whisker tool can be used to develop the graph:

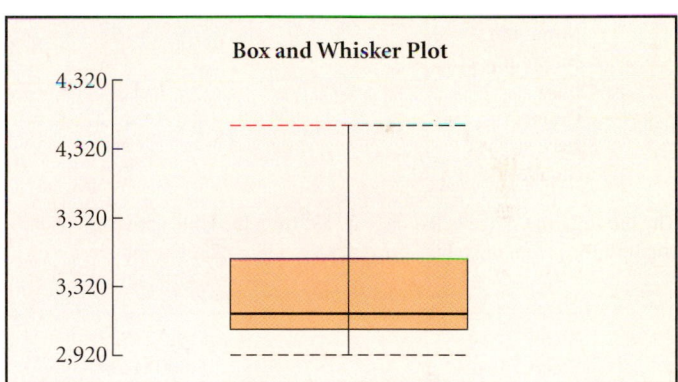

c Excel's Graph tool can be used to develop a line chart:

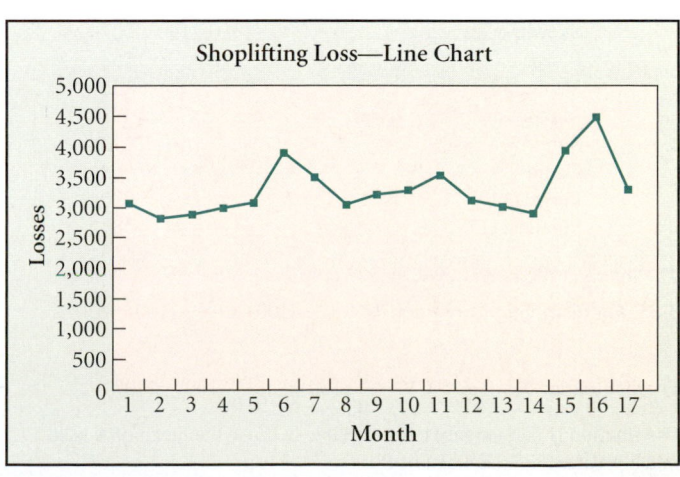

3-33 a Excel output

Credit Card Account Balance

Mean	753.68
Standard error	17.00202273
Median	737
Mode	600
Standard deviation	294.4836719
Sample variance	86720.63304
Kurtosis	−0.517456441
Skewness	0.113822027
Range	1394
Minimum	99
Maximum	1493
Sum	226104
Count	300
Largest (75)	974
Smallest (75)	544

The interquartile range = 974 − 544 = 430

b For males: Excel output

Credit Card Balances—Male

Mean	746.512931
Standard error	19.33632279
Median	738.5
Mode	1018
Standard deviation	294.5220941
Sample variance	86743.2639
Kurtosis	−0.605714694
Skewness	0.085179909
Range	1344
Minimum	99
Maximum	1443
Sum	173191
Count	232
Largest (58)	960
Smallest (58)	538

The interquartile range is the largest (58) from the table above minus the smallest (58) from the table above. 960 − 538 = 422. For females:

Credit Card Balances—Female

Mean	778.1323529
Standard error	35.80014705
Median	737
Mode	600
Standard deviation	295.2155754
Sample variance	87152.23595
Kurtosis	−0.199115911
Skewness	0.219080607
Range	1358
Minimum	135
Maximum	1493
Sum	52913
Count	68
Largest (17)	990
Smallest (17)	587

The interquartile range = 990 − 587 = 403.

3-35 For distribution A we get: $CV = \dfrac{\sigma}{\mu}(100) = \dfrac{100}{500}(100) = 20\%$.

For distribution B we get: $CV = \dfrac{\sigma}{\mu}(100) = \dfrac{4.0}{10.0}(100) = 40\%$.

Distribution B is relatively more variable because the mean of A is so much greater than the mean of B.

3-37 Distribution A: $z = \dfrac{50,000 - 45,600}{6,333} = 0.6948$;

distribution B: $z = \dfrac{40 - 33.40}{4.05} = 1.6296$. The value from distribution A is relatively closer to its mean.

3-39 a For population A: mean = 201.63, standard deviation = 37.75; for population B: mean = 1,013.63, standard deviation = 98.65 **b** For population A:

$$CV = \dfrac{37.75}{201.63}(100) = 18.72\%; \text{ for population B:}$$

$$CV = \dfrac{98.65}{1,013.63}(100) = 9.73\%. \text{ Because population A has the higher}$$

coefficient of variation, it is relatively more variable than population B.

3-41 a $z = \dfrac{x - \mu}{\sigma} = \dfrac{455 - 400}{30} = 1.833$ **b** $z = \dfrac{x - \mu}{\sigma} =$

$\dfrac{400 - 400}{30} = 0.00$

3-43 a Type A: $\bar{x} = \dfrac{\sum x}{n} = 2963/10 = 296.3$; $s^2 = \dfrac{\sum (x - \bar{x})^2}{n - 1}$

$= 536.1/(10 - 1) = 59.567$; $s = \sqrt{s^2} = \sqrt{59.567} = 7.718$. Type B:

$\bar{x} = \dfrac{\sum x}{n} = 2984/10 = 298.4$; $s^2 = \dfrac{\sum (x - \bar{x})^2}{n - 1} = 1352.4/$

$(10 - 1) = 150.267$; $s = \sqrt{s^2} = \sqrt{150.267} = 12.258$. Using the Tchebysheff's Rule, 89% of the observations should lie within this range. Type A: 273.146 − 319.45. Type B: 261.626 − 335.174. The technician is probably correct because for Type A at three standard deviations 274 would barely be in the range. **b** To be more conservative you should probably look at two standard deviations. Type A: 280.864 − 311.736. Type B: 273.884 − 322.916. **c** Based on the calculations in a and b there is a small chance that a Type B ball could go this far.

3-45 Plant 1: (810 − 700)/200 = 0.55 standard deviations; plant 2: (2600 − 2300)/350 = 0.86 standard deviations; plant 3: (1320 − 1200)/30 = 4 standard deviations. Plant 3 performed far better than the other plants on a relative basis.

3-47 a Yes, the data support the premise that cars will get better mileage on the highway than around town. The mean for highway (24.8) is higher than the mean for city (18.4) but there is not a lot of difference between the standard deviations. **b** Highway CV = 4.1778/24.8333 = 16.8%; city CV = 2.9548/18.4 = 16.1%. City driving has slightly less variability than highway driving. **c** $z = (24.8333 - 18.4)/2.9548 = 2.17$

3-49 The median would be preferred to the mean in data sets that have extremely high or low values that affect the mean. The median is also preferred as a measure of the center if a quantitative variable is measured on an ordinal scale.

3-51 By definition a sample is a subset of a population. The most different sample selected from a population will have a different mean because it includes different values on which the mean is calculated. The sample mean will rarely equal the population mean exactly.

3-53 Some problems are that it does not look at total hours taken. One student could have taken one class on campus and got an A so would have a 4.0 grade point average. Another student could have taken many hours and got all A's except for one or two B's and would have lower than a 4.0 grade point average. People might conclude that the first student is a better student than the second based only on grade point average.

3-55 The standard deviation is an average measure of the differences from the mean. The mean is considered to be the center of the data so this measures how spread out the data are from the mean.

3-57 a $\bar{x} = \dfrac{\sum x}{n} = 127/8 = 15.875$ **b** Median $= (13 + 16)/2 = 14.5$

c The modes are 12 and 16. **d** $s^2 = \dfrac{\sum (x - \bar{x})^2}{n - 1} = 346.875/(8 - 1) =$

49.5536; $s = \sqrt{s^2} = \sqrt{49.5536} = 7.0394$ **e** The extreme value does not affect the median or the mode. **f** In this case the median might be a better measure because you have an extreme outlier. **g** $Q3 = 16 + 0.75(17 - 16) = 16.75$

3-59 a $\bar{x} = \dfrac{\sum x}{n} = 371/15 = 24.7333$; median $= 20$; the median $<$ mean, which means the data are skewed right. **b** The mode is 19.
c The standard deviation is essentially an average of how the data are spread around the mean:

$s^2 = \dfrac{\sum (x - \bar{x})^2}{n - 1} = 1720.9333/(15 - 1) = 122.9238$;

$s = \sqrt{s^2} = \sqrt{122.9238} = 11.0871$ **d** Interquartile range $= 34 - 19 = 15$ **e** The box plot shows that the distribution is not symmetrical because the median line is not centered in the box but instead is located very close to the $Q1$ value.

3-61 a $\mu = \dfrac{\sum x}{N} = 10{,}605/20 = 530.25$; median $= (400 + 450)/2 = 425$ **b** The 33rd percentile is: $i = \dfrac{p}{100}(n + 1) = (33/100)(20 + 1) = 7$ or 7th observation $= 300$ **c** The first 6 oil wells will be closed, which are those producing at 75, 100, 200, 230, 250, 250.

3-63 a $\bar{x} = \dfrac{\sum x}{n} = 4373/12 = 364.4167$ **b** $s^2 = \dfrac{\sum (x - \bar{x})^2}{n - 1} =$

$183{,}288.9167/(12 - 1) = 16{,}662.6288$; $s = \sqrt{s^2} = \sqrt{16{,}662.6288} = 129.0838$
3-65 a Spokane–St. Louis $= (299 - 364.4167)/129.0838 = -0.5068$; Miami–Kansas City $= (502 - 443)/58 = 1.0172$. The agent was relatively closest to the mean for the Spokane–St. Louis route. **b** Spokane–St. Louis $= 129.0838/364.4167 = 0.3542$ or 35.42%; Miami–Kansas City $= 58/443 = 0.1309$ or 13.09%. The Spokane–St. Louis route has the largest relative variation.

3-67 a

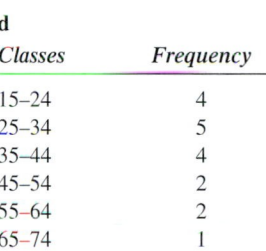

	Net Sales	Cap. Exp.	Curr. Debt	LT Debt	Equity
Average	1,413.06	67.90	112.72	279.75	415.12
Median	1,362.40	73.85	96.80	283.85	415.50
St. Dev.	262.77	15.08	85.51	65.05	69.88

b

Year	z-value Net Sales	z-value Cap. Exp.	z-value Curr. Debt	z-value LT Debt	z-value Equity
1988	−1.19	−1.16	−0.74	−0.77	−1.73
1989	−1.15	−0.96	−1.08	−1.06	−0.99
1990	−0.94	−0.63	−0.96	0.49	−0.73
1991	−0.52	0.34	−0.40	−1.11	−0.37
1992	−0.34	0.76	0.12	−1.21	0.33
1993	−0.05	0.54	−0.33	1.02	0.74
1994	0.44	1.31	1.18	1.45	1.07
1995	1.06	0.94	2.16	1.07	1.49
1996	1.22	0.45	−0.04	0.18	0.50
1997	1.48	−1.59	0.10	−0.05	−0.32

The years 1988 and 1989 are somewhat unique in that all the variables were below their means because all z-values are negative. In the same way 1994 and 1995 are unique in that all the variables were above their means.

3-69 a $\bar{x} = \dfrac{\sum x}{n} = 703/18 = 39.0556$ **b** Median $= (34 + 36)/2 = 35$

c $s^2 = \dfrac{\sum (x - \bar{x})^2}{n - 1} = 3726.944/(18 - 1) = 219.232$; $s = \sqrt{s^2} =$

$\sqrt{219.232} = 14.81$

d

Classes	Frequency
15–24	4
25–34	5
35–44	4
45–54	2
55–64	2
65–74	1

e

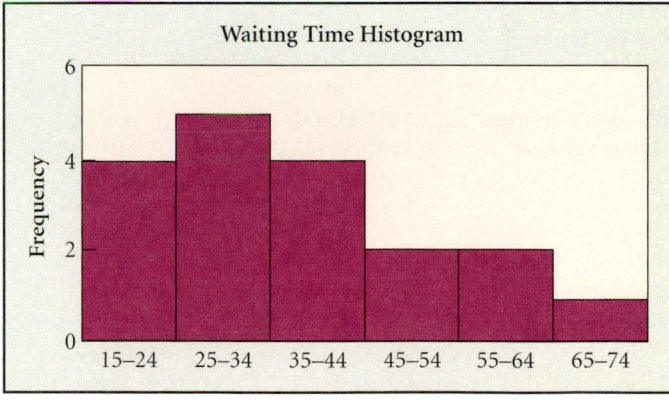

f

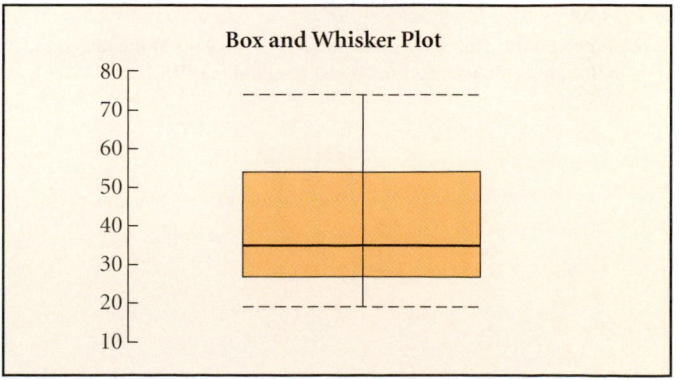

g 54 minutes

3-71 a Seed Type C produces the greatest average yield per acre.
b CV of Seed Type A = 25/88 = 0.2841 or 28.41%; CV of Seed
Type B = 15/56 = 0.2679 or 26.79%; CV of Seed Type C = 16/100 =
0.1600 or 16%; Seed Type C shows the least relative variability.
c Seed Type A: Approximately 68% will be within one standard deviation 88 ± 25 = 63 to 113; approximately 95% will be within two standard deviations 88 ± 2(25) = 38 to 138; approximately 100% will be
within three standard deviations 88 ± 3(25) = 13 to 163. Seed Type B:
Approximately 68% will be within one standard deviation 56 ± 15 = 41
to 71; approximately 95% will be within two standard deviations
56 ± 2(15) = 26 to 86; approximately 100% will be within three standard deviations 56 ± 3(15) = 11 to 101. Seed Type C: Approximately
68% will be within one standard deviation 100 ± 16 = 84 to 116;
approximately 95% will be within two standard deviations 100 ± 2(16)
= 68 to 132; approximately 100% will be within three standard deviations 100 ± 3(16) = 52 to 148. **d** Seed Type A because the 135 is
within two standard deviations. Because it has higher variability there is
a greater chance that it will produce 135. **e** Seed Type C because it has
a higher mean to begin and now the 115 would be within one standard
deviation.

3-73 b

Classes	Frequency
−6928.42 to −5077.00	1
−5076.99 to −3225.57	5
−3225.56 to −1374.14	11
−1374.13 to 477.29	7
477.30 to 2328.72	12
2328.73 to 4180.15	9
4180.16 to 6031.58	3
6031.59 to 7883.01	2

c Excel output

Difference	
Mean	**415.52**
Standard Error	436.0660531
Median	**621.5**
Mode	#N/A
Standard Deviation	**3083.452632**
Sample Variance	**9507680.132**
Kurtosis	−0.501771097
Skewness	0.177525892
Range	12960
Minimum	−5077
Maximum	7883
Sum	20776
Count	50

d $i = \dfrac{p}{100}(n + 1)$ so $29 = p/100(50 + 1)$ $p = 56.86$ or approximately

the 57th percentile. This shows that about 57% percent of the tax consultants in this study showed less tax owed than did the IRS.

3-75 a

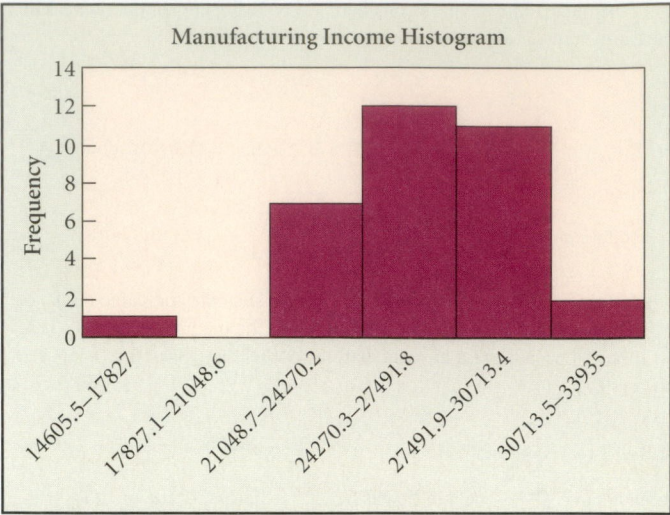

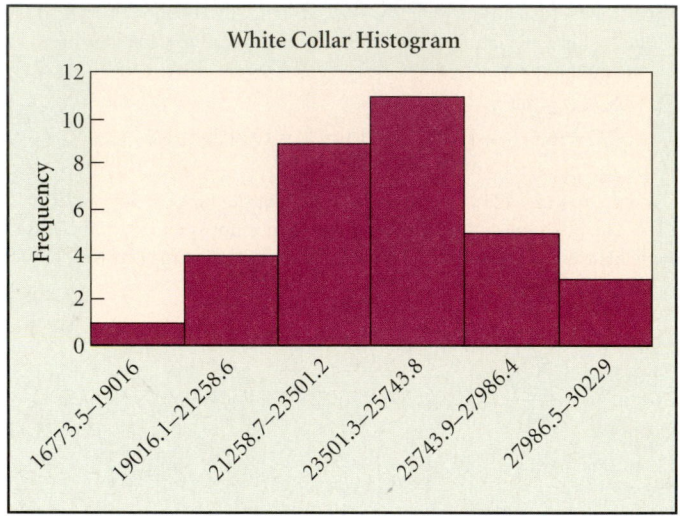

b

	Manufacturing	White Collar
Mean	26398.18	24117.06
Median	27204	24139
Mode	None	None

d City 22 is the only city that meets this criteria.
3-77 a The average 1997 median price is $122,344.
b

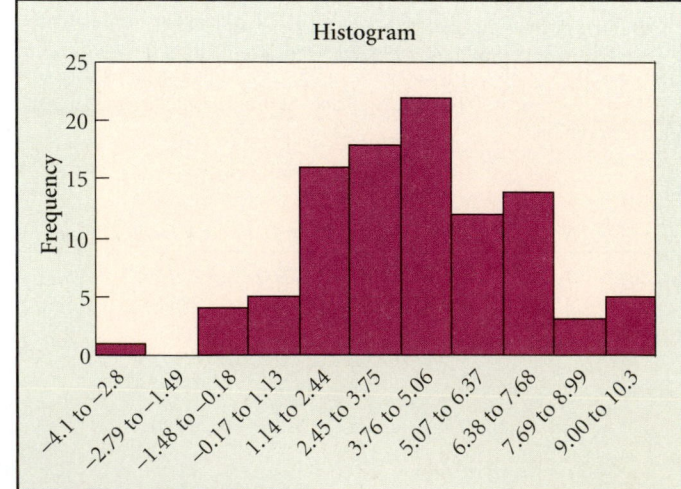

c

1993–98 Annualized Change

Mean	4.213
Median	4.15
Standard Deviation	2.545332627

d 9.76%. It appears very unlikely that you could obtain a quick profit and sell the house for $120,000.

CHAPTER 4

4-1 a $P(\text{male}) = 0.5075$ **b** $P(20\text{–}40) = 0.4716$ **c** $P(20\text{–}40 \text{ and male}) = 0.2545$ **d** $P(<20|\text{males}) = 0.2478$; $P(<20|\text{females}) = 0.3161$. Gender and age are not independent.

4-3 $P(\text{red}) = \frac{1}{4} = 0.25$.

4-5 $1 - P(\text{rain}) = 1 - 0.125 = 0.875$.

4-7 $P(\text{smoke}) = 0.30$

4-9 a $P(\text{early}) = 0.1875$ **b** $P(\text{Los Angeles}) = 0.5625$ **c** $P(\text{early given Los Angeles}) = 0.2222$. $P(\text{early}) = 0.125$

4-11 a $P(\text{female}) = 0.4643$ **b** Relative frequency **c** The events are not independent.

4-13 a Yes **b** No **c** Events cannot be both mutually exclusive and independent.

4-15 a $P(\text{Atlanta}) = 0.2182$ **b** $P(\text{wiring}) = 0.2091$ **c** $P(\text{Atlanta and wiring}) = 0.0727$ **d** $P(\text{day shift and Atlanta and cracked lens}) = 8/110 = 0.0727$

4-17 a $P(\text{dry}) = 0.50$ **b** $P(\text{rainy or cloudy and dry}) = 0.40 + 0.30 - 0.0 = 0.70$ **c** $P(\text{cloudy}|\text{dry}) = \dfrac{P(\text{cloudy and dry})}{P(\text{dry})} = \dfrac{0.30}{0.50} = 0.60$

4-19 This method will not work because the roulette wheel (if it is fair) has no memory and thus the outcomes are independent.

4-21 a $P(\text{matched}) = 2/3$ **b** $P(\text{both wrong}) = 1/9$

4-23 $P(\text{Michigan1 and Maryland2}) + P(\text{Maryland1 or Michigan2}) = 0.00072$

4-25 a 0.02060 **b** $P(G\text{-}G\text{-}G) = 0.03704$ **c** 0.00076; because this probability is so low that if it really did happen then the assignments are probably not made randomly.

4-27 This probability is $1 - [(0.2)(0.2)(0.2)(0.2)] = 0.9984$. They cannot get to 99.9% on color copies regardless of the configuration.

4-29 $P(\text{line1}|\text{defective}) = (0.05)(0.4)/0.0725 = 0.2759$; $P(\text{line2}|\text{defective}) = (0.10)(0.35)/0.0725 = 0.4828$; $P(\text{line3}|\text{defective}) = (0.07)(0.25)/0.0725 = 0.2413$; the unsealed cans probably came from Line 2.

4-31 $P(\text{clerk 1}|\text{defective}) = (0.02)(0.4)/0.02 = 0.4$; $P(\text{clerk 2}|\text{defective}) = (0.025)(0.3)/0.02 = 0.375$; $P(\text{clerk 3}|\text{defective}) = (0.015)(0.3)/0.02 = 0.225$; clerk 1 is most likely responsible for the boxes that raised the complaints.

4-33 Ten weeks can be covered by this schedule.

4-35 There is a total of 6 companies. **a** $P(\text{ace}) = 1/6 = 0.1667$ **b** $P(\text{win1 and win2}) = 0.0278$ **c** $P(\text{lose1 and lose2}) = (5/6)(5/6) = 0.6944$ **d** $P(\text{win1 and lose2}) + P(\text{lose1 and win2}) = (1/6)(5/6) + (5/6)(1/6) = 0.2778$ **e** $P(\text{win1 and lose2}) + P(\text{lose1 and win2}) + P(\text{win1 and win2}) = 0.1389 + 0.1389 + 0.0278 = 0.3056$ or $1 - P(\text{lose 1 and lose 2}) = 1 - 0.6944 = 0.3056$

4-37 $P(\text{free gas}) = 0.0003 + 0.00059 + 0.0005 = 0.00139$

4-39 a $P(\text{wiring}|\text{Atlanta}) = P(\text{wiring and Atlanta})/P(\text{Atlanta}) = 0.3333$ **b** $P(\text{Boise}|\text{return}) = 78/110 = 0.7091$; $P(\text{Atlanta}|\text{return}) = 24/110 = 0.2182$; $P(\text{Reno}|\text{return}) = 8/110 = 0.0727$

4-41 a $E(x) = 138$ **b** $\text{Var}(x) = 636$ **c** $\text{Std Dev}(x) = 25.219$

4-43 Expected value $= \$1.25 + -\$4.86 = -\$3.61$

4-45 For variable x: $E(x) = 225$; for variable y: $E(y) = 415$; then $E(x + y) = 225 + 415 = 640$

4-47 The covariance is 3,275. The relationship between the two variables is positive; $\sigma_x = \sqrt{9,875} = 99.37$; $\sigma_y = \sqrt{12,2751} = 110.79$; the correlation is: $\rho = \dfrac{\sigma_{xy}}{\sigma_x \sigma_y} = (3,275)/[(99.37)(110.79)] = 0.2975$.

4-49 a $E(x) = 2.885$ **b** 1.7725 **d** The coefficient of variation is: $CV = \dfrac{1.7725}{2.885}(100) = 61.44\%$ **e** 12 employees

4-51 The mean of the current plan is $53.40 with a standard deviation of $23.67. To determine the salary for $6 per hour you would need to assume 8 hours in a day, which would be a constant wage of $48. Because this is a constant $48 this would be the expected value of this pay plan. Employees would be better off staying with the $2 per car because it has an expected value of $53.40.

4-53 The relative frequency of occurrence approach takes the number of times the item of interest occurred and divides it by the total number of times the event or activity was done.

4-55 Classical probability assessment, sometimes referred to as *a priori* probability, is the method of determining probability based on the ratio of the number of ways the event of interest can occur to the total number of ways any event can occur when the individual elementary events are equally likely.

4-57 The probability assessment used here is the subjective probability method. Thus, each student could arrive at a different probability.

4-59 If the selection is made without replacement, the events for the two selections are dependent. **a** $P(D \text{ and } G) + P(G \text{ and } D) = 0.5333$ **b** $P(G \text{ and } G) = 0.3333$

4-61 a $e_1 = $ bid awarded; $e_2 = $ bid not awarded **b** $SS = (e_1, e_2)$ **c** $SS = (e_1, e_2, e_3, e_4, e_5, e_6, e_7, e_8)$

4-63 a $P(\text{win}) = 1/500 = 0.002$ **b** $P(\text{win}) = 3/500 = 0.006$ **c** Classical probability approach

4-65 a $P(\text{on time}) = 4900/10000 = 0.49$ **b** $P(\text{late}) = 4000/10000 = 0.40$ **c** $P(\text{early}) = (10000 - 4900 - 4000)/10000 = 0.11$

4-67 a $P(C \text{ and } C \text{ and } C) = 0.25 \times 0.25 \times 0.25 = 0.0156$ **b** $P(\text{Passing}) = 0.0156 + 0.0469 + 0.0469 + 0.0469 = 0.1563$ **c** $P(\text{Passing}) = 0.1250 + 0.1250 + 0.1250 + 0.1250 = 0.5000$.

4-69 a $E(x) = 750$; $E(y) = 100$ **b** $\text{Std Dev}(x) = 844.0972$; $\text{Std Dev}(y) = 717.635$ **c** $CV(x) = 844.0972/750 = 1.1255$; $CV(y) = 717.635/100 = 7.1764$

4-71 If two events are independent then the probability of both events occurring should be equal to the product of the two individual events, so if the two stocks are independent then $0.6(0.7) = 0.42$ which does not equal 0.15. Therefore, the two events are not independent.

4-73 $P(\text{Sales}) = 0.7 + 0.18 + 0.06 + 0.024 = 0.964$

4-75 a $P(\text{favor}) = 0.5958$ **b** $P(\text{office worker and against}) = 0.0875$ **c** They are not independent.

4-77 $P(AE|MC) = P(AE \text{ and } MC)/P(MC) = 0.2/(0.4 + 0.2) = 0.3333$

4-79 Find: $P(\text{Profit}|\text{NoGovernor}) = \dfrac{P(\text{Profit and NoGovernor})}{P(\text{NoGovernor})} =$

$\dfrac{(0.90)(0.20)}{(0.90)(0.20) + (0.10)(0.40)} = \dfrac{0.18}{0.22} = 0.82$. Thus, if the governor can't attend, the chances of a profitable conference drops from 0.90 to 0.82.

CHAPTER 5

5-1

x	$P(x)$
0	0.4096
1	0.4096
2	0.1536
3	0.0256
4	0.0016

5-3 a $P(x = 10) = 0.1171$ **b** $P(7 < x < 12) = 0.1797 + 0.1597 + 0.1171 + 0.0710 = 0.5275$ **c** $P(x \geq 12) = 0.0355 + 0.0146 + 0.0049 + 0.0013 + 0.0003 = 0.0566$

5-5 a $\dfrac{8!}{4!(8-4)!} = 70$ ways **b** $C_6^{10} = \dfrac{10!}{6!(10-6)!} = 210$ ways

c $C_3^{10} = \dfrac{10!}{3!(10-3)!} = 120$ ways **d** $C_7^{10} = \dfrac{10!}{7!(10-7)!} = 120$ ways

5-7 a $P(x=4) = 0.0768$ **b** $P(x \geq 4) = 0.0768 + 0.0102 = 0.0870$
c $E[x] = np = 5(0.40) = 2$; $SD[x] = \sqrt{npq} = \sqrt{5(0.40)(0.60)} = 1.0954$

5-9 a $P(x=5) = 0.0746$ **b** $P(x \geq 7) = 0.1124 + 0.0609 + 0.0271 + 0.0099 + 0.0030 + 0.0008 + 0.0002 = 0.2143$ **c** $E[x] = np = 20(0.30) = 6$ **d** $SD[x] = \sqrt{npq} = \sqrt{20(0.30)(0.70)} = 2.0494$

5-11 a $E(x) = \Sigma x P(x) = 0(0.4096) + 1(0.4096) + 2(0.1536) + 3(0.0256) + 4(0.0016) = 0.80$ **b** $E(x) = np = 4(0.20) = 0.80$

5-13 a $P(x = 5$ males$) = 0.1681$ **b** $P(x = 0$ males$) = 0.0024$

5-15 a $P(x \geq 2) = 1 - P(x \leq 1) = 1 - 0.7361 = 0.2639$ **b** $P(x \geq 2) = 1 - P(x \leq 1) = 1 - 0.5443 = 0.4557$

5-17 a $P(x = 5) = 0.0971$ **b** $P(x < 4) = P(x \leq 3) = 0.6626$ **c** $P(x > 2) = P(x \geq 3) = 1 - P(x \leq 2) = 1 - 0.3811 = 0.6189$

5-19 $E[x] = np = 6(0.67) = 4.02$

5-21 a Expected number $= 5(0.21) = 1.05$ **b** Variance $= 5(0.21)(0.79) = 0.8295$; standard deviation $= 0.9108$

5-23 a $P(x \leq 2) = 0.0746 + 0.3151 + 0.5987 = 0.9884$ **b** Suppose $p = 0.10$: $P(x \leq 2) = 0.1937 + 0.3874 + 0.3487 = 0.9298$ **c** Thus the plan is one-sided. It favors the supplier.

5-25 a It is a binomial distribution with $n = 3$, $p = $ probability of defective module. **b** $p = 0.05$; $P(x \geq 1) = 1 - P(x = 0) = 1 - 0.8574 = 0.1426$; yes it is larger. **c** For $n = 3$ the highest the p level can be such that the $P(x \geq 1) < 0.025$ is less than 0.01 (0.0084). At $p = 0.01$, $P(x \geq 1) = 1 - 0.9703 = 0.0297$ which is still slightly larger than the required 0.025 level. At $p = 0.0084$, $P(x \geq 1) = 0.02499$.

5-27 a $P(x = 5) = 0.1755$ **b** $P(x \leq 5) = 0.6160$ **c** $P(x \geq 3) = 1 - P(x \leq 2) = 1 - 0.12465 = 0.87535$

5-29 a Mean $= E[x] = \lambda t = 5(2) = 10$; standard deviation $= SD[x] = \sqrt{\lambda t} = 3.1623$ **b** $P(x \leq 3) = 0.0076 + 0.0023 + 0.0005 + 0.0000 = 0.0104$

5-31 Hypergeometric distribution

5-33 $P(2,2,6) = \dfrac{C_2^{10} \cdot C_2^{15} \cdot C_6^{15}}{C_{10}^{40}} = \dfrac{45 \cdot 105 \cdot 5{,}005}{847{,}660{,}528} = 0.0279$

5-35 a $P(x = 0) = 0.000123$ **b** $P(x > 14) = P(x \geq 15) = 1 - P(x \leq 14) = 1 - 0.9585 = 0.0415$ **c** $P(x < 9) = P(x \leq 8) = 0.4557$ **d** There is only a 4.15% chance of finding 15 or more errors if the claim is actually true. Students will probably conclude that the error rate is higher than 3 per 400.

5-37 $P(x \geq 1) = 1 - P(x = 0)$; $P(0) = \dfrac{C_{4-0}^{20-4} \cdot C_0^4}{C_4^{20}} = \dfrac{1{,}820 \cdot 1}{4{,}845} = 0.3756$; $1 - 0.3756 = 0.6244$

5-39 a $0.0058 + 0.0019 + 0.0278 = 0.0355$ **b** $P(0,3,1) = 0.0218$ **c** $P(0,2,2) = 0.0709$

5-41 a $P(x > 18.7) = P(z > (18.7 - 15)/2.5) = P(z > 1.48) = 0.5 - 0.4306 = 0.0694$ **b** $P(z > $ some value$) = (100 - $ 90th percentile$) = 0.1$; $z = 1.28$; $1.28 = (x - 15)/2.5$; $x = 18.2$ is the 90th percentile **c** $P(-2 < z < 2) = 0.4772 + 0.4772 = 0.9544$

5-43 a $P(0.00 < z \leq 2.33) = 0.4901$ **b** $P(-1.00 < z \leq 1.00) = 0.3413 + 0.3413 = 0.6826$ **c** $P(1.78 < z < 2.34) = (0.4904) - (0.4625) = 0.0279$

5-45 a $P(x \geq 8.5) = 0.50 - 0.1293 = 0.3707$ **b** $P(x \geq 6.5) = 0.50 + 0.1293 = 0.6293$ **c** $P(x \geq 9.5) = 0.50 - 0.2486 = 0.2514$ **d** $P(3.0 \leq x \leq 5.5) = 0.4332 - 0.2486 = 0.1846$

5-47 a $z = 3.00$; $z = \dfrac{x - \mu}{\sigma}$; $3.00 = \dfrac{x - 10.5}{4.087}$; $x = 22.76$ **b** $-1.96 = \dfrac{x - 10.5}{4.087}$; $x = 2.49$

5-49 a $z_{.37} = -1.13$; $z = \dfrac{x - \mu}{\sigma}$; $-1.13 = \dfrac{23 - \mu}{9.3}$; $\mu = 33.51$ **b** P(at least four out of five are 1 standard deviation below the mean) $= 1 - P$(0 of four > 1 standard deviation below the mean); $P(z < -1.00) = 0.50 - 0.3413 = 0.1587$; $P(z \geq -1.00) = 1 - 0.1587 = 0.8413 = P(\geq 1$ standard deviation below mean); P(0 of four 1 standard deviation or more below mean) $= P$(all 4 are at or above 1 standard deviation below the mean) $=$

$0.8413 \times 0.8413 \times 0.8413 \times 0.8413 = 0.5010$; P(at least 1 out of four 1 standard deviation or more below the mean) $= 1 - 0.5010 = 0.4990$

5-51 $z_{.25} = -0.675$; $-0.675 = \dfrac{17 - 22}{\sigma}$; $\sigma = 7.407$

5-53 a The average cost is 0.4232 million or \$423,200. **b** The average number of firefighters is 136.29 or 137. The standard deviation is the square root of $563.42 = 23.74$. **c** The z-value for 75% is 0.675; $0.675 = $ (firefighters $- 137)/23.74$; 153.02 or 154 firefighters. **d** $P(x < 160) = P(z < (160 - 137)/23.74) = P(z < 0.97) = 0.5 + 0.3340 = 0.8340$

5-55 a $P(x > 85) = P(z > (85 - 72)/4) = P(z > 3.25) = $ essentially 0 percent **b** $P(x > 82) = P(z > (82 - 72)/4) = P(z > 2.5) = 0.5 - 0.4938 = 0.0062$ **c** The number of fliers is actually a discrete variable. The normal distribution assumes that the value can take on an infinite number of possible outcomes.

5-57 a $P(x > 16.7) = 0.5 - 0.4772 = 0.0228$ **b** The mean would need to be 15.8. **c** $2.575 = (16.7 - 16)/$ standard deviation; std dev $= 0.2718$ **d** Because you want 16-ounce drinks it would probably be better to have your mean ounces be 16 and adjust the standard deviation.

5-59 a $15.62 + 2(0.35) = 16.32$ **b** $P(x > 16.32) = 0.5 - 0.4772 = 0.0228$ **c** $P(x > 16.32) = 0.5 - 0.3186 = 0.1814$; $P(x > 2|n = 3, p = 0.1814) = P(z > [2 - (3)(0.1814)]/\sqrt{(3)(0.1814)(1 - 0.1814)} = P(z > 2.18)$ which is $0.5000 - 0.4854 = 0.0146$.

5-61 a $z = \dfrac{x - \mu}{\sigma} = \dfrac{7.50 - 4.11}{1.37} = 2.48$; $P(x > \$7.50) = 0.50 - 0.4934 = 0.0066$ **b** $-1.645 = \dfrac{3.50 - \mu}{1.37}$; $\mu = \$5.75$

5-63 With a probability of no more than 5%, $z = -1.645$; $-1.645 = (3.5 - $ mean$)/0.5$; the mean would have to be 4.32 inches

5-65 a

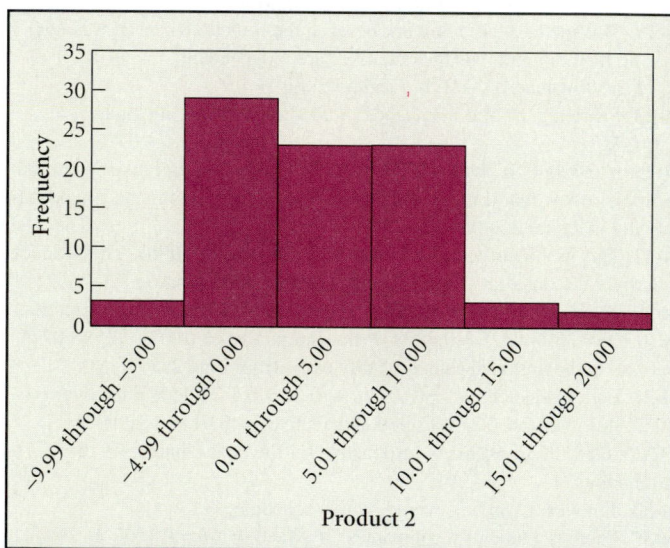

Product 2

It does not appear that Product 2 is as close to normal distribution as Plan 1 was. **b** Students can use Excel's descriptive statistics to determine the mean and standard deviation. Excel output

Product #2	
Mean	2.584337349
Standard Error	0.539795898
Median	2.4
Mode	−1.9
Standard Deviation	**4.917774678**
Sample Variance	24.18450779
Kurtosis	−0.045617579
Skewness	0.480907671
Range	23.7
Minimum	−6.6
Maximum	17.1
Sum	214.5
Count	83

c $P(x < -12) = 0.5 - 0.4985 = 0.0015$ **d** No, this would not be an appropriate claim.

5-67 a

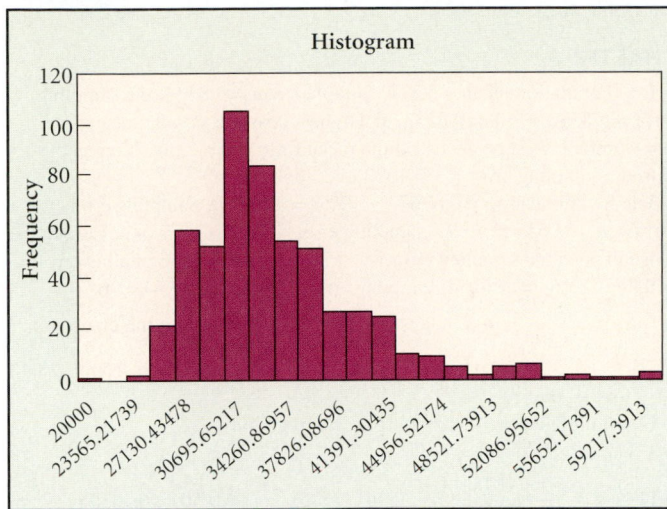

It could be considered approximately normally distributed.

b Students can use Excel's descriptive statistics feature to make these calculations. Excel output

Household Annual Income

Mean	**32801.09489**
Standard Error	266.1365661
Median	31000
Mode	30000
Standard Deviation	**6230.097282**
Sample Variance	38814112.14
Kurtosis	3.044243192
Skewness	1.481126946
Range	41000
Minimum	20000
Maximum	61000
Sum	17975000
Count	548

c $P(x > 40,000) = 0.5 - 0.3770 = 0.1230$ **d** The income cutoff would be $23,581.36.

5-69 a $P(x > 50) = (60 - 50)/(60 - 20) = 0.25$ **b** $P(x = 45) = 0$; you cannot find the probability of a specific value in a continuous distribution. **c** $P(25 < x < 35) = (35 - 25)/(60 - 20) = 0.25$ **d** $P(x < 34) = (34 - 20)/(60 - 20) = 0.35$

5-71 a $P(x > 200) = 200/300 = 0.67$ **b** $P(150 < x < 300) = 150/300 = 0.50$ **c** $P(180 < x < 260) = 80/300 = 0.2667$

5-73 a

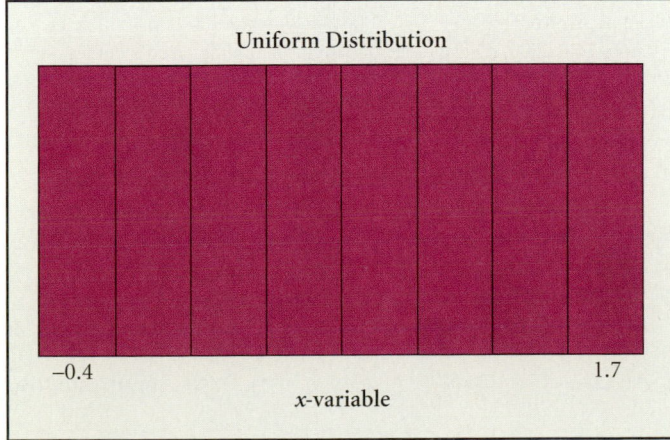

b $P(x > 0) = (1.7 - 0.0)/(1.7 - 0.40) = 1.7/2.10 = 0.8095$

5-75 a $P(0.20 \le x \le 0.60) = P(x \le 0.60) - P(x < 0.20)$; $P(x \le 0.60) = 1 - 0.8607 = 0.1393$; $P(x < 0.20) = 1 - 0.9512 = 0.0488$; $P(0.20 \le x \le 0.60) = 0.1393 - 0.0488 = 0.0905$ **b** $P(x > 4) = 1 - P(x \le 4) = 1 - (1 - 0.3679) = 0.3679$ **c** $P(x > 0.30) = 0.9277$

5-77 a $P(x < 7) = (7 - 5)/(8.5 - 5) = 2/3.5 = 0.5714$; the probability of the growth being less than 7 inches is more than 50%, so the model would probably overstate the actual pine tree growth. **b** $P(x > 6) = (8.5 - 6)/(8.5 - 5) = 0.7143$; if they use this as the constant growth rate they will probably understate the actual pine tree growth.

5-79 $\lambda = 12/\text{hour} = 0.2$ per minutes; $P(x < 4) = 1 - e^{-(.2)(4)} = 1 - 0.4493 = 0.5507$

5-81 a $\lambda = 1/4000 = .00025$; $P(x < 2100) =$ EXPONDIST(2100,0.00025,true) = 0.4084; yes, because this is a pretty high probability of a failure at less than 2100. **b** $100,000(0.4084) = 40,840$

5-83 If sampling is done without replacement then the probability of an outcome changes because the total outcomes decrease by 1 each time an item is removed. However, if the total outcomes are large the change in the probability will be so small it would still be acceptable to use the binomial distribution.

5-85 As the sample size is increased for a given level of the probability of success, p, the probability distribution becomes more symmetric, or bell-shaped.

5-87 The mean and the variance of the Poisson distribution are the same so if you reduce one you will also be reducing the spread, which is the variance.

5-89 To calculate the probability of a continuous distribution you must calculate the area under the curve. A single point has no area so the probability of a specific value must be zero.

5-91 a $f(x) = 1/(0.80 - 0.40) = 2.5$

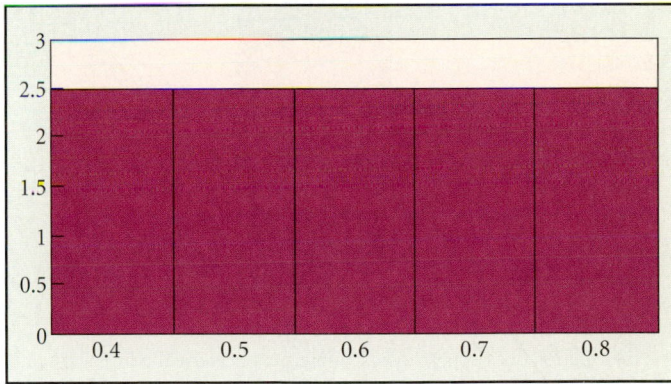

b $P(x < 0.65) = (0.65 - 0.4)/(0.8 - 0.4) = 0.625$ **c** $P(x > 0.7) = (0.8 - 0.7)/(0.8 - 0.4) = 0.25$ **d** $P(0.6 < x < 0.75) = (0.75 - 0.6)/(0.8 - 0.4) = 0.375$ **e** $(0.8 - 0.4)(0.9) = 0.36$ so $0.4 + 0.36 = 0.76$ which is the 90th percentile

5-93 a $P(x > 8) = 1 - P(x \le 8) = 1 - 0.9319 = 0.0681$ **b** $P(3 \le x \le 6) = 0.1404 + 0.1755 + 0.1755 + 0.1402 = 0.6376$ **c** $P(x < 3|\text{mean} = 2.5) = P(x \le 2) = 0.5438$

5-95 a $P(x = 0) = 0.6065$ **b** $P(x < 3) = 0.6065 + 0.3033 + 0.0758 = 0.9856$ **c** Mean = 0.5(3) = 1.5; $P(x = 0) = 0.2231$ **d** $P(x \ge 5) = 1 - P(x \le 4) = 1 - 0.9998 = 0.0002$. Because the probability of this occurring is so small if the mean error is actually 0.5 then you would conclude that the mean error is actually higher than 0.5.

5-97 a $P(x \ge 5) = 0.0250 + 0.0036 + 0.0002 = 0.0288$ **b** $np = 7(0.3) = 2.1$

5-99 $n = 15, p = 0.10$; **a** $P(x < 7) = P(x \le 6) = 0.9997$ **b** $P(x = 0) = 0.2059$

5-101 a Because the mean and median are different, this cannot be a normal distribution. **b** It would be possible for the mean to be $700 and the standard deviation to be $600. However, because an account balance cannot likely be negative, a distribution with mean = $700 and standard deviation equal to $600 is most likely not a normal distribution because we would expect data within ± 3 standard deviations.

5-103 a Minimum level should be 12.96 or 13 gallons **b** $P(x < 13) = P(z < -0.17) = 0.5 - 0.0675 = 0.4325$
5-105 a $P(x > 4.90) = P(z > 0.36) = 0.5 - 0.1406 = 0.3594$ **b** $P(x < 6.25) = P(z < 1.59) = 0.5 + 0.4441 = 0.9441$ **c** $P(3.25 < x < 5.75) = P[(3.25 - 4.5)/1.1 < z < (5.75 - 4.5)/1.1] = P(-1.14 < z < 1.14) = 2(0.3729) = 0.7458$
5-107 a $E[x] = np = 10(0.10) = 1.0$ **b** $SD[x] = \sqrt{npq} = \sqrt{10(0.10)(0.90)} = \sqrt{0.9} = 0.9487$
5-109 a The trim saw length should be set to 10' 5.4675". **b** The standard deviation should be 0.892"
5-111 $P(x > 74) = P(z > 1.14) = 0.5 - 0.3729 = 0.1271$; $P(x > 90) = P(z > 2.29) = 0.5 - 0.489 = 0.011$
5-113 a $P(5.85 < x < 6.15) = P(-1.5 < z < 1.5) = 2(0.4332) = 0.8664$; because this is less than 99% Bryce Brothers should not purchase this machine. **b** 0.058 inch
5-115 a $P(x \geq 4) = 1 - P(x \leq 3) = 1 - 0.9130 = 0.0870$ **b** The expected number = $5(0.4) = 2.0$
5-117 a $P(x < 20) = 1 - e^{-(20)(.05)} = 1 - 0.3679 = 0.6321$ **b** $P(x > 30) = e^{-(30)(.05)} = 0.2231$ **c** $P(30 < x < 60) = P(x < 60) - P(x < 30) = 0.9502 - 0.7769 = 0.1733$
5-119 One way to determine if you think the problem is with the disks is to observe the results from other operators. If similar results occur you could conclude it is the disk. If other operators are not having this problem then you could probably conclude that it is the operator.
5-121 a

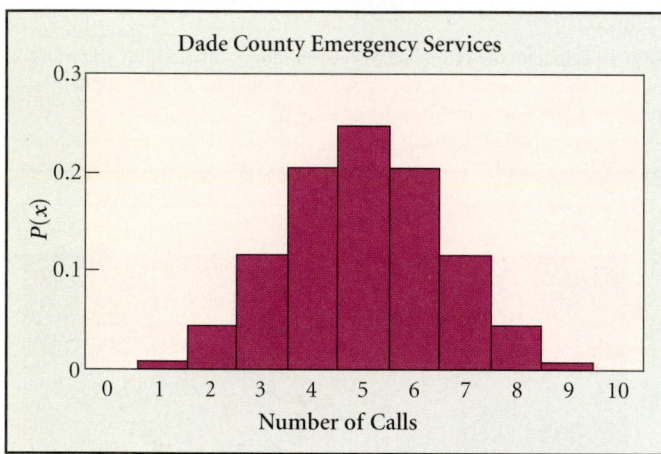

The distribution does appear to be symmetrical because the probability is equal to 0.5.
b

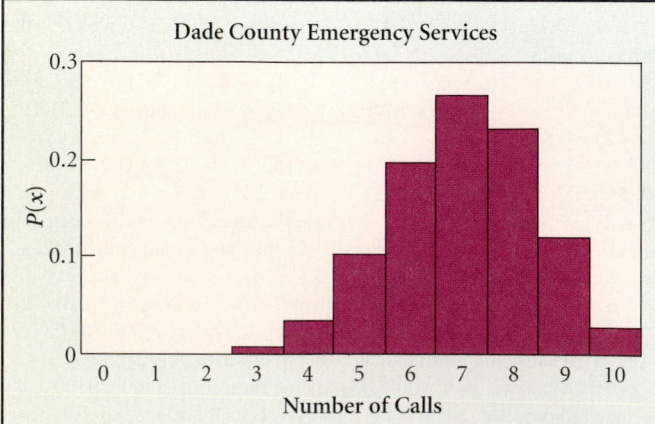

As the probability moves away from 0.5 in either direction the distribution will become skewed, which is the case in this problem.

5-123 a $P(x < 90) = P(x \leq 89) = 0.4168$ **b** $P(x > 10) = 1 - P(x \leq 10) = 1 - 0.5832 = 0.4168$ **c** $P(x = 78) = 0.0002$
5-125 a $P(x < 10) = 0.5 - 0.4279 = 0.0721$ **b** This allows you to have a log with a diameter of 9.375. $P(x < 9.375) = 0.5 - 0.4525 = 0.0475$

CHAPTER 6

6-1 a Population mean = 5.8 **b** Sample mean = 5.8333; the sampling error = $5.8333 - 5.8 = 0.0333$. **c** Highest possible sample mean for $n = 6 = 8.6667$; lowest possible sample mean for $n = 6 = 2.6667$; range of extreme sampling error = -3.1333 to 2.8667
6-3 a Sampling error = $216.67 - 177.64 = 39.03$ **b** Sampling error = $101.67 - 177.64 = -75.97$; sampling error = $310.0 - 177.64 = 132.36$; the range in potential sampling error is -75.97 to 132.36. **c** Sampling error = $110.8 - 177.64 = -66.84$; sampling error = $254.0 - 177.64 = 76.36$
6-5 a $\mu = \dfrac{864}{20} = 43.20$ days **b** $\bar{x} = 41.20$ days; sampling error = $41.20 - 43.20 = -2$ days **c** The range in sampling error is from -28.4 days to 40.4 days.
6-7 Sampling error = $17.06 - 16.9 = 0.16$ gallon.
6-9 The sample mean = 40.9.
6-11 a $z = \dfrac{970 - 1,000}{\dfrac{200}{\sqrt{5}}} = -0.34$; $P(z < -.34) = 0.50 - 0.1331 = 0.3669$ **b** $z = \dfrac{970 - 1,000}{\dfrac{200}{\sqrt{10}}} = -0.47$; $P(z < -0.47) = 0.50 - 0.1808 = 0.3192$ **c** The probability of extreme sampling error is reduced when the sample size is increased because the sampling distribution is less variable.
6-13 a $P(x > 450) = 0.1587$ **b** $P(\bar{x} > 450) = 0.0418$ **c** As the sample size increases the standard deviation of the sampling distribution is reduced. This means the spread of the sampling distribution is reduced.
6-15 a Sampling error = $24.69 - 24.90 = -0.21$ **b** $z = \dfrac{24.69 - 24.9}{\dfrac{1.30}{\sqrt{40}}} = -1.02$; $P(z \leq -1.02) = 0.50 - 0.3461 = 0.1539$
6-17 $P(\bar{x} > 200) = 0.5 - 0.4984 = 0.0016$
6-19 a $P(\bar{x} < 31) = 0.5$ **b** Standard error = 0.86 **c** To reduce the standard error the company could increase the sample size.
6-21 a $P(\bar{x} > 15) = 0.1762$ **b** We can quite safely say that the original assumptions are false.
6-23 a $P(\bar{x} > 0.392) = 0.0082$ **b** You should conclude that the sample is not representative of the population if the true population thickness is 0.375. On the other hand you might conclude that because the probability of this observed result is so low, the standards are not being satisfied.
6-25 a Mean = 468.89; standard deviation = 804.12
6-27 $z = \dfrac{450 - 0}{\dfrac{2000}{\sqrt{200}}} = 3.18$; $P(z > 3.18) = 0.50 - 0.50 \cong 0.0$
6-29 a 0.8000 **b** Sampling error = $0.4667 - 0.8000 = -0.3333$ **c** Range of sampling error = $(0.3333 - 0.8000) \text{ ——— } (1.0000 - 0.8000) = -0.4667$ to 0.2000 **d** The range of extreme sampling error becomes $(0.6667 - 0.8000) \text{ ——— } (1.000 - 0.8000) = -0.1333$ to 0.2000.
6-31 a $\sigma = \sqrt{\dfrac{0.65(1 - 0.65)}{100}} = 0.0477$; $z = \dfrac{0.63 - 0.65}{\sqrt{\dfrac{0.65(1 - 0.65)}{100}}} = -0.42$; $P(z < -0.42) = 0.50 - 0.1628 = 0.3372$ **b** $z = \dfrac{0.63 - 0.65}{\sqrt{\dfrac{0.65(1 - 0.65)}{200}}} = -0.59$; $P(z < -0.59) = 0.50 - 0.2224 = 0.2776$
6-33 $z = \dfrac{0.33 - 0.30}{\sqrt{\dfrac{0.30(1 - 0.30)}{60}}} = 0.51$; $P(z > 0.51) = 0.50 - 0.1950 = 0.3050$

6-35 a $z = \dfrac{0.42 - 0.40}{\sqrt{\dfrac{0.40(1 - 0.40)}{1000}}} = 1.29; P(z < 1.29) = 0.50 + 0.4015 = 0.9015$

b $z = \dfrac{0.44 - 0.40}{\sqrt{\dfrac{0.40(1 - 0.40)}{1000}}} = 2.58; P(z > 2.58) = 0.50 - 0.4951 = 0.0049$

6-37 a $p = 35/300 = 0.1167$ **b** $P(p \geq 0.1167) = 0.0096$

6-39 a $P(p < 0.68) = 0.1635$

6-41 a $P(\text{Medicare}) = 116/138 = 0.8406$ **b** $P(p > 0.8406) = 0.117$

6-43 a The $P(>55) = 47/200 = 0.235$ **b** $P(p \leq 0.235) = 0.0222$

6-45 A sampling distribution is made up of all possible values that a particular estimator can take for a population.

6-47 Sampling error is the difference between the population mean and a particular sample mean. Because the distribution of sample means centers on the population mean, the estimate of the spread of the sampling distribution also estimates the average amount by which the sample mean differs from the population.

6-49 The sampling distribution of the sample mean will have less dispersion than the population because the means cannot take on values as extreme as those in the population.

6-51 a The true population mean is 405.55. The mean of the sample means should be the same as the population mean. **b** sigma = 159.83

6-53 The population mean = 56.78; The population standard deviation: $9.6 = \text{sigma}/\sqrt{400}$; sigma = 192

6-55 If the population is normally distributed, the distribution of all possible sample means will also be normally distributed.

6-57 a The mean of the sampling distribution will be 68; it is the same as the population mean. The standard deviation for the sampling distribution of the mean is $12/\sqrt{100} = 1.2$. **b** For $n = 100$, the standard deviation is 1.2 and for $n = 500$, the standard deviation is 0.537.

6-59 a The reduction is a factor of $1 - 1/\sqrt{2}$. **b** $P(z > 2.5) = 0.5 - 0.4938 = 0.0062$

6-61 a The mean of the sampling distribution will be \$21,500 and the standard deviation will be $1700/\sqrt{200} = \$120.21$. **b** The mean would be \$21,500 and the standard deviation would be $1700/\sqrt{60} = \$219.47$.

c $P(\bar{x} > 21300) = 0.8186$

6-63 a $P(\bar{x} < 26) = 0.0367$ **b** $P(\bar{x} < 28) = 0.1867$

6-65 a $P(\bar{x} \leq 24.25) = 0.0228$ **b** $P(\bar{x} \geq 34) = 0$

6-67 a $P(19500 < x < 22000) = 0.3161$ **b** $P(19500 < \bar{x} < 22000) = 0.8413$

6-69 $P(\bar{x} \geq 31.14) = 0.0401$

6-71 a $P(\bar{x} > 120.2) = 0.0668$ **b** $P(\bar{x} < 119.73) = 0.0212$ **c** $P(\bar{x} > 120.3) = 0.0122$ **d** You need to calculate the probability that a board would be more than 1.5 different from 120. $P(z > 1.5/0.8) = P(z > 1.88) = 0.5 - 0.4699 = 0.0301$. Because you are looking for either 1.5 larger or smaller than the mean the probability would be the same. The probability that any one board would be more than 1.5 different is then $(0.0301)(2) = 0.0602$. Because they are ordering 1000 boards, the expected number of boards that would be different would be $(0.0602)(1000) = 60.2$. Therefore it is not a good proposition for the company.

6-73 a Sampling error **b** $P(p \leq 0.28) = 0.0143$

6-75 a $p = 18/49 = 0.367; (p < 0.367) = 0.121$ **b** The maximum sampling error we might expect is $0.6632 - 0.45 = 0.2132$.

6-77 a $p = 250/625 = 0.40; P(p \geq 0.4) = 0.0606$ **b** $P(p < 0.5) = 0.9964$

6-79 a $P(p \geq 0.3) = 0.0655$ **b** $P(p \geq 0.3) = 0.3121$

6-81 $P(0.25 < p < 0.29) = 0.6876$

6-83 a The sample proportion of business plan customers is 0.74. **b** $P(p \geq 0.74) = 0.1093$

CHAPTER 7

7-1 a $t = 2.0595$ **b** $t = 1.6973$ **c** $t = 2.6245$ **d** $t = 2.8784$ **e** $t = 1.3253$ **f** $t = 1.7459$

7-3 a $102.36 \pm 1.645(1.26/\sqrt{17}); 101.8573 \text{———} 102.8627$ **b** $56.33 \pm 1.7247(22.4/\sqrt{21}); 47.8995 \text{———} 64.7605$

7-5 a $e = \pm2.33(6.58/\sqrt{12}); \pm4.4258$ **b** $e = \pm2.0860(2.33/\sqrt{21}); \pm1.0606$ **c** $e = \pm1.28(15.6/\sqrt{500}); \pm0.8930$

7-7 a $e = \pm2.681(15.6/8\sqrt{13}); \pm 11.6593$ **b** $e = \pm2.575(3.47/\sqrt{25}); \pm1.7871$ **c** $e = \pm2.33(2.356); \pm5.4895$

7-9 $92.2 \pm 2.2622(15.562/\sqrt{10}); 92.2 \pm 11.1326; 81.0674 \text{———} 103.3326$

7-11 a Point estimate $= \bar{x} = \$4.22$ **b** $4.22 \pm 1.96(2.59/\sqrt{200}); 4.22 \pm 0.359; \$3.861 \text{———} \$4.579$

7-13 a $54.5 \pm 1.96(14.0/\sqrt{200}); 52.5597 \text{———} 56.4403$ per car **b** $(52.5597)(0.25)(200) \text{———} (56.4403)(0.25)(200); \$2,627.99 \text{———} \$2,822.02$ **c** The margin of error is comprised of the critical value, the standard deviation of the population or sample, and the sample size. If you decrease the confidence level (i.e., from 90% to 80%) you will decrease the margin of error. If you decrease the standard deviation you will decrease the margin of error. If you increase the sample size you will decrease the margin of error.

7-15 a $1.2 \pm 1.96(0.5/\sqrt{200}); 1.1307 \text{———} 1.2693$ **b** $1.2 \pm 1.645(0.5/\sqrt{200}); 1.1418 \text{———} 1.2582$ **c** The interval in part b is more precise, and, because it is narrower it may be more useful in decision making.

7-17 a $311 \pm 1.645(72/\sqrt{144}); 301.13 \text{———} 320.87$ **b** If you decrease the confidence level (i.e., from 90% to 80%) you will decrease the margin of error. If you increase the sample size you will decrease the margin of error.

7-19 a $67 \pm 1.7709(14.5285/\sqrt{14}); 67 \pm 6.8762; 60.1238 \text{———} 73.8762$ **b** No **c** (1) It does look like heart rates did increase because the interval estimate for the mean heart rate, $P(z \geq (67 - 55)(14.5285/\sqrt{14})) = P(z \geq 3.09) = 0.50 - 0.50 = 0$

7-21 a $2.505 \pm 1.645(1.5071/\sqrt{200}); 2.3297 \text{———} 2.6803$ **b** If you decrease the confidence level (i.e., from 90% to 80%) you will decrease the margin of error. If you increase the sample size you will decrease the margin of error.

7-23 a $268.4359 \pm 1.9913(50.8955/\sqrt{78}); 256.9605 \text{———} 279.9113$; corrosion: $274.1333 \pm 2.0452(54.0196/\sqrt{30}); 253.9623 \text{———} 294.3043$

7-25 $\dfrac{(1.96^2)(40^2)}{2.5^2} = 983.44 = 984$

7-27 $\dfrac{(1.645^2)(246.667^2)}{60^2} = 45.73 = 46$

7-29 a. $\dfrac{(1.645^2)(900^2)}{40^2} = 1,369.9 = 1,370$ **b** $\dfrac{(1.96^2)(900^2)}{40^2} = 1,944.8 = 1,945$; the percentage change is equal to a 41.97% increase.

7-31 a The margin of error can be decreased by either decreasing the confidence level, or decreasing the population standard deviation, or some combination of both. **b** If the confidence level is increased for a given size sample, the margin of error will be increased. **c** Both confidence level and margin of error can be decreased at the same time by increasing the required sample size or by reducing the population standard deviation.

7-33 $n = (1.645)^2(0.80)^2/(0.2)^2 = 43.29$ or 44

7-35 a $n = (1.96)^2(200)^2/(50)^2 = 61.4656$ or 62 so you would need to sample $62 - 40 = 22$ more **b** \$620 with pilot: savings of $\$1390 - \$620 = \$770$

7-37 $\dfrac{(2.33^2)(1.91^2)}{0.10^2} = 1,980.5 = 1,981$; the additional required sample size is $1,981 - 88 = 1,893$ items.

7-39 a $6,1780.7018 \pm 1.96(35,620.9230/\sqrt{171}); 56,441.6617 \text{———} 67,119.7419$; because \$67,500 is outside the confidence interval the promotion was probably not a success. **b** $n = (1.96)^2(35,620.9230)^2/(2,135.616)^2 = 1,068.75$ or $1,069 - 171$ current = 898 additional **c** He would need to change the confidence level.

7-41 $0.30 \pm 1.96(\sqrt{[(0.3)(1 - 0.3)]/400}); 0.2551 \text{———} 0.3449$

7-43 $0.1833 \pm 1.645(\sqrt{[(0.1833)(1 - 0.1833)] / 300})$; $0.1833 \pm .0367$; 0.1466 ——— 0.2200

7-45 $\dfrac{2.33^2(0.22)(1 - 0.22)}{0.03^2} = 1,035.1 = 1,036$; additional items needed $= 1,036 - 50 = 986$

7-47 a $\dfrac{1.96^2(0.70)(1 - 0.70)}{0.03^2} = 896.37 = 897$ **b** $\dfrac{1.96^2(0.30)(1 - 0.30)}{0.03^2}$ $= 896.37 = 897$

7-49 $\bar{p} = 88/300 = 0.2933$; $0.2933 \pm 1.44(\sqrt{[(0.2933)(1 - 0.2933)] / 300})$; 0.2554 ——— 0.3312

7-51 $\bar{p} = 22/50 = 0.44$; $n = 1.645^2(0.44)(1 - 0.44)/(0.05)^2 = 266.71$ or $267 - 50$ pilot sample $= 217$ more

7-53 a $0.10 \pm 1.645(\sqrt{[(0.10)(1 - 0.10)] / 130})$; $0.10 \pm .0433$; 0.0567 ——— 0.1433 **b** Reduce the confidence level or take a larger sample size.

7-55 a $\dfrac{1.96^2(0.50)(1 - 0.50)}{0.03^2} = 1,067.1 = 1,068$

b $0.18 \pm 1.96(\sqrt{[(0.18)(1 - 0.18)] / 1,068})$; 0.18 ± 0.0230; 0.1570 ——— 0.2030

7-57 a $0.7144 \pm 1.96(\sqrt{[(0.7144)(1 - 0.7144] / 900}) = 0.6849$ ——— 0.7439 **b** If the proportion in the eastern states is 0.75, they should use a different ratio for the western states. The interval estimate for the western states does not include 0.75. **c** $1.96(\sqrt{[(0.7144)(1 - 0.7144] / 900}) = 0.0295$ **d** The options available to reduce the margin of error are to reduce the confidence level or to increase the sample size.

7-59 a $0.23 \pm 1.645(\sqrt{[(0.23)(1 - 0.23)] / 499})$; 0.1990 ——— 0.2610 **b** The point estimate would be 0.23 and the margin of error would be 0.031.

c $e = \sqrt{\dfrac{z^2(p)(1 - p)}{n}} = \sqrt{\dfrac{1.645^2(0.23)(1 - 0.23)}{300}} = 0.04$

7-61 The margin of error for a proportion is $z\sqrt{[(\bar{p})(1 - \bar{p})] / n}$. The only thing that is going to change is the numerator ($\bar{p})(1 - \bar{p}$). The larger the numerator, the larger the margin of error.

7-63 This is not correct. The average number of miles people commute is a single value. Therefore it has no probability.

7-65 a $\bar{x} = \$178$ **b** $1.96(271 / \sqrt{48}) = 7.6383$ **c** 170.3617 ——— 185.6383

7-67 a $1,345.78 \pm 1.96(257.90 / \sqrt{300})$; $\$1,316.5959$ ——— $\$1,374.9641$ **b** Increasing the sample size and/or decreasing the confidence level. **c** We typically think of the smallest and largest values being three standard deviations from the mean. Using this assumption the smallest population mean as specified by the confidence interval we get the lowest price to be $\$1,316.60 - 3(257.90) = \$542.90$; and the largest price would be $\$1,316.60 + 3(257.90) = \$2,090.30$ However, if we assumed that the population mean was at the upper limit of the confidence interval then the smallest value might be $\$1,374.96 - 3(257.90) = \$601.26$ and the largest price would be $\$1,374.96 + 3(257.90) = \$2,148.66$. **d** approximately normally distributed

7-69 $\dfrac{1.96^2 7^2}{1^2} = 188.24 = 189$

7-71 $n = 1.88^2(0.5)(1 - 0.5)/(.04)^2 = 552.25$ or 553

7-73 $11.9991 \pm 1.96(0.2002 / \sqrt{5000})$; 11.9936 ——— 12.0046; the confidence interval does include the 12 ounces.

7-75 a $0.7 \pm 1.96\sqrt{[(0.7)(1 - 0.7)] / 1024}$; 0.6719 ——— 0.7281

b $1.96\sqrt{[(0.5)(1 - 0.5)] / 1024}$; 0.0306

7-77 c The population mean is 63668.5714. At a 90% confidence interval you would expect 90% of your 10 samples, which would be 9.

7-79 a $\bar{p} = 546/758 = 0.7203$; $0.7203 \pm 1.96\sqrt{[(0.7203)(1 - 0.7203)] / 758}$; 0.6883 ——— 0.7523 **b** Number of males $= 758 - 316 = 442$; number of males who have gambled $= 546 - 187 = 359$; $\bar{p} = 359/442 = 0.8122$; $0.8122 \pm 2.575\sqrt{[(0.8122)(1 - 0.8122)] / 442}$; 0.7644 ——— 0.8600

c $\bar{p} = 22/442 = 0.0498$; $0.0498 \pm 1.96\sqrt{[(0.0498)(1 - 0.0498] / 442}$; 0.0295 ——— 0.0701

7-81 a $0.625 \pm 2.575\sqrt{[(0.625)(1 - 0.625)] / 64}$; 0.4692 ——— 0.7808 **b** Student answers will vary but one approach might be that because 50% is within the range of the confidence interval they may want to produce half mint and half plain.

CHAPTER 8

8-1 a $H_O: \mu \leq 20$; $H_A: \mu > 20$ **b** $H_O: \mu = 50$; $H_A: \mu \neq 50$ **c** $H_O: \mu \geq 35$; $H_A: \mu < 35$ **d** $H_O: \mu \leq 87$; $H_A: \mu > 87$ **e** $H_O: \mu \leq 6$; $H_A: \mu > 6$

8-3 a If $\bar{x} > 205.2344$, reject H_O, if $\bar{x} \leq 205.2344$, do not reject H_O; if $z > 1.645$, reject H_O, if $z \leq 1.645$, do not reject H_O **b** Because $z = 1.41 < 1.645$, do not reject H_O; because $204.5 < 205.2344$, do not reject H_O **c** The alternative hypothesis

8-5 a If $\bar{x} < 3966.2775$, reject H_O, if $\bar{x} \geq 3966.2775$, do not reject H_O; if p-value < 0.05, reject H_O, if p-value ≥ 0.05, do not reject H_O **b** Because $3980 > 3966.2775$, do not reject H_O, because p-value $= 0.1635 \geq 0.05$, do not reject H_O **c** The two research hypotheses that could have produced the null and alternative hypotheses are: the population mean is less than 4,000; the population mean is at least 4,000

8-7 a Type I error **b** Type II error **c** Type I error **d** Type II error

8-9 a p-value $= 0.0182$ **b** p-value $= 0.0322$ **c** p-value $= 0.2005$ **d** p-value $= 0.9803$

8-11 a Decision rule: If $\bar{x} < 4,158.4$, reject H_O, if $\bar{x} > 4,741.6$, reject H_O; otherwise, do not reject **b** Because $\bar{x} = 4,475.6$ is $> 4,158.4$ and $< 4,741.6$, do not reject the null hypothesis.

8-13 a $H_O: \mu \geq 30,000$; $H_A: \mu < 30,000$ **b** Because $z = -1.00 > -1.645$, do not reject the null hypothesis.

8-15 a $H_O: \mu \leq 6$ days; $H_A: \mu > 6$ days **b** Because $2.7406 > 1.96$, reject H_O **c** p-value $= 0.0031$; because $0.0031 < 0.025$, reject the null hypothesis. **d** If $\bar{x} > 6.4649$, reject the null hypothesis; otherwise, do not reject.

8-17 a $H_O: \mu \leq 4,000$; $H_A: \mu > 4,000$ **b** Because $t = 1.2668 < 1.7959$ there is insufficient evidence to reject the null hypothesis.

8-19 a $H_O: \mu \geq 40$, $H_A: \mu < 40$ **b** Because $z = -0.8052 > -1.28$ do not reject H_O and conclude that the average age is not less than 40. **c** Type II error

8-21 a $H_O: \mu = 0.75$ inch, $H_A: \mu \neq 0.75$ inch **b** Because $z = 0.9496 < 2.58$, do not reject H_O **c** If $\bar{x} < 0.7413$, reject the null hypothesis, if $\bar{x} > 0.7586$, reject the null hypothesis; otherwise, do not reject the null hypothesis **d** Type II error

8-23 a $z_\alpha = 1.645$; $= 0.40 + 1.645\left(\sqrt{\dfrac{0.40(1 - 0.40)}{150}}\right) = 0.4658$

b $z_\alpha = -1.28$; $= 0.70 - 1.28\left(\sqrt{\dfrac{0.70(1 - 0.70)}{200}}\right) = 0.6585$

c $z_\alpha = 1.645$; $= 0.85 \pm 1.645\left(\sqrt{\dfrac{0.85(1 - 0.85)}{100}}\right) = 0.7913$ and 0.9087

8-25 p-value $= 0.1902$; because $0.1902 > 0.07$, do not reject the null hypothesis.

8-27 a Because $0.27 < 0.3103$, do not reject the null hypothesis **b** Because $0.7024 < 1.645$, do not reject.

8-29 a $H_O: p \geq 0.70$, $H_A: p < 0.70$; because $z = -1.5275 > -1.645$, do not reject. **b** A Type II error in this problem would mean that the proportion of students passing the test is actually less than 0.70 but the sample results lead the administrators to believe that it is actually 70% or better. This would mean that a test that must be too difficult would continue to be administered.

8-31 a $H_O: p \geq 0.01$, $H_A: p < 0.01$; because $z = -0.7107 > -1.645$ do not reject. **b** 0.0075 ± 0.006; 0.0015 ——— 0.0135

8-33 a $H_O: p \leq 0.30$, $H_A: p > 0.30$ **b** Because $z = 0.9258 < 1.28$, do not reject the null hypothesis.

8-35 a $H_O: p \leq 0.50$, $H_A: p > 0.50$ **b** Because $z = 5.889 > 1.645$, reject the null hypothesis.

8-37 a H_O: $p \le 0.80$, H_A: $p > 0.80$ **b** Because $z = 2.5 > 1.28$, reject and conclude that the proportion of calls answered within 5 minutes is greater than 80%. **c** 0.8410 ——— 0.9590; consistent

8-39 a Use Excel's Pivot Table—use percent of rows option and group handicaps as shown below. Note there are 67 golfers with handicaps of 20 or more.

Count of Club Status	Club Status		
USGA Handicap	Copy	Original	Grand Total
0–19.99	27.31%	72.69%	100.00%
20.00–39.98	25.37%	74.63%	100.00%
Grand Total	26.87%	73.13%	100.00%

H_O: $p \ge 0.40$; H_A: $p < 0.40$ **b** Because $z = -2.4444 < -1.645$, reject H_O

8-41 a Beta = 0.4922 + 0.3078 = 0.80 **b** Power of the test = 1 − 0.80 = 0.20 **c** The power increases, and beta decreases, as the sample size increases. We could also increase alpha because alpha and beta are inversely related. **d** Because $\bar{x} = 1.23$ then $1.0938 < 1.23 < 1.3062$, do not reject H_O.

8-43 a $\bar{x}_\alpha = 4{,}350 - 1.645(200 / \sqrt{100})$; $\bar{x}_\alpha = 4{,}317.10$; beta = 0.5 + 0.4192 = 0.9192 **b** Power = 1 − 0.9192 = 0.0808 **c** The power increases, and beta decreases, as the sample size increases. We could also increase alpha because alpha and beta are inversely related. **d** Because $\bar{x} = 4{,}337.5 > 4{,}317.1$, do not reject the null hypothesis.

8-45 H_O: $\mu \ge 18.0$, H_A: $\mu < 18.0$ **a** Beta = 0.50 − 0.4985 = 0.0015 **b** Beta = 0.50 −0.1480 = 0.352 **c** The probability of a Type II error would be smaller. **d** The probabilities of Type II errors would be reduced for larger sample sizes.

8-47 a Beta = 0.8686 **b** No changes needed.

8-49 A Type I error occurs when the decision maker rejects a true null hypothesis. A Type II error occurs when a false null hypothesis is accepted.

8-51 The critical value is the cut-off point or demarcation determining the rejection regions in a hypothesis test. It may be expressed in terms of a value of the sample mean or as a z-value.

8-53 The probability of committing a Type I error is denoted by alpha (α) and is usually specified by the decision maker. The choice of alpha reflects the cost of making a Type I error.

8-55 You use the population proportion to calculate the standard error. If you were testing that the population proportion were 0 then the standard error would be 0. This would make it impossible to make a logical calculation.

8-57 a H_O: $\mu \le 100$, H_A: $\mu > 100$; because $z = 1.98 > 1.28$, reject H_O **b** $\bar{x} = 109.051$

8-59 a H_O: $\mu \ge 20$, H_A: $\mu < 20$; because $-6.3586 < -1.645$, reject H_O. **b** $P(z < -6.36) = 0.50 - 0.50 = 0$; this is called the p-value.

8-61 a H_O: $\mu \le 10$, H_A: $\mu > 10$; because $1.56 < 1.645$, do not reject H_O. **b** 9.9181 ——— 10.7219

8-63 a H_O: $\mu \le 3$, H_A: $\mu > 3$ research from Union perspective **b** If $z > 2.33$ reject H_O, otherwise do not reject H_O. **c** Because $z = 1.98 < 2.33$, do not reject H_O.

8-65 a H_O: $\mu \ge 40$, H_A: $\mu < 40$ **b** Because $z = -3.3334 < -1.28$, reject H_O.

8-67 a H_O: $\mu \le 417$, H_A: $\mu > 417$ **c** Because $z = 0.80 < 1.645$, do not reject H_O.

8-69 a H_O: $\mu \le 3$, H_A: $\mu > 3$; because $t = 3.35 > 1.7291$, reject and conclude that the mean exceeds 3 tries.

8-71 a H_O: $\mu \ge 10$, H_A: $\mu < 10$ **b** Decision rule: If $z < -1.28$, reject H_O; otherwise do not reject H_O. **c** Because $z = -1.3944 < -1.28$, reject H_O and conclude that the average savings is less than 10 ounces. **d** Type I error

8-73 a H_O: $\mu \le \$3$, H_A: $\mu > \$3$ **b** Because $z = 0.6108 < 1.645$, do not reject H_O. **c** The consumer group would be more concerned with a Type I error. The company would be more concerned with a Type II error.

8-75 a H_O: $p \le 0.30$, H_A: $p > 0.30$; because $2.1602 > 1.28$, reject H_O. **b** 0.3138 ——— 0.4262; $156.90 ——— $213.10

8-77 H_O: $\mu \ge 25{,}000$, H_A: $\mu < 25{,}000$; because $z = -1.8461 < -1.645$, reject H_O.

8-79 H_O: $p \le 0.35$, H_A: $p > 0.35$; because $1.0377 < 1.645$, do not reject H_O.

CHAPTER 9

9-1 a 13.541 ——— 16.459 **b** 12.933 ——— 17.067

9-3 a 329.297 ——— 358.703 **b** 331.827 ——— 356.173 **c** A lower confidence level gives a more precise, narrower interval. However, the chances of an interval not containing the true population mean are increased.

9-5 a −25.49 ——— 17.49 **b** −34.439 ——— 26.439

9-7 a −0.1043 ——— 2.7043

9-9 −20.8069 ——— 38.6011; these results do not suggest that the manager needs to focus on one location or the other.

9-11 a −48.1297 ——— 111.3687 **b** The interval includes the value 0.

9-13 a 946.9545 − 854.7143 = 94.2402; no **b** 48 ——— 136.5 **c** 63.7 ——— 120.8

9-15 a 1.6461 ——— 3.3539; yes **b** Company A: $\bar{x} = 41.0813$; Company B: $\bar{x} = 38.4184$

9-17 The hypotheses are: H_O: $\mu_1 = \mu_2$, H_A: $\mu_1 > \mu_2$; $t = -0.0479$, do not reject H_O.

9-19 a The hypotheses are: H_O: $\mu_1 \le \mu_2$, H_A: $\mu_1 > \mu_2$; reject H_O if $t < -2.0227$ or $t > 2.0227$. **b** $t = -0.4058$, do not reject H_O.

9-21 a The hypotheses are: H_O: $\mu_1 = \mu_2$, H_A: $\mu_1 \ne \mu_2$; the Decision Rule is: if $z > 1.96$ or $z < -1.96$, reject H_O; otherwise do not reject H_O. **b** Because $5.630 > 1.96$, reject H_O.

9-23 a If the difference is Sample 1 − Sample 2, the hypotheses are: H_O: $\mu_d \ge 0$, H_A: $\mu_d < 0$ **b** $t = -3.64$; because $-3.64 < -1.3968$, reject H_O. **c** −2.1998 ——— −0.7122. This confidence interval does not contain 0.

9-25 H_O: $\mu_F - \mu_M \le 1$, H_A: $\mu_F - \mu_M > 1$; because $z = 1.6136 < 1.645$, do not reject H_O and conclude that the difference is not greater than 1.

9-27 a H_O: $\mu_N - \mu_O \le 0$, H_A: $\mu_N - \mu_O > 0$; because $z = 2.2907 > 1.28$, reject H_O and conclude that the new cartridge will result in a longer lasting product. **b** 2.537 ——— 15.463; yes

9-29 a H_O: $\mu_B - \mu_A \le 0.35$, H_A: $\mu_B - \mu_A > 0.35$; because $t = 0.8781 < 2.4286$, do not reject H_O. **b** You have to assume independent samples, and that each population has a normal distribution.

9-31 a H_O: $\mu_D - \mu_S \le 0$, H_A: $\mu_D - \mu_S > 0$; because $t = 3.0853 > 1.6909$, reject H_O and conclude that the children who have been in day care have a higher mean time in interactive situations than the stay-at-home children. **b** Type I error

9-33 a H_O: $\mu_d = 0$, H_A: $\mu_d \ne 0$; because $t = -0.1526 > -2.1448$, do not reject H_O. **b** Yes **c** −8.0302 ——— 6.9636; yes

9-35 Because $z = -1.82 < -1.645$, reject H_O.

9-37 a Because $z = 2.4059 > 2.05$, reject H_O. **b** p-value = 0.00800, which is less than $\alpha = 0.02$.

9-39 a $n_1\bar{p}_1 = 0.62(745) = 462 > 5$; $n_1(1 - \bar{p}_1) = 745(1 - 0.62) = 283 > 5$; $n_2\bar{p}_2 = 0.49(455) = 223 > 5$; $n_2(1 - \bar{p}_2) = 455(1 - 0.49) = 232 > 5$. Because both are greater than 5, the normal approximation is appropriate. **b** H_O: $p_1 - p_2 = 0$, H_A: $p_1 - p_2 \ne 0$; because $z = 4.414 > 1.96$, reject H_O.

9-41 0.1832 ——— 0.3000

9-43 Calculated chi-square test statistic = $1.0377 > 3.8415$, do not reject H_O and conclude that response to question 1 is independent of question 2.

9-45 a $z = 1.82$. The critical value for a two-sided hypothesis test is 1.96. There is not enough evidence to indicate a difference. **b** Calculated chi-square test statistic = $3.339 > 3.8415$; conclude that the data indicate the proportion of bad calls is the same for each official. **c** $\chi^2 = 3.339 \approx (1.82)^2 = z^2$

9-47 a H_O: type of car owned is independent of union membership, H_A: type of car owned is not independent of union membership; calculated chi-square test statistic = $27.9092 > 3.8415$, reject H_O. **b** Use Excel's CHITEST function to find 0.0000001271442.

9-49 a Calculated chi-square = 2.3536 < 9.4877; conclude gender and citations issued are independent. **b** 0.39241

9-51 a Because calculated chi-square = 61.5267 > 15.5073, reject H_O and conclude that strike length tolerance is not independent of time with company. **b** $z = -3.53$, do not conclude the proportion is larger for the first group.

9-53 Calculated chi-square = 11.1167 > 9.21035, reject H_O and conclude type of accident and shift are not independent.

9-55 Calculated chi-square = 30.2753. The p-value = 0.00003484.

9-57 H_O: $\mu_W - \mu_O = 0$, H_A: $\mu_W - \mu_O \neq 0$; because p-value = 0.3738 > 0.05, do not reject H_O.

9-59 Because $z = -2.4237 < -1.96$, reject H_O and conclude that there is a difference in graduation rates.

9-61 Because $z = 1.8464 > 1.28$, reject H_O.

9-63 a You must assume that the populations are normally distributed. **b** H_O: $\mu_A - \mu_B \leq 0$, H_A: $\mu_A - \mu_B > 0$; because $t = 0.4544 < 1.7823$, do not reject H_O.

9-65 a $n_m \bar{p}_m = (81/280)(280) = 81 > 5$; $n_m(1 - \bar{p}_m) = 280(1 - 0.2893) = 199 > 5$; $n_w \bar{p}_w = (74/280)(280) = 74 > 5$; $n_w(1 - \bar{p}_w) = 280(1 - 0.2643) = 206 > 5$ **b** H_O: $p_m - p_w = 0$, H_A: $p_m - p_w \neq 0$; because $z = 0.6611 < 1.645$, do not reject H_O.

9-67 a Because calculated chi-square = 172.50 > 16.9190, conclude "taxable income" and "taxes paid" are not independent. **b** As income increases the amount of taxes paid increases.

9-69 a Because p-value = $(0.5 - 0.3051)2 = 0.3898 > 0.05$, do not reject H_O. **b** A Type I error would be if there is no difference but we concluded there was a difference. A Type II error would be if there is a difference but we concluded there was not a difference.

9-71 a H_O: $\mu_{BB} - \mu_S \leq 0$, H_A: $\mu_{BB} - \mu_S > 0$ **b** Because $z = -1.7502 < 2.33$, do not reject H_O.

9-73 a H_O: $\mu_M - \mu_F = 0$, H_A: $\mu_M - \mu_F \neq 0$; if $z > 1.96$ or $z < -1.96$, reject H_O; otherwise do not reject H_O. Because $z = 0.7771 < 1.96$, do not reject H_O.

9-75 a H_O: $p_U - p_G \leq 0$, H_A: $p_U - p_G > 0$; because $z = 1.66 > 1.645$, reject H_O. **b** $0.4333 \pm 1.96\sqrt{\dfrac{0.4333(0.5667)}{60}} = 0.4333 \pm 0.1254 = 0.3079 \text{——} 0.5587$

Graduate minimum/maximum number of seats = 500(0.3079) = 154 to 500(0.5587) = 279

$0.575 \pm 1.96\sqrt{\dfrac{0.575(0.425)}{80}} = 0.575 \pm 0.1083 = 0.4667 \text{——} 0.6833$

Undergraduate minimum/maximum number of seats = 2000(0.4667) = 934 to 2000(0.6833) = 1,367

CHAPTER 10

10-1 a $\chi^2 = 16.919$ **b** $\chi^2 = 32.8523$ **c** $\chi^2 = 16.919$

10-3 a Because $\chi^2 = 20.25 > 18.5493$, reject the null hypothesis. **b** Because $\chi^2 = 50.75 > 42.5569$, reject the null hypothesis.

10-5 a Because $\chi^2 = 25.3333 < 30.1435$, do not reject H_O and conclude that the population variance is less than 300. **b** Because $\chi^2 = 17.1267 < 21.0641$, do not reject H_O.

10-7 a H_O: $\sigma^2 \leq 2{,}025$, H_A: $\sigma^2 > 2{,}025$ **b** Because $\chi^2 = 28.1481 > 27.2036$, reject the null hypothesis.

10-9 a H_O: $\mu = 0$, H_A: $\mu \neq 0$; because $t = 1.1597 < 2.2010$, do not reject H_O. **b** H_O: $\sigma^2 \leq 4$, H_A: $\sigma^2 > 4$; because $\chi^2 = 68.1655 > 19.6752$, reject H_O. **c** From parts a and b airlines should conclude that on the average the planes arrive on time but with variance greater than 4.

10-11 H_O: $\mu \leq 14.25$, H_A: $\mu > 14.25$; because $z = 2.8553 > 1.645$, reject H_O. H_O: $\sigma^2 \geq 41.4736$, H_A: $\sigma^2 < 41.4736$; because $\chi^2 = 204.0936 > 136.2992$, reject H_O and conclude that the population variance is greater than or equal to 41.4736. Thus, the standard deviation has not been reduced.

10-13 a $F = 3.619$ **b** $F = 3.106$ **c** $F = 3.051$

10-15 a If the calculated $F > 2.865$, reject H_O; otherwise, do not reject H_O. **b** Because $F = 1.1995 < 2.865$, do not reject H_O.

10-17 a If the calculated $F > 3.858$, reject H_O; otherwise, do not reject H_O. **b** Because $F = 0.46390 < 3.858$, do not reject H_O.

10-19 H_O: $\sigma_d^2 = \sigma_w^2$, H_A: $\sigma_d^2 \neq \sigma_w^2$; because $F = 2.7778 < 3.284$, do not reject H_O.

10-21 H_O: $\sigma_A^2 = \sigma_B^2$, H_A: $\sigma_A^2 \neq \sigma_B^2$ because $F = 1.4833 < 3.0274$, do not reject H_O.

10-23 H_O: $\sigma_c^2 \leq \sigma_n^2$, H_A: $\sigma_c^2 > \sigma_n^2$; because $F = 1.445 < 2.276$, do not reject H_O.

10-25 a H_O: $\sigma_A^2 \leq \sigma_T^2$, H_A: $\sigma_A^2 > \sigma_T^2$; because $F = 2.0818 < 2.534$ do not reject H_O. **b** You would have rejected a true null hypothesis, which is a Type I error. You could decrease the alpha level to decrease the probability of a Type I error or you could increase the sample sizes.

10-27 H_O: $\sigma_A^2 = \sigma_Z^2$, H_A: $\sigma_A^2 \neq \sigma_Z^2$; because $F = 1.2129 < 2.231$, do not reject the null hypothesis.

10-29 H_O: $\sigma^2 \leq 0.90^2$, H_A: $\sigma^2 > 0.90^2$; because $\chi^2 = 42.451 > 38.885$, reject the null hypothesis.

10-31 H_O: $\sigma_1^2 \leq \sigma_2^2$, H_A: $\sigma_1^2 > \sigma_2^2$; because $F = 1.0582 < 1.599$, do not reject the null hypothesis.

10-33 H_O: $\sigma^2 \geq 29.2^2$, H_A: $\sigma^2 < 29.2^2$; because $\chi^2 = 26.826 < 29.788$, reject the null hypothesis.

10-35 H_O: $\sigma_N^2 \geq \sigma_C^2$, H_A: $\sigma_N^2 < \sigma_C^2$; because $F = 2.109 > 1.748$, reject the null hypothesis.

10-37 H_O: $\sigma^2 \leq 3{,}900^2$, H_A: $\sigma^2 > 3{,}900^2$; because $\chi^2 = 202.5424 < 224.9568$, do not reject the null hypothesis.

10-39 a H_O: $\sigma_{1998}^2 \leq \sigma_{1997}^2$, H_A: $\sigma_{1998}^2 > \sigma_{1997}^2$; because $F = 1.4263 < 9.2766$, do not reject the null hypothesis. **b** H_O: $\sigma_{\text{Dept}}^2 \leq \sigma_{\text{Misc}}^2$, H_A: $\sigma_{\text{Dept}}^2 > \sigma_{\text{Misc}}^2$; because $F = 1.132 < 4.8759$, do not reject the null hypothesis.

10-41 a H_O: $\sigma_H^2 \geq 2.5^2$, H_A: $\sigma_H^2 < 2.5^2$; H_O: $\sigma_{SD}^2 \geq 2.5^2$, H_A: $\sigma_{SD}^2 < 2.5^2$; H_O: $\sigma_B^2 \geq 2.5^2$, H_A: $\sigma_B^2 < 2.5^2$; H_O: $\sigma_R^2 \geq 2.5^2$, H_A: $\sigma_R^2 < 2.5^2$; H_O: $\sigma_{TW}^2 \geq 2.5^2$, H_A: $\sigma_{TW}^2 < 2.5^2$; $\chi_H^2 = \dfrac{(n-1)s^2}{\sigma^2} = 19.2005 > 15.6587$, do not reject; $\chi_{SD}^2 = \dfrac{(n-1)s^2}{\sigma^2} = 23.0552 > 15.6587$, do not reject; $\chi_B^2 = \dfrac{(n-1)s^2}{\sigma^2} = 11.4861 < 15.6587$, reject; $\chi_R^2 = \dfrac{(n-1)s^2}{\sigma^2} = 19.7802 > 15.6587$, do not reject; $\chi_{TW}^2 = \dfrac{(n-1)s^2}{\sigma^2} = 12.8191 < 15.6587$, reject; if $\chi^2 < 15.6587$, reject the null hypothesis. **b** H_O: $\sigma_{TW}^2 \leq \sigma_B^2$, H_A: $\sigma_{TW}^2 > \sigma_B^2$; because $F = 1.1160 < 1.7019$, do not reject the null hypothesis.

10-43 a H_O: $\sigma^2 \geq 10^2$, H_A: $\sigma^2 < 10^2$; because $\chi^2 = 29.1577 < 32.2676$, reject the null hypothesis. **b** H_O: $\sigma_{P/C}^2 = \sigma_{IS}^2$, H_A: $\sigma_{P/C}^2 \neq \sigma_{IS}^2$; because $F = 1.0801 < 1.8163$, do not reject the null hypothesis and conclude that there is no difference in the variability of sales between the two sales channels.

10-45 a H_O: $\sigma_B^2 \leq 1.5^2$, H_A: $\sigma_B^2 > 1.5^2$; because $\chi^2 = 45.0477 < 59.3035$, do not reject the null hypothesis. **b** H_O: $\sigma_{AS}^2 \leq \sigma_E^2$, H_A: $\sigma_{AS}^2 > \sigma_E^2$; because $F = 1.2027 < 1.5653$, do not reject the null hypothesis.

CHAPTER 11

11-1 a 7

b

Source	SS	df	MS	F
Between Samples	1,745	6	290.833	14.667
Within Samples	4,759	240	19.829	
Total	6,504	246		

c H_O: $\mu_1 = \mu_2 = \mu_3 = \mu_4 = \mu_5 = \mu_6 = \mu_7$, H_A: at least two population means are different **d** F-critical = 2.8778 (Minitab), $F = 14.667 > 2.8778$ reject H_O

11-3 a $H_0: \mu_1 = \mu_2 = \mu_3$, H_A: at least two population means are different **b** $SSB = 53.444$ **c** $SSW = 33.592$
d
ANOVA

Source of Variation	SS	df	MS	F	p-value
Between Groups	53.44444	2	26.72222	11.93252	0.000792
Within Groups	33.59167	15	2.239444		
Total	87.03611	17			

11-5 a
ANOVA

Source of Variation	SS	df	MS	F
Between Groups	55.6	2	27.8	7.419635
Within Groups	101.164	27	3.746815	
Total	156.764	29		

F-critical $= 3.3541$; reject H_0.
b No change.
11-7
ANOVA

Source of Variation	SS	df	MS	F
Between Groups	7620	3	2540	16.08667
Within Groups	12000	76	157.8947	
Total	19620	79		

$F = 16.08667 > 2.7249$ reject H_0.
11-9 a Because $0.00001 < 0.05$ reject H_0. **b** Recommend Car 2.
c $461.76 —— $786.84
11-11 a Because $5.5342 > 2.8661$ reject H_0. **b** Recommendation: Display Type A or Display Type C.
11-13 a
ANALYSIS OF VARIANCE

Source	DF	SS	MS	F	p-value
Blocks	9	8346.3	927.4	10.56	0.000
Groups	2	248.3	124.1	1.41	0.269
Error	18	1580.4	87.8		
Total	29	10175.0			

b $H_0: \mu_{b1} = \mu_{b2} = \mu_{b3} = \mu_{b4} = \mu_{b5} = \mu_{b6} = \mu_{b7} = \mu_{b8} = \mu_{b9} = \mu_{b10}$, H_A: not all block means are equal; because $10.56 > 2.456$ reject H_0. **c** p-value $0.269 > 0.05$ do not reject H_0. **d** Multiple comparisons are not necessary.
11-15 a 7 **b** 15 **c** 3.638 **d** Blocking was effective.
e 10.2601 **f** $10.2601 > 2.2086$ reject H_0.
11-17 a Because $7.656659 > 3.098393$ reject H_0. **c** Because $26.6951 > 3.2874$ reject H_0.
f
LEAST SIGNIFICANT DIFFERENCE (LSD)   293.112167

	Mean Difference	Absolute Mean Difference	Significant?
D1–D2	263.33	263.33	No
D1–D3	−555	555	Yes
D1–D4	−835	835	Yes
D2–D3	−818.33	818.33	Yes
D2–D4	−1098.33	1098.33	Yes
D3–D4	−280	280	No

11-19 b Because $952.6155 > 1.8673$ reject H_0. **c** Because the p-value $= 2.68E{-}10$ reject H_0. **d** Store 2 has the highest average prices.
11-29 Because p-value $= 0.3477 > \alpha = 0.05$ do not reject.

11-31 a Because the p-value $= 8.74E{-}30 < 0.05$ reject H_0.
b

	Absolute Difference	Critical Range	Significant?
Wichita–Little Rock	5773.64	1504.719	yes
Little Rock–Tulsa	1157.57	1504.719	no
Tulsa–Memphis	1774.17	1504.719	yes

c 98
11-33 b Because $1.542 > 1.4829$ conclude that blocking was effective.
c Because $28.38721 > 3.0892$ reject H_0 and conclude that at least two populations means are different. **d** Center 3 takes the greatest amount of time to handle calls.
11-35 a $H_0: \mu_1 = \mu_2 = \mu_3$, H_A: not all means are equal **b** Because $0.3858 < 4.7476$ conclude there is no difference. **c** 0.680554
d $P(t > 0.6059) = 0.2727$

CHAPTER 12

12-1 A very weak curvilinear relationship.
12-3 Because the two variables have a negative linear relationship as x increases y will decrease.
12-7 a A fairly strong positive relationship. **b** 0.847065. **c** Because $3.5638 > 2.5706$, reject H_0 and conclude the correlation coefficient is not 0. **d** Type I error.
12-9 a A fairly strong positive linear relationship. **b** Because p-value is essentially $= 0 < 0.1$, reject H_0.
12-11 a No **b** Probably
12-13 a Almost no linear relationship. **b** -0.1087. **c** Because p-value $= 0.3825 > 0.025$, do not reject the null hypothesis.
12-15 a $R^2 = 0.568498$ **b** (1) $\hat{y} = 58.7246 + 12.9410(0) = 58.7246$; (2) the y-intercept
12-17 a $\hat{y} = 19.75 - 0.08346(10) = 18.9154$ **b** (1) $\hat{y} = 19.75 - 0.08346(117.22) = 9.9668$
12-19 a A weak positive linear relationship. **b** $r = 0.6239$; because $t = 2.2580 < 3.3554$, do not reject H_0. **c** (1) $\hat{y} = 0.9772 + 0.0034(x)$
12-21 $r = 0.9963$; because $t = 34.7774 > 2.2622$, reject H_0.
12-23 a $\hat{y} = 1,096.7502 + 4.6585(x)$ **b** Because $-2.3060 < 0.7846 < 2.3060$, do not reject H_0. **c** Type II
12-25 a A positive linear relationship. **b** $r = 0.7658$ **c** $\hat{y} = -7203.81 + 185.3649(x)$ **d** $\hat{y} = \$17,449.7217$; residual $= 20278 - 17,449.7217 = 2,828.2783$ **e** Because $F = 39.6979 > 7.6357$, reject H_0.
12-27 a A positive linear relationship. **b** $r = 0.2283$ **c** $\hat{y} = 4.5225 + 0.0000001239(x)$; because p-value $= 0.20135 > .05$, do not reject H_0.
12-29 a The p-value $= 0.0000 < 0.10$, therefore reject H_0.
b $0.7925 —— 1.0573$; it does contain 1.
12-31 a $-17858.6143 —— -17853.3857$

b $1.7341(6.6677)\sqrt{\dfrac{1}{20} + \dfrac{(80 - 67.2)^2}{145,789}} = 2.614339$

12-33 b $400.48 —— 1623.52$ **c** $249.38 —— 762.71$
12-35 a $\hat{y} = -4.7933 + 1.0488x$ **b** $\hat{y} = 100.09$ **c** $82.2671 —— 117.9129$ **d** $95.0939 —— 105.0861$
12-37 a $\hat{y} = 18.8378$ **b** Confidence interval lower limit $= 16.25832354$; confidence interval upper limit $= 21.10019247$ **c** Prediction interval lower limit $= 12.33289554$; prediction interval upper limit $= 25.02562048$ **f** The confidence interval is found by finding the confidence interval of the slope coefficient and multiplying it by the difference in weight. The lower 90% $= 13.3 \times 135.318 = 1799.73$, the upper 90% $= 13.3 \times 235.412 = 3130.98$
12-41 The student is correct.
12-45 a A positive linear relationship **b** 0.9389 **c** Because $t = 11.57 > 2.1009$, reject H_0.
12-47 Because $1.9082 < 2.3376$, do not reject H_0.
12-49 a $0.0148 —— 0.0152$ **b** No **c** Because $122.95 > 1.98$, reject H_0.

12-51 b $\hat{y} = 1219.8035 + (-9.1196)(x)$ **c** Lower 90%: $25 \times -22.7314 = -568.285$; upper 90%: $25 \times 4.4922 = 112.305$ **d** Because $F = 1.5 < 5.117$, do not reject H_O.

12-53 a A possible positive linear relationship **b** $\hat{y} = 66.7111 + 10.6167(x)$

12-55 a 0.7059 **b** Because $t = 3.8598 > 1.3406$, reject H_O.

12-57 Multiplying 0.0002385 ——— 0.0008175 by 10,000 gives: 2.385 ——— 8.175

12-59 a Lower 95%: $50 \times 7.5673 = 378.365$; upper 95%: $50 \times 11.8416 = 592.08$ **b** No **c** Confidence interval lower limit = 2115.458156; confidence interval upper limit = 2687.465486

12-61 a 105.7397 ——— 116.2603 **b** 87.2979 ——— 134.7021

12-63 3.4358 ——— 3.4922

CHAPTER 13

13-1 a Holding x_2 constant and increasing x_1 by one unit, the average y is estimated to increase by 4.14 units. $b_2 = 8.72$. This implies that, holding x_1 constant and increasing x_2 by one unit, the average y is estimated to increase by 4.14 units. **b** 107.71

13-3 a $\hat{y} = 10.437 + 1.3108x_1$ **b** $\hat{y} = -29.83 + 3.500x_2$
c $\hat{y} = -21.82 + 0.7513x_1 + 2.4357x_2$

13-5 No

13-7 a Excel Output

	Calls Received	Ads Placed Previous Week	Calls Received the Previous Week	Airline Bookings
Calls Received	1			
Ads Placed Previous Week	0.5843589	1		
Calls Received the Previous Week	0.654483	0.709017466	1	
Airline Bookings	0.5339732	0.360694798	0.219988054	1

b Calls Received − Ads Placed Previous Week—indicates a weak positive linear relationship; Calls Received − Calls Received Previous Week—indicates a weak positive linear relationship; Calls Received − Airline Bookings—indicates a weak positive linear relationship. A multiple regression model is possible, but the relations are not strong.
c $\hat{y} = -93.0196 + 36.0196$ (Ads); $\hat{y} = -18.3280 + 1.0679$ (Calls); $\hat{y} = 27.4730 + 0.1206$ (Bookings) **d** The second model has the largest F-value, the highest R^2, and the smallest s^2.

13-9 a A positive linear relationship between team win/loss percentage and attendance; a positive linear relationship between opponent win/loss percentage and attendance; a positive linear relationship between games played and attendance; no relationship between temperature and game attendance. **b** A significant relationship between game attendance and team win/loss percentage and games played. Therefore, a multiple regression model could be effective.
c Excel output

	Coefficients	Standard Error	t-Stat	p-value
Intercept	14122.24086	4335.791765	3.25713079	0.007637823
Team Win/Loss %	63.15325348	14.93880137	4.227464568	0.001418453
Opponent Win/Loss %	10.09582009	14.31396102	0.705312811	0.49528028
Games Played	31.50621796	177.129782	0.177870811	0.862057676
Temperature	−55.4609057	62.09372861	−0.89318047	0.390882768

d 77.53% **e** p-value = 0.00143, conclude the overall model is significant. **f** For team win/loss percentage the p-value = 0.0014 < 0.08 significant; for opponent win/loss percentage the p-value = 0.4953 > 0.08 not significant; for games played the p-value = 0.8621 > 0.08 not significant; for temperature the p-value = 0.3909 > 0.08 not significant **g** 1184.1274

h

	VIF
Team win/loss percentage and all other x	1.57
Temperature and all other x	1.96
Games played and all other x	1.31428258
Opponent win/loss percentage and all other x	1.50934547

The low VIF values indicate multicollinearity is not a problem.
i Excel output

	Lower 95%	Upper 95%
Intercept	4579.222699	23665.25902
Team Winn/Loss %	30.27315672	96.03335024
Opponent Win/Loss %	−21.40901163	41.6006518
Games Played	−358.3540008	421.3664367
Temperature	−192.12835	81.20653863

13-11 a 3 **b** $y = \beta_0 + \beta_1 x_1 + \beta_2 x_2 + \beta_3 x_3 + \beta_4 x_4 + \varepsilon$; $x_1 = \{1$ for level 1, 0 otherwise$\}$; $x_2 = \{1$ for level 2, 0 otherwise$\}$; $x_3 = \{1$ for level 3, 0 otherwise$\}$

13-13 $x_4 = 1$ if gas water heater, 0 otherwise; $x_5 = 1$ if constructed before 1974, 0 otherwise; $y = \beta_0 + \beta_1 x_1 + \beta_2 x_2 + \beta_3 x_3 + \beta_4 x_4 + \beta_5 x_5 + \varepsilon$

13-17 a $x_2 = 1$ if manufacturing, 0 otherwise; $x_3 = 1$ if service, 0 otherwise; $\hat{y} = -586.2556 + 22.8611(x_1) + 2302.2670(x_2) + 1869.8130(x_3)$
b $F = 5.3934 > 4.3468$ the model is significant **c** p-value for hours = 0.4613 **d** $\hat{y} = 71 + 2689(x_2) + 2127(x_3)$ **e** 495.8326 ——— 4882.16

13-19 b $\hat{y} = 9.398 + 0.5181x$. Not significant. **c** $\hat{y} = -5.445 + 3.8509x - 0.14793x^2$ not significant; better R^2.

13-21 b $\hat{y} = 4.937 + 1.2643x$ significant **c** $\hat{y} = -25.155 + 18.983 \ln x$ significant; better fit

13-23 a $\hat{y} = 2902.965 + 12.263x$; $\hat{y} = -1070.398 + 293.483x - 4.536x^2$ **b** The simple linear model is not a significant model; the 2nd order model is a significant model. **c** No. **d** The 2nd order model

13-25 a $\hat{y} = 5.9023 + 2.8426x - 0.8049x^2$ **b** $r = 0.9477$ significant
c $\hat{y} = -4.9533 + 3.8123x$ **d** The nonlinear model was shown in part a and has a higher R-square.

13-27 a Price = $207311.77 - 2192.3367$ (age) + 6.8385 (age sq)
c Price = $205722.97 - 1856.76$ (age)

13-29 a

	y	x_1	x_2
x_1	−0.088		
	0.765		
x_2	0.062	−0.366	
	0.834	0.198	
x_3	0.383	−0.128	0.129
	0.176	0.664	0.660

Cell Contents: Pearson correlation, p-value
b $\hat{y} = 26.19 + 0.42x_3$ with a high alpha to enter. **c** $\hat{y} = 27.9 - 0.035x_1 - 0.002x_2 + 0.412x_3$

13-31 a $\hat{y} = -18.33 + 1.07x_2$ **b** There is one independent variable (x_2) and one dependent variable (y).

13-33 a Team win/loss percentage **b** Only one step occurred in this model. **c** No other variables are significant. **d** The model is significant with a p-value of 3.2237E-05. The team win/loss percentage is significant with a p-value of 3.2237E-05.

13-35 a $\hat{y} = 5.494 + 1.2213x$ **b** Yes. p-value = 0.002

c

RESI1	SRES1
−7.82146	−2.07346
3.51475	0.85039
5.40844	1.20642
2.52340	0.55140
0.63835	0.14135
−3.46796	−0.82305
−0.79552	−0.23246

No significant evidence.

13-37 a $\hat{y} = 16.928 + 0.286x$ **b** No

c

RESIDUAL OUTPUT

Observation	Predicted y	Residuals	Standard Residuals
1	21.49957134	−6.499571341	−0.594099288
2	22.35676669	−2.356766687	−0.215422424
3	23.7854256	4.214574403	0.385237044
4	24.92835273	−9.928352725	−0.907510199
5	26.07127985	8.928720147	0.816137866
6	27.49993876	−7.499938763	−0.685538791
7	29.21432945	25.78567055	2.356962899
8	34.07176975	−9.071769749	−0.829213446
9	37.21481935	−5.214819351	−0.476665352
10	38.35774648	1.642253521	0.150111691

Perhaps increasing variance.

13-41 a Excel output

	Coefficients	Standard Error	t Stat	p-value
Intercept	14122.24086	4335.791765	3.25713079	0.0076378
Team Win/Loss Percentage	63.15325348	14.93880137	4.227464568	0.0014185
Opponent Win/Loss Percentage	10.09582009	14.31396102	0.705312811	0.4952803
Games Played	31.50621796	177.129782	0.177870811	0.8620577
Temperature	−55.4609057	62.09372861	−0.89318047	0.3908828

c The plot of residuals does not appear to have a pattern, therefore the constant variance assumption has apparently not been violated. **d** The plot of the residuals against time shows a systematic variation about zero, indicating that the residuals are dependent. **e** Based on the normal probability plot, which is almost a straight line, we can assume the model error terms are approximately normally distributed.

13-43 a The residuals do not exhibit a constant variance. When Days^2 is small the variance of the residuals is large and decreases as Days^2 increases. **b** The residuals seem to possess a normal distribution. **c** Within 1 standard deviation = 9/16 = 56.25%; within 2 standard deviations = 16/16 = 100%; within 3 standard deviations = 16/16 = 100%; because there are 68.75% within one standard deviation and 100% within two standard deviations, the residuals appear to be normally distributed.

13-51 Excel output

	Coefficients	Standard Error	t Stat	p-value
Intercept	21.48048774	10.53116151	2.039707	0.066137
Case Analysis Score	2.363993584	1.183937188	1.996722	0.071203
Written Presentation Score	1.531347982	1.773536135	0.863443	0.406327
Oral Presentation Score	3.807380091	2.493027189	1.527212	0.154937

13-53 a The calculated F is 16.6931 > 3.5874, so conclude that the overall regression model is significant. **b** Improve oral presentation skills because this is the most highly correlated of the three independent variables.

13-55 a The R^2 is 0.8199. This factor is measured by SSR/TSS. **b** Job rating $= 21.4805 + 2.3640(9.1) + 1.5313(9.4) + 3.8074(9.3) = 92.7959$ **c** -2.3722 ———— 5.4349; effect could be 0 because this interval contains 0.

13-57 a $R^2 = 0.8448$; because $F = 13.6076 > 3.4780$, conclude that the overall model is significant.

b

	Coefficients	Lower 95%	Upper 95%
Intercept	-125307.8062	-194563.0421	-56052.6
Pages x_1	175.8963214	87.28373715	264.5089
Competing Books x_2	-1573.777885	-6020.812614	2873.257
Advertising Budget x_3	1.591706487	0.601381026	2.582032
Age of Author x_4	1613.747496	221.1082826	3006.387

c The critical t-value would be ±2.2281.

	Coefficients	Standard Error	t Stat	p-value
Intercept	-125307.8062	31082.09519	-4.031510921	0.002393684
Pages x_1	175.8963214	39.76976966	4.422864977	0.001288354
Competing Books x_2	-1573.777885	1995.851361	-0.788524595	0.448679286
Advertising Budget x_3	1.591706487	0.444463005	3.581190042	0.005001797
Age of Author x_4	1613.747496	625.0234231	2.581899232	0.027327123

Competing books not significant.

d The interval is: $175.8963 \pm 2.2281(39.7698)$; 87.2852 ———— 264.5074

13-59 There appears to be a negative linear relationship between age and purchases; there appears to be a slight positive linear relationship between purchases and family income; based on the scatter plot it is difficult to detect any pattern of relationship between family size and purchases; there does not appear to be any relationship between age and family income; there appears to be a slightly positive linear relationship between age and family size; there seems to be little correlation between income and family size.

13-61 It had the highest correlation with average monthly purchases.

13-63 The interval is: $0.000329 - 0.003653$.

13-65 Issues to address: (1) Did the adjusted R^2 increase?; (2) Did the standard error decrease?; (3) For a model that will be used for forecasting purposes, is the added variable significant?; (4) Does the introduction of the new variable into the model introduce a high level of multicollinearity?

13-73 $x_7 = 1$ if NYSE, 0 otherwise, $x_8 = 1$ if NASDAQ, 0 otherwise; if both are 0, the designation is OTC.

Excel output

	Growth %	Sales	EPS	Profits	Last Yr Price	P/E Ratio	x_7	x_8	Stk-Price
Growth %	1								
Sales	-0.09866	1							
EPS	0.358471	-0.15644	1						
Profits	-0.1172	0.744225	-0.01751	1					
Last Yr Price	-0.16851	0.505016	0.214602	0.668754	1				
P/E ratio	0.00722	0.27566	0.150827	0.1032	0.0857454	1			
x_7	0.006398	0.209664	-0.03129	0.143019	0.2176906	-0.10315	1		
x_8	-0.09525	-0.09168	-0.22298	-0.07548	0.00200916	0.09867	-0.16479	1	
Stk-Price	-0.07107	0.201503	0.447163	0.507966	0.65544737	0.306452	0.024908	-0.07927	1

The best predictors would be the ones most highly correlated with the stock price.

GLOSSARY

Adjusted R-squared—A measure of the percentage of explained variation in the dependent variable that takes into account the relationship between the sample size and the number of independent variables in the regression model.

Aggregate Price Index—An index that is used to measure the rate of change from a base period for a group of two or more items.

All-inclusive classes—A set of classes that contains all the possible data values.

Alternative hypothesis—The hypothesis that includes all population values not covered by the null hypothesis. The alternative hypothesis is deemed to be true if the null hypothesis is rejected.

Aptness—The degree to which a regression model satisfies the basic assumptions of multiple regression, including the following.
1. The relationship between the dependent and independent variables is linear.
2. The variance of the model errors is constant over the range of the values of the independent variables.
3. The model errors are independent from observation to observation.
4. The model errors are normally distributed.

Arithmetic mean, or average—The sum of all the values divided by the number of values.

Autocorrelation—Correlation of the error terms (residuals) occurs when the residuals at successive points in time are related.

Average—The sum of all the values divided by the number of values.

Balanced design—An experiment has a balanced design if the factor levels have equal sample sizes.

Bar chart—A graphical representation of a categorical data set in which a rectangle or bar is drawn over each category or class. The length of each bar represents the frequency or percentage of observations, or some other measure associated with the category. The bars may be vertical or horizontal. The bars may all be the same color or they may be different colors depicting different categories. Additionally, multiple variables can be graphed on the same bar chart.

Base period index—The time-series value to which all other values in the time series are compared. The index number for the base period is defined as 100.

Between-sample variation—Dispersion among the factor sample means is called the *between-sample variation*.

Binomial probability distribution characteristics—A distribution that gives the probability of x successes in n trials in a process that meets the following conditions.
1. A trial has only two possible outcomes: a success or a failure.
2. There is a fixed number, n, of identical trials.
3. The trials of the experiment are independent of each other. This means that if one outcome is a success, this does not influence the chance of another outcome being a success.

4. The process must be consistent in generating successes and failures. That is, the probability, p, associated with a success remains constant from trial to trial.
5. If p represents the probability of a success, then $(1 - p) = q$ is the probability of a failure.

Box and whisker plot—A graph that is composed of two parts: a box and the whiskers. The box has a width that ranges from the first quartile to the third quartile. The whiskers extend to the right and to the left of the box a distance of 1.5 times the distance between the first and third quartiles. A vertical line through the box is placed at the median.

Business statistics—A collection of tools and techniques that are used to convert data into meaningful information in a business environment.

Census—An enumeration of the entire set of measurements taken from the whole population.

Central limit theorem—For simple random samples of n observations taken from a population with mean μ and standard deviation σ, regardless of the population's distribution, provided the sample size is sufficiently large, the distribution of the sample means, $\bar{x}$, will be approximately normal with a mean equal to the population mean $(\mu_{\bar{x}} = \mu)$ and a standard deviation equal to the population standard deviation divided by the square root of the sample size $\left(\sigma_{\bar{x}} = \dfrac{\sigma}{\sqrt{n}} \right)$. The larger the sample size, the better the approximation to the normal distribution.

Certainty—A decision environment in which the results of selecting each alternative are known before the decision is made.

Class boundaries—The upper and lower values of each class.

Class width—The distance between the lowest possible value and the highest possible value for a frequency class.

Classical probability assessment—The method of determining probability based on the ratio of the number of ways the event of interest can occur to the number of ways *any* event can occur when the individual elementary events are equally likely.

Closed-end questions—Questions that require the respondent to select from a short list of defined choices.

Cluster sampling—A method by which the population is divided into groups, or clusters, that are each intended to be mini-populations. A simple random sample of m clusters is selected. The items selected from a cluster can be selected using any probability sampling technique.

Coefficient of determination—The portion of the total variation in the dependent variable that is explained by its relationship with the independent variable. The coefficient of determination is also called R-squared and is denoted as R^2.

Coefficient of partial determination—The measure of the marginal contribution of each independent variable, given that other independent variables are in the model.

Coefficient of variation—The ratio of the standard deviation to the mean expressed as a percentage. The coefficient of variation is used to measure the relative variation in data.

Completely randomized design—An experiment is completely randomized if it consists of the independent random selection of observations representing each level of one factor.

Composite model—The model that contains both the basic terms and the interaction terms.

Conditional probability—The probability that an event will occur *given* that some other event has already happened.

Confidence coefficient—The confidence level divided by 100%—that is, the decimal equivalent of a confidence level.

Confidence interval—An interval developed from sample values such that if all possible intervals of a given width were constructed, a percentage of these intervals, known as the confidence level, would include the true population parameter.

Confidence level—A percentage less than 100 that corresponds to the percentage of all possible confidence intervals, based on a given sample size, that will contain the true population parameter.

Contingency table—A table used to classify sample observations according to two or more identifiable characteristics. It is also called a *cross-tabulation table*.

Continuous data—Data whose possible values are uncountable and which may assume any value in an interval.

Continuous random variables—Random variables that can assume any value in an interval.

Convenience sampling—A sampling technique that selects the items from the population based on accessibility and ease of selection.

Correlation coefficient—A quantitative measure of the strength of the linear relationship between two variables. The correlation ranges from -1.0 to $+1.0$. A correlation of ±1.0 indicates a perfect linear relationship, whereas a correlation of 0 indicates no linear relationship.

Correlation matrix—A table showing the pairwise correlations between all variables (dependent and independent).

Critical value—The value of a statistic corresponding to a given significance level. This cutoff value determines the boundary between those samples resulting in a test statistic that leads to rejecting the null hypothesis and those that lead to a decision not to reject the null hypothesis.

Cross-sectional data—A set of data values observed at a fixed point in time.

Cumulative frequency distribution—A summary of a set of data that displays the number of observations with values less than or equal to the upper limit of each of its classes.

Cumulative relative frequency distribution—A summary of a set of data that displays the proportion of observations with values less than or equal to the upper limit of each of its classes.

Cyclical component—A wave-like pattern within the time series that repeats itself throughout the time series and has a recurrence period of more than one year.

Data array—Data that have been sorted in ascending or descending order.

Decision tree—A diagram that illustrates the correct ordering of actions and events in a decision-analysis problem. Each act or event is represented by a branch on the decision tree.

Degrees of freedom—The number of independent data values available to estimate the population's standard deviation. If k parameters must be estimated before the population's standard deviation can be calculated from a sample of size n, the degrees of freedom are equal to $n - k$.

Demographic questions—Questions relating to the respondents' own characteristics, backgrounds, and attributes.

Dependent events—Two events are dependent if the occurrence of one event impacts the probability of the other event occurring.

Dependent variable—A variable whose values are thought to be a function of, or dependent on, the values of another variable called the *independent variable*. On a scatter plot, the dependent variable is placed on the y axis and is often called the response variable.

Discrete data—Data whose possible values are countable.

Discrete random variable—A random variable that can assume only a countable number of possible values.

Dummy variables—A variable that is assigned a value equal to either zero or one, depending on whether the observation possesses a given characteristic.

Elementary events—The most rudimentary outcomes resulting from a simple experiment.

Equal-width classes—The distance between the lowest possible value and the highest possible value in each class is equal for all classes.

Event—A collection of elementary events.

Expected value—The mean of a discrete probability distribution. The average value when the experiment that generates values for the random variable is repeated over the long run.

Expected-value criterion—A decision criterion that employs probability to select the alternative that will produce the greatest average payoff or minimum average loss.

Experiment—A process that produces a single outcome whose result cannot be predicted with certainty.

Experimental design—A plan for performing an experiment in which the variable of interest is defined. One or more factors are identified to be manipulated or changed so that the impact (or influence) on the variable of interest can be measured or observed.

Experiment-wide error rate—The proportion of experiments in which at least one of the set of confidence intervals constructed does not contain the true value of the population parameter being estimated.

Exponential smoothing—A time-series and forecasting technique that produces an exponentially weighted moving average in which each smoothing calculation or forecast is dependent on all previous observed values.

Factor—A quantity under examination in an experiment as a possible cause of variation in the response variable.

Forecasting horizon—The number of future periods covered by a forecast. It is sometimes referred to as *forecast lead time*.

Forecasting interval—The frequency with which new forecasts are prepared.

Forecasting period—The unit of time for which forecasts are to be made.

Frequency distribution—A summary of a set of data that displays the number of observations in each of the distribution's distinct categories or classes.

Frequency histogram—A graph of a frequency distribution with the horizontal axis showing the classes, the vertical axis showing the frequency count, and (for equal class widths) the rectangles having a height equal to the frequency in each class.

Independent events—Two events are independent if the occurrence of one event in no way influences the probability of the occurrence of the other event.

Independent samples—Samples selected from two or more populations in such a way that the occurrence of values in one sample has no influence on the probability of the occurrence of values in the other sample(s).

Independent variable—A variable whose values are thought to impact the values of the *dependent variable*. The independent variable, or explanatory variable, is often within the direct control of the decision maker. On a scatter plot, the independent variable, or explanatory variable, is graphed on the x axis.

Interaction—The case in which one independent variable (such as x_2) affects the relationship between another independent variable (x_1) and a dependent variable (y).

Interquartile range—The interquartile range is a measure of variation that is determined by computing the difference between the third and first quartiles.

Least squares criterion—The criterion for determining a regression line that minimizes the sum of squared residuals.

Left-skewed data—A data distribution is left skewed if the mean for the data is smaller than the median.

Levels—The categories, measurements, or strata of a factor of interest in the current experiment.

Line chart—A two-dimensional chart showing time on the horizontal axis and the variable of interest on the vertical axis.

Linear trend—A long-term increase or decrease in a time series in which the rate of change is relatively constant.

Margin of error—The amount that is added and subtracted to the point estimate to determine the endpoints of the confidence interval.

Maximax criterion—An optimistic decision criterion for dealing with uncertainty without using probability. For each option, the decision maker finds the maximum possible payoff and then selects the option with the greatest maximum payoff.

Maximin criterion—A pessimistic (conservative) decision criterion for dealing with uncertainty without using probability. For each option, the decision maker finds the minimum possible payoff and selects the option with the greatest minimum payoff.

Mean—A numerical measure of the center of a set of quantitative measures computed by dividing the sum of the values by the number of values in the data.

Median—The median is a center value that divides a data array into two halves. We use $\tilde{\mu}$ to denote the population median and M_d to denote the sample median.

Minimax regret criterion—A decision criterion that considers the results of selecting the "wrong" alternative. For each state of nature, the decision maker finds the difference between the best payoff and each other alternative and uses these values to construct an opportunity-loss table. The decision maker then selects the alternative with the minimum opportunity loss (or regret).

Mode—The mode is the value in a data set that occurs most frequently.

Model—A representation of an actual system using either a physical or a mathematical portrayal.

Model diagnosis—The process of determining how well a model fits past data and how well the model's assumptions appear to be satisfied.

Model fitting—The process of determining how well a specified model fits past data.

Model specification—The process of selecting the forecasting technique to be used in a particular situation.

Moving averages—The successive averages of n consecutive values in a time series.

Multicollinearity—A high correlation between two independent variables such that the two variables contribute redundant information to the model. When highly correlated independent variables are included in the regression model, they can adversely affect the regression results.

Mutually exclusive classes—Classes that do not overlap so that a data value can be placed in only one class.

Mutually exclusive events—Two events are mutually exclusive if the occurrence of one event precludes the occurrence of the other event.

Nonstatistical sampling techniques—Those methods of selecting samples using convenience, judgment, or other nonchance processes.

Normal distribution—The normal distribution is a bell-shaped distribution with the following properties:

1. It is *unimodal*; that is, the normal distribution peaks at a single value.
2. It is *symmetrical*; this means that the two areas under the curve between the mean and any two points equidistant on either side of the mean are identical. One side of the distribution is the mirror image of the other side.
3. The mean, median, and mode are equal.
4. The normal approaches the horizontal axis on either side of the mean toward plus and minus infinity ($\pm\infty$). In more formal terms, the normal distribution is *asymptotic* to the x-axis.
5. The amount of variation in the random variable determines the width of the normal distribution.

Null hypothesis—The statement about the population value that will be tested. The null hypothesis will be rejected only if the sample data provide substantial contradictory evidence.

One-tailed test—A hypothesis test in which the entire rejection region is located in one tail of the sampling distribution. In a one-tailed test, the entire alpha level is located in one tail of the distribution.

One-way analysis of variance—An analysis of variance design in which independent samples are obtained from k levels of a single factor for the purpose of testing whether the k levels have equal means.

Open-end questions—Questions that allow respondents the freedom to respond with any value, words, or statements of their own choosing.

Opportunity loss—The difference between the actual payoff that occurs for a decision and the optimal payoff for the same state of nature.

Paired samples—Samples that are selected in such a way that values in one sample are matched with the values in the second sample for the purpose of controlling for extraneous factors. Another term for paired samples is dependent samples.

Parameter—A measure computed from the entire population. As long as the population does not change, the value of the parameter will not change.

Pareto principle—80% of the trouble comes from 20% of the causes.

Payoff—The outcome (profit or loss) for any combination of alternative and state of nature. The payoffs associated with all possible combinations of alternatives and states of nature constitute a *payoff table*.

Percentiles—The pth percentile in a data array is a value that divides the data set into two parts. The lower segment contains at least $p\%$, and the upper segment contains at least $(100 - p)\%$, of the data. The 50th percentile is the median.

Pie chart—A graph in the shape of a circle. The circle is divided into "slices" corresponding to the categories or classes to be displayed. The size of each slice is proportional to the magnitude of the displayed variable associated with each category or class.

Pilot sample—A sample taken from the population of interest of a size smaller than the anticipated sample size that is used to provide an estimate for the population standard deviation or population proportion.

Point estimate—A single number, determined from a sample, that is used to estimate the corresponding population parameter.

Population—The set of all objects or individuals of interest or the measurements obtained from all objects or individuals of interest.

Population proportion—The fraction of values in a population that have a specific attribute.

Power—The probability that the hypothesis test will reject the null hypothesis when the null hypothesis is false.

Probability—The chance that a particular event will occur. The probability of an event will be a value in the range 0 to 1. A value of 0 means the event will not occur. A probability of 1 means the event will occur. Anything between 0 and 1 reflects the uncertainty of the event occurring. The definition given is for a countable number of events.

p-Value—The probability (assuming the null hypothesis is true) of obtaining a test statistic at least as extreme as the test statistic we calculated from the sample. The p-value is also known as the *observed significance level*.

Qualitative data—Data whose measurement scale is inherently categorical.

Quantitative data—Measurements whose values are inherently numerical.

Quartiles—Quartiles in a data array are those values that divide the data set into four equal-sized groups. The median corresponds to the second quartile.

Random component—Changes in time-series data that are unpredictable and cannot be associated with a trend, seasonal, or cyclical component.

Random variable—A variable that assigns a numerical value to each outcome of a random experiment or trial.

Range—The range is a measure of variation that is computed by finding the difference between the maximum and minimum values in a data set.

Ratio data—Data that have all the characteristics of interval data but also have a true zero point (at which zero means "none").

Regression hyperplane—The multiple regression equivalent of the simple regression line. The plane has a different slope for each independent variable.

Regression slope coefficient—The average change in the dependent variable for a unit increase in the independent variable. The slope coefficient may be positive or negative, depending on the relationship between the two variables.

Relative frequency—The proportion of total observations that are in a given category. Relative frequency is computed by dividing the frequency in a category by the total number of observations. The relative frequencies can be converted to percentages by multiplying by 100.

Relative frequency of occurrence—The method that defines probability as the number of times an event occurs divided by the total number of times an experiment is performed in a large number of trials.

Research hypothesis—The hypothesis the decision maker attempts to demonstrate to be true. Because this is the hypothesis deemed to be the most important to the decision maker, it will not be declared true unless the sample data strongly indicate that it is true.

Residual (prediction error)—The distance between the y-coordinate of an (x,y) point and the estimate of that y-coordinate produced by the regression line.

Right-skewed data—A data distribution is right skewed if the mean for the data is larger than the median.

Sample—A subset of the population.

Sample space—The collection of all elementary outcomes that can result from a selection, decision, or experiment.

Sampling distribution—A distribution of the possible values of a statistic for a given-size random sample selected from a population.

Sampling error—The difference between a value (a statistic) computed from a sample and the corresponding value (a parameter) computed from the population.

Scatter diagram—A two-dimensional graph of plotted points in which the vertical axis represents values of one variable and the horizontal axis represents values of the other. Each plotted point has coordinates whose values are obtained from the respective variables.

Scatter plot—A two-dimensional plot showing the values for the joint occurrence of two variables. The scatter plot may be used to graphically represent the relationship between two variables. It is also known as a scatter diagram.

Seasonal component—A wave-like pattern that is repeated throughout a time series and has a recurrence period of at most one year.

Seasonal index—A number used to quantify the effect of seasonality in time-series data.

Seasonally unadjusted forecast—A forecast made for seasonal data that does not include an adjustment for the seasonal component in the time series.

Significance level—The maximum allowable probability of committing a Type I statistical error. The probability is denoted by the symbol α.

Simple random sample—A sample selected in such a manner that each possible sample of a given size has an equal chance of being selected.

Skewed data—Data sets that are not symmetric. For skewed data, the mean will be larger or smaller than the median.

Spurious correlation—When a correlation exists between two seemingly unrelated variables, the correlation is said to be a spurious correlation.

Standard deviation—The standard deviation is the positive square root of the variance.

Standard normal distribution—A normal distribution that has a mean = 0 and a standard deviation =1. The horizontal axis is scaled in z-values that measure the number of standard deviations a point is from the mean. Values above the mean have positive z-values. Values below the mean have negative z-values.

Standardized data values—The number of standard deviations a value is from the mean. Standardized data values are sometimes referred to as z-scores.

States of nature—The possible outcomes in a decision situation over which the decision maker has no control.

Statistic—A measure computed from a sample that has been selected from a population. The value of the statistic will depend on which sample is selected.

Statistical inference tools—Tools that allow a decision maker to reach a conclusion about a population of data based on a subset of data from the population.

Statistical sampling techniques—Those sampling methods that use selection techniques based on chance selection.

Stratified random sampling—A statistical sampling method in which the population is divided into subgroups called *strata* so that each population item belongs to only one stratum. The objective is to form strata such that the population values of interest within each stratum are as much alike as possible. Sample items are selected from each stratum using the simple random sampling method.

Structured interview—Interviews in which the questions are scripted.

Student's *t*-distribution—A family of distributions that is bell-shaped and symmetric like the standard normal distribution but with greater area in the tails. Each distribution in the *t*-family is defined by its degrees of freedom. As the degrees of freedom increase, the *t*-distribution approaches the normal distribution.

Subjective probability assessment—The method that defines probability of an event as reflecting a decision maker's state of mind regarding the chances that the particular event will occur.

Symmetric data—Data sets whose values are evenly spread around the center. For symmetric data, the mean and median are equal.

Systematic random sampling—A statistical sampling technique that involves selecting every kth item in the population after a randomly selected starting point between 1 and k. The value of k is determined as the ratio of the population size over the desired sample size.

Tchebysheff's theorem—Regardless of how data are distributed, *at least* $(1 - 1/k^2)$ of the values will fall within k standard deviations of the mean.

Test statistic—A function of the sampled observations that provides a basis for testing a statistical hypothesis.

Time-series data—A set of ordered data values observed at successive points in time.

Total quality management—A journey to excellence in which everyone in the organization is focused on continuous process improvement directed toward increased customer satisfaction.

Total variation—The aggregate dispersion of the individual data values across the various factor levels is called the *total variation* in the data.

Two-tailed test—A hypothesis test in which the entire rejection region is split into the two tails of the sampling distribution. In a two-tailed test, the alpha level is typically split evenly between the two tails.

Type I error—*Rejecting* the null hypothesis when it is, in fact, true.

Type II error—*Failing to reject* the null hypothesis when it is, in fact, false.

Unbiased estimator—A characteristic of certain statistics in which the average of all possible values of the sample statistic equals a parameter.

Uncertainty—A decision environment in which the decision maker does not know what outcome will occur when an alternative is selected.

Unstructured interview—Interviews that begin with one or more broadly stated questions, with further questions being based on the responses.

Variance—The population variance is the average of the squared distances of the data values from the mean.

Variance inflation factor—A measure of how much the variance of an estimated regression coefficient increases if the independent variables are correlated. A VIF equal to 1.0 for a given independent variable indicates that this independent variable is not correlated with the remaining independent variables in the model. The greater the multicollinearity, the larger the VIF.

Variation—A set of data exhibits variation if all the data are not the same value.

Weighted mean—The mean value of data values that have been weighted according to their relative importance.

Within-sample variation—The dispersion that exists among the data values within a particular factor level is called the *within-sample variation*.

INDEX

Values of t for Selected Probabilities

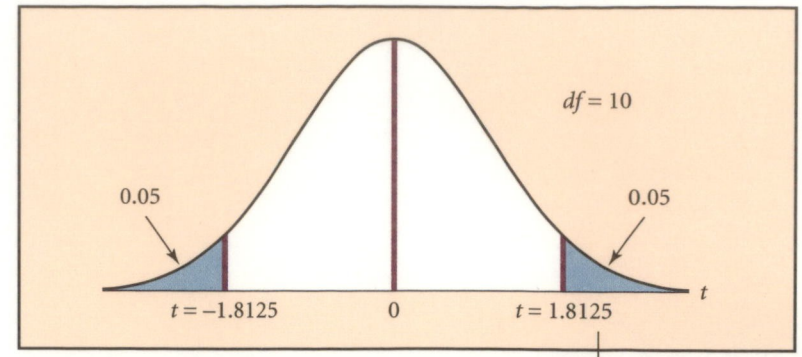

Probabilites (Or Areas Under t-Distribution Curve)

Conf. Level	0.1	0.3	0.5	0.7	0.8	0.9	0.95	0.98	0.99
One Tail	0.45	0.35	0.25	0.15	0.1	0.05	0.025	0.01	0.005
Two Tails	0.9	0.7	0.5	0.3	0.2	0.1	0.05	0.02	0.01
d.f.					*Values of t*				
1	0.1584	0.5095	1.0000	1.9626	3.0777	6.3137	12.7062	31.8210	63.6559
2	0.1421	0.4447	0.8165	1.3862	1.8856	2.9200	4.3027	6.9645	9.9250
3	0.1366	0.4242	0.7649	1.2498	1.6377	2.3534	3.1824	4.5407	5.8408
4	0.1338	0.4142	0.7407	1.1896	1.5332	2.1318	2.7765	3.7469	4.6041
5	0.1322	0.4082	0.7267	1.1558	1.4759	2.0150	2.5706	3.3649	4.0321
6	0.1311	0.4043	0.7176	1.1342	1.4398	1.9432	2.4469	3.1427	3.7074
7	0.1303	0.4015	0.7111	1.1192	1.4149	1.8946	2.3646	2.9979	3.4995
8	0.1297	0.3995	0.7064	1.1081	1.3968	1.8595	2.3060	2.8965	3.3554
9	0.1293	0.3979	0.7027	1.0997	1.3830	1.8331	2.2622	2.8214	3.2498
10	0.1289	0.3966	0.6998	1.0931	1.3722	1.8125	2.2281	2.7638	3.1693
11	0.1286	0.3956	0.6974	1.0877	1.3634	1.7959	2.2010	2.7181	3.1058
12	0.1283	0.3947	0.6955	1.0832	1.3562	1.7823	2.1788	2.6810	3.0545
13	0.1281	0.3940	0.6938	1.0795	1.3502	1.7709	2.1604	2.6503	3.0123
14	0.1280	0.3933	0.6924	1.0763	1.3450	1.7613	2.1448	2.6245	2.9768
15	0.1278	0.3928	0.6912	1.0735	1.3406	1.7531	2.1315	2.6025	2.9467
16	0.1277	0.3923	0.6901	1.0711	1.3368	1.7459	2.1199	2.5835	2.9208
17	0.1276	0.3919	0.6892	1.0690	1.3334	1.7396	2.1098	2.5669	2.8982
18	0.1274	0.3915	0.6884	1.0672	1.3304	1.7341	2.1009	2.5524	2.8784
19	0.1274	0.3912	0.6876	1.0655	1.3277	1.7291	2.0930	2.5395	2.8609
20	0.1273	0.3909	0.6870	1.0640	1.3253	1.7247	2.0860	2.5280	2.8453
21	0.1272	0.3906	0.6864	1.0627	1.3232	1.7207	2.0796	2.5176	2.8314
22	0.1271	0.3904	0.6858	1.0614	1.3212	1.7171	2.0739	2.5083	2.8188
23	0.1271	0.3902	0.6853	1.0603	1.3195	1.7139	2.0687	2.4999	2.8073
24	0.1270	0.3900	0.6848	1.0593	1.3178	1.7109	2.0639	2.4922	2.7970
25	0.1269	0.3898	0.6844	1.0584	1.3163	1.7081	2.0595	2.4851	2.7874
26	0.1269	0.3896	0.6840	1.0575	1.3150	1.7056	2.0555	2.4786	2.7787
27	0.1268	0.3894	0.6837	1.0567	1.3137	1.7033	2.0518	2.4727	2.7707
28	0.1268	0.3893	0.6834	1.0560	1.3125	1.7011	2.0484	2.4671	2.7633
29	0.1268	0.3892	0.6830	1.0553	1.3114	1.6991	2.0452	2.4620	2.7564
30	0.1267	0.3890	0.6828	1.0547	1.3104	1.6973	2.0423	2.4573	2.7500
40	0.1265	0.3881	0.6807	1.0500	1.3031	1.6839	2.0211	2.4233	2.7045
50	0.1263	0.3875	0.6794	1.0473	1.2987	1.6759	2.0086	2.4033	2.6778
60	0.1262	0.3872	0.6786	1.0455	1.2958	1.6706	2.0003	2.3901	2.6603
70	0.1261	0.3869	0.6780	1.0442	1.2938	1.6669	1.9944	2.3808	2.6479
80	0.1261	0.3867	0.6776	1.0432	1.2922	1.6641	1.9901	2.3739	2.6387
90	0.1260	0.3866	0.6772	1.0424	1.2910	1.6620	1.9867	2.3685	2.6316
100	0.1260	0.3864	0.6770	1.0418	1.2901	1.6602	1.9840	2.3642	2.6259
250	0.1258	0.3858	0.6755	1.0386	1.2849	1.6510	1.9695	2.3414	2.5956
500	0.1257	0.3855	0.6750	1.0375	1.2832	1.6479	1.9647	2.3338	2.5857
∞					See Normal Distribution				

Fourth Edition

HUMAN RESOURCE MANAGEMENT

An Experiential Approach

H. John Bernardin
Department of Management, International Business, and Entrepreneurship
Florida Atlantic University

McGraw-Hill
Irwin

Boston   Burr Ridge, IL   Dubuque, IA   Madison, WI   New York   San Francisco   St. Louis
Bangkok   Bogotá   Caracas   Kuala Lumpur   Lisbon   London   Madrid   Mexico City
Milan   Montreal   New Delhi   Santiago   Seoul   Singapore   Sydney   Taipei   Toronto

I dedicate this edition to pilot Hugh Thompson Jr. who died in 2006. William Eckhardt, who served as chief prosecutor for the My Lai courts-martial said this about Thompson: "When you have evil, sometimes, in the midst of it, you will have incredible, selfless good. And that's Hugh Thompson."

John Bernardin (January 7, 2006)

HUMAN RESOURCE MANAGEMENT: AN EXPERIENTIAL APPROACH

Published by McGraw-Hill/Irwin, a business unit of The McGraw-Hill Companies, Inc., 1221 Avenue of the Americas, New York, NY, 10020. Copyright © 2007 by The McGraw-Hill Companies, Inc. All rights reserved. No part of this publication may be reproduced or distributed in any form or by any means, or stored in a database or retrieval system, without the prior written consent of The McGraw-Hill Companies, Inc., including, but not limited to, in any network or other electronic storage or transmission, or broadcast for distance learning.

Some ancillaries, including electronic and print components, may not be available to customers outside the United States.

This book is printed on acid-free paper.

2 3 4 5 6 7 8 9 0 QPD/QPD 0 9 8 7

ISBN 978-0-07-298725-6
MHID 0-07-298725-1

Editorial director: *John E. Biernat*
Executive editor: *John Weimeister*
Editorial assistant: *Heather Darr*
Associate marketing manager: *Margaret A. Beamer*
Media producer: *Benjamin Curless*
Project manager: *Dana M. Pauley*
Production supervisor: *Debra R. Sylvester*
Coordinator freelance design: *Artemio Ortiz Jr.*
Media project manager: *Lynn M. Bluhm*
Cover design: *Pam Verros*
Typeface: *10/12 Times Roman*
Compositor: *GTS, New Delhi, India Campus*
Printer: *Quebecor World Dubuque Inc.*

Library of Congress Cataloging-in-Publication Data

Bernardin, H. John.
    Human resource management: an experiential approach / H. John Bernardin.—4th ed.
        p. cm.
    Includes bibliographical references and index.
    ISBN-13: 978-0-07-298725-6 (alk. paper)
    ISBN-10: 0-07-298725-1 (alk. paper)
    1. Personnel management—United States. I. Title.
HF5549.2.U5 B456 2007
658.3—dc22   2005057676

www.mhhe.com

ABOUT THE AUTHOR

H. John Bernardin is University Research Professor and the Adams Professor of Management in the College of Business at Florida Atlantic University in Boca Raton. He earned his Ph.D in industrial/organizational psychology from Bowling Green State University and is the former director of doctoral studies in I/O psychology at Virginia Tech. He is past Chair of the Division of Personnel/ Human Resources of The Academy of Management. Dr. Bernardin was editor of *Human Resource Management Review* and has served on the editorial boards of numerous journals, including the *Academy of Management Review, Human Resource Management Journal,* and the *Journal of Organizational Behavior.* He is the author of six books and over 100 articles related to human resource management. His paper on employment discrimination was cited as the best paper of the year by the Society of Human Resource Management. Dr. Bernardin has consulted for many of the most successful companies in the world and he has served as an expert witness in numerous employment discrimination lawsuits. He was denied stardom in the NHL because of that lame "no double runners" rule. He narrowly missed a Nobel Prize in 2006 for his "Put a penny in, take a penny out" invention.

PREFACE

The fourth edition of *Human Resource Management* continues with the dual goals of providing theoretical and experiential approaches to the study of human resource management while focusing on the enhancement of student competencies shown to be predictive of a student's ability to obtain and maintain employment. Students are given the conceptual background and content necessary to understand the relevant issues in HRM. In addition, they participate in individual and group exercises that require the application of chapter content to specific problems designed to develop critical personal competencies.

This new edition continues with the basic experiential approach but changes have been made to improve the text. First, more emphasis is placed on the implications of HRM issues and policies for general managers who apply HRM policy but also who have a profound effect on the success or failure of HRM. Second, more attention is paid to the implications of HRM for small business, where all HRM functions may rest with personnel also performing a myriad of other small business activities and with no formal training in HRM. I continue to point out discrepancies between HRM findings from research and the practice of HRM. I am happy to report that many of these discrepancies are closing as more HR specialists become aware of research on "high-performance work systems" and the growing body of literature linking particular HRM practices to corporate success.

Perhaps the most important improvement in the book is in the writing. An extra effort has been made to simplify and improve the writing and the transitions from chapter to chapter. This text remains the only HR book that attempts to directly link student learning experiences in HRM with assessed competencies judged by experts to be essential for graduating business students. Research on college of business graduates has been critical of the readiness of business graduates for work, noting deficiencies in a number of areas, including communication skills, analytical thinking, decision-making ability, and leadership potential. While other experiential texts are available, this is the first to attempt to provide adequate coverage of the subject matter in each of the vital areas of HRM while preparing the student to "learn by doing." This is also the first attempt among HRM texts to provide a research-based methodology for the assessment of the critical competencies and to provide a process by which students may evaluate the extent to which they have improved their competencies as they progress through the course.

All the experiential exercises in this book were designed to enhance some or all of the critical personal competencies in the context of HRM subject matter. Participation in experiential exercises requires the application of the HRM knowledge expected of practicing managers and HR generalists. The experiential exercises were developed so as to facilitate greater learning through class interaction and projects. There is usually an individual writing component to the exercise followed by group interaction and consensus building. A study by Dr. Richard Light at Harvard University found that this approach to education is superior to other pedagogical options. While it may have something to do with the particular way I lecture, my 30 years of experience in teaching strongly support Dr. Light's research.

Successful completion of these field-tested exercises, combined with the assessment processes described in Appendix C, should foster student development in all the areas experts believe to be critical in preparing business students for their first "real jobs."

Studies show that the majority of business graduates will ultimately manage or supervise employees. Research in this area shows that the two areas that prove to be the most challenging for managers are performance management and dealing with an increasingly diverse workforce in the context of equal employment opportunity law. My objective in this book is to emphasize knowledge and direct experience in these areas without compromising treatment of the other domains of HRM.

Procedures are available in this text to require students to evaluate their own performance and that of peer group members after completion of most of the experiential exercises. As discussed in Chapter 7 (Performance Management and Appraisal), this multirater approach provides more valid information about performance and a useful frame of reference for monitoring performance improvements. Research also shows that the more experience a person has had with the performance management process, the more effective that individual is in fulfilling this important managerial responsibility.

Exercises and discussion questions have been incorporated that require the student to consider equal employment opportunity laws in particular HRM contexts. So, unlike the standard HRM text that may cover EEO issues in one chapter, this book compels the student to weigh the EEO implications of HRM activities such as job analysis (Chapter 4), downsizing programs (Chapters 5 and 12), personnel selection processes (Chapter 6), employee training and development (Chapter 8), performance appraisal (Chapter 7), compensation (Chapters 10 and 11), and other major HRM activities.

The most significant and contentious issues of the day are considered head-on in this text. For example, among the controversial topics covered in experiential exercises are ethnic score differences on employee screening devices, affirmative action programs and preferential treatment, the outsourcing of work overseas, binding arbitration agreements, sexual harassment policies, employment-at-will, random drug testing with no probable cause, smoking in the workplace, CEO and executive compensation, and equal pay for work of comparable worth.

Another distinctive feature of this book is that some chapters were written by experts in the HRM field. Experts were selected on the basis of their experience, knowledge, and research accomplishments in a particular area of HRM and/or their experience with well-tested, experiential exercises that foster learning in a critical HRM content area. Since HRM is strongly influenced by a number of disciplines (e.g., law, economics, psychology, sociology, strategic management), expertise was sought to represent these varied orientations. I believe the finished product represents a broader perspective than a book prepared by an author from only one of those disciplines.

New "Critical Thinking Applications" (Appendix A) that concern some of the most important and timely issues of the day also have been added. Interwoven in each chapter of the book is an underlying theme of improving quality and increasing competitive advantage with more effective HRM practices compatible with the new research on "high-performance work systems."

ACKNOWLEDGMENTS

A number of people have made valuable contributions to this book. First, we would like to thank the various editors and staff members with whom we have worked at McGraw-Hill. We also would like to acknowledge the many reviewers from various universities and colleges who provided helpful comments and suggestions: Jarold Abbott and Barry Axe, Florida Atlantic University; Steven E. Abraham, State University of New York at Oswego; Debra A. Arvanites, Villanova University; Dan Braunstein, Oakland University; Robert L. Cardy, Arizona State University; Herschel N. Chait, Indiana State University; Joan G. Dahl, California State University, Northridge; Randy L. DeSimone, Rhode Island College; William L. Eslin, Glassboro State College; John Fielding, Roger Williams University; Robert Figler, University of Akron; Cynthia Fukami, University of Denver; David Gilmore, University of North Carolina–Charlotte; Roger Griffith, Georgia State University; Nancy Johnson, University of Kentucky; John Kammeyer-Mueller, University of Florida; Katherine Karl, Western Michigan University; John F. P. Konarski, Florida International University; Jack Kondrasuk, University of Portland; Jacqueline Landau, Suffolk University; Robert M. Madigan, Virginia Polytechnic Institute; A. Amin Mohamed, Indiana University of Pennsylvania; Herff L. Moore, University of Central Arkansas; Joseph Morrell, Aquinas College; Paul Poppler, Bellvue University; James S. Russell, Lewis and Clark College; Janet Stern Solomon, Towson State University; Lee Stepina, Florida State University; Charles M. Vance, Loyola Marymount University; Susan C. Wajert, College of Mount St. Joseph; Richard A. Wald, Eastern Washington University; Elizabeth C. Wesman, Syracuse University; Kenneth M. York, Oakland University; and Mary D. Zalesny, University of Missouri–St. Louis.

Contributors of chapters or portions of chapters were Jennifer Robin, David O. Ulrich, Joyce E. A. Russell, Barbara A. Lee, Scott A. Snell, Chris Hagan, Monica Favia, Michael M. Harris, Barbara K. Brown, Joan E. Pynes, P. Christopher Earley, Diana Deadrick, Philip J. Decker, Barry R. Nathan, Jeffrey S. Kane, Sabrine Maetzke, Lee P. Stepina, James R. Harris, Alan Cabelly, E. Brian Peach, M. Ronald Buckley, Nancy Brown Johnson, Joseph G. Clark Jr., Roger L. Cole, Harriette S. McCaul, Fred E. Schuster, Thomas Becker, Susan M. Stewart, and Peter Villanova. Contributors of experiential exercises were Sue A. Dahmus, Jeffrey D. Kudisch, Jennifer Bowers, David Herst, Barry Axe, Marilyn A. Perkins, Lori Spina, Jarold Abbott, Mary E. Wilson, Joan E. Pynes, Peter Villanova, M. Ronald Buckley, Robert W. Eder, J. R. Biddle, Patrick Wright, James A. Breaugh, Barbara Hassell, Lee P. Stepina, James R. Harris, Jeffrey S. Kane, Richard Peters, Roger L. Cole, Christine M. Hagan, Scott A. Snell, Ann M. Herd, Larry A. Pace, Caroline C. Wilhelm, Sheila Kennelly-McGinnis, Stephanie D. Myers, Paul Guglielmino, Lucy Guglielmino, Fred E. Schuster, E. Brian Peach, Brenda E. Richey, Steven M. Barnard, Steve Long, Lillian T. Eby, Jennifer Robin, Sharon L. Wagner, Richard G. Moffett III, Catherine M. Westerberry,

Esther J. Long, Joseph G. Clark Jr., Susan M. Stewart, Nancy Brown Johnson, Karen Preston, and Renee Fitzgerald.

Many colleagues have provided enormous assistance on this edition—by contributing their comments on earlier drafts, reviewing exercises, or furnishing extensive reference materials. I appreciate the efforts of Lauren Lispi, Danielle Adams, Bryan Anderson, Jennifer Robin, Joseph Clark, Stephen H. Gaby, Lynn B. Curtis, Laura A. Davenport, Aaron T. Fausz, David Herst, Jeffrey D. Kudisch, Ann Rigel, and (especially) Christine Hagan and Jennifer Bowers.

Special thanks to Renee Fitzgerald for work on just about everything.

John Bernardin

BRIEF TABLE OF CONTENTS

TABLE OF CONTENTS

PART

III Developing Human Resource
Capability 171

7 Performance Management and Appraisal 172

8 Training and Development 192

PART

IV Compensating and Managing
        Human Resources 251

Human Resource Management and the Environment

1

STRATEGIC HUMAN RESOURCE MANAGEMENT IN A CHANGING ENVIRONMENT

OVERVIEW

In the 2004 Presidential campaign, the *American Prospect* magazine ran an assessment of President Bush's fitness for office based on an analysis of his handwriting. Sheila Kurtz of the Graphology Consulting Group analyzed a few cursive notes written by the president and opined that Mr. Bush was "exquisitely sensitive to anyone who might direct criticism his way" and that the President might have too much "tenacity" and that "when a person has so much tenacity it's very hard for them to change. They stick to what they believe . . . it can severely interfere with their flexibility, productivity, and imagination in all areas." She went on to describe his handwriting as depicting "a narrow-minded or tunnel-mindedness . . . and that means that he takes in almost nothing else but what he already knows into his decision making."[1]

When I shared this assessment with undergraduate human resources classes recently, about a third of students thought the evaluation was "dead on accurate," another third thought it was absolutely wrong, and another third didn't have an opinion at all. Within the last group, about half the students expressed great skepticism about the ability to assess personality, aptitude, or anything else important using a person's handwriting. It is this group of students who are "dead-on accurate." Research clearly shows that handwriting is not a valid means of assessing anything important (except for your handwriting!).

The assessment of presidential candidates is not the only place you will find the use of invalid assessment methods. *Inc.* magazine, one of the most popular magazines for U.S. small business, ran a story extolling the benefits of using graphology to hire managers.[2] The article reported that the use of graphology was on the increase and that the method was very effective for selecting managers and salespersons. Sound research in human resource management (HRM) has determined that companies would do just about as well picking names out of a hat to make personnel decisions.[3]

Skilled HRM specialists help organizations with all activities related to staffing and maintaining an effective workforce. Major HRM responsibilities include work design and job analysis, training and development, recruiting, compensation, team-building, performance management and appraisal, worker health and safety issues, as well as identifying or developing valid methods for selecting staff.

Research by academics who study and teach HRM is devoted to identifying the most effective and efficient methods for meeting these HRM responsibilities. **A recurring theme of this book is that the most effective HRM programs, policies, and practices are those that are developed in deference to research in HRM.** Our view is that practicing HRM often ignores the sound research about policy, practice, or people that is available to help make decisions. Instead, organizations often adopt an HRM procedure because competitors are using it (this was a main theme of the *Inc.* article).

The author had a conversation with a business owner who had hired his 145-person sales staff based on graphology reports (at $75 per report) and the answer to a single question he posed in an interview. When questioned about the validity of these methods, he described one terrible salesman he had hired out of desperation in a tight labor market despite a graphologist's report that said the "small writing with little slant indicated he may be too introverted for sales work." He lamented that "If only I had listened to the handwriting expert; I wasted a bundle training the guy!" Those of us who teach statistics refer to this type of "research" as a "man who statistic." When you discuss the overwhelming evidence showing that smoking causes cancer, someone might offer the counterargument that "I knew a man who smoked three packs a day and lived to be 90." Needless to say, this is not the way to do research. There are good ways to do research and good ways to assess the effects of programs and activities. Sound measurement is a key to effective management. Remember the old adage: if it's not measured, it's not managed. What does someone's handwriting measure?

Many HRM systems and activities are not subjected to systematic measurement. Many organizations do not assess either the short- or long-term consequences of their HRM programs or activities. Another recurring theme of our book is that **measurement and accountability are key components to organizational effectiveness and competitive advantage.** Good measurement, allied with business strategies, will help organizations select and improve all of their HRM activities and provide a much stronger connection between HRM activities and organizational effectiveness.

Stanford University professor Jeffrey Pfeffer considers measurement to be one of the keys to competitive advantage. His book *Competitive Advantage Through People* cites measurement as one of the 16 HRM practices that contribute the most to competitive advantage.[4] Pfeffer's views were echoed and expanded in the popular text *The Balanced Scorecard* by Harvard professor Robert Kaplan and consultant David Norton.[5] Kaplan and Norton stress that "if companies are to survive and prosper in information age competition, they must use measurement and management systems derived from their strategies and capabilities" (p. 21). Their "balanced scorecard" emphasizes much more management attention to "leading indicators" of performance that predict the "lagging" financial performance measures. The "balance" reflects the need to measure short- and long-term objectives, financial and nonfinancial measures, lagging and leading indicators, and internal and external performance perspectives.

A new book entitled *The Workforce Scorecard* by Professors Mark Huselid, Brian Becker, and Dick Beatty

extends research on the "balanced scorecard" to a comprehensive management and measurement system to maximize workforce potential.[6] These authors show that the traditional financial performance measures such as return on equity, stock price, and return on investment, the "lagging indicators," can be predicted by the way companies conduct their HR. HR practices are the "leading indicators" that predict subsequent financial performance measures. Unfortunately, research indicates that only a small percentage of HRM programs or activities are subjected to analysis. The good news, however, is that the percentage is at least going up. Measurement is essential for American business in the 21st century!

One prophetic study defined the vision of human resources for the 21st century. HRM activities must be (1) responsive to a highly competitive marketplace and global business structures, (2) closely linked to business strategic plans, (3) jointly conceived and implemented by line and HR managers, and (4) focused on quality, customer service, productivity, employee involvement, teamwork, and workforce flexibility.[7]

The status of HRM is improving relative to other potential sources of competitive advantage for an organization. Professor Pfeffer notes that "traditional sources of success (e.g., speed to market, financial, technological) can still provide competitive leverage, but to a lesser degree now than in the past, leaving organizational culture and capabilities, derived from how people are managed, as comparatively more vital."[8]

You are likely to manage people at some point in your career. Research shows that the manner in which you conduct the human resource responsibilities of your management job will be a key to your effectiveness. We believe that the knowledge and experiences provided by this book will make you a more effective manager. The thesis is that the most effective HRM programs, policies, and practices are those that keep the organization's mission and strategic plan in mind. All HRM activities should be evaluated in this context using "leading indicator" performance measures.

OBJECTIVES

After reading this chapter, you should be able to

1. *Describe the field of HRM and its potential for creating and sustaining competitive advantage.*
2. *Describe discrepancies between actual HRM practices and recommendations for HRM practice from research.*
3. *Describe the major activities of HRM.*
4. *Explain important trends relevant to HRM, including globalization of the economy, new technology and the Internet, the increasing role of regulations and*

lawsuits, the changing demographics of the workforce, and the growing body of research linking particular HRM practices to corporate performance.

5. *Emphasize the importance of measurement for effective and strategic HRM.*
6. *Understand what is meant by competitive advantage, and why it is important for organizations.*

What Is Human Resource Management?

The human resources of an organization consist of all people who perform its activities. In a sense, *all* decisions that affect the workforce concern the organization's HRM function. **Human resource management** concerns the personnel policies and managerial practices and systems that influence the workforce. Regardless of the size—or existence—of a formal HRM or Personnel Department (many small businesses have no HRM department), the activities involved in HRM are pervasive throughout the organization. Line managers, for example, will spend more than 50 percent of their time involved in human resource activities such as hiring, evaluating, disciplining, and scheduling employees.

The effectiveness with which line management performs HRM functions with the tools, data, and processes provided by HRM specialists is the key to competitive advantage through HRM. This principle generalizes from very small businesses to the very largest global enterprises. Dr. James Spina, former head of executive development at the Tribune Company, really put things in perspective about the role of HRM. He said, "The HRM focus should always be maintaining and, ideally, expanding the customer base while maintaining and, ideally, maximizing profit. HRM has a whole lot to do with this focus regardless of the size of the business, or the products or services you are trying to sell."

Those individuals classified within an HRM functional unit provide products and services for the organization. These products and services may include the provision of, or recommendation for, systems or processes that facilitate organizational restructuring, job design, personnel planning, recruitment, hiring, evaluating, training, developing, promoting, compensating, and terminating personnel. A major goal of this book is to provide information and experiences that will improve the student's future involvement and effectiveness in HRM activities.

While HR can create and sustain competitive advantage, some would argue that HR is often more a weakness than a strength. A recent *Fast Company* article summarizes a 2005 survey that only 40 percent of employees thought their companies were doing a good job retaining high-quality workers and only 41 percent thought performance evaluations were fair. A mere 58 percent of respondents reported their job training as favorable. A majority said they had few opportunities for advancement and they had little idea how to advance in the first place. About half of those surveyed below the managerial level believed their companies took a genuine interest in their well-being.

HRM and Corporate Performance

A growing body of research shows that progressive HRM practices can have a significant effect on corporate performance. Studies now document the relationship between specific HR practices and critical outcome measures such as corporate financial performance, productivity, product and service quality, and cost control. Many of the methods characterizing these so-called **high-performance work systems** (HPWS) have been researched and developed by the HRM academic community. Figure 1-1 presents a summary of this research.[9]

HPWS is a term used to describe a collection of HR practices or characteristics designed to enhance employees' competencies and productivity so that employees can be a reliable source of competitive advantage. Research shows that "firm competitiveness can be enhanced by high-performance work systems." A summary of this research found that a one standard deviation of improved assessment on a HPWS measurement tool increased sales per employee in excess of $15,000 per employee, an 8 percent gain in labor productivity.[10]

Recall our critical remarks earlier about handwriting analysis. Figure 1-1 states that validated selection

---

FIGURE 1-1   Characteristics of High-Performance Work Systems

- Large number of highly qualified applicants for each strategic position.
- The use of validated selection and promotion models/procedures.
- Extensive training and development of new employees.
- The use of formal performance appraisal and management.
- The use of multisource (360 degree) performance appraisal and feedback.
- Linkage of merit increases to formal appraisal processes.
- Above-market compensation for key positions.
- High percentage of entire workforce included in incentive systems.
- High differential in pay between high and low performers.
- High percentage of workforce working in self-managed, project-based work teams.
- Low percentage of employees covered by union contract.
- High percentage of jobs filled from within.

Source: B. Becker, M. Ulrich. *The HR Scorecard* (Boston: Harvard Business School Press, 2001). Reprinted with permission.

and promotion systems are related to higher productivity and reduced costs. The term *validated* means that the method has actually been shown to predict something important. If you're using a method to select managers or sales personnel, a "validated" method is a method shown to actually predict managerial or sales success. While graphology is no way to assess personality, there are valid methods for predicting future employee performance based on the assessed characteristics of job candidates.

Better training and development programs and team-based work configurations improve performance and job satisfaction and decrease employee turnover. Particular incentive and compensation systems also translate into higher productivity and performance. The fair treatment of employees results in higher job satisfaction, which in turn facilitates higher performance, lower employee turnover, reduced costs, and a lower likelihood of successful union organizing.

Greater demands are now being made on HRM practitioners to respond to contemporary trends in the business environment. Today, the most effective HRM functions are conceptualized in a business capacity, constantly focusing on the strategy of the organization and the core competencies of the organization. HRM specialists must show how they can make a difference for the company's bottom line. Costs and efficiencies are a necessary criterion for evaluating recommendations from research in HRM.

Many corporate strategy specialists maintain that the key to sustained competitive advantage is building and sustaining core competencies within the organization and maintaining flexibility in order to react quickly to the changing global marketplace and the advances in technology. One primary role of HRM practitioners should be to facilitate this process.

DISCREPANCIES BETWEEN ACADEMIC RESEARCH AND HRM PRACTICE

While HRM executives and managers are more educated and professional than in the days when they were in charge of personnel, the level of knowledge in practicing HRM is another story. Many companies hire MBAs for HRM jobs when not even a single HRM course is required in the typical curriculum for an MBA. The 190,000-member Society for Human Resource Management (SHRM, see www.SHRM.org), which established the Human Resource Certification Institute, formally recognizes human resource professionals who have demonstrated particular expertise in HR. As of 2006, over 70,000 HR professionals hold the Professional in Human Resources (PHR), the Senior Professional in Human Resources (SPHR), and the Global Professional in Human Resources (GPHR) designation.

HRM practitioners need to pay more attention to academic research. There is a great deal of carefully crafted academic research that is highly relevant to HRM practice. Figure 1-2 presents a few examples of discrepancies between the current state of HR practice and what the

---

FIGURE 1-2 Sample of Discrepancies between Academic Research Findings and HRM Practices

Academic Research Findings	HRM Practice
RECRUITMENT	
Quantitative analysis of recruitment sources using yield ratios can facilitate efficiencies in recruitment.	Less than 10% calculate yield ratios. Less than 25% know how.
STAFFING	
Realistic job previews can reduce turnover.	Less than 20% of companies use RJPs in high-turnover jobs.
Weighted application blanks reduce turnover.	Less than 30% know what a WAB is; less than 1% use WABs.
Structured, behavioral, or situational interviews are more valid.	45% of companies use structured interviews.
Use actuarial model of prediction with multiple measures.	Less than 5% use actuarial model.
Graphology is invalid and should not be used.	Use is on the increase in the United States.
PERFORMANCE APPRAISAL	
Do not use traits on rating forms.	More than 70% still use traits.
Train raters (for accuracy, observation bias).	Less than 30% train raters.
Make appraisal process important element of manager's job.	Less than 35% of managers are evaluated on performance appraisal.
COMPENSATION	
Merit-based systems should not be tied into a base salary.	More than 75% tie merit pay into base pay.
Gainsharing is an effective PFP system.	Less than 5% of companies use it where they could.

Source: H. J. Bernardin. "A Survey of Human Resource Practices," Working Paper, 2005.

academic literature clearly recommends. One recent study reinforced this "knowledge gap."[11] HR professionals were given a 35-item test that assessed the extent of their HR knowledge. The test was scored on findings from academic research, which would likely be covered in any basic HR course like this one. Items were developed where there was little or no argument on the correct answer within the academic community. The average grade for the nearly 1,000 HR professionals was "D." On numerous items, over 50 percent of the HR professionals got the answer wrong!

Throughout the book, we intend to emphasize the most glaring discrepancies between the way HRM is actually being practiced and what academic research has to say about particular practices. The failure on the part of practicing HRM personnel to either be aware of the research or understand it is a problem that can have a profound effect on an organization's bottom line, such as return on equity, profit, profit growth, and stock price. Although line management plays a critical role in the successful implementation and execution of HRM programs, these programs are typically either developed or purchased by HRM specialists.

Many HR activities such as payroll, recruitment, and pre-employment screening are now outsourced to organizations that specialize in these areas. The number of consulting organizations specializing in HR activities has increased substantially in the last 10 years. There are now Web-based HR products and services in almost every major functional area and full-service HR online department. An organization's HR specialist must have the necessary knowledge and skills to be able to identify the best and most cost-effective of these HR products and services for a particular situation.

HRM professionals should possess up-to-date knowledge about the relative effectiveness of the various programs and activities related to HR planning, training and development, compensation, performance management, selection, information systems, equal employment opportunity/diversity, labor relations, recruitment, and health and safety issues. HRM professionals also should be capable of conducting their own research to evaluate their programs and program alternatives. Unfortunately, recent evidence suggests that HR professionals adopt many programs based either on effective marketing from the plethora of vendors selling HR materials and programs or simply on what other companies are doing. While some consideration may be given to the leading-indicator research described in Figure 1-1, greater weight seems to be given to slick marketing programs and simply what others are doing. When "bottom line" questions arise later on—as they inevitably do—HR departments are caught off guard because costly and relatively ineffective programs have been adopted. A careful study of the program with evaluative criteria linked to strategic goals might reveal negligible or no impact. Again, if you don't measure it, you can't manage it.

Many HR professionals are not even trained to ask the right questions and conduct the appropriate study of a given HR program or activity. The author had a conversation with a VP of HR of a Fortune 500 company. He had a Big-Ten MBA and was convinced that one particular test was the best way to hire retail sales personnel. The basis for his position was conversations with other poorly informed HRM MBAs who were using the test. This is no way to evaluate a selection method. Another HR vice president for a retailer adopted an expensive computerized testing program that the publisher claimed would reduce employee turnover by 50 percent. The VP did not request the research that purported to document this effect and later admitted that although he ultimately made the decision to adopt the test, he was unqualified to assess the test's usefulness since he could not even ask fundamental measurement questions that should be the focus of any evaluation of such a product or service. In addition, although the retailer had been using the test for over two years, it apparently never occurred to him to evaluate the extent to which the test actually did reduce turnover in his organization. A Connecticut police department used an intelligence test to screen for officers but eliminated candidates if their scores were too high. Their argument was that highly intelligent officers would get bored and quit. They had no evidence to support their theory and conceded that their leaders were all selected from within the organization. This kind of theory should be tested first and its unintended consequences carefully examined before implementation!

One of the great values of academic research is the objective evaluation of activities or programs using well-controlled experimental designs, which allow for unambiguous assessments of effects. For example, *Buros Mental Measurements Yearbook* is a reference source that publishes evaluations of tests written by qualified academics who have no vested interest in the tests themselves. Over 2,000 tests have been reviewed and the reviews can be downloaded from the *Buros* Web site for $15 per test (http://buros.unl.edu/buros/jsp/search). Many HRM professionals who adopt tests do not know that this very useful text even exists.

THE ACTIVITIES OF HUMAN RESOURCE MANAGEMENT

Figure 1-3 presents a listing of the most commonly performed activities by HRM professionals. These HRM activities fall under five major domains: (1) Organizational Design, (2) Staffing, (3) Performance Management and Appraisal, (4) Employee and Organizational Development, and (5) Reward Systems, Benefits, and Compliance.

Although the activities subsumed under these domains are conceptually interdependent, in practice of course they are not. Nevertheless many organizations pursue the various activities as if they had no implications

FIGURE 1-3	Major Activities of Human Resource Management

ORGANIZATIONAL DESIGN

Human resource planning based on strategy
Job analysis/work analysis
Job design
Information systems

STAFFING

Recruiting/interviewing/hiring
Affirmative action/diversity
Promotion/transfer/separation
Outplacement services
Induction/orientation
Employee selection methods

PERFORMANCE MANAGEMENT AND APPRAISAL

Management appraisal/management by objectives/strategy execution
Productivity/enhancement programs
Customer-focused performance appraisal
Multirater systems (360°, 180°)

EMPLOYEE TRAINING AND ORGANIZATIONAL DEVELOPMENT

Management/supervisory development
Career planning/development
Employee assistance/counseling programs
Attitude surveys
Training delivery options
Diversity programs

REWARD SYSTEMS, BENEFITS, AND COMPLIANCE

Safety programs/OSHA compliance
Health/medical services
Complaint/disciplinary procedures
Compensation administration
Wage/salary administration
Insurance benefits administration
Unemployment compensation administration
Pension/profit-sharing plans
Labor relations/collective bargaining

building, computerization, and worker-machine interfaces also fall under this domain.

Organizational and work design issues are almost always the first ones that should be addressed whenever significant change is necessary because of changing economic conditions, new technologies, new opportunities, potential advantages, or serious internal problems. Design issues usually drive other HR domains such as selection, training, performance management, and compensation.

Economic downturns can provide an opportunity for a more serious evaluation of the organization's strategy and its competitive position. But there are clearly effective and ineffective approaches to organizational design.

Corporate downsizing, outsourcing, and reengineering efforts often begin with human resource planning in the context of a strategic plan and an analysis of how the work is performed, how jobs and work units relate to one another, and, of course, cost analysis. These decisions can be critical for the long-term survival of a struggling company. Research shows that layoffs designed to derive a short-term "cost savings" may foster an increase in market value in the short run but that investors often lose all of this value plus considerably more. We will cover the issues of HR design, planning, downsizing, and restructuring in Chapters 4 and 5.

After the organization is structured and jobs are clearly defined in terms of the necessary knowledge, skills, and abilities and how jobs and work relate to one another, positions must be staffed. Recruitment, employee orientation, selection, promotion, and termination are among the functions that fit into the **staffing** domain. Of the HR activities within this domain, selection and termination are probably the two most likely affected by the regulation and litigation we discuss in Chapter 3. Chapter 6 will cover the critical area of selection. We will focus on termination in Chapter 12.

The **performance management** domain includes assessments of individual, unit, or other aggregated levels of performance to measure, and improve, work performance. Chapter 7 will deal with these subjects, which, like selection, are also the focus of numerous lawsuits. A lawsuit can occur if the organization maintains that an employee was terminated, not promoted, or not given a merit raise because of performance, and the employee believes the negative personnel action was because of his or her gender, race, religion, age, disability, or some other characteristic. An employee also can claim an unlawful discharge based on an alleged contract or implied contract violation and even make a claim for pre-emptive retaliation. Obviously, merit pay systems require accurate measures of employee performance.

Employee training and organizational development programs are concerned with establishing, fostering, and maintaining employee skills based on organizational

for any of the other domains. For example, many organizations have reduced or eliminated health care benefits without consideration of the impact of the new compensation package on staffing and employee retention. In addition, all domain activity must be weighed in the context of the new global environment and contemporary legal interpretation.

Acquiring human resource capability should begin with organizational design and analysis. **Organizational design** involves the arrangement of work tasks based on the interaction of people, technology, and the tasks to be performed in the context of the mission, goals, and strategic plan of the organization. HRM activities such as human resources planning, job and work analysis, organizational restructuring, job design, team and employee needs. Activities include specialized training for jobs or management functions, career development, and self-directed learning. Chapters 8 and 9 cover these vital areas.

Reward systems, benefits and compliance have to do with any type of reward or benefit that may be available to employees. Direct and indirect compensation, merit pay, profit sharing, health care, parental leave programs, vacation leave, and pensions are among the critical areas within this domain. The activities also include the myriad of compliance requirements facing organizations from local, state, and federal agencies. Labor law, health and safety issues, and unemployment policy are three other major areas within this domain. These are covered in Chapters 10 and 11.

This domain also concerns managing employment relationships, labor relations law and compliance, and procedures designed to maintain good working relationships between employees and employers. This may include the negotiation of collective bargaining agreements, which require employers to negotiate with unionized workers over the conditions of employment. We cover these areas in Chapters 12 and 13.

Employee health and safety issues are also subsumed under this domain and include compliance with laws and regulations concerned with the work environment and the effects of health and safety policy and practice on workers and the "bottom line." Our focus will be health and safety policy as a leading indicator of HR effectiveness. This area is explored in Chapter 14.

TRENDS ENHANCING THE IMPORTANCE OF HRM

As we have said, there is an increasing realization that the manner in which organizations conduct their HR activities will help create and sustain a competitive advantage. The contemporary trends and challenges in the business environment necessitate that even greater attention be given to the human resources of an organization. Let us examine these trends next and relate each to particular HRM activities. Figure 1-4 presents a summary of major current trends.

The most significant trend is the increasing globalization of the economy and a growing competitive work environment with a premium on product and service quality. One of the most important factors affecting globalization and the growth of transnational corporations is the goal of reducing the cost of production, labor costs being the most significant for U.S. companies. But as we discuss in Chapter 2, market-seeking behavior is now as important a motivator of globalization as the search for low-cost productivity.

Another major trend is the unpredictable but inevitable power of technology to transform HRM. There is a need to be more flexible today because of the incredible

---

FIGURE 1-4   Major Trends Affecting HRM

TREND 1: THE INCREASED GLOBALIZATION OF THE ECONOMY
Opportunity for global workforce and labor cost reduction
Increasing global competition for U.S. products and services
Opportunity for expansion that presents global challenges for HR

TREND 2: TECHNOLOGICAL CHANGES, CHALLENGES, AND OPPORTUNITIES
Great opportunities presented by Web-based systems
New threats: privacy, confidentiality, intellectual property

TREND 3: THE NEED TO BE FLEXIBLE IN RESPONSE TO CHANGING BUSINESS ENVIRONMENTS
Outsourcing/downsizing/temps/reengineering
Technological changes that require it

TREND 4: INCREASE IN LITIGATION RELATED TO HRM
Federal, state, and municipal lawsuits on the increase
Wrongful discharge; negligent hiring, retention, referral

TREND 5: CHANGING CHARACTERISTICS OF THE WORKFORCE
Growing workforce diversity, which complicates HRM
Labor shortages/aging workforce

---

pace of change in markets and technology. HRM can facilitate this flexibility. The growth and proliferation of lawsuits related to HR practice and changes in workforce characteristics also have had a big impact on HRM. So is the fact that many in the workforce are ill-equipped with the necessary knowledge, skills and abilities, and job requirements to do their jobs well.

Trend 1: The Increased Globalization of the Economy

In his excellent new book *The World Is Flat: A Brief History of the Twenty-First Century,* Thomas Friedman described the next phase of globalization.[12] An Indian software executive told him how the world's economic playing field is being leveled. So-called barriers to entry are being destroyed. A company (or even an individual) can compete (or collaborate) from almost anywhere in the world. Over 400,000 American tax returns were prepared in India in 2005. Says Jerry Rao, Indian entrepreneur, "any activity where we can digitize and decompose the value chain, and move the work around, will get moved around. Some people will say, 'Yes, but you can't serve me a steak.' True, but I can take the reservation for your table sitting anywhere in the world." Rao's 2006 plans were to collaborate with an Israeli company that can transmit MRI and CAT scans through the Internet so Americans can get a second opinion very quickly (and relatively cheaply). When you order a Big Mac at the McDonald's on Route 55 in Cape Girardeau, Missouri, the person taking the order is at a call center in India.

There is no question that the increasing globalization of most of the world's economies will affect HRM. It is predicted that most of the largest U.S. companies soon will employ more workers in countries other than the United States and the growth for most major corporations will derive from off-shore operations. With technological advances, one of the strongest trends is the development of a worldwide labor market for U.S. companies. In their quest for greater efficiencies and reduced costs, American companies can now look globally to get work done. While this opportunity stands to decrease the cost of labor, the process of HRM is more complicated. Of course, U.S. workers will resist this trend through union and political activity.

Globalization also should foster greater competition and more concern over productivity and cost control. The recent woes of GM and Ford are clear illustrations. One important reason for the recent increased interest in HRM is the perceived connection between HRM expertise and productivity. A growing portion of corporate America has come to the realization that competing in an increasingly global environment requires constant vigilance over productivity and customer satisfaction. A smaller but growing percentage of managers recognize the importance of human resources in dealing with these issues. Indeed, a great deal of the recent corporate downsizing can be linked to some technological improvement and estimates of productivity improvements with both HR and the interacting technological changes. Bank of America, American Express, Coca-Cola, and General Electric have successfully followed a formula of cutting personnel costs while investing in automated equipment and more efficient facilities. The recent plant closures by Ford and GM are examples.

U.S. exports now generate about one in six American jobs, an increase of over 20 percent in just 10 years. McDonald's opened its first non-U.S. restaurant in Canada in 1967. Their total sales outside of the United States contributed over 50 percent of the operating income of the firm in 2005. Two-thirds of its new stores are now opened outside of the United States each year. While McDonald's has moved more quickly than other U.S. firms, many other U.S. firms are now expanding rapidly in terms of both new countries and new markets. The majority of new restaurants opened by Burger King and KFC, for example, are now in an international market. The majority of new stores opened by Wal-Mart are now opened outside of the United States.

Another response to increasing global competition is restructuring/downsizing, as described earlier. Coca-Cola, Ford, Sears, AT&T, CBS, DuPont, GM, Kodak, Xerox, and IBM are among the many corporate behemoths that have reduced their workforces by more than 10 percent in the last decade. Many HRM specialists are experts in organizational restructuring and change procedures. They have expertise in downsizing and outsourcing options that can reduce labor costs. They may also conduct vocational counseling for those who are displaced or assist in developing new staffing plans as a result of the restructuring.

As we will describe in more detail in later chapters, HRM specialists also are asked to help in a legal defense against allegations of discrimination related to corporate downsizing. Ford settled two discrimination lawsuits related to downsizing efforts. In an attempt to compete more effectively against Geico and Progressive, Allstate Insurance converted all of its 15,200-member sales force to independent contractors. To continue as contractors, the agents had to sign a waiver that they would not sue Allstate for discrimination. The result was a costly age discrimination lawsuit brought against Allstate. The law can impose constraints on companies trying to cut costs through labor.

Trend 2: Technological Changes, Challenges, and Opportunities

The second trend is the rate of change in technology. More organizations are now evaluating their human resources and labor costs in the context of available technologies, based on the theory that products and services can be delivered more effectively (and efficiently) through an optimal combination of people, software, and equipment, increasing productivity. Instead of speaking to a customer service representative at Bank of America to discuss your account, you can interact with an automated system via the Internet or an automated teller machine (ATM) or through an 800 number. The program is designed to handle almost any problem about which you would inquire. With the automated system, BOA is able to shed customer service representatives, thereby reducing labor costs. As more people use their automated services and ATMs, there is less need for supervision. Customers, as a result, pay less in service charges and may earn more interest on their money. As these automated systems evolve, customers ultimately could be more satisfied with the service, even though they are not dealing with an actual person. HRM specialists participate in the development and execution of user testing programs to assess the design of the automated interface.

Today, with the assistance of HR, more companies are evaluating the role of organizational structure, technology, and human resources with the goal of providing more and higher-quality products and services to the customer at a lower price. This pricing is at least partially achieved by controlling the cost of labor while not losing the focus on meeting customer definitions of quality. Of course, the ultimate goal of for-profit organizations is to maximize profit margins while sustaining perceived customer value. HR has a great deal to offer in this endeavor.

While the potential is there, HR specialists are often ignored. Technological advances and offshoring are of course related. A recent survey found that only 35 percent of respondents reported that HR was involved in the offshoring process from an early stage, although HR does typically play a major role in restructuring the organization's workforce as a result of offshoring. Says Jennifer Schramm, manager of workplace trends and forecasting at the Society of Human Resource Management (SHRM.org) "from training HR professionals from offshore sites in the home organization's corporate culture and policies, to developing strong channels of communication between global satellite offices, HR's involvement is crucial in effectively managing cross-border human capital . . . HR's role in boosting productivity through human capital and workplace culture, even as the scope of the workplace extends across the globe and spans very different cultures, will continue to grow."[13]

Technology is revolutionizing many HRM activities. Most organizations now use software packages to aid in recruitment and personnel management. Many HR activities are tracked electronically, such as turnover, performance appraisals, and training. Managers from different departments, states, or even countries can readily access the HR system and update employment files. Software packages are easily customized to fit a specific organization's HR activities.

Technology has also changed the speed with which HR communicates with employees. HR can draft and e-mail a companywide memo to all employees within a single hour. In addition, employees can instantly communicate with Human Resources. Many companies have created intranet sites. These Web sites provide employees with a variety of information, such as health care benefits and proposed changes. HR is now able to communicate with employees at the speed of light.

The advent of technology has created a variety of concerns for management. Employee privacy and intellectual property rights are increasingly cited as major ones. With computer attacks occurring worldwide, ensuring confidentiality of employee data is a growing concern, and liability of an organization in the event of security breaches is still unclear.[14]

Protecting intellectual property is vital for all organizations, especially emerging technology and research and development organizations. As a result, organizations are developing electronic communication policies that clearly outline permitted electronic activities, uses of employer systems, and monitoring of employees files, such as e-mail. Many companies have banned cellular cameras and instant messaging because of the increased risk of intellectual property theft.

Although still rare, the following scenario is already here for some companies: A manager or supervisor gets authorization to hire someone. The manager goes into a "node" on the Internet and completes a standardized job description for the new position that establishes critical information regarding the job, including the necessary knowledge, ability, skills, and other critical characteristics. The job description is then used to conduct a "key word" computer search of a potential applicant pool in order to match the requirement of the job with the standardized resumes in the database. Out pops a number of potential candidates for the job. The manager then immediately sends out the job vacancy announcement to all of the potential candidates in the database through electronic mail. Interested candidates respond back via e-mail. The manager then selects the "short list" of candidates who would compete for the job.

The same job analysis information also could be used to construct or retrieve job-related tests or questions for an employment interview. The manager might even have a Web camera and could conduct the testing and "face-to-face" interviewing of the candidates as soon as the contact is made (assuming the candidate also has access to a camera-based computer). This process of going from describing the job to actually interviewing candidates could take less than a day. HR is playing a key role in getting these systems up and running.

Some of the most successful high-tech companies today rely on the Internet for fast, convenient, and efficient recruiting of their core personnel. Even the CIA and the FBI do recruiting on the Internet (try www.odci.gov/cia if you'd like to be a spy).

Trend 3: The Need to Be Flexible in Response to Changing Business Environments

Being innovative and responsive to changing business environments requires great flexibility. The trend toward the "elastic" company is affecting the HR function, too. As more companies focus on their *core competencies*—essentially, what they do best and what is the essence of their business—they outsource other work, use temporary or leased employees or independent contractors to perform services or work on specific projects even at the professional level, and replace personnel with new technology. These so-called modular companies such as Nike and Dell Computers can be highly successful if they have reliable vendors and suppliers and, of course, a hot product. HR consultants have been instrumental in helping companies discover their core competencies and then developing optimal work design and HR strategies. HR departments themselves are not exempt from this trend toward outsourcing. The result has been a proliferation of consulting firms that compete for HR-related projects and programs previously performed within the company. Consulting is now a thriving business for HRM.

Outsourcing trends along with the Internet, software, and consulting options have reduced the size of many HR departments and have the potential for making them more efficient and more effective. How lean can you get in HR? Nucor, a steel company with 6,000 employees, has an HR staff of four at its headquarters. Most of the HR work is farmed out to HR consultants. Some experts argue that the most efficient and perhaps most effective HRM departments select the best and least costly outside contractors for HRM products and services, make certain these products or services are being used properly, and then evaluate and adapt these products and services to make certain they are working effectively and efficiently.

One trend in the United States is toward hiring temporary employees through a temporary employment agency such as Spherion, Kelly Services, or Manpower. These organizations provide companies with skilled and unskilled employees on an "as needed" basis and take care of all aspects of the hiring, placement, and assessment of those employees. This trend toward outsourcing some of the personnel function supports the thesis of many experts that the HRM functions must be very lean in structure so that companies can react quickly to the changing world. Many HRM departments now assess the need for any expense, personnel included, in the context of the primary functions of the organization and its competitive strategy. So, if companies can maintain a leaner and more cost-effective structure by outsourcing, where will that leave the HR department in the future? A 2005 survey found that 94 percent of large companies reported they were outsourcing at least one human resources activity. Most employers indicated that they plan to expand HR outsourcing to include training and development, payroll, recruiting, health care, and global mobility.[15]

Keith Hammonds, executive editor of *Fast Company,* predicts companies will "farm out pretty much everything HR does. The happy rhetoric from the HR world says this is all for the best: Outsourcing the administrative minutiae, after all, would allow human resources professionals to focus on more important stuff that's central to the business. You know, being strategic partners."[16] Hammond argues that most HR people are not equipped to take on this more important, strategic responsibility because they don't know enough about the business.

Trend 4: Increase in Litigation Related to HRM

In addition to the growing concerns over productivity, changes in technology, and increases in global competition, another important trend affecting the status of HRM is the proliferation of regulations and lawsuits related to personnel decisions. As predicted by one cynical statistician, by the year 2010, there will be more lawyers in this country than people. While this is obviously a joke, there is no question that the proliferation and creativity of lawyers have helped to foster our highly litigious society. There is no sign of this activity letting up in the near term. In fact, federal lawsuits charging violations of labor laws have increased faster (up over 125 percent since 1991) than any other area of civil rights legislation. Jury awards have gotten much bigger in recent years. In 2005, 24 percent of judgments against companies were

$1 million or more. In 1994, the percentage of such awards was only 7 percent.

In general, these laws and regulations reflect societal responses to economic, social, or political issues. For example, the Civil Rights Act of 1964, which prohibits job discrimination on the basis of race, sex, color, religion, or national origin, was passed primarily in response to the tremendous differences in economic outcomes of blacks versus whites. The 1990 Americans with Disabilities Act (ADA) was passed to promote equal opportunity for disabled Americans. Other examples are the proliferation of state laws regarding corporate acquisitions and mergers, laws protecting AIDS victims and homosexuals from employment discrimination, and even regulations regarding family leave benefits and the design of video display terminals.

Organizations are bound by a plethora of federal, state, and local laws, regulations, executive orders, and rules that have an impact on virtually every type of personnel decision. There are health and safety regulations, laws regarding employee pensions and other compensation programs, plant closures, mergers and acquisitions, new immigration laws, and a growing number of equal opportunity laws and guidelines. Today's HRM professionals and line managers must be familiar with the ADEA, OFCCP, OSHA, EEOC, ADA, FLSA, NLRA, and ERISA—among many other acronyms. Each represents a major regulatory effort. Organizations spend considerable time and expense in order to comply with these laws and regulations and/or to defend allegations regarding violations. Line managers who do not understand the implications of their actions in the context of these laws can cost a company dearly. Line managers may also be personally liable.

Sometimes companies learn the hard way. Abercrombie and Fitch settled a race discrimination lawsuit in 2005 for $40 million. Texaco and Coca-Cola settled similar for over $165 million each. Baker and McKenzie, the largest law firm in the United States, was assessed $3.5 million in punitive damages for sexual harassment committed by one partner at the firm. The EEOC settled a similar suit with Honda of America for $6 million. Westinghouse Electric Corporation agreed to a $35 million settlement in an age discrimination suit involving 4,000 employees affected by the company's reorganization. Ford recently agreed to a $10.6 million settlement in an age discrimination case. Morgan Stanley settled a sex discrimination case for $54 million. Wal-Mart remained mired in a massive sex discrimination lawsuit over pay and promotions when this book went to press.

Trend 5: Changing Characteristics of the Workforce

Several trends regarding the future of the American workforce underscore the challenges to and the importance of the human resource function. Compared to 10 years ago,

American workers are more ethnically diverse, more educated, more cynical toward work and organizations, getting older, and, for a growing number, becoming less prepared to handle the challenges of work today. The composition of the workforce is changing drastically and these changes are affecting HRM policies and practices.

Increasing diversity creates the need for more diverse HRM systems and practices and increases the probability of litigation. It is estimated that by 2010 only 15 percent of the U.S. workforce will be native-born white males. A greater proportion of women and minorities have entered the workforce and are beginning to move into previously white, male-dominated positions, including managers, lawyers, accountants, medical doctors, and professors. Nearly 90 percent of the growth in the U.S. workforce from 1995 to 2005 came from women, immigrants, African-Americans, and people of Hispanic or Asian origin. In addition, there are more dual-career couples in the labor force. The "typical" U.S. worker in the past was a male—often white—who was a member of a single-earner household. Fewer than 20 percent of today's employees fit this description. In March 2005, an estimated 10.9 percent of the U.S. population was foreign born. The rapid increase in the foreign-born population from 9.6 million in 1970 to 30 million in 2005 reflects the very high rate of international migration.[17]

The retirement of the baby-boomer generation, those born between 1946 and 1964, is expected to create a smaller workforce and to decrease economic output. However, some experts maintain that enough baby boomers will remain in the workforce to make up for any shortfall of workers. Because of the larger numbers of workers over the age of 40, age discrimination litigation is expected to increase; moreover, a 2005 Supreme Court age discrimination ruling to be discussed in Chapter 3 changed the burden of proof needed to prove age discrimination and should increase the amount of litigation. Also, the workforce under the age of 40 is expected to acquire more family life responsibilities. The "sandwich generation," those born between the baby-boomer generation and generation X, will be expected to juggle both child care and elder care demands. This is a concern HR must address in the coming years.

As a result of these changes in workforce composition, organizations are having to develop and implement programs on diversity, more flexible work schedules, better training programs, child and elder care arrangements, and career development strategies, so that work and non-work responsibilities can be more easily integrated. Building and sustaining a quality workforce from this diversity is a great challenge for HR.

While increasing diversity translates into a greater probability of EEO legal actions, many experts also argue that the diversity of the workforce must match the population or the organization is vulnerable to public criticism that can hurt the business. It is little wonder that most large U.S. companies include a goal of increasing the diversity of their workforce as a priority for the new year. As we will discuss in later chapters, the diversity goals of corporations can have an impact on the less diverse but older part of the workforce, particularly in downsizing situations. Such scenarios create great difficulties for corporations.

All of these trends are having a profound effect on the way HR is conducted. The changing demographics and cultural diversity of the workforce, the increased number of lawsuits and regulations, and the growing demands on American workers in the context of a paramount need to improve U.S. productivity and establish a competitive edge all create a situation that will challenge HRM professionals and line management. Yet through better coordination with organizational planning and strategy, human resources can be used to create and sustain an organization's advantage in an increasingly competitive world.

There is no question that the intense and growing competition has placed greater pressure on organizations to carefully examine their costs. Edward Lawler, a prominent management author and consultant, states, "All staff departments are being asked to justify their cost structures on a competitive basis . . . head-count comparisons are being made by corporations to check the ratio of employees to members of the HR department."[18]

Whether the organization is facing increasing international competition or simply more intense pressure to improve the bottom line, HR has a great opportunity to meet new and old challenges as a business partner. Lawler sees the most pressing need in the area of corporate strategy. "The HR function must become a partner in developing an organization's strategic plan, for human resources are a key consideration in determining strategies that are both practical and feasible."[19] This HR partnership must evolve out of the major activities of the HR function. We believe the key to this partnership is good, strategic measurement.

THE IMPORTANCE OF HRM MEASUREMENT IN STRATEGY EXECUTION

In an excellent new book entitled *The Workforce Scorecard: Managing Human Capital to Execute Strategy,* Professors Mark Huselid, Brian Becker, and Dick Beatty argue that of all the controllable factors that can affect organizational performance, a workforce that can execute strategy is the most critical and underperforming asset in most organizations.[20] Measurement is front and center in their prescription for a more effective workforce. They outline three challenges organizations must take on to maximize workforce potential in order to meet strategic objectives: (1) view the workforce in terms of contribution rather than cost; (2) use measurement as a tool for differentiating contributions to strategic impact; and (3) hold line and HR management responsible for getting the workforce to execute strategy.

Their measurement strategy calls for the development of a "workforce scorecard" that evolves from six general steps an organization needs to take. Figure 1-5 summarizes this process: (1) identify critical and carefully defined outcome measures that really matter; (2) translate the measures into specific actions and accountabilities; (3) employees receive detailed descriptions of what is expected and how improvements can be facilitated; (4) identify high and low performing employees and establish differentiated incentive systems; (5) develop supporting HR management and measurement systems; and (6) specify the roles of leadership, the workforce, and HR in strategy execution (go to www.theworkforcescorecard.com for more detail).

Huselid, Becker, and Beatty propose three challenges for successful workforce measurement and management (see Figure 1-5). The "perspective" challenge asks whether management fully understands how workforce behaviors affect strategy execution. The "metrics" challenge asks whether they have identified and collected the right measures of success. Finally, the "execution" challenge asks whether managers have the access, capability and motivation to use the measurement data to communicate strategy and monitor progress.

Human resource activities, practices, and research typically focus on a relatively small number of criteria or outcome measures. These measures can be fined-tuned on the quality of their measurement and the extent to which they are related to customer satisfaction and then long-term profitability and growth. Much of the research in HRM and many of the criteria used to assess management practices focus on employee satisfaction. Figure 1-6 presents a simple model that illustrates why there is (and should be) such a focus. There is a connection between these things. Throughout the book, many studies will be referenced that establish some relationship between an HR practice or HR policy or employee characteristics (e.g., employee satisfaction) and one or more of "bottom-line" criteria such as profit or customer satisfaction. For example, in an excellent study of the relationship between employee attitudes and corporate performance measures in almost 8,000 business units and 36 companies, strong and reliable correlations were found between unit-level employee job satisfaction and job engagement and critical business-unit outcomes, including profit. "Engagement" in this study had to do with, among other things, the level of employee satisfaction regarding working conditions, recognition and encouragement for good work, opportunities to perform well, and commitment to quality. The authors estimated that those business units in the top quartile on the job engagement scale had, on average, from $80,000 to $120,000 higher monthly revenues or sales. Can HRM practices facilitate higher engagement? Absolutely! It is clear that changes in HRM practices that serve to increase employee satisfaction and engagement can increase critical business-unit outcomes.[21]

We should also be interested in how the various criteria relate to one another. For example, another recent review showed a strong relationship between a construct known as "organizational commitment" and both job performance and employee turnover. Employees with higher levels of "organizational commitment" were more likely to be better performers and also stay with the company longer.[22] Obviously, managers will want to know how more "committed" or "engaged" employees can be found or developed. The author knows one CEO who was highly critical of academic research because it focused so much attention on variables like "engagement" and "commitment" or even " job satisfaction." He referred to these as "softies" and not relevant to the bottom line. In fact, an abundant literature now exists which documents that such "softies" are indeed strong correlates of bottom-line accounting and financial measures of organizational performance. A key to effective HR policy and practice is measuring such "softies" and understanding how they do relate to critical bottom-line measures like cost and profit and customer satisfaction.

FIGURE 1-5	Steps and Challenges for Developing a Workforce Scorecard

STEPS

1. Identify critical and carefully defined outcome measures related to strategic objectives.
2. Translate the measures into specific actions and accountabilities.
3. Develop and communicate detailed descriptions of what is expected. Determine how (or if) improvements can be facilitated.
4. Identify high and low performing employees. Establish differentiated incentive systems.
5. Develop supporting HR management and measurement systems of selection, formal performance appraisal, promotion, development, and termination practices.
6. Specify the roles of leadership, the workforce, and HR in strategy execution.

CHALLENGES

Perspective challenge—Does management fully understand how workforce behaviors affect strategy execution?

Metrics challenge—Has the organization identified and collected the right measures of success?

Execution challenge—Does management have access to the data and the motivation to use the data in decision making?

Source: Adapted from M. A. Huselid, B. E. Becker, and R. W. Beatty, *The Workforce Scorecard: Managing Human Capital to Execute Strategy* (Boston: Harvard Business School Press, 2005).

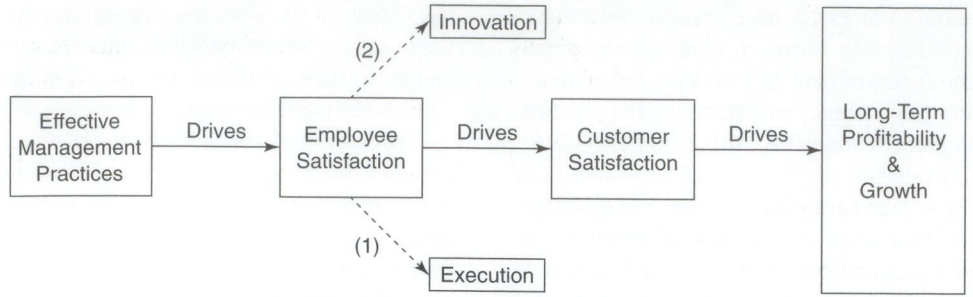

Figure 1-6   **The Chain of Relationships Linking Management Practices to Employee Satisfaction, Customer Satisfaction, and Long-Term Profitability and Growth**

Source: Cascio, W. (2005). From business partner to driving business success: the next step in the evolution of HR management. *Human Resource Management,* 44, p. 162. Reprinted with permission of John Wiley & Sons.

Organizations should certainly strive to satisfy their employees with good pay, good supervision, and good, stimulating work. But the model presented in Figure 1-6 also helps keep measures of employee job satisfaction in perspective. Employee satisfaction is related to customer satisfaction. So is cost. Customers are often particularly impressed with low cost. Wal-Mart does so well not because their employees are happy but because their products are on average 14 percent cheaper than their competitors'. The author would be a lot happier if his university salary was doubled! You'd probably be unhappy if your tuition was raised (again).

The key is linking measurement to strategic goals. "Thinking strategically means understanding whether the measurement system you are considering will provide you with the kinds of information that will help you manage the HR function strategically."[23] This linkage creates the connection between leading indicators and lagging indicators. Let us turn to illustrations of recent HRM activities directed at these criteria.

Frito-Lay had a problem with job vacancies in key positions, which they believed had a direct effect on sales. They instituted a training and development program through their HRM division to cross-train workers for several jobs in an effort to reduce "down time" from employee vacancies and provide more opportunities for employees to move up. The "down time" could be operationally defined in terms of dollars and the training program saved the company $250,000 in the first year.

AMC Theaters developed a battery of applicant tests to identify individuals most likely to perform more effectively and to stay with the company longer. The reduction in turnover saved the company over a half million dollars in five years. Blockbuster Video tried an applicant test that purported to help reduce employee theft and developed a new performance management system for all employees. They estimated savings at $450,000. Owens-Corning Fiberglas trained all of its managers in statistical quality analysis as a part of their total quality management program. Trainees were made accountable for

improving the quality at Owens-Corning and the program worked. Reduction of rejected materials saved over a million dollars. John Hancock Insurance installed a new managerial pay-for-performance system in order to increase regional sales and decrease employee turnover. J. Walter Thompson developed a new incentive system to promote creative advertising ideas from its consumer research and accounting units. RJR Nabisco replaced a fixed-rate commission with a new compensation system for its advertisers, which linked ad agency compensation to the success of the campaign. Concerned about the quality of one managerial level, Office Depot developed a managerial assessment center to select their district managers. They then determined the extent to which the quality of management improved as a function of the new screening method.

Turnover is a serious problem for many service industries and especially fast-food. Many consultants just write it off as part of the business. David Brandon, CEO of Domino's Pizza, did a study inside Domino's, the results of which surprised his top management team.[24] He found that the most important factor related to the success (or failure) of any individual store was not marketing, or packaging, or neighborhood demographics. It was the quality of the store manager. Store managers had a great deal to do with the employee turnover, and turnover had a great deal to do with store profit. Domino's calculated that it costs the company $2,500 each time an hourly employee quits and $20,000 each time a store manager quits. Mr. Brandon focused on reducing the 158 percent turnover rate among all employees. Domino's implemented a new and more valid test for selecting managers and hourly personnel, installed new computerized systems for tracking and monitoring employee performance and output, and developed a much more focused pay-for-performance system for all managers. As of 2006, the program was a great success by all counts. Turnover was way down, store profit was up, and the stock price was doing well in an otherwise difficult market. Brandon clearly showed how important HRM is to the bottom line. Attracting and keeping good employees, measuring and monitoring performance, and rewarding strategically important outcomes are all keys. Obviously, all of this has to translate into good (and cheap) pizza. Long-term profitability and growth is driven by customer satisfaction and that's mainly a function of the quality and cost of the products and services. Research clearly shows HRM practice and employee satisfaction are in the "chain of relationships."

In the past, HRM interventions were rarely linked to financial measures or cost figures in order to show a reliable financial benefit. This inability to link such HRM practices to the big picture might explain why personnel departments in the past have had so little clout. While marketing departments were reporting the bottom-line impact of a new marketing strategy in terms of market share or sales volume, personnel could only show that absenteeism or turnover was reduced by some percentage, rarely assessing the relationship between these reductions and a specific financial benefit. Stanford professor Jeffrey Pfeffer summed it up: "In a world in which financial results are measured, a failure to measure human resource policy and practice implementation dooms this to second-class status, oversight neglect, and potential failure. The feedback from the measurements is essential to refine and further develop implementation ideas as well as to learn how well the practices are actually achieving their intended results."[25]

Developing clear criteria linked to strategic goals is critical for managerial success and should be a major driver of HR policy. Some experts argue that HR should quarterback the development and administration of a "management by measurement" system, ensuring all functional business units are subscribing to the guidelines for sound, strategic measurement. Allowing business units to develop and administer "leading indicator" measures can result in the measurement of criteria more linked to making that unit (and particular managers) look good rather than the strategic goals of the unit. HR can help with sound measurement.

But what is sound measurement? One HR executive laid the groundwork with this definition: "The most effective employees are those who provide the highest possible quantity and quality of a product or service at the lowest cost and in the most timely fashion, with a maximum of positive impact on co-workers, organizational units, and the client/customer population." This statement of effectiveness also applies to particular HR programs, products, and services and all functional business units. In evaluating an outsourced recruiting effort, an HR VP provided the following criterion for evaluation: "Give me a large pool of highly qualified candidates, give me this list as quickly as possible, and don't charge me much when you're doing it." The details of the measurement system (e.g., the quantity and quality of what products/services?) must be linked to strategic goals. These details are critical. We will focus on these criteria throughout the book.

The most effective organizations get down to specifics about all important criteria and these are directly linked to key objectives or desired outcomes for the organization. This prescription applies to HR as for any other business function. Wayne Keegan, VP of HR for toymaker ERTL in Diresville, Iowa, clearly represented the bottom line for HR: "HR managers should strive to quantify all facets of HR to determine what works and what doesn't."[26]

What works and doesn't work should focus on the "big picture." The most effective organizations are driven by measurement strategies perhaps conceptualized by HR specialists and applied to HR functions but, more important, applied throughout the workforce. HR can (and should) help senior management develop and focus on key workforce measures that derive from organizational strategy. The most effective organizations develop a set of "top tier" measurement tools that reflect and integrate the company's strategic goals. As Mark Huselid and his colleagues put it, "There should be no gap between what is measured and what is managed." Linking workforce success at the individual and unit level to the most critical business outcomes is a key to competitive advantage.

COMPETITIVE ADVANTAGE[27]

Competitive advantage refers to the ability of an organization to formulate strategies that place it at a favorable position relative to other companies in the industry. Two major principles describe the extent to which a business has a competitive advantage. These two principles are perceived customer value and uniqueness.

Customer Value

Competitive advantage occurs if customers perceive that they receive more value from their transaction with an organization than from its competitors. Ensuring that customers receive value from transacting with a business requires that all employees be focused on understanding customer needs and expectations. This can occur if customer data are used in the designing of products or service processes and customer value is used as the major criterion of interest. Some companies conduct value chain analysis that is designed to assess the amount of added value produced by each position, program, activity and unit in the organization. The value chain analysis can be used to refocus the organization on its core competencies and the requirements of the customer base.

Customers not only perceive but actually realize value from Wal-Mart in the form of price. The products and services are available in convenient stores and average prices are 14 percent lower than its competitors. While there are many reasons Wal-Mart can price goods lower than competitors (e.g., economies of scale, price control pressures on suppliers, technology on products bought and sold, cheaper imports), low labor cost is certainly one factor. Sales clerks earn substantially less at Wal-Mart compared to unionized workers doing essentially the same work for competitors. Health care benefits are estimated to be 30 percent less than coverage for workers within the same industry.

Wal-Mart's strategy to be a price leader and its obsession with cost control have the potential for trouble. The company has been mired in various labor-related lawsuits in recent years, all of which may be related to controlling costs. They paid a huge fine in 2005 for contracting with a company that employed illegal aliens, have been sued numerous times for violating labor laws, including firing people for union organizing efforts, and have been found guilty of violating the Fair Labor Standards Act regarding overtime. While they are the largest employer in the United States, the rate of complaints related to their HR practices is high.

Value to Abercrombie & Fitch is related to creating and sustaining an image for its mostly teen customers. A&F went for an all-American look and it certainly worked. They are the largest teen retailer in the United States with over 600 stores and over a billion dollars in revenues. Their clothes are certainly not cheaper than competitors. A&F is clearly promoting image as a part of its definition of value. But just like Wal-Mart's cost control/price strategy, A&F's "image" strategy created big trouble for the company. In a discrimination lawsuit settled for $40 million in 2005, A&F was accused of favoring white job applicants and employees. A&F agreed to change some of its marketing strategy as a part of the settlement.

Customer Value and Corporate Social Responsibility (CSR)

The notion of customer value is more complicated than it may seem to the uninitiated. Many customers seek out products and services at least to some extent as a function of the reputation of the organization selling the product or service in matters not directly related to the cost or quality of the particular product or service. One of the reasons companies (and politicians) wrap themselves around the Olympics every four years is they believe that the basic sense of American pride and excellence that goes with the Olympics tends to rub off onto the company. Research in marketing shows that perceptions of product quality are positively affected by affiliation with the Olympics. Thus, at least the theory is that customer value is affected by this connection. Likewise, the reputation of companies' environmental policies affects the decision making of some consumers as well as the use of child labor or pitiful labor conditions in international facilities. When Kathy Lee Gifford was accused of exploiting child labor in Honduran clothing plants, some consumers avoided her line of clothing. Nike was accused by the chairman of the

Made in the USA Foundation of using child labor in Indonesia to make its athletic shoes. Nike's business was affected to the extent that consumers consider these allegations when they buy sneakers. Jesse Jackson launched a boycott against Mitsubishi to "encourage" the company to put more women and minorities in executive positions.

Some companies obviously believe that their perceived corporate social and environmental responsibility figures into the complicated calculation of value. There is evidence that companies are under increasing pressure to behave in a socially responsible manner. While there are a variety of definitions of corporate social/environmental performance (CSP), there is debate over the extent to which (or whether) a positive image of CSP is related to corporate financial performance. One recent and large-scale review of the literature on this subject has provided compelling data that CSP does affect the bottom line. The results suggested that "corporate virtue in the form of social responsibility and, to a lesser extent, environmental responsibility is likely to pay off."[28] Perhaps Wal-Mart already knew this. Have you noticed the many ads on TV informing the public about all their good deeds?

Many college students are now involved in tracking the manufacturing process for their school paraphernalia. The United Students Against Sweatshops (USASNET. ORG) is an organization of students from over 200 universities affiliated with the Worker's Rights Consortium. The WRC conducts investigations of manufacturing plants, issues reports, and proclaims boycotts for certain university products such as hats or T-shirts if plants do not meet its standards for wages and safety. This movement is growing and has already had some major successes.

Many consumers use "Newman's Own" products (as in actor Paul Newman) not only because they like the products but because all profits are donated to "educational and charitable purposes." (Go to newmansown.com.) Sure, Newman's Sockarooni spaghetti sauce is tasty. But does the taste account for all of the customer value when the sauce typically costs almost twice as much as other sauces? Customer value can be complicated. Jesse Jackson and Burger King were well aware of this when Burger King agreed to special financing and support for minority-owned franchises. Most people do not live and die for a Whopper. Knowledge regarding Burger King's policy toward minorities could affect the fast-food decision.

So an organization's CSP reputation regarding issues such as corporate ethics or corporate social responsibility, pro-family policies, or affirmative action/diversity practices can go into the "customer value" assessment. This, of course, underscores the importance of the communications domain for particular HR activities. For years, Dow Chemical in Midland, Michigan, had a negative reputation on college campuses because of napalm, a chemical agent they produced that was used in the Vietnam war. Dow had a terrible time recruiting chemists and other vital professionals because of this one product. Dow launched a public relations campaign to enhance its reputation. They focused their advertising on the many agricultural products that they produced and marketed. The result was a profound improvement in Dow's ability to recruit on college campuses. Obviously, Dow's ability to recruit and retain the best chemists was vital to their competitiveness.

While consumers undoubtedly place greater weight on the product or service itself they are considering, there is no question that "customer value" can include tangential variables such as corporate responsibility, environmental impacts, diversity policies, and political issues. One hot issue related to the complicated equation of "customer value" is the way a company treats its employees. Activist consumer groups, by calling attention to corporate greed, may foster more social responsibility by simply affecting the complicated variable of the customer value equation.

The reputation of a company regarding how it treats its employees can also affect the size of the pool of candidates for any job within the organization. Organizations work hard to make the list of the "most admired" companies with which to work because it does help attract more qualified workers. The ratio of the number of qualified applicants to the number of positions is a "high performance work system characteristic." (see again Figure 1-1).

At SAS, a North Carolina computer software company with over 9,000 employees, it all started with free M&Ms every Wednesday. The SAS HR strategy is clearly designed to attract the best programmers and to keep the SAS workforce happy. The strategy has worked. They sold over a billion dollars of analytical software to retailers like Victoria's Secret and the U.S. military in 2005 alone. SAS has never had a losing year and has never laid off a single employee! Says Jim Goodnight, the founder of the company, "If employees are happy, they make the customers happy. If they make the customers are happy, they make me happy." SAS is always ranked very high in *Fortune* magazine's best companies to work for (go to Fortune.com or SAS.com for their current rank). SAS offers a myriad of benefits you don't find at many companies. They have a Work/Life Center made up of social workers who help SAS employees solve life's problems like elder care and college selection for SAS kids. They'll even have someone pick up and deliver your dry cleaning! Says Jeff Chambers, director of HR, "We do all these things because it makes good business sense," saving staff time. SAS claims a turnover rate differential of 3 percent at SAS versus 20 percent at competitors (true even in the heat of the 90s' dot-com craze!). That 17 percent savings in turnover was estimated to save SAS $60–70 million annually. While some companies treat employees as costs or necessities, Jim Goodnight regards his SAS employees as the best investments he ever made. "Ninety-five percent of my assets drive out the front gate every evening. It's my job to bring them back."

There is hard and growing evidence that treating employees well will translate into better financial performance. A recent study showed that positive employee relations served as an "intangible and enduring asset and . . . a source of sustained competitive advantage at the firm level."[29] The study found that companies that made the "100 Best Companies to Work for in America" list had much more positive employee attitudes toward work and significant financial performance advantages over competitors. The advantage is self-sustaining. Once companies make the list, the quality and quantity of its applicants for key positions goes up and thus the quality of its new hires improves!

Maintaining Uniqueness

The second principle of competitive advantage derives from offering a product or service that your competitor cannot easily imitate or copy. For example, if you open a restaurant and serve hamburgers, and a competitor moves in next to you and also serves hamburgers that taste, cost, and are prepared just like yours, unless you quickly offer something unique in your restaurant, you may lose a large part of your business to your competitor. Your restaurant needs to have something that is unique to continue to attract customers. Competitive advantage comes to a business when it adds value to customers through some form of uniqueness. The author of this book works in Boca Raton, Florida, one of the great resort areas of the world (and a golfer's paradise). This location enables his university to attract top faculty and student talent from around the world—clearly a competitive (and unique) advantage.

Apple computer has a great history of getting in focus and staying in focus to meet and exceed customer demands, some of which the customer may not have even thought of. One example of this Apple strategy is the iPod. Says Apple VP Phillip Schiller, the iPod development was about how many songs it holds, how quickly songs can be transferred and how good the sound is in the context of the design. These were the essential questions the customer was asking regarding MP3 players. The uniform whiteness, even the headphones, certainly contributed to the product's iconic status. But as one devoted iPod owner put it, "If it didn't load up fast, store a lot and, above all, sound good, I probably would have stuck with my Walkman for a while longer."[30]

Sources of Uniqueness

The key to any business's competitive advantage is to ensure that uniqueness lasts over time. Three traditional avenues exist to offer customers uniqueness. These include businesses having capabilities in finances or economics, strategy or product, and technology or operations. In addition to these sources, businesses may offer customers uniqueness through a nontraditional capability, namely, organizational processes. The four mechanisms for offering uniqueness are described below. First, **financial or economic capability** derives from an advantage related to costs; when a business is able to produce a good or service cheaper than someone else. If, in your hamburger restaurant, you have received a financial gift from family or friends to build the restaurant, without repayment of the gift, you may be able to charge less for your product than a competitor who borrowed money from a bank or financial institution. Your cheaper-priced hamburger would then become a source of uniqueness that customers value. Toyota and Honda do not have anywhere near the "legacy" costs that Ford and GM Rave (pension and health care commitments to retirees). This is a clear financial advantage for their competitors.

The question of what is unique about a product or service is almost always asked and answered in the context of the usually overriding "cost" question. Wal-Mart's source of uniqueness is rather simple: They have what we want and it's cheaper! For most people and for almost any product or service, the assessment of the product or service is done in the context of price or cost, at both a relative and an absolute level. One early reviewer of the iPod took a look at the $400 initial price tag and suggested that the name might be an acronym for "Idiots Price Our Devices"! But, despite its pricey introduction, the iPod overwhelmed the other MP3 players and acquired what pop star Moby referred to as an "insidious revolutionary quality . . . it becomes a part of your life so quickly that you can't remember what it was like beforehand." Now that's uniqueness![31]

The second source of uniqueness comes from having **strategic or product capability.** That is, a business needs to offer a product or service that differentiates it from other products or services. The iPod is a clear example. In the hamburger wars, each restaurant has attempted to offer unique products and services to attract customers. Salad bars, taco bars, kiddie meals, and $30 breakfasts with giant rodents named Mickey and Minnie are all examples of restaurants attempting to make their product unique and appealing to customers. The possession of a patent for a critical drug is an advantage for a pharmaceutical company.

A third source of uniqueness for a business is a **technological or operational capability.** That is, a business can have a distinctive way of building or delivering its product or service. In the hamburger restaurant, the different methods of preparing the hamburgers may distinguish restaurants from each other (broiled versus flame-grilled). Customers may prefer one technological (cooking) process over another, and thus continue to patronize one restaurant. In more complex businesses, technological capability may include research and development, engineering, computer systems and/or software, and manufacturing facilities. Microsoft has thrived in this area by getting consumers to purchase

and get comfortable with one of their products so they are more attracted to future products related to their technological capability. Google is a great example of unique technological and operational capability.

A fourth source of uniqueness aiding a company in seeking competitive advantage may be derived from **organizational capability.** Organizational capability represents the business's ability to manage organizational systems and people in order to match customer and strategic needs. In a complex, dynamic, uncertain, and turbulent environment (e.g., changing customers, technology, suppliers, relevant laws and regulations), organizational capability derives from the organization's flexibility, adaptiveness, and responsiveness. In a restaurant, organizational capability may be derived from having employees who ensure that when customers enter the restaurant, their customer requirements, their needs, are better met than when the customers go to a competitor's restaurant. That is, employees will want to ensure that customers are served promptly and pleasantly, and that the food is well prepared.

HR systems need to be put in place that not only maximize organizational capability but exploit any other potential sources of uniqueness. Organizations with serious problems on the organizational capability side of the ledger can fail to exploit other potential sources of competitive advantage. The cultural problems after the merger of Chrysler and Daimler-Benz are a good illustration of this interaction. Despite a solid financial situation and highly regarded products, DaimlerChrysler was troubled for years by difficulties in integrating the two distinctly different organizational cultures.

With increased globalization and the need for strategic alliances, organizational capability is a key to sustained competitive advantage as companies expand their businesses around the world. Take McDonald's as one example of a successful global expansion with needs for challenging strategic alliances. McDonald's has restaurants in over 115 countries, but expansion to some areas of the world pose special challenges. Their marketing determined that they could sell the Big Macs in Saudi Arabia. Here's the line-up for the Saudi Big Mac: two all beef patties from Spain, the special sauce from the United States, lettuce from Holland, cheese from New Zealand, pickles from the United States, onions and sesame seeds from Mexico, the bun from Saudi wheat, sugar and oil from Brazil, and the packaging from Germany. Organizational capability enables McDonald's to pull this integration off and the result is a highly popular and profitable product. Globalization will necessitate more of these challenging arrangements. HR will have a lot to do with making them a success through enhanced organizational capability.

HR systems help determine how people are recruited, hired, trained, motivated, treated, evaluated, paid, and integrated into the organization. As we discussed earlier, research now shows that organizational capability in the form of particular HR activities is a reliable predictor of the corporate financial performance. HR activities and processes such as those defining the "leading indicator" high-performance work systems are illustrations of organizational capability as a source of competitive advantage. The ability to attract and retain those individuals with the skills to establish or maintain all potential sources of uniqueness should be a part of any "management by measurement" system.

SUMMARY

Human resource management is to some extent concerned with any organizational decision that has an impact on the workforce or the potential workforce. The trends we describe in Chapter 1 underscore the importance of HR to meet the challenges of the 21st century. While there is typically a human resource or personnel department in middle to large corporations, line management is still primarily responsible for the application of HRM policies and practices. There are critical competencies for general management and HRM professionals. An organization needs both competent personnel trained in HRM and motivated managers who recognize the importance of HRM activities and apply the best procedures. HR managers are more likely to convince line managers of the value of HR programs by focusing on "leading indicator" measurements, which can be linked to the lagging financial indicators that are more clearly understood by management. Personnel/HR functions are often perceived by line managers to be out of step with the real bottom-line outcome measures for the organization. The most effective human resource departments are those in which HRM policy and activities are established and measured in the context of the mission and strategic objectives of the organization. HRM should assist management in the difficult task of integrating and coordinating the interests of the various organizational constituencies, with the ultimate criterion being to enhance the organization's competitive position by focusing on meeting or exceeding customer requirements and expanding the customer base.

Competitive advantage is the key to success for most businesses. To attain competitive advantage, businesses need to add value for customers and offer uniqueness. Four capabilities provide a business's uniqueness: financial, strategic or product, technological or operational, and organizational. To sustain competitive advantage, organizational capability should be emphasized and, ideally, in the context of the other sources of uniqueness. Organizational capability derives from a business's HRM practices.

The view of HRM outlined in this chapter provides a foundation for integrating HRM activities into the organization's mission and goals. We have emphasized that HRM professionals should be actively involved in building more competitive organizations through the HRM domains. One necessary competency for both line managers and HRM professionals is an understanding of the role of globalization in HR policy and practice. We will explore this critical area in the next chapter.

DISCUSSION QUESTIONS

1. Describe the changing status of HRM. What factors have led to these changes?

2. How do productivity concerns influence organizational policies and procedures regarding HRM activities?

3. Describe the major HRM activities conducted in an organization. Provide an example of each from a company with which you are familiar.

4. What impact should the composition of the workforce have on HRM practices or activities? What future trends do you see that will influence HRM activities? Why is the growing cultural diversity of the workforce a management challenge?

5. Why is the support of line management critical to the effective functioning of HRM practices in an organization? Provide some suggestions to ensure that this support is maintained.

6. Why does the number of qualified applicants for each strategic position relate to corporate effectiveness? How can HRM enhance this?

7. What are the sources of uniqueness that can aid a company in seeking competitive advantage?

8. Explain how Ford and GM have a competitive disadvantage related to financial capability.

2

THE ROLE OF GLOBALIZATION IN HR POLICY AND PRACTICE*

O V E R V I E W

In Chapter 1, we described the importance of aligning Human Resource (HR) programs with the business strategy. This means that as organizations change, HR policies and programs must adapt as well. One of the major challenges facing businesses today is the increasing globalization of the world economy and competition.

Thomas Friedman's critically acclaimed new book on globalization, *The World Is Flat: A Brief History of the Twenty-First Century,* describes the next phase of globalization.[1] Technological and political forces have facilitated a global, Web-based "playing field" that allows for multiple types of collaboration regardless of geography, distance, and even language. Morgan Stanley estimates that from 1995 to 2005, cheap imports from China have saved American consumers over $600 billion. They have probably saved U.S. companies much more than that. Wal-Mart imported $18 billion worth of goods in 2004 from its 5,000 Chinese suppliers (that's 80 percent of Wal-Mart's 6,000 suppliers!). While India and China are clearly threats to the developed world, Tom Friedman argues that they represent great opportunity. The net effect will add millions of consumers to the world economy.

Over the past 50 years, world output increased by more than 600 percent, and world trade grew by 1,500 percent.[2] In 1950, world exports totaled $53 billion. In 1996, they were estimated to be over $5.1 trillion, accounting for 18 percent of the world's $29 trillion economy. Between 1990 and 2000, world trade increased almost 7 percent per year.[3] The World Bank now estimates that global trade accounts for half of all of the world's gross national product (GNP). Six out of 10 firms say they have at least one foreign company among their top five competitors.[4]

The same explosive growth has occurred in foreign direct investment (FDI). Foreign direct investment involves the control of a company through its ownership by a foreign company or foreign individuals. This growth was most dramatic in the last decade.[5] One expert indicates that about 63,000 companies worldwide have FDIs.[6]

Another strong trend is the creation of offshore professional and operations centers, regardless of where the final work product is ultimately marketed. Many U.S. and European software manufacturers now have facilities in India to take advantage of the high concentration of computer skills in that country and the low cost of labor. Traditionally, business facilities were strategically located in order to be close to suppliers or customers, and/or within trade alliance borders. Today, however, the use of private satellite links, e-mail, fax machines, and the World Wide Web has made workers from all over the world very accessible. Even customer service facilities are being located overseas, particularly when there is a sufficient supply of productive workers who are willing to work for relatively low pay.

*Contributed by Christine M. Hagan.

Global recruitment and staffing are now the rage. As a consumer, you may be unaware that your X-rays may be read by someone in India, that your software is repaired by specialists in Ireland, that your airline reservations were booked with a customer service rep in Jamaica, or that your insurance claims were processed in the Philippines. Technology now allows a great deal of even service work to move offshore where labor costs are less than in the United States. Workers can (and do) telecommute across continents.

Why are so many organizations today under pressure to expand their business interests beyond their national boundaries? Major reasons include access to additional resources (including skilled workers), lower costs, economies of scale, favorable regulations and tax systems, direct access to new and growing markets, and the ability to customize products to local tastes and styles. In addition, the rise of regional trade alliances (such as NAFTA and the European Union) is another important reason explaining why organizations have increasingly internationalized. Later in this chapter, we will describe some of the problems associated with the rise of regional trade alliances, such as the "banana wars" and Mexico's "screwdriver factories."

These trends are not expected to slow over the next several years. Let's take a brief look at a few examples. Founded in 1901 and headquartered in Cleveland, Ohio, TRW is a $17 billion global company, employing more than 110,000 individuals in 35 countries, half of whom are non-U.S. employees. TRW conducts about 65 percent of its business in the automotive field and 35 percent in space, defense, and information technology. More than 40 percent of its revenues come from international operations.[7]

McDonald's opened its first non-U.S. restaurant in Canada in 1967. By 2002, their total sales outside of the United States represented 58 percent of their operating income.[8] In fact, every three hours, a new McDonald's opens somewhere on earth.[9] Two-thirds of these new stores are outside of the United States.

Coca-Cola and Wal-Mart are two other great examples of the potential presented by the global economy. With operations in more than 200 countries, Coke derives over 70 percent of its operating income from overseas operations. In 1991, Wal-Mart first ventured offshore in a joint venture in Mexico. They are now the largest retailer in Canada and Mexico and have over 1,100 stores in nine countries.

This global expansion presents great challenges for HRM. When McDonald's entered into a joint venture with the Moscow city council, the company placed a help-wanted ad and received about 27,000 Russian applicants for its 605 positions. It sent six Russian managers to its Hamburger University outside Chicago, Illinois, for six months of training and another 30 managers for several months of training in Canada or Europe.[10] It also needed to overcome significant problems obtaining high-quality

supplies, most of which were perishable. Ultimately, McDonald's opened a $40 million food-processing center about 45 minutes from its first Moscow restaurant.[11]

An estimated 80 percent of Coca-Cola employees are non-U.S. personnel.[12] Coke now has six largely autonomous regional groups (North America, Europe, Eastern Europe/Mideast, Africa, Latin America, and the Pacific Region). In addition, they have established a global service staff of 500 people who are trained to go anywhere in the world to offer advice and expertise concerning operational and customer service problems. These team members are paid U.S. wages, even though many of them are not from the United States.

The majority of Fortune 500 companies are now multinational in that some portion of their business (and profits) is derived from overseas operations.[13] Many of our largest, most prestigious companies, including IBM, Exxon, and Microsoft, derive more than half of their revenues from overseas business. With the immense market potential overseas, particularly in Asia, this figure is likely to get even higher for many U.S. corporations. It is estimated that by 2020, the six largest world economies will be the United States plus five Asian economies: China, Japan, India, Indonesia, and a united Korea. Along with this success will come great demand for products and services for the new middle classes of these countries. In 2000, about one-third of the sales of Fortune 500 companies came from outside the United States.[14]

Of course, global expansion is not reserved for U.S. companies. Many organizations headquartered in Europe and Asia have expanded their global reach over the last decade or so. In fact, chances are better than ever that you may work for a foreign corporation in your own community. Consider that the majority of 2001 Hondas driven in the United States were actually manufactured in the United States. In the last 10 years, more than 200 German businesses established direct investments in North and South Carolina alone. Most Mercedes and BMW cars driven in the United States are now assembled in the United States. Nokia, the cell phone giant from Finland, employs over 1,000 foreign workers in Finland and over 60 percent of its 53,000 employees are non-Finns working all over the world. Philips, the electronics multinational, employs 83 percent of its workforce outside of its headquarters in the Netherlands. The Roche Group, the Swiss pharmaceutical giant, has 88 percent of its workforce outside of Switzerland.[15] Today, an estimated 4.9 million U.S. citizens work in U.S. affiliations of foreign-owned corporations.[16]

In addition, your company is now more likely than ever before to have some type of business partnership with a foreign corporation. Earlier we mentioned that McDonald's opened its first restaurant in Russia through a joint venture with the Moscow city council. Businessland, one of the largest U.S. dealers of personal computers, moved into Japan with the help of Japan's four largest electronics firms. There are estimates that over 80 percent of U.S. businesses could successfully market their products or services overseas provided that they had the required knowledge of foreign markets.[17] Since U.S. markets are regarded as mature or "soft" in many product lines, international markets appear to offer potential for substantial growth. Today, over 95 percent of the world's population lives outside of the United States.[18] That's a lot of Coke, Big Macs, and even Vegamatics!

There is also a higher probability than ever before that you will have an overseas assignment. A 1997 study by the National Foreign Trade Council estimated that there are more than 250,000 Americans on overseas assignments and that that number is expected to increase in the future.[19]

Even if you don't ever work for a foreign-owned firm, or for a U.S. firm with significant foreign investments, experts tell us that all organizations today are affected by the global economy. Even small businesses are using foreign-made materials or equipment, are competing with foreign firms, and are selling their products and services in foreign markets.[20]

As we discussed in Chapter 1, this inevitable globalization of the world's business presents challenges and opportunities for human resources professionals. The purpose of this chapter is to describe and discuss the implications of this increasing globalization for HR activities.

OBJECTIVES

After reading this chapter, you should be able to

1. *Know the different ways companies may engage in international commerce.*
2. *Learn the different international business strategies.*
3. *Know how international human resource management (IHRM) differs from traditional, domestic HRM.*
4. *Understand the different IHRM strategies.*
5. *Learn the trends relating to international job assignments.*
6. *Understand the issues and trends relating to the development of globally competent business leaders.*

HOW DO COMPANIES ENGAGE IN INTERNATIONAL COMMERCE?

Organizations conduct international business in a variety of ways. Each of these forms of international commerce has implications for human resource strategies and tactics. An effective HR professional recognizes the range of choices that each of these international business forms (or combinations of these forms) offers. In this section, we will review the different ways firms may internationalize. Then we will describe some of the ways that HR practices may facilitate and advance these business goals.

When a firm simply wants to sell its products and services in foreign marketplaces, it may choose to **export.** Most companies that export do so in order to increase sales and revenues. For some companies, particularly companies with high research and development costs, exporting is necessary in order to spread these costs over a larger sales volume. Companies may also export in order to relieve excess capacity. Some companies export as a form of diversification because they are concerned that their domestic markets may be maturing. Finally, some companies export because they believe that they lack the necessary knowledge to directly do business effectively on foreign shores. In this case, exporting may be the first step toward a more aggressive international strategy. Baskin-Robbins followed this approach with its entry into Russia. In 1990, it began shipping ice cream to that country from its company-owned plants in Texas and Canada. Over the next five years, the company opened 74 retail outlets with Russian partners, carefully observing the likes and dislikes of local consumers. Finally, in 1995, Baskin-Robbins opened its first, full-service ice cream plant in Moscow.[21] Companies that choose to export may directly sell their products in a foreign market, or they may do business through third parties that specialize in facilitating importing and exporting, called **intermediaries.**

There is little risk in exporting: relatively low investment is involved and a decision to withdraw from a market can be made and executed very quickly. Exporting, however, has several disadvantages, including the high cost of transportation and the difficulty of finding good distributors. Tariffs and quotas are also a major problem when goods or services enter a country that is part of a regional pact or a free-trade area. For example, products created within the European Union (EU) move from country to country within the Union tariff-free. The same products and services imported from countries outside the Union typically pay tariffs upon entry. This increases the cost of the product and often places "outside" organizations at a competitive disadvantage. The banana trade provides an interesting example. During the 1990s, when Caribbean bananas were exported to EU countries, they were subject to tariffs and quotas. However, bananas grown in Martinique and Guadeloupe were not subject to these tariffs because those particular islands were still provinces of France and, therefore, enjoyed insider status within the EU.[22] The wars were officially ended by treaty in 2001.[23]

Similarly, extensive rules were required in order to regulate so-called screwdriver plants in Mexico. Capitalizing on Mexico's membership in the North American Free Trade Agreement (NAFTA), companies in other parts of the world were shipping virtually finished goods to plants in Mexico where, typically, a screwdriver was the only tool needed to complete the assembly. Then, the exporting country would assert that the product had been "manufactured" in Mexico and, therefore, would qualify for favorable tariff treatment within NAFTA. Since most of these goods ended up in the United States and Canada, these NAFTA members were particularly worried about the loss of tariff revenues and the loss of jobs to non-NAFTA countries whose goods might qualify for treatment as though they had been created within the NAFTA region. As a result, NAFTA contains complex rules of origin that specify how much and what type of assembly qualifies an item as having actually been produced within the NAFTA area. For example, NAFTA's rules of origin specify that for an automobile to qualify as a North American product, 62.5 percent of its value must be created in Canada, Mexico, or the United States. Similarly, to protect textile industry jobs, clothing and other textile products must use North American–produced fibers in order to benefit from NAFTA's preferential tariff treatment.

Another means of entering a foreign market is **licensing.** In this approach, one firm, called the licensor, leases the right to use its intellectual property to another firm, called the licensee, in exchange for a fee. Intellectual property typically includes patents, formulas, patterns, copyrights, trademarks, brand names, methods, and procedures. Licensors are usually required to provide technical information and assistance, and the licensee is obliged to use the rights responsibly and effectively, and to pay the agreed-upon fees. Heineken, for example, is exclusively licensed to manufacture and sell Pepsi-Cola in the Netherlands. To implement this agreement, Pepsi either provides Heineken with its formula or agrees to supply the cola syrup. Heineken then adds carbonated water, packages it in appropriate containers, and sells it in the Netherlands. Under the conditions of the license agreement, Pepsi cannot enter into a similar agreement with another firm to sell Pepsi in the Netherlands, and Heineken cannot alter the product, nor can it begin duplicating other Pepsi products (such as Lays Potato Chips) without a separate agreement.

Franchising is a special form of licensing. One of the fastest-growing forms of international business activities today, a franchise agreement allows an independent organization, called the franchisee, to operate a business under the name of another, called a franchisor, in return for a fee. Franchising typically allows the franchisor more control over the franchisee and provides for more ongoing support from the franchisor to the franchisee than is the case in the typical licensing agreement. For instance, a franchisor may provide ongoing services such as advertising, training, quality assurance programs, and reservation systems (for airline or hotel operations).

Fast-food chains such as McDonald's, Dairy Queen, Domino's Pizza, and KFC have franchised restaurants worldwide.

On the plus side, licensees (and franchisees) receive access to a business that has an established product and operating system plus a good reputation. Licensors (and franchisors) get the opportunity to expand internationally with very limited knowledge about local markets. In addition, over time, each party to the agreement learns valuable information from the other: franchisees learn how to operate a successful business; franchisors learn quickly about the marketplace. On the negative side, both parties typically share the revenues, while neither party has full decision-making authority. Disputes about the terms and conditions of the agreement can become a problem. Of course, in some areas of the world, patents and copyrights are not protected, so a particular company could find its intellectual property duplicated and sold everywhere. This has been particularly problematic in the computer software and the music industries in Asia and Eastern Europe. In addition, licensors (and franchisors) must make certain that the required technical skills are available to support the quality of the product or service. McDonald's, for example, spent considerable resources teaching Russian farmers how to grow potatoes that would meet their standards.

Some firms may choose to use a specialized strategy to participate in international business without making direct, long-term investments. Nike engages in **contract manufacturing** when it outsources the creation of its athletic footwear to numerous factories in southeast Asia. This permits Nike to focus its efforts on product design and marketing, rather than production. Contract manufacturing typically means that the organization gives up a major amount of control over the processes, and this may lead to quality problems or other surprises. Nike has suffered considerable negative publicity about the working conditions employed by its contractors in the factories manufacturing its products. (See Critical Thinking Application 2.A.)

Another specialized international business strategy involves **management contracts.** In this form of business, one company sells its management (and sometimes technical) expertise to a company in another area of the world. BAA of Britain, for example, operates the Indianapolis Airport under a 10-year management contract and provides retail services management at the Air Mall in the Pittsburgh Airport.[24] Similarly, major airlines such as Delta, Air France, and KLM often sell their management expertise to small state-owned airlines headquartered in developing countries.[25] Other benefits may become available to organizations that seek managerial partners. For instance, when Sheraton Corporation signs a contract to manage a hotel facility overseas, it usually includes access to and use of its international reservation system.[26]

All of the above approaches enable an organization to internationalize its business interests without actually investing in foreign factories or facilities. Of course, some firms prefer to enter international markets through actual ownership of business. We mentioned earlier that when an organization directly owns part of or an entire business in a foreign market, this form of commerce is called **foreign direct investment (FDI).** Often, FDI follows a period in which an organization seeks to learn about and understand a particular market or region using one of the lower-risk entry alternatives, such as exporting, licensing, franchising, or contracting. Although FDI involves much greater risk, it also means increased managerial and operational control, and it ultimately may mean greater profitability if the venture is successful. One common approach to FDI is to identify an appropriate organization with which to "partner." Such an **alliance** allows an organization to make direct investment very gradually while sharing its risk with a knowledgeable, experienced other party. Sometimes, partners enter into **joint ventures,** which involve creating a new, separate company that is owned jointly by the venture partners. Joint venture partners can be privately owned companies, government agencies, or government-owned companies. For instance, Suzuki Motors Corporation of Japan teamed with the government of India to produce an efficient, small-engine car specifically for the Indian marketplace.[27] Sometimes, organizations enter into joint ventures as defensive moves. Caterpillar (U.S.) and Mitsubishi (Japan) created a joint venture to improve each's competitive position against joint rival Komatsu (Japan).[28] General Mills (U.S.) and Nestlé (Switzerland) created Cereal Partners Worldwide (CPW) to combat Kellogg's 50 percent market share of the global cereal industry and, in particular, their considerable domination of the European cereal marketplace.[29]

The major disadvantage to joint ventures is the potential for conflict between the partners. This potential is increased considerably when each partner owns 50 percent of the venture. Common areas of conflict include future investments and the sharing of future profits. Joint ventures with local governments also create challenges particularly when the government's motives and priorities are considerably different from those of its business partner. This situation occurs most often in industries considered to be culturally sensitive or important to national security such as broadcasting, infrastructure projects, and defense.[30]

When companies agree to partner with one another, but do not set up a separate entity, they have formed a **strategic alliance.** Such alliances can be set up between an organization and its suppliers, its customers, and its competitors. Strategic alliances share most of the same advantages as joint ventures and some experts regard joint ventures as a form of strategic alliance. Strategic alliances permit organizations to share risk and expenses, particularly related to research and new product development. They also enable each partner to tap into (and, ultimately, benefit from) the strengths of the other. Disadvantages tend to center on the possibility that each is helping to create a future competitor. Thus, organizations are advised to protect their core competencies from the other, which may mean that trust and communication become problematic.

Of course, some organizations prefer the high risk of **sole ownership** of operations in foreign countries in order to ensure that they have full decision-making authority and operational control. In such cases, organizations would rather not audit the practices of franchisees or manage the compromises that shared alliances tend to create. Such businesses may take the form of start-up operations (that is, built from scratch), or they may be carried out through acquisition. Acquisitions involve the purchase of an already-up-and-running business with an existing group of suppliers and customers. As a result, growth in foreign markets through acquisitions tends to allow a firm to enter and compete in a new market more quickly than it would if it created a start-up operation. General Electric's 1990 acquisition of Tungsram, a lighting company in Hungary, is an example of this. The acquisition occurred just as communist rule was being eliminated in Eastern Europe. General Electric wanted to learn how to do business in this part of the world. Tungsram was willing to be acquired in order to access Western capitalism and management practices. Some assert that GE's acquisition was a defensive response to the earlier acquisition of Westinghouse's lamp division (GE's traditional rival in its domestic market) by Philips Electronics of Holland. As GE's then–lighting chief, John Opie, indicated, "Suddenly we have bigger, stronger competition. They're invading our market, but we're not in theirs. So, we're immediately put on the defensive."[31] Within a year of acquiring Tungsram, GE Lighting also acquired Thorn EMI in Great Britain and created a joint venture with Hitachi that would allow entry into the Asian market. As a result of these efforts, GE Lighting's business focus quickly shifted. In 1988, GE Lighting got less than 10 percent of its sales from outside the United States; within five years, more than 40 percent of GE Lighting's sales were coming from abroad. In this case, the speed of GE Lighting's internationalization was facilitated by its use of an acquisition strategy.

Exporting Work

Earlier we mentioned the recent trend toward businesses creating **offshore professional and operations centers.** Either as a form of sole ownership or as a strategic alliance, these centers involve the exporting of the work itself to places on the globe in order to obtain competitive advantage by leveraging combinations of such factors as workforce skills, cultural similarities, costs, time, and government policies, regardless of where the work product is ultimately marketed. A good case in point is India, which has been the recipient of many U.S. technical and customer service jobs over the past several years. Among developing countries, the Indian workforce is comparatively well-educated and speaks English. Upon achieving independence from Great Britain in 1947, India adopted a democratic political system, although its economic system involved significant government planning and intervention. Over the past 10 years, however, the Indian government's regulation of and involvement in private business matters has been steadily declining in order to specifically encourage foreign direct investment. At the same time, the cost of living in India is much lower than in developed countries, which means that the relative cost of labor is extremely attractive for Western companies.

When the World Bank surveyed 150 prominent U.S. and European computer hardware and software manufacturers, India's programmers were ranked first out of eight countries, well ahead of Ireland, Israel, Mexico, and Singapore. In fact, one in four software engineers in the world is of Indian origin. With average annual programmer salaries in India of approximately $3,000 per year, no wonder companies such as Hewlett-Packard, IBM, Texas Instruments, Honeywell, and Motorola employ skilled technical workers there.[32] (Of course, this pay could rise significantly and rapidly as the demand for Indian programmers grows and the country continues to develop economically.) In addition to competent workers at advantageous costs, organizations also are benefiting from time advantages, by increasingly using international teams of skilled programmers in the United States, Western Europe, and India who pass the work to the next team as each location's workday ends. This permits around-the-clock product development and/or troubleshooting to be done, a huge benefit in industries in which competitive advantage is influenced by "first-to-market" capability.

Customer service facilities are also increasingly moving from the United States to India. Customer service representatives at one call center in India are taught to speak English with midwestern accents in order to fend off consumer concern about the use of foreign customer service centers by U.S. companies. Each Indian customer representative is also provided a "U.S. biography" that is used when conversations with customers become personal.[33] The net result of these trends is lower labor costs for American companies, and thus greater profits. Of course, it also means the increased shipment of previously American jobs overseas and the continued stagnation of middle-class wages in this country.

Summary

In summary, then, there are a broad variety of approaches organizations may take to internationalizing their business ranging in risk and degree of involvement from an export strategy to sole ownership of foreign facilities. Each of these approaches has substantially different implications for human resource professionals. When companies engage in exporting, licensing, or contract manufacturing, the major challenges may be primarily related to operations, marketing, and legal issues. HR issues may be affected only on a secondary basis. For instance, in Chapter 1, we mentioned the increasing importance of a company's reputation and the way it relates both to consumers and to potential (or current) employees. When Nike's reputation suffers because of the labor conditions used by its contract facilities, HR professionals may find that it is increasingly difficult to attract, retain, and motivate qualified and high-performance employees.

On the other hand, when companies engage in management contracts or franchising, the terms and conditions of the agreement will affect the degree of HR involvement and challenge. Certainly, as McDonald's has franchised foreign restaurants, it has maintained an extremely strong role in the training and development of workers at all levels. However, when McDonald's directly owns and operates a restaurant on foreign shores, the HR challenge increases exponentially to include all the HR domains described in Chapter 1. In general, the HR challenge increases as the degree of an organization's international involvement increases. Thus, sole ownership of foreign subsidiaries presents the highest level of HR involvement and challenge.

The HR challenge also is affected by such things as the degree of cultural similarity among a firm's business holdings and the degree of internationalization of a firm, both of which we will discuss later in this chapter. In the next section, we will describe the managerial strategies that firms may implement and the way they influence HR issues.

INTERNATIONAL BUSINESS STRATEGIES

Organizations with foreign direct investments (FDI) tend to choose among three general international management strategies. In a **multilocal** strategy, a business is managed as a collection of relatively independent operating organizations, each of which is focused on a particular domestic market. Multilocal businesses tend to be very decentralized: Each division is free to customize its own products, create its own advertising and promotion campaigns, and utilize whatever production techniques best serve the customers. Kraft, Unilever, and Cadbury Schweppes are good examples of organizations that are more interested in meeting the needs of their local customers than they are in taking advantage of the economies of scale that result from a more centralized or regionalized approach to doing business. In these situations, HR practices also tend to be decentralized and are focused on the policies and practices that fit best with the particular situation.

An **export** corporation tends to view the world as a single marketplace and strives to create standardized goods or services that will meet the needs of customers everywhere. This type of organization tends to be the antithesis of the multilocal business. While multilocal companies believe that consumers in each country, or region, are fundamentally different in their tastes and preferences, export organizations believe that consumers are basically the same worldwide. Export companies tend to seek economies of scale by concentrating production in a handful of highly productive factories and creating global advertising and marketing campaigns. As a result, export organizations tend to be centralized and, typically, power and responsibility are vested in the headquarters of the company. This approach has been adopted by many of the Japanese companies such as Sony and Matsushita, who design their products with the world in mind. In these organizations, HR programs also tend to emanate from the headquarters office, and policies will tend to be reasonably consistent. For example, in these organizations, pay amounts will differ from country to country (based on local practices), but the way jobs are valued may be very similar. Burger King, for example, uses a single job evaluation plan throughout its worldwide operations, but publishes many different pay scales, based on local or regional pay practices.

The third international business strategy is a **global** approach, which tries to combine the benefits of an export orientation and multilocal organizations. These businesses try to achieve global-scale efficiencies, while remaining locally responsive to their customers. Ford Motor Company has tried to employ this approach. Ford tends to have a single manager responsible for global engine and transmission development. Other managers have similar responsibilities for worldwide design and development, production, and marketing. But each manager is also responsible for ensuring that the Ford product is tailored to meet local customer tastes and preferences. From an HR perspective, these types of companies also will tend to contain a mix of policies and programs that are applied uniformly, with many that are locally created, modified, and managed because of their ability to attract, retain, and motivate qualified workers in a particular setting.

What Influences the Type of International Strategy a Firm Will Choose?

Precisely which of the above international strategies a business chooses is influenced by three factors. First, issues in a country's general environment make a difference. A country's general environment tends to affect all organizations in a similar way. A particular country's economic, legal, political, and sociocultural systems, plus diversity in language and religious beliefs, are all examples of general environment issues. For example, the increasing cultural diversity of the U.S. workforce and

the general aging of the population are sociocultural factors that foreign companies would typically consider before they located operations in the United States. The low unemployment rate that characterized the U.S. economy during the late 1990s was a major factor influencing whether Asian, European, and Latin American companies would open subsidiaries here and what particular business and HR strategy they would implement. Political instability in a particular world region is obviously a major influence on all businesses in the region.

The second factor that influences a company's choice of strategy is the company's task environment, typically those forces that are directly related to the industry within which a firm operates. Such issues as cost pressures, the intensity of competitive rivalry, the ease with which organizations may enter or leave the industry, and the degree of power over the company maintained by suppliers and customers are all examples of a firm's task environment. Harvard professor Michael Porter argues that such characteristics of an organization's industry are among the most important factors that influence the choice of which international strategy to implement. Porter addresses two types of international industries.[34] In **multilocal industries,** competition in each country, or region, is essentially independent of the competition in other regions. In multilocal industries, business policies and practices can be as centralized or as decentralized as management prefers. In this situation, the organization may choose to manage a portfolio of businesses, each with its own policies and practices. Such multilocal industries include retailing, many consumer food products, wholesaling, life insurance, consumer finance, and caustic chemicals. At the other end of the continuum is the **global industry** in which a firm's competitive position in one country is significantly affected by its position in other countries. Global industries require high integration among units in order to leverage gains and to achieve overall competitive advantage. It is difficult to operate in a decentralized fashion in a global industry because of the high need for coordination. Yet, HR professionals in these organizations must find the appropriate balance between global competitiveness and local responsiveness. Global industries include commercial aircraft, semiconductors, copiers, automobiles, and watches.

The third factor that influences choice of international strategy is the internal strengths or weaknesses of the organization. Relevant internal factors include an organization's culture, the expertise of its management staff, the sophistication of its information systems, and the ability to detect and respond to consumer trends. In many cases, these are critical assets that add value within the firm. Organizational capability is an important internal strength and, as we indicated in Chapter 1, may be a source of sustainable competitive advantage for an organization, thus influencing its readiness to pursue a particular international strategy.

DOMESTIC VERSUS INTERNATIONAL HR

How do creating and providing HR services in an organization that is actively international differ from the HR role in a firm that is essentially rooted within the borders of a single nation? HR activities all relate to the procurement, allocation, and utilization of people. Thus, the particular activities may not be all that different regardless of where they are performed or whom they cover. Experts assert that what differentiates domestic HR from international HR is the complexity involved in operating in different countries with different cultures, politics, and laws and regulations.[35] Operating in different countries means that individuals must work with different national governments, different legal systems, under widely different economic conditions, with people of diverse cultures and values, and suppliers and customers over vast geographical distances.[36] Figure 2-1 presents a summary of HRM activities and challenges related to international joint ventures.

In Chapter 3, we will describe the broad array of employment laws that regulate organizations that operate within the United States. But this isn't all there is! Later in the text, you will be introduced to the extensive legal rules governing pay and benefits (Chapter 10), labor relations (Chapter 13), and worker health and safety (Chapter 14). When a foreign firm moves into the United States, they must be expert at understanding and applying legally defensible HR policies and practices. One recent study indicated that the amount of U.S. work-related legislation combined with the litigious orientation of Americans in general places foreign companies at a competitive disadvantage here that they must overcome if they are to be successful.[37] But the reverse is also true. Most developed countries and many emerging economies have a broad framework of work-related legislation. The effective HR professional must understand the implications of such legislation in relevant areas of the world and must have a solid grasp of the costs relating to compliance.

In addition to the legal complexity of operating internationally, other factors affect the level of difficulty involved in operating HR on an international basis.[38] First, the degree of cultural difference influences the complexity of HR and managerial challenges. Culture has been defined as "a system of values and norms that are shared among a group of people and that when taken together constitute a design for living."[39] Studies indicate that culture affects the policies and practices of HRM and that a major reason that international assignments fail is culture shock, or the expatriate's inability to adjust to a different cultural environment.[40]

Experts suggest that a third issue that increases the complexity in managing HR internationally is an organization's degree of foreign investment in relation to its domestic investment. The United States is both the largest national economy and the largest national consumer market in the world. Thus, businesses have had many options concerning growth and expansion (e.g., introducing new products, entering new market segments, finding new uses for existing products, etc.). When U.S. organizations enter foreign markets, they often stumble and fall because they lack experience in effectively operating and managing foreign businesses. Wal-Mart is a great example of a company that has struggled through a number of missteps in its thrust to internationalize. While they are successful in Canada and Mexico now, they started out on very shaky ground. Their problems in Germany persist despite considerable investment.

Organizations headquartered in Switzerland (e.g., Nestlé, ABB, Roche Pharmaceuticals) have tended to plan for growth by internationalizing, since the Swiss domestic market is so small. Such growth, then, is fundamentally based on the organization's ability to effectively manage foreign operations and foreign workers, and organizations tend to plan for this eventuality. In the United States, we have traditionally measured complexity based on size. *Fortune*'s annual Global 500 list identifies the largest 500 international organizations in the world based on total revenues. Using this measure, the U.S. headquarters 189 (or 38 percent) of the world's largest international corporations. On the other hand, the United Nations Conference on Trade and Development (UNCTAD), which tracks industrial development around the world, measures the degree of internationality among firms, based not on *how much* an organization directly invests in

FIGURE 2-1	Unique HRM Challenges in International Joint Ventures
HR Activity	**HRM Challenges**
Staffing	Host country may demand staffing policies contrary to maximizing profits.
Decision making	Conflicts among diverse constituent groups; complexity of decision processes.
Communication	Interpersonal problems due to geographical dispersion and cultural differences.
Compensation	Perceived and real compensation differences.
Career planning	Perceptions regarding value of overseas assignments; difficulties in reentry.
Performance management	Differences in standards; difficulties in measuring performance across countries.
Training	Special training for functioning in international joint venture (IJV) structure.

FIGURE 2-2	Top 10 Organizations Based on UNCTAD's Transnationality Index, 2002		
Company		**Country**	**Industry**
1. NTL, Inc.		United States	Communication services
2. Thomson Corp.		Canada	Media, publishing
3. Holcim AG		Switzerland	Construction equipment
4. CRH Plc		Ireland	Lumber, building materials
5. ABB		Switzerland	Machinery and equipment
6. Roche Group		Switzerland	Pharmaceuticals
7. Interbrew SA		Belgium	Beverages
8. Publicis Groupe SA		France	Business services
9. News Corp.		Australia	Media
10. Philips Electronics		Netherlands	Electrical and electronic equipment

Source: *World Investment Report 2004: The Shift towards Services.* Available at www.UNCTAD.org/wir.

or derives from its foreign business assets, but rather on the *proportionate share* of an organization's overall business that foreign investment and commerce represent. According to UNCTAD, it is considerably more complex to manage a business and its people when the resources are deployed in various ways all over world than it is to manage just a big organization. The UNCTAD index is based on a composite of three ratios: (1) foreign assets to total assets, (2) foreign sales to total sales, and (3) foreign employment to total employment. NTL, Inc. (United States) tops the UNCTAD transnationality list with an overall index of 99.1. What? So you've never heard of NTL, Inc.—the telecommunications powerhouse specializing in telephone, television, and broadband services? That's probably because 100 percent of its sales come from *outside* the United States. In fact, the only tie between NTL and the United States that we could find was 208 employees reportedly located in its world headquarters in New York City.

Ranking second is Thomson Corporation (Canada) with a transnationality index of 97.9 based on the fact that 97.7 percent of its assets and its sales and 98 percent of its employees are located in other countries. Figure 2-2 illustrates the top 10 organizations in terms of UNCTAD's transnationality index. Other than that blockbuster U.S. firm NTL, one can't help but notice the conspicuous absence of any other U.S.-based organization on the top-10 list. In fact, you have to go all the way down to number 27 to find Coca-Cola. Figure 2-3 identifies the 20 "most international" U.S. firms. Thus, the UNCTAD approach to organizational complexity would suggest that, as the degree of a company's internationalization increases, the complexity of the HR challenge increases exponentially.

Another issue (perhaps somewhat related to the above issue) is the attitude of senior management toward international operations. If senior management lacks an international orientation and considers its foreign subsidiaries as nothing more than "outposts" of the home office, the overall importance of internationalization is diminished. Thinking can become very parochial, as managers focus on domestic issues and assume that inter-

national issues are identical to those at home. Regardless of the reason, this failure to recognize differences between domestic and international operations frequently creates problems in foreign business units.[41] This failure often limits the problem-solving capacity of the firm and increases the difficulty of successfully operating offshore.

FIGURE 2-3	The 20 "Most International" U.S. Companies, 2002		
Company		**TNI Rank**	**Industry**
1. NTL, Inc.		1	Communication services
2. Coca-Cola		27	Beverages
3. AES Corp.		32	Utility
4. ExxonMobil		41	Petroleum
5. Chevron Texaco		50	Petroleum
6. McDonald's		51	Restaurants
7. Procter & Gamble		59	Diversified
8. Dow Chemical		61	Chemicals
9. IBM		62	Electrical and electronic equipment
10. Ford Motor		67	Motor vehicles
11. Pfizer		68	Pharmaceuticals
12. Hewlett-Packard		70	Electrical and electronic equipment
13. Motorola, Inc.		74	Machinery and equipment
14. Alcoa		77	Metal and metal products
15. Abbott Labs		79	Pharmaceuticals
16. DuPont		81	Chemicals
17. General Electric		84	Electrical and electronic equipment
18. Johnson & Johnson		91	Pharmaceuticals
19. ConocoPhillips		92	Petroleum
20. Philip Morris		93	Diversified

Source: Based on UNCTAD's Transnationality Index—TNI. *World Investment Report 2004: The Shift towards Services.* Available at www.UNCTAD.org/wir.

In summary, then, IHRM is generally more complex than domestic HR because it crosses a number of different systems, including different political systems, economic systems, and legal systems. However, when cultures are very similar, the challenge may not be as difficult as when cultures vary considerably from one another. In addition, when businesses move into the international arena earlier in their history, perhaps because of domestic market size constraints, they build important internal capabilities that may be more difficult to develop later in a firm's experience curve. Finally, when senior managers adopt a multicultural mindset, their international ventures are more likely to be successful.

In the next section, we will turn our attention to the different strategic approaches that may be used when procuring, deploying, and utilizing people on an international basis.

INTERNATIONAL HR STRATEGIES

International firms choose among four general HR management strategies although many use different strategies for different situations. First, in the **ethnocentric** approach, foreign subsidiaries have little autonomy, operations are typically centralized, and major decisions are made at the corporate headquarters. Although rank-and-file workers are probably locals, key positions in foreign subsidiaries are typically held by management who are moved to the assignment by or from the company headquarters. Individuals who are residents of the organization's home country who are sent offshore on assignment are called **parent-country nationals** (PCNs). Toyota, for example, typically sends a team of Japanese executives to oversee the start-up of a new operation in the United States. Many organizations in the United States manage foreign operations using the same basic format. Research suggests that companies follow this approach because they believe that their management and human resource practices are a critical core competence that provides competitive advantage to the firm.[42] Within this type of strategy, pay for the local workers will tend to be based on the local marketplace. Pay for the management team, particularly if they are PCNs, will tend to be related to the home country. One expert described the traditional mindset about managing overseas operations of U.S. companies as being related to two questions: "Who's the best U.S. person to handle this job?" and "What will it take to get him or her there?"[43] In ethnocentric situations, training and development efforts will tend to be focused on ensuring that the local workers possess the necessary knowledge, abilities, skills, and other characteristics (KASOCs) to perform effectively.

When organizations adopt a **polycentric** philosophy, they tend to treat each subsidiary as a distinct entity with some level of decision-making authority. This approach suggests that parent company HR management systems should not be imposed on overseas affiliates since these operations face considerably different legal, social, and cultural conditions.[44] Thus, subsidiaries will be encouraged to craft policies and procedures that will work most effectively based on the particular situation and locale. Within this strategy, subsidiaries are typically led by talented individuals who have proven themselves in the local marketplace. However, there is very little movement of talent from assignment to assignment, and foreign talent is rarely promoted to key positions at headquarters. Individuals who are residents of countries in which a foreign subsidiary is located are called **host-country nationals** (HCNs). During the early stages of internationalization, HCNs tend to fill middle- and lower-level positions. As time progresses, and the organization builds up management experience, it is increasingly common to see HCNs replace PCNs in key management positions. Many organizations specifically target promising HCNs for training and development initiatives. This is at least partly because HCNs are considerably less expensive than PCNs. As with other HR policies, pay in polycentric organizations will tend to be based on local marketplace trends. In polycentric settings, training and development efforts begin to focus on preparing talented locals (HCNs), particularly in developing countries, for future managerial positions and challenges.

When a company chooses to pursue a **geocentric** managerial approach, it strives to integrate its businesses. In these organizations, relationships between headquarters and foreign subsidiaries tend to be extremely collaborative, with each participant contributing important information, perspective, and decision-making factors. Organizations begin considering themselves to have a **global** workforce that can be deployed in a variety of ways, throughout the world. Key positions tend to be filled by the most qualified individual, regardless of national origin. In other words, individual differences in nationality are not as important as individual differences in talent. Geocentric organizations may still rely heavily on HCNs to fill most of their entry-level and operating jobs, but key jobs will tend to be filled by HCNs, PCNs, or **third-country nationals** (TCNs). TCNs are residents of a different country than the parent country or the host country. Thus, when IBM (a U.S. company) transfers an Australian to a position in its Singapore office, they are using a TCN.

Like the staffing patterns, compensation plans in geocentric organizations will tend to be based on the concept of a "global marketplace." Pay differences will focus less on an individual's country of origin. Instead, pay will begin to consider the value of this particular work to the organization, at this particular time, in this particular setting, by a person with these particular credentials. Training and development will be especially important in geocentric organizations because of the importance of developing a globally competent group of managers. Investments will be made in sending talented individuals from all corners of the globe to all corners of the organization, including to developmental positions in corporate headquarters.

The **regiocentric** managerial approach may be thought of as a scaled-down version of the geocentric model in that it tends to appoint people to positions within general regions of the world. Thus, European subsidiaries would tend to be managed by Europeans, while Asian subsidiaries would tend to be managed by Asians. When this approach is used, there tends to be limited movement between corporate headquarters and regions. However, there typically is a strong regional headquarters that is vested with considerable power to manage its operations. Such regional headquarters work very collaboratively and independently with the subsidiaries within the region. Some organizations may use the regiocentric approach as an interim step on their way to a geocentric philosophy. As indicated earlier, Coca-Cola is regionally managed, although it maintains a group of global troubleshooters. In the regiocentric management model, the staffing, compensation, and training strategies also generally would relate to regional norms.

What Influences the Choice of IHRM Strategy?

The selection and implementation of an IHRM strategy are very similar to the process used when an organization decides upon its business strategy. A variety of factors must be carefully assessed, including the general environment, the industry environment, and the firm's internal strengths and weaknesses. However, as we described in Chapter 1, the development of an HR strategy also involves careful consideration of the firm's strategy.

For example, earlier we described a multilocal firm as one that is primarily targeted at local responsiveness. As such, it tends to be a decentralized collection of relatively independent operating organizations. Many such organizations would find a polycentric IHRM strategy to effectively respond to its need for local focus. However, if the firm was anticipating rapid growth in the near future and was concerned about sufficient supply of local talent to meet the upcoming managerial challenges, a regiocentric strategy might provide an improved opportunity to identify and develop the necessary local talent. If the availability of qualified talent on a regional basis was uncertain, the organization might find that a geocentric or even an ethnocentric strategy could provide an effective transition that would enable a firm to transfer the necessary managerial and operational know-how from talented parent-country or third country nationals to local country nationals. The decision concerning which IHRM strategy to implement also may be influenced by the cost pressures within an industry. Firms with high cost pressures may find that the polycentric strategy—with its high level of decentralization—requires so much duplication of functions and services that the strategy is not economically feasible. The key point is that IHRM strategies do not necessarily "match" firm strategies. This is because the particular elements of the firm's environments that indicate what products and services the firm should create do not necessarily consider critical IHRM issues, such as the supply of and demand for labor in a particular area of the world, its relative cost, and its skill level. In Chapter 5, we will describe the HR planning process and the way it relates to both domestic and international businesses.

INTERNATIONAL BUSINESS ASSIGNMENTS

International businesses need international expertise. International job rotation has long been recognized as a key tool for developing such expertise.[45] Yet, foreign job assignments create important HR challenges. In this section, we will describe the use of expatriates and their advantages and disadvantages, and we will note contemporary trends concerning international job assignments.

Employees who are placed in an assignment outside their home country are called **expatriates.** Traditionally, most expatriates have been parent country nationals (PCNs) assigned by the home office to lead and manage overseas expansions for two reasons.[46] First, top management doubted whether local talent was up to the challenge of managing a business unit. Second, top management wanted to "mold" offshore affiliates into its own culture and practices. Today, organizations report a shift away from using PCNs and increasing their reliance on host-country nationals (HCNs) and third-county nationals (TCNs) to fill its managerial ranks. This is particularly true as multinational organizations move toward a geocentric managerial philosophy. In addition, governments often exert pressure to fill increasing numbers of managerial positions with HCNs.[47] Today, organizations report using international assignments in order to achieve one or more of the following goals.

First, international assignments are a key element in developing management teams that are globally focused and globally competent. The global leadership challenge is discussed later in this chapter. Second, expatriate assignments encourage high levels of coordination and control among business units. This is especially important when an organization internationalizes by acquiring or creating widely dispersed production and marketing facilities, then integrating them with the rest of the overall business. Expatriates possess knowledge about the way the overall company operates, its long-term goals, and its problem solving resources that may enable them to identify and capitalize on synergies, while noting duplications of effort.

Third, international business requires high levels of internal communication, both information sharing and information exchange, because of geographical distances, cultural diversity, complex supply and demand conditions, and other similar pressures. Such information sharing is key to effective strategic and tactical decision making. While e-mail and other technological developments facilitate interpersonal contact, global assignments provide the opportunity to work side by side and to

FIGURE 2-4	Comparative Illustration of HR Challenges		
Description of Challenge	**U.S. Firms Reporting Challenges**	**European Firms Reporting Challenges**	**Japanese Firms Reporting Challenges**
Difficulty attracting high-performance managers for offshore assignments	21%	26%	44%
Poor relationships between parent country nationals (PCNs) and host country nationals (HCNs)	13%	9%	32%
HCNs reporting frustration about advancement opportunities	8%	4%	21%
High turnover among HCNs	4%	9%	32%
Lack of PCNs skilled in international management	29%	39%	68%
Few PCNs interested in accepting offshore assignments	13%	26%	26%
Reported PCN adjustment problems upon completion of offshore assignment	42%	39%	24%

Adapted from R. Kopp. "International Human Resource Policies and Practices in Japanese, European, and United States Multinationals," *Human Resource Management*, 33, no. 4, (Winter 1994), pp. 58–99.

develop relationships of collaboration and trust over an extended period of time. Such relationships do not end after the expat "returns home" (or goes on to the next assignment). The continuous exchange of rich information, particularly when people share competitive, marketplace, and technological information, may enable an organization to seize opportunities and respond to challenges more quickly and effectively.

In spite of their strategic value, managing an effective program of international assignments presents huge challenges. First, expatriates tend to be costly, since they are usually compensated based on home country practices. In addition to base salary, organizations typically pick up costs relating to relocation, cost-of-living allowances, special family benefits (such as housing and school), and any costs relating to protection against threats of terrorism. Organizations also invest significant time and resources preparing individuals and their families for international assignments. Such preparation may include cross-cultural and language training. Recently, as the number of dual-income families increased in the United States, international HR deals have expanded to include "trailing spouse" benefits. Deals typically include direct assistance in locating a position for the spouse, paying the search firm fee when a position is located, or actually paying the spouse's salary until suitable employment can be located. If no suitable employment can be found, the company often continues to subsidize the spouse for lost wages. In other words, costs can mount quickly when an organization's expansion plans call for the extensive use of expatriates. One estimate indicates that the cost of a manager triples as soon as he steps into a foreign country.

Second, there is a high level of expatriate assignment failure. Traditionally, "failed" assignments were those in which the expatriate left the assignment prematurely. It is estimated that 10–20 percent of assignments are failures

based on this definition. The most common factors relating to assignment failure are partner dissatisfaction, family concerns, and inability to comfortably adapt.[48] Of full-term assignments, it is estimated that an additional 33 percent of expatriates are ineffective in performing their international assignment.[49] Figure 2-4 reports the results of a survey of Japanese, European, and U.S. firms concerning key problems with international job assignments.

Third, organizations report increased difficulty in retaining expatriates after completion of an overseas assignment. One study indicates that 25 percent of expatriates terminate employment with the organization within two years of repatriation.[50] Consultants add that anecdotal evidence leads them to place that turnover rate closer to 50 percent.[51] Why is there such turnover following an experience that should deliver a clear benefit to both the company and the individual? One reason is a reported lack of concern on the part of organizations about repatriation adjustment. Apparently, most organizations think that "repatriation" means calling the mover and buying the return airline tickets. Yet, "reverse culture shock" is a very real thing,[52] and fewer than 20 percent of organizations report even discussing repatriation when an individual agrees to accept an international assignment. In addition, expatriates and repatriates are increasingly reporting frustration with perceived career opportunities when the international assignment is complete.

It is also interesting to note that the length of overseas assignments is declining. In 1996, 32 percent of such assignments lasted more than three years. In 1999, 23 percent of assignments were this long. In 2003, 70 percent of international assignments lasted for one year or less. Cost and family pressures were the major reasons given for the decline in duration. Today, four types of expatriate assignments are identified. **Short-term assignments,** described as "something longer than a business trip," are increasingly popular. Typically, these are project-oriented assignments with the worker staying in a hotel and the family remaining behind at home. The second type are considered to be **developmental assignments** that are increasingly considered to be a necessity for a high-potential fast-tracker in many large international companies. **Strategic assignments** involve persons with special skills who are moved to become a country manager in an unfamiliar area. For example, an individual may be sent to Korea because an organization is planning an expansion and wants a complete immersion in learning the marketplace, in relationship-building, and in understanding the way business is conducted. A **long-term assignment** is similar to the traditional expatriate role. Typically, they involve start-ups, or an ongoing managerial presence to resolve major problems, and would typically be taken by a "career expatriate."[53]

This changing philosophy about international assignments may mean that such assignments become more available to women. Today, although women occupy an estimated 50 percent of the U.S. middle-management labor pool, they represent only 18 percent of the expatriate pool. One study indicated that, when actually offered an international assignment, 80 percent of women accepted the offer, while only 71 percent of men did. Yet, women are rarely offered international assignments. Two surveys indicated that women were left out because of managerial beliefs that women were not as globally mobile as men, and that supervisors were very worried about crime overseas as well as cultural biases against women in some areas of the world.[54] Thus far, studies have failed to find a rational foundation for these beliefs.

Even though the use of expatriates may be slowing, expatriates continue to occupy a critically important position in organizations' international expansion and management development strategies. One recent survey provided a snapshot of the characteristics of the "typical" expatriate in 2003:

- 17 percent of current expats were hired specifically to fill their present international assignment.
- 40 percent of expats were between 40 and 49 years of age, followed by 30 to 39 years (26 percent), then 50 to 59 years (21 percent).
- 60 percent are married; 86 percent of their spouses accompanied them on the assignment; 51 percent brought children.
- 50 percent of the spouses were employed full-time before the assignment; 16 percent were employed during the assignment.

A recent meta-analysis of the expatriate literature revealed some surprising effects.[55] While expatriate adjustment was found to be sensitive to many stressors, some of the most obvious predictors such as previous overseas experience and host country language ability

had negligible effects. Spouse–family adjustment, role clarity, and expat relational skills were potent predictors of assignee adjustment and success.

The U.K., United States, and China are the most active destinations; China, Japan and the United States are considered to be the most challenging assignments; for the first time in this survey's 11-year history, the United States appears on this "Most Challenging" list. Chief issues cited—by both expats and program administrators—relate to time delays, immigration restrictions, and general inconvenience. Most attribute this to security measures designed to protect against terrorism threats.

Figure 2-5 summarizes expert recommendations for successful international assignments. In summary, then, international business assignments provide critical opportunities and resources to organizations as they internationalize. Although the traditional use of expatriates, particularly parent-country nationals, continues to be popular, their costs are increasingly under scrutiny. Firms are investing more resources in third-country nationals and other developmental programs in order to increase the managerial potential of local workers.

GLOBAL LEADERSHIP CHALLENGES

As organizations internationalize, there is an increasing sense that managing global operations involves a particular expertise that is separate and distinct from traditional U.S. domestic managerial technology. Today, organizations are increasingly committed to developing management teams that are globally focused. According to management guru Rosabeth Moss Kanter, global management skills are becoming a major core competence for future business leaders.[56] In some organizations, considerable global experience is recognized as a major strategic imperative. At General Electric, for example, an individual will not advance beyond a particular level without significant experience managing overseas operations. Each of the final candidates in the search for GE CEO Jack Welsh's replacement had spent considerable time working outside the United States during the past decade or so. Richard Waggoner was promoted to president and CEO of General Motors after he successfully turned around GM's South American operations. Avon appointed Charles Perrin as CEO largely based on the global business expertise he demonstrated at Duracell. Recently appointed leaders at Campbell's Soup, Ford, Gillette, Tupperware, Goodyear, and General Mills all spent significant time in major offshore assignments.[57] *The Wall Street Journal* reports that, in 1996, 28 percent of executive-level searches required individuals with significant overseas management experience.[58] Yet, progress is slow. A 2001 study reported that only 22 percent of U.S. international firms were led by CEOs with international experience, and that only half that percentage (11 percent) of other top management team

FIGURE 2-5	Three Steps to Getting Payback from Expat Investments
Step	**Specific Considerations**
Step 1: Send people for the right reasons	Specifically what do we want to achieve? • Response to immediate business demands? • Generating new knowledge? • Developing global capability? • Some combination of the above?
Step 2: Send the right people	Technical skills are needed plus • Communication skills • Cultural flexibility • Broad social skills • "Cosmopolitan orientation" • Collaborative negotiation style

Step 3: Finish the assignment the right way	Create straightforward processes to smooth transition
	• Start planning *early*
	• Involve the expat in reentry planning
	• Find suitable job—focus on direct application of new knowledge and skills
	• Prepare expat for social adjustment realities
	  • Family's readjustment
	  • Mentors may be gone, reassigned
	  • Transition from "in-charge leader" to "fitting back in" or "starting over again" in new international assignment

Source: Reprinted by permission of *Harvard Business Review*. From "The right way to manage expats," by J. S. Black & H. B. Gregerson, 77(2), 52–63. Copyright © 1999 by the Harvard Business School Publishing Corporation, all rights reserved.

members had international experience. The most common international experience was in Canada. In the coming years, it is expected that this trend will continue and that the nature of the international experience will become more diversified.[59]

A Conference Board study of executives in 33 countries indicated that the most important HR goal for the coming years is to develop solid global leadership teams.[60] Some argue that the lack of global management bench strength in many organizations has limited business's ability to implement global growth strategies.[61] In other words, the stage was ready for major expansion, but the supply of effective, well-trained leadership talent was short of the mark.

A Fortune 200 global consumer products company provides a good illustration of the challenge.[62] In the early 1990s, the organization had approximately 60 "globally competent" managers: that is, knowledgeable, effective, well-rounded individuals who could be sent anywhere on the globe to run an operation. Estimates indicated that this was a shortfall of 30–35 people if the company was going to be able to implement its strategic growth plans during the next five years. Why the shortfall? First, the organization realized that they had grown faster internationally over the past five years than they anticipated. In the early 1990s, they had opened facilities in 25 new locations, primarily in developing markets, including Eastern Europe, Africa, and Asia. Second, a third of this current globally competent team was nearing

retirement age. In addition, the firm was having difficulty maintaining its high-potential employees. As investments were being made in developing global capabilities, individuals were being scooped up by other organizations (including many competitors). Most of these high-potential individuals were part of dual-career, high-potential families and they were not particularly interested in expatriate duty, especially in the organization's high growth areas such as the Ukraine, Nigeria, and Vietnam. In addition, many of the developmental attempts seemed to be "hit or miss" propositions, since the firm had never really articulated exactly what a globally competent leader was. Finally, HR development specialists expressed ongoing frustration because the KASOCs for successful global managers seemed to be changing while developmental efforts were taking place. Review of the popular press would suggest that this organization's experience is not unusual.

Exactly what is a globally competent leader? A variety of answers have been offered. One expert describes three key skills relating to globally competent managers and leaders. First, they are integrators who see beyond obvious country and cultural differences. Second, they are diplomats who can resolve conflicts and influence locals to accept world standards or commonalities. Next, they are cross-fertilizers who recognize the best from various places and adapt it for utilization elsewhere.[63] Another expert cites three knowledges as being critical. First, globally competent managers have an in-depth understanding of world markets: their potentials and their problems. Second, they master all elements of the global supply chains and distribution channels. Finally, they skillfully embrace cultural diversity.[64] In general, it appears as though the need for global leadership is clear. Exactly what one is and how one is developed is much less clear.[65]

One of the difficulties in agreeing about the attributes of effective global skills may be related to the evolution taking place in the way people think about the management roles in global settings in general. One expert asserts that management is currently in the fourth stage of an evolving process of international management philosophy and practices.[66] During early internationalization efforts, companies typically relied on domestic leadership style, at least partly because they didn't see a reason for managing differently. The traditional assumption was that companies achieved competitive advantage by noting and exploiting marketplace discontinuities. For example, if an organization spotted an unfilled need for a particular type of product or service, or noted a rapid improvement in a culture's standard of living, and a dearth of middle-class products, the ability to rush in and produce the desired goods or services could create a windfall for the company. Mostly these were temporary opportunities, however, because other organizations would imitate a successful campaign and drive the price down, and eventually the market would return to a balanced state. This thinking, then, assumed that international success was based on operational capability and marketing savvy, rather than any particular adaptation of managerial style.

During the second stage, international operations began falling short of expectations, and issues of "How should this facility be managed?" arose. Emerging from this thinking was a general consensus that effective management style varied based on the particular situation and setting. Usually referred to as contingency theory, leaders began to examine the applicability of different managerial styles and mindsets, seeking the one that "fit" best, given a specific situation. In the third stage of international managerial development, the spotlight increased its focus on management practices, but thinking shifted away from a pure "it depends on the situation" attitude, and began examining the way managerial roles and styles need to be altered and adjusted to meet the needs of a particular cultural setting. A wealth of cross-cultural managerial literature emerged, including such bestsellers as *Kiss, Bow or Shake Hands* and *Riding the Waves of Culture*.[67] Today, the interest in cross-cultural management and contingency theory continues, but there is an increasing belief that global business leadership needs an overarching managerial philosophy that considers the collection of situations, challenges, and styles as its primary frame of reference.

A review of the popular literature suggests that the most widespread (and perhaps faddish) approach to global leadership development currently in use is a "competency model." This thinking assumes that effectiveness in global leaders is based on the degree to which individuals possess particular knowledges, abilities, skills, and other characteristics (KASOCs), such as "customer

---

FIGURE 2-6	General Components of a Global Mindset
Component	**Description/Illustration**
Global data bank	Maintaining relevant, current, "hard" data about countries, regions
Market knowledge	What are the top 20 markets in our industry?
	What are a key country's defining historic moments?
	What are a key country's defining cultural moments?
	What is the economic system and performance of a key market?
	What is the key country's political system?
	What are the relevant business practices in a key country?
	What are the major geographic features of the key country?
Understanding the global superstructure	Same questions as required for market knowledge, but applied to critical regions.
Global economic system	Appreciation for and knowledge of the "interconnected economy"; that is, the system that connects the world and covers trade and finance, the world capital markets, and the major trade areas.
Cross-cultural skills	Competence in effectively interacting with managers from many countries or cultures.
	Foreign language skills.
	Understanding nonverbal communication commonalities.
	Appreciation for culture-based nuances in communication techniques.
Cultural roots	Global mindsets require grounding in a home culture for personal balance.
Spirit of generosity, magnanimity	Giving others the opportunity to proceed and to define own directions.

Source: JEANNET, JEAN-PIERRE, MANAGING WITH A GLOBAL MINDSET, 1st Edition, © 2000. Adapted with permission of Pearson Education, inc., Upper Saddle River, NJ.

orientation," "building alliances," and "intellectual capacity." However, critics of this approach assert that these competencies are often subjectively derived, poorly defined, and related to an individual's basic traits, rather than learned behavior. In addition, some organizations have too many competencies and they overlap considerably. For example, Chase Manhattan identifies 250 competencies that comprise effective global leadership. In addition, little research has been conducted to investigate whether measures of individual competencies can predict actual performance, domestically or internationally. In Chapter 1 we emphasized the need to measure the effects of HR interventions. Competency models are nice. Good measurement is absolutely necessary.

The term *global mindset* is frequently seen these days in the popular press. Global mindset is more a general description of the need for all organizational decision makers to think well beyond domestic issues. One European expert indicates:

> The idea of the global mindset as a roving globetrotter is probably overblown, and clearly, managers possessing, or aspiring to a global mindset need to come equipped with a globalized database, or some factual knowledge that is different from the domestic mindset. Furthermore, they need to be able to view the world differently. And, finally, their thinking patterns, responses, and cognitive skills differ sharply from a traditional domestic or even multi-domestic mindset.[68]

Figure 2-6 lists the general components of this global mindset according to this expert.

In summary, then, developing global leaders and global mindsets will be a continuing challenge faced by HR professionals probably both in the short term as well as over the long term.

SUMMARY

Business and commerce are increasingly crossing national, regional, and continental borders. Some organizations have expanded their marketplaces; some organizations have extended their operations; some organizations operate globally. Even if you never work for an international organization, the global economy affects the marketplaces and the operational environments of most business, even small domestic organizations. In this chapter, we described and discussed the way that this expansion affects human resource practices.

When organizations decide to focus attention outside their national borders, there are a variety of approaches that may be taken. Such choices range in risk and degree of involvement from simply exporting goods and services to sole ownership of foreign facilities. Each of these approaches may present very different HR challenges, ranging from providing technical advice and expertise all the way up to (and including) providing in-depth, comprehensive management services and job-related training to people who live in developing parts of the world.

Once a firm decides on the basic format of its expansion, it then must choose its basic management strategy. In a multilocal strategy, each individual operating unit is relatively independent and focuses on its own domestic market. At the other end of the spectrum, global organizations tend to create outputs that will meet the needs of customers everywhere. A global strategy focuses on local responsiveness while still achieving considerable large-scale economies and efficiencies. In general, the more "international" a company's strategy, the more complex are its human resource systems. However, such differences can be further complicated when they involve major cultural differences, when organizations move offshore late in their life cycle, and when senior management views foreign operations as being "generally the same as" their domestic operations.

International organizations tend to choose among four general HR strategies. In ethnocentric organizations, offshore operations have little autonomy, major decisions are made at corporate headquarters, and managers are often moved to assignments from the home country (parent-country nationals).

At the other end of the spectrum is the polycentric strategy in which each subsidiary is empowered to make important decisions concerning its own operations and markets. When this approach is adopted, employees tend to have stable assignments and rarely move from location to location. The geocentric HR strategy tends to balance the two philosophies: relationships between headquarters and foreign subsidiaries tend to be collaborative, with each participant contributing important inputs. The partnership found in the geocentric HR strategy often gives rise to a global workforce that can be deployed as needed in various areas throughout the world. A scaled-down version of this philosophy is the regiocentric approach in which the world is viewed as a collection of areas in which people and resources may move fluidly, but cross-regional movement may be the exception rather than the rule. Some organizations use a regiocentric approach as a stepping stone to a global philosophy. In deciding on which international HR management (IHRM) strategy to consider, a company typically considers a variety of factors, including the general environment, an organization's industry characteristics, the business's strategy, and the firm's internal strengths and weakness. In other words, the process of choosing an IHRM philosophy is very similar to the process of deciding which business strategy an organization will choose to pursue.

Traditionally, U.S. organizations have used key management talent and international job rotation as a means for developing and deploying strategic capability during efforts to internationalize business. Yet, such job rotation creates huge cross-cultural challenges, and the record of expatriate success has been increasingly called into question. At this time, two trends are emerging: (1) the widespread reliance of U.S. companies on their own expatriate managers to build effective businesses abroad is decreasing and (2) expatriate job rotation is increasingly being used to aid in the development of global capability, rather than primarily as a tool for transplanting specific home-country business, managerial, and HR practices. In other words, international job rotation is increasingly being used as a developmental assignment for an organization's managerial talent, rather than as a way of creating "satellite offices" or "home-country clones."

The development of effective global leadership continues to be a major challenge for organizations. Most international companies view such development as critical to their long-term effectiveness in international marketplaces. There is little question that business leaders everywhere in the world have a great deal to learn about the way to establish, build, and leverage subsidiaries in foreign countries in order to fully deliver strategic capabilities and organizational excellence.

DISCUSSION QUESTIONS

1. Why do you think businesses internationalize? Which forces are most influential and which are secondary forces?

2. Think of three or four organizations with which you are familiar. How have they been affected by the globalization of business? Make sure you consider both direct and indirect influences. If they have not been particularly affected, what are some of the reasons for their insulation from the trend?

3. Think about two businesses: (1) a manufacturer of athletic gear and (2) a property and casualty insurance company. How might the internationalization of each of these companies differ from one another? What factors might account for these differences? Choose one company and pretend that you're the HR director. How would you figure out the "right" way to manage this international expansion?

4. How do differences in international HR management (IHRM) strategies affect the relative importance of each of the HR domains?

5. What are the advantages and disadvantages of using home-country, host-country, and third-country nationals? Under what specific circumstances might an organization choose to utilize third-country nationals?

3

THE LEGAL ENVIRONMENT OF HRM: EQUAL EMPLOYMENT OPPORTUNITY

OVERVIEW

Chapter 1 briefly summarized the regulatory environment in which HRM is practiced today and Chapter 2 discussed this environment in the context of the globalization of the economy. Many experts in HRM have noted that the legal environment is a critical component of the external environment for HRM and that legal considerations are a primary force shaping staffing policies and the growth of manufacturing and even service facilities outside the United States. Indeed, legal and regulatory studies related to labor issues and labor costs are often cited as the main reason that some jobs (and facilities) are moved offshore.

There are a plethora of federal, state, and local laws and regulations that can be the basis of a lawsuit against an employer for actions related to labor relations, workers' compensation, unemployment compensation, wages, health and safety in the workplace, whistleblower's protection, retirement, employee benefits, rights of privacy, and protection against unjust dismissal. We will consider the most important of these laws when we address the various HRM activities in the chapters to follow.

No other area of the regulatory environment has had such a profound effect on HRM as the laws related to equal employment opportunity (EEO). Surveys of perceived discrimination in the workplace underscore the importance of EEO law for

HRM practice. A 2005 Gallup Poll found that 15 percent of all workers perceived they had been subjected to discrimination.[1] Over 31 percent of Asians reported incidents of discrimination (the largest ethnic group percentage) with 26 percent of African Americans reporting incidents. Other noteworthy statistics: 22 percent of white women perceived discrimination versus 3 percent of white men; 20 percent of Hispanic men reported discrimination versus 15 percent of Hispanic women.[2]

Such findings, combined with the increasing diversity of the workforce, translate into an increasing rate of legal activity related to personnel decisions. We will concentrate our discussion in this chapter on federal EEO law since most work areas of HRM can be affected by the EEO laws and the regulations we are about to discuss. The processes by which employers recruit, hire, place, evaluate, transfer, train, promote, compensate, monitor, lay off, and terminate employees can fall under the close scrutiny of the courts and regulatory agencies based on some form of EEO legislation. There are numerous state and local laws that also affect HRM practice. For example, California has a number of state-specific laws and added two major laws on HR issues in 2006.

The purpose of this chapter is to provide an overview of the legal environment with particular emphasis on equal employment opportunity laws and regulations. We will provide descriptions of the most important laws in EEO and the legal interpretations of those laws. We will conclude with a discussion of the implications of these laws in the global environment and likely future trends related to EEO.

OBJECTIVES

After reading this chapter, you should be able to

1. *Understand the legal issues affecting HRM activity and the various laws related to equal employment opportunity and employment discrimination.*
2. *Identify potential problems in HRM policy and practice as related to equal employment opportunity laws.*
3. *Understand the importance of judicial interpretation in EEO law.*
4. *Understand the implications of EEO law in the international context.*
5. *Know the future trends related to EEO law and their implications for practice.*

We have discussed the trend of increasing litigation that has had an impact on virtually all aspects of HRM. Let's start out with some recent cases that represent fairly typical legal actions today. Figure 3-1 presents some examples of cases that reflect this trend.

As we discussed in Chapter 1, the rate of litigation related to workplace activity is on the increase despite the fact that practicing managers should know more about the legal

implications of their behavior than managers did 20 or even 10 years ago.[3] As we discussed in Chapter 1, the jury verdicts have grown substantially in recent years with 24 percent of verdicts resulting in awards of $1 million or more.

One of the reasons for the increase in legal activity is that there is an increase in the legal options and theories available to someone who feels he or she has been treated unfairly in the workplace. One review summarized the "piecemeal evolution of the U.S. employment law system" as follows:

[E]mployees are now statutorily protected from workplace discrimination on the basis of race, color, sex, religion, national origin, age, union status, disability, marital status, and in some places, sexual preference, smoking habits, personal appearance, height and weight, political affiliation, arrest and conviction records, and even the method of birth control they chose. Simultaneously, courts have applied long-standing common law to recognize torts of wrongful discharge, negligent and intentional infliction of emotional distress, breach of contract, invasions of privacy, fraud, defamation, and negligent hiring, retention, training and supervision. Employment law further affords employees the right to a minimum wage and to overtime pay, the right to a safe and healthful workplace, and the right to benefits of social security, unemployment insurance, worker's compensation, family and medical leave, and proper administration of their pension. Thus, U.S. employment law is a broad patchwork of federal and state statutory rights, common law rights, and administra-

---

FIGURE 3-1   Examples of the Increased Litigation Trend

- A federal judge certified a class of 1.6 million women in a Title VII lawsuit against Wal-Mart.
- A federal judge threw out the minimum test score requirement imposed by the NCAA for college athletic eligibility, ruling that the SAT or ACT score requirement had "an unjustified disparate impact against African-Americans."
- Seven Muslim security workers filed a complaint with the EEOC alleging they were fired because they refused to remove their hijabs while at work.
- The EEOC settled a lawsuit for $8.5 million against Ford and the United Auto Workers (UAW) on behalf of African Americans denied apprenticeships based on a written application test.
- Lockheed Martin Corporation agreed to pay $13 million to settle claims of age discrimination brought by former employees of Martin Marietta.
- Bus drivers in Indianapolis challenged the mandatory retirement age of 55 under the Age Discrimination in Employment Act.
- Target Stores was sued for using a psychological test to screen applicants for security guard positions that the plaintiffs regarded as an invasion of privacy.
- A jury found Circuit City guilty of racial discrimination after plaintiffs' attorneys argued promotion decisions were made under an "excessively subjective" personnel system.
- A California jury awarded a college instructor $2.75 million after San Francisco State University turned him down for tenure because he was white.
- Women working for Home Depot claimed that the company discriminates against women in its selection of supervisors.
- A supervisor was sued by a former employee who claimed the supervisor libeled him in a reference check.
- Ford settled a reverse discrimination lawsuit related to their downsizing efforts.
- African Americans working for Coca-Cola claimed racial discrimination in the manner in which the company promoted people. The case settled for $196 million.
- A terminated employee sued his former employer for disability discrimination citing his clinical depression as a disability.

tively created rights that can be implicated by almost any managerial decision that affects employees.[4]

The cases listed in Figure 3-1 illustrate this summary. Most Americans work under the **employment-at-will** doctrine that stipulates that both employer and employee can terminate a working relationship at any time and for any reason other than those characteristics or situations explicitly covered by law. As illustrated by the summary above, these characteristics and situations are expanding greatly.

There are more and more challenges to the employment-at-will doctrine today and plaintiffs are winning large judgments against employers under creative legal theories related to contract or tort law. For example, courts have ruled that an **implied contract** exists by the actions or statements of the employer. Statements in employment documents and manuals are often used to define the contract. But the use of a theory such as a violation of the implied contract or other exceptions to the employment-at-will doctrine depends on the particular state. (Employment-at-will is discussed in detail in Chapter 12.)

We will discuss the trends in litigation related to specific HR practices when we cover a particular HRM activity. But what you should know at the outset is that the practice of human resources is a litigious minefield with more "mines" being planted in the form of new laws or regulations and the judicial acceptance of new legal theories of unfair or injurious employment practice.

This expansion of new legal theories, combined with the changing demographics of the workforce (an aging, more diverse workforce), strongly supports the proposition that the legal "minefield" will be more heavily mined in the future. Practicing HRM specialists need to know where the mines are. HRM researchers can shed light on issues related to the legality of certain HRM practices.

We will first enter perhaps the most contentious of the minefields: equal employment opportunity law. We will bring up other legal issues as they relate to particular HR activities when we discuss those particular activities throughout the text.

EQUAL EMPLOYMENT OPPORTUNITY LAW

Prior to the civil rights movement of the early 1960s, employment decisions often were made on the basis of an applicant's or worker's race, gender, religion, or other characteristics unrelated to job qualifications or performance. And across racial groups, women earned less than men, even in identical jobs.

The laws we will discuss in this chapter were designed to punish employers that used such criteria as race, gender, disability, or age to exclude certain persons from employment or from certain employment benefits. They also were designed to restore the unfairly treated worker to the position she or he would have held absent the discrimination. Our focus will not be on punishment, however, but on preventing unfair treatment and the legal vulnerability of managers under the civil rights laws.

What Is Employment Discrimination?

Employment discrimination occurs in a variety of ways and there are a number of methods for seeking redress through the courts. While the legal definition of **discrimination** differs depending on the specific law, it can be broadly defined as *employment decision making or working conditions that are advantageous (or disadvantageous) to members of one group compared to members of another group.* The decision making can apply to personnel selection, admission to training programs, promotions, work assignments, transfers, compensation, layoffs, punishments, and dismissals. The conditions also can pertain to the work atmosphere itself. For example, a common lawsuit today concerns allegations of sexually harassing behaviors at work that place an individual in an offensive or intimidating environment.

What Are the Major Sources of EEO Redress?

Figure 3-2 presents a summary of illegal discriminatory practices. Of the many sources of redress that are available, the most frequently used sources are **federal laws: Title VII of the 1964 U.S. Civil Rights Act** (CRA), the **Age Discrimination in Employment Act of 1967** (ADEA), and the **Americans with Disabilities Act of 1990** (ADA). (See Figure 3-3 for some excerpts from Title VII.) Most of the states and many municipalities also have their own fair employment laws.

All claims of discrimination under CRA, ADEA, and ADA must first be filed with the EEOC, which received over 75,000 claims of discrimination in 2005 (check out their Web site at www.eeoc.gov). The highest percentage of claims of discrimination are for race, gender, age, disability, national origin, and religion (in that order). Unfortunately, claims of discrimination are up for all of these areas. National-origin lawsuits represented 11 percent of Title VII claims in 2005 and this includes suits from resident aliens. Aliens who are eligible to work in the United States are covered by Title VII.[5]

The 1991 amendment to Title VII of the Civil Rights Act and the increasing diversity of the workforce have increased the number of lawsuits brought under Title VII. This amendment added compensatory and punitive damages as remediation for violations of the law, thus creating a greater financial incentive for plaintiffs and plaintiffs' attorneys to pursue these cases. Also, Title VII now covers employees of U.S. companies working abroad.

Equal employment laws similar to Title VII exist in 41 states as well as Washington, D.C., and Puerto Rico. There are also state and local laws that vary on the legality of certain personnel practices. For example, as of

FIGURE 3-2   Discriminatory Practices

Under Title VII of the Civil Rights Act of 1964, the Americans with Disabilities Act (ADA), and the Age Discrimination in Employment Act (ADEA), it is illegal to discriminate in any aspect of employment, including:

- Hiring and firing
- Compensation, assignment, or classification of employees
- Transfer, promotion, layoff, or recall
- Job advertisements
- Recruitment
- Testing
- Use of company facilities
- Training and apprenticeship programs
- Fringe benefits
- Pay, retirement plans, and disability leave
- Other terms and conditions of employment

Discriminatory practices under these laws also include:

- Harassment on the basis of race, color, religion, sex, national origin, disability, or age.
- Retaliation against an individual for filing a charge of discrimination, participating in an investigation, or opposing discriminatory practices.
- Employment decisions based on stereotypes or assumptions about the abilities, traits, or performance of individuals of a certain sex, race, age, religion, or ethnic group, or individuals with disabilities.
- Denying employment opportunities to a person because of marriage to, or association with, an individual of a particular race, religion, national origin, or an individual with a disability. Title VII also prohibits discrimination because of participation in schools or places of worship associated with a particular racial, ethnic, or religious group.

Employers are required to post notices to all employees advising them of their rights under the laws EEOC enforces and their right to be free from retaliation. Such notices must be accessible, as needed, to persons with visual or other disabilities that affect reading.

Note: Many states and municipalities also have enacted protections against discrimination and harassment based on sexual orientation, status as a parent, marital status and political affiliation. For information, please contact the EEOC District Office nearest you.

TITLE VII

Title VII prohibits not only intentional discrimination, but also practices that have the effect of discriminating against individuals because of their race, color, national origin, religion, or sex.

National Origin Discrimination

- It is illegal to discriminate against an individual because of birthplace, ancestry, culture, or linguistic characteristics common to a specific ethnic group.
- A rule requiring that employees speak only English on the job may violate Title VII unless an employer shows that the requirement is necessary for conducting business. If the employer believes such a rule is necessary, employees must be informed when English is required and the consequences of violating the rule.

The Immigration Reform and Control Act (IRCA) of 1986 requires employers to assure that employees hired are legally authorized to work in the U.S. However, an employer who requests employment verification only for individuals of a particular national origin, or individuals who appear to be or sound foreign, may violate both Title VII and IRCA; verification must be obtained from all applicants and employees. Employers who impose citizenship requirements or give preferences to U.S. citizens in hiring or employment opportunities also may violate IRCA.

Additional information about IRCA may be obtained from the Office of Special Counsel for Immigration-Related Unfair Employment Practices at 1-800-255-7688 (voice), 1-800-237-2515 (TTY for employees/applicants) or 1-800-362-2735 (TTY for employers) or at http://www.usdoj.gov/crt/osc.

Religious Accommodation

- An employer is required to reasonably accommodate the religious belief of an employee or prospective employee, unless doing so would impose an undue hardship.

Sex Discrimination

Title VII's broad prohibitions against sex discrimination specifically cover:

- Sexual harassment—This includes practices ranging from direct requests for sexual favors to workplace conditions that create a hostile environment for persons of either gender, including same sex harassment. (The "hostile environment" standard also applies to harassment on the bases of race, color, national origin, religion, age, and disability.)

(Continued)

FIGURE 3-2   *(Continued)*

- Pregnancy based discrimination—Pregnancy, childbirth, and related medical conditions must be treated in the same way as other temporary illnesses or conditions.

Additional rights are available to parents and others under the Family and Medical Leave Act (FMLA), which is enforced by the U.S. Department of Labor. For information on the FMLA, or to file an FMLA complaint, individuals should contact the nearest office of the Wage and Hour Division, Employment Standards Administration, U.S. Department of Labor. The Wage and Hour Division is listed in most telephone directories under U.S. Government, Department of Labor or at http://www.dol.gov/esa/whd_org.htm.

AGE DISCRIMINATION IN EMPLOYMENT ACT

The ADEA's broad ban against age discrimination also specifically prohibits:

- Statements or specifications in job notices or advertisements of age preference and limitations. An age limit may only be specified in the rare circumstance where age has been proven to be a *bona fide* occupational qualification (BFOQ).
- Discrimination on the basis of age by apprenticeship programs, including joint labor-management apprenticeship programs.
- Denial of benefits to older employees. An employer may reduce benefits based on age only if the cost of providing the reduced benefits to older workers is the same as the cost of providing benefits to younger workers.

EQUAL PAY ACT

The Equal Pay Act (EPA) prohibits discrimination on the basis of sex in the payment of wages of benefits, where men and women perform work of similar skill, effort, and responsibility for the same employer under similar working conditions. Note that:

- Employers may not reduce wages of either sex to equalize pay between men and women.
- A violation of the EPA may occur where a different wage was/is paid to a person who worked in the same job before or after an employee of the opposite sex.
- A violation may also occur where a labor union causes the employer to violate the law.

TITLES I AND V OF THE AMERICANS WITH DISABILITIES ACT

The ADA prohibits discrimination on the basis of disability in all employment practices. It is necessary to understand several important ADA definitions to know who is protected by the law and what constitutes illegal discrimination:

Individual with a Disability

An individual with a disability under the ADA is a person who has a physical or mental impairment that substantially limits one or more major life activities, has a record of such an impairment, or is regarded as having such an impairment. Major life activities are activities that an average person can perform with little or no difficulty such as walking, breathing, seeing, hearing, speaking, learning, and working.

Qualified Individual with a Disability

A qualified employee or applicant with a disability is someone who satisfies skill, experience, education, and other job-related requirements of the position held or desired, and who, with or without reasonable accommodation, can perform the essential functions of that position.

Reasonable Accommodation

Reasonable accommodation may include, but is not limited to, making existing facilities used by employees readily accessible to and usable by persons with disabilities; job restructuring; modification of work schedules; providing additional unpaid leave; reassignment to a vacant position; acquiring or modifying equipment or devices; adjusting or modifying examinations, training materials, or policies; and providing qualified readers or interpreters. Reasonable accommodation may be necessary to apply for a job, to perform job functions, or to enjoy the benefits and privileges of employment that are enjoyed by people without disabilities. An employer is not required to lower production standards to make an accommodation. An employer generally is not obligated to provide personal use items such as eyeglasses or hearing aids.

Undue Hardship

An employer is required to make a reasonable accommodation to a qualified individual with a disability unless doing so would impose an undue hardship on the operation of the employer's business. Undue hardship means an action that requires significant difficulty or expense when considered in relation to factors such as a business's size, financial resources, and the nature and structure of its operation.

Prohibited Inquiries and Examinations

Before making an offer of employment, an employer may not ask job applicants about the existence, nature, or severity of a disability. Applicants may be asked about their ability to perform job functions. A job offer may be conditioned on the results of a medical examination, but only if the examination is required for all entering employees in the same job category. Medical examinations of employees must be job-related and consistent with business necessity.

(Continued)

FIGURE 3-2   *(Continued)*

Drug and Alcohol Use

Employees and applicants currently engaging in the illegal use of drugs are not protected by the ADA when an employer acts on the basis of such use. Tests for illegal use of drugs are not considered medical examinations and, therefore, are not subject to the ADA's restrictions on medical examinations. Employers may hold individuals who are illegally using drugs and individuals with alcoholism to the same standards of performance as other employees.

THE CIVIL RIGHTS ACT OF 1991

The Civil Rights Act of 1991 made major changes in the federal laws against employment discrimination enforced by EEOC. Enacted in part to reverse several Supreme Court decisions that limited the rights of persons protected by these laws, the Act also provides additional protections. The Act authorizes compensatory and punitive damages in cases of intentional discrimination, and provides for obtaining attorneys' fees and the possibility of jury trials. It also directs the EEOC to expand its technical assistance and outreach activities.

FIGURE 3-3   **Excerpts from Title VII of the Civil Rights Act of 1964**

SECTION 703

(a) It shall be an unlawful practice for an employer
    (1) to fail to hire or to discharge any individual, or otherwise to discriminate against any individual with respect to compensation, terms, conditions, or privileges of employment, because of such individual's race, color, religion, sex, or national origin; or (2) to limit, segregate, or classify employees or applicants for employment in any way which would deprive or tend to deprive any individual of employment opportunities or otherwise adversely affect status as an employee, because of such individual's race, color, religion, sex, or national origin.

(e) Notwithstanding any other provision of this title,
    (1) it shall not be an unlawful employment practice for an employer to hire and employ those employees . . . on the basis of religion, sex, or national origin in those certain instances where religion, sex, or national origin is a bona fide occupational qualification reasonably necessary to the normal operation of that particular business or enterprise . . .

(h) Notwithstanding any other provision of this title, it shall not be an unlawful employment practice for an employer to apply different standards of compensation, or different terms, conditions, or privileges of employment pursuant to a bona fide seniority or merit system, or a system which measures earnings by quantity or quality of production or to employees who work in different locations, provided that such differences are not the result of an intention to discriminate because of race, color, religion, sex, or national origin, nor shall it be unlawful employment practice for an employer to give and act upon the results of any professionally developed ability test provided that such test, its administration or action upon the results is not designed, intended, or used to discriminate because of race, color, religion, sex, or national origin . . .

(j) Nothing contained in this title shall be interpreted to require any employer . . . to grant preferential treatment to any individual or to any group because of the race, color, religion, sex, or national origin of such individual or group on account of an imbalance which may exist with respect to the total number or percentage of persons of any race, color, religion, sex, or national origin employed by any employer . . . in comparison with the total number or percentage of persons of such race, color, religion, sex, or national origin in any community, State, section, or other area, or in the available work force in any community, State, section, or other area.

SECTION 704

(a) It shall be an unlawful employment practice for an employer to discriminate against any employees or applicants for employment . . . because the employee or applicant has opposed any practice made an unlawful employment practice by this title, or because he or she has made a charge, testified, assisted, or participated in any matter in an investigation, proceeding, or hearing under this title.

2006, 10 states, the District of Columbia, and over 165 cities and counties had laws prohibiting employment discrimination based on sexual orientation. Bills are pending and already may have passed in other states (see www.aclu.org for up-to-date data). Most laws cover actual and perceived homosexuality. Several state laws include all orientation, including heterosexuals and bisexuals. Some states also provide additional protection beyond the ADA opposing discrimination against people who are HIV positive or are victims of AIDS.

What Is the Cost of Violating EEO Laws?

The costs can be substantial, not only because of direct expenses related to litigation, but also a company's reputation. In certifying the largest class in an employment discrimination lawsuit, a federal judge concluded that promotion decisions at Wal-Mart were "excessively subjective." Testimony in the case indicated that the company imposed only a current "above average" performance evaluation and a willingness to relocate as minimal requirements for promotion. The selection of employees for the management training program was a "tap on the shoulder process" with evidence that jobs were posted only on occasion.

Women's total earnings at Wal-Mart were 5 percent to 15 percent less than men's total earnings in similar jobs. About 65 percent of hourly employees are women but women hold only 33 percent of management positions. Women take 4.38 years from date of hire to be promoted to assistant manager while men take only 2.86 years. Women take 10.12 years to reach the store manager level while men take only 8.64 years. An expert witness also used "external benchmarking" in showing that Wal-Mart lagged far behind the retail industry in rates of women in managerial positions The court concluded that gender was a significant variable in explaining these discrepancies. This conclusion led to the certification of a class of 1.6 million women in the Title VII lawsuit.

Employers are now well aware of how costly violations of EEO laws can be. In a much-publicized case in 2005, Abercrombie & Fitch settled a Title VII suit for $40 million. Morgan Stanley agreed to pay $52 million to end a sex discrimination suit in 2005. The firm was accused by the EEOC of a pattern of discrimination that denied women opportunities for promotions and higher salaries. Another $2 million was set aside for a training program directed at gender-based discrimination. Home Depot settled a class-action lawsuit alleging sex discrimination for $65 million. The federal government is not immune from charges of discrimination. The Department of Justice settled a lawsuit against the Voice of America for $108 million and the Social Security Administration settled a race discrimination lawsuit for $7.75 million in 2002. The "jury is still out" (so to speak) on the huge class action, sex discrimination lawsuit against Wal-Mart.

With some 20 percent of jury verdicts at $1 million or more, organizations try to be more careful about their personnel practices, with monitoring systems and EEO offices and training programs for personnel decision makers and supervisors. HRM specialists and labor attorneys are active in conducting training and research in areas related to EEO.

One major component of training programs is simply making personnel decision makers aware of EEO laws. Let us follow this approach by introducing you to the major laws that account for most of the regulation and litigation in EEO. We present these laws in the same order as the frequency with which they are used as a source of redress in employment discrimination claims. Remember that there are many other laws related to HRM psychology and HRM practice. These laws will be introduced when we cover the most relevant HRM activity in the text.

TITLE VII OF THE CIVIL RIGHTS ACT OF 1964

The Civil Rights Act was signed by President Johnson in 1964, and was amended by the **Equal Employment Opportunity Act** in 1972 and the **Civil Rights Act of 1991.** Title VII deals specifically with discrimination in employment and prohibits discrimination based on race, color, religion, sex, or national origin. Figure 3-3 provides major excerpts from Title VII. The Act covers all employers having more than 15 employees except private clubs, religious organizations, and places of employment connected to an Indian reservation.

What Is the EEOC?

The **U.S. Equal Employment Opportunity Commission (EEOC),** an agency of the U.S. Department of Labor, was created to monitor and enforce compliance with several laws, including Title VII. The EEOC can file Title VII suits against organizations for violations of the law. The EEOC also issues interpretive regulations regarding employment practices (see www.eeoc.gov to review these guidelines). Among the many regulatory interpretations issued by the EEOC are the **Uniform Guidelines on Employee Selection Procedures** that provide recommendations for employment staffing, the **Interpretative Guidelines on Sexual Harassment**, and the **Policy Guidance on Reasonable Accommodation Under the Americans with Disabilities Act.** HRM specialists participated in the development of these guidelines. While these guidelines are not law, the courts often use them to evaluate claims in a case.

The EEOC also requires that most employers with 100 or more employees submit an annual **EEO-1** form. Figure 3-4 presents the form. Changes to Section D have been proposed to take effect in 2007 (get an update at http://www.eeoc.gov). Data from these forms are used to identify possible patterns of discrimination in particular organizations or segments of the workforce. The EEOC may then take legal action against an organization based on these data.

The EEOC offers a mediation program that is available at no cost to the parties. Mediation is an informal process in which a neutral third party assists the opposing parties to reach a voluntary, negotiated resolution of a charge of discrimination. The decision to mediate is completely voluntary for the charging party and the employer. Mediation gives the parties the opportunity to discuss the issues raised in the charge, clear up misunderstandings, determine the underlying interests or concerns, find areas of agreement and, ultimately, to incorporate those areas of agreements into resolutions. A mediator does not resolve the charge or impose a decision on the parties. Instead, the mediator helps

Joint Reporting Committee

- **Equal Employment Opportunity Commission**
- **Office of Federal Contract Compliance Programs (Labor)**

EQUAL EMPLOYMENT OPPORTUNITY

EMPLOYER INFORMATION REPORT EEO—1

Standard Form 100
(Rev. 3/97)

O.M.B. No. 3046-0007
EXPIRES 10/31/99
100-214

Section A—TYPE OF REPORT

Refer to instructions for number and types of reports to be filed.

1. Indicate by marking in the appropriate box the type of reporting unit for which this copy of the form is submitted (MARK ONLY ONE BOX).

   (1) ☐ Single-establishment Employer Report

Multi-establishment Employer:
(2) ☐ Consolidated Report (Required)
(3) ☐ Headquarters Unit Report (Required)
(4) ☐ Individual Establishment Report (submit one for each establishment with 50 or more employees)
(5) ☐ Special Report

---

2. Total number of reports being filed by this Company (Answer on Consolidated Report only) _____

Section B—COMPANY IDENTIFICATION (To be answered by all employers)	OFFICE USE ONLY
1. Parent Company	
a. Name of parent company (owns or controls establishment in item 2) omit if same as label	a.
Address (Number and street)	b.
City or town State ZIP code	c.
2. Establishment for which this report is filed. (Omit if same as label)	
a. Name of establishment	d.
Address (Number and street) City or Town County State ZIP code	e.
b. Employer Identification No. (IRS 9-DIGIT TAX NUMBER)	f.
c. Was an EEO–1 report filed for this establishment last year? ☐ Yes ☐ No	

Section C—EMPLOYERS WHO ARE REQUIRED TO FILE (To be answered by all employers)

☐ Yes ☐ No	1.	Does the entire company have at least 100 employees in the payroll period for which you are reporting?
☐ Yes ☐ No	2.	Is your company affiliated through common ownership and/or centralized management with other entities in an enterprise with a total employment of 100 or more?
☐ Yes ☐ No	3.	Does the company or any of its establishments (a) have 50 or more employees AND (b) is not exempt as provided by 41 CFR 60–1.5, AND either (1) is a prime government contractor or first-tier subcontractor, and has a contract, subcontract, or purchase order amounting to $50,000 or more, or (2) serves as a depository of Government funds in any amount or is a financial institution which is an issuing and paying agent for U.S. Savings Bonds and Savings Notes?

If the response to question C-3 is yes, please enter your Dun and Bradstreet Identification number (if you have one): ☐☐☐☐☐☐☐☐☐

NOTE: If the answer is yes to questions 1, 2, or 3, complete the entire form, otherwise skip to Section G.

Figure 3-4   EEO-1 Form

SF 100 Page 2

Section D—EMPLOYMENT DATA

Employment at this establishment—Report all permanent full-time and part-time employees including apprentices and on-the-job trainees unless specifically excluded as set forth in the instructions. Enter the appropriate figures on all lines and in all columns. Blank spaces will be considered as zeros.

JOB CATEGORIES		OVERALL TOTALS (SUM OF COL. B THRU K)	MALE					FEMALE				
			WHITE (NOT OF HISPANIC ORIGIN)	BLACK (NOT OF HISPANIC ORIGIN)	HISPANIC	ASIAN OR PACIFIC ISLANDER	AMERICAN INDIAN OR ALASKAN NATIVE	WHITE (NOT OF HISPANIC ORIGIN)	BLACK (NOT OF HISPANIC ORIGIN)	HISPANIC	ASIAN OR PACIFIC ISLANDER	AMERICAN INDIAN OR ALASKAN NATIVE
		A	B	C	D	E	F	G	H	I	J	K
Officials and Managers	1											
Professionals	2											
Technicians	3											
Sales Workers	4											
Office and Clerical	5											
Craft Workers (Skilled)	6											
Operatives (Semi-Skilled)	7											
Laborers (Unskilled)	8											
Service Workers	9											
TOTAL	10											
Total employment reported in previous EEO-1 report	11											

NOTE: Omit questions 1 and 2 on the Consolidated Report.

1. Date(s) of payroll period used: 2. Does this establishment employ apprentices?
                                                                            1 ☐ Yes   2 ☐ No

Section E—ESTABLISHMENT INFORMATION (Omit on the Consolidated Report)

1. What is the major activity of this establishment? (Be specific, i.e., manufacturing steel castings, retail grocer, wholesale plumbing supplies, title insurance, etc. Include the specific type of product or type of service provided, as well as the principal business or industrial activity.)

OFFICE USE ONLY
g.

Section F—REMARKS

Use this item to give any identification data appearing on last report which differs from that given above, explain major changes in composition of reporting units and other pertinent information.

Section G—CERTIFICATION (See Instructions G)

Check one
1 ☐ All reports are accurate and were prepared in accordance with the instructions (check on consolidated only)
2 ☐ This report is accurate and was prepared in accordance with the instructions.

Name of Certifying Official	Title	Signature	Date
Name of person to contact regarding this report (Type or print)	Address (Number and Street)		
Title	City and State	ZIP Code	Telephone Number (Including Area Code)	Extension

All reports and information obtained from individual reports will be kept confidential as required by Section 709(e) of Title VII.
WILLFULLY FALSE STATEMENTS ON THIS REPORT ARE PUNISHABLE BY LAW, U.S. CODE, TITLE 18, SECTION 1001.

Figure 3-4   (*Continued*)

the parties to agree on a mutually acceptable resolution. The mediation process is strictly confidential. In 2005, the EEOC and McDonald's USA signed an agreement to mediate workplace disputes prior to an EEOC investigation or potential litigation when a charge of discrimination is filed with the federal agency in some regions of the U.S. This mediation partnership was the 90th such national or regional agreement between the EEOC and a large employer (mainly Fortune 500 companies). The EEOC oversees approximately 12,000 mediations annually.

Under the terms of such agreements, all eligible charges of discrimination filed with the Commission naming McDonald's as the employer will be referred directly to the mediation unit. As of 2005, expanding mediation was a key component of the EEOC current plan to improve their operational efficiency.

What Is Not Prohibited by Title VII?

Title VII does not prohibit discrimination based on seniority systems, veterans' preference rights, national security reasons, or job qualifications based on test scores, backgrounds, or experience, even when the use of such practices may be correlated with the race, gender, color, religion, or national origin. Title VII also does not prohibit **bona fide occupational qualifications (BFOQs)** or discriminatory practices whenever these practices are "reasonably necessary to the normal operation of the organization." For example, a BFOQ that excludes one group (e.g., males or females) from an employment opportunity is permissible if the employer can argue that the **"essence of the business"** requires the exclusion, that is, when business would be significantly affected by not employing members of one group exclusively.

What if a company had data showing customers clearly prefer employees with certain protected class characteristics? Pan American Airways tried this argument in *Diaz v. Pan America*. They presented data showing the vast majority of their customers (overwhelmingly male) preferred female flight attendants. The Supreme Court said that customer preference was not a legally defensible reason to discriminate.

In general, the position of the courts regarding BFOQs favors judgments about the performance, abilities, or potential of specific individuals rather than discrimination by class or categories. The court has said that the BFOQ exception to Title VII is a narrow one, limited to policies that are directly related to a worker's ability to do the job and the essence of the business.

How Do You File a Title VII Lawsuit?

If an individual believes that he or she has been a victim of illegal discrimination and wishes to pursue a claim through the legal system, the complaint must first be filed with an office of the EEOC. The EEOC guideline for filing a charge is presented in Figure 3-5.

What Legal Steps Are Followed in a Title VII Case?

The Supreme Court has established the legal steps to be followed in a Title VII action through the federal court system. Although the plaintiff retains the "burden of proof," a model is used such that the burden of producing evidence shifts from the plaintiff to the defendant and back to the plaintiff. Initially the complainant or plaintiff has the burden to show that a **prima facie** case of discrimination exists. Prima facie means "presumed to be true until proven otherwise"; the plaintiff must show that there is a high likelihood that a violation of EEO law has occurred. After the plaintiff produces sufficient evidence to establish a prima facie case, the burden of producing evidence shifts to the employer or defendant, who must provide some proof of a legitimate, nondiscriminatory reason for the employment decision. Finally, the burden of producing evidence shifts back to the plaintiff to either show that the reason given was a pretext for discrimination or that an alternate practice, less discriminatory in its effect, would achieve the employer's purpose equally well. Title VII cases can be brought under either (or both) of two theories: **disparate treatment** and **disparate impact.** The steps to follow for each are illustrated in Figure 3-6.

What Is Disparate Treatment?

Plaintiffs can demonstrate a prima facie case by showing disparate treatment, the most frequently used theory. According to the procedures established in the 1973 *McDonnell Douglas v. Green* Supreme Court case, plaintiffs must show that an employer treats one or more members of a protected group differently.[6] For example, the use of different criteria for promotion depending on the candidate's sex would constitute disparate treatment. Female applicants who were not hired by a firm might show that the employer asked them questions about their marital status or child care arrangements that were not asked of male applicants.

In disparate treatment cases, the Supreme Court established that the burden is on the plaintiff to prove that the employer *intended* to discriminate because of race, sex, color, religion, or national origin.[7]

One special form of disparate treatment is **retaliation.** Employers cannot retaliate against employees who file EEO charges or parties who testify on behalf of plaintiffs in such cases. Retaliation accounted for 24 percent of Titles VII charges in 2005.

What Is Disparate Impact?

According to procedures established in the 1971 *Griggs v. Duke Power* case,[8] plaintiffs can show that an employer's practices had a disparate impact on members of a protected group by showing that the employment procedures (e.g., tests, interviews, credentials) had a disproportionately negative effect on members of a protected group. Impact cases are often established as **class action** cases in which a judge can certify a class of people who

FIGURE 3-5	Filing a Charge of Employment Discrimination

Note: Federal employees or applicants for Federal employment should see Federal Sector Equal Employment Opportunity Complaint Processing.

WHO CAN FILE A CHARGE OF DISCRIMINATION?

- Any individual who believes that his or her employment rights have been violated may file a charge of discrimination with EEOC.
- In addition, an individual, organization, or agency may file a charge on behalf of another person in order to protect the aggrieved person's identity.

HOW IS A CHARGE OF DISCRIMINATION FILED?

- A charge may be filed by mail or in person at the nearest EEOC office.
- Individuals who need an accommodation in order to file a charge (e.g., sign language interpreter, print materials in an accessible format) should inform the EEOC field office so appropriate arrangements can be made.
- Federal employees or applicants for employment should see Federal Sector Equal Employment Opportunity Complaint Processing.

WHAT INFORMATION MUST BE PROVIDED TO FILE A CHARGE?

- The complaining party's name, address, and telephone number.
- The name, address, and telephone number of the respondent employer, employment agency, or union that is alleged to have discriminated, and number of employees (or union members), if known.
- A short description of the alleged violation (the event that caused the complaining party to believe that his or her rights were violated).
- The date(s) of the alleged violation(s).
- Federal employees or applicants for employment should see Federal Sector Equal Employment Opportunity Complaint Processing.

WHAT ARE THE TIME LIMITS FOR FILING A CHARGE OF DISCRIMINATION?

All laws enforced by EEOC, except the Equal Pay Act, require filing a charge with EEOC before a private lawsuit may be filed in court. There are strict time limits within which charges must be filed:

- A charge must be filed with EEOC within 180 days from the date of the alleged violation, in order to protect the charging party's rights.
- This 180-day filing deadline is extended to 300 days if the charge also is covered by a state or local antidiscrimination law. For ADEA charges, only state laws extend the filing limit to 300 days.
- These time limits do not apply to claims under the Equal Pay Act, because under that Act persons do not have to first file a charge with EEOC in order to have the right to go to court. However, since many EPA claims also raise Title VII sex discrimination issues, it may be advisable to file charges under both laws within the time limits indicated.
- To protect legal rights, it is always best to contact EEOC promptly when discrimination is suspected.
- Federal employees or applicants for employment should see Federal Sector Equal Employment Opportunity Complaint Processing.

WHAT AGENCY HANDLES A CHARGE THAT IS ALSO COVERED BY STATE OR LOCAL LAW?

Many states and localities have antidiscrimination laws and agencies responsible for enforcing those laws. EEOC refers to these agencies as "Fair Employment Practices Agencies (FEPAs)." Through the use of "work sharing agreements," EEOC and the FEPAs avoid duplication of effort while at the same time ensuring that a charging party's rights are protected under both federal and state law.

- If a charge is filed with a FEPA and is also covered by federal law, the FEPA "dual files" the charge with EEOC to protect federal rights. The charge usually will be retained by the FEPA for handling.
- If a charge is filed with EEOC and also is covered by state or local law, EEOC "dual files" the charge with the state or local FEPA, but ordinarily retains the charge for handling.

HOW IS A CHARGE FILED FOR DISCRIMINATION OUTSIDE THE UNITED STATES?

U.S.-based companies that employ U.S. citizens outside the United States or its territories are covered under EEO laws, with certain exceptions. An individual alleging an EEO violation outside the U.S. should file a charge with the district office closest to his or her employer's headquarters. However, if you are unsure where to file, you may file a charge with any EEOC office. For answers to common questions about how EEO laws apply to multinational employers, please see:

- The Equal Employment Opportunity Responsibilities of Multinational Employers
- Employee Rights When Working for Multinational Employers

FIGURE 3-6   Evidence and Proof in Title VII Cases

Evidence Burden	Disparate Treatment	Disparate Impact
Plaintiff's initial burden (prima facie case)	He or she belongs to the discriminated-against group. He or she applied and was qualified. He or she was rejected. The position remained open to applicants with equal or fewer qualifications.	Unequal impact of the practice(s) in question on different groups (e.g., 80% rule violation)
Defendant's rebuttal burden	Articulate a "legitimate nondiscriminatory reason for the rejection."	Demonstrate that the challenged practice is job-related for the position in question and consistent with business necessity.
Plaintiff's burden in response	Show that the stated reason is a pretext by demonstrating, e.g.: • The employer doesn't apply that reason equally to all. • The employer has treated the plaintiff unfairly before. • The employer engages in other unfair employment practices. OR Show the plaintiff's group membership was a factor in the rejection decision.	Show that a less discriminatory and equally valid alternative practice or method does exist.
Defendant's burden in response	Show that the decision would have been the same even if it had not taken plaintiff's group membership into account.	

Source: From *Federal Regulation of Personnel in Human Resource Management,* 21st edition, by Ledvinka. Reprinted with permission of South-Western, a division of Thomson Learning: www.thomsonrights.com. Fax 800.730.2215.

make similar claims against a company. For example, the plaintiffs in the *Wal-Mart* case were certified as a class before the rest of the case was pursued. Such impact is considered unintentional but illegal discrimination if the employment practice is not shown to be "job related."

Whether or not the employer had good intentions or didn't mean to discriminate is irrelevant to the courts in this type of lawsuit. After the plaintiff shows evidence of adverse or disparate impact, the employer must carry the burden of producing evidence of "business necessity" and "job relatedness" for the employment practice. Finally, the burden shifts back to the plaintiff, who must then show that an alternative procedure is available that is equal to or better than the employer's practice and has less adverse impact.

HRM specialists are very much involved in this important area. The concept of "job relatedness" as defined in *Griggs* is very similar to the concept of validity developed by industrial psychologists.

How Do You Determine Disparate or Adverse Impact?

One common "yardstick" recommended (and used) by the EEOC in the Uniform Guidelines and adopted in numerous court cases for determining disparate or adverse

impact is the **four-fifths rule** (also known as the 80 percent rule). This rule means that a selection rate (number selected/number considered) for a protected group cannot be less than four-fifths or 80 percent of the selection rate for the group with the highest selection rate. For example, the City of Columbus, Ohio, used a paper-and-pencil, multiple-choice examination to screen applicants for its firefighter positions. While 84 percent of the whites passed the examination, only 27 percent of the blacks did. Using the four-fifths rule, 80 percent of the white selection rate is 67 percent ($.8 \times .84$). Since the 27 percent selection rate for blacks was less than 67 percent, the test was determined to have an adverse impact on blacks.

The 80 percent or Four fifths rule derives from the EEOC's **Uniform Guidelines on Employee Selection Procedures.** However, it is not the only statistical measure of adverse impact that can be used to establish prima facie evidence of discrimination. The make-up of a work force can also be compared to population or industry data (e.g., a geographical area is 15 percent Hispanic while only 3 percent of workers for Company X in that same area are Hispanic. In the class action, sex discrimination lawsuit against Wal-Mart, the plaintiffs presented data showing 58 percent of managers in general merchandising were women while only 32 percent of Wal-Mart's managers were women. Plaintiffs (or the EEOC) can also analyze the extent to which a protected class possesses a particular credential or years of experience versus a majority group.

Remember that these statistical data only establish prima facie evidence of discrimination. The employer still has the opportunity to prove "job relatedness" and/or "business necessity."

The disparate impact theory has been used in a great many cases involving "neutral employment practices" such as tests, entrance requirements, particular credentials, or physical requirements. For example, in 2005, a class of African Americans who were denied apprenticeships at Ford using the test score requirements applied the 80 percent rule to show that the proportion of African Americans meeting the minimum requirements was less than 80 percent of the rate of whites.

The Civil Rights Act of 1991 is unclear as to precisely what an employer must demonstrate; it simply says that the employer must demonstrate *"that the challenged practice is job related for the position in question and consistent with business necessity."* There is a great deal of litigation over just what both employees and the organizations they sue must demonstrate under the CRA of 1991.

HRM specialists and academics often find themselves on both sides of a court case, attacking (and defending) the validity evidence and the statistics presented to support or refute a theory of discrimination and claims of "job relatedness."

Prior to 1991, organizations attempted to avoid statistical adverse impact by interpreting test scores based on the ethnicity of the test taker. Called **race norming** and even practiced by the U.S. Department of Labor, the exact raw scores on the same test were interpreted (and converted) depending on whether the test taker was white, Latino, or African American. The practice of race (and gender) norming was outlawed by the Civil Rights Act of 1991.

How Does an Employer Prove "Job Relatedness"?

There is a large body of case law that provides legal definitions of the term *job related*. The major case in this area is *Griggs v. Duke Power*, in which the Supreme Court struck down the use of an employment test and a high school educational requirement for entry-level personnel selection. Such practices were judged to be discriminatory because they excluded a disproportionate number of blacks from employment, and because the employer could not show that the hiring requirements were "job related," or related to performance on the job. As the court noted, if an employment practice cannot be shown to be related to job performance, and that practice operates to exclude a disproportionate number of protected class members, then the practice is prohibited.

Since the *Griggs* decision was rendered in 1971, there have been many cases that have focused on job-relatedness

issues. In *Albemarle Paper Company v. Moody* (1975), the Supreme Court clarified the job-relatedness defense, requiring a careful job analysis to identify the specific knowledge, skills, and abilities necessary to perform the job or a study that shows a clear statistical relationship between applicant test scores (or a particular credential) and their job performance.[9] In *Connecticut v. Teal* (1982), the Supreme Court declared that the job-relatedness argument must be applied to *all* steps of a multiple-hurdle selection procedure.[10] Winnie Teal had been denied promotion to a supervisory position because of a low score on a written exam that was the first hurdle of the promotion process. When the final promotion decisions were made, the "bottom line" decisions (i.e., who was actually promoted) actually favored African Americans. But the Court said that the "bottom line" is *not* an acceptable legal defense in such a case.

Evidence of a significant correlation between test scores and job performance is considered ideal to support an argument of job relatedness. HRM specialists conduct such studies routinely to evaluate the use of a test or selection procedure. What if a study exists showing that the test being challenged has validity for the same or similar jobs? So a company is sued based on the disparate impact theory and must establish the "job relatedness" of the test. The company does not have enough data to conduct an internal study. Could the company "borrow" a validity study based on data collected in several other organizations? Called **validity generalization** (VG) studies, there are now many such studies based on the correct assumption that the mean of several correlational studies is probably a stronger basis for concluding that there is a valid relationship between test scores and job performance. The most recent review on this issue concludes that the courts have been that impressed with VG evidence but certainly, in order to "borrow" validity in this manner, the organization needs to demonstrate that the job connected to the lawsuit is similar to the jobs under study in the VG study. In addition, the VG study should present sufficient detail on the individual studies that led to the inference that the test was valid.[11] Even with VG evidence, however, it is unclear whether the exclusive use of "borrowed" validity in the form of a VG study will meet the "job relatedness" burden for organizations.

Once the defendant has presented acceptable evidence of job relatedness, the case is not necessarily over. The EEOC takes the position that where two or more selection procedures are available which serve the user's "legitimate interest in efficient and trustworthy workmanship," and which are equally valid for a given purpose, the user should use the procedure which has been demonstrated to have the lesser adverse impact. Thus, the plaintiffs could present evidence that an alternative method exists and that its use would result in less (or no) adverse impact. This step in the process could even apply to the use a particular "cut-off" score for a test (e.g., 70 percent is passing).

Another critical case related to "disparate impact" theory is *Watson v. Ft. Worth Bank & Trust* (1988). Clara Watson was denied a promotion based on an interview. The critical question that the Supreme Court ultimately addressed was whether "impact" theory could be used in "subjective" employment practices such as interviews and performance appraisals (the *Griggs* and *Albemarle* cases concerned "neutral employment practices" such as credentials or test scores). In a unanimous decision, the Court allowed "disparate impact" theory for subjective employment practices. This decision is of course critical for the Wal-Mart Title VII class action, sex discrimination lawsuit where women maintain that the "subjective" method of selecting and promoting managers was discriminatory.

What Constitutes Sexual Harassment under Title VII?

Over 15,000 claims of sexual harassment were filed with the EEOC in 2005 alone. Under Title VII, sexual harassment, like racial and ethnic harassment, is illegal since it constitutes discrimination with respect to a person's conditions of employment. These conditions can refer to psychological and emotional workplace conditions that are coercive or insulting to an individual. The EEOC has published guidelines for employers dealing with sexual harassment issues (go to www.eeoc.gov). According to the Guidelines, sexual harassment is defined as

> unwelcome sexual advances, requests for sexual favors, and other verbal or physical conduct of a sexual nature constitute sexual harassment when (1) submission to such conduct is made either explicitly or implicitly a term or condition of an individual's employment, (2) submission to or rejection of such conduct by an individual is used as the basis for employment decisions affecting such individual, or (3) such conduct has the purpose or effect of unreasonably interfering with an individual's work performance or creating an intimidating, hostile, or offensive working environment.

A growing number of sexual harassment complaints are filed by males. However, harassment of an employee because of sexual orientation does not constitute illegal harassment under Title VII (it probably does under applicable state or local laws prohibiting discrimination based on sexual orientation).

In 1986, the Supreme Court in *Meritor Savings v. Vinson* stated that it was not necessary for the plaintiff to establish a causal relationship or **quid pro quo** between the rejection of sexual advances and a specific personnel action such as a dismissal or a layoff.[12] Rather, it was only necessary for the plaintiff to establish that the harassment created unfavorable or hostile working conditions for him or her. Any workplace conduct that is "sufficiently severe or pervasive to alter the conditions of employment and create an abusive working environment" constitutes illegal sexual harassment.[13]

The Supreme Court has since provided further clarification on this and other harassment issues. In *Harris v. Forklift* (1993), Theresa Harris was asked to remove coins from her boss's front pocket, was asked to go to the Holiday Inn to "negotiate" her raise, and was exposed to hundreds of other disgusting suggestions and behaviors.[14] A lower court determined that Harris had not suffered emotionally from the harassment and thus a hostile working environment was not created. The Supreme Court disagreed, stating that the psychological effect was unnecessary and that only a "reasonable person" needed to find it hostile or abusive. The Court also provided some guidance for the lower courts in determining a hostile working environment. The frequency of the behavior or verbal abuse, its severity, the extent to which it is threatening or humiliating, and whether the abuse interferes with the employee's work performance all may be considered in making the determination of hostile working environment.

Research on the judicial outcomes of sexual harassment claims identified the following correlates of favorable legal outcomes for the claimant: (1) when the harassment involved physical contact of a sexual nature, (2) when sexual propositions were linked to threats or promises of a change in the conditions of employment, (3) when the claimant notified management of the problem before filing charges, (4) when the claims are corroborated, and (5) when the organization had no formal policy toward sexual harassment that had been communicated to its employees.[15]

The Civil Rights Act of 1991 provides for compensatory and punitive damages (in addition to back pay) of up to $300,000 for companies with over 500 employees. That's $300,000 per complaint. The price tag for sexual harassment can be even much higher under state laws that have no ceilings on compensatory or punitive damages.

What Is the Employer's Liability in Sexual Harassment Cases?

Two 1998 Supreme Court decisions provided clarification on employer liability for sexual harassment by supervisors. In *Burlington Industries, Inc. v. Ellerth* and *Faragher v. City of Boca Raton,* the Court said that the employer is always liable when a hostile environment is created by a supervisor that results in a tangible employment action (e.g., termination).[16] However, the employer may not be liable when there is no tangible employment action if it can be shown that the employer exercised "reasonable care" in preventing and correcting the harassing behavior and the plaintiff failed to take advantage of corrective opportunities that were available. This so-called **affirmative defense** clearly indicates that organizations should have sexual harassment policies in place and communicated to all employees.

Regarding co-workers, the employer will be liable if someone in authority knew or should have known of the harassment and did nothing to stop it. The courts are generally clear that this rule applies to any kind of harassment: racial, ethnic, or religious. Employers also may be liable for behaviors committed by nonemployees, clients, temporary employees, or outside contractors in the workplace if they knew or should have known about the acts and didn't take appropriate action. Essentially, the courts have made it clear that an organization is liable for sexual harassment when management is aware of the activity yet does not take immediate and appropriate corrective action.

Thus, an employer is not always liable for sexual harassment. For example, a company is less likely to be found liable under the following conditions: (1) There is a specific policy on harassment that an employee violated, (2) there is a company grievance procedure that the complainant did not follow, and (3) the grievance procedure allows the complainant to bypass the alleged harasser in filing the violation. The policy has to be acceptable. A policy that requires that a complaint be made through an immediate supervisor (with no alternatives) is not an acceptable policy. But a good harassment policy (any type of harassment) can give an employer legal protection. In *Farley v. American Cast Iron Pipe*, the 11th Circuit Court of Appeals, established that once an employer has promulgated an effective antiharassment policy, it is incumbent upon the employees to utilize the procedural mechanisms established by the company specifically to address problems and grievances.

What Steps Should a Company Follow Regarding Sexual Harassment?

Because of the steady increase in Title VII litigation regarding sexual harassment, the following "affirmative defense" strategies have been recommended for organizations: (1) Develop a written policy against sexual harassment, including a definition of sexual harassment and a strong statement by the CEO that it will not be tolerated (some courts have concluded that an employer without a harassment policy is sanctioning a hostile environment); (2) conduct training to make managers aware of the problem (required in Massachusetts California, Connecticut, and Maine); (3) inform employees that they should expect a workplace free from harassment, and what actions they can take under Title VII if their rights are violated; (4) detail the sanctions for violators and protection for those who make any charges; (5) establish a grievance procedure for alleged victims of harassment; (6) investigate claims made by victims; and (7) discipline violators of the policy.[17] On this last point, companies must be careful. Individuals can claim "unlawful termination" and have prevailed in cases where they show that they were not treated fairly in the investigation or the hearing that led to the dismissal. Judgments have been in the millions. The person being accused of sexual harassment deserves as fair a treatment as that which was afforded the accuser. Miller Brewing executive Jerold MacKenzie was awarded over $26 million after he was fired "for sexually harassing" a female employee by describing an episode of the *Seinfeld* show. The sexual harassment policy should stipulate that the policy applies to same-sex harassment as well. The Supreme Court ruled unanimously in 1998 that same-sex harassment was illegal under the CRA.[18] Figure 3-7 presents a summary of employer liability for harassment.

The California law mandating sexual harassment training for all supervisors of employers with 50 or more employees took effect in 2006. The law sets specific standards for the training. The training must be conducted via "classroom or other effective interactive training" and include the following topics: (1) Information and practical guidance regarding the federal and state statutory provisions concerning the prohibition against and the prevention of sexual harassment; (2) Information about the correction of sexual harassment and the remedies available to victims of sexual harassment in employment; and; (3) practical examples aimed at instructing supervisors in the prevention of harassment, discrimination, and retaliation. An example of an interactive training program that probably complies with the new training law was developed by the California State University system. Go to http://www.calstate.edu/gc/AntisexualHarassmentTraining/ and you can go through the entire program and earn a certificate.

What Is Affirmative Action?

Although there is no one generally recognized definition, **affirmative action** has to do with the extent to which employers make an effort through their personnel practices to attract, retain, and upgrade members of the protected classes of the 1964 Civil Rights Act or persons with disabilities. Affirmative action may refer to several strategies, including actively recruiting underrepresented groups in a firm, changing management and employee attitudes about various protected groups, eliminating irrelevant employment practices that bar protected groups from employment, and granting preferential treatment to protected groups. The term *affirmative action* has been replaced with *diversity* programs and policies, but the actual HRM activities defining the old affirmative action programs and the new diversity programs are very similar. The issue of affirmative action and how it is carried out has been identified as a source of trouble between HRM professionals and line managers. Whether or not preferential treatment can or should be granted based on protected class characteristics is at the heart of the trouble. Diversity is a complex term. The 1990 census

FIGURE 3-7   **Employer Liability for Harassment by Supervisors**

1. When does harassment *violate federal law*?

   Harassment violates federal law if it involves discriminatory treatment based on race, color, sex (with or without sexual conduct), religion, national origin, age, disability, or because the employee opposed job discrimination or participated in an investigation or complaint proceeding under the EEO statutes.

   Federal law does not prohibit simple teasing, offhand comments, or isolated incidents that are not extremely serious. The conduct must be sufficiently frequent or severe to create a hostile work environment or result in a "tangible employment action," such as hiring, firing, promotion, or demotion.

2. Does the guidance apply *only to sexual harassment*?

   No, it applies to all types of unlawful harassment.

3. When is an employer legally responsible for harassment by a supervisor?

   An employer is always responsible for harassment by a supervisor that culminated in a tangible employment action. If the harassment did not lead to a tangible employment action, the employer is liable unless it proves that: (1) it exercised reasonable care to prevent and promptly correct any harassment; and (2) the employee unreasonably failed to complain to management or to avoid harm otherwise.

4. Who qualifies as a *"supervisor"* for purposes of employer liability?

   An individual qualifies as an employee's "supervisor" if the individual has the authority to recommend tangible employment decisions affecting the employee or if the individual has the authority to direct the employee's daily work activities.

5. What is a *"tangible employment action"*?

   A "tangible employment action" means a significant change in employment status. Examples include hiring, firing, promotion, demotion, undesirable reassignment, a decision causing a significant change in benefits, compensation decisions, and work assignment.

6. How might harassment culminate in a tangible employment action?

   This might occur if a supervisor fires or demotes a subordinate because she rejects his sexual demands, or promotes her because she submits to his sexual demands.

7. What should employers do to *prevent and correct harassment*?

   Employers should establish, distribute to all employees, and enforce a policy prohibiting harassment and setting out a procedure for making complaints. In most cases, the policy and procedure should be in writing.

   Small businesses may be able to discharge their responsibility to prevent and correct harassment through less formal means. For example, if a business is sufficiently small that the owner maintains regular contact with all employees, the owner can tell the employees at staff meetings that harassment is prohibited, that employees should report such conduct promptly, and that a complaint can be brought "straight to the top." If the business conducts a prompt, thorough, and impartial investigation of any complaint that arises and undertakes swift and appropriate corrective action, it will have fulfilled its responsibility to "effectively prevent and correct harassment."

8. What should an antiharassment *policy* say?

   An employer's antiharassment policy should make clear that the employer will not tolerate harassment based on race, sex, religion, national origin, age, or disability, or harassment based on opposition to discrimination on participation in complaint proceedings.

   The policy should also state that the employer will not tolerate retaliation against anyone who complains of harassment or who participates in an investigation.

9. What are important *elements of a complaint procedure*?

   The employer should encourage employees to report harassment to management before it becomes severe or pervasive.
   The employer should designate more than one individual to take complaints, and should ensure that these individuals are in accessible locations. The employer also should instruct all of its supervisors to report complaints of harassment to appropriate officials.
   The employer should assure employees that it will protect the confidentiality of harassment complaints to the extent possible.

(Continued)

| FIGURE 3-7 | *(Continued)* |

10. Is a complaint procedure adequate if employees are instructed to report harassment to their immediate supervisors?

   No, because the supervisor may be the one committing harassment or may not be impartial. It is advisable for an employer to designate at least one official outside an employee's chain of command to take complaints, to assure that the complaint will be handled impartially.

11. How should an employer *investigate* a harassment complaint?

   An employer should conduct a prompt, thorough, and impartial investigation. The alleged harasser should not have any direct or indirect control over the investigation.

   The investigator should interview the employee who complained of harassment, the alleged harasser, and others who could reasonably be expected to have relevant information. Before completing the investigation, the employer should take steps to make sure that harassment does not continue. If the parties have to be separated, then the separation should not burden the employee who has complained of harassment. An involuntary transfer of the complainant could constitute unlawful retaliation. Other examples of interim measures are making scheduling changes to avoid contact between the parties or placing the alleged harasser on non-disciplinary leave with pay pending the conclusion of the investigation.

12. How should an employer *correct harassment*?

   If an employer determines that harassment occurred, it should take immediate measures to stop the harassment and ensure that it does not recur. Disciplinary measures should be proportional to the seriousness of the offense.

13. Does an employee who is harassed by his or her supervisor have any *responsibilities*?

   Yes. The employee must take reasonable steps to avoid harm from the harassment. Usually, the employee will exercise this responsibility by using the employer's complaint procedure.

14. Is an employer legally responsible for its supervisor's harassment if the *employee failed to use* the employer's complaint procedure?

   No, unless the harassment resulted in a tangible employment action or unless it was reasonable for the employee not to complain to management. An employee's failure to complain would be reasonable, for example, if he or she had a legitimate fear of retaliation. The employer must prove that the employee acted unreasonably.

15. If an employee complains to management about harassment, should he or she wait for management to complete the investigation before *filing a charge* with EEOC?

   It may make sense to wait to see if management corrects the harassment before filing a charge. However, if management does not act promptly to investigate the complaint and undertake corrective action, then it may be appropriate to file a charge. The deadline for filing an EEOC charge is either 180 or 300 days after the last date of alleged harassment, depending on the state in which the allegation arises. This deadline is not extended because of an employer's internal investigation of the complaint.

included five categories for ethnicity. The 2000 census included 63 categories.

Contractors and subcontractors with more than $50,000 in government business and 50 or more employees are not only prohibited from discriminating, but also must take affirmative action to ensure that applicants and employees are not treated differently as a function of their sex, religion, race, color, and national origin.

Section 503 of the Rehabilitation Act requires federal contractors to take affirmative action to employ and advance qualified people with disabilities. Under Executive Order 11246, contractors and subcontractors are required to develop a written affirmative action plan that is designed to ensure equal employment opportunity. These plans are monitored by the Office of Contract Compliance Programs (OFCCP) in the U.S. Department of Labor (www.dol.gov).

What Is the Legal Status of Affirmative Action?

Federal courts can order involuntary affirmative action programs or organizations can implement voluntary affirmative action without court mandate. Given the recent personnel changes on the Supreme Court, the legality of such programs is now more questionable than ever. As either part of a judicial decision or the negotiated settlement of a lawsuit, a court also can order targeted quota hiring. For example, as a part of a negotiated settlement with the U.S. Forest Service in 1994, a California federal judge ordered the Forest Service to hire a set number of females over a prescribed period of time. The Forest Service had to submit an annual report on compliance with the quota and was subject to punitive action for failure to comply.

In 1979, the Supreme Court in *U.S. Steelworkers v. Weber* approved Kaiser Aluminum's voluntary affirmative action plan because it did not "unnecessarily trammel" the interests of majority employees and it was a temporary measure that would cease when blacks reached parity with their representation in the labor market. Lower courts reviewing subsequent challenges to voluntary affirmative action programs have used the *Weber* test to ascertain their legality.[19]

It has been argued that affirmative action is appropriate only as a remedy for past discrimination against specific individuals. The Supreme Court had opposed this narrow application in early decisions. The 1987 Supreme Court ruling in *Johnson v. Santa Clara Transportation Agency* provided some clarity to the remedies that have been pursued under affirmative action and equal employment opportunity.[20] According to the court, organizations may adopt voluntary programs to hire and promote qualified minorities and women to correct a "manifest imbalance" in their representation in various job categories, even when there is no evidence of past discrimination. This was the first time that the Supreme Court explicitly ruled that women as well as blacks and other minorities can receive preferential treatment. The decision also affects the most common employment situation in the United States today: work situations where it is difficult or impossible to prove past discrimination, but a statistical disparity exists in the number of females and minorities in certain occupations relative to population statistics. Even that decision emphasized that "manifest imbalance" meant substantial, inexplicable differences in workforce representation. The decision also emphasized that preferential treatment may only be granted when job candidates are judged to be "equally qualified."

While the majority of the Supreme Court decisions have favored affirmative action and most forms of preferential treatment, there now appear to be some important qualifiers on their appropriateness. These qualifiers include (1) affirmative action plans should be "narrowly tailored" to achieve their ends with a timetable for ending the preferential practice, (2) class-based firing or layoff schemes are too harsh on the innocent and inappropriate in most circumstances, and (3) preferential personnel practices of any kind are appropriate only in employment situations where there is a prior history or indication of past discrimination. Also unclear is the literal meaning of *prior discrimination*. In its earlier decision in *U.S. Steelworkers v. Weber,* the Supreme Court said it was acceptable to use affirmative action programs to remedy "manifest racial imbalance" regardless of whether an employer had been guilty of discriminatory job practices in the past.

In two cases involving the University of Michigan in 2004, the Supreme Court provided some clarity to the issue of affirmative action and college admissions. Both Michigan cases (*Gratz v. Bollinger*; *Grutter v. Bollinger*) addressed the question of whether racial preference programs unconstitutionally discriminate (based on the equal protection clause of the Constitution) against white students.[21]

The Court ruled that race can be a factor in college admissions since a social value may be derived from greater "diversity" in the classroom. However, race cannot be an "overriding" factor in admissions decisions. While these twin decisions only directly applied to public universities, the decisions are likely to have implications for private schools, other governmental decision making, and perhaps the business world. The impact of both decisions is that schools have dropped fixed or rigid, point-based systems for admission. Justice Sandra Day O'Connor, writing for the majority in the law school admissions test (*Grutter*), stated that the Constitution "does not prohibit the law school's narrowly tailoring use of race in admissions decisions to further a compelling interest in obtaining the educational benefits that flow from a diverse student body."[22] Justice O'Connor retired in 2006. The Supreme Court is likely to revisit this issue soon.

What Is Required before a Company Embarks on a Voluntary Affirmative Action/Diversity Program?

The courts have clarified criteria for *voluntary* affirmative action plans. For voluntary plans, it has been suggested that they (1) be designed to eradicate old patterns of discrimination, (2) not impose an "absolute bar" to white advancement, (3) be temporary, (4) not "trammel the interests of white employees," (5) be designed to eliminate a "manifest racial imbalance," and (6) show preference only from a pool of equally qualified candidates. For involuntary affirmative action programs, it was suggested that preferential treatment is legal when it (1) is necessary to remedy "pervasive and egregious discrimination"; (2) is used as a flexible benchmark for court monitoring, rather than as a quota; (3) is temporary; and (4) does not "unnecessarily trammel the interests of white employees."

Despite the apparent legal protection for voluntary affirmative action plans, managers must tread very carefully to avoid "reverse discrimination" lawsuits. Race- or gender-conscious employment decisions made in the absence of an AA plan may result in a successful claim of reverse discrimination by a rejected majority applicant or employee. Even when OFCCP-approved AA programs exist, managers must ensure that all individuals meet the stated job requirements and that affirmative action plans are carefully drafted and followed. The most difficult and legally troublesome issue related to AA is when (and if) a protected class characteristic may be considered relative to the qualifications of the job candidates.

Is Affirmative Action Still Necessary?

There is an argument that AA is now unnecessary because equal employment opportunity already exists. Women and minorities strongly disagree with this argument. A three-year study conducted by a bipartisan federal commission in 1996 concluded that women and minorities still face barriers to their advancement: the so-called **glass ceiling.** The glass ceiling refers to the lack of women and minorities in top managerial positions. The various diversity programs are designed to break down some of these barriers. Go to www.ilr.cornell.edu for the Glass Ceiling Commission archives.

There is no question that the general public is opposed to preferential treatment when it is defined as taking a protected class characteristic such as race or gender into account in making a staffing decision. People tend to favor affirmative action in terms of recruitment, training opportunities, and attention to applicant qualifications. They tend to oppose preferential treatment and any form of quota staffing. The state of California amended their Constitution in 1996 when they approved Amendment 209, which explicitly outlaws any preferential treatment for California public agencies. (The language of the amendment is almost identical to Section 703J of the 1964 Civil Rights Act but with less ambiguity.) The state of Washington also adopted a similar provision and other states are considering such amendments.

THE AGE DISCRIMINATION IN EMPLOYMENT ACT OF 1967, AMENDED IN 1978 AND 1986

The Age Discrimination in Employment Act (ADEA) was designed to prohibit age discrimination in employment decisions (e.g., hiring, job retention, compensation, and other terms and conditions). The law applies to workers over the age of 39. The ADEA applies to employers with 20 or more employees, unions of 25 or more members, employment agencies, and federal, state, and local governments. There were almost 18,000 claims of age discrimination in 2005, up 26 percent from 1999. While it has been difficult for claimants to win ADEA cases, the 2005 Supreme Court decision in *Smith v. Jackson* might make it easier for plaintiffs to win ADEA cases and is likely to increase the number of cases filed. The Court allowed the use of "disparate impact" theory for ADEA cases.

What Is Required to Establish Prima Facie Evidence of Age Discrimination?

Similar to Title VII cases, there are certain requirements for establishing a prima facie case of age discrimination. These include showing that (1) the employee is a member of the protected age group (40 or older); (2) the employee has the ability to perform satisfactorily at some absolute or relative level (e.g., relative to other employees involved in the decision process or at an absolute standard of acceptability); (3) the employee was not hired, promoted, or compensated, or was discharged, laid off, or forced to retire; and (4) the position was filled or maintained by a younger person (just younger, not necessarily under age 40). The second condition is the biggest challenge for the plaintiff and is usually the one where the

plaintiff falls short in establishing a prima facie case due to the usual subjectivity in comparing individuals.[23] Of course, a detendent can rebut all claims based on other data or critiques of the plaintiffs' evidence.

Once a prima facie case has been established based on the evidence presented by the plaintiff, the defendant must then present evidence that "reasonable factors" other than age were the basis of the personnel decision. At this point, appearing to be untruthful or incomplete in communications could be costly for employers.

One of the most common scenarios for litigation under ADEA concerns the termination of an employee because of alleged poor performance. For example, in *Mastie v. Great Lakes Steel Corp.* (1976), the employer maintained that Mr. Mastie had been discharged in reduction-in-force efforts because of his poorer performance relative to other employees.[24] Mr. Mastie presented personnel records reflecting an exemplary performance record and a history of merit-based salary increases. However, the court found for the employer and said that the controlling issue should be whether age was a *determinative* factor in the personnel decision, not the "absolute accuracy" or correctness of the personnel decision. Several other courts have established that it is not the role of the court to "second guess" employers in their personnel decisions—that is, did they really discharge the poorest performer or hire the very best person? *A critical question in ADEA litigation is whether age was a "determinative factor" in a personnel decision.* It is the plaintiff's responsibility to establish this as fact, which makes it difficult for plaintiffs to win such cases.

In his 2005 majority opinion *in Smith v. Jackson*, Justice John Paul Stevens wrote that employers must show an age-neutral "business necessity" for their actions. The Court thus shifted the burden to employers once evidence is presented, usually statistical, showing "prima facie" discrimination. But as *Fortune* magazine put it so delicately, "there usually is a 'business necessity' for dumping workers over 50." That "business necessity" is cost reduction. Older workers tend to make more money than what it would cost the employer to get the same work done today.

Is it a violation of the ADEA to eliminate health care benefits for workers who are under the age of 50? The Supreme Court recently ruled in *General Dynamics Land Systems v. Cline* that the ADEA does not prohibit an employer from practicing "reverse age discrimination" where older workers are favored over younger workers who are over 39.

Can Employers Claim Age as a Bona Fide Occupational Qualification (BFOQ)?

Greyhound Bus Lines survived a court challenge to their rule that they would accept no applicants over 40 years of age to drive their buses. The company successfully contended that age was a bona fide occupational qualification

(BFOQ) since it was related to the safe conduct of the busline.[25] Other cases have supported the use of age as a BFOQ. *In general, if public safety is relevant and the employee must be in good physical condition, the courts have supported the use of age requirements, both in terms of entry-level positions and, more commonly, mandatory retirement for certain jobs.* Congress specifically exempted public safety personnel, allowing mandatory retirement for police officers and firefighters (usually 55 years of age). The courts have generally recognized age ceilings as legal BFOQs, but only when the employer can demonstrate that (1) physical fitness, and especially good aerobic fitness, is important to the job and (2) the employer applies the same physical fitness standards to employees under 40 as well as to older employees. The EEOC provides the following rules for the imposition of BFOQs: (1) the age limit is reasonably necessary for the business, (2) all or almost all individuals over the age are unable to perform adequately, or (3) some people over the age have a disqualifying characteristic (e.g., health) that cannot be determined independent of age.

One managerial implication is to determine if it is in the employer's best interests to impose an age ceiling or mandatory retirement. In the early 1990s, a 54-year-old pilot successfully crash landed a 737, saving hundreds of lives. He celebrated his retirement only a few weeks later.

Pilots have challenged a Federal Aviation Administration rule requiring them to retire at age 60. The appeal was backed by Southwest Airlines, which argued that the airline was denied some of its best pilots "at the peak of their careers." They cited FAA data showing older pilots are "as safe as and in some cases safer than their younger colleagues." In 2005, the Supreme Court declined to hear the appeal by the pilots and the mandatory retirement age still stands.

THE AMERICANS WITH DISABILITIES ACT OF 1990 (ADA)

In 1990, Congress passed the Americans with Disabilities Act, which extends the rights and privileges disabled employees of federal contractors have under the Rehabilitation Act of 1973 to virtually all employees. Figure 3-8 presents a summary of the ADA, some excerpts from the law, and a list of the EEOC ADA Enforcement Guidelines and Policy Documents. You can retrieve these documents at eeoc.gov. Keep in mind, however, that EEOC Guidelines are only guidelines and are subject to judicial interpretation. For example, in 2002, the EEOC had to amend its guidelines on "reasonable accommodation" based on a Supreme Court ruling. The EEOC also issues new regulations, so be sure to monitor the EEOC Web site for changes. The EEOC received over 15,000 charges of disability discrimination in fiscal year 2004. They resolved almost 17,000 charges and recovered almost $48 million in monetary benefits for charging parties (not including benefits derived through litigation).

The ADA provides that qualified individuals with disabilities may not be discriminated against by a private-sector organization or a department or agency of a state or local government employing 15 or more employees, *if the individual can perform the essential functions of the job with or without reasonable accommodation.* Reasonable accommodations are determined on a case-by-case basis and may include reassignment, part-time work, and flexible schedules. They also may include providing readers, interpreters, assistants, or attendants. No accommodation is required if an individual is not otherwise qualified for the position. The EEOC *Policy Guidance on Reasonable Accommodation Under ADA* suggests the following process for assessing reasonable accommodation:

1. Look at the particular job involved; determine its purpose and its essential functions.
2. Consult with the individual with the disability to identify potential accommodations.
3. If several accommodations are available, preference should be given to the individual's preferences.

Public facilities such as restaurants, doctor's offices, pharmacies, grocery stores, shopping centers, and hotels must be made accessible to the disabled unless undue hardship would occur for the business. It is not clear, however, how exactly organizations will show "undue hardship," although the law suggests that a reviewing court compare the cost of the accommodation with the employer's operating budget.

The three areas of disability that are the most common for the claims are various mental difficulties (e.g., depression), headaches, and backaches. The most common personnel action has been termination. While some claims of mental duress and headaches are undoubtedly legitimate, there is no question that some people have taken advantage of the ambiguity in the law to make costly and unwarranted claims.

What Is Legal and Illegal under ADA?

The EEOC approved enforcement guidelines on pre-employment disability-related inquiries and medical exams under ADA. The guidelines state that "the guiding principle is that while employers may ask applicants about the ability to perform job functions, employers may not ask about disability." For example, a lawful question would be: "Can you perform the functions of this job with or without reasonable accommodation?" But it is unlawful for an employer to ask questions related to a disability, such as "Have you ever filed for worker's compensation?" or "What prescription drugs

FIGURE 3-8	A Summary of the ADA; Excerpts from ADA; Guidelines Available at eeoc.gov

DISABILITY DISCRIMINATION

Title I of the Americans with Disabilities Act of 1990 prohibits private employers, state and local governments, employment agencies and labor unions from discriminating against qualified individuals with disabilities in job application procedures, hiring, firing, advancement, compensation, job training, and other terms, conditions, and privileges of employment. The ADA covers employers with 15 or more employees, including state and local governments. It also applies to employment agencies and to labor organizations. The ADA's nondiscrimination standards also apply to federal sector employees under section 501 of the Rehabilitation Act, as amended, and its implementing rules.

An individual with a disability is a person who:

- Has a physical or mental impairment that substantially limits one or more major life activities.
- Has a record of such an impairment.
- Is regarded as having such an impairment.

A qualified employee or applicant with a disability is an individual who, with or without reasonable accommodation, can perform the essential functions of the job in question. Reasonable accommodation may include, but is not limited to:

- Making existing facilities used by employees readily accessible to and usable by persons with disabilities.
- Job restructuring, modifying work schedules, reassignment to a vacant position.
- Acquiring or modifying equipment or devices, adjusting or modifying examinations, training materials, or policies, and providing qualified readers or interpreters.

An employer is required to make a reasonable accommodation to the known disability of a qualified applicant or employee if it would not impose an "undue hardship" on the operation of the employer's business. Undue hardship is defined as an action requiring significant difficulty or expense when considered in light of factors such as an employer's size, financial resources, and the nature and structure of its operation.

An employer is not required to lower quality or production standards to make an accommodation; nor is an employer obligated to provide personal use items such as glasses or hearing aids.

Title I of the ADA also covers:

- *Medical examinations and inquiries*—Employers may not ask job applicants about the existence, nature, or severity of a disability. Applicants may be asked about their ability to perform specific job functions. A job offer may be conditioned on the results of a medical examination, but only if the examination is required for all entering employees in similar jobs. Medical examinations of employees must be job related and consistent with the employer's business needs.
- *Drug and alcohol abuse*—Employees and applicants currently engaging in the illegal use of drugs are not covered by the ADA when an employer acts on the basis of such use. Tests for illegal drugs are not subject to the ADA's restrictions on medical examinations. Employers may hold illegal drug users and alcoholics to the same performance standards as other employees.

It is also unlawful to retaliate against an individual for opposing employment practices that discriminate based on disability or for filling a discrimination charge, testifying, or participating in any way in an investigation, proceeding, or litigation under the ADA.

Need More Information?

The law:

- Titles I and V of the ADA

The regulations:

- 29 C.F.R Part 1630
- 29 C.F.R Part 1640
- 29 C.F.R Part 1641

EEOC Enforcement Guidances and Policy Documents:

- Selected list

See also:

- The Family and Medical Leave Act, the ADA, and Title VII of the Civil Rights Act of 1964
- The ADA: A Primer for Small Business
- Your Responsibilities as an Employer
- Your Employment Rights as an Individual with a Disability
- Job Applicants and the ADA
- Small Employers and Reasonable Accommodation
- Work at Home/Telework as a Reasonable Accommodation
- Obtaining and Using Employee Medical Information as Part of Emergency Evacuation Procedures

(*Continued*)

FIGURE 3-8   *(Continued)*

- How to Comply with the Americans with Disabilities Act: A Guide for Restaurants and Other Food Service Employers
- Questions and Answers about:
  - Diabetes in the Workplace and the ADA
  - Epilepsy in the Workplace and the ADA
  - Persons with Intellectual Disabilities in the Workplace and the ADA

EXCERPTS FROM ADA

(a) General Rule. No covered entity shall discriminate against a qualified individual with a disability because of the disability of such individual.

(b) Construction. As used in subsection (a), the term "discrimination" includes:

  (1) limiting, segregating, or classifying a job applicant or employee in a way that adversely affects the opportunities or status of such applicant or employee because of . . . disability . . .

  (2) participating in a contractual or other arrangement or relationship that has the effect of subjecting a qualified applicant or employee with a disability to the discrimination prohibited by this title . . .

  (5) not making reasonable accommodations to the known physical or mental limitations of a qualified individual who is an applicant or employee, unless such covered entity can demonstrate that the accommodation would impose an undue hardship on the operation of the business of such covered entity, and;

  (7) using employment tests or other selection criteria that screen out or tend to screen out an individual with a disability or a class of individuals with disabilities unless the test or other selection criteria, as used by the covered entity, is shown to be job-related for the position in question and is consistent with business necessity.

(c) Medical Examinations and Inquiries.

  (1) In general. The prohibition against discrimination as referred to in subsection (a) shall include medical examinations and inquiries.

Definitions

(2) Disability. The term "disability" means, with respect to an individual:

  (A) a physical or mental impairment that substantially limits one or more of the major life activities of such individual;

  (B) a record of such an impairment, or;

  (C) being regarded as having such an impairment.

Definitions

(7) Qualified Individual with a Disability. The term "qualified individual with a disability" means an individual with a disability who, with or without reasonable accommodation, can perform the essential functions of the employment position that such individual holds or desires.

(8) Reasonable Accommodation. The term "reasonable accommodation" may include:

  (A) making existing facilities used by employees readily accessible to and usable by individuals with disabilities, and;

  (B) job restructuring, part-time or modified work schedules, reassignment to a vacant position, acquisition or modification of equipment or devices, appropriate adjustment or modifications of examinations, training materials or policies, the provision of qualified readers or interpreters, and other similar accommodations for individuals with disabilities.

(9) (A) In general. The term "undue hardship" means an action requiring significant difficulty or expense.

  (B) Determination. In determining whether an accommodation would impose an undue hardship on a covered entity, factors to be considered include:

    (i) the overall size of the business:

    (ii) the type of operation, and;

    (iii) the nature and cost of the accommodation.

Defenses

(b) Qualification Standards. The term "qualification standards" may include a requirement that an individual with a currently contagious disease or infection shall not pose a direct threat to the health or safety of other individuals in the workplace.

Illegal Drugs and Alcohol

(a) Qualified Individual with a Disability. For purposes of this title, the term "qualified individual with a disability" shall not include any employee or applicant who is a current user of illegal drugs . . .

(b) Authority of Covered Entity. A covered entity:

  (1) may prohibit the use of alcohol or illegal drugs at the workplace by all employees;

  (2) may require that employees shall not be under the influence of alcohol or illegal drugs at the workplace;

  (3) may require that employees behave in conformance with the requirements established under "The Drug-Free Workplace Act" (41 U.S.C. 701 et seq.) [See Chapter 14.];

  (4) may hold an employee who is a drug user or alcoholic to the same qualification standards for employment or job performance and behavior that such entity holds other employees . . .

(c) Drug Testing.

  (1) In general. For purposes of this title, a test to determine the use of illegal drugs shall not be considered a medical examination.

do you take?" or "Have you ever been treated for mental illness?"

After an employer has made an offer and an applicant requests accommodation, the employer may "require documentation of the individual's need for, and entitlement to, reasonable accommodations."

There has been a great deal of litigation under ADA since the law took effect for most employers and the Supreme Court has been very much involved in attempting to clarify the law and its implications. Perhaps the most important issue is what constitutes a disability under ADA.

Bonnie Cook was a 300-pound Rhode Island woman who was rejected for an attendant's job at a school for the mentally retarded. She sued claiming her obesity was a disability under ADA. The EEOC has taken the position that only severely obese people are covered by ADA (weight in excess of 100 percent of the norm for a particular height) or if their weight can be linked to a medical disorder. The courts have deferred to the EEOC's position on this matter.

The Supreme Court has clarified the definition of a covered disability under ADA. People whose impairments can be alleviated by medication or glasses are not disabled under ADA.[26] According to a unanimous 2002 Supreme Court in *Toyota v. Williams,* a disability under ADA means the worker must be unable to perform "activities that are of central importance to most people's daily lives, such as walking, seeing and hearing."[27]

PREGNANCY DISCRIMINATION ACT OF 1978

In 2005, the EEOC received over 4,500 complaints about pregnancy discrimination. The Pregnancy Discrimination Act (PDA) prohibits employment practices that discriminate on the basis of pregnancy, childbirth, or related medical conditions (e.g., abortion). This means that a woman is protected from being fired or refused a job or promotion simply because she is pregnant or has had an abortion. She also cannot be forced to take a leave of absence as long as she is able to work. What about refusing to hire a woman because she may become pregnant soon? Can't do that either. An employer may not use potential pregnancy as a basis for a decision. Pregnant women must be treated in the same manner as other applicants (or employees) with similar abilities. Like the ADA, the PDA stipulates that an employer cannot refuse to hire a pregnant woman if she can perform the essential functions of the job. What about a pregnant woman who freely admits that she plans to take a leave three months after her starting date? Surely this is a "job-related" reason to not hire her. While this may be costly to the employer, in fact the employer cannot consider either her pregnancy or her impending leave in a hiring decision.

Under the law, women are not guaranteed the same job or, indeed, any job when they return from their pregnancy leave. However, most U.S. companies have adopted either a "same job," "comparable job," or "some job" policy for women who wish to return to work. The employer must adopt such a policy with consideration to the disparate treatment theory of Title VII, and pregnancy should be treated like any other disability. In other words, if other employees on disability leave are entitled to return to their jobs when they are able to work again, then so should women who have been unable to work due to pregnancy.

The Act also requires that employers must provide benefit coverage for pregnancy as fully as for other medical conditions. In other words, a woman unable to work for pregnancy-related reasons is entitled to disability benefits or sick leave on the same basis as other employees unable to work for medical reasons.

The PDA does not prohibit states from requiring additional benefits for pregnant employees. The Supreme Court, for example, upheld a California law that required employers to provide up to four months' unpaid pregnancy disability leave with guaranteed reinstatement, even though disabled males were not entitled to the same benefit. In Chapter 10, we will discuss the **Work and Family Leave Act,** which was passed into federal law in 1994. This law provides additional protection related to pregnancy. Figure 3-9 presents a summary of the PDA.

ARE EXPATRIATES COVERED BY FEDERAL EEO LAWS WHEN THEY ARE ASSIGNED TO COUNTRIES OTHER THAN THE UNITED STATES?

Figure 3-10 presents guidelines to help multinational employers determine their obligations under EEO laws. In general, the Civil Rights Act, the ADEA, and the ADA all have **extraterritoriality.** This means that an American working for an American corporation on foreign soil is covered by these laws. With some exceptions, the laws also apply to resident aliens working for foreign companies on U.S. soil.

Many U.S. companies have branches, subsidiaries, or joint venture partners in Western Europe (and, increasingly, in Eastern Europe as well). U.S. multinationals have considerable experience with the various regulatory systems of Western European countries, some of which require national-level collective bargaining and others of which have relatively little labor regulation. The situation was simplified in 2003 when the European Union adopted standards regarding most labor issues.

What Are Employee Rights When Working for Multinational Employers?

What EEO laws apply to an American working for a foreign company operating in the United States or in another

FIGURE 3-9   Pregnancy Discrimination

The Pregnancy Discrimination Act is an amendment to Title VII of the Civil Rights Act of 1964. Discrimination on the basis of pregnancy, childbirth, or related medical conditions constitutes unlawful sex discrimination under Title VII, which covers employers with 15 or more employees, including state and local governments. Title VII also applies to employment agencies and to labor organizations, as well as to the federal government. Women who are pregnant or affected by related conditions must be treated in the same manner as other applicants or employees with similar abilities or limitations.

   Title VII's pregnancy-related protections include:

- *Hiring*—An employer cannot refuse to hire a pregnant woman because of her pregnancy, because of a pregnancy-related condition or because of the prejudices of co-workers, clients, or customers.
- *Pregnancy and maternity leave*—An employer may not single out pregnancy-related conditions for special procedures to determine an employee's ability to work. However, if an employer requires its employees to submit a doctor's statement concerning their inability to work before granting leave or paying sick benefits, the employer may require employees affected by pregnancy-related conditions to submit such statements.

   If an employee is temporarily unable to perform her job due to pregnancy, the employer must treat her the same as any other temporarily disabled employee. For example, if the employer allows temporarily disabled employees to modify tasks, perform alternative assignments or take disability leave or leave without pay, the employer also must allow an employee who is temporarily disabled due to pregnancy to do the same.

   Pregnant employees must be permitted to work as long as they are able to perform their jobs. If an employee has been absent from work as a result of a pregnancy-related condition and recovers, her employer may not require her to remain on leave until the baby's birth. An employer also may not have a rule that prohibits an employee from returning to work for a predetermined length of time after childbirth.

   Employers must hold open a job for a pregnancy-related absence the same length of time jobs are held open for employees on sick or disability leave.

- *Health insurance*—Any health insurance provided by an employer must cover expenses for pregnancy-related conditions on the same basis as costs for other medical conditions. Health insurance for expenses arising from abortion is not required, except where the life of the mother is endangered.

   Pregnancy-related expenses should be reimbursed exactly as those incurred for other medical conditions, whether payment is on a fixed basis or a percentage of reasonable-and-customary-charge basis.

   The amounts payable by the insurance provider can be limited only to the same extent as amounts payable for other conditions. No additional, increased, or larger deductible can be imposed.

   Employers must provide the same level of health benefits for spouses of male employees as they do for spouses of female employees.

- *Fringe Benefits*—Pregnancy-related benefits cannot be limited to married employees. In an all-female workforce or job classification, benefits must be provided for pregnancy-related conditions if benefits are provided for other medical conditions.

   If an employer provides any benefits to workers on leave, the employer must provide the same benefits for those on leave for pregnancy-related conditions.

   Employees with pregnancy-related disabilities must be treated the same as other temporarily disabled employees for accrual and crediting of seniority, vacation calculation, pay increases, and temporary disability benefits.

It is also unlawful to retaliate against an individual for opposing employment practices that discriminate based on pregnancy or for filing a discrimination charge, testifying, or participating in any way in an investigation, proceeding, or litigation under Title VII.

Need More Information?

The law:

- Title VII of the Civil Rights Act

The regulations:

- 29 C.F.R Part 1604

The EEOC has also issued guidance on:

- The Family and Medical Leave Act, the Americans with Disabilities Act, and Title VII of the Civil Rights Act of 1964

---

country? Figure 3-11 presents a summary of these rights. In general, all three laws apply to the American company and protect the American worker. However, an American working for a foreign company on foreign soil is not protected.

HRM specialists working in these various contexts must be well aware of the various laws and their applications. A great resource is the global forum of the Society of Human Resource Management (www.SHRMglobal.org).

FIGURE 3-10	The Equal Employment Opportunity Responsibilities of Multinational Employers

The globalization of business activity has resulted in employers from around the world assigning increasing numbers of personnel internationally. The following general guidance is intended to help multinational employers determine their obligations under U.S. equal employment opportunity laws (EEO laws).

OPERATIONS IN THE UNITED STATES OR U.S. TERRITORIES

Multinational employers that operate in the United States or its territories—American Samoa, Guam, the Commonwealth of the Northern Mariana Islands, Puerto Rico, and the U.S. Virgin Islands—are subject to EEO laws to the same extent as U.S. employers, unless the employer is covered by a treaty or other binding international agreement that limits the full applicability of U.S. antidiscrimination laws, such as one that permits the company to prefer its own nationals for certain positions.

OPERATIONS OUTSIDE THE UNITED STATES AND U.S. TERRITORIES

Companies Based in the U.S.

Employers that are incorporated or based in the U.S. or are controlled by U.S. companies and that employ U.S. citizens outside the United States or its territories are subject to Title VII, the ADEA, and the ADA with respect to those employees. U.S. EEO laws do not apply to non-U.S. citizens outside the U.S. or its territories.

How to Determine Who Is a U.S. Employer

An employer will be considered to be a U.S. employer if it is incorporated or based in the United States or if it has sufficient connections with the United States. This is an individualized factual determination that will be based on the following relevant factors:

- The employer's principal place of business, i.e., the primary place where factories, offices, and other facilities are located.
- The nationality of dominant shareholders and/or those holding voting control.
- The nationality and location of management (the officers and directors of the company).

How to Determine Whether a Company Is "Controlled" by a U.S. Employer

Employers operating outside the United States are covered by Title VII, the ADEA, and the ADA only if they are controlled by a U.S. employer. Whether a company is controlled by a U.S. employer is also an individualized determination, which will be based on the following relevant factors:

- Whether the operations of the employers are interrelated.
- Whether there is common management.
- Whether there is centralized control of labor relations.
- Whether there is common ownership or financial control.

Foreign Laws Defense

U.S. employers are not required to comply with the requirements of Title VII, the ADEA, or the ADA, if adherence to that requirement would violate a law of the country where the workplace is located. For example, an employer would have a "Foreign Laws Defense" for a mandatory retirement policy if the law of the country in which the company is located requires mandatory retirement.

A U.S. employer may not transfer an employee to another country in order to disadvantage the employee because of his/her race, color, sex, religion, national origin, age, or disability. For example, an employer may not transfer an older worker to a country with a mandatory retirement age for the purpose of forcing the employee's retirement.

WHAT U.S. EEO LAWS COVER

The federal EEO laws enforced by the EEOC are Title VII of the Civil Rights Act of 1964 (Title VII), the Age Discrimination in Employment Act (ADEA), the Americans with Disabilities Act (ADA), and the Equal Pay Act (EPA). These laws prohibit covered employers from discriminating on the bases of race, color, sex, national origin, religion, age, and disability. Examples of conduct prohibited include:

- *Discriminatory employment decisions*—Title VII, the ADEA, and the ADA prohibit discrimination in all aspects of the employment relationship including recruitment, hiring, assignment, transfer, firing, layoffs, and other conditions or privileges of employment.
- *Discrimination in compensation and benefits*—Title VII, the ADEA, and the ADA prohibit discrimination in compensation based on race, color, sex, national origin, religion, age, and disability. In addition, the EPA prohibits pay discrimination between men and women who are performing substantially equal work. Although the EPA does not apply outside the United States, such claims are covered by Title VII, which also prohibits discrimination in compensation on the basis of sex.
- *Harassment*—Title VII, the ADEA, and the ADA also prohibit offensive conduct that creates a hostile work environment based on race, color, sex, national origin, religion, age, and disability. Employers are required to take appropriate steps to prevent and correct unlawful harassment and employees are responsible for reporting harassment at an early stage to prevent its escalation.

(Continued)

FIGURE 3-10   *(Continued)*

• *Retaliation*—Title VII, the ADEA, the ADA, and the EPA prohibit employers from retaliating against employees because they have opposed unlawful discrimination or participated in a discrimination related proceeding.

Need More Information?

For more detailed information, including a comprehensive discussion of these and other issues, please see:

• EEOC's Web site at www.eeoc.gov for detailed information on EEO laws. Go to "Laws, Regulations and Policy Guidance" for Compliance Manual Sections and Enforcement Guidance.
• EEOC Enforcement Guidance, "Application of Title VII and the Americans with Disabilities Act to Conduct Overseas and to Foreign Employers Discriminating in the United States" (1993).
• EEOC Policy Guidance, "Application of the Age Discrimination in Employment Act of 1967 and the Equal Pay Act of 1963 to American Firms Overseas, Their Overseas Subsidiaries, and Foreign Firms" (1989).
• EEOC Policy Guidance: "Analysis of the sec. 4(f)(1) 'foreign laws' defense of the Age Discrimination in Employment Act of 1967."

To be automatically connected to an EEOC field office, call 1-800-669-4000 or TTY 1-800-669-6820. For more information on EEO law in other countries, see:

• Directorate General for Employment and Social Affairs for the European Union, http://www.europa.eu.int/comm/employment_social/fundamental_rights/index_en.htm
• Canadian Human Rights Commission http://www.chrc-ccdp.ca
• UK Equal Opportunities Commission http://www.eoc.org.uk
• UK Disability Rights Commission, http://www.drc-gb.org
• UK Commission on Racial Equality, http://www.cre.gov.uk
• Hong Kong Equal Opportunity Commission http://www.eoc.org.hk

FUTURE TRENDS IN EEO

The issue of affirmative action will be at the forefront of litigation and legislation. With the plaintiffs' recent successes in much publicized cases and the huge jury verdicts and settlements, an increasing number of class-action lawsuits are likely. The number of ADEA cases also are expected to increase because of the Supreme Court ruling in *Smith v. Jackson* allowing "disparate impact" theory, and the increasing proportion of workers who are over 39 and therefore eligible to sue.

An interesting case to watch in this regard is the case the EEOC joined in 2005 on behalf of lawyers demoted by the law firm of Sibley, Austin, Brown and Wood, all of whom were over the age of 50. At the same time, the chairman of the firm's executive committee was quoted in newspapers saying that the new organizational structure should create greater opportunities for the firm's younger lawyers in the future. The EEOC's John Hendrickson called this the most "in your face admission of age discrimination" he's seen in years. The law firm argued that it was exempt for the ADEA because all demoted attorneys were equity partners (or owners) and that the ADEA doesn't protect owners. The Court disagreed with this argument and declared that these individuals should be considered employees not partners since only a very few people in the firm actually participated in important decisions made at the firm and that the 30 demoted individuals had no say in their demotions. This case is very

interesting, particularly in the context of arguments made in the 2005 *Smith v. Jackson* Supreme Court decision regarding "disparate impact." But what if the law firm presents data showing the older lawyers generate considerably less income than the younger lawyers? Their salary could be much higher while their billable hours are many fewer. So Sibley et al. gets more productivity from its younger employees. Isn't this a reasonable (and legal) alternative explanation for their actions?

Employment practices liability insurance should become more common in the years ahead although premiums already have increased substantially because of the increased risk of large jury verdicts. A growing area of business-related insurance, some policies make stipulations about how HRM should be practiced as a condition of coverage. Providing training in EEO laws is often one such condition. Requiring alternative dispute resolution as a condition of employment is another recommended HRM policy that has gained in popularity.

Alternative Dispute Resolution: An Employer Reaction to Increased Litigation

One of the strongest trends with regard to management reaction to increased litigation is in the area of **alternative dispute resolution.** As discussed earlier, many large employers have entered mediation agreements with the EEOC in an effort to expedite the resolution of

FIGURE 3-11	Employee Rights When Working for Multinational Employers

As the workplace grows more global and mobile, increased numbers of employers have international operations, resulting in more international assignments of their employees. The following provides general guidance concerning employees' rights under the United States' equal employment opportunity laws (U.S. EEO laws) when working for multinational employers.

WORK IN THE UNITED STATES AND U.S. TERRITORIES

All employees who work in the U.S. or its territories—American Samoa, Guam, the Commonwealth of the Northern Mariana Islands, Puerto Rico, and the U.S. Virgin Islands—for covered employers are protected by EEO laws, regardless of their citizenship or work authorization status. Employees who work in the U.S. or its territories are protected whether they work for a U.S. or foreign employer.

Example:

Kim is a Chinese citizen working in the Commonwealth of the Northern Mariana Islands for a Chinese manufacturer of women's attire. Kim's manager threatens Kim with losing her job if she does not comply with his sexual demands. Kim is protected by U.S. EEO laws because she works in a U.S. territory. The employer can be held liable for sexual harassment.

WORKING FOR NON-U.S. EMPLOYERS IN THE U.S.

The only exception to the rule that employees working in the U.S. are covered by federal EEO laws occurs when the employer is not a U.S. employer and is subject to a treaty or other binding international agreement that permits the company to prefer its own nationals for certain positions.

Example:

ABC Communications is an Egyptian company doing business in the U.S. Under a "friendship, commerce and navigation treaty" ("FCN") between the U.S. and Egypt, Egyptian companies operating in the U.S. are authorized to hire Egyptian citizens for executive positions. Thomas, a U.S. citizen, alleges that he was subjected to national origin discrimination when he was denied a position as Vice President of Legislative Affairs in favor of Menkure, who is an Egyptian citizen. ABC Communications admits that it favored Menkure because he is an Egyptian citizen and can successfully assert the FCN treaty as a defense.

However, if Menkure were not an Egyptian citizen but a citizen of the U.S. or a third country, ABC would not have the treaty as a defense because the treaty authorizes a preference only for Egyptian citizens.

WORK OUTSIDE THE UNITED STATES

Individuals who are not U.S. citizens are not protected by U.S. EEO laws when employed outside the U.S. or its territories. Consult your embassy to determine whether EEO laws for other countries exist and whether they apply to your situation.

U.S. citizens who are employed outside the U.S. by a U.S. employer—or a foreign company controlled by an U.S. employer—are protected by Title VII, the ADEA, and the ADA.

Example:

Isaac is an African-American U.S. citizen working in Africa for a U.S. employer as a customer service manager. Isaac alleges race discrimination after he was transferred to a less desirable and less public position. The new position involved a loss of pay and lack of upward career mobility opportunities. The employer admitted that it transferred Isaac because its predominantly white customers did not want to deal directly with nonwhites. Customer preference is never a defense to violations of U.S. EEO law. The transfer violates Title VII.

Whether a Company Is a U.S. Employer or Controlled by a U.S. Employer

An employer will be considered a U.S. employer if it is incorporated or based in the United States or if it has sufficient connections with the United States. Several factors help determine whether a company has sufficient connections with the U.S., including the company's principal place of business and the nationality of its dominant shareholders and management. Whether a foreign company is controlled by a U.S. employer will depend on the interrelation of operations, common management, centralized control of labor relations, and common ownership or financial control of the two entities. For more information, see http://www.eeoc.gov/docs/threshold.html#2-III-B-3-c

Foreign Laws Defense

U.S. employers are not required to comply with the requirements of Title VII, the ADEA, or the ADA if adherence to that requirement would violate a law of the country where the workplace is located.

(Continued)

FIGURE 3-11 (*Continued*)

Example:

Sarah is a U.S. citizen. She works as an assistant manager for a U.S. employer located in a Middle Eastern Country. Sarah applies for the branch manager position. Although Sarah is the most qualified person for the position, the employer informs her that it cannot promote her because that country's laws forbid women from supervising men. Sarah files a charge alleging sex discrimination. The employer would have a "Foreign Laws" defense for its actions if the law does contain that prohibition.

An American employer cannot transfer an employee to another country in order to disadvantage the employee because of race, color, sex, religion, national origin, age, or disability. For example, an employer may not transfer an older worker to a country with a mandatory retirement age for the purpose of forcing the employee's retirement.

WHAT U.S. EEO LAWS COVER

The federal EEO laws enforced by the EEOC are Title VII of the Civil Rights Act of 1964 (Title VII), the Age Discrimination in Employment Act (ADEA), the Americans with Disabilities Act (ADA), and the Equal Pay Act (EPA). These laws prohibit covered employers from discriminating on the bases of race, color, sex, national origin, religion, age, and disability. Examples of conduct prohibited include:

- *Discriminatory employment decisions*—Title VII, the ADEA, and the ADA prohibit discrimination in all aspects of the employment relationship, including recruitment, hiring, assignment, transfer, firing, layoffs, and other conditions or privileges of employment.
- *Discrimination in compensation and benefits*—Title VII, the ADEA, and the ADA prohibit discrimination in compensation based on race, color, sex, national origin, religion, age, and disability. In addition, the EPA prohibits pay discrimination between men and women who are performing substantially equal work. Although the EPA does not apply outside the United States, such claims are covered by Title VII, which also prohibits discrimination in compensation on the basis of sex.
- *Harassment*—Title VII, the ADEA, and the ADA also prohibit offensive conduct that creates a hostile work environment based on race, color, sex, national origin, religion, age, and disability. Employers are required to take appropriate steps to prevent and correct unlawful harassment and employees are responsible for reporting harassment at an early stage to prevent its escalation.
- *Retaliation*—Title VII, the ADEA, the ADA, and the EPA prohibit employers from retaliating against employees because they have opposed unlawful discrimination or participated in a discrimination related proceeding.

FILING A CHARGE

If you believe that you have been discriminated against, you may file a charge with the EEOC. An individual alleging an EEO violation outside the U.S. should file a charge with the district office closest to his or her employer's headquarters. However, if you are unsure where to file, you may file a charge with any EEOC office. For information on filing a charge of discrimination see *How to File a Charge of Employment Discrimination*. Charges may be filed in person, or by phone, mail, or facsimile.

Example:

Isaiah is a U.S. citizen working in Canada for a U.S. employer that is headquartered in New York and has an office in Detroit, Michigan. Isaiah alleges a failure to accommodate his religious beliefs. Although the charge will be processed by the New York District Office because it is closest to his employer's headquarters, Isaiah may file the charge in any convenient EEOC office.

---

employment disputes. A growing number of companies have adopted **mandatory arbitration** to settle all claims related to employment. They cite the provisions of the Civil Rights Act of 1991 that allows alternative dispute resolution as an alternative to litigation. Although mandatory arbitration is controversial, and is opposed by the EEOC, many companies have nevertheless adopted mandatory arbitration as policy. It is estimated that, as of 2005, 10 percent of the U.S. workforce nows works under such policy.

Mandatory arbitration requires employees and job applicants to sign a contract in which they agree to binding arbitration in order to resolve virtually any dispute related to their employment. So, let's say you feel you were a victim of gender discrimination. With the mandatory arbitration policy, the complaint must be submitted to an arbitration association such as the American Arbitration Association for a hearing and binding decision. If you refused to sign an arbitration agreement, a company could decide to not hire you and, in most states, could fire you if you refused to sign a newly imposed policy.

The courts have in general supported arbitration as an alternative to litigation in settling employment disputes. Given the likely increases in most forms of EEO litigation, arbitration may prove to be advantageous to all concerned.

Another trend may be an increase in the EEO complaints filed by Muslims, Arabs, Sikhs, and others whose religion may require certain types of dress. Although formal complaints to the EEOC were still quite low as of 2006, the EEOC has issued guidelines about the workplace rights of Muslims, Arabs, South Asians, and Sikhs under all EEO laws (see eeoc.gov).

SUMMARY

Despite the confusing array of laws and regulations on EEO, the underlying principle is clear. EEO simply means individuals should be given an equal opportunity in employment decisions. EEO does not mean preferential treatment for one individual over another because of race, color, sex, religion, national origin, age, or disability. For instance, white males have won racial and sex discrimination suits against organizations that have violated Title VII for hiring less-qualified minorities or women. The EEO laws clearly state that treatment at work and opportunity for work should be unrelated to the race, sex, and other personal characteristics of individual workers.

Remember that we have only discussed EEO law in this chapter and that there are numerous other federal, state, and local laws and labor regulations that can be the basis of a lawsuit. In the applicable chapters, we will discuss labor and collective bargaining law, workers' compensation, unemployment compensation, wages, health and safety legislation, whistleblower's protection, retirement, employee benefits, rights of privacy, protection against unjust dismissal, and other potentially legal issues for employers.

One Implication of Increased Litigation: Better HRM Practices

While the trend of increasing litigation and resultant settlements and jury verdicts can create competitive problems for U.S. employers in a global economy, many of the regulations and guidelines for HR practice, particularly EEO laws, actually encourage more effective HRM practices and underscore the need for HRM expertise. One large retailer specified that applicants for a district manager job had to have a minimum of five years' experience as a district manager from some other retailer. This job specification created a disadvantage for women and minorities who may have been denied opportunities throughout the retail industry and thus could not have accumulated the required experience. This is an illustration of the glass-ceiling effect,[28] which refers to invisible barriers for women that serve as obstacles to moving up the corporate ladder. In addition, an internal study showed that years of previous experience was unrelated to performance as a district manager. The company was thus vulnerable to a lawsuit and, based on their own study, would have great difficulty proving the five-year specification was related to job success. The specification also forced the company to compensate the district manager job at a higher rate and made it much more difficult to recruit. This combination of facts seems to lead to a simple conclusion: change the job specification and reduce the number of years of experience required to be considered for the job. Sometimes, many times, EEO laws and regulations and effective HR practices go hand in hand.

The point is that the legality of human resource practices is often related to the effectiveness of human resource practices as well. Remember our discussion of "validated" selection procedures as characteristic of "high performance work systems."

Validated means the procedures actually predict what the employer intends for them to predict. This is all EEO law requires regarding the burden on an organization after adverse impact is established.

Organizations thus would do well to evaluate all of their HR policies and practices in the context of the laws and case law and adjust those practices accordingly after their internal assessment. The result just might be more legally defensible and more effective HR policies. The old adage, an ounce of prevention is worth a pound of cure, really applies to the legal issues related to HR.

While the implications of HR-related litigation may be confusing, there can be no question that managers will be on relatively safer ground if they adhere to the following strategy with regard to employment practices: (1) monitor personnel decisions to ensure there is no evidence of disparate treatment or a disproportionate impact caused by particular personnel practices; (2) if there are disparities, determine whether the practices causing the disparity are essential for the business and/or are job related; and (3) eliminate the practices if they are not job related or replace them with practices that do not cause such a disparity or less of a disparity. Not only will such a strategy protect managers from EEO claims, it also will lead to better and more cost-effective personnel decisions. HRM specialists have the expertise to assist organizations to pursue these strategies.

In general, most would agree that EEO legislation has had positive effects on the occupational status of minorities and females. An additional benefit is that EEO laws and the threat of EEO litigation have forced managers to "clean up their act" with regard to personnel policy and practice. While the paperwork may be voluminous and the compliance requirements may seem ominous, there can be little question that EEO laws and regulations have fostered a fairer system of employment opportunity and a more systematic and valid process for personnel decisions. The efforts of managers in this regard are critical to organizational effectiveness and their mistakes can be extremely costly. Personnel practices may be the most heavily regulated area of organizational life today. HRM specialists in staffing issues cannot learn too much about this vital area.

In the following chapters, we will have much more to say about labor legislation and employment practices. The importance of EEO issues for virtually all HRM activities cannot be overstated. Students should consider the implications of the Civil Rights Act, the ADEA, the PDA, the ADA, and the myriad of other federal, state, and local laws when we discuss topics such as job analysis and design (Chapter 4), planning and recruitment (Chapter 5), personnel selection (Chapter 6), performance appraisal (Chapter 7), training and development (Chapter 8), and compensation (Chapter 10).

We also must emphasize that the content of this chapter is more likely to go out of date faster than any of the others in this book. In the volatile area of EEO, current, state-of-the-art knowledge is a competitive advantage for any organization. Make sure your knowledge in this area is indeed current.

DISCUSSION QUESTIONS

1. In terms of EEO, how can customer requirements or preferences be used in the process of hiring people?

2. Given the great economic incentives for plaintiffs' attorneys today, why is the EEOC even necessary? Why can't a person simply be allowed to sue without the involvement of the EEOC?

3. Describe the procedures required to file a discrimination lawsuit under the disparate impact and disparate treatment theories. How is adverse impact determined? Provide a scenario illustrating evidence of adverse impact in an employment decision.

4. Based on your reading of the major EEO laws, what information should an employer include in a personnel policies and procedures manual given to all employees?

5. Should the ADA be amended to restrict claims? Should the ADA be repealed? Justify your positions.

6. What steps would you take to prevent ADEA cases after a major restructuring or reduction in force?

7. Would you be less likely to join an organization that required you to agree to binding arbitration regarding labor disputes and to waive your right to a jury trial?

8. Should Title VII of the Civil Rights Act be amended to include sexual orientation? Justify your position.

II

Acquiring Human Resource Capability

4

WORK ANALYSIS AND DESIGN

OVERVIEW

Among the HR prescriptions cited in Chapter 1 as predictive of corporate performance was the use of "validated" selection tests to hire people, the use of formal performance appraisal, and the percentage of the workforce working in self-managed work teams. These prescriptions require some form of work or job analysis. An analysis of work is considered a building block for most HR systems in organizations. Corporate restructuring processes, quality improvement programs, human resource planning, job design, recruitment strategies, training programs, succession planning, and compensation systems are among the other HR activities that are based on work analysis. Let us not forget the importance of job analysis in the legal context we discussed in Chapter 3.

Work analysis, a term within which we include traditional job analysis and job design, provides the basic information that leads to specific products used or actions taken by management to create and sustain **organizational capability.** While sometimes a highly formal system involving trained analysts and standardized instruments and other times a more informal process, work analysis should be the first step for actions within most of the functional areas of HR. Consider the following scenarios to illustrate the point:

General Cinema is interested in the development of a screening test for theater manager positions. They want to be certain that the test is legally defensible and "job related" and emphasizes the most important elements of the job. Having also read the previous chapter in this book on

equal employment opportunity (EEO), the consultant recommends two methods of work analysis to gather information. Why two methods?

The State of Virginia passed a law mandating that state employee pay be based on performance. However, there was a need for the development of a new performance appraisal system. The first step in the development of the appraisal system was the use of the critical incident method to identify the critical outcomes and behaviors for each position to be evaluated. Why?

Two laboratory technicians have similar job experience and education, but are employed at different local hospitals. One technician makes $5,000 more per year than the other. The lower-paid employee asks her HR department to review her pay based on the external compensation market. What information will the hospital need in order to establish fair compensation?

The Monsanto Corporation has many jobs that stipulate specific physical requirements (e.g., must be able to lift 75 lbs.). The company is concerned that some of the requirements are unnecessary and may be in violation of the Civil Rights Act or the Americans with Disabilities Act. Will a work analysis help?

A division of Ford Motor Company decided to adopt autonomous work groups (AWGs) to reconfigure a factory floor. Teams rather than individuals would be assigned specific tasks. The teams would divide up the work, which was as clearly defined and standardized as in typical American factories, but all team members would be expected to be able to perform any of the work tasks. What information did the HR department at Ford need in order to help redesign jobs into these AWGs?

The James River Corporation uses a standardized job analysis questionnaire known as the Position Analysis Questionnaire (PAQ) to identify the best written tests to determine admission to their pipe fitter and millwright apprenticeship programs. They attempt to establish the "job relatedness" of the tests using the results from the Position Analysis Questionnaire. How will the Questionnaire help?

Pratt and Whitney, the jet engine division of United Technologies, seeks to improve its competitiveness through the elimination of activities no longer essential to the business and the improvement of existing job functions in the context of customer requirements. Can work analysis help them?

The state of Maryland asked the consulting firm of Booz, Allen, and Hamilton to determine the necessary knowledge, skills, and abilities required to perform certain social work positions for the state. The study led to the reclassification of many positions, stipulating that only a Bachelor's degree should be required to do the work rather than a Master's in Social Work. Could the reclassification save the state money?

The city of Ft. Lauderdale, Florida, updates all of its job descriptions by identifying the "essential functions" of each job according to the Americans with Disabilities Act and incorporating this language into new job descriptions. How does this serve them?

The city of Chicago loses a lawsuit because it cannot justify a particular passing score on a test used to screen firefighter applicants.

Work analysis information is needed for each of these situations to assist organizations in achieving certain objectives. Job descriptions and job specifications are needed to attract and select qualified (but not overqualified) employees and evaluate compensation systems. Job standards and performance criteria are used to evaluate employee and/or unit performance; job factors are needed to group jobs to assess wage and salary systems; and tasks and context factors are examined to redesign and evaluate jobs, restructure organizations, develop succession planning, and stay on the right side of the law. Almost all programs of interest to human resource specialists and other practitioners whose work pertains to organizational personnel depend on work analysis results.[1]

This chapter describes the importance of work analysis for the field of HRM. Our discussion will center on the purposes for work analysis as well as the major approaches for collecting data.

The nature of work is changing and traditional work arrangements exist alongside contingent workers, independent contractors, outsourced activities, and work teams. But while the world of work may be changing, the basics of work analysis can (and should) be the cornerstone of HR activities. Good work analysis increases the probability that the "deliverables" from the

HR suppliers will meet the requirements of their customers both internal and external. This applies whether jobs are becoming more elastic and less static and even if we don't call them jobs anymore but rather projects or roles.

OBJECTIVES

After reading this chapter, you should be able to

1. *Understand what work analysis is and what its major products are.*
2. *Explain the purposes and uses for work analysis data.*
3. *Compare and contrast methods for collecting data.*
4. *Describe commonly used and newer methods for conducting work analysis, including O*NET.*
5. *Explain how work analysis information is applied to job design efforts.*
6. *Understand that different procedures emphasize different kinds of information that may be more or less useful for different HRM functions.*
7. *Conduct and prepare a work analysis report.*

WHAT IS WORK ANALYSIS?

Work analysis is a systematic process of gathering information about work, jobs, and the relationships among jobs.[2] Figure 4-1 presents a chronology of the steps to be undertaken in a comprehensive (and effective) work analysis. Please note that this approach should focus on (and begin with) customer requirements and meeting customer demands. Thus, the focus is on internal and especially external customers to first identify the critical products, services, or

FIGURE 4-1	The Chronological Steps in Effective Work Analysis
Step	**Critical Questions**
1	What are the required outcomes/measures for assessing strategy execution (e.g., customer requirements for products/services derived from the strategic plan)?
2	What are necessary, critical, essential tasks, activities, behaviors required to meet or exceed the requirements established at step 1? What are the relative importance, frequency, and essentiality of these tasks for achieving measures at step 1?
3	What are the necessary knowledges, skills, abilities and other characteristics or competencies required to perform the activities at step 2?
4	How should jobs/work be defined? Where does the work get done to maximize efficiency/effectiveness? Do we use individual jobs, work teams, independent contractors, full-time/part-time? Do we outsource?

performance outcomes that are required of the supplier. This list of carefully defined products and services should then be the frame of reference for the rest of the steps in the analysis of that supplier's job, starting with the major tasks or activities necessary to achieve the required outcomes defined by the customers. The required outcomes as defined by customers are derived from the strategic planning of the organization.

General Cinema, for example, required a cost-effective and job-related test that would help identify persons most likely to be effective theater managers. The product to be delivered by HR was the test and the internal customers were managers who would have to make the hiring decisions. Of course, the main frame of reference of the manager must be the external customer, the ticket buyers.

Once the products are defined and the tasks and activities have been identified, the relative importance, relative frequency, or essentiality with which the various tasks are performed can be assessed. Remember that word *essentiality*. Many methods now require the determination of *essential functions* for jobs because of the language of the Americans with Disabilities Act (see Chapter 3 discussion).

Next, the critical **knowledges, abilities, skills, and other characteristics** (or **KASOCs**) necessary to perform the tasks must be identified. KASOCs are also called "competencies." This step is roughly equivalent to **competency modeling,** which we discuss later. **Knowledge** refers to an organized body of information, usually of a factual or procedural nature applied directly to the performance of a function. For example, computer programmers may need knowledge of specific languages such as Java. Your instructor in this class should obviously have knowledge of research and practice in human resource management.

An **ability** refers to a demonstrated competence to perform an observable behavior or a behavior that results in an observable product. Police officers, for example, are required to possess the physical ability to apprehend and detain a suspect or the cognitive ability to understand and complete arrest forms. Vigilance may be such an ability. For example, while the ability to perform as an airport baggage checker may not require high levels of cognitive ability, the ability to be vigilant in a fairly boring task may be a critical ability, especially post-9/11. NFL quarterbacks should possess high levels of cognitive ability to be able to read (and react quickly) to defense formations.

A **skill** is a competence to perform a learned, psychomotor act, and may include a manual, verbal, or mental manipulation of data, people, or things. So, in the case of an officer, she or he must demonstrate an acceptable level of driving skill or skill in operating and maintaining a weapon.

Finally, **other personal characteristics** include personality characteristics, attitudes, or physical or mental competencies needed to perform the job. Even something as simple as being courteous to civilians plays an important role in determining how well officers perform

their jobs. When officers are unable to empathize with crime victims, are callous in treating witnesses, or are impulsive and destroy evidence at a crime scene, they demonstrate some shortcoming on personal characteristics that affect their job performance. Being able to tolerate the belligerence of customers and control one's temper may be critical in certain circumstances. Being able to work in teams is another example of a critical characteristic for many jobs today. An analysis could conclude, for example, that armed security guards must not have a history indicating psychiatric problems.

As you can tell from these examples, the *products* of competencies or KASOCs are typically easy to observe and serve as the basic units of observation for analysis.[3] For example, the customer of the computer programmer requires a Java program that meets certain specifications. Knowledge of a computer language such as Java can be determined from an interview, responses to a written test, the possession of a certain license, or graduation from a certain class or by observing an individual attempt to program. The knowledge required to teach a class in human resource management can be determined based on the possession of certain credentials (e.g., Ph.D. in human resource management or industrial/organizational psychology) or through an interview or test.

Establishing that someone requires driving skill to perform a job is somewhat more difficult in that an interview or written test does not afford an opportunity to observe the series of behaviors that demonstrate the application of this knowledge domain in the job environment. The latter would seem to require observations of actual motor vehicle operation.

What Are the Major Goals for Work Analysis?

As you've probably gathered by now, much of the success (i.e., validity) of work analysis efforts is a function of the accuracy of the inferences one draws about the job from observations, interviews, and/or questionnaire data gathered through work analysis. One underlying objective of work analysis is to minimize the inferential leaps required to arrive at a conclusion. The context for work analysis should always be critical outcome measures that define strategy. Toward this end, the following are offered as goals one should strive for in the course of work analysis:[4]

1. *One objective of work analysis should be the description of observables.* Often the behavior or competency necessary for performing the job is not observable but the products or outcomes, kinds of materials or work aids used, and the people included in the decision process can be reported. Work analysis should focus on observable behaviors and work outcomes. A *job description* is the usual product of this analysis.

2. *Work analysis should describe work behavior independent of the personal characteristics of*

particular people who perform the job. Quite simply, work analysis describes how a job is performed and focuses on the position, not the person doing the work. **Performance appraisal** is used to describe how well individuals perform their jobs. The actual performance appraisal instrument may have been developed from work analysis and should be linked to the job description.

3. *Work analysis data must be verifiable and reliable.* The organization should maintain records of the data, document all decisions that are data-based, and be able to justify every job analysis judgment. The data must be reliable, indicating that different sources agreed on judgments about the work. Recall the importance of job analysis in EEO litigation and, in particular, in establishing job relatedness. The City of Chicago recently lost a lawsuit because the particular passing score on a hiring test (which caused adverse impact against African Americans) was not justified by job analysis.[5]

Do We Really Need All the Specificity in Formal Job Analysis?

Most American workers have a detailed job description that describes their work. This approach is not without critics. In Japan, for example, new employees are typically hired without a job description or specifications. Japan places much greater reliance on in-house training and job rotation to foster a versatility in the skills of each new employee. Japanese managers think job descriptions can be harmful to their team-building approach to management. Many experts in job design and organizational restructuring embrace this view and believe job descriptions should be written for units or teams with all team members responsible for (or at least qualified to perform) all unit functions or activities. Individual job descriptions are thought to be detrimental to work group effectiveness. However, as discussed in Chapter 3, job descriptions may be needed for legal reasons and can be written in such a way as to facilitate a team-oriented approach to work processes.

Highly detailed job descriptions are very common in Europe where they are frequently required by regulation or union agreement. Every employee at the Volvo plant in Sweden, for example, has a detailed job description based on a quantitative job analysis even though the assembly process at Volvo is team-based rather than the traditional assembly line.

While work analysis is often used to derive specific information about particular jobs, as we stated above, the method can be used for organizations. Work analysis data can be aggregated to the unit or function level so that the end products such as job descriptions or job specifications are defined at the team level rather than for particular positions. Often this approach to defining the job in terms of team member competencies is coupled with skill-based pay systems where individuals are compensated on their potential to perform multiple tasks as opposed to a limited set of tasks specific to a job. So, a team member may be expected to perform the tasks of another who is absent, rotate task assignments with others as needed, and provide additional expert opinion on task processes or products. In this way, the team member is cross-trained to perform a number of different tasks, perhaps even all of those involved in a specific work process. In other words, no one has a monopoly on a set of tasks as the responsibility for performance of these tasks is shared by team members.

So what's the answer to the question about the value of specificity? Unfortunately for those seeking "specificity" in this answer, it really depends on the context! While in many situations organizations can retrieve general job descriptions right off the Internet, there are other situations where great detail in the job description and job specifications may be required. For example, had a job analysis existed with greater specificity in the Chicago lawsuit mentioned above regarding a particular passing score that caused adverse impact, it might have helped the city in its defense.

What Is the Legal Significance of Work Analysis?

There has been strong interest in job analysis since passage of the Civil Rights Act, the ADA, and subsequent court rulings and government guidelines. As we discussed in Chapter 3, the "Uniform Guidelines on Employee Selection Procedures (see eeoc.gov) and the Supreme Court decisions in *Griggs v. Duke Power* and *Albemarle Paper Company v. Moody* emphasized the importance of demonstrating the job relatedness of employer selection systems. One way to do this is by conducting a thorough work analysis to justify personnel job specifications such as passing scores on tests or particular credentials for the job.

There are a great number of court cases that focus on the results of (or the nonexistence of) a job analysis. For example, many women have filed lawsuits contesting the physical ability tests (e.g., push-ups, sit-ups) mandated for entry into police or firefighters' academies. They often claim "adverse impact" since a greater proportion of women than men are disqualified as a result of such tests. The Chicago case focused on a particular passing score on a written test that caused adverse impact.

There also have been a number of lawsuits filed on behalf of older workers who lost their jobs because of a mandatory retirement age. For example, an Indianapolis bus driver used the ADEA to challenge the mandatory retirement age of 55 (he lost). In this case, job analysis data were introduced at trial to support the age limit. The American Association of Retired Persons has been active in challenging mandatory retirement ages using job analysis data.

As discussed in Chapter 3, statistics can be used to establish prima facie evidence of discrimination under the disparate impact theory of Title VII. The burden of proof then rests with the employer to show that the selection device or job specification (e.g., the test, test score, educational requirement) is "job related" or a "business necessity." We have alluded to the recent Chicago lawsuit in which a job analysis might have helped the defendant. The particulars are as follows: In 2005, the City of Chicago lost a class action lawsuit brought by the African American Fire Fighters League. The plaintiffs contested the adverse impact of an entrance exam and, in particular, the use of a particular cutoff score to screen applicants. The court argued that the city did not provide sufficient information about the job-relatedness of the test and the particular cutoff score. Job analysis methods can be used to provide a justification for a particular cutoff score.

Firefighter candidates in Dallas, Texas, were required to scale a fence six feet in height in a prescribed amount of time. Since a higher percentage of women were unable to scale the fence than men, the court asked the city to show how scaling a fence six feet in height was job-related. The city presented data that demonstrated that the average fence in the jurisdiction was six feet in height and that scaling fences was a frequent activity that must be performed by competent firefighters.

Legal challenges to job specifications involving physical attributes (e.g., strength, speed) and mental attributes have increased since the Americans with Disabilities Act took effect in 1990. The ADA specifies that employers must make "reasonable accommodations" that would allow qualified disabled workers to perform the "essential functions" of the job. According to the EEOC, these accommodations may include physical renovations to the job.

What Are the Major Work Analysis Products?

There are numerous products that can be derived from work analysis. The most frequent and commonly used products include "job descriptions" and "job specifications." **Job descriptions** define the job in terms of its content and scope. Although the format can vary, the job description may include information on job duties, tasks, activities, behaviors and/or responsibilities. An identification of critical internal and external customers, equipment to be used on the job, working conditions, relationships with co-workers, and the extent of supervision required is also typical in a job description. Figure 4-2 presents an example of a job description for a compensation manager. In a sense, you can think of a job description as being a report of the job situation. Job descriptions are often summarized in classified employment ads and, more recently, available on the Internet through various job placement services. Go to www.online.onetcenter.org for over 1,000 job descriptions.

Job specifications consist of the KASOCs needed to carry out the job tasks and duties. Specific educational requirements (e.g., Ph.D., MD, MBA, Ed.D., MSW), certifications or licenses (e.g., CPA, CFP), or other qualifications (e.g., years of experience) are often listed in job specifications. Cutoff scores on tests are also job specifi-

cations. Figure 4-2 presents an example of the job specifications for a compensation manager. You will note that a college degree in personnel, human resources, industrial psychology, or a related field is required for the compensation manager job. Job specifications detail the specific KASOCs or competencies required. Work analysis should be the basis of each specification.

Job specifications often are contested in court because they have adverse impact against groups protected by EEO laws. Certainly job specifications that result in adverse impact against groups covered by EEO legislation should be derived from a thorough analysis. Where data are available in company records that shed light on the relationship between a given job specification and some measure of effectiveness, these data should certainly be used. A regional manager of a 500 store clothing retailer decided that all of his 200 assistant managers should have college degrees. Research from the HR Department indicated there was no correlation between having or not having a college degree and performance as a store manager. In addition, HR determined the degree specification caused adverse impact. The manager was persuaded to change his mind.

Unnecessary job specifications can translate into higher labor costs. The state of Maryland, as we mentioned in the chapter opening, was concerned about the number of state positions that required a Master's in Social Work (MSW), a requirement that necessitated a higher starting salary. The consulting firm of Booz, Allen, and Hamilton conducted work analysis of these jobs and determined the extent to which the knowledge acquired by the MSW was essential for these jobs. In addition, since many positions had some MSW-trained occupants and others doing the same work with only a Bachelor's degree, the consultant firm also could study whether the more advanced degree was related to better performance on the job (it wasn't). Booz, Allen recommended that the MSW job specification be dropped for these positions. The state saved millions of dollars by dropping the higher degree requirement and was able to recruit from a much larger pool of potential candidates.

Many business schools now stipulate that a Ph.D. is required for any faculty position although it is conceivable that a candidate with an MBA would be less costly and perhaps as (or more) effective as an instructor of undergraduate students. Job specifications such as reading level, formal education requirements, and the like must be established at a level that reflects the minimum necessary for job entry. Establishing specifications at too high a level often results in adverse impact and can hinder diversity and affirmative action goals. For this reason, such practices are closely scrutinized by the courts. The so-called glass-ceiling effect in certain industries may to some extent be caused by job specifications that block women from many key positions because they lack certain credentials or experience.

FIGURE 4-2 **Job Description and Job Specifications for a Compensation Manager**

Job Title: Compensation Manager   DOT Code: 166.167–022

Reports to:

Job Description

Responsible for the design and administration of employee compensation programs. Ensures proper consideration of the relationship of salary to performance of each employee and provides consultation on salary administration to managers and supervisors.

Principal Duties and Responsibilities:

1. Ensures the preparation and maintenance of job descriptions for each current and projected position. Prepares all job descriptions, authorizing final drafts. Coordinates periodic review of all job descriptions, making revisions as necessary. Educates employees and supervisors on job description use and their intent by participation in formal training programs and by responding to their questions. Maintains accurate file of all current job descriptions. Distributes revised job descriptions to appropriate individuals.
2. Ensures the proper evaluation of job descriptions. Serves as chair of Job Evaluation Committee, coordinating its activities. Resolves disputes over proper evaluation of jobs. Assigns jobs to pay ranges and reevaluates jobs periodically through the Committee process. Conducts initial evaluation of new positions prior to hiring. Ensures integrity of job evaluation process.
3. Ensures that Company compensation rates are in accordance with the Company philosophy. Maintains current information concerning applicable salary movements taking place in comparable organizations. Obtains or conducts salary surveys as necessary. Conducts analysis of salary changes among competitors and presents recommendations on salary movements on an annual basis.
4. Ensures proper consideration of the relationship of salary to the performance of each employee. Inspects all performance appraisals and salary reviews, authorizing all pay adjustments.
5. Develops and administers the performance appraisal program. Develops and updates performance appraisal instruments. Assists in the development of training programs to educate supervisors on using the performance appraisal system. Monitors the use of the performance appraisal instruments to ensure the integrity of the system and proper use.
6. Assists in the development and oversees the administration of all bonus payments up through the Officer level.
7. Researches and provides recommendations on executive compensation issues.
8. Coordinates the development of an integrated HR information system. Assists in identifying needs; interfaces with the Management Information Systems Department to achieve departmental goals for information needs.
9. Performs related duties as assigned or as the situation dictates.

Job Specifications

Required Knowledges, Skills, and Abilities:

1. Knowledge of compensation and HRM practices and principles.
2. Knowledge of job analysis procedures.
3. Knowledge of survey development and interpretation practices.
4. Knowledge of current performance appraisal issues for designing, implementing, and maintaining systems.
5. Skill in conducting job analysis interviews.
6. Skill in writing job descriptions, memorandums, letters, and proposals.
7. Skill in making group presentations, conducting job analysis interviews, and explaining policies and practices to employees and supervisors.
8. Skill in performing statistical computations including regression, correlation, and basic descriptive statistics.
9. Ability to conduct meetings.
10. Ability to plan and prioritize work.

Education and Experience Requirements:

This position requires the equivalent of a college degree in personnel, human resources, industrial psychology, or a related degree, plus 3–5 years' experience in Personnel, 2–3 of which should include compensation administration experience. An advanced degree in Industrial Psychology, Business Administration, or Personnel Management is preferred.

Work Orientation Factors:

This position may require up to 15 percent travel.

For example, requiring an advanced degree and a minimum number of years of previous experience are examples of job specifications that could hinder the ability of women or minorities to even compete for a job—and those specifications may have been set arbitrarily. It is in an organization's best interest to determine whether a particular job specification is really necessary for success on a job. After all, more education or more years of experience almost always translate into higher salaries and more difficulty recruiting. Organizations should

FIGURE 4-3   Products of Job Analysis Information

Job Description. A complete job description should contain job identification information, a job summary, the job duties, accountabilities, and job specification or employment standards information.

Job Classification. Job classification is the arrangement of jobs into classes, groups, or families according to some systematic schema. Traditional classification schemes have been based on organizational lines of authority, technology-based job/task content, and human behavior–based job content.

Job Evaluation. Job evaluation is a procedure for classifying jobs in terms of their relative worth both within an organization and within the related labor market. Job evaluation is used to determine compensation.

Job Design/Restructuring. Job design deals with the allocation and arrangement of organizational work activities and tasks into sets where a singular set of activities constitutes a "job" and is performed by the job incumbent. Job restructuring or redesign consists of reallocation or rearrangement of the work activities into different sets.

Job Specifications. Personnel requirements and specifications for a particular job are the personal knowledge, skills, aptitudes, attributes, and traits that are required for successful performance. Job specifications may be identified as minimum qualifications, as essential characteristics, or as desirable specifications. Cutoff scores on tests, credentials, licenses, degrees, previous experience are all job specifications.

Performance Appraisal. Performance appraisal is a **systematic** evaluation of employee job performance by their supervisors or others who are familiar with their performance. Job analysis is used to develop the criteria or standards for the appraisal.

Worker Training. Training is a systematic, intentional process of developing specific skills and influencing behavior of organizational members such that their resultant behavior contributes to organizational effectiveness.

Worker Mobility/Succession Planning. Worker mobility (career development and pathing) is the movement of individuals into and out of positions, jobs, and occupations. From the perspective of the individual, both self-concepts and social situations change, making the process of job/occupational choice continuous due to growth, exploration, establishment, maintenance, and decline.

Efficiency. Improving efficiency in jobs involves the development of optimal work processes, and design of equipment and other physical facilities with particular reference to work activities of people, including work procedures, work layout, and work standards.

Safety. Similar to efficiency, improving safety in jobs involves the development of optimal work processes and safe design of equipment and physical facilities. However, the focus is on identifying and eliminating unsafe work behaviors, physical conditions, and environmental conditions.

Human Resource Planning. Human resource planning consists of anticipatory and reactive activities by which an organization ensures that it has and will continue to have the right number and kind of people at the right places, at the right times, performing jobs that maximize both the service objectives and/or profit of the organization. It includes the activities by which an organization enhances the self-actualization and growth needs of its people and allows for the maximum utilization of their skills and talents.

Legal/Quasi-Legal Requirements. Laws, regulations, and guidelines established by government agencies (e.g., EEOC, OFCCP, OSHA) have set forth requirements related to one or more of the job analysis products or purposes listed above.

Source: Adapted from R. A. Ash, "Job Analysis Questionnaire (PAQ)," in *The Job Analysis Handbook for Business, Industry and Government*, ed. S. Gael vol. II, pp. 826–827. Reprinted with permission.

constantly monitor their specifications. Larger companies often have the data available to be able to assess the correlation between job specifications and important outcomes like performance. If the data are available, they really need to test the validity of job specifications.

In addition to job descriptions and job specifications, work analysis is used for a variety of purposes and products for both the private and the public sector, particularly in larger organizations (see Figure 4-3). Smaller businesses are less likely to use formal approaches for conducting job analyses and less likely to even use formal job descriptions. In larger organizations, including state and federal government agencies, personnel are hired, trained, and classified as job analysts. In these positions, their primary duty is to perform work analyses for **job classification** and **job evaluation.** A great deal of their work today concerns legal compliance and, in particular, compliance

with the ADA. For example, as we mentioned at the start of the chapter, job analysts employed by the city at Fort Lauderdale, Florida, developed a new job analysis method that incorporated ADA language such as "essential functions."

Work analysis also is used for recruitment and selection purposes in a large number of companies. For example, General Cinema developed a test and a structured interview using the *Management Position Description Questionnaire,* a standardized job analysis instrument, and the **critical incident technique.** Exxon Corporation and AT&T employ a standardized questionnaire to analyze their jobs in order to develop or identify personnel selection tests for their entry-level employees. The City of New York and the Monsanto Corporation also use a job analysis method to establish very specific physical requirements for certain jobs.

Work analysis is used to **redesign jobs** and how jobs relate to one another. Pratt and Whitney, a division of United Technologies, conducted work analysis as a part of a corporatewide restructuring effort. Motorola Corporation and Ford used a standardized, task-based instrument known as the *Job Diagnostic Survey* to collect the necessary information to develop work teams. Numerous organizations also use work analysis to develop training curricula.

While work analysis is typically used to derive specific information about particular jobs, as we stated above, the method can be used to describe projects, work teams, or units so that the end products such as job descriptions or job specifications are defined at the team level rather than for particular positions. Often this approach to defining the job in terms of team member competencies is coupled with skill-based pay systems where individuals are compensated on their potential to perform multiple tasks as opposed to a limited set of tasks specific to a job. So, a team member may be expected to perform the tasks of another who is absent, rotate task assignments with others as needed, and provide additional expert opinion on task processes or products. In this way, the team member is cross-trained to perform a number of different tasks, perhaps even all of those involved in a specific work process. In other words, no one has a monopoly on a set of tasks as the responsibility for performance of these tasks is shared by team members.

What Are the Major Methods of Work Analysis?

There are a variety of methods used to collect information about jobs including observation, performance of the job, interviews, critical incidents, diaries, and organization records, including customer complaints and questionnaires. Figure 4-4 presents a list of the various data collection methods available along with some of their relative advantages and disadvantages. As noted, an analyst, most often the supervisor for the position under study, can simply observe the job and record his or her observations. The analyst also can actually perform the job. Many corporations now require high-level managers to spend time performing jobs where there is personal contact with the customer. Blockbuster Video, for example, makes their managers work the cash register on weekends and Xerox Corporation sends its top managers on sales calls. The basic idea is to better understand the customer's perspective on the business. Individual or group interviews can be conducted with incumbents, supervisors, or subordinates for the position under study. Incumbents or observers can be asked to maintain a diary or record critical incidents regarding their performance or behavior on the job. Available records of work activities or other relevant information such as job descriptions, an organizational chart, and policies and procedures manuals can be reviewed by the analyst to have background data on the job. Relevant job

descriptions can also be retrieved from the Internet through O*NET, a product of the United States Department of Labor.[6]

Questionnaires or checklists also can be completed by incumbents, supervisors, clients, or subordinates. Respondents can be asked to list the major tasks they perform as well as to rate the importance, frequency, time spent, or "essential" nature of each task. Respondents also can indicate how important a specific knowledge, skill, or ability is for completing the tasks. Methods are available for determining the importance of job tasks. A variety of standardized questionnaires exist for conducting job analyses and some of the more commonly used ones are described in a later section. Questionnaires are also available through O*NET.

The methods described in Figure 4-4 should be augmented with organizational data directly relevant to the purposes for doing the work analysis. For example, in the state of Maryland study of social workers described earlier, one of the primary purposes of the study was to determine whether a graduate degree was really essential for the actual work being done. Fortunately, the state of Maryland had performance data on social workers and could thus conduct a study correlating educational level (e.g., MSW or not) with job performance. This data analysis was used along with the results of a standardized job analysis instrument to recommend dropping the advanced degree in social work as a necessary credential for employment.

What Are the Dimensions on Which Work Analysis May Vary?

Work analysis methods can vary along several dimensions including (1) the types of information provided, (2) the forms in which job information is illustrated, (3) the standardization of the analysis, and (4) the sources of job information.[7] Each of these dimensions is described below.

Types of Information

Work analysis methods can solicit a variety of types of information. Some approaches are called **task-** or **job-oriented** methods since they indicate the tasks or duties required to perform the job. For example, "performing cardiopulmonary resuscitation" is considered an important task for a nurse. Similarly, "study and evaluate state-of-the-art techniques to remain competitive and/or lead the field" may be considered an essential task for a member of the management information systems (MIS) staff. Task/job-oriented approaches can be distinguished from the other two approaches we will discuss by their identification or, at least, implication of an end-product. That is, task/job-oriented approaches tend to stress "what gets done on the job." These approaches typically produce quite detailed descriptions of the objectives for each job. As a result, they are very good for fine-grained analysis

FIGURE 4-4   **Common Job Analysis Data Collection Methods**

Collection Method	Advantages	Disadvantages
Observation: Direct observation of job duties, work sampling or observation of segments of job performance, and indirect recording of activities (e.g., film).	Allows for a deeper understanding of job duties than relying on incumbents' descriptions.	Unable to observe mental aspects of jobs (e.g., decision making of managers, creativity of scientists); may not sample all important aspects of the job, especially important yet infrequently performed activities (e.g., use of weapons by police officers).
Performing the Job: Actual performance of job duties by the analyst.	Analyst receives first-hand experience of contextual factors on the job including physical hazards, social demands, emotional stressors, and mental requirements; useful for jobs that can be easily learned.	May be dangerous for hazardous jobs (e.g., firefighters, patrol officers) or unethical/illegal for jobs requiring licensing or extensive training (e.g., medical doctor, psychologist, pharmacist); analyst may be exposed only to frequently performed activities.
Interviews: Individual and group interviews with job incumbents, supervisors, subordinates, clients, or other knowledgeable sources.	Information on infrequently performed activities, and physical and mental activities can be collected; use of multiple sources instead of one source can provide a more comprehensive, unbiased view of the job.	Value of the data is dependent on the interviewers' skills and may be faulty if they ask ambiguous questions; interviewees may be suspicious about the motives for the job analysis (e.g., fearful it will alter their compensation) and distort the information they provide.
Critical Incidents: Descriptions of behavioral examples of exceptionally poor or good performance, and context and consequences in which they occur.	Since observable and measurable behaviors are described, the information can be readily used for performance appraisal and training purposes; may provide insights into job expectations as defined by incumbents.	Descriptions of average or typical behavior are typically not collected so the data may be less inclusive of the entire job domain; time-consuming to gather the incidents.
Diaries: Descriptions of daily work activities by incumbents.	Written in terms familiar to incumbents and supervisors so the data may be easier to use (e.g., in developing performance appraisal measures); may provide insights into the reasons for job activities.	Time-consuming to document; may be biased accounts; may not include mental activities (e.g., innovativeness) or a representative account of all activities.
Background Records: Data mining review and analysis of relevant materials and data including: organizational charts, O*NET, company training manuals, organizational policies and procedures manuals, existing job descriptions, correlational studies relating work variables (e.g., job specifications) to important outcomes.	Provides analyst with job information that assists in developing interview questions or questionnaires; provides useful contextual information for the job; is relatively easy to collect/and analyze; can help determine the value of job specifications.	May not provide complete information and generally needs to be supplemented with data collected using other methods; may be outdated materials; usually provides limited information on specific KASOCs required as well as importance ratings of tasks.
Questionnaires: Structured forms and activity checklists (PAQ, JDS, MPDQ, JCQ) as well as open-ended or unstructured questions (see www.onetcenter.org/questionnaires.html for downloadable questionnaires on abilities, background, education and training, knowledge, skills, work context, and work style).	Commercially available questionnaires are generally less expensive and quicker to use than other methods; can reach a large sample of incumbents or sources, which allows for a greater coverage of informed individuals; responses often can be quantified and analyzed in a variety of meaningful ways (e.g., comparisons can be made across jobs or departments for compensation or selection purposes); can be integrated with O*NET database.	Questions may be interpreted incorrectly; difficult to assess how respondents interpreted questions; response rate may be low, making the results less generalizable; often expensive and time-consuming to develop, score, or analyze; open-ended questions are difficult to quantify and require content analysis that is time-consuming.

FIGURE 4-5 Job Analysis Approach and HR Function Matrix

	Human Resource Function				
Job Analysis Method	Job Redesign	Personnel Selection	Compensation	Training	Performance Appraisal
Job/task	+	0	+	+	+
Person/worker	0	+	+	+	+
Trait/competency-based	0	+	0	0	−

+ = The approach is well-suited for meeting the information requirements of this function.
0 = The approach provides useful information for this function but should not be used in isolation.
− = The approach defeats the aims of this function by providing largely useless information.

of jobs but often are too specific to allow for useful comparisons across jobs.

Other methods such as the Position Analysis Questionnaire (PAQ) are considered to be **person- or worker-oriented** approaches since information is more focused on the KASOCs or behaviors (e.g., decision making, communicating) needed to perform the tasks satisfactorily. In the nurse example, a person-oriented analysis may determine that "knowledge of disorders of the circulatory system" is critical for competent nursing. These approaches provide less detailed information than the job/task-oriented approach but tend to provide better information for the purpose of comparing jobs and identifying job specifications.

Finally, **trait-oriented** approaches such as **threshold traits analysis** focus more on the latent traits (physical and mental abilities and sometimes personality or temperament) a worker must possess in order to perform the required behaviors that lead to specific ends. These approaches detail the job specifications necessary for job success. In a sense they generate a prototype of the ideal job incumbent. They ask, "Who can perform these behaviors?" Oftentimes several approaches are combined into a more comprehensive analysis. As you can imagine, it makes little sense to ask "Who can perform these behaviors?" without first answering the questions: "What behaviors are performed?" and "For what ends?" In fact, some courts have ruled that detailed task analysis must precede any attempt to identify critical competencies or job specifications.[8]

Almost all systematic work analysis methods collect data on the machines, tools, and work aids used. More complete analyses also include records of contextual factors of the job (e.g., physical working conditions, environmental hazards, contact with co-workers). Some methods also provide information on work performance standards (e.g., quality and quantity standards, error analysis) and specific customer requirements. These latter pieces of information are essential to support personnel decisions based on performance appraisal such as terminations, assignment to training, or promotion.

The last paragraph has probably already clued you into the fact that different approaches to work analysis are better suited to supporting different HRM functions and providing necessary products and that the wisest strategy is to support one approach through the use of at least a second, somewhat different approach. Figure 4-5 provides a convenient approach and HRM function matrix to better illustrate this idea. As you can tell from this figure, trait- or competency-oriented approaches are well-suited for identifying KASOCs for personnel selection purposes. Also, trait-oriented approaches are useful for identifying skill requirements for skill-based job evaluation plans. Note that job/task-oriented approaches are the best method for job redesign efforts whereas both job/task- and person/worker-oriented approaches are better suited for performance appraisal development than is the trait approach. In fact, the trait approach receives a "−" for this function as it is uniquely tailored to invite employee grievance and subsequent employer liability for personnel decisions based on trait appraisal.

The Form of Job Information

Work analysis information can be presented in qualitative or quantitative form depending on the method used. Most methods are **qualitative** in the sense that the job is described in a narrative, nonnumerical manner and results in verbal or narrative descriptions of job information. The critical incident technique (CIT), discussed later, is an example of a qualitative method. Other methods such as the O*NET questionnaires, PAQ, and the MPDQ are **quantitative** and provide descriptive information in numerical form. Common examples include a listing of tasks and ratings of the relative frequency, essentiality, or importance with which they are performed and descriptions of the production or error rates per time period. In most cases, work analyses include both quantitative and qualitative information.

The Standardization of the Work Analysis Content

Many HRM professionals have created a uniform or consistent method for work analysis. Some methods, for example, have a set number of questions or items to which responses are required. The job analyst may be asked to write the major objectives of the position, the most important or essential tasks or functions to be performed, the KASOCs that an occupant should have for the position, the major work products or outcomes, and the critical internal or external customers for the products or services. The quantitative approaches are more standardized. The PAQ, for example, has standard content for all the jobs that are under study. Other methods have a standardized content (listing of tasks) for a group of similar jobs, but another list may be used for a different set of jobs.

Another component of the standardization process is the response format. Many methods are completed using computer sheets, direct entry through a computer diskette, or, most recently, through the Internet. Many questionnaires can be completed online with near instant results for the job analyst.

Recall our discussion of the elasticity of work itself and how jobs change so rapidly. So, the recommendation here is not to have too much faith in an already standardized measure since many jobs, their duties, and necessary worker competencies can change dramatically. Who would have envisioned just 15 years ago that clerical jobs would have so much of their job activity centered on the computer or that automobile assembly plants would require computer competencies to the extent they do today? As a more vivid example for you, think about how the role of human resource assistant has changed from the days when most jobs in the personnel office were largely clerical and centered around payroll issues.

Sources of Job Information

There are a number of potential sources for information about a job. Cameras can be used to observe tasks and a variety of recording devices can be used to assess employees' physiological reactions. For a number of cultural and labor relations reasons, the use of physiological monitoring devices is more frequently used in Sweden and Germany for studying jobs suspected of taxing worker stamina than in the United States. The most common source for information is job incumbents and supervisors for the job under study. Other possibilities include job analysts or specialists trained to conduct job analyses, outside observers or consultants, subordinates to the job under study, clients or customers, or persons simply in a good position to observe the job as it is performed. Most agencies of the federal government have job analyst positions whose major responsibility is analysis of other agency jobs. Obviously, more sources of information will probably more fully capture a job on a project.

WHAT ARE THE MOST USEFUL FORMAL APPROACHES TO WORK ANALYSIS?

There are a great number of formal approaches available today. One of the best sources of information on traditional job analyses is the two-volume *Job Analysis Handbook for*

Business, Industry, and Government. The handbook describes 18 different job analysis methods in use today.[9] A very readable text for novices is *Everything You Always Wanted to Know about Job Analysis,* authored by one of the leading authorities in the field.[10] We will concentrate our discussion on methods that have been used to accomplish a specific purpose.

Position Analysis Questionnaire (PAQ)

The **Position Analysis Questionnaire (PAQ)** is a standardized questionnaire that assesses activities using 187 items in six categories.[11] These are

1. *Information input*—where and how does the worker obtain the information needed to perform the job? (e.g., use of visual or sensory input).
2. *Mental processes*—what reasoning, planning, decision-making, or information-processing activities are necessary to perform the activities?
3. *Work output*—what physical activities are performed, and what tools are used?
4. *Relationships with other people*—what relationships with other people are required to perform the job? (e.g., negotiating, performing supervisory activities).
5. *Job context*—in what physical and social contexts is the work performed? (e.g., hazards, stress).
6. *Other job characteristics*—what other activities or characteristics are relevant to the job? (e.g., apparel required, work schedule, salary basis).

Sample items for each of the six PAQ categories are presented in Figure 4-6. Items on the PAQ are rated using several different scales including importance, amount of time required, extent of use, possibility of occurrence, applicability, and difficulty.[12] The PAQ can be completed in about two-and-one-half hours. An on-line scoring form is now available (www.paq.com). Each job is scored on 32 dimensions, and a profile is constructed for the job. Norms are provided so that the job profile can be compared to profiles of benchmark jobs. Usually, a computer printout is prepared for each job that illustrates the job dimension scores and profile, estimates of aptitude test data (e.g., the average scores expected for incumbents on standardized tests), and job evaluation points for compensation purposes. Figure 4-7 presents a printout from a PAQ analysis of a job analyst's job. This printout identifies "G" or general intelligence as the most valid factor underlying job performance as a job analyst and even recommends particular tests (e.g., Wonderlic) that can be used to measure "G" intelligence. The .33 "Predictive Validity Coefficient" is the estimated correlation between scores on a general intelligence or cognitive ability test and job performance. This correlation indicates that the construct of general

FIGURE 4-6 | Sample Items from the PAQ

POSITION ANALYSIS QUESTIONNAIRE (PAQ)

1 INFORMATION INPUT

1.1 Sources of Job Information

Rate each of the following items in terms of the extent to which it is used by the worker as a source of information in performing the job.

Code	Extent of Use (U)
N	Does not apply
1	Nominal, very infrequent
2	Occasional
3	Moderate
4	Considerable
5	Very substantial

1.1.1 Visual Sources of Job Information

1 | U | Written materials (books, reports, office notes, articles, job instructions, signs, etc.)

2 | U | Quantitative materials (materials that deal with quantities or amounts, such as graphs, accounts, specifications, tables of numbers, etc.)

3 | U | Pictorial materials (pictures or picturelike materials used as *sources* of information, for example, drawings, blueprints, diagrams, maps, tracings, photographic films, x-ray films, TV pictures, etc.)

2 MENTAL PROCESSES

2.2 Information Processing Activities

In this section are various human operations involving the "processing" of information or data. Rate each of the following items in terms of how *important* the activity is to the completion of the job.

Code	Importance to This Job (I)
N	Does not apply
1	Very minor
2	Low
3	Average
4	High
5	Extreme

39 | I | Combining information (*combining,* synthesizing, or integrating information or data from two or more sources to establish new facts, hypotheses, theories, or a more complete body of *related* information, for example, an economist using information from various sources to predict future economic conditions, a pilot flying aircraft, a judge trying a case, etc.)

40 | I | Analyzing information or data (for the purpose of identifying *underlying* principles or facts by *breaking down* information into component parts, for example, interpreting financial reports, diagnosing mechanical disorders or medical symptoms, etc.)

49 | S | Using mathematics (indicate, using the code below, the highest level of mathematics that the individual must understand as required by the job)

Code | Level of Mathematics
N | Does not apply.
1 | Simple basic (counting, addition and subtraction of 2-digit numbers or less).
2 | Basic (addition and subtraction of numbers of 3 digits or more, multiplication, division, etc.)
3 | Intermediate (calculations and concepts involving fractions, decimals, percentages, etc.)
4 | Advanced (algebraic, geometric, trigonometric, and statistical concepts, techniques, and procedures usually applied in standard practical situations).
5 | Very advanced (advanced mathematical and statistical theory, concepts, and techniques, for example, calculus, topology, vector analysis, factor analysis, probability theory, etc.)

3 WORK OUTPUT

3.6 Manipulation/Coordination Activities

Rate the following items in terms of how important the activity is to completion of the job.

Code	Importance to This Job (I)
N	Does not apply
1	Very minor
2	Low
3	Average
4	High
5	Extreme

93 | I | Finger manipulation (making careful finger movements in various types of activities, for example, fine assembly, use of precision tools, repairing watches, use of writing and drawing instruments, hand painting of china, etc., usually the hand and arm are *not* involved to any great extent).

94 | I | Hand-arm manipulation (the manual control or manipulation of objects through hand and/or arm movements, which may or may not require continuous visual control, for example, repairing automobiles, packaging products, etc.)

(continued)

FIGURE 4-6 *(Continued)*

RELATIONSHIPS WITH OTHER PERSONS

4 RELATIONSHIPS WITH OTHER PERSONS

This section deals with different aspects of interaction between people involved in various kinds of work.

Code	Importance to This Job (I)
N	Does not apply
1	Very minor
2	Low
3	Average
4	High
5	Extreme

4.1 Communications

Rate the following in terms of how *important* the activity is to the completion of the job. Some jobs may involve several or all of the items in this section.

4.1.1 Oral (communicating by speaking)

99 | I | Advising (dealing with individuals in order to counsel and/or guide them with regard to problems that may be resolved by legal, financial, scientific, technical, clinical, spiritual, and/or other professional principles).

100 | I | Negotiating (dealing with others in order to reach an agreement or solution, for example, labor bargaining, diplomatic relations, etc.)

4.3 Amount of Job-required Personal Contact

112 | S | Job-required personal contact (Indicate, using the code below, the extent of job-required contact with others, individually or in groups, for example, contact with customers, patients, students, the public, superiors, subordinates, fellow employees, official visitors, etc.; consider *only* personal contact which is definitely *part* of the job).

Code	Extent of Required Personal Contact
1	Very infrequent (almost no contact with others is required)
2	Infrequent (limited contact with others is required)
3	Occasional (moderate contact with others is required)
4	Frequent (considerable contact with others is required)
5	Very frequent (almost continual contact with others is required)

5 JOB CONTEXT

5.1 Physical Working Conditions

This section lists various working conditions. Rate the average amount of time the worker is exposed to each condition during a *typical* work period.

Code	Amount of Time (T)
N	Does not apply (or is very incidental)
1	Under 1/10 of the time
2	Between 1/10 and 1/3 of the time
3	Between 1/3 and 2/3 of the time
4	Over 2/3 of the time
5	Almost continually

5.1.1 Outdoor environment

135 | T | Out-of-door environment (subject to changing weather conditions).

6 OTHER JOB CHARACTERISTICS

6.4 Job Demands (cont.)

172 | I | Following set procedures (need to follow specific set procedures or routines in order to obtain satisfactory outcomes, for example, following check-out lists to inspect equipment or vehicles, following procedures for changing a tire, performing specified laboratory tests, etc.)

173 | I | Time pressure of situation (rush hours in a restaurant, urgent time deadlines, rush jobs, etc.)

Source: E. J. McCormick and P. R. Jeanneret, "Position Analysis Questionnaire (PAQ)," in *The Job Analysis Handbook for Business, Industry and Government* ed. S. Gael, Vol. II, pp. 826–827. Reprinted with permission.

FIGURE 4-7 Option 4A: Job Profile—Part 1

IDENTIFICATION INFORMATION

PAQ Number: 002335
Organization: DOTPAQ
Job Title: JOB ANALYST
Dept/Unit: ADMIN SPEC
Analyst(s): AVERAGE/DB
Completed: 01/91
Dot Number: 16626701B N
Dot Coded By: ORGANIZATION
Processed: 08/20/91

Organization Number: 1
Group #: 2335   Record #: 0001
NUMBER OF ANALYSTS/TYPE
Incumbents: Analysis:
Supervisors: Unknown:
WORKFORCE ANALYSTS (optional)
Number of Job Incumbents: 39
% FM: % WH: %BL:
% HS: % TO:

JOB EVALUATION, FLSA EXEMPTION AND JOB PRESTIGE PREDICTIONS

Equation(s) Used to Calculate Job Evaluation Points
(2)
816

Job Evaluation Points:
Reported Median Monthly Compensation:
Probability this Job is EXEMPT from the Fair Labor Standards Act: 1.000
Job Prestige Score: 55.1

SELECTED PAQ ITEMS

#	NAME	RATING	MEANING
20	Near Visual Acuity	2.9	Moderate Detail
46	Education (Level or Equiv)	3.5	College Degree
47	Job-Related Experience	2.8	1 Year to 3 Years
48	Training (Time to Learn Job)	2.7	6 Months to 1 Year
49	Using Mathematics (Level)	3.2	Intermediate
87	Level of Physical Exertion	1.2	Very Light
134	Supervision Received	2.8	General Direction

PAQ ITEMS WITH HIGHEST PERCENTILE SCORES

#	NAME	RATING	%ILE
46	Education	3.5	88
133	Staff Functions	2.5	88
103	Interviewing	2.9	87
88	Siting	3.6	77
49	Using Mathematics	3.2	76
107	Writing/Composing	2.8	75
39	Combining Information	2.8	70
134	Supervision received	2.8	67
114	Middle Management/Staff Personnel	2.8	67
132	Coordinates Activities	1.5	65
40	Analyzing Information or Data	2.8	65
117	Semiprofessional Personnel	2.3	65
36	Decision Making	3.2	64
47	Job-Related Experience	2.8	63
41	Compiling	2.9	63
104	Routine Information Exchange	3.1	63
186	Job Structure	3.1	63
150	Strained Personal Contacts	1.7	62
118	Clerical Personnel	2.6	61
37	Reasoning in Problem Solving	3.1	59
12	Behavior	2.2	59
113	Executive/Officials	1.7	58
149	Frustrating Situations	2.2	58
152	Interpersonal Conflict Situations	1.5	57
38	Amount of Planning/Scheduling	3.0	57
116	Professional Personnel	1.7	54
99	Advising	2.0	53
112	Job-Required Personal Contact	3.8	53
48	Training	2.7	53
1	Written Materials	3.4	51
153	Non-Job-Required Social Contact	2.6	50
101	Persuading	1.4	48
61	Machines/Equipment	1.4	48
105	Nonroutine Information Exchange	1.5	48
32	Inspecting	2.2	47
106	Public Speaking	0.5	47
102	Instructing	1.7	47
35	Estimating Time	2.1	47

TEST PREDICTIONS

GATB TESTS* / *General Aptitude Test Battery	Predicted Score Range Low	Avg	High	Prob. of Use	Predictive Validity Coefficient	SIMILAR TESTS	Predicted Score Range Low	Avg	High
G-Intelligence	102	115	128	.93	.33	— Adaptability	17	20	25
						Learning Abilt	37	43	49
						Wonderlic P'T	19	26	33
V-Verbal Aptitude	99	113	127	.37	.27	EAS-Verbal	13	18	22
						PTI-Verbal	24	33	40
						SET-Verbal	24	37	46
						DAT-Verbal Rsn	*	*	
						DAT-LU Sentenc	*	*	
						DAT-LU Speling	*	*	
N-Numerical Apt.	100	113	127	.60	.28	Arith Fundmnl	31	36	40
						Arithmtc Index	40	47	53
						EAS-Numerical	25	34	43
						FIT-Arithmetic	28	34	39
						PTI-Numerical	14	20	24
						SET-Numerical	28	40	50
						DAT-Numrcl Abil	*	*	
S-Spatial Apt.	92	109	126	.16	.18	EAS-Spatial	17	27	34
						FIT-Assembly	8	11	14
						Mn Ppr Frm Brd	42	50	57
						DAT-Space Rltn	*	*	
P-Form Percept.	94	111	128	.19	.18	— None			
Q-Clerical Percpt.	101	116	131	.50	.23	EAS-Visual Spd	83	96	111
						Mn Clrcl-Names	113	136	165
						SET-Clerical	*	*	
						DAT-Clercl Spd	28	34	42
K-Motor Coord.	95	112	129	.20	.17	— None			
F-Finger Dexterity	81	101	120	.01	.15	— None			
M-Manual Dexterity	83	104	124	.07	.14	— None			

(* Test scores correlated well with GATB scores, but norms were unavailable)

MYERS-BRIGGS TYPE INDICATOR (MBTI) (est. % of incumbents with high score on):

Extraversion	54	Sensing	52	Thinking	50	Judgment	62
Introversion	46	Intuitive	48	Feeling	48	Perception	38

intelligence and the tests that measure it are valid predictors for this job (and the most valid of those considered) based on the PAQ database.

The extensive research that has been conducted with
the PAQ makes it one of the most useful of the standardized job analysis instruments, particularly for selection
and compensation purposes. For example, PAQ results
were used to first select a particular test and then to
successfully support an argument of **job relatedness** in a
Title VII case involving a cognitive ability test that had
caused adverse impact at the James River Corporation.[13]
The approach is also excellent for small businesses with
little or no expertise in human resources. Considerable
research supports the use of the PAQ. However, the PAQ
must usually be completed by a trained job analyst rather
than incumbents since the language in the questionnaire
is difficult and at a fairly high reading level. The instrument also lacks the specificity that can be gained by a
questionnaire developed within the company for one or
more particular positions or one adapted from the O*NET.

As with almost all questionnaires, results must be
interpreted with caution and with consideration of the
"hidden agendas" of the source of the data. The PAQ was
administered to a graphic artist of a specialty mail-order
firm. The graphic artist job was part-time and paid about
50 cents per hour above minimum wage. The job entailed
creating original stencils for use in casting and dying. The
current incumbent had approximately six months' experience at the job and was taking courses part-time at a local
community college. PAQ analysis of the job revealed that
the job required a Ph.D. in art history or related areas and
that compensation appropriate for the work approximated
$55,000 per year! This result can be explained in large
part by a number of factors. First, in the course of the
analysis, answers were recorded just as the incumbent
provided them to the analyst despite observations of the
work performed that indicated the incumbent was grossly
exaggerating the behavioral requirements of the job. And
perhaps more importantly, there had been a rumor in this
organization that the job analyses were to be used to revise current compensation practices. The lesson here is
that the organizational context can strongly influence the
validity of work analysis.

Management Position Description Questionnaire (MPDQ)

Although the PAQ has been used to study managerial positions, other instruments are more suitable for executive and
managerial jobs. For example, the PAQ Web site recommends the *Professional and Managerial Questionnaire,*
specifically designed for executive, professional, and managerial jobs. The most heavily researched of such instruments is the **Management Position Description Questionnaire (MPDQ)** is a standardized instrument designed
specifically for use in analyzing managerial jobs. The

274-item questionnaire contains 15 sections, one of which
is presented in Figure 4-8.[14]

Two-and-one-half hours are required to complete
the entire MPDQ. In most sections, respondents (usually
the managers above the position under study) are asked
to indicate how significant each item is to the position.
For example, they may state that "contact with clerical
staff" is of substantial significance to the position. A
computer program generates eight reports including a
management position description, a position-tailored
performance appraisal form, and a group comparison report, among others.[15] The data provided by this report
are particularly valuable for determining areas of emphasis in hiring, training, and staff development. For example, Office Depot relied on the MPDQ results to develop
assessment center exercises to be used in hiring its district managers. Figure 4-8 also presents a portion of their
results. General Cinema relied on the MPDQ to construct a job-related, behavioral interview and a test for
theater managers. MPDQ results, however, will not tell
you whether a particular job specification is necessary
for any given position. For example, Office Depot
dropped their new requirement that associate store managers have college degrees not based an MPDQ results
but rather a study showing no correlation between a
graduate college degree and manager performance.

Competency Modeling

Although the term is confusing and, some would argue,
describes a process similar to job analysis, most experts
contend that **competency modeling** is focused more on
how objectives are accomplished than on what is accomplished. In addition, the process of competency modeling
is usually concentrated on managerial positions and
should be more closely linked to business goals and
strategies. Competency modeling attempts to identify
and define the individual competencies that are common
or core for an occupational group or the organization as a
whole. By contrast, job analysis methods such as the PAQ
and the MPDQ attempt to draw distinctions across jobs.
The most common purpose for competency modeling is to
derive performance management and training programs.

Software now available for competency modeling
through PeopleSoft, SAP, and Oracle is very popular as
the starting point for comprehensive enterprisewide resource planning systems. Try www.Haygroup.com for a
popular competency modeling approach.

The focus on core competencies to drive HR systems
and applications is very popular today despite the general
lack of rigor in the derivation of the so-called competencies. The integration of the measurement rigor characteristic of methods such as the PAQ and the MPDQ with this
focus on core competencies for HR applications should
make competency modeling a more effective method for
whatever purpose the data are collected.

FIGURE 4-8	Sample Portion of MPDQ

MANAGEMENT POSITION DESCRIPTION

NAME:	B. B. BARKER		ORGANIZATION:	CDBA
EMPLOYEE I.D.:	222		SUPERVISOR:	D. D. DUNCAN
POSITION TITLE:	MANAGER		SUPERVISOR'S TITLE:	MANAGER
FUNCTIONAL AREA:	HUMAN RESOURCES		% OF JOB DESCRIBED:	90%
SUPERVISORY LEVEL:	SUPERVISOR		DATE COMPLETED:	9/11/84

I. GENERAL INFORMATION

A. HUMAN RESOURCE RESPONSIBILITIES

—Management responsibility for **7** employees:

    5 (71%) Full Time—Salaried Exempt

    2 (28%) Part Time—Salaried Nonexempt

—**7** report directly and **0** report on a dotted line basis.

    —Highest direct subordinate: **SR. PROGRAMMER**

—**No** geographically separate facilities managed directly.

B. FINANCIAL RESPONSIBILITIES

—No annual operating budget.

—Sales for last fiscal year: **$ 78,000.**
—Sales objective for current fiscal year: **$ 220,000.**

—Revenue for last fiscal year.   **$ 275,000.**
—Revenue objective for current fiscal year: **$ 230,000.**

II. POSITION ACTIVITIES

A. DECISION MAKING

Decision Making: **5%** of jobholder's time is spent on this function and it is **VERY IMPORTANT** to this position.

—Related activities and their significance:

Significance	Item No.	Activity
CRUCIAL	5	Consider the long-range implications of decisions.
CRUCIAL	8	Make decisions in new/unusual situations without clear guidelines on basis of precedent/experience.
CRUCIAL	11	Make critical decisions under time pressure.
CRUCIAL	18	Process and evaluate a variety of information before making a decision.
CRUCIAL	21	Make decisions that significantly affect customers/clients.
SUBSTANTIAL	4	Make decisions concerning the future direction of operations.
SUBSTANTIAL	7	Consider legal or ethical constraints, as well as company policy or goals, when making decisions.
SUBSTANTIAL	12	Make major product/program/technology/marketing decisions in implementing strategic business plan.
SUBSTANTIAL	14	Make decisions without hesitation when required.
MODERATE	1	Evaluate the costs/benefits of alternative solutions to problems before making decisions.

(continued)

| FIGURE 4-8 | *(Continued)* |

SIGNIFICANCE

THE DUTIES OF THIS POSITION REQUIRE YOU TO:

_____ 1. Define areas of responsibility for supervisory/managerial personnel.

_____ 2. Schedule activities of subordinates on a day-to-day basis to maintain steady work flow.

_____ 3. Interact face-to-face with subordinates on an almost daily basis.

_____ 4. Delegate work and assign responsibility to subordinates.

_____ 5. Facilitate the completion of assignments when subordinates are unable to meet commitments.

_____ 6. Provide detailed instructions to subordinates when making assignments.

_____ 7. Coach subordinates on technical aspects of the job.

_____ 8. Provide on-the-job training for employees.

_____ 9. Frequently review and provide feedback concerning the accuracy and efficiency of subordinates' work.

_____ 10. Motivate employees through interpersonal interactions rather than through external incentives (e.g., pay, promotion, status, etc.).

_____ 11. Motivate subordinates to improve performance through a process of goal setting and positive reinforcement (i.e., incentives).

_____ 12. Work with subordinates to identify and correct weaknesses in performance.

_____ 13. Conduct formal performance appraisals with subordinates.

_____ 14. Develop executive-level management talent.

_____ 15. Establish formal career development plans with employees.

_____ 16. Implement career development and management succession plans.

_____ 17. Identify the training needed for employees to acquire the skills/knowledge necessary for advancement and ensure that the appropriate training is obtained.

_____ 18. Work with employees in highly emotional situations concerning personal or career problems.

_____ 19. Arbitrate conflicts between supervisors and employees.

_____ 20. Investigate and/or settle employee grievances/complaints.

_____ 21. Take necessary action to prevent and/or resolve alleged discriminatory practices.

_____ 22. Interpret, administer, and enforce personnel policies and practices (e.g., employee benefits, training or education reimbursement, affirmative action).

_____ 23. Interpret and administer union contract agreements in the supervision of subordinates.

_____ 24. Interview and hire individuals for approved positions.

Competency modeling is a very popular form of work analysis today. A competency has been defined as an "underlying characteristic of a person which results in effective and/or superior performance on the job" or as a "cluster of related knowledge, skills and attitudes that affects a major part of one's job (a role or responsibility), that correlates with performance on the job, and that can be measured against well-accepted standards."[16] Competencies are essentially no different than KASOCs but competency modeling tends to stay more focused on organizational strategy goals and important outcomes measures.

The use of competencies as a fundamental building block of organizations and the people they employ is increasingly popular. It is estimated that over 75 percent of companies have some form of competency-based application. This competency modeling has exploded onto the field of human resources.[17] One study reported that over 500 articles were published on the topic between 1995 and 2003. It is estimated that firms spend $100 million per year developing, implementing, and revising competency models. One popular, two-level competency model distinguishes "can-do competencies" (skills and knowledge derived from education and experience) from "will-do competencies" (personality and attitudinal characteristics that reflect an individual's willingness to perform).[18]

In one recent study of retail management, competencies were defined as clusters of measurable and relevant behaviorally based characteristics or capabilities of people.[19] The capabilities were described as descriptors reflecting abilities to perform specific work activities and included specific skills or specific knowledge. The goal was to define all competencies with specific, observable, and verifiable descriptors that were reliably and logically classified together.

The researchers used a variety of methods and data to derive competencies for assessment. First, they used the **Critical Incident Technique** for associate and store manager jobs. They also reviewed company records, performance assessment criteria, and conducted correlational studies of the relationship between store managers' characteristics (KASOCs). Next, they interviewed subject matter experts (SMEs) and administered a questionnaire that derived ratings of the importance of various managerial tasks, activities, behaviors, knowledge, skills and abilities for retail management positions within the company.

Four groups of SMEs, who participated in the refinement of the company's mission/vision statement, the derivation of a competitive strategy, and the initial development of core competencies to meet strategic business goals, drafted and refined a list of competencies based on both the strategic business goals for the company and the questionnaire results. The descriptor content for each competency was then refined into the list of competencies. A different group of SMEs was then asked to evaluate the "relative importance" weights for each competency and "relative predictive" weights for each competency. Seven competencies were identified as "core" or "generalizable" competencies such that each was judged to be a critical and independent underlying competency for successful performance at two levels of management. These categories were: Technical knowledge, Oral Presentation/Communication, Written Communication, Interpersonal Skills, Planning and Organizing, Decision Making, and Leadership. These competencies were judged to be important for and representative of relatively stable and important work activities for retail management jobs within the organization. Figure 4-9 presents the "Planning and Organizing" competency. The core competencies and their descriptors formed the basis for the development of tools for assessing job candidates for managerial positions.

While competency modeling is popular and there are a number of so-called validated models available for managerial jobs, this approach usually does not help determine what *specific* job specifications to require for a particular job or assignment. For example, the typical competency modeling process would require an inferential leap to determine how particular competencies relate to particular educational credentials or the number of years of experience, the types of specifications most often written into want ads and provided to recruiters for searches. In general, much like our discussion in Chapter 3 regarding validation and job-relatedness, the recommendation here would be to use whatever data you have to assess particular job specifications. If it's possible to correlate a particular job specification with job performance (if you have the data available), do the study. If EEO difficulties (e.g., 80 percent rule violations) should arise because of a particular job specification that has been used to screen job candidates, the plaintiffs will make every attempt to conduct such a study.

Driven by the availability of vendor software, many companies use competency modeling to evaluate the performance of their managers. The performance appraisals are then used to make important decisions about these managers. The problem here is the difficulty in distinguishing between competencies and psychological traits. For example, the managerial competencies utilized by the American Management Association include self-confidence, positive regard, self-control, spontaneity, stamina, and adaptability. Jaguar Cars reported complaints from managers who received low performance ratings on the "integrity" competency as a part of the performance appraisal process. Office Depot evaluates its store managers on their "personal maturity." Store managers often disagreed with ratings indicating they needed to work on their personal maturity. Ratings on these types of competencies can cause the legal difficulties we covered in Chapter 3 when ratings are used to make important personnel decisions about people such as promotions, terminations, or raises. Assessments of competencies

FIGURE 4-9 Behavioral Expectation Scale for Planning and Organizing Competency

Based on what you know of _____ knowledge, skills and abilities, plus his (her) relevant performance on the job, indicate what level of competence you would expect for this person at the store manager level.

This manager could be expected to:

7- create a *detailed* plan for achieving all strategic results with a level of precision that facilitates the setting and meeting of *very clear, appropriate and attainable* objectives

6-

5-

4- establish clear strategies that are tied to specific objectives for all occasions in which such strategies are needed with a level of precision that facilitates the setting and meeting of mostly *clear, appropriate and attainable* objectives.

3-

2-

1- create an *ambiguous plan (or no plan at all)* for achieving the most important strategic results. The level of precision would *probably be as much of a hindrance* as a help to the setting and meeting of *clear, appropriate and attainable* objectives

Source: Hagan, C. H., Konopaske, R., Bernardin, H. J. & Tyler, C. L. (In press). The criterion-related validity of 360-degree, top down and customer-based competency assessments using assessment center performance as the criterion: A competency modeling approach. *Human Resource Management.*

should be clearly distinguished from measures of performance on any given job.

O*NET

The Occupational Information Network or O*NET provides an automated database for collecting, describing, and presenting reliable and valid occupational information. It could be considered an alternative to traditional job analysis. O*NET is now the federal government's primary source of information about occupations (see Figure 4-10 for a summary of what O*NET can do). O*NET uses multiple descriptors to reveal "multiple windows" on the world of work that can be used to address different uses for the information. For example, O*NET uses "generalized work activities," which are broader than traditional task statements so that the same descriptors can be used across jobs. Because of the many intended uses for O*NET, the descriptors for each job include tasks, behaviors, abilities, skills, knowledge, styles, and work context.

O*NET is based on a six-domain content model that attempts to provide a descriptive framework for describing jobs in greater detail. Figure 4-11 presents the content

model and major categories within each of the six domains of the model. All of the questionnaires used to describe work using the O*NET model can be completed by job incumbents, which will be the primary source of information about work. Unlike many popular methods (e.g., PAQ), the reading level for the questionnaires allows for most incumbents to participate. All questionnaires can be downloaded from the O*NET Web site (onetcenter.org).

One of the many unique features of O*NET is that it classifies jobs according to worker personality and dispositional styles. Jobs are classified according to seven general style categories and 17 subcategories. The seven style categories are achievement orientation, social influence, interpersonal orientation, adjustment, conscientiousness, independence, and practical intelligence. This information can be useful for the development of selection procedures for hiring employees and for vocational counseling.

O*NET is the most comprehensive methodology for describing occupations and workers. Preliminary work and research with O*NET have been positive. One recent study showed O*NET data can help practitioners identify useful tests for employee selection.[20] Many companies now use O*NET to download basic job descriptions (there are over

FIGURE 4-10   What Is O*NET?

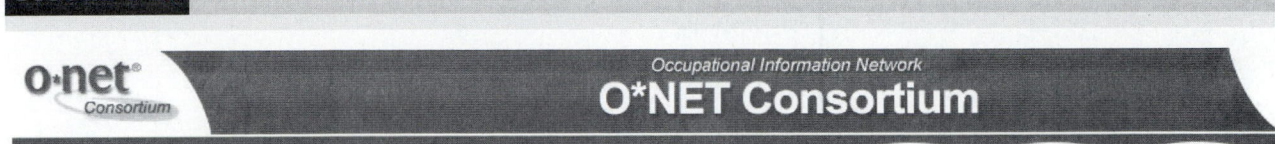

O*NET, the Occupational Information Network, is a comprehensive database of worker attributes and job characteristics. As the replacement for the *Dictionary of Occupational Titles (DOT),* O*NET will be the nation's primary source of occupational information.

O*NET is being developed as a timely, easy-to-use resource that supports public and private sector efforts to identify and develop the skills of the American workforce. It provides a common language for defining and describing occupations. Its flexible design also captures rapidly changing job requirements. In addition, O*NET moves occupational information into the technological age.

As the basis for enhanced product development, the O*NET database can serve as the engine that drives value-added applications designed around core information. It provides the essential foundation for facilitating career counseling, education, employment, and training activities. The database contains information about knowledges, skills, abilities (KSAs), interests, general work activities (GWAs), and work context. O*NET data and structure will also link related occupational, educational, and labor market information databases to the system.

O*NET may be used to:

- Align educational and job training curricula with current workplace needs.
- Create occupational clusters based on KSA information.
- Develop job descriptions or specifications, job orders, and resumes.
- Facilitate employee training and development initiatives.
- Develop and supplement assessment tools to identify worker attributes.
- Structure compensation and reward systems.
- Evaluate and forecast human resource requirements.
- Design and implement organizational development initiatives.
- Identify criteria to establish performance appraisal and management systems.
- Identify criteria to guide selection and placement decisions.
- Create skills-match profiles.
- Explore career options that capitalize on individual KSA profiles.
- Target recruitment efforts to maximize person-job-organizational fit.
- Improve vocational and career counseling efforts.

WHAT IS THE FOUNDATION OF O*NET?

Common Language

O*NET offers a common language for communication across the economy and among workforce development efforts. It provides definitions and concepts for describing worker attributes and workplace requirements that can be broadly understood and easily accepted. Using comprehensive terms to describe the KSAs, interests, content, and context of work, O*NET provides a common frame of reference for understanding what is involved in effective job performance.

The goal of O*NET's common language is straightforward: "improve the quality of dialogue among people who communicate about jobs in the economy, generate employment statistics, and develop education and training programs." It provides the shared foundation of language upon which to build private and public sector workforce development efforts. Employer hiring requirements will have the same meaning for human resource practitioners, workers, education and training developers, program planners, and students.

Conceptual Framework

The conceptual foundation of O*NET is called the Content Model. The Content Model provides a framework for classifying, organizing, and structuring O*NET data.

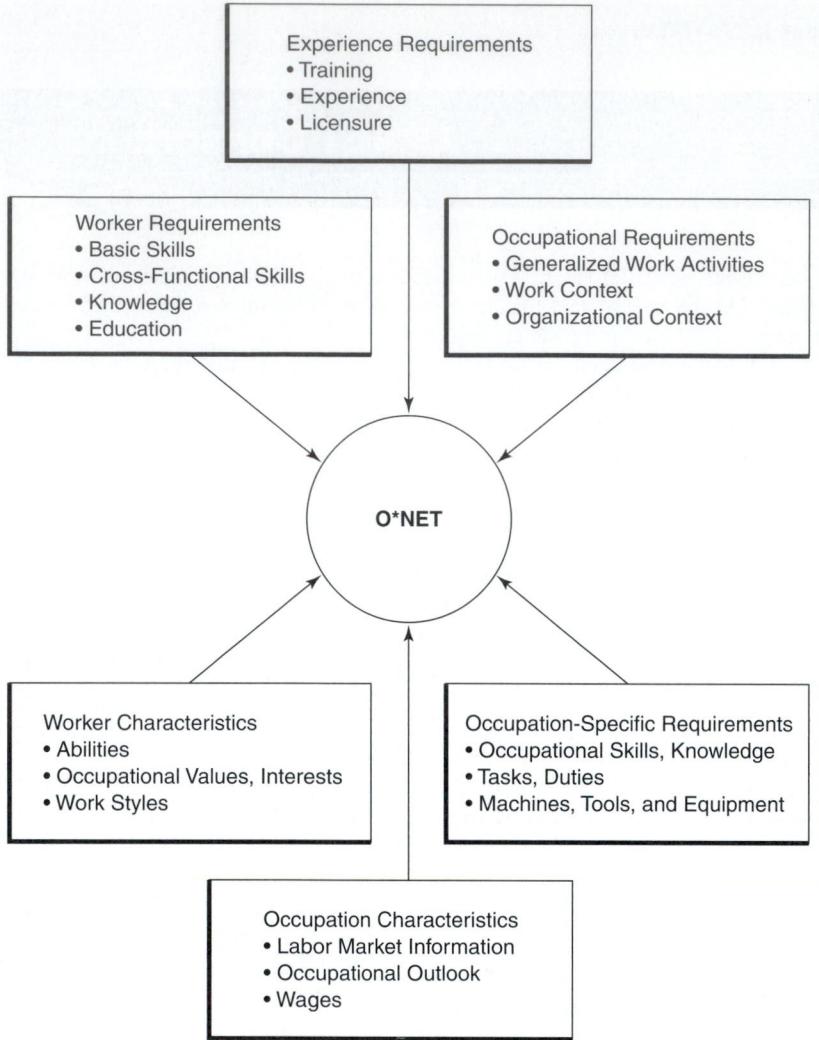

Figure 4-11   O*NET Content Model

Source: N. G. Peterson, et al. "Understanding Occupational Information Network (ONET): Implications for Practice and Research," *Personnel Psychology* 54 (2001), p. 58. Reprinted by permission of Blackwell Publishing.

1,000 job descriptions). Figure 4-12 presents a portion of the job description for human resources managers retrieved from O*NET. Occupational data, including salary information, are also available. The information is obviously a great start on a detailed job description for any HRM job. Completion of the work context questions will add useful detail. The O*NET database also provides very useful compensation data (see Figure 4-12).

Critical Incident Technique (CIT)

The critical incident technique is a qualitative approach for obtaining specific, behaviorally focused descriptions of work or other activities. The technique originally was developed as a training needs assessment and performance appraisal tool.[21] In this regard, individuals recalled and reported specific behavioral examples of incidents that reflected exceptionally good or exceptionally poor performance. A critical incident should possess four characteristics. It should be *specific,* focus

on *observable* behaviors that have been exhibited on the job, describe the *context* in which the behavior occurred, and indicate the *consequences,* outcomes or products of the behavior. A critical incident also must be sufficiently detailed so that knowledgeable people will picture the same incident as it was experienced by the individual.[22] One vivid example of a critical incident characterizing extremely poor performance was provided by a police officer in describing an ex-partner. He wrote, "while on duty, this officer went out of his assigned duty area, went into a bar, got drunk, and had his gun stolen."

A critical incident report references actual behavior in a specific situation with no mention of traits or judgmental inferences. The following is an example of a well-written critical incident. "I observed an employee looking through the scrap tub. Shortly later, she came to me stating that someone had thrown a large piece of cast iron piston into the scrap tub. We salvaged this piston and, a short time later, used this piece to make a pulley for a very urgently

FIGURE 4-12   **Job Prescription from O*NET**

Related Links | OnLine Help | Home

SUMMARY REPORT FOR: 11-3040.00—HUMAN RESOURCES MANAGERS

Plan, direct, and coordinate human resource management activities of an organization to maximize the strategic use of human resources and maintain functions such as employee compensation, recruitment, personnel policies, and regulatory compliance.

   Sample of reported job titles: Human Resources Manager, Director of Human Resources, HR Director (Human Resources Director), Employee Benefits Manager, Employee Relations Manager.

View report: Summary   Details   Custom

Tasks | Knowledge | Skills | Abilities | Work Activities | Work Context | Job Zone | Interests | Work Styles | Work Values | Related Occupations | Wages & Employment

Tasks

- Administer compensation, benefits and performance management systems, and safety and recreation programs.
- Identify staff vacancies and recruit, interview and select applicants.
- Allocate human resources, ensuring appropriate matches between personnel.
- Provide current and prospective employees with information about policies, job duties, working conditions, wages, opportunities for promotion and employee benefits.
- Perform difficult staffing duties, including dealing with understaffing, refereeing disputes, firing employees, and administering disciplinary procedures.
- Advise managers on organizational policy matters such as equal employment opportunity and sexual harassment, and recommend needed changes.
- Analyze and modify compensation and benefits policies to establish competitive programs and ensure compliance with legal requirements.
- Plan and conduct new employee orientation to foster positive attitude toward organizational objectives.
- Serve as a link between management and employees by handling questions, interpreting and administering contracts and helping resolve work-related problems.
- Plan, direct, supervise, and coordinate work activities of subordinates and staff relating to employment, compensation, labor relations, and employee relations.

Knowledge

Personnel and Human Resources—Knowledge of principles and procedures for personnel recruitment, selection, training, compensation and benefits, labor relations and negotiation, and personnel information systems.

English Language—Knowledge of the structure and content of the English language including the meaning and spelling of words, rules of composition, and grammar.

Customer and Personal Service—Knowledge of principles and processes for providing customer and personal services. This includes customer needs assessment, meeting quality standards for services, and evaluation of customer satisfaction.

Administration and Management—Knowledge of business and management principles involved in strategic planning, resource allocation, human resources modeling, leadership technique, production methods, and coordination of people and resources.

Law and Government—Knowledge of laws, legal codes, court procedures, precedents, government regulations, executive orders, agency rules, and the democratic political process.

Clerical—Knowledge of administrative and clerical procedures and systems such as word processing, managing files and records, stenography and transcription, designing forms, and other office procedures and terminology.

Education and Training—Knowledge of principles and methods for curriculum and training design, teaching and instruction for individuals and groups, and the measurement of training effects.

Economics and Accounting—Knowledge of economic and accounting principles and practices, the financial markets, banking and the analysis and reporting of financial data.

Psychology—Knowledge of human behavior and performance; individual differences in ability, personality, and interests; learning and motivation; psychological research methods; and the assessment and treatment of behavioral and affective disorders.

Mathematics—Knowledge of arithmetic, algebra, geometry, calculus, statistics, and their applications.

Skills

Active Listening—Giving full attention to what other people are saying, taking time to understand the points being made, asking questions as appropriate, and not interrupting at inappropriate times.

Management of Personnel Resources—Motivating, developing, and directing people as they work, identifying the best people for the job.

(continued)

FIGURE 4-12 *(Continued)*

Reading Comprehension—Understanding written sentences and paragraphs in work related documents.

Writing—Communicating effectively in writing as appropriate for the needs of the audience.

Speaking—Talking to others to convey information effectively.

Negotiation—Bringing others together and trying to reconcile differences.

Time Management—Managing one's own time and the time of others.

Social Perceptiveness—Being aware of others' reactions and understanding why they react as they do.

Critical Thinking—Using logic and reasoning to identify the strengths and weaknesses of alternative solutions, conclusions or approaches to problems.

Monitoring—Monitoring/assessing performance of yourself, other individuals, or organizations to make improvements or take corrective action.

Abilities

Oral Comprehension—The ability to listen to and understand information and ideas presented through spoken words and sentences.

Oral Expression—The ability to communicate information and ideas in speaking so others will understand.

Written Comprehension—The ability to read and understand information and ideas presented in writing.

Written Expression—The ability to communicate information and ideas in writing so others will understand.

Speech Recognition—The ability to identify and understand the speech of another person.

Speech Clarity—The ability to speak clearly so others can understand you.

Problem Sensitivity—The ability to tell when something is wrong or is likely to go wrong. It does not involve solving the problem, only recognizing there is a problem.

Deductive Reasoning—The ability to apply general rules to specific problems to produce answers that make sense.

Inductive Reasoning—The ability to combine pieces of information to form general rules or conclusions (includes finding a relationship among seemingly unrelated events).

Originality—The ability to come up with unusual or clever ideas about a given topic or situation, or to develop creative ways to solve a problem.

Work Activities

Establishing and Maintaining Interpersonal Relationships—Developing constructive and cooperative working relationships with others, and maintaining them over time.

Communicating with Supervisors, Peers, or Subordinates—Providing information to supervisors, co-workers, and subordinates by telephone, in written form, e-mail, or in person.

Making Decisions and Solving Problems—Analyzing information and evaluating results to choose the best solution and solve problems.

Staffing Organizational Units—Recruiting, interviewing, selecting, hiring, and promoting employees in an organization.

Getting Information—Observing, receiving, and otherwise obtaining information from all relevant sources.

Judging the Qualities of Things, Services, or People—Assessing the value, importance, or quality of things or people.

Resolving Conflicts and Negotiating with Others—Handling complaints, settling disputes, and resolving grievances and conflicts, or otherwise negotiating with others.

Guiding, Directing, and Motivating Subordinates—Providing guidance and direction to subordinates, including setting performance standards and monitoring performance.

Evaluating Information to Determine Compliance with Standards—Using relevant information and individual judgment to determine whether events or processes comply with laws, regulations, or standards.

Coaching and Developing Others—Identifying the developmental needs of others and coaching, mentoring, or otherwise helping others to improve their knowledge or skills.

Work Context

Telephone—How often do you have telephone conversations in this job?

Indoors, Environmentally Controlled—How often does this job require working indoors in environmentally controlled conditions?

Structured versus Unstructured Work—To what extent is this job structured for the worker, rather than allowing the worker to determine tasks, priorities, and goals?

Contact With Others—How much does this job require the worker to be in contact with others (face-to-face, by telephone, or otherwise) in order to perform it?

Electronic Mail—How often do you use electronic mail in this job?

Spend Time Sitting—How much does this job require sitting?

Freedom to Make Decisions—How much decision making freedom, without supervision, does the job offer?

Importance of Being Exact or Accurate—How important is being very exact or highly accurate in performing this job?

Face-to-Face Discussions—How often do you have to have face-to-face discussions with individuals or teams in this job?

Letters and Memos—How often does the job require written letters and memos?

FIGURE 4-12 *(Continued)*

Job Zone Title	Job Zone Four: Considerable Preparation Needed
Overall experience	A minimum of two to four years of work-related skill, knowledge, or experience is needed for these occupations. For example, an accountant must complete four years of college and work for several years in accounting to be considered qualified.
Job training	Employees in these occupations usually need several years of work-related experience, on-the-job training, and/or vocational training.
Job zone	Many of these occupations involve coordinating, supervising.
Examples	Managing, or training others. Examples include accountants, chefs and head cooks, computer programmers, historians, pharmacists, and police detectives.
SVP range	(7.0 to < 8.0)
Education	Most of these occupations require a four-year bachelor's degree, but some do not.

Interests

Enterprising—Enterprising occupations frequently involve starting up and carrying out projects. These occupations can involve leading people and making many decisions. Sometimes they require risk taking and often deal with business.

Social—Social occupations frequently involve working with, communicating with, and teaching people. These occupations often involve helping or providing service to others.

Conventional—Conventional occupations frequently involve following set procedures and routines. These occupations can include working with data and details more than with ideas. Usually there is a clear line of authority to follow.

Work Styles

Concern for Others—Job requires being sensitive to others' needs and feelings and being understanding and helpful on the job.

Attention to Detail—Job requires being careful about detail and thorough in completing work tasks.

Integrity—Job requires being honest and ethical.

Initiative—Job requires a willingness to take on responsibilities and challenges.

Independence—Job requires developing one's own ways of doing things, guiding oneself with little or no supervision, and depending on oneself to get things done.

Persistence—Job requires persistence in the face of obstacles.

Dependability—Job requires being reliable, responsible, and dependable, and fulfilling obligations.

Stress Tolerance—Job requires accepting criticism and dealing calmly and effectively with high stress situations.

Leadership—Job requires a willingness to lead, take charge, and offer opinions and direction.

Self Control—Job requires maintaining composure, keeping emotions in check, controlling anger, and avoiding aggressive behavior, even in very difficult situations.

Work Values

Achievement—Occupations that satisfy this work value are results oriented and allow employees to use their strongest abilities, giving them a feeling of accomplishment. Corresponding needs are Ability Utilization and Achievement.

Independence—Occupations that satisfy this work value allow employs to work on their own and make decisions. Corresponding needs are Creativity, Responsibility and Autonomy.

Related Occupations

11-3011.00	Administrative Services Managers
11-9111.00	Medical and Health Services Managers
11-9131.00	Postmasters and Mail Superintendents
13-1073.00	Training and Development Specialists

Wages and Employment

Location	Pay Period	2003 10%	25%	Median	75%	90%
United States	Hourly	$19.03	$24.86	$33.82	$45.15	$58.71
	Yearly	$39,600	$51,700	$70,300	$93,900	$122,100
Florida	Hourly	$18.94	$23.78	$31.78	$41.65	$53.65
	Yearly	$39,400	$49,500	$66,100	$86,600	$111,600

Source: Bureau of Labor Statistics, Occupational Employment Statistics Survey; Florida Agency for Workforce Innovation.

FIGURE 4-12   *(Continued)*

State and National Trends

Human resources managers, which includes **Compensation and Benefits Managers; Human Resources Managers, All Other; Training and Development Managers.**

United States	Employment		Percent Change	Job Openings[1]
	2002	2012		
Human resources managers	202,200	241,600	+19%	7,350

Florida	Employment		Percent Change	Job Openings[1]
	2002	2012		
Human resources managers	6,040	7,570	+25%	260

[1]Job Openings refers to the average annual job openings due to growth and net replacement.

needed job." The following example does *not* qualify as a well-written critical incident: "The employee completely lacked initiative in getting the job done. While there was plenty of opportunity, I couldn't count on her to deliver." This incident mentions a trait (initiative), does not describe either the situation or the employee's behavior in any detail, and is judgmental in nature.

The critical incident technique has been used to study a variety of jobs such as those of airline pilots, air traffic controllers, research scientists, dentists, industrial foremen, life insurance agents, sales clerks, retail managers, and college professors. One major purpose of the use of CIT is to develop performance appraisal systems. CIT is also an excellent approach for the development of customer satisfaction instruments. Customers provide the examples of effective and ineffective customer service that are then used to develop a standardized customer service evaluation instrument. Burger King, Office Depot, and Continental Bank used the critical incident method to develop a performance appraisal instrument used by "professional customers" to assess compliance with company regulations regarding customer service. The CIT is also very useful for developing highly detailed selection procedures such as assessment centers or behavioral interviews. Office Depot developed their district manager assessment methods using both MPDQ and critical incident results.

Job Compatibility Questionnaire (JCQ)

The **Job Compatibility Questionnaire (JCQ)** was designed as a work analysis method to be used in the development of personnel selection instruments and intervention strategies.[23] Unlike other work analysis methods, the JCQ gathers information on all aspects of the work experience that are thought to be related to employee performance, absences, turnover, and job satisfaction. The underlying assumption of the JCQ is that the

greater the compatibility between a job applicant's preferences for work characteristics and the characteristics of a job as perceived by job incumbents, the more likely that the applicant will stay in the job longer and be effective. The primary goal of the JCQ methodology is to derive perceptions of job characteristics from incumbents' perspectives and to develop selection instruments capable of assessing the extent to which job applicants' preferences are compatible with these perspectives. The selection instrument derived from the JCQ is designed to predict and ultimately increase the level of employee effectiveness. In addition, the instrument can be used to redesign jobs to increase group effectiveness and decrease absences and turnover.

The JCQ is a 200-item instrument that measures job factors that have been shown by previous research to be related to one or more effectiveness criteria (e.g., performance, turnover, absenteeism, job satisfaction). Items cover the following job factors: task requirements, physical environment, customer characteristics, co-worker characteristics, leader characteristics, worker compensation preferences, dispositional factors, task variety, job autonomy, physical demands, and work schedule.

The JCQ is administered to job incumbents, who are asked to indicate the extent to which each JCQ item is descriptive of the job. Thus, an incumbent is asked to indicate on a five-point scale how descriptive each item is of his/her job. A sample list of characteristics is presented below:

Working alone all day.

Having different projects that challenge the intellect.

Staying physically active all day.

Working at my own pace.

Being able to choose the order of my work tasks.

Working under the constant threat of danger.

Having to copy or post numerical data all day.

Having to make public speeches.

Working under extreme time pressure.

Having an opportunity to be creative at work.

The average time required to complete the JCQ is 30 minutes and can be reduced by removing items and factors that clearly do not apply to the job under study. There is also a provision for adding important characteristics that are not covered on the JCQ such as those that may characterize organizational culture or climate. Responses from incumbents on the JCQ are used to derive a selection instrument with a scoring key. The selection instrument items come directly from the items on the JCQ. The details of this process are discussed in Chapter 6.

Research indicates that the tests that evolve from the JCQ do a good job in predicting retention for low-wage jobs such as customer service representatives, theater personnel, security guards, telephone interviewers, and counter personnel.[24] The JCQ is usually nested within a comprehensive test that also assesses applicants on their job-related aptitudes. The JCQ has not been validated (or used) for higher level jobs (e.g., managerial) and is not recommended for such positions.

The JCQ also can be used to redesign jobs. For example, at Tenneco Corporation, responses to the JCQ indicated strong preferences for a pay-for-performance system and a more stable work schedule. These work characteristics, shown to be related to employee turnover, were changed at relatively little cost and turnover was reduced by 14 percent, saving Tenneco over $3 million over three years.

The Job Diagnostic Survey (JDS)

One of the direct applications of work analysis has been for job design and redesign efforts. This has been particularly true in recent years with the increasing interest in the quality of employees' work life, the team-oriented concept, and the principle of worker "empowerment." In general, most of these efforts have focused on redesigning jobs by enriching them. Such enrichment entails providing more meaningful work, greater responsibility, and greater worker autonomy.[25] One of the most well-known and researched job enrichment approaches is the **Job Characteristics Model,** which uses the **Job Diagnostic Survey (JDS).**[26] Over 200 studies have investigated the validity and utility of this approach.[27] Figure 4-13 presents the Job Characteristics Model.

What Is the Job Characteristics Model?

The Job Characteristics Model emphasizes enhancing the intrinsic aspects of an employee's work to increase satisfaction and performance. The model states that workers will be more motivated and satisfied, produce better quality work, and have less absenteeism and turnover to the extent that they experience three psychological states. These states are (1) the belief that their *work is meaningful,* (2) that they have *responsibility for the outcomes* of their work, and (3) that they *receive feedback on the results* of their work. These psychological states can be enhanced by designing the job with consideration of five core characteristics. These characteristics are skill variety,

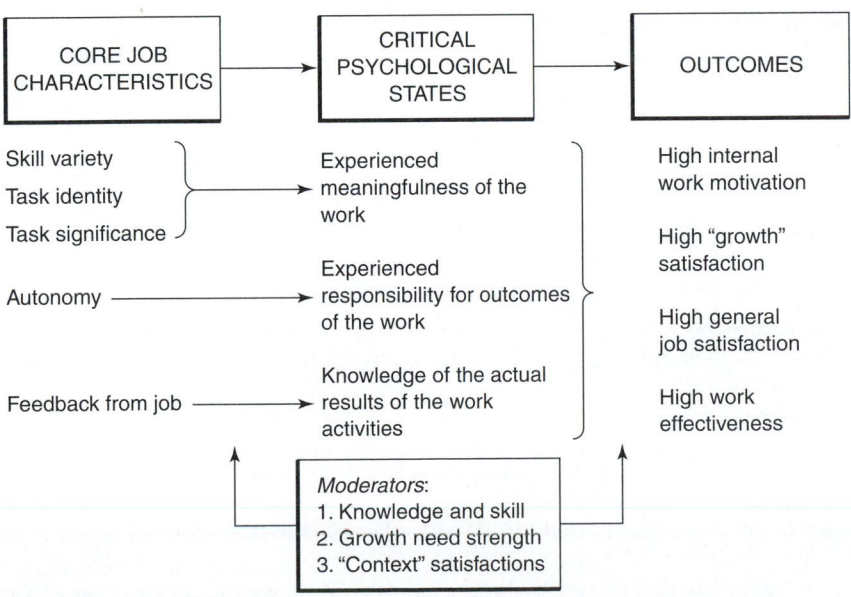

Figure 4-13 Job Characteristics Model

Source: Reprinted from Organizational Behavior and Human Decision Process, Vol. 16, 1996, pp. 250–279, Hackman et. al., Copyright 2007, with permission of Elsevier.

task identity, task significance, autonomy, and feedback and are defined below:

Skill variety refers to the extent to which a job requires the use of a variety of skills, activities, and abilities in order to complete the work.

Task identity is the extent to which job incumbents can complete a whole and identifiable task (e.g., doing a job from beginning to end with a visible outcome).

Task significance is the extent to which the job has a substantial impact on the lives or work of other people.

Autonomy is the extent to which the job gives incumbents discretion, independence, and freedom in scheduling and planning work procedures.

Feedback from the job itself is the extent to which carrying out the work activities results in incumbents receiving clear and direct knowledge about how well they are performing.

The JDS, a 21-item questionnaire, is used to assess employees' perceptions of the degree to which each of the five core characteristics is present in their job.[28] Figure 4-14 presents some items from the JDS.

The most comprehensive review of the Job Characteristics Model found that it is generally valid but that JDS responses are more highly related to worker outcomes such as job satisfaction than to specific work outcomes such as productivity, absenteeism, or job turnover.[29]

Multimethod Job Design Questionnaire (MJDQ)

A more comprehensive method for studying work and the design of jobs is the **Multimethod Job Design Question-**

naire **(MJDQ).**[30] The MJDQ is a 48-item instrument that asks job incumbents to evaluate the motivational, mechanistic, biological, and perceptual-motor approaches to measuring work. The primary purpose is to redesign work to facilitate more effective performance and higher worker satisfaction. The motivational components comprise factors related to enriching and enlarging jobs to make them more intrinsically motivating. The mechanistic component emphasizes task specialization and skill simplification. The biological components focus on the physical and environmental requirements of the job. The perceptual-motor approach concerns the design of jobs to accommodate the physical and mental limitations of workers. The limited research with the MJDQ as a diagnostic work design tool is positive with scores representing the four approaches shown to be related to important work outcomes such as efficiency and job satisfaction. The most recent research indicates it may be better to conceptualize work along more than the four dimensions originally proposed.[31]

What Is Strategic Job Analysis?

Before closing this section on work and design methods, let's review how job analyses can be conducted in situations where jobs don't already exist such as when a new small business is started or where jobs are changing dramatically, as might result from restructuring or workplace reengineering.

In instances where a job is being created or where an organization is undergoing significant strategy evaluation, work analysis takes on a rather predictive bent in that the idea is to describe a job through the anticipated tasks that need to be performed in order to meet organizational goals. This approach has been termed **strategic job analysis** as it intends to forecast what a job may be like in a new environment with new strategic goals, new

---

FIGURE 4-14 **Sample Questions from the JDS, an Instrument Designed to Measure the Key Elements of the Job Characteristics Theory Model**

1--------2--------3---------4--------5--------6---------7

Very little   Moderately   Very much

1. To what extent do managers or co-workers let you know how well you are doing on your job?
2. In general, how significant or important is your job? That is, are the results of your work likely to significantly affect the lives or well-being of other people?
3. How much autonomy is there in your job?
4. To what extent does your job involve doing a "whole" and identifiable piece of work?
5. How much variety is there in your job? That is, to what extent does the job require you to do many different things at work using a variety of your skills and talents?
6. To what extent does your job require you to work closely with other people (either clients or people in related jobs in your organization)?
7. To what extent does doing the job itself provide you with information about your work performance? That is, does the actual work itself provide clues about how well you are doing—aside from the feedback co-workers or managers may provide?

Source: Reprinted by permission of Select Press.

technologies, increased customer contact, or expanded duties. Briefly, conducting a strategic job analysis involves the following steps:[32]

1. If the job currently exists, then a conventional job analysis procedure is used to describe it in detail. If the job isn't in existence yet, then subject matter experts (SMEs) and primary customers of the job's intended services are brought together to identify the tasks that constitute the job based on the new strategic plan. O*NET can be consulted to identify any existing jobs that are similar and can further inform job design.

2. Incumbents and/or SMEs discuss how changes to the job such as new technology or increased contact with external customers will change the tasks making up the job and how the job is performed.

3. Detailed descriptions of the job's tasks and the required KASOCs necessary for successful performance are generated by SMEs and others familiar with the job and the expected changes.

4. The results of the analysis of the projected job are compared to those of the current job to identify differences in tasks and KASOCs.

5. The comparison provides information relevant to developing performance standards, training content, KASOCs for personnel selection, the need for supervision and management, and the relationship between jobs (internal customers and suppliers).

The utility of this approach depends on how accurately the SMEs and other participants anticipate changes in the job or in anticipating what a job created from scratch may be like when actually performed by someone. This approach requires widespread involvement from organizational members, often from different functional areas. In addition, when the job change issue is one of introducing new technology, it may be necessary to involve the hardware or software manufacturer in the analysis of job changes. While more focused on tasks, this approach is similar to *competency modeling*.

What Is Work Process Mapping?

Work Process Mapping (WPM) is a tool used with increasing frequency, as it has proven to be an important supplement to traditional text-based job descriptions. At Columbia Forest Products, WPM is an important tool of the skill-based, work-team approach the company is adopting. Through WPM, the company hopes to better identify coordinated sequences of activities that lend themselves to work-team organization and also to assist in identifying skills and competencies needed to staff process teams.

Processes have increasingly been the target of continuous improvement programs as they provide multiple targets of opportunity for improvement, including quality, operational efficiency, cost, customer service, and com-

petitive advantage. Processes will become even more important as units of analysis as more organizations adopt work-team-based methods of organizing work. Processes lend themselves to coordinated effort and team building because they include a clear terminal goal, multiple skills and competencies to complete, and interdependence among value-added stages of the work.

WPM applies a simplified version of flowcharting to describe work processes. Oftentimes it can be performed by incumbents with some modest training. A work process map produces a picture of how people do their work to achieve specific aims.[33] Just as there are many possible paths you may choose to get to school and many landmarks you may pass along the way, there are many paths to getting work done and several features of the path that clue you to how far along you are on your work assignment. A work process map illustrates these alternative paths and the key features along the way. WPM literally involves drawing a map of the work process to illustrate the tasks and decisions (processes) that need to take place to transform inputs to outputs (see Figure 4-15).

The first step in process mapping is to select the individuals who would serve as the mapping team. They should be knowledgeable about the work and consist of 5–10 members. Groups are preferred over an individual because more people can provide more information about alternatives.

Second, a *process* must be selected for mapping. Processes are activities ordered in a sequence of steps that produce value to internal and/or external customers. Processes include activities such as order processing, product development, and shipping. Processes consist of several activities but culminate in a final product or aim. At each step of the process, each employee receives work, adds value, and directs the work to another worker or group of workers. In our case, we'll create an abbreviated map of the work analysis process used in a small toy manufacturing organization.

FIGURE 4-15 Work Process Mapping

Inputs	Process	Outputs
Purpose	I. Determine purpose	Job descriptions
Agents	II. Define customers and requirements	Performance standards
Sources	III. Identify agents, sources, methods, and resources	Appraisal format
Methods	IV. Develop job analysis protocol	
Resources	V. Collect job information	
	VI. Compile data	
	VII. Analyze and interpret data	
	VIII. Compose report	

The next step involves defining the process and involves identifying the output, internal and external customers, customer requirements, positions that allocate resources to sustain the process, suppliers, stakeholders, and process boundaries (starting and ending points of the process).

The fourth step involves mapping the primary process, which represents the primary sequence of work activities necessary to complete the process. Note that there may be parallel processes occurring that are also related to sustaining or speeding up the primary process, much as a clerk bags your groceries while a cashier rings up your purchases. In the case of work analysis process at our toy manufacturer, the primary process begins with defining the purpose of the work analysis (setting performance standards) as this determines the products that result (appraisal forms and/or production and attendance standards) and the type of analysis to be performed (task- and/or behavior-based methods). This is followed by identifying work analysis agents, whether in-house or external consultants, the resources necessary to complete the project, the specific methods to be used (interviews and questionnaires to collect task information and collect critical incident data), and the sources of analysis information such as job incumbents and supervisors. For brevity, we've included the other sequences in the process map shown in Figure 4-15 and now proceed to discuss steps five and six in the mapping effort.

Step five involves mapping alternative paths that may be followed to produce the output. Not everyone does things the same way and there may be occasions where a number of contingencies do not allow the primary process to proceed as intended. In our situation, it may be that a poor response rate to the task inventory questionnaire requires a second administration or that the poor quality of the critical incidents signals a need for conducting a workshop with information sources to produce data that are more useful. Oftentimes these alternative paths are triggered by some quality control decision point, the unavailability of resources, or different customer specifications for a product. At step six, inspection points are mapped and several of these already may have been identified from the mapping of alternative paths.

At step seven, the map is subject to close study and further refinement. At this point, specific performance standards may be included for different subprocesses, such as adopting a questionnaire return rate standard of 50 percent or a standard of 200 useable critical incidents. Of course, the standards also can be more precise, such as better defining what *usable* refers to with respect to the critical incident data.

The coupling of strategic job analysis and work mapping can go a long way to reducing the ambiguity involved in understanding the work required of new or restructured (reengineered) positions. However, neither is sufficient as a work analysis method, but rather they serve as supplementary tools for conventional job analysis methods. Strategic job analysis is borne out of necessity for specific situations where little information about a job exists or the job is changing radically. Work process mapping is an enabler in that it makes more understandable what is occurring in the course of a work process. Both require careful attention to internal and external customer specifications, include worker participation in the work analysis, and are relatively novel developments that have become increasingly common in a short period of time.

AUTONOMOUS WORK GROUPS (AWG) OR SELF-MANAGING TEAMS

Work process mapping is often the first step an organization takes if work teams are being considered or a major redesign or reengineering effort is under way. Autonomous work groups (also known as self-managing work teams) are employee groups given a high degree of decision-making responsibility and behavioral control for completing their work. Usually, the team is empowered or given the responsibility for producing the entire product or service. A team essentially replaces the boss by taking over responsibilities for scheduling, hiring, ordering, and firing. AWGs represent an application of the Job Characteristics Model we discussed earlier.

DaimlerChrysler and Corning are examples of major manufacturing facilities with work teams. At the Procter & Gamble plant in Lima, Ohio, which makes Liquid Tide, Downy fabric softener, and Biz bleach, teams are responsible for their own safety, production targets, quality goals, and improvements in customer service. Team meetings occur at every shift change, and the teams reorganize themselves as they deem necessary.

AWGs are also catching on in the services sector. Using a service quality audit, managers and quality-improvement teams at Ritz-Carlton Hotels identify errors and determine their frequency, assign costs of fixing (or not fixing) the errors, and identify steps to prevent them.

AWGs usually elect an internal leader. Management may appoint an external leader or coordinator as well. The external leader serves primarily as a facilitator rather than as a supervisor and, where the organization is converting to AWGs, may facilitate relationships among AWGs. He or she may assist the group members in receiving feedback on the quality and quantity of their performance as well as make any structural changes in the team design. The coordinator is also responsible for helping the team acquire needed resources (e.g., equipment) and technical assistance.

Self-managing teams may be involved in a number of different activities, including

- Recording quality control statistics.
- Making scheduling assignments.
- Solving technical problems.
- Setting group or team goals.
- Resolving internal conflicts.
- Assessing group or team performance.
- Making task assignments to group or team members.
- Preparing a budget.
- Training team members.
- Selecting new members.
- Allocating pay raises for members.

Suggestions for Using AWGs or Self-Managing Work Teams

For AWGs or self-managing work teams to be effective, training is critical. Training is necessary for team members on a variety of human relations skills, such as problem solving, group dynamics, conflict resolution, cooperation and participation, and technical skills such as statistical quality control and budget preparation. Training is also necessary for managers in their new roles as facilitators.

The Effectiveness of AWGs or Self-Managing Work Teams

The overall effects of AWGs on productivity have been mixed. It often takes up to two years for some of the positive effects of AWGs to materialize. Managers need to be patient in expecting results and should guarantee job security to enable employees to feel comfortable taking risks and being creative and innovative.

There are many success stories. Based on the way in which the plant was reorganized into only three levels (one plant manager, 10 managers, and about 350 technicians working in teams), the Ohio Procter & Gamble plant was 30 percent more productive. At Pacific Bell, employees on craft, clerical, and engineering self-managed teams reported higher productivity and performance and satisfaction with their jobs, work units, and growth potential as compared to similar traditional work groups. At Ritz-Carlton, the quality audit found that the most common error at the front desk at one hotel was not posting late charges on a guest's bill, which cost the hotel an estimated $250,000 per year.

Employees report that team membership provides them with more autonomy, flexibility, skill variety, training opportunities, and financial benefits (e.g., group-based bonuses). It is not surprising then that firms have found members of AWGs experience higher job satisfaction and morale.

IS THERE BIAS AND INACCURACY IN WORK ANALYSIS DATA?

There has been considerable research on the extent to which work analysis data are subject to inaccuracy or bias.[34] Most of this research has focused on potential sex biases in job evaluation for setting pay rates.[35] Job evaluation is another product of job analysis that can create considerable trouble for a company *or* result in a rational and reasonable pay system. Briefly, the research to date indicates that work analysis is generally free of gender and racial bias.[36] In other words, the race or gender of the job analyst doesn't seem to matter in terms of results. However, courts have been critical of the racial/sexual composition of committees responsible for conducting work analysis and deriving job specifications. A job specification stipulated by an all-white-male panel of job experts that ultimately resulted in adverse impact could be subject to a more problematic legal challenge because of the composition of the panel. A more diverse panel of subject matter experts is strongly recommended by the EEOC and experts familiar with EEO law.

There also has been some research investigating whether the source of the job information influences the nature of the data collected. In general, incumbents tend to assign more importance to their jobs than do supervisors or trained analysts.[37] There is evidence that incumbents and supervisors agree more about the tasks performed than they do about the attributes that are required to perform the job well.[38] There is also evidence that those who know more about a job tend to make more reliable and accurate judgments.[39] Naive raters do not provide work analysis data equivalent to the information provided by experts of the job.[40] However, there is no support for the view that incumbents who are more effective at their jobs provide different information about their jobs than do low performers.[41] Surprisingly, there is no research comparing customer perspectives with those of incumbents or supervisors. A recent study found that ratings on the frequency of tasks performed and the importance of tasks performed provided the most reliable data across different types of raters (e.g., incumbents, experts).[42] Another study found that expert ratings of job specifications in the form of specific KASOCs may be more transportable across organizations and that the idiosyncrasies of particular raters contributed the most to unreliability in the ratings.[43] Another recent study found that Hispanics perceived bi-lingual language skills as significantly more important than non-Hispanics and that the Hispanic point-of-view was more compatible with the view of actual customers. Bottom line: Get more experts for more reliable assessments of job specifications and/or competencies and how they relate to strategy execution. And strive for customers' views too.

More research is needed to explore possible sources of bias in work analysis data and the processes involved in deriving work analysis. Such research may reveal better methods for gathering and integrating work analyses to enhance their accuracy and usefulness.

HOW DO YOU CHOOSE THE BEST WORK ANALYSIS METHOD?

A number of studies have examined the relative effectiveness of specific methods. For example, one study asked experienced job analysts to indicate the extent to which four methods accomplished the various purposes for job analysis.[44] In addition, they were asked to evaluate the amount of training required to use the method, the sample sizes required for deriving reliable results, and the cost to administer and score the method. The results indicated that, of the methods evaluated, if the purpose is to generate a job description or to do job classification or job design, a good method is the PAQ. CIT is probably not as good for job classification purposes. The best method for job evaluation is the PAQ. The PAQ was also the best method for identifying specific tests to use for hiring. If the purpose of the analysis is to develop a performance appraisal instrument, detailed and job-related interview questions, or training programs, the recommended method is CIT. No method is ideal in terms of legal compliance, including ADA compliance. For companies in need of highly detailed information about a job, the development of their own job analysis method is probably preferable to an "off-the-shelf" type such as the PAQ, which would not

give you the level of detail in describing the job, perhaps a critical issue if you are developing a training program.

Experts agree that organizations should use their own data whenever possible to determine whether particular job specifications (e.g., a particular level of education or experience) are related to critical criteria such as job performance.

O*NET has a wealth of information that can be used effectively by organizations to accomplish most of the major purposes for which you do work analysis. The job descriptions you can retrieve from the Web site are a great start on a number of the work analysis products discussed in this chapter (if not finished products) and you can even retrieve up-to-date salary information for your particular jobs and geographical areas. And it's all free! You can also download detailed questionnaires that can be adapted for whatever purposes you have in mind.

Experts also agree that the choice of work analysis method depends upon the purposes to be served by the data and the desired product. There is no "one best way" to conduct work analysis. The purposes for the data and the practicality of the various methods for particular organizations must be considered. The most definitive finding from the research on the relative effectiveness of the various methods is that multiple methods of analysis should be used whenever possible. For example, a quantitative approach such as the PAQ should probably be augmented by a qualitative approach such as the CIT, which can provide more specific information about jobs than what can typically be derived from the quantitative methods.

SUMMARY

Jobs are important to people because they have surplus meaning beyond just providing a paycheck necessary to sustain their economic survival. People ask a lot of their jobs, as they become better educated and develop rising expectations about what jobs should supply. As a result of technology and the flattening of organizational structures, jobs are no longer the static entities they once were thought to be. Work has become more dynamic and the lines distinguishing the responsibilities of one job from another continue to blur. Recent research on job performance has shown that there are some generic dimensions of work behavior that apply across a broad spectrum of jobs while others that are more task-based are very specific to a limited set of jobs. Generic work behaviors influence the performance of virtually any job,[45] honesty or integrity, goal attendance, treating co-workers with respect, and maintaining good personal hygiene. The idea of generic work behaviors opens the possibility for more direct comparisons of employee performance regardless of the specific tasks for which employees are responsible. It also challenges the traditional idea that jobs and job performance can be neatly compartmentalized.

Yet one of the aims of work analysis is to identify differences between jobs so that selection tests, levels of compensation, training and development efforts, and performance standards are demonstrably relevant to job success. An

increasing burden on work analysis today is to describe jobs in sufficient detail so that differences between them are recognized and appropriate criteria for personnel decisions result. At the same time, work analysis should be flexible enough to be applied to the study of jobs as they change in response to technological demands and the organization of projects and work. Detailed work analysis products is also considered to be a critical element of any possible outsourcing effort. Research on successful and unsuccessful outsourcing projects shows that one key variable is the specificity in the job description and the determination of the key outcomes from the customer perspective.[46]

The once traditional idea of "the job" is under challenge as more organizations adopt project-based work assignments. Work analysis remains an essential tool for HR professionals despite contemporary changes in the world of work and the new "team" orientation within many companies. There has been much discussion in the popular press about the "de-jobbing" of organizations.[47] In fact, formal job analysis may be even more significant in the context of a turbulent work environment and a more comprehensive work analysis. Regardless of the elasticity of the job, projects, and tasks, work analysis should be a starting point in the design of most HR systems including restructuring, human resource planning, reengineering of recruitment strategies, selection processes, training and career development programs, performance appraisal systems, customer-based appraisal, job design efforts, compensation plans, and health and safety compliance and improvements. Even project-based employment requires hiring, training, compensation, and performance appraisal functions. The need to describe the work a prospective employee or contractor will perform before hiring still presupposes an inventory of the likely situational demands and worker competencies required to fulfill this broader mission.

Work analysis helps to ensure that HR systems will be professionally sound. As noted in Chapter 3, HR systems that involve personnel decisions such as selection, pay, promotion, and terminations should be based on a determination of the important job duties and KASOCs necessary for successful job performance. Even if the legal mandate did not exist, effective HR practice dictates the linkage between these HR activities and work analysis.

While many contemporary management gurus preach that job descriptions promote individualism to the detriment of unit effectiveness, we believe that work analysis can facilitate more effective group and unit effectiveness through clearer definitions of responsibilities and a determination of the relative importance of tasks and working relationships between positions and individuals and how all are related to customer requirements. Job descriptions do not have to say, and they rarely ever say, that the incumbent will perform only those tasks defined on the description regardless of circumstances. To the extent that job descriptions foster an "it's not my job" philosophy of work and a deviation in attention away from customer requirements, the gurus are right. The trick is to develop and use work analysis with customer requirements as the focus.

Although static unchanging jobs may be obsolete, work analysis as a tool for understanding and describing work activities will remain an essential HR competency for the foreseeable future. As we cover the various HR functional areas in the chapters to follow, we will address in more detail how work analysis is used to supply internal and external customers with the very best and most efficient HR products.

DISCUSSION QUESTIONS

1. What is meant by conducting a work analysis? How might you convince top managers of the importance of conducting work analysis?

2. Do you believe having highly detailed job descriptions for every position can interfere with group effectiveness? If so, is there anything that can be done?

3. For each of the following HR systems, what type of analysis is needed to develop a professional and legally defensible system?
   a. Training program for new employees.
   b. Selection system.
   c. Performance appraisal system.
   d. Compensation system.
   e. Job design.

4. Describe the advantages and disadvantages of using interviews, observation, and questionnaires for collecting work analysis.

5. How might you involve customers in the development of job descriptions and job specifications? Are there any constraints on what customers can stipulate in job specifications?

6. Do PAQ data provide sufficient argument for "job-relatedness"? Explain.

7. How would you use O*NET for developing job descriptions and specifications?

8. A fast growing small business decides to hire a human resources manager for the first time. What steps should be taken next?

5

HUMAN RESOURCE PLANNING AND RECRUITMENT*

OVERVIEW

Kathryn Connors, the vice president of human resources at Liz Claiborne, described the ideal role for HR in strategic planning: "Human resources is part of the strategic planning process. It's part of policy development, line extension planning and the merger and acquisition process. Little is done in the company that doesn't involve us in the planning, policy or finalization stages of any deal."[1] Unfortunately, as we discussed in Chapter 1, the extent of involvement of human resources in strategic planning as practiced by Liz Claiborne is still rather unusual. While more companies now link HR planning to strategic planning, the linkage is usually focused mainly on the reduction of labor costs with limited consideration of other elements related to HR.[2] The typical practice is for an HRM unit to receive forecasting plans to reduce overhead by reducing labor costs. The role of HR is to devise the HR strategy for implementing the plan. One indication that the strategy/planning process of HRM may not be ideal is the announcements of massive layoffs at General Motors (30,000 workers'), Ford (30,000), Kmart, Delta Airlines, Lucent Technologies, IBM, and General Electric in recent years. How did these companies come to be overstaffed by so many workers? Amazon.com's layoffs may be an example of more strategic HR planning involving business forecasting, customer demand, and labor force needs and options. They laid off 1,800 workers based on a thorough study of projected sales. Another company with great HR planning processes is Southwest Airlines. While all other airlines were laying people off after September 11, Southwest transferred people, cut overtime, and changed some assignments. Not a single Southwest employee was laid off. This may still be true.

In terms of competitive advantage in the global economy, however, the "good" news is that most foreign competitors also conduct their HR planning and recruitment in a more reactive manner rather than as a fully integrated system. Particularly, given the greater HR constraints in reacting to business problems placed on foreign competitors, especially European, there is opportunity for HR-based competitive advantage for U.S. companies.

HR planning (HRP) should be an integral part of competitive strategy. The most effective approach to staffing, whether adding workers or eliminating them, is to assess staffing needs with a focus on meeting customer requirements and expanding the customer base.

One important element of HR planning today is a consideration of outsourcing to reduce costs. As exposed in a recent survey, HR should be much more involved in assessing outsourcing and offshoring options. Says Jennifer Schramm, manager of workplace trends and forecasting at the Society of Human

*An early version of this chapter was written by Scott A. Snell and Monica Favia.

Resource Management (SHRM.org), "The participation of HR professionals in offshoring is necessary from the beginning stages of exploring the idea of offshoring as a viable option to the implementation stage. . . HR should be involved in spearheading the country selection process—investigating the most viable offshore labor force—and then in orchestrating the recruitment of qualified staff."[3] The survey shows limited HR involvement in this process.

The goal for organizations of all sizes is quite simple: Keep the cost of labor as low as possible while meeting (or exceeding) customer demand and, if this is a part of the strategic plan, expanding the customer base. The realization of this goal for HR practice is obviously much more difficult. The goal also can be applied to the internal customers who require products or services from internal suppliers, including HRM staff. For example, an internal customer could be a district manager in retail who must hire a store manager for one of the stores in the district. One option could be to use an external headhunter group that specializes in retail, or perhaps the company relies on internal recruiters to compile a list of qualified candidates. Obviously, the company is very interested in the cost of the recruiting effort and the district manager may be particularly interested in filling the position quickly with someone who requires little or no training.

Two of the most important aspects of staffing are HRM planning and recruitment. Planning is the forecasting of HR needs in the context of strategic business planning. The human resource planning process of the past was typically reactive, with business needs defining personnel needs. However, with major changes in the business environment and increasing uncertainty, many organizations have adopted a longer-term perspective, integrating human resource planning with strategic business planning centered on a consideration of core business competencies.

Recruitment is the process of attracting applicants for the positions needed. This process *should* be fully integrated with the HR planning process and other HR activities, especially the selection process. Recruitment and other HRM activities are interdependent. For example, recruitment success affects selection success and the use of certain selection procedures can affect recruitment success.

This chapter provides an overview of the planning and recruitment process. We will discuss the relationship between planning, recruitment, and the other HRM functions; the process of downsizing and reengineering or restructuring; the various sources available for recruiting and their relative effectiveness; the advantages and disadvantages of internal and external recruiting; and the role of equal employment opportunity in the planning and recruitment process.

OBJECTIVES

After reading this chapter, you should be able to

1. *Understand the importance of HRP to the organization.*
2. *Identify the six steps in the HRP process.*
3. *Identify the methods by which an organization can develop forecasts of anticipated personnel demand and understand labor markets.*
4. *Understand how an organization can stay apprised of and evaluate its personnel supply and, if necessary, implement a downsizing program.*
5. *Determine which recruitment methods are best for given situations, including the role of the Internet.*
6. *Understand the pros and cons of internal versus external recruiting.*
7. *Know the most important features of recruitment advertising.*
8. *Know the EEO implications of recruitment and planning.*

EFFECTIVE HUMAN RESOURCE PLANNING

Organizations that integrate strategy with HR planning and recruitment have an HR competitive advantage. Recruitment planning should flow directly from HR planning. Figure 5-1 presents a model of this relationship. Effective HRP closes the gap from the current situation to a desired state of affairs in the context of the organization's strategy. The process for determining this match is outlined in Figure 5-2. Effective HRP should involve (1) environmental scanning, (2) labor analysis, (3) supply analysis, (4) gap analysis, (5) action programming, and (6) evaluation. We examine each of these below.

Step One: Environmental Scanning

Environmental scanning helps HR planners identify and anticipate sources of problems, threats, and opportunities that should drive the organization's strategic planning. Scanning provides a better understanding of the context in which HR decisions are/will be made. Both an external and an internal environmental scan are critical for effective planning.

While there can be (and often are) situations with ambiguous problems, threats, and opportunities, the probability of reducing or eliminating the ambiguity is increased by a more thorough environmental scan. The idea here is to at least attempt to turn a threat into an opportunity with information. In general, the greater the amount of relevant information that managers have about a problem, the more likely that problem can be turned into an opportunity. Both external and internal

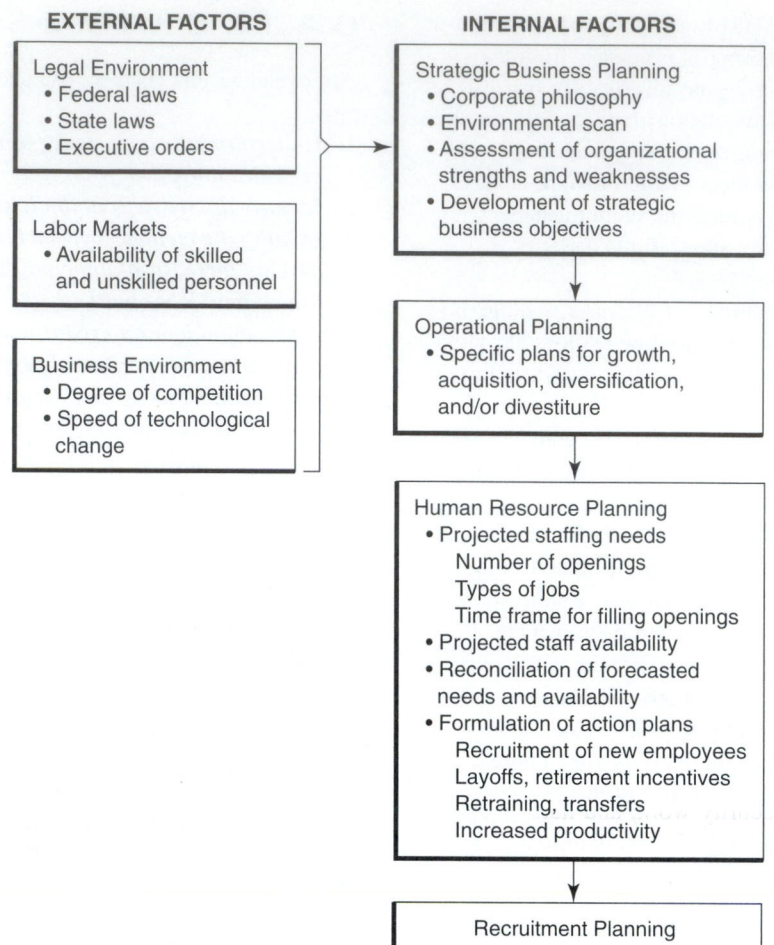

EXTERNAL FACTORS

Legal Environment
- Federal laws
- State laws
- Executive orders

Labor Markets
- Availability of skilled and unskilled personnel

Business Environment
- Degree of competition
- Speed of technological change

INTERNAL FACTORS

Strategic Business Planning
- Corporate philosophy
- Environmental scan
- Assessment of organizational strengths and weaknesses
- Development of strategic business objectives

Operational Planning
- Specific plans for growth, acquisition, diversification, and/or divestiture

Human Resource Planning
- Projected staffing needs
    - Number of openings
    - Types of jobs
    - Time frame for filling openings
- Projected staff availability
- Reconciliation of forecasted needs and availability
- Formulation of action plans
    - Recruitment of new employees
    - Layoffs, retirement incentives
    - Retraining, transfers
    - Increased productivity

Recruitment Planning

Figure 5-1   Simplified Model of External and Internal Factors That Influence Recruitment

Source: Simplified Model of External and Internal Factors That Influence Recruitment. Adapted from *Employee Recruitment: Science and Practice* by James Breaugh. Reprinted by permission of the author.

FIGURE 5-2   Steps for Effective HR Planning

1. **Environmental scanning.** Identify and anticipate sources of threats and opportunities, scanning the external environment (competitors, regulation) and internal environment (strategy, technology, culture).
2. **Labor demand forecast.** Project how business needs will affect HR needs, using qualitative methods (e.g., Delphi, nominal) and quantitative methods (trend analysis, simple and multiple linear regression analysis).
3. **Labor supply forecast.** Project resource availability from internal and external sources.
4. **Gap analysis.** Reconcile the forecast of labor supply and demand.
5. **Action programming.** Implement the recommended solution from step 4.
6. **Control and evaluation.** Monitor the effects of the HRP by defining and measuring critical criteria (e.g., turnover costs, breakeven costs of new hires, recruitment costs, performance outcomes).

environmental scans are critical for this information. Amazon is a good example here, as we suggested earlier. They closed a large and costly customer service center in Seattle despite projections of 20 to 30 percent sales growth because their study of global labor options told them they could meet their sales growth projections with a far less costly customer service center in India. Numerous other companies have turned to offshoring and outsourcing to save money.

Environmental scanning pursued for the purposes of HR planning should not lose sight of the fact that the frame of reference for such scanning should always be on strategic goals with a customer focus. A large law firm in Atlanta was losing young associates, many of whom in exit interviews complained about "burnout" and conflicts with partners and more senior associates. The turnover rate spiked coincidental with the loss of two major clients and almost 400 billable hours a week. While the loss of the associates was obviously important, the customer/client problem was more important. It turned out that the two were related in that partners were sending more work to associates. The clients were increasingly unhappy with work products, were then complaining before finally firing the law firm altogether. For any HR problem, an environmental scan should always keep the "big picture" in mind. What specifically are the customer complaints? Can we fix a systemic problem that may be causing customer problems, problems that translate into an HR problem like high turnover? Reducing customer complaints may take care of the HR problem or sharply reduce it. Military recruiting problems in 2005 were probably not so much related to recruiting procedures or style, pay, benefits, etc. It's probably mainly a "big picture" issue.

Understanding the Labor Market for HR Planning

One critical component of environmental scanning for HR planning and recruitment is an understanding of the relevant labor market. Labor market conditions influence HR planning in terms of both the number and types of available employees. In a loose **labor market,** qualified recruits are abundant. However, many labor markets are extremely tight. For example, there are shortages in numerous cutting-edge technologies such as optics and laser technology as well as shortages in unskilled labor areas such as child care, security work, and nursing home assistance. Tight markets limit the availability of labor, drive up the price of those employees who are selected, and even limit the extent to which the organization can be selective in its hiring procedures. Most private security guard companies use psychological tests for screening mainly because of fears of negligent hiring lawsuits. In fact, because of the level of competition in this area, the demand for services, and the tight labor market for largely unskilled labor, these companies cannot be very selective in hiring people despite what the tests may predict.

The relevant labor market for an employer is defined by occupation, geography, and employer competition. Obviously, the job and the skills or job specifications play the greatest role in the definition of the relevant labor market and the ease (or difficulty) with which positions can be filled. The labor market is affected by geography but, because of technology, not nearly as much as in the past. Offshoring is having a significant impact on the definition of a labor market. Competing employers are the third factor defining the labor market. The number and type of employers seeking similarly qualified personnel or offering similar compensation in the same location also can serve to define the labor market. Google and Microsoft are now rivals. They compete for the same rare talent and try hard to recruit employees directly from their rivals.

The Global Labor Market/Offshoring

The technological and communications revolution has really changed the relationship between geography and labor supply. Says Thomas L. Friedman, author of *The world is flat,* "globalization has collapsed time and distance and raised the notion that someone anywhere on earth can do your job, more cheaply."[4] As discussed in Chapter 2, an international division of labor has emerged. The world is now the labor market for many skilled and unskilled jobs. The outsourcing of the manufacturing/assembly process to a foreign location is now commonplace in most industries. The chances are also much greater now than just a few years ago that the customer service representative you speak with over the phone or who processes your Internet order is sitting a long way from U.S. soil. According the National Association of Software and Service Companies in India, customer service business is expected to increase to 200,000 employees and $5 billion by 2008. One call center in Bangalore, 247customer.com, founded in 2000, includes several Fortune 500 companies and a major telecommunications company. General Electric and British Airways have large phone banks in India and are expanding this function because of the low cost and low turnover of personnel and the quality of the work. As of 2006, entry-level customer service representatives in India earn between $3,000 and $4,000 per year, a good salary by India's standards, which probably explains the low turnover. The total savings estimates for U.S. companies for this critical work is between 20 and 40 percent.

What also is becoming more common is that *skilled* labor is being "offshored" to lower-paid, overseas workers as well. Dallas-based software company I2 Technologies runs software centers in Bombay and Bangalore. The programming costs are estimated to be about one-third of the cost of an American programmer. However, this difference could change rapidly as the demand for Indian programmers grows. The consulting firm McKinsey and Company reports that by 2008, new jobs in accounting, software development, and transcribing will generate 800,000 new jobs and $17 billion in revenue for India.

India is by no means the only attractive offshoring destination. Figure 5-3 presents the results of a study conducted by A. T. Kearney that derived an index of the most attractive countries for offshoring based on cost, the economic and political environment, and each country's human capital.

E-mail, fax machines, private satellite links, and the World Wide Web have made workers from all over the world accessible and have expanded the labor market for U.S. companies. The result is lower labor costs for American companies and (usually) greater profits; the shipment of more American jobs overseas; and the continued stagnation of middle-class wages in this country. Rick Younts, executive vice president for international operations at Motorola, claims more than lower wages as the reason Motorola hires Asian programmers. U.S.-based

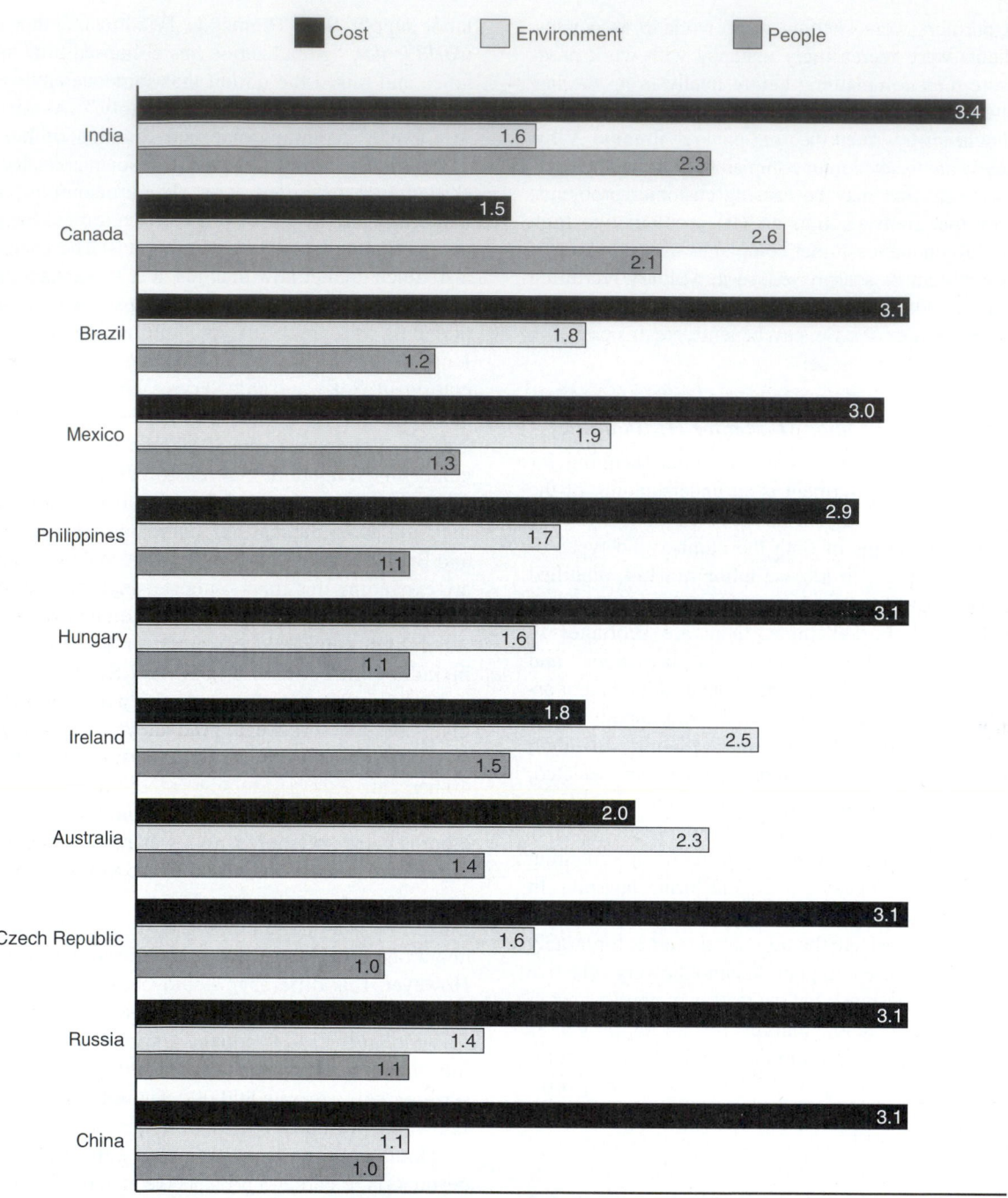

Figure 5-3 Composite Offshoring "Attractiveness" Scores by Country*

Note: Higher scores indicate higher levels of attractiveness.

*Scoring methodology reviewed and confirmed by leading industry analysts.

Source: Composite Offshoring "Attractiveness" Scores by Country. Copyright AT Kearney (2005). All rights reserved. Reprinted with permission.

programmers can work on a project during the day and then e-mail their work to Asian counterparts who can work on it while the U.S.-based programmers are sleeping. Younts estimates a 40 percent reduction in time to completion because of this work schedule. Companies that do not take advantage of the global labor market for labor will be at a competitive disadvantage as long as consumers do not place a heavy

weight on the extent to which a product or service involves American workers.

One of the leading worldwide outsourcing firms is California-based Elance, which charges a fee for vendors to compete on "Requests for Proposals" submitted through their Web site. Elance claims over 50,000 registered and qualified professionals in more than 100 categories of work (e.g., software design, writing, Web site design, sales and marketing, management and finance, training and development, legal) are ready to bid on a project proposal which is submitted to www.Elance.com. With bids, you also receive credentials, work samples and a performance assessment on previous projects. Elance claims that companies have saved "over 60%" by outsourcing their projects through Elance. The service is free to outsourcing organizations.

U.S. companies are now outsourcing their legal work offshore. The leading firm in this area is Michigan-based Lexadigm Solutions that offers legal research conducted by Indian lawyers at substantially lower fees (see www.lexadigm.com). The Lexidigm Web site states that "by hiring India-based attorneys, we are able to take advantage of the large wage disparity between Indian attorneys and their U.S. counterparts, and our rates reflect this cost advantage. We are also able to be extremely selective in our hiring practices. Each of our India-based Research Specialists has graduated from one of the top five law schools in India, practiced law for at least three years, received extensive legal training from U.S. attorneys, and passed Lexadigm's rigorous legal research and writing exam. In addition, a large percentage of our India-based attorneys have legal degrees from reputable U.S. law schools."

Since labor can constitute as much as 80 percent of operating expenses, and since most businesses compete at least partly on a price/cost basis, managing the labor market and the cost of labor is a crucial HR activity (the great increase in the proportion of adjunct professors at most universities is a good example of this). Companies usually look at labor first when their corporate performance measures do not meet expectations. Recall our discussion in Chapter 1 about the need to be flexible in this dynamic and more global economy. Compared to European countries, flexibility regarding labor reductions and cost cutting is relatively common in the United States. American companies certainly have a competitive advantage over European countries as they compete on price.

The trend line for offshoring American jobs is clearly up and for a growing number of professional service jobs. A. T. Kearney, a financial services company, estimates that they will move about a half million jobs offshore by 2008. These jobs include high-level financial analyst positions. Some experts predict that the greatest growth in offshoring will be for services requiring higher skill levels.

The differences in compensation between U.S. workers and offshored options are, at least for now, considerable. Three million U.S. manufacturing jobs have been lost since 2000. General Motors had the worst year of its existence in 2005, announcing layoffs of 30,000 jobs (17 percent of its American workforce). Every time a car comes off a U.S. assembly line, GM loses $1,100. Said

CEO Rick Wagoner at a 2005 GM board meeting, "We're reenergizing our global sourcing efforts . . . our move to a global product development system, accompanied by the emergence of excellent supply capabilities in lower cost markets, provide us with some real cost savings opportunities." GM is clearly looking to China where labor costs are much lower (the average hourly rate for a U.S. GM factory worker is $54 per hour versus $5.50 for a Chinese autoworker; the average worker in China makes about $100 per month).

Of course, there should be more to outsourcing than saving on labor costs. A 2005 report by DiamondCluster International, a global management consulting firm, found that 51 percent of U.S. buyers of outsourcing services are dissatisfied with the service providers and terminating contracts early. "The blame cannot be heaped solely on the shoulders of providers," said Tom Weakland, who heads up an outsourcing advisory consulting practice. "Many buyers are now several years into at least one outsourcing relationship, but they still lack effective measures to gauge the success of their outsourcing initiatives, which are critical for knowing and getting what you want." Many companies report that because of quality problems, "companies are learning that the tremendous cost-savings outsourcers have been promising are actually difficult to achieve. And they are learning more about the cost of losing good people and the value of their institutional knowledge." Outsourcing buyers report that the greatest risks of outsourcing include the increased complexity of managing relationships, reduced operational effectiveness, and lower quality of output from their outsourcing providers.

Affirmative Action/Diversity Programs and the Law: A Problem, Threat, or Opportunity?

As discussed in Chapter 3, **government regulations** also influence HR planning and must be considered in any environmental scan. Equal employment opportunity legislation such as Title VII of the Civil Rights Act, the 1991 Civil Rights Act, the Age Discrimination in Employment Act, the 1990 Americans with Disabilities Act, and Executive Order 11246 require that companies pay close attention to the manner in which they treat protected class individuals. Section 706(G) of the Civil Rights Act allows a judge to order an affirmative action program if the employer is found guilty of intentional discrimination. We return to this issue since diversity goals are an important part of HR planning and recruitment for most large U.S. corporations and government in general.

Hiring to promote a diverse workforce will probably remain a complicated issue because of the confusing state of the EEO case law, particularly in situations in which organizations embark on some form of preferential treatment as a part of a voluntary diversity or affirmative action program. The most contentious situation is one in which the employer shows some form of preferential treatment toward members of one group when there is no proven history of discrimination, and no court-ordered requirement. What organizations can and cannot do under a voluntary affirmative action or diversity program is unclear.

The ambiguity and potential illegality seems to occur when preferential treatment is shown toward members of groups by placing at least some weight on a job candidate's gender or ethnicity. The controversy lies in whether such a characteristic should ever be considered and, if so, to what extent. The safest strategy for an organization today is to meet diversity goals by increasing the recruitment effort to attract women and minorities and, once the pool of candidates is established, ignore the gender or ethnicity of members of the pool and concentrate on only the job-related credentials of the candidates. The issue of diversity and affirmative action also comes up when companies are downsizing.

Recent out-of-court settlements with Texaco, Coca-Cola, Home Depot, Office Depot, and Circuit City have included provisions where managers would be accountable for meeting diversity goals. Yet these goals can be problematic when companies entertain downsizing options and consider maintaining the diversity goals they had attained when they conceptualize the downsizing steps. This was clearly illustrated in an age discrimination and Title VII lawsuit against the Ford Motor Company. The plaintiffs maintained preferences were shown to women and minorities during the downsizing.

Despite the legal confusion, organizations are continuing their efforts to promote diversity in their workforces. Walt Disney, for example, has minority hiring targets "at every level," according to Marc Pacala, Disney's general manager. Kentucky Fried Chicken maintains separate lists of minority candidates for its executive positions. Xerox continues with its "balanced workforce" program, which has measurable diversity hiring goals for all levels of management. In 2005, Wal-Mart began a diversity program that holds managers responsible (and pays them) for meeting "diversity" goals.

Despite the legal controversy, one survey found that 70 percent of Fortune 500 companies engage in race-based hiring while only 14 percent said they hired by merit alone.[5] The diversity issue is here to stay. Figure 5-4 presents some data and projections that illustrate trends in the U.S. workforce and U.S. businesses. Figure 5-5 presents a summary of research and implications for diversity initiatives. Specific recommendations are made to make diversity programs more effective.

The United States Office of Contract Compliance's Revised Order #4 (see www.OFCCP.gov) describes affirmative action activities and several actions an employer

FIGURE 5-4	The Growing Diversity of the U.S. Workforce and U.S. Work

- The fastest-growing labor force age group is 45–64 years of age.
- Workers aged 25–34 will decline by almost 3 million by 2008.
- As of 2005, over 50 percent of the U.S. workforce consisted of women, nonwhites, ethnic minorities, and immigrants.
- Women will constitute 48 percent of the labor force by 2008.
- Hispanics as a percentage of the U.S. workforce will be 14 percent by 2008 (estimated to be 19.5 million by 2008).
- African Americans as a percentage of the U.S. workforce will hold steady at 12 percent by 2008.
- Asians, Native Americans, Alaska Natives, and Pacific Islanders will constitute 6 percent of the U.S. workforce by 2008.
- In 2000, women held 43 percent of executive, managerial, and administrative jobs.
- As of 2000, Hispanics owned 1.2 million businesses and employed more than 1.3 million people.
- As of 2000, women made up 38 percent of U.S. business owners.
- As of 2000, African Americans owned over 800,000 businesses.
- Service jobs will constitute 88 percent of U.S. jobs by 2008.

Source: U.S. Bureau of Labor Statistics, Employment Projections, 1998–2008.

may take to "improve recruitment and increase the flow of minority or female applicants." One recommendation is to contact sources such as the Urban League, the Job Corp, and colleges with high minority enrollment. For example, most major U.S. corporations actively recruit at Florida A&M in Tallahassee, Florida, a predominantly African American university with an excellent business school.

Step Two: Labor Demand Forecast

In one survey, 24 percent of small businesses indicated that the "lack of qualified workers" posed a serious threat to their survival.[6] Many entrepreneurs in the survey indicated that labor shortages were preventing them from expanding their businesses and that such shortages made any type of planning more difficult. Over half of the respondents who had labor shortages had stepped up recruitment efforts and sought assistance from temporary employment agencies just to meet current demand for products or services. In the same year, over 30 percent of the largest U.S. companies actually reduced the size of their workforce despite a strong economy and, for many companies, record profits.

FIGURE 5-5	Research and Implications for Diversity

Gaps between Diversity Rhetoric and Research

1. Increased diversity does not necessarily improve the talent pool.
2. Increased diversity does not necessarily build commitment, improve motivation, or reduce conflict.
3. Increased group-level diversity does not necessarily lead to improved performance.
4. Increased diversity does not necessarily improve organizational performance.

Implications of Research and Theory

1. Benefits of diversity are contingent on the situation.
2. Successful diversity programs are based on meeting specific goals.
3. Diversity initiatives should be framed as strengths and opportunities with individual merit emphasized over numerical measures.
4. Diversity programs are more likely to be successful when employees identify with their work teams and organizations rather than with whichever diverse social groups they are drawn from.

Actions Organizations Can Take to Manage Diversity Effectively

1. Build senior management commitment and accountability.
2. Conduct a thorough needs assessment of people, jobs, and the organization.
3. Develop a well-defined diversity strategy tied to business results.
4. Emphasize team building and group-process training.
5. Establish metrics and evaluate the effectiveness of diversity initiatives.

Source: Adapted from M. E. A. Jayne and R. L. Dipboye, "Leveraging Diversity to Improve Business Performance: Research Findings and Recommendations for Organizations," *Human Resource Management* 43 (2004) pp. 409–424.

FIGURE 5-6	Advantages and Disadvantages of Forecasting Methods

Method		Advantages	Disadvantages
QUALITATIVE			
Delphi	• Experts go through several rounds of estimates • No face-to-face meetings	• More futuristic • Incorporates future plans	• May ignore data • Subjective • Time consuming
Nominal	• Face-to-face discussion	• Group exchanges facilitate plans	• May ignore data • Subjective
QUANTITATIVE			
Markov	• Incorporates past data for time period	• Data-driven	• Need adequate historical data
Regression	• Regress staffing needs onto key variables	• Data-driven • Actuarial • Learning curve	• Large and representative sample needed • Difficult to understand
Trend analysis	• Required staffing matched to desired outcomes	• Futuristic • Actuarial • Use business	• Many assumptions • Required factors

A forecast of labor demand derives from a projection of how business needs will affect HR. Each of the environmental forces discussed above is likely to exert pressure on HR demand—both in terms of the number and types of employees required, as well as the number and types of jobs utilized. The HR planner must anticipate these needs, add focus to an otherwise confusing array of possibilities, and set priorities for conflicting goals. Labor demand forecasting methods fall into two categories: qualitative and quantitative. As each category embraces certain assumptions, a combination of the two is preferred. Figure 5-6 presents a summary of the most common methods.

Qualitative Methods

The simplest method for projecting labor demand is a **centralized** approach in which the HR department examines the current business situation and determines staffing requirements for the rest of the firm. While this approach is simple, it can be inaccurate. A top-down approach assumes that the central HR office has an accurate understanding of the business as well as the needs of each unit or function. In large complex firms, these assumptions typically do not hold. A more preferred method involves a **decentralized** process[7] wherein each unit or functional manager subjectively derives his/her own staffing needs. These projections are aggregated to create an overall composite forecast for the company.

At jet engine maker Pratt & Whitney, for example, top management set a goal of 30 percent cost reduction for each functional unit after a study at competitors' overhead. Unit managers were asked to conduct job analysis of each job under their jurisdiction and, after analysis, to submit proposals for workload reduction and other cost-reduction options. A procedure was established to present the various reduction options including a method for the presentation of a rationale if the manager failed to make the 30 percent target reduction.

Other firms have experimented with formalized problem-solving methods such as the **Delphi technique** to minimize interpersonal and jurisdictional conflicts.[8] The Delphi technique avoids face-to-face group discussion by the use of an intermediary. Experts take turns at presenting a forecast statement and assumptions. The intermediary passes on the forecasts and assumptions to the others. Revisions are then made independently and anonymously by the experts. The intermediary then pools and summarizes the judgments and gives them to the experts. This process is continued until a consensus forecast emerges or until the intermediary concludes that more than one perspective must be presented. In comparison with linear regression analysis (discussed below), the Delphi technique has been shown to produce better one-year forecasts, but there can be difficulties in reaching consensus on complex problems.[9]

The full Delphi process can take considerable time. For example, the Gap, a clothing retailer, took over four months to forecast the number of buyers needed for the next year using a Delphi method. The use of networked computers can do much to reduce the time for Delphi forecasting.

The **nominal group technique** is similar to the Delphi method. However, experts join at a conference table and independently list their ideas in writing.[10] The experts then share their ideas with the group in turn. As the ideas are presented, a master list of the ideas is compiled so that everyone can refer back to them. The ideas are discussed and ranked by member vote.

Quantitative Methods

Quantitative methods are based on the assumption that the future is an extrapolation from the past. **Trend analysis** incorporates certain business factors (e.g., units produced, revenues) and a productivity ratio (e.g., employees per unit produced). For example, Pratt & Whitney calculated 16 jet engines per factory worker and almost 20 support, marketing, and management personnel for every 100 factory workers. Their external environmental scanning data indicated more favorable ratios for General Electric, Pratt's chief competitor. By projecting changes in the business factor and/or the productivity ratio, we can forecast changes in the labor demand. There are six steps in trend analysis:

1. Find the appropriate business factor that relates to the size of the workforce.
2. Plot the historical record of that factor in relation to the size of the workforce.
3. Compute the productivity ratio (average output per worker per year).
4. Determine the trend.
5. Make necessary adjustments in the trend, past and future.
6. Project to the target year.[11]

The use of the appropriate business factor is critical to the success of trend analysis.[12] Learning curves assume that the average number of units produced per employee will increase as more units are produced. Such an increase is expected because workers learn to perform their tasks more efficiently over time. Learning curves are evident in virtually all industries. For example, in the automotive industry, learning curves for new models improve by over 50 percent through the life of the model. At Pratt, the learning curve for one particular engine exceeded 60 percent from startup to the final production year. The business factor, of course, should be directly related to the essential purpose for the business. Universities typically use student enrollment by discipline, hospitals use patient-days, manufacturers typically use output needs, and retailers use sales adjusted by inventory.

Regression analysis uses information from the past relationship between the organization's employment level and some important success criterion known to be related to employment. For example, companies can establish a statistical relationship between sales or work output and level of employment. Such a relationship, however, also is influenced by the learning curve. Learning curves can be studied and used to make more accurate projections of future employment levels. More complicated quantitative methods can improve accuracy by incorporating operational constraints (e.g., budgets, mix of labor) into the models. Through this elaboration, it is possible to forecast demand under varying business scenarios. While our discussion of labor demand may suggest that planners attempt to establish a singular forecast, the outcome of this process is typically a set of potential scenarios. A scenario is a multifaceted portrayal of the mix of business factors in conjunction with the array of HR needs. As such, each scenario/forecast is an elaborate set of "if–then" statements; that is, "if" the business context presents us with scenario A, "then" our labor demand forecast would be B. Ideally, HR planning is as comprehensive as possible to provide leeway for a wide variety of business activities. Next, we discuss labor supply forecasts that reveal some of the constraints placed on business planning.

Step Three: Labor Supply Forecast

Whereas the labor demand forecast projects HR needs, the labor supply forecast projects resource availability. This step of HR planning is vital in that it conveys an inventory of the firm's current and projected competencies. This skill base sets an upper limit on the commitments and challenges the firm can undertake (all else being equal). From a problem-solving perspective, labor supply represents the "raw materials" available to address problems, threats, and opportunities. Supply forecasts are typically broken down into two categories: **external supply** and **internal supply.**

Internal Supply

Internal labor supply consists of those individuals and jobs currently available within the firm. Information on personnel is maintained in Human Resource Information Systems (HRIS). Although many systems are available, Peoplesoft is probably the most popular. They have a human capital management, Web-based HRIS system that includes a competency or skill inventory. Data from this system are used to make projections into the future based on current trends. These trends include not only the number and kinds of individuals in each job, but also the flow of employees in, through, and out of the organization. Specifically, a skills or competency inventory includes an assessment of the knowledge, skills, abilities, experience, and career aspirations of each of the present workers. This record should be updated frequently and should include changes such as new competencies, degree completions, and changed job duties.

These inventories also aid in the internal recruitment process. If these inventories are not updated, present employees may be overlooked for job openings within the organization.[13] This may result in increased search costs in addition to dissatisfaction among employees who were overlooked. Accordingly, internal supply forecasts must take into account the company's current practices pertaining to hiring, firing, transfer, promotion, development, and attrition. Performance appraisal and/or competency-based assessment should be a part of any personnel/skills inventory.

Succession planning and replacement charts also are used by some companies to identify individuals to fill a given slot if an incumbent should leave. These techniques are most useful for individual-level problems with short-term planning time horizons. There are over 300 computerized HRIS now available, many of which include skills inventories. The General Electric Company and Dunn and Bradstreet, for example, have used electronic data files on their employees for years as an aid for internal promotions and for required EEO reports. Pratt used an HRIS system to project successions, early retirements, future openings, and overstaffing problems.

Two of the most important concerns regarding the use of electronic databases for personnel are privacy rights and security problems. The latter issues can be handled with the right systems and software provisions. The privacy issue is much more difficult. Many states and many countries have privacy laws and regulations that may pertain to the use, content, and access of the HRIS.

More complicated transition models such as **Markov analysis** are used for long-range forecasts in large organizations. Markov analysis uses historical information from personnel movements of the internal labor supply to predict what will happen in the future. An estimate is made of the likelihood that persons in a particular job will remain in that job or be transferred, promoted, demoted, terminated, or retired using data collected over a number of years. Probabilities are used to represent the historical flow of personnel through the organization, a "transition matrix" is formed from these probabilities, and future personnel flows are estimated from this matrix.[14] Figure 5-7 presents Markov data from one division of Progressive Tool and Industries, one of the largest tool companies serving the automotive industry (Progressive designs and manufactures the tooling for assembly lines). The transition probability matrix presents percentages or probabilities of employee movement through four positions within the division. These data were retrieved from personnel records and averaged over a five-year period. The matrix shows that 70 percent of the assemblers remain in the position after one year with a turnover (quit or fired) rate of 20 percent. The matrix also shows that 80 percent of the more skilled machinist

FIGURE 5-7 Markov Analysis at Progressive Industries

	A	M	F	S	Exit
Assemblers (A)	.70	.10			.20
Machinists (M)	.05	.80	.10		.05
Foreman (F)		.10	.75	.05	.10
Supervision (S)			.05	.90	.05

	Staffing Levels	A	M	F	S	Exit
Assemblers (A)	250	175	25			50
Machinists (M)	120	6	96	12		6
Foremen (F)	40		4	30	2	4
Supervision (S)	20			1	18	1
Forecast		181	125	43	20	61

jobs are retained after one year with only a 5 percent turnover rate. These data were used by Progressive to plan their recruiting strategy based on their projected contracts. The data indicated a strong need to evaluate the assembler job to determine the causes of the high turnover rate and the need to concentrate recruiting at that level in anticipation of shortages of assemblers in the coming year when contracts were expected to expand.

Both Eaton Corporation[15] and Weyerhaeuser[16] have used Markov analysis successfully in their forecasts. However, two attempts at Corning Glass proved unsuccessful because the transition probabilities were unreliable.[17] A minimum of 50 people in each job of the transition matrix is recommended to ensure adequate reliability in forecasting. At Progressive, for example, projections for oversupplies of foremen were based on small numbers and proved to be relatively inaccurate. More research is needed on Markov analysis to determine the key variables affecting its accuracy. Variables such as unemployment rate, changes in competitor status, and business plans or customer demand that differ significantly from the situation when the probabilities were established will have a profound effect on the usefulness of the Markov projections for the future.

External Supply

External supply consists of those individuals in the labor force who are potential recruits of the firm (including those working for another firm). The skill levels being sought determine the relevant labor market. The entire country (or world) may be the relevant labor market for highly skilled jobs whereas for unskilled jobs, the relevant labor market is usually (but not always) the local community. Determining the relevant labor market also will determine what type of recruiting approach should be used. Several governmental and industrial reports (e.g., Bureau of Labor Statistics, Public Health Service, Northwestern Endicott Lindquist Report) regularly forecast the supply of labor and make estimates of available workers in general job and demographic categories. These forecasts are also extrapolations into the future based on current trends.

What Is the Immigration Reform and Control Act (IRCA) of 1986?   The labor pool should be a legal pool. While there is a global market for many jobs today, some jobs just have to be done in person (i.e., the worker is in the United States). The IRCA requires that every U.S. employer, no matter how small, not hire or continue to employ aliens who are not legally authorized to work here. In 2004, it is estimated that the U.S. Border Patrol intercepted over 900,000 illegal immigrants. Another 700,000 are thought to have made it through into the United States. For the most part, these people are flooding over mostly our southern borders to work in the United States illegally. Employers are supposed to verify the identity and work authorization of every new employee and to sign an I-9 form attesting to the legal status

of each worker. Financial penalties for noncompliance can be harsh (from $100 to $1,000 per employee) and criminal penalties are possible. The use of illegals is rampant in some American industries as enforcement of the law is limited and criminal penalties are rarely enforced. Law-abiding companies in some industries such as construction can have difficulty competing on price against the cheaters. One roofing-business owner in Florida reported that he couldn't adequately staff his business without illegals and that he certainly couldn't compete in bidding jobs without low-wage illegals. "In addition, he reported that he "saves a ton" on worker's compensation expenses when he uses "illegals."

There are major problems with the current I-9 form system. President Bush has recommended the implementation of a mandatory electronic verification program for I-9 information and worker eligibility.

What Are the Immigration Options for U.S. Employers?   Another employment option for U.S. employers is legally importing workers through work visas. The H-1B visa program allows employers to hire highly skilled or specialized foreign workers for temporary jobs in the United States. The program is designed for skilled workers in high demand and was capped at 58,200 for 2006. An employer must file a labor condition application with the Department of Labor attesting to several items, including payment of prevailing wages for the position and the working conditions offered. Under current law, an alien can only be on H-1B status for six years at a time (go to http://uscis.gov for more detail). The legal limit of H-1B visas was reached for 2006 before the fiscal year even began.

Employers can also hire foreign workers to temporarily work in the United States or to receive training. Employers must file a petition for temporary foreign employees. There are many categories of temporary workers and the categories vary by the maximum time such an employee may stay. One controversial program for temporary employees is the Intracompany Transferee **L-1 classification.** The purpose of these visas is to allow foreign companies to transfer employees into the United States. The number of these visas has risen in recent years. Unlike the H-1B visa, employers do not have to pay L-1 workers prevailing wages. Aliens with "specialized knowledge" or managerial responsibilities who are transferred to the United States by a foreign employer to work for the parent company in the United States qualify for L-1 visa status.

While the United States Citizenship and Immigration Service has specific definitions for "specialized knowledge," "managerial," and "executive" classes, there are accusations that the L-1 program has been abused to the detriment of the American worker. (There may have been changes in this law since publication of this book.) At present, L-1 workers can stay in the United States for a maximum of seven years. Critics charge that L-1 visas are now used by foreign companies to bring workers into the United States who then do contract work for American companies, at times to replace American workers. There have even been accusations that American workers trained the L-1 contract workers before the Americans were fired. In 2005 there were 135,000 L-1 visa holders in the United States. However, there is little research on whether American workers really lost jobs because of the program.

Step Four: Gap Analysis

Gap analysis is used to reconcile the forecasts of labor demand and supply. At a minimum, this process identifies potential shortages or surpluses of employees, skills, and competencies. In addition, however, planners can review several environmental forecasts with alternative supply and demand forecasts in order to determine the firm's preparedness for different business scenarios in the context of business objectives. From a problem-solving perspective, gap analysis is used to pair up potential strengths and opportunities with solutions in order to evaluate how the firm might attack the future. This decision-making process involves (1) search for alternative solutions, (2) evaluation of alternatives, and (3) choice of solutions.

Is There an Optimal Way to Downsize or Restructure?

This type of gap analysis has been used in employee downsizing or reengineering programs for a majority of the Fortune 1,000, even some of the most successful and profitable. More than 75 percent of the Fortune 1,000 firms have implemented downsizing programs since 2000.[18] The evidence on the effects of downsizing is mixed. Strategic downsizing and restructuring can clearly be effective in improving a firm's position but strategic downsizing is more than just "cost reduction." Figure 5-8 presents a summary of the research evidence.

One expert echoes the latest research showing that restructuring by downsizing does not necessarily make a company more profitable. In an excellent book entitled

FIGURE 5-8   Summary of Research on Downsizing and Outcome Variables

1. No consistent relationship between downsizing and postdownsizing financial performance.
2. Other cost-saving measures may be more effective (e.g., attrition).
3. Even when payroll is reduced, restructuring charges may offset benefit.
4. Costs to replace downsized employees can be high and wipe out temporary reduction in payroll.
5. Costs connected with negative effect on survivors should be incorporated into calculation of effects.
6. Net effect of downsizing on dollar costs is uncertain.
7. Layoffs may depress post-layoff accounting returns.
8. Large sample studies indicate a general negative effect of layoff announcements on market-adjusted equity values.
9. Reductions framed as restructuring or consolidation tend to realize positive response in equity value.
10. Early retirement programs tend to realize positive response.

Source: W. McKinley, J. Zhao, and K. G. Rust, "A Sociocognitive Interpretation of Organizational Downsizing," *Academy of Management Review* 25 (2000), pp. 227–243.

"Responsible Restructuring," Professor Wayne Cascio presents a strategy for optimal restructuring.[19] Figure 5-9 presents Dr. Cascio's prescriptions for enhancing the effectiveness of restructuring and downsizing. He makes a convincing argument that his approach can be an opportunity to focus on the most important elements (and people) of the organization where it has (or could have) a sustained competitive advantage.[20]

Most companies implemented downsizing as a reaction to loss of market share, increased competition, or lower productivity GM and Ford are examples here. Most also looked at downsizing as simply a workforce reduction process rather than a restructuring or reengineering of jobs in the context of corporate strategy or planning. As one CEO put it, "We lost the organization in the process . . . we

FIGURE 5-9   Enhancing the Effectiveness of Employment Restructuring and Downsizing

1. Carefully consider the rationale behind employment downsizing.
2. Consider the virtues of stability.
3. Before making any final decisions about downsizing, executives should make their concerns known to employees and seek their input.
4. Top management should lead by example, and use downsizing as a last resort.
5. If employment downsizing is unavoidable, be sure that employees perceive the process as fair and make decisions in a consistent manner.
6. Communicate regularly and in a variety of ways in order to keep everyone abreast of new developments and information.
7. Give survivors a reason to stay and prospective new hires a reason to join.
8. Train employees and their managers in the new ways of operating.
9. Examine carefully all management systems in light of the change of strategy or environment facing the firm.

Source: Adapted from W. F. Cascio and P. Wynn, "Managing a Downsizing Process," *Human Resource Management* 43 (2004), pp. 425–436.

basically fired people and called it re-engineering . . . we jumped on the re-engineering bandwagon without understanding its destination." Another CEO was even more disillusioned with job cutting posing as reengineering. "We cut costs, ruined quality and eliminated more customers than employees. . . . Re-engineering has replaced strategic thinking around here."

The most effective reengineering efforts are an opportunity to create or improve the company's competitive advantage through restructuring, overhead reduction, and more effective performance management with constant focus on the core competencies of the organization and the current and/or future customer base. The process can create a frame of mind that could be sustained after the major downsizing effort is complete. The idea is to create and maintain a "lean and mean" mentality in management that would be sustained long after the specific downsizing goals were met and always in the context of meeting (or exceeding) customer requirements with measurement criteria that best define this customer focus. Reengineering that focuses on the core competencies of the organization and the core business and its customers can help support a clear and compelling organizational strategy. But as strategy expert Darrell Rigby puts it, "Cutting people whose experience is vital to the creation of customer value will never create superior results."

Over 100,000 IBM employees have taken early retirement since their first major downsizing effort in 1988. While the program helped IBM maintain its company policy of never laying off a single full-time employee, IBM lost some of its best employees who opted for one of the attractive termination programs. One major downsizing program focused on offering early retirement to only noncritical employees, terminating marginal employees for cause, and offering less attractive transfer options to those who were not needed in their current jobs. One of their biggest problems in achieving their downsizing goals, however, was their performance appraisal system, which did not provide enough useful data to take performance-based actions.

There are many approaches to downsizing and some may be required due to union agreements. AT&T "selected" current employees for the new positions based on new job descriptions created by the overhaul of their divisions. The skilled-based résumés and the performance appraisals of the "applicants" for the new jobs were assessed in the context of the labor demands projected based on the new corporate strategy. Voluntary buyouts were one part of the options AT&T used to close the gap in their supply and demand for labor.

One survey of 1,600 chief executives and senior managers by Bain and Company, a Boston-based strategy firm, found that executives viewed a customer focus as the framework for downsizing.[21] This focus included increasing an understanding of customer needs, increasing the customer base, and increasing product and service quality. Of course, the relationship between labor costs and pricing is almost always on the top of the list in terms of customer focus. But the list must be longer than just cutting payroll to save money.

Downsizing that is not done in the context of this customer focus will merely exchange old problems with new ones. Many firms that have gone through radical downsizing in recent years have come to realize how important the connection is between customer needs and any form of organizational restructuring, including downsizing.

As indicated in Figure 5-9, some of the problems associated with downsizing (or rightsizing) can be minimized with good planning and strategy. In addition to examining performance data and redeployment options, such planning may include *outplacement* services for employees who have lost their jobs. Outplacement can involve job coaching, résumé preparation, placement services, and interview training. Every AT&T employee who was not selected for the restructured company was given access to a resource center that provided job counseling and access to job postings within the company and at other companies. Such outplacement services are now available in Europe and even in Japan where Japanese companies are faced with a need to downsize as well. It is generally believed that offering outplacement services to employees who have lost their jobs will reduce the probability of a lawsuit, such as a claim of age discrimination. (There is actually no definitive study on the subject.)

Professor Cascio asks, "Could it be that there is virtue in stability?" He reports that 80 of the 100 companies that made *Fortune*'s 2002 list of the "100 Best Companies to Work For" avoided layoffs in 2001; 47 of them had some form of policy barring layoffs. And remember there is a relationship between that list of the "best companies" to work for and actual corporate financial performance.[22]

These prescriptions for effective (and very limited) downsizing do not necessarily rule out strategic termination. A strong argument can be made that having the very best people in the most important strategic positions is a key to strategy execution. Former GE CEO Jack Walsh often talks about having "A" players in the strategic "A" positions and that having "C" players in such positions can kill strategic execution. HR planning should emphasize the placement of the most qualified individuals in the most important positions. Strategic planning may also include a careful look at and action regarding those employees who could be replaced with more effective individuals.

What Are Some Alternative or Additional Solutions?

As discussed above, in HRP there are likely to be multiple scenarios that are worthy of consideration. Environmental scanning and labor forecasts identify a range of possible options. At this stage, the range of possibilities can be increased by seeking input from executives, line managers, employees, customers, and consultants in a "brainstorming" process. A qualitative approach such a *Delphi* can be used at this point as well.

As part of their HR planning process and after a thorough job analysis, pharmaceutical giant Upjohn asks line managers to answer four basic questions:

1. How does each job relate to the strategic plan of the work unit?
2. Are there alternatives to a full-time job that should be considered to accomplish the same objectives (e.g., temporary workers, part-time employees, independent contractors, job sharing, telecommuting, employee leasing, consultants, overtime)?
3. What are the projected costs of each job?
4. What specific impact will the job have on critical and clearly defined effectiveness criteria?

What Is the Role of Temporary Employment?

More and more companies have been asking similar questions regarding their workforce and coming up with rather creative answers. One of the strongest trends in this country is the use of creative labor arrangements. Temporary employment, part-time workers, telecommuters, job sharing, and employee leasing are among the most popular solutions to labor cost control and fluctuating demand. With employee leasing, a leasing company assumes complete responsibility for the employee, including pay and benefits. The major disadvantage for the employer is a loss in some control over the employee. This loss of control, of course, could affect the effectiveness of employees' performance, which could have a direct impact on the customer. There are few studies that compare the performance, productivity, absence rates, or any other criteria of permanent versus leased employees.

Another significant trend in creative HR planning is the use of permanent part-time employees.[23] For years, IBM's policy of maintaining a 10 percent part-time workforce enabled the company to maintain a labor pool in line with the business cycle and to preserve their sacrosanct policy of no layoffs. They have now increased the percentage to 20 percent and outsourced many functions, including a large share of their HRM functions. Many other companies, particularly in service, are now following suit. Ryder Trucks, UPS, and Wal-Mart are among the major companies now maintaining a sizable percentage of their workforce with part-time status. According to the Bureau of Labor Statistics, 33 percent of the U.S. workforce worked part-time in 2004. Two-thirds of this group were women.

While working parents consider part-time employment a good thing, women's groups such as the National Organization for Women (NOW) decry the trend as fostering a marginal employment policy characterized by low wages and no benefits. But companies that have adopted policies of permanent part-time staff for many job classifications report substantial cost savings and relatively little difficulty in recruiting and retaining a capable staff.

What Is Job Sharing?

Job sharing divides a single job between two or more workers. American Express has adopted this policy for their customer service representatives and reduced their employee turnover rate and recruitment costs significantly.

More employers also are hiring temporary help, particularly in clerical data processing and industrial jobs. The National Association of Temporary Services reported a growth rate in temporary employment in excess of 30 percent. While employers generally report that temporaries are typically hired for emergencies, an increasing number of companies report considerable cost savings as well with "temps" judged to be as productive as permanent employees.[24]

Technology has facilitated job sharing. Projects no longer have to stop at the end of the American workday. This is especially evident in the IT industry. Americans finish their workday and then turn over a project to computer programmers in India or Dubai who work while the Americans sleep. Needless to say, this 24-hour attention helps companies hit deadlines.

What Is Telecommuting?

Technology enables work to be done from almost anywhere. *The Wall Street Journal* reported that 19 million Americans telecommuted as of 2001. The number is surely much higher today as traffic becomes more problematic, the cost of gas continues to rise, and telecommunications technology improves. Telecommuting is an alternative work arrangement allowing workers to work at home or in some other location other than the employer's physical premises. When properly implemented, the evidence of its effectiveness and efficiency is quite strong. Companies are able to attract and retain effective workers with considerable cost savings.[25]

Is There a Conflict between Downsizing and Diversity Goals?

One of the more complicated issues regarding a major downsizing is the potential conflict between downsizing efforts and programs aimed at promoting workforce diversity. Ciba-Geigy, the pharmaceutical company, had a diversity challenge as a part their retention process. In the assessment of employee performance, managers were asked to value a diverse organization by "proactively considering diversity in this process." After the initial retention decisions were made, "HR challengers will review retention decisions with respect to diversity . . . and to test for adverse impact." HR compared diversity data after the initial retention decisions to predownsizing data. According to documents in a lawsuit, "the result of this analysis may lead to a possible further challenge." Several older Ciba-Geigy employees who were fired maintained that the "diversity challenges" resulted in discrimination against older workers since they were not a part of the diversity programs. Given the current state of EEO law regarding preferential treatment, if the plaintiffs could show that race or gender were actually considered in the retention process and that this consideration affected the status of older workers, would the older workers prevail in an ADEA case? This is a tough call and probably would depend on the process that was followed after the internal audit. If the plaintiff could show that performance ratings were simply changed because of statistical adverse impact and changed in such a way as to avoid the adverse impact and that this process changed the status of some workers over the age of 39, the older workers probably would prevail.

Organizations that undergo downsizing while attempting to maintain any diversity or affirmative action accomplishments should try to avoid showing preferential treatment on the basis of any protected class characteristic. It is possible (and advisable) to actually evaluate past performance or even potential performance without even considering a protected class characteristic. While conducting adverse impact analysis such as hypothetical violations of the 80 percent rule is certainly recommended, violations of the guidelines should lead to a serious evaluation of the job relatedness of the decision-making system, not the simple adjustment in ratings as a consequence of a protected class characteristic in order to avoid a violation of the 80 percent rule.

Step Five: Action Programming

Action programming is the final step of HRP that takes the adopted solution and lays out the sequence of events that need to be executed to realize the plan. In the previous four steps of HR planning, the task was to derive a solution that best addresses the issues identified through environmental scanning and labor forecasts in the context of the strategic plan. The purpose of action programming is to make certain that those decisions become reality. In general, there are two aspects of programming: internal and external.

Internal Programming

Many of the solutions in HRP rest on actions inside the firm with the current workforce. For routine issues, in particular, bureaucratic adjustments in HR practices can be easily programmed internally (e.g., job design/assignments). GM's action regarding its engineers is one such example. In addition, for some uncertain areas, adaptive adjustments such as training, career planning, promotions, and compensation design can be made internally.

These are the adaptive requirements many companies follow because of labor shortages in key areas. Taking a closer look at organizational design around changing technologies is one such example.

External Programming

Other solutions in HRP require going outside the firm to interact with constituencies in the environment (e.g., labor unions, competitors, etc.). In particular, when plans require drastically different competencies from what employees currently possess and/or the time frame for change is quite short, the firm likely will need to recruit from the outside labor market. Motorola's experience with the coordinated efforts of U.S. and Indian programmers is one example of reacting to new time frames.

Step Six: Control and Evaluation

Control and evaluation monitor the effectiveness of human resource plans over time. Deviations from the plans are identified and actions are taken. The extent to which human resource objectives have been met is measured by the feedback from various outcomes. It has been suggested that, essentially, long-range planning activities require the attainment of short-run objectives. Examples include performance or productivity data, turnover costs, workforce reduction effects from early retirement programs, break-even costs of new hires, and analysis of costs of recruits compared to the training and development costs of existing employees. Obviously, actual staffing levels compared to projected levels should be evaluated for accuracy. Doing evaluations such as cost–benefit analysis makes it easier to determine whether long-run planning objectives will be met.

The issue of evaluation of planning can be considered along with the evaluation of recruitment efforts since the criteria used for the evaluations are often the same. We will discuss this later in the chapter. The critical consideration here should be the identification of the vital measurement criteria, which will provide for an assessment of the HR planning implementation in the context of the business strategy. Regarding outsourcing and employee leasing, the most fundamental criterion should be cost savings but always in the context of meeting customer requirements.

When HR planning involves adding to the labor force, the organization must rely on the recruitment function to meet its employment needs. The whole point of the planning exercise is to provide the optimal number and quality of employees to meet internal and external customer requirements. If the gap analysis determines that employees are needed, that is where recruitment comes in. We will deal with this vital HR function next.

THE RECRUITMENT FUNCTION: PUTTING HRP INTO ACTION

Moving from HRP to recruitment is essentially a process of translating broad strategies into operational tasks. The major responsibility for this process typically rests within the HRM department, although most tasks are shared with line managers. While HR managers are responsible for determining recruitment policy, ensuring EEO compliance, training, and evaluating the recruiters, many organizations such as Oracle, IBM, and Procter & Gamble actively involve line managers and employees as recruiters. As mentioned above, conflict between HR and line managers can occur when their priorities diverge. For example, line managers may be more concerned about filling a position quickly (i.e., when the new employee is needed) while HR managers may be more concerned about affirmative action guidelines or complying with EEO regulations. Their goals should be the same: hiring the most qualified person(s) when needed and without violating any laws or regulations.

Figure 5-10 presents a model of the organizational recruitment process.

Recruitment, Other HR Activities, and Organizational Attractiveness

Recall the statement earlier about the interdependent nature of recruiting with other HR activities and the reputation of the organization. Decisions regarding employee testing,

work policies and programs, compensation, benefits and corporate image all can have an impact on recruiting. One large retailer required high-level managerial candidates to travel to the company headquarters (for some, over 2,000 miles) to go through a two-day assessment center that was only offered at headquarters. Because of these requirements, many experienced managers who were working for other companies dropped out of the pool of candidates because they didn't have the time to commit to a two-day assessment center with two additional days of travel to the national headquarters. As another example, the 2,900-room Opryland Hotel in Nashville had difficulty attracting housekeepers, kitchen helpers, and laundry workers. They put in a seven-day-a-week child care center and a bus service to transport workers. The two new employee benefits increased the number of applicants by 35 percent.

A company institutes a comprehensive drug-testing program that includes random drug testing with no probable cause for all employees. The company does not consider how the broader pool of candidates might view this and merely assumes that the policy will have an impact only by deterring applicants who would be most likely to use drugs. Another company installs a binding arbitration policy for all employee–employer disputes. A new employee must sign off on the policy as a condition of employment. Once again, the company does not consider the effect of this new policy on the ability to recruit and retain the most qualified applicants. Another company decides to reduce indirect compensation by reducing health benefits for new employees and increasing the premium. They have

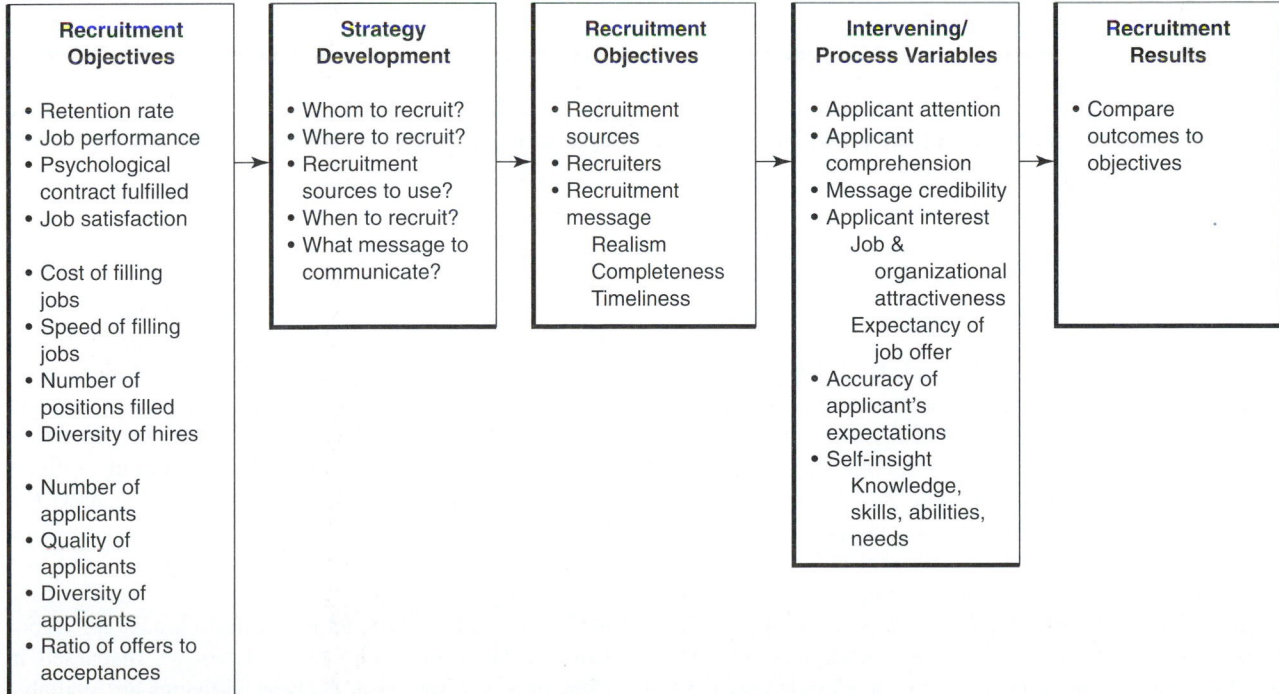

Figure 5-10   A Model of the Organizational Recruitment Process

Source: Breaugh and Starke, *Journal of Management* "Research on Employee Recruitment: So Many Studies, So Many Questions," Vol. 26. p. 408. Copyright (2000) by Sage Publications. Reprinted by permission.

no idea what the change in policy will do to their ability to recruit. They find out later that recruitment costs have gone up along with the rate of offer rejections. They finally conduct an actual cost–benefit study of their change in policy and discover that in fact the company lost money because of the interactive effect of the policy on staffing and the retention of valuable employees. Recruitment, selection, and personnel policies are indeed interdependent.

Of course, recruitment and human resource planning should be done with the assumption that consideration be given to where the work is performed. Technology now allows employers to consider many more options for getting the job done. Along with telecommuting, as discussed earlier, more companies are now turning to offshoring and the outsourcing of work, particularly work that is strategically less important and can be done for less.

"Geography is history" says Raman Roy, chairman of Wipro Spectramind, one of India's fast growing customer service companies.[26] Over 400,000 American tax returns were prepared in India in 2005, most of them by SurePrep, headquartered in Bangalore. Indian tax preparers are paid between $300 and $400 per month versus $3,000 to $4,000 per month in the United States. In 2005, SurePrep did work for more than 150 American accounting firms. Morgan Stanley now has Indian stock analysts and Dell sends customer calls to India (estimated savings of around 50 percent on compensation). Says Jerry Rao, Indian entrepreneur, "Any activity where we can digitize and decompose the value chain, and move the work around, will get moved around." Even when you place an order at the window of a McDonald's today, you may be interacting with an Indian in Bangalore. It is estimated that 400,000 American jobs went to China, Russia, and India between 2001 and 2004. See again Figure 5-3 for offshoring "attractiveness" scores by country.

For jobs with high turnover rates, as stated earlier, consideration should also be given to telecommuting where a customer call "center" isn't a center at all. When you call JetBlue to make a reservation, 100 percent of the time you're talking to a Utah housewife working from her home. There is growing evidence that turnover rates and overall costs can be sharply reduced with this approach to work.

Recruitment can clearly be made harder or easier by a whole host of factors, as we said above. The state of the economy, the supply and demand for particular KASOCs or competencies, and HR policies and practices are all important. Of course, the attractiveness of the organization from the perspective of potential job candidates is also critical. This attractiveness factor is also related to many factors that go into an organization's reputation, as we have said. As discussed in Chapter 1, an organization's reputation in terms of its effectiveness or as a "socially responsible" employer can clearly affect recruitment. Google may now be the leader in IT applications because of their reputation. Even Microsoft is losing employees to Google perhaps

because of their upstart rival's recent accomplishments (and stock price!). No doubt an organization's reputation as a great place to work with an optimistic outlook and a stable history, as a company with great potential for growth, or as a socially responsible company will make a recruiter's job a whole lot easier. Have you noticed how many ads are on television now extolling the virtues of Wal-Mart as a great place to work and how much Wal-Mart is doing for the local community? This PR campaign is probably to some extent a response to the negative news about Wal-Mart in these same areas. Obviously, Wal-Mart wants its reputation to attract and keep good workers and, of course, great (and many) customers.

The Three Essential Steps for Recruitment Planning

Based on the gap analysis, an organization should have a fairly good idea of their overall recruitment or downsizing needs. This information must be operationalized and communicated to others who will be taking the action. Three essential steps for translating future needs into specific operational terms are (1) work analysis, (2) time lapse data, and (3) yield ratio.

Work Analysis

Recruiters and HR planners rely on two aspects of work analysis information to identify the critical skills for which they will recruit. First, job descriptions provide an outline of the responsibilities, duties, and tasks to be performed by the potential employee. Second, the job specifications outline the knowledge, skills, and abilities required of the applicant. In general, the more specific the recruitment design, especially in terms of job specifications, the more efficient and effective it is, assuming of course that the specificity is important for the job. Poorly designed recruiting is more expensive and takes longer.

For example, job specifications are sometimes written that are not essential for the job and are sometimes unnecessary and costly. One retailer stipulated three years' experience as a store manager in order to be eligible for consideration as a store manager for the company. The VP of operations drew up specifications unilaterally and based on his "sense" of what was required in the job. The result was a small pool of applicants, higher advertising costs, and fewer females and minorities who were eligible for consideration.

Work analysis information that accurately reflects the requirements needed for the job can have a direct impact on the effectiveness of any recruitment and planning effort. Work analysis information can also be used in a downsizing effort as jobs are restructured based on the new organizational structure or individuals are repositioned based on a new strategy. As we discussed in Chapter 4, specific work analysis strategies are available for writing job descriptions and specifications based on an organization's competitive strategy.

Work analysis can also determine where work should be done for maximum efficiency. Office Depot cut 900 call center jobs and then contracted with Willow CSN Corp. in Miramar, Florida, to provide the "home-based" service to customers. Technology now allows for telecommuting where most (or all) work is performed at home. Alston and Byrd, an Atlanta-based law firm, allows lawyers considerable latitude in determining when to go into the office and when to stay home and work. With their entire law library now online and many other communication vehicles available, lawyers don't miss a beat on productivity and they avoid the horrendous Atlanta traffic.

The need for accurate job descriptions and job specifications is particularly critical for Web-based recruiting of any kind. There are numerous examples of Internet recruiting that can quickly get you an overwhelming number of résumés, the vast majority of which are irrelevant to the jobs you are trying to fill.

While HRP provides the number of jobs needed and job analysis provides the requirements of the jobs, management must know when to start a recruiting process and how extensive the search should be. This is where time lapse data and yield ratios come in.

Time Lapse Data

Time lapse data (TLD) provide the average time that elapses between points of decision making in recruiting. For example, if the recruitment plan calls for newspaper advertisements, records may reflect that the job is ultimately filled an average of two months after publication of the ad. Thus, the ad should be placed at least two months before the job has to be filled. Data also may be available on the time lapse between interviews and offers, and offers and acceptances. When combined with yield ratios, the TLD can provide useful information for planning a recruitment effort.

Time lapses have been reduced for some companies taking advantage of the automated recruiting options available through the World Wide Web. Most of the country's largest newspapers now have job listings services on the Internet. Careerjournal.com is an online job board that allows employers to post positions on multiple Web sites. Currently, there are over 150 sites that "partner" to cover many job specialties.

Yield Ratios or Percentage

A yield ratio for any recruiting step reflects the number of candidates available at a step compared to a previous step. For example, a series of newspaper ads may result in 1,000 applications for employment. Of these 1,000 applications, 100 are judged to meet some minimum qualifications, (to be in the "ball game" so to speak). Thus, the yield "ratio" at this initial stage is 10 percent. Of the group of 100 candidates, 50 accepted invitations to be interviewed (yield ratio is 50 percent for this stage); of the 50, 10 were given job offers (20 percent yield ratio).

Assuming the labor market has not changed dramatically from when the yield ratios were derived and that similar methods of recruiting are to be used (e.g., advertising in the same papers, using a Web service or a headhunter), the ratios can be used as the basis for planning future recruitment efforts. By going backwards from the calculated yield ratios, the recruiter can estimate how many applicants will be necessary in order to fill a certain number of positions. The recruiter then can adjust the recruiting effort accordingly with more (or less) advertising, more (or fewer) trips to college campuses, more "Monster" ads, and so on.

The use of time lapse data and yield ratios is another area where there is a wide gap between what academic texts and scholarly research recommend and the extent to which such data are collected in organizations to drive future recruitment planning. While almost every scholar on the subject recommends a recruitment evaluation process that includes yield ratios to assist decision makers in efficient recruitment planning, few companies actually collect these data as a part of a recruitment evaluation.

Recruitment is a never-ending process for many jobs where there are critical shortages of highly specialized skills. As we discussed above, there are tight labor markets for many occupations and indications that markets will get even tighter, particularly for knowledge-intensive jobs. Many hospitals recruit for nurses on a continuous basis because they are constantly understaffed. Advertisements for nurses today often promise not only high pay, but more of a say in their jobs and hospital management, bonuses of $3,000 or more for signing up, bonuses for staying on the job a certain length of time, flexible work schedules, child care, and free tuition for advanced courses. Some employers even offer maid service and free housing for nurses who are willing to work at various locations based on demand. Many high-tech manufacturing firms recruit for engineers and computer programmers year round as well.

Some companies have difficulty filling even the unskilled positions.[27] The fast-food industry, for example, beset by turnover rates in excess of 200 percent (two incumbents for every job in one year), often advertises and takes applications for counter personnel throughout the year for many locations. Many companies have mobile recruiting units that visit high schools and shopping malls to solicit applications. McDonald's cooperates with the American Association of Retired Persons to attract senior citizens for hard-to-fill counter-personnel positions. Burger King offered a $6,000 signing bonus in 2005 to attract workers back to New Orleans after Hurricane Katrina. AMC theaters also concentrates on senior citizens for its ticket takers and counter personnel. Chemical Bank in New York must interview 50 applicants to find one who can be successfully trained as a teller. In general, the changing demographics of our workforce and the changing nature of the demands of the work indicate that recruitment will be more challenging in the years to come. Despite 5.2 percent unemployment in 2005, many companies still reported difficulties in recruiting unskilled workers in many geographical areas.

The Two Sources of Recruiting: Internal and External

There are two general sources of recruiting: internal and external. Internal recruiting seeks applicants for positions from among the ranks of those currently employed. With the exception of entry-level positions, most organizations try to fill positions with current employees. Figure 5-11 summarizes the advantages and disadvantages of each.

Advantages and Disadvantages of Internal and External Recruitment

There are several major advantages of internal recruiting. First of all, it is considerably less costly than external recruiting. Second, organizations typically have a better knowledge of internal applicants' skills and abilities than that which can be acquired of candidates in an external recruiting effort. Through performance and competency assessment, decision makers typically will have much more extensive knowledge of internal candidates and thus make more valid selection decisions. The third advantage to internal recruiting is that an organizational policy of promoting from within can enhance organizational commitment and job satisfaction. These variables have been shown to be correlated with lower employee turnover rates and higher productivity. A policy of internal recruiting is one component of **high-performance work systems (HPWS),** which we introduced in Chapter 1. Companies that practice internal recruiting are more likely to be successful financially than companies that rely on

external recuiting for top talent. Ted LeVino, senior vice president at GE, argues that their internal recruiting policy has fostered stability and continuity in the managerial ranks of the company. Bank of America has a policy in which newly hired college grads receive a career planning guide that describes the typical timetable for progression within the company for their best employees.

One of the great advantages of detailed job analysis is that succession planning programs can be developed so that management (and employees) can have a good idea of the sources for internal recruiting. At Ford, for example, associates complete a competency-based job analysis describing their current knowledge and skills required for their present job and what knowledge or skills they would like to acquire. These responses are then linked to particular vacancies within the company, descriptions of which already have been completed by managers of the vacant positions.

There are disadvantages to internal recruiting as well. Continuity is not always such a good thing. If the organization has decided to change its business strategy, for example, entrenched managers are probably not the "change masters" you want. One theory of internal recruiting is that the approach simply promulgates the old ways of doing things; that creative problem solving may be hindered by the lack of new blood or a sort of "managerial inbreeding." However, there is no solid research that supports the belief that internal recruiting stifles creativity and innovative thinking, and one recent study at a Fortune 500 company found just the opposite.

One well-documented managerial blunder is to irrationally stay committed to an initial course of action, particularly if you initiated the action. Irrational commitment, misdirected persistence, and escalation bias are more likely when internal versus external recruiting is emphasized, especially if the internal candidates were personally involved in a particular course of action.[28] For example, one U.S. company faced new competition to an established product line from a foreign competitor. The senior managers, all of whom had been at the company for at least 15 years and had great ownership in the product and how it was marketed, agreed to deal with the new competition as they had always dealt with competition— by competing on price. This manner was unfortunately out of step with the upstart competitor's strategy, which included competing on price. The result was a disaster for the company with over 30 percent of their workforce laid off because of a loss of market share. A new manager might have been better able to conduct a more rational analysis of the situation.

Entrenched managers sometimes have difficulty understanding that time and money already invested are "sunk costs" and should therefore not be considered in future planning. Managers who had something to do with a present course of action seem to have more difficulty in understanding this.

Figure 5-11	**Advantages and Disadvantages of Internal versus External Recruiting**	
Recruitment	Advantages	Disadvantages
Internal	Better assessment of candidates	Creates vacancies
	Reduces training time	Stifles diversity
	Faster	Insufficient supply of candidates
	Cheaper	
	Motivates employees	
External	Increases diversity	Expensive
	Facilitates growth	Slower
	Can save training time	Less reliable data
	New/novel problem solving	Stifles upward movement of personnel

Some organizations complain of unit raiding where divisions may compete for the same people. GM, for example, reported raiding of the best design engineers from one division by another despite an agreement that such recruiting was not in the best interests of the company. Raiding is quite common in universities for clerical positions where position descriptions can be written in such a way that a secretary can move to another department because the new position pays more.

A third possible disadvantage of internal recruiting is that politics probably have a greater impact on internal recruiting and selection than does external recruiting. Thus, while more job-related information may be known about internal candidates, personnel decisions involving internal candidates are more likely to be affected by the political agendas of the decision makers and are also more likely to be contested legally than external staffing decisions.

One survey of high-level federal government managers revealed that the easiest way to get rid of a troublesome employee was to evaluate that employee so positively that the employee would be more likely to get an employment opportunity out of the unit (either within or outside of the same agency). The "Peter Principle" states that we rise to our level of incompetence. This survey found that, at least in the federal government, once we reach our level of incompetence, our boss may actually try to get us moved up a notch above our level of incompetence in order to get rid of us with the least amount of paperwork. In other words, things may be even worse than the "Peter Principle."[29] HR managers must constantly monitor very tightly defined job descriptions or job specifications. While this may constitute well-focused recruiting based on precisely what the organization requires, it also can mean that a position has been "wired" for an internal candidate. An effective HR manager should be capable of making the distinction. The manager writing the job description and job specifications should be required to stipulate why highly specific credentials or areas of expertise are required in the context of the organization's or unit's strategic plan.

Internal recruiting programs should be carefully integrated with other HR functions. Effective HR succession planning, job analysis, personnel selection, and performance appraisal are all important for an effective system that can fill required positions with the most qualified personnel in the shortest amount of time. Administrators of such programs should be knowledgeable about EEO legislation and litigation as numerous lawsuits have been filed related to internal recruiting and placement decisions. (Recall the huge Wal-Mart sex discrimination case.)

While most large companies have formal succession plans at the managerial level, a much lower percentage of small to medium size firms have formal systems.[30] A job-posting system can enhance the effectiveness of internal recruiting. Job posting is a process where announcements of positions are made available to all current employees through company newsletters, bulletin boards, and so on. Surprisingly, only a small percentage of organizations have formal systems of job posting for vacant positions within the organization.[31] When properly implemented, job-posting systems can substantially improve the quality of the job placements that are made within an organization and protect the organization from EEO problems (this issue is related to Wal-Mart's problems). The most effective job-posting systems take advantage of a corporate intranet where employees can access information about job openings through their connected computers. Many sophisticated human resource information systems (HRIS) are now available with competency-based, succession planning data.

External Recruitment Sources

External recruiting concerns recruitment from outside the organization. Most scholars argue that one of the biggest advantages of external recruiting is that the approach can facilitate the introduction of new ideas and thinking into corporate decision making. The new blood comes with no ownership of past strategies that can hinder an objective assessment of future strategy. A major disadvantage of external recruiting is that the introduction of new personnel may have a negative impact on work group cohesion and morale. Also, new personnel from outside the organization typically take longer to learn the ropes of the job. Another possible disadvantage is that external recruiting can be very costly. For example, companies have paid in excess of $100,000 to executive search firms for locating a single, high-level manager. Figure 5-12 presents some examples of ads for professional and executive global positions.

The Internet has had a profound impact on the cost and the time involved in recruiting personnel, including that of managers. Most Fortune 1,000 companies now post available jobs on their Web sites and more and more skilled employees are applying for these jobs through these sites. A formal job posting system for both internal and external recruiting can also give an employer some protection against legal claims based on simple "progression" statistics (e.g., nonsupervisory positions vs. supervisory positions by race or gender).

The final disadvantage of external recruiting is that you typically have less data on external candidates. There is thus a need for good assessment procedures that can be used instead of reliable performance data on the candidate. Good assessment procedures can be costly and bad assessment procedures can be downright deceptive. (Remember the survey of federal managers regarding how to be rid of incompetent employees.) Inflated letters of recommendation or confidential interviews also could land a job for a troublesome employee in a job outside of the organization. (This is probably the main reason that letters of reference have limited validity; there may actually be an incentive on the part of evaluators to inflate references in order to move a job candidate out of an organization.)

FIGURE 5-12 Ads for Global Executive and Professional Positions

INTERNATIONAL PROFESSIONALS

In today's dynamic global environment, there are exceptional opportunities for individuals whose experience and skills equip them to live and work overseas. There are currently positions available to men and women throughout a wide spectrum of professional fields, including the sciences, engineering, information and computer systems, economics/finance, education, marketing, business, or management. If you have worked abroad in any of these areas, you have a definite advantage in securing an exciting new overseas career.

These worldwide positions are being offered to people who are already confident and at home in foreign locations. You must be self-reliant and have the integrity to work without direct supervision. Reporting will require excellent verbal and written communications skills, and you must be conversant in at least one foreign language. Advanced degrees are preferred; a bachelor's degree in an appropriate area is a minimum requirement for consideration.

We represent international employers who will pay all fees associated with your selection process. They require that all applicants be U.S. citizens (Legal Permanent Residents also may apply). These positions are open to individuals of all racial and ethnic backgrounds. Compensation and benefits are commensurate with your demonstrated qualifications. For consideration under strict confidentiality, send your résumé and a letter describing your credentials. As we are a third party and not an employer, no phone calls from applicants will be accepted. We will respond only to those applicants who are of interest to our clients.

CAREER SYSTEMS INTERNATIONAL
P.O. Box 15788, Dept. IP-96/27
Philadelphia, PA 19103
Representing equal opportunity employers.

Manager-Expatriate Programs

Philips Electronics North America Corp., a global consumer and electronic business with a significant number of employees on worldwide expatriate assignments, has an excellent career opportunity in Manhattan for a pro-active professional with 5–8 years' human resources expertise to design, develop, implement, and manage the expatriate program. This fundamental position will advise personnel on expatriate and immigration policies/procedures; develop worldwide compensation programs; implement program changes; and serve as an international liaison.

To qualify, you must have 4+ years' immigration/expatriate and supervisory experience, plus a B.A. in business, human resources, or related discipline is highly beneficial. Top-notch organizational, technical, business, interpersonal, and communication skills are essential.

We offer a competitive salary/benefits package and a stimulating work environment. For confidential consideration, please send résumé to:
Human Resources/JM, Philips Electronics North America Corp., 100 East 42nd Street, New York, NY 10017. FAX:
EOE M/F/D/V. Principals only.

PHILIPS

What Methods Are Available for External Recruiting?

There are several methods available for external recruitment:

Walk-ins/Unsolicited Applicant Files The most common and least expensive approach for candidates is direct applications where job seekers submit unsolicited material (e.g., a résumé) or simply show up in person seeking employment. Direct applications also can provide a pool of potential employees to meet future needs. While direct applications are particularly effective in filling entry-level and unskilled positions, some organizations, because of their reputations or because of their geographical locations, compile excellent pools of potential employees from direct applications for skilled positions.

E-Span Interactive Employment Network provides a résumé database that is accessible from several online service providers. The Network is used by most Fortune 1,000 companies and search firms. Careerbuilder.com is an effective online source for small business. For $389, a company can post one position and access, the Web site claims, 20 million "candidates".

The reputation of the company has a great deal to do with the usefulness and size of the pool of unsolicited applicants and résumés. Organizations such as Google, Coca-Cola, SAS, Microsoft, GE, IBM, the *New York Times,* and Harvard University receive thousands of unsolicited applications every year. Many excellent candidates can be found in this pool. One of the reasons that companies actively campaign to make one or more of the many top 10 lists of the "best companies to work for" is because the rate of unsolicited résumés is directly related to this honor.

Not only do unsolicited résumés reduce the cost of recruiting, they also increase the probability of hiring the very best employees. The *New York Times* has led the world in Pulitzer Prize winners for years. They spend very little time recruiting the future Pulitzer winners; the best writers just know where to work.

Many companies now scan résumés or applications and then conduct key-word computer searches to quickly get to a reasonable short list of candidates when positions become available. Software now exists to match fairly detailed job specifications with résumé information. The result is usually a much more efficient (and faster) recruiting effort. Monster's "TARGET Reach" filters résumés by a company's criteria (e.g., experience, location, education).

Referrals   Some organizations have formal systems of employee referral for occupations with great demand. Pratt & Whitney, for example, pays current employees a $2,000 bonus if electrical engineers who are referred are ultimately hired and work for the company for at least one year. While formal systems of referral are more effective in attracting interested applicants, there is also some evidence that the quality of the applicants is less than that which results from an informal system of referrals. Microsoft is presently offering referral incentives to its employees for Internet experts of all shapes and sizes.

Referrals by friends and family have been found to increase job tenure (and decrease voluntary job turnover). The "referred" job candidates tend to have a more realistic understanding of the job when they take it and thus have more accurate expectations about the job and the organization. But before we get too excited about an employee referral program, let's not forget about Abercrombie and Fitch. A&F encouraged its mostly beautiful but also mostly white sales staff to recruit its beautiful customers and friends to become sales personnel. The result was a Title VII race discrimination lawsuit that A&F settled for $40 million in 2005.

The extensive use of employee referrals can thus cause EEO problems. In *EEOC v. Detroit Edison,* the court concluded that: "the practice of relying on referrals by a predominantly white workforce rather than seeking new employees in the marketplace for jobs was discriminatory."[32] Of course, this may not be a problem if the workforce is diverse to begin with, if the organization relies on other methods of recruiting as well, or if the organization offers a referral program that specifically targets minorities and women. Coca-Cola and Disney are among the many large corporations that offer targeted referral programs, another of the recommendations from the OFCCP Revised Order #4. Coca-Cola agreed to target African Americans in recruiting as a part of their recent out-of-court race discrimination settlement.

Advertising   A third common method for recruiting is advertising. Advertising can range from a simple classified ad to an elaborate media campaign through radio or television to attract applicants. The approach can be quite versatile in its ability to provide information about job opportunities while targeting specific labor markets in particular geographical areas. While the majority of advertising is in newspapers, many organizations go beyond the typical newspaper ads for tight labor markets. You have undoubtedly seen one of the commercials extolling the virtues of starting your "career" in our armed forces. Merrill Lynch, GTE, and Dow Chemical are also among the companies that use television to attract applicants for hard-to-fill positions.[33] Some budgets for classified print ads have been cut because of the Internet. Diane Schlageter, director of employment for Adobe Systems in San Jose, says Adobe has dropped its ad budget by 60 to 70 percent in favor of Internet recruiting. "A half-page ad in the San Jose *Mercury News* may be $15,000 to $18,000. You can do a lot of stuff online for that amount of money," says Schlageter.[34] As we discuss below, employer advertising on the Web is now the norm.

Most experts agree that advertising through any media (including the Internet) should contain the following information:

1. The job content (primary tasks and responsibilities).
2. A realistic description of working conditions, particularly if they are unusual.
3. The location of the job.
4. The compensation, including the fringe benefits.
5. Job specifications (e.g., education, experience).
6. To whom one applies.[35]

Since advertising can be very expensive, record keeping on the successes of the various media sources can help to identify the approaches with the biggest potential payoff for future recruiting. Figure 5-13 presents a summary of some of the advantages and disadvantages of the various media options. A section to follow will examine on-line recruiting.

EEO considerations are also critical for advertising.[36] A men's clothing retailer decided to target younger men with their new fall line. As part of that effort, they advertised

FIGURE 5-13	Advantages and Disadvantages of Recruitment Media	
Medium	**Advantages**	**Disadvantages**
Internet	Global reach Fast processing Relatively inexpensive Appeals to youth Technologically savvy More information about job	Many unmotivated applicants EEO/Diversity problems Not effective for low-skilled jobs Spam class (if e-mail)
Newspapers/Magazines	Local audience Tailored to audience Specialty outlets Good circulation Good yield ratios for low-skilled jobs	Often ignored/not seen Expensive Long lead time
Direct Mail	Can be well-targeted with good list	Expensive (for better mailing lists) Very long lead time
Televison/Radio	Targeted locally More attention to Ad Can attract people not seeking a job	Very expensive Longest lead time Less information regarding jobs

Source: Adapted from "Planning for Recruitment Advertising: Part II," by B. S. Hodes, copyright 1983.

for "young, energetic" assistant managers at the same time they were firing a 48-year-old man who had been with the company for 10 years. An ADEA lawsuit resulted in an out-of-court settlement in excess of $100,000. Obviously, a person knowledgeable about EEO laws should review all ad copy for potential legal problems.

There are several excellent outlets for targeted advertising to minorities and women. Monster.com allows job seekers to search for positions using diversity organizations as a search criterion (see http://diversity.monster.com). Most highly regarded African American universities have Web sites that post résumés of new graduates. Many universities place their ads in a newspaper known as *Black Issues* in an effort to attract more minority applicants.

Employment Agencies Employment agencies are used by many companies for identifying potential workers. There are publicly funded agencies that provide free placement services and private agencies that charge either the employee or the employer for a placement or referral. The major functions of these agencies are to increase the pool of possible applicants and to do preliminary screening. Private agencies are most effective when (1) the organization has had difficulty in building a pool of qualified applicants, (2) the organization is not equipped to develop a sophisticated recruitment effort, (3) there is a need to fill a position quickly, (4) the organization is explicitly recruiting minorities or females, and (5) the organization is attempting to recruit individuals who are not actively seeking employment.[37]

There are about 2,400 federally funded but state-run employment agencies under the U.S. Training and Employment Service (USTES). All persons drawing unemployment compensation must apply through one of these agencies. The most recent approach to job placement under USTES is to attempt a matching of applicants' aptitudes and interests with the requirements of the job. In general, neither employers nor employees are satisfied with the service that is offered, but efforts are being made to improve the service.[38]

Search Firms Search firms are private companies that help employers find and hire employees. These firms used to specialize in executive recruiting and placement, but there are now many specialized firms for specific occupations (e.g., IT, nursing, psychologists) and full-service companies that handle all aspects of recruiting. A growing number of companies now use employment process outsourcing (EPO), also known as recruitment process outsourcing (RPO). These are search and recruiting firms that can handle all or a part of a company's recruiting. EPOs are the fourth-largest component of HR being outsourced and the fastest growing, according to Allan Schweyer, executive director of the Human Capital Institute (HCI). InSearch Worldwide Corp. surveyed 300 HR executives about professional-level EPO and found that more than 30 percent of companies are doing at least some recruitment outsourcing.

In selecting a search firm, experts recommend the following criteria:

1. The firm should recruit in a specific industry.
2. The firm pays its sales personnel based on the completion of an assignment.

3. The firm uses primary data sources rather than secondary sources such as computerized lists of potential candidates and association directories.

4. Firms that also do outplacement services are not recommended (outplacement is professional services for terminated employees that may include placement in another job). Many socially responsible organizations are turning to outplacement programs to assist terminated employees, especially after major downsizing actions.

5. Ensure the firm provides a placement guarantee, typically 30, 60, or 90 days. This gives the organization a specified amount of time to review the employee on the job and receive a refund if a candidate's skills do not meet the requirements of the organization.

6. The firm should also have a recruitment strategy in writing. You would not allow a contractor to build your house without a blueprint so why would you allow a search firm to staff your organization without a specific plan. This defined process also ties back to your placement guarantee.[39]

7. The firm should not charge a fee to candidates. Charging a fee to candidates limits the number of qualified candidates the search firm can draw on, thereby dramatically limiting the pool of qualified candidates.

8. The firm should be able to provide references from both clients and candidates who have used their services in the past.

Many search firms now specialize in "targeted" recruiting for many jobs.[40] Recruitment in a specific industry helps ensure the search firm understands the specific needs of the organization and industry, thereby increasing the probability the candidate placement will be a success. One of the largest firms is DHR International, which for one fee provides a list of candidates whose credentials match job specifications and, for an additional fee, completes the search process. AON Consulting specializes in human resource management practices in Russia, including job recruiting and job placement.

A good source for identifying a qualified search firm is Recruiterlink.com. This Web site helps managers who are responsible for identifying qualified search firms which specialize in over 50 areas such as CEO search, financial services, consumer products, information technology, marketing, and telecommunications. Recruiterlink.com has a database of over 400 executive headhunters, from some of largest firms such as Korn/Ferry to so-called "boutique" recruiters. These recruiters specialize in jobs starting at annual salaries of $125,000. Recruiters pay a $500-a-year fee to be included in the database.

At this Web site, an organization's representative identifies a specialty area, provides geographic specifications (including international), the average salary handled, and other criteria. A list of potential recruiters is then provided with fees and recent experiences/assignments. This is all free to the "searcher" of the search firm.

In addition to negotiating fees, many organizations are developing partnerships with a select group of search firms, known as preferred vendors. The goal of the preferred vendor relationship is that the search firm is better able to match candidates not only on job specifications but also on fit to the organization's culture. In addition, the partnership allows organizations to maintain control over how the organization's open positions are marketed since the search firm has intimate knowledge of the company. The partnership relationship is often mutually beneficial to both parties since the company receives highly qualified candidates and the recruiter has inside knowledge of the "unwritten" needs of the organization.

The fees for search firms can be very high, with estimates ranging from 20 to 50 percent of the first-year salaries of the individuals placed. The reviews on the effectiveness of search firms are mixed. According to one review, 50 percent of the fulfilled job searches take twice as long to fill as promised. Less than 50 percent of contracts to fill positions are ever fulfilled.[41] More search firms are now charging a flat rate rather than a percentage of salary. Says one recruiter, "By charging a flat rate, we are able to remain objective in presenting candidates to the client. We do not show only the high-priced candidates; we show the most qualified." Many companies have begun to demand the flat-fee approach because of the tendency of percentage-based recruiters to recommend high-priced candidates.[42] A sliding scale fee structure can be negotiated so that as the total number of placements increases the fee percentage decreases.

Campus Visits One major source of recruiting for professional and managerial positions is the college campus.[43] Numerous organizations, and, in particular, the larger organizations, send recruiters to campuses once or twice a year to inform graduates and future graduates about career opportunities. One survey found that 59 percent of all managers and professionals with less than three years' experience were hired through college recruiting.[44] There is no question that college recruiting is successful at filling vacancies. There is a question as to the extent to which the vacancies are filled with people most likely to be successful within the organization. Some companies report turnover rates in excess of 50 percent for new college graduates after only one year.

The cost of college recruiting can be enormous. Estimates now run as high as $6,000 per hired graduate.[45] Despite this substantial cost, program evaluation is rarely done and little attention is placed on recruiting processes. When evaluation has been done, the criterion for evaluation was simply filled vacancies or number of offers accepted rather than a measure of the quality of those who are recruited or retention rates. Recruiters often receive little guidance on interviewing procedures, despite evidence that the interviewing format is important for the accuracy of the predictions that are made.

The recruiting process should commence long before there are any visits to the campus. Recruiters should get familiar with the university and university personnel before their visit. Job descriptions and specifications should be mailed to the campus before the recruiter arrives.

Another good strategy is to set up internship programs through the university. In general, the most effective college recruiting efforts are those that facilitate a long-term relationship with the college through a variety of cooperative programs between the school and the organization. Again, record keeping on past experience will be very helpful in planning future campus recruiting. Campus.monster.com and internshipprogram.com are great sources for internships. Both sites help students locate internships by geography, industry, and salary.

Some companies use videoconferencing at college campuses. This allows for interviewing that is much more cost effective than traditional face-to-face interviewing. The extent to which videoconferencing is an effective approach to recruiting is another empirical question. There is now a need to compare the effects (and costs) of campus visits with recruiting (and interviewing) through the Internet. Most college graduates are now capable of going on-line and may not be adversely affected by highly efficient, computerized recruiting and interviewing.[46]

One of the largest recruiters of college graduates is the federal government. Research on the ability of the government to attract the most qualified graduates is not encouraging. One survey found only 38 percent of graduates interested in careers with the federal government. The private sector was viewed as offering more prestige and power than the public sector.[47] The research also indicated that the government could do a much better job recruiting graduates by more on-campus visits and a concerted effort at dissolving their negative public image. If anything, the public image has actually gotten worse in recent years.

Two other sources for recruiting that should be mentioned are professional associations and computerized services. The first is professional societies or associations within specialized areas. College faculty for management departments, for example, are often recruited through the Academy of Management (www.aomonline.org) and other academic associations. The Society of Human Resource Management now has a placement service available for jobs in all aspects of HR (SHRM.org).

Newly minted MBAs and companies seeking project-related help should consult mbaglobalnet.com. As of 2005, this site charged the employer $225 to post a job for 60 days on the career center. The site then e-mails members new jobs every Tuesday. In addition, the site provides a project worker hiring service and charges 15 percent of the contract. MBAs register on the site for free.

Electronic Recruiting on the World Wide Web

One survey suggested that over 80 percent of organizations use the Web to recruit.[48] Electronic job descriptions and résumés are now retrievable from numerous recruitment Web sites. Monster.com and Hotjobs.yahoo.com are two of an estimated 5,000 job boards on the Web. Figure 5-14 presents a list of some of the major sites and the costs to the employer.

The most popular job site is Monster.com, which claims to have more than 500,000 jobs in its databank. *Forbes* magazine named Monster the best job hunting site on the Web based on its design, navigation, content, speed, and customization. As of May 2005, Monster has over 46.4 million searchable résumés, with an average of 45,000 to 50,000 résumés being added daily and over 1.1 million job postings. There are many niche sites on the Web too. Computer-related specialists should check out techies.com or dice.com. There are specialty sites for pharmacists, toxicologists, and even highly paid executives (sixfigures.com).

An estimated 94 percent of global 500 companies are now posting jobs on their own Web sites. Some companies accept only online applications. When Hewlett-Packard was looking for an engineer with specific programming skills and five years' experience who could speak Spanish, the software screened the résumés and identified three applicants who met these specifications. While the efficiency of this approach should be obvious, some problems with the software as it reads the résumés can create errors in the search and eliminate applicants who otherwise would have survived at least the initial screening. For example, if you misspell a key word, you could be out of luck.

Excellent software tracking is now available. Resumix Inc., for example, contains 10 million terms related to various industries, including terms such as *application design* and *general ledger* for specialized programmer and accounting applications. Some companies report substantial savings in recruiting and advertising due to this type of software tracking system. HP claims to have over 330,000 résumés in its database. Needless to say, they avoid a paperwork nightmare with the "virtual recruiter" system. They recently received over 100,000 résumés in the staffing of 1,400 new hires.

Recruiting in the very near future may go something like this for most large companies:

1. A line manager completes a standardized job analysis questionnaire on the Internet identifying employment needs for the unit; the questionnaire may include job location and other details of the job in addition to the critical job specifications.
2. The completed questionnaire is then automatically converted into a job posting on the Internet and matched with a current database of "candidates" whose credentials are entered using the same terminology as the job analysis.

FIGURE 5-14 **Recruitment Web site Comparisons**

Web sites	Search Options	Job Search Database	Ease of Use for Searcher	Costs for One-Time Posting	Employer Benefits
Monster.com	Location Industry/Job Keyword Employer	**Position/Title**—click and view job description **Company**—search by company name to see all job postings **Posted date**—sorted by most recent; can limit date range **Salary**—not searchable; must click job description to view	• Site easy to use • Can search by company from basic search	1 job/60 days/ $365	• Online database search • Track statistics of each job posting • Search agents (automatically generated list of potential candidates) • International postings available • Company profiles • Diversity section • Likely one of the most recognized job boards by job seekers
Hotjobs.yahoo.com	Location Industry/Job Keyword Employer	**Position/Title**—click and view job description **Company**—click and view all job postings from specific company **Posted date**—sorted by most recent; can limit date range **Salary**—searchable in advanced search; must click job description to view	• Site easy to use • Can search by company; requires change in search option • Search by industry/job was easy to use since further specified state and city	1 job/30 days/ $275	• Online database search • Unlimited job posting changes permitted • Track statistics on each job posting • E-mail potential candidates • Jobs can be posted in U.S. and Canada • Company profile
Careerbuilder.com	Location Industry/Job Keyword Employer	**Position/Title**—click and view job description **Company**—click and view all job postings (must conduct a search first) **Posted date**—sorted by most recent; can limit date range **Salary**—searchable in advanced search; listed on search results page	• Site easy to use • Can search by company; requires change in search option • Site moderately easy to navigate • Cannot search for positions from home page	1 job/30 days/ $365	• Online database search • Additional services such as prescreened candidates, background checks, career fairs • International postings available • Company profile
Employmentguide.com	Location Industry/Job Keyword Employer	**Position/Title**—click and view position **Company**—click and view all positions by employer (sorted alphabetically) **Posted date**—sorted by most recent: cannot limit date **Salary**—not searchable or provided separately	• Site moderately easy to navigate • Cannot search for positions from home page	1 job/30 days/ $250	• Online database search • Entry level to middle management positions (hourly and nonexempt positions)

(continued)

FIGURE 5-14	(Continued)

Web sites	Search Options	Job Search Database	Ease of Use for Searcher	Costs for One-Time Posting	Employer Benefits
Careerjournal.com	Location Industry/Job Keyword Employer	**Position/Title**—click and view position **Company**—click and view all job postings **Posted date**—sorted by most recent; cannot limit date **Salary**—not searchable or provided separately	• Site moderately easy to navigate • Cannot search for positions from home page	1 job/30 days/ $299	• Online database search (300,000+ résumés) • Diversity career fairs • Brief company overview (Briefing Book) • Partnership with 150+ media sources so positions are posted to additional sites • International job postings
Flipdog.com	Location Industry/Job Keyword Employer	**Position/Title**—click and view position **Company**—click and view all job postings **Posted date**—sorted by most recent; cannot limit date **Salary**—does not include a separate section listing salary	• Site moderately easy to navigate • Advanced search method is interactive and may be confusing for novice job board users	1 job/30 days/ $125	• Online database search • International job postings
America's Job Bank www.ajb.dni.us	Location Industry/Job Keyword	**Position/Title**—click and view job description **Company**—click and view all positions by employer (once original search has been completed) **Posted date**—sorted by most recent **Salary**—not searchable but is listed in the search results	• Site easy to navigate	Free	• Provided by the U.S. Department of Labor • Online database search • Jobs are posted in the U.S. only • Company profile

Source: Contributed by Renee Fitzgerald.

3. A list of candidates is identified based on the match of job specifications with job credentials.

4. Almost instantaneously, the line manager has a list of minimally qualified candidates with whom s/he can interact.

5. A testing and interview format (with job-related questions), in compliance with all EEO guidelines, is derived from the same job analysis information completed at Step 1.

6. Using the testing/interview material, additional data are collected on the candidates through e-mail and/or Web camera and a list of top candidates is compiled.

Note that we used the word *candidates* first rather than *applicants* because résumés of qualified persons may be retrieved from Web databases and personnel Web sites and these potential candidates may or may not be interested in a particular job opportunity. They are simply alerted to the new job and then decide whether they wish to become applicants. A new and hot HR position today is "Internet" or "cyber" recruiter. These folks are specialists in locating and placing people off job websites. Many also coordinate all Web recruiting activities for companies. There are already 18,000 members of the Association of Internet Recruiters (see Recruitersnetwork. com). One of these cyber recruiters boasts that he can access the résumé of every IBM employee.

It is clear that the Internet has great potential for expediting the recruiting process. The scenario above should be contrasted with the typical methods of recruiting we described above. Of course, the Internet approach depends on potential job applicants being aware of this convenient approach and amenable to the process. A great place to start to research your Web options is the online directories such as the Riley Guide (www.airsdirectory. com), which provides loads of free information and links to numerous recruitment sites.

A great Web site for college students is www.campus. monster.com. The site has internships, résumé services, and job listings for students and partnerships with over 1,000 universities. Monster's site is a comprehensive source for first-time job seekers with excellent information on valuable internships.

A major concern for organizations is reaching diversity candidates online. The digital divide between white users and minorities is a concern of many HR practitioners. According to the Pew Internet & American Life Project, 58 percent of whites have access to the Internet whereas only 43 percent of African Americans and 50 percent of Hispanics have Internet access. Yet, the yearly Internet adoption rate is growing rapidly in African American and Hispanic households. There is also evidence that African Americans and Hispanics are more likely to search for jobs online than whites. In 2000, of those seeking work, 41 percent of Hispanics, 36 percent of Whites, and 50 percent of African Americans

surveyed said they had used to the Internet to look for information about a job.[49]

What Method of Recruiting Is Most Effective?

There have been few studies that have compared the effects of different methods for recruitment. The criteria that have been used in these studies also differ and include cost per hire, number of résumés, time lapse from recruiting to filling the vacancy, interview/invitation ratio, applicant performance on the job, and job tenure or turnover. A recent emphasis also has been placed on minority hiring patterns as a function of the recruiting effort and relative to population statistics and census data on potential employees. These comparisons may be critical if EEO litigation is pending. The EEOC has stated that the definition of an "applicant" depends upon the user's recruitment and selection procedures. The concept of an applicant is that of a person who has indicated an interest in being considered for hiring, promotion, or other employment opportunities. This interest might be expressed by completing an application form, or might be expressed orally, depending on the employer's practice or through the Internet and related electronic technologies only. According to the EEOC, in order for an individual to be an applicant in the context of the Internet and related electronic data processing technologies, the following must have occurred: (1) the employer has acted to fill a particular position; (2) the individual has followed the employer's standard procedures for submitting applications; and (3) the individual has indicated an interest in the particular position.

Figure 5-15 presents a list of some of the most important criteria that could be used to evaluate different approaches to recruiting and the extent to which companies collect such data.

One excellent study emphasizes the importance of "attraction outcomes" as a recruitment outcome that

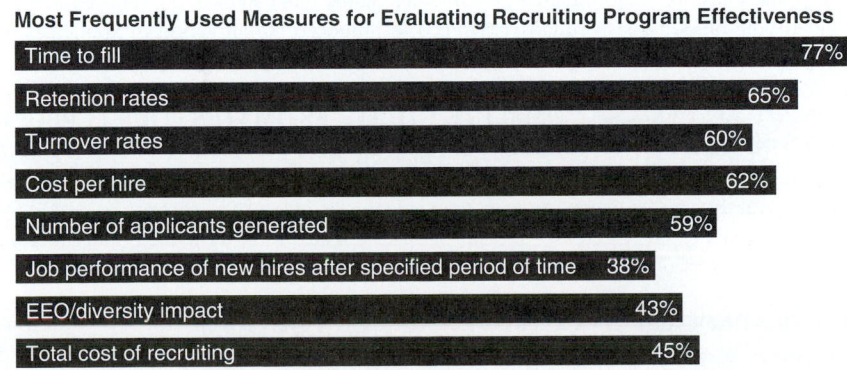

Most Frequently Used Measures for Evaluating Recruiting Program Effectiveness

Measure	Percent
Time to fill	77%
Retention rates	65%
Turnover rates	60%
Cost per hire	62%
Number of applicants generated	59%
Job performance of new hires after specified period of time	38%
EEO/diversity impact	43%
Total cost of recruiting	45%

Figure 5-15   Criteria for Evaluating Recruitment Activities and the Extent to Which They Are Measured
Source: Bernardin, H. J. (2006). A survey of SHRM member recruiting practices and criteria for evaluation.

should be emphasized when evaluating recruitment practices. Attraction outcomes emphasize (and measure) the quality of the applicant pool as a function of the recruitment source. The authors argue that "adopting methods for evaluating attraction outcomes may be the single most valuable step organizations can take toward improving recruitment effectiveness."[50] They emphasize a more systematic measurement process that includes detail on the methods used to screen candidates. Figure 5-16 presents their seven-step plan for assessing attraction outcomes. Their plan includes estimates of the economic yield or utility from each source. Yield ratios are important but there should be close scrutiny of the criteria used to qualify candidates from one recruitment step to the next. Obviously, a recruitment source that yields a high propor-

tion of "qualified" candidates is important but a more fine-tuned analysis will provide more useful definitions of "qualified" that include comparative "scores" on these qualified candidates.

The Discrepancy between Research and Practice

Unfortunately, there is little systematic research on the effects of recruiting options using any of these criteria. Despite calls for systematic research on the effects of various approaches to recruiting, few companies have strategic measurement criteria for evaluating recruitment and recruitment sources. One survey found that only 48 percent of companies even had a formal system for evaluating their recruiting. Only 38 percent look at the job performance of new hires relative to

---

FIGURE 5-16   **Assessing Attraction Outcomes: A Step-by-Step Overview**

STEP 1: IDENTIFY POSITIONS TO ASSESS

Description: Organizations may choose not to develop scores to evaluate recruitment outcomes for all positions. Those positions where assessment of attraction outcomes is likely to be of greatest value are jobs that generate several new hires and attract large numbers of applicants.

STEP 2: IDENTIFY CURRENT SCREENING METHOD AND DETERMINE CURRENT PROPERTIES

Description: Organizations need to identify the current selection methods used at each step in the recruitment process.

STEP 3: DETERMINE STRATEGY FOR ADAPTING CURRENT SCREENING METHOD TO PRODUCE SCORES FOR EACH APPLICANT AND ADAPT CHANGES

Description: Depending on what screening method is currently used, the amount of deviation between current recommended practices and the development of comparable scores for each candidate.

STEP 4: ASSESS ATTRACTION OUTCOMES

Description: Assess each applicant using the device developed in Step 3. Scores for all applicants in the applicant pool should be evaluated, including those that have left the pool by withdrawing themselves from consideration or because they were hired during the appropriate time period (defined by the organization).

STEP 5: MATCH RECRUITMENT ACTIVITIES TO RECRUITMENT PHASES AND ESTIMATE RECRUITMENT COSTS

Description: In order to evaluate the cost effectiveness of various recruitment practices, recruitment costs must be identified and mapped to the appropriate phase of recruitment (i.e., attraction, status maintenance, gaining job acceptance). Estimate costs of attraction by identifying all activities primarily designed to influence the attraction of applicants to this position, not general recruitment costs.

STEP 6: ESTIMATE INPUT VALUES AND COMPLETE UTILITY ESTIMATES (THIS IS REQUIRED TO COMPLETE EVALUATIONS THAT INCORPORATE BOTH COST AND BENEFIT CONSIDERATIONS)

Description: To be able to use utility analysis to convert differences in quality scores to dollars, several values need to be estimated. These include the validity of screening devices, the standard deviation of performance in dollars for the job in question, the number of individuals to be selected or the subset of candidates to be evaluated, and the average expected tenure of candidates in their positions once hired.

STEP 7: EVALUATE THE ADEQUACY OF CURRENT SCREENING DEVICES

Description: Organizations may decide that alternative screening devices may be more appropriate due to their cost, validity, adverse impact rate, or other properties of the scores they generate.

Source: Adapted from K. D. Carlson, M. L. Connerley, and R. L. Mecham, "Recruitment Evaluation: The Case for Assessing the Quality of Applicants Attracted," *Personnel Psychology* 55 (2002), pp. 461–490.

recruitment source. Only 43 percent evaluate recruiting sources in terms of EEO or diversity issues. Obviously, the tracking of vital criteria such as is essential in determining the relative effectiveness of the various recruiting options.

In general, the limited comparative studies on recruitment methods suggest that the more informal methods (e.g., walk-ins, referrals) are more likely to lead to longer job tenure than the more formal sources, such as newspaper ads. The Internet now exceeds newspaper ads in generating a large number of applicants for a position compared to the other methods. Another study found that people who had worked for the organization earlier had superior performance records, longer job tenure, and better attendance.[51]

Many problems in recruiting may be a consequence of the way in which recruiters are rewarded. You may recall the Army recruiting scandals in 2005. One recruiter in Colorado, working under a specific "head count" quota, produced a "Faith Hill High School" diploma for a dropout who was actually not eligible. Research has shown that those criteria that pertain to direct costs of recruiting to the organization are the ones on which recruiters are typically evaluated.[52] For example, recruiters for a large manufacturing company in the South are compensated in relation to a "cost per hire" measure or what one staff member refers to as the "warm body" phenomenon. This emphasis on cost figures may explain the general lack of systematic research relating recruiting methods to higher-level criteria such as work quality. In the context of affirmative action, those persons assigned to meet specific EEO goals or timetables often are evaluated on the extent to which they meet the goals or timetables and not the extent to which the positions have been filled with qualified personnel or whether those individuals are successfully retained. The conflicting incentives of recruiters and line management can cause problems when the time comes to make job offers.

The effectiveness of the various methods of recruiting also has been shown to vary as a function of particular method characteristics. In general, research allows us to construct an ideal recruiter: strong interpersonal skills, extensive knowledge of the organization, and enthusiasm for the organization, the job, and the candidates. College recruiting is apparently enhanced when the recruiter is between the ages of 30 and 55, is perceived to have stature in the company (line managers are preferred to professional recruiters), and is verbally fluent with good interpersonal skills and an extensive knowledge of the company and the particular job.[53] The success of any recruiting effort, however, is more dependent on the job (and offer) characteristics themselves. College students place the greatest weight on pay, fringe benefits, and the type of work. Recruiters often underestimate the importance of such factors relative to others.[54]

Figure 5-17 presents a summary of the latest research findings on recruitment and practical applications.

What Are the Effects of the Internet?

Despite its great potential, the Internet is not necessarily a panacea for all organizations and all jobs. The track record to date is not all that impressive. One CEO of a marketing development company said, "Unless you're looking for programmers in some cutting-edge technology, you're kind of out of luck." While others would certainly disagree with such a sweeping conclusion, there is limited empirical evidence showing Web-based recruiting to be superior to other recruiting options for the most important criteria for assessing the recruitment effort. A 2001 survey found that 50 percent of Internet job hunters indicated that their searches seldom or never led to an interview that matched their skills.[55] Only 12 percent credit the Internet when they find a job. A 2005 survey found that most small computer-related businesses regarded Internet recruiting as "useful." Less than 50 percent of respondents from all other sectors regarded it as useful.[56]

The Internet will certainly give you a lot of résumés and fast. But whether the Internet facilitates the faster hiring of better people at relatively lower cost has not yet been determined except with isolated case studies, usually involving technological jobs. Darlene Chapin, Recruiting Director for Cheetah Technologies in Florida, claims Internet recruiting for programmers has made the process much more efficient. Even so, she says, Web-based staffing should be a supplement not a replacement for traditional recruiting such as newspaper ads, college outreach, job fairs, and headhunters.

One of the major problems reported with Internet recruiting is the volume of résumés received, the so-called résumé overload. Many recruiters simply download all the "applications." While this type of recruiting will surely get you more applications and faster, the process can get quite inefficient without a strategy for classifying, rating, or ranking résumés based on a matching process between job specifications and candidates' KASOCs or competencies.

More companies are now using online structured approaches to screening that require applicants to submit biographical information according to a specific format. The format allows for an automatic "scoring" of biographical and other information and thus a classification scheme for candidates. This "artificial intelligence" approach allows for greater control over information gathering and storage and has the potential for better decision making. One discrepancy between academic research and personnel practice is the clear finding in research that statistical or actuarial decision making based on the valid weighting of different sources of information about job candidates results in more effective staffing decisions compared to the way personnel decisions are normally made where an evaluator forms a general impression based on an overall

FIGURE 5-17   **Recruitment Research and Practical Applications**

Research Finding	Practical Applications
Recruitment sources affect the characteristics of applicants attracted.	Use sources such as referrals (e.g., from current employees) that yield applicants less likely to turnover and more likely to be better performers.
Recruitment materials have a more positive impact if they contain more specific information.	Provide applicants with information on aspects of the job that are important to them, such as salary, location, and diversity.
Organizational image influences applicants' initial reactions to employers.	Ensure all communications regarding an organization provide a positive message regarding the corporate image and the attractiveness of the organization as a place to work.
Applicants with a greater number of job opportunities are more attentive to and more influenced by early recruitment activities than those with fewer opportunities (i.e., less marketable individuals).	Ensure initial recruitment activities (e.g., Web site, brochure, on-campus recruiting) are as attractive to candidates as later activities.
Recruiter demographics have a relatively small effect on applicants' attraction to the organization.	Worry less about matching recruiter/applicant demographics and more about the content of recruiting messages and the organization's overall image in terms of diversity.
Realistic job previews (e.g., brochures, videos, group discussions that highlight both the advantages and the disadvantages of the job) reduce subsequent turnover.	Provide applicants with a realistic picture of the job and organization, not just the positives.
Applicants will infer job and organizational information based on the organizational image projected and their early interactions with the organization if the information is not clearly provided by the organization.	Provide clear, specific, and complete information in recruitment materials so that applicants do not make erroneous inferences about the nature of the job or the organization as an employer.
Recruiter warmth has a large and positive effect on applicants' decisions to accept a job.	Individuals who have contact with applicants should be chosen for their interpersonal skills.
Applicants' beliefs in a "good fit" between their values and the organization's influence their job-choice decisions.	Provide applicants with accurate information about what the organization is like so that they can make accurate fit assessments.

Source: Adapted from Ryan A. M. and Tippins N. T. (2004). Attracting and selecting: What psychological research tells us. *HUMAN RESOURCE MANAGEMENT, 43* p. 311. Reprinted with permission of John Wiley & Sons.

evaluation of the information about candidates. When done properly, "artificial intelligence" can lead to more intelligent decision making. One study reported a 270 percent increase in productivity using an automated résumé scoring system. One expert recommends the following strategies for processing résumés: (1) Optimize the e-mail system by pushing candidates to particular job folders; (2) Use auto-response e-mails with valid, prequalifying questions or conditions (certain required job specifications); (3) Drive candidates to apply online at your Web site so valid scores can be derived based on relevant biographical, competency-based information; and (4) Use an outsourced staffing or résumé screening service.[57] This expert is also the co-founder of a company called PeopleBonus that offers this very service (check out their Web site).

Two Philosophies of Recruiting: Flypaper versus Matching

The traditional philosophy of recruiting has been to get as many people to apply for a job as possible. The idea is based on trying to obtain the lowest possible selection ratio given a fixed recruiting cost. A **selection ratio (SR)** is the proportion of job openings to applicants. An SR of .10 means there are 10 applicants for every job opening. A lower selection ratio is generally more desirable because it enables the organization to choose job candidates from a larger pool, thereby increasing selectivity. Research on **High-Performance Work Systems,** which we introduced in Chapter 1, clearly shows that more successful firms have a significantly lower selection ratio than less successful firms.

This assumption holds true as long as the cost of recruiting and subsequent screening is not exorbitant and applicants for the job are at least minimally qualified. In general, selection ratios go down when companies are admired by the working public. For example, the number of job applicants is up for most of *Fortune* magazine's "most admired" companies (e.g., Google, FedEx, SAS, Southwest Airlines, Procter & Gamble) relative to competitors that did not make the list.

Unfortunately, the war in Iraq has had a negative effect on military recruiting. In 2005, the Army achieved only 73 percent of its recruiting goals. Even the Marine Corps was facing recruiting strains. The percentage of new Army recruits who are black has fallen significantly since the Iraq war. Army research has determined that some of the decline is due to the unpopularity of the war in Iraq among blacks.

Of course, what is critical is that the increases in the applicant pool reflect at least minimally qualified applicants. Many companies express disappointment with Web-based recruiting because of the labor involved in processing a larger collection of résumés, many of which are not really a close match to the requirements of the job. In circumstances where the "quality" of the candidates is most important and along with the attraction of people who are more likely to stay longer, the "matching" philosophy of recruitment may be more efficient.[58] A persuasive argument can be made that matching the needs of the organization to the needs of the applicant will enhance the recruitment process. The result will be a workforce that is more likely to stay with the organization longer and perform at a higher level of effectiveness for a longer period of time. In the context of this matching philosophy, a process of realistic recruitment is recommended. An important component of realistic recruiting is a **realistic job preview (RJP).** RJPs provide the characteristics of the job to applicants so they can evaluate the compatibility of this realistic presentation of the job with their own work preferences. St. Petersburg, Florida, police recruits are shown a video depicting the realistic life of a St. Petersburg police officer. Recruits are told that each arrest they make entails hours of paperwork. RJPs can result in a self-selection process that screens people most likely to have difficulty on the job. Those applicants who are hired after being exposed to an RJP are also better able to cope because of more realistic expectations about the job.[59] It is said that RJPs "vaccinate" applicants by lowering their unrealistic expectations and bringing them more in line with actual work conditions.

Many companies doing international work provide extensive RJPs for potential expatriates and their families. Bechtel, the giant construction company, provides a 60-minute video of life in Saudi Arabia that engineers and their spouses view before they make a commitment for a one-year assignment. Research on realistic recruiting shows lower rates of employee turnover for employees recruited with RJPs, particularly for more complex jobs, and higher levels of job satisfaction and performance at the initial stages of employment. RJPs are more beneficial for organizations hiring at the entry level, when there are low selection ratios (i.e., many applicants per position), and under conditions of relatively low unemployment (i.e., where people have more job options). Otherwise, the approach may increase the cost of recruiting by increasing the average time it takes to fill each position.[60] RJPs are developed using job analysis information. The critical incident technique is particularly effective for developing RJPs. RJPs also could be incorporated in job postings on the Internet to facilitate the self-selection process.

Another approach to staffing that fits into the matching philosophy is the use of the **Job Compatibility Questionnaire (JCQ)** we discussed in Chapter 4 and will illustrate in the next chapter.[61] The JCQ provides a quantitative match between job applicant preferences and the actual characteristics of a job, including compensation system characteristics, benefits, work schedule, and, of course, the characteristics of the actual work to be performed. The JCQ has also been used to construct a realistic job preview. A study of customer service representatives at one Tribune Company newspaper found that the combination of JCQ as a selection device plus the RJP after the job offer was conveyed reduced voluntary turnover by 35 percent and increased the job satisfaction of the workforce.[62] An instrument such as the JCQ also could be incorporated into a standardized job analysis method for downloading from the Internet.

Understanding the Recruits

Effective recruiting requires that the organization know what potential applicants are thinking and what their needs and desires are regarding all major characteristics of the job. For example, how important are the various elements of the fringe benefit package? Are applicants interested in special work schedules, child care, particular work locations? Organizations also need to be keenly aware of how candidates search for jobs. What outlets do they rely on for job information? To what extent do they rely on outside referral agencies for job placement? Should recruitment be restricted to specific geographical areas based on the search behavior of potential candidates? At least some answers to these questions can be gathered over time based on the past recruiting successes and failures of the organization. Recruitment is one area of HRM where a computerized system of detailed, record keeping would be most beneficial for recruiting efforts in the future. Unfortunately, most organizations rely on recruiter "hunches" to make decisions and do little to organize their past recruiting efforts in such a way that systematic research could help to determine their future strategies. Research indicates that these "hunches" are not particularly accurate.[63]

Human Resource Planning and Recruitment for Multinational Corporations

The majority of Fortune 500 companies are now multinational in nature in that some portion of their business (and profits) are derived from overseas operations. As discussed in Chapter 2, some of our largest, most prestigious companies (e.g., IBM, GE, McDonald's, Coca-Cola) derive close to (or over) 50 percent of their revenues from overseas business. Unfortunately, with few exceptions, the relationship between HR planning and strategic planning for international ventures is even weaker than for U.S. operations despite the fact that many experts regard human resource issues as even more important to the success of an overseas operation than domestic operations. Efforts are being made to enhance the recruiting and success of expatriates. As shown in Figure 5-18, some companies are responding by consolidating the external hiring requirements and gaining expertise in overseas staffing needs.

As discussed in Chapter 2, international HRM is more complicated than domestic HRM. All of the planning

and recruitment are more unpredictable because of the importance of volatile environmental and political issues in the host country that can affect the overseas operations. For example, after considerable success penetrating the Japanese market, Milwaukee-based Harley-Davidson has had to respond to considerable political pressure directed at restricting their growth in Japan. The pressure is affecting their forecasts of market penetration in Japan.

Terrorism is something taken seriously all over the world. Before September 11, 2001, terrorism was a particular problem with regard to overseas assignments. Needless to say (and unfortunately), the concern Americans feel when they ponder overseas assignments regarding

---

FIGURE 5-18 **International HR Jobs**

Director, Global eRecruiting

International, Munich, Germany

Allianz AG, a global leader in the financial services arena, seeks a highly motivated individual to lead an international team responsible for creating and implementing a comprehensive eRecruiting and employment branding plan and incorporating multiple segmented lead generation tactics that ensure a consistent candidate experience with Allianz and its affiliates.

Requirements:

At least 8 years of Marketing and/or branding experience (project management) in financial services or insurance fields. Recruiting-related marketing experience preferred.

Significant project management experience.

Demonstrated leadership and relationship management abilities.

Sourcing strategist who has developed a total approach to generating leads in a similar environment desired.

Proficient in Internet utilization and Web analysis.

Ability to conduct and report on relevant research

Bachelor's Degree and/or MBA (e.g., business, economics marketing) or equivalent.

Work experience abroad (6-month minimum).

HR Director

International, Riyadh, Saudi Arabia

New position reporting to COO for one of the world's largest jewelry manufacturing facilities located in Riyadh, SA. Approximately 3,000 employees in seven (7) locations throughout Saudi Arabia. Will be responsible for the development of an effective HR program, building all systems including core competencies and organizational values. Ideal candidate will be fluid in the language, culture, and customs/laws of Middle Eastern manufacturing operations. Excellent salary and benefits package to include housing allowance and relocation. Submit resume to:

HR Director

International, Toronto, Canada

We are one of Forbes' 200 Best Small Companies (www.edumgt.com) for the third year in a row. With proprietary colleges throughout the U.S., we have recently acquired three post-secondary institutions. specializing in information technology, located in Halifax, Toronto, and Vancouver. We seek a Director of Human Resources for the three locations, to be based in Toronto headquarters.

The Director of Human Resources is a position of leadership within our organization. We seek a seasoned generalist who is familiar with start-ups or acquisitions, and who is able to successfully guide employees through change. The incumbent will possess the ability to integrate HR into key business operations, and to assist senior executives in building an infrastructure with all levels of management, staff, and faculty. Particular emphasis will be placed on organizational development, staffing, compensation, benefits, employee relations, training, and knowledge of provincial employment laws within a tri-site environment.

The successful candidate will possess a broad understanding of HR practices and policies, a minimum Bachelors degree in business, human resources management, or related field and at least seven (7) years of parallel experience in HR management. Some travel will be necessary in order to serve each of the locations.

The environment is challenging and very fast-paced, as well as student- and employee-centered. We offer a competitive salary and benefits, with enormous opportunities for advancement. For immediate consideration, your résumé and salary history may be sent via e-mail attachment to

---

Source: From Stayskal, "Army Recruiters Having Tough Time Meeting Goals." By Tribune Media Services. Reprinted by permission of TMS Reprints.

potential problems may now be shared by workers of other nations who are considering assignments to U.S. cities. The implications of the European Community remain unclear in terms of many HRM activities. With few exceptions (e.g., Poland, Yugoslavia), the current state of the economies of most east European nations makes planning and market forecasting for these new potential markets extremely tenuous. As of 2005, the state of European Union human resource laws and regulations is unclear.

Almost all other HRM activities (e.g., staffing, performance management, reward systems and compliance, and employee development) are more difficult and unpredictable in overseas operations not only because of environmental volatility but because many of the methods within each of these domains that have proven effective in U.S. settings do not necessarily work for international staffing, performance management, and the other domains. The U.S. insurance industry, for example, puts considerable weight on biographical information in the selection of insurance agents. The validity of the method for predicting sales success, discussed in Chapter 6, has never been studied for overseas sales and thus may not apply in the hiring of expatriate Americans, in-country nationals, or third-country nationals.

Within the rewards/compliance domain of HRM activities, issues related to family, housing, dependent care and schooling, spouse employment, taxation, and health care all tend to complicate the international HRM function. These issues also make the economic and psychological implications of errors in international HRM to be relatively greater than for domestic assignments.[64]

One study identified the critical issues affecting planning and recruitment aspects of international HRM.[65] The major challenges were:

1. Identifying top managerial talent early in the process.
2. Identifying criteria for success in overseas assignments.
3. Motivating employees to take overseas assignments.
4. Establishing a stronger connection between the strategic plan of the company and HR planning.

Few experts would argue with the contention that these challenges are more difficult with international planning and recruitment. The third challenge, motivating employees to take overseas assignments, is no longer a problem. One survey, for example, found that a majority of managers indicated that a foreign assignment was helpful for one's career.[66] Repatriation policies often are not adequate to meet the needs of returning expatriates. Lawrence Buckley, Personnel Manager for GE, for example, says the "re-entry process isn't as smooth as we would like it to be." He states that GE is making progress in this area but that it is "still a problem for us and U.S. industry in general."[67] Whereas many managers still perceive overseas assignments as a banishment of sorts, corporations now place more and considerable weight on

overseas experience as a requirement for high-level executive assignments. For example, Honeywell, Allied-Signal, and Rohm & Haas all require overseas assignments prior to senior management placement. With the increased sophistication of international communications and the growing importance of international operations for corporate strategy, studies showing managers perceiving a loss of visibility at headquarters due to overseas assignments probably apply less today than only a few years ago.

Underlying all HRM challenges is the strategic position of the multinational corporation regarding the relationship of the overseas operation to the parent company.[68] The recruitment strategy for overseas assignments is directly tied to this strategic position. U.S. companies may recruit and select from one (or more) of three sources:

1. The pool of U.S. personnel who would be expatriated to the foreign assignment.
2. The pool of candidates from the country of the overseas operations.
3. Candidates from all nationalities.

Ethnocentrism, the policy of using *only* home-country executives for overseas assignments, really only makes sense either financially or strategically when the company is just starting the operation. Otherwise, the disadvantages of this approach outweigh the advantages. Japanese companies with this philosophy applied to U.S. operations have encountered a number of problems, including a proliferation of equal employment opportunity lawsuits and, in particular, age discrimination cases as Japanese companies replace American managers over the age of 40 with sometimes younger and very often Japanese managers. The use of nationals in overseas operations can reduce language and cultural problems, the need for expensive training programs, and, of course, the tremendous cost of placing expatriates and their families in overseas assignments. This is becoming more common for American companies.[69]

Japanese women may be one major pool of highly skilled workers that American companies could tap for penetration into Japanese markets. Japanese females are still subjected to considerable employment discrimination in their own country and are attracted to U.S. corporations for this reason. The geocentric policy of hiring the best person regardless of nationality is the formal policy of choice for most large U.S. corporations but is certainly not without its problems since such a management team may have more difficulties communicating with each other and understanding the subtle implications of cultural differences.

For corporations maintaining a close strategic relationship to the overseas division (as opposed to a philosophy of autonomous operations), the most common strategy for managerial recruitment and job placement for U.S.

companies is a balance between expatriates and nationals. Sales and production personnel are typically recruited from the national pool. Companies that have a "hands off" managerial philosophy to autonomous foreign operations they may have acquired or developed typically use expatriates in coordination with nationals until the parent company is comfortable with the operation and profits of the foreign division are acceptable. Most of the expatriates may then be recalled to reduce the overhead of the operation.

SUMMARY

Human resource planning (HRP) seeks to place the right employees in the right jobs at the right time and at the lowest possible cost, thereby providing the means for the organization to pursue its competitive strategy and fulfill its mission. Planning improves the organization's ability to create and sustain competitive advantage and to cope with problems, threats, and opportunities arising from change—technological, social, political, and environmental. HRP and all of its derivatives should always keep the future customer in focus. Reengineering or downsizing programs that lose this focus ultimately may have a negative impact on the organization. HRP systematically attempts to forecast personnel demand, assess supply, and reconcile the two. Personnel demand can be assessed using qualitative methods such as the Delphi technique and quantitative methods. Internal supply may be forecast by using human resources information systems (HRIS), replacement charts, and Markov analysis. Internal shortages are resolved through training and/or recruitment. This information is used in action planning to develop human resource strategy. HRP is an ongoing process where control and evaluation procedures are necessary to guide HRP activities. Deviations from the plan and their causes must be identified in order to assess whether the plan should be revised. Most labor market analysis should now be done with a global contact and the possibility that work can be done almost anywhere.[70]

Recruitment is the process of finding and attracting applicants who are interested in and qualified for position vacancies. The Internet has had more of an impact on this HR function than any other. Recruitment should encompass both the attraction and the selection of the most qualified personnel. The ideal recruitment program is one in which a sufficient number of qualified applicants are attracted to and ultimately accept the positions in an efficient manner. Unfortunately, the typical assessment of recruitment policies, programs, and personnel in the past has focused on simply whether positions were filled and the cost and speed of filling positions rather than evaluating the quality of the personnel who were hired and placed. The most recent writing on recruitment, however, has placed a greater emphasis on the quality dimension of the recruiting effort. There is increasing evidence that the various approaches to recruiting result in different outcomes for the organization. The evaluation of recruiting programs in the future is thus more likely to focus on the quality dimension of the people who are hired in addition to the "body count" criteria that are more typically used. We have emphasized the quality criterion in this chapter and the need to establish a match between job seekers' needs and desires for certain job characteristics and that which the organization can offer.

DISCUSSION QUESTIONS

1. How should HR planning involve a comparison to competitors? What critical data are required?
2. Why is planning an important activity? What are some of the advantages of effective planning?
3. Some organizations do thorough job analysis first and then human resource planning as part of a restructuring process. What approach makes more sense to you?
4. Discuss the possible pros and cons of the two qualitative methods of forecasting labor demand presented.
5. If actual performance of the human resource plan differs from desired performance, what remedial steps might you use?
6. Employee referral is a popular method of recruiting candidates. What are its advantages and disadvantages?
7. What are the advantages and disadvantages of the various external recruitment sources?
8. How do human resource planning and recruitment complement each other?
9. Suppose a key employee has just resigned and you are the department manager. After you have sent your request to personnel for a replacement, how could you help the recruiter find the best replacement?
10. Discuss the advantages and disadvantages of using Web-based recruitment.

6

PERSONNEL SELECTION*

O V E R V I E W

It sounds simple: Match employees with jobs. Researchers have made this task easier by developing selection methods that successfully predict employee effectiveness. Still, there is a void between what research indicates and how organizations actually do personnel selection. Real-world personnel selection is replete with examples of methods that have been proven to be ineffective or inferior to other methods.

Personnel selection (and retention) is a key to organizational effectiveness. The most successful firms tend to use methods that accurately predict future perform-ance. We also are interested in selecting employees who will not only be effective, but who will work for us as long as we need them, and who will not engage in counterproductive behavior such as vio-lence, substance abuse, avoidable accidents, and employee theft.

A multiple-hurdle process involving an application, reference and background checks, various forms of standardized testing, and some form of interview is the typical chronology of events for selection, particularly for external hiring decisions. Internal decisions, such as promotions, are typically done with less formality. *Selection is the process of gathering and assessing information about job candidates and ultimately making decisions about personnel.* The process applies to both entry-level personnel decisions and decisions regarding promotions, transfers, and even job retention as part of corporate downsizing efforts.

This chapter will introduce you to selection, describe some of the most popular types of screening procedures,

review the research evidence on each, and discuss the social and legal implications of selection methods. We will first provide an overview of selection and the typical steps employed in the process. We will then introduce you to the various selection approaches in their usual order of use: First, we will review application and biographical blanks; next, we will review the use of background and reference checks; then we will review the various forms of standardized tests that purport to assess applicants' KASOCs. Finally, the chapter will conclude with a discussion of the use of more sophisticated selection procedures, such as assessment centers, performance testing and work samples, and drug and medical tests in the preemployment selection process. Our context for this discussion will be the legal implications of the various personnel practices and areas where there are clear discrepancies between what typically happens and what academic research indicates. This is certainly one chapter where the discrepancies between findings in academic research and actual practice are quite great.

O B J E C T I V E S

After reading this chapter, you should be able to

1. *Understand the concepts of reliability, validity, and utility.*
2. *Understand the validity evidence for various selection methods.*
3. *Discuss approaches to the more effective use for application blanks,*

*An early version of this chapter was written by Michael M. Harris and Barbara K. Brown.

reference checks, biographical data, and the interview in order to increase the validity and legal defensibility of each.

4. *Discuss the approaches available for drug testing.*
5. *Review the validity of different approaches to interviewing.*
6. *Discuss how the various types of candidate information should be integrated and evaluated.*

Wackenhut Security had its share of selection challenges. Although recruitment efforts and a sluggish economy attracted a large number of applicants for its entry-level armed and unarmed security guard positions, new contract opportunities developed after the September 11, 2001, tragedy and new concern was raised about the quality of its personnel. The turnover rate for some positions exceeded 100 percent—meaning, the quit rate in one year exceeded the number of positions. Wackenhut Security also was dissatisfied with the quality of its supervisory personnel.

The company contracted with BA&C (Behavioral Analysts and Consultants), a Florida psychological consulting firm that specializes in selection problems and personnel selection. Wackenhut asked BA&C to develop a new personnel selection system for entry-level guards and supervisors. Underlying this request was a need for Wackenhut to improve its competitive position in this highly competitive industry by increasing sales and contracts, decreasing costs, and, perhaps most important, making certain their security personnel could measure up.

The company, which already compensated its guards and supervisors more than others in the industry, wanted to avoid an increase in compensation in these areas. The company estimated that the cost of training a new armed guard was about $1,800. With several hundred guards quitting in less than a year, the company often failed to even recover training costs in sales. Wackenhut needed new selection methods that could increase the effectiveness of the guards and supervisors and identify guard applicants most likely to stay with the company.

You will recall from Chapter 4 that job analysis should identify the knowledge, abilities, skills, and other characteristics (KASOCs) that are necessary for successful performance and retention on the job. In this case, BA&C first conducted a job analysis of the various guard jobs to get better information on the KASOCs required for the work. After identifying the critical KASOCs, BA&C developed a reliable, valid, and **job-related** weighted application blank, screening test, and interview format.

The process of selection varies substantially from company to company. While Wackenhut initially used only a high school diploma as a job specification, an application blank, a background check, and an interview by someone in personnel, other companies have used more

---

FIGURE 6-1   Steps in the Development and Evaluation of a Selection Procedure

JOB ANALYSIS/HUMAN RESOURCE PLANNING
Identify knowledge, abilities, skills, and other characteristics (KASOCs) (aka: competencies)
Use a competency model tied to strategy orientation

RECRUITMENT STRATEGY: SELECT/DEVELOP SELECTION PROCEDURES
Review options for assessing applicants on each of the KASOCs: Standardized tests (cognitive, personality, motivational, psychomotor)
Application blanks, biographical data, background, reference checks, accomplishment record
Performance tests, assessment centers, interviews

DETERMINE VALIDITY FOR SELECTION METHODS
Criterion-related validation
Expert judgment (content validity)
Validity generalization

DETERMINE WEIGHTING SYSTEM FOR SELECTION METHODS AND RESULTANT DATA

---

complex methods to select employees. American Protective Services, for example, the company that handled security for the Olympics, used a battery of psychological and aptitude tests along with a structured interview.

As with the job analysis and the recruitment process, personnel selection should be directly linked to the HR planning function and the strategic objectives of the company. The mission goal of the Marriott Corporation is to be the hotel chain of choice of frequent travelers. As part of this strategy, the company developed a selection system designed to identify people who could be particularly attentive to customer demands. Wackenhut also had a major marketing strategy aimed at new contracts for armed security guards who would be extremely vigilant. They needed a legal selection system that could identify people most likely to perform well in this capacity.

Figure 6-1 presents a chronology of events in the selection process and the major options available for personnel selection. The previous chapters on job analysis, planning, and recruitment have gotten us to the point of selecting job candidates based on information from one or more selection methods. We will review each of these methods in this chapter. But keep in mind the focus should be on selecting or developing tools that will provide valid assessments on the critical KASOCs, competencies, or job specifications most important for strategy execution. So, the job analysis should identify the strategically important KASOCs or competencies. Then, particular selection methods (or tools) should be adopted to assess these *job specifications.*

SELECTION METHODS: ARE THEY EFFECTIVE?

Our review includes a summary of the validity of each major approach to selection and an assessment of the relative cost to develop and administer each method. Three key terms related to effectiveness are **reliability, validity, and utility.** While these terms are strongly related to one another, the most important criterion for a selection method is *validity.* Remember our discussion of the research on **High-Performance Work Systems.** One of the HR practices shown to be related to corporate performance was the percentage of employees hired using "validated selection methods."[1] The essence of the term *validity* is the extent to which a selection method predicts one or more important criteria. While the most typical criterion of interest to selection specialists is job performance, companies also may be very interested in other criteria such as how long an employee may stay on the job or whether the employee will steal, be violent, or be involved in accidents. But before we address the validity of a method, let's look at one of the necessary conditions for validity: the reliability of measurement.

What Is Reliability?

A necessary condition in order for a selection method to be valid is that it first be *reliable.* Reliability concerns the consistency of measurement. This consistency applies to the scores that derive from the selection method. These scores can come from a paper-and-pencil test, a job interview, a performance appraisal, or any other method that is used to make decisions about people. The CIA uses a very long multiple-choice test as an initial screening device for job applicants to be agents. If applicants were to take the test twice three weeks apart, their scores on the test would stay pretty much the same (the same thing can be said for SAT scores). The level of reliability can be represented by a correlation coefficient. Correlations from 0 to 1.0 show the extent of the reliability. Generally, reliable methods have reliability coefficients that are .8 or higher, indicating a high degree of consistency in scores. No selection method achieves perfect reliability, but the goal should be to reduce error in measurement as much as possible. If raters are a part of the selection method, such as job interviewers or on-the-job performance evaluators, the extent to which different raters agree also can represent the reliability (or unreliability) of the method.

Remember how we cast serious doubts upon graphology (or handwriting analysis) in Chapter 1? This method of selection is used by some U.S. companies and even more European firms. One problem with this method is that it is not even reliable, much less valid. If the same handwriting sample was given to two graphologists, they would generally not agree on scores on various employment-related attributes (e.g., drive, creativity, intelligence). Even if they did agree this does not necessarily mean that their assessments are valid.

More reliable tests tend to be longer. One of the reasons the SAT, the GRE, the GMAT, and the LSAT seemingly take forever to complete is so these tests will have very high reliability (and they do). But while high reliability is a necessary condition for high validity, high reliability does not ensure that a method is valid. The SAT may be highly reliable, but do scores on the SAT predict anything important such as how well you actually will perform in college? This question addresses the *validity* of the method.

What Is Validity?

The objective of the Wackenhut Security Consultants was to develop a reliable, valid, legally defensible, user-friendly, and inexpensive test that could predict both job performance and long job tenure for security guards. The extent to which the test was able to predict an important criterion was an indication of the *test's validity.* The term *validity* is close in meaning but not synonymous with that critical legal term *job relatedness*, which we discussed in Chapters 3 and 4. **Empirical** or **criterion-related validity** involves the statistical relationship between performance or scores on some predictor or selection method (e.g., a test or an interview) and performance on some criterion measure such as on-the-job effectiveness (e.g., sales, supervisory ratings, job turnover, employee theft). At Wackenhut, a study was conducted in which scores on their proposed screening test were correlated with job performance and job tenure. Such a study would strongly support an argument of job relatedness.

The statistical relationship is usually reported as a correlation coefficient. This describes the relationship between the predictor and measures of effectiveness (also called criteria). Correlations from -1 to $+1$ show the direction and strength of the relationship. Higher correlations indicate stronger validity. Assuming that the study was conducted properly, a significant correlation between a method's scores and some important criterion could be offered as a strong argument for the job relatedness of the method if the method resulted in adverse impact against a protected class. Figure 6-2 presents a summary of the empirical validity evidence for the various selection tools, the cost of their development and administration, and group differences by ethnicity.

The higher the correlation, the more predictive (and valid) the selection method. The correlation also can be used to calculate the financial value of a selection method, using a *utility* formula, which can convert **correlations** into dollar savings or profits that can be credited to a particular selection method. A method's utility depends on its validity but other issues as well. For example, recall our discussion of **selection ratio** in Chapter 5. Selection ratio is the number of positions divided by the

FIGURE 6-2   Selection Tools, Cost for Development and Administration, and Group Differences

Tool	Validity[a]	Costs (Development/ Administration)[b]	Group Differences[c]
Cognitive ability tests measure mental abilities such as logic, reading comprehension, verbal or mathematical reasoning, and perceptual abilities, typically with paper-and-pencil or computer-based instruments.	.51	Low/low	B/W: −1.0 H/W: −.5 A/W: .2 W/M: 0
Structured interviews measure a variety of skills and abilities, particularly noncognitive skills (e.g., interpersonal skills, leadership style, etc.) using a standard set of questions and behavioral response anchors to evaluate the candidate.	.51	High/high	B/W: −.23 H/W: −.17
Unstructured interviews measure a variety of skills and abilities, particularly noncognitive skills (e.g., interpersonal skills, leadership style, etc.) using questions that vary from candidate to candidate and interviewer to interviewer for the same job. Often, specific standards for evaluating responses are not used.	.31	Low/high	B/W: −.32 H/W: −.71
Work samples measure job skills (e.g., electronic repair, planning and organizing), using the actual performance of tasks that are similar to those performed on the job. Typically, work samples use multiple, trained raters and detailed rating guides to classify and evaluate behaviors.	.54	High/high	B/W: .38
Job knowledge tests measure bodies of knowledge (often technical) required by a job, often using formats such as multiple-choice questions or essay-type items.	.48	High/low	B/W: .38
Conscientiousness measures the personality trait "conscientiousness," typically with multiple-choice or true/false formats.	.31	Low/low	B/W: −.06 H/W: −.04 A/W: −.08 W/M: .08
Biographical information measures a variety of noncognitive skills and personal characteristics (e.g., conscientiousness, achievement orientation) through questions about education, training, work experience, and interests.	.35	High/low	B/W: −.78 for grades B/W: −.27 biodata H/W: .08 biodata W/M: −.15 biodata
Situational judgment tests measure a variety of noncognitive skills by presenting individuals with short scenarios (either in written or video format) and ask what would be their most likely response or what they see as the most effective response.	.34	High/low	B/W: −.61 on paper and pencil B/W: −.43 on video H/W: −.26 on paper and pencil H/W: −.39 on video W/M: .26 on paper and pencil W/M = .19 on video

FIGURE 6-2	*(Continued)*			

Integrity tests measure attitudes and experiences related to a person's honesty, dependability, trustworthiness, and reliability, typically with multiple-choice or true/false formats.	.41	Low/low	B/W: −.04 H/W: .14 A/W: .04 W/M: .16	
Assessment centers measure knowledge, skills, and abilities through a series of work samples/exercises that reflect job content and types of problems faced on the job, cognitive ability tests, personality inventories, and/or job knowledge tests.	.37	High/high	Varies by exercise; −.02 to −.58	
Reference checks provide information about an applicant's past performance or measure the accuracy of an applicant's statements on the résumé or in interviews by asking individuals who have previous experience with a job candidate to provide an evaluation.	.26	Low/low	??	

[a]Validity values range from 0 to 1.0, with higher numbers indicating better prediction of job performance.

[b]The labels "high" and "low" are designations relative to other tools rather than based on some specific expense level.

[c]Values are effect sizes expressed in standard deviation units. Higher numbers indicate a greater difference; negative values mean the first group scores lower. B/W is black/white difference; H/W is Hispanic/white difference; A/W is Asian/white difference; W/M is female/male difference.

Source: Adapted from Ryan, A. M. & Tippins, N. T. (2004). "Attracting and selecting: What psychological research tells us." HUMAN RESOURCE MANAGEMENT, 43, pp. 307–308. Reprinted with permission of John Wiley & Sons.

number of applicants for those positions. A test with perfect validity will have no utility if the selection ratio is 1.0 (one applicant per position). This is why recruitment and other HR issues such as compensation are so important for personnel selection. Valid selection methods only have great utility for an organization when that organization can be selective based on the scores on that method. There's almost no point in developing and administrating a highly valid selection method if you have to hire anyone who took the test. This was a problem for the military in 2005 and perhaps later.

Content validity assesses the degree to which the content of a selection method represents (or assesses) the requirements of the job. A knowledge-based test for "Certified Public Accountant" could be considered to have content validity for an accounting job. Subject matter experts are typically used to evaluate the compatibility of the content of a test with the actual requirements of a job (e.g., is the knowledge or skill assessed on the test compatible with the knowledge or skill required on the actual job?). Such a study also can be offered as evidence of job relatedness, but the study should follow the directions provided by the Supreme Court in *Albemarle v. Moody* (see Chapter 3) and, just to be safe, comply with the *Uniform Guidelines on Employee Selection Procedures* (UGESP). (See www.eeoc.gov for details on the UGESPs.) **Validity generalization** invokes evidence from past studies on a selection method that is then applied to a new and similar jobs and settings.

What Is Utility?

Utility concerns the economic gains derived from using a particular selection method. The basic formula involves estimating the increase in revenue as a function of the use of the selection method after subtracting the cost of the method. As we said above, good utility requires low selection ratios and thus is related to the ability of the organization to attract a large number of qualified applicants for each position they need to fill.

Selection methods with high validity but that cost relatively little are the ideal for utility. Before contracting with BA&C, Wackenhut Security had studied the options and was not impressed with the validity or utility evidence reported by the test publishers, particularly in the context of the $10–$15 cost per applicant. This was the main reason Wackenhut decided to develop its own methods.

BA&C investigated the validity of its proposed new selection systems using both criterion-related and content-validation procedures. This dual approach to validation provides stronger evidence for job relatedness. The BA&C study strongly suggested that new methods of personnel selection should be used if the company hoped to increase its sales and decrease the costly employee turnover. The resulting analysis showed substantial financial benefit to the company if it adopted the new methods for use in lieu of the old ineffective procedures. The first method BA&C considered was the application blank.

APPLICATION BLANKS AND BIOGRAPHICAL DATA

Like most companies, Wackenhut first required a completed application blank requesting standard information about the applicant, such as previous employment history, experience, and education. Often used as an initial screening method, the application blank, when properly used, can provide much more than a first cut. However, application blanks, as with any other selection procedure used for screening people, falls under the scrutiny of the courts for possible EEO violations. HR managers should be cautious about using information on an application blank that disproportionately screens out protected class members, and they must be careful not to ask illegal questions. The passage of the **Americans with Disabilities Act (ADA),** for example, states that application blanks should not include questions about an applicant's health, disabilities, and worker's compensation history.

Application blanks obviously can yield information relevant to an employment decision. Yet, it is often the weight—or lack of weight—assigned to specific information by particular decision makers that can seriously undermine their usefulness. Decision makers often disagree about the relative importance attached to information on application blanks. For instance they might disagree about the amount of education or experience required. Wackenhut required a bachelor's degree in business or a related discipline for the supervisory job. This criterion alone, however, should not carry all the weight. Wackenhut's personnel staff made no effort to develop a uniform practice of evaluating the information on the forms. They did not take into consideration indicators such as the fact that an applicant lives 20 miles from the workplace. This may indicate that, relative to other responses, the candidate is more likely to quit as soon as another job comes along that is closer to home.

A Discrepancy between Research and Practice: The Use of Application and Biographical Data

What companies do to evaluate application blank data and biographical information and what research suggests are worlds apart. Decision makers rarely use a uniform approach to evaluate data. Scholarly research clearly shows, with adequate data available, the best way to use and interpret application blank information is to derive an objective weighting system.[2] The system is based on an empirical research study, resulting in a **weighted application blank (WAB),** with the weights derived from the results of the research. By empirical study, we mean the responses from the application blanks are statistically related to one or more important criteria such that the critical predictive relationships can be identified. For example, BA&C was able to show that where a security guard lived relative to his assigned duties was indeed a significant predictor of job turnover. Another useful predictor was the number of jobs held by the applicant during the past three years. Figure 6-3 shows some examples from a WAB.

The process of statistically weighting the information on an application blank enhances use of the application blank's information and improves the validity of

---

FIGURE 6-3   Examples of WAB and BIB

WAB EXAMPLES

How many jobs have you held in the last five years?
(a) none (0); (b) 1 (+5); (c) 2–3 (+1); (d) 4–5 (−3); (e) over 5 (−5)

What distance must you travel from your home to work?
(a) less than 1 mile (+5); (b) 1–5 miles (+3); (c) 6–10 miles (0); (d) 11–20 miles (–3); and (e) 21 or more miles (−5)

BIB EXAMPLES

How often have you made speeches in front of a group of adults?

How often have you set long-term goals or objectives for yourself?

How often have other students come to you for advice?

How often have you had to persuade someone to do what you wanted?

How often have you felt that you were an unimportant member of a group?

How often have you felt awkward about asking for help on something?

How often do you work in "study groups" with other students?

How often have you had difficulties in maintaining your priorities?

How often have you felt "burnt out" after working hard on a task?

How often have you felt pressured to do something when you thought it was wrong?

Source: C. J. Russell, J. Matson, S. E. Devlin, and D. Atwater, "Predictive Validity of Biodata Items Generated from Retrospective Life Experience Essays," *Journal of Applied Psychology* 75 (1990), pp. 569–580. Copyright © 1990 by the American Psychological Association. Reproduced with permission.

---

the whole process. The WAB simply is an application blank that is scored—similar to a paper-and-pencil test. It provides a score for each job candidate and makes it possible to compare the score with that of other candidates. For example, the numbers in parentheses for the WAB examples in Figure 6-3 were derived from an actual study showing particular responses were related to job tenure.

Biographical information blanks (BIB) are similar to WABs except the items of a BIB tend to be more personal with questions about personal background and life experiences. Figure 6-3 shows examples of items from a BIB for the U.S. Navy. BIB research has shown the method can be an effective tool in the prediction of job turnover, job choice, and job performance. In one excellent study conducted at the Naval Academy, biographical information was derived from life-history essays, reflecting accomplishments that were then written in multiple-choice format (see Figure 6-3).[3] BIB scoring is also derived from a study of how responses relate to important criteria.

WABs and BIBs have been used in a variety of settings for many types of jobs. WABs are used primarily for clerical and sales jobs. BIBs have been used successfully in the military and the insurance industry. Many insurance companies, for example, use a very lengthy BIB to screen their applicants. Check out www.e-Selex.com for an online biodata testing service.

The **accomplishment record** is an approach similar to a BIB. Job candidates are asked to write examples of their actual accomplishments, illustrating how they had mastered job-related problems or challenges. Obviously, the problems or challenges should be compatible with the problems or challenges facing the organization. The applicant writes these accomplishments for each of the major components of the job. For example, in a search for a new business school dean, applicants were asked to cite a fund-raising project they had successfully organized. HRM specialists evaluate these accomplishments for their predictive value or importance for the job to be filled. Accomplishment records are particularly effective for managerial, professional, and executive jobs.[4] In general, research indicates that methods such as BIBs and accomplishment records are more valid than credentials. For example, having an MBA versus only a Bachelor's degree is not a particularly valid predictor of successful management performance. What an applicant has accomplished in past jobs or assignments is a more valid approach to "leadership" assessment.

How Do You Derive WAB or BIB or Accomplished Record Weights?

To derive the weights for WABs or BIBs, you ideally need a large (at least 150) representative sample of application or biographical data and criterion data (e.g., job tenure and/or performance) of the employees in the position under study. You then can correlate responses to individual parts of the instrument with the performance data. If effective and ineffective employees responded to an item differently, responses to this item would then be given different weights, depending on the magnitude of the relationship. Weights for the accomplishment record are usually derived by expert judgment for various problems or challenges.

Research supports the use of WABs, BIBs, and the accomplishment record in selection. The development of the scoring system requires considerable work, but it is worthwhile because the resulting decisions are often superior to those typically made based on a subjective interpretation of application blank information. However, since you need a large sample size to validate results, the WAB technique will probably be useful only for jobs with many incumbents.

What if you can't do the empirical validation study? Might you still get better results using a weighted system, in which the weights are based on expert judgment? Yes. This approach is superior to one in which there is no uniform weighting system and each application blank or résumé is evaluated in a more holistic manner by whoever is evaluating it.

REFERENCE CHECKS AND BACKGROUND CHECKS

More than 80 percent of companies do some form of reference or background check.[5] The goal is to gain insight about the potential employee from people who have had previous experience with him or her. An important role of the background check is to simply verify the information provided by the applicant regarding previous employment and experience. This is a good practice, considering research indicates that between 20 and 25 percent of job applications include at least one fabrication.[6] Fear of **negligent hiring** lawsuits is a related reason employers do reference and background checks. A negligent hiring lawsuit is directed at an organization accused of hiring incompetent (or dangerous) employees. One HMO was sued for $10 million when a patient under the care of a psychologist was committed to a psychiatric institution and it was later revealed that the psychologist was unlicensed and lied about his previous experience.

A second purpose for reference checks is to assess the potential success of the person for the new job. Reference checks provide information about a candidate's past performance and are also used to assess the accuracy of information provided by candidates. However, HR professionals should be warned: a proliferation of lawsuits has engendered a great reluctance on the part of evaluators to provide anything other than a statement as to when a person was employed and in what capacity. These lawsuits have been directed at previous employers for defamation of character, fraud, and intentional infliction of emotional distress. This legal hurdle has prompted many organizations to stop employees from providing any information about former employees other than dates of employment and jobs. Turnaround is fair play—at least litigiously. Organizations are being sued and held liable if they do not give accurate information about a former employee when another company makes such a request. The bottom line appears simple: Tell the truth. There are laws in several states that provide protection for employers who provide candid and valid evaluations of former employees.

What Are the Legal Implications of Doing Background Checks on Job Candidates?

Employers often request consumer reports or more detailed "investigative consumer reports" (ICVs) from a consumer credit services as a part of the background check. If this is so, employers need to be aware of state laws related to background checks and **The Fair Credit Reporting Act (FCRA),** amended in 2005, a federal law that regulates how such agencies provide information about consumers. State laws vary considerably on background checks. Experts maintain that it is legally safest to comply with the laws of the states where the job candidate resides, where the reporting agency is incorporated, and the employer has its principal place of business. In general, in order to abide by the FCRA or state law, four steps must be followed by the employer: (1) Give the job candidate investigated a notice in writing that you may request an investigative report, and obtain a signed consent form; (2) Provide a summary of rights under federal law (individuals must request a copy); (3) Certify to the investigation company that you will comply with federal and state laws by signing a form they should provide; and (4) Provide a copy of the report in a letter to the person investigated if a copy has been requested or if an adverse action is taken based on information in the report.

One of the problems with letters of reference is that they are almost always very positive while there is some validity, it is low in general (.26). One approach to getting more useful (and valid) distinctions among applicants is to construct a "letter of reference" or recommendation that is essentially a performance appraisal form.[7] One can construct a rating form and request that the evaluator indicate the extent to which the candidate was effective in performing a list of job tasks. This approach offers the added advantage of deriving comparable data for both internal and external job candidates, since the performance appraisal, or reference data, can be completed for both internal and external candidates.

With this approach, both internal and external evaluators must evaluate performances on the tasks that are most important for the position to be filled. An alternative approach asks the evaluator to rate the extent of job-related knowledge, skill, ability, or competencies of a candidate. These ratings can then be weighted by experts based on the relative importance of the KASOCs or competencies for the position to be filled. This approach makes good sense whenever past performance is a strong predictor of future performance. For example, when selecting a manager from a pool of current or former managers, a candidate's past performance as a manager is important. Performance appraisals or promotability ratings, particularly those provided by peers, are a valid source of information about job candidates. However, promotability ratings made by managers are not as valid as other potential sources of information about candidates, such as performance tests and assessment centers.

Employers should do their utmost to obtain accurate reference information despite the difficulties. If for no other reason, a good-faith effort to obtain verification of employment history can make it possible for a company to avoid (or win) negligent hiring lawsuits.

PERSONNEL TESTING

Surveys indicate that between 15 and 20 percent of organizations use some form of ability or knowledge testing to make selection decisions.[8] Many companies now use aptitude or cognitive ability tests to screen applicants, bolstered by considerable research indicating the tests are valid for virtually all jobs in the U.S. economy. The dilemma facing organizations is this: While mental or cognitive ability tests have been shown to be valid predictors of job performance, they can create legal problems because minorities tend to score lower.

Corporate America also is increasing its use of various forms of personality or motivational testing—in part due to the body of evidence supporting the use of certain methods, concern over employee theft, the outlawing of the polygraph test, and potential corporate liability for the behavior of its employees. Lawsuits for negligent hiring and negligent retention, for example, attempt to hold an organization responsible for the behavior of employees when there is little or no attempt to assess critical characteristics of those who are hired. Domino's Pizza settled a lawsuit in which one of its delivery personnel was involved in a fatal accident. The driver had a long and disturbing psychiatric history and terrible driving record before he was hired.

Cognitive ability tests are the most frequently used paper-and-pencil tests in use today. These tests attempt to measure mental, clerical, mechanical, or sensory capabilities in job applicants. You are probably familiar with these cognitive ability tests: the Scholastic Aptitude Test (SAT), the American College Test (ACT), and the General Mental Ability Test (GMAT). Cognitive ability tests, most of which are administered in a paper-and-pencil or computerized format under standardized conditions of test administration, are controversial. On the average, African Americans and Hispanics score lower than whites on virtually all of these tests; thus, use of these tests can affect employment and other opportunities for minorities (see Figure 6-2).

We will address the critical issue of test score differences as a function of ethnicity later in the chapter. Let us begin our discussion with a definition of cognitive ability testing and provide brief descriptions of some of the most popular tests. Then we will review the validity evidence for these tests. We will conclude with a focus on the legal aspects of cognitive ability testing in the context of the latest research, ethnic score differences, and case law.

What Is a Cognitive Ability Test?

Cognitive ability tests measure one's aptitude or mental capacity to acquire knowledge based on the accumulation of learning from all possible sources. Such tests are often distinguished from **achievement tests,** which attempt to measure the effects of knowledge obtained in a standardized environment (e.g., your final exam in this course could be considered a form of achievement test). Cognitive ability or aptitude tests are typically used to predict future performance. Examples are the SAT and ACT, which were developed to measure ability to master college-level material. Having made this distinction between achievement tests and cognitive ability tests, however, we hasten to point out that in practice there isn't a clear distinction between these two classes of tests. Achievement tests can be used to predict future behavior and all tests measure some degree of accumulated knowledge. **Knowledge-based tests** assess a sample of what is required on the job. If you are hiring a computer programmer, a cognitive ability test score might predict who will learn to be a computer programmer; yet, you would benefit more with an assessment of actual programming knowledge. Knowledge-based tests are easier to defend in terms of job relatedness and are quite valid (.48). They can be expensive to develop.

There are hundreds of mental or cognitive ability tests available. Some of the most frequently used and highly regarded tests are the Wechsler Adult Intelligence Scale, the Wonderlic Personnel Test, and the Armed Services Vocational Aptitude Battery. In addition, many of the largest U.S. companies have developed their own battery of cognitive ability tests. AT&T evaluates applicants for any of its nonsupervisory positions on the basis of scores on one or more of its 16 mental ability subtests—the weights given to a particular test depend on the particular job and the validation results. Knight-Ridder, the communications giant, has a battery of 10 aptitude tests, some of which are even used to select newspaper carriers.

There are hundreds of cognitive ability tests available for commercial use. The **Wechsler Adult Intelligence Scale** is one of the most valid and heavily researched. A valid and more practical test is the **Wonderlic Personnel Test.** The publisher of this test, first copyrighted in 1938, has data from more than 3 million applicants. The Wonderlic consists of 50 questions, covering a variety of areas including mathematics, vocabulary, spatial relations, perceptual speed, analogies, and miscellaneous topics. Here is an example of a typical mathematics question: "A watch lost 1 minute 18 seconds in 39 days. How many seconds did it lose per day?" A typical vocabulary question might be phrased as follows: "Usual is the opposite of: a. rare b. habitual c. regular d. stanch e. always." An item that assesses ability in spatial relations would require the test taker to choose among five figures to form depicted shapes. Applicants have 12 minutes to complete the 50 items. The Wonderlic will cost an employer from $1.50 to $3.50 per applicant depending on whether the employer scores the test. The Wonderlic is used by the National Football League to provide data for potential draft picks (the average score of draftees is one point below the national population).[9]

You may remember the Wonderlic from our discussion of the Supreme Court ruling in *Griggs v. Duke Power* (discussed in Chapter 3) and *Albemarle v. Moody.* In *Griggs,* scores on the Wonderlic had an adverse impact against African Americans (a greater proportion of African Americans failed the test than did whites); and Duke Power did not show that the test was job related. Despite early courtroom setbacks and a decrease in use following the *Griggs* decision, according to the test's publisher, the use of the Wonderlic has increased in recent years.

What Are Tests of Specific Ability?

A variety of tests also have been developed to measure specific abilities, including specific cognitive abilities such as verbal comprehension, numerical reasoning, and verbal fluency, as well as tests assessing mechanical or clerical ability, physical or psychomotor ability, including coordination and sensory skills. The most widely used mechanical ability test is the **Bennett Mechanical Comprehension Test (BMCT).** First developed in the 1940s, the BMCT consists mainly of pictures depicting mechanical situations with questions pertaining to the situations. The respondent describes relationships between physical forces and mechanical issues. The BMCT is particularly effective in the prediction of success in mechanically oriented jobs.

While there are several tests available for the assessment of clerical ability, the most popular is the **Minnesota Clerical Test (MCT).** The MCT requires test takers to quickly compare either names or numbers and to indicate pairs that are the same. The name comparison part of the test has been shown to be related to reading speed and spelling accuracy, while the number comparison is related to arithmetic ability.

Physical, psychomotor, and sensory/perceptual are classifications of ability tests used when the job requires particular abilities. Physical ability tests are designed to assess a candidate's muscular strength, movement quality, and cardiovascular endurance. Scores on physical ability tests have been linked to accidents and injuries. One study found that railroad workers who failed a physical ability test were much more likely to suffer an injury at work. Psychomotor tests assess processes such as eye-hand coordination, arm-hand steadiness, and manual dexterity. Sensory/perceptual tests are designed to assess the extent to which an applicant can detect and recognize differences in environmental stimuli. These tests are ideal for jobs that require workers to edit or enter data at a high rate of speed. For example, Bank of America uses a battery of these tests to screen applicants for checking account data entry.

As we discussed in Chapter 3, the validity of physical ability tests has been under close scrutiny lately, particularly with regard to their use for public safety jobs. Many lawsuits have been filed on behalf of female applicants applying for police and firefighter jobs who had failed some type of physical ability test, such as push-ups, sit-ups, or chin-ups. In fact, the probability is great for adverse impact against women when a physical ability test is used to make selection decisions.[10] Sensory ability testing concentrates on the measurement of hearing and sight acuity, reaction time, and psychomotor skills, such as eye and hand coordination. Such tests have been shown to be related to quantity and quality of work output and accident rates.

Are There Racial Differences in Test Performance?

Many organizations discontinued the use of cognitive ability tests because of the Supreme Court ruling in *Griggs*. Despite fairly strong evidence that the tests are valid and increased use by U.S. businesses, the details of the *Griggs* case illustrate the continuing problem with the use of such tests. The Duke Power Company required new employees either to have a high school diploma or to pass the Wonderlic Personnel Test and the Bennett Mechanical Comprehension Test. Fifty-eight percent of whites who took the tests passed, while only 6 percent of African Americans passed. According to the Supreme Court, the Duke Power Company was unable to provide sufficient evidence to support the job relatedness of the tests or the business necessity for their use. Accordingly, the High Court ruled that the company had discriminated against African Americans under Title VII of the 1964 Civil Rights Act. As we discussed in Chapter 3, the rationale for the Supreme Court's decision gave rise to the theory of disparate impact.

The statistical data presented in the *Griggs* case are not unusual. African Americans, on average, score significantly lower than whites on cognitive ability tests; Hispanics, on average, fall about midway between average African American and white scores.[11] See Figure 6-2 for a summary of group differences as a function of selection tool options. Thus, under the disparate impact theory of discrimination, plaintiffs are likely to establish adverse impact based on the proportion of African Americans versus whites who pass such tests. If the *Griggs* case wasn't enough, the 1975 Supreme Court ruling in *Albemarle Paper Company v. Moody* probably convinced many organizations that the use of cognitive ability tests was too risky. In *Albemarle*, the Court applied specific and difficult guidelines to which the defendant had to conform in order to establish the job relatedness of the particular test. The *Uniform Guidelines in Employee Selection Procedures*, as issued by the Equal Employment Opportunity Commission, also established rigorous and potentially costly methods to be followed by an organization to support the job relatedness of the test if adverse impact should result. Current interest in cognitive ability tests was spurred by the research on **validity generalization**, which strongly supported the validity of these tests for virtually all jobs and projected substantial increases in utility for organizations that use the tests. The average validity of such tests was reported to be .51.[12] (See Figure 6-2.)

Some major questions remain regarding the validity generalization results for cognitive ability tests: Are these tests the most valid method of personnel selection across all job situations or are other methods, such as biographical data and personality tests, more valid for some jobs that were not the focus of previous research? Are there procedures that can make more accurate predictions than cognitive ability tests for some job situations? Are cognitive ability tests the best predictors of sales success, for example? (Remember the Unabomber? He had a Ph.D. in math from the University of Michigan. How would he do in sales?) Another issue is the extent to which validity can be inferred for jobs involving bilingual skills. Would the Wonderlic administered in English have strong validity for a job, such as a customs agent, requiring the worker to speak in two or more languages? Bilingual job specifications are increasing in the United States. Invoking the "validity generalization" argument for this type of job based on research involving only the use of English is somewhat dubious. The validity of such tests to predict performance for these jobs is probably not as strong as .5.

Another issue concerns the extent to which other measures can enhance predictions beyond what cognitive ability tests can predict. Generally, human performance is thought to be a function of a person's ability, motivation, and personality. The highest estimate of the validity of cognitive ability tests is about .50. This means that 25 percent of the variability in the criterion measure (e.g., performance) can be accounted for by the predictor, or the test. That leaves 75 percent unaccounted for. Industrial psychologists think the answer lies in measures of one's motivation to perform, personality, or the compatibility of a person's job preferences with actual job characteristics.

Would a combination of methods—perhaps, a cognitive ability test and a personality or motivational test—result in significantly better prediction than the cognitive ability test alone? Research indicates that a combination of cognitive and motivational tests may lead to a more comprehensive assessment of an individual.[13] These tools add what is known as "*incremental validity*" in the prediction of job performance. In general, cognitive ability and job knowledge tests are valid but additional (and valid) tools can add validity to the prediction. Accordingly, the use of other tests that address the motivational components of human performance, in addition to a cognitive ability or knowledge-based test, can help an organization make better decisions. We will discuss these measures shortly.

Why Do Minorities Score Lower than Whites on Cognitive Ability Tests?

This question has interested researchers for years; yet there appears to be no clear answer. Most HRM experts now generally take the view that these differences are not created by the tests, but are most related to inferior educational experiences. But the problem is not a defect or deficiency in the tests per se. The critical issue for HRM experts is not how to modify the test itself, but how to use the test in the most effective way. A panel of the National

Academy of Sciences concluded that cognitive ability tests have limited but real ability to predict how well job applicants will perform, and these tests predict minority group performance as well as they predict the future performance of nonminorities. In other words, the tests themselves are not to blame for differences in scores. Obviously, the dilemma for organizations is the potential conflict in promoting diversity while at the same time using valid selection methods that have the potential for causing adverse impact.[14]

How Do Organizations Deal with Race Differences on Cognitive Ability Tests?

The use of top-down selection decisions based strictly on scores on cognitive ability tests is likely to result in adverse impact against minorities. One solution to this problem is to set a cutoff score on the test so as not to violate the 80 percent rule, which defines adverse impact. Scores above the cutoff score are then ignored and selection decisions are made on some other basis. The major disadvantage of this approach is that there will be a significant decline in the utility of a valid test because people could be hired who are at the lower end of the scoring continuum, making them less qualified than people at the upper end of the continuum who may not be selected. Virtually all of the research on cognitive ability test validity indicates that the relationship between test scores and job performance is linear; that is, *higher test scores go with higher performance and lower scores go with lower performance.* Thus, setting a low cutoff score and ignoring score differences above this point can result in the hiring of people who are less qualified. So, while use of a low cutoff score may enable an organization to comply with the 80 percent adverse impact rule, the test will lose considerable utility.

Another approach to dealing with potential adverse impact is to use a **banding** procedure that groups test scores based on data indicating that the bands of scores are not significantly different from one another. The decision maker then may select anyone from within this band of scores. Research shows that banding procedures have less effect on adverse impact than the characteristics of the applicant pool. Banding only has a big effect on adverse impact when minority preference within a band is used for selection. This approach is controversial and legally questionable.[15]

The use of cognitive ability tests obviously presents a dilemma for organizations. Evidence indicates that such tests are valid predictors of job performance across a wide array of jobs (see Figure 6-2). Employers who use such tests enjoy economic utility with greater productivity and considerable cost savings. However, selection decisions that are based solely on the scores of such tests will result in adverse impact against African Americans and Hispanics. Such adverse impact could entangle the organization in

costly litigation and result in considerable public relations problems. If the organization chooses to avoid adverse impact, the question becomes one of either throwing out a test that has been shown to be useful in predicting job performance or keeping the test and reducing or eliminating the level of adverse impact. Does such a policy leave a company open to reverse discrimination lawsuits by whites who were not selected for employment—their raw scores on the test were higher than scores obtained by some minorities who were hired? Many organizations, particularly in the public sector, have abandoned the use of cognitive ability tests in favor of other methods, such as interviews or performance tests, which result in less adverse impact and are more defensible in court.

However, many other cities and municipalities have opted to keep such tests and then employed some form of banding in the selection of their police and firefighters primarily in order to make personnel decisions that do not result in statistical adverse impact.

Researchers and practitioners are very interested in how to select the most effective candidates while meeting diversity goals and minimizing (or eliminating) adverse impact. Figure 6-4 presents a summary of common practices used to reduce adverse impact, the degree of support in research, and the research findings.

What Is Personality/Motivational/ Dispositional Testing?

While research supports the use of cognitive ability tests for personnel selection, virtually all HRM professionals regard performance as a function of both ability and motivation. Scores on ability tests say little or nothing about a person's motivation to do the job. We can all think of examples of very intelligent individuals who were unsuccessful in many situations (we're back to the Unabomber!). Most of us can remember a classmate who was very bright but received poor grades due to low motivation. The general validity of cognitive ability tests for predicting sales success is rather low and much could be done to improve prediction.

Most personnel selection programs attempt an informal or formal assessment of an applicant's motivation, attitudes, or disposition through psychological testing or a job interview. Some of these assessments are based on scores from standardized tests, performance testing such as job simulations, or assessment centers. Others are more informal, derived from an interviewer's gut reaction or intuition. This section will review the abundant literature on the measurement and prediction of motivation, disposition, and personality using various forms of testing.

There is an increased use of various types and formats for personality or motivational testings, including paper-and-pencil types, video and telephone testing, and, most recently, online testing. Some organizations place great weight on personality testing for employment decisions. BA&C, the company working with Wackenhut

FIGURE 6-4   Practices Used to Reduce Adverse Impact

Common Practices to Reduce Adverse Impact	Degree of Support for Practice in Literature	Research Findings
Target recruitment strategies toward qualified minorities.	+	Characteristics of the applicant pool (e.g., proportion of minorities, average score levels of minorities) have the greatest effect on rates of adverse impact; changing these characteristics through targeted recruitment should help reduce adverse impact. However, simply increasing numbers of minorities in the pool will not help unless one is increasing numbers of qualified recruits.
Use a selection system that focuses on predicting performance in areas such as helping coworkers, dedication, and reliability, in addition to task performance.	+	If the overall performance measure weights contextual performance (e.g., helping, reliability) more than task performance and the tests in a battery are uncorrelated, a test battery designed to predict this definition of overall performance will have smaller levels of adverse impact. Weighting task performance less than contextual performance in the overall performance measure will make cognitive ability less important in hiring and will lead to less adverse impact.
Use a tool with high adverse impact and good validity in combination with a tool with low adverse impact to reduce the overall adverse impact of the system.	0/−	The degree to which adverse impact is reduced by combining tools with lower adverse impact is greatly overestimated; reductions may be small or the combination may actually increase adverse impact.
Provide orientation and preparation programs to candidates.	0	Coaching and orientation programs have little effect on size of group differences but are well received by examinees.
Remove cognitive ability testing from the selection process.	+/0	Using only noncognitive predictors (e.g., interview, conscientiousness, biodata) will lead to significantly reduced adverse impact, but significant black/white differences will remain. Also, cognitive ability tests are among the most valid predictors of job performance, and their removal may result in a selection system that is less effective.
Use banding of test scores.	0	The use of banding has less effect on adverse impact than the characteristics of the applicant pool. Substantial reduction of adverse impact through banding only occurs when minority preference within a band is used for selection (i.e., preferential selection is employed).
Use tools with less adverse impact as screening devices early in the selection process and those with greater adverse impact as later hurdles in the process.	+/0	Using tools with less adverse impact as screening devices early in the process and those with greater adverse impact later in the process will aid minority hiring if the selection ratio is low, but will not have much effect if the selection ratio is high (i.e., few applicants per position).
Change the more negative test taking perceptions of minority test takers about test validity, thereby increasing motivation and performance.	0	May provide a very small reduction in adverse impact.

FIGURE 6-4 *(Continued)*

Identify and remove culturally biased test items.	0	Research suggests that clear patterns regarding what items favor one group or another do not exist and that removal of such items has little effect on test scores; however, item content should not be unfamiliar to those of a particular culture and should not be more verbally complex than warranted by job requirements.
Use other modes of presenting test stimuli than multiple-choice, paper-and-pencil testing (e.g., video).	0	Changes in format often result in changes in what is actually measured and can be problematic; in cases where a format change was simply that (e.g., changed format without affecting what was measured), there was no strong reduction in group differences.
Use portfolios, accomplishment records, and performance assessments (work samples) instead of paper-and-pencil measures.	+/0	Evidence suggests group differences may not be reduced by realistic assessments, and reliable scoring of these methods may be problematic. Well-developed work samples may have good validity and less adverse impact than cognitive ability tests.
Relax time limits on timed tools.	0	Research indicates that longer time limits do not reduce subgroup differences, and may actually increase them.

Source: Adapted from Ryan, A. M. & Tippins, N. T. (2004). "Attracting and selecting: What psychological research tells us," HUMAN RESOURCE MANAGEMENT, 43, pp. 312–313. Reprinted with permission of John Wiley & Sons.

Security, does psychological screening for hundreds of companies using specialized reports based on the five-factor model (FFM) of personality. One of the most popular personality assessment tools is the "Caliper Profile," developed by the Caliper Corporation (www.calipercorp.com). Their Web site claims 25,000 clients. Avis uses the Caliper Profile to hire salespeople.

Sears, Roebuck and Company, Standard Oil of New Jersey, and AT&T have used personality tests for years to select, place, and even promote employees. More companies today use some form of personality test to screen applicants for risk factors related to possible counterproductive behavior.

We will begin this section with a definition of personality and provide brief descriptions of some of the more popular personality tests. We will review the validity of these tests and provide an overview of relevant legal and ethical issues. We will conclude with a description of four relatively new personality tests that have shown potential as selection and placement devices.

What Is Personality?

While personality has been defined in many ways, the most widely accepted definition is that **personality** refers to an individual's consistent pattern of behavior. This consistent pattern is composed of psychological traits. Many researchers subscribe to a five-factor model (FFM) for describing personality.[16] These so-called "Big Five" personality factors are as follows: (1) **introversion/extra-**

version (outgoing, sociable); (2) **emotional stability;** (3) **agreeableness**/likability (friendliness, cooperative); (4) **conscientiousness** (dependability, carefulness); and (5) **openness to experience** (imaginative, curious, experimenting). There are several tests that measure the FFM. (Try http://users.wmin.ac./UK/~buchant/ for a free online "Big Five" test.)

Two relatively new characterizations of personality are **Emotional Intelligence (EI)** and **Core Self-Evaluations (CSE).** EI is considered to be a multidimensional form or subset of social intelligence or a form of social literacy. There are many definitions and many different instruments that purport to measure EI. One definition is that EI is a set of abilities that enable individuals to recognize and understand their own emotions and those of others in order to guide their thinking and behavior to help them cope with the environment. A recent review of EI revealed an average validity of .23 in the prediction of performance. EI was also found to have low correlations with cognitive ability (.22), agreeableness (.23), and extraversion (.34) of the Big Five. Obviously, EI is another construct measure to consider in the development of (or selection of) a testing battery for job candidates.[17]

CSE is a broad and general personality trait composed of four heavily researched traits: (1) self-esteem (the overall value that one places on oneself as an individual); (2) self-efficacy (an evaluation of how well one can perform across situations); (3) neuroticism (the tendency to focus on the negative); and (4) locus of control (the

FIGURE 6-5	**Some Examples of Personality/ Dispositional/Motivational Tests**

PROJECTIVE TECHNIQUES AND INSTRUMENTS

Thematic Apperception Test (TAT)
Miner Sentence Completion Scale (MSCS)
Graphology (Handwriting analysis)
Rorschach Inkblot Test

SELF-REPORT INVENTORIES—EXAMPLES

The NEO Personality Inventory (FFM)
Personal Characteristics Inventory
Gordon Personal Preference Inventory
Myers-Briggs Type Indicator
Minnesota Multiphasic Personality Inventory (MHPI)
California Personality Inventory (CPI)
Sixteen Personality Factors Questionnaire (16 PF)
Hogan Personality Inventory
Job Compatibility Questionnaire (JCQ)
Emotional Intelligence (e.g., EI Scale)
Core Self-Evaluation Scale (CSES)
Caliper Profile

extent to which one believes s/he has control over life's events). The core self-evaluation is a basic assessment of one's capability and potential.

There is some research that investigated the extent to which these new measures add predictive value (or incremental validity) beyond the Big Five or other selection tools. In general, this research indicates useful incremental validity for these measures beyond the big five and other selection models or tools. For example, research with a new instrument that purports to measure (CSE) shows scores on the scale are correlated with job performance and that CSE has incremental validity over the five-factor model.[18]

There are literally thousands of personality tests available that purport to measure hundreds of different traits or characteristics. (Go to www.unl.edu/buros/ for a sample). We will review the basic categories of personality testing next. Figure 6-5 presents a list of some of the most popular tests and methods.

How Do We Measure Personality?

Personality tests can be sorted into two broad categories: projective tests and self-report inventories. Of course, we also can use the interview and data from other sources such as performance appraisals as a means for assessing personality characteristics or competencies as well. **Projective tests** have many common characteristics, the most significant of which is that the purpose and scoring procedure of the test are disguised from the test taker. One of the most famous projective tests is the **Rorschach Inkblot Test,** which presents a series of inkblots to respondents who must then record what they see in each one.

While numerous projective tests exist, the **Miner Sentence Completion Scale (MSCS)** is one of the few such tests specifically designed for use in the employment

setting. Its aim is to measure managers' motivation to manage others.[19] And the test appears to work. The test consists of 40 incomplete sentences, such as "My family doctor . . . ," "Playing golf . . . ," and "Dictating letters . . . ." The test taker is instructed to complete each sentence. According to the developer of these tests, the way in which an applicant completes the sentences reflects his or her motivation along seven areas. These areas are capacity to deal with authority figures, dealing with competitive games, handling competitive situations, assertiveness, motivation to direct others, motivation to stand out in a group, and desire to perform day-to-day administrative tasks. On the downside, the MSCS is expensive and there isn't a great deal of validity evidence to support its use.

Another projective test that has been used occasionally for employment purposes is the **Thematic Apperception Test,** or **TAT,** a test that typically consists of a series of pictures that depict one or more persons in different situations. Test takers are asked to describe who the people are and what is happening in the situation, which is somewhat ambiguous and open to interpretation. The test taker then determines the outcome of the situation. Although a variety of scoring systems have been developed for interpreting a test taker's responses, one of the most popular approaches involves rating the responses with regard to the test taker's need for power (i.e., the need to control and influence others), achievement (i.e., need to be successful), and affiliation (i.e., the need for emotional relationships). Like the MSCS, the TAT has been used primarily for managerial selection and the limited research indicates some validity as a predictor of managerial and entrepreneurial success.

One form of projective test (which we alluded to previously) that has received considerable attention recently is **graphology,** or handwriting analysis. With this approach, a sample of your handwriting is mailed to a graphologist who (for anywhere from $10 to $50) provides an assessment of your intelligence, creativity, emotional stability, negotiation skills, problem-solving skills, and numerous other personal attributes. According to some writers, graphology is used extensively in Europe as a hiring tool. *The Wall Street Journal* and *Inc.* magazine have reported an increase in the use of the method in the United States since 1989. As described in *The Wall Street Journal,* "With the government pulling the plug on the polygraph, and employers clamming up on job references and liabilities from negligent hiring, it is one alternative managers are exploring in an effort to know whom they are hiring." While the use of the method may be increasing, there is no compelling evidence that the method does anything but provide an assessment of penmanship. The only published studies on the validity of graphology have found no validity for the approach.[20]

Self-Report Personality Inventories

Self-report inventories, which purport to measure personality or motivation with the respondent knowing the purpose and/or the scoring procedure of the test, are more popular today than projective techniques. Some instruments screen applicants for aberrant or deviant behavior (e.g., the MMPI), others attempt to identify potentially high performers, and others, particularly more recently developed tests, are directed at specific criteria such as employee theft, job tenure/turnover, accident proneness, or customer orientation.[21]

Self-report inventories typically consist of a series of short statements concerning one's behavior, thoughts, emotions, attitudes, past experiences, preferences, or characteristics. The test taker responds to each statement using a standardized rating scale. During the testing, respondents may be asked to indicate the extent to which they are "happy" or "sad," "like to work in groups," "prefer working alone," and so forth.

One of the most popular and respected personality tests is the **Minnesota Multiphasic Personality Inventory (MMPI).** The MMPI is used extensively for jobs that concern the public safety or welfare, including positions in law enforcement, security, and nuclear power plants. The MMPI is designed to identify pathological problems in respondents, not to predict job effectiveness. The revised version of the MMPI consists of more than 566 statements: "I am fearful of going crazy." "I am shy." "Sometimes evil spirits control my actions." "In walking, I am very careful to step over sidewalk cracks." "Much of the time, my head seems to hurt all over." Respondents indicate whether the statement is true, false, or cannot say. The MMPI reveals scores on 10 clinical scales, including depression, hysteria, paranoia, and schizophrenia, as well as four "validity" scales, which enable the interpreter to assess the credibility or truthfulness of the answers. Millions of people, from at least 46 different countries, from psychotics to Russian cosmonauts, have struggled through the strange questions.

Litigation related to negligent hiring often focuses on whether an organization properly screened job applicants. Failure to use the MMPI in filling sensitive jobs has been cited in legal arguments as an indication of negligent hiring—although not always persuasively. Unfortunately, some companies are damned if they do and damned if they don't. Target stores negotiated an out-of-court settlement based on a claim of invasion of privacy made by a California job candidate who objected to a few questions on the MMPI being used to hire armed guards. Had one of the armed guards who was hired used his or her weapon inappropriately (and Target had not used the MMPI), Target could have been slapped with a negligent hiring lawsuit.

Another popular instrument is the **16 Personality Factors (16PF),** which provides scores on the factors of the FFM, plus others. In addition to predicting performance, the test is used to screen applicants for counterproductive behavior, such as potential substance abuse or employee theft. AMC Theaters, C&S Corporation of Georgia, and the U. S. State Department are among the many organizations that use the 16PF to screen most employees.

Although there are many instruments available, the **NEO Personality Inventory** is one of the most reliable and valid measures of the FFM.[22] Another very popular instrument for employee development but that is not considered a good selection instrument is the **Myers-Briggs Type Indicator (MBTI).**[23]

What Is the Validity of Personality Tests?

Potentially useful personality tests exist among a great number of bad ones, making it difficult to derive general comments regarding their validity. Some instruments have shown adequate validity while others show no validity at all. One instrument with a good track record for selecting managers is the MSCS. A review of 26 studies involving the MSCS found an average validity coefficient of .35.[24] In general, the validity is lower for personality tests than for cognitive ability tests.

The latest review of the FFM found that **Conscientiousness** and **Emotional Stability** had useful predictive validity for all jobs but that Conscientiousness had the highest validity (see Figure 6-2). Extraversion, agreeableness, and openness to experience had useful predictive validity but for only certain situations.[25] For example, extraverted workers are more effective in jobs with a strong social component, such as sales and management. More Agreeable workers are more effective team members. People with high scores on Openness to Experience are more receptive to new training. A particular combination of FFM factors also can predict important criteria. Research involving the FFM and managerial performance shows that Conscientiousness (.25), Extraversion (.21), and Emotional Stability (.24) are useful predictors of managerial success.[26]

Why do personality tests have such low validity relative to cognitive ability? Experts have given a number of explanations for the low (but useful) validity of such tests in the employment context. First, applicants can "fake" personality tests so their personality as reflected on the tests was compatible with the requirement of the job.[27] Second, some proponents of personality testing have asserted that most of the validity studies involving personality tests are poorly designed with very small sample sizes. These experts contend that more carefully designed research would demonstrate higher validity for personality tests. Research shows the weight given to personality factors should derive from a job analysis of criterion-related validation research.

Another possible explanation is that behavior is to a great extent determined situationally, making stable personality traits unpredictable for criteria, such as job performance or employee turnover. Recall some of the examples of items from personality tests listed earlier in this chapter—note that most of the examples are not specific to the workplace; in fact, most of them are quite general. Research in other areas has found that behavior is dependent on the situation. A person who is friendly in outside work might be less sociable in the work setting. In order to enhance predictability, personality assessment should involve more than one method (e.g., tests, interviews). Personality assessment could be more specific to the workplace and target particular criterion measures of interest, such as employee theft, honesty or integrity, or job retention/turnover. Let us examine these newer approaches next.

Approaches to the Prediction of Particular Criteria

Some forms of personality, dispositional, or motivation assessment attempt to focus on either particular problems or criteria characteristic of the workplace. Examples are the prediction of voluntary turnover and the prediction of employee theft. Another instrument attempts to measure job compatibility in order to predict turnover. Other new instruments are designed for particular employment issues, such as customer service, violence, or accident proneness.

Predicting (and Reducing) Voluntary Turnover

Employee turnover can be a serious and costly problem for organizations. You may recall the discussion of Domino's Pizza. They found that the cost of turnover was $2,500 each time an hourly employee quit and $20,000 each time a store manager quit. Among other things, Domino's implemented a new and more valid test for selecting managers and hourly personnel that was aimed at predicting both job performance and voluntary turnover. As of 2005, the program was a great success on all counts. Turnover was down, store profits were up, and the stock was doing well in an otherwise difficult market. Attracting and keeping good employees was a key factor in their turnaround. There are numerous other examples of companies that have expensive and preventable high levels of turnover that can be reduced with better HR policy and practice. Recall the discussion of SAS, the North Carolina software company. Even at the height of the so-called "high tech" bubble in the late 90s, SAS had turnover rates that were well below the industry average. Attracting and keeping good employees is considered a key to the SAS success story.

One recent study revealed guidlines regarding methods that have been shown to be effective at reducing voluntary turnover.[28] A summary of the findings merged with previous research on turnover is presented in Figure 6-6. This most recent research drew several conclusions. First, voluntary turnover is less likely if a job candidate is referred by a current employee or has friends or family working at the organization. Candidates with more contacts within the organization are apt to better understand the nature of the job and the organization. Such candidates probably have a more realistic view of the job that may provide a "vaccination effect" that lowers expectations, thereby preventing job dissatisfaction and turnover (realistic job previews can also do this). Also, current job holders are less likely to refer job candidates who they feel are less capable or those who (they feel) would not fit in well with the organization's culture.

Another argument for an employee referral system is that having acquaintances within the organization is also likely to strengthen an employee's commitment to the firm and thus reduce the probability that he or she will leave. Of course, this argument also applies to the employee who made the referral.

Another reliable predictor of voluntary turnover is tenure in previous jobs. In general, if a person has a history of short-term employment, that person is likely to quit again. This tendency may also reflect a lower work ethic (lower Conscientiousness), which is correlated with organizational commitment and turnover. As discussed earlier, tenure in previous jobs, measured in a systematic manner as a part of a weighted application blank (WAB), is predictive of turnover. Intention to quit is also a solid predictor of, and perhaps the best predictor of, quitting. Believe it or not, questions on an application form such as "How long do you think you'll be working for this company?" are quite predictive of voluntary turnover. Prehire dispositions or behavioral intentions, derived from questions such as this one or from interview questions, work quite well. Measures of the extent of an applicant's desire to work for the organization also predict subsequent turnover. However, almost all of the research on WABS, has involved entry-level and nonmanagerial positions so its applicability to managerial positions is questionable. This is not true for biodata (or BIBs). Disguised-purpose attitudinal scales measuring self-confidence and decisiveness have been shown to predict turnover for higher level positions as well, including managerial positions. Answers to questions such as "How confident are you that you can do this job well?" and "When I make a decision, I tend to stick to it" did predict turnover quite well. In addition, there was no evidence of adverse impact against protected classes using these measures. This research also revealed that disguised-purpose measures added incremental validity to the prediction of turnover beyond what could be predicted by biodata alone.

Another example of a disguised purpose dispositional measure is the *Job Compatibility Questionnaire* (JCQ). We discussed the JCQ in Chapters 4 and 5. The JCQ was developed to determine whether an applicant's preferences-for-work characteristics match the characteristics of the job.[29] One theory is that the compatibility of preference with the job will predict job tenure and performance. Test takers are presented groups of items and are instructed to indicate which item is most desirable and which is least desirable. As we discussed in Chapter 4, the items are grouped based on a job analysis that identifies those characteristics that are common to the job(s) to be filled. Here is an example of a sample group: (a) being able to choose the order of my work tasks, (b) having different and challenging projects, (c) staying physically active on the job, (d) clearly seeing the effects of my hard work. The items are grouped together in such a way that the scoring key is hidden from the respondent, reducing the chance for faking.

FIGURE 6-6	Predictors of Voluntary Turnover

1. *Rely on employee referrals*

   Voluntary turnover is less likely if a job candidate is referred by a current employee or has friends or family working at the organization.

   Candidates with more contacts within the organization are apt to better understand the nature of the job and the organization.

   Having friends or family within the organization prior to hire is likely to strengthen the employee's commitment to the firm and reduce the likelihood that he or she will leave.

2. *Put weight on tenure in previous jobs*

   A past habitual practice of seeking out short-term employment predicts future short-term employment.

   Short-term employment may reflect a poor work ethic, which is correlated with lack of organizational commitment and turnover.

3. *Measure intent to quit*

   Intention to quit is one of the best (if not the best) predictors of turnover.

   Despite their transparency, expressions of intentions to stay or quit before a person starts a new position are an effective predictor of subsequent turnover. (e.g., how long do you plan to work for the company?)

4. *Measure the applicant's desires/motivations for the position*

   New employees with a strong desire for employment will require less time to be assimilated into the organization's culture.

5. *Use disguised-purpose dispositional measures*

   High self-confidence should respond more favorably to the challenges of a new environment.

   Employees with higher confidence in their abilities are less likely to quit than those who attribute their past performance to luck.

   Decisive individuals are likely to be more thoughtful about their decisions, more committed to the decisions they make, and less likely to leave the organization.

   Decisiveness is a component of the personality trait of Conscientiousness from the five-factor model.

   Decisiveness affects organizational commitment and, indirectly, turnover.

Source: Adapted from M. R. Barrick and R. D. Zimmerman, "Reducing Voluntary, Avoidable Turnover through Selection," *Journal of Applied Psychology* 90 (2005), pp. 159–166.

Studies involving customer service representatives, security guards, and theater personnel indicate that the JCQ can successfully predict employee turnover for low-skilled jobs. In addition, no evidence of adverse impact has been found. BA&C incorporated the JCQ in their test for security guards.[30] The JCQ has never been used or validated for managerial positions.

Predicting Employee Theft

More than five million job applicants took some form of honesty or integrity test in 2005. These tests are commonly used for jobs in which workers have access to money, such as retail stores, fast-food chains, and banks. Honesty tests have become more popular since the polygraph, or lie detector, test was banned in 1988 by the Employee Polygraph Protection Act. This federal law outlawed the use of the polygraph for selection and greatly restricts the use of the test for other employment situations. There are some employment exemptions to the law, such as those involving security services, businesses involving controlled substances, and government employers.

Most honesty tests contain items concerning an applicant's attitude towards theft. Sample items typically cover beliefs about the amount of theft that takes place, asking test takers questions such as the following: "What percentage of people take more than $1.00 per week from their employer?" The test also questions punitiveness towards theft: "Should a person be fired if caught stealing $5.00?" The test takers answer questions reflecting their thoughts about stealing: "Have you ever thought about taking company merchandise without actually taking any?" Other honesty tests include items that have been found to correlate with theft: "You freely admit your mistakes." "You like to do things that shock people." "You have had a lot of disagreements with your parents." Many banks and retail establishments use honesty tests for employee screening.

The validity evidence for honesty tests is fairly strong, with no adverse impact. Still, critics point to a number of problems with the validity studies. First, most of the validity studies have been conducted by the test publishers themselves; there have been very few independent validation studies. Second, very few of the criteria-related validity studies use employee theft as the criterion. A report by the American Psychological Association concluded that the evidence, albeit limited, supports the validity of some of the most carefully developed and validated honesty tests. The most recent studies on honesty tests support their use.[31]

Predicting Accident Proneness

Accidents are a major problem in the workplace, causing deaths, injuries, and expense. Preemployment testing is one strategy some companies have turned to in an effort to lower accident rates. One test developed to predict (and prevent) accidents is the Safety Locus of Control (SLC), which is a paper-and-pencil test containing 17 items assessing attitudes towards safety. A sample item is as follows: "Avoiding accidents is a matter of luck." The limited validity studies have been encouraging. Such studies have been conducted in several different industries, including transportation, hotel, and aviation. In addition, these investigations indicate no adverse impact against minorities and women.[32]

Predicting Customer Service

The **Service Orientation Index (SOI)** was initially developed as a means of predicting the helpfulness of nurses' aides in large, inner-city hospitals.[33] The test items were selected from three main dimensions: patient service, assisting other personnel, and communication. Here are some examples of SOI items: "I always notice when people are upset" and "I never resent it when I don't get my way." Several other studies of the SOI involving clerical employees and truck drivers have reported positive results as well.

How Do You Establish a Testing Program?

Establishing a psychological testing program is a difficult undertaking—one that should involve the advice of an industrial psychologist. HR professionals should follow these guidelines before using psychological tests:

1. Most reputable testing publishers provide a test manual. Study the manual carefully, particularly the adverse impact and validity evidence. Has the test been shown to predict success in jobs similar to the jobs you're trying to fill? Have adverse impact studies been performed? What are the findings? Are there positive, independent research studies in scholarly journals? Have qualified experts with advanced degrees in psychology or related fields been involved in the research?

2. Check to see if the test has been reviewed in *Mental Measurements Yearbook (MMY)*. Published by the Buros Institute of the University of Nebraska, the MMY publishes scholarly reviews of the test by qualified academics who have no vested interest in the tests they are reviewing. You can also download Buros test reviews on line at www.unl.edu/buros. You can retrieve reviews by test name or by category (e.g., achievement, intelligence, personality).

3. Ask the test publishers for the names of several companies that have used the test. Call a sample of them and determine if they have conducted any adverse impact and validity studies. Determine if legal actions have been taken related to the test; if so, what are the implications for your situation?

4. Obtain a copy of the test from the publisher and carefully examine all of the test items. Consider each item in the context of ethical, legal, and privacy ramifications. Organizations have lost court cases because of specific items on a test.

Proceed cautiously in the selection and adoption of psychological tests. Don't be wowed by a slick test brochure; take a step back and evaluate the product in the same manner you would evaluate any product before buying it. Be particularly critical of vendors' claims and remember that you might be able to assess personality and motivation by other means. If you decide to adopt a test, maintain the data so that you can evaluate whether the test is working. In general, it is always advisable to contact someone who can give you an objective, expert appraisal.

DRUG TESTING

Drug abuse is one of the most serious problems in the United States today, with productivity costs in the billions and on the rise. Drug abuse in the workplace also has been linked to employee theft, accidents, absences, use of sick time, and other counterproductive behavior. Detected amphetamine use doubled between 2000 and 2004. Methamphetamine is the most commonly used form of amphetamine today. To combat this growing problem, many organizations are turning to drug testing for job applicants and incumbents. One survey found 87 percent of major U.S. corporations now use some form of drug testing.[34]

While some of the tests are in the form of paper and pencil examinations, the vast majority of tests conducted are clinical tests of urine or hair samples. Ninety-six percent of firms refuse to hire applicants who test positive for illegal drug use, methamphetamines, and some prescription drugs (e.g., oxycontin). While the most common practice is to test job applicants, drug testing of job incumbents, either through a randomized procedure or based on probable cause, is also on the increase.

The most common form of urinalysis testing is the immunoassay test, which applies an enzyme solution to a urine sample and measures change in the density of the sample. The drawback of the $20 (per applicant) immunoassay test is that it is sensitive to some legal drugs as well as illegal drugs. Due to this problem, it is recommended that a positive immunoassay test be followed by a more reliable confirmatory test, such as gas chromatography. The only errors in testing that can occur with the confirmatory tests are due to two causes: positive results from passive inhalation, a rare event (caused by involuntarily inhaling marijuana), and laboratory blunders (e.g., mixing urine samples). Hair analysis is a more expensive but also more reliable and less invasive form of drug testing. Testing for methamphetamine use is more difficult since the ingredients pass through the body quickly.

Positive test results say little regarding one's ability to perform the job, and most testing gives little or no information about the amount of the drug that was used, when it was used, how frequently it was used, and whether the applicant or candidate will be (or is) less effective on the job.

The legal implications of drug testing may have changed significantly since this chapter was written. Currently, drug testing is legal in all 50 states for pre-employment screening and on-the-job assessment; however, employees in some states have successfully challenged dismissals based solely on a random drug test. For those employment situations in which a collective-bargaining agreement has allowed drug testing, the punitive action based on the results is subject to arbitration. One study found that the majority of dismissals based on drug tests were overturned by arbitrators.[35] Among the arguments against drug testing are that it is an invasion of privacy, it is an unreasonable search and seizure, and it violates the rights of due process. Most experts agree that all three of these arguments may apply to public employers, such as governments, but do not apply to private industry. State law is relevant here since some drug testing programs have been challenged under privacy provisions of state constitutions. With regard to public employment, the Supreme Court has ruled that drug testing is legal if the employer can show a "special need" (e.g., public safety). We will explore the matter of drug testing in more detail in Chapter 14.

Is Testing an Invasion of Privacy?

Some have critiqued the widespread use of employment tests on the grounds that these procedures may be an invasion of an individual's privacy and produce information that will affect an individual's employment opportunities. Some types of selection methods that seem particularly prone to these concerns are drug tests and honesty/integrity tests.[36] Questions on tests or interviews that are political in nature are also illegal in some states. Experts in the field of employment testing who support the use of these types of selection procedures have responded to the challenges in a number of ways. First, various professional standards and guidelines have been devised to protect the confidentiality of test results. Second, almost any interpersonal interaction, whether it be an interview or an informal discussion with an employer over lunch, involves the exchange of information. Thus, advocates of employment testing contend that every selection procedure comprises some invasion of the applicant's privacy. Finally, in the interests of high productivity and staying within the law, organizations may need to violate an individual's privacy to a certain degree. Companies with government contracts are among those that are obliged to maintain a safe work environment and may need to require drug testing and extensive background checks of employees.

There are those who will continue to voice concern over the confidentiality and ethics of employment testing, particularly as computer-based databases expand in scope and availability to organizations. It also is likely that there will be increasing calls for more legislation at federal, state, and local levels to restrict company access to and use of employment-related information.

PERFORMANCE TESTING/WORK SAMPLES[37]

Despite making valuable contributions to employee selection, paper-and-pencil tests have their problems and limitations. The validity of cognitive ability tests is clear. Unfortunately, the potential legal implications that stem from their use is considerable. As we discussed, the validity of paper-and-pencil measures of applicant motivation or personality is not nearly as impressive. Many experts suggest that the prediction of job performance can be enhanced through performance testing or work samples that involve samples of actual or simulated job tasks and/or behaviors. There is also evidence that the use of such tests can result in less adverse impact than cognitive ability tests (see Figure 6-2).

Performance testing is usually more complex than paper-and-pencil testing in that behavioral responses are required by test takers that are similar to the responses required on the job. A **work sample** consists of tasks representing the type, complexity, and difficulty level of the activities that are required on the job. Applicants must demonstrate that they possess the necessary competencies or skills needed for successful job performance. The most obvious example of a work sample is a word processing test for clerical personnel. More complex examples attempt to simulate what managers must do on the job. **Assessment centers,** for example, often entail several work samples or simulations of on-the-job behaviors typically exhibited by managers.

The objective of performance testing is to assess candidates' ability to do the job. Thus, applicants for clerical positions may be required to take word processing (typing) tests or demonstrate proficiency in shorthand or filing. These exercises are work samples because word processing, shorthand, and filing are representative of the tasks a clerical worker might be asked to perform, and applicants are expected to possess these skills at the time of the interview. A performance test is relatively more effective because of the overlap between the tasks/activities required in the test situation and the tasks/activities required for the actual job. Requesting that clerical applicants demonstrate shorthand skills is effective only if shorthand skills are required for the position. To ensure that performance tests are tailored to match the important activities of the job, HR professionals should develop the performance test from the tasks, behaviors, and responsibilities identified in a job analysis (see Chapter 4).

Another form of performance testing is the **Situational Judgment Test (SJT).** This test consists of a number of job-related situations presented in written, verbal, or visual (video) form. Unlike a traditional work sample, SJTs present hypothetical situations and ask respondents how they would respond. Here's an example of an SJT question: [38]

A customer asks for a specific brand of merchandise the store doesn't carry. How would you respond?

A. Tell the customer which stores carry that brand, but point out that your brand is similar.

B. Ask the customer more questions so you can suggest something else.

C. Tell the customer that the store carries the best merchandise available.

D. Ask another associate to help.

E. Tell the customer which stores carry the brand.

Questions:

1. Which of the options above do you believe is the best under the circumstances?

2. Which of the options above do you believe is the worst under the circumstances?

Research on SJTs is quite positive. (See Figure 6-2 for validity and group differences.) A recent review showed that SJT showed incremental validity above cognitive ability, personality (using the Five-Factor Model), and job/training experiences measures.[39]

The performance testing process should be standardized as much as possible with consistent and precise instructions, testing material, conditions, and equipment. All of the candidates must have the same time allotment to complete tests, and there must be a specific standard of performance by which to compare the applicants' efforts. To illustrate the point, a minimum passing score for a typing exam might be set at 40 words a minute with two errors. This standard would apply to all the applicants. Today, performance tests are available through the Internet. One large retailer had candidates for its district manager position complete a performance test over a Web site. Once responses are made through the Web site, trained assessors conduct interviews that focus on the candidates' responses.

Although the research is limited, that which exists tends to support proctored, Web-based testing.[40] Studies involving SJTs, biodata, and personality measurement using the five-factor model indicate that proctored, Web-based testing has positive benefits relative to paper-and-pencil measures. There is a need for more comparative research between Web-based testing and the traditional paper-and-pencil approach.

What Is an Assessment Center?

An assessment center is a collection of many of the selection tools already discussed. The use of multiple techniques and a standardized process of data collection certainly contributes to the validity of the method (see Figure 6-2). Unlike most of the research on cognitive ability tests, most of the validity evidence on assessment centers is from studies of management positions. These centers use trained observers and a variety of techniques to make judgments about behavior, in part, from specially developed assessment simulations. Assessors typically test job candidates with a collection of performance tests that simulate the work environment. Some centers also use paper-and-pencil tests as part of the assessment process. At the Center for Creative Leadership in Greensboro, North Carolina, managers complete a battery of cognitive and personality tests and receive subordinate and peer assessments prior to their participation in the four-day assessment center.

Private sector organizations, educational institutions, military organizations, public safety, and other governmental agencies have used the assessment center method to identify candidates for selection, placement, and promotion. Most organizations use assessment centers for supervisory or managerial positions. There have been many applications of the method for nonadministrative positions such as sales personnel, vocational rehabilitation counselors, planning analysts, social workers, personnel specialists, research analysts, firefighters, and police officers. One of the advantages of the approach for managerial selection is that internal and external candidates can go through the assessment center for a direct comparison of the candidates, as they participate in the performance testing.

Among the numerous organizations that use the assessment center method for selection are the FBI, AT&T, IBM, Ford, Office Depot, Xerox, Procter and Gamble, the Department of Defense, the CIA, and the Federal Aviation Administration. Assessment centers are expensive, with costs ranging from a low of about $200 for each candidate to as much as $6,000 for upper-level managerial selection.

With the typical assessment center method, information about an employee's strengths and weaknesses is provided through a combination of **performance tests,** which are designed to simulate the type of work to which the candidate will be exposed. A team of trained assessors observes and evaluates performance in the simulations. The assessors compile and integrate their judgments on each exercise to form a summary rating for each candidate being assessed.

Assessment centers tend to vary in terms of length of the assessment process (one day to one week), the ratio of assessors to those being assessed, the extent of assessor training, and the number and type of assessment instruments and exercises that are used to assess candidates.[41]

All assessment centers call for an assessment of job dimensions or competencies. United Technology evaluates managers on the following dimensions: oral presentation, initiative, leadership, planning and organization, written communication, decision making, and interpersonal skills. **Dimensions** are clusters of behaviors that are specific, observable, and verifiable and can be reliably and logically classified together. The dimension "written communication" was defined by United Technology as the following: "clear expression of ideas in writing and in good grammatical form." United Technology breaks down behavioral examples of written communication as: "Exchanges information/reports with superior regarding the day's activities. Completes all written reports and required forms in a manner that ensures the inclusion of all data necessary to meet the needs of the personnel using the information. Uses appropriate vocabulary and avoids excessive technical jargon in required correspondence." Figure 6-7 presents a set of dimensions and their definitions as used in an assessment center for selecting supervisors. There are essentially no differences between "competencies" and dimensions as they are typically defined.

The assessment dimensions and exercises are developed from the results of a job analysis. The exercises allow assessors to observe, record, classify, and evaluate relevant job behaviors. Some of the most common assessment exercises are in-baskets, leaderless group discussions, oral presentations, and role-playing. We will review each of these next.

In-Basket

The in-basket consists of a variety of materials of varying importance and priority that typically would be handled by a manager the organization is trying to hire. Candidates are asked to imagine that they are placed in the position and must deal with a number of memos and items accumulated in their in-baskets. Assessors give them background information about the unit they are managing and they must deal with the in-basket materials in a limited amount of time. After writing their responses to the memos, the candidates are interviewed by trained assessors who review the "out-basket" and question the actions taken. In-baskets are typically designed to measure oral and written communication skills, planning, decisiveness, initiative, and organization skills.

Leaderless Group Discussion

Candidates assemble in groups of three to six people after individually considering an issue or problem and making

specific recommendations. While a leader is not designated for the group, one usually emerges in the course of the group interaction. Two or more assessors observe the interaction as the group attempts to reach consensus on

---

FIGURE 6-7   Assessment Center Dimensions

Leadership: To direct, coordinate, and guide the activities of others; to monitor, instruct, and motivate others in the performance of their tasks; to assign duties and responsibilities and to follow up on assignments; to utilize available human and technical resources in accomplishing tasks and in achieving solutions to problems; to follow through within organizational guidelines.

Interpersonal: To be sensitive to the needs and feelings of others; to respond empathetically; to consistently display courtesy in interpersonal contacts; to develop rapport with others; to be cognizant of and respect the need in others for self-esteem.

Organizing and Planning: To create strategies for self and others to accomplish specific results; to utilize prescribed strategies; to fix schedules and priorities so as to meet objectives; to coordinate personnel and other resources; to establish and utilize follow-up procedures.

Perception and Analysis: To identify, assimilate, and comprehend the critical elements of a situation; to identify alternative courses of action; to be aware of situational or data discrepancies; to evaluate salient factors and elements essential to resolution of problems.

Decision Making: To use logical and sound judgment in use of resources; to adequately assess a situation and make a sound and logical determination of an appropriate course of action based on the facts available, including established procedures and guidelines; to select solutions to problems by weighing the ramifications of alternative courses of action.

Oral and Nonverbal Communication: To present information to others concisely and without ambiguity; to articulate clearly; to use appropriate voice inflection, grammar, and vocabulary; to maintain appropriate eye contact; to display congruent nonverbal behavior.

Adaptability: To modify courses of action to accommodate situational changes; to vary behavior in accordance with changes in human and interpersonal factors; to withstand stress.

Decisiveness: To make frequent decisions; to make decisions spanning many different areas; to render judgments, take action, and make commitments; to react quickly to situational changes; to make determinations based on available evidence; to defend actions when challenged by others.

Written Communications: To present and express information in writing, employing unambiguous, concise, and effective language. To use correct grammar, punctuation, and sentence structure; to adjust writing style to the demands of the communication.

the issue. Assessors typically use the leaderless group discussion to determine oral communication, stress tolerance, adaptability, leadership, and persuasiveness. Some graduate schools now use the leaderless group discussion to select doctoral students for their business and other graduate programs.

Oral Presentation

In the brief time allowed, candidates plan, organize, and prepare a presentation on an assigned topic. An assessment center developed by IBM requires candidates for sales management positions to prepare and deliver a five-minute oral presentation in which they present one of their hypothetical staff members for promotion, and then defend the staff member in a group discussion. IBM uses this exercise to evaluate aggressiveness, selling ability, self-confidence, resistance, and interpersonal contact.[42]

Role-Playing

For this common assessment center exercise, candidates assume the role of the incumbent and must deal with a subordinate about a performance problem. The subordinate is a trained role-player. Another example is to have candidates interact with clients or individuals external to the organization, requiring them to obtain information or alleviate a problem. Vocational rehabilitation counselor candidates who apply for jobs with the Massachusetts Rehabilitation Commission assume the role of a counselor who is meeting a client for the first time. The candidate has the responsibility of gaining information on the client's case and establishing rapport with the client. Figure 6-8 presents summary descriptions of four exercises used in an assessment center to select store managers in a retail environment.

How Are Assessments Done?

Assessors who have received extensive training on assessment center methodology evaluate all of the candidates in an assessment center—usually 6 to 12 people—as they perform the same tasks. Assessors are trained to recognize designated behaviors, which are clearly defined prior to each assessment.

Assessors are often representatives from the organization who are at higher levels than the candidates being assessed. This is done to diminish the potential for contamination, which may result from an assessor allowing prior association with a candidate to interfere with making an objective evaluation. Some assessment centers use outside consultants and psychologists as assessors.

Different assessors observe assessment center candidates in each exercise. The assessors are responsible for observing the actual behavior of the candidate during each exercise and documenting how each candidate performed.

FIGURE 6-8 **Description of Assessment Center Exercises**

Customer Situation: A large equipment user (a select national account) has been experiencing recent problems involving a particular piece of equipment, culminating in a systems down situation. Problems with the equipment could include software, and parts received to fix the equipment are damaged.

The participant will be required to review information about the problem for 30 minutes and generate potential courses of action. Participants will then meet in groups to devise a consensus strategy for dealing with the problem. Assessors should expect a plan of action from the participants and may probe the participants for additional contingency plans. The participants will have 45 minutes to discuss the customer problem and develop a strategy.

Employee Discussion: In this exercise the participant must develop a strategy for counseling a subordinate (a senior customer service engineer) who has been experiencing recent performance problems. The participant will have 30 minutes to review information regarding the technician's declining performance over the last few months.

The participant will then have 15 minutes to prepare a brief report on the individual with recommendations for submission to the district manager. The participant will then meet with two assessors to discuss the strategy.

In-Basket: In this exercise, the participant will assume the role of a newly transferred branch manager. The participant will have 90 minutes to review information related to various issues (technical developments, equipment maintenance specifications, customer information, etc.). The participant will be instructed to spend this time identifying priorities and grouping related issues, as well as indicating courses of action to be taken. The participant will then take part in a 15-minute interview with an assessor to clarify the actions taken and logic behind decisions made.

Problem Analysis: In this exercise the participant will be required to review information on three candidates and provide a recommendation on which of the three should be promoted to a branch manager position. The participant will have 90 minutes to review information and prepare a written recommendation.

The participants will then meet in groups to derive a consensus recommendation for the district manager.

After the participants complete all of the exercises, the assessors typically assemble at a team meeting to pool their impressions, arrive at an overall consensus rating for each candidate on each dimension, and derive an overall assessment rating.

There is recent evidence that assessment centers can be broken down to make them more efficient. Research shows that you probably do not have to assemble candidates together at a "center,"; performance tests completed online and follow-up interviews by trained assessors reveal essentially the same results as the more typical assessment centers.

What Is the Validity and Adverse Impact of Assessment Centers and Other Performance Tests?

There is a scarcity of well-done, criterion-related validity studies on assessment centers. With a few exceptions, assessment center validity studies focus on administrative positions such as managers and supervisors with positive correlations.[43] The method also has proved to be valid for law enforcement personnel.[44] In general, the validity of assessment centers is strong (see Figure 6-2), particularly for managerial positions.[45]

While the validities reported for assessment centers are generally not as high as those reported for most cognitive ability tests, decisions made from assessment centers appear to be substantially more defensible in court and result in less adverse impact than cognitive ability tests. The method is ideal when a company has both internal and external candidates. Most companies use assessment centers as one of the last steps in a selection process where both internal and external candidates are being considered. People who are assessed by the assessment center method or performance tests perceive the procedure to be fair and job related, making them less likely to take legal action.

Performance Appraisals/ Competency Assessment

The use of competencies as a fundamental building block of organizations and the people they employ is increasingly popular and is often used as the basis for personnel decisions within an organization. Remember that a policy of promotion from within the organization (based to some extent on past performance in other jobs) is **a High Performance Work System Characteristic.** But there is little research on the validity of performance-based competency assessment or performance appraisal in general for predicting performance at a higher level. Does high performance in Job A, for example, (at least as rated by supervisors, co-workers, or others) predict performance in Job B? Many companies now use some form of multirater or 360-degree assessment process to measure competencies. (Remember that 360 appraisal is also considered one of those high performance work system characteristics.) Appraisal data can often be found in human resource information systems (HRIS) and used for succession planning. PeopleSoft's most popular HRIS, for example, includes a Web-based competency-appraisal system, the data of which is maintained on each employee and helps companies do succession and career planning.

But how does 360 appraisal or, for that matter, appraisal from any rating source compare on its ability to predict later performance compared to some of these other tools just described? Is 360 appraisal data, or peer assessment, or supervisory assessment as good as (or better than) assessment centers or testing, for example? One recent study in a retail environment addressed this issue comparing the levels of criterion-related validity and the extent of statistical adverse impact against minorities with three popular methods.[46] Data based on top-down (supervisory) performance appraisals, a 360 competency-based appraisal system, and a traditional assessment center were correlated with subsequent job performance of retail store managers. The assessment center and 360 systems had the highest levels of predictive validity while the "top-down" managerial assessment was significantly lower (.30 for ACs and 360 versus .13 for "top-down"). The 360 data and the assessment center also resulted in less adverse impact than the "top-down" method. Evidence for the incremental validity of 360 appraisal data above the AC data was also found. While this one study showed practical usefulness for the 360 appraisal as a source of data for personnel decisions, these data are obviously problematic if both internal and external candidates are being considered since no 360 data would be available for the external candidates. However, you should not ignore useful (and valid) information because some candidates do not have it. Use whatever valid data you have but, if possible, try to obtain the full complement of data on all candidates. This is one advantage of assessment centers for higher-level staffing decisions. When you have external candidates competing against internal candidates for managerial positions, assessment centers create a "level playing field" of valid sources of information about the candidates.

INTERVIEWS[47]

While the use of paper-and-pencil tests and performance tests has increased, the employment interview continues to be the most common personnel selection tool. Primarily due to its expense, the interview is typically one of the last selection hurdles used after other methods have reduced the number of potential candidates. The manner in which interviews are conducted is not typically conducive to high validity for the method. But there is clear evidence that interviews, when done properly, can be quite valid.

One of the bigger discrepancies between HRM research and practice is in the area of interviewing. Research provides clear prescriptions for interviewing the right way and this way is clearly at odds with the way it is typically done. Figure 6-9 presents the most important discrepancies between research and practice as related to interviewing. Even academic institutions, from which the vast majority of this research is derived, do not usually practice what they preach when it comes to selecting a new faculty member or administrator.

FIGURE 6-9 Discrepancies between Research and Practice for Employment Interviews	
What Does Research Say?	**What Is the Practice?**
Use job analysis to derive questions	Less than 20% of companies use job analysis
Monitor interview data for adverse impact	Less than 15% of companies do
Validate interview format/content	Less than 20% of companies do
Train interviewers	Less than 25% do
Weight dimensions based on job analysis	Less than 5% do
Use structured, situational, or behavioral interview	Only 40% do
Use formal interview rating system	Only 21% do
Use more than one interviewer	Only 50% do
Use statistical model to combine data from other sources	Less than 5% use actuarial model

Almost every student eventually will take part in a job interview. Nearly 100 percent of organizations use the employment interview as one basis for personnel selection. Even some universities now use interviews to select students for graduate programs. Dartmouth, Carnegie-Mellon, and The Wharton School at the University of Pennsylvania routinely interview applicants for their prestigious MBA programs. Many companies now provide extensive training programs and specific guidelines for interviewers. As Tom Newman, director of training at S. C. Johnson & Son, Inc., said, interviewing is now "much more of a science." This "science" clearly pays off as research shows greater validity for more systematic interviewing. Mobil Oil, Radisson Hotels International, the Marriott Corporation, and Sun Bank are among many of the companies with extensive programs to prepare their interviewers.

What Factors Affect the Employment Interview?

A veritable plethora of research has been devoted to the employment interview. This research has focused on the attributes of the applicant, the attributes of the interviewer, extraneous variables that affect interview results, interview formats, and, of course, the validity of interviews related to all of these things.

In the context of the interview, the attributes of the applicant refer to characteristics that influence an interviewer's attention and impression of the applicant. Voice modulation, body language, posture, interviewee anxiety and visible characteristics such as sex, weight, ethnicity, and physical attractiveness are among the factors that might influence the interviewer's judgments about a job applicant. A common phenomenon here is "stereotyping," in which an impression about an individual is formed due to his/her group membership rather than any individual attributes. **Stereotyping** involves categorizing groups according to general traits and then attributing those traits to a particular individual once the group membership is known. Although stereotypes are a common and convenient means of efficiently processing information, they can be a source of bias when people attribute traits they

believe to be true for an entire group to one member—without considering that person as an individual

The interviewer's personal characteristics also can influence his/her ability to make decisions. Personal values and previously learned associations between certain information cues and decision responses might influence one's decision-making process. One type of perceptual influence due to the interviewer's personal characteristics is a "similar-to-me" attribution, meaning the interviewer forms an impression due to his/her perceived similarity between an applicant and himself/herself. This perceived similarity might be based on the interviewer's attitudes, interests, or group membership, thus causing certain information, or individuals, to be placed in a more favorable light than others. The danger is that these judgments of similarity can cause rating errors; they might not be relevant to the particular job for which the interview is being conducted.

Factors such as stress, background noise, interruptions, time pressures, decision accountability, and other conditions surrounding the interview also can influence interviewers' attention to information. An important factor is the amount of information the interviewer has prior to the actual interview session. Little background information about the job may cause distortion in the decision-making process because of resulting irrelevant or erroneous assumptions about job requirements. This lack of job information causes the interviewer to rely on his/her assumptions about what the job requires. These can be inconsistent across different interviewers or across different interview sessions. Rating errors occur because interviewers collect non-job-related information and use the information to make decisions.

Applicant, interviewer, and situation attributes can potentially bias one's decision-making process and result in erroneous evaluations during the interview. In response to the problems of interviewer bias and the high cost of face-to-face interviews, many companies conduct computer interviews to screen applicants. The next time you're in a Blockbuster Video, check out the "Employment Center," a computer workstation where you complete a job application online and take an employment test. Telecomputing Interviewing Services in San Francisco lists more than 1,500 clients that conduct computer interviews for mostly entry-level jobs. Bloomingdale's hired all of its personnel for its Miami store using computer interviewing that questions applicants about work attitudes, substance abuse, and employee theft. As Ellen Pollin, personnel manager at Bloomingdale's, puts it, "The machine never forgets to ask a question and asks each question in the same way." Other companies are using videoconferencing to interview employees, particularly managerial prospects. Merrill Lynch and Texas Instruments claim considerable cost savings with no loss in validity using videoconferences.

Citizens Bank of Maryland reduced interviewer involvement by combining a short, structured interview with a video developed especially for tellers and customer service representatives. The video provides a realistic job preview that describes the positive and negative features of the job and then tests applicants on job-related verbal, quantitative, and interpersonal skills. The test is completed on a computer and is scored for $29. Citizens Bank reports a significant drop in turnover with this method compared to turnover rates when hiring decisions were based on an unstructured interview (i.e., in which interviewers have no formal set of questions to ask).

Structured and standardized interviewing is growing in popularity. Perhaps the biggest company in this business is the Gallop Organization (visit gallop.com and find "talent-based hiring" for a description). Gallop conducted a huge study of management behavior, described in the best seller "Now, Discover Your Strengths."[48] Gallop associates conducted over 1.7 million interviews from 101 companies from 63 countries. One result of this research was a structured interview that is administered by telephone and then scored based on the taped transcript using a standardized rating form. This talent assessment tool is now used by, among many others, Disney, Toyota, Marriott, and Best Buy to help select managers and sales personnel. This nontraditional way to conduct an interview nonetheless resulted in the same level of validity as the more traditional approach.[49]

What Is the Validity of Employment Interviews?

The information obtained from the interview provides a basis for subsequent selection and placement decisions. The importance lies in the overall quality of those employment decisions based on interviews: How reliable is the interview information? How valid is that information for predictive purposes? That is, to what extent do interview judgments predict subsequent job performance?

The validity of the employment interview often has been hampered by perceptual factors such as first impressions, stereotypes, and lack of adequate job information. The interview procedure's validity also has been impaired by the underlying perceptual bias—especially due to factors such as different information utilization, different questioning content, and lack of interviewer knowledge regarding the requirements of the job to be filled. However, recent efforts to improve interview effectiveness indicate that certain types of interviews are more reliable and valid than the typical, unstructured format. For instance, interview questions that were based on a job analysis (see Chapter 4), as opposed to psychological or trait information, increase the validity of the interview procedure.[50] **Structured interviews,** which represent a standardized approach to systematically collecting and rating applicant information, have yielded higher reliability and validity results than unstructured interviews (.51 versus .31; see Figure 6-2). Research findings also suggest that the effectiveness of interview decisions can be improved by carefully defining what information is to be evaluated, by systematically evaluating that information using consistent rating standards, and by focusing the interview (and interview questions) on past behaviors and accomplishments in job-related situations. However, a recent study showed averaging across three or four *independent,* unstructured interviews is equivalent in validity to a structured interview done by one interviewer.[51]

With potential bias affecting employment interviews comes potential litigation. Many cases have involved the questions that are asked at the interviews. The employment interview is in essence a "test" and is thus subject to the same laws and guidelines prohibiting discrimination on the basis of age, race, sex, religion, national origin, or disability. Furthermore, the interview process is similar to the subjective nature of the performance appraisal process; hence, many of the court decisions concerning the use of performance appraisals also apply to the interview. The courts have not been kind to employers using vague, inadequate hiring standards; subjective, idiosyncratic interview evaluation criteria; or biased questions unrelated to the job. The courts also have criticized employers for inadequate interviewer training and irrelevant interview questions. In general, the courts have focused on two basic issues for determining interview discrimination: the content of the interview and the impact of those decisions.

The first issue involves discriminatory intent: Do certain questions convey an impression of underlying discriminatory attitudes? Discrimination is most likely to occur when interviewers ask non-job-related questions of only one protected group of job candidates and not of others. Women applying for work as truck drivers at Spokane Concrete Products were questioned about child care options and other issues not asked of male applicants. The court found disparate treatment against females and a violation of Title VII. An interviewer extensively questioned a female applicant of a bank about what she would do if her six-year-old got sick. The same interviewer did not ask that question of the male applicants. The applicant didn't get the job but did get a lawyer. The court concluded that this line of questioning constitutes sex discrimination.

The second issue pertains to discriminatory impact: Does the interview inquiry result in a differential, or adverse, impact on protected groups? If so, are the interview questions valid and job related? Discriminatory impact occurs when the questions asked of all job candidates implicitly screen out a majority of protected group members. Questions about arrests can have a discriminating impact on minorities. The Detroit Edison Company provided no training, job analysis information, or specific questions for its all-white staff of interviewers. The process could not be defended in light of the adverse impact that resulted from interview decisions.

In summary, the inherent bias in the interview and the relatively poor validity reported for unstructured interview decisions make this selection tool vulnerable to charges of discrimination. Employers need to quantify, standardize, and document interview judgments. Furthermore, employers should train interviewers, continuously evaluate the reliability and validity of interview decisions, and monitor interviewer decisions for any discriminatory effects. As we discussed earlier, many companies such as S. C. Johnson, Radisson Hotels, and ExxonMobil now have extensive training programs for interviewers. This training covers interviewing procedures, potential discriminatory areas, rating procedures, and role-plays.

The research evidence regarding the discriminatory effects of the interview is based on the stereotyping processes that affect female and minority job applicants. In the paragraphs that follow, we summarize the evidence, which is generally inconclusive.

Sex Discrimination

Although early research studies indicated that female applicants generally receive lower interview evaluations than male applicants, more detailed analyses suggest that this effect is largely dependent on the type of job in question, the amount of job information available to the interviewer, and the qualifications of the candidate. In fact, recent research suggests that females typically do not receive lower ratings in the selection interview; in some studies, females scored higher ratings than male applicants.

Race Discrimination

There is mixed evidence for racial bias in interviewer evaluations. Positive and negative results have been reported in the relatively few studies that have investigated race discrimination. There is some indication that African American interviewers rate African American applicants more favorably while white interviewers rate all applicants more favorably. One recent study of panel (three or more interviewers) interviews found the effects of rater race, and applicant race were small but that the racial composition of the panel had important practical implications in that over 20 percent of decisions would change depending on the racial composition of the interview panel. Black raters evaluated black applicants more favorably than white applicants only when they were on a predominantly black panel.[52]

Age Discrimination

Although the research indicates that older applicants generally receive lower evaluations than younger applicants, this effect is influenced by the type of job in question, interviewer characteristics, and the content of the interview questions (i.e., traits versus qualifications). The evidence for age bias is mixed and suggests that, as in sex bias, age bias might be largely determined by the type of job under study.

Disability Discrimination

Few studies have examined bias against disabled applicants. The evidence that exists suggests that some disabled applicants receive lower hiring evaluations but higher attribute ratings for personal factors such as motivation. Before any conclusions about disability bias can be made, more research needs to be conducted that examines the nature of the disability and the impact of situational factors, such as the nature of the job. (See Chapter 3 for a discussion of the ADA.)

Overall, the research evidence on discriminatory bias is insufficient to draw any firm conclusions. Employers, however, should examine their interview process for discriminatory bias, train interviewers about ways to prevent biased inquiries, provide interviewers with thorough and specific job specifications, structure the interview around a thorough and up-to-date job analysis, and monitor the activities and assessments of individual interviewers. Some interviewers, no doubt, are guilty of one or more of the discriminatory biases described above.

How Do We Improve the Validity of Interviews?

Many multinational corporations use successful overseas managers to develop and conduct interviews for the selection of managers for international assignments. These managers tend to understand the major requirements of such jobs better than managers who have no overseas experience. Many U.S. companies, including Ford, Nestlé, Procter & Gamble, Texaco, and Philip Morris, credit improvements in their expatriate placements to their interviewing processes, which involve experienced and successful expatriates who have had experience in the same jobs to be filled.

The **physical environment** for the interviews should be maintained consistently by providing a standardized setting for the interviews. The conditions surrounding the interview might influence the decision-making process; therefore, extraneous factors such as noise, temperature, and interruptions should be controlled. Some companies use computer interviewing to standardize the interview process and reduce costs.

There is a great need for interviewer training. Our previous discussion about the decision-making process indicates that interviewers need to be trained regarding how to evaluate job candidates, what criteria to use in the evaluation, how to use evaluation instruments, and how to avoid common biases and potentially illegal questions.

Johnson's Wax found that most interviewers had made their decisions about applicants after only five minutes. They trained their people to withhold judgment and gather information free of the first-impression bias. Companies should use workshops and group discussions to train interviewers on how to do the following:

1. Use job information: understand job requirements and relate these requirements to their questioning content and strategy.
2. Reduce rating bias: practice interviewing and provide feedback and group discussion about rating errors.
3. Communicate effectively: develop a rapport with applicants, "actively listen," and recognize differences in semantics.

This training should focus on the following:

1. Use of interview guides and outlines that structure the interview content and quantitatively rate applicant responses.
2. Exchange of information that focuses on relevant applicant information and provides applications with adequate and timely information about the job and company.

The content of the interview determines what specific factors are to be evaluated by the interviewers. The following are general suggestions based on legal and practical concerns; more specific content guidelines should be based on the specific organization and the relevant state and local laws.

1. Exclude traits that can be measured by more valid employment tests: for example, intelligence, job aptitude or ability, job skills, or knowledge.
2. Include motivational and interpersonal factors that are required for effective job performance. These two areas seem to have the most potential for both overall and interviewer validity. Interviewers should assess only those factors that are specifically exhibited in the behavior of the applicant during the interview and that are critical for performance in the job to be filled. Don't place too much weight on interviewee anxiety.
3. Match interview questions (content areas) with the job analysis data of the job to be filled and the strategic goals of the organization.
4. Avoid biased language or jokes that may detract from the formality of the interview, and inquiries that are not relevant to the job in question.

5. Limit the amount of preinterview information to information about the applicants' qualifications and clear up any ambiguous data. While knowledge of test results, letters of reference, and other sources of information can bias an interview, it is a good strategy to seek additional information relevant to applicants' levels of KASOCs.
6. Encourage note taking; it enhances recall accuracy.
7. Be aware of candidate impression management behaviors.

The format suggestions deal with how the interview content is structured and evaluated. These suggestions describe different types of interview procedures and rating forms for standardizing and documenting interviewer evaluations.

Interview questions are intended to elicit evaluation information; therefore, rating forms are recommended in order to provide a systematic scoring system for interpreting and evaluating information obtained from applicants. Based on the job analysis, the specified content of the interview, and the degree of structure for the procedure, rating forms should be constructed with the following features. First, the ratings should be behaviorally specific and based on possible applicant responses exhibited during the interview. Second, the ratings should reflect the relevant dimensions of job success and provide a focused evaluation of only the factors required for job performance. Third, the ratings should be based on quantitative rating scales that provide a continuum of possible responses. These anchors provide examples of good, average, and poor applicant responses for each interview question. The use of anchored rating forms reduces rater error and increases rater accuracy. This approach, using specific, multiple ratings for each content area of the interview, is preferred to using an overall, subjective suitability rating that is not explicitly relevant to the job. Figure 6-10 presents an example of an actual rating form.

What Are Major Types of Interviews?

A variety of interview formats are used today but most interviews are not standardized. While this lack of standardization has contributed to low reliability and validity of both overall interview decisions and the decisions of individual interviewers, improvements in the effectiveness of the procedure have been made based on the following types of interview formats.

Structured interviews range from highly structured procedures to semistructured inquiries. A highly structured interview is a procedure whereby interviewers ask the same questions of all candidates in the same order. The questions are based on a job analysis and are reviewed for relevance, accuracy, ambiguity, and bias. A semistructured interview provides general guidelines, such as an outline of either mandatory or suggested questions, and recording forms for note taking and summary ratings. In contrast, the

FIGURE 6-10 Sample Situational Interview Questions

1. A customer comes into the store to pick up a watch he had left for repair. The repair was supposed to have been completed a week ago, but the watch is not back yet from the repair shop. The customer is very angry. How would you handle the situation?

1 (low)	Tell the customer the watch is not back yet and ask him to check back with you later.
3 (average)	Apologize, tell the customer that you will check into the problem and call him or her back later.
5 (high)	Put the customer at ease and call the repair shop while the customer waits.[a]

2. For the past week you have been consistently getting the jobs that are the most time consuming (e.g., poor handwriting, complex statistical work). You know it's nobody's fault because you have been taking the jobs in priority order. You have just picked your fourth job of the day and it's another "loser." What would you do?

1 (low)	Thumb through the pile and take another job.
2 (average)	Complain to the coordinator, but do the job.
3 (high)	Take the job without complaining and do it.[b]

[a]Source: Jeff A. Weekley and Joseph A. Gier, "Reliability and Validity of the Situational Interview for a Sales Position," *Journal of Applied Psychology* 3 (1987), pp. 484–487. American Psychological Association. Reprinted with permission.

[b]Source: Gary P. Latham and Lise M. Saari, "Do People Do What They Say? Further Studies on the Situational Interview," *Journal of Applied Psychology* 4 (1984), pp. 569–573.

traditional, unstructured interview is characterized by open-ended questions that are not necessarily based on or related to the job to be filled. Interviewers who use either of the structured interview procedures standardize the content and process of the interview, thus improving the reliability and validity of the subsequent judgments.

Group/panel interviews consist of multiple interviewers who independently record and rate applicant responses during the interview session. With panel interviews, multiple ratings are combined usually by averaging across raters. The panel typically includes the job supervisor and a personnel representative or other job expert who helped develop the interview questions. As part of the interview process, the panel reviews job specifications, interview guides, and ways to avoid rating errors prior to each interview session. Procter & Gamble uses a minimum of four interviews for each position to be filled. The CIA uses a minimum of three interviews for each job candidate. The use of a panel interview reduces the impact of idiosyncratic biases that single interviewers might introduce, and the approach appears to increase interview reliability and validity. Many team-based production operations use team interviews to add new members and select team leaders. In general, there is greater validity in interviews that involve more than one interviewer for each job applicant.[53]

Situational or behavioral interviews require applicants to describe how they would behave in specific situations. The interview questions are based on the critical incident method of job analysis, which calls for examples of unusually effective or ineffective job behaviors for a particular job (see Chapter 4). For *situational* interviews, incidents are converted into interview questions and require job applicants to describe how they would handle a given situation. Each question is accompanied with a rating scale, and interviewers evaluate applicants according to the effectiveness or ineffectiveness of their responses.

Behavioral interviewing asks candidates to describe actual experiences they have had in dealing with specific, job-related issues or challenges. The Palm Beach County, Florida, school board asked the following question of all applicants for the job of high school principal: "Members of the PTA have complained about what they regard as overly harsh punishment imposed by one teacher regarding cheating on an exam. How would you handle the entire matter?" Another question had to do with a teacher who was not complying with regulations for administering standardized tests. The candidate was asked to provide a sequence of actions to be taken regarding the situation. The situational approach may be highly structured and may include an interview panel. In the case of Palm Beach County, three principals trained in situational interviewing listened to applicants' responses, asked questions, and then made independent evaluations of each response. The underlying assumption is that applicants' responses to the hypothetical job situations are predictive of what they would actually do on the job. This technique improves interviewer reliability and validity. Behavioral interviewing may involve probing beyond the initial answer. At GM's Saturn plant, employees are first asked to describe a project in which they participated as group or team members. Probing may involve work assignments, examples of good and bad teamwork, difficulties in completing the project, and other related projects.

While situational interviews are valid, the behavioral interviewing approach where candidates describe actual experiences or accomplishments with important job-related situations is more valid. While interview data should not be overemphasized, interviews will "contribute to the prediction at job performance over and above cognitive abilities and conscientiousness, as well as experience."[54]

COMBINING DATA FROM VARIOUS SELECTION METHODS

We have proposed a number of selection procedures in this chapter. BA&C, the consulting firm working with Wackenhut Security, recommended an accomplishment record for its supervisory job, which could be completed online. Applicants also could complete an "in-basket" on the Net. The next step involved Web-camera interviews between assessors and candidates, followed by a detailed structured and behavioral interview.

But how should the data from the different selection methods be combined so that a final decision can be made regarding the applicants to be selected? One way is to weigh scores from each approach equally after standardizing the data (standardizing means to convert scores to a common scoring key so that a particular score represents the same level of score). Each applicant would receive a standard score on each predictor, the standard scores would be summed, and candidates would then be ranked according to the summed scores. A similar approach calls for rank ordering candidates on each method and then averaging the ranks for each candidate (the top candidate would have the lowest average rank). Another approach is to weigh scores based on their empirical validity; that is, the extent to which each is correlated with the criterion of interest (e.g., sales, performance, turnover). A third approach is to rely on expert judgment regarding the weight that should be given to each selection method. Experts could review the content and procedures of each of the methods and give each a relative predictive weight that is then applied to applicant scores.

One of the "discrepancies" between research and practice is the clear academic finding that "actuarial" or "statistical" decision making is superior to "clinical" or "holistic" prediction. That means you should derive a formula based on the relative validity of different sources of information. This approach is superior to studying a lot of information and then making an overall "clinical" assessment (or prediction). If you can't use validity coefficients, using an average rank ordering process (across methods) is recommended and is superior to "clinical" judgment.

BA&C conducted an empirical validity study and derived weights based on the validity of each of the data sources. Structured, behavioral interviewing for only the top candidates was recommended based on the number of positions they had to fill. This multiple-step process saved time and money. Most companies that use a variety of different instruments follow a similar procedure by initially using the least expensive procedure (e.g., paper-and-pencil tests, biodata), and then using a set of procedures, such as performance tests, for those who do well in the first round. These companies only perform interviews on the top scorers from the second phase of testing. The CIA, the FBI, numerous insurance companies, and a number of the most prestigious graduate business schools follow a similar procedure. The Wharton School at the University of Pennsylvania does initial screening on the basis of the GMAT and undergraduate performance. The school then requests answers to lengthy essay test questions. If the student survives this hurdle, several faculty members conduct interviews with the student.

Interviewing, especially in this context, is perhaps the most important of the selection options for assessing the person–organization fit. Google, for example, interviews job applicants several times by as many as 20 interviewers. Toyota (USA) conducts a formal interview for its Georgetown, Kentucky, factory jobs. The interview results are combined with assessment center data, a work sample, and an aptitude test. The most effective selection systems integrate the data from the interview with other sources and weigh the information using the person–organizational fit model.

What are the legal implications of this multiple-step process? In the *Connecticut v. Teal* case (Chapter 3), Ms. Teal was eliminated from further consideration at the first step of a multiple-step selection process and claimed she was a victim of Title VII discrimination. The Supreme Court said that even if the company actually hired a disproportionately greater number of minorities after the entire selection process, the **job relatedness** of that first step must be determined because this was where Ms. Teal was eliminated.

One excellent example of the effectiveness of using multiple measures to predict is a recent study that focused on predicting college student performance.[55] Scores from a biographical instrument and a situational judgment inventory (SJI) provided incremental validity when considered in combination with standardized college-entrance tests (i.e., SAT/ACT) and a measure of big-five personality constructs. Also, racial subgroup mean differences were much smaller on the biodata and SJI measures than on the standardized tests and college grade point average. Female students outperformed male students on most predictors and outcomes with the exception of the SAT/ACT. The biodata and SJI measures clearly showed promise for selecting students with reduced adverse impact against minorities.

Individual assessment (IA) is a very popular approach for selecting managers although there has been little research to determine validity. This approach is almost always based on an overall assessment provided by one or more psychologists. The IA is based on information from several sources discussed in this chapter. A lengthy interview and psychological testing, often using projective measures, are almost always involved. The Tribune Company, for example, often uses the services of a company that (for $3,000 per candidate) provides a psychological report on the candidate's prospects based on scores on the 16PF personality test (which measures the Big-Five factors and others), a cognitive ability test, and a long interview with a psychologist who is basing the assessment on some prototype of the "ideal" manager. While the psychologist for this company could have used some statistical model for the final assessment based on the relative validity of the various sources of information about the candidates, like almost all IA, the report is based on a "holistic" or clinical assessment of the candidate as a "whole" where the psychologist studies all the information and then writes the report based on the impression formed. This is another example of the discrepancy between research and practice. The research clearly shows to use a statistical model based on the relative validity of the information. An excellent review of this approach to assessment was very critical of the method and concluded "the holistic approach to judgment and prediction has not held up to scientific scrutiny."[56]

Another issue is where you set the cutoff score in a multiple-cutoff system such as that recommended by BA&C. Where, for example, do you set the cutoff score for the paper-and-pencil tests in order to identify those eligible for further testing? Unfortunately, there is no clear answer to this important question. If data are available, cutoff scores for any step in the process generally should be set to ensure a *minimum* predicted standard of job performance is met. If data are not available, cutoff scores should be set based on a consideration of the cost of subsequent selection procedures per candidate, the legal defensibility of each step in the process, (i.e., job relatedness), and the adverse impact of possible scores at each step. As discussed in Chapters 3 and 4, cutoff scores can be at the center of litigation if a particular cutoff score causes adverse impact. As we pointed out, the city of Chicago lost a Title VII lawsuit in 2005 because the particular cutoff score used for the firefighters exam caused adverse impact and was not shown to be "job related" (*Lewis v. Chicago*, 98C5596).

Where the hiring of people who turn out to be ineffective is unacceptable, as, for example, in armed security positions at airports, the setting of a higher (more rigorous) cutoff score is clearly necessary.

PERSONNEL SELECTION FOR OVERSEAS ASSIGNMENTS

One expert on expatriate assignments tells the story of a major U.S. food manufacturer who selected the new head of the marketing division in Japan. The assumption made in the selection process was that the management skills required for successful performance in the United States were identical to the requirements for an overseas assignment. The new director was selected primarily because of his superior marketing skills. Within 18 months, his company lost 89 percent of its existing market share.[57]

What went wrong? The problem may have been the criteria that were used in the selection process. The selec-

tion criteria used to hire a manager for an overseas position must focus on more facets of a manager than the selection of someone for a domestic position. The weight given to the various criteria also may be different for overseas assignments. Besides succeeding in a job, an effective expatriate must adjust to a variety of factors: differing job responsibilities even though the same job title is used, language and cultural barriers that make the training of local personnel difficult, family matters such as spouse employment and family readjustment, simple routine activities that are frustrating in the new culture, and the lack of traditional support systems, such as religious institutions or social clubs. The marketing head in Japan, for example, spent considerable time during the first six months of his assignment simply trying to deal with family problems and to adjust to the new environment. This experience is hardly unique. As we discussed in Chapter 2, expatriate selection is a real challenge. One survey of 80 U.S. multinational corporations found that over 50 percent of the companies had expatriate failure rates of 20 percent or more.[58] The reasons cited for the high failure rate were as follows (presented in order of importance): (1) inability of the manager's spouse to adjust to the new environment, (2) the manager's inability to adapt to a new culture and environment, (3) the manager's personality or emotional immaturity, (4) the manager's inability to cope with new overseas responsibilities, (5) the manager's lack of technical competence, and (6) the manager's lack of motivation to work overseas. Obviously, some of these problems have to do with training and career issues.

Several of the factors listed above concern the process of selecting personnel for such assignments. The food manufacturer placed almost all the decision weight on the technical competence of the individual, apparently figuring that he and his family could adjust or adapt to almost anything. In fact, we now know that adjustment can be predicted to some extent, and that selection systems should place emphasis on adaptability along with the ability to interact well with a diverse group of clients, customers, and business associates. Surprisingly, few organizations place emphasis on so-called relational abilities in the selection of expatriates. One recent review found that despite the existence of useful tests and questionnaires, "many global organizations do not use them extensively because they can be viewed as overly intrusive."[59] Studies involving the Big Five show better cross-cultural adjustment with higher scores in "Openness to Experience" and stronger performance with high "Conscientiousness" scores.[60]

Of course, one critical question that must first be addressed is whether a corporation would be better off hiring someone from within the host country. Figure 6-11 presents a decision model that addresses this option. If the answer to this question is no, the model provides a chronology of the questions to be answered in the selection of an expatriate. If the answer is yes, the decision makers must be aware of any applicable host laws

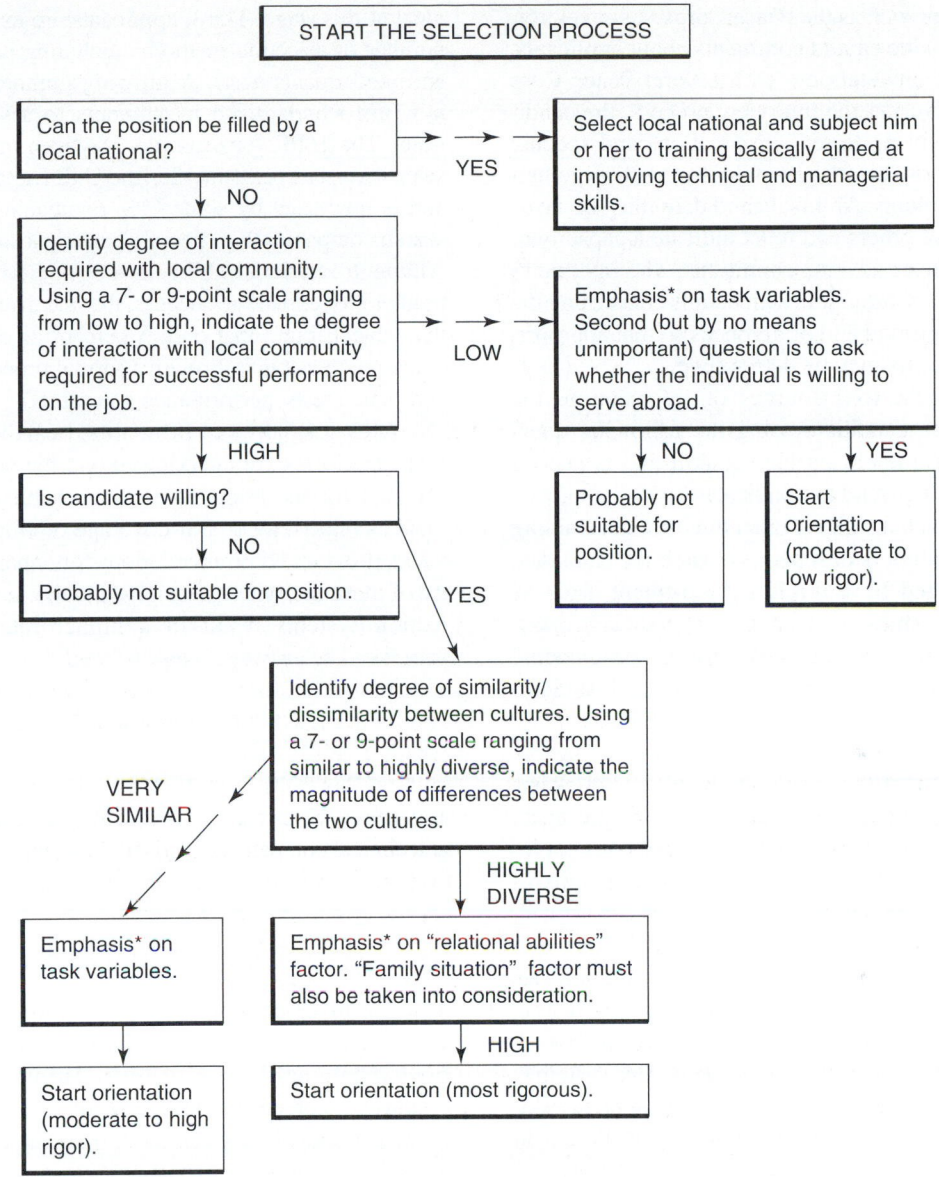

START THE SELECTION PROCESS

Can the position be filled by a local national?

YES → Select local national and subject him or her to training basically aimed at improving technical and managerial skills.

NO

Identify degree of interaction required with local community. Using a 7- or 9-point scale ranging from low to high, indicate the degree of interaction with local community required for successful performance on the job.

LOW → Emphasis* on task variables. Second (but by no means unimportant) question is to ask whether the individual is willing to serve abroad.

NO → Probably not suitable for position.

YES → Start orientation (moderate to low rigor).

HIGH

Is candidate willing?

NO → Probably not suitable for position.

YES → Identify degree of similarity/dissimilarity between cultures. Using a 7- or 9-point scale ranging from similar to highly diverse, indicate the magnitude of differences between the two cultures.

VERY SIMILAR → Emphasis* on task variables. → Start orientation (moderate to high rigor).

HIGHLY DIVERSE → Emphasis* on "relational abilities" factor. "Family situation" factor must also be taken into consideration.

HIGH → Start orientation (most rigorous).

* "Emphasis" does not mean ignoring the other factors. It only means that it should be the dominant factor.

Figure 6-11   Model of the Selection Process for Overseas Assignments

Source: Reprinted from R. L. Tung, "Selection and Training for Overseas Assignments," *Columbia Journal of World Business* 16, pp. 68–78 (1981). Reprinted with permission from Elsevier.

regarding personnel selection. In Poland and Sweden, for example, prospective employees must have prior knowledge of any testing and can prohibit the release of testing data to the company. Many European countries require union participation in all selection decisions for host nationals. Thus, companies may find that hiring host nationals is more problematic than going the expatriate route. Assuming that the host option is rejected, what steps should be followed to make better selection decisions about expatriates? Let us examine some organizations that select large numbers of expatriates successfully.

The Peace Corps has only about a 12 percent turnover rate (i.e., people who prematurely end their assignments).

Of the 12 percent, only 3 to 4 percent are attributed to selection errors. The Peace Corps receives an average of 5,000 applications per month. The selection process begins with an elaborate application and biographical data form that provides information on background, education, vocational preferences, and volunteer activity in the past. Second, the applicant must take a placement test to assess general intelligence and language aptitude. Third, college or high school transcripts are used for placement rather than screening. The fourth step requires up to 15 references from a variety of sources. Although the general tendency among references is to provide positive views of candidates, one study found that for sensitive positions such as the Peace Corps volunteer, references often provide candid comments about applicants. The final step is an interview with several Peace Corp representatives. During the interview process, the candidate is asked about preferred site locations and specific skills as well as how he or she would deal with hypothetical overseas problems. An ideal candidate must be flexible and tolerant of others and must indicate a capacity to get work done under adverse conditions. The interviews also provide Peace Corps staff with details concerning the candidate's background and preferences so that appropriate work assignments may be determined.

Based on these four sources of information, the screeners assess a candidate using the following questions: (1) Does the applicant have a skill that is needed overseas, or a background that indicates he or she may be able to develop such a skill within a three-month training period? This question is designed to match the candidate with a job required by a foreign government, such as botanist, small business consultant, or medical worker. (2) Is the applicant personally suited for the assignment? This question focuses on personality traits such as flexibility, conscientiousness, and emotional stability.

The weight to be given to expatriate selection factors differs as a function of the position to be filled. For example, a position that has an operational element requiring an individual to perform in a preexisting structure does not require strong interpersonal skills. However, a "structure reproducer," an individual who builds a unit or department, does need strong interpersonal skills. Thus, the selection system should focus on the cultural environment, job elements, and individual talents. The weights given to the various criteria should be determined by the individual job. A job analysis would be helpful in this regard. This system is exemplified by Texas Instruments (TI), a manufacturer of electronics and high-technology equipment based in Dallas. In seeking expatriates for start-up ventures, the company focuses on such issues as an individual's familiarity with the region and culture (environment), specific job knowledge for the venture (job elements), knowledge of the language spoken in the region, and interpersonal skills. TI uses several methods to make assessments on these dimensions, including the Five Factor Model.

Many companies emphasize the "manager as ambassador" approach since the expatriate may act as the sole representative of the home office. IBM and GE, for example, select people who best symbolize the esprit de corps of the company and who recognize the importance of overseas assignments for the company.

Our review of the most successful systems for selecting expatriates provides a set of recommendations for a selection system. First, potential expatriates are identified through posted announcements, peer and/or superior nominations, or performance appraisal data. Second, promising candidates are contacted and presented with an overview of the work assignment. A realistic job preview would be ideal at this stage. Third, applicants are examined using a number of selection methods, including paper-and-pencil and performance tests. A growing number of companies now use standardized instruments to assess personality traits. The 16PF, for example, has been used for years to select overseas personnel for the U.S. Department of State and is now used by some U.S. companies and executive search companies that specialize in expatriate assignments. Although relational ability is considered to be a major predictor of expatriate success, the one available survey on the subject found that only 5 percent of companies were assessing this ability through a formal process (e.g., paper-and-pencil tests, performance appraisals).

After a small pool of qualified candidates is identified, candidates are interviewed and the best matches are selected for the assignment. Successful expatriates are ideal as interviewers. Our coverage of employment interviews provides recommendations for enhancing the validity of these interview decisions. Do the more rigorous selection systems result in a higher rate of expatriate success? The answer is clearly "yes."

Two tests that have been shown to be useful (and valid) are the **Global Assignment Preparedness Survey** which assesses candidates on six dimensions, including cultural flexibility, and the **Cross-Cultural Adaptability Inventory** which focuses on the ability to adapt to new situations and interact with people different from oneself.[61]

SELECTION IN OTHER COUNTRIES

The use of employment tests in other countries of the world varies considerably as do the government regulations regarding the use of tests. Turning first to Asian countries, Korean employers report the use of employment tests extensively and more than any other country.[62] These tests tend to be written examinations covering English language skills, common sense, and knowledge of specific disciplines. A smaller percentage of Japanese companies use employment tests. Some Japanese companies use the Foreign Assignment Selection Test (FAST) to identify Japanese who are more likely to be successful expatriates in the United States. The FAST assesses cultural flexibility, sociability, conflict resolution style, and leadership style. Within Japan, however, most people are hired directly from the universities, and the prestige of the university attended is a major criterion for selection purposes. A survey of companies in Hong Kong and Singapore revealed little use of employment tests but there are a growing number of U.S. companies that have opened offices in Hong Kong. Aside from some use of clerical and office tests (e.g., typing), only two companies from these countries indicated use of any personality, cognitive ability, or related tests. Finally, recent evidence indicates China makes extensive use of employment testing, contrary to previous research.[63]

European countries have more controls on the use of tests for selection, but there is considerable variability in usage. Due to the power of unions in most European countries, employers have more restrictions on the use of tests for employment decisions, compared to the United States. A wide variety of employment tests appear to be used in Switzerland, including graphology and astrology, but in Italy selection tests are forbidden by law! In Holland, Sweden, and Poland, job applicants have access to all psychological test results and can choose to not allow the results to be divulged to an employer.[64]

Several surveys have given us clues about selection methods in England. One survey found that more than 80 percent of companies in England do some type of reference check and another found almost 40 percent had used personality tests and 25 percent had used cognitive ability tests to assess managers.[65] About 8 percent of the surveyed firms in England reported using this procedure occasionally.

In general, there is wide variation in the use of employment tests outside of the United States. While some countries have outlawed the use of tests (e.g., Italy), their use appears to be far more extensive in others (e.g., China, Korea). The United States and England appear to be major centers for research and development of employment tests. Japanese companies make extensive use of testing for their U.S. plants as well as for their expatriates.[66] Their Nissan plant in Tennessee relies on team assessment using a structured interview and a battery of cognitive ability tests to select new team members.

U.S. HRM specialists considering the use of tests outside of the United States to hire employees must be very familiar with laws and regulations within the country where the testing is being considered. These laws, regulations, and collective bargaining issues are very different across countries.

THE BOTTOM LINE ON STAFFING

Figure 6-12 presents a chronology of steps that should be followed based on solid research and legal considerations. You should note that effective selection requires effective recruiting. That recruiting should be done only when the organization has determined which KASOCs or competencies are required to execute strategic goals.[67]

FIGURE 6-12   The Bottom-Line Chronology on Staffing

1. DEFINE THE JOB WITH A FOCUS ON JOB SPECIFICATIONS (COMPETENCIES) COMPATIBLE WITH STRATEGIC GOALS AND EXECUTING THOSE GOALS

Action: Re-do job descriptions/specs
Define critical KASOCs/competencies

2. RECRUIT FROM A BROAD POOL OF CANDIDATES

Action: Lower selection ratio (increase number of qualified applicants for key positions) through better and more focused recruiting; for managerial positions, emphasize internal talent.

3. USE VALID INITIAL SCREENING DEVICES

Action: Develop or purchase most valid and most practical screening devices with the least adverse impact

Refer to Mental Measurements Yearbook (www.unl.edu/Buros) for test reviews

If using VG research to validate, make certain the VG study has sufficient detail to show similar jobs were studied.

Where more than one valid selection procedure is available, equally valid for a given purpose, use the procedure which has been demonstrated to have the lesser adverse impact

Develop weighting scheme for competencies and the information sources that purport to measure them (including interview data)

4. DO BACKGROUND/REFERENCE CHECKS

Action: Develop performance-based reference checking focused on KASOCs/competencies

5. USE BEHAVIORAL INTERVIEWING TECHNIQUE WITH STRUCTURED FORMAT OR INDEPENDENT MULTIPLE INTERVIEWERS ASKING BEHAVIORAL QUESTIONS

Action: Develop questions to assess KASOCs/competencies
Train interviewers on valid interviewing and legal issues
Derive a scoring system for interviews regardless of format

6. USE WEIGHTING SCHEME FOR INFORMATION

Action: Derive weighting scheme based on relative importance of KASOCs/competencies and relative validity of the sources of information on each critical KASOC/competency

7. EXTEND AN OFFER

Action: Offer should be in writing with the facts of the offer; train employees to avoid statements regarding future promotions, promises of long-term employment, etc.

Adapted from: Cascio, W. F. & Aguinis, H. (2005). Test development and use: New twists on old questions. *Human Resource Management, 44,* 219–236.

SUMMARY

Preemployment testing continues to be an important HRM responsibility. We have reviewed a number of commonly used tests, which vary in terms of their validity and legal implications. While cognitive ability tests are among the most valid measures, they also frequently result in adverse impact against minority groups. Conversely, many personality tests are safe from legal problems because they typically have no adverse impact, yet are less valid. Many companies also use preemployment drug tests. These tests are generally legal to use, but there are differences from state to state. There is evidence that drug tests will screen out less-effective employees. Reference checks may not be a particularly valid selection device; still, court decisions regarding negligent hiring lawsuits indicate that employers should do their best to check applicant references. Today, paper-and-pencil honesty tests are being used by a growing number of companies because of the restrictions on polygraph testing. Despite some political activity to amend the polygraph law by including a federal ban on these tests as well, research on these tests seems to support their use.

Assessment center and performance testing results are valid, job related, more legally defensible, but certainly more expensive than other selection techniques, including the employment interview. Assessment centers are ideal for managerial jobs with both internal and external candidates. There is evidence, that structured, behavioral interviewing conducted by more than one interviewer can increase the validity of interviews unless unstructured interviews are conducted independently by three or four interviewers.

Most companies use a variety of selection procedures, proceeding through the process in the order described in the model in Figure 6-1. Some organizations combine the information using a statistical or expert model, which enhances the accuracy of decision making. Unfortunately, most companies gather information from several sources (e.g., application blanks, cognitive and personality tests) and apply a subjective and unreliable weighting system to determine the rank of candidates for the positions to be filled. Almost all companies use an employment interview at some point in the selection process. These companies also tend to place entirely too much weight on the results of an unstructured interview.

The accuracy of interview decisions is limited by the information-processing capabilities of interviewers. Factors such as the characteristics of the applicant, the interviewer, and the situation can influence and distort the decision-making process, resulting in less-than-optimal interview decisions. Because employment interviews entail complex decision-making activities, interviewers often try to simplify that process and, in doing so, bias their decisions. This inherent bias poses both legal and practical implications for management. Overall organization performance can be affected because interviewer bias reduces the probability of selecting the highest-performing candidates.

The administrative guidelines described in this chapter help ensure that the validity of the interview is maximized while interviewer bias is minimized. In turn, the procedural guidelines define both the content and the method of the interview inquiry, providing a means of improving the overall effectiveness of the interview procedure. A final dilemma facing organizations that use the interview as a selection tool continues to be the issue of "functional utility": What is the unique contribution of the interview in the employment decision? This is a practical assessment of the usefulness of the interview based on a determination of which information is best collected through the interview process and whether interviewer decisions based on that information are consistent and accurate. In order to achieve any functional utility from the interview, organizations must evaluate their overall selection procedures and determine (1) what factors are best and most consistently evaluated during the interview and (2) whether other selection procedures can measure those identified factors as well as or better than the interview. Organizations also should focus on the purpose of selection interview. Interviews that attempt to assess candidate "fit" while simultaneously recruiting the candidate usually fail at both.

The most effective personnel selection systems place a great emphasis on the interaction of the person and the organization in the prediction of effectiveness. The "matching" model we presented in Chapter 5, for example, calls for an assessment of the applicant in the context of both job and organizational characteristics and a realistic assessment of the organization and the job by the applicant. This "matching" model is particularly effective in "high-involvement organizations" where employees have more latitude in the workplace. As stated at the outset of this chapter, the tools used for selection should ideally be the most valid for the particular KASOCs or competencies most important for strategic execution. This is the optimal "matching" model.

Labor attorney Rita Risser recommends that the "fairness factor" be kept in mind by line managers making hiring decisions.[68] The "fairness factor" is expressed in five questions that should be asked in every hiring decision: (1) Am I basing decisions solely on job-related criteria? (2) Am I treating people consistently? (3) Am I following organizational policy? (4) Am I communicating accurately and honestly? and (5) Should I consult with an HR specialist or a legal expert? Ms. Risser maintains managers who follow the "fairness factor" are more likely to make selection decisions that are free from bias or the perception of bias. Of course, the answers to the first four fairness questions should be "yes" and the importance of the answer to the fifth question about consulting an expert really depends on how knowledgeable the decision maker is about the legal implications of the action. At the most basic level, managers should know that it is either unlawful or potentially unlawful to do any of the following:

1. Base decisions on characteristics such as disability, religion, race, sex, age, or national origin. Some states and municipalities also offer protection for sexual orientation, marital status, and other characteristics.

2. Show prejudice in recruiting or advertising for or against persons with particular protected class characteristics.

3. Request information regarding mental and physical disabilities during the interview.

4. Use methods that cannot be shown to be job related or a business necessity and that cause adverse impact.

5. Make inquiries that reveal protected class characteristics. Questions dealing with place of birth, religious affiliations, citizenship of parents, and political views are examples of potentially troubling inquiries.

DISCUSSION QUESTIONS

1. Are cognitive ability tests more trouble than they are worth? Given that minorities are more likely to score lower on such tests, would it not be advisable to find some other method for predicting job success?
2. Why do you need tests of clerical ability? Couldn't you just rely on a typing test and recommendations from previous employers?
3. Under what circumstances would cognitive ability tests be appropriate for promotion decisions? Are there other methods that might be more valid?
4. If you were given a personality test as part of an employment application process, would you answer the questions honestly or would you attempt to answer the questions based on your image of the "correct" way to answer? What implications does your response have for the validity of personality testing?
5. Discuss the advantages and disadvantages of performance testing. Under what circumstances would such tests be most appropriate?
6. Given that the validity of assessment centers and work samples is not significantly greater than that reported for

cognitive ability tests, why would an organization choose the far more costly approach?
7. It has been proposed that students be assessed with work simulations similar to those used in managerial assessment centers. Assessments are then made on a student's competencies in decision making, leadership, oral communication, planning and organizing, written communication, and self-objectivity. What other methods could be used to assess student competencies in these areas?
8. What is stereotyping? Give examples of legal and illegal stereotypes.
9. Describe how an organization might improve the reliability and validity of the interview.
10. Contrast an unstructured interview with a situational or behavioral interview.
11. "The most efficient solution to the problem of interview validity is to do away with the interview and substitute paper-and-pencil measures." Do you agree or disagree? Explain.
12. Explain the difference between "actuarial" and "clinical" or "holistic" prediction.

III

Developing Human Resource Capability

CHAPTER

7

PERFORMANCE MANAGEMENT AND APPRAISAL*

OVERVIEW

As one review concluded, "the appraisal of performance appraisal is not good."[1] While most organizations report the use of formal systems of performance management and appraisal, the majority of those express considerable dissatisfaction with it.[2] Raters, ratees, and administrators have all expressed dissatisfaction with their appraisal systems.

All of the attention paid to performance appraisal is testimony to its potentially pivotal role in influencing organizational performance and effectiveness. Indeed, formal performance appraisal and multirater systems are components of high-performance work systems and have been linked to corporate financial performance.[3] Central to this linkage is the view that the most effective PM systems recognize that appraisal is not an end in itself; rather it is a critical component of a much broader set of human resource practices that are linked to business objectives, personal and organizational development, and corporate strategy.

Organizations are constantly searching for better ways to appraise performance. Pratt & Whitney, the jet engine division of United Technologies, and Blockbuster Video both made significant changes in their performance appraisal and management systems in three consecutive years. Ford installed a new and highly controversial system as part of a major restructuring effort because their old, highly regarded performance appraisal system resulted in such lenient ratings that few performance distinctions could be made among the workers and little evidence indicated that there were any ineffective workers.

When we recognize the potential value of performance appraisal as a part of **high-performance work systems,** we must also note that performance appraisal is the most heavily litigated personnel practice today.[4] Since the legal grounds for challenging appraisal systems are expanding, litigation can be expected to increase.

The growing diversity of the workforce increases the probability of legal and work-related difficulties. With greater proportions of women, members of minority groups, people of varying sexual orientation, employees with disabilities, and older workers in the labor force, unfairness and biases already present in appraisal systems, either real or perceived, may be magnified by greater diversity and differences between raters and ratees. Consequently, organizations will need to be increasingly scrupulous in encouraging fairness and objectivity in appraisal practices and personnel decisions.

The overall objective of this chapter is to provide recommendations for improving the effectiveness of performance management and appraisal in organizations. We also believe that there are major discrepancies between the way in which appraisal is *practiced* and the way in which experts say it *should* be done. We will emphasize these discrepancies throughout the chapter.

*Joyce Russell and Jeff Kane contributed to this chapter.

172

OBJECTIVES

After reading this chapter, you should be able to

1. *Understand the value and uses of performance appraisals in organizations and the prescriptions for effective appraisal.*
2. *Present a definition of performance and apply the definition to various jobs.*
3. *Discuss the legal implications of performance appraisal.*
4. *Explain the steps to follow when developing an appraisal system.*
5. *Describe the necessary steps for implementing an effective appraisal feedback system.*

Is there any hope for performance appraisal? We think so. Reviews of research, practice, and litigation related to appraisal have led to the recognition that there are some things that can be done to improve the effectiveness of appraisal systems.[5] The effects of appraisal and performance management systems will be more positive if and when certain prescriptions are followed that have generally *not* been heeded by practitioners. These prescriptions are

1. Precision in the definition and measurement of performance is a key element of effective appraisal.
2. The content and measurement of performance should derive from internal and external customers.
3. The PM system should incorporate a formal process for investigating and correcting for the effects of situational constraints on performance.

FIGURE 7-1 | **Prescriptions for Effective Performance Management**

1. Strive for as much precision in defining and measuring performance dimensions as is feasible.
   - Define performance with a focus on valued outcomes tied to strategic goals.
   - Outcome measures should be defined in terms of relative frequencies of outcomes.
   - Define performance dimensions by combining functions with aspects of value (e.g., quantity, quality, timeliness).
2. Link performance dimensions to meeting internal and external customer requirements.
   - Internal customer definitions of performance should be linked to external customer satisfaction.
3. Incorporate the measurement of situational constraints.
   - Focus attention on perceived constraints on performance.

Source: Adapted from H. J. Bernardin, C. Hagan, J. S. Kane, and P. Villanova, "Effective Performance Management: Precision in Measurement with a Focus on Customers and Situational Constraints," in *Performance Appraisal: State-of-the-Art Methods for Performance Management*, ed. J. Smither (San Francisco: Jossey-Bass, 1998).

Figure 7-1 presents these prescriptions, plus some specific recommendations subsumed under each of them.

As we discussed in Chapter 1, research shows that performance management, when done correctly, can (and does) affect corporate performance and the bottom line. In Chapter 4, we discussed the role of performance measurement as a focus in work and job design and analysis. In Chapter 5, we emphasized its role for succession planning and recruitment. In Chapter 6, we discussed its role in the evaluation and improvement of personnel selection systems. The identification and measurement of critical performance criteria are vital for improving an organization's competitive advantage through better products and services and greater responsiveness to customer requirements.

Performance management and appraisal practice have improved in recent years but still have a long way to go. Figure 7-2 presents a summary of findings concerning discrepancies between research and practice. We'll cover all these findings in the pages that follow.

HOW DO WE DEFINE PERFORMANCE AND WHY DO WE MEASURE IT?

Despite the importance of performance appraisal, few organizations clearly define what it is they are trying to measure. In order to design a system for appraising performance, it is important to first define what is meant by the term **work performance.** Although a person's job performance depends on some combination of ability, effort, and opportunity, it can be measured in terms of outcomes or results produced. *Performance is defined as the record of outcomes produced on specified job functions or activities during a specified time period.* For example, a trainer working for the World Bank was evaluated on her "organization of presentations," which was defined as "the presentation of training material in a logical and methodical order." The extent to which she was able to make such "methodical" presentations would be one measure of outcomes related to that function. Those outcomes were evaluated by the customers who received the training.

Obviously a sales representative would have some measure of actual sales as an outcome for a primary function of that job. Customer service is a likely candidate as another important function that would have very different outcome measures for defining performance. College professors are typically evaluated on three general work functions: teaching, research, and service. Performance in each of these three areas is defined with different outcome measures. Students are obviously one source of data to evaluate the quality of the teaching.

Performance on the job as a whole would be equal to the sum (or average) of performance on the major job functions or activities. For example, the World Bank identified eight job functions for their trainers (e.g., use of relevant examples, participant involvement, evaluation procedures). The functions have to do with the work that

FIGURE 7-2   Performance Management: Discrepancies between Research and Practice

Rating Content

Finding: Do not evaluate people on traits.
Practice: High percentage of employees still use traits as criteria.

Finding: Performance dimensions or criteria should be linked to job descriptions.
Practice: 60% of employers report strong linkage; 22% actually evaluate this.

Finding: Setting-specific, challenging goals results in higher performance.
Practice: 26% of managerial appraisal goals/objectives are specific.

Finding: Clearly distinguish among criterion aspects of performance (e.g., quality, quantity).
Practice: 14% of employers distinguish aspects of value by job function or goal.

Finding: Link individual performance dimensions to specific strategic goals.
Practice: 9% actually do this; 55% make the claim.

Rating Process

Finding: Employee participation in goal setting increases motivation, commitment, and performance.
Practice: 18% of nonmanagement positions set goals; 58% of management positions allow participation.

Finding: Specific feedback focuses attention on goals.
Practice: 37% of employees indicate they received specific feedback.

Finding: Establish tight link between goals attainment and rewards.
Practice: 41% of employees perceive a "close link" of goal attainment to rewards.

Finding: Train raters for common frame of reference (FOR).
Practice: 8% of employers use FOR; only 21% know what it is.

Finding: Train raters on giving negative feedback.
Practice: 27% of employers provide any such training.

Finding: Avoid training on rater error distributions—it can create other errors.
Practice: 41% of employers use rater error training.

Finding: Structured diary keeping increases reliability.
Practice: 5% of companies require diary keeping.

Finding: Train raters on cognitive errors like actor/observer bias.
Practice: 8% of employers know what this error is; 3% train on it.

Finding: Distinguish between ratings of person's characteristics and performance outcomes.
Practice: 46% of employers now rate on competencies and don't distinguish between performance and ratee potential, KASOCs, or competencies.

Administrative Uses

Finding: 360-degree appraisal data can reduce adverse impact in promotions.
Practice: 16% of companies that use 360 use it for decision making; 84% of companies rely on "top-down" appraisal for promotions.

Finding: Multi-rater appraisal has higher validity than "top down."
Practice: Less than 5 percent of companies use multi-rater appraisal for decision making.

Rating Results

Finding: Audit data for adverse impact against protected classes (including age).
Practice: 24% of companies do this annually; 63% have never done it.

Finding: Evaluate particular rater tendencies (e.g., ratings by ethnicity, gender, age).
Practice: 15% of companies calculate rating data by rater.

Finding: Reward raters for rating process adherence (e.g., precise criteria, good differentiation).
Practice: 27% of companies include performance management practices as critical component of managers' jobs.

Finding: Assess individual performance levels as related to aggregated, strategic goals.
Practice: 24% actually do this in any way; 58% make the claim.

Source: Adapted from H. J. Bernardin, "Survey of HR Practice: More Evidence on Discrepancies between Research and Practice." Manuscript under review, 2006. *Human Resource Management; See also,* M. London, E. M. Mone, and J.C. Scott, "Performance Management and Assessment: Methods for Improved Rater Accuracy and Employee Goal Setting." *Human Resource Management, 43,* 2004, pp. 319–336.

is performed and *not* the characteristics of the person performing. Unfortunately, many performance appraisal systems confuse measures of performance with measures, traits, or competencies of the person.

Let us emphasize this again: The definition of performance refers to a set of outcomes produced during a certain period of time, and does *not* refer to the traits, personal characteristics, or competencies of the performer. (See Critical Thinking Application 7-A.) We are not saying that there is no place for the measurement of competencies. Indeed, we think there is an important place! We believe, however, that there should be a clear distinction between the measurement of the person and his or her competencies or knowledge or potentiality and that person's performance. Competencies and performance are surely correlated but they are not the same thing.

What Are the Uses of Performance Data?

The information collected from performance measurement is most widely used for compensation, performance improvement or management, and documentation. As we discussed in previous chapters, performance data are also used for staffing decisions (e.g., promotion, transfer, discharge, layoffs), training needs analysis, employee development, and research and program evaluation.

Performance Management and Compensation

Performance appraisal information may be used by supervisors to manage the performance of their employees. Appraisal data can reveal employees' performance weaknesses, which managers can refer to when setting goals or target levels for improvements. Performance management programs may be focused at one or more of the following levels: individual performers, work groups or organizational subunits, or the entire organization. Data on performance should be collected at the appropriate level and over time to indicate trends.

To motivate employees to improve their performance and achieve their target goals, supervisors can use incentives such as pay-for-performance programs (e.g., merit pay, incentives, bonus awards). One of the strongest trends in this country is toward some form of pay-for-performance (PFP) system. We discuss this issue in Chapter 11. Obviously, effective performance measurement is critical for PFP systems to work.

Internal Staffing

Performance appraisal information is also used to make staffing decisions. As we discussed in Chapters 5 and 6, many organizations rely on performance appraisal data to decide which employees to move upwards (promote) to fill openings and which employees to retain as a part of "right-sizing" effort. Performance appraisals should also be the basis of terminations when the organization concludes performance fails to meet a minimum standard or, perhaps, the organization could do better without an employee.

One problem with relying on performance appraisal information to make decisions about job movements is that employee performance is typically only measured for the *current* job. If the job at the higher, lateral, or lower level is different from the employee's current job, then it may be difficult to estimate how the employee will perform on the new job if that new job requires significantly different competencies (or KASOCs). Assessments of these competencies can be done in a variety of ways, including judgments by supervisors, peers, and even subordinates. Of course, many organizations use assessment tools such as those described in Chapter 6.

Assessments of competencies or other worker characteristics using ratings by qualified rating sources such as supervisors and peers is a perfectly acceptable approach for internal staffing decisions and, in most cases, more valid than other approaches to assessment discussed in Chapter 6. However, such assessments should be distinguished from the measurement of performance. It is possible to apply "predictive weights" to performance appraisal data to use the data for promotional decisions. If a study establishes a linkage between effective performance on certain job dimensions at Job A with effective performance at Job B, then ratings on those dimensions could be given predictive weights. But it is not advisable to rely only on performance appraisal data to make promotional decisions since the jobs are undoubtedly different in some way and thus require somewhat different KASOCs or competencies.

Training Needs Analysis

Most firms use appraisal data to determine employees' needs for training or development. Hundreds of companies, including Microsoft, IBM, and Merck, now use multi-source raters (e.g., subordinates, peers, clients) to evaluate their supervisors or managers.[6] The results are revealed to each manager with suggestions for specific training and development (if needed). Honeywell, for example, has specific training modules based on appraisal ratings for several job functions.

Research and Evaluation

Appraisal data can also be used to determine whether various human resource programs (e.g., selection, training) are effective. For example, when Toledo, Ohio, wanted to know whether their police officer selection test was valid, they collected performance appraisal data on officers who had taken the test when they were hired so that test scores could be correlated with job performance.

LEGAL ISSUES ASSOCIATED WITH PERFORMANCE APPRAISALS

Since performance appraisal data are used to make many important personnel decisions (e.g., pay, promotion, selection, termination), it is understandable that appraisal is a major target of legal disputes involving employee charges of unfairness and bias.[7] There are several legal avenues a

FIGURE 7-3 Recommendations for Legally Sound Performance Appraisals

	Legal Theory	Suggestion for Limiting Potential Liability
Appraisal procedures		
• Should be standardized and uniform for all employees within a job group	Harassment or constructive discharge	Require employees to notify employer of any conditions related to job, job performance, or appraisals (for example, supervisor bias or improper conduct); establish and consistently follow procedures to promptly investigate and eliminate any such offending conditions or conduct by supervisors or other employees to avoid claim that employer tacitly accepted or approved of harassment
• Should be formally communicated to employees		
• Should provide notice of performance deficiencies and of opportunities to correct them		
• Should provide access for employees to review appraisal results		
• Should provide formal appeal mechanisms that allow for employee input		
• Should use multiple, diverse, and unbiased raters		
• Should provide written instructions and training for raters		
• Should require thorough and consistent documentation across raters that includes specific examples of performance based on personal knowledge	Age discrimination	Train supervisors to avoid age-loaded comments in verbal or written appraisals; update performance criteria as technology changes to avoid pretext claims when older workers are laid off for lack of newer skills
• Should establish a system to detect potentially discriminatory effects or abuses of the system overall		
Appraisal criteria	Disability discrimination	Review recommendations and appraisal results for evidence of perceived ("regarded as") discrimination; ensure that only essential functions are evaluated; train supervisors to identify reasonable accommodations in performance criteria and appraisal procedures on an interactive basis in a discrete and confidential manner
• Should be objective rather than subjective		
• Should be job-related or based on job analysis		
• Should be based on results or behavioral outcomes rather than traits		
• Should be within the control of the ratee	Defamation or misrepresentation	Establish procedures to control or avoid providing false performance information (favorable or unfavorable)
• Should relate to specific functions, not global assessments		
• Should be communicated to the employee	Negligence	Keep employees advised if performance is poor so they cannot contest discharge by claiming performance would have improved but for faulty evaluation process

person may pursue to obtain relief from discriminatory performance appraisals. As discussed in Chapter 3, the most widely used federal laws are Title VII of the Civil Rights Act and the Age Discrimination in Employment Act. However, there are numerous other possible sources of redress.

There are several recommendations to assist employers in conducting fair performance appraisals and avoiding legal suits. Figure 7-3 presents a summary of these recommendations.

Recall the discussion in Chapter 3 about adverse impact related to personnel decisions and court rulings regarding the "disparate impact" theory of discrimination and performance appraisal. The Supreme Court has ruled that adverse impact statistics such as the 80 percent rule can be used in Title VII and ADEA cases where performance appraisal was used to make decisions regarding who gets promoted (consider Wal-Mart's huge sex discrimination lawsuit), who gets terminated (think of Ford's 2001 age and race discrimination case related to its downsizing), who gets merit raises (back to Wal-Mart), and any other important personnel decisions. Prima facie evidence of discrimination in the form of an 80 percent rule violation is an excellent predictor of the outcome of court decisions against employers.

Organizations should audit their appraisal data to test for possible adverse impact effects long before they get sued. They might even avoid getting sued. Adverse impact statistics have even been used successfully in "disparate treatment" cases to support an individual's claim of race or gender discrimination. Such data can also be used by the employer to rebut such a claim if in fact there is no evidence of adverse impact. Bottom line for organizations: An organization is in trouble if it gets sued, there is a certified class of alleged victims (e.g., a class of females, minorities), and the organization has violated the 80 percent rule in its decisions based on using an appraisal system that adheres to few (or none) of the recommendations in Figure 7-3.

DESIGNING AN APPRAISAL SYSTEM

The process of designing an appraisal system should involve managers, employees, HR professionals, and both internal and external customers in making decisions about each of the following issues:

- Measurement content.
- Measurement process.
- Defining the rater (i.e., who should rate performance).
- Defining the ratee (i.e., the level of performance to rate).
- Administrative characteristics.

It is a challenge to make the correct decisions since no single set of choices is optimal in all situations. The starting point should be the strategic plan and objectives of the organization. The details of the plan should be reviewed in order to design an appraisal system consistent with the overall goals of the firm.

Measurement Content

Appraisal can be either person-oriented (focusing on the person who performed the behavior) or work-oriented (focusing on the *record of outcomes* that the person achieved on the job). Effective *performance* appraisal focuses on the record of outcomes and, in particular, outcomes directly linked to an organization's mission and objectives. Some Sheraton Hotels offer 25-minute room service or the meal is free. Sheraton employees who are directly connected to room service are appraised on the record of outcomes specifically related to this service guarantee. Lenscrafters guarantees new glasses in 60 minutes or they're free. Individual and unit performance are measured by the average time taken to get the new glasses in the customer's hands. These are outcomes. *In general, personal traits (e.g., dependability, integrity, perseverance, loyalty) should not be used when evaluating past performance since they are not measures of actual performance.* As personal characteristics of a performer, they may be correlates or predictors of performance but they are *not* measures of actual performance.

There are six categories of outcomes by which the value of performance in any work activity or work function may be assessed. These six criteria are listed and defined in Figure 7-4. Although all of these criteria may not be relevant to every job activity or job function, a subset of them will be. It is also important for organizations to

FIGURE 7-4	The Six Primary Criteria on Which the Value of Performance May Be Assessed

1. *Quality:* The degree to which the process or result of carrying out an activity approaches perfection, in terms of either conforming to some ideal way of performing the activity or fulfilling the activity's intended purpose.

2. *Quantity:* The amount produced, expressed in such terms as dollar value, number of units, or number of completed activity cycles.

3. *Timeliness:* The degree to which an activity is completed, or a result produced, at the earliest time desirable from the standpoints of both coordinating with the outputs of others and maximizing the time available for other activities.

4. *Cost-effectiveness:* The degree to which the use of the organization's resources (e.g., human, monetary, technological, material) is maximized in the sense of getting the highest gain or reduction in loss from each unit or instance of use of a resource.

5. *Need for supervision:* The degree to which a performer can carry out a job function without either having to request supervisory assistance or requiring supervisory intervention to prevent an adverse outcome.

6. *Interpersonal impact:* The degree to which a performer promotes feelings of self-esteem, goodwill, and cooperativeness among co-workers and subordinates.

recognize the relationships among the criteria. For example, sometimes managers encourage employees to push for quantity, without recognizing that quality may suffer or that co-workers might be affected. Likewise, they may focus on quality without emphasizing timeliness, cost effectiveness, or interpersonal impact.

We include "contextual or citizenship performance" in the "interpersonal impact" category of outcomes. A good "organizational citizen" is an employee who contributes beyond the formal role expectations of a job as might be detailed in a job description. Such employees are positively disposed to take on alternative job assignments, respond cheerfully to requests for assistance from others, are interpersonally tactful, arrive to work on time, and often may stay later than required to complete a task. Contextual performance operates to either support or inhibit technical production and can facilitate their translation into individual-, group-, and system-level outcomes.

Contextual performance contributions such as mentoring, facilitating a pleasant work environment, and compliance with organizational and subunit policies and procedures may have implications for several of the other outcome categories as well. If performance is defined at a more specific task or activity level, contextual performance also could be represented in the description of the function itself and combined with one or more of the value criteria (e.g., quality, quantity). For example, one model of "citizenship performance" includes "personal support" as a dimension and defines it by such behaviors as "helping others by offering suggestions, teaching useful knowledge or skills, and providing emotional support for their personal problems." We could certainly define outcomes in these areas according to quantity and quality values (e.g., how often is emotional support offered; how good was it?).

Measuring Overall Performance

While an overall rating approach where the rater does not distinguish among the criteria is surely faster than making assessments on separate criteria, the major drawback is that it requires raters to simultaneously perhaps consider as many as six different aspects of value and to mentally compute their average. The probable result of all this subjective reasoning may be less accurate ratings than those done on each relevant criterion for each job activity and less specific feedback to the performer. *In general, the greater the specificity in the content of the appraisal, the more effective the appraisal system regardless of the purpose for the appraisal system* (see again Figure 7-1).

The Measurement Process

There are three basic ways in which raters can make performance assessments: (1) they can make comparisons of ratees' performances, (2) they can make comparisons *among* anchors or performance level anchors and select one most descriptive of the person being appraised, and (3) they can make comparisons of individuals' performance *to* anchors. These are shown in simplified form in Figure 7-5.

FIGURE 7-5 Rating Format Options

COMPARISONS AMONG PERFORMANCES

Compare the performances of all ratees to each anchor for each job activity, function, or overall performance. Rater judgments may be made in one of the following ways:

- Indicate which ratee in each possible pair of ratees performed closest to the performance level described by the anchor or attained the highest level or overall performance. (Illustrative method: paired comparison)
- Indicate how the ratees ranked in terms of closeness to the performance level described by the anchor. (Illustrative method: straight ranking)
- Identify a predetermined percentage of employees as ineffective and highly effective. (Illustrative method: forced distribution)

COMPARISONS AMONG ANCHORS

Compare all the anchors for each job activity or function and select the one (or more) that best describes the ratee's performance level. Rater judgments are made in the following way:

- Indicate which of the anchors fit the ratee's performance best (and/or worst). (Illustrative method: CARS, forced choice)

COMPARISONS TO ANCHORS

Compare each ratee's performance to each anchor for each job activity or function. Rater judgments are made in one of the following ways:

- Whether or not the ratee's performance matches the anchor. (Illustrative methods: graphic rating scales such as BARS; MBO)
- The frequency with which the ratee's performance matches the anchor. (Illustrative methods: all summated rating scales such as BOS and PDA methods)
- Whether the ratee's performance was better than, equal to, or worse than that described by the anchor. (Illustrative method: Mixed standard scales)

Some of the most popular rating instruments representing each of these three ways are described in the next section.

Rating Instruments: Comparisons among Ratees' Performances

Paired comparisons, straight ranking, and forced distribution are appraisal systems that require raters to make comparisons among ratees according to some measure of effectiveness or simply overall effectiveness. Although controversial, employee comparison systems are growing in popularity to some extent because Jack Welch, GE's famous retired CEO, is a strong advocate of this approach.

Paired comparisons require the rater to compare all possible pairs of ratees on "overall performance" or some other, usually vaguely defined standard. This task can become cumbersome for the rater as the number of employees increases and more comparisons are needed. The formula for the number of possible pairs of employees is $n(n - 1)/2$, where n = the number of employees. *Straight ranking* or rank ordering asks the rater to simply identify the "best" employee, the "second best," and so forth, until the rater has identified the worst employee. For example, some NCAA rankings in football and basketball are based on a rank ordering of the teams by coaches and the press. Ranking systems are popular in research labs such as Sandia and Lawrence Livermore. Managers are forced to rank their subordinates in a 1 to *N* order based on performance.

Forced distribution usually presents the rater with a limited number of categories (usually five to seven) and requires (or "forces") the rater to place a designated portion of the ratees into each category. A forced distribution usually places the majority of employees in the middle category (i.e., with average ratings or raises) while fewer employees are placed in higher and lower categories.

Some organizations use forced distributions to assign pay increases while others require them to ensure that raters do not assign all of their employees the most extreme (e.g., highest) possible ratings. Ford adopted a forced letter grade system for each supervisor. Thus, only 10 percent of employees could receive an A grade while first 10 percent and then 5 percent had to receive a C grade. Employees who receive Cs were not eligible for a raise or a bonus and two C grades in a row could result in demotion and termination. A lawsuit was filed (and settled) with Ford in 2002 alleging that age and reverse race discrimination were caused by the new system.

In addressing GE shareholders former CEO Jack Welch stated, "A company that bets its future on its people must remove that lower 10 percent, and keep removing it every year—always raising the bar of performance and increasing the quality of its leadership."[8] Microsoft and Conoco also use forced distribution. It's not all good news for forced distribution. Enron had a GE-like system in place when the company collapsed. Recent research with forced distribution indicates that companies using forced distribution indicated superior differentiation among ratees, a primary purpose of the approach, but a lower overall evaluation of the appraisal system compared to other approaches.[9]

Rating Instruments: Comparisons among Performance-Level Anchors

Computerized adaptive rating scales (CARS) is a new and promising rating method that presents raters with pairs of behavioral statements reflecting different levels of performance on the same performance dimension.[10] For example, for the performance dimension entitled "Personal Support," raters could be asked to select one of the following two statements as most descriptive of a particular ratee:

1. Refuses to take the time to help others when they ask for assistance with work-related problems.
2. Occasionally takes the time to help others when they ask for assistance with work-related problems.

Based on the statement selected, additional statements are then paired through a computer program for subsequent rating. The new pair of behavioral statements would then

be selected, one of which was scaled by experts to be somewhat higher in effectiveness than the one first selected and the other of which was scaled to be somewhat below the level of effectiveness represented by the first statement selected. A rater's selection from this next pair of statements would then revise the estimate of the ratee's performance effectiveness level. Based on this new estimate, two new statements are selected by the computer program until the performance level can be measured reliably.

Laboratory research with CARS supported this method when compared to behaviorally anchored rating scales (BARS) and simple graphic rating scales.

Forced choice is another PA method that requires the rater to compare performance statements and select one (or more) as most descriptive. Unlike the CARS method, the forced choice method is specifically designed to reduce (or eliminate) intentional rating bias where the rater deliberately attempts to rate individuals high (or low) irrespective of their performance. The rationale underlying forced choice is that statements are grouped in such a way that the scoring key is not known to the rater (i.e., the way to rate higher or lower is not apparent). The rater is unaware of which statements (if selected) will result in higher (or lower) ratings for the ratee because all statements appear equally desirable or undesirable. For example, if you were asked to select the two statements that are most descriptive of your instructor for this class, which two would you select?

1. Is patient with slow learners.
2. Lectures with confidence.
3. Keeps the interest and attention of the class.
4. Presents objectives before each class session.

The statements are chosen to be equal in desirability in order to make it more difficult for the rater to pick out the ones that will give the ratee the highest or lowest ratings based on personal bias. However, only two of the items actually distinguish highly effective from ineffective performers. For the present case, items 1 and 3 have been shown to discriminate between the most effective and the least effective college professors. Items 2 and 4 did not generally discriminate between effective and ineffective performers. If you selected statements 1 and 3 as most descriptive of your instructor, then he or she would be awarded two points. This procedure would be used with each of the groups of statements to determine the total score for each ratee. Raters are not given the scoring scheme so they are unable to intentionally give performers high or low ratings. Research with forced choice is limited, but there is some evidence that deliberate bias can be reduced with this method. Unfortunately, raters do not like this method specifically because the scoring key is hidden.[11]

Rating Instruments: Comparisons to Performance-Level Anchors

Methods that require the rater to make comparisons of the employee's performance to specified anchors include

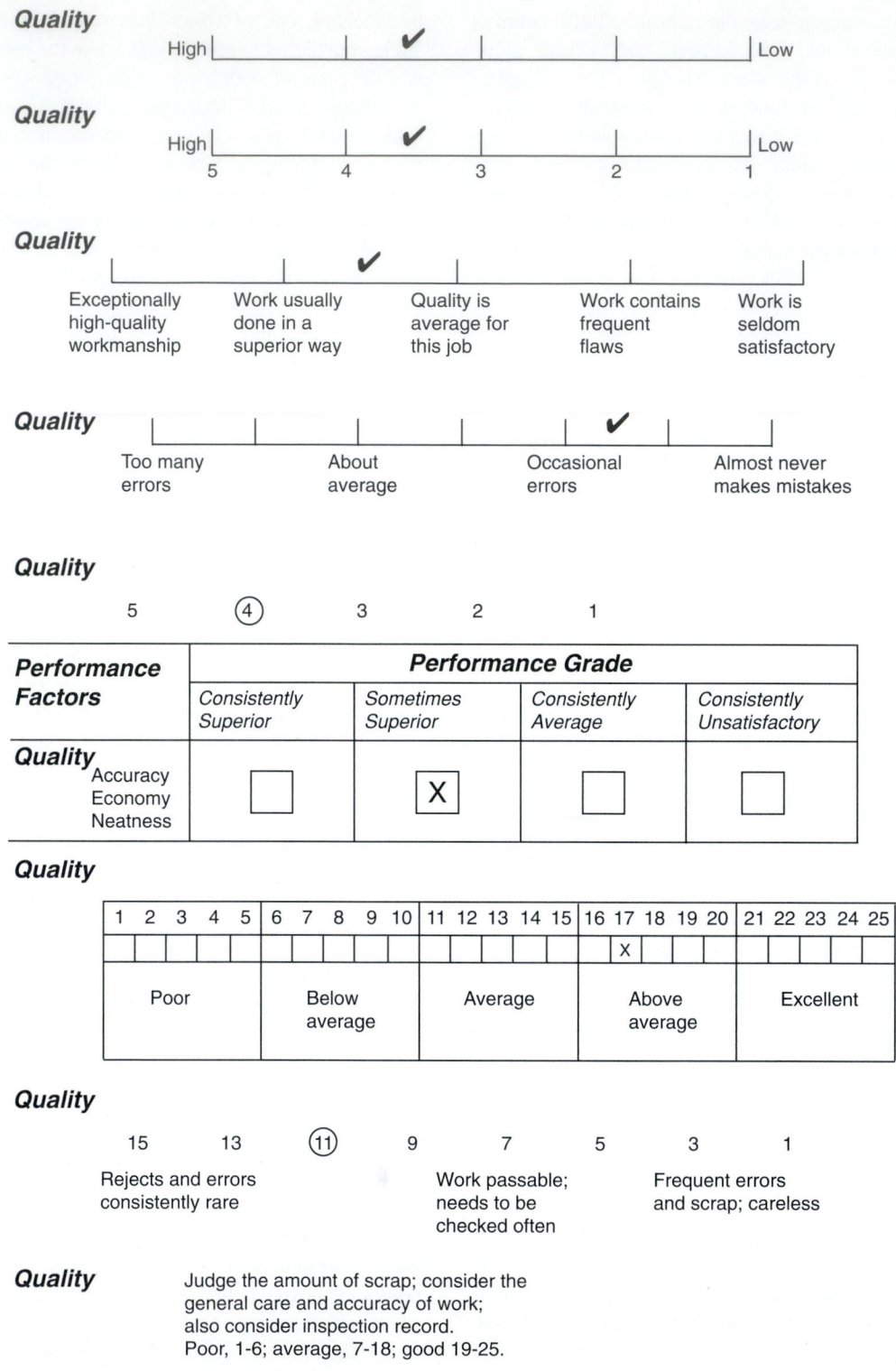

Figure 7-6   Examples of Graphic Rating Scales
Source: R. M. Guion, *Personnel Testing,* 1965, p. 98. Reprinted with permission.

graphic rating scales, behaviorally anchored rating scales (BARS), management by objectives (MBO), summated scales (e.g., behavioral observation scales (BOS), and performance distribution assessment (PDA)). *Graphic rating scales* are the most widely used type of rating format. Figure 7-6 presents some examples of graphic scales.

Generally, graphic rating scales use adjectives or numbers as anchors.

One of the most heavily researched types of graphic scales is *behaviorally anchored rating scales (BARS).* As shown in Figure 7-7, BARS are graphic scales with specific behavioral descriptions defining various points

Organizational skills: A good constructional order of material slides smoothly from one topic to another; design of course optimizes interest; students can easily follow organizational strategy; course outline followed.

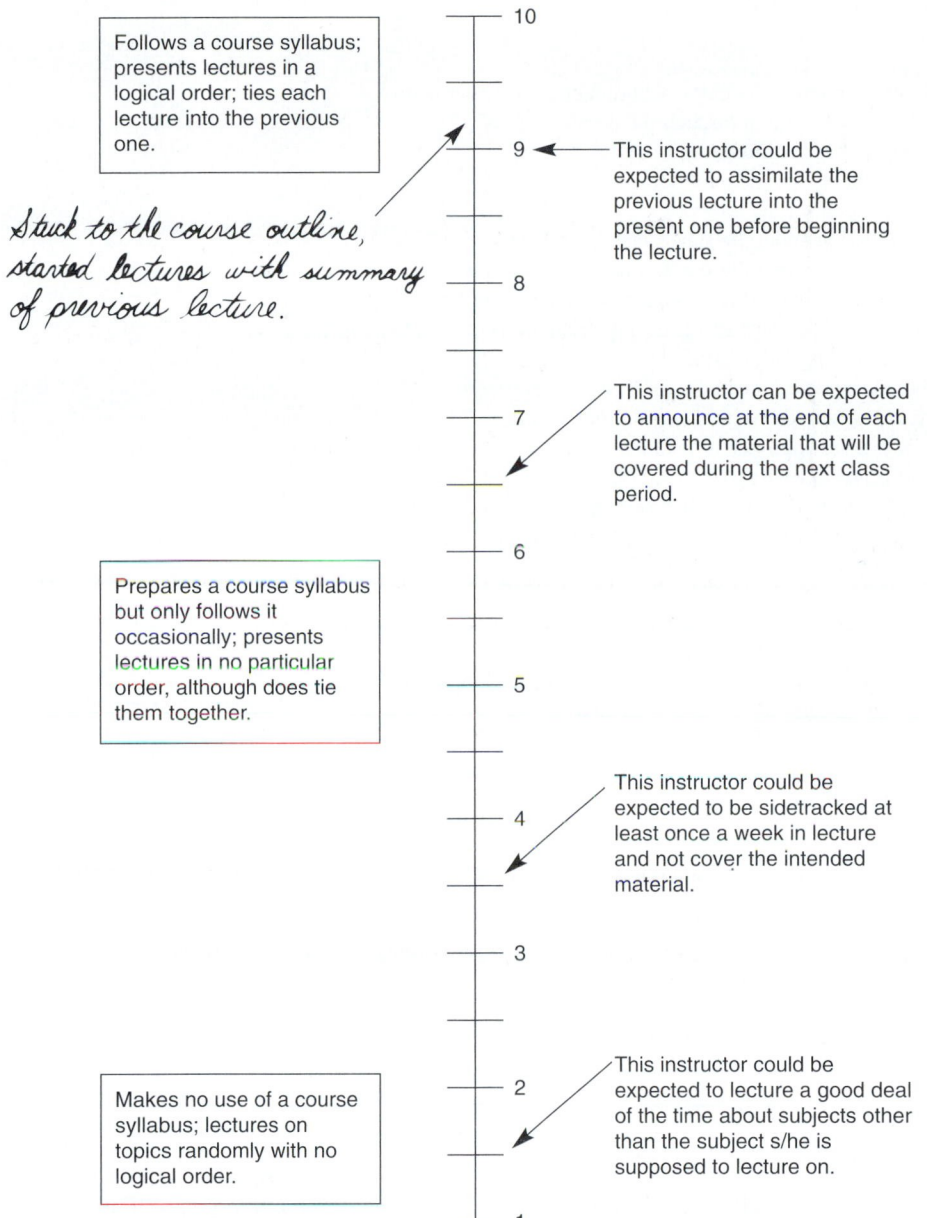

> Follows a course syllabus; presents lectures in a logical order; ties each lecture into the previous one.

Stuck to the course outline, started lectures with summary of previous lecture.

10

9 ← This instructor could be expected to assimilate the previous lecture into the present one before beginning the lecture.

8

7 This instructor can be expected to announce at the end of each lecture the material that will be covered during the next class period.

6

> Prepares a course syllabus but only follows it occasionally; presents lectures in no particular order, although does tie them together.

5

4 This instructor could be expected to be sidetracked at least once a week in lecture and not cover the intended material.

3

2 This instructor could be expected to lecture a good deal of the time about subjects other than the subject s/he is supposed to lecture on.

> Makes no use of a course syllabus; lectures on topics randomly with no logical order.

1

Figure 7-7   An Example of a Behaviorally Anchored Rating Scale

Source: From *Performance Appraisal: Assesing Human Behavior at Work* by Bernardin/Beatty, © 1984. Reprinted with permission of South-Western, a division of Thompson Learning: www.thomsonrights.com. Fax 800 730-2215.

along the scale for each dimension. The recommended rating method for BARS asks raters to record specific observations of the employee's performance relevant to the dimension on the scale.[12] For example, in Figure 7-7, the rater has written in "Stuck to the course outline, . . ." between points 9 and 10 on the left side of the scale. The rater would then select that point along the right side of the scale that best represents the ratee's overall performance

on that function. That point is selected by comparing the ratee's actual observed performance to the behavioral expectations that are provided as "anchors" on the scale. The rationale behind writing in observations on the scale prior to selecting an anchor is to ensure that raters are basing their ratings of expectations on actual observations of performance. In addition, the observations can be given to ratees as feedback on their performance. Research shows

FIGURE 7-8   A Summated Rating Scale

Directions: Rate your manager on the way he or she has conducted performance appraisal interviews. Use the following scale to make your ratings:

        1 = Always
        2 = Often
        3 = Occasionally
        4 = Seldom
        5 = Never

1. Effectively used information about the subordinate in the discussion.
2. Skillfully guided the discussion through the problem areas.
3. Maintained control over the interview.
4. Appeared to be prepared for the interview.
5. Let the subordinate control the interview.
6. Adhered to a discussion about the subordinate's problems.
7. Seemed concerned about the subordinate's perspective of the problems.
8. Probed deeply into sensitive areas in order to gain sufficient knowledge.
9. Made the subordinate feel comfortable during discussions of sensitive topics.
10. Projected sincerity during the interview.
11. Maintained the appropriate climate for an appraisal interview.
12. Displayed insensitivity to the subordinate's problems.
13. Displayed an organized approach to the interview.
14. Asked the appropriate questions.
15. Failed to follow up with questions when they appeared to be necessary.
16. Asked general questions about the subordinate's problems.
17. Asked only superficial questions that failed to confront the issues.
18. Displayed considerable interest in the subordinate's professional growth.
19. Provided general suggestions to aid in the subordinate's professional growth.
20. Provided poor advice regarding the subordinate's growth.
21. Made specific suggestions for helping the subordinate develop professionally.
22. Remained calm during the subordinate's outbursts.
23. Responded to the subordinate's outbursts in a rational manner.
24. Appeared to be defensive in reaction to the subordinate's complaints.
25. Backed down inappropriately when confronted.
26. Made realistic commitments to help the subordinate get along better with others.
27. Seemed unconcerned about the subordinate's problems.
28. Provided poor advice about the subordinate's relationships with others.
29. Provided good advice about resolving conflict.
30. When discussing the subordinate's future with the company, encouraged him/her to stay on.
31. Used appropriate compliments regarding the subordinate's technical expertise.
32. Motivated the subordinate to perform the job well.
33. Seemed to ignore the subordinate's excellent performance record.
34. Made inappropriate ultimatums to the subordinate about improving performance.

---

this form of feedback is effective at improving performance and that this particular BARS approach was more effective than other formats at improving performance.

The method of *summated scales* is one of the oldest formats and remains one of the most popular for the appraisal of job performance. One version of summated scales is behavioral observation scales (or BOS).[13] An example of a summated scale is presented in Figure 7-8. For this scale, the rater is asked to indicate how frequently the ratee has performed each of the listed behaviors.

Performance distribution assessment (PDA) is a more complicated rating method based on the theory that ratings should be made in the context of opportunities to perform at a certain level.[14] PDA is the only method that statistically incorporates constraints on performance into the measurement process. For example, in evaluating managers on the quality of their performance "monitoring" at Tiffany's of New York, their managers are asked to consider how many opportunities the manager had to "furnish information in response to an inquiry that was completely accurate with respect to central questions posed by the inquiry" and then to rate how frequently the manager achieved that level of performance. Although somewhat cumbersome in the rating method, PDA provides detailed documentation of constraints on performance and thus has the potential to remove those constraints over time. A Web-based PDA system is now available. (Try the demo at www.performance-sciences.com.)

Management by objectives (MBO) is a performance management and appraisal system that calls for a comparison between specific, quantifiable target goals and the actual results achieved by an employee. MBO is the most popular method of managerial appraisal.[15]

With MBO, the measurable, quantitative goals are usually mutually agreed upon by the employee and supervisor at the beginning of an appraisal period. During the review period, progress towards the goals is monitored. At the end of the review period, the employee and supervisor meet to evaluate whether the goals were achieved and to decide on new goals. The goals or objectives are usually set for individual employees or units and usually differ across employees (or units) depending on the circumstances of the job. For this reason, MBO has been shown to be useful for defining "individual" or unit performance in the context of strategic plans. As a motivational technique, as long as the objectives that are set are defined in specific terms using carefully defined criteria as listed in Figure 7-4, attainable as perceived by the performer while still being difficult, MBO is an effective approach to improving performance and motivating employees. Thus, precise definitions of quality and quantity, specifically linked to unit strategic goals, can make MBO a very effective PM system. But the criteria must be defined (and ultimately evaluated) with strategic goals in mind. MBO is not recommended as a method for comparing people or units unless the objectives that are set can be judged to be equally attainable in the context of potential situational constraints on performance, which we discuss in the next section.

What Is the "Bottom Line" on What It Is We Should Be Measuring?

You'll note if you look back at Figure 7-1 that one of the recommendations nested under strive for as much precision in defining and measuring performance as "feasible" is to measure content using ratings of **relative frequencies.** There are many options for rating behavior or performance outcomes. First of all, performance appraisal should focus on the *record of outcomes.* Let's pick on your instructor for a bit. Certainly "instruction" is a critical component (i.e., function) of his or her job. You are a type of "customer" who should be evaluating performance on that function (note prescription no. 2 in Figure 7-1 too). The most important criterion to define the "quality"of that instruction is probably how much you actually learn from this instruction. Perfection would then be a perfect score on some test of the knowledge you were supposed to acquire from this instruction. For a number of reasons, scores on such a test may not be a practical source of data and such data, with some exceptions, probably does not allow for comparisons on instructors for decision-making purposes.

Another way of getting at the "quality" of instruction is to have you (the customer) define levels of performance and then have you rate the extent to which the instructor meets or exceeds these levels of performance. Research says

when you do these ratings, your focus should be on how *frequently* (e.g., sometimes, 100 percent of the time, never) the instructor achieved this level of performance in the context of all the times the instructor had the opportunity to achieve at this level. Ratings of frequency are better than ratings of "intensity" (e.g., strongly agree/disagree) or satisfactoriness (e.g., how satisfied are with your instructor).

Here's an example of "perfection" as defined by students to evaluate "instruction": "Every time a lecture was given, I had a clear, unambiguous understanding of what it was s/he was trying to teach; no questions were needed to clarify the material presented." Let's say this defines the "perfection" level of performance for "instruction." Raters would make ratings of relative frequency on the "quality of instruction" dimension by rating how often the instructor hit this level of performance out of all the times s/he gave lectures (or did instruction). So, you might give your instructor 100 percent on this dimension level; that is, every time a lecture was given, you had a "clear, unambiguous understanding." Obviously, it is also possible that the rating here could be 0 percent! That's why we also need to define at least one other level of performance for "quality of instruction." Raters would then rate how frequently the instructor achieved this level of performance. Research on rating formats shows that ratings of relative frequency result in higher levels of reliability in ratings (across raters rating the same person) and that the people who receive feedback on their performance actually prefer frequency ratings to other feedback options. The PDA system is most compatible with this approach to appraisal.

Whatever is measured should obviously be vital to the strategic goals of the organization. Formal performance should clearly concentrate on reliable and valid measurement of outcomes that are directly linked to strategy goals and outcomes. One would hope that a strategic goal of your institution is superior instruction in every class. Sometimes the linkage between individual performance appraisal and the strategic objectives of the organization is very clear (a 100 percent score on "instruction" would be nice). In general, the more precision in measurement, the better the performance management and appraisal system regardless of its purpose. At the individual performer level, having performance dimensions that are derived from that performer's job description (or actually a part of it) makes a whole lot of sense. While some supervisors tend to ignore job descriptions, workers tend to look at job descriptions as contracts (i.e., this is why you're paying me).[16]

Control of Rating Errors

Performance ratings are subject to a wide variety of inaccuracies and biases referred to as rating errors. These errors occur in rater judgment and information processing and can seriously affect performance appraisal results. Unfortunately, many of these errors cannot be eradicated easily. The most common rating errors are leniency/severity, halo/horns effect, central tendency, fundamental attribution errors, representativeness, availability, and anchoring.

Leniency/Severity

Leniency occurs when ratings for employees are generally at the high end of the rating scale regardless of the actual performance of ratees. This error is considered deliberate. Surveys have identified leniency as the most serious problem with appraisals whenever they are linked to important decisions such as compensation, promotions, or terminations. Leniency is probably the main reason companies are turning to forced distribution where a certain percentage of employees must be rated as "C" or ineffective employees. Research shows leniency (or severity) in ratings is related to the characteristics of the *rater*.[17]

Leniency is probably the primary reason companies have turned to forced distribution systems such as the GE A, B, C system where managers have to put a certain percentage of subordinates into the "C" category. Jack Welch and many others argue that differentiation of employees by performance and making certain the most important positions in the organization (the "A" positions) are occupied by "A" players is a key toward competitive advantage. You do not want "C" or even "B" players in vital positions. Obviously, leniency error precludes an organization's ability to differentiate among employees and take action to reward the "A" players, move "C" performers out of key positions as soon as possible, and to try to develop the "B" into "A" players.

Halo/Horns Effect

Halo or "horns" effect occurs when a rater allows a rating on one dimension (or an overall impression) for an employee to influence the ratings he or she assigns to other dimensions for that employee. That is, the rater inappropriately assesses ratee performance similarly across different job functions, projects, or performance dimensions. This error is not deliberate.

Central Tendency

Central tendency occurs when ratings for employees tend to be toward the center (mid-point) of the scale regardless of the actual performance of ratees. This is also a deliberate error although much less common than leniency.

Fundamental Attribution Error/Actor-Observer Bias

The fundamental attribution error refers to the tendency to attribute observed behaviors to the disposition of the person being observed and to thereby underestimate the causal role of factors beyond the control of the performer.[18] This is related to the **actor-observer bias** and is a particular problem for performance appraisal because it tends to result in people being given insufficient credit for their successes and excessive blame for failures. People in general tend to make the exact opposite attributions for their *own* behavior: they tend to attribute their successes to their own competence and their failures to the influence of external factors beyond their control. The actor-observer bias is thus the tendency of observers to underestimate the effects of external factors and for performers to overestimate the effects of external factors on less than perfect performance. Rating systems that ask the rater to formally consider the possible constraints on performance have been shown to reduce the actor-observer bias.

Actor-observer bias is one of the major factors that causes perceptions of unfairness in appraisal decisions. Any student who has been graded on a group project may have experienced this problem in individual appraisal. Many conditions present in the job situation or work assignment can hold a person back from performing as well as he or she could. Some of these constraints include inadequate tools, lack of supplies, not enough money, too little time, lack of information, breakdowns in equipment, and not enough help from others. For example, truck inspectors may be limited in the number of trucks they can check for defects if they spend a considerable portion of their work day in court presenting testimony against offenders. They still may be held accountable, however, for inspecting a certain number of trucks despite these other job duties. If in a group project, one of your team members fails to retrieve vital information, the constraint could seriously hamper your ability to do your tasks. Situational factors that hinder an employee's job performance are called *situational constraints* and are described in Figure 7-9.[19]

FIGURE 7-9 **Possible Situational Constraints on Performance**

1. Absenteeism or turnover of key personnel.
2. Slowness of procedures for action approval.
3. Inadequate clerical support.
4. Shortages of supplies and/or raw materials.
5. Excessive restrictions on operating expenses.
6. Inadequate physical working conditions.
7. Inability to hire needed staff.
8. Inadequate performance of coworkers or personnel in other units on whom an individual's work depends.
9. Inadequate performance of subordinates.
10. Inadequate performance of managers.
11. Inefficient or unclear organizational structure or reporting relationships.
12. Excessive reporting requirements and administrative paperwork.
13. Unpredictable workloads.
14. Excessive workloads.
15. Changes in administrative policies, procedures, and/or regulations.
16. Pressures from coworkers to limit an individual's performance.
17. Unpredictable changes or additions to the types of work assigned.
18. Lack of proper equipment.
19. Inadequate communication within the organization.
20. The quality of raw materials.
21. Economic conditions (e.g., interest rates, labor availability, and costs of basic goods and services).
22. Inadequate training.

An appraisal system should consider the effects of situational constraints so that ratees are not unfairly downgraded for these uncontrollable factors. Rater training programs also should focus on making raters aware of potential constraints on employee performances and the tendency on the part of raters to commit this attributional error. Research shows training on the actor-observer bias can reduce the error and promote more agreement between the rater (observer) and the ratee (the actor).

Figure 7-10 presents an example of an appraisal method that considers the potential for this common error. With this method, raters and ratees must independently complete a performance dimension/constraint matrix. This approach places the focus squarely on discrepancies in perceptions of the effects of particular constraints.

In Figure 7-10, the list of constraints was recorded by the ratee (performer) who felt the constraint had a significant impact on her performance for a particular performance dimension. For example, this head of a Research and Development unit indicated that staff attendance at meetings was an indication of poor subordinate performance and that this constraint impeded performance on "Organizing and Conducting seminars." After the supervisor has reviewed the constraints and recorded his/her own assessment of the effects of the constraints, specific goals are set where the supervisor agrees to attend to some (or all) of the perceived constraints (e.g., supervisor will send out a memo strongly encouraging seminar attendance).

One recent study showed promise for "self-efficacy training for raters." Raters who were trained in giving negative feedback produced less lenient ratings than a control group. This training involved observing a successful rater, a simulated appraisal session with a "problem" employee, feedback on performance, and then coaching on how to conduct an appraisal discussion. Research shows that this approach to appraisal and training results in more effective appraisals, higher perceptions of procedural fairness, more agreement between raters and performers and, most important, higher unit performance.[20]

Representativeness

This error refers to the tendency to make judgments about people (or their performance) on the basis of their similarity to people who exhibited prominent or memorable levels on the attribute being judged, even though the similarity may have no causal connection to the attribute. For example, popular stereotypes may have given the rater an image that attractive people are more effective in groups.

When confronted with the task of rating someone on factors related to their group effectiveness, to the extent that the ratee possesses the *representative* trait (e.g., is attractive), the rater will tend to rate in accordance with this preconception rather than in accordance with actual observations.

The problem with this type of thinking is that it ignores the fact that although some prominent examples of people who performed at the upper or lower extremes of effectiveness may have possessed a certain characteristic like attractiveness, most of the people who possess such a characteristic do not so distinguish themselves and in fact the characteristic has no causative connection to actual performance.

This is a difficult tendency to overcome. Perhaps the best means of suppressing it is to use rating scales that are anchored with detailed descriptions of behaviors or outcomes.

Availability

This is a rule of thumb that some people use in judging the relative frequency of outcomes. Specifically, people tend to mistake the ease with which a category of outcomes can be recalled as an indication of its frequency of occurrence relative to other categories. The relevance to performance appraisal judgments should be obvious: since more extreme outcomes tend to be more memorable, raters will tend to attribute greater frequency to them than was actually the case. This results in such outcomes being given excessive weight in the formation of appraisal judgments. It has been found that negative events—instances of ineffective performance—seem to have the greatest availability in memory.

There is no easy solution to the availability problem either. It is possible that the mere act of making raters aware of their proneness to this type of error will cause them to make efforts to compensate for this tendency. However, there is no research to substantiate this possibility.

Anchoring

This error refers to the tendency to insufficiently alter a judgment away from some starting point when new information is received. Most of us start with some initial impression of any situation we encounter, or we form one very quickly after our initial immersion in a situation. This is very true of observations of other people's performances. Either from past experience, stereotyping, interpersonal affect, or reputation, we generally start off any period of observing another's performance with some initial impression or we form one very quickly. The problem that arises is that once an initial starting point, or anchor, is selected, we tend to resist being moved from this point by subsequent information that warrants movement. As a consequence, our final appraisal judgments will be much nearer to our starting points than they should be. This is an obvious source of unfairness in appraisals. A person's reputation or even his/her past performance, should not be a factor in how his/her performance during the period under consideration is judged.

Anchoring is a potent error. For example, if a person whom I regard as unreliable and untrustworthy told me that the performance of a new hire had been terrible on his/her last job, even though I had other sources of credible information, I could be affected by that person's opinion in evaluating the new hire. This anchoring effect

FIGURE 7-10 A Performance/Constraint Matrix (R&D Director)

Constraints	Performance Dimensions			
	Assisting Center Researchers	Generating Research Grants	Organizing and Conducting Seminars	Conducting Research
Absenteeism/turnover		a		
Slow procedures				
Clerical support		b		b
Supply shortage				
Excessive restrictions	c	d		
Working conditions				
Poor co-worker performance				
Poor subordinate performance			e	f
Poor manager performance				
Inefficient structure				
Excessive reporting requirements				
Workloads				
Change in administrative policy				
Co-worker pressure				
Change in work assignment	k, h	k, h	k, h	k, h
Lack of equipment				
Inadequate communication			i	
Raw material problem				
Economic conditions				j
Lack of (or poor) training				

Constraints

a. Loss of departmental secretary precluded proposal writing for two months

b. Secretary worked on unrelated project for two months

c. Grant support lifted from four recipients due to lack of funds

d. No money allotted for hiring grantsperson as promised

e. Staff rarely attended seminars although they were scheduled on payday

f. Staff member failed to do literature review in a collaborative research project

h. Given new responsibility for compensation policy and computer records (not on original job description)

i. Failure of management to provide written charge for compensation project resulted in time being wasted in clarification with divisions

j. Severe reduction in research budget has precluded three pilot projects that had great potential for external funding

k. Asked to conduct seminar at last moment due to funding problem; took 15 percent of my time away from all assignments

Goals

a. Proposed backup clerical support for excessive workloads; have plan by 3/1

b. Develop more detailed job description and chain of command for secretaries, that is, only one boss; submit plan by 3/1

c. Review committee will be made aware of total funds available

d. Conduct search to determine if part-time person can be identified; write announcement by 2/15

e. Send memo to staff encouraging attendance

h. Provide written charge in the future

i. Get commitment from management to attend all executive-level meetings

j. More active search for external dollars. Will review foundation interests; submit report by 4/1

k. Will do survey to determine what time would be most favorable; report attendance to director (will submit report in two months)

also applies to multirater systems. Supervisors, for example, can be inappropriately affected by the level of subordinates' initial self-ratings. Supervisors should make assessments before they review (and consider) self-ratings.

The origin of this problem again seems to be the holistic consideration of a person's performance on each rating factor rather than attending to the specific behaviors or outcomes that were exhibited. If rating scales are used that don't call for an overall judgment but rather elicit estimates of the frequencies with which the behaviors or outcomes anchoring each level occurred, we might overcome (or reduce) the problem of anchoring.

Rater Training

All of these errors can arise in two different ways: as the result of *unintentional* errors in the way people observe, store, recall, and report events or as the result of *intentional* efforts to assign inaccurate ratings. If rating errors are *unintentional,* raters may commit them because they do not have the necessary skills to make accurate ratings or the content of the appraisal is not carefully defined. Rater training can help.

Attempts to control unconscious, unintentional errors most often focus on rater training. Training to improve the rater's observational and categorization skills (called **frame-of-reference training**) has been shown to increase rater accuracy and consistency.[21] This training consists of creating a common frame of reference among raters in the observation process. Raters are familiarized with the rating scales, and are given opportunities to practice making ratings. Following this, they are given feedback on their practice ratings. They also are given descriptions of critical incidents of performance that illustrate outstanding, average, and unsatisfactory levels of performance on each dimension. This is done so they will know what behaviors or outcomes to consider when making their ratings.

Raters may commit rating errors *intentionally* for political reasons or to provide certain outcomes to their employees or themselves. For example, one of the most common intentional rating errors in organizations is leniency. Managers may assign higher ratings than an employee deserves to avoid a confrontation with the employee, to protect an employee suffering from personal problems, to acquire more recognition for the department or themselves, or to be able to reward the employee with a bonus or promotion. Although less common, managers also may intentionally assign more severe ratings than an employee deserves to motivate him or her to work harder, to teach the employee a lesson, or to build a case for firing the employee. There is strong evidence that leniency/severity is based on the stable personality characteristics of the rater. For example, more lenient raters tend to be higher on "agreeableness" and lower on "conscientiousness" from the Five-Factor Model of personality (see Chapter 6).[22]

While rater training has been shown to be effective at reducing unintentional rating bias, there is little evidence that any form of rater training, including *frame of reference* training, can help with deliberate, intentional bias.

Attempts to control intentional rating errors include hiding scoring keys such as through forced choice, using forced distribution or other forms of ratee comparison systems, requiring cross-checks or reviews of ratings by other people, using multirater systems, training raters on how to provide negative evaluation, and reducing the rater's motivation to assign inaccurate ratings. Unfortunately, none of these methods has proven to be reliably effective for controlling deliberate errors and biases.[23]

Most experts contend that the best way to control for deliberate bias on the part of an individual rater is to use more than one rater. In general, the mean rating compiled from ratings across all (or a sample) of qualified raters will result in less bias and more validity for the performance appraisal system. A "qualified" rater can be defined as any internal and external customer who is the recipient of the performers' products or services.[24]

Defining the Rater

Ratings can be provided by ratees, supervisors, peers, clients or customers, or high-level managers. While most companies still give the supervisor the sole responsibility for the employee's appraisal, formal multirater systems are becoming quite popular.[25] A growing number of companies use formal self-assessments. The purpose is to encourage employees to take an active role in their own development. Upward appraisals (ratings by subordinates) are also on the increase.

With increasing frequency, organizations are concluding that multiple rater types are beneficial for use in their appraisal systems.[26] Ratings collected from several raters, also known as 360-degree appraisal systems, are thought to be more accurate, have fewer biases, are perceived to be more fair, and are less often the targets of lawsuits.[27] The use of 360-degree appraisal systems is one of the characteristics of **high-performance work systems,** which have been linked to superior corporate financial performance. There are numerous Web-based systems of 360-degree appraisal. Some are based on competency-based models of HR strategy.

The probable reason 360 is successful is that many of the rater types used (e.g., customers, peers) have direct and unique knowledge of at least some aspects of the ratee's job performance and provide reliable and valid performance information on some job activities. In fact, the use of raters who represent all critical internal and external customers contributes to the accuracy and relevance of the appraisal system.[28]

Many organizations use self-, subordinate, peer, and superior ratings as a comprehensive appraisal prior to a training program. The Center for Creative Leadership in

FIGURE 7-11   Recommendations for Implementing a 360-Degree Appraisal System

INSTRUMENT ISSUES

- Items should be directly linked to effectiveness on the job.
- Items should focus on specific, observable behaviors (not traits, competencies).
- Items should be worded in positive terms, rather than negative terms. Ratees, particularly employees, may be less likely to respond honestly to negative items about their boss.
- Raters should be asked only about issues for which they have firsthand knowledge (i.e., ask subordinates about whether the boss delegates work to them; don't ask peers since they may not know).

ADMINISTRATION ISSUES

- Select raters carefully by using a representative sample of people most critical to the ratee and who have had the greatest opportunity to observe his or her performance.
- Use an adequate number of raters to ensure adequate sampling and to protect the confidentiality of respondents (at least three per source).
- Instruct respondents in how the data will be used and ensure confidentiality.
- To maintain confidentiality, raters should not indicate their names or other identifying characteristics and surveys should be mailed back directly to the analyst in a sealed envelope.
- Alert and train raters regarding rater errors (e.g., halo, leniency, severity, attributional bias).

FEEDBACK REPORT

- Separate the results from the various sources. The ratee should see the average, aggregated results from peers, subordinates, higher-level managers, customers, or other sources that may be used.
- Show the ratee's self-ratings as compared to ratings by others. This enables the ratee to see how his or her self-perceptions are similar or different from others' perceptions.
- Compare the ratee's ratings with other norm groups. For example, a manager's ratings can be compared to other managers (as a group) in the firm.
- Provide feedback on items as well as scales so ratees can see how to improve.

FEEDBACK SESSION

- Use a trained facilitator to provide feedback to ratees.
- Involve the ratee in interpreting his or her own results.
- Provide an overview of the individual's strengths and areas for improvement.
- Provide feedback on recommendations and help him or her to develop an action plan.

FOLLOW-UP ACTIVITIES

- Provide opportunities for skill training in how to improve his or her behaviors.
- Provide support and coaching to help him or her apply what has been learned.
- Over time, evaluate the degree to which the ratee has changed behaviors.

Source: Modified from G. Yukl and R. Lepsinger, "360° Feedback," *Training*, December 1995, pp. 45–48, 50.

Greensboro, North Carolina, requires all participants in its one-week assessment center program to first submit evaluations from superiors, peers, and subordinates. These data are tabulated by the Center, and the feedback is reported to participants on the first day of the assessment center program. Participants consider this feedback to be among the most valuable they receive.

Many companies now use external customers as an important source of information about employee performance and for reward systems. The Marriott Corporation places considerable weight on its customer survey data in the evaluation of each hotel as well as work units within the hotels. Burger King, McDonald's, Domino's Pizza, and Taco Bell are among the companies that hire professional "customers" or "mystery shoppers" to visit specific installations to provide detailed appraisals of

several performance functions.[29] Critical Thinking Application 7-B focuses on this approach to appraisal.

Figure 7-11 presents a summary of recommendations for implementing a multirater/360-degree appraisal system.

Defining the "Ratee"

Many people assume that appraisals always focus on an *individual* level of performance. There are alternatives to using the individual as the ratee that are becoming more common in organizations as more and more firms (e.g., General Foods Corporation, Rohm & Haas, General Motors, Saturn, Westinghouse) shift to using more self-managed teams. Specifically, the ratee may be defined at the individual, work group, division, or organization-wide

about the actor-observer bias factor either. It is no wonder that raters are often hesitant about confronting poor performers with negative appraisal feedback and may be lenient when they do. Although pressure on managers to give accurate feedback and affect change may override a reluctance to give negative feedback, the pressure doesn't make the experience any more pleasant nor any less likely to evoke a leniency bias. Feedback to inform poor performers of performance deficiencies and to encourage improvement doesn't always lead to performance improvements.[33]

Many employees view their supervisors less favorably after the feedback and feel less motivated after the appraisal. The fear or discomfort experienced in providing negative feedback tends to differ across managers. One survey, known as the **Performance Appraisal Discomfort Scale (PADS),** showed that the level of discomfort felt by a rater was correlated with leniency.[34] As stated earlier, training raters on giving negative feedback can help facilitate this process.

To create a supportive atmosphere for the feedback meeting between the employee and supervisor, several recommendations exist. The rater should remove distractions, avoid being disturbed, and take sufficient time in the meeting. Raters seem to have trouble adhering to these guidelines. Raters should keep notes on effective and ineffective behavior as it occurs so that they will have some notes to refer to when conducting the feedback session (review the legal prescriptions we presented earlier). Raters should be informal and relaxed and allow the employee the opportunity to share his or her insights. Topics that should be addressed include praise for special assignments, the employee's own assessment of his or her performance, the supervisor's response to the employee's assessment, action plans to improve the subordinate's performance, perceived constraints on performance that require subordinate or supervisory attention, employee career aspirations, ambitions, and developmental goals. In sum, raters should provide feedback that is clear, specific, descriptive, job related, constructive, frequent, and timely.

SUMMARY

Performance appraisals have become an increasingly important tool for organizations to manage and improve the performance of employees, to make more valid staffing decisions, and to enhance the overall effectiveness of the firm's services and products. The design, development, and implementation of appraisal systems are not endeavors that can be effectively handled by following the latest fad or even by copying other organizations' systems. Instead, a new appraisal system must be considered a major organizational change effort that should be pursued in the context of improving the organization's competitive advantage. This means, like any such change effort, there will be vested interests in preserving the status quo that will be resistant to change, no matter how beneficial it may be for the organization. These sources of resistance to the change have to be identified and managed to build incentives for using a new appraisal system.

Once a well-designed system has been implemented, the work is still not done. An appraisal system has to be maintained by monitoring its operation through periodic evaluations. Only by keeping an appraisal system finely tuned will it enable managers to have a rational basis for making sound personnel decisions and for making the kinds of gains in productivity that are so critically needed in today's times. Performance management and appraisal should be an integral part of the strategic HR system. Data from this system should be a critical component at internal staffing decisions (promotion, retention, and termination).

Among the personnel decisions, some of the most important concern the organization's compensation system. The prescriptions we presented in Figure 7-1 and the findings discussed in Figure 7-2 should be helpful guidelines for improving any appraisal system. Effective performance appraisal also must be carefully integrated with other human resource domains, particularly compensation systems with a pay-for-performance component. Accurate appraisals also are critical for determining training needs. We turn to that subject next.

DISCUSSION QUESTIONS

1. Why has performance appraisal taken on increased significance in recent years?
2. As the workforce becomes more diverse, why does performance appraisal become a more difficult process?
3. Ford was accused of age discrimination based on the use of their forced-grading system. What evidence would you investigate to test this allegation?
4. Many managers describe performance appraisal as the responsibility that they like the least. Why is this so? What could be done to improve the situation?
5. Describe several advantages and disadvantages to using rating instruments that are based on comparisons among

ratees' performance, comparisons among anchors, and comparisons to anchors.
6. What steps would you take if your performance appraisal system resulted in disparate or adverse impact?
7. Under what circumstances would you use customer or client evaluation as a basis for appraising employees?
8. Why are so many companies using 360-degree feedback systems? What are the benefits of such a system?
9. Why should managers provide ongoing and frequent feedback to employees about their performance?
10. As a supervisor, how would you react to a forced distribution rating system?

8

TRAINING AND DEVELOPMENT*

OVERVIEW

Throughout this book we have referred to the empirical research linking particular human resource practices to corporate financial performance. The last chapter emphasized the critical role of performance measurement and management as characteristics of these "high-performance work systems."[1] This same body of research also points to the importance of training and development as contributors to the "bottom line" of corporate performance. Training has evolved substantially in recent years with evidence indicating more organizational investment in training and development. The 2004–2005 *workplace forecast* from the Society of Human Resource Management ranked the growth of computer-based, electronic learning as one of the top-10 most important trends in all HRM (see Figure 8-1).[2] Given the intense pressure to compete, improve quality and customer service, and lower costs, leading American companies have come to view training as a key to organizational survival and success. One recent review found that "many organizations are more likely to include training solutions as part of a systemwide change to gain competitive advantage"[3] Likewise, in countries around the world, training has become increasingly important to prepare workers for new jobs. For example, in Japan with the increasing numbers of women entering traditionally male factory jobs, more training is needed to help them learn the necessary skills. At Toyota Motor Corp. women have been given more training in everything from sexual harassment policies to skills for working on assembly lines.[4] Of course, some training is required for legal or regulatory reasons. For example, as of 2006, employers with 50 or more employees operating in California must provide sexual harassment training for all supervisors.[5]

Many employers view the skill level of their workforce as the top priority for planning. They worry that increasing technology is "de-skilling" 75 percent of the population. Their suggestion is continual training for employees. As Chuck Nielson, vice president of human resources at Texas Instruments, notes, "our challenge is creating an environment in which people love to learn." The company mandates a minimum of 40 hours of training per year. Peter Drucker, well-known management author, says the fastest-growing industry in the United States will be the continuing education and training of adults due to the replacement of industrial workers with knowledge workers.[6] International business scholars, Jeffrey Pfeffer and John Veiga cite training as an "essential component of high performance work systems" and a "source of competitive advantage." As one example, they described The Men's Wearhouse, a specialty retailer of men's tailored business attire, that attributes its success (its stock value has increased by 400 percent) to the emphasis it has placed on training. They built a 35,000-square-foot training center at their headquarters

*Contributed by Joyce E. A. Russell.

in Fremont, California, and put their "clothing consultants" through training and retraining at "Suits University."[7]

Organizations with exceptional training opportunities and programs also often make *Fortune* magazine's list of the "Best Companies to Work for," an honor that also translates into financial success. A recent study found that companies that made *Fortune's* list had 50 percent less turnover than their peers and returned about three times more money for stockholders.

Miami-based Baptist Health South Florida made the list in 2005 due mainly to the manner in which they invested in their people.[8] The hospital offers extensive training and tuition reimbursement for taking outside courses. Their "School at Work" programs prepares lower-level workers for college-level courses and more professional careers. They pay their employees to attend the classes and graduates can then take advantage of the hospital's tuition reimbursement benefits to take community college or university classes.

To become a leading-edge company, a firm will need to be more concerned with the types of programs they use to improve workplace learning and performance, not simply how much money they spend on training. A transformation of a firm's training efforts and other practices and systems that support training may be needed. For example, successful firms align their training with high-performance work practices (e.g., self-directed work teams, access to business information), innovative compensation practices (profit sharing, group-based pay), and innovative training practices (e.g., mentoring or coaching programs, training information systems).[9]

Not only must firms invest in the continual learning of workers in order to be competitive, but many companies are providing training to workers who are new to the workforce. Many companies also include an assessment of workforce trainability as part of their analysis for expansion and plant openings. Unfortunately, recent evidence indicates that many U.S. workers are not competing well on the trainability criterion. In 2005, Toyota selected Ontario, Canada, over the United States as the place for a new plant for its mini-S.U.V.s. They chose Canada over several U.S. states offering substantial financial incentives based to some extent on the relative trainability of Ontario's workforce. The president of the Automotive Parts Manufacturers' Association stated that the educational level in parts of the United States was so low that trainers for Japanese plants have to use "pictorials" to teach some illiterate workers how to use high-tech equipment. Other reports support the contention that auto companies with plants in parts of the United States are disappointed in the trainability of the U.S. workforce.[10]

Many firms provide life training in addition to skills training. When Marriott Hotels hires new workers, it enrolls them in a six-week training course, with classes on hotel duties and self-esteem and stress. At Burger King, basic training for starting restaurant jobs also includes Life 101 (e.g., teaching employees how to balance a checkbook, the importance of getting to work on time). Ecolab established partnerships with welfare-to-work community groups and started a training program at a Wisconsin plant to teach entry-level employees math, basic physics, and blueprint-reading skills.[11]

This chapter provides an overview of employee training. We will discuss the importance of training in the context of the organization's competitive strategy and the need to link training needs with the mission and goals of the organization. You will learn how to design and evaluate a training program and to tailor the training to particular situations.

OBJECTIVES

After reading this chapter, you should be able to

1. *Define what is meant by training, and describe why it is a critical function for corporations today.*
2. *Explain how to conduct a needs assessment, including performing organizational, task, and person analyses and deriving instructional objectives for a training program.*
3. *Know how to design a training program to facilitate learning.*
4. *Identify the critical elements related to transfer of training.*
5. *Compare and contrast the various techniques available for training, including their relative advantages and disadvantages, with particular emphasis on e-learning.*
6. *Identify criteria to use to evaluate training effectiveness.*
7. *Understand different experimental designs that can be used for evaluating training programs.*
8. *Understand the components of training programs for employee orientation, teamwork, information technology, diversity awareness, sexual harassment, creativity, and international assignments.*

DEFINING TRAINING AND DEVELOPMENT

Training is defined as any attempt to improve employee performance on a currently held job or one related to it. This usually means changes in specific knowledge, skills, attitudes, or behaviors. To be effective, training should involve a learning experience, be a planned organizational activity, and be designed in response to identified needs. Ideally, training also should be designed to meet the goals of the organization while simultaneously meeting the goals of individual employees. The term *training* is often confused with the term *development*. **Development** refers to learning opportunities designed to help employees

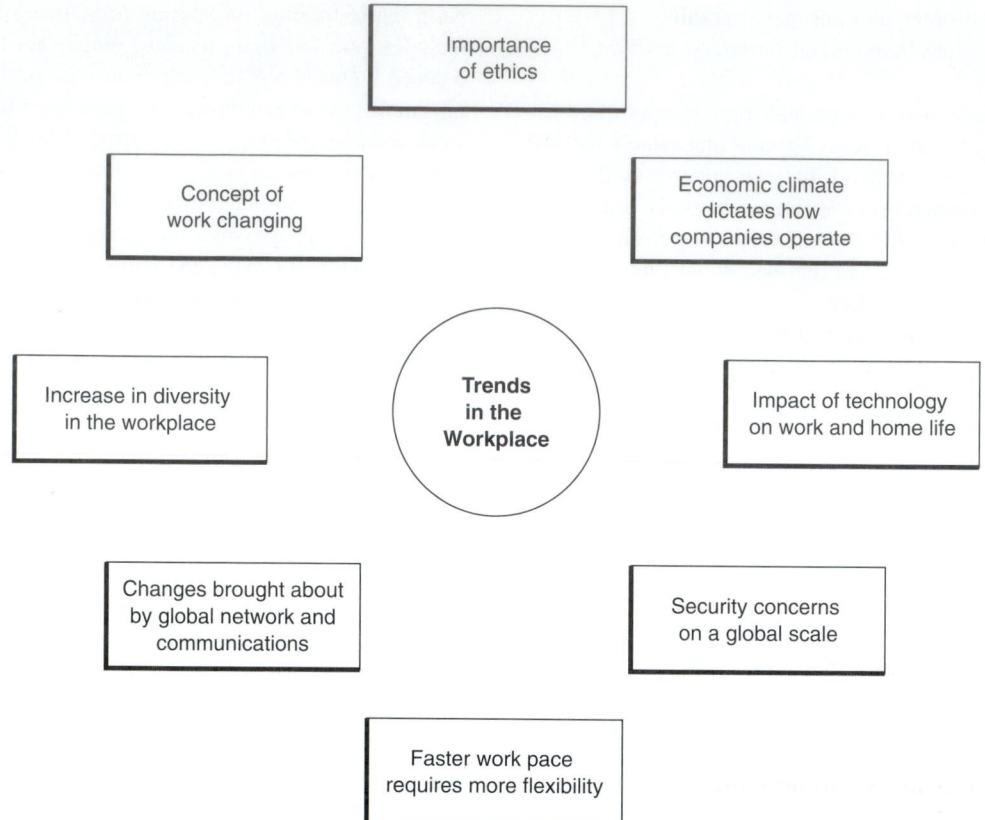

Figure 8-1 **Trends in the Workplace**

grow. Such opportunities do not have to be limited to improving employees' performance on their current jobs. At Ford, for example, a new systems analyst is required to take a course on Ford standards for user manuals. The content of this training is needed to perform the systems analyst job at Ford. The systems analyst, however, also may enroll in a course entitled "Self-Awareness," the content of which is not required on the current job. This situation illustrates the difference between "training" and "development."[12] The focus of "development" is on the long term to help employees prepare for future work demands, while "training" often focuses on the immediate period to help fix any current deficits in employees' skills. The most effective companies look at training and career development as an integral part of a "human resources development" (HRD) program carefully aligned with corporate business strategies.

EXTENT OF TRAINING AND DEVELOPMENT

U.S. organizations with more than 100 employees spent $51.4 billion on formal training for their employees in 2004.[13] The average percentage of payroll invested in learning in the ASTD Best Award Winner Companies ranged from 3.2 percent in 2002 to 4.16 percent in 2004. This was

considerably higher than Fortune 500 Companies and public sector firms that were also surveyed (i.e. average percentage of payroll 1.99 percent in 2004). The BEST award winners were defined as those organizations honored for their exceptional efforts to foster, support, and leverage enterprise-wide learning for business results. Common characteristics of BEST winning organizations were:

- High-level of investment in learning
- Measurement and demonstration of efficiency and effectiveness of the leadership function
- Alignment of learning with business needs and individual contemporary needs
- Provision of a broad range of internal and external formal and informal learning opportunities
- Chief-level involvement and support for learning
- Combination of learning with other performance improvement solutions[14]

As an example, Solectron Corporation, a worldwide provider of electronic manufacturing services, has focused its efforts on expanding its in-house training capabilities or in-sourcing, rather than utilizing more outsourcing for its training needs.[15] The proportion of courses designed, developed, and delivered by outside contractors has remained at about a third for the past few years (35 percent of courses are designed and developed by outside contractors and 26 percent are delivered by outsiders). These percentages are slightly higher for technical training programs.[16] Expenditure per employee group was greatest for customer service employees in 2003, with an average of 18 percent to that group. However, an average of 28 percent of learning expenditures went to employees with managerial responsibilities, including first-line supervisors (7 percent), middle managers (11 percent), senior managers (6 percent), and executives (4 percent).[17] Delivery of training via learning technologies increased, and the percentage of learning delivered in classrooms was 68 percent, showing a steady decrease since 1999 when it was 80 percent.[18]

Mercedes-Benz built a $30 million training center, called the Mercedes-Benz Institute, in its new $300 million plant in Alabama. The 100,000-square-foot center houses labs for teaching basic skills in welding, hydraulics, pneumatics, computer-aided design, measurement, and robotics. They set aside $60 million to send new workers to Germany for training.[19] Motorola mandates 40 hours of training per employee per year and has invested over $170 million in training.[20] Industries differ in their use of training. In 2003, the industry sectors with the highest levels of expenditure per employee were financial and technology, while those with the lowest expenditures were manufacturing durables and wholesaling and retail trade.[21]

Training has been viewed positively among employees. Approximately two-thirds of employees, regardless of age or gender, view the training they have received from their employers to be useful in helping them perform their current job duties. They were less enthusiastic about how well it has prepared them for higher-level jobs (about half were satisfied). They also viewed the training their employer provided as critical for determining whether or not they would stay with their current firm.[22]

Corporations are offering a variety of training programs to meet their organizational needs. These include content on IT and systems; processes, procedures and business practices; industry specific training; managerial or supervisory training; interpersonal skills; compliance; sales; executive development; basic skills; new employee orientation; customer service, and quality.[23] Figure 8-2 lists the most frequent types of training offered in 2003.

The importance of training is likely to continue in the future given recent trends in the workforce. As the United States shifts from manufacturing to service jobs, more workers are needed in service-based industries. In addition, increasing technology demands that current employees enhance their skills and technical sophistication. For example, U.S. Steel (USX) invested money in training for workers so that they would be able to use the new technology they implemented in its production processes. Similarly, Xerox spent about $7 million on its training center to assist its sales staff in gaining additional training to better meet customers' needs for handling documents.[24]

FIGURE 8-2	Most Frequent Types of Training Offered*

Type of Training	Percentage of Firms Offering
Computer systems/applications	96%
New hire orientation	96
Management development, nonexecutive	91
Technical training	90
Communication skills	89
Sexual harassment	88
Supervisory skills	88
Leadership	85
New equipment operation	85
Performance management/appraisal	85
Team building	82
Customer service	81
Product knowledge	79
Executive development	78
Safety	77
Computer programming	76
Personal growth	76
Managing change	75
Problem solving/decision making	75
Time management	74
Train-the-trainer	74
Diversity/cultural awareness	72
Hiring/interviewing	71
Strategic planning	69
Customer education	68
Quality/process improvement	65
Public speaking/presentation skills	62
Basic life/work skills	61
Ethics	61
Sales	55
Wellness	54

*Respondents were asked the extent to which they used these methods via classroom, via technology, via a blended approach, or do not provide. The figures shown here are for those who reported using any of the three means of providing training.

Employees at RJR Nabisco who have been confronted with new technology in their jobs are given the option of receiving retraining or early retirement.[25] Employees themselves are asking for additional training in using new technology.[26]

A SYSTEMS VIEW OF TRAINING

The basic process of training is illustrated in Figure 8-3. Three major steps are involved: assessment, development, and evaluation. The goal of the *assessment* phase is to collect information to determine if training is needed in the organization. If it is needed, it is then important to determine where in the organization it is needed, what kind of training is needed, and what specific knowledge, abilities,

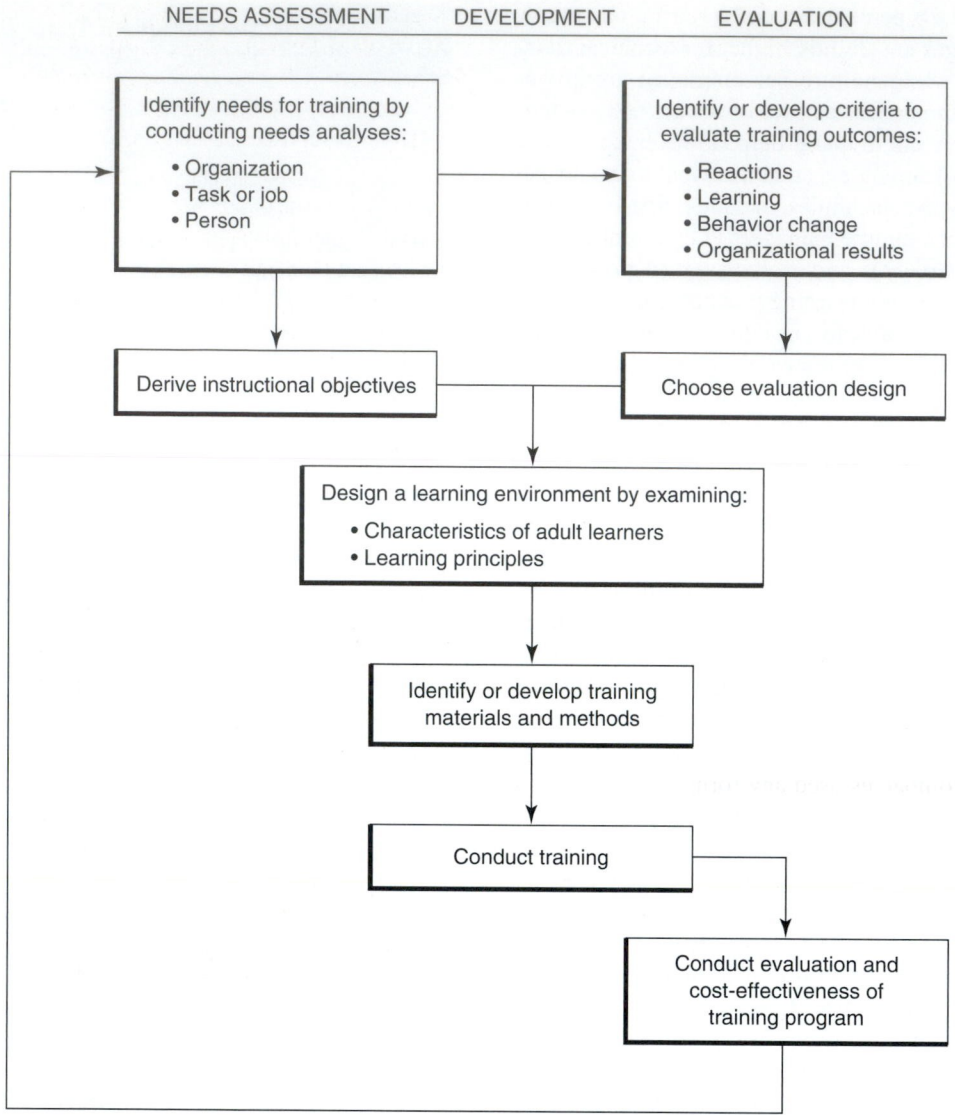

Figure 8-3   A Systems Model of Training

skills, or other characteristics (KASOCs) should be taught. This information is collected by conducting three types of analyses: at the organizational, job, and individual level of analysis. After the information is compiled, objectives for the training program can be derived.

The goal of the *development* phase of training is to design the training environment necessary to achieve the objectives. This means trainers must review relevant learning issues, including characteristics of adult learners and learning principles as they apply to the particular training and potential trainees under consideration. Also, trainers must identify or develop training materials and techniques to use in the program. Finally, after the appropriate learning environment is designed or selected, the training is conducted.

The goal of the *evaluation* phase is to examine whether the training program has been effective in meeting the stated objectives. The evaluation phase requires

the identification and development of criteria, which should include participants' reactions to the training, assessments of what they learned in the training program, measures of their behavior after the training, indicators of organizational results (e.g., changes in productivity data, sales figures, employee turnover, accident rates), and return on investments (ROI) or, as discussed in Chapter 6, utility analysis. An experimental design is chosen to assess the effectiveness of training. The choice of the criteria and the design are both made *before* training is conducted in order to ensure that training will be properly evaluated. After the training is completed, the program is then evaluated using the criteria and design selected.

Discrepancies between Research and Practice

Research in training is needed now more than ever before as the demand for training increases in organizations.[27] In addition, since much of the literature on training comes from a variety of scientific fields (e.g., industrial and organizational psychology, human resource development, cognitive psychology, anthropology, education, human factors, computer science), it is increasingly important to integrate the findings across those disciplines. Various fields in psychology even define training differently.[28]

Compared to other areas of HRM, practitioners have a fairly strong knowledge of some areas of training research.[29] A recent survey of training processes used in corporate America revealed some discrepancies between the academic recommendations regarding training program development and evaluation and the current state of the practice.[30] While larger companies were more likely to have done formal needs assessments, written specific instructional objectives, and evaluated the training with something other than a simple, post-training reaction questionnaire, the majority of all classes of respondents did none of these things. Small businesses rarely did any of these things as part of their training. Over 60 percent of all surveyed companies, regardless of company size, relied only on trainee reactions to assess the training, taken upon completion of the training, and had no systematic follow-up to further evaluate the training. Less than 10 percent of companies used any form of control group to evaluate the effects of the training. Over 50 percent of companies admitted that managerial training programs were first tried because some other company had been using them. As one training director put it, " A lot of companies buy off-the-shelf training programs just because they had heard or knew that a competitor was using the same training. Shouldn't we expect more data to determine training needs?"

Other scholars also have noted the gaps between research and practice in the training field. Practitioners[31] point out that research findings are often ignored and faddish programs are adopted with little proven utility. In addition, training needs assessments and evaluations are often rare despite their importance, and most training is informal even though this is not the best approach to use.

In order to address some of the gaps between research and practice, the American Society for Training and Development has initiated and published their ASTD 2005 Research-to-Practice conference proceedings. In this extensive report, they have included over 25 articles examining a variety of training issues such as evaluation efforts, learning transfer, e-learning, and designing programs. The intent of the proceedings is to share knowledge that will affect practice in the field.[32]

NEEDS ASSESSMENT

The first step in training is to determine that a need for training actually exists. An organization should commit its resources to a training activity only if the training can be expected to achieve some organizational goal. The decision to conduct training must be based on the best available data, which are collected by conducting a needs assessment. This needs analysis ideally should be conducted in the context of a human resource planning (HRP) program and timely and valid performance data. Companies that implement training programs without conducting a needs assessment may be making errors or spending money unnecessarily. For example, a needs assessment might reveal that less-costly interventions (e.g., personnel selection, a new compensation system, job redesign) could be used in lieu of training. Despite the importance of conducting needs assessments, few employers conduct such an analysis in the context of their strategic plans or any form of strength, weakness, opportunity, or threat analysis.

A **needs assessment** is a systematic, objective determination of training needs that involves conducting three primary types of analyses. These analyses are used to derive objectives for the training program. The three analyses consist of an organizational analysis, a job analysis, and a person analysis.[33] After compiling the results, objectives for the training program can be derived.

Many trainers suggest that a training need is any discrepancy between what is desired and what exists. Thus, one of the goals of the needs assessment is to note any discrepancies. For example, the World Bank recently determined through a needs assessment that many of its constituents from eastern Europe required training in transforming state-owned businesses into self-sustaining businesses. The organization contracted with a number of universities to develop and provide the necessary training.

Comparisons between the expected level of performance specified (from the job analysis) and the current level of performance exhibited (evident in the person analysis) may indicate performance discrepancies. The Sheraton Corporation, for example, specified that all hotel managers must be familiar with the implications of the 1990 Americans with Disabilities Act (ADA) for hotel operations (see Chapter 3). A test of the law was administered, and scores on the test were used as a basis for identifying those managers who needed training on the implications of the law. Performance discrepancies, however, should not be automatically interpreted as a need for training.[34] The analyst must determine whether the discrepancy is a skill or knowledge deficiency, thus requiring training. If, however, the required skill is present and performance is still lacking, then the problem may be motivational in nature and thus require some other type of organizational intervention (e.g., new reward or discipline system).

Organizational Analysis

An organizational analysis tries to answer the question of *where* the training emphasis should be placed in the company and what factors may affect training. To do this, an examination should be made of the organizational goals, personnel inventories, performance data, and climate and efficiency indices. This examination should ideally be conducted in the context of the labor supply forecast and gap analysis. Organization system constraints that may hamper the training process also should be explored. Training does not exist in a vacuum and the context in which it occurs has an impact on whether individuals will learn.[35] Many companies rely on very detailed surveys of the workforce to determine training needs as part of the planning effort. Motorola and IBM, for example, conduct annual surveys that assess particular training needs in the context of the company's short- and long-term goals.

The review of short- and long-term goals of the organization and any trends that may affect these goals is done to channel the training towards specific issues of importance to the firm (e.g., international expansion, improved customer satisfaction, increased productivity). For example, after Merrill Lynch pleaded guilty to a number of fraudulent business practices, the new chief executive officer (CEO) ordered training in business ethics for all employees. To reduce layoffs, IBM retrained hundreds of employees to be sales representatives. Not only was IBM able to minimize layoffs, but the larger sales staff was able to attack another corporate goal: to improve customer satisfaction.

Data from a human resource information system (HRIS) can reveal projected employee mobility, retirements, and turnover. The more sophisticated inventories also can indicate the number of employees in each KASOC or competency group, which can then be compared to what is needed based on the gap analysis of the HR planning process. For example, the Ford Manufacturing Systems Division decided to change to a new programming language for future support work. The first step it took was to determine the extent to which current staff was sufficiently skilled in the new language. The HRIS quickly revealed how many of the staff had at least basic knowledge of and experience with the new language.

A review of climate and performance efficiency data is important to identify problems that could be alleviated with training.[36] Climate indices are quality-of-work-life indicators and include records on turnover, grievances, absenteeism, productivity, accidents, attitude surveys, employee suggestions, and labor–management data (e.g., strikes, lockouts). Job satisfaction indexes provide data on employee attitudes toward the work itself, supervision, and co-workers. Performance data should be the specific record of important outcomes over a specific period of time. A record of competency assessment could be useful data as well. Multirater data should be maintained here as well. Efficiency indexes consist of costs of labor, materials, and distribution; the quality of the product; downtime; waste; late deliveries; repairs; and equipment utilization. These data are examined to find any discrepancies between desired and actual performance.

It is also important to identify any organization system constraints on training efforts. For example, if the benefits of training are not clear to top management, they may not plan and budget appropriately for training. Consequently, the training program may not be properly designed or implemented. Omni Hotels requires senior executives to attend training programs to ensure that they are supportive of the training that lower-level managers receive. In addition, the training staff makes sure that the training is tailored to Omni so that trainees can more readily see the value of the training.[37]

Organizational analysis should test hypotheses about training needs. You're testing theories related to strategy execution. For example, a retail marketing manager received a complaint from a vendor that the sales staff did not understand the advantages at a particular product. The manager then "mined" the customer survey and complaint database to determine the extent to which product knowledge of the sales staff was a problem. (He was able to determine that the complaint may have been an isolated event.)

Job Analysis

A job analysis tries to answer the question of *what* should be taught in training so that the trainee can perform the job satisfactorily. As discussed in Chapter 4, a job analysis should document the tasks or duties involved in the job as well as the KASOCs (or competencies) needed to carry out the duties. When conducting a job analysis to determine training needs, both a *worker-oriented* approach, which focuses on identifying behaviors and KASOCs, and a *task-oriented* approach, which describes the work activities performed, should be used. The critical incident technique (CIT) is particularly valuable because it provides considerable detail on the job and the consequences of specific work behaviors. A task-oriented approach is beneficial in identifying specific training objectives that are used in curriculum development and program evaluation. Ideally more than one method of job analysis should be used to determine training needs. If interviews or questionnaires are used and discrepancies exist between what a supervisor says is an important job duty and what an employee states, these discrepancies should be resolved before any training programs are designed.[38]

Person Analysis

A person analysis attempts to answer the question of *who* needs training in the firm and the specific type of training needed. To do this, the performance of individuals, groups, or units on major job functions (taken from the performance appraisal data) or assessments of KASOCs or competencies are compared to the desired levels. Many companies use self-assessments in this process. For example, Ford determined the training needs for a new computer language based on a self-assessment questionnaire distributed to the staff. At the managerial level, many organizations (e.g., IBM, AT&T, Federal Express, the World Bank, and the Federal Aviation Administration) use peers and subordinates to provide performance information about their managers. Knight-Ridder uses a 360-degree appraisal system to determine training needs. Managers receive "competency" ratings from customers, peers, subordinates, and their managers. At Ford, each supervisor is responsible for completing an individual training plan for each subordinate. The plan is developed jointly by the supervisor and the subordinate. The two decide on the courses that should be taken and the time frame for completion. The goal is for each employee to reach a certain level of proficiency considered necessary for current and future tasks. Many organizations in the service sector rely on customers for information about sales personnel. Bloomingdale's, for example, uses "paid" customers to assess the sales techniques of probationary employees. The data are then used to determine the appropriate managerial intervention to take with the employee (e.g., training, discipline, new compensation).

Performance discrepancies are used to indicate areas needing attention. It is important to determine whether any discrepancies are due to a lack of KASOCs, which KASOCs are missing, and whether they can be developed in employees through training. Individuals may lack the necessary skills or perceive themselves as lacking the skills (i.e., they may lack confidence in their abilities). In these cases, training may be needed. In other situations, employees may have the skills yet lack the needed motivation to perform, and other action may be called upon (e.g., changes in the reward system, discipline). Employees also can be tested on the desired behaviors using a performance test such as those discussed in Chapter 6. If they can perform the duties satisfactorily, the organization will know that skills training is not required. The U.S. Navy,

for example, uses miniature training and testing in order to determine skill level prior to comprehensive training. Pratt & Whitney and Office Depot are among the many companies that use an assessment center to measure supervisory skills judged to be critical based on its goals. Person analysis can also be used to assess trainability; whether the individual is capable of benefiting from the training and who, among candidates, might benefit the most. We discuss trainability later on the chapter. Research is clear that individual difference variables such as cognitive ability and motivation to learn are related to trainability and the extent someone will learn.[39]

Techniques for Collecting Needs Assessment Data

A variety of techniques have been suggested for conducting a needs assessment and for collecting data to use in the organizational, job, and person analyses. Figure 8-4 lists these techniques. Some techniques (e.g., work sampling) can be used for more than one type of analysis. Thus, efforts to coordinate and integrate results are recommended.

Deriving Instructional Objectives

After completing the three types of analyses in the needs assessment, the training professional should begin to develop instructional or learning objectives for the performance discrepancies identified. Instructional objectives describe the performance you want trainees to be able to exhibit. Well-written learning objectives should contain observable actions (e.g., time on target; error rate for things that can be identified, ordered, or charted), measurable criteria (e.g., percentage correct), and the conditions of performance (e.g., specification as to when the behavior

FIGURE 8-4 Data Sources Used in Training Needs Assessment

Organizational Analysis	Job/Task Analysis	Person Analysis
Organizational goals and objectives	Job descriptions	Performance appraisal data
HRIS data	Job specifications or task analysis	Work sampling
Skills/Competency inventories	Performance standards	Interviews
Organizational climate indexes	Performing the job	Performance tests
Efficiency indexes/Performance data	Work sampling	Tests (KASOCs)
Changes in systems or subsystems (e.g., equipment)	Reviewing literature on the job	Attitude surveys
Management requests	Asking questions about the job	Training progress charts/checklists
Exit interviews	Training committees/conferences	Assessment centers
Management-by-objectives or work planning systems	Analysis of operating problems	Critical incidents
	O*NET data	Self-efficacy measures

Source: Modified from M. L. Moore and P. Dutton, "Training Needs Analysis: Review and Critique," *Academy of Management Review* 3 (1978), pp. 534–538. Used with permission.

should occur). Some sample learning objectives for a training program with sales employees are:

- After training, the employee will be able to smile at all customers even when exhausted or ill, unless the customer is irate.
- After training, the employee will be able to calculate markdowns on all sales merchandise (e.g., 30 percent markdown) correctly 100 percent of the time.

Although training programs can be developed without deriving learning objectives, there are several advantages to developing them. First, the process of defining learning objectives helps the trainer identify criteria for evaluating training programs. For example, specifying an instructional objective of a 20 percent reduction in waste reveals that measures of waste may be important indicators of program effectiveness. Second, learning objectives direct trainers to the specific issues and content to focus on. This ensures that trainers are addressing important topics that have been identified through strategic planning. Also, learning objectives guide trainees by specifying what is expected of them at the end of training. Finally, specifying objectives makes the training department more accountable and more clearly linked to other human resource activities, which may make the training program easier to sell to line managers.

DEVELOPMENT OF THE TRAINING PROGRAM

After a needs analysis has been conducted and the staff is confident that training is needed to address the performance problem or to advance the firm's strategic mission, the training program is developed. This can be done by an in-house training staff or by outside consultants. Many firms now even design and manage their own corporate training centers. Some of the 400 companies that have their own corporate universities include Toyota, Ford, Disney, GE, Union Carbide, IBM, Home Depot, Xerox, Motorola, Phillips Petroleum, McDonald's, Black & Decker, Aetna Life & Casualty, Kodak, and Goodyear Tire & Rubber.[40] To develop the program, the trainer should design a training environment conducive to learning. This can be done by setting up preconditions for learning and arranging the training environment to ensure learning. Following this, the trainer should examine various training methods and techniques to choose the combination most beneficial for accomplishment of the instructional objectives of the training program.

Designing a Learning Environment for Training

To design a training program in which learning will be facilitated, trainers should review the basic principles of how individuals learn. Learning principles should be reviewed and integrated into the design of the training program and materials. Also, issues of how to maximize

transfer of new behaviors back to the job should be addressed. Finally, trainers should design their programs to meet the needs of adults as learners, which means understanding how adults best learn. For example, adult learners want to set their own goals for training since they see themselves as capable of self-direction. In addition, they often enjoy experiential learning techniques and self-directed learning more than conventional informational techniques. They are problem-centered and are more receptive to training that enables them to solve problems of particular interest to their situation. They want to be able to apply the training they receive to their day-to-day work experiences and are less interested in the program if they cannot see a direct application to their work situation.[41]

Preconditions of Learning

Trainees must be ready to learn before they are placed in any training program. To ensure this, trainers should determine whether trainees are **trainable** (i.e., whether they have the ability to learn and are motivated to learn). In addition, trainers should try to gain the support of trainees and their supervisors prior to actually implementing the program. This is particularly important for training in sensitive areas such as diversity and gender and race discrimination.

Trainability

Before the learner can benefit from any formal training, he or she must be trainable or ready to learn. This means the trainee must have both the ability and the motivation to learn. To have the ability, the trainee must possess the skills and knowledge prerequisite to master the material. One way to determine this is to give trainees a performance test or work sample (i.e., an example of the types of skills to be performed on the job) and measure how quickly they are able to learn the material or how well they are able to perform the skills. Assessing trainees' ability to learn is of increasing concern to corporate America. In view of the increasing technological knowledge required in most jobs, many Americans are not being educated at a level compatible with the requirements of most entry-level jobs. This situation appears to be getting worse in the United States since the entry-level jobs of the future are being "up-skilled" while the pool of qualified workers is shrinking. (Recall the comment earlier about Toyota's 2005 decision to open a new plant in Canada and not the United States.)

It has been estimated that over 30 million workers in the United States are functionally illiterate, meaning that they cannot read or write well enough to perform their job duties. Sun Oil, Campbell Soup, and Digital Equipment work with state and local governments in partnership programs to help address literacy issues among the workforce.[42] Research clearly shows that employees with higher cognitive ability and basic math and reading skills are more trainable.[43]

It's not enough that trainees have the ability to learn the skills; they must also have the desire or motivation to learn. Research also finds that employees who are more conscientious, more oriented toward learning, less anxious, and younger are more trainable.[44] One way to assess motivation to learn is to examine how involved they are in their own jobs and career planning. The assumption is that those individuals who are more highly involved will have higher motivation to learn.[45] It is also important to assess the attitudes and expectations of trainees regarding training since their views will most likely affect their reactions to the program and the amount they learn.[46] For example, employees who choose to attend training learn more than those who are required to attend.[47] Some companies link successful completion of training programs and acquired skills with compensation. At Ford, employees must select 40 hours of training from a list of options. An employee must fulfill the 40 hours to qualify for merit pay.

Given the increasing use of distance learning formats, it is also important to assess learners' readiness to participate in online learning. The readiness of learners to enter into distance learning environments may play a critical role in increasing their course-completion and program-retention rates. Thus, a tool, the **E-learning Readiness Self-Assessment** has been designed to provide a quick, yet comprehensive analysis of preparedness for success in an online training program. It addresses questions about the learner's access to technology, online skills, motivation, online audio, Internet skills, and views about training success.[48]

Gaining the Support of Trainees and Others

If trainees do not see the value of training, they will be unlikely to learn new behaviors or use them on their jobs. Trainees should be informed in advance about the benefits that will result from training. If they see some incentives for training, it may strengthen their motivation to learn the behaviors, practice them, and remember them. To gain the support of trainees for the training program, the trainer must point out the intrinsic (e.g., personal growth) and extrinsic (e.g., promotion) benefits of attending training. At Saturn, employees are strongly encouraged to receive skills training. In fact, 5 percent of their yearly compensation is based on the amount of training they receive.

In addition to garnering the support of trainees for training, the support of their supervisors, co-workers, and subordinates should be sought. For example, if the trainees' supervisors are not supportive of training, then they may not facilitate the learning process (e.g., allow employees time off for training, reward them for using new skills). Likewise, if their peers or subordinates ridicule them for attending training, they may not be motivated to attend training programs or to learn. Trainers can improve the likelihood of acquiring others' support for training by getting their opinions on the content of training, the location, and the times. At Patapsco Valley Veterinary Hospital located in Ellicott City, Maryland, staff members are consistently asked for their opinions on the most convenient times to hold training sessions. In addition, the owners of the practice set a positive example by attending the training sessions themselves and by rewarding employees for participating in training and using their new skills on the job.

Conditions of the Learning Environment

After ensuring the preconditions for learning are met, trainers should build a training environment in which learning is maximized. To do this, trainers need to decide how to best arrange the training environment by addressing the issues below.

Whole versus Part Learning

Research has shown that when a complex task is to be learned, it should be broken down into its parts if this can be done. Trainees should learn each part separately, starting with the simplest and going on to the most difficult. However, part learning should be combined with whole learning; that is, trainees should be shown the whole performance so that they know what their final goal is. The training content should be broken down into integrated parts, and each part should be learned until it can be performed accurately. Then a trainee should be allowed to put all the parts together and practice the whole task. One method that combines part and whole learning is called *progressive part learning.* In this approach, the trainees learn one part, then learn and practice that first part along with a second part, then learn and practice the first and second parts along with a third part, and so on. This might be used if the topics to be taught are somewhat interdependent (e.g., a communications course that involved sessions on active listening, being assertive, using nonverbals).

Massed versus Spaced Practice

Practice is important for trainees to learn a new skill or behavior. Trainers also can observe the practice sessions and provide feedback to the trainees to correct their mistakes. Spaced practice (i.e., practicing the new behavior and taking rest periods in between) is more effective than massed practice (practicing the new behavior without breaks), especially for motor skills. For example, it would be easier for you to learn how to play golf by having a lesson on putting and then going out to practice putting, rather than learning how to do all of the possible golf shots (e.g., putting, chipping, pitching, driving, etc.) and then going out to play. If a learner has to concentrate for long periods of time without some rest, learning and retention may suffer. It's a little like cramming for an examination: rapid forgetting sets in very soon. Consequently, spaced practice seems to be more productive for long-term retention and for transfer of learning to the work setting. Of course, it takes longer for spaced practice than for massed practice so trainees may resist it (e.g., they may be less receptive to attending four half-day workshops than two full-day sessions). Tasks that are difficult and complex seem to be performed better when massed practice is provided first, followed by briefer sessions with more frequent rest periods.[49]

Overlearning

Overlearning (i.e., practicing far beyond the point of performing the task successfully) can be critical in both acquisition and transfer of knowledge and skills. Generally, overlearning increases retention over time, makes the behavior or skill more automatic, increases the quality of the performance during stress, and helps trainees transfer what they have learned back to the job setting.[50] Overlearning is desirable in a program when the task to be learned is not likely to be immediately practiced in the work situation and when performance must be maintained during periods of emergency and stress. For example, overlearning skills for driving or flying may be important so that in a crisis situation the individual will be able to quickly remember what actions should be taken. Pat Head Summitt, rated as one of the top coaches in collegiate basketball, believes in the importance of overlearning, which she calls "discipline." She has her nationally ranked team, the Tennessee Lady Volunteers, practice their plays over and over again in preparation for critical games.[51]

Figure 8-5 presents a summary of the research on the trainee characteristics and work environment variables shown to be related to relatively more training success and training transfer.

FIGURE 8-5	**Predictors and Correlates of Trainability**

TRAINEE CHARACTERISTICS RELATED TO GREATER TRAINING SUCCESS

High cognitive ability
High basic reading and math skills
Oriented toward learning
Less anxious
High-conscientiousness (from the Five Factor Model-see Ch. 6)
High-achievement motivation
Self-efficacy/confidence in success
High motivation to learn
Perceive training as relevant to job/career
Value outcomes (learning)

WORK ENVIRONMENT CORRELATES OF TRANSFER

Opportunity to perform trained tasks
Positive climate for learning
Reinforce importance of continuous learning
Time and opportunity for training and practice

Source: Adapted from Arthur, W., Bennett, W., Jr., Edens, P., & Bell, S. (2003). Effectiveness of training in organizations: A meta-analysis of design and evaluation features. *Journal of Applied Psychology,* **88,** 234–245.

Goal Setting

Goal setting can help employees improve their performance by directing their attention to specific behaviors that need to be changed. If employees set specific, challenging goals, they can reach higher levels of performance. For example, research has shown that goal setting has led to an average increase of 19 percent.[52] Goal setting improves performance because it affects four mechanisms: (a) it directs and focuses a person's behavior, (b) it increases an individual's effort towards attaining the goal, (c) it encourages an individual to persist on the goal or work harder and faster to attain it, and (d) it enables an individual to set specific strategies for attaining the goal.[53] Training programs should include specific, yet challenging goals so trainees can reach higher levels of performance or greater mastery of the training material. Trainees should be encouraged to set public goals and to record their accomplishments to ensure greater transfer of their training skills.

Knowledge of Results

For trainees to improve performance, they need to receive timely and specific feedback or knowledge of results. Feedback serves informational and motivational purposes. It tells trainees how discrepant their performance is from the desired performance and what particular skills or behaviors they need to correct. Also, it can motivate them to meet their performance goals once they see that they are coming close to accomplishing them. Trainers should build into the training environment opportunities for providing feedback to trainees. For example, the trainer could give pop quizzes to trainees during the session and call out the correct answers. Trainees could quickly score their work to see how well they are doing in the session and what they need additional learning or practice in. Sometimes trainees can provide feedback to one another (e.g., observers can be used in role-plays to provide feedback to role-players).

Attention

Trainers should try to design training programs and materials to ensure that trainees devote attention to them. They can do this by choosing a training environment that is comfortable to trainees (e.g., that has good temperature, lighting, seats, plenty of room, snacks) and free from distractions (e.g., phone calls, interruptions from colleagues). This is becoming increasingly more critical and challenging as trainees bring in more and more technology (e.g., blackberries, cell phones; laptops) into the classroom. No matter how motivated trainees are, if the environment is not comfortable to work in, trainees will have difficulty learning. Trainers also should make sure that trainees are familiar with and have accepted the learning objectives. They can do this by asking trainees to describe how accomplishing the objectives will resolve problems on the job. If trainees are able to translate learning objectives into relevant job issues, they may pay more attention to the training sessions.

Retention

The ability to retain what is learned is obviously relevant to the effectiveness of a training program. Many factors have been found to increase retention. If the material presented is meaningful to trainees, they should have an easier time understanding and remembering it. Trainers can make the content meaningful by (1) presenting trainees with an overview of what is to be learned so that they will be able to see the overall picture, (2) using examples, concepts, and terms familiar to the trainees (e.g., use medical terms and examples when training doctors and nurses), and (3) organizing the material from simple to complex (e.g., teach someone how to serve before you teach him/her strategies in tennis). Retention also can be enhanced by rehearsal or requiring trainees to periodically recall what they have learned through tests.

Using Learning Principles to Develop Training Materials

The learning principles described above should be considered not only when designing the training environment but also when developing training materials. Any materials used with trainees should be able to stimulate them into learning and remembering the information. To ensure that this occurs, trainers need to make sure that the learning principles are built into their training materials. For example, the materials should provide illustrations and relevant examples to stimulate trainees. In addition, the objectives of the material should be clearly stated and a summary should be provided.[54]

Transfer of Training

The ultimate goal of a training program is that the learning that occurs during training be transferred back to the job. Research strongly supports the view that the post-training climate will affect whether training influences behaviors or results on the job. To maximize transfer, the following suggestions have been offered.[55] These include ideas for the training session itself as well as for the employee once he or she has returned to the job:

1. Maximize the similarity between the training context and the job context. That is, the training should resemble the job as closely as possible. At GE, for example, the "action-learning" process focuses on real business problems.
2. Require practice of the new behaviors and overlearning in training.
3. Encourage trainees to practice skills on their jobs in between training sessions. For example, the executive education programs conducted by the Robert H. Smith School of Business for its corporate clients (e.g., Entergy, Lockheed Martin) often require "homework assignments" such as customer-value projects, organizational systems projects, and individual leadership development plans in between attendance at sessions. The assignments encourage trainees to apply their new skills in the workplace, using an *action learning model.*
4. Include a variety of stimulus situations in the practice so trainees will learn to generalize their knowledge and skills. Coach Pat Summitt sets up grueling basketball game schedules with top-ranked teams so that the Lady Vols will play in a variety of situations and be ready for the NCAA playoffs each year.
5. Label or identify the important features of the content to be learned to distinguish the major steps involved.
6. Develop, and have available on the job, job aids to remind employees of the key action steps necessary on the job. For example, Alcoa uses job aids in many of its manufacturing jobs.
7. Make sure that the general principles underlying the specific content are understood in training.
8. Ensure that there is a supportive climate for learning and for transferring new behaviors. This can be done by building managerial support (emotional and financial) for training, providing trainees with the freedom to set personal performance goals, and encouraging risk-taking among trainees. One study used 505 supermarket managers from 52 stores and found that the work environment, measured by training climate and learning culture, was directly related to the transfer of trained behaviors.[56] It is also important to encourage peer support since this type of support has been shown to influence transfer of training skills.[57]
9. Build the trainee's self-efficacy for learning and using the new skills. Self-efficacy is a feeling of control and accomplishment; that you can control your own destiny. It has been shown to be related to learning using a sample of Navy warfare officers in midlevel managerial positions. In addition, encourage trainees to develop an action plan including specific measurable goals.[58]
10. Once back on the job, employees should be given opportunities to demonstrate that they can use the new skills. For example, one study of plane mechanics from the Air Force found that after training they were given opportunities to perform only about half of the tasks they learned in training.[59] Likewise, in a study of university employees, it was found that situational constraints (e.g., adequate resources, time) limited the amount that trainees could transfer new skills to the work environment.[60]
11. Encourage continual learning by employees. They should realize that one-time training in an area is not sufficient to maintain effective skills. Retraining also may be needed to update skills.

Relapse Prevention

Sometimes despite trainers' best efforts to get individuals to transfer what they have learned back to the job, it is difficult for trainees to maintain new behaviors or skills over a long period. They encounter high-risk situations and revert back to their old habits. Most people experience relapses after learning new behaviors. Think about all the times you or someone you know went on a diet or started an exercise program. Perhaps you were quite successful sticking to the plan after attending a training program (e.g., Weight Watchers). Then, one weekend you go on a trip with friends. Next thing you know you are eating lots of snacks and ignoring your exercise plan. This is a relapse. The same thing often happens to employees after they have attended a training program. For example, a manager learns how to control his temper in training, yet the first time returning back to the job he encounters an irate employee and he screams at the person. **Relapse prevention** is needed to assist trainees.[61] This model emphasizes the learning of a set of self-control and coping strategies when the trainee is faced with high-risk situations.[62]

Employees should be made aware of the relapse process itself by informing them there are some situations that make it difficult for trainees to use their new behaviors. For example, they may be faced with peers or supervisors who are not supportive of their new skills.[63] They should learn to identify and anticipate high-risk situations they will face when returning from training. They should be instructed on how to cope in these situations. Teaching these issues should increase trainees' self-efficacy so that they can effectively use their new training skills back on the job.

Choosing Methods for the Training Program

Training methods can be divided into two categories:

1. Methods that are primarily informational or transmittal in nature; that is, they use primarily one-way communication in which information is transmitted to the learners.
2. Methods that are experiential in nature; that is, the learner interacts with the instructor, a computer/simulator, customers, or other trainees to practice the skill.

FIGURE 8-6 | Informational Training Methods

Uses	Benefits	Limitations
LECTURE		
Gaining new knowledge	Equally good as programmed instruction and television	Learners are passive
To present introductory material	Low cost	Poor transfer
	Reaches a large audience at one time	Depends on the lecturer's ability
	Audience is often comfortable with it	Is not tailored to individual trainees
AUDIOVISUALS		
Gaining new knowledge	Can reach a large audience at one time	Is not tailored to individual trainees
Gaining attention	Allows for replays	Must be updated
	Versatility	Passive learners
	Can reduce trainer, travel and facility costs	
INDEPENDENT STUDY		
Gaining new knowledge	Allows trainees to go at their own pace	Expensive to develop a library of materials
Completing degree requirements	Minimizes trainers' time	Materials must be designed to adjust to varying reading levels
Continuous education	Minimizes costs of development	Performance depends on trainee's motivation
		Is not applicable for all jobs
E-LEARNING		
Gaining new knowledge	Convenient	Expensive to develop
Pretraining preparation to ensure that all trainees have similar backgrounds	Allows trainees to go at their own pace	Is not easily applicable for all tasks (e.g., cognitive tasks, verbal, psychomotor)
	Can guarantee mastery at a specified level	Does not lead to higher performance than lectures
	Encourages active trainee involvement	
	Provides immediate feedback to trainees	

Some of the major methods including their uses, benefits, and limitations are described below and in Figures 8-6 and 8-7. Electronic learning or e-learning can be both on informational and an experiential method of training.

Most training programs utilize several training techniques since no one approach is best suited for every purpose. In fact, there has been increased interest in the use of blended training approaches in organizations. This often means the integration of classroom and e-learning training approaches.[64] IBM's international sales training program includes both classroom and on-the-job training (OJT), which is given over one year. AMC Theatres uses videotapes, detailed training manuals,

FIGURE 8-7	Experiential Training Methods	
Uses	**Benefits**	**Limitations**
ON-THE-JOB TRAINING		
Learning job skills	Good transfer	Depends on the trainer's skills
Apprenticeship training	Limited trainer costs	and willingness
Job rotation	High trainee motivation since training is relevant	May be costly due to lost production and mistakes
		May have frequent interruptions due to job demands
		Often is haphazardly done
		Trainees may learn bad habits
E-LEARNING		
Gaining new knowledge	Self-paced	Trainees may have difficulties
Drill and practice	Standardization of training over time	using computers
Individualized training	Feedback given	Limited opportunities for trainee interaction
	Good retention	Less useful for training interpersonal skills or psychomotor tasks
	Convenient	
	Can reduce costs	
EQUIPMENT SIMULATORS		
To reproduce real-world conditions	Effective for learning and transfer	Costly to develop
For physical and cognitive skills	Can practice most of the job skills	Sickness can occur
For team training		Requires good fidelity
GAMES AND SIMULATIONS		
Decision-making skills	Resembles the job tasks	Highly competitive
Management training	Provides feedback	Time-consuming
Interpersonal skills	Presents realistic challenges	May stifle creativity
CASE STUDY OR ANALYSIS		
Decision-making skills	Decision-making practice	Must be updated
Analytical skills	Real-world training materials	Criticized as being unable to teach general management skills
Communication skills	Active learning	Trainers often dominate discussions
To illustrate diversity of solutions	Good for developing problem-solving skills	
ROLE-PLAYING		
For changing attitudes	Gain experience of other roles	Initial resistance of trainees
To practice skills	Active learning	Trainees may not take it seriously
To analyze interpersonal problems	Close to reality	
BEHAVIORAL MODELING		
To teach interpersonal skills	Allows practice	Time-consuming
To teach cognitive skills	Provides feedback	May be costly to develop
To teach training/teaching skills	Retention is improved	
	Strong research evidence	
SENSITIVITY TRAINING		
To enhance self-awareness	Can improve self-concept	May be threatening
To allow trainees to see how others see them	Can reduce prejudice	May have limited generalizability to job situations
	Can change interpersonal behaviors	

and OJT programs to train ushers and concession personnel. To determine which combination of methods to select for a particular training program, a developer should first clearly define the purpose of and the audience for the training. In addition, an assessment of the resources available to conduct the training is necessary. This will mean examining the staff, materials, and budget capable of handling the training demands. It is also important to consider whether the focus will be on skill acquisition, maintenance, or generalization of the skill to other areas.[65]

At a minimum, the training methods selected should (1) motivate the trainee to learn the new skill, (2) illustrate the desired skills to be learned, (3) be consistent with the content (e.g., use an interactive approach to teach interpersonal skills), (4) allow for active participation by the trainees to fit with the adult learning model, (5) provide opportunities for practice and overlearning, (6) provide feedback on performance during training, (7) be structured from simple to complex, (8) encourage positive transfer from the training to the job, and (9) be cost effective. In many cases, trainers will use several different techniques. For example, teaching supervisors how to give performance feedback may first begin with a lecture or overview of the performance appraisal process, followed by small-group discussions or videotapes depicting effective coaching, and then role-plays to have supervisors practice their feedback skills.

Informational Methods

Informational methods are used primarily to teach factual material, skills, or attitudes. Generally, they do not require the trainee to actually experience or practice the material taught during the training session. Some of the more commonly used informational techniques include lectures, audio and video media, and self-directed learning (SDL) methods. E-learning is one of the most popular approaches today.

Lectures

The lecture method is the most commonly used technique for training employees and teaching students. A 2004 survey found that 85 percent of firms offer or still use a classroom with an instructor for some training.[66] The method is often supplemented with group discussions, audiovisual aids, motion pictures, or television. The approach also can vary in the degree to which discussion is permitted, since some lectures involve all one-way communication, while others may allow trainees to participate by asking questions or providing comments. Despite the criticism of this method, recent research shows lecture-based training is quite an effective way to facilitate the transfer of theories, concepts, procedures, and other factual material.[67] In addition, a meta-analysis of the effects of lecture, modeling, and active participation on the performance of older trainees found that all three methods had positive effects on learning and skill measures.[68]

Audio and Video Media

A variety of audiovisuals are available to trainers including films, videos, slides, overheads, audiotapes, flip charts, and chalkboards. As of 2004, one survey found the following usage rates (often or always used) for various media: CD-ROM/DVD/diskettes (60 percent), videotapes (56 percent), teleconferencing (25 percent), videoconferencing (19 percent), satellite/broadcast TV (8 percent), and audiocassettes (5 percent).[69] Videoconferencing has gained in popularity as costs have become more affordable for employers and different systems have become more compatible. The staff of Greenberg Traurig, an international law firm, set up a videoconference system that is used almost constantly to share information and multimedia presentations in the 375-attorney firm.[70] FedEx Kinko's has videoconferencing facilities available at over 150 U.S. locations, with costs of about $225 per hour.[71] Other firms using videoconferencing include JCPenney, IBM, AT&T, and Texas Instruments. Often, these multimedia approaches are used to supplement other training techniques, including lectures and self-directed learning methods. They can address a variety of topics such as motivational techniques, EEO issues, performance appraisal interviews, leadership skills, and teamwork.

Self-Directed Learning (SDL) Methods

Several informational methods for training are considered to be SDL approaches because the trainee takes responsibility for learning the necessary knowledge and skills at his or her own pace. A wide range of decisions can be given to the trainee, including the topic of study, objectives, resources, schedule, learning strategy, type and sequence of activities, and media. In most cases, trainees work without direct supervision, set their own pace, and are allowed to choose their own activities, resources, and learning environments. Generally, the training department's role is to provide assistance by establishing learning centers with available materials and by having trained facilitators on hand for questions. Larger companies such as Motorola, Sunoco, and Office Depot have been successful in setting up such centers and encouraging self-directed learning by employees. In these centers, trainees can be given self-assessment tools or instruments.

The advantages of SDL include (1) reduced training time, as compared to more conventional methods (e.g., lecture); (2) more favorable attitudes by trainees compared to conventional techniques; (3) more consistent with an adult learning approach; (4) minimal reliance on instructors or trainers; (5) mobility (i.e., a variety of places can be used for training); (6) flexibility (i.e., trainees can learn at their own pace); (7) consistency of the information taught to all trainees; and (8) cost savings. There are also several disadvantages, including

(1) high developmental time for course materials and extensive planning requirements, (2) difficulties in revising and updating materials, and (3) limited interactions with peers and trainers.

Research indicates that employees with high levels of readiness for SDL as measured by the Self-Directed Learning Readiness Scale (SDLRS) were more likely to be higher-level managers, to be outstanding performers,[72] to possess greater creativity,[73] and to have a higher degree of life satisfaction.[74] Also, employees who were outstanding performers in jobs requiring high levels of creativity or problem solving or involving high levels of change were more likely to have high SDLRS scores. In addition, employees with higher SDLRS scores were successful in relatively unstructured learning situations in which more responsibility rests on the learners.[75]

A variety of SDL approaches are available. Two of the more commonly used techniques include independent study and various forms of e-learning. **Independent study** requires a trainee to read, synthesize, and remember the contents of written material, audio or videotapes, or other sources of information. The training or personnel department can develop a library of materials for trainees to use in teaching themselves at their own pace about various skills or knowledge. Companies such as Coors, Digital Equipment Corporation, Kraft, and U.S. Gypsum utilize extensive self-study materials for their sales employees.[76] Trainees also can design their own training curriculum by opting for correspondence courses or enrolling in independent study courses at local schools or on the Web. Generally, in these programs, trainees are required to master the content on their own without direct supervision.

E-learning is typically (although not always) an individualized learning method that allows for study of material online. For example, UBS uses an e-based program to train new stockbrokers. Most programs build in the important learning principles by (1) specifying what is to be learned (i.e., the behavioral objectives); (2) breaking down the learning topic into small, discrete steps; (3) presenting each step to the trainee and requiring him or her to respond to each step of the learning process (i.e., by reading each part); (4) testing the trainees' learning at each step (i.e., by responding to questions); (5) providing immediate feedback to the trainee on whether his or her response was correct or incorrect; and (6) testing the level of skill or knowledge acquired at the end of the training module. E-learning has replaced "programmed instruction" in training classification but is based on the same principles.

Experiential Methods

Experiential methods are often used to teach physical and cognitive skills and abilities. These techniques include OJT, computer-based training (CBT), equipment simulations, games and other simulations, case analyses, role-playing, and behavior modeling. In addition, a variety of electronic training-delivery media and distance learning techniques have increased in their usage as instructional/experiential methods.

On-the-Job Training

Approximately 90 percent of all industrial training is conducted on the job.[77] OJT is conducted at the work site and in the context of the job. Often, it is informal as when an experienced worker shows a trainee how to perform the job tasks. The trainer may watch over the trainee to provide guidance during practice or learning. For example, sales employees use coaching calls where a senior sales person coaches a new sales employee. Five steps are utilized:[78]

1. Observation of the new employee.
2. Feedback obtained by the new employee.
3. Consensus (i.e., the coach and the new employee arrive at an agreement as to the strengths and weaknesses of the sales call).
4. Rehearsal of a new sales call.
5. Review of the employee's performance.

Although OJT is often associated with the development of new employees, it also can be used to update or broaden the skills of existing employees when new procedures or work methods are introduced.[79] In some cases, the trainer may be a retired employee. For instance, at Corning Glass Works, new employees are paired with retirees for a brief on-the-job introduction regarding the company culture and market data. Following this, they are exposed to formal classroom and field training.[80] Many companies combine OJT with formal classroom training. At McDonald's, after a three-hour induction, new employees are partnered with a buddy who is a member of the training squad.[81] Dow Chemical alternates sales employees between classroom training at corporate headquarters and OJT experiences in the field for a year. Similarly, Wang Laboratories spends up to nine months alternating salespeople from company headquarters and field offices. Restaurant employees at the Hard Rock Café are trained by OJT and the use of job aids (i.e. training materials). Workers view this approach very favorably.[82]

OJT is best used when one-on-one training is necessary, only a small number (usually fewer than five) employees need to be trained, classroom instruction is not appropriate, work in progress cannot be interrupted, a certain level of proficiency on a task is needed for certification, and equipment or safety restrictions make other training techniques inappropriate. The training should emphasize equipment or instruments that are to be used, as well as safety issues or dangerous processes. For example, Quality Commercial Services, located in Westminster, Maryland, uses OJT effectively with its staff of construction workers to teach electrical wiring, dry walling, reading engineering blueprints, and painting, among other things.

Apprenticeship programs often are considered OJT programs because they involve a substantial amount of OJT, even though they do consist of some off-the-job training. Typically, the trainee follows a prescribed order of coursework and hands-on experience. The Department of Labor regulates apprenticeship programs and many require a minimum of 144 hours of classroom instruction each year, as well as OJT with a skilled employee.[83] Many professions (e.g., medicine) or trades require some type of apprenticeship program that may last anywhere from two to five years. Some of the most common occupations to offer apprenticeship programs include electricians, carpenters, plumbers, pipe fitters, sheet-metal workers, machinists, tool-and-die makers, roofers, firefighters, bricklayers, cooks, structural-steel workers, painters, operating engineers, correction officers, and mechanics.[84] In Europe, apprenticeships are still one of the most likely ways for individuals to gain entry into skilled jobs, while in the United States only 2 percent of high school graduates enter apprenticeship programs.[85] This is a problem for the U.S. workforce since the pool of qualified skilled labor for future jobs has been shrinking. In France in one apprenticeship program alone, there are currently 4,200 apprentices with the Association des Compagnons du Devoir (elite artisans responsible for restoring historical sites such as Notre Dame Cathedral and Arc de Triomphe). Restricted to men, they begin as young as 15 and undertake up to nine years of lessons, community chores, and hands-on training with 6,500 companies that have contracts with them. They train for an additional two years and have to complete a personal building project. Only one in 10 typically survives the apprenticeship period and is allowed to join the ranks of Compagnons.[86]

Another commonly used technique for OJT training is **job rotation,** which involves moving employees from one job to another to broaden their experience. Many U.S. companies are showing greater interest in having their employees be able to perform several job functions so that their workforce is more flexible and interchangeable. For example, in the automobile industry today, it is fairly common to see employees being trained on two or more tasks (e.g., painting and welding). This is done at GM's Saturn plant in order to relieve employees' boredom as well as make the company less dependent on specialized workers. GE requires all managerial trainees to participate in an extensive job rotation program in which the trainees must perform all jobs they will eventually supervise. This helps managers develop a broader background required for future managerial positions. At Lockheed Martin, a leadership development program was established for new HR college recruits. They are rotated to a variety of HR departments (e.g., recruiting, selection, compensation) to gain broader experiences as HR professionals. Black and

Decker provides a 3-year job rotation program for its new MBA employees entering into its financial development program.

Computer-Based Training (CBT)/E-Learning

The 2004–2005 workplace forecast conducted by the Society of Human Resource Management ranked e-learning as the second most important science and technology trend that will affect the workplace.[87] The survey also found that when used effectively, e-learning has been able to deliver training for large numbers of employees at reduced costs and that there was an increased usage of e-learning during an economic downturn. Another recent study found that Web-based instruction was more effective than classroom instruction for teaching declarative knowledge and procedural knowledge. Interestingly, they also noted that trainees were more satisfied with Web-based classes that had higher levels of human interaction than lower levels. When trainees were not given the opportunity to interact with others during Web-based courses, they preferred classroom instruction.[88] One leading provider of CBT software, CBT Group, has deals with Cisco Systems, IBM, Informix, Microsoft, Netscape Communications, Novell, Oracle, PeopleSoft, SAP, and Sybase, among others.

Effective computer skill training is vital to organizational productivity. One recent study demonstrated that the behavior modeling approach to computer skill training could be improved by incorporating **symbolic mental rehearsal** (SMR). SMR is a specific form of mental rehearsal that establishes a cognitive link between visual images and symbolic memory codes. The authors recommend that practitioners use SMR for improving the effectiveness of computer skill training.[89]

Chunking refers to chopping computer-based training into its smallest parts and sending them through a network so that learners receive just the instruction they need when they need it. Spring Corporation chunks CBT on the corporate intranet and is one of the leaders in using training over the intranet.[90] The most popular processing software packages (e.g., Microsoft Word) use CBT to introduce learners to the use of the software. The U.S. Armed Forces use CBT extensively for training many of their technicians. In fact, the military and NASA have numerous advanced technologies such as intelligent tutoring systems and virtual reality that are used for training purposes.[91] In some CBT programs, trainees interact directly with computers to actually learn and practice new skills. This is done similarly to the PI system and is called computer-assisted instruction (CAI). For example, Dialect Interactive Lectures (DIALECT) are university lectures that have been converted into multimedia-based digital learning material. DIALECT use animation, computer simulations, and hyperlink facilities to guide students through lectures.[92]

CBT has the advantage of being self-paced, standardized, self-sufficient, easily available, and flexible. This is particularly important in today's fast-paced environment, where organizations cannot afford for employees to be away from the job for large amounts of time. In fact, many employees view it as a proven way to save time and money while delivering consistent content.

Electronic training-delivery media involve some of the fastest growing instructional methods. The latest round of CBT-oriented software offers revolutionary ways in which interactive training is developed and delivered. Multimedia training programs often feature text, graphics, sound, pictures, videos, simulations, and hypertext links that enable trainees to structure their own learning experiences.[93] In 2005, it has been reported that over $500 million has been spent on Web conferencing with the figure expected to top $3 billion by 2011. Most CBT systems support links to the Internet and to corporate intranets. Internet-based e-learning has emerged as a cost- and time-efficient way to address many companies' training needs. The recent SHRM survey found very positive results in terms of user reactions and efficiencies.[94] Given these trends, it is clear that traditional training methods will continue to decline as electronic delivery techniques increase in usage. This is particularly true of more innovative firms that use a greater variety of learning technologies for training.[95]

Distance Learning Programs

Online education is the fastest growing sector of the education market. Online learners are predicted to go from 3 million in 2001 to more than 6 million by 2006.[96] Many resources now exist for designing and implementing distance learning programs.[97] In addition, a comprehensive list of vendors is provided by the Distance Education Clearinghouse Web site (http://www.uwex.edu/disted).

Companies such as Banco national de Mexico, one of the oldest and largest banks in Mexico, graduated its first class of 11 executives from a global MBA degree from San Diego–based National University that is a distance learning program. The company found that enabling managers to complete the coursework without having to leave their work or homes was beneficial.[98] Research on the effectiveness of distance education programs has only begun.[99] In general, offering training or educational programs over the Internet enables employees to access high-quality education at their own pace.[100] They have access to class material, conduct research without traveling, and have dialogs with professors and classmates via e-mail, bulletin boards, and chat rooms. Some programs use videoconferencing or transmit lectures via satellite. In this regard, they may have an easier time juggling careers and families.[101] Numerous firms have successfully used distance learning programs for their employees, including Ford, AT&T, EDS, MCI Communications, U.S. Department of Defense, Tennessee Valley Authority, United Technologies Corporation, Lockheed Martin, and Lucent Technologies.[102] Organizations have reported the following benefits for distance learning programs:[103]

- A fast, effective way to train global employees.
- Increased the impact and productivity of dollars invested in training and education programs.
- Reduced travel costs and made time formerly spent traveling available for more productive uses.
- Allowed for the training of more people, more often, in sessions that are easier to schedule and coordinate.
- Offered the ability to add students and instructors as needed without incurring significant additional expenses.
- Delivered a consistent message that can be disseminated quickly companywide.
- Provided real-time updates and just-in-time information access.
- Delivered to both work and home sites that are convenient for trainees.
- Offered live interactive programs delivered to multiple networked sites for group learning.
- Is learner-centered and enabled students to have more control over the pacing and sequencing of the learning experience.
- Offered easy access to learning resources.

One recent article provides a set of research-based principles for "learner control" training in the e-learning environment. "Learner control generally refers to 'a mode of instruction in which one or more key instructional decisions are delegated to the learner.'" Simply put, trainees have greater control over their training, such as pace, materials covered, and sequence.[104] Figure 8-8 presents the guidelines for more effective e-learning.

Equipment Simulations

Some training may involve machines or equipment designed to reproduce physiological and psychological conditions of the real world that are necessary in order for learning and transfer to occur. For example, driving simulators or flight simulators often are used to train employees in driving or flying skills. Another example of a simulation is the FireArms Training System (FATS), which is used by more than 300 law enforcement agencies in the United States.[105] In this simulation, officers are confronted with a number of everyday work situations (e.g., fleeing felons) on a video screen. The military uses virtual reality simulators for training of war game demonstrations. One exercise, called the Synthetic Theater of War, links tactics, techniques, and processes of modern systems to illustrate battles.[106] Equipment simulators also are relied on to a great deal in training for space missions (e.g., astronaut training). While many of these simulations are extremely costly, some have become more affordable. In addition, using simulators for training is only

FIGURE 8-8   Guidelines for Learner Controlled Training in E-Learning

PREPARING TRAINEES FOR LEARNER-LED INSTRUCTION

Guideline #1: Understanding Learner Control Is Half the Battle

- Instruct employees about areas they can control and how this increased control can increase learning.

- The perception of control can increase learning.

Guideline #2: Give It Time

- Typical learner-controlled training tasks last from 30 to 60 minutes.

- "Provide trainees with enough time to learn how to use learner control and with suggested completion times for each section of the training task."

- Ten or more separate training sessions are recommended as users become more familiar with the system as time progresses.

Guideline #3: Calibrate Expectations

Ensure trainees understand the training will be challenging. Adult users often perceive learning as an easy process and when confronted with the challenge of training they may become frustrated.

DESIGNING LEARNER-CONTROLLED TRAINING

Guideline #4: Offer Help

- Offer self-tests and feedback so trainees can self-regulate the number of examples to view and the amount of practice items to complete.

Guideline #5: What's Good for One Trainee May Not Be Good for Another

- "Trainees who are high in ability, prior experience, and motivation may benefit the most from learner control."

- "Create programs that provide trainees high in learning ability [also known as 'g'] and prior experience with more learner control options than trainees low in ability and prior experience."

- Motivation: "When trainees are made aware of the organizational objectives of the training they are often more motivated to successfully complete the training program."

Guideline #6: More Isn't Necessarily Better

- Match learner control to the amount of control needed for effective instruction and training objectives.

- Structure training tasks based on trainees' learning preferences.

Guideline #7: "Skipping" Is Better than "Adding"

For optional/additional training material, use the word "skip" additional instruction rather than "add" additional material.

Guideline #8: Keep It Real

Increase meaningfulness of training by using familiar contexts and examples.

Guideline #9: Footprints Help ("You Are Here")

Provide trainees with a 'map' to track their training progress.

Guideline #10: Keep Each Instructional Segment Self-Contained

- Each section should be short and concise.

- Trainees should not have to revisit a previous section to complete the current section.

Guideline #11: Share Design Control

- Obtain user preferences from trainees prior to training; i.e., does the user prefer having multiple windows open during the training session?

- "Allow the trainees to stop, pause, or restart the program where they wish."

Guideline #12: Be Consistent

- "Keep the font size and color as well as the background color consistent from one instructional segment to another."

Guideline #13: Create Smooth Transitions

Have clear relationships between training segments.

CREATING WORKPLACE CONDITIONS THAT FACILITATE SUCCESSFUL LEARNER-LED INSTRUCTION

Guideline #14: Promote It

Supervisors can improve learner-controlled effectiveness by setting difficult but attainable goals regarding the level of skill mastery and encouraging the trainees to use their new obtained skills on the job.

Guideline #15: Make It Matter

Ensure that trainees judge the incentive to participate in training is attainable but also valuable.

Guideline #16: Organizational Climate Matters

Organizations with climates that encourage employee participation, empowerment, and autonomy may find it easier to implement learner-controlled training programs.

Source: Adapted from Renée E. DeRouin, Barbara A. Fritzsche, and Eduardo Salas, (2004). "Optimizing E-Learning: Research-Based Guidelines for Learner-Controlled Training," *Human Resource Management* 43, pp. 147–162. Reprinted by permission of John Wiley & Sons.

a fraction of the cost of using the real equipment to train employees.

Games, Simulations, and Outdoor Experiential Programs

Some training programs rely on the use of a variety of games, nonequipment simulations, or outdoor experiential programs. In fact, these instructional techniques appear to be gaining in popularity with hundreds of different types of games available for teaching technical, managerial, professional, or other business-related skills. In 2004, 21 percent of organizations often used games or simulations, and 10 percent used computer-based games or simulations.[107] Some of the more common games include in-baskets and business games. Most games are used to teach skills such as decision making as well as analytical, strategic, or interpersonal skills. Business games typically require trainees to assume various roles in a company (e.g., president, marketing vice president) where they are given several years' worth of information on the company's products, technology, and human resources and asked to deal with the information in a compressed period of time (several weeks or months). They make decisions regarding production volumes, inventory levels, and prices in an environment in which other trainees are running competitor companies. The most successful business games keep the focus on specific corporate objectives or problems such as profits, customer service, or labor costs. One very popular cross-functional simulation is *The Marketplace Business Simulation.* Working in teams, trainees must assume various roles in the start-up of a firm in the microcomputer industry. The teams work over a compressed period of time to play 2 to 3 years in the game. Performance is measured on a number of short- and long-term metrics (e.g., financial, marketing, human resource). Numerous levels and variations of the game are available depending on the expertise and backgrounds of the trainees. The simulation has been used all over the world as a capstone, integrative experience to an MBA or undergraduate program as well as by organizations (e.g., Nextel, Hughes Network Systems).[108]

In-baskets are used to train managerial candidates in decision-making skills by requiring them to act on a variety of memos, reports, and other correspondence that are typically found in a manager's in-basket. As we discussed in Chapter 5, participants must prioritize items and respond to them in a limited time period. In-baskets are often included in assessment centers. For example, the method is used as one component of the week-long executive development program at the Center for Creative Leadership.

Outdoor experiential programs have gained in popularity as training methods for teams. In 2004, 20 percent of firms often or always used experiential programs and estimates of over $100 million are spent annually on them.[109] Firms such as *Outward Bound* and *Higher Pursuits* have developed a variety of outdoor activities and challenge courses (e.g., rope courses, canoeing trips, hiking trips) that can be used to help employers build stronger teams. By placing a work unit in a challenge course or physical activity, the coaches or counselors can observe how the team works together and can debrief them and provide feedback on issues of communication, conflict, and trust.

Case Analyses

Most business students are very familiar with case analysis, a training method often used in management training to improve analytical skills. In 2004, 43 percent of firms with over 100 employees often or always used case studies for employee and management training.[110] Trainees are asked to read a case report that describes the organizational, social, and technical aspects of some organizational problem (e.g., poor leadership, intergroup conflict). Each trainee prepares a report in which he or she describes the problems and offers solutions (including potential risks and benefits). Working in a group, trainees may then be asked to justify the problems they have identified and their recommendations. The trainer's role is to facilitate the group's learning and to help the trainees see the underlying management concepts in the case. One variation to the traditional case method is called a living case. This has trainees analyze a problem that their organization is currently facing.[111]

Role-Playing

In a role-playing exercise, trainees act out roles and attempt to perform the behaviors required in those roles. Role-plays are commonly used in training, and in 2004, 34 percent of the firms reported often or always using them for training.[112] This method is often used to teach skills such as oral communication, interpersonal styles, leadership styles, performance feedback reviews, and interviewing techniques. In the popular MBA course, "Executive Power and Negotiations," at the University of Maryland's Robert H. Smith School of Business, students participate in role-plays every class period to enhance their negotiating skills across a variety of situations (e.g., receiving jobs, raises and promotions, international deals, ethical dilemmas). Similarly, in the EMBA course on Leadership and Human Capital, executives are videotaped while role-playing and given feedback on their skills. At the *Chicago Tribune,* trainees are assigned the role of a supervisor giving performance appraisal feedback to a subordinate, while other trainees play the role of the subordinate. Xerox uses role-plays in some of its training programs to teach managers how to develop a culturally diverse workforce. Role-plays are very common components of sexual harassment training programs.

Behavior Modeling

Behavior modeling is quickly growing as a technique for training with managers on interpersonal and supervisory skills. Many large companies such as Exxon, Westinghouse, and Union Carbide use this approach. Based on Bandura's theory of social learning,[113] the method consists of four consecutive components: (1) *attention* (watching someone perform a behavior usually through videotapes), (2) *retention* (processes to help the trainee retain what was observed), (3) *motor reproduction* or behavioral rehearsal (using role-plays to practice new behaviors), and (4) *motivation* or feedback/reinforcement (receiving feedback on the behaviors performed). The success of this approach to training is based on the notion that many of us learn by observing others. For example, suppose you have just taken a job as a sales representative. You may spend some time watching the techniques used by other reps to get ideas for how to perform the job. If you practice the behaviors you have observed and get feedback from the "models" or others, your learning should be enhanced. Generally, trainees should observe predominately positive examples of the behaviors if the goal is to get them to reproduce the behaviors. At the U.S. Naval Construction Battalian at Gulfport, Mississippi, the use of behavior modeling resulted in superior retention of knowledge, transfer of learning, and end-user satisfaction.[114]

Behavioral modeling is an excellent approach for training trainers and educators where a "master" teacher can serve as the model for the future trainer or teacher or someone who is having difficulties in the classroom. For example, many graduate programs assign a new grad student to a "star" professor who is teaching a course that the grad student will teach in the near future.

EVALUATION

Evaluation involves the collection of information on whether trainees were satisfied with the program, learned the material, and were able to apply the skills back on the job. It may be important to determine whether trainees are capable of exhibiting the appropriate level of a skill (e.g., do new supervisors know all of the organization's policies and procedures?). It may be important to know whether or not trainees have changed their behavior and if the change was due to training (e.g., do supervisors complete the necessary paperwork for disciplining an employee more so after the training than before it was conducted). Further, it may be critical to know that if the organization places a new group of supervisors in the same training program that they will also improve their learning or behaviors. Evaluation efforts can be designed to answer these various questions or issues.[115]

Evaluation ensures that programs are accountable and are meeting the particular needs of employees in a cost-effective manner. This is especially important today, as organizations attempt to cut costs and improve quality. Without evaluation, it is very difficult to show that training was the reason for any improvements. As a result, management may reduce training budgets or staffs in times of financial hardship. While most companies recognize the importance of evaluation, few actually evaluate their training programs.[116] Many successful firms that emphasize training do so almost as a *matter of faith* and because of their belief in the connection between people and profits.[117] A review of Fortune 500 companies found that only a small number conduct sound evaluations of their programs.[118] One study of more than 40 organizations identified IBM, Motorola University, Florida Power & Light's Nuclear Division, and the AT&T School of Business as the companies with the best training evaluation practices.[119] Despite these accolades, companies still have difficulties fully measuring the effects of their training investments. Some firms, such as GE, believe that new ways must be used to evaluate training programs. They use surveys to realign training as needed and examine returns in the form of tangible and intangible business results, increased consumer satisfaction, and career development for GE workers.[120]

Types of Criteria

In a recent survey of learning executives (e.g., HR executive, CEO, Chief Learning Officers) 67 percent stated that their most pressing issue was establishing a link between learning and organizational performance. A secondary concern reported by 49 percent was establishing ROI or value for learning.[121] Thus, trainers should try to collect five types of data when evaluating training programs: measures of reactions, learning, behavior change, organizational results, and return on investment (ROI) utility. The first four of these criteria are widely used to evaluate corporate training programs, and the last, ROI,[122] has recently been added as another important source of evaluation data.[123]

- *Reactions*—trainees' attitudes toward the training program, instructor, facilities, and so forth.
- *Learning*—changes in knowledge by trainees or level of knowledge reached after training.
- *Behavior*—changes in job performance or level of job performance reached after training.
- *Results*—changes in organizational measures (e.g., productivity, turnover, absences) due to training.
- *ROI*—monetary value of the results (benefits of training minus costs of training; expressed as a percentage).

Although most organizations rely on reactive measures as the sole basis for evaluating their training, scores on reactive measures say very little about the more important criteria. As one recent review put it, "There is very little reason to believe that how trainees feel about or whether they like a training program tells researchers much, if anything, about (a) how much they learned from the program (*learning criteria*), (b) changes in their job-related behaviors or performance (*behavioral criteria*), or (c) the utility of the program to the organization (*results criteria*). This is supported by the lack of relationship between reaction criteria and the other three criteria." Yet, reaction measures are the most widely used evaluation criteria in applied settings. For instance, in the American Society of Training and Development 2003 *State-of-the Industry Report*, 75 percent of the organizations surveyed reported using reaction measures, compared with 41, 21 and 11 percent for learning, behavioral, and results, respectively.[124] There is however, some good news. In a comprehensive meta-analysis of 162 training evaluation studies, it was found that the average or mean effect sizes for training interventions (across all topics and methods used) were fairly large. This reveals that reactions, learning, behavior, and results criteria should lead to meaningful positive changes in the organizations.[125]

Reactions

Reaction measures are designed to assess trainees' opinions regarding the training program. Using a questionnaire, trainees are asked at the end of training to indicate the degree they were satisfied with the trainer, subject matter and content, the materials (books, pamphlets, handouts), and the environment (room, breaks, meals, temperature). It is important to assess trainees' satisfaction with multiple aspects of a training program and not just their overall satisfaction.[126] Also, they may be asked to indicate the aspects of the program they considered to be most valuable and least useful to them. You have probably been asked to complete a reaction form or course evaluation instrument for some of your classes.

Favorable reactions to a program do not guarantee that learning has occurred or that appropriate behaviors have been adopted. In fact, there is little correlation between reactions and *other criteria*. However, it is important to collect reaction data for several reasons: (1) to find out how satisfied trainees were with the program, (2) to make any needed revisions in the program, and (3) and to ensure that other trainees will be receptive to attending the program. Trainees should be given ample time at the end of the session to complete the reaction form. Also, trainers should assess trainees' reactions several months after the program to determine how relevant trainees felt the training was to their jobs. An example of a reaction form is presented in Figure 8-9.

Learning

Learning measures assess the degree to which trainees have mastered the concepts, knowledge, and skills of the training. Typically, learning is measured by paper-and-pencil tests (e.g., essay-type questions, multiple choice), performance tests, and simulation exercises. These measures should be designed to sample the content of the training program. Trainees should be tested on their level

of understanding before and after training to determine the effect of training on their knowledge. Figure 8-10 presents two examples of performance tests used to assess learning. Figure 8-11 presents a more commonly used type of learning measure. Regarding learning criteria, trainee learning appears to be a necessary but insufficient prerequisite for changes in behavior, improvements in actual on-the-job performance, and "bottom-line" results.

Behaviors/Performance

Behavioral criteria are measures of actual on-the-job performance and can be used to identify the effects of training on actual work performance. Issues pertaining to the transfer of training are also relevant here. Behavioral criteria are typically operationalized by using supervisor ratings or objective indicators of performance. Although learning and behavioral criteria are conceptually linked, researchers have had limited success in empirically demonstrating this relationship. This is because behavioral criteria are susceptible to environmental variables that can influence the transfer or use of trained skills or capabilities on the job. For example, the posttraining environment may not provide opportunities for the learned material or skills to be applied or performed.

Behaviors of trainees before and after training should be compared to assess the degree to which training has changed their performance. This is important because one of the goals of training is to modify the on-the-job behavior or performance of trainees. Behaviors can be measured by relying on the performance evaluation system to collect ratings of trainees both before and after training. For example, trainees of the Federal Aviation Administration must submit subordinate evaluations of their supervisory behavior prior to attending the national training center in Florida. Subordinates also submit evaluations of the same supervisors' behavior six months after the training. To determine whether or not the supervisors' skills have improved due to training, the performance evaluations they received from their subordinates before and after completion of training are compared. A variety of performance appraisal measures can be used to assess behavioral changes of trainees. These were described in detail in Chapter 7. Figure 8-12 presents a sample behavioral measure.

Organizational Results

The purpose of collecting organizational results is to examine the impact of training on the work group or entire company. Data may be collected before and after training on criteria such as productivity, turnover, absenteeism, formal complaints/lawsuits, accidents, grievances, quality improvements, scrap, sales, and customer satisfaction. The trainer will try to show that the training program was responsible for any changes noted in these criteria. This may be difficult to do without a careful design and data

FIGURE 8-9 An Example of a Trainee Reaction Questionnaire

Evaluation Questionnaire

(Please return this form *unsigned* to the Training and Development Group)

1. Considering everything, how would you rate this program? (Check one)

Unsatisfactory _____ Satisfactory _____ Good _____ Outstanding _____

Please explain briefly the reasons for this rating you have given:

2. Were your expectations: exceeded _____ matched _____ fallen below _____? (Check one)

3. Are you going to recommend this training program to other members of your department?

Yes _____ No _____ If you checked "yes," please describe the job titles held by the people to whom you would recommend this program.

4. Please rate the relative value (1 = very valuable; 2 = worthwhile; 3 = negligible) of the following components of the training program to you:

Videocassettes _____   Role-playing exercises _____
Workbooks _____   Small group exercises _____
Small group discussions _____ Lectures _____
Cases _____   Readings, articles _____

5. Please rate the main lecturer's presentation (1 = not effective; 2 = somewhat effective; 3 = very effective) in terms of:

Ability to communicate _____
Emphasis on key points _____
Visual aids _____
Handout materials _____

6. Please rate the following cases, readings, and videocassettes by placing a checkmark in the appropriate column:

	Excell.	Good	Fair	Poor
Overcoming Resistance to Change				
Reviewing Performance Goals				
Setting Performance Goals				
Handling Employee Complaints				
Improving Employee Performance				
Slade Co.				
Superior Slate Quarry				
McGregor's Theory X and Y				
Henry Manufacturing				
First Federal Savings				
Claremont Industries				

7. Was the ratio of lectures to cases (check one): High _____ OK _____ Low _____?

8. Were the videocassettes pertinent to your work? (check one)

To most of my work? _____
To some of my work? _____
To none of my work? _____

9. To help the training director and the staff provide further improvements in future programs, please give us your frank opinion of each case discussion leader's contribution to your learning. (Place your checkmarks in the appropriate boxes.)

	Excellent	Above Average	Average	Below Average	Poor
DAVIS					
GLEASON					
LAIRD					
MARTIN					
PONTELLO					
SHALL					
SOMMERS					
WILSON					
ZIMMER					

10. How would you evaluate your participation in the program? (check)

Overall workload: Too heavy _____ Just right _____ Too light _____
Case preparation: Too heavy _____ Just right _____ Too light _____
Homework assignments: Too heavy _____ Just right _____ Too light _____

11. What suggestions do you have for improving the program?

_____

_____

Source: WEXLEY, KENNETH N.; LATHAM, GARY P.; DEVELOPING AND TRAINING HUMAN RESOURCES IN ORGANIZATIONS, 2nd Edition, © 1991. Reprinted by permission of Pearson Education, Inc. Upper Saddle River, NJ.

FIGURE 8-10 | Examples of Learning Performance Tests

MECHANICS

"You have in front of you a gear reducer, a line shaft, bearings, and coupling. I want you to assemble and adjust the proper alignment so that the finished assembly is right-hand (or left-hand) driven assembly. Set the coupling gap 1/8 inch apart. You do not have to put the grid member in place or fasten the coupling covers. After you are finished, I will ask you where and how the grid member should go in. You will have 45 minutes to complete this job."

PAINTERS

"I want you to boost yourself up about 10 feet off the floor using this boatsman chair, and then tie yourself off so that you don't fall. After that, I would like you to hook this spraygun to the air supply, set the regulator to the correct pressure, and then spray this wall."

Source: WEXLEY, KENNETH N.; LATHAM, GARY P.; DEVELOPING AND TRAINING HUMAN RESOURCES IN ORGANIZATIONS, 2nd Edition, © 1991. Reprinted by permission of Pearson Education, Inc. Upper Saddle River, NJ.

FIGURE 8-11 | Learning Measure

SAMPLE ITEMS FROM A MGIC TEST TO EVALUATE SUPERVISOR KNOWLEDGE

1. T or F   When preparing a truth-in-lending disclosure with a financed single premium, mortgage insurance should always be disclosed for the life of the loan.

2. T or F   GE and MGIC have the same refund policy for refundable single premiums.

3. T or F   MGIC, GE, and PMI are the only mortgage insurers offering a nonrefundable single premium.

4. _____   Which one of the following is not a category in the loan progress reports?
   a. Loans approved
   b. Loans-in-suspense
   c. Loans denied
   d. Loans received

5. _____   Which of the following do not affect the MGIC Plus buying decision?
   a. Consumer
   b. Realtor
   c. MGIC underwriter
   d. Secondary market manager
   e. Servicing manager

6. _____   The new risk-based capital regulations for savings and loans have caused many of them to:
   a. Convert whole loans into securities
   b. Begin originating home equity loans
   c. Put MI on their uninsured 90s

Source: Reprinted with permission of the publisher. From *Evaluating Training Programs: The Four Levels.* Copyright © 1996 by Kirkpatrick, Barrett-Koehler, Inc. San Francisco, CA. All rights reserved. www.bkconnection.com

FIGURE 8-12 | Sample Survey Behavioral Measure

Instructions: The purpose of this questionnaire is to determine the extent to which those who attended the recent leadership program have applied the principles and techniques that they learned back on the job. The survey results will help us to assess the effectiveness of the program. Please circle the appropriate response for each question.

5 = Much more   4 = Some more   3 = The same
2 = Some less   1 = Much less

	Time and Energy Spent after the Program Compared to Time and Energy Spent before the Program				
Understanding and Motivating					
1. Getting to know my employees	5	4	3	2	1
2. Listening to my subordinates	5	4	3	2	1
3. Praising good work	5	4	3	2	1
4. Talking with employees about their families and interests	5	4	3	2	1
5. Asking subordinates for their ideas	5	4	3	2	1
6. Managing by walking around	5	4	3	2	1
Orienting and Training					
7. Asking new employees about their past experiences, etc	5	4	3	2	1
8. Taking new employees on a tour of the department and facilities	5	4	3	2	1
9. Introducing new employees to their coworkers	5	4	3	2	1
10. Being patient with employees	5	4	3	2	1

Source: Reprinted with permission of the publisher. From *Evaluating Training Programs: The Four Levels.* Copyright © 1996 by Kirkpatrick, Barrett-Koehler, Inc. San Francisco, CA. All rights reserved. www.bkconnection.com

collection strategy, since many other factors could explain the changes detected. For example, changes in dollar sales could be due to a new pay system rather than to a sales training program. An evaluation using a results measure (pharmacy sales) was conducted for a training program designed for pharmacy technicians at 2,000 Walgreen stores. Sales for pharmacies where technicians had received 20 hours of classroom training and 20 hours of OJT were $9,500 greater annually than those for pharmacies where technicians received only OJT.

Results criteria (e.g., productivity, sales, company profits) are the most distal and macro criteria used to evaluate the effectiveness of training. Results criteria are frequently operationalized by using utility analysis estimates. As discussed in Chapter 6, utility analysis provides a methodology to assess the dollar value gained by engaging in specified personnel interventions including training.

The Effectiveness of Organizational Training

As noted earlier, a recent meta-analysis determined the effectiveness of organizational training.[127] While the effects differed as a function of the type of criteria used to evaluate the training, the overall effect of the training was comparable to (or larger) than those reported for other organizational interventions, such as the effects for performance appraisal and feedback, management by objectives, and goal setting on productivity.

Testing for the effect of skill or task characteristics was intended to shed light on the "trainability" of particular skills and tasks. For both learning and behavioral criteria, the largest effects were obtained for training that included both cognitive and interpersonal skills, followed by psychomotor skills. Where results criteria were used in the study, the largest effect was obtained for interpersonal skills and the smallest for psychomotor skills. A medium effect was obtained for cognitive skills or tasks.

The study also examined the effectiveness of training delivery methods as a function of the skill or task being trained. The magnitude of the effect sizes was generally favorable and ranged from medium to large regardless of delivery methods or skill type. As an example of this, even the findings for the much-maligned lecture method were positive. Findings were generally favorable for lectures across all skill or task types and evaluation criteria. The results suggest that organizational training is generally effective. Furthermore, the authors also suggest that the effectiveness of training appears to vary as a function of the specified training delivery method, the skill or task being trained, and the criterion used to operationalize effectiveness.[128]

Comparisons of the effect sizes for learning criteria versus behavioral and results criteria showed a substantial decrease in effect sizes from learning to the other criteria. The authors concluded that the effect may have been due to the fact that the manifestation of training learning outcomes in job behaviors and organizational results may be a consequence of the favorability of the posttraining environment for the performance of the learned skills. "Environmental favorability" is defined as the extent to which the transfer or work environment is supportive of the application of new skills and behaviors learned or acquired in training. Thus, learned skills will not be demonstrated as behaviors or performance if workers are denied the opportunity to perform them; the social context and favorability of the posttraining environment play a critical role in determining whether the trained skills are transferred to the job.

Assessing the Costs and Benefits of Training

A variety of methods can be used to assess the value of training. We have mentioned calculations of *ROI* and *utility analysis.* No matter which approach is used, costs and benefits associated with training must be estimated. Some **costs** that should be measured for a training program include (1) one-time costs such as needs assessment costs, salaries and benefits of training designers, purchase of equipment and media (computers, videos, handouts, distance learning techniques), program development costs, evaluation costs for the first offering of the program; (2) costs associated with each training session such as trainers' costs (e.g., salaries and benefits, travel, lodging, meals) and facilities rental; and (3) costs associated with trainees including trainee wages during training, travel, lodging, and meals for trainees during training, and nonreusable training materials.

It is important to compare the **benefits** of the training program with its costs. One benefit that should be estimated is the dollar payback associated with the improvement in trainees' performance after receiving training. This is often difficult to approximate. Since the results of the experimental design will indicate any differences in behavior between those trained versus those untrained, the trainer can then estimate for that particular group of employees (e.g., managers, engineers) what this difference is worth in terms of the salaries of those employees. Often, the amount gained per trainee per year is multiplied by the number of persons trained. Another factor that should be considered when estimating the benefits of training is the duration of the training's impact; that is, the length of time during which the improved performance will be maintained. While probably no programs will show benefits forever, those that do incur longer-term improved performance will have greater value to the organization.

Return on Investment (ROI)

Given the increasing amount of money that firms budget on training, it is imperative that companies be able to estimate the return on investment (ROI) that training provides them. To do this, firms should assess the costs and benefits associated with their programs. In one study of several training programs at a pharmaceutical firm it was found that the managerial training programs had an average ROI of 45 percent, while the sales and technical training programs had an average ROI of 156 percent.[129] At Ford, all training programs are evaluated against the criterion of product line profitability. A tracking system shows costs and revenue for training facilities and individual courses.[130] The basic ROI formula is as follows:

$$\text{ROI } (\%) = \frac{\text{Net program benefits}}{\text{Program costs}} \times 100$$

For example, at an 18-week literacy program for entry-level electrical and mechanical assemblers at Magnavox Electronics Systems Company, the results were impressive. The benefits (productivity and quality) were $321,600 while the costs were only $38,233. Thus, the ROI is calculated as

741 percent. This means that for each dollar invested, Magnavox received $7.41 over the cost of the program.[131]

$$ROI = \frac{\$321,600 - \$38,233}{\$38,233} \times 100 = 741\%$$

When making ROI calculations, it is important to use reliable and credible sources and to be conservative when estimating benefits and costs for training. It is also important to involve management when deciding on what is an acceptable ROI as a target goal for the training.[132] For example, British Airways has utilized training to become one of the most profitable airlines in the world. Before training begins, a tangible value for the training investment is set, reflecting how much improvement in customer satisfaction is to be expected if training is successful.[133]

Utility Analysis

Another approach that can be used when calculating the value of training is a utility model. See Chapter 6 for a review of utility. This is difficult but may be important for showing top management the value of training for the organization. Utility is a function of the duration of a training program's effect on employees, the number of employees trained, the validity of the training program, the value of the job for which training was provided, and the total cost of the program. Utility analysis measures the economic contribution of a program according to how effective it was in identifying and modifying behavior.[134] Because the calculations involved in a utility analysis are based on subjective estimations, this model has not yet gained widespread acceptance by trainers as a practical tool for evaluating return on training investments.[135]

Designs for Evaluating Training

After determining the criteria to use in evaluating the training program, the trainer should choose an experimental design. The design is used to answer two primary questions: (1) whether or not a change has occurred in the criteria (e.g., learning, behavior, organizational results) and (2) whether or not the change can be attributed to the training program. Designs employ two possible strategies to answer these questions. The first is to compare the trainee's performance before and after participation in training. This is done to see what changes may have occurred in learning, behavior, or organizational results. While this is important for answering the question of whether change has taken place, it is deficient in answering the question of whether the change can be attributed to the training program since the criteria may have changed for a number of reasons. Answering the second question requires a design comparing the changes that occurred in the trainees with change that occurred in another group of employees who did not receive the training (e.g., a control group), yet are similar to the training group in important ways (e.g., similar job titles, rank, geographical location). The most effective experimental designs use both strategies (i.e., before–after measures and a control group) and are better able to answer both questions. Some of the more commonly used designs for training evaluation are described below.[136]

One-Shot Posttest-Only Design

In many organizations, training is designed and conducted without prior thought given to evaluation. For example, a plant manager may decide to put all the employees in a safety training course. After the course is completed the manager decides to evaluate it. At this point, the design would look like the one below:

TRAINING ⟶ MEASURE

Any of the four types of criteria (e.g., reactions, learning, behavior, organizational results) could be used as the "after" measures. It would be difficult, however, to know what, if any, changes occurred since no "before" measure (e.g., pretest) was made. In addition, because the results may not be compared with those of another group who did not receive training, it would not be possible to say whether any change was due to the training. If, however, the primary goal was to make sure that the trainees reached a certain mastery level, then the design might still be appropriate (e.g., the trainees reached a 95 percent safety goal).

One-Group Pretest–Posttest Design

Another design for evaluating the training group on the criteria is to measure the group before and after the training. This design is as follows:

MEASURE ⟶ TRAINING ⟶ MEASURE

This design can assess whether a change has occurred for the training group in the criteria (e.g., learning, behavior) that is useful. Unfortunately, it is not able to tell for sure whether or not the change is due to training, since there is no control group. A change that is detected could have been caused by the introduction of new equipment, a new manager, revised pay systems, or a number of other reasons. If the trainer is going to use this design, it is important to document other events that have occurred during the measurement period to determine the most likely explanations for any detected changes.

Posttest-Only Control Group Design

A much stronger design for assessing the effectiveness of a training program is shown here:

GROUP 1: R: TRAINING ⟶ MEASURE

GROUP 2: R: NO TRAINING ⟶ MEASURE

In this design, two groups are used and individuals are **randomly assigned** (R) to either group (i.e., an individual has an equal chance of being put in either group 1, the training group, or group 2, the control group). The use of random assignment helps to initially equalize the two groups. This is important to ensure that any differences between the two groups after training are not simply caused by differences in ability, motivation, or experience. The posttest-only control group design is useful when it is difficult to collect criteria measures on individuals prior to offering them the training. For example, the trainer may believe that giving individuals a pretest, such as a learning test, may overly influence their scores on the posttest, which might be the same learning measure. Another trainer may not have time to give pre-measures. Individuals are randomly assigned to the two groups, and their scores on the posttest are compared. Any differences on the posttest can be attributed to the training program since we can assume the two groups were somewhat equal before training. It would be beneficial to make sure the employees from the control group are placed in a training program later so that they have similar opportunities.

Pretest–Posttest Control Group Design

Another powerful design that is recommended for use in training evaluation is as follows:

> **GROUP 1: R: MEASURE ————→**
> **TRAINING ————→ MEASURE**
>
> **GROUP 2: R: MEASURE ————→**
> **NO TRAINING ————→ MEASURE**

Individuals1 are randomly assigned to the two groups. Criteria measures are collected on both groups before and after the training program is offered, yet only one group actually receives the training (group 2 is the control group). Comparisons are made of the changes detected in both groups. If the change in group one is significantly different than the change in group two, we can be somewhat certain that it was caused by the training. The two features that make this a stronger design are the *randomization* of people into the groups, and the use of a *control group*. These aspects enable us to determine (1) if a change occurred and (2) whether the change was due to training. Since many organizations will want all of the employees in both groups to receive the training, the training can be offered to group 2 at a later time.

Multiple Time-Series Design

Another design recommended for use in training evaluation is shown below:

> **GROUP 1: R:**
> **MEASURE → MEASURE → MEASURE →**
> **TRAINING → MEASURE → MEASURE →**
> **MEASURE**
>
> **GROUP 2: R:**
> **MEASURE → MEASURE → MEASURE →**
> **NO TRAINING → MEASURE → MEASURE →**
> **MEASURE**

In this design, individuals are randomly assigned to either of two groups, and the criteria measures (learning, behavior,

results) are collected at several times before and after the training has been offered. This design allows us to observe any changes between the two groups over time or any trends in performance. If the effects of training held up over several months, this design would offer stronger support for the program. Of course, this design might be more costly or difficult to implement since it requires taking measurements of individuals multiple times.

Benchmarking Training Efforts

To conduct a thorough evaluation of a training program, training departments can benchmark their practices against the best in the industry. They can compare their training department to leading-edge companies in terms of (1) training activities (e.g., percent of payroll spent on training, average training hours per employee, training dollars spent per employee, percent of employees trained per year, training staff per 1,000 employees), (2) training results (e.g., average percent of positive trainee ratings per year, average percent of satisfied trainees, average percent gain in learning per course, average percent of improvement in job performance, cost savings as a ratio of training expenses, revenues per employee per year, profits per employee per year), and (3) training efficiency (e.g., training costs per student hour, time on task).[137] The American Society for Training and Development (ASTD), provides conferences and sessions each year where HR and training professionals can learn strategies from the ASTD BEST award winners. Some of the 2005 recipients included Booz Allen Hamilton, Caterpillar, Lockheed Martin Corp., HP, IBM, Intel Corp., QUALCOMM, and Schwan Food Company. See www.astd.org for more information.

PLANNING FOR TRAINING EFFECTIVENESS IN ORGANIZATIONS

One recent review on training concludes that "We must do a better job of linking training outcomes to organizational and business outcomes, and do so while involving organizational decision makers."[138] Four guidelines are offered for training professionals on planning "collaborative" interventions that are more likely to affect business objectives. Figure 8-13 presents these guidelines.

SPECIAL TRAINING PROGRAMS

Employee Orientation Programs

In 2005, most firms provide some types of employee orientation where new employees are informed about their roles and responsibilities (i.e., what is expected of them) in an effort to ease their transition to the firm. The trend seems to be continuing as more firms have been placing their new employees in orientation programs to familiarize them with their supervisors and co-workers, the company policies and procedures, the requirements of their

---

FIGURE 8-13   **Collaborative Planning for Training**

Guideline: Develop a theory of impact

Goal:	Link evaluation and measurement to unique capabilities and/or strategic initiatives of the organization.
Strategies:	• Identify business results that matter to the organization.
	• Link training outcomes to measures of organizational effectiveness.
	• Link measures of organizational effectiveness to job-level knowledge and skills.
Tools:	• Scan internal and external environment to determine organization-level strategic initiatives.
	• Develop logic models or causal models linking training to organizational impact.
	• Involve decision makers in long-term planning for training.

Guideline: Reframe the point of evaluation from proof to evidence

Goal:	Establish reasonable expectations from decision makers about the type of evidence that will demonstrate training success.
Strategies:	• Distinguish between proof and evidence in the minds of decision makers.
	• Identify required levels of evidence to show training success
	• Frame expectations for evaluation outcomes in the minds of decision makers.
Tools:	• Clarify the purpose for evaluation or intended use of information.
	• Clarify costs of evaluation as a function of evaluation rigor.
	• Involve decision makers in planning for training evaluation.

Guideline: Isolate the effects of training

Goal:	Eliminate or reduce counterarguments to claims that training is effective.
Strategies:	• Demonstrate linkage between training and organizational effectiveness.
	• Choose appropriate research designs.
Tools:	• Use control groups and pretests whenever possible.
	• Use trend lines or staggered start dates for training when more sophisticated research designs are unavailable.
	• Use the internal referencing strategy when other research designs are unavailable.

Guideline: Establish accountability for training

Goal:	Improve the impact of training on individual and organizational effectiveness by involving all organizational members in the planning of training.
Strategies:	• Increase motivation to train in trainees.
	• Increase support by peers and supervisors on the job.
	• Increase organizational support for training.
Tools:	• Use evidence of past training success to enhance motivation of future trainees.
	• Clarify the relationship between training and organizational effectiveness, and train supervisors in post-training support behaviors.
	• Involve decision makers in planning for training.

Source: Kraiger K., Casper W. J. (2004). Collaborative training for training impact. *Human Resource Management*, 43, p. 343. Reprinted with permission from John Wiley & Sons.

---

jobs, and the organizational culture. The intent is to increase an employee's job satisfaction and to reduce turnover. Unfortunately, most of these programs are not properly planned, implemented, or evaluated. All too often new employees are given a brief introduction to the company and are then left to learn the ropes by themselves. Often this leads to feelings of confusion, frustration, stress, and uncertainty among new employees.[139] In fact, job satisfaction is often related to an employee's orientation.[140] If employee dissatisfaction leads to turnover, this can be quite costly for the firm. For example, at Merck & Company, turnover cost has been estimated to range from 1.5 to 2.5 times the annual salary paid for a job.[141]

Generally, the objectives of an employee orientation program are threefold: (1) to assist the new employee in adjusting to the organization and feeling comfortable and positive about the new job; (2) to clarify the job requirements, demands, and performance expectations; and (3) to get the employee to understand the organization's culture and quickly adopt the organization's goals, values, and behaviors.[142] A Realistic Orientation Program for New Employee Stress (ROPES) has been suggested as the model.[143] Employees would be given realistic information about the job and the organization, general support and reassurance from managers, and help in identifying and coping with the stresses of the job. This should reduce turnover of new employees, resulting in savings for the company.[144] Corning Glass Works developed an orientation program for all of its new employees to help them make the transition to the company, their specific jobs, and the community. They were able to reduce voluntary turnover among new hires by 69 percent after two years.[145]

Most orientation programs consist of three stages: (1) a general introduction to the organization, often given by the HR department; (2) a specific orientation to the department and the job typically given by the employee's immediate supervisor; and (3) a follow-up meeting to verify that the important issues have been addressed and employee questions have been answered.[146] This follow-up meeting usually takes place between a new employee and his or her supervisor a week or so after the employee has begun working. A follow-up meeting is very important because often new employees may feel uncomfortable seeking out a supervisor regarding any questions they face. A supervisor or a human resources representative should meet with the employee to be sure that he or she is effectively "learning the ropes" of the organization. At PricewaterhouseCoopers, new employees participate in an extensive two-week orientation program with employees and managers from offices throughout the world and address topics such as team building, benefits, ethics, computers, and client relations. Following this, new employees are assigned a coach and a resource manager who assist them with their career progress and job assignments.

The orientation program used by the Disney Corporation for employees of Walt Disney World in Orlando, Florida, follows this multiple-stage format in most respects. Individuals begin their employment by attending a one-day program, "Disney Traditions II," which describes the history of the organization and the values of the culture. On this first day, employees are also taken on a tour of the facilities. On the second day, they are provided with descriptions of the policies and procedures. The third day, OJT begins with an assigned buddy who is an experienced coworker. Buddies spend anywhere from two days to two weeks showing new employees their job duties and providing feedback as they attempt to perform the tasks. As a result of participating in the orientation program, employees express less confusion with their new jobs.[147] We will discuss this issue in greater depth in Chapter 12.

The training department should be actively involved in planning, conducting, and evaluating orientation programs. They also should enlist the support of senior employees to serve as mentors to new employees. Also, supervisors should be called on to help orient new employees to the workforce and should receive training on how to do this. In the follow-up meeting, supervisors should be required to complete a checklist, indicating that they have discussed with new employees the major issues of concern. Employees should sign the checklist to confirm that they have received the orientation information.

Evaluation of the orientation program is the responsibility of the human resource department.

Training for Teams

Training techniques can be chosen for individual level training or for training that is conducted for work teams. With the increasing popularity of teams in organizations,[148] it is common for employers to send their teams to training sessions. For example, Hewlett-Packard started its team members on a two-week training and orientation program to familiarize everyone with the existing processes and the needs of the business.[149] Likewise, Allied Signal sent their maintenance teams from the Garrett Engine Division to a two-day course in team building. Cummins Engine Company places improvement teams through a five-day training program that is based on an action learning model (classroom and OJT training).[150] GE sends entire teams to participate in business games, all of which deal with real GE strengths, weaknesses, opportunities, and threats (SWOT analysis).

Team training often focuses on teaching members how to work more effectively or efficiently in teams. Some topics include team building, problem solving, running effective meetings, managing stress, managing productivity, appraising team members' performance, and managing conflict. Trust building is also an important component of the training.[151] Employers offer training in problem solving, meeting skills, communication skills, handling conflict, roles and responsibilities, quality tools and concepts, and evaluating team performance.[152] In general, trainers use a variety of training techniques when conducting team training such as information-based, demonstration-based (videos), and practice-based (role-plays) methods.[153] In some cases, "ropes" or challenge courses are used to build stronger, more cohesive teams.[154] At Patapsco Valley Veterinary Hospital, employees participate in team building training sessions, including outdoor challenge activities, to further enhance communication, trust, and collaboration among the team of veterinarians, vet technicians, and receptionists. They also cross-train their team of technicians and receptionists to provide greater flexibility in staffing for the firm.

Often, teams are formed with individuals from various functional areas (e.g., marketing, finance, sales, production). These **cross-functional teams** may require training in other disciplines to help them understand what is involved in other functional areas (called multi-skilling or cross-training). This has been used in the military,[155] in high-technology firms,[156] and in assembly plants.[157] Generally, job rotation may be used or individuals may receive training from their peers on other disciplines. For example, peer trainers have been used at T. J. Maxx, a national retail chain, and at Xerox.[158] In fact, sometimes unstructured or informal learning from peers is more effective than structured classroom training.[159] Peers are helpful in socializing new employees, reducing stress, and helping newcomers establish satisfying social relationships.[160] The benefits of cross-training are that it may provide employees with more skill variety or interesting tasks, allow for more flexibility in getting the work done when teammates are absent, and help workers to better understand the entire work process.[161] It may be important to clarify expectations of cross-training during an employee's orientation to the firm in order to set a realistic preview of the job.[162]

Information-Technology Training

As employers adopt more sophisticated hardware and software systems, it has become increasingly more important to provide relevant training to use these systems effectively.[163] Training on using computers consumes an increasing part of all formal training provided by U.S. employers, whether the firm has 100–500 employees or over 10,000 employees. For example, Pricewaterhouse-Coopers offers its employees (consultants) a number of technical training and computer-based training courses so that they will continue to be on the cutting edge of business. One problem facing employers today is the shortage of competent people to provide IT training. In fact, many firms are relying on informal peer learning to deliver the necessary IT training.[164] A 2004 survey indicated that 26 percent of firms had a separate technology-based training budget.[165]

Diversity Awareness Training

Managing diversity effectively is one of the greatest challenges for organizations over the next century.[166] Many firms throughout the world face discrimination claims from immigrants, women, older workers, gays, lesbians, various racial and ethnic groups, those with physical disabilities, and those of varying religious affiliations. In addition, different values, attitudes, and behaviors of generations (e.g., baby boomers, Generation Y) or types of workers (blue collar vs. white collar) have implications for the management and training necessary to use with these groups.[167] Some employers have been proactive about hiring more diverse employees to mirror the population. For example, Pitney Bowes CEO Michael Critelli cites diversity as "a business necessity."[168] Other firms, however, have minimized diversity issues, and subsequently have faced discrimination suits (e.g., State Farm Insurance with gender bias; Denny's Restaurant with racial bias).[169] Research on diversity issues has increased.[170] In addition, training for increasing awareness of the diverse workforce has become more prevalent in organizations, and a variety of different programs exist.[171]

Diversity awareness programs have been developed for a variety of reasons, including improving the productivity and competitiveness of the firm, changing attitudes and stereotypes, reducing conflict, improving communication and work relationships, enhancing creativity, and improving the progress and satisfaction of women, minorities, and others into upper management positions.[172] When Texaco settled a race discrimination lawsuit, it agreed to put its 29,000 employees through a two-day workshop on race, gender, and culture. Texaco has tripled the number of workshops it offered each month and hired an additional 27 consultants. The workshops focus on four broad areas: creating a diverse workforce, managing a diverse workforce, creating an environment that values a diverse workforce, and leveraging diversity into a competitive business advantage.[173] Fannie Mae's training and development programs to support the professional development of its employees resulted in an upper management that is now over 50 percent women and minority.[174] At Merck and Mead Corporation, male executives participate in workshops to change their attitudes toward women and to sensitize supervisors to the needs for balancing work and family. AT&T boasts one of the nation's most progressive diversity programs.[175] Chase offers a comprehensive diversity program for all its employees including awareness training and skill building. Similarly, ExxonMobil has a training program called Internal Resource Education that is an intense team-based course conducted in three one-week segments.[176] American Express created a program called Diversity Learning Labs for training.[177] Texas Instruments requires that all employees take the firm's Valuing Individuals class at least once, preferably within their first year of being hired.[178]

To assist in the placement and advancement of employees with disabilities, the EEOC has written material and a video on hiring and developing individuals with disabilities. In recent years, researchers have offered suggestions for assisting employees with disabilities to become more effectively socialized in organizations.[179] Sears became a model by benchmarking the practices of other firms and then adopting them to their own workplace.[180] Some firms (e.g., Xerox, American Express, Disney) have offered diversity training programs to reduce discrimination due to disability.

One factor shown to be highly related to the adoption and perceived success of diversity training programs has been top management support and participation.[181] American Express formed a high-level diversity council to guide and drive the company's diversity efforts. Likewise, at Hewlett-Packard, the diversity initiatives are driven by the Diversity Leadership Council, which is comprised of senior executives. Along with top managers, immediate supervisors and peers must support and reinforce diversity programs. In addition, trainees should be rewarded for positive changes in their behaviors.[182]

Other factors determining whether or not a company adopts a diversity training program include whether the firm is large, has a high strategic priority of diversity relative to other competing objectives, has the presence of a diversity manager, and has in place a large number of other diversity-supportive policies.[183] Other research has shown the perceived success of diversity training programs to be related to mandatory attendance for all managers, long-term evaluation of training results, managerial rewards for increasing diversity, and a broad definition of diversity in the organization.[184] Apple South's president, S. Kirk Kinsell, states that diversity management can only be successful when it is "integrated fully—that is, made a part of all customer, vendor and employee programs."[185]

Sexual Harassment Training

Most large firms now offer training on sexual harassment issues. In California, training on sexual harassment is mandatory for all supervisors. All different types of organizations have been accused of sexual harassment, from manufacturing (e.g., Mitsubishi Motor Manufacturing of America) to pharmaceuticals (e.g., Astra Pharmaceuticals) to the military (Navy Tailhook incident), where suits were filed, and managers were subsequently fired or reassigned.[186] Training on sexual harassment issues has increased dramatically. The Federal Aviation Administration introduced a training program to respond to women's complaints of harassment.[187] Training has increased in organizations in part due to two 1998 Supreme Court cases. As discussed in Chapter 3, these cases left employers even more vulnerable to sexual harassment lawsuits, and the Court clarified what employers could do to protect themselves against liability. In *Faragher v. City of Boca Raton* (1998), the Court sent a message to employers that they must be proactive about sexual harassment by developing a policy and by training employees on it. The city of Boca Raton had a policy on sexual harassment, but did little to communicate it to employees. In *Burlington Industries Inc. v. Ellerth* (1998), the Supreme Court emphasized that employees with sexual harassment claims should communicate them through existing channels in the company before filing suit. Kimberly Ellerth had not done this. This case pointed out the importance of training employees on the sexual harassment policies and procedures that should be followed when making claims.

Most larger firms (over 100 employees) have policies on sexual harassment, but they often do not clearly communicate or train their employees on these policies. Companies such as Texas Instruments and Motorola, however, have provided sexual harassment training classes for a number of years.[188] Some firms have hired outside consultants to conduct the training, while others rely on their own training staffs to develop and deliver the courses.

Training on sexual harassment should include a description of the firm's policy including[189]

- A statement indicating the firm's strong opposition to sexual harassment.
- Definitions of sexual harassment, using examples relevant to employees' jobs. Enough detail should be given so employees understand what "quid-pro-quo" harassment is as well as what constitutes a "hostile environment."
- The procedure for reporting harassment (e.g., reporting to the HR director, installing an anonymous hot line).
- The procedure that will be used to investigate claims and that protects whistleblowers.
- Descriptions of punishments for offenders, regardless of their level in the organization.

Many organizations now use e-learning for their sexual harassment training.

Creativity Training

As organizations become more competitive in today's global marketplace, they have recognized the need for employees to become more innovative. They have tried to instill a spirit of risk taking and innovativeness among employees by providing them with creativity training. Using experiential exercises and brainstorming techniques, trainers try to get trainees to think "outside the box." In some cases, the training has been shown to be effective. For example, Frito-Lay indicated that creative problem-solving training saved the firm more than $500 million from 1983 through 1987.[190] 3M tries to provide a supportive culture and safe environment for risk-taking entrepreneurship. The firm seems to be successful since it has achieved its goal of consistently getting 30 percent of sales from products less than four years old. New employees are pushed to learn about the "nourishing and ruthless environment" by taking a class in risk taking. They attend with their supervisors yet are taught that they need to be willing to go against their supervisors.[191]

A recent meta-analysis of 70 studies found that well-designed **creativity training** programs do induce gains in creativity performance across criteria, settings, and populations.[192] The successful programs were more likely to focus on the development of cognitive skills and the heuristics involved in skill application, using realistic exercises.

Training for International Assignments

Most multinational firms predicted that their number of expatriates would increase to better position their firms for global competition.[193] Due to the increasing use of expatriate assignments, training should not be considered as a one-shot program but, rather, as a life-long endeavor to learn about other cultures. To do this, companies will have to invest more heavily in training programs.[194] As one expert stated, "The key to successfully competing in the global marketplace may be staffing key expatriate positions with accomplished/ skilled leaders."[195] Thus, U.S. firms have begun to realize that to be successful in their overseas projects, they need to better prepare individuals to work in international assignments. Studies document the high rate of expatriate failures ranging from 25 percent to 50 percent.[196] These early returns can be costly for firms with respect to goodwill, reputation, and finances. In many cases, the difficulties encountered by expatriates have been blamed on inadequate training programs. For example, Honeywell surveyed 347 managers who lived abroad or traveled regularly and found that increased training was cited as critical for executives and employees assigned overseas. Cross-cultural training has been found to reduce the severity of culture shock and reduced the time necessary for managers to adjust to the culture, reach a level of cultural proficiency, and become effective and productive in their assignments.[197]

Training and orientation for international assignments are more common today. It is estimated that 50 percent of companies that sent employees overseas were conducting pre-training and orientation.[198] Other countries, such as Japan, are more committed to the importance of training for international assignments. This may explain the low (less than 10 percent) failure rate cited for most of Japan's multinational corporations. In Japanese firms, overseas training is typically conducted over a one-year period where international assignees are taught about the culture, customs, and business techniques of the host country.[199]

A growing number of U.S. firms have shown a strong commitment to international training and orientation,[200] although increasingly more companies are outsourcing expatriate training.[201] Federal Express sends future expatriates and their families on "familiarization" trips, which also serve as "realistic job previews." Over 70 percent of companies now pay for similar trips. Gillette is a leader in this area with international assignments as a part of its junior trainee program. The objective of the program is to build careers with a global perspective.[202] American Express provides U.S. business school students summer jobs in a foreign location. Colgate-Palmolive trains recent graduates for multiple overseas assignments. Many large international companies also have established health care policies for traveling executives. One new topic for discussion in recent training programs has been safety issues due to increased violence experienced by businesspeople working in foreign countries.[203]

Skills Needed by International Assignees

To design effective training programs to better prepare U.S. managers and employees for assignments overseas, it is important to understand the kinds of skills they will need for international assignments. As we discussed in Chapter 6, in addition to good technical skills, individuals who will be working overseas need to be adaptable and have skills in languages and an understanding of social customs, cultural values, codes of conduct, and motivation and reward systems in the host country.[204] For Middle

Eastern assignments, for example, Bechtel places great emphasis on the importance of religion in the culture. Also, expatriates need assistance in the practical aspects of foreign assignments (e.g., housing, schools, currency, and health issues). Visits to the country can aid in reassuring employees and their families about their home, hospitals, dentists, and schools. Training programs should include expatriates and their families, particularly in cultures where women are excluded culturally from doing a variety of things during the day. For instance, in Saudi Arabia, women have many restrictions about dress and proper behaviors.

Before presenting several specific examples of cross-cultural training programs, it is useful to discuss how cultural training differs from traditional training. Cultural training focuses on several goals,[205] including

1. Communication—Expatriates will need to understand and communicate directly and through nonverbal means in order to listen to the concerns and motives of others.
2. Decision making—They will have to develop conclusions and take actions on the basis of inadequate, unreliable, and conflicting information, and to trust their feelings, impressions, and facts.
3. Commitment—They will need to become involved in relationships and inspire confidence in others.
4. Ideals—They will have to value the causes and objectives of others from a radically different social environment.
5. Problem solving—They will have to make decisions needed to achieve common goals.

Understanding cultural influences at the individual level is the key to understanding cultural influences in the workplace. Cultural self-knowledge is critical for this understanding.[206] A three-level construct called "cultural intelligence" has been proposed where a person's self-efficacy through social interaction in cross-cultural settings plays a key role in the subsequent effectiveness of such interactions. High self-efficacy results in the initiation of cross-cultural interactions which persist in the face of early failures. In addition, individuals with high self-efficacy engage in problem solving in order to master required skills.[207]

There are several examples of cross-cultural training programs used by organizations. For instance, ARAMCO, a Saudi Arabian corporation, uses an extensive orientation program for employees and their families. The program includes practical housekeeping information such as local transportation, shopping, day-to-day finances, and comparisons of the beliefs and customs of the Saudi and American people. The International Development Agency's predeparture program for overseas volunteers has several objectives, including the following: communicate respect, be nonjudgmental, display empathy, practice role flexibility, and tolerate ambiguity. Research on cross-cultural training indicates expatriates perform better and are more satisfied with their assignments after such training.[208]

Training Techniques

To acquire the skills necessary to be successful in an international assignment, a variety of training techniques can be used. Procter & Gamble uses several methods to refine language skills and to improve intercultural awareness among international assignees.[209] Their "P&G College" for new and mid-level managers emphasizes globalization issues. In any program developed, it is recommended that the international assignee and his or her family be actively involved in the training to ease the transition and build a supportive environment. It is further suggested that the training should be led by people who have served in the specific country and that the training should begin a year before the employee's move to that country. This is often not done, however, as many companies try to squeeze the training into the last six weeks.[210] To teach employees about area studies or the host country's environment (e.g., geography, climate, political system, customs, religion, labor force, economy, etc.) and the company's international operations, *informational* approaches such as lectures, reading material, videotapes, and movies can be effectively used. One technique, the cultural assimilator, was designed as a programmed learning technique to test trainees' knowledge of cultural differences and their understanding of these issues for effective functioning in a foreign culture.[211] To teach trainees about the host country's norms, values, and interpersonal styles so that they will be able to effectively understand and negotiate with host individuals, *experiential* approaches may be beneficial. These might include role-playing and simulations (simulations specific to the culture). Using both a cognitive approach to training (e.g., cultural assimilator) and an experiential approach (e.g., behavior modeling) together has been tried for cross-cultural training. With U.S. government managers, it was discovered that using both techniques together revealed higher performance than using either technique alone.[212]

Field experiences are recommended to provide a more in-depth view of the host country's customs, values, and behaviors. These experiences can take a variety of forms, including (1) short family trips to the host country, (2) informal meetings with other American families that have lived in the host country, (3) minicultures (i.e., the family visits a multicultural environment in the United States such as an ethnic neighborhood), and (4) host-family surrogates (i.e., a U.S. family from a background similar to the host country has the expatriate family stay with them for a period of time so they can observe the customs). The value of such experiences is to provide a realistic preview of what is to be expected in the overseas position.[213] Finally, *language skill* classes and cassettes are recommended for use in developing skills in interpersonal communication and the day-to-day dealings that the family will encounter in the host country. In a 12-country study of 3,000 executives, respondents from many countries viewed foreign language skills as critical to a firm's competitive advantage.[214] This should include not only verbal communication skills, but also nonverbal messages and meanings.

Training for Inpatriates

In addition to providing training for expatriates, U.S. firms are increasingly providing training for foreign nationals who are coming to the United States to work. For example, SC Johnson Wax has been bringing employees into the United States for the past 10 years. Eli Lilly and Company brings in about 20 people a year, typically in the fields of science, finances, and marketing. Their training needs are very similar to those of expatriates. To help them adjust, the following tips are offered:[215]

1. Make sure the spouse and children are content with the new location.
2. Make the necessary arrangements to process Social Security numbers in order to help them get a driver's license, bank account, and credit cards.
3. Provide training with U.S. managers on dealing with people from the other culture.
4. Help them establish credit in the new country.
5. Use relocation counselors to help them with real estate, schools, stores, community activities, and other information to help them get settled.
6. Provide assistance to accompanying spouses (e.g., jobs, educational reimbursements, career guidance, etc.).
7. Provide cross-cultural training to inpatriates and U.S. employees.
8. Offer competitive compensation.
9. Provide language training for employees and their spouses and children.

SUMMARY

Over the years, training has become increasingly popular as a tool for increasing employee and managerial performance in organizations. Most organizations and governmental agencies provide some formal training, and spend millions of dollars doing so. Successful training depends upon a systematic approach involving a careful needs assessment, solid program design, and thorough evaluation of results. Training programs should not be designed as quick fixes for every organizational problem, nor should they rely on faddish techniques. Instead, training should be designed to meet the particular needs of the organization and its employees. It should be viewed as a *continuous learning* endeavor by employees and managers to stay current

9

CAREER DEVELOPMENT*

OVERVIEW

The workplace has changed. The business environment is highly turbulent and complex, resulting in terribly ambiguous and contradictory career signals. Individuals, perhaps in self-defense, are altering some of their career-related attitudes and behaviors and becoming ambivalent about their desires and plans for career development. The traditional psychological contract in which an employee entered a firm, worked hard, performed well, was loyal and committed, and thus received ever-greater rewards and job security has been replaced by a new contract based on continuous learning and identity change. In short, the organizational career is dead, while the protean career or boundaryless career is alive and flourishing.[1]

Not that long ago, individuals believed that there was *only one* occupation for which each person was best suited, that the best career decision would be made when a person was *young,* and that once a field was chosen the choice was *irreversible.* They also believed that *interests* were more important in determining career choices than were skills and aptitudes, and that individuals who were successful in a career only moved *upwards.*[2] Today, fewer people subscribe to these assumptions about careers.

> The career as we once knew it—
> as a series of upward moves, with
> steadily increasing income, power,
> status, and security—has died.
> Nevertheless, people will always
> have work lives that unfold over
> time, offering challenge, growth,
> and learning. So, if we think of
> the career as a series of lifelong
> work-related experiences and
> personal learnings, it will never die.[3]

The career of the 21st century is measured by continuous learning and identity changes rather than by chronological age and life stages. With downsizings, delayerings, right-sizings, restructurings, and layoffs, the covenant employees used to believe in between the employer and employee seems null. Jack Welch, former CEO of General Electric, said there is a one-day contract between employer and employee, in which all that counts is the current value that each party contributes to the relationship. Of course, Jack Welch also strongly believed in providing opportunities at GE for developing and challenging employees.[4]

Interestingly, in a 2005 online survey, 44 percent of senior HR executives predicted that as many as half of their employees would be looking for jobs once the economy improves. Similarly, in the SHRM 2004 U.S. Job Recovery and Retention Poll,[5] they noted that 75 percent of those who were currently employed were either actively or passively job searching. Employees with less than 5 years of work experience and those with 11–20 years of experience, were the most likely to be searching for jobs. These findings are of great concern to HR professionals since the defections at their firms could lead to difficulties in serving customers and achieving organizational goals.

Thus, there is ever greater interest in career development, and trainers have never before faced so many challenges in meeting the needs of individual employees

*Contributed by Joyce E. A. Russell.

and organizations in designing career systems. To cope in today's turbulent times, it has become increasingly important for both organizations and employees to better address career needs. This chapter describes some current career-related issues of relevance to practicing managers. We begin by describing what individuals and organizations can do to address some of the changing career forces. We then define some of the key career concepts and models, and describe some of the issues involved in designing career development systems in organizations. We describe the various components of career systems and how career systems can be coordinated with other programs in organizations. Finally, we review career issues for a number of targeted groups of employees.

OBJECTIVES

After reading this chapter, you should be able to

1. *Describe the new changes taking place in the workplace and what implications these have for individuals and organizations.*
2. *Define organizational career development and the reasons for understanding career development.*
3. *Understand the importance of integrating career development programs with other organizational systems (e.g., training, selection, recruitment).*
4. *Identify the steps in designing career development systems.*
5. *Describe the components of career development systems.*
6. *Understand how to design career programs for various target groups of employees such as fast-track employees, entrenched employees, supervisors, executives, women, minorities, employed spouses and parents, teams, repatriates, and others.*

DEFINITIONS

While most people think the term **career** means "advancement" in an organization, a broader view of career defines it as an "individually perceived sequence of attitudes and behaviors associated with work-related activities and experiences over the span of a person's life."[6] In other words, the term *career* has an *internal* focus and refers to the way an individual views his or her career and has an *external* or objective focus and refers to the actual series of job positions held by the individual.[7] Understanding career development in an organization requires an examination of two processes: how individuals plan and implement their own career goals (career planning) and how organizations design and implement their career development programs (career management). These

processes are illustrated in Figure 9-1. As noted, **career planning** is a deliberate attempt by an individual to become more aware of his or her own skills, interests, values, opportunities, constraints, choices, and consequences. It involves identifying career-related goals and establishing plans for achieving those goals.[8] **Career management** is considered to be an organizational process that involves preparing, implementing, and monitoring career plans undertaken by an individual alone or within the organization's career systems.[9]

A **career development system** is a formal, organized, planned effort to achieve a balance between individual career needs and organizational workforce requirements.[10] For example, the organization has certain needs for staffing and employees have needs to effectively utilize their personal skills. A development system is a mechanism for meeting the present and future human resource needs of the organization. Stanford professor Pfeffer looks at formal systems of career development as a key to competitive advantage. Says Pfeffer, "Career systems that emphasize promotions from within not only promote advantages in terms of managing the employment relationship but also make it more likely that strategies for achieving competitive advantage through people will be understood and pursued."[11] A career planning system coordinated with an organization's staffing system will foster a well-integrated system.

Career development practices are designed to enhance the career satisfaction of employees and to improve organizational effectiveness.[12] It may be difficult, however, to completely integrate individual and organizational career efforts because the rate at which an individual grows and develops may not parallel an organization's needs. For example, many of the baby boomers in the workforce are interested in advancing in their present positions, yet are finding those positions to be more scarce given the thinning out of management jobs in organizations due to downsizings. As a result, baby boomers held an average of 10.2 jobs from the ages of 18 to 38.[13] With all of the recent changes in organizations (e.g., downsizings, mergers, divestitures), it has become even more important to try to integrate the needs of employers with those of employees.

This chapter emphasizes the importance of understanding career development in organizations by examining the interaction of individual and organizational career processes. Of particular value is an understanding of the role HR managers must play to design career development systems. One model focuses on a dynamic interaction of the individual and the organization over time through a "matching" process. If the matching process works well, the organization and the individual will benefit. The organization may experience increased productivity, higher organizational commitment, and long-range effectiveness, and the employee may have greater satisfaction, security, and personal development.[14]

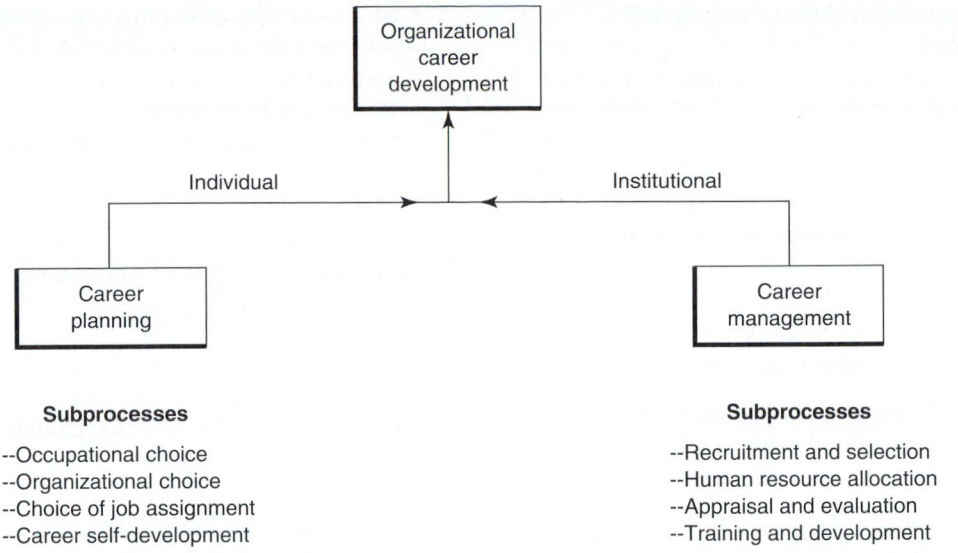

Subprocesses

--Occupational choice
--Organizational choice
--Choice of job assignment
--Career self-development

Subprocesses

--Recruitment and selection
--Human resource allocation
--Appraisal and evaluation
--Training and development

Career: The sequence of a person's work-related activities and behaviors and associated attitudes, values, and aspirations over the span of one's life.

Organizational career development: The outcomes emanating from the interaction of individual career planning and institutional career management processes.

Career planning: A deliberate process for (1) becoming aware of self, opportunities, constraints, choices, and consequences; (2) identifying career-related goals; and (3) programming of work, education, and related developmental experiences to provide the direction, timing, and sequence of steps to attain a specific career goal.

Career management: An ongoing process of preparing, implementing, and monitoring career plans undertaken by the individual alone or in concert with the organization's career system.

Figure 9-1   A Model of Organizational Career Development

Source: T. G. Gutteridge, "Organizational Career Development Systems: The State of the Practice," in *Career Development in Organizations*, D. T. Hall and associates. Copyright © John Wiley & Sons Inc., 1986. Reprinted with permission of John Wiley & Sons, Inc.

IMPLICATIONS OF WORKPLACE CHANGES FOR INDIVIDUALS AND ORGANIZATIONS

What Should Individuals Do?

Given the changing views of careers in organizations, what should individuals do to be prepared for future jobs and why is this important? Assuming salary is a good measure of career advancement, one recent review provides some helpful guidelines for predicting future success.[15] In terms of what an individual can control, the most important predictors of future salary are (in order of importance): (1) education level; (2) political knowledge and skills; (3) work experience; (4) hours worked and; (5) sponsorship by a colleague. The following tips are offered for individuals regarding their careers.

- The focus today should be on an individual's *employability.* Individuals should not worry about holding onto a specific job, but rather should make sure they have developed the competitive skills needed in the marketplace. They need to have *portable competencies.*[16]

- Employees need to *take more control of their careers* than they ever have before and look out for their own best career interests.[17]

- Employees must develop new and better personal skills of *self-assessment and career planning,* especially because organizations do not have the resources to completely plan individuals' careers.[18] The protean or boundaryless career is one that is driven by the person, not the organization. Pursuing this career requires a high level of self-awareness and personal responsibility.

- Individuals need to *set career goals and clearly define* what they are interested in (e.g., talents, preferences).

- Especially during the early career period, employees need to maintain a *technical specialty.* They must, however, be careful not to become obsolete or too narrow in terms of their functional expertise.

- Individuals must invest in *reputation building* or image enhancement to illustrate success and suitability for jobs.[19]

- Individuals will need to develop their *collaboration skills* because the use of project teams in organizations will continue to increase.[20]

- Employees will need to develop multiple *networking and peer learning* relationships.

- The new career will be a continuous learning process and necessitates that the individual develop self-knowledge, *adaptability, and flexibility.* Individuals

will need to be adaptable to changing job requirements.[21]
- Employees need to periodically *solicit feedback* and appraise how they are doing relative to their career goals.
- Individuals need to commit to *lifelong learning* to keep their skills relevant, whether by additional schooling or taking on new assignments.

What Should Organizations Do?

Organizations likewise need to become more active in implementing career development programs. Companies are designing career programs in efforts to decrease employee turnover, prevent job burnout and obsolescence, and improve the quality of employees' work lives. In addition, child care, concierge services, and other employee support programs will increase as employers compete to attract and keep qualified employees in what is predicted to be the most severe shortage of skilled labor in history. The top concerns among employees' today are: burnout, lack of career growth, feeling disconnected from the firm, and a general distrust or lack of confidence in leadership's ability to drive the organization forward.[22] A number of organizations such as Chevron, CIGNA, Sears Information Services, Texaco, Turner Broadcasting, Internal Revenue Service, and Marriott International participated in a conference specifically to share their strategies for creating a career-resilient workforce.[23] A few recommendations for organizations are provided below:[24]

- It is the employee's responsibility to manage his or her own career, yet it is the employer's responsibility to provide employees with the *tools and opportunities* to enhance their skills. The end result should be a career-resilient workforce, one that has self-reliant workers who are capable of reinventing themselves to keep up with the fast pace of organizational changes.[25]
- Create an *environment for continuous learning* by supporting and rewarding employee development and learning (e.g., professional associations, training, schooling). Some organizations such as Motorola, Ford, and Intel are especially effective at this.[26]
- Provide *opportunities for self-assessment.* Have career counselors and career resource centers available.
- Provide opportunities for additional *training,* including orientation, core training, and computer-based training.[27]
- Have managers trained as coaches and mentors to assist employees.
- Assist employees with striking *balances between their work and nonwork* lives (e.g., child care, elder care, flexible work arrangements).
- Use *reward systems* that support the organization's career development strategy.

- Make sure the career programs are *integrated with other human resource programs* (e.g., training, performance appraisal, selection).
- Before using outsourcing, try to *redeploy* the current workforce to teach them the new skills needed.

IMPORTANCE OF UNDERSTANDING CAREER DEVELOPMENT

Today's competitive business environment has forced organizations to restructure and downsize, resulting in fewer hierarchical levels and traditional promotional opportunities for employees. At the same time, there is increased pressure to improve productivity or risk falling prey to larger corporations. The creation of new technologies has required that individuals update their skills or else become outdated.

A number of organizational change initiatives could have unintended and undesired consequences for individuals. These include the following:

- **Downsizing**—jobs are cut from the organization.
- **Delayering**—jobs are reclassified more broadly, yet old reporting lines exist to maintain managerial control.
- **Decentralizing**—responsibilities are reassigned from the corporate centralized function to functions in each location or at lower levels.
- **Reorganizations**—company may be refocusing around core competencies.
- **Cost-reduction strategies**—the same work is done with fewer resources.
- **IT innovations**—how the work is done is altered due to advances in information technology.
- **Competency measurement**—skill sets required of employees are redefined or measured in different ways.
- **Performance-related pay**—pay is linked to performance and used as a motivator.

Figure 9-2 depicts some of the organizational change initiatives, their effects on jobs and careers, their psychological impact on individuals, and the necessary strategies to remedy or mitigate the negative effects.[28]

Understanding career development is also important today due to the changing workforce. Current labor force changes have included a greater proportion of older workers, working mothers, and members of the baby-boom generation who are competing for a limited number of jobs. In addition, employees have changed their values such that now they want more self-fulfillment in work and to be in charge of managing their own career planning. They want opportunities for growth in their careers, and to expand their knowledge and skills. They also demand well-balanced lives in which comparable value is placed

---

FIGURE 9-2   **Organizational Change Initiatives and Their Effects on Careers and Individuals**

Organizational Change Form	Effects on Jobs and Careers	Psychological Impact on Individuals	Remedial and Mitigating Strategies
Downsizing	Job security	Anxiety	Openness and involvement
Delayering	Plateauing	Lowered self-esteem	Delegation and self-management
Decentralization	Segmentation and fragmentation	Competitive behaviors	Team building and mobility
Reorganization	Displacement	Frustration	Self-appraisal and pathfinding
Cost-reduction	Work intensification	Stress	Time and task management
IT innovation	Deskilling	Lowered self-efficacy	Reskilling
Competency measurement	Obsolescence	Self-defense	Coaching and mentoring
Performance-related pay	Individualism and politics	Low trust behaviors	Team-based objectives and feedback

Source: N. Nicholson, "Career Systems in Crisis: Change and Opportunity in the Information Age," *Academy of Management Executive* 10, no. 4 (1996), p. 43.

---

on work, family, and leisure.[29] Generation X employees have different values. They seem less interested in climbing the corporate ladder, acquiring fancy titles, or spending their careers in one type of work or job. Rather, they want to explore and do different kinds of jobs where they can express their own individual values.[30]

Social changes have included increased societal pressures on organizations to be more responsible. For example, corporations are now more likely to offer child care programs, flexible work scheduling, and parental leave time. In addition, as discussed in Chapter 3, litigation concerning employment opportunity through laws such as the Age Discrimination in Employment Act, the Americans with Disabilities Act, the Civil Rights Act, and the Equal Pay Act has placed more responsibility on companies to avoid discrimination in their career development programs.

A greater emphasis now will be placed on designing and implementing relevant career systems in organizations. Organizations will have to find more creative ways for people to develop since employees will not be able to rely on organizational growth to provide career opportunities (e.g., promotions). The line manager may experience greater pressure to provide career counseling to employees, and HR managers may be called upon to offer training for managers in career coaching skills.[31] For example, the Coca-Cola and Ford career systems require training for all managers in how to conduct career development discussions with employees in the context of performance appraisal. The intent is to make managers more accountable for the development of their employees.[32]

DESIGNING CAREER DEVELOPMENT SYSTEMS

An effective career development system attempts to integrate a series of individual career planning and organizational career management activities that involve the employee, management, and the organization. For example, most corporations with career programs (e.g., Lincoln Electric, Wal-Mart, IBM, Bell Atlantic, Xerox) involve career assessment by the employee with the manager serving as a facilitator and the organization providing a supportive environment. HR specialists can help organizations determine if their firm has a culture that supports career development by administering the Career Development Culture Index provided in Figure 9-3. Low scores reflect ineffective (or nonexistent) career development systems. High scores reflect an effective system likely to correlate with lower voluntary turnover rates.

Benefits of Career Development Systems

Some of the benefits of a career development system for employees, managers, and the organization are presented in Figure 9-4. As shown, managers can benefit from career development programs by being better able to communicate with and develop their staff. Employees also may benefit from a career development system by acquiring a deepened appreciation for their own skills and career possibilities and assuming a greater responsibility for managing their own careers. The organization may gain from a career development system by increased employee loyalty, improved communication throughout the organization, lower turnover rates, and strengthened human resource systems. For example, the Federal National Mortgage Association reduced turnover of its sales force by 50 percent after instituting a supervisory training program on career planning.

To maintain the career development program, it is essential to integrate the career program into the organization's ongoing employee training and development strategy. The program also should be evaluated to determine revisions and to win the continued support of top

FIGURE 9-3 Twenty Questions: A Career Development Culture Index

Instructions: If your answer is yes to a question, make a check mark in the space to the left of the number of that item. See scoring instructions at the end of the exercise.

_____ 1. Does senior management use work assignments and work relationships to develop employees?

_____ 2. Do they do it consciously or intentionally for developing people (as opposed to doing it only for business purposes)?

_____ 3. Are these career development activities part of the business plan for the employee's unit?

_____ 4. Is the organization's purpose expressed in human terms with which employees can identify?

_____ 5. Does top management value employee development?

_____ 6. Is career development owned by senior line management (as opposed to being seen as owned by HR)?

_____ 7. Is diversity actively promoted by senior line management?

_____ 8. Is employee development done by senior line management for the explicit purpose of supporting the business strategy?

_____ 9. Are new forms of employee mobility being used (such as cross-functional, cross-business teams)?

_____ 10. Is personal development or self-knowledge (for example, 360-degree feedback) promoted?

_____ 11. Is career development part of the overall corporate strategy?

_____ 12. Is there a strong succession planning process, which puts emphasis on development as well as identification?

_____ 13. Do employees have significant input to plans for their future development and assignments?

_____ 14. Does career development include opportunities for risk and learning (adaptability)?

_____ 15. Does career development include personal (identity) learning as well as task learning?

_____ 16. Do most people here believe that career development should also take family and personal balance needs into account?

_____ 17. Is there general agreement in management about whether historical career development approaches are appropriate for the future?

_____ 18. Is it relatively easy for employees to access information about other job opportunities in the company?

_____ 19. Are employees encouraged to be empowered and self-directed in their careers?

_____ 20. (The acid test): Are individual employees aware of your organization's career development activities?

Scoring:

Add up the number of checks (symbolizing "yes" to the item).

Key: 17 or more checks . . . . Outstanding

10–16 . . . . Good

6–9 . . . . Fair

<5 . . . . Work needed!

Source: Z. B. Leibowitz, C. Farren, and B. L. Kaye, *Designing Career Development Systems.* Copyright © John Wiley & Sons 1986. Reprinted with permission of John Wiley & Sons, Inc.

FIGURE 9-4 Benefits of a Career Development System

Managers/Supervisors	Employees	Organization
Increased skill in managing own careers	Helpful assistance with career decisions	Better use of employee skills
Greater retention of valued employees	Enrichment of present job and increased job satisfaction	Dissemination of information at all organization levels
Better communication between manager and employee	Better communication between employee and manager	Better communication within the organization as a whole
More realistic staff and development planning	More realistic goals and expectations	Greater retention of valued employees
Productive performance-appraisal discussions	Better feedback on performance	Expanded public image as a people developer
Greater understanding of the organization	Current information on the firm and the future	Increased effectiveness of personnel systems
Enhanced reputation as a people developer	Greater personal responsibility for career	Clarification of goals of the organization

Source: Z. B. Leibowitz, C. Farren, and B. L. Kaye, *Designing Career Development Systems.* Copyright © John Wiley & Sons 1986. Reprinted with permission of John Wiley & Sons, Inc.

FIGURE 9-5	Indicators of Career Program Effectiveness

Goal Attainment

Achievement of prespecified individual and organizational objectives on qualitative as well as quantitative dimensions

Individual	Organizational
Exercise greater self-determination	Improve career communications between employees and supervisors
Achieve greater self-awareness	Improve individual/organizational career match
Acquire necessary organizational career information	Enhance organization's image
Enhance personal growth and development	Respond to EEO and affirmative action pressures
Improve goal-setting capability	Identify pool of management talent

Actions or events completed

1. Employee use of career tools (participation in career workshops, enrollment in training courses)
2. Career decisions conducted
3. Employee career plans implemented
4. Career actions taken (promotions, cross-functional moves)
5. Management successors identified

Changes in performance indexes

1. Reduced turnover rates
2. Lower employee absenteeism
3. Improved employee morale
4. Improved employee performance ratings
5. Reduced time to fill job openings
6. Increased promotion from within

Attitudes/perceptions

1. Evaluation of career tools and practices (participant's reaction to career workshop, supervisor's evaluation of job-posting system)
2. Perceived benefits of career system
3. Employees' expression of career feelings (responses to career attitude survey)
4. Evaluation of employee career planning skills
5. Adequacy of organizational career information

Source: T. G. Gutteridge, "Organizational Career Development Systems: The State of the Practice," in *Career Development in Organizations*, D. T. Hall and associates. Copyright © John Wiley & Sons Inc., 1986. Reprinted with permission of John Wiley & Sons, Inc.

management. Figure 9-5 illustrates some of the criteria that may be used to evaluate the program or indicate success. As noted, success can be measured by individual and organizational goal attainment, the actions that are completed (e.g., use of career tools), and any changes in performance measures and attitudes.

Research on the effectiveness of career development programs is sparse, yet promising. One study found that 44 percent of administrators of career development programs for Fortune 500 companies regarded them as "very helpful."[33] IBM evaluated the effectiveness of its career development workshop and found improvements in the participants' abilities and responsibilities for their own career planning. They also discovered that employee perceptions of better job opportunities (defined as opportunities to use new and different skills) had increased substantially.[34] Pratt & Whitney reported that its turnover rate for new engineers had decreased by 25 percent after instituting a career development program.

Of course, measures of program success may vary depending on whom you are asking in the organization. Employees, managers, organizations, and the HR staff may differ in the specific factors they view as indicative of program success. For example, employees may say that a career program is effective if it organizes a way for them to plan and manage their career interests or offers them opportunities to discuss their career decisions with their supervisors. Managers may view a career program as successful if it offers them staffing flexibility or helps them to identify pools of qualified employees to meet forecasted openings. Organizations may find a program to be useful if it increases the attractiveness of the organization to potential employees (recruits) or raises the motivation and productivity of current employees. Finally, the HR staff may determine that a program is successful if it has credibility or enhances the reputation of the career or training department with line managers.[35]

COMPONENTS OF CAREER DEVELOPMENT SYSTEMS

A variety of career components (i.e., activities and tools) exist for use in organizations. HR managers should be familiar with these components since they often serve as internal or external consultants responsible for designing the career development system. Some of the activities described are *individual career planning* tools and others are commonly used for *organizational career management*.[36] In general, the most effective career development programs will use both types of activities.

A variety of career development activities are available for use. Some of the more popular ones are listed in Figure 9-6. These programs were cited as having the greatest positive impact on employees' job satisfaction, communication, retention, work motivation, and their views or image of the company as well as their commitment to the firm.[37] No matter what tools are used for career development, it is important that employees develop an individualized career development plan. For example, Raychem requires every person to have a learning or development plan.[38]

Career development programs are effective retention tools and are quickly becoming an employee expectation. Larger corporations began to develop CD programs in the late 1980s and early 1990s, and they are beginning to appear in smaller firms. Organizations recognize that they can link their career programs to specific business objectives while developing their employees to meet their goals. At the same time, the employees are kept abreast of changing technology, and are developing Career-Related Skills. In addition, these programs tell employees that the organization values and respects them by investing in their future career growth.[39]

Self-Assessment Tools

Self-assessments are usually among the first techniques implemented by organizations in their career development efforts. Thus, it is important for managers to become familiar with the different self-assessment and career exploration instruments available. Typically, individuals completing self-assessment exercises for career-planning purposes go through a process where they think through their life roles, interests, skills, and work attitudes and preferences. They try to plan their short- and long-term goals, develop action plans to meet those goals, and identify any obstacles and opportunities that might be associated with them.[40] Hewlett-Packard employees at the Colorado Springs Division complete a variety of self-assessment exercises including a written self-assessment, vocational interest tests (e.g., Strong Interest Inventory), and 24-hour diaries before meeting with their managers for career counseling.[41] Six months after the course, 40 percent of the participants had planned internal career moves and 37 percent had already advanced to new positions in the firm. Of those, 74 percent stated that the career-development program played a critical part in their job change. Two tools often used to assist individuals in their self-assessments include career-planning workshops and career workbooks.

FIGURE 9-6   Types of Organizational Career Development Interventions

Self-assessment tools
   Career planning workshops
   Career workbooks
Individual counseling
Information services
   Job-posting systems
   Skills inventories
   Career ladders and paths
   Career resource centers
Organizational assessment programs
   Assessment centers
   Psychological testing
   Promotability forecasts
   Succession planning
Developmental programs
   Assessment centers
   Job rotation programs
   Tuition refund plans
   Internal training programs
   External training seminars
   Formal mentoring programs
Career programs for special target groups
   Fast-track or high-potential employees
   Terminated employees (outplacement programs)
   Supervisors and managers
   Senior-level executives
   Professional employees
   Technical employees
   Women
   Minorities
   Employees with disabilities
   New employees (early-career issues)
      Employee orientation programs
      Anticipatory socialization programs
      Realistic recruitment
   Middle-career and older-career issues
      Programs to combat obsolescence or plateauing
      Workshops on older-worker issues
      Preretirement programs
      Incentives for early retirement
   Programs to assist employed spouses and parents
      Policies on hiring couples
      Work–family programs
      Part-time work
      Job-sharing programs
      Relaxed policies on transfers and travel
      Flexible work arrangements
      Paid maternity/paternity leave
      Child-care services
      Adoption benefits

Career-Planning Workshops

After individuals complete their self-assessments, they may share their findings with other individuals in career workshops. For example, General Electric provides career training to its engineering staff followed by periodic meetings to share results.[42] In general, most workshops use experiential exercises in a structured, participative group format to educate individuals on how to prepare and follow through on their career strategies. A group format allows participants to receive feedback from others so they can check the reality of their plans and consider other alternatives. In addition, workshops are beneficial in helping employees gain greater self-awareness and insight and learn more about career opportunities in the organization. TVA offered career planning workshops to many of its employees, and employees found them to be helpful in better understanding their career needs and insights.[43] At NASA Goddard Space Flight Center, career awareness workshops are conducted to educate employees about alternative career paths and to provide counseling to them. Eli Lilly and Company in Indianapolis uses workshops with executives and managers to give them feedback on their own career concepts and motives, as well as advice on how to provide career counseling to their subordinates.[44]

Career Workbooks

Career workbooks consist of questions and exercises designed to guide individuals to figure out their strengths and weaknesses, job and career opportunities, and necessary steps for reaching their goals. One popular example of a generic career workbook is the annual book "What Color Is Your Parachute?"[45] Individuals use this manual to learn about their career possibilities since it provides suggestions for job hunting and making career changes. Many workbooks are tailor-made for a particular company and can be completed in several sessions. If "homegrown" workbooks are used, they should contain a statement of the organization's career policy, a description of the career options in the organization, and the strategies available for obtaining career information. The workbooks also should illustrate the organization's structure, career paths, and job qualifications for jobs along the career ladders.[46]

Check out the self-assessment tool available through O*NET. In Chapter 4, we discussed the model that was the basis for the O*NET development (go to www.onetcenter.org). There are also other Internet-based career services available for free, often through university and corporate career centers. These are useful for finding jobs, posting résumés, networking, and learning about careers. For example, the Talent Alliance is an Internet-based resource cosponsored by member companies that provides support for the self-initiated, self-paced, career exploration. Personal inventory tools prompt self-discovery of leadership style, motivation, technical skills, and work context.[47]

Individual Counseling

One common career development activity is career counseling. Individual career counseling is to help employees discuss their career goals in one-on-one counseling sessions using workbooks and other self-assessment exercises.[48] Discussions of the employees' interests, goals, current job activities and performance, and career objectives often occur. Because the counseling sessions often are conducted on a one-on-one basis, they may be very time-consuming and not as cost-effective as other career development methods.

Generally, career counseling is provided by the human resource, training, or career department, although some organizations hire professional counselors and others use line managers as career counselors. PricewaterhouseCoopers assigns all employees, including partners, coaches to assist them in job-related and career concerns. If supervisors are used in career-counseling sessions, they should be given clearly defined roles and training in career issues, performance evaluation, listening, and communication skills. In addition, they should be required to meet with their subordinates on a consistent basis to review career goals and plans and to assist employees in developing their career objectives. Supervisors also should be instructed that part of their job is to help employees develop. In addition, they should be rewarded for their efforts as career coaches to encourage them to devote the necessary time to this role. For example, at Federal National Mortgage Association and Baxter Health Care Corporation, managers' bonuses are directly linked to the career development programs for women and minorities. Both companies identify key females and minorities early in their careers and develop specific plans for acquiring the necessary skills in advancement. In general, supervisors can be valuable sources of career information for employees. Some tips for helping managers be more effective as coaches include those below:[49]

- Practice active listening and paraphrasing to make sure you truly understand what the employee is saying.
- Support the employee's learning by asking him or her about the actions he or she has taken and how successful they were.
- Help the employee work on easier career goals first, then more difficult ones.
- Help the employee write out scripts and role-play possible scenarios (e.g., interviewing for jobs).
- Provide positive feedback as employees take relevant career actions (e.g., attending career workshops).

Information Services

Internal communication systems often are used by organizations to alert employees to employment opportunities at all levels including upward, downward, and lateral moves. They also may be used to keep ongoing records of employees' skills, knowledge, and work experiences and preferences. These records are valuable for pointing out possible candidates for job openings in the company.

Several systems commonly used for compiling and communicating career-related information include job-posting systems, skills inventories, career ladders and paths, and career resource centers.

Job-Posting Systems

Job-posting systems are commonly used by companies to inform employees about openings in the organization using Web sites, bulletin boards, newsletters, computer systems (e-mail), and other company publications. While they serve an informational purpose, postings also may be useful as a motivational tool. They imply that the organization is more interested in selecting employees from within the company than outside the organization. This is a sound strategy since one of the "High Performance Work Characteristics" is a policy of promoting managers from within the organization. Guidelines for effective job-posting systems include

- Posting all permanent promotion and transfer opportunities for at least one week before recruiting outside the organization.
- Outlining minimum requirements for the position (including specific training courses).
- Describing decision rules that will be used.
- Making application forms available.
- Informing all applicants how and when the job was filled.

It is also important that all employees have access to the job postings. At Ford, a training matrix is available for each job family in which specific courses are linked as optional or recommended for particular job classification. Raychem has created an internal network, called Internal Information Interview Network, of more than 360 people within the firm who are willing to talk with any employee who wants to learn more about their job.[50] Company intranets can also be useful for ensuring all employees have access to job postings. Employees can simply login to the site, view positions by job title and location, and apply for the position immediately. The use of an intranet can also be particularly useful when a collective bargaining agreement requires job openings be made available to employees before hiring outside the organization.

Skills Inventories

Skills inventories are company files of data on employees' skills, abilities, experiences, and education that are often computerized. They may contain comprehensive records of employees' work histories, qualifications, education degrees and major fields of study, accomplishments, training completed, skill and knowledge ratings, career objectives, geographical preferences, and anticipated retirement dates.[51] Skills inventories are created to help organizations know the characteristics of their workforce so they can effectively utilize employees' skills. They also reveal shortages of critical skills, which

is useful for indicating training needs. AT&T has a department, Resource Link, that operates as an internal temporary services unit to meet the variable workforce needs of the company's business units and divisions.[52]

Career Ladders and Career Paths

Organizations usually map out steps (job positions) that employees might follow over time. These steps are used to document possible patterns of job movement including vertical or upward moves and lateral or cross-functional moves. Illustrations of career paths and ladders are helpful for answering employees' questions about career progression and future job opportunities in the organization. For example, General Motors groups jobs by job families such as HR, engineering, clerical, systems professional, and so forth, to show employees the career possibilities in each of the various job fields. ARCO (Atlantic Richfield Company) has a lot of lateral movement for positions. They make special arrangements for employees who want to shift career paths.[53]

Typically, the description of a career path or ladder illustrates a career plan complete with the final goal, intermediate steps, and timetables for reaching the goal. In addition, the qualifications necessary to proceed to the next position are specified as is any minimum time required prior to advancing. For example, in an academic position, the path may look like Instructor → Assistant Professor → Associate Professor → Professor. At a consulting firm, the path may look like Consultant → Senior Consultant → Manager → Partner. An employee may be required to spend a minimum amount of time in each level and gain increasing responsibilities before moving to the next higher level.

Common in many organizations is the development of career paths for "fast-track" employees that outline the series of career moves that will prepare them for upper management. In recent years, many companies have developed multiple or dual career paths.[54] This is becoming more common in firms hiring professional employees (e.g., scientists, engineers). Previously, if an engineer wanted to advance in a firm, he or she had to eventually move into a management position to move up the corporate ladder. Today, many organizations (e.g., National Security Agency) offer dual career ladders so that technical employees and professionals can advance either through a management track or a scientist track. This enables them to remain in a technical, professional field yet still be able to advance in the firm to a higher status and higher-paying position.

Career Resource Center and Other Communication Formats

One of the least expensive approaches for providing career information is setting up a career resource center. A center consists of a small library set up to distribute career development materials such as reference books, learning guides, videos, and self-study tapes. Universities are well known for having career centers where students can obtain company brochures and videos and career books and gain access to computers to research firms on the Internet. Kodak has three internal career services, "Kodak Career Services," which consist of a career library of tapes, books, and career counselors.[55] Other methods for communicating organizational career information and programs may include the use of flyers, brochures, newsletters, and manuals. Today, with the increasing use of computers, many firms are placing career resource information on their company's intranet. The program at PricewaterhouseCoopers, called MYC or Managing Your Career, enables employees to directly ask questions about career issues. Sun Microsystems, Apple Computer, and Raychem have centers set up with career specialists where employees 0can work on self-assessments, receive counseling, check on internal and external ob openings, and attend seminars on networking or interviewing. Their centers are highly visible and easily accessible, which conveys to employees that the firms want their career centers to be used. Other companies have formed partnerships to enable their employees to receive career assistance.

Organizational Assessment Programs

Assessment programs consist of methods for evaluating employees' potential for growth and development in the organization. For example, Johnson & Johnson has used career assessment to facilitate the staffing and development of special "tiger teams," which are formed to speed up the development of high-priority, new products.[56] Some of the more popular assessment programs include assessment centers, psychological testing, 360-degree appraisal, promotability forecasts, and succession planning.

Assessment Centers

In addition to their use as decision-making tools, assessment centers are popular as developmental tools. One survey found that 43 percent of surveyed firms used assessment centers as part of their career development programs.[57] AT&T, JCPenney, Sears Roebuck & Co., IBM, GE, TVA, Bendix, and Pratt & Whitney are among the companies using assessment centers for development as well as employee decision making.[58] "Assessment centers are particularly predictive of 'advancement criteria' such as career progress, salary advancement, long-term promotion, and potential development." As described in Chapter 6, participants of an assessment center engage in a variety of situational exercises including tests, interviews, in-baskets, leaderless group discussions, and business games. Their performance on these exercises is evaluated by a panel of trained raters

(usually middle- to upper-level managers), and they are given in-depth developmental feedback on their strengths and weaknesses. This feedback is often very useful for improving their own insights about their skills and for helping them outline realistic future career goals and plans.

Psychological Assessment

Diagnostic tests and other inventories may be used for self-assessment or with career counseling. They consist of written tests and questionnaires that help individuals determine their vocational interests, personality types, work attitudes, and other personal characteristics that may reveal their career needs and preferences. In addition to O*NET, among useful tools are the Strong Vocational Interest Inventory, the Myers-Briggs Type Indicator, various measures of the Big-Five personality factors, and the Kuder Preference Schedule, which assess preferences for certain jobs and job characteristics.

Promotability Forecasts

Forecasts are used by the organization to make early identifications of individuals with exceptionally high career potential. Once individuals are identified, they are given relevant developmental experiences (e.g., attending conferences, training) to groom them for higher positions. Several companies now have such programs for women and minorities in an effort to get greater female and minority representation at higher managerial levels. Others, such as AT&T, track the progress of high-potential managers and provide them with developmental assignments.[59]

It is important that promotability forecasts do not exclude employees based upon factors protected under Title VII, such as age, sex, or race. HR must be diligent in ensuring that all employees are treated fairly and equally. The 80 percent rule discussed in Chapter 3 is a good internal auditing measure for assessing potential legal trouble with forecasting.

Succession Planning

Succession planning involves having senior executives periodically review their top executives and those in the next-lower level to determine several backups for each senior position. This is important because it often takes years of grooming to develop effective senior managers. There is a critical shortage in companies of middle and top leaders for the next five years. Organizations will need to create pools of candidates with high leadership potential.

In the next five years as the baby boomers begin retiring, developed nations will see a 15 percent drop in the number of people of "key leader age." HR must begin planning how to fill these key positions in the near future. Microsoft is being proactive by not only recruiting top talent but aggressively promoting "high potential" employees; matching leaders with positions; providing challenging cross-function experiences; and rewarding employees who bring the greatest value to the organization.[60]

In addition to executive level succession planning, organizations can use succession planning for mid- to upper-level management positions. Management succession can create a career ladder for employees and can be a planning reprieve for the anticipated brain drain as the baby boomers retire. Organizations benefit from increased employee commitment, increased retention, and higher corporate performance.[61]

Succession planning is usually restricted to senior-level management positions and can be informal or formal. For informal succession planning, the individual manager identifies and grooms his or her own replacement. This is more prevalent in smaller firms. In fact, one survey of 800 small business owners found that only 25 percent have a succession plan and that only 50 percent of them have even written it down.[62] Succession planning for family businesses seems to be especially important for the firm to remain successful.[63]

Formal succession planning involves an examination of strategic (long-range) plans and HR forecasts and a review of the data on all potential candidates. The objective is to identify employees with potential and increase managerial depth as well as promoting from within the company. In addition, it includes determining and clarifying the requirements of the managerial position and developing plans for how future managerial requirements will be met. It involves behavioral profile matching between the individual managers' skills, behavioral flexibility, and adaptability and the organization's future needs as depicted by the organization's strategic plan.[64] In one study of Fortune 500 firms with succession plans, components used in the plans included identification of high-potential employees, updated lists of possible replacements, performance appraisals of all employees, and individual development plans and management development programs. Additionally, the factors rated as most important in selecting specific candidates for grooming included past job performance, past positions or prior employment, perceived credibility, area of expertise and career path, and values and attitudes.[65]

There are many benefits of having a formal succession planning system. In a survey of Fortune 500 firms, succession planning programs were perceived to have a positive impact on an organization's profitability, organizational culture, and organizational efficiency.[66] Some of the general benefits of a succession planning program are listed in Figure 9-7.

Regardless of what type of succession planning program is used (formal or informal), most successful programs obtain the support and commitment of top managers.[67] For example, Schwan Foods, one of the recipients of ASTD's BEST Awards, credits its success in building future leaders to the CEO who expresses a strong commitment to employee training and leadership development.[68] Usually, committees of top managers

---

FIGURE 9-7	**Benefits of Formal Succession Planning**

- Provides a specific connection to business and strategic planning.
- Provides a more systematic basis to judge the risks of making particular succession and development moves.
- Assists in developing systematized succession plans that fit with a distinct trend to codify, wherever possible, more general and comprehensive corporate planning actions.
- Reduces randomness of managerial development movements.
- Helps to anticipate problems before they get started—and thereby avoids awkward or dysfunctional situations.
- Increases managerial depth, which can be called on as needed.
- Provides a logical approach for locking succession planning into the process of human resource planning—connecting formats (data, timing) with process (judgments, discussions, analyses).
- Facilitates integration of the many components of human resource planning after having done many of these separately in the past.
- Improves the identification of high-potential and future leaders.
- Exploits the use of computer power or capabilities to improve succession planning formats and processes further.
- Broadens the use of cross-functional development techniques to improve competencies and quality of decision making.
- Stimulates inquiry into the fit of succession planning with the philosophy of the organization.
- Improves internal promotion opportunities.
- Overcomes the limitations of reactive management approaches and goes to planned management of managerial positions.
- Establishes a logical basis for choices among qualified candidates.
- Improves fulfillment of EEO objectives.
- Makes informal but critical criteria (e.g., "fit") more explicit.

Source: E. H. Burack, *Creative Human Resource Planning and Applications: A Strategic Approach,* 1988, p. 167. Reprinted with permission.

---

work together to identify high-potential candidates and then outline developmental activities for them. They also may include a formal assessment of the performance and potential of candidates and written individual developmental plans for candidates. Of course, with the current turbulent times in organizations (i.e., with downsizings, layoffs, mergers), some argue that it is foolish to spend a lot of time on succession planning efforts or identifying candidates for jobs that may not even exist in the future.[69] In addition, the firm's strategic goals may change, making some candidates, previously groomed for top positions, no longer the right choice.[70] For example, AT&T and IBM relied on succession-planning procedures that resulted in having the right kinds of leaders for the wrong times.[71] The individual's own aspirations for moving into senior management positions have only recently been considered when making succession plans, despite the obvious importance of this.[72] It is clear that each organization has to weigh the pros and cons of providing a succession-planning system. In general, in most organizations, a succession-planning system seems to be highly beneficial.[73]

Developmental Programs

Developmental programs consist of skills assessment and training programs that organizations may use to develop their employees for future positions. Development programs can be internal and run by the human resource staff, or be offered externally in the form of seminars and workshops. DuPont offers in-house seminars on various job functions and hands out a list of employee contacts with whom individuals can follow up to find out more about various job functions.[74] Other corporations have three- to four-year training programs at lower levels to groom employees for subsequent managerial positions.[75] One survey of 12 leading companies found that they agreed on the criteria for a successful executive development process: (1) extensive CEO involvement, (2) a clearly stated development policy, (3) CEO development linked to the business strategy, (4) an annual succession- planning process and on-the-job developmental assignments, and (5) line management responsibility for the program.[76]

Some commonly used programs for development include assessment centers, job rotation programs, in-house training programs, and tuition-refund or assistance plans. Xerox and 3M use many of these programs to develop their employees.[77] In some cases, organizations (e.g., Pacific Bell) provide college credit to an employee when he or she has completed courses offered by the firm (e.g., training or human resource courses).[78] In addition to assessment centers, discussed earlier, 360-degree feedback systems are useful for helping employees better understand their strengths and weaknesses for managerial jobs. Many companies (e.g., GE) also use job rotation programs that enable employees to develop a broader base of skills (cross-functional training) as part of the managerial training program. Apple Computer lets people sample jobs by filling in for employees who are on sabbaticals.[79] Some firms, such as Xerox, American Express, and Wells Fargo & Co., use sabbaticals to enable employees to get paid while working for charitable organizations. In this way, employees come back to their jobs refreshed and possessing new skills.[80] Most Fortune 500 companies cover expenses for job-related and career-oriented courses taken at colleges. They also offer internal programs on a variety of topics including technical training and interpersonal skills.

Mentoring

Another developmental program gaining in popularity is mentoring.[81] Mentoring consists of establishing formal relationships between junior and senior colleagues or peers.[82] These relationships contribute to career functions (e.g., sponsorship, coaching, and protection of the colleague; exposure to important contacts and resources; assignment of challenging work) and to psychosocial functions (e.g., role modeling, counseling, acceptance and confirmation of the colleague, friendship).[83]

Some recent meta-analyses of the effects of mentoring on objective (e.g., promotions, compensation) and subjective (e.g., career satisfaction) outcomes was supportive of claims associated with the benefits of mentoring, particularly for career satisfaction but also revealed that the magnitude of the effects associated with objective career outcomes were quite small. One study[84] found that human capital (individuals' educational, personal, and professional experiences) and sociodemographic predictors (gender, race, marital status, age) generally displayed stronger relationships with objective career success, and organizational career sponsorship (the extent to which employees receive sponsorship from senior-level employees, training and skill development opportunities, and organizational resources) and stable individual differences (e.g., cognitive ability, the "big five," proactivity, and locus of control) were generally more strongly related to career satisfaction. Among the strongest predictors of subsequent salaries were hours worked, work experience, political knowledge and skills, career sponsorship, training and skill opportunities, gender (favoring males), and cognitive ability.

Another recent meta-analysis was "generally supportive of the benefits associated with mentoring, but effect sizes associated with objective outcomes were small. There was also some indication that the outcomes studied differed in the magnitude of their relationship with the type of mentoring provided (i.e., career or psychosocial)."[85] The researchers also found that objective career success indicators, such as compensation and promotion, were more highly related to career mentoring than to psychosocial mentoring. Career mentoring behaviors such as sponsorship, exposure and visibility, coaching, and protection are more related to the enhancement of the task-based elements of work that are more strongly related to promotions and salary. The authors argue that the degree of mentoring provided does not play as large a role in objective career success as does the presence of a mentor while degree is more strongly related to career satisfaction.

Some of the companies with formal mentoring programs include Federal Express, Merrill Lynch, and The Jewel Companies.[86] Bank of America's program uses "quad squads" that consist of a mentor and three new hires (a male, a female, and a racial minority group member). Some organizations institutionalize like-to-like mentoring relationships (e.g., Hispanic mentors with Hispanic protégés) to better assist individuals in assimilating to the organization's culture.[87] Despite the benefits of mentoring programs for both mentors and protégés, they are still not used in many law firms or consulting agencies.[88]

CAREER PROGRAMS FOR SPECIAL TARGET GROUPS

Career development programs often are put into effect to meet the unique needs of particular employees. Although many different groups and issues may be targeted for career development, some of the more common programs are those that focus on fast-track employees, outplacement issues, entrenched employees, supervisors, women and minorities, new employees, late-career employees, and employed spouses and parents.

Fast-Track Employees

Organizations often identify "stars" or individuals with high career potential and place them on a fast track for upward moves in the company. AT&T, for example, uses assessment centers for the early identification of managerial talent. These specially recruited and selected employees are given rapid and intensive developmental opportunities in the company.[89] The identification and development of these employees requires organizations to exert extra recruitment efforts and to monitor career progress of these employees frequently. Organizations must provide considerable feedback, training, and counseling, as well as offer quicker job changes and more challenging job assignments, particularly during the employees' first few years on the job.

Managers who are responsible for identifying and developing fast-track employees should be recognized for their efforts if they are to take their responsibilities seriously. For example, Baxter Health Care links managers' bonuses to the early identification and development of promising female employees. At Eli Lilly, managers assess their employees and make decisions about their career potential and offer them opportunities for development. Similarly, Northern Telecom has a program that identifies fast trackers and helps them to develop a variety of skills that go beyond their own technical expertise.[90]

Outplacement Programs

Outplacement programs assist terminated employees in making the transition to new employment. Generally, outplacement programs involve individual counseling sessions with external or internal counselors where individuals are able to share their feelings about being let go. The programs also may contain financial counseling. In addition, workshops may be used to show individuals how to become successful job seekers by teaching them how to identify their skills and abilities, develop résumés, and interview with prospective employers. Outplacement programs stressing the importance of self-confidence and individual career planning may be particularly beneficial for middle- or late-career employees who have been laid off. This is because many older people were forced into involuntary retirement, often with insufficient skills and financial assets.[91] The programs should help laid-off employees deal with their anger, depression, stress, grief, or loss of self-esteem associated with the job loss. Many terminated employees suffer changes in their mental health. The programs also should encourage them to develop support networks. If an organization is going to use downsizing, the following recommendations can make it less traumatic and more fair:[92]

- Be fair in implementing layoffs; spread them throughout the organizational ranks, not just among lower-level employees.
- Allow employees to leave with dignity; if possible, allow them to leave of their own accord.
- Help those displaced find new jobs.
- Avoid belittling laid-off employees.
- Be cautious when hiring outside executives; educate them on the internal morale.
- Keep employees informed about the company's goals and expectations.
- Set realistic expectations.
- Use ceremonies to reduce anger and confusion and convey to employees what is going on.

Outplacement programs have been shown to benefit employees by helping them cope with the shock and stress associated with losing a job, and by helping them find jobs faster than they could on their own. This also may lower the likelihood that they will take legal action (sue) the firm for laying them off. In addition, a firm that offers outplacement programs may be viewed more positively by the "survivors," which could help improve their morale and reduce fears of job insecurity.

In some cases, employees are given the option of "job sharing" or reduced workweeks. This enables employees to keep their jobs, although with fewer hours and less pay. The organization also benefits since it helps them reduce their labor costs and overtime as well as retain valuable expertise and knowledge about the company. AT&T developed an innovative program, called Resource Link, that consists of an internal contingent of displaced managers and professionals who can be assigned to temporary projects of 3 to 12 months' duration. This gives project managers the assistance they need without hiring permanent staff. The program has been so popular that some employees have volunteered to be assigned to the unit to gain exposure to different parts of the business.[93] One recent study looked at almost 2,000 managers and executives using an outplacement company. Controlling for past salary, severance, and demographics, results demonstrated that displaced managers and executives participating in programs that demonstrated higher levels of outplacement support had a greater likelihood of reemployment, and had higher salaries in new jobs than individuals participating in programs with lower levels of outplacement support.[94]

It is also important to provide some assistance to survivors. Their attitudes will be influenced in large part by how fairly they thought the layoffs were done. Often the morale of those remaining hits an all-time low, confidence is shaken, and communication and trust are fragmented. In many cases, survivors will have increased workloads and job responsibilities due to the loss of personnel. They may experience work overload and stress, and could benefit from counseling and realistic information about the firm's future and their future role with the company.[95] It is critical that a firm address the needs of the remaining employees if it is to be competitive.

A number of recommendations have been offered for fostering the successful redeployment of displaced workers due to restructurings and downsizings. Figure 9-8 lists some of these suggestions.

Entrenched Employees

Due to the large number of organizational restructurings and downsizings, many employees stay with their organization to keep their jobs, but do not stay as committed or attached to them as their employers would like. In fact, Gallup reported that one of every three workers would choose a different career if given the chance to start over. These employees have become entrenched in their careers. They stay in the job because of their investments, psychological preservation, and a perception that there are few career opportunities. To eliminate the potentially adverse consequences of entrenchment, organizations can take some of the following steps:[96]

- Offer generous severance pay packages to fund employees' explorations into new careers.
- Encourage portability of benefits such as pension funds and accrued time off.
- Provide ongoing career counseling and outplacement assistance to attend classes while still employed.
- Offer tuition reimbursement and time off for employees to attend classes.
- Implement staged retirement programs.
- Give employees time to rotate to other positions in the organization to explore other career options.

FIGURE 9-8 Roles for Executives and Managers to Foster the Successful Redeployment of Displaced Workers

To build career resilience

- Enhance and maintain value of current employees (continuous learning environment)
- Foster a culture of entrepreneurship internal to the organization by rewarding creative new ideas and self-management
- Assign people to teams and work processes rather than to single, unifunctional jobs
- Adopt continuous improvement programs based on employee participation
- Partner with regional universities and colleges and government and community agencies to develop support systems for displaced workers
- Train people in areas that create or add value through problem solving and support
- Form new initiatives and joint ventures

To build career insight

- Offer assessment and feedback processes to help people better understand their strengths and weaknesses
- Provide problem-focused (in addition to symptom-focused) training to teach the unemployed job search skills, entrepreneurship, and realistic expectations
- Conduct human resource forecasting to inform and direct organizational initiatives. This entails conducting job analyses for positions that do not yet exist and communicating the results as input to individual and organizational planning. Moreover, scenarios of likely environmental trends and organizational strategies can be constructed as ways to envision different sorts of change and its implications
- Assist federal and state programs for reemployment and coping that recognize individual (e.g., age, profession, malleability) and regional economic factors

To build career identity

- Fund and implement outside redeployment efforts stemming from restructuring (outplacement)
- Support the professional development of all functional specialities; develop job families and career paths within speciality areas
- Train employees in multiple skills and use these different skills in role assignments
- Join with other organizations and agencies in the community to create new economic opportunities (e.g., participate in job fairs)

Source: M. London, "Redeployment and Continuous Learning in the 21st Century: Hard Lessons and Positive Examples from the Downsizing Era." *Academy of Management Executive,* 10, no. 4 (1996) p. 76.

- Allow employees to phase out of jobs and not automatically eliminate them.
- Emphasize the importance of learning and development throughout the organization.

- Encourage employees to think about career-planning issues.
- Extend portability of medical coverage and other insurances for 18–24 months.

Supervisors and Career Counseling

Supervisors are increasingly being called upon to play a greater role in managing the career progress of their employees. They may serve as coach, advisor, performance appraiser, and referral agent. In a profile of the superior CEO, working with people (coaching, growing and developing people, leading teams) was listed as one of the top eight qualities needed.[97] To be effective in these roles, they should be trained as career coaches and mentors to help subordinates develop and implement their career plans in one-on-one counseling sessions.[98] Further, they should be instructed on how to integrate counseling into their performance appraisal and selection activities. AT&T has one such program in place for training supervisors in career counseling, performance-appraisal skills, and mutual goal setting with subordinates.

Executive Coaching

Executive coaching has recently arisen as a popular method for career and leadership development of managers.[99] See the Web site of the International Coach Federation (www.coachfederation.org). Executive coaching is described as a practical, goal-focused form of personal one-to-one learning for executives.[100] An executive meets with a coach who may be an internal career counselor or an external consultant.

In the coaching session, the coach and executive typically discuss the results of a 360-degree assessment of the executive (see Chapter 7) or some other performance review, which describes his or her strengths and areas for improvement.[101] The coach works individually with the leader to improve performance, develop or refine behaviors, and devise strategies for enhancing his or her career and preventing derailment. Meetings are held to establish career development plans and to follow up and assist executives on their career progress.

Coaching has become popular because it does not require much of a disruption to the executive's schedule, and it provides individualized, targeted, flexible, just-in-time development for executives on the run.[102] Texas Commerce Bank uses coaches for its senior 25 executives. Since executive coaching is so new, few studies evaluating its effectiveness currently exist. One study revealed that participants in an executive coaching program viewed it as very valuable and that they had changed their behaviors. In another study, most executives rated their executive coaching experience as very

satisfactory. Most leaders like coaching because they receive direct one-on-one assistance from a respected person, they don't have to leave their offices, it fits within their time frames, and they can see fast results if they are dedicated to it.[103]

Programs for Women, Minorities, and Employees with Disabilities

With the increasing numbers of women, immigrants, minorities, and people with disabilities entering the workplace, employers have recognized the importance of assisting these employees with their career needs.[104] The primary issues facing employers are recruiting and selecting diverse employees, promoting them, and retaining them in the organization. To adhere to EEO or affirmative action guidelines, some organizations are supporting minority recruitment, selection, and training efforts (see Chapter 5). They also are providing additional feedback, educational opportunities, counseling, and career management seminars to meet the unique needs of these groups.[105] These practices are designed to help these employees compete for management positions.[106] For example, top managers at Xerox and Kodak encourage the development of networks and support groups for women and minority groups (e.g., African Americans, Hispanics). Avon has no glass ceiling since women are groomed for top jobs. As of 1997, four of the top eight officers were women, four of the 11-member board were women, and more than 40 percent of its global managers were women.[107]

Some firms (e.g., Corning, Wal-Mart, Gannett Company) have started tying managers' bonuses to their success at meeting EEO or upward mobility goals for women's progress.[108] At both Motorola and Procter & Gamble, executives are held accountable for recruiting and developing women and minorities.[109] Tenneco established a women's advisory council to help identify the barriers that kept women from advancing into management. As a result, more women were able to move into Tenneco's upper management ranks. Other companies, including Dow Chemical Company, Honeywell, Polaroid, and GE Silicone, also have solicited assistance and advice from women's groups in the recruitment, mentoring, and advancement of women.[110]

Catalyst is one of the most prominent nonprofit organizations called upon to assist firms in their efforts to capitalize on the talents of their female employees and maximize opportunities for women in management positions. Recently, they published a book on creating women's networks in organizations. They document the successful networking efforts by companies such as Dow Chemical, Bausch & Lomb, Kodak, and Kimberly-Clark.[111] Networks are an effective system for assisting employees with career issues and addressing their unique concerns (e.g., social isolation, discrimination, glass ceiling).[112] The benefits of these networks include serving as advisors to senior management and human resource staff regarding issues for the particular population (e.g., women, minorities), providing support, providing career development assistance, and helping the organization to change.[113]

Some firms have focused on trying to retain their female employees. One way that some have tried to do this is by showing a commitment to the health of their female employees. Each year, *Working Woman* magazine rates the healthiest companies for women. The best firms have implemented practices such as: increasing insurance coverage to help women affected by depression and providing employee assistance services; prenatal services; health resource centers; work-exercise programs; in vitro treatments; screenings for blood pressure, cholesterol, breast cancer, and osteoporosis; medical libraries; stress prevention programs; and counseling. Then companies have lowered their insurance costs because they prevented more serious illnesses from developing.

The so-called opt-out revolution is receiving a great deal of media attention. This is a term that describes the trend of highly trained and educated women, mostly mothers, choosing to drop out of the job market to devote more attention to the family. A recent review examines this trend and presents a "kaleidoscope" career model that fits concerns for life balance and challenge with the demands of parenting. "Like a kaleidoscope that produces changing patterns when the tube is rotated and its glass chips fall into new arrangements, women shift the pattern of their careers by rotating different aspects in their lives to arrange their roles and relationships in new ways."[114] The review also presents guidelines on how women can increase career success and how organizations can improve the workplace so as to attract and retain valuable women.

Programs for New Employees (Early-Career Issues)

When an employee first starts working in a company, he or she generally has been exposed to some type of recruitment effort and company orientation. Or if the employee has worked part-time for a company or served in an internship program, he or she has been socialized regarding the unique characteristics of the job and organization. These initial employment programs may be valuable mechanisms to familiarize the employee with the career policies and procedures of the organization.

Employee Orientation Programs

Orientation programs for new employees help reduce anxieties since they provide information on organizational policies, procedures, rules, work requirements, and sources of information. Orientation programs also may be used to educate employees about any career programs, career paths, and opportunities for advancement. For example, Texas Instruments has developed an orientation program to address the unique concerns of new employees regarding career options.[115] The program includes a realistic job preview, an introduction to the formal mentoring program, a bibliography of readings relevant to career planning, and a guideline for career planning based on a study of Texas Instrument employees.

Anticipatory Socialization Programs

Socialization programs (e.g., internships, cooperative education programs) are beneficial for individuals to develop accurate, realistic expectations about their chosen career field and about the world of work. Socialization through peer support in organizations and universities is also beneficial for reducing stress.[116] By working for an organization part-time or for several months, individuals may learn how well they are suited to the particular job or organization. This knowledge may help them gain a better sense of responsibility, maturity, and self-confidence about work. Frito-Lay, IBM, Procter & Gamble, and Saturn are some of the many companies that hire interns and then make permanent offers if those internships are successful experiences.

Realistic Recruitment

As discussed in Chapter 5, when job applicants are given a realistic, balanced, accurate view of the organization and the job (i.e., provided with positive and negative information), they experience less reality shock, dissatisfaction, and turnover.[117] This is true for new employees as well as current employees who are transferring to new jobs in the organization. To meet career development needs, job applicants should be informed in realistic job previews about the skills required of various positions in the organizations and their own readiness and aptitude for those positions. 360-degree performance feedback also could be used to provide them with information about their own skills relative to other jobs in the firm. These data should assist them in developing their future career goals and action plans.

Programs for Late Career and Retirement

In recent years, the number of older workers has increased because of the aging of the baby-boom generation. With the increasing corporate restructurings, many of these older employees have lost their jobs. Some firms have opted to use early retirement for their older employees rather than retraining and redeploying them. And more employees have been choosing to retire early. As a result, late-career and retirement issues have become increasingly important to organizations.[118]

Some organizations offer programs to help supervisors increase their awareness of issues facing late-career employees. It is critical that employers handle retirement issues effectively since they affect not only the retirees, but also the morale of the remaining staff. Generally, supervisors are instructed on the changing demographics of the workforce, laws regarding older employees, stereotypes and realities of the aging process, and strategies for dealing with the loss of older employees who retire (i.e., the loss in their departments of expertise and skills). Supervisors also may be taught to develop action plans for enhancing the performance of their older workers. These plans involve giving older workers more concrete feedback, allowing them to serve as mentors, and providing them with training and cross-training opportunities. It is important that managers help employees deal with career plateaus so they can continue to be challenged and productive.[119] It is also critical that older employees are aided in their transition to retirement. To do this, many companies have instituted retirement planning programs.

The focus of preretirement workshops is to help preretirees understand the life and career concerns they may face as they prepare for retirement. Topics that may be discussed include health, finances, making the transition from work to retirement status, safety, housing and location, legal affairs, time utilization, Social Security, second careers, use of leisure time, and problems of aging. Often, individual counseling and group workshops are used, and efforts are made to tailor the programs to the needs of the participants and their spouses. Another type of assistance given to preretirees may be for education such as the Retirement Education Assistance Plan available to potential retirees at IBM.

It is also important to offer flexible work schedules for late-career employees. Some do not want to quit their jobs but want to cut back the number of hours they work so they can enjoy their hobbies, go back to school, travel, or spend more time with their families. Polaroid gave its older employees the option to share jobs rather than be laid off. Many companies, such as McDonald's, Home Shopping Network, Aetna, Prudential, GEICO, and Monsanto, have hired older employees to work part-time or for temporary jobs. This has been beneficial due to the critical shortage of young people to hire. In fact, a study by the Society for Human Resource Management found that over 80 percent of firms that aggressively recruited and hired older employees found them to be more amenable than younger individuals for working part-time.[120] As employees age, it is going to be imperative for organizations in the United States, and in other parts of the world, to make good use of the expertise and talent residing in their older employees if they are to remain competitive.

Programs to Assist Employed Spouses and Parents

Society has seen increasing numbers of working mothers and two-income households. Recent reports have indicated that 90 percent of working adults expressed a concern about not spending enough time with their family. In addition the total number of hours worked by employees have increased continuously over the last 20 years.[121] In recent years, organizations have been much more interested in developing family-responsive policies. These are programs designed to alleviate individual conflict between work and family. Several organizational trends in these practices are

- Increasing use of flexible work schedules, and training for managers in implementing the schedules.
- More openings of on-site child-care centers.
- A greater number of companies (e.g., Xerox, Motorola) setting aside monies employees can use for paying child-care costs or buying a first home.
- Greater use of paid leaves for fathers and adoptive parents.
- More programs that set goals for advancing women into senior management positions, and increasing numbers of companies holding managers accountable for meeting these goals.
- Continued support and funding for American Business Collaboration for Quality Dependent Care, which is a $100 million, six-year commitment that participating companies have made to improve and expand child and elder care in their communities.

In recent years, organizations have become more interested in helping individuals to face demands from their work and family roles. Employers are beginning to realize that these individuals may experience role conflict and difficulties dealing with travel, child care, household tasks, job transfers, and relocations, and may have trouble determining priorities for their various roles and responsibilities. This may be especially true for dual-career couples since each partner has a high level of commitment to his or her career. In fact, it was reported that couples prior to having children and couples without children reported having the happiest marriages.[122] Couples with children reported the least contentment when their children were teenagers.

Policies on Hiring Couples and Relocation Assistance

Many employees, particularly members of dual-career couples, have expressed less willingness to accept relocation offers from their employers. In a large-scale study of U.S. firms, spouse willingness to relocate was shown to be the most important factor related to employee willingness to relocate.[123] It is not surprising then that some organizations have already begun offering relocation assistance to the spouses of their employees.[124] Companies, however, vary in the amount and type of assistance provided to spouses and employees considering relocations. It ranges from no assistance at all to locating jobs for spouses. One study found that 50 percent of U.S. firms provide job-related assistance to a "trailing spouse." For example, Unisys pays up to $500 to a spouse to help with résumé writing and job hunting.[125] Motorola provides assistance to dual-career couples by finding jobs for spouses of employees who take international assignments. Both the spouse and the expatriate were found to view the policy positively.[126] Johnson & Johnson offers personal counseling and job search information to relocating families. Some companies (ConAgra, Burlington Northern Santa Fe Railway) have hired relocation consultants and firms to assist them in planning the relocation of large numbers of employees. They also involved employees throughout the planning process.[127]

Some firms have altered their policy on nepotism to allow hiring both spouses. They may still, however, keep the rule that an employee cannot work under the direct supervision of his or her spouse. There are a number of benefits to hiring both spouses including lower recruiting and relocation costs for the employer, and it encourages employees to remain with the firm or to accept intraorganizational moves or transfers. It also helps employers who are trying to hire for branches in a remote geographical area. Of course, one downside is that if one of the spouses wants to leave the firm, the other may also leave.

Work–Family Programs

Organizations are becoming more involved in designing programs to help employees manage their work–family role conflict by providing a place and procedure for discussing conflicts and coping strategies.[128] Organizations also are changing their practices for recruitment, travel, transfers, promotions, scheduling hours, and benefits to meet the needs of the larger numbers of dual-career couples. For example, General Electric and Procter & Gamble require fewer geographic moves in order to advance.

DuPont has been very active in providing assistance to their more than 3,500 dual-career couples and has developed more flexible employment plans to accommodate the family demands of both male and female employees. DuPont also trains its supervisors to be more sensitive to family issues, allows longer parental leave for fathers and mothers, and has instituted adjustable work schedules. Mobil Oil provides flexible work schedules, a proposed part-time option, childbirth and other leaves, and a national network of child care information.

Flexible Work Arrangements

Employers have been adopting a number of flexible work arrangements in order to assist employees. Some of these include flextime, job sharing, part-time work, compressed workweeks, temporary work, and work at home (telecommuting). These programs enable employees to address their work and family concerns and reduce their potential stress or conflict between their various life roles. Of the 100 rated the best for working mothers, 54 have established training programs to educate managers on how to implement alternative work arrangements. Some of these companies include Aetna, TRW, Texas Instruments, SAS Institute, Sara Lee Corporation, and Prudential.

Telecommuting

As discussed in Chapter 5, telecommuting is growing in popularity,[129] although research on its effects is mixed.

Recent research suggests a curvilinear relationship between the extent of telecommuting and job satisfaction. Satisfaction appears to plateau at more extensive levels of telecommuting, but task interdependence and job discretion are related to satisfaction. It is estimated that between 7.5 million and 15 million workers now telecommute three to four days a week.[130]

A third of the companies from one survey offered employees the option of working at home, and many gave them modern-equipped computers linking them to the office. Home-based work is used primarily by firms in industries such as education, professional work, consulting, business, repair, and social-service occupations. Gandalf Technologies, a computer networking company, allows employees to telecommute from home several days a week. AT&T lets many of its employees telecommute at least part of the week from home via computer. Some difficulties with telecommuting are communication problems with other employees, limited access to necessary supplies and equipment, and family interruptions. Another issue is how to supervise such workers. Many United States companies now have, on-call operations that are handled by part-time employees working at home.[131] Today, many of these problems are getting resolved due to a greater reliance on technology (e.g., Internet) for getting work done.

There are a number of benefits to telecommuting. For instance, IBM has saved considerable money on office space by going mobile through telecommuting, "hoteling" (being assigned to a desk via a reservations system), and "hot desking" (several people using the same desk at different times). About 10,000 employees share offices with four people on average. Many studies show that people's strategic planning skills go up when they telecommute since they have uninterrupted time to think clearly. In fact, it has been estimated that people who work at home are 5 to 20 percent more productive because they have fewer distractions.[132] It may be important to provide orientation or training to educate employees and managers on the rules of telecommuting.

Maternity and Paternity Leave

With the passage in 1993 of the Family and Medical Leave Act (FMLA), employers with more than 50 employees are required to allow 12 weeks of unpaid leave from work for either parent following the birth, adoption, or severe illness of a child. By 1996, more companies were offering financial aid for *adoption*. Two-thirds of the top-rated 100 companies for working mothers provided this benefit (e.g., Eli Lilly offers up to $10,000).

Despite these advances, some unresolved issues and obstacles facing pregnant employees still exist. With pressures at work, they may be rushed by their bosses through maternity leave or denied comparable jobs or promotions when they return to their jobs.[133] The workplace culture may emphasize overtime work to such a degree that employees are discouraged from taking advantage of maternity or paternity leave policies. In addition, employees may be anxious about taking time off due to fears of losing their jobs in this era of downsizings.

Job pressures also bear great risks for pregnant women. One study found that women lawyers who worked more than 45 hours a week were three times more likely to experience a miscarriage in the first trimester of pregnancy than were women who worked less than 35 hours a week. Pregnant employees also may face stereotypes from their colleagues who believe they will lose interest in their jobs or quit. But a study of 140 bank employees found that their performance actually increased during pregnancy. In addition, it was noted that 80 percent of women return to work after maternity leave. Cigna HealthCare in Hartford, Connecticut, developed a training program to debunk stereotypes about pregnant women and to help managers be supportive in dealing with pregnant employees. A few tips follow:[134]

- Discuss and reach agreement with a pregnant employee on how her work will be covered during her leave.
- Discuss with co-workers worries they have about covering for a woman on leave. Make sure the work is distributed fairly.
- Be patient with new mothers' efforts to balance their expanded responsibilities.
- Weigh short-term scheduling hassles against the long-term benefits of retaining an employee.

Child Care and Elder Care Services

Today, employees must concern themselves with child care while they are at work. In addition, many are discovering that they need to care for their parents or older members of their families. *Elder care* may be of great concern to employees, particularly if their parents suffer from health problems (e.g., Alzheimer's disease, heart conditions, depression). Firms providing elder care as a benefit to employees include Gannett Co., First Union Corporation, General Motors Corporation, Eddie Bauer, The DuPont Merck Pharmaceutical Company, Corning, and Deloitte & Touche LLP.[135]

Generally, employers find it beneficial to provide child care assistance to employees. They may find greater morale, easier recruitment of parents, lower turnover, and tax savings.[136] When employers assisted employees with child care or elder care concerns, these employees did not have to use company time to make phone calls, visit doctors, and so on. DuPont reported savings of $6.78 for every dollar spent on resource and referral, and Aetna reported $3.59 in savings per dollar spent.[137] Marriott reported savings in reduced turnover with its "Associate Resource Line," a toll-free hot line with bilingual social workers who provide advice on child care and elder care issues among other things.

Some employers (e.g., Bankers Trust New York Corporation, Merrill Lynch & Co.) have opened backup centers to help employees who run into problems with their child care arrangements.[138] First Tennessee Bank opened a center for mildly sick children to cut down on employee absences when parents had to stay home with sick children. The center has saved the company considerable money. Other companies have sponsored public schools at their work sites. American Bankers Insurance Group spent $2.4 million to build a satellite public school on its 84-acre corporate campus. The company paid $146,000 in 1996 toward the school's operation. Parents can visit their children at lunchtime and after school. The company believes it has seen some payback: the turnover rate has been reduced from 13 percent to 5 percent for employees with children in the school.[139]

Effectiveness of Programs

Businesses that offer flexible schedules, part-time or alternative work options, work–family conflict seminars, and telecommuting are not just being nice to their employees. These programs have an impact on the bottom line. They have been shown to increase employees' loyalty, thereby reducing turnover and absenteeism and increasing organizational productivity.[140] One survey of 2,376 pregnant women in 80 communities across the United States found that those in the most accommodating companies in terms of health insurance, sick days, job-protected leave, flexible scheduling, and supervisor understanding were more satisfied with their jobs, took fewer sick days, worked more on their own time, worked later into their pregnancies, and were more likely to return to work.[141]

One survey of 75 large corporations found increased commitment to the job, higher morale, higher productivity, superior job performance, and reduced absenteeism.[142] Programs such as flextime, job sharing, and part-time work seem to be the most effective and least costly in terms of keeping employees and increasing productivity. Neuville Industries, a 575-employee sock manufacturer in North Carolina, found that with its work–family programs (on-site day care center, flextime, emergency backup child care) turnover was half (45 percent a year) the industry average (80 to 100 percent at other plants). At Aetna Health Plans, telecommuting has increased productivity of claims processed by 29 percent. The firm also is saving $12,000 per year in office space. Deloitte & Touche allowed reduced hours for partners and the opportunity for employees to be made partner while working part-time, and this has decreased turnover 8 percent between 1993 and 1995. Also, more women were made partners.

Career Development Issues with Teams

More U.S. firms are using teams as the unit of work. Much discussion has centered on the organizational practices that are needed with teams (e.g., selection systems, training programs, performance appraisal systems, rewards).

Much less attention, however, has been devoted to the career development issues relevant to teams. Teams, however, can be quite important to the career development and progress of members. Members can serve as role models for one another and teach each other new skills and competencies. This should lead to greater staffing flexibility for the organization. Similarly, teams can identify training needs for members. For instance, at Cadillac, each plant and staff unit has a training needs analysis that specifies the KSAs needed to meet quality goals.[143] In addition, rotating assignments among members enables individuals to gain a diverse set of skills. Further, by evaluating team member performance, developmental plans can be established for each member. Teams can serve as a powerful way in which individuals enhance their career-related skills.

Repatriates[*]

One recent article on the "boundaryless" trend[144] examined the perceived impact of an international assignment on career advancement and the effectiveness of expatriate career management systems. The majority of expatriates viewed their international assignment as an opportunity for professional development and career advancement but with skepticism that the assignment would be helpful for advancement within their own companies. As we discussed in Chapter 8, more organizations have been offering training for expatriates to prepare them for overseas assignments. While this is important, it is also critical to offer some developmental opportunities for repatriates to prepare them for their return back to the firm after an overseas assignment. It has been estimated that 15 to 40 percent of repatriates leave the company within 12 to 18 months of their return from overseas assignments. Many organizations find themselves losing valuable, highly skilled employees simply because the repatriation process was handled poorly.[145] While more commonplace in Japanese and European firms, repatriate programs often do not exist in American firms. One survey revealed that only 30 percent of American companies reported any type of repatriation program for managers reentering the domestic organization.[146] This may explain why American managers who are repatriates have more difficulties adjusting than their Japanese and European counterparts.[147]

Often the difficulties associated with reentry are not anticipated by an employee, his or her family, or the organization. Most American repatriates experience considerable adjustment problems and "re-entry shock" upon their return to their firm.[148] They report having difficulty getting back to high levels of productivity. If they have been abroad for a long time, they may be technologically obsolete.[149] Problems often occur because the organization does not realize that the repatriate needs assistance in readapting to work-related and nonwork-related routines. Because the person is coming "home," issues such as reverse culture shock often are not addressed.[150] The foreign experience may have changed the employee's attitudes and beliefs in a profound way. The changes may have occurred so subtly that the employee does not initially recognize these internal changes. Repatriates often are not given enough time to become reacclimated to life in the United States. Some experts state that it may take as long as 18 months for them to readjust.[151] Repatriates often report feeling disoriented from their communities and co-workers.

Repatriates report frustration with their organizations' limited attempts to place them back in permanent assignments.[152] Many complain that they are penalized for taking international assignments because they are placed in lower-level positions than their peers when they return. They may find that they have been passed over for promotion opportunities. In one survey of 56 U.S.-based multinational firms, 56 percent said a foreign assignment was detrimental or immaterial in one's career, 47 percent said the repatriates are not guaranteed jobs with the organization upon completion of the assignment, and 65 percent reported that the foreign assignment was not integrated into their overall career planning. In addition, only 20 percent considered the organization's repatriation policies adequate to meet repatriates' needs.[153] In a more recent survey, expatriates reported low satisfaction and serious concerns for their company's repatriation program and policies. They experience major setbacks in their careers upon their return home. This is not surprising since most organizations do not fully utilize the new skills and experiences that repatriates bring back to their firms. Managers often are not sure how to establish career paths or ladders for those taking an international assignment.[154]

The following is a list of problems repatriates may face within their companies:[155]

- Feeling out of place in the corporate culture of the home office.
- Receiving little, if any, guidance regarding the career opportunities available upon their return.
- Being passed over for promotions that go to co-workers who did not go abroad.
- Receiving lower salaries than they were while they were on the international assignment.
- Not being able to effectively utilize the new skills that were acquired while abroad; not receiving support for using those skills.
- Not receiving recognition for the work that was completed during the international assignment.
- Losing the social status that was obtained while being a key employee at the foreign office.

For a repatriation program to be effective, it must be part of an overall organizational philosophy that values continued productive employment of international

---

[*]Contributed by Sabine Maetzke and Joyce E. A. Russell.

employees. The organization must be committed to addressing all phases of repatriation beginning with a pretraining program to prepare employees before they leave on their assignments. The career or training staff must be willing to take on the role as a "repatriation advocate" to help the company and the employees. They also can keep records of the international assignments and reasons employees leave assignments early or leave the company early. In addition, many companies have set up permanent offices in other countries. Information should be collected that can address cultural, communication, and job-related issues faced by most employees in that region of the world. Linkages between the type of assignment held and the difficulties experienced with returning to the home office should be documented. By using this information, the career staff can more accurately determine the specific career needs repatriates need.

For a repatriate transition to be successful, several career development practices are recommended:[156]

- A year before they return they should begin a repatriation program.
- Once back to the firm, retraining and reorientation should be provided to help them learn of any new changes in their job, department, corporate culture, or organization.

- Repatriates should be given opportunities to use the experiences and skills they gained from the international assignments.
- They should be given definite assignments, and these assignments should be clearly linked to their career paths.
- Mentors should be provided to repatriates to help them cope with their transition.
- Ongoing career management should be provided to them.
- Assistance in housing and compensation should be provided to ease their transition.

Taken together, these practices should reduce the stress and disorientation experienced by repatriates as well as improve the quality and quantity of their performance. Additionally, repatriates may become more committed to the firm and opt to remain there.

A 2004 study[157] showed that while operational technical sophistication, use of standard practices at home, technical orientation of the individual, and increased responsibility and promotion all positively contributed to expatriate satisfaction, repatriate satisfaction was mainly influenced by the difficulty in finding a suitable position upon repatriation. The technical orientation of the individual, especially, had important implications for repatriation success.

SUMMARY

Career development programs must be integrated with and supported by the existing HR programs in the organization if they are to be successful. Career programs and HR programs are linked to the degree they help each other meet individuals' growth needs and organizations' staffing needs. 3M has established a career resources department to better integrate its career programs, performance appraisal process, and HR planning systems. Similarly, Boeing developed a program called CAREERS, which is linked with its other HR programs.[158] Individuals should refer to performance appraisal information and illustrations of organizational career paths to help them in career planning. This information may help employees evaluate their strengths and weaknesses and set goals based on possible career alternatives. Supervisors also should be able to use performance appraisal data to assist employees in developing realistic career plans. In Coca-Cola's career program, managers are given training to provide such guidance.[159]

Career or job changes by employees should be based on an understanding of organizations' job descriptions, job posting systems, and selection policies. The continued development of employees and rewards for their performances should be founded on organizational training and development systems and compensation plans. Finally, organizational career information and planning systems should be developed to be consistent with the organizations' strategic plans and existing forecasting systems, skills inventories, and succession plans.

Coordinated, integrated efforts of the career staff, employees, managers, and organizations are the key to success in career development. Career development programs must be concerned with organizational and individual effectiveness over the short and long run. It is the responsibility of the career staff to work with management to ensure that career programs are integrated with the HR functions and are routinely evaluated. It is, however, the responsibility of management to view career development as necessary to an effective HR system. Managers must be willing to work with career professionals to formulate new strategies for career development and to provide support to them as they design and implement new career development programs.[160] Finally, it is the responsibility of the individual to create his or her own career opportunities. The following quote provides some advice for individuals as they attempt to navigate their way through their careers:

> Careers in today's world are what you make them. The apparent boundaries in a department are also your platforms for further opportunity. Organize your employment around your professional and social networks. . . . Don't wait for formal training, but make sure the colleagues you surround yourself with sustain new learning for you, and try to reciprocate for them. Look after yourself, but don't be afraid to trust and to build trust around you. Remember that who you are and what you achieve will always be embedded in your relationships with others.[161]

DISCUSSION QUESTIONS

1. Should organizations adopt formal career development policies and programs? How do these programs affect their ability to be flexible in terms of staffing? How do they influence their ability to recruit employees?

2. What is the role of EEO in career development? What is the role of the training or career staff in designing and implementing career development programs?

3. Recently, the role of managers has changed and today more are being called to be career "coaches" for their employees. What suggestions would you give to a manager about what that new role involves?

4. Describe several career development programs that would be useful for individuals planning on making a career or job change. Suppose they have worked in one field for 10 years (e.g., engineering) and have decided to switch jobs (e.g., teaching or management). How should they prepare for this change?

5. What is the value of self-assessment for individual career planning and organizational career management? Why should employees seek feedback from others regarding their job performance and career plans? How could performance appraisal information (360-degree appraisal) be used to assist individuals in career development?

6. Why is it important to integrate career development programs with other programs in organizations (e.g., performance appraisal, training, selection, compensation)? Offer some suggestions for how this can be done.

7. Should organizations make special efforts to deal with career-family issues through part-time work, job sharing, flextime, relocation assistance, and other programs? Should they also have special programs in place for employees who are not married or parents?

8. With the increasing number of organizations experiencing downsizings and layoffs, it has become critical that they have career programs in place to assist outplaced employees. What suggestions would you offer for the types of assistance that are needed in outplacement programs?

9. Companies are increasingly expecting their employees to take international assignments, and yet they are not providing much career development for them while they are away and when they return. Why is this important to do? What recommendations would you offer?

10. How can companies use career programs to retain their most talented employees? What career programs would keep you employed at a particular firm?

Compensating and Managing Human Resources

10

COMPENSATION: BASE PAY AND FRINGE BENEFITS*

OVERVIEW

The Tribune Company developed a new performance management system, closely following the prescriptions provided in Chapter 7. At an orientation session in which the new system was introduced to management, the first several questions had to do with the relationship between the new system and pay. Pay is very important to people and very important to organizations. Research on high-performance work systems indicates that characteristics of a firm's compensation system are strongly related to corporate financial performance.[1]

The term **compensation** refers to all forms of financial returns and tangible benefits that employees receive as part of an employment relationship. As the business environment becomes increasingly complex and global, the challenge to create and maintain effective compensation programs, given cost constraints, also requires greater professional expertise, organizational understanding, creativity, and vision than ever before.

During the last decade, three key trends in compensation have occurred. First, there has been a dramatic increase in the diversity of compensation strategies and practices. Not too long ago, employees received a base salary (which the organization probably described as being "competitive") and a set of preestablished benefits (which the organization probably described as being "comprehensive"). Today, firms are providing variable pay, hiring bonuses, lump-sum recognition bonuses, group incentive plans, broad-based success-sharing programs, plus a broader and more flexible selection of employee benefits.

The second noteworthy trend has been a significant rise in pay inequity.[2] In the last decade, chief executives' average compensation has more than tripled. The average corporate chieftain now earns in a single day more than the typical U.S. worker earns in a year. According to one expert, "U.S. CEOs are far and away the highest paid CEOs in the world. Yet, from a long-term perspective, and compared to CEOs in other countries, they cannot be considered the very best performers."[3] In 1974, the CEO of a large American corporation earned an estimated 35 times what a factory worker earned. By 1990, that figure had increased to 120 times; by 1998 that figure increased to 326 times; by 2004, the gap was 431 to 1. Of course, this increase far exceeded the average growth in corporate revenues, growth in value, or the cost of living. In fact, a study of 1,500 U.S. companies found that, between 1992 and 2002, every 1 percent increase in total compensation for each of the top five executives predicted a .22 percent decrease in shareholder return over the next year, and a .12 percent decline over the coming three years.[4] Pay increases for CEOs appeared to be coming under more scrutiny by late 2001, as the economy slowed and as corporate scandals involving executive behavior and accounting irregularities came to light. In the first quarter of 2004, 40 percent of the proposals to be voted on at annual shareholder meetings related to executive

*Contributed by Christine M. Hagan.

pay—a 19 percent increase over the prior two-year period. Even so, in 2004, CEO pay climbed 12 percent while the wages for average American workers increased by an estimated 2 percent.[5]

Third, pay programs are increasingly being used to communicate major change and realignment in organizations, particularly during and after major downsizing and reengineering efforts. As IBM began to rebuild itself in the late 1990s, one of the key tools for change was a complete redesign of the pay system. It scrapped its traditional approach to evaluating work and its pay grade structure. It reduced the number of different jobs from 5,000 to fewer than 1,200. It significantly increased the percentage of an individual's pay that was directly related to performance and created pay-at-risk programs at all levels in the organization (a big first for IBM!).[6] Although HR and compensation experts continued to design and develop the framework of the pay program, significant day-to-day administration of the program was transferred to line managers, making compensation more of a management tool than an HR program. Compensation experts have traditionally argued the importance of directly aligning business strategies and compensation programs. This past decade, however, has seen a rethinking of the role that compensation programs play in supporting, communicating, and even leading the way to new organizational values and performance norms.

As a result, compensation programs are in a state of transition. Organizations are experimenting with different types of structures; they are allocating money differently to programs; they are questioning the traditional (rather rigid) approach to compensation program design; and they are looking for innovative ways to "get more" for their investment in compensation.

Does pay matter? Research suggests that reward systems can influence a company's success in three ways.[7] First, the amount of pay and the way it is packaged and delivered to employees can motivate, energize, and direct behavior. IBM's compensation program redesign (described above) was directly targeted at changing the way IBMers thought about their work, focused their energies, and directed their performance. Second, compensation plays an important role in an organization's ability to attract and retain qualified, high-performance workers. Unless applicants find job offers to be appropriate in terms of the amount and type of compensation, they may not consider employment with a particular firm. In other words, compensation strategies and practices can shape the composition of a workforce and the competencies and capabilities they will bring to the organization and ultimately influence firm performance level and effectiveness. This is especially important for firms operating in tight, high-expertise labor markets. Microsoft, for example, sets out to hire a certain percentage of the top technical talent that graduates each year. In addition to investing heavily in recruiting and

selection activities, they offer job candidates a generous sign-on bonus, a competitive base salary, stock options, and a flexible benefits programs, which allows individuals to select the programs and coverage that they both need and value most.

Finally, the cost of compensation can influence firm success. On average, the overall cost of labor is estimated to be 70 percent of a firm's total costs.[8] Within the United States, firms that wish to pursue a strategy based on cost leadership must find ways to reduce those costs without sacrificing quality. Organizations that compete in global marketplaces have greater cost-competitor pressures. The average hourly wage for a U.S. production worker in 2000 was $19.86, which ranked 12th highest among the 29 industrialized countries of the world. In Europe, the average cost of a production worker in 2000 was $18.50 (in U.S. dollars). In Mexico, the average in 2000 was $2.46.[9]

In summary, then, the strategy and structure of compensation programs have important implications for businesses and their ability to create and sustain competitive advantage.

Does compensation matter to individual workers? Recent discussions suggest that money motivates people on two basic dimensions. The instrumental meaning of money relates directly to what money buys: better houses, better educations for children, better vacations, clothes, and cars. The symbolic meaning of money concerns how wealth is viewed by ourselves and within our society in general. In the United States, "rich" is usually equated with "successful," "intelligent," "diligent," and "highly motivated," while "poor" tends to be equated with "failure," "unmotivated," "uneducated," perhaps "lazy" and "slovenly." One recent discussion of the issue pointed to all the money-oriented slang expressions used in our culture as an indication of the value of material possessions: "put your money where your mouth is," "crime doesn't pay," "paying the piper," "hitting pay dirt," "you get what you pay for," and "there is no free lunch."[10]

In job situations, money motivates behavior when it rewards people in relation to their performance or contributions, when it is perceived as being fair and equitable, and when it provides rewards that employees truly value.[11] Recent research supports the belief that U.S. workers prefer pay that is based on their own performance—not the performance of the team, group, or company. In one particular study, employees reporting the strongest preference for individualized rewards were also the highest-performing employees.[12] Research also indicates that employee satisfaction with pay is correlated with organizational commitment and trust in management, while it is inversely related to absenteeism and lateness, seeking alternative employment opportunities, terminating employment with the organization, pro-union voting, and incidents of theft.[13] It is also interesting to note that the particular components of pay have different value to different people. For example, research indicates that younger people tend to focus predominantly on cash compensation. As people age, however, their preference tends to shift to benefits and workplace flexibility.[14] It should be no surprise that life stage, career stage, and individual circumstances create differences in compensation preferences.

What makes an employee satisfied with pay? First of all, research indicates that individuals differ in the way in which they conceptualize pay satisfaction.[15] Research also indicates that pay satisfaction is a function of the comparisons of an individual's input–outcome ratio with his or her perceptions about the input–outcome ratios of referent others. In other words, people compare themselves to others focusing on two variables: inputs and outcomes. Inputs refer to individuals' characteristics (e.g., education, previous work experience, special licenses), effort (e.g., how long they persist in solving a problem), and performance (e.g., number of units produced). Outcomes are what people get out of their jobs (e.g., pay, promotion, recognition). It's important to note that these comparisons are based on perceptions, rather than on any objective, or quantifiable, measures of actual inputs and outcomes. Also important is that these judgments are made in terms of ratios—that is, relationships of "equal to," "greater than," or "less than." Pay satisfaction occurs when people perceive that they are paid appropriately in relation to others. When employees feel underpaid, they are dissatisfied and may withhold effort or engage in the negative behaviors mentioned above. What happens when these comparisons suggest that a worker is overpaid? Originally, researchers hypothesized that individuals would feel guilty and would work harder or smarter in order to close the gap. More recent evidence suggests that employees whose comparisons and perceptions indicate that they are overpaid tend to rethink their comparisons in order to find a more equitable balance.

Does compensation matter at the societal level? Over the course of history, societies that produced more also enjoyed higher standards of living. This means that its citizens enjoyed higher qualities of life, including better transportation systems, higher levels of education, more luxuries, better health care, and more time off.[16] In addition, however, governments tend to use such standards of living as platforms for social change. Legislation such as the Fair Labor Standards Act (which includes the minimum wage and child labor rules), the Employee Retirement Income Security Act (ERISA), the Equal Pay Act (EPA), the Pregnancy Discrimination Act, and the Age Discrimination in Employment Act (ADEA) are aimed at ensuring that people are treated justly and that the poorer and less powerful members of society are protected from flagrant abuse. Former President Bill Clinton championed legislation to limit the tax deductibility of excessive executive compensation.

Remember that organizations deduct the compensation they pay to employees as a "business expense" when they calculate their taxes. Excessive compensation to high-level employees, then, actually reduces the amount of taxes paid by a corporation. Who makes up the shortfall? Clinton's law limited an organization's deduction to $1 million for the compensation it paid to any individual in any year unless the pay was specifically and explicitly based on performance. Considering the continued escalation of executive compensation even after that law was passed, some argue today that the law should specifically exclude the deductibility of *any* compensation to an individual above a certain dollar amount per year, regardless of the basis for the payment.[17]

At the same time, many argue that the relatively high cost of U.S. labor, in general, is the principal reason that the United States has trouble competing globally in certain industries. Some assert that industry setbacks can be traced to product price increases necessitated by the unreasonable wage and benefits demands of its workers.

In summary, then, an effective compensation system typically has the following characteristics:

1. It enables an organization to attract and retain qualified, competent workers.
2. It motivates employee performance, fosters a feeling of equity, and provides direction to their efforts.
3. It supports, communicates, and reinforces an organization's culture, values, and competitive strategy.
4. Its cost structure reflects the organization's ability to pay.
5. It complies with government regulations.

Compensation is divided up into two parts. **Cash compensation** is the direct pay provided by employers for work performed. Cash compensation has two elements: base pay (e.g., hourly or weekly wages plus overtime pay, shift differential, uniform allowances) and pay contingent on performance (e.g., merit increases, incentive pay, bonuses, gainsharing). **Fringe compensation** refers to employee benefits programs. Fringe compensation also has two dimensions: legally-required programs (e.g., social security, workers' compensation) and discretionary programs (e.g., health benefits, pension plans, paid time off, tuition reimbursement). This chapter covers base pay programs and fringe benefits. Pay that is contingent on performance will be covered in Chapter 11.

As indicated earlier, compensation systems are in a state of transition. Traditional designs focus primarily on attracting and retaining qualified workers and complying with government regulations. Newer pay models balance these concerns with increased attention to motivating and directing performance and to aligning pay with achieving important firm effectiveness goals.

OBJECTIVES

After reading this chapter, you should be able to

1. *Understand the traditional model for base pay programs.*
2. *Know the basic approaches to job evaluation.*
3. *Know the contemporary trends in compensation.*
4. *Know the role of government in compensation.*
5. *Understand the various forms of fringe compensation, including the government-mandated programs.*
6. *Understand the different types of pension plans.*
7. *Understand the complexities of international compensation.*

CASH COMPENSATION: BASE PAY

The traditional model for structuring base pay programs has existed in its relatively unchanged form for more than 50 years.[18] In the 1800s business owners knew their employees, their performance, and their financial needs, and individual pay was established on that basis. As businesses grew, bureaucracies were created to provide structure, organization, and direction. Professional managers replaced business owners, while rapidly growing hierarchies distanced them from most workers. Efficiency and effectiveness became the most important business objectives. In the late 1800s, Frederick Taylor designed a formal, systematic way of assigning pay to jobs while helping a steel company identify methods for improving productivity. His methodology came to be called **job evaluation.**

In the following sections, we will describe the traditional approach to base pay administration, examine some recent trends in base pay program design, and discuss the government's role in shaping employer practices in the cash compensation area. Figure 10-1 depicts and summarizes the steps involved in creating and installing a traditional compensation plan.

THE TRADITIONAL APPROACH TO COMPENSATION

What Is Internal Equity?

Job evaluation is defined as the process of assessing the value of each job in relation to other jobs in an organization. Traditional compensation programs use job evaluation to create **internal equity** among jobs. Internal equity means that individual employees perceive that their position is treated fairly within a pay program in relation to other jobs in the organization.

Job evaluation focuses on the duties and responsibilities assigned to a *job*. It's important to note that traditional job evaluation does not directly consider the credentials or characteristics of the *person* who occupies the job, or the quality or quantity of the individual's performance.

Traditional job evaluation is described as an objective procedure that measures the complexity of the work, the amount of responsibility, and the level of effort required of each position in relation to other positions in the organization. Traditional job evaluation typically results in a hierarchy of jobs ranked in order of their relative value to the firm.

Traditional job evaluation typically involves three steps. During step one, job analysis is conducted. You will recall from the discussion in Chapter 4 that job analysis is the process of collecting and evaluating relevant information about jobs. During this step, job descriptions are usually drafted (or updated) and job specifications (KASOCs) are identified. See Chapter 4 for a full discussion of the methods and techniques for collecting information about job analysis. Step two involves actually rating the job. Once again, you may recall from Chapter 4 that some standardized approaches to job analysis, particularly O*NET and the Position Analysis Questionnaire provide information relating to compensation. However, most organizations use some form of job evaluation specifically developed for use in determining pay. Step three involves carefully reviewing the job evaluation results. This is typically done by arranging jobs in hierarchical order using the job evaluation results. At this point, it is important to study the evaluations in relation to one another. Consider this something of a "sore thumbing" process that looks at the final results of the job evaluation and identifies positions that don't appear to fit best where the job evaluation plan has placed them. This is also the stage in which evaluators should try to identify judgmental biases that may have crept into the evaluation process.

Job Evaluation Methods

Three basic job evaluation approaches are most common: job ranking, job classification, and point-factor plans. Each of these methods is described and explained below. A summary of the approaches is provided in Figure 10-2.

The oldest, fastest, and simplest method of job evaluation, **job ranking** involves placing jobs in order from most valuable (or most important or most difficult) to least valuable (or least important or least difficult) using a single factor such as job complexity or the importance of the job to the firm's competitive advantage. This method typically looks at each job as a whole and does not examine the tasks that make up the job. Although it is the simplest method, ranking is seldom the recommended approach.[19] Typically, the ranking factor is not well-defined so that the resultant hierarchy is very difficult to explain to employees. In addition, since the approach focuses on the total job, often the highest-level duty becomes the basis for the evaluation. Finally, the ranking approach provides no information concerning *how much* more valuable one job is in relation to another, or how the KASOCs of one job relate to those of another. This could

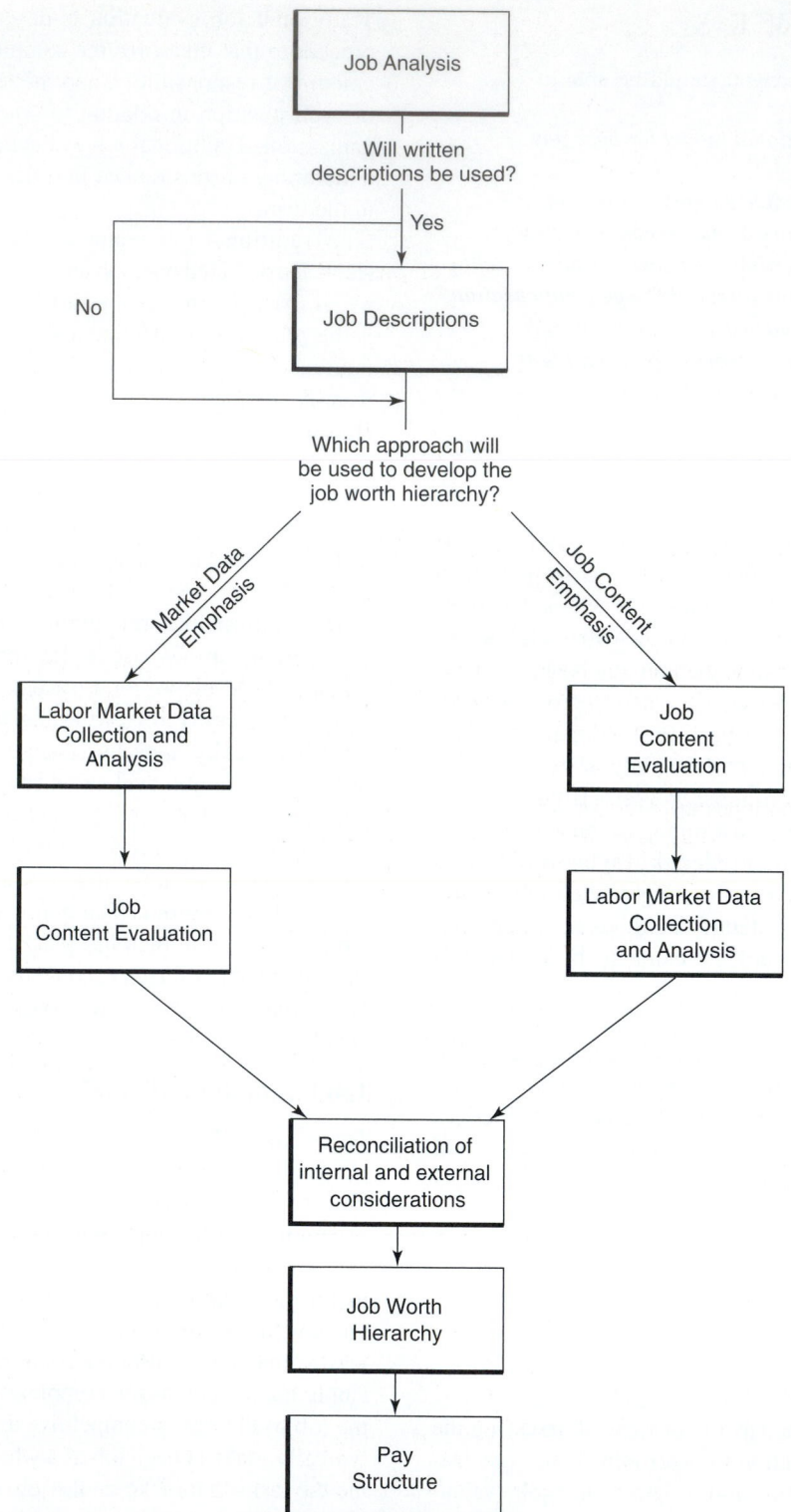

Figure 10-1   The Traditional Approach to Compensation

Source: Reprinted from "Elements of Sound Base Pay Administration," 2nd edition © 1998, with permission from WorldatWork, 14040 N. Northsight Blvd., Scottsdale, AZ 85260; phone (877) 951-9191; fax (480) 483-8352; www.worldatwork.org. © 2005 WorldatWork. Unauthorized reproduction or distribution is strictly prohibited.

	FIGURE 10-2	Summary of Three Traditional Job Evaluation Methods		

Method	Procedure	Advantages	Disadvantages
Ranking	Rank order whole jobs for worth or compare pairs of jobs	Simplest method; inexpensive, easy to understand	Only general rating of "worth"—not very reliable; doesn't measure differences between jobs
Classification	Compare job descriptions to preestablished grade descriptors	Simple, easy to use for large numbers of jobs; one rating scale	Ambiguous, overlapping grade descriptors
Point factor	Reduce general factors to subfactors; give each factor weights and points; "score jobs"; use points to determine grades	More specific and larger numbers of factors; off-the-shelf plans available (e.g., Hay Plan); more precise measurements	Time-consuming process; more difficult to understand; greater opportunity to disagree

	FIGURE 10-3	Grade Descriptors for Federal Job Classification System-Serving as a Yardstick in Job Rating

Grade GS-1

Includes all classes of positions the duties of which are to perform, under immediate supervision, with little or no latitude for the exercise of independent judgment, the following: (1) the simplest routine work in office, business, or fiscal operations; or (2) elementary work of a subordinate technical character in a professional, scientific, or technical field.

Grade GS-18

Includes all classes of positions the duties of which are: (1) to serve as the head of a bureau. This position, considering the kind and extent of the authorities and responsibilities vested in it, and the scope, complexity, and degree of difficulty of the activities carried on, is exceptional and outstanding among the whole group of positions of heads of bureaus. (2) To plan and direct, or to plan and execute, new or innovative projects.

be a key drawback for an organization that is committed to employee development, internal mobility, cross-training programs, and career ladders.

The **job classification** method was originally developed, and continues to be used, by the federal government. Here, each job is measured against a preexisting set of job classes that have been designed to cover the full range of work that would be performed by federal government employees. In other words, broad descriptions are designed in advance to reflect the characteristics of the jobs that would be placed at each level in that system. Job classification, then, involves comparing a specific position to these generic descriptors and deciding which level fits best. Figure 10-3 presents the generic descriptors for two job levels within the federal job classification system. The classification system is relatively inexpensive and easy to administer.[20] But as the number and diversity of positions grow, it is increasingly difficult to write level descriptors in advance that will cover the full range of jobs. When specific level descriptors don't exist, the classification method becomes unclear and difficult to communicate to workers. In addition, like the ranking method, it is difficult to know how much difference exists between job levels. Finally, in any whole job rating system, one must be

cautious about the same type of rater errors that can creep into job evaluation and performance appraisal (see Chapter 7). For example, a halo-type error might be committed when a rater is overwhelmed by one particular element of a job.

Under a **point-factor plan,** a variety of factors are the basis for determining relative worth. Point-factor plans are the most widely used approach to job evaluation in the United States and in Europe. In choosing factors, the organization decides: "What particular job components do we value? What job characteristics will we pay for?" Companies should choose factors for a job evaluation plan that are based on the organization's strategy, that reflect the type of work performed, and that are generally acceptable to its stakeholders. Skill, effort, responsibility and working conditions are the most common factors found in point-factor plans.[21] Figure 10-4 presents a summary of the three major factors within the **Hay plan,** which is the most popular point-factor plan.

After the factors are identified and described, they are usually weighted because all factors are probably not equally important to an organization. For example, factors such as responsibility, decision making, and mental effort tend to be more heavily weighted than physical

FIGURE 10-4 Major Factors of the Hay Plan

Know-How	Problem Solving	Accountability
Sum total of every kind of skill, however acquired, required for acceptable job performance. Know-how has three subfactors:	Original "self-starting" thinking required by the job for analyzing, evaluating, creating, and reasoning. Problem solving has two subfactors:	Answerability for action and for the consequences of the action; the measured effect of the job. Accountability has three subfactors:
1. Practical procedures, specialized techniques.	1. The thinking environment in which problems are solved.	1. Freedom to act (personal control).
2. Ability to integrate and harmonize the diversified functions of management.	2. The thinking challenge of the actual problems typically encountered by the position.	2. The impact of the job on end results (direct versus indirect).
3. Interpersonal skills.		3. Magnitude—the general dollar size of areas most affected by this job.

FIGURE 10-5 Example of Degree Statements for the Factor "Physical Requirements"

FACTOR: PHYSICAL REQUIREMENTS

This factor appraises the physical effort required by a job, including its intensity and degree of continuity. Analysis of this factor may be incorrect unless a sufficiently broad view of the work is considered.

Degree

1. Light work involving a minimum of physical effort. Requires only intermittent sitting, standing, and walking. (10 Points)
2. Repetitive work of a mechanical nature. Small amount of lifting and carrying. Occasional difficult working positions. Almost continuous sitting or considerable moving around. (20 Points)
3. Continuous standing or walking, or difficult working positions. Working with average-weight or heavy materials and supplies. Fast manipulative skill in almost continuous use of machine or office equipment on paced work. (30 Points)

A higher degree rating for a job translates into a greater number of job evaluation points.

effort or working conditions. Next, degree statements must be constructed. Sometimes called factor scales, these are statements of the extent to which the factor is present in any given job. Figure 10-5 illustrates a typical degree statement for the factor "Physical Requirements." When a position's evaluation is complete, the point scores on each factor are totaled. The more valuable a job is, the higher its total point score.

Unlike job ranking, point-factor plans do not rank jobs in an organization purely based on a comparison of one against another, and they do not rely on a rater's perception of the whole job. Instead, each job is examined concerning the degree to which each factor is present. In this way, the point-factor plan is similar to the classification approach in that it uses an external standard, evaluating each job in relation to that standard. Unlike the classification system, however, the point-factor approach breaks jobs down into component parts and assigns point values for various characteristics. In a point-factor plan, a job's relative worth is the sum of the numerical values for each degree within each factor.

A job hierarchy is derived by ranking jobs by their total point score.

Point-factor job evaluation is typically conducted within a **job family** in order to establish internal equity. Thus, the job hierarchy is established within each family. While definitions differ a little, a job family is essentially a group of jobs having the same basic nature of work (e.g., clerk, teacher, engineer) but requiring different levels of skill, effort, responsibility or working conditions (e.g., entry versus senior level). Families can be groupings of related jobs with common vocations or professions in that they have similar market characteristics, related key behaviors, and a continuum of knowledge, skills, and abilities. A family can also be made up of jobs involving work of the same nature, but requiring different skill and responsibility levels. For example, Maintenance Worker and Senior Maintenance Worker are in the same job family. So the idea is to conduct point-factor job evaluation within a family so as to establish internal equity among the jobs within the family and then use benchmark jobs within that family to set rates according to the external market.

Point-factor plans have a number of advantages.[22] The written evaluation enables an organization to trace, analyze, and document differences among jobs. Such differences can be the foundation for training, development, and career progression programs. The fact that jobs are broken down into parts and evaluated using the same criteria over and over again limits the opportunity for rater bias to enter the process. Finally, when explaining job evaluation to employees, point-factor plans tend to have a high level of integrity. On the other hand, point-factor plans are expensive to design or buy and they are time-consuming to install and maintain. Some consultants assert that point-factor plans should be administered by evaluation committees consisting of line operating managers.[23] The time and cost of such commitments must be considered.

In summary, an organization chooses a job evaluation approach that it believes will best meet its needs and systematically evaluates each job within or against that standard. Within a traditional compensation plan, the goal involves creating not only an internally equitable program, but also one that is externally competitive. The next group of activities focuses on considering pay practices in the marketplace so that the organization may effectively compete for qualified workers.

What Is External Equity?

The process of pricing jobs involves identifying the compensation provided by other organizations for jobs similar to yours. When your pay practices are similar to the practices of other organizations competing for the same talent, then your program is said to be **competitive,** or **externally equitable.** When we concern ourselves with external equity, we shift our focus from an administrative value system to an economic one. Thus, one should not expect the results of job surveying and the results of job evaluation to match one another.[24] In fact, some small companies bypass the time and expense of job evaluation and go straight to the marketplace to find the wage information they need in order to set pay. This is called a **market pricing** approach. Some authors say the use of this approach is one of the fastest-growing trends in U.S. industry today.[25] Others assert that it is not an effective method for two reasons. First, most companies have some unique jobs that are more effectively priced in relation to other jobs within an organization than they are to similar jobs in the external marketplace. Second, the strategic importance of jobs within a particular company may be misstated if compared only with the external labor market. See Critical Thinking Application 10-A for further consideration of this issue in reference to executive pay.

The principal tool for establishing external equity is salary surveys. Most organizations utilize some sort of survey information in order to approximate the prevalent pay practices in their particular marketplace. Within a traditional compensation program, comparing an organization's practices to those of the marketplace typically involves three steps: (1) planning the data collection activities, (2) collecting the survey information, and (3) analyzing the information.

Planning to survey involves choosing which jobs will be surveyed. Typically, organizations survey **benchmark** positions. Benchmarks are well-known jobs, with many incumbents, that are strategically important and are structured in such a way that one would expect to find them in the general marketplace. Next, the organization should decide what sources it will use for gathering market data. The least expensive and the quickest approach is to obtain data from public sources, such as local chambers of commerce, the U.S. Department of Labor, and various other state and local agencies. Another alternative is to purchase a survey from a consulting firm. These are more expensive than local or government surveys, but they are usually of higher quality. Third, an organization can conduct its own survey or can contract with an outside firm to conduct such a survey on its behalf. This is the most expensive of the three options, but it typically provides the highest quality of information, since the company sponsoring the survey decides who will be invited to participate, which jobs will be covered, and the extent of the information that will be gathered. Check out salary.com, SalaryExpert.com, careerjournal.com or the *Occupational Outlook Handbook* at stats.bls.gov for information related to benchmarking.

The activities involved in actually collecting survey data depend on whether the organization decides to purchase survey information or to sponsor its own survey. During this phase, it is important to make certain that job content is carefully matched to survey descriptions and that the information gathered is of the highest quality possible. If an organization is buying an existing survey, it must make certain that the data represent the **relevant market.** As discussed in Chapter 5, the geographical pool is expanding for many jobs. Internet recruiting and other improvements in technology now make it possible to consider regional, national, and global labor marketplaces in order to locate the best job candidates and/or the most cost-effective candidates. Effective surveys tend to go beyond base pay and provide information concerning all elements of compensation (e.g., eligibility for incentive pay and bonuses, time-off provisions, benefits provided). Finally, good surveys provide information in addition to practices relating to existing workers and will include salary ranges, hiring ranges, practices concerning signing bonuses, and other similar information.

In terms of analyzing market data, practices vary widely among organizations.[26] Some organizations look at competitor pay data only very generally, using average salaries or median starting salaries, or some other index that it believes to be meaningful, to guide its decision making about its own pay policies. Other organizations invest considerable time, effort, and money analyzing data using least-squares regression analysis to aggregate data across jobs and across companies. An organization should choose the type and the depth of the analysis based on its own individual needs, the complexity of its marketplace, the amount of time the organization can afford to allocate to the project, the professional expertise that is available within the organization, and the resources that it is able and willing to spend for outside advice and assistance.[27]

In general, organizations tie their pay practices for most positions to the market average, although there are situations when organizations choose to pay above or below average based on their strategy or goals. For example, Merck, the highly successful pharmaceutical company, allows its research and development division to go above market for researchers with particular specialties that are compatible with its goals. Organizations that are willing to train entry-level workers may find that they can pay below market for such positions.

Developing the Pay Structure

How an organization structures its base salary program is primarily a matter of organizational philosophy, although marketplace practices are often important to consider in highly competitive situations. In structuring a program, several options are available. First, an organization can use a single rate structure in which all employees performing the same work receive the same pay rate. Second, an organization can use a tenure-based approach that focuses on how long an individual has been employed in a particular job. Third, some organizations use a combination of a tenure-based plan and a merit-based plan. For example, employees begin at a fixed rate, progress to higher rates during their first year based on time in the job, then any additional pay increase is awarded solely on the basis of performance. Yet another option would be a pay system based on productivity. An individual who is paid only a sales commission is an example of this. A fifth and increasingly popular option could be some form of base pay with an incentive opportunity, either based on individual, team, unit, or company performance. Finally, many organizations combine elements of these approaches to create their own formal program. The most common traditional pay structure involves grouping similar jobs into pay grades and assigning a salary range, with a minimum, midpoint, and maximum.[28] The use of pay grades simplifies program administration. Rather than hundreds (or thousands) of unique pay rates, grouping jobs into grades typically means 10 to 25 pay grades (depending on company type and size). Pay ranges, as opposed to pay rates, provide increased flexibility that enables managers to consider particular job-related characteristics of individual employees or job candidates. In traditional programs, employees typically progress through pay ranges based on a combination of tenure and merit.

In summary, then, this traditional pay model focuses on internal equity (through job evaluation), external equity (through market surveying), and some reconciliation of these to arrive at a final pay structure that fits well with the organization's strategy and goals and that will enable the organization to attract and retain qualified employees. As indicated earlier, this general approach has dominated compensation practice for the past 50 years.

Assessing the Traditional Approach to Pay

Over the past decade or two, new forms of pay programs have cropped up. Many of these represent a considerable break from this traditional approach. Before describing these trends, it is useful to look at why organizations are interested in experimenting with new approaches.[29]

First, the basic nature of work is changing. Globalization, competitive pressures, the unpredictable business environment, the shift from a manufacturing to a service economy, and the drive towards quality have influenced the way work is structured, performed, and supervised. Today, key issues are worker empowerment, team-based processes, and a coaching style of supervision. Jobs are more fluid and more broadly defined. Traditional job description tasks are being replaced by more general worker roles. When IBM reduced the number of different jobs it utilized from more than 5,000 to fewer than 1,200, it was responding to these same pressures by "generalizing" and broadening work. However, traditional job evaluation was built on a different work philosophy. Many traditional job evaluation programs place great value on specialty knowledge and the dollar value of areas managed. Few, if any, traditional job evaluation plans explicitly consider customer service challenges, responsibility for quality, or working successfully within and across teams as valuable dimensions of jobs. Thus, some argue that traditional job evaluation plans reward the wrong things.

Second, the traditional approach assumes that paying competitively is a primary goal of a compensation system. To this end, compensation experts within organizations tend to be "outwardly focused," monitoring competitor practices, adopting those that appear to be successful, using surveys to identify appropriate levels of pay. As discussed in Chapter 1, this element of compensation management may actually encourage "trendy, faddish thinking." In contrast to this traditional mindset, successful companies today are trying to differentiate themselves from others in the marketplace. Critics of the traditional approach urge compensation experts to "focus inwardly" on what will motivate, direct, and energize performance given the strategy and goals of the individual organization.

Third, critics argue that traditional plans create "entitlement mindsets" on the part of employees. Annual base salary increases and similar pay scale adjustments foster an expectation among employees that pay only moves in one (upward) direction. Organizations in

FIGURE 10-6	A Comparison of Three Contemporary Approaches to Pay		
Approach	**Description**	**Advantages**	**Disadvantages**
Broadbanding	Replaces traditional narrow salary ranges (40–60 percent spread) with fewer, wider bands (200–300 percent spread)	More consistent with downsized, flatter organizational structures Breaks down previous structural pay barriers among jobs to facilitate empowerment, teamwork, etc. Greater flexibility; more useful managerial tool	Traditional cost control in pay structure is lost Job pricing may be more difficult May be more difficult to communicate to employees
Pay for knowledge	Employees paid on basis of either (1) degree of specific knowledge they possess or (2) an inventory of skills	Encourages workforce flexibility and enhanced competence Fewer supervisors needed as employees improve knowledge and skill Fosters sense of individual empowerment about pay	Pay costs may get out of control Unused skills may get rusty Creating and maintaining skill and competency menus take time and effort Do we pay for inputs or outcomes?
Team pay	Any form of compensation contingent on group membership or team results	Reinforces concepts of teams, empowerment May better communicate and support organization's culture and goals	May demotivate top individual performance Few existing plans; beginning to emerge

highly competitive situations may not be able to absorb these continuous increases in fixed costs.

One strength of the traditional approach is that it conveys a sense of orderliness, rationality, fairness, and objectivity to the process of ranking job value within an organization. Job evaluation plans, especially point-factor plans, identify the particular factors that are valued in an organization. Despite this systematic foundation, the traditional compensation process provides numerous opportunities for bias, rater errors, and other forms of distortion and controversy.[30] Many have argued, for example, that traditional compensation programs have been biased against jobs traditionally held by women. Referred to as the comparable worth dilemma, traditional plans have been criticized for measuring internal job worth and then relying on market survey information to establish actual pay. The net result is that some jobs could be rated quite high in terms of their job content using a job evaluation plan, but paid comparatively low if the market undervalues their contribution. Comparable worth supporters argue that this occurs frequently because the marketplace is discriminatory. The prestigious National Academy of Science drew this conclusion in 1981.[31] Proponents of comparable worth legislation argue that waiting for an economic market adjustment is too slow and that it ignores a basic inequity in our society. We will discuss the comparable

worth equity issue in the section on government compliance later in this chapter.

In summary, there are a variety of reasons the traditional internal equity/external competitive approach to compensation has been called into question. In the next section, we will describe some of the noteworthy efforts in this direction. Figure 10-6 illustrates the characteristics of three contemporary pay approaches that are described and discussed below.

Current Trends in Salary Administration

Broadbanding

Broadbanding is an approach to base pay that is receiving considerable attention in the business press.[32] In theory, it is considered to be more consistent with the broader, downsized, flatter organizations that exist today. Broadbanding involves consolidating existing pay grades and ranges into fewer, wider bands. While a traditional pay range might be $30,000–45,000 (i.e., 50 percent spread from minimum to maximum), a job band could be $25,000–75,000 (i.e., 300 percent spread). Broadbanding provides greater flexibility in setting pay rates, and it provides considerably more latitude in defining work and in moving people around within an organization. Northern Telecom clustered more than 34 pay grades into 10 bands and replaced 19,000 job titles with approximately

200 generic job titles. General Electric collapsed 30 pay grades covering administrative, executive, and professional employees into five broad bands.

Hewitt Associates studied the experience of 106 organizations that replaced traditional pay grades with broad bands by conducting focus groups that included affected employees, the managers responsible for administering the new plans, and top organizational executives.[33] Employee groups asserted that broadbanding encourages developmental and lateral career moves and facilitates cross-functional teams because differences in titles, levels, and salaries are minimized. Managers agreed with these observations and added that they liked the greater flexibility the approach provided in setting and managing pay. Executives viewed bands as a mechanism that could be molded to support a business's organizational style, strategy, and vision. An American Compensation Association study of broadband organizations found that 78 percent considered the approach to be effective.[34]

Insufficient research has been conducted to date to indicate whether broadbanding is a long-term, effective pay model.[35] Traditionally, narrow pay grades and ranges place upper limits on an individual's earnings. Some experts argue that broadbanding could increase payroll costs without specifically fostering corresponding increases in worker productivity. Some argue that broadbanding is appropriate for higher-level positions only.

Pay for Knowledge, Competencies, or Skills

In these types of plans, employees are paid on the basis of either the degree of specific, technical knowledge they hold or an inventory of knowledge and/or skills that they possess.[36] These plans are based on the assumption that knowledge, skill, or competence will be translated into improved employee performance and, ultimately, superior organizational effectiveness. Advocates assert that such plans can increase worker productivity and product quality, while decreasing absenteeism, turnover, and accident rates. One estimate of the popularity of the approach is that as many as 40 percent of large organizations use this approach, but only for a very small percentage of their workforce. Paying for knowledge has long been a viable pay strategy in scientific, technical, and professional disciplines in which expertise and innovation were sources of competitive, albeit intangible, advantage. Business schools, for example, typically pay considerably more for an assistant professor with a Ph.D. than for an instructor with an MBA. Similarly, unionized professions, such as teachers and nurses, have strongly favored pay based on education and experience. These plans are based on the assumption that professional competence increases with training and longevity. As technology continues to move forward at its rapid pace, such plans are increasing in popularity.

The most modern application of this thinking can be found in organizations designing and implementing skills-based pay. Originally found in new, nonunion manufacturing organizations, interest in this approach has grown considerably. Although it is not used as widely as its publicity might indicate (only 5 percent of U.S. organizations are believed to have implemented some version of the approach), its influence has been felt in some industries, such as pharmaceuticals and telecommunications. In a typical skills-based pay plan, the array of knowledges or skills that the organization values becomes like a pay menu. Employees begin at an entry-level rate. Incremental pay increases are awarded as employees demonstrate knowledge, or mastery, of specific, additional skills. Three types of potentially useful skill enhancements have been identified: (1) skill depth is increased when employees learn more about specialized areas, enhancing their ability to solve difficult problems and moving along a career track to becoming an expert, or master; (2) skill breadth is improved when employees learn more and different tasks, or jobs, in the organization; (3) self-management skills are increased when employees improve their abilities to organize and schedule work, to supervise work quality, and to perform other administrative tasks.

Supporters argue its merits: (1) the cross-training and acquisition of knowledge can create a flexible, empowered workforce; (2) fewer supervisors are needed; and (3) programs encourage employees to take responsibility for and control over their own development and their own compensation growth. Opponents assert that, first, potentially higher individual pay costs may be uneconomical unless they are offset by higher worker productivity. Second, unless skills are used regularly, they become rusty, although the pay for the skill may continue indefinitely. Third, depending on the growth and direction of the organization, employees can still reach the top of the skills-based pay scale, resulting in the same frustration that these plans are designed to remedy. Fourth, one very controversial issue is whether organizations should pay for inputs (e.g., individual credentials) or outcomes (e.g., performance). Skills-based pay represents paying for inputs. In contrast, some organizations believe that the best response to rising costs in uncertain environments is to put increasing amounts of pay at risk, that is, paying for outcomes, for the attainment of real individual, group, or organizational goals. Paying for knowledge, competence, or skills suggests that credentials hold potential performance value. When organizations pay on this basis, they should do so understanding that they are assuming the risk that these credentials will ultimately improve performance.

Team Pay Plans

With the wide growth in the use of teams within organizations has come discussion concerning how team members should be compensated. There appears to be a general consensus that teams require a different compensation approach than work that is organized for and performed by individuals. However, there currently appear to be more questions than answers.[37] In a 1995 study of 230 large U.S. organizations, Hay Associates reported that 80 percent were satisfied with their use of teams, but that only 40 percent were satisfied with the related pay program.

One group of experts argues that it is important to distinguish between behaviors that a company values (as in teamwork) versus a true organizational form (as in teams). In addition, at least five types of teams have been identified: management teams, work teams, quality circles, virtual teams, and problem-solving teams. In sorting through the types and uses of teams, three criteria have been suggested as a basis for determining whether a team is a candidate for some kind of customized form of pay: (1) the team is the ongoing, relatively permanent form of work organization in use; (2) the work is truly interdependent; and (3) the team shares responsibility for its own decision making concerning its work.

Some experts recommend that team organizations use broadbanding in combination with incentive profit-sharing plans based on team results (see the next chapter). Depending on the environment, a division and/or organizational component may be added to the incentive plan as well. Some organizations report the use of pay for knowledge systems, particularly skills-based pay, as a compensation approach for teams.

Government Influence on Compensation Issues

In Chapter 3, you read about equal employment opportunity regulations that were enacted by the federal government to positively influence social change. The government also provides a legal framework about direct compensation within which organizations must operate. These rules ensure that minimum operating standards of fairness and humanity are applied to compensation matters in the employer–employee relationship.[38] Figure 10-7 summarizes the principal provisions of the most important federal regulations governing pay. Of course, as with most HRM activities, the reader should be aware that state, county, and local laws also may regulate pay policies.

The Fair Labor Standards Act

The broadest, most comprehensive legislation that affects base pay programs is the Fair Labor Standards Act (FLSA). Enacted in 1938, the law focuses on three main areas: minimum wage, overtime pay, and child labor rules. In 1963, the Equal Pay Act (EPA) amended the FLSA to include a prohibition against pay differentials based on gender. The Act also requires that employers maintain detailed records of time worked and pay received by each employee. The record-keeping requirement is used to determine whether or not an organization has complied with the law.

The **minimum wage** law places a bottom limit on what an employer may pay. When the law was passed in 1938, the minimum wage was $.25. As of 2005, the federal minimum wage for *covered nonexempt* employees is $5.15 an hour. However, many *states* (and some cities) also have minimum wage laws, some of which are indexed. Where an employee is subject to both the state (or city) and federal minimum wage laws, the employee is entitled to the higher of the two minimum wages. An employer of a tipped employee is required to pay only $2.13 an hour in direct wages if that amount plus the tips received equals at least the federal minimum wage, the employee retains all tips, and the employee customarily and regularly receives more than $30 a month in tips. Some states also have minimum wage laws specific to tipped employees. Visit the Department of Labor Web site (dol.gov) for a state-by-state breakdown of minimum wage law. A minimum wage of $4.25 per hour applies to workers under the age of 20 during their first 90 days of employment as long as their work does not displace other workers. After 90 days of employment, the employee must receive a minimum wage of $5.15 per hour.[39]

FIGURE 10-7	Summary of Federal Laws Affecting Direct Compensation
Laws	**Provisions**
Fair Labor Standards Act (FLSA) of 1938	Sets minimum wage ($5.15 per hour in 2005), overtime pay requirements, and rules governing child labor (states can increase rate)
Equal Pay Act (EPA) of 1963	Men and women must be paid the same when they hold "substantially equal" jobs in terms of skill, effort, responsibility, and working conditions (some exceptions apply)
Davis-Bacon Act of 1931	Workers employed in construction industry must be paid at the prevailing local pay rate when working on government contracts.
Walsh-Healey Act of 1936	Workers employed in organizations providing goods to federal offices and projects must be paid the prevailing local rate for such work
Services Contract Act of 1965	Workers providing services to government offices and projects must be paid the prevailing local rate for such work

There has been much discussion about whether minimum wage laws represent too much government involvement in the private sector and whether a minimum wage is healthy for an economy.[40] Those in favor of the regulation argue that a minimum wage is necessary to ensure that employers do not take unfair advantage of workers. Opponents argue that the law actually puts people out of work because employers tend to eliminate jobs as the cost of doing business rises.

FLSA's **overtime** provisions establish 40 hours as the standard workweek and require that employers pay workers at least 1.5 times their regular hourly rate for all work in excess of 40 hours in any workweek (hence the expression, time-and-one-half). Effective in September 2004, the FLSA rules concerning who is covered under its overtime provisions were changed. There were two reasons generally given for the changes, depending on an individual's perspective. Many argued that the 1938 FLSA was designed to regulate the payment of wages in an industrial economy, and that it has failed to do so effectively in the current services economy. These arguments cited the lack of flexibility in the FLSA rules that limited, for example, the degree to which working long hours during one pay period could be offset by shortened work hours in subsequent pay periods (without incurring a liability for overtime pay, of course). Others argued that the law was changed to help businesses escape the consequences of their wrongdoing. In 2004, the Department of Labor estimated that litigation filed by employees claiming that their employer had not paid them properly for overtime work was costing companies $2 billion per year. Since 2001, courts have ruled against such organizations as Starbucks ($18 million), Perdue Farms ($10 million), T-Mobile ($4.8 million), and Bank of America ($4.1 million). By mid-2004, Wal-Mart faced close to 40 separate lawsuits concerning nonpayment of overtime and denial of state-mandated breaks to workers. One case alone involved 64,000 Wal-Mart workers in Minnesota.

The new rules may be summarized as follows:

- Any workers earning less than $455 per week (an annual equivalent of $23,660) are subject to FLSA overtime provisions regardless of the type of work they do. In other words, these employees must be paid at the rate of time-and-one-half for all hours worked in excess of 40 in a workweek.
- Workers earning more than $455 weekly may be eligible for exemption from the FLSA overtime pay provided that the nature of the work they perform meets particular criteria for exemption. Job titles do not serve as a basis for the exemption.
- As was the case previously, exemptions are available for "executive," "administrative," and "professional" work and for certain types of "outside sales" positions. The 2004 changes simplify the criteria that must be met in order to be "exempt" from overtime pay.

- The revised FLSA rules provide a "shortcut" exemption from overtime eligibility which applies if a worker is considered to be "highly compensated" (i.e., earning $100,000 per year or more).
- The new rules add a provision for businesses to begin excluding computer-related workers from overtime eligibility provided that they earn at least $455 per week, or $27.63 per hour (if part-time). No highly compensated shortcut exemption is provided for workers in computer-related occupations.

The **child labor** provisions restrict the employment of children by organizations. Employees must be at least 18 years old to perform any kind of hazardous work; at least 16 years old to work in manufacturing, mining, and transportation positions; and at least 14 years old to perform work in most other jobs. In spite of these clear regulations, an Associated Press investigation (1997–1998) followed 165 children working illegally in 16 states, from New Mexican chile fields to a sweatshop in New York City. The investigation found that the work products of these children ended up in such places as JCPenney, Pillsbury, Wal-Mart, ConAgra, Campbell Soup, and Newman's Own. (Most of these companies launched major investigations when told that their suppliers illegally employed children.) One labor economist estimates that 290,200 children were employed unlawfully in the United States in 1998; 59,600 of these children are believed to be below the age of 14.[41]

The FLSA was amended in 1963 to include the **Equal Pay Act** (EPA). This provision requires that men and women be paid the same when they hold "substantially equal" jobs in terms of skill, effort, and responsibility and are performed under the same working conditions. It also provides for a few exceptions. When pay differences are traceable to differences in job tenure, quality or quantity of performance, or individual differences in education or experience—provided that the pay system actually recognizes and rewards these factors—pay differences between men and women are permitted. The filing of a claim under the EPA does not preclude pursuing a claim under Title VII. This can be important because the Civil Rights Act contains no provision stipulating job similarity. Plaintiffs who can establish that they have been paid a lower rate due to gender, race, religion, or national origin are eligible for judicial relief under Title VII, regardless of the job's similarity to other work. (See Critical Thinking Application 10-B). Figure 10-8 presents a summary of the EPA and other forms of compensation discrimination.

Prevailing Wage Laws

Several federal laws have been designed to make certain that workers employed on government contracts receive fair wages relative to other local workers. The three most important laws are the **Davis Bacon Act of 1931,** the **Walsh-Healey Act of 1936,** and the **Services Contract Act of 1965** and they cover federal contracts for construction,

FIGURE 10-8 Equal Pay and Compensation Discrimination

EQUAL PAY ACT

The Equal Pay Act requires that men and women be given equal pay for equal work in the same establishment. The jobs need not be identical, but they must be substantially equal.

It is job content, not job titles, that determines whether jobs are substantially equal. Specifically, the EPA provides:

Employers may not pay unequal wages to men and women who perform jobs that require substantially equal skill, effort and responsibility, and that are performed under similar working conditions within the same establishment. Each of these factors is summarized below:

Skill—Measured by factors such as the experience, ability, education, and training required to perform the job. The key issue is what skills are required for the job, not what skills the individual employees may have.

Effort—The amount of physical or mental exertion needed to perform the job.

Responsibility—The degree of accountability required in performing the job.

Working Conditions—These encompasses two factors: (1) physical surroundings like temperature, fumes, and ventilation; and (2) hazards.

Establishment—The prohibition against compensation discrimination under the EPA applies only to jobs within an establishment. An establishment is a distinct physical place of business rather than an entire business or enterprise consisting of several places of business.

Pay differentials are permitted when they are based on seniority, merit, quantity or quality of production, or a factor other than sex. These are known as "affirmative defenses" and it is the employer's burden to prove that they apply. In correcting a pay differential, no employee's pay may be reduced. Instead, the pay of the lower-paid employee(s) must be increased.

TITLE VII, ADEA, and ADA

Title VII, the ADEA, and the ADA prohibit compensation discrimination on the basis of race, color, religion, sex, national origin, age, or disability. Unlike the EPA, there is no requirement under Title VII, the ADEA, or the ADA that the claimant's job be substantially equal to that of a higher-paid person outside the claimant's protected class, nor do these statutes require the claimant to work in the same establishment as a comparator.

---

goods, and services, respectively. Typically, prevailing wage levels have been equal to union wage levels, which, in effect, creates a higher minimum wage for federally funded projects. At the same time, these regulations ensure that large federal projects, awarded on the basis of competitive bids, do not create a decline in an area's wage rates. President Bush issued an executive order in 2005 suspending the Davis Bacon Act for federal contractors rebuilding in designated areas after Hurricane Katrina; thus allowing contractors to pay below the prevailing wage.

Pay Equity or Comparable Worth Policy

One contemporary pay topic concerns the policy of comparable worth or pay equity we introduced earlier in the chapter. First enunciated in 1934 and adopted as policy in 1951 by over 100 nations (not the United States), a comparable worth or pay equity policy requires a pay structure that is strictly based on an internal assessment of job worth (i.e., a job evaluation process). It has been proposed as a means of eliminating gender and racial discrimination in the wage-setting process.

Pay equity assumes that the traditional method of achieving equity within, *but not between,* job families is inherently unfair. The theory of "within but not between" assumes, for example, that clerical jobs are compared to

each other, that skilled trades jobs are compared to each other, and that professional jobs are compared to each other. The problem with this assumption is that jobs are typically not compared across job families. Thus, a skilled trade job evaluated at 400 points on a point-factor plan might be paid 20 percent higher than a clerical job receiving the same number of points, due to different labor market rates. In Washington state, for example, the average wages of women were 20 percent lower than men for jobs found to have the same number of job evaluation points. Thus, jobs in the clerical families may have shared equitable pay, but they were systematically lower than wages paid to men in traditionally male-dominated jobs, such as skilled trades. Advocates of comparable worth maintain that the labor market undervalues the economic worth of jobs performed predominantly by women and minorities.

Traditionally, the lower-paid job families include many women's jobs. For a number of reasons, job families with a large proportion of "female-dominated" jobs (defined in most comparable worth studies as jobs where more than 70 percent of the incumbents are women) have been compensated at a lower rate than have job families with many "male-dominated" jobs. According to the Bureau of Labor Statistics, in fact, 80 percent of U.S. female workers are employed in occupations in which at least 70 percent of all employees are women.[42]

Opponents to comparable worth pay policies present three arguments against the issue. First, they argue that there is no legal mandate to pay comparable worth salaries. Second, they argue that a comparable worth approach would mean inflating salaries and that most companies could not afford to do this and stay in business. In the state of Washington, for example, it was estimated in 1986 that providing a pay plan based on comparable worth carried an annual cost of $400 million. Third, opponents argue that if women really want to advance in terms of salary, they can do so by preparing themselves to enter traditionally male-dominated jobs where they will enjoy the same pay—a right that is protected legally. This argument relies on an assumption that, over time, as women migrate away from lower-paid jobs because they can obtain more lucrative pay in other careers, the pay for such traditionally female work will rise to reflect the worker shortage.

There is little question that differences between male and female wages are reduced under a comparable worth policy. Women in Sweden, for example, earn 92 percent of what men earn under a long-standing pay equity program. The United Kingdom, Ireland, Switzerland, and Australia provide additional examples of wage gap decreases after pay equity programs were implemented. No country in the world pays women as much as men. (Sri Lanka, just southeast of India, leads the world in this regard, paying women, on average, 96 percent of what men earn.)

The Fair Pay Act, mandating a comparable worth policy for federal employees, was introduced in Congress in 2005. While passage of such legislation in the United States is highly unlikely, the influence of unions and the successes at the state and local levels to legislate and bargain for the policy is likely to continue. As of 2005, according to the National Committee on Pay Equity, 20 states have some form of pay equity policy for segments of the workforce. Seven states have comprehensive pay equity policies for all or almost all employees who work for those states. Bills have been introduced in over 25 state legislatures since 2000. Check out www.pay-equity.org for recent activity.

The Wage Gap

At the Wage Equity Day festivities in April 2005, several speakers made reference to the "wage gap" between men and women. According to the Bureau of Labor Statistics, despite over 40 years of the Equal Pay Act, women earn 78.5 cents for every dollar earned by a man. Says Connecticut Congresswoman Rosa DeLauro, one of the co-authors of the Fair Pay Act, "No matter how hard women work or whatever they achieve in terms of advancement in their own profession and degree, they will not be compensated equitably." But a new book disputes the arguments attributing the wage gap to discrimination. Says Warren Farrell, author of *Why Men Earn More,* the wage gap exists primarily because of the type of work women choose and the number of hours worked.[43]

Farrell compared the starting salaries of men and women with Bachelor's Degrees in 26 categories of employment, from investment bankers to dieticians. Women are paid equally in one category; in every other category, their starting salaries exceed men's. A female investment banker's starting salary is 116 percent of a man's. A female dietician's is 130 percent; that is, $23,160 compared to $17,680. Another argument he makes is that women often prefer jobs with shorter and more flexible hours in order to accommodate family responsibilities. For example, women generally favor jobs that involve little danger, no travel and good social skills. These jobs generally pay less. Another reason men earn more is that they work more hours per week. According to the Bureau of Labor Statistics, full-time men work about 45 hours a week versus 42 for women. Women choose to avoid particularly dangerous jobs that pay well. Over 92 percent of occupational deaths are men. Of course, women have a legal right to enter dangerous professions, the most dangerous of which are over 95 percent male.

Other Compliance Issues

As indicated earlier, many states and localities have their own regulations that cover workers in addition to those covered by the federal legislation. Human resource professionals must stay educated on these matters and be prepared to ensure that their organization complies with such laws. Often legislation covers areas with which business management would rather not concern itself. Such issues as maintaining records that document compliance with the overtime provisions of the FLSA or documenting the basis for a particular position's exemption from coverage under the overtime provisions of FLSA are not issues that are foremost in the minds of most CEOs. However, the cost of noncompliance can be extremely high and can include back pay awards, penalties, and interest. One method that has been recommended to assist HR professionals is the compliance audit. This is an analysis of employee records and organizational policies, communications, and practices to ensure that both the letter and the spirit of the laws are being followed. This audit is an abbreviated form of the audit that would be conducted by a federal compliance officer if the organization were under review. The audit pinpoints problem areas so they can be proactively addressed.

In this section, we have examined the general methods and processes used by organizations to establish pay programs. We discussed the traditional approach, which may still be very effective in some organizations, and we noted some recent trends. In addition, we briefly looked at the way the government involves itself in base pay issues. In the next section, we shift our emphasis away from wage and salary payments to the area of employee benefits.

FRINGE COMPENSATION: EMPLOYEE BENEFITS

Employee benefits focus on maintaining (or improving) the quality of life for employees and providing a level of protection and financial security for workers and for their family members. Like base pay plans, the major objective for most organizational fringe compensation programs is to attract, retain, and motivate qualified, competent employees.

Research supports the importance of the benefits package in applicants' job selection process.[44] Recent research, for example, shows that women are particularly attracted to a company with a strong pro-family fringe compensation package. These packages become relatively more important when the unemployment rate is low and the competition for qualified workers is high. However, employees tend to grossly underestimate the cost of benefits to the organization. For example, one study found that current employees estimated the cost of benefits to the organization was 12 percent of payroll when the actual cost was 31 percent.[45] Organizations are now working harder to better explain the cost of the benefit package to employees.

Three important trends characterize employee benefit plans as they exist in organizations today.[46] First, over the past several decades, the popularity of employee benefits has increased significantly. In 1929, benefits offered to employees averaged 3 percent of payroll; by 1950, the number had risen to 16 percent; by 2003, the cost of benefits was about 39 percent of payroll.[47] Second, while benefit plans initially were quite uniform, recent years have seen considerable variation in the type of benefits offered. The third trend is the increased flexibility employees have these days in selecting their own benefit coverages.

The rise in the popularity of employee benefit programs is attributable to a variety of forces. During World War II, the War Labor Board (WLB) excluded employee benefit improvements from wage stabilization controls because such benefits were "on the fringe of wages," so benefit program improvements were not expected to be inflationary. Since then, benefits have grown largely due to favorable federal tax policies.[48]

Three general types of tax advantages relate to employee benefit programs, provided that the plans comply with certain rules. First, employers are allowed **tax deductions** for the costs of benefit programs. In this way, the cost of benefits is treated in the same way as direct payroll costs. Second, employees receive many benefit plans, as well as some plan payouts, on a **tax-free** basis. For example, when an employer offers a health care plan, three things typically occur: (1) the organization deducts the cost of the plan from its earnings for tax purposes; (2) employees are not taxed on the cost of the plan that the employer has provided to them; (3) employees are not taxed on the reimbursement they receive under the terms

of the plan for covered services. Particularly when individual tax rates are rising significantly, these tax advantages make employee benefit programs attractive alternatives to direct pay for many employees. The third tax advantage is that some benefits are **tax-deferred.** For example, when an employer sets aside pension money for an individual, taxes are not paid on that money (or the investment earnings on the money) until the money is actually withdrawn by the employee, presumably during retirement. Similarly, when an employee makes certain types of contributions to a company 401(k) program, those contributions are typically made on a pretax basis, any employer contributions are not taxable to the individual, nor is any interest accumulation taxable until the employee begins actually withdrawing the money. Liberal loan provisions and rollover options permit the delay of taxes even longer. Thus, favorable tax treatment has made employee benefits a worthwhile investment both for organizations and for individual workers.

While employee benefit programs were at one time quite uniform, there is now considerable variance. Benefit programs vary as a consequence of the organization's human resource philosophy, its size, its location, the type of business, the industry, and the type of job that an individual holds.[49] Some companies such as Stride Rite, Johnson Wax, Procter & Gamble, and Merck have a strong pro-family orientation to their benefit package with options such as family care leave, child and elder care support, dependent care accounts, adoption benefits, alternative work schedules, and on-site day care. In general, larger companies offer a wider array of benefits.[50] Across large, medium, and small organizations, benefit programs for professional and technical employees tend to be the most comprehensive, followed by those for clerical and sales employees, and then for blue-collar and service employees.[51]

A growing number of U.S. companies now offer flexible, or cafeteria-style, benefit plans.[52] With the increasing diversity of the workforce, cafeteria plans are particularly valued by the two-income family because duplicate coverage can be replaced with other valuable benefits, such as increased time off or child care allowances. Cafeteria plans are not new. Decades ago, organizations were reluctant to implement them for two reasons: (1) the increased administrative complexity created by managing a large variety of possible benefit combinations across an entire workforce and (2) the concern that benefit costs might rise dramatically when employees are allowed to opt out of coverages that they would be unlikely to use and replace those programs with benefits that they might use extensively. Over the past decade, however, the increased sophistication in user-friendly computer software and consulting firms that have built considerable track records assisting companies with these plans have supported the rapid growth of cafeteria plans, and this growth is expected to continue for the foreseeable future.

Categories of Employee Benefits

As we said earlier, fringe benefits may be divided into legally required programs and discretionary benefits. Discretionary benefits include (1) employee welfare programs; (2) long-term capital accumulation programs; (3) time-off plans; and (4) employee services.

Legally Required Programs

Five benefits programs are required by federal law. Social Security, unemployment insurance, and workers' compensation are basic income continuity programs. In other words, they provide payments when an individual is not working. The Consolidated Omnibus Budget Reconciliation Act (COBRA) and the Family and Medical Leave Act (FMLA) focus primarily on employees' right to maintain their employee benefits, specifically their health care benefits. The FMLA allows workers to take job-protected, unpaid time off to care for themselves or a family member. According to the Department of Labor, almost 17 percent of U.S. workers reported having used the FMLA in the past 18 months. The DOL was considering revisions to the law in 2005. Figure 10-9 summarizes the principal provisions concerning legally-required benefits.

Social Security Under the Social Security program, eligible individuals are covered by a comprehensive program of retirement, survivor, disability, and health benefits. Individuals are eligible for Social Security retirement benefits in the form of monthly payments when they reach the stipulated age under the program, and provided they have worked long enough to qualify for benefits.

Disability Social Security benefits are comparable to retirement benefits and are provided only when a disability is expected to endure for at least one year, or is expected to result in death. In addition, individuals must be disabled for six months before they qualify for payments. Survivor benefits may be available to a worker's beneficiaries, depending on their length (and recency) of employment.

The Medicare program provides health care benefits to nearly all United States citizens aged 65 or older regardless of whether or not they have worked. Medicare is also available to individuals receiving Social Security disability benefits after a specified period of time. Medicare Part A covers hospital costs. Part B is a voluntary and contributory supplement covering medical expenses. Part C (passed in 1997) provides new health care coverage options to Medicare recipients including managed care plans, medical savings accounts, and the like. In addition, many states offer Medigap insurance for an extra fee to fill the unpaid gaps in coverage under Medicare Parts A, B, and C.

Employers and employees share equally the cost of providing Social Security coverage to individuals. The tax paid by employers and employees is based on the Federal Insurance Contributions Act (FICA). In 2005, the tax for the retirement, survivor, and disability portion of the Social Security program was 12.4 percent of the first $90,000 earned by an employee. Half this amount (6.2 percent) was paid by the employer; the other half was paid by the employee through payroll deduction. In 2001, the Medicare portion of the Social Security program cost 2.9 percent (with the same employer–employee split). Since 1994, all compensation paid to an employee has been subject to the Medicare tax.

At the time of this writing, there was concern about whether the current Social Security program could meet its future obligations. When the program was established in 1938, there were 39 workers for each retiree. In 1950, there were 16 workers paying in for each retiree. Today, there are about 3.5 workers for each Social Security beneficiary. Over the next 20 years, baby boomers will bring

FIGURE 10-9	**Summary of Federal Laws Affecting Indirect Compensation**
Laws	**Provisions**
Social Security Act of 1935	Requires that companies cover employees under comprehensive program of retirement, survivor, disability, and health benefits (OASDHI). In addition, requires that employers pay taxes to cover benefits payable to workers who are out of work "through no fault of their own."
Workers' Compensation Laws	Requires that employers finance variety of benefits (i.e., lost wages, medical benefits, survivor benefits, and rehabilitation services) for employees with work-related illnesses or injuries on "no-fault" basis.
Federal Unemployment Tax Act (FUTA)	Requires that employers pay taxes to cover laid-off employees for up to 39 weeks (additional extensions possible).
Consolidated Omnibus Budget Reconciliation Act (COBRA)	Requires employers to provide access to health care coverage in particular instances when coverage would otherwise be terminated. Cost of coverage may be completely passed on to worker. Administrative record-keeping fee also may be charged.
Family and Medical Leave Act of 1993 (FMLA)	Requires employers to continue providing health care coverage to employees who are on FMLA leave (up to 12 weeks per year for specified family emergencies) on same basis as it was provided before the leave.

retiree numbers to record-breaking levels. In anticipation of possible funding problems, Congress is currently considering action to shore up the system. Options under discussion include raising the Social Security payroll tax, increasing (or eliminating) the wage base on which the social security tax is paid ($90,000 in 2005), reducing Social Security benefits, or creating some form of individual retirement accounts.

Unemployment Insurance   The unemployment insurance program in the United States is jointly managed by the federal government and the states. The program is designed to encourage employers to stabilize their workforces, and it provides emergency income for workers when they are unemployed.[53] The federal unemployment tax is 6.2 percent on the first $7,000 of wages. However, in the majority of states, an employer's tax rate is adjusted up or down from this standard, depending on the number of their former employees who collect unemployment benefits. This "experience-rated" approach to the unemployment tax is designed to ensure that firms that create the unemployment pay at least their fair share of the costs in supporting individuals who are out of work.

In terms of payouts under the unemployment program, the individual states decide how much to pay, how long to pay, and on what basis they will pay. The average unemployment benefit, which is determined by the individual's previous wage earnings, is about $212 per week. In general, employees who are covered under FUTA (the Federal Unemployment Tax Act), and whose employment is terminated, are eligible to receive unemployment payments for up to 26 weeks. A 1970 amendment permitted an extension of these benefits, usually for an additional 13 weeks. Such Supplemental Unemployment Benefits (SUBs) are usually triggered when a state's unemployment rate exceeds a particular level. Since late 2001, when the economy weakened, President George W. Bush has approved three additional 13-week extensions, permitting unemployment recipients up to 65 weeks of benefits. To be eligible to receive benefits, the worker must have been employed previously in an occupation covered by the insurance, must have been dismissed by the organization (but not for misconduct), must be actively seeking work, and (in all states but Rhode Island and New York) may not be unemployed due to a labor dispute.

Workers' Compensation Insurance   Unlike unemployment compensation insurance, workers' compensation (WC) programs are managed solely by the states with no direct federal involvement or mandatory standards. Typically, workers' compensation provides for medical expenses and pay due to lost work time in cases where the illness or injury is work related. The primary purpose of workers' compensation programs is to provide for benefits to injured or ill workers on a no-fault basis

and thus to eliminate the costly lawsuits that would otherwise clog the legal system and disrupt employer–employee relations.[54]

The first laws for handling occupational disabilities and death were enacted in 1910, and they have existed in all states since 1948. Employers are fully responsible for the cost of the coverage, and they may not require any employee contributions. To facilitate the consideration of claims, most states have established workers' compensation boards or commissions. In most states, employers are free to select their own carriers to insure the risk (or to self-insure the risk), investigate claims, and process payments. More will be said about workers' compensation programs in Chapter 14.

Consolidated Omnibus Budget Reconciliation Act of 1985 (COBRA)   This law was enacted in order to provide current and former employees, and their eligible dependents, with a temporary extension of group health insurance when coverage would otherwise be lost. When it is the employee whose coverage is lost (e.g., layoff or other form of termination), the individual has the right to continue medical coverage for up to 18 months. When a dependent's coverage is lost (e.g., due to the death of the worker, divorce, or reaching the maximum age for a dependent child), the covered individual is entitled to continue the coverage for a maximum of 36 months. In all cases, the individual pays the full cost of the coverage and organizations have the option of adding a 2 percent surcharge to cover administrative costs.

Family and Medical Leave Act of 1993 (FMLA)   FMLA entitles all eligible employees to receive unpaid leave for up to 12 weeks per year for specified family and medical emergencies relating to self, spouse, parents, and children. When the employee returns to work, the act requires the employer to place the individual in the same or an equivalent job, with the same pay, benefits, and conditions of employment. During the leave, the employer is required to continue to provide coverage under the health care program on the same basis as it was provided before the leave. In other words, if the cost of the insurance was shared between the employer and employee, the employer can continue to require such cost contributions. If an employee on a leave fails to live up to his or her financial obligations to the plan (e.g., payment within 30 days), the employer may drop the employee –after giving at least 15 days' notice. Supervisors may have personal liability for violations of the FMLA. California offers paid family leave as of 2004.

Discretionary Plans: Employee Welfare Programs

The benefits of greatest concern to both employees and employers in this category are health care plans. Also included in this category are survivor benefits, which include all types of life insurance.

Health Care Plans   In 2004, nearly all large, private industry employers (100 workers or more) in the United States offered protection under a health care program. Sixty percent of smaller companies offered such coverage. Employees paid an average of 18 percent of the health care premiums (on average, $67.57 per month) for single coverage and 31 percent of the cost for family coverage (on average, $264.59 per month).[55]

A disturbing contemporary trend is the dropping of health care benefits for workers and retirees. Can an employer drop health care benefits for workers who are under the age of 50 while maintaining them for retirees? The Supreme Court recently ruled in *General Dynamics Land Systems v. Cline* that the Age Discrimination in Employment Act does not prohibit an employer from practicing "reverse age discrimination" where older workers are favored over younger workers who are over 39.

Health Care Management Tools   Four other health care management tools are increasingly popular: (1) wellness programs, (2) personal responsibility clauses, (3) periodic health care plan audits, and (4) managed care plans. **Wellness programs** are typically used in two ways: (1) to educate employees to make informed decisions about their lifestyles and their health care and (2) to challenge employees' belief that employers are responsible for their health and for paying all their medical care costs. One survey found that 76 percent of respondents had wellness plans in place.[56] Wellness programs will be discussed further in Chapter 14.

Personal responsibility clauses are based on the principle that if employees or their dependents take personal risks, then they should bear additional responsibility for the costs arising from resulting illness or injury. The two most targeted behaviors for plan incentive or disincentive strategies are smoking and seat belt use.

Health care plan audits focus on carefully tracking plan utilization and costs in order to determine whether the organization's health care spending is generally effective.[57] Audits include examining claims to ensure that benefits are paid accurately and within acceptable time frames, conducting employee surveys about health care and lifestyle issues, tracking which providers are widely used (for the purpose of possibly negotiating volume discounts), and making certain that when more than one insurance plan is in effect (e.g., coverage under a spouse's plan), benefit payments are correctly coordinated.

Managed care continues to grow. Popular approaches include **health maintenance organizations (HMOs)** and **preferred provider organizations (PPOs).** HMOs are organizations comprised of health care professionals who provide services on a prepaid basis. PPOs are usually hospitals and health care professionals that offer reduced rates based on a contractual arrangement with the organization.

Government Regulation of Health Care Programs
The Employee Retirement Income Security Act of 1974 (ERISA) is the most comprehensive piece of employee benefits legislation ever enacted in the United States.[58] It was passed because many retiring workers were not getting the benefits that had been promised to them over their working lifetimes.[59] Earlier in this chapter, we described the tax advantages enjoyed by company-sponsored benefit plans. In order to qualify for this favorable treatment, however, an employee benefit plan must be "qualified," that is, the plan must be in full compliance with all provisions of ERISA. ERISA primarily affects pension plans, but health care programs are subject to certain provisions.

Under ERISA, health care plans must be set forth in written documents that clearly describe the terms of the plan. Employees are entitled to detailed information concerning their health care plan and the state of its financing. Each year, organizations are required to submit annual reports concerning the state of the plan and to send a summary of the annual report to all plan participants. In 1996, ERISA was revised to include The Health Insurance Portability and Accountability Act (HIPAA). The Act, which applies to all employers offering group health plans, significantly reduced an employer's ability to deny or limit coverage for preexisting conditions, or to require higher premiums based on an individual's medical condition. Effective in 2003, health care privacy rules were implemented that require health care entities (plans, providers, etc.) to obtain a patient's written consent before releasing any health care information. In order to obtain consent, the Act requires full disclosure about how and for what purpose such medical information will be used.

Under the Age Discrimination in Employment Act (ADEA), employer health plans must offer the same benefits to employees aged 65 and older (and their spouses, if applicable) as the plan provides to younger employees. (Traditionally, organizations moved employees at age 65 onto Medicare and provided a Medicare Supplement policy. This practice has been outlawed under these ADEA provisions.) The Pregnancy Discrimination Act of 1978 requires that pregnancy and pregnancy-related disabilities be treated the same as other illnesses or disabilities. Employers who offer health care plans, temporary disability plans, and sick leave are now legally required to include pregnancy as a covered condition. As mentioned earlier, both COBRA and FMLA are primarily aimed at preserving health care benefits for individuals.

Life Insurance   One of the oldest and most common forms of employee benefit is group life insurance. In 2004, 60 percent of full-time workers in the United States were covered under company-provided life insurance programs. More than half of those programs based benefits on a fixed multiple of earnings. The most common multiple is 1.0 times earnings (59 percent of plans), followed by 2.0 times earnings (25 percent of plans).[60] Group life insurance typically provides coverage to all employees of an organization without physical examinations, with premiums typically based on the group characteristics.[61]

Discretionary Plans: Long-Term Capital Accumulation Plans

A pension is a payment to a retired employee based on the extent and level of employment with the organization. The term *long-term capital accumulation plan* is the generic name for any program that seeks to systematically set aside money during one's working lifetime, primarily for use during one's retirement. This category includes not only pensions, but also 401(k) programs, thrift and other savings programs, traditional profit-sharing plans, and a large variety of similar arrangements.

In 1994, it was estimated that 53 percent of U.S. private industry workers participated in company-based pension plans. In 2004, that number had declined to 49 percent. Medium and large employers are one-and-one-half times more likely to provide pensions programs than small companies.[62]

The Major Pension Plans   There are two types of plans: defined benefit plans and defined contribution plans. A **defined benefit plan** (DB) guarantees a specific retirement payment based on a percentage of preretirement income. Typically, the amount is based on years of service, average earnings during a specified time period (e.g., last five years), and age at time of retirement. The typical target benefit in a defined benefit plan is to replace approximately 50 percent of an individual's final average pay.[63] A small but growing percentage of defined benefit plans (approximately 5 percent) are indexed to adjust pensions for inflation.[64] In a defined benefit plan, the employer funds employees' pensions over their working lifetimes. An employer's commitment to an employee is for a particular payout, at a particular time, based on a formula specified by the plan. Defined benefit programs typically involve significant administrative fees, particularly for actuarial services, to ensure that the plan is financed appropriately under ERISA requirements. In addition, defined benefit plans are required to purchase insurance with the **Pension Benefit Guarantee Corporation** (PBGC), which acts like the FDIC by insuring pension moneys in the event that the company goes bankrupt (or is otherwise unable to meet its promised obligation).

In 2005, United Airlines, under bankruptcy protection, was granted permission to terminate its employee pension plans that would have obligated United to pay $3.2 billion in pension payouts over five years. The Pension Guaranty Benefit Corporation assumed responsibility for the 134,000 people who were part of the pension plans. The result of the takeover will significantly lower pension checks for United retirees with projected obligations to the PGBC of around $10 billion. Experts worry that other companies will opt to dump their pension obligations on the already deeply indebted PGBC.

Many large companies cut their pensions in 2005 and 2006 according to Watson Wyatt Worldwide, a compensation consulting firm. Eleven percent of these firms either discontinued their pension plans altogether or froze benefits to workers. It is estimated that defined benefit plans fell about $350 billion into arrears in 2005. How did this happen? Companies lobbied for and received lax regulations on how to calculate pension obligations, estimating returns on pension investments twice as high as they actually returned. Companies do this so they can use more revenue to report as earnings. They of course have the PBGC to fall back on to bail them out if they cannot meet real pension obligations. Unfortunately, as of 2006, the PBGC had a $23 billion deficit, mainly because of the pension obligations they've already assumed and because companies do not pay sufficient premiums to adequately fund this federal insurance agency. While a bailout by Congress may have already occurred, the problem could have been alleviated by simply raising premiums and holding companies actually responsible for the promises they have made to their employees. As of 2005, the system had essentially rewarded mismanagement and the double-crossing of American workers while companies orchestrate ill-conceived mergers and acquisitions and pay their executives obscene salaries.

In a **defined contribution** (DC) plan, an employer provides a specific dollar amount (typically a percent of base salary) that is paid into an individual's account each period. The most common DC plan is the 401(k) plan which is named after the section of the internal revenue code which regulates these plans. In a typical 401(k) plan, employees defer a percent of pay (subject to certain limitations) that is fully or partially matched by the company. Employees choose among investment options and, typically, may take the vested portion of the account with them if they leave employment before they are eligible to retire (vesting refers to the point in time when pension monies set aside by a company become the actual property of that individual).

In a 401(k) plan, the employer makes no promise to an employee about a pension amount: an individual's pension is the account balance at the time of retirement. As a result, administrative costs are lower under 401(k) programs (and other DC plans) than they are under traditional DB plans, and plan communication is simplified. DB plans have been more common historically than DC plans, but recent concerns about cost uncertainties pushed many companies to replace their DB plans with the simpler, less expensive DC plans. In 2006, IBM announced that it would freeze pension benefits for its American employees beginning in 2008 and offer 401(k) plans in the future. Among the many companies that have recently frozen pension plans for employees are Verizon, Hewlett-Packard, Motorola, and Sears. In 1990, similar numbers of employees were covered under DB plans (35 percent) and DC plans (35 percent). By 2004, the percent of employees covered under DB plans declined to 21 percent while the number of employees covered under DC plans rose to 42 percent. United switched its current employees from a defined benefit plan to a defined contribution plan (401(k)). In fact, the number of employees participating in 401(k) plans since 1995 has more than doubled. Figure 10-10 presents (0k) the trends.

Another popular form of DC plan is the Employee Stock Ownership Plan (ESOP). In an ESOP, the company contributes stock, rather than cash, to employee accounts.

While the number of employees participating in 401(k) plans has more than doubled in the past 10 years . . .

Active participants (in thousands)

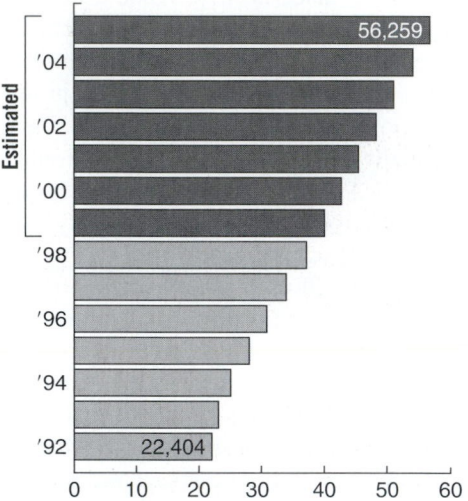

. . . fewer employees are receiving a defined benefit pension as many small businesses drop their pensions.

Active participants in single employer plans (in millions)

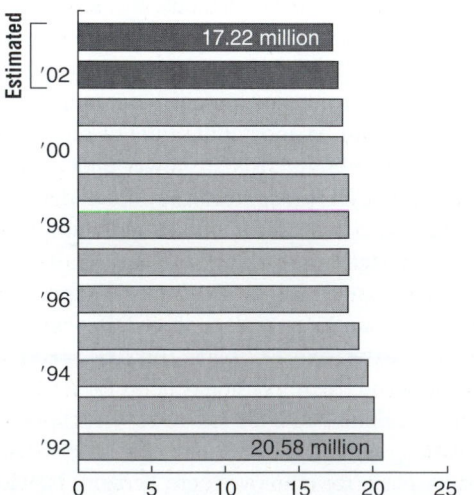

Figure 10-10   Retirement Plan Trends

Sources: Pension Benefit Guaranty Corp., Employee Benefit Research Institute. Reprinted with permission.

Individual allocations are typically based on a person's level of earnings. At the time of retirement, an employee participating in an ESOP receives cash that is directly based on the value of the underlying stock at that time. Some 401(k) plans include company stock as one of the possible investment choices. When this occurs, employees who choose to invest their account balance heavily in the company's stock are, in effect, converting their 401(k) plan into an ESOP. Enron's 401(k) program provides a good example. Because of the enormous success of Enron in its heyday, many employees bypassed 19 other investment options, choosing instead to invest their 401(k) account balances in Enron stock. When the company crashed and burned, employee 401(k) balances were wiped out. Critics have, since, argued that organizations should limit the amount of 401(k) money that can be directly invested in the company's stock (unless, of course, the plan is specifically designed to be an ESOP). Other forms of DC plans include traditional profit-sharing plans, thrift and savings plans, Section 403(b) tax-deferred annuity plans (for education institutions and/or private tax exempt organizations), and Section 457 plans (for government employees).

Government Role in Pension Plans   As mentioned earlier, the **Employee Retirement Income Security Act** (ERISA, 1974) regulates employee pension plans. The requirement that defined benefit plans purchase insurance through the PBGC is an ERISA rule. Since establishment of this rule, more than 1,500 pension plans have resorted to the PBGC in order to meet their pension commitments.[65] ERISA has passed extensive rules concerning the way pension funds may be invested (in general, using a "prudent man" rule focusing on capital preservation), has broadened participation rules (people at all levels in the organization typically enter a plan after only one year of employment), and liberalized vesting rules (after two to three years, at least a portion of the company contribution belongs to the employee). Before ERISA, many pension plans had no vesting provisions; if you weren't working for the company the day you retired, you were not entitled to any benefit.

Other nonbenefits legislation has significantly influenced pension plan provisions. The Civil Rights Act of 1964 and subsequent amendments, which prohibit discrimination on the basis of gender, outlawed pension differences between men and women even if such distinctions were based on real life expectancy differences. Today, most plans use unisex tables that combine the life expectancy rates of men and women.[66] Amendments to the Age Discrimination in Employment Act (ADEA) outlawed mandatory retirement ages and forbade any differences in treatment for individuals who were above a plan's "normal" retirement age. (Years ago, plans typically "froze" individual pensions on employees' 65th birthdays and did not permit them to earn any additional pension credit even if they worked beyond the age of 65. ADEA has outlawed this practice.)[67]

Discretionary Plans: Time-Off Programs

The cost of paid time off represents one of the highest benefit costs for employers today.[68] In March 2004, the cost of paid time off amounted to 6.7 percent of total hourly compensation. According to the United States Bureau of Labor Statistics (BLS), 90 percent of full-time workers receive paid vacation (average 9 days per year); 89 percent receive paid holidays (average 8 days per year); 70 percent receive paid sick leave; 77 percent receive pay for jury duty; and 54 percent receive paid military leave.[69] Of course, multinationals must comply with the laws of the host country for its citizens.

Long-term disability (LTD) coverage typically provides for the replacement of at least some income in the event that an individual contracts a long-term illness or sustains an injury that prevents him/her from working. In small organizations, 20 percent of organizations cover full-time workers with some form of protection. In medium and large organizations, 43 percent of organizations report covering full-time workers in LTD programs.[70]

Discretionary Plans: Employee Services

Although there are a variety of programs, the most common employee services are education programs, employee assistance programs, employee recognition programs, and child care. We will briefly discuss each of these below.

Education Programs   Many organizations have educational programs for their employees that range from literacy programs to tuition refunds for college or graduate school. According to BLS, 72 percent of medium and large U.S. firms offer job-related tuition plans and 36 percent of small organizations offer job-related tuition assistance.[71] In addition, some companies are helping their workers cope with educating their kids. Aluminum Co. of America, for example, hands out over 200 scholarships a year to employees' children.

Employee Assistance Programs and Mental Health Care   Employee assistance programs (EAPs) typically provide counseling, diagnosis, and treatment for substance abuse, family and marital problems, depression, and financial and other personal difficulties. EAPs are used by about 70 percent of Fortune 500 companies with about one-third of U.S. employees having access to the programs. Other companies simply cover treatment for mental disorders within their health care programs. EAPs tend to be cheaper and more effective than simple reimbursement.[72] We will discuss EAPs in more detail in Chapter 14.

Employee Recognition Programs   A growing number of organizations offer awards to employees for extended service, work-related achievements, and suggestions for improving organizational effectiveness. Awards are often in the form of gifts and travel rather than cash. Suggestion systems offer incentives to employees who submit ideas that result in greater efficiency or profitability for the company. According to the National Association of Suggestions Systems, employees were awarded almost $128 million for suggestions in one year.

Child Care   A growing number of companies also are offering various forms of child care benefits. There is evidence that this benefit can reduce employee absences, improve recruitment, and help retain valuable employees.[73] A small but growing number of companies offer on-site centers. Dominion Bankshares in Roanoke, Virginia, reported decreased absences among its 950 employees since its on-site day care center was established. With a variety of government financial incentives now available, and considerable political activity on the subject, there is every reason to believe that child care will become quite common as an employee benefit in years to come. Child care assistance is usually included in cafeteria-style benefit programs.

There is a growing recognition that illness among employees' children can be costly to the company in terms of absenteeism, tardiness, and work stress. AT&T invested in sick bays through hospitals and child care centers. Hoffman-LaRoche and Hughes Aircraft offer sick child care to employees' children through convenient medical centers. The 3M Company covers up to 78 percent of the fees for home health care for kids.

COMMUNICATING THE BENEFITS PROGRAM

As we indicated earlier in the chapter, most employees have little understanding of the costs involved in a benefits program. While ERISA requires that plan and cost information be routinely distributed to benefit participants, most employees know very little about how to value such programs, particularly relative to the programs offered by others. Yet, if an organization's benefits are supposed to be a key tool for attracting and retaining competent workers, this type of understanding would seem to be of paramount importance.

Over the past decade or so, companies have focused attention on improving the information they provide to employees about their benefits. The goals in benefits communication should be to clearly explain the coverages that are available under the plan and to present the value of the benefit package to current and future employees. Today, many employers provide counseling for employees to enhance their understanding of the benefits program and have stepped up their investment in benefits-related recruitment literature. One very popular tool is the Benefits Statement, which is a periodic report customized for and distributed to each individual employee identifying his/her coverages and providing very specific cost information on each such program. Other methods used to explain benefits include paycheck inserts, employee publications, posters, and audio/video recorded messages.

When organizations implement flexible, or cafeteria, benefits, they typically find that they must step up their investment in employee benefits education. When employees are given choices about which coverages to select and which to decline, organizations should feel comfortable that employees are making these selections based on an educated understanding of each benefit option. At Citicorp, for example, 56,000 employees are exposed to software, videos, seminars, and several other teaching tools that explain their flexible benefit program. Each Citicorp employee receives a printout of benefits compared to the previous year, a computer disk, and a workbook that explains how to determine the tax and "out-of-pocket" implications of the benefit options. Each year, the University of Miami holds a two-day, on-campus benefits fair in which every benefits provider stands ready to give whatever information employees need in order to make their benefit selections for the coming year. Providers include claims processors, representatives from each health care provider (every HMO sends a team of representatives to explain their programs to individuals), and each of the five firms that invest pension funds. The university takes the opportunity to combine the benefits fair with a health fair and provides free flu shots, tests cholesterol levels, and provides other information relating to wellness issues. In addition, at the end of the year, the university sends every employee a personalized benefits statement itemizing and describing an individual's coverages and their costs to the university.

INTERNATIONAL COMPENSATION

With over 100,000 U.S. companies now involved in some type of global venture, it is estimated that over 60 million workers are employed overseas by U.S. companies. More than 75 percent of the employees of Gillette work outside the United States and more than 70 percent of profits come from overseas sales. In Chapter 2 we discussed the HR strategies that companies use to help guide an organization's expansion overseas (i.e., ethnocentric, polycentric, geocentric, regiocentric). We also discussed three types of workers (i.e., parent-country nationals, host-country nationals, and third-country nationals). McDonald's now has over 10,000 restaurants in over 100 countries, and the vast majority of the employees are host-country nationals. The expansion of retail giants such as Wal-Mart, Home Depot, and Office Depot into foreign markets has followed this same pattern.

While the discussion here focuses on executive and professional compensation for multinational corporations, there is no question that labor costs (both cash compensation and benefits), play a major role in corporate decisions regarding plant and operations openings, closings, and locations. Virtually no teddy bears are made on U.S. soil today because they can be produced at a fraction of the cost in a developing country such as Haiti or Honduras. The costs of total compensation plus ancillary regulation are the main reasons manufacturing and even some service organizations have moved from the United States.

To fully realize their growth potential, U.S. companies must staff their international operations with personnel who are technically competent, culturally proficient, and cost-effective. In the early stages of globalization, when managers were needed for overseas operations, companies often chose successful managers from company headquarters and enticed them to spend time establishing and building such operations. The main HR goal was ensuring that these managers were "kept financially whole" through a series of complex allowances plus special incentives and benefits.

As organizations have become more proficient in effectively managing global overseas operations, two trends have emerged. First, the availability of well-trained, competent, host-country nationals prepared to manage businesses within their borders has increased. As organizations have achieved access to larger, broader markets by globalizing, many host countries have increased the number of jobs in their economy, improved their standards of living, and benefited from transfers of technology. One form of technological transfer has involved the improved ability on the part of host-country nationals to direct and manage enterprises. In addition, in almost all cases, it's cheaper to employ host-country nationals than to use expatriates, particularly if the reference point for expatriate compensation is the United States, Germany, or a similar country that has both high management salaries and a strong currency.[74] AT&T estimates that expatriate managers cost three times as much as host-country nationals. And yet, the assignment failure rate among expatriates is considerably higher than the failure rate for host-country nationals.[75] AT&T, like so many other American companies, has seen its overseas business increasing, but it has reduced the number of expatriates, replacing them with host-country nationals.

The second trend involves the growing recognition that managing global operations involves a particular expertise that is different from traditional U.S. managerial technology. No longer is an international "tour of duty" simply an assignment. No longer is sending over an American manager in order to supervise operations and resolve problems based on the "American way" considered to be an effective solution. Instead, organizations are increasingly committed to developing management teams that are globally focused. In some organizations, considerable global experience is recognized as a major strategic imperative. At General Electric, for example, an individual will not advance beyond a particular level without significant experience managing overseas operations. Each of the final candidates in the search for Jack Welch's replacement had spent considerable time working outside the United States during the past decade or so. *The Wall Street Journal* reports that, in 1996, 28 percent of executive-level searches required individuals with significant overseas management experience.[76] According to management guru Rosabeth Moss Kanter, global management skills are becoming a major core competence for future business leaders. Such leaders will be globally skilled as (1) integrators, who will see beyond obvious cultural country and cultural differences; (2) diplomats, who can resolve conflicts and influence locals to accept world standards or commonalities; and (3) cross-fertilizers, who recognize the best from various places and adapt it for utilization elsewhere.[77]

The result is that international compensation programs, like base pay programs, are in a state of transition as their emphasis shifts. Typical questions asked these days include: "When should we utilize a host-country national versus someone from someplace else?" "How much can we afford to spend in order to provide developmental opportunities for high-potential employees?" "How should we integrate third-country and host-country nationals with parent-country nationals in order to develop a world-class, global workforce?" The answers to these questions have strong implications for compensation practices. Yet, little formal research is available to guide compensation policy and practice in global settings.[78]

Two traditional approaches exist in the area of international compensation: (1) the going-rate approach and (2) the balance sheet approach.[79] In the going-rate, or market-rate, approach, pay is linked to the prevailing pay in the local area. Burger King, for example, uses a standardized job evaluation instrument (translated into eight languages) and a standard pay structure for its restaurants. However, personnel in different countries receive different pay based on market surveys conducted within each country. In general, this approach is very similar to the general compensation model described earlier in this chapter (i.e., conduct job evaluation, review pay surveys, create a final structure). However, the going rate also can be used for expatriates. When using the approach, however, the organization must carefully consider its relevant market and the reference points it will use. For example, a Japanese bank operating in New York City, using a management team from Japan, would need to decide whether its reference point would be local U.S. salaries, other Japanese competitors in New York, all foreign banks operating in the area, or other Japanese expatriates in the region.

The traditional approach used by U.S. companies for compensating expatriates is the balance sheet approach, in which the goal is "to keep the expatriate whole." This usually means that pay equity focuses on other home-country colleagues and compensating the individual for the additional costs of an international assignment. What happens to third-country nationals? Traditionally, companies headquartered in the United States used U.S. pay practices as the reference point for U.S. expatriates and home country practices as the reference points for third-country nationals. This most certainly saves money, but it can create serious pay inequities when expatriates from different home countries work together.[80]

A newer, emerging approach resolves this dichotomy by developing an international pay scale that ties all expatriate pay to some common reference point. This approach means that pay remains relatively equivalent regardless of the location of a particular assignment, or the home country of a particular expatriate. This approach further standardizes international compensation and moves it away from an individual, case-by-case focus.[81]

Three factors typically influence an organization's approach to international pay design, particularly when expatriates are used.[82] First, the expected length of the assignment influences the type and amount of special benefits and allowances. Assignments lasting less than one year, typically, do not require major modifications to domestic pay practices. Second, the degree of mobility expected of the expatriate influences practices. Assignments that require the employee to move from one foreign location to another will probably require greater incentives to offset family disruptions. Third, the desired reference point to be used for pay equity purposes makes a difference in pay program design. Some companies are beginning to use host-country pay levels (i.e., the going-rate approach described above) and extending them to expatriates on long-term assignments, because they believe that it facilitates an individual's integration into foreign countries and avoids obvious pay inequities within local work groups.

Compensation for international assignments typically has four components, each of which is explained below: (1) base salary, (2) foreign service inducements, (3) allowances, and (4) benefits.

Base Salary

In international compensation, base salary represents the amount of cash compensation that will be provided to an individual each pay period, plus it often serves as a reference point for calculating other allowances. Base salary may be paid in parent- or host-country currency. If parent-country currency is used, the organization must monitor fluctuations in the exchange rate (since the expatriate will be required to exchange the money in order to make local purchases). If host-country currency is used, the organization must monitor the country's inflation rate and changes in the cost of living (to ensure that the expatriate's purchasing power does not inappropriately erode).

Foreign Service Premiums

Foreign service premiums are monetary payments above and beyond base salary that companies offer in order to encourage employees to accept expatriate assignments. Such premiums typically apply to assignments that extend beyond a year. Foreign service premiums tend to range between 5 and 40 percent of base pay.[83] Companies typically disburse premiums to expatriates through periodic lump-sum payments in order to remind the individual that the payment is directly tied to the international assignment.[84]

Hardship premiums are used to compensate expatriates for exceptionally hard living and working conditions in some foreign locations. Many organizations refer to the U.S. Department of State schedule that uses three criteria in identifying hardship: (1) difficult living conditions due to inadequate housing, isolation, inadequate transportation facilities, and lack of food or consumer services; (2) physical hardship relating to extreme climates, high altitudes, and the presence of dangerous conditions that might affect physical and mental well-being; and (3) unhealthy conditions, such as diseases and epidemics, lack of public sanitation, and inadequate health facilities. In the late 1990s, the State Department identified 150 places as hardship locations. Hardship allowances range from 5 to 25 percent of base salary. Like foreign service premiums, organizations tend to provide them in periodic lump-sum payments. Danger pay compensates employees for their willingness to work in politically unstable places. Figure 10-11 is a sample of some hardship and dangerous locations and the percent differential paid for working in these areas.[85]

Allowances

There is great variation in the types of allowances that are used in international compensation. Changes in **purchasing power** due to inflation and **exchange rate** fluctuations (both mentioned earlier) are typically handled with cash allowances. Most organizations provide some type of **housing** allowance in order to provide a level of comfort to the international worker. Depending on the company and the country, housing allowances range from company-provided housing (mandatory or optional), to a fixed-dollar cash bonus, to a cash allowance calculated as a percentage of base salary. **Educational** allowances provide for a variety of needs and are mainly focused toward the expatriates' children. Possible allowances include the cost of private or boarding schools, language class tuition, books and supplies, room and board, and uniforms. **Relocation** allowances typically cover moving, shipping, and storage charges; temporary living expenses; subsidies for major appliance or car purchases; and lease-related charges. Increasingly, organizations are providing special **spouse assistance** to help offset income lost by an expatriate's spouse as a result of relocating abroad. Allowances include cash payments equivalent to the spouse's former wages, assistance in locating suitable employment in the new location (e.g., paying search fees), and continuing supplements if the spouse's income is less than previously earned. Many companies also offer **home leave** allowances in order to encourage the maintenance of ties with family and friends. Such allowances usually cover all expenses relating to visits back to the home country (usually, two trips per year).

Benefits

In many ways, expatriate benefits are a bigger problem in international compensation than pay. Employee benefits and the related tax issues vary considerably from country to country. Key questions that an organization needs to ask itself when dealing with the benefits of expatriates include: "Should we keep expatriates in parent-country programs, even if we do not get a tax deduction for it?" "Can we legally enroll the individual in the host-country benefits and make up the differences in actual coverage?" "What should we do about Social Security issues?" Within the European Union, Social Security is portable. It is not in most other places in the world.

Most U.S. expatriates remain under their parent-country's benefit plan. In countries where employees may not opt out of **Social Security** (or other mandatory pension) coverage, the firm will typically cover this expense.

One particularly challenging international compensation problem involves **taxation**.[86] For U.S. expatriates, an assignment overseas often means that they will be double-taxed—both in the country of assignment and in the United States. Most organizations choose between two strategies for managing taxes on behalf of their expatriates. In the **tax equalization** approach, firms withhold taxes based on the home-country tax obligation and pay all taxes in the host country. The **tax protection** approach involves the employee paying all taxes up to the amount he would pay in the home country. Under this approach, considering the tax credit for foreign earned income provided by the United States, if taxes in the foreign country are less than those that would have been paid in the United States, the international employee gets to keep the windfall.

FIGURE 10-11	U.S. Department of State Indices of Hardship Differentials and Danger Pay—January 2005	
City, Country	**Hardship Differential**	**Danger Pay**
Kabul, Afghanistan	25%	25%
Minsk, Belarus	25	—
Beijing, China	20	—
Bogota, Colombia	5	15
Santo Domingo, Dominican Republic	20	—
Tallinn, Estonia	5	—
Athens, Greece	5	—
Port-au-Prince, Haiti	25	15
Bombay, India	20	—
Jerusalem	10	20
Antananarivo, Madagascar	25	—
Mexico City, Mexico	15	—
Islamabad, Pakistan	20	25
Lima, Peru	15	—
Warsaw, Poland	5	—
Moscow, Russia	15	—
Riyadh, Saudi Arabia	25	25
Freetown, Sierra Leone	25	—
Ankara, Turkey	10	—
Caracas, Venezuela	15	—

Source: www.state.gov/m/a/ais/gtrpt/2005/42.178.html. Accessed May 14, 2005.

SUMMARY

Because of the importance that compensation holds for their lifestyle and self-esteem, individuals are very concerned that they be paid a fair and competitive wage. Organizations are concerned with pay, not only because of its importance as a cost of doing business, but also because it motivates important decisions of employees about taking a job, leaving a job, and performance on the job.

When designing base salary compensation plans, it is important that an organization choose an approach that is in alignment with its organizational philosophy and that supports its organizational goals. In some cases, the traditional approach to pay still provides the best answer. This approach involves the use of a job evaluation plan (to measure internal job worth and to foster internal equity), the review of market salary data (to identify externally competitive practices), and the reconciliation of these two in the form of a final pay structure. Due to the basic changes in organizations today and the new global challenges and opportunities, there is a growing search for new compensation approaches in the hope that they will better focus employees on achieving organizational goals. Such new approaches to pay include broadbanding, pay for knowledge (or skills-based pay), and team pay plans. To date, however, the relative effectiveness of these new approaches remains to be tested.

Employee benefits programs continue to grow and expand, although there are considerable variations in the benefits that are offered by organizations. Benefits mainly have been directed at assisting employees in maintaining a particular lifestyle and providing for their long-term welfare and security. The rise of flexible (or cafeteria) benefit plans suggests the importance of considering individual preferences, the increasing diversity of the workforce, and lifestyle realities when structuring an employee benefits program.

The government's goal concerning its regulation of pay and benefits is to ensure that discrimination does not exist and that certain minimum levels of fairness are maintained in compensation programs. A number of federal, state, and local laws regulate compensation. In addition, regulation is aimed at managing the delicate balance between tax revenue maximization and maintaining the positive social forces that tax-favored employee benefit plans have contributed to society.

Base pay programs and fringe benefit programs must be assessed for the extent to which they attract, retain, and motivate the workforce relative to major competitors. The cost of labor is critical to corporate performance and must be constantly monitored to determine whether costs can be reduced with no loss in the quality of products or services necessary for fulfilling the organization's strategy. By the same token, when required skills for competitive advantage are in great demand, companies that do not respond with competitive pay packages will lose out and end up cutting their labor costs at the expense of organizational capability. While America's most admired companies such as Coca-Cola, Mirage Resorts, United Parcel Service, and Microsoft all take steps to control and (at times) reduce their labor costs, they also make certain that their compensation packages attract, retain, and motivate the key personnel they require to maintain their admirable status.

Regardless of which particular compensation program is chosen, organizations need the capacity to measure individual or group results so that such performance may be reflected in pay. In the next chapter, we consider the methods that are used to reward employees for their contributions to an organization. As we shall see, these decisions are by no means easy, but when combined with other components of compensation, an effective pay-for-performance program can be a powerful tool with which to attract, retain, and motivate a high-quality workforce. Almost all the companies named in *Fortune*'s 2000 rating of America's most admired companies have compensation systems with relatively more pay at risk in the form of stock awards for its key employees. We will discuss this growing component of American compensation next.

DISCUSSION QUESTIONS

1. Research CEO pay on the internet (try www.aflcio.org/ paywatch and Graef Crystal's columns at www.bloomberg.com/columns). Has CEO pay changed since the scandals of 2002? Identify persons you believe to be the most overpaid and underpaid.

2. It has been proposed that HR managers should be more involved with compensation committees charged with determining executive pay packages. How should HR be involved?

3. What is more important for organizational effectiveness— internal equity or external equity? Explain your answer.

4. Pay expert Ed Lawler says pay the person, not the job. Explain what you think he means and how that would work.

5. What is broadbanding and what does the latest research say about its effects?

6. The Fair Pay Act has been proposed, mandating a comparable worth policy for federal employees. Research this legislation and take a position.

7. A constant political debate is whether the minimum wage should be increased. Research this topic and justify your position on the topic.

8. Workers' compensation programs and the FMLA have proven to be problematic laws for employers. Research these laws to determine the recent controversies and proposed solutions.

9. Research the current trends in defined contribution versus defined benefit programs. From the employer's perspective, what program is preferable and why? Now, consider the employee's perspective.

10. What is the most typical pay policy for expatriate assignments? How would you determine the entire pay package?

11

PAY FOR PERFORMANCE*

O V E R V I E W

As Harvard professor Rosabeth Moss Kanter put it, "America is . . . already well on its way to transforming the meaning of the paycheck . . . the most important trend in pay determination has actually been the loosening relationship between job assignment and pay level."[1]

Professor Kanter's remarks were prophetic for 21st century compensation. As we discussed in Chapter 10, a strong trend in compensation administration over the last 10 years is the installation of various forms of pay-for-performance (PFP) systems. The term *pay-for-performance* is a little misleading since many incentive systems now award something other than pay for desired performance. Luxury cruises, golf outings, and trips to Las Vegas are common parts of incentive programs. We will use the PFP term, but you should understand that company stock, vacation trips, and outings are also used to recognize and reward desired performance. In general, these PFP systems put more employee pay at risk and do indeed loosen the relationship between assignments and pay levels. This loosening at least theoretically provides more flexibility for organizations.

Controlling labor costs and increasing productivity through the establishment of clearer linkages between pay and performance are considered to be a key human resource management (HRM) component of competitive advantage. In addition, increased concerns over productivity and meeting customer requirements have prompted renewed interest in methods designed to motivate employees to be more focused on meeting (or exceeding) customer requirements and increasing productivity. What better way to do this than by establishing a closer connection between meeting such requirements and compensation? Research has found characteristics of PFP systems to be major elements of "high-performance work systems" (HPWS) and linked PFP to firm performance, particularly when the PFP system is closely aligned with the company's strategic objectives and a high percentage of employees participate in the plan.[2]

But many firms jump on the PFP bandwagon without thoroughly understanding the potential difficulties and limitations of PFP systems. The most recent review of the vast literature concluded that "the evidence on PFP is generally positive. To be sure, there are some very important caveats: pay is not the only important motivator in organizations, and PFP programs can yield serious, unintended negative results. Nevertheless, it can also deliver powerful improvements in performance.[3]" There are clear guidelines to follow and failure to follow them can doom a PFP system.[4] And there are many classic failures. Harvard professor Kevin Murphy summarized the research on PFP nicely: "Business history is littered with firms that got what they paid for."[5] Sears had a very clear PFP system in which mechanics were paid bonuses as a percentage of repair receipts. Receivables went up,

---

*E. Brian Peach and M. Ronald Buckley contributed to this chapter.

mechanics got higher pay, and 41 states indicted Sears for fraud. Columbia Hospitals is probably another example of getting what you pay for in a PFP system. When you can increase your profits by "gaming" a government entitlement system like Medicare, the government just might think the "gaming" constitutes fraud. Paying teachers for higher student test scores invites "teaching to the test" or worse unless proper safeguards are put in place. New York State discovered internal e-mails blasting companies that Merrill Lynch analysts were pushing as "strong buys." Merrill settled a lawsuit for $100 million in 2002. Morgan-Stanley lost a similar lawsuit in 2005 when a Florida jury determined that they were fraudulently pushing Sunbeam stock with full knowledge it was overpriced. They were assessed $1 billion in punitive damages. Needless to say, organizations need to be very careful about setting up the performance measures used for the PFP system.

In the best-seller *Freakonomics,* authors Levitt and Dubner put it this way: "For every clever person who goes to the trouble of creating an incentive scheme, there is an army of people, clever and otherwise, who will inevitably spend even more time trying to beat it. Cheating may or may not be human nature, but it is certainly a prominent feature in just about every human endeavor. Cheating is a primordial economic act: getting more for less. So it isn't just the boldface names—inside-trading CEOs and pill-popping ballplayers and perk-abusing politicians-who cheat. It is the waitress who pockets her tips instead of pooling them. It is the Wal-Mart payroll manager who goes into the computer and shaves his employees' hours to make his own performance look better. It is the third grader who, worried about not making it to the fourth grade, copies test answers from the kid sitting next to him."[6]

PFP systems are very common for executives, mostly in the form of stock options that have been lavished on top executives. While a few studies have found that executive pay is generally tracking with corporate performance, there are many more studies documenting the obscenely exorbitant pay for CEOs. CEO pay rose 570 percent from 1990 to 2000 versus 37 percent in average workers' salaries.[7] Most of the increase in CEO pay is due to the PFP components of the pay package and, in particular, stock options. Compensation that is overloaded with stock options will drive affected executives to focus on stock price and driving the stock price up using whatever chicanery is available.

Many of our most successful companies have endeavored to establish a stronger connection between employee pay and strategic goals. Federal Express, for example, won the prestigious Baldrige Award in 1990 and was cited for the clear linkage it established between worker pay and customer satisfaction data. Stanford Professor Pfeffer, whose research we discussed in Chapter 1, identified a successful PFP system as a key to the success of some of the most profitable companies in the United States.[8] Lincoln Electric Welding is one such company. Pfeffer attributes Lincoln Electric's success to its incentive management program (lincolnelectric.com). But he also emphasizes that their PFP system could only be pulled off in the context of a particular management system and philosophy, a system based on great trust between workers and management.

One survey of the largest United States companies found that 90 percent connect at least part of some employees' pay to performance.[9] Among the many companies that have implemented some form of PFP system for nonmanagerial employees in recent years are General Motors (GM), the Tribune Company, Blockbuster Video, Coca-Cola, Burger King, Office Depot, Mirage Resorts, United Parcel Service (UPS), Federal Express, Grumman, and Wal-Mart. GM, for example, put more than 26,000 workers on a merit pay system after abandoning across-the-board increases. Wendy's and Office Depot even have bonus systems based on assessments conducted by "mystery shoppers" (see Chapter 7). One survey of 2,719 midsize companies found that 30 percent of companies paid lump-sum bonuses averaging 3.5 percent of annual salary.[10]

The purpose of this chapter is to review the major types of PFP systems and to discuss their relative advantages and disadvantages. The determinants of effective PFP systems are described first, followed by an exploration of questions of fairness and practicality regarding PFP. Next, the major problems associated with PFP will be reviewed. The second part of the chapter reviews the major types of PFP and the problems with measuring performance.

OBJECTIVES

After reading this chapter, you should be able to

1. *Understand the determinants of effective PFP systems.*
2. *Identify the critical variables related to the selection of the most appropriate PFP systems.*
3. *Review the evidence on the effectiveness of different PFP systems.*
4. *Determine the relative advantages and disadvantages of the various PFP systems.*

PFP systems come in all shapes and sizes. One of the most important considerations is the level-of-performance measurement. The most common type of PFP is to tie pay to individual performance in a merit pay system. However, in an effort to promote teamwork, a growing number of companies now tie pay to unit or group performance, and others tie pay to organizational or company performance.

Within each of these three general categories, however, there are numerous approaches. As we discussed in Chapter 7, the accurate measurement of performance and the linkage of the performance measures to the strategic goals of the organization are the keys to successful PFP efforts.

DOES PFP WORK?

A special issue of the *Harvard Business Review* included a note from the editors that identified two major themes of the special issue. One of those themes was that "while traditional rewards and punishments can, if ill managed, severely damage motivation, they have little beneficial effect under even the best of circumstances." Stanford scholar Jeff Pfeffer called the notion that people work for money a "myth."[11] In fact, experts in the area of PFP have concluded, "these claims are simply inconsistent with the voluminous evidence, based on hundreds of studies."[12] While experts provide a number of important "contingencies" or conditions which are related to the relative effectiveness of PFP, "the usefulness of money as well as its many symbolic meanings suggests that, far from being a mere low order motivator, pay can assist in obtaining any level on Maslow's motivational hierarchy, including social esteem and self-actualization." A study of "high performance work systems" found certain types of PFP systems and characteristics were correlated with stronger firm performance.[13] Many firms have developed new forms of incentive programs despite arguments that pay for performance doesn't work.[14]

PFP systems can (and clearly do) work and they are important for attracting and keeping top talent. But there are contingency factors that research has shown can affect important outcomes related to pay and the importance attached to pay by workers. Figure 11-1 presents a summary of the most important contingencies. You will note that the characteristics of the employee matter (e.g., extroverts place more value on pay than introverts; high performers are more receptive to and also more critical of PFP systems) as do the characteristics of the pay system itself. For example, changes to pay systems, particularly without employee input, can have a significant negative impact. One study found over a 100 percent increase in employee theft after the company cut pay by 15 percent with no explanation. Also, while pay will have little effect where people receive similar pay increases despite large differences in performance, dramatic changes in performance can occur when pay is made more contingent on performance. Regarding marginal utility, there is evidence that being "under market" has a stronger motivational impact than does the positive effect of being "above market." People often reject offers simply because of the pay. Pay is probably relatively more critical in terms of job choice than in decisions to quit because pay is one of the few characteristics people can know with certainty before taking a job. Once you've had a job for a while, other factors like the quality of supervision will have a strong impact.

The bottom line on the effects of PFP systems is that PFP systems can be effective if they are tailored to particular work situations and strategies and contribute to high-probability estimates by employees concerning

---

FIGURE 11-1	Examples of Contingency Factors Affecting Pay Importance
Individual Difference Contingencies	**Situational Contingencies**
1. Pay is more important to extroverts than to introverts.	1. Pay is more important in job choice when pay varies widely across employers than when pay is relatively more uniform.
2. Receiving performance-based pay is more important to high academic achievers than to others.	2. There is a declining marginal utility to additional increments of pay.
3. High-performance employees appear to be particularly sensitive to whether their higher performance is rewarded with above-average pay increases, while low performers prefer low-contingency pay systems.	3. The salience or "importance" of pay is likely to rise after *changes* are made to pay systems. Employees are particularly sensitive to pay *cuts*.
4. Pay appears to be more important to men than to women.	4. Employee reactions to changes in pay depend heavily on communication of the *reasons* for pay policies and changes.
5. People with high need for achievement and higher feelings of self-efficacy prefer pay systems that more closely link pay to performance.	5. Pay is probably more important in job choice than in decisions to quit.
	6. Pay will do little to motivate performance in systems where people receive similar pay increases regardless of individual or firm performance. However, dramatic changes in performance can occur when pay is made more contingent on performance.

Source: Adapted from S. L. Rynes, B. Gerhart, and K. A. Minette, "The Importance of Pay in Employee Motivation: Discrepancies between What People Say and What They Do." *Human Resource Management* 43 (2004), pp. 381–394.

their effort and their performance and desired outcomes. **Expectancy/Instrumentality theory** (see Figure 11-3) particularly when combined with **goal-setting,** has a great deal of predictive power in understanding the value of PFP systems.

Domino's Pizza claimed an increase in sales in excess of 20 percent after implementing a complicated PFP system. International Business Machines (IBM) reported a 200 percent increase over 10 years in productivity in manufacturing—an increase that IBM attributes to its PFP system. One survey reported improved output from two out of three companies using some form of PFP when incentives were provided for meeting specific performance targets.[15] The evidence is strong that PFP systems are effective when what an organization is actually rewarding is highly compatible with its strategic objectives and execution.[16]

WHAT ARE THE DETERMINANTS OF EFFECTIVE PFP SYSTEMS?

Although pay is generally regarded as a motivator, organizations often are confronted with unique sets of issues and problems related to PFP and therefore must develop strategies to deal with them. The most important determinants of effective PFP are summarized in Figure 11-2.

Expectancy/Instrumentality theory explains why more pay leads to higher performance and why the connection is often not all that strong. Motivation is a function of the perception a worker has about the likelihood that more effort will lead to higher performance and that higher performance will lead to valued outcomes like more money. Of course, performance is also a function of a worker's (or student's) knowledge, skills, and abilities. A worker's perception of the critical effort to performance relationship is to some extent a consequence of that worker's self-assessment of his or her KASOCs as related to the work. In addition, if workers believe that

FIGURE 11-2 Determinants of Effective PFP Systems

1. Worker values outcomes (money, prizes).
2. Outcome is valued relative to other rewards.
3. Desired performance must be measurable.
4. Worker must be able to control rate of output or quality.
5. Worker must be capable of increasing output or quality.
6. Worker must believe that capability to increase exists.
7. Worker must believe that increased output will result in receiving a reward.
8. Size of reward must be sufficient to stimulate increased effort.
9. Performance measures must be compatible with strategic goals for short and long term.

situational constraints beyond their control have more to do with performance than their own effort or competencies, their perception of the likelihood that effort will lead to higher performance will be very low (see points 4–6 in Figure 11-2). While the determinants presented in Figure 11-2 can increase the likelihood of an effective PFP system, all are not required for an effective PFP system. Figure 11-3 presents the critical probabilities that have the most to do with the success or failure of any PFP system.

Increases in pay as a reward for increases in performance must be valued by the specific employee or work unit for which the PFP plan is intended—and must be valued highly relative to other rewards. Occasionally group norms or cultural values de-emphasize money or at least differential rewards for differential outputs. Unions, for example, have traditionally opposed pay systems based on individual or unit-level output, such as piece-rate incentive systems. A major reason for this is doubt by workers that increased productivity will result in increased pay. Some unions (e.g., the United Auto Workers, the Communication Workers of America, and the Teamsters) have become more receptive to PFP systems in recent years when trust is established between the union and management. Ford's profit-sharing plan resulted in each of the over 125,000 eligible Ford employees receiving an average of $3,100 in 1999. There was no profit from 2000 to 2005 and thus no profit-sharing. The Teamsters supported a profit-sharing plan for UPS workers in its 1997 collective bargaining agreement. At GM's Saturn plant, UAW members work for a salary (about $45,000 per year), with 20 percent of the amount fluctuating up or down since it is tied to assessments of car quality, productivity, and profits. These examples are certainly exceptions rather than the rule. In general, unions favor only organization-wide or plant-based PFP systems and not individual PFP systems, which the unions maintain will inevitably pit worker against worker. When the state of Florida mandated an individual merit pay system for teachers, the American Federation of Teachers (AFT) worked diligently to promote regulations regarding the merit pay process which ultimately led to the demise of the system. Within two years, the state had rescinded the individual PFP program.

Some companies regard individual PFP systems as contrary to their team-oriented philosophy of management and organizational culture. United Technologies is an example of one company that espouses this view. Its PFP reward system uses only aggregated methods of rewards in which unit and company-wide performance measures are the basis of the awards.

The organization must identify those measures of performance (e.g., outputs, products, services, behaviors, cost reductions) that are most compatible with their strategic goals and execution. For example, increased output may be desirable only in situations in which there

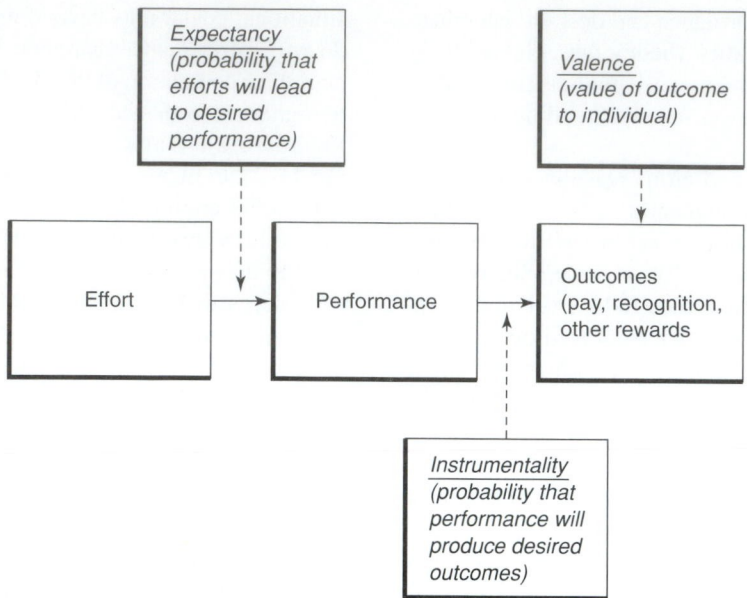

Figure 11-3   Expectancy/Instrumentality Theory

is customer demand for more of the product. Needless to say, the organization should tie pay only to those aspects of value that are critical for the organization. You may recall from Chapter 7 that we distinguished among six aspects of value in the measurement of performance. While most organizations place equal weight on the quality and the quantity of a worker's performance, some companies have a clear preference for one of these aspects over the other. The PFP system should establish a reward system for those aspects of value that are compatible with the strategic goals of the *organization*. For example, retailers often offer incentives for the sale of certain merchandise that is overstocked. Inventory control and sales projections drive the time for the incentive system. Marriott's strategic goal was to be the "hotel of choice" for business travelers. It established a telephone survey of their patrons' experience and then tied the customer satisfaction data to bonuses. Home Depot outsources all of its *home* installations, but it does a follow-up survey to customers of the recommended installers in order to determine whether they were pleased with the service. A favorable review gets the vendor a small bonus while an unfavorable review could jeopardize the priority rank of the outsourcing company. The proper emphasis on criteria can be tricky but can make or break a PFP system. Inspectors working for the Federal Emergency Management Agency were paid *per* inspection in 2004 after a hurricane in Florida. The result was a whole lot of fraudulent inspections leading to over $10 million in awards for damages that didn't occur.

Perhaps encouraged by the *Valdez* oil spill in Alaska and Exxon's woeful response, Conoco made environmen-

tal issues a major strategic priority. Environmental criteria became a component of its incentive system for top managers. Xerox Corporation places great emphasis on customer service and now uses customer survey data as a criterion in its bonus system. According to Xerox's president, it is possible that an executive of a profitable unit would not get a bonus at all if the customer survey data indicated poor performance. The Aluminum Company of America now emphasizes improvements in safety records as a part of its managerial bonus system. Merrill Lynch was concerned about the loss of new brokers who had recently completed their expensive 17-week training program. The company installed a straight salary system with deferred commission contingent on two years of service. All commission was lost if the executives quit prior to two years. The new incentive system also included a $100,000 bonus for brokers who stayed with the company for 10 years. Workers at a Monsanto Corporation chemical plant in Louisiana can earn bonuses for meeting goals that include reducing injuries and preventing emissions from escaping into the environment. Texaco places considerable weight on diversity issues in its PFP plans for executives as a partial response to the settlement of a class-action racial discrimination lawsuit. Executives were evaluated and paid based on their ability to keep and develop minorities and women. Wal-Mart installed a similar program in 2005 in the context of the mammoth class-action, sex discrimination lawsuit (see pages 408–410 for detail).

Successful PFP systems recognize that all of the determinants presented in Figure 11-2 are intimately related. For example, to determine the nature of a reward that should be offered for an increased level of effort, a firm must know the relative importance of money to its typical worker, the increased value to the firm of any given performance increase, the worker's perception of the increased effort required, and the likelihood of receiving the reward. Money also fails to motivate if the required level of extra effort results in unacceptable fatigue to the worker or prevents the worker from enjoying a valued social life. All of the determinants are more likely to occur with more worker involvement in the development of the PFP system. Employee participation in the development will enhance acceptance of the plan. The personal characteristics of employees can also affect results. As discussed earlier research indicates that PFP systems are more attractive to individuals who are stronger performers and higher in achievement orientation, academic achievement, and self-efficacy. Also, high performers are the most likely to seek out other employment if they do not feel they have been recognized with financial rewards.[17]

WHAT ARE THE MAIN PROBLEMS WITH PFP PROGRAMS?

There are many potential problems with PFP systems. Figure 11-4 presents a summary of the problems judged by experts to be most responsible for the failure of such systems. PFP systems can be expensive to develop and maintain. In addition to the initial cost of establishing standards and rates, changes in procedures, equipment, and product may require revision of any existing standards and reward structures. In many cases a revision of the compensation system will be viewed with suspicion. Historically, some short-sighted firms have taken advantage of changes in the production process to reduce the amount of reward for any given level of effort. General Motors established what it thought were challenging

FIGURE 11-4	**Reasons for the Failures of PFP Systems**

1. Poor perceived connection between performance and pay.
2. The level of performance-based pay is too low relative to base pay. The cost of more highly motivating programs may be prohibitive.
3. Lack of objective, countable results for most jobs, requiring the use of performance ratings.
4. Faulty performance appraisal systems, with poor cooperation from managers, leniency bias in the appraisals, and resistance to change.
5. Union resistance to such systems and to change in general.
6. Poor connection between PFP outcomes and corporate performance measures.

production targets for a Michigan plant and let workers go home when the targets were achieved, GM then increased the targets when it found workers were able to go home early. Such actions had a long-term negative effect on worker responses to PFP systems. Again, the more worker involvement in pay plan changes, the greater the acceptance of the changes.

Many problems can arise in a PFP system that relies on performance appraisals. One frequent problem is that workers do not feel that their rewards are closely linked to their performance, a critical component of expectancy instrumentality theory. This low probability often occurs when employees believe that the performance measure does not accurately reflect their performance. As we discussed in Chapter 7, employees often have inflated ideas about their performance levels, which translate into unrealistic expectations about rewards as well. One study found that the majority of workers who were rated even slightly less than the highest level (e.g., 8 on a 9-point scale) were more dissatisfied than satisfied with the rating. Those with even larger discrepancies between their self-assessments and their supervisor's ratings were more dissatisfied with their merit pay increase.[18] Given these beliefs, a large portion of the workforce may receive performance ratings below their expectations, and rewards will likely fall short of expectations. As discussed in Chapter 7, there can be a perception of bias in the process even if such bias does not exist. To the extent that workers perceive that the performance measurement component of the PFP system is biased or invalid, the perceived connection between pay and performance will be undermined and the PFP system will be less effective. This is a common problem when performance is measured by ratings. Some experts on PFP go so far as to say that if performance must be measured by ratings, PFP is not worth the trouble. One such expert concluded that when ratings must be used, "the approach is so flawed that it is hard to imagine a set of conditions which would make it effective."[19] While this conclusion may be overly pessimistic, there is no denying that PFP systems based on ratings of performance can be problematic. In one of the largest Title VII class-action lawsuits, it was alleged that Coca-Cola discriminated against African Americans in the manner in which it evaluated personnel and awarded merit increases. Companies should not contemplate PFP until they have great faith in their performance measurement system.

Many PFP plans have failed because the performance measure that was rewarded was not related to the performance objectives of the entire organization as a whole and to those aspects of performance that were most important to the organization. For example, a PFP system may put inordinate emphasis on the quantity of output when the organizational emphasis is on quality improvement or cost effectiveness. As one expert in compensation put it, "Misaligned pay strategy not only fails to add value, it produces high costs . . . as well as inappropriate and misdirected behavior."[20] The organization must constantly ensure that the aspects of value that are emphasized in the appraisal and PFP system are the same ones that are the priority of the organization.

Recall from our discussion of performance appraisal in Chapter 7 that it is possible to weight performance dimensions (which are combinations of job functions with aspects of value: quantity, quality, timeliness, need for supervision, effects on constituents, and cost). This weighting process should reflect the strategic plan of the unit and the organization. Unfortunately, the typical measurement process for PFP systems is far more haphazard than this. In fact, one survey found that the majority of workers who were paid on a PFP system had little understanding of the criteria for performance measurement.[21]

The organization also should ensure that workers are capable of increasing their performance. You may recall the discussion in Chapter 7 regarding constraints on performance. An employee working on an assembly line or operating a machine with a preset speed may not have the opportunity to increase the quantity of performance. For higher pay to result in higher performance, workers must believe in (and be capable of) higher levels of performance. When workers believe that performance standards exceed their capabilities, they will not expend extra effort.

One of the most common problems with PFP systems is that an insufficient amount of money is available for meritorious performance. There is some indication that this situation may be improving. While a 1990 survey of 459 firms found that the most effective workers received 8 percent increases, while lower-rated workers received around 5 percent, another study found that more money was available for PFP with greater differentiation among workers.[22]

One study found that the most effective computer programmers received an additional $17 per month more than satisfactory workers on annual salaries of about $40,000. Says one expert on the subject, this difference is "hardly enough to push someone to excel."[23] While experts differ on the subject, the lowest level recommended is between 10 and 15 percent of base salary for the money to be considered significant and for the PFP system to be effective.[24] Digital Equipment Corporation used a range of 0 to 30 percent, and Westinghouse has a range of 0 to 19 percent, but most companies are at lower levels. At Continental Bank, for example, an employee earning $3,000 per month who worked and achieved the very highest performance appraisal was eligible for the highest PFP award of 5 percent, which increased earnings $150 per month (before taxes). Most employees who were surveyed on the PFP system didn't think the amount of money involved in the PFP system was worth the extra effort. When subjective measures of performance are used (ratings), pay is rarely seen as sufficiently differentiated, especially among high performers.

WHAT ARE THE LEGAL IMPLICATIONS OF PFP?

As we discussed in Chapter 10, all decisions regarding compensation, including all that are derived from PFP systems, are subject to complaints using the same sources of redress we have discussed throughout the book. PFP systems have been challenged for more subtle forms of alleged discrimination. For example, as we discussed in Chapter 7, situational constraints on performance can affect the basic fairness and equity of the PFP system. They also have been the basis of Title VII actions. An office furniture retailer terminated a female employee for failure to meet a sales quota in a difficult territory. She argued that her opportunity to meet the quota was severely restricted by situational constraints that were beyond her control and that men were not so constrained. She also argued that benefits such as providing sample products that were made available to the male sales personnel were deliberately denied her. Her complaint resulted in a large out-of-court settlement. The current huge Wal-Mart class action sex discrimination case alleges discrimination in the pay system.

HOW DO YOU SELECT A PFP SYSTEM?

In designing a PFP system, three major questions should be asked:

1. Who should be included in the PFP system?
2. How will performance be measured?
3. Which incentives will be used?

The process for developing the characteristics of a performance appraisal system apply to the first two questions, which were discussed in Chapter 7.

Who Should Be Included in a PFP System?

In general, all groups should be included in a PFP system, with one critical condition: the PFP system should be developed with specific groups and conditions in mind. The "devil" is in the details of PFP systems, so production workers, middle management, salespeople, engineers, professionals, or senior executives and top management should probably have different systems. Many companies use very different PFP systems for different jobs. For example, McDonald's has eight different PFP systems for various classes of employees. IBM has six different systems. Many companies have different PFP systems as a function of their organizational and unit-level strategies, with some form of market share measurement for a start-up product or service, and cost cutting for a more established product or service line. Some companies use a variety of different PFP systems for the same job families. For example, AMOCO has an individual merit pay system, a unit-level PFP measurement, and an employee stock ownership program (ESOP) for the same employees.

Other companies have reward systems that are compatible with an egalitarian culture that attempts to minimize the distance between people at different levels in the organizational hierarchy. Digital Equipment Corporation, for example, has only one reward system for all employees. In general, however, American workers prefer individual PFP systems where they can control their own destinies. Great deference should be given to this preference unless a compelling argument can be made that individual PFP systems will foster a competition among employees that will interfere with meeting company or unit-level strategic objectives.

So the bottom line is that you should try to involve as many workers in a PFP system as possible, but each system should be tailored to particular work situations. Organizations should avoid PFP systems that promote individual competition among workers that interferes with meeting major corporate or unit-level objectives.

What Are the Rewards in a PFP System?

Cash payments, percentage increases in base pay, and numerous noncash prizes are still the most common rewards for performance. While these incentives are flexible and well suited to short-run objectives, stock award and stock options are an approach for meeting long-run objectives. Stock options are becoming more common for lower-level employees and are a bigger percentage of the raise for lower-level managers. In addition to quarterly bonuses based on "mystery shopper" data, Wendy's also awards stock to employees for performance and time on the job.

Another company with an employee stock ownership plan is Publix Super Markets. This highly successful privately held company made *Fortune's* 2005 list of "Great Companies To Work For." Its stockholders are the 125,000 workers. If you work more than 1,000 hours per year at Publix and work more than one year, you get Publix stock. Publix "associates" clearly have a sense of ownership in the company. Says Publix spokesperson, Anne Hendricks "Put yourself in the place of a Publix associate: If you see areas where you can eliminate waste, you're going to do it, because you're going to see it in your next dividend check."

Options are typically additions to upper-management pay that also include a cash bonus. Many of the U.S. Fortune 500 companies offer some form of stock option for executives. Although there are several types of stock options, the most popular today are incentive options that give an executive the right to purchase stock at a specified price within a designated time period. The price is lower than the market price. If the company does well and the stock price goes up, everyone is happy. Actually, some CEOs made out all right even if the stock price went down as corporate boards awarded new options and lowered exercise prices. Options have developed a bad reputation lately due to the numerous examples of corporate executives making millions exercising options just before a stock headed south.

Many highly successful companies offer options to low-level employees. For example, some experts argue that Federal Express has low turnover among its drivers and maintains a union-free environment at least to some extent because these employees own a part of the company. The average CEO earned $9.84 million in 2004 with almost 75 percent of that figure in the form of exercising their stock options.[25]

One reason for the past popularity of stock options was that companies were not required to report stock options as an expense. However, a new accounting rule proposed in 2005 would require that stock options be reported as an expense. As a result, many organizations are reconsidering their current stock option plans. The National Center for Employee Ownership estimates that at least 40 percent of publicly traded companies with stock option plans are reconsidering stock options and as many as a third may discontinue stock options in the next few years.[26] Dell cut options for employees by 60 percent, CDW no longer grants options to nonmanagerial employees, and McDonald's is scaling back its stock option compensation plans. In addition, many organizations, such as Microsoft, ExxonMobil Corp., and insurer Progressive Corp., have stopped granting options altogether. If enacted, the 2005 accounting rules are likely to dramatically decrease the use of options.

While the size of CEO paychecks continued to grow in 2004 (a 12 percent increase) the form of the pay package is changing. Pressed by institutional investors and the controversy over expensing options, stock options made up only 31 percent of CEOs' compensation (down from 69 percent in 2001). The obvious problem with stock options is that they can provide senior executives with incentives that may not be in the best interests of long-term shareholders.

A Discrepancy between Research and Practice

With regard to actual *pay* for performance, another strong trend today is a PFP system in which the performance-based pay is not permanently tied to an employee's base pay. In fact, experts have been recommending this approach for years, mainly because the size of the bonus that can be offered can be greater and the cost to the organization in the long run is far less (a bonus that goes in your base salary is in your base salary forever).[27] Compensation experts maintain that base pay should be tied to expected levels of work and that PFP should be tied to performance that exceeds that level. Workers are more likely to exceed that level if the performance–outcome connection is stronger. This connection is typically stronger with bonus-based systems. Many companies pay lump sums based on corporate profits, and the lump sum does not increase an employee's base salary. As we mentioned previously, GM's Saturn plant operates on a 20 percent rate of "risk" for all salaried workers, with no tie-in to the base salary. Champion International pays managers based on growth in earnings per share of stock relative to the stock of the 15 major competitors. The bonus awarded to the 12 senior managers is not tied to the managers' base pay. Federal Express managers have "small spot" awards of $100 that are available for unusual achievement. For example, one "small spot" award was given to a driver who went well beyond the call of duty to deliver a package when the weather would have been a justifiable excuse. Home Depot has a holiday, bonus-based system available to all employees and awards deep discounts on Home Depot products.

The long-term costs of PFP systems that are tied into base pay can be enormous. For example, the state of Florida awarded $5,000 increases to the base pay of 797 faculty based on the quality and quantity of undergraduate teaching they had performed up to three years earlier. The conservative amortized cost of the 797 $5,000 awards was $148.2 million over 20 years. Remember this was for work already performed. No evidence was ever presented that the program actually increased either the quality or the quantity of undergraduate teaching. Many of these outstanding professors no longer teach at all but still get over $5,000 per year for great teaching they did 10 years earlier! Bottom-line: PFP should be bonus-based and not tied to base pay.

Should You Use Individual, Group, or Company-Level PFP?

As we discussed in Chapter 7, the major issues are the extent to which output is controlled at the group or individual level, whether individual contributions can be measured, and the extent to which teamwork among unit members would be affected by the PFP system.

At Champion, for example, earnings are compared only to the company's major competitors so as to control for factors beyond the influence of the managers, such as inflation, interest rates, and general state of the economy. Managers perceive this relative comparison to be fairer than comparisons to absolute earnings, which are more susceptible to changes in the general state of the economy. (Recall our discussion of constraints on performance and the importance of perceived constraints on the critical probability statements in expectancy/instrumentality theory: If I believe factors beyond my control have more to do with performance outcomes than my own effort, my motivation to try harder will diminish.) In general, PFP

systems are more effective when specific worker contributions can be clearly measured. If individual contributions cannot be measured reliably, then the smallest number of workers whose performance is determined to be important (e.g., related to strategic objectives) and, of course, measurable would constitute the incentive group or unit.

An organization may choose to use a group plan even when it is possible to measure output on an individual basis. Individual PFP plans can increase competition among workers and may reduce cooperation and teamwork. As two experts put it, "when companies change the dynamics of work from structure driven—organized around individual role and functions—to process-driven—often organized around teams—they should change the reward system to support those new dynamics."[28] Workers will be less likely to assist their co-workers if such an effort will adversely affect their own production rate or potential rewards. If teamwork and cooperation are important, but team members are competing for a *set number or amount of awards,* a group or unit-based system is preferable. For example, at the GM Saturn plant in Tennessee, while individual measurement was possible on a number of important outcome measures, an individual PFP system was thought to be contrary to the company's team-oriented approach to production. Thus, Saturn's UAW-endorsed PFP system is based strictly on unit-level and company-wide measures of performance. One health care products manufacturer designed its work teams around project teams for 50 product development employees. But they maintained their old compensation system with job classes, individual performance appraisal, and merit pay. The compensation system turned out to be dysfunctional for the new project-based job structure.

When Should Team-Based PFP Be Used?

A growing number of organizations now use some form of team bonus. One survey of Fortune 1,000 companies found that 70 percent of companies now use some form of team bonus, with 17 percent of these organizations applying bonuses to at least 40 percent of their employees.[29] **Team-based PFP** is a better approach particularly when it is part of a comprehensive team-based model of HRM and compensation. For example, the job evaluation process would place more emphasis on the work products of the team with less emphasis on individual job descriptions. The focus of the pay structure in general is on objectives and results *of the team.* The performance appraisal and career development systems also focus on team performance and contributing to team performance by new skill acquisition. However, the performance appraisal system usually includes peer assessment and great weight is given to the extent to which employees contribute to team performance. These individual assessments, however, are usually only used as developmental tools and not directly tied to pay. All other forms of reward and recognition programs also place emphasis on the team. Company-wide recognition programs, for example, should also focus on team performance and team contribution to the company's strategic goals. Reactions to team-based approaches depend on individual team-member characteristics. For example, one study found that people who are more collectivist in their orientation (high on the "Agreeableness" factor of the Big Five, for example) tend to prefer team-based rewards.[30]

There are many examples of individually based PFP systems even where teamwork is critical. Great professional athletes are always paid a premium for their greatness despite the need for teamwork. Remember, the critical issues regarding the level of aggregation of the performance measures (individual, group, organization) are identifying and measuring performance criteria that the organization seeks to increase or improve in its strategic plan and then linking pay to performance on those measurements. When the pool of award or merit money is not fixed or set among team members, combining individual and group systems may be the most motivating. A 2005 review summed it up this way: "Both individual and group-based pay plans have potential limitations. Individual-based plans may generate too little cooperation when work is highly interdependent and may be seen as unfair when system factors rather than individual effort and ability determine performance. In contrast, group-based plans can weaken incentive effects via "free-rider" problems, which generally increase with group size. "Free riders" are workers who benefit from group-based pay but who don't do their share of the work. Group-based plans can also result in detrimental sorting effects if high achievers go elsewhere to have their individual contributions recognized and rewarded."[31]

Now that we've introduced the major factors that should be considered in designing a PFP system, let's look at the individual, group, and company-based systems in some detail.

INDIVIDUAL PFP PLANS: MERIT PAY AND INCENTIVE SYSTEMS

Individual PFP systems can be divided into merit pay systems and incentive systems specifically tied to production rates. **Merit pay plans** are the most common and perhaps the most troublesome of PFP systems because performance is typically measured by ratings done by supervisors. **Incentive plans** rely on some countable result or results to be used as a basis for setting the PFP rate. These are also known as piece-rate systems. **Sales incentive plans** set certain commissions for sales of specified products or services. We will examine each of these methods next.

What Are Merit Pay Plans?

Merit pay plans call for a distribution of pay based on an appraisal of a worker's performance. The merit pay is usually folded into the base pay of the recipient and is usually granted as a percentage of a worker's base pay. At the Tribune Company, for example, 4 percent merit money was distributed to individual units (e.g., TV and radio stations, newspapers owned by the Tribune). Unit heads then distributed 4 percent to department heads, who had a total pool of 4 percent of their payroll to distribute among the workers. Obviously, the bigger the pool of meritorious workers, the smaller the average percent that could be granted.

Surveys indicate that workers prefer merit pay plans that link individual performance with desired outcomes. At least compared to straight pay with no tie-in to performance, workers in general prefer merit pay plans even after they've been granted what they regarded as less than satisfactory raises based on the plan. But many studies have found little relationship between merit pay plans that rely on performance appraisals by supervisors to measure performance and important organizational outcomes, such as productivity increases or cost reductions.

As you review the reasons for the failure in PFP systems in Figure 11-4, you will see that many of these reasons are unfortunately characteristic of merit pay systems. The most serious problem is the failure to create a clear linkage between employee performance and pay. The performance appraisal system and the evaluators of performance are mainly responsible for this problem. There are several factors related to the appraisal system that contribute to this breakdown in the linkage between pay and performance. The fundamental problem is with measuring performance, a problem compounded in service industries in which individual performance is more difficult to measure. Another cause of the measurement problem is the lack of skill of those who do the appraisals. As we discussed in Chapter 7, this lack of skill is often manifested in *leniency* bias in the ratings. Leniency causes ratings to be so bunched at the high end of the rating scale that very little distinction can be made between superior and other performances. The result is twofold: (1) a merit pay system in which the amount of the merit pay is relatively trivial because so many individuals are judged to be eligible and (2) a system in which the best performers perceive their merit pay as a gross inequity because the system is supposed to be based on merit.

Although we discussed leniency in Chapter 7, the discussion of methods designed to reduce leniency bias bears repeating, since leniency is so critical to the effectiveness of any merit pay system based on performance appraisal. One approach that is clearly growing in popularity is to impose a forced-distribution rating or ranking system in which the number of people rated at the highest level is controlled (recall our discussion of Ford's system in Chapter 7). Raters tend to dislike these approaches. One recent study conducted by pay guru Ed Lawler found negative results for forced-distribution systems. Among his theories for the results was "when employees in a work area compete with each other for ratings, knowing there is always a percentage at the bottom who will be forced out, it creates fear and selfishness. People are much less likely to help each other, train each other, share information, and operate as an effective team. In today's flatter, knowledge work–driven, more team-based organizations, excessive internal competition can take a significant toll on organizational performance."[32]

Many quality improvement experts maintain that pay should not be linked to performance, particularly at the individual level. Deming, the most highly regarded of the quality gurus before he died in 1995, believed that performance appraisal fosters competition among individual workers and diverts attention away from systems related to the quality of the product or service. We will discuss this issue more thoroughly in Chapter 12.

Despite Deming's comments, most individuals prefer to be paid on the basis of some measure of their own performance. The problem is creating the linkage when the criteria are ambiguous. The merit pay principle is easy when criteria are available that are countable (e.g., not rated by supervisors) and important (linked to the strategic plan of the organization or unit or to specific customer requirements). Although most jobs do not easily provide objective criteria, and firms thus rely on ratings, alternatives to ratings are available. As we discussed in Chapter 7, ratings by internal and external customers on the extent to which their expectations are met could be a preferable alternative to supervisory ratings. Studies have found that including some measure of customer satisfaction as one of the outcome measures has a positive effect on sales, profits, and customer satisfaction.[33] Federal Express conducts customer-related performance reviews every six months. Although they have problems, merit pay systems are still widely used. In addition to the recommendations presented in Chapter 7 for sound performance appraisal systems, Figure 11-5 presents a set of recommendations for the use of individual merit pay systems.

What Is Incentive Pay?

Incentive pay is based on units produced and provides the closest connection between individual effort or performance and individual pay. There are two types of individual incentive systems based on nonrated output: the **piece-rate system** and the **standard hourly rate.** Many variations of piece work have been used over the years, but most share common characteristics. A firm using the piece-rate system will determine an appropriate amount of work to be accomplished in a set period of time (e.g., an hour) and then define this as the standard. (Recall from our discussion in Chapter 4 that job analysis methods can be used to establish work standards.) Then, using either internal or external measures, a fair rate is set for this period of time. The piece rate is then calculated by dividing the base wage by the standard. Today, to comply

---

| **FIGURE 11-5** | **Recommendations for Merit Pay Plans** |

1. Use a bonus system in which merit pay is not tied to the base salary.
2. Maintain a bonus range from 0 to 20 percent for lower pay levels and from 0 to 40 percent for higher levels.
3. Pay attention to the process issues of the merit pay plan. Involve workers in decision making and maintain an open communication policy.
4. Take performance appraisal seriously. Hold raters accountable for their appraisals, and provide training.
5. Focus on key organizational factors that affect the pay system. Information systems and job designs must be compatible with the performance measurement system.
6. Include group and team performance in evaluation. Evaluate team performance where appropriate, and base part of individual merit pay on the team evaluation use multiple rates if possible.
7. Consider special awards separately from an annual merit allocation that recognizes major accomplishments.

Source: Recommendations for Merit Pay Plans. Adapted from E. E. Lawler, *Strategic Pay,* San Francisco, Copyright © 1990. Reprinted by permission of John Wiley & Sons Inc.

---

with regulations such as the minimum wage, piece-rate plans usually include an hourly wage and a piece-rate incentive.

The basic piece rate is the oldest and most common wage incentive plan. The earliest approach, popular in textile and apparel mills, was called **straight piece work.** In this approach, a worker was paid per unit of production. Used in early American times when work was done at home on the piece-rate system, the piece-rate approach is still popular today, particularly with the increased use of electronic monitoring of performance. Data processing personnel, customer service representatives, and some clerks, for example, are paid based on a specific formula tied to the finished product or the number of customers served or processed.

International Piece-Rate Pay

The piece-rate pay method is also very common in factories around the world, particularly in textile factories where (typically) young women are paid by the piece of clothing produced. Nike, Ralph Lauren, Liz Claiborne, and Tommy Hilfiger maintain that the hourly rate they pay with the piece-rate system complies with the minimum wage laws of the country. For example, in 2005 Nike paid the following wages in *full compliance with the minimum wage requirements of the respective countries:* 20 cents an hour in Vietnam; 30 cents an hour in Haiti; and 48 cents an hour in Indonesia. According to Medea Benjamin of Global Exchange, a San Francisco world labor watchdog group, these hourly rates do not even get the employees three decent meals a day. Nike, Liz

Claiborne, Reebok, and numerous other companies signed onto a "Code of Conduct" of the Fair Labor Association that put some controls on the pay and treatment of international workers. With regard to wages, however, compliance with the minimum wage laws of the host country is all that is stipulated.

The basic piece rate provides a production incentive based on paying only for what is actually produced. A simple piece-rate approach often results in production variability that can disrupt the flow of product to customers. **Production variability** occurs because employees may be willing to forgo extra effort on some days when they are tired, bored, or ill, but will work especially hard on other days when they need some extra money. Frederick Taylor developed the **differential rate** as a response to the variation potential in piece-rate systems.[34] Taylor's differential rate had two piece rates: one for performing below standard and a higher rate for meeting or exceeding the standard, thus encouraging workers to at least meet the standard. One major advantage of piece-rate systems is that they are easy to understand. They are useful in labor-intensive industries such as textiles or agriculture, where individual production can be reliably measured. Migrant workers who harvest fruit and vegetables are often paid by unit of production.

Lincoln Electric, a Fortune 500 Ohio company, is cited as *the* success story regarding piece-rate pay. In fact, Stanford's Jeff Pfeffer considers Lincoln to be one of corporate America's greatest success stories, citing Lincoln's piece-rate system as a primary reason for their success.

Except for some industries like textiles, individual piece-rate systems are less popular now than they were 20 years ago as a growing number of jobs are team-based or are in areas such as the service sector, which often precludes the establishment of a clear standard for determining the rate of production and the piece rate. Piece-rate incentive systems in their various forms tend to work better when the situation is repetitive, the pace is under the direct control of individual workers, there is little or no interaction or cooperation required among workers, and the results can be easily measured or counted. But even for companies in which incentive systems would seem to work, there is often trouble. The major problem with incentive systems is that an adversarial relationship can develop between workers and management. Workers make every effort to maximize their financial gains by attempting to manipulate the system of setting rates, setting informal production norms, and filing grievances regarding rate adjustments. Lincoln, for example, had great difficulty implementing this system in some of its international plants when they expanded in the 90s. Plants in Germany and Brazil were ultimately shut down. The highly acclaimed management system apparently does not automatically transfer across the world.

There are numerous examples of worker attempts to sabotage piece-rate incentive systems. One expert on pay systems tells the story of how a sales force selling baby foods in South Florida kept secret their highly successful efforts at selling the food to senior citizens because they feared that their method would be rejected by management.[35]

Unfortunately, most jobs outside of sales and straight assembly work do not have a reliable measure of production or performance. Another problem is that adjustments in the standard are required whenever there is a significant change in the machinery or production methods. Finally, work group norms can develop that will restrict the productivity of any one individual. Employees may worry that high earnings under the PFP system will result in an adjustment of the standard. Also, some workers may worry that high productivity may ultimately translate into layoffs or terminations if inventories get too large.

Some banks have piece-rate systems for data entry jobs in which individuals entering check amounts have virtually no interaction with coworkers: workers control the rate of data entry and the computer tallies the rate of production. One bank reported a 30 percent increase in production after installing a piece-rate system for data entry personnel.[36] Many telephone reservationists, whose performance is closely monitored by computer, also are paid by piece rate. Many of the reservationist services left the United States because lower piece-rates can be set on foreign soil.

The adversarial relationship that quickly develops between workers and management can be reduced or eliminated if workers participate in the rate-setting process through task forces. Says one expert, "if they do not involve employees, there is a good chance that the employees will find a way to get involved—for example, by organizing a union."[37]

Standard Hourly Rates

Standard hourly rates differ from piece-rate systems in that the production standard is expressed in time units. Using job analysis, the standard time for a given task is established and the organization then sets a fair hourly wage rate. The standard rate for any task is the wage rate times the standard. For example, if the standard time for a task is four hours and the fair hourly wage is $10, the standard rate is $40. The worker receives the $40 standard rate of pay regardless of the length of time it takes to complete the task. A common example is auto body repair. A customer is given an estimate based on a standards book listing the time required to repair various parts of a car and the hourly wage rate. Insurance companies use a similar book to check the accuracy of the estimate.

In some standard hourly plans, the rate varies with output. For example, the **Halsey plan**,[38] developed in 1891 by Frederick Halsey, divided between employer and worker the savings realized from performing a task in less than the standard time. Halsey believed that sharing the rewards with management would reduce the likelihood that management would increase the standard as worker output increased. Although Halsey proposed a one-third worker and two-thirds organization split, today his plan is more commonly known as the **"Halsey 50-50 plan,"** because savings are equally divided.

When managers are considering an incentive system, they must take into account the firm's organizational strategy, culture, and position in the marketplace. Incentive plans in manufacturing are advisable if there are (1) high labor costs, (2) a high level of cost competition in the marketplace, (3) relatively slow advances in technology, (4) a high level of trust and cooperation between labor and management and (5) individuals can control or affect the rate of production.[39]

The loss of U.S. jobs conducive to individual incentive systems, particularly in the manufacturing sector, combined with the trend toward more team-based work systems, indicates that the decline in individual incentive systems in the United States based on rates of production will continue.

What Are Sales Incentive Plans?

Performance-based sales incentive plans have been found to increase sales over time.[40] Sales incentive plans share many of the characteristics of individual incentive plans, but there are also unique requirements. Both the determinants of employee control over output and measurability of performance have added dimensions for sales. Because an output measure can be easily established as the level of sales, in dollars or units, a common assumption is that salespeople are paid strictly on the volume of product sold. In many cases, however, employers expect salespeople to perform duties beyond strictly sales. Like any PFP system for a job with many important performance dimensions, if sales duties include customer training, market analysis, and credit checks, then the PFP system should involve complex measures of performance that include these dimensions along with sales data. Thus, a critical first step for a sales incentive program, as for all other incentive programs, is to determine what aspects of performance are most important to the firm. The next step is to decide on the methods of measurement and the appropriate levels of compensation. To motivate employees to increase customer satisfaction, many companies now incorporate client- or customer-based survey results into their sales compensation systems to underscore the need for nurturing customer relations as well as selling products and services.[41]

Approximately 75 percent of salespeople are on a commission-based, incentive plan.[42] **Commission plans** pay the salesperson directly on sales data. Although simple in concept, commissions can become complex. Ordinarily, commissions are a percentage of the dollar value of sales. However, the percentage can increase, decrease, or be constant in relation to changes in sales volume,

depending on the nature of the product and its market. Commissions should provide sufficient incentive to the salesperson without adding too much to product cost. Because commissions can be highly variable over time, some firms protect salespeople from low sales periods by using a **draw-plus commission system.** At JCPenney, for example, a salesperson can draw against an account up to a predetermined limit during slack periods. During periods of higher commissions, the draw account is repaid from commissions in excess of the draw limit. A draw is essentially an interest-free loan to the salesperson, repayable when commissions exceed the draw limit. Another common sales incentive plan uses commissions in conjunction with a salary. The base salary serves as a guaranteed minimum wage, and the commissions are an incentive to sell. Inclusion of salary as part of compensation is useful when the firm requires the salesperson to perform activities other than sales.

Many variations of sales compensation exist. Bonuses for a specific product and bonuses for sales levels are common. In each case, the reward should be tied to a specific performance that is of value to the firm and that justifies the additional expense. Sales incentive programs may have equity problems that differ from a manufacturing situation. Operators of similar machines face the same workplace challenge, but salespeople with different territories may experience different levels of opportunity and challenge.

Most companies now have databases that enable them to establish and sustain a fair sales incentive program through the maintenance of the sales history of particular territories. For example, Steelcase offers greater incentives for new business in low-volume territories where their analysis indicates greater competition. Information systems now provide more sophisticated incentive systems that can promote equity among the sales force.

Stockbrokers often receive a large percentage of their pay based on commissions from stocks. This situation is considered the underlying cause of considerable litigation by brokers' customers who claim this conflict of interest led to brokers pushing poor stocks that paid high commissions.

Many companies now offer rewards other than money as recognition for sales performance. Trips and prizes, which can be purchased by the company at a price considerably less than the cost of cash-only incentive programs, are quite common as a form of sales commission today, particularly in insurance, real estate, and the tourism industry. JM Family Enterprises provides trips to the Bahamas on the company yacht, haircuts, and massages as part of their awards system for top performers.

What Are Bonuses?

Bonuses are one-time payments based on performance. They have the advantage of not adding permanently to the base wage and can be given based on either rated or non-rated output measures. Bonuses also can be based on individual or group-based measures. Some workers prefer them to merit pay plans because they get the money all at once and it looks like a larger sum. Fifty dollars every two weeks does not have the same impact as a single payment of $1,300. In general, bonuses are more effective because they allow for larger one-time awards without the amortized effect of tying pay-for-performance into base pay.

WHAT ARE GROUP INCENTIVE PLANS?

There are three major types of group-based incentive plans: **profit sharing, gain sharing,** and **employee stock option plans.** Profit sharing distributes a portion of corporate profits among designated employees. Gain sharing divides a portion of cost reductions or productivity increases between groups covered by the plan. Stock option plans distribute stocks and stock options to employees based on corporate performance measures such as return on equity.

All three types are designed to establish a link between pay and performance, but performance is measured at the group, unit, or company level. Many PFP systems combine individual PFP systems with some form of group incentives. Recall the discussion of Lincoln Electric, which combines the piece rate method with profit sharing for all employees. In general, as expectancy/instrumentality theory would predict, group-based systems are at least theoretically less motivating because individual employees typically do not perceive a strong connection between their efforts and performance.

All three of the group plans have increased in the last few years, and the majority of gain-sharing plans in the United States were introduced in the past 20 years. Manufacturing organizations are more likely to adopt group plans than are service-oriented firms. Group plans are generally preferable to individual plans under the increasingly popular team-based approaches to production or service, although, as we discussed in Chapter 7, this depends principally on the ability to sort out individual contributions to important outcomes.

Successful group incentive plans require the same determinants as individual plans. The measures differ in that a group plan must be based on a measure of group performance or productivity. The use of group plans is particularly effective when cooperation and teamwork are essential and when a goal of the system is to enhance the feeling of participation. Group plans are most useful when tasks are so interrelated that it is difficult (or impossible) to identify a measure of individual output. The size of the "group" can range from two people to plantwide or companywide. The smaller the group, the more a worker will identify individual effort as affecting group performance.

Group PFP plans require special considerations. First, there is potential for conflict when all group members receive the same reward regardless of individual input. Second, strong group norms that control output can inhibit group efforts. Third, the variable compensation distribution formula must meet the **Fair Labor Standards Act** requirements for calculating overtime pay.[43] However, there is increasing evidence that group incentives increase productivity.[44]

What Is Profit Sharing?

Profit sharing is designed to motivate cost savings by allowing workers to share in benefits of increased profits. As we discussed in Chapter 10, retirement income for employees is frequently linked to a profit-sharing plan. Rewards can be periodic cash disbursements or deposits to an employee account. Either a predetermined percentage of profit or a percentage above a certain threshold is allocated to a pool (e.g., 10 to 25 percent). This pool is disbursed to employees on the basis of some ratio, usually related to their wage. Most companies now have options from which the employee may select a particular profit-sharing plan compatible with his or her long-range plans. Profit sharing has been criticized as being remote and perceptually unrelated to individual performance, but research indicates that it produces generally positive results. Many firms also use profit sharing as a tool to control employee turnover. At Johnson & Johnson, the allocation is distributed in equal increments over a period of years, and an employee sacrifices remaining distributions by leaving the firm before the period is up. Obviously, some of the incentive value of profit sharing for higher performance is lost when it is used in this fashion. In general, profit sharing works best as an incentive when the group size is small enough that employees believe they have some impact on group profitability.

The typical profit-sharing plan uses profits to fund retirement plans and is thus advantageous for tax purposes. However, some companies pay annual bonuses based on company profits. Anderson Windows, for example, has a profit-sharing pool that has paid employees up to 84 percent of their annual salary. This approach gives Anderson greater flexibility during hard times since company costs go down when company performance goes down. Given the relatively lower base pay for its employees, Anderson could afford to retain more employees and weather the storm.

While employees generally approve of profit sharing, they get testy when their base pay is affected in a negative way by profit-sharing provisions. When DuPont Corporation announced that there would be 4 percent cuts in the base pay of all its 20,000 employees due to poor sales in the fibers division, worker dissatisfaction was so high that the profit-sharing plan was scrapped. If the company was profitable, workers would have earned an additional 12 percent above their base pay under the plan. The major reason for the dissatisfaction with the system was the lack of perceived connection between worker performance and company profits. UAW workers at Caterpillar struck the company partially because they wanted an increase in base salary and a decrease in the risk of the profit-sharing plan. One UAW contract for the 4,700 Saturn workers scaled back the profit-sharing component of the innovative wage accord. Poor sales at Saturn had a great deal to do with the union's position. As GM stock headed south in 2005, more employees and unions also complained about their diminishing retirement plans when they were so closely tied to company stock price.

Profit sharing can be seen as a way to align the goals of management and employees. When employees perceive profit sharing favorably, commitment to the organization and trust in management tend to increase, thus "encouraging employees to exert maximum effort, share information, and invest in firm-specific training that may not be valued outside the firm."[45] Profit sharing draws on the core ideas from expectancy theory and organizational justice theory. Studies have reported increases in productivity between 7 and 9 percent. However, workers' beliefs that they have sufficient control to contribute to the profitability of the organization are critical to the success of profit-sharing programs.

A recent study concluded that "when profit sharing is perceived as both an opportunity for individual input to the organization's success and a reflection of the organization's desire to treat employees fairly, higher levels of commitment follow. Structuring profit-sharing systems to enhance perceptions of input (e.g., some portion of the profit sharing based on individual contribution to performance) and reciprocity (e.g., some portion based on years of service) appears to be advantageous."[46]

What Is Gain Sharing?

As team performance becomes increasingly important in our society, gain sharing is becoming a popular approach to motivate higher levels of group productivity. While there are subtle differences among various PFP programs classified as "gain sharing," all of them essentially deal with worker involvement and the process of sharing in the financial benefits of reducing costs or increasing productivity. One survey found that gain sharing is the second most important topic among human resource managers.[47]

More gain sharing plans were instituted in the mid-1980s than in the previous 50 years,[48] and almost 40 percent of Fortune 1000 firms rely on some form of gain sharing.[49] Gain sharing plans either try to reduce the amount of labor required for a given level of output (cost saving) or increase the output for a given amount of labor (productivity increase). The method for determining the standard production rate and the incentive rate must be clearly defined. Gain sharing plans generally are based on the assumption that better cooperation among workers and between workers and managers will result in greater

effectiveness. Successful plans require an organizational climate characterized by trust across organizational levels, worker participation, and cooperative unions. An organized employee suggestion system is also characteristic of almost all gain sharing plans. To maximize cost saving and productivity increases, there must be employee involvement in the plan development and execution. A successful gain sharing plan requires workers and management to work toward a common goal. Gain sharing encounters difficulty when management downgrades employee input or unions adopt a strong adversarial position. Like profit sharing, instrumentality can be low since employees may not perceive a strong connection between their performance and desired outcomes.

Gain sharing plans can get complicated. Measures of productivity can be (and often are) adapted to particular situations. For example, one firm uses both the labor/sales ratio and the cost-of-quality/sales ratio as financial measures. Another firm uses savings on warranty costs as a measure for its engineers and designers. As one expert puts it, "The financial measures of performance have great educational value in spurring employee understanding of business fundamentals . . . financial measures tend to closely parallel overall firm performance."[50]

All types of gain sharing plans use a productivity ratio to capture labor's contribution to value added. The differences among them tie in how labor's cost is calculated for the numerator and how organizational output is measured for the denominator.

Gain sharing plans are different from profit sharing in two major ways:

1. Gain sharing is based on a measure of productivity, not profit.
2. Gain sharing rewards are given out frequently, whereas profit sharing is annual and often tied to a retirement plan as deferred payment.

What Are the Four Approaches to Gain Sharing?

There are four basic approaches to gain sharing, although there is considerable variation within these categories. The four approaches are the Scanlon plan, the Rucker plan, the IMPROSHARE plan, and Winsharing. In addition to the productivity ratio, other issues influence the selection of a gain sharing plan. One of the most important aspects of a PFP system, strength of reinforcement, is roughly equal for the four methods. A summary of the issues to be considered in selecting a plan is provided in Figure 11-6.

The **Scanlon plan,** the most common gain sharing plan, measures the relationship between the sales value of production and labor costs. Like all gain sharing options, employee participation is an important component of this approach. Screening committees are used to evaluate cost-saving suggestions from employees with labor cost savings serving as the incentive. Savings are measured by

FIGURE 11-6	Factors to Consider in Designing a Gain Sharing Program

1. **Performance and financial measures.** The bonus formula must be perceived as reasonable, accurate, and equitable.

2. **Plant or facility size.** Plants with fewer than 500 employees are ideally suited to gain sharing, while plants with over 2,000 employees are not.

3. **Types of production.** Plants with highly mixed types of production will find it difficult to introduce gain sharing because the measurement process is so complicated.

4. **Workforce interdependence.** Highly integrated work units are ideal for gain sharing.

5. **Workforce composition.** Some workforces may not be as motivated by financial incentives.

6. **Potential to absorb additional output.** Initial increase in productivity must be useful to the organization and must not entail negative consequences for the workforce (e.g., layoffs).

7. **Potential for employee efforts.** Can employee efforts actually affect productivity to a significant extent, or does automation (or other factors) impede worker effects?

8. **Present organizational climate.** An initial level of trust is required.

9. **Union–management relations.** Union should be an active partner in program development.

10. **Capital investment plans.** Don't install gain sharing if large capital investments are planned.

11. **Organized employee suggestion system.** Do not downgrade or ignore employee input.

Source: Reprinted from Gain Sharing: Do It Right the First Time by M. Schuster, M.I.T. *Sloan Management Review* Winter 1987, pp. 17–25, by permission of publisher. Copyright © 2006 by Massachusetts Institute of Technology. All rights reserved.

a monthly calculation of the ratio of payroll to sales value of production compared to baseline data.

The Scanlon plan is the oldest form of gain sharing.[51] Developed by Joseph Scanlon, a steelworker, a union official, and later a professor at the Massachusetts Institute of Technology, the plan was originally devised to keep the La Pointe Steel Company from going bankrupt. The plan received wide public attention because of a *Life* magazine article published in 1946. At the time, its unique aspects were (1) rewarding the group for suggestions by individuals in the group; (2) joint labor–management committees designed to propose and evaluate labor-saving suggestions; and (3) a worker reward share based on reduced costs, not increased profits.

Scanlon plans require a considerable commitment by workers and management to cooperate in the development and maintenance of the program. While the track record for Scanlon plans is mixed, there are some great success stories. One paint manufacturer in Texas reported a 78 percent increase in production over its 17-year history of using a Scanlon plan.[52] The keys seem to be employee trust, understanding, and contributions to improvements. For example, a Levi's executive from its Blue Ridge, Georgia, plant described their highly successful Scanlon plan this way: "A formal method for having all organizational members contribute ingenuity and brainpower to the improvement of organizational performance . . . and improvement of relations across functional groups and levels of the organizational hierarchy."[53]

The **Rucker plan** is another successful group incentive system. While similar to Scanlon, the Rucker formula includes the value of all supplies, materials, and services. The result is a bonus formula based on the value added to the product per labor dollar. Thus, an incentive is created to save on all inputs, including materials and supplies. The advantage of Rucker over Scanlon is the linkage of rewards to savings other than labor savings, plus greater flexibility. The disadvantage is that concepts such as value added and the adjustments for inflation make the Rucker plan more difficult to understand and explain compared to the Scanlon plan.

A third category of gain sharing is **IMPROSHARE,** which stands for "improved productivity through sharing."[54] IMPROSHARE is similar to Scanlon except that the IMPROSHARE ratio uses standard hours rather than labor costs. Engineering studies or past performance data are used to specify the standard number of hours required to produce a base production level. Savings in hours result in reward allocation to workers. IMPROSHARE "rewards all covered employees equally whenever the actual number of labor hours used to produce output in the current week or month is less than the estimated number it would have taken to produce the current level of output in the base period."[55] IMPROSHARE is easy to administer and employees have no difficulty understanding the formula.

Winsharing combines gain sharing with profit sharing.[56] Winsharing is based on the rational proposition that if your PFP system results in more product being produced than can be sold, your PFP system needs some alterations. Winsharing takes the market demand into consideration. Winsharing payouts are based on whether group performance is achieved relative to business goals. Financial performance in excess of the goals is split evenly between workers and the company. Winsharing differs from profit sharing because group performance measures are used that are independent of profit measures. Whirlpool in Benton Harbor, Michigan, has been operating on a Winsharing program since 1988 with a productivity gain of 19 percent since it put in the system.[57]

What's the Bottom Line on Gain Sharing?

Research has found numerous benefits from gain sharing plans, including improved productivity and quality.[58]

Kendall-Futuro, a health-care products company, improved both TQM and JIT performance with gain sharing. The Volvo-GM plant at Orrville, Ohio, completed its fifth year of TQM implementation through gain sharing in 1997.[59] The company reports strong success so far. Other major companies offering gainsharing plans include Georgia Pacific, Huffy Bicycle, Inland Container, Eaton Corp., TRW, and General Electric.[60] Gain sharing is evolving from a simple productivity concept into a family of measures all designed to improve performance.[61] Whirlpool instituted such a family that featured gain sharing. The Board of Directors receives stock options when targets are met. Senior managers can receive up to 100 percent of base salary as annual stock options. Whirlpool eliminated profit sharing and instituted a plant-level gain sharing plan known as winsharing that increased worker performance as well as knowledge about shareholder value.[62]

Success of gain sharing plans in general depends on significant involvement and support by high-level management, actual employee participation and understanding, and realistic employee and (if applicable) union expectations.[63] Companies that are reluctant to involve unions in strategic planning also will have difficulty with gain sharing programs. There is also considerable evidence that group size affects gain-sharing results. For example, doubling the number of employees covered from 200 to 400 was associated with a 50 percent drop in the average productivity gain.[64]

One review of Scanlon, Rucker, and IMPROSHARE plans concluded that:

1. IMPROSHARE is easier for workers to comprehend.
2. With IMPROSHARE workers have more control over physical productivity.
3. IMPROSHARE does not require management to reveal sensitive corporate financial information.

The advantages of Scanlon and Rucker plans over IMPROSHARE are that:

1. Workers actually share in the financial risks of the company (appealing to management).
2. The Scanlon plan typically allows for more integration with problem-solving processes.

A well-controlled study of IMPROSHARE found that productivity continues to rise sharply after the initial introduction of the plan for at least three years. After three years few gains occur and productivity begins to plateau at the higher level (likely because slack has been eliminated and further changes may require dramatic production process changes).[65]

What Are Employee Stock Option Plans?

As discussed earlier, many companies use employee stock options plans to compensate, retain, and attract employees. These plans are contracts between a company and its employees that give employees the right to buy a specific number of the company's shares at a fixed price within a certain period of time. Employees who are granted stock options hope to profit by exercising their options at a higher price than when they were granted.

Employee Stock Options Plans should not be confused with the term *"ESOPs," or Employee Stock Ownership Plans,* which are retirement plans. An employee stock ownership plan (ESOP) is a retirement plan in which the company contributes its stock to the plan for the benefit of the company's employees. With an ESOP, you never buy or hold the stock directly.

The Securities and Exchange Commission presents the following example of a stock option plan on its Web site: an employee is granted the option to purchase 1,000 shares of the company's stock at the current market price of $5 per share (the "grant" price). The employee can exercise the option at $5 per share—typically the exercise price will be equal to the price when the options are granted. Plans allow employees to exercise their options after a certain number of years or when the company's stock reaches a certain price. If the price of the stock increases to $20 per share, for example, the employee may exercise his or her option to buy 1,000 shares at $5 and then sell the stock at the current market price of $20.

Companies sometimes revalue the price at which the options can be exercised. This may happen, for example, when a company's stock price has fallen below the original exercise price. Companies revalue the exercise price as a way to retain their employees. Many of our nation's largest companies have option plans (e.g., Anhauser-Busch, Lockheed, JCPenney, Texaco, Procter & Gamble, Avis, Polaroid).[66]

As of 2001, the National Center for Employee Ownership (www.NCEO.org) estimates that up to 10 million employees receive stock options. Other research confirms this trend. Research by Joseph Blasi at Rutgers University found that 97 of the top 100 e-commerce companies offer options to most or all employees. A 2003 World-at-Work study showed that options are popular in all kinds of public companies, with 15 percent of public companies offering options to most or all employees.[67] In principle, options sound like a terrific idea: companies sell stock to workers in order to give them a financial stake in the company. Stock allocations are made to the employee's account based on relative base pay.

Research results on the effects of stock options are unclear. A recent review concluded that "few of the studies have found strong and significant effects."[68] However, options tend to work better when combined with extensive employee involvement and problem solving. A popular method designed to replace fixed compensation costs with variable wages and benefits, options give the organization greater flexibility in response to a competitive environment. Santa Fe Railway reduced employee pay in 1990 for the first time in the company's 122-year history. The pay cuts were replaced with stock options that resulted in bonus checks for all 2,400 salaried employees. Some employees received checks in excess of $100,000. Needless to say, Santa Fe employees are now very happy with the new incentive system. Behlen Manufacturing has had great success in using a blend of base pay, gain sharing, profit sharing, and options to support its organizational goals. There are also some sad stories indicating options are no panacea. At Burlington Industries, employees bought out the company only to watch the stock plummet to less than half its purchase value.

One review drew the following conclusions and implications for options.[69]

1. Since stock options are distributed differentially in proportion to performance or contribution they may be perceived as more equitable than profit or gain sharing, particularly by employees seeking some sense of control or ownership in the company.
2. Options might generate weaker levels of work motivation and subsequent performance than good merit pay systems as their ultimate value is determined, at least in part, by market forces over which the employee has no control.
3. Consequently, the eventual value (or even anticipated ownership component) of stock options may turn out to be less proportionate to actual employee contribution or performance than expected. The result can be relatively stronger perceptions of inequity and lower instrumentality.

MANAGERIAL AND EXECUTIVE INCENTIVE PAY

In a 2006 editorial, the *New York Times* concluded that "there is no shortage of numbers and studies detailing the widening gap between what American companies pay workers and the millions of dollars those same companies pay top executives."[70] Correlational research generally supports the use of long-term reward systems for executives, which are directly tied to the long-term strategic goals of the firm. Incentives for managers and executives can have a significant impact upon the fortunes of an organization.[71] In general, executive incentive plans are linked either to net income, some measure of return on investment, or total dividends paid. These incentives are paid in the form of bonuses, not permanently tied to base pay, and the awarding of stock options. Even *The Wall Street Journal* concedes that things are out of control. In a lengthy exposé entitled "Pay for No Performance," the article documents the loss in linkage between pay and performance.[72]

CEO pay rose dramatically again in 2004 despite the fact that for years now only CEOs themselves and the occasional compensation consultant (who benefits directly from larger pay packages) are actually defending the packages. One of the highest-paid CEOs of late is George David of United Technology, one of the largest military contractors. The wars in Iraq and Afganistan are the most probable reasons for UT's strong performance, not anything this man has done. He earned over $88 million in 2004 and over $70 million in 2003. The expected total direct compensation (TDC = the sum of base salary, annual bonus, and the grant value of stock options, restricted stock, and other long-term incentives) increased 17.1 percent in 2004. Another obscene example of war profiteering is David Brooks, CEO of DHB Industries, a bulletproof vest manufacturer. Mr Brooks made $70 million in 2004 compared to $525,000 in pre-Iraq war 2001.

War profiteering aside, the increase in CEO pay is largely due to higher annual bonuses to over $7 million per year. Net income for the Mercer 350 rose a median of 23 percent in 2004, after a 19.2 percent rise in 2003.[73] One trend is the movement away from stock options and toward other long-term awards. A total of 273 companies awarded stock options to CEOs in 2004, compared to 278 in 2003 and 295 in 2002—a gradual decline of 7.5 percent over the two years. But 166 CEOs received restricted stock grants in 2004, compared to 138 in 2003 and 104 in 2002—a 59.6 percent jump over the same period.

Rank certainly has its privileges. A 2002 special report in *BusinessWeek* concluded that "during the past two years, as the market cratered, executives went right on raking in the dough—as nearly 200 companies swapped or repriced their stock options. "It's just way off the charts," says portfolio manager Jennifer Ladd, who is fighting for lower executive pay.[74] Management guru Peter Drucker argued that no CEO should earn more than 20 times the company's lowest-paid employee. He reasoned that if the CEO took too large a share of the rewards, "it would make a mockery of the contributions of all the other employees in a successful organization."

A large portion of executive compensation is now tied to meeting earnings goals. According to a *Forbes* magazine editorial, "Accepted accounting principles are an art, not a science. Give a smart boss the incentive to do it, and he can push the earnings envelope to the limit—or beyond." Delphi, OfficeMax, Qwest, and WorldCom are companies that heaped big performance-based bonuses on their bosses but subsequently had to restate earnings lower after accounting shenanigans were discovered. Paying for performance "has vastly increased the number of accounting disasters," says Paul Hodgson, a senior research associate at the Corporate Library, a corporate-governance research firm in Portland, Maine. According to a 2003 study by the comptroller of New York State, between 1995 and 2002, when companies were increasingly tying bonuses to earnings, the number of earnings restatements increased from 44 to 240.[75]

Are There Documented Negative Consequences to Widening Pay Dispersion?

While there has been considerable writing about the negative consequences of the widening dispersion between CEO pay and the pay of others, little research has shown a relationship between dispersion and subsequent performance decrements or higher turnover. The problem of pay dispersion may be more acute in more technologically intensive industries where executives are encouraged to be entrepeneurially aggressive and they often are compensated very well based on their performance. However, intensive teamwork and coordination are often required for the development of high-tech products or services, thus indicating the need for a PFP system with more of a team or corporate-level orientation. One study found that pay dispersion in high-tech firms is predictive of subsequent performance decrements.[76] Pay dispersion tends to diminish communication, increase status gaps, and foster aggressive competition for advancement to lucrative top posts within a company. The same effect was found for low-technology firms, but the effect was not as profound. We believe this is the first evidence to clearly document the deleterious effects of exorbitant CEO pay.

Should You Use Short- or Long-Term Measures of Performance?

A principal distinction between managerial and executive incentives is the time horizon of the performance measure that is the basis of the incentive. Although more lower-level managers are being awarded stock options, they typically have incentives based on short-term measures. Top executives have both short- and long-term performance incentives. Managers and executives have a wider area of discretion in making decisions that affect the firm. As a consequence, the PFP system is designed to reinforce a sense of commitment to the organization. Most managers receive bonuses related to profit. The amount is usually awarded as a percentage of their base pay, although there is a trend toward awarding lump sums not tied to the base pay. As higher profitability thresholds are attained, the manager receives bigger bonuses. The bonus structure for any given manager often depends on the relative contributions of all managers, with the assessment of relative contribution made at a higher level. This method suffers from the drawbacks discussed previously regarding profit sharing for individuals. Many managers might feel that they have a negligible impact on organization profits. As the link between performance and pay becomes weaker, the reward loses incentive value. The link can be strengthened by clearly defining performance standards, while basing the amount of the reward on corporate profitability.

Executives and their boards should be concerned with the long-term viability of the firm. There are many situations in which a decision option can have a conflicting impact on a firm's short- and long-run profitability. Investing in research and development (R&D) will depress short-term profit but should lead to maintenance of a long-run competitive position. Cutting back on services provided may add to short-run profits but damage market share in the long run.

Long-term rewards focus on future profitability. The most popular approach is based on appreciation of stock value using various stock purchase plans.[77] Almost 100 percent of the 500 largest industrials had stock option plans in 2000, up from 52 percent in 1974.[78] However, as discussed earlier, the new accounting rules on options, have reversed this trend.

A stock option plan gives an executive the right to purchase a stock, over a specified period, at a fixed price. The theory is that if the executive is prudent and hardworking, the stock price will go up. If the stock price does increase, the executive can purchase it at the lower fixed price, effectively receiving as a bonus the difference between the fixed purchase price and the higher market price. Congress periodically revises legislation controlling the awarding of stock options. These limitations have typically affected only options exceeding $100,000 per year.

Although take-home pay wasn't too shabby without them, CEO salaries have gone through the roof through abuse of stock options. Numerous experts endorsed the use of options on the assumption that executives would profit when shareholders profited. However, while this incentive system worked well for awhile, from 2001 through 2002, "shareholders lost their shirts, but executives went right on raking in the dough."[79] Many companies awarded huge option grants despite terrible corporate performance by any reputable measure. Many companies simply adjusted performance goals for no particular reason. According to a stinging *BusinessWeek* exposé, almost 200 companies swapped or repriced stock options "to enrich members of a corporate elite who already were among the world's wealthiest people. When CEOs can clear $1 billion during their tenures, executive pay is clearly too high. Worse still, the system is not providing an incentive for outstanding performance."[80] But similar things were written in the early 1990s that led to a toothless law regarding executive pay. Although there are many excellent Web sites, pay expert Graef Crystal's columns at www.bloomberg.com provide the most objective treatment on executive pay.

There are many variations on stock options. *Stock appreciation rights* (SARs), for example, do not involve buying stock. Having been awarded rights to a stock at a fixed price for a specified period, the executive can call the option and receive the difference between the fixed and market prices in cash. *Restricted stock plans* give shares as a bonus, but with restrictions.[81] The restrictions may be that the executive cannot leave the company or sell the stock for a specified time. *Performance share plans* award units based on both short- and long-term measures. These units are later translated into stock awards. Other incentive stock option plans are part of retirement packages. These may include profit-sharing and stock bonus plans. In both cases, employers pay into a retirement fund based on corporate profits. Recent evidence suggests that stock incentives may not be effective.[82]

Executive incentives of the future are more likely to be tied to long-term corporate performance, which may involve qualitative assessment of performance along with corporate financial performance. New products and service lines, environmental impact assessments, and new territorial penetration are some of the long-range measures that may be used to assess executive performance. For example, McDonald's, Burger King, and General Electric (GE) place considerable weight on their long-term growth in the European sector as a basis for compensating senior management. The trend in executive compensation is against heavy reliance on stock prices as a basis for compensating executives, since such reliance would promote short-term perspectives to the detriment of the long-term strategic plan of the organization.

What about the Corporate Board Room? How Should Directors Be Paid?

Corporate boards have been called "America's last dirty little secret."[83] They have very lucrative and comprehensive compensation packages that are rarely linked to corporate performance. One study found companies with outside directors who owned substantial stock holdings were less likely to overpay their CEO and, more importantly, presided over superior corporate performance.[84]

HOW DO COMPANIES KEEP ENTREPRENEURS AND PROMOTE INTRAPRENEURS?

Under the current competitive pressures and the great opportunity for launching new businesses, many companies are attempting to retain entrepreneurial mavericks within the corporate umbrella and promote intrapreneurial thinking.[85] For example, many high-tech firms are funding employee ventures by using innovative compensation schemes. At IBM, employees can submit business plans for IBM risk capital. Employees can negotiate a share of the profits from an idea that they may have otherwise pursued on the outside.[86] The basic principle of entrepreneurial pay is that the employee places a major portion of salary at risk, with the percentage of employee ownership of the venture determined by the portion of salary at risk.

The potential for large returns replaces many of the standard perks expected by employees. Payoffs may have a variety of bases, from profits produced by the venture to increases in parent company stock value. Although such payoffs may be less than if the venture were truly independent, the risk for the venture employee is also more limited. In addition, there is the support and expertise available from the parent. American Telephone and Telegraph (AT&T), for example, wanted to increase the risk its people were willing to take in entrepreneurial efforts. Three venture approaches were offered, corresponding to the levels of risk the venture employee was willing to take.

Many companies have adopted special award programs for major accomplishments. Microsoft, IBM, Amoco, Xerox, and Bell South, for example, have programs in which the awards can exceed $100,000 for R&D discoveries. American Express has $10,000 awards for "exceptional performers." These special programs are independent of any other PFP systems within the company.

WHAT ARE THE MANAGERIAL IMPLICATIONS FOR PFP PROGRAMS?

A well-designed PFP system should lead to lower costs, higher profits, and a higher degree of individual or group motivation, which thus requires less supervision. Introduction of a well-designed PFP system can provide a more accurate estimate of labor costs as well as prompt workers to make more effective use of their time, supplies, and equipment. Using a mix of plans often has the best results. These same general principles also apply to small business. Research has clearly established that involving employees in the process of developing or changing a PFP system will ultimately lead to more effective results. Figure 11-7 presents three strategic positions to make PFP systems more effective. Once again, sound measurement is the key.

PFP systems are more complicated than lock-step, straight compensation. There are numerous challenges that must be met. Emphasizing one measure can lead to

---

FIGURE 11-7 | **Three Strategic Positions for Pay Systems**

1. **Pay the person.** People should be paid according to their individual market value—both internal and external. Pricing a job (not the individual) is not good enough. Need to measure knowledge, skills, and competencies of individuals against the external market.

2. **Pay-for-performance approach needs to translate business strategy into measures that can be used for reward system.** Individual, team-based, and business-based PFP systems all should have a place in any single organization for any single person.

3. **Individualize the reward system.** Individualize the system to fit characteristics of persons the organization wants to attract and retain. Avoid one-size-fits-all PFP system.

Source: FERRIS, GERALD R; BUCKLEY, M. RONALD; FEDOR, DONALD B., HUMAN RESOURCE MANAGEMENT; PERSPECTIVES, CONTEXT, FUNCTIONS, AND OUTCOMES, 4th, © 2002. Adapted by permission of Pearson Education, Inc., Upper Saddle River, NJ.

reduced performance levels in other measures. A strong focus on output or quantity can reduce quality, which could lead to increased costs in quality control. In addition, a focus on output could jeopardize safety. Remember our discussion in Chapter 7 about the definition of performance and the various aspects of value. A PFP system should reward all important dimensions of performance. An overemphasis on one dimension or one aspect of value such as quantity will result in a deemphasis on other aspects such as quality.

A second challenge is the increased overhead expense of installing and maintaining the PFP system. Unless the production process is very stable, maintenance costs for PFP systems can be substantial and consultants in this area are very expensive. A third challenge is the difficulty in setting standards that accurately reflect task requirements and are perceived as fair. This problem can be greater when a system adds new processes or equipment, as workers will be suspicious of new standards. A fourth challenge is that there will be resistance to any change involving employee compensation, particularly when base pay is affected. Unions have been born out of attempts to radically alter compensation systems. In addition to the typical fear of anything new, workers may oppose change to avoid being victimized by new rates and standards. The final challenge is that PFP systems are more likely to be subject to legal actions for possible discrimination.

Management may resist change because of the expense of revising the pay system, the time required to do more valid performance measurement, and the difficulties that develop in defending PFP decisions. Finally, variations in pay due to performance differences may lead to conflict, a potential problem in a team or process-oriented work setting focused on the external customer. When measures are explicit and objective, some conflict will occur. When methods are subjective or ambiguous, as with the typical performance appraisal system, significant reward differences may not be perceived as justified, resulting in even greater conflict. Let's not forget the warning from *Freakonomics* author. Incentive systems invite cheating. Close monitoring is required.

SUMMARY

The PFP system must support the competitive strategy and values of the organization. If the strategy emphasizes entrepreneurial activity and independent effort, individual PFP systems become increasingly important and effective. Incentive systems must be compatible with organizational values. Closed, secretive cultures do not mix well with performance incentives. Openness and trust are necessary if employees are to accept the standards and believe in the equity of the rewards. Lincoln Electric's much touted piece-rate system would probably not be successful without the other elements of the Lincoln management, a system based on mutual trust and a fair distribution of the products of hard work. Organizational culture clearly affects the nature of incentives selected and, in the end, the effectiveness of the system. Individual PFP plans are preferable when individuals contribute important criteria that can be clearly measured and teamwork is not seriously undermined by the process of individual performance measurement and rewards. Highly interdependent jobs or groups will dictate group or organizational-based PFP plans.

As one expert on the subject has put it, "Paying for performance will not solve all of the motivational problems associated with the new workforce and strong national competition. However, it can be an important part of a total performance management system that is designed to create a highly motivating work environment."[87] There is no question that money *is* a motivator. A key question is, Motivation for what? Following the measurement principles we presented in Chapter 7 for defining performance is a critical step in linking the performance appraisal, performance management, and pay-for-performance system.

The bottom line remains that for any PFP system to work, rewards valued by the worker must be clearly linked to outcomes valued by internal and, most important, external customers. Virtually all of the research on high-performance work systems supports the view that proper PFP systems can help to create and sustain a competitive advantage. The evidence supports the value of carefully designed PFP systems. When the focus is on organizations that follow academic guidelines for development and maintenance, PFP systems look like a winner. A 2005 review of the vast literature provided a great "bottom-line" summary: "Every pay program has its advantages and disadvantages. Programs differ in their sorting and incentive effects, their incentive intensity and risk, their use of behaviors versus results, and their emphasis on individual versus group measures of performance. Because of the limitations of any single pay program, organizations often elect to use a portfolio of programs, which may provide a means of reducing the risks of particular pay strategies while garnering most of their benefits. For example, using only an individual incentive program could result in unacceptably high levels of competitive behavior and focus on overly narrow objectives. On the other hand, relying exclusively on gain sharing could result in the underrewarding of high individual performers, thus risking their attraction, motivation, and retention. However, offering a mix of these different programs offers the possibility that the advantages of each can be captured, while minimizing the disadvantages."[88]

Chapter 12 will turn to other HRM systems and characteristics that can contribute to the productivity and the competitive advantage of the organization.

DISCUSSION QUESTIONS

1. Deming and others think PFP is a bad idea. What do you think?
2. Why is trust so important for PFP systems?
3. When is a group-based PFP system better than an individual system?
4. Some experts argue that a corporation's board of directors should be paid only with stock options. What do you think?
5. How would you go about combining individual and group-based PFP systems?
6. Some experts believe that if you have to use performance appraisals as the main source of data for a PFP system, you shouldn't bother with the PFP system. What do you think?
7. Under what conditions (if any) should a company install a forced-distribution rating system for PFP?

12

Managing the Employment Relationship*

OVERVIEW

According to the proceedings of a relatively recent court case, an employee handbook was presented to an employee after he had been working at an organization for several months. From the employee's perspective, two sections of the handbook implied an employment contract. The first section outlined the job security of individuals in the industry, although it made no mention of job security within this particular organization. The second section was the organization's disciplinary policy, which outlined specific circumstances and behaviors that were subject to discipline, up to and including termination. Upon his termination, the employee sued the organization, claiming that these two sections of the handbook constituted an implicit contract. The employee won the suit on the basis of the disciplinary policy published in the employee handbook. Because he was terminated for an act that was not explicitly outlined in the disciplinary policy, the court ruled that the employer violated an implicit contract. The court ruled that employee handbooks represent choices for the organization to implement contracts or modify existing contracts with every employee.[1]

This case bears upon several issues relevant to the subject of this chapter, the organization's attempts to create and manage its relationships with employees. The situation described above illustrates an instance of the internal and external forces by which an employment relationship is formed, namely,

organizational policies and procedures on the one hand and employment law on the other. Specifically, the case deals with organizational entry and exit—the beginnings and endings of an employment relationship. We touched on various aspects of the employment relationship in Chapter 3 when we described major employment laws, in Chapter 5 when we discussed recruitment, in Chapter 6 on selection processes, in Chapter 7 on performance management, and even in Chapter 10 on compensation theory and practice. Chapter 12 provides a more complete description of the elements of the employment relationship that affect specific HR activities.

You may recall the discussion of SAS, the highly successful North Carolina computer software company. SAS has never had a losing year and has never laid off a single employee. SAS founder Jim Goodnight, puts it simply: "If employees are happy, they make the customers happy. If they make the customers happy, they make me happy." SAS has a voluntary turnover rate that is substantially below their competitors (3 percent per year versus 20 percent for the industry). Jeff Chambers, Director of HR, estimates that SAS saves between $60 and $70 million annually because of this 17 percent advantage.

Numerous studies now document that there is a reliable causal relationship between employee attitudes in the form of their commitment to the organization, their satisfaction with the job, their

*Contributed by Jennifer Robin.

perceived engagement with and trust in the firm, and their perceptions of fairness and justice at work and vital customer outcomes such as satisfaction and repeat business translating into better financial performance. One study showed that positive employee relations served as an "intangible and enduring asset and . . . a source of sustained competitive advantage at the firm level."[2] Another recent study found that "employee satisfaction and engagement are related to meaningful business outcomes." Of course, good employee attitudes evolve from good personnel policy. One excellent study found that the level of employee satisfaction regarding working conditions, the recognition and encouragement they receive for their good work, the opportunities provided to help them perform well, and the commitment to product or service quality all contributed to the business units' "bottom line." Business units with more progressive HR policies had higher monthly revenue.[3]

Thus, concern for perceptions of organizational justice or measuring job satisfaction should be of interest even to the "hard-liners" focused on the bottom line. Having engaged, committed, and satisfied employees can certainly help you get there. The HR policies described on the pages to follow can facilitate more positive employee attitudes.

O B J E C T I V E S

After reading this chapter, you should be able to

1. *Explain the concept of organizational justice and how it relates to all aspects of relationship building with employees.*
2. *Understand how actions taken at organizational entry help to build the employment relationship.*
3. *Know the major laws and legal doctrines governing the employment relationship.*
4. *Show familiarity with the complexities of employee handbooks, some current issues, and ways to avoid lawsuits.*
5. *Understand policies and procedures associated with discipline and grievances.*
6. *Explain the various ways that an employee can exit an organization and the measures organizations can take to make this parting of ways a more positive experience for all involved.*

INTRODUCTION

HR professionals are managers by virtue of their directing many critical projects and ongoing efforts in organizations. Perhaps the most important thing an HR professional helps to "manage" is the relationship the organization has with each employee. While many of the elements of this relationship are established through policies, procedures, and processes common to every employee, contingencies also

must be established to accommodate each unique relationship an individual develops.

This chapter discusses the actions organizations take to establish and maintain positive associations with their employees, starting with the mechanisms associated with organizational entry, then the ways of maintaining an ongoing relationship, and, lastly, how to effectively accomplish organizational exit. Each of these establishes expectations and responsibilities for the employee's performance while making the employee aware of his or her rights as a member of the organization. The fundamental basis for this exchange of rights and responsibilities is "organizational justice."

Organizational Justice

Justice, or fairness, is thought to exist when people receive those things they believe they deserve based upon their contributions. While there are obvious moral imperatives to treat employees in a fair and just manner, there are more instrumental reasons as well. Research has shown that perceptions of justice impact organizational outcomes such as productivity, absences and turnover, accident rates and health costs, and theft from the organization.[4] It is clear that fairness and justice should be the bedrock of any relationship an organization establishes with an employee.

That being said, it is important to recognize that justice is a *perception* on the part of an individual. No matter how much time and effort practitioners and leaders in organizations spend in an attempt to create perceptions of justice, these perceptions are ultimately impossible to manipulate fully. In other words, one will likely never create a situation in which everyone enjoys the satisfaction of perceived justice. Illustrative of this is a study in which individuals were asked how a lump sum of money should be distributed within the organization. The lowest level of employees believed the money should be divided *equally* among all employees, while managers thought this money should be divided *based upon departmental inputs.*[5] This study shows that differences in justice perceptions exist between distinct employee groups such as managers and employees; imagine the differences in perceptions of justice that undoubtedly exist between each individual employee! Two types of organizational justice are considered here, both of which are relevant when considering the employment relationship.

Distributive justice requires equity in the allocation of rewards or penalties given by the organization. In other words, a relationship that is "distributively just" is one in which the ratio of inputs to outcomes for one individual are equitable to that of another. Typically we hear of distributive justice with regard to pay, which is one obvious component of the organization–employee relationship. But distributive justice pertains to other policies as well. For instance, employees in organizations are often awarded varying amounts of paid vacation. An employee with only two weeks of paid vacation may resent his or her colleague's receipt of three weeks of paid vacation, particularly when both employees work equally hard. Because the perceived ratio of inputs to outcomes is not equal (in this case, the inputs are equal while the outcomes are not), perceptions of distributive *injustice* result for this individual.

Although distributive justice is an important concept, procedural justice is even more basic to the establishment of relationships with employees. **Procedural justice** results from a perception of fair rules, laws, or policies that allocate valued rewards and punishments. This type of justice refers to the underlying manner in which policy was established and its fair execution. To continue with our example, the number of paid vacation days may be awarded to each employee on the basis of his or her tenure. Perhaps three weeks' paid vacation is awarded to an employee for 15 years of continuous service, while those with 5 to 10 years of service receive two weeks of paid leave. If an employee felt deserving of three weeks' paid leave after only 5 years of service, he or she would perceive procedural *and* distributive injustice. In other words, this individual is dissatisfied with the way in which his or her number of vacation days is calculated as well as with the ultimate number of vacation days received.

Conversely, the individual may be unhappy that he or she receives only two weeks' vacation but respects and understands the organization's policy. He or she may be unhappy with the *amount* of paid leave received (i.e., distributive injustice) but feels as though the amount of paid leave was arrived at by an appropriate procedure (i.e., procedural justice). In this situation, the individual still may have overall feelings of fairness. Said another way, "perceived procedural fairness may help mitigate the effects of perceived unjust outcomes."[6] Given this, one can see why procedural justice is crucial to the efficient operation of the organization. Some suggest that an employee's repeated interpretation of policies and procedures as fair builds trust in the organization, which subsequently allows more leeway in terms of employee reactions to its more negative distributive decisions (e.g., low pay increases).[7]

Research shows that perceived fair treatment has significant effects not only on worker attitudes (e.g., job satisfaction and commitment to the organization), but on specific individual behaviors, including absenteeism and citizenship behavior. In addition, research has demonstrated associations between perceived justice and individual work performance. A recent study in the hotel industry illustrated the strengths of these relationships. The authors concluded that the "results of this study show that fair policies and treatment of employees in organizations may increase an organization's capability to address the needs of its customer base. Fair treatment of employees appears to translate into both employee retention and enhanced customer service, as employees are more committed to the organization and its goals and both employee retention and customer service satisfaction affect profitability. Interventions aimed at the fairness climate thus seem likely to improve organizational performance. Research supports a trickle-down model of organizational justice in which employee perceptions of fairness are related to their organizational commitment, which influences customer reactions to employees."[8]

Ethics Programs

An interesting twist on the notion of justice and fairness is formalized ethics programs. As a complement to an employer's specific attempts to be fair, formalized **ethics programs** are designed primarily to ensure honest, fair, and responsible actions *on the part of employees*. Ethical thinking programs usually emphasize four elements:

1. Respect the customs/rituals of others.
2. Think of yourself and the organization as a part of the larger society.
3. Try to evaluate a situation objectively and evaluate the anticipated and unintended consequences of each possible action.
4. Consider the welfare of others as much as is feasible.

Why ethics programs, you may ask? While organizational policy or legal obligation binds employees to specific behavior in most instances, these programs attempt to ensure that employees will *always* act in a manner that is ethical and fair to the organization. Accordingly, benefits of formalized ethics programs are reduced employee misconduct and added protection against lawsuits brought against the organization. Relevant to the latter benefit, the Federal Sentencing Guidelines of 1991 include steeper consequences for federal criminal misconduct if an organization does not have formalized ethics programs in place.[9]

Ethics programs appear to be working overall. In the 2003 National Business Ethics Survey, the Ethics Resource Center notes that employees are reporting violations more than ever. In 1994, 48 percent of employees responded that they have reported violations; in 2003, that percentage rose to 65 percent. The likelihood of reporting is directly related to the nature of the program. Programs with the highest likelihood of reporting were those that included a written statement, training, advice lines, and reporting systems.[10]

The most important component of the ethics program may be managerial support and role modeling. It seems that a formalized ethics program in and of itself is not enough to ensure that employees behave in an ethical manner. At any rate, the trend shows that organizations are feeling at liberty to demand fair and ethical employee behavior, just as the organization attempts to provide the same through its policies, procedures, and practices.

Some ethics programs are innovative in communicating expectations in employee relationships. Lockheed Martin uses an ethics game in which employees test their ethics knowledge and problem-solving skills through 34 scenarios. Dilbert™ and Dogbert™, popular characters created by Scott Adams, serve as the subjects in the scenarios, creating a sense of play that is hard to replicate in instructor-led presentations of ethics information. Lockheed Martin distributes a self-paced, interactive CD recapitulating the ethics information, as well as a calendar and a computer screensaver outlining the company's "twelve building blocks of trust."[11] As another example, Texas Instruments uses formal training and a 14-page booklet to communicate its expectations for ethical behavior. At the back of the booklet is a tear-out, wallet-sized card that includes tips for diagnosing the ethical implications of situations. The card contains the following:

- Is the action legal?
- Does it comply with our values?
- If you do it, will you feel bad?
- How will it look in the newspaper?
- If you know it's wrong, don't do it!
- If you're not sure, ask.
- Keep asking until you get an answer.[12]

In sum, justice, fairness, and ethics, on the part of both the organization and the employee, are fundamental to the employment relationship. We now turn to specific organizational actions that help to build and foster this relationship. Those actions that are common at the outset of the relationship, or at the stage known as "organizational entry," are discussed first.

ORGANIZATIONAL ENTRY

The employment relationship likely begins when an individual enters the selection process for a position or contract with an organization. It is here that individuals begin to form expectations as to how they will be treated. The most fundamental questions at this early stage are the individual's employment status and work arrangement.

Employment Status

As we discussed in Chapter 5, there is a strong trend in the United States toward the use of contingent workers, including part-time, temporary, contract, and leased workers. The temporary help industry provides in excess of 3 million workers today, a 300 percent increase since 1991. But should a temporary worker be considered an employee or an independent contractor? The distinction between these two classifications is not always clear, while the implications may be crucial to the establishment of a healthy employment relationship. Organizations can avoid large tax liabilities by classifying workers as contractors rather than employees, and many costly benefits of employment (e.g., health insurance, retirement plans, stock options) are made available only to employees of the organization. Undoubtedly, it affords clear financial advantage to classify employees as contractors. However, the mere labeling of employees as contractors is not sufficient; several facets of the employment relationship need to be considered in making this distinction.

In determining if the worker should be considered an employee or a contractor, a full assessment of the circumstances of the working relationship is needed, although the focus is often on a few key areas. Specifically, it is important to assess the worker's "right to control." The right to control is simply the extent of the employer's supervision over the manner and means of doing the work. If the worker has complete control over the manner and means of accomplishing the end result, he or she is likely in a contract relationship. Alternatively, if a supervisor can dictate the means by which the worker accomplishes tasks, the worker should be classified as an employee. The extent to which the worker must follow established HR policies and practices, including disciplinary and grievance programs, is also important. If the worker must strictly adhere to these policies and procedures, the worker is likely to be considered an employee rather than a contractor. Other important issues in determining the fundamental nature of the worker's status include length of employment, tax treatment, method of payment, level of the worker's economic dependency on the employer, whether the employer trains the worker, who controls the work schedule, and whether benefits are paid.

Two recent cases illustrate the complexity of this seemingly simple question. Microsoft arranged a contract agreement with its computer programmers, as did Time-Warner with its free-lance writers. In both cases, the courts ruled that the companies had misclassified the workers as independent contractors, thus precluding the employees from participating in benefits and stock option plans. While the courts concluded that the misclassification was not intentionally illegal, the courts ordered immediate participation of all misclassified workers in these programs. It is clear that misclassification in order to avoid tax liability and paying benefits can result in big penalties, unnecessary legal fees, and time-consuming litigation.

Flexible Work Arrangements

Another crucial question at this early stage is that of the work arrangement. Specifically, will the new employee work a traditional schedule (i.e., eight hours per day, five days per week, 50 weeks per year), or one that is less rigid? One survey of 521 of the nation's largest firms indicated that more than 90 percent offered alternative work schedules ranging from flextime to job sharing to summers off.[13] These programs are designed to help employees balance their work and nonwork lives by allowing workers to adopt more flexible work schedules. Some of the more popular programs include flextime, permanent part-time work, job sharing, and compressed workweeks.

Flextime

Nearly 30 percent of U.S. firms now offer some version of flextime. **Flextime** means that the employee can choose his or her work schedule within some limits. Generally, most employees are required to be at work during some "core" period of time, often in the middle of the day. In most instances, the core period is between 10 A.M. and 2 P.M. About 15 percent of employers make 9 A.M. to 3 P.M. their core period, while another 28 percent make 9 A.M. to 4 P.M. their core period.

Flextime has been shown to be effective in relieving work–family conflict among private-sector employees.[14] In addition, the federal government's survey of 325,000 employees who participated in a flextime program demonstrated that 90 percent of them believed the program was at least somewhat important for resolving their work–family conflicts.[15] Flextime has been shown to be related to less tardiness, absenteeism, and sick leave taken by employees and to increases in productivity and quality of work.[16]

One disadvantage associated with flextime is the difficulty in scheduling meetings and trying to locate employees. Also, it may require the use of time clocks, which are often perceived by employees as a managerial control mechanism. Moreover, flextime may not be appropriate for all jobs. Where tasks are highly interdependent, such as on a manufacturing assembly line, it may be more difficult to administer.

Today, some firms are expanding on the idea behind flextime. For instance, Barrios Technology offers flexible work hours and flexible workplaces (flexplace). Flexplace offers employees the option of working at home or in a satellite office closer to home. As discussed in Chapter 5, **telecommuting** is a popular option that enables employees to work at home using computers, video displays, and phones to transmit letters and completed work back to the office. At Pacific Bell, 70 percent of the employees working at home reported higher job satisfaction.[17]

Permanent Part-Time Work

Another relatively recent work arrangement is the use of permanent part-time work. While part-time work has always been available on a temporary basis for some jobs, it has only recently been applied on a permanent basis to professional jobs. Among the companies offering permanent part-time work are AT&T, Barrios Technology, Digital Equipment Corporation, DuPont, UPS, Arthur Andersen, and Herman Miller. While little research is available on the effectiveness of these changes, research in some firms has shown that part-timers were more productive than full-timers and had lower absenteeism.[18] Moreover, a Catalyst study of 2,000 managers (both full-time and part-time) showed that 78 percent of full-time professionals and 98 percent of part-time professionals agreed that offering part-time work encourages employee retention.[19]

Job Sharing

Job sharing is when two people divide the responsibilities for a regular, full-time job. For example, one person may work mornings, while the other person works in the evenings. Job sharing provides the organization with more staffing flexibility and enables the firm to attract and keep good employees. In addition, one early study found that each person does closer to 80 percent of the work of a full-time employee, rather than the expected 50 percent.[20] Employees also favor job-sharing programs because it allows them to reduce their work hours while still keeping their professional skills up to date.[21] Check out www.jobsharing.com for an online job sharing service.

Compressed Workweeks

Yet another innovative arrangement allows employees to work fewer days during the week, with longer hours per day worked. For example, employees could work four 10-hour days instead of five 8-hour days. This type of work schedule has been an option for years for some occupations such as firefighters, police officers, nurses, hair stylists, and technicians. Today, it is being used in other occupations and firms including tellers at Citibank and operators at US Sprint.[22] Using compressed workweeks has a number of benefits for both employees and employers. This arrangement, like other flexible arrangements, allows employees to better accommodate their other life demands so they are not forced to leave the firm. Employee morale and productivity are higher, and tardiness and absenteeism are lower.[23] In addition, the organization can make better use of its equipment and resources. There are some drawbacks, though. Understaffing, scheduling meetings, and coordinating team projects are three common problems. One of the most serious concerns is the increased employee fatigue brought on by working longer hours in one given day.

Once a worker's employment status and work arrangement are clear, the organizational entry time period is crucial for companies to establish the underpinnings of a positive and productive relationship. Next, we discuss two ways in which organizations do this: realistic job previews and socialization/orientation programs.

Realistic Job Previews

Establishing a relationship with employees may begin before the individual is actually hired by the organization. As we discussed in Chapter 5, an organization may choose to provide **realistic job previews** (RJPs), which are presentations of relevant, balanced, and unbiased information about the organization, the job, and the conditions under which the job candidate will work.[24] More traditional recruitment would focus solely upon the positive aspects of the job, often overoptimistically describing the conditions of employment. This has been called the "flypaper approach" because its goal is to attract as many candidates as possible. The flypaper approach is less desirable because, while some candidates ultimately will enjoy and accept the working conditions, others will not and will most probably leave the organization.[25]

Early employee turnover is often the result of misinformation about the job's requirements; thus, informing applicants of the realities of the job is necessary. Research has shown that RJPs can reduce the voluntary turnover in an organization 5 to 10 percent.[26] Four mechanisms are hypothesized to be at work here.[27] First, RJPs lower expectations to appropriate levels. It is commonly known that high expectations are often met with disappointment and dissatisfaction. By lowering expectations, RJPs guard against this disillusionment on the part of new employees. Secondly, RJPs can help the employee to create coping mechanisms for the stressful aspects of the job. If these stressful conditions are anticipated, it is more likely that they will be adequately handled. Third, RJPs convey honesty on the part of the organization; the candidate with negative as well as positive information is less likely to feel he/she was seduced into a job by way of dishonesty on the part of organizational agents. Finally, RJPs allow for candidates to withdraw from the process voluntarily if the job doesn't meet their standards or fulfill their specific career goals.

Thirty percent of organizations surveyed by SHRM reported using RJPs as a selection technique for nonmanagerial jobs.[28] There are several ways to conduct realistic job previews. Information provided by recruiters and interviewers, videotapes, job samples, and candid conversations with job incumbents are some of the methods used. By conducting RJPs, the organization takes advantage of an opportunity to communicate the relevant employee rights and responsibilities before the candidate is actually hired. Although more specific information and detailed instructions will surface over the course of the candidate's actual employment with the organization, RJPs allow the candidate first insight into relevant organizational policies and procedures.

Of course, the downside of RJPs is that the organization may have to recruit a larger number of job candidates. The process of self-selection facilitated by RJPs usually eliminates some highly qualified candidates who ultimately may have thrived in the position. Indeed, the most qualified candidates are probably the ones with the most job opportunities as well. By virtue of the negative aspects of the job presented in the RJP, these high-potential applicants may narrow the number of employment options they have. Also, including the negative aspects of a job in an RJP does not give the organization license to ignore these aspects. If there are stressful or otherwise unpleasant elements of a job, the organization should endeavor to reduce these such that the RJP can be

more positive and thus attract more candidates to stay in the applicant pool.

Socialization and Orientation

Socialization is the process by which an individual comes to appreciate the values, abilities, expected behaviors, and social knowledge essential for assuming an organizational role and for participating as an organization member. Accordingly, socialization is commonly thought of as a learning process. Individuals learn how to operate within the explicitly (i.e., policies and procedures) and implicitly (i.e., cultural) expressed environments. Moreover, socialization takes place over time; it is not a discrete event. It may take months, even years, for employees to become fully adjusted to the organization's working environment.

Orientation is a term used for the organizationally sponsored, formalized activities associated with an employee's socialization into the organization. While realistic job previews may be employed primarily to reduce involuntary turnover and only indirectly inform employees of their rights and responsibilities, orientation activities have the specific purpose of doing so. Orientation programs often include informational training sessions on topics relevant to the newcomer (e.g., key policies and procedures, corporate vision and mission, and compensation and benefits), site tours, and interactions with various organizational members. Orientation programs also may include the assignment of the individual to a mentor, a practice that has been shown to provide the most insight about organizational (i.e., systemwide) information, more than that of co-workers, supervisors, and objective referents such as policy manuals.[29] Sears Roebuck and Company recently reduced the turnover rate by more than half, from approximately 17.5 percent to 7.5 percent. Mentoring was cited as a chief reason for that decline.[30]

Organizationally sponsored orientation programs are part of what is called **institutionalized socialization.** This type of socialization is formal; that is, each member of the organization receives the same, sequential, fixed information upon organizational entry. On the other hand, **individualized socialization** is tailored to each individual employee; one employee's induction into his or her organizational role may be very different from that of his or her peers if organizationally sponsored programs are not provided. Most often, an employee is socialized with some of both tactics. The degree to which the organization uses either institutionalized or individualized tactics depends upon many factors. For instance, the number of employees hired is likely to affect the time and effort placed upon an institutionalized program. If the organization is very small, it may be more efficient to rely primarily upon individualized socialization.

Research has shown that the more formalized the program, the more success in reducing role ambiguity, role conflict, and intentions to quit.[31] Corning Glass Works found that new hires were 69 percent more likely to be with the company after three years when they completed a formalized orientation program rather than being left on their own to sort out the job.[32] It seems that these types of orientation programs most successfully communicate knowledge about the organization and the individual's role within the larger system. Individualized tactics, however, have been shown to be related to innovation and would obviously provide more immediately relevant (i.e., just-in-time) information.[33] Moreover, this informal socialization may be used to complement and solidify what is learned in formal training.[34] Ultimately, it is best to rely upon both types of socialization tactics, using orientation programs and other formalized actions to assure that individuals have requisite general knowledge, while using more individualized tactics to communicate details and encourage creativity and process improvement on the job. Renaissance Worldwide, a Massachusetts-based consulting firm, does just this. New hires spend time in a corporate orientation program sponsored by the Human Resources department. Here, general information on such things as benefits and paid leave are provided. Then, the new hire spends time with his or her manager, learning group strategies and goals, the relationships among all group members, and other job-specific information.[35]

As with RJPs, some unique employee orientation techniques have been utilized by organizations. Southwest Airlines uses some of its employee orientation time to complete necessary paperwork, but Southwest also asks employees to complete a form listing their hobbies and clothing sizes. This information is then used to celebrate employees' birthdays and anniversaries with tailor-made presents.[36] At the end of their orientation program, Ernst & Young employees receive a customized employee handbook, likened to the "triptik" provided by some travel organizations. This customized guidebook tells employees what they're responsible for learning and where they're responsible for learning it over the subsequent six to nine months.[37] Finally, one software company takes action to begin socializing employees before they arrive for their first day. Specifically, a four-step program is used by this company and recommended to others in order to make new employees feel at home:

1. Mail a personal note of welcome to new employees.
2. Send employee handbooks, information on benefits, maps and other information on the area, company programs, and a résumé of work projects being accomplished by department personnel.
3. Personally call the new employee to answer any questions he or she may have regarding the materials already sent.
4. Call the new employee the night before the first workday.[38]

As with any HR intervention, care must be taken to design a program that reaps the benefits described above without causing further confusion, helplessness, or information overload, which may inadvertently create disenchantment with the organization. One expert cautions against the following:

- Using too much valuable orientation time to complete paperwork.
- Giving too much information too quickly.
- Giving information that is irrelevant to adjusting to the position and the organization.
- Scaring the employee by spending an inordinate amount of time discussing the negative aspects of the job.
- Using lectures and videos rather than methods that allow for two-way communication.
- Limiting orientation to the first day at work.
- Selling the organization.[39]

The last point, selling the organization, can be a serious problem if the sales pitch includes false or misleading information. One New York lawyer won a lawsuit against her former law firm after they laid her off less than three months after recruiting her with a plethora of inflated financial information about the firm (this is known as promissory estoppel).

Once an employee has completed the initial stages of socialization, he or she begins to perform the roles associated with the position he or she fills in the organizational structure. The next section discusses the tactics organizations can use to form an ongoing, productive, and positive relationship with each of its employees.

THE ONGOING RELATIONSHIP

Consider for a moment all of the personal relationships you maintain. To some people, you are a family member—child, parent, grandchild, grandparent, and so on. To others, you are a friend, confidant, tennis partner, neighbor, or acquaintance. Perhaps you are also a significant other, a spouse, or a life partner. Consider now all of the ways in which you sustain these relationships. You may have some general rules when it comes to the important people in your life; you may always send cards for birthdays, for instance. But you also must be prepared to relate differently to others depending upon the role you fill in their lives and changes that occur over time.

Now consider the employment relationship. The employee is related to an *entity,* not a person, which presents some obvious differences. However, we are still calling this association a *relationship.* As with your personal relationships, the organization must have mechanisms in place to handle both the portions of the relationship that are common to all employees (e.g., most policies and procedures) and those that deal with each employee's unique situation. As you can imagine, such things as an employee's tenure, health, and violation of rules and regulations may require an organization to alter the relationship. For instance, an employee with 5 years' tenure may receive two weeks' paid vacation, while the employee receives three weeks of paid leave when he or she reaches 15 years of tenure. Each organization will establish its own policies, procedures, and contingencies. We provide a brief overview of the ways in which the ongoing employment relationship can be managed.

Internal forces influencing the working relationship are the employees themselves (through participation programs) and organizationally established policy and procedure. Also in this section, employee discipline and grievance procedures are discussed. First, though one of the most important influences upon the ongoing relationship is not determined by the organization at all: the external legal environment.

External Forces: Law

The external forces governing the employment relationship are employment laws. Not only is it a good business practice to ensure fair dealing with employees, but organizations are legally bound to do so in some cases. Labor and selection laws are discussed in Chapter 3 and elsewhere in the book, but four types of legal doctrine and legislation are particularly relevant to the established employment relationship.

Employment-at-Will

The **employment-at-will** doctrine is a common-law standard that states that a private institution has the right to terminate its employees, with or without just cause, in the absence of a written contract. Proponents of the employment-at-will doctrine argue that individuals often exercise this right; they may resign from the organization at any time without providing reasons or rationale for doing so. An organization having the ability to terminate employees at will simply introduces mutuality into this facet of the relationship. It is important to note that employment-at-will does not exist when there is either a contract (implied or explicit) or a collective bargaining agreement. Of course, it also cannot be invoked when the true underlying reason for the employment action was discriminatory. For instance, as we learned in Chapter 3, an organization may not terminate an employee because of race, sex, disability, age, pregnancy, or religion. In addition, as we will discuss in the next chapter, employees have strong protection for union activity.

There are three additional major exceptions to the employment-at-will doctrine that are recognized by states. However, it should be recognized that the adoption of these exceptions, and indeed the strength of adoption of the doctrine itself, differs from state to state. For instance, six states adopt all of the exceptions listed below, while four states do not adopt any.[40] Although not a universal statute, this doctrine and the exceptions listed below provide legal guidance for much of the relationship between employers and employees, as is noted below and throughout this chapter. The three common exceptions to employment-at-will are[41]

1. *Public policy:* Terminations that violate a state's public policy are prohibited. This exception is particularly relevant to whistleblowing, discussed further in the next section. State laws also may preclude terminations based upon the filing of workers' compensation claims or reporting a wrongful act.

2. *Implied contracts:* It is unlawful to terminate an individual if an implied contract of employment exists. This exception is most relevant to policy and procedure manuals distributed by the organization. See "Employee Handbooks as Implied Contracts" later in this chapter.

3. *Covenant of good faith and fair dealing:* It is unlawful to terminate an employee without just cause or for malicious reasons. Only 11 states have adopted these specific "good faith and fair dealing" provisions.

Because "wrongful termination" suits are quite common, HR professionals should be aware of the common law governing employment in their state. Further, to avoid such wrongful termination lawsuits, organizations should take steps to ensure that terminations are substantiated by documentation and that they follow a standard procedure. Moreover, some suggest that organizations should actually take responsibility for educating employees as to the meaning of employment-at-will. When surveyed on this issue, a full 83 percent of respondents thought that a satisfactory employee could not lawfully be fired in order for the organization to replace her with someone at a lower wage.[42] Of course, abiding by employment-at-will principles, this practice is probably acceptable. It seems that most employees have little understanding of their employment rights provided under law. As discussed later in the chapter, most experts recommend that at the very least, employee handbooks include a clear stipulation that the employer is an "employment-at-will" organization.

Whistleblowing

One practice protected by various federal, state, and local laws is **whistleblowing,** or reporting misconduct to persons who have the power to take action.[43] By definition, whistleblowing can be internal (e.g., to the supervisor or HR department) or external (e.g., to the media, legislators, or professional organizations) reporting of wrongdoing. However, those cases that represent "whistleblowing" to most people are those in which the whistleblower reported information externally. One example is that of Dr. Jeffrey Wigand, the subject of the 1999 movie *The Insider* starring Russell Crowe as Dr. Wigand. Dr. Wigand, former vice president for research and development for the tobacco company Brown and Williamson (B&W),

discovered that a flavoring used in B&W tobacco was a serious carcinogen. After reporting this discovery to the president of the firm, Dr. Wigand was fired. Dr. Wigand then spoke to investigators at the Food and Drug Administration, testified in several state lawsuits against the tobacco industry, and was interviewed for the CBS program *60 Minutes*. Since the whistleblowing incident, Dr. Wigand claims he experienced retaliation in several forms: he was fired, physically threatened, and received negative publicity since his public reports.[44] While most instances of whistleblowing are not this extreme, it is important to recognize the legal obligations of organizations when faced with reports of internal wrongdoing.

Unfortunately, those legal obligations are complex and vary from state to state. Employees are not uniformly protected against retaliation from whistleblowing; however, many constitutional, federal, and state laws can protect employees based upon the nature of their actions. The First (i.e., Freedom of Speech) and Fourteenth (i.e., Due Process) Amendments prohibit government officials from retaliating, as do more minor federal laws specific to the incident such as the Clean Air Act, the Occupational Safety and Health Act (OSHA), the Civil Service Reform Act, and the False Claims Act. Moreover, 44 states have a clear "public policy" exception to their employment-at-will doctrine, 42 states have specific whistleblowing protection for public employees, and 19 states have whistleblowing protection for private employees.[45] At any rate, organizations should be aware of the specific laws protecting its employees, and they should take measures to promote internal reporting. These measures help the organization to avoid costly litigation and public relations problems. Anonymous reporting policies and established lines of communication for reports of misconduct may encourage employees to report misconduct internally so that it can be handled internally.

It is important to realize that certain employee obligations may restrict divulging information which is in no way whistleblowing and thus not protected as such. For instance, employees have a duty to protect confidential information. This is called a **covenant of nondisclosure,** and the formal policy regarding such conduct often appears in the employee handbook. In 2005, the Supreme Court of Missouri held that "an employee and a new employer may be liable for damages to a former employer if the employee engages in direct competition while still employed." Nondisclosure agreements protect trade secrets and other information privileged by the organization. Organizations also can mandate a certain degree of employee loyalty through **noncompete agreements.** These agreements are contractual arrangements with employees that restrict their acceptance of employment with an industry competitor upon voluntarily leaving the current organization. Courts are not always receptive to these agreements, and most states have statutes that govern their enforceability. In general, these statutes ask whether there is a legitimate business interest in the enforcement

of the noncompete agreement and whether the agreement is not excessive in terms of the restrictions on the employee, the time limit of the agreement, and its geographic scope.[46] While there is a trend toward more restrictive contracts, such covenants are not favored, and are indeed more carefully scrutinized in the courts when a person's abilities to earn a living and better himself or herself are restricted.

Privacy

There has been a great deal of legal activity related to privacy in the wake of September 11, 2001. Before this date, the federal Privacy Act of 1974 established protection against the use of employment records for purposes other than business functioning. Applying only to federal organizations, this statute allows employees to review, amend, and bring civil suit for misuse of their employment records. Many states have similar laws for private-sector employees, covering both personnel files and any information about an employee's medical condition. It is important to recognize, though, that the enforcement and stringency of privacy law varies from jurisdiction to jurisdiction. However, records such as performance appraisals, disciplinary actions, and formal complaints are typically deemed confidential in the courts. In many states, an employer may be liable for invasion of privacy if the employer publicly discloses a private fact that is objectionable to a reasonable person and is not a legitimate public concern. Some states (e.g., New York, California) have clear restrictions on the business use of information concerning off-duty conduct such as political or union activities, including revealing these activities to prospective employers. The Electronic Privacy Information Center at www.epic.org provides a summary of privacy laws for each state.

In the case of medical information, HR departments may have a surprising amount of documentation. For instance, records may include results from physicals, Family and Medical Leave Act information, documentation of accommodations required under the Americans with Disabilities Act, and records from Employee Assistance Programs. Because of the highly sensitive nature of the information, it is recommended that these records be kept separate from the personnel files and that access to their contents be highly restricted.[47]

Particularly relevant to the issue of privacy is the use of HR information systems (HRIS). While computerized storage of data aids the HR professional, it also allows for easy access to sensitive information by unwanted individuals. Moreover, information in HRIS is often keyed from written documents, making the databases susceptible to errors. It is recommended that organizations enact procedures to periodically confirm the accuracy of information. Moreover, organizations should remind employees to update key information in order to capture relevant information changes such as marriage or an increase or decrease in the number of dependents reported. Likewise, supervisors should be reminded to update records with disciplinary actions, complaints, and terminations.[48] Finally, anyone with access to sensitive information, be it in a file or an HRIS, should be warned that the information is confidential and that breach of the confidentiality is a serious offense that may result in termination.[49]

Records that may be relevant to terrorism investigations are the exception to this rule. The Providing Appropriate Tools Required to Intercept and Obstruct Terrorism (PATRIOT) Act of 2001 allows government officials access to business records and transactions. In some cases, officials are allowed to conduct surveillance in the workplace. While the constitutionality of this law is still being tested in the courts, it appears that organizations are now to be held simultaneously responsible for balancing employee privacy concerns and governmental requests for information.

It is obvious that employers are now faced with a serious predicament. Aside from the legal obligation to do so, organizations should be concerned for the basic respect of an employee's privacy by limiting the amount of information gathered to that which is needed to carry out the business function. However, this respect for privacy must now be balanced with a desire (and obligation) to cooperate with the government in its antiterrorism efforts. Antiterrorism efforts aside, methods by which the information is gathered, stored, utilized, and distributed should be in a manner considerate of employee privacy.

Privacy and the Job Applicant   Employers often request consumer reports or more detailed "investigative consumer reports" (ICVs) from a consumer credit services as a part of the background check. If this is so, employers need to be aware of The Fair Credit Reporting Act (FCRA), amended in 2005, a federal law that regulates how such agencies provide information about consumers. Under the FCRA, employers must receive approval from an applicant that any consumer document can be secured and must provide such an approval in writing to the consumer credit agency. If the employer decides to reject the applicant based to some extent on the report, the applicant must be provided a copy of the report before the employer takes any formal action regarding the applicant.

The FCRA may also apply to internal investigations of suspected employee misconduct. Under 2005 amendments, employers do not have to give advance notice of an investigation to employees. However, employers do have to provide a summary of the nature of the information provided that led to any adverse action such as a termination.

Privacy versus Employer Rights   Can an employer impose rules regarding the off-duty behavior of employees? While there are exceptions, the general answer to this question is yes. "If you test positive for tobacco, you can't work here." So says Howard Weyers, CEO of WEYCO, Inc., a Michigan health care company. Mr. Weyers's policy applies to all smoking regardless of when, where, or how often you do it. His rationale is quite simple. He says smokers cost him too much money. According to the Center for Disease Control, a smoker will cost a company an average of $3,400 in lost productivity and health care cost every year. While 28 states and the District of Columbia have passed laws protecting smokers, in general, Mr. Weyers has the legal right to impose such a rule on his employees. But Lewis Maltby of the National Workrights Institute says the no smoking rule is the "first step on a slippery slope . . . If you smoke, or you drink, if you eat too much junk food, you're promiscuous. What comes next?"

Military Rights

With the United States involved in protracted wars in Iraq and Afghanistan, more reserve and national guard units are being called to active duty. Today, nearly half of U.S. military members are reservists. Many reservists may be on active duty for six months or longer and are unsure of their rights concerning their job and benefits.

The federal Uniformed Services Employment and Reemployment Rights Act (USERRA) establishes the rights of reservists and the National Guard to return to work at the end of their service. The USERRA applies to all employers regardless of their size and protects those serving in the U.S. reserve forces of the Army, Navy, Marine Corps, Air Force, Coast Guard, Public Health Service Commissioned Corps, and the National Guard. While on active duty, employees must receive all benefits available to other employees on comparable leaves of absence. Employees also may use accrued vacation while on leave but cannot be forced to do so. While the law does not require employers to pay a worker on active duty, many employers pay the difference between a worker's regular salary and his or her military pay.

Worker Adjustment and Retraining Notification Act (WARN)

As we discussed in Chapter 5, the Worker Adjustment and Retraining Notification Act (WARN), enacted in 1989, requires organizations to give affected employees 60 days' written notice when a plant will close or when mass layoffs are expected. WARN covers employers with more than 100 full-time employees, and its compliance is required when there will be an employment loss of six months or more. Go to www.doleta.gov for the details of WARN.

Evidence shows that the overall timeframe of notification before plant closings has slightly increased as a result of this law.[50] However, in many individual instances, the WARN Act does not protect workers with a 60-day notice. Particularly in the case of unforeseen circumstances, many cases have been filed in which courts have ruled on the side of employers. For instance, when a General Dynamics contract with the U.S. Navy was suddenly cancelled, the courts ruled that the 17-day notice the company provided to its workers was adequate.[51] Similarly, a court ruled that the owners of the Atlantis Casino in New Jersey did not violate the WARN Act when the New Jersey Casino Control Commission unexpectedly ordered the casino's closing.[52]

Internal Forces: Employee Surveys

Beyond the external legal forces that govern the ongoing working relationship to some extent, there are two major internal forces that must be considered. The first of these is the influence of the employees themselves. Particularly in cases where formalized participation and involvement programs exist, the employees may have the power to make suggestions, become involved in management decision making, and provide feedback to the organization and its leaders. Generally, it is believed that involving employees in decision making will result in improved job attitudes and cooperation and reduced turnover, absenteeism, and grievances. In practice, organizations involve their employees in actual decision making to varying degrees; many use such tactics as quality circles, autonomous work teams, and high-involvement initiatives to engage employees and include them in decision making. Fundamental to these initiatives, however, is the solicitation of employee feedback. Virtually all organizations gather feedback from their employees, and most often this is accomplished through employee survey systems.

A growing body of research shows that employee feedback programs are effective in increasing an organization's productivity and product and service quality. In the case of the human resource function, organizational productivity and quality are influenced indirectly through the satisfaction and support that the HR programs give to each employee. Feedback provided by employees, then, can help the human resource function evaluate its programs and take corrective action where needed—either through initiating programs to address shortcomings or discontinuing programs that are not well received.

Survey results reveal an organization's strengths and weaknesses and provide a means for comparing results against norms established by data from other organizations as well as against internal norms established in other departments. An example of a typical employee survey and definitions of the factors that are assessed are shown in Figures 12-1 and 12-2. Go to www.employeesurveys.com for online tailored employee surveys.

In addition to their evaluation purpose, employee surveys also may be used to facilitate planned organization change and team building based on feedback and discussion of the survey data, thus improving the employment relationship over time. Companies often begin the review of survey data by comparing the organization's data against outside or internal norms to establish an initial benchmark. If the same survey is repeated in subsequent years, it becomes especially valuable to compare data in a given year with the data from previous years. Analyzing the trend of data over several years is a particularly powerful tool for understanding what is going on in the organization. Many companies combine attitude surveys with 360-degree appraisals (see Chapter 7) for a more comprehensive perspective.

Many organizations also find it useful to compare the data (and trends) for different units across the organization to pinpoint specific parts of the organization where particular issues or concerns may be arising. This approach facilitates the development of action strategies specific to individual parts of the organization as well as other action strategies relevant for the entire organization. Survey data also promote the early identification of difficulties and permit timely response before minor concerns become major issues. In this way, feedback from employees changes the ongoing employment relationship. It is hoped that these changes are iterative improvements to the association between the organization and its employees.

Attitude surveys are used most effectively as part of a comprehensive assessment and intervention strategy. The focus is often on the business unit and the manager or supervisor of the unit. Companies use the same survey questions in order to establish interpretive and predictive data. For example, researchers at the Gallup organization conducted focus groups across several industries to determine the characteristics of successful employees and managers. They focused on the importance of the managers' influence over the "engagement level" of employees and their job satisfaction with their companies. They found that the specific facet of job satisfaction most related to job performance was satisfaction with the supervisor. "Engagement" in the Gallup research refers to a worker's involvement, satisfaction and enthusiasm for work. Gallup uses a set of 12 key questions and maintains a huge database from hundreds of companies. For example, workers are asked to indicate how satisfied they are with their company in terms of encouraging their development and providing opportunities and the necessary information and equipment to do the job. One excellent study focused on these "engagement" scores and profit data of business units and found a difference of approximately 1 to 4 percentage points in profitability for high engagement units and from $80,000 to $120,000 higher monthly revenue or sales (and for one organization, the difference was more than $300,000). The authors concluded that "employee satisfaction and engagement are related to meaningful business outcomes at a magnitude that is important to many organizations and that these correlations generalize across companies."[53]

Since 1994, Wal-Mart has surveyed its associates annually as part of the "Grass Roots survey program." Like the Gallup survey, the purpose of the Grass Roots program is to assess employees' perceptions on work-related issues. Results are calculated by store, and the top three concerns are posted at each store. Store Managers are expected to meet with their employees to discuss concerns and to develop action plans to address them. Responses are also

FIGURE 12-1	Example of an Employee Opinion Survey

HUMAN RESOURCES INDEX

The objective of this survey is to determine how members of this organization feel about the effectiveness with which the organization's human resources are managed. The survey provides you an opportunity to express your opinions in a way that is constructive. Your views will be valuable in assisting the organization to evaluate and improve its performance.

The survey is to be done anonymously. Please **do not put your name** on the response sheet or identify your responses in any way. Responses can in no way be traced to any individual. The frank and free expression of your own opinions will be most helpful to the organization.

Listed below are a series of statements. After you have read each statement, please decide the extent to which the statement describes your own situation and your own feelings, using the following scale:

A) almost never
B) not often
C) sometimes (i.e., about half the time)
D) often
E) almost always

Then, using a No. 2 pencil, darken the appropriate box on the response sheet. For example, if you believe that the statement is true "sometimes," darken block C on the answer sheet next to the number corresponding to the indicated statement.

Questions 65 and 66 should be answered in **pencil** on the back of the **response sheet.**

When you have completed the survey, please return the response sheet and this survey form in accordance with the directions in the cover letter.

IN THIS ORGANIZATION:

1. There is sufficient communication and sharing of information between groups.
2. The skills and abilities of employees are fully and effectively utilized.
3. Objectives of the total organization and my work unit are valid and challenging.
4. The activities of my job are satisfying and rewarding.
5. I have received the amount and kind of training that I need and desire to do my job well.
6. Leadership in this organization is achieved through ability.
7. Rewards are fairly and equitably distributed.
8. First-level supervision is of a high quality.
9. Management has a high concern for production and effectively communicates this concern.
10. My job provides ample opportunity for a sense of individual responsibility.
11. There is a sense of loyalty and belonging among members of this organization.

- •
- •
- •

63. By and large, most members of this organization are sensitive, perceptive, and helpful to one another.
64. In general, complete and accurate information is available for making organizational decisions.

---

65. The things I like best about this organization are: _____
66. The things I would most like to change are: _____

Source: Fred E. Schuster, Professor of Management, Florida Atlantic University, Boca Raton, FL 33431. Copyright © 1977. Reprinted with permission.

used to calculate an "Unresolved People Index" (which was originally called the Union Potential Index) to identify stores at risk of union organizing activity. Stores scoring high on the index are targeted for intervention by company management with expertise in avoiding union organizing. The stores are then surveyed again subsequently to assess whether there was any improvement after the intervention. The survey process was actually used against Wal-Mart in the recent sex discrimination lawsuit. An expert witness testified that while the survey is "an efficient mechanism for assessing employees' perceptions about barriers to equal opportunity associated with gender . . . [it] has never been

used to assess employees' perceptions on issues such as whether they have been treated unfairly due to gender (or race) or the firm's commitment to diversity. Nor have the results of Grass Roots Surveys ever been analyzed by gender or race in order to assess perceived discriminatory barriers."

Internal Forces: Employee Handbooks

An organization's published policies and procedures (i.e., employee handbooks) are the second of the two major internal forces governing the employment relationship. Generally stated, the purpose of policies and procedures

FIGURE 12-2	Factor Definitions from an Employee Survey

1. **Reward system** (RWD): compensation, benefits, perquisites, and other (tangible and intangible) rewards.

2. **Communication** (COM): flow of information downward, upward, and across the organization.

3. **Organization effectiveness** (OE): level of confidence in the overall abilities and success of the organization; how well the organization achieves its objectives.

4. **Concern for people** (PLP): the degree to which the organization is perceived of as caring for the individuals who work for it.

5. **Organization objectives** (OO): the extent to which individuals perceive the organization to have objectives that they can understand, feel proud of, and identify with.

6. **Cooperation** (COP): the ability of people throughout the organization to work effectively together to achieve shared goals.

7. **Intrinsic satisfaction** (IS): rewards that people receive from the work itself (sense of achievement, pride in a job well done, growth and development, feeling of competence).

8. **Structure** (STC): rules and regulations, operating policies and procedures, management practices and systems, the formal organization structure and reporting relationships.

9. **Relationships** (REL): feelings that people have about others in the organization.

10. **Climate** (CLM): the atmosphere of the organization, the extent to which people see it as a comfortable, supportive, pleasant place to work.

11. **Participation** (PAR): opportunity to contribute one's ideas, to be consulted, to be informed, and to play a part in decision making.

12. **Work group** (WG): feelings about the immediate group of people with whom one works on a daily basis.

13. **Intergroup competence** (ITG): the ability of separate work groups to work smoothly and effectively together to accomplish shared objectives.

14. **First-level supervision** (FLM): confidence that members of the organization have in the competence and integrity of first-line supervisors.

15. **Quality of management** (QM): confidence that members of the organization have in the competence and integrity of middle and higher management.

Source: Fred E. Schuster, Professor of Management, Florida Atlantic University, Boca Raton, FL 33431. Copyright 1977. Reprinted with permission.

is to establish the guidelines by which the organization and the employee contribute to the mutual relationship. Many companies end up in court because of their handbooks. Others survive in court for the same reason.

Thus, the creation and distribution of an employee handbook should not be taken lightly; however, there is often disagreement about what purposes a handbook should serve. Lawyers often will recommend that the handbook be filled with legal disclaimers, many of which can alienate or confuse the employee or candidate. Employee relations specialists may recommend that the handbook include warm and cuddly human relations statements that may end up implying more job security than the employer intended. Neither extreme is desirable, and bad employee handbooks may be worse than no handbook at all. It is important to carefully consider each and every aspect of content in an employee handbook. Go to www.HR-Guide.com for online help on developing employee handbooks.

In their handbook on handbooks, *Inc.* magazine notes that employee handbooks should be used to communicate company policies and procedures, establish the mutual agreements between the employee and the organization while avoiding contractual language, explain the company's philosophy, excite and motivate the employees about their jobs, and convey a broader sense of the company mission and vision.[54] Guidelines for writing a handbook and what to include in it are presented in Figure 12-3. One key guideline regarding handbooks is that they should be evaluated regularly for possible revision. Most handbooks that have not been revised in the last few years may have failed to address numerous federal, state, and local laws, regulations, and executive orders that may be directly relevant to the employment relationship. Among the more pressing issues that organizations now face in the way of establishing policy are sexual harassment, Internet and computer usage, dispute resolution programs, performance monitoring, trade secrets and noncompete clauses, smoking in the workplace, cell phone policy, personal appearance, nepotism, employee dating, and conflicts of interest. The Web site for the Society of Human Resource Management (shrm.org) provides model policies for most of these issues and several online articles about good and bad employee handbooks.

Many organizations now maintain their handbooks on the company intranet. This affords easy accessibility for all parties and allows for efficient changes and immediate notice of such changes through e-mail. In addition, the contents of employee handbooks often differ depending on the particular classification or status of the worker and the location of the workers. Remember our discussion earlier regarding employment status and work arrangements. Therefore, electronic copies offer a much more efficient means of providing such tailored information.

Handbooks also should reflect the conditions of employment for particular states or countries. Furthermore, it may be necessary to provide a copy of the handbook in languages other than English. Regardless of the format of the handbook (e.g., hard copy, intranet only), there should always be a provision for an acknowledgment of the receipt of the handbook. We will discuss this issue later since it is so important. Additionally, two specific policies of importance are sexual harassment and technology usage.

FIGURE 12-3	**Guidelines for Writing a Handbook**

- Prepare a list of all the policies you think your company needs. Review the list with your management group and with supervisors who will be using these policies.
- Pull out all the policies you now have and review them, bringing them up to date and discarding those that aren't needed.
- When writing policies, be brief and eliminate trite and verbose language. Keep them short and concise.
- Because some courts have ruled that employee handbooks and policy manuals can be considered employment contracts, it is important to insert a clause that states the handbook or manual should not be considered an employment contract and that employment is a strictly "at-will" relationship. You may wish to obtain more specific language from an attorney.
- Keep the language simple. If it is too technical, people won't read it.
- Don't undercut your supervisors' or managers' authority. You are paying them to manage, so give them the opportunity to do so.
- Write policies that are realistic for your size and type of business.
- Avoid redundancy—don't cover the same ground in two policies.
- Be sure your policies conform to local, state, and federal laws.
- Leave the lengthy details of benefit programs to a benefit handbook; don't include them in the policies.
- Be careful not to sound "preachy" by using condescending or patronizing language.
- Do not use sexist language.

WHAT TO INCLUDE IN AN EMPLOYEE HANDBOOK

- Accidents/injuries
- Alcohol or Drug Use
- At-will statement
- Benefits
- COBRA issues
- Company Rules
- Complaint/ADR Procedures
- Confidentiality Agreement
- Dating policy
- Demotion
- Disciplinary Action and Warning Notices
- Dress codes, protective clothing
- Drug testing
- Educational Assistance
- Emergency procedures
- Employee Assistance
- Employee Suggestions
- Employer/employee rights
- Employment Procedures
- Equal Employment Opportunity
- Ethical statements/policy
- Exit Interviews
- External Communication
- Falsification of Records
- Flexible Time Off
- Flextime
- FMLA
- Funeral Time Off

- Garnishments
- Grievance Procedure/Rights
- Holidays
- Jury Duty Time Off
- Layoffs
- Leaves
- Lockers/personal property
- Maternity Leave of Absence
- Military Leave of Absence
- Nepotism policy
- Non-compete agreements
- Non-disclosure covenants
- Open door policy
- Organizational Bulletins
- Orientation Sessions
- Overtime
- Ownership of Patents, Inventions, Royalties
- Pay Days
- Performance Appraisal
- Personal Leave of Absence
- Personal Time Off
- Pre-employment Physical Exam
- Pregnancy
- Professional Memberships
- Promotions/job postings
- References
- Relocation
- Rest areas

- Right to amend Handbook
- Safety Administration
- Safety/OSHA issues
- Separation Pay
- Service Awards
- Sexual Harassment/other harassment
- Smoking
- Solicitation
- Suggestions
- Support of Recreational Activities
- Telephone/cell phone/ e-mail/Internet/intranet Use
- Temporary Employees/status/ I-9 forms
- Terminations
- Testing
- Time Cards
- Training Programs
- Transfers
- Unemployment Compensation
- Vacation
- Violence policy
- Visitors
- Voting
- Warning System
- Whistleblowing policy
- Worker's Compensation
- Work Week

Source: Adapted and updated from M. F. Cook, "Personnel Policies and Employee Communications: Handling New Issues in Today's Work Environment," *New Directions in Human Resources: A Handbook* (Englewood Cliffs, NJ: Prentice Hall, 1987).

Sexual Harassment Policies

Like other issues that have been covered in this chapter, addressing sexual harassment in the workplace makes both conceptual and legal sense for organizations. Because sexual harassment is one of the most extreme examples of employee disrespect, perceptions of injustice and emotional reactions to harassment undermine work performance and organizational efficiency. As we discussed in Chapter 3, the Supreme Court has ruled that formally stated policies could protect organizations from lawsuits even when a supervisor sexually harassed an employee unbeknownst to the organization.[55] In short, one of the first actions an HR professional should take upon entering a new organization is to verify the presence of a sexual harassment policy. If one does not exist there, create one! In California, both a policy and mandatory training are the law for all employers. The policy must be published in the handbook.

A sexual harassment policy should demonstrate management's understanding of the issue and express commitment to eliminating its existence. Likewise, the construction of the policy should encourage employees to come forward with complaints. A good sexual harassment policy should include information on the purpose of the policy, the legal and behavioral definitions of sexual harassment, the importance of the problem, reporting procedures and organizational actions such as investigations and discipline, and names and phone numbers for individuals to report complaints.[56]

Technology Usage Policies

Just as employers regulate such things as usage of the telephone, office supplies and equipment, and other company property, some are finding it increasingly necessary to regulate such things as Internet and e-mail. In 1998, it was reported that 41 percent of organizations had restricted Internet access for employees, while only 17 percent had unrestricted access.[57] As you may expect, concerns of privacy and confidentiality are at issue. It is important that employers ask themselves if a reasonable expectation of privacy exists with the usage of the Internet and e-mail at work. If so, courts may determine that monitoring of e-mail and Internet usage is a violation of privacy.

In general, however, employers can monitor e-mail and Internet activity when these activities are conducted with the employer's equipment, particularly when a specific policy is in place concerning the proper usage of the technology. Excessive personal usage of the Internet and e-mail is obviously counterproductive and may be of particular concern when it infringes upon the organization's morals and values. For example, one recent study found that 20 percent of male U.S. workers access at least one pornographic site per week while at work. Employers are allowed to monitor and stop such behavior.

Employee handbooks should present technology usage policies in such a way that employees are very clear about their rights and responsibilities when creating, accessing, and disseminating information from the work environment.[58] Relatedly, handbooks should include a policy on cell phone use at work, including both personal and company-provided phones. Employers can be judged culpable for the reckless behavior of employees who talk on their cell phones while driving or performing other potentially dangerous tasks. Such culpability can be reduced if an employee handbook clearly prohibits such behavior.

Employee Handbooks as Implied Contracts

One of the most important components of any employee handbook is a statement that makes clear the fact that the contents of the employee handbook should not be construed as evidence of an implicit or explicit employment contract.[59] In the context of an employee handbook, an implicit contract could mean that an employee's failure to engage in specified circumstances and behaviors outlined in the discipline and termination policies serve as an unwritten guarantee of job security. Most organizations ask that employees sign a document stating that they have read the policy and procedure handbook and that they accept that its contents are not legally binding. As in the court case mentioned in this chapter's "Overview," employers can be sued for wrongful termination on the basis of the contents of an employee handbook.

In fact, any management employee's verbal comments to employees about the duration of employment also may serve as an implicit contract.[60] For instance, managers should not state that employment will continue as long as the employee abides by the policies and procedures contained in the employee handbook. Courts in about 30 states have adopted the "implied contract" exception to the employment-at-will doctrine. Consequently, courts could very well rule for the employee in any case in which it is determined that an implied contract of employment is in effect.

A sample statement that attempts to release the handbook from interpretation as a contract is presented below. Simply put, handbooks should introduce the concept of employment-at-will. However, whether this statement has any legal significance depends upon many factors, including other statements made by the employer that are relevant to the allegation and the state court's interpretation of the employment-at-will doctrine.

SAMPLE DISCLAIMER

This manual is not to be construed as a contract. Employees of Company X are employed on an at-will basis, meaning that either the employee or Company X may terminate the employment relationship at any time, with or without notice. Nothing contained in this manual is intended to provide or guarantee employment for a specific period of time, nor does this manual create any type of employment contract. Within the limits allowed by law, Company X reserves the right to amend, modify, or cancel this manual, as well as any and all of the various policies, procedures, guidelines, standards, benefits, and programs outlined within, whenever it deems appropriate.

Interestingly, while organizations must take care to avoid certain language for fear of wrongful termination suits, other handbook language can actually protect organizations in court. That is, if the court finds that a handbook is considered to be an implied contract, then its contents are binding for both employers *and* employees. For instance, a Continental Airlines employee contested his termination on the grounds that the airline had incorrectly counted his absences in violation of the implied contract, or the handbook. The U.S. Court of Appeals reversed a $200,000 verdict against Continental when it ruled that there are both benefits and responsibilities associated with a handbook that creates an implied contract. The handbook stipulated that the employee must use a formal internal appeals process to contest personnel actions, an action that the terminated employee did not take. Thus, employees can have certain "implied" obligations under a handbook as well.

Violations of Policy/Discipline

As the adage goes, "Rules were made to be broken." While you, in the role of an officer of the organization, may not want employees to live by this creed, undoubtedly there will be violations of the policies set forth for appropriate conduct. It is for this reason that discipline policies and guidelines must be enacted. Many differences exist in the actions that organizations deem necessary as recourse for violations of policy, some of them being very fundamental differences. Specifically, while some may choose a discipline approach, others may focus more upon punishment for the misconduct.[61] **Punishment** is the provision of a negative consequence following a behavior. It is focused upon the past and penalizes undesirable behavior. On the other hand, **discipline** is more future oriented; its goal is to point the way to more positive and productive behavior rather than to penalize the person for his or her mistakes. Although different organizational cultures will undoubtedly support different blends of punishment and discipline, the goal of these policies should be to improve productivity. Therefore, a discipline approach is ultimately more desirable.

Before any discipline takes place, organizational members should attempt to diagnose the problem to be sure that the employee is to blame for the incident. In courts of law, organizations are held responsible for a thorough investigation. Individuals have won large judgments against their former employers when they failed to conduct such investigations prior to termination. Particular attention should be paid to allegations of serious misconduct such as sexual harassment. When investigating a possible violation of policy, employees may be entitled to representation at the associated hearings or meetings. According to a 2000 decision by the National Labor Relations Board against the Epilepsy Foundation of Northeast Ohio, union and nonunion employees have the right, upon request, to the presence of a co-worker during an investigatory interview. Although it's unclear whether this ruling will be sustained over time, two things are clear at the time of this writing: It is the employee's responsibility to request that a co-worker or representative be present and the meeting must involve solely investigation and not discipline or termination. See www.nlrb.gov., 331, no. 92 (2000).

Even when the employee is to blame, a causal analysis should be done to determine the best tactics for preventing the misconduct in the future. Briefly, one should determine if the problem resulted from misunderstanding, lack of knowledge, or motivation. If an employee does not *understand* why his or her behavior was inappropriate, communicate with the employee. If the employee does not *know how* to perform properly, train the employee. Finally, if the employee is not *motivated* to perform correctly, look for systems/issues that can be changed. Ultimately, motivation issues may be the hardest to address, but cases of misconduct are a good opportunity to examine motivational factors in the workplace.

While the investigation and/or the causal analysis may uncover information that lessens the need to hold the employee fully accountable, discipline is the appropriate action in most cases. For discipline, the guiding principles are generally the same as the bases for selection decisions:

1. Decisions should be based on job-related criteria; that is, behavior that is being disciplined should have a direct impact upon job or organizational performance.
2. Employees should be treated consistently.
3. Company policy should be followed; any deviation from company policy due to mitigating circumstances should be clearly documented and rationalized.
4. Communication to all involved should be accurate and honest, but confidentiality should be maintained when appropriate.

If possible, a legal expert (e.g., an HR specialist or lawyer) should be consulted before an actual decision is made.

Of course, if employees continue to violate policy, discipline should become more and more severe, a practice often called **progressive discipline.** Organizations often respond to misconduct first with some minimal warning, followed by more severe punishments up to and including termination or discharge. An example of a progressive disciplinary program is:

- Verbal warning.
- Written warning copied to supervisor's file.
- Written warning copied to HR file.
- Suspension or demotion.
- Termination.

The severity of the misconduct should be taken into account when an organization determines the appropriate disciplinary actions along the progressive discipline continuum. If it is found that an employee has stolen large amounts of money from the operating budget, the organization is likely to exercise termination and even press criminal charges. This situation should not be handled merely with a verbal warning. Lateness, on the other hand, lends itself more readily to a multiple-step, progressive discipline approach. Specific actions that result in deviations from strict progressive discipline should be outlined in an employee handbook. However, the wording of these policies should not be exclusive. In other words, the specific actions leading directly to termination should be provided as examples, not a definitive listing of reasons one may be terminated. The latter approach makes the discipline policy susceptible to charges of an implicit contract, putting the organization at risk for a wrongful termination suit.

While setting limits is important, enforcement is paramount. Obviously, ignoring cases of misconduct allows problem employees to perform at a level of decreased productivity and efficiency. However, failing to use established discipline policies also may have indirect effects. First, management may lose credibility in the eyes of other employees if it does not carry out policies that have been explicitly set forth. Furthermore, the morale of other employees may be diminished by their having to make up for poor productivity on the part of one underperforming employee. Much of the literature on sound management and talent retention discusses the sensitivity of employees to these issues. As one source put it: "Many good employees leave because they don't see recurring labor problems handled by their managers."[62]

Of course, a discipline policy should allow for exceptions to progressive discipline given certain offenses. In particular, employees also should be given an opportunity to disclose a medical reason for the problem. If such disclosures are made, a lawyer or HR specialist should be consulted to determine the Americans with Disabilities Act or Family Medical Leave Act implications of the matter. Remember our discussion of reasonable accommodation regarding the ADA (see Chapter 3). The ADA is particularly relevant for drug and alcohol use policies. Recovering alcoholics and recovering drug users are protected by the law; thus, employees who are participating in legitimate rehabilitation programs are covered. The ADA does not protect active or illegal users.

Grievances

As astute as an organization may be in establishing policies and practices that allocate rewards and distribute punishments fairly, employees may have cause to challenge decisions made on the part of the organization. Most typically, this is executed by way of a formally established grievance procedure. A grievance can be defined in many ways; as such, an organization establishing a grievance policy should define the term succinctly. Some organizations limit grievances to treatment by a supervisor, while others state that a grievance may be filed against the administration or interpretation of a company policy, but not against the policy itself.[63] The simplest way to define **grievance** may be

to say that it is a formal, written complaint about the way in which the employment relationship is being carried out.

Most decisions resulting from formal grievances are specific to the individual filing the complaint, but grievances can be made on behalf of a group of affected employees. At any rate, grievance procedures are important because of the seriousness of claims of unfair treatment, but also because they increase acceptance of an organization's policies and procedures. Thibaut and Walker have noted that employees evaluate policies as more fair and just when they believe that they have control over the process of implementing and administering organizational decisions.[64]

In unionized organizations (see Chapter 13), the grievance procedure is usually elaborate, drawing on stewards and other union leaders to argue the grievance if it is not rectified through written procedures. In nonunionized organizations, the extensiveness of the grievance procedure varies, although there is a trend for detailed procedures in large organizations. Among the most informal procedures are general open-door policies and commitment on the part of supervisors and managers to promote fair dealing with employees. The problem with these generalized mechanisms to handle employee grievances is that virtually all executives say that they adopt an open-door policy. Moreover, they are more popular with professional employees; manufacturing employees may prefer a more explicit system.[65]

More formalized grievance procedures in nonunionized organizations often include some sort of peer review process.[66] Peer reviews are typically done by a group of organizational members using a process described in the employee handbook. The procedure for submitting a grievance and processing a grievance and the degree to which the peer decision is binding must be established. Research has found that peer review systems are generally well accepted by managers and executives and that they actually motivate supervisors to perform better so as to avoid a peer review.[67]

Finally, nonunion grievance procedures may provide for formal mediation and arbitration as final steps, much as in the procedures in unionized organizations. In this case, complaints are often first heard by an external mediator who attempts to settle the dispute. If the mediation fails, binding arbitration may follow. With binding arbitration, the complaint is heard by arbitrators (usually from one to three arbitrators), and decisions are then legally binding. Most companies rely on organizations such as the American Arbitration Association (see AAA.org), which can handle both the mediation and the arbitration process. In general, research that has examined arbitration as a dispute resolution tactic is positive from both the employer and the employee perspectives. The most recent evidence indicates that employees are more likely to prevail in arbitration than in fully litigated cases. Moreover, employees typically do not abuse the system with frivolous disputes, and employers can further assure this by limiting in the employee handbook the issues available for arbitration. Arbitration typically reviews the execution of an established company policy, not the policy itself.[68]

Despite generally positive reviews, arbitration agreements and stipulations can be complex in practice. As this is an area of heavy legal activity, the laws in this area are changing rapidly. In one court case, an employee of Y-3 Holdings in California signed an acknowledgment form that she had received, understood, and agreed to the terms in the company handbook that included a description of the binding arbitration agreement. The California Appeals Court ruled that the employee's signature on the acknowledgment form did not necessarily pertain to the arbitration agreement. Bottom line: Employers should obtain specific documentation of the employee's understanding and agreement regarding the arbitration policy itself and not just an acknowledgment of the contents of the handbook. Figure 12-4 presents an outline of a comprehensive (and successful) dispute resolution program. There are many options to dispute resolution.

As can be seen, there are many mechanisms that an organization may use to maintain the employment relationship. In fact, there are many other programs that also help to keep the working relationship healthy (i.e., work–family programs, award programs, employee suggestion programs) that were not discussed due to space constraints. Next, an inevitable event in the employment relationship is discussed: organizational exit. As with those practices that maintain the employment relationship, organizational exit should be conducted in a way that is fair, productive, and satisfactory to all involved.

ORGANIZATIONAL EXIT

Organizational exit can take many forms. Simply defined, **organizational exit** is the dissolution of the employment relationship. Four distinct forms of exit are discussed here.

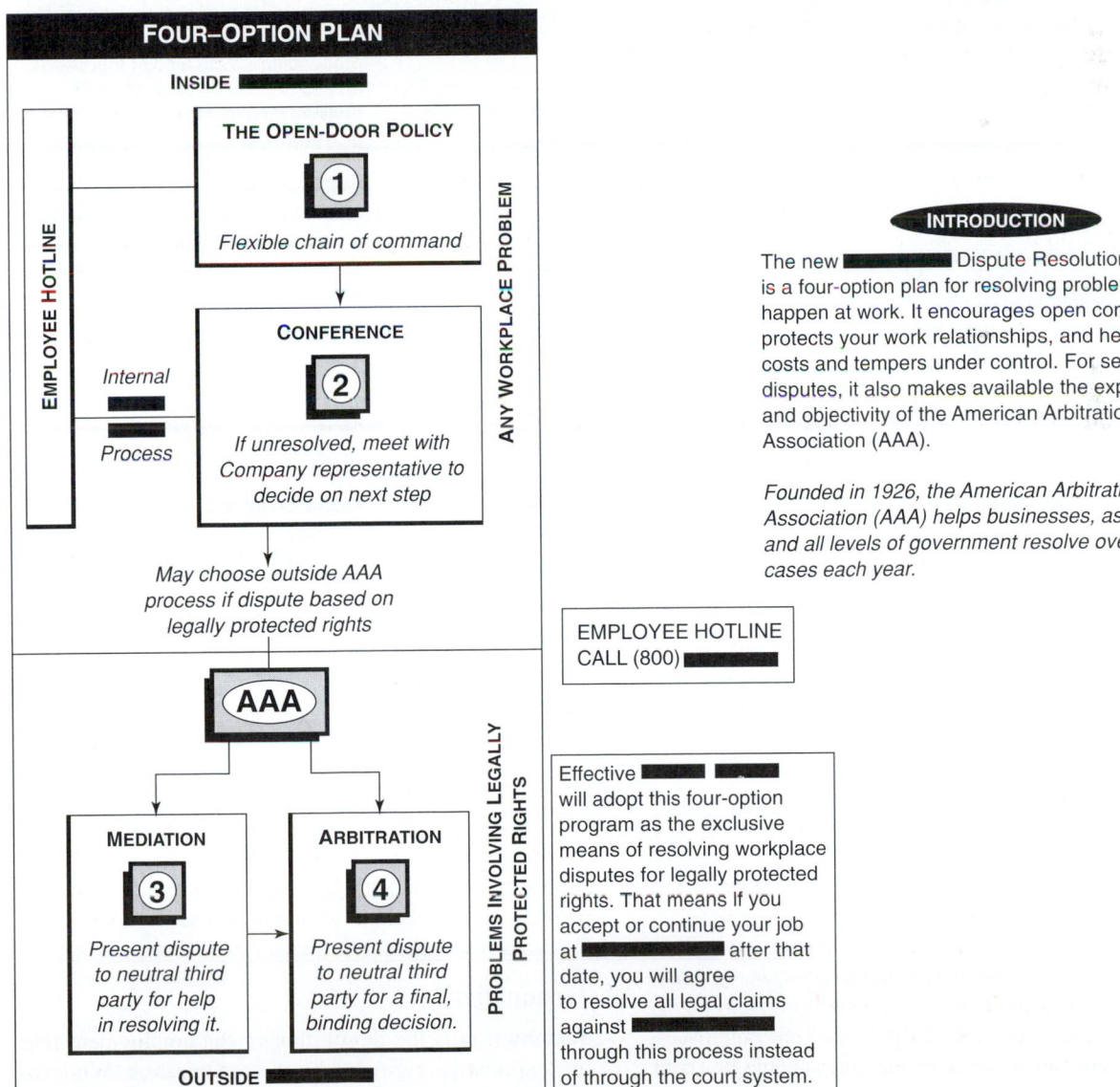

Figure 12-4 Sample Dispute Resolution Program (*continued*)

FOUR OPTIONS— AN OVERVIEW

Option One—The Open-Door Policy helps you solve your problem early through the **Chain of Command.** Discuss it with Business Unit Personnel or Corporate Employee Relations. An **Employee Hotline,** (800) ████████, puts you in touch with a confidential Adviser who can also help you. If you think your problem is serious enough, you may want to request a **Legal Consultation.** If approved, ████████████ will pay for most of it.

Option Two—The Conference is the next step if your problem is still unresolved. You can sit down with a Company representative and the Program Administrator to decide what process you would like to use to settle your dispute. If both parties agree, an inhouse resolution process can be arranged. If your dispute involves a legally protected right, such as protection from discrimination or harassment, you may prefer to go to mediation or arbitration through AAA.

Option Three—Mediation lets you and the Company discuss your legal dispute with a neutral third party, AAA. The neutral party or mediator can listen to both sides of the story and help you work it out together. To use AAA, you pay a processing fee of $50. *Mediation is only for disputes involving legally protected rights.*

Option Four—Arbitration lets you present your legal dispute to a neutral third party, AAA, for a final decision. The arbitrator will decide your case after hearing arguments from both sides. AAA can make an award just like a judge in the court system. To use AAA, you pay a fee of $50, unless you have already paid it for mediation. *Arbitration is only for disputes involving legally protected rights.*

QUESTIONS AND ANSWERS

 How does the new Open-Door Policy differ from the old one?

For the first time in the history of the Company, the Open-Door Policy has been put into writing. Both old and new Open-Door Policies call for resolving workplace disputes through the Chain of Command. Improvements to the Policy include an Employee Hotline, the opportunity to talk with an Adviser, and, if approved, a legal consultation for serious legal disputes. ████████████ will be training all of its managers and supervisors in how to use the new program.

 What do I do if the supervisor I approach ignores the Open-Door Policy?

If the first person you approach under the Open-Door Policy doesn't help you, proceed immediately to another level of supervision in the Chain of Command. You may also want to call the Employee Hotline at (800) ████████████ or call your Business Unit Personnel Manager or Employee Relations.

 What happens if my supervisor starts to make things difficult for me after I complain?

Take your problem to a higher level in the Chain of Command, or to an Adviser through the Employee Hotline. The Adviser will help you decide on a strategy for handling your problem or refer you to someone in the Chain of Command.

 Can I use the ████████ Dispute Resolution Program to solve any problem that happens at work?

You may use Options One, the Open-Door Policy, and Two, the Conference, to address any workplace dispute.

Options Three and Four, the AAA process, can be used to resolve only those problems or disputes involving legally protected rights, such as discrimination for age, sex, or religion; on-the-job harassment; or being asked to commit unlawful acts.

 How does arbitration differ from a court trial?

With arbitration, the decision is final; except under rare circumstances, it may not be reversed by subsequent proceedings. With a court trial decision, an appeal may be filed, causing endless delays. Also, an arbitration proceeding is usually much more informal than a case in court. The biggest difference, however, lies in the reasonable cost of arbitration. Because arbitration is faster and less formal, it ends up costing much less to prepare the case for both the employee and the employer.

 If I don't like the arbitrator's decision, can I appeal it through the court system?

Arbitration awards are final, binding, and may be enforced under the law, with only limited appeals allowed through the courts.

Figure 12-4 *(Continued)*

Sometimes the organization originates an individual's exit, as in *Termination;* at other times, the individual does so, as in *resignation* (or voluntary turnover) and *retirement.* Still other times, the organization institutes large-scale organizational exit by engaging in downsizing and *layoffs.* In all instances, this marks the end of the formalized employee–employer relationship; however, measures should be taken to make the separation as amicable as possible while maintaining productivity, learning from the experience, and perhaps making changes to organizational policies, procedures, and practices as a result.

Termination

Termination is the dissolution of the employment relationship that is originated by the organization. While we know that termination can happen for any reason as provided by the employment-at-will doctrine, it occurs most often for poor performance and misconduct. In general, termination for poor performance occurs when an employee consistently fails to meet a minimum standard or fails to meet a specific goal, objective, standard, or quota. Consistent unauthorized absences and tardiness are also common reasons for termination. Failure to follow organization policy or procedure is yet another reason for termination. More broadly, the reasons for termination often vary according to the level the employee occupies within an organization. Lower-level employees are most often terminated due to job performance, insubordination, or failure to comply with written policies and procedures. Managers and other higher-level employees are often fired when there is a lack of fit or a personality characteristic that has resulted in negative organizational outcomes.[69]

Consistency is a driving force of employee acceptance of dismissal practices. Termination should not be used for vague or unsubstantiated reasons, and documentation (e.g., discipline records, performance appraisals) should inform the decision to terminate an employee.[70] It is of the utmost importance that employers make every attempt to apply rules consistently. Recall our discussion of the legal prescriptions for performance appraisals in Chapter 7. One of the best predictors of the outcomes of cases favorable to the employer is consistent application of the policy. Consistency also helps to establish the perception of procedural justice discussed above. These perceptions of fairness at termination are extremely important. If employees feel as if they were treated fairly, they are less likely to file wrongful termination claims. Moreover, adequate notice on the part of the employer and the provision of aid in finding a new job have been shown to increase feelings of justice at termination.[71] Although we have spoken periodically about the separate legal and psychological reasons for maintaining a fair employment relationship, here one can see that the two are clearly linked.

Although retaining an ineffective employee often undermines the performance of the work group and the organization, termination often is cited as one of the most troubling aspects of a manager's job. The HR department is often heavily involved when an employee is to be terminated. In some cases, HR managers handle all of the details involved when terminating an employee. In other cases, it is incumbent upon the employee's direct supervisor to carry out the termination; however, it is typically not without support from the HR department and (oftentimes) legal clearance. At the very least, HR may provide coaching and training on how to effectively handle termination meetings. Undoubtedly, when managers talk about the difficulty of terminations, they are often referring to the termination meeting itself, the face-to-face interaction with the employee to be terminated. Compiling recommendations from trade magazines in several industries,[72] the best practices for before, during, and after this meeting appear Figure 12-5.

FIGURE 12-5 Guidelines for Conducting Terminations

Before the meeting:
- If you have doubts about terminating the employee, consult corporate counsel.
- Document each level of progressive discipline.
- Investigate serious misconduct before terminating the employee.
- Prepare severance packages and the final paycheck.
- Recognize that the task before you is not an easy one, but that the actions you take can minimize potential negative consequences.
- Consider the timing of the termination, taking care to schedule the meeting at the best time of day for the employee.
- Give the employee a chance to disclose a medical reason.
- Have HR review situation to make certain termination abides by law, company policy, and collective bargaining agreement.
- If this is a group layoff, review compliance with WARN and ADEA.

During the meeting:
- Consider having a witness present if anger and mistrust surround the termination.
- Maintain full control of the meeting. Don't allow the employee to blame others or report the misconduct of co-workers at this time.
- Get to the point quickly:
  —The employee has been fired.
  —Outline severance, ongoing benefits, and noncompete agreements.
  —Develop a consistent story to be relayed to other employees and agree upon the contents of any future recommendation letters.
  —Tell the employee that he or she is no longer responsible for duties at the organization. Rather, he or she should focus upon the job search.
- Do not end the meeting with an apology. Rather, shake the employee's hand and wish him/her well in the future.

After the meeting:
- Update personnel files.
- Document any agreements.
- Arrange for exit services such as outplacement, benefits, or severance.
- Review job descriptions and discipline policies. Could the termination have been prevented if either were more clear or descriptive? If so, consider making those revisions.
- Shut down access to premises and equipment.

Resignation/Voluntary Turnover

Ask an HR manager what his/her organization's turnover rate is, and you are likely to be answered first with a groan or a sigh. It seems the turnover statistic (i.e., the rate at which employees voluntary resign from their position within the organization) is never at a level that is acceptable given the operating environment and the organization's goals and growth strategies. In a recent survey, 52 percent of managers said that they had a problem retaining high-performing employees.[73] As a more vivid example, you may recall the debate over the federalization of baggage checkers at airports after September 11, 2001. Proponents of federalizing this job noted the very high turnover rate of the baggage checkers as an indication of inevitably poor job performance. Some of the larger airports reported turnover rates of baggage checkers that were higher than 100 percent (that's complete turnover in one year and then some!).

Though it seems counterintuitive, some degree of resignation and turnover is probably beneficial, as it allows the organization to renew itself and invites its practices to be critically examined from another point of view. However, too much turnover is problematic and predictive of corporate financial problems. The high-performance work systems research we have alluded to so often throughout the book presents data showing superior corporate financial performance for organizations with

relatively lower turnover. One reason for the negative financial impact may be the high cost of replacing employees. The U.S. Department of Labor estimates that it costs approximately one-third of a new employee's salary to replace the employee, and some say that this figure is more like one-half.[74] Consider that the time consumed in exiting the employee while recruiting and hiring another is substantial. And any efficiencies gained by way of intact internal and external customer relationships are undermined when an employee voluntarily resigns.[75] For these reasons, organizations typically take action to investigate the reasons for employee turnover and ultimately attempt to minimize its occurrence. Figure 12-6 presents the cycle of failure for a service company due to the connection between high turnover and quality of service. Figure 12-7 presents a model that illustrates the determinants of voluntary turnover.

Throughout this book we have suggested ways to minimize unnecessary employee turnover. The use of more valid selection procedures we covered in Chapter 6 is one approach. Creating and sustaining fair relationships with employees that are considerate of procedural and distributive justice issues will help build commitment to the organization. Giving employees realistic job

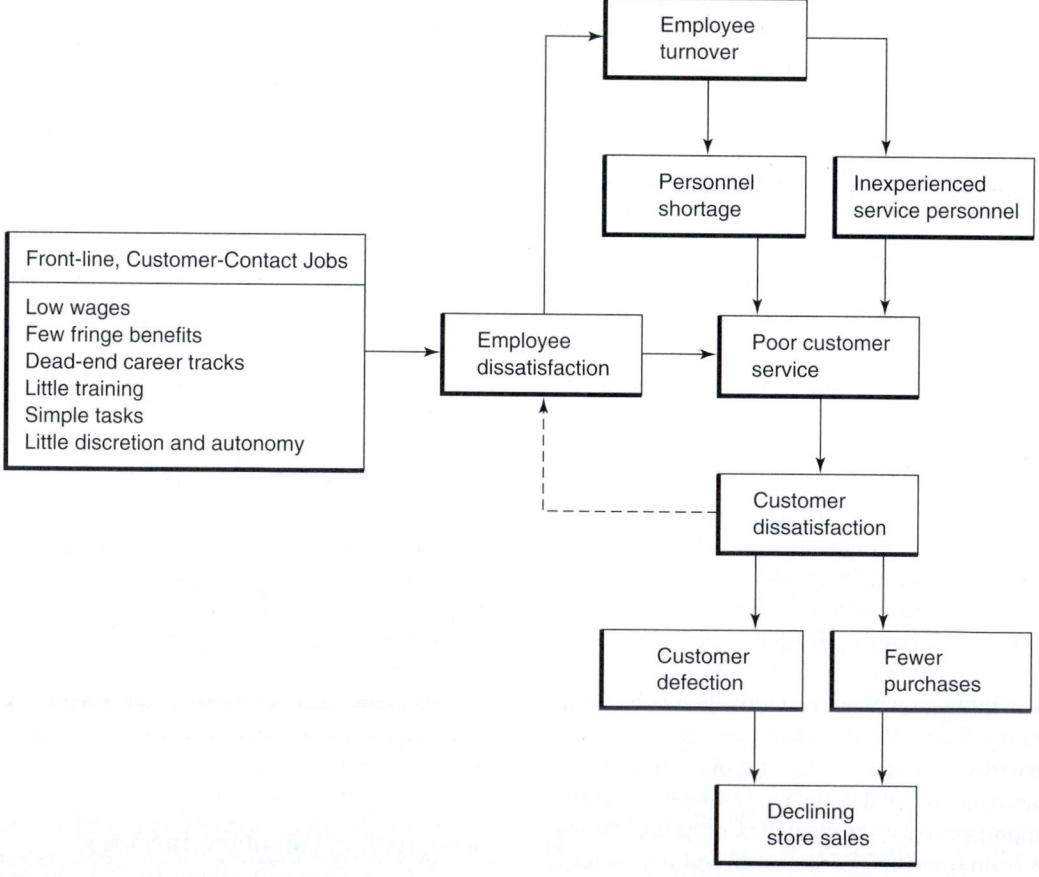

Figure 12-6   Cycle of Failure in Service Company
Source: P. W. Hom and R. W. Griffeth, *Employee turnover.* Cincinnati, OH: SouthWestern, 1992, p. 24. Reprinted with permission from the author.

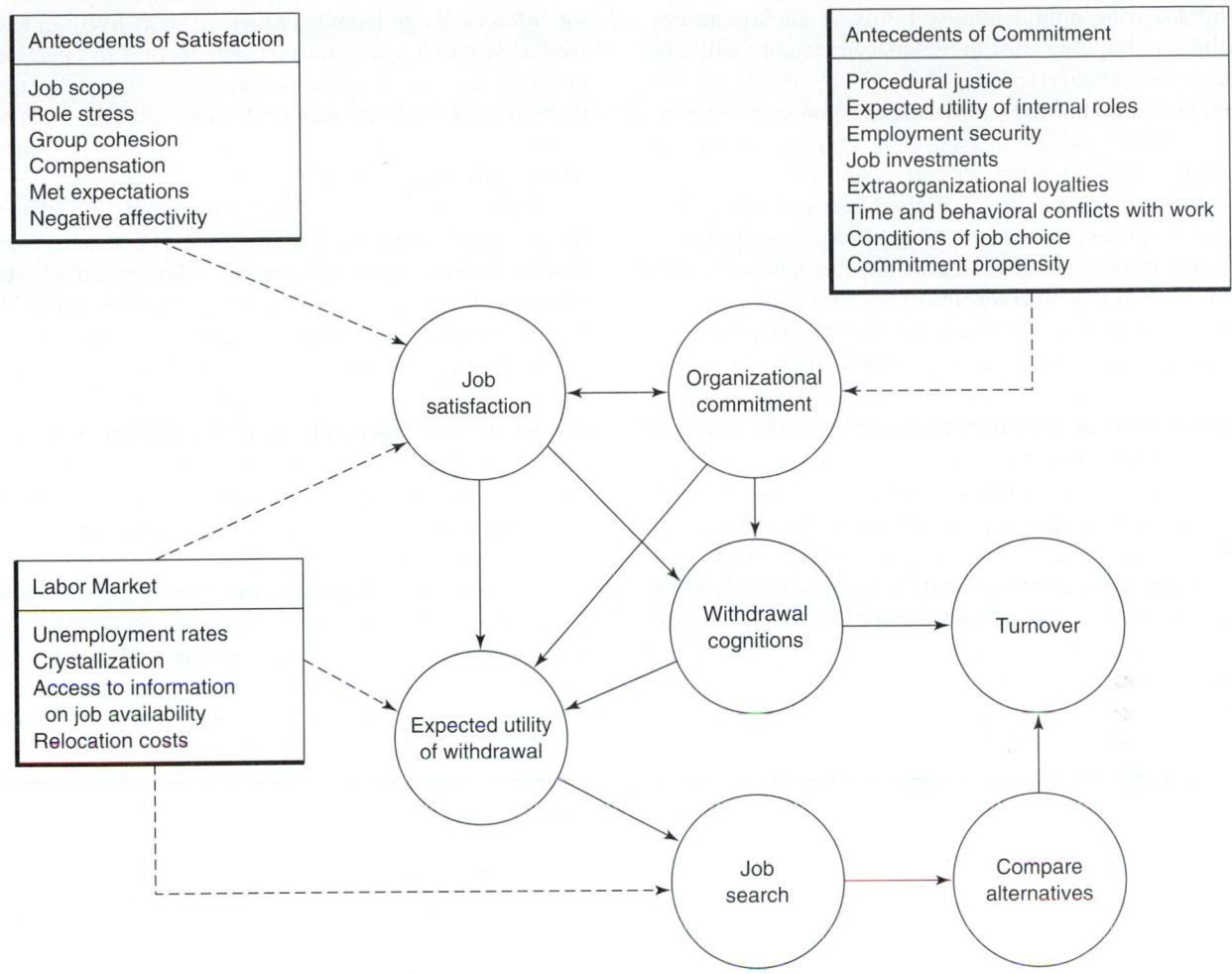

Figure 12-7   Integrative Model of Turnover Determinants
Source: P. W. Hom and R. W. Griffeth, *Employee turnover*. Cincinnati, OH: SouthWestern, 1992, p. 108. Reprinted with permission from the author.

previews and ensuring that they are socialized appropriately will facilitate appropriate expectations. Policies and procedures that produce productive, efficient, and positive relationships with employees are also critical. Other recommendations from various experts include:

- Provide a safe and secure work environment in which the employee does not feel threatened.
- Provide feedback to employees.
- Ensure that employees are managed properly by providing management training and feedback.
- Provide pay and benefits commensurate with other organizations in your industry.
- Provide flexible working hours and family-friendly policies.
- Provide opportunities for growth and development, and, where possible, advancement.
- Involve employees in business matters and keep them abreast of company happenings.
- Don't send the message that employees are expendable.[76]

When employees do leave, organizations often conduct **exit interviews** or distribute **post-employment surveys** in order to assess the reasons for voluntary turnover. Using either the face-to-face or survey technique, individuals in the organization attempt to uncover the reasons for the employee's departure. The content of exit interviews and surveys is quite varied across companies. They may cover any of the following: reasons for leaving, satisfaction with the job, the quality of management, perceived opportunities for advancement, and the adequacy of pay, training, and performance appraisals.[77] Much like employee surveys, this information allows organizations to assess how well their retention strategies are working, update benefits and other programs, and discontinue programs that are not well-accepted by employees. Moreover, it may send a message to employees that their opinions are valued, even as they leave the organization.[78] It is often recommended that exit interviews be conducted by someone who was only indirectly related to the employee while he or she was working in the organization, perhaps even an external consulting firm. Assuring confidentiality by using such measures while also building trust in the interview likely will produce more candid responses.[79] One study has shown that both fear of blame and concern that responses will not be held confidential are reasons that employees are not truthful in exit interviews.[80]

Some organizations do not conduct exit interviews. At the very least, though, most organizations keep tabs on the rate of turnover. One way to calculate a turnover rate is to consider it as a percentage of the total number of employees. In other words, the turnover rate is the number of turnovers divided by the average total number of workers. Other firms calculate the mean or median length of tenure of employees. In some industries, such as retail and food service, turnover is stunningly high. One study commissioned by Coca-Cola showed that the median tenure of employees working in supermarkets was only 148 days.[81] On the other hand, the SAS institute (ranked #3 in *Fortune*'s 2002 best places to work[82]) has a turnover rate of only 3 percent.[83] (Go to www.fortune.com for its current standing.)

Downsizing and Layoffs

We discussed downsizing and layoffs in Chapter 5 when we covered HR planning. We focus here on the impact upon the employment relationship of these activities. While a **layoff** refers to the *tactical,* physical action of eliminating redundant skills in the organization, **downsizing** is the name given to the overall organizational *strategy* to which the layoff may contribute. These terms (as well as various others) are often interpreted in a similar manner: "downsizing" is often used to refer to the elimination of jobs associated with the overall strategy. The term *rightsizing,* having a meaning similar to downsizing, appeared in many popular press articles during the 1990s. The expression does not enjoy widespread use, likely because it is a thinly veiled euphemism for massive job loss. The term *layoff* typically is reserved for manufacturing employees, but is formally defined as above, which would pertain to an employee at any level. At any rate, we focus here on the effects such events have upon individual employees and the associated organizational actions regardless of the terminology one prefers. Because of its popularity in current HR publications, the term *downsizing* is used here.

The Causes and Effects of Downsizing and Layoffs

In some cases, downsizing is undertaken to reduce labor costs and streamline organizational operations. In other cases, downsizing results from mergers and acquisitions in which the resulting company is plagued with redundant functions. At any rate, organizations are often not realizing all of the cost benefits they hoped to receive from downsizing because they must replace functions, either by hiring consultants or training those that remain on the

job. Moreover, productivity gains are short-lived; in fact, they are more a reflection of the reduction in operating expenses than they are true output advances. Finally, motivation and morale are damaged, which can have indirect effects upon both the productivity and economic consequences discussed above.[84]

Indeed, downsizing can have devastating effects upon individual employees, both those that have been downsized and those that haven't, who are called **survivors.** Specifically, downsized employees probably face many emotions. Their initial response may be one of shock, anger, relief, or escapism. Eventually, these employees need to confront the tasks of becoming reemployed without succumbing to frustration and self-doubt.[85] Organizational actions, discussed in the next section, can help employees avoid such emotions by preparing them for the transition to a new job, a new organization, or a new career.

Even for those employees that do not lose their jobs as a result of downsizing, serious psychological consequences can occur. David Noer, who has written several books on the topic, notes that the emotional reactions of survivors are much like those of individuals who were downsized.[86] Indeed, a content analysis of those that survived a downsizing showed that experienced emotions included anger, anxiety, cynicism, resentment of upper management, and resignation, mixed with some hope.[87] There are tangible consequences in the workplace that survivors must deal with as well. Many times, organizations cut the staff positions they need to devise a new "leaner" strategy and vision, so expected benefits from such drastic actions are never realized.[88] Also, the energies and stress levels of survivors are stretched particularly thin, given that the survivors are now expected to accomplish the additional work of those that have been released from the organization.

It should be noted that there are some instances of positive individual outcomes as a result of downsizing. Due to relief from surviving the cuts or the heightened awareness of performance that a downsizing brings, individual effort after a downsizing may actually increase.[89] The degree to which overall outcomes are positive or negative, however, depends upon organizational measures taken to execute the downsizing efforts.

Organizational Measures

Organizational actions and policy for dealing with downsizing should be geared toward maintaining goodwill to those directly affected by the downsizing and toward reassuring and maximizing productivity among the survivors. It has been shown in several studies that the manner in which an organization executes the reduction in employees affects levels of bitterness and dissatisfaction felt by both layoff victims and survivors.[90] For instance, advanced notice of the downsizing has been shown to reduce negative feelings.[91] Indeed, there is agreement on this among many authors' recommendations for successful downsizing.[92]

Additionally, some form of outplacement assistance for downsized workers is quite common and recommended to amicably end the employment relationship. **Outplacement programs** are simply those that help discharged employees find new jobs. Outplacement efforts may include the provision of information to affected employees concerning continuation of benefits and compensation, announcements to other employers via personal contact or broader-scale advertising concerning availability of skilled workers, career and job-seeking counseling, and training on the development of résumés and interview skills. While these efforts obviously help the employee through the downsizing experience, they benefit organizations by reducing legal risks, reducing severance pay and unemployment compensation, preserving morale among survivors, and maintaining a positive public image.[93] The oldest (and largest) of outplacement firms is Challenger, Gray & Christmas (www.challengergray.com), which claims a median placement time of 3.2 months versus an average of 5 months for the industry.

In sum, organizations must take actions to remedy the situation for both downsized employees and survivors. But must a large number of employees be relieved during times of economic need? If an organization considers other alternatives before downsizing its employees, employees may perceive the layoffs as more of a business necessity, thus harboring less bitterness and dissatisfaction as a result. One alternative to layoffs is **worksharing programs,** in which employees voluntarily reduce the number of hours or days per week they work in order to cut labor costs while maintaining their gainful employment. Organizations also could limit the availability of vacation and overtime and redistribute workers to needed areas through transfers.[94] The disadvantage of these alternatives is that it decreases costs associated with wages alone, not health or other benefits. However, these costs could provide some degree of immediate financial gain.

Other alternatives would decrease the size of the workforce, but less disruptively. For instance, organizations could limit the inflow of employees, often called a **hiring freeze.** Also, several organizations offer **early retirement packages** as a tactic to reduce the number of employees in the workforce. These packages often include incentives for retiring such as bonuses, full benefits before they are earned through tenure, or supplemental income until the employee is able to receive full Social Security benefits.[95] Ford had a very successful early retirement program in 2001 and 2002 probably due to the extra incentives offered to those who took the early retirement plan. Again, though, these measures are not without disadvantages. Hiring freezes and early retirement packages are very blunt cutting tools when it comes to downsizing. In other words, organizations utilizing these measures could be left with a number of vacancies in key areas while having a surplus of workers in functions and jobs considered redundant.

Retirement

Retirement has been defined as an exit from an organizational position or career path of considerable duration taken by individuals after middle age and taken with the intention of reduced psychological commitment to work thereafter.[96] After the Age Discrimination in Employment Act repealed mandatory retirement, retirement is a voluntary decision for nearly all Americans—at least those living and working within the United States. Organizations headquartered in the United States that employ workers overseas may be subject to different laws and regulations. For example, a U.S. company does not violate the ADEA if an American worker is forced to retire at the age of 65 under a German collective bargaining agreement that stipulates mandatory retirement.

While some liken retirement to turnover because of its willfulness, the two concepts have been clearly distinguished.[97] Where retirement signals a decreased involvement in work, turnover does not. Because of its unique nature, it is worthwhile to consider the reasons for which individuals decide to retire. Retirement is influenced by both personal characteristics and economic concerns. Specifically, government policies, individual and family characteristics, and the organization's policies all affect an individual's decision to retire.[98] Figure 12-8 presents a model of the influences upon this decision.[99] At any rate, the organization has an influential part in the retirement decision. We turn now to those organizational actions that help maintain a positive relationship with retiring employees.

Organizational Actions

While many adjustments to retirement are incumbent upon the employee, organizations are adopting more and more practices to facilitate the transition to non- or reduced-working life. Specifically, more flexible retirement plans allow employees to phase into retirement more slowly, preventing the shock that often comes with the end of work. Examples include part-time work, longer vacation periods or sabbaticals, altering the content of the job, accepting a demotion, and second-career assistance. It stands to reason that more flexible retirement plans (i.e., those that offer a variety of alternatives for reducing the amount of time that is worked) may help employees successfully adjust to the change. When employees are allowed to choose the path to retirement that is most workable given some unique combination of these considerations, a more successful transition can be expected.

Some organizations are transitioning employees to retirement by using them as volunteers and ambassadors for their own social programs. Corporations such as

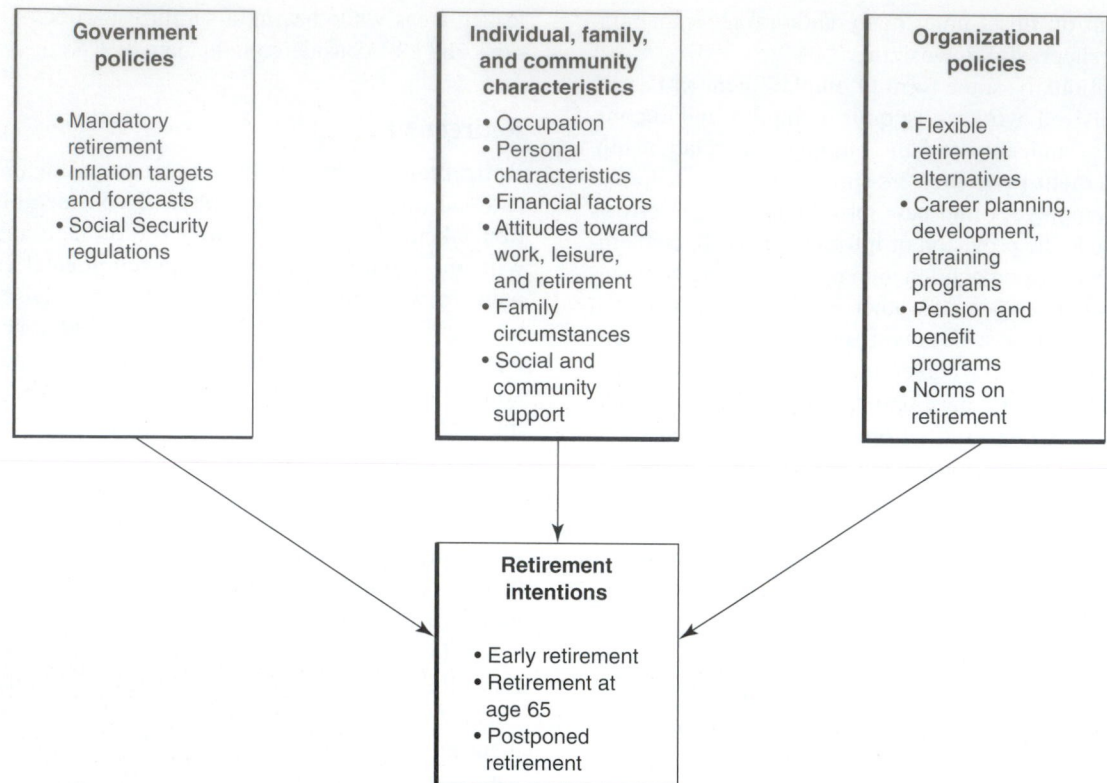

Figure 12-8   Influences on the Retirement Decision
Source: B. Rosen and T. H. Jerdee, *Older Employees: New Roles for Valued Resources*, p. 143. Reprinted with permission.

American Express Financial Services, Amoco Corporation, The Gillette Company, and H. J. Heinz Company are doing so.[100] Specifically, these retired employees participate in volunteer activities in the name of their former employer, providing a win-win situation for all involved. The retiree benefits from continued interaction with others in a helping role, continued affiliation with the organization, and contact with the larger community. The organization reaps obvious public relations and visibility benefits.

Typically, even if organizations do not provide flexible retirement options and/or other creative transition programs, they offer some sort of informational programs intended to ease the transition into retirement. These programs may include information on both the economic and social concerns facing retiring workers. It is recommended that these programs be conducted in small groups to build social networks around the retirement decision.[101] In fact, spouse participation is encouraged.[102] Finally, it is recommended by many that the transition to retirement begin years before the actual date of departure from the organization. One recommendation is that attendance at retirement programs should begin at least five years prior to retirement and should continue for some time after.[103] These types of transition programs should be the very least that organizations consider offering in addition to the monetary benefits associated with retirement.

SUMMARY

Managing the employment relationship is a little-talked-about function of the HR department. While this may be the case, it is not because the employment relationship is less important than selection, training, or performance appraisal. Rather, *all* human resource functions are crucial to maintaining the employment relationship; it is a broad function that permeates the entirety of the HR professional's job. In other words, perceptions of fairness and justice are not limited to the organizational actions discussed in this chapter. An employee will consider his or her entire employment experience when forming perceptions of fairness.

That being said, some functions of the HR department are carried out for the sole purpose of building and maintaining the employment relationship. Realistic job previews and socialization programs provide employees with information needed to begin forming a relationship with their employer. Next, the maintenance of the relationship is governed by the external force of employment law and internal forces such as employee handbooks. Legal issues are employment-at-will, whistleblowing, privacy, the Worker Adjustment Relocation Notification Act, are many more. HR professionals must help to create an operating environment perceived as fair and just while always considering and integrating the legal environment. The HR department must create, maintain, and review employee handbooks, discipline policies, and grievance systems. Privacy issues concerning employee records must be balanced against government antiterrorism requirements. Finally, employers must manage the exit of their employees, be it voluntary or involuntary, a single case or a mass layoff.

In sum, one can see that employee relationships are a delicate balancing act: Organizational concerns for productivity must balance individual concerns for justice, legal doctrine must balance internal procedure, and the uniqueness of each employee must balance the efficiencies gained when establishing blanket policy. Any actions that an organization takes to create and maintain relationships with its employees must consider each of these competing forces. This is not an easy task at any given moment, let alone in the changing work environment we discussed in Chapter 1. However, keeping the employment relationship in balance will undoubtedly lead to productivity and efficiencies that would not be gained otherwise.

DISCUSSION QUESTIONS

1. A CEO once told an HR consultant that organizational justice is a "touchy feely concept not related to anything important." If you were the HR consultant, what would you say?

2. Should realistic job previews be applied to overseas assignments? If so, how would you go about constructing a realistic job preview for such an assignment? Pick one country and do a draft of an RJP for an assignment there.

3. The "covenant of good faith and fair dealing" as related to employment-at-will implies that excellent performance over an extended period of time grants the performer a right to be terminated only for "just cause." But only 11 states have adopted this exception to employment-at-will. Research your state and take a position on whether your state should join the 11 or drop the exception.

4. Should companies have the right to monitor all Internet "surfing" at work? How would you react if a company stipulated that no personal surfing is allowed and, if discovered, could result in termination?

5. How does a binding arbitration agreement work? Should companies be allowed to adopt a binding arbitration requirement for its current employees in which employees surrender their right to litigate employment disputes through the court system? Explain your answer. What is the current state of the law regarding arbitration?

6. Should companies purchase software that shuts down all access terminated employees have to company equipment, credit cards and premises as soon as the termination takes effect? Why would a company need to purchase such software?

7. To what extent would you be attracted to an organization that offered a variety of work arrangements such as flextime, telecommuting, four-day work weeks, and job sharing?

13

LABOR RELATIONS AND COLLECTIVE BARGAINING*

OVERVIEW

Issues related to organizational justice and practices related to employee discipline and grievances are major factors in the employment relationship and have a great deal to do with why employees join unions. Unions are organizations that represent employees' interests to management on almost all critical HR issues. The topics covered in Chapters 10 and 11 have to do with increasing productivity and performance through compensation practices. Unions generally resist such efforts and prefer greater stability and equality in workers' paychecks. This resistance may have something to do with the negative attitudes business students have toward unions and certainly contributes to the antipathy that management has toward organized labor.

Although some believe that unions have become an institution of the past, there is some evidence that attitudes toward unions may be improving. A 2002 Gallup survey of Americans found that 65 percent approved of unions while only 28 percent disapproved.[1] The approval rate is up compared to 1995 responses. There is also evidence that unions are now more supportive of innovative pay-for-performance systems and productivity enhancement programs such as quality circles and work team designs.[2]

Management students today often learn the "ideal" way to manage firms' human resources, making it difficult for them to comprehend the adverse working environments that led to (and still lead to) unionization. People in the early part of the 20th century often worked under conditions many of us cannot fathom: "dark, satanic mills," with workweeks of at least 60 hours and with no provisions for safety, illness, vacations, or retirement.[3] The union's role in improving these conditions is clear. While the goal of unions today in the United States is still to improve working conditions and increase workers' economic status, the need and effects are more subtle than they were during the early years of unions.

The United States has legislation governing wages and hours, equal employment opportunity (EEO), family and medical leave, pensions, mergers, Social Security, and health and safety. Almost all U.S. workers benefit from this legislation, which probably would not be law were it not for the past political clout and successes of the unions. But this legislative success also fosters a feeling among American workers that unions may not be needed. The relatively clean service industry, not the harsh factories and coal mines, provide for a substantial proportion of present-day U.S. employment. Most workers today face mental rather than physical strains, which makes the need for a union less clear. Nonetheless, service work often pays low wages with few benefits and is (some argue) in need of union protection.

Union membership in the United States has dropped substantially over the last 30 years and in 2004 was estimated to be 12.5 percent of wage and salary

*Contributed by Nancy Brown Johnson

workers. Figure 13-1 presents a summary of union members in 2004, membership by industry and occupations, demographic characteristics, earnings, and membership rates across the states (it was 35 percent in 1945).[4] Unions are nonetheless an important influence upon workers and firms—both union and nonunion. The AFL-CIO, which represents over 9 million workers, has 53 national and international union affiliates in the United States.[5] Go to www.aflcio.org for links to all affiliated unions. The largest union is the National Education Association with over 2,500,000 members. As we discussed in Chapter 2, increased globalization also may necessitate stronger consideration of international labor relations. Although Starbucks in the United States has almost no union representation for its U.S. employees, when Starbucks expanded to Italy and Sweden, management had to be well informed about labor relations in those countries, where a much higher percentage of workers are unionized.[6] The online Georgetown University law library (www.ll.georgetown.edu) is an excellent source for international labor relations.

Worker–management relationships are strongly affected by the presence of unions. HR decisions, such as compensation, promotion, discipline, demotion, and termination, require union involvement. In general, management must handle personnel matters with the union rather than with each individual employee. As discussed in Chapters 10 and 11, unions have a great influence over pay structure and the compensation system in general. Nonunion firms also concern themselves with union activities because they usually desire to maintain their nonunion status. To do so, firms must be aware of unions and their history, their goals, their influences upon firms, and the legal issues binding both sides. Obviously, the working conditions, wages, and terms of employment of unionized firms have an effect on the way in which nonunion employers manage their HR in order to maintain nonunion status.

This chapter will begin with a discussion of what factors affect employee decisions to join unions. We will then review the major legislation affecting the labor movement and management today. The factors and procedures related to union organizing also will be covered. We then discuss collective bargaining and the methods that unions and organizations employ to achieve their goals. The chapter will close with a discussion of the contemporary labor movement in the context of increased globalization.

O B J E C T I V E S

After reading this chapter, you should be able to

1. *Understand why people join unions.*
2. *Understand the basic elements of labor law.*

3. *Understand collective bargaining as a tool for labor negotiation.*
4. *Identify the bases of power in collective bargaining related to both unions and management.*
5. *Describe current trends and issues in labor relations.*
6. *Understand the state of labor relations in other countries.*

Most business students today hold a negative view of the American labor movement. Unions are often viewed as antimanagement, striving to control or even reduce productivity, while demanding higher wages and ironclad protection for workers regardless of their performance. Indeed, the law requires management to meet and confer with union representatives when formulating policy and making decisions regarding virtually all important elements of HRM. The presence of a union or efforts to organize workers require HR expertise in labor relations. A lot can go wrong when managers have limited knowledge of labor law and organizing strategy. Management also should use HR specialists to negotiate and renegotiate labor contracts. But there is no question that some knowledge of labor law and collective bargaining is critical in any work environment where union organizing efforts are serious. Management also should understand why workers would contemplate giving up part of their paycheck to be represented by a union. Let's turn to that issue first.

WHY DO WORKERS JOIN UNIONS?

Understanding unions and why people organize is important for managers whether or not their organization is unionized. As discussed in Chapter 12, perceptions of organizational justice, job satisfaction, and perceptions of fair pay likely deter union organizing drives.

There are three general reasons why workers join unions: (1) dissatisfaction with the work environment, including working conditions, compensation, and supervision; (2) a desire to have more influence in affecting change in the work environment; and (3) employee beliefs regarding the potential benefit of unions. Figure 13-2 presents a summary of the major determinants.

Workers' dissatisfaction with their jobs and, in particular, dissatisfaction with their wages, benefits, and supervision are most related to the tendency to vote for a union.[7] One surprising finding is that the work itself does not seem to be strongly related to union voting. The best predictors in several studies are satisfaction with pay, working conditions, and supervision rather than the work itself. Satisfaction with first-line supervision appears to be particularly important as well as concerns regarding job security.

A second general reason for joining unions is a belief that there are no other options for either gaining more influence at the workplace or finding employment elsewhere. In general, to the extent that management has mechanisms for employees to voice their concerns about HRM policy,

FIGURE 13-1   Union Members in 2004

In 2004, 12.5% of wage and salary workers were union members, the union membership rate has steadily declined from a high of 20.1% in 1983, the first year for which comparable union data are available.

HIGHLIGHTS FROM 2004 DATA

- About 36% of government workers were union members in 2004, compared with about 8% of workers in private-sector industries.
- Two occupational groups—education, training, and library occupations and protective service occupations—had the highest unionization rates in 2004, at about 37% each. Protective service occupations include fire fighters and police officers.
- Men were more likely to be union members than women (14% versus 11%).
- Black workers (15%) were more likely to be union members than were white (12%), Asians (11%), or Hispanic or Latino workers (10%).

MEMBERSHIP BY INDUSTRY AND OCCUPATION (2004)

- Local government workers had the highest union membership rate (41%).
- Among major private industries, transporation and utilities had the highest union membership rate, at 25%. Construction (15%), information industries (14%), and manufacturing (13%) also had higher-than-average rates.

OTHER DEMOGRAPHIC CHARACTERISTICS OF UNION MEMBERS

- Union membership rates were highest among workers 45 to 54 years old (17.0%) and were lowest among those ages 16 to 24 (4.7%).
- Full-time workers were more than twice as likely as part-time workers to be union members.

UNION REPRESENTATION OF NONMEMBERS

About 1.6 million wage and salary workers were represented by a union on their main job in 2004, while not being union members themselves.

EARNINGS

- Full-time wage and salary workers who were union members had median usual weekly earnings of $781, compared with a median of $612 for nonunion workers.
- Four states had union membership rates over 20%: New York (25%), Hawaii (24%), Michigan (22%), and Alaska (20%).
- Membership rates below 6% are: North Carolina and South Carolina (3%), Arkansas and Mississippi (also under 5%), and Florida was at 6% in 2004.
- The largest numbers of union members lived in California (2.4 million) and New York (2.0 million). About half (7.8 million) of the 15.5 million union members in the U.S. lived in six states (California, New York, Michigan, Illinois, Pennsylvania, and Ohio).

Source: Bureau of Labor Statistics (www.bls.gov)

there is less tendency on the part of workers to favor unionization. A formal grievance procedure as discussed in Chapter 12, for example, which has been used successfully by employees, can deter union activity since workers perceive that there are alternatives to unions as an approach to correcting problems at work. Workers are much more likely to join a union if they perceive that they have little or no influence on important matters at work.

The third critical reason for joining unions is that employees believe that unions can actually improve conditions and, in particular, can have an impact at their own workplace. In general, this belief is driven by the extent to which unions represent workers in any particular industry or occupation. A worker who perceives that unions are more likely to help solve problems in the workplace is more likely to vote for unionization.

Companies attempt to influence employees' beliefs about unions. Campaign tactics by management include written communications, meetings, threats, and actions against union supporters. These can negatively affect workers' votes for unionization. Companies often use consultants who specialize in refuting the claims of union organizers and presenting horrendous scenarios if the union should prevail. It is estimated that there are over 1,000 such firms and an additional 1,500 private consultants in the union prevention or "busting" business (check out www.tbqlabor.com for one example of such a firm). Union tactics, although less often examined, also influence workers' willingness to join unions. One study found that unions that conducted a rank-and-file organizing strategy were more likely to win certification.[8] Such a strategy involves reliance on a slow underground person-to-person campaign that involves using employees themselves to organize the campaign.

While most Americans believe unions can improve things at work, many are generally hostile to unions. They think unions protect ineffective workers, abuse their

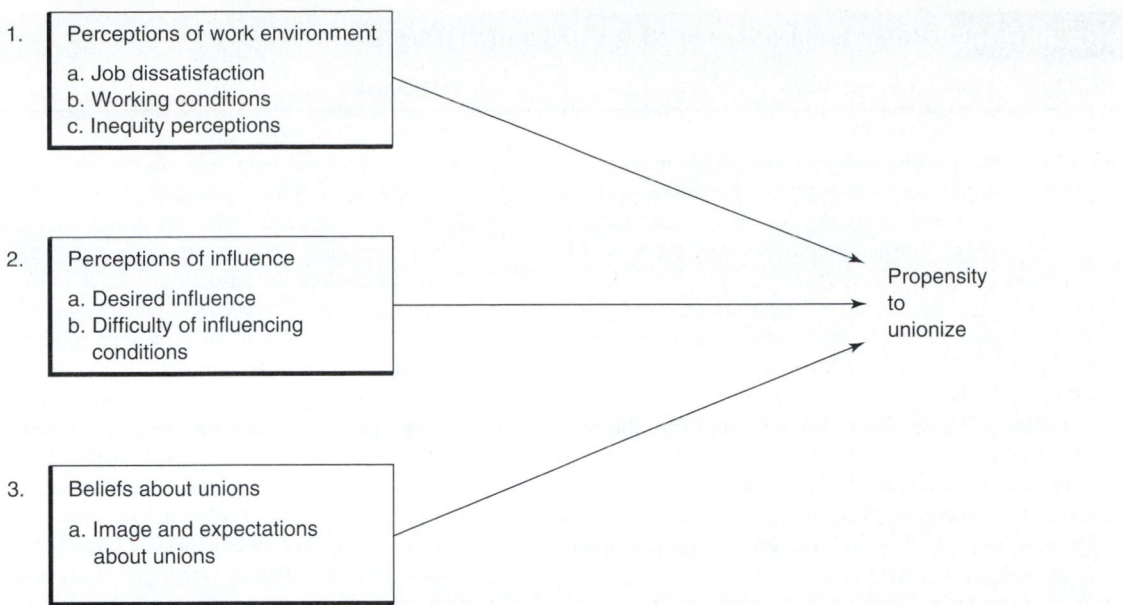

Figure 13-2   Determinants of Propensity to Join Unions
Source: T. Kochan, *Collective bargaining and industrial relations*. Homewood, IL: Richard D. Irwin, 1980, p. 144. Copyright © The McGraw-Hill Companies.

power through strikes, are corrupt, and impede productivity improvement programs. One study found that knowing an employee's general opinion about unions in these areas was a strong predictor of how an employee would vote for union representation.[9] Most business students aspire to management positions. There is no question that management prefers a nonunion environment. The focus of unions on the so-called bread-and-butter issues such as wages, benefits, and job security is viewed by management as constraining.

THE LEGAL ENVIRONMENT OF LABOR RELATIONS

Figure 13-3 highlights the two major federal laws affecting labor relations in the United States. The National Labor Relations Act, also known as the Wagner Act, was designed to protect workers' rights to organize and join unions. The Taft-Hartley Act was designed to place limits on some of the powers of unions. Of course, state laws may also play a role in union organizing efforts. For example, 22 states now have "right-to-work" laws, which allow workers to work in an establishment under a collective bargaining agreement without having to join a union.

National Labor Relations Act (NLRA)

The *National Labor Relations Act* (NLRA), also known as the Wagner Act, became law during the great depression of 1935. The NLRA formally recognized workers' rights to organize and bargain collectively with representatives of their own choosing. To enforce that right, the NLRA described what constituted unfair labor practices

by employers. Prohibited activities included forbidding employers from (1) interfering with employee representation and collective bargaining rights; (2) dominating or interfering with the affairs of unions; (3) discriminating in regard to hiring, retention, or any employment condition against workers who engage in union activity or who file unfair labor practice charges; and (4) not bargaining in good faith with employee representatives. Further, the act established the National Labor Relations Board (NLRB) to enforce the *Wagner Act* and to conduct representation elections. Essentially, the goal of the NLRB is to regulate the *processes* of organizing and collective bargaining, not necessarily the *outcomes*. As an independent federal agency (see www.nlrb. gov), the two primary functions of the NLRB are (1) to prevent and correct unfair labor practices and (2) to administer certification and decertification elections to determine whether workers choose to be represented.

When an unfair labor practice (ULP) charge is filed, a field office conducts an investigation to determine whether there is reasonable cause to believe the NLRA was violated. If the Regional Director determines that the charge lacks merit, it is dismissed. A dismissal may be appealed to the General Counsel's office of the NLRB. If the Regional Director finds reasonable cause to believe a violation of the law has been committed, that office of the NLRB seeks a voluntary settlement to remedy the alleged violations. If the settlement efforts fail, a formal complaint is issued and the case goes to a hearing before an NLRB Judge. The judge issues a written decision that may be appealed to the five-member NLR Board in Washington for a final agency determination. The Board's decision is subject to review in a U.S. Court of Appeals.

FIGURE 13-3 Major Implications of NLRA and Taft-Hartley Act

NLRA	Taft-Hartley
MANAGEMENT CANNOT:	UNIONS CANNOT:
Interfere with, restrain, or coerce employees in the exercise of their rights to organize, bargain collectively, and engage in other activities for their mutual aid or protection (e.g., threaten employees with the loss of a job if they vote for the union).	Restrain or coerce employees in the exercise of their right to join or not join a union.
Dominate or interfere with the formation or administration of any labor organization or contribute financial or other support to it.	Restrain or coerce an employer in the selection of his or her bargaining or grievance representative.
Encourage or discourage membership in any labor organization by discrimination with regard to hiring or tenure or conditions of employment, subject to an exception for valid union-security agreements.	Cause or attempt to cause an employer to discriminate against an employee due to membership or nonmembership in a union, subject to an exception for valid union-shop agreements.
Discharge or otherwise discriminate against an employee because he or she has filed charges or given testimony under the Wagner Act.	Refuse to bargain collectively (in good faith) with an employer if the union has been designated as a bargaining agent by a majority of the employees.
Refuse to bargain collectively with representatives of the employees; that is, bargain in good faith.	Induce or encourage employees to stop work in order to force an employer or self-employed person to join a union or to force an employer or other person to stop doing business with any other person (secondary boycott).
	Induce or encourage employees to stop work in order to force an employer to recognize and bargain with the union where another union has been certified as a bargaining agent (strike against a certification).
	Induce or encourage employees to stop work in order to force an employer to assign particular work to members of the union instead of to members of another union (jurisdictional strike).
	Charge an excessive or discriminatory membership fee as a condition to becoming a member of the union.
	Cause or attempt to cause an employer to pay for services that are not performed or not to be performed (featherbedding).

Source: Adapted with permission from J. J. Kenny and L. G. Kahn, *Primer of labor relations.* Washington, DC: Bureau of National Affairs, 1989, pp. 1–3. Reprinted with permission from BNA Books.

About 30,000 ULPs are filed each year and about one-third are found to have merit. Over 90 percent are settled. The NLRA also empowers the NLRB to petition a federal district court for an injunction to temporarily prevent unfair labor practices by employers or unions and to restore the status quo, pending the full review of the case by the Board. The NLRA also *requires* the Board to seek a temporary federal court injunction against certain forms of union misconduct, principally involving "secondary boycotts" and certain forms of picketing.

Some academic experts maintain that many of the most recent NLRB rulings are contrary to the goals of the NLRA. For example, the NLRB overturned a Clinton-era ruling that gave nonunion employees the right to have a colleague accompany them to an investigative or disciplinary ruling involving a colleague (known as the Weingarten rule). The NLRB reversed a 1990s ruling granting graduate students the right to unionize. The NLRB also ruled that a company claiming "financial distress" did not have to share financial information with the union during contract negotiations.

The Taft-Hartley Act

The Taft-Hartley Act of 1947 was designed to limit the power of unions by regulating labor activities allowed under the NLRA. Labor called this amendment to the NLRA the "slave labor bill." Taft-Hartley amended the NLRA by describing what constituted unfair labor practices by unions, including (1) restricting the usage of the strike, including granting the president of the United States the power to issue an injunction against a strike; (2) restricting unions from interfering with workers' right to organize; and (3) prohibiting union discrimination against workers who did not want to participate in union activities, including strikes.

The Taft-Hartley Act provided states with the option of enacting right-to-work legislation. Right-to-work laws declare that union security agreements that require membership as a condition of employment are illegal. As of 2005, 22 states have enacted right-to-work laws.[10] To aid in the peaceful settlement of contractual disputes, the *Federal Mediation and Conciliation Service* (FMCS) was established and provided emergency dispute provisions for the settlement of strikes affecting national health and safety (see www.fmcs.gov). Thus, the Taft-Hartley Act further restricted union activity. One purpose of the FMCS is to provide trained representatives to assist in labor negotiations.(see www.fmcs.gov).

Other Important Labor Laws

The Landrum-Griffin Act

In the late 1950s, the U.S. Senate held hearings investigating and exposing union corruption that ultimately resulted in the 1959 Landrum-Griffin Act. Designed to protect workers from their unions, Landrum-Griffin, also an amendment to the NLRA, provided for the employee "bill of rights," union filing of annual financial statements with the Department of Labor, and the requirement that unions hold national and local officer elections every five years and three years, respectively. The main purpose of Landrum-Griffin was to allow for the monitoring of the internal activity of unions. Union officials were now accountable for union spending, union elections, and other activities.

The Railway Labor Act of 1926

The Railway Labor Act was jointly crafted by both labor and management in the railroad industry. Airline workers became covered in 1935. The focus of the law is upon avoiding prolonged strikes whenever possible. In recent years, negotiations in the airline industry have been quite protracted spanning over several years. On the other hand, strikes have been averted for the most part. The president does have the right to intervene to preclude a strike which he did in the case of United Airlines in 2001.

The Civil Service Reform Act (CSRA) of 1978

While similar to the NLRA in its provisions but applicable only to federal employees, the CSRA prohibits wage negotiations (they're set by Congress) and strikes. The CSRA also established the Federal Labor Relations Authority (FLRA) as an independent agency within the executive branch of the government. The FLRA has authority similar to the NLRB. (See www.flra.gov.)

HOW DO WORKERS FORM UNIONS?

The process of organizing workers can be lengthy. Typically, the steps are as follows:

1. Either union membership is solicited by the employees who contact a union or a union might conduct an organizing drive.
2. At least 30 percent of employees must sign **authorization cards** that stipulate that a particular union should be their representative in negotiating with the employer (see Figure 13-4 for an example).
3. The NLRB is petitioned to conduct an election.
4. Assuming the authorization cards are in order, the NLRB sets a date for the election.
5. A secret ballot representative certification (RC) election is held, which requires that a majority of eligible voting workers accept the union.

FIGURE 13-4	Sample Union Authorization Card

Date . . . . 20 . . . .

STRICTLY CONFIDENTIAL

Office & Professional Employees International Union, Local 153, AFL-CIO
265 West 14th Street, New York, NY 10011

I hereby authorize Office & Professional Employees International Union, Local 153, AFL-CIO, to represent me and to petition the National Labor Relations Board to conduct a secret ballot election among the staff.

Name . . . . Tel. No. . . . .
(Please print)

Address . . . .
(Zip Code)

Present Employer . . . .

Present Employer's Address . . . .

Position . . . . Dept. . . . .

Signature . . . .

CONFIDENTIAL

Source: Office & Professional Employees Union, New York, NY.

NOTICE TO EMPLOYEES

FROM THE
National Labor Relations Board

A PETITION has been filed with this Federal agency seeking an election to determine whether certain employees want to be represented by a union.

The case is being investigated and NO DETERMINATION HAS BEEN MADE AT THIS TIME by the National Labor Relations Board. IF an election is held Notices of Election will be posted giving complete details for voting.

It was suggested that your employer post this notice so the National Labor Relations Board could inform you of your basic rights under the National Labor Relations Act.

YOU HAVE THE RIGHT under Federal Law

- **To self-organization**
- **To form, join, or assist labor organizations**
- **To bargain collectively through representatives of your own choosing**
- **To act together for the purposes of collective bargaining or other mutual aid or protection**
- **To refuse to do any or all of these things unless the union and employer, in a state where such agreements are permitted, enter into a lawful union-security agreement requiring employees to pay periodic dues and initiation fees. Nonmembers who inform the union that they object to the use of their payments for nonrepresentational purposes may be required to pay only their share of the union's costs of representational activities (*such as collective bargaining, contract administration, and grievance adjustments*).**

It is possible that some of you will be voting in an employee representation election as a result of the request for an election having been filed. While NO DETERMINATION HAS BEEN MADE AT THIS TIME, in the event an election is held, the NATIONAL LABOR RELATIONS BOARD wants all eligible voters to be familiar with their rights under the law IF it holds an election.

The Board applies rules that are intended to keep its elections fair and honest and that result in a free choice. If agents of either unions or employers act in such a way as to interfere with your right to a free election, the election can be set aside by the Board. Where appropriate the Board provides other remedies, such as reinstatement for employees fired for exercising their rights, including backpay from the party responsible for their discharge.

NOTE:

The following are examples of conduct that interfere with the rights of employees and may result in the setting aside of the election.

- **Threatening loss of jobs or benefits by an employer or a union**
- **Promising or granting promotions, pay raises, or other benefits to influence an employee's vote by a party capable of carrying out such promises**
- **An employer firing employees to discourage or encourage union activity or a union causing them to be fired to encourage union activity**
- **Making campaign speeches to assembled groups of employees on company time within the 24-hour period before the election**
- **Incitement by either an employer or a union of racial or religious prejudice by inflammatory appeals**
- **Threatening physical force or violence to employees by a union or an employer to influence their votes**

Please be assured that IF AN ELECTION IS HELD every effort will be made to protect your right to a free choice under the law. Improper conduct will not be permitted. All parties are expected to cooperate fully with this Agency in maintaining basic principles of a fair election as required by law. The National Labor Relations Board, as an agency of the United States Government, does not endorse any choice in the election.

NATIONAL LABOR RELATIONS BOARD
an agency of the
UNITED STATES GOVERNMENT

THIS IS AN OFFICIAL GOVERNMENT NOTICE AND MUST NOT BE DEFACED BY ANYONE

FORM NLRB-666 (5-90)   ★U.S. GOVERNMENT PRINTING OFFICE: 1941-312-471751356

Figure 13-5   NLRB Election Notice
Source: National Labor Relations Board.

The goal of the NLRB is to maintain an environment in which workers can make an uncoerced decision regarding the certification election. Figure 13-5 presents an example of an NLRB election notice.

Many unions now use the Internet to conduct the authorization step (for an example, try walmartworkerslv.com/authorization). Many employers do not get very involved in union prevention activities until step 2 because they are often not aware of the union organizing efforts until this step has been reached. Regardless, managers should have a thorough understanding as to what behaviors are lawful and unlawful under the NLRA.

If a majority vote is received for the union, the NLRB certifies the union and the union is then recognized as the exclusive bargaining unit for the workers. The union then enters negotiations with the employer. If a majority do not accept the union, another certification election cannot be held for 12 months. In fact, in recent years, the majority of union representation votes have been lost by the union. Even after a union is certified negotiations often break down. A high percentage of certified unions never obtain a contract.

Employers also get involved after a union vote and may work toward a representation decertification (RD), which also is conducted by the NLRB at least 12 months after a certification vote. While the petition for an RD must be made by the rank-and-file workers, management also is allowed, in the rare case of union misconduct, to initiate a decertification drive. Usually, decertification elections are specifically barred when a labor contract is in effect. The number of NLRB elections declined in 2004 to under 3,000 and lower than the rate in 2002. Unions won about 54 percent of the votes. Decertification elections were 15 percent of elections in 2004 (these were 4 percent of elections in 1960).

Traditionally, unions organize workers through campaigns. Bottom-up campaigns begin when workers become dissatisfied with some aspect of their work and contact a union to request organization. Top-down campaigns are initiated by the union as part of a strategy to increase their representation in the area or industry. In order to gain worker support unions employ a variety of tactics including worker-to-worker campaigns, increasing internal pressure tactics, and community involvement.[11] Their goal is to help build a sense of injustice and a belief that the union can effectively remedy the wrong.[12]

Management typically counters the union campaigns with a campaign of their own. They can communicate with the workers citing the harmful effects of unions and hold "captive audience meetings" where workers must listen to management discuss their reasons for not wanting a union. In regulating the campaign process, the goal of the NLRB is to promote an environment in which workers feel free to vote their conscience whether or not it is for or against unions. By law, workers should not be subject to threats or intimidation from either the union or management. Management violations include promising wages or firing workers for union activity. In recent years, management has often employed consultants who specialize in refuting the claims of union organizers as well as more aggressive management tactics. Often the result is management violating the NLRA and engaging in such tactics as illegally firing workers for union activity. Despite the illegality of these actions, there is evidence that many companies engage in these activities as the penalties for these actions are weak.[13]

Many unions feel that they do not have a level playing field in union organizing drives and the regulation of election conduct. Thus, they will avoid elections where possible. Recently, some unions have been successful at obtaining what are known as neutrality agreements from management. These agreements often contain provisions in which management agrees to recognize the union if a majority of the workers sign authorization cards and they waive their rights to wage a countercampaign. Management will typically agree to a neutrality clause when the union and management have a preexisting relationship such as collective bargaining agreement at another location.

THE EFFECTS OF UNIONS

Workers join unions to improve their wages, working conditions, and job security. This section presents opinions regarding whether or not unions actually do provide these improvements and what these effects mean for firm performance. Estimates of union and nonunion wage differentials range from 3 percent (utilities) to 52 percent (construction). The private sector percent difference was 22 percent in 2004. Unions also have a positive fringe benefit effect. In general, those who are usually paid the least tend to benefit the most from unionization. Studies show that younger workers, nonwhites, people living in the South and the West, and blue-collar workers seem to gain the most from unionization. Interestingly, little apparent difference exists between the wage gains from unionization for males and females. Research on public-sector unions shows a 22 percent pay differential for public-sector employees represented by unions versus public-sector employees not represented. In 2004, full-time wage and salary union workers had median weekly earnings of $781, compared with a median of $612 for workers not represented by unions.[14]

Variations in union wage effects across industries partially occur due to the union's ability to take "wages out of competition." Wages can be taken out of competition in several ways. First, labor demand may be relatively insensitive to wage changes (inelastic). That is, consumers will absorb the increased labor costs without offsetting employment effects. The extent of union organization in a particular market also can affect union power. More unionized markets have greater union/nonunion wage differentials because of less nonunion wage competition. The extent of bargaining coverage further augments this effect. This coverage can take several forms. For example, one union may bargain for the entire market—so that all union firms in the industry have virtually identical contracts. In the auto industry, the UAW bargains with one of the big automakers and then uses this contract as a pattern for remaining settlements. This strategy has become less effective as nonunionized automakers have gained market share. A union negotiating simultaneously with numerous employers, such as in steel and coal, provides another example of extensive industry coverage. A union that bargains at the plant level has much less power than those that negotiate on a broader basis.

Union advocates maintain that the "collective voice" of unions reduces worker quit rates, thereby leading to retention of experienced workers, lowering a firm's training costs, and raising its productivity. Another side benefit is that management is forced to become more efficient when faced with the necessity of providing higher wages to unionized employees.

This suggests that unions may actually have positive effects on management. If so, why does management strenuously resist unions? Are they behaving rationally? Or do they resist unions only because unions threaten their decision-making autonomy? Two theories exist regarding the unions' effects upon firms' productivity. On one hand, productivity is predicted to decrease in unionized firms because unions create resource misallocation and demand restrictive work rules. In contrast, the collective voice view predicts that productivity gains may occur because the union wage effect causes firms to manage better, employ better-quality labor, substitute capital for labor, and reduce voluntary turnover, leading to the development of a more experienced and better-trained labor force.

The evidence is mixed regarding the effects of unions on organizational productivity. Unions tend to have a negative effect on productivity when there is relatively greater conflict between the union and management. Stanford professor Jeffrey Pfeffer summed up the confusing evidence on unions and productivity this way: "The effects of unions depend very much on what management does."[15] Positive productivity effects generally tend to be found in competitive industries with higher union wage effects (i.e., where firm survival apparently depends upon offsetting the higher wage costs with increased productivity). One review of the research concluded that, in general, productivity remains higher in union establishments than in nonunion establishments. This conclusion is controversial and the subject of much debate.[16] The researchers concluded that when unions and management are working for a "bigger pie" as well as fighting over their relative share, the result is higher productivity. Under conditions of poor labor–management relations, where the focus is on taking a bigger share of the same size pie, the result is usually lower productivity. What of the argument that unions raise wages to noncompetitive levels and have thus seriously affected the ability of some U.S. industries to compete? One surprising study of 134 industries concluded that "heavily unionized industries are not found to have lost any more to imports nor gained any more in exports than comparable U.S. industries . . . industrial concentration appears to be a significant disadvantage."[17] This means that U.S. industries facing a more globally competitive environment after less domestic competition tended to have more difficulty competing *regardless of union status.*

If unions do improve productivity, how can management behave rationally by resisting unions? Apparently union productivity effects do not sufficiently outweigh the negative impact of unions on accounting profits and stock prices. Studies show that unionization negatively affects accounting profits and shareholder wealth. For example, shareholder wealth decreases during union organizing campaigns and strikes, and increases during concession bargaining.[18] In addition, unions do not seem to change the overall firm value, but they do redistribute the firm's economic profits from the stockholders to the workers. Research on "high performance work systems" establishes a closer relationship between the absence of labor unions and corporate financial performance.[19]

Unions and Quality of Worklife Issues

As we discussed in Chapter 12, quality of worklife issues (QWL) came to the forefront in the 1980s and play an important role in the labor–management relationship. Some QWL programs such as job redesign efforts, upward communication, team-based work configurations, and quality circles (QCs) have elicited a variety of union responses.[20] Overt hostility and resistance characterize some unions' reactions to QWL programs. A significant faction of the UAW membership at the Saturn plant, for example, strongly opposes the negotiated worker involvement programs. These members fear that management intends to use these programs to circumvent the union and the collective bargaining relationship. Other members cautiously indicate that they prefer the collective bargaining process to QWL programs but will support QWL programs if there is no attempt to bust the union or interfere with the collective bargaining process. Many have argued that union support remains critical for successful implementation of QWL programs. One study cited management neglect in inviting union participation early enough, or not at all, as a contributing factor to many failures of QWL programs.[21] Generally, in union settings, management is seen as more careful in evaluating the decision to implement a QWL program than in firms where a union is not present.[22]

The UAW has noted that the goods that workers manufacture and the services they provide must succeed in the marketplace (with good quality) in order to ensure long-term job and income security for workers. They further note that UAW workers have everything to gain by demanding that employees work to achieve the highest possible product and service quality. This means that QWL programs can be quite important as well as training, up-to-date equipment, and quality materials and resources. These will enable employees to achieve first-rate quality in goods and services and better guarantee their own future employment.[23]

There is limited research on the effects of QWL efforts in union settings. Two studies found that QWL programs did not have any effect upon the firm's economic performance.[24] However, more recent research found that unionized firms had more gains from employee participation than did nonunion firms.[25] Other research has shown that QWL programs can improve the firm's industrial relations.[26] Some early research has, however, elicited evidence that QWL programs may negatively influence perceptions of unions. One study found that participants in employee involvement programs felt that these were better at resolving differences than collective bargaining. Similar individuals not in those programs maintained preference toward collective bargaining.[27] In addition, nonunion companies that encourage communication and participation programs have been successful in maintaining nonunion status.[28]

Firms must be cautious in their implementation of nonunion work teams because of legal concerns regarding violations of the NLRA prohibition regarding company unions. The NLRA states that it is unlawful for an employer "to dominate or interfere with the formation or administration of any labor organization or contribute financial or other support to it." In the 1994 *Electromation* case, the U.S. Court of Appeals upheld the National Labor Relations Board's ruling that management committees addressing employee dissatisfaction with absenteeism and attendance bonuses represented illegal employer domination.[29] However, the facts of this case suggest that management had established these committees to avoid unionization. Research on QWL is relatively new and these findings are preliminary; however, they suggest that QWL programs may have an important influence upon the labor–management environment.

Union Effects on Worker Satisfaction

Better wages, benefits, and improved working conditions would seem to predict that union workers also would be more satisfied than nonunion workers. But evidence points to the contrary. Supervision, coworkers, and job content create more dissatisfaction for union workers than for nonunion workers. Only pay provides more union satisfaction.[30] This may result from unions encouraging members to voice their dissatisfaction rather than to quit. Voluntary turnover rates are substantially lower under unions. Alternatively, union workers may feel compelled to stay because of the "golden handcuffs" of better wages, health insurance, and working conditions: they may feel that they cannot afford to quit when they are dissatisfied. The most recent research indicates that union membership has no effect on either general job satisfaction or intention to quit.[31]

Unions and HRM

There can be no question that with a union HRM decisions are more constrained. In unionized organizations, the union itself gives employees a voice in the development of work rules. Termination is generally for cause only. Total compensation is almost always higher. Staffing and performance management activities are often subject to

collective bargaining. There's no question that management must clearly justify their reasons for termination when unionized.

COLLECTIVE BARGAINING*

Collective bargaining occurs when representatives of a labor union meet with management representatives to determine employees' wages and benefits, to create or revise work rules, and to resolve disputes or violations of the labor contract. For almost 16 million workers, collective bargaining represents the primary process for determining their wages, benefits, and working conditions. Despite the decline in unions and their membership in recent years, it is unlikely that either unions or collective bargaining will ever disappear. In fact, there is recent evidence that union activity is surging in some occupations (e.g., nursing) and developing in others (physicians).

Organizations and unions need to maintain knowledge of bargaining strategies and guidelines in order to successfully represent their interests. Knowledge of labor relations and collective bargaining is important for HRM specialists and general managers. In fact, it is difficult to separate labor relations as a human resource (HR) function from the many other HR functions. For example, labor relations is closely tied to HR planning since the labor contract generally stipulates policies and procedures related to promotions, transfers, job security, and layoffs. The area of HR where a knowledge of collective bargaining is probably most critical is compensation and benefits, since almost all aspects of wages and benefits are subject to negotiation.

Collective bargaining should be viewed by both the union and management as a two-way street. This means that the basic interests of management must be protected as well as the rights of employees. Both sides have a responsibility to each other. For example, unions should not expect management to concede to issues that ultimately would impair the company's ability to stay in business. Likewise, management must recognize the rights of employees to form unions to argue for improved wages and working conditions.

The Labor Contract

A labor contract is a formal agreement between a union and management that specifies the conditions of employment and the union–management relationship over a mutually agreed upon period of time (typically two to three years, but up to five years). The labor contract specifies what the two parties have agreed upon regarding issues such as wages, benefits, and working conditions. The process involved in reaching this agreement is a complex and difficult job requiring a willingness from both sides

*This section was written by Roger L. Cole and Joseph G. Clark, Jr.

to reconcile their differences and compromise their interests. This process is also bound to certain "good-faith" guidelines that must be upheld by both parties.

The Taft-Hartley Act of 1947 (section 8d) states: "to bargain collectively is [to recognize] . . . the mutual obligation of the employer and representative of the employees to meet at reasonable times and confer in good faith with respect to wages, hours, and other terms and conditions of employment, . . . or the negotiation of an agreement, or any question arising thereunder, and the execution of a written contract incorporating any agreement reached if requested by either party, . . . such obligation does not compel either party to agree to a proposal or require the making of a concession."[32] Thus, the law requires that the employer negotiate with the union once the union has been recognized as the employees' representative. Good-faith bargaining is characterized by the following events:

- Meetings for purposes of negotiating the contract are scheduled and conducted with the union at reasonable times and places.
- Realistic proposals are submitted.
- Reasonable counterproposals are offered.
- Each party signs the agreement once it has been completed.

Good-faith bargaining does not mean that either party is required to agree to a final proposal or to make concessions.

The National Labor Relations Board further defines the "duty to bargain" as covering bargaining on all matters concerning rates of pay, wages, hours of employment, and other conditions of employment.[33] "Mandatory" issues for bargaining include wages, benefits, hours of work, incentive pay, overtime, seniority, safety, layoff and recall procedures, grievance procedures, and job security. "Permissive" or "nonmandatory" issues have no direct relationship to wages, hours, or working conditions. These might include changes in benefits for retired employees, performance bonds for unions or management, and union input into prices of the firm's products. Permissive issues can be introduced into the discussion by either party; however, neither party is obligated to discuss them or include them in the labor contract.

Issues in Collective Bargaining

The major issues discussed in collective bargaining fall under the following four categories:[34]

1. **Wage-related issues.** These include such topics as how basic wage rates are determined, cost-of-living adjustments (COLAs), wage differentials, overtime rates, wage adjustments, and two-tier wage systems.
2. **Supplementary economic benefits.** These include such issues as pension plans, paid vacations, paid holidays, health insurance plans, dismissal pay, reporting pay, and supplementary unemployment benefits (SUB).
3. **Institutional issues.** These consist of the rights and duties of employers, employees, and unions, including union security (i.e., union membership as a condition of employment), check-off procedures (i.e., when the employer collects dues by deduction from employees' paychecks), employee stock ownership plans (ESOPs), and quality-of-worklife (QWL) programs.
4. **Administrative issues.** These include such issues as seniority, employee discipline and discharge procedures, employee health and safety, technological changes, work rules, job security, and training.

While the last two categories contain important issues, the wage and benefit issues are the ones that receive the greatest amount of attention at the bargaining table. In recent years, however, issues of job security have become increasingly important as bargaining items.[35] In addition, the unions have adapted to a variety of workplace changes and have played an important role in defining public policies. For example, they have been active in negotiating family-friendly contract provisions such as child care, elder care, domestic partnership benefits, and paternity leaves. They also have been involved in promoting health and safety protections for their members.[36]

Types of Bargaining

Bargaining between labor and management can take several different forms. Three of the most common are distributive, integrative, and concessionary bargaining. Distributive bargaining is the most common type of bargaining and involves zero-sum negotiation. In other words, one side wins and the other side loses. Union employees may try to convince management that they will strike if they don't get the wages or working conditions they desire. Management, in turn, may be willing to try to ride the strike out, especially if they have cross-trained other workers or have external replacements to fill in for those on strike. In distributive bargaining, unions and management have initial offers or demands, target points (e.g., desired wage level), resistance points (e.g., unacceptable wage level), and settlement ranges (e.g., acceptable wage level).

Integrative bargaining is similar to problem-solving sessions in which both sides are trying to reach a mutually beneficial alternative (i.e., a win-win solution). Both the employers and the union try to resolve the conflict to the benefit of both parties. One example might consist of providing retraining opportunities to employees to avoid having to lay off workers. Plant safety and incentive pay systems are other programs that involve collaborative efforts between management and employees. Another name for this type of bargaining has been called "interest-based bargaining." The objective is for both parties to find the common ground between them, to build relationships, and to eliminate the adversarial elements of traditional bargaining. This was used when a public electric and water utility, Salt River Project, located in Phoenix, Arizona, was experiencing tension with the International Brotherhood of Electrical Workers (IBEW) Local 266. To resolve an impasse in communications, they tried using a new approach, interest-based bargaining. Both sides shared information about their interests and concerns and they created a list of possible solutions to best meet everyone's needs.

Concessionary bargaining involves a union's giving back to management some of what it has gained in previous bargaining. Why would labor be willing to give back what it worked so hard to obtain? Usually such a move is prompted by labor leaders who recognize the need to assist employers in reducing operating costs in order to prevent layoffs and plant closings. Thus, it is often economic adversity that motivates concessionary bargaining. A good example is the agreement between GM and the International Union of Electric Workers that granted GM around-the-clock operations, wage and benefit concessions for new hires, and a two-week mass vacation. The concessions were made to save over 3,000 jobs at a plant in Ohio. In some cases, despite a financial crisis, the union may not be willing to concede. This may be because the union does not view management's arguments as credible. Thus, the degree of trust between management and the union may influence the extent to which concessionary bargaining occurs. Recent evidence suggests that it is not clear whether concessions even help the firm financially.

What kinds of concessions are sought by employers? Often they relate to wages and benefits (e.g., health insurance and pensions); for example, putting a cap on increases in compensation or increasing the premium. For example, in return for wage concessions, the union may receive a gain-sharing plan that links compensation with performance data, or some form of profit-sharing or stock ownership. Other demands made by unions in return for concessions include restrictions on work rules, transfers of work, subcontracting, and plant closures; getting advance notice of shutdowns and severance pay; and transfer rights for displaced employees.

Conducting Labor Contract Negotiations
Preparing for Negotiations

Because of the complexity of the issues and the broad range of topics discussed during negotiating sessions, a substantial amount of preparation time is required. To prepare for negotiations, one must have a planning strategy. Negotiating teams typically begin data gathering for the next negotiation session immediately after a contract is signed. Preparation includes reviewing and diagnosing the mistakes and weaknesses from previous negotiations and gathering information on recent contract settlements in the local area and industrywide (e.g., comparative

industry and occupational wage rates and fringe benefits). Preparation also includes gathering data on economic conditions, studying consumer price indices, determining cost-of-living trends, and looking at projections regarding the short-term and long-term financial outlook. Internal to the firm, data such as minimum and maximum pay by job classification, shift work data, cost and duration of breaks, an analysis of grievances, and overtime data are almost always of interest to both sides. Often unions and large corporations have research departments that collect necessary data for negotiations. Management is likely to come armed with data regarding grievances and arbitration, disciplinary actions, transfers, promotions, layoffs, overtime worked, individual performance measures, and wage payments.

During the preparation phase of contract negotiations, employers develop a written plan covering its bargaining strategy. The plan takes into account what the employer considers the union's goals to be and the degree to which it is willing to concede on various issues. Such a plan is useful to the negotiators because it helps them to identify the relative importance of each issue in the proposal.

Both the union and management send their negotiating teams to the bargaining table. The union's negotiating team generally consists of local union officials, union stewards, and one or more specialists from the national union staff. Management's negotiating team usually consists of one or more production or operations managers, a labor lawyer, a compensation specialist, a benefits specialist, and a chief labor relations specialist, who heads the team.

Meetings in Contract Negotiations

One of the most important objectives of early bargaining meetings is to establish a climate for negotiations. In other words, determining whether the tone of the negotiations is going to be one of mutual trust with "nothing up our sleeves," one of suspicion with a lot of distortion and misrepresentation, or one of hostility with a lot of name calling and accusations. Also, early meetings are used to establish the bargaining authority of each party and determine rules and procedures that will be used throughout the negotiation process. Both parties try to avoid disclosing the relative importance they attach to each proposal so that they will not have to pay a higher price than is necessary to have the proposal accepted. Generally, each side tries to determine how far the other is willing to go in terms of concessions, and the minimum levels each is willing to accept. It is best not to establish a position that is too extreme, nor one that is too inflexible. For instance, "take it or leave it" proposals are typically ineffective. One of the best examples of a "take it or leave it" philosophy of bargaining was at General Electric from the 1940s to the 1970s. During this period, GE's policy was that

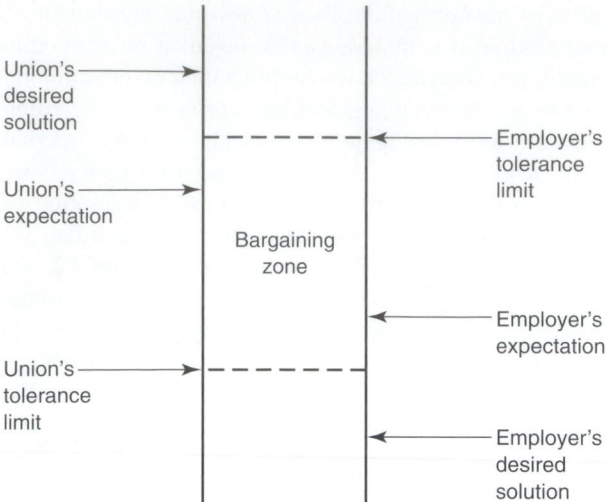

Figure 13-6   Desires, Expectations, and Tolerance Limits That Determine the Bargaining Zone

Source: From Psychology of Union–Management Relations, 1st edition by Stagner/Rosen. © 1966. Reprinted with permission of Wadsworth, a division of Thomson Learning: www.thomsonrights.com. Fax 800 730-2215.

management initially brought to the bargaining table its final proposal. The unions obviously viewed this as unethical and illegal (lack of good-faith bargaining). The Supreme Court ruling supported the unions and found them guilty of bad-faith bargaining based upon their "take-it-or-leave-it" policy combined with other tactics designed to circumvent the union. Thus, GE eventually relinquished this policy.

Successful negotiations are contingent upon each side remaining flexible. It is hoped that the end result will be a "package" representing the maximum and minimum levels acceptable to each of the parties. The bargaining zone, which is illustrated in Figure 13-6, is the area bounded by the limits that the union and employer are willing to concede. If neither the union nor management is willing to change its demands enough to bring them within the inside boundaries of the bargaining zone, or if neither is willing to extend the limits to accommodate the other's demands, then negotiations reach impasse.

The union team is first to present its initial proposals. Usually, the original union proposal demands more than it expects to end up with (i.e., excessive demands in terms of changes in, additions to, and deletions from the previous contract), which will allow leverage for trading off for management concessions. The management negotiating team then states the management case, often presenting unrealistic counterproposals and data supporting the view that union workers are treated well. The early meetings are often characterized by both parties remaining far apart on the issues; however, as negotiations proceed, there is generally movement

toward a pattern of agreement. As topics are discussed and considered, mutual concessions are offered, counterproposals are made, and eventually a tentative agreement is reached.

When a tentative agreement is reached, in most cases, the union members vote on the contract. If it is approved, the contract is ratified; if it is voted down, more negotiating takes place. The next step involves the actual drafting of a formal document, attempting to keep it in simple, clear, and concise terms. In fact, however, most contracts are difficult to read and some sections are virtually incomprehensible for the rank and file (e.g., most often sections on seniority and grievance procedures). The last step is the actual signing of the agreement by the representatives of the union and management. The typical labor agreement defines the responsibilities and authority of unions and management and stipulates what management activities are not subject to union authority (e.g., purchasing and hiring).

Resolving Bargaining Deadlocks and Impasse Resolution

If neither the organization nor the union is willing to remain flexible and make concessions, then negotiations reach a deadlock or impasse that can eventually result in a strike on the part of the union or a lockout on the part of management. So how can these breakdowns in negotiations be avoided? One way is to delay consideration of the more difficult issues until the latter stages of bargaining and, for the time being, to simply agree to disagree on the tougher decisions. The easier questions can be considered in the beginning, thus giving both sides a feeling of making progress. Another way to avoid breakdowns in negotiations is for each side to be prepared to offer propositions and to accept alternative solutions to some of the more controversial issues.

If the two parties are unable to compromise and resolve a deadlock, then they have the option of calling in a **mediator,** a neutral third party who reviews the dispute between the two parties and attempts to open up communication channels by suggesting compromise solutions and concessions. Mediation is based upon the principle of voluntary acceptance. This means that mediators act as go-betweens between the parties to help clarify the issues but that they have no conclusive power or authority to impose or recommend a solution. In fact, either party may accept or reject the mediator's recommendations. The Federal Mediation and Conciliation Service (FMCS) was established by the Taft-Hartley Act. Mediators perform their services for free and mediate about an average of 15,000 labor disagreements per year.[37]

Sometimes government intervention is necessary to resolve deadlocks. This is generally in cases where a work stoppage would threaten the national security or the public welfare. For example, one of the provisions of the

Taft-Hartley Act is a national emergency strike provision that gives the president of the United States the power to stop a strike if it imperils national health or safety.

The Union's Economic Power in Collective Bargaining

The basis for the union's power in collective bargaining is economic and generally takes one of three forms: striking the employer, picketing the employer, or boycotting the employer.[38]

Striking the Employer

One tool a labor union can use to motivate an employer to reach an agreement is to call a strike. A strike is simply a refusal on the part of employees to perform their jobs. Strikes occur when the union is unable to obtain an offer from management that is acceptable to its members. Strikes are rare. According the Bureau of Labor Statistics 17 major work stoppages began during 2004 and one major work stoppage continued from 2003, idling 170,700 workers and resulting in 3.3 million workdays of idleness. Comparable figures for 2003 were 14 stoppages, 129,200 workers idled, and 4.1 million workdays of idleness.[39]

Before a union goes on strike, it must first assess the consequences of a strike and its members' willingness to make the sacrifices and endure the hardships (e.g., lost pay) that are part of striking. Even when the union perceives the strike as necessary, employees may not be willing to strike. Factors such as loyalty to the organization and commitment to the job have been shown to differentiate workers who are willing to strike and those who are not.[40] Another part of this assessment also involves determining whether or not the employer can continue operating by using supervisory and nonstriking employees.

There are a number of risks to the union and its members attached to striking. For one, replacement employees can vote the union out in an NLRB-conducted decertification election. Also, a strike can result in a loss of union members. The public also may withdraw its support from union members and often does.

The power of the strike to pressure management has been seriously diminished during the past decades. Automation, recent court rulings, and a growing number of unemployed workers willing to serve as replacements have helped management. After Congress passed the Wagner Act in 1935, workers' rights to organize and to strike were guaranteed. However, the 1938 Supreme Court ruling in *NLRB v. Mackay Radio & Telegraph*[41] weakened this right by permitting the permanent replacement of economic strikers by management.[42] The use of replacement workers seriously undermines the economic pressure that strikes once had. Even though this court decision was made in 1938, it was not until the 1980s that the ruling was frequently applied. A recent example is the Northwest Airlines strike by its machinists. Northwest had replacement workers ready to go the very first day of the strike action by the Aircraft Mechanics Federal Association. Many workers who went on strike have found that their jobs were not waiting for them when the strike ended.[43]

Since President Reagan hired nonunion workers to replace air-traffic controllers in 1981, management's hiring of nonunion members has been a regular and successful strikebreaking weapon. Nonetheless, it appears that in some industries strikes lessen the value of struck firms and enhance the value of their competitors.[44]

Picketing the Employer

Another basis for union power is the picket. The picket is used by employees on strike to advertise their dispute with management and to discourage others from entering or leaving the premises. Picketing usually takes place at the plant or company entrances. It can result in severe financial losses for a firm and eventually can lead to a shutdown of the plant if enough employees refuse to cross the picket line. Picket lines can become very emotional at times, especially when employees or replacements attempt to cross them. These people may become the target of verbal insults and sometimes even physical violence. Companies hire security firms to protect nonstriking and replacement workers.

Boycotting the Employer

Boycotting involves refusing to patronize an employer—in other words, refusing to buy or use the employer's products or services. As an incentive to employees to honor the boycott, heavy fines may be levied against union members if they are caught patronizing an employer who is the subject of a union boycott. The union hopes that the general public also will join the boycott to put additional pressure on the employer.

Generally, there are two types of boycotts: the primary boycott and the secondary boycott. The primary boycott involves the refusal of the union to allow members to patronize a business where there is a labor dispute. In most cases, these types of boycotts are legal. A secondary boycott refers to the union trying to induce third parties, such as suppliers and customers, to refrain from any business dealings with an employer with whom it has a dispute. This type of boycott, as provided for under the Taft-Hartley Act, is illegal.

The Employer's Power in Collective Bargaining

Employers may come to the bargaining table with their own base of power. Foremost is their ability to determine how to use capital within the organization. This enables them to decide whether and when to close down the company, the plant, or certain operations within the plant; to transfer operations to another location; or to subcontract out certain jobs. All these decisions must be made in accordance with the law. This means that management must be sure that its actions are not interpreted by the National Labor Relations Board (NLRB) as attempting to avoid bargaining with the union.

If an employer is confronted with a strike by one or more of its unions, then the firm must weigh the costs associated with enduring the strike against the costs of agreeing to the union's demands. There are a number of considerations the employer must take into account: (1) how the employer's actions will affect future negotiations with the union, (2) how long the firm and the union can endure a strike, and (3) whether business can continue during the strike. Today, employers are more able to endure strikes than they were in the past. This is because the permanent hiring of replacements has greatly weakened the power of the strike. Research finds that the use of replacement workers usually prolongs strikes.[45]

In general, union members themselves are less willing to support a strike, and without strike unity, the power of the strike is negligible. Also, technological advances have increased some employers' ability to operate during a strike with a substantially reduced staff. Strikes in the public sector are illegal in most states, although walkouts have occurred in some states where strikes are illegal. Federal employees cannot strike pursuant to the 1978 Civil Service Reform Act.

The lockout is another source of power for the employer. A **lockout** is basically a shutting down of operations, usually in anticipation of a strike. The lockout also can be used to fight union slow-downs, damage to property, or violence within the plants. Generally, lockouts are not used very often because they lead to financial revenue losses for the firm. Many states allow employees to draw unemployment benefits, thus weakening the power of the lockout.

Administration of the Labor Contract

The earlier part of this chapter dealt with the negotiation of the labor contract. In this part of the chapter, we will address the application and interpretation of the labor agreement. Despite the incredible amount of time and effort that goes into negotiating and carefully writing the contract, most are written in such broad, ambiguous terms that a great deal of interpretation is required in order to put the contract to work. Most rank-and-file union workers do not clearly understand the labor contract.

Most of the problems associated with the interpretation or application of the labor contract are resolved at the lower levels of the **grievance** procedure (i.e., between the supervisor and the union steward). Grievance procedures and the time limits associated with them are generally spelled out in the contract for the purpose of reaching quick, fair, and equitable solutions to contract problems. Unresolved grievances proceed progressively to higher and higher levels of management and union representation. If the grievance procedure fails (i.e., the grievance reaches a deadlock or stalemate), most contracts stipulate that the final step will be binding **arbitration.** Arbitration involves bringing in a third party, an impartial outsider mutually agreed upon by both parties, to decide the controversy. In the following section, both the grievance procedure and the arbitration process will be reviewed. Figure 13-7 illustrates what these processes look like.

Grievance Procedure

When an employee believes that the labor agreement has been violated, the employee files a grievance. A grievance is a formal complaint regarding the event, action, or practice that violated the contract. The grievance procedure serves a number of purposes.[46] The primary purpose is to determine whether the labor contract has been violated. Also, the grievance procedure is designed to settle alleged contract violations in as friendly and orderly a fashion as possible, before they become major issues. Other purposes of the grievance procedure include preventing future grievances from arising, improving communication and cooperation between labor and management, and helping to obtain a better climate of labor relations. The grievance procedure also helps to clarify what often is not clear in the contract (e.g., defining lawful or unlawful conduct). Grievance procedures generally establish the following: (1) how the grievance will be initiated, (2) the number of steps in the process, (3) who will represent each party, and (4) the specified number of working days within which the grievance must be taken to the next step in the hearing. Failure to comply with time limits may result in forfeiture of the grievance.[47]

Resolution of Grievances

In most cases the labor contract stipulates that the employee's grievance be expressed orally or in writing to the employee's immediate supervisor. One advantage of expressing the grievance in written form is that it reduces the chance that differing versions of the grievance will be circulated. It also forces the employee to approach the grievance in a comparatively rational manner, thus helping to eliminate or reduce the likelihood of trivial complaints or feelings of hostility. Generally, the grievance is processed through the union steward, who will discuss it with the employee's supervisor.

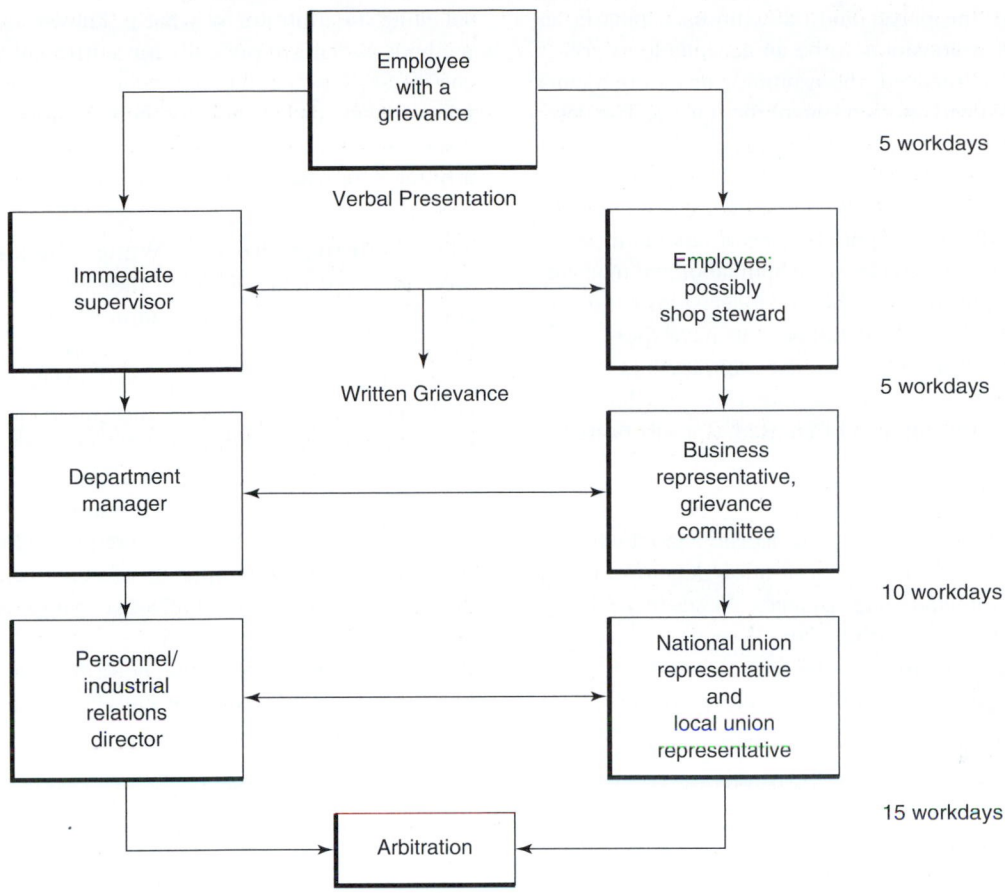

Figure 13-7   A Grievance Procedure
Source: A Grievance Procedure R. E. Allen and T. J. Keaveny, *Contemporary Labor Relations,* 2nd ed., p. 530. Reprinted with permission of the author.

Most grievances are settled early in the process. Settlement generally occurs after an employee has either presented his or her grievance in writing to the supervisor or appealed to the next higher level. An early settlement is contingent, however, on each side being willing to listen to the other side and discuss the problem in a rational and objective manner. Settlement can be hampered if both sides enter the procedure with an attitude of "win-lose" as opposed to "win-win."

When a grievance does not get settled in the first or second step, it goes to a higher level, often to company representatives (e.g., a general superintendent) and union representatives (e.g., a grievance committee). These representatives meet to further discuss the grievance and try to reach a solution agreeable to all. In most cases, the burden of proof in a grievance proceeding is on the union. Sometimes a mediator will be brought in to help resolve the grievance. The mediator's role in a grievance resolution is much the same as in contract mediation (i.e., to get the two parties to communicate and to offer compromise solutions). The mediator's role is not to establish which side is right or wrong. His or her recommendations and suggestions can be accepted or rejected by either party. The role of the mediator, as will be seen later, is much

different from that played by the arbitrator, whose decisions are final and binding.

Arbitration Process

While there is no law that forces parties to include arbitration in their labor agreements (either party can refuse to incorporate any arbitration provisions), approximately 96 percent of all labor agreements in the United States do provide for arbitration as the final step in the grievance procedure. In the majority of grievances filed, arbitration is not necessary since resolutions are usually made during lower-level discussions. In fact, arbitration should be the last resort after all other options in the grievance process have failed. Since both parties share the cost of arbitration, there is a financial disincentive to rely upon it. Arbitration involves bringing in an impartial third party (referred to as the *arbitrator* or *adjudicator*), who is mutually agreed upon by both parties to break the deadlock between the union and management. Unlike the mediator's role of providing *recommended* solutions, the arbitrator's role is to make a ruling that is "final and binding upon both parties."

Major League baseball is one organization that uses binding arbitration in salary determination. In this form of negotiation, the player and the team each puts in an offer for what it considers to be an acceptable salary. If no agreement is reached, the arbitrator hears arguments from both sides and chooses one of the figures. The decision reached then becomes binding to both the player and the team.

Arbitration is generally not used as a method of breaking a deadlock in negotiating a new labor contract in the private sector. This is because both labor and management would prefer to make their own decisions regarding conditions of employment rather than have these decisions made by a third party (i.e., the arbitrator). However, because most public-sector workers do not have the right to strike, arbitration is often used as a substitute for the strike.

The Decision to Arbitrate The decision about whether or not to take a grievance to arbitration depends upon a number of factors and circumstances. At least two things might happen before arbitration becomes necessary: (1) the union could withdraw the grievance or (2) the employer could give in. If neither of these happens, then both sides must take into account whether or not the case is important enough to justify the costs in terms of time, money, and effort. They also should determine what the chances are for a favorable ruling.

According to the duty of fair representation doctrine, unions cannot ignore their legal obligation to provide assistance to their members who are pursuing a grievance. Even if the union knows that an employee's case is weak, it often pursues the case to demonstrate its commitment to its members. In addition, management cannot refuse to arbitrate unresolved grievances if the labor contract contains an arbitration clause.

Selection of the Arbitrator Most labor agreements state that union and management will select an arbitrator from a panel of names submitted by either the FMCS or the American Arbitration Association (AAA). Neither party is, however, obligated to use either service. One of these organizations will provide the two parties with a list of names (usually seven) from their roster of arbitrators. The two parties will then agree upon an arbitrator through a process of elimination or some other mutually acceptable procedure. Many labor contracts stipulate a procedure for appointing an arbitrator. In some cases, a *permanent* arbitrator may be appointed under the terms of the labor agreement. The advantages of using a permanent arbitrator are that it saves time in the selection process, the arbitrator is already familiar with the contract and the current state of labor relations in the company, and there is a greater likelihood of uniformity in decisions because there tends to be more consistency in the interpretation of the contract. The other option for

selecting an arbitrator is what is known as the "ad hoc method," which simply calls for a different arbitrator for each case. Despite the fact that the selection process takes longer, the ad hoc method is more popular precisely because the parties are not stuck with the same arbitrator for every case.

The Arbitration Process While arbitration hearings are considered quasi-judicial, they are less formal than court proceedings. The arbitration hearing begins with a submission agreement, either oral or written, that describes the issues to be resolved through arbitration. Once the issues are presented, it is up to each of the parties to educate the arbitrator about relevant issues, facts, evidence, and arguments. The arbitrator does not play the role of fact finder; however, he or she does have the right to question witnesses or to request additional facts. Interestingly, union complaints of employers' failures to disclose information for collective bargaining purposes have increased.

Arbitrators are not bound by formal rules of evidence like those used in a court of law. For example, hearsay evidence may be introduced as long as it is identified as such. In addition, throughout the arbitration proceedings, a court recorder may be present to prepare a transcript of the hearing.

Basis for the Arbitrator's Decision and Award

After hearing all of the evidence, the arbitrator writes his or her opinion supporting the decision and award. This includes providing written rationale for the decision (i.e., an explanation for why the decision was made the way it was). The written opinion of the arbitrator presents the basic issues of the case, the pertinent facts, the position and arguments of each party, the merits of each position, and the reasons for the case. As a rule of thumb, the arbitrator has 30 days in which to consider the evidence and to prepare a decision.

A fair decision and award must be based strictly upon the contract if relevant contract language exists. Also, they should be based upon an accurate assessment and interpretation of the contractual clauses of the labor agreement. The contract is the final authority. That is why the contract language is so important; it should be as clear-cut and precise as possible. Unfortunately, contractual language usually is unclear and ambiguous and has many different meanings. When contract language is silent, such factors as past practice, negotiation history, and other relevant laws play an important role in the arbitrator's decision.

In reaching a decision, an arbitrator must decide if the employee was accorded due process. The arbitrator must also determine whether the employer had just cause for any actions taken against the complainant.

One final consideration for the arbitrator is to make sure that his or her decision is not based upon precedents established in previous cases, but rather on the facts of the current case. The arbitrator's awards should be clear and to the point. If the union receives the award, the arbitrator should state explicitly what actions the employer must take to comply with the provisions of the contract.

Criticisms of the Arbitration Process

Probably the criticisms heard most often about arbitration relate to costs and delays. Arbitration can be both expensive and time-consuming. However, supporters of arbitration will counter that argument with the fact that the costs associated with strikes and lockouts are even greater. The average fee for an arbitrator now typically exceeds $2,000 per day, plus expenses. These costs include all the arbitrator's expenses such as hotel, travel, and meals; his or her time to analyze and write up the case and opinion; and other miscellaneous costs such as those associated with lawyers and stenographers.

A few strategies have been found to reduce the costs of arbitration. These include developing a system to ensure that only grievances of high importance to the union and employer end up in arbitration, using arbitrators from the local area, consolidating grievances into one hearing, and having the arbitrator issue an award without providing a detailed written opinion.

The arbitration process is also frequently criticized for being too time-consuming. Cases often become backlogged due to arbitrators' busy schedules. Also, the actual hearings get drawn out because of the need to read lengthy transcripts or briefs. Finally, the writing of the opinion is very time-consuming. Several things can be done to cut down on this excessive time. These include using new arbitrators with smaller case loads, creating a permanent panel of arbitrators from which to choose, and cutting out transcripts and posthearing briefs (i.e., having the arbitrator take his or her own notes).

Some employers try to reduce arbitration time and costs by using a form of expedited arbitration sometimes referred to as *miniarbitration*. Miniarbitration requires that a hearing be held within 10 days after an appeal is made. Also, arbitration hearings are completed in one day, the arbitrator's decision must be made within 48 hours after the close of the hearing, there are no transcripts or briefs, and the fee is paid for only the hearing day. Miniarbitration is not always appropriate, but it generally works well with simple, routine cases. Another alternative is a process called *grievance mediation,* which combines aspects of both mediation and arbitration. It is much less formal than arbitrations, with no briefs or cross-examinations of witnesses.

CURRENT AND FUTURE U.S. TRENDS IN LABOR RELATIONS

Union Membership

The future of unions in the United States is unclear. There can be no question that political power at the state and federal levels has diminished. Legislation dealing with how unions can spend members' dues will be on many state legislative agendas. Republicans tend to support "paycheck protection" ballot initiatives that give union members more say in how their money is spent. With the unions suffering from declining membership and unfavorable legislation, a new movement has begun within the union leadership to place greater emphasis on union organizing.

Five of the largest **AFL-CIO** affiliates formed a separate coalition in 2005 in order to focus on organizing. The **Change to Win Coalition** is composed of unions that were very unhappy with the leadership of AFL-CIO President John Sweeney, who was reelected in 2005. The new coalition is made up of the **Service Employees International Union,** the **United Food and Commercial Workers Union, Unite Here,** the **Laborers' International Union,** and the **International Brotherhood of Teamsters.** The coalition maintains that the AFL-CIO has spent too much money on politics and not nearly enough to organize new members. The five unions represent 5 million workers. The Coalition pledges to devote 75 percent of its income to organizing.

Unions continue to challenge team-based productivity improvement programs as violations of NLRA. They have successfully blocked the Republican-supported Teamwork for Employees and Management (TEAM) Act. A ruling by the NLRB upheld a claim by the union at DuPont's largest chemical plant that the company's quality circles (QCs) constituted an employer-dominated labor organization and thus violated NLRA as an unfair labor practice. A similar ruling also affected Electromation, Inc. These rulings make the environment unclear as to the continued formation of employee committees and have left many organizations wary of testing empowerment programs in a union environment. Of course, QCs are still legal if first agreed to as part of a collective bargaining contract.

The widening wage gap also suggests that workers on the lower rung of the economic ladder feel more inequity and may be willing to risk jobs for economic gain. Contingent workers also may feel a sense of inequity relative to those in more standardized work arrangements with whom they are working side-by-side. These factors suggest that workers may be more receptive to unions than when working conditions were more favorable and equitable. In 2000, the NLRB extended the rights guaranteed by the NLRA to temporary and other contingent workers although these unions must reside in a separate bargaining unit.[48] There are over 35 million temporary workers.

Unions are gaining support among women, minorities, and immigrants.[49] Since the rate of women and minorities entering the workforce is higher than the rate for white males, this represents a bright spot for the future of unions. In fact, one highlight for unions in the early part of the 21st century is the increase in the number of women who joined unions and the growth of unionism among nurses, a fast-growing occupation with critical real (and projected) shortages.

Most experts predict that if union representation is to increase, the focus of organizing must be on clerical workers, data processors, salespersons, nurses, auditors, financial services, child care workers, computer technicians, and other major occupations of the service sector. In many of these jobs, women represent the majority of workers. Interestingly, while the total of union membership declined in the 1990s, the number of women who belong to unions increased in the 90s relative to the 80s. Overall, as of 2004, 11.1 percent of working women were union members, compared to 13.8 percent of male workers. From the perspective of union organizers, while this signifies improvement and expansion, there is still a long way to go.

A prime and successful target of late has been nursing home employees who toil at very difficult and physically taxing jobs at slightly more than the minimum wage. The Service Employees International Union won the right to represent 75,000 home care workers in Los Angeles County in 2000. Workers reported that they voted in the union to raise their wages from $5.75 and gain health insurance and vacation time. This is the single largest gain for unions anywhere since the first auto contracts were signed over 70 years ago. Unions even won 25 of 37 elections in the South for health care workers and over 75 percent of elections across the country in the late 90s.[50]

Many physicians are unionizing against health maintenance organizations due to low fees, excessive patient loads, and increased interference in what physicians believe to be their decision making regarding medical treatment.[51] The Federation of Physicians and Dentists now claims over 40,000 members as of 2005.[52]

There are few recent and successful union organizing efforts. In 2005, Hollywood casting directors (the people who pick the actors) voted to become Teamsters. Says Gary Zuckerbroad, a casting director and organizer who weeds out auditioning actors, "Every other major craft in the entertainment industry is unionized. Casting directors get no residuals—writers do." But a key question in this case is whether casting directors, given their jobs and as independent contractors, are even protected by the NLRA. Are they management since they participate in hiring the actors? Teamsters represent over 4,000 location

manager and studio drivers; they will probably refuse to cross picket lines.

The trend in recent court rulings and NLRB decisions is certainly not favorable for unions. "The cumulative effect is to decrease the capability of unions to organize" says Theodore St. Antoine, former Dean of University of Michigan Law School and professor of labor law. These rulings, the anti-union political power in Washington (and elsewhere), plus the growing conservatism of the federal judiciary should make labor organizing even more difficult and, given the decline in unions in most sectors of the U.S. economy, things have apparently gone from quite bad to nearly catastrophic in terms of union organizing.

As of 2005, no American Wal-Mart worker belonged to a union. Wal-Mart's prices are 14 percent lower than its competitors for lots of reasons (e.g., economies of scale, price control pressures on suppliers, technology on products bought and sold, cheaper imports). Low wages are certainly another factor. Sales clerks in some areas of the United States earn substantially less at Wal-Mart than unionized workers doing essentially the same work for competitors. Health care benefits are estimated to be 30 percent less than coverage for workers within the same industry. There is no doubt that Wal-Mart will continue to be a high priority target for union organizing.

There is a lot at stake for managers too. Research shows that managers who preside over a successful union organizing effort are much more likely to be fired and not promoted. Many former Wal-Mart managers, for example, have reported that they were warned they would be fired if any part of their workforce even authorized an election.

Public-Sector Union Membership

While private-sector union membership has been dropping, public-sector, or government employees', unionization has been on the increase. Public-sector employees generally have less bargaining power than private-sector employees. This is because unions often have to negotiate or bargain with more than one person or group. Also, many governmental entities prohibit striking. Colorado and Florida, for example, forbid striking by any state employee, including teachers. However, many state employees in midwestern states have maintained the right to strike. Visit the Web site of the National Education Association (nea.org) for a study of teacher salaries as a function of the right to strike.

The most sophisticated (and successful) of the service sector unions has been the American Federation of State, County, and Municipal Employees (AFSME), which emphasizes workplace dignity and safety, pay equity programs (comparable worth), resistance to performance and electronic monitoring, and career development. AFSME, an affiliate of the AFL-CIO, has 1.3 million members. According to the *Philadelphia Inquirer*, "AFSME seems to represent labor's future. A majority of its members are women, nearly a quarter of them are minorities, and more than half are younger than 40."[53]

Mergers and Acquisitions

A common occurrence today is for a new company to buy a failing (or failed) business. What then are the legal obligations of the new company with regard to active collective bargaining agreements? Federal labor law addresses the duties of the new employer to recognize and bargain with the predecessor's union. In the 1987 case *Fall River Dyeing & Finishing Corp. v. NLRB*, the U.S. Supreme Court established that when (1) a successor employer shows "substantial continuity" in business operations, (2) the bargaining unit is appropriate (performing essentially the same jobs under the same working conditions), and (3) the predecessor employed a majority of the new employer's workers, then the successor employer is required to recognize and bargain with the predecessor union.[54] However, there is no duty imposed on the successor employer to hire the predecessor's workers unless the failure to hire them was based upon their union status. Also, the successor is not legally required to adopt an old collective bargaining agreement that was made with the predecessor.

Union lobbyists have been successful in passing legislation regulating mergers and acquisitions. According to the Investor Responsibility Research Center, 39 states now have some form of antitakeover statute. This legislation typically requires a lengthy waiting period for completion of a takeover or the approval by the corporation's board of directors. Legislation enacted in Massachusetts is considered the most favorable for unions. Hostile takeovers in Massachusetts require approval by the board of directors, and a long waiting period is stipulated for the takeover. Workers laid off within two years of the takeover get severance pay, and new management must recognize all existing collective bargaining agreements.

Retraining Provisions

Mergers and acquisitions, downsizing, and deregulation have all imposed great threats to job security, particularly for union workers. One of the key ways that unions have begun to deal with this threat is through retraining provisions in collective bargaining agreements. For example, job security has become a prime concern of unions in the deregulated and technologically changing telecommunications industry.

Some unions have cooperated with management to enhance employee development in order to limit downsizings and maintain jobs. Model programs have been initiated in the past by the United Auto Workers with Ford and GM and the Communications Workers of America with AT&T. These programs were jointly funded by management and the union. They were designed to help employees prepare for re-employment in the face of layoffs or to help workers gain more marketable skills that could be used within or outside the firm.[55]

Employee Benefits

With declining membership and the need to attract women, unions have emphasized health care and family-oriented benefits in recent years.[56] For example, unions such as the American Federation of Teachers (AFT), the Amalgamated Clothing and Textile Workers Union, the International Ladies Garment Workers Union, the Communication Workers of America, and the National Union of Hospital and Health Care Employees have taken active roles in child-care and family-leave issues. These and other unions were instrumental in the passage of the Family and Medical Leave Act discussed in Chapter 10. In some cases, the union lobbies for child care funds from the state legislature, and in some cases the union is directly involved in supporting child care centers.[57] The UAW and Ford jointly operate child care resource and referral centers in many locations.

A Proposal to Reinvent U.S. Trade Unionism

Experts on U.S. unionism drafted a proposal in 2005 with the goal of revitalizing the union movement.[58] They prefaced their list of recommendations with the following context: "The economic and political changes over the last thirty years both in the United States as well as globally have resulted in a far more hostile environment for labor unions specifically and for working people generally. In this context, contrary to the spirit of A. Philip Randolph's notion that the essence of trade unionism is social uplift, the trade union movement is rarely looked to today as a voice of progress and innovation, or a consistent ally of progressive social movements."

After much discussion, this consortium of experts concluded: "The current situation necessitates a new approach to strategy, tactics, and fundamentally, the vision of trade unionism. This is more than the production of new mission statements, but instead rests on the necessity to rethink the relationship of the union to its members, to the employer(s), to government, to U.S. society as a whole, and to the larger *global village*. Can the union . . . rise to the challenge of being a means to confront injustice, or is the union condemned to be solely an institutional mechanism to lessen the pain of contemporary capitalism on those fortunate to be members of organized labor?" Figure 13-8 presents a summary of their strategy for reinventing trade unionism in the United States. They have an uphill battle.

FIGURE 13-8   A Strategy for Reinventing Trade Unionism in the 21st Century

1. **There is a need for a vision that includes, but is not limited, to organizing the unorganized:** There must be massive organizing of the unorganized.

2. **The union movement must be unapologetically pro-public sector and pro-public service.**

3. **The union movement must stand for the expansion of democracy:** Organized labor must stand AND fight for an expansion of democracy beyond the limits of formal legality.

4. **We must have a U.S. union movement structure suited to advancing organizing of the unorganized workers:** The question of the shape and structure of the U.S. union movement cannot be driven by a concern about jobs for the officers and staffs of the current unions.

5. **The union movement must reshape its political program to focus on the needs of the working class:** The union movement has made the repeated mistake of assuming that it can tell its members how to vote, and that the Democratic Party structure will automatically represent their interest.

6. **The union movement must organize in the South and Southwest:** There is a direct (though not exclusive) relationship between union membership and one's tending to vote in one's own economic interests.

7. **State federations and central labor councils must be democratic, inclusive, young and audacious:** Too many central labor councils and state federations are disconnected from the realities that their members face and most of the working class.

8. **The union movement needs real membership education:** It is presumptuous to think that either organized or unorganized workers will blindly follow or adhere to a certain point-of-view without providing them with a coherent and up-to-scale mechanism by which they can access information.

9. **The U.S. union movement must build both global union partnerships and solidarity with others fighting global injustice.**

Source: Adapted from K. Bronfenbrenner, D. DeWitt, B. Fletcher, et al., "Future of Organized Labor in the U.S.: Reinventing Trade Unionism for the 21st Century," *Monthly Review Online*, February 2005.

INTERNATIONAL ISSUES

There are several unique characteristics of the U.S. labor relations system relative to systems in most other countries.[59] Among the most significant are the following:

1. In the United States, unions have exclusive representation (i.e., there is representation by only one union for any given job in the United States). In Europe, more than one union, often with religious and political affiliations, may represent the same workers.

2. In the United States, the government plays a passive role in labor relations and dispute resolution, characterized by regulating the process, not the outcomes. In Western and Eastern European countries, Australia, Canada, and Latin America, the role of the government is much more active.

3. In the United States, there is generally an adversarial relationship between the union and management, while in most other countries the relationship is much more conciliatory and cooperative.

4. Collective bargaining in the United States is more decentralized (i.e., agreements are negotiated primarily at the local level). Unions in Europe, Japan, and Canada rely primarily on macro-negotiation by industry.

5. In the United States, unions place a high emphasis on economic issues such as wages, benefits, and job security, while in other countries (e.g., France), the unions emphasize political issues to a greater degree. Swedish unions emphasize both economic and political issues. For example, the Swedish model is considered humane since their goal is to replace unemployment benefits by a guarantee of work or training for long-term unemployed people. In China, unions have very little political or economic power and great difficulty in organizing workers.

In several countries, trade unions influence firm economic and financial decisions by including worker representatives as members on the supervisory boards. In Germany, workers are represented at the plant level in work councils and at the corporate level through **codetermination.** Work councils are committees that have representatives from both employees and managers. They have responsibility for the governance of the workplace, including hiring and firing workers, training issues, and overtime.[60] Codetermination is usually associated with Germany because, there, a full-parity system was established in the steel and coal industry. Labor and management are equally represented on the supervisory or corporate boards of these companies. Some form of codetermination also can be found in other industries in Germany. Since 1976, German law has required companies with over 2,000 employees to have the same numbers of management and worker representatives on the supervisory board (usually comprised of 11 members including the chair, who is chosen by the other 10 members). The decisive vote is cast by the "neutral" chair in tie situations. AEG-Telefunken, a German appliance and machinery company, provides a good example of the codetermination principle: AEG (today a division of DaimlerChrysler) was in deep financial trouble in the early 1980s. Surprisingly, the chair cast the deciding vote in favor of the labor representatives' proposal to persuade the government to provide more aid.[61]

When making union comparisons across countries, it is important to recognize that even within a country there may be marked differences among their unions. In Germany today, two of the biggest unions are IG Metall with over two million members representing cars and electronics and IG Chemie with over one million members representing chemicals. Their approaches to union issues are quite different even though both were established in 1890–1891. The main goal of IG Metall is to fight for better benefits, wages, and hours even if it means losing members as companies lay off workers. On the other hand, IG Chemie recently signed an agreement that allows employers who are in trouble to cut wages of up to 10 percent in return for job security. IG Metall has a similar agreement in the former East Germany, but so far has not been willing to allow a similar system in western Germany.[62]

The head of the works council at the Hamburg factory of Daimler Benz Aerospace (DASA), Hans-Gunter Eidtner, was able to persuade the IG Metall union to eliminate overtime pay so that employees would not lose their jobs. German workers seem more eager to compromise given the large number of people out of work (4.3 million). In fact, as in the United States, employers are increasingly making deals with workers that improve productivity and flexibility. Most of the companies negotiate concessions with the works councils at individual factories then gain approval (often reluctantly) from national unions. Companies in eastern Germany have an easier time making deals and cutting labor costs since the unions are less powerful than in western Germany. Some of the agreements reached in Germany are similar to those reached in the United States where employees are expected to make some concessions in order to help out struggling companies.[63] Some of these are listed below:

- At Bayer, the chemical union agreed to reduce bonuses, eliminate an employee share-purchase program, and introduce flexible work hours over three years.
- At Volkswagen, the union agreed to a two-tier wage system and temporary employees will earn 10 percent less than current employees.
- Workers at the Hanover tire plant for Continental will increase their workweek by 75 minutes and make other concessions worth about $20 million.
- At Deutz, a machinery maker, employees will accept a second year of pay cuts and will receive up to $11 million in Deutz stock.

U.S. Managers and Unions

A lack of understanding of union structure and the underlying social dimension is often cited as a major cause of difficulties for expatriate American managers of multinational corporations. While American managers tend to

have an antiunion orientation in their management style, unions carry considerably more clout in other countries. This attitude often can result in serious (and quick) trouble. For example, Johnson & Johnson's joint venture with a German pharmaceutical company ran into difficulties at the start because Johnson & Johnson managers apparently did not recognize the importance of the work councils at German plants and the practical implications of codetermination for the manufacturing process. Codetermination also stipulates that a labor director be treated as a manager who is charged with attending to worker concerns. Labor directors have great influence in Germany and often participate in corporate strategic planning. The management board is elected by the supervisory board and must include a labor director who is approved by labor representatives. Johnson & Johnson's expatriate managers did not recognize the significance of the labor director in the daily operation of the joint venture plants. Consequently, the firm experienced problems on matters related to work rules, productivity measures, and job responsibilities.

Similar cases of difficulties for expatriate managers have been noted in Japan, where joint consultation systems are very common yet very alien to American managers. Over 75 percent of Japan's largest employers have a joint consultation system in which employee groups meet monthly with management to discuss policy, production, personnel issues, and even financial matters. Although not as common as in large companies, consultation systems and participative management systems are becoming more common for small and medium-sized Japanese companies as well. Japan has **enterprise unions** in which most firms have a single union with virtually all job families in the same union. For instance, in large firms such as Toyota, Toshiba, and Hitachi, workers in each company are organized into a union. This ensures that the union's loyalty will not be divided among different companies. There is no clear distinction between labor and management. In fact, many Japanese executives started their careers as union members, were promoted to leadership positions in the union, and then moved into management jobs in the same company. Thus, they have an appreciation for the perspective of labor and management. There is considerable trust between labor and management. Bargaining is done by the central organization during the "spring offensive" with details negotiated at the individual company.

Figure 13-9 presents the percentage of employees who are unionized around the world as of 2005. Union membership was lower in the United States (13 percent) than in many countries. For example, union participation was highest in Sweden (81 percent). While many Central and South American countries have a higher percentage of workforce union membership (e.g., Mexico, Argentina, Brazil), there is no guaranteed right to collective bargaining. Unions in Central and South America are generally very political.

Union membership is decreasing in many European countries. In Great Britain, for example, membership has

FIGURE 13-9	Unionization around the World

	Percent
United States	13%
Australia	28
Canada	30
France	31
Germany	26
Ireland	44
Italy	34
Japan	22
Korea	12
Mexico	32
Netherlands	29
Spain	11
Sweden	81
United Kingdom	30

Source: http://www.ilr.cornell.edu/library/research/QuestionOfTheMonth/ archive/laborUnionsAcrossTheWorld.html. Accessed October 3, 2005.

dropped about 15 percent in the last 15 years. Unions there are closely tied to the Labour Party and can be militant. Wildcat strikes, for example, are illegal in the United States, but are a more common form of protest in Britain.[64]

The effects of unions and labor law on MNCs varies widely with European unions having high standards regarding wages, employment-at-will and the ability to globally integrate operations and that in many developing countries labor unions and labor laws provide very little protection of workers and their rights.[65] Ford plants in Germany can only be closed after an extended period of consultation with affected parties. Many European countries impose stiff fines for terminating employees, even if the layoffs are temporary.

Another problem for MNCs is the inability to integrate optimal manufacturing operations across borders because powerful labor unions exert strong political pressure. The result of this suboptimization is higher manufacturing costs. The influence of the German Metal Workers' union on GM operations is often cited as a case in point.

The pro-labor Organization for Economic Cooperation and Development in Paris has issued "Guidelines for MNCs" that attempt to guarantee the same basic social and labor relations rights for all workers. However, union attempts to develop uniform standards for MNCs have not proven very fruitful to date. As noted earlier, the National Labor Relations Board enacted in the United States in 1935 was designed to enable workers to exert pressure on companies to achieve fair wages and address poor working conditions. In most cases, the NLRA has been applied to U.S. firms located in the States.[66] It has not been extended to U.S. firms located in other countries, despite the fact that some argue that this would be advantageous for employers and unions. Some of the possible benefits would include

providing some stability for corporations and unions dealing in the global labor market, discouraging multinational firms from establishing facilities in foreign countries that have poor working conditions and weak labor standards, and allowing unions to use legal means to exert economic pressure on firms without worrying about whether they will flee to underdeveloped countries.[67]

The National Labor Committee, a coalition formed in 1983 of 25 of the member unions of the AFL-CIO to monitor conditions in Central America, has alleged that some companies have contracted with offshore manufacturers that use child labor, maintain sweatshops, and severely underpay their employees. It also contends that U.S. firms have a duty to monitor their offshore contractors to ensure that they are not acting unethically or illegally. This means that U.S. firms should perform self-checks, adopt a code of conduct for their offshore operations, communicate the code and monitor compliance with it, and train managers to ensure that they understand the code and enforce it.[68]

Global Collective Bargaining and Productivity

A 2003 World Bank study entitled "Unions and Collective Bargaining: Economic Effects in a Global Environment" concluded that union members, and other workers covered by collective agreements in industrial as well as in developing countries, get significantly higher average wages than workers who are not affiliated with a trade union.[69] The wage differential was larger in the United States (15 percent) than in most other industrial countries (5 to 10 percent). The report, which reviewed more than a thousand studies on the effects of unions and collective bargaining, found that bargaining coordination between workers' and employers' organizations in wage setting and other aspects of employment (for example, working conditions) was an influential determinant of a country's economic performance.

Union membership reduced wage differences between skilled and unskilled workers and also between men and women. In some countries such as Germany, Japan, Mexico, South Africa, and the United Kingdom, unionized women workers have a greater pay advantage over their nonunionized counterparts than unionized men. In the United States and the United Kingdom, unionized nonwhite workers tend to get a higher wage markup than white workers. In Mexico and Canada, unions have been found to reduce the discrimination against indigenous people.

What should be clear from this brief discussion of international labor relations is that we can make very few generalizations about labor relations across borders. The role of government, social agendas, religious affiliation, and underlying political and economic issues must be understood before one can thoroughly understand the diversity of international labor relations.

SUMMARY

As a result of the changes taking place in the size and composition of the workforce, the advances in technology, and the increased competition from foreign businesses, the future of unions and the collective bargaining system is uncertain. Some have predicted that the days of unions are over unless they incorporate these changes into their collective bargaining strategies. There is little doubt that unions must be willing to be flexible and to adapt to the changes taking place. Unions must find a way to attract the new entrants into the labor force such as women, minorities, and immigrants—if they are to survive.

What does the future hold for unions and collective bargaining? Some critics of conventional collective bargaining say that the current system cannot survive because it is inefficient, ineffective, excessively time-consuming, and characterized by exaggerated opening demands and inflated counterproposals.

NLRB interpretive decisions tend to track with the political party in power. NLRB was controlled by Democrats during the eight years of the Clinton administration (1992–2000) and the decisions tended to be pro-union. Decisions under George W. Bush have tended to be more pro-business. The NLR Board has five seats. The President appoints members to five-year terms; Republicans have held the majority of seats most recently. While all NLRB interpretative decisions are subject to federal judicial interpretation of the NLRA, the federal judiciary has gotten more conservative and pro-business as well. Managers in nonunion environments must be aware that many of the rights provided to union workers also extend to nonunion workers under the National Labor Relations Act. For example, in 2004 the NLRB found that nonunion employees no longer had what were commonly known as "Weingarten rights" in which nonunion workers could have a co-worker attend an investigative review. Prior to this 2004 reversal, managers were obligated to allow an employee to have a co-worker attend an investigatory review. At least as of the date of this publication, "Weingarten rights" for nonunion employees are out.[70]

Cooperation and collaboration are the words being used to describe contract negotiations today. This is true in the United States and in other countries. Collaboration can take many forms. For example, management can create committees on which employees are represented [e.g., shop committees, department committees, quality circles (QCs)]. Also, there has been a movement toward greater cooperation in handling disciplinary problems and resolving grievances.

Unions and collective bargaining will continue to play an important role in the lives of American workers as long as they are able to help workers overcome dissatisfaction with management and to meet their economic needs. Greater cooperation between labor and management is needed to make organizations more effective and competitive. In some industries, that cooperation may be necessary in order to survive.

The major labor development in 2005 was the formation of the Change to Win Coalition which broke from the AFL-CIO. The two major unions of the new Coalition are the Teamsters and the Service Employees International Union (SEIU). Over 4 million workers left the 13 million strong AFL-CIO to join the Coalition, Other members of the Change to Win Coalition are the Laborers' International Union of North America, the United Farm Workers, and the United Brotherhood of Carpenters and Joiners of America, which is not in the AFL-CIO.

The breakup may do even more damage to unions by reducing the AFL-CIO's clout. Says Robert Reich, secretary of Labor under former President Bill Clinton. "It's very bad news in the short term . . . a fundamental principle in the union movement is that in unity there's strength. The reverse is also true. In disunity there's weakness." But Anna Burger, the first chairperson of the Coalition says labor will reverse its long slide as a social and political force by focusing on the nation's lowest-paid workers. Certainly, SEIU has been very successful organizing such groups as home health care and child care workers, building service workers and private security workers, all heavily female and minority. The jury is still out as to whether the newly formed Coalition can take advantage of the SEIU's successful organizing techniques and apply them to other unions.

Time will tell about the comeback of unions in the 21st century. Some experts are predicting a resurgence with new, aggressive leadership and a more sympathetic ear from middle-class workers, women, and minorities. The widening gap between executive pay and the average worker is contributing to renewed sympathy and greater receptivity to union arguments. The political power, however, is certainly on the side of business and against unions in the United States.

DISCUSSION QUESTIONS

1. Should public employees be allowed to strike?
2. What are the major effects of unions on compensation?
3. Why do unions sometimes have a positive impact on productivity?
4. If unions are to survive, what do you think they will have to do to attract and maintain members?
5. Should companies be allowed to hire workers based on their attitudes toward unions?
6. Why is it advantageous for both the union and management to remain flexible during collective bargaining negotiations?
7. Describe the sources of power brought to the bargaining table by union and management.
8. Describe how union and management might prepare for labor negotiations. How are their preparations similar and different?
9. Should the government be allowed to intervene on strikes that are not a threat to national security or public welfare, in order to expedite their resolution? Why or why not?
10. How might a multinational corporation better prepare itself for dealing with the differing union environments in other countries?
11. Compare and contrast unions in the United States, Germany, and Japan. How are they similar and different? What can they learn from one another?

14

EMPLOYEE HEALTH AND SAFETY*

OVERVIEW

Employers, unions, employees, and government agencies have a great and growing interest in health and safety issues related to the workplace. With the number of work-related injuries, illnesses, and deaths, it is no surprise! According to the National Safety Council, each workday a fatality occurs every two hours and a debilitating injury occurs every two seconds. Industrial accidents cost the U.S. economy an estimated $120.7 billion per year. However, there is some indication that injury and illness statistics look more favorable in recent years. For example, while 5,575 fatal work injuries in the United States were recorded in 2003, this figure is 337 less than for the average of 1998–2002. Fatal injuries among Hispanic and Latino workers also fell compared to 2000 data. There were almost 4.5 million recorded cases of nonfatal incidents of occupational injury or illness in 2003 compared to almost 6 million in 2000.[1] These indications of improvements should be interpreted with caution. First of all, the government changed its criteria for reporting nonfatal injuries. Second, studies indicate that reported accidents represent only about half of all accidents.[2] There is growing speculation that illegal immigrants are doing more of our most dangerous work and many deaths and injuries are not reported.

Examples of the costs to individual employers are immense as well. General Motors (GM) was fined $1.94 million for safety violations by the Occupational Safety and Health Administration (OSHA). One of the largest meatpackers, John Morrell and Co. of Sioux Falls, South Dakota, was cited by OSHA and assessed a $4.33 million fine for safety violations. According to the federal agency, more than 800 of the 2,000 employees at the plant sustained "serious and sometimes disabling injuries." The rate of injuries at the plant was 652 times more than the rate of injuries for businesses in general. USX, the giant steel company, was fined $7.3 million for numerous violations of safety, health, and recordkeeping, including 58 "willful" hazards. Criminal charges and convictions against management for willful neglect of worker health and safety are now quite common.

Despite these disturbing statistics, safety issues have not been a priority to students or researchers in management. However, the events of September 11, 2001, and the terrorist threats that continue provide a new focus on at least some aspects of employer responsibilities regarding their role in worker safety. This chapter will review the costs of employee injuries, illnesses, and deaths and the regulatory environment that seeks to improve work safety and health. Human resource professionals should understand these issues so they can take a proactive stance in managing employee health and safety. Considerable attention will be given to the role of the Occupational Safety and Health Administration Act of 1970 and the federal regulations that have

*Contributed by Susan M. Stewart, University of Puget Sound and, Harriette McCall.

been issued regarding this law. OSHA is responsible for establishing and enforcing occupational health and safety standards and for inspecting and issuing citations to organizations that violate these standards. OSHA is without question one of the greatest legislative accomplishments of organized labor, and research on its effectiveness will be reviewed in this chapter. The final portion of the chapter will cover contemporary issues related to employee health and safety and will discuss some of the controversial steps organizations are taking to improve their employee health, safety, and performance records (e.g., drug testing, antismoking policies, threat management teams, employee assistance, and wellness programs).

OBJECTIVES

After reading this chapter, you should be able to

1. *Understand the extent and costs of employee accidents, illnesses, and deaths on the job.*
2. *Discuss the role of workers' compensation programs for job-related injuries and illnesses.*
3. *Describe legal issues related to health and safety.*
4. *Explain the functions of OSHA and review research on the effectiveness of this act and related regulation.*
5. *Discuss recent approaches that have been used to improve workplace safety and health.*
6. *Review contemporary issues and programs that seek to improve worker health and safety, including drug testing, antismoking policies, threat management teams, stress management interventions, employee assistance programs, and employee wellness programs.*

Ferguson-Hall Co. Inc., an excavation contractor, really felt the costs of a workplace accident in 2006. One of its employees died after the bank of an unprotected 8 1/2-foot deep water line excavation collapsed on him. The U.S. Labor Department's Occupational Safety and Health Administration (OSHA) sought the maximum fine after an inspection found that the excavation had no cave-in protection. OSHA cited Ferguson-Hall for an alleged willful violation of safety standards that require collapse protection. There could be more trouble for Ferguson-Hall managers as well.

State prosecutors have argued successfully for criminal prosecution of managers who cause injury or illness to employees.[3] For example, three senior managers of Film Recovery Systems in Illinois received 25-year sentences for recklessly exposing their employees to toxic cyanide fumes. Five senior executives of Chicago Magnet Wire Company were prosecuted for causing illnesses by allowing workers to be exposed to hazardous chemicals. A supervisor at Jackson Enterprises in Michigan was con-

victed of involuntary manslaughter for an employee's death.[4] The list goes on.

The death and accident figures presented above vary substantially as a function of the industry, occupation, and organization size. Moderate-sized organizations (50 to 100 employees) have higher accident rates than smaller or larger companies. This may be because moderate firms cannot offer extensive safety programs or cannot closely supervise their employees. According to the Bureau of Labor Statistics (BLS), the industries with the highest number of fatalities in 2005 were construction, transportation and public utilities, agriculture, forestry, and fishing, services, and the retail trade.

While the current statistics are disturbing, they do not compare to the early days of industrial growth in the United States. The Industrial Revolution was born with little concern for employee health or safety. Working conditions were often so unbearable and serious injuries were so pervasive that employees began to demand that management implement safeguards. Union activity emphasized improving employee working conditions. Today, many older Americans suffer because of the conditions to which they were exposed at work decades ago. For example, 49 workers from a foundry in Michigan got tuberculosis because of their exposure to silica at the foundry in the 1940s (silica is a glassy material found in sand). There are thousands of other examples.

Despite the work-related injuries, illnesses, and deaths that occur each year in this country, U.S. health and safety standards are superior to those in most developing parts of the world. In most other countries that maintain reliable data on the subject, injury and illness figures are even more alarming than those in the United States. Most developing countries have very basic safety laws and few resources for safety enforcement. In addition, they have antiquated equipment and limited training available to employees about safety issues. These developing countries are often so in need of economic development that they accept any industry, even those that have the potential for significant harm. This presents serious ethical questions for firms operating in the developing nations. However, in many European countries with strong national unions, safety law enforcement mechanisms are often ranked higher than those in the United States. The rankings are as follows: Sweden, former East Germany, Finland, former West Germany, United Kingdom, and the United States. In countries such as the Netherlands, France, Belgium, Denmark, and Luxembourg, legally mandated employee safety committees give workers more control over workplace safety issues.[5]

Without question, the American workplace is safer today than it was 60 years ago, but there is still considerable room for improvement. One modern day issue being addressed includes the use of **chemical hazards.** More than 30 million workers are potentially exposed to one or more chemical hazards per year. There are an estimated

650,000 existing hazardous chemical products, and hundreds of new ones are introduced annually. Most have never been tested for toxicity, and no regulatory restraints affect their use. New materials, composed of exotic combinations of plastics, carbons, and other substances are introduced into the workplace at an alarming rate, with little knowledge of their interactive effects on worker health.

Another growing problem is **repetitive strain injury** (RSI), the so-called disease of the new millennium. Since 1990, cases of RSI have increased by 80 percent. RSI is an umbrella term for a number of overuse injuries affecting the soft tissues (muscles, tendons, and nerves) of the neck, upper and lower back, chest, shoulders, arms, and hands. RSI is an occupational injury that occurs from continuous and repetitive physical movements, such as assembly-line work or data entry. Typically arising as aches and pains, these injuries can progress to become crippling disorders that prevent sufferers from working or leading normal lives. The most frequently hit area with this disorder is in the wrist and is called carpal tunnel syndrome. Carpal tunnel syndrome accounts for one-third of workplace injuries in the United States and costs about $20 billion yearly. In 2005, the median days away from work were highest for cases of carpal tunnel syndrome. Median days away from work—the key measure of severity for occupational injuries and illnesses—designates the point at which half the cases involved more days and half involved fewer days. For carpal tunnel syndrome, the median was 27 days. The average worker's compensation claim for carpal tunnel syndrome is about $17,000.

Workers today also suffer more subtle forms of health problems at work. Research concludes that workplace stress, for example, has reached epidemic proportions due to company restructuring, increased work demands, layoffs, downsizing, conflicts with family obligations, and the continuing threat of terrorism.[6] Chronic and long-term stress is commonly referred to as **job burnout**. Job burnout is a particular type of stress that tends to be experienced by workers in specific areas such as police work, customer service centers, health care, education, and the airline industry. Job burnout is costing U.S. industry billions of dollars. One estimate revealed that almost $90 billion is lost each year due to burnout and its related implications (i.e., emotional exhaustion, poor performance, absenteeism). Prolonged stress, along with fatigue, drugs, exposure to harmful chemicals, and disorders, can result in worker errors that are the cause of most workplace accidents.[7]

In addition to the obvious effects of pain, suffering, and a decreased quality of life, the impact of injuries and illnesses on productivity is enormous. In 2003, there were approximately 1.3 million cases of injuries or illnesses related to work that involved days away from work. Wage and productivity losses, medical expenses, and administrative expenses amounted to over $100 billion, with approximately 2 percent of payroll used for disability pay-

ments through workers' compensation. Indirect costs to the employer, including the monetary value of time lost by workers, replacing workers, damage to company equipment or property, and the cost of time required to investigate incidents (i.e., written reports), amounted to over $10 billion.[8] The bottom line work-injury cost is in excess of $200 billion per year. One study reported that employees who had suffered accidents were unsatisfied with their jobs and had higher levels of job tension and lower organizational commitment and faith in management.[9] Given these facts, the interest in health and safety issues by employees, employers, unions, and government agencies is understandable.

COMMON WORKPLACE INJURIES AND DISEASES

Employees are subjected to a number of on-the-job injuries each day. The most costly lost-time workers' compensation claims by cause of injury are for those resulting from motor-vehicle accidents, followed by injuries from a fall or slip. Injuries are usually caused by overexertion such as picking up heavy objects, falling, being struck by objects, or hyperextending a limb. Back problems are very common among sedentary white-collar workers. Merrill Lynch is one company that has moved aggressively with a comprehensive program directed at back injuries. They purchased ergonomically designed office equipment for their 70,000 white-collar workers. Workers can request an audit of their workspace to determine its ergonomic soundness. The comprehensive program seems to be working.

It can be difficult for employers to detect the cause of certain diseases. For example, an individual may suffer a hearing loss due to working in a plant with an extremely high noise level or for other reasons not related to the workplace. In fact, more and more supervisors are beginning to worry about the effects of noise on employee health, morale, and productivity. Some adverse effects caused by persistent loud noise include constriction of blood vessels to the brain and other key organs, damage to the nervous system, and triggering of seizures among epileptics. One study of typical open-office noise found elevated urinary epinephrine levels and motivational deficits related to typical open-office noise.[10] OSHA's prescribed standard for acceptable noise levels in the workplace is 85 decibels. Unfortunately, many work settings today have daily noise levels well over the OSHA standard. Workers who are most at risk of noise pollution include factory workers, jackhammer operators, and printing-press operators. For effective noise management, supervisors should take worker complaints about noise seriously and act on them and rotate workers so that no one worker has lengthy exposure to loud noises. In addition, to avoid litigation, employers must introduce and enforce safety regulations in the workplace.

Many employee illnesses also are caused by food poisoning. A likely source of infections is the plant or office lunchroom, where improperly handled food can contaminate tabletops and work surfaces. Another threat is from food that employees bring from home. In the workplace, it is important to provide employees with refrigerated food storage and disposable utensils, plus a sink and paper towels for cleanup. Housekeeping personnel should make sure to use germicides or disinfectants rather than liquid soap.[11]

LEGAL ISSUES RELATED TO HEALTH AND SAFETY

Many laws are designed to protect workers from illness and injury. The Michigan foundry referred to earlier now must abide by strict OSHA standards regarding silica emissions. As evidenced by the fines against GM, John Morrell and Company, USX, and others discussed above, penalties are imposed for violating these laws and regulations. Under OSHA rules, employees now have a "right to know" about hazards to which they may be exposed at work. Companies are now required to issue a **hazard communication** to their workers when they may be exposed to certain hazardous chemicals. Under OSHA, employees can refuse to work and be supported by the law when certain unsafe conditions exist. Employers need to keep equipment, machinery, and the workplace in good, safe working order.[12]

In some states, if a fatality occurs from a willful violation of safety rules, company officials can serve time in prison and pay substantial fines. In addition, as one state attorney general said, "The workplace offers no refuge from criminal laws."[13] Prosecutors are now charging employers and supervisory personnel with involuntary manslaughter for negligence regarding workplace safety. This type of criminal prosecution can involve much heavier penalties.

In addition to this legal pressure, many employers seek a safe working environment because they wish to foster a high quality of work life (QWL) for their employees. Other employers recognize the costliness of accidents, illnesses, and injuries and endeavor to reduce these costs as much as possible through a variety of health and safety programs.

The major legislation related to health and safety, the steps that organizations have taken to reduce accidents and injuries, and the major contemporary issues that affect employee health and safety are reviewed below. Following this, the major controversies of the day such as AIDS policies, drug testing, antismoking positions, and responses to workplace violence are examined.

Workers' Compensation

As we discussed in Chapter 10, **workers' compensation** is a federally mandated insurance program developed on the theory that work-related accidents and illnesses are costs of doing business that should be paid for by the employer and passed on to the consumer. The direct cost of claims to U.S. businesses has been around $70 billion annually. Workers' compensation is based on the concept of **liability without fault,** which provides that workers who are victims of work-related injury or illness are granted benefits regardless of who is responsible for the accident, injury, or illness. This means that if an organization participates in the workers' compensation system, a worker may not sue the employer for negligence, even if the injury was clearly the employer's fault. On the other hand, even careless or accident-prone workers are generally covered by workers' compensation, and injuries that are the result of co-workers' negligence also are covered. Some state laws, however, deny benefits if the worker was under the influence of alcohol or controlled substances (illegal drugs) when the injury occurred.

What Employers Need Workers' Compensation Coverage and What Are the Costs?

While workers' compensation laws differ across the states, the basics are about the same. Figure 14-1 presents the highlights of the law as they apply to employers and employees. Keep in mind that state law stipulates the detail. Thus, for example, whether a worker can make a claim for psychological stress at work depends on the state (in most states, the worker cannot). Employers, including governments, with a small number of full-time or part-time employees (four is the average) are required to carry workers' compensation insurance. Employers typically purchase an insurance policy from an agent representing a company approved by a state regulatory agency. These premiums can be pricey and the rates differ across the states (and the industry). Some employers pay in access of $4 per $100 of payroll. The rate is partially determined by the firm's health and safety record. Across the United States, it is the employer's responsibility to pay the entire premium for this coverage.

Again, while the law differs across the states, employers typically do not have to pay for the first few days of disability (usually 7) but if time of the disability extends to over a set number of days (usually 21), the employer would be obligated to pay for the first 7 days as well. In terms of lost work, the benefit check is paid at about two-thirds of the average weekly wage.

What Injuries or Diseases Are Covered?

The law covers all accidental injuries and occupational diseases arising out of and in the course and scope of employment. This includes diseases or infections resulting from such injuries. Visit the Web site of the National Council on Compensation Insurance (NCCI) for more detail. State laws differ on what conditions are not covered. In general, the law does not provide compensation

---

FIGURE 14-1 | Highlights of Workers' Compensation Law

Employers' Responsibilities	Employees' Issues
Employers with a small number of full-time or part-time employees (4 is the average) must carry insurance.	Must report injury or illness as soon as possible (usually not later than 30 days).
Must report the injury to the carrier within about 7 days after their knowledge.	Can report the injury to the insurance company if the employer doesn't comply.
Typically pay 100% of the policy from a company approved by a state regulatory agency.	Must typically choose a doctor from a list provided by the insurance company.
Covers all accidental injuries and occupational diseases related employment.	The employer is generally not required to hold a job open for a victim.
Although there are exceptions, workers' compensation does not pay for mental stress or "pain and suffering" from such a condition.	It is unlawful to fire someone for filing or a claim.
Compensation is not paid if the injury was caused by the employee's willful intention to injure or kill him or herself or another or if the injury was caused primarily because the employee was intoxicated or under the influence of drugs.	Reemployment services are available to help employees return to work. Services include vocational counseling, transferable skills analysis, job-seeking skills, job placement, on-the-job training, and formal retraining.
Compensation must still be paid when an employee refuses to obey safety rules.	If a claim is denied, an employee can get an attorney or work with a state agency. A petition for benefits must usually be filed within two years of the original decision.

---

for any of the following conditions: (1) a mental or nervous injury due to stress; (2) a work-related condition that causes an employee to have fear or dislike for another individual because of the individual's race, color, religion, sex, national origin, age, or handicap; and (3) "pain and suffering" from the condition.

An employer cannot sue an injured worker for causing the accident nor can an injured worker sue the employer for an injury. This trade-off makes it possible for injured workers to receive immediate medical care, at no cost to the injured worker, without any consideration for who was at fault, the employer or the employee. In civil law, negligence must be established through litigation before any compensation is awarded. In general, compensation is not paid if the injury is caused by the employee's willful intention to injure or kill him or herself or another or if the injury is caused primarily because the employee is intoxicated or under the influence of drugs. If an injured worker refuses to submit to a test for drugs or alcohol, the employee may forfeit eligibility for benefits.

Compensation must still be paid, although in a reduced amount (e.g., 25 percent) even when the employee refuses to use safety equipment like a hard hat or safety goggles or refuses to obey a safety rule. Compensation will still be paid, but partial wage replacement may be reduced if the employee knew about the safety rule prior to the accident and failed to observe the rule, or if the employee knowingly chose not to use safety equipment where the employer had directed the use. There is great variability in payouts for injuries; even today, injuries to

body parts are worth different amounts in different states.

When a worker is injured on the job or develops a disabling occupational disease, the worker must file a claim, either with the company or its insurance carrier (or in some states, with a state agency), to request workers' compensation benefits. In most states, benefits begin after a short waiting period (two to 14 days) and include a wage replacement payment (a percentage of the worker's salary) and a reimbursement of medical costs. The employer (or its insurance carrier) may require the injured worker to be treated by a doctor selected by the company.

Employers may contest a worker's compensation claim if they believe (1) the injury (or illness) is not a result of the work, (2) the employee is capable of performing the job despite the injury or illness, or (3) the employee has made a fraudulent claim. Other issues that may involve a challenge to a worker's compensation claim include heart attacks, strokes, or other stress-related problems. In some states, the law places the burden on the employee to prove that the disabling condition was a result of work effort or work-related stress and would not have occurred otherwise.

Disputes related to workers' compensation are common. Many states have established dispute resolution agencies in an attempt to resolve the dispute more quickly. For example, the state of Florida established the Employee Assistance and Ombudsman Office (EAO), which requires injured workers, employers, and medical providers to file a request for assistance with this agency for a mandatory dispute resolution period. Some employees are challenging the no-fault assumptions of the workers' compensation system, arguing that an employer who knowingly exposes workers to hazardous substances or dangerous working conditions should not be protected from negligence lawsuits. In most instances, the courts have ruled that all employer conduct short of an "intentional wrong" will fall under the rubric of workers' compensation. However, there are some exceptions to this general rule. One state court ruled that a company that withholds information from employees regarding the development of a serious occupational disease could be sued for negligence and fraud.[14]

The fact that a company may have violated an OSHA standard will not necessarily remove the protection of workers' compensation. The no-fault provisions of the system (with the above-noted exception) make irrelevant the issue of whether the employer or the worker was to blame. The worker gets medical treatment and a portion of his or her wages; the employer is insulated from litigation in return for paying the workers' compensation benefits.

If a worker becomes disabled due to a job-related accident or illness, the employer may be obligated under the 1990 Americans with Disabilities Act (ADA) to provide "reasonable accommodations" for that worker, assuming the disability qualifies as a disability under the ADA. This accommodation might include job restructuring or reassignment. However, the injury must qualify as a disability under the ADA.

While provisions of workers' compensation laws, such as the premium imposed, encouraged employers' efforts to improve their health and safety records, the effects of such provisions were not very impressive. Many states took matters into their own hands to do more in this area. Between 1911 and 1948, each state passed a workers' compensation law. This created a myriad of rules and regulations, which resulted in a lack of uniformity in policies and regulations across the states. This prompted political pressure from numerous constituencies, particularly unions, for a federal law aimed primarily at the reduction and prevention of occupational fatalities, injuries, and illness. The result of the pressure was passage of the Occupational Safety and Health Act in 1970.

The Occupational Safety and Health Administration Act

The **Occupational Safety and Health Administration (OSHA)** was created in 1970 within the U.S. Department of Labor. It was designed to reduce occupational diseases and on-the-job injuries. The official mission of OSHA is "to ensure worker safety and health in the United States by working with employers and employees to create better working environments." OSHA has helped to cut workplace fatalities by more than 60 percent and occupational injury and illness rates by 40 percent. At the same time, U.S. employment has doubled from 56 million workers at 3.5 million worksites to more than 115 million workers at 7.2 million sites. In fiscal year 2005, OSHA had more than 2,220 employees, including 1,100 inspectors. The agency's appropriation is about $468 million. The 2003 data compiled by OSHA indicated a decline from 2002 data to 5.0 cases per 100 workers, with 4.4 million injuries and illnesses among private-sector firms. About 32 percent of work-related injuries occurred in goods-producing industries and 68 percent in services. Figure 14-2 presents a summary of the various agencies and functions that derive from OSHA.

There were 5,559 worker deaths in 2003, a slight increase from 2002, accounted for by 114 additional deaths among self-employed workers and 61 more through workplace violence. The fatality rate of 4.0 deaths per 100,000 workers remained the same from 2002 to 2003. Fatalities related to highway incidents, falls, and electrocutions declined while homicides and deaths related to fires and explosions and contact with objects or equipment increased (go to www.osha.gov for the latest figures). According to the National Safety Council (www.nsc.org), between 1912 and 2003, unintentional work deaths (per 100,000 workers) were reduced 93 percent from 21 to 1.5.

FIGURE 14-2 The Basics of OSHA and Worker Safety

Agencies under the Occupational Safety and Health Act of 1970	Agency Actions
Occupational Safety & Health Administration	Issue standards; conduct inspections, citations, variances
Occupational Safety & Health Review Commission (OSHRC)	Review citations; abatement
U.S. Court of Appeals	Render decision on contested citations
National Institute for Occupational Safety and Health (NIOSH)	Conduct research
State Agencies (22 states) (Arizona, California, Hawaii, Indiana, Iowa, Kentucky, Maryland, Michigan, Minnesota, Nevada, New Mexico, New Jersey, New York, North Carolina, Oregon, South Carolina, Tennessee, Utah, Vermont, Virginia, Washington and Wyoming)	Standards; enforcement / Train Compliance Safety and Health officers (COSHOs)

The NSC proclaimed 2005 to be the start of a "promising trend" in the adoption of safety as a "core corporate value" among an increasing number of corporate leaders. In 2005, the National Safety Council sponsored the 17th World Congress on Safety and Health at Work to call greater attention to international safety issues. As noted previously while the workplace is safer in the United States and many other industrialized countries, there is no question that worker health and safety is of relatively less concern in developing nations.

Specifically, the purpose of OSHA is to accomplish the following:

1. Encourage employers and employees to reduce workplace hazards and to implement new or improve existing safety and health programs.
2. Provide for research in occupational safety and health to develop innovative ways of dealing with occupational safety and health problems.
3. Establish "separate but dependent responsibilities and rights" for employers and employees to achieve better safety and health conditions.
4. Maintain a reporting and recordkeeping system to monitor job-related injuries and illnesses.
5. Establish training programs to increase the number and competence of occupational safety and health personnel.
6. Develop mandatory job safety and health standards and enforce them effectively.
7. Provide for the development, analysis, evaluation, and approval of state occupational safety and health programs.

Coverage of the OSHA Act of 1970, which includes virtually all employers and their employees in the United States, is provided either directly by federal OSHA or through an OSHA-approved state program. OSHA seeks to assist the majority of employers who want to do the right thing while focusing its enforcement resources on sites in more hazardous industries—especially those with high injury and illness rates. Less than 1 percent of inspections—about 300—came under the agency's Enhanced Enforcement Program, designed to address employers who repeatedly and willfully violate the law. Strong enforcement has helped to increase alleged violations by more than 10 percent over the past five years, including an increase of 14 percent in alleged willful violations since 2003. At the same time, injuries and illnesses continue to decline significantly.

State Health and Safety Plans

OSHA encourages states to create their own safety and health programs for workers, thus largely superseding enforcement, compliance, and outreach through federal OSHA, although the federal agency has responsibility for approving and monitoring state plans. In return, the law allows states to receive up to 50 percent of their plan's operating costs in grant form from the agency. Twenty-two states have chosen to develop and operate their own occupational safety and health compliance programs for private- and public-sector employees (see Figure 14-2 for a list of the states). Four others operate programs that cover public employees only. OSHA has responsibility for approving and monitoring state plans. State plans must set job safety and health standards that are "at least as effective as" comparable federal standards. State plans must adhere to stringent guidelines, such as conducting inspections to enforce standards, covering public employees, and running safety training and education programs. Says one expert, "State plans give the states flexibility to build occupational safety and health programs around a state's geographic, economic, political and cultural peculiarities. Loggers in Oregon, for instance, are faced with struck-by hazards because the trees are pulled off slopes. In North Carolina, tree felling is the biggest hazard to workers."[15]

Under the Bush Administration, OSHA is focusing on three strategies: (1) strong, fair and effective enforcement; (2) outreach, education and compliance assistance; and (3) partnerships and cooperative programs. It should be noted that OSHA devoted considerable time and expense at "ground zero" of the World Trade Center tragedy. Nearly 400 OSHA staffers monitored conditions at the work site to ensure the health and safety of all workers in the area. OSHA conducted over 100 air samples in the area and found that all samples fell below the OSHA standard for asbestos. They also tested the area for dioxin, metals, volatile organic compounds, carbon monoxide, silica, and freon. They provided respirators and other personal protection equipment. During that same time period, OSHA issued an Anthrax Matrix that provided guidelines for equipment and workspaces and assessed risk for anthrax exposure. OSHA's role continues to be assistance and consultation.

Standards

OSHA is responsible for developing enforceable safety standards. The noise and asbestos standards are two examples. It is the employers' responsibility to become familiar with the standards applicable to their establishments and to ensure that employees have and use personal protective gear and equipment when required for safety. Where OSHA has not promulgated specific standards, employers are responsible for following the act's general duty clause.

The general duty clause states that each employer "shall furnish . . . a place of employment which is free from recognized hazards that are causing or are likely to cause death or serious physical harm to his [or her] employees." This means that if a workplace situation involves foreseeable danger of potential injury, the employer is required to eliminate or reduce that danger through redesign, new equipment, or training workers about safety.

In 1989, OSHA greatly expanded its role in protecting workers from hazardous materials. Maximum exposure limits were set for 164 substances, and limits were tightened for 212 others. The limits cover the maximum amount of time a worker can be exposed to specific substances during an eight-hour workday. Among the substances regulated for the first time were cotton dust, wood dust, grain dust, gasoline, acrylic acid, tungsten, and welding fumes. OSHA also cut maximum exposure limits for carbon monoxide, chloroform, and hydrogen. In addition to exposure to hazardous materials, it is also important to examine the protective clothing worn by employees. Choosing the appropriate protection level and material of personal protective apparel is critical.

Employers may ask for a temporary (up to one year) **variance** from a standard when they cannot comply with a new standard by its effective date. OSHA may grant a permanent variance from a standard when an employer can demonstrate that it has alternatives in place that protect employees as effectively as compliance with the standard would.

Generally, a variance is an exception to compliance with some part of a safety and health standard granted by OSHA to an employer. For example, sometimes employers may not be able to comply fully and on time with a new safety or health standard because of a shortage of personnel, materials, or equipment. Or employers may prefer to use methods, equipment, or facilities that they believe protect employees as well as or better than OSHA standards. In situations like these, employers may apply to OSHA for a variance. There are four types of variances: *temporary, permanent, experimental,* and *national defense.*

Recordkeeping and Reporting

Before OSHA became effective, no centralized and systematic method existed for monitoring occupational safety and health problems. Statistics on job injuries and illnesses were collected by some states and by some private organizations. With OSHA came the first basis for consistent, nationwide procedures—a vital requirement for gauging safety problems and solving them.

Employers with 11 or more employees must maintain records of occupational injuries and illnesses as they occur. The records permit the Bureau of Labor Statistics to compile data, to help define high-hazard industries, and to inform employees of the status of their employers' record. OSHA provides a free 24-hour hot line for reporting workplace safety or health emergencies.

Recordkeeping forms must be maintained for five years at the establishment and must be available for inspection by representatives of OSHA. The Injury and Incident Report (Form 301) must be completed within seven days once a recordable work-related injury or illness has occurred. The Log of Work Related Injuries and Illnesses (Form 300) is used to classify work-related injuries and illnesses and to note the severity of each case. The Summary (Form 300A) provides the totals for the year in each category. Figure 14-3 presents a summary of employer obligations as outlined by the U.S. Department of Labor.

Keeping records of accidents is important not only to meet compliance issues, but also for identifying ergonomic problems in the workplace. Records should be kept not only for visible traumas, but also for musculoskeletal injuries such as strained backs, pulled limbs, and RSIs. Analyzing these records can identify areas where poor manual handling or ergonomics cause work-related injuries. Statistics on absences are also valuable and enable organizations to draw comparisons between their firm and others. Unfortunately, many firms do not keep very detailed absence records, if they keep any.

Defining Occupational Injury or Illness

An **occupational injury** is any injury, such as a cut, fracture, sprain, or amputation, that results from a work-related accident or from exposure involving a single incident in the work environment. An **occupational illness** is any abnormal condition or disorder, other than one resulting from an occupational injury, caused by exposure to environmental factors associated with employment. Included are acute and chronic illnesses or diseases that may be caused by inhalation, absorption, or ingestion of or direct contact with toxic substances or harmful agents. Alcoholism has even been considered an occupational illness in a case involving an employee who developed an alcohol-related problem as a result of the socializing responsibilities associated with his job.

All occupational illnesses must be recorded, regardless of severity. All occupational injuries must be recorded if they result in the following:

- Death (must be recorded regardless of the length of time between the injury and death).
- One or more lost workdays.
- Restriction of work or motion.
- Loss of consciousness.
- Transfer to another job.
- Medical treatment (other than first-aid).

In 2002, OSHA installed several changes to the definitions of injury and illness cases recorded by employers. These new definitions of course resulted in changes in occupational injury and illness statistics provided by the Bureau of Labor Statistics. As one example, in one change, the old definition considered the application of a butterfly bandage to be medical treatment and a recordable case; the new definition considers such treatment to be first-aid and not recordable.[16]

Workplace Inspection

To enforce its standards, OSHA is authorized under the act to conduct workplace inspections. Every establishment covered by the act is subject to inspection by OSHA compliance

An Overview: Recording Work-Related Injuries and Illnesses

The Occupational Safety and Health (OSH) Act of 1970 requires certain employers to prepare and maintain records of work-related injuries and illnesses. Use these definitions when you classify cases on the Log. OSHA's recordkeeping regulation (see 29 CFR Part 1904) provides more information about the definitions below.

The *Log of Work-Related Injuries and Illnesses* (Form 300) is used to classify work-related injuries and illnesses and to note the extent and severity of each case. When an incident occurs, use the *Log* to record specific details about what happened and how it happened. The *Summary* — a separate form (Form 300A) — shows the totals for the year in each category. At the end of the year, post the *Summary* in a visible location so that your employees are aware of the injuries and illnesses occurring in their workplace.

Employers must keep a *Log* for each establishment or site. If you have more than one establishment, you must keep a separate *Log* and *Summary* for each physical location that is expected to be in operation for one year or longer.

Note that your employees have the right to review your injury and illness records. For more information, see 29 Code of Federal Regulations Part 1904.35, *Employee Involvement*.

Cases listed on the *Log of Work-Related Injuries and Illnesses* are not necessarily eligible for workers' compensation or other insurance benefits. Listing a case on the *Log* does not mean that the employer or worker was at fault or that an OSHA standard was violated.

When is an injury or illness considered work-related?

An injury or illness is considered work-related if an event or exposure in the work environment caused or contributed to the condition or significantly aggravated a preexisting condition. Work-relatedness is presumed for injuries and illnesses resulting from events or exposures occurring in the workplace, unless an exception specifically applies. See 29 CFR Part 1904.5(b)(2) for the exceptions. The work environment includes the establishment and other locations where one or more employees are working or are present as a condition of their employment. See 29 CFR Part 1904.5(b)(1).

Which work-related injuries and illnesses should you record?

Record those work-related injuries and illnesses that result in:

▸ death,
▸ loss of consciousness,
▸ days away from work,
▸ restricted work activity or job transfer, or
▸ medical treatment beyond first aid.

You must also record work-related injuries and illnesses that are significant (as defined below) or meet any of the additional criteria listed below.

You must record any significant work-related injury or illness that is diagnosed by a physician or other licensed health care professional. You must record any work-related case involving cancer, chronic irreversible disease, a fractured or cracked bone, or a punctured eardrum. See 29 CFR 1904.7.

What are the additional criteria?

You must record the following conditions when they are work-related:

▸ any needlestick injury or cut from a sharp object that is contaminated with another person's blood or other potentially infectious material;
▸ any case requiring an employee to be medically removed under the requirements of an OSHA health standard;
▸ tuberculosis infection as evidenced by a positive skin test or diagnosis by a physician or other licensed health care professional after exposure to a known case of active tuberculosis.

What is medical treatment?

Medical treatment includes managing and caring for a patient for the purpose of combating disease or disorder. The following are not considered medical treatments and are NOT recordable:

▸ visits to a doctor or health care professional solely for observation or counseling;
▸ diagnostic procedures, including administering prescription medications that are used solely for diagnostic purposes; and
▸ any procedure that can be labeled first aid. *(See below for more information about first aid.)*

What do you need to do?

1. Within 7 calendar days after you receive information about a case, decide if the case is recordable under the OSHA recordkeeping requirements.

2. Determine whether the incident is a new case or a recurrence of an existing one.

3. Establish whether the case was work-related.

4. If the case is recordable, decide which form you will fill out as the injury and illness incident report.

   You may use *OSHA's 301: Injury and Illness Incident Report* or an equivalent form. Some state workers compensation, insurance, or other reports may be acceptable substitutes, as long as they provide the same information as the OSHA 301.

How to work with the Log

1. Identify the employee involved unless it is a privacy concern case as described below.

2. Identify when and where the case occurred.

3. Describe the case, as specifically as you can.

4. Classify the seriousness of the case by recording the **most serious outcome** associated with the case, with column J (Other recordable cases) being the least serious and column G (Death) being the most serious.

5. Identify whether the case is an injury or illness. If the case is an injury, check the injury category. If the case is an illness, check the appropriate illness category.

U.S. Department of Labor
Occupational Safety and Health Administration

Figure 14-3   Summary of Employer Obligations

safety and health officers (COSHOs), who are chosen for their knowledge and experience in the occupational safety and health field, and who are trained in OSHA standards and in recognition of safety and health hazards.

Under the act, "upon presenting appropriate credentials to the owner, operator, or agent in charge," a COSHO is authorized to carry out the following:

- "Enter without delay and at reasonable times any factory, plant, establishment, construction site or other areas, workplace, or environment where work is performed by an employee of an employer."
- "Inspect and investigate during regular working hours, and at other reasonable times, and within reasonable limits and in a reasonable manner, any such place of employment and all pertinent conditions, structures, machines, apparatus, devices, equipment and materials therein, and to question privately any such employer, owner, operator, agent, or employee."

OSHA's highest priorities for inspections are to first go to imminent danger situations and actual fatal accident sites. Next, it inspects workplaces with valid employee complaints or target industries (those with high rates of accidents). Finally, it performs random inspections and reinspections of various work sites.[17] OSHA conducted over 39,000 inspections in 2004, almost 80 percent of which were directed at hazardous works sites and to investigate complaints or serious injuries or fatalities. Over 50 percent of inspections are directed at the construction industry.

With very few exceptions, inspections are conducted without advance notice. In fact, alerting an employer in advance of an OSHA inspection can bring a fine of up to $1,000 and/or a six-month jail term. If an employer refuses to grant admittance to the COSHO, or if an employer attempts to interfere with the inspection, the act permits appropriate legal action.

Based on a 1978 U.S. Supreme Court ruling in *Marshall v. Barlow's Inc.*,[18] OSHA may not conduct warrantless inspections without an employer's consent. It may, however, inspect after acquiring a judicially authorized search warrant based on administrative probable cause or on evidence of a violation. Employers are not required to allow inspectors to observe all work areas nor are they required to provide all requested documents. Warrants and administrative subpoenas may be necessary.

If employees are represented by a recognized bargaining representative, the union ordinarily will designate an employee representative to accompany the compliance officer. Similarly, if there is a plant safety committee, the employee members of that committee will designate the employee representative. OSHA requires that employees—whether represented by a union or not—have a right to select a representative for the inspection. OSHA regulations require that the inspector consult with a "reasonable number of employees" if no representative is designated.

Inspection Tour   After the opening conference in which the scope of the inspection is stipulated, the COSHO and accompanying representatives proceed through the establishment and inspect work areas for compliance with OSHA standards. The route and duration of the inspection are determined by the compliance officer. If an employer is concerned about an apparent expansion of the inspection from what was said at the opening conference, another opening conference may be requested to discuss the expansion. At that point, the employer can demand a warrant. While talking with employees, the compliance officer makes every effort to minimize work interruptions. The compliance officer observes conditions, consults with employees, takes instrument readings, examines records, and may even take photos or videotape (this is for recordkeeping purposes and employers may request that confidentiality be maintained).

Employees are consulted during the inspection tour. The compliance officer may stop and question workers, in private if they so desire, about safety and health conditions and practices in their workplaces. All employees are protected, under the act, from discrimination from their employer for exercising their safety and health rights.

Records and postings are checked. The compliance officer inspects records of injuries, illnesses, and deaths that the employer is required to keep. He or she checks to see that a copy of the totals from the last page of OSHA Form 300 have been posted.

Closing Conference   After the inspection tour, a closing conference is held between the compliance officer and the employer or the employer's representative. This is the time for free discussion of problems and needs—a time for frank questions and answers.

The compliance officer discusses with the employer all unsafe conditions observed on the inspection and indicates all apparent violations for which a citation may be issued or recommended: (1) a description of the violation; (2) the proposed financial penalty, if any; and (3) the date by which the hazard must be corrected. The employer is then informed of appeal rights. The OSHA Appeals Commission hears appeals regarding citations. That judgment also can be appealed to the U.S. Court of Appeals for that geographical area.

While OSHA looks for violations of all types, they rely on their extensive data to look for certain violations. In 2004, the most frequently found violations concerned scaffolding, fall protection, and hazard communications.

OSHA provides an abatement period, which is the amount of time the employer has to fix the problem. Employers are rarely given more than 30 days to make the stipulated improvements. However, longer periods may be granted if the employer must make major changes or order new equipment or parts that will not arrive within 30 days. Requests for extensions can be made to the area OSHA representative.

The compliance officer explains that OSHA area offices are full-service resource centers that provide a number of services such as training speakers and technical materials on safety and health matters. The compliance officer also explains the requirements of the Hazard Communications Standard, which requires employers to establish a written, comprehensive hazard communication program that includes provisions for container labeling, material safety data sheets, and an employee training program. (Employers have been cited for over 60,000 violations of the Hazard Communications Standard since 1985.) Employers are required to certify to OSHA that they have corrected workplace hazards cited by the agency.[19]

Citations and Penalties

After the compliance officer reports his or her findings, the area director determines what citations, if any will be issued, and what penalties, if any, will be proposed. Citations inform the employer and employees of the regulations and standards alleged to have been violated and of the proposed length of time set for their abatement. The employer will receive citations and notices of proposed penalties by certified mail. The employer must post a copy of each citation at or near the place a violation occurred, for three days or until the violation is abated, whichever is longer. Figure 14-4 presents a summary of the penalty options OSHA will consider.

These are the types of violations that may be cited and the penalties that may be proposed:

- *Other than Serious Violation*—A violation that has a direct relationship to job safety and health, but probably would not cause death or serious physical harm. A proposed penalty of up to $7,000 for each violation is discretionary.
- *Serious Violation*—A violation where there is substantial probability that death or serious physical harm could result and that the employer knew, or should have known, of the hazard. A mandatory

penalty of up to $7,000 for each violation is proposed. A penalty for a serious violation may be adjusted downward, based on the employer's good faith, history of previous violations, the gravity of the alleged violation, and size of business.
- *Willful Violation*—A violation that the employer knowingly commits or commits with plain indifference to the law. The employer either knows that what he or she is doing constitutes a violation, or is aware that a hazardous condition existed and made no reasonable effort to eliminate it. Penalties of up to $70,000 may be proposed for each willful violation, with a minimum penalty of $5,000 for each violation. A proposed penalty for a willful violation may be adjusted downward, depending on the size of the business and its history of previous violations. Usually, no credit is given for good faith.

If an employer is convicted of a willful violation of a standard that has resulted in the death of an employee, the offense is punishable by a court-imposed fine or by imprisonment for up to six months, or both. A fine of up to $250,000 for an individual, or $500,000 for a corporation, may be imposed for a criminal conviction.
- *Repeated Violation*—A violation of any standard, regulation, rule, or order where, upon reinspection, a substantially similar violation can bring a fine of up to $70,000 for each such violation. To be the basis of a repeated citation, the original citation must be final; a citation under contest may not serve as the basis for a subsequent repeated citation.
- *Failure to Abate Prior Violation*—Failure to abate a prior violation may bring a civil penalty of up to $7,000 for each day the violation continues beyond the prescribed abatement date.

Additional violations for which citations and proposed penalties may be issued upon conviction are:

- Falsifying records, reports, or applications can bring a fine of $10,000 or up to six months in jail, or both.

FIGURE 14-4 **Employer Penalties for OSHA Violations**

Violation	Description	Penalty
Other than serious violation	Violation not capable of causing death or serious injury	Fine up to $7,000 per violation (discretionary)
Serious violation	Substantial probability that death or serious physical harm could result and that the employer knew, or should have known, of the hazard	Fine up to $7,000 per violation (mandatory)
Willful violation	Intentional (knowing) violation	Possible criminal penalties; fines up to $10,000 per violation
Repeat violation and or failure to correct the violation	Finding of similar violation; failure to correct violation	Fine up to $70,000 per violation; up to: $7,000 per day if violation continues

- Violations of posting requirements can bring a civil penalty of up to $7,000.
- Assaulting a compliance officer, or otherwise resisting, opposing, intimidating, or interfering with a compliance officer while they are engaged in the performance of their duties is a criminal offense, subject to a fine of not more than $5,000 and imprisonment for not more than three years.

Citation and penalty procedures may differ somewhat in states with their own occupational safety and health programs. Employees may request an informal conference with OSHA to discuss any issues raised by an inspection, citation, notice of proposed penalty or employer's notice of intention to contest.

In 2004, the "top five" violations of OSHA standards were related to (in order of the number of violations): (1) scaffolding (8,682 violations); (2) hazard communication; (3) fall protection; (4) lockout/control of hazardous energy respiratory protection; and (5) electrical wiring. The top "willful violations" in addition to these five were: protection systems—excavation, noise exposure, permit violations for confined spaces, and machine guarding.

Services Available

Consultation Assistance Free consultation assistance is available to employers who want help establishing and maintaining a safe and healthful workplace. Largely funded by OSHA, the service is provided at no cost to the employer. As part of this service, no citations are issued, no penalties are imposed, and information is kept confidential. Besides helping employers to identify and correct specific hazards, consultation can include assistance in developing and implementing effective workplace safety and health programs with emphasis on the prevention of worker injuries and illnesses. Training and education services also can be provided.

Voluntary Protection Programs Voluntary protection programs (VPPs) represent one component of OSHA's effort to extend worker protection beyond the minimum required by OSHA standards. When combined with an effective enforcement program, VPPs, expanded on-site consultation services, and full-service area offices can expand worker protection to help meet the goals of the OSHA. VPP participants establish and maintain excellent safety records and programs that are recognized by OSHA as models for their industries. The cooperative interaction with OSHA gives companies the opportunity to provide OSHA with valuable input on health and safety issues and to provide the industry with effective models of excellence in health and safety.

Unlike other companies, VPP participants are not subject to routine OSHA inspections. Establishing and maintaining OSHA-endorsed programs following the VPP model are reflected in significantly lower injury rates for participating companies. For example, the average VPP worksite has a days-away-from-work rate of 52 percent below the average for its industry. These sites typically do not start out with such low rates. Reductions in injuries and illnesses begin when the site commits to the VPP approach to safety and health management and the challenging VPP application process. Among the members of the VPP programs is the New Holland, Michigan Ford Motor Company plant. Ford reported a 13 percent increase in productivity since joining the VPP program and a 16 percent drop in scrapped product that had to be re-worked.

The VPP program was revised in 2000 to allow previously ineligible employers, especially small businesses, to raise the health and safety achievement levels expected of participants. OSHA expects VPP sites to participate in outreach programs that assist other workplaces and help OSHA accomplish its goals. Visit OSHA's outstanding website for more details on this program.

The three VPPs—Star, Merit, and Demonstration—are designed to perform the following functions:

- Recognize outstanding achievement of those who have successfully incorporated comprehensive safety and health programs into their total management systems.
- Motivate other companies to achieve excellent safety and health results in the same outstanding way.
- Establish a relationship between employers, employees, and OSHA that is based on cooperation rather than coercion.

The Star program, OSHA's most demanding and the most prestigious VPP, is open to an employer in any industry who has successfully managed a comprehensive safety and health program to reduce injury rates below the industry's national average. Specific requirements for the program include systems for management commitment and responsibility; hazard assessment and control; and safety planning, rules, work procedures, and training that are in place and operating effectively.[20]

The Merit program, also open to any industry, is primarily a stepping stone to Star program participation. A company with a basic safety and health program that is committed to improvement and has the resources to do so within a specified time period may work with OSHA to meet merit qualifications.[21]

The Star Demonstration program is designed for worksites with Star level quality safety and health protection to test alternatives to current Star eligibility and performance requirements. Promising and successful projects are considered for changes to Star requirements.

Training and Education OSHA's area offices are full-service centers offering a variety of informational services such as speakers, publications, audiovisual aids on workplace hazards, and technical advice. The OSHA Training Institute in Arlington Heights, Illinois, provides basic and advanced training and education in safety and health for federal and state compliance officers; state consultants; other federal agency personnel; and private-sector employers, employees, and their representatives. Institute courses are also offered to the public and cover areas such as electrical hazards, machine guarding, ventilation, and ergonomics.

Employer Responsibilities under OSHA

As an employer, you must abide by these OSHA guidelines:

- Meet your general duty responsibility to provide a workplace free from recognized hazards that are causing or are likely to cause death or serious physical harm to employees and comply with standards, rules, and regulations issued under the act.
- Familiarize yourself and employees with mandatory OSHA standards and make copies available to employees for review upon request.
- Examine workplace conditions to ensure they conform to applicable standards.
- Minimize or reduce safety and health hazards.
- Ensure that employees have and use safe tools and equipment (including appropriate personal protective equipment) and that such equipment is properly maintained.
- Employ color codes, posters, labels, or signs in several languages to warn employees of potential hazards.
- Establish or update operating procedures and communicate them so that employees follow safety and health requirements.
- Provide medical examinations when required by OSHA standards.
- Report to the nearest OSHA office within 48 hours of any fatal accident or one that results in the hospitalization of five or more employees.
- Keep OSHA-required records of work-related injuries and illnesses and post a copy of the totals from the last page of OSHA Form 300 during the entire month of February each year.
- Post, at a prominent location within the workplace, an OSHA poster informing employees of their rights and responsibilities.
- Provide employees, former employees, and their representatives access to the Log and Summary of Occupational Injuries and Illnesses (OSHA Form 300) at a reasonable time and in a reasonable manner.
- Cooperate with the OSHA compliance officer by furnishing names of authorized employee representatives who may be asked to accompany the compliance officer during an inspection.
- Refrain from discriminating against employees who properly exercise their rights under the act.

- Post OSHA citations at or near the work site involved. Each citation, or citation copy thereof, must remain posted until the violation has been abated or for three working days, whichever is longer.

Although OSHA does not cite employees for violations of their responsibilities, each employee "shall comply with all occupational safety and health standards and rules, regulations, and orders issued under the act" that are applicable.

Employee Rights under OSHA

Employees have a right to seek a safe workplace without fear of punishment. That right is spelled out in Section 11(c) of the act. All employees are covered except workers who are self-employed and public employees in state and local government.

The law says employers shall not punish or discriminate against workers for exercising the following rights:

- Complaining to an employer, union, OSHA, or any other government agency about job safety and health hazards.
- Filing safety or health grievances.
- Participating on a workplace safety and health committee or in union activities concerning job safety and health.
- Participating in OSHA inspections, conferences, hearings, or other OSHA-related activities.

If an employee is exercising these or other OSHA rights, the employer is not allowed to discriminate against that worker in any way, such as through firing, demotion, transferring the worker to an undesirable job or shift, or threatening or harassing the worker.

In *Whirlpool v. Marshall,* the Supreme Court ruled in 1981 that although there is no specific language in the law about walking off a job, employees who have a reasonable apprehension of death or serious injury may refuse to work until that safety hazard is corrected. The employer may not discipline or discharge a worker who exercises this right, although the employer is not required to pay the worker for the hours not worked.[22]

Workers believing they have been punished for exercising safety and health rights must contact the nearest OSHA office within 30 days of the time they learn of the alleged discrimination. A union representative can file the complaint for the worker. The worker does not have to complete any form. Any OSHA staff member will complete the forms after asking what happened and who was involved.

Following a complaint, OSHA investigates the organization. If an employee has been illegally punished for exercising safety and health rights, OSHA asks the employer to restore that worker's job earnings and benefits. If necessary, and if it can prove discrimination, OSHA takes the employer to court. In such cases, the worker does not pay any legal fees. If a state agency has an OSHA-approved state program, employees may file their complaint with either federal OSHA or the state agency under its laws.

Employees also have these additional rights under OSHA:

- Review copies of appropriate OSHA standards, rules, regulations, and requirements that the employer should have available at the workplace.
- Request information from your employer on safety and health hazards in the area, on precautions that may be taken, and on procedures to be followed if an employee is involved in an accident or is exposed to toxic substances.
- Request the OSHA area director to conduct an inspection if you believe hazardous conditions or violations of standards exist in your workplace.
- Have your name withheld from your employer, upon request to OSHA, if you file a written and signed complaint.
- Learn about OSHA actions regarding your complaint and have an informal review, if requested, of any decision not to inspect or to issue a citation.
- Have your authorized employee representative accompany the OSHA compliance officer during the inspection tour.
- Respond to questions from the OSHA compliance officer, particularly if there is no authorized employee representative accompanying the compliance officer.
- Observe any monitoring or measuring of hazardous materials and have the right to see these records, as specified under the act.
- Have your authorized representative, or yourself, review the Log and Summary of Occupational Injuries (OSHA Form 300) at a reasonable time and in a reasonable manner.
- Request a closing discussion with the compliance officer following an inspection.
- Submit a written request to the National Institute for Occupational Safety and Health (NIOSH) for information on whether any substance in your workplace has potentially toxic effects in the concentration being used, and have your name withheld from your employer, if you so request.
- Receive notification from your employer if he or she applies for a variance from an OSHA standard, testify at a variance hearing, and appeal the final decision.
- Submit information or comment to OSHA on the issuance, modification, or revocation of OSHA standards and request a public hearing.

The Effects of OSHA

OSHA has had a profound impact on employer actions regarding health and safety issues. The establishment of formal safety committees, improved equipment and machinery, improved medical facilities and staff, and, in general, greater emphasis on safety and prevention are among the major changes that are the direct result of OSHA.

OSHA has been used as the "poster child" for excessive governmental regulation since Ronald Reagan attacked the agency when he ran for president. Republicans in particular who attack "big government" argue that OSHA regulations seriously hinder productivity and increase costs. Critics argue that OSHA is often meddling in areas where there is enough protection for workers at the state level through workers' compensation and by companies on their own because it's in their best interest to keep workers safe and healthy. The classic cartoon in Figure 14-5 illustrates this anti-OSHA attitude. Says ABC network's John Stossel, OSHA is made up of "a bunch of clueless busybodies trying to micromanage everybody's life." James Knott, owner of a Massachusetts manufacturing facility, is not a big fan of OSHA. He says OSHA has never been helpful about anything. "They send their inspectors around who invent complaints and then they would like you to pay them money; they're extortionists."[23] But what most critics of OSHA ignore is that while OSHA and its inspectors have made mistakes along the way in issuing regulations and citations, companies have appeal processes. For example, Mr. Knott had particular problems regarding an OSHA inspector's recommendation under the "General Duty Clause" that he extend the height of a fence. Mr. Knott could have appealed this recommendation to the Occupational Safety and Health Review Commission (OSHRC) or requested a variance to an OSHA regulation or standard. If Mr. Knott lost at the OSHRC level, he could also contest the citation to the U.S. Court of Appeals. There are many options for organizations against OSHA "complaint inventions" and the arbitrary imposition of any provision of the law.

It is very difficult to evaluate the effects of OSHA using data on injuries, accidents and fatalities. We mentioned the changes to the reporting rules for injuries in 2002. These new definitions of course resulted in changes in occupational injury and illness statistics provided by the Bureau of Labor Statistics. Using the new definitions, the BLS reported that there were 4.7 million nonfatal injuries and illnesses in private-industry workplaces in 2002, resulting in a rate of 5.3 cases per 100 equivalent full-time workers. While these data follow the trend of declining cases and rates seen throughout the past decade, because of the change in definition they cannot be compared with data from prior years.

Some may also cite the decline in construction injuries as an illustration of OSHA's positive effects. Workers' compensation claims dropped more than 15 percent

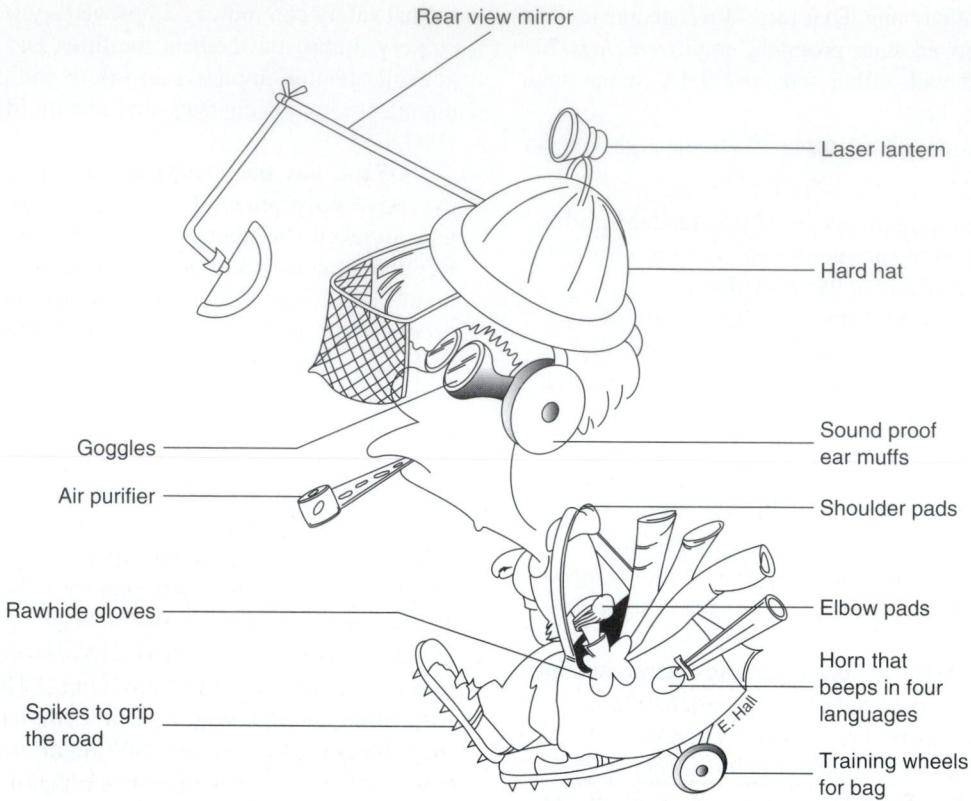

Figure 14-5   Newspaper Carrier after OSHA
Source: Copyright © 2006 by E. Hall. Reprinted with permission.

in 2004 and 2005. (See Figure 14-6.) Construction is a high priority industry for OSHA because of their reported injury rate. OSHA did do more inspections in this industry than any other in those same two years. There's another possible explanation for the decline in reported injuries. Fewer injuries may be reported. Why would that be? Down in Florida after five hurricanes in 2004, roofers were in high demand. As one contractor put it, "I couldn't staff my jobs without illegal immigrants; and I probably couldn't get any bids given what my competition is up to." Illegal immigrants who fall off the roof tend not to make workers' compensation claims. Their bosses tend not to submit the injury data to OSHA. Statistics always need to be interpreted in context!

OSHA also has come under fire from safety experts for trivial fines—at times, only in the hundreds of dollars. Two months before the horrendous Phillips Petroleum explosion in 1989, OSHA neglected to conduct a complete inspection of the plant after an accident killed one worker. OSHA does have some power to ask the Justice Department to prosecute employers who intentionally or negligently injure their employees, but critics of OSHA have maintained that state prosecutions are necessary because few employers have been charged under federal law. Fines for violations that led to a fatality are quite small. For example, in one state, less than 20 percent of fines for death-related citations exceeded $10,000.

Subsequent to September 11, 2001, OSHA devoted considerable (and valuable) resources to the World Trade Center site. As a result and with no additional funding, many of their other activities were reduced in scope and magnitude. While OSHA under President Clinton had renewed, and some say misguided, vigor, OSHA under President George W. Bush has had more limited goals and claimed accomplishments. While enforcement and fines increased under President Clinton, there were fewer inspections and fines under Bush.[24]

OSHA can use its subpoena powers to have employees testify under oath about safety violations. Business executives can face jail terms for their behavior and policies regarding the health and safety of their workers. State Supreme Courts in New York, Illinois, and Michigan have already ruled that employers can face criminal charges and prison. The renewed zeal has created a fearful perspective among employers. As one expert put it, "For the first time, the cost of ignoring OSHA has become greater than the cost of complying."[25] Initiatives such as special emphasis programs on silica and nursing homes have enabled OSHA to do a better job of getting to the most hazardous workplaces.[26]

The key question, however, is whether having OSHA in place has reduced workplace deaths, accidents, or injuries. The data regarding fatalities are clear, but the extent to which the OSHA laws and regulations are related

Although construction is one of the most dangerous industries to work, the number of workers' compensation claims has dropped more than 15 percent in the past two years.

Workers' compensation petitions

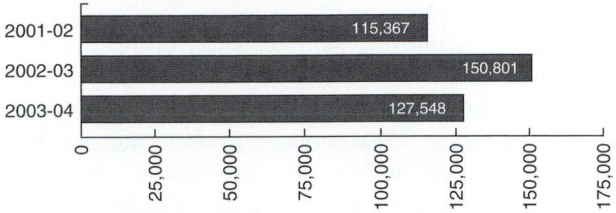

2001-02	115,367
2002-03	150,801
2003-04	127,548

NONFATAL INJURIES

Of the 4.1 million nonfatal injuries in the workplace in 2003, construction ranks fourth in occupational injuries.

FATAL INJURIES

In 2003, construction had the most fatalities with 1,126, but still ranked only fourth among industry fatality rates.

Workplace injuries, by industry
Ranked by percent

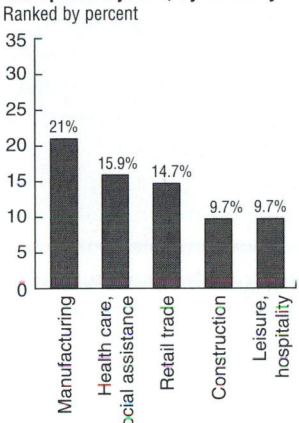

Top five industry fatality rates
Per 100,000 employees

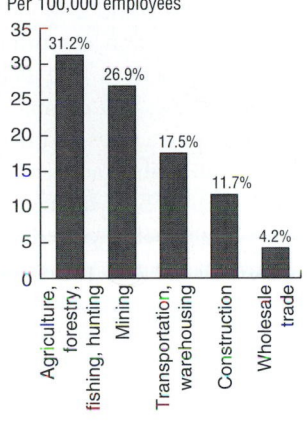

Figure 14-6   Construction Injuries
Sources: Bureau of Labor Statistics, Office of the Judges of Compensation

to these findings is not clear. Workplace deaths went from 21 per 100,000 in 1912 to only 4 per 100,000 in 2004.[27] However, while this trend has been steady, the same trend line of reduced fatalities existed even before OSHA was passed in 1970. There has been a decrease in the rate of injuries and illnesses involving lost work days from 1984 to 2004. But there has been an increase in total injuries and illnesses since 1984, mainly due to reports of RSI.[28] Nearly two-thirds of all workplace injuries are some form of RSI with over 350,000 cases reported in 2004.

Another criticism of OSHA is that its focus is almost exclusively on unsafe working conditions and managerial responsibility; however, virtually no attention is given to employee behavior and responsibility. Because of this lack of attention, most experts agree that the impact of OSHA on accident rates will be moderate. Experts generally agree that more attention must be paid to behaviors and attitudes.[29] GM, for example, reported that in 1976 it was spending $15 per car to comply with OSHA regulations, but there had been no positive impact on accident rates as a function of the regulations. GM claimed that many accidents were a consequence of improper behavior by employees.[30] Other experts maintain that the long-term

impact of OSHA will be overwhelmingly positive because of the increased knowledge of hazardous substances discovered through OSHA activities. For example, critical information about a great number of carcinogens such as PCBs, cotton dust, asbestos, and vinyl chloride can be directly linked to OSHA research. The banning of asbestos in 1989 would probably not have occurred had it not been for OSHA research.

The right-to-know provisions of OSHA also should have a positive impact on company health and safety records. These provisions specify the employees' right to know if they are working with unsafe substances, how to work with them safely, and how to administer first aid if workers come in contact with toxic chemicals. These provisions also require that a "material safety data sheet" be provided with each chemical used. This form provides all necessary information about the substance, what precautions to take, and how to treat any injury associated with its use.

Unions take a much more positive position on the effects of OSHA and have been at the forefront in advocating many of the preventative provisions of OSHA. For example, over 20,000 workers are trained annually in the recognition and control of work hazards. Still, unions favor more aggressive enforcement that is more uniform across the country and a faster process for the development of new standards. Unions have worked very hard on behalf of its members to control RSI.[31]

PROGRAMS TO REDUCE ACCIDENTS AT WORK

Organizations have tried a variety of strategies directed at reducing or eliminating unsafe behaviors at work. These programs can be classified into four general areas: personnel selection, employee training, incentive programs, and safety rules and regulations. Health and safety guru E. Scott Geller has 50 key principles to a total safety culture, a subset of which is presented in Figure 14-7. All four general areas are covered by these principles.[32] Views by top management toward safety are very important and vary across cultures. In general, plants are safer in the United States, Japan, and the European Union.[33] The Worker Rights Consortium, a student "watchdog" group that evaluates working conditions at facilities all over the world, evaluates non-U.S. manufacturing facilities using OSHA standards and regulations. Good communication is vital to successful safety and health programs and to business in general. Employee participation and involvement in safety issues and programs are critical for successful programs.[34] In addition, research has shown that management's demonstration of concern after an employee's injury creates a "halo effect" that can aid the worker's recovery and speed return to work. Also, workers who experienced the halo effect expressed more

FIGURE 14-7	Some Key Principles of a Total Safety Culture

1. Safety should be internally, not externally, driven.

2. Culture changes require people to understand the principles and how to use them.

3. A total safety culture requires continuous attention to factors in three domains: environment, behavior, and person.

4. Don't count on common sense for safety improvement.

5. Safety incentive programs should focus on process rather than outcomes.

6. People view behavior as correct to the degree they see others doing it.

7. On-the-job observation and interpersonal feedback are key to total safety culture.

8. Behavior is directed by activators and motivated by consequences.

9. People compensate for increases in perceived safety by taking more risks.

10. Stressors lead to positive stress or negative distress, depending on appraisal of personal control.

11. When people feel empowered, their safe behavior spreads to other situations.

12. Numbers from program evaluations should be meaningful to all participants.

Source: Adapted from Geller, E. S. (1996). *Working Safe: How to Help People Actively Care for Health and Safety*. Radnor, PA: Chilton Book Company. (Dr. Geller has 50 principles.)

satisfaction with their treatment from the firm and were less likely to seek a lawyer.[35]

With the growth of at-home workers, OSHA took an interest in health and safety conditions in the home, but this interest passed with the change in administration in 2000. The 1992 Management of Health and Safety at Work Regulations require that employers carry out a risk assessment of home workers.[36]

One excellent new study focused on high-performance work systems (HPWS) and applied the "commitment" and "high involvement" principles of HPWS to improving workplace safety.[37] They argue that safety should be considered a performance variable much like production, profits, sales, quality control, or customer complaints. They found strong support for the hypothesis that a high-performance work system will improve workplace safety by increasing employee trust in management and perceived safety climate. A company achieves this level through selective hiring, extensive training, and team-based structures and decision making. Specifically, they found individual safety knowledge, safety motivation, safety compliance, and safety initiatives were all related to safety incidents (i.e., injuries requiring first-aid and near misses). The research confirmed the importance of organizational factors in ensuring worker safety.

Selective Hiring

Selective hiring focuses on the fit between employees and their work environment. This is achieved through the "selective exclusion" of high-risk employees. High-risk applicants are defined as those who have histories of drug addiction or alcoholism, and those with low levels of emotional maturity and trustworthiness. Researchers in this area argue, "Organizations committed to occupational safety will attend closely to how they hire new personnel and will incorporate the value of occupational safety into their employee-selection processes to achieve a better fit." They also called for the use of work teams in the selection of future members which could also improve safety levels—"requiring applicants to go through several rounds of interviews in which the organization's values are conveyed could also enhance occupational safety."[38] Although research examining the relationship between selection practices and occupational safety is sparse, research shows that companies with more safety-focused selection procedures had lower injury rates.

We describe "accident-prone" people as those who inadvertently hurt themselves or destroy something at work. Is it possible to predict accident proneness? If so, we might change our personnel decisions to select those people who are less likely to be in accidents. Organizations such as Domino's Pizza, Greyhound, and every police department in the nation would love to be able to avoid employing individuals with a knack for traffic mishaps. Unfortunately, while there have been numerous attempts to identify careless, accident-prone people, the evidence really boils down to three general findings: (1) older employees are safer than younger ones (regardless of job tenure); (2) physical characteristics, such as hearing and vision, are related to accident rates when they are critical aspects of a job; and (3) a record of accidents or driving citations does predict similar activity in the future. Chapter 6 described some tests that have potential for the prediction and prevention of employee accidents. Related tests should identify applicants who don't use drugs and are honest, value-driven, customer-oriented, respectful, and responsive to authority—in short, "safe" employees. More research is needed in this area.

Safety Training

In some organizations, there exist only informal safety training procedures. In these situations, a new employee may be given a brief orientation to company policy including safety issues; spend a day or two with a supervisor or lead person; and is then expected to work safely. Research indicates that a formal system of safety training is much more effective. In addition, because safety programs are so costly, it is important to be able to show that the programs save the firm money.

Research clearly shows that workers who receive more safety training suffer fewer work-related injuries than others. The most effective training "allows employees to acquire greater competencies to control their work, leading them to perform their jobs more safely. To be maximally effective, training must extend beyond the mere provision of knowledge related to how to do one's job safely. Employees must also be empowered to use new skills following training."[39]

Companies that place more emphasis on worker safety have seen benefits from their actions. One study found that climate perceptions in the form of supervisory safety practices significantly predicted injuries requiring medical attention.[40] When managers pay more attention to safety issues and reward employees for safety-related behaviors, accidents are reduced. Another study suggests that interactive approaches to training may be the best way to get employees to really understand safety issues. At TrueTime Inc., the safety staff gives a brief review of the company's safety procedures to the employees each year at the company meeting. Each employee is then given a custom, randomly generated quiz. Employees have to seek answers to the questions by checking source materials and glossaries, studying the policies, and examining reports. This encourages employees to take an active learning approach to learning about the firm's safety procedures.

OSHA has issued "voluntary training guidelines" for employers that provide a framework for the development, administration, and evaluation of training programs. These guidelines are especially helpful for organizations that have no expertise in formal training development and evaluation. One study supported the use of accident simulations as a training method.[41] In addition, providing training sessions in several languages increases the chance of compliance by the millions of workers for whom English is a second language. The message on safe work practices and job hazards needs to get through to everyone.

OSHA standard requires training for employees who operate powered industrial trucks. The training rule covers nearly 1.2 million employees who drive trucks in general industry and for maritime employers. There are over 800,000 powered industrial trucks operating in the workplace. As of 2003, statistics indicate that about 500 workers are killed each year in incidents related to industrial truck operations and nearly 47,000 suffer injuries that result in lost workdays. Approximately 20 to 25 percent of those incidents are partly due to inadequate training. The cost for employers to comply with the rule is estimated to be approximately $35 million in the first year and $20 million annually each year thereafter. Compliance will ultimately save employers between $8 million and $42 million annually in property damage and $770,000 paid as a result of lawsuits involving workers injured in forklift accidents that could be attributed to deficiencies in training.[42]

Training programs are typical in industries with serious accident problems. For example, the construction industry employs only 5 percent of the workforce yet has the highest lost-time injury rate of any major industry (it accounts for 20 percent of all occupational fatalities). As a result, some contractors include the cost of supplying safety equipment and employee training in their bids.[43] Training programs also exist in public safety arenas. For example, in the restaurant industry, training is used to educate restaurant employees about food illnesses. This is critical because as many as 9,000 people die annually in the United States and an estimated nine million become sick from illnesses transmitted by restaurant food.[44]

Most training programs generally focus on hazards at work, safety rules and regulations, and safe and unsafe work behaviors. For example, one study describes a bakery that developed a detailed behavior observation code of safe and unsafe behaviors.[45] Participants in the safety program were then shown slides of the unsafe and safe behaviors. Goals were set for increasing the percentage of safe behaviors, and a feedback chart was set up for monitoring group performance. Supervisors also were trained in giving positive reinforcement for safe work behaviors. The training and monitoring increased the percentage of safe behaviors more than 20 percent.

Today, when developing training programs, human resource professionals should recognize the aging of the workforce and be sure that training addresses changes in workers' strength, size, flexibility, and stamina. The National Institute on Aging's Gerontology Research Center recommends that employers use routine medical checkups to determine employee health initially and then track positive or negative changes in work ability.[46] Training should be adjusted to fit the needs of the aging workforce. In addition, with the increasing numbers of corporate downsizings, it is important to be sure that a core set of employees (who will be with the company for some time) are trained in safety procedures. In high-turnover facilities, long-term training for all employees is impractical. However, it is possible to find long-term employees who are interested in worker safety and health. These employees can be the core group who are able to train new employees as they enter the organization.[47]

Many manufacturers use a peer review process to improve safety records. The objective is to shape behavior with immediate and constant feedback and positive reinforcement. At Alcoa, all workers must submit safety suggestions and are rewarded for good ones. Production-line workers can stop the line at any time if they spot a safety problem. Other companies employ industrial psychologists and engineers to study the worker–machine interface. At DuPont Corporation, engineers observe workers and then redesign valves and install key locks to reduce accidents. At Monsanto's Pensacola, Florida, plant, psychologists used the critical incident technique (CIT) of job analysis. Experts drew "cause trees" to identify the root causes of the less-than-obvious problems. If a worker slipped on oil, for example, the root cause was not oil but the failure of maintenance to attend to an oil leak. A safety scorecard also was prepared, and workers reviewed processes to check for "shortcuts and deviations," which ultimately predict trouble. Safe workers win recognition at weekly safety meetings, and free lunches and promotions have been tied to safety records. As a result of this comprehensive approach to safety, Monsanto's record improved from 6.5 to 1.6 lost-time injuries per hundred workers in the five years of the program.

Safety training is important not only for employees, but also for supervisors. Workplace health and safety efforts cannot succeed without the support and efforts of supervisors. In general, supervisors must know (1) about any hazards in their area of supervision and any hazards that may affect their subordinates when traveling outside their area of supervision; (2) what safety procedures and devices are needed to safely carry out the jobs in their departments; (3) about safety rules, policies, procedures, and programs that have been developed; and (4) what is required under all applicable occupational health and safety legislation.[48] Supervisors also should be aware of safety rules associated with contractors. For example, companies that hire contractors who fall short on safety procedures may find themselves jointly liable when workers are injured. A key factor in determining contractor status and employer liability is who supervises outside employees working under a specific contract. Management should assume that the company could have some liability for anything that occurs on the property. Thus, a firm would be wise to make a contractor's health and safety record a factor in the selection process when contractors are hired.[49]

Teamwork, Supervision, and Decentralized Decision Making

Teamwork and decentralized decision making should benefit employee performance and safety performance by fostering higher group cohesion. The quality of supervisor–employee relationships, as well as cohesion with the work group are the best predictors of the tendency to comply with safety rules. Working in teams also causes workers to feel more responsible for their own and each other's safety. One study found that a sense of belongingness to a group and personal control was related to the propensity to actively care for co-worker safety. Teamwork and decentralized decision making should also provide workers who are more familiar with the work situation greater opportunities for control. Research in chemical plants and with manufacturing teams support this view. It is also argued that teams should enhance occupational safety when they promote the sharing of ideas that result in better solutions. Flight crews performed more effectively as groups in dangerous situations than when they were formed in a hierarchical structure with the captain at the top of the chain of command.

Incentive Systems

Today, safety incentives are a hotly competitive and growing segment of the highly profitable corporate incentive industry. Even small incentives can change employees' attitudes.[50] As discussed in Chapter 11, many employers use safety contests where company units compete with one another for cash or prizes. Other contests are set up so that each unit competes with its own safety record. If a lower number of accidents occur over a period of time, an award is given. At DuPont, directors give safety awards and workers win cash prizes if their units remain accident-free for six months. These prizes are only one part of their safety philosophy. As part of an overall safety management that focuses on injury prevention and a goal of zero accidents and injuries, DuPont has used many forms of recognition to increase awareness of safety excellence.[51] At Kodak, volunteer observers take turns supervising peers and providing token awards (e.g., free soft drinks). Summer construction workers at Colorado State University started driving more safely when the city began offering the incentive of small coolers for carrying meals.[52] At Hunter Industries, a sprinkler manufacturer, the safety and health coordinator created a three-level safety incentive program. Level one involves mandatory safety activities; level two includes wellness and self-enrichment activities; and level three includes community involvement. Based on the program, the company has met total regulatory compliance for the past three years and has reported improved work habits and cost savings.[53]

There has been little systematic research on incentive systems for accident reduction. Some research, however, suggests that safety programs help offset the high cost of health insurance benefits, workers' compensation claims, and lost-time injuries.[54] Bulova Corporation of Woodside, New York, has a guide for setting up a successful safety incentive program.[55]

When awards are substantial, failure to report accidents is a possibility. For example, offering safety prizes of significant worth (e.g., new car, tropical vacation) may provide employees with an incentive not to report injuries.[56] To decrease occupational accidents, safety programs must be run and promoted effectively. First, it is necessary to determine what types of behaviors are to be controlled. Next, the human resource professional must prioritize the behaviors and then develop a plan and the appropriate rewards. For example, one common program used by many firms is safety bingo. Monthly drawings and quarterly drawings are also popular, as are special contests.[57]

Safety Rules

Most companies now publish employee handbooks with formal rules and regulations that stipulate what employees can and cannot do in the workplace. Unfortunately, many of these rules and regulations are too general to be effective. The most effective employee safety handbooks are those that carefully describe the steps to be taken on the job to ensure maximum safety. For each step, potential dangers are identified to alert the worker. In addition to specificity in the rules, it is also critical to get workers to read and comprehend safety handbooks. Some companies require that employees pass a test about safety-related issues before they begin work.

No matter how thorough the training, safety rules will be meaningless if they are not enforced. There are, unfortunately, numerous cases where a worker ignored a safety rule and was injured, or when a supervisor ordered workers to ignore a safety rule. Consistent enforcement of safety rules, with discipline for infractions, will benefit management in several ways. First, it will send a clear message to employees that the company takes safety seriously. Second, it should reduce injuries. Third, a company may be able to avoid an OSHA citation if it can demonstrate that it complied with relevant OSHA standards (or the general duty clause), that it trained its workers properly, and that the injury was the result of a worker's intentional refusal to adhere to work rules. Documentation of consistent discipline for work rule violations would be necessary for a company to avoid OSHA liability. Safety committees comprised of management and nonmanagement employees can be used to enforce safety rules. Committee members can identify safety hazards and devise solutions to safety problems. In addition, they can organize safety training courses or workshops to increase employees' awareness of safety issues.

CONTEMPORARY ISSUES RELATED TO HEALTH AND SAFETY

AIDS and the Workplace

As human immunodeficiency virus (HIV) and acquired immune deficiency syndrome (AIDS) continue to plague millions of Americans, numerous organizations are becoming more vulnerable to the tremendous loss exposure associated with the increasing presence of these diseases in the workplace.[58] According to the Centers for Disease Control (CDC), two or three employees in all U.S. companies with a workforce of at least 300 people suffer from AIDS or have dependents, spouses, significant others, or friends with the disease. AIDS is now one of the leading causes of death for people between the ages of 25 and 44, with the majority of the U.S. workforce in this age group. The CDC reported that over 18,000 Americans died of the disease in 2003. The virus has spread to over 40 million people worldwide, with most of those people in their prime working years. AIDS has become a critical health care issue for employers and employees alike, with corporations incurring increasing costs related to the growing number of AIDS cases. Overall, AIDS-related

corporate expenses include the patient's health insurance, disability benefits, employee life insurance, and pension costs. They also include the costs of hiring and training replacements and the costs of any lawsuits. The cumulative costs of treating AIDS exceeded $15 billion in 2000. The estimated losses in productivity were over $65 billion.

AIDS victims are now protected by a variety of state and local laws that prohibit discrimination against disabled people. As discussed in Chapter 3, AIDS has typically been defined as a legal disability under the Rehabilitation Act of 1973, which prohibits discrimination against the disabled by federal contractors, and is covered by the 1990 Americans with Disabilities Act (ADA). The ADA protects the jobs of people with AIDS-related disabilities and helps keep them in the workforce. Few jobs exist where having HIV or AIDS prohibits an employee from performing essential job functions. However, should such a situation occur, employers must make reasonable accommodations for the employee under the ADA (e.g., equipment changes, workstation modifications, flexible work schedules). With appropriate and reasonable accommodations, there is no reason people with HIV and AIDS cannot continue to work for many years.

Businesses must be careful to abide by the ADA when hiring. They cannot ask job candidates about their HIV or AIDS status, nor can they require HIV testing on a preemployment or pre-offer basis. Upon the extension of an offer, however, employers may require an HIV test or pose questions concerning the prospective employee's HIV status, as long as all applicants in a particular job category are treated similarly. Of course, test results must be treated confidentially. A positive HIV test result cannot prompt a job revocation unless the employer can demonstrate that the individual poses a direct health threat to coworkers or customers that cannot be eliminated through reasonable accommodations. Such arguments are extremely difficult to make and customer or potential coworker preference data cannot be used to justify such a position. Overall, management should be very familiar with the organization's AIDS policy and training should be provided to ensure that all employees understand the policy and its implications. OSHA has excellent guidelines on its website for formulating a policy and training personnel.

Managers and human resource professionals should understand the legal implications of HIV and AIDS in the workplace because many claims of AIDS-related discrimination cases have been filed. In a typical case, the Florida Commission of Human Relations ruled that a teacher who was fired because he had AIDS was a victim of disability discrimination. The teacher was awarded almost $200,000. Another example was when an HIV-positive physician sued Philadelphia's Mercy Health Corporation for discrimination when he was barred from performing invasive medical procedures unless his patients signed a consent form that disclosed his HIV status. The doctor sued (and won) under Section I of the ADA, which prohibits discrimination in employment, and Section III, which prohibits public facilities from discriminating against people with disabilities.

In July 1992, OSHA passed its Bloodborne Pathogen Standards, which state that all workplaces with employees that could be "reasonably anticipated" to contact blood or body fluids must comply. Under these guidelines, OSHA takes the position that there is no such thing as a risk-free population. According to these OSHA standards, employers must write an "exposure control plan," which details the procedure for identifying individuals at risk and how the organization will comply with the standards; "universal precautions," which detail how blood and body fluids are handled; and "cleaning protocols," which detail the location of cleaning supplies and the handling of cleaning wastes. Furthermore, employers must provide "personal protective equipment" such as gloves, masks, mouth guards, and smocks for workers who might come in contact with blood and other bodily fluids; "communicate the presence of hazards," which places warning labels and signs for restricted areas; educate and train employees of OSHA standards; and keep records as evidence that companies are complying. Employers who violate the regulations are subject to OSHA penalties.

OSHA mandates that businesses have a comprehensive HIV/AIDS policy and communicate the plan throughout the workplace. One survey found that only one-third of large and mid-size companies have formal HIV/AIDS policies.[59] The CDC AIDS Clearinghouse provides businesses with information on policy formation, employee education, manager and supervisor training, volunteerism, and family education in a kit titled "Business Response to AIDS." This kit helps companies develop specific policies and programs to deal with AIDS-related work issues. Most major companies take the position that AIDS-afflicted employees should be treated the same as other employees as long as they can perform their jobs. The Bank of America allows coworkers to transfer from departments where there are AIDS victims, but there has not been a single request to date. This is undoubtedly because the bank has provided a great deal of information about the disease to its employees and about the very low risk of transmission in the workplace. Through 2000, the CDC has not found a single case of AIDS transmission based on casual contact at work. The CDC believes that AIDS-afflicted employees do not have to be isolated or restricted from any work area, although there is much debate about possible restrictions in hospitals, food service, and dental settings. Caution is suggested for health care workers and patients or clients who may be exposed to blood, mucous membranes, or lesions.

Levi Strauss and IBM have been at the forefront in the development of a comprehensive AIDS-awareness program. The educational component of the Levi Strauss program includes informative brochures, a manager's guide to treating AIDS-afflicted employees, a policy manual, and a guidebook for policy makers. The company also provides an opportunity for employees to meet with medical professionals to discuss HIV/AIDS issues in more detail.[60] Since the enactment of the program, Levi Strauss has not incurred any lawsuits, employees refusing to work with AIDS-afflicted employees, or requests for reassignment. The IBM policy is to encourage AIDS-afflicted employees to work as long as they are capable and to ensure their privacy.

Drugs in the Workplace

It is not necessary to remind students that the abuse of controlled substances is a serious social problem—one that plagues employers as well as law enforcement agencies. The Substance Abuse and Mental Health Services Administration estimated that drug abuse costs U.S. businesses $102 billion annually in lost productivity, accidents, absenteeism, turnover, medical claims, and thefts.[61] Other reported consequences of drug abuse include increased on-the-job violence, workforce irritability, fistfights, and job mistakes. Employees using drugs are 3.6 times more likely to be involved in on-the-job accidents than other employees, and more liability insurance–covered accidents are caused by drug-impaired employees. This may be because today's drug users are relying more on amphetamines (e.g., crystal methedrine), which accelerates their systems, turning them from "recreational users" into "volatile abusers." Previously, employees had relied more on depressants such as alcohol and marijuana.[62] Of course, alcohol abuse still leads to a number of workplace symptoms including unexcused and frequent absences, tardiness and early departures, fights with employees, on-the-job accidents, and poor judgments.

As discussed in Chapter 6, many companies have responded to the drug crisis with a drug testing program. In one such company, personal injuries reportedly dropped from 15.5 per year before random urine testing to 5.8 per year five years after initiating the program. **The Drug Free Workplace Act of 1988** requires federal contractors to provide a drug-free workplace. Under the law, employers must educate employees about the risks of drug use and establish penalties for substance abuse. Furthermore, organizations must have specific policies on substance abuse, establish awareness programs, and notify employees and applicants that a drug-free state is a condition of employment. In response, U.S. companies have increasingly turned to drug testing both as a screening device for job applicants and as a means of evaluating current employees.

An American Management Association (AMA) survey found that 78 percent of all companies test at least some employees and applicants for drug abuse.[63] The firms that participated in the survey stated the rise in drug testing was due to the following factors:

- Department of Transportation (DOT) and Department of Defense (DoD) regulations that, with local and state legislation, mandated testing in certain job categories.
- The practical effects of the Drug Free Workplace Act of 1988.
- Court decisions that recognize an employer's right to test both employees and job applicants in the private sector.
- Action by insurance carriers to reduce accident liability and control health costs.
- Corporate requirements that vendors and contractors certify that theirs is a drug-free workplace.

According to the AMA survey, over 70 percent of companies conduct random drug testing of current employees. Motorola, for example, recently ordered all of its U.S. employees to undergo random drug testing at least once every three years, with more frequent testing for employees with positive test results. A Kansas City manufacturer of food processing equipment used a private undercover drug agent to monitor drug use. In a drug "sweep," she found that two dozen workers were either using or dealing drugs. The icing on the cake was the internal theft of a $16,000 piece of equipment. The agent found that an employee had sold it for $800 to buy drugs. Investigators are doing the same thing at a number of other companies that are suffering financial and behavioral consequences from employee drug abuse.[64]

Before a company initiates drug testing, the following questions should be addressed: Why do we want this program? Do we have a problem with drugs in our company? What will we do with the results of drug tests? Can our current discipline policy handle violations of this policy? How much will the program cost? Can we afford it? Will it affect morale? Should it be a punitive or rehabilitative program? Only after these questions are answered satisfactorily should a company consider implementing drug testing.

Some companies use five approaches to drug testing: preemployment screening, random testing of current employees, "reasonable cause" testing in response to performance problems, return-to-duty testing after drug treatment or suspension, and postaccident testing. Science makes it possible to ascertain if a person has ingested a controlled substance, and more and more companies are joining the ranks of those who at least test applicants for the presence of drugs. The AMA survey found that 77 percent of the companies that responded test all new hires for drugs in preemployment physical examinations. Surprisingly, workers are quite tolerant of testing. The aforementioned survey found 60 percent of those questioned supported random drug testing of current employees with no probable cause.[65]

Two questions that science has not yet been able to answer, however, are exactly how much of a controlled substance an individual must ingest to be impaired and just what impaired means. For example, most states have set a 0.10 percent blood alcohol level to establish impairment by alcohol; a similar standard does not exist for controlled substances. While some employers declare that a drug test result showing any amount of a controlled substance will be grounds for rejecting an applicant or discharging a worker, other employers have set some level as the threshold for an assumption that the employee is impaired. Computerized tests are now available to help employers determine whether workers in safety-related jobs are impaired. One test operates like a videogame and takes less than a minute to determine eye–hand coordination and reaction time. Old Town Trolley Tours of San Diego, California, uses the test to assess drivers.

Because of the lack of a standard for impairment, combined with the manner in which the presence of drugs is usually ascertained, many employment decisions made on the basis of positive drug test results have been legally challenged. The latest analysis indicates that urine is the most widely used specimen in the detection of drugs and offers about a 1–3 day window of detection. Hair analysis offers the largest window of detection (from 7 to 100+ days) while saliva analysis may be useful in determining very recent drug use (1–36 hours). Sweat analysis is another option that could be useful for the continuous monitoring of drug use (1–14 days). Drug testing has become a fast, convenient process with the development of point-of-collection drug testing devices.[66]

So does workplace drug testing reduce drug use? One recent large scale study says yes, it does. Drug testing programs are clearly achieving one of the desired effects: deterring drug use.[67]

Although there are no federal laws regulating drug testing, drug testing programs have been challenged using a number of legal theories. Private-sector employers generally have been able to successfully defend their drug testing programs in court, but there are a number of exceptions. In California, for example, the court ruled that Southern Pacific wrongfully fired a computer programmer when she refused to provide a random-test urine specimen. Another California court ruled that Kerr-McGee Chemical Corporation violated a worker's privacy by requiring her to submit to a drug test. However, other California decisions have supported drug testing. Lower courts in Michigan and Texas have sided with employers on random urinalysis, while a court in New Jersey found for the plaintiff. Utah is the only state that clearly permits drug testing of employees and applicants and authorizes firing employees who refuse to be tested. Maine explicitly allows testing for "probable cause," but limits random testing to safety-sensitive jobs.

Public employers are bound by the Fourth Amendment of the U.S. Constitution, which forbids "unreasonable" searches and seizures. However, even characterizing a urine test as either a search (of the urine) or a seizure (of body fluids) has not legally established that drug testing by public employers is unconstitutional. Supreme Court decisions now permit public employers to use drug testing for employees engaged in jobs where public safety is an issue, such as railroad engineers, U.S. Customs agents, and nuclear power plant workers. Private-sector employers, however, are not bound by the Fourth Amendment, and challenges must be based on contract claims or "public policy" grounds.

This does not mean, however, that a company should establish a drug testing program without concern for potential legal consequences. Unionized employers must bargain with the union about the procedures to be used, according to the National Labor Relations Board (NLRB). Nonunionized employers must consider that not all positive drug results indicate that the employee is presently impaired or has even ingested a controlled substance, as the ingestion of innocuous substances (poppy seeds, quinine water) may result in a positive test result. At a minimum, the company should make sure its program includes the following components:

- Notice to employees (or applicants) that drug testing will be conducted and the procedures to be used.
- An opportunity for the individual to disclose which prescription or over-the-counter drugs he or she is currently taking as well as other information that might skew the test results.
- A careful chain of custody to ensure that samples are not lost, mixed up, or switched.
- A dignified but secure method of collecting samples.
- Confirmation of all positive drug results with more sensitive tests.
- The opportunity for the individual to have the sample retested at his or her own expense.
- Confidentiality of test results.

In developing a drug testing policy, a company must determine what, if any, substances are permissible. For example, will a positive reading for marijuana be treated the same way as a positive reading for heroin? If testing is performed on current employees, will it be done only "for cause" (for example, after an accident or if a supervisor determines that an employee appears impaired) or randomly without cause?

Potential legal claims to drug testing in the public sector include Fourth Amendment challenges to the testing. This occurs if there was no reasonable cause to conclude that the employee had ingested controlled substances or if the drug testing represented a violation of the employee's constitutional due process rights. This may occur if the employee is discharged without being given an opportunity to challenge the test results. All employers may face charges of defamation (if test results become known to anyone but those who need the information); contract claims (for currently employed workers); and claims of discrimination against workers with disabilities (e.g., if the employee is a recovering drug abuser).

Human resource managers are well advised to consult with legal counsel before developing a drug testing program. Model programs that have withstood litigation are available, and an attorney can advise managers of any state laws that may affect the way the program is designed or administered.

Smoking in the Workplace

One of the most volatile issues for human resource professionals today is a company's position on smoking. Growing information about the adverse effects of second-hand smoke has led some people to call for a ban on smoking in the workplace. The U.S. Environmental Protection Agency reported that secondhand smoke causes 3,800 lung cancer deaths per year and classified it as a "class A" life-threatening carcinogen, a rating used only for substances (i.e., asbestos, radon, benzene) proven to cause cancer in humans. The Centers for Disease Control estimates that cigarette smoking costs the national economy at least $50 billion a year in direct medical expenses. This number does not include costs due to increased absenteeism or decreased productivity.[68] The costs of property fires ($500 million per year) and additional cleaning required because of smoking ($4 billion per year) are also significant. The American Heart Association reported that passive smoking is the third greatest preventable cause of death in the United States.

Nonsmoking employees can file workers' compensation and disability claims and legal suits against companies where smoking is not restricted. For example, the Wisconsin Labor and Industry Review Commission awarded an employee $23,400 in workers' compensation benefits because her eight-year exposure to secondhand smoke resulted in a permanent disability. The California Compensation Insurance Fund paid $85,000 in damages to an employee who suffered a heart attack from her exposure to smoke at work. In addition, a federal hearings examiner awarded a widower $21,500 a year for life to compensate for his wife's death due to lung cancer believed to be caused by her job as a Veterans Administration nurse on a hospital ward where heavy smoking was common.

The U.S. Environmental Protection Agency's "Guide to Workplace Smoking Policies" recommends that employers create ventilated smoking lounges to separate smokers from nonsmokers. A growing number have developed restrictive policies ranging from the use of designated smoking areas to banning smoking in the workplace to requiring nonsmoking as a condition of employment. One study found that smokers in a nonsmoking organization reduced the number of cigarettes smoked per work shift and decreased levels of nicotine and carbon monoxide. Thus, work-site smoking restrictions may promote meaningful reductions in tobacco exposure and consequent health risks.

Section 654(a) of OSHA states that the "general duty" of employers is to provide places of employment "free of recognized hazards that are causing or likely to cause death or serious physical harm to his/her employees." OSHA has never successfully developed regulations regarding indoor air quality that includes tobacco smoke. Yet, given that the surgeon general's report now documents the effects of sidestream smoke and the EPA places tobacco smoke in the top tier of known carcinogens, the OSHA obligation to take action seems obvious. While the approval of new federal laws is under review, many states and municipalities have enacted antismoking laws.[69] A New Jersey state law, for example, prohibits discrimination in hiring, pay, and working conditions against smokers "unless the employer has a rational basis for doing so." Unfortunately, it is now up to employers to determine what constitutes a "rational basis." Are higher health care costs a rational basis? The state of New York has one of the most sweeping laws regarding protections for nonsmokers. Employers must adopt and post a written policy on smoking that must include smoke-free work and eating areas.

Growing evidence that health care costs more for smokers than nonsmokers is prompting some companies to levy additional charges on smokers and offer incentives for quitting. Provident Indemnity Life Insurance Co. offers nonsmokers 33 percent discounts on health and life insurance. At Mahoning Culvert in Youngstown, Ohio, smokers who are attempting to quit contribute 50 cents a day to a pool that accumulates for one year. To that pool of $182.50, the company adds $817.50 to reward each smoker who manages to quit for a year. An additional $500 is given the second year. Other companies have drawings for prizes and other incentives to encourage employees to quit smoking. Some companies have taken the punitive route. Lutheran Health Systems, a Fargo, North Dakota, hospital and nursing home chain, charges smokers a 10 percent premium on their health insurance. U-Haul International deducts $5 every other week from the paychecks of smokers. Several fire departments have imposed deadlines by which smoking firefighters must quit or be terminated. Particularly in hazardous work environments where the risks of cancer are great (e.g., daily exposure to chemical fumes), companies are more likely to impose no-smoking rules. While insurance premiums and increased health care costs are major reasons for employers' move toward a smoke-free workplace, pressure by nonsmokers has also contributed to the development of formal no-smoking policies at many organizations. One survey found that 85 percent of organizations surveyed indicated they had prohibited or restricted workplace smoking.[70]

A seven-step plan has been proposed for the development of a smoking policy:[71]

1. Top management should make a commitment to the development of a smoking policy.
2. Pertinent state and local laws should be reviewed.
3. Unions should be involved (if applicable).
4. The smoking policy should be tailored to particular work situations or stations.
5. A committee of smokers and nonsmokers from a cross-section of the workforce should be formed.
6. The workforce should be surveyed to determine attitudes toward smoking and toward possible smoking policies.
7. A proposed policy should be circulated throughout the workplace. Enforcement of policy violations on a consistent basis will encourage employee compliance.

Violence in the Workplace

Violence had infiltrated all aspects of American life long before September 11, 2001. The workplace appears to be no safe haven from the threat or reality of violence, and research suggests that both the frequency and severity of work-related violence are increasing. Workplace violence, often perpetrated by disgruntled employees, has reached epidemic proportions. Estimates indicate that more than 1.9 million violent workplace crimes occur each year with half of these infractions caused by employees or former employees. About 10 percent of these violent workplace crimes involve offenders armed with handguns. An American Management Association survey of 311 organizations found that almost 25 percent indicated at least one employee had been attacked or killed on the job since 1990.[72] A Society for Human Resource Management (SHRM) survey found that of more than 1,000 employers, 48 percent had experienced at least one violent incident in the last year.[73]

Homicide is the second leading cause of fatal occupational injury in the United States and the leading cause of death. Homicides are surpassed only by motor vehicle crashes as a cause of job-related deaths.[74] In 2004, the number of work-related homicides increased from 2000. The statistics on extreme cases of workplace violence (e.g., murder, rape) are disturbing. The trend may get worse because now over 40 states have legalized the possession of concealed weapons.[75] Employers, however, can ban concealed weapons in the workplace. If they do, there should be a written policy that is communicated to all employees and is contained in an employee handbook or in the policies and procedures manual.

Employers have an obligation to protect workers from violence under the "general duty clause" of OSHA.

OSHA can (and has) issued citations for preventable violence in the workplace. In addition, a legal cause of action for negligent hiring or retention may be determined if the employer hires or retains an employee with a history of violence or who acts in a negligent manner. The European Commission's definition of workplace violence includes "incidents where persons are abused, threatened, or assaulted in circumstances relating to their work, involving an explicit challenge to their safety, well-being, or health." The Manufacturing, Science, and Finance Union has outlawed workplace bullying. According to the law, if an employer fails to adequately address a complaint from an employee about bullying, the employer could be subject to civil proceedings. In general, as awareness of the problem increases, employers are installing various security systems and training employees to avoid or diffuse incidents.[76]

Human resource professionals must be aware of the many forms of less severe violence (see Figure 14-8) that is occurring and must be taken seriously.[77] Although no method exists that can perfectly predict a violent employee, the growing number of workplace homicides has made it possible to construct a profile of the typical perpetrator (see Figure 14-9). While violent employees may not have all the profile characteristics, most have a majority of them.

OSHA issued the first federal guidelines regarding workplace violence on March 14, 1996. The guidelines, which are not mandatory, recommend that social service and health care employees carefully assess security issues that may result in workplace violence. About 66 percent of all those assaulted in the workplace are health care and social service employees. While OSHA's initial

---

FIGURE 14-9 **Violent Employee Profile**

PRIMARY CHARACTERISTICS

- White middle-aged male
- Holds a white- or blue-collar position, possibly as department head, manager, or supervisor
- History of violence towards others
- Abuses illicit drugs
- Weapon owner and/or served in the military
- Extremely withdrawn, a "loner"
- Few interests outside of work
- Constantly disgruntled, a "troublemaker"
- Perceives unfairness, injustice, or malice in others

SECONDARY CHARACTERISTICS

- Overreacts to corporate changes
- Suffers from interpersonal conflict
- Recently fired or laid off, or perceives soon will be
- Argumentative/uncooperative
- Extremist opinions and attitudes
- Makes sexual comments or threats of physical assault
- Disobeys company policies and procedures/has difficulty accepting authority
- May sabotage equipment and/or property
- Steals

Note: Most individuals prone to violence will possess a majority of these traits.

Source: S. M. Burroughs and J. W. Jones, "Managing Violence: Looking Out for Trouble," *Occupational Health and Safety,* April 1995, pp. 34–37.

---

guidelines focus on these industries, another set of guidelines is being prepared to protect workers in the night retail industry, which also is disproportionately victimized by violence. In general, OSHA's guidelines state that a workplace violence prevention program should include the elements of any good safety and health program, which are management commitment, employee involvement, work-site analysis, hazard prevention and control, and training and education.[78]

Consequences

It is clear that employee violence costs companies dearly. There is the immediate cost of human suffering, pain, and possibly the precious loss of life. The effect of workplace violence on traumatized employees, families of employees, and coworkers is difficult to put into exact financial terms. Beyond human losses, the organization itself becomes a victim of workplace violence. The National Safe Workplace Institute estimates that workplace violence costs employers approximately $4 billion a year.[79] Rising health care costs, higher workers' compensation fees, and increased legal expenditures are a few of the significant consequences. For example, in 1994, insurers paid $12 million to settle lawsuits by parents of four teenage girls who were murdered during a robbery

---

FIGURE 14-8 **Levels of Workplace Violence**

MODERATELY INJURIOUS

- Property damage, vandalism
- Sabotage
- Pushing, fistfights
- Major violations of company policy
- Frequent arguments with customers, co-workers, or supervisors
- Theft

HIGHLY INJURIOUS

- Physical attacks and assaults
- Psychological trauma
- Anger-related accidents
- Rape
- Arson
- Murder

Source: S. M. Burroughs and J. W. Jones, "Managing Violence: Looking Out for Trouble," *Occupational Health and Safety,* April 1995, pp. 34–37.

at an Austin, Texas, I Can't Believe It's Yogurt store where the girls worked. In the aftermath of a violent incident, the organization usually pays for medical and post-trauma stress treatments, lost wages due to increased absences, increased security and property damage, and investigations, which may include the use of outside experts such as management consultants. Another cost component is the loss of employee productivity. Revenue losses from disruption in work progress, turnover, and the diminished public image of the organization may result in reduced sales potential and lower stock value.

Violence Prevention Programs

Taking specific actions to prevent workplace violence can create a security-conscious organizational culture, thereby potentially reducing a company's exposure to violent employee crime. These prevention programs involve screening potential employees, communicating your company's commitment to nonviolence through policies and procedures, training and educating supervisors and workers, building a threat management team with the aid of employee assistance programs, and implementing security measures.

Preemployment Screening Human resource professionals can reduce the potential for violent incidents and negligent hiring claims by using comprehensive preemployment screening procedures. Such procedures can usually detect service-oriented employees with strong interpersonal skills, as opposed to excessively violent and aggressive workers. Scientifically based paper-and-pencil or computerized tests can serve as a baseline assessment for measuring future changes in an employee's behavior. Such tests typically measure the likelihood that an applicant is prone to abusive, argumentative, or hostile workplace behavior. To obtain credible information about a high-risk applicant, a valid measure of violence potential that complies with professional guidelines should be chosen. Research shows that well-validated instruments can detect applicants who possess a history of violent behavior who, once hired, may become counterproductive employees.

The optimum preemployment screening program will combine testing with employment verification (if there's a gap in work history, find out why), reference checks, criminal record checks, drug testing, and structured interviews. Interviewers should be educated to ask questions that may elicit responses indicating a candidate's likelihood for future violent outbursts. It is useful to design a standard assessment form to ensure candidates are compared consistently. Examples of structured interview questions include the following:

- Tell me about a time at work when you were so angry that you yelled at a supervisor or fellow employee.
- Were you ever angered to the point where you felt like yelling at someone, even though you didn't?

- Did you ever actually push or hit someone who made you really angry?
- Did you ever yell at or hit an obnoxious customer?
- Would any of your past supervisors or co-workers remember a situation where you yelled at or hit anybody?

To avoid potential litigation, have the preemployment screening process, including structured interview questions, reviewed by an expert in human rights legislation. This will ensure that the department keeps within any legal restrictions. Furthermore, such processes may provide necessary information about the candidate should that person become violent after being hired and file a discrimination suit under the ADA, which protects people with mental impairments. There is a strong overlap between violent behavior and mental illness. The evidence gathered about the individual at the front end may help the charged organization to show that it tried to avert preventable violence to maintain a safe work environment. One or two hours of legal advice in advance could make the world of difference. A small employer could easily spend $100,000 on litigation related to claims of negligent hiring.

Policies and Procedures By sending a strong message about the company's commitment to workplace safety, employees will feel more secure about reporting statements or behaviors that they perceive as threatening. One way to encourage such reports is to require employees to read and sign a "Zero Tolerance for Violence Policy" prohibiting the use of weapons, harassment, and verbal or physical threats on the job. Under this policy, employees will feel obligated to notify the human resource or security department regarding threats or violent encounters. A survey by SHRM revealed that 73 percent of respondents had a written policy addressing rules and regulations about weapons in the workplace, 59 percent said they have a written policy addressing violent acts in the workplace, and 39 percent do not have a written policy. Some companies offer a confidential hot line or website through which reports can be made. A zero-tolerance policy will be effective only if the human resource or security departments have the reputation for promptly handling matters seriously and with concern for all employees involved. As part of this policy, security procedures (e.g., visitors should wear ID badges) and planned escape routes should be identified and emergency phone numbers should be published. This way employees can refer to these important policies and procedures to know exactly what is expected of them.

Training and Education Most employees do not become violent without displaying some early warning signs or symptoms. Therefore, employees and supervisors should learn to recognize and respond to highly stressed individuals and violent incidents and use nonconfrontational response techniques to defuse potential problems. Supervisors must learn to recognize workers who display signs of extreme stress and whose work deteriorates significantly. Employees who begin to display irresponsible and inappropriate behaviors such as chronic absenteeism and lateness, grievances and complaints, and overt anger and resentment also should be monitored. Too many tragic situations occur because warning signs go unnoticed, suspicious acts never get reported, or reported information is ignored. It is in these cases that a situation explodes and workers shake their heads and wonder how they could have missed such obvious signs.

Management can help ease a frustrating work environment by giving employees an outlet to air their grievances without fear of reprisal. When possible, managers should take action to resolve the complaints. Establishing trust, cooperation, creativity, and internal teamwork will encourage mutual respect and allow for the development of team problem-solving skills. Basic interpersonal skills such as listening, giving positive encouragement, and learning to be prepared for change should be part of any program.

Employee assistance programs (EAPs) provide specific programs designed to help employees with personal problems. EAPs are a resource to intervene with violent employees, but they are only one way in which human resource departments can help. Training and education programs should incorporate stress management, active coping techniques, and drug abuse awareness. Employers can make educational materials available to employees and their families to help them identify and handle harassment, domestic abuse, substance abuse, and other emotional problems. Companies can even provide voluntary self-defense training and classes in personal safety and security to teach employees how to reduce their chances of being victimized.

Companies where violence has previously occurred need to be especially aware of situations that could lead to employee anger or frustration because that workplace is already perceived by employees as unsafe. Workplace violence should be an ongoing topic of company meetings, workshops, newsletters, and new-hire orientation classes.

Handling layoffs and terminations is a highly sensitive area that requires special training because certain employees may become hostile after a dismissal. A person charged with this responsibility needs to remain neutral when disciplining or terminating employees. In return, employees should have the opportunity to submit written grievances or appeals about their termination or any other pertinent issues. Consideration should be made as to how the dismissal is conducted. Some managers recommend using only one room during the process. The affected individual should remain in the room while meeting with the manager, human resource representative, and outplacement counselor. This prevents the person from moving around the building and possibly causing a scene.

After a dismissal, confidential psychological counseling should be offered as well as outplacement services such as vocational counseling and job search or résumé-writing assistance. It is critical that keys, identification badges, and access cards are collected. Following up with an employee after termination is a good idea because violent acts typically occur within one week after an ex-employee has threatened to retaliate. This follow-up may be in the form of a structured exit interview where the former employee can vent his or her feelings or a simple phone call to find out how the person is doing.

Threat Management Teams   Most experts agree that in addition to formal policies and procedures, companies need to form a threat management team. A **threat management team** is responsible for translating workplace violence policies into action, with particular emphasis on prevention. Typically this team is staffed with individuals from both inside and outside the company including a human resource professional, a psychologist, a lawyer, a security guard, and a key front-line manager who is capable of supervising a tense situation. A strong negotiator also can be part of the team.

The first task of the team is to conduct an initial risk assessment to determine if a threat is serious enough to justify deployment of the team and its resources. Risk assessment involves collecting personnel data to identify past and present problems with the employee posing the threat. Based on such assessment, the team then develops an initial action plan. This phase involves mobilizing the resources needed to intervene in the situation and planning additional steps.

The team should outline the scope of activities and operations that it will cover and set criteria for convening and reporting incidents to law enforcement and the media. Before extreme violence hits, the team must establish a relationship with local police and designate a spokesperson to deal with press reports. A formal procedure for investigating threats also must be defined. Some companies bring in an expert to evaluate the threat objectively and to guide action after the investigation.

Threat management teams also plan escape routes, coordinate medical and psychological care of injured victims, train employees to administer emergency aid to victims, and organize transportation for employees who are in no condition to drive following an incident. Employees and their families must be kept informed during the crisis and immediately thereafter. Therefore, a team member will be responsible for telephoning families to provide updates of victims' conditions, answering payroll or use-of-sick-leave questions, and other necessary matters. Primary and refresher training criteria should be set for all team members. It is recommended that a company develop crisis scenarios against which the threat management team can practice its response. The team also can prepare news releases and potential question-and-answer lists before a crisis occurs.

Security   Workplace violence can be prevented in some cases by employing security measures. Often these are used to protect employees and employers from violent people outside the organization (e.g., former employees). In this area, much can be accomplished at little cost. For example, a threat management team member can arrange regular police checkups and rearrange offices and furniture to provide escape routes that are accessible to employees who, because of their positions, may be obvious targets of disgruntled persons. Limited and controlled access, security awareness briefings, surveillance cameras, and silent alarms all can help reduce employee vulnerability. Making high-risk areas visible to more people and installing good external lighting are two more strategies. In short, the company should make it difficult for anyone to engage in violence.

As stated earlier, the goal of the OSHA Act of 1970 is "to ensure, so far as possible, every working man and woman in the nation safe and healthful working conditions." By law it is every organization's responsibility to prevent workplace violence from occurring and to be prepared to handle it should a situation arise. If a violent incident occurs on a company's premises, and inquiries show an absence of reasonable preventive efforts, the company could be held liable. While it is unrealistic to believe that a company can eliminate the threat of workplace violence, proper precautions can increase employee protection.

Video Display Terminals

Over 30 million Americans now work with video display terminals (VDTs). Many workers who spend considerable time in front of VDTs complain of eye fatigue and irritation, blurred vision, headaches, dizziness, and various muscular and wrist problems. Some VDT users have reported complicated or failed pregnancies. While one California study found that pregnant women who worked at VDTs for 20 hours or more a week had twice the risk of miscarriage as other clerical workers, a larger, more recent study sponsored by the federal government found no relationship between long exposure to VDTs and miscarriage.[80] Unions such as the American Federation of State and Municipal Employees (AFSME) are now demanding that pregnant women be allowed to switch to jobs not involving VDTs. Although there is no denying that electric and magnetic fields can influence biological processes, the critical question related to VDTs is the extent to which exposure is harmful. More research is urgently needed on this topic.

Employees should be properly trained in using ergonomic work methods and equipment to reduce the visual and muscular problems associated with VDTs. Visual problems can be minimized by correcting seat levels and angles, by using monitors that control contrast and brightness or have antiglare screens, and by lowering light levels in places where VDTs are used. People who work as little as two hours a day in front of a computer monitor can develop "computer vision syndrome," the symptoms of which include eye strain, blurred vision, headaches, and dry, irritated eyes. Specially designed glasses are available to reduce this syndrome. Muscular and wrist problems can be reduced by using adjustable chairs, keyboard support equipment, and physical therapy for the eyes, hands, wrists, shoulders, and back. The World Health Organization (WHO) has adopted a standard that states workers should sit at least three feet away from the back of a terminal (where the radiation is generated).

OSHA issued a VDT workstation checklist (see Figure 14-10) in 2000 designed to help workers and employers identify, analyze, and control hazards related to VDT tasks. The checklist is a very useful guideline for companies with potential VDT injuries such as repetitive strain injuries.

While evidence on the physical effects of VDTs has been questioned, the psychological stress related to work with VDTs is well documented, because workers are concerned that increased usage could affect their health or offspring. It seems that the speed with which technology has evolved has not been matched by the dissemination of knowledge about health and safety issues related to its use.[81]

Repetitive Strain Injuries (RSI)

It is estimated that over one million people are afflicted by ergonomic injuries each year at an annual cost of at least $50 billion with workers' compensation claims of $20 billion. Repetitive strain injuries (RSIs) such as carpal tunnel syndrome are now a very common workers' compensation claim in jobs involving essentially the same movements over and over again. Digital Equipment lost a large class action lawsuit in 1996 for RSI injuries a jury concluded had been caused by the design of their VDT keyboards. Similar lawsuits against several manufacturers are now pending.

Ergonomics is the science of designing work space and equipment to be as compatible as possible with the physical and psychological limits of people. OSHA put an ergonomics standard in place in 2000 that they estimated would prevent 4.6 million RSI injuries in the first 10 years. The standard was repealed by Congress under George W. Bush's administration. Business groups such as the Chamber of Commerce strongly oppose an ergonomics standard, claiming OSHA had seriously underestimated the cost of compliance. OSHA, however, may issue a voluntary standard and provide guidance on what companies and industries can do

FIGURE 14-10   VDT Workstation Checklist

Instructions: Evaluate the workstation by answering yes or no to the following statements related to working conditions, the chair, keyboard/input device, monitor, work area, and accessories

WORKING CONDITIONS

The workstation is designed or arranged for doing VDT tasks so it allows the employee's . . .

		Y	N
A.	**Head** and **neck** to be about upright (not bent down/back).	—	—
B.	**Head, neck,** and **trunk** to face forward (not twisted).	—	—
C.	**Trunk** to be about perpendicular to floor (not leaning forward/backward).	—	—
D.	**Shoulders** and **upper arms** to be about perpendicular to floor (not stretched forward) and relaxed (not elevated).	—	—
E.	**Upper arms** and **elbows** to be close to body (not extended outward).	—	—
F.	**Forearms, wrists,** and **hands** to be straight and parallel to floor (not pointing up/down).	—	—
G.	**Wrists** and **hands** to be straight (not bent up/down or sideways toward little finger).	—	—
H.	**Thighs** to be about parallel to floor and **lower legs** to be about perpendicular to floor.	—	—
I.	**Feet** to rest flat on floor or be supported by a stable footrest.	—	—
J.	**VDT tasks** to be organized in a way that allows employee to vary VDT tasks with other work activities, or to take micro-breaks or recovery pauses while at the VDT workstation.	—	—

SEATING

The chair . . .

		Y	N
1.	**Backrest** provides support for employee's lower back (lumbar area).	—	—
2.	**Seat width** and **depth** accommodate specific employee (seatpan not too big/small).	—	—
3.	**Seat front** does not press against the back of employee's knees and lower legs (seatpan not too long).	—	—
4.	**Seat** has cushioning and is rounded/has "waterfall" front (no sharp edge).	—	—
5.	**Armrests** support both forearms while employee performs VDT tasks and do not interfere with movement.	—	—

KEYBOARD/INPUT DEVICE

The keyboard/input device is designed or arranged for doing VDT tasks so that . . .

		Y	N
6.	**Keyboard/input device platform(s)** is stable and large enough to hold keyboard and input device.	—	—
7.	**Input device** (mouse or trackball) is located right next to keyboard so it can be operated without reaching.	—	—
8.	**Input device** is easy to activate and shape/size fits hand of specific employee (not too big/small).	—	—
9.	**Wrists** and **hands** do not rest on sharp or hard edge.		

MONITOR

The monitor is designed or arranged for VDT tasks so that . . .

		Y	N
10.	**Top line** of screen is at or below eye level so employee is able to read it without bending head or neck down/back. (For employees with bifocals/trifocals, see next item.)	—	—
11.	**Employee with bifocals/trifocals** is able to read screen without bending head or neck backward.		
12.	**Monitor distance** allows employee to read screen without leaning head, neck, or trunk forward/backward.	—	—
13.	**Monitor position** is directly in front of employee so employee does not have to twist head or neck.	—	—
14.	**No glare** (e.g., from windows, lights) is present on the screen that might cause employee to assume an awkward posture to read screen.	—	—

WORK AREA

The work area is designed or arranged for doing VDT tasks so that . . .

		Y	N
15.	**Thighs** have clearance space between chair and VDT table/keyboard platform (thighs not trapped).	—	—
16.	**Legs** and **feet** have clearance space under VDT table so employee is able to get close enough to keyboard/input device.	—	—

FIGURE 14-10	*(Continued)*

ACCESSORIES Y N

17. **Document holder,** if provided, is stable and large enough to hold documents that are used. — —
18. **Document holder,** if provided, is placed at about the same height and distance as monitor screen so there is little head movement when employee looks from document to screen. — —
19. **Wrist rest,** if provided, is padded and free of sharp and square edges. — —
20. **Wrist rest,** if provided, allows employee to keep forearms, wrists, and hands straight and parallel to ground when using keyboard/input device. — —
21. **Telephone** can be used with head upright (not bent) and shoulders relaxed (not elevated) if employee does VDT tasks at the same time. — —

GENERAL Y N

22. Workstation and equipment have sufficient adjustability so that the employee is able to be in a safe working posture and to make occasional changes in posture while performing VDT tasks. — —
23. VDT workstation, equipment, and accessories are maintained in serviceable condition and function properly. — —

PASSING SCORE = "YES" answer on all "working postures" items (A–J) and no more than two "NO" answers on remainder of checklist (1–23).

to reduce RSIs. They issued such a standard in 1990 for the meatpacking industry and many companies from other industries have adopted the guidelines.

OSHA can cite employers for hazards that may cause RSIs. Although a specific OSHA rule may never be implemented, OSHA can use the general duty clause of the law. Pepperidge Farm has been fined $310,000 based on an inspection of a Pennsylvania plant. In the appeal of the fine, a judge ruled that OSHA could use the general duty clause for the reported RSI. But OSHA has a limited number of inspectors, and ergonomics-related investigations are very labor intensive. There was some OSHA activity related to RSI in 2005 under the general duty clause of OSHA.

California is the only state with its own safety standards designed to protect workers from repetitive motion injuries such as carpal tunnel syndrome. These regulations require improved working conditions if employees suffer nerve, muscle, or joint injuries as a consequence of repetitive motion. Workers also can demand that employers at least consider wrist guards, adjustable tables, increased breaks, and job rotation as ways of combating the injuries. The workstation checklist in Figure 14-10 would be an excellent diagnostic tool.

While there is no ergonomics standard, OSHA has done considerable research that focused on musculoskeletal injury. One recent study investigated a trial of the "best practices" musculoskeletal injury prevention program designed by OSHA to safely lift physically dependent nursing home residents. The results were quite impressive with significant reductions in resident handling injury incidence, workers' compensation costs, and lost workday injuries after the intervention. The "best practices" prevention program significantly reduced injuries for full-time and part-time nurses in all age groups and all lengths of experience in all study sites.[82]

Occupational Stress

The shock of seeing a highly regarded National League umpire collapse and die on the field at Cincinnati's Riverfront Stadium on opening day of the 1996 baseball season turned the sports world's attention to questions about wellness and stress on the job. An autopsy established that Jerry McSherry, 51, died of severe coronary artery disease. He had an enlarged heart and a reoccurring weight problem. Richie Phillips, the head of the umpires' union, reported that Jerry brought "a lot of stress onto himself."

The description sounds both familiar and universal. Rising stress levels have been blamed on work stressors such as the threat of terrorism, the information age, widespread layoffs, global competition, as well as violent crime, immigration, or any other modern threat Americans zero in on. The stress levels on our soldiers and civilians were extremely high in 2005 with numerous ill effects, including violence among our own troops. The new initiatives to make organizations more competitive and productive also have great potential to increase stress in workers. What is the main culprit of stress? According to a survey conducted in 2000, over 50 percent of respondents blamed their stress levels on "having to work more than 12 hours a day to get the job done."[83] This is a pervasive national problem. A 1999 United Nations survey found that Americans work more hours than any other industrialized nation.

Stress is making workers sick, increasing the potential for violence at work, and affecting productivity and accident rates. One in 10 workers reports that workers have come to blows because of work stress. Forty-two percent report verbal abuse at the office. Twenty-three percent say they have been driven to tears at work. Fourteen percent report that they work with equipment damaged from workplace rage. One in eight workers says he/she has called in sick because of stress and 20 percent have quit a job because of stress. Job stress also can lead to alcohol and drug use and is a frequently cited problem in workers' compensation claims. Problem drinkers file five times more compensation claims and use three times more accident benefits than nonabusers.[84] Job stress costs corporate America an estimated $200 billion annually in absenteeism, lost productivity, accidents, and medical insurance. Worse, stress is contributing to the deaths of hundreds of workers every year. The highest concentration of deaths occurred among operators, fabricators, laborers, and service workers. The most common day of the week when fatal heart attacks occur, not surprisingly, is Monday.

Job stress has been defined as a "situation wherein job-related factors interact with a worker to change his or her psychological and/or physiological condition such that the person is forced to deviate from normal functioning."[85] Stress is considered to be a major problem for workers in today's turbulent and highly competitive environment, with its emphasis on cost control, reduced labor expense, and higher productivity. Stress should be distinguished from a **stressor,** which is the object or event that causes the stress. For example, the speculation that work with VDTs may be hazardous could be considered a stressor that may cause stress in some employees. Exposure to secondhand smoke, which may cause cancer, now serves as a stressor for many nonsmoking workers. Figure 14-11

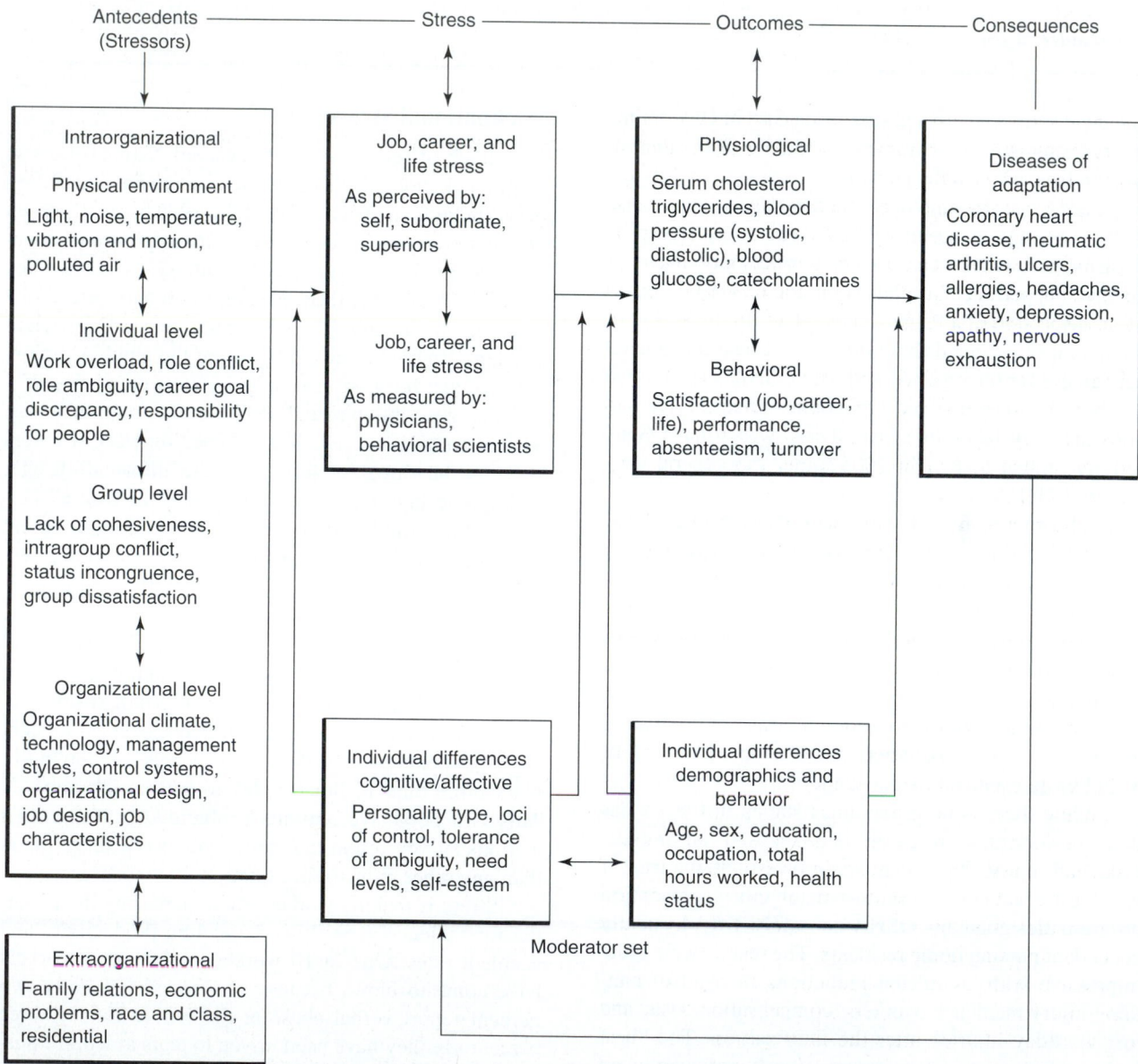

Figure 14-11   A Model for Organizational Stress Research
Source: J. M. Ivancevich and M. T. Matteson, *Stress and Work: A management perspective.* 1980. Reprinted with permission.

presents a model of the antecedents, outcomes, and consequences of stress. Stressors can be found in the physical environment due to lighting or noise problems, temperature, or polluted air. We know that these potential stressors can have an interactive effect such that, for example, temperature combined with a noisy environment may cause even greater stress than the two sources independently.

Prolonged exposure to certain job demands has been linked to several measures of mental and physical stress as well as productivity problems and absenteeism. **Job demands** have been defined as psychological stressors, such as working too hard or too fast, having too much to do (role overload), or having conflicting demands from several sources (role conflict).[86] An individual may perceive role conflict when pressures from two or more sources are exerted such that complying with one source creates greater problems regarding another source. For example, workers may try to maintain a high quality standard while simultaneously trying to meet a very difficult quantity standard, or managers may attempt to hit a quota for production while reducing labor costs. Also, employees in matrix organizational structures may experience role conflict if they have two bosses: one in charge of their "line" job and one in charge of the "project" job or team they have been assigned to. Another source of stress is **role ambiguity,** in which workers simply do not understand what is expected on the job or where what is expected is contrary to what they think should be done. An example of role ambiguity occurs when a boss is vague about an employee's responsibilities or the time frame in which the employee has to complete specific tasks. Research on role ambiguity and conflict is plentiful. As in other areas related to stress, the reactions to the stressors tend to vary widely depending on an individual's characteristics. For example, people with Type A personalities suffer more stress and experience a greater number of health problems than do Type B people. Type A people tend to do just about everything quickly (walk, talk, eat) and have little tolerance for people who go at a more moderate pace.[87] Research also shows that people with more "proactive" personalities are more able to control stressful situations and handle job demands.[88] A "proactive" personality exhibits a tendency to initiate and maintain actions that can alter the surrounding environment.

Other sources of individual stress include conflicts between job obligations and family obligations. Women in particular tend to experience this conflict. "Family responsibilities can place tremendous pressure on women. When both husband and wife have careers, the wife is often expected to keep her housekeeping role in addition to her work role. . . . More and more Superwomen are now questioning their multiple roles. With this uncertainty comes more conflict and stress."[89] Dual-career couples, in particular, face increasing time pressures as they try to balance work and family responsibilities. As discussed in Chapter 9, many corporations are aware of this extra burden on women and are providing employment options designed to reduce this source of stress. Companies such as DuPont, Merck, and General Mills offer family leave, flexible work schedules, and on-site day care. One review of 80 studies found reduced turnover, absenteeism, and increased productivity in companies that help employees balance work with family obligations.[90] For example, Xerox, Tandem Computers, and Corning Inc. enabled their employees working in teams to develop their own schedules that would meet their personal needs while addressing their work demands. They found a decrease in absenteeism and the teams became more effective, self-directed, and independent.[91] Concern for their personal safety is an additional significant stressor for women. Some companies now provide coping-skills training including self-defense programs. Research shows that such training increases women's perceived self-efficacy regarding the ability to exercise self-defense. Such coping skills could help alleviate stress at work.[92]

The role of the manager in alleviating stress appears to be critical. Recent research documents that stress levels are on the rise and that the primary sources of stress are work-family conflicts. Organizations that help employees cope with these roles report less stress and reductions in workers' compensation claims, medical expenses, and voluntary termination. Ensuring that work-family policies are created in a just manner through employee surveys can help create procedures that are representative of all groups' concerns and are consistent across persons and time. However, "the leader who enacts those procedures must be supportive—even the best parental leave procedure cannot overcome supervisors who forbid their employees from using it."[93]

The work group, unit, or organization can be a stressor as well, aside from the issues of role ambiguity and conflict. Particularly in this era of downsizing or "rightsizing," many U.S. corporations are feeling the competitive crunch by making hard decisions to reduce overhead costs. Supervisors and managers are being asked to make hard personnel decisions regarding employee cutbacks. As a result, employees worry more now that their jobs may be on the line. Jobs affected by recent major changes are generally stressful. If a company was purchased, has gone through a layoff or downsizing, has imposed mandatory overtime, or has undergone a major reorganization, the employees, regardless of rank, are likely to have high levels of stress. Of course, the events of September 11, 2001 and the continuing threat of terrorism have exacerbated the normal sources of stress at work.

Some jobs are more likely to cause stress than others. Air traffic controllers, for example, report higher rates of ulcers, chest pains, and headaches than other workers and after only three years of work! Nurses and teachers also report high and increasing levels of stress. While high-level executives lament their stressful responsibilities, the evidence regarding stress-related illnesses does not support the belief that higher-level management jobs are more stressful than other jobs. In fact, one large-scale study found that rates of coronary heart disease were greater at lower management levels.[94] Researchers hypothesize that stress is a function of high job demands in combination with low control at work. So when an individual has little authority to make decisions in a highly demanding job, the most negative aspects of stress should be expected.[95] There is also evidence that coping responses to stressors and control differ as a function of culture.[96]

Because stress and fatigue cannot be measured by biochemical testing, some employers have turned to testing an employee's ability to perform a safety-sensitive job. These job performance exams are generally computer-based and check an employee's visual acuity, coordination, and reaction time. Even though such exams were developed nearly 40 years ago by NASA to check the performance skills of astronauts, the technology was first made available to the general public just a few years ago. An example of a test is one that measures responses while the test subject tries to keep a diamond-shaped cursor aligned with the center of the computer screen. The cursor moves randomly and quickly, so the subject's responses must be fast and accurate. This test takes 30 seconds to complete and employees have eight chances to match or beat their baseline score. If they fail, then the employer can reassign them for the day or request that they take the day off.

A relatively new term for one type of stress is **burnout,** which is a reflection of emotional exhaustion, depersonalization, and reduced personal accomplishment. While originally meant to reflect an emotional reaction in people who often work closely with people, burnout can be found both within as well outside human-services occupations. Burnout is common among police officers, teachers, social workers, and nurses. People experiencing burnout may develop cynical attitudes toward their jobs and clients and may feel emotional exhaustion, depersonalization, and a sense of low personal accomplishment or control.[97] However, burnout is not inevitable in these jobs. A stress reduction program for public school teachers found that the effects of burnout could be reduced using positive feedback about teacher competencies.[98]

Recent research also shows that attempts to decrease job demands and increase job control should be directed at specific job situations and not occupational groupings. Interventions tailored to redesigning particular jobs have proven effective. Interventions will be most successful if they are "tailor-made to address the most important job demands and job resources in specific working environments."[99]

To address stress-related issues and other employee concerns in the United Kingdom, the Working Time Directive became effective in November 1996. This directive contains specific rules relating to all workers, additional rules for those working at night, and general rules on health and safety. The time that an employee spends at work is restricted to 48 hours a week, averaged over a period of up to four months.[100]

As noted in Figure 14-11, there are psychological, physiological, and behavioral consequences of stress. However, reactions to the same stressors vary greatly with the individual. Although individual reactions are difficult to predict, it is known that some people can handle tremendous amounts of stressors without any manifest stressful reactions. For example, people with more proactive personalities are less susceptible to stress under demanding work conditions. Other people fall apart, become violent, or turn to drugs or alcohol. Psychological stress may be manifested in anxiety, depression, irritability, and hostility and also may have physiological consequences such as high blood pressure, numbness, fatigue, and heart problems. Of course, the stress also may affect work performance, work attendance, and accident rates. These consequences can have profound (and costly) organizational consequences, including union organizing, workers' compensation, poor work products, and legal problems. McDonald's Corporation, for example, was held liable for a fatal crash caused by a 19-year-old who had worked a double shift. More recently, a social worker was paid damages after a legal battle to prove that his job caused him to have two nervous breakdowns, brought on by stress and his "impossible workload."

There are different types of stress. While most people assume that stress is always bad for workers and that organizations should always find methods for preventing or reducing it, some research actually shows the opposite effect—that stress can have desirable consequences. Some dimensions of stress are associated with *positive* work outcomes. One study of executives found that stress related to the challenging or rewarding aspects of work was related to positive outcomes while stress which associated with hindering or constraining job experiences was negative. Challenge-related stress was correlated with job satisfaction and less job search, and hindrance-related stress was associated with more job search and less job satisfaction.[101] A more recent study found similar effects but also that both types of stress were positively related to psychological strain.[102]

Figure 14-12 provides a framework of specific intervention programs and the stress outcomes that they may be directed toward. The three intervention targets in the figure correspond to (1) changing the degree of stress potential in a situation by reducing the intensity or number of stressors present, (2) helping employees to modify their appraisal of potentially stressful situations, and (3) helping employees to cope more effectively with the consequences of stress. Stress management and reduction programs are common in industry today. At Motorola, for example, programs emphasize exercise, nutrition, relaxation techniques, time management, and self-awareness. Cigna Corporation provides

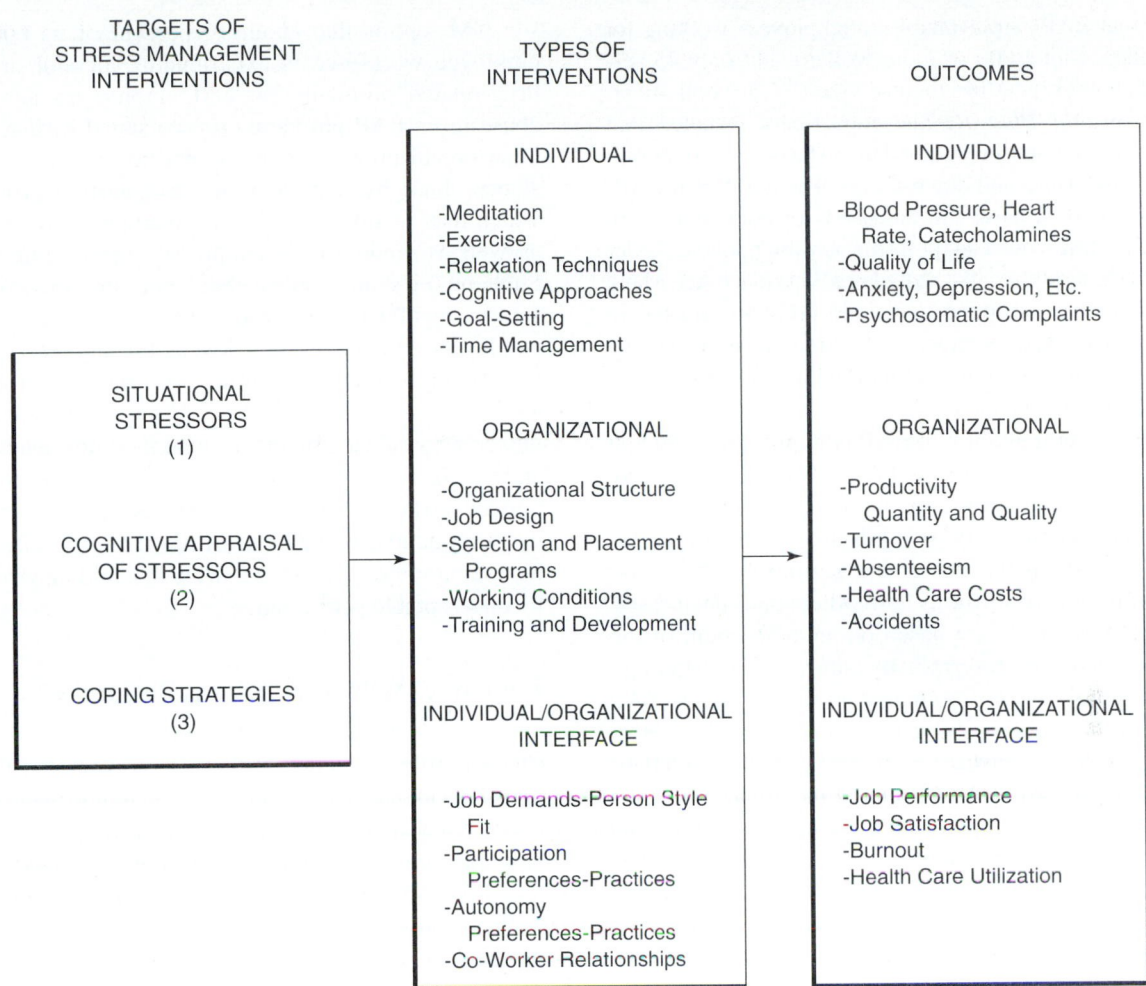

TARGETS OF
STRESS MANAGEMENT
INTERVENTIONS

TYPES OF
INTERVENTIONS

OUTCOMES

INDIVIDUAL

-Meditation
-Exercise
-Relaxation Techniques
-Cognitive Approaches
-Goal-Setting
-Time Management

INDIVIDUAL

-Blood Pressure, Heart
  Rate, Catecholamines
-Quality of Life
-Anxiety, Depression, Etc.
-Psychosomatic Complaints

**SITUATIONAL
STRESSORS
(1)**

**COGNITIVE APPRAISAL
OF STRESSORS
(2)**

**COPING STRATEGIES
(3)**

ORGANIZATIONAL

-Organizational Structure
-Job Design
-Selection and Placement
  Programs
-Working Conditions
-Training and Development

ORGANIZATIONAL

-Productivity
  Quantity and Quality
-Turnover
-Absenteeism
-Health Care Costs
-Accidents

**INDIVIDUAL/ORGANIZATIONAL
INTERFACE**

-Job Demands-Person Style
  Fit
-Participation
  Preferences-Practices
-Autonomy
  Preferences-Practices
-Co-Worker Relationships

**INDIVIDUAL/ORGANIZATIONAL
INTERFACE**

-Job Performance
-Job Satisfaction
-Burnout
-Health Care Utilization

Figure 14-12   Stress Management Interventions: Targets, Types, and Outcomes
Source: J. M. Ivancevich, M. T. Matteson, S. M. Freedman, and J. S. Phillips, Worksite stress management interventions. *American Psychologist,*
February 1990, pp. 252–261. Reprinted with permission.

employees with breaks during which they can relax with new age music, meditation, and stretches or increase their energy level by listening to a tape of empowering thoughts or getting up and moving to upbeat music. Cigna even has a massage therapist who will come to an employee's desk to soothe tense neck muscles. Other organizations have attempted to reduce physical stressors by redesigning the workplace. A survey conducted in 2000 found that 12 percent of Americans indicate that they work in a cubicle "like the cartoon character Dilbert." Work space is another important variable related to stress.

Role ambiguity and role conflict often can be reduced by interventions following a job analysis and survey research. Studies point to immediate supervisors as a primary source of stress among workers. Survey data may help to pinpoint unit-level problems before they result in serious organizational difficulties such as termination, absences, and disabilities. Many organizations incorporate their stress reduction programs into comprehensive

employment assistance programs. We will examine these programs next.

Employee Assistance Programs

EAPs are programs designed to assist employees with performance problems. EAPs are a growing form of employee benefit that provides help to millions of U.S. employees for a variety of problems related to performance. Although cost estimates of EAPs exceed $750 million, most organizations report the programs to be very cost effective. For example, executives at Banc One Financial Services receive in-office counseling. Lucent Technologies also set up its own internal counseling divisions to coach difficult workers. In San Francisco, companies pay Noon-Time University $8,000 for six three-hour lunchtime training sessions for 20 to 24 employees. There are over 10,000 organizations with formal EAPs treating job stress, alcoholism, and other forms of drug abuse, marital and emotional difficulties, and financial problems. One survey found that EAPs are available to employees working for companies with 1,000 or more workers, but only 45 percent of all workers utilize their services.[103] One poll of *Employee Benefit Plan Review* subscribers revealed that 32 percent of employees turned to EAPs because of corporate restructurings and downsizings. The number of EAPs has increased because the thousands of companies with federal contracts must adopt formal antidrug policies under the provisions of the 1988 Drug Free Workplace Act. Many EAPs also are equipped to handle problems related to AIDS and workplace violence. In addition, EAPs can be designed to provide physical help with controlling blood pressure, weight, and smoking.

The general goal of an EAP is to provide treatment for employees who are having problems so they can return to normal, productive functioning on the job. While the vast majority of EAPs are in large organizations, even small businesses are getting involved with EAPs through consortiums with other small businesses. Most EAP referrals are based on an assessment of job performance and referrals by supervisors, although many employees also volunteer to attend EAPs. EAP staff often provide training for managers and supervisors on making "constructive confrontations" with their employees regarding work-related deficiencies. Supervisors are thus exempted from trying to diagnose the causes of a problem. Getting at the cause of the performance problem is left to professionals (e.g., people with graduate degrees in psychology and social work), who are trained to make such diagnoses and treat people accordingly. Most EAPs are based on the principle of voluntary participation. Labor unions generally support drug counseling and EAPs but oppose coercion to participate in such programs as a condition of employment, as well as opposing drug testing of any kind.[104]

An EAP is typically run by an outside health service organization, with an average cost of about $35 per employee per year. The limited data on the effects of EAPs are quite positive. EAP advocates estimate that for every dollar spent, organizations recover from three to five dollars because of increased productivity, decreased insurance costs, and reduced workers' compensation claims and sick leave. Adolph Coors Company reported savings of $6 for every $1 spent on the EAP. AT&T reported a savings of almost $600,000 as a result of its EAP activities. In one study of 110 employees, 85 percent of poor performers were judged to be no longer poor after the EAP. The rate of improvement for all participants was 86 percent. There was a significant decrease in the number of accidents in which these individuals were involved. Absenteeism also went down, as did visits to the medical department. In short, at least for this sample of AT&T workers, the EAP was a great success.[105] United Airlines estimates that for every $1 spent for its EAP, it realizes savings of $16.35 through reduction in employee absences.[106]

GM reports that about 10 percent of its 600,000-employee workforce is experiencing alcohol or other drug-related problems, so GM emphasizes substance abuse in its EAP programs. As we stated earlier, many other organizations have responded to problems of substance abuse by implementing drug testing programs, which may involve entry-level screening for drug usage as well as random drug testing of current employees. Such policies are controversial but, in most circumstances, legal. Under the doctrine of employment at will, employers may dismiss employees for any reason other than those covered by statute (e.g., race, sex, religion, age, national origin, disability). Firing a nonunion employee who fails a drug test is legal in almost every state and has been done thousands of times. However, most human resource management experts take the position that termination should be a last resort after an attempt at intervention through an EAP, which should be prompted by unacceptable performance.

Employee Wellness or Fitness Programs

Due to the staggering health care costs described in Chapter 10, many companies have set up wellness, fitness, or health management programs for employees. While EAPS are designed to treat employee problems, wellness programs are designed to prevent problems. One survey found that 75 percent of large employers participated in wellness programs. Unions also have been increasingly involved in promoting health and safety protections for their members.[107]

Wellness is defined as a "freely chosen lifestyle aimed at achieving and maintaining an individual's good health."[108] Companies have discovered that the best way to reduce health care costs is to keep employees healthy. In general, healthy employees are more productive than unhealthy ones. Research shows that employees who set specific, obtainable goals related to improving their health often increase their perceived control and confidence to overcome barriers to performing healthy behaviors.[109] As long as goals are reasonable and employees experience success in their first few attempts at reaching their goals, a motivational change is brought about by this mastery. This motivational change involves increasingly higher levels of control and confidence, especially over work-related barriers (i.e., work piling up while the employee uses release time to exercise).

One problem with wellness programs is that healthy people tend to take advantage of the programs while those most in need stay away. Incentive programs can help encourage those most needy employees. One survey found that 39 percent of employers offer incentives to participate in wellness programs. Workers get rewarded for meeting health-related wellness criteria. Most large U.S. corporations offer some form of formal wellness programs involving health assessment, exercise planning, counseling or support groups, stress management, weight control, and smoking cessation. Some insurance companies offer reduced rates for organizations with organized wellness programs.[110] At New York Telephone, the wellness program focuses on the following major areas of health: smoking cessation, cholesterol reduction, alcohol abuse control, fitness training, stress management, and cancer screening. New York Telephone reported a savings of almost $3 million in reduced absences and medical treatment because of its wellness program. Kimberly-Clark offers a variety of health-related programs, including an exercise routine available at the fitness center on the premises, weight control consultation, blood pressure analysis and treatment, and nutritional advice. These programs are available to the company's entire workforce, and 88 percent of employees are enrolled in one or more of the programs. While the cost is high (about $435 per employee per year), the director of the program is certain the bottom line will support its effectiveness. There are many other success stories. IBM, Johnson & Johnson, Tenneco, Campbell Soup, and Xerox all report success with their fitness and wellness programs. One Xerox work location provides a soccer field, an Olympic-size pool, two gyms, tennis courts, a weight room, and over 2,000 acres of running space. Johnson & Johnson reports savings of $378 per employee as a result of its comprehensive wellness program, which it now also administers for 60 other companies. The goals of the program are basic: stop smoking, eat fruit and fewer fatty foods, get some exercise, and buckle up.[111]

The effectiveness of Pacific Bell's FitWorks health promotion program was assessed in four of its construction sites. The results of the one-year study found that employees who had access to physical training equipment had lower heart rates after step tests, greater lower-body muscular endurance, and greater flexibility than those who did not work out.[112] John Alden Financial has found that corporate wellness programs boost productivity, lower health care costs, and help firms attract and retain top-quality employees.[113] This organization's wellness activities include a health fair, an employee-published cookbook of nutritious recipes, numerous sports clubs, substance abuse prevention campaigns, an in-house fitness center, and many health-related seminars and workshops. Provided below are some tips for launching wellness programs based on the experience of John Alden Financial and other corporate members.[114]

- Start small: Launch simple programs such as blood pressure and cholesterol screening or distribute information about nutrition to employees.
- Delegate responsibility: Let employees plan and implement activities and conduct a survey to assess employees' health and recreational interests.
- Schedule activities around the workday: Schedule events before work, during lunch, or after work so the activities do not take employees away from their regular duties.
- Learn from other companies: Find out what other firms in the area or industry have done and learn from their experiences.
- Take advantage of community services: Many local health agencies and nonprofit organizations provide health screenings and information for free.

SUMMARY

Top management is taking a more active role in improving the health and safety of workers. Figure 14-13 summarizes the managerial steps for improving the work environment as recommended by one expert.[115]

The first step (affirming management commitment) means that management must make resources available for health and safety issues. Research shows that plants with superior health and safety records spend more money on health and safety. In addition to management commitment to safety, it is also crucial to have employee participation. This can be done by empowering employees to take ownership in the safety of the organization.[116] The second step for improving the work environment calls for a clearly established policy and results-oriented set of objectives for health and safety. Third, managers should perform planned and unplanned inspections of work sites to assess compliance. Fourth, as the safety manager at DuPont states, "When plant managers begin to audit people and their actions, dramatic changes occur... audits foster fewer unsafe acts." Managers also should establish an atmosphere in which employees feel comfortable reporting unsafe working conditions so that all potential hazards can be identified. Managers must form a

FIGURE 14-13	**Eight Essential Steps in Improving the Work Environment**

1. Affirm management's commitment to a safe and healthy environment.
2. Review current safety objectives and policies.
3. Conduct periodic evaluations and inspections of the workplace.
4. Identify potential and existing work hazards in the areas of safety and health.
5. Identify the employees at risk.
6. Make the necessary improvements in the workplace.
7. Prepare and conduct preventive programs.
8. Monitor the feedback results and evaluate costs.

Source: S. Greenfield, "Management's Safety and Health Imperative: Eight Essential Steps to Improving the Work Environment." *Minerva Occasional Paper Series (2.9).* Cincinnati, OH: Xavier University, 1989.

partnership designed to maximize employee safety and health and acknowledge that a trained, safe workforce is the most productive workforce an employer can have.[117] The fifth step is to identify particular employees at risk so that appropriate training and policies can be developed. The development of an employee database or the use of a comprehensive personnel inventory (see Chapter 5) could assist with this effort. The sixth step for enhancing managerial attention is to make corrections in the work environment based on the research and employee data analysis. This may include a number of preventive measures. With the proliferation of complaints regarding carpal tunnel syndrome and related stress symptoms, this step may include ergonomics or work station redesign. Where the job situation contributes to an unsafe environment, management should take the appropriate action. The seventh step calls on management to prepare and conduct preventive programs. Aggressive antidrug policies, EAPs, threat management teams, and wellness programs are examples. The final step is for management to evaluate actions and feed the results back to employees. An assessment of the monetary value of health and safety programs is one necessary component of this step. Many companies report considerable savings from such programs.

Gillette saved over $1.2 million from its health and safety programs. Procter & Gamble reported direct cost savings in excess of $1.5 million. A. M. Castle & Company in Franklin Park, Illinois, started a safety program in 1980. Since then it has reported fewer injuries and reduced lost time, as well as significant cost savings for the company. In addition, employees are involved in the program, which covers a wide range of health and safety issues, including alcohol and drug abuse, fleet safety, and equipment maintenance.[118] Exeter Healthcare, Inc., implemented a program called PEPS—Patient/Resident, Employee, Plant Safety. It took place in four phases: program development, implementation, outcome analysis, and program enhancements. Within the first eight months of the program, patient/resident falls were reduced 40 percent in one quarter, with further reductions in following quarters. Exeter's work-related costs were far below what was ever anticipated, and work injuries and related costs showed an 85 percent drop in one year.[119] Milliken & Company's emphasis on employee participation in safety has elevated the textile firm to unrivaled status in American industry. Of Milliken's 55 U.S. facilities, 30 have been judged good enough for inclusion in OSHA's elite voluntary protection program. The basic belief of the programs is that all incidents can be prevented. Star status is awarded to those sites that excel

in these areas: management commitment and planning, hazard assessment, hazard correction and control, safety and health training, association awareness/ownership participation, and safety and health process assessments. One of the most recent Star designees is Milliken's New Holland Plant in Gainesville, Georgia.[120]

More companies are developing formal health and safety policies, and management is now more likely to be held accountable for accident rates and other health-related measures. In the next century, even greater interest in the subject and more programs that focus on employee behavior are likely. Drug testing, antismoking programs, threat management teams, EAPs, and wellness programs hold promise as methods that can contribute to a more productive and healthy workforce.[121]

Employee health and safety are issues of importance not simply in the United States. Most other countries have some policies on these issues, and their rules are changing to reflect greater concerns among employees for injuries and illnesses. For example, in Ireland, in 1989 the Safety, Health, and Welfare Work Act was enacted. This set out provisions for establishment of the National Authority for Occupational Safety and Health to promote, encourage, and foster the prevention of accidents and injury to health at work. Under the act, the employer's duties are to provide (1) a safe place at work, (2) safe equipment, and (3) personal protective equipment. These efforts initially cost the companies money, but over the long term have reduced premiums, absenteeism, and claims against the firms.[122] In Britain, an important case occurred in 1994: *Walker v. Northumberland County Council* extended the common-law duty of an employer to provide a safe system of work for employees in terms of mental as well as physical health.[123] In Canada, the city of Toronto recently began a new program for its workforce of approximately 7,000. The goal of the new initiative is the successful return to work for employees with psychological disabilities (e.g., suffering from work-related stress). Toronto now provides a wide range of rehabilitation services for injured and ill employees.[124]

For U.S. human resource professionals, a key element of human resource management in a foreign country is employee morale. Companies operating in harsh and high-threat locations can maintain good morale and prevent unnecessary turnover by providing safe working and living conditions as well as basic comforts. Human resource professionals can prepare their employees if they have analyzed the working conditions in the other country and have developed plans to deal with potential illnesses or injuries.[125]

DISCUSSION QUESTIONS

1. Why is a 20-year-old with three years of experience more likely to be involved in an accident than a 30-year-old with three years of experience? After you develop your theory for this fact, explain how companies can intervene to reduce (or wipe out) the effect.

2. How could you as a manager develop a strategy for increasing employees' motivation to work more safely?

3. Devise a training program and a policy directed at in-creasing the physical fitness of your employees. Take a position on smoking, alcohol use, and other health-related matters and state whether you would make the programs mandatory.

4. Do you think managers should be held criminally liable for health and safety violations? Should they go to jail for such violations? If so, under what conditions? If not, why not?

5. Do you support a policy of random drug testing for all employees? Explain. Would you be less attracted to an organization that required random drug testing with no probable cause?

6. Should a company be allowed to prohibit smoking or drinking alcohol on or off the job for its employees? Explain your answer.

7. Given the accumulated evidence on the effects of smoking, why hasn't OSHA taken steps to regulate smoking and second-hand smoke in the workplace?
8. What kinds of work-related factors affect employees' stress levels? What recommendations would you offer a company to manage the stress of its employees?
9. Compare and contrast employee assistance and wellness programs. What is the value of each for an organization?
10. Why has violence in the workplace become a larger problem for organizations? What recommendations would you offer to a company to ensure that it does not experience violence? Be specific.

RECOMMENDED INTERNET SITES

AFL-CIO	http://www.aflcio.org/home.htm
Bureau of Labor Statistics	http://www.bls.gov/
Centers for Disease Control and Prevention	http://www.cdc.gov/
Department of Labor	http://www.dol.gov/
Employment and Training Administration	http://www.doleta.gov/
Environmental Protection Agency	http://www.epa.gov/
Equal Employment Opportunity Commission	http://www.eeoc.gov/
FedWorld	http://www.fedworld.gov/
National Institute for Occupational Safety & Health	http://www.cdc.gov/niosh/homepage.html
National Safety Council	http://www.nsc.org/
Occupational Safety and Health Administration	http://www.osha.gov/
Occupational Safety and Health Resources	http://www.osh.net/
Office of Personnel Management	http://www.opm.gov/
Worker Rights Consortium	http://www.wrc.org

APPENDIX A

Critical Thinking Applications

CRITICAL THINKING APPLICATION 1-A

What Do You Know about HRM?[1]

Directions

Answer each of the following True or False questions. Skip the item if you have no idea whether the statement is true or false.

Name _____

T or F

_____ 1. Leadership training is ineffective because good leaders are born, not made.

_____ 2. The most important requirement for an effective leader is to have an outgoing, enthusiastic personality.

_____ 3. Once employees have mastered a task, they perform better when they are told to "do their best" than when they are given specific, difficult performance goals.

_____ 4. Companies with vision statements perform better than those without them.

_____ 5. Companies with very low rates of professional turnover are less profitable than those with moderate turnover rates.

_____ 6. If a company feels it must downsize employees, the most profitable way to do it is through targeted cuts rather than attrition.

_____ 7. In order to be evaluated favorably by line managers, the most important competency for HR managers is ability to manage change.

_____ 8. On average, encouraging employees to participate in decision making is more effective for improving organizational performance than setting performance goals.

_____ 9. Most managers give employees lower performance appraisals than they objectively deserve.

_____ 10. Poor performers are generally more realistic about their performance than good performers are.

_____ 11. Teams with members from different functional areas are likely to reach better solutions to complex problems than teams from a single area.

_____ 12. Despite the popularity of drug testing, there is no clear evidence that applicants who score positive on drug tests are any less reliable.

_____ 13. Most people overevaluate how they will perform on the job.

_____ 14. Most errors in performance appraisals can be eliminated by providing training that describes the kinds of errors managers tend to make and suggesting ways to avoid them.

_____ 15. Lecture-based training is generally superior to other forms of training delivery.

_____ 16. Older adults learn more from training than younger adults.

_____ 17. The most important determinants of how much training employees actually use on their jobs is how much they learned during training.

_____ 18. Training for simple skills will be more effective if it is presented in one concentrated session than if it is presented in several sessions over time.

_____ 19. The most valid employment interviews are designed around each candidate's unique background.

_____ 20. Although people use many different terms to describe personalities, there are really only four basic dimensions of personality, as captured by the Myers-Briggs Type Indicator (MBTI).

_____ 21. On average, applicants who answer job advertisements are likely to have higher turnover than those referred by other employees.

_____ 22. Being very intelligent is actually a disadvantage for performing well on low-skilled jobs.

_____ 23. There is very little difference among personality inventories in terms of how well they predict an applicant's likely job performance.

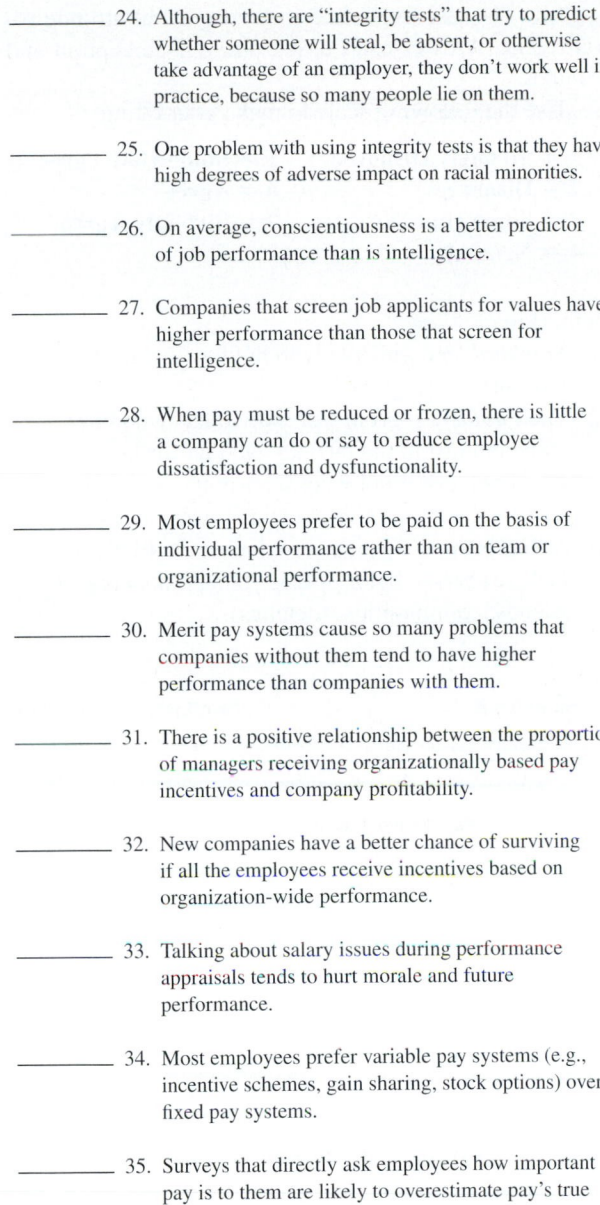

_____ 24. Although, there are "integrity tests" that try to predict whether someone will steal, be absent, or otherwise take advantage of an employer, they don't work well in practice, because so many people lie on them.

_____ 25. One problem with using integrity tests is that they have high degrees of adverse impact on racial minorities.

_____ 26. On average, conscientiousness is a better predictor of job performance than is intelligence.

_____ 27. Companies that screen job applicants for values have higher performance than those that screen for intelligence.

_____ 28. When pay must be reduced or frozen, there is little a company can do or say to reduce employee dissatisfaction and dysfunctionality.

_____ 29. Most employees prefer to be paid on the basis of individual performance rather than on team or organizational performance.

_____ 30. Merit pay systems cause so many problems that companies without them tend to have higher performance than companies with them.

_____ 31. There is a positive relationship between the proportion of managers receiving organizationally based pay incentives and company profitability.

_____ 32. New companies have a better chance of surviving if all the employees receive incentives based on organization-wide performance.

_____ 33. Talking about salary issues during performance appraisals tends to hurt morale and future performance.

_____ 34. Most employees prefer variable pay systems (e.g., incentive schemes, gain sharing, stock options) over fixed pay systems.

_____ 35. Surveys that directly ask employees how important pay is to them are likely to overestimate pay's true importance in actual decisions.

[1]Rynes, S. Colbert, A. and Brown, K. (2002). HR professionals' beliefs about effective human resource management practices: Correspondence between research and practice. *Human Resource Management, 41,* 149–174. Reprinted with permission of John Wiley & Sons.

CRITICAL THINKING APPLICATION 1-B*

Corporate Social Responsibility and Human Resources Management

It seemingly took the recent spate of financial accounting scandals to more strongly deliver the message of Corporate Social Responsibility (CSR) to both business leaders and the general public. Much like the Savings and Loans (S&L) fiasco during the eighties, the demise of super-corporations like Enron and WorldCom taught us all a very important lesson; it costs to be bad. While the threat of bankruptcy and criminal action may have scared some CEOs into implementing CSR, others are attempting to use CSR to their advantage. Recent surveys conducted in the United States suggest that managers no longer treat CSR as a "necessary evil," but are inclined to believe that effective CSR management can lead to improved financial performance.[1]

CEOs are now increasingly looking for ways in which social performance and reputation can benefit the organization financially, either through lowered costs and/or increased sales revenue. For example, firms are using their rankings on lists like *Forbes*'s annual "100 Best Companies to Work For" to attract and select the most qualified and loyal employees. CSR has also become a marketing tool for many businesses eager to sell themselves to a socially conscious public which rewards good ethics, employee relations, and environmental management with increased purchasing and brand loyalty.

Buoyed by recent evidence that suggests effective Corporate Social Performance leads to financial growth, firms are attempting to leverage the value of social responsibility by creating CSR strategies that target all operations and functions of the organization, including Human Resources Management (HRM).[2]

With specific respect to HRM, both managers and academics are seeking to tie CSR to personnel selection and employee retention. Since both functions are critical elements in HRM, the ability of CSR to promote them adds to the strategic value of HRM to the firm. For example, firms which are deemed to be socially responsible are potentially more attractive to potential applicants because of their enhanced reputation and social desirability. Increased interest and desire to work at the company give the organization not only a greater pool of applicants from which to choose but perhaps a criterion on which to select its employees; compatibility with the corporate culture of social responsibility. For CSR strategies to be implemented effectively, employees must relate to the CSR values of the firm which promote the management of multiple stakeholder relationships and a commitment to goals beyond the financial bottom line.

Once employees are hired, CSR also helps to facilitate and sustain the employee–firm relationship. Most CSR firms recognize their employees as primary stakeholders, and therefore commit themselves to the preservation of mutually beneficial relationships.[3] Also, because of similarity between personal and organizational values, employees of firms that practice superior CSR are expected to identify more closely and strongly with the goals and ideals they work for, thereby leading to decreased absenteeism and turnover. Therefore, a commitment to CSR leads to a commitment to employee well-being which benefits the firm through cost reduction skill development, and the retention of valuable employees.

While the benefits of CSR to HRM seem feasible, most organizations do not formally use CSR to match applicants' attitudes or dispositions regarding salient issues as a hiring tool. The lack of research in this area may be caused by the lack of measurement tools that assess the compatibility of applicants' attitudes or preferences regarding CSR and the corporate positions on the same CSR issues. Since CSR is normally treated as a business-level issue, there has been little effort to formally gauge employee attitudes toward stakeholder commitment, environmental protection, and social concern. However, because of the inherent need for qualified and committed employees to effectively implement strategy, it seems the onus is squarely on those firms which are undertaking or plan to undertake CSR strategies to find ways of more formally incorporating it into their HRM policies. It is only then that firms will fully enjoy the benefits of "doing good."

Name _____

Exercise Questions

The first 10 questions are adaptations from a popular CSR instrument intended to elicit the attitudes of managers to CSR. The last five relate to your general attitude toward CSR. Answer each based on your perception and attitudes.

Use the following scale to make your ratings:

1 = Strongly Disagree	**5 = Somewhat Agree**
2 = Disagree	**6 = Agree**
3 = Somewhat Disagree	**7 = Strongly Agree**
4 = Neutral	

Definitions

1. *Stockholders*—people who hold financial shares of a business.
2. *Stakeholders*—groups or individuals who have some interest in the business and its welfare (stockholders, employees, consumers, communities, societies, natural environment, governments).
3. *Social groups*—groups to which an individual believes he/she belongs (e.g., family, network of friends, communities, societies).

	Strongly Disagree	Disagree	Somewhat Disagree	Neutral	Agree	Somewhat Agree	Strongly Agree
1. The primary role of business is to increase the wealth of STOCKHOLDERS.	1	2	3	4	5	6	7
2. STOCKHOLDERS are the most important stakeholder group to organizations.	1	2	3	4	5	6	7
3. The interest and rights of a firm's STOCKHOLDERS are more important than the interests of other stakeholder groups.	1	2	3	4	5	6	7
4. Businesses should only be concerned with meeting financial and economic objectives.	1	2	3	4	5	6	7
5. Organizations have a responsibility to **all** STAKEHOLDER groups, not just its STOCKHOLDERS.	1	2	3	4	5	6	7
6. All STAKEHOLDER groups are **equally** important and should be considered when making business decisions.	1	2	3	4	5	6	7
7. A business should treat all its STAKEHOLDERS fairly.	1	2	3	4	5	6	7
8. Businesses should always act in the best interests of society and the natural environment.	1	2	3	4	5	6	7
9. Some STAKEHOLDER groups are more important than others.	1	2	3	4	5	6	7
10. Only persons and environments directly related to the organization should be the concern of business.	1	2	3	4	5	6	7
11. I do consider the CSR of a company when I consider buying a product or service.	1	2	3	4	5	6	7
12. I would consider the CSR of an organization as I search for a job.	1	2	3	4	5	6	7

13. I have extensive knowledge about the CSR of companies from which I buy products or services.	1	2	3	4	5	6	7
14. I only consider price and quality when I buy a product.	1	2	3	4	5	6	7
15. I would buy and sell stock based on the CSR reputation of the firm.	1	2	3	4	5	6	7

*Contributed by Richard Peters.
[1]Simms, J. (2002). "Business: Corporate Social Responsibility—You know it makes sense." *Accountancy*, 1311.
[2]This evidence comes from a meta-analysis which shows a positive correlation between CSR and firm financial performance (Orlitzky, M., Schmidt, F. L., and Rynes S. L. 2003. Corporate social and financial performance: A meta-analysis. *Organization Studies, 24*(3), 403–410).
[3]Waddock, S. A., Bodwell, C., and Graves, S. B. (2002). Responsibility: The new business imperative. *Academy of Management Executive, 16*(2), 132–148.

CRITICAL THINKING APPLICATION 1-C

Resolution: Close Down the Human Resources Department

A great deal of research indicates that it is line management that will determine whether or not human resources can create and sustain a competitive advantage for organizations. While HR staff develop, purchase, and administer HR activities, the proper use of these activities by line management has the most to do with their effectiveness. *Fortune* magazine's Thomas Stewart argues that outsourcing those HR functions that can be outsourced will ultimately save the company money and thus facilitate a competitive advantage through reducing costs.[1] This cost reduction could then increase profits and/or help the company compete on price.

Some HR departments are already responding by outsourcing many functions traditionally done by full-time employees. Compensation and executive recruiting are two of a growing number of areas that are more likely to be outsourced.

Stewart argues that an in-house HR department will probably cost the company much more money and since it's line management (not the HR staff) that really determines HR effectiveness, the use of outsourced personnel to perform certain HR activities should have little impact on effectiveness. For example, instead of using full-time HR staff to develop and implement a new performance management system, the company could contract with a company to do this work.

Stewart refers the reader to the Washington, D.C.–based Corporate Leadership Council, which concluded that indirect compensation (benefits), personnel recordkeeping, and employee services such as outplacement and retirement counseling, and health and safety issues (drug testing, wellness programs, workers' compensation) could all be outsourced to save money.

Stewart goes beyond the Council's recommendation. He argues that many HR functions can now be purchased from vendors with considerable savings and no loss in quality. For example, recruiting can be done through "head-hunters" now for even low-level jobs. Personnel testing, performance management, and pay-for-performance systems can be purchased from consulting firms with impressive expertise in these areas. He cites Nucor Steel, which has an HR staff of four for its 6,000-person operation. Nucor farms out most of its HR work.

Stewart is not the only one critical of HR. Says Keith Hammonds, deputy editor of *Fast Company,* in a 2005 article diplomatically entitled "Why We Hate HR," after close to 20 years of hopeful rhetoric about becoming 'strategic partners' with a 'seat at the table' where the business decisions that matter are made, most human-resources professionals aren't nearly there. They have no seat, and the table is locked inside a conference room to which they have no key. HR people are, for most practical purposes, neither strategic nor leaders."[2]

Hammond asks "Why are annual performance appraisals so time-consuming—and so routinely useless? Why is HR so often a henchman for the chief financial officer, finding ever-more ingenious ways to cut benefits and hack at payroll? Why do its communications—when we can understand them at all—so often flout reality? Why are so many people processes duplicative and wasteful, creating a forest of paperwork for every minor transaction?

Mr. Hammond pointed to a 2005 survey which found that only 40 percent of employees thought their companies were effective at retaining high-quality workers. Only 41 percent thought performance evaluations were fair and 58 percent rated their job training as favorable. Most respondents said they had little opportunity for advancement—and that they didn't know how to move up in their organization. Hammond also recommends serious downsizing and outsourcing of HR functions.

Assignment

Generate a list of reasons why there may be another side to this story. What key questions would you want to ask Mr. Stewart and Mr. Hammonds regarding outsourcing? Compile a list of advantages and disadvantages to outsourcing that could help a company make thoughtful decisions regarding HR.

[1]Stewart, T. A. (January 15, 1996). Taking on the last bureaucracy. *Fortune,* pp. 105–108.
[2]Hammonds, K. H. (2005) Why we hate HR. *Fast Company*, 97 (August), 40–43.

CRITICAL THINKING APPLICATION 2-A

What Is the Origin of Your University Apparel?[1]

Chapter 2 discusses the issues, problems, and advantages related to the use of offshore facilities for manufacturing. We've probably all heard Jay Leno take a crack at Nike about working conditions in the overseas "sweatshops" where Nike products are made. You may be wearing a shirt or hat right now with your university logo on it. Do you have any idea where the apparel was manufactured and under what conditions?

On March 25, 2002, 12 students at Florida State University were arrested by FSU campus police for demonstrating in an area not designated for free speech. These students were members of United Students Against Sweatshops (USAS) and were protesting a recent decision by University President Sandy D'Alemberte to not join the Worker Rights Consortium (WRC), an organization initiated by the USAS that monitors factories worldwide to ensure humane working conditions.[2]

The USAS is an international student movement that fights for sweatshop-free working conditions in factories around the world. Students from more than 30 schools started the organization in 1998. These students wanted to increase awareness of workers' rights issues and coordinate efforts between campuses to address workers' rights as a greater force. A part of the plan was to develop an organization that monitors production facilities. That plan resulted in the Worker Rights Consortium.[3]

The Worker Rights Consortium was started in October 1999 by the USAS.[4] Its purpose is to "assist in the enforcement of manufacturing Codes of Conduct adopted by colleges and universities . . . to ensure that factories producing clothing and other goods bearing college and university names respect the basic rights of workers." The organization is supported by affiliation fees from each member school in the amount of 1 percent of the previous year's gross licensing revenues (with a minimum of $1,000 and a maximum of $50,000).[5]

Since its inception, the WRC has had success both domestically and abroad. At Mexmode, a textile factory in Atlixco, Mexico, the WRC and the USAS pressed Nike to allow the workers to form an independent labor union with voluntary membership.[6] Additionally, the WRC issued a negative report regarding New Era Cap Co. near Buffalo, New York. The report resulted in some schools canceling contracts with New Era and others pushing for the company to resolve its struggle with its employees.[7] This pressure resulted in a resolution between the workers and New Era.[8]

As of June 2005, there were over a hundred colleges and universities participating in the WRC. Essentially, these schools joined the Consortium out of concern for the conditions under which their school paraphernalia (hats, sweats, shirts, etc.) are produced. The USAS initiated the WRC as a response to the inadequacy of the Fair Labor Association (FLA).[9]

The Fair Labor Association was established after a Clinton administration initiative in response to growing public concern about humane working conditions, especially in Third World countries. The FLA is a partnership of manufacturers, educational institutions, consumer groups, and human rights organizations started in 1996 that monitors production factories and enforces humane standards. Its purpose is to improve factory working conditions in the United States and abroad. The FLA monitors the factories of participating companies and makes decisions about how to rectify existing problems.[10]

The FLA has been successful in its attempts. For example, at the BJ&B/Yupoong facility in Villa Altagracia, Dominican Republic, the FLA recently resolved a dispute issued on behalf of 20 workers dismissed for supporting the organization of a union. The day after the complaint was filed, FLA reps arrived at the plant for inspection. The issue was resolved with the dismissed workers being rehired.[11]

However, the USAS and other parties believe the FLA's system has problems. In a report to the Faculty Senate Steering Committee, the Committee on Apparel Licensing stated that the FLA monitoring system is "fundamentally flawed." Among these flaws are a small percentage of facilities are monitored, the participating companies choose their monitors and the factories to be monitored, monitors are restricted by confidentiality, the process is slow, and the FLA voting structure favors the manufacturers over the workers.[12]

Dara O'Rourke, a professor of environmental and labor policy at M.I.T., is displeased with the FLA's choice of monitoring companies, particularly PricewaterhouseCoopers. Professor O'Rourke has inspected over 100 factories for various international organizations and claimed "PwC's monitoring efforts are significantly flawed." O'Rourke adds, "PwC's audit reports glossed over problems of freedom of association and collective bargaining, overlooked serious violations of health and safety standards, and failed to report common problems in wages and hours." PwC's Randy Rankin commented, "I think we do very good work in this field, and we're contributing to improving conditions on behalf of our clients."[13]

On April 9, 2002, the FLA board approved changes to the FLA monitoring system, perhaps in response to the numerous critiques. The FLA will now randomly choose which factories will be monitored and also will choose the monitoring company. Additionally, the visits will be unannounced and reports will be posted on the FLA Web site. The FLA believes these changes will improve its system.[14] However, all of this changes little since almost half of the FLA board is comprised of company representatives and the voting structure still favors the manufacturers.

This is the situation that the leadership at Florida State walked into. The FSU Faculty Senate Steering Committee formed a committee in Spring 2000 to study the issue of apparel licensing for FSU paraphernalia. After researching the issue, the committee submitted a report in spring 2001 recommending the university join the WRC.[15] The FSU student government also passed a resolution supporting WRC membership. Nonetheless, the FSU president rejected the proposal.[16] Since FSU is already a member of the FLA (one of the 17 original universities to join), D'Alemberte is apprehensive about spending 1 percent of the university's licensing revenues ($17,000–$21,000 annually) on a redundant measure. Additionally, he believes that if FSU were to support human rights organizations financially, there are other organizations such as the Lawyers Committee for Human Rights and Amnesty International that might be more deserving.[17]

However, FSU would have much more influence on manufacturer behavior through the WRC. It would not be merely financial support, but the power to cancel licensing contracts. With a championship athletics program, FSU's business is important to any manufacturer. That is the support the WRC wants from FSU. This would be quite different from supporting most other human rights organizations.

The issue of worker rights abroad is growing to the point of rivaling worker rights issues in the United States. As the economy becomes more global, conditions in workplaces around the world become more transparent. The FLA was one of the first responses to the opposition people brought against manufacturers for unfair treatment of employees. However, the USAS was not satisfied with the FLA's approach to rectifying workplace problems and created the WRC. Colleges and universities are now faced with choosing between the FLA and WRC (though membership in both is permitted).[18]

Assignment

Take a position on whether FSU should have joined the WRC. Conduct a Web search to determine the current state of the controversy. Assuming your instructor doesn't provide the information, conduct research on your campus to find out where most of your campus paraphernalia is produced and what companies have the licensing agreements. Find out whether the supplier is cleared by the FLA and/or the WRC. Is your school affiliated with either the FLA or the WRC? Is there a USAS chapter active on your campus? Go into the websites of the USAS and the WRC and review their mission statements and past accomplishments. What is your opinion about the intervention of such organizations as the FLA, WRC, and USAS? Would you consider joining the USAS? Do you think your university should join the WRC if it doesn't belong already?

Relevant organizations with Web addresses: USAS, www.usasnet.org; WRC, www.workersrights.org; FLA, www.fairlabor.org; Global Exchange, www.globalexchange.org; Human Rights Watch, www.hrw.org; International Labour Organization, www.ilo.org; Sweatshop Watch, www.sweatshopwatch.org; Verité, www.verite.org.

[1]Contributed by Mike Ryan.
[2]Twelve Florida State Students Arrested in Protest. (March 26, 2002). Sun-Sentinel.com, accessed June 11, 2002 (http://www.sun-sentinel.com/news/local/florida/sfl-0326fsu_protest.story).
[3]United Students Against Sweatshops Web site, accessed June 6, 2002 (http://www.usasnet.org/who/history.shtml).
[4]Marklein, M. B. (October 20, 1999). Sweatshop Foes Form Alliance of Universities. *USA Today*, accessed June 10, 2002 (http://www.usasnet.org/resources/articles/NLC/USAToday10-20-99.html).
[5]Worker Rights Consortium Web site, accessed June 13, 2002 (http://www.workersrights.org).
[6]Thompson, G. (October 8, 2001). Mexican Labor Protest Gets Results. *New York Times*.
[7]Hats Off: A U.S. Cap Company Gets a Hard Look from Universities. *The Wall Street Journal Online*, accessed June 13, 2002 (http://www.workersrights.org/wsj.pdf).
[8]Williams, F. (June 6, 2002). New Era Cap, Union Reach Deal to End Strike. *The Buffalo News*, accessed June 13, 2002 (http://www.workersrights.org/buffalo_news_6.5.02.pdf).
[9]A Renewed Analysis of the Fair Labor Association. USAS Web site, accessed June 10, 2002 (http://usasnet.org/old/oldsite/organizing/info/flacritique.pdf).
[10]Fair Labor Association Web site, accessed June 13, 2002 (http://www.fairlabor.org/html/summary.html).
[11]FLA Facilitates Key Agreement to Re-Hire Workers Under Third Party Complaint Process. (January 28, 2002). Fair Labor Association website, accessed June 13, 2002 (http://www.fairlabor.org/html/press.html#Press012902).
[12]Committee Report on Apparel Licensing to FSU Faculty Senate Steering Committee. (March 28, 2001).
[13]Greenhouse, S. (September 28, 2000). Report Says Global Accounting Firm Overlooks Factory Abuses. *New York Times,* accessed June 11, 2002 (http://www.hartford-hwp.com/archives/26/073.html).
[14]Changes to the FLA: A Comparison of the Old and New System. Fair Labor Association Web site, accessed June 13, 2002 (http://www.fairlabor.org/html/new_fla_comparison.html).
[15]Committee Report on Apparel Licensing to FSU Faculty Senate.
[16]Twelve Florida State Students Arrested.
[17]Yeager, M. (March 4, 2002). Sweatshop Campaign by Students Comes to Head, *Tallahassee Democrat,* accessed June 12, 2002 (http://www.tallahassee.com/mld/democrat/news/local/2786363.htm).
[18]Worker Rights Consortium Web site.

CRITICAL THINKING APPLICATION 2-B

International HR: How about a Cuppa?[1]

Starbucks (www.starbucks.com) opened its first location in 1971 in Seattle's Pike Place Market. By 1987, with the backing of local investors, Il Giornale acquired Starbucks' assets and changed its name to Starbucks Corporation with 17 locations. One year later, Starbucks introduced a mail-order catalog with service to all 50 states and expanded to 33 locations. Starbucks built a new roasting plant in 1990 and opened its 84th location. In 1991, Starbucks became the first U.S. privately owned company to offer a stock option program that included part-time employees and started offering coffee in airport locations. Nineteen ninety-two saw Starbucks complete its initial public offering trading on the Nasdaq under the symbol "SBUX."

By 1995, Starbucks had formed an alliance with Canadian bookstore Chapters Inc. and Starbucks Coffee International formed a joint venture with SAZABY Inc.

to develop Starbucks coffeehouses in Japan. Its 676 locations began selling compact discs. One year later, Starbucks Coffee International opened locations in Japan, Hawaii, and Singapore. In just five years, Starbucks opened its 300th Japanese location. Also in 1996, Starbucks Coffee Japan introduced a stock option program for its full- and part-time partners and successfully implemented an IPO.

Starbucks locations in 2005 total 5,240. By the end of 2006, Starbucks plans to open in China, Argentina, Brazil, Chile, Colombia, Peru, and Venezuela. Starbucks currently has existing partnerships with the following markets:

Australia	Lebanon	Qatar
Austria	Malaysia	Saudi Arabia
Bahrain	Mexico	Singapore
Canada	New Zealand	South Korea
Germany	Oman	Spain
Greece	People's	Switzerland
Hawaii	Republic of	Taiwan
Hong Kong	China (Beijing)	Thailand
S.A.R.	People's	United Arab
Israel	Republic of	Emirates
Japan	China (Shanghai)	United Kingdom
Kuwait	Philippines	United States

Starbucks does not sell individual franchises or subfranchises. Starbucks Coffee Company either will operate its coffeehouses directly (or through a local subsidiary) or will enter into a business agreement with a company or group of individuals. This company or group is granted the right to develop and operate coffeehouses throughout a defined region. Their development strategy adapts to different markets addressing local needs and requirements.

Starbucks currently uses three business strategies: joint ventures, licenses, and company-owned operations. Starbucks' global success would not be possible without their international partners, who share in their values and commitment to bringing the Starbucks Experience to customers worldwide.

They choose their partners based on:

Shared values and corporate culture

Strong multiunit retail/restaurant experience

Dedicated human resources

Commitment to customer service

Quality image

Creative ability, local knowledge, and brand-building skills

Strong financial resources

Assignment

So what are the critical HR issues with regard to Starbucks' international goals? What are the key questions that must be asked once research has determined the market is going to be profitable in a particular country? In terms of the HR domains discussed in Chapter 1, what answers are required before getting too far along in plans to open another location? Write down what you regard as the top five most important questions for which you need answers. Select a country that you believe would be a good opportunity for a Starbucks location. Then think about the variables you considered in selecting that country. Write down those variables.

[1] Contributed by Mary E. Wilson.

CRITICAL THINKING APPLICATION 3-A

Are Dreadlocks Protected under Title VII?

Christopher Polk was a delivery employee for FedEx when he listened to a Lord Jamal music video rapping about Rastafarian beliefs in the sanctity of dreadlocks. Such dreadlocks, permanently interlocked strands of hair, were worn by African chieftains 6,000 years ago. Polk became a Rastafarian and grew shoulder length locks to symbolize his new religious path. Dreadlocks are now quite fashionable and worn by many who do not practice Rastafarianism.

But Polk's new hair style violated FedEx grooming policy of a "reasonable style." After several internal rounds of problem solving, FedEx ordered Polk to cut his hair or be assigned to a job with no direct customer contact and lower pay. He refused and was terminated. He sued under Title VII, claiming religious discrimination. Six other FedEx employees lost their jobs for the same reason. These are not isolated cases. Police departments, prison authorities, retailers and schools have also been sued after refusing to allow dreadlocks that are not covered at work.

In general, courts have allowed employers to impose their own grooming standards providing that such standards are applied uniformly or fairly. For example, when Afros were all the rage, an employer could be accused of not applying a grooming policy fairly if Afros were banned but long hair or ponytails were allowed for men. But there was no religious basis to these hairstyle cases. Although limited, the legal track record for hair styles based on religion versus grooming policy is more favorable to plaintiffs like Mr. Polk. For example, Sikh men have won lawsuits based on their religion that requires them to wear their beards.

Assignment

Should Mr. Polk and others be allowed to violate a grooming policy on the basis of a religious proclamation on the sanctity of dreadlocks? Why or why not? If you answer "yes," is there any point where you would draw the line in terms of company policy regarding appearance and the religious implications of dress? Does FedEx have a right to impose a reasonable grooming policy based on customer reactions to personnel appearances?

CRITICAL THINKING APPLICATION 3-B

Allegations of Religious Discrimination

In 2004, the Equal Employment Opportunity Commission (www.eeoc.gov) received 2,466 charges of religious discrimination, resolved 2,676 religious discrimination charges, and recovered $6 million in monetary benefits for charging parties and other aggrieved individuals (not including monetary benefits obtained through litigation). Title VII of the Civil Rights Act of 1964 prohibits employers from discriminating against individuals because of their religion in hiring, firing, and other terms and conditions of employment. Title VII covers employers with 15 or more employees, including state and local governments. It also applies to employment agencies and to labor organizations, as well as to the federal government.

Under Title VII:

Employers may not treat employees or applicants less—or more—favorably because of their religious beliefs or practices. For example, an employer may not refuse to hire individuals of a certain religion, may not impose stricter promotion requirements for persons of a certain religion, and may not impose more or different work requirements on an employee because of that employee's religious beliefs or practices.

Employees cannot be forced to participate—or not participate—in a religious activity as a condition of employment.

Employers must reasonably accommodate employees' sincerely held religious beliefs or practices unless doing so would impose an undue hardship on the employer. A reasonable religious accommodation is any adjustment to the work environment that will allow the employee to practice his or her religion. Flexible scheduling, voluntary substitutions or swaps, job reassignments and lateral transfer, and modifying workplace practices, policies and/or procedures are examples of how an employer might accommodate an employee's religious beliefs.

An employer is not required to accommodate an employee's religious beliefs and practices if doing so would impose an undue hardship on the employer's legitimate business interests. An employer can show undue hardship if accommodating an employee's religious practices requires more than ordinary administrative costs, diminishes efficiency in other jobs, infringes on other employees' job rights or benefits, impairs

workplace safety, causes co-workers to carry the accommodated employee's share of potentially hazardous or burdensome work, or if the proposed accommodation conflicts with another law or regulation.

Employers must permit employees to engage in religious expression if employees are permitted to engage in other personal expression at work, unless the religious expression would impose an undue hardship on the employer. Therefore, an employer may not place more restrictions on religious expression than on other forms of expression that have a comparable effect on workplace efficiency.

Employers must take steps to prevent religious harassment of their employees. An employer can reduce the chance that employees will engage unlawful religious harassment by implementing an anti-harassment policy and having an effective procedure for reporting, investigating, and correcting harassing conduct.

It is also unlawful to retaliate against an individual for opposing employment practices that discriminate based on religion or for filing a discrimination charge, testifying, or participating in any way in an investigation, proceeding, or litigation under Title VII.

Assignment

Consider each of the four scenarios below and answer the questions after each one.

1. Muhammad, who is Arab American, works for XYZ Motors, a large used car business. Muhammad meets with his manager and complains that Bill, one of his co-workers, regularly calls him names like "camel jockey," "the local terrorist," and "the ayatollah," and has intentionally embarrassed him in front of customers by claiming that he is incompetent. How should the superior respond?

2. Three of the 10 Muslim employees in XYZ's 30-person template design division approach their supervisor and ask that they be allowed to use a conference room in an adjacent building for prayer. Until making the request, those employees prayed at their workstations. What should XYZ do?

3. Susan is an experienced clerical worker who wears a hijab (head scarf) in conformance with her Muslim beliefs. XYZ Temps places Susan in a long-term assignment with one of its clients. The client contacts XYZ and requests that it notify Susan that she must remove her hijab while working at the front desk, or that XYZ assign another person to Susan's position. According to the client, Susan's religious attire violates its dress code and presents the "wrong image." Should XYZ comply with its client's request?

4. Anwar, who was born in Egypt, applies for a position as a security guard with XYZ Corp., which contracts to provide security services at government office building. Can XYZ require Muhammad to undergo a background investigation before he is hired?

CRITICAL THINKING APPLICATION 4-A

Can PAS Defend Its Test in Court?

Personnel Assessment Systems was asked to develop a job-related and valid screening test to hire armed and unarmed security guards for a large corporation. The job analysis method is described below. Supervisors were asked to complete the following form:

Required Abilities and Characteristics Rating Form

Personnel Assessment Systems is studying security officer jobs in several companies to develop a valid battery of tests for hiring decisions. As part of our research, we are asking you for some information about the kinds of abilities and other characteristics required for effective performance in the entry-level security job with which you are most familiar. In the space below please write in the job title of the security job under study. Then fill in the information requested below on your experience performing and supervising this particular job.

Take a minute to think about the duties performed by security officers in this position and the kinds of abilities and characteristics they should have. On the following pages, we have listed a number of abilities and characteristics that may be necessary for performing as a security officer. Please read each one and decide how important you feel this ability or characteristic is to perform the *essential functions* of the security officer job. Use the following scale to make your ratings:

0—Neither useful nor necessary to perform one or more of the essential functions of the job at a minimally acceptable level

1—Useful but not necessary to perform one or more of the essential functions of the job at a minimally acceptable level

2—Necessary to perform one or more of the essential functions of the job at a minimally acceptable level

All of the following abilities and characteristics were assessed as "essential functions" (2s) by 75 percent or more of supervisors who were asked to complete the job analysis form.

Ability or Characteristic

Color vision: ability to distinguish red, yellow, blue, and green colors

Normal peripheral visual field (150°–180°)

Visual acuity: ability to distinguish small details from a complex background; ability to read indicator numbers from a normal viewing distance

Depth perception

Auditory acuity: ability to hear changes in pitch or loudness of equipment noises; ability to distinguish spoken language from a noisy background

Tactual acuity: ability to feel heat or vibrations in equipment

Sense of smell

Ability to read and comprehend blueprints, schematics, diagrams, or structures

Ability to respond appropriately under stress

Emotional stability

Analytical ability: ability to reason way through problems; detect trends, plan actions in a logical, orderly manner

System comprehension: ability to comprehend entire systems and how they function; ability to foresee system implications of malfunctions or of own actions; ability to *anticipate* required future conditions in numerous interacting systems

Ability to retain and recall information

Attention to detail: ability to perceive and interpret small details

Conscientiousness in checking and caring for equipment

Ability to add, subtract, multiply, and divide whole numbers, decimals, fractions

Ability to comprehend, use, and/or compute logs, powers, trigonometry, scientific notation

Ability to follow complex sequence of activities

Ability to control one's temper

Ability to remain calm in difficult situations

Ability to stay alert for possible unlawful activities

Ability to follow directions carefully

Ability to reason with multiple concepts and operations

Ability to identify clerical errors quickly

Ability to detect rule violations

Based on these job analysis results, PAS developed a test, a portion of which is presented below, that would be administered to job applicants. PAS then developed a "suitability" scoring procedure for the test, including the following:

Suitability for *responding to stressful aspects* of the job such as reacting quickly in dangerous situations, always controlling one's temper, remaining emotionally in control under difficult circumstances and dealing with difficult individuals.

The applicant's responses indicate (below average, average, above average) likelihood that the applicant will react appropriately and effectively in stressful situations.

Suitability for *interacting with clients, customers, and others* such as being friendly with customers/clients; always being courteous, treating all people the same regardless of their race, gender, age, national origin or disability, and being able to effectively communicate with different types of clients and customers.

Portion of Security Officer Test

Format: Job applicants must indicate whether each statement is TRUE OR FALSE about them:

1. Most of the time, I feel life has let me down.
2. I used to steal a lot when I was young.
3. I'm almost always angry to some extent.
4. I would like to be a police officer.
5. People from different races are more different than the same.
6. I like to jump from job to job.
7. I have trouble understanding written material.
8. I often feel things are out of my control.
9. Almost everyone I know is luckier than I.
10. I drink liquor or beer almost every day.
11. At times, I just want to punch someone.
12. Kids who are bad deserve to be spanked.
13. I dislike most of the people I know.
14. Things are out of my control most of the time.
15. I often lose my self-control.
16. I have a little problem with alcohol.
17. Everybody should be allowed to carry a handgun.
18. I cannot tolerate others' mistakes.
19. I'm almost always happy.
20. Stealing from an employer is acceptable if the employer cheats you.
21. I skipped over 20 days of school in my last year of high school.
22. I tend to get quite irritable when I'm tired.
23. I have great difficulty sleeping.
24. I enjoy watching a good fight.
25. Police officers deserve respect.
26. If I got this job, I'd probably keep it for about six months.
27. I've gotten into more than 15 physical fights in my life.
28. Success in life is mainly due to luck.
29. I've been drunk more than five times in my life.
30. I can tolerate a great deal before I get upset.
31. If I am hired for this job, I'll almost certainly keep it for over a year.
32. I almost always reach personal goals I set for myself.
33. If I am in charge, things have to be done my way or I'll quit.
34. I tend to get angry when I am criticized in a group.
35. When a person gets annoyed with me, I quickly get annoyed back.
36. I fear big government.
37. I don't believe in gay marriage.
38. I get depressed often.
39. Sometimes I am not in the mood to see anyone.
40. I get angry often.
41. I have fewer friends than most people.
42. Most people think I am too emotional.
43. I often get angry too quickly with people.
44. Daring and foolish things are fun to do.
45. I feel I am an outgoing, social person and fun to be with.
46. Marijuana should be legalized.

Assignment

Based on your understanding of the law and the job analysis results, can the company use this test to screen applicants? Are there specific test items that are (or may be) legally problematic? What (if any) other information do you need about the job analysis, the test, or anything else to be able to take a definitive position on whether the company should use the test? Do you regard any of these questions as an invasion of privacy? If so, which items?

CRITICAL THINKING APPLICATION 4-B

What to Do with Job Diagnostic Survey Results

Assignment

If you have a full-time job, complete the entire questionnaire and score it using the directions in Appendix A (page 406). Then answer the discussion questions. If you do not have a full-time job, ask someone you know to complete the JDS.

Job Diagnostic Survey

This questionnaire was developed as part of a Yale University study of jobs and how people react to them. The questionnaire helps to determine how jobs can be better designed, by obtaining information about how people react to different kinds of jobs.

On the following pages you will find several different kinds of questions about your job. Specific instructions are given at the start of each section. Please read them carefully. It should take no more than 25 minutes to complete the entire questionnaire. Please move through it quickly.

The questions are designed to obtain *your* perceptions of your job and *your* reactions to it. There are no trick questions. Your individual answers will be kept completely confidential. Please answer each item as honestly and frankly as possible.

Thank you for your cooperation.

SECTION ONE

This part of the questionnaire asks you to describe your job, as *objectively* as you can.

Please do *not* use this part of the questionnaire to show how much you like or dislike your job. Questions about that will come later. Instead, try to make your descriptions as accurate and as objective as you possibly can.

A sample question is given below.

A.   To what extent does your job require you to work with mechanical equipment?

1-------------2-------------3-------------4-------------5------------(6)------------7

Very little; the job requires   Moderately   Very much; the job requires
almost no contact with   almost constant work with
mechanical equipment of   mechanical equipment.
any kind.

You are to *circle* the number which is the most accurate description of your job.

If, for example, your job requires you to work with mechanical equipment a good deal of the time—but also requires some paperwork—you might circle the number six, as was done in the example above.

If you do not understand these instructions, please ask for assistance. If you do understand them, begin now.

1.   To what extent does your job require you to *work closely with other people* (either "clients," or people in related jobs in your own organization)?

1-------------2-------------3-------------4-------------5-------------6-------------7

Very little; dealing with   Moderately; some dealing   Very much; dealing with
other people is not at all   with others is necessary.   other people is an absolutely
necessary in doing the job.   essential and crucial part of
                                                                      doing the job.

2.   How much *autonomy* is there in your job? That is, to what extent does your job permit you to decide *on your own* how to go about doing the work?

1-------------2-------------3-------------4-------------5-------------6-------------7

Very little; the job gives me   Moderate autonomy; many   Very much; the job gives
almost no personal "say"   things are standardized and   me almost complete responsibility
about how and when the   not under my control, but I   for deciding how and when
work is done.   can make some decisions   the work is done.
                                    about the work.

3.   To what extent does your job involve doing a *"whole" and identifiable piece of work?* That is, is the job a complete piece of work that has an obvious beginning and end? Or is it only a small *part* of the overall piece of work, which is finished by other people or by automatic machines?

1-------------2-------------3-------------4-------------5-------------6-------------7

My job is only a tiny part of   My job is a moderate-sized   My job involves doing the
the overall piece of work;   "chunk" of the overall piece   whole piece of work, from
the results of my activities   of work; my own contribution   start to finish; the results of
cannot be seen in the final   can be seen in the final   my activities are easily seen
product or service.   outcome.   in the final product or
                                                                      service.

4. How much *variety* is there in your job? That is, to what extent does the job require you to do many different things at work, using a variety of your skills and talents?

1-------------2-------------3-------------4-------------5-------------6-------------7

Very little; the job requires me to do the same routine things over and over again.

Moderate variety.

Very much; the job requires me to do many different things, using a number of different skills and talents.

5. In general, how *significant or important* is your job? That is, are the results of your work likely to significantly affect the lives or well-being of other people?

1-------------2-------------3-------------4-------------5-------------6-------------7

Not very significant; the outcomes of my work are *not* likely to have important effects on other people.

Moderately significant.

Highly significant; the outcomes of my work can affect other people in very important ways.

6. To what extent do *managers or co-workers* let you know how well you are doing on your job?

1-------------2-------------3-------------4-------------5-------------6-------------7

Very little; people almost never let me know how well I am doing.

Moderately; sometimes people may give me "feedback"; other times they may not.

Very much; managers or co-workers provide me with almost constant "feedback" about how well I am doing.

7. To what extent does *doing the job itself* provide you with information about your work performance? That is, does the actual *work itself* provide clues about how well you are doing—aside from any "feedback" co-workers or supervisors may provide?

1-------------2-------------3-------------4-------------5-------------6-------------7

Very little; the job itself is set up so I could work forever without finding out how well I am doing.

Moderately; sometimes doing the job provides "feedback" to me; sometimes it does not.

Very much; the job is set up so that I get almost constant "feedback" as I work about how well I am doing.

SECTION TWO

Listed below are a number of statements which could be used to describe a job.

You are to indicate whether each statement is an *accurate* or an *inaccurate* description of *your* job.

Once again, please try to be as objective as you can in deciding how accurately each statement describes your job—regardless of whether you like or dislike your job.

Write a number in the blank beside each statement, based on the following scale:

How accurate is the statement in describing your job?

1	2	3	4	5	6	7
Very Inaccurate	Mostly Inaccurate	Slightly Inaccurate	Uncertain	Slightly Accurate	Mostly Accurate	Very Accurate

_____ 1. The job requires me to use a number of complex or high-level skills.

_____ 2. The job requires a lot of cooperative work with other people.

_____ 3. The job is arranged so that I do *not* have the chance to do an entire piece of work from beginning to end.

_____ 4. Just doing the work required by the job provides many chances for me to figure out how well I am doing.

_____ 5. The job is quite simple and repetitive.

_____ 6. The job can be done adequately by a person working alone—without talking or checking with other people.

_____ 7. The supervisors and co-workers on this job almost *never* give me any "feedback" about how well I am doing in my work.

_____ 8. This job is one where a lot of other people can be affected by how well the work gets done.

_____ 9. The job denies me any chance to use my personal initiative or judgment in carrying out the work.

_____ 10. Supervisors often let me know how well they think I am performing the job.

_____ 11. The job provides me the chance to completely finish the pieces of work I begin.

_____ 12. The job itself provides very few clues about whether or not I am performing well.

_____ 13. The job gives me considerable opportunity for independence and freedom in how I do the work.

_____ 14. The job itself is *not* very significant or important in the broader scheme of things.

SECTION THREE

Now please indicate how *you personally feel about your job.*

Each of the statements below is something that a person might say about his or her job. You are to indicate your own personal *feelings* about your job by marking how much you agree with each of the statements.

Write a number in the blank for each statement, based on this scale:

How much do you agree with the statement?

1	2	3	4	5	6	7
Disagree Strongly	Disagree	Disagree Slightly	Neutral	Agree Slightly	Agree	Agree Strongly

_____ 1. It's hard, on this job, for me to care very much about whether or not the work gets done right.

_____ 2. My opinion of myself goes up when I do this job well.

_____ 3. Generally speaking, I am very satisfied with this job.

_____ 4. Most of the things I have to do on this job seem useless or trivial.

_____ 5. I usually know whether or not my work is satisfactory on this job.

_____ 6. I feel a great sense of personal satisfaction when I do this job well.

_____ 7. The work I do on this job is very meaningful to me.

_____ 8. I feel a very high degree of *personal* responsibility for the work I do on this job.

_____ 9. I frequently think of quitting this job.

_____ 10. I feel bad and unhappy when I discover that I have performed poorly on this job.

_____ 11. I often have trouble figuring out whether I'm doing well or poorly on this job.

_____ 12. I feel I should personally take the credit or blame for the results of my work on this job.

_____ 13. I am generally satisfied with the kind of work I do in this job.

_____ 14. My own feelings generally are *not* affected much one way or the other by how well I do on this job.

_____ 15. Whether or not this job gets done right is clearly *my* responsibility.

SECTION FOUR

Now please indicate how *satisfied* you are with each aspect of your job listed below. Once again, write the appropriate number in the blank beside each statement.

How satisfied are you with this aspect of your job?

1	2	3	4	5	6	7
Extremely Dissatisfied	Dissatisfied	Slightly Dissatisfied	Neutral	Slightly Satisfied	Satisfied	Extremely Satisfied

_____ 1. The amount of job security I have.

_____ 2. The amount of pay and fringe benefits I receive.

_____ 3. The amount of personal growth and development I get in doing my job.

_____ 4. The people I talk to and work with on my job.

_____ 5. The degree of respect and fair treatment I receive from my boss.

_____ 6. The feeling of worthwhile accomplishment I get from doing my job.

_____ 7. The chance to get to know other people while on the job.

_____ 8. The amount of support and guidance I receive from my supervisor.

_____ 9. The degree to which I am fairly paid for what I contribute to this organization.

_____ 10. The amount of independent thought and action I can exercise in my job.

_____ 11. How secure things look for me in the future in this organization.

_____ 12. The chance to help other people while at work.

_____ 13. The amount of challenge in my job.

_____ 14. The overall quality of the supervision I receive in my work.

SECTION FIVE

Now please think of the *other people* in your organization who hold the same job you do. If no one has exactly the same job as you, think of the job which is most similar to yours.

Please think about how accurately each of the statements describes the feelings of those people about the job.

It is quite all right if your answers here are different from when you described your *own* reactions to the job. Often different people feel quite differently about the same job.

Once again, write a number in the blank for each statement, based on this scale:

How much do you agree with the statement?

1	2	3	4	5	6	7
Disagree Strongly	Disagree	Disagree Slightly	Neutral	Agree Slightly	Agree	Agree Strongly

_____ 1. Most people on this job feel a great sense of personal satisfaction when they do the job well.

_____ 2. Most people on this job are very satisfied with the job.

_____ 3. Most people on this job feel that the work is useless or trivial.

_____ 4. Most people on this job feel a great deal of personal responsibility for the work they do.

_____ 5. Most people on this job have a pretty good idea of how well they are performing their work.

_____ 6. Most people on this job find the work very meaningful.

_____ 7. Most people on this job feel that whether or not the job gets done right is clearly their own responsibility.

_____ 8. People on this job often think of quitting.

_____ 9. Most people on this job feel bad or unhappy when they find that they have performed the work poorly.

_____ 10. Most people on this job have trouble figuring out whether they are doing a good or a bad job.

SECTION SIX

Listed below are a number of characteristics which could be present on any job. People differ about how much they would like to have each one present in their own jobs. We are interested in learning *how much you personally would like* to have each one present in your job.

Using the scale below, please indicate the *degree* to which you *would like* to have each characteristic present in your job.

> Note: The numbers on this scale are different from those used in previous scales.

4	5	6	7	8	9	10
Would like having this only a moderate amount (or less)			Would like having this very much			Would like having this *extremely* much

_____ 1. High respect and fair treatment from my supervisor.

_____ 2. Stimulating and challenging work.

_____ 3. Chances to exercise independent thought and action in my job.

_____ 4. Great job security.

_____ 5. Very friendly co-workers.

_____ 6. Opportunities to learn new things from my work.

_____ 7. High salary and good fringe benefits.

_____ 8. Opportunities to be creative and imaginative in my work.

_____ 9. Quick promotions.

_____ 10. Opportunities for personal growth and development in my job.

_____ 11. A sense of worthwhile accomplishment in my work.

SECTION SEVEN

People differ in the kinds of jobs they would most like to hold. The questions in this section give you a chance to say just what it is about a job that is most important to *you*.

For each question, two different kinds of jobs are briefly described. You are to indicate which of the jobs you personally would prefer—if you had to make a choice between them

In answering each question, assume that everything else about the jobs is the same. Pay attention only to the characteristics actually listed.

Two examples are given below.

JOB A			*JOB B*	
A job requiring work with mechanical equipment most of the day			A job requiring work with other people most of the day	
1	2	(3)	4	5
Strongly Prefer A	Slightly Prefer A	Neutral	Slightly Prefer B	Strongly Prefer B

If you like working with people and working with equipment equally well, you would circle the number 3, as has been done in the example.

*   *   *   *   *   *   *   *   *   *   *   *   *   *

Here is another example. This one asks for a harder choice—between two jobs which both have some undesirable features.

JOB A			*JOB B*	
A job requiring you to expose yourself to considerable physical danger.			A job located 200 miles from your home and family.	
1	(2)	3	4	5
Strongly Prefer A	Slightly Prefer A	Neutral	Slightly Prefer B	Strongly Prefer B

If you would slightly prefer risking physical danger to working far from your home, you would circle number 2, as has been done in the example.

Please ask for assistance if you do not understand exactly how to do these questions.

JOB A			*JOB B*	
1. A job where the pay is very good.			A job where there is considerable opportunity to be creative and innovative.	
1	2	3	4	5
Strongly Prefer A	Slightly Prefer A	Neutral	Slightly Prefer B	Strongly Prefer B

JOB A			*JOB B*	
2. A job where you are often required to make important decisions.			A job with many pleasant people to work with.	
1	2	3	4	5
Strongly Prefer A	Slightly Prefer A	Neutral	Slightly Prefer B	Strongly Prefer B

JOB A		*JOB B*	

3. A job in which greater responsibility is given to those who do the best work.

A job in which greater responsibility is given to loyal employees who have the most seniority.

1	2	3	4	5
Strongly Prefer A	Slightly Prefer A	Neutral	Slightly Prefer B	Strongly Prefer B

4. A job in an organization which is in financial trouble—and might have to close down within the year.

A job in which you are not allowed to have any say whatever in how your work is scheduled, or in the procedures to be used in carrying it out.

1	2	3	4	5
Strongly Prefer A	Slightly Prefer A	Neutral	Slightly Prefer B	Strongly Prefer B

JOB A		*JOB B*	

5. A very routine job.

A job where your co-workers are not very friendly.

1	2	3	4	5
Strongly Prefer A	Slightly Prefer A	Neutral	Slightly Prefer B	Strongly Prefer B

6. A job with a supervisor who is often very critical of you and your work in front of other people.

A job which prevents you from using a number of skills that you worked hard to develop.

1	2	3	4	5
Strongly Prefer A	Slightly Prefer A	Neutral	Slightly Prefer B	Strongly Prefer B

7. A job with a supervisor who respects you and treats you fairly.

A job which provides constant opportunities for you to learn new and interesting things.

1	2	3	4	5
Strongly Prefer A	Slightly Prefer A	Neutral	Slightly Prefer B	Strongly Prefer B

JOB A		*JOB B*	

8. A job where there is a real chance you could be laid off.

A job with very little chance to do challenging work.

1	2	3	4	5
Strongly Prefer A	Slightly Prefer A	Neutral	Slightly Prefer B	Strongly Prefer B

9. A job in which there is a real chance for you to develop new skills and advance in the organization.

A job which provides lots of vacation time and an excellent fringe benefit package.

1	2	3	4	5
Strongly Prefer A	Slightly Prefer A	Neutral	Slightly Prefer B	Strongly Prefer B

JOB A

JOB B

10. A job with little freedom and independence to do your work in the way you think best.

A job where the working conditions are poor.

1----------------------------2----------------------------3----------------------------4----------------------------5

| Strongly Prefer A | Slightly Prefer A | Neutral | Slightly Prefer B | Strongly Prefer B |

JOB A

JOB B

11. A job with very satisfying teamwork.

A job which allows you to use your skills and abilities to the fullest extent.

1----------------------------2----------------------------3----------------------------4----------------------------5

| Strongly Prefer A | Slightly Prefer A | Neutral | Slightly Prefer B | Strongly Prefer B |

12. A job which offers little or no challenge.

A job which requires you to be completely isolated from co-workers.

1----------------------------2----------------------------3----------------------------4----------------------------5

| Strongly Prefer A | Slightly Prefer A | Neutral | Slightly Prefer B | Strongly Prefer B |

SECTION EIGHT

Biographical Background

1. Sex: Male _____   Female _____

2. Age (check one):

_____ under 20   _____ 40–49

_____ 20–29   _____ 50–59

_____ 30–39   _____ 60 or over

3. Education (check one for highest level attained):

_____ Grade School

_____ Some High School

_____ High School Degree

_____ Some Business College or Technical School Experience

_____ Some College Experience (other than business or technical school)

_____ Business College or Technical School Degree

_____ College Degree

_____ Master's or Higher Degree

4. What is your brief job title? _____

Appendix A   Scoring Key for the Job Diagnostic Survey

The scoring manual for the Job Diagnostic Survey (JDS) is presented below. For each variable measured by the JDS, the questionnaire items that are averaged to yield a summary score for the variable are listed.

***

I. JOB CHARACTERISTICS.
  A. *Skill variety.* Average the following items:
      Section One: #4
      Section Two: #1
                     #5 (reversed scoring—i.e., subtract the number entered by the respondent from 8)
  B. *Task identity.* Average the following items:
      Section One: #3
      Section Two: #11
                     #3 (reversed scoring)
  C. *Task significance.* Average the following items:
      Section One: #5
      Section Two: #8
                     #14 (reversed scoring)
  D. *Autonomy.* Average the following items:
      Section One: #2
      Section Two: #13
                     #9 (reversed scoring)
  E. *Feedback from the job itself.* Average the following items:
      Section One: #7
      Section Two: #4
                     #12 (reversed scoring)
  F. *Feedback from agents.* Average the following items:
      Section One: #6
      Section Two: #10
                     #7 (reversed scoring)
  G. *Dealing with others.* Average the following items:
      Section One: #1
      Section Two: #2
                     #6 (reversed scoring)

II. EXPERIENCED PSYCHOLOGICAL STATES. Each of the three constructs are measured both directly (Section Three) and indirectly, via projective-type items (Section Five).
  A. *Experienced meaningfulness of the work.* Average the following items:
      Section Three: #7
                       #4 (reversed scoring)
      Section Five: #6
                       #3 (reversed scoring)

  B. *Experienced responsibility for the work.* Average the following items:
      Section Three: #8, #12, #15
                       #1 (reversed scoring)
      Section Five: #4, #7
  C. *Knowledge of results.* Average the following items:
      Section Three: #5
                       #11 (reversed scoring)
      Section Five: #5
                       #10 (reversed scoring)

III. AFFECTIVE OUTCOMES. The first two constructs (general satisfaction and internal work motivation) are measured both directly (Section Three) and indirectly (Section Five); growth satisfaction is measured only directly (Section Four).
  A. *General satisfaction.* Average the following items:
      Section Three: #3, #13
                       #9 (reversed scoring)
      Section Five: #2
                       #8 (reversed scoring)
  B. *Internal work motivation.* Average the following items:
      Section Three: #2, #6, #10
                       #14 (reversed scoring)
      Section Five: #1, #9
  C. *Growth satisfaction.* Average the following items:
      Section Four: #3, #6, #10, #13

IV. CONTEXT SATISFACTIONS. Each of these short scales uses items from Section Four only.
  A. *Satisfaction with job security.* Average items #1 and #11 of Section Four.
  B. *Satisfaction with compensation (pay).* Average items #2 and #9 of Section Four.
  C. *Satisfaction with co-workers.* Average items #4, #7, and #12 of Section Four.
  D. *Satisfaction with supervision.* Average items #5, #8, and #14 of Section Four.

V. INDIVIDUAL GROWTH NEED STRENGTH. The questionnaire yields two separate measures of growth need strength, one from Section Six (the "would like" format) and one from Section Seven (the "job choice" format).
  A. *"Would like" format* (Section Six). Average the six items from Section Six listed below. Before averaging, subtract 3 from each item score; this will result in a summary scale ranging from one to seven. The items are:
  #2, #3, #6, #8, #10, #11

B. *"Job choice" format* (Section Seven). Each item in Section Seven yields a number from 1-5 (i.e., "Strongly prefer A" is scored 1; "Neutral" is scored 3; and "Strongly prefer B" is scored 5). Compute the need strength measure by averaging the twelve items as follows:
#1, #5, #7, #10, #11, #12 (direct scoring)
#2, #3, #4, #6, #8, #9   (reversed scoring—i.e., subtract the respondent's score from 6)
Note: To transform the job choice summary score from a 5-point scale to a 7-point scale, use this formula: $Y = 1.5X - .5$.

C. *Combined growth need strength score.* To obtain an overall estimate of growth need strength based on both "would like" and "job choice" data, first transform the "job choice" summary score to a 7-point scale (using the formula given above), and then average the "would like" and the transformed "job choice" summary scores.

VI. MOTIVATING POTENTIAL SCORE.

$$\text{Motivating potential score (MPS)} = \left[\frac{\text{Skill variety} + \text{Task identity} + \text{Task significance}}{3} \right] \times \text{Autonomy} \times \text{Feedback from the job}$$

Discussion Questions

1. Conduct research on the Job Diagnostic Survey and the Job Characteristics Model and after receiving information on how to interpret your score, make some predictions about the implications of your score for important work outcomes.

2. Play the role of an HRM consultant. Explain how you would use the JDS results to facilitate changes in the design of work. What steps would you take to ensure you are receiving accurate information?

CRITICAL THINKING APPLICATION 5-A

Recruiting on the Internet[1]

The iLogos Research (www.iLogos.com), a consulting firm, Global 500 Web site Recruiting: 2003 Survey found 94 percent of the firms are using corporate career Web sites. iLogos estimates in 2004–2005 the Global 500 career Web site adoption rate will reach nearly 100 percent since the current late-adopters will catch up with technology.[2]

The 2002 iLogos study, *Where the Jobs Are: Fortune 500 Job Postings on Careers Web Sites and Major Job Boards,* found that 81 percent of Fortune 500 companies are posting job openings on their own career Web sites (e.g., www.starbucks.com/aboutus/hotjobs.asp) compared with 51 percent for Monster (www.monster.com), 43 percent for HotJobs (www.hotjobs), and 22 percent for CareerBuilder (www.careerbuilder.com). The study stated the total number of available positions on Fortune

500 corporate career Web sites was found to be approximately 75,000 compared with roughly 25,500 for Monster, 13,200 for CareerBuilder, and 7,800 for HotJobs (The numbers for 2006 are much higher for all three sites).[3]

As discussed in Chapter 5, recruiters complain that the Web has increased the number of résumés they must now sift through. Despite the additional work it creates, many recruiters prefer online recruiting due to the cost savings. One 1998 study of 45 Fortune 500 companies by iLogos Research revealed that the hiring cycle was shortened by 9 percent by posting jobs online. If the company took only online applications or résumés, it saved the average company another 12 percent, and when those applications or résumés were screened electronically, the company saved another 9 percent for an overall savings of 30 percent.[4] This is impressive considering speed is essential when it comes to winning top talent. As Peter Cappeli said in his "On-Line Recruiting" article for *Harvard Business Review,* "the first company to make contact often gains a huge advantage."[5]

Some companies may experience even higher returns. Dow Chemical (http://www.dow.com/careers/index.htm) actually saved 62 percent in the time it takes to fill a job by accepting applicants only online. It also saves 26 percent on its costs-per-hire average and reduced recruiting staff by 40 percent worldwide.[6]

With HRM becoming a more strategic and integral component of the competitive advantage equation, the adage of "first to market" can now be considered "first to talent." One of the ways a company can find its talent faster is in an efficient sorting tool. A hiring management system (HMS) tends to automate the process by standardizing the application in order to screen and track the candidate quickly. Although standardizing limits the applicant to the choice on the pull-down boxes, it can help companies track the application. Tracking can calculate how long it takes to fill a job or how long it takes for that new hire to become productive, giving the manager essential feedback on which employees are more productive based on the standardized information from the application.

In addition to the time, the average cost per hire through online recruiting is $152 compared with $1,383 using traditional methods like temporary agencies, according to a report by Thomas Weisel Partners.[7] Some experts argue that the practice of online recruiting using the best methods delivers better candidates, lowers hiring costs, and gives companies a competitive advantage. In fact, at companies such as Microsystems (www.sun.com/corp_emp/), Microsoft (http://www.microsoft.com/careers/default.mspx), and Unisys (http://www.unisys.com/about_unisys/careers/index.htm), online recruiting is second in securing new hires. Employee referral programs are still more efficient.[8]

As you probably know by going into your own college or university's Web site, schools at all levels are recruiting online. Even the federal government recruits online (www.usajobs.opm.gov/). So it is highly probable that you will be filling out an online application or submitting your résumés online. In addition to completing an online application, you may be asked to do a Net interview. The typical Net interviews may use digital conferencing equipment. Some recruiters are using video résumés. "I think it's a great idea. I can get a better feel for communication skills and the type of role people are looking for," says Jean Moss, HR manager for Symagery Microsystems (www.symagery.com).[9] The applicant has a one- to two-minute faux interview for the video résumé. The video file is then attached to the résumé file and e-mailed or posted on the job board. The interviews "help tell if the candidates are people you could work with and how they carry themselves in an interactive situation," says Kirsten Watson, president and CEO of HireTopTalent (www.hiretoptalent.com/videohandshake/index.shtml).[10]

Assignment

1. Would you be more or less attracted to an organization that used online recruiting only? Explain your answer.
2. How do you feel being limited to "what's in the box" (see www.dow.com/careers/index.htm as an example) on a standardized application?
3. Are there any methods described in Chapter 5 that could be adapted for online screening?
4. What are the legal implications for using a standardized application?
5. Would you be more or less attracted to an organization that required a video résumé? Explain your answer.

[1]Contributed by Mary Wilson. Updated 2006, by Renee Fitzgerald
[2]iLogos Research (2003). *Global 500 website recruiting: 2003 survey.*
[3]iLogos Research (2002). *Where the jobs are: Fortune 500 job postings on career web sites and major job boards—summary, p. 5.*
[4]iLogos Research (1998). *Achieving results with Internet recruiting,* pp. 10–11.
[5]Cappeli, P. (2001). "On-line recruiting." *Harvard Business Review, 79*(3), 139–147.
[6]Gill, J. (2001). *Now hiring. Apply online.* www.businessweek.com/careers/content/ju12011/ca20010718_003.htm.
[7]JobTipLotto.com. *Editorial—new & unique method of finding a job.* http://www.alamedajtl.com/html/news/editorial.html.
[8]McCool, J.D. (2002). *Adventures in online recruiting.* www.thestandard.com/article/0.1902.15665.00.html?body_page=2.
[9]www.hiretoptalent.com/videohandshake/index.shtml.
[10]Click here for sneak preview. (2002). *Profit, 21*(1), 69.

CRITICAL THINKING APPLICATION 5-B

Hi, I'm in Bangalore (but I Can't Say So)

In a *New York Times* article entitled "Hi, I'm in Bangalore (but I Can't Say So)," Mark Landler describes the training for customer service center workers in India.[1] "Hi, my name is Susan Sanders, and I'm from Chicago," said C. R. Suman, who is actually from India and is sitting in Bangalore as she talks with an American caller regarding a service offered by a U.S. telecommunications company. Part of Ms. Suman's training at Customer Asset, the Indian call center, is to "fake it" as an American. She not only receives considerable dialect training so callers think they are speaking with a midwesterner, she also is given instructions to lie to the caller about where she is from and where she is at the time of the call. "Susan's" parents are Bob and Ann, she has a brother Mark, and she attended the University of Illinois. Ms. Suman's training includes an episode of *Friends* in which she is supposed to learn the "in" phrases. Defenders of this practice maintain that customers are troubled if they find out that the company representative with whom they are dealing is over 8,000 miles away. Ms. Suman earns about $2,500 per year for full-time work with Customer Asset.

Assignment

What do you see as the major advantages and disadvantages of contracting with an overseas customer call center? What do you see as the advantages and disadvantages of allowing this outsourced organization to lie to your customers about who they are and where they are? Is it unethical to contract with such an organization? What if Customer Asset presented data showing American callers are more satisfied with the call service they receive from the "fake" Americans than from call center associates who admit they are Indians sitting in India? Would you be more accepting of this practice if data showed customers feel more secure about transactions if they feel they are interacting with an American? Do a Net search to determine what the salary would be of a customer service representative working in the United States.

[1]Landler, M. (March 21, 2001). Hi, I'm in Bangalore (but I can't say so). *New York Times* (http://NYTimes.qpass.com/qpass-archives/).

CRITICAL THINKING APPLICATION 5-C

Is Wal-Mart Guilty of Gender Discrimination?

Wal-Mart is the largest private employer in the United States and the world's largest retailer. Through its Wal-Mart and Sam's Club divisions, it operates over 3,000 stores across the country, encompassing every state. There are so many Wal-Mart locations in the United States that, according to Wal-Mart, the average store is within 30 miles of the next Wal-Mart store. In the United States, Wal-Mart employs nearly one million "associates," Wal-Mart's term for its hourly employees. In its last fiscal year, it had sales exceeding $191 billion. It claims that it has 100 million customers each week.

In 2000, Betty Dukes filed a sex discrimination claim against Wal-Mart. Dukes claimed that after six years of hard work and excellent performance reviews, she was denied the training Wal-Mart required to enable her to advance to a higher, salaried position. The lawsuit, *Dukes vs. Wal-Mart Stores, Inc.* (see www.walmartclass.com), was eventually expanded to represent 1.6 million women, comprising both current and former employees. As of January, 2006, the lawsuit was the largest civil rights class-action suit in history.

The plaintiffs charge Wal-Mart with discriminating against women in promotions, pay, and job assignments, in violation of Title VII of the 1964 Civil Rights Act. In a new book, "Selling Women Short: The Landmark Battle for Workers' Rights at Wal-Mart," journalist Liza Featherstone reviews the lawsuit. As described in Salon.com, Ms. Featherstone "paints a picture of Wal-Mart as a hypocritical, falsely pious, exceptionally greedy corporation that creates a massive sinkhole for working women."[1] Female employees from many stores across the United States claim they were repeatedly passed over for promotions, made to endure sexist comments from male co-workers, and paid significantly lower salaries for doing the same amount of work (or more).

The plaintiffs made the following claims:

1. Through its Wal-Mart and Sam's Club divisions, it is the industry leader not only in size, but also in its failure to advance its female employees. There are two workforces at Wal-Mart. By far the largest workforce is female, which comprises over 72 percent of the hourly sales employees, yet only one-third of management positions. This workforce is predominantly assigned to the lowest paying positions with the least chance of advancement. The other workforce is male. This workforce is the reverse image of the female workforce—it comprises less than 28 percent of the hourly sales workers, yet holds two-thirds of all store management positions and over 90 percent of the top Store Manager positions. This disparate distribution of the genders is the result of purposeful discrimination and of practices that serve no reasonable business purpose yet have a disproportionate impact on women.

2. The class action lawsuit was brought by present and former Wal-Mart employees on behalf of themselves and all other similarly situated women who have been subjected to Wal-Mart's continuing policies and practices of gender discrimination. Plaintiffs, and the class that they represent, charge that Wal-Mart discriminates against its female employees by advancing male employees more quickly than female employees, by denying female employees equal job assignments, promotions, training and compensation, and by retaliating against those who oppose its unlawful practices.

3. Wal-Mart employs uniform employment and personnel policies throughout the United States. All of its stores are linked by state-of-the-art electronic and video communications, through which all stores regularly report payroll, labor and other employment data. Regardless of division, there are uniform policies for employees, uniform "orientation" procedures, uniform salary, assignment, pay, training, and promotion policies. All stores are regularly audited for compliance with these uniform, companywide policies and procedures.

4. The vast majority of Wal-Mart store employees are hourly paid sales associates, who report to department heads. Each store has a number of assistant managers who have different functional responsibilities, one or more "co-managers" and a store manager. District and regional managers supervise the stores.

5. Few objective requirements or qualifications for specific store assignments, promotions, or raises exist. Salaries are supposed to conform to general company guidelines, but store management has substantial discretion in setting salary levels within salary ranges for each employee. Salaries are also adjusted based on performance reviews, which are largely based on subjective judgments of performance. Plaintiffs are informed and believe that Wal-Mart policy prohibits employees from exchanging information about their salary levels.

6. The hourly sales workforce at Wal-Mart is predominantly female, representing over 72 percent of all hourly employees. Yet, male and female employees are not evenly distributed among the departments in the store. In some departments and positions, such as furniture, garden, electronics, hardware, sporting goods, guns, produce, and stocking, males are disproportionately assigned. In other departments, such as front-end cashier, customer service, health and beauty aids, cosmetics, housewares, stationery, toys, layaway, fabrics and clothes, women are disproportionately assigned. Plaintiffs are informed and believe that the male-dominated departments and jobs are better paid and offer greater opportunities for advancement than the female-dominated positions and departments.

7. Male employees are more likely than female employees to obtain "cross-training" in other departments or to receive training and support to enter into departments that would aid their advancement.

8. Plaintiffs are informed and believe that female employees are paid less than male employees who perform substantially similar work, with similar or lesser skills and experience. Plaintiffs are further informed and believe that segregated assignment patterns exacerbate such unequal pay, because men are more likely to be assigned to departments that pay better than departments to which women are assigned.

9. Although women comprise the substantial majority of all hourly employees, the source from which

most managers are drawn, their representation in management is the polar opposite. Women hold only about one-third of the positions that Wal-Mart identifies as management. However, even this figure overstates the proportion of female managers in true management positions. Thus, the "one third" of management positions held by women includes traditionally "female" positions, such as assistant managers whose primary responsibility is supervising cashiers, and the lowest level of managers. Plaintiffs are informed and believe that women comprise less than 10 percent of all Store Managers and approximately 4 percent of all District Managers. There are few, if any, female Regional Managers. There is only one woman among the 20 executive officers of the company. Plaintiffs are informed and believe that even when women are promoted, on average they are advanced later, and then more slowly, than similarly situated male employees.

10. The workforce profile of Wal-Mart does not reflect the industry or the profile of its largest competitors. In fact, although it is the largest discount retailer in the country, it lags far behind its competitors in the promotion of women. Thus, while Wal-Mart's store management is only about one-third female, among its 20 top competitors, women comprise over 56 percent of management, even though the proportion of hourly workers that are female at these companies is comparable to Wal-Mart. These differences are consistently found around the country. Moreover, these differences are longstanding. In fact, female representation among managers at Wal-Mart is at a substantially lower level today than the level of representation among Wal-Mart's competitors in 1975.

11. This pattern of unequal assignments, pay, training, and advancement opportunities is not the result of random or nondiscriminatory factors. Rather, it is the result of an ongoing and continuous pattern and practice of intentional sex discrimination in assignments, pay, training and promotions, and reliance on policies and practices that have an adverse impact on female employees that cannot be justified by business necessity, and for which alternative policies and practices with less discriminatory impact could be utilized that equally serve any asserted justification. These policies and practices include, without limitation:

a. Failure to consistently post job and promotional openings to ensure that all employees have notice of and an opportunity to seek advancement or more desirable assignments and training.

b. Reliance upon unweighted, arbitrary and subjective criteria utilized by a nearly all male managerial workforce in making assignments, training, pay, performance review and promotional decisions. Even where Wal-Mart policy states objective requirements, these requirements are often applied in an inconsistent manner and ignored at the discretion of management.

c. Reliance on gender stereotypes in making employment decisions such as assignments, promotions, pay, and training.

d. Pre-selection and "grooming" of male employees for advancement, favorable assignments and training.

e. Maintenance of largely sex-segregated job categories and departments.

f. Deterrence and discouragement of female employees from seeking advancement, training, and favorable assignments and pay.

g. Paying female employees lower compensation than similarly situated men.

h. Assigning women to lower paying positions, and positions with lesser advancement potential than those given to men, and advancing women more slowly than similarly situated male employees.

i. Providing less training and support to female employees and managers than that given to male employees and managers.

j. Harassing female employees interested in advancement and subjecting them to a hostile work environment.

k. Requiring, as a condition of promotion to management jobs, that employees be willing to relocate, often to significantly distant stores, and applying this policy to require frequent and substantial relocations of its managers without any reasonable business justification. Plaintiffs are further informed and believe that the relocation policy is applied disparately between male and female employees, to the disadvantage of female employees.

l. Retaliating against female employees who have complained either internally or externally about Wal-Mart's treatment of its female employees. Wal-Mart maintains a companywide, toll-free telephone number, which it encourages employees to use if they have a problem or complaint in their store or with store management. Plaintiffs are informed and believe that Wal-Mart retaliates against women who use this number to report discrimination, sexual harassment, or other unfair working conditions.

Assignment

Conduct research on the *Dukes et al. v. Wal-Mart* case and determine the present status. What arguments and/or evidence did Wal-Mart present to argue against the gender discrimination claims. Based on what you have reviewed, was Wal-Mart guilty of gender discrimination as alleged? Try to take a definitive position and then justify that position with specific evidence or arguments. If you are unsure, what specific information do you need to be able to render a verdict in this case? Setting aside the alleged illegalities, what specific HR practices could Wal-Mart improve to make their HR more effective and (perhaps) to lower the likelihood of such Title VII lawsuits in the future?

[1]Pikul, C. (2004, November 22). Women vs. Wal-Mart. Salon.com

CRITICAL THINKING APPLICATION 6-A

What Privacy Do We Have in the Workplace?[1]

Currently debated privacy issues have included drug testing, medical information kept on employees and family members credit history and certain questions on personality tests. Employers have maintained records on employees since the employer/employee relationship was first established. Research on personnel recordkeeping has revealed that as the employer/employee relationship changed, the level and amount of information collected on employees also changed. Employers had personal knowledge of employees in the 1800s, could vouch for the employees' integrity, and could observe the personal patterns of behaviors (going to church, etc.). The amount of information kept in files was not as important because of the face-to-face interaction.[2] In order to hire the right person, limit negligent hiring claims, and provide employee benefits, companies need to keep extensive dossiers on employees. The management (sharing and disclosing) of those dossiers was the subject of a report by the U.S. Privacy Protection Commission investigation established by the Privacy Act of 1974. Survey data was collected in 2005 to determine corporate privacy policies.[3]

The Commission recommended the following as fair information practices:

- Acquire only relevant information.
- Consider pretext interviews unacceptable methods of gathering information.
- Use no polygraph or lie detector tests in employment.
- Allow and encourage employees to see and copy records pertaining to them.
- Keep no secret records.
- Establish a procedure for challenging and correcting erroneous reports.
- Use information only for the purpose for which it was originally acquired.
- Transfer no information without the subjects' authorization or knowledge.
- Destroy data after their purpose has been served.[4]

The results of the survey revealed that the majority of companies still do not have formal policies that follow the Commission's guidelines in regard to disclosure and access. Informing and evaluating the recordkeeping system are being done by most companies. However, many companies surveyed are still shy of following the Commission's recommendations. The survey results are listed below:

Policy to inform employees of routine disclosure?	56%
Personal access to records?	34%
Policy of evaluating record system?	65%
Inform employees on types of records maintained?	82%
Inform employees of how information is used?	58%
Inform individual of collecting information?	66%[5]

Based on the information provided by the Commission and subsequent surveys as well as information from Chapter 3 on job relatedness, evaluate and justify your reaction to the following questions:

You have just come from a job interview in which you were asked the following questions in a personality screening test for a homeland security position. The company has assured you that your answers will be strictly confidential and that emotional stability (which this test proports to test) is essential for the job. You realize that this position is a high-stress and safety-sensitive job, yet it seems that some of these questions are not job relevant.

1. I enjoy social gatherings just to be with people.
2. The only interesting part of the newspaper is the "funnies."
3. Our thinking would be a lot better off if we would just forget about words like "probably," "approximately," and "perhaps."
4. I usually go to the movies more than once a week.
5. I looked up to my father as an ideal man.
6. I liked *Alice in Wonderland* by Lewis Carroll.
7. When a person "pads" his income tax report so as to get out of some of his taxes, it is just as bad as stealing money from the government.
8. Women should not be allowed to drink in cocktail bars.
9. I think Lincoln was greater that Washington.
10. I feel sure there is only one true religion.
11. I am embarrassed by dirty stories.
12. Maybe some minorities get rough treatment, but it is no business of mine.
13. I fall in and out of love rather easily.
14. I wish I were not bothered by thoughts about sex.
15. My home life was always happy.
16. Only a fool would ever vote to increase his own taxes.
17. When a man is with a woman, he is usually thinking about things related to her sex.
18. I hardly ever feel pain in the back of my neck.
19. I have no difficulty starting or holding my urine.

20. My sex life is satisfactory.
21. I am very strongly attracted to members of my own sex.
22. I used to like "drop-the-handkerchief."
23. I've often wished I were a girl (or if you are a girl) I've never been sorry that I'm a girl.
24. I go to church almost every week.
25. I believe in the second coming of Christ.
26. I believe in life hereafter.
27. I've never indulged in any unusual sex practices.
28. I believe my sins are unpardonable.[6]

Assignment

Should the company be allowed to ask such questions? Think of all issues that you considered in taking a position *or*, if you aren't sure what your position is, what additional information do you need? How would the company prove the job relatedness of such a test? When must the company prove the job relatedness of the test?

[1]Contributed by Mary E. Wilson
[2]Linowes, D. F., and Spencer, R. C. (1996). Privacy in the workplace in perspective. *Human Resource Management Review, 6* (3), 165–182.
[3]Benardin, H. J. (2005). *Privacy in the workplace.* Unpublished survey.
[4]Ibid., pp.177–178.
[5]Ibid.
[6]Taken from Psychscreen, a screening tool used by Target stores based on the Minnesota Multiphasic Personality Inventory (MMPI) and the California Personality Inventory (CPI). Source: Alderman, E., and Kennedy, C. (1995). *The right to privacy.* New York: Alfred A. Knopf.

Critical Thinking Application 6-B

The Measurement of Personality Traits[1]

Overview

Research supports the proposition that stable personality characteristics are related to not only success in particular occupations but also job and life satisfaction. The purpose of this exercise is to provide a profile of your personality based on valid measures of personality.

As discussed in Chapter 6, the "Big Five" factor structure has gained widespread acceptance by personality researchers and has greatly influenced the research into individual differences. There is also strong evidence that personality measures have utility in providing vocational and career guidance. It is clear that certain Big Five factors and their combinations are correlated with career choice, success, and satisfaction. More recent research supports the validity of core self-evaluations and Emotional Intelligence.

Objectives

After completing this exercise, you should be able to:

1. Understand how your personality as measured could be related to occupational success.
2. Critique the measures for their usefulness in other HR domains.

Part A. The Big Five (Five Factor Model)

Instructions   Prior to class, answer the 50 questions below. Based on your answers, a profile from the "Big Five" personality factors will be presented. Your instructor will provide the general interpretation of the profile based on your answers.

Answer each question as honestly as you can. The accuracy of your profile depends on honest responses that reflect your true feelings and not how you would like to feel or act.

For each question, try to answer either "yes" or "no." If you cannot decide how to answer, record your answer as "unsure." If your answer to the question is "yes," put a "1" in the space provided to the left of the item number. If your answer is "unsure," put a "2" in the space provided. If your answer is "no" to the question, put a "3" in the space provided.

Put 1 if your answer is "yes," 2 if your answer is "unsure," and 3 if your answer is "no."

NAME _____

_____ 1. Do you worry about most things?

_____ 2. Are you anxious about your life most of the time?

_____ 3. Do you consider yourself to have low self-esteem?

_____ 4. Are you often depressed?

_____ 5. Are you often embarrassed by your behavior?

_____ 6. Do you feel inferior to most people you know?

_____ 7. Do you often give in to temptations?

_____ 8. Do you have trouble making decisions?

_____ 9. Do you feel vulnerable in many situations?

_____ 10. Do you have difficulty in stressful situations?

_____ 11. Do you prefer working in groups?

_____ 12. Do you really enjoy talking with people?

_____ 13. Do you think you would be good in sales?

_____ 14. Do you prefer being around people more than being alone?

_____ 15. Do you prefer work that involves more interaction with people?

_____ 16. Do you consider yourself outgoing?

_____ 17. Would you describe yourself as shy?

_____ 18. Do you tend to dominate most conversations?

_____ 19. Do you often emerge as a leader in a group?

_____ 20. Do you enjoy sports that most people consider to be risky?

_____ 21. Do you like intellectual challenges?

_____ 22. Do you like associating with people who stimulate your mind?

_____ 23. Do you really enjoy good poetry or reading the classics?

_____ 24. Do you have a very active fantasy life?

_____ 25. Are you tolerant of different lifestyles?

_____ 26. Do you like to debate controversial issues of the day?

_____ 27. Do you always like to hear the other side of an issue?

_____ 28. Do you often select reading as a leisure activity?

_____ 29. Do you often find yourself daydreaming?

_____ 30. Are you fascinated by art and artists?

_____ 31. Do you have difficulty telling people how you really feel?

_____ 32. Do you trust most people?

_____ 33. Do you think most people are honest?

_____ 34. Do you enjoy a good argument?

_____ 35. Would you describe yourself as stubborn?

_____ 36. Do you prefer cooperating over competing?

_____ 37. Do you like to put people in their place when they deserve it?

_____ 38. Do you consider yourself superior to most people you know?

_____ 39. Would most people describe you as courteous?

_____ 40. Do you hate giving people bad news about themselves?

_____ 41. Do you do well at most things you try?

_____ 42. Do most people consider you to be highly competent?

_____ 43. Do you like to carefully plan things?

_____ 44. Do you have a clear set of objectives when you work?

_____ 45. Do you consider yourself very well disciplined?

_____ 46. Do you always honor the commitments you have made?

_____ 47. Do you consider yourself to be highly effective in your work?

_____ 48. Do you try to do the best that you can every time?

_____ 49. Do you consider yourself well organized?

_____ 50. Do you stick with a job until you're finished?

To Score Your Responses

For items 17, 34, 35, 37, and 38 only, change a "1" response to a "3" and change a "3" response to a "1." All other items are scored using the number you have entered (1, 2, or 3). Add up the scores for the Big Five factors as follows:

Score

_____ 1. **ANXIOUS VS. RELAXED** (also known as Emotional Stability or Neuroticism) (items 1–10)

_____ 2. **EXTROVERTED-INTROVERTED** (items 11–20)

_____ 3. **EXPERIMENTAL VS. CONVENTIONAL** (or openness to experience) (items 21–30)

_____ 4. **AGREEABLE VS. SKEPTICAL** (items 31–40)

_____ 5. **CAREFREE VS. CONSCIENTIOUS** (items 41–50) (Conscientiousness)

Your instructor will provide the interpretation of your profile.

Part B. The Core-Self-Evaluations Scale (CSES)[2]

Instructions   Presented below are several statements about you with which you may agree or disagree. Using the response scale below, indicate your agreement or disagreement with each item by placing the appropriate number on the line preceding that item.

1	2	3	4	5
Strongly Disagree	Disagree	Neutral	Agree	Strongly Agree

_____ 1. I am confident I get the success I deserve in life.

_____ 2. Sometimes I feel depressed. (r)

_____ 3. When I try, I generally succeed.

_____ 4. Sometimes when I fail I feel worthless. (r)

_____ 5. I complete tasks successfully.

_____ 6. Sometimes, I do not feel in control of my work. (r)

_____ 7. Overall, I am satisfied with myself.

_____ 8. I am filled with doubts about my competence. (r)

_____ 9. I determine what will happen in my life.

_____ 10. I do not feel in control of my success in my career. (r)

_____ 11. I am capable of coping with most of my problems.

_____ 12. There are times when things look pretty bleak and hopeless to me. (r)

TO SCORE: Reverse score items with r (even numbered items) (1=5, 2=4, 3=3, 4=2, 5=1). Mark that above and then add up your total and divide by 12.

YOUR MEAN SCORE = _____

Part C. The EMOTIONAL INTELLIGENCE (EI) Scale

Instructions Consider the next set of statements and rate whether you agree or disagree. With each statement, using the response scale below, indicate your agreement or disagreement by placing the appropriate number on the line preceding that item. Use the same scale to make your ratings.

1	2	3	4	5
Strongly Disagree	Disagree	Neutral	Agree	Strongly Agree

_____ 1. I have a good sense of why I have certain feelings most of the time.

_____ 2. I have good understanding of my own emotions.

_____ 3. I really understand what I feel.

_____ 4. I always know whether or not I am happy.

_____ 5. I always know my friends' emotions from their behavior.

_____ 6. I am a good observer of others' emotions.

_____ 7. I am sensitive to the feelings and emotions of others.

_____ 8. I have a good understanding of the emotions of people around me.

_____ 9. I always set goals for myself and then try my best to achieve them.

_____ 10. I always tell myself I am a competent person.

_____ 11. I am a self-motivated person.

_____ 12. I would always encourage myself to try my best.

_____ 13. I am able to control my temper and handle difficulties rationally.

_____ 14. I am quite capable of controlling my own emotions.

_____ 15. I can always calm down quickly when I am very angry.

_____ 16. I have good control of my emotions.

_____ ADD UP YOUR RESPONSES FOR ITEMS 1–16.

To perform my job well, it is necessary for me to:

_____ 17. Spend most of my work time interacting with people (e.g., customers, colleagues, and other workers in the organization).

_____ 18. Spend a lot of time with every person whom I work with.

_____ 19. Hide my actual feelings when acting and speaking with people.

_____ 20. Be considerate and think from the point of view of others.

_____ 21. Hide my negative feelings (e.g., anger and depression).

_____ ADD UP YOUR RESPONSES FOR ITEMS 17–21.

Your instructor will give you data to help you interpret these scores. Answer one final question. True or false: The Big Five, the CSES and the EI scale have no practical value because real job candidates would fudge their responses; thus undermining the validity of the scores. Be prepared to discuss (AND DEFEND) your answer.

[1]Contributed by Kathleen Bernardin.
[2]Judge, T. A., Erez, A., Bono, J. E., and Thoresen, C. J. (2003). The core self-evaluations scale: Development of a measure. *Personnel Psychology, 56,* 303–331.

CRITICAL THINKING APPLICATION 7-A

Should We Measure Competencies in Performance Appraisal?

One strong trend in performance appraisal in the assessment of so-called competencies. Competencies have been defined as bundles of knowledges, skills, or abilities. Many of these "competencies" look a lot like the old traits that have been condemned in a plethora of articles on appraisal. As an illustration, the managerial competencies used by the American Management Association include self-confidence, positive regard, self-control, spontaneity, stamina, and adaptability.[1]

Some argue that performance appraisal should first focus on *the record of outcomes* that the person (or persons) actually achieved on the job; a focus on actual performance first. Diagnostics (or causal theories) can come later. There is nothing wrong with assessing what qualities a person possesses, but that should not be confused with measuring performance.[2] We can assess the extent to which a person possesses certain technical skills through ratings by those familiar with a person's skills (although it would probably be better to use some form of test). It is the manifestation of those skills on the job in the form of outcomes that constitutes performance. We can assess Shaquille O'Neal's psychomotor skills, his height, his hand size, his anxiety level, all of which may be predictors or correlates of his performance. But his foul shooting in 2005 was 48 percent and that is one measure of his performance.

Many companies use a software program that gives ratings on a competency labeled "integrity." Some appraisal experts would suggest that an elimination of such "competency" labels would help focus the managers' attention on actual behavior and the outcomes that result from the behaviors. Another popular software package calls for evaluations of managers on their "personal maturity." Needless to say, store managers often disagree with ratings indicating they need work on their "personal maturity."

Assignment

When is it appropriate to measure competencies? Describe an appraisal system in which the purposes for the appraisal system were accomplished when the system called for assessments of personal competencies as opposed to a record of performance outcomes.

---

[1]Parry, S. B. (July 1996). The quest for competencies. *Training*, pp. 48–53.
[2]Hagan, C. H., Konopaske, R., Bernardin, H. J. & Tyler, C. L. (In press). The criterion-related validity of 360-degree, top down and customer-based competency assessments using assessment center performance as the criterion: a competency modeling approach. *Human Resource Management*.

CRITICAL THINKING APPLICATION 7-B

The Role of Mystery Shoppers in Performance Appraisal[1]

The retail industry has made noteworthy efforts in soliciting customer feedback through its use of mystery shopping. Typically, this involves contracting with an organization to provide anonymous individuals who periodically shop the store, evaluating and reporting about the experience from a customer's viewpoint. Mystery shoppers usually review a predetermined menu of variables for each store they shop, based on criteria established by the retail organization. At the Limited and the Gap, for example, mystery shoppers follow a script to test the extent to which store employees adhere to their training regarding customer interactions.

The use of mystery shopping has become very popular. One contractor reported a professional shopping staff of 8,800 and a business that was growing at the rate of 50 percent per year.[2] Many organizations, including Burger King, Neiman Marcus, Hyatt Hotels, Hertz Auto Rentals, Barney's New York, and Revco Drug Stores, have had extensive experience using mystery shoppers to obtain customer-based information.

Office Depot converts its mystery shopping data into a customer satisfaction index, which also includes customer complaints. The index is reported to each store manager once a month. The data, aggregated across the year, become a key determinant of each manager's annual appraisal, bonus, base salary increase, and objectives for the next appraisal cycle.

One survey[3] reported that a high percentage of retail and service companies use customer data for decision making, and 71 percent reported supplementing customer surveys with mystery shoppers. While recent case studies describe the value of mystery shopping,[4] little research has examined the validity or reliability of mystery shopping data. Two recent studies found that "mystery shopper" data was correlated with assessment center performance[5] and overall store performance[6] among retail managers. Since efficiency data are easiest to identify and contract out, mystery shoppers may be focusing on issues such as determining the length of time it takes an associate to approach them, or how long they await final service delivery, or the number of times the telephone rings before it is answered, or the number of different individuals that become involved when a customer request strays from the norm. These measures are effective customer measures *only* when they capture information that real customers value highly. In other words, if an organization's source of competitive advantages is price, or convenience, or uniqueness of service features, or value in relation to competitors, then the above efficiency measures may create an inaccurate, or a mixed, signal to employees about the performance efforts that are really valued.

Assignment

Pick a job in which "mystery shoppers" might provide helpful and unique data. Describe how you would develop the system and incorporate data from this system into the performance-appraisal system. Also, could your university use "mystery shoppers"? If you think it could, should it and what would the "shoppers" look for?

---

[1]Contributed by Christine M. Hagan.
[2]Helliker, K. (November 30, 1994). Smile: That cranky shopper may be a store spy. *The Wall Street Journal*, p. B1.
[3]Wilson, A. M. (2002). Attitudes towards customer satisfaction measurement in the retail sector. *International Journal of Market Research*, *44*, 213–222.
[4]Hagan, C. & Bernardin, H. J. (2003). Customer feedback as a critical performance dimension. In A. Miles and P. Perrewe (Eds.) *New Directions in Human Resource Management*, pp. 1–27.
[5]Hagan, C. H., Konopaske, R., Bernardin, H. J. & Tyler, C.L. (In press). The criterion-related validity of 360-degree, top down and customer-based competency assessments using assessment center performance as the criterion: a competency modeling approach. *Human Resource Management*.
[6]Tyler, K. & Bernardin, H. J. (2003). Predictive validity and adverse impact: A comparison of three managerial selection methods. *Best Papers of the Academy of Management: HRF* 1–6. Paper presented at 2003 AOM meeting, Vancouver, Canada.

CRITICAL THINKING APPLICATION 7-C

Allegations of Age and Race Discrimination against Ford Motor Company

Nine white-collar workers at Ford Motor Company filed a multimillion-dollar age discrimination lawsuit against the automaker, a challenge to the company's controversial employee evaluation process.

In addition, another group of salaried Ford employees filed a Title VII class action age and reverse discrimination suit against the Dearborn-based company in federal district court. The claims came as some Ford employees complained that President Jacques Nasser was attempting to sweep out older workers. Nasser had said he wanted to build a younger, more diverse management that would embrace new technology in rapid change while better reflecting Ford's customer base.

At issue in both cases was Ford's forced distribution appraisal system for its top 18,000 managers and executives. Under Ford's new policy, instituted to replace the old appraisal system, 10 percent of employees had to receive A grades, 80 percent had to get Bs, and 10 percent received Cs.

Those who received Cs were not eligible for a raise or bonus and a C grade two consecutive years was grounds for demotion or termination. Lawyers for the nine employees who filed suit claimed Ford was using the grading scale to systematically weed out older workers. They asked the court to prohibit further use of this system. "We believe Ford is using this system to get rid of older workers," said Morgan Bonanny, a lawyer for the plaintiffs. "Our hope is to stop this program before anyone else gets hurt."

Ford spokesman Edward Miller said the grading system—referred to internally as the performance management process—does not take an employee's age into account. "It's designed to be fair to everybody," he said. "We want all our people to contribute at higher levels, but the age of a worker shouldn't be a consideration." While Ford is not the only major company using a forced-distribution system, the automaker had been among the most vocal in promoting and defending the approach.

Some within Ford maintain that the grading system struck a nerve at Ford because its conservative corporate culture traditionally favored the promotion of long-time, loyal managers—often white males. The new system has meant that many veteran white-collar workers were being passed over for promotion by younger managers.

The lawsuit claimed that the plaintiffs unfairly received poor evaluations that led to economic loss, embarrassment, and mental anguish. The workers sought several million dollars in damages.

One of the plaintiffs in the case said he had a history of good reviews in his 23-year career as a Ford engineer. He was chosen to participate in the Ford six sigma quality improvement program. Ford had said the six sigma program was intended only for top employees.

But then he was informed he would receive a C grade and was eligible for a raise or bonus. He claims his supervisor could not tell him specifically where his performance came up short. He said he first noticed that the culture had changed for older workers after he returned from a six-year Ford assignment in Germany. "There was this pervasive fear," he said. "At our age it was reality—you don't get promoted."

A separate Title VII class-action lawsuit also was filed against Ford on behalf of several current employees. The plaintiffs in this case, all white, claimed they were unfairly given C ratings in the last year on annual performance report reviews. In addition, each of the men is between 40 and 50 and is considered at a leadership level at Ford. The lead attorney planned to cite several diversity programs at Ford as well as public comments made by the CEO and other company executives as proof that the automaker is making personnel decisions based on race and age.

Ford has increasingly made diversity a top priority for managers in recent years. At the same time, it has become a hot-button issue among employees. The top 300 managers were asked to outline a plan to increase the diversity in their organization. Part of the executives' bonuses hinged on how well they accomplished these goals. *Fortune* magazine recently rated Ford the country's 30th best company for minorities. No other automaker made the top 50. "Increasing diversity is a major goal," Ford's Miller said. "We want to be inclusive. But the evaluations are based totally on job performance."

Assignment

How would you test the theories of discrimination in these complaints? Play the role of consultant to Ford and write a one-page memo recommending and justifying the data and documentation that should be analyzed? Your memo should also include an evaluation of the forced distribution rating system and refer to research on its effects. Ford would also like your opinion as to whether the plaintiffs in the ADEA (age) case can use a "disparate impact" theory to define prima facie discrimination.

CRITICAL THINKING APPLICATION 7-D

Performance Appraisal Characteristics Questionnaire

Assignment

Think of a work situation in which your organization uses performance appraisal as a basis for any type of personnel decision (e.g., promotions, reductions-in-force, transfer, lay-off, pay, discharge). Select a situation with which you are very familiar or ask an acquaintance to answer the questions. Respond to each of the items below in this context. Select *unsure* if you do not understand a question.

Check one per question

Yes	No	Unsure	Does your organization . . .
___	___	___	1. Violate the 80% rule in the decisions from the performance appraisal data?
___	___	___	2. Use procedures for appraisal and the resultant personnel decisions that do not differ as a function of the race, sex, national origin, religion, or age of those affected by such decisions?
___	___	___	3. Use objective or countable (nonrated) performance data?
___	___	___	4. Have a formal system of review or appeal for situations in which the rated individual disagrees with a rating?

_____	_____	_____	5.	Use more than one independent evaluator of performance?
_____	_____	_____	6.	Use a formal, standardized system for the personnel decision?
_____	_____	_____	7.	Make certain evaluators have had ample opportunity to observe rate performance (if rating must be made)?
_____	_____	_____	8.	Avoid ratings on traits such as dependability, drive, aptitude, or attitude?
_____	_____	_____	9.	Validate the performance appraisal data with other data?
_____	_____	_____	10.	Communicate specific performance standards to employee?
_____	_____	_____	11.	Provide written instructions on how to complete the performance evaluations?
_____	_____	_____	12.	Evaluate employees on specific work dimensions rather than a single overall or global measure?
_____	_____	_____	13.	Require behavioral documentation for extreme ratings (e.g., critical incidents)?
_____	_____	_____	14.	Provide employees with an opportunity to review their appraisals?
_____	_____	_____	15.	Train personnel decision makers on laws regarding discrimination?

CRITICAL THINKING APPLICATION 8-A

Workplace Diversity Training[1]

What is workplace diversity? The answer to this question may be the first step in initiating diversity training in the workplace. Whether to include only the protected groups under Title VII or to broaden the definition to include the "invisible" minorities, such as individuals with mental disabilities, substance abuse conditions, or various sexual orientations, may be a factor specific to the organization or the company's location.

Once diversity has been defined, the next question to address is: what is it about workplace diversity that is important for the organization? Some organizations that have looked to diversity training to "sensitize" employees to the differences of cultures and biases have been greeted with multimillion-dollar settlements from the "sensitizing." Lucky Stores supermarket chain in California was ordered to pay $90 million in damages to over 20,000 women after airing sex and racial stereotypes in a workshop designed to increase sensitivity.[2] Jeffrey Mello asserts that a "best practice" workplace diversity initiative relates that program with the overall strategy of the organization, "such as meeting the changing needs of customers and/or expanding markets both domestically and abroad."[3] A strong argument is made that a "solid business case increases the likelihood of obtaining the leadership commitment and resources needed to successfully implement diversity initiatives."[4]

It may be that what is important to an organization is capital conservation. Organizations like Mazda North America Inc., Archer Daniels Midland Co., Arkansas Human Services Department, Texaco, JC Penney, and Baker and McKenzie were all ordered to pay in the millions of dollars that some say a "best practice workplace diversity" program would have avoided.[5] According to EEOC, the total monetary benefits in 2004 alone was over $50 million.[6]

The next question is what is to be trained? The damages in court cases are awarded based on behavior and instances of illegal conduct. San Diego Gas & Electric Company and Wal-Mart were ordered to pay $3 million and $5 million, respectively, to employees who were subjected to illegal conduct. At the power company, a black former employee had been called "nigger," "coon," and "boy" and was threatened by a co-worker in the presence of a manager to "beat his black ass." He also had racial and sexual graffiti written about him on the men's room walls. SDG & E did not stop or discipline the transgressions. A woman stockroom clerk was subject to comments concerning her anatomy and unwelcome attempts to kiss her by her supervisor at Wal-Mart. Wal-Mart was ordered to pay even though the company has a strong sexual harrasement policy because the store manager did nothing to stop the harassment after the employee complained.[7]

How is the training going to be done? Careful planning and designing will prevent problems such as poor attendance and nonownership of diversity management. A division executive of a major insurance firm declined to send his managers to the company's diversity training. His response was a blunt "if there's a problem, just tell us what you want us to do. Don't waste our time with this diversity stuff."[8]

Finally, how will the diversity training be evaluated? Accounting for the benefits, which may include increased productivity due to incident-free workdays (much like accident-free workdays promoted by OSHA), enhanced public opinion about the organization, or recruitment and retention of valued diverse employees, is crucial to an effective workplace diversity program.

Assignment

You have been asked to design a diversity training program for incoming freshmen at your school. Try to answer the questions presented above in this context. Develop a method for the training program. Do a Web search to identify online diversity programs. Using Kirkpatrick's model (discussed in Chapter 8), give one example of each of the four types of data for evaluation that you would use to either evaluate your own new program or a ready-made online program.

[1]Contributed by Mary E. Wilson.
[2]Murray, K. (August 1, 1993). The unfortunate side effects of "diversity training." *New York Times*, p. F5.
[3]Mello, J. A. (1996). The strategic management of workplace diversity initiatives: Public sector implications. *International Journal of Public Administration, 19*(3), 425–447.
[4]Robinson, G., and Dechart, K. (1997). Building a business case for diversity. *Academy of Management Executive, 11*, 21–31.
[5]DB Pargman Diversity Training website, www.dbpargman.com/lawdiversity.htm, accessed July 23, 2002.
[6]The U.S. Equal Employment Opportunity Commission. (2001). *EEOC Litgation Statistics, FY 1992 through FY 2001*, eeoc.gov/stats/litigation.html, accessed July 23, 2002.
[7]Paskoff, S. A. (August 1996). Ending the workplace diversity wars. *Training, 33*(8), 42–47.
[8]Ibid., p. 43.

CRITICAL THINKING APPLICATION 8-B

Sexual Harassment Training[1]

Sexual harassment is a form of sex discrimination that violates *Title VII of the Civil Rights Act of 1964.* Title VII applies to employers with 15 or more employees, including state and local governments. It also applies to employment agencies and labor organizations. Unwelcome sexual advances, requests for sexual favors, and other verbal or physical conduct of a sexual nature constitutes sexual harassment when this conduct explicitly or implicitly affects an individual's employment, unreasonably interferes with an individual's work performance, or creates an intimidating, hostile, or offensive work environment.

Sexual harassment can occur in a variety of circumstances, including, but not limited to the following:

The victim as well as the harasser may be a woman or a man. The victim does not have to be of the opposite sex.

The harasser can be the victim's supervisor, an agent of the employer, a supervisor in another area, a co-worker, or a non-employee.

The victim does not have to be the person harassed but could be anyone affected by the offensive conduct.

Unlawful sexual harassment may occur without economic injury to or discharge of the victim.

The harasser's conduct must be unwelcome.

It is helpful for the victim to inform the harasser directly that the conduct is unwelcome and must stop. The victim should use any employer complaint mechanism or grievance system available.

When investigating allegations of sexual harassment, The Equal Employment Opportunity Commission (EEOC) looks at the whole record: the circumstances, such as the nature of the sexual advances, and the context in which the alleged incidents occurred. A determination on the allegations is made from the facts on a case-by-case basis.

Prevention is the best tool to eliminate sexual harassment in the workplace. Employers are encouraged to take steps necessary to prevent sexual harassment from occurring. They should clearly communicate to employees that sexual harassment will not be tolerated by providing sexual harassment training to their employees and by establishing an effective complaint or grievance process and taking immediate and appropriate action when an employee complains.

It is also unlawful to retaliate against an individual for opposing employment practices that discriminate based on sex or for filing a discrimination charge, testifying, or participating in any way in an investigation, proceeding, or litigation under Title VII.

As of 2006, employers operating in California must comply with state law AB 1825, mandating sexual harassment prevention training for supervisors. If an employer has 50 or more employees, including independent contractors and temps, they must abide by the law. A "Supervisor" is "any individual having the authority . . . to hire, transfer, suspend, lay off, recall, promote, discharge, assign, reward, or discipline other employees, or the responsibility to direct them, or to adjust their grievances, or effectively to recommend that action, if, in connection with the foregoing, the exercise of that authority is not of a merely routine or clerical nature, but requires the use of independent judgment." Thus, even employees who merely have input into personnel decisions, but who are not themselves final decision makers, may be considered "supervisors" who must receive training. The law mandates two hours of sexual harassment prevention training to supervisory employees every two years. The training can be interactive, computer-based training.

An employer's compliance with AB 1825 does not automatically protect them from liability for sexual harassment of any current or former employee or applicant. A claim that training did not take place does not automatically result in the liability of an employer for harassment. Plaintiffs may argue, however, that the failure to meet the new training mandates is partial evidence of an employer's failure to take all reasonable steps to prevent harassment.

Advocates of the new law claim that the training will change behavior and reduce sexual harassment in the workplace. Some experts claim the EEOC stipulates that employers should periodically train employees. Under *Farragher v. Boca Raton,* if employers do train employees and an employee makes a claim, using an "affirmative defense" argument, the employer may be able to avoid liability even if the alleged bad conduct occurred. In 2003, California's Supreme Court adopted a slight variation of the affirmative defense for lawsuits brought under the state Fair Employment and Housing Act (FEHA). Under the FEHA, an employer is strictly liable for a harassing manager. However, a company may still avoid financial responsibility if it has effectively trained employees on its anti-harassment policy. Finally, in 1999, the US Supreme Court, (followed by California) stated that if employees win a claim for harassment or discrimination, employers can avoid punitive damages if they show a good faith effort to comply with the law by training employees. Some experts maintain that policy statements and handbook subject matter are not enough.

Under AB 1825, the training must include information and practical guidance regarding federal and state laws that prohibit sexual harassment, including prevention and correction of harassment, and remedies available to victims. The statute specifically requires employers to use practical examples aimed at instructing supervisors in the prevention of harassment, discrimination, and retaliation.

Assignment

1. Visit the following Web site of California State University (CSU) and go through the antisexual harassment training program http://www.calstate.edu/gc/AntiSexualHarassmentTraining/sh-page1.shtml

2. Make sure you enter your name when you are asked and be sure to make a copy of your training certificate once you have gone through the training. Bring your certificate to class.

3. After you have completed the questionnaire, propose reactive results, behavioral, and outcomes measures that could be used to assess the effects of the CSU interactive training program. Write specific examples. Answer the other questions as well.

The first page of the site will say the following:
Welcome to the CSU Office of General Counsel's Web-Based Training on "Sexual Harassment: Understanding Your Rights and Responsibilities." As a starting point, let's review the CSU's policy on sexual harassment:

"The California State University (CSU) is committed to maintaining a work environment where every employee, applicant, and independent contractor is treated with dignity and respect. CSU will not tolerate unlawful harassment based on race, color, religion, national origin, ancestry, age, sex, sexual orientation, marital status, veteran status (as defined by the Vietnam-Era Veterans' Readjustment Assistance Act of 1974, as amended), physical disability, mental disability, or medical condition."

This training is intended to help you understand and comply with CSU's policy prohibiting sexual harassment. Whether this is your first training or just a refresher, we hope you find it interesting and informative.

Written Assignment

4. After you have completed the training and received your certificate, answer the questions that follow and bring your responses to class along with the certificate.

NAME _____

For each scenario below, indicate whether you agree or disagree that what is described constitutes illegal sexual harassment. Use the following scale to make your judgment:

> 1=Strongly Disagree; 2=Disagree; 3=Unsure;
> 4=Agree; 5=Strongly Agree

_____ 1. A supervisor lets a subordinate know that he/she will be laid off unless he/she gives in to the supervisor's sexual advances.

_____ 2. A supervisor suggests that he/she can help a subordinate get a promotion if the subordinate gives in to the supervisor's sexual advances.

_____ 3. A professor implies that if a student engages in sexual activity, he/she will give the student a better grade.

_____ 4. Jake supervises a staff of ten people. He holds required staff meetings every Thursday. For the past six months, Jake has reserved the first ten minutes of each staff meeting for what he calls a "morale builder," during which the staff exchanges the latest jokes. The jokes are often of a sexual nature. Jake's behavior constitutes sexual harassment.

_____ 5. A customer makes repetitive unwelcome sexual advances to a staff member. The staff member complains to her supervisor. The customer's behavior constitutes illegal sexual harassment and the company may be liable.

_____ 6. Several male employees sabotage the work of a female co-worker because she is a woman.

_____ 7. A male employee constantly stares at a particular female employee for long periods of time while she is working. She tells him to stop, but he keeps staring.

_____ 8. While having dinner with friends, Michelle was introduced to Sid, chair of the department. Both were attracted to each other, and before the evening was over, Sid and Michelle agreed to a date. Sid and Michelle had a wonderful time when they went out the first time. During the evening, Michelle told Sid she hoped to be admitted to his department as a graduate student and land a position as a teaching assistant. Sid told her she should send him a copy of her application and he would take care of it. Michelle was admitted to the program and got a TA position. However, she soon found she had little time for socializing and felt Sid was too demanding. When Michelle didn't want to see Sid one weekend, he insisted that she "owed him." Michelle then told Sid that, from then on, their relationship was to be strictly professional. Sid still kept calling, hanging around outside her classes, and putting notes in her campus mailbox. Michelle begged him to stop, but he didn't, so she began avoiding him by staying away from campus as much as possible. Michelle is still a victim of sexual harassment even though her relationship with Sid had been consensual.

_____ 9. A guy hangs suggestive pictures of Pamela Anderson on his wall in full view of female co-workers.

_____ 10. A guy comments that he thinks a co-worker's "rack" has gotten bigger.

_____ 11. Kerry worked as an admissions and records technician. During her initial training, she met Sterling, another trainee. Soon after, Sterling began to pester Kerry with unnecessary questions, hang around her desk and pressure her to have lunch with him alone. She consistently refused. Then he started asking her to have drinks with him after work. Each time, Kerry put him off. One day, Sterling handed her a note that said, "I cried over you last night and I'm totally drained today. I have never been in such turmoil." Kerry was shocked and frightened. She left the room, but Sterling followed, saying, "I really care for you, Kerry. Please talk with me!" Kerry called in sick the rest of that week.

That weekend, Sterling stuck a romantic card with a three-page letter in Kerry's home mailbox. One part of the letter said: "I really care for you and know that you are worth knowing with or without sex. I have enjoyed you so much over these past few months. Watching you. Experiencing you from oh so far away. Admiring your style and élan. I'll write again soon." Kerry became frantic and filed a grievance alleging sexual harassment. Sterling's actions constitute sexual harassment.

_____ 12. As she is entering the classroom, Sandy walks by the desk of her friend Bob, who is leaning over the desk to place his books underneath. She pats him on his behind with her hand, and says, "Nice butt." He looks up, horrified, and asks her to keep her hands to herself. She apologizes, and it never happens again. This is still an example of hostile environment sexual harassment.

_____ 13. Stanley has a crush on his co-worker, Lisa. He asks her for dates several times, but she always says no. The last time Stanley asks, she tells him she isn't interested and wants him to stop asking her out. Although he stops asking her out, he starts watching her all the time. He stares at her when she's at her desk. He stares at her when she walks around the office. He seems to watch her every move. When she catches him staring at her (and sometimes checking out her body), he doesn't bother to look away, he just keeps looking. This goes on for months. This constitutes sexual harassment.

_____ 14. Tom is a university employee. His department has a new student assistant, Suzi, who is an attractive, vivacious junior. Tom shows interest in her, but Suzi doesn't seem interested. One evening when Tom is working late on a presentation for the Trustees, Suzi stops by after an evening class to pick up some papers she left at her desk. As she walks by, he stands up and grabs her, tries to kiss her, and when she protests and attempts to get away, he fondles her breast and says, "Come on, you know you want me." Suzi escapes his grasp, runs away, and is so upset that she never returns to work in the department. This is an example of hostile environment sexual harassment.

_____ 15. Jane, an administrative assistant in the Sociology Department at CSU Tahoe, files a lawsuit against the University and John, a Sociology Professor, alleging that John has sexually harassed her for years, repeatedly asking her to go out with him even though she has told him she is not interested, making sexually suggestive comments to her when no one else is around, etc. No one else in the department or campus administration has seen or heard any of this, and nobody but Jane and John know anything about it. Assuming Jane's claim is true, the University can be held liable for John's conduct.

_____ 16. Brittany is a student in the Accounting Department. One day she visits Samantha, Chair of the Accounting Department, and tearfully tells her that Steven, an Accounting Professor, gave her an "F" in one of her courses because she wouldn't continue seeing him romantically. Samantha is sympathetic and calms Brittany down, promising to try to resolve the matter informally with Steven. Samantha later speaks with Steven about the situation, but that's all she does. Samantha does not pass the information on to anyone else at the University. Brittany later files a sexual harassment lawsuit. The University can be held liable for Steven's conduct, even though Samantha spoke to him about it.

_____ 17. Fred and Mary share office space as support technicians in the Information Technology Office. Fred occasionally uses his office computer to look at Web sites that feature scantily clad women. Mary has told him she finds that sort of thing offensive, but he does it anyway. Sometimes he even draws her attention to the pictures and comments on the women's physiques. Fed up, Mary finally files a sexual harassment claim against both Fred and the University. Fred can be held personally liable for the offending conduct.

_____ 18. In the previous scenario, after Mary sues Fred for sexual harassment, he asks the University to provide a lawyer to defend him in the lawsuit. The University must provide Fred a lawyer to defend him in the lawsuit because the offending conduct took place at work.

For items 19–27, do you agree or disagree that the described behavior constitutes sexual harassment? (Use the same 5 point scale.)

_____ 19. A secretary enters the boss' office and says "You wanted me?" the boss says, "Of course I want you. But let's stick to the work at hand."

_____ 20. Telling a blond female the following joke, "How can you tell a blond is enjoying sex? She drops her nail file."

_____ 21. Whistling at a woman who is walking in a hallway.

_____ 22. Female says to a male co-worker "Hey, ya big stud. How's it hanging today?"

_____ 23. A male co-worker writes numerous notes expressing a sexual interest in a male worker.

_____ 24. A boss massages the shoulders of his secretary as she types.

_____ 25. A male co-worker asks a woman out on dates on numerous occasions despite always being rejected.

_____ 26. As he is entering the classroom, Bob walks by the desk of his friend Sandy, who is leaning over the desk to place her books underneath. He pats her on her behind with his hand, and says, "Nice butt." She looks up, horrified, and asks him to keep his hands to himself. He apologizes, and it never happens again. This is still an example of hostile environment sexual harassment.

_____ 27. Tom is a member of Jake's staff. He never participates in the "morale builders" and generally avoids them by arriving ten minutes late to staff meetings. Jake calls Tom into his office. He tells Tom that his habit of arriving late is unacceptable and warns him that he will receive a written reprimand the next time he is late. Tom tells Jake that the reason he arrives late is because he finds the dirty joke sessions offensive. Jake just repeats his warning. Tom is a victim of sexual harassment.

_____ 28. Supervisor Stanley Lopata shows favoritism in assignments and raises to his lover, Chris Jayjo. Lopata displays no objectionable behavior to any of his subordinates. His subordinates may still have a sexual harassment claim.

5. Answer the following questions:
   A. If you were assessing the effectiveness of the CSU interactive training, what criteria would you use?
   B. How does this type of training compare to alternative training approaches that could have been used to comply with the law?
   C. Give at least one specific example of a reactive measure, a learning measure, a behavioral measure, and results measure that could be used to assess the CSU training you just went through.
   D. What type of evaluative measure is the questionnaire you just completed? Is it reactive, learning, behavioral, or results? What is your opinion of the quality of this measure?
   E. What organizational analysis did the state have which led to this legislation? You may either state some theories or find information to justify your answer.
   F. If you were working for the state of California charged with evaluating the effects of state law AB 1825 legislation, what specific evaluative criteria would you use?

[1]Contributed by Jennifer Bowers.

CRITICAL THINKING APPLICATION 9-A

Careers and Corporate Social Responsibility[1]

Research shows that your perceptions and opinions about the importance of corporate social responsibility can affect your attitudes toward potential and current employers. Conduct an Internet search on corporate social responsibility and social performance. Look for definitions of the term and choose a definition most compatible with your philosophy. Identify examples of firms that appear to be displaying socially responsible behavior based on this definition and other companies that seem to be illustrating irresponsible behaviors.

Assignment

Your research should attempt to identify the following:

1. The types of behavior that are indicative of socially responsible and irresponsible actions.
2. The real and potential difficulties faced by organizations in their attempts to manage social responsibility.
3. Provide suggestions for how organizations can evaluate their corporate social performance.
4. Outline a general plan for how an organization should conduct a corporate social audit.

Provide an explanation for why the behavior is indicative of socially responsible or irresponsible behavior. In addition, describe the consequences of the behavior for the employee workforce and for any clients or customers or the general public. Consider the extent to which you would weigh corporate social responsibility in your career planning and job choice. Which of the socially responsible actions identified do you think would be most resisted by management? Why? How could this resistance be addressed?

[1]Contributed by Joyce E. A. Russell and Lillian T. Eby.

CRITICAL THINKING APPLICATION 9-B

O*NET Skills Search

O*NET is the Occupational Information Network and is available to all users free of charge. O*NET is a primary source of occupational information and can facilitate career counseling, education, employment, and training activities by governments and organizations. The database contains information about knowledges, skills, abilities (KSA), interests, general work activities (GWA), and work context. O*NET data and structure also links related occupational, educational, and labor market information databases to the system. Among many other things, O*NET can accomplish the following: 1. Facilitate employee training and development initiatives; 2. Develop and supplement assessment tools to identify worker attributes; 3 Create skills-match profiles; 4. Explore career options that capitalize on individual knowledge, skill and ability profiles; and 5. Improve vocational and career counseling efforts.

The Skills Search function is designed to help people use their skill set to identify occupations for exploration. You select a set of skills from six broad groups of skills to create a customized skill list. You begin by selecting Skills from one or more of the six skill groups identified: Basic Skills, Complex Problem Solving Skills, Resource Management Skills, Social Skills, Systems Skills, and Technical Skills. The figure below is what you will see when you have the appropriate page of the O*NET Web site to start your skills search.

Source: O*NET OnLine
Skills Search

Select skills from one or more of the six skill groups below. Start by selecting as many skills as you have or plan to acquire. (See *Skills Search* for more details.)

Basic Skills | Complex Problem Solving Skills | Resource Management Skills | Social Skills | Systems Skills | Technical Skills

Basic Skills

Developed capacities that facilitate learning or the more rapid acquisition of knowledge

- Active Learning—Understanding the implications of new information for both current and future problem solving and decision making.
- Active Listening—Giving full attention to what other people are saying, taking time to understand the points being made, asking questions as appropriate, and not interrupting at inappropriate times.
- Critical Thinking—Using logic and reasoning to identify the strengths and weaknesses of alternative solutions, conclusions or approaches to problems.
- Learning Strategies—Selecting and using training/ instructional methods and procedures appropriate for the situation when learning or teaching new things.
- Mathematics—Using mathematics to solve problems.
- Monitoring—Monitoring/Assessing performance of yourself, other individuals, or organizations to make improvements or take corrective action.
- Reading Comprehension—Understanding written sentences and paragraphs in work-related documents.
- Science—Using scientific rules and methods to solve problems.
- Speaking—Talking to others to convey information effectively.
- Writing—Communicating effectively in writing as appropriate for the needs of the audience.

Complex Problem Solving Skills

Developed capacities used to solve novel, ill-defined problems in complex, real-world settings

- Complex Problem Solving—Identifying complex problems and reviewing related information to develop and evaluate options and implement solutions.

Resource Management Skills

Developed capacities used to allocate resources efficiently

- Management of Financial Resources—Determining how money will be spent to get the work done, and accounting for these expenditures.
- Management of Material Resources—Obtaining and seeing to the appropriate use of equipment, facilities, and materials needed to do certain work.
- Management of Personnel Resources—Motivating, developing, and directing people as they work, identifying the best people for the job.
- Time Management—Managing one's own time and the time of others.

Social Skills

Developed capacities used to work with people to achieve goals

- Coordination—Adjusting actions in relation to others' actions.
- Instruction—Teaching others how to do something.
- Negotiation—Bringing others together and trying to reconcile differences.
- Persuasion—Persuading others to change their minds or behavior.
- Service Orientation—Actively looking for ways to help people.
- Social Perceptiveness—Being aware of other's reactions and understanding why they react as they do.

Systems Skills

Developed capacities used to understand, monitor, and improve socio-technical systems

- Judgment and Decision Making—Considering the relative costs and benefits of potential actions to choose the most appropriate one.
- Systems Analysis—Determining how a system should work and how changes in conditions, operations, and the environment will affect outcomes.
- Systems Evaluation—Identifying measures or indicators of system performance and the actions needed to improve or correct performance, relative to the goals of the system.

Technical Skills

Developed capacities used to design, set-up, operate, and correct malfunctions involving applications of machines or technological systems

- Equipment Maintenance—Performing routine maintenance on equipment and determining when and what kind of maintenance is needed.
- Equipment Selection—Determining the kind of tools and equipment needed to do a job.

- Installation—Installing equipment, machines, wiring, or programs to meet specifications.
- Operation and Control—Controlling operations of equipment or systems.
- Operation Monitoring—Watching gauges, dials, or other indicators to make sure a machine is working properly.
- Operations Analysis—Analyzing needs and product requirements to create a design.
- Programming—Writing computer programs for various purposes.
- Quality Control Analysis—Conducting tests and inspections of products, services, or processes to evaluate quality or performance.
- Repairing—Repairing machines or systems using the needed tools.
- Technology Design—Generating or adapting equipment and technology to serve user needs.
- Troubleshooting—Determining causes of operating errors and deciding what to do about it.

Assignment

Assignment: Go To http://online.onetcenter.org/skills/ and complete the online skills match using all six skills groups. Retrieve your O*NET feedback printing the summary report for those jobs with the highest skills match. Bring this to class. In addition, investigate the O*NET Web site and find answers to the following questions:

1. What is an O*NET-SOC code? Explain what a standard occupational classification is.
2. Explain the process that was used to match your skills to a particular job? (how does the system do the match?)
3. What is an SVP rating?
4. What is a job zone?
5. Could an employer use the skills match to make hiring decisions or develop hiring criteria? For example, should an employer require all applicants to do the skills match and then determine whether the job the employer is trying to fill appears in the skills match feedback?
6. Were the jobs identified for you as compatible with your skills search really compatible with your interests and aspirations? Explain your answer.
7. Are there any other options in the O*NET web site that could provide useful vocational advice? Could you use the "find occupations" option at http://online.onetcenter.org/?

CRITICAL THINKING APPLICATION 10-A

Defending Corporate Executive Pay

According to Graef Crystal, named the "foremost authority on executive compensation" by *Fortune* magazine, "The modern American CEO is a cross between an ancient pharaoh and Louis XIV—an imperial personage who almost never sees what the little people do, who is served by bootlicking lackeys, who rules from posh offices, who travels in the modern equivalent of Cleopatra's barge, the corporate jet, and who is paid so much more than the ordinary worker that he hasn't the slightest clue as to how the other 99.9 percent of the country lives."[1]

In 2004, the total CEO compensation for America's 500 biggest corporations was $3.3 *billion* (versus $3.1 billion in 2002). Go to Forbes.com for more current figures. Reuben Mark, CEO of Colgate-Palmolive, "earned" $148 million despite an utterly mediocre year for the company. George David, CEO of United Technology, one of the largest military contractors, earned over $70 million in both 2003 and 2004. Check the aflcio.org Web site for the latest figures.[2]

In 2004, the average CEO of a Fortune 1000 company received $9.84 million in total compensation, according to a study by compensation consultant Pearl Meyer & Partners for *The New York Times*. This represents a 12 percent increase in CEO pay over 2003. In contrast, the average nonsupervisory worker's pay increased just 2.2 percent to $27,485 in 2004.

There are so many examples of corporate greed and illustrations of this greed in situations that seem to indicate incompetent performance. Kmart gave CEO Charles Conaway a $9.5 million severance package at the same time they were laying off over 22,000 workers and owed creditors millions. Conaway had already earned millions while Kmart was heading toward bankruptcy. According to the AFL-CIO, the CEO of Hershey Foods made over $22 million in 2001 while the company increased health care costs for its employees. The contrast in the treatment of the Hershey workers with the CEO's runaway pay may have had a lot to do with the 2002 strike against the company.

Coca-Cola's board set challenging goals in 2000 in order for CEO Doug Daft to be eligible for one million performance-based shares. But in May 2002 the board changed the goals to reflect lower earnings targets. He also received an 18 percent raise (to $1.5 million), a bonus of $3.5 million, and one million option grants. Share price of Coca-Cola stock fell 23 percent during this period of time and revenues were unchanged from the previous year. Still, Mr. Daft was cited for his "highly effective leadership."

Along with obscene amounts of compensation, CEOs who are "retired" get pretty cushy deals too! Coca-Cola finally had enough of Mr. Daft's "leadership" and in 2004 and paid him more than $36 million as a severance package. As part of his severance agreement, Daft's successor, M. Douglas Ivester, received a six-year consulting agreement worth $675,000, office space, furniture, supplies, a company car, home security service and club dues. In total, Ivester's retirement package was reportedly worth $119 million. Steven Heyer, Coca-Cola's former president and COO, received a severance package reportedly worth at least $24 million after only three years on the job. Jack Stahl, also a former president and COO of Coca-Cola, received a severance package reportedly worth more than $25 million.

Stock options give executives the benefits of share price increases with none of the risks if the share price declines. Executives have made huge sums from exercising stock options even if their company later collapses (e.g., Enron). Stock options can reward short-term decisions that are not in the long-term interest of the company or its shareholders.

Amgen Chairman and CEO Kevin Sharer must not think his own company's stock is a good investment. As of February 2005, he held only $2 million in actual shares through a family trust. He holds zero shares of stock outright, although he has been employed as an Amgen executive since 1992. Sharer cashed out more than $42 million in stock option exercises for the past five years. During that same period, Amgen's stock price has gone down. For every dollar invested in Amgen Common Stock as of December 31, 1999, total shareholder return equaled just 6.8 cents for the entire five-year period. The board of directors adopted a stockholding requirement for Amgen executives. Under this policy, Amgen's CEO is required to hold five times his salary. However, this stock ownership guideline does not go into effect until December 2007. And this salary multiple represents only a tiny fraction of Sharer's total equity compensation.

"Stock option grants have become so large over the last decade that executives have become wealthy by selling just a fraction of their holdings during a stock-price run-up that turns out to be fleeting," according to George Akerlof, a UC Berkeley economist.[3] "When you give executives too much compensation in the form of stock options, they tend to concentrate too much attention on the stock price and there is a perverse incentive to raise the stock price, particularly when the chief executive wants to exercise his own options."[4]

The Financial Accounting Standards Board proposed requiring companies to expense stock options beginning June 15, 2005. This change was opposed by the new head of the Securities and Exchange Commission. In addition, more than 750 companies have started voluntarily expensing the cost of stock options. As a result, many companies have started paying their CEOs with actual shares of stock only if they meet performance benchmarks.

Defenders of CEO pay argue that executive pay is set based on studies of the pay of CEOs in the industry and that pay is approved by the corporate board. As one board member put it, "if we don't pay him what the market pays, we'd lose him and then watch what happens to our stock price." Another line of argument is that CEO pay is not really out of line relative to star athletes or entertainers. Opposition to expensing stock options argue that many companies rely on options to attract and retain executives and that options are not really a cash expense like salaries and bonuses.

Assignment

What is your view on executive pay? Conduct an Internet search on the latest analysis of executive pay and the current status of the standard. Take a position on expensing stock options. What of the argument that pay is priced based on the external market (the principle of external equity)? What about the argument that CEO pay should match that of movie stars or stars of the NBA or Major League Baseball.

[1]G. Crystal, *In search of excess.* New York: Norton, 1991, p. 3.
[2]Cited in www.aflcio.org/executivepaywatch.
[3]Leonhardt, D. (April 7, 2002). Tell the good news. Then cash in. *New York Times,* pp. 1, C3.
[4]*Ibid*

CRITICAL THINKING APPLICATION 10-B

Illegal Pay Discrimination, Bad Pay Policy, or Both?

The following letter was written by Ms. Julia Kate, a female associate, and addressed to the director of the clinical counseling center.

> Dear Dr. Boseman:
> The purpose of this letter is to request an assessment of my salary in the context of my performance and responsibilities and the salary levels that have been set for three staff members recently hired by the Counseling Center. In the past year, the Center hired one Ph.D at $10,000 more than I earn and two unlicensed counselors at almost my identical salary rate.
>
> I believe my salary is extremely low given the following facts: (1) My job performance has been rated at the highest level for all six years I have been on staff; (2) the recently hired Ph.D, a male, had no experience and performs the identical work I perform; (3) the recently hired M.Ed., a male, who is paid at the same level as I, had no experience in counseling. As you know, with the exception of the referrals to which I refer below, assignments of clients to staff members are based strictly on space available and not the possession of a particular staff member's credentials.
>
> While I recognize that credentials do translate into higher salaries for persons performing identical work, so too do other credentials such as the possession of an applicable license and qualifications and experience in supervising graduate student interns. I receive no additional compensation for this license despite the fact that it enables me to supervise interns while the two Masters' level associates hired do not possess such a license and thus cannot (and do not) supervise students. I have supervised graduate students since 1997. In addition, I have a Masters in Social Work (MSW), a terminal degree that, as a credential, has far more external marketability than the degrees possessed by the two new hires.
>
> I am also the designated specialist who receives all referrals from the county regarding sexual assault

and rape. I have had to use my expertise in this highly sensitive area on several occasions.

Rational (and legal) compensation systems set and adjust pay levels based on a number of factors, including the credentials, experience, supervisory responsibilities, and, of course, the job performance of the incumbents. Based on these factors, my salary is difficult to explain, especially when compared to the new staff of the Counseling Center.

Thank you for considering these issues. I look forward to your response. Ms. Kate

Assignment

Write a one-page position paper. Is this a violation of the EPA? What about Title VII? If you cannot take a position, stipulate what specific additional information you need. Conduct a Web search to determine whether you can find pay data that are relevant to the claims in the letter. The legal implications aside, what should Dr. Boseman do? Does Ms. Kate have a case?

CRITICAL THINKING APPLICATION 10-C

Legal or Illegal Compensation Plan?[1]

The city of Tampa, Florida approved a revised pay plan granting raises to all city employees in the Police and Fire Departments. The stated purpose of the plan was to "attract and retain qualified people, provide incentives for performance, maintain competitiveness with other public sector agencies and ensure equitable compensation to all employees regardless of age, sex, race and/or disability."

A revision of the plan, which was motivated, at least in part, by the City's desire to bring the starting salaries of police officers up to the regional average, granted raises to all police officers and police dispatchers. Under the provisions of the plan, officers and dispatchers with fewer than five years tenure received proportionately greater raises than employees who had more than five years tenure. Although some officers over the age of 40 had less than five years of service, most of the older officers had more.

Within the police department there were five basic jobs included: police officer, master police officer, police sergeant, police lieutenant, and deputy police chief. The police officer is the entry level, or lowest ranked position in the hierarchy. Each of these positions was divided into a series of steps and half-steps. The salary for each job was based on a compensation survey conducted in comparable communities in the Southeast. As is typical in most organizations, the majority of personnel were in the three lowest ranks, and in each of the ranks there were officers both under and over the age of 40. Each employee was assigned to a position within the range that was equal to the lowest step that would give him or her a minimum 2 percent raise. The few officers in the two highest ranks were all over 40.

All of the officers received increases in their pay. Criteria for granting increases was applied consistently and without regard to the age of the employee. The officers in the two highest ranked jobs received raises that were higher in dollar amount than the more junior positions. However, because the base salaries for these positions are higher, the relative percentage increase was smaller.

Thirty police officers and public safety dispatchers over the age of 40 filed suit pursuant to the Age Discrimination in Employment Act (ADEA). They are members of the class complaining of the "disparate impact" of the award.

The plaintiffs' evidence established two principal facts: First, almost two-thirds (66.2 percent) of the officers under 40 received raises of more than 10 percent while less than half (45.3 percent) of those over 40 did. Second, the average percentage increase for the entire class of officers with less than five years of tenure was higher than the percentage for those with more seniority. Because older officers tended to occupy more senior positions, on average they received statistically significant, smaller increases when measured as a percentage of their salary. The City's explanation for the differential was the need to raise the salaries of junior officers to make them competitive with comparable positions in the market.

Assignment

Can the older workers use "disparate impact" theory in their age discrimination claim? Based on the facts above, is the city of Tampa guilty of unlawful discrimination against older workers? Explain your answer. What is your view of the methods they used to adjust pay rates?

[1]Contributed by Karen Preston.

CRITICAL THINKING APPLICATION 11-A

The Case For and Against Pay-for-Performance Systems[1]

If you want employees to perform at a higher level, you can motivate them to excel by tying their compensation to a particular performance index. After all, the way to influence employees is through the wallet. Right? According to Alfie Kohn, author of four books and professional business lecturer, this is not the case.[2] Drawing from Frederick Herzberg's motivation theory, Kohn claims that financial incentives cannot motivate employees to improve their performance; however, the absence of financial incentives can create employee dissatisfaction or demotivation. For example, if your salary was cut, you would become frustrated and might seek another source of employment, but if you received a raise, you wouldn't improve your performance over the long haul. Sure, you might become exceptionally productive right before your evaluation for your yearly bonus or right after you received a raise, but not when looking at the big picture. At best, pay-for-performance (PFP) incentives motivate employees to *temporarily* alter their behavior; they do not encourage any lasting changed behavior. In fact, once the reward is taken away, employees will revert back to their old patterns of behavior.

So, according to this argument, PFP incentives are generally ineffective, temporary employee bribes. "Jump through these hoops and you'll get this" is the inevitable philosophy behind reward systems. Employees are reduced to mere objects controlled by the wiles of manipulative bosses. Surprisingly enough, a rewarding system is not much different from a punishing system; not receiving a reward has a similar effect to being punished. For every employee who "wins" (receives an award), there is an employee who "loses" (does not receive an award). With increased emphasis on self-managed work teams and quality work circles, competition and hostility among workers over who secured the largest reward is the last thing a U.S. firm needs. Employees will abandon risk taking, innovation, and creativity—the key ingredients for competitive advantage—in an attempt to minimize challenges and maximize their personal wealth. In the worst-case scenario, employees will engage in unethical or illegal behavior just to finesse a greater payoff. Therefore, the emphasis shifts from employees excelling at their jobs to excelling at the incentive-winning game. Recent examples may include Morgan Stanley and Adelphia. PFP incentives, Kohn argues, do not motivate employees to improve their performance; "they motivate [them] to get rewards."

Charles M. Cummings, senior compensation consultant at William M. Mercer, Inc., has refuted Kohn's "blanket condemnation of incentive plans," citing that properly constructed pay-for-performance systems can be successful.[3] Cummings finds fault with Kohn's premise that PFP systems reduce employees to simple objects trying to take a bite off the golden carrot dangling in front of their noses. Such manipulative and highly ineffective systems are found only in "hierarchical, tradition organizations" and are not representative of the way PFP systems should be designed nor of the way these systems are now being built. Furthermore, in such a traditional organization, employees are largely performing specialized tasks that do not directly affect the firm's bottom line. Rather, they have to rely on their supervisors to integrate their tasks into a meaningful, profitable whole. Without a feeling of worth to the organization, it is little wonder that employees will lack *intrinsic* (inner) motivation and have to be "bribed" by their bosses to perform their meaningless jobs. Cummings suggests that more firms today are shifting to *team-based PFP plans* (e.g., profit sharing, gain sharing) rather than *individualistic plans* (e.g., the ill-fated merit pay), which Kohn describes in his argument. Team-based PFP plans not only help employees comprehend their significance to the organization as a whole but also provide the intrinsic motivation necessary for optimum job performance. (Participants in quality work circles, self-managed

work teams, and the like will experience this intrinsic motivation because they can see the fruits of their labors with results that hit the bottom line.)

Contrary to Alfie Kohn's assumption, Cummings believes that "most people have a need to have their achievements acknowledged by others." Because employees are being respected for their accomplishments with a properly designed and implemented PFP system, they will generate "goodwill and commitment" towards the organization. These feelings are much different from the feelings of ill will that Kohn describes. A proper PFP system can be very successful in an organization and can attain a competitive advantage through loyal and motivated workers.

Assignment

Consider the arguments above and take a position. Do you agree with Kohn or Cummings? Are there situations in which the opposing position would ever apply? What does the latest research indicate regarding this question? Think of a real-life example to support the position you have taken.

---

[1]Contributed by Lauren J. Lispi.
[2]Kohn, A. (September–October 1993). Why incentive plans cannot work. *Harvard Business Review*, pp. 54–63.
[3]Cummings, C. M. (May–June 1994). Incentives that really do motivate. *Compensation and Benefits Review*, pp. 38–40.

CRITICAL THINKING APPLICATION 11-B

The Prediction of Rating Error[1]

Assignments

Presented below are three instruments, the scores of which are related to rating behaviors by supervisors. Complete Parts A, B and C. Your instructor will provide interpretive information.

Part A. The Performance Appraisal Discomfort Scale (PADS)

Research indicates that the people who commit leniency bias tend to commit it across rating situations (e.g., no matter whom they are rating).[2] In essence, some people feel relatively more discomfort in giving negative feedback than others. The PADS is an instrument that assesses the level of discomfort in giving feedback. Because of the anticipated discomfort, raters are more likely to take steps to avoid the discomfort if they can do so. Thus, as supervisors, they are more likely to rate with leniency in order to avoid the discomfort that may result from giving a more accurate but more critical review.[3] Complete the PADS below and score it as directed. Your instructor will provide the interpretation of the score.

The PADS[4] Indicate the degree of discomfort you would feel in the following situations. Answer as candidly as possible for what is true for you. Use the following scale to write in one number in the blank to the left of each item: 5 = high discomfort; 4 = some discomfort; 3 = a little discomfort; 2 = very little discomfort; 1 = no discomfort at all.

_____ 1. Telling an employee who is also a friend that he or she must stop coming into work late.

_____ 2. Telling an employee that his or her work is only satisfactory, when you know that he or she expects an above satisfactory rating.

_____ 3. Conducting a formal performance appraisal interview with an ineffective employee.

_____ 4. Telling an employee who has problems in dealing with other employees that he or she should do something about it (take a course, read a book, etc.).

_____ 5. Telling a male subordinate that his performance must improve.

_____ 6. Having to terminate someone for poor performance.

_____ 7. Being challenged to justify an evaluation in the middle of an appraisal interview.

_____ 8. Being accused of playing favorites in the rating of your staff.

_____ 9. Recommending that an employee be discharged.

_____ 10. Telling an employee that his or her performance can be improved.

_____ 11. Warning an ineffective employee that unless performance improves, he or she will be discharged.

_____ 12. Telling a female employee that her performance must improve.

To Score   Add up your ratings on the 12 items. The maximum score is 60; minimum score is 12.

Assignment   To what extent do you agree with the interpretation of your score that has been provided? Do you see any practical value in the PADS? Could a company use PADS scores for any type of personnel decision making? Can you think of any changes that could be made to make this research have more practical value?

Part B. PADS—Forced Choice

Consider each pair of statements and select the one described behavior that you feel more confident in performing effectively. Circle a or b.

1. a. Responding to a complaint from a customer who demands a full refund because a store associate provided erroneous information about a product.

   b. Informing an employee who is also a friend that he must stop coming into work late.

2. a. Developing an advertising or sales promotion strategy for a new service you are offering in the store.

   b. Conducting a formal performance appraisal interview with an ineffective employee.

3. a. Informing an employee that his performance was only satisfactory when he believes it was above average.

   b. Providing detailed comparative information about a new product line to a potential customer.

4. a. Informing an employee that his performance has to improve.

   b. Representing the company at a charity event at which you have to make a speech.

5. a. Representing the company in an arbitration dispute with a supplier.

   b. Having to terminate an employee for poor performance.

6. a. Serving the company as a technical specialist on software options for a potential external customer.

   b. Telling an employee who has problems in dealing with other people that he should do something about it.

7. a. Being challenged to justify an evaluation in the middle of an appraisal interview.

   b. Preparing a detailed report about market trends and new products and new competitors for the district manager.

8. a. Interviewing a customer to determine the nature of a complaint.

   b. Telling an employee that her performance must be improved.

9. a. Negotiating with a distributor over a marketing emphasis or a pricing issue.

   b. Recommending that an employee be discharged.

10. a. Warning an ineffective employee that performance must improve.

    b. Negotiating with a government official over discounts and terms of credit.

Assignment.   If your instructor has provided the scoring key, assess to what extent you agree with the interpretation of this score? Could this instrument be used for personnel selection or training?

Part C. Trust in the Appraisal Process Survey

(Note: This instrument is most predictive completed by a supervisor who conducts formal performance appraisal as part of his/her job.)[5]

Using the following rating format, respond to each of the questions below as they relate to the manner in which the typical supervisor/rater conducts performance appraisals in your organization. If you do not work, have someone who does complete the survey.

Use this Scale:

0—Strongly Disagree; 1—Disagree; 2—Undecided/ Unsure; 3—Agree; 4—Strongly Agree

The typical supervisor/rater in my unit/division:

_____ 1. Rates subordinates' performances higher than they really deserve.

_____ 2. Recognizes that higher than deserved ratings will have no major consequences for him/her.

_____ 3. Feels personally responsible for the performance of his/her work group.

_____ 4. Is reluctant to give negative evaluations to people.

_____ 5. Seeks mostly to just "keep the peace" with his/her employees regarding performance ratings.

_____ 6. Feels uncomfortable giving performance ratings.

_____ 7. Purposely inflates ratings.

_____ 8. Looks at "average" performance ratings as "damning with faint praise."

_____ 9. Recognizes that there are more likely to be negative consequences for him/her if tough but fair ratings are given rather than lenient ones.

_____ 10. Uses performance appraisal to gain approval for himself/herself.

_____ 11. Will rate fairly and honestly.

_____ 12. Rates higher because s/he feels other raters are inflating their ratings.

_____ 13. Sticks fairly close to the "bell curve" in his/her ratings.

_____ 14. Will distort ratings to get a better deal for his/her subordinates.

_____ 15. Inflates ratings so his/her work group will be happy.

Items 11 and 13 are reverse scored (0=4, 1=3; 2=2; 3=1; 4=0). Add up the points and give yourself a total score.

Assignment What do you suppose this instrument measures? Does it predict anything important?

---

[1]Contributed by Jarold Abbott.
[2]Kane, J. S., Bernardin, H. J., Villanova, P., and Peyrefitte, J. (1995). The stability of rater leniency: Three studies. *Academy of Management Journal, 38,* 1036–1051.
[3]Villanova, P., Bernardin, H. J., Dahmus, S., and Sims, R. (1993). Rater leniency and performance appraisal discomfort. *Educational and Psychological Measurement, 53,* 789–799.
[4]Adapted from Abbott, J., and Bernardin, H. J. (1983). *The development of a scale of self-efficacy for giving performance feedback.* Unpublished manuscript. Florida Atlantic University, Boca Raton, FL 33431.
[5]Copyright 1981 H. John Bernardin. May be used with permission.

CRITICAL THINKING APPLICATION 11-C

Can We (and Should We) Apply the Lincoln Electric Method?

The sign on the front door at Lincoln Electric in Cleveland, Ohio, says it all: "No admittance prior to 30 minutes before the start of work." That's right. Lincoln Electric, a highly successful maker of welding machinery, has to keep workers from starting early! How does it motivate workers?

Although some unionists compare it to "sweatshops," this Fortune 500 company pays its 3,000 employees according to the piece-rate system. Workers are simply paid for what they produce. Except for a two-week vacation and a pension, workers earn only what they produce according to a piece-rate formula. According to CEO Don Hastings, the average Lincoln worker earns over $60,000 based on the piece-rate system, a rate he claims is the highest salary for a factory worker in the world.

Some other company policies are also unusual. First, Lincoln still maintains a lifetime employment policy. It has never laid off a worker, even during recessionary times when it had a 40 percent reduction in sales volume. Second, it distributes substantial bonuses to workers based on company performance; some workers earned over $40,000 in bonuses in 2004. Third, the base pay of the CEO is only about seven times that of the average annual wage of a factory worker (CEO Hastings argues that trust is critical for this process to work and that obscene executive salaries ruin trust). His bonus is a direct function of company profits and fluctuates just like the workers' bonuses do. Hastings credits this trust with the incredible cooperation Lincoln got from its Cleveland plant when international ventures turned sour in the early 90s. Workers stepped up production and exceeded all targets during difficult times with factories in Brazil and Germany.

Although Hastings has called the Lincoln method "barbaric," the workers seem to love the company or at least the money. But according to the late Dan Lacey, who was editor of *Work Place Trends,* a pro-union newsletter, using the piece-rate method to improve American productivity is like saying we "have to improve transportation in America so let's whip the horses a little harder."

Chapter 7 discussed different aspects of value in performance. If the piece rate pays a worker for a quantity produced, what happens to quality? At Lincoln, workers are paid only for pieces that meet carefully defined specifications. If there is a quality problem with a piece, workers are responsible for the correction. And what about teamwork? Lincoln also uses performance appraisals that reveal a letter grade for each worker's dependability, quality, output, and cooperation. The straight A workers get the highest bonuses.

The executives and factory workers at Lincoln agree that management is overhead. Their philosophy is "every worker must be a manager, and every manager must be a worker . . . in self-management is found the true meaning of efficiency, because nothing increases overhead as quickly and nonproductively as extra layers of management."[1] The workers are also heavy stockholders; over 80 percent of the workers own stock and the stock is closely held by the Lincoln family, the workers, and several foundations. The year-end profit sharing probably breaks the record for distribution. An average of over 40 percent of Lincoln's pre-tax income goes to the employees.[2]

Assignment

Does the Lincoln system generalize to many other work situations? Think of one work setting in which you think the piece-rate method might work. Generate a list of the key contingencies that may be related to the success of a piece-rate system in that setting.

Also, in addition to the piece-rate method, to what extent are the other characteristics of the Lincoln compensation and management systems critical for Lincoln's success? (As of 2005, Lincoln had still maintained its lifetime employment record.) Do you think a CEO's pay relative to that of the producers of the goods and services is critical for establishing and maintaining employee trust? Do you think trust is important? Expectancy theory says nothing about trust. Or does it? Also, is this a work setting for Type A personalities or so-called workaholics only?

---

[1] Handlin, H. C. (1992). The company built upon the golden rule: Lincoln Electric. In B. L. Hopkins and T. C. Mawhinney (eds.), *Pay for performance: History, controversy, and evidence.* New York: Haworth Press, p. 156.
[2] Chilton, K. W. (November/December 1994). Lincoln Electric's incentive system: A reservoir of trust. *Compensation & Benefits Review,* pp. 29–34.

CRITICAL THINKING APPLICATION 11-D

Should Teacher Pay Be Tied to Student Test Scores?

Governor Mitt Romney of Massachusetts proposed large increases in state spending on education to take effect in 2006 that included provisions for merit pay tied to the classroom performance for public school teachers in his state. The merit pay could add $5,000 or more to a teacher's annual salary. "The ability to close the achievement gap is the civil rights issue of our generation," Mr. Romney said in an interview, noting his concern over student test scores.[1]

As of 2005, *Arizona, Florida, Iowa, New Mexico* and *North Carolina* have various forms of merit pay for teachers that award classroom performance. Other states are moving in that direction although there is considerable resistance from teacher unions, which almost always fight merit pay proposals and programs. Minnesota has also proposed an extra $2,000 per year that would be based on student achievement. Some cities have also pursued merit pay for their teachers. A Denver, Colorado ballot initiative was approved in 2005 that will raise property taxes

$25 million a year to be used for a teacher pay initiative that included in performance-based bonuses and salary increases. The common thread behind these initiatives and programs is the tie-in between classroom performance and teacher pay. The American Board for Certification of Teacher Excellence (www.abcte.org) has been working on a model merit pay plan for all states.

Among the criticisms of teacher merit pay are the criteria for eligibility. Some programs restrict eligibility to only those who teach certain classes (e.g., science and math) and those who are at the top as measured by classroom test score improvement. In Massachusetts, there was great resistance to the proposals. Arranging deck chairs on the Titanic is how one scholar has described merit pay for teachers. Catherine A. Boudreau, president of the Massachusetts Teachers Association (www.massteacher.org), a branch of the National Education Association calls Governor Romney's proposals "short on substance, long on politics." She describes merit pay plans as "inequitable, divisive and ineffective." Kathleen A. Kelley, president of the Massachusetts Federation of Teachers (www.mfteducator.org) said that Mr. Romney's plan was developed with no input from the education community. In response to this criticism. Mr. Romney said "You know I would just love it if you could just throw out all the special interests from education."

Assignment

Conduct research on teacher merit pay. What does research say about the subject? What do teacher unions say about the subject? How have teachers been paid in the past and what has been the role of classroom performance? Generate a list of potential problems with teacher merit pay tied to classroom performance and then possible solutions to those problems. Where is your state on this subject?

---

[1] *Janofsky,* M. (2005, October 4). Teacher Merit Pay Tied to Education Gains. (www.NYtimes.com)

CRITICAL THINKING APPLICATION 12-A

Employment-at-Will[1]

Chapter 12 discussed the employment-at-will doctrine and its impact upon organizational initiatives and practices (i.e., employee handbooks, termination). The chapter also discussed the circumstances under which an employee may file a lawsuit in some states. This exercise affords you the opportunity to research perceptions of this doctrine and your own state's laws. Kim[2] asserts that workers appear to systematically overestimate protections provided to them by the law, particularly with regard to employment-at-will. Defenders of the at-will doctrine argue that workers have full information to enter into an at-will contract with their employers, while critics of the doctrine suggest that workers do not have such information.

Furthermore, the critics note, employers are in a powerful position when it comes to negotiating an (implicit or explicit) employment contract as organizations essentially support the livelihood of individual workers.

In a study investigating how well workers understand the employment-at-will doctrine, Kim found that, on the whole, many individuals erroneously deemed terminations for no "good reason" as unlawful, when in fact they were legal based upon the employment-at-will doctrine. For instance, 89 percent of workers surveyed believe that an employee cannot be lawfully terminated for simple reasons of personal dislike. This is in fact lawful as long as EEO laws are not violated.

No matter what your stance is on the issue, it is an interesting question as to whether workers tend to correctly estimate their job security under employment-at-will. The following exercise guides you through a replication of Kim's study and asks that you further research employment-at-will in your state. Moreover, this exercise asks that you argue either for or against training employees as to the meaning of employment-at-will.

Assignment

A study was discussed in which individuals were asked their perceptions of employment-at-will. Specifically, they were asked to define the concept and they were presented with a scenario in which they were to determine if a termination was lawful. Do a similar "study" by asking 10 people the following questions.

1. Define employment-at-will.
2. Can an employer legally fire someone who was performing satisfactorily merely to replace her with someone at a lower wage?
3. Can an employer legally fire someone who refuses to participate in illegal billing practices?
4. Can an employer legally fire someone who has been accused of stealing, even if the employee can prove that he or she is not the culprit?

The results from the entire class will then be compiled.

1. How many individuals correctly defined employment-at-will?
2. How many people correctly answered "yes" to the scenario presented in question number two? (In Kim's study, only 17.8 percent of the individuals surveyed answered "yes").
3. How many people correctly answered "no" to the scenario presented in question number three? (In Kim's study, 87.2 percent correctly answered "no").
4. How many people correctly answered "yes" to the scenario presented in question number two? (In Kim's study, 10.4 percent of respondents correctly answered "yes").
5. What are some alternative explanations for your results? That is, are there reasons other than

familiarity with employment-at-will (or lack thereof) that could have produced your results?
6. If your results are markedly different from those reported by Kim, what alternative explanations could there be?

What is employment-at-will in your state? What relevant statutes and common-law decisions can you find using the library at your campus, legal resources, and the Internet? Some individuals believe that organizations should formally train employees as to the meaning of employment-at-will. Do you agree with this statement? Who is responsible for this training and how should it be executed?

[1]Contributed by Jennifer R. D. Robin.
[2]Research based on Kim, P. (1997). Bargaining with imperfect information: A study of worker perceptions of legal protection in an at-will world. *Cornell Law Review, 83,* 105.

CRITICAL THINKING APPLICATION 12-B

Developing Organizational Policy and a Code of Ethics[1]

Most large companies have developed codes of ethics and strict policy stipulations regarding employee behavior. The recent events regarding Enron, Merrill Lynch, Tyco, WorldCom, Morgan Stanley, HealthSouth, and Andersen Accounting have stirred even more activity in this area. The information on policy and ethics is typically disseminated to employees during orientation when they join the firm and is included in the company handbook. It may be provided in the form of rules of conduct regarding professional demeanor, dress, working hours, and statements on EEO and affirmative action. Guidelines for whistle-blowing or reporting problems with conduct, health, safety, sexual harassment, discrimination, use of drugs or alcohol on the job, theft, fraud, Internet usage, or other grievances also may be included. While the information in the company policies manual often serves as a firm's ethics code, it may not be labeled as such.

Assignment

Do research to identify a company you are familiar with where you can borrow the firm's policies and procedures handbook or retrieve it through the Internet. Write a brief description of the company you have chosen. Identify the code of ethics for employee behavior and what (if any) policy exists regarding ethics and employee behavior. What issues are addressed? How confident do you feel in the company's code of ethics? What, if any, changes would you make in the organization's code of ethics? Why? Outline the changes you would make.

1. Identify the important components of an organizational code of ethics.
2. Design a plan for implementing an ethical code in a company.

3. Provide suggestions for how an organization can monitor compliance with its code of ethics.
4. Provide an outline of what the code of ethics should look like.
5. How does the company monitor the system to be sure that the policy and code of ethics were being adhered to? What suggestions would you make to the firm if supervisors were not enforcing the ethical codes (e.g., allowing unsafe behaviors to go unreported)?

Does the handbook and/or should an employee handbook deal with the following issues?

1. A strict no-smoking policy for all employees on or off the job and a requirement that employees should report breaches of this policy to HR.
2. Absolute proscriptions against any Internet surfing that is not business-related.
3. A warning that computer usage will be monitored for surfing violations and performance measurement. The company warns new hires up front that electronic performance monitoring is routine and should be expected.
4. A strict prohibition against the use of personal cell phones. Only emergency calls are allowed during work hours. A warning also is included in the handbook about the possibility of telephone monitoring by management.
5. A strong statement from the CEO that employees are expected to participate in the United Way program and that the goal is 100 percent participation.
6. A statement that all employment disputes will be resolved through a mediation and arbitration process and that this requirement is a condition of employment and continued employment.
7. A strict statement that the employer and employee have an "at-will" relationship and that no matter what anyone working for the company may have said, the "at-will" condition still stands.
8. A strict statement prohibiting any relatives of employees from working for the company.

Would you be comfortable working for an organization with a policies and procedures handbook you reviewed? Generate a list of the advantages and disadvantages. How would you feel if a firm for whom you work implemented the other policies described?

[1]Contributed by Joyce E. A. Russell and Lillian T. Eby.

CRITICAL THINKING APPLICATION 13-A

Unionizing FedEx[1]

In a world of more competition and higher profits and shareholders return on investment, unionizing does not seem to make sense. Or does it? Some employees at Federal Express have been trying to unionize since 1991. The pilots were successful in 1993. The ground employees have sought unionization at various sites for the six years it took for the National Labor Relations Board to rule that Federal Express continues to be covered under the Railway Labor Act. This prevented the local sites from unionizing because the election to unionize has to be conducted at all sites within a given job category simultaneously. As of the date of publication of this text, FedEx ground employees were not unionized.

As of 2005, The International Brotherhood of Teamsters has not emphasized organizing FedEx workers because of the difficulty created by the ruling regarding the Railway Labor Act. The U.S. Department of Labor continues to consider Federal Express to be a cargo airline and, at the time of that DOL ruling, almost all of FedEx's freight was carried at some point by an aircraft. The RLA requires that a union organize on a companywide basis. The IBT has an active Airline Division, and represent workers at a lot of RLA regulated airlines (e.g., Northwest and Airborne Express). Over 25 percent of surveyed Teamster members in 2005 believed that organizing FedEx should be a priority for the Teamsters.

FedEx pilots, about 4,000, are now covered under Air Line Pilots Association (ALPA). ALPA represents approximately 66,000 pilots in collective bargaining agreements.

Despite the fact that FedEx employees earn less than their unionized counterparts at UPS, FedEx continues to be awarded one of the best places to work by several publications and organizations. FedEx is also a *Fortune* Globally Admired Company.

FedEx continues its aggressive policy of no unionization. When employees in their Antigua location went on strike on August 23, 1999, the company terminated all its employees and closed the office two days later on August 25 after over 12 years.[2] They had contracted with Parcel Plus to continue FedEx servicing customers. FedEx still hires independent contractors. Approximately 31 percent of FedEx's total employment is direct. The majority of employment is indirect (i.e., independent contractors).[3] Some question the classification of those employees as independent contractors. Independent contractors have control over their work and the way they conduct that work. FedEx is very specific on what is required to be one of their independent contractors down to how you and your truck need to look.

A UPS strike cited part-time and subcontract work as grievances so that the Teamsters negotiation of UPS contracts included a "no shift of package delivery work to part-timers" clause and "no subcontracting of feeder work except during peak season, and then only if local union agrees" clause. Teamsters' organizers and FedEx employees who are pro-union believe that those issues and wage differential are the reasons for unionizing.

Assignment

You are a newly hired FedEx employee. Based on what you know about FedEx and its competitors, would you sign a card to certify a union at FedEx? If yes, explain what information weighed the heaviest in your decision. If no, is there additional information you need to help you make your decision? Compile a list of questions you believe to be vital for your decision? If no and you request no further information, explain what information weighed the heaviest in that decision.

[1]Contributed by Mary E. Wilson
[2]*The Daily Observer.* Thursday, August 26, 1999. FedEx Quits Antigua, All Workers Fired. Also see http://members.aol.com/BobKutchko/UnionPride2/page6.html, accessed July 2002.
[3]SRI. (2001). Global Impact of FedEx on the New Economy. http://www.fedex.com/us/about/download/economy/sri_exec_summary.pdf?link=4, 30, accessed July 2002.

CRITICAL THINKING APPLICATION 13-B

Do You Support Striker Replacement Legislation?

The labor movement first started to suffer major setbacks in the 1980s when management started hiring replacement workers with the intent of disarming organized labor while continuing to remain productive. In actuality, the hiring of new permanent workers to replace striking employees was sanctioned by the Supreme Court in 1935. However, this policy was not widely practiced until the federal air traffic controllers strike in 1981. President Reagan's firing and replacement of 12,000 union workers was certainly one impetus for this practice becoming widely used and accepted. Also cited as a factor in this widespread practice of hiring permanent replacement workers was the wave of corporate mergers and leveraged buyouts. As a result of these financial megadeals, some argue that management no longer placed high value on a long-term workforce with stable community roots.

Congress has proposed legislation to prohibit employers from hiring permanent replacement workers during a strike. As part of this legislative package there is also a section prohibiting management from giving employment preference to employees willing to cross the picket line in order to return to work. President Clinton supports this legislation.

The Workplace Fairness Act was designed to protect the interests of those employed under collective bargaining agreements. The law would amend the National Labor Relations Act and make it an unfair labor practice to offer or grant the status of permanent replacement employee to an individual for performing bargaining unit work for the employer during a labor dispute between the employer and the labor organization that is acting as the collective bargaining representative involved in the dispute.

It also would be an unfair labor practice to offer or grant an individual any other employment preference based on the fact that such an individual performed bargaining unit work, or indicated a willingness to perform such work during a labor dispute, over an individual who was an employee at the commencement of the dispute, who in connection with such dispute has exercised the right to join, to assist, or to engage in other concerted activities for the purpose of collective bargaining.

Assignment

Choose one of the following two positions and be prepared to justify it.

Pro Position

In general, supporters of the new law believe that legislation is necessary to rebalance the relationship between labor and management in contract disputes. Supporters further contend that this imbalance leans heavily toward management, thus enabling unfair practices through this power. Reflection of this belief is manifested in the declining rates of unionization, decreasing strike activity, inadequate contract settlements, and a new propensity of employers actively hiring permanent replacement workers. These effects, they maintain, send a message to employees that if they strike, they will lose their jobs.

Con Position

The essence of the opponent's argument is that by empowering striking employees with the right to displace their permanent replacements would guarantee that there would never be labor/management balance. They feel this act would place unequal power in the union's hands in the context of bargaining over contract terms. Furthermore, opponents of the law contend that prohibiting the hiring of permanent replacements would force many small businesses to close down operations because attracting temporary replacement employees can be extremely difficult (especially in rural areas).

CRITICAL THINKING APPLICATION 14-A

Can Health and Safety Behavior Be Predicted?

Companies are very interested in assessing job applicants for their potential to behave in certain ways. This is particularly true for jobs that may be considered highly stressful, dangerous, or challenging. Complete the questionnaire below.

Respond to each statement using the following scale:

1 = Strongly Disagree; 2 = Disagree; 3 = Unsure; 4 = Agree; 5 = Strongly Agree

_____   1. People tell me I eat too fast.

_____   2. I like to do something else while I'm watching TV.

_____ 3. I usually eat breakfast on the run or not at all.

_____ 4. I am late for many of my appointments.

_____ 5. I have trouble waiting on line for anything.

_____ 6. I like to really "dig into" school or work assignments.

_____ 7. I have trouble finding time to go food shopping.

_____ 8. My normal meal lasts less than 20 minutes.

_____ 9. Most of my day is filled with problems that need solutions.

_____ 10. I usually try to reduce stress as soon as I feel it.

_____ 11. I got into fights a lot as a kid.

_____ 12. People sometimes refer to me as a "roughneck."

_____ 13. I often feel like punching someone's lights out.

_____ 14. Some people just deserve physical punishment.

_____ 15. I often got spanked as a kid.

_____ 16. I think there are times when a good beating is in order.

_____ 17. I enjoy getting drunk and a little out of control.

_____ 18. I have never been mad at a member of my family.

_____ 19. I enjoy watching a good fistfight.

_____ 20. I have never gotten mad or upset.

_____ 21. I really like to speed when I'm driving.

_____ 22. I've gotten my share of speeding tickets.

_____ 23. I like to weave in and out on a crowded highway.

_____ 24. I like to drive well above the speed limit.

_____ 25. Most people drive fast.

_____ 26. I am constantly on the lookout for new ways to improve my life.

_____ 27. I feel driven to make a difference in my community, and maybe the world.

_____ 28. I tend to let others take the initiative to start new projects.

_____ 29. Wherever I have been, I have been a powerful force for constructive change.

_____ 30. I enjoy facing and overcoming obstacles to my ideas.

_____ 31. Nothing is more exciting than seeing my ideas turn into reality.

_____ 32. If I see something I don't like, I fix it.

_____ 33. No matter what the odds, if I believe in something, I will make it happen.

_____ 34. I love being a champion for my ideas, even against others' opposition.

_____ 35. I excel at identifying opportunities.

Assignment

Evaluate what you think the various parts of this questionnaire are attempting to measure (and predict). Specifically,

1. What do items 1–10 measure?
2. What do items 11–17 and 19 measure?
3. What do items 21–25 measure?
4. What do items 26–35 measure?
5. What do items 18 and 20 measure?

Do you think your responses predict anything about you? What evidence should an organization have before this instrument is used for personnel selection? What would be your reaction if you were told you were not hired based on your responses to this questionnaire?

CRITICAL THINKING APPLICATION 14-B

The Measurement of Stress at Work

There are many causes of stress at work; some issues or situations are more stressful than others. Follow the directions below for some insights into the relative potency of work situations for causing stress at work.

Assignment

Consider your current job, a job you once had, or ask an acquaintance to help out. You or your cooperating acquaintance should get one work situation in mind.

Section I—Environmental Stress
Step 1: Stress Procedures
A. Circle the number of the items that apply to this particular work situation.
   1. The company where you work recently was purchased by another company.
   2. Layoffs (or "downsizing") have occurred in the past year.
   3. Your department or employer has had a recent major reorganization.
   4. Employees expect that the company will be sold or relocated.
   5. Employee benefits were significantly cut recently.
   6. Mandatory overtime is frequently required.
   7. Employees have little control over how they do their work.
   8. Consequences of making a mistake on the job are severe.
   9. Workloads vary greatly.
   10. My work is machine-paced or fast-paced.

11. Employees must react quickly and accurately to rapidly changing conditions.
12. Personal conflicts on the job are commonplace.

A. Subtotal for Items 1–12 (number circled × 3) =

A = _____

B. Circle any of the next 10 items that apply to the work situation.
   1. Few opportunities for advancement are available.
   2. Employees deal with lots of red tape to get things done.
   3. Staffing, money or technology is inadequate.
   4. Pay is below the going rate.
   5. Sick and vacation are below normal.
   6. Employees are rotated among shifts.
   7. New machines or ways of working have been introduced.
   8. Noise or vibration levels are high, or room temperatures keep changing in work areas.
   9. Employees generally are isolated from one another.
   10. Performance of work units generally is below average.

B. Subtotal for these 10 items (number of circled items × 2) =

B = _____

C. Circle any of the following that apply.
   1. There are few or no windows or natural lighting.
   2. Employees have little or no privacy.
   3. Meal breaks are unpredictable.
   4. Work is either sedentary or physically exhausting.

C. Subtotal for these questions (number of circled items (0–4)

C = _____

D = Total points for stress procedures (add the three subtotals) =

_____ A

_____ B

_____ C

D = A + B + C = _____ (stress producers)

Step 2: Stress Reducers   Many employers recognize that work produces stress and take steps to relieve or counteract it. Circle those items that apply to the work situation that is the focus of your analysis.

1. Management takes significant action to reduce stress.
2. Mental health benefits are provided in employees' health insurance coverage.

3. Employer has formal employee-communications program.
4. Employees are given information regularly on how to cope with stress.
5. Employees have current and clear job descriptions.
6. Management and employees talk openly with each other.
7. Employees are free to talk with one another.
8. Employer offers exercise and other stress-reduction classes.
9. Employees are recognized and rewarded for their contributions.

E. Subtotal for 3-point questions (number of circled items × 3) =

E = _____

Follow the same procedure for the next 8 items.

1. Work rules are published and are the same for everyone.
2. Child-care programs are available.
3. Employees can work flexible hours.
4. Perks are granted fairly, based on a person's level in the organization.
5. Employees have access to the technology they need.
6. Employees receive training when assigned new tasks.
7. Employer encourages work and personal-support groups.
8. Employees have a place and time to relax during the workday.

F. Subtotal for these questions (number of circled items × 2) =

F = _____

Now just circle any additional items from the remaining five.

1. An employee assistance program is available.
2. Employees' work spaces are not crowded.
3. Employees can put up personal items in their work areas.
4. Management appreciates humor in the workplace.
5. Elder care programs are available.

G. Subtotal for these questions (number circled × 1) =

G = _____

Add up the stress-reducing points, if any.

H. Total points for stress reducers (add the three subtotals) =

Now subtract them from the total in Step D.

D – H = _____(this is the level of Environmental Stress; your instructor will provide the score interpretation)

Section II—The Role of Roles

This questionnaire concerns how you (or your cooperating acquaintance) feel about this same work situation. Use the following scale to answer each item.

7 = Very false; 6 = False; 5 = Somewhat false; 4 = Neither true not false; 3 = Somewhat true; 2 = True.

_____ 1. I have clear, planned goals and objectives for my job.

_____ 2. I know that I have divided my time properly.

_____ 3. I know what my responsibilities are.

_____ 4. I know exactly what is expected of me.

_____ 5. I feel certain about how much authority I have on the job.

_____ 6. Explanation is clear of what has to be done.

_____ 7. I have to do things that should be done differently under different conditions.

_____ 8. I receive an assignment without the resources to complete it.

_____ 9. I have to buck a rule or policy in order to carry out an assignment.

_____ 10. I work with two or more groups who operate quite differently.

_____ 11. I receive incompatible requests from two or more people.

_____ 12. I do things that are apt to be accepted by one person and not by others.

_____ 13. I receive an assignment without adequate materials to execute it.

_____ 14. I work on unnecessary things.

Add up your responses to items 1–6 _____ This is your Role Ambiguity Score.

Add up your responses to items 7–14 _____ This is your Role Conflict Score.

Your instructor will provide interpretations of these scores.

APPENDIX B

Chapter Exercises

Chapter 1 Exercises

EXERCISE 1.1

An Interview with an HRM Specialist

Overview

Chapter 1 presents an overview of the major activities of HR professionals today. As noted, HRM practitioners serve a variety of roles in organizations and are often classified as personnel directors, personnel managers, or HRM staff members. Individuals specializing in specific HRM job activities may be working in departments of training, labor relations, equal employment opportunity/affirmative action, compensation, or personnel research.

Learning Objectives

After completing this exercise, you should be able to

1. Describe the major HRM responsibilities and activities of HRM professionals.
2. Explain some contemporary problems or difficulties encountered in HRM work.
3. Derive a list of major job activities useful for understanding the HRM domains.

Procedure

Part A: Individual Interviews

Step 1. Read Chapter 1, paying particular attention to the discussion of HRM activities.

Step 2. Identify a practicing HRM or personnel professional or a line manager charged with HR activities and conduct a short interview to gather information about the person's job, his or her background, the organization, and the major job-related problems confronting the individual. An attempt should be made to interview a senior-level HR employee of the organization (e.g., the vice president of human resources or personnel director) either by phone or in person or a line manager who has significant HR

responsibilities. Form 1.1.1 should be used as a format for conducting the interview and recording responses.

Part B: Group Discussions

Step 1. Students should assemble in class in groups of about six and review each individual report. The group should then identify common problems identified by the HR professionals. The characteristics of the organization also should be considered in the context of the problems. For example, are there any clear differences in problems confronting HRM professionals from service versus manufacturing organizations, or public- versus private-sector organizations? Students should have a clear understanding of the HRM professional's position and reporting relationships within the organization. The group also should attempt to identify the HRM activities discussed in Chapter 1 that are most related to the problems discussed. The problems should be assessed in the context of the trends discussed in Chapter 1. The group also should discuss the professional's views of how line management views the personnel function (e.g., cooperative, adversarial).

Step 2. A spokesperson should be designated to report each group's findings. After all spokespersons have presented their list of activities and difficulties, the class should suggest HRM strategies and programs that could address the problems raised. Trends related to the relationship between line management and HRM professionals also should be discussed.

FORM 1.1.1
INTERVIEW FORMAT FOR HRM PROFESSIONALS

Interviewer's Name _____   Interview date _____

Interviewee's Name _____   Company _____

1. How would you describe your organization? (e.g., public versus private, size, service/manufacturing, union/nonunion, major competitors, international business, growing, stagnant, downsizing).

2. What is your position title?

3. *a.* How many months/years have you occupied this position?

   b. How many months/years have you been employed by this company?

4. *a.* Briefly, describe your background (education, previous experience).

   b. Which aspects of your background are most directly related to your current job duties?

Name _____

    5.   *a.*   How many employees do you directly supervise?

           b.   To whom do you report? What is his or her job title?

    6.   Describe the organization's human resource or personnel department. How many employees are in the department? What are their main job duties if different from yours?

    7.   What do you regard as your three most significant job responsibilities? Be as specific as possible.

Name _____

8. What do you regard as the three most significant and specific HR challenges or difficulties you face in your current job responsibilities? For each, briefly describe the steps you have taken (or are planning to take) to deal with each of the problems.

Challenges   **Action Strategies**

9. Describe your relationship with line management or if you are in line management, describe your relationship with HR. In general, how would you characterize the relationship (supportive, adversarial, cooperative)? Explain your answer. Give an example of where your interaction with either line management or HR was not favorable. Describe these circumstances in detail. How was the problem resolved? Give an example of a favorable interaction. Describe these circumstances in detail.

EXERCISE 1.2

An Assessment of Customer Satisfaction and the Relationship to HRM Activities

Overview

Chapter 1 described a variety of new challenges and trends confronting organizations today, many of which include concerns about productivity, product service and quality, and customer satisfaction.

As a practicing manager or an HRM specialist, you are likely to be asked to meet the human resource challenges related to productivity and/or customer satisfaction. Nine out of every 10 jobs are predicted to be in the services sector in the next 20 years. Productivity figures reflect a generally slow rate of productivity growth for many services industries. Assessments of product and service quality are also unfavorable, and customer service indexes are low in many segments of the services sector, although they have improved in recent years.

Chapter 1 presents an argument and cites research that shows human resource activities have the potential to enhance customer satisfaction, increase productivity, and improve product and service quality. We emphasized that the most effective HRM programs are those in which the focus is always on the ultimate criterion of customer satisfaction. This exercise will focus on those HRM efforts that are customer oriented and will generate discussion about steps that can be taken to improve customer satisfaction.

Learning Objectives

After completing this exercise, you should be able to

1. Identify some specific examples of how HRM can affect customer satisfaction.
2. View customer satisfaction from an HRM perspective such as the impact of employee attitudes, the diversity of worker characteristics, and the job skills gap and how you as a manager or HRM specialist could improve customer satisfaction through HRM activities.
3. Identify HRM activities that may be useful for tackling problems related to customer satisfaction.

Procedure

Part A: Individual Analysis

Think back over an experience you have had with any products or services. It could even be experiences related to your interaction with the university. Write two examples of what you regard as excellent customer service and two you regard as poor customer service regarding those products or services. Write the negative examples on Form 1.2.1 and the positive examples on Form 1.2.2.

After describing each experience, review the HRM activities discussed in Chapter 1 and form hypotheses as to what particular domains or activities may have been primarily responsible for the excellent or poor customer service. Generate a list of the possible causes. Be creative in your hypotheses and attempt to go beyond simple theories such as a "training" problem as the cause. Bring the completed forms to class for discussion.

On Form 1.2.3, write what you regard as your five absolute favorite products or services that you have actually purchased in any area. This can be any product, large or small, cheap or expensive. In the space provided, write a short explanation of why you regard each particular product or service as your favorite. Bring Form 1.2.3 to class.

Part B: Group Analysis

Approximately six people should be designated to discuss responses on Form 1.2.1 while the same number of students are designated as observers of the group. If possible, each observer should be assigned to observe the group performance of only one group participant. The observer should review the participant's Form 1.2.1 before group discussion. Each observer should use Form 1.2.4 as the context for observing group participation of the participant to whom he or she has been assigned. *Observers should review the directions for observation before the observation period. Form 1.2.4 should be completed by the observer immediately after group discussion is completed while the participant is completing Form 1.2.5 (self-assessment).*

All members of the first discussion group should also read each other's Form 1.2.1 and attempt to discern trends in the incidents. For example, was the dissatisfaction mainly caused for poor product or service quality? Was the product or service representative incompetent and not knowledgeable about the product or service? After identifying any trends in the dissatisfaction, discuss the HRM activities proposed as the major causes of the poor customer service. Generate a list of the most important HRM activities the group believes to be directly or indirectly responsible for the customer service problems. The group should attempt to reach consensus on the top three HRM activities that could be directed at correcting the customer service problems.

After about 15 minutes of discussion, each observer should evaluate the participant's performance in the group and each participant should complete the self-assessment on Form 1.2.5. The pairs should then switch roles and the new discussion group should discuss the responses on Form 1.2.2, also attempting to identify the major HRM activities thought to be the causes of the excellent customer services that were provided and the extent to which HRM was responsible relative to other organizational functions. The second group can use the first group's analysis as a starting point. Again, the group should attempt to reach consensus on the top three HRM activities thought to be responsible for the positive customer satisfaction.

Part C: Self- and Observer Assessment and Feedback Session

After completing the second group exercise, participants should make a self-assessment using the rating scale on Form 1.2.5 while the observer is completing Form 1.2.4. After Forms 1.2.5 and 1.2.4 are completed, students should pair off and take turns reviewing their respective self- and observer assessments. Discussion should then center on each individual's performance in the group, the written responses, areas of strength or weakness, and the rationale of their respective positions regarding HRM activities.

FORM 1.2.1

Name _____   Group _____

Think of two situations in which you felt very dissatisfied with the customer service you received. Describe each circumstance in some detail and consider the causes of the service in terms of possible HRM activities. What were you expecting and what did you receive? Answer the questions below for each situation:

1. Describe the organization (e.g., fast food, department store, university setting).
   Situation 1

   Situation 2

2. Describe the incident and the poor service in some detail.
   Situation 1

   Situation 2

3. What do you regard as the major causes for your dissatisfaction? To what extent do you believe HRM activities were related to the dissatisfaction? Specifically, which activities are most related to the customer service problem and how could HRM improve the service?
   Situation 1

   Situation 2

Name _____   Group _____

Think of two situations in which you felt very satisfied with the customer service you received. Describe each circumstance in some detail and consider the causes of the service in terms of possible HRM activities. What were you expecting and what did you receive?

1.   Describe the organization (e.g., fast food, department store, university setting).
     Situation 1

     Situation 2

2.   Describe the incident and the good service in some detail.
     Situation 1

     Situation 2

3.   What do you regard as the major causes of your customer satisfaction? To what extent do you believe HRM activities were related to your satisfaction? Specifically, which activities do you believe to be most related to the customer service you have received?
     Situation 1

     Situation 2

FORM 1.2.3
WHAT ARE YOUR FAVORITE PRODUCTS OR SERVICES?

Name _____

1. What do you regard as the most favorite product or service you have ever purchased? Explain why you regard this product or service so highly (be specific).

What (if any) role did human resources have in making this product or service so good?

2. What do you regard as the least favorite product or service you have ever purchased? Explain why you regard this product/service so poorly (be specific).

Do you think human resources had anything to do with the lack of regard you have for this product/service?

FORM 1.2.4
OBSERVER ASSESSMENT FORM

Observer's name _____ Discussant's name _____ Group _____

Directions for observation: Get familiar with the 10 behaviors or activities listed below. Observe your designated discussant on the extent to which he or she exhibited these behaviors. *Rate the extent to which the participant exhibited the behaviors described below. Make your ratings in the space provided. Use the following scale to make your ratings:*

1. Not at all

2. To a little extent

3. To some extent

4. To a great extent

5. To a very great extent

x. Does not apply

To what extent did the participant

_____ 1. Help establish a clear course of action to complete the work?

_____ 2. Speak effectively in the group?

_____ 3. Argue persuasively for a point of view?

_____ 4. Present a point of view concisely?

_____ 5. Write clearly and concisely?

_____ 6. Show sensitivity to other group members?

_____ 7. Stimulate and guide group members toward resolution of the assignment?

_____ 8. Listen carefully to other opinions and suggestions?

_____ 9. Analyze all pertinent information carefully before taking a position?

_____ 10. Display a willingness to state a position in a complex situation?

FORM 1.2.5

SELF-ASSESSMENT FORM

Name _____

Rate the extent to which you exhibited the behaviors described below in the group. Make your ratings in the space provided. Use the following scale to make your ratings:

1. Not at all

2. To a little extent

3. To some extent

4. To a great extent

5. To a very great extent

x. Does not apply

To what extent did you

_____ 1. Help establish a clear course of action to complete the work?

_____ 2. Speak effectively in the group?

_____ 3. Argue persuasively for a point of view?

_____ 4. Present your point of view concisely?

_____ 5. Write clearly and concisely?

_____ 6. Show sensitivity to other group members?

_____ 7. Stimulate and guide group members toward resolution of the assignment?

_____ 8. Listen carefully to other opinions and suggestions?

_____ 9. Analyze all pertinent information carefully before taking a position?

_____ 10. Display a willingness to state a position in a complex situation?

EXERCISE 1.2
ASSESSMENT QUESTIONS

Name ————————————————————   Group ————————————————————

1. Describe the experience you had in providing feedback on your designated discussant's performance. To what extent did you feel comfortable in that role?

2. How might that role be improved with better directions, better assessment devices, etc.?

3. How did you feel about receiving feedback on your group performance? To what extent did you find the feedback helpful? How might that process be improved?

4. Did this exercise give you a better understanding of the relationship between HRM-related activities and customer satisfaction? Explain your answer.

EXERCISE 1.3

Human Resource Issues at Valley National Bank*

Overview

Chapter 1 introduced you to the human resource issues that HRM professionals and general managers must deal with if they are to assist the organization in becoming competitive and in meeting its goals. This exercise enables you to further develop your analytical skills as you assess the human resource issues affecting competitiveness at Valley National Bank.

Learning Objectives

After completing this exercise, you should be able to

1. Identify human resource issues that may affect organizational effectiveness and competitiveness.
2. Develop strategies for dealing with human resource concerns.

Procedure

Part A: Individual Analysis

Step 1. Read Chapter 1, paying particular attention to the human resource domains in the context of the discussion on competitive advantage.

Step 2. Read the background information on Valley National Bank provided in Exhibits 1.3 and 1.3.1. Identify the human resource issues facing the vice president's department and under which of the HR domains (e.g., Organizational Design, Staffing, Performance Management and Appraisal) each issue belongs. Outline some strategies for dealing with these issues. Develop a rank-ordered *chronological* priority list of the first three issues that require your attention. Provide a written justification for your recommendations. Enter your rank orderings and justifications in the space provided on Form 1.3.1. **Answer the assessment questions *before class* as well.**

Part B: Group Discussions

Step 1. In groups, identify what you believe to be the potential competitive advantage(s) of the accounting department. Review all individual 1.3.1 forms and the assessment questions and determine the human resource issues of greatest concern to the accounting department. Reach a consensus on the chronology of the top three issues that can affect the Bank's competitive advantage. Discuss why these issues must be resolved if the department is to assist the Bank in becoming more competitive. Identify the benefits and drawbacks to each recommendation. Reach consensus on the assessment questions as well.

Step 2. A representative from each group should present the consensus recommendations and rationale to the rest of the class.

Part C: (Optional)

Students should complete the self- and peer assessment instrument.

*Contributed by Dave Ulrich.

EXHIBIT 1.3

BACKGROUND INFORMATION FOR VALLEY NATIONAL BANK

RECENT BANK HISTORY

Valley National Bank is a relatively young financial institution with close to $10 billion in assets, although it shortly will acquire another bank to bring its size up to about $12 billion in assets. As a whole, there is a wealth of technical talent in the company, yet most of the experiences have been developed within the confines of $1 and $2 billion institutions. The managers and employees have not had much collective experience managing a $12 billion company. Senior managers currently recognize they must make some critical strategic decisions regarding the future of the bank if they are to remain competitive in the next decade.

Accounting Department

The vice president of accounting reports directly to the senior vice president of management accounting, who in turn reports to the controller of the company (see the condensed organizational chart in Exhibit 1.3.1). The vice president, Suzanne Roberts, was promoted into her current position to manage a department that the previous manager had let get out of control. Her job is to provide accounting software to line and staff management throughout the organization so that managers might be able to make better decisions in the daily operations of their respective departments. The software, although difficult to implement, has proven to be very useful in institutions with postures of high growth. The information provided by the programs is financial in nature and, for the most part, is the type of information that VNB bankers are not used to receiving. Therefore, her current charge is twofold: to educate the company in the use of the new software so that the bank ultimately benefits in terms of bottom-line results and to use the software to identify those sectors of business in which the bank does exceptionally well so that better and more focused strategic decisions can be made.

As challenging as her stated primary job responsibilities are, Ms. Roberts believes that another issue she currently faces is getting the right people in the right places in her department so that they can accomplish their goals. When she came into the department, she quickly concluded that some of the best contributors in the department were also the lowest-paid employees.

Bob Phillips was the former manager of the department. Through a merger, he came to Valley National Bank to manage the department, having had experience supervising two people at his previous position.

In his role as vice president of accounting, he was asked to supervise about 10 people. Over two years, things got so out of hand that his employees did not know what they were supposed to do, except in emergency situations, which seemed to be happening every day. Performance reviews of employees were late by up to six months. Naturally, employee morale was very low and attitudes toward the company became hardened. Good people quit the bank or transferred to other departments. Finding replacements for these individuals was done poorly; often the first person who walked in for the interview was hired. Today, there are several people working for the department who probably should never have been hired. Unfortunately, their options are such that it probably pays for them to stay rather than voluntarily leave.

Bob lacked the organizational and planning skills needed to effectively manage his people. In addition, his weak interpersonal skills have created hard feelings among employees in the department. He usually can arrive at a very good financial/accounting solution to a problem and has an extensive knowledge of all *major* software programs. However, he has a difficult time working with other people to implement his solutions.

Needless to say, some employees resent that Bob is still paid a good salary and given a good title to go with his reduced responsibilities. Ms. Roberts believes the company should sever its ties with Bob, but other external factors make this choice difficult. For example, Bob has faced some very severe personal and health problems since transferring to Valley National Bank.

Carla Goodman previously worked for Bob for about 15 years. When the accounting department at Valley National was established, she was placed in charge of several people and given a promotion of two pay-grade levels. This decision proved to be disastrous because she could not (or would not) accept the responsibility of supervising and reviewing people. She was quickly relieved of these duties, but her salary grade level remained intact so that today she is overpaid for her overall responsibilities. Her title is such that it implies a lower pay level in the company, but it fools no one. She is average as a technical worker and understands the flow of transactions well. Currently, Ms. Roberts often has Carla working by herself because she doesn't make very good impressions with people. She tends to openly criticize the company, which draws concerns from other employees in the department. In fact, on occasion, she and Bob resort to shouting matches to

EXHIBIT 1.3.1

ORGANIZATIONAL CHART

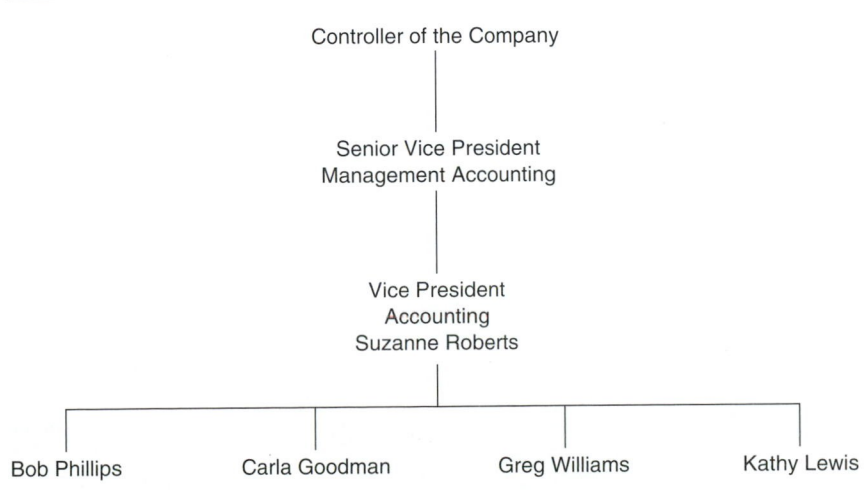

EXHIBIT 1.3 (*Continued*)

get their respective points across to each other. Ms. Roberts received an anonymous note reporting possible sexual harassment issues between Carla and another employee.

Greg Williams has been with the company about eight years and has worked for Ms. Roberts for about 2.5 years in various capacities. He has progressed in a very normal fashion in the bank, however, he has seen younger people such as Ms. Roberts move ahead of him on the organizational ladder. He expresses concern that his career may be leveling off unless something dramatic happens. He is not the quickest person to catch onto things in a technical sense, and he has a difficult time interacting effectively with people. This reduces his chances for a promotion. In general, he is a conscientious, mild-mannered employee who doesn't normally complain about things. He is good at taking orders, but not very good at handing them out.

Kathy Lewis is the most promising employee in the department today in terms of future potential within the company. She is technically sharp, with considerable knowledge of the new information systems, and has shown some promise in the effective management of people. She has been an employee of the company for a number of years and worked for Bob at the previous bank before the merger. She understands his odd nature. Her skills allow her to get more done than most people, and she is willing to put in extra hours to get things done. She did announce her resignation from the company at one time because of the mounting problems with the department, but a senior vice president talked her into staying by implying changes would be made sometime. Kathy is probably worth more to the bank than her current salary indicates, especially in light of the salaries of Bob and Carla. The normal guidelines should allow her to catch up in the next one to two years. She probably could also gain from receiving experience in other departments, but Ms. Roberts recognizes that she could not afford to let Kathy go because of the lack of depth with the other employees.

Overall, things are probably not as bad as they may appear to be. Ms. Roberts, however, does get concerned from time to time about the general lack of depth in the department as Mr. Jack Richter, Valley National Bank president, looks to the department to help the bank become more competitive. Ms. Roberts has met with Mr. Sterrett of the HRM Department, who has recommended that Bob be terminated immediately but that Carla should be retained because she could file a sex discrimination lawsuit. Sterrett also recommends that Carla's pay should be cut immediately.

FORM 1.3.1

PRIORITY LIST OF HRM ISSUES
_____

Name _____   Group _____

First issue in need of attention:

   Justification:

   Action to be taken:

   What is the HR domain (e.g., Organizational Design, Staffing, etc.)?

Second issue in need of attention:

   Justification:

   Action to be taken:

   What is the HR domain?

Third issue in need of attention:

   Justification:

   Action to be taken:

   What is the HR domain?

Name _____   Group _____

List the potential internal strengths at Valley National.

List the potential internal weaknesses at Valley National.

List the potential external opportunities at Valley National.

List the potential external threats at Valley National.

EXERCISE 1.3
ASSESSMENT QUESTIONS

Name _____   Group _____

1. Do you agree or disagree with the recommendations of Mr. Sterrett? Explain your position. Is it lawful to cut employees' pay as Mr. Sterrett recommends?

2. What other information would be helpful in preparation for recommending action to be taken?

EXERCISE 1.3 (*Continued*)

3.   What steps would you take to determine the legality of your action?

4.   What is potentially "unique" about VNB and how could the "uniqueness" give the bank a competitive advantage?

5.   Among the major activities of HRM (see Figure 1-3), what domain usually drives other HR domains when significant organizational change is necessary?

Chapter 2 Exercises

EXERCISE 2.1

International HR Strategies: The Derivation of Policy*

Overview

Chapter 2 discusses the issue how to staff various forms of overseas operations. Review the discussion in the chapter on the issues affecting decisions about the use of expatriates, the upfront training costs, the cultural orientation costs, and the high level of assignment failure. Consider the information provided in the case and take positions on each question posed.

Learning Objectives

After completing this exercise, you should be able to

1. Understand some of the complexities of international HRM.
2. Provide recommendations for decisions related to staffing and compensating international operations.

3. Outline the key issues that should be considered in dealing with expatriates and repatriates.

Procedure

Part A: Individual Analysis

Step 1. Read the attached background material on LeBert Graphics provided in Exhibit 2.1.1.

Step 2. Assume the role of consultant to the vice president of HR and respond to the issues he has raised. Prepare concise, written responses for each issue and point out any contingencies that should be considered. Answer the questions presented on Form 2.1.1.

EXHIBIT 2.1.1

William O'Dell, vice president for human resources at LeBert Graphics (LG), a fast-growing software development firm headquartered in Boston's Route 128 technology belt, was visiting the firm's first overseas subsidiary, LeBert Graphics Bangalore, Ltd. (LGB). The visit had been going well, but a recent lunch with his good friend, Ashok Rao, had left him troubled. Rao was one of many Indian expatriates who had migrated to the United States in the 1980s. He had been with LG for a number of years and had recently accepted an assignment to return to his hometown to head up the firm's new development lab. O'Dell was thankful to have him there—not just because of his development skills, but because he hoped he would serve as a cultural broker between headquarters and local employees.

During lunch, Rao noted how the city had changed. Rao had decided not to return to Bangalore after college in the United States because of the lack of opportunities. Now the city was booming, and computer software was the driving force. Neighbors in the technology park where LG had located included Siemens Components and Hitachi Asia.[1] The nature of the industry had changed too. Initially, foreign firms had employed Indian workers for basic programming. Although cheap, these employees did not always have the training or skill levels seen in their American counterparts. No longer. There were still large pools of these competent, but not exceptional employees. Recruiting for the new operations, however, he found many of the applicants had technical skills that would equal those of any of their Boston staff.[2] These were the employees they needed for the software development operations.

The market had changed in other ways too. Today, the best of these software engineers had more options. Because of a worldwide shortage, there were a host of firms looking for skilled engineers. An engineer could work for the local operations of a foreign firm, on temporary assignment basis in the United States or Europe, or could find a place in one of the many local, start-up firms.[3] Some had great success

starting their own software firms in the United States. While the same range of opportunities might not exist for those with more basic skills, the growth in foreign investment and start-ups in Bangalore also gave these employees many attractive options locally.

At first, the conversation appeared casual, the reminiscences of an old friend. However, Rao also had mentioned a conversation he had overheard in which one of the brightest engineers in the development unit had complained to a coworker that although he was a principal engineer on a joint Boston–Bangalore project, his American counterpart was receiving over four times his salary. On reflection, O'Dell was convinced that Rao had been attempting to draw his attention to an issue that was important to some of the Indian staff.

O'Dell's initial reaction had been, "Of course, that's why we located in Bangalore in the first place." Technology skills were abundant and pay rates for software engineers were a fraction of those in Boston. Moreover, the pay levels reflected the fact that productivity in the programming unit was not always up to U.S. standards. On reflection, he realized that the issue was much more complex.

On one hand were the economics. Cost savings not achieved now might be lost forever. Manufacturing firms that had moved operations to low-cost, offshore sites often had found that the benefits were partly illusory. Wages were low, but at times so was productivity. Employees were often willing, and with appropriate training, supervision, and equipment, productivity levels would rise. However, as these employees became more productive, they also became more attractive to other employers. Moreover, as the economy in these regions developed, there was often a shift in the exchange rate. Salaries rose locally, but because of exchange rate effects, they rose even more in U.S. dollars. Firms using contractors might shift to another, lower-cost site. Such shifts could be disruptive, however, and were even more difficult when the firm had invested directly in the overseas location.

It would be simpler, O'Dell thought, if the firm were in Bangalore for the short term. LG's interests in Bangalore had changed dramatically over the past year, however. LG had been using an Indian subcontractor to outsource basic programming for years. Individual pay levels had not concerned them directly. The Indian firm handled all issues related to recruitment, performance evaluation, and compensation. Recently, LG had decided both to bring the programming in-house (by acquiring the Indian firm) and to open a software development lab.

*Contributed by Brenda E. Richey, Associate professor and Chair, Department of Management, International Business and Entrepreneurship, Florida Atlantic University.
[1]Ristelhueber, R. (April 1997). Bangalore builds a high-tech future. *Electronic Business Today, 23*(4), 20.
[2]Stremlau, J. (November 1996). Bangalore: India's Silicon City. *Monthly Labor Review, 119*(11), 50–51.
[3]Leung, J. (June 1996). Brains fuel technology: Boom town. *Asian Business, 32*(6), 28–34.

EXHIBIT 2.1.1 (*Continued*)

The decision to move the operation in-house reflected a desire for greater control. It would allow greater emphasis on quality, especially after they trained the programmers to more closely meet the company's special needs. The decision to open the software development lab represented an even more dramatic shift. The new lab operation could take advantage of the rapidly developing skills of the Indian engineers, particularly in "hot jobs" for which there was a worldwide shortage. Moreover, the fast-growing Asian markets held real potential for LG. This required the development of programs that met the special needs of their Asian customers. At first the technology would originate in Boston, but substantial local adaptation was required. Later, the lab should stand alone in developing programs for the region and possibly the world market. These efforts required day-to-day interaction and teamwork between engineers at both locations. Soon the projects would require short-term transfers of personnel between facilities.

The discussion reminded him of a project he had left on his desk before the trip: developing a compensation plan for the revamped India operations. The project had not focused on compensation levels, but it had raised related questions. What type of compensation package was appropriate? Should they follow local custom as to vacations and leave? Should the generous stock option and pension plans, available to employees in Boston, be extended to these operations?

Custom and government regulation varied substantially from one nation to the next. In some nations, pensions were part of a government social security system; in others they were provided by firms. In some nations they were not required at all. Even something as simple as "monthly pay" differed: In Singapore a typical compensation package paid the employee by the month for 13, instead of 12, months.[4]

These were just a few of the differences O'Dell had run across in research for the project. The list could go on forever. No wonder compensation systems, like other aspects of human resource management, traditionally had been one of the most "local" aspects of a multinational's operations. Local wage scales were used, and the firms tended to follow local custom in regard to vacations, pensions, and other aspects of the compensation package. But with engineers of similar skill levels working together on a daily basis, how long would these distinctions be possible? Might some of these engineers be hired in the United States? Would LG offer different packages based on the facility they were assigned to? How would that affect recruiting? And what about the engineers transferred to Boston for six months: should they receive a different package while on tour? For the programmers doing more routine work, the issues might not be as complex but were still important. Considering the cost of the training planned for the Bangalore staff, it was vital to keep these employees on board and motivated despite the many opportunities open to them.

While the focus was on India for now, the firm also had considered opening subsidiary operations in Russia and Brazil. His project was the first step in an effort to decide the extent to which the firm's performance review and compensation plans should be integrated globally. The issue did not just concern the employees abroad. At home, some concern had been expressed about the long-term outlook. Software engineers were hot now, but in 10 years would the salaries reflect a lower, global scale? And would all the jobs be overseas? The opportunities abroad were exciting but had brought their share of headaches.

---

[4]Learning to manage host-country nationals. (March 1995). *Personnel Journal, 74*(3), 60–67.

Name _____   Group _____

1. How does culture affect the role of pay as a motivating force for workers? Would this issue be raised differently in the United States?

2. What would be the advantages and disadvantages of using the existing LG compensation package in India? How might it differ from a more typical Indian package? What additional information would O'Dell need to make this decision?

3. What other human resource issues might O'Dell need to be concerned about? Prepare a list and explain how they might interact.

4. How do these issues relate to the strategic choices that the firm has made? Does the analogy to a manufacturing firm seem appropriate?

EXERCISE 2.2
Going Global with Marriott Corporation*

Overview

In 2005, Marriott Corporation employed approximately 235,000 employees. From 1987 through 2005, Marriott had been one of the most successful firms in the United States, with 10 percent compounded growth in both sales and return on equity. They had established a strong presence in a variety of service-related industries: hotels, airline food service, business food service, family dining, and contract services. A key to Marriott's success in each of their lines of business came from Marriott's deserved reputation of providing outstanding service to guests and customers. As a result of their excellent service, the Marriott Corporation was considered by customers around the world as the "preferred provider" or the provider customers thought of first when making lodging or food choices.

Marriott's goal for the first decade of the 21st century was a major emphasis on global expansion. Along with being the "provider of choice," Marriott needed to become the "employer of choice" for international assignments. It was felt that if Marriott could not continue to attract, retain, and manage their employees in their overseas operations, then their rapid growth would slow down. Managing employees and becoming the international employer of choice was not an option; it was seen as central to business success and should be directly linked to the "provider of choice" emphasis. For example, one of Marriott Corporation's central challenges has been to ensure that all overseas operations are staffed with the most qualified and cost-effective employees who will join and stay in the business. In the past, Marriott had some problems with expatriate attrition and performance and difficulties in repatriation as well.

Learning Objectives

After completing this exercise, you should be able to

1. Identify a number of specific HRM practices that can be pursued by Marriott to create and sustain its goal to be the international "employer of choice."
2. Understand the connection between the goal to be the international "employer of choice" and the "provider of choice."

Procedure

Individual Analysis

1. Before class, generate a list of four actions the organization can take that will directly contribute to their goals regarding making Marriott the international employer of choice in the most efficient manner. Bear in mind that competitive advantage does entail labor costs, so your recommendations must be made in the context of estimated relative costs for the various actions the organization could take. Rank order the four actions.
2. Try to think of international opportunities and policies to which you would be attracted as a recent college graduate. How could Marriott gather information to meet its objectives in the context of cost control, the "provider of choice" emphasis, competitive advantage, and total customer satisfaction in their overseas operations? If your instructor has not assigned a country or region, identify one country where Marriott has a hotel and develop an HRM strategy for attracting and retaining the most qualified staff. Prepare your list of four key HRM actions on Form 2.2.1 and provide a concise written justification for your rank ordering of actions. What competitive-advantage principles did you consider in compiling your priority list? Explain how you would go about researching the problems with expatriate attrition, performance and difficulties in repatriation as well.

Group Exercise

1. In groups of about six people, exchange your priority lists so that all group members have had an opportunity to review each one. Attempt to reach consensus on a rank-ordered list of four specific actions the Marriott Corporation should take to contribute to its goal of becoming the international "employer of choice" in the context of the "provider of choice" emphasis. How could the HRM systems contribute to the "employer of choice"?
2. A group leader will be designated who will present the consensus view of the group. Discussion should focus on the extent to which the various groups agree on the priority list of Marriott activities.
3. Students should complete the Assessment Questions after group discussion (Form 2.2.2).

*Contributed by Dave Ulrich

FORM 2.2.1

PRIORITY LIST FOR MARRIOTT'S GLOBAL GOALS

Name _____   Group _____

Priority #1:
   Justification:

Priority #2:
   Justification:

Priority #3:
   Justification:

Priority #4:
   Justification:

Explain how you would go about researching the problems with expatriate attrition, performance and difficulties in repatriation.

EXERCISE 2.2
ASSESSMENT QUESTIONS—FORM 2.2.2

1. To what extent do the recommendations made by your group generalize to organizations other than Marriott? If they do not generalize, why not?

2. To what extent are the recommendations unique to international expansions and international operations?

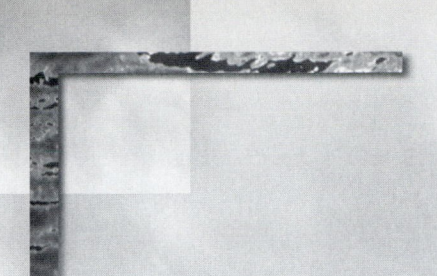

Chapter 3 Exercises

EXERCISE 3.1

Zimpfer v. Palm Beach County

Overview

Chapter 3 presented you with a variety of laws affecting HRM. One of those laws was the Age Discrimination in Employment Act (ADEA). The following case requires you to apply your understanding of the ADEA to provide some suggestions for Palm Beach County.

Learning Objectives

After completing this exercise, you should be able to

1. Identify the critical issues associated with age discrimination cases.
2. Provide recommendations for a plaintiff filing an age discrimination case and for the employer in defending EEO practices.
3. Outline policies that organizations should adopt to reduce the probability of age discrimination or claims of age discrimination.

Procedure

Part A: Individual Analysis

Step 1. Read the attached background material on Palm Beach County provided in Exhibit 3.1.1.

Step 2. Assume the role of the HR director and respond to the issues described below. Answer each question on Form 3.1.1.

Part B: Group Analysis

Step 1. In groups, attempt to reach consensus on the four questions. Each student should review each other student's Form 3.1.1 before the discussion.

Step 2. The instructor will designate one (or more) representatives to present each group's consensus position.

EXHIBIT 3.1.1

BACKGROUND MATERIAL FOR PALM BEACH COUNTY

Palm Beach County has requested your opinion regarding an alleged violation of the Age Discrimination in Employment Act. Mr. Bryce Zimpfer, age 52, has been an employee of the county for 16 years in the employee relations area. The Department of Human Resources posted a job vacancy for employee relations manager (see Exhibit 3.1.2) and Mr. Zimpfer applied for the position. The department filled the position with Mr. Brad Merriman, age 33, an outside applicant with less experience in employee relations than Mr. Zimpfer.

After filing a timely complaint with the EEOC, Mr. Zimpfer retained Ms. Lynn Szymoniak, an attorney who is now attempting to reach a settlement with the division's legal staff. In preparation for these negotiations, the attorney asked an industrial psychologist, Dr. Marcy Josephs, to examine the résumés of the job applicants and submit a report as to whether Mr. Zimpfer was more qualified for the position than Mr. Merriman. Dr. Josephs submitted a report and concluded that on the basis of her résumé analysis, Mr. Zimpfer was more qualified for the position than Mr. Merriman (see Exhibit 3.1.3).

EXHIBIT 3.1.2

JOB VACANCY

POSITION DESCRIPTION: EMPLOYEE RELATIONS MANAGER

NATURE OF WORK

This is professional personnel and labor relations work developing and managing programs and activities to enhance relationships between management and employees; to promote employee satisfaction, well-being, and quality of work life; to develop greater productivity in the workforce; and to achieve sound labor/management working relationships. Work is of a highly responsible nature, requiring considerable independent judgment and decision making. Work is performed under the direction of the Director, Employee Relations and Personnel, and is reviewed through conferences, reports, and results achieved.

EXAMPLES OF WORK

Initiates and manages programs that aim to improve communication and participation. These may be employee orientation meetings, committees, attitude surveys, suggestion boxes, awards programs, newsletters, newspapers, handbooks, benefits brochures, and other media such as posters or payroll stuffers that communicate policies and practices to employees.

Develops programs that monitor and detect employees' dissatisfactions with policies or working conditions. These include adequate complaint and grievance procedures, communication of these to employees, and adequate follow-up with management to resolve problems.

Initiates procedures for reviewing adverse actions taken by supervisors to ensure that such actions are fair. Investigates the facts of the case and determines whether any disciplinary action is appropriate. Directs and trains supervisors in discipline and discharge procedures.

Develops and monitors performance review systems, employee assistance programs, incentive/awards programs, quality circles, and others whose purpose is to motivate workers toward greater productivity.

Initiates programs to improve the quality of supervision, primarily training programs to improve knowledge of effective supervisory practices. May develop and present training programs for supervisors. May write and disseminate supervisors' handbooks or manuals.

Assists the Director in interpreting the provisions of labor contracts to supervisors. May conduct supervisory training sessions in contract administration.

Reviews and recommends policy and benefit changes to the Director that are needed to enhance employee/management relations.

Audits and approves personnel actions when applicable to ensure compliance with policies.

May supervise counselors or specialists in carrying out these employee relations activities.

Performs related work as required.

REQUIRED KNOWLEDGE, SKILLS, AND ABILITIES

- Thorough working knowledge of federal and state laws affecting public personnel administration and labor relations.
- Thorough knowledge of merit system principles and policies.
- Knowledge of organization and functions.
- Knowledge of the principles of management and supervision.
- Ability to organize work and supervise professional staff.
- Ability to write and interpret correspondence and reports.
- Ability to speak to a wide variety of groups and present ideas effectively.
- Ability to deal tactfully and persuasively with staff, employees, supervisors, administrators, and union officials.
- Ability to conduct personal and investigative interviews.
- Ability to interpret complex legal cases and documents.
- Ability to conduct independent research and analysis.

MINIMUM ENTRANCE REQUIREMENTS

Graduation from an accredited college or university with major course work in Human Resources Management, Industrial Relations, or Labor Relations, or closely related field; considerable progressively responsible experience in employee or labor relations; or any equivalent combination of related training and experience.

EXHIBIT 3.1.3

CULLEN & SZYMONIAK, P.A.

ATTORNEYS-AT-LAW

1030 Lake Avenue

Lake Worth, Florida 33460

(561) 585-4666

MARK A. CULLEN   October 25   LYNN E. SZYMONIAK

Marcy M. Josephs, Ph.D.
10475 Northwest Michigan Avenue
Birmingham, Michigan 48275

Dear Dr. Josephs:

I am very pleased that you are available to assist us with the Bryce Zimpfer case. Please find enclosed the following documents:

1. The job announcement, announcing the position of Employee Relations Manager;

2. A job description for the position of Employee Relations Manager;

3. Copies of the newspaper ads announcing this position;

4. A Referral List listing the candidates chosen for an interview for the position of Employee Relations Manager;

5. The resumes, cover letters, and applications of the applicants listed on the referral list; and

6. The application and resume of Bryce Zimpfer.

Based on your review of the above documents, please advise me:

1. Whether Mr. Zimpfer's qualifications equalled or exceeded the qualifications of the applicants selected for an interview; and

2. In particular, whether Bryce Zimpfer's qualifications equalled or exceeded the qualifications of J. Brad Merriman—the candidate ultimately selected for the position.

The experts' reports are to be exchanged on this case on November 12. Thank you again for your assistance.

Yours truly,

LYNN E. SZYMONIAK, ESQ.
Enclosures

EXHIBIT 3.1.4

MARCY MILLER JOSEPHS, PH.D.

INDUSTRIAL PSYCHOLOGIST

10475 NORTHWEST MICHIGAN AVENUE

BIRMINGHAM, MICHIGAN 48275

November 13

Lynn E. Szymoniak, Esq.

Cullen & Szymoniak, P.A.

1030 Lake Avenue

Lake Worth, FL 33460

Dear Ms. Szymoniak:

The purpose of this letter is to respond to your request for expert opinion in matters related to Bryce Zimpfer. In your letter of October 25, you requested that I render an opinion regarding the following:

1. Whether Mr. Zimpfer's qualifications equalled or exceeded the qualifications of the applicants selected for an interview; and
2. In particular, whether Bryce Zimpfer's qualifications equalled or exceeded the qualifications of J. Brad Merriman—the candidate ultimately selected for the position.

In rendering my opinion, I have reviewed the following documents:

1. The job announcement from Palm Beach County announcing the position of Employee Relations Manager;
2. A job description for the position of Employee Relations Manager;
3. Copies of the newspaper ads announcing this position;
4. A Referral List prepared, listing the candidates chosen for an interview for the position of Employee Relations Manager;
5. The resumes, cover letters, and applications of the applicants listed on the referral list; and
6. The application and resume of Bryce Zimpfer.

Based on my review of the aforementioned documents, I have the following opinions:

1. Mr. Zimpfer's qualifications equalled or exceeded the qualifications of several of the applicants selected for an interview; and
2. Mr. Zimpfer's qualifications exceeded the qualifications of Mr. J. Brad Merriman.

The following is a description of the procedure I followed to arrive at these opinions:

EXHIBIT 3.1.4 (*Continued*)

1. Based on a reading of the job announcement, the job description and the newspaper ad, I constructed three applicant/work requirement matrices for purposes of assessing applicant qualifications with regard to program/activities, work examples, and required knowledge, skills, and abilities (KSAs). See Figures 1, 2, and 3. The first column of each matrix represents the critical work requirements of the job as reflected in the job announcement, etc.

2. I read each resume and recorded those work requirements with which each applicant had experience or requisite KSAs. I performed this task on three occasions (for the three matrices), each time evaluating the resumes in random order.

3. I performed the identical task described in Step 2 five days later with no reference to the completed matrices from Step 2. Thus, I made two independent evaluations of each of the three work requirement matrices.

4. I examined the discrepancies in the applicant/requirement cells of each matrix from the Step 2 and Step 3 evaluations and reviewed the resumes for purposes of reconciling the disagreements. The totals in the last row of Figures 1, 2, and 3 reflect the final evaluations I have made of each candidate after reconciling the few discrepancies between the Step 2 and Step 3 evaluations.

5. The opinions rendered above with regard to Mr. Zimpfer are based on the final evaluations of the three matrices.

The matrix analysis on which I have based my opinions represents a content-valid and objective approach to the evaluation of applicant resumes. It is far superior in terms of validity and reliability to a nonquantitative evaluation procedure which calls for a global evaluation of the applicants in terms of suitability for a multifaceted job.

Sincerely,

Marcy M. Josephs, Ph.D.
MMJ:im

EXHIBIT 3.1.4 (*Continued*)

FIGURE 1

PROGRAMS AND ACTIVITIES ANALYSIS

Programs/Activities	Zimpfer	Atkinson	Bender	Bledsoe	Merriman	Schwab
Performance appraisals	X	X		X	X	
Employee assistance	X		X			X
Employee benefits	X	X	X	X	X	
Employee publications	X		X			X
Counseling and discipline	X				X	
Grievance procedures	X		X	X	X	
Attendance and leave policy	X			X		
Layoff policy	X				X	
Unemployment compensation						
Contract administration	X	X	X	X	X	
Totals	9	3	5	5	6	2

FIGURE 2

WORK SAMPLE ANALYSIS

Examples of Work	Zimpfer	Atkinson	Bender	Bledsoe	Merriman	Schwab
Employee orientation	X		X			X
Attitude surveys	X		X			
Suggestion boxes					X	
Awards program			X			
Newsletters	X		X			
Handbooks						
Benefits brochure	X	X				
Grievance procedures	X		X	X		
Disciplinary action			X	X		X
Supervisory training	X	X	X	X		X
Interpreting labor contracts		X	X		X	X
Policy and benefits	X	X	X	X	X	X
Audits and approves personal actions				X		
Totals	7	4	9	5	3	5

FIGURE 3

KNOWLEDGE, SKILLS, AND ABILITIES ANALYSIS

	Zimpfer	Atkinson	Bender	Bledsoe	Merriman	Schwab
State and federal law	X	X	X	X	X	X
Ability to speak to variety of groups	X		X	X		X
Conduct interviews	X	X	X		X	X
Interpret complex legal cases and documents						X
Conduct independent research	X		X			X
Totals	4	2	4	2	2	5

Name _____   Group _____

1. Was Mr. Zimpfer a victim of illegal age discrimination according to the ADEA and case law? Why or why not? Cite relevant court cases to justify your position.

2. What (if any) further evidence should be ascertained before the county fully understands the legal implications of its actions?

3. What action do you recommend that the county take in this matter?

4. What policies should the county adopt to reduce the possibility of age discrimination suits in the future?

5. In the same year that Zimpfer was rejected, Palm Beach County filled only 4 percent of managerial positions with persons over 55 years of age and only 16 percent with persons over 39. Do these data indicate illegal discrimination using disparate impact theory? Should Zimpfer's lawyer use disparate impact theory for his claim of age discrimination? Is Palm Beach County vulnerable to a future ADEA lawsuit using a disparate impact theory? What critical Supreme Court ruling is relevant to this question?

EXERCISE 3.2

Goebel et al. v. Frank Clothiers

Overview

Many Title VII cases involve the presentation of statistical evidence that is alleged to indicate illegal discrimination. The purpose of this exercise is to review the statistical evidence presented and to assess the implications of the data for the organization.

Learning Objectives

After completing this exercise, you should be able to

1. Calculate adverse impact for a selection procedure.
2. Provide recommendations for a plaintiff filing a race discrimination case, and for the employer in defending EEO practices.
3. Understand the burden of proof issues related to Title VII cases.

Procedure

Part A: Individual Analysis

Step 1. Read the attached background material on *Goebel et al. v. Frank Clothiers* provided in Exhibit 3.2.1.

Step 2. Assume the role of the HR director and respond to the issues described below. Please prepare concise, written responses for the legal division of Frank Clothiers. Answer the questions presented on Form 3.2.1.

Part B: Group Analysis

Step 3. In groups of about six, members should attempt to reach consensus on issue #1. A rationale for the position should be developed that includes relevant court citations.

Step 4. The instructor will designate one member from each group to present the group position and rationale.

Step 5. Students should complete Self and Peer assessments of each of their fellow group members.

EXHIBIT 3.2.1

GOEBEL ET AL. v. FRANK CLOTHIERS

A division of Frank Clothiers had 36 openings for assistant store manager last year (see Exhibit 3.2.2) and, as part of their voluntary affirmative action program, filled the vacancies with 16 African Americans, 10 Hispanics, and 10 whites. The selection process was a multiple-hurdle approach that began with an application form and a test of basic verbal and math skills called the Wonderlic Personnel Test (WPT). Applicants who scored 25 (out of 50) or higher on the test were then given an interview by the store managers. Based on the interview performances, the vacancies were filled.

The numbers of African Americans, Hispanics, and whites who passed the test were as follows:

Test Scores	African Americans	Hispanics	Whites
Number scoring 25 or higher	25	28	74
Number scoring less than 25	26	20	29
Totals	51	48	103

Dennis Goebel, one of the African-American applicants who scored 19 on the test, filed suit on behalf of all African-American applicants who failed the exam. Mr. Goebel claimed race discrimination based on Title VII of the Civil Rights Act of 1964.

Frank Clothiers has argued that more African-Americans were actually hired than any other protected class. Thus, the company asserts, there is obviously no racial discrimination in the selection process.

EXHIBIT 3.2.2

ASSISTANT MANAGER JOB DESCRIPTION (FRANK CLOTHIERS)

SUMMARY

Under general direction from the store manager, provides some administrative and functional supervision of a store unit, including inventory control, sales and returns, vendor relations, cash management, and related reporting. May supervise regular and/or temporary customer service and stock management staff.

Duties and Responsibilities:

1. Assists in managing the operation of a store unit, including purchasing of supplies and books, special orders, receiving and shipping, and return of overstocked or defective merchandise.

2. Supervises personnel which typically includes recommendations for hiring, firing, performance evaluation, training, work allocation, and problem resolution.

3. Prepares drafts of purchase requisitions, and related paperwork including annual budgets and accounts payable; monitors expenditures and revenue; makes periodic scheduled and ad hoc reports of store activity.

4. Through the store manager, helps to develop and control department budgets; researches and compiles administrative reports for personnel, payroll, and trade organization surveys for cost estimation and budget review.

5. Helps to coordinate some department marketing activities.

6. Assists in year-end inventory utilizing computer to check for theft and shrinkage.

7. May oversee or manage the operation of auxiliary services such as vending machines or student service areas.

8. Uses systems and processes to establish and maintain records for the operating unit.

9. Assists with the implementation of policies and procedures consistent with those of the organization to ensure efficient and safe operation of the unit.

10. Performs miscellaneous job-related duties as assigned.

Minimum Job Requirements:
High school diploma or GED.

Knowledge, Skills, and Abilities Required:
- Ability to gather data, compile information, and prepare reports.
- Skill in the use of personal computers and related software applications.
- Ability to prepare routine administrative paperwork.
- Ability to communicate effectively, both orally and in writing.
- Ability to supervise and train employees, to include organizing, prioritizing, and scheduling work assignments.
- Skill in examining and re-engineering operations and procedures, formulating policy, and developing and implementing new strategies and procedures.
- Ability to receive, stock, and/or deliver goods.
- Employee development and performance management skills.
- Skill in the use of computers, preferably in a PC, Windows-based operating environment.
- Skill in budget preparation and fiscal management.
- Ability to foster a cooperative work environment.
- Knowledge of procurement rules and regulations.
- Knowledge of retail advertising, sales promotion and/or visual merchandising techniques.
- Strong interpersonal and communication skills and the ability to work effectively with a wide range of constituencies in a diverse community.
- Ability to develop and maintain recordkeeping systems and procedures.
- Knowledge of retail floor merchandising and stock control procedures.

Working Conditions and Physical Effort:
- Work is normally performed in a typical interior/office work environment.
- No or very limited physical effort required.
- No or very limited exposure to physical risk.

Name _____   Group _____

1. Were Mr. Goebel and other African-American applicants victims of racial discrimination because of the hiring policies of Frank Clothiers? Explain your position and cite all relevant Supreme Court decisions. If you cannot take a definitive position, explain what specific information you require to be able to take a position.

2. Is there evidence of disparate impact against African Americans in the decisions that were made? On what basis did you arrive at this position?

Name _____   Group _____

3. If disparate impact is evident, what steps should the defendant take next? Provide specific recommendations.

4. An associate of the Personnel Department proposes that Frank should continue to use the examination but that the test scores should be interpreted by the ethnic classification of the test taker. For example, raw scores on the exam would be converted to percentages *within ethnic classification*. With such a procedure, African Americans taking the test who receive the exact raw score as whites would receive a higher percentage score on the exam because of the within-ethnic interpretation. He argues that this procedure would enable Frank to continue using a valid and useful test while avoiding adverse impact. (Mr. Goebel would have advanced to the interview with this approach.) Take a position on this recommendation.

5. Gordon Howe, a white male, scored 48 on the WPT and was interviewed but not hired. Does Mr. Howe have a possible Title VII lawsuit? What additional data are relevant to this question? Can "disparate impact" theory be used in cases involving subjective selection processes like interviews?

EXERCISE 3.3

A Case of Illegal Sexual Harassment?*

Overview

It is critical that employers and employees be very familiar with how sexual harassment is defined in the courts and what situations constitute illegal behavior. This exercise challenges you to think about some of these issues.

Learning Objectives

After completing this exercise, you should be able to

1. Define what is meant by illegal sexual harassment.
2. Understand the key provisions of a sexual harassment policy.
3. Outline the policies the organization should adopt to prevent charges of sexual harassment in the future.

Procedure

Part A: Individual Analysis

Step 1. Read the attached background material in Exhibits 3.3.1 and 3.3.2. You have been hired as a consultant to render opinions on the legal standing of Bowman, Idaho, and of Putnam County. Read each exhibit carefully.

Step 2. Answer the questions that apply to each case. Answer each question on Form 3.3.1. Questions 3 and 4 apply to both cases.

Part B: Group Analysis

Step 1. In groups of about six people, students shall attempt to reach consensus on the four questions. Each student should review each other student's Form 3.3.1 prior to the discussion.

Step 2. The instructor will designate one (or more) representatives to present each group and consensus position.

EXHIBIT 3.3.1
COMPLAINT OF MS. SMITH

Ms. Kathleen Smith worked part-time as a park recreation counselor for the city of Bowman, Idaho. Her immediate supervisor was Jack McKenna. She has brought an action against Mr. McKenna and the city alleging that the city and Mr. McKenna created a "hostile working atmosphere" by subjecting Ms. Smith to repeated and uninvited requests for dates and (later) lewd remarks and offensive speech. Ms. Smith had never met or spoken with the superintendent of recreation for the city.

Ms. Smith never complained about her treatment to higher management while employed and did not file a formal complaint under the city's sexual harassment policy guidelines because she feared retaliation. She did complain to a co-worker who also witnessed some of the incidents. The co-worker did inform Mr. Al Kaline, the Bowman HR manager. However, no action was taken by the city since, Bowman's city manager argues, pursuant to the city's sexual harassment guidelines, no formal complaint was made and the alleged incidents had occurred over six months earlier.

The city included the antidiscrimination/harassment policy in its employee handbook, which was given to all employees. Each employee signed a document that the handbook was received. In addition, each employee was required to complete an on-line sexual harassment course as a condition of employment.

The guidelines were clear on the procedure to follow if one felt that he or she has been a victim of discrimination and/or sexual harassment. The guidelines stipulated that all formal claims of harassment must be submitted to the employee's immediate supervisor with a designated HR representative informed at the same time. The complaint must be filed within six months of the alleged events.

Ms. Smith claimed that Mr. McKenna had asked her out on dates on numerous occasions. These propositions were made in the employee lounge while they were alone and, on other occasions, in front of other Bowman employees. Mr. McKenna would later maintain that Ms. Smith dressed in a provocative manner and she should therefore expect "to be asked out."

In the period in which the alleged sexual harassment took place, the following personnel actions were taken in the recreational unit:

Percent Salary Increases for the Year	
All counselors	5.8% (average)
Ms. Smith	8.5%

Christmas Bonuses	
All counselors	$250 (average)
Ms. Smith	$500

Promotions to Head Counselor
Total: 4 (including Ms. Smith)

When questioned about his knowledge of events, Mr. Kaline stated that "there was clearly no evidence that refusal to submit to sexual advances was related to any negative action against Ms. Smith. She is a good employee and is recognized as such through merit increases, bonuses, and promotions. Also, Ms. Smith did not follow the city's policy on filing harassment complaints. Thus, no further action should (or could) be taken."

*Contributed by Jennifer Bowers.

EXHIBIT 3.3.2

Mr. Joseph Nixon worked as an aide to Putnam County Commissioner Diane Richards. Mr. Nixon reported directly to Commissioner Richards. Mr. Nixon, along with another commissioner's aide, Michael Whitman, filed a claim of sexual harassment against Commissioner Richards and the Putnam County Board of County Commissioners.

According to Mr. Nixon and Mr. Whitman, Commissioner Richards pressured them into sexual relations, threatening to have them fired if they did not agree. Over a period of 18 months, Mr. Nixon and Mr. Whitman on separate occasions engaged in sexual activities with Commissioner Richards. During this period, Mr. Nixon traveled with Commissioner Richards to several commission-related meetings. Mr. Nixon alleges that Commissioner Richards insisted that they share hotel accommodations while on these trips. Hotel documentation substantiates this claim. Additionally, Mr. Nixon alleges that Commissioner Richards invited him to her home several times while her husband and family were absent.

Furthermore, Mr. Nixon and Mr. Whitman were involved in a romantic relationship with each other. Mr. Nixon alleges that Commissioner Richards demanded that he end his relationship with Mr. Whitman or he would be fired. According to Mr. Nixon, when he refused to end the relationship, Commissioner Richards terminated him. It is the policy of Putnam County Board of County Commission that commission aides serve at the pleasure of the appointing commissioner. Commissioner Richards claims that Mr. Nixon was terminated because of poor job performance and leaving the work areas for hours without permission.

It should also be noted that prior to Mr. Nixon's tenure with the Putnam County Board of County Commissioners, Mr. Nixon and Commissioner Richards were involved in a romantic relationship. Initially, Commissioner Richards denied having any sexual relationship with either of the plaintiffs. However, six months after the charges were filed Commissioner Richards admitted having a romantic relationship with Mr. Nixon before he was hired and during his tenure as a commission aide. She also admitted having a sexual relationship with Mr. Whitman. However, Commissioner Richards claims that in both instances, the relationships were agreed to by the men.

Mr. Nixon and Mr. Whitman further allege that the county administrator and other commission employees were aware of the relationships. While the county has a sexual harassment policy, there is no formal training provided to commission employees or commissioners. The policy is included in the New Employee Handbook which is given to every new employee.

Name ————————————————————————   Group ————————————————————————

1. Does the alleged sexual harassment in Bowman constitute a violation of Title VII? Explain your answer. If you are not ready to take a definitive position, explain what information you require.

2. Do the alleged charges brought against Putnam County constitute a violation of Title VII? Is the County liable? Explain your answer. What changes, if any, should the County make to prevent charges of sexual harassment in the future?

3. For both cases: Could (or should) the organizations institute a no-dating policy that would explicitly prohibit dating between supervisors and subordinates? Is such a policy legal?

4. In both cases, what if the plaintiffs were contingent or leased employees? Would the City and County still be liable for Title VII violations?

Exercise 3.4

Reverse Discrimination or Legal Affirmative Action?

Overview

Chapter 3 presents considerable detail on Title VII of the Civil Rights Act and the evolution of affirmative action programs. The purpose of this exercise is to introduce some of the complexities and ramifications of affirmative action programs. Two real cases are described that involve allegations of reverse discrimination.

Objective

After completing the exercise, you should be able to

1. Understand the variables that must be considered when determining the legality of affirmative action programs.
2. Know the conditions under which the sex (or race) of an employee may be taken into consideration for personnel decisions.

Procedure

Part A: Individual Analysis

Each student should study the cases presented in Exhibits 3.4.1 and 3.4.2 and take positions as required. First, read Exhibit 3.4.1. Then complete the assessment questions presented on Form 3.4.1. Next, read Exhibit 3.4.2 and complete Form 3.4.2.

Part B: Group Analysis

Step 1. In groups of no more than six, students should review each student's completed forms and then attempt to reach consensus on a position. Once the consensus is reached, each group should adopt a group position. One group member will be asked to present the group's position to the rest of the class.

Step 2. After completing step 1, each student should complete a self- and peer evaluation form for all group members.

EXHIBIT 3.4.1

JONES V. PURPLE CABS

After four tough years working on the road for the Purple Cabs, Diane Harrison applied for a less-strenuous desk job as a road dispatcher. At that time not one of the California company's 238 skilled positions was held by a woman. Harrison knew, however, that two years earlier, the company had enacted a voluntary affirmative-action policy designed to correct that imbalance.

Harrison has 18 years' clerical experience and four years as a road maintenance worker. Another candidate for the position, Edward Jones, had 11 years as a road yard clerk (clerical position) and four years as a road maintenance worker. He also had previous experience as a dispatcher in private employment.

The position of road dispatcher required four years of dispatcher or road maintenance work experience with the county. Twelve employees applied for the job. Nine were judged to be minimally qualified and interviewed by a two-person board. Seven of the applicants scored about 70 and were certified as eligible for selection. Jones scored 77 and Harrison ranked next with 73. At a second interview, three supervisors recommended that Jones be promoted. At the second interview, one male panel member described Harrison as a rabble-rousing, "skirt-wearing" troublemaker.

The local supervisor picked Jones, but the company's affirmative-action coordinator recommended Harrison. When she got the job, Jones got a lawyer. Jones claimed he was a victim of reverse discrimination and filed suit under Title VII of the 1964 Civil Rights Act.

POSITIONS

A. The Purple Cab plan is consistent with Title VII's purpose of eliminating the effects of past employment discrimination. Given the obvious imbalance in the skilled craft division and given the commitment to eliminating such imbalances, it was appropriate to consider as one fact the sex of Ms. Harrison in making its decision. Thus, the Court should decide in favor of Purple Cab.

B. To decide against Mr. Jones is to complete the process of converting Title VII from a guarantee that race or sex will not be the basis for employment determinations, to a guarantee that it often will. Ever so subtly, we effectively replace the goal of a discrimination-free society with the quite incompatible goal of proportionate representation by race and by sex in the workplace. Thus, the court should decide in favor of Mr. Jones.

Name _____   Group _____

1. What position do you support? (A or B). What is the basis for your answer (e.g., a court decision, the language of Title VII, EEOC Guidelines)?

2. Given the actual wording in section 703J of Title VII (see Figure 3-3, page 42), which seems to explicitly prohibit preferential treatment, how can an organization show preference to women as in this case? Doesn't position B seem more compatible with Section 703j?

3. To what extent did you take into consideration the great disparity in the number of male and female dispatchers? What conditions are necessary for an organization to show preferential treatment based on a protected class characteristic?

4. To what extent did you consider the qualifications of the candidates in taking your position? Did they have to be equally qualified? What if Jones had an interview score that was 10 points higher than Harrison?

5. Would you have a different opinion in this case if the defendant was a public agency in the state of California? Explain your answer.

EXHIBIT 3.4.2

TAXMAN V. PISCATAWAY TOWNSHIP

In 1975, the Board of Education of the Township of Piscataway, New Jersey, developed an affirmative action policy applicable to employment decisions. The board's affirmative action program, a 52-page document, was originally adopted in response to a regulation promulgated by the New Jersey State Board of Education. That regulation directed local school boards to adopt "affirmative action programs" to address employment as well as school and classroom practices and to ensure equal opportunity to all persons regardless of race, color, creed, religion, sex, or national origin. In 1983 the board also adopted a one-page "policy," entitled "Affirmative Action–Employment Practices." It is not clear from the record whether the policy superseded or simply added to the program, nor does it matter for purposes of this appeal.

The 1975 document states that the purpose of the program is "to provide equal educational opportunity for students and equal employment opportunity for employees and prospective employees" and "to make a concentrated effort to attract . . . minority personnel for all positions so that their qualifications can be evaluated along with other candidates." A 1983 document states that its purpose is to "ensure [ ] equal employment opportunity . . . and prohibit [ ] discrimination in employment because of [, inter alia,] race . . ."

The operative language regarding the means by which affirmative action goals are to be furthered is identical in the two documents. "In all cases, the most qualified candidate will be recommended for appointment. However, when candidates appear to be of equal qualification, candidates meeting the criteria of the affirmative action program will be recommended." The phrase "candidates meeting the criteria of the affirmative action program" refers to members of racial, national origin, or gender groups identified as minorities for statistical reporting purposes by the New Jersey State Department of Education, including African Americans. The 1983 document also clarifies that the affirmative action program applies to "every aspect of employment including . . . layoffs . . ."

The board's affirmative action policy did not have "any remedial purpose"; it was not adopted "with the intention of remedying the results of any prior discrimination or identified underrepresentation of minorities within the Piscataway Public School System." At all relevant times, African-American teachers were neither "underrepresented" nor "underutilized" in the Piscataway School District workforce. Indeed, statistics in 1976 and 1985 showed that the percentage of African-American employees in the job category that included teachers exceeded the percentage of African-Americans in the available workforce.

In May 1989, the board accepted a recommendation from the superintendent of schools to reduce the teaching staff in the Business Department at Piscataway High School by one. At that time, two of the teachers in the department were of equal seniority, both having begun their employment with the board on the same day nine years earlier. One of those teachers was plaintiff Sharon Taxman, who is white, and the other was Debra Williams, who is African-American. Williams was the only minority teacher among the faculty of the Business Department.

Decisions regarding layoffs by New Jersey school boards are highly circumscribed by state law; nontenured faculty must be laid off first, and layoffs among tenured teachers in the affected subject area or grade level must proceed in reverse order of seniority. Seniority for this purpose is calculated according to specific guidelines set by state law. Thus, local boards lack discretion to choose between employees for layoff, except in the rare instance of a tie in seniority between the two or more employees eligible to fill the last remaining position.

The board determined that it was facing just such a rare circumstance in deciding between Taxman and Williams. In prior decisions involving the layoff of employees with equal seniority, the Board has broken the tie through "a random process which included drawing numbers out of a container, drawing lots, or having a lottery." In none of those instances, however, had the employees involved been of different races.

In light of the unique posture of the layoff decision, Superintendent of Schools Burton Edelchick recommended to the board that the affirmative action plan be invoked in order to determine which teacher to retain. Superintendent Edelchick made this recommendation "because he believed Ms. Williams and Ms. Taxman were tied in seniority, were equally qualified, and because Ms. Williams was the only African-American teacher in the Business Education Department."

While the Board recognized that it was not bound to apply the affirmative action policy, it made a discretionary decision to invoke the policy to break the tie between Williams and Taxman. As a result, the Board "voted to terminate the employment of Sharon Taxman, effective June 30, 1988 . . ."

At her deposition, Paula Van Riper, the board's vice president at the time of the layoff, described the board's decision-making process. According to Van Riper, after the board recognized that Taxman and Williams were of equal seniority, it assessed their classroom performance, evaluations, volunteerism, and certifications and determined that they were "two teachers of equal ability" and "equal qualifications."

At his deposition Theodore H. Kruse, the board's president, explained his vote to apply the affirmative action policy as follows:

A. Basically I think because I had been aware that the student body and the community which is our responsibility, the schools of the community, is really quite diverse and there—I have a general feeling during my tenure on the board that it was valuable for the students to see in the various employment roles a wide range of background, and that it was also valuable to the workforce and in particular to the teaching staff that they have—they see that in each other.

Asked to articulate the "educational objective" served by retaining Williams rather than Taxman, Kruse stated:

A. In my own personal perspective I believe by retaining Ms. Williams it was sending a very clear message that we feel that our staff should be culturally diverse, our student population is culturally diverse and there is a distinct advantage to students, to all students, to be made—come into contact with people of different cultures, different background, so that they are more aware, more tolerant, more accepting, more understanding of people of all background.

Q. What do you mean by the phrase you used, culturally diverse?

A. Someone other than—different than yourself. And we have, our student population and our community has people of all different background, ethnic background, religious background, cultural background, and it's important that our school district encourage awareness and acceptance and tolerance and, therefore, I personally think it's important that our staff reflect that too.

Following the board's decision, Taxman filed a charge of employment discrimination with the Equal Employment Opportunity Commission. Attempts at conciliation were unsuccessful, and the United States filed suit under Title VII against the board in the United States District Court for the District of New Jersey. Taxman intervened, asserting claims under both Title VII and the New Jersey Law Against Discrimination.

Following discovery, the board moved for summary judgment and the United States and Taxman cross-moved for partial summary judgment only as to liability. The district court denied the board's motion and granted partial summary judgment to the United States and Taxman, holding the board liable under both statutes for discrimination on the basis of race. *United States v. Board of Educ. of Township Piscataway* 832 F.Supp. 836, 851 (D.N.J.1993).

EXHIBIT 3.4.2 (*Continued*)

A trial proceeded on the issue of damages. By this time, Taxman had been rehired by the board and thus her reinstatement was not an issue. The court awarded Taxman damages in the amount of $134,014.62 for back pay, fringe benefits, and prejudgment interest under Title VII. A jury awarded an additional $10,000 for emotional suffering under the NJLAD. The district court denied the United States' request for a broadly worded injunction against future discrimination, finding that there was no likelihood that the conduct at issue would recur, but it did order the board to give Taxman full seniority reflecting continuous employment from 1980. Additionally, the court dismissed Taxman's claim for punitive damages under the NJLAD.

In relevant part, Title VII makes it unlawful for an employer "to discriminate against any individual with respect to his compensation, terms, conditions, or privileges of employment" or "to limit, segregate, or classify his employees. . . in any way which would deprive or tend to deprive any individual of employment opportunities or otherwise affect his status as an employee" on the basis of "race, color, religion, sex, or national origin." [FN6] 42 U.S.C. 2000e-2(a). For a time, the Supreme Court construed this language as absolutely prohibiting discrimination in employment, neither requiring nor permitting any preference for any group.

In 1979, however, the court interpreted the statute's "antidiscriminatory strategy" in a "fundamentally different way," holding in the seminal case of *United Steelworkers v. Weber,* 443 U.S. 193, 99 S.Ct. 2721, that Title VII's prohibition against racial discrimination does not condemn all voluntary race-conscious affirmative action plans. In *Weber,* the court considered a plan implemented by Kaiser Aluminum & Chemical Corporation. Prior to 1974, Kaiser hired as craftworkers only those with prior craft experience. Because they had long been excluded from craft unions, African Americans were unable to present the credentials required for craft positions. Moreover, Kaiser's hiring practices, although not admittedly discriminatory with regard to minorities, were questionable. As a consequence, while the local labor force was about 39 percent African American, Kaiser's labor force was less than 15 percent African American and its crafts workforce was less than 2 percent African American. In 1974, Kaiser entered into a collective bargaining agreement that contained an affirmative action plan. The plan reserved 50 percent of the openings in an in-plant craft-training program for African American employees until the percentage of African American craft-workers in the plant reached a level commensurate with the percentage of African-Americans in the local labor force. During the first year of the plan's operation, 13 craft-trainees were selected, seven of whom were African American and six of whom were white.

Thereafter, Brian Weber, a white production worker, filed a class-action suit, alleging that the plan unlawfully discriminated against white employees under Title VII. The plaintiffs argued that it necessarily followed that the Kaiser plan, which resulted in junior African-American employees receiving craft training in preference to senior white employees, violated Title VII. The district court agreed and entered a judgment in favor of the plaintiffs; the Court of Appeals for the Fifth Circuit affirmed.

The Supreme Court, however, reversed, noting initially that although the plaintiffs' argument was not "without force," it disregarded "the significance of the fact that the Kaiser-USWA plan was an affirmative action plan voluntarily adopted by private parties to eliminate traditional patterns of racial segregation." The Court then embarked upon an exhaustive review of Title VII's legislative history and identified Congress's concerns in enacting Title VII's prohibition against discrimination—the deplorable status of African Americans in the nation's economy, racial injustice, and the need to open employment opportunities for African Americans in traditionally closed occupations. Against this background, the court concluded that Congress could not have intended to prohibit private employers from implementing programs directed toward the very goal of Title VII—the eradication of discrimination and its effects from the workplace:

> It would be ironic indeed if a law triggered by a nation's concern over centuries of racial injustice and intended to improve the lot of those who had "been excluded from the American dream for so long,"110 Cong. Rec. 6552 (1964) (remarks of Minnesota Senator Hubert Humphrey), constituted the first legislative prohibition of all voluntary, private, race-conscious efforts to abolish traditional patterns of racial segregation and hierarchy.

The court found support for its conclusion in the language and legislative history of section 2000e-2(j) of Title VII, which expressly provides that nothing in the act requires employers to grant racial preferences. According to the Court, the opponents of Title VII had raised two arguments: the act would be construed to impose obligations upon employers to integrate their workforces through preferential treatment of minorities, and even without being obligated to do so, employers with racially imbalanced workforces would grant racial preferences. Since Congress addressed only the first objection and did not specifically prohibit affirmative action efforts, the Court inferred that Congress did not intend that Title VII forbid all voluntary race-conscious preferences. The court further reasoned that since Congress also intended "to avoid undue federal regulation of private businesses," a prohibition against all voluntary affirmative action would disserve this end by "augment[ing] the power of the Federal Government and diminish[ing] traditional management prerogatives . . ."

The court then turned to the Kaiser plan in order to determine whether it fell on the "permissible" side of the "line of demarcation between permissible and impermissible affirmative action plans." The Court upheld the Kaiser plan because its purpose "mirror[ed] those of the statute" and it did not "unnecessarily trammel the interests of the [nonminority] employees":

> The purposes of the plan mirror those of the statute. Both were designed to break down old patterns of racial segregation and hierarchy. Both were structured to "open employment opportunities for Negroes in occupations which have been traditionally closed to them." 110 Cong. Rec. 6548 (1964) (remarks of Sen. Humphrey).

At the same time, the plan does not "unnecessarily trammel" the interests of the white employees. The plan does not require the discharge of white workers and their replacement with new black hires. Nor does the plan create an absolute bar to the advancement of white employees; half of those trained in the program will be white. Moreover, the plan is a temporary measure; it is not intended to maintain racial balance, but simply to eliminate a manifest racial imbalance.

Name _____   Group _____

1. Was Ms. Taxman a victim of illegal discrimination under Title VII? Explain your answer, citing pertinent cases and discussion.

2. What does the term "manifest imbalance" mean to you? Is there "manifest imbalance" in this case?

3. What is the most important Supreme Court case that justifies your position?

4. If you decided for Ms. Taxman, what do you propose as the remedy? If Ms. Taxman had been awarded the job, would Ms. Williams have had redress through Title VII? Explain your answer, citing any applicable case law.

5. Should Universities be allowed to take race into consideration in admissions decisions in order to foster a more diverse student body? What is the current state of the law regarding this issue?

EXERCISE 3.5

Joseph Garcia v. Hooters
Cameron v. LaVeille Maison

Overview

What is allowable as a BFOQ? The Supreme Court has said that BFOQs are allowable if they are "reasonably necessary to the normal operation of that particular business." What if a business has a competitive strategy that appeals to a particular segment of the population that has certain strong preferences for services to be provided by the establishment? (Recall the discussion of the *Pan Am v. Diaz* Supreme Court case). The 1991 decision in *UAW v. Johnson Controls* stated that the exception to Title VII in the form of BFOQs applies only to policies that involve the "essence of the business." The purpose of this exercise is to present two cases with characteristics that are hardly unique for the industry. We will ask you to take a position as to the legality of a company policy that the company claims falls under the "business essence" or BFOQ exception to Title VII.

Learning Objectives

After completing this exercise, the student should be able to

1. Understand the conditions under which a BFOQ or an "essence of the business" argument is a legal defense.
2. Know the role of customer preference in Title VII cases.
3. Consider the implications of the cases for related policies.

Procedure

Step 1. Prior to class, read the case histories in Exhibit 3.5.1 and answer the questions on Form 3.5.1.

Step 2. In groups of about six people, each student should review the other group member responses and then attempt to reach group consensus on each of the questions. One person should be designated as the group spokesperson and the group position should be presented.

EXHIBIT 3.5.1

JOSEPH GARCIA V. HOOTERS

Hooters Restaurants had a competitive strategy of appealing to the young, affluent male population through a number of features. Large-screen television for sports events, happy hours, sports celebrity events, and very attractive waitresses were part of their strategy. Joseph Garcia was a waiter from Chicago who had worked at similar restaurants for over 10 years. He heard from a friend that Hooters was hiring. However, he was told he would have to apply in person. When he showed up at one of the establishments, he was told that they in fact were not hiring. He learned a few weeks later that an attractive female had been hired at the same restaurant. He filed a timely claim with the EEOC.

CAROL CAMERON V. LAVEILLE MAISON

LaVeille Maison is a five-star restaurant in East Cupcake, Michigan. Carol Cameron, a waitress with over 10 years' experience in "upscale" restaurants and an esoteric knowledge of wine, applied for a job at LaVeille Maison at a period when the restaurant was hiring waiters in preparation for the heavy winter season. The restaurant only employs waiters and makes the argument that five-star French restaurants traditionally employ only waiters. After learning that LaVeille Maison had hired three new waiters, Ms. Cameron filed a timely Title VII lawsuit against the restaurant.

Name _____   Group _____

1. Was Mr. Garcia a victim of illegal sex discrimination? Explain your answer in some detail based on your understanding of BFOQs.

2. Was Ms. Cameron a victim of sex discrimination?

3. In principle, do you see these cases as the same in terms of your interpretation of legal BFOQs, business necessity, "essence of the business," or "job relatedness"?

4. What if, in doing a background check on Ms. Cameron, it is discovered that Ms. Cameron had quit a previous employer complaining that she had developed carpal tunnel syndrome. Could management use this information and reject Ms. Cameron on this basis?

EXERCISE 3.6

Hiring a Bank Teller*

Overview

Chapter 3 discusses the numerous laws that can affect the process of selecting employees. The purpose of Exercise 3.6 is to consider these laws in the context of a hiring situation.

Learning Objectives

After completing the exercise, you should be able to

1. Recognize the relevance of particular laws for specific situations.
2. Consider the major provisions and key concepts of those laws as they apply to a specific situation.

Procedure

Part A: Individual Analysis

Prior to class, read Chapter 3 and the scenario below and complete Form 3.6.1. Make sure that you understand each question.

Part B: Group Analysis and Class Discussion

In groups of about six, students should review each member's Form 3.6.1 and then attempt to reach consensus on key questions from the form as designated by the instructor. Class discussion will focus on key laws and provisions.

Scenario

Applicant Background

Anna has multiple sclerosis. Up until 10 months ago she was able to walk with the aid of a cane. Now she uses a wheelchair to get about but she can stand, unassisted, for very short periods of time. She has recent work experience as a cashier in a local cafeteria, which went out of business a few weeks ago. She worked part time at the cafeteria for six years and was highly regarded by the manager and staff as a pleasant, hard-working person. Anna left when the establishment closed. Before that, she worked part time as a concierge in a local hotel for five years. She speaks fluent English and Spanish. Her credit rating and background are impeccable and she has excellent references.

Anna answered the following advertisement in her local newspaper for the position of bank teller with a very large, well known bank in the southeast:

TELLER (P/T)
The ideal candidate must be available to work a flexible schedule. Good communication skills, positive customer service attitude, and professional manner a must. Qualified candidates must have min. 1 year recent cash handling experience; 6 month teller experience preferred. Bilingual (Eng/Span) preferred. We offer a pleasant working environment, competitive salary. Call Monday after 9:00 A.M.

Anna called and, after answering a few basic questions about her previous work experience, spoke with Dave, the location manager. He asked her some additional questions about money handling. Dave asked her to come in for an interview.

Bank Background

This bank is a small branch office in a community of 25,000 people. The manager likes to maintain a pool of five tellers and Dave attempts to schedule them around peak times to best serve the customers. Competition is fierce with five other banks to serve the community. High customer service is a driving force in the organization. The bank's success depends on quality service delivery. The manager prides himself in leading the competition in customer service. Tellers perform a variety of tasks at their stations and also cover the drive-thru window. The drive-thru window station is two steps below the rest of the floor. Historically, the manager has had difficulty finding qualified people who are bilingual to fill this vacancy.

The Interview

Anna arrives for her appointment 15 minutes early. She is anxious to make a good impression and needs to get back into the workforce. She has many ideas and thoughts about how to perform the job.

Dave is under pressure to fill this slot. He has not been impressed by the previous applicants. He is impressed with Anna's résumé and her references. Her work experience appears to be more than adequate. Dave does not know that Anna uses a wheelchair and he has never interviewed a disabled person. Dave's secretary escorts Anna into Dave's office.

Dave: So, you must be Anna. I'm Dave, the branch manager. Come on in.

Anna: Thank you. I hope I'm not too early.

Dave: No, not at all. Let's begin the interview, shall we? You indicated on the phone that your previous job was that of a cashier in a cafeteria, correct?

Anna: Yes, that's right. I usually worked the peak shift from 8:00 A.M. until 2:00 P.M. on my designated days. In addition to the usual register duties, such as keeping track of my cash balance, I also was responsible for the writing and placement of the daily specials menu boards, iced beverage stock count, and the general care and cleanliness of the condiments/register area.

*Contributed by Lori Spina.

Dave: Tell me, Anna, how did you manage to work at a register for six hours?

Anna: Well, I usually took a break after the coffee break crowd left but before the lunch crowd arrived. I have multiple sclerosis but I have no fatigue issues.

Dave: That's not exactly what I meant. I mean, well, let's talk about the job here as teller. All tellers here have to work their own stations and share the drive-thru station. They don't only sit or stand at their stations. They also have to run for signature cards and research items. When a customer arrives at the drive-thru, whichever teller is free first automatically moves to that station. During peak times it gets pretty hectic behind the counter. It's hard to imagine your being able to keep up with all of this. We cannot afford to slow the pace.

Anna: If you are asking me how I would be able to perform under the situation you described, I have some ideas about how I can work both stations. I thought about this after we scheduled the interview, and I think that there are some practical ways to work it.

Dave: I'm glad that you've thought about this ahead of time. That is quite commendable. But on to another demand of the job. We are very proud of our customer service record. In fact, we enjoy the best customer service reputation in the community. We deliver quality work in a timely manner. We know that our customers don't want to waste time waiting in line. So we strive to meet their needs. And we deliver what they have come to expect, great service. That's why we schedule for peak times, even though the hours are somewhat irregular for employees. How do you see yourself fitting into our environment?

Anna: I understand the flexible schedule and don't mind working that way. In fact, after we spoke on the phone to set up this interview, I spoke with a teller at my bank so as to understand what you meant in the ad by a flexible schedule. Also, I don't believe that there was ever a complaint about the quality of my work or my not being able to keep up with the work flow when I worked at the cafeteria. I am very quick with transactions and I enjoy meeting the customers. I got to know most of the regulars pretty well at the cafeteria.

Dave: Well, I think this about wraps up the questions that I have. Is there anything else that I can answer for you before we finish up?

Anna: Do you want to know about my ideas for doing the job?

Dave: I think that might be a bit premature. We can talk about that if you are one of the finalists for the job. Anything else?

Anna: No, I think I am about finished here. Thanks for the appointment.

Dave: Certainly, we will let you know of our decision soon. Good bye.

Anna: Good bye.

Dave is in a quandary. He realizes that Anna is qualified for the position but he does not know how to approach the issue of her using a wheelchair. No other candidate to date is as experienced with both money handling and the language skills as she. The main office wants Dave to make a decision within the next two to three days. The prospects for the remaining interviews do not look promising. Dave decides to interview everyone who has applied before making a decision.

Over the next two days Dave talks to two of his best friends. They are professionals in their fields and are managers as well. Dave still has not interviewed anyone as highly qualified as Anna, but has reservations about hiring her. Dave's friend, Ben, is in real estate and owns a small firm. Ben advises Dave to follow his gut feeling and not take the risk. Carl, an insurance actuary, advises Dave that Anna's MS could get much worse. Carl's main point is that the adjustments to the work environment could be costly and affect customers down the road.

Dave decides to hire another person, Nancy. Even though Nancy does not speak Spanish fluently, Dave decides that she can get by and, if necessary, use another teller to handle intricate transactions in Spanish. Dave feels that he has made the right decision and secretly hopes that he does not lose another teller in the near future.

Anna receives a letter of thanks from Dave, who states that she is not going to get the job. Anna feels that she did not have the opportunity to explain her ideas about performing the job. She wrestles with the thought of legal action. After a few days she contacts an attorney to discuss the incident. The attorney recommends that they file suit against Dave and the bank.

Name _____   Group _____

1. Does Anna have a case here? What are the critical variables?

2. Under the ADA, what is a qualified individual with a disability?

3. What critical terms related to the ADA must be considered in considering the legal implications of Dave's decision? How do they apply in this case?

Name _____   Group _____

4. Can expense or cost be a variable when considering "reasonable accommodation"?

5. What about Carl's point that multiple sclerosis is a progressive disease and that Anna will almost certainly get worse, thus creating potential problems of absenteeism and health care costs. Can Dave consider this issue in his decision?

6. Could Dave ask Anna about the nature or severity of her disability? Could he ask her about ability to perform certain job functions?

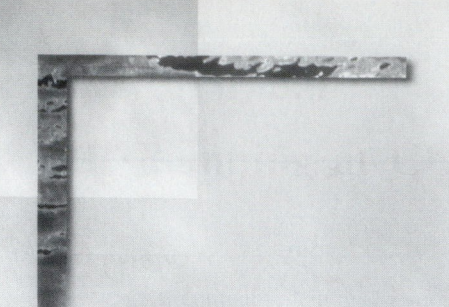

Chapter 4 Exercises

EXERCISE 4.1

Writing a Position Description

Overview

This exercise shows you how to write a position description (PD) that describes either a job you have, have had, or, if you have never worked, the job of someone else. As stated in Chapter 4, job or position descriptions are used for a number of personnel decisions. Many organizations start with job descriptions when they do restructuring and job design. Job descriptions are routinely used to set and adjust wage rates. The information also can be used to assist in recruitment efforts or develop selection devices, work teams, or performance-appraisal systems. To serve HR purposes most effectively, the PD must be current and accurate and it must be consistent with the goals and objectives of the organization, particularly in terms of customer requirements.

Learning Objectives

After completing this exercise, you should be able to

1. Identify the key components of job descriptions.
2. Prepare a position description report, including data on position objectives, tasks and duties, supervision and guidance, contacts, services and products provided to critical customers, and job qualifications or specifications.
3. Understand the purposes to be served by the position description.

Procedure

Part A: Individual Assignment: Completion of the Position Description

Before class, read the general guidelines for completing the position description (Exhibit 4.1.1). Then complete Form 4.1.1, the position description. Prior to class, students should also complete the Assessment Questions.

Part B: Peer Review

Students should bring their completed Form 4.1.1 to class. Students should be paired off and first review their respective position descriptions. Each student should serve as an examiner to try to interpret the PD of the other person. The examiner should try to sum up what is involved in the job and whether clear task statements have been written. The incumbent should clear up any confusion about job duties, requirements, and job specifications. Any needed changes to the PD should be made directly on Form 4.1.1. The discussion also should focus on any job specifications for the job, particularly those that may cause adverse impact. The examiner also should focus on the identification of the customers with whom the incumbent has contact for products or services that derive from this position and determine whether certain tasks on which the incumbent spends considerable time may be unnecessary in terms of the needs of the internal and external customers. The examiner should continue to seek clarification until he or she is confident the position description is as good as it can be. The examiner should then sign Form 4.1.1 in the space provided.

EXHIBIT 4.1.1

GENERAL GUIDELINES FOR COMPLETING THE POSITION DESCRIPTION

The position description should be written in your own words—it should not be written in technical "classified language." Basically the position description should be a collection of the tasks that add up to the total work assignment. All major work activities that are performed in the job should be described. The tools and equipment used should be mentioned. Also include the decisions made in performing the job, the outcomes, the products or services, and the relevant customers for each.

Samples of completed position descriptions for the jobs of public health nurse, mechanic helper, and human resources manager are also provided in Exhibits 4.1.2, 4.1.3, and 4.1.4. Review these samples as you read these instructions. Note the various sections to the position description (see Form 4.1.1).

PART I: COMPILING ORGANIZATIONAL INFORMATION

Step 1. Following the items listed in Part I (Organizational Information) state the name of the incumbent, the date, and the official job title. In item 5, you should state the working title if this title is different from the official title. Often, employees are given working titles for use. For example, a supervisor on a road crew may officially be a highway maintenance engineer.

Step 2. If possible, ask a supervisor or a personnel officer to complete the information requested from the other items listed in Part I.

Step 3. After reviewing the instructions, complete the items of Form 4.1.1, Part II: Position Information. This is the most important part of the position description because it provides information on the position's duties.

PART II: POSITION INFORMATION

Item 11—Objective

Item 11 asks you to state the chief objective of the position. This statement should be no more than two to three sentences. It should state why it is important that the tasks and duties that make up the job are performed. In writing item 11, it may help you to think of this statement as a definition of the position, or perhaps the essential aspect of the job. For example, the objective of a *child welfare supervisor* may be: "To orientate new caseworkers located in local courts, detention homes, and children's institutions by planning and teaching classes and seminars on social casework principles." This example of a position's main objective was used because: (1) It was *brief* (has no more than several lines); (2) it was *descriptive* (states the main tasks and duties of the position without giving detailed information); (3) it gives the reader an *overview* (what to expect in the more detailed listing of tasks); and (4) it states the *main purpose* for why the position exists.

EXHIBIT 4.1.1 (*Continued*)

Item 12—Tasks and Duties

In this section, you are to identify the tasks and duties that are performed in the job. Read the instructions for item 12 on Form 4.1.1 and write down the tasks on a separate sheet of paper. After you have completed this, arrange the tasks in order of the most important task first and finish with the least important task of the position. When these tasks are listed, decide the percent that each task requires of the total working time. Be sure these percentages total to 100. Writing all the tasks and duties of the position is difficult. Outlined below are some guidelines that should help. Following these are some examples of good and poor task statements.

1. Use action verbs to start each task statement, such as compiles, enters, totals, balances, writes, answers, telephones, or interviews. Avoid nondescriptive verbs such as prepares, conducts, coordinates, processes, or assists—these verbs do not tell the reader what you are really doing.

2. Use task statements to explain: What is done? What actions are you performing? To what or to whom? What is the purpose of this task? What references, resources, tools, equipment, or work aids are you using? Do you write reports? Do you train and supervise employees?

3. Try to group closely related tasks together. This grouping of tasks will help you more clearly define and explain to the reader what you are responsible for in your position.

4. It is important to include all the major tasks and duties of your position. It is not necessary to include minor things such as "sits in chair, pulls open drawer, takes out a pen from desk, begins to write."

EXAMPLES OF GOOD AND POOR TASK STATEMENTS

Poor	Good
Ensures that all daily cash is accounted for.	Balances cash in register by comparing it with the total on the register tape; locates and corrects errors in order to account for all cash receipts; writes totals on cash report for approval by head cashier.
Assists with the inspection of construction projects.	Inspects construction operations (erosion control, asphaltic concrete paving, painting, fencing, sign placement); compares visual observations with the construction specifications and plans.
Trains subordinate employees.	Instructs employees under his/her supervision in company policies, office procedures, applicable state and federal laws, and firm report preparation to facilitate improved job performance; distributes firm reading materials, schedules work assignments, and leads staff meetings.

Item 13—Supervision and Guidance

Item 13 asks you to state what work actions and/or decisions are made *without* first getting a supervisor's approval. This decision making is an important element in the evaluation of the job. In answering this question, consider the following examples:

1. If you are a clerk typist, you may edit a memorandum that was drafted by your supervisor in order to make it more grammatically correct.

2. If you are a clerk, you may set up your own filing procedures and reorganize your section's files.

You also may want to list any procedural manuals, laws, and/or standards that are used as guides in the work.

Item 14—Contacts

In many positions, contact with other people is a necessary part of the job. Item 14 requests that you list any contacts you have with individuals, customers, or organizations. Also state the purpose of these contacts, how often they occur (e.g., daily, weekly), and whether they are inside or outside the organization.

Item 15—Most Important Service or Product/Internal and External Customers

Item 15 requests a listing of the most important services or products that are expected from this position and an identification of the internal and external customers who receive them (not by name, just category). Note that managers or supervisors should not be considered customers and their demands may require tasks to be performed that detract from your attention to more important customers (e.g., external customers). Demands from managers should be linked to other internal or external customers.

Item 16—Entry Requirements/Job Specifications

Item 16 asks for information on the KASOCs that an employee must possess on the *first* day of the job. This information will be used in recruiting new employees. There are four sections to be answered.

1. *Knowledge, abilities, skills, and other personal characteristics:* State the KASOCs that a new employee must bring to the position. Use the definitions provided in Chapter 4.

2. *Special licenses, registration, or certification:* Identify occupational certifications or licenses, if any, that an applicant must hold to comply with laws or regulations.

3. *Education or training:* State the educational background or area of study that would provide the knowledge required for entry into the position.

4. *Experience:* State the level and type of experience an applicant should have to be qualified to fill the position. Examples might include "journey level carpentry with experience in remodeling interiors" or "supervisory experience."

EXHIBIT 4.1.2

PUBLIC HEALTH NURSE POSITION DESCRIPTION

PART I: ORGANIZATIONAL INFORMATION

1. Name (last, first, middle):
   Black, Sandy C.

2. Date:
   Nov. 12

3. Job title:
   Public Health Nurse

4. Position number:
   123456

5. Working title if different:

6. Agency:

7. Work location (county or city) and location code:

8. Agency code:

9. Title and position number of immediate supervisor:

10. Organizational unit:

PART II: POSITION INFORMATION

11. Objective of the position: To ensure that state employees are in good health by providing public health services.

12. Tasks and duties:

Percent of Total Working Time	Work Tasks and Duties
25%	Evaluates employees' or potential employees' physical condition by taking medical histories and examining the employee using diagnostic tools, such as stethoscope and otoscope, and interprets the results of laboratory tests.
25%	Treats work-related injuries to reduce absenteeism by administering medication and vaccines under the clinical guidance of a physician.
15%	Meets routinely with staff to review existing clinical services in order to improve them.
20%	Reviews accident reports to identify health and safety hazards. Analyzes causes of accidents and makes recommendations to management for eliminating hazards.
5%	Develops programs to educate employees on health-related issues. Uses self-prepared or programmed lesson plans, films, and other audiovisual materials.
5%	Orders supplies to maintain an adequate inventory. Completes requisition forms and sends them to the planning or supply room.
5%	Answers requests for medical status of employees from insurance companies or personnel staff by discussing results of examinations and current medical status over the telephone or by completing medical forms.
100%	

13. Describe work actions and/or decisions you make *without* prior approval and the extent of advice and guidance received from your supervisor:
    I decide how to treat minor injuries—giving first aid. I determine if a laboratory test is within acceptable limits. I plan educational programs.

EXHIBIT 4.1.2 (*Continued*)

14. Contacts:

Contacts	Purpose	How Often	Inside/Outside Organization
Employees	Perform physicals, treat injuries, and obtain information on the workplace	Daily	Inside
Insurance companies	Provide medical claim information	Weekly	Outside
Benefits staff (DPT)	Provide information for worker's compensation claims	Monthly	Inside

15. The most important service or product provided:

Contact with and treatment of employees.

16. Qualifications for entry into the position:

A. KASOCs:

Ability to obtain personal information from people and to determine if they are being truthful. Knowledge of nursing services in the employment setting.

B. Special licenses, registration, or certification:

RN

C. Education or training (cite major area of study):

Nursing

D. Level and type of experience:

Experience in providing nursing services to a wide variety of people.

17. I understand the above statements, and they are complete to the best of my knowledge.

Sandy C. Black
Employee's Signature

Nov. 12
Date

Connie Brown
Examiner's Signature

November 13
Date

EXHIBIT 4.1.3

MECHANIC HELPER POSITION DESCRIPTION

PART I: ORGANIZATIONAL INFORMATION

1. Name (last, first, middle):

Green, Chris M.

2. Date:

3. Job title:

Mechanic Helper

4. Position number:

5. Working title if different:

6. Organization:

7. Work location (county or city) and location code:

8. Agency code:

9. Title and position number of immediate supervisor:

10. Organizational unit:

EXHIBIT 4.1.3 (Continued)

PART II: POSITION INFORMATION

11. Objective of the position:

   To maintain highway construction equipment in good operating condition by inspecting and repairing equipment, when necessary.

12. Tasks and duties:

Percent of Total Working Time	Work Tasks and Duties
25%	Inspects highway equipment to identify any operating problems by visually checking and listening to the equipment.
25%	Repairs highway equipment, cars, dump trucks, and small engines needed to perform road maintenance work by overhauling motor transmissions and differentials, replacing axles, springs, and wheel bearings using small motorized shop equipment, hand tools, and shop repair manuals.
20%	Maintains equipment to prevent breakdowns by installing spark plugs, starters, distributor caps; changing oil; and greasing equipment using standard mechanic tools.
15%	Tunes up and analyzes gasoline engines to locate minor problems and provide for optimum engine performance by using the Peerless Engine Analyzer.
15%	Helps other mechanics by gathering tools and parts, purchasing, and picking up parts at local suppliers and moving equipment from one place to another as directed by the foreman.
100%	

13. Describe work actions and/or decisions you make *without* prior approval and the extent of advice and guidance you receive from your supervisor.

   I decide how to repair the equipment. If the work is going to take more hours than planned, I tell my supervisor.

14. Contacts:

Contacts	Purpose	How Often	Inside/Outside Organization
Supply stores	Pick up parts or supplies.	Weekly	Outside

15. The most important services or products provided and the customers:

   Perform repair work as assigned. Customer is car owner.

16. Qualifications for entry into the position:

   A. KASOCs:

      Knowledge of gasoline-powered engines.

      Ability to drive equipment.

      Ability to read and follow instructions in repair manual.

   B. Special licenses, registration, or certification:

      Apprentice license for mechanic

   C. Education or training (cite major area of study):

      Heavy equipment mechanics

   D. Level and type of experience:

17. I understand the above statements, and they are complete to the best of my knowledge.

Chris M. Green

Employee's Signature

April 19

Date

Bobby Diangela

Supervisor's Signature

_4-20_

Date

EXHIBIT 4.1.4

HUMAN RESOURCES MANAGER

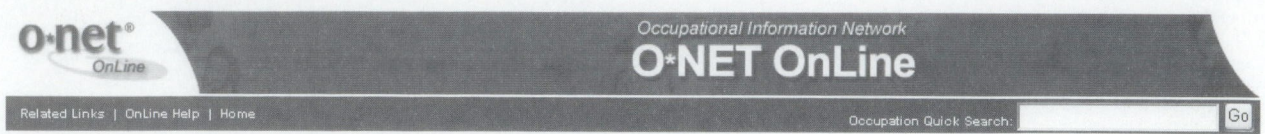

Related Links | OnLine Help | Home

Occupation Quick Search: [   ] Go

SUMMARY REPORT FOR

11-3040.00 - Human Resources Managers

Plan, direct, and coordinate human resource management activities of an organization to maximize the strategic use of human resources and maintain functions such as employee compensation, recruitment, personnel policies, and regulatory compliance.

Sample of reported job titles: Human Resources Manager, Director Of Human Resources, HR Director (Human Resources Director), Employee Benefits Manager, Employee Relations Manager

View report:	**Summary**	Details	Custom

Tasks | Knowledge | Skills | Abilities | Work Activities | Work Context | Job Zone | Interests | Work Styles | Work Values | Related Occupations | Wages & Employment

Tasks

- Administer compensation, benefits and performance management systems, and safety and recreation programs.
- Identify staff vacancies and recruit, interview and select applicants.
- Allocate human resources, ensuring appropriate matches between personnel.
- Provide current and prospective employees with information about policies, job duties, working conditions, wages, opportunities for promotion and employee benefits.
- Perform difficult staffing duties, including dealing with understaffing, refereeing disputes, firing employees, and administering disciplinary procedures.
- Advise managers on organizational policy matters such as equal employment opportunity and sexual harassment, and recommend needed changes.
- Analyze and modify compensation and benefits policies to establish competitive programs and ensure compliance with legal requirements.
- Plan and conduct new employee orientation to foster positive attitude toward organizational objectives.
- Serve as a link between management and employees by handling questions, interpreting and administering contracts and helping resolve work-related problems.
- Plan, direct, supervise, and coordinate work activities of subordinates and staff relating to employment, compensation, labor relations, and employee relations.

Knowledge

Personnel and Human Resources—Knowledge of principles and procedures for personnel recruitment, selection, training, compensation and benefits, labor relations and negotiation, and personnel information systems.

English Language—Knowledge of the structure and content of the English language including the meaning and spelling of words, rules of composition, and grammar.

Customer and Personal Service—Knowledge of principles and processes for providing customer and personal services. This includes customer needs assessment, meeting quality standards for services, and evaluation of customer satisfaction.

Administration and Management—Knowledge of business and management principles involved in strategic planning, resource allocation, human resources modeling, leadership technique, production methods, and coordination of people and resources.

Law and Government—Knowledge of laws, legal codes, court procedures, precedents, government regulations, executive orders, agency rules, and the democratic political process.

Clerical—Knowledge of administrative and clerical procedures and systems such as word processing, managing files and records, stenography and transcription, designing forms, and other office procedures and terminology.

Education and Training—Knowledge of principles and methods for curriculum and training design, teaching and instruction for individuals and groups, and the measurement of training effects.

Economics and Accounting—Knowledge of economic and accounting principles and practices, the financial markets, banking and the analysis and reporting of financial data.

Psychology—Knowledge of human behavior and performance; individual differences in ability, personality, and interests; learning and motivation; psychological research methods; and the assessment and treatment of behavioral and affective disorders.

Mathematics—Knowledge of arithmetic, algebra, geometry, calculus, statistics, and their applications.

EXHIBIT 4.1.4 (*Continued*)

Skills

Active Listening—Giving full attention to what other people are saying, taking time to understand the points being made, asking questions as appropriate, and not interrupting at inappropriate times.

Management of Personnel Resources—Motivating, developing, and directing people as they work, identifying the best people for the job.

Reading Comprehension—Understanding written sentences and paragraphs in work related documents.

Writing—Communicating effectively in writing as appropriate for the needs of the audience.

Speaking—Talking to others to convey information effectively.

Negotiation—Bringing others together and trying to reconcile differences.

Time Management—Managing one's own time and the time of others.

Social Perceptiveness—Being aware of others' reactions and understanding why they react as they do.

Critical Thinking—Using logic and reasoning to identify the strengths and weaknesses of alternative solutions, conclusions or approaches to problems.

Instructing—Teaching others how to do something.

Abilities

Oral Comprehension—The ability to listen to and understand information and ideas presented through spoken words and sentences.

Oral Expression—The ability to communicate information and ideas in speaking so others will understand.

Speech Clarity—The ability to speak clearly so others can understand you.

Speech Recognition—The ability to identify and understand the speech of another person.

Written Comprehension—The ability to read and understand information and ideas presented in writing.

Written Expression—The ability to communicate information and ideas in writing so others will understand.

Deductive Reasoning—The ability to apply general rules to specific problems to produce answers that make sense.

Problem Sensitivity—The ability to tell when something is wrong or is likely to go wrong. It does not involve solving the problem, only recognizing there is a problem.

Inductive Reasoning—The ability to combine pieces of information to form general rules or conclusions (includes finding a relationship among seemingly unrelated events).

Near Vision—The ability to see details at close range (within a few feet of the observer).

Work Activities

Establishing and Maintaining Interpersonal Relationships—Developing constructive and cooperative working relationships with others, and maintaining them over time.

Communicating with Supervisors, Peers, or Subordinates—Providing information to supervisors, co-workers, and subordinates by telephone, in written form, e-mail, or in person.

Making Decisions and Solving Problems—Analyzing information and evaluating results to choose the best solution and solve problems.

Staffing Organizational Units—Recruiting, interviewing, selecting, hiring, and promoting employees in an organization.

Getting Information—Observing, receiving, and otherwise obtaining information from all relevant sources.

Judging the Qualities of Things, Services, or People—Assessing the value, importance, or quality of things or people.

Guiding, Directing, and Motivating Subordinates—Providing guidance and direction to subordinates, including setting performance standards and monitoring performance.

Resolving Conflicts and Negotiating with Others—Handling complaints, settling disputes, and resolving grievances and conflicts, or otherwise negotiating with others.

Evaluating Information to Determine Compliance with Standards—Using relevant information and individual judgment to determine whether events or processes comply with laws, regulations, or standards.

Coaching and Developing Others—Identifying the developmental needs of others and coaching, mentoring, or otherwise helping others to improve their knowledge or skills.

Work Context

Telephone—How often do you have telephone conversations in this job?

Indoors, Environmentally Controlled—How often does this job require working indoors in environmentally controlled conditions?

Structured versus Unstructured Work—To what extent is this job structured for the worker, rather than allowing the worker to determine tasks, priorities, and goals?

Contact With Others—How much does this job require the worker to be in contact with others (face-to-face, by telephone, or otherwise) in order to perform it?

Electronic Mail—How often do you use electronic mail in this job?

Spend Time Sitting—How much does this job require sitting?

EXHIBIT 4.1.4 (*Continued*)

Freedom to Make Decisions—How much decision making freedom, without supervision, does the job offer?

Importance of Being Exact or Accurate—How important is being very exact or highly accurate in performing this?

Face-to-Face Discussions—How often do you have to have face-to-face discussions with individuals or teams in this job?

Letters and Memos—How often does the job require written letters and memos?

Job Zone

Title	Job Zone Four: Considerable Preparation Needed
Overall Experience	A minimum of two to four years of work-related skill, knowledge, or experience is needed for these occupations. For example, an accountant must complete four years of college and work for several years in accounting to be considered qualified.
Job Training	Employees in these occupations usually need several years of work-related experience, on-the-job training, and/or vocational training.
Job Zone Examples	Many of these occupations involve coordinating, supervising, managing, or training others. Examples include accountants, human resource managers, computer programmers, teachers, chemists, and police detectives.
SVP Range	(7.0 to < 8.0)
Education	Most of these occupations require a four-year bachelor's degree, but some do not.

Interests

Enterprising—Enterprising occupations frequently involve starting up and carrying out projects. These occupations can involve leading people and making many decisions. Sometimes they require risk taking and often deal with business.

Social—Social occupations frequently involve working with, communicating with, and teaching people. These occupations often involve helping or providing service to others.

Conventional—Conventional occupations frequently involve following set procedures and routines. These occupations can include working with data and details more than with ideas. Usually there is a clear line of authority to follow.

Work Styles

Attention to Detail—Job requires being careful about detail and thorough in completing work tasks.

Concern for Others—Job requires being sensitive to others' needs and feelings and being understanding and helpful on the job.

Integrity— Job requires being honest and ethical.

Independence—Job requires developing one's own ways of doing things, guiding oneself with little or no supervision, and depending on oneself to get things done.

Initiative—Job requires a willingness to take on responsibilities and challenges.

Dependability—Job requires being reliable, responsible, and dependable, and fulfilling obligations.

Persistence—Job requires persistence in the face of obstacles.

Stress Tolerance—Job requires accepting criticism and dealing calmly and effectively with high stress situations.

FORM 4.1.1

THE POSITION DESCRIPTION

PART I: ORGANIZATIONAL INFORMATION

    1.   Name (last, first, middle):

    2.   Date:

    3.   Job title:

    4.   How many people in organization have this title?

    5.   Working title if different:

    6.   Organization:

    7.   Work location (county or city)

    8.   Division within organization:

    9.   Title of immediate supervisor:

    10.   Organizational unit:

PART II: POSITION INFORMATION

    11.   State the chief *objective* of the position in a brief statement:

    12.   Before filling out the next section, think about the *tasks and duties* performed in the position. Consider the time spent on the tasks and duties, how important they are to achieving the objective of the position, and the processes or ways in which these tasks and duties are performed. After considering these aspects of the position, state the tasks and duties that are performed in the position.

        • State the *most important* duty first and finish with the *least important* duty of the position.
        • Calculate the percent that each duty requires of the total working time. Be sure these percentages total 100.
        • Include *all* tasks, duties, and functions that are performed *except* those that occupy 2 percent or less time, unless they are considered very important.

Percent of Total Working Time   **Work Tasks and Duties**

13. What work actions and/or decisions are made *without* prior approval? To what extent are the advice and guidance from a supervisor received? State examples of the type of supervisory advice and guidance that are received as well as actions or decisions made without prior approval.

14. List and explain the *contacts,* if any, both within and outside the organization, that are a routine function of the work. Do not list contacts with supervisors, co-workers, and subordinates.

Contacts	Purpose	How Often	Inside/Outside Organization

15. What are the most *important* services or products expected from an incumbent in the position described and who are the customers with these expectations?

Most Important Service/Product: **Customer:**

Second Most Important:

Third Most Important:

Fourth Most Important:

16. What are the *qualifications for entry* into this position:

    A. What KASOCs should a new employee bring to this position?

    B. Special licenses, registration, or certification:

    C. Education or training (cite major area of study):

    D. Level and type of experience:

17. I understand the above statements, and they are complete to the best of my knowledge.

_____   _____
Employee's Signature   Date

_____   _____
Supervisor's Signature (optional)   Date

_____   _____
Examiner's Signature   Date

EXERCISE 4.1
ASSESSMENT QUESTIONS

Name _____

1. Could you use this job analysis to determine essential functions on the job? How could this be done?

2. When preparing the job description, why is it important to list the critical customers for the products or services and the major tasks and duties of the job? Are there tasks that could be excluded with little or no effect on critical customers?

3. How often should a position description form be updated? Explain your response.

4. Explain how your job description could be used to evaluate your performance or to develop methods for hiring people for the position. Do you think having a highly detailed job description is actually counterproductive for certain jobs? Explain your answer.

EXERCISE 4.1 (*Continued*)

5.   How could the O*NET be used for developing job descriptions?

6.   You are assigned the task of writing a position description for a personnel recruiter. How would you proceed?

EXERCISE 4.2

The Use of the Critical Incident Technique to Analyze the Job of University Professor

Overview

The critical incident technique is heralded as one of the best job analysis methods for the development of performance appraisal systems and training programs. You will recall from the chapter discussion that experts in job analysis rated critical incidents as one of the best for these purposes. The purpose of this exercise is to write and critique critical incidents representing the performance of college instructors. The incidents will ultimately be used to develop an appraisal system for professors.

Learning Objectives

After completing this exercise, you should be able to

1. Know the difference between a good and a bad critical incident.
2. Critique incidents and revise them for purposes of appraisal development.
3. Understand the procedures to be followed in developing work functions from the critical incident technique.

Procedure

Part A: Individual Project

Before class, review the section in the chapter on the criteria for useful critical incidents. Using copies of Form 4.2.1, write five critical incidents (one per form) based on observations and experiences you have had with college instructors. Write at least two examples of effective performance and two of ineffective performance. Also, prior to class, complete the assessment questions.

Part B: Group Analysis and Discussion

Step 1. Students should be paired off. Each should read and critique incidents written by the other student using the criteria for usefulness presented in the text. Incidents that fail to meet the criteria should be rewritten after consultation with the writer. Make sure each incident is written in the same format (i.e., specific incident or single behavior, active voice, behavioral verb, visible, the action's context, and the results or outcomes of the incident). Be specific.

Step 2. In groups, the incidents written by group members should be subjected to a "content analysis." The content analysis identifies common themes or "functions" of behavior. The term *function* implies a category of events or incidents that fit together conceptually. For example, one such function for university professors might be "grading and testing procedures." Students will write many incidents pertaining to the way in which grades are assigned and tests are administered and scored. These incidents might all fit into a function perhaps called "grading and testing procedures." Another example of a function might be "communication skills" where examples of effective and ineffective communication skills are presented. Both positive and negative incidents can fit into the same function as long as they describe something pertaining to that function.

Each group member should read through all the incidents looking for consistencies or common themes running through the ways in which professors perform well or poorly. The group should first develop a methodology to sort incidents into piles representing functions. After the initial sorting, group members should go back through the remaining unsorted examples and try to identify new and different functions underlying these. Continue this process until as many functions are identified as are needed to represent all incidents. Label each of the functions with a short phrase.

After the group members agree on functions, they should then agree into what function each incident belongs and record that function on Form 4.2.1 in the space titled "Possible function label." One group member should then write the function titles on the blackboard and indicate the number of critical incidents that represented each function.

Step 3. The overlap of the functions developed by each group should be determined through class discussion, and the class should attempt to conclude with from 7 to 15 functions that represent all the functions generated for all groups. Function titles should be merged or rewritten to accommodate all perspectives and short definitions of each function should be written.

Step 4. Students should be regrouped and then given sets of critical incident forms. Each incident should be linked to one of the class functions identified at Step 3. After group discussion and consensus is reached, the function title should be written on each form in the section titled "Final function label."

FORM 4.2.1

CRITICAL INCIDENT FORM

Think back over your observations of various college professors. Try to recall noteworthy examples and things professors did that illustrate either unusually effective or ineffective performance. Write one example on each form.

    1.   What were the circumstances leading up to this example?

    2.   Describe exactly what was done that qualifies the example as either effective or ineffective.

    3.   What were the results or outcomes of the professor's actions? (Be specific.)

Possible function label _____

Final function label _____

Your name _____

Incident number _____

Group number _____

EXERCISE 4.2
ASSESSMENT QUESTIONS

Name _____   Group _____

1. How could the critical incidents be used to prepare professors for teaching assignments?

2. The book describes the critical incident method as one of the best for developing performance-appraisal systems. How do you propose to get from the incidents and job functions to an actual performance-appraisal system for evaluating professors?

3. Why are results or outcomes requested with CIT? What could be done with these data?

EXERCISE 4.3

Job Analysis at CompTech

Overview

Chapter 4 discusses the purposes of job analysis and the derivation of the job description and job specifications as critical products. This exercise explores the methods that could be used to assess job specifications, to solve HR problems, and to consider the implications of the actions recommended.

Learning Objectives

After completing this exercise, you should be able to

1. Evaluate the processes that could be followed to assess job specifications.
2. Consider the legal and practical implications of the job specifications based on the methods you have recommended and the particular specifications you recommend.
3. Evaluate the best methods for developing training programs based on job analysis information.
4. Explore the use of job analysis to identify problems of high employee turnover.

Procedure

Part A: Individual Analysis

Before class, read the scenario presented below and answer the questions on Form 4.3.1. In the space provided, write down any questions for which you need answers in order to take a definitive position on any of the issues.

Part B: Group Analysis

In groups, students should review each member's Form 4.3.1 and then attempt to reach consensus on the requested positions. You are allowed to ask the professor only three questions, so decide what additional information is most important in order for you to address the most critical issues. A designated group spokesperson will present the positions of the group. Class discussion will focus on the positions taken.

Scenario

CompTech is a large retailer of computer products. With 442 stores in the United States and a plan for 70 more stores within two years, CompTech is the fastest growing computer retailer in the United States. The company's most important strategic objective is to meet customer requirements and expand the customer base into small-business workstations in order to build a long-term relationship. You have been retained to develop a plan for a "CompTech University" that will provide training for all store managers before taking over a store. In addition, you have been asked to evaluate the

hiring process for store managers, to assess problems, and to suggest solutions.

CompTech, in competition with the other retailers, has had some difficulty recruiting store managers and the problem appears to have worsened in recent years. In addition, its turnover rate of store associates is higher than the average in retail although it is offering competitive pay packages. Exhibit 4.3.1 presents the breakdown of management vacancies at CompTech, plus an ethnic and gender breakdown. The retailer's orientation in the past has been to hire experienced store managers from outside the company (approximately 60 percent of store managers are hired from outside the company). However, district managers, responsible for from 8 to 13 stores in a geographical area, are given great discretion in the methods and criteria they use to hire store managers (including job specifications). The company has had to employ a costly employment agency to locate managerial candidates along with an expensive advertising/recruiting campaign, with frequent ads in *The Wall Street Journal* and the *New York Times*. The problem has become more acute in areas with an abundance of retail outlets where retail store managers are in great and increasing demand.

Jamie Carlyle, the vice president of human resources, has specific requests and would like you to consider two issues in particular:

1. Many district managers have required an MBA or at least three years' experience as a store manager as a condition of employment as a store manager. Carlyle would like you to devise a method for evaluating these job specifications in particular. What method of analysis do you recommend?
2. Carlyle wants to include training modules for store manager at CompTech University. How would you conduct a job analysis of the store manager job to determine what specific KASOCs are essential or critical for the job?

EXHIBIT 4.3.1

COMPTECH MANAGER DEMOGRAPHICS

	Assistant Manager	Associate Manager	Store Manager	District Manager
WM*	612	405	282	25
WF	292	164	56	8
BM	135	85	31	2
BF	115	41	15	0
HM	93	42	19	3
HF	41	20	10	0
Vacancies	20	12	30	3

*W, B, H, M, F represent white, black, hispanic, male, and female.

3. Carlyle is interested in a more "job-related" approach to selecting managers. How do we proceed with this objective?

4. Carlyle discovers that there is no formal job description for any retail management position. How should she proceed?

Carlyle is not certain how to go about addressing the most important HRM issues as they relate to CompTech's strate- gic plan and would like your advice on this issue as well. Finally, Carlyle welcomes any opinions regarding the manner in which CompTech is filling managerial positions and any issues related to HRM problems and CompTech's objectives. Use Form 4.3.1 to respond to these issues.

Name _____   Group _____

1. What are the current job specifications for the store manager job? Based on the information you have (or could have), how would you assess the validity of these specifications? What approaches or methods would you use? (You can propose particular statistical analysis, particular job analysis methods, or both; be specific.)

2. What hypotheses or proposals do you have so far regarding CompTech's strategic position? What do you regard as the critical strengths and weaknesses based on the data you have?

3. Carlyle is giving strong consideration to hiring a full-time personnel recruiter (CompTech has never employed such a specialist). Assuming she has decided to hire such a person, how should she proceed?

4. If CompTech decides to drop the MBA requirement, what possible effects could such a change in policy have on other human resource activities? What possible advantages do you see by keeping the MBA?

5. Carlyle is partial to the use of the PAQ to set job specifications. What is your position on the use of the PAQ for this purpose relative to other job analysis methods?

6. Given Carlyle's interest in the training program and the "job-related" selection tests, what job analysis method should be used for the development of these HR products?

7. Could Carlyle use the O*NET to address any issues? If so, what could she learn?

8. Do you see any potential EEO issues that should be considered at CompTech? Explain your answer with as much detail as possible.

Chapter 5 Exercises

EXERCISE 5.1

A Turnover Problem at the *Fort Lauderdale Herald**

Overview

The chapter discusses the importance of using data for better human resource planning and recruitment. The employee "matching" model is described. This exercise presents data from a newspaper that document the problems the company is having recruiting and retaining employees. Your job is to use the data as a basis for recommendations for improving the process and reducing the turnover problem for the company.

Objectives

After completing this exercise, you should be able to

1. Know how to calculate and use yield ratios for planning.
2. Know how an HR problem (e.g., turnover) can be solved most efficiently and effectively using approaches to HR planning and recruitment.

Procedure

Part A: Individual Analysis

Prior to class, read the background data on the *Fort Lauderdale Herald.* Using the additional information that is provided, think about the implications of this information for HR planning and recruitment at the newspaper. Then answer the questions on Form 5.1.1.

Part B: Group Analysis

In groups, members should review each other's responses and then attempt to reach consensus on the three recommendations to go forward to the director. Analyze those recommendations in the context of the problems, the potential effects on other HR programs, and the cost of implementation. Justify any specific recommendations with relevant research. A group spokesperson will then be designated to present the group consensus recommendations.

Scenario

The Fort Lauderdale Herald is located in southern Florida, one of the fastest-growing regions in the United States. Because of the increased migration, subscriptions to the paper have risen sharply. The newspaper's increased circulation has created a need for more Customer Service Representatives. In addition, competition in the area has increased with two new papers and the expansion of a Miami paper into the metropolitan area.

The advertisement for customer service representatives states the following:

> The position qualifications are: knowledge of MS Word or Word Perfect; typing 35 WPM; filing; experience in customer contact and answering telephones; referring customer calls to supervisor; some selling of additional services and calls for nonpayment of bills.

The starting salary for Customer Service Reps is $8.50 an hour for a 30-hour workweek. Customer Service Reps work six days per week in 5-hour shifts. The reps do not receive any fringe benefits.

Customer Service Reps spend a majority of the work day talking on the telephone with subscribers or potential subscribers regarding new accounts, renewing and expanding subscriptions, delivery, or other problems with the newspaper. Billing errors consume approximately 30 percent of the rep's time. The reps spend the remainder of their time responding to customer complaints, such as late, improper, or nondelivery of the paper, and soliciting new business through cold calls or calling subscribers for up-selling purposes. The most common complaints are: "the newspaper was supposed to be delivered at 7:00 AM, but did not arrive until 9:00"; "the paper was thrown in a puddle and can't be read"; "the paper was thrown in my neighbor's yard"; and so forth. Most of the subscribers who call are not friendly when registering their complaints. A 1999 study determined that automating the complaint process was more likely to foster nonpayment of subscription service and more cancellations.

While the newspaper has successfully recruited new Customer Service Reps, turnover in the position is very high. The Director of Human Resources has prepared the recruitment data shown in Exhibit 5.1.1. The data show that the company screened 633 applicants to produce 78 people who accepted a job offer. Within six months, 51 percent of new hires resigned from the newspaper. Exit interviews with departing Customer Service Reps revealed many reasons why they were dissatisfied with the job (see Exhibit 5.1.2).

*Contributed by Renee Fitzgerald

EXHIBIT 5.1.1

DATA ON RECRUITMENT SOURCES FOR CUSTOMER SERVICE REPRESENTATIVES, LAST 3 YEARS

Recruitment Source	Total # Applicants	Potentially Qualified	Interview	Qualified & Offered Job	Accepted Job	Six-month Survival	Recruitment Cost (Total)
Local Web site	450	32	20	17	11	5	$200.00
Newspaper ads	115	78	64	56	53	24	465.00
Walk-in applicants	31	20	14	9	7	3	295.00
Public employment agency	37	19	7	7	7	6	250.00
Totals	633[a]	149[b]	105	89[c]	78	38	1,210.00

[a]341 whites, 177 blacks, and 115 Hispanics
[b]91 whites, 43 blacks, and 15 Hispanics
[c]64 whites, 20 blacks, and 5 Hispanics

Name —————————————————————— Group ——————————————————————

Ms. Adalyn Saline, the Director of Human Resources, has asked you to analyze the recruitment and selection process and the related data and to make recommendations. She also requests the yield ratios for each step in the recruitment/screening process. Use this form to record your answers.

1. What are yield ratios for each step in the recruitment and selection process? What are the implications of these ratios for future hiring?

2. What are the advantages and disadvantages of the various recruiting methods used by the *Fort Lauderdale Herald?* (Use the data in Exhibit 5.1.1 and Chapter 5 discussion.) Where should they focus their recruitment efforts in the future?

3. Recommend at least three HR planning/recruitment/selection strategies designed to do any of the following: (1) improve customer satisfaction; (2) increase the efficiency of the customer service function (Ms. Saline encourages you to be as creative in your thinking as possible); and (3) increase the tenure of the Customer Service Reps. (or decrease the need for them).

4. What additional studies or data are necessary given the data presented in Exhibit 5.1.1? (Ms. Saline is very interested in potential legal issues.)

EXHIBIT 5.1.2

MOST FREQUENTLY GIVEN EXPLANATIONS FOR CUSTOMER SERVICE REP TURNOVER (LAST 3 YEARS)

- All customer service reps are required to work on Saturday and Sunday from 7:00 A.M. to 1:00 P.M.
- Seventy-five percent of calling customers are irate at things over which the customer service reps have no control.
- Customer service reps must sit for long periods of time, talking with customers on the phone. Physical movement is restricted.
- Customer service reps have little contact with coworkers.
- The work environment is noisy and hectic.
- Customer service reps have not been properly trained to respond to billing complaints.
- Cold Calls for subscriptions result in 78 percent hang-ups.
- Reps receive no additional remuneration for soliciation successes.
- Supervisors monitor a sample of calls taken each day, and often contradict what the customer service reps say to customers.
- Customer service reps don't like cold calls.
- Customer service reps don't like calling people at dinner time.

EXERCISE 5.2
Permalco's Recruiting Challenge

Overview

Chapter 5 describes the human resource planning (HRP) process and the relationships among resource planning, recruiting, and other human resource activities. Recruiting candidates who will be top performers for an organization requires good planning, targeted strategies, and supportive human resource processes. This exercise formulates a strategy for a company that faces the challenge of recruiting production leaders during a time of change and downsizing.

Learning Objectives

After completing this exercise, you should be able to analyze a company's recruiting challenge and

1. Identify the company's problems, threats, and opportunities.
2. Identify the impact of other human resource processes on recruiting.
3. Suggest logical, efficient recruiting solutions.

Procedure

Part A: Individual Analysis

Before class, read the scenario below. Answer the questions on Form 5.2.1.

Part B: Group Analysis

Working in groups, review each student's answers to Form 5.2.1. Formulate a recruiting plan for Permalco. Include in your plan

1. Short-term and long-term strategies.
2. Measures of success.
3. Sources of candidates.
4. Recruiting techniques.
5. Recommendations for changes to other human resource systems.

Scenario

Tracy Johnson threw open the doors of the storeroom supply cabinet and grimaced at the disarray. She pulled out a few old brochures, dusted them off, and closed the cabinet doors. Shaking her head, she noted that at least half of the people pictured in the brochure were no longer with Permalco.

As she emerged from the storeroom into the aluminum smelting plant, she stuffed her long brown hair under her hard hat and donned her safety glasses. Although the early spring weather was cool, the plant was sweltering. Her heavy safety boots clattered against the brick walkway. Here and there someone was tending carbon-lined shells, called pots, where alumina is dissolved into a molten chemical bath. It still amazed her that the electric current that entered the pot and separated the alumina into oxygen and aluminum was so strong that a paper clip chain on the pot would stand straight up like a flagpole. Ahead of Tracy, a crew was siphoning molten metal into a large container called a crucible. The flames and smoke from the pot seemed like hell, but the computer-generated voice from the loudspeaker chanting, "Pot 8. Anode Effect. Pot 8. Anode Effect," reminded Tracy that the smelter was a high-tech facility.

"Hey, sweet thing, how come you don't visit me more often?" shouted Cyrus "Hound Dog" Palmer. Although sexist comments from the crews bothered her, she knew she could accomplish more if she played along. "Hound Dog, I couldn't stand the excitement," retorted Tracy, continuing on her way. She heard the rest of the crew laughing at Cyrus.

Tracy's office was in an area outside the smelter. She had a few minutes to prepare an agenda for the first meeting of the recruiting team. Tracy glanced out the dirty window as a crucible hauler roared by and shook her desk. She recalled her first exposure to Permalco. Permalco's booth at her college career fair proudly displayed pictures of young engineers at work in various parts of Permalco's Landon Works, a smelter located in the mountains of western North Carolina. Landon's recruiter, a young man with a lovely southern accent, was animated as he spoke about Landon Works and Permalco. "The salary and benefits are top notch. You'll have opportunity to advance and transfer to other divisions. You're a mechanical engineer?" Tracy nodded. "We're installing a fume control system in the plant now. It's like playing with Tinker Toys. You'll love it."

And she did. Permalco had recently modernized Landon Works, and Tracy loved working on the high-tech equipment. However, she had accepted an entry-level position at Landon with the thought that she would be able to transfer to a facility closer to a metropolitan area. Although she loved the people in the community, she found it hard to meet other young professionals. Her dream of moving beyond Landon died when the CEO made each division a separate business. She didn't even hear about position openings anymore.

She sighed. The worst part was that after eight years she was worried about her job. Landon had recently laid off 30 percent of its employees, mainly young people.

She walked to the conference room at the end of the trailer. Carbon dust from the plant blanketed the steel table and mismatched chairs. She had just finished writing the agenda on the flip chart when the other members of the recruiting team walked in.

Elizabeth Gomez and Jim Brownwell found seats around the table. Elizabeth pulled off her hard hat to reveal dark hair plastered to her forehead. "I've been taking pot temperature readings all day. I swear I drank two gallons of water from the fountain in the hall. And it's not even summer yet."

Jim responded, "Switch to the graveyard shift. Even though you don't have a life, at least it's cooler." Elizabeth laughed.

Jim turned to Tracy, "Can you believe after all the layoffs we're looking for people again? Are the managers crazy?"

"Yes, what is going on, Tracy?" asked Elizabeth.

Tracy paused before she spoke. "There's no doubt about it. This is a challenge. As the managers look at the people in our line organization, they believe there are not enough people to fill our future production leadership positions. They have asked us to begin a recruiting effort focused on future leaders. They asked for both of you because you are good performers and they feel you can talk in a motivated way about opportunities at Permalco."

"Opportunities at Permalco?" snapped Jim. "How can I talk about opportunities when I'm not sure about my future?"

"How many people do they want to hire, Tracy?" asked Elizabeth, sighing.

"Two people this year, if we find people that meet our standards. We need to continue feeding the pipeline with good candidates each year. And by the way, our recruiting focus will be on females and minorities."

Tracy leaned toward them. "Remember, when we were hired, Permalco looked for the best engineer. The engineer with the highest grade point average. The managers hoped that engineers would emerge who had the desire and skills to be a production leader. That strategy won't work today. We must look for a special person. The person who wants to be a leader. The person who was the captain of the football team or head cheerleader.

President of the fraternity or sorority. The person whose gleam in his or her eye says, 'I want to make the million dollar decisions.'"

Jim shot back, "Yeah, the person who wants to do shift work for five years. Shift work used to be a temporary developmental assignment—a way to pay your dues before moving up the ladder. Since the layoffs there isn't anywhere for the production supervisors to go. They're stuck. The good salary and benefits have handcuffed them to Landon."

Elizabeth spoke. "I'm concerned, too. This plant is not the ideal place for a female or a minority. If I hadn't married Bill I imagine I would have left for a different company by now. There are no other Hispanic professionals in the entire town! That's one of the reasons why so many minorities have left Landon."

Tracy nodded, "You're both frustrated with this project. I am, too. But we're going to need people in these critical positions in a few years. Starting now gives us ample time to bring the right people in and develop them. Are you ready to put together a recruiting strategy for the plant manager? By Friday?"

Jim and Elizabeth reluctantly nodded. Tracy grabbed a flip chart marker. "So, where are we going to find these special people?"

"Tracy, you remember what it's like on campus," recalled Elizabeth. "The qualified minorities have been targeted by the large firms before their sophomore year. And for females the competition is intense, too. I had at least three summer internship offers each year. How are we going to attract the top students?"

Jim replied, "Campus isn't the only source of candidates, Elizabeth. Permalco hired me through a recruiting firm when I was leaving the military. Once you've been on a submarine for three months, shift work is no big deal."

Tracy smiled as she began to record the ideas on the flip chart.

FORM 5.2.1

Name _____   Group _____

1. Identify the SWOT at Permalco as related to recruiting production leaders?

2. What information must the team gather before it can formulate a recruiting strategy?

3. How might the short-term and long-term recruiting strategies differ?

4. What sources of candidates should the team consider?

5. What recruiting strategy has the highest probability of paying off for the team?

6. When planning the recruiting strategy, what other HR systems must the team consider?

7. What challenges face the recruiting team because of the focus on females and minorities?

EXERCISE 5.3*

Recruiting at Julia Richter's "Dressed for Success"

Overview

A proper recruiting plan is more than putting a résumé online. As an HR professional, you must think through the entire recruiting process. This exercise presents a typical company expansion with a need for staffing a new location.

Learning Objectives

After completing this exercise, you should be able to

1. Identify the essential steps in recruitment planning.
2. Suggest logical and efficient recruiting solutions.
3. Identify recruiting methods that promote diversity.

Procedure

Part A: Individual Analysis

Prior to class, read the background information on *Dressed for Success* in the scenario below. Think about the implications of this information for a current recruitment plan. Then answer the questions at the end of the exercise.

Part B: Group Analysis

In groups, members should review each other's recruitment plan, recruitment tools, and diversity recruitment tools. Reach a consensus on the best plan and tools for each question. Justify your recruitment tools with relevant research.

Scenario

Dressed for Success is a chain of clothing boutiques, located throughout the southeastern U.S.A. The chain has been in operation for 15 years and has seven stores. The stores sell a variety of women's designer clothes, shoes, and accessories. The owner has recently decided to expand operations into the Miami South Beach area. The new store will require a Store Manager and a minimum of five Sales Associates.

You have just (been) hired as the new Manager of Human Resources, responsible for (among many other things) ensuring adequate staffing levels at all store locations. The Fort Lauderdale store will open in four months. The Store manager will need 30 days to train, staff, and prepare the store for opening day.

The owner, Ms. Julia Richter, has given you the following KASOCs for each position:

Store Manager: 4-year college degree; 5 years' retail sales experience; minimum of 2 years' management experience.

Sales Associate: Minimum of 1 year sales experience (retail preferred); experience in upscale retail sales; and knowledge of designer apparel. Ms. Richter emphasizes that these KASOCs "seemed to work in the other stores."

The Store Manager will oversee all daily operations of the store. The position duties include: sales, preparation of daily sales and deposit report, maintaining store displays, inventory management, customer service, and also hiring, training, retain and supervising store employees. The Store Manager will receive a base salary of about $50,000 per year plus profit sharing.

The Sales Associates will be the front line sales staff. The position duties include: sales, customer service, restocking merchandise, and helping track inventory supplies. Associates will receive about $9.50 per hour plus 5 percent commission on individual sales.

Assignment

Develop a recruitment plan for both the Store Manager and Sales Associate positions. Provide a specific chronology of events. Address the following: (1) What three recruiting/advertising methods do you recommend for *Dressed for Success?* Ms. Richter specifically requests information about the costs and benefits of online recruiting and/or the use of a "headhunter" for the Store Manager job. She requests that you do research on this issue and take a firm position. Does the Internet provide any information about the compensation being considered for these jobs? (2) Ms. Richter is also concerned about diversity. What recruitment methods should be implemented to help increase diversity in the organization? (3) Ms. Richter wants your opinion of the salary levels she has set. Conduct Internet research to determine if what she is recommending is appropriate. She also wants to know if formal job descriptions should be written for the store manager job and the human resources manager. Write Ms. Richter a memo that addresses these issues.

[Handwritten notes: "o SALERY.COM o " Expert.com } WAGES"]

*Developed by Renee Fitzgerald.

EXERCISE 5.4
HR Planning at COMPTECH*

Overview

How does a company plan and respond to its human resource needs? What are the steps necessary to ensure that the company will have the right people in the right jobs? As stated in Chapter 5, HR planning is the forecasting of human resource needs in accordance with the company's strategic business planning. Proactive HR planning can be used to more effectively implement business strategies and react more swiftly to threats and challenges that may be encountered. For this exercise you will create such a plan for the profiled company, COMPTECH, INC.

Learning Objectives

After completing this exercise, you should be familiar with the process of HR planning, including:

1. Using an environmental scan to identify internal and external strengths, weaknesses, opportunities, and threats.
2. Conducting labor supply forecasts, labor demand forecasts, gap analysis, action planning, and controlling and evaluating the HR plan as it unfolds.
3. Tying all aspects of the HR plan together so that they work seamlessly with the business at hand.

Procedure

Part A: Individual Analysis

Before class, read the COMPTECH, INC. scenario and answer the questions on Form 5.4.1.

Part B: Group Analysis

The class should break into groups and then formulate an HR plan for COMPTECH.

1. Each group should take one of the five steps in HR planning: environmental scanning, labor demand forecasting, labor supply forecasting, gap analysis, and action planning.
2. Each group should meet and determine issues relevant to their assignment, and possible strategies for facing those issues.
3. After meeting separately, groups will then collaborate to complete an HR plan for COMPTECH, INC.

Scenario

BACKGROUND

Founded in 1980 by two "downsized" IBM software engineers, Maryland-based COMPTECH is credited by many analysts as being the inventor of the personal computer superstore concept. COMPTECH is the leader in the discount computer retail sales industry and America's largest personal computer retail outlet. The company operates over 350 stores in the United States and Canada and employs over 10,000 full-time associates.

HISTORY

When Jordan Green and Kyle Brown lost their positions at IBM in 1980, the wave of corporate downsizings in the United States had just begun. Green and Brown received generous severance packages from IBM and decided to go it on their own rather than begin second careers in another corporate environment. Working out of Green's home, they marketed themselves as "computer odd jobbers," primarily through word of mouth among friends and associates. Their first contract was to handle the weekend relocation of a small architectural firm owned by one of Jordan's tennis partners.

The partners set to work on a Friday afternoon, confident that neither would miss their Sunday morning tee time. Unfortunately, the job proved to be more complicated than it would have been inside IBM's corporate headquarters. Reconfiguring the client's network in the new location required several additional port hubs and LAN adapters. The nearest retail outlet was 60 miles away and would not open until Monday at 10:00 A.M. Green and Brown recognized a need for a retail personal computer outlet to cater to small businesses and self-employed professionals. That weekend, COMPTECH was born.

The first COMPTECH retail store was opened in Somers, New York in 1981 in leased warehouse space. The concept was promoted as a one-stop-shopping center for personal computer needs. The store carried personal computer equipment of all kinds and also offered installation, maintenance, training, and specialized technical services. Within six months, Green and Brown had a staff of eight and were looking for space to open a second location.

After opening their fifth store in the Northeast, the partners decided to expand nationwide. With financial backing from a venture capital group, they moved into every region of the United States During the next 12 years, COMPTECH experienced an average growth rate of 27 new stores per year. In 1990, the company acquired a chain of computer stores in Canada. By 2006, COMPTECH employed over 10,000 personnel across the U.S. and Canada.

COMPTECH went public in 1990 at $2.00 a share—by 1994, the stock was selling at $27.00 per share. In 2006, COMPTECH realized gross annual sales in excess of $10 billion. Exhibit 5.4.1 shows the company's domestic market share lead among its top competitors.

*Contributed by David Herst.

EXHIBIT 5.4.1

2005 U.S. PERSONAL COMPUTER RETAIL SALES

Competitor	Gross Sales ($ billions)
Dell.com	15
COMPTECH	10
Manufacturer Direct Sales	8
Warehouse Chains	7
Mail Order Companies	5
Retail Chains	3
Small Computer Stores	2
Total	50

While the company's meteoric rise was sparked by the growth in the work-at-home market and decreasing prices for personal computers, the unique strategy of combining a warehouse atmosphere with the highest levels of customer service must be credited as well. The company continues to build on that winning strategy.

In 2000, COMPTECH introduced its Newcomer's Club for customers buying their first computers. For a flat fee of $75, the customer receives installation service and a one hour in-home orientation training session. The newcomer's club helped boost personal computer sales by 5 percent nationwide during the holiday season. Last year, the company announced its trade-in program for personal computers. Customers will receive a credit of $250.00 towards the purchase of a new COMPTECH computer package when they trade in their old computer–no matter what make, year, or type. The computer packages consist of a computer, monitor, printer, scanner, and a small digital camera. COMPTECH is considering the possibility of developing warehouse type outlets for sales of the used computer components.

Shrinking margins on computer hardware and the success of the newcomer's club have prompted COMPTECH to expand into consumer services. This year the company plans to offer a service to install wireless home networking. A deal with the local cable and telephone companies to resell broadband Internet access has been in the works. COMPTECH plans on bundling the network installation with the reselling of broadband services. Management is also considering a comprehensive program aimed at the fast-growing telecommuting market. In addition, COMPTECH is pushing the high-margin printer cartridge business, but is finding it hard to compete with online stores such as Dell.com, which has an advantage in overhead.

COMPTECH continues to expand geographically, with plans to enter the South American, Eastern European, and perhaps Chinese markets in the next three years. COMPTECH plans to sell some of the used computers collected through the trade-in program in these emerging markets, as well as offer state-of-the art equipment for the upscale buyer. The company has also developed a state-of-the-art Web site. Of the 150 million American households with computers, 120 million are equipped with modems and connected to the Internet. Of these, 40 million have high speed, or broadband, Internet access. Because of low overhead associated with online sales, COMPTECH continues to push its Web-based store. The potential for online services, such as real-time computer assistance and online computer training for small businesses, are additional opportunities that the company is considering.

The COMPTECH Organization
THE RETAIL OPERATION

Because COMPTECH strives to maintain uniformity in each of the retail stores, layout and appearance are very similar from store to store and region to region. Corporate headquarters is responsible for planning and choosing models for store presentation; retail managers have little discretion in terms of merchandising approaches. Monthly floor plans for the stores are developed by corporate merchandising and distributed through the district managers. The stores, which range in size from 15,000–20,000 square feet, are brightly lit and project a high-tech efficiency look. The product line includes a wide variety of personal computers, peripherals, printers, and software. In 2006, the average COMPTECH retail store stocked about 3,500 kinds of computer and computer-related items. Sales were divided among product categories as follows:

Product Group	Percent of 2006 Revenues
Stationary Personal Computers	30%
Portable Personal Computers	22
Printers	18
Software	12
Peripherals	10
Technical Services	8

HUMAN RESOURCES

The organization structure that evolved at COMPTECH is very similar to most other large retail operations in the United States. Green is supported by seven Senior Vice Presidents (SVP's) in various functional areas as well as Vice Presidents (VP's) for Human Resources and Legal Services. The five Regional Vice Presidents (RVP's) are responsible for the Northeast, Southeast, Midwest, Northwest, and Southwest. Under each regional vice president are the District Managers (DMs). There are approximately 35 district managers. Each district manager is responsible for approximately 10 stores. Exhibit 5.4.2 shows COMPTECH's organizational structure for its U.S. operations.

EXHIBIT 5.4.2

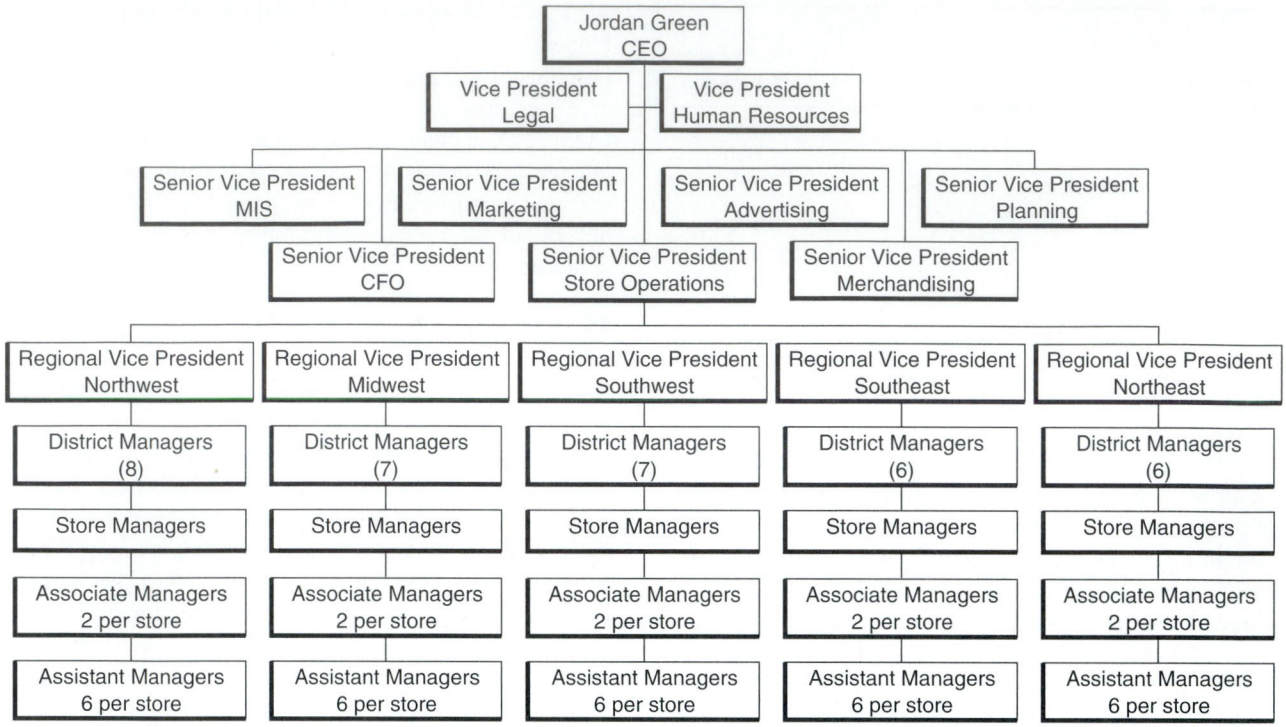

THE VICE PRESIDENTS

Vice presidents provide expert advice and strategic input to the president according to their functional area. They make sure that COMPTECH's information systems, marketing, store operations, advertising, merchandising, planning, and financing are all considered when developing and maintaining the business plan. They are directly responsible for providing expert knowledge within each functional area to the CEO on COMPTECH's strengths, weaknesses, opportunities, and threats. They are a vital part of both creating and implementing COMPTECH's business strategy.

THE REGIONAL VICE PRESIDENTS

Regional vice presidents (RVP) are responsible for developing strategies and goals for the region and helping the district managers develop implementation plans and schedules. They work closely with the vice presidents to determine overall business strategy, and to implement the strategy once it has been created. Regional vice presidents are directly responsible for all stores in their geographic area. They are also given some decision authority to pursue strategies tailored to their region.

THE DISTRICT MANAGER JOB

The job of the district manager is to participate in the development of the regional and district strategy, communicate corporate directives, and supervise and monitor store operations. DMs and regional vice presidents work together to develop implementation plans for marketing, budgeting, and purchasing. The DM has full responsibility for ensuring that the plans are implemented at the store level by communicating directives and monitoring progress of store management.

DMs screen, select, and evaluate all store managers and associate managers and conduct regular inspections of all the stores within the district. The DM is responsible for following up on monthly store performance reports to identify problem areas, develop plans, and solutions. The DMs oversight function is carried out primarily through conducting regular on-site visits, or "DM Audits" at each of the stores, and are an important component of the store managers' annual evaluations. The district manager is also responsible for selecting and evaluating the performance of all other management level personnel in the district.

THE STORE MANAGER JOB

The store manager (SM) provides the administrative and functional supervision of a store unit, including inventory control, sales and returns, vendor relations, cash management, and related reporting. The SM supervises all regular and/or temporary customer service and stock management staff. In addition, the SM manages the operation of a store unit, including purchasing of all supplies, special orders, receiving and shipping, and return of overstocked or defective merchandise. Finally, the store manager supervises personnel which typically include recommendations for hiring, firing, performance evaluation, training, work allocation, and problem resolution.

ASSOCIATE MANAGERS

Associate managers (AM) typically work as a second-in-charge to the store manager. They assist in the day-to-day running of the store by monitoring departments, conducting hiring interviews, evaluating sales associates, supervising assistant managers, conducting training, and scheduling employee shifts. They are also responsible for monitoring inventory levels and implementing sales initiatives.

ASSISTANT MANAGERS

Assistant managers run different departments within each store. They may be in charge of portable computers, software, networking, corporate sales, or customer service. Their primary functions include providing service to customers within their specialized area, monitoring trends, and advising the store manager on day-to-day operations within the store.

SALES ASSOCIATES

Sales associates are the first-line customer service and sales representatives for COMPTECH. They greet customers, assist them in making purchasing decisions, and advise them on their computer needs.

The company is known for its progressive human resource practices and emphasis on employee training. All COMPTECH sales associates receive a minimum of three weeks intensive training on COMPTECH's entire product line before joining the floor sales staff. Sales associates receive a base salary as well as incentive pay based on their sales performance. COMPTECH employees earn 10 percent more than their peers in similar organizations. Approximately 90 percent of the workforce at COMPTECH are full-time employees. Turnover in new stores averages about 40–50 percent for the first few months and then generally averages out to about 30 percent per year. A breakdown of employee trends since 2000 is presented in Table 5.4.1.

INDUSTRY CHALLENGES

Personal computer hardware has been the mainstay of COMPTECH's product line. The PC equipment market has matured, however, and further growth from that segment is not expected. Purchases of personal computers have begun to level off in the United States and growth is tied primarily to replacement sales. Many imitators have entered COMPTECH's market. BESTPRICE, a national retail chain offering computers and other electronic products as well as appliances, has been threatening COMPTECH's position in several key markets for some time. Other warehouse chains and even large retail department stores are expanding their personal computer departments. This is to say nothing of online direct sales companies such as Dell.com, who dominate the PC market in the United States. Finally, new technological developments, including access to rented disk time through telecommunications providers, are slowing the growth of the personal computer market.

Increasing competition and reduced revenues and profits have led to intense rivalry and price competition among computer retailers in the United States, and competition is increasing abroad as domestic companies begin to look beyond their home markets for new opportunities. The U.S. price wars that began in 1991 continue unabated, with suppliers forced to slash list prices, cut dealer margins and introduce lower-cost lines aimed at the home-user market.

Another trend that has had a negative impact on COMPTECH's business is the increasing tendency of computer manufacturers to use alternative channels for distribution of their product. Mail order catalogues, television home shopping channels, direct customer sales through third-party (e.g., Dell.com), manufacturer Web sites, and telemarketing operations are becoming common distribution mechanisms for PC's.

TABLE 5.4.1	Employee Staffing Trends 2000–2006						
Position	Staffing Levels	Sales Associate	Assistant Manager	Associate Manager	Store Manager	District Manager	Organizational Exit
Sales Associate	10,000	7,162	58				2,780
Assistant Manager	1,300		1,005	123			172
Associate Manager	780[a]		16	686	24		54[i]
Store Manager	450[b]			9	408	7	26[ii]
District Manager	42[c]				3	35	2[iii]

[a] 580 whites, 110 blacks, 90 Hispanics.
[b] 360 whites, 40 blacks, 50 Hispanics.
[c] 32 whites, 6 blacks, 4 Hispanics (2 DMs became RVPs).
[i] 10 whites, 32 blacks, 12 Hispanics.
[ii] 4 whites, 6 blacks, 16 Hispanics.
[iii] 0 whites, 1 black, 1 Hispanic.

The decline in growth of the personal computer equipment business has serious implications for COMPTECH. Meeting the challenge of competing in this environment means that every store must carefully monitor and match the price points of its competitors. The evolving multimedia technologies must be fully supported at each store, which could require significant employee retraining. The retail stores must generate growth through sales of peripherals, consumer and small business computer services, and perhaps most importantly, maintain their customer base by providing a flawless level of customer service. Attracting and retaining qualified technical personnel is vital to COMPTECH's success.

The challenge for COMPTECH is to find a way to sustain its growth without sacrificing its record of excellence in service. COMPTECH's corporate goal is to achieve 4–5 percent same-store gains in sales during each of the next five Fiscal Years. In the United States, small business sales/support and technical services are expected to be an important component of that growth.

Name _____   Group _____

1. What are the major SWOTs at COMPTECH? Use information from the chapter to determine the internal issues that will need attention. Review recent business trends in the retail computer sales sector and in the labor market in general (both domestic and foreign) to help you complete the environmental scan.

2. Determine the external labor supply available this year in five different states by using statistics from the Bureau of Labor Statistics (Web site www.bls.gov) or some other source. Employment statistics can be found at the State and Local Employment link under the Employment and Unemployment section. *HINT*: After clicking on the link, scroll down until you see the link for Create Customized Tables. These will help you find the applicable statistics.

3. What type, or types, of HR planning analysis do you propose for the data presented in Table 5.4.1? How do you propose to assess the internal trends in employee movement? Indicate what positions will require more training/retention efforts and which will require greater recruitment/selection efforts.

Name _____   Group _____

4. How would you use gap analysis for dealing with immediate HR issues and for HR planning?

5. COMPTECH executives set the goal of increasing the diversity of COMPTECH but there was no specificity to the goal. They have requested that you provide a game plan for achieving this goal. Provide a chronological outline of your strategy.

6. Given all of the data presented in the case, what is your chronological HR action plan for COMPTECH, INC?

Chapter 6 Exercises

EXERCISE 6.1

Should Tenneco Use the Wonderlic Test?

Overview

Although cognitive ability tests have been shown to be valid, they are likely to result in adverse impact against minorities because of test score differences. Recall our discussion in the text regarding the Wonderlic Personnel Test. The purpose of this exercise is to have the student consider the options available for dealing with the problem of a test that will probably cause adverse impact.

Learning Objectives

After completing this exercise, you should have a better understanding of the implications of the use of cognitive ability tests and should be capable of developing and articulating a rationale for the use of specific methods of selection.

Procedure

Part A: Individual Analysis

Before class, read the scenario presented below regarding the Tenneco Corporation and answer the questions on Form 6.1.1. Be prepared to defend your position in group discussion.

Part B: Group Analysis

In groups, each student should review the written responses of other members to the questions on Form 6.1.1. The group should then attempt to reach consensus on each of the questions. A written group response should be developed for each of the questions, and a group spokesperson should be designated to present the group's positions on the use of the test.

Scenario

Tenneco Corporation is considering the use of the *Wonderlic Personnel Test* (see www.wonderlic.com/products) as part of its selection process for assistant store managers. Each assistant store manager has management responsibilities for one convenience store. Responsibilities include complete supervision of at least 15 employees, including hiring, firing, and scheduling; budgetary matters; inventory; vendor deliveries; and customer issues. Tenneco hopes to maintain a policy of promotion from within and thus administered the Wonderlic to 400 store employees. A consultant from the Wonderlic Company recommends a particular minimum score of 24 for the assistant manager job. Based on the recommended passing score, the rate of passing (scoring at the minimum or higher) based on the ethnicity of the job candidates was as follows: Whites: 75 percent passed; Black: 51 percent passed; Hispanics: 58 percent passed; Asian or Pacific Islander: 83 percent passed; American Indian/Alaskan Native: 70 percent passed. The five-week training program at Tenneco headquarters has room for only 40 managerial trainees. The training is required for promotion to assistant store manager. As a new HRM personnel specialist, you have been asked to recommend a specific policy for the use of the Wonderlic and other possible selection procedures. Answer each of the questions on Form 6.1.1.

Name _____   Group _____

1. Assuming that only 40 candidates are to be selected for the training program, is adverse impact likely against minorities if the Wonderlic Personnel Test is used as the sole basis for entry into the training? Explain your answer.

2. Given your response to Question 1, what are the policy options for this situation? What policy do you recommend that Tenneco adopt for the use of the Wonderlic? Defend your response by considering the job situation, the need for further research, legal and social implications, and *alternative methods of selection*. Provide a detailed recommendation and rationale for action. If you take a position to drop the use of the Wonderlic, how do you propose to identify the 40 candidates?

3. What if you conducted a PAQ analysis that indicated that the Wonderlic was a valid test to use for this job? Do you believe that this result establishes the legality of the Wonderlic? Given that the Wonderlic consultant recommended the particular passing score, is Tenneco on safe legal ground if candidates are selected based on that Wonderlic passing score?

4. Could Tenneco convert each raw score on the Wonderlic to a percentile based on the ethnicity of the test taker? How might such a policy affect adverse impact? Is it legal?

5. Tenneco is also considering a Bachelor's degree in business as a required job specification. Do you agree or disagree with this requirement? Explain your answer.

6. Another suggestion is to review the *Wonderlic* test and to remove all culturally biased questions to eliminate the adverse impact. Do you agree with this suggestion? Explain your answer.

EXERCISE 6.2

Hiring a Plant Manager at Dynamo Industries*

Overview

Personnel selection decisions are typically made based on a collection of information from several sources. An organization may have test scores, previous performance appraisals, interview ratings, biographical information, and other data on the candidates. This exercise gives the student a feel for making a final recommendation based on such a collection of data. In addition, through the group interaction, students should gain an understanding of the process involved in a leaderless group discussion.

Your assignment is to review candidate credentials for the plant manager positions at Dynamo Industries in Pittsburgh.

Learning Objectives

After completing this exercise, you should be able to

1. Distinguish candidate information that is valuable and should be considered in the decision from that which should be ignored.
2. Articulate your rationale for decisions.
3. Suggest ways in which the selection process could be improved.
4. Understand the dynamics of a leaderless group discussion.

Procedure

Part A: Individual Analysis

Before class, review the material presented below. Assume the following:

You are the vice president of personnel. You are to write a report (a one-page executive summary followed by *no more* than two pages of supporting information) that includes the following:

a. A rank ordering of your top three choices for the Pittsburgh job based on the information you have now.
b. An *in-depth* discussion of how this rank ordering was reached (a rationale for some candidates being ranked higher than others and for others not being ranked). As part of this analysis, comment on the recommendation by the Ad Hoc committee on Diversity that Mr. Jackson should be hired since he meets the minimum qualifications and Dynamo has an affirmative action program.
c. A discussion of how the selection process for hiring a plant manager should be changed in the future (e.g., additional selection devices to use,

additional information to gather, sources to drop or change). Be specific in your recommendations.
d. A request for whatever additional information you would like to have regarding the process or the candidates, or issues that should be considered that could affect your rank-orderings. Your instructor may stipulate that requests for additional information may be e-mailed prior to the class meeting.

This report will be sent to the vice president of production and to the president of Dynamo Industries. Bring this report to class.

Part B: Group Analysis

Groups should be charged with reaching a consensus on the rank ordering of the top four candidates. Each member should be given an opportunity to review the others' written reports. The instructor will designate the time to be allotted to this process and will provide additional information on request. In addition, each group should reach consensus on the changes to be made for hiring the plant manager in the future.

Scenario

Dynamo Industries is a medium-sized manufacturer of small electrical motors headquartered in St. Paul, Minnesota. The firm employs 9,800 people. Dynamo Industries has plants in St. Paul; Columbus, Ohio; Atlanta; San Diego; Pittsburgh; Providence, Rhode Island; and Little Rock, Arkansas. All these plants are unionized, although the power of the respective unions varies greatly.

Recently, the company has been trying to hire a new plant manager (see job description in Exhibit 6.2.1) for the Pittsburgh plant (plant managers report directly to the vice president of production). Although Dynamo Industries has experienced slightly above-average growth and profit compared to its competitors, the Pittsburgh plant has been a trouble spot. Over the past three years, production costs there have been extremely high and there has been labor strife (e.g., numerous work slowdowns, an excessive number of grievances filed). The most recent Pittsburgh plant manager was terminated, although by mutual agreement, the company stated he left for a better job with another company. Because of the importance of the plant manager position, Dynamo Industries has used several expensive selection devices. These devices are detailed below. After a thorough recruitment effort (both within and outside the company) and some initial screening, the list of job candidates has been reduced to eight names. Exhibit 6.2.2 contains extensive information on each of the eight candidates.

*Contributed by James A. Breaugh.

Dynamo Industries does not have an established philosophy for filling job openings. In the past, it has favored promotion from within the company. However, the vice president of production was hired externally. Dynamo has no policy on lateral transfers. In the recent past, such transfers have been rare. The key issue seems to be whether the company benefits from the transfer.

EXHIBIT 6.2.1

PLANT MANAGER JOB DESCRIPTION

(Written by the vice president of production)

The plant manager (PM) is ultimately responsible for the operating efficiency of the entire plant. In fulfilling his/her responsibilities, the PM regularly consults with subordinate supervisory personnel (the PM frequently delegates duties). A plant manager must be somewhat knowledgeable of production methods and the capabilities of equipment. Some of the activities the plant manager is directly or indirectly involved in include

1. Procuring materials.
2. Maintaining the plant.
3. Controlling quality.
4. Using manpower.
5. Establishing budgets.
6. Revising production schedules because of equipment failure or operation problems.
7. Consulting with engineering personnel concerning the modification of machinery to improve production quantity, the quality of products, and employee safety.
8. Conducting hearings to resolve employee grievances.
9. Participating in union–management contract negotiations.
10. Ensuring safety.
11. Establishing community relations.

EXHIBIT 6.2.2

BACKGROUND INFORMATION ON THE CANDIDATES

1. *George Martin*—age 44. Education: B.A., University of Wisconsin; M.A. (Industrial Relations), Cornell University. He is a plant manager of a relatively small (580 nonunion employees) plant (located in Cleveland) of one of Dynamo's competitors. Martin has held that job for the past six years. He has been with that company for 14 years. No reference information was gathered because Martin was concerned about his present employer's reaction.

2. *Tony Caciopo*—age 59. Education: high school graduate. He is an assistant plant manager (Providence). Caciopo has been with Dynamo for 24 years. He has been assistant plant manager in Providence for the past 10 years. He had a severe heart attack four years ago but appears to have recovered. Ten years ago, he was offered a job as plant manager by Dynamo but turned it down because of health problems his wife was having.

3. *Kathy Joyce*—age 36. Education: B.A., Indiana University. She is currently plant manager of the Little Rock plant. She desires a lateral transfer because it would enhance job opportunities for her husband. Joyce has been with Dynamo for five years. She has been plant manager at Little Rock for two years.

4. *Barry Fein*—age 49. Education: associate degree (2 years) from Morehead State University. Until two months ago, Fein was plant manager at a large, unionized textile plant. Two months ago, the company Fein worked for discontinued this product line and he was let go. Fein had been with his former company for 20 years and was plant manager for 5 years. His letters of reference were excellent.

5. *Ron Jackson*—age 33. Education: B.A., Howard University; M.B.A., Northwestern. He is currently an assistant plant manager at the Pittsburgh plant. He has been with the company for four years; he has been assistant plant manager for two years. He has served as acting plant manager at Pittsburgh for the past two months.

6. *Jay Davis*—age 46. Education: B.A., Harvard; M.B.A., Harvard. He is currently assistant plant manager (Atlanta). Davis has been with Dynamo for 10 years; the past 7 years he has been assistant plant manager (6 years in St. Paul, the past year in Atlanta).

7. *Frank Hall*—age 58. Education: B.S. (chemistry), Duke University. He is currently vice president for production for one of Dynamo's major competitors. He says he seeks a demotion so that he is required to travel less. He has been vice president of production for six years. Before that, he was a plant manager for 12 years. The plant was organized. No reference information is available. However, he has received outstanding reviews in trade publications for his performance as vice president.

8. *Tom Doyle*—age 36. Education: B.A., Williams College; M.B.A., University of Chicago. For the past two years, Tom has worked as a special assistant to the vice president of production. Before this he was an assistant PM for two years and a PM (Little Rock) for three years. Tom was the youngest PM ever appointed at Dynamo. He was very ineffective as a PM and after three years was removed from this position.

EXHIBIT 6.2.3
PERSONALITY PROFILE

Each of the eight candidates was examined by a psychiatrist. In addition to interviewing each candidate, the psychiatrist utilized personality tests (e.g., 16PF, the Myers-Briggs Type Indicator, and the Thematic Apperception Test) in drawing the following conclusions.

CANDIDATES' RATINGS

	High	**Medium**	**Low**
Ability to handle stress	Martin Caciopo Davis	Joyce Jackson Fein Doyle	Hall
Ability to resolve conflict	Joyce Davis Caciopo	Martin Doyle Hall	Fein Jackson
Interpersonal skills	Martin Joyce	Hall Jackson Caciopo	Davis Fein Doyle
Most likely to succeed as a plant manager	Martin Caciopo Davis	Joyce Doyle Hall Jackson	Fein

EXHIBIT 6.2.4
INTERVIEWERS' RATINGS

	Vice President Production	**Vice President Personnel**	**Columbus Plant Manager**	**Atlanta Plant Manager**
George Martin	6.5	6	5.5	4
Tony Caciopo	5	5.5	4.5	6
Kathy Joyce	6	6.5	5	5.5
Barry Fein	4	4	3	4
Ron Jackson	5	5.5	4.5	5
Jay Davis	4.5	5	3.5	6.5
Frank Hall	6.5	7	Interviewer on vacation day of interview	4
Tom Doyle	5.5	6	4.5	6

Note: Each of the interviewers went through a one-day interview training program. The vice president of production's interviews averaged three hours in length. The other interviews averaged 60 minutes in length. Interview ratings were made on a seven-point scale (1 = poor candidate . . . 7 = excellent candidate). All interviews were semistructured.

EXHIBIT 6.2.5

INTELLIGENCE TESTS AND HANDWRITING
ANALYSES

Candidate	Intelligence Test	Handwriting Rating
George Martin	119	+3
Tony Caciopo	116	+1
Kathy Joyce	141	−1
Barry Fein	122	0
Ron Jackson	114	+2
Jay Davis	148	+2
Frank Hall	112	+3
Tom Doyle	125	+3

Note: The intelligence test (Wechsler Adult Intelligence Scale) given by
Dynamo Industries is commonly used for selecting candidates for
management. Individuals scoring below 115 tend not to do well in managerial
jobs. Standard error equals 3.5.

   The handwriting analyst rated the plant manager candidates in terms of
their likelihood of success as the Pittsburgh plant manager (−3 = very poor
prospect . . . +3 = very strong prospect).

EXHIBIT 6.2.6

PROMOTABILITY RATINGS, PERFORMANCE RATINGS, AND WORK SAMPLE SCORES

Candidate	Promotability	Performance	Work Sample Score
George Martin	Not available	NA	19.5
Tony Caciopo	6	5	15.5
Kathy Joyce	5	6	18.5
Barry Fein	NA	NA	18.5
Ron Jackson	5.5	6	18
Jay Davis	7	7	16.5
Frank Hall	NA	NA	19
Tom Doyle	5.5	6	17.5

Note: A promotability rating was made as part of the annual performance review (7 = ready for immediate promotion . . . 1 = should not be promoted). The
performance rating ranges from 1 = poor performance . . . 7 = exceptional performance. As part of the selection process, all applicants went through a series of
work sample tests (i.e., in-basket, leaderless group discussion, and production planning exercise). Scoring was done by trained raters from the personnel department
(20 = highest possible score).

EXERCISE 6.3

What Questions Can You Ask in an Interview?*

Overview

Chapter 6 describes the potential legal liability inherent in the employment interview. Given the subjective nature of the process and the discretion interviewers typically exercise in the interview, there is great opportunity for biases that could be interpreted as violations of any number of state, federal, or local laws on equal opportunity. This exercise explores the potential legal implications of a number of questions often posed by interviewers. The student may want to review Chapter 3 before attempting this exercise.

Learning Objectives

After completing this exercise, you should be able to

1. Identify those interview questions that are of questionable legality.
2. Know the major laws that may affect the interview process.

Procedure

Part A: Individual Analysis

Before class, check whether each question on Form 6.3.1 is acceptable or should be avoided during an employment interview. For those questions that you consider to be illegal or *potentially* illegal, in the space below the question, provide a justification for your position, citing an applicable law or regulation where appropriate. Rewrite any questions that could yield useful information. Also, before class, do the Assessment Questions (page 542).

Part B: Group Analysis

In groups, students should compare responses on each item and decide on a group response and justification for each. The items should then be divided among the students so that each group member is prepared to present the group position on the set of items. Also, the group should compose a response to each of the assessment questions for this exercise. Class discussion will focus on group responses to each item and possible discrepancies in the correct answers.

---

*Contributed by Robert W. Eder and M. Ronald Buckley.

Name _____   Group _____

Question Is Acceptable	Question Should Be Avoided	
_____	_____	1. Would you mind if I called you by your first name?
_____	_____	2. Are you a citizen of the United States?
_____	_____	3. Are you married or do you live with someone?
_____	_____	4. Have you ever been arrested?
_____	_____	5. What professional societies do you belong to?
_____	_____	6. What kinds of people do you enjoy working with the most?
_____	_____	7. Are you planning to start a family soon?
_____	_____	8. How long do you expect your husband will remain here before changing jobs?
_____	_____	9. I can't help but notice the great shape you've kept yourself in. How do you do it?
_____	_____	10. We're looking for someone who can relate effectively with college students; you're 52?
_____	_____	11. Have you ever been convicted of a crime (beyond traffic violations)?
_____	_____	12. Will your family or personal obligations interfere with your ability to keep the hours of this job?
_____	_____	13. How does your military experience relate to this job?
_____	_____	14. What are your religious beliefs?

_____   _____   15. How do you feel about getting personally involved with someone at work?

_____   _____   16. Would you be willing to work on Yom Kippur?

_____   _____   17. How long have you lived around here?

_____   _____   18. Are you a smoker or a nonsmoker?

_____   _____   19. Are you a homosexual?

_____   _____   20. What plans do you have for taking care of the children if you get this job?

_____   _____   21. Do you consider yourself handicapped in any way?

_____   _____   22. Is there any history of chronic illness in your family?

_____   _____   23. One of your references mentioned that you have a history of depression. Is this still a problem?

_____   _____   24. Given that you are in a wheelchair, how do you think you'll be able to do this work?

_____   _____   25. Do you think marijuana should be legalized?

_____   _____   26. Do you believe that corporate management has too much political power?

_____   _____   27. Do you support gay marriage?

_____   _____   28. Have you ever belonged to a labor union?

_____   _____   29. Do you have any family members (parents, siblings) who belong (or have belonged) to labor unions?

_____   _____   30. Are you willing to work without your hijab (head scarf)? It might offend our customers.

EXERCISE 6.3
ASSESSMENT QUESTIONS

Name _____

1. How would you design a training program so that future interviewers would understand what can and cannot be asked in an employment interview?

2. If your organizational research had clearly established (with data) that women with children under the age of five are more likely to be absent from work than others, could the company then use this information to make decisions?

3. How would you design a structured, situational, or behavioral interview for an overseas assignment? Based on the evidence, is the situational or the behavioral more valid?

EXERCISE 6.3 (*Continued*)

4.   Discuss the ethical and legal implications of asking applicants about the health history of family members. Setting aside the possible legal issues, should a company take family health into consideration when evaluating an applicant?

5.   Relative to alternative methods of selection, what role should an interview play in the selection of retail assistant managers? If you use more than one method, how would you go about weighing the information?

6.   A colleague suggests that you do not have to develop a structured, behavioral interview as long as you get at least three colleagues to do independent, unstructured interviews and then evaluate candidates. Do you agree with the colleague?

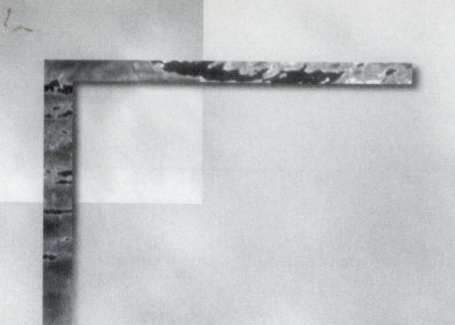

Chapter 7 Exercises

EXERCISE 7.1

Performance-Appraisal Feedback: A Role-Play Exercise*

Overview

As described in Chapter 7, the performance-appraisal process is a key human resource management function. The face-to-face performance feedback session can be an important part of this process because it allows the rater and ratee to thoroughly discuss the appraisal ratings. It also enables them to derive some developmental suggestions to improve the ratee's performance. This exercise provides an opportunity to role-play a face-to-face performance feedback session.

Learning Objectives

After completing this exercise, you should be able to

1. Understand and apply general guidelines for providing performance feedback.
2. Understand and apply guidelines for the observation of behavior.
3. Evaluate the effectiveness of a performance-appraisal feedback session.

Procedure

Part A: Analysis

Step 1. Each student should read Exhibits 7.1.1, 7.1.2, and 7.1.3 before class. Based on the discussion in Chapter 7, write a one-page critique on the performance form and the extent to which it will help with the feedback process.

Step 2. In class, the instructor will set up teams of three individuals. You will be assigned one of three roles: feedback giver, recipient, and observer of the feedback giver. If you have been assigned the role of feedback giver (Chris Williams), then carefully review Exhibit 7.1.1 and make notes about the content and message of the feedback

you will give to one of your subordinates, Jesse Anderson. Also, review Exhibit 7.1.2, the guidelines for providing feedback. If you have been assigned the role of feedback recipient, then you are Jesse Anderson, the subordinate. Your supervisor, Chris Williams, will be setting up a meeting to discuss your performance. If you have been assigned the role of observer, you should review Exhibits 7.1.2 and 7.1.3 so you can accurately observe and take notes on the feedback giver's behavior in the appraisal session.

Part B: Role-Play

The person assuming the role of Chris Williams, the supervisor, will call Jesse Anderson, the subordinate, into Chris's office and provide the feedback to Jesse in about 15 minutes. The observer will take notes during the feedback session.

Part C: Feedback

After the role-play has been completed, the observer should share his or her observations with the feedback giver. The intent is to give some constructive and positive information to the feedback giver to enhance that person's appraisal skills in the future. Feedback recipients also may want to offer their own perspectives on how comfortable they felt with the feedback session and whether or not they felt motivated to improve their performance after receiving the feedback.

Part D: Class Discussion

The class as a whole should discuss the types of behaviors they observed that were characteristic of effective and ineffective appraisal sessions. The instructor could chart their responses.

---

*Contributed by Sharon L. Wagner, Richard G. Moffett III, and Catherine M. Westberry.

EXHIBIT 7.1.1

PERFORMANCE-APPRAISAL FORM

SOUTHEAST BANK AND TRUST (CONFIDENTIAL)

Name of Employee:	*Jesse Anderson*	Date:	12/5/98
Name of Supervisor:	*Chris Williams*	Dept:	S-2

Directions: Please rate each factor based on observed behaviors. Answer as honestly and accurately as you can. Provide comments for especially poor or outstanding performance.

Job knowledge: Technical knowledge required to perform the job; skills in implementing policies and procedures; effectively using resources and equipment.

1	(2)	3	4	5
Unsatisfactory	Marginal	Acceptable	Above average	Outstanding

Comments: Has occasionally used the wrong equipment, seems to be uninformed about some of the company's procedures.

Interpersonal skills: Works well with others; displays helpfulness and cooperation with internal and external customers; effectively handles conflict of interests and difficult customers.

1	2	3	(4)	5
Unsatisfactory	Marginal	Acceptable	Above average	Outstanding

Comments: Coworkers and customers have consistently commented on how Jesse gets along with most everyone. A number of situations have arisen in the department that Jesse was instrumental in resolving.

Work quality: The quality of the work including aspects of completeness and thoroughness; adherence to company and organizational standards.

(1)	2	3	4	5
Unsatisfactory	Marginal	Acceptable	Above average	Outstanding

Comments: Has turned in several projects that needed considerable revisions and rework.

Reliability: Can be counted on to attend meetings punctually; turn in assignments when due; and volunteer to assist others in projects.

(1)	2	3	4	5
Unsatisfactory	Marginal	Acceptable	Above average	Outstanding

Comments: Has missed most departmental meetings; has consistently come to work late in the past few months; is difficult to find when help is needed on projects.

Quantity of work: Meets company and departmental standards for production.

1	2	(3)	4	5
Unsatisfactory	Marginal	Acceptable	Above average	Outstanding

Comments: Productivity has been acceptable.

EXHIBIT 7.1.2

GUIDELINES FOR PROVIDING PERFORMANCE-APPRAISAL FEEDBACK

1. Inform the employee about the purpose of the meeting. Describe the procedure that you will be following. Attempt to establish rapport with the ratee. You may want to inform the ratee that you may be taking some notes (i.e., ask if that is OK).

2. Focus on describing the ratee's behaviors. Avoid evaluating or blaming the ratee.

3. Be sure to indicate effective behaviors (i.e., praise the employee's strengths) as well as ineffective behaviors. Probe for specific causes of the employee's problem areas (e.g., why s/he believes s/he has a particular performance problem).

4. Be sure to make specific references to the appraisal form and ratings.

5. Discuss specific plans of action for improving the employee's deficiencies.

6. Jointly set developmental goals for the employee. Make sure you reach agreement with the employee regarding performance expectations and goals.

7. Strive to make your nonverbal behavior match your verbal message (i.e., maintain eye contact, maintain good posture, avoid use of uhs and uhms).

8. Provide feedback on each behavioral dimension, giving clear behavioral examples of performance to support the ratings.

9. Periodically check the ratee's understanding of the feedback you provide.

10. Answer any questions fully and politely. Remember that the only useful feedback is high-quality feedback.

11. Summarize the content of the feedback session.

12. Set a date for a future meeting to assess progress toward the goals.

13. Keep in mind that feedback directed at the *person* and away from the *task* will *decrease* the effectiveness of the feedback.

14. Feedback designed to be demoralizing is most likely to have detrimental effects.

15. Negative feedback focused on the *task* (not the *person*) can have positive effects a performance.

EXHIBIT 7.1.3

GUIDELINES FOR OBSERVING BEHAVIOR

1. Focus on observing the behavior of the rater, and, secondarily, the behavior of the ratee (i.e., how he/she responds to the rater).

2. Record the behaviors you observe (i.e., things that the role-players do and say). Don't make judgments about the behaviors. For example, write "sat back in his chair with his arms folded," rather than "acted uninterested."

3. Try to record verbatim statements from the role-player whenever possible, particularly statements that indicate exceptionally good or poor performance.

4. In addition to recording statements made by the role-players, be sure to observe and record nonverbal behavior, tone of voice, eye contact, body posture (e.g., leaning forward to show interest).

EXERCISE 7.2

The Heartland Greeting Cards Consulting Problem*

Overview

Employee turnover is a costly problem for employers. After spending considerable money recruiting, selecting, and training employees, it is costly to have to replace them. Sometimes the selection process is faulty, allowing the wrong candidates to be accepted and subsequently leave the firm. Other times, the performance-appraisal system is ineffective at providing valuable feedback to employees, and they become dissatisfied and leave the firm. The current exercise builds from material presented in Chapters 7 and 6. Students will have the opportunity to use job analysis information to refine the company's selection and performance-appraisal systems.

Learning Objectives

After completing this exercise, you should be able to

1. Review job specification and job analysis information to determine the important attributes that a selection tool should be based on.
2. Design a performance-appraisal system given job analysis information and critical organizational goals for the position.

Procedure

Part A: Individual Analysis

Step 1. Read the background information on the company and the job provided in Exhibit 7.2.1. Also, review the job analysis information provided for the merchandiser job provided in Exhibit 7.2.2.

Step 2. Referring back to Chapter 6, offer some ideas for selection tools that can be used to determine if applicants possess the job specifications. Complete Form 7.2.1.

Step 3. Offer some ideas for the performance appraisal system that can be used for the merchandiser position. Complete Form 7.2.2.

Part B: Group Analysis

In groups, discuss your recommendations for the selection and performance-appraisal systems. As a group, consolidate your ideas and draft plans for the selection and complete performance-appraisal systems. Be prepared to share your group's ideas with the class. Ask the instructor for information that could affect the positions you take.

EXHIBIT 7.2.1

COMPANY BACKGROUND INFORMATION

Heartland Greeting Cards, Inc., is a national greeting card company that is based out of St. Louis, Missouri. Heartland provides cards, stationery, gift wrap, and party favors to drug, grocery, and retail stores. One of Heartland's main competitors is Hammonds Greeting Cards, which has its own specialty stores as well as accounts in department stores and drugstores. Patriot Greeting Cards, Heartland's other major competitor, also has accounts in department, drug, and grocery stores, and it has recently moved into direct competition with Hammonds by opening its own specialty stores. Heartland has not yet entered into this arena, so it must keep its existing accounts and open new accounts to survive. The competition between these three companies is intense. A common tactic is for one company's sales representative to visit a store with a competitor's account and point out deficiencies in the existing service. Heartland's selling point is "no inventory in the store" guarantee.

The greeting card merchandiser is the employee who interacts most with the store managers (the manager responsible for all the store operations) and store customers. Therefore, it is crucial that each merchandiser maintain his or her card department in top condition to keep the store manager happy.

EXISTING SELECTION PROCEDURES

Most job applicants for the greeting card merchandiser position are recruited through employee referrals. Local newspaper ads are the other major source of applicants. Heartland has experienced the most success with employee referrals. Heartland has always had a serious problem with employee turnover and suspects that poor selection practices may be part of the problem.

EXISTING PERFORMANCE-APPRAISAL SYSTEM

Currently, Heartland has no formal performance-appraisal system. A greeting card merchandiser's performance is evaluated by unannounced spot checks conducted by the area manager (a Heartland employee who manages 23 merchandisers who service 70 stores in a 65-mile radius). These spot checks are often as infrequent as once every three weeks and usually occur when the greeting card merchandiser is not in the store. The merchandiser receives no feedback as to the results of these checks unless there is a problem. Merchandisers often cite lack of feedback about their performance on the job as a major source of frustration. You suspect that the lack of feedback also may be contributing to Heartland's high turnover rate.

---

*Contributed by Esther J. Long.

EXHIBIT 7.2.2

JOB ANALYSIS

Job Title: Greeting card merchandiser   **D.O.T Code:** 299.367-014

Duties Comprising a Routine Service Call

(Conducted two to five times a week per store depending on each store's sales volume and seasonal demand.)
1. Contacts the store manager to discuss any problems and determine if any new merchandise has arrived.
2. Checks in all new merchandise according to store procedure so that all items on the invoice are accounted for.
3. Unpacks all new merchandise and prices the soft goods (stationery, party favors, gift wrap, etc.) with a price gun.
4. Returns all cards and merchandise to their designated holders and puts new merchandise on display so that reorder needs can be determined to uphold the "no inventory in the store" guarantee.
5. Orders new merchandise as needed according to Heartland's company procedures and documents any such orders.
6. Fills all empty pockets with discontinued or "extra" cards and merchandise so that a "well-stocked" appearance is maintained.
7. Dusts and cleans card fixtures.

Seasonal Duties

1. Orders seasonal merchandise (e.g., Christmas, Valentine's Day), so it arrives just in time to display on the dates determined by Heartland's company headquarters in St. Louis.
2. Sets up all seasonal displays promptly (there is no place to store excess inventory) and replenishes them as needed.
3. Takes down all seasonal displays the day after the season ends and replaces them with novelty displays.
4. Takes inventory of all leftover seasonal goods and prepares a credit voucher for the store using the SMI forms.
5. Packages all merchandise that needs to be returned to headquarters and mails it.

SUPERVISION RECEIVED

Proximity	Frequency
Visual	Constant
Physical separation	Hourly
Geographical separation X	Daily
	Weekly
	Less than weekly X

Personal Contacts

Brief contact on a daily basis with store managers and occasionally with other store employees. No contact with other Heartland employees except the area manager.

Work Schedule

Hours vary according to the number of stores one is responsible for (usually a minimum of two), sales volume for a particular store, and seasonal demand. Work must be performed during the stores' regular operating hours. A merchandiser sets his or her own work schedule.

Physical Demands

Standing	X	Note: Must stand for up to three hours at a time.
Walking	X	
Crawling	X	
Stooping	X	
Kneeling	X	
Reaching	X	
Lifting	X	

Physical Environment

Indoors	X	Note: Typically a merchandiser services two or more stores. A person must provide his or her
Outdoors		own transportation from one store to the next.
Other	X	

EXHIBIT 7.2.2 (*Continued*)

Organizational Goals	Job Performance Criteria
1. Heartland's "no inventory in the store" promise is upheld while maintaining a well-stocked appearance.	• New merchandise is on order when a pocket contains less than three items. • No more than 5 percent of the pockets are empty at any given time. • Only merchandise that has arrived within the past four days can be found in the stockroom. Exception: seasonal displays may arrive one week in advance of assembly date. • No inventory is in the under stock drawers except for duplicates that do not fit on the displays.
2. Each store receives the services described in its contract with Heartland Greeting Cards.	• Layout of card department corresponds with blueprint of layout contracted for (training by the area manager is necessary to read the greeting card department blueprints). • Seasonal merchandise is set up according to the procedures provided in Heartland's service manual by Heartland's designated deadline.
3. No lost customer accounts due to poor customer service.	• Contacts store manager every time a service call is made and resolves any problems that may arise. • Is courteous to store manager, employees, and customers. • Prices all soft goods (e.g., stationery, wrapping paper) according to store procedures. • Follows all store procedures (these may vary from store to store) for checking in merchandise, doing inventory, and returning merchandise. • Fixtures are kept clean and displays are free of stray merchandise from other departments. • Seasonal displays are removed within two days of the end of the season. • Leftover seasonal merchandise is inventoried, packaged, and returned to headquarters within one week of the end of the season.

FORM 7.2.1

DESIGN OF A SELECTION INSTRUMENT

Identify at least one selection method that could be used to assess whether a candidate possesses each of the job specifications listed below. Refer back to Chapter 6 for guidance and the material presented in Exhibits 7.2.1 and 7.2.2.

Job specifications (minimum qualifications)

1. Mathematical ability to carry out calculations involving addition, subtraction, multiplication, and division of three digits or more including fractions and decimals. Note: Mathematical computations must be carried out when checking in merchandise or completing inventory. Calculators may be used.
    Assessment method:

2. A 12th-grade reading level in English. Note: The service manual is written at the 12th-grade reading level.
    Assessment method:

3. Ability to attend to details. Note: To minimize the in-store inventory, the company blueprint for each display must be followed precisely. Each set of cards has a pocket where it is supposed to be displayed (the numerical codes on the back of the cards must match the codes on the pocket labels).
    Assessment method:

4. Ability to carry out company procedures while adapting to situational needs. Note: A person must have the ability to make snap decisions on the spot.
    Assessment method:

5. Ability to resolve customer (i.e., store manager) complaints while maintaining good will.
    Assessment method:

6. Basic body mobility (e.g., ability to bend, reach, lift) and ability to stand for up to three hours at a time. Note: A person with a disability (in a wheelchair) could be accommodated.
    Assessment method:

7. Ability to work alone with no supervision for weeks at a time.
    Assessment method:

8. Must provide own transportation to all stores.
    Assessment method:

FORM 7.2.2

DESIGN OF A PERFORMANCE-APPRAISAL SYSTEM

Name _____   Group _____

Your assignment is to develop plans for a comprehensive performance-appraisal system for the merchandiser job at Heartland Greeting Cards. Decisions you must make include the following:

1. Who should be responsible for evaluating the greeting card merchandiser's performance?

2. What rating format(s) will allow you to incorporate the job performance criteria identified in the job analysis directly into the rating form? Explain your answer. Prepare a sample rating form. Write one rating item. Be sure to include the complete rating scale.

3.   What techniques do you recommend to ensure that the greeting card merchandiser is provided with accurate and timely feedback concerning his or her performance. Explain your answer.

4.   What other components of the PA system will help make it more legally defensible? Explain your answer.

EXERCISE 7.3
Price Waterhouse v. Hopkins

Overview

This exercise familiarizes students with an important Supreme Court case related to performance appraisal and the implications of the case in terms of appraisal system development, implementation, and administration.

Learning Objectives

After completing this exercise, you should be able to

1. Understand the importance of performance appraisal for EEO litigation.
2. Suggest methods of performance appraisal that are legally defensible and will result in the most valid results for the organization.
3. Understand what methods could be used to make staffing (e.g., promotion) decisions.

Procedure

Part A: Individual Analysis

Step 1. You have been retained as a consultant to advise Price Waterhouse on matters related to a lawsuit against it and methods that could be adopted to prevent further legal action against the company.

Review the actual case, which is summarized in Exhibit 7.3.1.

Step 2. Prepare a one-page report to the vice president of human resources for Price Waterhouse that addresses the following issues: (1) Explain in detail whether you believe that Hopkins was a victim of illegal discrimination; (2) the steps that can be taken with the method of selecting partners to prevent a reoccurrence of this problem. Include a critique of the current system and specific recommendations for change. Be sure to include recommendations for how performance is evaluated for partners and how appraisal data are used for making promotion decisions. Also, complete Form 7.3.1 and bring it to class.

Part B: Group Analysis

In small groups, review the written recommendations of each group member and reach consensus on the specific recommendations you would propose for changing the system. Each group member should review responses to Form 7.3.1. One group representative should present the findings to the class.

EXHIBIT 7.3.1

BACKGROUND CASE INFORMATION ON PRICE WATERHOUSE

At Price Waterhouse, a nationwide professional accounting partnership, a senior manager becomes a candidate for partnership when the partners in the local office submit his or her name as a candidate. All the other partners in the firm are then invited to submit written comments on each candidate—either on a long or a short form, depending on the partner's degree of knowledge about the candidate. Not every partner in the firm submits comments on every candidate. After reviewing the comments and interviewing the partners who submitted them, the firm's admissions committee makes a recommendation to the policy board. This recommendation will be that the firm either accept the candidate for partnership, put the application on hold, or deny the promotion. The policy board then decides whether to submit the candidate's name to the entire partnership for a vote, to hold the candidacy, or to reject the candidate. The recommendation of the admissions committee and the decision of the policy board are not controlled by fixed guidelines: A certain number of positive comments from partners will not guarantee a candidate's admission to the partnership, nor will a specific quantity of negative comments necessarily defeat the application. Price Waterhouse places no limit on the number of persons it will admit to the partnership in any given year.

Ann Hopkins had worked at Price Waterhouse's Office of Government Services in Washington, D.C., for five years when the partners in that office proposed her as a candidate for partnership. Of the 662 partners at the firm at that time, 7 were women. Of the 88 persons proposed for partnership that year, only 1—Hopkins—was a woman. Forty-seven of these candidates were admitted to the partnership, 21 were rejected, and 20—including Hopkins—were held for reconsideration the following year. Thirteen of the 32 partners who had submitted

comments on Hopkins supported her bid for partnership. Three partners recommended that her candidacy be placed on hold, eight stated that they did not have an informed opinion about her, and eight recommended that she be denied partnership.

In a jointly prepared statement supporting her candidacy, the partners in Hopkins' office showcased her successful two-year effort to secure a $25 million contract with the Department of State, labeling it "an outstanding performance" and one that Hopkins carried out "virtually at the partner level." Despite Price Waterhouse's attempt at trial to minimize her contribution to this project, District Court Judge Gesell specifically found that Hopkins has "played a key role in Price Waterhouse's successful effort to win a multimillion-dollar contract with the Department of State." Indeed, he went on, "none of the other partnership candidates at Price Waterhouse that year had a comparable record in terms of successfully securing major contracts for the partnership."

The partners in Hopkins' office praised her character as well as her accomplishments, describing her in their joint statement as "an outstanding professional" who had a "deft touch," a "strong character, independence, and integrity." Clients appear to have agreed with these assessments. At trial, one official from the State Department described her as "extremely competent, intelligent," "strong and forthright, very productive, energetic and creative." Another high-ranking official praised Hopkins' decisiveness, broadmindedness, and "intellectual clarity"; she was, in his words, "a stimulating conversationalist." Evaluations such as these led Judge Gesell to conclude that Hopkins "had no difficulty dealing with clients and her clients appear to have been very pleased with her work" and that she "was generally viewed as a highly competent project leader who worked long hours, pushed

EXHIBIT 7.3.1 (*Continued*)

vigorously to meet deadlines and demanded much from the multidisci-plinary staffs with which she worked."

On too many occasions, however, Hopkins' aggressiveness ap-parently spilled over into abrasiveness. Staff members seem to have borne the brunt of Hopkins' brusqueness. Long before her bid for part-nership, partners evaluating her work had counseled her to improve her relations with staff members. Although later evaluations indicate an improvement, Hopkins' perceived shortcomings in this important area eventually doomed her bid for partnership. Virtually all the partners' negative remarks about Hopkins—even those of partners supporting her—had to do with her "interpersonal skills." Both "supporters and opponents of her candidacy," stressed Judge Gesell, "indicated that she was sometimes overly aggressive, unduly harsh, difficult to work with, and impatient with staff."

There were clear signs, though, that some of the partners reacted negatively to Hopkins' personality because she was a woman. One partner described her as "macho"; another suggested that she "over-compensated for being a woman"; a third advised her to take "a course at charm school." Several partners criticized her use of profanity; in re-sponse, one partner suggested that those partners objected to her swearing only "because it is a lady using foul language." Another sup-porter explained that Hopkins "had matured from a tough-talking somewhat masculine hard-nosed manager to an authoritative, formida-ble, but much more appealing lady partner candidate." As Judge Gesell found, the reasons for the policy board's decision to place her candi-dacy on hold were to improve her chances for partnership. Thomas Beyer advised, Hopkins should "walk more femininely, talk more fem-ininely, dress more femininely, wear makeup, have her hair styled, and wear jewelry."

Dr. Susan Fiske, a social psychologist and associate professor of psychology at Carnegie-Mellon University, testified at the trial that the partnership selection process at Price Waterhouse was likely influenced by sex stereotyping. Her testimony focused not only on the overtly sex-based comments of partners but also on gender-neutral remarks, made by partners who knew Hopkins only slightly, that were intensely critical of her. One partner, for example, boldly stated that Hopkins was "universally disliked" by staff, and another described her as "con-sistently annoying and irritating"; yet these people had very little direct contact with Hopkins. According to Fiske, Hopkins' uniqueness (as the only woman in the pool of candidates) and the subjectivity of the eval-uations made it likely that sharply critical remarks such as these were the product of sex stereotyping—although Fiske admitted that she could not say with certainty whether any particular comment was the result of stereotyping. Fiske based her opinion on a review of the sub-mitted comments, explaining that it was commonly accepted practice for social psychologists to reach this kind of conclusion without hav-ing met any of the people involved in the decision-making process.

In previous years, other female candidates for partnership also had been evaluated in sex-based terms. As a general matter, Judge Gesell concluded, "Candidates were viewed favorably if partners be-lieved they maintained their femininity while becoming effective pro-fessional managers"; in this environment, "to be identified as a 'women's libber' was regarded as a negative comment." In fact, the judge found that in previous years "one partner repeatedly commented that he could not consider any woman seriously as a partnership candi-date and believed that women were not even capable of functioning as senior managers—yet the firm took no action to discourage his com-ments and recorded his vote in the overall summary of the evaluations."

Judge Gesell found that Price Waterhouse legitimately empha-sized interpersonal skills in its partnership decisions and also found that the firm has not fabricated its complaints about Hopkins' interper-sonal skills as a pretext for discrimination. Moreover, he concluded, the firm did not give decisive emphasis to such traits only because Hopkins was a woman, although there were male candidates who lacked these skills but were admitted to partnership. The judge found that these male candidates possessed other positive traits that Hopkins lacked. The judge went on to decide that some of the partners' remarks about Hopkins stemmed from their view of the "proper behavior of women," and that Price Waterhouse had done nothing to disavow re-liance on such comments. In fact, Price Waterhouse had given cre-dence and effect to partners' comments that resulted from sex stereotyping.

Source: Price Waterhouse v. Hopkins, 490 U.S. 228, 99 S. Ct. 1775, 49 FEP Cases 954 (1989).

Name _____   Group _____

1. What legal statute applies to this case?

2. What additional data or information would be helpful in order for you to take a definitive position on Hopkins?

3. What steps would you take at Price Waterhouse to prevent a similar legal problem in the future?

4. Is gender stereotyping illegal? If so, does Hopkins prevail in this case?

5. If gender stereotyping is an acceptable legal theory of discrimination, does the theory apply to discrimination against gay people under Title VII? Give an example of what you regard as illegal discrimination against a gay person using this theory.

6. What specific steps would you take to improve the validity and legal defensibility of the partner selection process?

EXERCISE 7.4

Performance Appraisal at Darby Gas & Light*

Overview

HR professionals are often asked to critique current systems and modify them to meet the changing needs and objectives of the organization. Often, they also are asked to design programs to train raters on using the appraisal systems. This exercise enables you to critique an appraisal system and offer your suggestions for how it should be changed. It also allows you to make some recommendations for a rater training program based on a needs assessment.

Learning Objectives

After completing this exercise, you should be able to

1. Critique an appraisal system and offer suggestions for revisions.
2. Interpret the findings from a needs assessment report.

Procedure

Part A: Individual Analysis

Step 1. Before class, read the background information on the firm presented in Exhibit 7.4.1. Review the appraisal form currently being used by the firm as illustrated in Exhibit 7.4.2.

Step 2. A survey was administered to managers and to employees at Darby Gas & Light. They were asked to indicate the types of rater training for supervisors that would be most beneficial. Results from the survey are reported in Exhibit

7.4.3. Review these findings. Respond to the questions listed in Form 7.4.1.

Part B: Group Analysis

In class, your group will be asked to revise the Darby form and performance-appraisal system.

EXHIBIT 7.4.1

BACKGROUND INFORMATION
FOR DARBY GAS & LIGHT

Steve Shakely is the CEO of a moderately sized public utility, Darby Gas & Light. He employs about 250 professionals (e.g., engineers, systems analysts) and support staff, including 25 managers. His firm recently started using a new appraisal system that consists of yearly formal reviews between managers and subordinates using the rating form illustrated in Exhibit 7.4.2. All employees are rated by their immediate supervisor once a year, and these ratings are used to make administrative decisions (e.g., promotions, merit increases, transfers, terminations, demotions). Mr. Shakely has hired you as an external consultant to review the appraisal form and offer your recommendations for the form and the system. The 25 managers are not formally evaluated.

Mr. Shakely also is interested in your plans for a rater training program. The managers have never received any formal training in conducting appraisal interviews with their subordinates. The firm's HR director, Linda James, recently surveyed the managers and 100 of the employees to assess the areas in which supervisors needed training for completing appraisals and for conducting feedback sessions. A summary of her findings is presented in Exhibit 7.4.3. The numbers indicate the percentages of managers and employees who agreed that supervisors needed training in those areas.

*Contributed by Joyce E. A. Russell.

EXHIBIT 7.4.2

EMPLOYEE EVALUATION FORM

DARBY GAS & LIGHT

Employee's name _____   SSN _____

Supervisor's name _____   SSN _____

Date of review: _____   Date of feedback: _____

Instructions:
This appraisal form is to be used with all employees of Darby Gas & Light, including supervisors. Raters should circle one number on the scales below to indicate the employee's level of performance on the dimension and should provide comments of the employee's performance on that dimension. Dimensions marked with an asterisk must be evaluated for all supervisory employees. After completing the ratings for the employee, be sure to schedule a feedback session with the employee to review the ratings.

1. JOB KNOWLEDGE   1   2   3   4   5
         low   average   high

Comments: _____

_____

2. DECISION MAKING   1   2   3   4   5
         low   average   high

Comments: _____

_____

3. *MOTIVATING OTHERS   1   2   3   4   5
         low   average   high

Comments: _____

_____

4. DEPENDABILITY   1   2   3   4   5
         low   average   high

Comments: _____

_____

5. *LEADERSHIP   1   2   3   4   5
         low   average   high

Comments: _____

_____

6. PROBLEM SOLVING   1   2   3   4   5
         low   average   high

Comments: _____

_____

7. COMMUNICATION   1   2   3   4   5
         low   average   high

Comments: _____

_____

EXHIBIT 7.4.2 (*Continued*)

8. *PLANNING AND ORGANIZING	1 low	2	3 average	4	5 high

Comments: _____

_____

9. TEAMWORK/COOPERATION	1 low	2	3 average	4	5 high

Comments: _____

_____

10. *EMPLOYEE DEVELOPMENT	1 low	2	3 average	4	5 high

Comments: _____

_____

11. PROFESSIONAL DEVELOPMENT	1 low	2	3 average	4	5 high

Comments: _____

_____

12. APPEARANCE AND WORK HABITS	1 low	2	3 average	4	5 high

Comments: _____

_____

EXHIBIT 7.4.3

SURVEY RESULTS ABOUT SUPERVISOR APPRAISAL TRAINING NEEDS

Area for Training	Percent Who Agreed Training for Supervisors Was Needed	
	Managers	**Subordinates**
	($N = 20$)	($N = 100$)
Giving specific, constructive criticism to employees	50%	15%
Giving specific, positive feedback to employees	10	50
Identifying available training opportunities for employees	40	40
Identifying employees' skills	40	45
Setting goals for employees' future performance	15	30
Conducting a career development session with employees	10	50
Assigning ratings for employees' performance	10	15
Understanding situational constraints on subordinates' performance	15	75
Administering rewards for good performance	15	55
Administering discipline for poor performance	45	15
Dealing effectively with employees who get upset in the feedback session	60	50
Providing timely praise	15	60
Identifying career paths for employees	40	50

Name _____   Group _____

1. After reviewing Exhibit 7.4.2, list what you regard as the major problems with the Darby appraisal system. Make specific recommendations about changing the system and cover what you regard as all aspects of the system.

2. What revisions to the rating form would you suggest? What particular methods (formats) discussed in Chapter 7 do you recommend?

3. Suppose the firm wants to use the current form for employee feedback (i.e., to provide feedback to employees on their strengths and weaknesses). Do you think the instrument will be useful for this purpose? Why or why not? What, if any, revisions would you suggest so that the form can be used for employee development?

Name _____   Group _____

4. Suppose Darby has used this form to both promote people and make merit pay adjustments. Suppose also that Darby has been informed that six African Americans have claimed discrimination based on promotion and pay policies. What (if any) advice can you give the company? What specific data should Darby evaluate in the context of these claims?

5. Based on the survey data and what you know about performance appraisal, what areas are most important for a rater training program? Any particular rating errors or biases clearly in need of attention based on the survey data?

6. Self-ratings with this system are almost two points higher than supervisory appraisals on average. Should supervisors review self-appraisals before they evaluate performance? Explain your answer based on possible rating errors.

Name ————————————————————— Group —————————————————————

7. Steve just read a Jack Welsh book (former CEO of GE) and Jack likes "forced distribution." What should you tell Steve about this rating method?

8. Should the managers be formally evaluated? If so, describe the system you recommend.

9. A performance appraisal "guru" said to use ratings of "relative frequency." What does this mean? Give an example.

EXERCISE 7.5

The Development of a Performance Appraisal System for Instructors*

Overview

The purpose of this exercise is to explore the concept of performance. You will discover that multiple activities determine overall performance and that various criteria can be applied to these activities to create a set of performance dimensions. You will follow several steps to construct a performance appraisal form that could be used to assess your instructors. Finally, you will examine the variability of performance and include this in your assessment of performance.

Learning Objectives

After completing this exercise, you should be able to

1. Have a better understanding of the multidimensionality of performance.
2. Know how to construct measurable performance dimensions.
3. Understand the steps involved in the development of an appraisal system.

Procedure

Step 1. Prior to class, complete Parts A, B, and C, below.

Part A: The Multidimensionality of Performance Assessment

What leads you to believe that your instructors perform well or poorly in your courses? Do their lectures entirely determine your rating? Are there other outcomes that influence your rating? In other words, is performance multidimensional?

Which of the following activities would you consider to be relevant in rating an instructor's overall performance? To show how important each of these is, divide up 100 percentage points among these to show how much you think each one should be weighted (one or more may be given a weight of zero).

_____ Lecture organization

_____ Oral explanation

_____ Providing examples

_____ Conducting exercises

_____ Using audiovisual media

*Contributed by Jeffrey S. Kane.

_____ Grading

_____ Course-related advising and feedback

_____ Classroom interaction

100% Total

Enter the activity weight in the space provided in Exhibit 7.5.1.

Part B: Determining Performance Criteria

The value of an instructor's performance in each of the above activities can be considered from several different perspectives. For example, we might consider performance on grading from the perspectives of its quality and timeliness. Each of these perspectives is called a "criterion." The examples that follow illustrate some of the criteria on which performance in these instructor activities can be evaluated. You are to decide which of these combinations of an activity and a criterion are appropriate to include.

For example, the cell "quality of grading" in Exhibit 7.5.1 refers to *how well* or how accurately the instructor graded exams, assignments, etc. The cell "timeliness of grading" refers to *how quickly* the exams or assignments were graded. These two aspects of grading determine how an instructor did in the grading category overall. Obviously, an instructor could have accurately graded the exams and achieved a perfect rating on quality of grading but not done so well on the timeliness of grading those exams. Conversely, another instructor could have graded the exams promptly but perhaps not graded the exams so that they accurately reflected students' achievement.

Another example is "interpersonal impact of course-related advising and feedback," which refers to whether the instructor gave you encouragement and confidence in overcoming your difficulties in the course as opposed to making you feel that further effort would get you nowhere. Another example might be "quantity of classroom interaction," which would refer to the number of times the instructor asked a question or invited comments during the class.

Your role is to select the cells of the matrix in Exhibit 7.5.1 which would be relevant to assessing an instructor's performance. Each of the categories to the left is referred to as an "instructor activity" or job function and the criteria on which performance can be valued are listed across the top under the heading of "criteria." Place an X in each cell you select as relevant for any activity given a weight greater than zero in Part A.

EXHIBIT 7.5.1

MATRIX OF INSTRUCTOR ACTIVITIES AND CRITERIA

Name _____   Group _____

			Criteria				
Instructor Activity	**Activity Weight***	**Quality**		**Quantity**	**Timeliness**	**Interpersonal Impact**	
Lecture organization	_____	Wt: #1	1	1	1	1	
		Wt: #2	2	2	2	2	
Oral explanation	_____	Wt: #1	1	1	1	1	
		Wt: #2	2	2	2	2	
Providing examples	_____	Wt: #1	1	1	1	1	
		Wt: #2	2	2	2	2	
Conducting exercises	_____	Wt: #1	1	1	1	1	
		Wt: #2	2	2	2	2	
Using audiovisual media	_____	Wt: #1	1	1	1	1	
		Wt: #2	2	2	2	2	
Grading	_____	Wt: #1	1	1	1	1	
		Wt: #2	2	2	2	2	
Course-related advising and feedback	_____	Wt: #1	1	1	1	1	
		Wt: #2	2	2	2	2	
Classroom interaction	_____	Wt: #1	1	1	1	1	
		Wt: #2	2	2	2	2	

*Must total 100%

Part C: Weighting of Performance Dimensions

The cells you have chosen are referred to as *performance dimensions*. Each performance dimension consists of the combination of a job activity and a criterion. Next, you will need to look at each row of the matrix and assign weights that reflect the relative importance of each of the relevant criteria in determining performance on the activity as a whole. Do this by distributing 100 points among the criteria you designated as relevant to each activity. For example, if the only two criteria for grading were quality and timeliness, perhaps the importance of these would be equally split, 50 and 50. If quality were seen as more important, perhaps the numbers would be 60 and 40. Enter these percentages in the space labelled Wt. #1 for the "grading" row.

Once you have assigned numbers to each of the *relevant* performance dimensions in the matrix, multiply each number by the numbers that were determined in Part A of this exercise (the activity weights). Let's say that you

assigned "grading" a 30 in Part A, and further, you set the relative importance of "quality of grading" at 60 and "timeliness of grading" at 40. The weight of each of these performance dimensions in the matrix (as a percentage of the whole matrix) would be:

Quality of grading   = 30% × 60% = 18%
Timeliness of grading = 30% × 40% = 12%

Fill in the weights for the rest of the performance dimensions in the matrix in the space labelled Wt. #2. These percentages will add up to 100 percent.

Step 2. In small groups, students should compare their individual results from Parts A to C and develop a strategy for determining a group response. Once the group has developed a strategy, a response should be derived and assignments should be made for the derivation of descriptors in Part D.

Part D: Creation of PLDs

The next step is to create statements that exemplify levels of performance for each of the performance dimensions the group chose as appropriate to rate. In order to determine how well or poorly the instructor performed on any of these performance dimensions, one must first identify what exemplifies good performance and what exemplifies poor performance.

Statements used as anchors at the ends and middle of a good-bad continuum must clearly state the behavior or result that constitutes each of these three scale points. These statements are referred to as *performance level descriptors* (PLDs). These PLDs would be placed at the 1, 3, and 5 points of a 1 to 5 scale.

Each group should create PLDs for the end and middle points of the scale for each of the performance dimensions assigned by the instructor. Write out the PLDs and put them at the appropriate points on a 1 to 5 scale. Exhibit 7.5.2 presents examples of PLDs for three performance dimensions.

Step 3. After the scales have been completed for each performance dimension, the instructor will present a sample of the scales for practice ratings. Part E should be completed by each student.

Part E: Performance as a Distribution

Think of the performance of an instructor whom you've had the opportunity to observe. Have you noticed that he or she doesn't *always* present organized lectures and may not *always* return your exams at the next class session, *always* provide a lot of examples in class, or *always* explain the subject matter in a clear and understandable manner?

The instructor's performance is likely to vary from day to day depending on his or her ability and the amount of effort exerted. Motivational state, physical health, amount of sleep, distractions in the environment, and other phenomena produce variations in behavior that determine your impression of the person's overall performance.

When you created the 1 to 5 scales in Part D, you may have realized that an instructor's performance didn't always fit at one level. If you had to rate someone on these scales and put a check mark at only one point along the scale, you'd do so with the realization that sometimes the instructor did better than that level and sometimes worse than that level. Further, instructors differ in how consistently they achieve their "typical" levels of performance.

In order to capture the full picture of a person's performance, it is necessary to show how the performance was distributed across the levels of outcomes described by a rating scale such as the scales you have created. This can be done by specifying the percentage of times that an instructor achieved each level of performance, out of all the times that the person was required to perform that activity. The result, called a *performance graph*, is illustrated in Exhibit 7.5.3.

Assume that this was the graph for timeliness of grading and that the outcome levels were defined as the number of class sessions that passed before the instructor returned the exams: 1, more than four class sessions; 2, four class sessions; 3, three class sessions; 4, two class sessions; and 5, the next class session. The graph would show that the person never delayed returning the exams more than four sessions, 10 percent of the time waited four sessions before returning the exams, 20 percent of the time waited three sessions before returning the exams, 40 percent of the time waited two sessions before returning the exams, and 30 percent of the time returned the exams at the next class session. These total to 100 percent.

For this part of the exercise, you are to make a performance graph out of the performance dimension scales that students created earlier, with the PLDs as anchors at either end of the scale and in the middle of the scale.

Now, think again of the instructor with whom you are familiar. What does the performance graph look like for each of the different performance dimensions for that person? Plot each performance graph independently of the other graphs, thinking only of the relevant anchors for that particular scale.

When you finish, look at the graphs as a group. Do you see any patterns emerging? Do you notice that the instructors are generally consistent in their behavior? Do some of the performance dimensions show more variation than others?

Look at particular groups of performance graphs—for example, all those relating to the same criterion. Are there patterns that show up when you look at all the "timeliness" graphs? (Is this person consistently late? Does he or she consistently procrastinate?) Do all the graphs having to do with "quality" show that the person does very high quality work? What about interpersonal impact? If so, what are the implications of this finding?

EXHIBIT 7.5.2

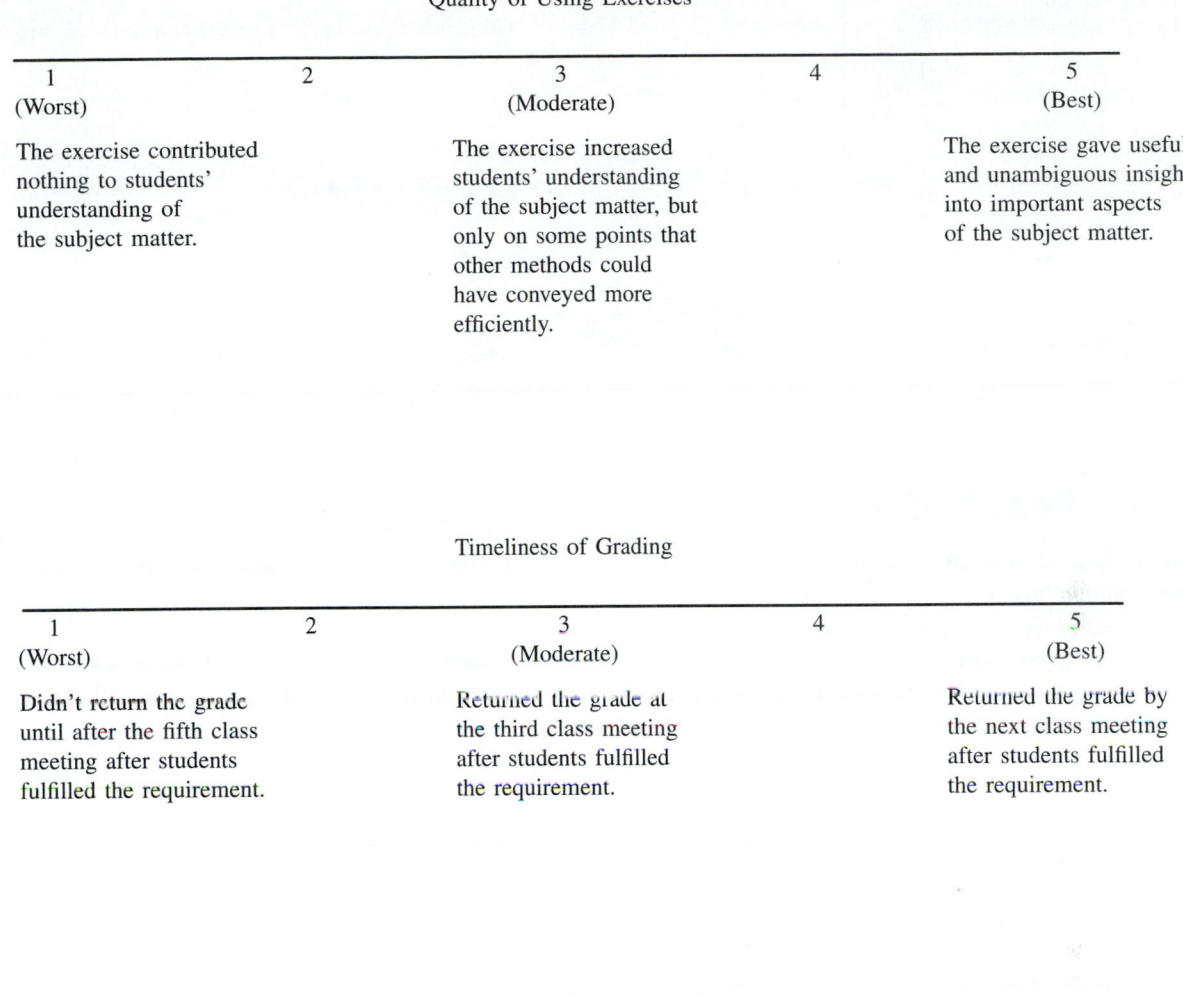

Quality of Using Exercises

1	2	3	4	5
(Worst)		(Moderate)		(Best)
The exercise contributed nothing to students' understanding of the subject matter.		The exercise increased students' understanding of the subject matter, but only on some points that other methods could have conveyed more efficiently.		The exercise gave useful and unambiguous insight into important aspects of the subject matter.

Timeliness of Grading

1	2	3	4	5
(Worst)		(Moderate)		(Best)
Didn't return the grade until after the fifth class meeting after students fulfilled the requirement.		Returned the grade at the third class meeting after students fulfilled the requirement.		Returned the grade by the next class meeting after students fulfilled the requirement.

Interpersonal Impact of Providing Examples

1	2	3	4	5
(Worst)		(Moderate)		(Best)
The example was offensive or demeaning to one or more of the students in the class.		The example was relevant but not particularly interesting or amusing.		The example was interesting and/or amusing, and generated a relaxed atmosphere in the class.

EXHIBIT 7.5.3

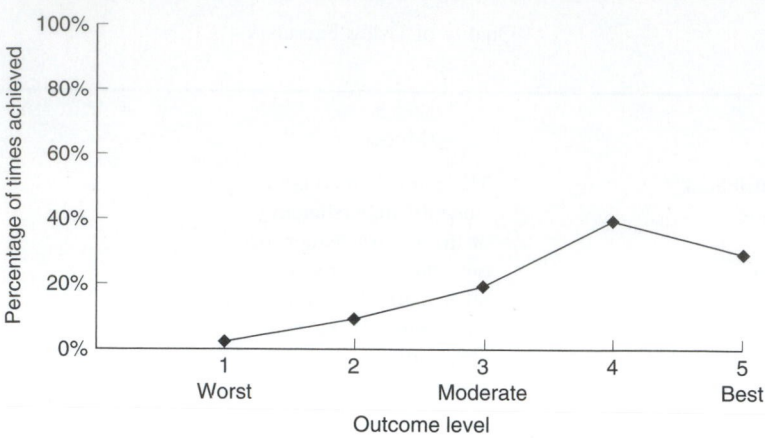

Part F: Calculating an Overall Mean Performance Score

Step 4. Next, an overall mean performance score will be calculated for the instructor. This calculation incorporates only the most basic parameter of performance, that of average (mean) performance. More sophisticated calculations of overall performance can take into consideration other relevant factors such as situational constraints on performance (things that prevented the instructor from performing as well as he or she could have done), as well as two additional parameters of performance: consistency of performance and avoidance of negative outcomes. The distributions depicted in the performance graphs are scored the same way that a grade point average is scored. Let's again use the example of the timeliness of grading. The distribution of the performance graph shown in Part E is as follows:

Level	Percentage
1	0
2	10
3	20
4	40
5	30

Multiply the level times the percentage to get an average percentage for each performance dimension, as follows:

$$1 \times 0\% = 0.00$$
$$2 \times 10\% = 0.20$$
$$3 \times 20\% = 0.60$$
$$4 \times 40\% = 1.60$$
$$5 \times 30\% = \underline{1.50}$$
$$3.90 \quad \text{total}$$

An average of 3.90 divided by a possible 5.0 is

$$3.90/5.00 = 0.78 \quad \text{or} \quad 78\%$$

Now, multiply the weight assigned to this performance dimension in Part C (which was 12 percent in the example) by the average of 78 percent which was just calculated:

$$12\% \times 78\% = 9.4\%$$

The instructor scores 9.4 percent for this dimension. Calculate all the other performance dimensions in exactly the same way. After making these calculations, add up the scores for all the performance dimensions to find the instructor's overall performance score.

Step 5. Group discussion should focus on the ability of students to make frequency judgments, the relative effectiveness of this type of appraisal relative to other types discussed in the chapter, the susceptibility of this type of performance appraisal to the various biases discussed in Chapter 7, and the criteria for evaluating the effectiveness of this performance appraisal system. Do the students feel that this approach to performance appraisal is superior to whatever form of appraisal they have used in the past to evaluate instructors? Would this be useful feedback for instructors? Finally, how would this approach work in industry?

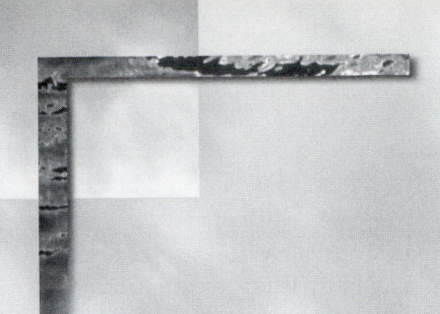

Chapter 8 Exercises

EXERCISE 8.1

Conducting a Needs Assessment*

Overview

To determine whether training is needed to address a particular area of concern in an organization (e.g., performance problem), it is first necessary to conduct a needs assessment. As stated in Chapter 8, a thorough needs assessment consists of an organizational analysis, job or task analysis, and a person analysis. This exercise gives the student practice in conducting a needs assessment.

Learning Objectives

After completing this exercise, you should be able to

1. Understand the various components of a needs assessment.
2. Develop items to conduct an organizational analysis, task analysis, and person analysis.
3. Interpret the results from a needs assessment, describing the implications for designing a training program.

Procedure

Step 1. Before coming to class, each person should review Chapter 8, paying particular attention to the section on needs assessment. Choose a job with which you are very familiar. Collect and review job analysis data (see Chapter 4). From this material, generate a list of "possible training topics" for an individual in that job (i.e., what are the different types of training that might be beneficial for performing that job). For example, if the job is a patrol officer, possible training topics might include handling firearms, dealing with domestic issues, arrest procedure, teamwork, stress management, legal issues, and investigation. You should generate as long of a list as possible (e.g., 40 to 50 topics).

Step 2. Using Form 8.1.1, interview employees (at least two) in the job you have chosen. Try to choose a representative sample of employees for the interviews. You may interview them individually or in a group.

Step 3. Summarize your findings from the needs assessment in a one-page report to the vice president of human resources. Offer *specific* recommendations regarding training for the job.

Step 4. Students will be paired. Form 8.1.1 should be exchanged and critiqued. Reviewers should evaluate the extent to which the responses to Form 8.1 provide guidelines for improving the training functions for this job.

*Contributed by Jeffrey D. Kudisch, Stephanie D. Myers, and Joyce E. A. Russell.

Job: _____   Organization: _____

Interviewer(s): _____   Date: _____

PART A: BACKGROUND INFORMATION OF INTERVIEWEE

Years in the job: _____   Years in the company: _____

Highest level of education completed: _____

PART B: ORGANIZATIONAL ANALYSIS (ATTITUDES AND CLIMATE FOR TRAINING)

From your perspective, what are the purposes of training?

How successful are current training programs in your firm for achieving these purposes?

If you asked a fellow worker to give his or her opinion regarding training in this firm, what would his or her response likely be?

Do you think trainees are motivated to attend training? Explain your response.

Do you think employees in your job experience any resistance toward attending training? Do you have any suggestions for minimizing this resistance?

What positive consequences are associated with successful completion of training (e.g., increased pay, greater promotional opportunities, recognition)? Are there any negative consequences associated with attending training (e.g., loss of production, loss of status among peers)?

Do you think it is difficult for trainees to apply the skills they learned in training once they return back to the job? Why or why not?

For training programs you have attended, are you asked to provide your reactions to the programs? Are you given learning tests before and after training to assess a change in your learning?

PART C: TASK AND PERSON ANALYSIS
Describe the major duties of your job. Rank these in terms of importance.

Take a moment to think about an individual who is especially effective at your job. What knowledges, abilities, or skills does this person possess? Can these skills be enhanced through training?

Looking ahead over the next five years, do you foresee any additional job demands being added to the current responsibilities in your job? If so, what additional skills or abilities will be needed to meet these demands?

Note to the interviewer: Hand the list of "possible training topics" to the interviewee(s). Give them the following instructions.
   Step 1.   After looking over the list, circle those 10 areas that are most critical to successful performance in your job.
   Step 2.   Of the 10 items you identified, check those areas in which training would be beneficial to your job performance.

Reviewer's Name_____

Comment on the extent to which this needs assessment provides guidelines for meeting training needs.

EXERCISE 8.2

Rainyday Insurance Adjusters Company*

Overview

Often in organizations, new equipment may be installed without designing or offering the appropriate amount or type of training. As a result, productivity and job satisfaction of employees may decline, causing business losses for a firm. In some cases, the training problems also may be related to other problems in the organization (e.g., communication, management issues). It is the HR professional's job to diagnose the nature of the problems and offer realistic, timely recommendations. This exercise provides the student with some case information and has the student diagnose the problems with the company and offer recommendations for addressing those problems.

Learning Objectives

After completing this exercise, you should be able to

1. Understand how to interpret partial needs assessment information to determine the next steps that must be taken in collecting additional information.
2. Use needs assessment information to develop plans for designing or implementing training.

Procedure

Part A: Individual Analysis

Step 1. Read the background material presented in Exhibit 8.2.1. Note that you have been hired by the CEO to help the company interpret its problems and to draft some recommendations. In the first few days, you have collected some information, which is contained in the exhibit.

Step 2. Complete the questions found in Form 8.2.1.

Part B: Group Analysis

Step 1. In groups, discuss your responses to Form 8.2.1.

Step 2. As a group, reach consensus on what the company's problems are. Then outline a short-term plan (within the month) and a longer-term plan (over the next six months) to address those problems. Make sure your group includes the timeline for when each recommendation should be implemented and what the benefits and drawbacks are to each suggestion.

*Contributed by Steven M. Barnard and Joyce E. A. Russell.

EXHIBIT 8.2.1

BACKGROUND INFORMATION ON RAINYDAY INSURANCE ADJUSTERS COMPANY

Based in South Florida, Rainyday Insurance Adjusters is a medium-sized company with 135 employees and seven managers. They process the claims of insurance holders who have experienced various misfortunes (e.g., hurricanes, floods). Their primary job is to determine the amount to be paid out and process the paperwork for some of the smaller insurance agencies in the area so that final payments can be issued. Although the company is only eight years old, it has done quite well and has seen a large increase in business. It has a reputation for quality work and quick turnaround on claims. Because customers are often eager to move on after misfortunes strike, Rainyday has built a loyal following by the insurance agencies that depend on it. Delayed claims often cost these companies time and money when they have to interact with continuous customer complaints.

To accommodate the increase in customers, six months ago, Rainyday expanded its office in the current building and upgraded all its equipment to make the company more efficient and to allow workers to process claims more quickly. In particular, computers were upgraded to facilitate speedier turnaround and higher capacity from claims processors. The new computers represent a large investment the company cannot afford to underutilize. Since installation of the computers, Rainyday has experienced a number of problems with voluntary turnover among claims processors as well as decreased productivity and increased errors.

Recently, the CEO of Rainyday, Rebecca Stephens, hired you as a consultant to help determine what, if any, training needs the claims processors have. There are 85 processors in the claims department. On your first day, you talked with several employees in the claims department. Fran, one of the more senior claims processors, has been with the company since it started eight years ago. He has become increasingly dissatisfied since the new computers arrived. As he remarked to you, "The managers told us the new computers would make our jobs easier, but they have been nothing but trouble. We spend half of our time printing out the forms and then we have to go back and correct errors on them. Also, some of the newer claims processors have been bugging me to show them how to fill out the forms. I don't have time for that, and besides, they should have learned it themselves in all those hotshot computer classes they have taken. On top of all that, my manager, Paula, stops by every day and tells us we all need to work faster because we are getting behind. I'm telling you, I have had it. I'm about to join the others and quit."

After your conversation with Fran, you decide that before you start drafting an action plan for the training program, you had better meet with Fran's manager to get her perspective. Paula seems friendly enough and is very open about what she thinks are the reasons for the problems. "Ever since we got the new computers, we have been having problems. Errors have increased, productivity has gone down, and we have had a lot of employees quit. At first, I thought it was just the new computers, but I also noticed a lot of bickering among the claims processors. It seems the more senior processors have resented the new hires, perhaps because some of their buddies quit the firm." After further inquiry, Paula mentioned that when the new computers arrived, she offered to send everyone to the local high school to take a computer class that would teach them how to use the computers and the software. The class was offered early in the morning (6:30 A.M. to 8:00 A.M.) so employees could take the class and still make it to work only one hour later than they normally arrived. They could get to work by 8:30 A.M., which was one hour after their normal start time. Paula also told employees they would be paid for the hour of work they missed. As she noted to you, "I was surprised that the employees did not seem more excited about the idea of the training. In fact, a number of employees told me that they did not want to be going to school with a bunch of teenagers and said they would just train themselves."

After talking with Paula, you asked her to point you in the direction of one of the newer employees who had been experiencing conflicts with the more senior employees. You reserved a conference room and met with Malcolm. He was very talkative and had a lot to complain about, especially regarding the older employees. "I'm having a pretty tough time here. After I took those computer classes at the high school, the computers have been really easy to work with, but I'm still having trouble filling out the claims forms. One of the senior employees, Randall, is supposed to help me, but he seems too busy. I think that he and the other old-timers are just jealous that some of the newer employees know the shortcuts on the computer. It's kind of funny watching them try to format their claims; they get so frustrated because they don't have a clue how to work the computers. I told a few of them I would show them, but they said they didn't need help from 'a youngster.' Fine by me; I have plenty to do."

After meeting with Malcolm, you realize that things don't sound too good. Because of the delays in the work by the claims processors, customers have been complaining to the insurance companies. Consequently, the firms are threatening to drop Rainyday. With all of their expansion efforts, Rainyday needs customers now more than ever. The CEO said to you as you were leaving for the day, "If things don't improve soon, we may be out of business." She encouraged you to develop a training program or whatever you think would help to improve the productivity of the claims department.

FORM 8.2.1

BASED ON THE INFORMATION YOU REVIEWED IN EXHIBIT 8.2.1, RESPOND
TO THE FOLLOWING QUESTIONS.

Name _____   Group _____

1. What do you see as the major problems at Rainyday Insurance Adjusters Company?

2. What are the causes of those problems?

3. What steps should be taken to better understand the performance problems at Rainyday? That is, what would you do to conduct a more thorough needs assessment to better pinpoint the problems?

4. Provide several suggestions for addressing the problems in the claims department at Rainyday.

EXERCISE 8.3

Backwoods Mail Order Company*

Overview

HR professionals are often contacted by an organization to design and deliver a training program to meet a specific problem in the organization (e.g., declining productivity, increasing customer complaints). In some cases, the organization has already conducted a needs assessment and has some idea of what the specific problem is. The HR professional may be asked to review the needs assessment findings and design a training program to meet the specified needs or goals. This exercise provides you with information about a company and the needs assessment findings in order to design a training program.

Learning Objectives

After completing this exercise, you should be able to

1. Review results from a training needs assessment and design a training plan to address the needs, detailing training objectives, training techniques to use, and the length of training.
2. Outline an evaluation plan to assess the effectiveness of the training program.

Procedure

Part A: Individual Analysis

Step 1. Before coming to class, read Exhibit 8.3.1, which contains the background information on Backwoods Mail Order Company as well as information about the needs assessment that has already been conducted.

Step 2. Complete the questions found on Form 8.3.1.

Part B: Class Discussion and Small Group Analysis

Step 1. As a class, review responses to Form 8.3.1. Discuss the learning objectives of the training program, the training techniques to be used, the duration of the training, and the plan for evaluating the training.

Step 2. In groups, write out ideas for the types of questions that should be included in a reaction form of the training. Each group should draft its own reaction form and share the form with the class.

*Contributed by Steve Long.

EXHIBIT 8.3.1

BACKGROUND INFORMATION ON BACKWOODS MAIL ORDER COMPANY

Backwoods is a telephone and mail order company that specializes in camping supplies and outdoor clothing. Gerald Banks is the operating manager of Backwoods' customer service department. He is interested in training his 40 employees in the customer orders group to be more effective in filling customers' orders, more helpful in answering customer questions, and more polite in dealing with customer problems and complaints. To familiarize you with the company and the job of customer order representative, an organizational chart and job description are provided below.

BACKWOODS ORGANIZATIONAL CHART

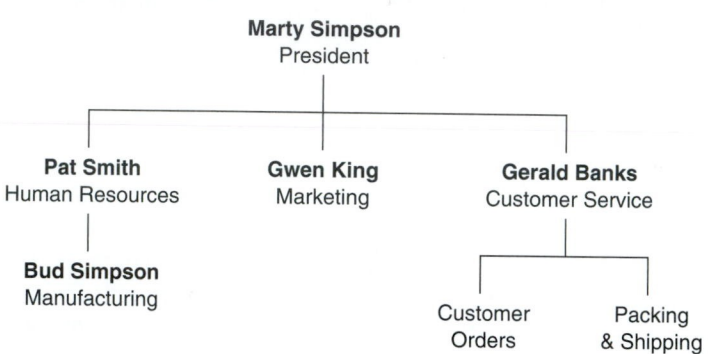

CUSTOMER SERVICE DIVISION

The customer service department consists of 40 employees and four supervisors in the customer orders group and 32 employees and three supervisors in the packing and shipping group. Employees are evenly divided into two shifts: a day shift (7 A.M. to 3 P.M.) and a night shift (3 P.M. to 11 P.M.). Employees in the customer orders group handle incoming calls from customers and record customers' orders on a central computer system that checks the availability of each item ordered. Orders are then transmitted to the shipping department, where shipping clerks pull the items from inventory and pack them for overnight delivery.

JOB DESCRIPTION FOR CUSTOMER ORDER REPRESENTATIVES

- Takes customer orders by telephone or direct mail.
- Answers customer questions about product prices, sizing, colors, features, and availability.
- Assists customers on the phone in determining equipment or clothing needs based on season, climate, or use requirements.
- Enters phone and mail orders into on-line order processing computer system.
- Processes returned merchandise, completes a defective merchandise form for quality assurance, and routes serviceable merchandise for repackaging.
- Handles customer complaints about problems or defects in merchandise, wrong sizes, or mistakes on customers' orders (wrong products delivered).
- Responds to questions about orders from employees in the shipping and handling group.

THE TRAINEES

The trainees will consist of the 40 employees in the customer order group as well as their four supervisors. Customer service employees earn about $7 per hour, and supervisors earn about $9 per hour. All employees must receive training, yet service must still be available to customers (i.e., you cannot put everyone through the training at the same time of the day or there will be no one to handle incoming calls from customers).

PROBLEMS IDENTIFIED BY A NEEDS ASSESSMENT

- The majority of merchandise returns (78 percent) are due to problems in size, features, and/or color selection.
- The majority of these errors (54 percent) result from mistakes in entering the order data correctly into the computer system.
- Many of the errors in sizing or features could be avoided if customer service representatives were more knowledgeable about the products' sizing and features (e.g., certain items run larger than standard sizing).
- Incorrect labeling and inventory of products are responsible for fewer than 8 percent of order errors.
- Customer order representatives have never been formally trained in dealing with customer complaints.
- The customer order work area is cluttered and noisy.

GOALS FOR THE TRAINING

- Reduce merchandise returns due to data entry problems.
- Improve the attitude of customer order representatives.
- Help customer order representatives to really understand product features and sizing (e.g., suitable climate range for a sleeping bag).
- Create a positive image of Backwoods Company to customers and employees.
- Reduce sizing errors by having representatives check customer knowledge of differently sized items (e.g., that jacket runs large).
- Encourage representatives to check with mail-order customers on difficult handwriting or potential problems with item sizing or features.

Name _____   Group _____

Based on the background information provided in Exhibit 8.3.1, respond to the following questions.

    1.   Write several clear, measurable objectives for the training to be delivered to the employees in the customer order group.

FBo 11-09

    2.   Develop a recommendation for the training plan that includes the training techniques that should be used and the length of training.

    3.   Offer a plan for evaluating the training program. Describe the criteria that will be used and the design you will employ.

EXERCISE 8.4

The Development and Evaluation of a Training Program for Graduate Student Instructors

Overview

A common practice, particularly in larger, research-oriented universities, is to give graduate students who have limited training in teaching complete responsibility for teaching an undergraduate class. Thus, while graduate students may possess adequate knowledge to cover the subject matter, many have had little (or no) training in organizing a class, teaching techniques, testing, grading, and so on. This exercise develops a training program for graduate students and proposes a design for evaluating the training.

Learning Objectives

After completing this exercise, you should be able to

1. Outline the steps to be followed in the conceptualization, development, and evaluation of a training program.
2. Discuss the advantages and disadvantages of the various training techniques and the evaluation design options.
3. Develop an approach to determine who should receive the training.

Procedure

Part A: Individual Preparation

Step 1. Before class, review the memo in Exhibit 8.4.1 from the university provost. As a member of the task force to develop and evaluate a new training program, your first assignment is to develop an outline of the steps to be followed to develop the most effective (and practical) training program for graduate student instructors.

Step 2. On Form 8.4.1, write a chronology of the steps you will follow to complete the assignment. Pay close attention to what the Provost has requested in the memo.

Part B: Group Analysis

Step 1. In groups of four to six students, each member should review each other member's response on Form 8.4.1

Step 2. The group should attempt to reach consensus on the chronology of events and the position to be taken on the issues raised by the provost. One group member should take careful notes to represent the consensus and all aspects of the training program, the design of evaluation, and the criteria to be used as a part of the evaluation process.

Part C: Class Discussion

One member of each group should present the group's recommendations for the steps to be followed for the training program. Class discussion will follow on the areas where the groups agree and disagree. An attempt should be made to reach consensus on all major points that must be addressed by the task force.

Part D: Self- and Peer Evaluation

Complete a self- and a peer evaluation form based *only* on the performance in the exercise.

EXHIBIT 8.4.1
THE PROVOST'S MEMO REQUESTING YOUR RECOMMENDATIONS

TO: Students

FROM: Jack Richter, University Provost and Eminent Scholar

SUBJECT: Charge to the Training Task Force

Congratulations on your appointment to the Training Task Force. As you may know, there have been a number of concerns raised about the quality of teaching by graduate students at our university. While the graduate students are highly motivated to teach, most of the students have received very little training or preparation prior to teaching their undergraduate classes. Your job as part of the task force is as follows: (1) to determine if there really is a need for such training (request any data you may need to test the theory that graduate students are not adequately prepared to teach); (2) if there is a need, to outline the objectives and the content of the training; (3) to state which future instructors should receive the training (i.e., all future instructors or only those who fail to meet some imposed standard); (4) to identify the specific techniques that are recommended to be used (e.g., lecture, role-plays); and (5) to provide a plan for ensuring that the training will be effective and cost effective. Specify the criteria and experimental design that should be used for evaluation. Keep in mind that I am very familiar with training methodology and prefer *detailed* suggestions on a strategy. (I know in general what organizational, task/job and person analysis is.) Also, while keeping costs in mind, consider whether the program should be expanded to other instructors/professors. What should we examine as we consider whether we need to train, what we should train, and who should be trained?

   Prior to the group meeting, take a position on each of the issues I have raised (and any others you can think of) and provide a *detailed* chronology using Form 8.4.1. Also, answer the specific questions on Form 8.4.1.

I look forward to our meeting.

FORM 8.4.1

CHRONOLOGY OF STEPS FOR TRAINING PROGRAM DEVELOPMENT & EVALUATION

Name _____   Group _____

Assignment   **Detailed and Chronological Description of Action to be Taken**

    Step   1.

                 2.

                 3.

                 4.

                 5.

Critical Questions Related to the Assignment:

1.   What data should we study (or collect) to determine whether this training is needed?

2.   If we do training, what specific experimental design do you recommend and what evaluative criteria should we use?

3.   A colleague has recommended using the *Self-directed Learning Readiness Scale.* Why would we do this? What does this scale predict?

4.   What specific types of training should be used? *Be specific.*

Exercise 8.5

Self-Directed Learning Assessment*

Overview

Chapter 8 discussed the increasing importance of continued learning as a training technique for use with employees bombarded with technological advances. More companies are holding employees responsible for knowledge of these advances, and employees are realizing that they must continue to learn on their own if they are to avoid obsolescence. For example, in one study employees in the aerospace industry reported spending twice as much time on Self-Directed Learning (SDL) projects as did other employees. In the following exercise, you will learn more about the impact of learning preferences in the workplace. You will complete the *Self-Directed Learning Readiness Scale* (SDLRS) which assesses your own learning preferences.

Learning Objectives

After completing this exercise, you should be able to

1. Estimate your own learning preferences.
2. Describe ways of incorporating SDL into the training process.

Procedure

Part A: Individual Analysis

Prior to class, read Chapter 8, and complete the questionnaire in Form 8.5.1 and answer the questions that follow. Bring Form 8.5.1 to class.

Part B: Group Analysis

Step 1. After your instructor has provided the scoring key and norms for the questionnaire, work in groups of five or six to share your scores with one another and discuss your views on the validity and usefulness of the measure. How could a company use this instrument as part of its training or selection program?

Step 2. Provide some ideas for increasing the level of readiness among employees for SDL. Assume that you are a manager and you want to encourage SDL among your employees. Describe several strategies you might use to get them to manage their own learning.

Part C: Class Discussion

As a class, discuss the importance of using SDL approaches to the continuing training of employees. Explain the relative advantages and disadvantages of these approaches over other, more conventional training techniques (e.g., lecture, films).

---

*Contributed by Paul Guglielmino and Lucy Guglielmino.

LEARNING PREFERENCE ASSESSMENT

Name _____ Group _____

Instructions: The following items are sample items taken from the SDLRS. The measure is designed to assess your learning preferences and your attitudes toward learning. Using the scale below, write in one number for each item on the blank to the left of the item. Answer as candidly as possible. There are no right or wrong answers.

　　1 = Almost never true of me. I hardly ever feel this way.
　　2 = Not often true of me. I feel this way less than half of the time.
　　3 = Sometimes true of me. I feel this way about half of the time.
　　4 = Usually true of me. I feel this way more than half of the time.
　　5 = Almost always true of me. There are very few times when I don't feel this way.

_____　1. I know what I want to learn.

_____　2. When I see something that I don't understand, I stay away from it.

_____　3. If there is something I want to learn, I can figure out a way to learn it.

_____　4. If I discover a need for information that I don't have, I know where to go to get it.

_____　5. In a classroom situation, I expect the instructor to tell all class members exactly what to do at all times.

_____　6. I can learn things on my own better than most people.

_____　7. Even if I have a great idea, I can't seem to develop a plan for making it work.

_____　8. In a learning experience, I prefer to take part in deciding what will be learned and how.

_____　9. Difficult study doesn't bother me if I'm interested in something.

_____　10. If there is something I have decided to learn, I can find time for it, no matter how busy I am.

_____　11. If I can understand something well enough to get by, it doesn't bother me if I still have questions about it.

_____　12. The people I admire most are always learning new things.

_____　13. I don't like it when people who really know what they're doing point out mistakes that I am making.

_____　14. I try to relate what I am learning to my long-term goals.

_____　15. I am capable of learning for myself almost anything I might need to know.

_____　16. I'm better than most people at trying to find out things I need to know.

_____　17. I become a leader in group learning situations.

_____　18. I don't like challenging learning situations.

_____　19. It's better to stick to the learning methods that we know will work instead of always trying new ones.

_____　20. I want to learn more so that I can keep growing as a person.

Questions:

1. What does the SDLRS predict?

2. Could a company use scores on this instrument to make staffing decisions or to select particular people for training?

Chapter 9 Exercises

EXERCISE 9.1

Attitudes about Older People*

Overview

As noted throughout this book, the workforce is aging. This is due primarily to three factors: (1) the increasing life expectancy of individuals, (2) the aging of the large number of baby boomers, and (3) the decline in birthrates over the past two decades. The aging of the workforce raises the issue of how individuals view older adults and older employees. That is, what stereotypes do they have about older adults and what are the consequences of these views for older workers. This exercise helps you in understanding your own views about older workers.

Learning Objectives

After completing this exercise, you should be able to

1. Be aware of the facts of aging.
2. Understand your own views and perceptions of older individuals.
3. Understand how stereotypes about older individuals may influence individuals' behaviors toward them in the workplace.

Procedure

Part A: Individual Analysis

Step 1. Complete Form 9.1.1. Bring your responses to class to be scored.

Step 2. Score your responses in class.

Part B: Group Analysis

Step 1. As a class, address the issues associated with each item on the questionnaire.

Step 2. Address the following questions:

A. To what extent did the class possess erroneous facts about aging workers?

B. Why did they possess these inaccurate pictures about older adults?

C. What are the consequences of stereotypes of older adults for the workplace?

D. What recommendations would you make for correcting these stereotypes in the workplace? What type of training programs do you recommend and how would you evaluate them?

*Contributed by Barbara Haskell.

FORM 9.1.1
AGING QUIZ

Name _____   Group _____

Directions. For each item, respond by answering **True** or **False** in the space provided on the left. Be candid in choosing the response that best tells what you believe.

_____   1. The majority of older people (past age 65) are senile (i.e., have defective memories, are disoriented, or are demented).

_____   2. All five senses tend to decline in old age.

_____   3. Most older people have no interest in, or capacity for, sexual relations.

_____   4. Lung capacity tends to decline in old age.

_____   5. The majority of older people feel miserable most of the time.

_____   6. Physical strength tends to decline in old age.

_____   7. At least one-tenth of the aged are living in long-stay institutions (i.e., nursing homes, mental hospitals).

_____   8. Aged drivers have fewer accidents per person than drivers under 65.

_____   9. Most older workers cannot work as effectively as younger workers.

_____   10. About 80 percent of the aged are healthy enough to carry out their normal activities.

_____   11. Most older people are set in their ways and unable to change.

_____   12. Older people usually take longer to learn something new.

_____   13. It is almost impossible for most older people to learn new things.

_____   14. The reaction time of most older people tends to be slower than the reaction time of younger people.

_____   15. In general, most older people are pretty much alike.

_____   16. The majority of older people are seldom bored.

_____   17. The majority of older people are socially isolated and lonely.

_____   18. Older workers have fewer accidents than younger workers.

_____   19. Over 20 percent of the U.S. population is now age 65 or over.

_____   20. Most medical practitioners tend to give low priority to the aged.

_____   21. The majority of older people have incomes below the poverty level (as defined by the federal government).

_____   22. The majority of older people are working or would like to have some kind of work to do (including housework and volunteer work).

_____   23. Older people tend to become more religious as they age.

_____   24. The majority of older people are seldom irritated or angry.

_____   25. The health and socioeconomic status of older people (compared to younger people) in the future will probably be the same as now.

_____   26. Older workers get along well with other employees.

_____   27. Older workers are less productive than younger workers.

_____   28. The costs of health care for an older worker are lower than those for a younger, married worker with several children.

_____   29. Older workers are absent more often because of age-related infirmities and above-average rates of illness.

_____   30. Mental abilities (e.g., verbal, numerical, reasoning skills) remain stable into the seventies.

Source: Palmore, E. (1977). Facts on aging: A short quiz. *Gerontologist,* 17, 315–320. Copyright © The Gerontological Society of America. Reproduced by permission of the publisher.

EXERCISE 9.2

Career Development Self-Assessment Exercise

Overview

Most career development programs in organizations use self-assessment exercises. In fact, these exercises may be the first activities employees participate in that help them to better understand their personal career interests and goals. Self-appraisal is important for enhancing self-awareness. It generally requires the collection of data about yourself, such as your values, interests, and skills, and the determination of goals and action plans for life and career planning. As an employee you might want to engage in a self-assessment exercise for career planning purposes. As an HR professional, you might be asked to develop a self-assessment exercise to use with employees for career planning purposes. Examples of some of the possible activities that may be included in a self-assessment exercise are included in this exercise.

Learning Objectives

After completing this exercise, you should be able to

1. Understand your values, skills, interests, experiences, and life and career preferences.
2. Be able to describe your immediate goals, the associated benefits and risks, and the skills you may need to develop to meet your goals.
3. Understand some of your own work attitudes and preferences and the issues associated with making career decisions and changes.
4. Be able to describe some of the activities used in a self-assessment exercise.

Procedure

Part A: Individual Analysis

Step 1. Complete the self-assessment exercise in Form 9.2.1 before coming to class. Be as candid as possible in your responses.

Step 2. Each individual should answer the assessment questions listed in Form 9.2.2.

Part B: Group Analysis

As a class, address the following issues:

A. Discuss the importance of using a self-assessment as a career planning tool. Describe how a self-assessment may be beneficial for individual growth and development as well as for organizational HR purposes (e.g., staffing, training).
B. Explain how you might use a self-assessment tool as part of a career development system you design for an organization.

FORM 9.2.1

CAREER SELF-ASSESSMENT INSTRUMENT

Name _____

PART A: VALUES AND EXPERIENCES

1. Describe the roles in your life that are important to you. Examples might include your work or career, family life, leisure, religious life, community life, and volunteer activities. Explain why these roles are important to you. Indicate how important each role is to your total life satisfaction. Assign a percent to each role (0 to 100 percent) so that the total adds up to 100 percent.

2. Describe your background and experiences, including
    a. *Education.* List the names of technical schools or colleges you have attended. List degrees earned or to be earned and your major or minor.

    b. *Work experience.* List any jobs you have held, including part- and full-time jobs, voluntary jobs, internships, cooperative education (co-ops).

    c. *Skills.* Describe any skills that you possess that you feel would be valued in the workplace.

    d. *Extracurricular activities.* Describe any nonwork activities that you engage in for personal development or recreational pursuits.

    e. *Accomplishments.* Summarize any recognition you have received that is related to your education, work experience, skills, or extracurricular activities.

3. Read the following list of skills. Put a + next to those you feel you are particularly strong in and circle those you would like to develop more thoroughly in the future.

    Communication (written or oral communication, listening skills)

    Management skills (supervising, persuading others, planning, organizing, delegating, motivating others)

    Interpersonal skills (working effectively with others)

    Team building (working effectively with groups or teams)

    Creativity (innovativeness, generating ideas)

    Training skills (ability to teach skills and knowledges to others)

    Mathematical skills (computation ability, budgeting, accounting proficiency)

    Sales/promotion (ability to persuade, negotiate, influence)

    Scientific skills (investigative abilities, researching, analyzing)

    Service skills (handling complaints, customer relations)

    Office skills (word processing, filing, bookkeeping, recordkeeping)

4. Rate yourself on each of the following personal qualities or work characteristics. Write one response for each characteristic, using the following scale: 1, very low; 2, low; 3, average; 4, high; 5, very high.

_____ Emotional maturity   _____ Dependability in completing work

_____ Initiative/independence   _____ Flexibility and open-mindedness

_____ Punctuality   _____ Perseverance/willingness to work

_____ Ability to handle conflict   _____ Ability to set and achieve goals

_____ Ability to plan, organize, and determine work priorities   _____ Tolerance for ambiguous, unusual, or different ideas or situations

_____ Ability to work with others   _____ Ability to lead projects

_____ Willingness to do more than is expected (to go above and beyond requirements)   _____ Integrity in work (honesty)

       _____ Ability and interest in coaching others as needed

_____ Tolerance for changes in assignments or team members   _____ Ability and interest in supporting or recognizing others' contributions

PART B: WORK ATTITUDES AND PREFERENCES

1. Describe an ideal job for you. What would it be like? Describe the activities, people, rewards, and other features that would be a part of your job experience.

2. Think about the ideal job you described above. Rank the following values or attributes in terms of how important they are for you in your work (1 = most important; 12 = least important).

Values/Conditions	Rank
Independence or autonomy	_____
Financial reward or affluence	_____
Sense of achievement or accomplishment	_____
Helping others	_____
Creating something	_____
Equality, fairness	_____
Loyalty	_____
Job security	_____
Pleasant working conditions	_____
Friendships at work	_____
Variety of tasks	_____
Opportunities for promotions	_____

3.   What talents do you wish to use in your work?

4.   What type of working relationship with other people do you prefer? That is, do you prefer working alone or with other people? Do you enjoy working with a few people you know well or helping people you don't know?

5.   What type of physical work setting is desirable to you (e.g., office, outdoors, plant facility, working at home)?

6.   How much freedom and independence do you want in your work? For example, do you want to set your own hours? Determine your own projects? How much guidance or structure by others do you need in your work (i.e., do you need others to outline the scope of your projects and provide deadlines)?

7.   Think of one time when you felt like a real professional. What were you doing or what had you just done? Why was this achievement meaningful?

PART C: GOALS AND ACTION PLANNING

1.   Describe your career goals for the next several years.

2.   What specific things will you need to do to meet your goals?

3.   What internal and external obstacles might you encounter along the way toward achievement of your goals?

4.   Describe any skills or assistance you will need to meet your goals.

5.   How much commitment do you have to your goals? Explain.

1. What did you learn about yourself that you did not realize before?

2. How important are your career and work in your total life? Why is this important for you to realize?

3. How can completing a self-assessment assist you in preparing a résumé or interviewing for a job?

4. What will you do to follow up on this self-assessment?

EXERCISE 9.3

Career Development at TechnoChip Computers*

Overview

As noted in Chapter 9, career development has become an increasingly more important topic with which HR professionals need to be familiar. Organizations have adopted more career programs and have changed the role of managers to reflect more of a coaching function than a traditional supervisory job. As organizations change in terms of structure (more teams, flattening managerial hierarchies), HR professionals face greater pressures in designing effective career programs to meet the needs of a new, more diverse workforce. This exercise presents you with a case that you will need to analyze in order to design a career development system that can be used with the firm's employees.

Learning Objectives

After completing this exercise, you should be able to

1. Analyze a case to determine the career issues of importance for employees and the types of career programs that are currently in use.
2. Recommend career development tools that can be used for various types of employees and issues.

Procedure

Part A: Individual Analysis

Step 1. Read the background information about the company in Exhibits 9.3.1, 9.3.2, and 9.3.3.

Step 2. Complete the questions found in Form 9.3.1.

Part B: Group Analysis

Step 1. In teams of about five or six people, review each person's responses to the questions found in Form 9.3.1.

Step 2. Discuss your responses and reach consensus on the appropriate career development tools to implement in the sales division at TechnoChip Computers. Be sure to address the following issues:

a. What is the timeline for implementation of your ideas and recommendations for career interventions?

b. What are the potential drawbacks as well as advantages to your recommendations?

EXHIBIT 9.3.1

BACKGROUND INFORMATION ON TECHNOCHIP COMPUTERS

TechnoChip Computers is a nationwide computer manufacturing and sales organization. Annual corporate revenue is in excess of $3 billion. Headquarters are located in Troy, Michigan, and there are branch offices in 100 cities across the United States. There are three main divisions within the organization: product development and research, manufacturing and distribution, and sales. This project will focus on the sales division.

TechnoChip has experienced increased competitive pressure in the past three years. This has mainly come from the diversification of products offered in the computer marketplace and rapid technological advancements. While a leader in the computer industry, TechnoChip's annual sales have declined in the past several years, most notably in the past two. Some key indicators of corporate performance are listed below.

Performance Criteria	1999	2000	2001	2002
Annual sales	3.5	3.4	3.2	2.9
Growth of customer base (new customers)	1%	1%	−3%	−5%
Retention of existing customer base	90%	88%	82%	78%
Customer satisfaction	65%	64%	62%	60%

Notes: Annual sales indicated in billions. Growth of customer base measured as a percentage change from previous year, with positive values indicating an increase and negative values indicating a decrease. Customer satisfaction percentages indicate the percent of customers rating service and product quality "very good" or "good."

---

*Contributed by Lillian T. Eby and Joyce E. A. Russell.

EXHIBIT 9.3.1 (*Continued*)

To remain competitive in the years ahead, the new CEO of the sales division, Bryan Williams, and a core staff of organizational representatives have refined the mission and strategic objectives for the organization. Their revised mission statement is presented below.

Mission Statement of TechnoChip Computers: Sales Division

Increase TechnoChip's shareholder value and remain the undisputed leader in the computer industry through:

- Satisfying customer needs and exceeding customer expectations
- Improving productivity through employee empowerment and quality principles
- Hiring, developing, and retaining top employees

Strategic Objectives for TechnoChip Computers: Sales Division

- Grow the existing customer base 3 percent annually over the next five years.
- Develop specialized sales teams to offer customized service to existing customers.
- Increase customer perceptions of product quality and customer service. Specifically, by 2007, 90 percent of customer satisfaction ratings should be in the "very good" to "good" category.
- Increase customer retention so that in five years, customer retention rates are at 96 percent.
- Increase employee perceptions that TechnoChip is the employer of choice. Key indicators of this will be turnover rates, job satisfaction, and commitment to the organization.

To accomplish the strategic objectives, TechnoChip decided to reorganize work around segmented sales teams in the sales division, instead of continuing the current practice of having individuals try to sell computers to all types of markets. It was believed that the change to teams would allow sales representatives to better meet customer needs by becoming experts in a particular business market. In the new system, sales reps would be better able to develop long-term relationships with customers because they would be servicing the same customers each year. This approach greatly differed from the "old" way of doing things, where sales reps serviced different customers every year. TechnoChip is also embracing employee empowerment by allowing the teams considerable latitude in decision making, work scheduling, and productivity management.

The change to teams occurred six months ago. Within each division, teams were created consisting of 4 to 13 members. Each team was formed to specialize in a particular business segment, and the size of the teams was determined based on the relative size of the business segments. To illustrate this work arrangement, the structure of the Newark, New Jersey, sales division is presented below.

Business Segment	Percentage of Total Market Sales	Number of team Members
Mainframe computers	15%	10
Management information systems (hardware & software)	35	21
Educational computers and software	10	8
International computer systems	10	8
Personal computers	30	19

NATURE OF THE JOB

Sales representatives can consist of telephone sales representatives who are primarily responsible for calling customers and on-site reps who make actual visits to meet with customers. Each team consists of several telephone reps and several on-site reps. Team members' duties and responsibilities are highly interdependent with one another. Sales calls (phone or on-site) to a customer are typically made by a team of individuals, each of whom has expertise in a certain function (e.g., installation, software, hardware). All team members are expected to have basic knowledge of each other's jobs. For instance, if Allie specializes in installation, then she also needs to have expertise in software and hardware for the particular business segment. In this sense, the teams are expected to be cross-functional. In addition, all team members are responsible for having knowledge specific to their business segment. This is necessary for customer expectations to be exceeded. This can be obtained in a variety of ways, including attending seminars, subscribing to trade journals, and reading current business articles.

CHARACTERISTICS OF THE SALES FORCE

Each city has a sales force of approximately 50 employees, although in larger cities, the sales force may have as many as 80 employees. The total sales force consists of about 7,000 sales reps (4,000 telephone sales reps; 3,000 on-site sales reps) and about 200 managers and 650 team leaders. At least 40 percent of the sales representatives have college degrees and the rest have high school degrees or some college. The average age of a sales rep is about 32, with most reps anywhere from 21 to 58 years old. The average tenure with the company is about 8 years, with most ranging from 1 year to about 25 years of service with TechnoChip.

In the new team environment, former managers have been renamed team leaders or coaches. This individual works side-by-side with the team and acts as a resource for the team by obtaining support for new ideas and facilitating team decision making. The organization is just starting to examine the training needs of its team leaders to help them in their new role as coach. An organizational chart is presented in Exhibit 9.3.2.

OTHER ONGOING INITIATIVES

Consistent with the mission statement, other efforts also have been made to increase employee perceptions of empowerment. This includes instituting a formal suggestion system and starting quality action teams to solve divisionwide problems (similar to quality circles). In addition, in the past three months, the sales division, in all locations, has implemented an employee survey system to collect feedback from employees about their views on the changes and other suggestions. The findings from this survey are presented in Exhibit 9.3.3.

EXHIBIT 9.3.2

ORGANIZATIONAL CHART FOR SALES DIVISIONS AT TECHNOCHIP COMPUTERS

EXHIBIT 9.3.3

SURVEY RESULTS FROM SALES DIVISION

GENERAL RESULTS

Sales representatives responded to a survey in which they indicated whether they were satisfied, neutral, or dissatisfied with various aspects of their jobs. The results for some of the issues are noted below:

- **Job content plateauing:** 55 percent of all sales reps reported *not* feeling plateaued with respect to the nature of the job. In other words, they felt that they were given interesting work and it was not mundane or routine; 10 percent were neutral; and 35 percent felt that they were plateaued and were doing boring work. Telephone sales reps were much more likely to indicate that they were plateaued or bored than were on-site sales reps.
- **Satisfaction with job challenges:** 58 percent of all sales reps reported that they were satisfied with the challenges on their job (i.e., feelings of worthwhile accomplishments, personal growth and development); 12 percent were neutral; and 30 percent reported being dissatisfied with the degree of challenge provided by their jobs. Telephone reps were much more likely than on-site reps to indicate they were dissatisfied.
- **Autonomy:** 70 percent of all sales employees agreed that they were given autonomy in completing their work; 20 percent were neutral; and 10 percent disagreed that they were given autonomy in doing their work. Telephone reps were more likely to indicate they were not given autonomy than were on-site reps.
- **Participation in decision making:** 60 percent of all sales reps agreed that they participated in decision making; 20 percent were neutral; and 20 percent disagreed.
- **Job security:** 55 percent of all sales employees agreed that they were satisfied with their job security or felt secure about their jobs; 10 percent were neutral; and 35 percent felt insecure (or fearful about losing their jobs). No differences were detected between on-site and telephone sales reps in their perceived job security.
- **Promotional opportunities:** 25 percent of all sales reps were satisfied with their chances for promotion or felt that the promotion process was a fair one; 15 percent were neutral; and 60 percent were dissatisfied with the promotion system in place. Note that sales reps could be promoted only one level higher than their current position to the position of team leader. No differences were detected between on-site and telephone sales reps.
- **Career guidance and development system:** 20 percent of all sales reps indicated they were satisfied with the career guidance and development provided to them by the company; 10 percent were neutral; and 70 percent reported being dissatisfied. No differences were detected for telephone or on-site reps.
- **Coaching system:** 25 percent of all sales reps indicated they were satisfied with the coaching provided by their team leader; 10 percent were neutral; and 65 percent reported being dissatisfied. No differences were detected for telephone and on-site reps. Note that 90 percent of all reps reported liking their team leaders. They did, however, feel that their team leaders did not devote enough time to coaching them or providing career assistance.
- **Team leaders' perspective on coaching:** 100 percent of all team leaders felt they did not have enough time to do all their job duties. All indicated that they did not have enough time to coach sales reps. Further, they indicated that in their performance appraisals, their bosses emphasized meeting sales quotas and never mentioned "coaching sales reps" or "career development of reps" as important job duties of team leaders.
- **Role clarity:** 80 percent of all sales reps reported that their roles were clear and that they knew what their job duties were; 10 percent were neutral; and 10 percent reported their roles were not clear. No differences were detected among on-site and telephone sales reps. Seventy-five percent of all team leaders reported that their roles were *not* clear; 10 percent were neutral; and 15 percent felt their roles were clear.
- **Job-induced tension:** 45 percent stated they experienced job-induced tension, while 10 percent were neutral; and 45 percent stated they did not experience job-induced tension. Job-induced tension refers to stress created by the work (having too much to do; conflicts at work; thinking about work-related problems off-duty; experiencing physical symptoms of stress such as ulcers, fatigue, headaches). On-site sales reps were more likely to report higher levels of job-induced stress than were telephone sales reps. Team leaders also reported high levels of job-induced tension.
- **Work–family conflict:** 60 percent of all sales reps indicated they experienced work–family conflict or stress; 15 percent were neutral; and 25 percent reported they did not experience work–family conflict or stress. On-site reps were much more likely to report experiencing work–family stress than were telephone sales reps due to all the traveling the on-site reps do.

Name _____   Group _____

1. For each of the following groups of employees in the sales division at TechnoChip Computers, first identify their career-related concerns as noted from the survey results. Then provide some recommendations for each group to meet career or job-related needs.
    A. Telephone sales employees:
        1. Concerns:

        2. Recommendations:

    B. On-site sales employees:
        1. Concerns:

        2. Recommendations:

    C. Team leaders:
        1. Concerns:

        2. Recommendations:

2. Describe the advantages and disadvantages to your recommendations as well as a timeline for when they should be implemented.

3. How would you assess whether the programs you have recommended for employees are perceived positively or improve attitudes after they are implemented? (Hint: Review the evaluation section in Chapter 8.) Should additional surveys be conducted with sales employees and their team leaders? If so, how often and what types of questions should be asked? What would you do with those data?

4. Review TechnoChip's mission statement, strategic objectives, and the survey feedback results. Based on what you learned in Chapter 8, identify the training needs for each of the following groups of employees:
    A. Telephone sales employees:

    B. On-site sales employees:

    C. Team leaders:

5. For each specific training need you identified above, what types of training methods would be appropriate to incorporate into the training? (Hint: Review the description of training methods and techniques in Chapter 8.)

6. Some of the employee attitude problems TechnoChip is facing may be due to the fact that when current employees were hired the job was very different than it is today. What steps can TechnoChip management take before hiring future sales employees and team leaders to be sure the applicants have a realistic assessment of what the job is like? (Hint: Think about what you learned in the previous chapters about job analysis, recruiting, and selecting employees.)

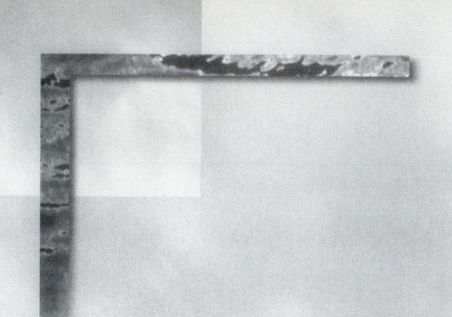

Chapter 10 Exercises

EXERCISE 10.1

Problems in the Pay System*

Overview

Chapter 10 discusses the importance of internal and external equity in structuring an effective pay program. This exercise describes a situation in which perceived inequities exist and the organization is already realizing the effects of these perceptions.

Learning Objectives

After completing the exercise, you should be able to

1. Determine the critical variables that must be considered in assessing the fairness of a pay system.
2. Assess the weights to be given to data related to internal and external equity.
3. Develop a system that can more closely monitor the effects of pay on critical personnel data.

Procedure

Part A: Individual Analysis

After reading the chapter and before class, read the scenario and all exhibits and then answer the questions on Form 10.1.1.

Part B: Group Analysis

In groups of about six, students should first review all of their respective Forms 10.1.1 and then attempt to reach consensus on the questions. The group should prepare a concise, written response to each of the questions on Form 10.1.1.

Scenario

Denise Nance is the director of the Computer Center/User Assistance (CCUA) department of a large manufacturing company in the rural Southeast. Last year's revenue was $23.5 million. Profit was in line with expectations.

Recently, a serious problem has developed in her division. A growing percentage of her employees have left the company in the past year, which has affected unit productivity and costs. While turnover in her department has always been a problem, things appear to have gotten out of hand. Until now, turnover had run around 20 percent per year for lower division staff personnel and 15 percent per year for middle division employees.

However, in the past three months, CCUA has lost five data processors (50 percent of the total) and six (75 percent) computer analysts. Previously, Ms. Nance had no policy regarding exit interviews or turnover control, but informal discussions with the individuals who

have left has led to the hypothesis that many employees leave because they feel they are underpaid.

To complicate matters, Ms. Nance's supervisor, Julie Linquist, the vice president in charge of technical services, is becoming increasingly concerned about the costs associated with the human resource function at CCUA. Exhibit 10.1.1 presents a recent memo from Ms. Linquist to Ms. Nance concerning the problem.

Following Ms. Linquist's orders, Ms. Nance conducted phone interviews with 12 former employees (the only ones available) and distributed questionnaires to her current workforce.

The survey results indicated a number of interesting findings, which are summarized in Exhibit 10.1.2. The dominant reason for individuals leaving CCUA was pay. The current workforce also indicated strong dissatisfaction with current pay levels. Although the survey was not limited to data processing IIs and computer analyst Is, both Ms. Nance and Ms. Linquist believe that these two positions are of particular concern. Responses from both current and past employees from both job classifications were similar to those of the entire sample.

The data processor II position currently carries a salary range of $11.00 to $12.70 per hour. The average actual pay of the seven incumbents is $12 per hour ($24,960 per year based on their 40-hour workweek). In addition, employees receive 40 hours of paid leave for the first year with an increase of 5 hours every 1,000 hours of service. Health insurance plus basic life insurance are provided by the company at a cost of $950 per year per employee. CCUA usually employs 10 DP IIs, but the current level is only 7.

The computer analyst I position currently carries a salary range of $25,500 to $32,500. The average actual salary paid to the eight incumbents is $31,500. Paid leave for CA IIs is 9 days for the first year of service increasing by 2 days for every following year with a limit of 21 days of paid leave. Health and life insurance coverage costs the company $950 per year per employee.

Recruitment costs for data processor IIs is $450 and $850 for computer analyst Is. Costs are low for the DP IIs because they have been obtained, primarily, from the local marketplace. Entry-level individuals are hired 75 percent of the time and the organization spends considerable resources to train them. By contrast, the computer analysts are recruited from the regional market. Prime candidates typically possess either considerable experience in a similar position or a college degree in information systems management with light, but related, part-time (or summer) work experience.

Ms. Nance budgets $255,490 for data processing IIs and $293,984 for computer analysts. The company is in

*Contributed by James R. Harris and Lee P. Stepina.

the sixth month of its fiscal year. During this fiscal year, the CCUA department has been using a 3.5 percent salary increase budget to reward its performers and to keep pace with the marketplace.

Ms. Nance obtained a pay survey conducted by Decision Sciences, Inc., a reputable, information systems consulting firm. The data are depicted in Exhibit 10.1.3.

A compensation analyst at DSI has suggested that, based on the verbal descriptions provided by Ms. Nance, the data processor II position would probably most closely match the survey's "data processor" position, while CCUA's computer analyst I job is most comparable with the survey's "junior analyst and programmer" position.

EXHIBIT 10.1.1

```
To: Denise Nance, Director of CCUA

From: Julie Linquist, Vice President Technical Services

Re: Personnel Problems


I don't know what's going on down there but Jon Anderson of placement services just informed me that
you requested another listing for a data processing person and another computer analyst. According
to my records, that's the fifth DP person and the sixth computer analyst you have lost this year! It
costs a lot of money to hire new people. This is obviously not the pattern that I want to see from
your department. I want you to investigate this immediately.

I want you to contact the individuals who you lost and find out why they left. I also want you to
talk to the employees who are still there and find what, if anything, could potentially be causing
the problem. Let's get this problem cleared up now.
```

EXHIBIT 10.1.2

SURVEY RESULTS

All items scaled 1 (satisfied) to 5 (dissatisfied).

Current Employees	Mean	SD
Supervision	2.1	1.6
Working conditions	1.9	1.8
Task characteristics	3.0	2.1
Pay	4.2	0.5
Benefits	4.3	1.1
Work hours	3.1	.9
Physical conditions	1.4	1.5
General satisfaction	3.9	0.7

Employees Who Left	Mean	SD
Supervision	1.9	1.5
Working conditions	2.4	1.7
Task characteristics	3.7	2.0
Pay	4.8	1.1
Benefits	4.5	0.6
Work hours	3.0	2.0
Physical conditions	1.7	0.5
General satisfaction	4.2	1.2
Reasons for leaving:		
Not enough money	83.3%	
Spouse left area	8.3%	
Child care problems	8.3%	

EXHIBIT 10.1.3

EXCERPT FROM DECISION SCIENCES

Title	Average Weighted Salary	Mfg/ Consumer	Mfg/ Industrial	Banking	Other Financial Services	DP Services	Wholesale Distribution
IS Management							
CIO/VP	106,864	128,611	100,741	124,318	109,130	157,500	130,000
Manager/supervisor	65,811	83,333	74,821	76,500	67,143	60,000	57,143
End-User Support							
Manager end-user computing	56,808	74,167	62,667	57,500	58,500	55,000	48,750
Information center manager	54,346	56,667	60,833	56,818	53,500	63,333	49,000
PC specialist support	38,058	40,000	48,077	39,211	36,250	37,000	38,636
LAN manager	45,880	55,000	52,857	46,000	46,000	52,000	52,000
WP supervisor	36,538	55,000	42,500	32,600	34,000	40,000	34,000
Systems Analysis/Programming							
Manager	65,357	83,182	63,913	68,611	64,286	66,364	72,000
Senior systems analyst and programmer	50,345	50,714	53,333	52,143	51,471	56,250	52,000
Systems analyst and programmer	43,220	44,000	43,462	45,250	42,647	48,750	60,455
Intermediate analyst and programmer	37,517	40,000	38,571	37,750	38,000	38,125	40,000
Junior analyst and programmer	35,156	33,750	40,714	35,000	32,143	37,500	32,875
Application/Operating Systems Programming Manager	64,481	79,000	67,667	68,529	71,765	68,750	66,667
Senior applications/operating sys. prog.	52,434	55,000	55,938	52,353	56,000	55,000	53,125
Applications/operating sys. prog.	44,419	48,571	46,250	46,176	46,563	46,429	40,000
Intermediate applications/operating sys. prog.	37,150	42,500	40,000	35,000	38,636	35,000	37,500
Junior applications/operating sys. prog.	29,709	30,000	32,500	29,615	30,455	30,000	28,750
Data Com/Telecom/Connectivity							
Network manager (LAN-WAN)	57,546	63,750	59,643	59,643	72,500	57,222	58,333
Telecommunications manager	57,136	58,750	66,111	59,231	67,500	63,125	60,000
Communications specialist	42,276	37,000	43,000	41,667	46,818	40,000	43,750
Database manager/administrator	61,077	71,000	60,500	64,643	70,385	52,500	62,000
Database analyst	48,194	52,000	55,000	46,000	51,250	42,500	47,500
Microcomputer/workstation manager	44,500	35,000	55,000	46,818	43,750	47,500	43,750
Data processor	27,500	26,000	29,000	28,000	26,500	26,000	27,000

EXHIBIT 10.1.3 (*Continued*)

Government	Medical/ Legal	Trans./ Utilities	Education	Construction/ Mining	Other	Average Salary by Company Revenue ($ Million)				
						Less than $200	$200– $499	$500– $4,999	$5,000– $19,999	$20,000+
71,731	64,500	114,167	103,571	76,667	101,600	82,292	84,697	104,844	128,780	129,700
51,739	42,500	66,667	51,250	52,000	65,104	50,204	61,094	68,534	75,811	73,269
53,750	—	63,462	49,000	43,750	54,310	47,200	46,667	58,871	62,593	60,857
47,500	40,000	61,364	46,000	—	51,500	43,529	46,250	56,957	60,741	56,071
30,455	27,143	41,071	31,429	30,000	38,250	36,053	31,600	39,405	40,429	40,833
42,500	40,000	44,500	34,000	40,000	45,833	42,368	46,667	48,519	46,250	46,172
36,667	40,000	40,000	25,000	25,000	38,846	32,500	40,000	36,667	38,235	37,000
55,294	40,000	67,105	50,000	62,500	65,814	58,958	53,421	65,288	71,216	68,261
45,926	40,000	52,750	40,000	46,000	49,375	46,935	46,250	49,500	53,784	52,843
38,571	35,000	42,727	32,500	40,000	41,667	45,000	39,464	42,750	43,663	44,692
31,316	25,000	39,000	32,500	40,000	38,448	35,000	38,333	38,256	36,250	38,500
32,500	30,000	40,313	30,000	30,000	33,913	37,500	36,000	33,529	33,750	36,667
53,333	47,500	66,875	47,500	62,500	62,027	51,667	51,250	66,395	70,789	68,889
47,105	—	56,875	45,000	47,500	50,286	43,947	46,667	52,391	55,429	57,206
37,500	40,000	47,000	36,000	55,000	43,500	41,500	37,273	44,390	45,571	46,562
33,571	—	38,846	32,500	—	36,250	40,000	30,455	38,448	35,556	39,444
23,125	—	37,273	25,000	26,000	26,875	30,000	26,875	30,192	29,038	31,176
49,231	47,500	68,750	40,000	55,000	60,000	46,154	61,667	54,630	80,000	64,500
46,429	—	54,231	43,750	55,000	55,556	41,538	48,333	57,000	82,258	61,852
36,786	—	49,000	36,250	55,000	41,071	39,000	33,182	39,189	45,825	47,857
51,786	—	69,000	55,033	70,000	55,962	47,778	51,364	60,000	66,818	66,765
42,143	—	50,000	40,000	55,000	46,136	46,000	46,429	46,207	48,500	50,781
43,000	40,000	47,600	40,000	—	38,848	35,714	43,750	45,000	44,412	47,941
25,000	28,000	25,500	25,000	—	28,000	25,000	27,000	28,000	28,500	29,000

Name _____   Group _____

You have been retained as a consultant to evaluate the situation and make recommendations for action. Ms. Nance wants your positions on the following:

1. Are the CCUA department's current pay practices concerning data processor IIs and computer analyst Is externally equitable (i.e., competitive)? Explain your answer.

2. What specific action, if any, do you recommend be taken now? Be specific and justify your recommendations as fully as possible.

3. What specific strategy(ies) do you recommend for the future so that these types of problems can be anticipated and (it is hoped) avoided.

4. As is often the case in business, we typically find that we must make decisions, or recommendations, on the basis of incomplete, imperfect information. What additional information in this situation would have enabled you to improve the quality of your recommendations?

5. Conduct a Web search (O*NET?) to determine how accurate the data are in Exhibit 10.1.3 for the systems analyst/programmer job title. Summarize your findings below, citing the relevant Web site(s) and the methods of the pay survey. What are the outsourcing options for the data processing and computer analyst jobs? Locate pay data for outsourcing options.

EXERCISE 10.2

Should the State Adopt a Pay Equity Policy?

Overview

The chapter discusses the controversial issue of pay equity or comparable worth. Many U.S. states and municipalities and over 100 countries have adopted some form of pay equity policy for government workers. Ontario, Canada has mandated pay equity for all public and private employers. Many collective bargaining writs now place great emphasis on pay equity adjustments based on studies that find evidence of gender- or race-based inequities in the pay system. This exercise examines the issues and implications of pay equity for public and private employers. Students will review the summary of a pay equity study.

Learning Objectives

After completing the exercise, you should be able to

1. Understand the major components of a pay equity study.
2. Anticipate some of the advantages and disadvantages of a pay equity policy.
3. Discuss the implications of pay equity adjustments on market rates and private-sector employment.

Procedure

Part A: Individual Analysis

Congratulations! You have been appointed to the State University Task Force on Compensation. Your assignment is to review the report (Exhibit 10.2.1) submitted by a consulting firm under contract to an ad hoc committee of the state legislature. After reviewing state compensation information and conducting a pay equity study, the consulting firm made specific recommendations to the legislature. As a member of the task force, your job is to take a position on each of the recommendations. On Form 10.2.1, state your position and provide a justification in the space provided. Answer all of the questions on Form 10.2.1.

Part B: Group Analysis

In groups, students should attempt to reach consensus on the recommendations. Each group should prepare concise justifications for its recommendations.

EXHIBIT 10.2.1

EXECUTIVE SUMMARY OF PAY EQUITY STUDY

The underlying theory of pay equity is that the wages for female- and minority-dominated occupations are artificially depressed due to historical bias against the value of "women's work." The goal of pay equity studies is to use objectively measured criteria to examine the relative value of all jobs to an employer in an effort to correct for any gender- and race-based undervaluation.

Crucial to pay equity policy is the recognition that jobs that require equivalent or *comparable* skill, effort, responsibility, and working conditions should be compensated equally. Once implemented, pay equity policy assures that an employer's classification and compensation systems are administered and maintained objectively and fairly.

Pay equity studies are typically conducted using point-factor job evaluations but with comparisons across job families. In the most common approach, known as "policy-capturing," benchmark jobs for major job families are evaluated using a point-factor job evaluation method and current salaries are then statistically related to the factors and the points. A statistical equation emerges that derives the weights for the factors rated in the study which best predicts the actual salary for the benchmark jobs (based on the job factors). For example, the predictive weight for "knowledge" might be three times as great as the weight for "supervisory responsibilities," which in turn may be twice as predictive as "budget authority." This equation is derived from the study of major job families. Then, if it's a gender equity study, female-dominated job families (jobs with 70 percent or more women) are identified and the overall equation is used with the point-factor results to "predict" the salaries for the female-dominated families. Now, a perfectly fair system would find that when the overall equation attempts to predict the salaries for the female dominated jobs, the predictions closely match actual salaries. But what typically happens is that when the points applied to the female-dominated job families are inserted in the predictive equation, the result is an estimate of salary that is substantially higher than the salary the female-dominated job families are actually earning. Females in the female-dominated jobs are thus "underpaid" when their real pay is compared to their "predicted" pay based on the overall pay "policy." A pay equity policy would use the predictive equation from all job families and adjust the female-dominated jobs to match the salaries that are predicted. This would be considered pay equity.

To accomplish the above objective, we examined a representative sample of 300 families in the career service system. This served as the basis of our analysis in determining objectively what job content characteristics the state values when setting pay. The question that guided this study is, in setting pay rates, does the state value work differently (and perhaps in a biased manner) for male-dominated jobs as opposed to female- and minority-dominated jobs? In other words, is there a difference in monetary return for jobs with similar characteristics and requirements?

The state utilizes a position classification system whereby positions are consolidated into job families and these families are assigned to pay grades. This study was designed to provide a model of "equitable compensation" for the state that is based largely on its current pay policy. Using this model, the analysis shows which classes are underpaid due to the influence of female or minority dominance of the job. The recommendations, if adopted, will bring female- and minority-dominated classes in line with equitable compensation.

The approach utilized for this study was *policy capturing*. Through policy capturing, the relative worth to the state of all jobs in a system is evaluated. As a first step a compensation model is developed in which specific job content features, such as the number of persons supervised, the level of education, the level of analytic reasoning, and the years of prerequisite experience are grouped into compensable factors. Each of the 300 job families is then evaluated in terms of relevance of each factor. Exhibit 10.2.2 presents a portion of the methodology used to evaluate compensable factors. As described above, these factors are then weighted in such a way that they statistically "predict" the current wage structure for the 300 families. In other words, the weights for each compensable job content characteristic are derived from a statistical model that makes explicit what is currently valued implicitly within an organization across all job families and jobs. The relationship between compensable factors and how they are paid thus becomes clear. The ability of each compensable factor to predict salary level is derived through policy capturing. Pay equity adjustments are indicated when this statistical relationship is violated simply because the jobs are performed by a high percentage of females and minorities. This methodology was selected because it does not impose outside standards for fair compensation on the state. Rather, it looks at the current compensation policy and simply adjusts the existing system in instances where its own standards are not met. Policy capturing techniques thus allow the state to adjust its salary grades to eliminate any influence of gender or race bias without radically altering its basic philosophy of compensation.

FINDINGS

As a result of the above analysis, it was determined there is substantial undervaluation of female- and minority-dominated classes in the Career Service System. A model of equitable compensation has been developed to adjust for the resulting pay inequities.

Another objective of this study was to assess the cost of correcting gender- or race-based pay inequities for the purpose of budget planning by the legislature. The total cost to the state for making pay equity adjustments to the female- and minority-dominated classes is estimated to be $75,552,000. An implementation model is recommended that suggests an appropriations schedule of $9,552,000 for the first year and $16,500,000 for the next four years to adjust base-pay rates.

The wage-setting process in the state is not structured in a way that facilitates the maintenance of internal equity. This is primarily because there is no quantitative job evaluation system tied to a unified wage structure that would keep future inequities from occurring. Women and minorities are underrepresented in job classes at the upper end of the wage structure.

EXHIBIT 10.2.2

PART OF POINT FACTOR JOB EVALUATION METHOD

1. Prerequisite knowledge
   - 11   Doctorate, law, medical, or other degree beyond master's
   - 10   Master's
   - 9   Some graduate education, but no degree
   - 8   B.A. or B.S.
   - 7   Two- or three-year college degree
   - 6   Some business or vocational school courses (such as typing, nursing, or drafting), *after* finishing high school or G.E.D.
   - 5   Some college
   - 4   High school or G.E.D.
   - 3   Some business or vocational courses (such as typing, nursing, plumbing, or drafting) but no G.E.D. or high school degree
   - 2   Some high school
   - 1   Elementary school
   - 0   None

2. Experience
   - 5   5 years or equivalent
   - 4   4 years
   - 3   3 years
   - 2   2 years
   - 1   1 year
   - 0   None

3. Supervision
   - 4   Major program or department
   - 3   Second-line supervision—supervises supervisors
   - 2   First-line supervision—hire, fire, discipline, promote
   - 1   Does not supervise, but coordinates, plans, and schedules, may be team leader or occasional supervisor
   - 0   Does not supervise

4. Mathematics
   - 3   Complex mathematics (statistics, advanced trig, and algebra)
   - 2   Basic math
   - 1   Basic arithmetic
   - 0   None

5. Special certification or license
   - 1   Yes
   - 0   No

6. Writing
   - 10   Technical, legal, scholarly, or policy analysis of length and creativity
   - 9   Formal reports or manual, technical reports/manual, more routine
   - 8   Monthly or annual reports, programs or work plans, technical specs, reports for others to review
   - 7   News releases, speeches
   - 6   Case histories
   - 5   Editing writing of others
   - 4   Writing original letters or memos
   - 3   Taking or writing minutes, dictation
   - 2   Writing (including patient records)
   - 1   Simple recording, tallying
   - 0   None

7. Information gathering
   - 6   Deciding what information should be gathered (policy decisions)
   - 5   Deciding how information should be gathered (design and planning decisions)
   - 4   Conducting complex information gathering—not routine
   - 3   Conducting data analysis under other's supervision—including lab tests
   - 2   Cataloging or classifying information
   - 1   Collecting or tallying information
   - 0   None

EXHIBIT 10.2.2 (*Continued*)

8. Recordkeeping
    4   Maintains records and files where confidentiality is required
    3   Maintains detailed client, patient, or inmate records, weekly or monthly
    2 Prepares and maintains files and records such as personnel, technical, financial
    1 Prepares and maintains daily records such as logs, supply inventory, medical charts, daily calendar
    0 None

 9. Organize/prioritize work
    5 Set work objectives for agency
    4 Responsible for organizing and prioritizing work in unit
    3 Responsible for organizing and prioritizing work of projects
    2 Organize and prioritize own work and schedule appointments for others (not limited to coworkers)
    1 Organize own work only
    0 No responsibility for organizing work

10. Training/teaching (integral part of job)
    5 Developing and implementing educational programs at the state level for employees at educational agencies
    4 Other employees
    3 Clients, inmates, patients
    2 Students
    1 Training/teaching on occasion
    0 None

11. Budget authority
    5 Determine budget priorities for major department
    4 Set budget for division within major department
    3 Propose or prepare budget or financial projection for unit
    2 Propose or prepare budget or financial projection for individual projects (includes assembling data)
    1 Authority to spend budgeted money
    0 No budget authority

12. Laws, policies, regulations, administrative codes	Yes	No
a. Develop agency position and defend laws or administrative codes	_____	_____
b. Draft laws or administrative codes for agency use	_____	_____
c. Ensure compliance with law, regulation, or administrative codes with public	_____	_____
d. Ensure compliance within or across agencies	_____	_____
e. Interpret administrative codes and regulations in order to carry out job responsibilities (i.e., determining eligibility or safety compliance)	_____	_____

Name _____   Group _____

1. The state legislature should appropriate $75,552,000 to cover the costs of the pay equity adjustments indicated by this study.
    Agree _____ Disagree _____ Unsure _____. If you are unsure, what additional information do you require before you take a position?

    Justification:

2. The policy-capturing analysis established that there is a violation of the Equal Pay Act.
    True _____ False _____

    Explain your answer:

3. Based on the Supreme Court ruling in *Johnson v. Santa Clara Transportation,* the state should establish an affirmative action program for women and minorities because such groups are underrepresented in job classes at the upper end of the wage structure. The program should allow the state to take gender and/or minority status into consideration when making decisions about hiring or pay.
    Agree _____ Disagree _____

    Justification:

4. The results of the "policy capturing" study established that there is a violation of Title VII.
    True _____ False _____

    Explain your answer:

5. If the state follows the recommendations, what impact could the policy have on private-sector compensation?

6. To create internal equity faster and more cheaply, the consultants could have recommended reducing the pay of "overpaid" jobs or workers. Please comment.

7. Explain exactly how the pay equity study determined that female-dominated jobs were "underpaid" and that some male-dominated jobs were found to be "overpaid." What does the term *policy capturing* mean in terms of this pay equity study?

EXERCISE 10.3

Developing an Employee Benefits Program*

Overview

Chapter 10 provides an overview of types of employee benefits programs. The following exercise describes a new business start-up and some key decisions that need to be made if this organization is going to succeed with its planned "preferred employer" strategy.

Learning Objectives

After completing the exercise, you should be able to

1. Determine the critical issues that must be considered when designing an employee benefits program.
2. Identify the trade-offs that are made when choosing from a wide variety of benefits alternatives.
3. Decide how to judge the effectiveness of a benefits program.

Procedure

Part A: Individual Analysis

After reading the chapter and before coming to class, read the scenario and all exhibits and then answer the questions on Form 10.3.1.

Part B: Group Analysis

In groups, students should first review all their forms 10.3.1 and then attempt to reach consensus on the questions. The group should prepare a concise, written response to each question on Form 10.3.1.

Scenario

USA Credit is a major financial services organization with growing interests in the private label credit card area. The organization began three years ago when it successfully acquired the credit card portfolios of five major U.S. retailers that were interested in outsourcing their programs. Since then, the organization has grown to a $1.5 billion business covering 25 retailers with a total of 6 million cardholders. Since its founding, USA Credit has targeted medium-sized retailers that like the customer closeness associated with having their own credit card but lack the technical expertise to effectively manage an accounts receivable business. USA Credit's business plan projects that it will double in size in the next two to three years. In addition, it plans to develop a bank card product and aggressively market it to small financial institutions that need this service to compete with the "megabanks" moving into their neighborhoods.

Traditionally, the business has used one of two organization models in its credit card relationships, depending on the needs and the sophistication of the retail client. With its earliest acquisitions, USA Credit simply subcontracted the credit and collections function and staffed the store-based credit offices with its own personnel who processed customers' applications for credit, accepted payments, and assisted customers in the resolution of billing questions and problems. As the business grew, regional processing centers became the more efficient model, facilitated by sophisticated information systems. In recent acquisitions the on-site credit offices have been replaced with a bank of telephones tied directly to the regional processing center. In addition, there is a payment drop box for customer payments and an attractive kiosk containing applications and assorted credit-related information. Recent customer surveys indicate elimination of the traditional, staffed credit office has had no effect on customer satisfaction. In addition, retailers express a neutral attitude concerning whether or not there is a staffed, on-site office. Their major concerns focus on (1) increasing the number of credit card customers; (2) maintaining accurate billing information that is summarized in attractively designed monthly statements to customers; and (3) maximizing collection efforts.

Since its founding, USA Credit's offices (both store-based and regional) have been staffed with part-time employees working 20–25 hours per week. Most employees are full-time students, mothers of school-age children, and senior citizens. Employees have been paid wages similar to those offered by other entry-level employers in the area, such as fast-food restaurants and retailers. No employee benefits have been offered, except those required by law.

Several months ago, USA Credit's top management team decided its future goals would best be met by establishing a national service center to replace the regional and in-store credit offices. The firm's information technology is more than capable of supporting such a shift and executives believe that this would effectively position the company for the expected short-term growth, as well as a long-term plan to expand into Mexico and Canada. They wish to attract a full-time workforce in order to provide stability and a level of professionalism as new accounts are added and as strategic services are expanded. Estimates are that the center would initially employ 75 customer service associates and 4 to 7 other individuals, such as managers and technical specialists. If business grows according to plan, the number of customer service associates is expected to double over the next few years.

A lengthy search has been conducted using a cross-functional managerial team, which included Andy

*Contributed by Christine M. Hagan.

Wolfson, USA Credit's HR manager. After months of research, the team recommended locating the center on a two-acre lot just northeast of Las Vegas, Nevada. Real estate values are excellent in the region, the profile of the local worker is very appealing, the tax situation is favorable, and state and local political and community organizations welcome the opportunity to sponsor the opening of a solid, reputable, growing business such as USA Credit. Last week, the recommendation was unanimously approved for implementation. Groundbreaking is scheduled for next month.

Andy Wolfson's main challenge is to assemble an HR plan. A key element of this involves designing a compensation and benefits program for the customer service associates. In addition to its state-of-the-art information systems technology, the competence and courtesy of its associates are expected to be major sources of competitive advantage. If USA Credit is going to continue to be successful in this upcoming growth period, it will be because it didn't lose focus on current customers and the customer service associates at the national service center would be critical contributors to this effort. Andy has requested a variety of information from knowledgeable sources concerning the employee marketplace and the practices of other area businesses. Exhibit 10.3.1 is a copy of a memo concerning local conditions that sums up the vast majority of information that he has compiled from other sources. Based on this information, he has sent a preliminary proposal to the corporate vice president for administration. Exhibit 10.3.2 is a copy of the vice president's response. Working with a number of consultants and with local insurance companies, Andy has developed a list of possible benefit choices and their costs, which are itemized in Exhibit 10.3.3.

EXHIBIT 10.3.1

To: Andy Wolfson, HR Manager

From: Andrea Birch, Senior Consultant
       Human Resources Concepts, Inc.

As requested, I reviewed the information you provided concerning the Customer Service Associate positions planned for your Nevada Service Center.

First, let me tell you that I think you'll be pleased with your decision to locate here. Gambling casinos/hotels are our foremost employers, accounting for 55 percent of the total jobs in the area. Second are tourist-related organizations such as small rental car companies, local motels, and restaurants. From the worker's point of view, these businesses are very cyclical and there is little job security. However, good casino workers are paid very well, both in base salary as well as tips. Needless to say, employee benefit programs are very meager.

It is my belief that, if you position yourself as a solid financial services company with a pleasant, stable work atmosphere, you will have no difficulty finding skilled, reliable workers. In particular, you would represent an excellent opportunity for a "casino spouse" whose concern for stable employment and a comprehensive benefits package—with particular emphasis on spouse and family options—is an important factor in choosing and staying with a job. Even if one or more benefits were contributory, access to the coverage would be valuable to these workers.

Thus, in a market that would normally call for hourly wages of $11.00 and up, we believe that your Customer Service Associate positions could be filled with competent employees in the $10.00 to $10.50 per hour range if the benefits plan were attractive.

As requested, I am also pleased to provide you with some local information concerning paid time off in this area. Most organizations in this market provide two weeks of vacation after one year of service and increase this to three weeks after five years. Typically, firms located here offer 7 to 10 days' sick leave per year and 5 to 7 paid holidays. Be aware, however, that there is quite a bit of variance across organizations relating to these practices.

I'll call you next week so that we can identify the next step in this process.

EXHIBIT 10.3.2

To: Andy Wolfson, HR Manager

From: Xavier Ortenzio, VP Corporate Administration

I applaud your efforts to date in constructing a "preferred employer" HR strategy for our National Service Center. Having reviewed the copy of the Birch memo concerning the worker marketplace in Las Vegas, I heartily support your recommendations.

Our original estimates called for a total compensation package for Customer Service Associates of $13.75 to $14.00 per hour. We arrived at this figure including a 28 percent rate for fringe benefits. "Fringe benefits" was broadly defined to include mandatory coverages, time off, and various other programs.

Your recommendation—that this amount be redistributed by reducing the average hourly pay rate to $10.50 and by increasing the fringe benefit amount to 38 percent of base rate—makes sense.

I also have no strong feelings about whether or not some benefits require employee contributions— provided that this would not interfere with our "preferred employer" strategy. In addition, I read in yesterday's newspaper that cafeteria benefits are becoming increasingly popular. Would such an approach offer us any advantages?

In any event, consider this your go-ahead to draft your benefits program as outlined above. I look forward to receiving your final recommendations and anticipate a speedy Executive Committee approval. The successful staffing and management of the National Service Center is critical to USA Credit's business strategy, future growth, and overall success.

EXHIBIT 10.3.3

LIST OF POSSIBLE BENEFITS

Benefit	Cost (Unless, where specified, all costs are annual rates)
FICA	
Social Security	6.2% on first $90,000 earned by individual
Medicare	1.45%
FUTA (Federal Unemployment Tax)	.8% on first $7,000 earned by individual
Workers' compensation	$1.50 for every $100 of total payroll
State disability	Not required in Nevada

	Employee Only	Employee and Family	
Health care insurance program			
High plan	$4,000	$6,000	
Medium plan	3,500	4,850	
Low plan	2,700	4,000	
HMO	2,400	3,000	
Dental plan			
Regular plan	650	1,300	
HMO dental	480	900	
Vision care	150	230	
Prescription drug	350	625	
Life insurance			
1 year's salary			$400
2 years' salary			650
3 years' salary			1,000
Dependent life ($5,000 for spouse; $1,000 per child)			250
Pension plan			
Defined benefit			4.5%
Defined contribution			3.0%
Tuition reimbursement			.7%
Employee assistance program			.5%
Child care subsidy			3.5%
Paid vacation			$62 per day
Paid holidays			$57 per day
Paid sick leave			$52 per day
Long-term disability			
High plan (full salary after five consecutive days absent due to illness)			$1,000
Low plan (60 percent of salary after 10 consecutive days absent due to illness)			$550

Name _____   Group _____

You have been retained as a consultant to Andy Wolfson.

1. Structure a benefits program that you think would be most effective for the customer service associates to be hired by USA Credit. Assume an average wage of $10.50 per hour and a workweek of 40 hours. A benefits budget of 38 percent of salary has been approved. If needed, assume that 70 percent of the customer service associates will require family coverage.

2. What were the trade-offs you made in deciding on your recommendations?

3. Assume that Andy Wolfson is interested in a cafeteria benefits approach. He has heard, however, that when people are permitted to select their own coverages, unit costs may rise (called "adverse selection"). In other words, in cafeteria benefits, the averaging effect of users versus nonusers across employee populations declines as people opt out of programs that they are not likely to use in favor of benefits that they are very likely to use. How might Andy deal with this problem in designing a cafeteria benefits plan?

Name _____   Group _____

4. What additional information concerning this situation would have enabled you to provide better recommendations?

5. How will you decide whether or not your benefits program is an effective one? Describe the procedure that you would use. What specific criteria would you use?

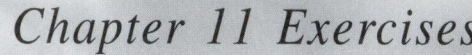

Chapter 11 Exercises

EXERCISE 11.1

The Design of a PFP System for Mega Manufacturing*

Overview

This exercise evaluates the feasibility of different approaches to PFP given the strategic plan of the organization. As discussed in the chapter, the effectiveness of the PFP system depends on a number of factors. This exercise will give the student the opportunity to consider some of these factors in proposing an ideal PFP system.

Learning Objectives

After completing this exercise, you should be able to

1. Identify the key organizational variables that should be considered in the development and/or revision of a PFP system.
2. Understand the role and importance of other HRM activities (e.g., job analysis, performance appraisal) in the development of a PFP system.

Procedure

Part A: Individual Analysis

Step 1. Before class, read the scenario.
Step 2. You have been retained as a consultant who must report to Ellen Lennett, director of incentive program development at Mega Manufacturing corporate headquarters. You will be working with the Kanto division. You have been asked to address the five issues raised on Form 11.1.1. Respond to each of the issues and recommend a specific program that supports both Mega's incentive policy and Kanto's situation. Your recommendation should consider *at least* the five points. Also, prior to class, complete the Assessment Questions.

The two memos in Exhibits 11.1.1 and 11.1.2 may be relevant to the recommendations you will make. Ellen Lennett has received the notes, one from Don Walker, vice president, compensation and benefits, and the other from Bill Idrey, a compensation specialist she sent to help the Kanto personnel department.

Part B: Group Analysis

Step 1. In groups, each member should review the individual reports and take notes on the most important points. Each member also should devise his or her own strategy for identifying the best group response to make for each of the five questions presented in Form 11.1.1 plus any additional issues the group considers to be relevant. The group also should devise a list of key questions that must be answered by management before a firm position can be taken on the elements of the PFP system.
Step 2. One group member should be designated to make a five-minute presentation of the group's position before the rest of the class. A "free for all" discussion should then focus on the various recommended plans.

Scenario

Mega Manufacturing International is a large diversified company with its corporate headquarters in Boston and manufacturing plants, research and development facilities, and distribution and marketing centers in the United States and around the world. Mega Manufacturing is pursuing a long-range strategy of producing high technology products for three markets: military, industrial, and retail consumer. Because of the intense competitive pressures in its chosen arenas, Mega Manufacturing believes it must obtain the maximum effort from its personnel. In support of this belief, Mega Manufacturing has adopted a policy of paying for performance (PFP). Typically, many of its divisions have incentives comprising a substantial portion of executive pay (40 percent to 150 percent of base pay possible in various types of incentives) and a significant portion of supervisory and employee compensation (5 percent to 25 percent possible).

To expand its capabilities in the new electronic surface-mount technology, Mega Manufacturing acquired GW Industries, which had several plants producing high-quality surface-mount electronic parts. The Kanto assembly plant was part of GW Industries; however, it was an older plant producing electronic parts for an industrial process rapidly approaching obsolescence. Although the products were produced on an assembly line, individual workers had relatively little contact with each other, and the skills required were relatively low. Kanto had been a profitable operation for GW, but Mega Manufacturing has to switch Kanto to a different product and process or close the plant.

Kanto has a reputation for paying average to below-market wages, but it was viewed as a dependable and stable employer with a good benefits package. As a consequence, Kanto has had a stable and loyal workforce; but with the buyout of GW and the consequent uncertainty surrounding Kanto's future, there has been talk of unionizing and some of the more skilled employees are known to be seeking other jobs.

Mega has decided to offer Kanto the opportunity to manufacture an extremely complex switching device for a military contract. Although the total manufacturing

*Contributed by E. Brian Peach and M. Ronald Buckley.

process is complex, it can be broken into steps, with each step consisting of individual skills that can be learned relatively quickly. Groups of individuals, each with a specific skill, will have to work closely together to achieve the required quality levels for each step in the switching device assembly. The nature of the process is such that each individual will have to take an active interest in the success of the assembly or the device will be unsatisfactory.

The two memos in Exhibits 11.1.1 and 11.1.2 may be relevant to the recommendations you will make. Ellen Lennett has just received the following notes, one (Exhibit 11.1.1) from Don Walker, vice president, compensation and benefits, and the other (Exhibit 11.1.2) from Bill Idrey, a compensation specialist whom Ms. Lennett sent to help the Kanto personnel department.

EXHIBIT 11.1.1

```
TO:        Ellen Lennett
SUBJECT:   Kanto incentive program
FROM:      Don Walker
```

Ellen,

We need to give Kanto some more help on setting up its incentives to adequately support the new switching assembly process. We cannot allow the conversion process to delay our completing switching assemblies as there is a large late delivery penalty. Also, Bids and Contracting apparently goofed and bid too low on the contract to maintain our usual margins. It appears we have to make up 3% somewhere.

EXHIBIT 11.1.2

```
TO:        Ellen Lennett
SUBJECT:   Kanto Incentive Program
FROM:      Bill Idrey
```

Just a quick note to advise you of some early problems I'm encountering.

1. The employees are learning the new skills, but the supervisors are having trouble (resisting?) learning the necessary composite skills.

2. The parts we're getting from our Indonesian plant will sometimes test OK individually, but not work in the final assembly. It apparently is not feasible to test the intermediate assembly steps.

3. Although job analysis says the steps and tasks are essentially equal, two of the assembly steps are perceived as being more important and thus as having higher status by the workers.

4. Robert Horne, the plant manager, is complaining that the new final quality check supervisor, Beatrice Inggold, is too strict and will slow down production.

5. Engineers from Design & Fabrication come in and watch, occasionally making suggestions, but I'm darned if I can see what they are contributing.

Name ———————————————————— Group ————————————————

1. Is an incentive program appropriate? Explain your position.

2. If so, should there be one, two, or several plans?

3. Who should be included?

4. What should be the basis for incentive payments?

5. What kind of incentives should be included?

EXERCISE 11.1
ASSESSMENT QUESTIONS

1.   What were the key variables you considered in your selection of an individual- or group-based PFP system?

2.   What changes in organizational characteristics would seriously affect your recommendations?

3.   What circumstances would lead you to conclude that a PFP system would not be in the best interests of the organization?

EXERCISE 11.2

Pay for Performance at Dee's Personalized Baskets

Overview

This exercise provides an opportunity for the student to develop a framework for a PFP system, training for the program, and a framework for the evaluation of the system. The problem is common to many organizations. As discussed in Chapter 11, while pay for performance is the preferred method of compensation for most jobs, there are many problems with such systems, including the apparent inability on the part of evaluators to be critical in their evaluations. Many experts on PFP systems maintain that this is the major problem with most PFP systems in operation today that use ratings as the basis for measurement. This exercise is designed to allow the student to construct a PFP system that would minimize such problems.

Learning Objectives

After completing this exercise, you should be able to

1. Consider different PFP options.
2. Evaluate the relative advantages and disadvantages of the different approaches to PFP.
3. Consider the various issues related to training for PFP, including transfer, relapse, and cost.
4. Develop an evaluation design that can assess the effects of the PFP system.

Procedure

Part A: Individual Analysis

Before class, read the background material on Dee's Personalized Baskets presented in Exhibit 11.2.1. Answer the questions on Form 11.2.1.

Part B: Group Analysis

Step 1. Assume the role of a team of HR consultants to consider the development of a PFP system. In addition, you have been asked to develop a managerial training program to prepare managers for the new PFP system. You also have been asked to evaluate the effectiveness of the PFP system.

Step 2. Among the critical issues that your team should address include those listed on Form 11.2.1. Review each consultant's responses on Form 11.2.1. Discuss each response and prepare a plan to deal with each.

Step 3. Prepare a short presentation for the vice president that covers your team's ideas regarding the design of the PFP system. Remember that management will weigh heavily both your recommendations as well as your plan for implementation.

EXHIBIT 11.2.1

BACKGROUND MATERIAL FOR DEE'S PERSONALIZED BASKETS

Nancy Harrison, HRM vice president of Dee's Personalized Baskets in Orlando, Florida, is disturbed by lagging productivity figures and problems of product quality and high turnover. She is intrigued by the results of a recent attitude survey of her employees. She has decided to experiment with some form of PFP system of compensation. The company's current system of compensation pays either straight hourly rates to nonsupervisory personnel or straight salary to all supervisory/managerial/sales personnel with a year-end bonus that is a percentage of base pay as determined by the board. The attitude survey results indicated employees believed that they would work harder if they perceived a stronger tie between their level of effort and their pay. Most of the 200 employees who would be part of the new pay system prepare individual baskets of gifts (perfumes, fancy soaps, fancy foods, wine, etc.), which are ordered by customers for clients and potential clients.

There are two distinct elements of the business. The largest and most reliable part of the business is partnerships with several of the largest hotels in the area to provide high-volume baskets for hotel rooms usually commensurate with the start of a convention. The convention contracts average around 300 baskets and have a profit margin of about 8 percent (the baskets retail for an average of $9.50). These high-volume baskets are produced by most of the assemblers who work around the supplies of goodies that typically go into the baskets (snacks, fruit, candy, hotel amenities). A growing and more profitable part of the business is much larger and more expensive baskets that retail for an average of $94 with a profit margin averaging 16 percent. The baskets are usually thematic and tailored to the particular situation or proclivities of the recipient. This part of the business represents about 20 percent of the business but a goal is to expand in this area. Design and assembly of these baskets requires some artistic talent. There is a sales staff of three who currently work on straight salary.

Few respondents to the survey felt that they were recognized in any significant way for working harder than others. People most disturbed by the failure to recognize greater effort were the same people who indicated they were more likely to seek other employment. The turnover rate has increased for three straight years and Dee's has lost some good people. The organization has a performance-appraisal system, but the ratings are generally very high. For the last performance-appraisal period, the average rating of effectiveness made by the 20 supervisors was 7.5 on a 9-point rating scale (with 9 representing "highly effective" performance).

Name ———————————————————————   Group ———————————————————————

1. What type(s) (if any) of PFP system(s) do you recommend for Dee's? Be as specific as possible and consider all jobs. What (if any) additional information would help you develop the most effective PFP system? (You may take a position against all PFP systems but make sure you explain why.)

2. Describe the chronology of steps for implementing the PFP system or explain why you are opposed to a PFP system for this situation.

3. What is your experimental design for evaluating the effectiveness of the PFP system?

Name _____   Group _____

    4.   What specific criteria will you use to evaluate the effects? Provide some examples of criteria.

    5.   What is measured using the PADS? What role (if any) should this score play in the PFP system or training raters for the system?

    6.   How would you address the high turnover rate? Could this problem be related to compensation?

Chapter 12 Exercises

EXERCISE 12.1

An Approach to Downsizing

Overview

Chapter 12 discusses the role of corporate restructuring and downsizing that has occurred in the United States in recent years. Many management experts maintain that overhead reduction and downsizing are required in order for U.S. corporations to remain competitive. The purpose of this exercise is to assess the effectiveness of downsizing strategies used by a phosphate company and a pharmaceutical company.

Learning Objectives

After completing this exercise, you should have

1. A better understanding of different approaches to downsizing and the advantages and disadvantages of each.
2. Knowledge of the potential problems that can develop with downsizing programs.

Procedure

Part A: Individual Analysis

Step 1. Prior to class, review the two scenarios below and the notes related to the downsizing/restructuring processes. Complete forms 12.1.1 and 12.1.2 prior to class. The phosphate company notes were taken by Rosemary Richter, the company president's secretary, who attended the management meeting in which the president (Abbott) announced the need to downsize (Exhibit 12.1.1). Answer the relevant questions on Form 12.1.1.

Step 2. You also have been asked to review the documents that were prepared pursuant to a downsizing/restructuring program by Brooks Pharmaceutical. While Brooks had to reduce its workforce, management was very interested in retaining those personnel with the best performance records and also those who had been hired as a part of their diversity program. Study these documents and prepare questions of clarification so as to help you understand the entire process of restructuring. On Form 12.1.2, comment on the effectiveness of this restructuring process and point out any potential restructuring scenarios that could pose difficulties for Brooks.

Part B: Group Analysis

Step 1. In groups of about six people, attempt to reach consensus on the Form 12.1.1 answers. Organize a group response to items 2 and 3. The instructor will designate one presenter.

Step 2. The group also should generate a list of questions regarding the downsizing and restructuring at Brooks. Prepare scenarios that could indicate future legal difficulties for Brooks.

EXHIBIT 12.1.1
NOTES FROM DOWNSIZING MEETING[1]

CONFIDENTIAL

STAFF MEETING NOTES

Meeting called by company president Jarold Abbott. All unit managers attended.

The purpose of the meeting was to provide an assessment of the financial situation and the need to take immediate action. We should make preparations for a full unit manpower review (UMR) and "show and tell" that will reduce our manpower by about one-half. We will use UMR, a performance appraisal of each employee, to "clean house." New organization charts are to be drawn up as if we are running all out and then taking every bit of the "fat" out. "Show and tell" will be a reduction in force from half rate to one-third rate. (In preparing the organization charts for the UMR and the "show and tell," early retirement is an area to look at. I will distribute a list of employees who would be eligible for a program we are considering.) This is a snapshot look of the company. Concern has been expressed regarding the seniority system that we have used in past reductions in force. This time, we need to make decisions based on future needs and potential. If a less senior person has more potential, that person should be retained. This applies to all employees, not just management. Possible transfers should be considered based on a skills match.

We presently have some 30 people in the hourly ranks between 60 and 65 and some 22 people on salary between 55 and up. We want to reduce hourly by 200 people and salary by 60. People 55 and up will probably be eligible for the early program being considered.

ADMINISTRATIVE

Presently there are three people in the Traffic area. Smith states that at present rates, this is one person too many. This department can function with the supervisor and one clerk, with possibly one-half person from another area in accounting assisting when workload is high.

The purchasing supervisor's position is a training slot. He handles most of the contracts and fills in as a buyer for vacation relief for purchasing agents and storekeeper. He spends a great deal of time supervising warehouse to improve purchasing and warehousing. Jones stated the warehouse is where we should "stash" maintenance supervisors as storekeepers and storage superintendents. Three people could be used here assuming no warehouse coverage on third shift.

Cost Accounting

Messenger can go. Records retention part of that function could possibly be shared by inventory clerk, data processing clerk, or property control clerk.

Laboratory

Laboratory will be reorganized with a reduction of seven people.

Projects

Herz supervises project engineers and handles special projects. He, with Andrews, will head up the wet rock grinding study. Three senior project engineers. Valk is handling the absorbing tower and pump tank project. Naberhaus is working on rock wetting project and special projects for production. Wischmeyer is an electrical engineer.

Plant Engineering

Konopnicki supervising plant engineers with heavy emphasis on vibration analysis and mechanical failures.

One senior plant engineer (Lamb).

Two plant engineers I (Broussard and Martin). Martin learning vibration analysis and working with Konopnicki. Broussard expert on rubber lining materials.

Three development engineers (Stanton, Neff, and Chamberlin). Neff will be transferred to Projects Group and Stanton reassigned to Maintenance. Consider eliminating chief plant engineer position and returning Konopnicki to senior plant engineer.

Process

Andrews supervises process engineers and makes sure that environmental government regulations in force. Andrews will also be working on wet rock grinding study.

One chemist I (Riddle). Does all forms on governmental regulations, pond water balances, and any special DAP projects.

Two process engineers I (Marrone and Katzaras). Marrone will temporarily fill in for Andrews. Katzaras working on cogeneration project.

One engineer II (Stone). DAP projects.

Environmental Engineering

One supervisor and three technicians who keep track of governmental sampling.

Ken to draw up organization chart that reflects number of people he needs with no capital projects and operating at one-third rates (interface with Production and Maintenance). Possibly eliminate chief plant engineer and move to Maintenance. Project can cover both areas.

PRODUCTION

Presently the Production department is structured with four production superintendents and four area superintendents. At one-third rates, Persons would like to restructure to combine Areas I and IV and Areas II and III. This would eliminate two superintendents, keeping four area superintendents. Possibly eliminating area superintendent in Area IV (Price), who will be interviewing for position at Hardee County. Four shift supervisors can be eliminated at one-third rates who will become guards under Industrial Relations. Some early retirement may be offered.

MAINTENANCE

The department is now staffed by two general superintendents and one superintendent over planning and coordination. The area superintendent position in Area III could be eliminated (Garcia is retirement age) and the planner (Card) could be moved over to pick up contractors. One maintenance clerk also can be eliminated. At one-third rates, #2 and #3 shifts in Area I. Eliminate #3 shift in Area II and possibly shift #1. McDuffie will draw up an organization chart as if Goebel, Garcia, and Lopata were to retire.

[1] Notes taken by Rosemary Richter.

Name _____   Group _____

1. How do you evaluate this approach to workforce reduction? What (if anything) did Abbott do right and what did he do wrong? What additional information do you need about the downsizing effort in order to fully understand the process?

2. Three months after this meeting, Garcia (age 58) and Lopata (age 55) were discharged. Based on the information provided, were Garcia and Lopata victims of age discrimination? Explain your answer. If necessary, what specific, additional information do you require before you can take a position? Provide a set of "if–then" propositions (e.g., if I know "X", then "Y" follows).

Name _____   Group _____

3. Must the company adhere to the WARN Act? How do they meet this obligation?

4. How would you evaluate the fairness of this approach to downsizing? What are some examples of possible difficulties with distributive and procedural justice?

5. How would you have handled this situation? What would you have done differently? Provide a chronology of steps. Would you use an outplacement service?

EXHIBIT 12.1.2

KEY CONSIDERATIONS IN BROOKS RESTRUCTURING

- New sales structure.
- No relos for reps and DL/minimal relocations for Rls and Als.
- Key job requirements and past performance.
- Maintenance of organizational diversity.

- Role of tenure in retention process.
- Role of customer constancy.
- Role of bumping.
- Role of pooling.
- Retention of our strongest leaders.
- Retention of identified successor candidates.

To: Managers
From: Moro Hipple
Subject: The HR Diversity Challenge Process
Goal: To follow through with our operating principles. Valuing a diverse organization—by proactively considering diversity in our restructuring process.

Stages/dates in the process:

- Preliminary ratings   6/5
- Rating sheet discussion   6/6–6/7
- Management/HR review   6/22–6/24
- Adverse impact analysis/challenges   6/28
- Final ratings for decisions   7/1

Rating sheet discussions at the area offices:

- These discussions must include a representative from human resources who will challenge decisions and ensure the integrity of the process.
- HR challengers will receive a report prior to arrival at the area office that details diversity data for personnel in the area.

Management/HR Review:

- HR challengers will review retention decisions with respect to diversity. HR challenger will ensure the integrity/objectivity/documentation of the process.

Impact analysis:
The final structure will be assessed against the predownsizing structure to test for adverse impact (80 percent rule).

- A report will be generated by HR indicating predownsizing(current) diversity data assessed by area and position for comparison to the new organization.

The result of this analysis may lead to a possible further challenge.

To: All Employees
From: David Brooks, CEO
Subject: Equal Employment Opportunity
Date: February

On behalf of the management of Brooks Pharmaceuticals Division, I wish to reaffirm our commitment to equal employment opportunity. It is Brooks' policy to provide equal employment opportunity to all individuals without regard to race, color, religion, age, sex, national origin, Vietnam Era veteran, or disability status. This priority covers all phases of employment, including but not limited to recruiting, hiring, training, promoting, placement, demotion, or transfer; layoff, termination, or recall; rates of pay or other forms of compensation, fringe benefits; the use of all facilities; and participation in all Company-sponsored employee activities. We impose only valid requirements to ensure that employment and promotional decisions are made in accordance with equal employment opportunity.

I have appointed Moro Hipple, senior vice president of Human Resources, to coordinate, implement, monitor, and report on the effectiveness of the Pharmaceuticals Division's Affirmative Action Program. All managers and supervisors are charged with the responsibility of ensuring that any discrimination in employment is avoided. All employees are expected to recognize this policy and cooperate with its implementation.

Our affirmative action plans and programs have been developed to help us achieve full utilization of our human resources. We have made substantial progress in equal opportunity in recent years and with your continued support we will continue to move forward.

Name _____   Group _____

1. Based on what you know so far, evaluate the Brooks approach to workforce reduction? What did Brooks do right and what did they do wrong?

2. What additional information do you need about the downsizing effort at Brooks in order to fully understand the legal implications of its restructuring?

3. One month after the restructuring, Brooks is informed by the EEOC that, thus far, four complaints have been filed against Brooks for age discrimination in the process. What data should you examine in order to determine the possibility of discrimination? Should Brooks be concerned about an ADEA claim based on the disparate impact theory?

EXERCISE 12.2

Compududes Considers Arbitration Options for Employee Disputes*

Overview

As discussed in Chapter 12, there has been a rapid "privatization" of the employment dispute resolution process in the American workplace. Supreme Court rulings have allowed employers to move away from costly, time-consuming litigation by adopting alternative dispute resolution (ADR) procedures for both existing employees and new hires. The American Arbitration Association reports that it currently provides ADR services for over 500 employers with five million employees. In 2001, the Supreme Court in *Circuit City v. Adams* determined that an employer can insist on the submission of an employment dispute to arbitration as a condition of employment.

One critical issue is the choice of appropriate ADR program characteristics and the effects of such characteristics on employees' attitudes. ADR programs vary from traditional mediation and arbitration to more unusual techniques such as "mock trials." There are two crucial issues for employers. The first issue is the choice between mediation, arbitration, or some combination. With mediation, the disputing parties attempt to resolve the issue themselves with the assistance of a neutral third party. Arbitration requires the parties to present their case to a neutral third party who then will make a determination on the issues. Many companies use some combination of the two for their ADR procedure.

The second issue is whether ADR procedures should be voluntary or mandatory. Voluntary ADR programs give the parties the option to select ADR, generally after the dispute has arisen; mandatory programs stipulate in advance that all disputes that arise in the course of employment will be referred to mediation and/or arbitration. Employer-imposed ADR programs may provide for any combination of these characteristics.

Learning Objectives

After completing of this exercise, you should have

1. An understanding of different approaches to ADR.
2. Knowledge of the differences in attitudes toward the ADR options and the implications of those attitudes.

Procedure

Part A: Individual Analysis

Prior to class, review the four ADR options presented in Exhibit 12.2.1 in the context of the scenario presented. Complete your ratings for each of the options on Form 12.2.1. In the space provided, make any comments regarding the options.

Part B: Group Analysis

In groups of about six people, calculate ratings for each option and then, representing the interests of Compududes, attempt to reach consensus on the policy to adopt or decide that none of the options should be adopted. If you reject all options, derive an alternative program. The group also should generate a list of questions regarding the ADR program options, their implementation, and the AAA.

*Contributed by Catherine Tyler.

EXHIBIT 12.2.1

You are a recent college graduate who has just started a paid internship with Compududes, a computer retailer. You receive the following e-mail from the HR department:

Compududes is considering four new policies for resolving problems that happen at work and that cannot be resolved through the "open door policy," which allows any employee to discuss any work-related problem with the manager of the department. Each proposed new policy encourages open communication, protects your work relationships, and helps keep costs and tempers under control. For serious, legal disputes, the new policy makes available the experience and objectivity of the American Arbitration Association (AAA). The AAA helps businesses, associations, and all levels of government resolve disputes. Thus, for any labor dispute such as sexual harassment or possible discrimination claims, we would like to involve the AAA.

We would like your opinion about the four options we are considering. Make your ratings of the four options on Form 12.2.1.

Option #1: The **voluntary mediation** ADR program: If you fail to resolve your disputes through the "open door policy," you may voluntarily elect to involve the AAA in resolving the dispute. This neutral body or mediator can listen to both sides of the story and help you work it out together. To use AAA, you will pay a $50 processing fee.

Option #2: The **mandatory mediation** option: If you fail to resolve your dispute through the "open door policy," the AAA will then be asked to attempt to resolve the dispute. This neutral body or mediator can listen to both sides of the story and help you work it out together. For the use of AAA, you will pay a $50 processing fee.

Option #3: The **voluntary mediation plus voluntary binding arbitration** option: If you fail to resolve your dispute through the "open door policy," you may voluntarily elect to involve the AAA. This neutral body or mediator can listen to both sides of the story and help you work it out together. To use AAA, you will pay a $50 processing fee.

If you fail to resolve the dispute to *your satisfaction* through mediation, you may elect to present your dispute to AAA for binding arbitration. The arbitration will decide your case after hearing arguments from both sides. With arbitration, the decision is final, binding, and enforced under the law, with only limited appeals allowed through the courts. The decision to go to arbitration is voluntary.

Option #4: The **mandatory mediation plus binding arbitration** option: If you fail to resolve your dispute through the "open door policy," the AAA will then attempt to resolve the dispute through mediation. This neutral body or mediator can listen to both sides of the story and help you work it out together. For the use of AAA, you will pay a $50 processing fee.

If you fail to resolve the dispute through mediation, your dispute will then be automatically presented to the AAA for binding arbitration. The AAA arbitration will decide your case after hearing arguments from both sides. With arbitration, the decision is final, binding, and enforced under the law, with only limited appeals allowed through the courts.

FORM 12.2.1

Name _____   Group _____

Review the four ADR options the company is considering. Rate the extent to which you agree or disagree with each policy using the following scale:
  Strongly disagree = 1; Disagree = 2; Undecided = 3;
  Agree = 4; and Strongly agree = 5

Options
1   2   3   4

___ ___ ___ ___   1. The procedure described is fair to all.

___ ___ ___ ___   2. The procedure is advantageous to management.

___ ___ ___ ___   3. I trust management at this organization.

___ ___ ___ ___   4. This option makes me more motivated to work here.

___ ___ ___ ___   5. The outcomes from this option should favor management.

___ ___ ___ ___   6. This option is fair for any labor dispute, including union-organizing issues.

Conduct a Web search and learn what you can about the AAA and ADR. From the employee's and employer's perspectives, what are the critical issues that should be considered? What changes would you make to any of the options to increase their fairness to all parties? Does the plaintiff have any other options after losing an arbitration case?

EXERCISE 12.3

Handling an Employee's Termination*

Overview

Chapter 12 discussed employee discipline and termination. Several issues are involved when an employee is performing below standards to the point that it is necessary to terminate the employment relationship. This exercise puts you in the role of HR professional and asks that you go through several steps leading up to the termination of an employee.

Learning Objectives

After completing this exercise, you should be able to

1. Experience the process by which HR professionals handle requests for termination by line managers and supervisors in the organization.
2. Make decisions on crucial issues involved in the termination process.
3. Develop an understanding of the sensitivity and gravity of the termination process.

Procedure

Part A: Individual Analysis

Step 1. Read the scenario and the accompanying exhibits associated with the termination of a customer service representative. Then, follow these steps to ensure that the termination is carried out appropriately:

1. The first step is to investigate the situation to make sure the supervisor's claims are true. Who will you contact? What questions will you ask? What precautions should you take to assure that your investigation is confidential and legally appropriate?
2. Ensure that the necessary documentation is in place based upon the discipline policy and your expertise as an HR manager.
3. Assume that the termination is in fact warranted. Managers typically hold termination meetings at

*Contributed by Jennifer Robin.

The Daily Register, but it is not unheard of for the HR department to conduct this meeting. Given the available information, who should conduct the meeting? What steps will you take to prepare the manager and/or yourself for this meeting? Prepare an agenda for the termination meeting.

4. The Daily Register has some guidelines for severance packages, benefits, and outplacement services, but they are very informal and typically decided upon on a case-by-case basis. In this situation, what would you recommend for Jeanette?

Step 2. Write a one-page memo in which you take a position an each question raised in step 1.

Part B: Group Analysis

Step 1. In groups, each member should review the memos of all other members. Each group should attempt to reach consensus an each question.

Scenario

You've been working with The Daily Register, a regional newspaper, for the last 12 months in the HR department. Your supervisor, the HR manager, is leaving for vacation tomorrow. With impeccable timing, one of the sales managers, Paul White, has submitted the paperwork for terminating one of his employees. The sales department is responsible for soliciting and securing advertisers for the newspaper. Paul maintains that Jeanette Landis has failed to reach sales goals for the last six months despite numerous attempts at discipline. Furthermore, Jeanette has threatened to file a lawsuit if The Daily Register terminates her employment. The HR manager delegates the handling of the termination to you. The documents sent by Paul, documents that you've received in HR, Jeanette's job description, and the company's discipline policy appear in the Exhibits 12.3.1 through 12.3.6.

EXHIBIT 12.3.1

Return-path:	<pwhite@ourcompany.com>
Content-return:	allowed
Date:	Wed, 11 Apr 15:45:01 −0400
From:	"Paul White" <pwhite@ourcompany.com>
Subject:	Termination
To:	you@ourcompany.com

HR Staff:

I have sent the necessary materials to your office to fire one of my customer service reps, Jeanette Landis. I've been pulling my hair out trying to get her to sell something for the past 6 months, but she can't do it! She repeatedly misses her sales goals by a huge margin due to her laziness and stupidity. I need to be rid of her as soon as possible so I can get an employee in here that can do the job. I could suspend her next, but I doubt it will help. Can you give me the go-ahead so I can show her the door? I know I was reluctant to fire my old high school buddy last year, but I will *gladly* hold this termination meeting.
Paul

EXHIBIT 12.3.2

From Paul's file:

Performance Appraisal
Name: Jeanette R. Landis
Position: Customer Service Representative
Last Review: **Review Period:** 12.6   **to** 6.6
Job knowledge: Employee's ability to understand the required duties, responsibilities, skills, and procedures.

Rating: Exceeds Requirements
Comments: Jeanette has an excellent understanding of the requirements of her job. She has been instrumental in training new staff members this period.

Quality of Work: The degree to which the employee's work is accurate, complete, and conforms to *The Daily Register* and supervisor requirements.

Rating: Meets Requirements
Comments: The sales Jeanette makes are processed appropriately. She reports them to me in an acceptable fashion, and she maintains customer
    accounts adequately.

Productivity: Employee produces a large volume of work, is timely, and meets all deadlines.

Rating: Unsatisfactory
Comments: Jeanette does not make new sales. Rather, she maintains customer orders for the same ad, run on the same day, for the same cost. She
    does not make attempts to win new customers or grow current accounts. This area needs severe improvement. It is recommended that Jeanette
    repeat sales training.

Organizational Skills: Employee uses time effectively, sets priorities, and demonstrates initiative on projects.

Rating: Needs Improvement
Comments: Jeanette should be using time to increase her customer base. Despite discussions this quarter, no evidence of this is present. She is not a
    high initiative person.

Communication Skills: The employee's ability to convey ideas and information effectively and appropriately to others.

Rating: Exceeds Expectations
Comments: Jeanette is extremely articulate. Other Customer Service Representatives solicit her opinion on ad content on a regular basis.

Overall Rating: Needs Improvement
Recommended Performance Raise: N/A (Commission sales)

Supervisor Signature: _____   **Date:** _____

Employee Signature: _____   **Date:** _____

EXHIBIT 12.3.3

From Paul's file:

Record of Disciplinary Action
Name: Jeanette Landis
Position: Customer Service Representative
Date: 10.2
Reason for Action: Jeanette has failed to meet sales goals for the second month in a row. We have discussed the reasons for her performance, and she
has assured me that she will meet them next month. At this time, no further training is needed.
Disciplinary Action Taken: Documented verbal warning

Supervisor Signature: _____   **Date:** _____

Employee Signature: _____   **Date:** _____

HR Signature (if necessary): _____   **Date:** _____

EXHIBIT 12.3.4

From your files (copies also provided from Paul):

Record of Disciplinary Action
Name: Jeanette Landis
Position: Customer Service Representative
Date: 3.3
Reason for Action: Jeanette has again failed to reach sales goals. In December, it was recommended that she attend sales training. She has failed to schedule this training and has not made improvements in her sales as established last month. If she fails to schedule training within the next 30 days, she understands that further steps will be taken.
Disciplinary Action Taken: Written warning copied to HR.

Supervisor Signature: _____

Employee Signature: _____

HR Signature (if necessary): _____

EXHIBIT 12.3.5

The Daily Register
Disciplinary Policy
The Daily Register attempts to provide the resources, training, and information required for individuals to perform their jobs successfully. If for any reason, performance is not up to the standards set by the employee handbook, job description, or direct supervisor, the employee shall be disciplined as follows.

    If an employee has committed a minor infraction, the following steps will be taken:

1. A verbal warning will be given and will be documented, signed by the employee, and placed in the supervisor's file.
2. A written warning will be documented, signed by the employee and filed with the supervisor.
3. A written warning will be documented as in step two, but also copied to the HR manager. This warning becomes a permanent part of the employee's file.
4. A third offense is grounds for suspension.
5. Upon the fourth offense, the individual may be terminated.

Minor Infractions:

Excessive personal telephone calls and long distance calls without approval, misuse of office supplies or equipment, excessive and unapproved absences and/or tardiness, misuse of leave time, failure to reach performance standards.

A major infraction will be examined on an individual basis and may be grounds for immediate termination and/or legal action. Examples of infractions include the following:
Major Infractions:

Breach of confidentiality, falsifying records, embezzlement, violation of Drug Free Workplace or firearms policies, sexual harassment.

EXERCISE 13.1
Organizing a Union*

Overview

Research shows that management often neither anticipates nor understands the motivation of employees to organize into unions. This exercise explores an organizing effort from the perspectives of labor and of management.

Learning Objectives

After completing this exercise, you should be able to

1. Understand the process of starting a union organizing effort.
2. Know the steps involved in the certification process.
3. Be able to consider employee and employer reactions to a union organizing effort.
4. Know the laws and regulations that govern the process of union organizing from management's perspective.

Procedure

Part A: Individual Analysis

Step 1. Before class, read the scenario below and follow the directions of the assignment.

Step 2. Each student will be assigned to either the union organizer role or the general manager role. Each role requires you to write a letter to be used in your arguments. These arguments are described in Exhibit 13.1.1.

Part B: Group Analysis

Step 1. Form small groups in which members are grouped by like assignment (e.g., all union organizers together and all general managers together). The members should first review one another's letters and outlines. One letter should be selected as the most effective, then edited, and submitted as the group response. Each group also should derive a chronology of steps to be taken by the union organizer to Mr. Cameron.

Step 2. A representative from each group should write the chronological steps on a blackboard or flip chart so that comparisons across groups can be made. The writer of the most effective letter from each group should then read the letter to the class. Discussion should center on the most important elements for each side and the legal implications of various strategies proposed.

Scenario

You are a customer service representative for American Rental Car (ARC), a national rental car company. Recently, the employees at the three installations in the southeastern United States, which are managed by the general manager, Scott Cameron, have experienced dissatisfaction. No raises have been given in over a year; employee benefits are sparse; employees' preferences have not been considered in the assignment of work schedules or installations; and an automated employee monitoring system has been implemented.

Many of the 100 full-time employees have been talking about unionization, although many have yet to be convinced that unionization provides the best answer. The average age of the 100 employees is 29; there are 58 females and 41 minorities. Some employees strongly believe that a union can address some of the workers' concerns. Consequently, they have contacted the Customer Service Reps of America (CSRA) for help in organizing the southeastern region of ARC. Despite numerous attempts, the CSRA has been successful in organizing only three other ARC installations nationwide because the firm engages in a very tough (and often questionably legal) campaign to stop any union organizing efforts. Before the CSRA will send an organizer to your location, it wants to be persuaded that enough employees back the union to merit the expense. Thus, it has suggested that as a first step someone write a letter to the workers convincing them of the benefits of unionization and enlisting their support.

*Contributed by Nancy Brown Johnson.

EXHIBIT 13.1.1

UNION ORGANIZER ROLE

Write a letter to your co-workers about the factors involved in the case. You remember from the chapter why people join unions and the benefits of membership, and you want to be sure to include these factors in your letter. Yet you know that your fellow workers will still wonder why the possible costs of unionization (e.g., union dues, getting fired, being permanently assigned to the midnight shift, and being harassed by their supervisor) are worth the benefits. From your speech class you know the importance of providing answers to counterarguments if you wish to effectively persuade your coworkers to support the union.

Prepare a chronological outline for the union organizing effort covering what steps or procedures are to be followed, what data you should gather, what to look for in management's reaction, and what to do if management does not respond fairly. Also, prepare a chronological outline of what you anticipate to be management's reaction to the union organizing effort (i.e., the steps that management will take through the course of the organizing effort).

GENERAL MANAGER ROLE

Assume the role of Scott Cameron and draft a letter to your three supervisors and six assistant supervisors stipulating what can and cannot be done regarding the union organizing effort. For example, you were just informed that one of the supervisors, Meredith Sterrett, has already begun to establish a "paper trail" on one union sympathizer so he can be terminated for poor performance if "things get out of hand." She also told an employee that if a CSRA representative showed up at her installation, she would "call the cops and have him arrested for trespassing." She recently refused to hire a black female applicant because both of the applicant's parents were members of a union. She also fired an employee because she found out he was a paid union organizer. You will need to respond to Ms. Sterrett's actions. You should also prepare an outline of a meeting to be held regarding the union organizing effort and what the firm should do regarding worker concerns. Also, prepare a chronology of steps management should take in response to the organizing effort.

EXERCISE 13.2*

Unions, Labor Law, and Managerial Prerogatives

Overview

Research indicates that general attitudes toward unions are strongly correlated with a number of workplace behaviors. These attitudes, sometimes based on limited facts about unions and their actual effects, can have a profound effect on a number of reactions in the workplace. Research also shows that expectancies regarding union behavior and activities can affect subsequent negotiations and managerial behaviors toward union activity. From the workers' perspective, attitudes also can affect reactions to union organizing efforts, perceptions of the extent to which unions can affect workers' pay and working conditions, and job attractiveness.

This exercise assesses attitudes toward unions in general and the extent to which these attitudes are grounded in fact. Discussion will center on the implications of the attitudes for union–management relations.

Learning Objectives

After completing this exercise, you should be able to

1. Understand the implications of preconceived attitudes toward union–management relations and managerial behavior.
2. Know some of the myths and truths about the effects of unions.
3. Adopt a more objective perspective on the subject of unions.

Procedure

Part A: Individual Analysis

Before reading Chapter 13 and before class, complete the questionnaire in Form 13.2.1. Then read Chapter 13 and conduct research on the statements in the exercise (your instructor may designate certain statements). For example, find research pertinent to the relationship between unions and productivity. Bring summaries of this research to class. Retain but cross out any of your original ratings and replace them with your "more educated" judgments. Next, visit Web sites related to the National Labor Relations Act and labor law (e.g., www.dol.gov). Try to answer the questions on Form 13.2.2. Bring this form to class.

Part B: Group Analysis

In groups of about 6, your instructor will instruct you to reach consensus on certain items on the two forms. Groups should prepare a short presentation for certain designated items.

*Contributed by Barry Axe

Name _____   Group _____

With regard to unions in the United States today, use the following scale to indicate your opinion about each statement:

5 = Strongly agree
4 = Agree
3 = Undecided
2 = Disagree
1 = Strongly disagree

_____   1. U.S. productivity would be much higher if it weren't for unions.

_____   2. Unions protect incompetent workers so long as they belong to the union.

_____   3. Unions interfere with management attempts to increase productivity.

_____   4. Unions are corrupt.

_____   5. Unions are mainly responsible for the adversarial relationship that exists between unions and management.

_____   6. Union wages are not competitive in a global economy.

_____   7. Union rules and regulations stifle attempts to improve the quality of our products or services.

_____   8. Unions are a big help to workers.

_____   9. Unions are violent during strikes.

_____   10. More protection is needed for replacement workers who are threatened and harassed by striking unionists.

_____   11. The United States could be more competitive if we could get rid of unions.

_____   12. Big labor has excessive political power in Washington.

_____   13. Unions are undemocratic in their organizational structure.

_____   14. Union workers are less satisfied with their wages and benefits than are nonunion workers.

_____   15. Unions tend to oppose pay-for-performance (PFP) systems.

_____   16. Companies should be allowed to screen people based on their general attitudes toward unions.

_____   17. Union wages have outpaced nonunion wages over the last 10 years.

_____   18. Management should be allowed to hire replacement workers immediately after a strike action.

_____   19. I would join a union if I thought it might help me.

Answer Questions 20–24 as directed. Put your answer in the space provided.

_____   20. In general, I feel: (1) positive, (2) neutral, or (3) negative toward unions.

_____   21. I would vote "yes" if a union election were held in my workplace tomorrow: (1) definitely yes, (2) probably yes, (3) not sure, (4) probably not, (5) definitely not.

_____   22. Employees who have a union are better off than those who don't. (1) Employees are better off; (2) Employees are worse off; (3) There is no difference; (4) I'm not sure.

_____   23. It would be good for the country if more workers had union representation. (1) Good for the country; (2) Bad for the country; (3) Depends; (4) Not sure.

_____   24. Employees are more successful in getting problems resolved with their employer when they bring these problems up as a group rather than as individuals. (1) More successful as a group; (2) More successful as individuals.

Name ———————————————————   Group ————————————————————

CIRCLE T (true) or F (False) for each item. Note the special instructions for #37.

1. T   F   Managers do not have to worry about the NLRA if the workers they manage are not in a union.

2. T   F   Nonunion workers cannot go on strike.

3. T   F   A company can adopt a no pro-union shirt rule.

4. T   F   A manager can invoke the "employment-at-will" doctrine and fire a nonunion worker who complains about too much overtime.

5. T   F   A manager can invoke the "employment-at-will" doctrine and fire an employee who refuses to obey an order the employee feels is unsafe.

6. T   F   A manager can fire an employee who fails to use the company complaint process and walks off the job in protest of working conditions.

7. T   F   A manager can fire an employee who refuses to work an overtime shift.

8. T   F   A manager can fire an employee who voices a complaint in an offensive or disruptive manner.

9. T   F   A company may include a rule in its Handbook that prohibits employees from discussing their wages.

10. T   F   Managers can bar off-duty employees entry to parking lots and other nonworking areas.

11. T   F   Managers can bar its off-site employees from access to an employer's faciltities.

12. T   F   A manager can fire an employee who makes disparaging remarks about the employer in a newspaper article.

13. T   F   An employer can ban all nonbusiness e-mail correspondence among employees.

14. T   F   Because of the employment-at-will doctrine, managers do not necessarily have to apply work rules consistently.

15. T   F   A manager can appoint nonunion subordinates to a committee to discuss working conditions.

16. T   F   A manager can fire a nonunion employee who is picketing a store during off-duty hours for purposes of organizing the workers.

17. T   F   A manager can fire an employee if the manager finds out that the employee is a paid union organizer.

18. T   F   A manager can refuse to hire a job applicant if the manager knows the applicant is a union member.

19. T   F   An employer can adopt a no "moonlighting" policy if it the employer is concerned about paid union organizers being hired.

20. T F   An employer can refuse to hire an overqualified individual if management knows the individual is sympathetic to unions.

21. T F   An employer can refuse to hire an applicant who violates a company rule forbidding disclosure by applicants of "protected activity" such as union organizing.

22. T F   A manager is allowed to tell employees that strikes are "inevitable" if there is a union.

23. T F   A manager can say that the store or plant will shut down if a union is voted in.

24. T F   A manager can ask employees questions about where they stand on unions.

25. T F   An employer can promise increases in employee benefits during an organizing campaign.

26. T F   An employer can impose a "no solicitation" rule at work stipulating absolutely no union organizing activities during all work hours on company property.

27. T F   An employer can allow anti-union activity during work hours while disallowing pro-union activity.

28. T F   An employer can allow charities to distribute material while not allowing a union to distribute information.

29. T F   An employer can ban pro-union buttons or insignia during working hours.

30. T F   An employer can ban union material from a bulletin board that allows Red Cross solicitations.

31. T F   An employer can ban pro-union screen-savers on the employer's computer.

32. T F   A manager is allowed to say wages and benefits are not paid during a strike.

33. T F   A manager is allowed to say unemployment insurance is unavailable during a strike.

34. T F   A manager is allowed to say that only strike benefits are available to workers who picket.

35. T F   A manager is allowed to say "my eyes are on you and you'd better watch your step" to a pro-union employee.

36. T F   A manager can hire "permanent replacement workers" during a strike action and these replacements need not be displaced when the strike ends.

Wal-Mart surveys its employees annually as part of its "Grass Roots" program. The survey is designed to assess employees' perceptions on work-related issues. Results are tabulated by store, and the top three concerns are posted at each store. Formerly known as the Union Potential Index, the Unresolved People Index (UPI) is used to identify stores at risk of union organizing activity.

37. T F   The use of the UPI is legal under the NLRA? Explain your answer below. If your answer is "No," describe at least one situation where the use of the survey would be illegal under the NLRA.

EXERCISE 13.3

The Baseball Strike: An Example of Collective Bargaining*

Overview

We have seen how important collective bargaining is to the resolution of differences between unions and management. Achieving consensus between the two parties is a long and taxing process, often leaving both sides feeling bitter and cheated. Rarely does a collective bargaining session leave both sides feeling good about the overall outcome of the negotiations. Collective bargaining also requires a great deal of preparation and the willingness to be flexible on the issues under debate.

This exercise introduces the collective bargaining process and the difficulties that can arise from the advancement of differing agendas by two parties. This is a team exercise, and each team should attempt to represent its side in good faith and with as much realism as possible. Discussion will probably center on reactions to the differing situations presented in the exercise.

Learning Objectives

After completing this exercise, you should

1. Understand the difficulties that can arise from two-party negotiations.
2. Understand the preparation involved in collective bargaining.
3. Be able to prepare an argument for the advancement of goals in a collective bargaining situation.
4. Be capable of understanding the process of reaching agreement in negotiations.

Procedure

Step 1. Two teams should be formed—one representing the baseball players union and the other representing the team owners. A student also should be selected as a mediator.

Step 2. The owners and players should be given a few minutes to read over their guidelines and discuss a plan of action. The mediator should read both briefings.

Step 3. The players should present their proposal to the owners, who then provide a counteroffer. Negotiations should continue until 25 minutes have elapsed or a decision is reached.

Step 4. Use of the mediator is optional. If one side asks for mediation, all parties must agree before he or she may be brought in to assist the bargaining. The final decision must still be made by both the owners and the players. The mediator can only provide suggestions or guidelines and help to facilitate the process.

Step 5. Following completion of the exercise, complete Form 13.3.1.

EXHIBIT 13.3.1
BASEBALL PLAYERS' BRIEFING

You represent the National Baseball Player's Union (NBPU). All players from all Major League teams must belong to the union and pay annual dues. Therefore, you represent 700 active players plus players who have paid dues but are currently in the minor leagues and the interests of retired players nationwide. Your primary goals in the negotiations are salary, pension benefits for retiring players, term requirements for benefits, and revenue-sharing issues. The environment with the owners has been difficult in the past. Your union has been forced to strike on three occasions, and lockouts by the owners have occurred on five occasions. The primary issues have shifted over the years, but bargaining has always been fierce and resentment has been high. The owners average a personal wealth of $350 million. Gross revenues from all ballparks average $25 million in ticket sales, $10 million in concession sales, and $22 million in merchandise sales. This does not include licensing rights, city parks, television rights, and other sources of owner income. As the players, the centers of attention, you simply want your fair share of the pie. Your agenda for the coming negotiations is as follows:

- An increase in the minimum salary from $500,000 to $600,000 (citing the similar raises the Canadian Hockey Alliance and the World Roundball Federation both received in their most recent contracts).
- A decrease in the minimum Major League service to earn a pension from five years to three years.
- A decrease in the no-trade rule from 10/5 to 7/3 (currently, a player who has been in the majors for 10 years and with the same team for 5 can veto being traded elsewhere).
- An increase in pension benefits for retired players from 25 percent of the minimum salary to 50 percent of the minimum.
- The ability for "marquee" players (i.e., All-Stars, MVPs) to negotiate revenues into their contracts (i.e., a percentage of the ticket sales, etc.) without having to wait for them to be offered by the owners.

These are the basics, but other needs may arise as the negotiations draw near. A poll of the players in the union has shown that the minimum salary increase and the no-trade stipulation are the most popular issues. The poll also stated that the players are *very* willing to strike to get what they want. They are still unhappy about the last round of negotiations, in which the owners got the upper hand.

*Contributed by Joseph G. Clark Jr.

EXHIBIT 13.3.2
BASEBALL OWNERS' BRIEFING

You represent the men and women who own Major League Baseball teams in the American Baseball League (ABL). Your primary goal in this negotiation is to keep your shirt. The average salary of a Major League player is $3.1 million. The average team salary is $55 million. Other costs to consider are equipment, travel, pensions, bonuses, stadium rental and city fees, insurance, stadium staff (i.e., groundskeepers, concessions, security, etc.), and taxes. Many owners are barely solvent. If salaries and benefits continue to increase at the current pace, some owners in smaller cities will be forced to sell to corporate alliances, which will surely ruin the integrity of the game. Negotiations with the players' union are always fierce. There is usually a lot of name calling, slander, and bad feelings from the players. This time, something *must* be done to curb the salaries or else the entire sport may be in serious trouble. The owner's agenda is as follows:

- Lower the current league minimum salary.
- Increase the minimum league service to earn a pension from five years to seven years.
- Obtain an agreement to at least a five-year contract, rather than the usual three-year contract.
- Obtain a stipulation that the players will not file for arbitration until after a new agreement takes effect (thus minimizing trades and revenue losses during the period when we don't know the future of our own financial status).
- The right to perform surprise drug testing on randomly selected or suspected players (with a stipulation for provision of drug and alcohol rehabilitation to be jointly provided by the players' union and the owners).
- The right to renegotiate player-vetoed trades to allow them to proceed (a player who has been in the majors for 10 years and with the same team for 5 can veto being traded elsewhere).

These are the key points, but other issues may arise as the negotiations draw nearer. Remember that the future of the game relies on our ability to stay out of bankruptcy court. A poll of the owners has shown that the salary and trade issues are seen as the most important issues (we simply cannot give up any more money). The poll also revealed that a majority (but not all) of the owners are willing to lock the players out if that is the only option. They are still very upset about the last round of talks, in which the players gained a definite victory.

Name _____   Group _____

    1.   What were the terms of the final agreement negotiated between the two sides?

    2.   What were the difficulties that arose while trying to reach an agreement?

    3.   What role can you see the mediator playing during bargaining of this type?

4. During collective bargaining, discussions can become heated. Did this occur during the exercise and, if so, how was this resolved?

5. In the future, what techniques for bargaining might both sides try to better gain their objectives?

Chapter 14 Exercises

EXERCISE 14.1

The Development of a Company Smoking Policy

Overview

One of the most controversial health issues is smoking in the workplace. Smoking has been taken for granted in most work settings. Little consideration has been given to either (1) the effects of the smoking on the health of both smokers and nonsmokers or (2) the potential cost to the organization. This is so even though smoking is a known cause of cancer, heart disease, and generally bad health. As discussed in Chapter 14, many states now have legislation mandating smoke-free work environments, while some states have taken steps to protect smokers' rights.

Learning Objectives

After completing this exercise, you should be able to

1. Understand the interpersonal dynamics of policy development, particularly policy that significantly affects (and changes) the work environment.
2. Use negotiating skills in relation to your positions on a controversial matter that has no "correct answer."
3. Use your writing skills in an attempt to assuage readers who may not be easily persuaded to agree with your position.

Procedure

Part A: Individual Analysis

Before class, read the scenario and respond as directed. Conduct a Web search to determine the current state of the law and pending legislation related to smokers' and non-smokers' rights.

Part B: Group Analysis

Step 1. Assemble in groups and compare your developmental strategies. Attempt to reach consensus on the correct approach to take in the formulation of the policy. List all the variables that should be considered and all questions of clarification that must be answered.

Step 2. Either students will be paired off or each student should review all the group members' reports and provide constructive suggestions for improving them. The critiques should focus on the drafts rather than starting from scratch. The feedback from the students should then be used in preparing a second letter. Each student group should select one edited letter considered to be the best.

Step 3. The consensus-derived strategy should then be presented to the rest of the class and the selected letter should be read. Subsequent discussion should focus on the likely reactions of the major constituencies of the law firm and the overall impact of the new policy.

Scenario

You have been appointed to a committee charged with the development of a smoking policy for the clerical staff of a law firm. Several of the younger secretaries and some attorneys have complained about smoke in the work area, which is a large room (2,000 square feet with average ventilation) housing 30 secretaries. Many of the law partners prefer to hire only nonsmokers in the future, and some take the position that current employees who smoke should be told they must quit within six months or they will be terminated. Ten of the secretaries smoke, seven of whom have worked for the firm for over 10 years. Two of the seven have disabilities and have some difficulty getting around. Up to now, all employees have been free to smoke any time and any place they choose.

You have been asked to develop a policy. What steps should you follow in formulating a policy? Review the options, which range from taking no action to imposing a strict ban on smoking for all employees either on or off the job. You also have been asked to take a position on a possible policy specifying that new employees must be nonsmokers and that current employees must stop smoking within six months. Assume you have followed the steps of the developmental plan and are ready to draft a policy. Draft a short letter that explains the policy to all employees including the secretaries. What procedures should be followed for establishing a firm policy? What action should be taken for those who choose to violate the policy? What (if any) additional data do you need to make a specific recommendation? Is it legal to impose an absolute prohibition against smoking (both on and off the job)?

EXERCISE 14.2

The Development of an Antidrug Policy*

Overview

As a result of the Drug Free Workplace Act, which went into effect in 1989, all federal contractors are required to provide their employees with a drug-free workplace. The act includes the following guidelines:

1. Furnish a policy statement prohibiting controlled substances in the workplace.
2. Notify employees (regular and contract) of the prohibition and the expected penalties for violating the policy.
3. Establish a drug-free awareness program.
4. Notify employees that conformance to the drug-free policy is a condition of employment.
5. Employees must notify the employer within five days if they are convicted of violating a criminal drug statute while in the workplace.
6. Contractors must notify the contracting agency of any such convictions.
7. For all employees convicted, the contractor must impose a sanction or require the completion of a substance-abuse treatment program.
8. Continue to make a good-faith effort to maintain a drug-free workplace.

Learning Objectives

After completing this exercise, you should be able to

1. Consider implications of different policies regarding drug testing.
2. Understand the options available for deterrence and enforcement of drug abuse and enforcement of an antidrug policy.

Procedure

Part A: Individual Analysis

Before class, read the scenario and respond as directed.

Part B: Group Analysis

In groups, each member should review the memos of all other members. Each group should attempt to reach consensus on the recommendation to the board. The recommendation must deal with all the issues raised above. Take a definitive position on random testing for all employees and on what specific steps should be taken if an employee tests positive.

Scenario

You are the manager of the HR department of a major federal contractor. Your responsibilities include implementing

*Contributed by Marilyn A. Perkins.

the drug-free workplace program mandated by the federal government. Your organization is responsible for conducting very costly and sensitive research. The machinery used in the research is complex and could be dangerous if not used properly. Some of the experiments being conducted are risky and could pose a hazard to the environment or a threat to national security. However, not all employees work with the dangerous machinery or on the sensitive experiments.

As part of the drug-free workplace, the position of the security department includes the following:

- Any employee with a substance-abuse problem should be reported to the security department, regardless of whether the substance abuse was detected by management or self-reported.
- Drug testing should be conducted for all individuals filling sensitive positions and randomly for the entire organization.
- All positive test results should be reported to the security department.
- All employees testing positive on the first test should be terminated.
- Any job applicant with a history of drug or alcohol abuse should not be hired.

The EAP representatives have reviewed the security department's position and disagree strongly with the proposed sanctions. In the EAP, 70 percent of the employees sent to employee counseling are self-referred. If the EAP is required to report the self-referrals to the security department, the EAP representatives argue, employees will not seek help from the EAP and will go untreated. The EAP representatives also contend that the termination sanction proposed by the security department is inhumane and may violate the Rehabilitation Act of 1973, the Americans with Disabilities Act, or inalienable rights of privacy. One board member has stated that mass drug testing as proposed "makes a mockery of the presumption of innocence and strongly implies that someone who refuses to submit to a test is guilty . . . the level of expectations of privacy is diminishing, and we are slowly surrendering our dignity."

The board of directors has requested that you, as a task force member, develop a response to both the security department and to the EAP representatives. Take into consideration the health and safety of the company as well as the rights of the employees. Consider the following components: the Drug Free Workplace Act, an employee's right to privacy, confidentiality of the drug-testing program, and access to the EAP. Prepare a memo to the board of directors in which you take a position on the matter (maximum of five pages). Be prepared to defend your position in group discussion.

EXERCISE 14.3

The Development of a Health and Safety Policy

Overview

Chapter 14 discusses the role of OSHA inspectors in pursuing violations of the 1970 OSHA Act. This exercise has you consider the implications of health and safety regulation for managerial activities.

Learning Objectives

After completing this exercise, you should be able to

1. Understand the steps that should be taken under OSHA regulation.
2. Know the rights that employers and employees have with regard to OSHA regulation.

Procedure

Part A: Individual Analysis

Read the following scenario before class. You have been retained as a consultant to implement compliance with OSHA. As a consultant, how would you approach the problem, and what kind of advice and help would you give? Complete Form 14.3.1 and bring it to class.

Part B: Group Analysis

In class, groups should review the completed 14.3.1 forms of individual members and attempt to reach consensus on all three aspects of the report. One group member should report the consensus recommendations to the rest of the class.

Scenario

Dynamic Duo, Inc., opened its manufacturing plant several months ago. The company is owned and operated by two enterprising business students, Jack Richter and Drew Saline, from Poedunk University in Poedunk, U.S.A. The company has 75 employees, most of whom work on the floor of the plant and handle the heavy equipment needed to manufacture widgets. One supervisor is in charge. Dynamic Duo, Inc., is concerned about safety, but the owners know almost nothing about OSHA.

Before you have had a chance to advise Dynamic Duo, the plant is visited by a compliance officer who simply enters the plant and conducts a tour, unaccompanied by either management or employees. At the end of the tour, the compliance officer presents Dynamic Duo with two citations. The Dynamic Duo owners call you in as a consultant and ask you what they should do next. The citations concern scaffolding and ergonomics problems.

Unfortunately for Dynamic Duo, soon after the compliance officer's visit, five employees are injured or become ill, all on the same day. One is seriously injured, having caught his hand in a conveyor. Another person fell off some scaffolding. Another has become mysteriously ill, and three others have suffered minor cuts. The owners call you in again and ask you whether they need to inform anybody of the accidents and the illness or to record them somehow. What else should you tell Dynamic Duo?

Name _____   Group _____

1. What questions would you ask Dynamic Duo's owners?

2. What legal steps would you recommend that Dynamic Duo take?

3. What advice would you give the owners concerning the company's obligations under OSHA to record accidents?

4. Visit www.OSHA.gov and determine if you can provide any additional information to help make the plant safer.

5. How could Dynamic Duo be issued a citation for an ergonomics violation? Jack Richter says, "I thought Bush got rid of that stupid regulation." What is your response?

EXERCISE 14.4

The Development of a Threat Management Team for a Workplace Violence Incident*

Overview

As described in Chapter 14, incidents of workplace violence are common in the United States. This exercise describes a situation in which the potential for a violent incident on the job is high. As members of a threat management team, students must decide how to recognize, report, and subsequently deal with the incident.

Learning Objectives

After completing this exercise, you should be able to

1. Recognize the warning signs and symptoms of a potentially violent situation in the workplace.
2. Record and report threatening behaviors.
3. Construct a plan for assessing an employee's potential for violence and recommend a course of action.

Procedure

Part A: Individual Analysis

Before class, read the scenario. Prepare a written answer to each of the questions presented on Form 14.4.1. Assume you actually observed the situation described in the scenario and complete the Violent Incident Report in Form 14.4.2.

Part B: Group Analysis

Working in groups of about six, review the individual written responses of all group members and develop a new intervention strategy that will handle the potentially violent situation and prevent others from happening. The group should act as a threat management team and reach consensus on the questions in Form 14.4.1.

Part C: Class Discussion and Assessment

Have one member from each group act as a spokesperson to describe the strategies developed by each threat management team. Discuss the feasibility of each team's plan. Recommendations of alternative plans should be addressed.

Scenario

Inside a large manufacturing plant in a suburban Midwestern city, a production manager, Rosalyn, just received word that she must lay off eight more people. It's the second time in the last six months that she's had to tell people they are no longer needed. Her head begins to pound and her heart races. She must prepare herself to handle the usual reactions of anger, disappointment, and resentment that will soon follow. This is the third time in the two years since Rosalyn has joined the company that she's had to give employees news about layoffs. It isn't easy, especially since, at age 31, she's younger than most of the employees. This time she's particularly afraid that one employee, named Roy, could become a physical threat to the workforce after hearing the news.

Roy is 49 and has worked at the plant for 23 years. He has a large family to support and hopes to remain an employee until retirement. Roy has a record of absenteeism and tardiness and is viewed as a "loner" by most of his co-workers. No one knows much about him except that he appears to have few interests outside of work besides the shooting range he frequently visits. Some workers have overheard him voicing extremist opinions and attitudes on a variety of issues. For the most part, people leave him alone to do his work.

As expected, Roy was not happy about the layoff. A few days after the layoff, he met with the production manager and a human resource professional to review the severance package offering. During this meeting, Roy began to speak angrily and at one point lost his temper. Shaking his finger at the production manager, he shouted, "I'll be back," and has since been spotted sitting in the parking lot in his truck. No one knows for sure what he's going to do.

Within the hour, Roy's file is on your desk. By the end of the day, you assemble the company's threat management team to assess the potential danger involved. You and the other team members review Roy's records, complete violent incident reports, and discuss options for handling the situation. All collected data will be analyzed and measured against an established criterion for dangerousness to determine whether Roy represents a clear and immediate threat to an identifiable target, namely Rosalyn, the production manager. A course of action must be developed.

*Contributed by Susan M. Stewart, University of Puget Sound.

Name _____   Group _____

1.   What warning signs or symptoms were displayed before Roy's blowup?

2.   Were proper immediate action(s) taken after this incident?

3.   Were time, money, and effort wasted or was a potential crisis averted in the meeting of the threat management team?

4.   Discuss five ways in which the threat management team could be more effective.

5.   What specific action(s) could be taken to create a security-conscious organizational culture at the manufacturing plant?

6.   What, if any, unique challenges may exist in this situation given the differences between Roy and Rosalyn, the production manager, in terms of gender, age, and tenure with the company?

7.   What, if any, ethical issues (e.g., privacy) are involved when members of a threat management team seek to identify and report potentially dangerous employees?

FORM 14.4.2
VIOLENT INCIDENT REPORT

Employees who have been victims of violence at work or have observed potentially violent incidents should complete this report as soon as possible. Upon completion, send a copy to your employer and to your threat management team contact person. Be sure to keep a copy for your records. Please print.

1. Identifying Information

Name: _____

Job title: _____

Employer: _____

Department/section: _____

2. Assailant/aggressor

_____ Worker

_____ Former worker

_____ Supervisor

_____ Customer

_____ Relative

_____ Girlfriend/boyfriend

_____ Spouse/ex-spouse

_____ Patient

_____ Student

_____ Resident

_____ Visitor

_____ Client

_____ Other (specify)

_____

Name (if known): _____

Age: _____

Gender: _____ Male _____ Female

Were you able to identify the assailant/aggressor as one who possessed potential for violence before this incident?

_____ Yes _____ No

If yes, what traits or characteristics did the assailant/aggressor possess? (Check all that apply.)

_____ Anger

_____ Aggressive/threatening

_____ Obsessive

_____ Withdrawn/"loner"

_____ Disgruntled/"troublemaker"

_____ Quiet

_____ Extremist attitudes or opinions

_____ Argumentative/uncooperative

_____ Interpersonal conflict

_____ Real or perceived emotional/mental disorders

_____ Other (explain) _____

3. Incident and injury Information

Date of incident: _____

Time: _____ (AM) ___ (PM) ___

Type(s) of violence observed (check all that apply):

_____ Gossip/rumors

_____ Verbal abuse/swearing

_____ Arguments with customers, coworkers, supervisors, or other employees

_____ Property damage/vandalism

_____ Fist-fight/physical altercation

_____ Theft

_____ Shooting

_____ Rape

_____ Stabbing

_____ Arson

_____ Murder

_____ Other (specify) _____

Type of weapon(s) used (check all that apply):

_____ Gun

_____ Knife

_____ Club/bat/pipe

_____ Fist

_____ No weapon involved

_____ Other (explain)

_____

Perceived motivation for the aggressive act (check all that apply):

_____ Firing

_____ Layoff

_____ Stress

_____ Feelings of unfairness, injustice, or malice by others

_____ Financial/legal difficulties

_____ Family/marital problems

_____ Emotional problems/mental illness

_____ Drug/alcohol abuse

_____ Personality conflict

_____ Violent criminal history

_____ Don't know/no knowledge of motive

_____ Other (specify) _____

_____

Medical attention/first aid obtained?   _____ Yes   _____ No

Workers' compensation forms completed?   _____ Yes   _____ No

Police called?   _____ Yes   _____ No

Reported to supervisor?   _____ Yes   _____ No

Action taken:

_____

_____

4. Other information

Was the assailant involved in any previous violent incidents with staff?   _____ Yes   _____ No

Are there any measures in place to prevent a similar incident?   _____ Yes   _____ No

Please provide any other information you think is relevant:

_____

_____

APPENDIX C

Assessment Guidelines for Self, Peer, and Designated Assessors

Appendix C presents the material necessary for assessments of your performance in the individual and group exercises. Your instructor has elected to use either (1) the "certified assessor" approach, in which certain students are designated to serve as assessors for specific exercises, or (2) the self/peer assessments, that are completed by group members at the conclusion of an exercise.

The certification process usually entails the designated assessors' being examined on the written responses to the exercise before the day on which the exercise is to be done in class. Assessors should receive specific feedback on their written responses and have a clear understanding of appropriate responses to the exercises.

Your instructor may elect to use the self/peer approach to assessment in addition to or as an alternative to the certified assessor approach. Regardless of the approach your instructor uses, students should become familiar with the competencies that are identified and defined in Figure C.2. Research has identified these competencies as critical for success in management. The exercises in this book are designed to enhance these competencies as you learn, integrate, and apply the HRM content of each chapter. Read the assessor job description in Figure C.1 before you begin. Your instructor may provide additional instructions regarding self and peer assessments.

Prior to Observation

1. Review the materials of the assigned chapter and the exercise to which you are assigned. Get very familiar with the recommended responses/answers and the five competencies defined in Figure C.2.
   A. Analytical thinking
   B. Leadership
   C. Oral communication; presentation
   D. Planning and organizing
   E. Written communication
2. Review the behavior examples for each competency to gain further understanding of each competency and how each is exhibited in group or written responses (see Figure C.2).

Instructions for Certified Assessors

After you are assigned to a group in class, review the exercise and competencies, including the behavioral examples for each competency. Before discussion begins, take a seat outside the circle of participants and do not discuss the exercise with group members. (You are strictly an observer/assessor.) Before discussion, quickly review each group member's individual exercise response. Make a note of the name of any group member who has not prepared a written response. Return the exercises to the participants.

3. Once discussion begins, observe the behavior of each discussant, keeping the competencies in mind as a frame of reference.
4. Record your observations on a plain sheet of paper, being careful to note who said what during discussion. Avoid any kind of evaluation at this point. (Do not use a complete sentence format.) Be as precise and complete as possible in recording your observations. Do not try to translate your observations into the competencies until the observation period is over. Your attention should be directed toward making accurate observations and keeping good notes.
5. At the conclusion of the discussion, collect all written responses and, if required, the group's written response. As you review your observations, assign a positive or negative value to each observation and determine what competency each observation illustrates. Next to each observation, enter the letter of the relevant competency, next to the + or – value.
6. Carefully review and critique each member's written responses, noting and correcting any misspellings, poor grammar, incomprehensible sentences, and so on.
7. Enter your name ("Observer") in the space provided. After reviewing the written responses and your notes on the discussion, summarize your observations in the space provided for feedback. The feedback should be constructive with (it is hoped) both positive and negative comments. Focus

FIGURE C.1

ASSESSOR JOB DESCRIPTION

The job of assessor will entail three major duties: observation, evaluation, and write-up. The actual tasks associated with each of these duties are listed below.

Observation

Watch participant activities and behaviors during an exercise.
Take notes on what is seen and/or heard.
Assign + or – value to each observation.
Classify notes according to predefined competencies.

Evaluation

Assign a numerical performance rating for each competency (based on notes taken).
Make an overall assessment.

Write-up (if assigned)

Collect all data on each student's performance for each competency.
Synthesize data for each competency.
Complete a final report, in narrative form, highlighting the participant's strengths and weaknesses.

---

on the way in which the member performed in the group and completed the exercise. Be sure to record your name and the name of the participant.

8. After recording your feedback for each participant, make a rating on each student's performance.

To Rate Performance

Use the following scale to make your rating:

    7 = Outstanding
    6 = Very good
    5 = Above average
    4 = Satisfactory
    3 = Below satisfactory
    2 = Well below satisfactory
    1 = Poor
    NO = Not observed

A very small percentage of students should be rated at the 7 level. *This rating is reserved for only the very best performance for that competency.* **Most ratings should be at or near the 4 level.** Usually, however, when observing a group of about six people, close to the full range of performance levels should be observed and therefore rated. Rate all participants on one competency and then proceed to the next competency. Using the same rating scale, make an overall assessment of each participant.

What If a Group Member Doesn't Participate?

How do you rate someone who says virtually nothing in the group exercise? The answer to this question depends on the particular competency. Inactivity in the group would constitute a low score for *leadership* and *planning* and *organizing*. Inactivity would probably necessitate a rating of "Not observed" (NO) for the other competencies.

FIGURE C.2

CRITICAL COMPETENCIES

Behavioral Examples

A. **Analytic Thinking:**   Identifying the fundamental ideas, concepts, themes or issues that help to integrate, interpret, and/or explain underlying patterns in a set of information or data.

Examples

Effective

"Let's take turns stating our solution to the problem. We'll write down the points we agree upon and come up with a set of solutions that everyone will be happy with. How does that sound to everyone? Who wants to write them down?"
Gather everyone's ideas, key in on main concept, look for consensus or pattern of responses.

Ineffective

Everyone talks at once, or one person dominates, or no one wants to talk. Instead, socializes with group members.
"We don't know what is wrong with the problem. Let's just put anything down to get a grade," or,
"I skipped that problem because I didn't understand it."

B. **Leadership:**   Utilization of appropriate interpersonal styles to stimulate and guide individuals or groups toward goal and/or task accomplishment.

Examples

Effective

"We've got a lot of great ideas, but we haven't heard from everyone yet. Let's write down what we have and then we'll add the rest of the ideas to our list."

Ineffective

"This case is just too complicated to come up with a solution. There is no way we can find the answer."
"I want to write down the solutions for everyone, that way my ideas will be sure to be included."

C. **Oral Communication; Presentation:**   Effective expression of ideas or viewpoints to others in individual or group situations (includes gestures, nonverbal communication, and the use of visual aids).

Examples

Effective

"I wrote down my thoughts on a solution to this problem. Let's take turns giving our ideas so that we can hear how everyone in the group feels about the problem. How does that sound to everyone? Who wants to go first?"

Ineffective

"I am not very good at speaking before a group. Let someone else who has more experience go first."
"I didn't come up with any ideas that the rest of the group hasn't already said. Take their ideas and write them down."

D. **Planning and Organizing:**   Establishing a course of action for self and/or others to accomplish specific goals; planning proper assignments of personnel and appropriate allocations of resources.

Examples

Effective

"Our assignment calls for three HRM objectives. Let's talk about each objective individually and reach a consensus for each one. Who will volunteer to write them down. We better hurry, we only have 20 minutes to come up with our final list."

Ineffective

"We have too many opinions to formulate a final list. There is no way that we can decide on the three objectives in 20 minutes."

E. **Written Communication:**   Clear expression of ideas in writing and in appropriate grammatical form.
Utilized appropriate vocabulary, proper grammar, and correct spelling. Writes legibly.

Examples

Effective

No spelling errors; few (if any) grammatical errors

Ineffective

Numerous spelling and grammatical errors

FIGURE C.3

STUDENT SELF-ASSESSMENT LOG—RATINGS

Name _____

Exer. #	Analytical Thinking	Leadership	Oral Communication, Presentation	Planning & Organizing	Written Communication	Overall Assessment
Average						

Use the following rating scale to make your self-assessment: 7 = outstanding; 6 = very good; 5 = above average; 4 = satisfactory; 3 = below satisfactory; 2 = well below satisfactory; 1 = poor.

FIGURE C.3

STUDENT SELF-ASSESSMENT LOG—RATINGS

Name _____

Exer. #	Analytical Thinking	Leadership	Oral Communication, Presentation	Planning & Organizing	Written Communication	Overall Assessment
Average						

Use the following rating scale to make your self-assessment: 7 = outstanding; 6 = very good; 5 = above average; 4 = satisfactory; 3 = below satisfactory; 2 = well below satisfactory; 1 = poor.

ENDNOTES

CHAPTER 1

1. Canfield, K. (2004, July 1). Analyze this. *The American Prospect Online.*

2. Bianchi, A. (1996, February). The character-revealing handwriting analysis. *Inc. Magazine,* 77–92.

3. Datta, D. K., Guthrie, J. P., and Wright, P. M. (2005). Human resource management and labor productivity: Does industry matter? *Academy of Management Journal, 48,* 135–145.

4. Pfeffer, J. (1994). *Competitive advantage through people.* Boston: Harvard Business School Press, p. 6.

5. Kaplan, R. S. and Norton, D. P. (1996). *The balanced scorecard.* Boston: Harvard Business School Press.

6. Huselid, M. A., Becker, B. E., and Beatty, R. W. (2005). *The workforce scorecard.* Boston: Harvard Business School Press.

7. Towers Perrin. (1992). Priorities for competitive advantage: An IBM study conducted by Towers Perrin.

8. See Pfeffer, *Competitive advantage through people,* p. 16.

9. Hammonds, K. H. (2005, August). Why we hate HR. *Fast Company,* p. 40.

10. Rynes, S., Colbert, A., and Brown, K. (2002). HR professionals' beliefs about effective human resource management practices: Correspondence between research and practice. *Human Resource Management, 41,* 149–174.

11. Plake, B. S., and Impara, J. C. (Eds.). (2001). *The Fourteenth Mental Measurements Yearbook.* Lincoln, NB: The University of Nebraska Press.

12. Friedman, T. L. (2005). *The world is flat: A brief history of the twenty-first century.* Boston: Farrar, Straus & Giroux.

13. Bernardin, H. J., Hagan, C., Kane, J., and Villanova, P. (1998). Effective performance management: Precision in measurement with focus on customers and situational constraints. In J. Smither (Ed.), *Performance appraisal: State-of-the-art in practice.* San Francisco: Jossey-Bass.

14. SHRM 2004–2005 *Workplace Forecast,* p. 47.

15. Stewart, T. (1996, January 15). Taking on the last bureaucracy. *Fortune,* 105–108.

16. Huselid, Becker, and Beatty, *The workforce scorecard.*

17. U.S. Bureau of the Census. (2005). Profile of the foreign-born population in the U.S. *Current Population Reports,* 23–206 (extrapolation).

18. Lawler, E. (1988, August). HRM: Meeting the new challenges. *Personnel,* 24.

19. Ibid.

20. Huselid, Becker, and Beatty, *The workforce scorecard.*

21. Van Rooy, D. L., and Viswesvaran, C. (2004). Emotional intelligence: A meta-analytic investigation of predictive validity and nomological net. *Journal of Vocational Behavior, 65,* 71–95.

22. Cooper-Hakim, A., and Viswesvaran, C. (2005). The construct of work commitment: Testing an integrative framework. *Psychological Bulletin, 131,* 241–259.

23. Becker, B. E., Huselid, M. A., and Ulrich, D. (2001). *The HR scorecard.* Boston: Harvard Business School Press.

24. White, E. (2005, February 17). To keep employees, Domino's decides it's not all about pay. *The Wall Street Journal,* pp. A1, A9.

25. Pfeffer, *Competitive advantage through people.*

26. Sheley, E. (1996, June). Share your worth: Talking numbers with the CEO. *HR Magazine,* 86–95.

27. An early version of this section was contributed by Dave Ulrich.

28. Orlitzky, M., Schimidt, F. L., and Rynes, S. L. (2003). Corporate social and financial performance: A meta-analysis. *Organization Studies, 24,* 403–411.

29. Fulmer, I. S., Gerhart, B., and Scott, K. S. (2003). Are the 100 best better? *Personnel Psychology, 56,* 965–993.

30. Walker, R. (2003, November 30). The guts of a new machine. *NewYorkTimes.com.*

31. Ibid.

CHAPTER 2

1. Friedman, T. L. (2005). *The world is flat: A brief history of the twenty-first century.* Boston: Farrar, Straus & Giroux.

2. Hill, C. W. (2005). *International business: Competing in the global marketplace.* New York: Irwin McGraw-Hill.

3. World Trade Organization. (2001). *International Trade Trends and Statistics.*

4. Ibid.

5. See Friedman, *The world is flat.*

6. Daniels, J. D., Radebaugh, L. H., and Sullivan, D. P. (2004). *International business: Environments and operations.* Upper Saddle River, NJ: Prentice Hall.

7. Cited in Neary, D. B. and O'Grady, D. A. (2000). The role of training in developing global leaders: A case study at TRW, Inc. *Human Resource Management, 39* (2-3), 185–193.

8. United Nations Conference on Trade and Development (UNCTAD). (2004). *World investment report 2002: The shift towards services.* Geneva: United Nations.

9. Czinkota, M. R., Ronkainen, I. A., and Moffett, M. H. (1999). *International Business*. NY: Harcourt Brace.

10. See Daniels et al., *International business*.

11. Ibid.

12. UNCTAD, *World investment report 2002*.

13. Konopaske, R., and Ivancevich, J. M. (2004). *Global management and organizational behavior*. Burr Ridge, IL: McGraw-Hill Irwin.

14. UNCTAD, *World investment report 2002*.

15. Ibid.

16. Griffin, R. W. and Pustay, R. W. (1999). *International business: A managerial perspective*. Reading, MA: Addison-Wesley.

17. Hallett, J. J. (1987). *Worklife visions*. Alexandria, VA: SHRM. pp. 45–46.

18. Zellner, W., Schmidt, C. A., Ihlwan, M., and Donley, H. (2001, September 3). How well does Wal-Mart travel? *BusinessWeek*, 82–84.

19. 1996 study by the National Foreign Trade Council and Windham International cited in Schell, M. S., and Solomon, C. M. (1997). *Capitalizing on the global workforce: A strategic guide to expatriate management*. Chicago, IL: Irwin, p. 174.

20. See Griffin and Pustay, *International business*.

21. Ibid.

22. Brown, C. (1996, August 12). Banana Split. *Forbes, 158* (4), 94–95.

23. Under a treaty signed in April, 2001, the European Banana Wars were brought to an official close when the EU agreed to relax many of its quotas, tariffs and restrictions. In exchange, the U.S. suspended several trade-related sanctions that it had levied in retaliation for the bananas. In addition to the banana-growing Caribbean provinces of France, colonies and provinces of EU countries in Africa and the Pacific Islands stood to gain considerable economic benefits from the tariffs and quotas on bananas imported from outside the EU. However, both Dole and Chiquita indicated that the wars had brought each of them to the brink of bankruptcy, since the majority of their growing fields were located outside the EU in South America and the Caribbean. This, in turn, was depressing regional and national economics in some areas of the western hemisphere. For further information, see Greitner, P. (2001). Europe, U.S. end banana dispute. *The Miami Herald*, April 12, p. C1.

24. Wild, J. J., Wild, K. L., and Han, J. C. Y. (2000). *International business: An integrated approach*. Upper Saddle River, NJ: Prentice Hall.

25. See Griffin and Pustay, *International business*.

26. Cited in Daniels, Radebaugh, and Sullivan, *International business*.

27. Cited in Wild, Wild, and Han, *International business*.

28. Ibid.

29. Knowlton, C. (1992, June 23). Europe cooks up a cereal war. *Fortune*.

30. Wild, Wild, and Han, *International business;* see also, Gong, Y., Shenkar, O., Luo, Y. and Nyaw, M. (2001). Role conflict and ambiguity of CEOs in international joint ventures: A transaction cost perspective. *Journal of Applied Psychology, 86,* 764–773.

31. Stewart, T. A. (1993, December 13). Welcome to the revolution. *Fortune,* 66.

32. Zubrzycki, J. (1997). Mastering software helps India youth snag foreign jobs. *The Christian Science Monitor,* November 10, p. D1. See also Bhargava, S. W. (1993). Software from India? Yes, it's for real. *BusinessWeek,* 77.

33. Landler, Mark (2001, March 21). Hi, I'm in Banglore (but I can't say so). *New York Times,* pp. A1, C4.

34. Porter, M. E. (1990). *The competitive advantage of nations.* New York: Free Press, 53.

35. Carmell, W. A. (2001, May–June). Application of U.S. antidiscrimination laws to multinational employers. *Legal Report,* 1–5; Dowling, P. J., Welch, D. E, and Schuler, R. S. (1999). *International human resource management: Managing people in a multinational context.* New York: ITP.

36. Sanyal, R. N. (2001). *International management: A strategic perspective.* Upper Saddle River, NJ: Prentice Hall.

37. Mezias, J. (2000). Do labor lawsuits represent a liability of foreignness for foreign subsidiaries operating in the United States? Paper presented at the twenty-first *Academy of Management Conference,* Toronto, Ontario.

38. See Dowling, Welch, and Schuler, *International human resource management*.

39. Hill, *International business,* p. 67. See also, Adair, W. L., Okumura, T., and Brett, J. M. (2001). Negotiation behavior when cultures collide: The United States and Japan. *Journal of Applied Psychology, 86,* 371–385.

40. Kraimer, M. L., Wayne, S., and Jaworski, R. A. (2001). Sources of support and expatriate performance: The mediating role of expatriate adjustment. *Personnel Psychology, 54,* 71–100; Ryan, A. M., McFarland, L., Baron, H. and Page, R. (1999). An international look at selection practices: Nation and culture as explanations for variability in practice. *Personnel Psychology, 52,* 359–392; Shaffer, M.A. and Harrison, D. A. (2001). Forgotten partners of international assignments: Development and test of a model of spouse adjustment. *Journal of Applied Psychology, 86,* 238–254.

41. Desatnick, R. L., and Bennet, M. L. (1978). *Human resource management in the multinational company.* New York: Nichols. See also Dowling, Welch, and Schuler, *International human resource management*.

42. Bird, A., Taylor, S., and Beechler, S. (1998). A typology of human resource management in Japanese multinational corporations: Organizational implications. *Human Resource Management, 37*(2), 159–172; see also Harzing, A. (2001). Who's in charge? An empirical study of executive staffing practices in foreign subsidiaries. *Human Resource Management, 40,* 139–158.

43. Overman, S. (2000). In Sync. *HR Magazine, 44*(4). 93–97; See also, Turban, D. B. Lua, C., Ngo, H., Chow, I. H., and Si, S. X. Organizational attractiveness of firms in the People's Republic of China: A person–organization fit perspective. *Journal of Applied Psychology, 86,* 194–206.

44. Ibid.

45. See Dowling, Welch, and Schuler, *International human resource management*.

46. For full discussion of the rationale for international business assignments, see Stroh, L. K., Black, J. S., Mendenhall, M. E., and Gregersen, H.B. (2005). *International*

assignments: An integration of strategy, research, and practice. Mahwah, NJ: Erlbaum.

47. GMAC Global Relocation Services. (2004, May). *Global relocation trends 2003/2004 survey report.* http.www.shrm.org/hrresources/surveys; See also, Garonzik, R., Brockner, J., and Siegel, P. A. (2000). Identifying international assignees at risk for premature departure: The interactive effect of outcome favorability and procedural fairness. *Journal of Applied Psychology, 85,* 13–20.

48. See GMAC, *Global relocation trends.*

49. For full discussion of international assignment success and failure, see Black, J. S., and Gregersen, H. (1999). The right way to manage experts. *Harvard Business Review, 77*(2), 52–63

50. See GMAC, *Global relocation trends.*

51. Ibid.

52. Johnson, C. (1999). Cutting down the days. *HR Magazine, 44*(4), 93–97.

53. Ibid.

54. Studies by the International Personnel Association (IPA) and Catalyst cited in Tyler, K. (2001). Don't fence her in. *HR Magazine, 46*(3), 70–77.

55. Bhaskar-Shrinivas, P., Harrison, D. A., Shaffer, M. A., and Luk, D. M. (2005). Input-based and time-based models of international adjustment: Meta-analytic evidence and theoretical extensions. *Academy of Management Journal, 48,* 257–281; see also, Au, K. Y., and Fukuda, J. (2002). Boundary spanning behaviors of expatriates. *Journal of World Business, 37,* 285–296; and Konopaske and Ivancevich, *Global management and organizational behavior.*

56. Kanter, R. M. (1995). *World class: Thinking locally in the global economy,* New York: Simon and Schuster, 88.

57. Carpenter, M. A., Sanders, G., and Gregersen, H. B. (2000). International assignment experience at the top can make a bottom line difference. *Human Resource Management, 39*(2 and 3), 277–285.

58. Lublin, J. S. (1996, January 29). On overseas stint can be a ticket to the top. *The Wall Street Journal,* p. B1.

59. Carpenter, M. A., Sanders, W. G., and Gregerson, H. B. (2001). Building human capability with organizational context: The impact of international assignment experience on multinational firm performance and CEO pay. *Academy of Management Journal, 44,* 493–511.

60. Csoka, L., and Hackett, B. (1998). *Transforming the HR function for global business success.* Report #1209-98-RR. New York: Conference Board.

61. Adler, N., and Bartholomew, S. (1992). Managing globally competent people. *Academy of Management Executive, 6*(3), 52–65.

62. Conner, J. (2000). Developing the global leaders of tomorrow. *Human Resource Management, 39*(2 and 3), 147–158.

63. Kanter, R. M. (1995). *World class: Thinking locally in the global economy,* New York: Simon and Schuster, 88.

64. Gregerson, H. B., Morrison, A. J., and Mendenhall, M. E. (2000). Guest editors' introduction. *Human Resource Management, 39*(2 and 3), 115–116.

65. Morrison, A. J. (2000). Developing a global leadership model. *Human Resource Management, 39*(2 and 3). 117–132.

66. Ibid.

67. Ibid.

68. Jeannet, J. (2000). *Managing with a global mindset.* London: Pearson Education Ltd., 189.

CHAPTER 3

1. Joyce, A. (2005, December 9). The bias breakdown: Asians and blacks lead in perceived discrimination at work. The Washington Post. D01.

2. Dobrzynski, J. H. (1995, September 12). Women more pessimistic about work. *The New York Times,* p. C2.

3. Dipboye, R. L. & Colella, A. (Eds.) (2005). *Discrimination at work.* Mahwah, NJ: Erlbaum.

4. Ferguson, T. W. (1996, November 4). Boss harassment. *Forbes,* 150-151; see also Holmes, S. A. (1996, November 17). Bias suit harbinger. *The New York Times,* 12; Kahan, S. C., Brown, B. B., Zepke, B. E., and Lanzarone, M. *Legal guide to human resources.* Boston: Warren, Gorham and Lamont.

5. See www.eeoc.gov. Summary statistics for 2005.

6. *McDonnell-Douglas v. Green* (1973). 411 U.S. 972 (U.S. Supreme Court).

7. *Texas Department of Community Affairs v. Burdine* (1981). 450 U.S. 248. (U.S. Supreme Court).

8. *Griggs v. Duke Power Company* (1971). 401 U.S. 424. (U.S. Supreme Court).

9. *Watson v. Fort Worth Bank and Trust* (1988). 487 U.S. 977 (5th Cir.); see also, Werner, J. M., and Bolino, M. C. (1997). Explaining U.S. Courts of Appeals decisions involving performance appraisal: Accuracy, fairness, and validation. *Personnel Psychology, 50,* 1–24.

10. *Albemarle Paper Co. v. Moody* (1975). 422 U.S. 405 (U.S. Supreme Court). Open to interpretation, the 1991 CRA requires that plaintiffs "demonstrate that each particular challenged employment practice causes a disparate impact, except that if the [plaintiff] can demonstrate to the court that the elements of [an employer's] decision-making process are not capable of separation for analysis, the decision-making process may be analyzed as one employment practice." Since most employers use multiple criteria to make selection, promotion, or similar decisions, disentangling the contribution of each criteron to the disparate impact is difficult.

11. *Connecticut v. Teal* (1982). 457 U.S. 440 (U.S. Supreme Court).

12. *Meritor Savings v. Vinsor* (1986). 477 U.S. 57. See also Bergman, M. E., (2002). The (Un)reasonableness of Reporting: Antecedents and Consequences of Reporting Sexual Harassment. *Journal of Applied Psychology, 87,* 230–242; see also, Segal, J. (1996). Sexual harassment: Where are we now? *HR Magazine, 41,* 68–73; For the finest writing on this and perhaps any subject, see Bernardin, L. (1994). Does the reasonable woman standard exist and does she have any place in hostile environment sexual harassment claims under Title VII after Harris? *Florida Law Review, 46,* 291–322; Lengnick-Hall, M. L. (1995) Sexual harassment research: A methodological critique. *Personnel Psychology, 48,* 841–864; Fisher, A. B. (1993, August 23). Sexual harassment: What to do. *Fortune,* 84–88; Johnson, C. (1995, May 17). Court cases give firms guidance on sexual harassment. *The Wall Street Journal,* p. B2.

13. Bradshaw, D. S. (1987). Sexual harassment: Confronting the troublesome issues. *Personnel Administrator, 32*(1), 51–53;

see also, Hoyman, M., and Robinson, R. (1980). Interpreting the new sexual harassment guidelines. *Personnel Journal, 59*(12), 996; *Meritor Savings Bank v. Vinson* (1986). 40 FEP Cases 1822 (U.S. Supreme Court); and Thornton, T. (1986). Sexual harassment: Discouraging it in the workplace. *Personnel, 63*(8), 18–26.

14. *Harris v. Forklift Systems* (1993). 114 S. Ct. 367, 370–77. See also, Fitzgerald, L. F., Gelfand, M. J., and Drasgow, F. (1995). Measuring sexual harassment: Theoretical and psychometric advances. *Applied Social Psychology, 17*(4): 425–445; Gutek, B. A. (1995). How subjective is sexual harassment? An examination of rater effects. *Basic and Applied Social Psychology, 17*(4), 447–467; Stockdale, M. S., Vaux, A., and Cashin, F. (1995). Acknowledging sexual harassment: A test of alternative models. *Basic and Applied Social Psychology, 17*(4), 469–496; Tang, T. L., and McCollum, S. L. (1996). Sexual harassment in the workplace. *Public Personnel Management, 25*(1), 53–58.

15. Terpstra, D. E., and Baker, D. D. (1992). Outcomes of federal court decisions on sexual harassment. *Academy of Management Journal, 35,* 181–190.

16. *Burlington Industries, Inc. v. Ellerth,* 524 U.S. 742 (1998); *Faragher v. City of Boca Raton,* 524 U.S. 775 (1998).

17. Laabs, J. (1995, July). What to do when sexual harassment comes calling. *Personnel Journal,* 42–53; see also, Lengnick-Hall, M. L. (1995). Sexual harassment research: A methodological critique. *Personnel Psychology, 48,* 841–863; Zigarelli, M. A (1994). *Can they do that? A Guide to your rights on the job.* New York: Lexington; See also, Block, R. N. and Wolkinson, B. (1996) *Employment law.* Cambridge, MA: Blackwell; see also, Sims, C. S. and Drasgow, F. (2002). *The effect of sexual harassment on attrition: Time dependent modeling.* Paper presented at the 17th Annual Conference of the Society for Industrial and Organizational Psychology, Inc., Ontario, Canada; Raver, J. L., and Gelfand, M. J. (2002). *Sexual harassment in work groups: An examination of group-level antecedents and consequences.* Paper presented at the 17th Annual Conference of the Society for Industrial and Organizational Psychology, Inc., Ontario, Canada; Wadlington, P. (2002). *The generalizability of a sexual harassment model across organizations.* Paper presented at the 17th Annual Conference of the Society for Industrial and Organizational Psychology, Inc., Ontario, Canada; Ritter, B. A. and Doverspike, D. (2002). *The changing nature of sexual harassment.* Paper presented at the 17th Annual Conference of the Society for Industrial and Organizational Psychology, Inc., Ontario, Canada; Wayne, S. et al. (2001). Is all sexual harassment viewed the same? *Journal of Applied Psychology, 86,* 179–187; *Psychology, 82,* 401–415.

18. *Oncale v. Sundowner,* Offshore Services, 523 U.S. 75 (1998).

19. *U.S. Steelworkers v. Weber,* 443 U.S. 193 (1979); see also LeRoy, M. H. and Schutz, J. M. (1995). *The legal context of human resource management: Conflict, confusion, and role conversion.* In Ferris, G. R., Rosen, S. D., and D. T. Barnum (Eds.) *Handbook of human resource management.* (pp. 143–158). Cambridge, MA: Blackwell.

20. *Johnson v. Santa Clara Transportation Agency,* 476 U.S. 267 (March 26, 1987). *Daily Labor Report,* pp. A1, D1–D19.

21. *Gratz v. Bollinger,* 539 U.S. 244 (2003); *Grutter v. Bollinger,* 539 U.S. 306 (2003).

22. *Grutter v. Bollinger.*

23. *Schwager v. Sun Oil Company of PA* (1979). 591 F.2d. 58 (10th Cir.).

24. *Mastie v. Great Lakes Steel Corp.* (1976). 424 F. Supp. 1299 (U.S. District Court, Michigan).

25. *Hodgson v. Greyhound Lines, Inc.* (1975). 419 U.S. 1122.

26. *Albertson's, Inc. v. Kirkingburg,* 527 U.S. 555 (1999); *Sutton v. United Airlines, Inc.,* 527 U.S. 471 (1999).

27. *Toyota Motor Manufacturing v. Ella Williams,* No. 00-1089, 534 U.S. 416 (2002).

28. www.dol.gov/glassceiling.

CHAPTER 4

1. Sanchez, J. I., and Levine, E. L. (1999). Is job analysis dead, misunderstood, or both? New forms of work analysis and design. In A. I. Kraut, and A. Korman (Eds.). *Evolving practices in human resources management.* San Francisco: Jossey-Bass, pp. 43–68; Edwards, J. R., Scully, and Brtek, M. D. (1999). The measurement of work: Hierarchical representation of the multimethod job design questionnaire. *Personnel Psychology, 52,* 305–334. See also Gael, S. (Ed.) (1988). *The job analysis handbook for business, industry and government, Vols. I, II.* New York: John Wiley and Sons; Peterson et al. (2000). Understanding work using the Occupational Information Network (O*NET): Implications for practice and research. *Personnel Psychology, 54,* 451–492.

2. See Sanchez and Levine (1999); see also Ash, R. A. (1988). Job analysis in the world of work. In S. Gael (Ed.) *The job analysis handbook for business, industry, land government: Vol. I* (pp. 3–13). New York: John Wiley and Sons.

3. Harvey, R. J. (1991). Job analysis. In M. D. Dunnette, and L. M. Hough (Eds.), *Handbook of Industrial and Organizational Psychology,* Vol. 2, 2nd Ed. (pp. 71–163), Palo Alto, CA: Consulting Psychologists Press.

4. Ibid.

5. Thompson, D. E., and Thompson, T. A. (1982). Court standards for job analysis in test validation. *Personnel Psychology, 35,* 865–874.

6. Go to http://online.onetcenter.org.

7. McCormick, E. J. (1976) Job and task analysis. In M. D. Dunnette (Ed.), *Handbook of industrial and organizational psychology* (pp. 651–696). Chicago, IL: Rand McNally.

8. *U.S. v. State of New York 21,* 473 F. Supp. 1103 (N.D.N.Y. 1979).

9. See Gael, *The job analysis handbook;* also see Spector, P. E., Brannick, M. T., and Coovert, M. D. (1989). Job analysis. In C. L. Cooper and I. T. Robertson (Eds.). *International Review of Industrial and Organizational Psychology.* (pp. 281–328). New York: John Wiley and Sons.

10. Levine, E. L. (1983). *Everything you always wanted to know about job analysis.* Tampa, FL: Mariner Publishing.

11. McCormick, E. J., and Jeanneret, P. R. (1988). Position analysis questionnaire. In S. Gael (Ed.), *The job analysis handbook for business, industry, and government: Vol. II* (pp. 825–842). New York: John Wiley and Sons.

12. McCormick, E. J., Jeanneret, P. R., and Mecham, R. C. (1972). A study of job characteristics and job dimensions as based on the Position Analysis Questionnaire (PAQ). *Journal of Applied Psychology, 56,* 347–368.

13. *Tayler v. James River Corporation* (November 16, 1989). CA-88-0818-T.C.

14. Page, R. C. (1988). Management position description questionnaire. In S. Gael (Ed.). *The job analysis handbook for business, industry, and government: Vol. II,* (pp. 860–879). New York: John Wiley and Sons.

15. Tornow, W. W., and Pinto, P. R. (1976). The development of a managerial job taxonomy: A system for describing, classifying, and evaluating executive positions. *Journal of Applied Psychology, 61,* 410–418.

16. Athey, T. R., and Orth, M. S. (1999). Emerging competency methods for the future. *Human Resource Management, 38,* 215–226; see also, Klemp, G. O. (Ed.). (1980). *The assessment of occupational competence.* Washington, D.C.: Report to the National Institute of Education.

17. Lievens, F., Sanchez, J. I., and DeCorte, W. D. (2004). Easing the inferential leap in competency modeling: The effects of task-related information and subject matter expertise. *Personnel Psychology, 57,* 881–904; see also, Lucia, A. D., and Lepsinger, R. (1999). *The art and science of competency models: Pinpointing critical success factors in organizations.* San Francisco: Jossey-Bass.

18. Schippmann, J. S. (1999). *Strategic job modeling: Working at the core of integrated human resources.* Mahwah, NJ: Erlbaum.

19. Hagan, C. M., Konopaske, R., Bernardin, H. J., and Tyler, C. L. (in press). Predicting assessment center performance with 360-degree, top-down, and customer-based competency ratings. *Human Resource Management.*

20. Jeanneret, P. R., and Strong, M. (2003). Linking O*NET job analysis information to job requirement predictors: An O*NET application. *Personnel Psychology, 56,* 465–492.

21. Flanagan, J. C. (1954). The critical incident technique. *Psychological Bulletin, 51,* 327–358.

22. Bownas, D., and Bernardin, H. J. (1988). The critical incident method. In S. Gael (Ed.) *The job analysis handbook for business, industry and government: Vol. II* (pp. 1120–1137). New York: John Wiley and Sons.

23. Bernardin, H. J. (1989). Innovative approaches to personnel selection and performance appraisal. *Journal of Management Systems, 1,* 25–76; see also Bernardin, H. J. (1987). Development and validation of a forced-choice scale to measure job-related discomfort among customer service representatives. *Academy of Management Journal* 30, 162–173.

24. Villanova, P., and Bernardin, H. J., (1990). Work behavior correlates of interviewer job compatibility. *Journal of Business and Psychology* 5, 179–195; Villanova, P., Bernardin, H. J., Johnson, D., and Dahmus, S. (1994). The validity of a measure of job compatibility in the prediction of job performance and turnover of motion picture theater personnel. *Personnel Psychology, 47,* 73–90.

25. Hackman, J. R., and Oldham, G. R. (1976). Motivation through the design of work: Test of a theory. *Organizational Behavior and Human Performance 16,* 250–279.

26. Hackman, J. R., and Oldham, G. R. (1980). *Work redesign.* Reading, MA: Addison-Wesley.

27. Fried, Y., and Ferris, G. R. (1987). The validity of the job characteristics model: A review and meta-analysis. *Personnel Psychology* 40, 287–322.

28. Hackman, J. R. and Oldham, G. R. (1975). Development of the Job Diagnostic Survey. *Journal of Applied Psychology 60,* 159–170.

29. See Fried and Ferris, The validity of the job characteristics model.

30. Campion, M. A., and Thayer, P. W. (1985). Development and field evaluation of an interdisciplinary measure of job design. *Journal of Applied Psychology, 70,* 29–43. See also, Campion, M. A. (1988). Interdisciplinary approaches to job design: A constructive replication with extensions. *Journal of Applied Psychology, 73,* 467–481. Edwards et al., The measurement of work. (1999).

31. See Edwards et al., The measurement of work. (1999).

32. Schneider, B., and Konz, A. (1989). Strategic job analysis. *Human Resource Management, 28,* 51–63.

33. Galloway, D. (1994). *Mapping work processes.* Milwaukee, WI: ASQC Quality Press.

34. Morgeson, F. P., and Campion, M. A. (1997). Social and cognitive sources of potential inaccuracy in job analysis. *Journal of Applied Psychology, 82,* 627–655.

35. Treiman, D. J., and Hartmann, H. J. (Eds.) (1981). *Women, work, and wages: Equal pay for jobs of equal value.* Washington, D.C.: National Academy Press.

36. See Gael, *The job analysis handbook.*

37. Cornelius, E. T. (1988). Practical findings from job analysis research. In S. Gael (Ed.), *The job analysis handbook for business, industry, and government: Vol. I.* (pp. 48–68). NewYork: John Wiley and Sons.

38. DeNisi, A. S., Cornelius, E. T., and Blencos, A. G. (1987). Further investigation of common knowledge effects on job analysis ratings. *Journal of Applied Psychology, 72,* 262–268.

39. Ibid.

40. Friedman, L. and Harvey, R. J. (1986). Can raters with reduced job descriptive information provide accurate Position Analysis Questionnaire (PAQ) ratings? *Personnel Psychology, 39,* 779–789.

41. Conley, P. R., and Sackett, P. R. (1987). Effects of using high-versus low-performing job incumbents as sources of job analysis information. *Journal of Applied Psychology, 72,* 434–437.

42. Dierdorff, E. C., and Wilson, M. A. (2003). A meta-analysis of job analysis reliability. *Journal of Applied Psychology, 88,* 635–646.

43. Van Iddelinge, C. H., and Putka, D. J. (2005). Modeling error variance in job specification ratings: The influence of rater, job, and organization-level factors. *Journal of Applied Psychology, 90,* 323–334.

44. Levine, E. L., Ash, R. A., Hall, H., and Sistrunk, F. (1983). Evaluation of job analysis methods by experienced job analysts. *Academy of Management Journal, 26,* 339–348.

45. Hunt, S. T. (1996). Generic work behavior: An investigation into dimensions of entry-level, hourly job performance. *Personnel Psychology, 49,* 51–84.

46. Rothman, J. (2003, September 15). 11 Steps to successful outsourcing. *Computer World online.*

47. Bridges, W. (1994, September 19). The end of the job. *Fortune.*

Chapter 5

1. Lawrence, S. (April 1989). Voice of HR experience, *Personnel Journal,* 70.

2. Cascio, W. F. (2002). *Responsible restructuring: Creative and profitable alternatives to layoffs.* San Francisco: Berrett-Koehler.

3. Schramm, J. (2005, March). HR's tech challenges. *HR Magazine online.*

4. Friedman, T. L. (2005). The world is flat: A brief history of the twenty-first century. Boston: Farrar, Straus, Giroux.

5. Cited in Kahlenberg, R. D. (1996). *The Remedy.* New York: Basic Books.

6. Bass, D. D. (2000). Survey of small business. *Nation's Business,* pp. 8–9.

7. Golden, K. A., and Ramanujam, V. (1985). Between a dream and a nightmare: On the integration of human resource management and strategic business planning processes. *Human Resource Management, 34,* 429–452; Walker, J. W. (1994). Integrating the human resource function with the business. *HR Planning, 17,* 59–77.

8. Delbecq, A. L., Van de Ven, A. H., and Gustafson, D. H. (1975). *Group techniques for progress planning: A guide to nominal and delphi processes.* Glenview, IL: Scott, Foresman.

9. Heneman, H. G., Judge, T. A., and Heneman, R. L. (2006). *Staffing organizations.* New York: McGraw-Hill.

10. See Delbecq, Van de Ven, and Gustafson, *Group techniques for progress planning.*

11. Wikstrom, W. S. (1971) *Manpower planning: Evolving systems.* New York: The Conference Board; see also Piskor, W. G., and Dudding, R. C. (1978). A computer-assisted manpower planning model. In D. T. Bryant and R. J. Niehaus (Eds.), *Manpower planning and organization design.* New York: Plenum Press, pp. 145–154. DeLuca, J. R. (1988). Strategic career management in non-growing volatile business environments. *Human Resource Planning, 11,* 49–62.

12. See Heneman, Judge, and Heneman, *Staffing organizations.*

13. Ibid.

14. Heneman, H. G., III, and Sandver, M. G. (1977). Markov analysis in human resource administration: Applications and limitations. *Academy of Management Review, 15,* 535–542.

15. Hooper, J. A., and Catelanello, R. E. (1981). Markov analysis applied to forecasting technical personnel. *Human Resource Planning, 4,* 41–47.

16. Buller, P. F., and Maki, W. R. (1981). A case history of a manpower planning model. *Human Resource Planning, 4,* 129–138.

17. Dyer, L. (1982). Human resource planning. In K. M. Rowland, and G. R. Ferris (Eds.), *Personnel management.* Boston: Allyn and Bacon.

18. Wellner, A. S. (2001, January). Focus on recruitment and hiring. *HR Magazine,* p. 87.

19. Cascio, *Responsible restructuring.*

20. Ibid.

21. Franklin, S. (1995, October 30). Downsizing realities revealed: American Management association survey tracks layoff patterns. *The News,* p. 8C.

22. Cascio, *Responsible restructuring.*

23. Hippel, C., Mangum, S. L., Greenberger, D. B., Heneman, R. L., and Skoglind, J. D. (1997). Temporary employment: Can organizations and employees both win? *Academy of Management Executive, 11*(1), 93–104.

24. Eng, S. (1995, December 11). Corporate compatibility: Having employer who shares your values is vital to job satisfaction. *The News,* pp. 10C, 11C; Krausz, M., Brandwein, T., and Fox, S. (1995, July). Work attitudes and emotional responses of permanent voluntary, and involuntary temporary-help employees: An exploratory study. *Applied Psychology: An International Review, 44*(3), 217–232.

25. Allen, D. G., and Renn, R. W. (2002). Telecommuting: Understanding and managing remote workers. In G. R. Ferris, M. R. Buckley, and D. B. Fedor (Eds.). *Human resource management: Perspectives, context, functions, and outcomes* (pp. 145–155). Upper Saddle River, NJ: Prentice Hall.

26. Friedman, *The world is flat.*

27. Slaughter, J. E., Zickar, M. J., and Highhouse, S. et al. (2004). Personality trait inferences about organizations: Development of a measure and assessment of construct validity. *Journal of Applied Psychology, 89,* 85–103. See also, Highhouse, S., Stanton, J. M., Reeve, C. L. (2004). Examining reactions to employer information using a simulated web-based job fair. *Journal of Career Assessment, 12,* 85–96; Brooks, M. E., Highhouse, S., and Russell, S. S. et al. (2003). Familiarity, ambivalence, and firm reputation: Is corporate fame a double-edged sword? *Journal of Applied Psychology, 88,* 904–914; Goltz, S. M., and Giannantonio, C. M. (1995). Recruiter friendliness and attraction to the job: The mediating role of interferences about the organization. *Journal of Vocational Behavior, 46*(1), 109–118; McDowell, E. (1996, July 5). Hotels are showing the job vacancy sign. *New York Times,* p. C2; Spina, V. (1995, July). Boosting your value in the workplace. *HR Magazine, 40*(7), 159–160.

28. Bazerman, M. H., and Neale, M. A. (1992). *Negotiating rationally.* New York: Free Press.

29. Peter, L. J., and Hull, R. (1969). *The Peter Principle.* New York: William Morrow.

30. Kleiman, L. S., and Clark, K. J. (1984). Recruitment: An effective job posting system. *Personnel Journal, 63,* 20, 22, 25. See also Taylor, M. S. and Schmidt, D. W. (1983). A process oriented investigation of recruitment source effectiveness. *Personnel Psychology, 36,* 343–354; Breaugh, J. A. (1981). Relationships between recruiting sources and employee performance, absenteeism, and work attitudes. *Academy of Management Journal, 24,* 142–147; Rynes, S. L., Heneman, H. G., III, and Schwab, D. P. (1980). Individual reactions to organizational recruiting: A review. *Personnel Psychology, 33,* 529–542; Rynes, S. L., and Miller, H. E. (1983). Recruiter and job influences on candidates for employment. *Journal of Applied Psychology, 68,* 147–154; Barber, A. E., Hollenbeck, J. R., Tower, S. L., and Phillips, J. M. (1994). The effects of interview focus on recruitment effectiveness: A field experiment. *Journal of Applied Psychology, 79*(6), 886–896; Rosse, J. G., Miller, J. L., and Stecher, M. D. (1994). A field study of job applicants' reactions to personality and cognitive ability testing. *Journal of Applied Psychology, 79*(6), 987–992; Saks, A. M., Leck, J. D., and Saunders, D. M. (September 1995). Effects of application blanks and employment equity on applicant reactions and job pursuit intentions. *Journal of Organizational Behavior, 16*(5), 415–430; Taylor, G. S. (1994). The relationship between sources of new employees and attitudes toward the job. *Journal of Social Psychology, 134*(1), 99–110.

31. See Heneman, Judge, and Heneman, *Staffing organizations;* see also Ashford, S. J., and Black, J. S. (1996). Proactivity during organizational entry: The role of desire for control. *Journal of Applied Psychology, 81*(2), 199–214.

32. *EEOC v. Detroit Edison* 515 F.2d 301 6th Cir. (1975). See also Schenkel-Savitt, S., and Seltzer, S. P. (1987–88). Recruitment as a successful means of affirmative action. *Employee Relations Law Journal, 13*(3), 465–470; Williams, M. L., and Bauer, T. N. (1994). The effect of a managing diversity policy on organizational attractiveness. *Human Factors, 36*(2), 315–326.

33. Hodes, B. S. (1982). *The principles and practice of recruitment advertising: A guide for personnel professionals.* New York: Frederick Fell; see also Bucalo, J. P. (1983). Good advertising can be more effective than other recruitment tools. *Personnel Administrator,* 73–79; Caldwell, D. F., and Spivey, W. A. (1983). The relationship between recruiting source and employee success: An analysis by race. *Personnel Psychology, 36,* 67–72; Decker, P. J., and Cornelius, E. T. (1979). A note on recruiting sources and job survival rates. *Journal of Applied Psychology, 64,* 463–464.

34. Raines, G. (1999, March 1). Online job searches take over classifieds. Reprinted from the *New York Times* in the *Boca Raton News,* p. 2B.

35. See Heneman, Judge, and Heneman, *Staffing organizations.*

36. National Research Council. (1989). *Fairness in employment testing.* Washington, DC: National Academy Press.

37. Dee, W. (1983). Evaluating a search firm. *Personnel Administrator, 28,* 41–43, 99–100.

38. See Heneman, Judge, and Heneman, *Staffing organizations.*

39. Fowler, E. M. (November 18, 1989). Recruiters refocusing techniques. *New York Times,* p. Y35; Savill, P. A. (June 1995). HR and Inova reengineer recruitment process. *Personnel Journal, 74*(6), 109–114.

40. Kristof, A. L. (1996). Person–organization fit: An integrative review of its conceptualizations, measurement, and implications. *Personnel Psychology, 49*(1), 1–49.

41. Dee, W. (1983). Evaluating a search firm. *Personnel Administrator, 28,* 41–43.

42. Fowler, Recruiters refocusing techniques.

43. Rynes, S. L., Orlitzky, M. O., and Bretz, R. D. (1997). Experienced hiring versus college recruiting: Practices and emerging trends. *Personnel Psychology, 50,* 309–339.

44. Lindquist, V. R., and Endicott, F. S. (2002). *Trends in the employment of college and university graduates in business and industry.* Evanston, IL: Northwestern University.

45. Hanigan, M. (1987). Campus recruiters upgrade their pitch. *Personnel Administrator, 32,* 56.

46. Cappelli, P. (March 2001). Making the most of on-line recruiting. *Harvard Business Review,* pp. 139–146.

47. U.S. Merit Systems Protection Board. (1988). *Attracting quality graduates to the federal government: A view of college recruiting.* U.S. Merit Systems Protection Board, Washington, DC.

48. Tessler, J. (1999, May 27). Web surfing is fast way to go job hopping. *The Wall Street Journal,* p. B12. See also Leonard, B. (2001, February 6). Online and overwhelmed. *HR Magazine.*

49. Spooner, E. D., and Raine, J. (2001, July 25) Hispanics and the Internet. Pew Internet and American Life Project. www.pewinternet.org.

50. Carlson, K. D., Connerley, M. L., and Mecham, R. I. (2002). Recruitment evaluation: The case for assessing the quality of applicants attracted. *Personnel Psychology, 55,* 461–490.

51. Gannon, M. J. (1971). Source of referral and employee turnover. *Journal of Applied Psychology, 55,* 226–228; Vecchio, R. P. (1995). The impact of referral sources on employee attitudes: Evidence from a national sample. *Journal of Management, 21*(5), 953–965.

52. Barber, A. E. (1998). *Recruiting employees.* Thousand Oaks, CA: Sage.

53. Bartol, K. M., and Martin, D. C. (1988). Recruitment source as a resource: The value of pay-related information to part-time job applicants. Paper presented at the Annual Meeting of the Academy of Management. See also Taylor, M. S., and Bergmann, T. J. (1987). Organizational recruitment activities and applicants' reactions at different stages of the recruitment process. *Personnel Psychology, 40*(2), 261–285; Taylor, M. S., and Sniezek, J. A. (1984). The college recruitment interview: Topical content and applicant reactions. *Journal of Occupational Psychology, 57;* Irving, P. G., and Meyer, J. P. (December 1994). Reexamination of the met-expectations hypothesis: A longitudinal analysis. *Journal of Applied Psychology, 79*(6), 937–949.

54. Ryan, A. M. and Tippins, N. T. (2004). Attracting and selecting: What psychological research tells us. *Human Resource Management, 43,* 305–318.

55. What do Internet job hunters say? (2001, May). *HR Magazine,* p. 45.

56. Who's using Internet recruiting? (1999, December). *Inc.,* p.156.

57. Krumwiede, J. (2003). Managing resume flow with artificial intelligence. SHRMForum (www.shrm.org/ema); see also, Cober, R. T., Brown, D. J., and Levy, P. E. (2004). Form, content, and function: An evaluative methodology for corporate employment Web sites. *Human Resource Management, 43,* 201–218.

58. Highhouse, S., et al. (2000). Assessing company employment image: An example in the fast food industry. *Personnel Psychology, 52,* 151–172; Heneman, Judge, and Heneman, *Staffing organizations;* Wanous, J. P. (1980). *Organizational entry: Recruitment, selection and socialization of newcomers.* Reading, MA: Addison-Wesley.

59. Hom, P. W., Griffith, R. W., Palich, L. E., and Bracker, J. S. (2000). Revisiting met expectations as a reason why realistic job previews work. *Personnel Psychology, 52,* 97–112; Premack, S. L., and Wanous, J. P. (1985). A meta-analysis of realistic job preview experiments. *Journal of Applied Psychology, 70,* 706–719; see also Popovich, P., and Wanous, J. P. (1982). The realistic job preview as a persuasive communication. *Academy of Management Review, 7,* 570–579; Dean, R. A., and Wanous, J. P. (1984). The effects of realistic job previews on hiring bank tellers. *Journal of Applied Psychology, 69,* 61–68; Meglino, B. M., DeNisi, A. S., and Ravlin, E. C. (1996). Effects of previous job exposure and subsequent job status on the functioning of realistic job preview. *Personnel Psychology, 46*(4), 803–810.

60. McEvoy, G. M., and Cascio, W. F. (1985). Strategies for reducing employee turnover: A meta-analysis. *Journal of Applied Psychology, 70,* 342–353.

61. Bernardin, H. J. (1989). Innovative approaches to personnel selection and performance appraisal. *Journal of Management Systems, 1,* 25–36.

62. Bernardin, H. J. (1989). The development of a scale of discomfort to predict employee turnover among customer

services representatives. *Academy of Management Journal, 30,* 162–173.

63. Breaugh, J. (1992). *Recruitment: Science and practice.* Cincinnati, OH: South-Western.

64. Dowling, P. J., Schuler, R. R. S., and Welch, D. E. (2000). *International dimensions of human resource management.* Boston: Wadsworth.

65. Dowling, P. J. (1989). Hot issues overseas. *Personnel Administrator, 34,* 68–72.

66. Lublin, J. S. (1996, January 29). An overseas stint can be a ticket to the top. *The Wall Street Journal,* pp. B1, B5; see also Moran, R., Stahl, H., and Steel, R. (1989). Survey of personnel managers at 56 international companies. Cited in O'Boyle, T. (1989, December 11). Grappling with the expatriate issue. *The Wall Street Journal,* pp. B1, B4.

67. Mendenhall, M. E., and Oddou, G. (1995). The overseas assignment: A practical look. In Mendenhall, M. E., and Oddoe, G. (Eds.), *Readings and cases in international human resource management.* Cincinnati, OH: South-Western, pp. 206–216.

68. Black, J. S., Gregersen, H. B., and Mendenhall, M. E. (1992). *Global assignments.* San Francisco: Jossey-Bass.

69. Bhaskar-Shrinivas, P., Harrison, D. A., Shaffer. M. H., and Luk, D. (2005). Input-based and time-based models of International Adjustment: Meta analytic evidence and theoretical extensions. *Academy of Management Journal 48,* 257–281.

70. Konopaske, R., and Ivancevich, J. M. (2004). *Global management and organizational behavior.* Burr Ridge, IL: McGraw-Hill Irwin.

CHAPTER 6

1. Huselid, M. A., Becker, B. E., and Beatty, R. W. (2005). *The workforce scorecard: Managing human capital to execute strategy.* Boston: Harvard Business School Press.

2. Cascio, W. F., and Aguinis, H. (2005). *Applied psychology in human resource management.* Upper Saddle River, NJ: Prentice Hall.

3. Russell, C. J., Mattson, J., Devlin, S. E., and Atwater, D. (1990). Predictive validity of biodata items generated from retrospective life experience essays. *Journal of Applied Psychology, 75,* 569–580. See also Kluger, A., Reilly, R. R., and Russell, C. J. (1991). Faking biodata tests: Are option-keyed instruments more resistant? *Journal of Applied Psychology, 76,* 889–896; Mael, F. A., Connerley, M., and Morath, R. A. (1996). None of your business: Parameters of biodata invasiveness. *Personnel Psychology, 49,* 613–619.

4. Hough, L. M., Keyes, M. A., and Dunnette, M. D. (1983). An evaluation of three alternative selection procedures. *Personnel Psychology, 36,* 261–276.

5. Click, J. (July 1995). SHRM survey highlights dilemmas of reference checks. *HR News,* p. 13.

6. Cascio and Aquinis, *Applied psychology in human resource management.*

7. Bernardin, H. J., and Beatty, R. W. (1984). *Performance appraisal: Assessing human behavior at work.* Boston: Kent-PWS.

8. Heneman, H. H., Judge, T. A., and Heneman, R. L. (2006). *Staffing organizations.* New York: McGraw-Hill.

9. Plaschke, B., and Alomond, E. (1995, April 21). Has the NFL draft become a thinking man's game? *Los Angeles Times.*

10. See Heneman, Judge, and Heneman, *Staffing organizations,* for reviews.

11. Roth et al. (2001). Ethnic group differences in cognitive ability in employment and educational settings. *Personnel Psychology, 54,* 297–330.

12. Schmidt, F. L., and Hunter, J. E. (1998). The validity and utility of selection methods in personnel psychology: Practical and theoretical implications of 85 years of research findings. *Psychological Bulletin, 124,* 262–274.

13. Oswald, F. L., Schmitt, N., Kim, B. H., Ramsay L. J., and Gillespie, M. A. (2004). Developing a biodata measure and situational judgment inventory as predictors of college student performance. *Journal of Applied Psychology, 89,* 187–207; see also, Cascio, W. F., and Aguinis, H. (2005). *Applied Psychology in human resource management.* Upper Saddle River, NJ: Prentice Hall.

14. Chan, D. (1997). Racial subgroup differences in predictive validity perceptions on personality and cognitive ability tests. *Journal of Applied Psychology, 82*(2), 311–320. See also Chan, D., Schmitt, N., DeShon, R. P., Clause, C. S., and Delbridge, K. (1997). Reactions to cognitive ability tests: The relationships between race, test performance, face validity perceptions, and test-taking motivation. *Journal of Applied Psychology, 82*(2), 300–310.

15. Ryan, A. M., and Tippins, N. T. (2004). Attracting and selecting: What psychological research tells us. *Human Resource Management, 43,* 305–318.

16. Barrick, M. R., Mount, M. K., and Judge, T. A. (2001). The FFM personality dimensions and job performance: Meta-analysis of meta-analyses. *International Journal of Selection and Assessment, 9,* 9–30; see also, Barrick, M. R., Stewart, G. L., and Piotrowski, M. (2002). Personality and job performance: Test of the mediating effects of motivation among sales representatives. *Journal of Applied Psychology, 87,* 43–51; Witt, L. A., Burke, L. A., Barrick, M. R., and M. K. Mount (2002). The interactive effect of conscientiousness and agreeableness on job performance. *Journal of Applied Psychology, 87,* 164–169.

17. Van Rooy, D. L., and Viswesvaran, C. (2004). Emotional intelligence: A meta-analytic investigation of predictive validity and nomological net. *Journal of Vocational Behavior, 65,* 71–95.

18. Judge, T. A., Erez, A., Bono, J. E., and Thoresen, C. J. (2003). The core self-evaluations scale: Development of a measure. *Personnel Psychology, 56,* 303–331.

19. Miner, J. B. (1985). Sentence completion measures in personnel research: The development and validation of the Miner Sentence Completion Scales. In H. J. Bernardin and D. Bownas (Eds.), *Personality testing in organizations.* New York: Praeger, pp. 145–176. See also Miner, J. B., Chen, C. C., and Yu, K. C. (1991). Testing theory under adverse conditions: Motivation to manage in the People's Republic of China. *Journal of Applied Psychology, 76,* 343–349.

20. Neter, E., and Ben-Shakhar, H. (1989). The predictive validity of graphological inferences: A meta-analytic study. *Personality and Individual Differences, 10,* 737–745; see also McCarthy, M. J. (1988, August 25). Handwriting analysis as a personnel tool. *The Wall Street Journal,* p. B1.

21. Bernardin, H. J., and Bownas, D. (1985). *Personality assessment in organizations.* New York: Praeger; see also Ones, D. S., Viswesvaran, C., and Reiss, A. D. (1996). Role of social desirability in personality testing for personnel selection: The red herring. *Journal of Applied Psychology, 81*(6), 660–679.

22. Costa, P. T., and McCrae, R. R. (1992). *Revised NEO Personality Inventory (NEO-PI-R) and NEO Five-Factor (NEO-FFI) Inventory Professional Manual.* Odessa, FL: Psychological Assessment Resources.

23. Gardner, W. L., and Martinko, M. J. (1996). Using the Myers-Briggs type indicator to study managers: A literature review and research agenda. *Journal of Management, 22*(1), 45–83.

24. Miner, Sentence completion measures in personnel research. See also Miner, Chen, and Yu, Testing theory under adverse conditions.

25. See Barrick et al. FFM personality dimensions and job performance.

26. Bernardin, H. J., Villanova, P., and Cooke, D. (2000). Conscientiousness and agreeableness as predictors of rating elevation. *Journal of Applied Psychology 85,* 232–237. See also Salgado, J. F. (1997). The five factor model of personality and job performance in the European community. *Journal of Applied Psychology, 82*(1), 30–43; Stewart, J. L. (1996). Reward structure as a moderator of the relationship between extraversion and sales performance. *Journal of Applied Psychology, 81*(6), 617–619.

27. McFarland, L. A., and Ryan, A. M. (2000). Variance in faking across noncognitive measures. *Journal of Applied Psychology, 85,* 812–821.

28. Barrick, M. R., and Zimmerman, R. D. (2005). Reducing voluntary, avoidable turnover through selection. *Journal of Applied Psychology, 90,* 159–166.

29. Bernardin, H. J. (1989). Innovative approaches to personnel selection and performance appraisal. *Journal of Management Systems, 1,* 25–36.

30. Bernardin, H. J., Hagan, C., Schubinski, M., and Johnson, D. (1997). The development and validation of the Security Officer Profile. *Security Journal, 8,* 195–200.

31. Sackett, P. R., and Wanek, J. E. (1996). New developments in the use of measures of honesty, integrity, conscientiousness, dependability, trustworthiness, and reliability for personnel selection. *Personnel Psychology, 49*(4), 787–795.

32. Jones, J. W., and Wuebker, L. (1985). Development and validation of the safety locus of control scale. *Perceptual and Motor Skills, 61,* 151–161; see also, Hunter, D. R. Measurement of hazardous attitudes among pilots. *International Journal of Aviation Psychology, 15,* 23–43.

33. Hogan, J., Hogan, R., and Busch, C. M. (1984). How to measure service orientation. *Journal of Applied Psychology, 69,* 167–173; see also, Homburg, C., and Stock, R. M. (2005). Exploring the conditions under which salesperson work satisfaction can lead to customer satisfaction. *Psychology & Marketing, 22,* 393–420; Grandey, A. A., Fisk, G. M., Mattila, A. S., Jansen, K. J., Sideman, I. A. (2005). Is "service with a smile" enough? Authenticity of positive displays during service encounters. *Organizational Behavior and Human Decision Processes, 96,* 38–55.

34. Zigarelli, M. A. (1995). Drug testing litigation: Trends and outcomes. *Human Resource Management Review, 5,* 267–288.

35. Geidt, T. (1985). Drug and alcohol abuse in the workplace: Balancing employer and employee rights. *Employer Relations Law Journal, 11,* 181–205. See also Faley, R. H., Kleiman, L. S., and Wall, J. (1988). Drug testing in public and private-sector workplace: Technical and legal issues. *Journal of Business and Psychology, 3,* 154–186; Murphy, K. R., Thornton, G. C., III, and Reynolds, D. H. (1990). College students' attitudes toward employee drug testing programs. *Personnel Psychology, 43,* 615–632; Crant, J. M., and Bateman, T. S. (1990). An experimental test of the impact of drug testing programs on potential job applicants' attitudes and intentions. *Journal of Applied Psychology, 75,* 127–131; Zigarelli, M. A. (1995). Drug testing litigation: Trends and Outcomes. *Human Resource Management Review, 5*(4), 267–288.

36. Linowes, D. F., and Spencer, R. C. (1996). Privacy in the workplace in perspective. *Human Resource Management Review, 6*(3), 165–182.

37. Schmitt, N., and Mills, (2001). Traditional tests and job simulations: Minority and majority performance and test validation. *Journal of Applied Psychology, 86,* 451–458.

38. Weekley, J. A., and Jones, C. (1999). Further studies of situational tests. *Personnel Psychology, 52,* 679–700.

39. Weekley, J. A., and Ployhart, R. E. (2005). Situational judgment: Antecedents and relationships with performance. *Human Performance, 18,* 81–104.

40. Potosky, D., and Bobko, P. (2004). Selection testing via the Internet: Practical considerations and exploratory empirical findings. *Personnel Psychology, 57,* 1003–1034: see also, Ployhart, R. E., Weekley, J. A., Holtz, B. C., and Kemp, C. (2003). Web-based and paper-and-pencil testing of applicants in a proctored setting: Are personality, biodata, and situational judgment tests comparable? *Personnel Psychology, 56,* 733–752; Xiao X., and Wang Z. M. (2004). Use new technology to design electronic assessment centers. *International Journal of Psychology, 39,* 439; Silvester, J., and Anderson, N. (2003). Technology and discourse: A comparison of face-to-face and telephone employment interviews. *International Journal of Selection and Assessment, 11,* 206–214; Taylor, P. J., Pajo, K., Cheung, G. W., Stringfield, P. (2004). Dimensionality and validity of a structured telephone reference check procedure. *Personnel Psychology, 57,* 745–772.

41. Thornton, G. C., III, and Byham, W. C. (1982). *Assessment centers and managerial performance.* New York: Academic Press. See also Fitzgerald, L. F., and Quaintance, M. K. (1982). Survey of assessment center in state and local government. *Journal of Assessment Center Technology, 5,* 9–19; Schneider, J. R., and Schmitt, N. (1992). An exercise design approach to understanding assessment center dimension and exercise constructs. *Journal of Applied Psychology, 77,* 32–41; Schmitt, N., Schneider, J. R., and Cohen, S. A. (1990). Factors affecting validity of a regionally administered assessment center. *Personnel Psychology, 43,* 1–12; Gaugler, B. B., and Rudolph, A. S. (1992). The influence of assessee performance variation on assessors' judgements. *Personnel Psychology, 45,* 77–98; Reilly, R. R., Henry, S., and Smither, J. W. (1990). An examination of the effects of using behavior checklists on the construct validity of assessment center dimensions. *Personnel Psychology, 43,* 71–84.

42. Kraut, A. I., and Scott, G. J. (1972). Validity of an operational management assessment program. *Journal of Applied Psychology, 56,* 124–129.

43. Bray, D. W., and Campbell, R. J. (1968). Selection of salesmen by means of an assessment center. *Journal of Applied Psychology, 52,* 36–41. See also McEvoy, G. M., Beatty, R. W., and Bernardin, H. J. (1987). Unanswered questions in assessment center research. *Journal of Business and Psychology, 2,* 97–111.

44. Pynes, J. E., and Bernardin, H. J. (1989). Predictive validity of an entry-level police officer assessment center. *Journal of Applied Psychology, 74,* 831–833.

45. Gaugler, B. B., Rosenthal, D. B., Thornton, G. C., III, and Benton, C. (1987). Meta-analysis of assessment center validity. *Journal of Applied Psychology, 72,* 493–511; Schippmann, J. S., Prien, E. P., and Katz, J. A. (1990). Reliability and validity of in-basket performance measures. *Personnel Psychology, 43,* 837–860.

46. Tyler, C., and Bernardin, H. J. (2003). Predictive validity and adverse impact: A comparison of three managerial selection methods. *Best Papers of the Academy of Management:* HR: F 1-6. Paper presented at the annual meeting of the Academy of Management, Vancouver, Canada.

47. An early version of this section was written by Diana Deadrick. See also Chen, C. C., and Chiu, S. F. (2005). Exploring boundaries of the effects of applicant impression management tactics in job interviews. *Journal of Management, 31,* 108–125; see also, Lievens, F., and De Paepe, A. (2004). An empirical investigation of interviewer-related factors that discourage the use of high structure interviews. *Journal of Organizational Behavior, 25,* 29–46; Maurer, S. D. (2002). A practitioner-based analysis of interviewer job expertise and scale format as contextual factors in situational interviews. *Personnel Psychology, 55,* 307–327. Christina, S. C., and Latham, G. P. (2004). The situational interview as a predictor of academic and team performance: A study of the mediating effects of cognitive ability and emotional intelligence. *International Journal of Selection and Assessment, 12,* 312–320.

48. Buckingham, M., and Clifton, D. (2001). *Now, discover your strengths.* New York: The Free Press.

49. Schmidt, F. L., and Rader, M. (2001). Exploring the boundary conditions for interview validity: Meta-analytic findings for a new interview type. *Personnel Psychology, 52,* 445–464.

50. Gatewood and Feild, *Human resource selection.* See also Douglas, J. A., Feld, D. E., and Asquith, N. (1989). *Employment testing manual.* Boston, MA: Warren, Gorham, Lamont; Bobocel, D. R., and Farrell, A. C. (1996). Sex-based promotion decisions an interactional fairness: Investigating the influence of managerial accounts. *Journal of Applied Psychology, 81*(1), 22–35; Howard, J. L., and Ferris, G. R. (1996). The employment interview context: Social and situational influences on interviewer decisions. *Journal of Applied Social Psychology, 25*(2), 111–136; Marlowe, C. M., Schneider, S. L., and Nelson, C. E. (1996). Gender and attractiveness biases in hiring decisions: Are more experienced managers less biased? *Applied Psychology, 81*(1), 11–21; Prewett-Livingston, A. J., Feild, H. S., Veres, J. G., III, and Lewis, P. M. (1996). Effects of race on interview ratings in a situational panel interview. *Journal of Applied Psychology, 81*(2), 178–186.

51. Schmidt, F. L., and Zimmerman, R. D. (2004). A counterintuitive hypothesis about employment interview validity and some supporting evidence. *Journal of Applied Psychology, 89,* 553–561; see also, Van Iddekinge, C. H., Raymark, P. H., Eidson, C. E., and Attenweiler, W. J. (2004). What do structured selection interviews really measure? The construct validity of behavior description interviews. *Human Performance, 17,* 71–93; Allen, I. D., Facteau, J. D., Facteau, C. L. (2004). Structured interviewing for OCB: Construct validity, faking, and the effects of suggestion type. *Human Performance, 17,* 1–24.

52. McFarland, L. A., Ryan, A. M., Sacco, J. M., and Kriska, S. D. (2004). Examination of structured interview ratings across time: The effects of applicant race, rater race, and panel composition. *Journal of Management, 30,* 435–452; see also, Harris, M. M., Lievens, F., Van Hoye, G. (2004). "I think they discriminated against me": Using prototype theory and organizational justice theory for understanding perceived discrimination in selection and promotion situations. *International Journal of Selection and Assessment, 12,* 54–65; Williamson, G., Campion, J. E., Malos, S. B., Roehling, M. V., and Campion, M. A. (1997). Employment interview on trial: Linking interview structure with litigation outcomes. *Journal of Applied Psychology, 82,* 900–912.

53. Schmidt, F. L., and Zimmerman, R. D. (2004). A counterintuitive hypothesis about employment interview validity and some supporting evidence. *Journal of Applied Psychology, 89,* 553–561; see also, McFarland, Ryan, Sacco, and Kriska, Examination of structured interview ratings across time.

54. Taylor, P. J., and Small, B. (2002). Asking applicants what they would do versus what they did do: A meta-analytic comparison of situational and past behaviour employment interview questions. *Journal of Occupational and Organizational Psychology, 75,* 277–294; see also, Huffcutt, A. I., Weekley, J. A., Wiesner, W. H., Degroot, T. G., and Jones, C. (2001). Comparison of situational and behavior description interview questions for higher-level positions. *Personnel Psychology, 54,* 619–644.

55. Oswald, F. L., Schmitt, N., Kim, B. H., Ramsay L. J., and Gillespie, M. A. (2004). Developing a biodata measure and situational judgment inventory as predictors of college student performance. *Journal of Applied Psychology, 89,* 187–207.

56. Highhouse, S. (2002). Assessing the candidate as a whole: A historical and critical analysis of individual psychological assessment for personnel decision making. *Personnel Psychology, 55,* 363–396.

57. Tung, R. L. (May 1987). Expatriate assignments: Enhancing success and minimizing failure. *The Academy of Management Executive,* pp. 118–125; see also Sprietzer, G. M., McCall, M. W., Jr., and Mahoney, J. D. (1977). Early identification of international executive potential. *Journal of Applied Psychology, 82*(1), 6–29.

58. Mendenhall, M., and Oddou, G. (1985). The dimensions of expatriate acculturation: A review. *Academy of Management Review, 19,* 39–47.

59. Konopaske, R., and Ivancevich, J. M. (2004). *Global management and organizational behavior.* Burr Ridge, IL: McGraw-Hill Irwin, p. 341; see also, Bhaskar-Shrinivas, P., Harrison, D. A., Shaffer, M. A., and Luk, D. M. (2005). Input-based and time-based models of international adjustment: Meta-analytic evidence and theoretical extensions. *Academy of Management Journal 48,* 257–281.

60. Konopaske and Ivancevich, *Global management and organizational behavior.* See also, Matsumoto, D., LeRoux, J. A., Bernhard, R., and Gray, H. (2004). Unraveling the psychological correlates of intercultural adjustment potential. *International Journal of Intercultural Relations, 28,* 281–309.

61. Konopaske and Ivancevich, *Global management and organizational behavior.*

62. Huo, Y. P., Huan, H. J., and Napier, N. K. (2002). Divergence or convergence: A cross-national comparison of personnel selection practices. *Human Resource Management, 41,* 31–44; Von Glinow, M. A., and Chung, B. J. (1990). Comparative human resource management practices in the United States, Japan, Korea, and the People's Republic of China. In A. Nedd, G. R. Ferris, and K. M. Rowland (Eds.), *Research in personnel and human resources management International human resources management* (suppl. 1). Greenwich, CT: JAI Press, pp. 153–171.

63. Latham, G. P., and Napier, N. K. (1990). Chinese human resource management practices in Hong Kong and Singapore: An exploratory study. In A. Nedd, G. R. Ferris, and K. M. Rowland (Eds.), *Research in personnel and human resources management: International human resources management* (Suppl. 1). Greenwich, CT: JAI Press, pp. 173–199.

64. Levy-Leboyer, C. (1994). Selection and assessment in Europe. In M. Dunnette and L. Hough (Eds.), *Handbook of industrial and organizational psychology.* Palo Alto, CA: Consulting Psychologists Press, pp. 173–190; see also Cascio, W. F., and Bailey, E. (1995). International HRM: The state of research and practice. In O. Shenkar (Ed.), *Global perspectives of human resources management.* Englewood Cliffs, NJ: Prentice Hall, pp. 15–36.

65. Huo, Y. P., Huan, H. J., and Napier, N. K. (2002). Divergence or convergence: A cross-national comparison of personnel selection practices. *Human Resource Management, 41,* 31–44; see also Shimmin, S. (1989). Selection in a European context. In P. Harriot (Ed.), *Assessment and selection in organizations.* Chichester, England: John Wiley and Sons, pp. 109–118.

66. Shackleton, V. J., and Newell, S. (1989). Selection procedures in practice. In P. Herriot (Ed.), *Assessment and selection in organizations.* Chichester, England: John Wiley and Sons, pp. 257–271.

67. Gould, J. (2002). *Leader's guide for the fairness factor: How to recruit, interview, and hire to maximize effectiveness and minimize legal liability.* Carlsbad, CA: CRM Films.

68. Ibid.

Chapter 7

1. Bernardin, H. J., Hagan, C., Kane, J. S., and Villanova, P. (1998). Effective performance management: A focus on precision, customers, and situational constraints. In J. Smither (Ed.), *Performance appraisal: The state of the art in practice.* San Francisco: Jossey-Bass, pp. 3–45; See also Wigdor, A. K., and Green, B. F. (Eds.). (1992). *Performance assessment for the workplace, vols. I and II: The technical issues.* Washington, DC: National Academy Press; Moravec, M., Juliff, R., and Hesler, K. (January 1995). Partnerships help a company manage performance. *Personnel Journal,* 105–108; Cardy, R. L., and Dobbins, G. H. (1994). *Performance appraisal: Alternative perspectives.* Cincinnati, OH: South-Western.

2. *The Wall Street Journal* (1996). Cited in *The Palm Beach Post* (December 15, 1996) p. 3F. See also Smith, B., Hornsby, J. S., and Shirmeyer, R. (1996). Current trends in performance appraisal: An examination of managerial practice. *SAM Advanced Management Journal, Summer,* 10–15; Antonioni, D. (1994). Improve the performance management process before discontinuing performance appraisals. *Compensation and Benefits Review, 26*(3), 29–32.

3. Huselid, M. A., Becker, B. E., and Beatty, R. W. (2005). *The workforce scorecard: Managing human capital to execute strategy.* Boston: Harvard Business School Press.

4. Bernardin, H. J., and Tyler, C. (2001). The legal and ethical implications of multirater appraisal systems. In A. Church et al. (Ed.), *The handbook of multisource feedback.* San Francisco, CA: Jossey-Bass, pp. 264–292; see also Austin, J. T., Villanova, P., and Bernardin, H. J. (2002). Legal requirements and technical guidelines involved in implementing performance appraisal systems. In G. R. Ferris, and M. R. Buckley (Eds.), *Human resources management: Perspectives, context, functions, and outcomes* (4th ed.). Englewood Cliffs, NJ: Prentice Hall, pp. 208–236; see also Bernardin, H. J., Hennessey, H. W., and Peyrefitte, J. (1995). Age, racial, and gender bias as a function of criterion specificity: A test of expert testimony. *Human Resource Management Review, 5,* 63–77.

5. See Bernardin et al., Effective performance management; see also Kane, J., and Kane, K. (1992). The analytic framework: The most promising approach for the advancement of performance appraisal. *Human Resource Management Review, 2,* 37–70.

6. Edwards, M. R., and Ewen, A. J. (1996). *360-degree feedback: The powerful new model for employee assessment and performance improvement.* New York: AMACOM. See also Edwards, M. R. (1990). Implementation strategies for multiple rater systems. *Personnel Journal, 69*(9), 130, 132, 134, 137, 139.

7. See Bernardin and Tyler, The legal and ethical implications of multirater appraisal systems.

8. Ableson, R. (2001, March 21). Companies turn to grades, and employees go to court. *New York Times* (www.NYTimes.com); see also Truby, M., and Garrett, C. (February 14, 2001). Workers accuse Ford of age bias. *Ford Global Clipsheet* (www.clipsheet.ford.com).

9. Lawler, E. E. (2003). Reward practices and performance management system effectivesness. *Organizational Dynamics, 32,* 396–404.

10. Borman, W. C., et al. (2001). An examination of the comparative reliability, validity, and accuracy of performance ratings made using computerized adaptive rating scales. *Journal of Applied Psychology, 86,* 965–973.

11. Bernardin, H. J. (2006). Another look at forced-choice scales to control intentional rating bias. Manuscript under review.

12. Bernardin, H. J., and Smith, P. C. (1981). A clarification of some issues regarding the development and use of behaviorally anchored rating scales. *Journal of Applied Psychology, 66,* 458–463.

13. Latham, G., and Wexley, K. (1977). Behavioral observation scales for performance appraisal purposes. *Personnel Psychology, 30,* 255–268.

14. Kane, J. S. (1986). Performance distribution assessment. In R. A. Berk (Ed.), *Performance assessment: Methods and*

applications. Baltimore: Johns Hopkins University Press, pp. 237–273.

15. Bretz, R. D., Jr., Milkovich, G. T., and Read, W. (1992). The current state of performance appraisal research and practice: Concerns, directions, and implications. *Journal of Management, 18,* 321–352.

16. See Bernardin et al., Effective performance management.

17. Kane, J. S., Bernardin, H. J., Villanova, P., and Peyrefitte, J. (1995). The stability of rater leniency: Three studies. *Academy of Management Journal, 38,* 1036–1051.

18. Bernardin, H. J. (1989). Increasing the accuracy of performance measurement: A proposed solution to erroneous attributions. *Human Resource Planning, 12,* 239–250.

19. Peters, L. H., and O'Connor, E. J. (1980). Situational constraints and work outcomes: The influence of a frequently overlooked construct. *Academy of Management Review, 5,* 391–397; Dobbins, G. H., Cardy, R. L., Facteau, J. D., and Miller, J. S. (1993). Implications of situational constraints on performance evaluation and performance management. *Human Resource Management Review, 3,* 105–128; Villanova, P., and Roman, M. A. (1993). A meta-analytic review of situational constraints and work-related outcomes: Alternative approaches to conceptualization. *Human Resource Management Review, 3,* 147–175.

20. See Bernardin, Increasing the accuracy of performance measurement.

21. Bernardin, H. J., et al. (2001). Frame of reference training: A twenty year follow-up. In G. Ferris (Ed.), *Research in personnel and human resources management.* JAI Press. See also Bernardin, H. J., and Buckley, M. R. (1981). A consideration of strategies in rater training. *Academy of Management Review, 6,* 205–212; Bernardin, H. J., and Pence, E. C. (1980). Rater training: Creating new response sets and decreasing accuracy. *Journal of Applied Psychology, 65,* 60–66; McIntyre, R. M., Smith, D. E., and Hassett, C. E. (1984). Accuracy of performance ratings as affected by rater training and perceived purpose of rating. *Journal of Applied Psychology, 69,* 147–156; Pulakos, E. D. (1984). A comparison of rater training programs: Error training and accuracy training. *Journal of Applied Psychology, 69,* 581–588; Pulakos, E. D. (1986). The development of training programs to increase accuracy with different rating tasks. *Organizational Behavior and Human Decision Processes, 38,* 76–91; Sulsky, L. M., and Day, D. V. (1994). Effects of frame-of-reference training on rater accuracy under alternative time delays. *Journal of Applied Psychology, 79*(4), 535–543.

22. Bernardin, H. J., Cooke, D., and Villanova, P. (2000). Conscientiousness and agreeableness as predictors of rating elevation. *Journal of Applied Psychology, 85,* 232–237.

23. Bernardin, H. J., and Villanova, P. (2005). Research streams in rater self-efficacy. *Group & Organization Management, 30,* 61–88.

24. Hagan, C., and Bernardin, H. J. (2003). Customer feedback as a critical performance dimension. In A. Miles and P. Perrewe (Eds.), *New Directions in Human Resource Management* (pp. 1–27).

25. See Bernardin and Tyler, The legal and ethical implications of multirater appraisal systems; Austin et al., Legal requirements and technical guidelines; Bernardin et al., Age, racial, and gender bias; see also Smither, J. W., London, M., Vasilopoulos, N. L., Reilly, R. R., Millsap, R. E., and

Salvemini, N. (1995). An examination of the effects of an upward feedback program over time. *Personnel Psychology 48,* 1–34; Atwater, L., Roush, P., and Fischthal, A. (1995). The influence of upward feedback on self- and follower ratings of leadership. *Personnel Psychology, 48,* 35–60; London, M., and Smither, J. W. (1995). Can multi-source feedback change perceptions of goal accomplishment, self-evaluations, and performance-related outcomes? Theory-based applications and directions for research. *Personnel Psychology, 48,* 803–839; Vinson, M. N. (1996). The pros and cons of 360-degree feedback: Making it work. *Training & Development, 50*(4), 11–12.

26. Antonioni, D. (1996). Designing an effective 360-degree appraisal feedback process. *Organizational Dynamics, 25*(2), 24–38.

27. See Bernardin and Tyler, The legal and ethical implications of multirater appraisal systems; Austin et al., Legal requirements and technical guidelines; Bernardin et al., Age, racial, and gender bias.

28. See Hagan and Bernardin, Customer feedback as a critical performance dimension.

29. Finn, A., and Kayande, U. (1999). Unmasking a phantom: A psychometric assessment of mystery shopping. *Journal of Retailing, 75,* 195–217; see also, Moriarty, H., McLeod, D., and Dowell, A. (2003). Mystery shopping in health service evaluation. *British Journal of General Practice, 53,* 942–946.

30. Alge, B. J., Ballinger, G. A., and Green, S. G. (2004). Remote control: Predictors of electronic monitoring intensity and secrecy. *Personnel Psychology, 57,* 377–410; see also, Alge, B. J. (2001). Effects of computer surveillance on perceptions of privacy and procedural justice. *Journal of Applied Psychology, 86,* 797–804.

31. Murphy, K. R., and Cleveland, J. N. (1991). *Performance appraisal: An organizational perspective.* Boston, MA: Allyn and Bacon.

32. Becker, T. E., and Klimoski, R. J. (1989). A field study of the relationship between the organizational feedback environment and performance. *Personnel Psychology, 42,*343–358.

33. Kluger, A. N., and DeNisi, A. (1996). The effects of feedback interventions on performance: A historical review, a meta-analysis, and a preliminary feedback intervention theory. *Psychological Bulletin, 119,* 254–284.

34. Villanova, P., Bernardin, H. J., Dahmus, S., and Sims, R. (1993). Rater leniency and performance appraisal discomfort. *Educational and Psychological Measurement, 53,* 789–799.

CHAPTER 8

1. Huselid, M. A., Becker, B. E. and Beatty, R. W. (2005). *The workforce scorecard: Managing human capital to execute strategy.* Boston: Harvard Business School Press.

2. SHRM 2004–2005 Workplace Forecast-A Strategic Outlook SHRM Research, June 2004.

3. Kraiger, K., McLinden, D., and Casper, W. J. (2004). Collaborative training for training impact. *Human Resource Management, 43,* p. 337; Goldstein, I. L., and Ford, J. K. (2002). *Training in organizations: Needs assessment, development, and evaluation* (4th ed.). Belmont, CA: Wadsworth.; see also, Noe, R. A., and Colquitt, J. A. (2002).

Planning for training impact: Principals of training effectiveness. In K. Kraiger (Ed.), *Creating, implementing, and maintaining effective training and development: State-of-the-art lessons for practice* (pp. 53-79). San Francisco: Jossey-Bass.

4. Thornton, E. (1999, April 19). Make way for women with welding guns. *BusinessWeek,* 54.

5. Johnson, M. W. (2005). California requires sexual harassment training. *SHRM Legal Report.* (2005, January–February), January–February, 1–3.

6. Drucker, P. F. (1994). The age of social transformation. *Atlantic Monthly, 274*(5), 53–80.

7. Pfeffer, J., and Veiga, J. F. (1999). Putting people first for organizational success, *Academy of Management Executive, 13*(2), 37–48.

8. Huselid, M. A., Becker, B. E., and Beaty, R. W. (2005). *The workforce scorecard: Managing human capital to execute strategy.* Boston: Harvard Business School Press.

9. Ibid.

10. Krugman, P. (2005, July 25). Toyota, Moving Northward New York Times Online.

11. Leonhardt, D., and Cohn, L. (1999, April 26). Business takes up the challenge of training its rawest recruits. *BusinessWeek,* pp. 30–32.

12. Nadler, L. (1984). Human resource development. In L. Nadler (Ed.), *The handbook of human resource development.* (pp. 1–47). New York: John Wiley and Sons.

13. Sugrue, B., and Kim, K. (2004). State of the Industry: ASTD's annual review of trends in workplace learning and performance. ASTD, pp. 1–24.

14. Schaaf, D. (1998). What workers really think about training. *Training, 35*(9), 59–66.

15. Williams, C. P. (1999). The end of the job as we know it. *Training & Development, 53*(1), 52–54, 56, 58–60.

16. Sugrue and Kim (2004). See also: Sugrue, B. and Deviney, N. (2005). Learning outsourcing, research report. ASTD.

17. Sugrue and Kim (2004).

18. Sugrue and Kim (2004).

19. Stamps, D. (1997). Communities of practice, *Training, 34*(2), 34–42.

20. Pfeffer, J., and Veiga, J. F. (1999). Putting people first for organizational success, *Academy of Management Executive, 13*(2), 37–48.

21. Sugrue and Kim (2004).

22. Schaaf, D. (1998). What workers really think about training. *Training, 35*(9), 59–66.

23. Sugrue and Kim (2004).

24. Gomez-Mejia, L. R., Balkin, D. B., and Cardy, R. L. (1995). *Managing human resources.* Englewood Cliffs: Prentice Hall.

25. Thornburg, L. (1992). Training in a changing world. *HR Magazine, 37*(8), 44–47.

26. Overman, S. (1993). Retraining our work force. *HR Magazine, 38*(10), 40–44. See also Schaat (1998).

27. Quinones, M. A. (1996). Training and development in organizations: Now more than over, *Psychological Science Agenda, 9*(2), 8–9.

28. Quinones, M. A., and Ehrenstein, A. (1997). Introduction: Psychological perspectives on training in organizations. In M. A. Quinones, and A. Ehrenstein (Eds) *Training for a rapidly changing workplace: Applications of psychological research* (pp. 1–10). Washington, DC: American Psychological Association.

29. Kraiger, K., McLinden, D., and Casper, W. J. (2004). Collaborative training for training impact. *Human Resource Management, 43,* 337.

30. Bernardin, H. J. (2005). Discrepancies between research and practice: Organizational training. Unpublished manuscript.

31. Goldstein, I. L., and Ford, J. K. (2002). *Training in organizations: Needs assessment, development, and evaluation* (4th ed.). Belmont, CA: Wadsworth.

32. Carliner, S., and Sugrue, B. (Eds.), (2005). *ASTD 2005 Research-to-practice conference proceedings.* ASTD.

33. Nadler, L. (1984). Human resource development. In L. Nadler (Ed.), *The handbook of human resource development.* (pp. 1–47). New York: John Wiley and Sons.

34. Mager, R. F., and Pipe, P. (1984). *Analyzing performance problems or "You really oughta wanna"*, 2nd ed. Belmont, CA: David Lake Publishing.

35. Quinones, M. A. (1997). Contextual influences on training effectiveness. In M. A. Quinones and A. Ehrenstein (Eds). *Training for a rapidly changing workplace: Applications of psychological research* (pp. 331–356). Washington, DC: American Psychological Association.

36. Nadler, L. (1984). Human resource development. In L. Nadler (Ed.), *The handbook of human resource development.* (pp. 1–47). New York: John Wiley and Sons.

37. Joinson, C. (1995). Make your training stick. *HR Magazine, 40*(5), 55–60; Salinger, R. D. (1973). *Disincentives to effective employee training and development.* Washington. DC: U.S. Civil Service Commission Bureau of Training.

38. Goldstein, I. L. (1993). *Training in organizations,* 3rd ed. Pacific Grove, CA: Brooks/Cole.

39. Colquitt, J. A., LePine, J. A., and Noe, R. A. (2000). Toward an integrative theory of training motivation: A meta-analytic path analysis of 20 years of research. *Journal of Applied Psychology, 85,* 678–707.

40. Blanchard, R. N., and Thacker, J. W. (1999). *Effective training: Systems, strategies, and practices.* Englewood Cliffs, NJ: Prentice Hall; Schaaf, D. (1990). Lessons from the '100 best'. *Training 27*(2), 18–20.

41. Burns, R. (1995). *The adult learner at work.* Sydney, Australia: Business and Professional Publishing; Sullivan, E., and Decker, P. (1988). *Effective management in nursing.* 2nd ed. Reading, MA: Addison-Wesley.

42. Lund, L., and McGuire, E. P. (1990). *Literacy in the workforce.* New York: The Conference Board; Rosow, J. M., and Zager, R. (1992). *Job-linked literacy: Innovative strategies at work: Part II. Meeting the challenges of change: Basic skills for a competitive workforce.* Scottsdale, NY: Work in America Institute.

43. Kraiger, K., McLinden, D., and Casper, W. J. (2004). Collaborative training for training impact. *Human Resource Management, 43,* 337–351.

44. Colquitt, J. A., LePine, J. A., and Noe, R. A. (2000). Toward an integrative theory of training motivation: A meta-analytic path analysis of 20 years of research. *Journal of Applied Psychology, 85,* 678–707.

45. Noe, R. A., and Schmitt, N. (1986). The influence of trainee attitudes on training effectiveness: Test of a model. *Personnel Psychology, 39,* 497–523.

46. Baldwin, T. T., and Magjuka, R. J. (1997). Training as an organizational episode: Pretraining influences on trainee motivation. In J. K. Ford (Ed.), *Improving training effectiveness in work organizations* (pp. 99–127). Mahwah, NJ: Lawrence Erlbaum Associates; Mathieu, J. E., and Martineau, M. W. (1997). Individual and situational influences on training motivation. In J. K. Ford (Ed.), *Improving training effectiveness in work organizations* (pp. 193–221). Mahwah, NJ: Lawrence Erlbaum Associates.

47. Baldwin, T. T., Magjuka, R. J., and Loher, B. T. (1991). The perils of participation: Effects of choice of training on trainee motivation and learning. *Personnel Psychology, 44*(1), 51–66; Hicks, W. D., and Klimoski, R. J. (1987). Entry into training programs and its effects on training outcomes: A field experiment. *Academy of Management Journal, 30*(3), 542–552; Higher Pursuits. For more information on team building, outdoor education, and wilderness adventures contact: Higher Pursuits, 211 3rd Avenue, Columbia, TN 38401, JSeufert@aol.com.

48. Leigh, D., and Watkins, R. (2005). E-learner success: Validating a self-assessment of learner readiness for online training. In S. Carliner, and B. Sugrue (Eds.), (2005). *ASTD 2005 Research-to-Practice Conference Proceedings,* pp. 121–131. ASTD.

49. Dobbins, G. H., Russell, J. E. A., Ladd, R. T., and Kudisch, J. D. (1995). The influence of general perceptions of the training environment on pretraining motivation and perceived training transfer. *Journal of Management, 21*(1), 1–25.

50. Driskell, J. E., Willis, R. P., and Copper, C. (1992). Effect of overlearning on retention. *Journal of Applied Psychology, 77,* 615–622.

51. Summitt, P. H. (1998). *Reach for the Summit: The definite dozen system for succeeding at whatever you do.* New York: Broadway Books.

52. Locke, E. A., and Latham, G. P. (1984). *Goal setting: A motivational technique that works.* Englewood Cliffs, NJ: Prentice Hall; Mealiea, L. W., and Latham, G. P. (1996). Skills for managerial success: Theory, experience, and practice. Chicago, IL: Irwin.

53. Latham, G. P., and Locke, E. A. (1991). Self-regulation through goal-setting. *Organizational Behavior and Human Decision Processes, 50,* 212–247.

54. Silber, K. H., and Stelnicki, M. B. (1987). Writing training materials. In R. L. Craig (Ed.), *Training and development handbook* (3rd ed., pp. 263–285). New York: McGraw-Hill.

55. Baldwin, T. T., and Ford, J. K. (1988). Transfer of training: A review and directions for future research. *Personnel Psychology, 41,* 63–105; Baldwin, T. T., and Magjuka, R. J. (1991). Organizational training and signals of importance: Linking pretraining perceptions to intentions to transfer. *Human Resource Development Quarterly, 2,* 25–36; Broad, M. L., and Newstrom, J. W. (1992). *Transfer of training: Action-packed strategies to ensure high payoff from training investments.* Reading, MA: Addison-Wesley; Ellis, H. C. (1965). *The transfer of learning.* New York: Macmillan. Kozlowski, S. W., and Salas, E. (1997). A multilevel organizational systems approach for the implementation and transfer of training. In J. K. Ford (Ed.). *Improving training effectiveness in work organizations.* Mahwah, NJ: Lawrence Erlbaum. Rouiller, J. Z., and Goldstein, I. L. (1993). The relationship between organizational transfer climate and positive transfer of training. *Human Resource Development Quarterly, 4,* 377–390.

56. Tracey, J. B., Tannenbaum, S. I., and Kavanagh, M. J. (1995). Applying trained skills on the job: The importance of the work environment. *Journal of Applied Psychology, 80,* 239–252.

57. Chiaburu, D. S. (2005). Individual and contextual predictors of learning transfer: An examination using structural equation modeling. In S. Carliner, and B. Sugrue (Eds.), (2005). *ASTD 2005 Research-to-Practice Conference Proceedings* (pp. 36–42). ASTD.

58. Morrison, R. F., and Branter, T. M. (1992). What enhances or inhibits a new job? A basic career issue. *Journal of Applied Psychology, 77,* 926–940. See also: Stevens, C. K., and Gist, M. E. (1997). Effects of self-efficacy and goal orientation training on negotiation skill maintenance: What are the mechanisms? *Personnel Psychology, 50,* 955–978; Chiaburu (2005).

59. Ford, J. K., Quinones, M. A., Sego, D., and Sorra, J. (1992). Factors affecting the opportunity to perform trained tasks on the job. *Personnel Psychology, 45,* 511–527.

60. Mathieu, J. E., Tannenbaum, S. I., and Salas, E. (1992). Influences of individual and situational characteristics on measures of training effectiveness. *Academy of Management Journal, 35,* 828–847.

61. Marx, R. D. (1982). Relapse prevention for managerial training: A model for maintenance of behavior change. *Academy of Management Review 7,* 433–441.

62. Marx, R. D. (1982).

63. Facteau, J. D., Dobbins, G. H., Russell, J. E. A., Ladd, R. T., and Kudisch, J. D. (1995). The influence of general perceptions of the training environment on pretraining motivation and perceived training transfer. *Journal of Management, 21*(1), 1–25. See also Chiaburu (2005).

64. Bersin, R. (2004). *The blended learning book: Best Practices, proven methodologies, and lessons learned.* San Francisco: Pfeiffer.

65. Gist, M. E. (1997). Training design and pedagogy: Implications for skill acquisition, maintenance, and generalization. In M. A. Quinones and A. Ehrenstein (eds). *Training for a rapidly changing workplace: Applications of psychological research,* 201–224. Washington, DC: American Psychological Association.

66. Dolezalek, H. (2004). Training magazine's 23rd annual comprehensive analysis of employee-sponsored training in the United States. *Training, 41*(10), 20–36.

67. Arthur, W., Bennett, W., Jr., Edens, P., and Bell, S. (2003). Effectiveness of training in organizations: A meta-analysis of design and evaluation features. *Journal of Applied Psychology, 88,* 234–245.

68. Callahan, J. S., Ki Kor, D. S. and Cross, T. (2003). Does method matter? A meta-analysis of the effects of training method on older learner training performance. *Journal of Management, 29*(5), 663–680.

69. Dolezalek (2004).

70. Jossi, F. (1998). Videoconferencing on the cheap. *Training, 35*(10), DL10–13, DL15, DL17–18, DL20.

71. FedEx KinKo's Videoconferencing (2005). Retrieved September 27, 2005 from http://www.fedex.com/us/customersupport/officeprint/faq/videoconf.html?link=4#topthree12.

72. Guglielmino, L. M., and Guglielmino, P. J. (1991). *Expanding your readiness for self-directed learning.* King of Prussia, PA: Organizational Design and Development.

73. Torrance, E. P., and Mourad, S. (1978). Some creativity and style of learning and thinking correlates of Guglielmino's Self-Directed Learning Readiness Scale. *Psychological Reports 43,* 1167–1171.

74. Sabbaghian, Z. (1979). *Adult self-directedness and self-concept: An exploration of relationship.* Doctoral dissertation. Ames: Iowa State University.

75. Durr, R. E. (1992). *An examination of readiness for self-directed learning and selected personnel variables at a large midwestern electronics development and manufacturing corporation.* Unpublished doctoral dissertation. Boca Raton, FL: Florida Atlantic University; Savoie, M. (1979). *Continuing education for nurses: Predictors of success courses requiring a degree of learner self-direction.* Unpublished doctoral dissertation. Toronto, Canada: University of Toronto.

76. Schaaf, D. (1990). Lessons from the "100 best."

77. Baron, J. M., Berger, M. C., and Black, D. A. (1997). *On-the-job training.* Kalamazoo, MI: Upjohn Institute; Phipps, P. A. (1996). On-the-job training and employee productivity. *Monthly Labor Review, 119*(3), 33.

78. Monoky, J. F. (1996). Master the coaching call. *Industrial Distribution, 85*(6), p. 112.

79. Cannell, M. (1997). Practice makes perfect. *People Management, 3*(5), 26–33.

80. Schaaf, D. (1990). Lessons from the '100 best'. *Training 27*(2), 18–20.

81. Cannell, M. (1997). Practice makes perfect. *People Management, 3*(5), 26–33.

82. Knight, J. (2000). The school of hard rocks. *Training,* August, 36–38.

83. Gitter, R. J. (1994). Apprenticeship-trained workers: United States and Great Britain, *Monthly Labor Review, 117*(4), 38–43. Reynolds, L. (1993). Apprenticeship program raises many questions. *HR Focus,* July, 1, 4.

84. Apprenticeship (1991–1992). *Occupational Outlook Quarterly,* Winter, p. 29.

85. McKenna, J. F. (1992, January 20). Apprenticeships: Something old, something new, something needed. *Industry Week,* pp. 14–20.

86. Resch, I. (1998, November 30). A medieval work ethic that still works. *BusinessWeek,* p. 30J.

87. SHRM 2004–2005 Workplace Forecast—A Strategic Outlook SHRM. Research. June 2004.

88. Sitzmann, T. M., and Wisher, R. (2005). The effectiveness of Web-based training compared to classroom instruction: A meta-analysis. In S. Carliner, and B. Sugrue (Eds.), (2005). *ASTD 2005 Research-to-Practice Conference Proceedings.* pp. 196–202. ASTD.

89. Davis, F. D., and Yi, M. Y. (2004). Improving computer skill training: Behavior modeling, symbolic mental rehearsal, and the role of knowledge structures. *Journal of Applied Psychology, 89,* 509–523.

90. Filipczak, B. (1996). Who owns your OJT? *Training, 33*(12), 44–49.

91. Steele-Johnson, D., and Hyde, B. G. (1997). Advanced technologies in training: Intelligent tutoring systems and virtual reality. In M. A. Quinones, and A. Ehrenstein (Eds). *Training for a rapidly changing workplace: Applications of psychological research* (pp. 225–248). Washington, DC: American Psychological Association.

92. Apostolopoulos, N., Albert, G., and Zimmerman, S. (1996). DIALECT—Network-based digital interactive lectures. *Computer Networks and ISDN Systems, 28*(14), 1873–1886.

93. *CFO-IT* (2005). Web conferencing: Your place and mine Vol 21, p. 14.

94. *SHRM 2004–2005 Workplace Forecast.*

95. Bassi, L. J., and VanBuren, M. E. (1999). Sharpening the leading edge. *Training & Development, 53*(1), 23–28, 30, 32–33.

96. Abboud, S. R. (2004). *Online education gets accolades; experts weigh in on distance learning.* In the National Center for Education Statistics report, Distance Education at Degree-Granting PostSecondary Institutions 2000–2001.

97. Chute, A. G., Thompson, M. M., and Hancock, B. W. (1999). *The McGraw-Hill handbook of distance learning: An implementation guide for trainers and human resources professionals.* New York: McGraw-Hill; Harrison, N. (1999). *How to design self-directed and distance learning.* New York: McGraw-Hill; Stadtlander, L. M. (1998). Virtual instruction; Teaching an online graduate seminar. *Teaching of Psychology, 25*(2), 146–148.

98. Donoho, R. (1998). The new MBA. *Training, 35*(10), pp. DL4–DL9.

99. Burgess, J. R. D., and Russell, J. E. A. (2003). The effectiveness of distance learning initiatives in organizations. *Journal of Vocational Behavior, 63,* 289–303.

100. Greengard, S. (1999). Web-based training yields maximum returns. *Workforce, 78*(2), 95; Hefner, D. (1996). The CBT revolution and the authoring engines that drive it. *CD ROM Professional, 9*(10), 46–65; Teas, D. (1996). The internet means opportunity. *Life Association News, 91*(3), 135–138.

101. Murphy, K. (1999, April 5). Welcome to the world of MBA.com. *BusinessWeek,* p. 120.

102. Lohman, J. S. (1998). Classrooms without walls: Three companies that took the plunge. *Training & Development, 52*(9), 38.

103. Burgess and Russell (2003); Chute, Thompson, and Hancock. *The McGraw-Hill handbook of distance learning.*

104. DeRouin, R. E. Fritzsche, B. A., and Sales, E. (2004). Optimizing e-learning: Research-based guidelines for learner-controlled training. *Human Resource Management, 43*(3), 147–162.

105. Geber, B. (1990). Simulating reality. *Training, 27*(4), 41–46.

106. Agres, T. (1997). VR for war games and for real. *R-and-D, 39*(2), 45–46.

107. Dolezalek (2004).

108. www.marketplace-simulation.com. See also: Cadotte, E. R., and Bruce, H. J. (Eds.), (2003). *The management of strategy in the marketplace.* Mason, OH: South-Western.

109. Dolezalek (2004). See also: Weaver, M. (1999). Beyond the ropes: Guidelines for selecting experiential training. *Corporate University Review, 7*(1), Jan/Feb, 34–37. See also: Williams, S. D., Graham, T. S., and Baker, B. (2003). Evaluating outdoor experiential training for leadership and team building. *Journal of Management Development, 22* (1/2), 45–59.

110. Dolezalek (2004).

111. Andrews, E. S., and Noel, J. L. (1986). Adding life to the case study method. *Training and Development Journal, 40*(2), 28–29.

112. Dolezalek (2004).

113. Bandura, A. (1986). *Social foundations of thought and action: A social cognitive theory.* Englewood Cliffs, NJ: Prentice Hall.

114. Simon, S. J., Grover-Varun, T., Teng, J. T., and Whitcomb, K. (1996). The relationship of information system training methods and cognitive ability to end-user satisfaction, comprehension, and skill transfer: A longitudinal field study. *Information Systems Research, 7*(4), 466–490.

115. Sackett, P. R., and Mullen, E. J. (1993). Beyond formal experimental design: Towards an expanded view of the training evaluation process. *Personnel Psychology, 46,* 613–627.

116. Salas, E., and Kosarzycki, M. P. (2003). Why don't organizations pay attention to (and use) findings from the science of training? *Human Resource Development Quarterly, 14*(4), 487–492.

117. Pfeffer, J., and Veiga, J. F. (1999). Putting people first for organizational success, *Academy of Management Executive, 13*(2), 37–48.

118. Clegg, W. H. (1987). Management training evaluation: An update. *Training & Development, 41*(2), 65–71.

119. Dixon, N. M. (1996). New routes to evaluation. *Training & Development, 50*(5), 82–85.

120. Abernathy, D. J. (1999). Thinking outside the evaluation box. *Training & Development, 53*(2), 19–23.

121. Sugrue, B., and DeViney, N. (2005). Learning outsourcing research report. ASTD/IBM Report, ASTD.

122. Alliger, G. M., and Janak, E. A. (1989). Kirkpatrick's levels of training criteria: Thirty years later. *Personnel Psychology, 42,* 331–342.

123. Phillips, J. J. (1997). *Handbook of training evaluation and measurement methods,* 3rd ed. Houston, TX: Gulf Publishing.

124. 2003 State of the Industry Report (2003). Alexandria, VA: ASTD.

125. Arthur, W., Bennett, W., Jr., Edens, P., and Bell, S. (2003). Effectiveness of training in organizations: A meta-analysis of design and evaluation features. *Journal of Applied Psychology, 88,* 234–245.

126. Brown, K. G. (2005). An examination of the structure and nomological network of trainee reactions: A closer look at "smilesheets." *Journal of Applied Psychology, 90,* 991–1001.

127. Geber, B. (1995). Does your training make a difference? Prove it! *Training, 32*(3), 27–34.

128. Arthur, W., Bennett, W., Jr., Edens, P., and Bell, S. (2003). Effectiveness of training in organizations: A meta-analysis of design and evaluation features.

129. Morrow, C. C., Jarrett, M. Q., and Rupinski, M. T. (1997). An investigation of the effect and economic utility of corporate-wide training. *Personnel Psychology, 50*(1), 91–119.

130. Laabs, J. J. (1996). Eyeing future HR concerns. *Personnel Journal, 75*(1), 28–30, 32, 34–37; Mathieu, J. E., and Leonard, R. L. (1987). Applying utility concepts to a training program in supervisory skills: A time-based approach. *Academy of Management Journal, 30,* 316–335.

131. Ford, D. (1994). Three Rs in the workplace. In J. Phillips (Ed.), *In action: Measuring return on investment,* vol. 1, 85–104. Alexandria, VA: American Society for Training and Development; Phillips, J. J. (1997). *Handbook of training evaluation and measurement methods,* 3rd ed. Houston, TX: Gulf Publishing.

132. Parry, S. B. (1996). Measuring training's ROI. *Training & Development, 50*(5), 72–77. See also Jacobs, R. L. (2005). Comparing the forecasted financial benefits of blended training, classroom training, and structured on-the-job training. In. S. Carliner, and B. Sugrue (Eds.), (2005). *ASTD 2005 Research-to-Practice Conference Proceedings.* pp. 106–111. ASTD.

133. Fitz-Enz, J. (1997). *The 8 practices of exceptional companies.* New York: AMACOM.

134. Schmidt, F. L., Hunter, J. E., and Pearlman, K. (1982). Assessing the economic impact of personnel programs on workforce productivity. *Personnel Psychology, 35,* 333–347.

135. Phillips, J. J. (1997). *Handbook of training evaluation and measurement methods,* 3rd ed. Houston, TX: Gulf Publishing.

136. Campbell, D. T., and Stanley, J. C. (1963). *Experimental and quasi-experimental designs for research.* Boston, MA: Houghton Mifflin.

137. Ford, D. J. (1993). Benchmarking HRD. *Training & Development, 47*(6), 36–41.

138. Kraiger, K., McLinden, D., and Casper, W. J. (2004). Collaborative training for training impact. *Human Resource Management, 43,* p. 337.

139. Feldman, D. C., and Brett, J. M. (1983). Coping with new jobs: A comparative study of new hires and job changers. *Academy of Management Journal, 26,* 258–272; Fisher, C. D. (1986). Organizational socialization: An integrative review. In K. M. Rowland, and G. R. Ferris (Eds). *Research in Personnel and Human Resources Management, 4,* 101–145.

140. Felon, I. A., and Pepermans, R. G. (1998). Exploring the relationship between orientation programs and current job satisfaction. *Psychological Reports, 83*(1), 367.

141. Solomon, J. (1988, December 29). Companies try measuring cost savings from new types of corporate benefits. *The Wall Street Journal,* p. B1.

142. Cook, M. F. (Ed.) (1992). *The AMA handbook for employee recruitment and retention.* New York: AMACOM.

143. Wanous, J. P. (1992). *Organizational entry.* 2nd ed. Reading, MA: Addison-Wesley.

144. Ibid.

145. McGarrell, E. J. (1984). An orientation system that builds productivity. *Personnel Administrator, 29*(10), 75–85.

146. Reed-Mendenhall, D., and Millard, C. W. (1980). Orientation: A training and development tool. *Personnel Administrator, 25*(8), 42–44.

147. London, M. (1989). *Managing the training enterprise: High-quality, cost-effective employee training in organizations.* San Francisco: Jossey-Bass.

148. See also, Russell, J. E. A., and DeMatteo, J. S. (2002a). Group dynamics, processes, and teamwork. In E. J. Cadotte and H. J. Bruce (Eds). *The management of strategy in the marketplace,* chapter 2. Southwest Publishing; Russell, J. E. A., and DeMatteo, J. S. (2002b). Managing the team to excellence. In E. J. Cadotte and H. J. Bruce (Eds). *The management of strategy in the marketplace,* chapter 12. Southwest Publishing.

149. Sherman, S. (1996, March 18). Secrets of HP's "muddled team." *Fortune,* 116–118, 120.

150. Taylor, D, and Ramsey, R. (1993). Empowering employees to "just do it." *Training & Development, 47*(5), 71–76.

151. Banker, R. D., Field, J. M., Schroeder, G., and Sinha, K. K. (1996). Impact of work teams on manufacturing performance: A longitudinal study. *Academy of Management Journal, 39,* 867–890. See also Salas, E., Burke, C. S., Bowers, C. A., Wilson, K. A. (2001). Team training in the skies: Does crew resource management (CRM) training work? *Human Factors, 43,* 641–674; Chen, G., Thomas, B., and Wallace, J. C. (2005). A multilevel examination of the relationships among training outcomes, mediating regulatory processes, and adaptive performance. *Journal of Applied Psychology, 90*(5), 827–841.

152. Wellins, R., and George, J. (1991). The key to self-directed teams. *Training & Development, 45*(4), 26–31.

153. Cannon-Bowers, J. A., and Salas, E. (1998). Team performance and training in complex environments: Recent findings from applied research. *Current Directions in Psychological Science, 7*(3), 83–87; Salas, E., and Cannon-Bowers, J. A. (1997). Methods, tools, and strategies for team training. In M. A. Quinones and A. Ehrenstein (Eds.), *Training for a rapidly changing workplace: Applications of psychological research* (pp. 249–279). Washington, DC: American Psychological Association.

154. Ames, L. (1991, July 21). An obstacle course: Lessons in teamwork. *The New York Times,* p. WC 2.

155. Cannon-Bowers, J. A., Salas, E., Blickensderfer, E., and Bowers, C. A. (1998). The impact of cross-training and workload on team functioning: A replication and extension of initial findings. *Human Factors, 40*(1), 92–101.

156. Hottenstein, M. P., and Bowman, S. A. (1998). Cross-training and worker flexibility: A review of DRC system research. *Journal of High Technology Management Research, 9*(2), 157.

157. Cottrill, M. (1997). Give your work teams time and training. *Academy of Management Executive, 11*(3), 87.

158. Filipczak, B. (1993a). Frick teaches Frack. *Training, 30*(6), 30–34; Filipczak, B. (1993b). Training budgets boom. *Training, 30*(10), 37–40, 42–43, 45, 47; Messmer, M. (1992). Cross-discipline training: A strategic model to do more with less. *Management Review, 81,* 26–28; Rickett, D. (1993). Peer training: Not just a low-budget answer. *Training, 30*(2), 70–72; Santora, J. E. (1992). Keep up production through cross-training. *Personnel Journal, 71*(6), 21–24.

159. Benson, G. (1997). Informal training takes off. *Training & Development, 51*(5), 93–94; Chao, G. (1997). Unstructured training and development: The role of organizational socialization. In J. K. Ford et al. (Eds.), *Improving training effectiveness in work organizations.* Mahwah, NJ: Lawrence Erlbaum Associates, 129–151; Chemers, M. M., Oskamp, S., and Costanzo, M. A., (Eds), (1995). *Diversity in organizations.* Newbury Park, CA: Sage. Leonard, B. (1998). Informal training of employees helps to boost productivity. *HR Magazine, 43*(2), p. 10; Stamps, D. (1997). Communities of practice, *Training, 34*(2), 34–42.

160. Allen, T. D., McManus, S. E., and Russell, J. E. A. (1999). Newcomer socialization and stress: Formal peer relationships as a source of support. *Journal of Vocational Behavior, 54,* 453–470.

161. Fisher, C. D., Schoenfeldt, L. F., and Shaw, J. B. (1999). *Human resource management,* 4th ed. Boston, MA: Houghton Mifflin; Kaeter, M. (1993). Cross-training: The tactical view. *Training, 30*(3), 35–39.

162. Parker, S. K., and Wall, T. D. (1997). 'That's not my job': Developing flexible employee work orientations. *Academy of Management Journal, 40*(4), 899.

163. Patterson, P. A., and Johann, B. (1998). Why new IT systems don't pay off. *Training, 35*(11), 64–72; Dzaidzo, E., Performance-based compliance training programs (1996). *ABA-Bank Compliance, 17*(3), 28.

164. Kiser, K. (1999). When those who 'do', teach. *Training, 36*(4), 42–48.

165. Dolezalek (2004).

166. Plummer, D. L. (1998). Approaching diversity training in the year 2000. *Consulting Psychology Journal: Practice and Research, 50*(3), 181–189.

167. Olesen, M. (1999). The diversity issue no one talks about. *Training, 36*(5), 46–56.

168. Cox, T., and Blake, S. (1991). Managing cultural diversity: Implications for organizational competitiveness. *Academy of Management Executive, 5*(3), 45–56.

169. Dass, P., and Parker, B. (1999). Strategies for managing human resource diversity: From resistance to learning. *Academy of Management Executive, 13*(2), 68–80.

170. Jordan, K. (1998). Diversity training in the workplace today: A status report. *Journal of Career Planning and Employment, 59*(1), p. 46.

171. Colombo, J. (June 12, 1997). A law school's diversity checklist, *The Wall Street Journal,* p. A18. See also Owens, D. M. (2005). Multilingual workforces: How can employees help employees who speak different languages work in harmony? *HR Magazine 50*(9), 125–128.

172. Russell, J. E. A., and Eby, L. T. (1993). Career assessment strategies for women in management. *Journal of Career Assessment, 1,* 267–293; Wentling, R. M., and Palma-Rivas, N. (1998). Current status and future trends of diversity initiatives in the workplace: Diversity experts' perspective. *Human Resource Development Quarterly, 9*(3), 235–253.

173. Gadsden, E. N. (1997, June 15). Teaching diversity awareness in the workplace. *Baltimore Sun,* pp. D1, D3; Mirabella, L. (1997, June 15). Helping staff be aware of diversity. *Baltimore Sun,* p. D1.

174. Diversity: America's strength, *Fortune,* June 23, 1997.

175. Dass, P., and Parker, B. (1999). Strategies for managing human resource diversity: From resistance to learning. *Academy of Management Executive, 13*(2), 68–80; Swisher, K. (1996). Coming out in corporate America. *Working Woman Magazine,* July/August, 50–53, 78, 80.

176. Diversity: America's strength, *Fortune,* June 23, 1997.

177. Dass, P., and Parker, B. (1999). Strategies for managing human resource diversity: From resistance to learning. *Academy of Management Executive, 13*(2), 68–80.

178. Ganzel, R. (1998). A guide to players in distance training. *Training, 35*(10), pp. DL4–DL22.

179. Putney, D. M., Russell, J. E. A., and Colvin, C. (1996). Factors related to the effective workplace socialization of people with disabilities. *Proceedings of the Southern Management Association,* Charleston, SC; Stone, D. L., and Colella, A. (1996). A model of factors affecting the treatment of disabled individuals in organizations. *Academy of Management Review, 21*(2), 352–401; Veves, J. G., and R. R. Simms (Eds). (1995). *Human resource management and the Americans with Disabilities Act.* Westport, CT: Quorum Books.

180. Dass, P., and Parker, B. (1999). Strategies for managing human resource diversity: From resistance to learning. *Academy of Management Executive, 13*(2), 68–80.

181. Jackson, S. E., and Ruderman, M. N. (Eds.). (1995). *Diversity in work teams: Research paradigms for a changing workplace.* Washington, DC: American Psychological Association; Larkey, L. K. (1996). Toward a theory of communicative interactions in culturally diverse workgroups. *Academy of Management Review, 21*(2), 463–491; Milliken, F. J., and Martins, L. L. (1996). Searching for common threads: Understanding the multiple effects of diversity in organizational groups. *Academy of Management Review, 21*(2), 402–433. Russell, J. E. A., Atchley, K. P., Eby, L. T., and Fausz, A. T., Attitudes of White Employees and Managers towards Diversity Issues, in *Proceedings of the Southern Management Association,* M. Schnake (Ed.). (1994). Valdosta, GA: Valdosta State University, 1994, pp. 466–471.

182. Ibid.

183. Rynes, S., and Rosen, B. (1995). A field survey of factors affecting the adoption and perceived success of diversity training. *Personnel Psychology, 48,* 247–270.

184. Chemers, M. M., Oskamp, S., and Costanzo, M. A., (Eds.), (1995). *Diversity in organizations.* Newbury Park, CA: Sage; Fine, M. G. (1995). *Building successful multicultural organizations: Challenges and opportunities.* Westport, CT: Quorum, Books; Gallos, J. V., and Ramsey, V. J. (Eds.), (1996). *Listening to the soul and speaking from the heart: The joys and complexities of teaching about workplace diversity.* San Francisco: Jossey-Bass; Hanover, J. M., and Cellar, D. F. (1998). Environmental factors and the effectiveness of workforce diversity training. *Human Resource Development Quarterly, 9*(2), 105–124; Herriot, P., and Pemberton, C. (1995). *Competitive advantage through diversity: Organizational learning from difference.* London, England: Sage; Kossek, E. E., and Lobel, S. A. (Eds.), (1996). *Human resource strategies for managing diversity.* Oxford, England: Basil Blackwell; Prasad, P., Mills, A. J., Elmes, M., and Prasad, A. (Eds.), (1996). *Managing the organizational melting pot: Dilemmas for workplace diversity.* London: Sage.

185. Hayes, J., and Prewitt, M. (1998, August 24). Operators explore diversity at 1st multicultural conference. *Nation's Restaurant News, 32*(34), pp. 3, 127.

186. Dass, P., and Parker, B. (1999). Strategies for managing human resource diversity: From resistance to learning. *Academy of Management Executive, 13*(2), 68–80.

187. Daniel, L. (1997, June 23). FAA offers new diversity training plan. *Federal Times, 33*(20), p. 6; Daniel, L. (1997). FAA tries again at diversity training. *Federal Times, 33*(21), 7.

188. Dass, and Parker. Strategies for managing human resource diversity; Ganzel, R. (1998). A guide to players in distance training. *Training, 35(10),* pp. DL4–DL22.

189. Mulligan, J., and Foy, N. (2003). Not in my company: Preventing sexual harassment. *Industrial Management, 45*(5), 26, 28–30.

190. Wise, R. (1991). The boom in creativity training. *Across the Board, 28,* 38–42.

191. Stewart, T. A. (1996, February 5). 3M fights back. *Fortune,* 94–99.

192. Scott, G., Leritz, L. E., and Mumford, M. D. (2004). The effectiveness of creativity training: A quantitative review. *Creativity Research Journal, 16,* 361–388.

193. Boles, M. (1997). How organized is your expatriate program? *Workforce, 76*(8), 21.

194. Aycan, Z. (1997). New approaches to employee management, vol. 4: *Expatriate management: Theory and research.* Greenwich, CT: JAl Press; Tung, R. L. (1998). A contingency framework of selection and training of expatriates revisited. *Human Resource Management Review, 8*(1), 23–37.

195. Harvey, H. G. (1996). Developing leaders rather than managers for the global marketplace. *Human Resource Management Review, 6,* 279–288

196. Dowling, P. J., and Schuler, R. S. (1990). *International dimensions of human resource management.* Boston, MA: PWS-Kent. See also: Jack, D. W., and Stage, V. C. (2005). Success strategies for expacts. *Training and Development 59*(9), 48–52.

197. Ronen, S. (1989). Training the international assignee. In I. L. Goldstein and Associates (Eds.), *Training and development in organizations* (pp. 417–453). San Francisco: Jossey-Bass.

198. *Training* (1997). 1997 Industry Report, *34*(10), 33–72.

199. Hogan, G. W., and Goodson, J. R. (1990). The key to expatriate success. *Training & Development, 44*(1), 50, 52.

200. Lubin, J. S. (1992, March 31). Younger managers learn global skills. *The Wall Street Journal,* p. B1.

201. Allerton, H. (1997). Survey says. *Training & Development, 51*(2), 7.

202. Lubin, J. S. (1996, January 29). An overseas stint can be a ticket to the top. *The Wall Street Journal,* pp. B1, B5.

203. Bensimon, H. (1998). Is it safe to work abroad? *Training & Development, 52*(8), 20–24.

204. Kemper, C. L. (1998). Global training's critical success factors. *Training & Development, 52*(2), 35.

205. Gudykunst, W. B., and Hammer, M. R. (1983). *Basic training and design: An approach to intercultural training.* In D. Landis and R. W. Brislin (Eds.), Handbook of intercultural training (Vol. 1, pp. 118–154). Elmsford, NY: Pergamon.

206. Earley, P. C. and Erez, M. (1997). *The transplanted executive.* New York: Oxford University Press.

207. Earley, C. P. (2002). Redefining interactions across cultures and organizations: Moving forward with cultural intelligence. In *Research in Organizational Behavior: An Annual Series of Analytical Essays and Critical Reviews,* ed. B. M. Staw, R. M. Kramer, pp. 271–99. Kidlington, UK: Elsevier.

208. Black, J. S., and Mendenhall, M. (1990). Cross-cultural training effectiveness: A review and theoretical framework for future research. *Academy of Management Review, 15*(1), 113–136.

209. Copeland, M. J. (1987). International training. In R. L. Craig (Ed.). *Training and development handbook* (pp. 717–725). New York: McGraw-Hill.

210. McCrea, J. (1997, July). Rx for expatriates. *World Traveler,* pp. 18–20, 22, 25–27.

211. Fiedler, F. E., Mitchell, T., and Triandis, H. C. (1971). The culture assimilator: An approach to cross-cultural training. *Journal of Applied Psychology, 55,* 95–102.

212. Harrison, J. K. (1992). Individual and combined effects of behavior modeling and the cultural assimilator in cross-cultural management training. *Journal of Applied Psychology, 77,* 952–962.

213. Tung, R. L. (1998). A contingency framework of selection and training of expatriates revisited. *Human Resource Management Review, 8*(1), 23–37.

214. Ibid.

215. Solomon, C. M. (1995a). HR's helping hand pulls global inpatriates onboard. *Personnel Journal, 74*(11), 40–49.

216. Galagan, P., and Wulf, K. (1996). Signs of the times. *Training & Development, 50*(2), 32–36.

217. Meister, J. C. (1998). Ten steps to creating a corporate university. *Training & Development, 52*(11), 38–43; Myers, S. D. (1997). *The role of person, outcome, environmental, and learning variables in training effectiveness.* Unpublished doctoral dissertation. Knoxville, TN: The University of Tennessee; Williams, C. P. (1999). The end of the job as we know it. *Training & Development, 53*(1), 52–54, 56, 58–60.

218. Meister, J. C. (1998). Ten steps.

219. Keith, J. D., and Payton, E. S. (1995). The new face of training. *Training & Development, 49*(2), 49–51.

CHAPTER 9

1. Arthur, M. B., Khapova, S. N., and Wilderom, C. P. M. (2005). Career success in a boundaryless career world. *Journal of Organizational Behavior, 26,* 177–202. See also, Parker P., Arthur M. B., and Inkson, K. (2004, June). Career communities: A preliminary exploration of member-defined career support structures. *Journal of Organizational Behavior, 25*(4), 489–514.

2. Osipow, S. H. (1986). Career issues through the life span. In M. S. Pallak and R. Perloff (Eds.), *Psychology and work: Productivity, change, and employment* (pp. 137–168). Washington, DC: American Psychological Association.

3. Hall, D. T., and Associates (Eds.). (1996). The career is dead—long live the career. San Francisco, CA: Jossey-Bass.

4. Hall D. T., and Chandler, D. E. (2005). Psychological success: When the career is a calling. *Journal of Organizational Behavior, 26,* 155–176; see also, Hall, D. (2002). *Careers in and out of organizations.* Thousand Oaks, CA: Sage. Charan, R., and Colrin, 6. (1999, June 21). Why CEOs fail. *Fortune 139*(12), 69–78. See also Welch, J. (2005). *Winning.* New York: Harper Collins.

5. Gurchiek, K. (2005). *Experts predict employee exodus, urge career development.* Retrieved September 29, 2005 from http://www.shrm.org/hrnewspublished/archives/CMS010953.asp. See also Burke, M. E., and Collison, J. (2004). *2004 U.S. Job Recovery and Retention Poll Findings* SHRM.

6. Hall, D. T. (1976). *Careers in organizations.* Glenview, IL: Scott, Foresman.

7. Hall, D. T. (1987). Careers and socialization. *Journal of Management, 13,* 301–321.

8. Hall, D. T., and Associates (1986). *Career development in organizations.* San Francisco, CA: Jossey-Bass.

9. Ibid.

10. Leibowitz, Z., Farren, C., and Kaye, B. (1986). *Designing career development systems.* San Francisco: Jossey-Bass.

11. Pfeffer, J. (1994). *Competitive advantage through people.* Boston. Harvard Business School Press.

12. Pazy, A. (1987). Sex differences in responsiveness to organizational career management. *Human Resource Management, 26,* 243–256.

13. Frequently Asked Questions (Online), U.S. Department of Labor, Bureau of Labor Statistics. Retrieved June 18, 2005, from http://www.bls.gov/nls/nlstaqs.htm#anch10.

14. Schein, E. H. (1978). *Career dynamics: Matching individual and organizational needs.* Reading, MA: Addison Wesley.

15. Ng, T. W. H., Eby, L. T., Sorensen, K. L., and Feldman, D. C. (2005). Predictors of objective and subjective career success: A meta-analysis. *Personnel Psychology, 58,* 367–408.

16. Managing your career: Special report. (1995, January 15). *Fortune,* pp. 34–78; Waterman, R. H., Waterman, J. A., and Collard, B. A. (1994). Toward a career-resilient workforce, *Harvard Business Review, 72*(4), 87–95; Arthur, M. B. (1994). The boundaryless career: A new perspective of organizational inquiry. *Journal of Organization Behavior, 15,* 295–309.

17. Callanan, G. A., and Greenhaus, J. H. (1999). Personal and career development: The best and worst of times. In A. Kraut and A. Korman (Eds.). *Evolving practices in human resource management: Responses to a changing world of work* (pp. 146–171). San Francisco: Jossey-Bass; Raelin, J. A. (1997). Internal career development in the age of insecurity. *Business Forum, 22*(1), 19.

18. Brousseau, K. R., Driver, M. J., Eneroth, K., and Larson, R. (1996). Career pandemonium: Realigning organizations and individuals. *Academy of Management Executive, 10*(4), 52–66; Buckner, M., and Slavenski, L. (1994). Succession planning. In W. R. Tracey (Ed.), *Human resources management and development handbook* (pp. 561–575). New York: AMACOM.

19. Greenhaus, J. H. and Callanan, G. A. (1994). *Career management* (2nd ed). New York: Dryden Press.

20. Allred, B. B., Snow, C. C., and Miles, R. E. (1996). Characteristics of managerial careers in the 21st century. *Academy of Management Executive, 10*(4), 17–27.

21. Callanan, G. A., and Greenhaus, J. H. (1999). Personal and career development: The best and worst of times. In A. Kraut and A. Korman (Eds.). *Evolving practices in human resource management: Responses to a changing world of work* (pp. 146–171). San Francisco: Jossey-Bass; Hall, D. T. (1996). Protean careers of the 21st century. *Academy of Management Executive, 10*(4), 8–16.

22. Gurchiek (2005). Montgomery, C. E. (1996). Organizational fit is key to job success. *HR Magazine, 41*(1), 94–96; Quinn, J. B., Anderson, P., and Finkelstein, S. (1996). Managing professional intellect: Making the most of the best. *Harvard Business Review,* March-April, 71–80.

23. Linking career development with the new corporate agenda: Strategies for creating a career-resilient workforce (1997, February). Conference sponsored by the National Career Development Association, Atlanta: GA.

24. Callanan, G. A., and Greenhaus, J. H. (1999). In A. Kraut and A. Korman (Eds.). *Evolving practices in human resource management: Responses to a changing world of work* (pp. 146–171). San Francisco: Jossey-Bass; Sullivan, S. E., Carden, W. A., and Martin, D. F. (1998). Careers in the next millennium: Directions for future research. *Human Resource Management Review, 8*(2), 165–185.

25. Waterman, R. H., Waterman, J. A., and Collard, B. A. (1994). Toward a career-resilient workforce, *Harvard Business Review, 72*(4), 87–95.

26. Callanan, G. A., and Greenhaus, J. H. (1999). In A. Kraut and A. Korman (Eds.). *Evolving practices in human resource management: Responses to a changing world of work* (pp. 146–171). San Francisco: Jossey-Bass.

27. Weber, P. F. (1999). Getting a grip on employee growth. *Training & Development, 53*(5), 87–94.

28. Nicholson, N., and De Waal-Andrews, W. (2005). Playing to win: Biological imperatives, self-regulation, and trade-offs in the game of career success. *Journal of Organizational Behavior, 26,* 137–154. See also Leana, C. R. (2002). The changing organizational context of careers. In D. C. Feldman (Ed.), *Work Careers: A developmental perspective.* (pp. 274–293). San Francisco: Jossey-Bass.

29. Gooding, G. J. (1988). Career moves—for the employee, for the organization, *Personnel, 65*(4), 112, 114, 116; London, M., and Mone, E. M. (1987). *Career management and survival in the workplace.* San Francisco, CA: Jossey-Bass.

30. Lancaster, L. C., and Stillman, D. (2002). *When generations Collide.* New York: Harper Business, Zemke, R., Raines, C., and Filipczak, B. (2000). *Generations at Work.* New York: AMACOM.

31. Souerwine, A. H. (1981). The manager as career counselor: Some issues and approaches. In D. H. Montross and C. J. Shinkman (Eds.), *Career development in the 1980's: Theory and practice* (pp. 363–378). Springfield, IL: Charles C. Thomas. See also Gurchiek (2005).

32. Slavenski, L. (1987). Career development: A systems approach. *Training & Development, 41*(2), 56–60.

33. Keller J., and Piotrowski, C. (1987). Career development programs in Fortune 500 firms. *Psychological Reports, 61*(3), 920–922.

34. Bardsley, C. A. (1987). Improving employee awareness of opportunity at IBM. *Personnel, 64*(4), 58–63.

35. Leibowitz, Z., Farren, C., and Kaye, B. (1986). *Designing career development systems.* San Francisco: Jossey-Bass.

36. Russell, J. E. A. (1991). Career development interventions in organizations. *Journal of Vocational Behavior, 38,* 237–287; Gutteridge, T. G. (1986). Organizational career development systems: The state of the practice. In D. T. Hall and Associates (Eds.), *Career development in organizations* (pp. 50–94). San Francisco, CA: Jossey-Bass; Meier, S. T. (1991). Vocational behavior 1988–1990: Vocational choice, decision-making, career development interventions, and assessment. *Journal of Vocational Behavior, 39,* 131–181.

37. Russell, J. E. A., and Curtis, L. B. (1993, April). *Career development practices and perceived effectiveness in Fortune 500 firms.* Paper presented at the annual meeting of the Society of Industrial and Organizational Psychology, San Francisco: CA.

38. Waterman, R. H., Waterman, J. A., and Collard, B. A. (1994). Toward a career-resilient workforce, *Harvard Business Review, 72*(4), 87–95.

39. Prochaska, S. T. (2002). *Designing organizational programs for employee career development.* SHRM.

40. Martin, J. (1997, January 13). Job surfing: Move on to move. *Fortune, 135*(1), 50–54.

41. Wilhelm, W. R. (1983). Helping workers to self-manage their careers. *Personnel Administrator, 28*(8), 83–89.

42. Jackson, T., and Vitberg, A. (1987). Career development, part 2: Challenges for the organization. *Personnel, 64*(3), 68–72.

43. Curtis, L. B. (1996). *An examination of factors related to the effectiveness of a career development workshop.* Unpublished doctoral dissertation. The University of Tennessee, Knoxville, TN.

44. Brousseau, K. R., Driver, M. J., Eneroth, K., and Larson, R. (1996). Career pandemonium: Realigning organizations and individuals. *Academy of Management Executive, 10*(4), 52–66.

45. Bolles, R. N. (2005). *What color is your parachute?* Berkeley, CA: Ten Speed Press.

46. Burack, E. H., and Mathys, N. J. (1980). Career management in organizations: *A practical human resource planning approach.* Lake Forest, IL: Brace-Park.

47. London, M. (2002). Organizational assistance in career development. In D. C. Feldman (Ed.). *Work careers: A developmental perspective* (pp. 323–345). San Francisco: Jossey-Bass.

48. Brown, S. D., and Lent, R. W. (2005). *Career development and counseling: Putting theory and research to work.* New York: Wiley.

49. Peters, H. (1996). Peer coaching for executives. *Training & Development, 50*(3), 39–41; Waldroop, J., and Butler, T. (1996). The executive as coach. *Harvard Business Review, 74*(6), 111–117.

50. See also Jansen, B. J., Jansen, K. J., and Spink, A. (2005). Using the Web to look for work—Implications for online job seeking and recruiting. *Internet Research—Electronic Networking Applications and Policy, 15*(1), 49–66.

51. Russell, J. E. A. (1991). Career development interventions in organizations. *Journal of Vocational Behavior, 38,* 237–287.

52. Smither, J. W. (1995). Creating an internal contingent workforce: Managing the resource link. In M. London (Ed.), *Employees, careers, and job creation: Developing growth-oriented human resource strategies and programs* (pp. 142–164). San Francisco: Jossey-Bass.

53. Brousseau, K. R., Driver, M. J., Eneroth, K., and Larson, R. (1996). Career pandemonium: Realigning organizations and individuals. *Academy of Management Executive, 10*(4), 52–66.

54. Leibowitz, Z. B., Kaye, B. L., and Farren, C. (1992). Multiple career paths. *Training & Development, 46*(10), 31–35.

55. Gutteridge, T. G., Leibowitz, Z. B., and Shore, J. E. (1993). *Organizational career development: Benchmarks for building a world-class workforce.* San Francisco, CA: Jossey-Bass.

56. Brousseau, K. R., Driver, M. J., Eneroth, K., and Larson, R. (1996). Career pandemonium: Realigning organizations and individuals. *Academy of Management Executive, 10*(4), 52–66.

57. Gutteridge, T. G., Leibowitz, Z. B., and Shore, J. E. (1993). *Organizational career development: Benchmarks for building a world-class workforce.* San Francisco, CA: Jossey-Bass.

58. Jansen, P. G., and Stoop, B. A. (2001). The dynamics of assessment center validity: Results of a 7-year study. *Journal of Applied Psychology, 86,* 741–753.

59. Rocco, J. (1991). Computers track high-potential managers. *HR Magazine, 36*(8), 66–68.

60. Gandossy, R., and Kao, T. (2004). Talent wars: Out of mind, out of practice. *Human Resource Planning, 27,* 4; ABI/INFORM Global. See also Behn, B. K., Riley, R. A., and Yang, Y. W. (2005). The value of an heir apparent in succession planning. *Corporate Governance—An International Review, 13*(2), 168–177; Biggs, E. L. (2004). CEO succession planning: An emerging challenge for boards of directors. *Academy of Management Executive, 18*(1), 105–107; Freeman, K. W. (2004). The CEO's real legacy. *Harvard Business Review, 82,* 51+.

61. Who's next in line? *Strategic Direction,* May 2004, 20, 6; ABI/INFORM Global.

62. Garrett, E. M. (1994, April). Going the distance. *Small Business Reports,* 22–30.

63. Greenberg, H. M., and Sidler, G. (1998, November). Succession planning: Easing the transition of your business. *Forum, 198,* p. 14–16.

64. Moses, J. L., and Eggebeen, S. L. (1999). Building room at the top: Selecting senior executives who can lead and succeed in the new world of work. In A. I. Kraut and A. Korman (Eds.), *Evolving practices in human resource management: Responses to a changing world of work* (pp. 201–225). San Francisco: Jossey-Bass.

65. Curtis, L. B., and Russell, J. E. A. (1993, April). *A study of succession planning programs in Fortune 500 firms.* Paper presented at the annual meeting of the Society of Industrial and Organizational Psychology, San Francisco, CA.

66. Curtis, L. B., and Russell, J. E. A. (1993, April). *A study of succession planning programs in Fortune 500 firms.* Paper presented at the annual meeting of the Society of Industrial and Organizational Psychology, San Francisco, CA.

67. Golden, E. (1998). Nothing succeeds like succession. *Across the Board, 35*(6), 36–41.

68. Barron, T. (2004). The link between leadership development and retention. *Training & Development, 58*(4), 58–65.

69. Walker, J. W. (1998). Do we need succession planning anymore? *Human Resource Planning, 21*(3), 9–11.

70. H. Kets de Vries, M. F. R. (1995). *Life and death in the executive fast lane.* San Francisco: Jossey-Bass.

71. Mills, D. Q. (1988). *The IBM lesson: The profitable art of full employment.* New York: Random House; Schlesinger, L. A., Dyer, D., Clough, T. M., and Landau, D. (1987). *Chronicles of corporate change: Management lessons from AT&T and its offspring.* San Francisco, CA: New Lexington Press.

72. Buckner, M., and Slavenski, L. (1994). Succession planning. In W. R. Tracey (Ed.). *Human resources management and development handbook* (pp. 561–575). New York: AMACOM.

73. Beeson, J. (1998). Succession planning: Building the management corps. *Business Horizons, 41*(5), 61–66.

74. Nusbaum, H. J. (1986). The career development program at DuPont's Pioneering Research Laboratory. *Personnel, 63*(9), 68–75.

75. Gaertner, K. N. (1988). Managers' careers and organizational change. *Academy of Management Executive, 11,* 311–318.

76. Fenwick-Magrath, J. A. (1988). Executive development: Key factors for success. *Personnel, 65*(7), 68–72.

77. Georgemiller, D. (1992, Winter). Making the grades: The ABCs of educational reimbursement. *The Human Resource Professional,* 16–19; Lesly, E. (1993, November 29). Sticking it out at Xerox by sticking together. *BusinessWeek,* p. 77.

78. Kurschner, D. (1996). Getting credit. *Training, 34*(6), 52–53.

79. Waterman, R. H., Waterman, J. A., and Collard, B. A. (1994). Toward a career-resilient workforce, *Harvard Business Review, 72*(4), 87–95. See also London (2002).

80. Dolan, K. A. (1996, November 18). When money isn't enough. *Forbes, 158*(12), 164–170.

81. Russell, J. E. A. (2004). *Mentoring Encyclopedia of Applied Psychology Vol 2,* 609–616. Russell, J. E. A., and Adams, D. M. (1997). The changing nature of mentoring in organizations: An introduction to the special issue on mentoring in organizations. *Journal of Vocational Behavior, 51*(1), 1–14.

82. Russell, J. E. A., and McManus, S. E. (in press) Peer mentoring and relationships. In B. R. Ragins and K. E. Kram. (Eds.), *The Handbook of Mentoring.* Sage, Eby, L. T. (1997). Alternative forms of mentoring in changing organizational environments: A conceptual extension of the mentoring literature. *Journal of Vocational Behavior, 51*(1), 125–144.

83. Kram, K. E. (1985). *Mentoring at work.* Glenwood, IL: Scott, Foresman; Kram, K. E. (1986). Mentoring in the workplace. In D. T. Hall (Ed.), *Career development in organizations* (pp. 160–201). San Francisco, CA: Jossey-Bass.

84. Ng, Eby, Sorensen, and Feldman, Predictors of objective and subjective career success: A meta-analysis. *Personnel Psychology, 58,* 367–408.

85. Allen, T. D., Eby, L. T., Poteet, M. L., Lentz, E., and Lima L. (2004). Career benefits associated with mentoring for protégés: A meta-analysis. *Journal of Applied Psychology, 89,* 127; See also Allen, T. D., Day, R., and Lentz, E. (2005). The role of interpersonal comfort in mentoring relationships. *Journal of Career Development, 31,* 155–169; Allen, T. D. (2005). Life balance: How to convert professional success into personal happiness. *Academy of Management Review, 30,* 196–198; de Janasz, S. C., Sullivan, S. E., and Whiting, V. (2003). Mentor networks and career success: Lessons for turbulent times. *Academy of Management Executive, 17,* 78–91; and Sullivan, S. E. (2003). Working identity: Unconventional strategies for reinventing your career. *Academy of Management Executive, 17,* 154–155.

86. Gunn, E. (1995). Mentoring: The democratic version. *Training, 32*(8), 64–67; Odiorne, G. S. (1985). Mentoring— An American management innovation. *Personnel*

Administrator, 30(5), 63–70; Rigdon, J. E. (1993, December 1). You're not all alone if there's a mentor just a keyboard away. *The Wall Street Journal,* p. B1.

87. Dass, P., and Parker, B. (1999). Strategies for managing human resource diversity: From resistance to learning. *Academy of Management Executive, 13*(2), 68–80.

88. Allen, T. D., Russell, J. E. A., and Maetzke, S. (1997). Formal peer mentoring: Factors related to protégé satisfaction and willingness to mentor others. *Group and Organization Management, 22*(4), 488–507; Russell, J. E. A., and Adams, D. M. (1997). The changing nature of mentoring in organizations: An introduction to the special issue on mentoring in organizations. *Journal of Vocational Behavior, 51*(1), 1–14.

89. Thompson, P., Kirkham, K., and Dixon, J. (1985). Warning: The fast track may be hazardous to organizational health. *Organizational Dynamics, 13,* 21–33.

90. Brousseau, K. R., Driver, M. J., Eneroth, K., and Larsson, R. (1996). Career pandemonium: Realigning organizations and individuals. *Academy of Management Executive, 10*(4), 52–66.

91. London, M. (1996). Redeployment and continuous learning in the 21st century: Hard lessons and positive examples from the downsizing era. *Academy of Management Executive, 10*(4), 67–79.

92. Tang, T., and Fuller, R. M. (1995). Corporate downsizing: What managers can do to lessen the negative effects of layoffs. *SAM Advanced Management Journal, 60*(4), 12–15, 31.

93. London, Redeployment and continuous learning in the 21st century.

94. Butterfield, L. D., and Borgen, W. A. (2005). Outplacement counseling from the client's perspective. *Career Development Quarterly, 53,* 306–316; see also Westaby, J. D. (2004). The impact of outplacement programs on reemployment criteria: A longitudinal study of displaced managers and executives. *Journal of Employment Counseling, 41,* 19–28.

95. Brockner, J., Konovsky, M., Cooper-Schneider, R., Folger, R., Martin, C., and Bies, R. J. (1994). Interactive effects of procedural justice and outcome negativity on victims and survivors of job loss. *Academy of Management Journal, 37,* 397–409; O'Neill, H. M., and Lenn, D. J. (1995). Voices of survivors: Words that downsizing CEOs should hear. *Academy of Management Executive, 9,* 23–34.

96. Carson, K. D., and Carson, P. P. (1997). Career entrenchment: A quiet march toward occupational death? *Academy of Management Executive, 11*(1), 62–75.

97. Charan, R., and Colvin, G. (1999, June 21). Why CEOs fail. *Fortune, 139*(12), 69–78.

98. Bell, C. R. (1996). *Managers as mentors: Building partnerships for learning.* San Francisco, CA: Berrett-Koehler Publishers. See also London (2002).

99. Kilburg, R. R. (Ed.). (1996). Executive coaching. *Consulting Psychology Journal: Practice and Research, 48*(2), 57–152; Smith, L. (1993, December 27). The executive's new coach. *Fortune, 128*(16), 126–134; Witherspoon, R., and White, R. P. (1996). Executive coaching: A continuum of roles. *Consulting Psychology Journal: Practice and Research, 48*(2), 124–133.

100. Bench, M. (2003). *Career coaching: An insider's guide.* Palo Alto, CA: Davies-Black. See also London (2002).

101. Facteau, C. L., Facteau, J. D., Schoel, L. C., Russell, J. E. A., and Poteet, M. L. (1998). Reactions of leaders to 360 degree feedback from subordinates and peers. *Leadership Quarterly, 9*(4), 427–448.

102. Hollenbeck, G. P., and McCall, M. W. (1999). Leadership development: Contemporary practices. In A. I. Kraut and A. Korman (eds). *Evolving practices in human resource management* (pp. 172–200). San Francisco: Jossey-Bass.

103. Edelstein, B. C., and Armstrong, D. J. (1993). A model for executive development. *Human Resource Planning, 16*(4), 51–64. Thach, L., and Heinselman, T. (1999). Executive coaching defined. *Training & Development, 53*(3), 35–39.

104. Johnson, R. S. (1997, August 4). The new black power. *Fortune, 136*(3), 46–82; Walker, B. A. (1996). The value of diversity in career self-development. In D. T. Hall and Associates (Eds.), *The career is dead—long live the career: A relational approach to careers.* San Francisco: Jossey-Bass.

105. Russell, J. E. A. (2005). Career counseling for women in management. In W. B. Walsh and M. Heppner (Eds.), *Handbook of Career Counseling for Women* (2nd ed). Mahwah, NJ: Lawrence Erlbaum.

106. Kalish, B. B. (1992). Dismantling the glass ceiling. *Management Review, 81*(3), 64; Keller, J. J. (1996, March 18). AT&T tries to put new spin on big job cuts. *The Wall Street Journal,* pp. B1, B6; Ragins, B. R. (1997). Antecedents of diversified mentoring relationships. *Journal of Vocational Behavior, 51*(1), 90–109; Catalyst (1999). Creating women's networks: A how-to-guide for women and companies. San Francisco: Jossey-Bass.

107. Morris, B. (1997a, March 17). Is your family wrecking your career (and vice versa)? *Fortune, 135*(5), 71–90; Morris, B. (1997b, July 21). If women ran the world. *Fortune, 136*(2), 74–79.

108. Trost (1989, November 22). New approach forced by shifts in population. *The Wall Street Journal,* pp. B1, B4; Russell, J. E. A. (2006). Career counseling for women in management. In W. B. Walsh and S. H. Osipow (Eds.), *Career counseling for women* (pp. 263–326). Hillsdale, NJ: Lawrence Erlbaum.

109. Digh, P. (1998). The next challenge: Holding people accountable. *HR Magazine, 43*(10), 63–69.

110. Dass, P., and Parker, B. (1999). Strategies for managing human resource diversity: From resistance to learning. *Academy of Management Executive, 13*(2), 68–80; Deutsch, C. H. (1990, December 16). Putting women on the fast track. *New York Times,* p. F 25.

111. Catalyst (1999). Creating women's networks: A how-to-guide for women and companies. San Francisco: Jossey-Bass.

112. Friedman, R. A. (1999). Employee network groups: Self-help strategy for women and minorities. *Performance Improvement Quarterly, 12*(1), 148–163; Leonard, B. (1999). Linking diversity initiatives. *HR Magazine, 44*(6), 60–64.

113. Catalyst (1999). Creating women's networks: A how-to-guide for women and companies. San Francisco: Jossey-Bass.

114. Mainiero, L. A., and Sullivan, S. E. (2005). Kaleidoscope careers: An alternate explanation for the "opt-out" revolution. *Academy of Management Executive, 19*(1), 106–123.

115. Feldman, D. C. (1988). *Managing careers in organizations.* Glenview, IL: Scott, Foresman.

116. Allen, T. D., McManus, S. E., and Russell, J. E. A. (1999). Newcomer socialization and stress: Formal peer relationships as a source of support. *Journal of Vocational Behavior, 54*, 453–470. See also Scandura, T. A. (2002). The establishment years: A dependence perspective. In D. C. Feldman (Ed.), *Work careers: A developmental perspective.* (pp. 159–185). San Francisco: Jossey-Bass.

117. Adkins, C. L. (1995). Previous work experience and organizational socialization: A longitudinal examination. *Academy of Management Journal, 38,* 839–862; Major, D. A., Kozlowski, S. W., Chao, G. T., and Gardner, P. D. (1995). A longitudinal investigation of newcomer expectations, early socialization outcomes, and the moderating effects of role development factors. *Journal of Applied Psychology, 80,* 418–431; Wanous, J. P. (1980). *Organizational entry: Recruitment, selection, and socialization of newcomers.* Reading, MA: Addison-Wesley.

118. Mirvis, P. H. (Ed.). (1993). Building a competitive workforce: Investing in human capital for corporate success. New York: Wiley; Mirvis, P. H., and Hall, D. T. (1996). Career development for the older worker. In D. T. Hall and Associates (Eds.). *The career is dead—long live the career: A relational approach to careers* (pp. 278–296). San Francisco: Jossey-Bass.

119. Allen, T. D., Poteet, M. L., and Russell, J. E. A. (1999). *Journal of Organizational Behavior,* 20, 1113–1137. Attitudes of managers who are "more or less" career plateaued. *Career Development Quarterly,* 47, 159–172; Allen, T. D., Russell, J. E. A., Poteet, M. L., and Dobbins, G. H. (in press). Learning and development factors related to perceptions of job content and hierarchical plateauing. *Journal of Organizational Behavior.* See also Beehr, T. A., and Bowling, N. A. (2002), career issues facing older workers. In D. C. Feldman (Ed.), *Work careers: A developmental perspective* (pp. 214–241). San Francisco: Jossey-Bass.

120. American Association of Retired Persons. (1993). *The older workforce: Recruitment and retention.* Washington, DC: Author.

121. Lockwood, N. R. (2003). Work/life balance: Challenges and Solutions. *HR Magazine, 48,* 2–10. Saltzstein, A. L., Ting, Y., and Saltzstein, G. H. (2001). Family-friendly balance and job satisfaction: The impact of family-friendly policies on attitudes of federal government employees. *Public Administration Review, 4,* 452–467.

122. Elias, M. (1997, August 12). Couples in pre-kid, no-kid marriages happiest. *USA Today,* p. D1.

123. Eby, L. T. (1996). *Intra-organizational mobility: An examination of factors related to employees' willingness to relocate.* Unpublished doctoral dissertation. The University of Tennessee, Knoxville, TN.

124. Eby, L. T., DeMatteo, J. S., and Russell, J. E. A. (1997). Employment assistance needs of accompanying spouses following relocation. *Journal of Vocational Behavior, 50,* 291–307.

125. Lublin, J. S. (1993, April 13). Husbands in limbo. *The Wall Street Journal,* pp. A1, A8.

126. Pellico, M. T., and Stroh. L. K. (1997). Spousal assistance programs: An integral component of the international assignment. In A. Zeynep (Ed.). *New approaches to employee management, Vol. 4: Expatriate management: Theory and research* (pp. 227–243). Greenwich, CT: JAI Press.

127. Mitchell, H. R., (1999). When a company moves: How to help employees adjust. *HR Magazine, 44*(1), 61–65.

128. Russell, J. E. A., and Burgess, J. R. D. (1998). Success and women's career adjustment. *Journal of Career Assessment,* 6(4), 365–387; See also Sutton, K. L., and Noe, R. A. (2005). Family-friendly programs and work-life integration: More myth than magic? In E. E. Kossek and S. G. Lambert (Eds.), *Work and Life Integration: Organizational, Cultural, and Individual Perspectives,* (pp. 151–169). Mahwah, NJ: Lawrence Erlbaum.

129. Golden, T. D., and Veiga, J. F. (2005). The impact of extent of telecommuting on job satisfaction: Resolving inconsistent findings. *Journal of Management, 31,* 301–318.

130. Wells, S. J. (1999). Using rush hour to your advantage. *HR Magazine, 44*(3), 27–32; Wilhelm, W. R. (1983). Helping workers to self-manage their careers. *Personnel Administrator, 28*(8), 83–89. See also Russell, J. E. A. (2003). Introduction: Technology and Careers. *Journal of Vocational Behavior, 63*(2), 153–158.

131. Wells, S. J. (1999). Using rush hour to your advantage. *HR Magazine, 44*(3), 27–32; Wilhelm, W. R. (1983). Helping workers to self-manage their careers. *Personnel Administrator, 28* (8), 83–89.

132. Warner, M. (1997, March 3). Working at home—The right way to be a star in your bunny slippers. *Fortune, 135*(4) 165–166.

133. Allen, T. D., and Russell, J. E. A. (1999). Parental leaves of absence: Some not so friendly family implications. *Journal of Applied Social Psychology, 29,* 166–191; See also Fried, M. (1998). *Taking time: Parental leave policy and corporate culture.* Philadelphia, PA: Temple University Press. See also: Kossek, E. E., and Lambert, S. G. (Eds.). (2005). *Work and life integration: Organizational, cultural, and individual perspectives.* Mahwah, NJ: Lawrence Erlbaum.

134. Shellenbarger, S. (1997, June 11). Employees, managers need to plan ahead for maternity leaves. *The Wall Street Journal,* p. B1.

135. Moskowitz, M. (October 1996). 100 Best companies for working mothers. *Working Mother Magazine,* 10, 70.

136. Goff, S. J., Mount, M. K., and Jamison, R. L. (1990). Employee supported child care, work/family conflict, and absenteeism: A field study. *Personnel Psychology, 43,* 793–810; Kossek, E. F. and Nichol, V. (1992). The effects of on-site child care on employee attitudes and performance. *Personnel Psychology, 45,* 485–509.

137 Lawlor, J. (1996, July/August). The bottom line on work-family programs. *Working Woman Magazine,* 54–56, 58, 74, 76.

138. Dolan, K. A. (1996, November 18). When money isn't enough. *Forbes, 158*(12), 164–170.

139. Ibid.

140. Bureau of National Affairs (1993). Measuring results: Cost-benefit analyses of work and family programs. *Employee*

Relations Weekly. Washington, DC: Bureau of National Affairs; Lawlor, J. (1996, July/August). The bottom line on work-family programs. *Working Woman Magazine, 54–56,* 58, 74, 76.

141. Rynes, S., and Rosen, B. (1995). A field survey of factors affecting the adoption and perceived success of diversity training. *Personnel Psychology, 48*(2), 247–270.

142. Lawlor, J. (1996, July/August). The bottom line on work-family programs. *Working Woman Magazine, 54–56,* 58, 74, 76.

143. Cianni, M., and Wnuck, D. (1997). Individual growth and team enhancement: Moving toward a new model of career development. *Academy of Management Executive, 11*(1), 105–115; Dumaine, B. (1991, June 17). The bureaucracy busters. *Fortune, 123*(13), 36–44.

144. Stahl, G. K., Miller, E. L., and Tung, R. L. (2002). Toward the boundaryless career: A closer look at the expatriate career concept and the perceived implications of an international assignment. *Journal of World Business, 37,* 216–227.

145. Allerton, H. E. (1997). Expatriate gaps. *Training & Development, 51*(7), 7–8; Harvey, M. G. (1989). Repatriation of corporate executives: An empitical study, *Journal of International Business Studies, 20,* 131–144; see also, Allen, D., and Alvarez, S. (1998). Empowering expatriates and organizations to improve repatriation effectiveness. *Human Resource Planning, 21*(4), 29–39.

146. Allerton, H. E. (1997). Expatriate gaps. *Training & Development, 51*(7), 7–8.

147. Tung, R. L. (1998). A contingency framework of selection and training of expatriates revisited. *Human Resource Management Review, 8*(1), 23–37.

148. Stroh, L. K., Gregersen, H. B., and Black, J. (1998). Closing the gap: Expectations versus reality among repatriates. *Journal of World Business, 33*(2), 111–125.

149. Engen, J. R. (1995). Coming home. *Training, 32*(3), 37–40.

150. Black, J. S., Gregersen, H. B., and Mendenhall, M. (1992). *Global assignments: Successfully expatriating and repatriating international managers.* San Francisco: Jossey-Bass; see also Solomon C. M., Navigating your search for Global Talent, *Personnel Journal, 99*(1), 94–95.

151. Feldman, D. C. (1991). Repatriate moves as career transitions. *Human Resource Management Review, 1*(3), 163–178.

152. Hegler, D. Views on the expatriate (December 11, 1989), *The Wall Street Journal,* p. B1.

153. Napier, N., and Patterson, R. (1991). Expatriate re-entry: What do expatriates have to say? *Human Resource Planning, 14*(1), 18–28.

154. Solomon, C. M. (1995b). Repatriation: Up, down, or out? *Personnel Journal, 74*(1), 28–35.

155. Finney, M. I. (1996). Global success rides on keeping top talent. *HR Magazine, 41*(4), 69–72; *Global Relocation Trends Survey Report* (1995, January). National Foreign Trade Council and Windham International.

156. Allerton, H. E. (2004). Expatriate gaps. *Training & Development, 51*(7), 7–8; Feldman, D. C. (1991). Repatriate moves as career transitions. *Human Resource Management Review, 1*(3), 163–178; Gregersen, H. B. (1992). Commitments to a parent company and a local work unit during repatriation. *Personnel Psychology, 45*(1), 29–54.

157. Morgan, L. O., Nie, W., and Young, S. T. (2004). Operational factors as determinants of expatriate and repatriate success.

International Journal of Operations & Production Management, 24, 1247–1268; see also Bossard, A. B., and Peterson, R. B. (2005). The repatriate experience as seen by American expatriates. *Journal of World Business, 40,* 9–28.

158. Greenhaus, J. H., and Callanan, G. A. (1994). *Career management* (2nd ed). New York: Dryden Press.

159. Slavenski, L. (1987). Career development: A systems approach. *Training & Development, 41*(2), 56–60.

160. Bennis, W. (1996). What lies ahead. *Training & Development, 50*(1), 75–79; Colby, A. G. (1995). Making the new career development model work. *HR Magazine, 40*(6), 150, 152; Thornburg, L. (1995). HR in the year 2010. *HR Magazine, 40*(5), 63–70.

161. Arthur, M. B., and Rousseau, D. (1996). A new career lexicon for the 21st century. *Academy of Management Executive, 10*(4), 28–39.

CHAPTER 10

1. Becker, B. E., Huselid, M. A., and Ulrich, D. (2001). *The HR scorecard.* Boston: Harvard Business School Press. See also, Lawler, E. E. (2002). Pay strategy: New thinking for the new millennium. In G. R. Ferris et al. *Human resource management.* Upper Saddle River, NJ: Prentice Hall, pp. 310–316; Rynes, S. L., and Bono, J. E. (2000). Psychological research on determinants of pay. In S. L. Rynes and B. Gerhart (Eds.), *Compensation in organizations: Current research and practice.* San Francisco: Jossey-Bass, pp. 3–31.

2. For full discussion of pay inequity issues, see Bergman, T. J., and Scarpello, V. G. (2001). *Compensation decision-making* (4th ed.). New York: Harcourt. See also Rynes and Bono, Psychological research on determinants of pay; Leonhardt, D. (April 16, 2000). Executive pay drops off the political radar. *New York Times;* Reingold, J., Melcher, R. A., and McWilliams, G. (April 20, 1998). Executive pay: Stock options plus a bull market made a mockery of many attempts to link pay to performance. *BusinessWeek,* pp. 71–90; Gilpin, K. A. (January 2, 1996). Workers are expected to push for more of the economic pie. *New York Times,* p. C20; Crystal, G. S. (1991). *In search of excess: The overcompensation of American executives.* New York: Norton.

3. Crystal, G. S., and Kay, I. T. (1997). Contrasting perspectives: CEO pay and the "efficient" marketplace. *CEO pay: A comprehensive look.* Scottsdale, AZ: American Compensation Association, p. 50.

4. Survey conducted by Joseph R. Blasi and Douglas L. Kruse, cited in Gretchen Morgenstern (2004, April 4). Option pie: Overeating is a health hazard. *New York Times,* p. B1.

5. For discussion of 2002–2004 trends, see McGeehan, P. (2004, April 4). Is CEO pay up or down? Both. *New York Times,* pp. BU1, 6; Morgenstern, G. (2004, April 4). Two pay packages, two different galaxies. *New York Times,* pp. BU1, 7; and Deutsch, C. (2005, April 4). My big, fat CEO paycheck. *New York Times,* pp. BU1, 12.

6. For full discussion of IBM, see Gerstner, L. V. (2002). Who says elephants can't dance? Inside IBM's historic turnaround. New York: Harper Business. See also Richter, A. S. (1998). Paying the people in black at Big Blue. *Compensation and Benefits Review, 30*(3), 51–59.

7. Gerhart, B. (2000). Compensation strategy and organizational performance. In S. L. Rynes and B. Gerhart (Eds.), *Compensation in organizations: Current research and practice*. San Francisco: Jossey-Bass, pp. 151–194.

8. Blinder, A. S. (ed). (1990). *Paying for productivity*. Washington, DC: Brookings Institution.

9. Bureau of Labor Statistics (2002). International comparisons of newly compensation costs, 2000. *bls.gov*.

10. Gupta, N., and Shaw, J. D. (1998). Let the evidence speak: Financial incentives are effective. *Compensation and Benefits Review, 30*(2), 28.

11. Martocchio, J. J. (2004). Strategic compensation: A human resource management approach (3rd ed.). Upper Saddle River, NJ: Pearson Prentice Hall.

12. LeBlanc, P. V., and Mulvey, P. W. (1998). How American workers see the rewards of work. *Compensation and Benefits Review, 30*(1), 24–34.

13. For a review of the pay satisfaction literature, see Heneman, H. G., III, and Judge, T. A. (2000). Compensation attitudes. In Rynes and Gerhart, *Compensation in organizations,* pp. 61–103.

14. Barber, A. E., and Bretz, R. D. (2000). Compensation, attraction and retention. In Rynes and Gerhart, *Compensation in organizations,* pp. 32–60.

15. Carraher, S. M. and Buckley, M. R. (1996). Cognitive complexity and the perceived dimensionality of pay satisfaction. *Journal of Applied Psychology, 81,* 102–109.

16. Henderson, R. I. (2000). *Compensation management in a knowledge-based world*. Upper Saddle River, NJ: Prentice Hall, pp. 6–7.

17. Paine, T. (January 4, 2000). Out-of-control CEO salaries: Should taxpayers subsidize them? *Common sense.*

18. For a full discussion concerning the history of compensation in organizations, see Rock, M. L. (1991). Looking back on forty years of compensation programs. In M. L. Rock and L. A. Berger (Eds.), *The compensation handbook: A state of the art guide to compensation strategy and design*. New York: McGraw-Hill, pp. 3–11. See also Wallace, M. J., and Fay, C. H. (1988). *Compensation theory and practices*. Boston: PWS-Kent; DeLuca, M. J. (1993). *Handbook of compensation management*. Englewood Cliffs, NJ: Prentice Hall.

19. For a full discussion of the advantages and disadvantages of job ranking, see Bureau of National Affairs. (2005). *Compensation*. Washington, DC: BNA. See also Berg, J. G. (1976). *Managing compensation*. New York: AMACOM; Sibson, R. E. (1990). *Compensation*. New York: AMACOM.

20. For a full discussion of the advantages and disadvantages of job classification, see Bureau of National Affairs, *Compensation;* Berg, *Managing compensation;* Sibson, *Compensation.*

21. For full discussion, see Martocchio, *Strategic compensation.* See also Milkovich, G. T., and Newman, J. M. (2005). *Compensation* (8th ed.). New York: McGraw-Hill/Irwin; and Sibson, *Compensation.*

22. For a full discussion of the advantages and disadvantages of point-factor job evaluation plans, see Bureau of National Affairs, *Compensation;* Berg, *Managing compensation;* Sibson, *Compensation.*

23. Kanin-Lovers, J. (1991). Job evaluation technology. In M. L. Rock and L. A. Berger (Eds.), *The compensation handbook: A state of the art guide to compensation strategy and design*. New York: McGraw-Hill, pp. 72–86. See also DeLuca, *Handbook of compensation management.*

24. Dolmat-Connell, J. (1994). Labor market definition and salary survey selection: A new look at the foundation of compensation program design. *Compensation and Benefits Review, 26*(2), 38–46. See also Lichty, D. T. (1991). Compensation surveys. In M. L. Rock and L. A. Berger (Eds.), *The compensation handbook: A state of the art guide to compensation strategy and design*. New York: McGraw-Hill, pp. 87–103. For full discussion of the economic forces in the labor market (both supply and demand sides) see Wallace and Fay, *Compensation theory and practices.*

25. For a full discussion concerning advantages and disadvantages of market pricing, see Gomez-Mejia, L. R., Balkin, D. B., and Cardy, R. L. (1995). *Managing human resources,* Englewood Cliffs, NJ: Prentice Hall. See also Brennan, J. P., and McKee, B. (1995). Structure-less salary management: A successful application of a modest approach. *Compensation and Benefits Review, 27*(2), 56–62; Sibson, *Compensation.*

26. See Milkovich and Newman, *Compensation.*

27. See Lichty, Compensation surveys; DeLuca, *Handbook of compensation management;* Sibson, *Compensation.*

28. See DeLuca, *Handbook of compensation management.* See also Martocchio, *Strategic compensation.*

29. For a full discussion concerning theoretical support for new compensation approaches, see Risher, H. (1997). The end of jobs: Planning and managing rewards in the new work paradigm. *Compensation and Benefits Review, 29*(1), 13–17. See also Cappelli, P. (1997). Re-thinking the nature of work. *Compensation and Benefits Review, 29*(4), 50–59; Lissy, W. E., and Morgenstern, M. L. (1994). Currents in compensation and benefits. *Compensation and Benefits Review, 26*(5), 10–18; Schuster, J. R., and Zingheim, P. K. (1992). *The new pay: Linking employee and organizational performance*. New York: Lexington Books; Bergel, G. I. (1994). Choosing the right pay delivery system to fit banding. *Compensation and Benefits Review, 26*(4), 34–38.

30. For a full discussion of bias in compensation programs, see Arvey, R. D. (1987). Potential problems in job evaluation methods and processes. In D. B. Balkin and L. R. Gomez-Mejia (Eds.), *New perspectives on compensation*. Englewood Cliffs, NJ: Prentice Hall, pp. 20–30. See also Cook, F. W. (1994). Compensation surveys are biased. *Compensation and Benefits Review, 26*(5), 19–22; Berg, *Managing compensation;* Bureau of National Affairs, *Compensation.*

31. Treiman, D. J., and Hartmann, H. (Eds.) (1981). *Women, work and wages: Equal pay for jobs of equal value*. Washington, DC: National Academy Press.

32. For a full discussion of broadbanding, see Martocchio, *Strategic compensation*. Also see Haslett, S. (1995). Broadbanding: A strategic tool for organizational change. *Compensation and Benefits Review, 27*(6), 40–46; Abosch, K. S. (1995). The promise of broadbanding. *Compensation and Benefits Review, 27*(1), 54–58; LeBlanc, P. V., and McInerney, M. (1994). Need a change? Jump on the banding wagon. *Personnel Journal, 73*(1), 72–82; Donnelly, K., LeBlanc, P. V., Torrence, R. D., and Lyon, M. A. (1992).

Career banding. *Human Resource Management, 31*(1–2), 35–43; Lissy and Morgenstern, Currents in compensation and benefits; Bergel, Choosing the right pay delivery system; Brennan and McKee, Structure-less salary management.

33. Hewitt study cited in Abosch, The promise of broadbanding.

34. ACA study cited in Lissy and Morgenstern, Currents in compensation and benefits.

35. For a discussion of broadbanding disadvantages, see Sibson, R. E. (1990). *New compensation plans: A consultant's report.* Vero Beach, FL: Sibson. See also Reissman, L. (1995). Nine common myths about broadbands. *HR Magazine, 40*(8), 79–88; Abosch, The promise of broadbanding; LeBlanc and McInerney, Need a change?

36. For a full discussion of pay-for-knowledge programs, including advantages and disadvantages, see Bennett, L. (1996). The C&BR board comments on compensation fads, custom pay plans, and team pay. *Compensation and Benefits Review, 28*(2), 67–75. See also Vogeley, E. G., and Schaeffer, L. J. (1995). Link employee pay to competencies and objectives. *HR Magazine, 40*(10), 75–81; Parent, K. I., and Weber, C. L. (1994). Case study: Does pay for knowledge pay off? *Compensation and Benefits Review, 26*(5), 44–50; Sibson, *New compensation plans;* Bergel, Choosing the right pay delivery system; Gomez-Mejia, Balkin, and Cardy, *Managing human resources.*

37. For a full discussion of teams and team-related pay, see Zingheim, P. K., and Schuster, J. R. (1995). First findings: The team pay research study. *Compensation and Benefits Review, 27*(6), 6–14. See also Cauldron. S. (1994). Tie individual pay to team success. *Personnel Journal, 73*(10), 40–47; Gross, S. E. (1995). *Compensation for teams: How to design and implement team-based reward programs.* New York: AMACOM; Dumaine, B. (September 15, 1994). The trouble with teams. *Fortune,* pp. 86–92; Lissy and Morgenstern, Currents in compensation and benefits; Bergel, Choosing the right pay delivery system.

38. See Wallace and Fay, *Compensation theory and practices.*

39. Hansen, F. (1998). Currents in compensation and benefits. *Compensation and Benefits Review, 30*(2), 9.

40. For a full discussion concerning minimum wage, see Hansen, F. (1998). Labor markets and compensation. *Compensation and Benefits Review, 30*(2), 21–25. See also Dunham, S. R. (1996, July 26). We interrupt this revolution to hike the minimum wage. *BusinessWeek,* p. 47; Norton, R. (1996, May 27). The minimum wage is unfair. *Fortune,* p. 53; Prasch, R. E. (1996). In defense of the minimum wage. *Journal of Economic Issues, 30*(2), 391–397; Laabs, J. J. (1996). Maximum debate over minimum wage hike—again. *Personnel Journal, 75*(6), 12; Bernstein, A. (1996, May 20). Commentary: A minimum wage argument you haven't heard before. *BusinessWeek,* 42.

41. Hansen, Currents in compensation and benefits, pp. 8–9.

42. BLS statistics cited in Milkovich and Newman, *Compensation.*

43. Farrell, W. (2005). *Why men earn more: The startling truth behind the pay gap—and what women can do about it.* New York: AMACOM Books.

44. Hart, D. E. and Carraher, S. M. (1995). The development of an instrument to measure attitudes toward benefits. *Educational and Psychological Measurement, 55,* 480–484; McCaffery, R. M. (1988). *Employee benefit programs: A total compensation perspective.* Boston: PWS-Kent. See also

Dreher, G. F., Ash, R. A., and Bretz, R. D. (1988). Benefit coverage and employee cost: Critical factors in explaining compensation satisfaction. *Personnel Psychology, 41,* 237–254; Barber, A. E., Dunham, R. B., and Formisano, R. A. (1992). The importance of flexible benefits on employee satisfaction: A field study. *Personnel Psychology, 45,* 55–76.

45. Bernardin, H. J. (1989). A survey of state employee attitudes toward benefits. Unpublished report to the Florida legislature.

46. See Bergman and Scarpello, *Compensation decision-making;* Martocchio, *Strategic compensation;* McCaffery, *Employee benefit programs.*

47. U.S. Chamber of Commerce Annual Benefits Surveys, 2000 and 2001.

48. See Martocchio, J. J. (2006). Employee benefits: A primer for human resource professionals (2nd ed.). New York: McGraw-Hill/Irwin; McCaffery, *Employee benefit programs;* Steinberg, A. T. (1995). Beyond the tax code: How employee needs are driving employee benefits design. *Compensation and Benefits Review, 27*(1), 29–32; Bureau of Labor Statistics. (1992, September). *Employee Benefits in a Changing Economy: A BLS Chartbook.* Washington, DC: U.S. Government Printing Office.

49. Morgenstern, M. L. (1996). Currents in compensation and benefits. *Compensation and Benefits Review, 28*(3), 10–15. See also Milkovich and Newman, *Compensation;* Martocchio, *Strategic compensation;* Bergman and Scarpello, *Compensation decision-making.*

50. Ibid.

51. Bureau of Labor Statistics. (1998, April). *Employee benefits in small, private establishments, 1996.* Washington, DC: U.S. Government Printing Office. See also Bureau of Labor Statistics. (1999, November). *Employee benefits in medium and large establishments, 1997.* Washington, DC: U.S. Government Printing Office.

52. Labor Letter. (1990, March 27). *The Wall Street Journal,* p. 1. See also Morgenstern, Currents in compensation and benefits; Milkovich and Newman, *Compensation;* Martocchio, *Strategic compensation;* Bergman and Scarpello, *Compensation decision-making.*

53. Bureau of National Affairs. (1994). *Compensation.* Washington, DC: BNA.

54. Rosenbloom, J. S., and Hallman, G. V. (1986). *Employee benefit planning.* Englewood Cliffs, NJ: Prentice Hall.

55. See Bureau of Labor Statistics. (2004, March). National Compensation Survey: Employee benefits in private industry in the United States. www.bls.gov.

56. For a full discussion of wellness programs, see Haltom, C. (1995). Shifting the focus from sickness to wellness. *Compensation and Benefits Review, 27*(1), 47–53. See also Povall, J. (1994). Wellness strategies: How to choose a health risk assessment appraisal. *Compensation and Benefits Review, 27*(1), 54–61.

57. For a discussion of health plan audits, see Reace, D. (1995). The collapse of health care reform—What now? *Compensation and Benefits Review, 29*(2), 69–74. See also Povall, Wellness strategies.

58. McGill, D. M., and Grubbs, D. S. (1989). *Fundamentals of private pensions.* Philadelphia, PA: University of Pennsylvania Press, p. 54.

59. For a full discussion of ERISA provisions, see Bureau of National Affairs. (1994). *Compensation.*

60. See note 55, Bureau of Labor Statistics.

61. Ibid.

62. Ibid.

63. See McGill and Grubbs, *Fundamentals of private pensions.* See also McCaffery, *Employee benefit programs.*

64. See note 51, Bureau of Labor Statistics.

65. See Bureau of National Affairs. (1994). *Compensation.*

66. Ibid.

67. Ibid.

68. See note 55, Bureau of Labor Statistics.

69. See note 55, Bureau of Labor Statistics.

70. See note 51, Bureau of Labor Statistics.

71. Ibid.

72. Winslow, R. (1989, December 13). Spending to cut mental health costs. *The Wall Street Journal,* p. B1.

73. Hansen, Currents in compensation and benefits; p. 9. See also Densford, L. E. (1987, May/June). Make room for baby: The employer's role in solving the day care dilemma. *Employee Benefits News,* pp. 19–38.

74. Dowling, P. J., Welch, D. E., and Schuler, R. S. (1999). *International human resource management: Managing people in a multinational context.* New York: ITP.

75. Swaak, R. A. (1995). Expatriate management: The search for best practices. *Compensation and Benefits Review, 27*(2), 21–29. Also see Martocchio, *Strategic compensation.*

76. Lublin, J. S. (January 29, 1996). An overseas stint can be a ticket to the top. *The Wall Street Journal,* p. B1.

77. Kanter, R. M. (1995). *World class: Thinking locally in the global economy.* New York: Simon and Schuster, p. 88.

78. See note 13, Heneman, and Judge, Compensation attitudes, p. 97.

79. See Dowling, Welch, and Schuler, *International human resource management.*

80. See ibid., p. 198.

81. See Bergman and Scarpello, *Compensation decision-making.*

82. See Martocchio, *Strategic compensation.*

83. See Dowling, Welch, and Schuler, *International human resource management.*

84. See Martocchio, *Strategic compensation.*

85. See ibid., p. 321.

86. See Dowling, Welsh, and Schuler, *International human resource management.*

CHAPTER 11

1. Kanter, R. M. (1989). *When giants learn to dance.* New York: Simon and Schuster, p. 232. See also Heneman, R. (1992). *Merit pay.* Reading, MA: Addison-Wesley.

2. Huselid, M. A., Becker, B. E., and Beatty, R. W. (2005). *The workforce scorecard: Managing human capital to execute strategy.* Boston: Harvard Business School Press; Becker, B. E., Huselid, M. A., and Ulrich, D. (2001). *The HR scorecard.* Boston: Harvard Business School Press. See also Becker, B. E., Huselid, M. A., Pickus, P. S., and Spratt, M. F. (1997). HR as a source of shareholder value: Research and recommendations. *Human Resource Management, 36,* 39–47. See also McDonald, D., and Smith, A. (1995, January/February). A proven connection: Performance management and business results. *Compensation and Benefits Review,* 59–64.

3. Rynes, S. L., Gerhart, B., and Parks, L. (2005). Personnel psychology: Performance evaluation and pay for performance. *Annual Reviews of Psychology, 56,* p. 571.

4. Collins, D. (1995, Summer). Death of a gain sharing plan: Power politics and participatory management. *Organizational Dynamics, 24*(1), 23–38. See also Lawler, E. E., III, and Cohen, S. G. (1992). Designing a pay system for teams. *American Compensation Association Journal, 1*(1), 6–19.

5. Murphy, K. (1994, June 13). Quoted in Fierman, J. The perilous new world of fair pay. *Fortune,* p. 58.

6. Levitt, S. D., and Dubner, S. J. (2005). *Freakonomics: A rogue economist explores the hidden side of everything.* New York: W. M. Morrow.

7. DeCarlo, S. (Ed.) (2005). Special report: CEO compensation. *Forbes,* www.Forbes.com/2005/ceoland.

8. Pfeffer, J. (1994). *HR for competitive advantage.* Boston: Harvard Business Press. See also Lawler, E. E. (1990). *Strategic pay.* San Francisco, CA: Jossey-Bass.

9. William Mercer Inc. (1996). Compensation planning survey. Unpublished report.

10. Anonymous. (2005). The most tangible assets. *Harvard Business Review, 81,* p. 8.

11. Pfeffer, J. (1998). Six dangerous myths about pay. *Harvard Business Review, 76,* 108–120.

12. Rynes, S. L., Gerhart, B., and Minette, K. A. (2004). The importance of pay in employee motivation: Discrepancies between what people say and what they do. *Human Resource Management, 43,* 381–394.

13. See Becker, Huselid, and Ulrich, *The HR scorecard;* Becker et al., HR as a source of shareholder value; McDonald, A proven connection. See also Gerhart, B., and Milkovich, G. T. (1992). Employee compensation: Research and practice. In M. D. Dunnette and L. M. Hough (Eds.), *Handbook of industrial and organizational psychology,* 2nd ed., vol 3. Palo Alto, CA: Consulting Psychologists Press; pp. 431–469.

14. See note 12; see also Kahn, A. (1993, September–October). Why incentive plans cannot work. *Harvard Business Review,* pp. 54–63. See also Bassett, G. (1996, January/February). Merit pay increases are a mistake. *Compensation and Benefits Review,* pp. 20–22.

15. Labor Letter. (1989, December 5). *The Wall Street Journal,* p. 1. See also Wright, P. (1994, May–June). Goal setting and monetary incentives: Motivational tools that can work too well. *Compensation and Benefits Review,* pp. 41–49.

16. Rynes, Gerhart, and Parks. Personnel psychology: Performance evaluation and pay for performance, 571–600.

17. Ibid.

18. Bernardin, H. J. (1992). An "analytic" framework for customer-based performance content development and appraisal. *Human Resource Management Review, 2,* 81–102.

19. Lawler, E. E. (1984). Pay for performance: A motivational analysis. *University of Southern California Report, G84-9(57),* p. 12. See also Wagner, J. A., III, Rubin, P., and Callahan, T. J. (1988). Incentive payment and non-managerial productivity: An interrupted time series analysis of magnitude and trend. *Organizational Behavior and Human Decision Processes, 42,* 47–74.

20. Lawler, E. E. (2002). Pay strategy: New thinking for the new millennium. In G. Furtz et al. (Ed). *Human Resource Management.* Upper Saddle River, NJ, Prentice Hall, pp. 308–316.

21. Bernardin, H. J., and Villanova, P. J. (1986). Performance appraisal. In E. Locke (Ed.), *Generalizing from laboratory to field research.* Boston, MA: D. C. Heath.

22. Tully, S. (November 1, 1993). Your paychecks get exciting. *Fortune,* p. 83.

23. Kay, I. (1990, August 9). Quoted in Labor Letter, *The Wall Street Journal,* p. 1.

24. Kanter, R. M. (January 1987). From status to contribution implications of the changing basis for pay. *Personnel,* pp. 12–24. See also Konrad, A. M., and Pfeffer, J. (1990). Do you get what you deserve? Factors affecting the relationship between productivity and pay. *Administrative Science Quarterly, 35,* 258–285.

25. Editorial (2006, January 2). Another Marie Antoinette moment. *NYTimes online.*

26. National Center for Employee Ownership, www.NCEO.org.

27. See Heneman, *Merit Pay.*

28. Sauner, A. M., and Hawk, E. J. (1994, July–August). Realizing the potential of teams through team-based rewards. *Compensation and Benefits,* pp. 24–33. See also Wageman, R. (March 1995). Interdependence and group effectiveness. *Administrative Science Quarterly, 40* (1), 145–180; Wright, P. M. (May/June 1994). Goal setting and monetary incentives: Motivational tools that can work too well. *Compensation and Benefits Review,* pp. 41–49; Zingheim, P. K., and Schuster, J. R. (November/December 1995). First Findings: The team pay research study. *Compensation and Benefits Review,* pp. 6–32.

29. Ledford, G. E., Lawler, E. E., and Mohrman, S. A. (1995). Reward innovations in *Fortune* 1000 companies. *Compensation and Benefits Review, 27,* 76–80. See also DeMatteo, J. S., and Eby, L. T. (August 1997). Who likes team rewards? An examination of individual difference variables related to satisfaction with team-based rewards. *Best papers proceedings,* Boston: Academy of Management, pp. 134–138.

30. See DeMatteo and Eby, Who likes team rewards?

31. Rynes, Gerhart, and Parks. *Personnel psychology:* Performance evaluation and pay for performance, 586.

32. Lawler, E. E. (2003). Reward practices and performance management system effectiveness. *Organizational Dynamics, 32,* 403.

33. Banker, R. D., Lee, S., Potter, G., and Srinivasan, D. (1996). Contextual analysis of performance impacts of outcome-based incentive compensation. *Academy of Management Journal, 39* (4), 920–948.

34. Taylor, F. W. (1967). *Principles of scientific management.* New York: Norton. See also Taylor, F. W. (1895). A piece rate system, being a step toward partial solution of the labor problem. *American Society of Mechanical Engineers, 16,* 856–883.

35. See Collins, Death of a gain sharing plan; Lawler and Cohen, Designing a pay system for teams.

36. Halsey, F. A. (1891). The premium plan of paying for labor. *Transactions, American Society of Mechanical Engineers, 12,* 755–764.

37. See Collins, Death of a gain sharing plan; Lawler and Cohen, Designing a pay system for teams.

38. See ibid.

39. Schwinger, P. (1975). *Wage incentive systems.* New York: Halsted.

40. Banker, R. D., Lee, S., and Potter, G. (1996). A field study of the impact of a performance-based incentive plan. *Journal of Accounting and Economics, 21*(2), 195–226.

41. Hauser, J. R., Simester, D., and Wernerfelt, B. (1994). Customer satisfaction incentives. *Journal of Marketing, 13*(4), 327–350. See also Johnson, *New York Times;* Heneman, *Merit Pay;* Bivins, J. (1989). Focus on compensation. *Stores, 71*(9), 25–30; Burns, K. C. (1992). A bonus plan that promotes customer service: Star performance—Bonus plan of Aetna Life and Casualty Co. *Compensation and Benefits Review, 24*(5), 15–20; Coopers and Lybrand. (1993). *Compensation planning for 1993.* New York: Coopers and Lybrand; Hills instills employee incentives to lure repeat business. (1993). *Discount Store News, 32*(9), 61. Kanter, R. M. (1989). The new managerial work. *Harvard Business Review, 67*(6), 85–92; Levy and Olive Garden restaurants introduce incentive plans to improve customer service (November 1992). *Restaurants and Institutions;* Schlesinger, L. A., and Heskett, J. L. (1991). The service driven service company. *Harvard Business Review, 69*(5), 71–81.

42. Henderson, R. I. (2000). *Compensation management,* 8th ed. Englewood Cliffs, NJ: Prentice Hall.

43. Mercile, K., and Lund, J. (August 1995). Variable compensation plans, overtime calculations and the Fair Labor Standards Act. *Labor Law Journal, 46*(8), 492–503.

44. Pritchard, R. D., Jones, S. D., Roth, P. L., Stuebing, K. K., and Ekeberg, S. E. (1988). Effects of group feedback, goal setting, and incentives on organizational productivity. *Journal of Applied Psychology, 73*(2), 337–358.

45. Coyle-Shapiro, J. A., Morrow, P. C., Richardson, R., and Dunn, S. R. (2002). Using profit sharing to enhance employee attitudes: A longitudinal examination of the effects on trust and commitment. *Human Resource Management, 41,* 423–439.

46. Ibid., 439.

47. Alexander Consulting Group. (1992). Health care costs, quality top lists of human resource concerns. *Employee Benefit Plan Review, 47*(3), 38–39; see also Welbourne, T. M., Balkin, D. B., and Gomez-Mejia, L. R. (1995, June). Gainsharing and mutual monitoring: A combined agency–organizational justice interpretation. *Academy of Management Journal, 38*(3), 881–899; Belcher, J. G., Jr. (May/June 1994). Gainsharing and variable pay: The state of the art. *Compensation and Benefits Review,* pp. 50–60.

48. Welbourne, T. M., and Gomez-Mejia, L. R. (July/August 1988). Gainsharing revisited. *Compensation and Benefits Review,* pp. 19–28.

49. Lawler and Cohen, Designing a pay system for teams.

50. Schuster, M. (1987, Winter). Gainsharing. Do it right the first time. *Sloan Management Review,* p. 23. See also Bullock, R. J., and Lawler, E. E. (1984). Gainsharing: A few questions, and fewer answers. *Human Resource Management, 23*(l), 23–40; Hatcher, L., and Ross, T. L. (1991). From individual incentives to an organization-wide gainsharing plan: Effects on teamwork and product quality. *Journal of Organizational Behavior, 12,* 169–183; Rollins, T. (May/June 1989). Productivity-based group incentive plans: Powerful, but use with caution. *Compensation and Benefits Review,* pp. 39–50.

51. Lesieur, F. (1958). *The Scanlon plan: A frontier in labor management relations*. New York: John Wiley and Sons.

52. Graham-Moore, B. (1990). 17 years of experience with the Scanlon plan: Desota revisited. In B. Graham-Moore and T. L. Ross (Eds.), *Gainsharing*. Washington, DC: Bureau of National Affairs, pp. 139–173.

53. Thigpen, P. (1994). Quoted in J. Pfeffer, *Competitive advantage through people*. Boston: Harvard Business Press, p. 62.

54. Fein, M. (1980). *An alternative to traditional managing*. Hillsdale, NJ: Mitchell Fein.

55. Kaufman, R. (1992). The effects of IMPROSHARE on productivity. *Industrial and Labor Relations Review, 45*, p. 312.

56. Schuster, J. R., and Zingheim, P. K. (1992). *The new pay: Linking employee and organizational performance*. New York: Lexington Books.

57. Wartzman, R. (1992, May 4). A Whirlpool factory raises productivity—and pay of workers. *The Wall Street Journal*, pp. A1, A4.

58. Scontrino, P. (1995, July–August). An effective productivity and quality tool. *Journal for Quality and Participation, 18*(4), 90–93. See also Reward Staff. (March 1994). Sharing the gains of improved performance. *Personnel Review, 23*(2), 47–49.

59. McAninch, L. (1995, November). Gainsharing creates an environment that supports TQM. *Management Accounting, 77*(5), 38–39.

60. Imberman, W. (1995, November). Is gainsharing the wave of the future? *Management Accounting, 77*(5), 35–38.

61. Belcher, J. G., Jr. (May/June 1994). Gainsharing and variable pay: The state of the art. *Compensation and Benefits Review, 26*(3), 50–60.

62. Hewitt Associates. (January/February 1995). Case studies: Whirlpool, Nike, Salomon and PSEG. *Compensation and Benefits Review*, pp. 71–76.

63. Kim, D. (April 1996). Factors influencing organizational performance in gainsharing programs. *Industrial Relations, 35*(2), 227–244.

64. Rynes, Gerhart, and Parks. Personnel psychology: Performance evaluation and pay for performance, 590.

65. Kaufman, R. T. (1992). The effects of IMPROSHARE on productivity. *Industrial & Labor Relations Review, 45*, p. 2.

66. Capell, K. (1996, July 22). Options for everyone. *BusinessWeek*, pp. 80–84.

67. National Center for Employee Ownership (www.NCEO.ORL). Web site.

68. Blasi, J., Conte, M., and Kruse, D. (1996). Employee stock ownership and corporate performance among public companies. *Industrial and Labor Relations Review, 50*, 63; see also Blasi, J. (1985). *Employee ownership: Revolution not ripoff*. New York: John Wiley and Sons; Florkowski, G. W. (1991). Profit sharing and public policy: Insights for the United States. *Industrial Relations, 30*, 96–115; Florkowski, G. W. (1987). The organizational impact of profit sharing. *Academy of Management Review, 12*, 622–636; Hammer, T. H. (1988). New developments in profit sharing, gain sharing, and employee ownership. In J. P. Campbell, R. J. Campbell, and Associates (Eds.), *Productivity in organizations*. San Francisco: Jossey-Bass; Klein, K. J.

(1987). Employee stock ownership and employee attitudes: A test of three models. *Journal of Applied Psychology [monograph], 72*, 319–332; Kruse, D. L. (1991). Profit-sharing and employment variability: Microeconomic evidence on the Weitzman theory. *Industrial and Labor Relations Review, 44*, 437–453; Pierce, J. L., Rubenfeld, S., and Morgan, S. (1991). Employee ownership: A conceptual model of process and effects. *Academy of Management Review, 16*, 121–144.

69. Kraizberg, E., Tziner, A., and Weisberg, J. (2002). Employee stock options: Are they indeed superior to other incentive compensation schemes? *Journal of Business and Psychology, 16*, 212–228.

70. Editorial (2006, January 2). Another Marie Antoinette moment. *NYTimes online*.

71. Crystal, G. S. (1984). Pay for performance: It's not dead after all. *Compensation Review, 3*, 24–25.

72. Lublin, J. S. (1998, April 9). Pay for no performance. *The Wall Street Journal*, pp. R1–R18.

73. DeCarlo, S. (Ed.) (2005). Special report: CEO compensation. *Forbes*, www.Forbes.com/2005/ceoland.

74. Byrne, J. A. (2002, May 6). How to fix corporate governance. *BusinessWeek*, pp. 69–78.

75. Ozanian, M. K., and MacDonald, E. (2005). Paychecks on steroids. *Forbes*, www.Forbes.com/2005/ceoland.

76. Hambrick, D. C., and Siegel, P. A. (1997). Pay dispersion within top management groups: Harmful effects on performance of high-technology firms. *Best paper proceedings*. Boston: Academy of Management, pp. 26–28.

77. Thompson, J. H., Smith, L. M., and Murray, A. F. (September/October 1986). Management performance incentives: Three critical issues. *Compensation and Benefits Review*, pp. 41–47.

78. Crystal, G. (2002, May 8). What's best when it comes to options accounting. Bloomberg.com.

79. Byrne, How to fix corporate governance.

80. Ibid.

81. Edelstein, C. M. (1981). Long-term incentives for management, Part 4. Restricted stock. *Compensation Review*, pp. 31–40. See also Kerr, J., and Bettis, R. A. (1987). Board of directors, top management compensation, and shareholder returns. *Academy of Management Journal, 30*, 645–665.

82. Byrne, How to fix corporate governance.

83. Dunlap, A. (1997, August 10). Final front in crusade for corporate reform. *New York Times*, p. F13.

84. Lublin, J. (1991, June 4). Are chief executives paid too much? *The Wall Street Journal*, p. B1.

85. Balkin, D. B., and Logan, J. W. (1988, January/February). Reward policies that support entrepreneurship. *Compensation and Benefits Review*, pp. 19–32. See also Kahn, L. M., and Sherer, P. D. (1990). Contingent pay and managerial performance. *Industrial and Labor Relations Review, 43*, 107S–120S.

86. See Collins, Death of a gain sharing plan; Lawler and Cohen, Designing a pay system for teams. See also Kerr, J., and Slocum, J. W., Jr. (1987). Managing corporate culture through reward systems. *Academy of Management Executive, 1*(2), 99–108.

87. See Collins, Death of a gain sharing plan.

88. Rynes, Gerhart, and Parks. Personnel psychology: Performance evaluation and pay for performance, 590.

CHAPTER 12

1. Adopted from Muhl, C. J. (2001). The employment-at-will doctrine: Three major exceptions. *Monthly Labor Review, 124*(1), 3–11.

2. Huselid, M. A., Becker, B. E., and Beatty, R. W. (2005). *The workforce scorecard: Managing human capital to execute strategy.* Boston: Harvard Business School Press.

3. Harter, J. K., Schmidt, F. L., and Hayes T. L. (2002). Business-unit-level relationship between employee satisfaction, employee engagement, and business outcomes: A meta-analysis. *Journal of Applied Psychology, 87,* 268–279.

4. Greenberg, J., and Colquih, J. A. (2006). *Handbook of Organizational Justice.* Mahwah, NJ: Erlbaum.

5. Lansberg, I. (1984). Hierarchy as a mediator of fairness: A contingency approach to distributive justice in organizations. *Journal of Applied Social Psychology, 14,* 124–135.

6. Sheppard, B. H., Lewicki, R. J., and Minton, J. W. (1992). *Organizational justice: The search for fairness in the workplace.* New York: Lexington Books.

7. Brockner, J. (2002). Making sense of procedural fairness: How high procedural fairness can reduce or heighten the influence of outcome favorability. *Academy of Organizational Management Review, 27,* 58–76.

8. Simons, T., and Roberson, Q. (2003). Why managers should care about fairness: The effects of aggregate justice perceptions on organizational outcomes. *Journal of Applied Psychology, 88,* p. 441.

9. Barrier, M. (1998). Doing the right thing. *Nation's Business, 86*(3), 32–38; Wells, S. J. (1999). Turn employees into saints? *HR Magazine, 44*(13), 48–58; Rafalko, R. J. (1994). Remaking the corporation: The 1991 U.S. sentencing guidelines. *Journal of Business Ethics, 13,* 625–636.

10. Ethics Resource Center (2003). National Business Ethics Survey Executive Summary. http://www.ethics.org/nbes2003/2003nbes_summary.html.

11. Greengard, S. (1997). Lockheed Martin is game for ethics. *Workforce, 76*(10), 51; Wells, Turn employees into saints?

12. Ibid.

13. Holcomb, B. (July 1991). Time off: The benefit of the hour. *Working Mother Magazine,* pp. 31–35.

14. Greenhaus, J. H., and Beutell, N. J. (1985). Sources of conflict between work and family roles. *Academy of Management Review, 10,* 76–88; see also Kush, K., and Stroh, L. (September–October 1994). Flextime: Myth or reality? *Business Horizons,* pp. 51–55; Bureau of National Affairs. (September 3, 1992). Flexible work schedules. *Bulletin to Management,* pp. 276–277.

15. Fernandez, J. P. (1986). *Child care and corporate productivity: Resolving family/work conflicts.* Lexington, MA: D. C. Heath and Co.

16. Sheppard, E. M., Clifton, T. J., and Kruse, D. (1996). Flexible work hours and productivity: Some evidence from the pharmaceutical industry. *Industrial Relations, 35,* 123–129; see also Nollen, S. (1977). Does flextime improve productivity? *Harvard Business Review, 56*(9/10), 12–22.

17. Holcomb, B. (July 1991). Time off: The benefit of the hour. *Working Mother Magazine,* pp. 31–35.

18. Fernandez, *Child care and corporate productivity.*

19. Catalyst. (2001). A new approach to flexibility: Managing the work/time equation. Available at *www.catalystwomen.org/press/factsheets/factspt.html,* visited August 24, 2001.

20. Closson, M. (October 25, 1976). Company couples flourish. *BusinessWeek,* p. 112.

21. Solomon, C. M. (September 1994). Job sharing: One job, double headache? *Personnel Journal,* pp. 88–96.

22. Greengard, S. (November 1995). Discover best practices through benchmarking. *Personnel Journal,* pp. 62–73. See also Schneier, C. E., and Johnson, C. (Spring/Summer 1993). Benchmarking: A tool for improving performance management and reward systems. *American Compensation Association Journal,* pp. 14–31.

23. Holcomb, Time off; Solomon, C. M. (August 1991). 24-hour employees. *Personnel Journal,* p. 56.

24. Wanous, J. P. (1992). *Recruitment, selection, orientation, and socialization of newcomers.* Reading, MA: Addison-Wesley.

25. Schneider, B., and Schmitt, N. W. (1986). *Staffing organizations,* 2nd ed. Glenview, IL: Scott, Foresman.

26. McEvoy, G. M., and Cascio, W. F. (1985). Strategies for reducing employee turnover: A meta-analysis. *Journal of Applied Psychology, 70,* 342–353; Premack, S. L., and Wanous, J. P. (1985). A meta-analysis of realistic job preview experiments. *Journal of Applied Psychology, 70,* 706–719; Wanous, J. P., and Colella, A. (1989). Organizational entry research: Current status and future directions. *Research in Personnel and Human Resource Management, 7,* 59–120.

27. Greenhaus, J. H., and Callanan, G. A. (1994). *Career management.* Fort Worth, TX: Dryden Press.

28. SHRM. (1997). Survey of Human Resource Trends [Online]. Available at *www.shrm.org/press/releases/default.asp?page=hrtrend2.htm,* visited April 11, 2001. 1997 Survey of Human Resource Trends.

29. Ibid.

30. Horowitz, A. (1999). Up to speed—fast. *Computerworld, 33*(7), 48.

31. Saks, A. M., and Ashforth, B. E. (1997). Organizational socialization: Making sense of the past and present as a prologue for the future. *Journal of Vocational Behavior, 51,* 234–279.

32. Ganzel, R. (1998). Putting out the welcome mat. *Training, 35*(3), 54–62.

33. Ibid.

34. Chao, G. T. (1997). Unstructured training and development: The role of organizational socialization. In J. K. Ford (Ed.), *Improving training effectiveness in work organizations.* Mahwah, NJ: Lawrence Erlbaum.

35. Ibid.

36. Ganzel, R. (1998). More than a handshake. *Training, 35*(3), 60.

37. Ganzel, Putting out the welcome mat.

38. Lindo, D. K. (1993). Orientation express. *Office Systems, 10*(11), 64–67.

39. Feldman, D. C. (1988). *Managing careers in organizations.* Glenview, IL: Scott, Foresman.

40. Muhl, C. J. (2001). The employment-at-will doctrine: Three major exceptions. *Monthly Labor Review, 124*(1), 3–11.

41. Ibid.; Walsh, D. J., and Schwarz, J. L. (1996). State common law wrongful discharge doctrines: Up-date, refinement, and rationales. *American Business Law Journal, 33,* 645–689.

42. Siegel, M. (1998). Yes, they can fire you. *Fortune, 138*(8), 301.

43. Miethe, T. D. (1999). *Whistleblowing at work.* Boulder, CO: Westview Press.

44. Ibid.

45. Ibid.

46. Gurchiek, K. (2005). Survey: No clear consensus on noncompete agreements. *HR Legal Reporter,* www.SHRM.org.

47. Ibid.; Flynn, G. (1995). Balance on the fine line of employee privacy. *Personnel Journal, 74*(3), 90–92.

48. Ibid.

49. Flynn, Balance on the fine line of employee privacy.

50. Addison, J. T., and Blackburn, M. L. (1994). The Worker Adjustment and Retraining Notification Act: Effects on notice provision. *Industrial and Labor Relations Review, 47,* 650–662.

51. Hatch, D. D., and Hall, J. E. (1999). Unforeseen circumstance precludes WARN notice. *Workforce, 78*(1), 107.

52. Muhl, C. J. (1999). WARN Act. *Monthly Labor Review, 122*(4), 45.

53. Harter, Schmidt, and Hayes. Business-unit-level relationship between employee satisfaction, employee engagement, and business outcomes, 279.

54. Ehrenfeld, T. (1993). The (handbook) handbook. *Inc, 15*(11), 57–64.

55. *Burlington Industries, Inc. v. Ellerth,* 524 U.S. 742, 118 S. Ct. 2257, 141 L. Ed. 2d 633 (1998), *aff'g* 123 F. 3d 490.

56. Webb, S. (1991). *Step forward: Sexual harassment in the workplace.* Winchester, VA: Master Media.

57. Abenathy, D. J. (1998). Who's watching the net? *Training & Development, 52*(11), 18.

58. Ibid.

59. Muhl, The employment-at-will doctrine; Rasmusson, E. (March 2001). Protective measures: Put policies in place to protect your company from employee lawsuits. *Working Woman Magazine,* p. 26; Flynn, G. (2000). Take another look at the employee handbook. *Workforce, 79*(3), 132–134.

60. Muhl, The employment-at-will doctrine.

61. Arvey, R. D., and Jones, A. P. (1985). The use of discipline in organizational settings. In B. M. Staw and L. L. Cummings (Eds.), *Research in organizational behavior,* Vol. 7. Greenwich, CT: JAI Press, pp. 47–82.

62. Raines, C. (1997). *Beyond generation X: A practical guide for managers.* Menlo Park, CA: Crisp Publications.

63. McCabe, D. M. (1997). Alternative dispute resolution and employee voice in nonunion employment: An ethical analysis of organizational due process procedures and mechanisms—the case of the United States. *Journal of Business Ethics, 16,* 349–356.

64. Thibaut, J., and Walker, L. (1975). *Procedural justice: A psychological analysis.* Hillsdale, NJ: Erlbaum.

65. Balfour, A. (1984). Five types of non-union grievance systems. *Personnel, 61,* 67–76.

66. McCabe, Alternative dispute resolution.

67. Tasini, J., and Houston, P. (September 15, 1986). Letting workers help handle workers' gripes. *BusinessWeek,* p. 82.

68. McCabe, Alternative dispute resolution.

69. Morin, W. J., and Yorks, L. (1990). *Dismissal.* New York: Drake Beam Morin.

70. Pinder, C. C. (1988). *Work motivation in organizational behavior.* Upper Saddle River, NJ: Prentice Hall.

71. Lind, E. A., Greenberg, J., Scott, K. S., and Welchans, T. D. (2000). The winding road from employee to complainant: Situational and psychological determinants of wrongful-termination claims. *Administrative Science Quarterly, 45,* 557–590.

72. Ensman, R. G. (1998). Firing line. *Office Systems, 15*(3), 67; Garron, R. S. (2001). Take action on poor performance. *InfoWorld. 23*(7), 69; Latack, J. C., and Kaufman, H. G. (1988). Termination and outplacement strategies. In M. London and E. M. Mone (Eds.), *Career growth and human resource strategies.* New York: Quorum Books; Marchetti, M. (1997). The fine art of firing. *Sales and Marketing Management, 149*(4), 67; Opperman, M. (1997). Firing a problem employee. *Veterinary Economics, 38*(5), 34–36.

73. Middlebrook, J. F. (1999). Avoiding brain drain: How to lock in talent. *HR Focus, 76*(3), 9–10.

74. Cole, C. L. (2000). Building loyalty. *Workforce, 79*(8), 42–48; Will, M. (2001). Protecting your company from high turnover. *Women in Business, 53*(2), 30–31.

75. Middlebrook, Avoiding brain drain; Will, Protecting your company from high turnover.

76. Breuer, N. (2000). Shelf life. *Workforce, 79*(8), 28–32; Cole, C. L. (2000). Building loyalty. *Workforce, 79*(8), 42–48; Middlebrook, Avoiding brain drain; Taylor, J. (April 1999). Avoid avoidable turnover. *Workforce,* Supplement, 6; Will, Protecting your company from high turnover.

77. Giacalone, R. A., Knouse, S. B., and Montagliani, A. (1997). Motivation for and prevention of honest responding in exit interviews and surveys. *Journal of Psychology, 131,* 438–448.

78. Lilienthal, S. M. (2000). Screen and glean: What do workers really think of your company? And if they leave, what can your firm learn from their departure? *Workforce, 79*(10), 71, 80.

79. Taylor, Avoid avoidable turnover.

80. Giacalone, Knouse, and Montagliani, Motivation for and prevention of honest responding in exit interviews and surveys.

81. Breuer, Shelf life.

82. Levering, R., and Moskowitz, M. (2001). The 100 best companies to work for. *Fortune, 143*(1), 148–168.

83. Wooldridge, A. (March 5, 2000). Come back, company man! *New York Times Magazine,* p. 6.82.

84. Cascio, W. F. (1993). Downsizing: What do we know? What have we learned? *Academy of Management Executive, 7,* 95–104.

85. Greenhaus, J. H., and Callanan, G. A. (1994). *Career management.* Fort Worth, TX: Dryden Press.

86. Noer, D. M. (1993). *Healing the wounds.* San Francisco, CA: Jossey-Bass.

87. O'Neill, H. M., and Lenn, D. J. (1995). Voices of survivors. Words that downsizing CEOs should hear. *Academy of Management Executive, 9,* 23–34.

88. Cascio, Downsizing.

89. Brockner, J. (1988). *Self-esteem at work.* Lexington, MA: Lexington Books; Pinder, C. C. (1988). *Work motivation in organizational behavior.* Upper Saddle River, NJ: Prentice Hall.

90. Brockner, J., Konovsky, M., Cooper-Schneider, R., Folger, R., Martin, C., and Bies, R. J. (1994). Interactive effects of procedural justice and outcome negativity on victims and survivors of job loss. *Academy of Management Journal, 37,* 397–409.

91. Ibid.

92. Baker, A. M. (Fall 1988). Lessons from the Maine experience. *Human Resource Management, 3,* 315–328; Feldman, D. C., and Leana, C. R. (Summer 1989). Managing layoffs: Experiences at the *Challenger* disaster site and the Pittsburgh steel mills. *Organizational Dynamics, 18*(1), 52–64; Noer, *Healing the wounds;* Pinder, *Work motivation in organizational behavior;* Settles, M. F. (1988). Humane downsizing: Can it be done? *Journal of Business Ethics, 7,* 961–963.

93. Latack, J. C., and Kaufman, H. G. (1988). Termination and outplacement strategies. In M. London and E. M. Mone (Eds.), *Career growth and human resource strategies.* New York: Quorum Books.

94. Feldman, D. C. (1995). The impact of downsizing on organizational career and employee career development opportunities. *Human Resource Management Review, 5*(3), 189–221.

95. Rosen, B., and Jerdee, T. H. (1985). *Older employees: New roles for valued resources.* Homewood, IL: Dow Jones-Irwin, p. 143.

96. Feldman, D. C. (1994). The decision to retire early: A review and conceptualization. *Academy of Management Review, 19,* 285–311.

97. Adams, G. A., and Beehr, T. A. (1998). Turnover and retirement: A comparison of their similarities and differences. *Personnel Psychology, 51,* 643–665.

98. Rosen and Jerdee, *Older employees,* p. 143; Talaga, J. A., and Beehr, T. A. (1995). Are there gender differences in predicting retirement decisions? *Journal of Applied Psychology, 80,* 16–28; Brown, M. T., Fukunaga, C., Umemoto, D., and Wicker, L. (1996). Annual review, 1990–1996: Social class, work, and retirement behavior. *Journal of Vocational Behavior, 49,* 159–189.

99. Rosen and Jerdee, *Older employees,* p. 143.

100. Gerbman, R. (1999). Reach out with retirees. *HR Magazine, 44*(7), 74–80.

101. Greenhaus and Callanan, *Career management.*

102. Siegel, S. R. (1981). Preparation for retirement in commercial banking firms. *The Banker's Magazine, 164*(5), 89–93.

103. Siegel, S. R. (March–April 1989). Preretirement programs in service firms. *Compensation and Benefits Review,* pp. 47–58.

CHAPTER 13

1. Klima, B. and McComb, C. (2002). Unions in the age of Enron, www.gallup.com

2. Peter Hart Research. (June 1999). Americans' attitudes toward unions. Peter Hart and Associates (www.aflcio.org/labor).

3. Schrank, R. (1979). Are unions an anachronism? *Harvard Business Review, 57,* 107–115. See also Flynn, G. (1997). How HR has weathered the changing legal climate. *Workforce, 76*(1), 159, 162.

4. www.bls.gov

5. See www.aflcio.org

6. www.nasdag.com/services. "Taking the world by storm," June 12, 2002.

7. Murray, M. K. (2001). The new economy and new union organizing strategies: Union wins in healthcare. *Journal of Nursing Administration, 31,* 339–343; see also Feared, J., and Greyer, C. R. (1982). Determinants of U. S. unionism: Past

research and future needs. *Industrial Relations, 21,* 1–32; Heneman, H. G., III, and Sandver, M. H. (1983). Predicting the outcome of union certification elections: A review of the literature. *Industrial and Labor Relations Review, 36,* 537–560; Curme, M. A., Hirsch, B. T., and Macpherson, D. M. (1990). Union membership and contract coverage in the United States, 1983–1988. *Industrial and Labor Relations Review, 44,* 5–33; Newton, L. A., and Shore, L. M. (1992). A model of union membership: Instrumentality, commitment, and opposition. *Academy of Management Review, 17,* 275–298.

8. Bronfenbrenner, K. (1997). The role of union strategies in NLRB certification elections. *Industrial and Labor Relations Review, 50*(2), 195–212.

9. Brett, J. M. (1980). Why employees want unions. *Organizational Dynamics, 8,* 47–59.

10. http://www.dol.gov/esa/programs/whd/state/righttowork.htm.

11. Bronfenbrenner, K., and Hickey, R. (2004). Changing to organize: A national assessment of union strategies. In Milkman, R., and Voss, K. (Eds.), *Rebuilding labor.* Ithaca, NY: Cornell University Press.

12. Kelly, J. (1998). *Rethinking industrialization: Mobilization, collectivization, and long waves.* London: Routledge; Johnson, N., and Jarley, P. (2004). Justice and union participation: An extension and test of mobilization theory. *British Journal of Industrial Relations 42* (3), 543–562.

13. Freeman, Richard B., and Kleiner, Morris M. (1990). Employer behavior in the face of union organizing drives. *Industrial & Labor Relations Review, 43,* 451–466; (1998). Morris, Charles J. A tale of two statutes: Discrimination for union activity under the NLRA and RLA. *Employment Rights and Policy Journal 327,* 329–30.

14. U.S. BLS (www.bls.gov).

15. Pfeffer, J. (1994). *Competitive advantage through people.* Boston: Harvard Business School Press, p. 163. See also Hirsch, B. T., (1991). Union coverage and profitability among U.S. firms. *Review of Economics and Statistics, 73,* 69–77.

16. Burton, J. F. (Ed.). (1985). Review symposium: What do unions do? *Industrial and Labor Relations Review, 38,* 244–263. See also Kramer, J. K., and Vasconcellos, G. M. (1996). The economic effect of strikes on the shareholders of nonstruck competitors. *Industrial and Labor Relations Review, 49*(2), 213–222; Beaumont, P. B., and Harris, R. I. D. (1996). Good industrial relations, joint problem solving, and HRM. *Industrial Relations Quebec, 51*(2), 391–406; GM local labor dispute spins out of control. (March 13, 1996). *The Wall Street Journal,* pp. B1, B3.

17. Karier, T. (1991). Unions and the U.S. comparative advantage. *Industrial Relations, 30,* 1.

18. Becker, B. E., and Olsen, C. A. (1987). Labor relations and firm performance. In M. M. Kleiner, R. N. Block, M. Roomkin, and S. W. Salsburg (Eds.), *Human resources and performance of the firm,* Madison, WI: Industrial Relations Research Association, pp. 43–86. See also Cutcher-Gershenfeld, J. (1991). The impact of economic performance on a transformation in workplace relations. *Industrial and Labor Relations Review, 44,* 241–260.

19. Becker, B., Huselid, M., and Ulrich, D. (2001). *The HR scorecard.* Boston, MA: Harvard Business Press.

20. Gershenfeld, W. J. (1987). Employee participation in firm decisions. In M. M. Kleiner, R. N. Block, M. Roomkin, and S. W. Salsburg (Eds.), *Human resources and performance of*

the firm. Madison, WI: Industrial Relations Research Association, 123–158. See also Ferman, L. A., Hoyman, M., Cutcher-Gershenfeld, J., and Savoie, E. J. (Eds.) (1991). *Joint training programs: A union–management approach to preparing workers for the future.* Ithaca, NY: ILR Press, School of Industrial and Labor Relations, Cornell University. Hammer, T. H., Curall, S. C., and Stern, R. N. (1991). Worker representation on board of directors: A study of competing roles. *Industrial and Labor Relations Review, 44,* 661–680.

21. Gold, C. (1986). *Labor management committees: Confrontation, cooptation, or cooperation?* Ithaca, NY: ILR Press.

22. Goll, I., and Hochner, A. (1987). Labor–management practices as a function of environmental pressures and corporate ideology in union and nonunion settings. *Proceedings of the Fortieth Annual Meeting of the Industrial Relations Research Association,* pp. 516–524. See also Miller, R. L. (1996). Employee participation and contemporary labor law in the U.S. *Industrial Relations Journal, 27*(2), 166–174.

23. The UAW continues its efforts to improve quality. (1996). *Quality Progress, 29*(7), 62–63.

24. Katz, H. C., Kochan, T. A., and Gobeille, K. R. (1984). Industrial relations performance, economic performance, and QWL programs: An interplant analysis. *Industrial and Labor Relations Review, 37,* 3–17. See also Katz, H. C., Kochan, T. A., and Weber, M. C. (1985). Assessing the effects of industrial relations systems and efforts to improve the quality of working life on organizational effectiveness. *Academy of Management Review, 28,* 509–526.

25. Cooke, W. N. (1994). Employee participation programs, group-based incentives and company performance: A union–nonunion comparison. *Industrial and Labor Relations Review, 47*(4), 594–609.

26. Steel, R. P., Jennings, K. R., Mento, A. J., and Hendricks, W. H. (August 1988). *Effects of institutional employee participation on industrial labor relations.* Paper presented at the meeting of the Academy of Management, Anaheim, CA.

27. Leana, C. R., Ahlbrandt, R. S., and Murrell, A. J. (1992). The effects of employee involvement programs on unionized workers' attitudes, perceptions, and preferences in decision making. *Academy of Management Journal, 35*(4), 861–873.

28. Feared, J., Lowman, C., and Nelson, F. D. (1987). The impact of human resource policies on union organizing. *Industrial Relations, 26,* 113–126.

29. *Electromation, Inc. v. NLRB,* 35 F. 3d 1148 (7th Cir. 1994).

30. Schwochau, S. (1987). Union effects on job attitudes. *Industrial and Labor Relations Review, 40,* 219–220.

31. Gordon, M. E., and DeNisi, A. S. (1995). A re-examination of the relationship between union membership and job satisfaction. *Industrial Relations Review, 48,* 222–236.

32. Lawyer, J. E. (1947). The United States Labor–Management Relations Act of 1947. *International Labor Review, 56*(2), 125–166.

33. McCulloch, F. W., and Bornstein, T. (1974). *The National Labor Relations Board.* New York: Praeger.

34. Extejt, M. M., and Lynn, M. P. (1996). Trends in computer use in collective bargaining. *Information and Management, 30*(3), 111–117; see also Issacharoff, S. (1996). Contracting for employment: The limited return of the common law.

Texas Law Review, 74(7), 1783–1812; Korman, R. (May 6, 1996). Court upholds job targeting. *ENR, 236*(18), 14; Lissy, W. E., and Morgenstern, M. L. (1996). Labor. *Compensation and Benefits Review, 28*(2), 14–15; Berreth, C. A. (January/February 1996). Workers' compensation laws enacted in 1995. *Monthly Labor Review, 119,* 59–72.

35. Blumenfeld, S. B., and Partridge, M. D. (Winter 1996). The long-run and short-run impacts of global competition on U.S. union wages. *Journal of Labor Research, 17*(1), 149–171.

36. Pynes, J. E. (1996). The two faces of unions. *Journal of Collective Negotiations in the Public Sector, 25*(1), 31–43.

37. www.fmcs.gov

38. Sunoo, B. P. (February 1995). Managing strikes, minimizing loss. *Personnel Journal,* pp. 50–60. See also Barlow, W. E., Hatch, D. D., and Murphy, B. (1996). Recent legal decisions affect you. *Personnel Journal, 75*(1), 100.

39. www.bls.gov

40. Tivendeel, J., and Watson, C. (1995). Attitudes toward unions as predictors of actual strike behavior. *Ergonomics, 38*(3), 534–538.

41. NLRBV. Mackay Radio & Telegraph (U.S. 1938)

42. *AFL-CIO Committee for Workplace Fairness.* (1990). Washington, DC: AFL-CIO. See also Budd, J. W. (1996). Canadian strike replacement legislation and collective bargaining: Lessons for the U.S. *Industrial Relations, 35*(2), 245–260.

43. Reuters. (2006, January 16). Northwest's machinists will vote on concessions. *International Herald Tribune online.*

44. DeFusco, R. A., and Fuess, J. R. (1991). The effects of airline strikes on struck and nonstruck carriers. *Industrial and Labor Relations Review, 44*(2), 324–333.

45. Schnell, J. F., and Gramm, C. L. (1994). The empirical relations between employers' striker replacement strategies and strike duration. *Industrial and Labor Relations Review, 47*(2), 189–206.

46. Dastmalchian, A., and Ng, I. (1990). Industrial relations climate and grievance outcomes. *Industrial Relations, 45,* 311–324. See also Salipante, P. F., and Bouwen, R. (1990). Behavioral analysis of grievances: Conflict sources, complexity and transformation. *Employee Relations, 12,* 17–22.

47. Sloan, A. A., and Whitney, F. (2002). *Labor relations.* Upper Saddle River, NJ: Prentice Hall.

48. M. B. Sturgis, Inc., 331 NLRB No. 173, 2000.

49. See Murray, The new economy and new union organizing strategies; Feared and Greyer, Determinants of U.S. unionism; Heneman and Sandver, Predicting the outcome of union certification elections; Curme, Hirsch, and Macpherson, Union membership and contract coverage; Newton and Shore, A model of union membership. See also Wells, M. J. (2000). Unionization and immigrant incorporation in San Francisco hotels. *Social Problems, 47,* 241–265.

50. Dzaidzo, E. (2000, June 4). Union making strides in health care. *Time,* p. 17.

51. www.aflcio.org

52. www.fpd.org

53. Quote from www.afsme.org/about/aff.108

54. Mace, R. F. (1988). The Supreme Court's labor law successorship doctrine after *Fall River Dyeing. Labor Law Journal, 39,* 102–109.

55. London, M. (1996). Redeployment and continuous learning in the 21st century: Hard lessons and positive examples from the downsizing era. *Academy of Management Executive, 10*(4), 67–79.

56. Auerbach, J. D. (1988). *In the business of child care.* New York: Praeger.

57. See Murray, The new economy and new union organizing strategies; Feared and Greyer, Determinants of U.S. unionism; Heneman and Sandver, Predicting the outcome of union certification elections; Curme, Hirsch, and Macpherson, Union membership and contract coverage; Newton and Shore, A model of union membership.

58. Bronfenbrenner, K., DeWitt, D., Fletcher, B., et al (2005, February). Future of organized labor in the U.S.: Reinventing trade unionism for the 21st century. *Monthly Review, Online.* (www.MonthlyReview.org)

59. See Sloan and Whitney, *Labor relations.*

60. Mills, D. G. (1989). *Labor–management relations.* New York: McGraw-Hill.

61. A Business International Research Report. (1982). *Managing manpower in Europe.* Business International Corporation. See also Hoerr, J. (February 1991). What should unions do? *Harvard Business Review,* pp. 30–45.

62. Steinmetz, G. (1997, June 12). One union accepts reality, breaking with inflexible past. *The Wall Street Journal,* p. A14. See also Steinmetz, G. (June 12, 1997). Germans falter in struggle to regain competitive edge. *The Wall Street Journal,* p. A14.

63. Woodruff, D. (July 28, 1997). The German worker is making a sacrifice: *BusinessWeek,* pp. 46–47.

64. Consultation on new strike restrictions. (1996, December). *IRS Employment Review,* pp. 5515–5516.

65. Dowling, P. J., and Schuler, R. S. (1999). *International dimensions of human resource management.* Boston: PWS-Kent.

66. See Sloan and Whitney, *Labor relations.*

67. Hammock, B. T. (1996). The extraterritorial application of the National Labor Relations Act: A union perspective. *Syracuse Journal of International Law and Commerce, 22,* 127–154.

68. Rolnick, A. L. (1997, February 3). Muzzling the offshore watchdogs. *Bobbin, 8*(6), 72–73.

69. World Bank (2003, Feb. 13). *Economics perform better in coordinated labor markets* (http://web.worldbank.org)

70. Greenhouse, S. (2005, January 2). Labor board's critics see a bias against workers. *New York Times Online.* (www.NYTimes.com)

CHAPTER 14

1. Bureau of Labor Statistics. (2003). *Workplace injury and illness summary and census of fatal occupational injuries.* Washington, D.C.: Department of Labor.

2. Health concerns dominate construction lecture. (1997). *Occupational Safety, 15*(1), 37.

3. Garland, S. B. (1989, February 20). This safety ruling could be hazardous to employer's health. *BusinessWeek,* p. 34.

4. Ibid. See also Bureau of National Affairs. (1989, July 24). Michigan Supreme Court rules OSH Act does not preempt state proceedings. *BNA's Employee Relations Weekly, 7,* 945.

5. *Health and Safety Statistics.* (2002). Geneva: International Labour Organization (ILO.org). See also Elling, R. H. (1986). The struggle for workers' health: A study of six industrialized countries. Farmingdale, NY: Baywood Publishing; Fisher, C. D., Schoenfeldt, L. F., and Shaw, J. B. (1996). *Human resource management.* Boston: Houghton-Mifflin Company.

6. Bureau of Labor Statistics. (2002). *Survey of work-related health.* Washington, DC: Department of Labor.

7. Leonard, B. (February 1996). Performance testing can add an extra margin of safety. *HR Magazine,* pp. 61–64.

8. National Safety Council. (2005). *Accident facts.* (www.NSC.org): National Safety Council; see also Hoskin, A. F. (May 1995). 1994 work-related deaths decline. *Safety and Health, 151*(5), 70–71; Labor Letter. (1991, June 13). *The Wall Street Journal,* p. 1; Karr, A. R. (1990, May 2). White House backs raising penalties levied by OSHA. *The Wall Street Journal,* p. A8.

9. Colburn, L. E. (1995). Defending against workers' compensation fraud. *Industrial Management, 37,* 1–2.

10. Evans, G., and Johnson, D. (2000). Stress and open office noise. *Journal of Applied Psychology, 85,* 779–783.

11. Elsberry, R. B. (1996). Food for thought on plant sanitation. *Electrical Apparatus, 49*(12), 42–43.

12. Atkinson, L. (1996). Avoiding safety walkouts. *HR Focus, 73*(10), 20.

13. Vlasic, B. (1989, July 23). Death in the workplace. *Detroit News,* p. 1.

14. Verespej, M. A. (1990, May 21). OSHA goes to court. *Industry Week,* 91–92; see also Redeker, J. R., and Tang, D. J. (April 1988). Criminal accountability for workplace safety. *Management Review,* 32–36; Glaberson, W. (1990, October 17). Court upholds prosecution of employer for job hazard. *New York Times,* p. A16.

15. Greene, M. V. (2005). State plans bring safety control home. NSC Web site. (www.NSC.org).

16. Wiatrowski, W. J. (2004). Occupational injury and illness: New recordkeeping requirements. *Monthly Labor Review, 127,* 10–24.

17. www.osha.gov; see also U.S. Department of Labor. (June 1975). *OSHA Inspections.* Programs and Policy Series, OSHA.

18. *Marshall v. Barlow's, Inc.,* 436 U.S. 307, 98 S. Ct. 1816, 56 L. Ed. 2d 305 (1978).

19. OSHA issues final rule requiring employers to certify hazard corrections. (1997). *BNAC Communicator, 15*(3), 10.

20. Occupational Safety and Health Administration. (2005). *Voluntary protection programs.* Washington, D.C.

21. Ibid.

22. *Whirlpool Corp. v. Marshall.* (1981, February 26). *Daily Labor Report.* Washington, DC: Bureau of National Affairs; Whirlpool Corp. v. Marshall, 445 U.S. 1, 100 S. Ct. 883, 63 L. Ed. 2d 154 (1980).

23. ABC News *20/20.* (1999). John Stossel, "Give me a break."

24. See www.osha.gov/inspections.

25. See Verespej, OSHA goes to court. See also Brooks, J. (1977). *Failure to meet commitments in the Occupational Safety and Health Act.* Washington, DC: U.S. Congress, Committee on Government Operations; Uzumeri, M. V. (1997). ISO9000 and other metastandards: Principles for management practice? *Academy of Management Executive, 11*(1), 21–36.

26. OSHA doing better job of finding most hazardous workplaces, acting administrator says. (1997). *BNAC Communicator, 15*(3), 29.

27. Bureau of Labor Statistics (2003). *Workplace injury and illness summary and census of fatal occupational injuries.* Washington, D.C.: Department of Labor.

28. Ibid.

29. Geller, E. S. (1996). *The psychology of safety: How to improve behaviors and attitudes on the job.* Radnor, PA: Chilton Book Company; Geller, E. S. (1994). Ten principles for achieving a total safety culture. *Professional Safety, 39*(9), 18–24; Guastello, S. J. (1993). Do we really know how well our occupational accident prevention programs work? *Safety Science, 16,* 445–463.

30. Ashford, N. A. (1977). Crisis in the workplace: Occupational disease and injury. *A Report to the Ford Foundation.* Cambridge, MA: MIT Press.

31. Schwartz, R. G., and Weinstein, S. M. (1996). Getting a handle on cumulative trauma disorders. *Patient Care, 30,* 118–120; Gangemi, R. A. (July 1996). Ergonomics: Reducing workplace injuries. *Inc.* p. 92.

32. Geller, E. S. (1996). *Working safe: How to help people actively care for health and safety.* Radnor, PA: Chilton Book Company.

33. Taylor, A. (1997). Danger: Rough road ahead. *Fortune,* pp. 114–118.

34. Pierce, F. D. (1996). 10 rules for better communication. *Occupational Hazards, 58*(5), 78–80.

35. It pays to be nice. (1997, June 12). *The Wall Street Journal,* p. A1.

36. How to get management and employees on board. (1996). *Occupational Health and Safety, 65*(1), 27.

37. Zacharatos, A., Barling, J., and Iverson, R. D. (2005). High-performance work systems and occupational safety. *Journal of Applied Psychology, 90,* 77–93.

38. Turner, N., and Parker, S. K. (2004). The effect of teamwork on safety processes and outcomes. In J. Barling and M. R. Frone (Eds.), *The psychology of workplace safety* (pp. 35–62). Washington, DC: American Psychological Association; see also Parker, S. K., Axtell, C., and Turner, N. (2001). Designing a safer workplace: Importance of job autonomy, communication quality, and supportive supervisors. *Journal of Occupational Health Psychology, 6,* 211–228.

39. Zacharatos, Barling, and Iverson. High-performance work systems and occupational safety, 78. See also Zohar, D. (2003). Safety climate: Conceptual and measurement issues. In J. C. Quick and L. E. Tetrick (Eds.), *Handbook of occupational health psychology* (pp. 123–142). Washington, DC: American Psychological Association.

40. Geller, E. S., Roberts, D. S., and Gilmore, M. R. (1996). Predicting propensity to actively care for occupational safety. *Journal of Safety Research, 27,* 1–8; see also Zohar, D. (2000). A group-level model of safety climate: Testing the effect of group climate on microaccidents in manufacturing jobs. *Journal of Applied Psychology, 85,* 587–596; Zohar, D. (2002). The effects of leadership dimensions, safety climate and assigned priorities on minor injuries in work groups. *Journal of Organizational Behavior, 23,* 75–92; Zohar, D. (2003). The influence of leadership and climate on occupational health and safety. In D. A. Hoffman and L. E.

Tetrick (Eds.), *Health and safety in organizations: A multilevel perspective* (pp. 201–230). San Francisco: Wiley.

41. Dunbar, R. (June 1975). Manager's influence on subordinate's thinking about safety. *Academy of Management Journal, 18,* 364–369.

42. OSHA rule requiring forklift training becomes final in September '97. (1997). *BNAC Communicator, 15*(3), 1, 28.

43. Nwaelele, D. D. (1996). Prudent owners take proactive approach. *Professional Safety, 41*(4), 27–29.

44. Van Houten, B. (1997). In the trenches. *Restaurant Business, 96,* 25–30.

45. Komaki, J., Barwick, K. D., and Scott, L. R. (1978). A behavioral approach to occupational safety: Pinpointing and reinforcing safe performance in a food manufacturing plant. *Journal of Applied Psychology, 63,* 434–445; see also Dehaas, D. (1996). The problem with training. *OH and S Canada, 12,* 4.

46. LeBar, G. (1996). The age(ing) of ergonomics. *Occupational Hazards, 58,* 32–33.

47. Breeding, D. C. (1996). Worker empowerment: A useful tool for effective safety management. *Occupational Health and Safety, 65*(9), 16–17.

48. Strahlendorf, P. (1996). What supervisors need to know? *OH and S Canada, 12*(1), 38–40.

49. Roughton, J. E. (1996). When contractors fall short. *Security Management, 40,* 68–71.

50. Laws, J. (1996). The power of incentives. *Occupational Health and Safety, 65*(1), 24–28.

51. Wilson, J. C. (1996). Employee well-being is the real prize. *Occupational Health and Safety, 65,* 168–169.

52. See Laws, The power of incentives.

53. Minter, S. G. (1996). Putting incentives to work. *Occupational Hazards, 58*(6), S7–S9.

54. Case study in safety. (1996). *Incentive, 170*(10), P22–P23.

55. Ibid.

56. See Wilson, Employee well-being is the real prize.

57. Swearingen, M. H. (1996). Do safety incentive programs really help? *Occupational Health and Safety, 65*(10), 164–165.

58. Oswald, E. M. (1996). No employer is immune: AIDS in the workplace. *Risk Management, 43,* 18–21.

59. Smith, J. M. (March 1993). How to develop and implement an AIDS workplace policy. *HR Focus,* p. 15.

60. Feuer, D. (June 1987). AIDS at work: Fighting the fear. *Training,* pp. 61–71; see also Elliott, R. H., and Wilson, T. M. (1987). AIDS in the workplace: Public personnel management and the law. *Public Personnel Management,* pp. 209–219; Breuer, N. L. (January 1992). AIDS issues haven't gone away. *Personnel Journal, 71,* 47–49; Elkiss, H. (1991). Reasonable accommodation and unreasonable fears: An AIDS policy guide for human resource personnel. *Human Resource Planning, 14,* 183–190; Brown, D. R., and Gray, G. R. (Summer 1991). Designing an appropriate AIDS policy. *Employment Relations Today, 18,* 149–155.

61. Kedjidian, C. B. (December 1995). Say no to booze and drugs in your workplace. *Safety and Health, 152*(6), 38–41. See also Labaton, S. (December 5, 1989). The cost of drug abuse: $60 billion a year. *New York Times,* pp. B1, B30; Zigarelli, M. A. (1995). Drug testing litigation: Trends and outcomes. *Human Resource Management Review, 5*(4), 267–288; Like, S. K.

(Winter 1990–1991). Employee drug testing. *Small Business Reports, 16*(3), 347–358; Lehman, W. E., and Simpson, D. D. (1992). Employee substance use and on-the-job behaviors. *Journal of Applied Psychology, 77*, 309–321.

62. Drug use on the job being probed. (July 5, 1996). *Baltimore Sun,* pp. 9c, 11c.

63. American Management Association. (1997). *The AMA handbook for developing employee assistance and counseling programs.* Washington, DC: AMA. See also Cunningham, G. (1994). *Effective employee assistance programs.* Palo Alto, CA: Sage Publications; Carroll, M. (1996). *Workplace counseling.* Palo Alto, CA: Sage Publications.

64. See Kedjidian, Say no to booze.

65. See AMA, *The AMA handbook.*

66. Dolan, K., Rouen, D., and Kimber, J. (2004). An overview of the use of urine, hair, sweat and saliva to detect drug use. *Drug and Alcohol Review, 23,* 213–217.

67. French, M. T., Roebuck, M. C., and Alexandre, P. K. (2004). To test or not to test: do workplace drug testing programs discourage employee drug use? *Social Science Research, 33,* 45–63.

68. deLisser, E. (July 8, 1994). U.S. health costs tied to smoking total $50 billion a year, CDC says. *The Wall Street Journal,* p. B3.

69. Litvan, L. M. (1994). A smoke-free workplace? *Nation's Business, 82,* 65; see also Winslow, R. (March 6, 1995). Will firms shift costs to smokers? *The Wall Street Journal,* pp. B1, B4; Rundle, R. L. (January 14, 1990). U-Haul puts high price on vices of its workers. *The Wall Street Journal,* p. B10; Beck, J. (February 1994). Helping workers breathe free. *Journal of Commerce and Commercial, 399*(28163), 8A.

70. Yandrick, R. M. (July 1994). More employers prohibit smoking. *HR Magazine,* pp. 68–71.

71. Smith, L. (August 9, 1993). Can smoking or bungee jumping get you canned? *Fortune, 128*(3), 92; see also Karr, A. R., and Gutfeld, R. (January 16, 1992). OSHA inches toward limiting smoking. *The Wall Street Journal,* pp. B1, B7; Bureau of National Affairs. (1991). *Employment guide.* Washington, DC: Bureau of National Affairs.

72. American Management Association. (1999). *Survey of workplace violence.* Washington, DC: AMA.

73. *www.shrm.org/* survey on violence. See also Epstein, B. D. (1996). Preventing workplace violence. *Provider, 22,* 71–72; see also Bureau of National Affairs. (April 26, 1993). Preventing workplace violence: Legal imperatives can clash. *Employee Relations Weekly, 11*(17), 451–452.

74. National Institute for Occupational Safety and Health. (2002). Violence: Occupational hazards in hospitals. Washington, DC: U.S. Government Printing Office.

75. Flynn, G. (1996). What can you do about weapons in the workplace? *Personnel Journal, 75*(3), 122–125.

76. Davies, E. (1996). How violence at work can hit employees hard. *People Management, 2*(18), 50–53.

77. Burroughs, S. M., and Jones, J. W. (April 1995). Managing violence: Looking out for trouble. *Occupational Health and Safety,* pp. 34–37.

78. Stage, J. K. (1997). Attack on violence. *Industry Week, 246*(4), 15–18.

79. Kinney, J. A., and Johnson, D. L. (1993). *Breaking point: The workplace violence epidemic and what to do about it.* Chicago: National Safe Workplace Institute.

80. Stevens, W. K. (March 14, 1991). Study backs safety of video terminals. *New York Times,* p. C21. See also Sullivan, J. F. (November 29, 1989). New Jersey acts on video terminals. *New York Times,* p. Y13; Gettings, L., and Maddox, E. N. (1989). Overview: When health means wealth. *Human resources yearbook.* Englewood Cliffs, NJ: Prentice Hall, pp. 6.1–6.4.

81. Fine, B. (1997). Coping with computers. *Safety and Health Practitioner, 15*(3), 42–43.

82. Collins, J. W., Wolf, I., Bell, J., and Evanoff, B. (2004). An evaluation of a "best practices" musculoskeletal injury prevention program in nursing homes. *Injury Prevention, 10,* 206–211.

83. Buffa, D. (November 16, 2000). Not enough hours in a day. *New York Post,* p. 3.

84. Madonia, J. F. (June 1984). Managerial responses to alcohol and drug abuse among employees. *Personnel Administrator, 8,* 134–139.

85. Beehr, T. A., and Newman, J. E. (1990). Job stress, employee health, and organizational effectiveness: A facet analysis, model and literature review. *Personnel Psychology, 31,* 665–699. See also Ivancevich, J. M., and Ganster, D. C. (1987). *Job stress: From theory to suggestion.* New York: Haworth; Schaubroeck, J., Ganster, D. C., and Fox, M. L. (1992). Dispositional affect and work-related stress. *Journal of Applied Psychology, 77,* 322–335.

86. Bruening, J. C. (1996). The ergonomics of the mind: Psychosocial issues in the office. *Managing Office Technology, 41,* 35–36.

87. Matteson, M. T., Ivancevich, J. M., and Smith, S. V. (1984). Relation of Type A behavior to performance and satisfaction among sales personnel. *Journal of Vocational Behavior, 25,* 203–214.

88. Parker, S., and Sprigg, C. A. (1999). Minimizing strain and maximizing learning: The role of job demands, job control, and proactive personality. *Journal of Applied Psychology, 84,* 925–929.

89. Loerch, K. J., Russell, J. E. A., and Rush, M. C. (1989). The relationship among family domain variables and work–family conflict for men and women. *Journal of Vocational Behavior, 35,* 288–308. See also Allen, T. D., Russell, J. E. A., and Rush, M. C. (1994). The effects of gender and leave of absence on attributions for high performance, perceived organizational commitment, and allocation of organizational rewards. *Sex Roles, 31,* 443–464; Chusmir, L., and Durand, D. (May 1987). Stress and the working woman. *Personnel,* pp. 38–43.

90. Conference Board. (1991). *Work schedules and productivity.* Atlanta: The Conference Board.

91. Azar, B. (1997). Quelling today's conflict between home and work. *APA Monitor, 28*(7), 1, 16.

92. Weitlauf, J., Smith, R. E., and Cervone, D. (2000). Generalization effects of coping-skills training: Influence of self-defense training on women's efficacy beliefs, assertiveness, and aggression. *Journal of Applied Psychology, 85,* 625–631.

93. Judge, T. A., and Colquitt, J. A. (2004). Organizational justice and stress: The mediating role of work-family conflict. *Journal of Applied Psychology, 89,* 403; see also, Vermunt, R., and Steensma, H. (2001). Stress and justice in organizations: An exploration into justice processes with the aim to find mechanisms to reduce stress. In R. Cropanzano (Ed.), *Justice in the workplace: From theory to practice* (vol. 2, pp. 27–48). Mahwah, NJ: Erlbaum.

94. Ganster, D. C., and Schaubroeck, J. (1991). Work stress and employee health. *Journal of Management, 17,* 235–271; Cartwright, S., and Cooper, C. L. (1997). *Managing workplace stress.* Palo Alto, CA: Sage Publications.

95. Cooper. C. L., and Robertson, I. T., (Eds.), *International review of industrial and organizational psychology.* Chichester, England: Wiley, pp. 235–280.

96. Schaubroeck, J., Lam, S. K., and Xie, J. L. (2000). Collective efficacy versus self-efficacy in coping responses to stressors and control: A cross-cultural study. *Journal of Applied Psychology, 85,* 512–525.

97. Gordes, C. L., and Dougherty, T. (1993). A review and integration of research on burnout. *Academy of Management Journal, 18,* 621–656.

98. Russell, D. W., Altmaier, E., and Velzen, D. V. (1987). Job-related stress, social support, and burnout among classroom teachers. *Journal of Applied Psychology, 72,* 269–274; see also Cherniss, C. (1992). Long-term consequences of burnout: An exploratory study. *Journal of Organizational Behavior, 13,* 1–11; McKeown, S. (1996). Stress: No quack cures, just sensible management. *Works Management, 49*(9), 60–63.

99. Demerouti, E., Bakker, A. B., Nachreiner, F., and Schaufeli, W. B. (2001). The job demands–resources model of burnout. *Journal of Applied Psychology, 86,* 512–517; see also Ganster, D. C., Fox, M. L., and Dwyer, D. J. (October 2001). Explaining employees' health care costs: A prospective examination of stressful job demands, personal control, and physiological reactivity. *Journal of Applied Psychology, 86,* 954–959.

100. Arkin, O. (1997). Time to take account of work, rest, and play. *People Management, 3,* 47–48.

101. Cavanaugh, M. A., Boswell, W. R., Roehling, M. V., and Boudreau, J. (2000). An empirical examination of self-reported work stress among U.S. managers. *Journal of Applied Psychology, 85,* 65–74.

102. Boswell, W. R., Olson-Buchanan, J. B., and LePine, M. A. (2004). Relations between stress and work outcomes: The role of felt challenge, job control, and psychological strain. *Journal of Vocational Behavior, 64,* 165–181.

103. Feldman, S. (February 1991). Today's EAPs make the grade. *Personnel, 68,* 3. See also Spangler, J. (June 29, 1992). Assistance available for those under stress. *Amoco Torch,* pp. 1–2.

104. Leonard, B. (July 1993). The tough decision to use confidential information. *HR Magazine,* pp. 72–75; see also Schultz, E. E. (May 26, 1994). If you use firm's counselors, remember your secrets could be used against you. *The Wall Street Journal,* p. C1.

105. Gaeta, E. Lynn, R., and Grey, L. (May 1982). AT&T looks at program evaluation. *EAP Digest,* pp. 22–31; see also Freudenheim, M. (November 13, 1989). More aid for addicts on the job. *New York Times,* pp. 27, 39.

106. See Feldman, Today's EAPs make the grade.

107. Pynes, J. E. (1996). The two faces of unions. *Journal of Collective Negotiations in the Public Sector, 25,* 31–43.

108. Health Insurance Association of America. (1983). *Your guide to wellness at the worksite.* Washington, DC: Health Insurance Association of America, p. 3.

109. Harrison, D. A., and Liska, L. Z. (1994). Promoting regular exercise in organizational fitness programs: Health-related differences in motivational building blocks. *Personnel Psychology, 47,* 47–71.

110. Wolfe, R. A., Ulrich, D. O., and Parker, D. F. (1987). Employee health management programs: Review, critique, and research agenda. *Journal of Management, 13,* 603–615; see also Erfurt, J. C., Foote, A., and Heirich, M. A. (1992). The cost-effectiveness of worksite wellness programs for hypertension control, weight loss, smoking cessation, and exercise. *Personnel Psychology, 45,* 5–27; Moore, T. L. (1991). Build wellness from an EAP base. *Personnel Journal, 70,* 104.

111. Helmer, D. C., Dunn, L. M., Eaton, K., Macedonio, C., and Lubritz, L. (1995). Implementing corporate wellness programs. *AAOHN Journal, 43,* 558–563; see also Erfurt, Foote, and Heirich. The cost-effectiveness of worksite wellness programs.

112. Petersen, C. (1996). Work-hardening program pays big dividends. *Managed Healthcare, 6*(12), 43.

113. Epes, B. (August 1995). Start an employee wellness program. *Training & Development,* pp. 12–13.

114. See Helmer et al., Implementing corporate wellness programs.

115. Greenfeld, S. (July 1989). Management's safety and health imperative: Eight essential steps to improving the work environment. *Occasional Paper 2.9.* Cincinnati, OH: Xavier University, Minerva Education Institute. See also LaBar, G. (1996). Safety gets down to business. *Occupational Hazards, 58*(8), 23–28; Geller, *The psychology of safety*; Geller, *Working safe*; Geller, Ten principles for achieving a total safety culture; Guastella, Do we really know how well our occupational accident prevention programs work?

116. Jonas, P. (1996). The missing letter in TQM. *Occupational Health and Safety, 65,* 18–19.

117. Nwaelele, O. D. (1996). Prudent owners take proactive approach. *Professional Safety, 41,* 27–29.

118. Lamb, M. R. (1996). Safety is all in a day's work at A. M. Castle. *Metal Center News, 36,* 42–50.

119. Palmer, M. (1996). Now it's safety first. *Nursing Homes, 45,* 29–36.

120. McCurry, J. W. (1996). Milliken and Co.: Textile's king of safety. *Textile World, 146,* 76–80.

121. Zacharatos et al., High-performance work systems and occupational safety.

122. Costello, A. (1996). Your health is your wealth. *Accountancy Ireland, 28,* 10–12.

123. Stress in the workplace. (May/June 1996). *British Journal of Administrative Management,* pp. 8–9.

124. Ritcy, S. (1996). Psychological job matching. *OH and S Canada, 12,* 50–56.

125. Pasquarelli, T. (1996). Dealing with discomfort and danger. *HR Magazine, 41,* 104–110.

Name Index

COMPANY INDEX

SUBJECT INDEX